Street by Street

ATER
IDON

n

of
ɔse
ad,
ıber

Ɔffice

Ɔirect.

Key to map pages ii-iii

Key to map symbols iv-1

Enlarged scale pages 2-19

Street by Street 20-285

Index – town & villages 286-288

Index – streets 289-406

Index – featured places 406-431

Mapping produced by the Cartographic Department of The Automobile Association. A01250.

A CIP Catalogue record for this book is available from the British Library.

Printed by Trento Srl, Italy.

Ref: GS040z

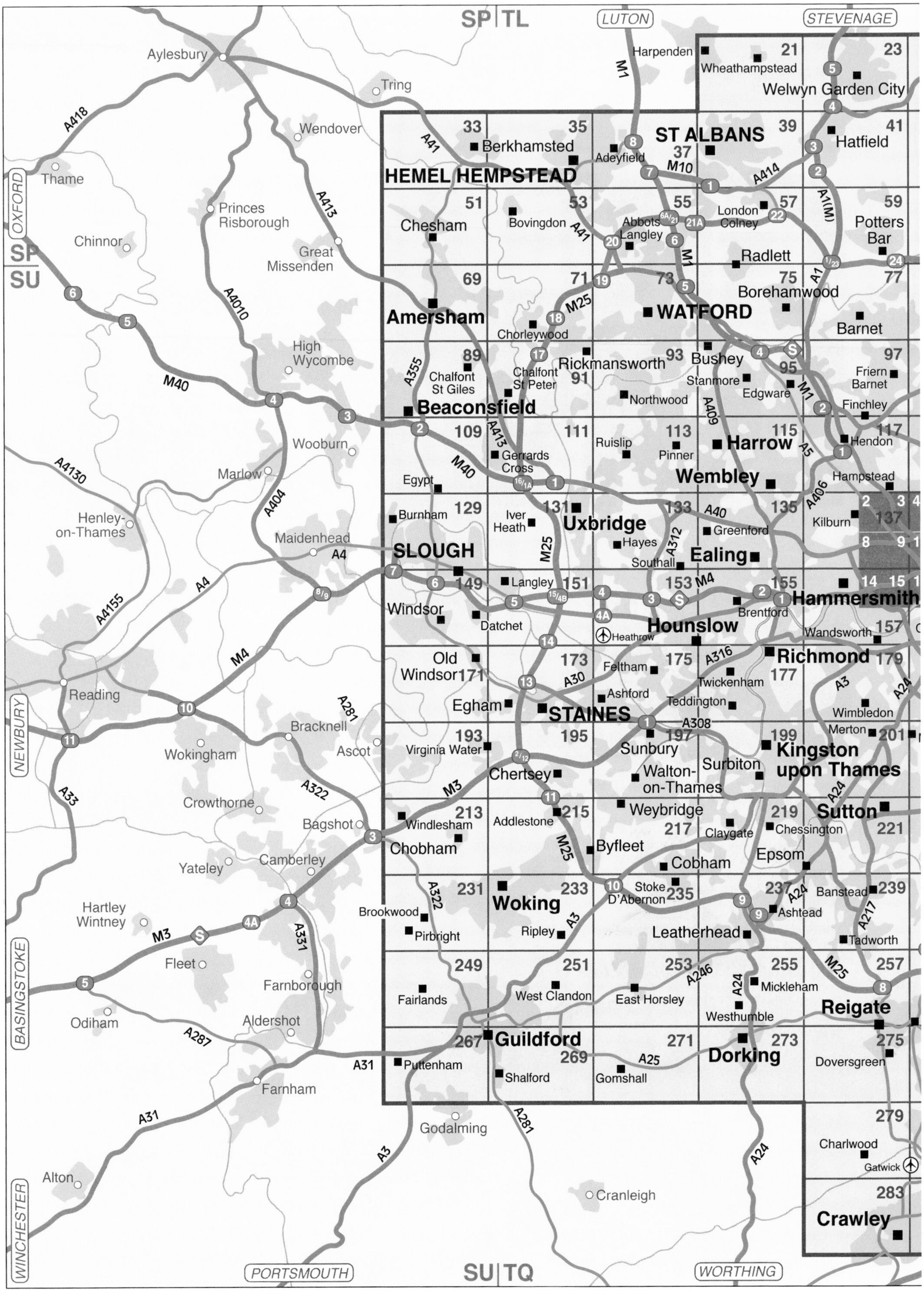
SP | TL
LUTON
STEVENAGE
OXFORD
SP
SU
NEWBURY
BASINGSTOKE
WINCHESTER
PORTSMOUTH
SU | TQ
WORTHING
Aylesbury
Tring
Harpenden
Wheathampstead
21
23
Welwyn Garden City
Wendover
33
Berkhamsted
35
Adeyfield
ST ALBANS
37
M10
39
Hatfield
41
HEMEL HEMPSTEAD
Thame
Princes Risborough
Chinnor
Great Missenden
51
Chesham
Bovingdon
53
Abbots Langley
55
London Colney
57
59
Potters Bar
Radlett
69
Amersham
71
73
WATFORD
75
Borehamwood
77
Barnet
Chorleywood
High Wycombe
89
Chalfont St Giles
Chalfont St Peter
Rickmansworth
91
93
Bushey
Stanmore
95
Edgware
97
Friern Barnet
Finchley
Northwood
Beaconsfield
109
111
Ruislip
113
Pinner
Harrow
115
117
Hendon
Wooburn
Marlow
Gerrards Cross
Egypt
Wembley
Hampstead
Henley-on-Thames
Burnham
129
Iver Heath
131
Uxbridge
133
135
Kilburn
137
Hayes
Greenford
Maidenhead
SLOUGH
Southall
Ealing
149
Langley
151
153
155
Hammersmith
Windsor
Datchet
Heathrow
Hounslow
Brentford
Wandsworth
157
Old Windsor
171
173
Feltham
175
177
Richmond
179
Reading
Ashford
Twickenham
Teddington
Egham
STAINES
Wimbledon
Bracknell
Wokingham
Ascot
193
Virginia Water
195
197
Sunbury
199
Kingston upon Thames
Merton
201
Chertsey
Walton-on-Thames
Surbiton
Crowthorne
213
Windlesham
Addlestone
215
Weybridge
217
Claygate
219
Chessington
Sutton
221
Bagshot
Chobham
Byfleet
Cobham
Epsom
Yateley
Camberley
231
Woking
233
Stoke D'Abernon
235
237
Banstead
239
Hartley Wintney
Brookwood
Ashtead
Pirbright
Ripley
Leatherhead
Tadworth
Fleet
249
251
253
255
257
Farnborough
Fairlands
West Clandon
East Horsley
Mickleham
Westhumble
Reigate
Odiham
Aldershot
267
Guildford
269
271
Dorking
273
275
Puttenham
Shalford
Gomshall
Doversgreen
Farnham
Godalming
279
Charlwood
Gatwick
Alton
Cranleigh
283
Crawley
A418
A41
A413
A4010
A355
M40
A4130
A404
A4
A4155
M4
A33
A281
A322
M3
A331
A287
A31
A3
M25
M1
A414
A1(M)
A1
A409
A5
A406
A40
A312
A30
A316
A308
A24
A217
A246
A25

Enlarged scale pages 1:10,000

6.3 inches to 1 mile

0 1/4 miles 1/2 3/4

0 1/4 1/2 kilometres 3/4 1 1 1/4

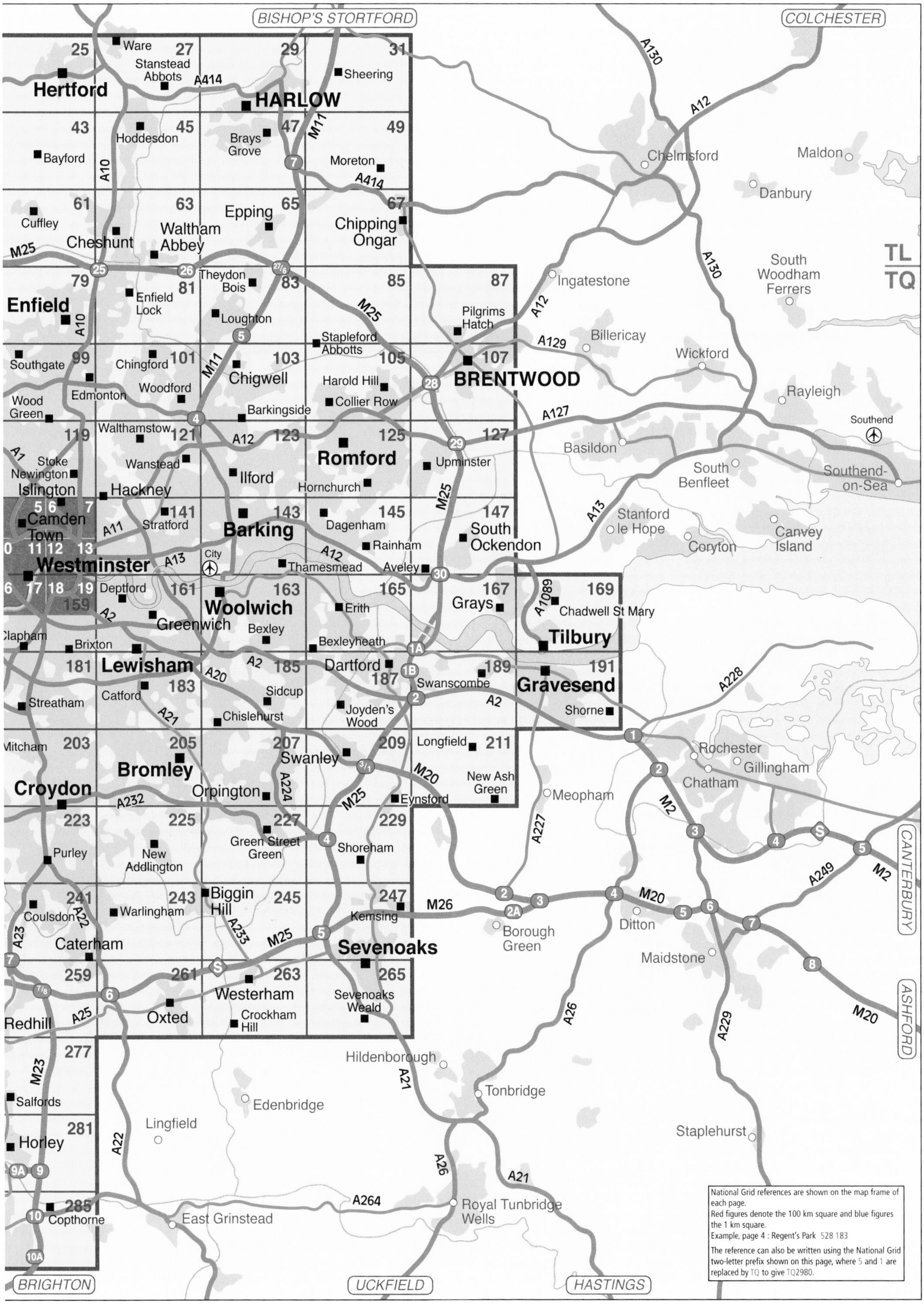
BISHOP'S STORTFORD
COLCHESTER
25
Ware
27
Stanstead Abbots
A414
29
31
Sheering
Hertford
HARLOW
43
Hoddesdon
45
Brays Grove
47
M11
49
Bayford
A10
7
Moreton
A414
A130
A12
Chelmsford
Maldon
Danbury
61
Cuffley
63
Epping
65
67
Chipping Ongar
Waltham Abbey
Cheshunt
M25
25
26
27/6
Theydon Bois
79
81
83
85
87
Enfield
Enfield Lock
Loughton
M25
Pilgrims Hatch
A12
Ingatestone
A130
South Woodham Ferrers
TL
TQ
5
Stapleford Abbotts
A129
Billericay
Wickford
Southgate
99
Chingford
101
M11
103
Chigwell
105
28
107
BRENTWOOD
Edmonton
Woodford
Harold Hill
Collier Row
Rayleigh
Wood Green
4
Barkingside
A127
Southend
119
Walthamstow
121
A12
123
125
29
127
Basildon
A1
Stoke Newington
Wanstead
Romford
Upminster
South Benfleet
Southend-on-Sea
Islington
Ilford
Hornchurch
Hackney
M25
A13
5
6
7
141
143
145
147
Stanford le Hope
Camden Town
Stratford
Barking
Dagenham
South Ockendon
Canvey Island
A11
Coryton
0
11
12
13
A12
Rainham
Westminster
A13
City
Thamesmead
Aveley
30
6
17
18
19
Deptford
161
163
165
167
A1089
169
Grays
Chadwell St Mary
159
Woolwich
Erith
A2
Greenwich
Bexley
Tilbury
Clapham
Bexleyheath
Brixton
1A
181
Lewisham
A2
185
Dartford
1B
189
191
A20
183
187
Swanscombe
Gravesend
Catford
Sidcup
2
A2
A228
Streatham
A21
Chislehurst
Joyden's Wood
Shorne
Mitcham
203
205
207
209
Longfield
211
1
Rochester
Swanley
3/1
M20
2
Gillingham
Bromley
Croydon
A224
New Ash Green
Chatham
A232
Orpington
M25
Eynsford
Meopham
M2
223
225
227
229
A227
3
Purley
New Addington
Green Street Green
4
Shoreham
S
4
5
CANTERBURY
A249
M2
241
243
Biggin Hill
245
247
2
3
4
M20
M26
2A
Coulsdon
A22
Warlingham
Kemsing
5
6
A23
A233
Ditton
Caterham
M25
5
Borough Green
7
Sevenoaks
Maidstone
7
S
8
259
261
263
265
7/8
6
Westerham
Sevenoaks Weald
ASHFORD
Oxted
A25
A26
M20
Redhill
Crockham Hill
A229
277
Hildenborough
M23
A21
Tonbridge
Salfords
Edenbridge
Lingfield
281
Staplehurst
Horley
A22
9A
9
A26
A21
285
A264
10
Copthorne
Royal Tunbridge Wells
East Grinstead
10A
BRIGHTON
UCKFIELD
HASTINGS
National Grid references are shown on the map frame of each page.
Red figures denote the 100 km square and blue figures the 1 km square.
Example, page 4 : Regent's Park 528 183
The reference can also be written using the National Grid two-letter prefix shown on this page, where 5 and 1 are replaced by TQ to give TQ2980.

3.2 inches to 1 mile

Scale of main map pages 1:20,000

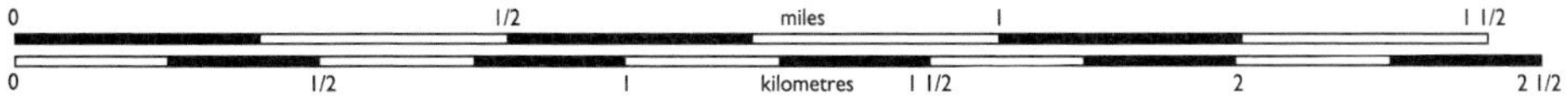
0
1/2
miles
1
1 1/2
0
1/2
1
kilometres
1 1/2
2
2 1/2

Symbol	Description
Junction 9	Motorway & junction
Services	Motorway service area
	Primary road single/dual carriageway
Services	Primary road service area
	A road single/dual carriageway
	B road single/dual carriageway
	Other road single/dual carriageway
	Minor/private road, access may be restricted
	One-way street
	Pedestrian area
	Track or footpath
	Road under construction
	Road tunnel
AA	AA Service Centre
P	Parking
P+	Park & Ride
	Bus/coach station
	Railway & main railway station
	Railway & minor railway station
	Underground station
	Light railway & station
	Preserved private railway
LC	Level crossing
	Tramway
	Ferry route
	Airport runway
	County, administrative boundary
	Mounds
93	Page continuation
7	Page continuation to enlarged scale
	River/canal, lake, pier
	Aqueduct, lock, weir
465 Winter Hill	Peak (with height in metres)
	Beach
	Coniferous woodland
	Broadleaved woodland
	Mixed woodland
	Park

Symbol	Meaning
	Cemetery
	Built-up area
	Featured building
	City wall
A&E	Hospital with 24-hour A&E department
PO	Post Office
	Public library
i	Tourist Information Centre
	Petrol station Major suppliers only
	Church/chapel
	Public toilets
	Toilet with disabled facilities
PH	Public house AA recommended
	Restaurant AA inspected
	Theatre or performing arts centre
	Cinema
	Golf course
	Camping AA inspected
	Caravan site AA inspected
	Camping & caravan site AA inspected
	Theme park
	Abbey, cathedral or priory
	Castle
	Historic house or building
Wakehurst Place NT	National Trust property
M	Museum or art gallery
	Roman antiquity
	Ancient site, battlefield or monument
	Industrial interest
	Garden
	Arboretum
	Farm or animal centre
	Zoological or wildlife collection
	Bird collection
	Nature reserve
V	Visitor or heritage centre
	Country park
	Cave
	Windmill
	Distillery, brewery or vineyard

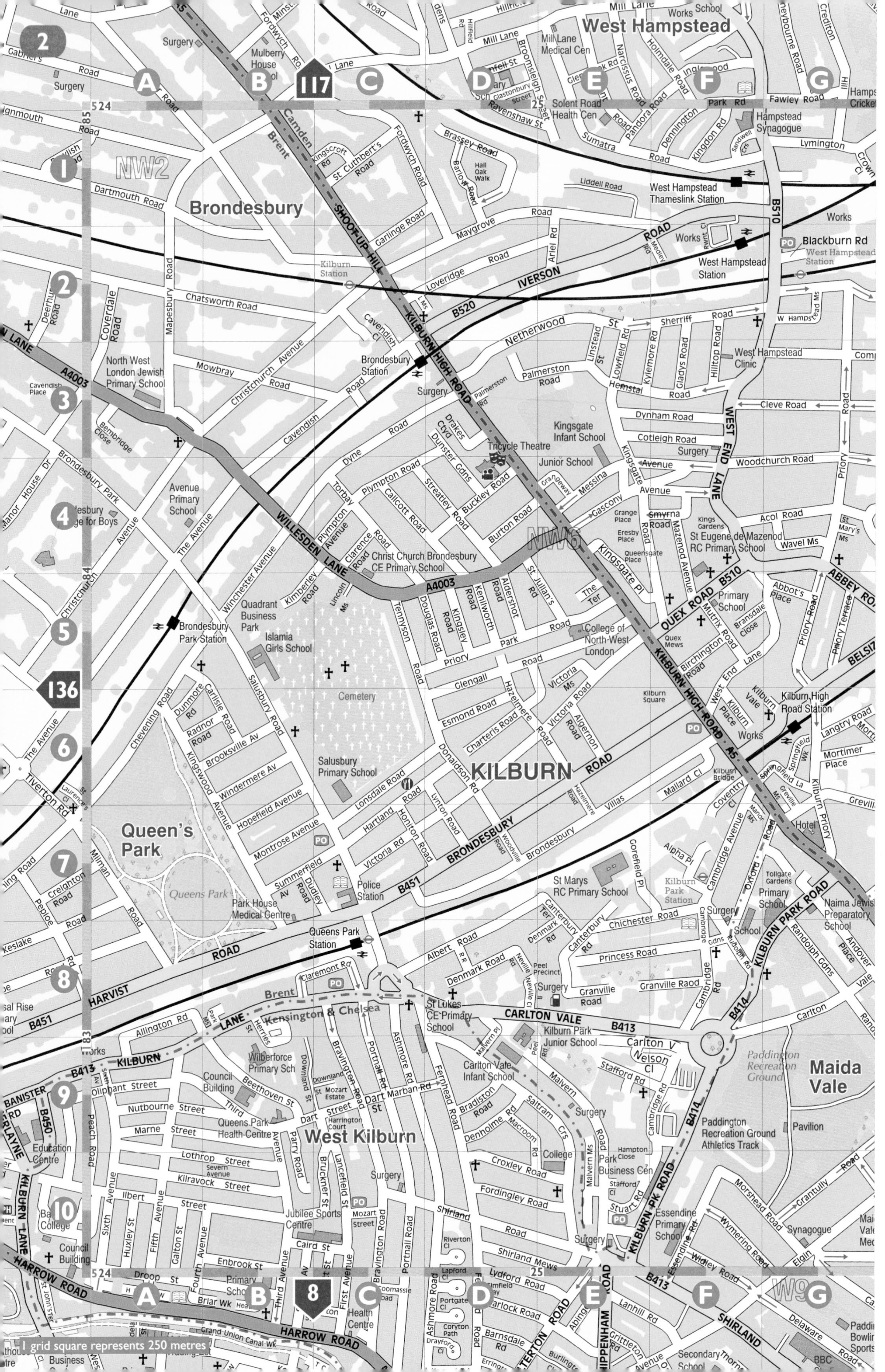
West Hampstead
Brondesbury
NW2
NW6
W9
KILBURN
West Kilburn
Queen's Park
Maida Vale
117
136
8
2
A
B
C
D
E
F
G
1
2
3
4
5
6
7
8
9
10
524
25
185
184
183
1 grid square represents 250 metres
Mill Lane
Mill Lane Medical Cen
Works
School
Solent Road Health Cen
Sumatra Road
Hampstead Synagogue
Lymington
Fawley Road
Park Rd
Ravenshaw St
Broomsleigh Street
Glastonbury Street
Narcissus Road
Holmdale Road
Pandora Road
Dennington
Kingdon Rd
Liddell Road
West Hampstead Thameslink Station
B510
Blackburn Rd
West Hampstead Station
Brassey Road
Hall Oak Walk
Barlow Road
Maygrove Road
Ariel Rd
IVERSON ROAD
Loveridge Road
B520
Sherriff Road
Netherwood St
Palmerston Road
Hemstal Road
West Hampstead Clinic
Dynham Road
Cotleigh Road
Cleve Road
Woodchurch Road
Priory Road
Acol Road
Wavel Ms
WEST END LANE
Surgery
Kingsgate Infant School
Junior School
Tricycle Theatre
Kingsgate Avenue
Messina Avenue
Gascony Avenue
Smyrna Road
Mazenod Avenue
St Eugene de Mazenod RC Primary School
QUEX ROAD
Quex Mews
Birchington Road
Mutrix Road
Primary School
Bransdale Close
Abbot's Place
ABBEY ROAD
Priory Terrace
Kilburn High Road Station
Kilburn Square
Kilburn Vale
Kilburn Place
Langtry Road
Mortimer Place
Springfield La
Kilburn Priory
Hotel
Greville
Kilburn Bridge
Coventry Cl
Mallard Cl
Manor Ms
Cambridge Avenue
Oxford Road
Tollgate Gardens
Primary School
Naima Jewish Preparatory School
KILBURN PARK ROAD
Randolph Gdns
Andover Place
B414
Kilburn Park Station
Alpha Pl
Gorefield Pl
St Marys RC Primary School
Chichester Road
Princess Road
Granville Raod
Granville Road
Peel Precinct
Carlton Vale
CARLTON VALE
B413
Kilburn Park Junior School
Nelson Cl
Carlton Vale Infant School
Stafford Rd
Paddington Recreation Ground
Paddington Recreation Ground Athletics Track
Pavilion
Morshead Road
Grantully Road
Wymering Road
Synagogue
Elgin
Essendine Rd
Essendine Primary School
Widley Road
Shirland Road
Shirland Mews
Saltram Crs
Malvern Road
Malvern Ms
College
Hampton Close
Park Business Cen
Stuart Rd
Croxley Road
Fordingley Road
Denholme Road
Bradiston Road
Macroom Rd
Fernhead Road
Ashmore Rd
Portnall Rd
Portnall Road
Bravington Road
Dart Street
Marban Rd
Downland St
Mozart Street
Mozart Estate
Jubilee Sports Centre
Caird St
Lancefield St
Bruckner St
Parry Road
Queens Park Health Centre
Wilberforce Primary Sch
Beethoven St
Council Building
Oliphant Street
Nutbourne Street
Marne Street
Lothrop Street
Severn Avenue
Kilravock Street
Ilbert Street
Enbrook St
Droop St
Briar Wk
Huxley St
Galton St
Sixth Avenue
Fifth Avenue
Fourth Avenue
Third Avenue
First Avenue
Peach Road
Education Centre
KILBURN LANE
HARROW ROAD
Grand Union Canal Wk
Business
BANISTER RD
B450
Allington Rd
Herries St
Brent
Kensington & Chelsea
Claremont Rd
KILBURN LANE
St Lukes CE Primary School
Albert Road
Denmark Road
Canterbury Road
Canterbury Ter
Queens Park Station
HARVIST ROAD
B451
Park House Medical Centre
Police Station
Summerfield Av
Dudley Road
Victoria Rd
Montrose Avenue
Hopefield Avenue
Windermere Av
Brooksville Av
Kingswood Avenue
Milman Road
Chevening Road
Dunmore Rd
Radnor Road
Carlisle Road
Salusbury Road
Salusbury Primary School
Cemetery
Islamia Girls School
Quadrant Business Park
Brondesbury Park Station
Lonsdale Road
Hartland Road
Honiton Road
Lynton Road
Donaldson Rd
BRONDESBURY ROAD
Brondesbury Villas
Woodville Road
Hazelmere Road
Charteris Road
Esmond Road
Glengall Road
Victoria Road
Victoria Ms
Algernon Road
Priory Park Road
Tennyson Road
Douglas Road
Kingsley Road
Kenilworth Road
Aldershot Road
St Julian's Road
The Ter
College of North-West London
Kingsgate Pl
KILBURN HIGH ROAD
A5
WILLESDEN LANE
A4003
Christ Church Brondesbury CE Primary School
Kimberley Road
Lincoln Ms
Clarence Road
Plympton Avenue
Plympton Road
Torbay Road
Callcott Road
Streatley Road
Buckley Road
Burton Road
Dunster Gdns
Drakes Ctyd
Dyne Road
Cavendish Road
Brondesbury Station
SHOOT-UP HILL
Kilburn Station
Garlinge Road
St Cuthbert's Road
Kingscroft Rd
Fordwych Road
Camden
Brent
Mulberry House School
Chatsworth Road
Dartmouth Road
Mapesbury Road
Mowbray Road
Christchurch Avenue
The Avenue
Avenue Primary School
North West London Jewish Primary School
Coverdale Road
Deerhurst Road
Cavendish Place
Bembridge Close
Brondesbury Park
Manor House Dr
Christchurch Avenue
Tiverton Rd
Creighton Road
Pepioe Road
Keslake Road
Gabriel's Road
Surgery

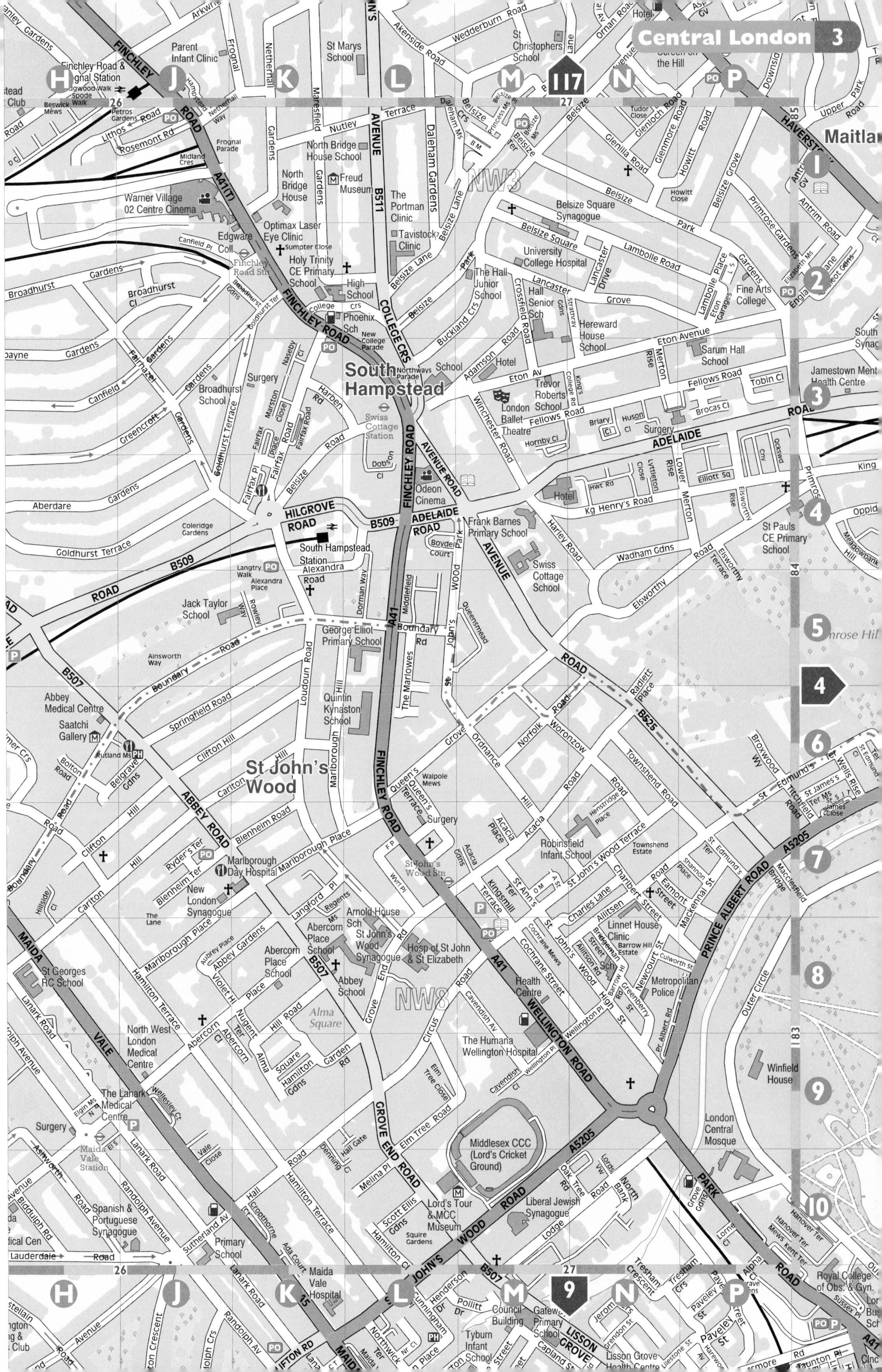
117
H
J
K
L
M
N
P
26
27
Finchley Road & Frognal Station
Parent Infant Clinic
St Marys School
St Christophers School
Akenside Road
Wedderburn Road
FINCHLEY ROAD
Frognal
Netherhall
Maresfield
Nutley Terrace
AVENUE
Daleham Gardens
Belsize Crs
Belsize Ms
Glenloch Road
Glenmore Road
Howitt Road
HAVERSTOCK
Maitla
Lithos Road
Rosemont Rd
Frognal Parade
Midland Cres
North Bridge House School
Freud Museum
North Bridge House
B511
The Portman Clinic
Belsize Lane
NW3
Glenilla Road
Belsize Grove
Primrose Gardens
Antrim Road
Warner Village 02 Centre Cinema
A41(T)
Optimax Laser Eye Clinic
Edgware Coll
Holy Trinity CE Primary School
Tavistock Clinic
Belsize Square Synagogue
Belsize Square
Belsize Park
Howitt Close
Lambolle Road
University College Hospital
Finchley Road Stn
Canfield Pl
Broadhurst Gardens
Broadhurst Cl
High School
The Hall Junior School
Lancaster Drive
Lambolle Place
Fine Arts College
College Crs
Phoenix Sch
New College Parade
COLLEGE CRS
Lancaster Grove
Hall Senior Sch
Hereward House School
Eton Garages
South Hampstead
Canfield Gardens
Fairhazel Gardens
Greencroft Gardens
Broadhurst School
Goldhurst Terrace
Surgery
Naseby Cl
Marston Close
Harben Rd
Swiss Cottage Station
Northways Parade
School
Adamson Road
Hotel
Eton Avenue
Merton Rise
Sarum Hall School
Jamestown Mental Health Centre
Eton Av
Trevor Roberts School
Fellows Road
Tobin Cl
Brocas Cl
London Ballet Theatre
Winchester Road
Briary Cl
Huson Cl
Surgery
ADELAIDE ROAD
Hornby Cl
Fairfax Road
Fairfax Place
Fairfax Pl
Belsize Road
Dobson Cl
AVENUE ROAD
Odeon Cinema
Hwt Rd
Lyttelton Close
Lower Merton Rise
Elliott Sq
Primrose
King
Aberdare Gardens
HILGROVE ROAD
ADELAIDE ROAD
B509
Kg Henry's Road
Elsworthy Rise
Oppidans
Coleridge Gardens
South Hampstead Station
Boydell Court
Frank Barnes Primary School
Harley Road
St Pauls CE Primary School
Meadowbank
Goldhurst Terrace
Alexandra Road
Langtry Walk
Alexandra Place
Swiss Cottage School
Wadham Gdns
Elsworthy Terrace
Hill
ROAD
Jack Taylor School
Rowley Way
Dorman Way
Middlefield
Park
Queensmead
Elsworthy Road
Primrose Hill
George Elliot Primary School
Boundary Rd
A41
Ainsworth Way
Boundary Road
The Marlowes
St John's Wood Park
Radlett Place
B507
Abbey Medical Centre
Saatchi Gallery
Springfield Road
Loudoun Road
Quintin Kynaston School
Woronzow Road
Norfolk Road
B525
Broxwood Way
Rutland Ms
Belgrave Gdns
Bolton Road
Clifton Hill
Marlborough Hill
Grove
Ordnance Hill
Townshend Road
St Edmund's Ter
Wells Rise
St John's Wood
ABBEY ROAD
Carlton Hill
Queen's Terrace
Walpole Mews
Surgery
Acacia Place
Acacia Road
Henstridge Place
Robinsfield Infant School
St John's Wood Terrace
Townshend Estate
St James's Ter Ms
Titchfield Road
A5205
Blenheim Road
Ryder's Ter
Marlborough Place
Marlborough Day Hospital
Blenheim Ter
New London Synagogue
St John's Wood Stn
Wyell Pl
Kingsmill Terrace
St Ann's Ter
Charles Lane
Charlbert Street
Eamont Street
Shannon Place
Mackennal St
PRINCE ALBERT ROAD
Macclesfield Bridge
Carlton
Hillside Cl
The Lane
Marlborough Place
Abbey Gardens
Langford Pl
Regents Ms
Arnold House Sch
Abercorn Place School
St John's Wood Synagogue
Hosp of St John & St Elizabeth
Allitsen Rd
Linnet House Clinic
Barrow Hill Estate
Culworth St
Cochrane Mews
Cochrane Street
MAIDA
St Georges RC School
Aubrey Place
Violet Hill
Abercorn Place School
B507
Abbey Road
Grove End Rd
NW8
Health Centre
A41
WELLINGTON ROAD
Metropolitan Police
Outer Circle
Newcourt St
Greenberry St
Lanark Road
North West London Medical Centre
Hamilton Terrace
Abercorn Cl
Nugent Ter
Alma Square
Hill Road
Alma Square
Cavendish Av
Circus Road
Wellington Pl
The Humana Wellington Hospital
Pr Albert Rd
Winfield House
VALE
Hamilton Gdns
Garden Rd
Elm Tree Close
Cavendish Cl
183
The Lanark Medical Centre
Wellesley Ct
Elgin Ms
Surgery
Maida Vale Station
Ashworth Road
Vale Close
GROVE END ROAD
Elm Tree Road
Hall Gate
Denning Cl
Middlesex CCC (Lord's Cricket Ground)
A5205
London Central Mosque
Melina Pl
Lord's Tour & MCC Museum
Oak Tree Rd
Lodge Road
North Bank
Lords Vw
Grove Gdns
PARK ROAD
Randolph Avenue
Spanish & Portuguese Synagogue
Hall Rd
Cropthorne Ct
Sutherland Av
Primary School
Scott Ellis Gdns
Squire Gardens
ST JOHN'S WOOD ROAD
Liberal Jewish Synagogue
Lorne Cl
Hanover Ter
Kent Ter
Lauderdale Road
Ada Court
Hamilton Cl
Maida Vale Hospital
Henderson Dr
Pollitt Dr
Council Building
B507
Gateway Primary School
Tresham Crescent
Paveley St
Royal College of Obs. & Gyn.
9
Randolph Crs
Clifton RD
Northwick Ter
Tyburn Infant School
LISSON GROVE
Lisson Grove Health Centre
Grendon St
Capland St
Taunton Pl
1
2
3
4
5
6
7
8
9
10
4
84
85

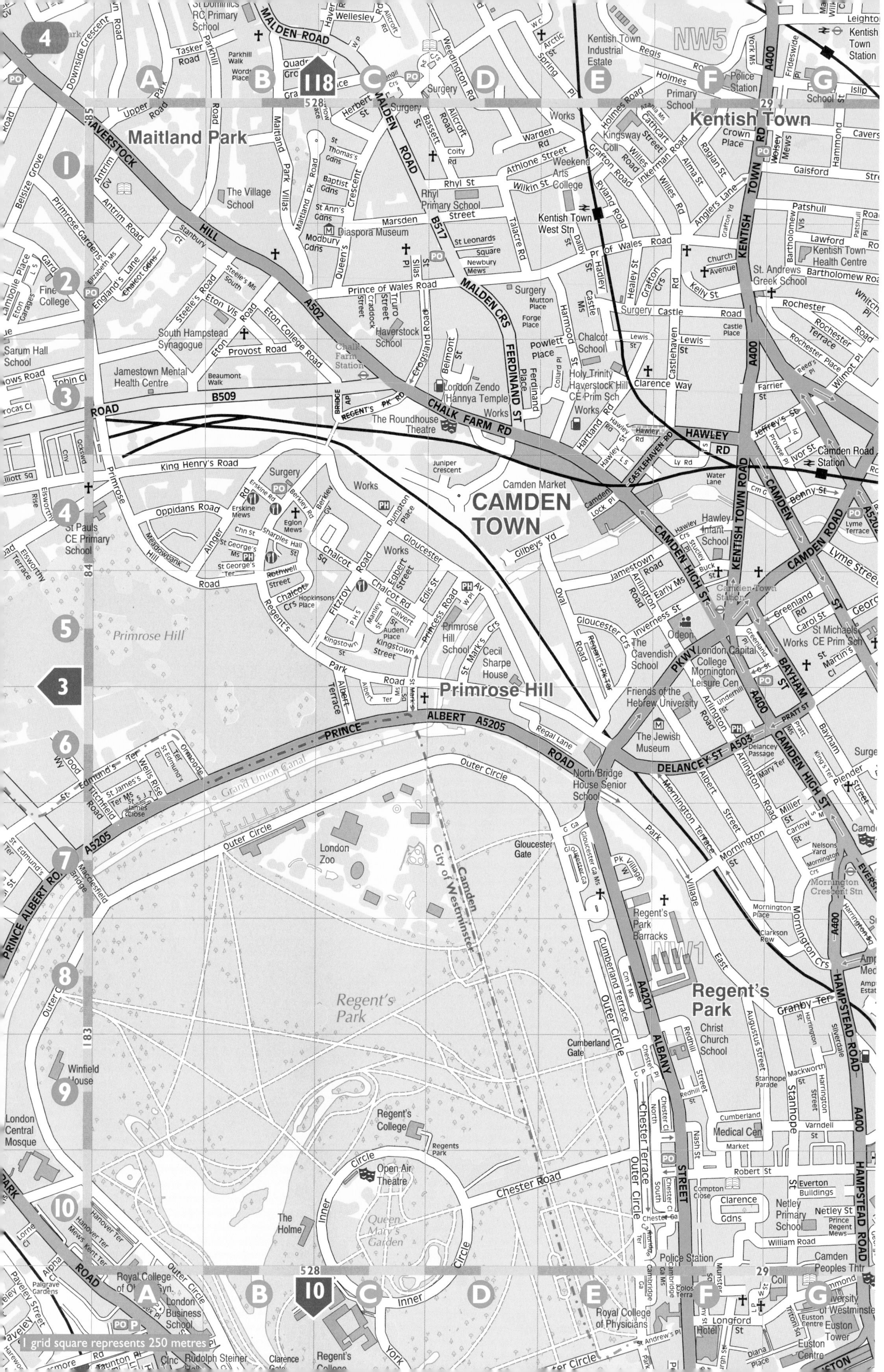
4
118
10
3
A
B
C
D
E
F
G
1
2
3
4
5
6
7
8
9
10
528
29
NW5
NW1
Maitland Park
Kentish Town
CAMDEN TOWN
Primrose Hill
Regent's Park
Primrose Hill
Regent's Park
HAVERSTOCK HILL
A502
MALDEN ROAD
B517
MALDEN CRS
FERDINAND ST
CHALK FARM RD
B509
ROAD
REGENT'S PK RD
BRIDGE AP
KENTISH TOWN ROAD
A400
KENTISH TOWN RD
CAMDEN HIGH ST
CAMDEN ROAD
CAMDEN ST
BAYHAM ST
HAWLEY RD
CASTLEHAVEN RD
PKWY
DELANCEY ST
A503
PRATT ST
PRINCE ALBERT A5205 ROAD
PRINCE ALBERT RD
A5205
ALBANY STREET
A4201
HAMPSTEAD ROAD
Outer Circle
Inner Circle
Chester Road
Grand Union Canal
City of Westminster
Camden
Upper Park Road
Tasker Road
Parkhill Walk
Wellesley
Weedington Rd
Herbert St
Bassett St
Allcroft Road
Coity Rd
Warden Rd
Athlone Street
Wilkin St
Rhyl St
Rhyl Primary School
Marsden Street
Diaspora Museum
Modbury Gdns
St Thomas's Gdns
Baptist Gdns
St Ann's Gdns
Queen's Crescent
Maitland Park Villas
Maitland Pk Road
The Village School
Antrim Gv
Antrim Road
Primrose Gardens
Belsize Grove
Elizabeth Ms
England's Lane
Chalcot Gdns
Stanbury Ct
Steele's Road
Steele's Ms South
Eton Vls
Eton Road
Eton College Road
Provost Road
South Hampstead Synagogue
Jamestown Mental Health Centre
Beaumont Walk
Sarum Hall School
Fine Arts College
Tobin Cl
King Henry's Road
Oppidans Road
Meadowbank
Erskine Rd
Erskine Mews
Eglon Mews
Berkley Rd
Berkley Gv
Chalcot Road
Chalcot Sq
Chalcot Crs
Sharples Hall St
Chn St
St George's Ms
St George's Ter
Rothwell Street
Hopkinsons Place
Fitzroy Road
Manley St
Calvert St
Auden Place
Kingstown Street
Egbert Street
Edis St
Gloucester Avenue
Dumpton Place
Princess Road
Primrose Hill School
Cecil Sharpe House
St Mark's Crs
St Mark's Sq
Albert Terrace
Albert Ter
Regal Lane
Prince of Wales Road
Truro Street
Cradock Street
Crogsland Road
Haverstock School
Chalk Farm Station
Belmont St
London Zendo (Hannya Temple)
The Roundhouse Theatre
Juniper Crescent
Camden Market
Camden Lock Pl
Gilbeys Yd
Oval Road
Jamestown Road
Arlington Road
Early Ms
Inverness St
Gloucester Crs
Regent's Pk Ter
The Cavendish School
Odeon
London Capital College
Mornington Leisure Cen
Friends of the Hebrew University
The Jewish Museum
Delancey Passage
Mary Ter
Albert Street
Mornington Terrace
Mornington St
Mornington Crescent Stn
Mornington Crs
Mornington Place
Clarkson Row
Camden Town Station
Camden Road Station
Kentish Town West Stn
Kentish Town Station
Kentish Town Industrial Estate
Kentish Town Health Centre
St. Andrews Greek School
Police Station
Holmes Road
Regis Road
Kingsway Coll
Cathcart Street
Willes Road
Inkerman Road
Alma St
Raglan St
Crown Place
Anglers Lane
Wolsey Mews
Gaisford St
Patshull Road
Lawford Rd
Bartholomew Road
Rochester Road
Rochester Terrace
Rochester Place
Wilmot Pl
Castle Road
Castle Place
Lewis St
Castlehaven Rd
Clarence Way
Farrier St
Jeffrey's St
Prowse Pl
Ivor St
Bonny St
Lyme Street
Lyme Terrace
Hawley Infant School
Hawley Crs
Buck St
Water Lane
Greenland Rd
Carol St
St Michael's CE Prim Sch
St Martin's Cl
Plender Street
Greenland Pl
Weekend Arts College
Talacre Rd
Harmood St
Hadley St
Healey St
Grafton Crs
Grafton Road
Rylands Road
Dalby St
Pr of Wales Road
St Leonards Square
Newbury Mews
Surgery
Mutton Place
Forge Place
Powlett Place
Chalcot School
Holy Trinity Haverstock Hill CE Prim Sch
Collard Pl
Hartland Rd
Hawley Ms
Works
St Pauls CE Primary School
Elsworthy Rise
Elsworthy Terrace
St Edmund's Ter
St James's Ter Ms
Wells Rise
Ormonde Ter
Titchfield Road
Macclesfield Bridge
London Zoo
Gloucester Gate
Gloucester Ga Ms
Pk Village
North Bridge House Senior School
Park Village East
Regent's Park Barracks
Cumberland Terrace
Cumberland Gate
Augustus Street
Redhill Street
Christ Church School
Granby Ter
Harrington Sq
Stanhope Parade
Stanhope Street
Mackworth St
Varndell St
Cumberland Market
Medical Cen
Robert St
Everton Buildings
Netley Primary School
Netley St
Prince Regent Mews
William Road
Camden Peoples Thtr
Clarence Gdns
Compton Close
Chester Terrace
Chester Pl
Chester Ga
Cambridge Ga
Police Station
Royal College of Physicians
Longford St
Hotel
Euston Tower
Euston Centre
Euston Centre
University of Westminster
Regent's College
Open Air Theatre
Queen Mary's Garden
The Holme
Winfield House
London Central Mosque
Hanover Ter
Hanover Ter Mews
Kent Ter
Royal College of Obs. & Gyn.
London Business School
Rudolph Steiner
Clarence
Regent's College
Palgrave Gardens
Paveley Street
Lorne Cl
Alpha Cl
St Andrew's Pl
1 grid square represents 250 metres

LEIGHTON ROAD
Leighton Place
Torriano Cottages
Torriano Primary School
Hampshire Street
Busby Place
Brecon Mews
Oseney Crs
Works
Bartholomew Road
Sandall Rd
Camden School for Girls
CAMDEN ROAD
A503
A5200
CAMDEN PK ROAD
Camden Square
Murray Mews
Camden Terrace
North Villas
South Villas
St Augustine's Road
Cantelowes Road
Marquis Road
St Paul's Crescent
Rochester Ms
Rochester Sq
Day Hosp
Stratford Villas
Cobham Ms
Spiritualist Temple
Agar Grove
St Pauls Ms
St Pauls Crs
Maiden Lane
Elm Friars Walk
Broadfield Lane
Allensbury Place
Springbank Walk
Bowmore Walk
Linkwood Walk
Rosebank Walk
Camley St
Cedar Way Industrial Estate
Barker Drive
Blakeney Close
Berghoit Ms
Rossendale Wy
Weavers Wy
Ploughmans Cl
Crofters Wy
Reapers Close
Cedar Wy
ROYAL COLLEGE STREET
College Place
Mandela Street
Pratt St
ST PANCRAS WAY
College Gv
A5202
Royal Veterinary College
Richard Cobden Primary School
Granary Street
Camley Street
St Pancras Hospital
Central School Speech & Drama
CROWNDALE ROAD
Blakeney Close
Goldington Crs
Oakley Sq
OAKLEY SQ
A400
Crowndale Hlth Cen
Chalton St
Unity Ms
Charrington St
Medburn St
Goldington St
Penryn St
Platt St
Purchese St
Cheney's Pl
Clyde Court
Hampden Close
Coopers Lane
Community School
Somers Town
Community Sports Cen
Edith Neville Primary School
PANCRAS ROAD
St Mary & St Pancras CE Primary School
Polygon Rd
Ossulston Street
Brill Place
Midland Rd
Cranleigh St
Bridgeway St
Werrington St
Aldenham St
EVERSHOLT STREET
Barnby Street
Ampthill Square
Maria Fidelis Convent Upper School
St Aloysius RC Infant School
Phoenix Rd
Drummond Crs
Doric Way
Churchway
Chalton St
Lancing St
Grafton Place
Elizabeth Garrett Anderson Hosp
A4200
Euston Station
Fire Station
National Temperance Hospital
Lower School
Cardington Street
Hotel
Starcross St
Cobourg St
Melton Street
Euston Street
A501
EUSTON ROAD
UPR WOBURN PL
Friends House
University College
Wellcome Institute
Gordon St
Gower Pl
Endsleigh Gdns
Taviton Street
Euston Square Station
Birkbeck Coll
Bloomsbury
British Library
St Pancras Station
St Pancras International Youth Hostel
Camden Town Hall & St Pancras Library
King's Cross Station
Battle Br Rd
Stanley Passage
Cheney Rd
Goods Way
Camley Street
Depot
YORK WAY
A5200
Camden
Islington
Brandon Road
Tileyard Rd
Vale Royal
Works
Brewery Road
Blundell Street
Market Road
Market Estate
York Way Estate
Robert Blair Primary School
Goodinge Close
Goodinge Hlth Centre
Corporation St
North Road
Primary School
Brecknock Primary School
Surgery
Cliff Road
Cliff Villas
Rowstock Gardens
Hungerford
Hilldrop
Belmore Lane
Surr Street
Hartham Close
Hanover Trading Est
Pleasance Theatre
Lairs Close
Fleece Wk
Shearling Way
Manger Road
Ewe Close
Yoke Cl
Caledonian Road Stn
N7
EW Fact/Emile Woolf Colleges
Piper Close
Georges Road
Watkinson Road
Mackenzie
Jupiter Way
Fortuna Close
Medical Centre
Vulcan Way
Burness Close
Lockhart Close
Sophia Close
Balmoral Grove
Knowledge Point School
Armour Close
Roman Way
Wellington Mews
HM Prison
A5203
THE DRIVE
CALEDONIAN ROAD
Bradley Close
Kerwick Close
Rydston Close
Sutterton St
Coniston Way
Bunning Way
Wheelwright St
Centurion Cl
Caledonian Road & Barnsbury Station
Barnsbury
Surgery
Lyon St
Offord Rd
Crescent St
Huntingdon Street
Thornhill Crs
Bridgeman Road
Thornhill Square
Hemingford Road
Richmond Crs
Richmond Avenue
Gifford Street
Tayport Close
Airdrie Close
Carnoustie Dr
Pembroke Street
Stranraer Way
Earlsferry Wy
Bemerton Estate
Rufford Street
Randell's Rd
Bingfield Street
Bingfield
Francis Walk
Cowdenbeath Path
Wheeler Gardens
Brydon Walk
Havelock Street
Bemerton Street
Outram Place
Vibart Walk
Lawrence Place
Delhi St
Twyford St
Surgery
Matilda Street
St Andrews Primary School
Everilda Street
Julius Nyerere Close
COPENHAGEN ST B514
Surgery
Boadicea St
Treaty St
True Buddha School
Muriel St
Blessed Sacrament RC Primary School
Edward Sq
Tiber Gdns
Copenhagen Primary School
Thornhill Br Whf
Carnegie Street
Charlotte Terrace
Barnsbury Estate
The London Canal Museum
New Wharf Rd
Lavina Gv
All Saints St
Killick Street Medical Centre
Crinan St
WHARFDALE ROAD
Calshot St
Wynford Road
Priory Green Estate
Rodney Street
Pentonville
Chalbury Walk
Elizabeth Garrett Anderson School
Railway St
Albion Yard
Balfe St
Caledonia St
Works
Omega Pl
Northdown Street
Killick Street
Southern Street
Primary School
Collier St
Cumming St
Cosmopolitan Coll
Donegal Street
Cynthia St
PENTONVILLE ROAD
A501
PENTON RISE
King's Cross Thameslink Stn
KING'S CROSS ROAD
Leeke St
Wicklow St
Britannia St
Field St
Weston Rise
Lorenzo St
Surgery
Kingsway College
GRAY'S INN RD
Royal National Throat Nose & Ear Hosp
Vernon Rise
Great Percy St
Prideaux Pl
Lloyd Square
Lloyd Baker St
Magistrates Court
Police Stn
Wharton St
Granville Sq
SWINTON STREET
ACTON STREET
Frederick Street
KING'S CROSS RD
Sage Way
Wells Square
Cubitt St
Fleet Sq
WC1X
St Chad's St
Birkenhead St
Crestfield St
Belgrove St
Argyle St
Argyle Square
Counterpoint Thtr
Water Rats Thtr
Argyle Street
Surgery
Euston
Midhope St
St Pancras
Whidborne St
Cromer St
Harrison Street
Sidmouth St
Regent Sq
Kingsway College
A5200
Mecklenburgh Sq
Seddon St
Pakenham St
Eastman Dental Hosp
Hotel
Cubitt St
GRAY'S
CALTHORPE ST
Mount Pleasant (Postal Sorting Office)
FARRINGDON
Primary
Tonbridge St
Judd St
B504
Thanet St
Surgery
Sandwich St
Cartwright Gdns
Leigh St
Hastings St
Bidborough Street
Mabledon Pl
University
Uni Coll Sch of Fine Art
Flaxman Ter
Duke's Rd
Hotel
Woburn Walk
WC1H
British Medical Association
Burton St
Tavistock Sq
Woolf Mews
Tavistock
Health Centre
Brunswick Medical Centre
Handel St
HUNTER ST
Brunswick Sq
Henrietta Ms
The Foundling Museum
Coram's Fields Playground
Mecklenburgh Square
Islington
Barnsbury Sq
Barnsbury Terrace
Barnsbury St
The Courtyard
Lofting Rd
Brayfield Ter
Ripplevale Grove
Malvern Ter
Barnsbury Road
Bewdley St
Copenhagen St
Dewey Rd
Denmark Gv
Maygood St
Risinghill St
Penton St
Penton Gv
Claremont Sq
Works
Cruikshank Street
Cumberland Gdns
Great Percy St
Lloyd Sq
Amwell St
Margery Street
Farringdon
Our Lady of the Sacred Heart School
Primary School
Westbourne Road
Ellington Street
Bride Street
Faraday Close
Davey Close
Cornelia Street
Barnsbury Gv
Barn School for Girls
Beech Tree Close
Papworth Gardens
Paradise Passage
Sheringham Rd
Crossley St
Thornhill Rd
ISLIN
Thornhill Rd

6
119
ISLINGTON
Canonbury
FINSBURY
Pentonville
St Luke's
Clerkenwell
N1
EC1V
WC1X
Highbury Grove School
Highbury & Islington Station
Highbury Corner
Highbury Corner Magistrates Court
Council Building
Canonbury Station
St Paul's Road
A1199
Liverpool Road
Upper Street
A1
Essex Road
A104
Essex Road Station
Canonbury Road
A1200
New North Road
Islington Town Hall
William Tyndale Primary School
Canonbury JMI School
Laycock Primary School
Barnsbury School for Girls
Almeida Theatre
Kings Head Theatre
Screen on the Green Cinema
Islington Green
The Business Design Centre
N1 Shopping Centre
Angel Station
Pentonville Road
A501
City Road
St John St
Goswell Road
Sadler's Wells Theatre
Lillian Baylis Thr
City University
Moorfields Eye Hospital
Museum of London
Eagle Whf Road
B144
Shepherdess Walk
Bath Street
Old Street
Old St Station
Lever Street
B502
Percival St
Rosebery Avenue
A401
Kingsway College
Mount Pleasant (Postal Sorting Office)
Finsbury Health Cen
Finsbury Leisure Complex
Hanover Primary School
London Open College
Canonbury Business Centre
Police Stn
Pentonville Police Stn
Consulate of Eritrea
Elizabeth Garrett Anderson School
Moreland Primary School
12
5
1 grid square represents 250 metres

Dalston
Kingsland
De Beauvoir Town
Haggerston
Hoxton
SHOREDITCH
BETHNAL GREEN
Haggerston Park
Shoreditch Park
Weavers Fields
KINGSLAND ROAD
KINGSLAND HIGH ST
SHOREDITCH HIGH ST
QUEENSBRIDGE ROAD
SOUTHGATE ROAD
BALLS POND ROAD
DALSTON LANE
GRAHAM ROAD
HACKNEY ROAD
COLUMBIA ROAD
OLD STREET
GREAT EASTERN STREET
CURTAIN ROAD
PITFIELD STREET
NEW NORTH ROAD
EAST ROAD
CALVERT AVENUE
GOSSET STREET
SQUIRRIES ST
WARNER PLACE
BETHNAL GREEN ROAD
CHESHIRE STREET
DUNBRIDGE STREET
OLD BETHNAL GN RD
CLUB ROW
A10
A104
A1208
A1209
A5201
B101
B102
B108
B118
B122
B135
E8
119
140
13
H
J
K
L
M
N
P
1
2
3
4
5
6
7
8
9
10
Dalston Kingsland Station
Kingsland Shop Cen
Colvestone Primary School
St Judes & St Pauls CE Primary School
De Beauvoir Primary School
Holy Trinity Primary School
Kingsland Health Cen
Metropolitan Business Cen
Queensbridge Infant School
Gayhurst Primary School
Laburnum Primary Sch
Haggerston Swimming Pool
Sebright Primary School
Whitmore Primary School
Burbage School
St Leonards Hospital
Hoxton Hall Community Thtr
Comprehensive School
Trans Atlantic College
Geffrye Mus
Haggerston School
Hackney City Farm
Hackney Community College
St John the Baptist CE Primary Sch
City Coll of Higher Education
Brick Lane Music Hall
Midway Mission Hosp
Virginia Primary Sch
Columbia Primary School
Bethnal Green Technology College
Tower Hamlets College
Lawdale Junior Sch
St Matthias CE Primary School
Shoreditch County Court
Boys School
The Liberty City Clnc
Hackney Downs

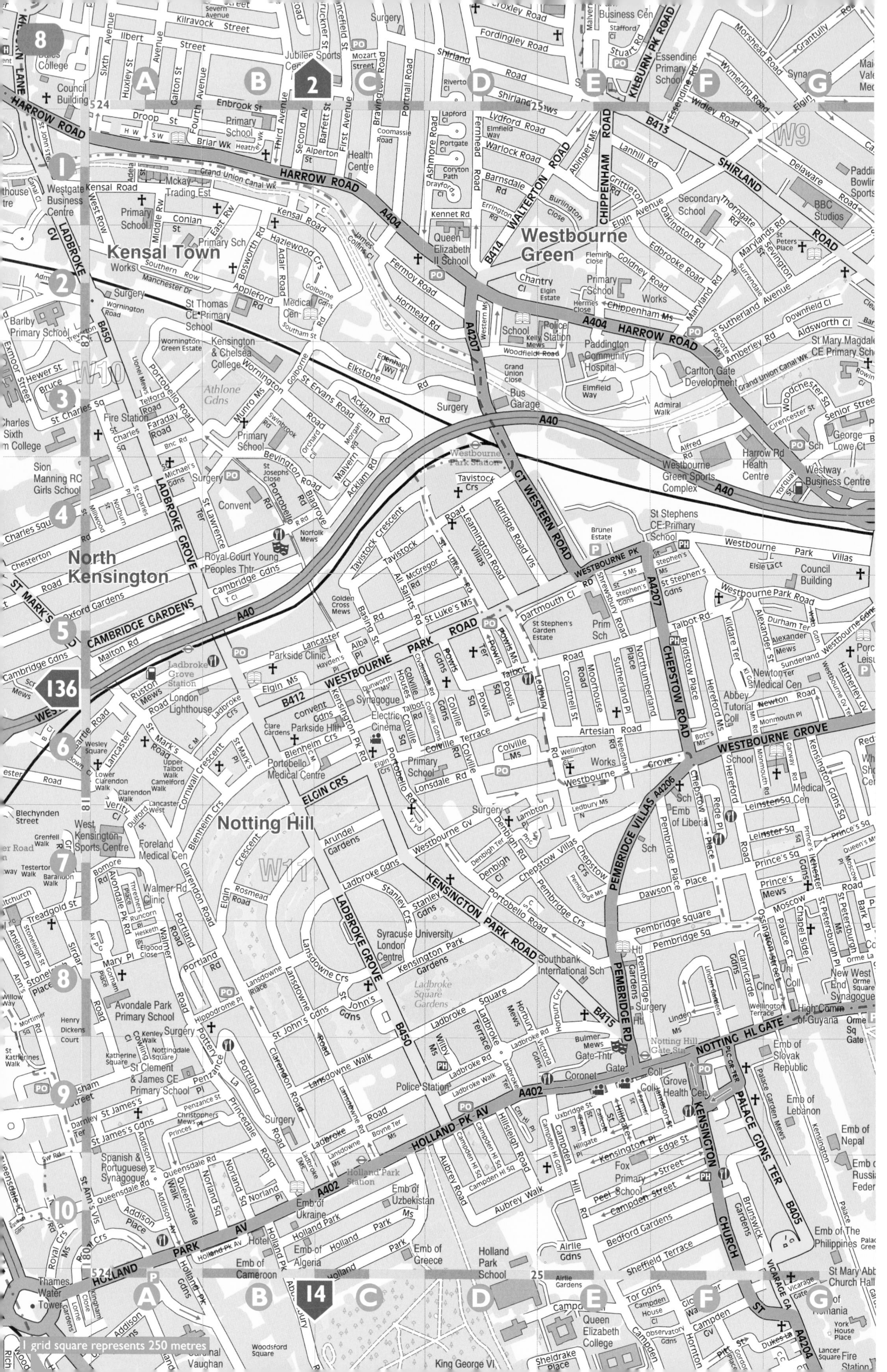
8
2
14
136
A
B
C
D
E
F
G
1
2
3
4
5
6
7
8
9
10
524
25
W9
W10
W11
Kensal Town
Westbourne Green
North Kensington
Notting Hill
HARROW ROAD
A404
A40
A4207
A4206
A402
B412
B413
B414
B415
B450
B405
A4204
LADBROKE GROVE
CAMBRIDGE GARDENS
ST MARK'S RD
GT WESTERN ROAD
WESTBOURNE PARK ROAD
WESTBOURNE GROVE
CHEPSTOW ROAD
PEMBRIDGE VILLAS
PEMBRIDGE RD
KENSINGTON PARK ROAD
ELGIN CRS
NOTTING HL GATE
HOLLAND PK AV
HOLLAND PARK AV
KENSINGTON CHURCH ST
PALACE GDNS TER
SHIRLAND ROAD
WALTERTON ROAD
CHIPPENHAM ROAD
KILBURN PK ROAD
Grand Union Canal Wk
Westbourne Park Station
Ladbroke Grove Station
Notting Hill Gate Stn
Holland Park Station
Kensington & Chelsea College
Paddington Community Hospital
Syracuse University London Centre
Ladbroke Square Gardens
Royal Court Young Peoples Thtr
Gate Thtr
Coronet
Electric Cinema
Westbourne Green Sports Complex
BBC Studios
Holland Park School
Queen Elizabeth College
Thames Water Tower
Avondale Park Primary School
Fox Primary School
1 grid square represents 250 metres

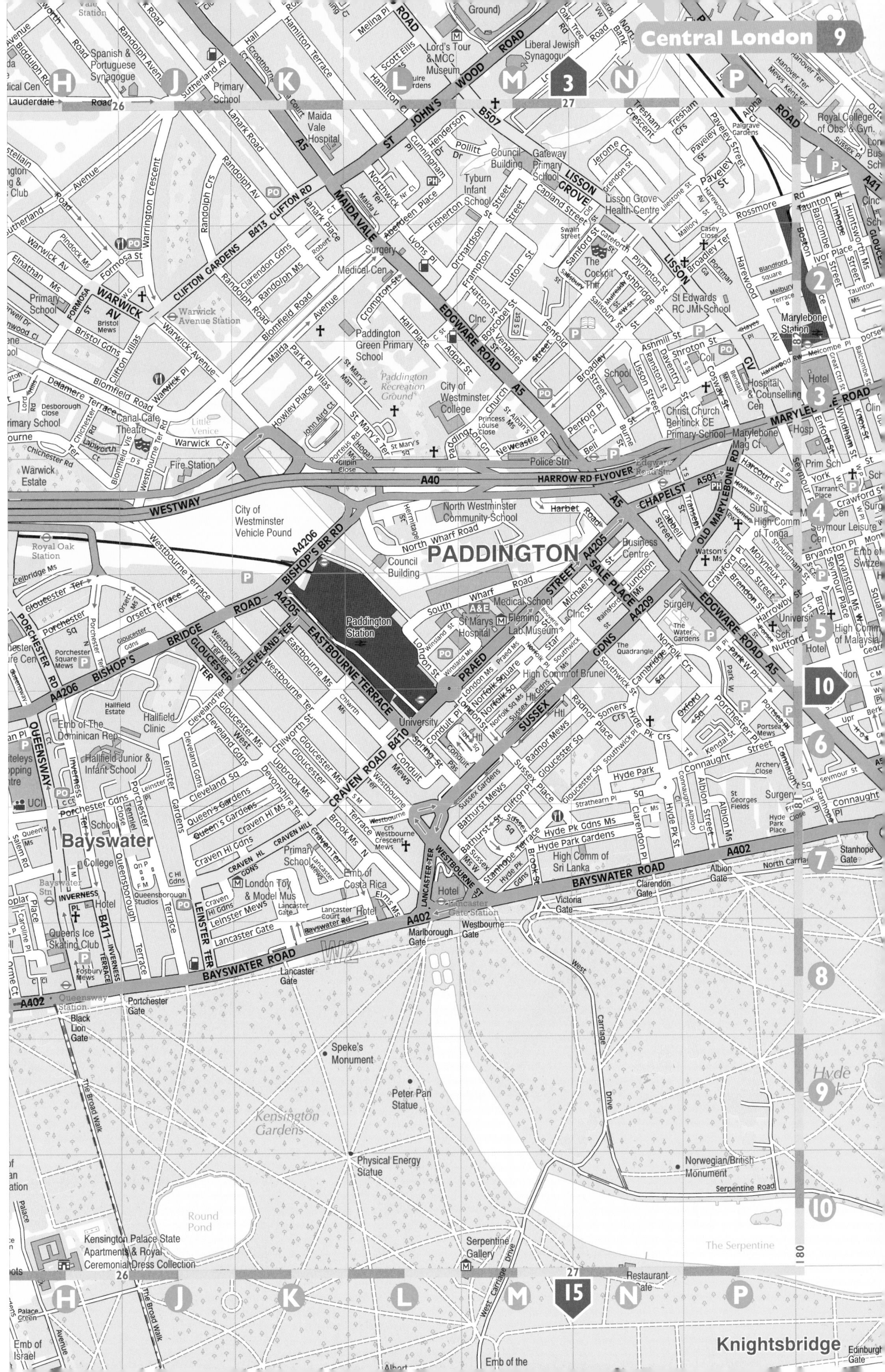
PADDINGTON
Bayswater
Knightsbridge
Kensington Gardens
Hyde Park
The Serpentine
Round Pond
W2
Paddington Station
Royal Oak Station
Warwick Avenue Station
Marylebone Station
Edgware Road Stn
Lancaster Gate Station
Queensway Station
Bayswater Stn
Maida Vale Hospital
Lord's Tour & MCC Museum
Liberal Jewish Synagogue
Spanish & Portuguese Synagogue
Primary School
Paddington Green Primary School
Paddington Recreation Ground
City of Westminster College
City of Westminster Vehicle Pound
North Westminster Community School
Council Building
Gateway Primary School
Tyburn Infant School
Lisson Grove Health Centre
The Cockpit Thtr
St Edwards RC JMI School
Christ Church Bentinck CE Primary School
Hospital & Counselling Cen
Marylebone Mag Ct
Police Stn
Fire Station
Canal Cafe Theatre
Little Venice
Warwick Estate
St Marys Hospital
Fleming Lab Museum
Medical School
Business Centre
The Water Gardens
The Quadrangle
High Comm of Brunei
High Comm of Tonga
High Comm of Malaysia
High Comm of Sri Lanka
Seymour Leisure Cen
Emb of The Dominican Rep
Emb of Costa Rica
Emb of Israel
Hallfield Estate
Hallfield Clinic
Hallfield Junior & Infant School
Queens Ice Skating Club
London Toy & Model Mus
Speke's Monument
Peter Pan Statue
Physical Energy Statue
Norwegian/British Monument
Serpentine Gallery
Kensington Palace State Apartments & Royal Ceremonial Dress Collection
The Broad Walk
West Carriage Drive
Serpentine Road
Restaurant Cafe
Marlborough Gate
Westbourne Gate
Victoria Gate
Albion Gate
Clarendon Gate
Stanhope Gate
Lancaster Gate
Black Lion Gate
Portchester Gate
Edinburgh Gate
WESTWAY
HARROW RD FLYOVER
A40
BISHOP'S BRIDGE ROAD
A4206
EASTBOURNE TERRACE
EDGWARE ROAD
A5
MAIDA VALE
ST JOHN'S WOOD ROAD
B507
LISSON GROVE
MARYLEBONE ROAD
OLD MARYLEBONE RD
A501
PRAED ST
A4209
SUSSEX GDNS
CRAVEN ROAD
B410
BAYSWATER ROAD
A402
QUEENSWAY
INVERNESS TERRACE
B411
LEINSTER TER
GLOUCESTER TER
CLEVELAND TER
WESTBOURNE TER
CLIFTON GARDENS
B413 CLIFTON RD
WARWICK AV
FORMOSA ST
PORCHESTER RD
SALE PLACE
CHAPEL ST
LANCASTER TER
H J K L M N P
3
15
10
26
27
1 2 3 4 5 6 7 8 9 10

10
4
528
29
A
B
C
D
E
F
G
1
2
3
4
5
6
7
8
9
10
9
16
Open-Air Theatre
Chester Road
Outer Circle
Inner Circle
Regent's College
Royal College of Obs. & Gyn.
London Business School
Rudolph Steiner Hall
Sherlock Holmes Mus
Madame Tussaud's
Planetarium
Marylebone Station
Lisson Grove
MARYLEBONE ROAD
MARYLEBONE
Royal College of Physicians
Park Square
International Community School
Royal Academy of Music
Central London Co-Court
Great Portland Street Stn
Royal National Orthopaedic Hosp
EUSTON ROAD
Euston Tower
Euston Centre
University of Westminster
British Telecom Twr
PADDINGTON ST
King Edward VII Hosp for Officers
Devonshire Hospital
Wallace Collection
PORTMAN SQUARE
BAKER STREET
GLOUCESTER PLACE
WIGMORE STREET
Wigmore Hall
Royal Society of Medicine
BBC & Visitor Centre
CAVENDISH PL
OXFORD ST
Oxford Circus Station
Bond Street Stn
Marble Arch Station
Marble Arch
CUMBERLAND GATE
Speakers Corner
West London Synagogue
West End Great Synagogue
Odeon
PARK LANE
Roosevelt Memorial
Grosvenor Square
Emb of USA
NEW BOND STREET
REGENT STREET
Palladium Thtr
Mayfair
Royal Institution (Faraday Museum)
Royal Academy of Arts
Burlington Arcade
PICCADILLY
Green Park Station
Green Park
Hyde Park
The Serpentine
Serpentine Road
South Carriage Drive
Apsley House, The Wellington Museum
Hyde Park Corner Stn
HYDE PK CORNER
Wellington Arch
Queen Mother Gate
Lancaster House
Spencer House
Albert Gate
Brook Gate
Grosvenor Gate
Stanhope Gate
Curzon St
A4202
A40
A41
A501
A5204
A4
1 grid square represents 250 metres

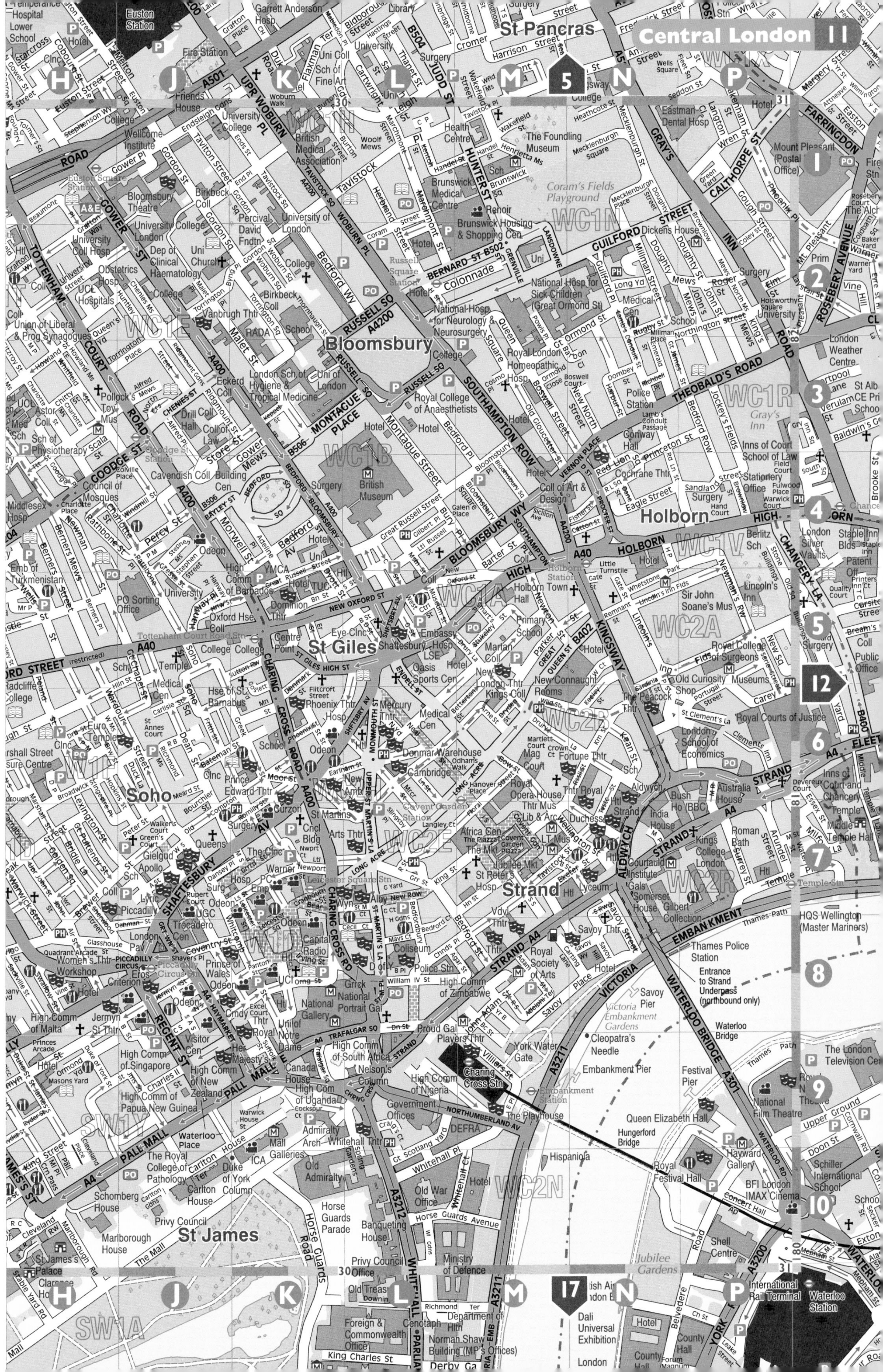
St Pancras
Euston Station
Bloomsbury
St Giles
Holborn
Soho
Strand
St James
WC1H
WC1N
WC1E
WC1B
WC1A
WC1R
WC1V
WC2A
WC2B
WC2H
WC2E
WC2R
WC2N
W1F
W1D
SW1Y
SW1A
The Foundling Museum
Coram's Fields Playground
University College London
University of London
British Museum
Russell Square Station
Goodge St Station
Tottenham Court Road Stn
Holborn Station
Covent Garden Station
Leicester Square Stn
Piccadilly Circus Stn
Charing Cross Stn
Embankment Station
Temple Stn
Waterloo Station
Sir John Soane's Mus
Royal Courts of Justice
London School of Economics
Royal Opera House
National Gallery
National Portrait Gal
Nelson's Column
Trafalgar Sq
Horse Guards Parade
Banqueting House
Ministry of Defence
Old War Office
Cleopatra's Needle
Victoria Embankment Gardens
Waterloo Bridge
Royal Festival Hall
Queen Elizabeth Hall
Hayward Gallery
National Film Theatre
BFI London IMAX Cinema
Jubilee Gardens
Hungerford Bridge
Somerset House
Courtauld Institute Gals
HQS Wellington (Master Mariners)
Thames Police Station
Entrance to Strand Underpass (northbound only)
EUSTON ROAD
TOTTENHAM COURT ROAD
GOWER ST
UPR WOBURN PL
WOBURN PL
SOUTHAMPTON ROW
KINGSWAY
ALDWYCH
STRAND
HIGH HOLBORN
NEW OXFORD ST
OXFORD STREET
CHARING CROSS ROAD
SHAFTESBURY AV
REGENT ST
HAYMARKET
PALL MALL
WHITEHALL
VICTORIA EMBANKMENT
GRAY'S INN ROAD
THEOBALD'S ROAD
GUILFORD STREET
CHANCERY LA
ROSEBERY AVENUE
FARRINGDON
H
J
K
L
M
N
P
1
2
3
4
5
6
7
8
9
10
12
17

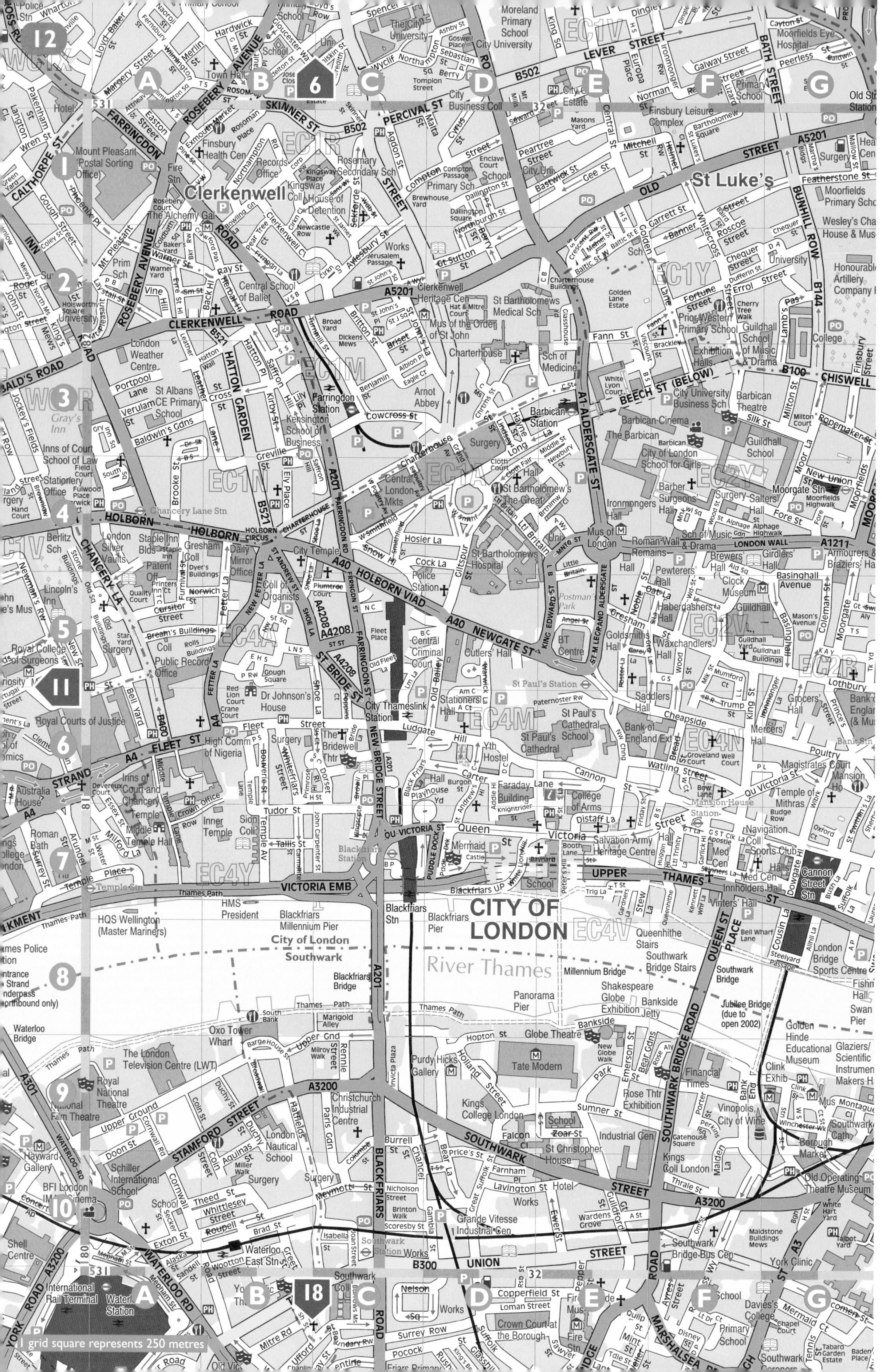

12
6
11
18
A
B
C
D
E
F
G
1
2
3
4
5
6
7
8
9
10
Clerkenwell
St Luke's
CITY OF LONDON
River Thames
City of London
Southwark
EC1R
EC1V
EC1M
EC1N
EC1A
EC1Y
EC2Y
EC2V
EC2R
EC4A
EC4M
EC4N
EC4Y
EC4V
WC1X
WC1R
WC1V
ROSEBERY AVENUE
FARRINGDON
SKINNER ST
PERCIVAL ST
CLERKENWELL ROAD
HOLBORN
HOLBORN CIRCUS
HOLBORN VIAD
NEWGATE ST
CHARTERHOUSE
FARRINGDON RD
FARRINGDON ST
NEW BRIDGE STREET
ST BRIDE ST
FLEET ST
STRAND
VICTORIA EMB
QU VICTORIA ST
UPPER THAMES ST
QUEEN ST PLACE
SOUTHWARK BRIDGE ROAD
SOUTHWARK STREET
STAMFORD STREET
BLACKFRIARS ROAD
WATERLOO RD
UNION STREET
OLD STREET
BUNHILL ROW
CHISWELL
BEECH ST (BELOW)
LONDON WALL
ALDERSGATE ST
ST M LE GRAND ALDERSGATE
KING EDWARD ST
CHANCERY LA
HATTON GARDEN
GOSWELL ROAD
ST JOHN STREET
LEVER STREET
BATH STREET
CALTHORPE ST
GRAY'S INN ROAD
THEOBALD'S ROAD
A5201
A201
A40
A4
A4208
A1211
A3200
B502
B521
B400
B100
B144
B300
Mount Pleasant Postal Sorting Office
Finsbury Health Cen
Farringdon Station
Barbican Station
Moorgate Stn
Chancery Lane Stn
City Thameslink Station
Blackfriars Station
Blackfriars Stn
Mansion House Station
Cannon Street Stn
Temple Stn
Southwark Station
Waterloo East Stn
Waterloo Station
International Rail Terminal
St Paul's Station
St Paul's Cathedral
St Bartholomews Hospital
St Bartholomew's The Great
Smithfield
Central London Mkts
Charterhouse
The Barbican
Barbican Theatre
Barbican Cinema
Guildhall
Guildhall School of Music & Drama
Museum of London
Bank of England Ext
Tate Modern
Globe Theatre
Shakespeare Globe Exhibition
Millennium Bridge
Blackfriars Bridge
Blackfriars Millennium Pier
Blackfriars Pier
HMS President
HQS Wellington (Master Mariners)
Royal National Theatre
National Film Theatre
The London Television Centre (LWT)
Oxo Tower Wharf
Waterloo Bridge
BFI London IMAX Cinema
Royal Courts of Justice
Inns of Court School of Law
Lincoln's Inn
Gray's Inn
Inner Temple
Middle Temple Hall
Central Criminal Court
Dr Johnson's House
City University
Moorfields Eye Hospital
Finsbury Leisure Complex
Golden Lane Estate
Honourable Artillery Company
Southwark Bridge
Jubilee Bridge (due to open 2002)
Golden Hinde Educational Museum
Borough Market
Southwark Cath
Clink Exhib
Financial Times
Vinopolis, City of Wine
Kings College London
Mermaid Theatre
College of Arms
Faraday Building
Salvation Army Heritage Centre
1 grid square represents 250 metres

SPITALFIELDS
Whitechapel
St George in the East
Wappin
OLD STREET
SHOREDITCH HIGH ST
CURTAIN ROAD
GREAT EASTERN STREET
COMMERCIAL STREET
CITY ROAD
BISHOPSGATE
WHITECHAPEL ROAD
COMMERCIAL ROAD
WHITECHAPEL HIGH ST
ALDGATE HIGH ST
HOUNDSDITCH
CAMOMILE ST
LONDON WALL
MINORIES
MANSELL ST
LEMAN ST
CABLE STREET
ROYAL MINT ST
EAST SMITHFIELD
THE HIGHWAY
TOWER HILL
LWR THAMES ST
TOWER BRIDGE APPROACH
TOWER BR RD
TOOLEY STREET
BERMONDSEY STREET
BOROUGH HIGH ST
KG WILLIAM ST
GRACECHURCH ST
CHESHIRE STREET
SCLATER STREET
BRICK LANE
VALLANCE RD
NEW ROAD
CANNON STREET ROAD
Liverpool Street Station
Aldgate Bus Station
Shoreditch Station
Spitalfields Market Hall
Tower of London
Tower Bridge
St Katharine Docks
St Katharine Pier
London Bridge Station
HMS Belfast
Greater London Authority Headquarters (City Hall)
Tower Millennium Pier
London Bridge City Pier
News International
City of London
Southwark
EC2A
EC2M
EC2N
EC3A
EC3V
EC3M
EC3R
EC3N
H
J
K
L
M
N
P
1
2
3
4
5
6
7
8
9
10
7
19
140
33
34
80
81
82

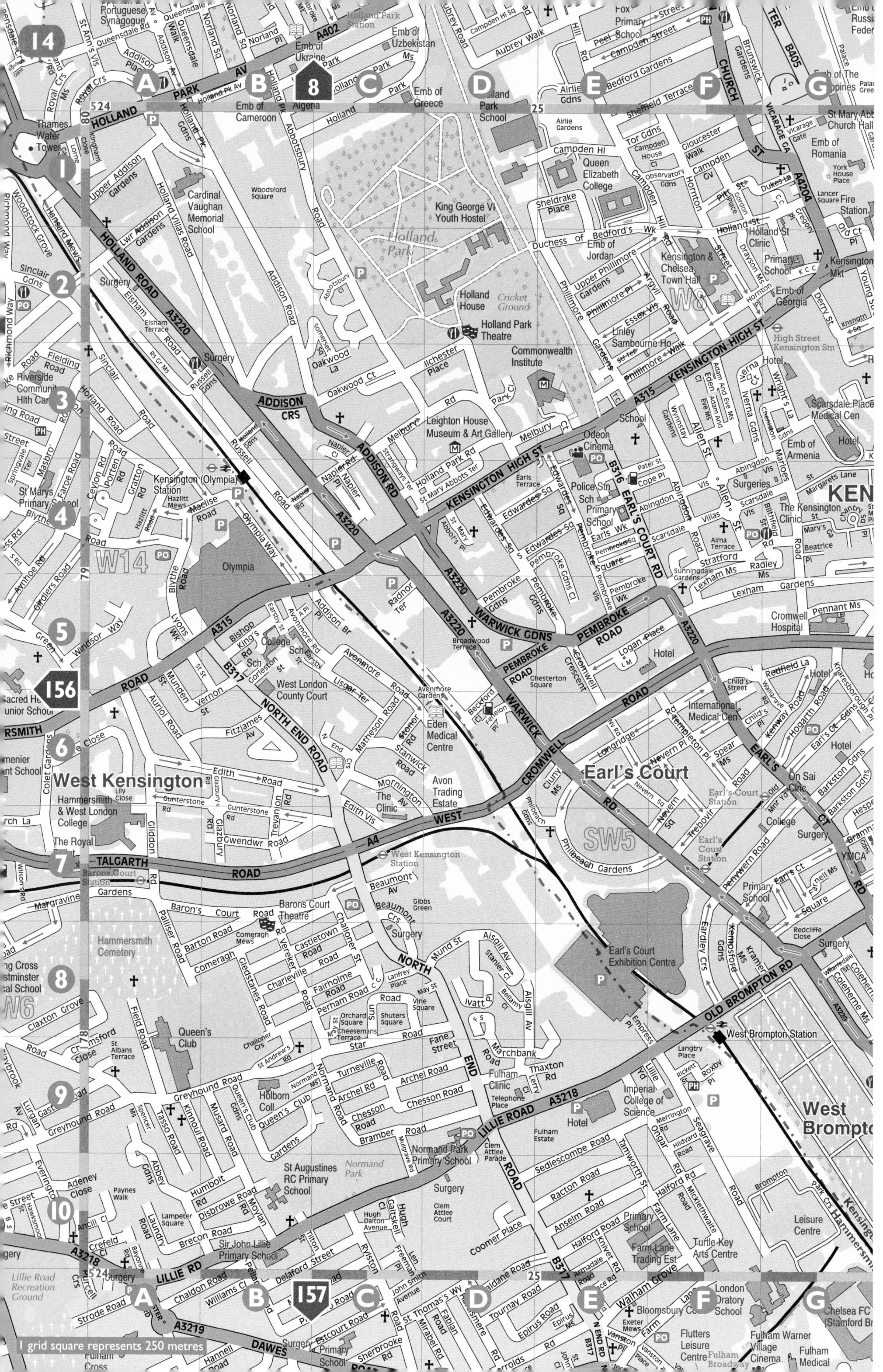

14
8
156
157
524
25
79
178
Holland Park Station
Emb of Uzbekistan
Emb of Ukraine
Emb of Algeria
Emb of Cameroon
Emb of Greece
Holland Park School
Portuguese Synagogue
Thames Water Tower
HOLLAND PARK AV
A402
Queensdale Rd
Norland Sq
Campden Hl Sq
Aubrey Walk
Fox Primary School
Peel St
Campden Street
Bedford Gardens
Sheffield Terrace
CHURCH ST
VICARAGE GA
A4204
B405
Emb of The Philippines
St Mary Abb Church Hall
Emb of Romania
York House Place
Lancer Square
Fire Station
Airlie Gdns
Campden Hl
Queen Elizabeth College
King George VI Youth Hostel
Holland Park
Cardinal Vaughan Memorial School
Woodsford Square
Upper Addison Gardens
Lwr Addison Gardens
Holland Villas Road
Addison Road
Abbotsbury Road
Holland House
Cricket Ground
Holland Park Theatre
Commonwealth Institute
Sheldrake Place
Duchess of Bedford's Wk
Emb of Jordan
Upper Phillimore Gardens
Phillimore Gardens
Kensington & Chelsea Town Hall
W8
Holland St Clinic
Primary School
Emb of Georgia
Kensington Mkt
High Street Kensington Stn
KENSINGTON HIGH ST
A315
Ilchester Place
Oakwood Ct
Leighton House Museum & Art Gallery
Melbury Rd
Odeon Cinema
Earls Terrace
Edwardes Sq
Police Stn
B316
EARL'S COURT RD
Abingdon Road
Allen St
Emb of Armenia
Scarsdale Place Medical Cen
Hotel
The Kensington Clinic
KEN
HOLLAND ROAD
A3220
Surgery
Sinclair Gdns
Sinclair Road
Elsham Road
Riverside Community Hlth Care
Hofland Road
St Marys Primary School
Kensington (Olympia) Station
Olympia
Olympia Way
ADDISON CRS
ADDISON RD
Russell Road
W14
Napier Rd
Radnor Ter
Blythe Road
Pembroke Road
Pembroke Gdns
Lexham Gardens
Stratford Rd
Cromwell Hospital
Pennant Ms
WARWICK GDNS
PEMBROKE ROAD
Logan Place
Hotel
A315
Bishop King's Rd
College
West London County Court
NORTH END ROAD
B317
Avonmore Road
Lisgar Ter
Matheson Road
Eden Medical Centre
Chesterton Square
WARWICK ROAD
CROMWELL ROAD
International Medical Cen
Earl's Court
Nevern Sq
Earl's Court Station
Barkston Gdns
College
Surgery
YMCA
West Kensington
Hammersmith & West London College
Edith Road
Gunterstone Rd
Gwendwr Road
Avon Trading Estate
The Clinic
WEST CROMWELL ROAD
A4
TALGARTH ROAD
West Kensington Station
Barons Court Station
SW5
Philbeach Gardens
Earl's Court Exhibition Centre
Margravine Gardens
Hammersmith Cemetery
Barons Court Theatre
Gibbs Green
Queen's Club
NORTH END
Old Brompton Rd
West Brompton Station
Redcliffe Square
Fulham Clinic
Imperial College of Science
Greyhound Road
Holborn Coll
LILLIE ROAD
A3218
Normand Park Primary School
St Augustines RC Primary School
Fulham Estate
Sedlescombe Road
Anselm Road
Farm Lane Trading Est
Turtle Key Arts Centre
West Brompton
Leisure Centre
Sir John Lillie Primary School
Lillie Road Recreation Ground
A3219
DAWES RD
Walham Grove
London Oratory School
Flutters Leisure Centre
Fulham Broadway
Fulham Warner Village Cinema
Chelsea FC (Stamford Br)
1 grid square represents 250 metres

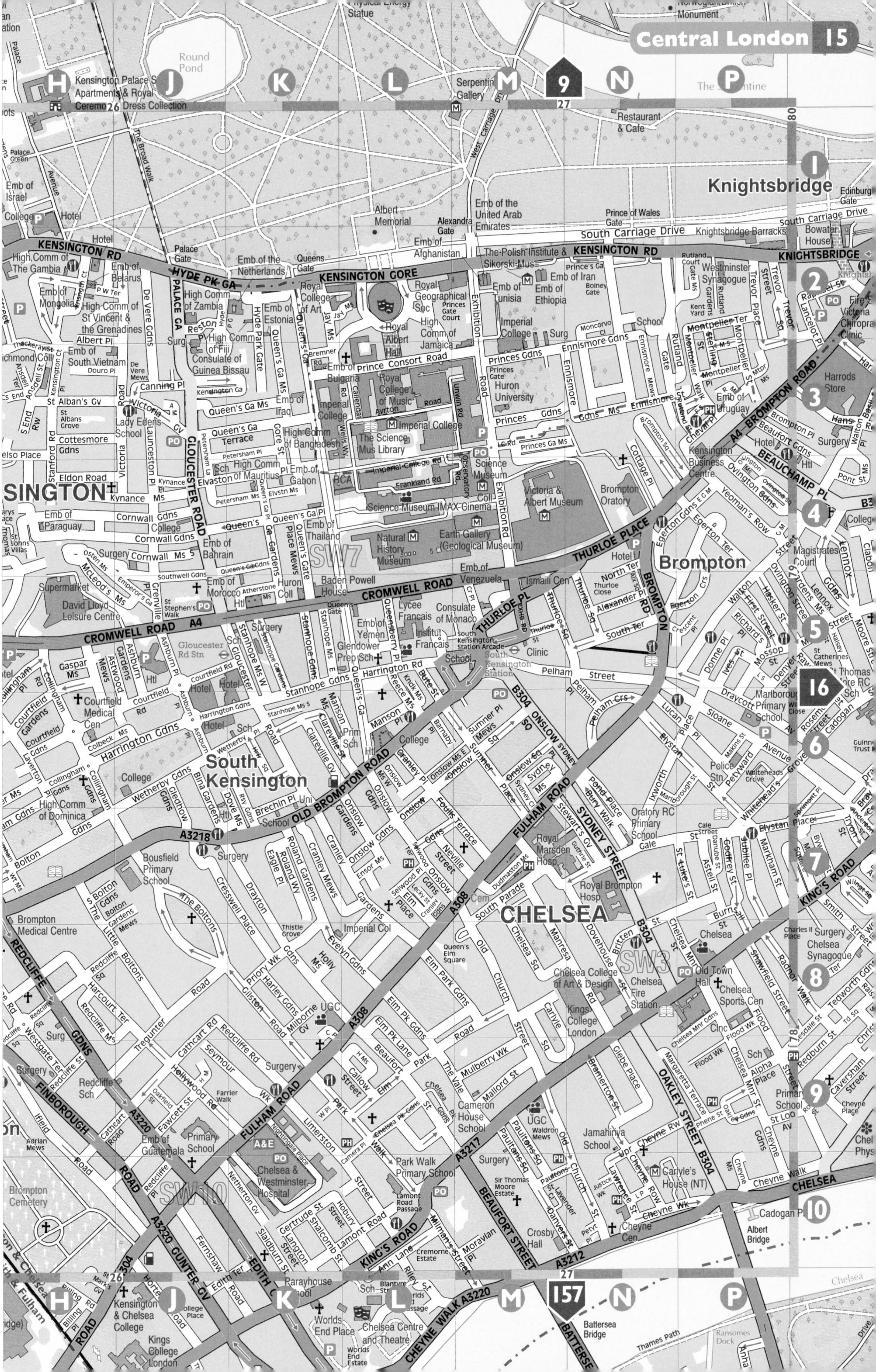
Round Pond
Physical Energy Statue
Norwegian/British Monument
Kensington Palace State Apartments & Royal Ceremonial Dress Collection
The Broad Walk
Serpentine Gallery
West Carriage Dr
The Serpentine
Restaurant & Cafe
Knightsbridge
Edinburgh Gate
Albert Memorial
Alexandra Gate
Emb of the United Arab Emirates
Prince of Wales Gate
South Carriage Drive
Knightsbridge Barracks
Bowater House
KENSINGTON RD
KNIGHTSBRIDGE
HYDE PK GA
KENSINGTON GORE
Palace Gate
Queens Gate
Emb of the Netherlands
Emb of Afghanistan
The Polish Institute & Sikorski Mus
Emb of Iran
Emb of Tunisia
Emb of Ethiopia
High Comm of The Gambia
Emb of Belarus
Emb of Mongolia
High Comm of St Vincent & the Grenadines
Emb of South Vietnam
High Comm of Zambia
High Comm of Fiji
Consulate of Guinea Bissau
Emb of Estonia
Royal College of Art
Royal Albert Hall
Royal Geographical Soc
High Comm of Jamaica
Imperial College
Westminster Synagogue
Harrods Store
Emb of Bulgaria
Prince Consort Road
Royal College of Music
Imperial College
The Science Mus Library
Emb of Iraq
High Comm of Bangladesh
High Comm of Mauritius
Emb of Gabon
Emb of Uruguay
Princes Gate Huron University
Ennismore Gdns
Kensington Business Centre
BROMPTON ROAD
BEAUCHAMP PL
Science Museum
Science Museum IMAX Cinema
Victoria & Albert Museum
Brompton Oratory
Natural History Museum
Earth Gallery (Geological Museum)
Emb of Thailand
SW7
Emb of Paraguay
Emb of Bahrain
Emb of Morocco
Emb of Venezuela
Ismaili Cen
THURLOE PLACE
Brompton
Magistrates Court
SINGTON
GLOUCESTER ROAD
CROMWELL ROAD
A4
Baden Powell House
Lycee Francais
Consulate of Monaco
Emb of Yemen
Institut Francais
Glendower Prep Sch
Supermarket
David Lloyd Leisure Centre
Gloucester Rd Stn
South Kensington Station
South Kensington Station Arcade
Clinic
Courtfield Medical Cen
Harrington Gdns
South Kensington
High Comm of Dominica
College
OLD BROMPTON ROAD
A3218
FULHAM ROAD
SYDNEY STREET
ONSLOW SQ
Royal Marsden Hosp
Oratory RC Primary School
Police Stn
Marlborough Primary School
Sloane Avenue
Bousfield Primary School
The Boltons
Brompton Medical Centre
Imperial Col
CHELSEA
Royal Brompton Hosp
SW3
Chelsea College of Art & Design
Chelsea Fire Station
Kings College London
Old Town Hall
Chelsea Sports Cen
Surgery Chelsea Synagogue
KING'S ROAD
REDCLIFFE GDNS
FINBOROUGH ROAD
Emb of Guatemala
Primary School
UGC
A308
Chelsea & Westminster Hospital
Brompton Cemetery
SW10
Park Walk Primary School
Cameron House School
Jamahiriya School
Carlyle's House (NT)
Sir Thomas Moore Estate
Crosby Hall
BEAUFORT STREET
OAKLEY STREET B304
Cheyne Cen
Cadogan Pier
Albert Bridge
CHELSEA
A3220
A3212
Kensington & Chelsea College
Kings College London
Worlds End Place
Chelsea Centre and Theatre
CHEYNE WALK A3220
BATTERSEA
Battersea Bridge
Ransomes Dock
Thames Path
Chelsea
H J K L M N P
9 16 157
1 2 3 4 5 6 7 8 9 10
26 27 78 79 80

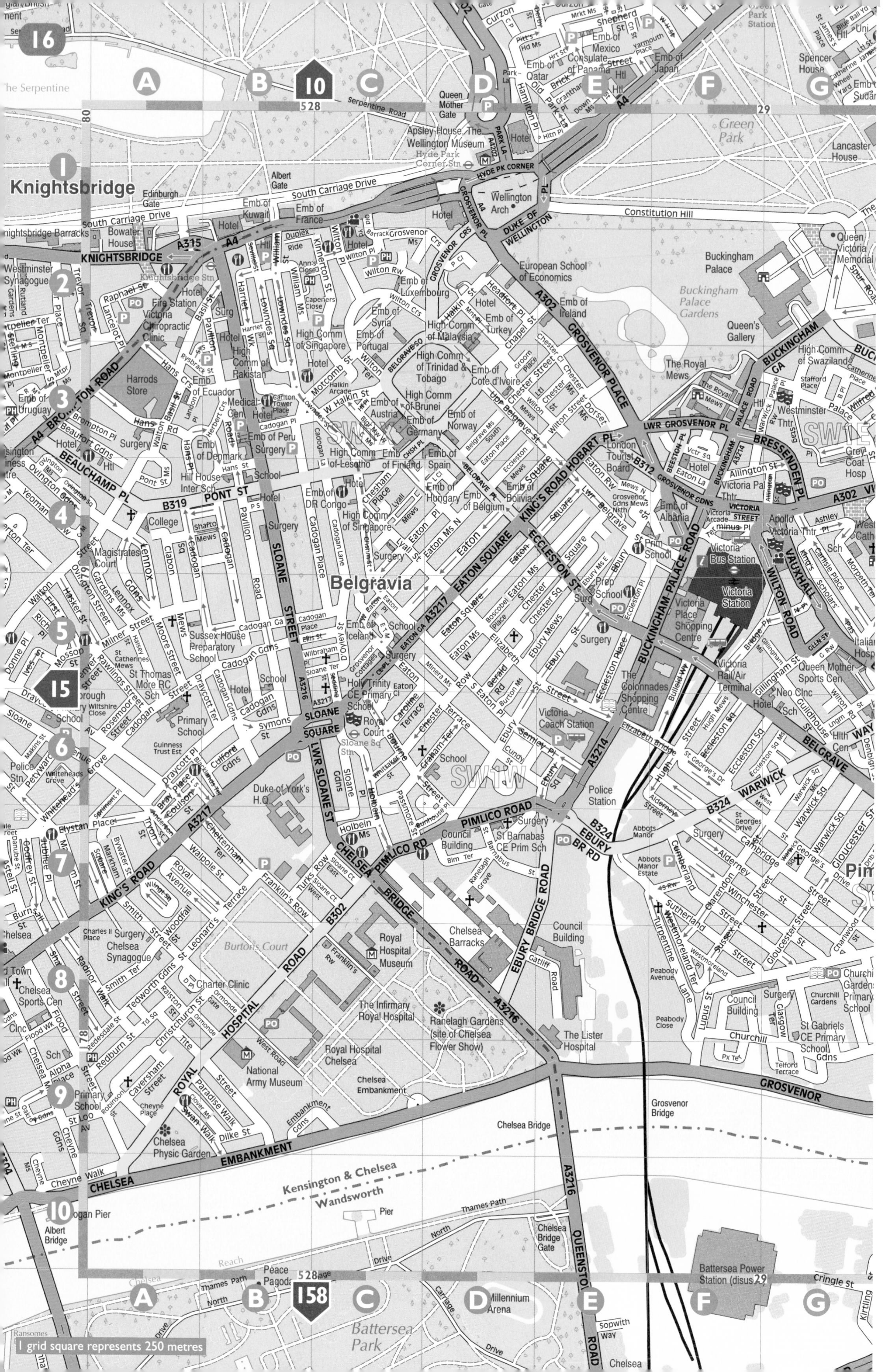

16
10
15
158
A
B
C
D
E
F
G
1
2
3
4
5
6
7
8
9
10
528
29
The Serpentine
Serpentine Road
Queen Mother Gate
Apsley House, The Wellington Museum
Hyde Park Corner Stn
HYDE PK CORNER
Wellington Arch
Constitution Hill
Green Park
Green Park Station
Spencer House
Lancaster House
Queen Victoria Memorial
Buckingham Palace
Buckingham Palace Gardens
Queen's Gallery
The Royal Mews
Knightsbridge
Knightsbridge Barracks
KNIGHTSBRIDGE
Knightsbridge Stn
South Carriage Drive
Albert Gate
Edinburgh Gate
Emb of Kuwait
Emb of France
Harrods Store
BROMPTON ROAD
BEAUCHAMP PL
PONT ST
SLOANE STREET
Belgravia
EATON SQUARE
KING'S ROAD
ECCLESTON ST
GROSVENOR PLACE
BUCKINGHAM PALACE ROAD
LWR GROSVENOR PL
BRESSENDEN PL
VICTORIA STREET
VAUXHALL
WILTON ROAD
Victoria Station
Victoria Bus Station
Victoria Coach Station
Victoria Place Shopping Centre
Victoria Rail/Air Terminal
The Colonnades Shopping Centre
European School of Economics
London Tourist Board
SLOANE SQUARE
Sloane Sq Stn
Royal Court
Holy Trinity CE Primary School
Duke of York's H.Q.
LWR SLOANE ST
PIMLICO ROAD
CHELSEA BRIDGE ROAD
EBURY BRIDGE ROAD
Chelsea Barracks
Royal Hospital Museum
The Infirmary Royal Hospital
Royal Hospital Chelsea
Ranelagh Gardens (site of Chelsea Flower Show)
Burton's Court
ROYAL HOSPITAL ROAD
National Army Museum
Chelsea Physic Garden
CHELSEA EMBANKMENT
Chelsea Embankment
The Lister Hospital
GROSVENOR
Grosvenor Bridge
Chelsea Bridge
Kensington & Chelsea
Wandsworth
Thames Path
Chelsea Bridge Gate
QUEENSTOWN ROAD
Battersea Power Station (disus
Millennium Arena
Battersea Park
Peace Pagoda
Albert Bridge
Cringle St
Chelsea Sports Cen
Chelsea Synagogue
Westminster Synagogue
Sussex House Preparatory School
Police Station
Council Building
St Barnabas CE Prim Sch
St Gabriels CE Primary School
Churchill Gardens
Queen Mother Sports Cen
BELGRAVE
WARWICK
Belgravia
1 grid square represents 250 metres

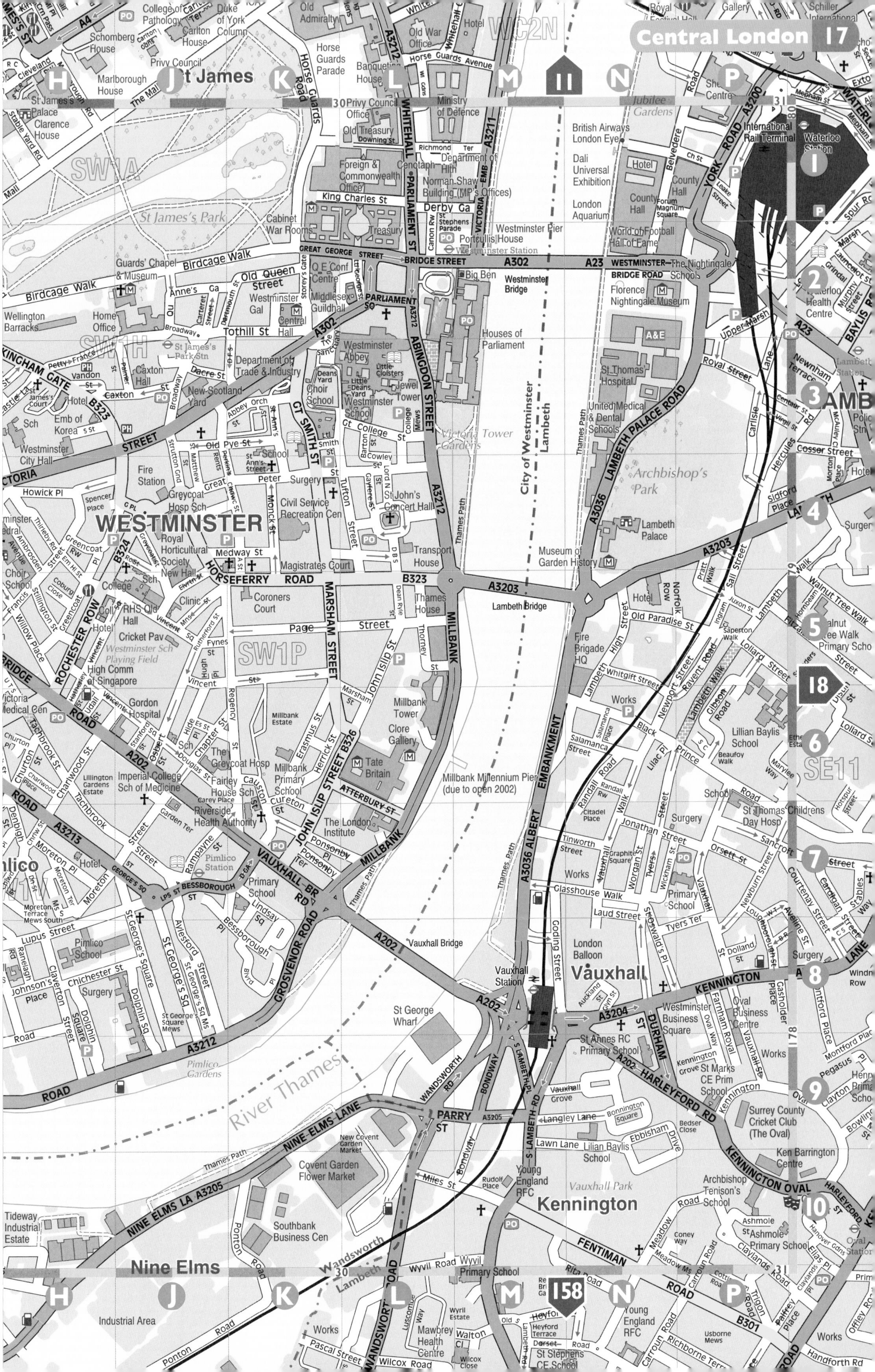
St James
SW1A
St James's Park
Birdcage Walk
Horse Guards Road
Horse Guards Parade
Whitehall
Parliament St
Ministry of Defence
Foreign & Commonwealth Office
King Charles St
Cabinet War Rooms
Treasury
Great George Street
Bridge Street
Westminster Bridge Road
Westminster Bridge
Big Ben
Houses of Parliament
Parliament Sq
Westminster Abbey
Jewel Tower
Abingdon Street
Victoria Tower Gardens
British Airways London Eye
Dali Universal Exhibition
London Aquarium
County Hall
Jubilee Gardens
Westminster Pier
Waterloo Station
International Rail Terminal
York Road
Florence Nightingale Museum
St Thomas' Hospital
Lambeth Palace Road
Archbishop's Park
Lambeth Palace
Museum of Garden History
Lambeth Bridge
City of Westminster
Lambeth
WESTMINSTER
Horseferry Road
Victoria Street
Tothill St
New Scotland Yard
Department of Trade & Industry
Home Office
Wellington Barracks
Marsham Street
SW1P
Millbank
Millbank Tower
Tate Britain
Clore Gallery
John Islip Street
Atterbury St
Vauxhall Bridge Rd
Millbank Millennium Pier (due to open 2002)
Albert Embankment
Vauxhall Bridge
River Thames
Pimlico
Pimlico Station
Grosvenor Road
Rochester Row
Vauxhall
Vauxhall Station
London Balloon
Kennington
Kennington Lane
Kennington Oval
Harleyford Rd
Surrey County Cricket Club (The Oval)
Vauxhall Park
Fentiman Road
South Lambeth Rd
Wandsworth Road
Nine Elms Lane
Nine Elms
Covent Garden Flower Market
New Covent Garden Market
St George Wharf
Parry St
Kennington Road
SE11
Lambeth Walk
18
158

18
12
17
159
A
B
C
D
E
F
G
1
2
3
4
5
6
7
8
9
10
531
32
79
78
80
LAMBETH
Newington
Walworth
The Borough
SE1
SE11
SE17
Waterloo Station
International Rail Terminal
Waterloo East Stn
Imperial War Museum
Geraldine Mary Harmsworth Park
Council Building
IWM Annexe
St George's Cathedral
St George's Cathedral RC Primary School
St George's Circus
South Bank University
Elephant and Castle Stn
Elephant & Castle Shopping Centre
Elephant and Castle Stn
Metropolitan Tabernacle
London Coll of Printing
Recreation Centre
Eden College
Newington Court Business Cen
Inner London Sessions Ho (Crown Court)
Newington Gardens
Crown Court at the Borough
Fire Brigade Mus
Borough Stn
Southwark Coroners Court
Lambeth North Station
Kennington Station
Oval Station
Surrey County Cricket Club (The Oval)
Ken Barrington Centre
Oval Ho Thtr
Armchair Theatre
Young Vic Theatre
Old Vic Theatre
Metropolitan Hospital
Churchill Clinic
Walworth Town Hall
The Cuming Museum
Police Station
Hinley Clinic
London College of Further Education
Lambeth County Court
Art School
Art College
The Michael Tippett School
Archbishop Sumners CE Primary School
Walnut Tree Walk Primary School
St Thomas Childrens Day Hosp
Newington Industrial Est
Elephant and Castle Industrial Est
Heygate Estate
Crampton Primary School
St Pauls CE Primary School
Keyworth Primary School
Aspen House School
John Ruskin Primary School
Robert Browning Primary Sch
Victory Primary School
Joseph Lancaster School
Geoffrey Chaucer School
St Peters CE Primary School
Faraday Gardens
Oval Business Centre
Henry Fawcett Primary School
St Joseph's RC Primary School
St John the Divine CE Primary
Johanna Primary School
Waterloo Health Centre
Friars Primary Foundation School
Girls School
WATERLOO RD
WESTMINSTER BR RD
BOROUGH ROAD
LAMBETH ROAD
KENNINGTON RD
KENNINGTON LANE
KENNINGTON PARK ROAD
KENNINGTON OVAL
CAMBERWELL NEW ROAD
NEWINGTON BUTTS
WALWORTH RD
NEW KENT ROAD
ST GEORGE'S RD
LONDON RD
SOUTHWARK BRIDGE RD
BOROUGH HIGH ST
GREAT DOVER STREET
NEWINGTON CSWY
MARSHALSEA RD
HARPER RD
UNION STREET
THE CUT
BLACKFRIARS ROAD
BAYLIS ROAD
ALBANY ROAD
CAMBERWELL
A3
A23
A201
A202
A215
A300
A301
A302
A3200
A3203
A3204
A2
B300
B301
B240
1 grid square represents 250 metres

Tower Bridge
Greater London Authority Headquarters (City Hall)
The Tower Bridge Experience
Tower Bridge Museum
Butlers Wharf Pier
Wapping Pier Head
Capital Wharf
Winston Churchill's Britain at War Exp
St Thomas' Hosp Operation Theatre
Guys Hospital
London Bridge Station
TOOLEY STREET
ST THOMAS ST
Magdalen St
Morgans Lane
Millennium Balloon
Shad Thames
Thames Path
Butlers Wharf
Des Mus
Bramah Tea & Coffee Mus
Tower Hamlets
Southwark
Chambers Wharf
Bermondsey Wall West
Providence Square
Chambers Street
Jacob St
Wolseley Street
Mill Street
Dockhead
Parkers Row
Jamaica Road
JAMAICA RD
DRUID ST
Druid Street
TOWER BR RD
A100
A200
CRUCIFIX LANE
BERMONDSEY STREET
Snowsfields
Guy St
Weston St
Kipling Estate
Leathermarket Gardens
Leathermarket Street
Fashion & Textile Design Museum
Tanner St
Tanner Street
Morocco St
LONG LANE
A2198
Staple Street
Tabard Garden Estate
Newham's Row
Caledonian Market
Works
Abbey Street
B202
ABBEY STREET
Maltby Street
Riley Road
Gedling Pl
St Saviour's Estate
Neckinger
Neckinger Estate
Enid St
Old Jamaica Bus Est
Old Jamaica Road
BERMONDSEY
Bermondsey Station
Scott Lidgett Crs
Dickens Estate
Arnold Estate
St James CE J&I School
Marine St
Thurland Rd
Voyager Bus Est
Spa Road
Dockley Road Industrial Est
Bermondsey Town Hall
Grange Walk
Grange Yd
GRANGE ROAD
The Grange
TOWER BRIDGE
Southwark Coll
Alice St
Decima St
Rothsay St
Webb St
Rich Industrial Estate
Crimscott Street
Pages Walk
Willow Walk
Mandela Way
Bricklayer Arms Industrial Estate
A2206
Boutcher CE Primary School
Alscot Rd
Alscot Rd Ind Est
Lucey Rd
Aylwin Girls School
Alma Junior & Infant School
Alexis Street
SOUTHWARK PARK ROAD
Southwark College
Blue Anchor La
Cherry Garden School
Abbey Gardens
Spa School
Longfield Estate
Fort Road
Balaclava Road
Alma Grove
Reverdy Road
Thorburn Square
Strathnairn St
Simms Road
Esmeralda Rd
Lynton Rd
Lynton Road
Beatrice Road
Paterson Park
St James's Road
Admiral Hyson Industrial Est
Oxley Close
Abercorn Wy
ROLLS ROAD
B204
Avondale Estate
Mawbey Estate
Marlborough Gv
Six Bridges Trading Estate
CATLIN STREET
Sherwood Gardens
ROTHERHITHE NEW RD
A2208
Sandgate Trading Est
Cantium Retail Park
North Peckham Civic Centre & Library
OLD KENT ROAD
A2
Council Building
DUNTON ROAD
B203
MANDELA WY
Superstore
Marcia Road
Madron St
Rowcross Street
Fire Station
Cooper's Road
Brodie St
TRAFALGAR AV
Nile Ter
Surgery
NEW KENT RD
Townsend Primary School
Surrey Square Primary School
Surrey Square Park
East Street
Flint Street
Aylesbury Estate
Thurlow St
Inville Road
Michael Faraday Primary School
Beaconsfield Road
Walworth Lower School
Walworth Upper School
ALBANY ROAD
Burgess Park
Burgess Park Lake
Cobourg Primary School
Cobourg Road
Loncroft Road
New Peckham Mosque
Neate Street
Wells Way
St George's Way
Winchcombe Business Cen
St Georges CE Primary School
Trinity College Cen
Gloucested Primary School
Cator Street
SUMNER RD
B215
Glengall Road
WILLOWBROOK R
Haymerle Road
Haymerle School
Horizon Industrial Estate
PECKHAM PARK ROAD
St Francis RC Primary School
Camelot Primary School
Livesey Museum
Bird In Bush Road
Commercial Way
SOUTHAMPTON WAY
B217
Burgess Industrial Park
Daniel Gardens
Nutt St
Garnies Cl
Rosemary
Hordle Promenade East
Willowbrook Estate
Radnor Rd
Lindley Estate
13
159
160
33
34
H J K L M N P
1 2 3 4 5 6 7 8 9 10

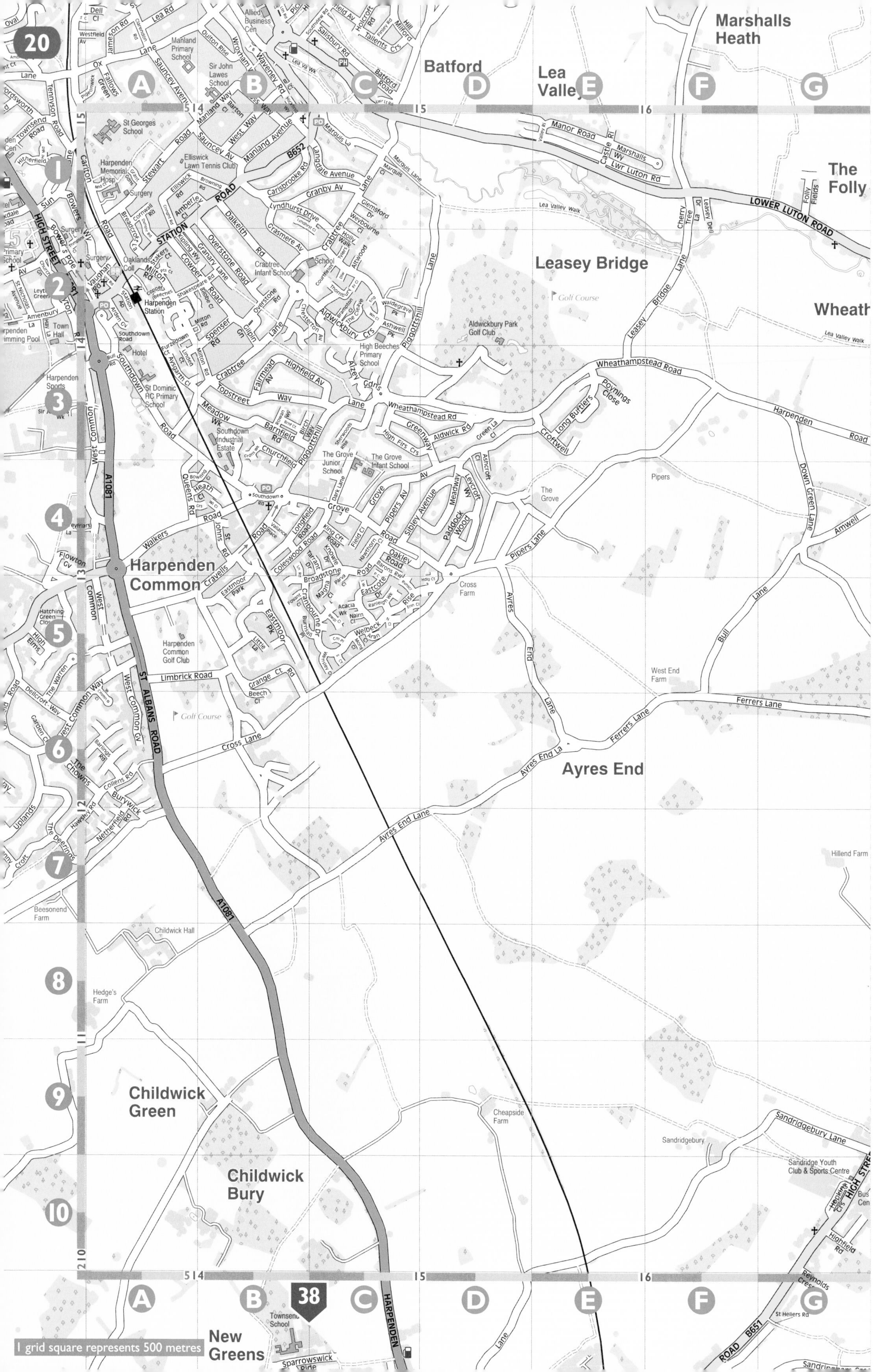
Marshalls Heath
Batford
Lea Valley
The Folly
Leasey Bridge
Wheath
Harpenden Common
Ayres End
Childwick Green
Childwick Bury
New Greens
LOWER LUTON ROAD
Lwr Luton Rd
Manor Road
Lea Valley Walk
Golf Course
Aldwickbury Park Golf Club
Wheathampstead Road
Harpenden Road
Pipers
The Grove
Down Green Lane
Amwell
Bull Lane
West End Farm
Ferrers Lane
Ayres End Lane
Ayres End La
Cross Farm
Pipers Lane
Hillend Farm
Cheapside Farm
Sandridgebury
Sandridgebury Lane
Sandridge Youth Club & Sports Centre
HIGH STREET
ROAD B651
St Heliers Rd
Reynolds Cres
Highfield Rd
ST ALBANS ROAD
A1081
HARPENDEN
West Common
West Common Gv
West Common Way
Limbrick Road
Cross Lane
Harpenden Common Golf Club
Childwick Hall
Hedge's Farm
Beesonend Farm
Townsend School
Sparrowswick Ride
HIGH STREET
STATION ROAD
Harpenden Station
Southdown Road
Southdown Industrial Estate
St Dominic RC Primary School
The Grove Junior School
The Grove Infant School
High Beeches Primary School
Crabtree Infant School
St Georges School
Harpenden Memorial Hosp
Elliswick Lawn Tennis Club
Manland Primary School
Sir John Lawes School
Allied Business Cen
Piggottshill Lane
Crabtree Lane
Walkers Road
Luton Road
Lea Valley Walk
Harpenden Sports
Town Hall
Harpenden Swimming Pool
Marquis Lane
Granby Av
Carisbrooke Rd
Manland Avenue
Wheathampstead Rd
Cravells
Eastmoor Park
Coleswood Road
Broadstone Road
Grove Road
Sibley Avenue
Cranbourne Dr
Welbeck Rise
A
B
C
D
E
F
G
1
2
3
4
5
6
7
8
9
10
514
15
16
210
11
12
13
14
15
38
1 grid square represents 500 metres

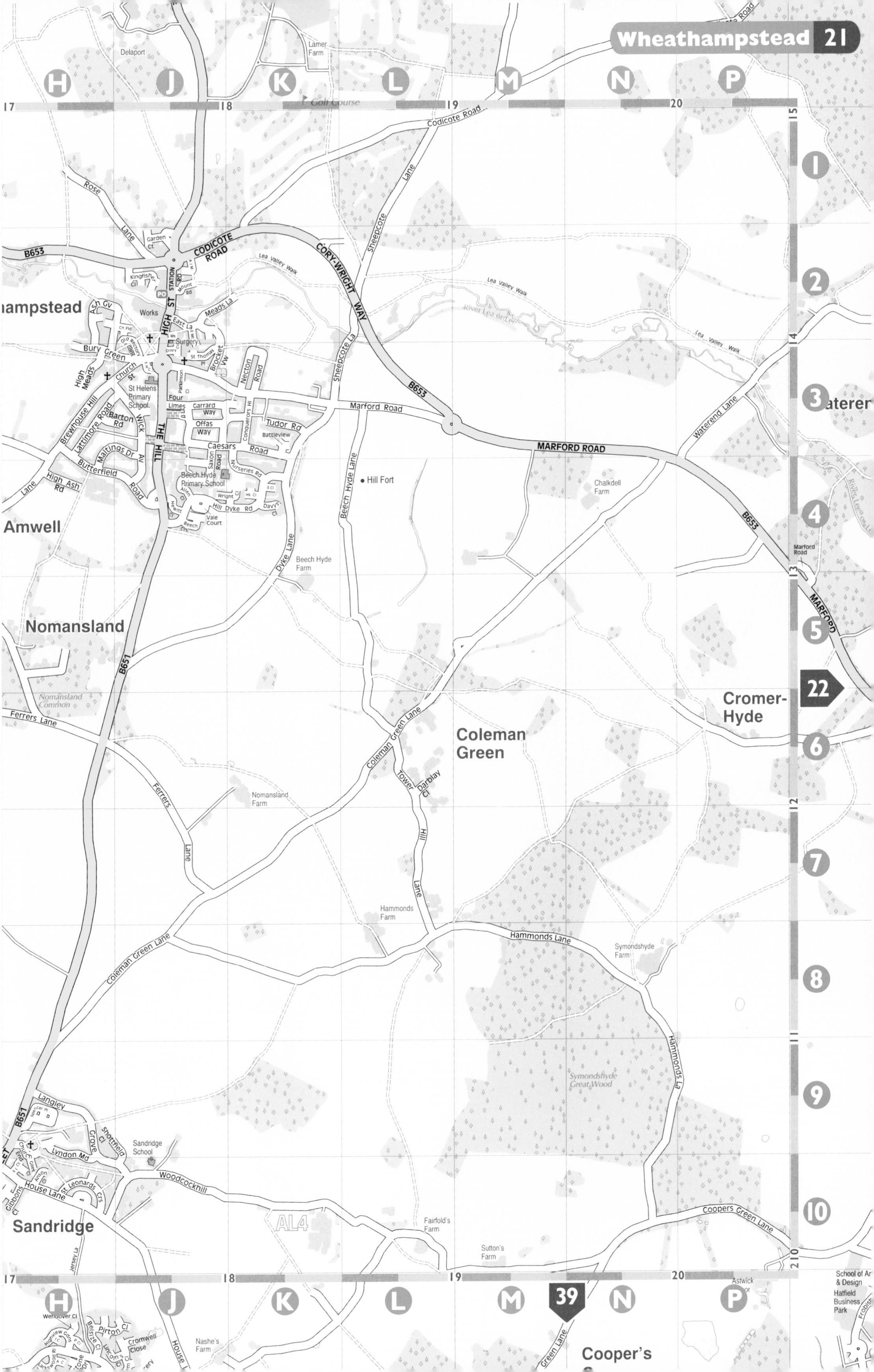
Delaport
Lamer Farm
Golf Course
Codicote Road
Rose Lane
Garden Ct
B653
CODICOTE ROAD
CORY-WRIGHT WAY
Sheepcote Lane
Lea Valley Walk
River Lea or Lee
Kingfisher Cl
STATION RD
Mount Rd
HIGH ST
Meads La
East La
Works
Surgery
Brocket Vw
Bury Green
Church St
High Meads
St Helens Primary School
Parkinson Cl
Necton Road
Sheepcote La
Four Limes
Garrard Way
Offas Way
Conquerors Hl
Tudor Rd
Battleview
Caesars Road
Brewhouse Hill
Lattimore Road
Barton Rd
Wick Av
Maltings Dr
Butterfield Road
THE HILL
Saxon Road
Nurseries Rd
Beech Hyde Primary School
Wright Cl
Hill Dyke Rd
Davys Cl
Vale Court
High Ash Rd
Lane
Marford Road
MARFORD ROAD
Hill Fort
Beech Hyde Lane
Chalkdell Farm
Waterend Lane
Marford Road
Dyke Lane
Beech Hyde Farm
Amwell
Nomansland
Nomansland Common
B651
Ferrers Lane
Ferrers Lane
Coleman Green Lane
Coleman Green
Cromer-Hyde
Tower Hill Lane
Darblay Cl
Nomansland Farm
Hammonds Farm
Hammonds Lane
Symondshyde Farm
Coleman Green Lane
Hammonds La
Symondshyde Great Wood
Langley Grove
Shottfield Cl
Lyndon Md
Church End
Sandridge School
Woodcockhill
House Lane
St. Leonards Crs
Gibbons
Sandridge
AL4
Fairfold's Farm
Sutton's Farm
Coopers Green Lane
Jersey La
Astwick
School of Art & Design
Hatfield Business Park
Wendover Cl
Pirton Cl
Cromwell Close
Nashe's Farm
House La
Green Lane
Cooper's
39
22
H J K L M N P
17 18 19 20
1 2 3 4 5 6 7 8 9 10
15 14 13 12 11 210

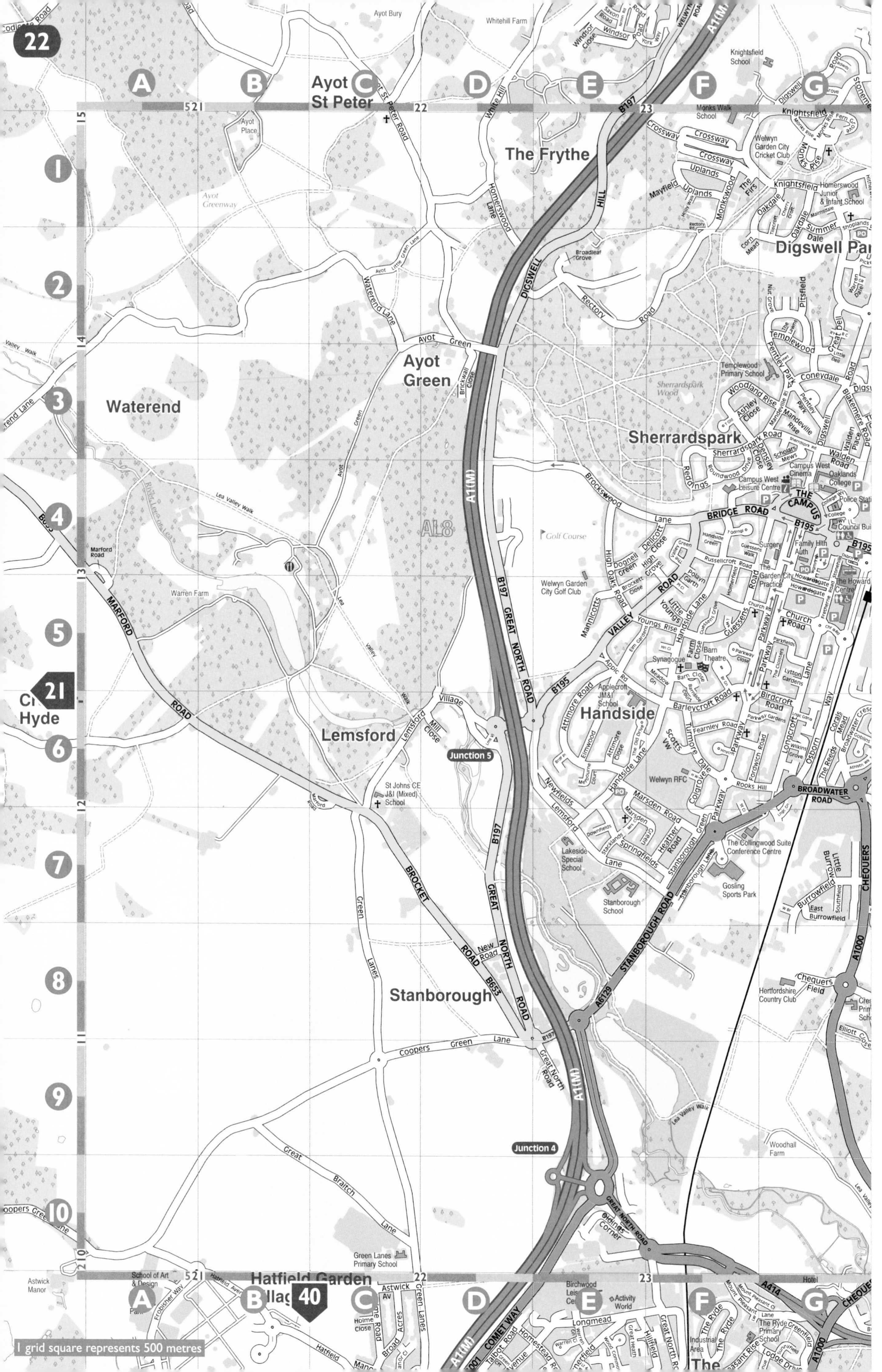
Ayot St Peter
Ayot Bury
Whitehill Farm
Ayot Place
Ayot Greenway
The Frythe
Knightsfield School
Monks Walk School
Welwyn Garden City Cricket Club
Homerswood Junior & Infant School
Digswell Park
Ayot Green
Waterend
Templewood Primary School
Sherrardspark Wood
Sherrardspark
Campus West Leisure Centre
Campus West Cinema
Oaklands College
THE CAMPUS
Police Station
Council Buildings
Family Hlth Auth
Surgery
The Garden City Practice
The Howard Centre
Lea Valley Walk
Marford Road
Warren Farm
AL8
Golf Course
Welwyn Garden City Golf Club
Synagogue
Barn Theatre
Applecroft JM&I School
Handside
Lemsford
Junction 5
St Johns CE J&I (Mixed) School
Welwyn RFC
Lakeside Special School
Stanborough School
The Collingwood Suite Conference Centre
Gosling Sports Park
Stanborough
Hertfordshire Country Club
Junction 4
Woodhall Farm
Green Lanes Primary School
Stanborough Road
Great North Road
Brocket Road
Marford Road
Digswell Hill
Valley Road
Bridge Road
Broadwater Road
Coopers Green Lane
Great Braitch Lane
Green Lanes
A1(M)
B197
B195
B653
A6129
A1000
A414
Astwick Manor
School of Art & Design
Hatfield Garden Village
Birchwood Leisure Centre
Activity World
Industrial Area
The Ryde Primary School
Hotel
40
21
1 grid square represents 500 metres

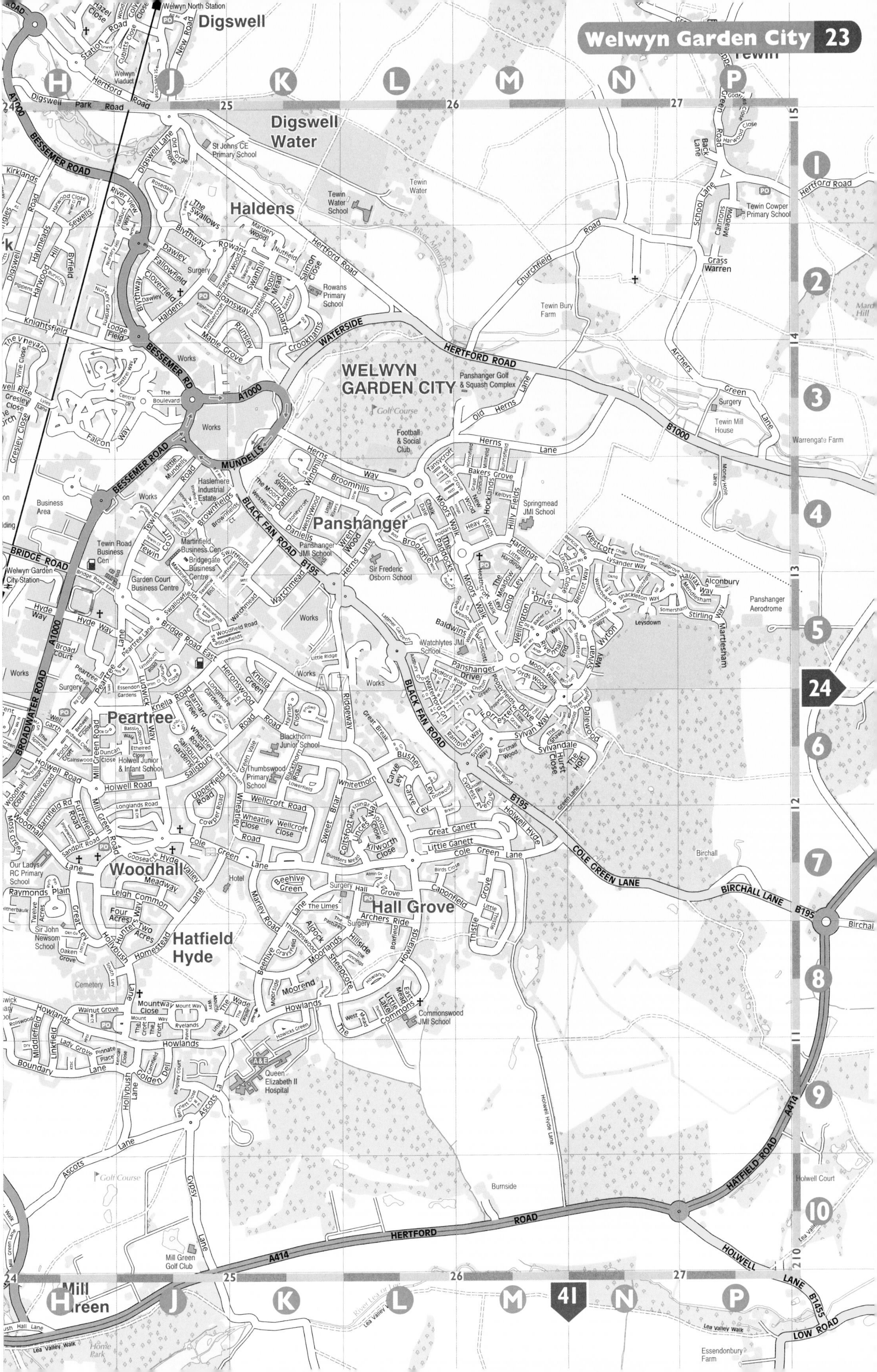
Digswell
Welwyn North Station
Digswell Water
Haldens
Tewin Water
Tewin Water School
St Johns CE Primary School
Rowans Primary School
WELWYN GARDEN CITY
Panshanger Golf & Squash Complex
Golf Course
Football & Social Club
HERTFORD ROAD
WATERSIDE
BESSEMER ROAD
A1000
MUNDELLS
BLACK FAN ROAD
B195
B1000
Panshanger
Panshanger JMI School
Sir Frederic Osborn School
Springmead JMI School
Watchlytes JMI School
Panshanger Aerodrome
Tewin Bury Farm
Tewin Cowper Primary School
Tewin Mill House
Warrengate Farm
Churchfield
Grass Warren
Archers Green Lane
Haslemere Industrial Estate
Business Area
Tewin Road Business Cen
Welwyn Garden City Station
BRIDGE ROAD
Bridgegate Business Centre
Garden Court Business Centre
Martinfield Business Cen
BROADWATER ROAD
Peartree
Holwell Junior & Infant School
Blackthorn Junior School
Thumbswood Primary School
Our Ladys RC Primary School
Sir John Newsom School
Woodhall
Hatfield Hyde
Hall Grove
Commonswood JMI School
Queen Elizabeth II Hospital
COLE GREEN LANE
BIRCHALL LANE
Birchall
Cemetery
Golf Course
Mill Green Golf Club
Mill Green
HERTFORD ROAD
A414
HATFIELD ROAD
HOLWELL LANE
B1455
LOW ROAD
Holwell Court
Burnside
Holwell Hyde Lane
Lea Valley Walk
Essendonbury Farm
Home Park
AL7
H J K L M N P
25 26 27
24 41

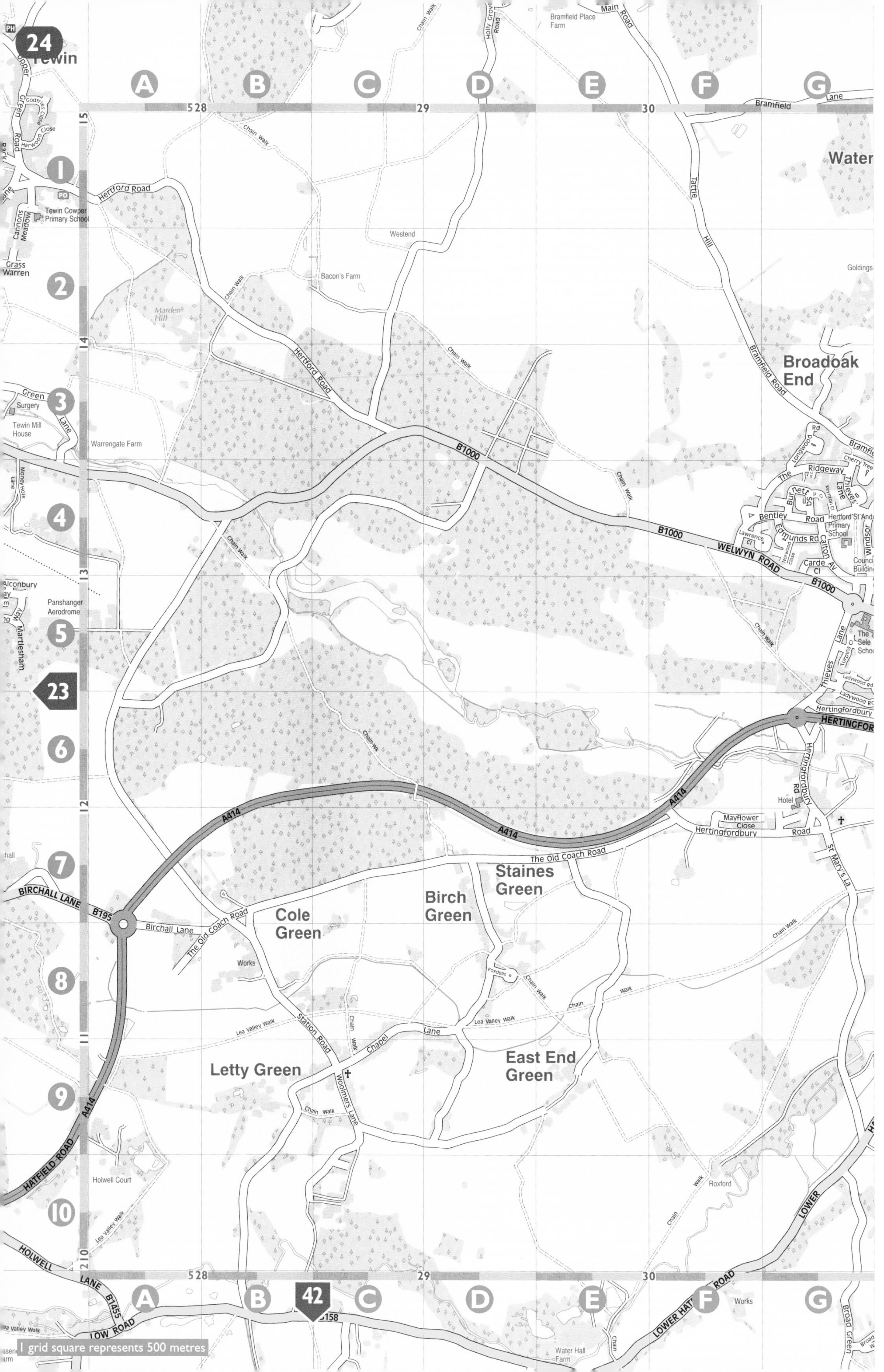

24
Tewin
23
42
A
B
C
D
E
F
G
1
2
3
4
5
6
7
8
9
10
528
29
30
15
14
13
12
11
210
Main Road
Bramfield Place Farm
Holly Grove Road
Chain Walk
Bramfield Lane
Water
Upper Green Road
Godfries Close
Harwood Close
Hertford Road
PO
Tewin Cowper Primary School
Cannons Meadow
Grass Warren
Westend
Bacon's Farm
Marden Hill
Tattle Hill
Goldings
Bramfield Road
Broadoak End
Green Lane
Surgery
Tewin Mill House
Warrengate Farm
Money Hole Lane
B1000
WELWYN ROAD
Longwood Rd
The Ridgeway
Thieves Lane
Burnett Sq
Bentley Road
Hertford St Andrew Primary School
Lawrence Cl
Edmunds Rd
Norwood Close
Calton Av
Carde Cl
Windsor
Council Building
Alconbury
Panshanger Aerodrome
Martlesham
The Sele School
Ladywood Rd
Hertingfordbury
HERTINGFORD
Hertingfordbury Rd
Hotel
Mayflower Close
Hertingfordbury Road
St Mary's La
A414
The Old Coach Road
Staines Green
Birch Green
Cole Green
BIRCHALL LANE
B195
Birchall Lane
Works
Foxdells
Lea Valley Walk
Station Road
Chapel Lane
Letty Green
East End Green
Woolmers Lane
HATFIELD ROAD
Holwell Court
Roxford
LOWER HATFIELD ROAD
HOLWELL LANE
B1455
LOW ROAD
B158
Water Hall Farm
Broad Green
1 grid square represents 500 metres

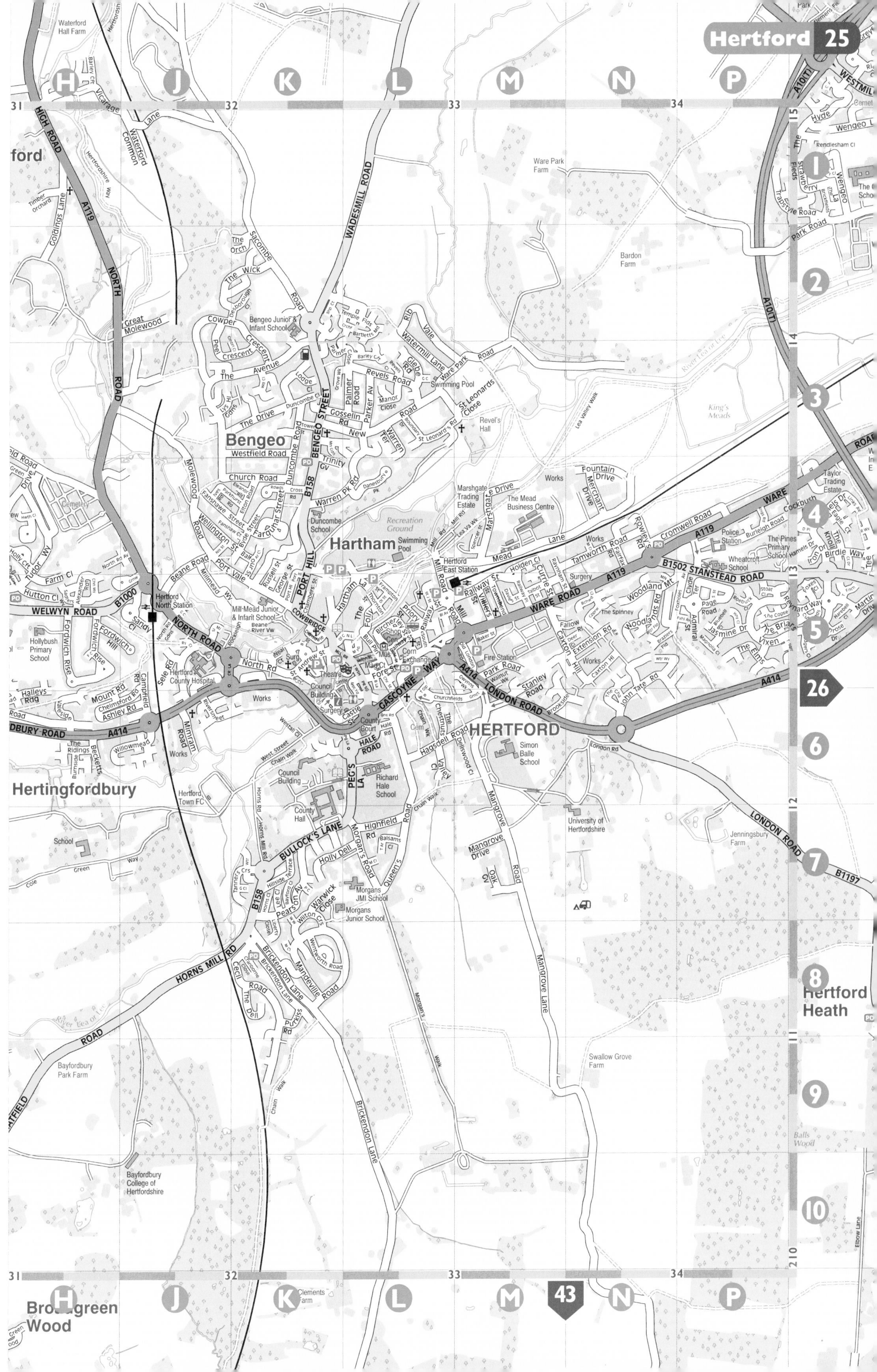
Bengeo
Hartham
HERTFORD
Hertingfordbury
Hertford Heath
Broadgreen Wood
Waterford Hall Farm
Waterford Common
HIGH ROAD
A119
NORTH ROAD
WADESMILL ROAD
Sacombe Road
BENGEO STREET
B158
PORT HILL
Ware Park Farm
Bardon Farm
Bengeo Junior & Infant School
Swimming Pool
Revel's Hall
King's Meads
River Lea or Lee
Lea Valley Walk
Westfield Road
Church Road
Duncombe School
Recreation Ground
Marshgate Trading Estate
The Mead Business Centre
Fountain Drive
Cromwell Road
Tamworth Road
Taylor Trading Estate
Police Station
The Pines Primary School
Wheatcroft School
B1502 STANSTEAD ROAD
WARE ROAD
Hertford East Station
Hertford North Station
WELWYN ROAD
B1000
Hollybush Primary School
Mill-Mead Junior & Infant School
Hertford County Hospital
A414
Council Building
Theatre
County Court
GASCOYNE WAY
LONDON ROAD
Fire Station
Simon Balle School
Richard Hale School
County Hall
HALE ROAD
PEG'S LA
BULLOCK'S LANE
Hertford Town FC
Morgans JMI School
Morgans Junior School
University of Hertfordshire
Jenningsbury Farm
B1197
Mangrove Road
Mangrove Lane
HORNS MILL RD
Brickendon Lane
Mandeville Road
Swallow Grove Farm
Bayfordbury Park Farm
Bayfordbury College of Hertfordshire
Balls Wood
Clements Farm
Elbow Lane
A10(T)
26
43
H J K L M N P
31 32 33 34
1 2 3 4 5 6 7 8 9 10

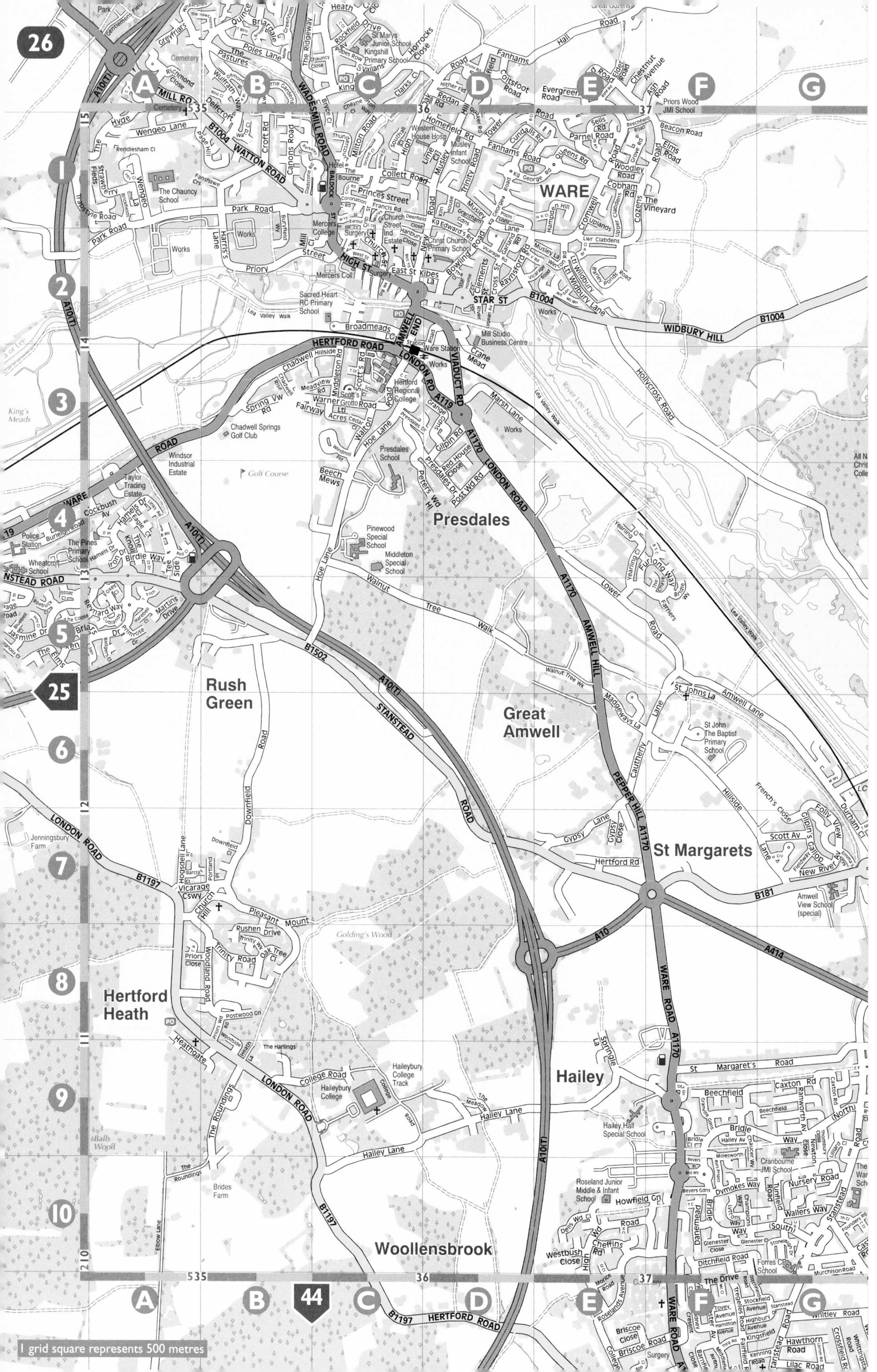
26
WARE
Presdales
Rush Green
Great Amwell
St Margarets
Hertford Heath
Hailey
Woollensbrook
WADESMILL ROAD
B1004 WATTON ROAD
HIGH ST
STAR ST
WIDBURY HILL
B1004
HERTFORD ROAD
AMWELL END
LONDON RD
A119
VIADUCT RD
A1170 LONDON ROAD
A1170 AMWELL HILL
PEPPER HILL
A1170
B1502 STANSTEAD ROAD
A10(T)
A10
A414
B181
WARE ROAD A1170
LONDON ROAD
B1197
B1197 HERTFORD ROAD
Park Road
Priory
Mill Street
Walnut Tree Walk
Hoe Lane
Downfield Road
Pleasant Mount
Hailey Lane
College Road
St Margaret's Road
Haileybury College
The Chauncy School
Chadwell Springs Golf Club
Windsor Industrial Estate
Hertford Regional College
Presdales School
Pinewood Special School
Middleton Special School
Mercers College
Sacred Heart RC Primary School
Ware Station
Mill Studio Business Centre
River Lee Navigation
Lea Valley Walk
Hollycross Road
Marsh Lane
St John The Baptist Primary School
Amwell View School (special)
Hailey Hall Special School
Roseland Junior Middle & Infant School
Cranbourne JMI School
Priors Wood JMI School
Golding's Wood
Golf Course
King's Meads
Jenningsbury Farm
Brides Farm
Balls Wood
25
44
A
B
C
D
E
F
G
1
2
3
4
5
6
7
8
9
10
535
36
37
15
14
13
12
11
210
1 grid square represents 500 metres

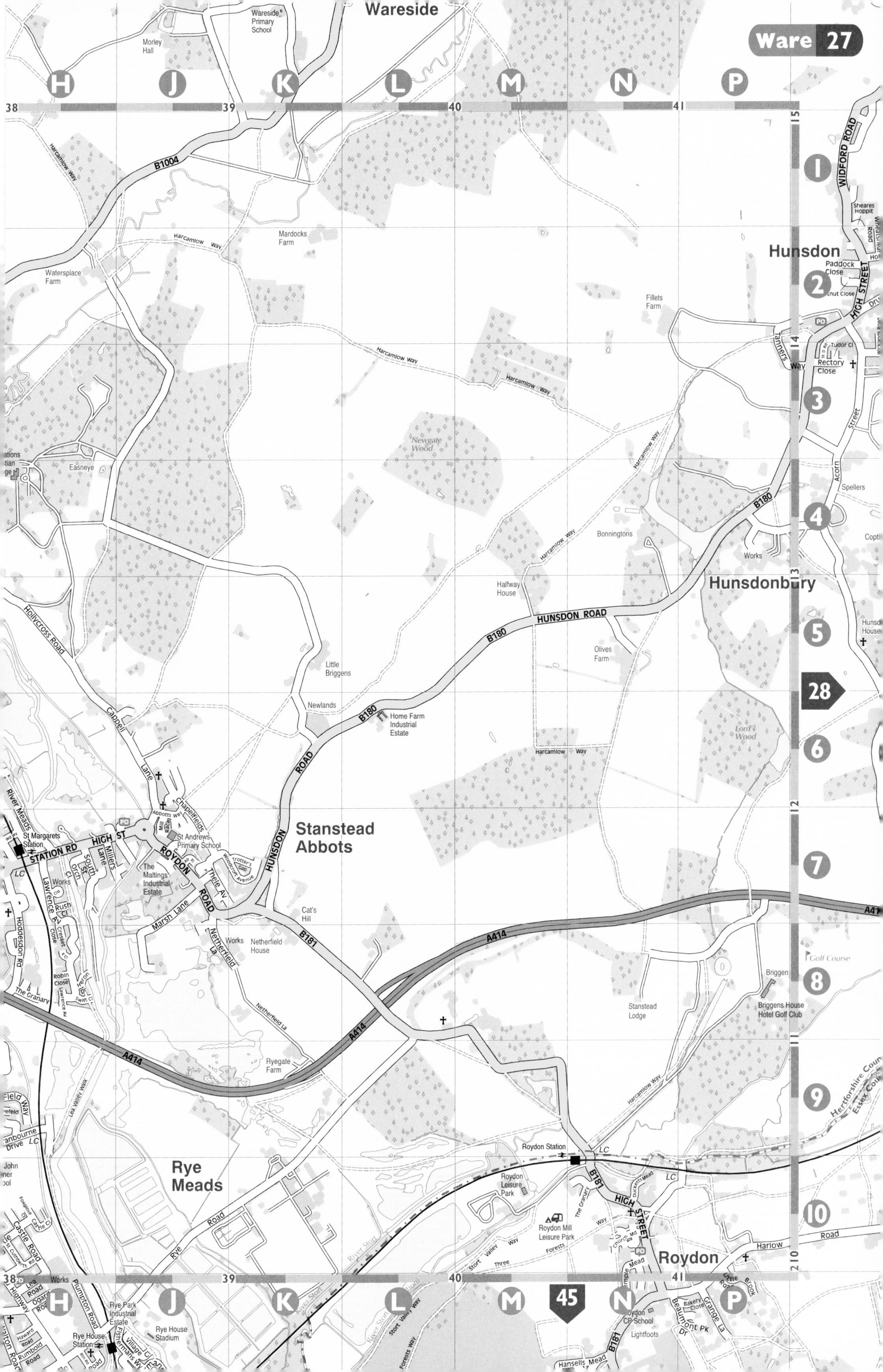

Wareside
Wareside Primary School
Morley Hall
B1004
Harcamlow Way
Mardocks Farm
Watersplace Farm
Easneye
Hunsdon
Paddock Close
Knut Close
HIGH STREET
WIDFORD ROAD
Sheares Hoppit
Fillets Farm
Tanners Way
Tudor Cl
Rectory Close
Newgate Wood
Acorn Street
Spellers
B180
Bonningtons
Works
Hunsdonbury
Halfway House
HUNSDON ROAD
Olives Farm
Hollycross Road
Capell Lane
Little Briggens
Newlands
Home Farm Industrial Estate
Lord's Wood
HUNSDON ROAD
Stanstead Abbots
Chapelfields
Abbotts Way
St Andrews Primary School
St Margarets Station
STATION RD
HIGH ST
ROYDON ROAD
The Maltings Industrial Estate
Marsh Lane
Netherfield La
Netherfield House
Cat's Hill
B181
A414
Golf Course
Briggens
Briggens House Hotel Golf Club
Stanstead Lodge
Ryegate Farm
Lea Valley Walk
Hertfordshire County
Essex County
Rye Meads
Rye Road
Roydon Station
Roydon Leisure Park
Roydon Mill Leisure Park
Stort Valley Way
River Stort
Roydon
Harlow Road
Rye Park Industrial Estate
Rye House Station
Rye House Stadium
Plumpton Road
Roydon CP School
Lightfoots
Hansells Mead
Beaumont Pk Dr
Grange La
Little Brook Road
Church Mead
H J K L M N P
38 39 40 41
1 2 3 4 5 6 7 8 9 10
15 14 13 12 11 210
28
45

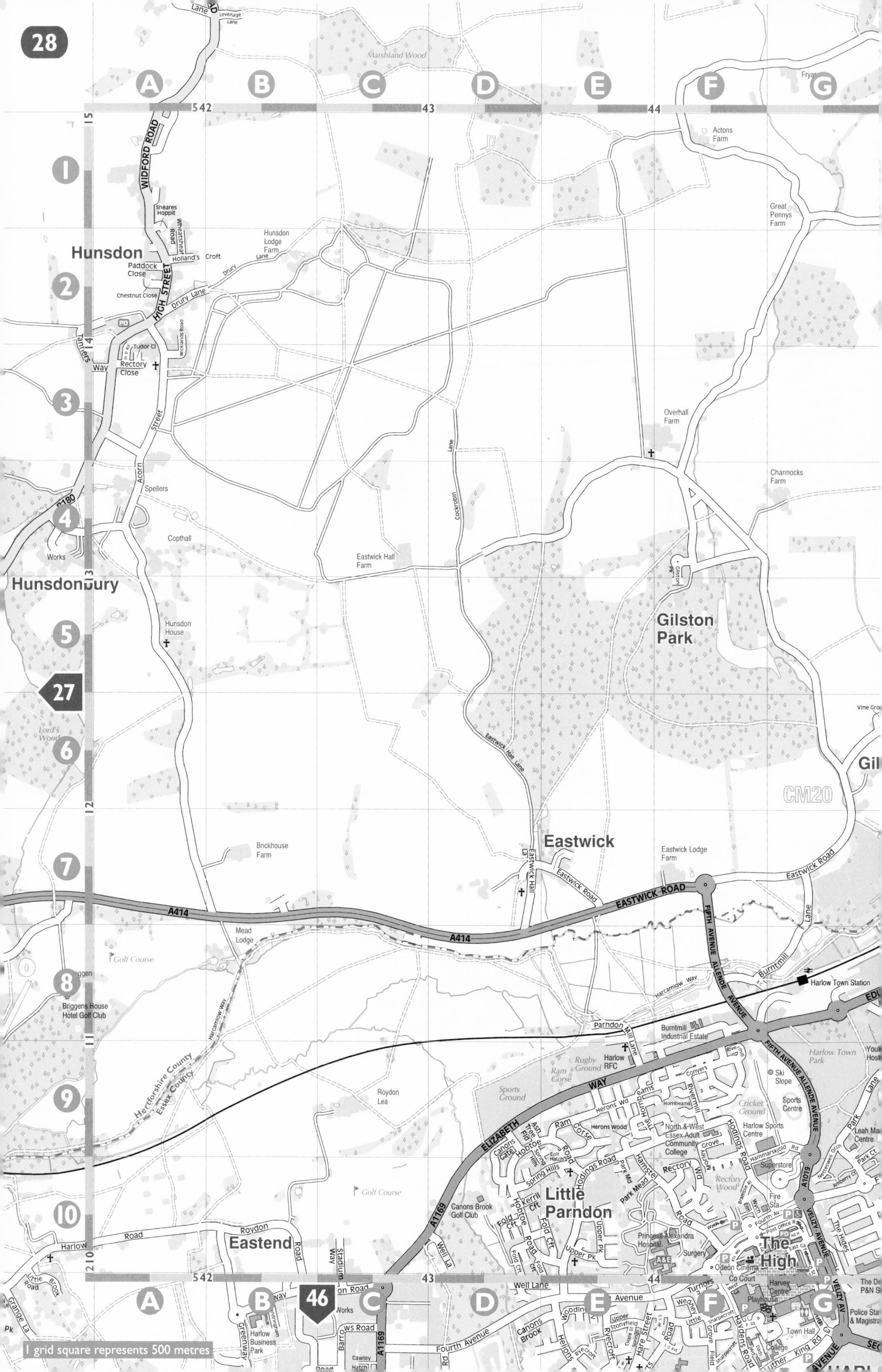
Marshland Wood
Levenage Lane
Fryan
Actons Farm
Great Pennys Farm
WIDFORD ROAD
Sheares Hoppit
Wheatsheaf Road
Hunsdon
Hunsdon Lodge Farm
Drury Lane
Holland's Croft
Paddock Close
Chestnut Close
HIGH STREET
PO
Tanners Way
Tudor Cl
Wicklands Road
Rectory Close
Acorn Street
Spellers
Copthall
Works
Hunsdonbury
B180
Overhall Farm
Channocks Farm
Cockrobin Lane
Eastwick Hall Farm
Gilston Pk
Gilston Park
Hunsdon House
Lord's Wood
Eastwick Hall Lane
CM20
Vine Cro
Gil
Brickhouse Farm
Eastwick
Eastwick Hall La
Eastwick Lodge Farm
Eastwick Road
EASTWICK ROAD
A414
Mead Lodge
Golf Course
Briggens House Hotel Golf Club
Harcamlow Way
Hertfordshire County
Essex County
FIFTH AVENUE
ALLENDE AVENUE
Burntmill Lane
Harlow Town Station
Parndon Mill Lane
Burntmill Industrial Estate
Rugby Ground
Harlow RFC
Ram Gorse
Harlow Town Park
Ski Slope
Sports Ground
Roydon Lea
ELIZABETH WAY
Herons Wd
Hornbeams
Rivermill
Conyers
Cricket Ground
Sports Centre
Herons Wood
North & West Essex Adult Community College
Hodings Road
Harlow Sports Centre
Hammarskjold Rd
Superstore
Leah Manor Centre
Park Ct
Canons Gate
Hobtoe Road
Spring Hills
Colt Hatch
Rectory Wd
Rectory Wood
A1019
VELIZY AVENUE
Golf Course
A1169
Canons Brook Golf Club
Little Parndon
Fold Cft
Park Mead
Hamstel Road
Fire Sta
Fourth Av
Post Office Rd
The Hides
Roydon Road
Harlow Road
Eastend
Well La
Upper Pk
Princess Alexandra Hospital
A&E
Surgery
Wych Elm
Odeon Cinema
The High
Co Court
Harvey Centre
Playhouse
Police Sta & Magistrates
Town Hall
College
King Rd
Stadium Way
Well Lane
Avenue
Turners
Harlow Business Park
Greenway
Works
Barrows Road
Cawley Hatch
Fourth Avenue
Canons Brook
Heltons
Ryecroft
Upper Stonyfield
Hare Street
Little Grove Field
Sharpecroft
Hadens Road
Grange La
27
46
542
43
44
A B C D E F G
1 2 3 4 5 6 7 8 9 10
1 grid square represents 500 metres

SAWBRIDGEWORTH
High Wych
Temple Fields
Old Harlow
Mark Hall North
Mark Hall South
Netteswell
Church Langley
Harlow Mill Station
Sawbridgeworth Station
The Manor of Groves Golf Club
Golf Course
Hoskins
Crumps
Claylane Farm
Carters
Jeffs
Bakers Farm
Sayes Park Farm
Rowney Farm
Redricks Farm
Pole Hole Farm
Aylmers Farm
Gibberd's Garden
Harlowbury
New Hall Farm
Hubbard's Hall
Pishiobury Park
Rowneybury
The Thomas Rivers Medical Centre
Thomas Rivers Medical Centre
Hertfordshire County
Essex County
Maple River Industrial Estate
Sarbir Industrial Park
Mead Industrial Park
Shenval Industrial Estate
The Oaks Industrial Estate
Oakwood Estate
UGC Cinema
Superstore
Works
Hotel
Mark Hall Cycle Museum
Mark Hall Comprehensive School
Tanys Dell Primary School
St Albans Primary School
Burnt Mill School
The Spinney Junior & Infant School
Broadfields Primary School
Harlow College
Harlowbury Primary School
Old Harlow Health Centre
Fawbert & Barnards (Undl) Primary School
Church Langley Primary School
Swimming Pool
Council Building
Clinic
Surgery
Eversley College
West Road
London Road
Cambridge Road
Harlow Road
Bonks Hill A1184
A1184
A414
Edinburgh Way A414
Edinburgh Way
B183 Gilden Way
First Av Mandela Av
High Wych Road
High Wych Lane
Redricks Lane
Eastwick Road
Harcamlow Way
River Way
Station Road
Netteswell Road
Howard Way
Mandela Avenue
First Avenue
Hobbs Cross Road
Churchgate Street
Ladyshot
Pishiobury Drive
Hart Road
Priory Avenue
Old Road
Watlington Road
Mulberry Green
Sheering Mill Lane
Sheering Road
Ridgeways
Minton Lane
Parsonage Leys
Maddox Rd
Longley Wood
Vicarage wood
Reservoir Road
Water Gardens

30
A
B
C
D
E
F
G
549
50
51
Sawbridgeworth Station
The Maltings Industrial Estate
Little Hyde Hall
Sawbridgeworth Road
Quickbury Farm
Harcamlow Way
Stort Valley Way
Lower Sheering
Gladwyns
Shrubbs
Sheering CE Primary School
Sheering
THE STREET
B183
Newhouse
Sheering Lower Road
B183 HARLOW ROAD
M11
Durrington Hall
Aylmers Farm
Sheering Hall
Wheelers Farm
High Lane
Harlow Road
29
Newman End
Campions
SHEERING ROAD
Housham Hall
Collin's Cross
Moor Hall Road
Matching Road
Churchgate Street
Churchgate CE Primary School
St Nicholas School
Feltimores
Harlow Tye
Matching Tye
Rainbow Road
Carter's Green
Matching Park
Housham Tye
Franklins Farm
Chalk Lane
Hobbs Cross
Hobbs Cross Road
Hubbard's Hall
Forest Way
New Way Lane
Faggotters Lane
Loyter's Green
Faggoters Farm
48
CM17
Roffey Hall
New Way
1 grid square represents 500 metres

Hatfield Heath
Ardley End
Manwood Green
Matching
Matching Green
Little Laver
CHELMSFORD ROAD
A1060
Lancasters
The Paddocks
Hill Farm
Friars
Friars Lane
Gibsons
Hatfield Grange
Pincey Brook
Forest Way
Matching Road
Downhall Road
Sparrow's Lane
Parvilles
Hotel
Stone Hall Farm
Kingstons Farm
Brick House
Potash Road
Stock Hall
Fairlands
Waterloo Farmhouse
Matching Green CE Primary School
Watermans End
Hull Green
Little Laver Road
Little Laver Hall
Brickles Wood
Cobbler's Pieces
Row Wood
Three Forests Way
Robins Acre
Blackcat
Pierce Williams
Lea Hall
Ongars
Hatfield Heath Primary School
Park Drive
Stort Valley Way
Colvers
Perryfield
Pond Lane
Clipped Hedge
The Shaw
Broomfields
Home Pastures
Cox Ley
Barley Close
Ardley Crescent
Watery Lane
H J K L M N P
1 2 3 4 5 6 7 8 9 10
52 53 54 55
49

32
50
A B C D E F G
1 2 3 4 5 6 7 8 9 10
493
94
95
10
09
08
07
06
205
Cow Roast
A4251
A41(T)
Wigginton Bottom
Hastoe
Buckland Common
Cholesbury
Heath End
Bellingdon
Icknield Way
Ridgeway
Fox Close
Road
Vicarage Road
Highfield Road
The Hollies
Common Field
School
The Firs
The Bit
Chesham Road
The Coppice
Osborne Way
Hemp Lane
Hemp
Hill Green Farm
Tinker's Lodge
Wick Road
Wick Farm
Marlin Hill
Lane
Crawley's Lane
Wiggington Bottom
Rossway Lane
Wood Row
Hamberlins
Kiln Farm
Tinkers Lane
Champneys
Shootersway
High Scrubs
Cholesbury Road
The Flats
Lodge Farm
Bedfordshire County
Buckinghamshire County
Shirelane Farm
Parrott's Farm
Parrott's Lane
Shire Lane
Tring Grange Farm
Rossway Home Farm
Cholesbury Lane
PH
Hawridge Common
Oak Lane
Braziers End House
Ray's Hill
Braziers End
Hawridge & Cholesbury CE Combined School
Hawridge Vale
Hill Farm
Gyles Croft
Cherry Tree
Peppett's Green
Bank Green
Wood Farm
Bank Farm
Cedar Grove
Hawridge Lane
Bellingdon Farm
Asheridge Farm
Two Gates Lane
Bloomfield Farm
Ramscote Lane
Ashotts Lane
Chartridge End
Savecroft
1 grid square represents 500 metres

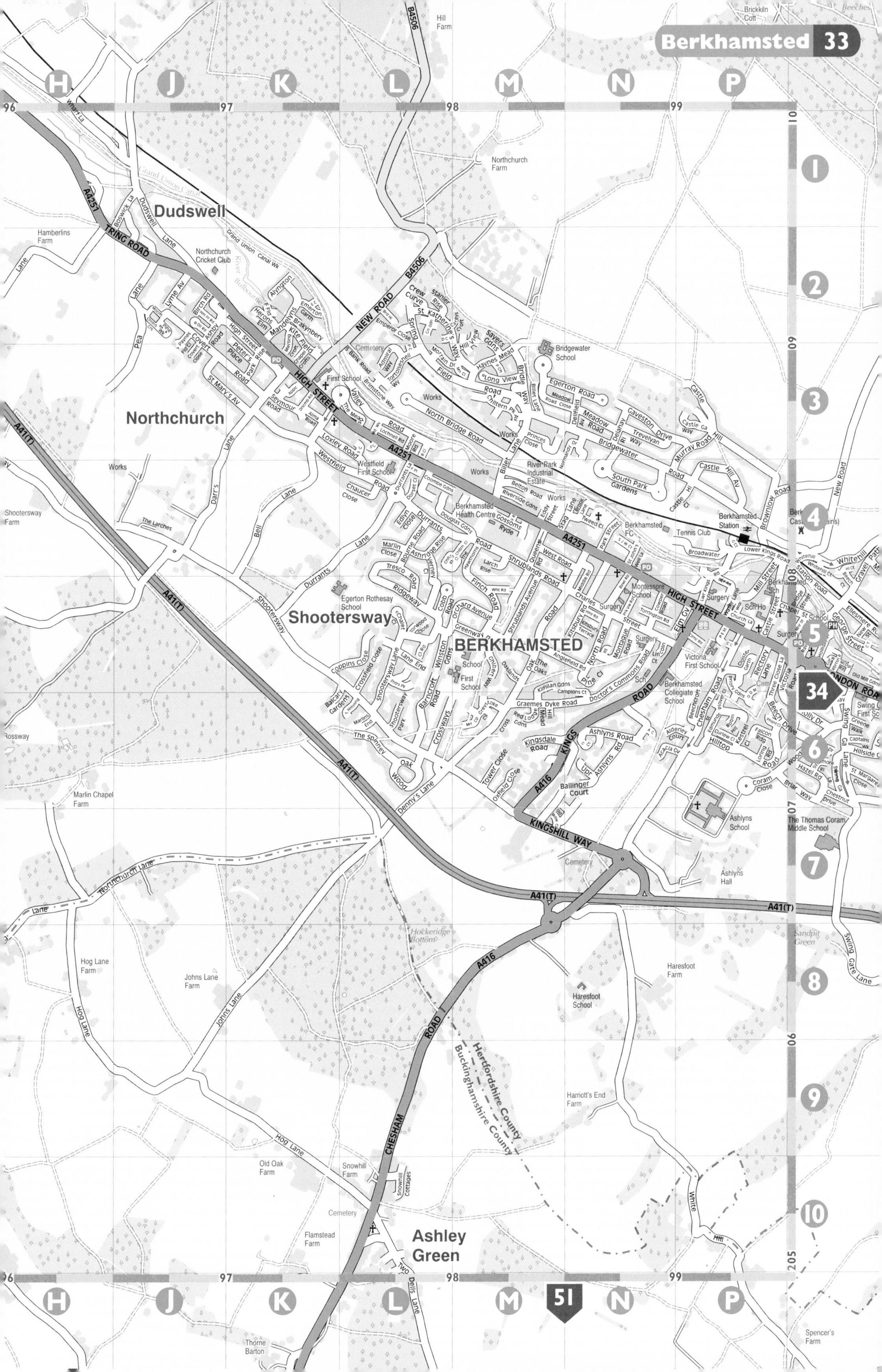
H
J
K
L
M
N
P
96
97
98
99
Dudswell
Northchurch
Shootersway
BERKHAMSTED
Ashley Green
Hill Farm
Brickkiln Cott
Northchurch Farm
Hamberlins Farm
Northchurch Cricket Club
Grand Union Canal
Grand Union Canal Wk
River Bulbourne
Wharf La
Boswick La
Dudswell Lane
TRING ROAD
A4251
NEW ROAD
B4506
HIGH STREET
Alyngton
Emerton Garth
Brakynbery
Mandelyns
Kite Field
Herons Elm
Birch Rd
Lyme Av
Lane
Pea Lane
Covert Road
Ashby Road
High Street
Peter's Place
Park Rise
St Mary's Av
Seymour Road
Alma Road
Cemetery
First School
Valley
The Meads
Bank Road
Admiral Way
Tortoiseshell Wy
Brimstone Way
Emperor Close
Spring Field
Crew Curve
Stanier Rise
St Katherine's Way
Hill View
Sayers Gdns
Morgan Cl
Haynes Mead
Long View
Bridle Way
Billet Lane
Bridgewater School
Egerton Road
Meadow Road Close
Delfield Av
Meadow Road
Gaveston Drive
Trevelyan Way
Delamay Rd
Bridgewater
South Park Gardens
Castle Hill
Castle Hill Av
Castle Ct
Murray Road
Castle Ga Way
Chiltern Pk Av
North Bridge Road
Works
Princes Close
Normandy Dr
River Park Industrial Estate
Belton Road
Riverside Gdns
Loxley Road
Westfield
Westfield First School
Lochnell Rd
Moore Rd
Durrants Rd
Coombe Gdns
Chaucer Close
Berkhamsted Health Centre
Douglas Gdns
Gossoms Ryde
Edyn Close
Durrants Lane
Marlin Close
Bourne Road
Ashridge Rise
Tresco Road
Ridgeway
Verney Cl
Larch Rise
Finch Road
Shrublands Road
Shrublands Avenue
Queens Road
West Road
Eddy Street
Stag Lane
Tweed Ct
Park Street
Berkhamsted FC
Tennis Club
Berkhamsted Station
Broadwater
Lower Kings Road
Brownlow Road
New Road
Montessore School
Charles Street
Surgery
Kitsbury Rd
Kitsbury Terrace
North Road
Montague Road
Torrington Rd
Cowper Road
Elm Gv
Egerton Rothesay School
Durrants Lane
Bell Lane
Darr's Lane
The Larches
Shootersway
Shootersway Farm
Chalet Cl
Orchard Avenue
Greenway
Cobb Road
Winston Gdns
Barncroft Road
Crossways
School
First School
Oaklands
The Oaks
Anglefield Rd
Pine Ct
Doctor's Commons Road
Kilfillan Gdns
Campions Ct
Graemes Dyke Road
Red Lodge Gdns
Mead Hill
Coppins Close
Crossfield Close
Shootersway Lane
Lane End
Shootersway Park
Balcary Gardens
The Spinney
Oak Wood
Denny's Lane
Tower Close
Oxfield Close
Kingsdale Road
KINGS ROAD
A416
Ashlyns Road
Ashlyns Rd
Upr Ashlyns Rd
Ballinger Court
Alderley Court
Acacia Gv
Berkhamsted Collegiate School
Victoria First School
Beechcroft Road
Chesham Road
Hilltop
Kestrel Cl
Falcon Rdg
Loring Rd
Coram Close
Briar Way
Chestnut Drive
Hazel Rd
Ashlyns School
Ashlyns Hall
The Thomas Coram Middle School
KINGSHILL WAY
Cemetery
A41(T)
Rossway
Marlin Chapel Farm
Northchurch Lane
Lane
Hog Lane Farm
Hog Lane
Johns Lane Farm
Johns Lane
Hockeridge Bottom
Haresfoot Farm
Haresfoot School
Sandpit Green
Swing Gate Lane
Hertfordshire County
Buckinghamshire County
CHESHAM ROAD
Harriott's End Farm
Old Oak Farm
Snowhill Farm
Snowhill Cottages
Cemetery
Flamstead Farm
White Hill
Dells Lane
Thorne Barton
Spencer's Farm
Berkhamsted Sch
Castle Street
Chapel St
Mill Street
Station Road
Whitehill
Ellesmere Rd
George Street
Surgery
Swing Gate Lane
Hillside Gdns
St Margarets Close
Swing First Sc
Greene Walk
Captains Wk
34
51
1
2
3
4
5
6
7
8
9
10
01
09
08
07
06
205

34
Frithsden Gardens
Brickkiln Cott
A
B
C
D
E
F
G
500
01
02
10
09
08
07
06
205
1
2
3
4
5
6
7
8
9
10
Frithsden
Vineyard
Nettleden Road
Frithsden Copse
Golf Course
Hollybush Cl
Browns Spring
Works
Olivers
End
Road
Water
Homefield
Vicarage Gdns
Vicarage
Road
The Hamlet
Briar Cl
Hedgeside
Common Gdns
The Front
The Back
School
The Common
Church Rd
Chestnut Cl
Rambling Wy
Rambling Way
The Laurels
Potten End
Berkhamsted Golf Club
Whybrow Gdns
Britwell Dr
The Common
Hempstead
Lane
Haresfoot Senior School
Gutteridge Farm
Little Heath
Little Heath Farm
Little Heath Lane
Berkhar
Shenstone Hl
Byways
Path
Hunters Pk
Lamerck Copse
Bracken Hl
New Road
Berkhamsted Castle (Remains)
Berkhamsted Station
Castle Hill Av
Lower Kings Road
Whitehill
Gilpin's Ride
Meadway
House
Lane
Bullbeggars Lane
Pouchen End Lane
Fields
Fields End
Station Road
Gravel Path
Millfield
Mill Street
Surgery
Sch Ho
Chapel St
School
George Street
Ellesmere Road
Grantham Ms
PH
PO
Ivy
Bank Mill
George St
LONDON ROAD
Victoria Road
Highfield Road
Curtis Way
Holly Dr
Swing Gate First School
Greene Walk
Captains Wk
Hillside Gdns
Lombardy Drive
Cedar Road
Bank
Mill
Lane
Bankmill Bridge
33
Chesham Road
Hilltop
Kestrel
Falcon
Woodlands Av
Oak Dr
Sycamore
Hazel Rd
St Margaret's Close
Hall Park
Hall Park Hill
Hall Park Gate
Fieldway
Upper Hall Park
Coram Close
Briar Way
Chestnut Drive
Ashlyns School
The Thomas Coram Middle School
Ashlyns Hall
River Bulbourne
Grand Union Canal
Works
Little Heath Lane
Pouchen End
Pouchen End Lane
Long Green
Broadway Farm
A41(T)
Sandpit Green
Swing Gate Lane
Pix
Farm
Lane
Sharpes Lane
Grand Union Canal Wk
Hotel
Sugar Lane
LONDON
ROAD
A4251
Bourne End
Bourne End La
Bottom Farm
Lower Farm
Bourne Gutter
Stoney La
Hotel
Upper Bourne End La
Vale Farm
Golf Course
Westbrook Hay Preparatory School
Westbrook Ha
Upper Bourne End Lane
Bourne End La
Little Hay Golf Complex
Hill
Spencer's
52
BOX
Bury Rise
B4505
Shothanger Wy
1 grid square represents 500 metres

Water End
Nettleden Road
Potten End Hill
Bigham's Park Farm
Rumblers Farm
Gaddesden Hall
Noake Mill
Wood Farm
Lovetts End Farm
Piccotts End
Grovehill
Barnctoft JMI School
Aycliffe Drive Primary School
Boxted Farm
Housewood End
Fennycroft Road
Link Rd
A4147
A4146
Leighton Buzzard Road
Gadebridge
Warners End
Highfield
Queensway
Hammerfield
Counters End
HEMEL HEMPSTEAD
Chaulden
Green End
Boxmoor
Two Waters
Station Road
London Road
Hemel Hempstead Station
Roughdown Common
Felden
Boxmoor Golf Club
Sheethanger Common
Apsley
Apsley Mills Retail Park
Apsley Station
Apsley Manor
Hyde Farm
Longcroft Farm
Highcroft Road
St Albans Road
A414
A4251
A41(T)
Hemel Hempstead General Hospital
Dacorum Sports Centre
Hemel Hempstead Town Cricket Club
Frogmore Road Industrial Est
Jupiter JMI School
Tudor Primary School
Belswains Infant School
Nash Mills Primary School
H J K L M N P
04 05 06
36
53

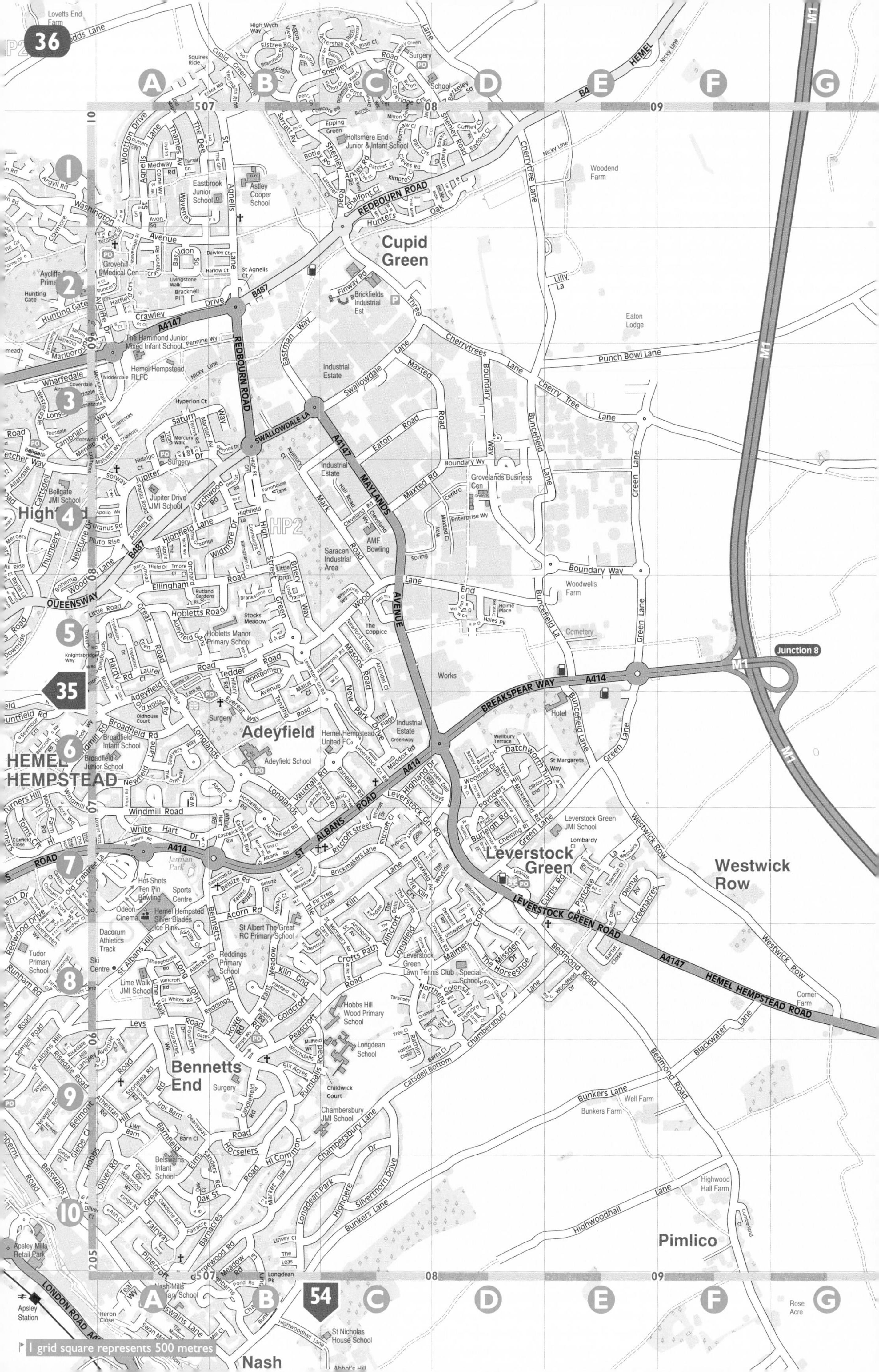

36
35
54
Cupid Green
Adeyfield
Leverstock Green
Westwick Row
HEMEL HEMPSTEAD
Highfield
Bennetts End
Pimlico
Nash
Lovetts End Farm
Woodend Farm
Eaton Lodge
Woodwells Farm
Highwood Hall Farm
Bunkers Farm
Well Farm
Corner Farm
Rose Acre
Junction 8
M1
A4147
A414
B487
REDBOURN ROAD
MAYLANDS AVENUE
BREAKSPEAR WAY
ST ALBANS ROAD
LEVERSTOCK GREEN ROAD
HEMEL HEMPSTEAD ROAD
QUEENSWAY
LONDON ROAD
Punch Bowl Lane
Cherry Tree Lane
Green Lane
Buncefield Lane
Bedmond Road
Westwick Row
Bunkers Lane
Highwoodhall Lane
Chambersbury Lane
Brickfields Industrial Est
Industrial Estate
Saracen Industrial Area
Grovelands Business Cen
Works
Hemel Hempstead United FC
Adeyfield School
Holtsmere End Junior & Infant School
Astley Cooper School
Eastbrook Junior School
Leverstock Green JMI School
Hobbs Hill Wood Primary School
Longdean School
Chambersbury JMI School
Belswains Infant School
Apsley Station
Apsley Mills Retail Park
St Nicholas House School
Cemetery
Hotel
1 grid square represents 500 metres

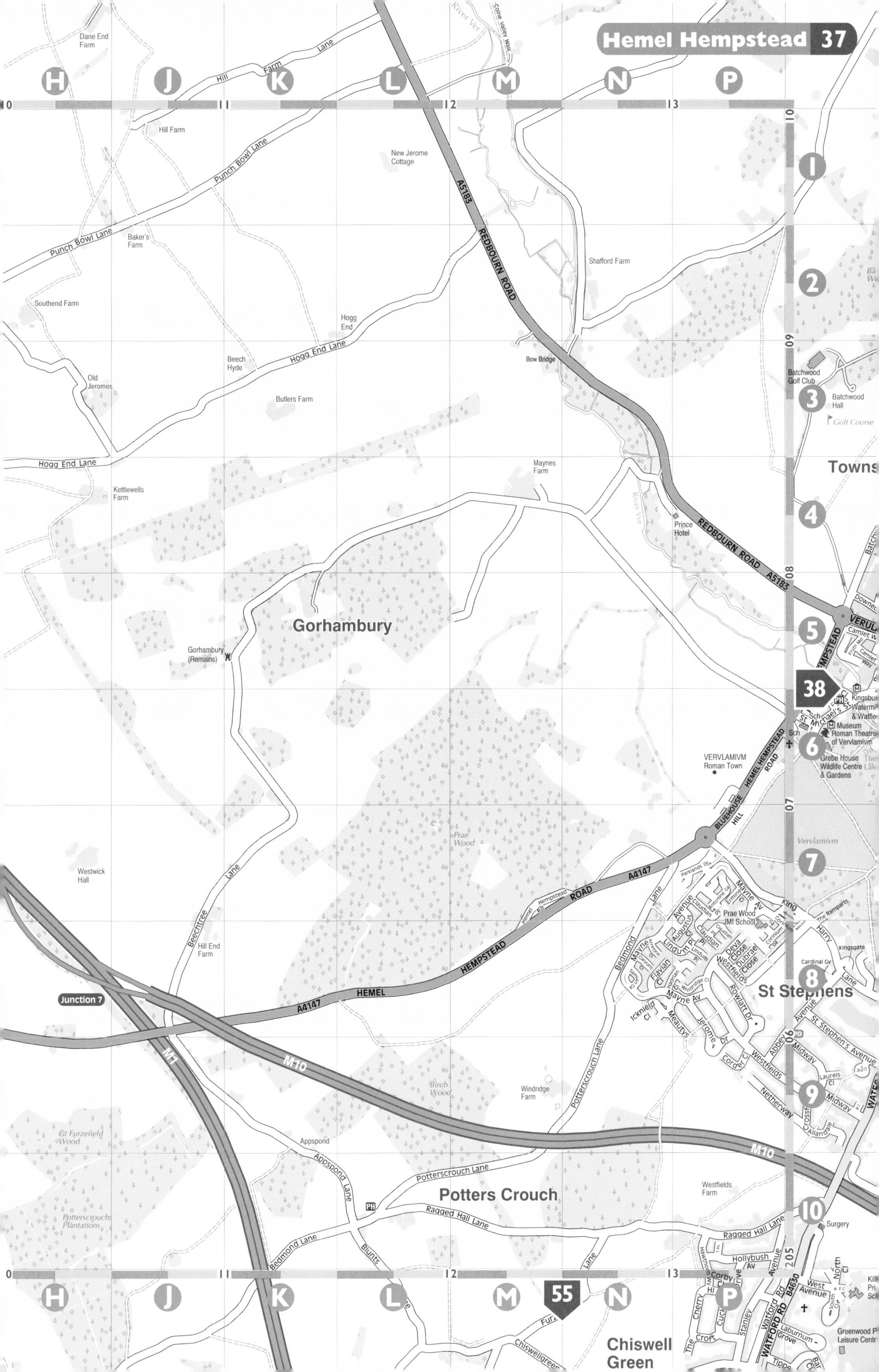
Dane End Farm
Hill Farm Lane
Hill Farm
Punch Bowl Lane
Baker's Farm
New Jerome Cottage
A5183
REDBOURN ROAD
River Ver
Colne Valley Walk
Shafford Farm
Southend Farm
Hogg End
Hogg End Lane
Beech Hyde
Old Jeromes
Butlers Farm
Bow Bridge
Batchwood Golf Club
Batchwood Hall
Golf Course
Kettlewells Farm
Maynes Farm
Prince Hotel
Gorhambury
Gorhambury (Remains)
VERVLAMIVM Roman Town
Kingsbury Watermill & Waffle
Museum
Roman Theatre of Verulamium
Grebe House Wildlife Centre & Gardens
BLUEHOUSE HILL
HEMEL HEMPSTEAD ROAD
Prae Wood
Vervlamivm
Westwick Hall
Beechtree Lane
Hill End Farm
A4147
HEMEL HEMPSTEAD ROAD
Junction 7
Prae Wood JMI School
St Stephens
M1
M10
Birch Wood
Windridge Farm
Potterscrouch Lane
Gt Furzefield Wood
Appspond
Appspond Lane
Potters Crouch
Westfields Farm
Ragged Hall Lane
Potterscrouch Plantations
Bedmond Lane
Blunts
Surgery
Chiswell Green
Chiswellgreen
WATFORD RD B4630
38
55

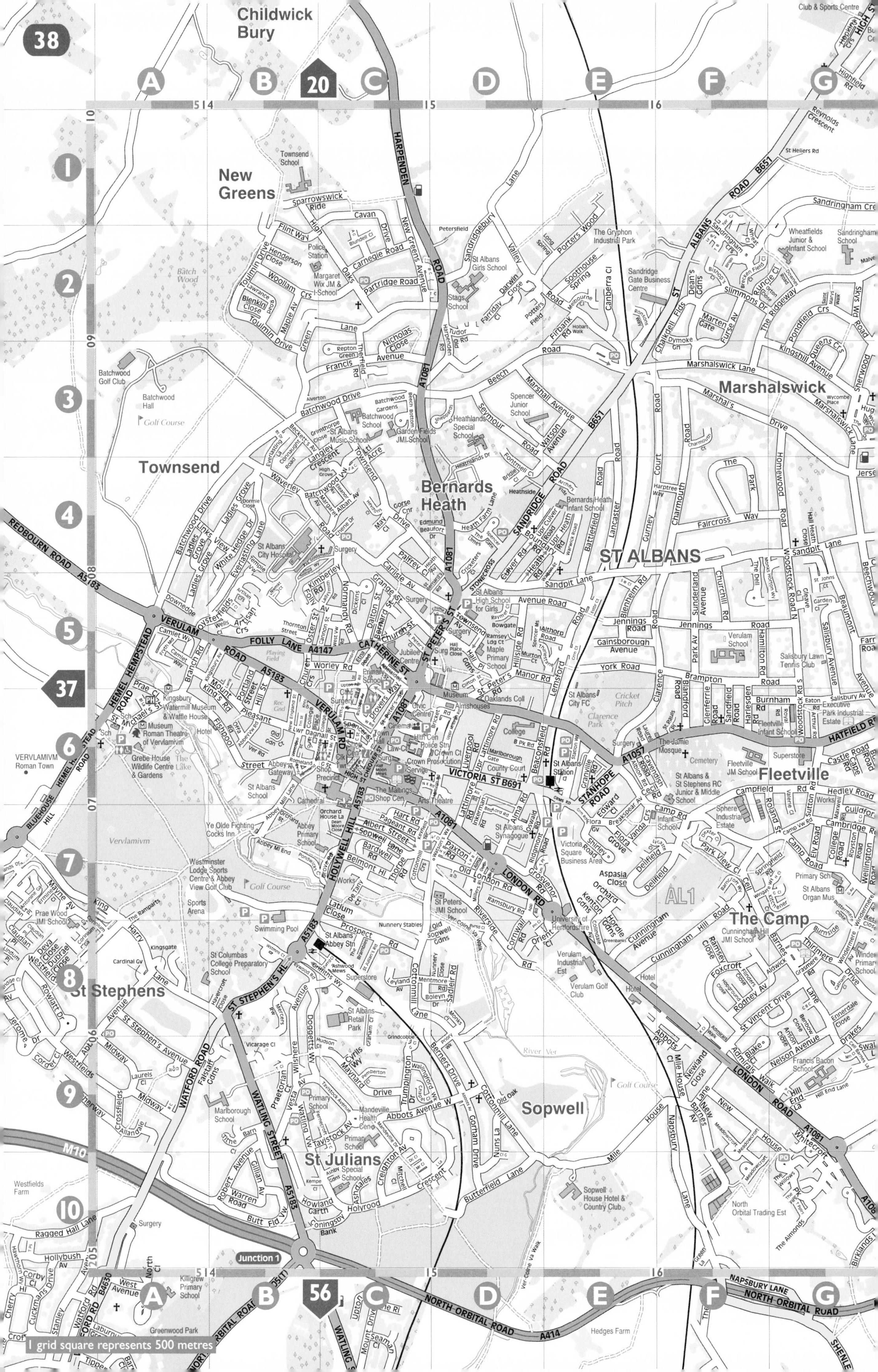
Childwick Bury
20
A
B
C
D
E
F
G
514
15
16
10
09
08
07
06
205
1
2
3
4
5
6
7
8
9
10
37
56
New Greens
Townsend School
Sparrowswick Ride
Cavan Drive
Flint Way
Henderson Close
Police Station
Toulmin Drive
Woollam Crs
Blenkin Close
Maple Av
Margaret Wix JM & I School
Carnegie Road
New Greens Avenue
Partridge Road
HARPENDEN ROAD
Petersfield
Sandridgebury Lane
St Albans Girls School
Stags School
Valley Road
Darwin Close
Porters Wood
The Gryphon Industrial Park
Soothouse Spring
Canberra Cl
Sandridge Gate Business Centre
Batch Wood
Batchwood Golf Club
Batchwood Hall
Golf Course
Townsend
Repton Green
Francis Rd
Nicholas Close
Avenue
Batchwood Drive
Batchwood School
St Albans Music School
Garden Fields JMI School
Heathlands Special School
Spencer Junior School
Beech Road
Seymour Road
Marshal Avenue
Watson Avenue
Marshalswick Lane
Marshalswick
Marshal's Drive
Wheatfields Junior & Infant School
Sandringham School
Sandringham Cre
ST ALBANS ROAD B651
Reynolds Crescent
St Heliers Rd
Highfield
Club & Sports Centre
Bernards Heath
SANDRIDGE ROAD
Bernards Heath Infant School
Battlefield Road
Lancaster Road
Gurney Court
Charmouth Road
Faircross Way
Homewood Road
Woodstock Road N
Sandpit Lane
ST ALBANS
St Albans City Hospital
Ladies Grove
Batchwood Drive
White Hedge Dr
Everlasting Lane
Kimberley Rd
Normandy Rd
Dalton St
Grange St
St Albans High School for Girls
Avenue Road
Jennings Road
Gainsborough Avenue
Verulam School
York Road
Brampton Road
Burnham Road
Salisbury Lawn Tennis Club
Salisbury Avenue
Executive Park Industrial Estate
Fleetville Infant School
HATFIELD RD
Fleetville
Fleetville JM School
Superstore
Castle Road
REDBOURN ROAD A5183
VERULAM ROAD A5183
FOLLY LANE A4147
CATHERINE ST
Playing Field
Jubilee Centre
Maple Primary School
Manor Rd
St Peter's St
Oaklands Coll
Almshouses
Museum
HEMEL HEMPSTEAD ROAD
Kingsbury Watermill Museum & Waffle House
Museum Roman Theatre of Verulamium
Grebe House Wildlife Centre & Gardens
The Lake
VERULAMIVM Roman Town
St Albans City FC
Cricket Pitch
Clarence Park
College
The Jamie Mosque
Cemetery
St Albans & St Stephens RC Junior & Middle School
St Albans Station
STANHOPE ROAD
VICTORIA ST B691
Civic Centre
Cinema
Hlth Cen
Police Stn
Crown Ct
Crown Prosecution Service
County Court
Arts Theatre
The Maltings Shop Cen
Cathedral
St Albans School
Abbey Gateway
HOLYWELL HILL A5183
LONDON RD A1081
St Albans Synagogue
Victoria Square Business Area
Camp Rd
Sphere Industrial Estate
Campfield Rd
Hedley Road
Cambridge Ro
Primary Sch
St Albans Organ Mus
Ye Olde Fighting Cocks Inn
Vervlamivm
Abbey Primary School
Westminster Lodge Sports Centre & Abbey View Golf Club
Golf Course
Sports Arena
Swimming Pool
Prae Wood JMI School
King Harry Lane
Kingsgate
Cardinal Gv
St Columbas College Preparatory School
Latium Close
Prospect Rd
Nunnery Stables
St Peters JMI School
Ramsbury Rd
Riverside
University of Hertfordshire
Verulam Industrial Est
Verulam Golf Club
Cunningham Avenue
Cunningham Hill JMI School
AL1
The Camp
Aspasia Close
Orchard Close
Hotel
St Albans Abbey Stn
Superstore
St Albans Retail Park
Cottonmill Lane
St Stephens
ST STEPHEN'S HL
St Stephen's Avenue
WATFORD ROAD
Marlborough School
Vicarage Cl
WATLING STREET A5183
Primary School
Mandeville Health Cen
Abbots Avenue W
Berners Drive
Cottonmill Lane
Gorham Drive
River Ver
Sopwell
Golf Course
Mile House Lane
Napsbury Lane
Newland Close
New Barnes Av
Meadowcroft
LONDON ROAD A1081
Whitecroft
Francis Bacon School
Nelson Avenue
St Vincent Drive
Drakes Drive
St Julians
Ashby Special Schools
Holyrood
Howland Garth
Coningsby Bank
Creighton Av
Crescent
Butterfield Lane
Sopwell House Hotel & Country Club
North Orbital Trading Est
The Almonds
M10
Westfields Farm
Robert Avenue
Warren Road
Butt Fld Vw
Ragged Hall Lane
Surgery
Junction 1
Hollybush Av
Killigrew Primary School
West Avenue
Greenwood Park
NORTH ORBITAL ROAD A414
Hedges Farm
NAPSBURY LANE
NORTH ORBITAL ROAD
SHENLEY
BLUEHOUSE HILL
1 grid square represents 500 metres

Sandridge
Woodcockhill
AL4
Fairfold's Farm
Sutton Farm
21
H
J
K
L
M
N
P
17
18
19
20
Astwick Manor
School of Art & Design
Hatfield Business Park
Hatfield Aerodrome
House Lane
St Leonards Crs
Jersey La
Wendover Cl
Pirton Cl
Cromwell Close
Nashe's Farm
Cooper's Green
Coopers Green Lane
Chiltern Road
Windmill Av
The Ridgeway
Sandringham Crescent
Craiglands
Beverley Gdns
Ripon Wy
Cheriton Cl
Tewin Close
Evans Grove
Chandlers Rd
Skyswood JMI School
Hazelmere Road
St John Fisher RC JMI School
Woodfield Wy
Meadow Close
Packhorse Close
Briar Road
Villiers Crs
Beech Farm
Oak Farm
Ellenbrook
Newgate Cl
Sandpit Lane
Barnfield Road
Buxton Cl
Ardens Way
The Ridgeway
St Albans Lawn Tennis Club
Oaklands Lane
North Drive
East Drive
Oaklands College
Oakwood JMI School
Beaumont School
Woodland Drive
Central Dr
Hazelwood Drive
Oakwood Drive
Elm Drive
Kay Walk
Wynchlands Crs
A1057
HATFIELD ROAD
Pinewood Cl
Cedarwood Dr
Cresford Cl
Sewell Cl
Firwood Av
Popefield Farm
St Albans Road West
Bramble Road
Poplars Close
Wilkin's Green Lane
Springfield Rd
Station Road
Smallford
Smallford Trail
Acrewood Way
Industrial Estate
Lyon Way
40
Hill End Lane
Colney Heath Lane
Hobbs Close
Swans Close
Nicholas Breakspear RC School
Brick Knoll Park
de-Havilland Aircraft Heritage Centre
Bramley Wy
Diana Dr
Camp Rd
Oxford Av
Hill End La
Highfield Lane
Puddingstone Dr
Smallford Farm
Sleapshyde
Sleapshyde Lane
Smallford Lane
Police Station
Sleapcross Gardens
A414
NORTH ORBITAL ROAD
Colney Heath JM&I School
Colney Heath
High St
Church Lane
Park Corner
Park La
High Street
Meadway
Tyttenhanger Green
Barley Mow Lane
Tyttenhanger
Nightingale Lane
Cemetery
Highfield Hall
Warren Farm
River Colne
Tyttenhanger Farm
LONDON ROAD
London Road
A1081
Alexander Rd
Five Acres
Oldfield Rd
Old Verulamians RFC
Coursers Road
Coursers Farm
57
1
2
3
4
5
6
7
8
9
10
10
09
08
07
06
205

40
22
58
39
A
B
C
D
E
F
G
1
2
3
4
5
6
7
8
9
10
Hatfield Garden Village
Astwick Manor
School of Art & Design
Hatfield Business Park
Hatfield Aerodrome
AL10
Frobisher Way Hatfield Business Park
Bishops Square Business Park
Ellenbrook
Nast Hyde
Hatfield Business Park
Galleria Shopping Centre
Birchwood Leisure Centre
Birchwood
The Ryde
Hatfield Station
Old Hat
Roe Green
HATFIELD
Oxlease
University of Hertfordshire
Junction 3
Junction 2
ORBITAL ROAD
ROEHYDE WAY
COMET WAY
GREAT NORTH ROAD
HERTFORD ROAD
ST ALBANS ROAD WEST
ST ALBANS ROAD EAST
QUEENSWAY
CAVENDISH WAY
SOUTH WAY
WELLFIELD ROAD
FRENCH HORN LA
Hatfield Leisure Centre
Hatfield House
Real Tennis Club
Cemetery
South Hatfield
Marshmoor
Bullen's Green
Colney Heath
Roestock
Welham Green
Welham Green Station
Alpha Business Park
Tollgate Farm
Warren Farm
Hazelgrove Primary School
Bishops Square Business Park
Potterells Medical Centre
1 grid square represents 500 metres

Mill Green
Mill Green Golf Club
Golf Course
Gypsy Lane
Burnside
Holwell Court
HATFIELD ROAD
A414
Holwell Lane
B1455
Lea Valley Walk
River Lea or Lee
Home Park
The Vineyard
Hillend Farm
Essendonbury Farm
Essendon Hill B158
Church St
Rectory Cl
School Lane
East View
Cottages
Essendon Primary School
High Road
West End
West End Lane
Bedwell Farm
Golf Course
Essendon Place
Bedwell Park
Hatfield London Country Club
Pope's Farm
Park Dairy
Coombe Wood
B158
Camfield Place
Cucumber Hall Farm
Woodside
Woodside Place
Wildhill
Wildhill Road
Woodside Lane
Hornbeam Lane
Kentish Lane
Warrenwood Park
AL9
Lower Woodside
Grubbs Lane
Westfield
Woodhill House
Woodfield Lane
Woodfield Farm
A1000
GREAT NORTH ROAD
Barbers Lodge Farm
Kentish Lane Farm
Fox's Lane
Bulls Lane
Bell Bar
Bell Lane
The Drive
Chancellors School
Ash Close
Pine
Upland
Brookmans Park Golf Club
H
J
K
L
M
N
P
23
42
59
24
25
26
27
1
2
3
4
5
6
7
8
9
10
05
06
07
08
09
10

42
24
41
60
A B C D E F G
1 2 3 4 5 6 7 8 9 10
528
29
30
Essendon
Little Berkhamsted
Bayford
Epping Green
Tylers Causeway
Newgate Street
Holwell Court
Roxford
Works
Water Hall Farm
Howe Green
Kennel Hall Farm
Bayford Hall
Culverwood House
Bayford Wood
Bayford Primary School
Essendon Primary School
Bedwellpark Farm
Golf Course
Essendon Place
Bedwell Park
Hatfield London Country Club
Bucks Farm
Bush Farm
Bedwell Lodge Farm
Cucumber Hall Farm
Woodcock Lodge
Epping House School
Ashendene Farm
Woodcock Lodge Farm
Coldharbour Farm
Barbers Lodge Farm
Ponsbourne Park
New Park Farm
Ponsbourne St Marys JMI School
HOLWELL
LOW ROAD
B1455
B158
LOWER HATFIELD ROAD
Broad Green
Bayford Lane
ESSENDON HILL B158
HIGH ROAD
Lea Valley Walk
Bedwell Avenue
Bedwell Av
School Lane
Chain Walk
Stockings Lane
Robins Nest Hill
Little Berkhamstead La
Little Berkhamstead Lane
Church Road
Goddards Cl
Bucks Alley
Ashendene Road
Cucumber Lane
Woodfield Lane
Tylers Causeway
New Park Road
New Pk Rd
Newgate Street Village
1 grid square represents 500 metres

Bayfordbury College of Hertfordshire
Broadgreen Wood
SG13
Clements Farm
Edwards Green Farm
Mangrove Lane
Dalmonds
Elbow Lane
Warren House
Bayford Green
Monks Green
Highfield Wood
Bayford Station
Fanshaws
Fanshaws Lane
Brickendon Lane
Brickendon
Cowheath Wood
Brickendon Grange Golf Club
Blackfan Wood
Golf Course
Broxbourne Wood
Pembridge Lane
Wood House Lane
Paradise Wildlife Park
Ettridge Farm
Claypits
Chain Walk
White Stubbs Lane
Ponsbourne Tunnel
Bencroft Wood
Emanual Pollards
Wormley West End
Path Short Valley Way
Westlea
West End Road
Wormley Wood
Holy Cross Hill
Beaumont Manor
Beaumont Road
Bread and Cheese Lane
Derry's Wood
Thunderfield Grove
Park Lane Paradise
Factory Fa
Ashendene Road
Lawrence
Tanfield Stud Farm
Brace Cl
Shambrook Rd
Bittern Close
Nightingale Rd
Dahlia Close
Darnicle Hill
Hammondstreet Road
Sadler
Bread & Cheese La
25
44
61
31
32
33
34
H
J
K
L
M
N
P
1
2
3
4
5
6
7
8
9
10
205
06
07
08
09
10

A
B
C
D
E
F
G
535
36
37
10
09
08
07
06
205
1
2
3
4
5
6
7
8
9
10
Woollensbrook
Brides Farm
Roundings
Elbow Lane
B1197
HERTFORD ROAD
Roseland Junior Middle & Infant School
Howfield Gn
Westbury Close
Cemetery
Briscoe Close
Briscoe Road
College Road
West Hill Road
Surgery
WARE ROAD
A1170
Dymokes Way
Nursery Road
Wallers Way
Stanstead
Ditchfield Road
Forres CP School
The Drive
Dorchester Av
Tovey Avenue
Stockfield Avenue
Highbury Road
Kingsfield
Whitley Road
Hawthorn Road
Crossfield Road
Lilac Road
Middlefield Road
Rye Road
Rye Park
Ryelands JMI School
River Avenue
Gladstone Road
Box Wood
Goose Green
Works
Westfield Community Primary School
Saffron Close
Goodwood Close
Cherry Tree Road
Westfield Road
Norris Rise
Cillocks Close
Hillside
Paddick Close
Winterscroft Road
EN11
Duke Street
DINANT LINK RD
Essex Road
Parrotts Field
Stortford Road
Dalmonds
Marsh Lane
Box Lane
Lord Street
A10(T)
Kennedy Avenue
Burnside
Langton Road
Brookside
Haslewood Junior School
Infant School
Bell Lane
Amwell Street
High Street
Brewery Road
Conduit Lane
Rosehill Close
Rose Vale
Norris Road
High Leigh
Hoddesdon Lawn Tennis Club
Lowfield Sports Ground
Brocket Road
Park Road
CHARLTON WAY
Lampits
St Augustines RC Primary School
Priory Close
Highfield Wood
Hoddesdonpark Wood
HODDESDON
Park View
Hoddesdon Health Centre
Civic Hall Cinema
Lowewood Museum
Yewlands Drive
Yew Walk
Yewlands
Sheredes School
Upper Marsh Lane
St Cross RC Primary School
Spitalbrook
Woodlands Drive
HIGH STREET
Admirals Walk
Cock Lane
Crabtree Wk
Warners Av
Sheredes Drive
Benford Road
Parkwood Close
Park Lane
The Avenue
St David's Drive
St Catharine's Road
Osborne Road
Meadway
Stratfield Drive
Springfields
New Road
The Rowans
Woodstock Road
Sutton Close
Mandeville Close
St Augustines Drive
St Michael's Road
Friarscroft
Monks Close
Alamein Close
Norris Groove
Gold Close
Sheriden Walk
Pulham Avenue
Carnaby Road
Bourne Close
Grosvenor Road
Mc Kenzie Road
The Paddock
Churchfields Lane
Churchfields
Broxbourne Station
43
STATION ROAD B194
Broxbourne
River Lea or Lee
Surgery
Church View
Mill Lane
Somerby Close
Borrell Close
Graham Av
Baas Lane
Allard Way
Cold Hall
HIGH ROAD BROXBOURNE
HIGH ROAD
Grenville Avenue
Trafalgar Avenue
Broxbourne Sports Club
Baas Hill
Baas Hill Close
Highfield Drive
Tudor Rise
Beverly Close
Broxbourne Primary School
Crownfield
Keysers Estate
Carneles Green
Spring Walk
Baas Manor Farm
Church Lane
The Broxbourne School
The Lawns Drive
Winford Drive
Keysers Road
Riverside Avenue
Great Meadow
Buttondene Crescent
Cozens Lane West
Cozens Lane East
Briarley Close
Ley Park CP School
Wormley West End
EN10
Bushby Avenue
Berners Way
Clayton Close
Green Lane
St Laurence Drive
Church Lane
Wormleybury
Wormley Primary School
Holy Cross Hill
HIGH ROAD WORMLEY
Lammasmead
Surgery
Works
Nazeing Marsh
The Croft
Pembroke Close
Westlea Road
Wharf Road
LC
Wormley
Elgin Road
Fairfield Dr
Oaklands Grove
Home Close
Macer's Lane
Huntingdon Close
Slipe Lane
King's Weir
Factory Farm
HIGH RD TURNFORD
New River
The Oval
The Springs
Mulberry Close
Park Lane Paradise
62
A10(T)
Turnford
West Side
B176
Longlands Primary School
Langridge
1 grid square represents 500 metres

26
43
62

Rye Meads
Roydon Leisure Park
Roydon
Harlow Road
High Street
B181
27
Rye Park Industrial Estate
Rye House Station
Rye House Stadium
Hoddesdon Industrial Estate
Optima Business Park
Trident Industrial Estate
New England Industrial Estate
Belcon Industrial Estate
The Lynch
Plumpton Road
Castle Road
Pindar Road
Essex Road
Bingley Road
Normandy Way
River Stort
Stort Valley Way
Three Forests Way
The Grove
Roydon CP School
Lightfoots
Hansells Mead
Park Fields
Kingsmead Close
Epping Road
Downe Hall
Didgemere Hall
Halls Green
CM19
B181 Epping
Ratty's Lane
Glen Faba Road
Low Hill Road
Netherhall Road
Chariton Mead Lane
Waterside Industrial Estate
Lea Valley Walk
Dobb's Weir
Dobb's Weir Road
Avenue Road
Blythe Road
Clyde Road
Derby Road
Eldon Road
Lee Valley Caravan Park
Nazeing Mead
Sedge Green
Barn Hill
Hamlet Hill
Reeves Lane
Roydon Hamlet
46
Hertfordshire County
Essex County
Broxbourne Sailing Club
Meadgate
Meadgate Road
Meadgate Works
Stoneshot Common
Hoe Lane
Betts Lane
Peck's Hill
Lake Road
North Street
Maplecroft Lane
John Eliot Close
Highland Road
Banes Down
Nursery Road
Shooters Drive
Palmers Grove
Western Road
Hillgrove Business Park
Old Nazeing Road
Elizabeth Close
Mayflower Close
Crooked Way
Hyde Mead
Nazeing CP School
Barnard Acres
Tovey Close
Pound Close
Middle Street
Lower Nazeing
Tatsfield Avenue
Nazeing
Back Lane
Nazeing Park School
Golf Course
Perry Hill
Curtis Farm
Nazeing Golf Club
Belchers
Belchers Lane
Bumble's Green
Paynes Lane
St Leonards
St Leonards Road
Laundry Lane
63
Waltham
Nazeing Long Green
Council Building
The Avenue
Bumbles Green Lane
Nazeing Gate
H
J
K
L
M
N
P
1
2
3
4
5
6
7
8
9
10
38
39
40
41
205

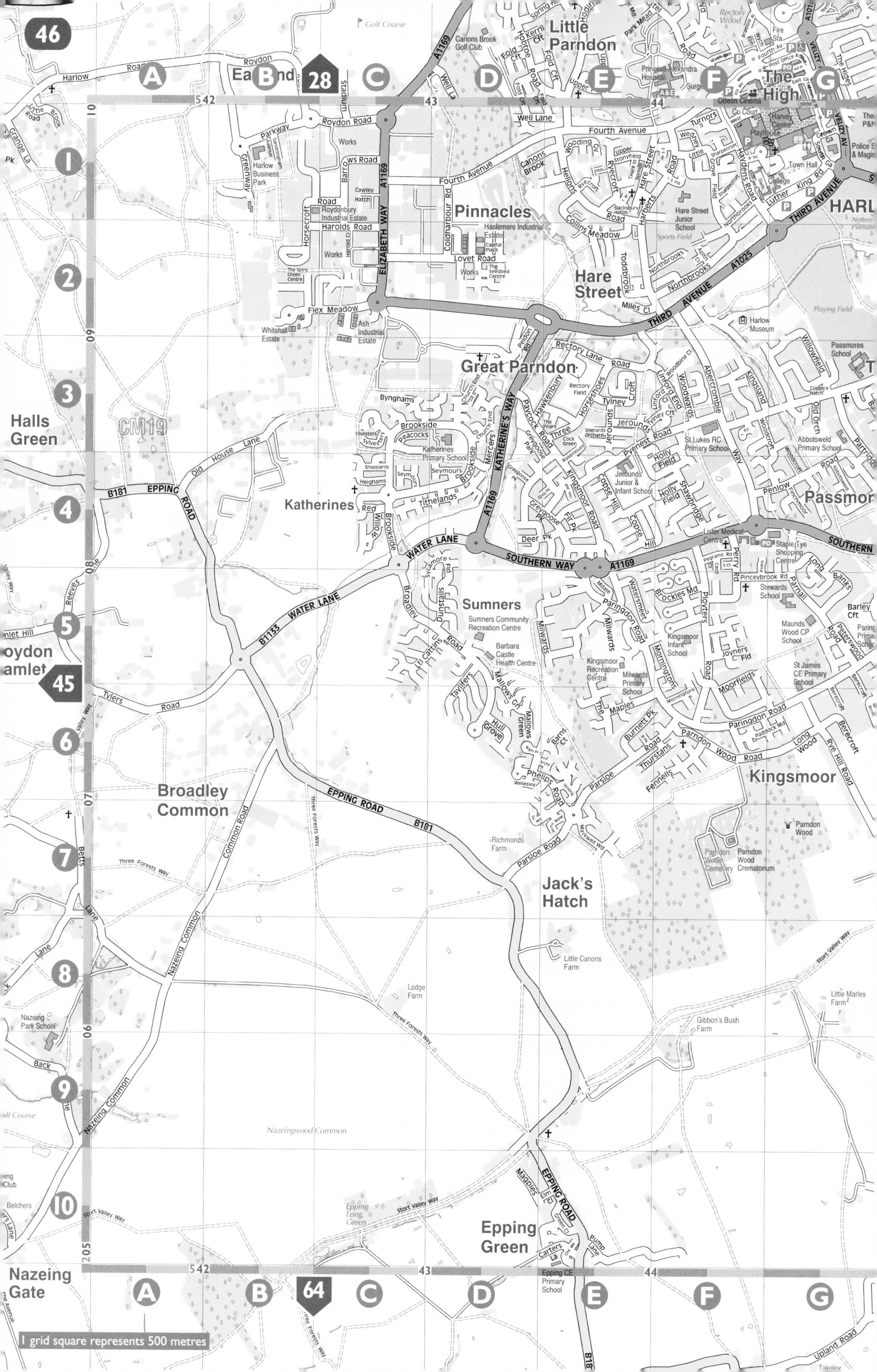
Golf Course
Roydon Road
Harlow Road
Eastend
28
Stadium
A
B
C
D
E
F
G
542
43
44
Little Parndon
Canons Brook Golf Club
Well La
Well Lane
Fourth Avenue
Princess Alexandra Hospital
A&E
Odeon Cinema
The High
Harvey Centre
Playhouse
Town Hall
College
Police Sta & Magis
Fire Sta
Rectory Wood
HARL
Parkway
Harlow Business Park
Greenway
Works
Barrows Road
Cawley Hatch
Roydonbury Industrial Estate
Horsecroft Road
Harolds Road
ELIZABETH WAY
A1169
The Spire Green Centre
Flex Meadow
Whitehall Estate
Ash Industrial Estate
Pinnacles
Haslemere Industrial Estate
Capital Place
Lovet Road
Coldharbour Rd
The Seedbed Centre
Canons Brook
Hare Street
Hare Street Junior School
Sports Field
Collins Meadow
Toddbrook
Northbrooks
THIRD AVENUE
A1025
Harlow Museum
Playing Field
Passmores School
Miles Cl
Rectory Lane
Great Parndon
Paycock Road
Hawkenbury
Horseshoes
Tylney Croft
Jerounds
Linford End
Woodwards
Abercrombie Way
Kingsland
Willowfield
Coppice Hatch
Abbotsweld Primary School
Partridge
Old Orch
Woodcroft
Penlow
Passmor
St Lukes RC Primary School
Pyenest Road
Holly Field
Jerounds Junior & Infant School
Copse Hill
Kingsmoor Road
Fir Pk
Greygoose Pk
Deer Pk
Rectory Field
The Friars
Sherards Orchard
Cock Green
Bynghams
Brookside
Peacocks
Katherines Primary School
Seymours
Sylvesters
Sheppards
Heighams
Tithelands
Church End
Mercers
KATHERINE'S WAY
Katherines
Red Willow
CM19
Halls Green
Old House Lane
B181
EPPING ROAD
WATER LANE
B1133
SOUTHERN WAY
Lister Medical Centre
Staple Tye Shopping Centre
Perry Rd
Pincey Brook Rd
Stewards School
Long Banks
Parnall
Barley Cft
Maunds Wood CP School
Petersweood
St James CE Primary School
Beresfort
Sumners
Sumners Community Recreation Centre
Sycamore Fld
Dunstalls
Broadley Road
Barbara Castle Health Centre
Ltl Cattins
Taylifers
Mallows Grn
Hull Grove
Barns Ct
Phelips Road
Wellesley
Millwards
Paringdon Road
Watersmeet
Brockles Md
Ploughers
Kingsmoor Infant School
Kingsmoor Recreation Centre
Millwards Primary School
Morningtons
The Maples
Burnett Pk
Joyners Fld
Moorfields
Paddock Md
Parndon Wood Road
Thurstans
Fennells
Long Wood
Rye Hill Road
Kingsmoor
Parndon Wood
Parndon Wood Cemetery
Parndon Wood Crematorium
Parsloe Road
Markwell Wd
Richmonds Farm
Jack's Hatch
Little Canons Farm
Stort Valley Way
Little Marles Farm
Gibbon's Bush Farm
Lodge Farm
Three Forests Way
Broadley Common
Common Road
Nazeing Common
Nazeingwood Common
Tylers Road
Reeves Cle
Roydon Hamlet
45
Betts Lane
Nazeing Park School
Back Lane
Belchers
Epping Long Green
Magpies
Epping Green
EPPING ROAD
Pump Lane
Carters La
Epping CE Primary School
64
Nazeing Gate
Upland Road
1 grid square represents 500 metres

Netteswell
The Dashes
Harlow College
Lavender Close
Broadfields Primary School
Whitewalts
Arkwrights
Parsonage Leys
Clinic
Long Ley
Maddox
Home Cl
Manston Rd
The Downs
Greenhills
Longley Wood
Howard Way
Quarry Springs
Ladyshot
Latton Hall Cl
Church Langley
Church Langley Primary School
Florence Nightingale Health Centre
Minton Lane
Chamberlain Cl
Aynsley Gdns
Mallards Rise
Ashworth Place
Rushton Grove
Sheldon Cl
Old Hall Rise
Ridgeways
Elwood
Doulton Cl
Chelsea Gdns
Davenport
Wedgewood Drive
Albert Gdns
Lane End
Malkin Dr
Church Langley Way
Tickenhall Dr
Westbury
Kiln La
Burley Hill
Coalport Cl
Pilkingtons
Bentley Drive
Fenton Grange
Belfield Gdns
Kiln Lane
Oaklands Dr
Abbey Dale
Works
Kingsdon Lane
Fullers Mead
London Road
The Gardiners
Victoria Cl
Hadley Gra
Second Av
Latton St
Pytt Fld
A1025 SECOND AVENUE
A1025
A414
Latton Street
St Marks RC Comprehensive School
St Andrews Meadow
Westfield
Tripton Road
Waterhoose Moor
Tendring Road
Church Leys
Brays Grove
Great Leylands
Purford Green
Sadlers Mead
Tumbler Road
Nicholls Fld
Manor Hatch Cl
Tilbury Road
Spencers Cft
Purford Green Primary School
Stile Cft
Tilbury Mead
Brays Grove School
Longfield
Primary School
Tracyes Rd
Tillwicks Rd
Little Brays
Industrial Estate
Brays Md
The Fortunes
Bushey Cft
Rushes Mead
Hook Field
Pawneys Road
Tilegate Road
Upper Hook
Yorkes
The Fairway
Primrose Field
Surgery
Community Clinic
A1169 SOUTHERN WAY
Pear Tree Md
Trotters Road
Spinning Wheel Md
Brookline
Latton House
Priory Ct
Hotel
Pynchons
Regency Ct
Upr Mealines
Wharley Hook
Tysea Road
Latton Bush Business Centre
Sakins Cft
The Readings
Latton Bush Recreation Centre
Commonside Road
Commonside School
Rundells
Radburn Cl
Latton Bush
Latton Green
Clarkhill
Fernhill
CM18
Five Acres
Coppins Cl
Carters Mead
Pinewood Cl
Hastingwood Business Cen
Potter Street
Potter Street Primary School
Southern Way
Chapel Flds
Chapel La
Church Rd
Hillside
Red Lion Lane
Red Lion Crescent
Perry Spring
Fullers Mead
Potters Fld
Sweyne
Potter Street
Harlow Common
Forest Way
Harlow Common
Latton Street
London Road
Park Av
Stort Valley Way
Harlow Park
Foster Street
Works
Mill Street
M11
LONDON ROAD
Latton Park
Junction 7
Hastingwood Road
PH
Glovers La
Glovers Farm
Hastingwood
48
Hilly Fld
Hawthorns
Cnr Meadow
Riddings Lane
Forest Way
Sort Valley Way
Lodge Hall
Gibb Cft
Sibneys Gn
Spruce Hill
Fern Hill Lane
Fernhill Cottage
Stewards
Mark Bushes
Dorrington Farm
Rundells
A414
CANES LANE
Canes Farm
Rye Hill
Rye Hill Road
Horseshoes Farm
Rivetts Farm
B1393
LONDON ROAD
Marles Farm
Rye Hill Road
Esgors
Orchard Farm
Crispey Brook
HIGH ROAD
Upland Road
Upper Clapton RFC
Blake Hall
Weald Hall
Weald Hall Lane
Hayley Manor Farm
Upland Road
Thornwood Common
Weald Hall Lane
Carpenters Arms La
Industrial Estate
Pinch Timber Farm
29
65
H
J
K
L
M
N
P
1
2
3
4
5
6
7
8
9
10
46
47
48

Hubbard's Hall
Hobbs Cross
30
Loyter's Green
Faggotters Lane
Faggoters Farm
Way Lane
New Way
CM17
Roffey Hall
M11
Ridgeways
Doulton Cl
Chelsea Gdns
Threshers Bush
Green Lane
New Way La
Foster Street
Works
Great Wilmores
Stort Valley Way
Tilegate Green
School Lane
Tilegate Road
Hall Farm
Magdalen Laver
Mill Street
Wynter's Farm
Hastingwood Road
Rolls Farm
Spencers Farm
Willow Pl
Wynter's Grange
Hastingwood
47
Humphreys
Greens Farm
Shonks Brook
Sewalds Hall Farm
Weald Lodge
Paris Hall
Glovers Farm
Kents Lane
Weald Bridge Road
Weald Bridge
Ashlyns Lane
Ashlyns
Canes Farm
CANES LANE
Golf Course
Little Weald Hall
North Weald Golf Club
A414
Wyldingtree
Rayley Lane
New House Farm
Tower Close
Bluemans End
St Andrews Close
Bluemans
Hows Mead
Vicarage Close
Vicarage Lane
Tyler's Green
HIGH ROAD
EPPING RO
Weald Hall
Weald Lane
Merlin Way
St Andrews CE Primary
66
Beamish Close
Oak Piece
Green Lane
Princes Close
B181
1 grid square represents 500 metres

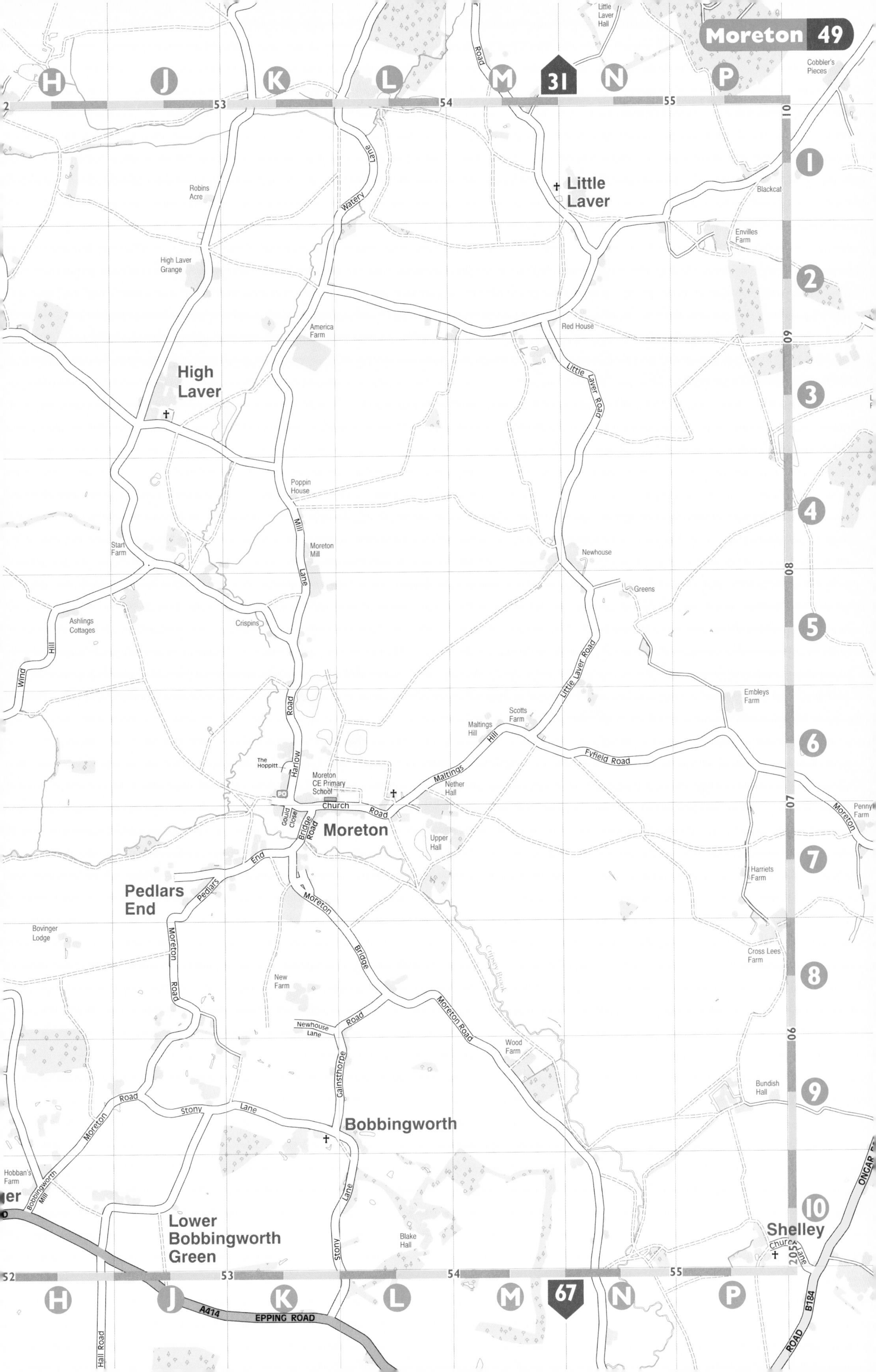
Little Laver Hall
Cobbler's Pieces
H
J
K
L
M
31
N
P
53
54
55
Robins Acre
Watery Lane
Road
Little Laver
Blackcat
Envilles Farm
High Laver Grange
America Farm
Red House
High Laver
Little Laver Road
Poppin House
Mill Lane
Moreton Mill
Start Farm
Newhouse
Greens
Ashlings Cottages
Crispins
Wind Hill
Embleys Farm
Scotts Farm
Maltings Hill
Harlow Road
The Hoppitt
Moreton CE Primary School
PO
Maltings Hill
Nether Hall
Fyfield Road
Church Road
Gould Close
Bridge Road
Moreton
Upper Hall
Moreton
Penny Farm
Pedlars End
Harriets Farm
Bovinger Lodge
Moreton Bridge
Cripsey Brook
Cross Lees Farm
Moreton Road
New Farm
Newhouse Lane
Road
Moreton Road
Wood Farm
Bundish Hall
Moreton Road
Stony Lane
Gainsthorpe Road
Bobbingworth
Hobban's Farm
Bobbingworth Mill
Lower Bobbingworth Green
Stony Lane
Blake Hall
Shelley
Church Lane
ONGAR
A414
EPPING ROAD
Hall Road
B184
ROAD
52
67
10
09
08
07
06
05
1
2
3
4
5
6
7
8
9
10

Bellingdon
Asheridge Farm
Chesham Road
Ramscote Lane
Chartridge End Farm
Ashotts Lane
Savecroft Farm
Widmore Farm
Widmore Cl
Asheridge
Tile's Farm
Copse Way
Broadview Farm
Mount Nugent
Great Hivings
Broadview Road
Hazeldene Farm
HP5
Cogdells Close
Cogdells Lane
Chartridge Combined School
Chartridge Grange Drive
Raymonds
Old Sax Lane
Chartridge Park Golf Club
Chartridge Lane
Buslins Lane
Greenway School
Greenway
Junior School
Chartridge
Westdean Lane
Great Hivings
Asheridge Road
Saxeway Business Centre
Golf Course
Ridgeway
Belmont Road
Windsor Road
Pednor Bottom
The Warren
Upland Avenue
Hivings Hill
Berkeley Avenue
Cross Meadow
Longfield Road
Pednor Bottom
Little Pednor Farm
Valley Vw
Darvell Drive
Asheridge Road Industrial Est
Poles Hill
Fair Leas
Pond Park
Milton Road
Pond Pk Road
Pulpit Cl
Chartridge Lane
Pednor Road
Chapmans Crescent
Deansway
Harries Cl
Chalk Hill
Bellingdon Road
Dellfield
Dorney End
Aylward Gardens
Elmtree Infant School
Works
Fire Station
Chiltern Link
Herberts Hole
Hollow Way
Little Hundridge Farm
Rose Acre
Beechcroft
Oak Field
Penn Av
Hampden Avenue
Lowndes Avenue
Chesham Park Community College
Webb Close
Stanley Avenue
Surgery
Bellingdon Rd
Park Road
Council Building
Drydell Lane
Little Hundridge Lane
Lowndes Park
Skottowes Pond
St Mary's Wy
Town Hall
Hundridge Manor
Bury Pond
The Bury
Church St
Chesham Road
B485
Pednormead End
Hawthorn Farm
B485
Browns Rd
Hyde House
Missenden Road
Rycroft Road
Chessbury Road
Germains Close
Daves Cl
Chessbury Rd
Delmeade Road
Junior School
Chesham Health Cen
Halfway House Farm
Fuller's Hill
Fuller's Close
Chesham United FC
Hyde Heath Road
White's Wood
Hydeheath Common
Hyde Heath
White House Farm
Bullbaiters Lane
Bromley La
Heath Rd
Hyde Heath Infant School
Fuller's Hill
Brays Lane
Cedar Rdg
Saunders End
Harvest Bank
Weedon Hill Farm
Weedon
Brays Close
Mayhall Farm
Winstone Close
Our Ladys School
The Beacon School
Oakway
A416
1 grid square represents 500 metres

Ashley Green
Flamstead Farm
Cemetery
Thorne Barton
Pressmore Farm
Chesham Vale
Nashleigh Farm
ASHLEY GREEN ROAD
NASHLEIGH HILL A416
Two Dells Lane
Grove Farm
Chesham Preparatory School
Orchard Leigh
Grove Lane
RUSHMERE LANE B4505
Hemming's Farm
Whelpley Hill Park
Whelpley Hill
Moors Farm
Lycrome Road
Lye Green
Deer Pk Walk
Brushwood Junior School
Brockhurst Farm
LYE GREEN ROAD
Jasonshill Farm
Jasons Hill
Buckinghamshire County
Hertfordshire County
Marchant's Farm
Ver Coine Va
Newtown
Hilltop
Howard Industrial Estate
BERKHAMSTEAD ROAD
BROAD STREET
Heritage House School
Codmore
Codmore Crescent
Warrender Road
B4505
ESKDALE AVENUE
Botley Road
Botley Lane
Birch Tree Grove
Grooms Cottages
Ley Hill School
Ley Hill
Ley Hill Cricket Club
Golf Course
Botley
Tylers Hill Road
Kiln Lane
Tyler's Hill
Blackwell Hall Lane
Chesham High School
Chesham Leisure Centre
Police Station
CHESHAM
Chesham Station
Dungrove Farm
Ashridge Lane
Ashridge Farm
Horse Hill
Meadhams Farm
Pinner Green
Prospect Industrial Estate
Chesham Community Hospital
Chessmount
Orchard House Industrial Estate
Waterside
Combined School
Pump Lane
Green Lane
Codmore Wood
White End Park
Great End
Latimer Road
Mill Close
Lower Bois
Cemetery
Chiltern Link
Broadwater Bridge
AMERSHAM ROAD
Frith Wood
Clifton Lawns
Chesham Bois CE Combined Sch
Blackwell Hall
Chess Valley Walk
H
J
K
L
M
N
P
33
52
69
96
97
98
99
05
04
03
02
01
200
1
2
3
4
5
6
7
8
9
10

Westbrook Ha
34
Little Hay
Golf Complex
Upper Bourne End La
Bourne End La
BOX
B4505
Bury Rise
Shothanger Wy
Spencer's
Farm
Hemming's
Farm
Whelpley
Hill Park
Grove Lane
Hill
Whelpley
Hill
Moors
Farm
HM
Prison
Duckhau
Farm
Hawkings
Wy
Newhouse Rd
The Bourne
Anson Close
Lancaster
Mitchell
Cl
Howard
Anne Close
Bushfield Road
HEMPSTEAD ROAD
Hotel
PH
Vicarage Lane
St Lawrence Cl
Granville Dene
Council
Building
Bovingdon
Primary
School
Church
Lane
Stoney Lane
High
Surgery
PO
Church St
BOVINGDON
Lane
Farm
Longcroft Lane
Copse Hi
Cl
CHESHAM
ROAD
B4505
Hyde Lane
Old Dean
Hamer Cl
Dinmore
Eastnor
Pembridge Cl
Ashridge
Ryder Cl
Rymill Close
Nye Wy
Lane
Orchard
Homefield
Yew Tree Dr
Austins
Mead
Chipperfield Rd
Arden Close
Farnham Cl
Green
Louise
Wk
Little Pk
Ver-Colne Valley Walk
Pudds
Cross
Bovingdon
Green
Lane
Green
Cl
Vw
Shantock
Hall
Lane
Bovingdon
Green
Hunters
PH
Waterlane
Farm
Water
Lane
Middle
Lane
Long Lane
Long Lane
Farm
Flaunden Lane
Cottingham
Farm
Marchant's
Farm
Maples
Farm
Shantock
Lane
Shantock
Hall
Meadow Way
Farm
Oxgate
Farm
Middle Lane
Venus
Hill
Holly
Hedges
Lane
Long Lane
Venus
Hill
New Maulden
Farm
Venus Hill
Farm
Flaunden Lane
Ley Hill
Cricket Club
Golf Course
Chesham & Ley Hill
Golf Club
Ashridge
Ashridge
Farm
Lane
Horse
Hill
Simon Dean's
Wood
Jay's
Hatch
Long
Lane
Hogpits Bottom
Hogpits
Bottom
PH
Woodman's
Wood
Lower
Plantation
Cherry Trees
Farm
Birch
Lane
Flaunden
Pinner
Green
Hockley Farm
Sharlowe's
Farm
PH
Flaunden
Hill
Whitedell
Farm
Rose Hall
Farm
Hall Lane
Wood
Road
Great White
End
Flaunden
Bottom
Hollin's
Hall
Moonshine Farm
Frith Wood
70
Flaunden
Bottom
Martin Tae
1 grid square represents 500 metres

Boxmoor Golf Club
Sheethanger Common
Golf Course
Felden Dr
Felden Lane
Sheethanger La
Featherbed
Manorville Road
King Edward St
Weymouth St
Cade Vw
Apsley
Apsley Retail
35
Two Waters JMI School
High Ridge Cl
Apsley Station
LONDON ROAD A4251
Golf Course
Nash Mills Primary Sc
Heron Close
Hyde Farm
Tower Farm
Highcroft Road
Bury Wood
Longcroft Farm
Longcroft Lane
Flaunden La
Apsley Manor Farm
Shendish Manor Golf Club
HP3
Valley Farm
Bulstrode Lane
Praisels Wood
A41(T)
Rucklers Lane
Works
Abbots Vw
Barnes Rise
Ladymeadow
Roundwood
Barnes Lod
Flaunden Lane
Nuffield Farm
Barnes Farm
Barnes Lane
Barnes La
Kings Langley Primary School
KINGS LANGLEY
Common
Bulstrode
Bulstrode Lane
Bulstrode Cl
Scatterdells Wood
Love La
Vicarage
Five Acres
Rudolf Steiner School
Hill
54
Tower Hill
Chipperfield Road
Balls Pond Farm
Megg Lane
Wayside
Whippendell Farm
Meggacres Farm
WD4
New Road
Tenements Farm
Stoney Lane
Tuffs Farm
Chipperfield House
Scatterdells Lane
Croft Fld
Croft Meadow
Croft End Rd
Croft Lane
Courtaulds
Langley Road
Whippendell Hill
Whippendell Bottom
Alexandra Rd
Braziers Farm
Chapel Croft
Pale Farm
The Street
Forge Cl
King's Lane
King's Cl
Havenfield
Chipperfield
Hotel
Chipperfield Junior & Infant School
Rockery Wood
Langley Ldg La
Langley Lodge Lane
Dunny Lane
Queen St
The Common
Rose Farm
Woodmans Farm
Windmill Hill
Chipperfield Common
Langley Lodge Farm
Belsize
Olleberrie Lane
Ltl Windmill Hl
Hollow Hedge
Penman's Green
Callipers Hall
Bucks Hill
Flaunden Lane
Belsize Farm
Poles Hill
Plough Lane
Hillmeads Farm
Jeffery's Farm
Quickmoor Lane
Rosehall Wood
Commonwood
Baytree Farm
Bucks Hill
Great Sarratt Hall
71
Moor Lane
Red Lion Lane
Sarratt
Great Westwood
H
J
K
L
M
N
P
03
04
05
06
1
2
3
4
5
6
7
8
9
10
200

54
36
53
72
Nash Mills
Ruckl rs Lane
KINGS LANGLEY
Bedmond
Pimlico
Abbots Langley
Hunton Bridge
Langleybury
Leavesden Green
Apsley Station
Apsley Mills Retail Park
Golf Course
Nash Mills Primary School
St Nicholas House School
Abbot's Hill School
Hyde Farm
Hart Hall Farm
Rose Acre
Highwood Hall Farm
Barnes Lodge
Barnes Farm
Kings Langley Primary School
Happy Valley Industrial Est
Kings Park Industrial Est
Sunderland Est
Council Building
Surgery
Rudolf Steiner School
Numbers Farm
Bedmond JMI School
Abbots Langley Primary School
Kings Langley Station
Home Park Industrial Estate
Station Footpath
Clapgate Farm
Junction 20
Langley Lodge Farm
Berrybushes Wood
Model Farm
St Pauls CE Primary School
Breakspeare School
Tanners Wood Primary School
Hill Farm Industrial Est
Great Westwood
HEMPSTEAD ROAD A4251
LONDON ROAD A4251
HIGH ST A4251
WATFORD ROAD
M25
A41(T)
Grand Union Canal
River Gade
Hyde Lane
Harthall Lane
Tom's Lane
Bedmond Road
Abbots Road
Gallows Hill
Langley Lodge Lane
Old House Lane
1 grid square represents 500 metres

Kings Langley
55
37
56
73
Potters Crouch
Potterscrouch Lane
Ragged Hall Lane
Bedmond Lane
Bluntts Lane
Potterscrouch Plantations
Chiswell Green
Chiswellgreen Lane
Furzebushes Lane
Watford Road
Tippendell Lane
Hollybush Av
Cherry Hl
Corby Cl
Cuckmans Drive
Stanley Avenue
The Croft
West Avenue
North Cl
Laburnum Grove
Barry Close
Greenwood Leisure Cent
Surgery
Bone Hill
Gardens of the Rose (Royal National Rose)
Daneswick
Sergehill
Sergehill Lane
Whitehouse Farm
Whitehouse Lane
Millhouse Lane
Millhouse Farm
Bell Lane
Searches Lane
Searches Farm
Noke Lane
Noke Farm
Holt Farm
Business Centre
Forge End
Long Fallow
Belvedere Gdns
Driftwood Avenue
Willow Way
Orchard Dell
Mayflower
Penman Cl
N Orbital Rd
A405(T) NORTH ORBITAL ROAD
Lye Lane
Tenterden House
Birchwood Wy
Applecroft
Hazel Road
Homewood Independent School
Tenements Farm
East Lane
Junction 21a
Junction 6a/21
M25
M1
Park Street Lane
Horseshoe Business Park
Five Acres Av
Oakwood
Oakridge
Ryall Cl
Reynard's Wy
Stratford Wy
Short Lane
Jordan's Way
Woodside Road
The Meads
Riding
Ashridge Drive
Larch Av
Broad Acre
Newlyn Close
The Uplands
Birch Copse
Jenkins Avenue
Wildwood Av
Pine Gr
Brackendene
West Riding
N Riding
South Riding
Oak Av
Lye Lane
Black Boy Wd
Works
Smug
Mount Pleasant
Mount Pleasant J & I School
Yule Cl
The Crs
St Lawrence Wy
Hamilton Cl
Rowan Cl
Hunters Ride
Claremont
Station Rd
Bricket Wood Station
Drop Lane
Bricket Wood
Ferndene
Ash Copse
Bucknalls Drive
Enid Cl
The Kestrels
Bricket Wood Common
Chequers Lane
Waterdale
Junction 6
Cem
East Lane
Woodside Road
High Elms Lane
Parmiters School
West Herts Crematorium
Cemetery
A405(T) NORTH ORBITAL ROAD ST ALBANS ROAD
St Michaels RC School
Francis Combe School
Garston Manor Special School
Primary School
Bucknalls Lane
Verdure Close
Tudor Mnr Gdns
Coates Way
Bridger Cl
Coates Way Prim Sch
Chichester Wy
Cranefield Drive
Kytes Dr
Mutchetts Cl
Little Munden Farm
School Lane
Leavesden Hospital
Abbotsford Medical Cen
College Road
Horseshoe Lane
Boundary Wy
Louvain Way
Poplars Close
Woodside
Infant School
Newhouse Crescent
Woodside Stadium
Watford Sports & Leisure Centre
Alban Wood Junior School
Albans Vw
Ganders Ash
Sheepcot La
Hill Farm Av
High Road
Woodgate
St Michaels Dr
Warner Village Cinema
Forest Road
Sheriff Wy
Leavesden Green Junior Middle & Infant School
Haines
Police Stn
KINGSWAY
NORTH ORBITAL ROAD
A405(T)
North Approach
Kingswood
Meadow Road
Hillingdon Road
Kingswood Road
Briar Road
Sheepcot Medical Cen
Crown Rise
St Albans Road
A412
ST ALBANS RD
Gaddesden Crs
Bovingdon Crs
Garston Drive Community Mental Health Centre
North Watford Hlth Clinic
Avon Cl
Kingsway Infant School
Garston
Garston Station
Garston JMI School
Stanborough School
North Watford Cemetery
Fern Way
Clarke Way
Rushton Avenue
First Avenue
Second Av
Third Av
Fourth Avenue
The Gossamers
Valley Walk

St Julians
Junction 1
38
North Orbital Trading Est
Sopwell House Hotel & Country Club
Killigrew Primary School
Greenwood Park Leisure Centre
NORTH ORBITAL ROAD A405(T)
WATLING STREET A5183
NORTH ORBITAL ROAD A414
NAPSBURY LANE
NORTH ORBITAL ROAD
SHENLEY LANE B5
Hedges Farm
Park Street
Park Street Station
Radlett Aerodrome
Napsbury Hospital
WATFORD ROAD B4630
WATFORD
How Wood
How Wood Station
AL2
Park Industrial Estate
Stroud Wood Business Cen
Park Street CE Primary School
St Albans Musical Museum
FROGMORE
Frogmore
Homewood Independent School
Hampden Place
RADLETT
M25
55
Smug Oak Green Business Cen
Horseshoe Business Park
Colney Street
Ventura Park
Old Parkbury
Smug Oak Lane
Smug Oak
Bricket Wood Station
Sports Centre
Works
HARPER LANE B556
Drop Lane
River Colne
Netherwyde Farm
Houndswood
Bricket Wood Common
Ver-Colne Valley Walk
Little Munden Farm
Hill Farm
A5183
Radlett Station
ROMAN ROAD
ALDENHAM ROAD
Radlett & Bushey Reform Synagogue
74
A B C D E F G
1 2 3 4 5 6 7 8 9 10
514 15 16
1 grid square represents 500 metres

LONDON COLNEY
Broad Colney
Shenleybury
Shenley
RADLETT
Cemetery
Highfield Hall
Old Verulamians RFC
Coursers Farm
Coursers Road
Bowmansgreen Farm
Riverside Industrial Estate
THE BELL ROUNDABOUT
Junction 22
Nature Reserve
Superstore
Salisbury Hall
Mosquito Aircraft Museum
Pastoral Centre
Manor Lodge School
Shenley Lodge
Clore Shalom School
Harperbury Hospital
Shenleybury Cottages
Combe Wood
Wild Farm
Shenley Hall
Shenley JMI School
Pursley Farm
Porters Park Golf Club
Golf Course
Southridge
Rabley Park Farm
Rectory Lane
Mimms Lane
Black Lion Hill
London Road
Radlett Lane
Shenley Lane
Harper Lane
Bell Lane
North Orbital Road
A414
A1081
B556
B5378
M25
WD7
39
58
75

Water End
South Mimms
Ridge
Dancers Hill
Walsingham Wood
Cobs Ash
Potwells
Mymmshall Wood
Redwell Wood
Hawkshead Wood
Coursers Farm
Redwell Wood Farm
Manor Lodge School
Southridge
Rabley Park Farm
Deeves Hall
Earl's Farm
Blanche Farm
Bignell's Corner
The Grange
North Mymms Cricket Club
Potterells Medical Centre
Potterells
Brookmans Station
Royal Veterinary College
New Cottages
Warrengate Farm
Mymms Hall
The Wroxham School
St Giles Primary School
Bridgefoot
Hotel
Service Centre
South Mimms Service Area
Junction 1/23
Tollgate Road
Dixons Hill Close
Dixons Hill Road
Station Road
Bradmore Lane
Abdale Lane
Swanland Road
Warrengate Road
Warrengate Lane
Coursers Road
Blackhorse Lane
St Albans Road
Cecil Road
Rectory Lane
Packhorse Lane
Mimms Lane
Earls Lane
Deeves Hall Lane
Crossoaks Lane
Blanche Lane
Greyhound Lane
Hamilton Close
Frowycke Crs
New Road
St Giles' Avenue
Brookside
Bignells Corner
Summerswood
Windmore Avenue
Deepdene
Wroxham Gardens
Ranworth Gdns
Ormesby Drive
Oulton Crescent
Mimms Hall Road
Kimptons Close
Kimptons Mead
Mutton Lane
Welham Manor
Mymmshall Brook
Catharine Bourne
River Colne
A1(M)
M25
B556
A
B
C
D
E
F
G
1
2
3
4
5
6
7
8
9
10
40
57
76
1 grid square represents 500 metres

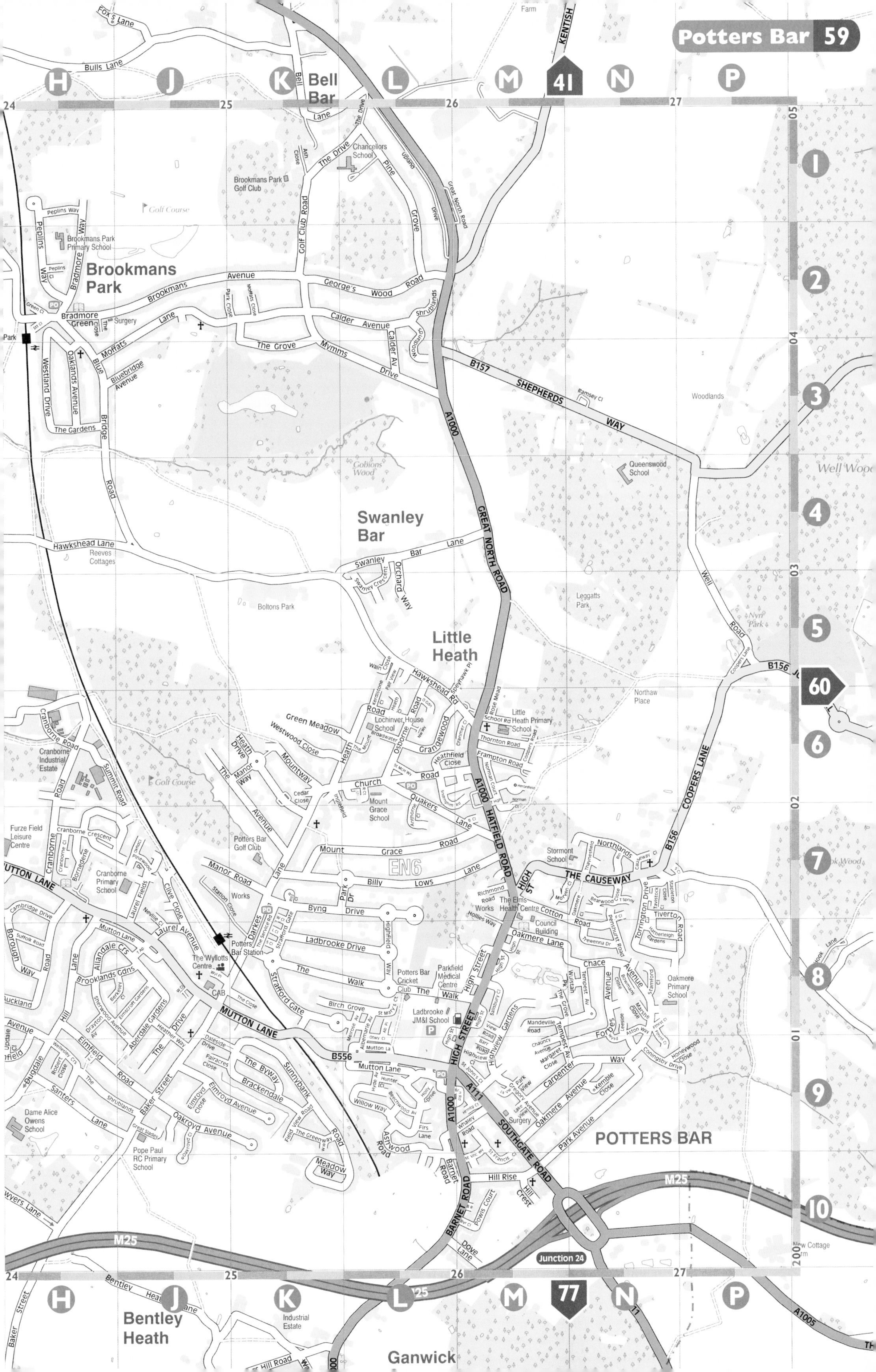

Bell Bar
Brookmans Park
Swanley Bar
Little Heath
POTTERS BAR
Bentley Heath
Ganwick
Bulls Lane
Fox's Lane
Bell Lane
KENTISH
Farm
Chancellors School
Brookmans Park Golf Club
Golf Course
Brookmans Park Primary School
Peplins Way
Peplins Way
Bradmore Way
Brookmans Avenue
George's Wood Road
Golf Club Road
Pine Grove
Upland Drive
Great North Road
The Drive
Ash Close
Park Close
Moffats Close
Shrublands
Calder Avenue
Calder Av
Woodlands Cl
Mymms Drive
The Grove
Moffats Lane
Bradmore Green
Green Cl
Surgery
Bluebridge Avenue
Oaklands Avenue
Westland Drive
The Gardens
Bridge Road
Blue Bridge Road
Park
B157
SHEPHERDS WAY
Ramsey Cl
Woodlands
Queenswood School
Well Wood
A1000
GREAT NORTH ROAD
Gobions Wood
Hawkshead Lane
Reeves Cottages
Swanley Bar Lane
Swanley Crescent
Orchard Way
Boltons Park
Leggatts Park
Well Road
Nyn Park
B156
Coopers Lane
COOPERS LANE
Northaw Place
Wain Close
Hawkshead Rd
Sparrowhawk Pl
Rose Mead
Little Heath Primary School
School Rd
Thornton Road
Frampton Road
Coopers Road
Kerdistone Close
Heath Road
Osborne Road
Lochinver House School
Broadwater
Grangewood
Heathfield Close
Cranmer Cl
Green Meadow
Westwood Close
Mountway
Heath Drive
The Manor Way
The Avenue
Church Road
Cedar Close
Mount Grace School
Quakers Lane
Norman Court
Heronfield
Cranborne Road
Cranborne Industrial Estate
Summit Road
Golf Course
Potters Bar Golf Club
Furze Field Leisure Centre
Cranborne Crescent
Cranborne Road
Cranborne Primary School
Mount Grace Road
EN6
Billy Lows Lane
A1000 HATFIELD ROAD
HIGH ST
THE CAUSEWAY
Northlands
Stormont School
Causeway Cl
Richmond Road
Works
Hollies Way
The Elms Health Centre
Council Building
Cotton Road
Oakmere Lane
Torrington Drive
Tiverton Road
Penshurst Road
Trewenna Dr
Chace Avenue
Tempest Av
Oakmere Primary School
Manor Road
Station Close
Works
Lane
Park Dr
Byng Drive
Highfield Way
Ladbrooke Drive
Darkes Lane
Potters Bar Station
Stafford Gate
The Walk
Potters Bar Cricket Club
Parkfield Medical Centre
High Street
The Walk
Ladbrooke JM&I School
Birch Grove
Mutton La
MUTTON LANE
B556
Mutton Lane
The Wyllotts Centre
CAB
The Close
MUTTON LANE
Cambridge Drive
Suffolk Road
Borough Way
Mutton Lane
Alandale Crs
Laurel Fields
Laurel Avenue
Clive Close
Neville Cl
Brooklands Gdns
Aberdale Gardens
The Drive
Auckland
Hill Lane
Emfield Road
The Shrublands
Santers Lane
Dugdale
Baker Street
Great Slades
Pope Paul RC Primary School
Dame Alice Owens School
Oakroyd Avenue
Elmroyd Avenue
Elmroyd Close
Dalesde Drive
Fairacres Close
The Byway
Brackendale
Sunnybank Road
Field View Road
The Greenway
Meadow Way
Hunter
Willow Way
Firs Lane
Ashwood Road
HIGH STREET
A1000
A111
SOUTHGATE ROAD
Whaley Road
Highview Gardens
Mandeville Road
Margaret Close
Temperest Av
Carpenter Way
Forbes Av
Aston Way
Coningsby Drive
Honeywood Close
Oakmere Avenue
Kemble Close
Park Avenue
Park View
Surgery
St Francis Cl
Barnet Road
BARNET ROAD
Hill Rise
Hill Crest
Powis Court
Dove Lane
M25
Junction 24
New Cottage Farm
A1005
Bentley Heath Lane
Baker Street
Industrial Estate
Hill Road
Dwyers Lane
H
J
K
L
M
N
P
1
2
3
4
5
6
7
8
9
10
24
25
26
27
05
04
03
02
01
200
41
60
77

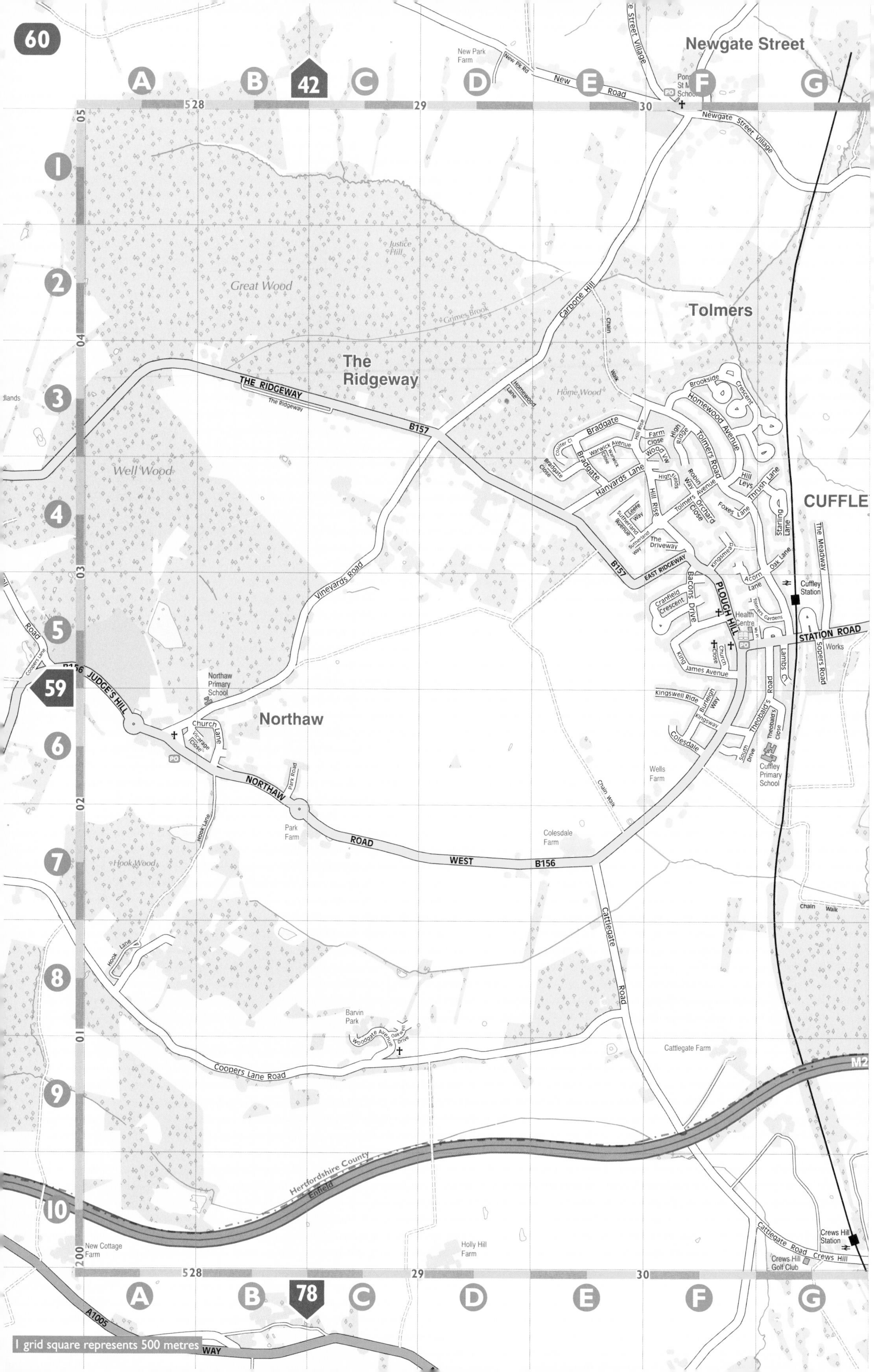
42
59
78
A
B
C
D
E
F
G
528
29
30
05
04
03
02
01
200
1
2
3
4
5
6
7
8
9
10
Newgate Street
New Park Farm
New Pk Rd
New Road
Street Village
Newgate Street Village
Great Wood
Justice Hill
Grimes Brook
The Ridgeway
THE RIDGEWAY
B157
Well Wood
Carbone Hill
Chain Walk
Homewood Lane
Home Wood
Tolmers
Brookside
Crescent
Homewood Avenue
Tolmers Road
Bradgate
Bradgate Close
Coulter Cl
Warwick Avenue
Hill Rise
Farm Close
High Ridge
Wood Vw
Hanyards Lane
Robin Way
Hill Leys
Thrush Lane
CUFFLE
Foxes Lane
Starling Lane
Leete Way
Sutherland Avenue
Sutherland Way
The Driveway
Tolmers Avenue
Orchard Close
Kingsmead
EAST RIDGEWAY
Oak Lane
Acorn Lane
Cuffley Station
The Meadway
Cranfield Crescent
Bacons Drive
PLOUGH HILL
Tolmers Gardens
Health Centre
STATION ROAD
Works
Sopers Road
Lambs Close
Church Close
King James Avenue
Kingswell Ride
Burleigh Way
Kingsway
Colesdale
Theobald's Road
Theobald's Close
South Drive
Cuffley Primary School
Vineyards Road
Road
Coopers Lane
B156
JUDGE'S HILL
Northaw Primary School
Northaw
Church Lane
Vicarage Close
PO
NORTHAW
Park Road
Park Farm
ROAD
WEST
Wells Farm
Chain Walk
Colesdale Farm
Hook Lane
Hook Wood
Cattlegate Road
Chain Walk
Barvin Park
Woodgate Avenue
Oakwell Drive
Coopers Lane Road
Cattlegate Farm
M25
Hertfordshire County
Enfield
New Cottage Farm
Holly Hill Farm
Cattlegate Road
Crews Hill Station
Crews Hill
Crews Hill Golf Club
A1005
WAY
1 grid square represents 500 metres

Hammond Street
Lucas End
GOFF'S OAK
Rosedale
Crews Hill
Cheshunt Common
Saint Lawrence Farm
Burleigh Farm
Tanfield Stud Farm
Beaumont Manor
Derry's Wood
Thunderfield Grove
Darnicle Hill
Hammondstreet Road
Newgatestreet Road
Ashendene Road
Bread and Cheese Lane
Park Lane Paradise
Appleby Street
Pear Tree Walk
Crouch Lane
Argent Way
Rags Lane
St James's Road
Andrew's Lane
Burton Lane
Goff's Lane
Cuffley Hill
B156
Millcrest Road
Robinson Avenue
Goffs Oak Primary School
Woodside Primary School
Flamstead End Infant School
Flamstead End Junior School
Fairfields Primary School
Goffs School
Bonneygrove Junior & Infant School
Andrews Lane Junior & Infant School
St Pauls RC Primary School
Colesgrove Manor
Halstead Hill
Silver Street
EN7
Cemetery
Woodgreen Farm
Barrow Lane
Beverley Gardens
Dark Lane
Lieutenant Ellis Way
B198
Broadfield Farm
Burnt Farm
Burntfarm Ride
Jones Road
Chain Walk
Oldpark Ride
Spring Farm
Theobalds Manor
Temple House
The Paddocks
Glasgow Stud
Sloemans Farm
Bullscross
Bulls Cross Ride
Hertfordshire County
Enfield
M25
Junction 25
Whitewebbs Road
Whitewebbs Lane
The Whitewebbs Museum of Transport & Industry
Theobalds Park
Cromwell Avenue
Churchgate Road
43
62
79
H J K L M N P
31 32 33 34
1 2 3 4 5 6 7 8 9 10

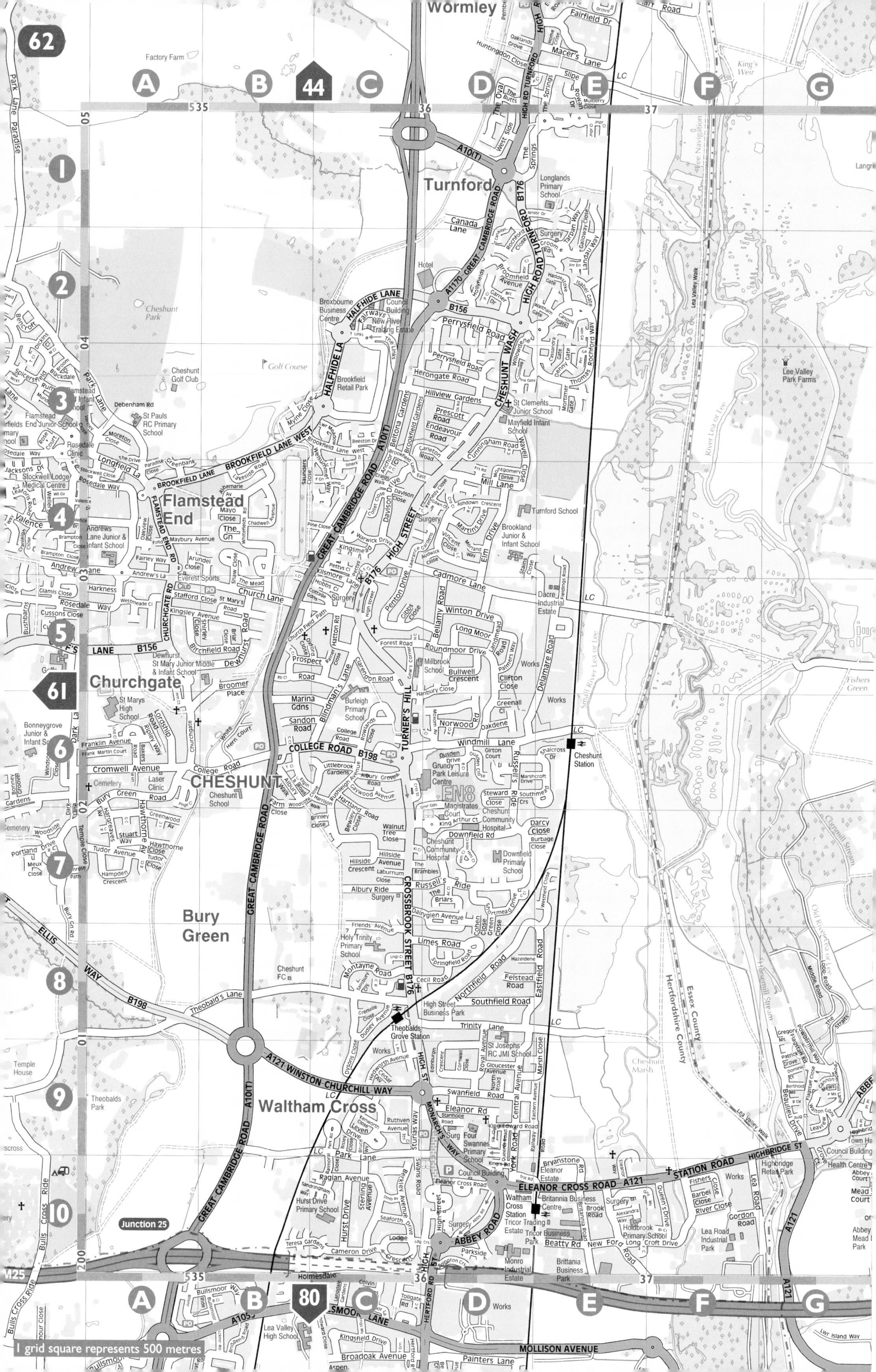

Wormley
Turnford
Flamstead End
Churchgate
CHESHUNT
Bury Green
Waltham Cross
EN8
Cheshunt Station
Theobalds Grove Station
Waltham Cross Station
Junction 25
M25
GREAT CAMBRIDGE ROAD
A10(T)
A1170 GREAT CAMBRIDGE ROAD
HIGH ROAD TURNFORD
B176
B156
B198
A121 WINSTON CHURCHILL WAY
ELEANOR CROSS ROAD A121
STATION ROAD
HIGHBRIDGE ST
HALFHIDE LANE
BROOKFIELD LANE WEST
BROOKFIELD LANE
CHESHUNT WASH
HIGH STREET
TURNER'S HILL
CROSSBROOK STREET B176
COLLEGE ROAD
CHURCHGATE RD
FLAMSTEAD END RD
THEOBALD'S LANE
ELLIS WAY
MONARCH'S WAY
ABBEY ROAD
HERTFORD RD
MOLLISON AVENUE
Park Lane Paradise
Bulls Cross Ride
Cheshunt Park
Cheshunt Golf Club
Golf Course
Brookfield Retail Park
Broxbourne Business Centre
New River Trading Estate
Longlands Primary School
St Clements Junior School
Mayfield Infant School
Turnford School
Brookland Junior & Infant School
Dacre Industrial Estate
Works
Grundy Park Leisure Centre
Cheshunt Community Hospital
Downfield Primary School
Burleigh Primary School
St Marys High School
Bonneygrove Junior & Infant School
Cheshunt School
Laser Clinic
Cemetery
Holy Trinity Primary School
Cheshunt FC
High Street Business Park
St Josephs RC JMI School
Four Swannes Primary School
Council Building
Hurst Drive Primary School
Britannia Business Centre
Tricor Trading Estate
Tricor Business Park
Monro Industrial Estate
Brittania Business Park
Holdbrook Primary School
Lea Road Industrial Park
Highbridge Retail Park
Lea Valley High School
Lee Valley Park Farms
Cheshunt Marsh
Small River Lea or Lee
River Lea or Lee
Old River Lea or Lee
Lea Valley Walk
Lee Navigation
Hertfordshire County
Essex County
Theobalds Park
Temple House
King's Weir
Fishers Green
Factory Farm
A B C D E F G
1 2 3 4 5 6 7 8 9 10
44
61
80
535 36 37
1 grid square represents 500 metres

Nazeing Gate
Nazeing Long Green
Claverhambury
Holyfield
Aimes Green
EN9
WALTHAM ABBEY
Upshire
Wood Green
Waltham Road
Laundry Lane
St Leonards Road
Marsh Hill B194
Coleman's Lane
Holyfield Road B194
Crooked Mile B194
Claverhambury Road
Galleyhill Road
Breach Barns Lane
Galleyhill Wood
Deerpark Wood
Warlies Park
Horseshoe Hill
Upshire Road
Honey Lane
Farm Hill Road
Sewardstone Road
Broomstick Hall Road
Monkswood Avenue
Parklands
Paternoster Hill
Woodgreen Road
Southend Lane
Old Shire Lane
Fernhall Lane
Felsteads
Galleyhill Green
Harold's Park Farm
Maynards Farm
Fernhall Farm
Home Farm
Breach Barns
Dallance House
Breaches Farm
Monkhams Hall
Hayes Hill Farm
Holyfield Hall Farm
Marsh Hill House
St Leonards
Pick Hill Farm
Upshire Primary School
King Harold GM School
Thomas Tallis School
The Leverton Primary School
Waltham Holy Cross Junior School
Howard Business Park
Cemetery
Waltham Abbey Gatehouse
Waltham Abbey Swimming Pool
M25
45
64
81

Nazeing Gate
Harold's Park
Maynards Farm
Fernhall Farm
Home Farm
Upshire
Horseshoe Hill
Copthall Green
Works
Wood Green
Stort Valley Way
Epping Long Green
Epping Green
EPPING ROAD
Magpies
Carters La
Epping CE Primary School
Three Forests Way
Parvills Farm
Hunter's Hall Farm
Gills Farm
Chambers Manor Farm
B181
Upland Road
Takeley Manor
Epping Upland
Cobbin's Bridge
Cobbin's Brook
Bury Farm
B182
Cobbinsend Road
Long Street
Fernhall Lane
Forest Way
Copped Hall
New Farm
Bell Common
Hotel
HIGH ROAD
M25
The Warren
Crown Hill
Lodge Road
Ambresbury Banks Fort
Centenary Walk
Theydon Road
Theydon Golf Club
Forest Side
Woodredon Farm
EPPING ROAD
Ltl Gregories Lane
Wansfell College
1 grid square represents 500 metres
46
63
82
A B C D E F G
1 2 3 4 5 6 7 8 9 10
542 43 44
05 04 03 02 01 200

Thornwood Common
Woodside
EPPING
Coopersale Common
Coopersale Street
Steward's Green
Fiddlers Hamlet
Ivy Chimneys
Mount End
NORTH BASSE
CM16
HIGH ROAD
B1393
THORNWOOD ROAD
EPPING ROAD
B181
LINDSEY STREET
HIGH STREET
THE PLAIN
PALMERS HILL
Upland Road
Weald Hall Lane
Woodside
Forest Glade
Silver Birch Av
Coopersale Common
Garnon Mead
Stonards Hill
Houblons Hill
Hobbs Cross Road
Mount Road
Banks Lane
Stewards Green Road
Brook Road
Bridge Hill
Ivy Chimneys Road
Bury Lane
Lwr Bury Lane
Bury Road
Station Road
Hemnall Street
Kendal Avenue
Harland Road
Tower Road
Regent Road
Crows Road
St John's Road
Coronation Hill
Beaconfield Road
Shaftesbury Road
Woodberry Down
Beulah Rd
Frampton Rd
Barnfield
James St
Lindsey St
Church Hill
Theydon Gv
Weddewood Cl
Rayfield
Clover Leas
Lincolns Fld
Sunnyside Road
Springfield
Centre Drive
Western Av
Broadoaks
Centenary Wk
The Orchards
Bower Vale
Bower Hill
Allnutts Road
Charles St
Warren Fld
Crossing Rd
Stewards Cl
Flux Lane
Great Gregories Lane
Lower Swaines
Chapel Rd
Albany Court
Bodley Cl
Ravensmere
Nicholl Road
Amesbury Rd
Madells
Theydon Pl
Beech Place
Highfield Pl
Tidy's Lane
Granville Rd
Fairfield Road
Winch View
Wood Meads
Duck Lane
Rowley Md
Brookfield
Carpenters Arms La
Weald Hall Lane
Chevely Close
Brickfield Rd
Laburnum Rd
St Alban's Rd
Vicarage Rd
Essex Way
Epping Forest Railway
M11
M25
Junction 27/6
Esgors
Orchard Farm
Hayleys Manor Farm
Upper Clapton RFC
Pinch Timber Farm
Blake Hall
Weald Hall
Industrial Estate
The Lower Forest
Wintry Park Farm
Club
Roughtallys
Golf Course
Woodlands
Gernon Bushes
The Limes Medical Centre
St Margarets Hospital
Works
Coopersale & Theydon Garnon CE Primary School
Epping County Infant School
St Johns School
Junior School
Council Building
Surgery
Police Station
Epping Sports Centre
Epping Station
Stonards Farm
Gaynes Park
Bower Hill Industrial Estate
Ivy Chimneys Primary School
The Epping Golf Club
Searles Hall
Council Building
Coopersale Hall School
Great Gregories Farm
Little Gregories
Peakes Farm
Garnish Hall
Dukes
Harewood Hill
H
J
K
L
M
N
P
47
66
83
45
46
47
48
05
04
03
02
01
200
1
2
3
4
5
6
7
8
9
10

NORTH WEALD BASSETT
Tyler's Green
Colliers Hatch
Toot Hill
Mount End
Bovin
North Weald Airfield
Roughtalley's Wood
Beachet Wood
Knightsland Wood
Tawney Common
Epping Forest Railway
Essex Way
Weald Hall Lane
Merlin Way
Church Lane
HIGH ROAD
EPPING ROAD
A414
B181
M11
Vicarage Lane
St Andrews CE Primary School
Queens Road
Oak Piece
School Green Lane
Princes Close
Beamish Close
Thornhill
The Limes Medical Centre
Lancaster Road
George Avey Cft
Blenheim Way
York Road
Wellington Rd
Dukes Ct
Station Road
Kiln Road
Pike Way
Hawks Hl
Park Cl
Club House
Roughtallys
Golf Course
Forest Glade
Woodlands
Cold Hall Farm
Ongar Park Hall
Mill Lane
Toot Hill Road
Epping Road
Does Farm
Cumley Road
Hill Crest Road
Freemans Farm
School Road
Toot Hill Golf Club
Blakes
Mount Farm
Banks Lane
Tawney Common
Tawney Lane
Woodhatch
Nickerlands
Cesslands
Berwick Lane
Berwick
Searles Hall
Peakes Farm
Little Tawney Hall
Coleman's Farm
Howfields
Gaynes
48
65
84
1 grid square represents 500 metres

Lower Bobbingworth Green
Shelley
Church Lane
Bobbingworth Mill
Stony Lane
A414 EPPING ROAD
Blake Hall Road
B184
FYFIELD ROAD
Water End Farm
Bilsdens Farm
Perrills
Brookfields
Moreton Road
Ongar War Memorial Hospital
Coles Close
Cripsey Avenue
Shortlands Avenue
Acres Avenue
Shelley Close
St Peter's Avenue
Queensway
Clare Mews
Ongar Leisure Centre
Shelley Primary School
Springfield Close
Council Building
High Road Ongar (Chelmsford Road)
CHELMSFORD ROAD
Lane
Penson's Lane
A128
Great Lawn
Great Stony School
The Johns
Mayflower Way
Rodings
Mark's Avenue
Barron's Close
Bowes Drive
Epping Forest Railway
Churchill Close
Onslow Gardens
Three Forests Way
Cemetery
Ongar & District Sports Club
Love Lane
Council Building
Essex Way
Bansons Way
Shakletons
Greensted House
Greensted Green
Greensted Road
Road
Ongar Health Centre
Banson's Lane
Superstore
Essex Way
Greensted
Log Church
HIGH STREET
CHIPPING ONGAR
Castle Street
Millbank Avenue
Fairbank Close
Glebe Road
Fairfield Road
Rodney Road
Works
Stanley Place
Turner's Close
Lodge Farm
The Borough
The Spinney
Clatterford End
Toot Hill Road
Mutton Row
Chipping Ongar Primary School
Woodland Way
Green Walk
COOPERS HILL A128
The Elms
Cloverley Road
Long Fields
Landview Gardens
Mead Walk
St James' Avenue
A128 BRENTWOOD RD
Stondon
Hallsford
Kettlebury Way
Hunters Md
Sandon Place
Marden Ash
Marden Ash House
Coleman's Farm
Clark's Farm
STANFORD RIVERS ROAD
BRENTWOOD ROAD
Gray's Farm
Stewarts
A113
Great Colemans
Langford Bridge
Littlebury Hall
Three Forests Way
ROMFORD ROAD
School Road
Stanford Rivers
Langford Bridge Farm
Old Rectory Road
Church Road
Bridge Farm
Park Wood
The Old Rectory
Garden Field
Works
Little End
LONDON ROAD
Kelvedon Hall
River Roding
Murrells Farm
Traceys Farm
H J K L M N P
49
85
53 54 55
1 2 3 4 5 6 7 8 9 10

Hyde Heath
Hyde Heath Infant School
White House Farm
Fuller's Hill
50
Weedon Hill Farm
Weedon Hill
Brays Close
Brays Green Lane
Harvest Bank
Westfield
Walnut Way
Mayhall Farm
Our Ladys Catholic Primary School
The Beacon School
Mantle's Farm
Chalk Lane
Weedonhill Wood
Amersham & Chiltern RFC
Weedon Lane
Lime Farm
South Bucks Way
Little Missenden
River Misbourne
Amersham o
Longfield
A413
Mantles Green
School Lane
Shardeloes
Amersham Town FC
St Marys CE Combined School
High Street
Little Shardeloes
Coldmoreham Yard
Cherry Lane
Mop End
Amersham Old Town
Shardeloes Farm
The Platt
Whielden Street
Hotel
Broadway
Woodrow High House
Second Wood
Whielden Lane
Curzon CE Primary School
School Lane
Chancellors
Penn Street
Woodrow
HP7
HP6
WHIELDEN LANE A404
New Road
Coleshill House
Chase Close
Tower Road
Coleshill Cricket Club
Works
Rushymead
Coleshill
Village Road
Meadow Cott Lane
Coleshill CE First School
Winchmore Hill Cricket Club
Penn House
Horsemoor
Nelson Cl
The Hill
Pond Close
Winchmore Hill
Barracks Hill
AMERSHAM ROAD
88
Fagnall Lane
Fagnall Farm
Chalk Hill
1 grid square represents 500 metres

Lower Bois
Chesham Bois
AMERSHAM
Amersham Common
Little Chalfont
H
J
K
L
M
N
P
51
70
89
97
98
99
200
99
98
97
96
195
1
2
3
4
5
6
7
8
9
10
Cemetery
Cresswell Road
Latimer Road
Mill Close
Broadwater Bridge
Frith Wood
Chesham Bois CE Combined School
Chess Valley Walk
Blackwell Hall
Blackwell Hall Lane
Hollow Way Lane
St Leonards Road
Bois Mill
Latimer Road
Chess Valley Walk
Bois Lane
Stubbs Wood
Elangeni Junior School
Chestnut Lane First School
North Road
South Road
Quill Hall Farm
Lane Wood
Latimer House
Latimer Park Farm
Stubbs End Cl
Chestnut Lane
Plantation Road
Quill Hall Lane
Raans Road
Woodside Road
A404
Chesham Road
A416
Sycamore Rd
Swimming Pool
Council Building
Woodside Junior School
Amersham Hill Cricket Club
Amersham Station
Fairview Industrial Est
Corinium Industrial Est
St Georges CE Infant School
St Georges Industrial Est
Stony Dean Special School
Amersham & Wycombe College
The Amersham School
White Lion Road
Bell Lane Combined School
Beechwood Avenue
Sandycroft Road
Elizabeth Avenue
Westwood Drive
Bedford Avenue
Chalfont and Latimer Sta
Chalfont Road
Dr Challoners High School
Surgery
Coke's Lane
Burtons Way
Loudhams Wood Lane
Highland Road
Station Road
Stanley Hill
Beech Grove
First Avenue
Superstore
Bury Farm
London Road West
A413
London Road East
South Bucks Way
River Misbourne
Finch Lane
Coke's Farm
Doggetts Wood Lane
B4442
Nightingales Lane
Rodgers Wood
Harewood Down Golf Club
Council Building
Quarrendon Farm
Pollards Park House
Harewood Downs House
Golf Course
Lower Bottom House Farm
Warren Farm
Amersham Road
HP8
Brentford Grange
Farm La
Upper Bottom House
Misbourne Farm

52
Latimer
Chenies
Chorleywood West
Latimer House
Latimer Park Farm
Flaunden Bottom
Martin Top Farm
Baldwin's Wood
Hollin's Hall
Valley Farm
Mill Farm
Mount Wood
River Chess
Chess Valley Walk
Chenies Place
Mountwood Farm
Chenies School
Hotel
Chenies Cricket Club
Latimer Road
Holloway Lane
Stony Lane
Flaunden Bottom
The Chess
The Grove
The Ridings
Spring Close
Frith Wood
A404
AMERSHAM ROAD
Chessfield Park
Church Grove
Amersham Way
Oakington Avenue
Chalfont and Latimer Station
STATION ROAD
Village Way
Little Chalfont Golf Club
Golf Course
Beechwood Avenue
Chandos Close
Westwood Drive
Westwood Close
Russell Close
Bedford Avenue
Elizabeth Avenue
Latimer Close
Cokes Lane
The Hawthorns
Loudhams Wood Lane
Burton's Way
Long Walk
Birkett Way
Park Gv
B4442
Doggetts Wood Lane
NIGHTINGALES LANE
Pollards Wood
Pollards Park House
Warren Farm
Lodge Lane
Lodge Farm
New Road
Burton's Farm
Burton's Lane
Burtons Lane
Roughwood Lane
Roughwood Park
Greenstreet Farms
Green Street
St Clement Danes School
Newhouse Farm
Whitelands Avenue
Carpenters Wood Drive
The Russell School
St Peters Way
Blacketts Wood Drive
Grovewood Close
Farm Road
Chalfont Lane
Chorleywood Health Centre
Chorleywood Station
Station Approach
Lower Road
South Road
Hillside Road
Berks Hill
Haddon Rd
Shire Lane
Burfield Rd
Dove Park
Quickley Lane
Quickley Rise
Heronsgate Road
Old Shire Lane
Bullsland Lane
Lawford Close
Stag Lane
Chorleywood Primary School
Furze View
Capell Road
Hubbards Rd
Clements Rd
Penn Way
Orchard Drive
Orchard Close
Greenbury Close
Homefield Rd
Darvell's Works
Chorleywood Common
Chorleywood Golf Club
Woodland Lane
The Swillett
Bullsland Farm
Long Lane
Heronsgate
Bradford Road
Stockport Road
1 grid square represents 500 metres
90
69

Commonwood
Bucks Hill
Great Sarratt Hall
53
H
J
K
L
M
N
P
04
05
06
200
99
98
97
96
195
1
2
3
4
5
6
7
8
9
10
72
91
Sarratt
Red Lion Lane
Moor Lane
Bucks Hill
Great Westwood
Bottom Lane
Buck's Hill Bottom
Tom's Hill
Dawes Lane
Downer Dr
Alexandra Rd
Sarratt School
Surgery
Church Lane
George Wy
Caroon Drive
Dimmocks Lane
Deadman's Ash Lane
Newhall Farm
Sarratt Road
Sarratt Bottom
Moor Lane
Templepan Lane
Yew Court Farm
White House
Chandler's Lane
M25
White Shack Lane
Chandler's Cross
Green End Business Centre
Micklefield Green
Goldingtons
PH
Church End
Chess Valley Walk
Sarratt Mill House
New Road
Rousebarn
Sarratt Road
Redhall Lane
Redhall
Marrocks
North Hill
Solesbridge Lane
Sarratt Lane
Cherry Walk
Chess Valley Walk
Beechengrove Wood
York House School
Ladywood Close
Whisper Wood
Loudwater Hts
Bridle Lane
Wagon Way
Lower Plantation
Loudwater
Little
Thurlwood House
A404
RICKMANSWORTH ROAD
Cemetery
Council Building
Solesbridge Close
The Readings
Solesbridge La
Chess Wy
Warwick Ct
Tollgate Cl
Wyatt's Road
Wyatt's Cl
Briery Fld
Christ Church School
Trout Rise
Farm La
River Chess
Sarratt Lane
Lodge Dr
Violet Way
Timber Rdg
Armitage Close
Loudwater Lane
Croxley Green
Chorleywood Common
Golf Course
The Paddocks
Beechwood
Marriott Terrace
High View
Junction 18
Troutstream Way
Overstream
Kingfisher Lure
Loudwater Drive
Rooks Hill
Chess Hill
Chess Cl
Chess Lane
Finch Green
Badgers Walk
Parkfield
Kennel Lane
EYWOOD
Dog
Haywood Park
Cottage Gdns
Cottage Dr
The Beeches
South Pk Av
Park Avenue
Chestnut Avenue
Clump
Loudwater Lane
Chess Valley Walk
Harewood
Hillpoint
Rasehill Close
Chorleywood Rd
CHORLEYWOOD ROAD
Lime Tree Wk
Lynwood Heights
Spencer Wk
WD3
The Drive
The Clump
The Drive
The Royal Masonic School
Old Barn Lane
The Orchard
On the Gn
Green La
Copthorne Road
Chess V Ri
Elmcote Way
Windmill Drive
SCOTS HILL
Cottage Close
Valley Road
Greenhills Cl
Highfield Close
Valley Road
The Mount
Goosefields
The Drive
ywood Bottom
Catlips Farm
Highfield Wy
Highfield
The Queen's Dr
Berry Lane
Edinburgh Dr
Arnett Hills Primary School
Upper Hill Rise
Arnett Close
Arnett Way
Beacon Way
Rickmansworth Sports Club
PARK ROAD
Lavrock Lane
Quickwood Cl
Oakfield
Ivinghoe Rd
Aldbury Rd
Chiltern
Coombe Hill Road
Beacon Way
Pheasants Way
Ridge Way
Meadow Way
Nightingale
RICKMANSWORTH
Chess Vale Walk
Park Rd
Caravan La
St Joan of Arc RC School
The Cloisters
Rickmansworth Station
Homestead Rd
Berry Way
The Greenway
Orchard
Council

Leavesden Green
Langleybury
St Pauls CE Primary School
Langleybury Lane
Lane
54
A
B
C
D
E
F
G
507
08
09
200
99
98
97
96
195
1
2
3
4
5
6
7
8
9
10
Great Westwood
Old House Lane
Buck's Hill Bottom
M25
Junction 19
Heath Wood
Templepan Lane
Yew Court Farm
White Shack Lane
Fir Tree Hill
Chandler's Cross
The Grove
The Grove Mill
Grove Mill Lane
Lees Wood
Rousebarn Lane
Harrocks Wood
Whippendell Wood
Redhall
71
Redheath
York House School
Golf Course
Gypsy Lane
Old Mill Road
Mill Road
WATFORD RD
A41(T)
NORTH WESTERN AVENUE GADE SIDE
North Western Av
Russell Lane
Greenbank Road
Minerva Drive
Goodwood Av
Hudson Cl
Leggatts Close
Orchard Primary School
Holy Rood Infant School
Holy Rood Junior School
River Gade
Grand Union Canal Walk
Works
Rosecroft Dr
Courtlands
HEMPSTEAD ROAD
Ridgeway
Denewood Cl
Nascot Wood Rd
Tunnel Wd Rd
Stanbury Av
Glen Way
Roughwood Cl
WD17
A411
Devereux Drive
Harford Drive
Cassiobury Drive
Bellmount Wood Avenue
Trefusis Walk
Lodge Sun Sports Club
Langley Way
Woodland Drive
Orchard Drive
Coningesby Drive
Capelvere Walk
Berceau Wk
Richmond Drive
De Vere Wk
Parkside Drive
The Gardens
Garden Close
Cassiobury Park
Watford Station
Cassiobury Park Avenue
Swiss Avenue
Shepherds Road
Metropolitan Station Approach
Watford Grammar School for Boys
A412
RICKMANSWORTH ROAD
Cherrydale
King Georges Av
Whippendell Road
Sydney Road
Hagden Lane
Tolpits Close
St Anthonys RC Junior School
Westfield School
TOLPITS LANE
A4145
Holywell
Holywell School
Chaffinch La
Ryde College
Greenhill Crescent
Ascot Road
Industrial Estate
Blackmoor Lane
Woodshots Meadow
Faraday Close
Hatters Lane
Caxton Way
Dwight Road
Wolsey Business Park
Moor Park Industrial Est
West Herts Golf Club
Lodge End
Links Way
Canterbury Way
Durrants Drive
Dover Way
Ludlow Way
Hastings Way
Richmond Way
Warwick Way
Baldwins Lane
Kenilworth Drive
Lewes Way
Norwich Way
Little Green Lane
Old Merchant Taylors Sports Club
Little Green Junior School
Lincoln Dr
Lincoln Way
Rochester Way
Manor Way
Grove Crs
Dugdales
Baldwins Lane
Legates Cl
Waterdell House
Little Green Lane
Thurlwood House
Loudwater Lane
Croxley Green
The Green
Sherborne Way
Winchester Way
Malvern Way
Malvern Way School
Claremont Crs
Girton Way
Winton Drive
Winton Crs
Lancing Way
Owens Way
Repton Way
Rugby Way
Dulwich Way
Fuller Way
Croxley Green
Old Barn Lane
The Orch
On the Gn
Green La
New Road
Barton Way
Dickinson Avenue
Surgery
Croxley Station
WATFORD ROAD
A412
Sycamore Rd
Mayfare
Valley Walk
Beechcroft Av
Oakleigh Drive
Grand Union Canal Walk
Copthorne Rd
Windmill Drive
Elmcote Way
Yorke Rd
Bateman Road
Harvey Road Primary Sch
Rickmansworth School
SCOTS HILL
Rickmansworth Sports Club
PARK ROAD
Frankland Road
Harvey Road
All Saints Lane
Lavrock Lane
Cottage Close
92
Works
River Gade
1 grid square represents 500 metres
RC School

Kingswood
Garston
North Watford
WATFORD
West Watford
Oxhey
Meriden
Otterspool
Aldenham
Watford Heath
NORTH ORBITAL ROAD
KINGSWAY
A405(T)
A41(T)
NORTH WESTERN AV
N WESTERN AV
COLNE WY
ST ALBANS ROAD
A412
M1
Junction 5
STEPHENSON WAY
A4008
BERRY WAY
HARTSPRING LANE
B462
ALDENHAM ROAD
BEECHEN GROVE
CASSIO ROAD
EXCHANGE RD
WIGGENHALL ROAD
WATERFIELDS WAY
A411
VICARAGE ROAD
HAGDEN LANE
EASTBURY ROAD
A4125
PINNER ROAD
LWR HIGH ST
CHALK HILL
LONDON ROAD
HIGH STREET
Garston Station
Watford North Stn
Watford Junction Station
Watford High Street Stn
Bushey Station
Watford General Hospital
Watford FC & Saracens RFC (Vicarage Road Stadium)
North Watford Cemetery
Vicarage Road Cemetery
West Hertfordshire College
University of Hertfordshire
International University
Bushey Hall Golf Club
Aldenham Golf and Country Club
Bushey Golf & Country Club
Hartspring Industrial Park
Colne Valley Retail Park
Watford Arches Retail Park
Harlequin Shopping Centre
WD24
WD23
WD18
55
74
93
H
J
K
L
M
N
P
1
2
3
4
5
6
7
8
9
10
11
12
13

56
73
94
A
B
C
D
E
F
G
1
2
3
4
5
6
7
8
9
10
514
15
16
200
99
98
97
96
195
Aldenham
High Cross
Round Bush
Batlers Green
Letchmore Heath
Patchetts Green
BUSHEY
Bushey
Caldecote Hill
University of Hertfordshire
Blackbirds Farm
Edge Grove
Edge Grove School
Aldenham Golf & Country Club
Golf Course
Delrow School
Fair Field Junior School
Infant School
Radlett Station
Radlett & Bushey Reform Synagogue
Surgery
Council Building
Cemetery
Radlett Infant School
Tabard RFC
Little Kendals Farm
Aldenham School
Slades Farm
Haberdash Boys' Scho
Haberdash Girls' Scho
Elstree Aerodrome
Hilfield Park Reservoir
Aldenham Country Park
Lismarrine Industrial Park
Rosary Priory High School
Immanuel College
Bushey Meads School
Meadow Wood School
Bournehall Junior & Infant School
Little Reddings Primary School
Bushey Golf Country Club
Hartspring Sports Centre
WD23
Crab Lane
Blackbirds Lane
Kemprow
Oakridge
High Cross
RADLETT ROAD
WATFORD ROAD
B462
HARTSPRING LANE
Church La
Hilfield Lane
Pegmire Lane
Summerhouse Lane
Grange Lane
New Rd
Common Lane
Back Lane
Aldenham Road
New Road
Loom Lane
The Ridgeway
Homefield Rd
Heyford Rd
Manor Ct
Gills Hill
Gills Hollow
Aldenham Avenue
The Pathway
Willow Way
Elm Walk
Craig Av
Orchard Cl
Loom Pl
Church Cl
COBDEN HILL
A5183
ROMAN ROAD
ALDENHAM RD
Station Rd
Park Rd
The Grove
Newlands Avenue
Shenley Hill
Canons Cl
Newberries Avenue
Craig Mt
Theobald St
Butterfly Lane
Hogg Lane
Dagger Lane
M1
NORTH WESTERN AVENUE ELTON WAY
A41(T)
NORTH WESTERN AVENUE
(TYLERS WAY)
N WESTERN AV (WATFORD BY-PASS)
ELSTREE ROAD
A411 ELSTREE ROAD
A411
A409
Hilfield La South
Little Bushey Lane
Sandy Lane
Berrygrove
OTTERSPOOL WAY
Farm Way
Cornfield Rd
Harcourt Rd
Mostyn Road
Coldharbour
Cotswold Avenue
Oundle Avenue
Pentland Rd
Chiltern
Kg George Av
Herne Road
Melbourne Rd
Herkomer Road
HIGH STREET
Caldecote Gdns
Woodfield
Richfield Road
1 grid square represents 500 metres

Shenley
JMI School
Newcome Road
Birchwood
New Road
B5378
WD7
Golf Course
Porters Park Golf Club
H
J
K
L
M
57
N
P
Hill
Faggots Cl
Shenley
Radlett Lane
18
19
20
London Road
Crossoaks Lane
200
Williams Way
RADLETT
Woodhall Lane
Wood Hall Farm
Woodhall La
B5378
1
2
3
4
5
6
7
8
9
10
Theobald Street
Lyndhurst
Silver Hill
Green Street
High Canons
Lane
Well End
Buckettsland
Cowley Hill
B5378
Redwood Rd
Stapleton Rd
Walshford Way
Retford Cl
Abbots Pl
Stanborough Road
Thirsk
The Campions
Parkside Prim School
Well End
Hertsmere Jewish Primary School
Radlett Preparatory School
Berwick Road
Morpeth Avenue
Stretton Wy
Allerton Rd
Allerton Cl
Aycliffe Road
Greenside
Woolmer Close
Reston Cl
Road
Haggerston Road
Rossington Av
Belford Rd
Torworth Rd
Theobald St
Wetherby Rd
Cromwell
Darrington Road
Sinderby Cl
Aycliffe
Leeming Road
Clifton Wy
Gateshead Road
Crown Road
Alban Crs
Odessey Rd
Cowley Hl
Hawksmoor Sch
Sports Centre
Potters Lane
Wilcox Cl
Denham Way
Alexandra Road
Kent Cl
Rowley Lane
Tallis Wy
Bairstow Cl
Stanley Gdns
Lyndhurst Middle School
Woodlands Prim Sch
Calshowe Road
Northfield Rd
Edulf Rd
Shenley Rd
Danziger Way
Lion Ct
Gate Close
Gregson Cl
Studio Way
Hancock Ct
Banks Rd
76
Merryfield School
Gateshead Road
Catterick Wy
Warenford Wy
Ranskill Rd
Norton Cl
Surgery
Cowley Hill Prim Sch
Road
Winstre Road
Broughinge Road
Gibbons Cl
Boyce Cl
Stevenage Crescent
Lombardy Way
Beech Drive
Linton Avenue
Croxdale Rd
Brook Cl
Hartforde Road
Borehamwood FC
Holmshill School
Thrift Farm Lane
Rutherford Close
Borehamwood
Surgery
Merryfield
Theobald St
Anthony Road
Ashdown Dr
Beechfield Cl
Haberdashers RUFC
Aberford Rd
Council Building
Meadow Rd
St Teresa's School
Oaklands College
Council Building
Elstree Way
Elstree Way Clnc
ELSTREE WY
A5135
ELSTREE WAY
York Crs
North Medburn Farm
WD6
Croxdale Road
Kingsley Av
Barton Wy
Chandos Road
Barton Wy
Road
Eldon Avenue
Fairbrook Medical Cen
Council Building
Bullhead Road
Manor Way
Works
Chester Road
Red Road
Theobald St
Elstree Studios
Maxwell Road
West Herts Business Centre
Manor Place Industrial Estate
Durham Rd
Road
Elstree Golf Club
Golf Course
BOREHAMWOOD
Gables Av
Stratfield Rd
Audley Rd
Maiden Rd
Essex Rd
Clarendon Rd
Grosvenor Rd
B5378
Kinetic Business Centre
Works
Park Crs
Links Dr
Boulevard 25 Retail Park
SHENLEY ROAD
Cardinal Av
Superstore
Hillside Avenue
Monksmead School
Kenilworth Dr
Kenilworth First School
Kenilworth Drive
Tykes Water Lake
Barham Avenue
Glenhaven Av
Drayton Rd
Mildred Av
Whitehouse Avenue
Hillside School
Thornbury Gdns
Manor Way
Featherstone Gardens
Buckingham Road
Elstree & Borehamwood Station
Holt Cl
Harkness Industrial Est
Station Rd
Works
Furzehill School
Oakwood Av
Woodlands Cl
Monksmead Rd
Bullhead Rd
Arundel Dr
Manor Way
Drive
Balmoral Dr
Home Farm
Blattner Close
LANE
B5378
Allum La
Nash Cl
Fir Tree Ct
Tauber Cl
Lodge Av
Deacons Cl
Cavendish Crs
Cedars Cl
Summerswood Primary School
Elmwood Avenue
Melrose Av
Tennison Av
Milton Dr
Graveley Avenue
Cleveland Crs
Cranes Way
Ripon Way
Elstree Hill N
ALLUM
Knowl Wy
Bishops Av
Grange Road
Hartfield Av
Deacon's Hill
Berkeley Cl
Ascot Cl
Hartfield Cl
Byron Av
Vale Av
Masefield Avenue
Furzehill Road
Burghley Avenue
Ashley Dr
Cemetery
The Rise
Shiremeade Rd
Wentworth Av
Sheraton Cl
Nicholas Road
Alwyn Cl
Clare Cl
Belmor
Summer Hl
Carrington Av
Carrington Gdns
Clydesdale Cl
Halter Close
Cob Close
Farriers
Works
Shetland Close
Retail Park
Surgery
Elstree
Lands End
St Nicholas Cl
School
Hertsmere Progressive Synagogue
BARNET LANE
LANE
BARNET LANE
Deacons Hts
London Loop
WATFORD ROAD
HIGH ST
A411
BARNET
Deacons Hill
Schubert Rd
Rodgers Cl
Delius Cl
Beethoven Rd
Sullivan Way
Elgar Close
Coates Rd
ELSTREE HILL SOUTH
A5183
Summer Gv
May Gdns
Fortune La
A5183
195
18
19
95
20
London Loop
Hyver Hill
A1(T)
BARNET
Centennial Avenue
Hotel
Edgwarebury
M1

Ridge
Crossoaks Lane
58
A B C D E F G
521 22 23
200 1 2 99 3 4 98 5 6 97 7 8 96 9 10 95
Service Centre
Bignells Corner
Hotel
South Mimms Services
Junction 1/23
Blanche Farm
M25
ST ALBANS ROAD
A1081
Dancers Hill
Summerswood Lane
Blanche Lane
A1(M)
Wash Lane
Dancers Hill
Dyrham Lane
Holmshill Lane
BARNET BY-PASS
A1(T)
Trotters Bottom
Golf Course
High Canons
Well End Road
Buckettsland Lane
Dyrham Park Country Club
Rowley Lane
Galley Lane
75
Potters Lane
Denham Way
Alexandra Road
Kent Cl
Studio Way
Pinewood Cl
Gate Close
Holmshill School
Oaklands College
Rutherford Close
Borehamwood Industrial Park
York Crs
A5135 ELSTREE WAY
ROWLEY LA
ELSTREE WAY
Works
Manor Place Industrial Estate
Chester Road
Warwick Road
Kenilworth First School
Kenilworth Drive
Newark Gn
NEWARK GN
Hertfordshire County
Barnet
Paddock Lane
Rowley Green
High Barnet
Christ Church CE Primary School
EN5
Byng Road
Foulds School
Cavendish Road
Old Fold View
Jennings Way
Kings Road
Grimsdyke Crescent
Queen Elizabeths Boys School
Granville Road
WOOD STREET
Arkley Lane
Laings Sports Ground
Golf Course
Buckingham Road
Norfolk Gardens
Howard Drive
Tempsford Avenue
Saffron Green Primary School
Wansford Park
Easton Gdns
Balmoral Drive
Ripon Way
Stirling Industrial Cen
Stirling Way
Arkley Golf Club
Rowley Green Road
Carrington Close
Chartridge Close
BARNET ROAD
A411
Hedgerow La
Hazel Mead
Garthland Drive
Quinta Drive
West End Lane
Barnet Hospital Chest Clinic
Barnet General Hospital
Wellhouse Lane
Cemetery
Spring Close
Whitings Hill Primary School
Chesterfield Rd
Arkley
Sports Ground
Barnet Gate
BARNET LANE
Shetland Close
Retail Park
Mays Lane
Partridge Cl
London Loop
96
Barnet Gate Lane
B552
Hyver Hill
Ducks Island
1 grid square represents 500 metres

M25
Junction 24
59
Bentley Heath
Bentley Heath Lane
Industrial Estate
Dancers Hill Road
Wagon Rd
A1000
BARNET ROAD
Ganwick Corner
Hertfordshire County
Enfield
STAGG HILL
A111
A1000
Spoilbank Wood
Wagon Road
Kitt's End
Kitt's End Road
Hadley Wood Primary School
Claremont Road
Helena Close
Courtleigh Avenue
Kingwell Road
Duchy Road
Hadley Wood
Hadley Wood Station
Lancaster Avenue
Crescent West
Crescent East
Beech Hill
Camlet Way
Hadley Wood Golf Club
Golf Course
HADLEY HIGHSTONE
Langley Row
Old Fold Manor Golf Club
Monken Hadley
Monken Hadley CE Primary School
St Marthas Convent Senior School
Pagitts Grove
Broadgates Avenue
Parkgate Avenue
Newman's Way
Greenbrook Av
Covert Way
Dury Rd
Hadley Wood Road
Monken Hadley Common
Enfield
Barnet
EN4
78
Cockfosters Road
Bakers Hill
ST ALBANS ROAD
HADLEY GREEN
Hadley Green Rd
Hadley
King George's Field
London Loop
The Crs
Latimer Rd
Clifford Road
Hadley Road
Woodville Road
Vincent Close
Tudor Road
Norfolk Rd
Bosworth Rd
East Barnet School
Livingstone Primary School
Westbrook Crescent
Lawton Road
Fordham Road
Park Road
The Spires Shopping Centre
Surgery
Police Station
Barnet Trading Estate
Queen Elizabeth Centre
Queen Elizabeth's Girls School
High Barnet Station
Barnet Museum
Barnet College
The Bull Theatre
HIGH ST
BARNET HILL
A411
Union St
Moxon Street
Meadway
Kingsmead
Potter's Road
Cromer Road JMI School
Leicester Road
Station Road
A110
East Barnet Road
New Barnet Stn
Red Rose Trading Estate
Cockfosters
Chipping Barnet
Old Court House Rec Gnd
Barnet Health Centre
New Barnet
Lyonsdown School
Barnet Synagogue
Longmore Avenue
B193
Barnet FC (Underhill)
Playing Field
Underhill
BARNET
Barnet Hill JMI School
Dollis Valley Way
Grasvenor Avenue Infant School
Prickler's Hill
Western Way
Northumberland Road
St Marys CE Primary School
Oakland CP School
East Barnet School
Ravenscroft School
97
Oakleigh Park Station
East Barnet
Church Hill Primary School
Oaklands Road
Golf Course

78
60
77
98
A
B
C
D
E
F
G
1
2
3
4
5
6
7
8
9
10
528
29
30
200
99
98
97
96
195
Hertfordshire Co.
Enfield
New Cottage Farm
Crews Hill Station
Cattlegate Road
Crews Hill Golf Club
A1005
THE RIDGEWAY
Botany Bay
East Lodge Lane
Botany Bay Cricket Club
Golf Course
London Loop
Hotel
Ferny Hill
Hadley Road
Hadley Wood Golf Club
COCKFOSTERS ROAD
A111
Oak Avenue
Mount View
High Oaks
EN4
University of Middlesex
Trent Country Park
Snakes Lane
Bournwell Close
Fairgreen
Games Road
Northfield Road
Cockfosters Sports Ground
Trent Park Cemetery
Southgate Compton Cricket Club
Cockfosters Station
ENFIELD RD
A110
Trent Park Golf Club
Lakeside
Lowther Drive
Merryhills Drive
Merryhills Clinic
Glenbrook S
Roundhill Dr
Rushey Hill
Lonsdale Drive
South Lodge Drive
Grosvenor Gdns
Prince George Av
Carlton Av
Oakwood Station
Westpole Avenue
Gloucester Gardens
Kent Drive
Southgate School
Sussex Way
BRAMLEY ROAD
Oakwood Medical Cen
Priory Close
Cockfosters
Ashurst
CAT HILL
Chestnut Grove
Museum of Domestic Design & Architecture
Middlesex University
Chicken Shed Theatre
Bramley Close
Homestead Paddock
De Bohun Primary School
Addison Av
The Fairway
Cowper Gardens
Reservoir Rd
Wolverton Wy
Lakenheath
Merrivale
Sheringham Avenue
Oakwood
Overton Road
Chaseville Park Road
Eversley Primary School
Chaseville Clinic
Oakwood Park Rd
Fountains Crs
East Barnet School
Oakland CP School
Windsor Drive
Ridgeway Avenue
Daneland
Mansfield Av
Vernon Crs
Oak Hill College
Canon Mohan Close
Pymmes Brook Trail
Brookhill Close
Pilgrim's Rise
Primary School
Surgery
Pleasant Way
Mount Road
Langford Crescent
Trent CE Primary School
Bevan Road
Heddon Court Avenue
Freston Gardens
Leys Gdns
Belmont
Evelyn Road
Norrys Close
Cedar Av
Lovelace Road
Dorchester Ct
Synagogue
Nursery Rd
Chelmsford Rd
Ivy Road
Salcombe School
Mayfair Ter
Winchmore
Highlands Av
Newsholme Dr
World's End
Tresilian Av
Pennington Dr
Holly Hill
Willow Walk
Park View
Church Hill
1 grid square represents 500 metres
N14

H
J
K
L
M
N
P
61
Hertfordshire County
M25
Crews Hill
Whitewebbs Road
The Whitewebbs Museum of Transport & Industry
Theobalds Park Road
Glasgow Stud
Burntfarm Ride
Chain Walk
Golf Course
Whitewebbs Lane
Bulls Cross Ride
Gilmour Close
Bullsmoor Lane
Capel Manor Primary School
Bulls Cross
University of London
Turkey Street
St Ignatius College
GREAT CAMBRIDGE ROAD
London Loop
St Johns CE Primary School
Strayfield Road
Flash Lane
Whitewebbs Park Golf Club
Clay Hill
EN2
Forty Hill
Forty Hill CE Primary School
Forty Hall Museum
The Kings Oak Private Hospital
Chase Farm Hospitals
Cemetery
Cook's Hole Road
Phipps Hatch Lane
Lavender Hill
Gordon Hill Station
Worcesters Primary School
Goat Lane
St George's Road
Russell Road
Hoe Lane
Carterhatch Lane
Lancaster Road
Baker Street
Chace Community School
Adath Yisroel Cemetery
Queen Elizabeth Stadium
Sports Centre & Swimming Pool
Donkey Lane
80
EN1
Enfield Playing Fields
Bishop Stopford School
Suffolks Primary School
Works
Gordon Road
St Georges RC Primary School
Trinity Street Infant School
Chase Side
Enfield Lower Grammar School
Enfield Town
Police Station
Civic Centre
Upper School
Grammar School
Chase Green Avenue
Slades Hill
A110 Windmill Hill
Enfield Chase Station
Church Street
Palace Gardens Shopping Centre
Cecil Road
Enfield Town Stn
St Annes Convent School
Southbury Road
George Spicer Primary School
Enfield FC
Kingsmead School
Superstore
A10(T)
A110
Southbury Station
Haslemere Business Centre
World's End
Enfield Golf Club
Old Park Road
Old Park Avenue
ENFIELD
Town Park
New River
London Road
Lincoln Road
Enfield Cricket Club
Martindale Ind Estate
Bush Hill Park
Recreation Ground
Main Avenue
Bush Hill Park Primary School
Martinbridge Industrial Estate
Great Cambridge Industrial Est
Grange Park Primary School
Grange Park
Grange Park Station
Bush Hill Park Golf Club
A105 Park Avenue
Village Road
Bush Hill Park Stn
Bush Hill Park Medical Cen
Edmonton Upper School
Ridge Avenue
Green Lane
Ridge Ho Clinic
99
N21
32
33
34
1
2
3
4
5
6
7
8
9
10
200
199
198
197
196
195

80
Junction 25
62
79
100
M25
GREAT CAMBRIDGE ROAD
A10(T)
BULLSMOOR LANE
A1055
MOLLISON AVENUE
HERTFORD ROAD
A1010
ELEANOR CROSS ROAD
A121
SOUTHBURY ROAD
NAGS HEAD ROAD
A110
LEA VALLEY ROAD
HERTFORD ROAD HIGH ST
NIGHTINGALE ROAD
MERIDIAN WAY
A112
SEWARDSTONE ROAD
Bulls Cross
Freezy Water
Enfield Lock
Enfield Wash
Enfield Highway
EN3
Brimsdown
Ponders End
King George's Reservoir
William Girling Reservoir
Turkey Street Station
Enfield Lock Stn
Brimsdown Station
Southbury Station
Ponders End Station
Waltham Cross Station
Enfield Crematorium
Lea Valley High School
Capel Manor Primary School
St Ignatius College
Albany School
Enfield College
Innova Business Park
Prince of Wales Primary School
Waterways Business Centre
Lee Valley Campsite
Tricor Trading Estate
Monro Industrial Estate
Riverside Industrial Estate
Lea Valley Walk
River Lea or Lee
Enfield
Essex County
I grid square represents 500 metres

Sewardstone
Lippitts Hill
High Beach
Gilwell Park
Sewardstonebury
Epping Forest
M25
A121
A112
A104
Junction 26
HONEY LANE
SEWARDSTONE ROAD
EPPING NEW ROAD
RANGERS ROAD
HIGH ROAD
Avey Lane
Mott Street
Lippitts Hill
Church Road
Manor Road
Cross Roads
Bury Road
Daws Hill
Hawes Lane
Butlers Drive
Godwin Close
Gilwell Lane
Woodman Lane
Hornbeam Lane
Farm End
Pynest Green Lane
Wellington Hill
Claypit Hill
Fairmead Road
Centenary Walk
Green Ride
Earl's Path
Warren Hill
Manor Road
Forest Way
Three Forests Way
London Loop
Golf Course
High Beech Golf Club
West Essex Golf Club
High Beech CE Primary School
Manor House
Wallsgrove House
Beach Hill Park
Epping Forest Conservation Centre
Whitehouse Plain
Long Hills
The Warren
Cemetery
Eastbrook End Cemetery
Hawkswood School & Centre
Essex County
Waltham Forest
Royal Epping Forest Golf Club
Queen Elizabeth Museum
Chingford
Oaklands School
Buckhurst Hill Reform Synagogue
Surgery
North Farm
Waltham Abbey Swimming Pool
The Leverton Primary School
Howard Business Park
Works
Hotel
Southend Lane
Sewardstone Road
Shernbroke Road
Honey Lane
Roundhills
Quinton Way
Lodge Lane
Beechfield Walk
Greenwich Wy
Sewardstone Way
South Way
Wood
H
J
K
L
M
N
P
63
101
82
39
40
41
200
99
98
97
96
195
1
2
3
4
5
6
7
8
9
10

82
Wood Green
64
81
102
A
B
C
D
E
F
G
1
2
3
4
5
6
7
8
9
10
Loughton
Debden Green
Theydon Bois
Piercing Hill
IG10
Epping Road
B1393
B172
Woodridden Hill
Epping New Road
A121
Golding's Hill
Lower Rd
Church Hill
Rectory Lane
A1168
Chigwell Lane
High Rd
Coppice Row
Crown Hill
Lodge Road
Ambresbury Banks Fort
Woodredon Farm
Great Monk Wood
Epping Forest Conservation Centre
Wansfell College
College of Teachers
Birch Hall
Ripley Grange
Debden House Residential Centre
Davenant Foundation School
Golf Course
Loughton Golf Club
The Hereward County School
St John Fisher RC Primary School
Thomas Willingale Primary School
Woodcroft School
Staples Road Junior & Infant School
Loughton Cricket Club
Eastbrook End Cemetery
Cemetery
Loughton Health Cen
Police Station
Loughton Mental Hlth Cen
Buckhurst Hill Reform Synagogue
Oaklands School
Forest Medical Centre
Roding Valley High School
Loughton Station
Debden Station
Epping Forest College Tertiary FE
Loughton Hall Clinic
Roding Valley High School
The Alderton Primary School
Oakwood Hill Industrial Est
Debden Sports Club
Council Building
Business Centre
Prospect Business Park
Junction 5
M11
River Roding
Home Farm
Rolls Park
North Farm
White Bridge
Three Forests Way
Centenary Walk
1 grid square represents 500 metres

Hall School
Junction 27/6
M25
Golf Course
Little Gregories
H
J
K
L
M
65
N
P
46
47
48
200
Peakes Farm
Dukes
Harewood Hill
Purlieu Way
Avenue
Heath Dr
Baldocks Rd
Theydon Bois Primary School
Orchard Drive
Elizabeth Drive
Buxton Road
Forest Drive
Slade End
Mead Barn
Theydon Bois Station
Council Building
Thrifts Md
Poplar Rw
The Green
Green Gld
Pakes Wy
Green Glade
Hill Road
Surgery
B172
Thrifts Hall Farm
Blunts Farm
Coopersale Lane
Garnish Hall
Theydon Garnon
Hobbs Cross
Hobbs Cross Rd
Hobbs Cross Road
M11
ABRIDGE ROAD
Cemetery
Hydes Farm
Abridge Golf & Country Club
Skinners Farm
Brook House
Theydon Park Road
Theydon Hall
Hill Farm
99
98
97
96
195
1
2
3
4
5
6
7
8
9
10
84
Epping Lane
Piggotts Farm
ONGAR ROAD
A113
Church Lane
Three Forests Way
Surgery
Patch Park
New Farm Drive
Pancroft
The Mead
The Poplars
Knights
Walk
Middle Boy
Spur Close
Field Cl
Alderwood Drive
Hoe Lane
Silver St
MKT Pl
LONDON ROAD
Abridge
Lambourne
Lambourne Primary School
Great Wood
Great Downs Farm
Turnours Hall
GRAVEL LANE
Marchings Farm
Bishop's Hall
New Road
St John's Farm
Hook Lane
Pudding Lane
Taylors Farm
Manor Road
103
Pettitts Hall
A1112
Young's Farm

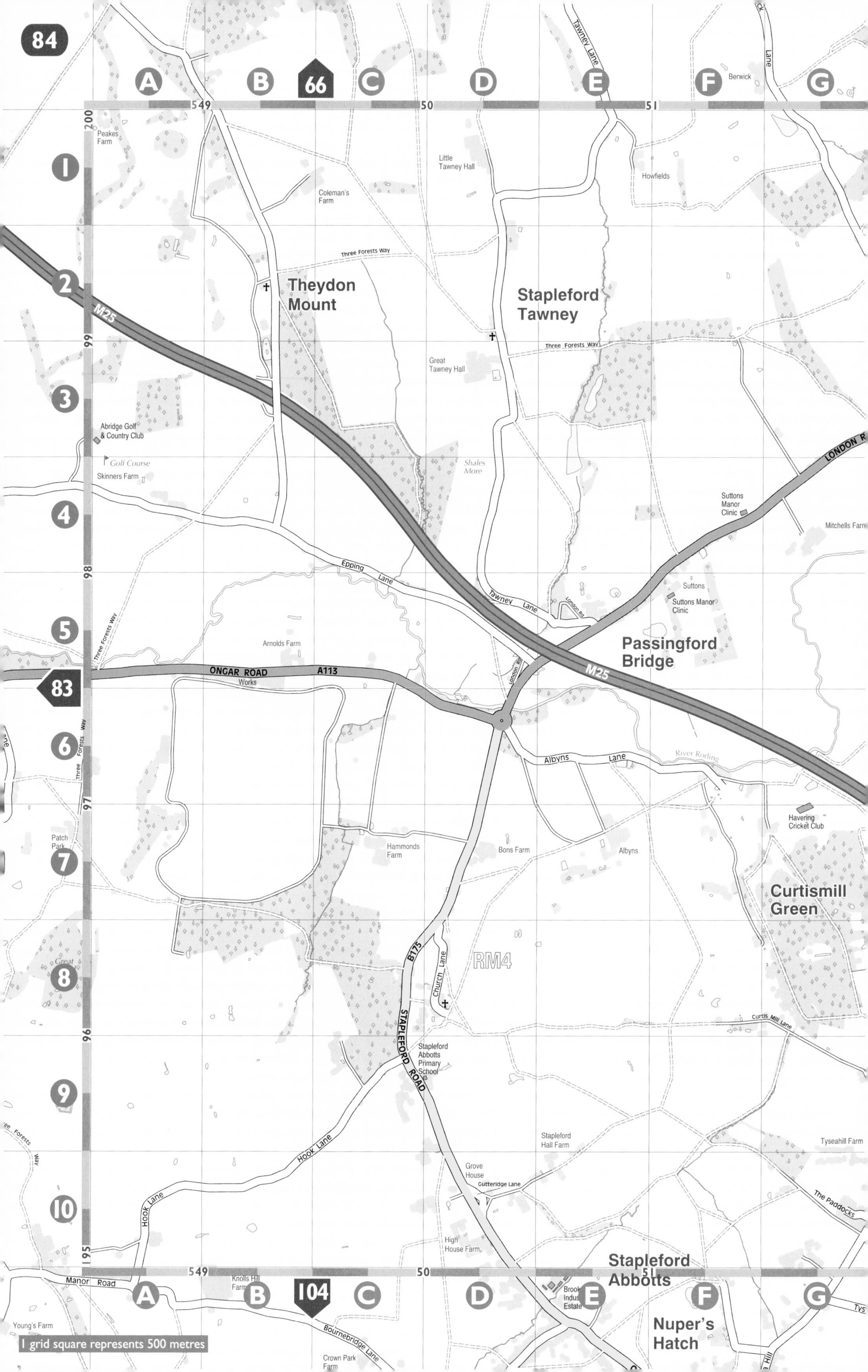
66
83
104
Theydon Mount
Stapleford Tawney
Passingford Bridge
Curtismill Green
Stapleford Abbotts
Nuper's Hatch
Peakes Farm
Coleman's Farm
Little Tawney Hall
Howfields
Berwick
Tawney Lane
Three Forests Way
Great Tawney Hall
Abridge Golf & Country Club
Golf Course
Skinners Farm
Shales More
Suttons Manor Clinic
Mitchells Farm
LONDON R
M25
Epping Lane
Tawney Lane
London Rd
Suttons
Arnolds Farm
ONGAR ROAD
A113
Works
Albyns Lane
River Roding
Havering Cricket Club
Patch Park
Hammonds Farm
Bons Farm
Albyns
Great
B175
Church Lane
RM4
Curtis Mill Lane
STAPLEFORD ROAD
Stapleford Abbotts Primary School
Hook Lane
Stapleford Hall Farm
Tyseahill Farm
Grove House
Gutteridge Lane
The Paddocks
High House Farm
Manor Road
Knolls Hill Farm
Brook Indus Estate
Young's Farm
Bournebridge Lane
Crown Park Farm
1 grid square represents 500 metres

The Old Rectory
Three Forests Way
LONDON ROAD
A113
Garden Field
Works
Little
67
Kelvedon Hall
River Roding
Murrells Farm
Traceys Farm
Germains Farm
Kelvedon
Aspen Wood
Berwick Lane
Wayletts
Beacon Hill
Lawns
Dudbrook Road
Navestock Hall Farm
Bois
Rose Hall Farm
Shonks Mill Road
Church Road
Howletts Hall
86
Mill Lane
Navestock Heath
Murthering Lane
Prince's Road
Sabine's Green
Old Road
Loft Hall
Sabines Road
Tan House Lane
Princes Gate
M25
Bower Farm
South Weald Common
Wheelers Lane
Brook Farm
Horseman Side
Dytchleys Road
Coxtie Green Road
Murthering Lane
Horseman Side
Weald Park Golf Club
Dytchleys
Jenkins Farm
Gilstead Hall
Golf Course
Waterhales
Curtis Mill Lane
Weald Brook
Frieze Hall
Golf Course
Watton's Green
Coxtie Green
105
Stapleford Abbotts Golf Club
Navestock Common
Asheton Farm
Goatswood
Havering Plain
H J K L M N P
1 2 3 4 5 6 7 8 9 10
52 53 54 55
200 99 98 97 96 195

Massey
A
B
C
D
E
F
G
Kelvedon Hall Lane
Kelvedon Grange
556
57
58
200
99
98
97
96
195
1
2
3
4
5
6
7
8
9
10
85
106
Chivers Road
Blackmore Road
Deatree Close
Hook
Hall Lane
Kelvedon Hall Lane
Pole's Wood
Mellow Purgess Farm
Germains Farm
Kelvedon Hatch Primary School
Beacon Hill
School Road
Church Road
Church Close
Mill Lane
Chandlers Walk
Eagle
Swan Lane
Kelvedon Hatch
A128
ONGAR ROAD
Beacon Hill Road
Dudbrook
Dudbrook Road
Bois Hall
Blackmore Road
Glovers Fld
Kelvedon Green
Elmtree Av
Stocksfield
Stocks Lane
Short Cft
Broad Meadow
Fox Hatch
Place Farm
Place Farm Lane
Church Lane
Doddinghurst Junior School
Doddingh
Dagwood
Dagwood Farm
Crown Road
Cow Farm
Cowes Farm
Frog Street
Warren Lane
Warren
Green Lane
Bentley Golf Club
Old Crown Lane
Solid Lane
Navestock Side
Golf Course
Prince's Road
Tan House Lane
Princes Gate
Navestock Side
St Pauls CE Primary School
Bentley
Ashwells
Crow Green
Wishfield Farm
Snakes Hill
Mores Lane
Mores La
The Mores
Ashwells Road
Well Lane
South Weald Common
Wheelers Lane
Pilgrim's Lane
Days Lane
Crow Gn
Coxtie Green Road
Warwick Place
Weald Park Golf Club
Dytchleys
Pilgrims Hall
Pilgrims Hatch
Mores Lane
Bellhouse Lane
Pilgrim's Lane
Crow Green Road
Crow Gn Lane
Lascelles Close
Hatch Road
Orchard Lane
Catherine Close
Coxtie Green Road
Apple Gate
Georges Drive
Coxtie Green
Gilstead Hall
Golf Course
Danbury Close
Danes Way
Priory Close
Balmoral Road
Larchwood Gardens
Pilgrims Hatch County Primary School
Broomwood Gdns
Ongar Rd
Kensington Road
Osborne Road
Windsor Rd
Elizabeth Rd
Bishop's Hall Rd
Sandpit Lane
Lincolns
Lincolns Lane
Frieze Hall
CM14
Langtons
Weald Park
A12(T)
Warescot Road
1 grid square represents 500 metres

Hook End
Peartree Green
Swallows Cross
Green Street
Hutton
Shenfield
Stubbers Farm
Hay Green
Hay Green Lane
Mill Lane
The Robins
Beehive
Whitelands
Honey Close
Hazel Chase
Glen
Field Kiln
Plovers Mead
Wyatts Gn La
Wyatt's Green Road
Wrights Lane
Church Lane
Widbrook
Priory Mead
Rectory Chase
Bakers Meadow
Brook Lane
Brook La
Middle Green
Harpers La
Parsonage Field
Peartree Lane
Lime Grove
Apple Tree Crescent
Willow Close
Peartree Close
Park Meadow
Doddinghurst Road
Days Lane
Mountnessing Lane
Pettits Lane
Wyatt's Green Road
Mountnessing Road
Thoby Lane
Thoby Priory
Works
Woodlands Farmhouse
Master Johns
St Anne's Road
Park Farm
Park Wood
America Farm
CM15
River Wid
Heard's Farm
Heard's Lane
Fitzwalters
Chainbridge Farm
Chelmsford Road
Lower Rd
Sumner's Farm
Palmer's Farm
Hall Lane
Brickhouse Farm
Canterbury Tye Hall
A12(T)
Fen Close
A1023
Chelmsford Road
Alexander Lane
Shenfield High School
Shenfield Sports Centre
Oliver Road
Rochford Av
Holmwood Av
Alwyne Av
Kilworth Avenue
Sebastian Avenue
Hunter Avenue
Crossways
Shenfield Cricket Club
St Marys CE Primary School
Sawyer's Hall
St Helens RC Junior School
Hedley Walter High School
Hutton Road
Rayleigh Road
A129
Community College
Long Ridings Junior & Infant School
Hutton All Saints CE Primary
Roxwell Gardens
Walton Gardens
Woodland Close
Arnolds Avenue
Colet Road
Whittington Road
Surgery
Surman Crescent
Tennyson Road
Byron Road
Cory Drive
Greyfriars
Newmans Drive
Burses Way
60
61
62
200
99
98
97
96
195
107

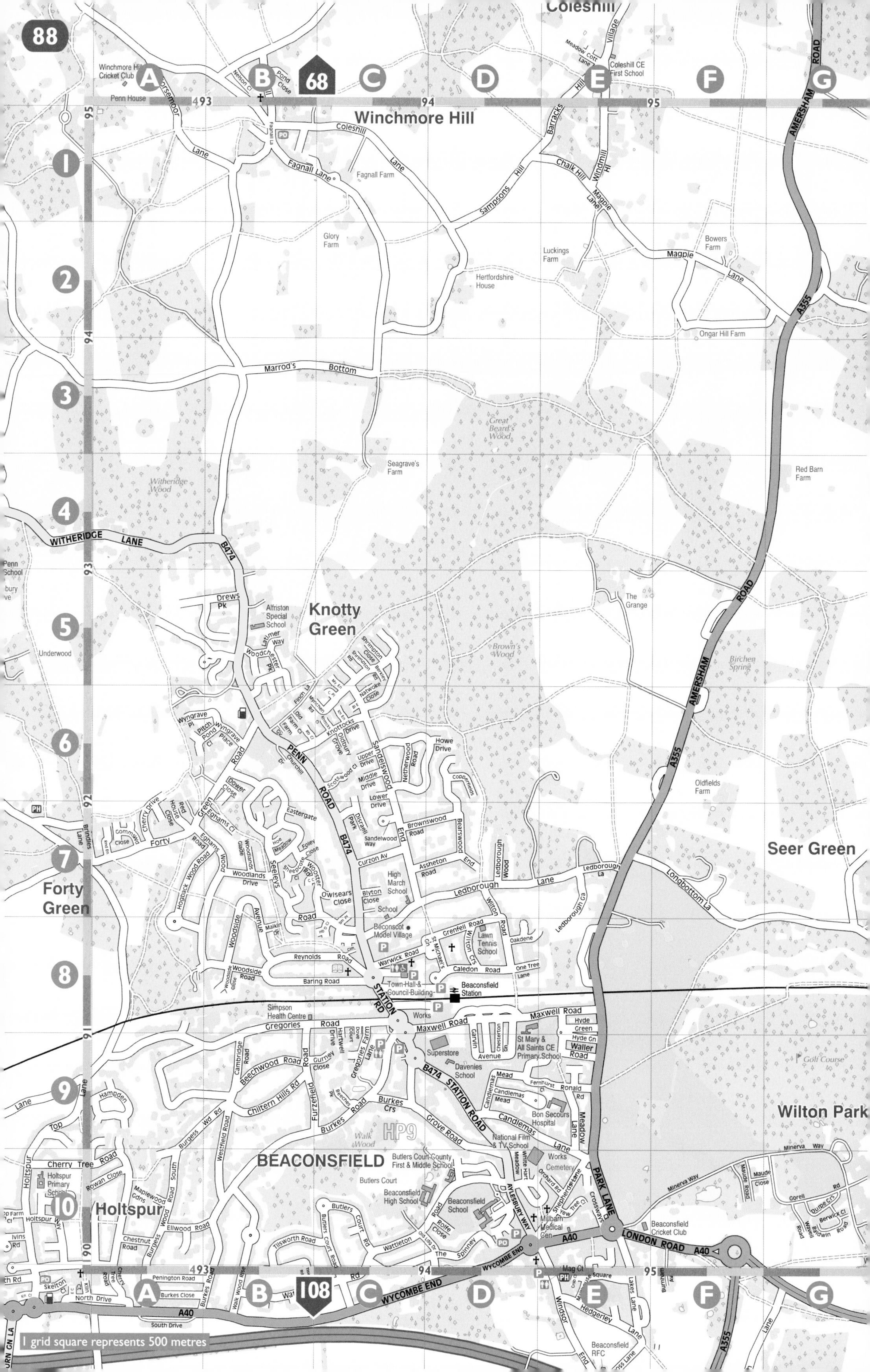
68
Coleshill
Winchmore Hill
Winchmore Hill Cricket Club
Penn House
Coleshill CE First School
Meadow Cott
Fagnall Farm
Fagnall Lane
Coleshill Lane
Sampsons Hill
Chalk Hill
Windmill Hl
Magpie Lane
Barracks Hill
Glory Farm
Luckings Farm
Bowers Farm
Hertfordshire House
Ongar Hill Farm
Marrod's Bottom
Great Beard's Wood
Seagrave's Farm
Red Barn Farm
Witheridge Wood
WITHERIDGE LANE
B474
Penn School
Drews Pk
Alfriston Special School
Knotty Green
The Grange
Underwood
Brown's Wood
Birchen Spring
AMERSHAM ROAD
A355
Oldfields Farm
Seer Green
Forty Green
Forty Lane
Brindles Lane
PENN ROAD
Eastergate
Sandelswood End
Brownswood Road
Bearswood End
Curzon Av
Assheton Road
High March School
Ledborough Lane
Ledborough La
Ledborough Ga
Longbottom La
Wilton Road
Woodlands Drive
Hogback Wood Road
Owlsears Close
Beconscot Model Village
Lawn Tennis School
Reynolds Road
Warwick Road
Grenfell Road
Caledon Road
Baring Road
Woodside Road
Town Hall & Council Building
Beaconsfield Station
Simpson Health Centre
Gregories Road
Maxwell Road
Works
St Mary & All Saints CE Primary School
Superstore
Davenies School
Golf Course
Beechwood Road
Chiltern Hills Rd
Furzefield
Burkes Road
Burkes Crs
B474 STATION ROAD
Grove Road
Candlemas Lane
Bon Secours Hospital
National Film & TV School
Wilton Park
Minerva Way
HP9
Walk Wood
BEACONSFIELD
Butlers Court County First & Middle School
Butlers Court
Beaconsfield High School
Beaconsfield School
Cemetery
PARK LANE
Holtspur
Holtspur Primary School
Cherry Tree Road
Rowan Close
Maplewood Gdns
Ellwood Road
Chestnut Road
Tilsworth Road
Wattleton Road
Millbarn Medical Cen
AYLESBURY WAY
Beaconsfield Cricket Club
LONDON ROAD A40
WYCOMBE END
493
94
95
108
Pennington Road
Burkes Close
North Drive
South Drive
A40
Mag Ct
Hedgerley Lane
Lakes Lane
Windsor End
Beaconsfield RFC
Skelton Cl
1 grid square represents 500 metres

H
J
K
L
M
69
N
P
97
98
99
HP8
Golf Course
Lower Bottom House Farm
Warren Farm
AMERSHAM ROAD
A413
Brentford Grange
Upper Bottom House
Misbourne Farm
The Vache
Stratton Chase
NIGHTINGALES LANE
Stockings Farm
Hill Farm House
Works
B4442
VACHE LANE
Gorelands
Highfield
Bottrells Lane
Dodds Lane
Silver Hill
Pheasant Hill
LONDON ROAD
CHALFONT ST GILES
Hodgemoor Woods
Chalfont St Giles Infant School
Milton Fields
Milton's Cottage
Surgery
Stylecroft
The Brow
Cromwell Cl
Outlook Drive
Woodbank Drive
Three Households
Dean Way
Bramble Mead
Narcot Road
Parsonage Road
Chalfont St Giles Junior School
Middle Meadow
Seymour Rd
Cemetery
Rawlings Lane
Widmer Farm
Highclere Farm Country Touring Park
Oakland Park Golf Club
Golf Course
Butlers Cross
Newbarn Lane
Newbarn
Rawlings Farm
The Lagger
Dibden Hill
90
Highlands Road
Orchard Road
Park Place
Manor Road
Chalfont Rd
Austens
Bowstridge
Hall Place
Jordans Quaker Meeting House
Wilton Lane
Jordans School
Grove Farm
Chalfont Grove
Windmill Farm
Long Grove
School Lane
Cemetery
Seer Green CE Combined School
Seer Mead
Vicarage Close
Bayne Hl
Jordans Way
Long Wd Drive
Meadowside
Seer Green Lane
Beech Lane
Copse Lane
Jordans
Narcot Lane
Chalfont St Peters Infant School
Lovel End
The Chalfonts Community College
Chalfont Leisure Centre
Calcot Medical Centre
Seer Green Station
Beaconsfield Golf Club
Farm Lane
Narcot Lane
Potkiln La
Stone Dean Farm
Layters Green
Glebe Road
Nicol Road
Gold Hill
Orchard Grove
Market Place
Holy Cross Convent School
Pond Lane
Layter's Green
Layter's Av
Layter's Cl
Criss Grove
Meadowcroft
Austenwood
Hill Rise
London Road A40
Potkiln Lane
Stampwell Farm
109
Austenwood
St Josephs CE Combined School
Maltmans Green School
Lewins Rd
Maltmans Lane

70
89
110
A
B
C
D
E
F
G
1
2
3
4
5
6
7
8
9
10
500
01
02
95
94
93
92
91
90
Roughwood Park
Warren
The Vache
Works
Nightingales Lane
B4442 Vache Lane
London Road
Pheasant Hill
Cromwell Cl
Surgery
Outlook Drive
Turners Wd Dr
Woodbank Drive
Stylecroft
The Brow
Valentine Way
High View
Highfield
Kings Close
Ashwells Way
Gorelands Lane
Gorelands
Deadhearn Lane
Chesham Lane
Ashwell's Farm
Philipshill Wood
Buckinghamshire County
Hertfordshire County
Shrubs Wood
Chiltern Open Air Museum
Buckinghamshire Chilterns University College
Newland Park
Shire Horse Centre
Old Shire Lane
Old Shire La Circular Walk
Chalfont Road
Bullsland Farm
The Swillett
Heronsgate
Heronsgate Road
Quickley Rise
Lawford Close
Stag Lane
Chorleywood Primary School
Long Lane
Bradford Road
Stockport Road
Nottingham Road
Cherry Tree La
Old Shire Lane Circular Walk
Bottom Wood
M25
Maple Cross
Horn Hill Court
Brawlings Lane
Brawlings Farm
Gables Close
Pheasant Wk
Foxdell Way
Micholls Avenue
Chalfont Common
Tate Road
Penn Caskell Lane
Rickmansworth Lane
Roberts Lane
Robert's Farm
Roberts Wood Drive
Copper Rdg
Ravensmead
Nortoft Road
Cross Lanes
Mid Cross Lane
Monument Lane
Cedars Close
Northdown Rd
The Paddock
Misbourne Cl
The Dell
Old Mead
Wheatley Way
Deanacre Close
Amersham Road
A413
Gravel Hill
South Bucks Way
Dibden Hill
Bowstridge
Windmill Farm
Deancroft Rd
Denham Lane
Garners Road
Denham Walk
Hillside
Highlands Lane
Highlands Close
Glynswood
Hedgerow
Copthall Corner
Copthall Lane
Robertswood Combined School
West Hyde Lane
Shire Lane
Chalfont Lane
Hornhill Road
Pollards
Bradbery
Long Wd
Horsleys
Ash Vale
Birch Drive
Maple Cross JMI School
Sunnyhill Road
Gravel Hill
Cemetery
CHALFONT ST PETER
Warren Farm
Nimmings Road
Joiners Lane
Chestnut Close
Chiltern Hill
Ellis Avenue
Halfacre Hill
Morris Close
Winkers Lane
Chalfont St Peters Infant School
Boundary Rd
Pennington Road
Field Way
Chalfont St Peter FC
Chalfont St Peter Junior School
Pinetree Cl
The Chalfonts Community College
Chalfont Leisure Centre
Glebe Road
Laurel Rd
Calcot Medical Centre
Surgery
Chalfonts & Gerrards Cross Hlth Clinic
Market Place
Orchard Grove
Gold Hill North
Gold Hill East
Gold Hill West
Holy Cross Convent School
Hogtrough Wood
Linden Drive
Lincoln Road
Woodside Hill
Lower Road
Croft Rd
Hill Rise
Meadowcroft
Penshurst Close
Austenwood Close
School Lane
Ashlea Road
Layter's Av
Layter's Cl
Layters End
Mopes Farm
South Bucks Way
Denham Lane
Old Shire Lane
St Josephs CE Combined School
Priory Rd
The Rowans
Lewins Rd
Maltmans Green
Austenwood Lane
Kingscote
SL9
Gerrards Cross Golf Club
Golf Course
Chalfont Park
Chalfont
1 grid square represents 500 metres

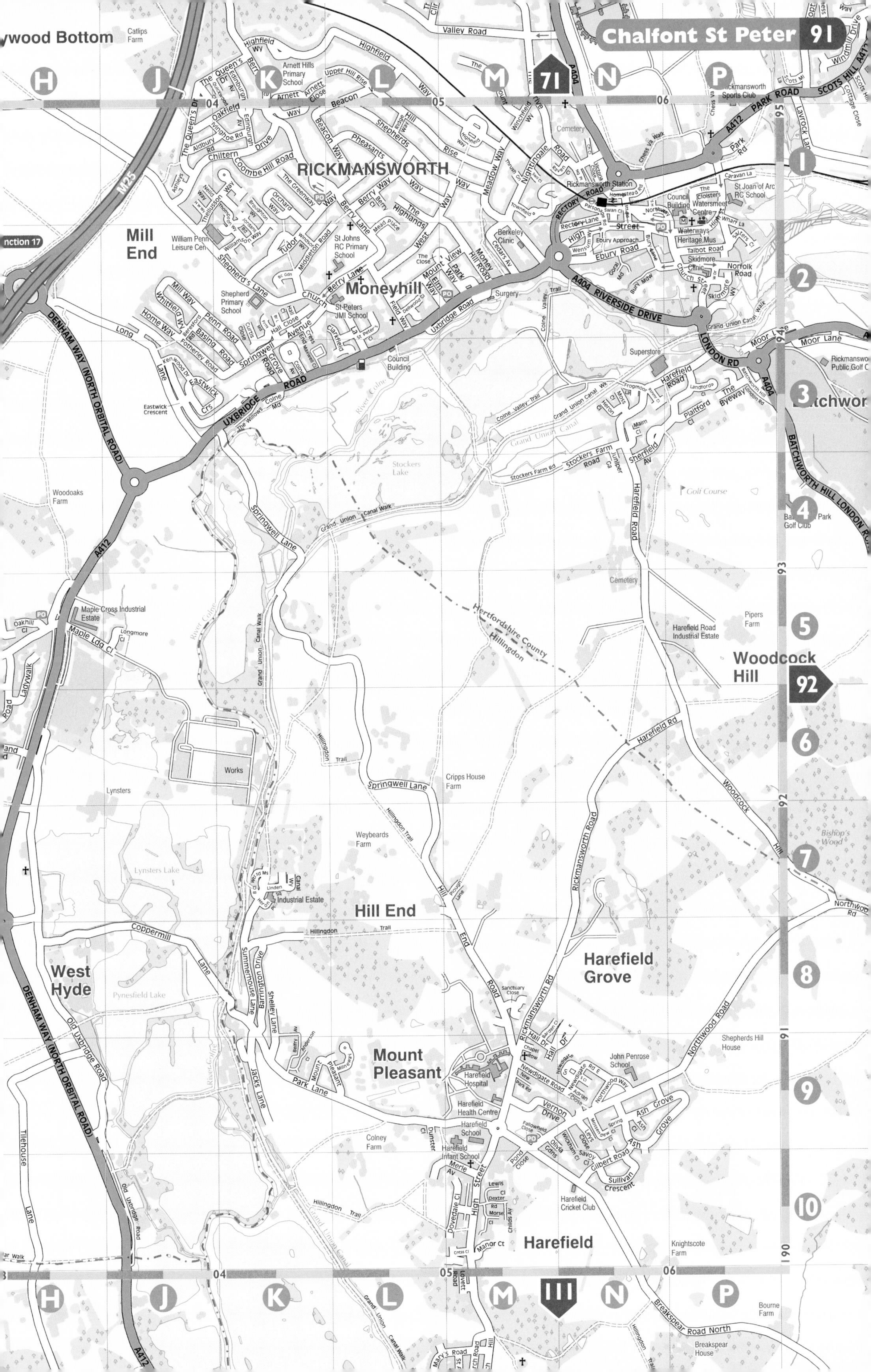

Chalfont St Peter 91
71
111
92
RICKMANSWORTH
Mill End
Moneyhill
Hill End
Harefield Grove
Mount Pleasant
West Hyde
Harefield
Woodcock Hill
Rickmansworth Station
Stockers Lake
Hertfordshire County
Hillingdon
Grand Union Canal
A404 RIVERSIDE DRIVE
UXBRIDGE ROAD
DENHAM WAY (NORTH ORBITAL ROAD)
A412
M25
Springwell Lane
Harefield Road
Rickmansworth Road
Northwood Road
Woodcock Hill
Breakspear Road North
Hill End Road
Coppermill Lane
Summerhouse Lane
Jacks Lane
Park Lane
Moor Lane
LONDON RD
PARK ROAD
SCOTS HILL
BATCHWORTH HILL LONDON ROAD
Harefield Hospital
Harefield Health Centre
Harefield School
Harefield Infant School
Harefield Cricket Club
John Penrose School
Shepherds Hill House
Knightscote Farm
Bourne Farm
Breakspear House
Colney Farm
Weybeards Farm
Cripps House Farm
Pipers Farm
Harefield Road Industrial Estate
Cemetery
Golf Course
Maple Cross Industrial Estate
Woodoaks Farm
Lynsters
Lynsters Lake
Pynesfield Lake
Works
Industrial Estate
Superstore
Council Building
William Penn Leisure Cen
Shepherd Primary School
St Johns RC Primary School
St Peters JMI School
Arnett Hills Primary School
Rickmansworth Sports Club
St Joan of Arc RC School
Watersmeet Centre
Waterways Heritage Mus
Berkeley Clinic
Skidmore Clinic
Surgery
Catlips Farm
Bishop's Wood
Batchworth Park Golf Club
Rickmansworth Public Golf Course
ywood Bottom
nction 17
H J K L M N P
04 05 06
95 94 93 92 91 190
1 2 3 4 5 6 7 8 9 10

72
91
112
A
B
C
D
E
F
G
1
2
3
4
5
6
7
8
9
10
507
08
09
95
94
93
92
91
90
Holywell
Batchworth
Woodcock
Batchworth Heath
Moor Park
Eastbury
NORTHWOOD
Northwood Hills
HA6
Rickmansworth Sports Club
Rickmansworth School
Harvey Road Primary Sch
St Joan of Arc RC School
Watersmeet Centre
Moor Park Industrial Est
Wolsey Business Park
Peerglow Industrial Est
Byfleet Industrial Est
Vale Industrial Est
Merchant Taylors School
Ryde College
Holywell School
Hampermill Lake
Rickmansworth Public Golf Club
Northwood Preparatory School
Moor Park Golf Club
Moor Park Station
Sandy Lodge Golf Club
Batchworth Park Golf Club
Golf Course
Eastbury Farm JMI School
Mount Vernon Hospital
Bishops Wood Hospital
Bishop's Wood
St Martins School
Holy Trinity School
London Bible College
Northwood Pinner Liberal Synagogue
St Helens School
Little St Helens School
Northwood United Synagogue
Police Station
Northwood Stn
Madison Bowl
Northwood Golf Club
Equestrian Centre
Denville Hall
Shepherds Hill House
Holland & Holland Shooting School
Copse Wood
Haste Hill Golf Club
Northwood Cemetery
Northwood FC
Bourne Farm
Poor's Field
WATFORD ROAD
PARK ROAD
TOLPITS LANE
MOOR LANE
Sandy Lodge Road
Sandy Lodge Lane
BATCHWORTH HILL LONDON ROAD A404
Batchworth Lane
Hertfordshire County
Hillingdon
RICKMANSWORTH ROAD A404
GREEN LANE
B469
A4180 DUCK'S HILL ROAD
DUCKS HILL ROAD
Northwood Rd
Jackets Lane
White Hill
Woodcock Hill
Grand Union Canal Walk
River Colne
River Gade
LONDON RD
HIGH STREET
A4125
SANDY LANE
Moor Park Road
Halland Way
The Avenue
Northgate
Rickmansworth Road
Westbury Road
Bishops Avenue
Eastbury Avenue
Grosvenor Road
Frithwood Avenue
Chester Road
Hallowell Road
Reginald Road
Copse Wood Way
Nicholas Way
The Broad Walk
Links Way
Kewferry Road
Sandy Lane
St Mary's Avenue
Bourne End Road
The Fairway
Crofters Road
1 grid square represents 500 metres

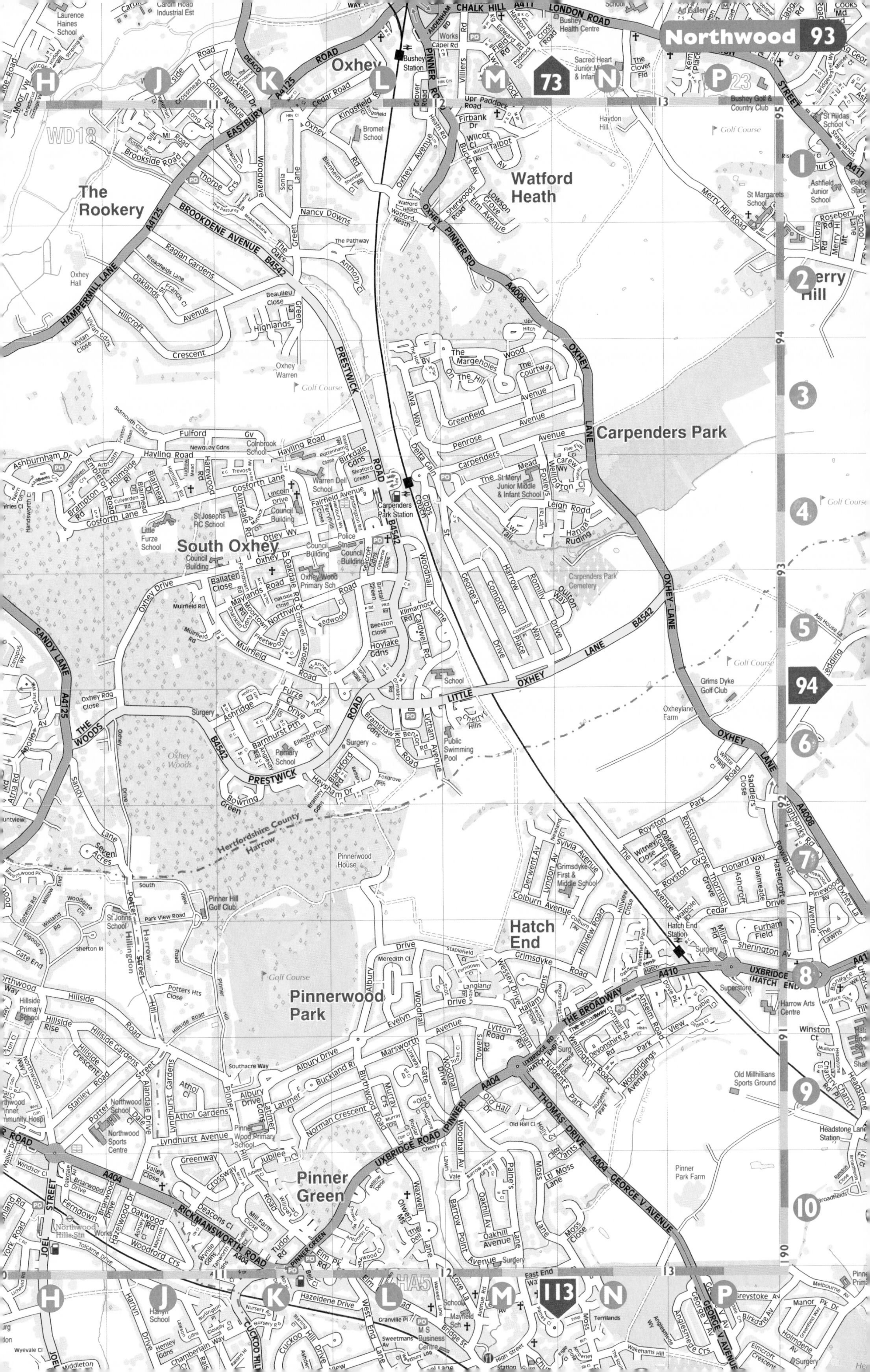

Northwood 93
73
94
113
Oxhey
Bushey Station
Watford Heath
The Rookery
Oxhey Hall
Oxhey Warren
Golf Course
Carpenders Park
Carpenders Park Station
South Oxhey
Oxhey Woods
Hertfordshire County
Harrow
Pinnerwood House
Hatch End
Hatch End Station
Pinnerwood Park
Pinner Green
Grims Dyke Golf Club
Oxheylane Farm
Old Millhillians Sports Ground
Pinner Park Farm
Headstone Lane Station
Harrow Arts Centre
Pinner Hill Golf Club
Northwood Hills Stn
Merry Hill
Bushey Golf & Country Club
WD18
HA5
PRESTWICK ROAD
OXHEY LANE
UXBRIDGE ROAD
RICKMANSWORTH ROAD
HAMPERMILL LANE
BROOKDENE AVENUE
EASTBURY ROAD
SANDY LANE
THE WOODS
ST THOMAS' DRIVE
GEORGE V AVENUE
PINNER ROAD
LONDON ROAD
CHALK HILL
JOEL STREET
THE BROADWAY

94
93
74
114
BUSHEY
Bushey Heath
Caldecote Hill
Merry Hill
Harrow Weald
Belmont
Wealdstone
WD23
HA7
HA3
A
B
C
D
E
F
G
1
2
3
4
5
6
7
8
9
10
A411 ELSTREE ROAD
ELSTREE ROAD
N WESTERN AV (WATFORD BY-PASS)
M1
SPARROWS HERNE
ELSTREE
HIGH ROAD
A4140
HEATHBOURNE ROAD
A409
MAGPIE HALL RD
COMMON ROAD
THE COMMON
STANMORE HILL
Warren Lane
Old Redding
BROOKSHILL
UXBRIDGE ROAD (HARROW WEALD)
UXBRIDGE RD (HARROW WEALD)
UXBRIDGE ROAD (STANMORE)
A410
A4008
OXHEY LANE
HIGH ROAD
HIGH ST
Stanmore Common
Harrow Weald Common
Hertfordshire County
Harrow
Golf Course
Bushey Golf & Country Club
Hartsbourne Golf & Country Club
Bentley Priory
Peterborough & St Margarets High School
Bentley Wood Girls School
Harrow Weald Cemetery
Weald College
Roger Bannister Sports Ground
Bannister Stadium
Harrow Arts Centre
Headstone Lane Station
Stanmore Golf Club
Royal National Orthopaedic Hospital
Harrow RFC
Harrow Heritage Museum
Salvatorian College
Immanuel College
Council Building
Primary School
Westwood School
Hartsbourne JMI School
St Johns CE Middle School
First School
Weald First & Middle School
Belmont First & Middle School
Cedars First School
Cedars Middle School
Hatch End High School
Shaftesbury School
Timbers Clinic
Hotel
Works
1 grid square represents 500 metres

Elstree
Deacons Hill
75
Edgware
Canons Park
Little Stanmore
QUEENSBURY
96
115
M1
Hertfordshire County
Barnet
Harrow
Junction 4
London Gateway (Scratchwood) Service Area
Brockley Hill Farm
Bury Farm
Edgwarebury Cemetery
Edgwarebury Park
Stone Grove Park
The Lake
Chandos Recreation Ground
Sports Ground
Golf Course
WATFORD ROAD
BARNET LANE
ELSTREE HILL SOUTH
A5 BROCKLEY HILL
EDGWARE WAY (WATFORD BY-PASS)
SPUR ROAD A410
LONDON ROAD
STONE GROVE A5
EDGWARE RD HIGH ST
STATION ROAD
HALE LANE
DEANSBROOK RD
DEAN'S LANE
BURNT OAK BROADWAY
MARSH LANE
HONEYPOT LANE
WHITCHURCH LANE
THE HYDE EDGWARE RD
Stanmore Station
Canons Park Station
Edgware Station
Burnt Oak Station
Queensbury Station
HA8
H J K L M N P
18 19 20
1 2 3 4 5 6 7 8 9 10

96
76
95
116
Barnet Gate
Ducks Island
Totteridge Green
Highwood Hill
Mill Hill
NW7
Burnt Oak
Holders Hill
Colindale
London Gateway (Scratchwood) Service Area
BARNET LANE
BARNET WAY (BARNET BY-PASS)
A1(T)
A411
B552
HENDON WOOD LANE
Mays Lane
London Loop
TOTTERIDGE COMMON
A5109
TOTTERIDGE
HIGHWOOD HILL
MARSH LANE
EDGWARE WAY (WATFORD BY-PASS)
A41(T)
WATFORD WAY (BARNET BY-PASS) A1(T)
SELVAGE LANE
HALE LANE
A5100
THE BROADWAY
DAWS LANE B1461
THE RIDGEWAY
M1
Mill Hill Broadway Station
Mill Hill County High School
Mill Hill Golf Club
St Marys Abbey
Belmont (Mill Hill Junior School)
St Pauls CE JMI School
Mill Hill School
The Mill Hill Cricket Club
Mill Hill Cemetery
Copthall School
Hendon Golf Club
Barnet Copthall Stadium
The Metro Golf Centre
Hasmonean High School
Junction 2
FIVE WAYS JUNCTION
GREAT NORTH WAY (BARNET BY-PASS)
WATFORD WAY
Royal Air Force Museum
Police Station
Grahame Park
Hendon College
BURNT OAK BROADWAY
A5 THE HYDE
Burnt Oak Station
Colindale Hosp
British Library Newspaper Library
Metropolitan Police Track (Hendon)
Metropolitan Police Training School, Hendon
Church Farm House Museum
St Georges Medical Cen
PARSON STREET B552
B552 HOLDERS HILL
A
B
C
D
E
F
G
1
2
3
4
5
6
7
8
9
10
21
22
23
95
94
93
92
91
90
1 grid square represents 500 metres

Underhill
Totteridge
Whetstone
East Barnet
Oakleigh Park
Woodside Park
FRIERN BARNET
North Finchley
FINCHLEY
Church End
Colney Hatch
East Finchley
Friary Park
Victoria Park
St Pancras and Islington Cemetery
Islington Crematorium
St Marylebone Crematorium
Finchley Golf Club
South Herts Golf Club
North Middlesex Golf Club
Woodside Park Golf Club
Finchley Memorial Hospital
Old Owens Sports Ground
Wingate & Finchley FC
Totteridge & Whetstone Stn
Woodside Park Station
West Finchley Stn
Finchley Central Stn
Oakleigh Park Station
LONGMORE AVENUE
A5109 TOTTERIDGE LANE
TOTTERIDGE VILLAGE
A1000 HIGH ROAD
OAKLEIGH ROAD NORTH
FRIERN BARNET ROAD
WOODHOUSE ROAD
A1003
BALLARDS LANE
A598
REGENT'S PK ROAD
DOLLIS RD
B1462
A504 EAST END ROAD
NORTH CIRCULAR ROAD
A406(T)
HIGH ROAD
GREAT NORTH ROAD
Dollis Valley Green Walk
N20
N12
N3
77
98
117
H
J
K
L
M
N
P
25
26
27
1
2
3
4
5
6
7
8
9
10

98
78
97
118
A
B
C
D
E
F
G
1
2
3
4
5
6
7
8
9
10
528
29
30
95
94
93
92
91
190
Oakwood
Southgate
Osidge
Brunswick Park
New Southgate
Palmers Green
Bowes Park
FRIERN BARNET
Colney Hatch
Muswell Hill
N14
N11
N22
N10
Middlesex University
Oakland CP School
Monkfrith Primary School
Church Hill Primary School
Sir Thomas Lipton Memorial Hospital
Osidge JMI School
West Grove Primary School
Salcombe School
Southgate Leisure Centre
Southgate Stn
Police Station
Crown Lane Clinic
Grovelands Priory Hospital
Bourneside Sports Club
Ashmole School
Southgate College
Brunswick Park JMI School
New Southgate Crematorium
New Southgate Cemetery
Southgate Cemetery
Walker Primary School
Greengrove College
Cannon Hill Clinic
Bowling Green
Broomfield Park
Boating Lake
Arnos Grove Stn
Brunswick Industrial Park
St Johns CE Primary School
St Pauls CE Primary School
New Southgate Station
New Southgate Pain Clinic & Medical Cen
New Southgate Industrial Est
Enfield School of Swimming
Broomfield School
Palmers Green & Southgate Synagogue
Brownlow Medical Cen
Friern Bridge Retail Park
Bounds Green Industrial Est
St Martin of Pores RC Primary School
Glencairn Sports Club
Bounds Green Health Cen
Bounds Green Stn
Bowes Park Stn
Hollickwood JMI School
Golf Course
College of North East London
Muswell Hill Golf Club
Rhodes Avenue Primary School
Greenfields Special School
Coppetts Wood Primary School
Coppetts Wood Hospital
Islington Crematorium
St Pancras and Islington Cemetery
Coldfall Wood
Alexandra Palace Ice Rink
Alexandra Palace Stn
Alexandra Park
Alexandra Palace (Historic Ho)
Middlesex University
The Business Cen
Olympia Industrial Est
Norfolk House School
The Compton School
OSIDGE LANE
RUSSELL LANE
OAKLEIGH ROAD NORTH
OAKLEIGH ROAD SOUTH
FRIERN BARNET ROAD
COLNEY HATCH LANE
BOWES ROAD
STATION ROAD
TELFORD RD N CIRCULAR RD
BOUNDS GREEN ROAD
DURNSFORD ROAD
WATERFALL ROAD
HIGH STREET
THE BOURNE
THE GREEN
CANNON HILL
ALDERMAN'S HILL
POWYS LANE
BROWNLOW ROAD
WILMER WAY
ALEXANDRA PARK ROAD
QUEENS AV
PARK AV
A111
A1003
A1004
A109
A1110
A406(T)
A504
B1453
B550
B1452
B106
1 grid square represents 500 metres

Bush Hill Park
79
Winchmore Hill
Lower Edmonton
EDMONTON
Upper Edmonton
100
WOOD GREEN
Noel Park
TOTTENHAM
119
Tottenham Hale
GREEN LANE
RIDGE AVENUE
VILLAGE ROAD
CHURCH STREET
GREAT CAMBRIDGE ROAD
HEDGE LANE
NORTH CIRCULAR
STERLING WAY (NORTH CIRCULAR)
ANGEL RD
FORE STREET
HIGH ROAD
THE ROUNDWAY
LORDSHIP LANE
BRUCE GROVE
WESTBURY AV
HERTFORD
THE GREEN
Pymmes Park
Edmonton Cemetery
Millfield Thtr
North Middlesex Hospital
Tottenham Hotspur FC (White Hart Lane)
Bruce Castle Museum
New River Stadium
Wood Green Station
White Hart Lane Station
Bruce Grove Stn
Silver Street Station
Edmonton Green Stn
Winchmore Hill Station
Turnpike Lane Station
Tottenham Hale Station

100
80
99
120
A
B
C
D
E
F
G
1
2
3
4
5
6
7
8
9
10
535
36
37
95
94
93
92
91
190
1 grid square represents 500 metres
William Girling Reservoir
Banbury Reservoir
Lockwood Reservoir
Upper Edmonton
Higham Hill
LEA VALLEY ROAD
MERIDIAN WAY
HERTFORD ROAD
NIGHTINGALE ROAD
FORE STREET
THE GREEN
MONTAGU ROAD
ANGEL RD A406(T) (NORTH CIRCULAR)
CONDUIT LANE
WATERMEAD WAY
WALTHAM WAY
HALL LANE
NEW ROAD
WALTHAMSTOW AVENUE (NORTH CIRCULAR)
CHINGFORD MOUNT ROAD
CHINGFORD ROAD
OLD CHURCH ROAD
MANSFIELD HILL
KINGS HEAD HILL
BILLET ROAD
BLACKHORSE LANE
BLACKHORSE ROAD
FOREST ROAD
Pickett's Lock La
Lee Valley Leisure Golf Club
Lee Valley Leisure Centre Camping & Caravan
Golf Course
UCI
Edmonton Green Stn
Edmonton Leisure Centre
Tottenham Park Cemetery
Angel Road Station
Northumberland Park Station
COOKS FERRY ROUNDABOUT
CROOKED BILLET ROUNDABOUT
Lee Valley Watersports Cen
Walthamstow Greyhound Stadium
Chingford RFC
Cemetery
Sir George Monoux College
Waltham Forest College
Hale Station
Enfield
Haringey
Waltham Forest
Lea Valley Walk
River Lee

H
J
K
L
M
N
P
81
39
40
41
Golf Course
Forest View
Royal Epping Forest Golf Club
Queen Elizabeth Museum
Chingford Station
Station Road
Chingford Green
Chingford
The Ridgeway
Kings Road
Whitehall Road
Larkshall Road
Larkshall Business Centre
Friday Hill
New Road
Hatch La
Chingford Hatch
Chingford Lane
Epping New Road
High Road
Buckhurst Hill
Lord's Bushes
Palmerston Rd
Queen's Road
Princes Road
Holly House Private Hospital
Woodford Wells
Bancrofts School
High Rd Woodford Green
Woodford Golf Club
Woodford Green Primary School
Jubilee Sports Ground
Hale End
Highams Park Station
Handsworth Hlth Clinic
Woodford County High School
Woodford Green Prep School
Woodford Station
Woodford
Broadmead Road
Woodford Green
Woodford New Road
Woodbridge High School
Southend Road (North Circular)
Southend Rd (North Circular Road)
South Woodford
George Lane
Chigwell Road
Junction 4
Woodford Trading Est
Unity Trading Estate
BUPA Roding Hospital
Walthamstow Business Cen
Forest Road
Fulbourne Road
Winchester Road
Hyland House School
South Woodford Station
Ray Lodge Primary School
Roding Valley
102
121
I
2
3
4
5
6
7
8
9
10
E4
E18
IG8
IG9

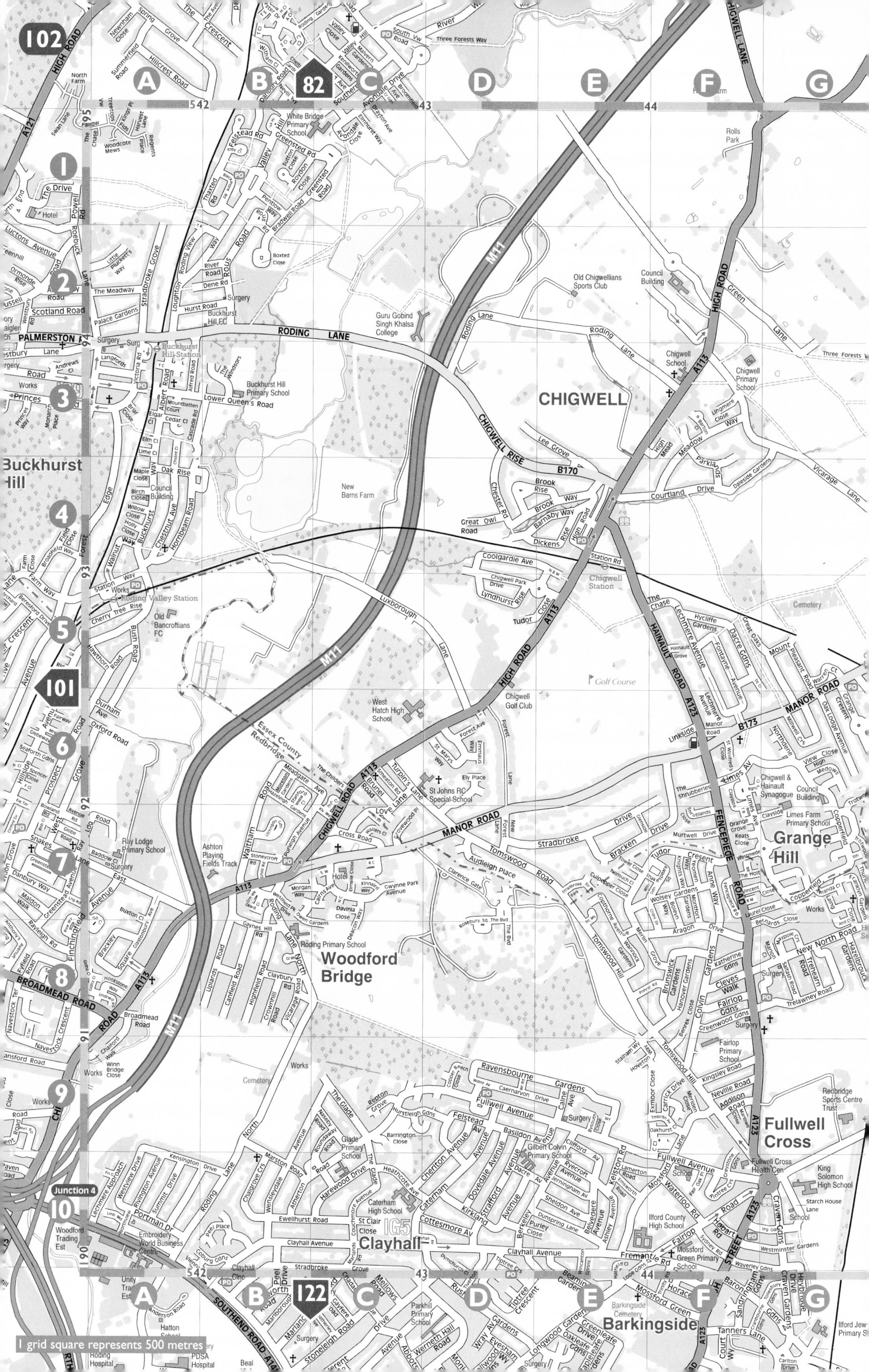
102
82
101
122
Buckhurst Hill
CHIGWELL
Grange Hill
Woodford Bridge
Fullwell Cross
Clayhall
Barkingside
M11
A113
A123
A121
B170
B173
HIGH ROAD
RODING LANE
CHIGWELL RISE
MANOR ROAD
CHIGWELL ROAD
HAINAULT ROAD
FENCEPIECE ROAD
BROADMEAD ROAD
SOUTHEND ROAD
PALMERSTON RD
CHIGWELL LANE
Buckhurst Hill Station
Roding Valley Station
Chigwell Station
Chigwell Golf Club
Golf Course
New Barns Farm
Old Chigwellians Sports Club
Guru Gobind Singh Khalsa College
Chigwell School
Chigwell Primary School
West Hatch High School
St Johns RC Special School
Buckhurst Hill Primary School
Ray Lodge Primary School
Roding Primary School
Limes Farm Primary School
Fairlop Primary School
Gilbert Colvin Primary School
Caterham High School
Glade Primary School
Ilford County High School
King Solomon High School
Redbridge Sports Centre Trust
Fullwell Cross Health Cen
Mossford Green Primary School
Barkingside Cemetery
Woodford Trading Est
Embroidery World Business Centre
Ashton Playing Fields Track
Old Bancroftians FC
Buckhurst Hill FC
Chigwell & Hainault Synagogue
Essex County
Redbridge
Cemetery
Junction 4
IG5
A
B
C
D
E
F
G
542
43
44
1 grid square represents 500 metres

H
J
K
L
M
83
N
P
46
47
48
Marchings Farm
Bishop's Hall
New Road
St John's Farm
Pudding Lane
Gravel Lane
Taylors Farm
Hoe Lane
Manor Road
Pettits Hall
A1112
Young's Farm
Lambourne End
Crabtree Hill
Brownings Farm
Miller's Lane
Harmes Farm
Billingsbourne
Three Forests Way
Chigwell Row
Chigwell Row Infants School
Essex County
Redbridge
Hainault Forest Country Park
Lambourne Road
B173
Vicarage Lane
Green Lane
IG7
Grove Lane
Chapel Lane
Lodge Close
Wells Park School
School Lane
Romford Road
Fox Burrows
Fox Burrow Road
Golf Course
104
Brocket Way
Manford Way
Coppice Primary School
Hainault Industrial Estate
Hainault Forest High School
Fowler Road
Works
Burnside Industrial Estate
Hog Hill
Hainault Forest Golf Club
Five Oaks Lane
Roebuck Road Trading Estate
Forest Road
Elmbridge Road
New North Road
John Bramston Primary School
Hainault
Kennylands Road
Whalebone Lane North
A1174
Forest Ind Park
Bracken Industrial Est
L P R Sports Club
Fairlop
Fairlop Waters
IG6
Hainault Road
Hainault Works
Hainault Farm
Collier Row
Northgate Ind Park
Marks Gate
Redbridge
Barking and Dagenham
Billet Road
1
2
3
4
5
6
7
8
9
10
95
94
93
92
91
90
123
Red House Farm
Marks Gate Junior School
Cemetery

84
124
103
Stapleford Abbotts
Nuper's Hatch
Havering-atte-Bower
Chase Cross
Collier Row
Rise Park
Marks Gate
Gidea Park
RM5
RM1
Grove House
Gutteridge Lane
High House Farm
The Paddocks
Mangi Road
Hook Lane
Knolls Hill Farm
Brook Farm Industrial Estate
Young's Farm
Bournebridge Lane
Crown Park Farm
OAK HILL ROAD
Tysea Hill
Crabtree Hill
Three Forests Way
B175 NORTH ROAD
Bower Farm
Bower Farm Road
Dame Tipping CE Primary School
Park Farm
Wellingtonia Avenue
Havering Country Park
Pinewood Road
ORANGE TREE HILL
Bower House
Golf Course
Havering Redbridge
River Rom
Carter Drive
Kiln Wood Lane
St Johns Road
Thistledene Av
Pinewood Primary School
B175 HAVERING ROAD
Havering Court Nursing Home
Immanuel School
Bower Park School
Gobions JMI School
Bedfords Park
B1459
Risebridge Chase
Lodge Lane
Five Oaks Lane
Firbank Road
Warden Av
Boxmoor Road
Clitheroe Road
Kingshill
Clockhouse Primary School
Burland Road
Ascension Road
Mount Pleasant Rd
CHASE CROSS ROAD
Gobions Avenue
Chelmsford Avenue
Risebridge Golf Club
ROMFORD ROAD B174
HOG HILL ROAD
COLLIER ROW ROAD
WHALEBONE LANE NORTH A1112
Collier Row FC
Northgate Ind Park
Crownfield Primary School
COLLIER ROW LANE B174
Mawney Rd
Rise Park Primary School
Pettits Lane
Heather Avenue
EASTERN AVENUE A12(T)
Marshalls Park School
Rise Park Boulevard
Pettits Bouvard
Primary School
Hubbinet Ind Est
St Peters Catholic Primary School
Birch Road
Birch Close
Forest Road
Kingston Hill Avenue
Billet Road
Cemetery
Barking and Dagenham Havering
1 grid square represents 500 metres

Waterhales
Watton's Green
Navestock Common
Stapleford Abbotts Golf Club
Asheton Farm
Goatswood Lane
Essex County
Havering
Church Road
Paternoster Row
Home Farm
Widdrington Farm
Noak Hill
Noak Hill Road
Manor Farm
Havering Plain
Wrightsbridge Road
Weald Road
St Vincent's Hamlet
Chequers Road
Lower Noke Close
Coxtie Green Road
Frieze Hall
M25
Broxhill Road
Cummings Hall La
Greenbank Cl
The Mount
Castle Close
Kynance Close
Wincanton Road
Tees Drive
Priory Road
Priory Grove
Dagnam Park
Havering College
Ingrebourne Primary School
Ashbourne Road
Whitchurch Road
Tring Gardens
Chudleigh Rd
Lindfield Road
Dagnam Park Drive
Brookside Primary School
Dycourts School
Kingswood School
Settle Road
Sedgefield Crescent
Swindon Lane
Wickford Dr
Sheffield Drive
Central Park Swimming Pool
The Health Centre
Harold Hill
Straight Road
Noak Hill Road
Lower Bedfords Road
Stanwyck Gardens
St Ursulas RC Junior School
RC Infant School
Hilldene Primary School
Chippenham Rd
Petersfield Av
Petersfield Avenue
Penrith Road
Stratton Road
Mead JM&I School
Gooshays Dr
Amersham Rd
Faringdon Avenue
Broadford Primary School
Camborne
Kingsbridge Road
RM3
Colchester Road
A12(T)
Eastern Avenue
Gallows Corner
Gidea Park Sports Ground
Golf Course
Main Road
A118
Harold Court Primary School
Havering Hospitals
Harold Wood Station
Harold Wood
Harold Wood Clinic
Shepherds Hill
Ingrebourne River
Ardleigh Green Primary School
Royal Liberty School
Romford Golf Club
RM2
Harold Wood JMI School
A127(T)
Southend Arterial Road
Ardleigh
85
106
125
H
J
K
L
M
N
P
1
2
3
4
5
6
7
8
9
10
53
54
55
95
94
93
92
91
190

86
105
126
A
B
C
D
E
F
G
1
2
3
4
5
6
7
8
9
10
556
57
58
95
94
93
92
91
90
St Vincent's Hamlet
Wealdside
Hou Hatch
Weald Park (Country Park)
Rochetts
Council Building
Brookweald Cricket Club
Halfway House Farm
Langtons
Sandpit Lane
Weald Road
St Peters CE Primary School
South Weald
Wigley Bush Lane
Weald Park Way
BRENTWOOD
Honeypot Lane
Cemetery
A12(T)
A1023
LONDON ROAD
BROOK STREET
Brook Street
Hotel
Spital Lane
Nag's Head Lane
Junction 28
M25
COLCHESTER ROAD
Maylands Golf Club & Country Club
Golf Course
Harold Park
Harold Court Primary School
Elms Industrial Estate
Harold Court
Bates Industrial Est
The Old Brickworks Business Centre
Harold Wood
Mascalls
Mascalls Lane
Boyles Court
Essex County
Havering
Dark Lane
Great Ropers Lane
Green Lane
WARLEY ROAD
B186
Great Warley
GREAT WARLEY STREET
Tylers Common
Shepherds Hill
Warley Road
Beredens Lane
Coombe Lodge
Hall Lane
Tomkyns Lane
Hole Farm
Ingrebourne River
Dagnam Park
Council Building
Pilgrims Hatch County Primary School
1 grid square represents 500 metres

Shenfield
Hutton Mount
Hutton
Ingrave
Little Warley
CM13
A12(T)
A1023
A128
B186
SHENFIELD ROAD
HUTTON ROAD
INGRAVE ROAD
BRENTWOOD ROAD
ONGAR ROAD
HIGH ST
KING'S ROAD
QUEEN'S RD
RAYLEIGH
Shenfield Station
Brentwood Station
Shenfield Common
St Helens RC Junior School
Hedley Walter High School
St Thomas of Canterbury Junior & Infant School
Anglia Polytechnic University
Brentwood Sports Ground
Ambulance Station
Fire Station
Superstore
Brentwood Theatre
Cinema
Chapel High Shopping Centre
Brentwood Sch
Cath of St Mary & St Helen
Infant School
Council Building
Ursuline Convent High School
Brentwood County High School
The Essex Nuffield Hospital
Brentwood Preparatory School
Brentwood Community Hospital
Shenfield Cricket Club
St Mary's CE Primary School
Community College
Hartswood Golf Club
Brentwood RFC
Hart's Wood
Golf Course
Woodman Road Cem
Warley Primary School
South Essex Health Authority
Warley Hill Business Park
Marillac Hospital
Barrack Wood
Dry Ski Slope
Holden's Wood
Pump Farm
Little Warley Lodge
Warley Lodge Hospital
Warley Park Golf Club
Roses Farm
Hatch Farm
Thorndon Country Park
Thorndon Park Golf Club
Ingrave Johnstone CE Primary School
Ingrave Hall
St Martins School
Childerditch Industrial Park
Eagle Way
Hartswood Road
Childerditch Lane
Magpie Lane
Warley Gap
Bird Lane
The Avenue
Middle Road
Hanging Hill Lane
Running Waters
Priest's Lane
Seven Arches Road
Little Warley Hall Lane
Home Farm Road
Childerditch Hall Drive
87
127
60
61
62
H
J
K
L
M
N
P
2
3
4
5
6
7
8
9
10
90
91
92
93
94
95

BEACONSFIELD
Holtspur
Cherry Tree Road
Rowan Close
Maplewood Gdns
Wood Road
South
Holtspur Way
Ellwood Road
Cherry Tree Road
Penington Road
Burkes Close
Burkes Road
Walk Wood Rise
Wattleton Rd
North Drive
South Drive
A40
WYCOMBE END
Butlers Court
Beaconsfield High School
Beaconsfield School
Butlers Court County First & Middle School
Rolfe Close
AYLESBURY WAY
Millbarn Medical Cen
Crossways
PARK LANE
LONDON ROAD
Beaconsfield Cricket Club
Minerva Way
Maude Road
Maude Close
Gorell Rd
Burnham Av
Hedgerley Lane
Lakes Lane
Windsor End
Beaconsfield RFC
Cross Lane
Malthouse Square
Mag Ct
WOOBURN GN LA
Cemetery
Broad Lane
A355
Pyebush Lane
Hyde Farm
Hall Barn
Junction 2
The Grove
Over's Farm
Rare Breeds Centre
Lillyfee Farm
Lillyfee Farm Lane
Burnham Road
Fairview House
Burtley Wood
Woodlands Hill
Dipple Wood
Woodlands Farm
A355 DORNEY HILL NORTH
Bower Wood
Green Common Lane
Odds Farm
Wooburn Common
Jennings Farm
DORNEY HILL SOUTH
Ship Hill
Sheepcote Farm
Pennlands Farm
Harehatch Lane
Hicknaham Farm
Abbey Park Lane
Abbey Park Farm
COLLINSWOOD ROAD
Hales Cott
Wooburn Common Road
Wood Lane
Boveney Wood Lane
Dropmore Infant School
Little Road
Dorney Wood Road
Beeches Way
Egypt Lane
Egypt Woods
Littleworth Common
Common Lane
Dropmore
Horseshoe Hill
Great Burnt Coppice
Egypt
Brook End Farm
Stewarts Drive
The Avenue
Beeches
Cabrook
Golf Course
Dropmore Road
Curriers Lane
Park Lane
Burnham Beeches (Nature Reserve)
Beeches
Lambourne Golf Club
Pumpkin Hill
Dorney Wood
Lord Mayors Drive
Sir Henry Peakes Drive
East Burnham Common
Bedford Drive
Green Lane
A B C D E F G
1 2 3 4 5 6 7 8 9 10
493 94 95
90 89 88 87 86 85
1 grid square represents 500 metres

88
128

89
110
129
Austenwood
St Josephs CE Combined School
Maltmans Green School
Maltmans Lane
Gayhurst School
Bull Lane
Milton Avenue
Latchmoor Avenue
Acrefield Road
Orchehill Avenue
South View Road
Layters Way
Bentinck Close
Bulstrode
Main Drive
Hotel
Top Park
Valley Way
GERRARDS CROSS
Camp Road
B416
Gerrards Sports C
Meadway Park
WINDSOR RD
Hedgerley Lane
Dukes Wood Drive
Dukes Kiln Drive
High Beeches
Birchdale
Howards Thicket
Howards Wood Dr
M40
Low Farm
Fulmer Chase
The Pickeridge
Hay Lane
Fulmer
Windmill Road
Stoke Common Road
Beeches Way
Stoke Common
Larchmoor Park
Frame Wood
Hollybush
Clevehurst Close
Vine Road
Fircroft Close
Neville Close
Hazel
Elderfield
Duffield Lane
Rickman's
LONDON ROAD A40
Porkin Lane
Stampwell Farm
Hotel
Mumfords Lane
Mumfords Farm
The Manor House
Siblet's Wood
OXFORD ROAD A40
Chiltern Hundreds
Bulstrode Park
Moat Farm
Slade Farm
Hedgerley Lane
Wapseys Lane
Hedgerley Green
Beaconsfield Common Lane
Andrew Hill La
Village Lane
RSPB Site
Hedgerley
Kiln Lane
Hedgerley Hill
Coppice Way
Stevenson Road
Gregory Rd
Jones Way
Elkins Road
Cottage Park Road
Old Nursery Court
Hedgerley Park
Hedgerley
Longfield
Parish Lane
Collum Green Road
Colley Hill Lane
Tara
Cemetery
Wood End Close
Woodland Glade
Romsey Drive
Heatherside Gdns
Gypsy Lane
Stoke Wood
Wood Stoke
Christmas Lane
One Pin Lane
Mount Close
Ashenden Walk
Holly Cl
Farnham Common Sports Club
Farnham Common Middle School
Sherbourne Walk
Crispin Way
Templewood Lane
Bracken Cl
Common Wood
Scott Close
Mayflower Way
Badgers Wood
Grange Gdns
Templewood La
Brockhurst Wood
Rosewood Way
Foxhollow Drive
Rowanhurst Dr
Temple Way
Orchard Gd
Dell Cl
Meadow
Farnham Common
Beeches Way
Forge Dr
Elm Close
B416
GERRARDS CROSS ROAD
H
J
K
L
M
N
P
97
98
99
90
89
88
87
86
185
1
2
3
4
5
6
7
8
9
10

110
90
109
130
A
B
C
D
E
F
G
500
01
02
1
2
3
4
5
6
7
8
9
10
90
89
88
87
86
185
GERRARDS CROSS
Higher Denham
Tatling End
Fulmer
Langley Corner
SL9
M25
M40
A413
A40
B416
B4163
Junction 16/1a
Hogtrough Wood
South Bucks Way
Denham Lane
Mopes Farm
Old Shire La
Croft Rd
Hill Rise
Rise Crs
School La
Meadowcroft
Cherrytree La
Penshurst Close
Austenwood Close
Austenwood La
School Lane
Ashlea Road
Austenway
Kingsway
Claydon Lane
Claydon End
Lower Road
Russell Hill
North Road
North Pk
Hitherway
Kingscote School
St Josephs CE Combined School
Jory Rd
The Rowans
Lewins Rd
Maltmans Green School
Maltmans Lane
South Side
Acrefield Road
The Greenway
Bull Lane
Milton Avenue
Gayhurst School
Latchmoor Way
Latchmoor Avenue
Latchmoor Grove
Orchehill Avenue
Oval Way
Norgrove Park
St Marys School
South Park Drive
Park Road
Amersham Road
Parkside
Park Crs
South Park
Surgery
Hotel
Chalfont Lodge
Gerrards Cross Golf Club
Golf Course
Chalfont Park
Coldharbour Farm
Oakend Wood
The Marish
Marish Lane
South View Road
Layters Way
Bentinck Close
Bulstrode Way
Orchehill Rise
Gerrards Cross Stn
Station Approach
Odeon Cinema
Station Rd
Oak End Way
Rouse Court
Mill Lane
Woodlands
Woodlands Close
Mirrie Lane
Over The Misbourne Road
Over The Misbourne
Isle of Wight Farm
Slade Oak Lane
Denham Golf Cl
Denham Golf Course Sta
Main Drive
Park
Hotel
Top Park
Woodbank Avenue
Donnay Close
Miller Place
West Common
Packhorse Road
Marsham Way
Fulmer Way
East Common
Marsham Lodge
Vicarage Way
Mill Lane
Hill Waye
Woodhill Avenue
Woodhill Av
Beech Waye
Moreland Drive
The Gerrards Cross CE School
Camp Road
Manor Lane
Manor Road
Deerhead Close
Pinewood Close
Gaviots Way
Gaviots Close
Gaviots Gn
Woodhill Farm
Oxford Road
Heusden Way
Amersham Road
Doggetts Farm Road
Middle Road
Upper Road
Lower Road
Works
Misbourne Meadows
Moor House Farm
Wayside Gdns
Gerrards Cross Sports Centre
Meadway Park
Windsor Road
Hedgerley Lane
Dukes Wood Avenue
Dukes Wood Drive
Dukes Ride
Dukes Cl
Coombe Vale
Cheyne Close
Fulmer Road
Fulmer Lane
Old Amersham Road
Neal Cl
Capswood Business Centre
Broken Gate Lane
Bakers Wood
Pinstone Way
Beta Works
Skylark Road
Hollybush Lane
Hollybush Farm
Denham Mount
Blacksmith's Lane
Mount Lane
Froggy Lane
Dukes Kiln Drive
Howards Thicket
Howards Wood Dr
High Beeches
Birchdale
The Glade
Dale Side
The Uplands
Uplands Close
St Huberts Close
St Huberts Cl
St Huberts Lane
Elmwood Pk
St Huberts
Fulmer Drive
The Oldhouse Farm
Alderbourne Manor
Hawk's Wood
Low Farm
Fulmer Chase
Hay Lane
Fulmer Infant School
Windmill Road
Alderbourne Lane
Beeches Way
Hawkswood Lane
Fulmer Rise
Cherry Tree Lane
Alderbourne Lane
Alderbourne Farm
Sevenhills Road
Fulmer Common Road
Pinewood Road
1 grid square represents 500 metres

Gerrards Cross
111
91
112
131
H
J
K
L
M
N
P
04
05
06
90
89
88
87
86
85
1
2
3
4
5
6
7
8
9
10
South Harefield
Denham Green
Denham
Baker's Wood
Willowbank
New Denham
UB9
NORTH ORBITAL ROAD
A412
DENHAM AVENUE A412
OXFORD ROAD
M40
A40
WESTERN AVENUE
A40(T)
A4020
Junction 1
Denham Station
Harefield Cricket Club
Bourne Farm
Breakspear Road North
Breakspear House
Park Lodge Farm
Harvil Road
Moorhall Road
Moorfield Road
Savay Farm
Savay Lane
Tilehouse Lane
Tilehouse Combined School
Martin Baker Sports Ground
Old Rectory Lane
Grand Union Canal Walk
Hillingdon Trail
Buckinghamshire County
Hillingdon
Widewater Business Centre
Highway Farm
Works
Golf Course
Uxbridge Golf Club
Buckinghamshire Golf Club
Court Drive
Denham Court Drive
South Bucks Way
Village Road
Council Building
Denham County Infant School
Cheapside Lane
Ashmead Lane
Mill Road
Lodore Green
Swakeleys Road
Warren Road
Vyners School
Copthall Farm
New House Farm
Field Road
Hollybush Lane
Southlands Road
Denham Road
Ivy House Farm
The Lea
Colne Valley Trail
Uxbridge Cricket Club
Uxbridge Swimming Pool
Dry Ski Slope
Park Road
B483
B467
Harefield Road
Education Centre
Knightscote Farm
Hangar Road
Denham Aerodrome
Bayhurst Country Park

Northwood Hills
Ruislip Common
RUISLIP
Newyears Green
West Ruislip
Ickenham
Ruislip Gardens
Bayhurst Wood Country Park
Breakspear Crematorium
Mad Bess Wood
Copse Wood
Park Wood
Poor's Field
Ruislip Lido
Haste Hill Golf Club
Northwood Cemetery
St Vincents Hospital
Kings College Sports Ground
Breakspear House
Bourne Farm
Youngwood Farm
Highway Farm
Copthall Farm
Uxbridge Golf Club
Ruislip Golf Club
West Ruislip Station
Ruislip Station
Ickenham Station
Ruislip Manor FC
Ruislip RFC
Hillingdon Borough FC
Compass Theatre
Ickenham Manor
Dry Ski Slope
Uxbridge Cricket Club
Uxbridge Swimming Pool
Vyners School
Breakspear Primary School
Glebe Primary School
The Douay Martyrs RC School
Ruislip Gardens Primary School
Sacred Heart RC Junior & Infant School
Bishop Ramsey CE School
Whiteheath Infant School
Whiteheath Junior School
Bishop Winnington-Ingram CE Primary School
Breakspear Road North
Breakspear Road South
Newyears Green Lane
Fine Bush Lane
Hillingdon Trail
Ducks Hill
Bury Street
High Street
Eastcote Road
Ickenham Road
Swakeleys Road
High Road Ickenham
Long Lane
Western Avenue
Harvil Road
Park Road
A4180
A40(T)
B466
B467
B483
A437
UB10
507
08
09
90
89
88
87
86
185
A
B
C
D
E
F
G
92
111
132

1 grid square represents 500 metres

Pinner Green
Pinner
Eastcote Village
Eastcote
North Harrow
Rayners Lane
Ruislip Manor
South Ruislip
South Harrow
Headstone
HA5
HA4
93
114
133
H
J
K
L
M
N
P
11
12
13
90
89
88
87
86
185
1
2
3
4
5
6
7
8
9
10
A404
RICKMANSWORTH ROAD
GEORGE V AVENUE
JOEL STREET
CUCKOO HILL
EASTCOTE ROAD
HIGH ROAD
IMPERIAL DRIVE
ALEXANDRA AVENUE
WEST END ROAD
VICTORIA ROAD
MANDEVILLE ROAD
PETTS HILL
A4180
A4090
A312
B466
B472
Pinner Station
Eastcote Station
Rayners Lane Station
Ruislip Manor Station
Ruislip Gardens Station
South Ruislip Station
North Harrow Station
Northolt Park Station
Northwood Hills Stn
Pinner Park Farm
Cemetery
Highgrove Swimming Pool
Eastcote Cricket Club
Harrow Town Cricket Club
The Roxbourne
Victoria Retail Park
Odyssey Business Park
Braintree Road Industrial Estate
Eastcote Industrial Est
Canada House Business Cen
Roxbourne Middle School
Newton Farm First & Middle School
Alexandra School
Field End Primary School
Deanesfield Primary School
Queensmead School
Bourne CP School
Heathfield School
Cannon Lane Primary School
Moriah Jewish Day School
Newnham Junior & Infant School
Bishop Ramsey CE School
Harlyn School
John Fisher School
Nower Hill High School
Reddiford School
West Lodge School
Longfield Primary School
Roxeth Manor First School
Earlsmead First & Middle School
Harrow Borough FC
Superstore
Works
Hillingdon
Ealing
Harrow
Northolt

114
94
113
134
A
B
C
D
E
F
G
1
2
3
4
5
6
7
8
9
10
Headstone
Wealdstone
Belmont
HARROW
Greenhill
West Harrow
Harrow on the Hill
North Wembley
Roxeth
South Harrow
Sudbury
HA1
HA2
HA3
Harrow Heritage Museum
Headstone Manor Recreation Ground
Harrow & Wealdstone Station
Harrow Crown Courts
Civic Centre
Harrow-on-the-Hill Station
St Georges Shopping Centre & Cinema
St Ann's Shopping Cen
Harrow College
West Harrow Station
North Harrow Station
Kenton Station
Northwick Park Station
Northwick Park Hospital & Clinical Research Centre
University of Westminster (Harrow Campus)
Northwick Park
Harrow School
Clementine Churchill Hospital
South Harrow Station
Sudbury Hill (Harrow Station)
Sudbury Hill Station
Sudbury & Harrow Road Station
Northolt Park Station
Whitmore High School
Vaughan First & Middle School
Harrow High School
Kenton Recreation Ground
Playing Fields
Golf Course
PINNER ROAD
GEORGE V AVENUE
STATION ROAD
SHEEPCOTE ROAD
KENTON ROAD
WATFORD ROAD
LOWER ROAD
BESSBOROUGH ROAD
NORTHOLT ROAD
SUDBURY HILL
GREENFORD ROAD
HARROW ROAD
WHITTON AVENUE
ALEXANDRA AVENUE
A404
A409
A4005
A312
A4090
A4127
B458
1 grid square represents 500 metres

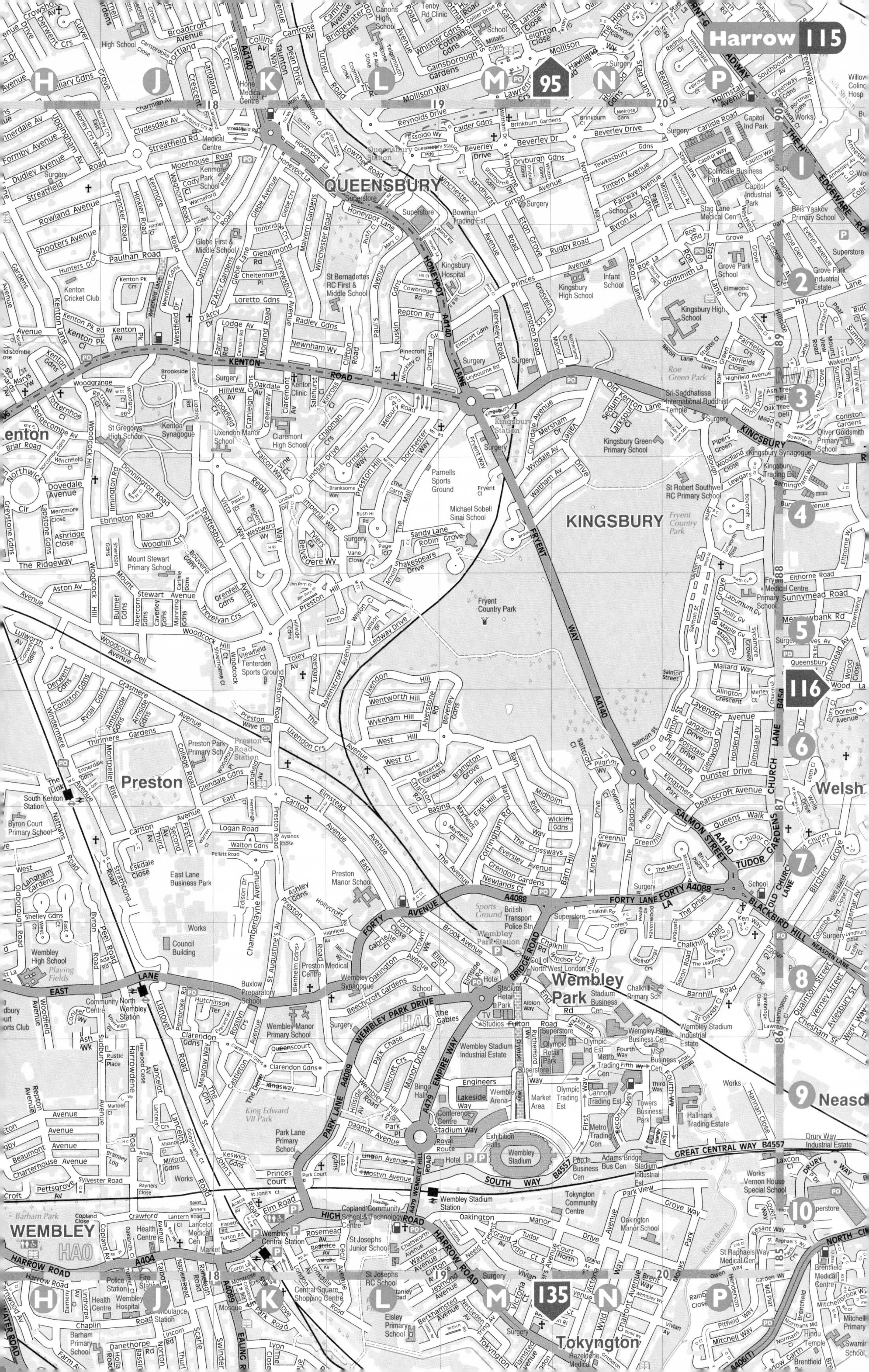

QUEENSBURY
KINGSBURY
Preston
Wembley Park
WEMBLEY
Tokyngton
Kenton
Welsh
Neasd
KENTON ROAD
HONEYPOT LANE
FRYENT WAY
SALMON STREET
FORTY AVENUE
FORTY LANE
EAST LANE
WEMBLEY PARK DRIVE
EMPIRE WAY
PARK LANE
HARROW ROAD
HIGH ROAD
SOUTH WAY
GREAT CENTRAL WAY
BRIDGE ROAD
CHURCH LANE
BLACKBIRD HILL
KINGSBURY ROAD
EDGWARE ROAD
NORTH CIRCULAR
WEMBLEY HILL ROAD
EALING ROAD
Fryent Country Park
Wembley Stadium
Wembley Arena
Kingsbury Station
Queensbury Station
Preston Road Station
Wembley Park Station
South Kenton Station
Wembley Central Station
Wembley Stadium Station
Kingsbury Hospital
King Edward VII Park
Barham Park
Roe Green Park
Colindale Business Park
Capitol Industrial Park
Wembley Stadium Industrial Estate
East Lane Business Park
A4140
A4088
A4089
A479
A404
B4557
B454
A406(T)
HA0
HA9
NW9
95
116
135
H
J
K
L
M
N
P
18
19
20
1
2
3
4
5
6
7
8
9
10
185
86
87
88
89
90

116
96
115
136
A
B
C
D
E
F
G
1
2
3
4
5
6
7
8
9
10
21
22
23
Colindale
The Hyde
HENDON
West Hendon
Welsh Harp
Dollis Hill
Neasden
Dudden Hill
WILLESDEN
NW9
NW4
NW2
Royal Air Force Museum
Colindale Station
British Library Newspaper Library
Metropolitan Police Track (Hendon)
Metropolitan Police Training School, Hendon
Hendon Central Station
Brent Cross Shopping Centre
Brent Cross Station
BRENT CROSS FLYOVER
West Hendon Playing Fields
Brent Reservoir
Junction 1
Gladstone Park
Recreation Ground
Hendon Park
Sunny Hill Park
Neasden Station
Cricklewood Station
Willesden Green Station
Kingsbury High School
Church Farm House Museum
Brent Arts Council
The Stables Gallery & Art Centre
Woodfield School
Hendon FC
WATFORD WAY
EDGWARE ROAD
THE HYDE
THE BROADWAY
NORTH CIRCULAR ROAD
COLINDEEP LANE
KINGSBURY ROAD
CHURCH ROAD
THE BURROUGHS
QUEEN'S ROAD
FINCHLEY LANE
BRENT STREET
PARSON STREET
STATION ROAD
CRICKLEWOOD BROADWAY
CHICHELE ROAD
WALM LANE
DUDDEN HILL LANE
NEASDEN LANE
BLACKBIRD HILL
OLD CHURCH LANE
CHURCH LANE
SALMON STREET
GREAT CENTRAL WAY
BARNET BY-PASS
GREAT NORTH WAY
HIGH ROAD
1 grid square represents 500 metres

East Finchley
Hampstead Garden Suburb
Golders Green
NW11
North End
Sandy Heath
West Heath
Child's Hill
Vale of Health
HAMPSTEAD
West Hampstead
Hampstead Heath
Maitland Park
Golf Course
Highgate Golf Club
Hampstead Golf Club
Kenwood House
Golders Green Station
Finchley Road & Frognal Station
West Hampstead Station
Royal Free Hospital
NORTH CIRCULAR ROAD
FALLODEN WAY
FINCHLEY ROAD
LYTTELTON ROAD
AYLMER ROAD
NORTH END ROAD
SPANIARDS ROAD
HEATH STREET
ROSSLYN HILL
HAVERSTOCK HILL
HENDON WAY
CRICKLEWOOD LANE
FORTUNE GN RD
GREAT NORTH ROAD
FORTIS GREEN
EAST END ROAD
REGENT'S PARK ROAD
97
118
137

118
98
117
138
A
B
C
D
E
F
G
1
2
3
4
5
6
7
8
9
10
528
29
30
Muswell Hill
Fortis Green
Cranley Gardens
Highgate
Hornsey
Crouch End
Upper Holloway
Dartmouth Park
Tufnell Park
Gospel Oak
Lower Holloway
Kentish Town
Maitland Park
Finsbury Park
Highgate Wood
Queen's Wood
Highgate Cemetery
Hampstead Heath
Parliament Hill
Alexandra Palace (Historic House)
Alexandra Park
Alexandra Palace Ice Rink
Alexandra Palace Stn
Highgate Station
Archway Stn
Upper Holloway Stn
Crouch Hill Station
Gospel Oak Station
Hampstead Heath Stn
Kentish Town Station
Kentish Town West Stn
Tufnell Park Station
MUSWELL HILL
PRIORY ROAD
PRIORY RD
HIGH STREET A504
FORTIS GREEN
QUEENS AV
MUSWELL HILL ROAD
ARCHWAY ROAD
NORTH HILL
HAMPSTEAD LANE
HIGHGATE HIGH STREET
HIGHGATE HILL
HOLLOWAY ROAD
JUNCTION ROAD
CAMDEN ROAD
FORTESS ROAD
KENTISH TOWN ROAD
HIGHGATE RD
MANSFIELD ROAD
AGINCOURT RD
FLEET RD
MALDEN ROAD
HAVERSTOCK HILL
BRECKNOCK ROAD
PARKHURST RD
HILLMARTON ROAD
CALEDONIAN ROAD
YORK WAY
TOTTENHAM LANE
CROUCH END HILL
CROUCH HILL
HORNSEY RISE
HORNSEY ROAD
HORNSEY LANE
PARK ROAD
CHERRY TREE HILL
AYLMER ROAD
GREAT NORTH ROAD
N6
N8
N10
N19
NW5
N7
1 grid square represents 500 metres

Noel Park
West Green
Tottenham Hale
South Tottenham
Harringay
Stroud Green
Stamford Hill
Upper Clapton
Finsbury Park
STOKE NEWINGTON
Highbury
Shacklewell
Canonbury
99
120
139
H
J
K
L
M
N
P
1
2
3
4
5
6
7
8
9
10
N4
N5
N15
N16
Finsbury Park Station
Manor House Station
Harringay Green Lanes Stn
Seven Sisters Station
Stamford Hill Stn
Stoke Newington Station
Rectory Road Station
Drayton Park Station
Tottenham Hale Station
South Tottenham Stn
Clissold Park
Abney Park Cemetery
Hackney Downs
Highbury Fields
SEVEN SISTERS ROAD
GREEN LANES
STAMFORD HILL
STOKE NEWINGTON HIGH STREET
BLACKSTOCK ROAD
HIGHBURY PARK
WEST GREEN ROAD
ST ANN'S ROAD
AMHURST PARK
LORDSHIP PARK
MANOR ROAD
CLAPTON COMMON
NORTHWOLD ROAD
BALLS POND ROAD
DALSTON LANE
GRAHAM ROAD

120
100
119
140
Higham Hill
WALTHAMSTOW
Upper Clapton
Walthamstow Marshes
Lea Bridge
Hackney Marsh
Clapton Park
Lower Clapton
Shacklewell
Hackney Downs
HACKNEY
Homerton
Hackney Wick
Temple Mills
Warwick Reservoir
Lockwood Reservoir
FOREST ROAD
FERRY LANE
BLACKHORSE ROAD
HOE STREET
MARKHOUSE ROAD
LEA BRIDGE ROAD
UPPER CLAPTON ROAD
LOWER CLAPTON ROAD
HOMERTON HIGH STREET
HOMERTON ROAD
CHURCH ROAD
RUCKHOLT ROAD
EASTWAY
DALSTON LANE
GRAHAM ROAD
WICK ROAD
E5
E10
E17
1 grid square represents 500 metres

South Woodford
101
Upper Walthamstow
Wood Street Station
Snaresbrook Crown Court
Snaresbrook Station
Redbridge
WANSTEAD
Wanstead Station
Leytonstone
Leytonstone Stn
Leytonstone High Road Stn
Aldersbrook
Leyton Midland Road Station
LEYTON
Forest Gate
Forest Gate Station
Wanstead Park Stn
Wanstead Flats
Manor Park Crematorium
Manor Park Station
Stratford New Town
122
141
E11
E18
E7
Whipps Cross Hospital
Wanstead Golf Club
Golf Course
Lincoln Island
Cemetery
Wanstead Hospital
Forest School
Leyton VI Form College
Langthorne Hospital
NORTH CIRCULAR ROAD
EASTERN AVENUE A12(T)
WOODFORD NEW ROAD
HOLLYBUSH HILL
NEW WANSTEAD
HERMON HILL
CHIGWELL ROAD
WHIPPS CROSS ROAD
LEA BRIDGE ROAD A104
BLAKE HALL ROAD
CENTRE ROAD A114
WOODFORD ROAD
ALDERSBROOK ROAD
HARROW ROAD
GROVE GREEN ROAD
HIGH ROAD LEYTON A112
LEYTONSTONE HIGH ROAD A11
ROMFORD ROAD A118
CHOBHAM ROAD A112
DAMES ROAD
BUSH ROAD A114
FOREST ROAD
H J K L M N P
1 2 3 4 5 6 7 8 9 10

122
102
121
142
A
B
C
D
E
F
G
1
2
3
4
5
6
7
8
9
10
Barkingside
Redbridge
Gants Hill
Cranbrook
Valentines Park
ILFORD
Manor Park
Little Ilford
Loxford
Clayhall
Wanstead Park
City of London Cemetery
City of London Crematorium
Ilford Golf Club
Clayhall Park
SOUTHEND ROAD A1400
NORTH CIRCULAR ROAD
A1400 WOODFORD AVENUE
EASTERN AVENUE A12(T)
EASTERN AV
CRANBROOK ROAD
HIGH STREET
ALDERSBROOK ROAD
FOREST DRIVE
ROMFORD ROAD
RABBITS RD
STATION RD
HIGH ST NORTH
ILFORD LANE
WINSTON WAY
ILFORD HILL
CHAPEL RD
HIGH ROAD
FANSHAWE AVENUE
LONGBRIDGE
BROWNING ROAD
Ilford Station
Manor Park Station
Woodgrange Park Stn
Redbridge Station
Gants Hill Station
Seven Kings High School
Valentine High School
Ilford County High School
Wanstead High School
Cranbrook College
1 grid square represents 500 metres

Marks Gate
Northgate Ind Park
103
Redbridge
Barking and Dagenham
Painters Road
Hainault Road
Red House Farm
Billet Road
Aldborough Hatch
Little Heath
Little Heath School
Marks Gate Junior School
Hlth Service Clinic
Cemetery
WHALEBONE LANE NORTH
A1112
A12(T)
EASTERN AVENUE
RM6
Newton Industrial Est
King George Hospital
Redbridge College
Ethel Davis School
Grove Primary School
Chadwell Heath Hospital
William Torbitt Junior & Infant School
Newbury Park (United) Synagogue
Seven Kings Park
Chadwell Heath
Warren Junior School
Warren Comprehensive School
BARLEY LANE
B177
Chadwell Heath School
Barley Lane Primary Sch
Blacksmith Close
Chadwell Heath Luncheon & Leisure Cen
Furze Infant School
HIGH ROAD
A118
Mirravale Trading Estate
Chadwell Heath Station
124
Goodmayes Retail Park
Goodmayes Station
Superstore
Independent School
Seven Kings
Seven Kings Stn
Seven Kings Health Cen
Kings Private Clinic
IG3
Mayfield School & College
Chadwell Heath Industrial Park
Eldenwall Industrial Est
Henry Green Primary School
Robert Clack School
GREEN LANE
A1083
GOODMAYES ROAD
Oak Tree Medical Cen
South Park Bus Cen
Goodmayes Park
Goodmayes
Becontree Primary School
Valence House Mus & Library
Becontree Day Hospital
RM8
Valence Park
Valence Circus
BENNETT'S CASTLE LANE
B191
Dagenham Chest Clinic
South Park Primary School
Mayespark Primary School
GOODMAYES LANE
LONGBRIDGE ROAD
A124
University of East London
Mayesbrook Park Arena
Barking FC
St Teresa RC Primary School
Roding Primary School
PORTERS AVENUE
A1153
Sydney Russell Comprehensive School
Becontree
Sidney Russell School
Fair Cross
East Barking Luncheon & Leisure Centre
Childs Welfare Clinic
Parsloes Park
Parsloes Primary School
143
Mayesbrook Park
Barking Abbey Comprehensive School
The Faircross Complementary Medical Cen
Ivyhouse Road
Dagenham
H
J
K
L
M
N
P
46
47
48
1
2
3
4
5
6
7
8
9
10
90
89
88
87
86
85

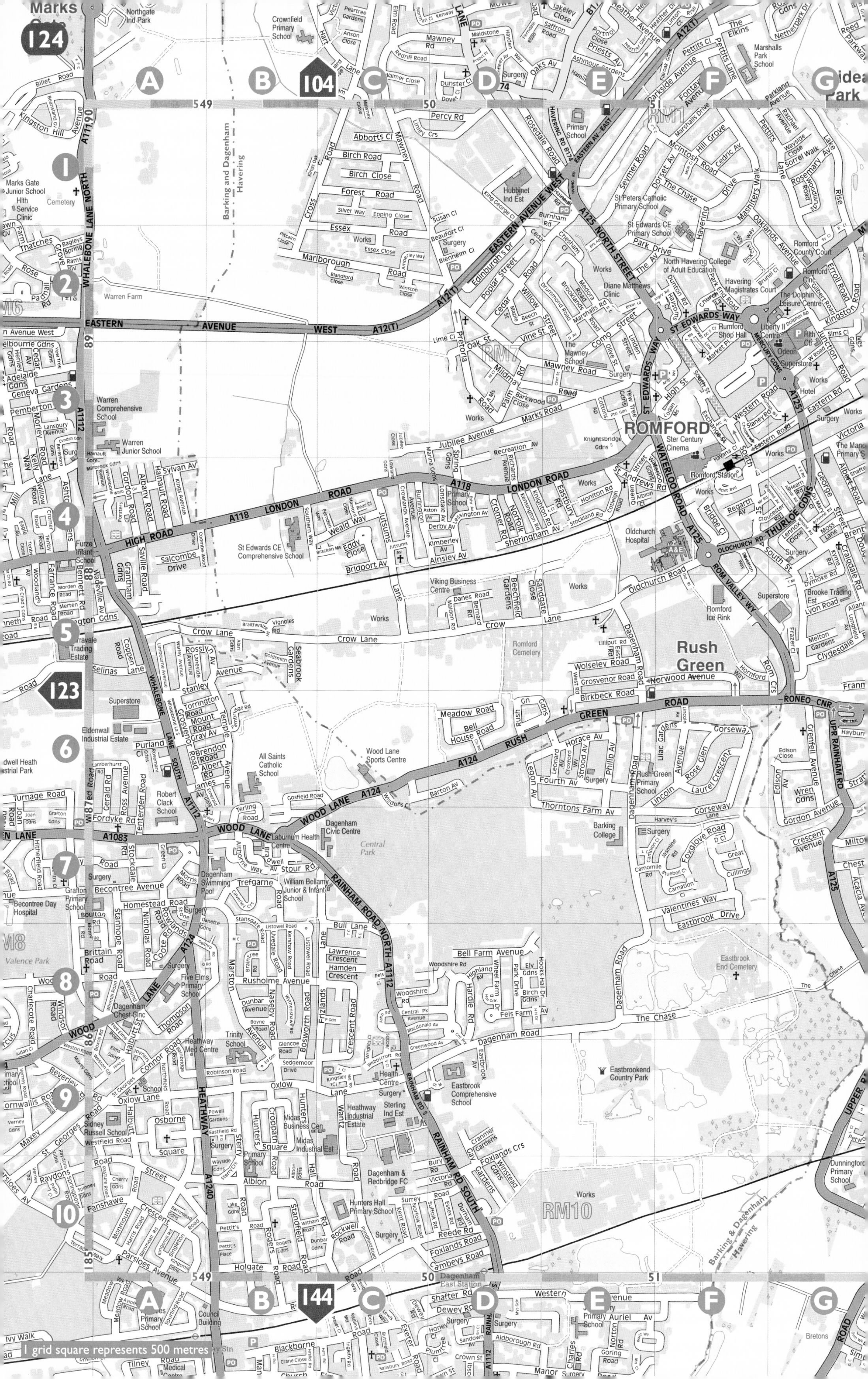

124
104
123
144
A
B
C
D
E
F
G
1
2
3
4
5
6
7
8
9
10
549
50
51
ROMFORD
Rush Green
RM7
RM10
EASTERN AVENUE WEST A12(T)
WHALEBONE LANE NORTH A1112
WHALEBONE LANE SOUTH A1112
HIGH ROAD
A118 LONDON ROAD
WOOD LANE A124
RUSH GREEN ROAD A124
WATERLOO ROAD A125
A125 NORTH STREET
ST EDWARDS WAY
RAINHAM ROAD NORTH A1112
RAINHAM RD SOUTH
HEATHWAY A1240
A1083
Crow Lane
Marks Road
Dagenham Road
The Chase
Romford Station
Oldchurch Hospital
Romford Cemetery
Central Park
Eastbrookend Country Park
Eastbrook End Cemetery
Dagenham Civic Centre
Wood Lane Sports Centre
St Edwards CE Comprehensive School
Warren Farm
Barking and Dagenham
Havering
Marks Gate Junior School
Romford Ice Rink
Ster Century Cinema
Dagenham East Station
1 grid square represents 500 metres

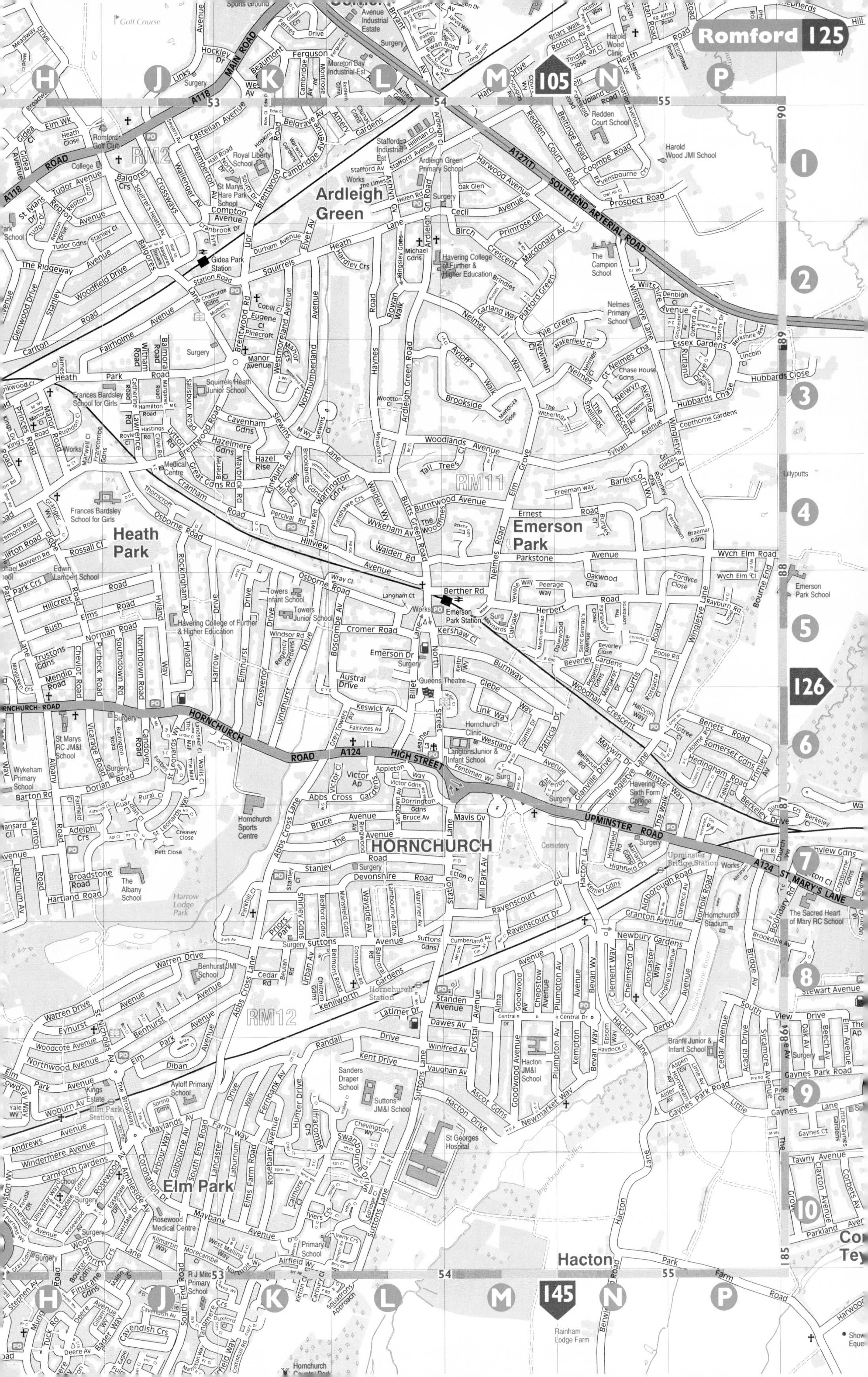
Ardleigh Green
Emerson Park
Heath Park
HORNCHURCH
Elm Park
Hacton
RM2
RM11
RM12
A127(T) SOUTHEND ARTERIAL ROAD
A118 MAIN ROAD
A124 HIGH STREET
HORNCHURCH ROAD
UPMINSTER ROAD
A124 ST MARY'S LANE
Gidea Park Station
Emerson Park Station
Hornchurch Station
Elm Park Station
Upminster Bridge Station
Queens Theatre
St Georges Hospital
Hornchurch Sports Centre
Harrow Lodge Park
Cemetery
Havering College of Further & Higher Education
Frances Bardsley School for Girls
Campion School
Hornchurch Stadium
Ingrebourne River
Ingrebourne Valley
Rainham Lodge Farm
105
126
145
H J K L M N P
1 2 3 4 5 6 7 8 9 10
53 54 55
185 86 87 88 89 90

126
106
125
146
A
B
C
D
E
F
G
1
2
3
4
5
6
7
8
9
10
556
57
58
90
89
88
87
86
185
1 grid square represents 500 metres
UPMINSTER
Cranham
Corbets Tey
Junction 29
M25
A127(T)
SOUTHEND ARTERIAL ROAD
B187
B1421
ST MARY'S LANE
CORBETS TEY ROAD
OCKENDON ROAD
Warley Road
Hall Lane
Tomkyns Lane
Beredens Lane
Coombe Lodge
Hole Farm
Folkes Lane
Front Lane
Moor Lane
Pike Lane
Codham Hall
Folkes Farm
Franks Farm
Westbury Farm
Broadfields Farm
Hobbs Hole
Chapmans Farm
Bird Lane
River Drive
Avon Rd
Lillyputts
Emerson Park School
Wych Elm Road
Bourne End
Hubbards Close
Tithe Barn Museum
Upminster Golf Club
Golf Course
Hall Mead School
Engayne Junior School
Cranham Health Cen
Surgery
Works
Upminster Station
Howard Road
St Lawrence Road
Station Road
The Sacred Heart of Mary RC School
Hornchurch Stadium
Upminster Primary School
Coopers Company & Coborn School
James Oglethorpe Primary School
Eaton Road
The Chase
Cranham Hall
Tudor Gardens
Cedar Gdns
Derham Gardens
Sunnyside Gardens
Argyle Gardens
Springfield Gardens
Stewart Avenue
Gaynes Park Road
Coniston Avenue
Cranston Park Avenue
Tawny Avenue
Gaynes School
Upminster Cemetery
South Essex Crematorium
Parkland Avenue
Meadowside Rd
Harwood Hall Lane
Harwood Hall
Farm Road
Manor Farm
Sunnings Lane
Stubbers (Outdoor Pursuits Centre)
Show Jumping
Church Lane School
Cranham Place
Waldegrave Gdns
Deyncourt Gardens
Ingrebourne Gardens
Ashburnham Gardens
Engayne Gardens
Courtenay Gardens
Grosvenor Gardens
Claremont Gdns
Everseigh Gdns
Esdaile Gdns
The Fairway
Holden Way
Marlborough Cl
Brookmans
Dorkins Wy
High Elms
Kings Gardens
Park Av
Heron
Swan Av
Nightingale Avenue
Kerry Drive
Limerick Gdns
Laburnham Gdns
Acacia Gdns
Fairholme Gdns
Queens Gdns
Rosebery Gardens
Roseberry Cl
Lexington Wy
Brunswick Av
Waycross Road
Macon Wy
Peterborough Av
Canterbury Av
Worcester Av
Winchester Av
Lichfield Terrace
Westbury Terrace
Ashvale Gdns
Rectory Gdns
Chester Av
Boyd Sch
Fleet Av
Fleet Cl
Severn Drive
Trent Avenue
Stour Wy
Pentire Cl
Isis Dr
Forth Road
Colne Valley
Humber Dr
Mersey Av
Chelmer Rd
Highview Gdns
Carlton Cl
Boundary Rd
Brookdale Av
Norfolk Road
Hornchurch Stadium
Ingrebourne River
Benets Rd
Somerset Gdns
Frimley Av
Berkeley Drive
Waltham Cl
Hurst

Magpie
Bird Lane
Warley Park Golf Club
Golf Course
Warley Hall Lane
Little Warley
Roses Farm
Childerditch Hall Drive
107
Little Warley Hall La
Childerditch Street
Childerditch Lane
Childerditch Industrial Park
Rectory Chase
Lane
Childerditch
Childerditch Hall Dr
Woodlands Preparatory School
Crossways
Kelrose Swimming Pool Centre
Little Warley Hall Lane
SOUTHEND ARTERIAL ROAD
A127
ARTERIAL ROAD
WARLEY STREET
B186
Thorndon Avenue
West Horndon Primary School
Nuttys Farm
Great Warley Hall
Church Lane
West Horndon
Cadogan Avenue
Dunmow Gdns
Freshwell Gdns
Fyfield Cl
Petresfield Way
Horndon Industrial Park
Works
West Horndon Station
Upminster Trading Park
St Mary's Lane
Monks Farm
Old Englands Farm
Field House
Tillingham Hall
Puddle Dock
Works
Dunnings Lane
Bury Farm
Thurrock
Havering
Clay Tye Farm
CLAY TYE ROAD
Blankets Farm
Fen Lane
RM14
Home Farm
Mar Dyke
White Post Farm
Corner Farm
Stone Hall
Golf Course
Fen Lane
Top Meadow Golf Club
OCKENDON ROAD
147
H J K L M N P
60 61 62
1 2 3 4 5 6 7 8 9 10
90 89 88 87 86 85

108
148
Burnham
East Burnham
Britwell
Cippenham
Lent Rise
Lent
Rose Hill
Lake End
SL1
Burnham Beeches (Nature Reserve)
East Burnham Common
Dorney Wood
Burnham Grove
East Burnham Park
Hunts Wood Farm
Snowball Farm
Lambourne Golf Club
Burnham Beeches Golf Club
Golf Course
Hotel
Hitcham House
Burnham Grammar School
Burnham Upper School
Lent Rise Combined School
St Peters CE Combined School
Burnham Health Centre
Burnham FC
Burnham Station
Lynch Hill School
Claycots School
Beechwood School
Caldicott School
Cippenham Infants School
Cippenham Junior School
Western House First School
Westgate School
Westgate Retail Park
Slough Trading Estate
Perth Trading Estate
Huntercombe Manor
Huntercombe Manor Hospital
Burnham Abbey
The Bharani Medical Centre
The Village Medical Centre
Taplow Health Centre
Superstore
Buckinghamshire County
Slough
Dropmore Road
Dorney Wood Road
Green Lane
Grove Road
Crow Piece Lane
Hawthorn Lane
Lord Mayors Drive
Sir Henry Peakes Drive
Crown Lane
Pumpkin Hill
Park Lane
Curriers Lane
Nashdom Lane
Wymers Wood Road
Taplow Common Road
Hitcham Lane
Farnham Lane
Long Furlong Drive
Whittaker Road
Northborough Road
Buckingham Avenue
Bath Road
A4
B3026
Lake End Road
Huntercombe Spur
Huntercombe Lane
M4
Allerds Road
Stomp Road
Burnham Lane
Lower Britwell Road
Priory Road
Lent Rise Road
Bath Road
Ipswich Road
Edinburgh Avenue
Dover Road
Dundee Road
Henley Road
1 grid square represents 500 metres

109
130
149
Farnham Common
Farnham Park
Farnham Royal
Hollybush Hill
Stoke Poges
Wexham Street
Stoke Green
Manor Park
Upton Lea
Salt Hill
SLOUGH
Chalvey
SL2
Beeches Way
Templewood
Grange Gdns
Rosewood Way
Langton's Meadow
Victoria Road
Parsonage Lane
Parson's Wood Lane
Purton Lane
Purton Court
Farnham Park Lane
BEACONSFIELD ROAD
Brockhurst Wood
Stoke Common
Frame Wood
Rickman's Lane
Duffield Lane
Vine Road
Fircroft Close
Clevehurst Close
GERRARDS CROSS RD
Elderfield Road
Hazell Way
Freemans Close
Pennylets Green
Bunby Road
Bells Green
Broom Hill
Cherry Orchard
Hollybush Hill
Sefton Paddock
Stoke Court
Stoke Poges County Middle School
Willow Park
Stoke Court Drive
Lakeside Drive
Rogers Lane
Surgery
Sefton Close
BELLS HILL
Stoke Poges School
School Lane
Hockley Lane
Chapel Lane
Framewood Road
Teikyo School
The Thames Valley Nuffield Hospital
Plough Lane
Tubwell Rd
Wexham Street
West End Lane
Elizabeth Way
Penn Meadow
Golf Course
Farnham Park Golf Club
Tithe Farm
Green Lane
Farthing Green Lane
GRAYS PARK ROAD
B416
PARK ROAD
Wexham Park Golf Club
Rowle Wood
Church Lane
Martin's Plain
Hampden Close
Buckland Gate
Galleons Lane
Rectory
The Cricket Club
Farnham Royal CE Combined School
Stoke Poges Golf Club
Stoke Park
Stoke Park House
Duffield Park
Bell Farm
Wrexham Park Hospital
A&E
St Anthonys RC Primary School
Wiltshire Avenue
Cornwall Avenue
Lancaster Avenue
Cumberland Avenue
Canterbury Avenue
The William Penn School
Penn Road
Fir Tree Avenue
Stoke Green
Stoke Place
The Cricket Club
Church Lane
Opal Court
Wexham Park Lane
Valley End
STOKE ROAD
Northern Road
Journeys End
Stoke Poges Lane
Salisbury Avenue
Warwick Avenue
Surrey Av
Essex Avenue
Kent Avenue
Norfolk Avenue
Hatton Avenue
Villiers Road
Beaumont Road
Staunton Road
Beechwood Road
Howard Avenue
Bryant Av
Granville Avenue
Whiteford Road
Church Grove
Wexham School
Wexham Woods
Norway Drive
Farm Crescent
Langewood
Manor Park Medical Centre
Baylis Court School
Hampshire Av
Gloucester Avenue
Godolphin Infant School
Warrington Av
Kirkwall Spur
Sumburgh Way
Renfrew Dr
Cromwell Drive
Hawthorne Crescent
Slough Crematorium
Slough Cemetery
Slough Town FC
Upton Lea
Almons Way
Mansel Close
Bell Close
Hillersdon
Moat Drive
Wexham Court Primary School
Knolton Way
Wexham Road
Devon Avenue
Sheffield Road
Godolphin Middle School
Waterbeach Road
Chester Road
Leiston Spur
Snape Spur
Mildenhall Road
Thurston Road
Littleport Spur
Mundesley Spur
Grant Av
St Ethelberts Catholic School
Arbour Vale Special School
The Normans
Winwood
Berry Field
Quinbrookes
Coftards
Melbourne Avenue
Sydney Grove
York Avenue
Belfast Avenue
Oatlands Drive
Herschel Grammar School
Hughenden Road
Aylesbury Crs
Aldborough Spur
Lismore Park
James Elliman School
St Josephs Catholic High School
Dunbar Cl
Borderside
Charles Gardens
The Frithe
Prestwood
Dawes Moor Cl
Holmdale
Northampton Avenue
Buckingham Avenue East
Redwood Gdns
Whitby Road
Sheeji Medical Centre
Baylis Business Centre
Oakley Crs
Leeds Road
Carmarthen Rd
Surgery
Elliman Avenue
Stokesay
Shaggy Calf Lane
The Sikh Temple
Mirador Crescent
Kendal Drive
Grasmere Av
Council Building
Carlisle Rd
Lake Avenue
Bradley Road
Montague Road
Belgrave Road
Shackleton Road
Myrtle Crs
Whitehaven
Keswick Court
Lea Junior School
Lea Infant School
Maple Crs
Glanmor Road
Elmwood Road
Broadmark Road
Hazlemere Rd
Preston Road
Beresford Avenue
Woodland Avenue
Sikh Temple
Baylis Road
Gilliat Road
Littledown Special School
Queens Rd
Greendale Mews
St Johns Road
Galloway Chase
Pauls Avenue
Grand Union Canal Walk
UXBRIDGE ROAD
Buckinghamshire County
Slough
Works
Salt Hill Way
Council Building
Ploughlees Lane
Pickfords Gardens
Sports Ground
Mill St
Grays Place
Stanley Cots
Bus Depot
Slough Station
Petersfield Avenue
Ind Est
Albion Close
The Business Village
Rochfords Gdns
Rochfords Gardens
Goodman Pk
Nursery Lane
Middlegreen Road
FARNHAM ROAD
A355
Salt Hill Avenue
Salt Hill Drive
Windmill Road
Salt Hill Park
Tennis Centre
Slough Museum
Town Hall
Blair Rd
Thames Valley University
Brunel Way
Superstore
Richmond Crs
Victoria Road
WELLINGTON ST
WELLINGTON STREET A4
A332
WILLIAMSTREET
Goodman Pk
Eastbridge
Slough Ice Arena
MONTEM LANE
LEDGER'S ROAD
Hillside
Burlington Avenue
Police Station
Mackenzie Street
High Street
Village Shopping Centre
UGC Cinema
The Observatory Shopping Centre
Council Building
Herschel Street
Chapel Street
Wexham Road
Alpha Street
UXBRIDGE RD
Clifton Rd
Sussex Place
Superstore
Fishguard Spur
Hawtrey Close
St Bernards Convent School
Fielding Gardens
Halkingcroft
Locke Gardens
Foxherne
Brackenforde
Sutton Avenue
Cherry Avenue
Downs
Hotel
Church St
Bourne Road
Worcester Gardens
Keel Drive
Hull Close
Cippenham
Sixth Form Walk
97
98
99
80
81
82
83
84
85
H
J
K
L
M
N
P
1
2
3
4
5
6
7
8
9
10

Langley Corner
Wexham Street
George Green
Middle Green
Shreding Green
Love Green
Iver Heath
Alderbourne Farm
Pinewood Film Studios
Teikyo School
Upton Lake
Rowley Wood
Rowley Farm
Blackpark Lake
Black Park Country Park
Langley Park Country Park
Langley Park
Park Lodge
Warren House
White Lodge
St Johns
Heath Lodge
Love Hill House Farm
Trenches Farm
Parsonage Farm
Iver Golf & Leisure Centre
Golf Course
Council Building
Langley Manor School
The Thames Nuffield Hospital
Wexham Park Golf Club
Bell Farm
Wrexham Park Hospital
Aysgarth Medical Centre
Iver Heath Hlth Centre
Iver Heath Primary School
First School
Surgery
Langley Station
Langley Business Cen
Industrial Estate
Middlegreen Trading Estate
Fulmer Common Road
Alderbourne Lane
Tree Cherry Lane
Pinewood Road
Pinewood Green
Pinewood Close
Peace Road
Black Park Road
Beeches Way
Queen's Drive
Rowley Lane
Framewood Road
Windmill
Sevenhills Road
M25
A412
Uxbridge Road
Slough Road
A4007
Church Road
Denham
Thornbridge Road
Ashford Rd
Heatherden Green
Parkway
Longstone Rd
Bangors Road N
Swallow Street
Swallowdale
Lower Md
Norwood
Martindale
Hardings Row
Coopers Row
The Close
Wood Lane Close
Wood Lane
Billet Lane
Bellswood Lane
Hollybush Lane
Honeysuckle Close
Lossie Dr
B470
Langley Park Road
Iverdale Cl
Mansion Lane
Hollow Hill Lane
Love Hill Lane
Trenches Lane
Avenue Drive
George Green Drive
Galleons Lane
Wexham Park Lane
Coronation Av
Rixon Cl
Post Office Lane
Homewood
George Gn Rd
Withy Croft
Middle Green
Middlegreen Rd
Nursery Lane
Pickford Dr
Pickford Drive
Orchard Way
Firs Dr
The Pippins
Morello
Grand Union Canal Walk
Union Canal Wk
Waterside Drive
Alderbury Road West
Alderbury Road
St Mary's Road
Halkingcroft
Brackenforde
Cherry Avenue
Mead Av
Goodman Pk
Opal Court
Church Grove
Wexham Woods
Buckinghamshire County
Slough
SL3
1 grid square represents 500 metres
110
129
150
A B C D E F G
1 2 3 4 5 6 7 8 9 10
500 01 02
85 84 83 82 81 80

Willowbank
New Denham
Uxbridge Moor
UXBRIDGE
Cowley
Cowley Peachy
Iver
Yiewsley
Thorney
DENHAM ROAD
SOUTHLANDS ROAD A412
OXFORD ROAD
A4020
HAREFIELD ROAD
PARK ROAD
ROCKINGHAM ROAD
HILLINGDON ROAD
HILLINGDON HILL
ST JOHN'S ROAD
SLOUGH ROAD
A4007
M25
COWLEY ROAD
HIGH STREET
HIGH ROAD
A408
IVER LANE
B470
HIGH ST
FALLING LANE A408
Palmer's Moor Lane
Packet Boat Lane
Grand Union Canal
Grand Union Canal Walk
Old Mill Lane
Ford Lane
Colne Valley Way
Ridge Way
Court Lane
Trout Lane
Cowley Mill Road
Station Road
Pield Heath Road
Kingston Lane
Royal Lane
Fairway Avenue
Warwick Rd
West Drayton Station
Iver Station
Brunel University
Uxbridge High School
RAF Uxbridge
Uxbridge College
Uxbridge Cricket Club
Uxbridge Swimming Pool
Uxbridge Common
Hillingdon Golf Club
Pavilions Shopping Cen
The Chimes Shopping Cen
Civic Centre
Uxbridge Station
Rockingham Recreation Ground
Uxbridge Works
Huntsmoor Park
Lyons Industrial Estate
Rainbow Industrial Estate
Trading Estate
Round Coppice Farm
Mansfield Farm
Moorwards
Coppins
SL0
UB8
H
J
K
L
M
N
P
04
05
06
85
84
83
82
81
80
1
2
3
4
5
6
7
8
9
10
111
132
151

132
112
131
152
A
B
C
D
E
F
G
1
2
3
4
5
6
7
8
9
10
507
08
09
85
84
83
82
81
80
UB10
UB11
WESTERN AVENUE
A40(T)
A437
Hillingdon Station
Ickenham Manor
Dry Ski Slope
Uxbridge Cricket Club
Uxbridge College
RAF Uxbridge
Tavistock Road
LONG LANE
Freezeland Wy
Granville Road
Richmond Avenue
Merton Avenue
Tudor Way
Sweetcroft Lane
Honeycroft Hill
North Hillingdon
Lynhurst Crescent
Gutteridge Wood
Hillingdon Trail
HILLINGDON
St Helens College
Oak Farm Junior & Infant School
Oak Farm Clinic
Acorn Medical Centre
American Community School
Harwood Drive
Court Drive
Ryefield Primary School
Sutton Court Road
St Bernadette's RC School
Golf Course
Hillingdon Golf Club
Sports Ground Pavilion
Swakeleys School
Abbotsfield School
Highfield School
Charville Lane
Charville Primary School
Hedgewood School
Goshawk Gardens
HILLINGDON HILL
UXBRIDGE ROAD
Uxbridge Cemetery
Bishophalt School
Hillingdon Primary School
A4020
Harrow View
Mellow Lane
Mellow Lane School
Hayes End
Hayes Park Junior & Infant School
Brook House FC
Pield Heath School
Hillingdon Hospital
Colham Green
HARLINGTON ROAD
Hillingdon Heath
HAYES
Moorcroft School
Wood End Green
Pronto Trading Estate
Uxbridge Co Court
The Beck Theatre
Hayes Cricket Club
The Hayes Manor School
Hayes Stadium
Wood End
Church Walk
Colham Manor Junior & Infant School
Evelyns School
STOCKLEY ROAD
A408
FALLING LANE
WEST DRAYTON ROAD
Judge Heath Lane
Mcmillan Clinic
Golf Course
Stockley Park Golf Club
DAWLEY ROAD
Botwell Common Road
Hayes FC
Hayes Social and Sports Club
Compton Road
Hayes Swimming Baths
Uxbridge FC
Whitehorn Place
Horton Road
Independent Industrial Est
Crown Business Cen
Furzeground Way
The Square
Yiewsley Health Centre
West Drayton Station
Grand Union Canal Wk
Warnford Industrial Est
Caxton Trading Est
Crown Trading Cen
Aberglen Industrial Est
Fairview Industrial Est
London Area Terminal Control Centre
1 grid square represents 500 metres

Hayes 133
113
134
153
H
J
K
L
M
N
P
11
12
13
1
2
3
4
5
6
7
8
9
10
85
84
83
82
81
80
Northolt
Northolt Aerodrome
Priors Farm
Hillingdon
Ealing
A40(T) WESTERN AVENUE
C & L Leisure Centre
Lime Trees Park Golf Club
Golf Course
WEST END ROAD
A4180
RUISLIP ROAD
Northolt Primary School
John Chilton School
Walford Secondary School
C & L Golf & Country Club
Downe Barns Farm
Dog Rose Ramble
Sharvel Lane
A312 CHURCH ROAD
UB5
Northolt Station
Northolt High School
Mandeville Special School
Willow Tree Primary School
Belvue School
Kelvin Ind Est
Belvue Business Cen
Greenford Industrial Estate
St Raphaels School
Downe Manor Primary School
Yeading Medical Centre
Viking Primary School
Gifford Primary School
Greenford High School
Grand Union Canal
RUISLIP ROAD B455
Yeading
THE PARKWAY A312
UB4
Belmore Primary School
Barnhill Community High School
Brookside School
The Willows
Superstore
Lady Margaret Primary School
Durdans Park School
Cranleigh Gardens Industrial Estate
Yeading Primary School
The Warren Medical Centre
Allenby Infant School
Dormers Wells School
Dormers Wells Medical Centre
Dormers Wells
Dormers Wells Primary School
UXBRIDGE ROAD A4020
Lombardy Retail Park
Uxbridge College
Elystan Business Cen
Hayes Bridge Retail Park
Hayes Town
Houston Business Park
Brook Industrial Est
Beaconsfield Road
Yeading FC
Blair Peach School
UXBRIDGE ROAD THE BROADWAY
SOUTHALL
UB1
Guru Nanak Medical Cen
Villiers High School
Southall Park
Barrett Ind Park
Hambrough Primary Sch
A3005 SOUTH ROAD
Minet Junior & Infant School
Silverdale Industrial Estate
Pump Lane Industrial Est
Trading Est
Provident Ind Est
Regent Business Cen
Chailey Industrial Est
Arches Business Cen
Middlesex Business Cen
Featherstone Industrial Est
Great Western Industrial Park
The Straight
Hortus Road

134
114
133
154
Sudbury
Northolt
GREENFORD
Dormer's Wells
Hanwell
West Ealing
UB6
W7
W13
UB1
A B C D E F G
1 2 3 4 5 6 7 8 9 10
514
15
16
85
84
83
82
81
80
WESTERN AVENUE
A40(T)
GREENFORD ROAD
A4127
RUISLIP ROAD
RUISLIP ROAD EAST
B455
UXBRIDGE ROAD
A4020
BROADWAY
ARGYLE ROAD
B456
B452
A4090
WHITTON AV WEST
MANDEVILLE ROAD
A312
Grand Union Canal
River Brent
Greenford Station
South Greenford Station
Perivale Station
Castle Bar Park Station
Drayton Green Station
West Ealing Station
Hanwell Stn
Northolt Station
Sudbury & Harrow Road Station
Sudbury Town Station
Horsenden Hill Golf Club
Perivale Park Golf Club
Perivale Park Athletics Track
Ealing Golf Club
Brent Valley Golf Club
West Middlesex Golf Club
Ealing Central Sports Ground
Gurnell Leisure Centre
Greenford Park Cemetery
City of Westminster Cemetery
Ealing Hospital
The Cardinal Wiseman ARC School Technology and Art College
Rockware Business Cen
Belvue Business Cen
Greenford Industrial Estate
Kelvin Ind Est
Perivale Industrial Park
Perivale Ind Park
Windmill Business Centre
West Ealing Business Centre
1 grid square represents 500 metres

Ealing 135
WEMBLEY
HA0
Tokyngton
Alperton
Lower Place
Park Royal
North Acton
West Acton
EALING
W5
W3
Acton
115
136
155
H
J
K
L
M
N
P
18
19
20
1
2
3
4
5
6
7
8
9
10
HARROW ROAD
EALING ROAD
BRIDGEWATER ROAD
NORTH CIRCULAR
WESTERN AVENUE
HANGER LANE
ALPERTON LANE
PARK ROYAL ROAD
HORN LANE
UXBRIDGE ROAD
GUNNERSBURY AVENUE
CASTLEBAR ROAD
THE BROADWAY
THE MALL
NEW BROADWAY
HIGH ST
SOUTH WAY
BRENTFIELD
HILLSIDE
VICTORIA ROAD
WALES FARM ROAD
Coronation Road
Wembley Stadium Station
Stonebridge Park Station
Alperton Station
Hanger Lane Station
Park Royal Stn
North Ealing Station
West Acton Station
Acton Station
Ealing Broadway Stn
Grand Union Canal
River Brent
Ealing Common
Central Middlesex Hospital
Pavilion Barclays Sports Ground
Ealing Cricket Club
Ellen Wilkinson School for Girls
Ealing Abbey Scriptorium
Pitshanger Manor Mus
Ealing Tertiary College
Ealing Film Studios
Walpole Park
Ealing Green
Thames Valley University
Acton Hospital
A40(T)
A406(T)
A4020
A404
A4000
A4005
B456
B4492

136
116
135
156
A
B
C
D
E
F
G
1
2
3
4
5
6
7
8
9
10
21
22
23
521
Dudden Hill
WILLESDEN
Church End
Willesden Green
Brondesbury Park
Harlesden
NW10
Kensal Rise
Kensal Green
College Park
North Acton
Old Oak Common
Wormwood Scrubs Park
North Kensington
East Acton
W12
Shepherd's Bush
W3
Acton
Acton Park
Roundwood Park
Cemetery
Grand Union Canal
Harlesden Station
Willesden Junction Station
Kensal Green Station
Kensal Rise Station
North Acton Station
East Acton Stn
White City Station
Shepherd's Bush Station
Acton Central Station
Willesden Green Station
Neasden Station
A406(T) NORTH CIRCULAR RD
A404 HILLSIDE
A404 HARROW RD
A4000 OLD OAK LA
A219 WOOD LANE
A40(T) WESTWAY
A40
A4020 UXBRIDGE ROAD
A4020 THE VALE
A407
A4088
B4492
B451
A3220 WEST CROSS ROUTE
SCRUBS LANE
VICTORIA ROAD
WESTERN AVENUE
HIGH ST HARLESDEN
CHURCH ROAD
DU CANE ROAD
ST QUINTIN AVENUE
WALM LANE
CHICHELE RD
MORTIMER RD
CHAMBERLAYNE
KILBURN LANE
LADBROKE GROVE
1 grid square represents 500 metres

Brondesbury
West Hampstead
South Hampstead
Kilburn
Queens Park
West Kilburn
Maida Vale
St John's Wood
Lisson Grove
Westbourne Green
Kensal Town
PADDINGTON
Notting Hill
Bayswater
Maitland Park
Primrose Hill
Hyde Park
Kensington Gardens
NW6
NW8
W9
W2
W11
W8
SW7
117
138
157
IVERSON ROAD
KILBURN HIGH ROAD
BELSIZE ROAD
FINCHLEY ROAD
ADELAIDE ROAD
AVENUE ROAD
PRINCE ALBERT ROAD
WELLINGTON RD
GROVE END ROAD
MAIDA VALE
ST JOHN'S WOOD ROAD
PARK ROAD
BRONDESBURY ROAD
CARLTON VALE
SHIRLAND ROAD
HARROW ROAD
WESTWAY
HARROW RD FLYOVER
EDGWARE RD
BISHOP'S BR RD
WESTBOURNE GV
BAYSWATER ROAD
HOLLAND PK AVENUE
KENSINGTON RD
KNIGHTSBRIDGE
Paddington Station
The Serpentine
Round Pond
Lord's Cricket Ground

138
118
137
158
4
5
10
11
A
B
C
D
E
F
G
1
2
3
4
5
6
7
8
9
10
528
29
30
Gospel Oak
Lower Holloway
Maitland Park
Kentish Town
CAMDEN TOWN
Primrose Hill
Barnsbury
London Zoo
Regent's Park
Somers Town
St Pancras
MARYLEBONE
Bloomsbury
St Giles
Soho
Mayfair
Strand
St James
Knightsbridge
Hyde Park
Euston Station
King's Cross Station
St Pancras Station
Charing Cross Stn
1 grid square represents 500 metres

Canonbury
Kingsland
Dalston
ISLINGTON
De Beauvoir Town
Hoxton
Haggerston
Pentonville
FINSBURY
SHOREDITCH
BETHNAL GREEN
Clerkenwell
St Luke's
SPITALFIELDS
CITY
LONDON
St George in the East
The Borough
River Thames
119
140
159

140
120
139
160
A
B
C
D
E
F
G
Temple Mills
Hackney Wick
HACKNEY
Homerton
Old Ford
South Hackney
BETHNAL GREEN
Globe Town
BOW
Bromley
Mile End
SPITALFIELDS
STEPNEY
Bow Common
Limehouse
Ratcliff
POPLAR
Shadwell
St George in the East
Wapping
Canary Wharf
Victoria Park
Tower Hamlets
Southwark
1 grid square represents 500 metres

Stratford New Town
STRATFORD
Forest Gate
121
Upton
Upton Park
Plaistow
Mill Meads
South Bromley
Blackwall
Silvertown
142
161
E13
E15
E16
West Ham Park
Memorial Recreation Ground
East London Cemetery
Canning Town Recreation Ground
Royal Victoria Dock
River Thames
Dome
Stratford Station
West Ham Station
Plaistow Station
Upton Park Station
Canning Town Station
East India Station
Royal Victoria Station
Custom House Station
Prince Regent Station
Blackwall Station
Forest Gate Station
ROMFORD ROAD
BARKING ROAD
NEWHAM WAY A13(T)
PRINCE REGENT LANE
NORTH WOOLWICH ROAD
LOWER LEA CROSSING
SILVERTOWN WAY
MANOR ROAD
STEPHENSON STREET
PLASHET ROAD
PORTWAY
GREEN STREET
UPTON LANE
STOPFORD ROAD
EAST INDIA DOCK ROAD
NORTHERN APPROACH
HIGH STREET
LEYTON ROAD
ANGEL LANE
WATER LANE
Newham General Hospital
West Ham United FC (Upton Park)
ExCeL Exhibition Centre
Royal Victoria Docks Watersports Centre
University of East London
East London RUFC
H J K L M N P
1 2 3 4 5 6 7 8 9 10
39 40 41

142
122
141
162
A
B
C
D
E
F
G
1
2
3
4
5
6
7
8
9
10
Ilford
Loxford
Plashet
Upton Park
EAST HAM
Wallend
Beckton
Custom House
Silvertown
North Woolwich
ROMFORD ROAD
BARKING ROAD
NORTH CIRCULAR ROAD
NEWHAM WAY
ROYAL DOCKS ROAD
WOOLWICH MNR WAY
ROYAL ALBERT WAY
CONNAUGHT BR
ALBERT RD
Royal Albert Dock
King George V Dock
London City Airport
River Thames
1 grid square represents 500 metres

Fair Cross
Becontree
RKING
Castle Green
Creekmouth
Thamesmead
River Thames
Barking Reach
Cross Ness
Margaret or Tripcock Ness
IG11
SE28
DA18
RIPPLE ROAD A123
RIPPLE ROAD
A13(T)
EAST HAM AND BARKING BY-PASS
LODGE AVENUE
A1153
PORTERS AVENUE
Renwick Road
River Road
Choats Road
Thames Road
Long Reach Road
Alfreds Way Industrial Est
Renwick Industrial Estate
Mayesbrook Park
Parsloes Park
Barking Abbey Comprehensive School
Barking Hospital
Upney Station
Becontree Station
Goresbrook Leisure Centre
Barking RUFC
Cemetery
Barking Ind Park
Thames View Clinic
Thames View Junior & Infant School
Riverside Industrial Est
Bankside Park Industrial Est
Trafalgar Business Centre
Anglian Industrial Estate
Balmoral Trading Estate
Buzzard Creek Industrial Estate
Barking and Dagenham
Newham
Bexley
Greenwich
CENTRAL WAY
CARLYLE ROAD
A2041
A2016
EASTERN WAY
WESTERN WAY
HARROW MANOR WAY
Woolwich Polytechnic School
Thamesmead Shopping Centre
Hawksmoor Primary School
Castilion Primary School
Bishop John Robinson CE Primary
Jubilee Primary School
Riverside Golf Club
Golf Course
St Margaret Clitherow RC Primary
Thamesmead Community College
Magistrates Court
Works
123
144
163
H J K L M N P
46 47 48
1 2 3 4 5 6 7 8 9 10
80 81 82 83 84 85

144
124
143
164
Dagenham
South Hornchurch
RM10
RM9
Dagenham Heathway Stn
Dagenham East Station
Dagenham Dock Station
HEATHWAY
A1240
A1306
NEW ROAD
A13(T)
A1112
RAINHAM RD SOUTH
DAGENHAM RD
RAINHAM ROAD
BALLARDS ROAD
B178
RIPPLE RD
A2016
Parsloes Avenue
Holgate Road
Reede Road
Western Avenue
Church Elm Lane
Oval Road North
Oval Rd South
Goresbrook Road
Chequers Lane
Thames Avenue
Sierra Drive
Choats Road
Hindmans Way
Thunderer Road
Kent Avenue
Fiesta Drive
Courier Road
Marsh Way
Frog Lane
Creek Way
Ferry Lane
Salamons Wy
Creekside
Norman Road
Crabtree Manorway North
Fisher's Way
Mulberry Way
Anderson Way
Power Station
Ford Industrial Park
Industrial Estate
Works
Merrielands Retail Park
Warner Village Cinema
Dagenham Superbowl
Suttons Business Park
Rainham Trading Est
Mudlands Estate
Manor Way Business Cen
Star Business Centre
Thamesview Business Cen
Lorimar Business Cen
Fairview Industrial Centre
Denver Industrial Est
Albright Industrial Estate
Industrial Estate Annexe
Kp Est
Capital Industrial Est
Belvedere Industrial Estate
Fordview Industrial Estate
Hornchurch Marshes
Halfway Reach
Frog Island
Jenningtree Point
Riverside Golf Club
Dagenham Priory Comprehensive School
William Ford CE Junior School
Parsloes Primary School
Godwin Primary School
St Peters RC Primary School
Marsh Green School
Beam Primary School
The Leys Primary School
Newtons Primary School
John Perry Primary School
Brittons School
Hunters Hall Primary School
Dagenham & Redbridge FC
Council Building
Beam River
Bretons
Hailey Road Business Park
Thamesmead
A B C D E F G
1 2 3 4 5 6 7 8 9 10
549 50 51
85 84 83 82 81 180
1 grid square represents 500 metres

Elm Park
Hacton
RAINHAM
Wennington
Rainham Marshes
Wennington Marshes
RM13
H
J
K
L
M
N
P
125
146
165
53
54
55
85
84
83
82
81
80
1
2
3
4
5
6
7
8
9
10
Carnforth Gardens
School
Ullswater Way
Langdale Gdns
Surgery
Rosewood
Ambleside Av
Coronation Dr
Rosewood Medical Centre
Maybank Aven
Morecambe Cl
West Malling Way
Northolt Wy
Airfield Wy
Primary School
Veny Crs
Suttons Lane
R J Mitchell Primary School
Astra Cl
Park Lane
Cavendish Av
Cavendish Crs
South End Road
Tangmere Crs
Oxford Cl
Airfield Way
Coltishall Rd
Mungo Park Road
Tuck Rd
Finucane Gdns
Boulter Gdns
Deere Av
Gilliam Wy
Bader Way
Fulmar Rd
Flight Av
Heron
School
Dowding Close
Hayes Dr
Surgery
Jersey Rd
Princes Park
South End Rd
Elmer Gardens
Grove Park Road
Gainsborough Road
Avelon Road
Gysfield Drive
Health & Welfare Clinic
Albyns Farm
Hornchurch Country Park
Squadrons Approach
Rainham Lodge Farm
Berwick Pond Road
Farm Road
Harwood
Show Equest
Gerpins Lane
Aveley Rd
Ltl Gerpins Rd
Berwick Ponds Farm
Berwick Pond Road
Berwick Manor
Gerpins Lane
Warwick Lane
Marsh View Industrial Estate
Cemetery
Upminster Rd N
North
Abbey Wood Lane
Mitchell Cl
Jordans Way
Berwick Road
Mygrove Rd
Mygrove Gdns
Durrants Cl
Parsonage Road
Briscoe Road
Cardinal Way
Lake Av
Giles Cl
Lakeside
Abbots Close
Thorn Lane
Farm Road
Parsonage Farm Primary School
King Edward Av
Fairview Avenue
Stoke Road
Avenue
Syracuse Av
Allen Road
Kenway
Surridge Cl
Glebe Road
Davies Cl
Police Station
Rainham Cem
Upminster Road
Surgery
Oreston Rd
Maclennan Av
Elder Way
Acer Av
Warwick Road
Imperial Trading Est
Todd Cl
Lamb's La N
Deans Trading Est
A1306
NEW ROAD
Penny Cl
Stirling Close
Wentworth Way
Anchor Dr
Hawthorn Av
South
Cloister Cl
Brights Av
Martin Dr
Orch Av
Arterial Av
Woodside Cl
Vincent Rd
The Glen
South Lane
Baillie Cl
Wantz La
Den Av
Lamb's
Chaffords School
Brady Primary School
South Hall Farm
Rainham Village Primary School
Glenwood Av
Ashwood Av
Upminster Rd
West Cl
Ingrebourne Road
Melville Road
Cowper Road
Rainham Hall NT
Surgery
BROADWAY
Surgery
Ellis Av
Venette Cl
WENNINGTON ROAD
Findon Gdns
Palliser Dr
Wilfred Av
Elizabeth Rd
Brookway
South Hall Drive
Penerley Road
Beechwood Gdns
Rothbury Av
Eastwood Drive
B1335
Stanhope Rd
Victory Rd
RAINHAM ROAD A125
Salette Primary School
Ingrebourne River
Launder's Lane
East Hall Lane
Church Lane
WENNINGTON ROAD B1335
The Gn
Wennington Hall Farm Business Centre
SANDY LANE
B1335
Sandy Lane Farm
Moor Hall
A13(T)
Ferry Lane Industrial Est
Coldharbour Lane
Purfleet Ind Park
Juliette Wy
Kerry Avenue
LONDON ROAD
Purfleet Ind Park
Havering
Thurrock
Aveley
Purflee

Corbets Tey
Harwood Hall
Show Jumping/ Equestrian Circuit
Upminster Cemetery
OCKENDON ROAD
B1421
B186
B186
Stubbers (Outdoor Pursuits Centre)
Manor Farm
Pea Lane
Pike Lane
M25
Havering
Thurrock
Church Lane
Gerpins Lane
Aveley Road
Sunnings Lane
Stubbers Lane
Dennises Lane
Dennises La
Dennis Road
Bramble Farm
Bramble Lane
Kemps Farm
Baldwins Farm
Warwick Lane
Farm Road
Harwood Hall Lane
Belhus Woods Country Park
Romford Road
West
Ockendon Station
Arisdale Avenue
Avontar Road
Daines Cl
Dalgien Drive
Arnton Road
Ardmore
Arcany
Ockendon School
Bonnygate Primary School
RM15
Woodacre Special School
Hamble Lane
Erriff Drive
Elmdon Rd
Ernan Rd
Elan Road
Easington Way
Annalee Road
Afton Drive
Humber Av
Loman Path
Dilkes Primary School
Dunkellin Wy
Council Building
Darenth Lane
Shaw Primary School
Barle Gdns
Health Centre
Belhus Park
Golf Course
Belhus Golf Club & Leisure Centre
Brets Farm
Kenningtons
Moor Hall
Usk Road
Ravel Gdns
Ravel Road
Surgery
Tamar Drive
Primary School
Teviot Avenue
Shannon Way
The Aveley School
Perry Wy
Nethan Drive
Humber Av
Gatehope Drive
Garron Lane
Fullarton Crs
Foyle Drive
Fairham Avenue
Danbury Crs
Holy Cross RC Primary School
Cawdor Avenue
Fortin Close
Fortin Way
Knightsmead Special School
Fyfield Drive
Fulbrook La
Stifford Rd
Somers Heath Primary School
Broxburn Drive
Carnach Gn
STIFFORD ROAD
Cherwell Grove
Works
LANE B1335
AVELEY BY-PASS
B1335
Aveley FC
AVELEY
Sandy Lane Farm
Rowan Grove
Mill Lane
St Michaels Cl
Martin Road
Dacre Crescent
Park Lane
B1335 STIFFORD ROAD
Toplands Av
Grange Road
Manor Close
Elm Rd
Blenheim Gdns
Lowlands Road
Stanford Gdns
Stifford Road
School House Aveley School
Junction 30
High Street
Purfleet Road
Surgery
Aveley Primary School
Arnhem Avenue
Hall Avenue
Health Centre
A13(T)
Love Lane
Kent View
Hall Road
Crescent Walk
Ship Lane
M25
145
126
166
A B C D E F G
1 2 3 4 5 6 7 8 9 10
85 84 83 82 81 180
556 57 58
1 grid square represents 500 metres

White Post Farm
Top Meadow Golf Club
Havering
Thurrock
Corner Farm
Fen Farm
Fen
OCKENDON ROAD
NORTH ROAD
B186
South Ockendon Hall
Cheelson Road
Wilsman Road
Nelson Road
Benyon Primary School
Surgery
Church Crs
Cliff Pl
Birch Crescent
Hornbeam Cha
Juniper Dr
Hazel Dr
Brandon Groves Avenue
Birch Cl
Holly Drive
Magnolia Cl
Medlar Drive
Sycamore Way
Laurel Dr
Poplar Cl
Mar Rd
Garth Rd
Aveley Medical Centre
Nursery Cl
Mollands Lane
Mollands La
Mollands Ct
SOUTH OCKENDON
SOUTH ROAD
Moss Rd
Oaklands Drive
Buckles Lane
Mar Dyke
Works
Medebridge Road
Green Lane
Springfield
Stifford Clays Road
Stifford Clays Farm
A13(T)
William Edwards School
Blackshots Lane
Goose Farm
Chelmer Dr
Cruick Avenue
Cullen Square
STIFFORD HILL
PILGRIMS LA
Back Lane
Works
Stifford Hill
High Road
Sherwood
Clockhouse Lane
North Stifford
Hotel
Well La
Marian Close
A1012
Crammavill Street
Prince Philip Avenue
Gourney Gv
Whitmore Avenue
Stifford Clays Primary School
Stifford Clays Health Cen
Blackthorn Rd
Oakway
Meadow Road
Fairway
Elmway
Leasway
The Firs
Fairfield Av
Ashley Gardens
Hogarth Road
Palins Way
Goddard Road
Fieldway
Chafford Way
Crawford Av
Harty Cl
Long Lane
Thurrock Athletic Stadium
Blackshots Leisure Centre
Deneholm Primary Schools
Highfield Gardens
Laird Avenue
Broadview Avenue
ARTERIAL ROAD NORTH STIFFORD
A1306
Dudley Close
Drake
Calshot Av
Catalina Av
Bark Burr Road
Lenthall
Lodge
Conrad Gdns
Conrad Close
Windsor Avenue
Chestnut Avenue
Connaught
Victoria
Crowstone Road
Hornsby
Blackshots
Orchard Dr
Edmund Rd
Ardleigh
Cobham
The Close
Regent Close
Culford
Haven
Dorset Fen
Hoblett
Stone Hall
Home Farm
127
167
RM14
60
61
62
85
84
83
82
81
80
H
J
K
L
M
N
P
1
2
3
4
5
6
7
8
9
10

128
170
Cippenham
Lake End
Dorney
Eton Wick
South Field
Boveney
Dedworth
Clewer Village
Oakley Green
Clewer Green
Clewer New Town
Rowing Lake
Dorney Common
Dorney Court
Boveney Court
Boveney Lock
River Thames
Thames Path
Royal Windsor Racecourse
Racecourse Yacht Basin
Windsor Marina
Sutherland Grange
Centrica HQ
Manor Farm
Tarbay Farm
St Leonards Farm
Down Place
M4
A308
A332
B3026 LAKE END ROAD
VILLAGE ROAD
COMMON B3026 ROAD
ETON WICK ROAD
MAIDENHEAD ROAD
WINDSOR ROAD
OAKLEY GREEN ROAD
DEDWORTH ROAD
CLARENCE ROAD
VALE RD B3025
IMPERIAL RD
B3175
B3022 ST LEONARDS
WINKFIELD B3022 ROAD
Buckinghamshire County
Slough
Windsor & Maidenhead
SL4
493
94
95
80
79
78
77
76
175
A
B
C
D
E
F
G
1
2
3
4
5
6
7
8
9
10

Salt Hill
Salt Hill Park
Slough Station
Thames Valley University
WELLINGTON ST
WELLINGTON STREET A4
A4 WELLINGTON STREET
Queensmere Shopping Centre
High Street
The Observatory Shopping Centre
UXBRIDGE ROAD
SLOUGH
Sutton Avenue
Langley
SUSSEX PL
LONDON ROAD
A4
Chalvey
Cippenham Lane
TUNS LANE
A355
MONTEM LANE
LEDGER'S ROAD
Burlington Avenue
Chalvey Road East
RAGSTONE ROAD B3027
WINDSOR ROAD A332
ALBERT STREET
MERE RD
YEW TREE RD A412
Upton Hospital
Slough Grammar School
Upton
Upton Court Road
Upton Court Park
Long Close School
Lascelles Road
Buckland Avenue
Park Lane
Castleview Combined School
M4
A332
SLOUGH ROAD
Agars Plough
Golf Course
DATCHET ROAD
The Myrke
B376
SLOUGH ROAD
Slough RFC
Ditton Park
B3026
POCOCKS LANE
Thames Valley Athletics Centre
Wallace Walk
ETON
Eton College
Common Lane
Cemetery
KEATS LANE
B3022 HIGH STREET
Romney Lock
Boatyard
Cricket, Hockey, Tennis and Rugby Clubs
Riding Court Farm
ETON ROAD
Whites Lane
150
MAJOR'S FARM
KING EDWARD VII AVENUE
B470
WINDSOR ROAD
Meadow Lane
The Brocas
Thames Path
Windsor Bridge
Windsor & Eton Riverside Station
Windsor & Eton Central Station
St Georges Preparatory School
Broad Water
Windsor Castle
Churchmead School
Datchet Sports Club
Datchet Golf Club
B470 LONDON RD
DATCHET
HORTON ROAD
DITTON ROAD
Datchet Common
Barry Avenue
Alexandra Gardens
Theatre Royal
THAMES STREET
HIGH ST
Royal Mews
Coach Museum
WINDSOR
River Thames
Datchet Station
Montagu Road
B3021 SOUTHLEA ROAD
Victoria Barracks
SHEET ST
Princess Christians Hosp
FRANCES ROAD
OSBORNE ROAD
KINGS ROAD
King Edward VII Hospital
Queen Elizabeth's Walk
The Home Park
Frogmore Drive
Frogmore House
Home Farm
Royal Mausoleum
Albert Bridge
Evergreen Oak Avenue
Royal Gardens
Shaw Farm
ALBERT ROAD
A308
A332
DATCHET ROAD
Ham Lane
Queen Anne's Gate
The Long Walk
Three Castles Path
Holly Drive
129
171
H J K L M N P
1 2 3 4 5 6 7 8 9 10
97 98 99
80 79 78 77 76 175

150
130
149
172
A
B
C
D
E
F
G
1
2
3
4
5
6
7
8
9
10
SLOUGH
Langley
Sutton
Brands Hill
Colnbrook
Datchet Common
Horton
Sunnymeads
The Queen Mother Reservoir
Wraysbury Reservoir
Langley Station
Sunnymeads Station
Junction 5
M4
A4 LONDON ROAD
LONDON RD
LONDON ROAD
COLNBROOK
B470 MAJOR'S FARM ROAD
MAJOR'S FARM RD
B376 HORTON ROAD
DITTON ROAD
WELLEY ROAD
STATION ROAD
HIGH STREET
Langley Road
Sutton Avenue
Downs Road
Middlegreen Road
Grand Union Canal Walk
Waterside Drive
Alderbury Road West
Alderbury Road
Meadfield Road
New Road
Parlaunt Road
Humber Way
Common Road
Sutton Lane
Hollow Hl Lane
Upton Court Road
Marlborough Road
Riding Court Road
Ditton Park Road
Datchet Road
Stanwell Road
Horton Road
Coppermill Road
Colne Valley Way
Buckinghamshire County
Slough
Windsor and Maidenhead
Surrey County
Langley Business Park
Langley Business Cen
East Berkshire College
Langley Grammar School
Langleywood School
Ryvers Combined School
Marish First School
Parlaunt Park Combined School
Foxborough Primary School
Holy Family RC School
Castleview Combined School
Colnbrook CE Combined School
Slough Community Mental Health Cen
Langley Health Centre
Middlegreen Trading Estate
Middlegreen Trading Est
Horton Trading Estate
Industrial Estate
Council Building
Iver Golf & Leisure Centre
Richings Park Golf & Country Club
Golf Course
Ditton Park
Riding Court Farm
Mildridge Farm
Manor Farm
Horton Lodge
Parsonage Farm
Trenches Farm
Cemetery
Hotel
1 grid square represents 500 metres

Langley 151
131
152
173
H J K L M N P
1 2 3 4 5 6 7 8 9 10
4 5 6
80 79 78 77 76 175
Grand Union Canal
Iver Station
Thorney
Thorney Park Golf Club
Golf Course
Richings Park Sports Club
Thorney House
St Leonards Walk
Thorney Mill Rd
Thorney Mill Road
Richings Way
Old Slade Lane
Old Slade La
The Poynings
The Ridings
Thorney Lane South
Somerset Way
Bathurst Walk
Syke Cluan
Syke Ings
Wellesley Avenue
St James Walk
North Pk
Main Dr
Colne Valley Way
Junction 15/4b
M25
M4
Buckinghamshire County
Hillingdon
Slough
Works
West Drayton
West Drayton Cricket Club
Cricketfield Road
St Catherines RC Primary School
Medical Centre
Longmead Primary School
The Closes Recreation Ground
Cemetery
Police Station
Primary School
Fairway Avenue
Coine Av
Lawn Avenue
Frays Avenue
Ferrers Avenue
Swan Road
Drayton Gdns
Old Farm Rd
Money La
The Green
Church Road
Church Close
Pippins Cl
Mill Road
St Martin's Cl
Frays Cl
Station Road
Bagley Close
West Drayton Park Avenue
Warwick Rd
Furzeham Road
Bellclose Road
Kingston Lane
Kings Rd
Porters
Thornton Av
Sipson Road
Laurel Lane
Rowan Road
Great Benty
Brambles
Harmondsworth Road
Wordsworth Way
Little Benty
Magnolia Street
Rosebary Close
Treeside Close
Lily Dr
Maxwell
London Area Control Centre
Independent Industrial Est
Yiewsley Centre
Harmondsworth
Harmondsworth Lane
Holloway Close
A3044
Hatch Lane
Moor Lane
Saxon Way
Accommodation Lane
Moorland Road
School Rd
Cambridge Cl
Candover Close
River Colne
Duke of Northumberland's River
Sipson
Airport Gate Business Centre
Lakeside Industrial Estate
Lakeside Road
Lakeside Industrial Estate
Colne Valley Way
Old Slade La
Tarmac Way
Speedbird Way
A4(T)
Colnbrook By-Pass
Bath Road
Skyport Dr
Zealand Av
Pinglestone Close
Coln Industrial Estate
Longford
Stanwell Moor Road
Bath Rd
Baysfarm Ct
Heathrow Cl
Western Perimeter Road
Northern Perimeter Rd (West)
Newton Rd
Newbury Rd
Northern
Poyle
Coleridge Crs
Dawley Ride
Winchester Cl
Rodney Way
Raymond Close
The Hawthorns
Pippins Sch
Coln Industrial Est
Galleymead Road
Colnbrook Sports Club
Daventry Cl
Poplar Cl
Mathisen Wy
Meadowbrook Cl
Poyle Road
Millbrook Wy
Colndale Road
Britannia Industrial Est
Willow Road
David Road
Polygon Business Cen
Mckay Trading Est
Prescott Rd
Blackthorne Road
Blackthorne Crs
Augustine Cl
Trident Industrial Est
Viscount Industrial Est
Newlands
Calder Way
Horton Rd
Junction 14
A3113 Airport Way
Horton Road
Leylands La
Colne Va Wy
Flintlock Cl
Spout Lane
Spout Lane North
Perry Oaks Dr
Wessex Road
Perry Oak Drive
Longford River
Bedfont Court
Burrows Hill Close
Western Perimeter Rd
Heathrow Airport
Terminal
Southern Perimeter Road
Heathrow World Cargo Centre
Shoreham Road (East)
Sandringham Rd
Seaford Rd
Vine Cl
Meadow View
Sheffield
Wraysbury

152
132
151
174
UB11
UB3
UB7
TW6
A
B
C
D
E
F
G
1
2
3
4
5
6
7
8
9
10
507
08
09
Sipson
Harlington
Heathrow Airport
Hatton
M4
Junction 4
Junction 4a
A4(T) BATH ROAD
BATH ROAD
HOLLOWAY LANE
SIPSON ROAD
STOCKLEY ROAD
DAWLEY ROAD
A437
N HYDE RD
STATION ROAD
HIGH STREET
HARLINGTON HIGH ST
GREAT SOUTH-WEST ROAD
A30(T)
Horton Road
Grand Union Canal Wk
Iron Br Road
Porters Way
London Area Terminal Control Centre
Heathpark Golf Club
Heathrow Primary School
Airport Gate Business Centre
Chambers Business Park
Imperial College Athletic Ground
William Byrd School
Harlington Community School
Pinkwell Primary School
Heathrow Medical Centre
Gravel Works
Sipson Lane
Harmondsworth Lane
Cranford Lane
Northern Perimeter Rd
HM Customs
BAA Heathrow Visitor Centre
Police Station
Fire & Ambulance Station
World Business Centre Heathrow
Eastern Business Park
Eastchurch Rd
Terminal 1
Terminal 2
Terminal 3
Arrivals
Departures
Control Tower
Queen's Building
Spectators Viewing Area
Heathrow Express Terminal
Airbus Coach Station
D'Albiac House
Heathrow World Cargo Centre
Terminal 4
West Drayton Station
Hayes & Harlington Station
Hatton Cross Stn
1 grid square represents 500 metres

Hayes Town
Hounslow
133
154
175
Southall Stn
North Hyde
Norwood Green
Heston
Cranford
HOUNSLOW
Hounslow West
North Feltham
UB2
TW5
TW4
Junction 3
Heston Services
M4
A312
A4020
A3005
A4127
A4(T)
A30(T)
A3063
A3006
A315
Uxbridge Road
Merrick Road
Norwood Road
North Hyde Rd
North Hyde Lane
Western Road
Bulls Bridge
Hayes Road
The Common
Wentworth Road
Convent Way
Southall Lane
Spitfire Way
Airlinks Golf Club
Golf Course
Air Links Industrial Estate
Church Road
Cranford Community College
Cranford Park
The Parkway
High Street
North Road
Vicarage Farm Road
Heston Road
Church Road
Upr Sutton La
Sutton La
Great West Road
Bath Road
Great South-West Road
The Causeway
Staines Road
Beavers Lane
Wellington Road North
Wellington Road South
Lampton Road
Jersey Rd
Heston Road
Hounslow Central Station
Hounslow West Station
Hounslow Cricket Club
Lampton Park
New Brentford Cemetery
Grand Union Canal
Hillingdon
Ealing
Hounslow
Osterley Lane
Tentelow
Hounslow Heath Golf Club
Reservoir
Fagg's Road
Whitton Road
Heston Swimming Baths
Heston Park Cricket Club
Springwell Infant School
Springwell Junior School
Berkeley Primary School
Heston Community School
Lampton School
Wellington Primary School
Hounslow Heath Infant School
Hounslow Heath Junior School
St Marks RC School
Community Primary School
Cranford Infant School
Cranford Junior School
The Cedars Primary School
Three Bridges Primary School
Featherstone School
Dairy Meadow Prim School
Havelock Primary School
Wolf Fields Primary School
Norwood Green Infant School
Rosary RC Primary School
Heston Junior School
Heston Infant School
The Andrew Ewing Prim School
The Orchard Junior School
Grove Primary School
Sybil Elgar School
Middlesex Business Cen
The Bridge Business Cen
Bullsbridge Industrial Estate
Brent Park Industrial Estate
Parkway Trading Estate
Heathrow International Trading Est
Wallbrook Business Cen
Sun Life Trading Estate
North Feltham Trading Est
Hounslow Business Park
The Treaty Centre
Civic Centre
Hounslow Heath Golf Club

154
134
153
176
Hanwell
West Ealing
W7
UXBRIDGE ROAD
BROADWAY
A4020
Ealing Hospital
Great Western Industrial Park
Three Bridges Business Centre
Grand Union Canal Walk
Middlesex Business Centre
The Bridge Business Cen
Norwood Green
TENTELOW LANE
WINDMILL LANE
BOSTON ROAD
A3002
Boston Manor Station
The Waterside Trading Cen
Boston Business Park
River Brent Business Park
Elthorne Park High School
River Brent
M4
Osterley Lane
Golf Course
Osterley Park House
Osterley Park
Wyke Green Golf Club
SYON LANE
B454
Centaurs Business Cen
Brentford End
Osterley
GREAT WEST ROAD
A4(T)
Osterley Station
Brunel University (Osterley Campus)
Syon Lane Station
Spring Grove
Lampton
SPRING GROVE ROAD
B363
LONDON ROAD
A315
Isleworth Station
TW7
Lampton Park
HOUNSLOW
Hounslow East Stn
Hounslow Central Station
HANWORTH ROAD
Woodlands
Inwood Park
TW3
Hounslow Station
TWICKENHAM ROAD
A310
SOUTH STREET
RICHMOND ROAD
A3004
ISLEWORTH
Isleworth Baths
Worton Hall Industrial Est
Ivybridge Retail Park
1 grid square represents 500 metres

Brentford
155
135
156
177
H
J
K
L
M
N
P
1
2
3
4
5
6
7
8
9
10
18
19
20
BRENTFORD
Kew
North Sheen
Mortlake
Grove Park
TW8
TW9
W4
SW14
Gunnersbury Park
Gunnersbury Park Museum
Kew Gardens (Royal Botanic Gardens)
Kew Palace
Palm House
Syon House
Syon Park
Old Deer Park
Royal Mid-Surrey Golf Club
River Thames
Junction 2
Junction 1
CHISWICK HIGH ROAD
GREAT WEST RD ELLESMERE
GUNNERSBURY AVE
KEW ROAD
KEW BR RD
MORTLAKE ROAD
LOWER RICHMOND ROAD
UPPER RICHMOND ROAD WEST
LWR MORTLAKE ROAD
CLIFFORD AVENUE
SANDYCOMBE ROAD
HIGH ST
HALF ACRE
SOUTH EALING RD
EALING ROAD
LITTLE EALING LANE
POPE'S LANE
ACTON LANE
WELLESLEY RD
Kew Bridge Station
Kew Gardens Stn
North Sheen Station
Gunnersbury Station
Brentford Stn
Chiswick Station
Mortlake Stn
Richmond Stn
Acton Town Stn
South Ealing Stn
South Acton Stn
Chiswick Park Station
Chiswick Bridge
Mortlake Crematorium
Hammersmith New Cemetery
Public Record Office Museum
Kew Retail Park
Marlborough Trading Estate
University of Westminster
Kew Bridge Steam Museum
The Musical Museum
Watermans Arts, Cinema & Theatre Centre
Hounslow
Richmond upon Thames
Ealing

156
136
155
178
Acton
Shepherd's Bush
Bedford Park
Acton Green
CHISWICK
HAMMERSMITH
Brook Green
W6
SW13
SW14
BARNES
Grove Park
Mortlake
East Sheen
Roehampton
Putney
Chiswick House
The Wetland Centre
River Thames
Richmond upon Thames
Hammersmith & Fulham
Wandsworth
Hounslow
UXBRIDGE ROAD
KING STREET
GREAT W ROAD
HAMMERSMITH FLYOVER
CHISWICK HIGH ROAD
GOLDHAWK RD
CASTELNAU
UPPER RICHMOND ROAD
LWR RICHMOND ROAD
MORTLAKE HIGH STREET
ROCKS LANE
HAMMERSMITH BR RD
SHEPHERD'S BUSH ROAD
1 grid square represents 500 metres

Knightsbridge
Kensington Gardens
Holland Park
KENSINGTON
Brompton
Earl's Court
South Kensington
West Brompton
Walham Green
Parsons Green
Sands End
WANDSWORTH
West Kensington
BATTE
River Thames
HOLLAND PK AVENUE
KENSINGTON HIGH ST
KENSINGTON RD
CROMWELL ROAD
WEST CROMWELL RD
BROMPTON RD
FULHAM ROAD
KING'S ROAD
NEW KING'S ROAD
WANDSWORTH BR ROAD
YORK ROAD
BATTERSEA BR RD
ALBERT BRIDGE ROAD
PUTNEY BRIDGE
ST JOHN'S HL
LATCHMERE ROAD
CHEYNE WK
137
15
14
158
179

158
138
16
17
157
180
A
B
C
D
E
F
G
1
2
3
4
5
6
7
8
9
10
528
29
30
St James
Knightsbridge
Brompton
Belgravia
WESTMINSTER
Pimlico
CHELSEA
Vauxhall
Kennington
Nine Elms
BATTERSEA
South Lambeth
CLAPHAM
Stockwell
SW1X
SW1A
SW1E
SW1H
SW1P
SW1V
SW1W
SW3
SW8
SW4
Buckingham Palace
Victoria Station
Constitution Hill
The Mall
St James's Park
Green Park
Hyde Park Corner
Queen Victoria Memorial
Houses of Parliament
Westminster Bridge
Lambeth Bridge
Vauxhall Bridge
Chelsea Bridge
Grosvenor Bridge
Lambeth Palace
Tate Britain
River Thames
Battersea Park
Battersea Power Station (disused)
New Covent Garden Market
Royal Hospital Chelsea
Ranelagh Gardens (site of Chelsea Flower Show)
National Army Museum
Chelsea Physic Garden
Queenstown Road Battersea Station
Wandsworth Road Station
Clapham North Stn
Clapham Common Station
Clapham High Street Stn
Clapham Junction Station
GROSVENOR PLACE
BUCKINGHAM PALACE ROAD
SLOANE STREET
VAUXHALL BR RD
BELGRAVE ROAD
GROSVENOR ROAD
CHELSEA EMBANKMENT
CHELSEA BR ROAD
ROYAL HOSPITAL ROAD
QUEENSTOWN ROAD
ALBERT BRIDGE ROAD
BATTERSEA PARK ROAD
NINE ELMS LANE
WANDSWORTH ROAD
LAVENDER HILL
CLAPHAM COMMON NORTH SIDE
CLAPHAM HIGH STREET
CLAPHAM ROAD
SOUTH LAMBETH ROAD
ALBERT EMB
LAMBETH PALACE RD
MILLBANK
VICTORIA ST
KNIGHTSBRIDGE
BROMPTON RD
PARK LANE
PICCADILLY
PALL MALL
WHITEHALL
1 grid square represents 500 metres

Lambeth 159
River Thames
Tower Bridge
City Pier
HMS Belfast
London Dungeon
Winston Churchill's Britain at War Experience
Vinopolis City of Wine
Wapping
Southwark
Tower Hamlets
139
160
181
18
19
H
J
K
L
M
N
P
1
2
3
4
5
6
7
8
9
10
32
33
34
The Borough
Borough Stn
London Bridge
Guys Hospital
BERMONDSEY
Imperial War Museum
LAMBETH
Newington
Elephant and Castle Stn
Elephant & Castle Shopping Cen
Walworth
Burgess Park
CAMBERWELL
Peckham
Peckham Rye Stn
Denmark Hill Stn
Kings College Hospital
The Maudsley Hosp
Loughborough Junction Stn
BRIXTON
Brixton Stn
East Dulwich Stn
North Dulwich Station
East Dulwich
SE1
SE5
SE15
SE17
SW9
SOUTHWARK STREET
TOOLEY STREET
BOROUGH HIGH ST
LONG LANE
GREAT DOVER STREET
TOWER BRIDGE ROAD
DRUID STREET
ABBEY STREET
JAMAICA RD
GRANGE ROAD
NEW KENT ROAD
OLD KENT ROAD
WALWORTH RD
KENNINGTON ROAD
KENNINGTON PARK ROAD
KENNINGTON LA
WESTMINSTER BR RD
WATERLOO ROAD
BLACKFRIARS RD
BOROUGH RD
ST GEORGE'S RD
LONDON RD
NEWINGTON BUTTS
ALBANY ROAD
CAMBERWELL RD
CAMBERWELL NEW ROAD
CAMBERWELL CHURCH ST
PECKHAM ROAD
PECKHAM HIGH ST
PECKHAM HILL STREET
RYE LANE
PECKHAM RYE
SOUTHAMPTON WY
DENMARK HILL
CHAMPION PK
GROVE LANE
DOG KENNEL HILL
EAST DULWICH RD
LORDSHIP LANE
COLDHARBOUR LANE
HERNE HILL
MILKWOOD ROAD
RAILTON ROAD
ROLLS ROAD
DUNTON ROAD
TRAFALGAR AV
SOUTHWARK PK RD

160
140
159
182
A
B
C
D
E
F
G
1
2
3
4
5
6
7
8
9
10
Wapping
Rotherhithe
Canary Wharf
Millwall
Deptford
New Cross Gate
New Cross
St Johns
Peckham
Nunhead
Ladywell
Brockley
Dulwich
SE16
SE8
SE14
SE15
SE4
River Thames
Southwark Park
Peckham Rye Park
Jamaica Road
Lower Road
Evelyn Street
Old Kent Road
Queen's Road
New Cross Rd
Lewisham Way
Westferry Road
Salter Road
Rotherhithe New Rd
Southwark Pk Rd
Drakefell Road
Nunhead Lane
Brockley Road
Loampit Hill
1 grid square represents 500 metres

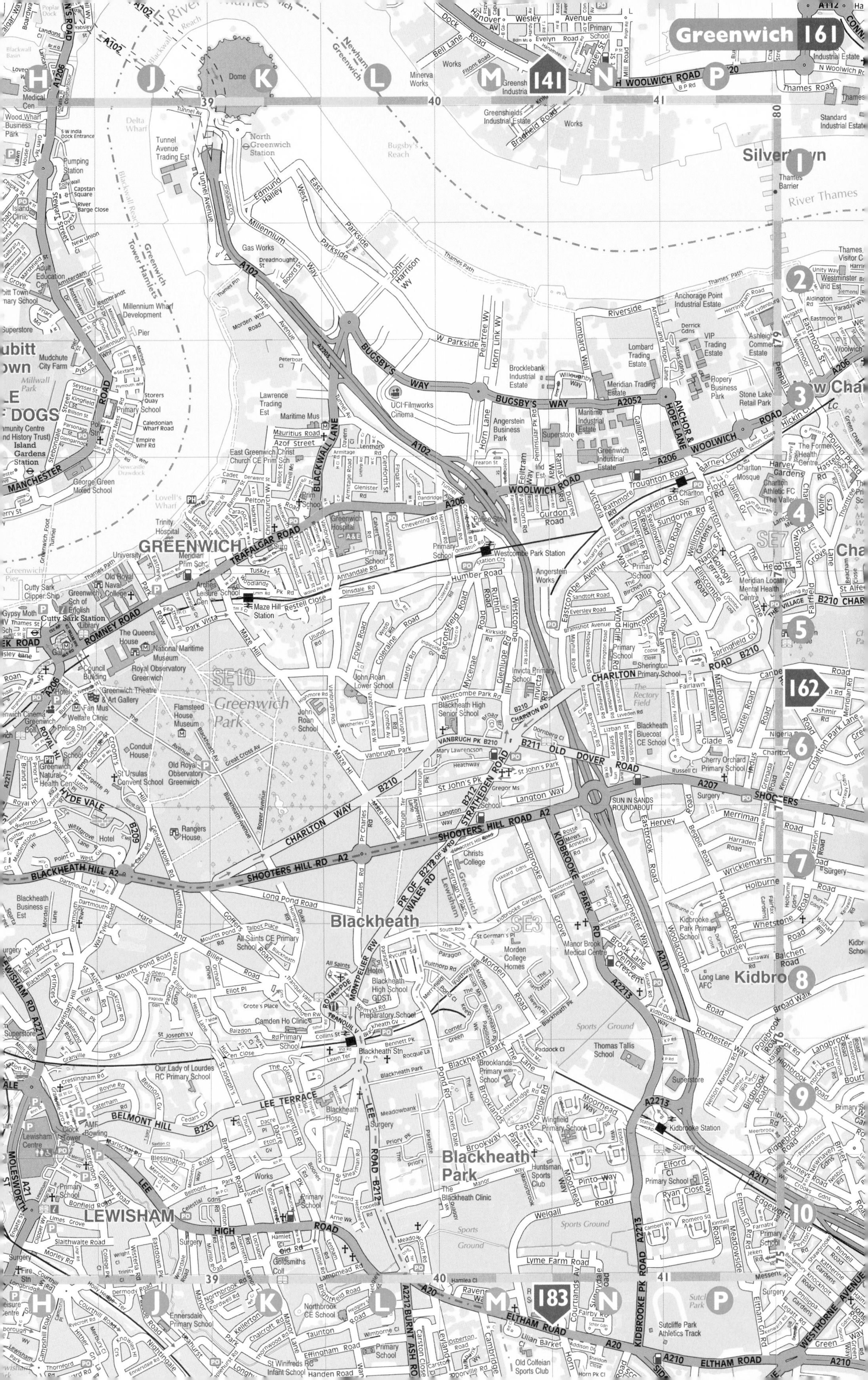
H
J
K
L
M
N
P
141
Dome
River Thames
Tunnel Av
North Greenwich Station
Tunnel Avenue Trading Est
Delta Wharf
Bugsby's Reach
Greenshields Industrial Estate
Bradfield Road
Works
Dock Road
Bell Lane
Minerva Works
Wesley Avenue
Evelyn Road
Primary School
Mill Road
Greensh Industria
WOOLWICH ROAD
Thames Road
N Woolwich Rd
Standard Industrial Estate
Silvertown
Thames Barrier
1
2
3
4
5
6
7
8
9
10
162
183
Thames Visitor C
Unity Wy
Westminster Ind Est
Tunnel Avenue
Edmund Halley
West
East
Millennium Way
Parkside
John Harrison Wy
Gas Works
Dreadnought St
Boord St
Thames Path
Millennium Wharf Development
Blackwall Reach
Greenwich
Tower Hamlets
Pier
Mudchute City Farm
Millwall Park
ISLE OF DOGS
Storers Quay
Primary School
Caledonian Wharf Road
Empire Whf Rd
Island Gardens Station
MANCHESTER ROAD
George Green Mixed School
Newcastle Drawdock
Lovell's Wharf
Trinity Hospital
Riverside
Anchor and Hope Lane
Anchorage Point Industrial Estate
Herringham Road
VIP Trading Estate
Ashleigh Commercial Estate
Lombard Trading Estate
Lombard Wall
Brocklebank Industrial Estate
Meridian Trading Estate
Ropery Business Park
Stone Lake Retail Park
W Parkside
Peartree Wy
Horn Link Wy
BUGSBY'S WAY
A2052
UCI Filmworks Cinema
Lawrence Trading Est
Maritime Mus
Mauritius Road
Azof Street
East Greenwich Christ Church CE Prim Sch
BLACKWALL LANE
A102
A206
Angerstein Business Park
Horn Lane
Maritime Industrial Estate
Superstore
Greenwich Industrial Estate
Gallions Rd
ANCHOR & HOPE LANE
WOOLWICH ROAD
Troughton Road
Charlton Stn
Charlton Mosque
Charlton Athletic FC (The Valley)
Harvey Gardens
The Former Health Centre
TRAFALGAR ROAD
GREENWICH
Meridian Prim Sch
Greenwich Hospital
A&E
Chevening Rd
Westcombe Park Station
Primary School
Annandale Rd
Humber Road
Angerstein Works
Eastcombe Avenue
Sandtoft Road
Eversley Road
Delafield Rd
Sundorne Rd
Priolo Road
Wellington Gardens
Charlton Church Lane
SE7
The Heights
Meridian Locality Mental Health Centre
THE VILLAGE
B210 CHARLTON
Cutty Sark Clipper Ship
Cutty Sark Station
Greenwich Sch of English
Old Royal Naval College
University
Arches Leisure Cen
Maze Hill Station
Restell Close
Dinsdale Rd
ROMNEY ROAD
Park Vista
The Queens House
National Maritime Museum
Royal Observatory Greenwich
Council Building
Greenwich Theatre & Art Gallery
Fan Mus
Welfare Clinic
Greenwich Cinema
Police Stn
SE10
Greenwich Park
Flamsteed House Museum
Conduit House
Old Royal Observatory Greenwich
Great Cross Av
St Ursulas Convent School
Greenwich Natural Health Cen
Rangers House
HYDE VALE
B209
John Roan Lower School
John Roan School
Maze Hill
Vanbrugh Park
Vanbrugh Flds
Coleraine Road
Foyle Road
Beaconsfield Road
Mycenae
Glenluge Rd
Westcombe Hill
Invicta Primary School
Westcombe Park Rd
Blackheath High Senior School
Charlton Rd
Highcombe
Sherington Primary School
CHARLTON ROAD B210
Springfield Gv
The Rectory Field
Blackheath Bluecoat CE School
Fairlawn
The Glade
Marlborough Lane
Cherry Orchard Primary School
VANBRUGH PK B210
OLD DOVER ROAD
B211
A207
SHOOTERS HILL
SUN IN SANDS ROUNDABOUT
Merriman Road
Hervey
Harraden Road
Wricklemarsh
Holburne
Kidbrooke Park Primary School
Whetstone
CHARLTON WAY
B210
STRATHEDEN ROAD
B212
St John's Pk
Langton Way
SHOOTERS HILL ROAD A2
SHOOTERS HILL RD A2
Christs College
BLACKHEATH HILL A2
Blackheath Business Est
Long Pond Road
Blackheath
PR OF WALES RD
St German's Pl
Kidbrooke Gardens
SE3
KIDBROOKE PARK RD
Rochester Way
Manor Brook Medical Centre
A2(T)
A2213
Long Lane AFC
Kidbrooke
All Saints CE Primary School
Talbot Place
Mounts Pond Road
Eliot Pl
Grote's Place
Camden Ho Clinic
Paragon
Morden College Homes
The Plantation
MONTPELIER RW
ROYAL PDE
TRANQUIL V
Blackheath High School GDST
Preparatory School
Blackheath Stn
Blackheath Park
Brooklands Primary School
Sports Ground
Thomas Tallis School
Superstore
Kidbrooke Station
Moorhead Way
Wingfield Primary School
Elford Cl
Primary School
Ryan Close
LEWISHAM RD A2211
Lewisham Centre
Clock Tower
Our Lady of Lourdes RC Primary School
LEE TERRACE
BELMONT HILL
B220
Blackheath Hosp
Meadowbank
Priory Pk
Blackheath Park
Huntsman Sports Club
The Blackheath Clinic
Pinto Way
Weigall Road
Sports Ground
Lyme Farm Road
LEWISHAM
HIGH ROAD
LEE ROAD B212
Goldsmiths Coll
Molesworth St
A20
ELTHAM ROAD
A210
Northcote CE School
Ennersdale Primary School
Sutcliffe Park Athletics Track
Sutcliffe Park
Old Colfeian Sports Club
A212 BURNT ASH RD
WESTHORNE AVENUE
Eltham Grn Rd
Meadowside
39
40
41
80
79
78
77
76
75

162
142
161
184
A
B
C
D
E
F
G
1
2
3
4
5
6
7
8
9
10
42
43
44
Silvertown
North Woolwich
River Thames
Newham
Greenwich
Woolwich Reach
Gallions Reach
King George V Dock
London City Airport
Thames Barrier
Thames Barrier Visitor Centre
Silvertown & City Airport Stn
North Woolwich Station
Old Station Museum
WOOLWICH FERRY
Thameside Industrial Estate
Standard Industrial Estate
Factory Road
ALBERT RD
PIER ROAD
CONNAUGHT RD
Hartmann Road
Drew Primary School
Storey Primary School
Woodman St
Royal Arsenal
Firepower (Museum of Artillery)
WOOLWICH CHURCH STREET
WOOLWICH HIGH ST
BERESFORD STREET
PLUMSTEAD ROAD
Woolwich Dockyard Stn
Woolwich Arsenal Station
Plumstead Station
New Charlton
Charlton
WOOLWICH
Plumstead
Charlton Athletic FC (The Valley)
Charlton House
Charlton Park
Museum of Artillery in The Rotunda
Military Barracks
Queen Elizabeth Hospital
Woolwich Common
JOHN WILSON ST
GRAND DEPOT ROAD
WOOLWICH COMMON
ACADEMY ROAD
HILLREACH B210
ARTILLERY PL
LITTLE HEATH B210
CHARLTON PK RD
SHOOTERS HILL ROAD
DOVER ROAD
Shooters Hill
Shooters Hill Golf Club
Memorial Hospital
Eltham Common
Jack Wood
Oxleas Wood
Eltham Park
Kidbrooke
Kidbrooke School
Broad Walk
WELL HALL ROAD
Rochester Way
Welling Way
Falconwood Station
A2(T)
ROCHESTER AVENUE
RELIEF ROAD
Eltham Station
Eltham Crematorium
University of Greenwich Sports Ground
The Pleasance
Eltham Warren Golf Club
Crown Woods School
BEXLEY ROAD
ELTHAM ROAD
Sutcliffe Park
SE7
SE18
1 grid square represents 500 metres

Thamesmead
Woolwich Polytechnic School
SE28
Western Way A2016
Eastern Way
New Acres Rd
Battery Rd
Kentlea Rd
Magistrates Court
Woolwich Crown Court
Harness Road
Purland Road
Nathan Way
Kellner Road
Boughton Road
Works
White Hart Road
North Road
Sewell Road
Ampleforth Road
Godstow Road
Harrow Manor Way
A2041
Hartslock
Seacourt Road
Tavy Clinic
Wolvercote Road
Kale Road
Yarnton Way
Thamesmead Community College
St John Fisher RC Primary School
Abbey Primary School
Lensbury Way
Overton Road
Lyndean Industrial Estate
Edington Rd
Abbey Wood School
Finchale Rd
Felixstowe Road
Mottisfont Road
Abbey Wood Station
Fendyke Road
Rushdene
Alsike
Parkway Primary School
Halifield Dr
Abbey Road
B213
Elstree Gardens
Kingswood Av
Lesnes Abbey
Lesnes Abbey Woods
Abbey Wood
Abbey Grove
Bracondale Road
Birkdale Road
Marmadon Road
Church Manor Way
Brookdene Road
Blithdale Road
McLeod Road
Federation Rd
Plumstead High Street
A206
Basildon Road
Bostall Hill
Woolwich Road
Knee Hill A2041
Plumstead Common
Winn Common Road
Bostall Woods
Abbey (rems of)
Green Chain Walk
Wickham Lane A209
West Heath
Bexley Coll
Bedonwell Primary School
Woodbrook Road
Cemetery
Madison Crs
Lansdowne Avenue
Plymstock Road
East Wickham
Okehampton Crescent
Axminster Crescent
St Michaels CE Primary School
East Wickham Primary School
Welling School
DA16
Wrotham Road
Swanley Road
Farnham Road
Preston Drive
Berkeley Avenue
Mayfair Avenue
Brampton Road
Brampton Primary School
Balliol Road
Somerhill Road
Welling Stn
Bellegrove Road
A207
Welling High Street
Welling
Park View Road
Crook Log
Broadway
Welling United FC
Bexley
Danson Park
Danson Road
Falconwood
Bexleyheath
Bexleyheath Station
East Rochester Way
A2(T)
Bexleyheath Golf Club
Upton Road School
DA6
DA17
DA18
164
143
185

164
144
163
186
A
B
C
D
E
F
G
1
2
3
4
5
6
7
8
9
10
549
50
51
80
79
78
77
76
75
DA18
DA17
DA8
DA7
DA6
Erith Marshes
Thamesmead Community College
East Thamesmead Business Park
Hailey Road Business Park
Capital Industrial Est
Belvedere Industrial Estate
Works
EASTERN WAY
A2016
PICARDY MANORWAY
Norman Road
North Road
Caldy Road
Yarnton Way
Waldrist Way
Mulberry Way
BRONZE AGE WAY
Fisher's Way
Belvedere Station
Erith & Belvedere FC
Elbourne Trading Estate
Belvedere Link Business Park
Sikh Temple
Parkway Primary School
GILBERT ROAD
PICARDY ST
LOWER ROAD
B213
B250
B253
Elstree Gardens
Kingswood Av
Upper Abbey Road
Belvedere Primary School
Woodside Sch
Capital Industrial Estate
Trinity Sch Belvedere
Bexley College
Fox House Rd
Belvedere
ERITH ROAD
A206
WOOLWICH ROAD
Holly Hill Road
FRASER ROAD
Hamlet International Industrial Estate
Europa Trading Estate
Erith Station
Erith
Riverside Swimming Centre
Erith Theatre Guild
Library & Mus
Business Centre
Superstore
Lessness Heath Primary School
Lessness Heath
Cemetery
Riverdale Road
A220
QUEENS ROAD
Christ Church Av
Park Crescent
Lesney Park Primary School
Erith & District Hosp
Northumberland Heath Medical Cen
Erith Stadium
Erith Sports Centre
Erith School
BEXLEY ROAD
Bedonwell Clinic
Bedonwell Primary School
Northumberland Heath
Colyers Lane Medical Centre
Colyers Primary School
Normandy Primary School
SOUTH ROAD
NORTHEND ROAD
Northend Primary School
North End Trading Est
Belmont Primary School
Primary School
Bursted Wood Primary School
St Thomas More RC Primary School
Barnehurst Station
Barnehurst
Barnehurst Public Pay & Play Golf Club
Golf Course
Bexleyheath Station
Upland Primary School
Bexleyheath School
Cemetery
Russell Park
Fire Stn
Amb Stn
London Transport Bus Depot
Pelham Primary School
Mayplace Primary School
PERRY STREET
A2000
Holmsdale Grove
Parkside Avenue
Eversley Avenue
Woodside Road
BROADWAY
A207
A221
ALBION ROAD
Bexleyheath Centre
Police Station
Shopping Centre
Civic Offices
Cineworld
Bexleyheath
WATLING STREET
Gravel Hill Primary School
St Columbas RC Boys School
Shenstone School
St Josephs RC Primary School
St Paulinus CE Primary School
CRAYFORD HIGH ST
ROMAN WAY
Bourne Road Industrial Park
Crayford Industrial Estate
Tower Retail Park
Medical Centre
GRAVEL HILL
Halcot Avenue
LONDON ROAD
Upton Road School
1 grid square represents 500 metres

A13(T)
145
Wennington Marsh
Havering
Thurrock
Purfleet Ind Park
Juliette Way
Kerry Avenue
LONDON ROAD
A1306
Aveley Marshes
Fanns Farm
LC
Milehams Industrial Estate
LONDON RD
RM
Water Lane
Surgery
Fanns Rise
Marlow Av
Thamley
Council Building
Marine Court
Centurion Way
Crusader Close
Chieftan Drive
Saladin
Comet
TANK HILL ROAD
Tank Lane
Purfleet Primary School
Beacon Hill Industrial Estate
A1090
Church Lane
Hotel
Works
Purfleet Station
Harrisons Wharf
Beacon Hill
Linnet
Oldharbour
Oldharbour Lane
Erith Rands
Havering
Bexley
River Thames
Crayford Ness
Landau Way
Darent Industrial Park
Dayton Drive
Maypole Crescent
Burnett Road
Ness Road
Purfleet
Works
Manford Industrial Estate
Bilton Road
Ray Lamb Way
Canada Road
Durlun Way
Jenningtree Rd
Sandpiper Dr
Longreach Rd
Beacon Rd
Widgeon Rd
Wallhouse Road
166
Long Reach
Dartford Marshes
Slade Green Primary School
Alderney Road
Hilden Dr
Brompton Dr
Green Road
Hollywood Wy
Fern Cl
Elm Road
Hazel Road
Hazel Dr
Rodeo Cl
Forest Rd
Leycroft Gdns
Cedar Rd
Slade Green FC
Slade Green Station
Moat Lane
Oak Rd
Slade Green
Darent Valley Path
Joyce Green Lane
Crayford Marshes
Kent County
Bexley
Howbury Lane
Works
Howbury Rd
Marsh Street
Crayside Industrial Estate
Kennet Road
A206 THAMES ROAD
Thames Road
Stour Rd
Medway Road
Maiden Lane
Russell Cl
Barnes Cray Primary School
Mayplace Avenue
Iron Mill Lane
Beech Walk
Mill Place
Geoffrey Whitworth Theatre
CRAYFORD WAY
Barnes Cray Rd
Barnes Cray
A206 UNIVERSITY WAY
Cemetery
McCudden Rd
Cornwall Rd
Joyce Green Lane
Strickland Av
Barnwell Rd
Chaucer Wy
Wodehouse Road
Henderson Drive
Wordsworth Way
Hall Road
Spielman Road
Welcome Av
Trevithick Drive
Browning Road
UNIVERSITY WY
Coleridge Rd
Shakespeare Rd
Temple Hill
Crayside Industrial Estate
DA1
Sandpit Road
Swan Business Park
Millside Industrial Estate
Burnham Trading Estate
Lawson Rd
Priory Rd
A2026 BURNHAM ROAD
Riverside Industrial Estate
Edmunds Rd
Primary School
Keyes Rd
Farnol Rd
Dickens Av
Hotel
187
Crayford
Victoria Industrial Park
Business Centre
Bus Garage
Central Rd
Surgery
Temple Hill Sq
Littlebrook Manor Way
Kingsley Av
Lansbury Crs
A282(T)
Acorn Industrial Park
Whitehill Rd
Swaisland Road
Chesterfield Dr
Wilmot Road
Priory Cl
Rayford
VICTORIA RD
Holy Trinity CE Primary School
Mayfair Rd
Savoy Road
Francis Rd

166
146
165
188
Junction 30
Junction 31
Junction 1a
Toplands Av
Grange Road
Manor Close
Blenheim Gdns
Lowlands Road
Dacre Crescent
Park Lane
Elm Rd
Dacre Avenue
Crescent Wy
Stanford Gdns
Stifford Road
School House
Aveley School
Surgery
Aveley Primary School
Works
Purfleet Road
Field Rd
Arnhem Avenue
Myrtle Grove
Beech Gv
Eastern Av
Church View
Health Centre
Central Av
Hall Road
Hall Ter
Love Lane
Kent View
Hall Road
Crescent Walk
Ship Lane
A13(T)
A13(T)
M25
Thurrock Service Area
Hotel
The Caravan Site
Causeway Bridge
South Way
Back La
Fanns Farm
London Road
A1306
Milehams Industrial Estate
Mar Dyke
RM19
London Rd
Water Lane
Surgery
Marlow Av
Fanns Rise
Tank Hill Road
Purfleet Primary School
Tank Lane
Beacon Hill Industrial Estate
Arterial Road Purfleet
Wood Av
North Road
Fondu Sports Club
Baron Close
Brimfield Rd
Armor Road
Stonehouse Lane
Dolphin Way
Purfleet By-Pass
Works
Purfleet Station
Botany Way
Beacon Hill Industrial Estate
Beacon Hill
Linnet Way
Oakhill Rd
A1090
London Road Purfleet
Joslin Rd
Mill Road
Purfleet
LC
Arterial Road West Thurrock
A1306
Cygnet View
Warner Village Cinema
Lakeside Shopping Centre
The Gallery at Lakeside
Lakeside Retail Park
Lakeside
Grebe Crest
UCI
Weston Avenue
A282(T)
B186
W Thurrock Wy
Chafford Hundred Station
Service Centre
Tunnel Industrial Estate
Central Av
Barclay Way
West Thurrock
West Thurrock Way
Heron Way
Trading Estate
Weston Avenue
The Glade Business Centre
Motherwell Way
RM20
Works
Eastern Av
Quarry Way
Hilltop Rd
Hilltop
Hillcrest Av
Cemetery
Sandy Lane
Tunnel Industrial Estate
Hotel
Mnr La
First Avenue
Second Avenue
Primary School
Park Av
St Clement's
Jubilee Rd
London Road
Thurrock Business Centre
Bridge View Industrial Est
West Road
Surgery
Schoolfield
Fox
Flint St
Elm Ter
Canterbury Way
Oliver Close
Oliver Road
Works
West Thurrock Marshes
Works
Works
Burnley Road
Watson Close
Works
Long Reach
Dartford Tunnel
Queen Elizabeth II Bridge
Stone Ness
Littlebrook Business Centre
Thurrock
Kent County
Stone Marshes
Bridge Close
Clipper Bvd West
Hotel
Clipper Bvd
University Wy
A206
Wodehouse Road
Wordsworth Way
Crescent
Coleridge Rd
Shakespeare Rd
Shaftesbury Lane
Hotel
Farnol Rd
Dunkin Rd
Dickens Av
Toll
Crossways Bvd
Victory Way
Anchor Boulevard
Galleon Bvd
Newton's Ct
Masthead Close
Capstan Ct
Schooner Ct
Clare Cswy
Crossways Boulevard
St Mary's Road
Charles Street
King Edward Rd
Superstore
Sara Crs
High Street
Station Rd
Kestner Industrial Est
Stone Crossing
Bell Close
Church Rd
Cooper Cl
Stone
Swallow Cl
Chalice Cl
Bishops
Cowley Av
Steele Av
Castle St
Providence St
Greenhithe for Bluewater Stn
A226
Surgery
Breakneck
Greenhithe
Cotton Lane
Littlebrook Manor Way
Tennyson Rd
Masefield Rd
Kingsley
556
57
58
80
79
78
77
76
75
A
B
C
D
E
F
G
1
2
3
4
5
6
7
8
9
10
1 grid square represents 500 metres

147
168
189
H
J
K
L
M
N
P
60
61
62
1
2
3
4
5
6
7
8
9
10
A13(T)
ARTERIAL ROAD NORTH STIFFORD A1306
ARTERIAL RD N STIFFORD
A1012
B186
Pilgrims La
Stifford
Long Lane
Chafford Hundred
The Chafford Hundred Medical Centre
South Stifford
Warren Primary School
Tudor Court Primary School
Stifford Primary School
Stifford Clays Primary School
Stifford Clays Health Cen
Deneholm Primary School
Blackshots Leisure Centre
Little Thurrock Primary School
The Grays School
Lawrence Trading Estate
Grays Business Centre
St Thomas Of Canterbury RC Primary School
Woodward Hts Tree Tops Special School
Grays Convent School
Quarry Hill Junior School
Quarry Hill Infant School
Titan Industrial Estate
Thameside Theatre
Grays Health Centre
Police Stn
County Court
Council Building
Grays Athletic FC
Globe Industrial Estate
Thameside Primary School
Manor Way Industrial Estate
Europa Trading Estate
Magnet Estate
Acorn Trading Centre
Grays Station
Dominoes Health Cen
ELIZABETH ROAD
HOGG LANE
LONDON ROAD
A126
ORSETT ROAD
PALMER'S AV
SOUTHEND ROAD
DERBY ROAD
STANLEY ROAD A126
CROWN ROAD
E THURROCK RD
BROADWAY
CLARENCE ROAD
SHERFIELD RD
A1013
LODGE
RM17
GRAYS
Broadness
St Clement's or Fiddler's Reach
Northfleet Hope
Works
Kent Kraft Industrial Estate
Northfleet Industrial Estate
Ebbsfleet Industrial Estate
Swanscombe Station
Manor Way
Pilgrims' Road
LONDON ROAD A226
GALLEY HILL ROAD
B259 HIGH STREET
STONEBRIDGE
Park Walls
College Road
Northfleet
Ness

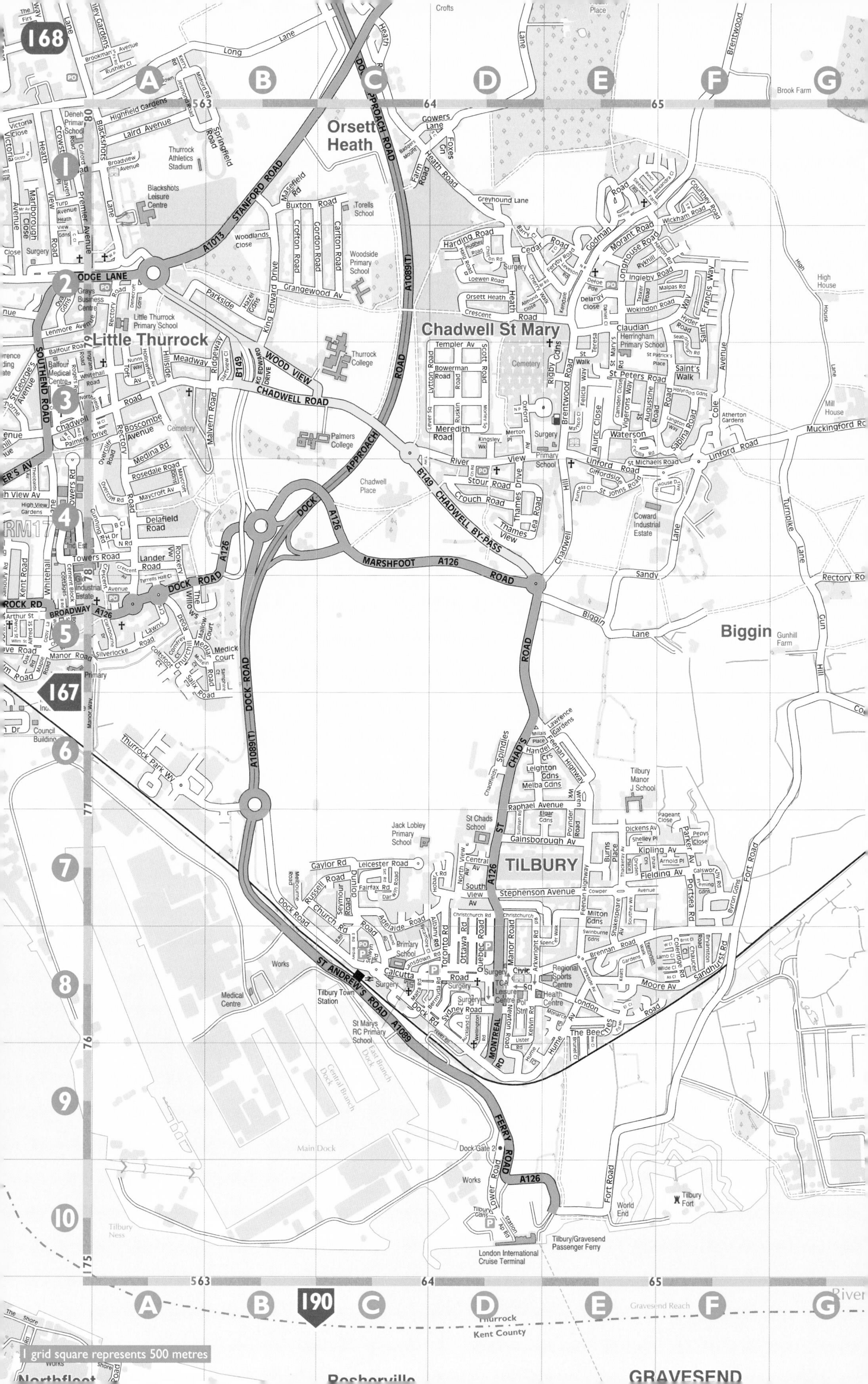
168
167
190
A
B
C
D
E
F
G
1
2
3
4
5
6
7
8
9
10
563
64
65
Orsett Heath
Little Thurrock
Chadwell St Mary
TILBURY
Biggin
Thurrock Athletics Stadium
Blackshots Leisure Centre
Torells School
Woodside Primary School
Thurrock College
Palmers College
Chadwell Place
Cemetery
Herringham Primary School
Coward Industrial Estate
Tilbury Manor J School
Jack Lobley Primary School
St Chads School
Tilbury Town Station
St Marys RC Primary School
Medical Centre
Works
Main Dock
Central Branch Dock
East Branch Dock
Dock Gate 2
Tilbury Fort
World End
Tilbury/Gravesend Passenger Ferry
London International Cruise Terminal
Tilbury Ness
Gravesend Reach
Thurrock
Kent County
Brook Farm
High House
Mill House
Gunhill Farm
STANFORD ROAD
A1013
DOCK APPROACH ROAD
A1089(T)
CHADWELL ROAD
B149
WOOD VIEW
MARSHFOOT
A126
ROAD
CHADWELL BY-PASS
DOCK ROAD
ST CHAD'S ROAD
ST ANDREW'S ROAD
A1089
FERRY ROAD
MONTREAL RD
SOUTHEND ROAD
BROADWAY
Linford Road
Muckingford Rd
Biggin Lane
Sandy Lane
Turnpike Lane
Gun Hill
Fort Road
Heath Road
Long Lane
Stephenson Avenue
Gainsborough Av
Civic Sq
Regional Sports Centre
Health Centre
Northfleet
Rosherville
GRAVESEND
1 grid square represents 500 metres

Linford
East Tilbury
Muckingford
West Tilbury
Low Street
Becksland
Thames Industrial Park
Industrial Park
Industrial Estate
Buckland
Bowaters Farm
Works
Coalhouse Fort
Coalhouse Point
West Tilbury Marshes
East Tilbury Marshes
East Tilbury Station
Bata Medical Centre
Surgery
Muckingford Road
Low Street Lane
Church Road
Station Road
Love Lane
Princess Margaret Road
Gordon Close
Linley Cl
Walton's Hall Road
Buckingham Hill Road
Holford Road
East Tilbury Road
Northumberland Road
Essex Gdns
Somerset Road
Stafford Close
Lower Crescent
Meadow Cl
Halt Drive
Beechcroft Av
Brindles Cl
Stenning Av
Alexandra Way
Queen Elizabeth Avenue
King George VI Avenue
Thomas Bata Av
Coronation Avenue
Queen Mary Av
Gloucester Av
Farm Road
Bata Av
Severn
Waldon
Bure
Solway
Colne
Clyde
Tweed
Arun
Trent
Shaw Road
RM18
LC

148
192
A
B
C
D
E
F
G
1
2
3
4
5
6
7
8
9
10
493
94
95
75
74
73
72
71
170
SU4
Legoland Windsor
St Leo Farm
St Leonards
St Leonard's Hill
Woodland Avenue
Gratton Drive
Chestnut Drive
Dower Park
Windsor & Eton
Prince Consort's Drive
Flemish Farm
Forest Park
WINKFIELD ROAD
B3022
Windsor Forest
Winkfield Place
Winkfield Plain
Barton Lodge
Drift Road
Forest Road
Cranbourne Chase
Cranbourne Tower
Ranger's Lodge
SHEET STREET ROAD
A332
Windsor Great Park
Cranbourne
Light Industrial Estate
Kingsmead
B383
MOUNTS HILL
Hatchet Lane
Forest Lodge
Forest Gate
Lime Avenue
The Village
Queen Anne's Close
Fernhill Park
Forest Farm
Holly Walk
Sandpit Gate
Woodside
Woodside Lane
B3034
LOVEL LANE
A330
Woodside Road
Hodge Lane
Wood End
Kiln Lane
Strood Lane
Home Farm
SUNNINGHILL ROAD
South Forest
Bracknell Forest
Windsor and Maidenhead
Duke's Lane
Three Castles Path
WINDSOR ROAD
Onslow Drive
Splash
Water Splash La
Cheapside CE Primary School
Dorian Dr
Pump La
Green La
1 grid square represents 500 metres

OLD WINDSOR
Beaumont
Bishopsgate
Englefield Green
Egham Wick
Runnymede (NT)
St Peters CE Middle School
Kings Court First School
St Johns Beaumont School
Bishopsgate School
Englefield Green County Infant School
St Jude's CE Junior School
St Cuthberts CE Primary School
Royal Lodge
Royal School
Cumberland Lodge
Great Meadow Pond
Savill Garden (Windsor Great Park)
The Savill Gardens
Parkside House
Obelisk Pond
Smith's Lawn
Bear's Rails
Woodside
Shaw Farm
Manor Farm Cottages
Royal Holloway College
American Community School
Albert Road
Straight Road
St Luke's Road
Burfield Road
Priest Hill
St Jude's Road
London Road
Crimp Hill
Ridgemead Road
Bishopsgate Road
Wick Lane
Kings Lane
Prospect Lane
Cooper's Hill Lane
Ham Lane
Church Road
Wharf Road
Ouseley Road
Windsor Road
Datchet Road
Three Castles Path
The Long Walk
Queen Anne's Ride
Windsor & Maidenhead
Surrey County
River Thames
A308
A328
A30
A332
B3021
TW20
149
172
193

150
171
194
A
B
C
D
E
F
G
1
2
3
4
5
6
7
8
9
10
Wraysbury Reservoir
Wraysbury
Wraysbury Primary School
Wraysbury Medical Centre
Wraysbury Station
Station Road
Douglas Lane
Old Station Lane
Tithe Lane
Coppermill Road
Windsor and Maidenhead
Surrey County
WELLEY RD
The Drive
Kingswood Creek
Ferry Drive
Hill View Road
King John's Cl
Old Ferry Drive
River Thames
Thames Path
Friary Road
Nursery Way
Fairfield Road
Fairfield Approach
Harcourt
The Green
Grange Cl
High St
WINDSOR ROAD
St Andrew's Cl
Oast House Cl
Old School Ct
Wharf Road
Ouseley Road
Carson Lane
Coppice Drive
Riverside
The Embankment
Magna Carta Lane
Mead Close
Magna Carta Lane
Vicarage La
STAINES ROAD
B376
Magna Carta Island
WINDSOR ROAD
A308
PRIEST HILL
A328
Cooper's Hill
Cooper's Hill Lane
Royal Holloway College
Runnymead Park
Kingswood Close
Kingswood Rise
Tite Hill
Spencer Gardens
Middle Hill
Lodge Close
Rushmere Pl
Alderside Walk
Kinburn Drive
Alder Cl
Parsonage Road
Harvest Road
Barnway
Barley Mow Road
St Jude's Cl
Torin Court
Willow Walk
Health Centre
Victoria Street
Albert Rd
Armstrong Road
South Road
Highfield Road
Penrose Court
The Retreat
St Cuthbert's Close
EGHAM HILL
Royal Holloway University of London
TW20
Bakeham Lane
Simons Walk
Prune Hill
St David's Drive
Roberts Way
LONDON ROAD
A30
Bagshot Road
ST JUDE'S ROAD
St Judes CE Junior School
Surgery
Junction 13
M25
A30(T)
Moor Lane
Works
Yeoveney Cl
Berkeley Cl
Feathers Lane
Sarsby Dr
Hythe End Road
Hythe End
Yard Mead
Thames Path
Ferry Lane
Hotel
WRAYSBURY ROAD
Gloucester Drive
Lammas Dr
Cemetery
EGHAM BY-PASS
Strode Street
Runnemede Road
Park Rd
Crown Street
HIGH STREET
THE AV
Police Stn
Strodes Coll
HIGH ST
CHURCH RD
Manor Farm La
Medical Cen
Egham Stn
Station Road
Grange Road
Limes Rd
Milton Rd
Spring Rise
The Crescent
North St
Rusham Road
Clarence Street
Osborne Rd
Ripley Av
Lynwood Av
Nightingale Shott
Manor Way
Whitehall Lane
Stroude Road
Fitzrobert Place
Manorcroft Primary School
EGHAM
Manorcroft Rd
New Wickham Lane
Clockhouse La E
THE GLANTY
THE CAUSEWAY
A308
Green Business Cen
Lovett Rd
Industrial Estate
Hawthorne Rd
New Rd
Chandos Rd
Mullens Road
Pooley Av
Pooley Green
Alexander Road
Rowan Avenue
VICARAGE ROAD
Egham Sports Centre
Mead Cl
College Av
Vicarage Ct
Egham Cricket Club
Egham Town FC
Pond Road
Pooley Gn Road
THORPE LEA ROAD
Glebe Road
Hythe Park Rd
The Hythe School
Wendover Road
Magna Carta School
Egham Hythe
Bishops Way
Langton Way
Stephen Cl
Devil's Lane
South Avenue
Park Avenue
Huntingfield Way
Thorpe Lea Primary School
Thorpe Lea
Avebridges Av
Ravendene Av
Warwick Avenue
THORPE LEA ROAD
Beta Way
Alpha Way
Thorpe Industrial
Milton Park
Bakeham Lane
Royal Holloway College
1 grid square represents 500 metres

Junction 14
M25
A3113 AIRPORT WAY
Spout Lane North
Works
STANWELL MOOR RD
Western Perimeter Rd
Southern Perimeter Road
151
Horton Road
Stanwell Moor
Stanwell
Stanwell Place
PARK ROAD
PARK RD
TOWN LA B378
TW19
King George VI Reservoir
Staines Reservoirs
Staines Moor
River Colne
Colne Valley Way
STANWELL MOOR ROAD A3044
Christ the King RC First School
St Marys CE Junior School
St Annes Primary School
St Davids Health Centre
Town Farm Primary School
Cemetery
Viola Avenue
Kingsway
Holywell Way
Explorer Av
Clare Road
Superstore
Ashford Hospital
A&E
Ashford Sports Club
174
A30(T) LONDON ROAD
STAINES BY-PASS
Kenilworth Road
Cumberland Road
Ashford High School
Ashford Clinic
St Davids School
Ashford Station
Clarendon Primary School
CHURCH ROAD
Shortwood Infant School
Parks Golf Courses & Sports Grounds
Shortwood Common
Ashford Park Primary School
Sandringham Dr
Queens Walk
Woodthorpe Rd
Chaucer Road
Wolsey Road
Chesterfield
Stanley Road
Tennyson Rd
STAINES
Two Rivers Retail Park
Arts Centre and Staines Theatre
Elmsleigh Centre Shopping Precinct
HIGH ST
LONDON ROAD
Police Stn
Oast House Centre
Staines Station
Staines & District Synagogue
Spelthorne Mus
Spelthorne Leisure Cen
Staines Prep School
Council Building
Indoor Sports Centre
Health Centre
Staines County Court
Knowle Green
Knowle Park Infant School
Youth Centre
Kingscroft School
Our Lady of the Rosary RC Primary School
STAINES BY-PASS A308
Brookside Avenue
Kingston Road
Kingston Crs
Cella Crs
FORDBRIDGE
KINGSTON ROAD
Ashford Manor Golf Club
The Matthew Arnold School
Commercial Road
Council Building
Elizabeth Avenue
Gloucester Crescent
Pavilion Gardens
Buckland Primary School
B377 ASHFORD ROAD
LALEHAM ROAD
B376
A320 CHERTSEY LANE
Staines Town FC
TW18
Wheatsheaf Lane
River Thames
Weir Place
Temple Gardens
195
04
05
06
75
74
73
72
71
70
H
J
K
L
M
N
P
1
2
3
4
5
6
7
8
9
10

Hatton
Terminal 2
152
Heathrow World Cargo Centre
Terminal 4
The British Museum Shop
Heathrow Terminal 4 Stn
Southern Perimeter Road
GREAT SOUTH-WEST ROAD
A30(T)
Hatton Road
The Marjory Kinnon School
Bedfont Junior & Infant School
Hillingdon
Hounslow
Court Farm Industrial Estate
Blackburn Trading Estate
St Marys CE Junior School
St Annes Primary School
West Bedfont
Longford River
Surrey County
East Bedfont
STAINES ROAD
A315
BEDFONT LANE
Bedfont Health Clinic
Grove Village Medical Cen
Southville Junior School
Fairholme Junior & Infant School
Clockhouse Industrial Estate
Ashford Sports Club
LONDON ROAD
Cemetery
Superstore
173
Bedfont Lakes Country Park
Industrial Estate
Edward Pauling School
Lower Feltham
HM Young Offender Institution
Feltham Hill Infant School
Feltham Hill Junior School
Ashford High School
St Davids School
CLOCKHOUSE LANE
B3003
Bedfont Industrial Park
Ashford Industrial Estate
Chattern Hill
ASHFORD ROAD
Ashford Station
Clarendon Primary School
TW15
Spelthorne Sixth Form College
Studholme Medical Cen
FELTHAM ROAD
CHURCH ROAD
Fordbridge Medical Cen
ASHFORD
St Michaels RC School
Echelford Primary School
CHERTSEY ROAD
A244
Felthamhill
Spelthorne Primary School
Spelthorne Clinic
Ashford Manor Golf Club
Golf Course
Ashford CE Primary School
KINGSTON ROAD
SCHOOL ROAD
STAINES ROAD WEST
Ashford Common
Littleton Common
Spelthorne Sports Club
Sunbury Common
Windmill Trading Estate
196
Sunbury Leisure Centre
Queen Mary Reservoir
1 grid square represents 500 metres

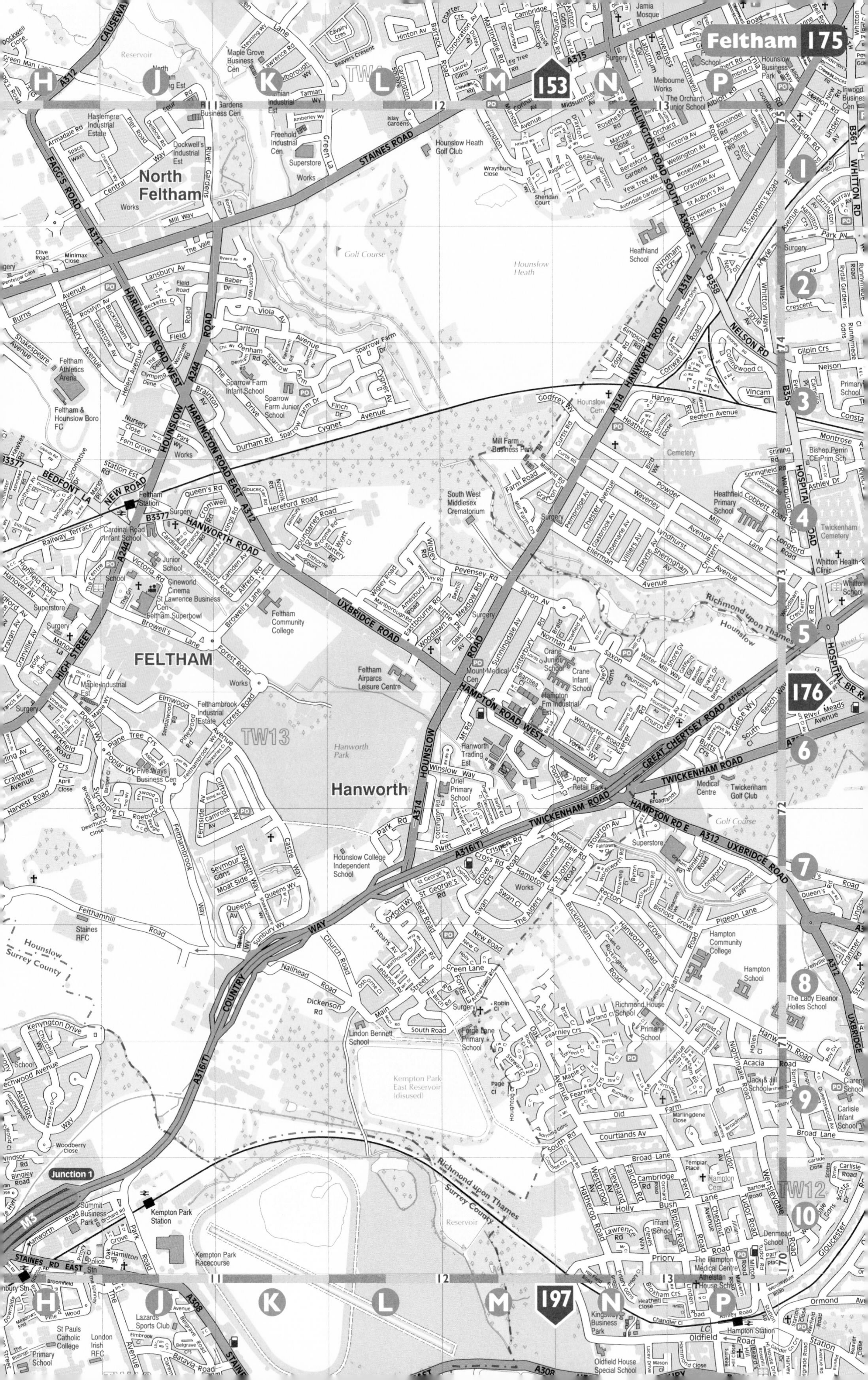
North Feltham
FELTHAM
Hanworth
TW13
TW12
Hounslow Heath
Golf Course
Hanworth Park
Kempton Park East Reservoir (disused)
Kempton Park Racecourse
Kempton Park Station
Feltham Station
Hampton Station
Junction 1
M3
STAINES ROAD
STAINES RD EAST
HANWORTH ROAD
HARLINGTON ROAD WEST
HARLINGTON ROAD EAST
HOUNSLOW ROAD
UXBRIDGE ROAD
HAMPTON ROAD WEST
GREAT CHERTSEY ROAD
TWICKENHAM ROAD
COUNTRY WAY
WELLINGTON ROAD SOUTH
HIGH STREET
NEW ROAD
BEDFONT LA
FAGG'S ROAD
HOSPITAL ROAD
NELSON RD
WHITTON RD
A312
A314
A316(T)
A244
A315
A3063
A308
B358
B3377
B361
Feltham Community College
Feltham Airparcs Leisure Centre
Hounslow College Independent School
South West Middlesex Crematorium
Hounslow Cem
Twickenham Cemetery
Twickenham Golf Club
Hampton Community College
Hampton School
The Lady Eleanor Holles School
Lindon Bennett School
Staines RFC
Richmond upon Thames
Surrey County
Hounslow
Reservoir
153
176
197
11
12
13
70
71
72
73
74
75

176
154
175
198
A
B
C
D
E
F
G
1
2
3
4
5
6
7
8
9
10
514
15
16
75
74
73
72
71
170
TW3
TW2
TW12
TW11
Whitton
TWICKENHAM
Cole Park
Strawberry Hill
Hampton Hill
TEDDINGTON
Hampton
Bushy Park
Eel Pie Island
Teddington Lock
Hounslow Business Park
Sikh Temple
Heath Business Cen
Hounslow Station
Chatsworth Junior & Infant School
Worton Hall Industrial Est
Victory Business Cen
Maswell Park Health Centre
Ivybridge Retail Park
Twickenham Stadium
Museum of Rugby & Twickenham Stadium Tours
Chase Bridge Primary School
Kneller Hall
Twickenham Trading Est
Richmond-upon-Thames College
NEC Harlequins RFC (The Stoop Memorial Ground)
Whitton Station
Twickenham Cemetery
Twickenham Stn
St Margarets Stn
St Margarets Business Centre
Richmond Adult & Community College
Civic Centre
Council Building
Mary Wallace Theatre
Waldegrave Girls School
Strawberry Hill Station
Strawberry Hill Golf Club
St James RC Primary School
St Marys University College
Fulwell Station
Fulwell Golf Club
Stanley Junior School
Teddington Cemetery
Twickenham Golf Club
Hampton Community College
The Lady Eleanor Holles School
St Clare Business Park
National Physical Laboratory
Teddington Memorial Hospital
Teddington Station
Teddington Swimming Pool
Teddington Business Park
Hampton Swimming Baths
Hampton Station
Bartons Cottage
King's Paddock
Collis Primary School
Sacred Heart RC Primary School
A316(T)
A305
A310
A311
A312
A313
A309
A3004
B358
B360
B361
WHITTON RD
CHERTSEY ROAD
HOSPITAL BR ROAD
STAINES ROAD
SIXTH CROSS ROAD
HAMPTON ROAD
WELLINGTON ROAD
FULWELL ROAD
UXBRIDGE ROAD
PARK ROAD
HIGH STREET
CHURCH ROAD
WALDEGRAVE ROAD
STRAWBERRY V
CROSS DEEP
HEATH ROAD
THE GREEN
KING ST
YORK ST
LONDON ROAD
ST MARGARET'S RD
TWICKENHAM RD
KINGSTON
BROAD ST
QUEEN'S ROAD
SANDY LANE
NELSON RD
KNELLER RD
1 grid square represents 500 metres

Twickenham 177
155
178
199
RICHMOND
Richmond Hill
St Margarets
Petersham
Ham
Kingston
Richmond Park
TW10
KT2
River Thames
Ham Common
Pen Ponds
Isabella Plantation
Sawyer's Hill
East Sheen Common
East Sheen Cemetery
Bog Lodge
Pembroke Lodge
Thatched House Lodge
The Richmond Golf Club
Marble Hill Park
Marble Hill House
Ham House (NT)
Deutsche Schule
The Russell School
Strathmore School
Star & Garter Home
Richmond College
Tiffin Girls School
Kingston University
Coombe Wood Golf Club
Holy Cross Preparatory School
Kingston Hospital
North Sheen Station
UPPER RICHMOND ROAD WEST
SHEEN ROAD
PETERSHAM ROAD
HAM GATE AVENUE
UPR HAM ROAD
RICHMOND ROAD
QUEEN'S ROAD
KINGSTON HILL
STAR AND GARTER HILL
COOMBE LANE WEST
COOMBE ROAD
PARK ROAD
TWICKENHAM ROAD
A307
A308
A305
A238
B352
B321
B322
B353
B351
B357

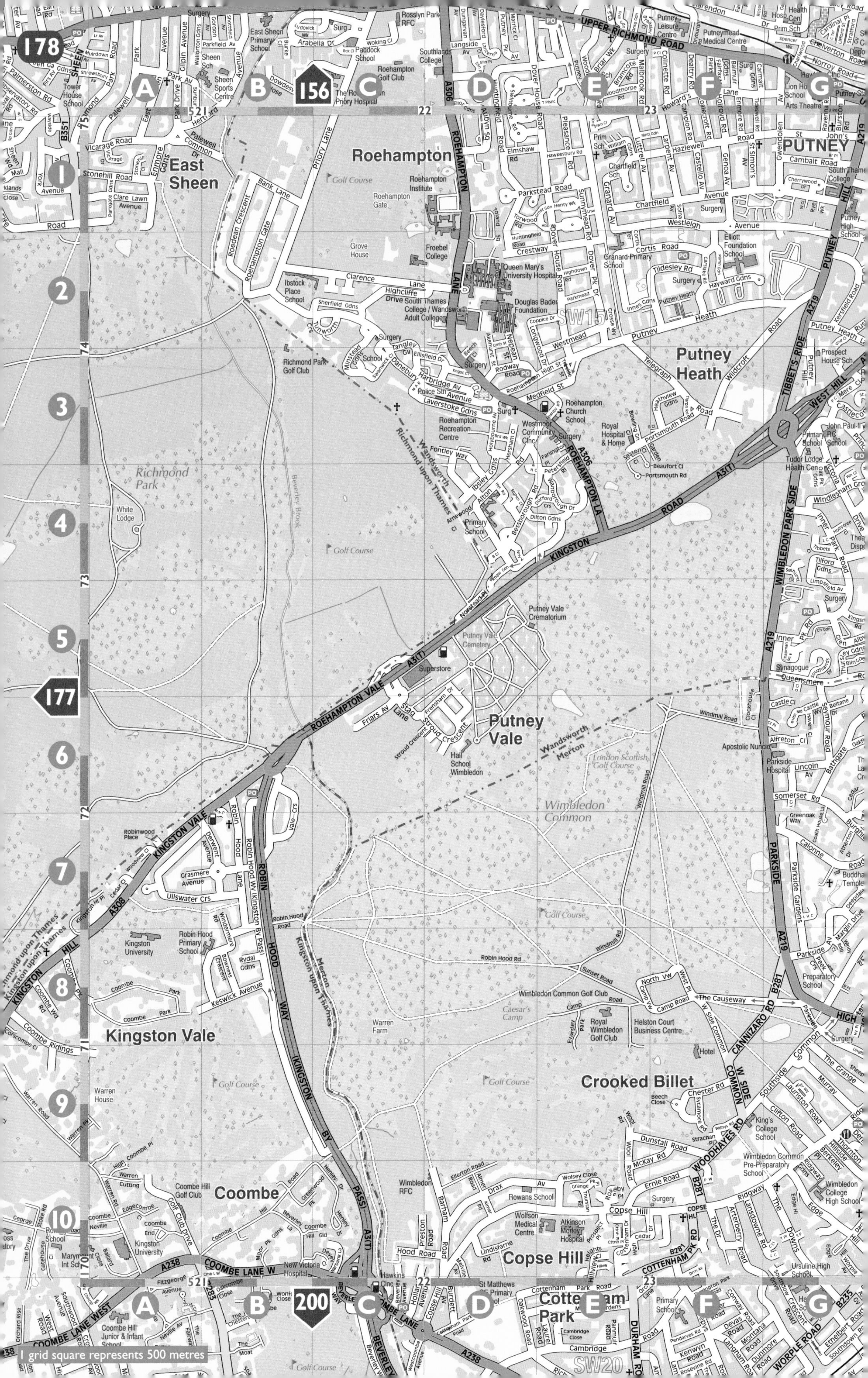
178
156
177
200
A
B
C
D
E
F
G
1
2
3
4
5
6
7
8
9
10
21
22
23
74
73
72
71
170
SHEEN
East Sheen
Sheen Sports Centre
East Sheen Primary School
Tower House School
Palewell Common Dr
Vicarage Road
Stonehill Road
Clare Lawn Avenue
Upper Richmond Road
Rosslyn Park RFC
Roehampton Golf Club
The Roehampton Priory Hospital
Southlands College
Roehampton
Roehampton Institute
Roehampton Gate
Golf Course
Roehampton Lane
Grove House
Froebel College
Queen Mary's University Hospital
Douglas Bader Foundation
Clarence Lane
Ibstock Place School
Roedean Crescent
Roehampton Gate
Bank Lane
Priory Lane
Highcliffe Drive
South Thames College / Wandsworth Adult College
Richmond Park Golf Club
Roehampton Recreation Centre
Roehampton High St
Medfield St
Roehampton Church School
Westmoor Community Clinic
Royal Hospital & Home
Portsmouth Road
Wandsworth
Richmond upon Thames
Richmond Park
White Lodge
Beverley Brook
Kingston Road
A3(T)
A306
Roehampton La
Putney Vale Crematorium
Putney Vale Cemetery
Superstore
Putney Vale
Roehampton Vale
Stroud Crescent
Hall School Wimbledon
Putney
PUTNEY
Putney Heath
SW15
Putney Heath
Tibbet's Ride
West Hill
Wimbledon Park Side
Parkside
A219
Queensmere
Windmill Road
London Scottish Golf Course
Wimbledon Common
Merton
Apostolic Nuncio
Parkside Hospital
Kingston Vale
Robin Hood Way (Kingston By Pass)
Robinwood Place
Grasmere Avenue
Ullswater Crs
Kingston University
Robin Hood Primary School
Kingston upon Thames
Keswick Avenue
Coombe Park
Robin Hood Rd
Wimbledon Common Golf Club
Caesar's Camp
Royal Wimbledon Golf Club
Helston Court Business Centre
Warren Farm
The Causeway
Crooked Billet
Cannizaro Rd
W Side Common
Kingston Vale
Coombe Ridings
Warren House
Warren Road
Coombe
Coombe Hill Golf Club
Golf Club Drive
Coombe Lane W
A238
New Victoria Hospital
Wimbledon RFC
Rowans School
Wolfson Medical Centre
Atkinson Morley's Hospital
Copse Hill
Cottenham Park
Cottenham Park Rd
Woodhayes Rd
King's College School
Wimbledon Common Pre-Preparatory School
Wimbledon College High School
Ursuline High School
Worple Road
Durham Rd
SW20
Coombe Hill Junior & Infant School
Coombe Lane West
Beverley Way
1 grid square represents 500 metres

River Thames
WANDSWORTH
Wandsworth Park
157
180
201
H
J
K
L
M
N
P
25
26
27
1
2
3
4
5
6
7
8
9
10
WANDSWORTH BRIDGE ROAD
RICHMOND RD
WEST HILL
SWANDON WY
ARMOURY WY
WANDSWORTH HIGH ST
FAIRFIELD ST
HUGUENOT PL
EAST HILL
N SIDE WANDSWORTH COMMON
BATTERSEA RISE
TRINITY RD
WINDMILL RD
SPENCER PARK
WOODWELL ST
BURNTWOOD LANE
GARRATT LANE
EARLSFIELD ROAD
MERTON ROAD
DURNSFORD ROAD
PLOUGH LANE
GAP ROAD
HAYDON'S RD
MERTON HIGH STREET
HIGH ST COLLIER'S WOOD
TOOTING HIGH STREET
UPPER TOOTING ROAD
MITCHAM RD
BOLINGBROKE GROVE
BELLEVUE RD
ST JAMES'S DRIVE
WIMBLEDON HL ROAD
THE BROADWAY
HARTFIELD RD
WORPLE ROAD
ALEXANDRA RD
KINGSTON ROAD
MERANTUM WY
CHRISTCHURCH RD
West Hill
SW18
Southfields
Earlsfield
Summerstown
Upper Tooting
SW17
Wandsworth Common
Wimbledon Park
Boating Lake
SW19
WIMBLEDON
South Wimbledon
Tooting Graveney
Collier's Wood
MERTON
Wimbledon Stadium
Lambeth Cemetery
Streatham Cemetery
Wandsworth Cemetery
HM Prison
St Georges Hospital
Springfield Hospital
Wimbledon Station
Wimbledon Park Station
Southfields Station
Earlsfield Station
Haydons Road Station
Wandsworth Common Station
South Wimbledon Station
Royal Hospital for Neuro-Disability
Roehampton Institute
Wimbledon Park Athletics Track
Wimbledon Park Golf Club
Central London Golf Club

180
158
179
202
A
B
C
D
E
F
G
1
2
3
4
5
6
7
8
9
10
28
29
30
CLAPHAM COMMON NORTH SIDE
Clapham Common
Clapham Park
Balham
Wandsworth Common
Streatham Hill
Streatham Park
Furzedown
STREATHAM
Streatham Vale
SW12
SW17
SW16
Tooting Bec Common
BALHAM HIGH RD
STREATHAM HIGH ROAD
UPPER TOOTING ROAD
MITCHAM ROAD
MITCHAM LANE
TOOTING BEC ROAD
POYNDERS ROAD
BRIXTON HILL
STREATHAM HILL
Clapham South Station
Balham Station
Streatham Hill Station
Streatham Stn
Streatham Common Station
Tooting Station
Wandsworth Common Station
1 grid square represents 500 metres

Streatham 181
159
182
203
BRIXTON
Herne Hill
East Dulwich
SE22
SE24
Brockwell Park
Dulwich Village
Knight's Hill
Tulse Hill
West Dulwich
SE21
Dulwich
SE27
West Norwood
Upper Sydenham
Crystal Palace
Norwood New Town
SE19
Upper Norwood
Herne Hill Station
North Dulwich Station
East Dulwich Stn
Tulse Hill Station
West Dulwich Station
Sydenham Hill Station
West Norwood
Gipsy Hill Station
Crystal Palace Station
Dulwich Picture Gallery
Dulwich College
Dulwich Park
Belair Park
Southwark Sports Ground
Marlborough Cricket Club
Lloyds Register Cricket Club
Dulwich & Sydenham Hill Golf Club
West Norwood Crematorium
Crystal Palace Museum
Crystal Palace Athletics Stadium
HALF MOON LANE
DULWICH COMMON
THURLOW PARK ROAD
NORWOOD ROAD
KNIGHT'S HILL
CROWN DALE
CENTRAL HILL
BEULAH HILL
CHURCH ROAD
CRYSTAL PALACE PDE
COLLEGE RD
LORDSHIP LANE
CROXTED ROAD
SOUTH CROXTED ROAD
DULWICH WOOD PARK
WESTWOOD
CRYSTAL PALACE PARK ROAD
ANERLEY HILL
ANERLEY ROAD
WESTOW HL
TULSE HILL
DULWICH ROAD
MILKWOOD ROAD
HERNE HILL
EAST DULWICH GROVE
H J K L M N P
32 33 34

182
160
181
204
Nunhead
Peckham Rye Park
East Dulwich
SE22
Honor Oak
Honor Oak Park
Brockley
Ladywell
SE4
SE23
Forest Hill
The Horniman Museum & Gardens
Catford Bridge Station
Bell Green
Lower Sydenham
Upper Sydenham
SE26
Bellingham
Crystal Palace
New Beckenham
PENGE
Sydenham Station
Forest Hill Station
Brockley
Honor Oak Park Station
Crofton Park Station
Ladywell Stn
Lower Sydenham Stn
New Beckenham Station
Penge East Station
Penge West Station
Crystal Palace Station
Bellingham Stn
Kent House Station
STANSTEAD ROAD
LONDON ROAD
LORDSHIP LANE A205
DARTMOUTH ROAD
KIRKDALE A2216
SYDENHAM ROAD
PERRY VALE
PERRY HILL
CATFORD HILL
CATFORD ROAD
BROCKLEY RISE
HONOR OAK PARK
FOREST HILL ROAD
CRYSTAL PALACE PARK ROAD
WESTWOOD HILL
HIGH ST
PARISH LANE
NEWLANDS PARK
GREEN LANE
BECKENHAM ROAD
SOUTHEND LANE
BROMLEY ROAD A21
SOUTHEND ROAD A2015
BECKENHAM HILL
LADYWELL ROAD
ADELAIDE AV
1 grid square represents 500 metres

161
184
205
LEWISHAM
Hither Green
Lee
CATFORD
SE13
SE12
SE6
BR1
Mottingham
Grove Park
Southend
Downham
Plaistow
Sundridge
Bromley Park
HIGH ROAD
ELTHAM ROAD
BURNT ASH ROAD
BURNT ASH HILL
WESTHORNE AVENUE
SIDCUP ROAD
BROWNHILL ROAD
ST MILDREDS ROAD
BARING ROAD
CHINBROOK ROAD
BURNT ASH LANE
BROMLEY ROAD
BROMLEY HILL
LONDON ROAD
KIDBROOKE PK ROAD
Hither Green Cemetery
Lewisham Crematorium
Sutcliffe Park
Sundridge Park Golf Club
Sundridge Park Station
Ravensbourne Station
Bromley North Station
Lee Station
Hither Green Stn
Grove Park Stn
Beckenham Place Park
Green Chain Walk

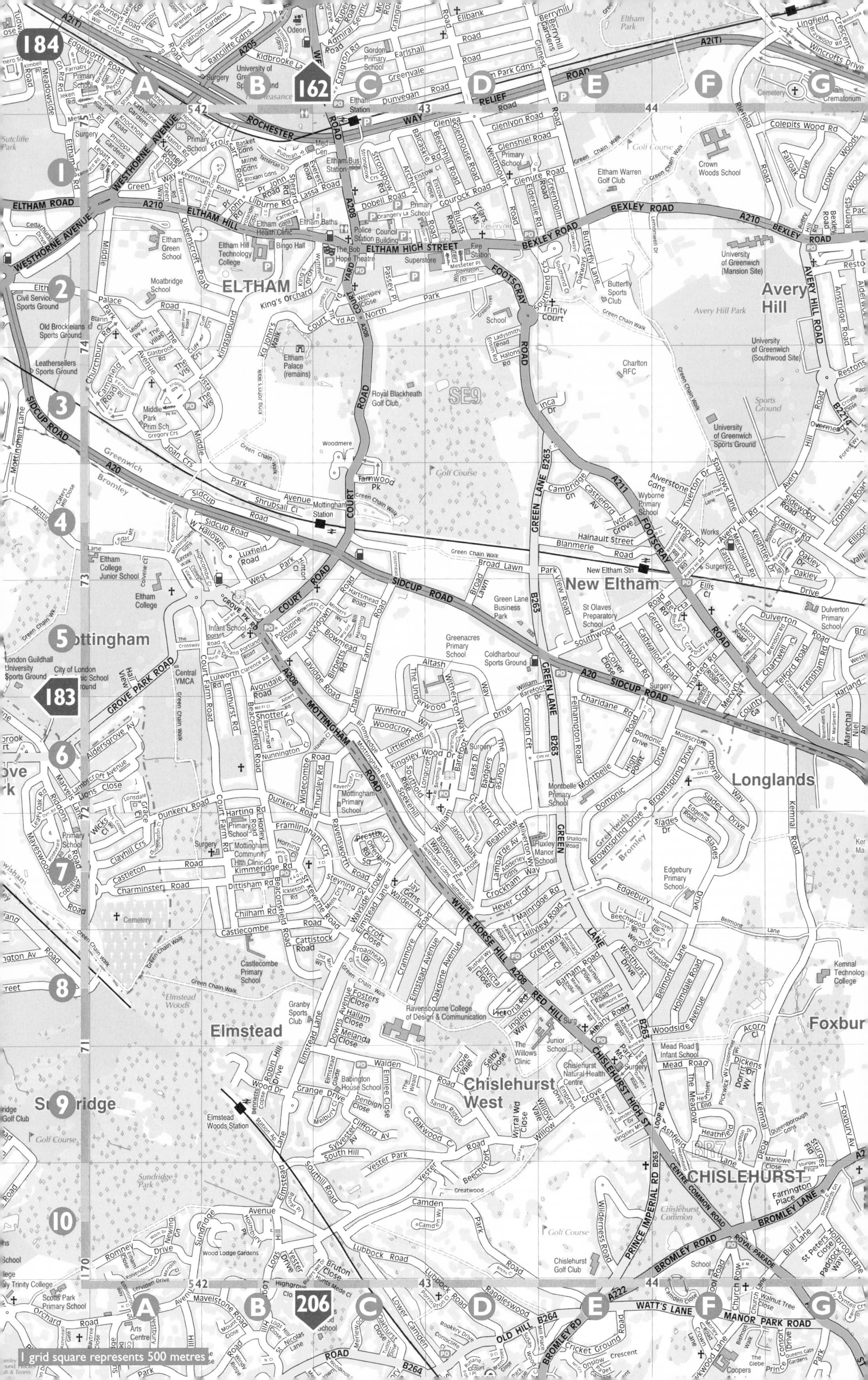
184
162
183
206
ELTHAM
New Eltham
Mottingham
Longlands
Avery Hill
Elmstead
Chislehurst West
CHISLEHURST
Foxbury
Sundridge
SE9
BR7
ELTHAM ROAD
ELTHAM HILL
ELTHAM HIGH STREET
BEXLEY ROAD
ROCHESTER WAY
ROCHESTER WAY RELIEF ROAD
WESTHORNE AVENUE
SIDCUP ROAD
COURT ROAD
FOOTSCRAY ROAD
GREEN LANE
MOTTINGHAM ROAD
WHITE HORSE HILL
RED HILL
CHISLEHURST HIGH ST
PRINCE IMPERIAL RD
CENTRE COMMON ROAD
BROMLEY ROAD
BROMLEY LANE
AVERY HILL ROAD
GROVE PARK ROAD
WATT'S LANE
MANOR PARK ROAD
Eltham Station
Mottingham Station
New Eltham Stn
Elmstead Woods Station
Eltham Palace (remains)
Royal Blackheath Golf Club
Eltham Warren Golf Club
Chislehurst Golf Club
Avery Hill Park
Eltham Park
Chislehurst Common
Sundridge Park
Elmstead Woods
Eltham Crematorium
Cemetery
University of Greenwich (Mansion Site)
University of Greenwich (Southwood Site)
University of Greenwich Sports Ground
Ravensbourne College of Design & Communication
Kemnal Technology College
Eltham College
Central YMCA
Green Chain Walk
1 grid square represents 500 metres

BEXLEY
Falconwood
Blackfen
SIDCUP
Foots Cray
Ruxley
Bexleyheath
DA15
DA14
DA6
163
186
207
H
J
K
L
M
N
P
46
47
48
75
74
73
72
71
70
1
2
3
4
5
6
7
8
9
10
EAST ROCHESTER WAY
A2(T)
BLACKFEN ROAD
A210
A221
DANSON ROAD
PENHILL ROAD
BLENDON ROAD
B2210
BRIDGEN ROAD B2210
HURST ROAD
A222
STATION ROAD
MAIN ROAD
A211
HIGH STREET
ELM ROAD
THE GREEN
A2001
CHISLEHURST RD
SIDCUP HILL
SIDCUP BY-PASS ROAD
A20(T)
CRAY ROAD
A224
FOOTS CRAY HIGH ST
MAIDSTONE ROAD
NORTH CRAY ROAD
A223
EDGINGTON WAY
PERRY STREET
HALFWAY STREET
B2214
Sidcup Station
Albany Park Station
Sidcup Golf Club
Chislehurst & Sidcup Grammar School
Rose Bruford College of Speech & Drama
Queen Marys Hospital
Lamorbey Park
Bexley Woods
Scadbury Park
Cemetery
Golf Course
Works
Superstore
Ruxley Corner Industrial Estate
Middlesex Hospital Sports Ground
Sidcup Sports Club
Frognal Corner
Ski Slope
Manor Farm

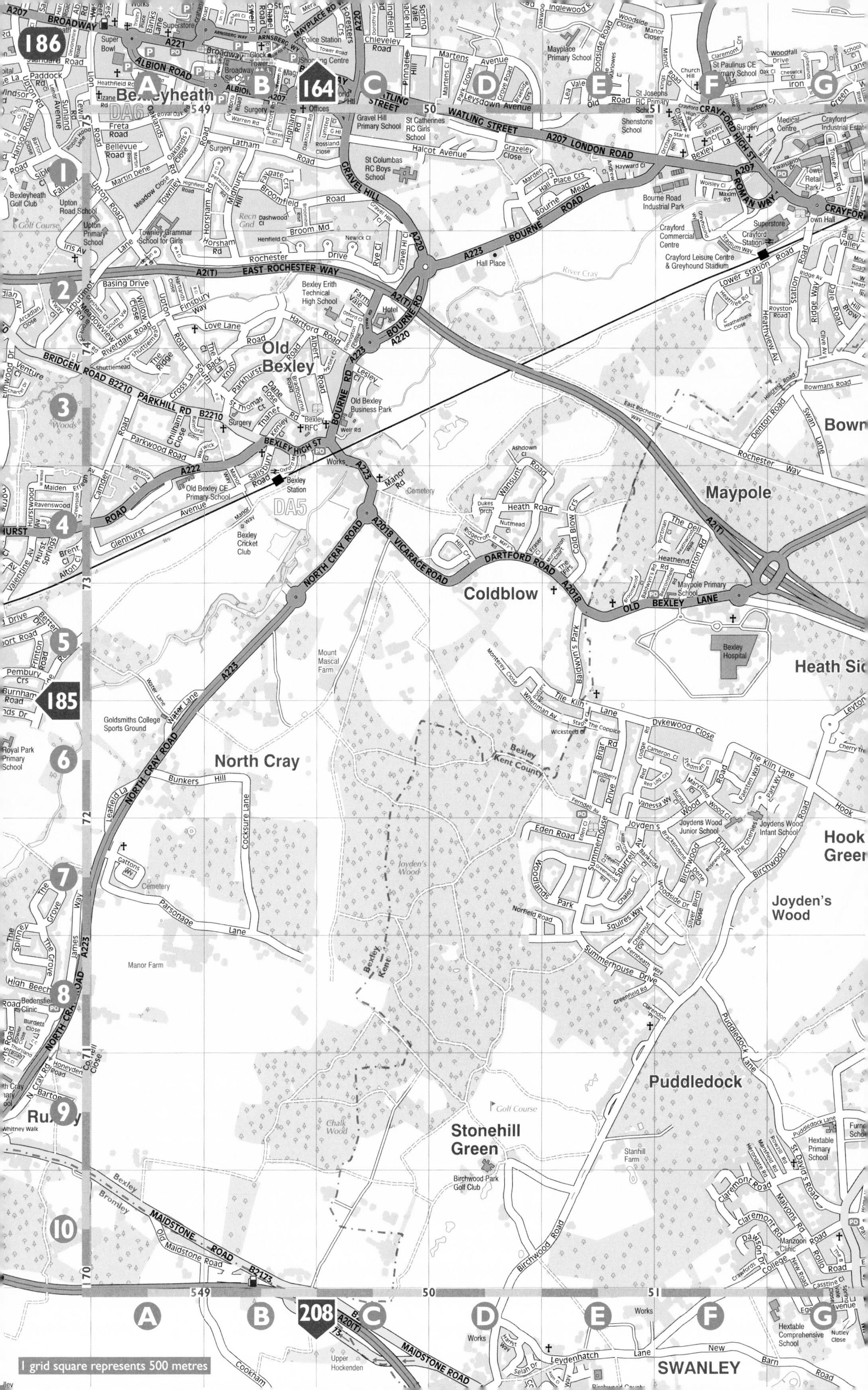
186
164
185
208
Bexleyheath
DA6
Old Bexley
DA5
Coldblow
Maypole
North Cray
Joyden's Wood
Puddledock
Stonehill Green
SWANLEY
Heath Side
Hook Green
A207 BROADWAY
ALBION ROAD
WATLING STREET
A207 LONDON ROAD
CRAYFORD HIGH ST
A2(T) EAST ROCHESTER WAY
A223 BOURNE ROAD
BRIDGEN ROAD B2210
PARKHILL RD B2210
BEXLEY HIGH ST
A222
A2018 VICARAGE ROAD
DARTFORD ROAD
OLD BEXLEY LANE
NORTH CRAY ROAD
A223
MAIDSTONE ROAD
B2173
GRAVEL HILL
A220
Bexley Station
Crayford Station
Bexley Hospital
Hall Place
Bexleyheath Golf Club
Birchwood Park Golf Club
Goldsmiths College Sports Ground
Bexley Cricket Club
Crayford Leisure Centre & Greyhound Stadium
Joyden's Wood
Chalk Wood
Mount Mascal Farm
Manor Farm
Stanhill Farm
A B C D E F G
1 2 3 4 5 6 7 8 9 10
549 50 51
1 grid square represents 500 metres

Crayford
Barnes Cray
Temple Hill
New Town
DARTFORD
Wilmington
Hawley
Clement Street
Hextable
Sutton at Hone
DA1
DA2
165
188
209
53
54
55
H
J
K
L
M
N
P
1
2
3
4
5
6
7
8
9
10
75
74
73
72
71
70
A206
A226
A2026
A2018
B2174
A225
B258
A296
A282(T)
A2(T)
M25
B260
DARTFORD ROAD
SHEPHERDS LANE
PRINCES ROAD
WEST HILL
SHEPHERDS LA
BURNHAM ROAD
VICTORIA ROAD
HIGHFIELD RD
INSTONE RD
LOWFIELD STREET
HAWLEY ROAD
CHURCH HILL
HIGH ROAD
BARN END LANE
TOP DARTFORD ROAD
EAST HILL
A296 PARK ROAD
THE BRENT
WATLING
MAIN ROAD
Dartford Station
Dartford Grammar School for Girls
NW Kent College of Technology
Dartford West Technology College
Westgate Primary School
Dartford Golf Club
University of Greenwich
Wilmington Grammar School for Girls
Wilmington Primary School
Wilmington Hall School
Wilmington Boys Grammar School
Rowhill School
Oakfield Primary School
Fairfield Pool & Leisure Centre
Central Park
Central Park Arena
Brooklands Lake
Leigh City Technology College
Dartford Heath
Leyton Cross
Superstore
Orchard Theatre
Priory Shopping Centre
Dartford FC
St Pauls CE Primary School
Sutton at Hone CE Primary School
Shirehall Road
Clement Street
Arnolds Lane
Church Road
Lower Road
Broad Lane
Goss Hill
Gildenhill Road
School Lane
Parsonage Lane
Royal Road
Darenth Road
Darenth Valley Path
River Darent

188
166
187
210
A
B
C
D
E
F
G
1
2
3
4
5
6
7
8
9
10
556
57
58
75
74
73
72
71
170
University Wy
Crossways Bvd
Anchor Boulevard
Victory Way
Galleon Bvd
Schooner Ct
Newton's Ct
Clare Cswy
Crossways Boulevard
St Mary's Road
Charles Street
Stone Crossing Station
Elizabeth Street
Cotton Lane
Junction 1a
Bell Close
Church Rd
Stone
DA9
High Street
Station Rd
Kestner Industrial Est
Greenhithe for Bluewater Stn
Greenh
London Road
A226
A206
A282(T)
Caveil Crescent
Coleridge Rd
Shakespeare Rd
Shaftesbury Lane
Farnol Rd
Dunkin Rd
Dickens Av
Littlebrook Manor Way
Tennyson Rd
Lansbury Crs
Attlee Dr
Ruskin Gv
Norfolk Cl
Bow Arrow Lane
St Vincents Rd
Bayly Road
Carlisle Road
Howard Rd
Shenley Road
School of Health
Invicta Road
Stone House Hospital
Cotton Road B3228
Brent Cl
Mile Stone Rd
The Brent
The Brent Primary School
Works
St John's Road
Hill House Road
Tollgate Rd
Alamein Gardens
Kirby Road
Wiltshire Cl
Jessamine Pl
Watling Street B2500
Parker Industrial Centre
Clarendon Gdns
Cadogan Av
Cemetery
Junction 1b
A296
Princes Road
Patterdale Rd
Fleet Road
Dartford FC
Oakland Rd
Queens Gdns
Princes Avenue
Teesdale Road
Lunedale Road
Lonsdale Crs
Weardale Avenue
Fleetdown Primary School
Fleet Downs
Darent Valley Hospital
A&E
Gore Road
Darenth Park Av
St Margarets Cl
Powell Av
Darenth Wood Road
Surgery
Carlton Av
Woodward Ter
Horns Cross
Hedge Place Road
Barnfield Cl
Plantation Cl
Stone Castle
Oak Rd
Acacia Rd
Elm Rd
Birch Pl
Hayes Road
Morgan Drive
Louvain Road
St James' Lane
B2174
Cliff Reach
Bluewater Parkway
Town Square Crs
Oak Tree Avenue
Bluewater Park
Showcase Bluewater
Lime Tree Av
Chestnut Av
B255
Bean Road
Mounts Road
Bean Lane
Farm Park
Leigh City Technology College
B260
Trolling Down Hill B260
Cemetery
A2(T)
Junction 2
DA2
Darenth Wood
Wood Lane
Bean
Turner Rd
Fallowfield
Green Street Green Road
Coombfield Drive
Sinclair Way
Bennett Way
Lordswood Cl
Collier Crs
Langlands Dr
Court Rd
St Lukes Cl
Ladywood Road
Hill Rise
Ridgeway
Lane End
Lords Wood
Shellbank Lane
Darenth Road South
Darenth Hill
Darenth
Darent Valley Path
Darenth Primary School
Green Street Green
B262
St Margaret's Road
St Margaret's
Roman Villa Road
Sutton Place
Parsonage Lane
Keith Av
Arnolds Lane
Cemetery
Church Road
Council Building
Main Road
A225
Sutton at Hone CE Primary School
Sutton at Hone
Gravel Rd
Balmoral Rd
Dartford FC
Russell Place
Barfield
Holmesdale Road
Grange Towers
Wood
Coopers Close
Shrubbery Rd
South Darenth
Gill's Road
Gill's Farm
Grubb Street
Greenstreet
Church Hill
1 grid square represents 500 metres

Swanscombe
Northfleet
Stonewood
Betsham
Southfleet
Hook Green
Westwood
Northfleet Green
DA10
DA11
167
190
211
H
J
K
L
M
N
P
60
61
62
75
73
72
71
170
1
2
3
4
5
6
7
8
9
10
LONDON ROAD A226
LONDON RD A226
GALLEY HILL ROAD
STONEBRIDGE ROAD
HIGH STREET
B259 HIGH STREET
STANHOPE RD
SOUTHFLEET ROAD
B259
A2(T)
A296
WATLING STREET
SPRINGHEAD RD
SPRINGHEAD ROAD
B2174
A2260
A226
HALL RD
PARK CORNER ROAD
STATION ROAD
B262
BETSHAM ROAD B262
BANKS HILL
B255
HIGHCROSS ROAD
WHITEHILL RD
Swanscombe Station
Northfleet Station
Swanscombe Business Centre
Galley Hill Industrial Estate
Kent Kraft Industrial Estate
Northfleet Industrial Estate
Ebbsfleet Industrial Estate
Kent Kraft Industrial Estate
Swan Valley Community School
The Sweyne Junior School
Lawn Primary School
Gravesend & Northfleet FC
St Josephs RC School
Council Building
Cemetery
Superstore
Spring Head
Northend
Mates Farm
Sedleys CE Primary School
Bea Primary School
Painters Ash Primary School
Works
Surgery
Tilbury Ness
New Barn Rd
New Barn Road
Dale Rd
Dale Road
Westwood Road
Sandy Lane
Warren Road
Red Street
Church St
Brakefield Road
Gloxinia Road
Rectory Meadow
Monks Wk
Hook Green Road
Hook Green Road
Banbury Villas
Broad Ditch Road
Downs Road
Hazells
Alkerden Lane
Milton St
Milton Rd
Manor Rd
Manor Road
Leonard Avenue
Durrant Way
Swanscombe Street
Pentstemon Drive
Broomfield Rd
Craylands La
Lewis Rd
Ames Road
Moore Rd
Broad Rd
Gunn Road
Park Road
Gasson Rd
Stanley Rd
Church Rd
Eglinton Rd
Castle Rd
Vernon Rd
Keary Road
Mounford Dr
Taunton Road
Lower Rd
Manor Way
Pilgrims Road
Lovers Lane
The Creek
The Shore
College Road
Park Walls
Grove Road
Station Road
Huntley Avenue
Hive La
Lawn Rd
Factory Rd
THE HILL
Granby Road
Portland Road
Waterdales
Mitchell Avenue
Gwynn Road
Fleet Road
Viking Rd
Pepper Hill
Roman Road
Clayood Lane
School Lane
Southfleet Road
Stonewood
Beacon Drive
Knockhall Road
Abbey Rd
Alexander Rd
Wakefield Rd
Swanscombe
Crayburne

168
189
A
B
C
D
E
F
G
1
2
3
4
5
6
7
8
9
10
563
64
65
75
74
73
72
71
170
Gravesend Reach
Thurrock
Kent County
GRAVESEND
Royal Terrace Pier
Gravesend Rowing Club
Gravesend Yacht Club
Northfleet
Rosherville
Perry Street
New House
Kings Farm
Singlewell
Istead Rise
Northfleet Green
Parrock F
DA11
Tilbury Ness
Tilbury Fort
World End
Works
A126
Tilbury/Gravesend Passenger
International Cruise Terminal
The Shore
Lawn Primary School
Gravesend & Northfleet FC
Crete Hall Road
Portland Road
Granby Road
A226 LONDON ROAD
OVERCLIFFE
Rosherville CE Primary School
Laburnum Gv
Lime Avenue
St Botolphs CE Primary School
THAMES WAY
A2260
DOVER ROAD
OLD ROAD EAST
OLD ROAD WEST
OLD RD EAST
St Josephs RC School
SPRINGHEAD RD
SPRINGHEAD ROAD
B2175
B261
Council Building
Cemetery
Superstore
Dover Road Primary School
Gravesend Grammar School for Girls
Gravesend Cricket Club
Wrotham Road Health Clinic
Imperial Business Est
Imperial Retail Park
Gravesend Stn
Civic Centre & Woodville Halls
Police Stn
Magistrates Court
St Georges Centre
Milton Road Business Park
MILTON ROAD
Canal Basin
Custom House
Industrial Estate
Guru Nanak Sports Club
Fleetway Sports Club
Parrock Avenue
Milton Hall Road
Convent Preparatory School
The Old Guild Theatre
Northfleet School for Boys
Cygnet Leisure Centre
Northfleet School for Girls
Waterdales
Mitchell Avenue
Colyer Road
Hall Road
Coldharbour Road
Sheares Green Primary School
Painters Ash Primary School
St Georges CE School
WROTHAM ROAD
A227
Mid Kent Golf Club
Golf Course
A2(T)
WATLING STREET
Watling Street
Kings Farm Junior School
Kings Farm Infant School
Ifield School
Southfields School
Singlewell Primary School
Church Road
Downs Road
Hazells
Ditch Road
Broad
Istead Rise
Wealdway
Superstore
Marks Sq
Harman Av
Brenchley Av
Orchard Avenue
Windsor Road
Singlewell Road
Cedar Avenue
Ash Road
Hillingdon Road
The Fairway
Dennis Road
Ascot Road
Central Road
Portland Avenue
Ferndale Rd
Malvina Av
Smarts Road
Ridgeway
Wilberforce Way
Codrington Crs
Kindown Court
Hever Court Road
The Hollies
1 grid square represents 500 metres

H
J
K
L
M
169
N
P
67
68
69
Thames
Saxon Shore Way
Shorne Marshes
Wharf Road
Mark Lane
Works
Works
Road
Waterton Av
Alexandra Rd
Lwr Range Rd
Mark La
Mark Lane
LC
Denton
Havengore Av
Artemis Cl
Shamrock Rd
Thistle Rd
Denton Ct Rd
Gerald Rd
Dickens Rd
Primary School
Ingoldsby Road
Dering Way
Farley Rd
Medbury Rd
Damigos Rd
North West Kent College of Technology
Rose Av
Abbey Road
Bellman Av
ROAD
B261
Lower Higham Road
Chalk
Copperfield Cl
Chalk
Vicarage Lane
Miller Road
Nickleby Rd
Havisham Rd
Orick Road
Villa Cl
Darenth Drive
Brooke Drive
Castle Lane
Lower Higham Road
Lower Higham Road
Lower Road
East Court Manor
Church Lane
Church La
Queen's Farm
Queen's Farm Road
Green Farm Lane
Green Farm
Forge Lane
Brown Rd
Rochester Rd
Lisle Cl
A226
ROCHESTER ROAD
ROCHESTER ROAD
Crescent
Jubilee Crescent
Hampton Crescent
Westcourt Primary School
West Court
Barr Road
Bourne Road
Thong Lane
Road
Surgery
St Gregory's Crescent
Medhurst Crs
Medhurst Gdns
Cruden Road
Freeman Way
St Chad's Dr
St Dunstan's Dr
St Hilda's Way
St Margaret's Crs
Hibernia Dr
Cervia Way
Raynehurst Junior School
Thamesview School
Calshot Way
Cambria Crs
Cerne Road
Dorset Crs
Betjana Dr
Verona Gdns
Kelso Dr
Clipper Crescent
Stornaway Strd
Crescent
Ariel Cl
Drive
Francis Avenue
The Rise
Volante Wy
Leander
Challenge Cl
Surgery
Cascades Leisure Centre
Southern Valley Golf Club
Golf Course
Riverview Park
Riverview Primary School
PO
Whinfell Way
Riverview Clinic
Thong La
Citrus Crs
Way
Imperial Drive
Britannia Drive
Sirdar Strd
Thelma Cl
Marling Way
Vanessa Wk
Vigilant Way
Hopewell Dr
Astra Drive
Gazelle Glade
Cienfuegos Gdns
Genesta Gld
Tower Cl
Marling Way
Fairfield
Michael Gdns
Wykeham Ct
Davy's Pl
DA12
Gravesend Road
GRAVESEND ROAD
A226
Burdett Av
Coutts Avenue
Crown Lane
Lane
Forge
Cob Drive
Shorne CE Primary School
Mill Hill Lane
The Street
Manor Fld
Surgery
Swiller's La
Shorne
Warren View
Lodge Ct
Upper Ifield
Shorne Ifield Road
Thong Lane
Thong
Tanyard Hill
Lane
Racefield Cl
Claylane Wood
Randall Wood
Shorne Ridgeway
Woodlands
The Ridgeway
Pondfield Lane
Bowesden Lane
Valley Dr
WATLING STREET
A2(T)
Henhurst Road
Thong Lane
WATLING STREET
A2(T)
Wood Park
Brewers Road
A2(T)
WATLING STREET
Pale Park
Henhurst
1
2
3
4
5
6
7
8
9
10
70
71
72
73
74
75

192
170
212
A
B
C
D
E
F
G
1
2
3
4
5
6
7
8
9
10
493
94
95
70
69
68
67
66
65
Cheapside
Sunninghill
Sunningdale
The Rise
Broomhall
South Ascot
Scotswood
SL5
Three Castles Path
Three Castles
Dukes Lane
Cheapside Road
Hilltop Close
Cheapside CE Primary School
Water Splash
Water Splash La
Pump La
Dorian Dr
Green La
Sunninghill Road
Golf Course
Ascot Farm
Royal Ascot Golf Club
New Mile Road
Silwood Cl
Tetworth Hall
Kier Park
Queens Hill Ri
Agincourt
Agincourt Pl
Carbery Lane
Works
Steeple Pt
Surgery
A329
London Road
A330
Queen's Rd
Course Rd
Ascot Station
Station Hill
Wells Lane
St Georges School
St George's Lane
Wells
Church Lane
Kingswick Cl
Shenstone Pk
Silwood Park
Imperial College of Science Technology & Medicine
Buckhurst Road
B383
Harewood
Buckhurst Lane
Hotel
Titness Park
Church Lane
Mill Lane
Oriental Road
Sunninghill Rd
Coombe Grange
Lower Village Road
Upr Village Rd
Marist Junior School
Marist Convent Senior School
Novello Theatre
Highclere
Kingswick Dr
Oliver Road
Victoria Road
Victoria Rd
Francis Chichester Cl
Elizabeth Gdns
Swinley CP School
Lyndhurst Rd
Porchester Rd
Truss Hill Road
Bowden Road
High St
Queen's Rd
King's Road
Heathfield Av
Larch Av
The Spinney
Avenue
Silwood Road
Civil Service College
Cemetery
Kiln Lane
Dale Lodge Road
Leacroft
Coworth Rd
Coworth Cl
High St
Church Road
Bedford Lane
Sandy Lane
Parkside Rd
Station Road
Holy Trinity CE Primary School
Woodend Drive
Cardwell Crescent
Norton Park
The Glade
St Mary's Hill
Bridge Road
Charters La
Fox Covert Cl
Bagshot Road
Cavendish Meads
Holmes Cl
Greyfriars Drive
Brockenhurst Road
Ravenswood
Hurstwood
Friary Rd
Monks Walk
Monks Dr
Monks Cl
St Francis RC Primary School
Horse Gate Ride
St Mary's Road
Hotel
Hancocks Mount
Wildewood
Heathermount
Heathermount School
Devenish Road
King's Beeches
Regents Wk
St Marys School Ascot
Park Drive
Park Crs
Rise Rd
Lynwood Crs
Beech Hill Rd
Galton Rd
Dry Arch Road
Oakdene
Charnwood
Broomhall Lane
Sunningdale School
Sunningdale Station
Cedar Dr
Sheridan Gra
Woodby Dr
Charters Road
Charters Wy
Hillhampton
Ballencrieff Rd
Pinecote Drive
Sunning Avenue
Hamilton Drive
Lady Margaret Road
Abbey Wd
Priory Close
Priory Road
Half Penny La
N End La
Broomfield Park
Redwood Dr
Onslow
Bridge View
Richmond Wood
Charters School
Broadlands Drive
Fireball Hill
The Covert
Hurst Lodge School
Fir Tree Cl
Field House Cl
Coronation Road
Earlywood
Earleydene
B3020
Grant Wk
Greenways Dr
Devenish Lane
Elm Pk
A30
London Rd
Sunningdale Ladies Golf Club
Golf Course
Cross Road
Hillside Pk
Whinshill Ct
Ridge Mount Road
Sunningdale Golf Club
Woodhall Lane
Westwood Road
Country Gardens Estate
Windlesham Hall
Windlesham Court
Snows Paddock
Bosman Dr
Windlesham Road
Ride
Court
Hawkes Leap
Leycester
Newark Road
Turpins Rise
Erl Wood Manor
Sunninghill Rd
Chertsey
B386
Cowarth
1 grid square represents 500 metres
GU20

Sunningdale 193
171
194
213
Englefield Green
Egham Wick
Obelisk Pond
Primary School
A30
LONDON ROAD
Royal Holloway College
Bakeham Lane
American Community School
Callow Hill
Wick Pond
The Valley Gardens
Temple Bungalow
Windsor and Maidenhead
Surrey County
Virginia Water
Blacknest
Sunninghill Mattenhurst
BLACKNEST ROAD
A329
Hotel
PH
B389
Pinewood Rd
Waterfall Cl
Woodside Wy
Christchurch CE Infant School
Stuart Wy
Waverley Dr
Quentin Wy
Spring Woods
Hollow Lane
VIRGINIA WATER
Woodlands Road West
Woodlands Rd
Woodlands Road East
Gorse Hill Road
Heath Rise
CHRISTCHURCH
Station Ap
Monks Road
Abbey Rd
Virginia Dr
Abbots Drive
Brock Way
Virginia Drive
Virginia Avenue
Badgers Hill
Nuns Walk
Oakwood Rd
Keepers
The Close
GU25
Coworth Park
Fort Belvedere
Wentworth Dr
Lindale Close
Chestnut Av
Pinewood Road
Stayne End
Lake Road
Wentworth Drive
Portnall Drive
Portnall Road
Meadow Road
North Drive
Wentworth Golf Club
Sherbourne Dr
Shepley End
West Drive
Shepley Dr
Firwood Rd
Shrubs Hill
Shrubs Hill Lane
Portnall Drive
Portnall Rise
Golf Course
Harpesford Av
Sundon Cres
Wellington Avenue
Woodshore Cl
Heatherside Dr
Drive
East
Hillside
Trumpsgreen Av
Crown Road
Cabrera Cl
Trumps Green
Oak Tree Cl
Bourneside
West Drive
South Drive
Beechwood Road
Knowle Gv Cl
Knowle Grove
Knowle Hill
Trumpsgreen Road
Corrie Gdns
M3
Longcross Station
Chobham Lane
Kitsmead Lane
Works
Burma Road
Barrowhills
CHOBHAM ROAD
Chobham Common
Tanglewood Cl
Holly Cl
Albury Cl
LONGCROSS ROAD
Longcross
B386
Flutters Hill
Staple Hill
Kitsmead La
H J K L M N P
1 2 3 4 5 6 7 8 9 10
97 98 99
70 69 68 67 66 65

194
172
193
214
TW20
GU25
KT16
Royal Holloway University of London
Royal Holloway College
Prune Hill
Bakeham Lane
Simons Walk
St David's Drive
Roberts Way
A30
LONDON
Thorpe Lea
THORPE LEA ROAD
New Wickham Lane
Wickham La
Stroude Road
Clockhouse La W
Avebridges Av
Wavendene Av
Warwick Avenue
Milton Park
Whitehall Lane
Stroude
Luddington Avenue
Hurst Lane
Whitehall Farm Lane
Edgell Cl
Lambly Hill
VIRGINIA WATER
Hollow Lane
Callow Hill
Woodlands Road West
Woodlands Rd
Woodlands Road East
Gorse Hill
Heath Rise
Heath Cl
Piper's End
Trotsworth Av
Morella Cl
Virginia Dr
B389
CHRISTCHURCH RD
CHRISTCHURCH ROAD
Station Ap
Monks Road
Abbey Rd
Station Par
Nuns Walk
Keepers Wk
The Close
Oakwood
Brock Way
Virginia Drive
Virginia Av
Badgers Hl
Virginia Water Station
PO Sorting Office
SANDHILLS LANE
Sandhills Ct
St Anns Heath Junior School
Whitehill Place
Holloway Dr
Upper Walk
Chapel Sq
Sandy Lane
Cypress Ct
Ridge Wy
Irvine Pl
The Orch
Stroude Road
The Lane
St Ann's Heath
Thorpe Cricket Club
Thorpe Green
GREEN ROAD
B388
Trumpsgreen Road
Bridge Lane
Lyne Lane
Lyne Rd
Mill Lane
Trumps Green
Trumps Green County Inf Sch
Beechmont Av
Cabrera Av
Bourne Rd
Hillside
Crown Rd
Trumpsgreen Av
Cabrera Cl
Home Farm Cl
Crown La
Furnival Cl
Tithe Cl
Oak Tree Cl
Knowle Gv Cl
Knowle Grove
Corrie Gdns
Trumps Farm
Lyne Road
Bottom Harrow Rd
Lyne Cl
Lyne Crossing Road
Farm Cl
Lyne Place Manor
M3
M25
Thorpe Industrial Park
Beta Way
Alpha Way
Delta Way
Omega Way
Crabtree Road
Egham Business Village
Sky Business Park
Ten Acre Lane
Cemetery
THORPE BY-PASS
Muckhatch La
Thorpe
Village Road
Western Av
Rosemary Lane
Midway Av
The Bence
Thorpe CE Infant School
Coldharbour Close
Coldharbour Lane
Yewtrees
Church Ap
The Gower
Longside Lake
Bourne Meadow
Green Road
MILL HOUSE LANE
The Bourne
Junction 2/12
THORPE
St Ann's Hill Road
St Ann's Hl Rd
Ruxbury Road
Almners Rd
Alm'ners Barn Farm
Lyne
Almners Road
Hardwick Lane
Kitsmead Lane
Barrowhills
Hersham Farm
Lyne & Longcross CE Infant School
Silverlands
B386
LONGCROSS ROAD
TRYS HILL
HOLLOWAY HILL
The Ashford & St Peters Hospital
A&E
Runnymede Hospital
France Farm
Stonehill Road
GUILDFORD
Accommodation Rd
Flutters Hill
Golf Course
Foxhills Golf Club
Fox Hills
Hillswood Drive
1 grid square represents 500 metres

173
196
215
H
J
K
L
M
N
P
04
05
06
1
2
3
4
5
6
7
8
9
10
70
69
68
67
66
165
Laleham
Abbey Mead
CHERTSEY
Chertsey Meads
Addlestonemoor
Hamm Moor
Penton Hook
Laleham Burway
Golf Course
Laleham Golf Club
Laleham Abbey
Abbey Chase
River Thames
Thames Path
Thames Side
M3
A320
A317
A318
B376
B375
B377
B387
B3121
CHERTSEY LANE
STAINES ROAD
ASHFORD ROAD
SHEPPERTON ROAD
THE BROADWAY
CHERTSEY BRIDGE ROAD
CHERTSEY ROAD
BRIDGE ROAD
WEIR ROAD
LONDON STREET
WINDSOR ST
GUILDFORD ST
EASTWORTH ROAD
CHERTSEY RD
WOBURN HILL
ST PETER'S WAY
WEYBRIDGE ROAD
HIGH STREET
STATION ROAD
ST ANN'S RD
FORDWATER ROAD
Laleham CE Primary School
Buckland Primary School
Staines Town FC
Thorpe Park
Works
Twynersh House
Chertsey Museum
Chertsey Town FC
Pyrcroft Primary School
Freemantles School
Chertsey Recreation Centre
Chertsey Station
Sir William Perkins School
Hanworth Business Park
Salesian College
Salesian RC School
Magistrates Court
Police Station
Council Building
Steppgates Community School
St Annes Catholic Primary School
Health Centre
Chertsey Cemetery
Addlestone Cemetery
Fordwater Trading Estate
Bourne Business Park
St George's College Track (under construction)
St Georges College
Woburn Park
Hamm Court
Meadowcroft County Infant School
Weybridge Business Park
St Pauls CE Primary School
Civic Offices
Superstore
Old Town Hall
Hotel
Shopping Precinct
Carlyle Business Centre
Gogmore Farm Park
Reed Place Business Park
Dockett Point
Sandgates
Shepperton Studios

196
174
195
216
Littleton Common
Sunbury Common
Queen Mary Reservoir
Charlton
Shepperton Studios
Littleton
Littleton CE Infant School
TW17
Shepperton Green
Upper Halliford
Upper Halliford Station
American Golf at Sunbury
Golf Course
Shepperton
Shepperton Station
Shepperton Business Park
St Nicholas CE First & Middle School
Thamesmead School
Saxon CP School
Lower Halliford
Halliford School
Bishop Duppas Park
Bishop Wand CE Secondary School
Springfield Primary School
Spelthorne Sports Club
Windmill Trading Estate
Sunbury Business Centre
Superstore
Rodd Estate
Longwood Business Park
Hotel
University Vandals RFC
River Thames
Reed Place Business Park
Dockett Point
Chertsey Meads
Hamm Court
Woburn Park
Walton-on-Thames Cricket Club
Weybridge Cricket Club
St James CE Primary School
Broad Water
Weybridge Hospital & Primary Care Centre
Council Building
Elmbridge Museum
Weybridge Business Park
Oatlands Park
Oatlands School
M3
B376
B375
B3366
A244
A317
A3050
STAINES ROAD WEST
LALEHAM ROAD
CHERTSEY ROAD
RENFREE WAY
GREEN LANE
HIGH STREET
RUSSELL RD
WALTON LANE
WALTON BRIDGE ROAD
UPR HALLIFORD ROAD
WINDMILL ROAD
GASTON BR ROAD
OATLANDS DRIVE
WEYBRIDGE ROAD
1 grid square represents 500 metres

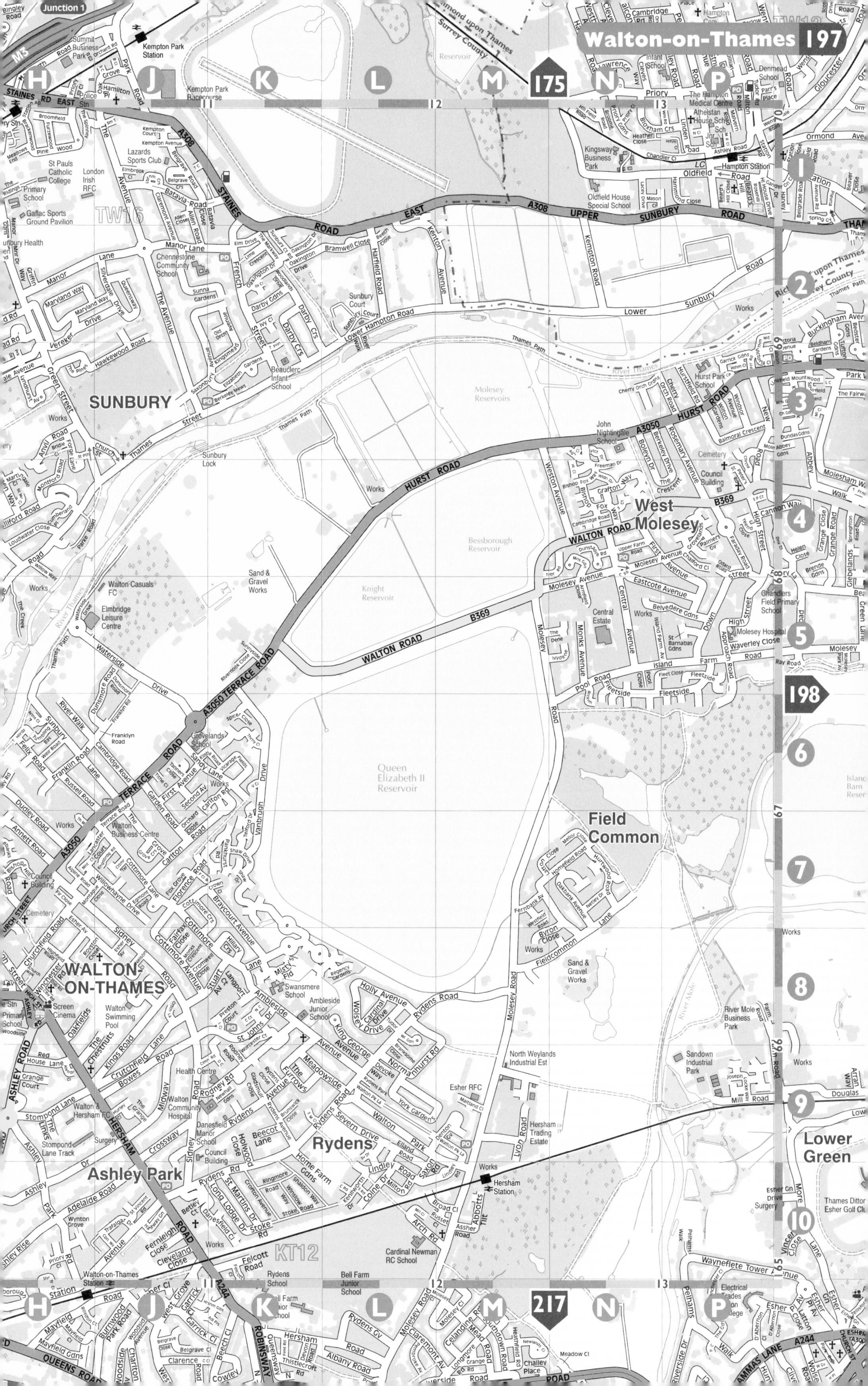
Junction 1
M3
Kempton Park Station
Kempton Park Racecourse
Reservoir
Surrey County
175
Hampton Station
Oldfield House Special School
Kingsway Business Park
A308 UPPER SUNBURY ROAD
STAINES ROAD EAST
Lazards Sports Club
St Pauls Catholic College
London Irish RFC
Gaflac Sports Ground Pavilion
TW16
Chennestone Community School
Sunbury Court
Lower Hampton Road
Lower Sunbury Road
Thames Path
River Thames
Molesey Reservoirs
SUNBURY
Sunbury Lock
Beauclerc Infant School
Hurst Park School
A3050 HURST ROAD
John Nightingale School
West Molesey
WALTON ROAD
B369
Bessborough Reservoir
Knight Reservoir
Sand & Gravel Works
Walton Casuals FC
Elmbridge Leisure Centre
Central Estate
Molesey Hospital
Chandlers Field Primary School
198
A3050 TERRACE ROAD
Grovelands School
Walton Business Centre
Queen Elizabeth II Reservoir
Field Common
Council Building
Cemetery
WALTON-ON-THAMES
Screen Cinema
Walton Swimming Pool
Swansmere School
Ambleside Junior School
River Mole Business Park
Sandown Industrial Park
North Weylands Industrial Est
Esher RFC
Hersham Trading Estate
Health Centre
Walton Community Hospital
Walton & Hersham FC
Stompond Lane Track
Danesfield Manor School
Rydens
Ashley Park
Hersham Station
Cardinal Newman RC School
KT12
Lower Green
Thames Ditton Esher Golf Club
Walton-on-Thames Station
Rydens School
Bell Farm Junior School
217
A244
QUEENS ROAD
ROBINSWAY

198
176
197
218
TW12
KT8
KT7
Hampton
Hurst Park
East Molesey
Thames Ditton
Giggshill
Weston Green
Lower Green
Hinchley Wood
ESHER
Bushy Park
Hampton Court Palace
Hampton Court Park
Hampton Court Station
Diana Fountain
Chestnut Avenue
Island Barn Reservoir
Sandown Park Racecourse
Thames Ditton & Esher Golf Club
Littleworth Common
Esher Station
Hinchley Wood Stn
Thames Ditton Station
River Thames
River Ember
River Mole
Thames Path
Richmond upon Thames
Surrey County
HAMPTON COURT ROAD
HAMPTON COURT WAY
HURST ROAD
THAMES STREET
WALTON ROAD
PORTSMOUTH ROAD
KINGSTON BY-PASS
EMBERCOURT ROAD
ESHER ROAD
EMBER LANE
STATION ROAD
WATTS ROAD
PARK ROAD
SANDY LANE
A308
A309
A3050
A307
A311
B3379
B364
B369
B358
Molesey Lock
East Molesey Cricket Club
Imber Court Trading Estate
Metropolitan Police FC
Grist Memorial Sports Club
Old Tiffinians Sports Ground
Esher College
Sandown Industrial Park
River Mole Business Park
1 grid square represents 500 metres

Kingston upon Thames
199
177
200
219
H
J
K
L
M
N
P
18
19
20
1
2
3
4
5
6
7
8
9
10
KT2
KT1
KT5
KT6
Norbiton
KINGSTON UPON THAMES
Berrylands
Tolworth
SURBITON
Old Malden
Hampton Wick Stn
Kingston Stn
Norbiton Station
Berrylands Station
Surbiton Station
Tolworth Station
Kingston Hospital
Kingston University
Kingsmeadow Athletics Centre
Kingstonian FC
Kingston Crematorium
Fairfield Industrial Estate
Surbiton Cemetery
Hogsmill River
Bentalls Shopping Centre
Eden Walk Shopping Centre
Kingsgate Business Centre
Canbury 2000 Bus Pk
Surbiton Business Centre
Kingston Business Cen
Hook Rise South Industrial Park
Corinthian Casuals FC
Red Lion Business Park
Tolworth Girls School & Centre for Continuing Education
Tolworth Recreation Cen
Knollmead Primary School
Grand Avenue Primary School
Christ Church CE Primary School
The Hollyfield School
Maple Infant School
St Matthews CE Primary School
Tolworth CP School
Our Lady Immaculate RC Primary School
Tolworth Tower
Holy Cross Preparatory School
Marymount Int Sch
Coombe Wood Golf Club
Richmond upon Thames
Kingston upon Thames
RICHMOND ROAD
QUEEN'S ROAD
KINGSTON HILL
COOMBE LANE WEST
COOMBE ROAD
CAMBRIDGE ROAD
A2043
A238
A308
A307
PORTSMOUTH ROAD
PENRHYN ROAD
HIGH STREET
HORSE FAIR
WOOD STREET
CROMWELL RD
FAIRFIELD NORTH
OLD LONDON RD
SURBITON HILL ROAD
EWELL ROAD A240
A240
BRIGHTON ROAD
VICTORIA ROAD
UPPER BRIGHTON ROAD A243
A243
HOOK ROAD
KINGSDOWNE ROAD
DITTON ROAD
CLAREMONT RD
B3363
MAPLE RD
HOOK UNDERPASS (KINGSTON BY-PASS)
KINGSTON BY-PASS
A3(T)
WARREN DRIVE NORTH
BROADWAY
ST MARK'S HILL
CHURCH GROVE
PARK ROAD
UPR TEDDINGTON RD
KINGSTON ROAD
WORCESTER PARK ROAD

200
178
199
220
Coombe
Copse Hill
Cottenham Park
SW20
New Malden
KT3
Raynes Park
Bushey Mead
West Barnes
Motspur Park
Old Malden
Worcester Park
KT4
North Cheam
Cannon Hill
Merton
Sutton
A B C D E F G
1 2 3 4 5 6 7 8 9 10
A238 COOMBE LANE W
COOMBE LANE WEST
KINGSTON BY PASS
BEVERLEY WAY
A3(T)
MALDEN WAY
KINGSTON ROAD
BURLINGTON ROAD
HIGH STREET
MALDEN ROAD
A2043
COOMBE ROAD
TRAPS LANE
WEST BARNES LANE
BUSHEY ROAD
A298
GRAND DRIVE
WORPLE ROAD
DURHAM ROAD
CENTRAL ROAD
CHEAM COMMON ROAD
LONDON ROAD
OLD MALDEN LANE
WORCESTER PARK ROAD
CHURCH ROAD
New Malden Stn
Raynes Park Station
Motspur Park Station
Malden Manor Station
Worcester Park Station
Malden Golf Club
Raynes Park Sports Ground
North East Surrey Crematorium
Morden Cemetery
Cuddington Cemetery
University of London Athletics Ground
LSE Sports Club
1 grid square represents 500 metres

Merton 201
Collier's Wood
MERTON
Merton Park
Morden
Morden Park
St Helier
Rosehill
Benhilton
The Wrythe
Carshalton
SM4
SM3
SM1
179
202
221
KINGSTON ROAD
MORDEN ROAD
MORDEN HALL ROAD
LONDON ROAD A24
CENTRAL ROAD
EPSOM ROAD
STONECOT HILL
MARTIN WAY
CROWN LANE
GREEN LANE
ST HELIER AVENUE
BISHOPSFORD ROAD
REIGATE AVENUE A217
OLDFIELDS ROAD
SUTTON COMMON ROAD
WRYTHE LANE
LONDON ROAD A217
WESTERN ROAD
CHRISTCHURCH RD
MERANTUM WAY
B285 DORSET ROAD
HARTFIELD ROAD
WORPLE ROAD
CRICKET GREEN
ANGEL HILL
ROSE HILL
HIGH STREET
ST DUNSTAN'S HILL
Morden Hall Park
St Helier Hospital
Sutton Cemetery
Morden South Station
St Helier Station
South Merton Station
Sutton Common Stn
Carshalton Station
Wimbledon Chase
H
J
K
L
M
N
P
1
2
3
4
5
6
7
8
9
10
25
26
27

202
180
201
222
Streatham Vale
Mitcham
CR4
Mitcham Common
Thornton Heath
Beddington Corner
Hackbridge
Beddington
Waddon
The Wrythe
Carshalton
Croydon Road
Mitcham Road
Carshalton Road
London Road
Beddington Lane
Windmill Road
Manor Road
Rowan Road
Streatham Road
Upper Green East
Cricket Green
Western Road
Mitcham Junction Station
Hackbridge Station
Norbury Station
Mitcham Golf Club
Golf Course
Beddington Park
Croydon Cemetery
Croydon Crematorium
Streatham Park Cemetery
South London Crematorium
Merton
Sutton
A217
A236
A239
A237
A23
B272
B277
B278
528
29
30
1 grid square represents 500 metres

Croydon 203
181
204
223
SE19
SE20
SE25
CR7
CR0
Upper Norwood
Norbury
Anerley
South Norwood
Selhurst
Woodside
Broad Green
Addiscombe
Wandle Park
CROYDON
Thornton Heath Station
Selhurst Station
Norwood Junction Stn
West Croydon Stn
East Croydon Station
Whitgift Shopping Centre
Drummond Shopping Centre
Mayday University Hospital
Croydon Mosque & Islamic Cen
Queen's Rd Cemetery
Wimbledon FC (Selhurst Park)
Crystal Palace FC (Selhurst Park)
Harris City Technology College
Addiscombe Cricket Club
Streatham & Croydon RFC
Kensington Ave Primary School
David Livingstone Primary School
Westwood High School for Girls
Spurgeons Coll
Heavers Farm Primary School
Follys End Christian High School
The BRIT School
GREEN LANE
LONDON ROAD
BRIGSTOCK ROAD
PARCHMORE ROAD
GRANGE ROAD
WHITEHORSE LANE
SOUTH NORWOOD HILL
HIGH STREET
PENGE ROAD
SELHURST ROAD
NORTHCOTE ROAD
WINDMILL ROAD
WELLESLEY ROAD
LOWER ADDISCOMBE ROAD
ADDISCOMBE ROAD
MORLAND ROAD
PORTLAND ROAD
WOODSIDE GREEN
SPRING LANE
ROMAN WAY
SUMNER ROAD
DUPPAS HILL ROAD
THE CROYDON FLYOVER
COOMBE ROAD
PARK LANE
FAIRFIELD RD
BARCLAY RD
CHEPSTOW ROAD
BEULAH HILL
CHURCH ROAD
A212
A215
A213
A222
A232
A235
A236
A23
B266
B273
B243
H
J
K
L
M
N
P
1
2
3
4
5
6
7
8
9
10
32
33
34
65
66
67
68
69
70

204
182
203
224
PENGE
Anerley
SE20
Elmers End
Eden Park
Upper Elmers End
Monks Orchard
Shirley
Upper Shirley
Spring Park
BECKENHAM
BR3
A
B
C
D
E
F
G
1
2
3
4
5
6
7
8
9
10
535
36
37
70
69
68
67
66
65
South Norwood Country Park
Beckenham Crematorium
Croydon Sports Arena
Ashburton High School
Bethlem Royal Hospital
Shirley Park Golf Club
Beckenham Hospital
Kelsey Park
Eden Park Station
Elmers End Station
Birkbeck Station
Clock House Station
Kent House Station
Beckenham Junction Station
Anerley Station
ANERLEY ROAD
CROYDON ROAD
ELMERS END ROAD
BECKENHAM ROAD
UPPER ELMERS END ROAD
LONG LANE
SHIRLEY ROAD
WICKHAM ROAD
ADDISCOMBE ROAD
PORTLAND ROAD
WOODSIDE GREEN
SPRING LANE
PENGE ROAD
SOUTH EDEN PK RD
LINKS WAY
HIGH ST
MANOR ROAD
BROMLEY ROAD
GREEN LANE
A214
A222
A213
A215
A232
A234
A2015
B230
1 grid square represents 500 metres

Bromley Park
Shortlands
Bromley
Park Langley
West Wickham
Hayes
Keston Mark
Keston
Masons Hill
Coney Hall
BR2
BR4
183
206
225
H
J
K
L
M
N
P
39
40
41
70
69
68
67
66
65
1
2
3
4
5
6
7
8
9
10
Ravensbourne Station
Shortlands Station
Bromley North Station
Bromley South Station
Sundridge Park Station
Hayes Station
West Wickham Station
Bromley Common
Norman Park
Hayes Common
Bromley FC
Norman Park Athletics Track
Old Bromlians Cricket Club
Langley Park Golf Club
Shortlands Golf Club
Civic Centre & Bromley Palace
The Glades Shopping Centre
The Pavilion Leisure Cen
Churchill Theatre
Bromley Hospital
Hayes Grove Priory Hospital
Wickham Theatre
Metropolitan Police Hayes Sports Club
Old Wilsonians Sports Club
Old Beckenhamian RFC
Park House RFC
St John Rigby Catholic College
Bromley College of Further & Higher Education
Ravens Wood School
Hayes School
Baston School
Hayes Primary School
Pickhurst Junior School
Pickhurst Infant School
Highfield Junior School
Highfield Infant School
Hawes Down Primary School
Glebe School
Coney Hill School
The Ravensbourne School
Raglan Primary School
Valley Primary School
Bishop Challoner School
Clare House Primary School
St Christophers School
Ashgrove School
Scotts Park Primary School
St Josephs Catholic Primary School
Holy Trinity College
Bromley College
Sloane Hospital
Widmore Centre
Chartwell Business Centre
Waldo Industrial Est
A21
A222
A232
A214
A2022
B228
B251
B265
B2212
Bromley Road
Beckenham Lane
Westmoreland Road
Hayes Lane
Hayes Road
Hayes Street
Masons Hill
Widmore Road
Kentish Way
Tweedy Road
High Street
Pickhurst Lane
Croydon Road
Glebe Way
Station Road
Addington Road
Baston Road
Hayes Way
Wickham Way
Tootswood Road
Mead Way
George Lane
Ridgeway
Warren Road
Homesdale Road
Bromley Common

184
205
226
Chislehurst
Widmore
Bickley
Bromley Common
Southborough
Petts Wood
Crofton
Keston Mark
Keston
Locksbottom
Bickley Park Cricket Club
Chislehurst Golf Club
Chislehurst Station
Bickley Station
Petts Wood Station
Chislehurst Caves
Jubilee Country Park
Bromley High School
Bromley College of Further & Higher Education
Bromley Golf Club
Southborough Primary School
St James RC Primary School
Coopers School
Ravens Wood School
Newstead Wood School for Girls
Darrick Wood Swimming Pool
Darrick Wood Primary School
Darrick Wood
Bullers Wood School
Scotts Park Primary School
Widmore Centre
Raglan Primary School
Bickley Park Prep School
Chartwell Business Centre
Waldo Industrial Est
Oakley House
Hawkwood Farm
Tongs Farm
Bromley Common
Golf Course
Cemetery
Bromley Hospitals
A222
A21
A232
A233
A208
B264
B265
BICKLEY ROAD
BICKLEY PARK ROAD
PAGE HEATH LANE
BROMLEY COMMON
HASTINGS ROAD
OAKLEY ROAD
CROYDON ROAD
CROFTON ROAD
SUMMER HILL
BROMLEY RD
OLD HILL
WATT'S LANE
MANOR PARK ROAD
PRINCE IMPERIAL RD
BROMLEY LANE
ROYAL PARADE
CHISLEHURST ROAD
HOMESDALE ROAD
FARNBOROUGH CO
BR2
1 grid square represents 500 metres

St Paul's Cray
Poverest
St Mary Cray
Derry Downs
Broom Hill
Ramsden
Goddington
ORPINGTON
Orpington Station
St Mary Cray Station
A224 SEVENOAKS WAY
CRAY AVENUE
A208 ORPINGTON ROAD
A208 CHISLEHURST ROAD
PERRY HALL ROAD
A223 HIGH STREET
A232 SPUR ROAD
STATION ROAD
A20(T)
A223 EDGINGTON WAY
CROCKENHILL ROAD
BLACKSMITHS LANE
MILL BROOK RD
B258
BR5
Scadbury Park
Ruxley Park Golf Centre
Cray Valley Golf Club
Golf Course
Ski Slope
Crayfields Business Park
Crayfield Industrial Park
Rectory Paddock School
Grays Farm Primary School
St Pauls Cray Health Clinic
Leesons Primary School
Murray Business Centre
Sevenoaks Way Industrial Estate
Springvale Retail Park
Orpington Retail Park
St Pauls Cray CE Primary School
Nugent Industrial Park
Ravensquay Business Centre
Manor Oak Primary School
Shawcroft School
Poverest Recreation Ground
Covet Wood
Perry Hall Primary School
Priory Gdns
Bromley Museum
The Priory
Walnuts Shopping Centre
Walnut Leisure Centre
Superbowl
College
Police Station
The Orpington Halls
Council Building
Priory School
Blenheim Junior & Infant School
Burwood School
St Olave's & St Saviour's Grammar School
Orpington Mental Health Centre
Bromley Hospitals
Cemetery
Superstore
Retail Park
Works
Surgery
H J K L M N P
46 47 48
1 2 3 4 5 6 7 8 9 10
70 69 68 67 66 65
185
208
227

186
207
228
A B C D E F G
1 2 3 4 5 6 7 8 9 10
549
50
51
70
69
68
67
66
65
SWANLEY
White Oak
Hockenden
Kevingtown
Crockenhill
Wested
BR8
MAIDSTONE ROAD
Old Maidstone Road
B2173
A20(T)
Upper Hockenden
Cookham Road
Golf Club
Golf Course
Birchwood Road
Works
Leydenhatch Lane
New Barn Road
Hextable Comprehensive School
Egerton Avenue
Birchwood County Primary School
LONDON ROAD
Alder Way
Northview
The Birches
Kettlewell Court
Haven Close
White Oak Primary School
St Bartholomews Hospital
SWANLEY LANE
Chapman's Lane
Hockenden Lane
Kent County
Bromley
Dale Road
Sermon Drive
Farm Avenue
Laburnum Av
Lynden Way
Hilda May Avenue
Sycamore Drive
Police Station
Swanley School
BARTHOLOMEW WAY
Superstore
Council Building
St Marys CE Primary School
HIGH ST
Park Road Industrial Estate
Star Lane
Bourne Wood
Sheepcote Lane
Swanley Station
Station Approach
GOLDSEL ROAD
Azalea Drive
Ladds Way
Phillip Avenue
Cranleigh Drive
High Firs Primary School
Pinks Hill
Glendale
Sheepcote Farm
Furness Swanley FC
Cross Road
Green Ct Road
Stones Cross
Shawcroft School
ROAD
B258
Crouch Farm
Crockenhill Primary School
GREEN COURT ROAD
Seven Acres
Cemetery
Eynsford Road
Gosenhill Farm
Petham Court
Bransell Close
CRAY ROAD B258
MAIN RD
Tylers Green Road
Old Chapel Road
Tudor Court
Church Road
Newports
Darns Hill
Harvest Way
Woodmount
Waldens
East Hall Road
Lane
Highcroft
Lone Barn
Daltons Road
Gorse Road
Crown Wood
Skeet Hill Lane
Skibbs Lane
Bromley
Kent County
Parkgate Road
Park Gate House
Hill
Lullingstone
1 grid square represents 500 metres

Swanley 209
187
229
210
H
J
K
L
M
N
P
53
54
55
1
2
3
4
5
6
7
8
9
10
70
69
68
67
66
65
Swanley Village
Farningham
EYNSFORD
Hulberry
DA4
Sutton at Hone
St Pauls CE Primary School
Hotham Close
Highlands Farm
Highlands
Anthonys Lane
Hill
Swanley
Village
Road
School Lane
Gildenhill Road
Church Road
Ship Lane
Wood Street
Park Lane
Dartford FC
Russell Place
Barfield
Balmoral Rd
Gravel Rd
Works
Long
Mead
Devon
Cedar Drive
Darent
Farningham Road Station
Homefield Farm
M25
Downsview Infant School
Parkwood Hall School
Beechenlea Lane
Manse Way
Mountain Hill
Abbots Close
LONDON ROAD
Mark Way
Moreton Industrial Estate
Button Street
Farningham Woods (Nature Reserve)
Calfstock Lane
Darent Valley Path
DARTFORD ROAD A225
Franks Lane
Valley Path
Pedham Place Industrial Estate
Teardrop Industrial Park
Junction 3/1
Hill Farm
Farningham Hill Rd
The Folly
Old Dartford Road
LONDON ROAD A20
MAIN ROAD
M20
Dartford Road
Wested Lane
High Street
Horton Way
Works
The Mill House
River Darent
Sparepenny Lane
Crockenhill Lane
Oliver Crescent
South Hall Cl
Hillside
White Post Hill
Surgery
Tilmans Mead
Alban Crescent
Beesfield Lane
EYNSFORD ROAD
A225
MAIN
Beesfield Farm
Old Mill Close
Mill Lane
Priory Lane
Priory Fields
Anthony Roper Primary School
Eynsford Castle
Eynsford Cricket Club
HIGH STREET
Tower Croft
Donkey Lane
Maplescombe Lane
Darent Valley Path
Riverside
Home Farm
Lullingstone Lane
STATION ROAD
Saddler's Park
Pollyhaugh
Bower Lane
Pollyhaugh Farm
St. Martins Drive
Birch Close
Lullingstone Roman Villa
Lullingstone Park Farm
Rise
Eynsford Station
PO
PH

210
Sutton at Hone
188
209
South Darenth
Horton Kirby
Grubb Street
Speed Gate
Farningham Station
Holmesdale Hill
Gill's Road
Gill's Farm
Shrubbery Road
East Hill
New Road
Station Road
Skinney Lane
Wilson Lane
Rabbits Farm
Rabbits Road
Gorringe Avenue
Horton Road
Horton Kirby CE Primary School
Stack Road
The Street
Rays Hill
Reynolds Place
Franks Lane
Mussenden Farm
Mussenden Lane
School Lane
Canada Farm Road
Beeches Farm
Eglantine Lane
Eglantine Farm
DARTFORD ROAD
A225
M20
Charton
Horton Wood
Three Gates Road
Grove Farm
Fawkham CE Primary School
Valley Road
MAIN ROAD
GORSE HILL
Beesfield Lane
Beesfield Farm
Donkey Lane
Maplescombe Lane
Gabrielspring Rd
Gabriel Spring Road (East)
Speedgate Hill
Sun Hill
Scratchers Lane
Colin Chapman Way
Brands Hatch Road
Fawkham Road
Rogers Wood Lane
Grandstand
Works
Council Building
Dartford FC
Russell Place
Holmesdale Road
Paddock Close
Montgomery Road
Coopers Close
The Grange
Towers Wood
Horton Kirby Trading Estate
Millstone Mews
Devon Road
Darent Mead
Cedar Drive
Mill Way
Glebe Pl
Forge Lane
Churchill Road
Lombard Street
Rashleigh Way
Saxon Pl
Darent Valley Path
A20
1 grid square represents 500 metres

Westwood
B255
Hook Green Road
WHITEHILL ROAD
189
H
J
K
L
M
N
P
60
61
62
70
69
68
67
66
65
1
2
3
4
5
6
7
8
9
10
MAIN ROAD B260
Works
West Shaw
Northdown Road
Rowans Close
Essex Road
Kent Road
Station Road
Hartley Road
Langafel Close
St Marys Wy
Oakwood Dene Wk
Longfield Station
Cavendish Square
Bramblefield Close
The Crs
Axton Chase School
Longfield
Dartford Hospital School
Langafel CE Primary School
Gorse Wood Road
Hottsfield
Quakers Close
Culcroft
Ash Road
Merton Av
Pitfield
Brambledown
Caxton Cl
Porchester Close
Well Field
Banckside
Larks Field
Gresham Avenue
Downs Valley
Woodland Avenue
Old Downs
Castle Hill
Fawkham Road
Dickens Close
Green Way
Church Road
Johns Cl
Gorse Way
Briars Way
Springcroft
Beechlands Close
Hartley Wood
Stack Lane
School
Hartley
Hartley Green
Broomfields
Culvey Cl
Carmelite Way
Cherry Trees
Hartley Primary School
Round Ash Wy
Oast Way
Conifer Av
The Warrens
St John's Lane
Hill Shaw
Billings
Grange Way
Berrylands
Manor Drive
Manor Lane
Fairby Lane
Corinthian Sports Club
Chantry Avenue
Tates Orchard
Manor Farm
Manor Road
MAIN ROAD B260
Nurstead Farm
Longfield Hill
Ryecroft
New Barn
New Barn Road
Ridgewood
Southfleet Avenue
Hart Shaw
Studley Crescent
Birch Close
Foxwood Way
Yew Tree Cl
Longfield Avenue
Orchard Close
Dene Drive
Nuthatch
Turnstone
Starling Close
Shearwater
Lapwings
Bentley Cl
The Gables
Woodlea
Poplars Close
Deerhurst Cl
Festival Avenue
Kenwood Avenue
Woodland Close
Fawkham Avenue
Pescot Avenue
The Drive
Hill View Road
The Hollies
Weird Wood
Oval
The Laurels
North Riding
Nurstead Avenue
Fairlight Cross
The Yews
Old
Pincroft Wood
Ferndene
Selbourne Close
Middleton Farm
Grange Lane
DA3
Ash Road
Hartley Bottom Road
Manor Lane
Fawkham Manor
Hospital
Milestone School
Caling Croft
Farm Holt
Chapel Wood Road
Chapel Wood
Church Road
Hartley Hill
Penenden
Bazes Shaw
Millfield La
Millfield
Aylands
Lane
Butchers Lane
New Ash Green Primary School
Surgery
Turner's Oak Shaw
New Ash Green
Idleigh Court
Idleigh Court Road
Coltstead
Centre Rd
Over Minnis
Lambardes
North Ash Road
Forstal
Spring Cross
West Yoke
Beechcroft Farm Industrial Estate
Ash Road
Punch Croft
Knights Cft
Redhill Road
Bowes Wd
Redhill Wood
New Street Road
Billet Hill
Ash Road

192
230
A
B
C
D
E
F
G
1
2
3
4
5
6
7
8
9
10
493
94
95
64
63
62
61
60
GU20
GU18
Junction 3
A30 LONDON ROAD
SUNNINGHILL RD
Eri Wood Manor
Snows Paddock
Bosman Dr
Windlesham Court
Snows Ride
Hawkes Leap
Poplar Avenue
SCHOOL ROAD
Inf Sch
Woodcote House School
Hatton Hill
Westwood Road
Hatton Hill
B386
KENNEL LANE
WINDLESHAM
UPDOWN HILL
CHERTSEY ROAD
Kings Lane
Ramsay Rd
Owen Rd
Kent Rd
Caldwell Rd
Oakwood Road
Heathpark Drive
Pine Grove
Edward Rd
Pound Lane
Church Road
Birch Hall
Rectory Lane
Hatch End
Graham Rd
Windmill Field
Thorndown Lane
Broadley Green
Hutton Cl
Orchard Hl
Ashleigh Farm
New
Works
Shepherds Lane
Valley End
Highams Lane
Valley End Road
Valley End CE Infant School
Valley End Cricket Club
Woodlands Lane
Windlesham Park
Windlesham Road
Westcroft Park
Twelve Oaks
M3
Rye Grove
Broadway Road
Industrial Estate
Windlebrook Farm
Hook Mill Lane
Oldhouse Lane
Halebourne House
Halebourne Lane
Halebourne Farm
Burnt Pollard La
A322
Guildford Road
Christie Cl
Lovells Cl
Coniston Ct
Grasmere Road
Ullswater Cl
All Saints Rd
Lightwater Village School
Junior School
The Ridgeway
Macdonald Road
Ridgeway Cl
Junction Road
Ambleside Road
Rydal Pl
Police Station
Birchwood Dr
Riverside Av
Glebe Rd
Marshwood Rd
Blackstroud Lane
Springfield
Heronscourt
Lightwater Meadow
Keswick Dr
Lightwater
Osborne Rd
Briar Av
Burdock Cl
Broom Fld
RED ROAD
LIGHTWATER
B311
Golf Course
Windlemere Golf Club
East
Windlesham
Hookstone Lane
Coldharbour La
A319
Streets Heath
Benner Lane
Fairfield Lane
Church Road
Gordons School
Malthouse Farm
Holy Trinity CE Primary School
New England
Tanglewood Ride
Birch Lane
Broad Street
Orchard Cl
Ashley Way
Cuckoo La
Revesby Cl
Brentmoor Road
Hook Lane
Donkey Town
Birch Platt
Rounce Lane
Priest Lane
Fenns Lane
Rufus Cl
Fuchsia Wy
Camellia Ct
Erica Ct
Acer Dr
Kerria Wy
GUILDFORD ROAD
High St
Meadow Way
Malthouse La
Commonfields
Jenner Drive
Gosden Rd
Sefton Cl
Fellow Green
Willow Gn
Kings Road
Beldam Bridge Road
The Oaks
Scott
Penn
West End
Oldhouse Lane
Westend Common
Lucas Green
Lucas Green Road
Ford Road
Works
Cedar Grove
Church
A322 GUILDFORD ROAD
Cowarth Park Sc
CHERTS
Woodcock
Brook
1 grid square represents 500 metres

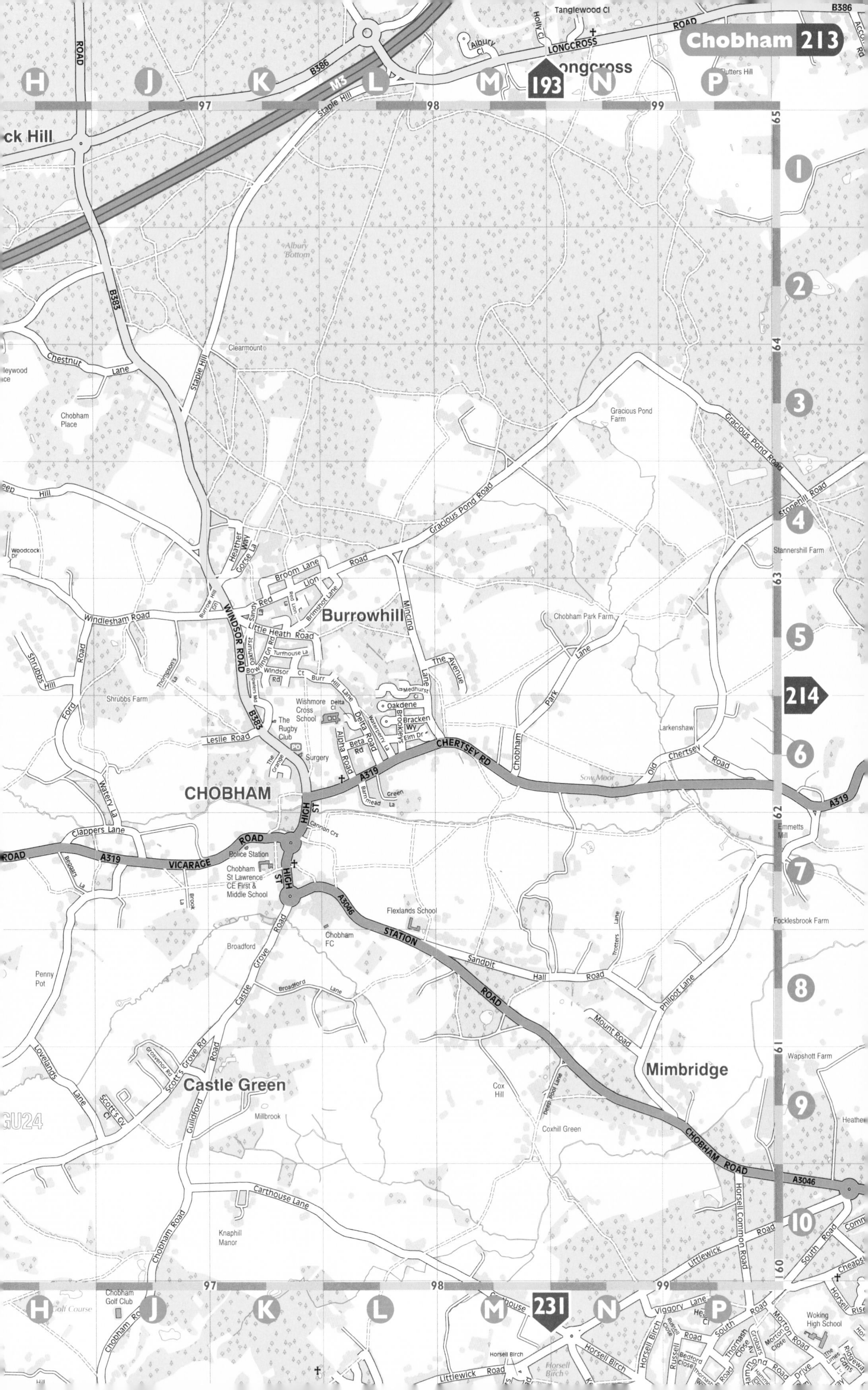
Tanglewood Cl
B386
ROAD
Holly Cl
Albury Cl
LONGCROSS
Longcross
193
Flutters Hill
H
J
K
L
M
N
P
97
98
99
M3
B386
Staple Hill
ck Hill
65
1
2
Albury Bottom
B383
Clearmount
64
Chestnut
Lane
leywood
Chobham Place
3
Gracious Pond Farm
Gracious Pond Road
Stonehill Road
4
Stannershill Farm
Hill
Gracious Pond Road
Woodcock Dr
Heather Way
Gorse La
Broom Lane
Road
Lion
Red Lion
Brimshot Lane
63
Burrowhill
Mincing Lane
Windlesham Road
Burrow Hill Grn
Sandy La
Red
WINDSOR ROAD
Little Heath Road
Chobham Park Farm
Park Lane
5
Shrubbs Hill
Ford Road
Thompson's La
Turfhouse La
Bowling Gn Rd
Windsor Ct
Rd
Burr Hill Lane
The Avenue
Shrubbs Farm
B383
Wishmore Cross School
Delta Cl
Medhurst Cl
Oakdene
Brookleys
Bracken Wy
Elm Dr
214
The Rugby Club
Leslie Road
Alpha Road
Beta Rd
Delta Road
Waterers La
Larkenshaw
Old Chertsey Road
6
CHERTSEY RD
Chobham
Sow Moor
A319
Surgery
The Grange
CHOBHAM
Watery La
Barrmead La
Green
HIGH ST
62
Emmetts Mill
A319
Clappers Lane
Cannon Crs
ROAD
ROAD
A319
VICARAGE
Police Station
Chobham St Lawrence CE First & Middle School
Beggars La
Brook La
HIGH ST
7
A3046
Flexlands School
STATION
Focklesbrook Farm
Broadford
Grove Road
Chobham FC
Trotters Lane
Sandpit
Hall
Road
Philpot Lane
8
Penny Pot
Castle
Broadford Lane
ROAD
Mount Road
Lovelands Lane
Grosvenor Rd
Scott's Grove Rd
Road
61
Wapshott Farm
Mimbridge
Castle Green
Cox Hill
Deep Pool Lane
Scott's Gv Cl
GU24
Millbrook
Guildford
Coxhill Green
9
Heather
CHOBHAM ROAD
A3046
Carthouse Lane
Chobham Road
Horsell Common Road
Road
10
South Road
Knaphill Manor
Littlewick
60
Cheapside
Horsell Rise
Chobham Golf Club
Golf Course
Chobham Rd
97
98
99
Carthouse
231
Viggory Lane
Heath Cl
South
Woking High School
Russell Close
Road
Horsell Birch
Littlewick Road
Horsell Birch
Bedford Close
Morton Close
Morton Road
Grobars
Thomas Close
Hill

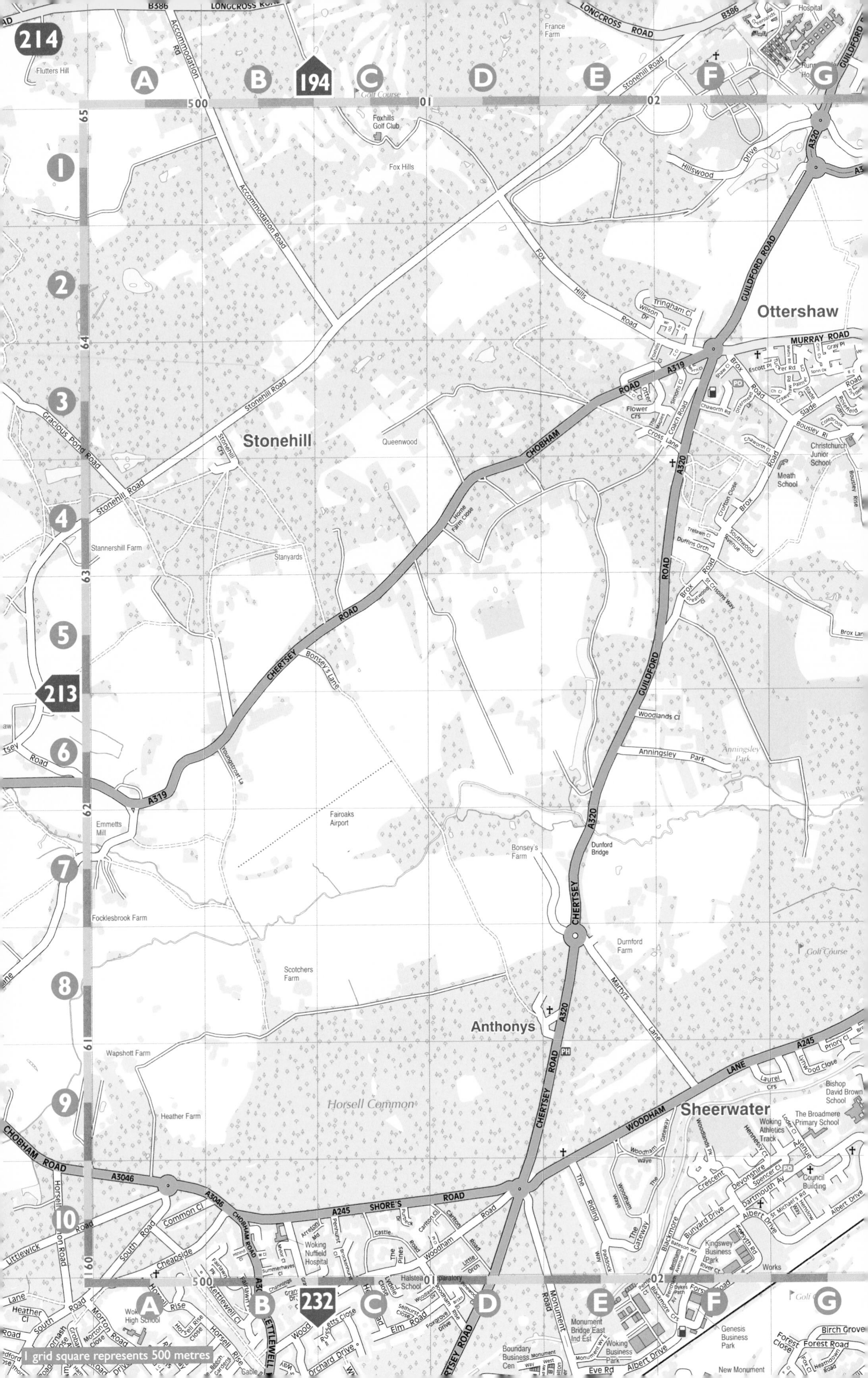
194
213
232
B386
LONGCROSS ROAD
Accommodation Rd
Flutters Hill
France Farm
Hospital
GUILDFORD ROAD
Golf Course
Foxhills Golf Club
Fox Hills
Stonehill Road
Hillswood Drive
A320
Accommodation Road
Fox Hills Road
Tringham Cl
Wilson Dr
Ottershaw
MURRAY ROAD
Gray Pl
Escott Pl
Brox Road
Slade Road
Rosefield Gdns
Bousley Ri
Chaworth Rd
Chaworth Cl
Christchurch Junior School
Meath School
Bousley Rise
Crofton Close
Southwood Avenue
Trelawn Cl
Duffins Orch
St Crispins Way
Brox Lane
Gracious Pond Road
Stonehill Road
Stonehill Crs
Stonehill
Queenwood
CHOBHAM ROAD
A319
Flower Crs
Coach Road
Cross Lane
Home Farm Close
Stannershill Farm
Stanyards
CHERTSEY ROAD
Bonsey's Lane
GUILDFORD ROAD
Woodlands Cl
Anningsley Park
Youngstroat La
Chertsey Road
Emmetts Mill
Fairoaks Airport
Bonsey's Farm
Dunford Bridge
Focklesbrook Farm
Durnford Farm
Golf Course
Scotchers Farm
Martyrs Lane
Anthonys
Wapshott Farm
Laurel Crs
Lynwood Close
Priory Cl
A245
Bishop David Brown School
Horsell Common
Heather Farm
Sheerwater
WOODHAM LANE
Woking Athletics Track
The Broadmere Primary School
CHOBHAM ROAD
A3046
Common Cl
SHORE'S ROAD
Woking Nuffield Hospital
Castle Road
Woodham Road
The Riding
Woodham Waye
The Gateway
Blackmore Crescent
Bunyard Drive
Devonshire Av
Dartmouth Av
Albert Drive
Council Building
Kingswey Business Park
Littlewick Road
South Road
Cheapside
Horsell Rise
Kettlewell Cl
KETTLEWELL
Halstead School
Monument Road
Monument Bridge East Ind Est
Woking Business Park
Genesis Business Park
Albert Drive
Forest Road
Forest Close
Birch Grove
New Monument
Eve Rd
Boundary Business Cen
Works
Elm Road
Orchard Drive
Morton Road
Heather Cl
1 grid square represents 500 metres

ADDLESTONE
Hamm Moor
New Haw
Row Town
Woodham
West Byfleet
BYFLEET
Brooklands
Pyrford
KT15
KT14
M25
A318
A317
A245
B3121
B385
B367
B382
B3121
Junction 11
ST PETER'S WAY
WEYBRIDGE ROAD
STATION ROAD
CHURCH ROAD
HIGH STREET
BRIGHTON ROAD
NEW HAW ROAD
BYFLEET ROAD
OYSTER LANE
PARVIS ROAD
WOODHAM LANE
SHEERWATER ROAD
OLD WOKING ROAD
OAKCROFT ROAD
SOPWITH DRIVE
BARNES WALLIS DR
SPINNEY HILL
Addlestone Station
Byfleet and New Haw Station
West Byfleet Station
Basingstoke Canal
River Wey Navigation
St Georges College
Abbeylands School
St Pauls CE Primary School
Holy Family RC Primary School
Sayes Court Junior School
Darley Dene Infant School
Grange CP School
Fullbrook School
West Byfleet Primary School
Byfleet CP School
St Marys CE Primary School
The Manor School
Camphill Industrial Estate
Brooklands Business Park
Waterside Trading Estate
Weybridge Business Park
Byfleet Industrial Estate
Sprint Industrial Estate
Byfleet Business Centre
Great Grove Farm
Rodwell Farm
Moated Farm Dr
West Byfleet Golf Club
Traditions Golf Club
West Hall
Civic Offices
Police Stn
Superstore
Superstores
195
216
233
04
05
06
65
64
63
62
61
60
H
J
K
L
M
N
P
1
2
3
4
5
6
7
8
9
10

216
196
215
234
A
B
C
D
E
F
G
1
2
3
4
5
6
7
8
9
10
507
08
09
65
64
63
62
61
60
WEYBRIDGE
Oatlands Park
Brooklands
St George's Hill
Whiteley Village
KT13
WEYBRIDGE ROAD
A317
BALFOUR RD
CHURCH ST
HIGH STREET
MONUMENT HILL
Monument Rd
OATLANDS DRIVE
A3050
HEATH ROAD
B374
B373
HANGER HILL
QUEENS ROAD
B372
ST GEORGE'S AV
SEVEN HILLS ROAD
B365
CAENSWOOD HILL
BROOKLANDS ROAD
PARVIS ROAD
A245
BYFLEET ROAD
PORTSMOUTH ROAD
A3(T)
FOXOAK HILL
SOPWITH DRIVE
Weybridge Station
Weybridge Hospital & Primary Care Centre
Elmbridge Museum
Heathside School
Brooklands College
Brooklands Museum
St Georges Business Park
Waterside Trading Estate
Cemetery
Manby Lodge Infant School
St James CE Primary School
Oatlands School
Walton Leigh School
Cleves Junior School
Burwood Park School & College
Notre Dame Preparatory School
Convent of Notre Dame
St George's Hill Golf Club
Golf Course
Cobham Bus Museum
Silver Mere
Silvermere Golf Club
Feltonfleet School
Foxwarren Park
Manor House
Painshill Landscape Garden
Pains Hill
St Marys CE Primary School
The Manor School
Hamm Court
Broad Water
River Wey
Service Centre
Connaught Drive
Wellington Way
Brooklands Lane
Egerton Road
Cavendish Road
Granville Road
Old Avenue
Golf Club Road
Camp End Road
Burwood Road
North Avenue
West Avenue
Octagon Rd
Circle Rd
Mill Lane
Redhill Road
Seven Hills Road (South)
Wisley
1 grid square represents 500 metres

Weybridge 217
197
218
235
Ashley Park
Hersham Station
Walton-on-Thames Station
KT12
Burwood Park
Hersham
West End
Claremont Park
Fairmile
Little Heath
OBHAM
Stoke D' Abernon
QUEENS ROAD
A317
QUEENSWAY N
A244 QUEENSWAY S
A244 ESHER ROAD
ROBINSWAY
A244
PORTSMOUTH ROAD
A307
STONY HILL
A3(T)
LAMMAS LANE
BETWEEN STREETS A245
HIGH ST
MILL RD
RIVER HL
A245
TARTAR HILL
Rydens School
Bell Farm Junior School
Cardinal Newman RC School
Electrical Trades Union College
Riverdene Industrial Est
Burhill Infant School
Police Station
Surgery
Works
Larkhall Close
Burvale Cemetery
Burvale Farm
Burhill Golf Club
Burhill
Golf Course
South Lodge Road
Burhill Road
Norwood Farm
Elveden Road
Norwood Farm Lane
Heywood
The American Community School
River Mole
West End Common
Sports Club
Claremont Fan Court School
Claremont Landscape Garden (NT)
Esher Common
Black Pond
Blackhills
Albany Cl
Meadway
Moore Place Golf Club
Fairmile Common
Waterford Cl
Hotel
Rugby Club
Queensgate
Reeds School
St Andrews Primary School
The Cobham Health Centre
Painshill Landscape Garden
Cobham Court
Turners Lane
Winterdown
Hawkshill Way
The Mount
Sandy Lane
Fairmile Lane
Oxshott Rise
Eaton Park Road
Littleheath
Woodside Rd
Roundhill Way
Spinney Cl
Brackenhill
The Ridings
Portsmouth Road
Denby Road
Icklingham Road
Leigh Hill Road
Freelands Road
Anvil Lane
Church Street
Towngate
Oxshott Way
Onslow Road
Eastwick Road
Kenwood Drive
Westcar Lane
Burwood Road
West End Lane
Esher Green
Wolsey Rd
Clive Rd
Hunting Cl
Drake's
Riverside Dr
Pelhams Walk
Molesey Road
Claremont Av
Thrupps Lane
Havers Av
Old Esher Rd
Brittain Rd
Ramornie Cl
Meadow Cl
Challey Place
Southdown Road
Celandine Rd
Rydens Gv
Albany Road
Hersham Rd
Thistlecroft Rd
Queensway
Cowley Crs
Beech Cl
Garrick Cl
West Grove
Clarence Cl
Charlton Av
Woodside Av
Burwood Park Road
Mayfield Gdns
Fisher Cl
Station Road
Adelaide Road
Ashley Park

218
198
217
236
Hinchley Wood
ESHER
Claygate
Oxshott
Claremont Park
KT10
KINGSTON BY-PASS
PORTSMOUTH ROAD
LAMMAS LANE
CLAREMONT LANE
COPSEM LANE
WARREN LANE
HIGH ST
LEATHERHEAD RD
FAIROAK LANE
A3(T)
A244
A307
A309
A243
B280
Thames Ditton & Esher Golf Club
Moore Place Golf Club
Surbiton Golf Club
Littleworth Common
Arbrook Common
Oxshott Heath
Prince's Coverts
Stoke Wood
Claygate Station
Oxshott Station
Hinchley Wood Stn
Esher Church School
Milbourne Lodge School
Claygate Primary School
Claremont Fan Court School
Reeds School
Bevendean Pre-Preparatory School
The Royal Kent CE Primary School
Danes Hill School
Electrical Trades Union College
Civic Centre
Loseberry Farm
Arbrook Farm
Sports Club
Surrey County
Kingston upon Thames
Claremont Landscape Garden (NT)
A B C D E F G
1 2 3 4 5 6 7 8 9 10
1 grid square represents 500 metres

H
J
K
L
M
N
P
18
19
20
199
220
237
1
2
3
4
5
6
7
8
9
10
65
64
63
62
61
60
HOOK UNDERPASS (KINGSTON BY-PASS)
A3(T)
KINGSTON BY-PASS
Hook
Chessington
KT9
KT19
EPSOM
The Wells
LEATHERHEAD ROAD
A243
HOOK ROAD
RUSHETT LANE
B280
CHRIST CHURCH ROAD
CHRIST CHURCH RD
CHESSINGTON ROAD
RUXLEY LANE
B284
DORKING RD A24
B2200
Moor Lane
Bridge Road
Cox Lane
Horton Lane
Long Grove Road
Chalky Lane
Green Lane
Thames Down Link
Kingston upon Thames
Surrey County
Chessington World of Adventures
Chessington Golf Club
Chessington Cricket Club
Barwell Business Park
Chessington North Stn
Chessington South Stn
Horton Country Park
Horton Park Farm
Park Farm
West Park Farm
West Park Hospital
Horton Hospital
St Ebba's Hospital
Horton Park Golf & Country Club
Epsom & Ewell High School
Danetree School
West Ewell Infant School
Moor Lane Junior School
Buckland Infant School
Lovelace Primary School
St Marys CE Primary School
Riverview CE Primary School
Stamford Green County Primary School
Kingswood House Sch
St Josephs Catholic Primary School
Epsom Common
Rushett Farm
Silverglade Business Park
Ebbisham Sports Club
Epsom Sports Club
Epsom Sta
Playhouse Theatre
Ashley Centre
Tolworth Girls School & Centre for Continuing Education
Tolworth Recreation Cen
Hook Rise South Industrial Park
Cemetery
Golf Course

220
200
219
238
A
B
C
D
E
F
G
1
2
3
4
5
6
7
8
9
10
521
22
23
Stoneleigh
West Ewell
Ewell
East Ewell
North Cheam
North Looe
EPSOM
KT19
KT17
Stoneleigh Station
Ewell West Station
Ewell East Station
Epsom Sta
Nonsuch Park
Nonsuch High School for Girls
Sutton
Surrey County
KINGSTON ROAD
EWELL-BY-PASS
CHESSINGTON ROAD
CHEAM ROAD
REIGATE ROAD
LONDON ROAD
EAST STREET
UPPER HIGH ST
ALEXANDRA ROAD
COLLEGE ROAD
WORCESTER PARK ROAD
MALDEN ROAD
HOOK ROAD
A240
A24
A232
A2022
B2200
B284
B290
Ewell Athletics Track
Epsom & Ewell High School
West Ewell Infant School
Riverview CE Primary School
Danetree School
St Ebba's Hospital
Blenheim High School
First Quarter Business Park
Longmead Industrial Est
Nonsuch Industrial Est
Kiln Park Business Centre
Epsom Business Park
Ewell Castle School
Ewell Grove Infant School
Bourne Hall Health Centre
St Clements RC Prim Sch
Surrey Co Council
North East Surrey College of Technology
Wallace Fields Junior School
Wallace Fields Infant School
Epsom College
The Downs Farm
Drift Bridge Farm
Surrey Institute of Art & Design
Playhouse Theatre
Ebbisham Sports Club
Epsom Sports Club
Epsom Ewell & St Helier NHS Trust
St Christophers School
Epsom Bowls
Ashley Centre Sh Precinct
The Old Cottage Hospital
Nonsuch Primary School
Cheam Leisure Cen
Linden Bridge School
Cuddington CP School
Auriol Junior School
Priest Hill
Howell Hill
1 grid square represents 500 metres

Benhilton
Carshalton
Cheam
SUTTON
Belmont
Carshalton Beeches
SM1
SM2
SM3
SM5
H
J
K
L
M
N
P
201
222
239
1
2
3
4
5
6
7
8
9
10
25
26
27
ST DUNSTAN'S HILL
A217
CHEAM ROAD
CARSHALTON ROAD
HIGH STREET
THE BROADWAY
STATION WAY
BELMONT RISE
BRIGHTON ROAD
B2230
B2218
SUTTON LANE
CROYDON LANE
A2022 WINKWORTH ROAD
B278
PARK HILL
THE BEECHES AV
WOODMANSTERNE ROAD
BURDON LANE
SANDY LANE
B283
Cheam Station
West Sutton Station
Sutton Station
Belmont Station
Carshalton Beeches Station
Carshalton Station
Banstead Station
Sutton United FC
Recreation Ground
Sutton General Hospital
Royal Marsden Hospital
Henderson Hosp
Queen Marys Hospital for Children
Sutton High School for Girls
Overton Grange School
The Avenue Primary School
Devonshire Primary School
Barrow Hedges Primary School
Seaton House School
Greenacre School for Girls
Oakland School
Banstead Downs Golf Club
Cuddington Golf Club
Golf Course
Banstead Downs
Oaks Park
Cemetery
Sutton
Surrey County
London Loop
Freedown Lane
The Warren
Banstead

222
202
221
240
A
B
C
D
E
F
G
1
2
3
4
5
6
7
8
9
10
528
29
30
65
64
63
62
61
60
Carshalton
Wallington
Bandonhill
South Beddington
Carshalton on the Hill
Carshalton Beeches
Woodcote Green
Little Woodcote
Woodcote
Clock House
Roundshaw
SM5
SM6
Beddington Park
CROYDON ROAD
A232
A237
A2022
B271
B272
B278
WOODCOTE ROAD
MANOR ROAD
STAFFORD ROAD
PLOUGH LANE
FORESTERS DRIVE
FOXLEY LANE
LITTLE WOODCOTE LANE
WOODMANSTERNE LANE
CARSHALTON ROAD
SMITHAM BOTTOM LANE
SMITHAM DOWNS RD
BRIGHTON ROAD
THE DRIVE
PARK HILL
PARK LANE
BOUNDARY ROAD
STANLEY PARK RD
RUSKIN ROAD
ACRE LANE
HIGH STREET
NORTH STREET
WEST STREET
POUND ST
Carshalton Station
Carshalton Beeches Station
Wallington Station
Reedham Station
Smitham Station
Queen Marys Hospital for Children
Oaks Park
Oaks Sports Centre
Woodcote Park Golf Club
Woodcote High School
Purley Sports Club
1 grid square represents 500 metres

CROYDON
South Croydon
Sanderstead
PURLEY
Purley Downs Golf Club
Croham Hurst Golf Club
Riddlesdown High School
Whitgift School
South Croydon Station
Sanderstead Station
Purley Oaks Stn
Purley Station
Riddlesdown Station
Kenley Stn
DUPPAS HILL ROAD A232
THE CROYDON FLYOVER A232
COOMBE ROAD
A212
PURLEY WAY A23
BRIGHTON ROAD
A235 BRIGHTON ROAD
SANDERSTEAD ROAD
B269 SANDERSTEAD HILL
UPPER SELSDON ROAD
ADDINGTON ROAD
LIMPSFIELD ROAD
RECTORY PARK A2022
A2022 MITCHLEY AVENUE
DOWNS COURT ROAD
GODSTONE ROAD
A22
CR2
CR8
203
224
241
H
J
K
L
M
N
P
32
33
34
65
64
63
62
61
60
1
2
3
4
5
6
7
8
9
10

224
204
223
242
Upper Shirley
Addington
Forestdale
Selsdon
Farleigh
Farleigh Court
CR2
COOMBE LANE
GRAVEL HILL
SELSDON PARK ROAD
KENT GATE WAY
A212
A2022
B275
B269
Shirley Church Road
Oaks Road
Croham Valley Road
Farley Road
Old Farleigh Road
Featherbed Lane
Court Wood Lane
Kingswood Way
Farleigh Court Road
Coloma Convent Girls School
Croydon Health Authority
Royal Russell School
Addington Palace
Addington Palace Golf Club
Gilbert Scott Primary School
Selsdon High School
John Ruskin College
Forestdale Primary School
Selsdon Primary School
Croydon High School
Selsdon Park Hotel Golf Club
Greenvale Primary School
Courtwood Primary School
The Addington Golf Club
Applegarth Primary School
Good Shepherd RC Primary School
Spring Park Primary School
Benson Primary School
Atwood Primary School
Farleigh Court Golf Club
Selsdon Wood
Nature Reserve
Frith Wood
Kings Wood
Croydon
Surrey County
Golf Course
Vanguard Way
London Loop
1 grid square represents 500 metres

205
Coney Hall
Keston
Nash
New Addington
Leaves Green
Fickleshole
226
243
A232
A2022
ADDINGTON ROAD
A233
B265
Layhams Road
North Pole Lane
Nash Lane
Jackass Lane
Fox Hill
Heathfield Road
Leaves Green Road
Main Road
Sheepbarn Lane
Jewels Hill
Saltbox Hill
Featherbed Lane
Blackman's Lane
Skid Hill
King Henry's Drive
Vulcan Way
Vulcan Business Cen
Addington Business Centre
Layhams Farm
Rouse Farm
High House Farm
Baston Manor
Keston Court
Heathfield College
Keston CE Primary School
St John Rigby Catholic College
Old Beckenhamian RFC
Wickham Theatre
New Addington Swimming Pools
Biggin Hill Airport
Bromley
Croydon
Skid Hill Farm
Biggin Hill Business Park
Concorde Business Park
Surex Swimming Pools

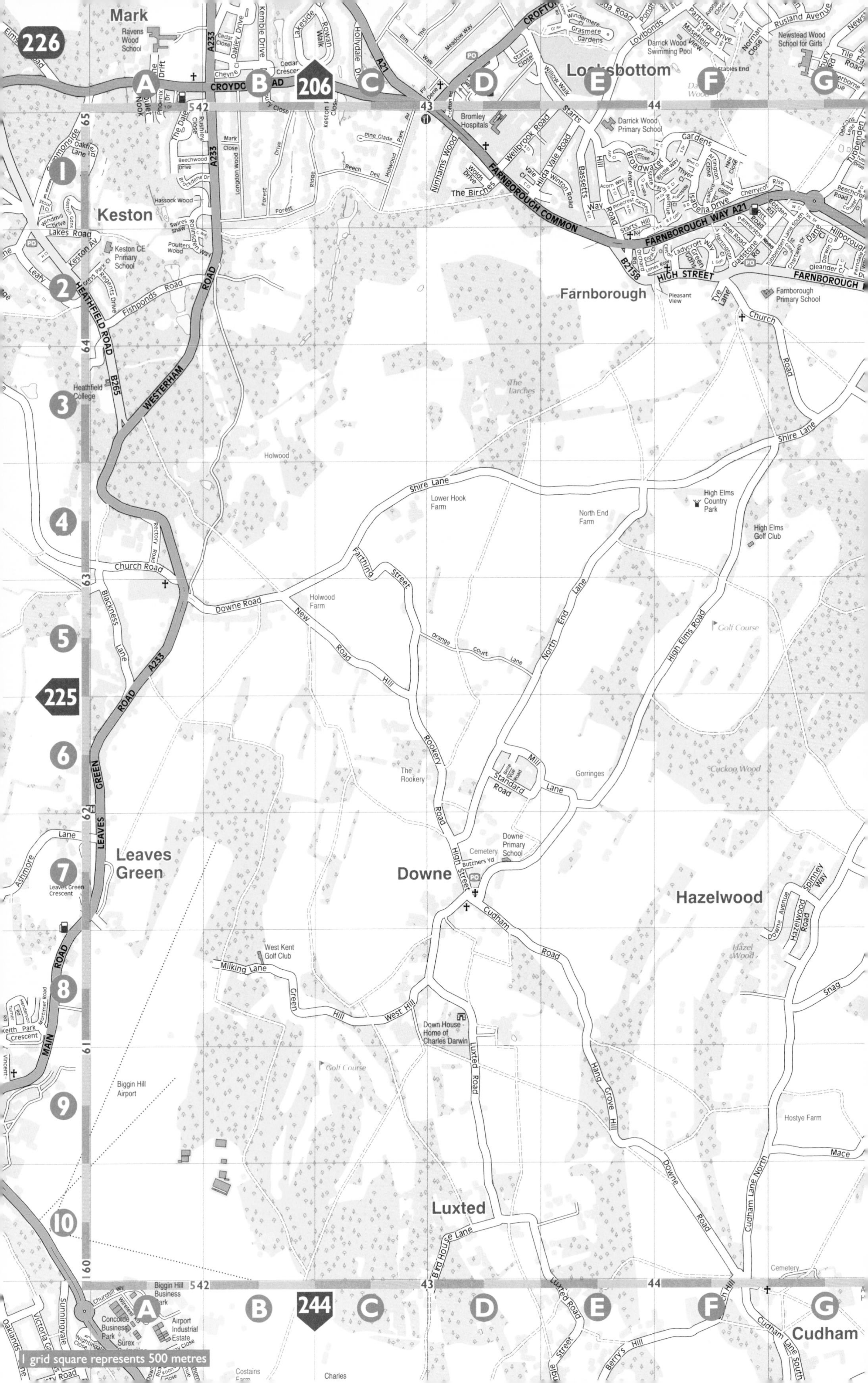
226
206
225
244
Mark
Ravens Wood School
Keston
Keston CE Primary School
Heathfield College
Locksbottom
Darrick Wood Swimming Pool
Newstead Wood School for Girls
Bromley Hospitals
Darrick Wood Primary School
Farnborough
Farnborough Primary School
FARNBOROUGH COMMON
FARNBOROUGH WAY A21
HIGH STREET
CROYDON ROAD
WESTERHAM ROAD
HEATHFIELD ROAD
B265
A233
A21
B2158
Holwood
Holwood Farm
Lower Hook Farm
North End Farm
High Elms Country Park
High Elms Golf Club
Golf Course
The Larches
Shire Lane
Church Road
Downe Road
New Road Hill
Farthing Street
Orange Court Lane
North End Lane
High Elms Road
Rookery Road
The Rookery
Standard Road
Mill Lane
Gorringes
Cuckoo Wood
Downe
Downe Primary School
Cemetery
Butchers Yd
High Street
Cudham Road
Hazelwood
Hazel Wood
Leaves Green
Leaves Green Crescent
LEAVES GREEN ROAD
MAIN ROAD
West Kent Golf Club
Milking Lane
Green Hill
West Hill
Down House - Home of Charles Darwin
Luxted Road
Hang Grove Hill
Downe Road
Biggin Hill Airport
Hostye Farm
Cudham Lane North
Luxted
Bird House Lane
Biggin Hill Business Park
Concorde Business Park
Airport Industrial Estate
Berry's Hill
Cudham
Cudham Lane South
Costains Farm
Charles
1 grid square represents 500 metres

ORPINGTON
Orpington Mental Health Centre
St Olave's & St Saviour's Grammar School
Goddington
207
Bromley Hospitals
Warren Road Primary School
Chelsfield Station
The Highway Primary School
Chelsfield Primary School
Chelsfield Park Hospital
Chelsfield
Maypole
Court Lodge
Chelsfield Lakes Golf Centre
Golf Course
Julian's Brimstone
Green Street Green
Rosenheath Close
Knockholt Station
228
Charmwood Farm
Pratt's Bottom
Stonehouse Farm
Pratts Bottom Primary School
Pratts Grove
Kent County
Bromley
Norsted Manor Farm
Fairtrough Farm
Halstead Place School
Halstead Primary School
Mace Farm
Rushmore Hill
The Washneys
Park Farm
New Years Wood
Curry Farm
Cacket's Farm
Blueberry Farm
Knockholt Pound
245
SEVENOAKS ROAD
HIGH STREET
A21
A223
A224
B2158
(ORPINGTON BY-PASS)
Warren Road
Worlds End Lane
Chelsfield Lane
Church Road
Chelsfield Hill
Stonehouse Lane
Charmwood Lane
Norsted Lane
Hookwood Road
Rushmore Hill
Fairtrough Road
Washneys Road
New Years Lane
Stubbs Hill
Randle's Lane
Deerleap Lane
Knockholt Road
The Chase
Homestead Road
Oxenden Wood Road
The Meadows
Bucks Cross Road
Cudham Lane North
BR6
H J K L M N P
46 47 48
65 64 63 62 61 60
1 2 3 4 5 6 7 8 9 10

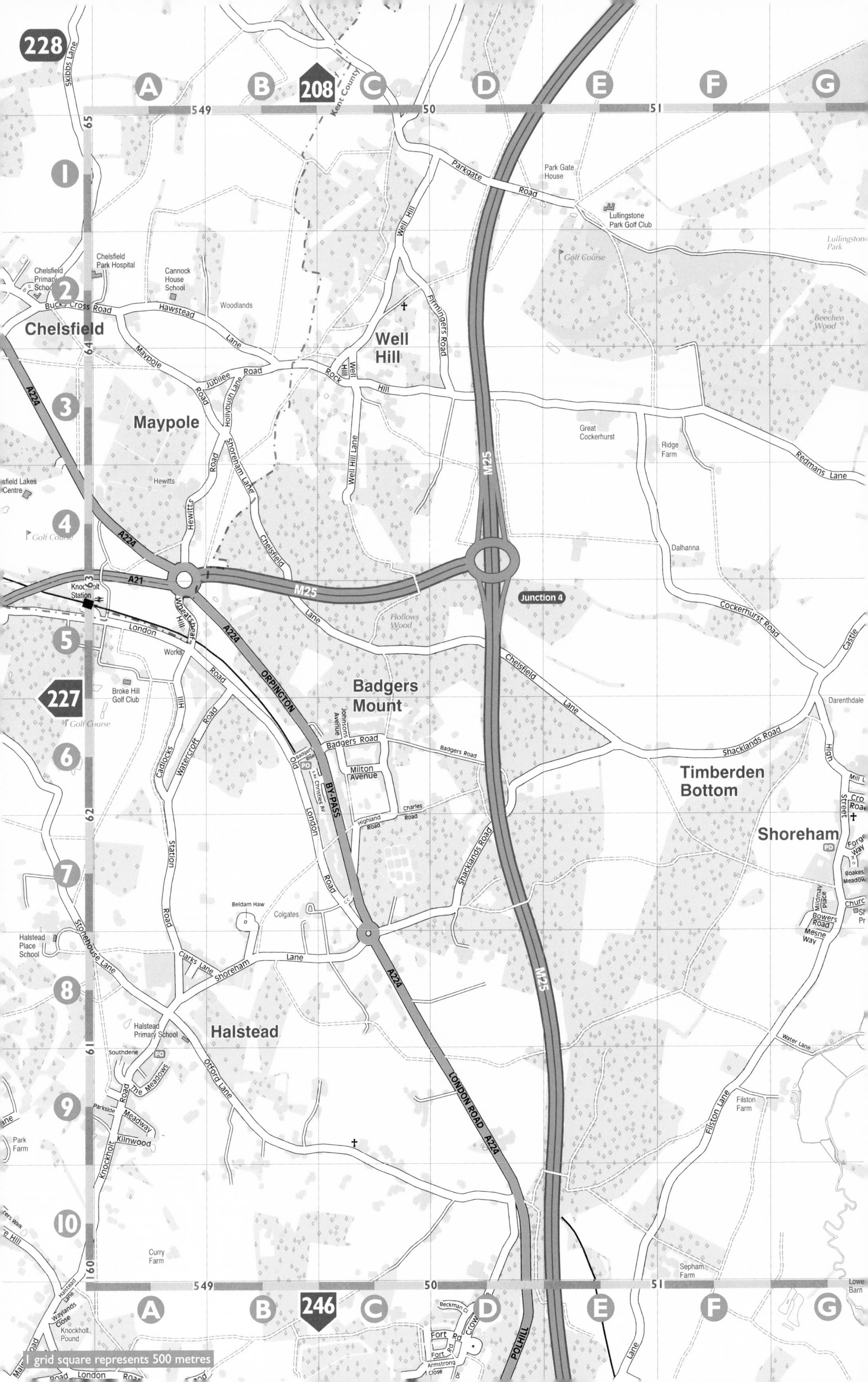
208
Kent County
A
B
C
D
E
F
G
549
50
51
65
64
63
62
61
60
1
2
3
4
5
6
7
8
9
10
Skibbs Lane
Parkgate
Road
Park Gate House
Lullingstone Park Golf Club
Lullingstone Park
Golf Course
Chelsfield Park Hospital
Chelsfield Primary School
Cannock House School
Woodlands
Bucks Cross Road
Hawstead
Lane
Chelsfield
Maypole
Jubilee
Road
Well Hill
Firmingers Road
Beechen Wood
Rock
Hill
Great Cockerhurst
Ridge Farm
Redmans Lane
Well Hill Lane
Hollybush Lane
Shoreham Lane
Hewitts
Hewitts Road
A224
A21
M25
Golf Course
Knockholt Station
Chelsfield
Lane
Junction 4
Dalhanna
Cockerhurst Road
Hollows Wood
Wheatsheaf Hill
London
Works
Road
227
Broke Hill Golf Club
Golf Course
ORPINGTON
BY-PASS
Badgers Mount
Johnsons Avenue
Badgers Road
Badgers Rise
Milton Avenue
Chelsfield
Lane
Castle
Darenthdale
Shacklands Road
Timberden Bottom
Shoreham
Charles Road
Highland Road
Christies Av
London
Road
Old
Cadlocks
Watercroft
Road
Station
Road
Shacklands Road
High
Street
Mill L
Cro Roa
Forge Way
Boakes Meadow
Mildmay Place
Bowers Road
Mesne Way
Church
Beldam Haw
Colgates
Halstead Place School
Stonehouse Lane
Clarks Lane
Shoreham
Lane
Halstead
Halstead Primary School
Southdene
The Meadows
Offord Lane
Water Lane
Filston Farm
Filston Lane
Parkside
Road
Meadway
Kilnwood
Knockholt
LONDON ROAD
A224
Park Farm
Curry Farm
Sepham Farm
Lowe Barn
246
Halstead Lane
Waylands Close
Knockholt Pound
Beckman Cl
Fort Rd
Fort
Crow
Armstrong Close
POLHILL
Lane
London
Road
1 grid square represents 500 metres

209
247
Lullingstone
Lullingstone Roman Villa
Darent Valley
STATION ROAD
A225
Saddler's Park
Pollyhaugh
Bower Lane
Pollyhaugh Farm
Birch Close
Eynsford Rise
Lullingstone Park Farm
Eynsford Station
Lullingstone Castle
Chalkhurst
Upper Austin Lodge Road
Darent Valley Path
Castle Road
Park House
Mapplescombe
Lower Austin Lodge
Bower Park Farm
Castle Farm
The Birches
Hog Wood
Upper Austin Lodge
Austin Lodge Golf Club
Preston Farm
East Hill
Ashen Grove Road
Golf Course
Dunstall Priory
Shoreham Station
Station Road
Darenth Valley Golf Club
Shoreham Place
Romney Street
Dunstall Farm
Magpie Bottom
East Hill Road
Goodbury Road
Eastdown
Fackenden Lane
Highfield
Clarkes Green Road
Birchin Cross Rd
Fernbank Farm
Rowdow La
Greenhill Wood
Greenhill Road
SHOREHAM ROAD
Hillydeal Road
Cross Road
Downs Way
North Downs Way
Lane
Otford Court
Shorehill Lane
Otford

West End
Lucas Green
Bisley
Sheets Heath
Brookwood
Pirbright
Bisley Common
Pirbright Common
Westend Common
Bisley Ranges
Bisley Camp
Cow Moor
Pirbright Camp
Alexander Barracks
Army Training Regiment
Furze Farm
Staffordlake
Miles Green
Goal Farm Golf Club
Golf Course
Stanley Pool
Mazamboni Farm
Pirbright Primary School
Knowl Hill School
Brookwood County Primary School
Brookwood Station
Military Cemetery
Brookwood Cemetery
Brookwood Bridge
Pirbright Lodge
White's Farm
Duchies
Works
Surgery
GUILDFORD ROAD
CONNAUGHT ROAD
BAGSHOT ROAD
DAWNEY HILL
SCHOOL LANE
GRANGE ROAD
GOLE ROAD
STANLEY HILL
Queens Road
Church Lane
Mill Lane
Chapel Lane
Rowe Lane
Cemetery Pales
Ford Road
Priest Lane
Lucas Green Road
Stafford Lake
Ben Well Road
The Ridgeway
Sheets Heath Lane
Brunswick Road
Vapery Lane
Limecroft Road
A322
A324
B3012
B3405
B3032
212
248
1 grid square represents 500 metres

Brookwood 231
213
232
249
H
J
K
L
M
N
P
97
98
99
Knaphill Manor
Carthouse Lane
Chobham Golf Club
Golf Course
Hill Place
Littlewick
Goldsworth Park
Goldsworth Park Trading Est
GU21
Horsell Birch
Littlewick Road
Horsell Birch
Kestrel Way
Viggory Lane
Woking High School
Horsell CE Junior School
Knaphill
Lynbrook
Barr's Lane
Chobham Road
Robin Hood Road
Beaufort Primary School
Goldsworth Park Health Centre
Lockfield Drive
A324
Amstel Way
The Winston Churchill School
St Johns CP School
Inkerman Way
Hermitage Road
Basingstoke Canal
St Hugh of Lincoln RCP School
First School
The Hermitage School
Woking St John's Crematorium
Council Building
St Johns
Hook Heath
Woking Golf Club
Goldsworth CP School
Surrey History Centre
Goldsworth Rd Industrial Est
Barnsbury County School
Mayford
Saunders Lane
Hook Heath Road
Worplesdon Hill
Worplesdon Golf Club
Blackhorse Road
Smart's Heath Road
B380
Berry Lane
Crastock Manor
Industrial Estate
Prey Heath
Prey Heath Road
Burdenshott Road
Worplesdon Station
Bridley Manor
Bagshot Road
A322
A320
Egley Road
Guildford Road
Havering Farm
Fox

214
231
250
Horsell
Woking High School
St Andrews School
Horsell CE Junior School
WOKING
Woking Station
Maybury
Mount Hermon
Kingfield
Old Woking
Westfield
Mayford
Cartbridge
Send
Pyle Hill
Sutton Green
GU22
Hoebridge Golf Centre
Roundbridge Farm
Sutton Green Golf Club
White House Farm
Lower Westfield Farm
Send Cricket Club
Winds Ridge Cemetery
Sendholme
Golf Course
River Wey
Genesis Business Park
New Monument School
Monument Bridge East Ind Est
Woking Business Park
Boundary Business Cen
Victoria Clinic
Maybury Infant School
Civic Offices
Council Building
Rhoda McGaw Theatre & Cin
New Victoria Theatre
Peacock Cinema
The Peacocks Shopping Centre
Wolsey Place Shopping Ctr
Goldsworth Rd Industrial Est
Surrey History Centre
Goldsworth CP School
Woking Community Hosp
Woking Hospice
Woking Leisure Centre
Woking Park
St Dunstans RC Primary Sch
Maybury Business Centre
Prins Willem-Alexander School
Hoe Bridge School
Hoe Bridge Works
St John the Baptist RC School
Woking College
Woking FC
Kingfield School
Barnsbury County School
Westfield Primary School
The St Martha Printing Works
St Bedes CE Junior School
Poundfield Gardens
Shah Jehan Mosque
Lion Retail Park
Halstead Preparatory School
Cable House School
A320
A3046
A245
A324
A247
B380
B382
CHERTSEY ROAD
CHOBHAM ROAD
KETTLEWELL HILL
LOCKFIELD DRIVE
GUILDFORD ROAD
WYCH HILL LANE
KINGFIELD ROAD
HIGH STREET
VICARAGE RD
OLD WOKING ROAD
SEND ROAD
EGLEY ROAD
WESTFIELD ROAD
LOOP ROAD
CLAREMONT AV
SHORE'S ROAD
1 grid square represents 500 metres

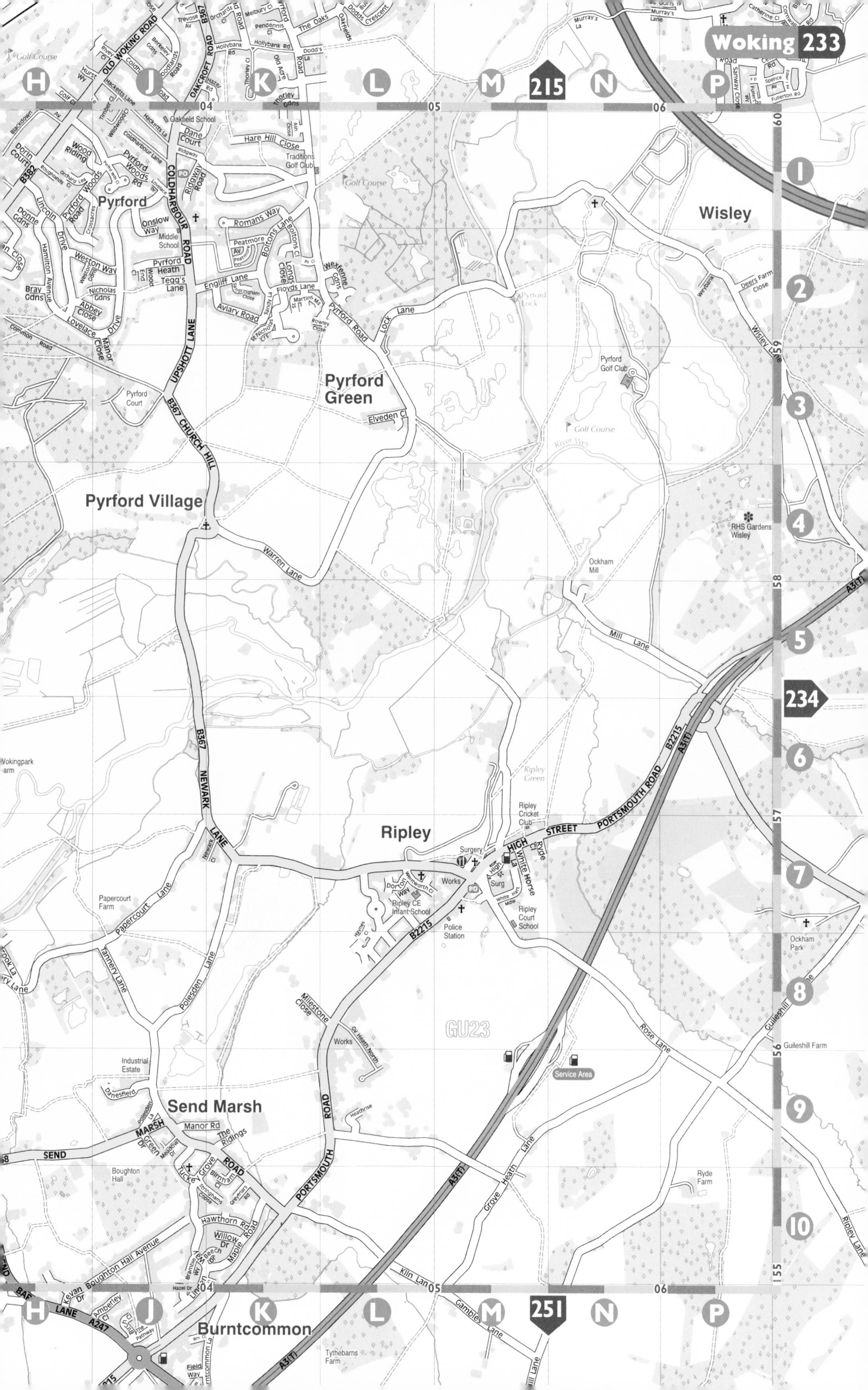

215
234
251
Pyrford
Pyrford Green
Pyrford Village
Wisley
Ripley
Send Marsh
Burntcommon
OLD WOKING ROAD
OAKCROFT ROAD
COLDHARBOUR ROAD
UPSHOTT LANE
B367 CHURCH HILL
B367 NEWARK LANE
Oakfield School
Traditions Golf Club
Golf Course
Pyrford Golf Club
RHS Gardens Wisley
Ockham Mill
Mill Lane
Wisley Lane
Lock Lane
Pyrford Road
Warren Lane
Elveden Cl
Romans Way
Engliff Lane
Aviary Road
Floyds Lane
Lincoln Drive
Hamilton Avenue
Weston Way
Lovelace Drive
Onslow Way
Middle School
Pyrford Heath
Tegg's Lane
Common Road
Pyrford Court
Papercourt Farm
Papercourt Lane
Tannery Lane
Polesden Lane
Industrial Estate
Danesfield
Manor Rd
The Ridings
SEND MARSH ROAD
Boughton Hall
Boughton Hall Avenue
Hawthorn Rd
Maple Road
Kiln Lane
Gambles Lane
Tythebarns Farm
PORTSMOUTH ROAD
B2215
A3(T)
HIGH STREET
Ripley Cricket Club
Ripley Green
Ripley Court School
Ripley CE Infant School
Police Station
Surgery
Works
White Horse La
Rose Lane
Grove Heath Lane
Milestone Close
Service Area
GU23
Ockham Park
Guileshill Farm
Ryde Farm
Ripley Lane
Hare Hill Close
Wokingpark Farm
A247
LANE

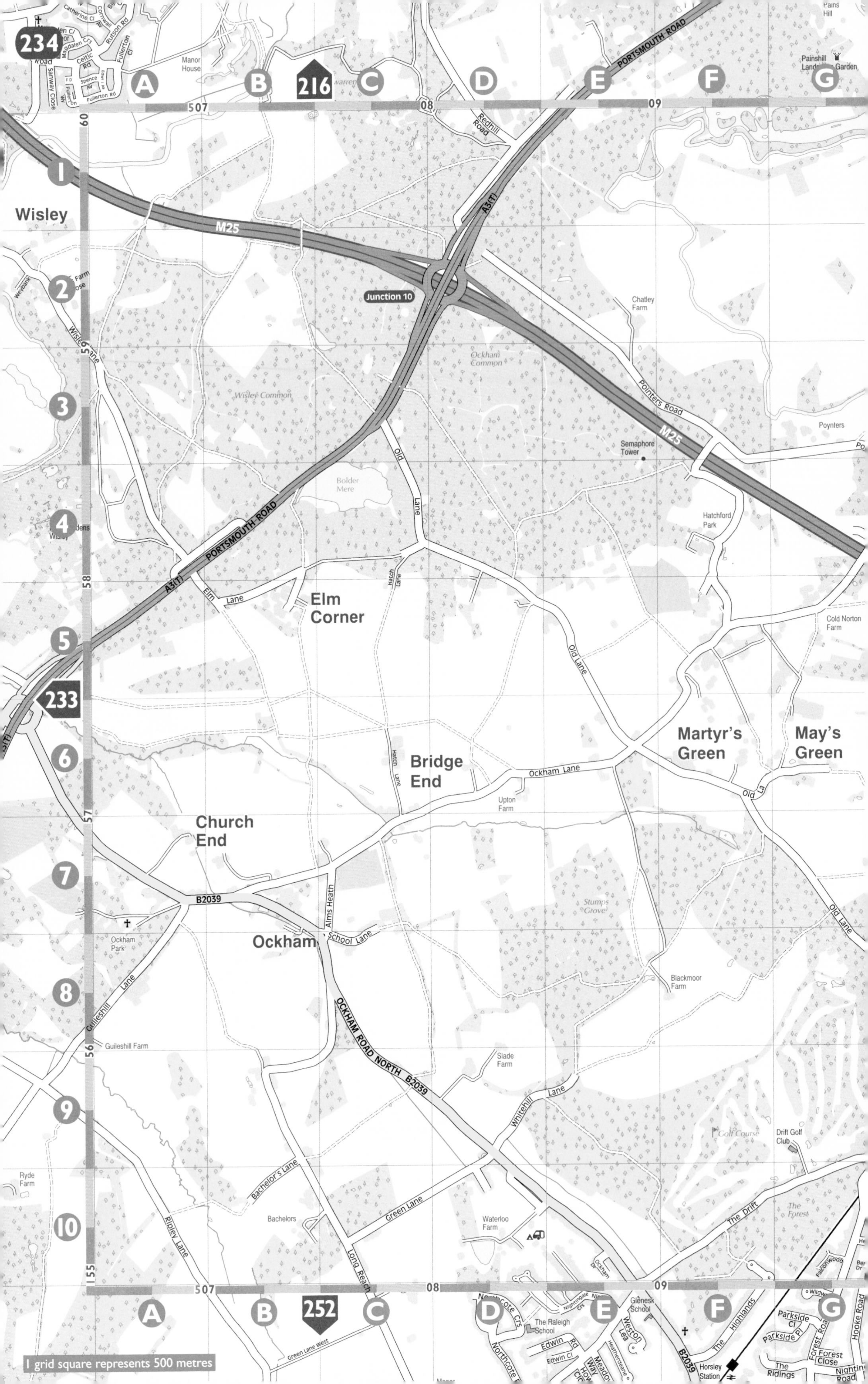
234
216
233
252
Wisley
Manor House
Warren
Pains Hill
Painshill Landscape Garden
PORTSMOUTH ROAD
Redhill Road
M25
A3(T)
Junction 10
Chatley Farm
Ockham Common
Wisley Common
Pointers Road
Poynters
Semaphore Tower
Bolder Mere
Old Lane
Hatchford Park
Elm Lane
Elm Corner
Hatch Lane
Cold Norton Farm
Martyr's Green
May's Green
Bridge End
Ockham Lane
Upton Farm
Old La
Church End
B2039
Ockham
Ockham Park
Alms Heath
School Lane
Stumps Grove
Blackmoor Farm
Guileshill Lane
Guileshill Farm
OCKHAM ROAD NORTH B2039
Slade Farm
Whitehill Lane
Golf Course
Drift Golf Club
The Forest
The Drift
Ryde Farm
Bachelor's Lane
Bachelors
Green Lane
Waterloo Farm
Ripley Lane
Long Reach
Green Lane West
Northcote Crs
The Raleigh School
Edwin Rd
Edwin Cl
Weston Lea
Glenesk School
The Highlands
Horsley Station
Parkside Cl
Parkside Pl
Forest Road
Forest Close
The Ridings
Hooke Road
Nightingale Road
Sanway Close
Fullerton Rd
Celtic Rd
Magdalen Cres
Rutson Rd
507
08
09
60
59
58
57
56
55
A
B
C
D
E
F
G
1
2
3
4
5
6
7
8
9
10
1 grid square represents 500 metres

COBHAM
Stoke D' Abernon
Little Heath
Downside
KT11
Cobham Park
Cobham & Stoke D'Abernon Station
Cemetery
Council Building
Manor House
Parkside School
Cobham Lodge
Downside Farm
St Matthews CE (Aided) Infant School
Yehudi Menuhin School
Bookham Lodge
Sheepbell Farm
Newmarsh Farm
Great Bookham Common
Little Bookham Common
Great Mornshill Wood
Effingham Junction Station
Effingham Common
Norwood Farm
Lower Farm
Effingham Cricket Club
Hotel
Bookham Station
Bookham Industrial Estate
Hinterland House
Thornet Wood
Eastwick Infant School
Surgery
A245
M25
STOKE ROAD
WOODLANDS
BETWEEN STREETS
HIGH ST
MILL RD
RIVER HL
Anvil Lane
Bridge Rd
Church Street
Plough Lane
Chilbrook Road
Downside Road
Cobham Park Road
Downside Common Road
Downside Common Rd
Deacon Close
Middleton Road
Horsley Road
Bookham Road
Cobham Road
Blundel Lane
Lodge Close
Knowle Park
Stoke Close
Evelyn Way
Tilt Road
Winston Drive
Station Rd
Fairmile Lane
Brooklands Cl
Oakshott Way
Avenue Road
Millhedge Close
Farmview
Elm Gv
Woodend Pk
Mizen Way
Bramble Ri
Leigh Hl
Banks Lane
Howard Road
Lower Farm Road
Maddox Pk
Church Road
Commonside
Merrylands Road
Meadow Lane
Sole Farm Road
Westfield Drive
Barclay Close
Langaller Lane
The Glade
Mark Oak Lane
253
236
217
H J K L M N P
1 2 3 4 5 6 7 8 9 10
11 12 13
55 56 57 58 59 60
KT23

236
218
235
254
A
B
C
D
E
F
G
1
2
3
4
5
6
7
8
9
10
514
15
16
60
59
58
57
56
155
Pachesham Park
Leatherhead Golf Club
Golf Course
Junction 9
KINGSTON ROAD
A243
LEATHERHEAD ROAD
A244
OXSHOTT ROAD
OXSHOTT
M25
WOODLANDS LANE
A245
WOODLANDS ROAD
RANDALLS ROAD
Hotel
Woodlands Park
Manor House
Tyrwhitt House
Dorincourt
Oaklawn Road
Pachesham Park Golf Centre
KT22
The Mounts
Superstore
Works
West Hill School
Therfield School
Infant School
Leatherhead Business Park
Crouch Industrial Estate
Council Building
Rydon Business Centre
Theatre Magenta
Plough Industrial Estate
Business Park
Industrial Estate
Leatherhead Station
Ryebrook Business Park
Woodville Junior School
Police Station
Sports Ground
LEATHERHEAD
Cemetery
Randalls Park
Falcon Wood
Kelvin Avenue
River Lane
Cobham Road
Emmerton Road
Mole Road
Monks Gn
Friars Orch
Sports Club
Cannon Way
Cannon Gv
Cannon Side
Raymead Way
Nutcroft Grove
Pound Crescent
Hilley Field Lane
Orchard Cl
The Street
Cobham Road
School Lane
Fetcham Village Infant School
Oakfield Junior School
Lower Road
Fetcham
Hawk's Hill
HAWK'S HILL
GUILDFORD ROAD
B2122
Ridgeway
Leatherhead Cricket Club
Leatherhead FC
Gym Club
Leatherhead Leisure Centre & Water Park
Thorncroft Manor
Fire Station
Leatherhead Industrial Estate
STATION RD
STATION AP
WATERWAY RD
Bridge St
Church St
High St
THE CRESCENT
CHURCH RD
DORKING ROAD
B2450
GIMCRACK HL
Vale Lodge
LERET WAY
The Swan Centre
Leatherhead Institute
Mark Oak Gate
Mark Oak Lane
Langaller Lane
Cobham Road
Sheepbell Farm
Yehudi Menuhin School
Eastwick Junior School
Eastwick Infant School
Surgery
Bocketts Farm Park
YOUNG STREET
A246
GUILDFORD RD
Salvation Place
River Mole
1 grid square represents 500 metres

H
J
K
L
M
N
P
The Wells
219
18
19
20
Epsom Common
The Forest
Ashtead Common
Caen Wood
Wood Field
Ashtead Station
Ashtead
Lower Ashtead
KT21
KT18
Woodcote Stud
Woodcote Park
Ashtead Park
City of London Freemans School
St Giles CE (Aided) Infant School
Greville Primary School
Ashtead Cricket Club
Ashtead Clinic
Infant School
Parsons Mead School
Ashtead Hospital
West Ashtead Primary School
St Peters RC Primary School
St Andrews RC School
Downsend School
Leatherhead Hospital
Woodlands School
St Marys CE Infant School
Chace Stud Farm
Thirty Acre Barn
Highlands Farm
Headley Court
Headley Park
Tyrrells Wood Golf Club
Tyrell's Wood
Golf Course
Fourfield Close
Hurst Farm
Downside Manor
Leatherhead Downs
Givons
Epsom Sports Club
Epsom Ewell & St Helier NHS Trust
Rosebery School
St Josephs Catholic Primary School
Hotel
The Durdans
Woodc
238
La
Va
Works
DORKING ROAD A24
EPSOM ROAD
THE STREET
LEATHERHEAD ROAD
A24
M25
LEATHERHEAD BY-PASS ROAD
REIGATE ROAD B2033
B2122
Thames Down Link
Headley Road
Green Lane
Park Lane
Chalk Pit Road
Walton Road
Hurst Lane
Tilley Lane
Clay Lane
The Drive
Pebble Lane
Downs Road
Wilmerhatch Lane
Farm Lane
Pleasure Pit Road
Rookery Hill
Crampshaw Lane
Grays Lane
Rectory Lane
Ottways Lane
Barnett Wood Lane
Woodfield Lane
Woodfield Rd
Craddocks Avenue
Newton Wood Road
Bramley Way
Overdale
Culverhay
Broadhurst
Woodlands Road
Wells Road
Greenway
The Greenway
Marneys Cl
Woodcote Green Road
Woodcote Side
Woodcote Park Road
Warren Hill
Oldfield Gardens
Harriotts Lane
West Farm Avenue
Taleworth Road
Uplands
Grange Road
Agates Lane
Skinners Lane
Glebe Road
Church Road
Greville Park Avenue
Stag Leys
1
2
3
4
5
6
7
8
9
10
60
59
58
57
56
155
255
MILL WAY

238
220
237
256
A
B
C
D
E
F
G
1
2
3
4
5
6
7
8
9
10
521
22
23
60
59
58
57
56
155
Woodcote
Langley Vale
Burgh Heath
Tadworth
Walton on the Hill
KT18
KT20
Epsom Downs
Walton Downs
Epsom Downs Racecourse
Epsom Downs Station
Tattenham Corner Station
Tadworth Station
Grandstand
Epsom Golf Club
Golf Course
Buckle's Gap
Epsom Cemetery
Great Burgh
Nohome Farm
Hurst Farm
Headley Park
Great Hurst Wood
Drift Bridge Farm
Castle House
Surrey Institute of Art & Design
St Martins CE Junior School
Epsom Sports Club
The Durdans
Council Building
Shawley Primary School
Merland Rise Primary School
Banstead Athletic FC
Banstead Sports Centre
Pitwood Park Industrial Estate
Tadworth Primary School
Chinthurst School
Vale Primary School
Tattenham Health Centre
Junior School
Infant School
Walton on the Hill CE Junior School
Bramley School
Walton Heath Golf Club
KING RD A24
A2022 COLLEGE ROAD
REIGATE ROAD A240
B284 YEW TREE BOTTOM ROAD
TATTENHAM CORNER ROAD
ASHLEY ROAD B290
DOWNS ROAD B289
BURGH HEATH ROAD
LONGDOWN LANE SOUTH B288
FIR TREE ROAD B291
EPSOM LANE NORTH B290
ASHURST ROAD B290
GREAT TATTENHAMS B2221
TADWORTH STREET B2220
B290 NEW ROAD
MERE ROAD
WALTON ST
CHEQUERS LANE
Langley Vale Road
Chalk Lane
Chalk Pit Road
Hurst Road
Hurst Lane
Walton Road
Ebbisham Lane
Motts Hill
Sandlands Road
Beech Lane
Grand Stand Road
M25
1 grid square represents 500 metres

BANSTEAD
Woodmansterne
Kingswood
Mugswell
A2022 WINKWORTH ROAD
B2217 HIGH STREET
B2217 SUTTON LA
BOLTERS LANE
B2219 HOLLY LANE
B2032
OUTWOOD LANE
WATERHOUSE LANE
BONSOR DRIVE
BRIGHTON ROAD
A217
ATTENHAM WAY
Oakland School
Palmersfield Road
Banstead County Primary School
Council Building
Priory School
Junior School
Banstead Clinic
St Annes Catholic Prim Sch
Banstead Village Clinic
Burghwood Clinic
Beacon School
Aberdour School
Rosehill Farm Meadow
Queen Elizabeth Foundation
Banstead Place
Queen Elizabeth Hospital
Banstead Wood
Ruffett Wood
Park Downs
Mint Farm
Woodmansterne Sports Club
Solomons Court
Chipstead Station
Chipstead Golf Club
Chipstead Bottom
Canons Farm
Perrotts Farm
Reads Rest Lane
Kingswood Station
Tudors Business Centre
Kingswood Warren
Kingswood Golf Club
Golf Course
Eyhurst Farm
Eyhurst Court
White Hill
Chipstead Lane
Reeves Rest
Rectory Road
Green Lane
Millfield Lane
Beechen Lane
Park Farm
Monkswell Lane
Pigeonhouse Lane
Southerns Lane
High Road
Markedge Lane
Hotel
Works
Stn Yard
The Longcroft Clinic
Woodmansterne Primary School
SM7
H J K L M N P
221
240
257
25 26 27
60 59 58 57 56 55
1 2 3 4 5 6 7 8 9 10

Clock House
Chipstead
Hooley
Coulsdon
222
258
239
Woodmansterne Primary School
Woodmansterne Sports Club
Woodmansterne Street
Rectory Lane
Manor Hill
B278
Longlands Avenue
Fryston Avenue
Whitethorn Avenue
Redford Av
Beechwood Avenue
Richmond Road
Grove Lane
Lynwood Av
Clifton Road
Bramley Avenue
Woodmansterne Road
Grove Wood Hill
The Chase
Warwick Road
Howard Road
The Avenue
Golf Course
Surgery
The Coulsdon Eye Clinic
Woodcote Gv Road
A237
Brighton Rd
Windermere Rd
Smitham Station
Malcolm Road
The Foot Health Cen
Station Approach
Edward Rd
Coulsdon South Station
Lion Gn Rd
Fourth Drive
Works
Smitham Primary School
Winifred Rd
Nutfield Road
Brigstock Rd
Alexander Road
Melrose Road
St Andrew's Road
Woodmansterne Station
Linden Av
Valley
Sherwood Road
Vincent Road
Coniston
Portnalls Rise
Chipstead Valley Road
B2032
Sandown Road
Lyndhurst Rd
Westleigh Avenue
Chipstead Close
Woodlands Grove
Parkside Gdns
Ridgemount Avenue
Portnalls Close
Portnalls Road
Rickman Hill
Chipstead Valley Primary School
Ravensbourne Trust
Hollymead Road
Bouverie Road
Lissoms Road
How Lane
Highwold
Chipstead Station
Chipstead Golf Club
Outwood Lane
Lackford Road
Station Ap
Stagbury Avenue
Court Hill
Lower Park Road
Chipstead Way
Pines Walk
Upper Pines
Manor Way
Hemsyhaw Av
Prestbury Cres
Lakers Rise
The Readens
Old Oak Av
Bourke Hill
Walpole Avenue
Hazel Way
Hazelwood Lane
Bridge Way
Yew Tree Close
Coulsdon Lane
Starrock Lane
Starrock Road
Shenfield Close
Woodfield Hill
Woodfield Close
Croydon
Surrey County
Starrock Wood
Tara Pk
Doghurst Lane
Vincents Close
High Road
Chipstead RFC
Castle Road
Elmore Road
Star Lane
Hogscross Lane
Church Lane
Broad Walk
Garden Wk
Noke Farm
Maple Way
Clover Hill
Church Lane Avenue
St Margaret's Rd
Forge Br La
Brighton Road
A23
Pretty Lane
London Rd North
Netherne Lane
Netherne La
Park Lane
Stoney Crft
Woodplace Lane
Woodplace Farm
CR5
The Netherlands
Winelmina Avenue
Woodplace Cl
Chartons Gardens
Downs Road
Westwood Rd
Fairdene
Reddown Road
Moorsom Wy
Dunstan Road
Ditches Lane
London Loop
Chaldon Way
Marlpit La
Marlpit Lane
B276
Marlpit Av
Coulsdon Rise
Redlands
Ullswater Crs
Ullswater Trading Estate
Industrial Estate
The Ullswater Business Park
Breakfield
Deepfield Way
Byron Avenue
Petersfield Crs
Hillars Heath Rd
Woodhatch Spinney
Rutherwick Rise
Birchfield Cl
Southlands
Byron Primary School
St David's
Stoneyfield Road
Bradmore Way
Mead Way
Coulsdon C.E. Primary School
Coulsdon Court Road
Coulsdon Road
B2030
Cearn Way
Hartley Down
Hartley Farm
Hartley Old Rd
Stoats Nest Rd
Drive
Tollers Farm
Ellis
The Gullet
Court Farm
Dean Farm
Dean Lane
Alderstead Heath
Alderstead Lane
Alderstead Farm
Glebe Road
London Road
Junction 7
Harps Oak
Oak Lane
Markedge Lane
Park Farm
Tollsworth Manor
528
29
30
60
59
58
57
56
155
1 grid square represents 500 metres

Kenley
Whyteleafe
Old Coulsdon
Caterham
Chaldon
A22 Godstone Road
B2030
B2031 Chaldon Road
B2208
Banstead Road
Coulsdon Road
Hillbury Road
Croydon Road
Rook Lane
Church Hill
High St
Townend
Kenley Stn
Whyteleafe Station
Whyteleafe South Station
Upper Warlingham Station
Caterham Station
Kenley Common
Coulsdon Common
Happy Valley Golf Club
Fryern Farm
Rook Farm
Six Brothers Field
East Surrey Museum
The Theatre on the Hill
Caterham Dene Hospital
De Stafford College
Coulsdon High School
Keston Infant School
Keston Junior School
Wattenden Primary School
Kenley Primary School
Whyteleafe Primary School
Hillcroft Primary School
Clifton Hill School
Audley Primary School
St Francis RC School
Sunnydown School
Marden Lodge Primary School
Warlingham School
St Peter & St Paul CE Primary School
Riddlesdown High Sch
Roke Primary School
Steyning Cl Primary School
London Loop
Tilling down Hill
223
242
259
H J K L M N P
32 33 34
55 56 57 58 59 60
1 2 3 4 5 6 7 8 9 10

242
224
241
260
A
B
C
D
E
F
G
1
2
3
4
5
6
7
8
9
10
535
36
37
60
59
58
57
56
55
Farleigh
Farleigh Court Road
Farleigh Court
Hamsey Green
Warlingham
Chelsham
Woldingham Garden Village
Woldingham
Primary School
Orchard Rd
Woodview Cl
Ellesmere Dr
Claremont Cl
Harewood Gdns
Asndown Gdns
Harewood Gdns
Kingswood Av
Hilton Way
Clyde Av
Princes Av
Wentworth Way
Hamsey Wy
Audley Dr
Kingswood Lane
London Loop
Kingswood Lodge
Tithepit Shaw La
Warlingham School
Hamsey Green Junior School
Martin Cl
Meadway
Trenham Drive
Verdayne Gdns
Hamsey Gn Gdns
Hamsey Green Infant School
Tithepit Shaw Lane
Batts Farm
LIMPSFIELD ROAD
B269
Crewe's Avenue
Crewe's Lane
Crewes House
Ward La
Church Road
Church La
Churchill Cl
Dane Rd
Warlingham Sports Club
Warlingham County Junior School
Old Farleigh Road
Farleigh Road
Farleigh Rovers FC
Harrow Gdns
Harrow Road
Daniels Lane
Parsonage Close
Cemetery
Warlingham Park Hospital
Warlingham Park School
Holt Wood
Vanguard Way
Chelsham Common Road
Chelsham Road
Greenhill Lane
Alexandra Rd
Sunny Bank
Farleigh Rd
Cranmer Gdns
Cranmer Cl
Glebe Rd
Elm Rd
Mint Walk
The Mdw
Boxwood Wy
Eglise Road
Warlingham RFC
B270
HILLBURY ROAD
Court Farm Rd
Oakley Road
Upper Warlingham Station
Westhall Rd
Shelton Avenue
Shelton Cl
WESTHALL RD
Chapel Rd
Warren Pk
Bond Rd
Linden Gv
Marks Rd
Marston Dr
Crowborough Dr
Mayes Cl
Redvers Rd
Leas Rd
Leas La
Birch Way
The Ct
Blanchman's Rd
Gresham Av
Eden Wy
John Fisher Sports Club
B269
Rogers Lane
Chelsham Place Farm
High La
Searchwood Road
Hillbury Close
Hillbury Gdns
Bayards
Hillside Rd
Tree Tops
The Mt
Ridley Road
Lime Gv
Larch Cl
Cedar Cl
Farm Road
LIMPSFIELD ROAD
Ledgers
Paddock Walk
Westhall Road
Homefield Road
Coneybury Cl
West View Road
Narrow La
Westhall Pk
Tydcombe Rd
Tandridge Rd
Tandridge Road
Beechwood Lane
Plantation Lane
Halliloo Farm
Slines Oak Road
Slines Oak
Barnard Road
Broadlands Dr
High Pines
Overhill
Landscape Road
Kooringa
Southview Rd
Succombs Pl
Baggers La
Butterfly Wk
Ashwood
Burnfield Dr
Bug Hill
Golf Course
High Lane
Slines New Road
Butlers Dene Road
Duke's Dene Golf Club
Dukes Hill
Beulah Wk
Beulah Walk
Hilltop Walk
Slines New Road
Bushes Rd
Succomb's Hill
A22
Stuart Road
Woldingham Road
Marden Lodge Primary School
Woldingham Road
Park Ley Road
Camp Rd
Upland Rd
Vanguard Way
Burntwood Lane
Birchwood House
Greenhill Av
Long Hill
Lunghurst Road
Tillingdown Hill
ROAD
Church Road
Station Road
Highfield Rd
Waltham Road
Abbots Wk
A22 CATERHAM-BY-PASS
CROYDON
Beechwood Rd
Park View Road
Long Hill
Woldingham Station
Woodlea Primary School
High Drive
Southdown Road
Station Road
Croft Rd
The Wold
Nethern Ct
Clare Court
Ulstan Cl
Park View
Church Road
Marden Park Farm
The Crs
Commonwealth Road
Mount Pleasant Rd
Road
The Green
Upper Court Road
Slines Oak Rd
Southfields
Crescent Rd
Timber Hl Rd
Tillingdown Farm
Marden Hillboxes Farm
Deerswood Cl
Tillingdown La
Church Road
Surgery
GODSTONE ROAD
Asprey Gv
Colliers
Greenwood Gdns
White Knobs Wy
B2030
Woldingham School
North Downs Golf Club
Northdown Road
Golf Course
Southview
1 grid square represents 500 metres

Fickleshole
225
244
261
BIGGIN HILL
Titsey
Ledgers Farm
Skid Hill Farm
Chelsham Court Farm
Beddlestead Farm
Beech Farm
Cheverells Farm
Norheads Farm
Oakland Primary School
Lusted Hall Farm
Clarks Lane Farm
Pilgrims Farm
Flint House
Titsey Park
Park Farm
Broom Bank
Scotshall Lane
Church Lane
Fairchildes Road
Skid Hill Lane
Hesiers Road
Hesiers Hill
Chelsham Court Road
Chelsham Lane
Beech Farm Road
Beddlestead Lane
Norheads Lane
CROYDON ROAD
B269
B2024
CLARKS LANE
TITSEY HILL
North Downs Way
Vanguard Way
White Lane
Approach Road
Pilgrims Lane
The Ridge
Lusted Hall Lane
Bromley
Surrey County
Oaklands Lane
Victoria Gardens
Sunningvale Avenue
Christy Road
Arthur Road
Kings Road
Beech Road
Highfield Road
Hillingdale
Melody Road
Scarborough Close
Sweveylands Road
Alexandra Road
Shallock Close
Crossways
Westmore Road
Redhouse Road
Ship Field Close
Surgery
MAIN ROAD
A233
Stock Hill
Lillie Road
Ninehams Road
Maesmaur Road
Edgar Road
Church Hill
Biggin Hill Business Park
Concorde Business Park
Swimming Pools
H
J
K
L
M
N
P
39
40
41
1
2
3
4
5
6
7
8
9
10
55
56
57
58
59
60

244
226
243
262
Luxted
Cudham
Berry's Green
Aperfield
South Street
Tatsfield
Hill Park
Biggin Hill Business Park
Concorde Business Park
Airport Industrial Estate
Surex Swimming Pools
Costains Farm
Charles Darwin School
Cudham CE Primary School
Biggin Hill Primary School
Cherry Lodge Golf Club
Golf Course
New Barn Farm
Southwood
Bombers Farm
Cudham Grange
Grays Farm
Hawley's Corner
Bromley
Kent County
Surrey County
Pilgrim House
TN16
Park Wood Golf Club
Betsom's Hill
Tatsfield Primary School
Tatsfield Court Farm
Hill School
Betsoms Farm
Gaysham Farm
Westerham Wood
Pilgrims Farm
Clarks Lane Farm
Court Lodge
Churchill CE Primary School
Clacket Lane Service Area
Police Station
Surgery
Cemetery
A233 MAIN ROAD
A233 WESTERHAM HILL
A233 LONDON ROAD
Jail Lane
Magnolia Drive
Church Road
Stock Hill
Berry's Hill
Berry's Green Road
Cudham Lane South
Newbarn Lane
Luxted Road
Single Street
Buckhurst Road
Grays Road
Silversted Lane
Tatsfield Lane
Rag Hill Road
Ricketts Hill Road
Cudham Road
Manor Road
Chestnut Avenue
Church Hill
Rectory Lane
Clacket Lane
Pilgrims Lane
North Downs Way
The Avenue
Parkwood Road
Palace Road
Paynesfield Road
John's Road
Maesmaur Road
Ninehams Road
Edgar Road
Old Lane
The Grove
Moselle Road
St Winifred's Road
Belvedere Road
Clarence Road
Woodbury Close
Edward Road
Aperfield Road
Nelson Close
Haig Road
Allenby Road
Village Green Avenue
Malan Close
Juniper Close
Old Tye Avenue
Hillcrest Road
Oaklands Lane
Victoria Gardens
Christy Road
Arthur Road
Sunningvale Avenue
Crossways
Westmore Road
Grove Road
Redhouse Road
Whitewood Cottages
Ship Hill
Borough Road
Barnfield Road
Hawthorne Avenue
Crossley Close
Lunar Close
Acer Road
Spruce Road
Kingsmead
Forge Road
Steeple Hts Dr
Lebanon Gdns
Falcons Close
Mount Pleasant
Lillie Road
Valley View
Foley Road
St Mary's Grove
Springholm Close
Sutherland Avenue
Hillside Road
Kemsley Road
Beech Avenue
Hurst Road
Haywood Rise
Force Green
542
43
44
60
59
58
57
56
155
A B C D E F G
1 2 3 4 5 6 7 8 9 10
1 grid square represents 500 metres

227
246
263
Curry Farm
New Years Wood
New Years Lane
Bromley
Kent County
Cacket's Farm
Cacket's Lane
Lett's Green
Shelleys
Shelleys Lane
Burlings
Burlings Lane
Horns Green
Knockholt
Knockholt CE Primary School
Main Road
The Mount
Stonelings Lane
Brasted Lane
Scott's Lodge
Viewlands Avenue
North Downs Way
The Nower
Brasted Hill Farm
Brasted Hill
Shootfield
Sundridge Hill Farm
Sundridge Hill
Sundridge Lane
Blueberry Farm
Blueberry Lane
Single's Cross Lane
Pound Lane
Randle's Lane
Rushmore Hill
Halstead Lane
Waylands Close
Knockholt Pound
Bond Close
Old Harrow Road
London Road
Ivy La
Chevening Lane
North Downs Way
Lord Chatham's Ride
TN14
Chevening Park
Ovenden Road
Combe Bank Farm
Court Lodge Farm
Hogtrough Hill
M25
Brasted Hill Road
Station Road
St Martins Mdw
Thorns Meadow
Coles Lane
Rectory Lane
Church Road
Combe Bank School
Combe Bank Drive
B2211
CHEVENING ROAD
B2211
Force Green
Park Farm
The Mill Works
Works
HIGH STREET
Elliotts Lane
The Carriageway
Brasted
A25 MAIN ROAD
PO
Manor Road
Woodside Road
Chapmans Road
Sundridge
Sundridge and Brasted CE Primary School
St Mary's Church Road
WESTERHAM ROAD
A25
A233
Chart Lane
Church Road
Heverswood
Birchfield Farm
Greystone Park
H
J
K
L
M
N
P
46
47
48
55
56
57
58
59
60
1
2
3
4
5
6
7
8
9
10

228
245
264
A
B
C
D
E
F
G
549
50
51
60
59
58
57
56
155
1
2
3
4
5
6
7
8
9
10
Chevening
Twitton
Dunton Green
Longford
Chipstead
Riverhead
Bessels Green
Sundridge
Dryhill
Sepham Farm
Lower Barn
North Downs Business Park
Star House
Morants Court Farm
Morants Court
Turvins Farm
Chevening Park
Chevening Cross
Chevening Primary School
Willow Farm
Broughton House
Hotel
Dunton Green Station
Dunton Green Primary School
Works
Infant School
Amherst School
Police Station
Salters Heath
Sundridge Place
Sundridge and Brasted CE Primary School
Junction 5
M25
M26
A224
A25
A21(T)
B2211
POLHILL
Harrow Road
London Road
Birchwood Lane
Star Hill Road
North Downs Way
Chevening Road
Main Road
Old
Waylands Close
Halstead Lane
Beckman Cl
Crow Drive
Fort Rd
Armstrong Close
Crow Dr
Lime Pit Lane
Star Hill Rd
SUNDRIDGE RD
MORANTS COURT ROAD
London Road
Filston Lane
Twitton Lane
Ivy House Lane
Pilgrims Way West
Twitton Meadows
Wickham Field
Telston Lane
Knighton Rd
Hale Lane
Dane Road
Willow
Darent Valley Path
SUNDRIDGE ROAD
B2211 OVENDEN ROAD
CHEVENING ROAD
WESTERHAM ROAD
MAIN ROAD
Dryhill Lane
Combe Bank Drive
Chapman
Road
LONDON ROAD
Glyn Davies Cl
Barretts Rd
Lennard Road
Hillfield Road
Station Road
Mill Rd
Milton Rd
Pounsley Road
Darenth La
Ryedale Ct
Chesterfield Drive
Baden Powell Rd
Bullfinch Lane
Orchard Rd
High Street
Chipstead Lane
Chipstead Park Close
Sandilands
Homedean Rd
Westerham Rd
Woodfields
Witches Lane
Barnfield Rd
WORSHIPS HILL
St Mary's Drive
AMHERST HILL
Shoreham Lane
BRADBOURNE
Marlborough Crescent
Lyndhurst Drive
The Close
Brittains Lane
Braeside Cl
Larkfield Rd
Bessels Meadow
Bessels Green Rd
COLD ARBOR RD
BACK LANE
The Square
St Mary's Church Road
Croft Way
Downsview Road
1 grid square represents 500 metres

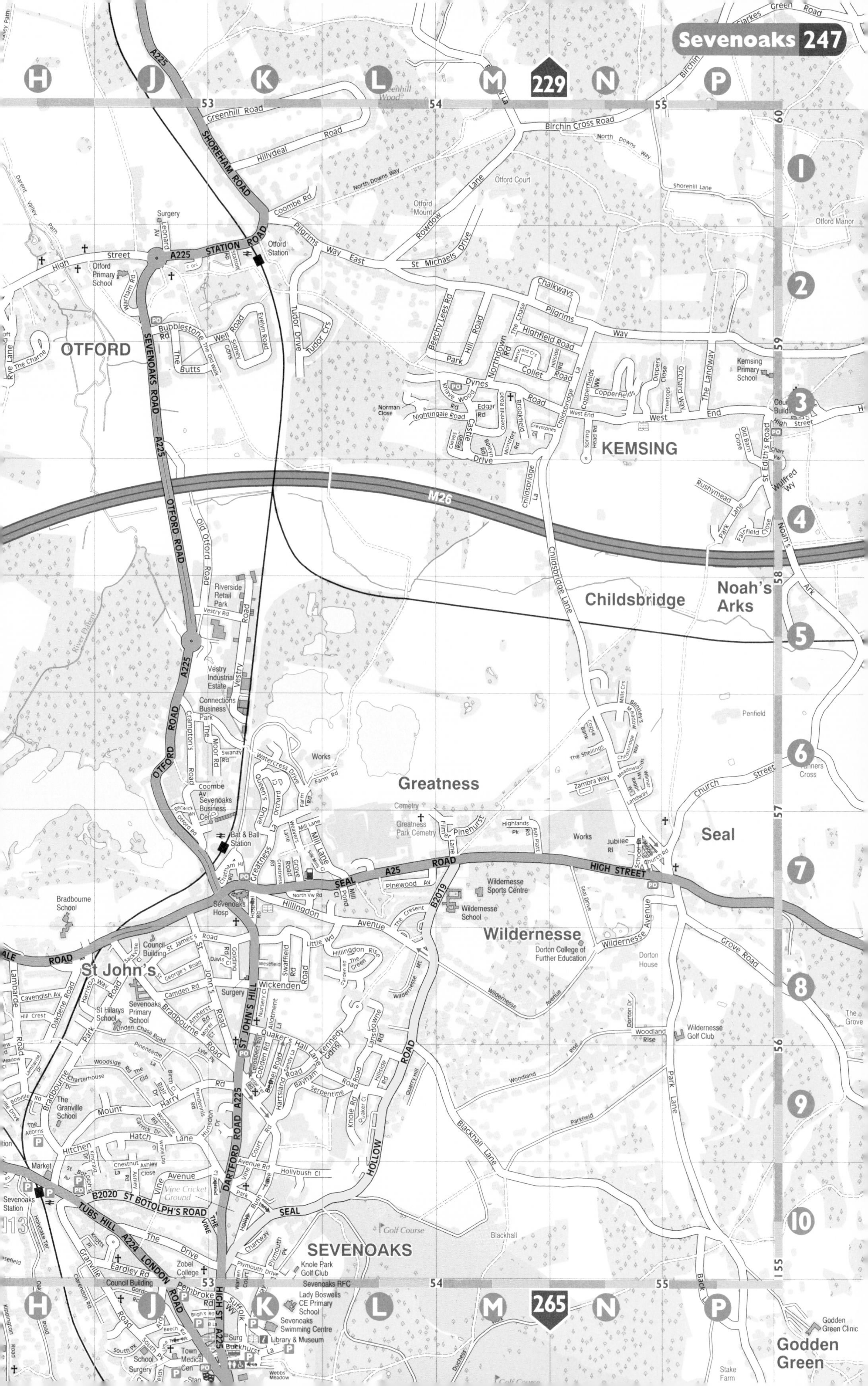

H
J
K
L
M
N
P
229
265
53
54
55
1
2
3
4
5
6
7
8
9
10
OTFORD
KEMSING
Childsbridge
Noah's Arks
Greatness
Seal
Wildernesse
St John's
SEVENOAKS
Godden Green
Shoreham Road
Station Road
Greenhill Road
Hillydeal Road
Coombe Rd
Birchin Cross Road
North Downs Way
Shorehill Lane
Otford Court
Otford Manor
Otford Mount
Rowdow Lane
Pilgrims Way East
St Michaels Drive
Otford Station
Surgery
Leonard Av
High Street
Otford Primary School
Warham Rd
Sevenoaks Road
Bubblestone Rd
The Butts
Well Road
Evelyn Road
Sidney Gdns
Tudor Drive
Tudor Crs
Darent Valley Path
Rye Lane
The Charne
Chalkways
Pilgrims Way
Highfield Road
The Chase
Beechy Lees Rd
Park Hill Road
Northdown Rd
Collet Road
Dynes Road
Knave Wood Rd
Nightingale Road
Norman Close
Edgar Rd
Castle Rd
Cleves Road
Boleyn Rd
Drive
Brookfield
Greystones Cl
Childsbridge La
Copperfields
Dippers Close
Treetops
Orchard Way
The Landway
West End
Spring Head Rd
Kemsing Primary School
Old Barn Close
St Edith's Road
Wulfred Wy
Rushymead
Park Lane
Fairfield Close
Noah's Ark
M26
A225
Otford Road
Old Otford Road
Riverside Retail Park
Vestry Rd
Vestry Road
Vestry Industrial Estate
Connections Business Park
Crampton's Road
The Moor Rd
Swanzy Rd
Coombe Av
Sevenoaks Business Centre
Berwick Wy
Otford Rd
Bat & Ball Station
River Darent
Watercress Drive
Works
Farm Rd
Queen's Drive
Orchard
Mill Lane
Cemetery
Greatness Park Cemetery
Filmer La
Pinehurst
Highlands Pk
Ash Platt
Jubilee Rl
Childsbridge Lane
Mills Crs
Bentley's Meadow
Copse Bank
The Shellings
Zambra Way
Penfield
Church Street
Tanners Cross
Seal Road
A25
High Street
Pinewood Av
Hillingdon Avenue
B2019
Wildernesse Sports Centre
Wildernesse School
Dorton College of Further Education
Dorton House
Wildernesse Avenue
Seal Drive
Grove Road
The Grove
Woodland Rise
Wildernesse Golf Club
Dorton Dr
Bradbourne School
Sevenoaks Hosp
Council Building
St James's Road
Davis
Golding
Westfield
Swaffield Rd
Wickenden Road
Hillingdon Rise
The Green
Lambarde Road
Cavendish Av
Oakdene Road
Harrison Way
Hill Crest
St Hilarys School
Sevenoaks Primary School
Camden Rd
Amherst
Bradbourne Road
Surgery
St John's Hill
Dartford Road
Quaker's Hall Lane
Kennedy Gdns
Lansdowne Rd
Hollow Road
Quarry Hill
Blackhall Lane
Woodland
Parkfield
Park Lane
Blackhall
Golf Course
Knole Park Golf Club
Sevenoaks RFC
Back La
Hollybush Cl
Chartway
Plymouth Drive
B2020 St Botolph's Road
Tubs Hill
A224 London Road
Vine Cricket Ground
The Vine
Sevenoaks Station
Market
Hitchen Hatch Lane
Mount Harry Rd
The Granville School
Chesnut Av
Ashley Close
Avenue
The Drive
Zobel College
Eardley Rd
Pembroke Rd
Council Building
High St A225
Suffolk Wy
Lady Boswells CE Primary School
Sevenoaks Swimming Centre
Library & Museum
Buckhurst La
Town Medical Cen
Surgery
School
Godden Green Clinic
Stake Farm
Duchess

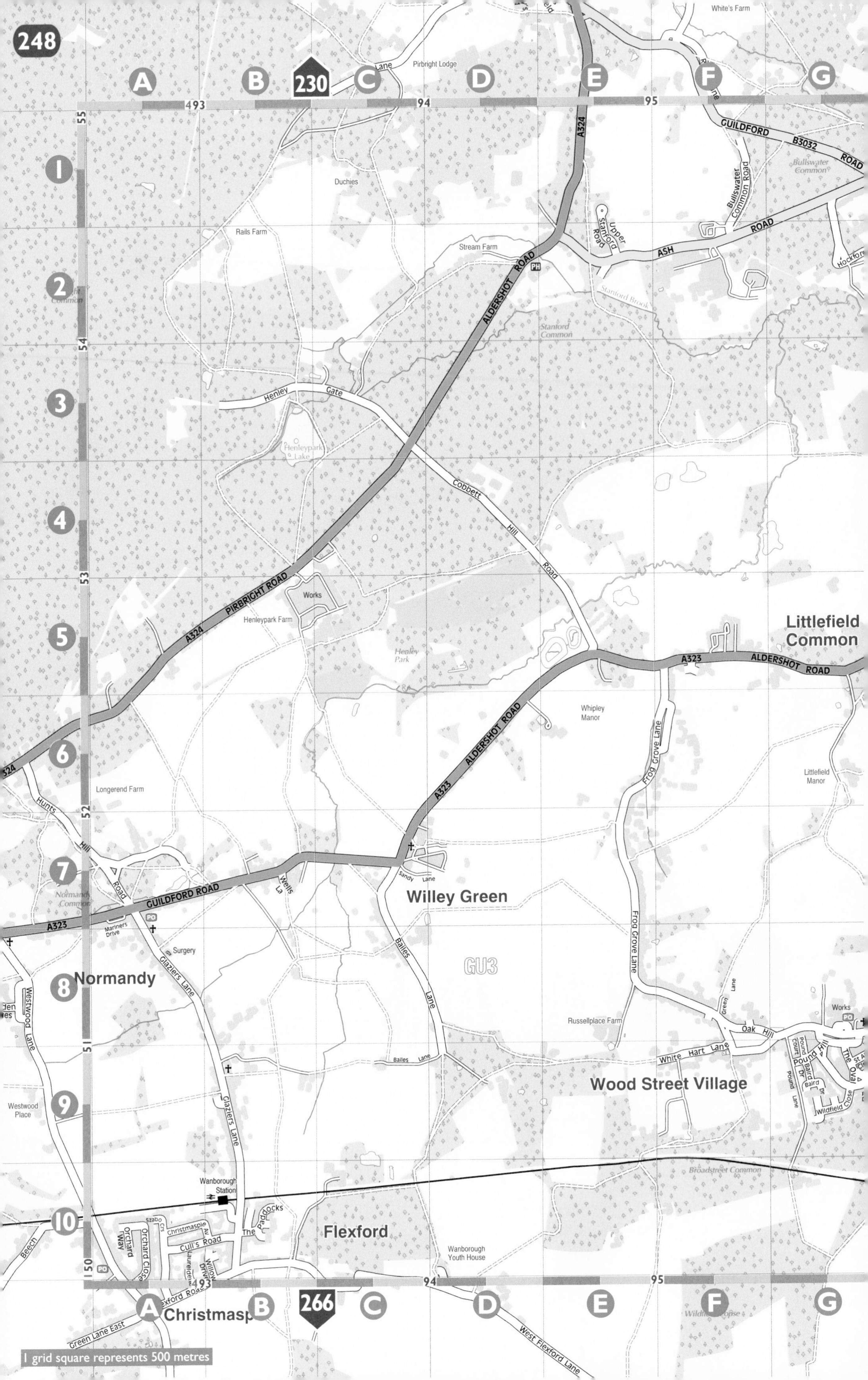
230
Pirbright Lodge
White's Farm
GUILDFORD B3032 ROAD
Bullswater Common
Bullswater Common Road
Upper Stanford Road
ASH ROAD
Hockford
Duchies
Rails Farm
Stream Farm
ALDERSHOT ROAD
A324
PH
Stanford Brook
Stanford Common
Henley Gate
Henleypark Lake
Cobbett Hill Road
PIRBRIGHT ROAD
Works
Henleypark Farm
Henley Park
Littlefield Common
A323 ALDERSHOT ROAD
Whipley Manor
Frog Grove Lane
Littlefield Manor
Longerend Farm
Hunts Hill Road
Normandy Common
GUILDFORD ROAD
Wells La
Sandy Lane
Willey Green
Mariners Drive
PO
Surgery
Normandy
Glaziers Lane
Westwood Lane
Bailes Lane
GU3
Russellplace Farm
Green Lane
Oak Hill
Works
White Hart Lane
Pound Court
Pound Lane
Baird Dr
Wildfield Close
The Oval
Wood Street Village
Westwood Place
Broadstreet Common
Wanborough Station
The Paddocks
Szabo Crs
Christmaspie Av
Orchard Way
Orchard Close
Cull's Road
Laurel Drive
Willow Drive
Flexford
Wanborough Youth House
Beech
Flexford Road
Christmaspie
266
Green Lane East
West Flexford Lane
Wildfield Copse
1 grid square represents 500 metres

Fox Corner
Worplesdon
Pitch Place
Jacobs Well
Slyfield
Bellfields
Stoughton
Fairlands
Rydeshill
Woodbridge Hill
Park Barn
Guildford Park
Worplesdon Station
Merrist Wood College
Roker Park Golf Club
Whitmoor Common
Hockley Lands
Woodcorner Farm
Norton Farm
Bridley Manor
Havering Farm
Golf Course
A322
A323
A320
A3(T)
A25
Goose Rye Road
Salt Box Road
Worplesdon Road
Aldershot Road
Broad Street
Woking Road
Guildford Road
Burdenshott Road
Holly Lane
Stoughton Road
Midleton Road
Woodbridge Road
Stoke Road
York Rd
Ladymead
University of Surrey
Guildford Cathedral
Royal Surrey County Hospital
The Guildford Nuffield Hospital
Cathedral Hill Industrial Estate
Guildford Business Park
Midleton Industrial Estate
Guildford Industrial Estate
Cemetery
River Wey
GU2
231
250
267

250
232
249
268
A
B
C
D
E
F
G
500
01
02
55
54
53
52
51
50
1
2
3
4
5
6
7
8
9
10
Send
Pyle Hill
Sutton Green
Send Grove
Jacobs Well
Slyfield
Bellfields
Burpham
Abbotswood
Bushy Hill
Merrow
GU1
Lower Westfield Farm
Cricket Club
Sendholme
Winds Ridge Cemetery
St Bedes CE Jun School
Whitmoor House
Cox's Farm
Ladygrove Farm
River Wey Navigation
Whitehouse Farm
Burpham Court Farm
Slyfield Industrial Estate
Council Building
Stoke Hill CP School
Weyfield Primary School
Burpham Foundation Primary School
Superstore
George Abbot School
Merrow Business Cen
Perram Works
Guildford Spectrum Athletics Stadium
Guildford Spectrum
Old Guildfordians RFC
Stoke Park
Guildford Lido
Guildford College of Further and Higher Education
Guildford High School
London Road Station
Tormead School
Pitfarm Lawn Tennis Club
Boxgrove Primary School
St Peters Catholic School
Merrow CE Infant School
Junior School
Merrow Clinic
Thorn Chase School
Guildford Golf Club
Royal Grammar Sch
Private Medical Clinic
Police Station
Woodbridge Business Park
Riverside Business Cen
Guildford Cricket Club
Odeon Multiplex
GUILDFORD ROAD
WOKING ROAD
A320
A3(T)
A25
A322
A246
A3100
B2234
CLAY LANE
LONDON RD
B2234 NEW INN LANE
PARK LANE
BOXGROVE ROAD
LADYMEAD
PARKWAY
STOKE ROAD
WOODBRIDGE ROAD
EPSOM ROAD
YORK RD
Sutton Green Road
Whitmoor Lane
Blanchards Hill
Runtley Wood Lane
Potters Lane
Vicarage Lane
Church Lane
Send Hill
Bull Lane
Clay Lane
Moorfield Road
Westfield Road
Woodlands Road
Merrow Lane
Orchard Road
Gosden Hill Road
Merrow Woods
Downside Road
1 grid square represents 500 metres

H
J
K
L
M
233
N
P
04
05
06
55
Burntcommon
Tythebarns Farm
Kiln Lane
Gambles Lane
Hungry Hill Lane
Hawthorn Rd
Willow Dr
Maple Road
Boughton Hall
Kevan Dr
Amberley Cl
BARNS LANE A247
LONDON ROAD
B2215
A3(T)
Field Way
Burntcommon La
Tythebarns Lane
Sussex Farm
Holride Farm
Silkmore Lane
Ripley Road
CLANDON ROAD
Highcotts Lane
Green Lane
The Spinney
A247
Malacca Farm
Lime Grove
Lime Cl
Woodstock
Dedswell Manor Farm
Felix Dr
Dedswell Drive
Oak Grange Road
Bennett Way
Clandon Station
Cason Wood
West Clandon
Surgery
Cotts Wood
THE STREET
PH
Meadowlands
Norcote Wood
252
Hatchlands Park (NT)
Back Lane
East Clandon
Clandon Regis Golf Club
Golf Course
New Park
The Street
School La
New Road
Epsom Road
Clandon CE Infant School
A246
Blake's Lane Farm
Temple Court
Clandon Park (NT)
Glebe Cottages
EPSOM ROAD A25
Staple Lane
High Clandon
A25
Clandon Downs
Old Scotland Farm
1
2
3
4
5
6
7
8
9
10
54
53
52
51
150
269
Trodd's Lane
Hotel
Netherlands
GU4

234
251
270
A
B
C
D
E
F
G
507
08
09
55
54
53
52
51
150
1
2
3
4
5
6
7
8
9
10
Bachelors
Green Lane
Waterloo Farm
The Drift
The Forest
Ripley Lane
Long Reach
Green Lane West
Jury Farm
Manor Farm
Northcote Crs
Northcote Road
The Raleigh School
Nightingale Crs
Nightingale Av
Edwin Rd
Edwin Cl
Meadow Way
Howard Close
Heatherdene
Weston Lea
Glenesk School
B2059
The Highlands
Horsley Station
Wildwood Cl
Parkside Cl
Parkside Pl
Forest Road
Forest Close
Hooke Road
The Ridings
Nightingale Road
Cobham Way
Station Ap
Thornleas Place
The Rise
The Chase
Norrels Dr
Farleys Cl
Woodside
Greta Bank
East Lane
Lollesworth Farm
Lollesworth Lane
Roundtree Farm
Kingston Avenue
The Medical Centre
Glendene Avenue
The Birches
High Park Av
High Park Av
Old Rectory La
Woodland Drive
Oakwood Dr
Oakwood Close
EAST HORSLEY
OCKHAM ROAD SOUTH
Frenchlands Hatch
Higher Dr
Pennymead Drive
Meadow Bank
Lynx Hill
Park Corner Dr
Lower Peryers
Manor Cl
Highfields
Pine Walk
Farm La
Farm Cl
Holmwood Close
Bishopsmead Close
Nomad Theatre
St Martins House Business Centre
Horsley Towers
St Martins
Fearn Cl
Fearn Road
Longhurst
KT24
Slikmore Lane
Kingston Lane
Silkmore Lane
Ricksons La
Tintells La
Kenyons
West Horsley
The Street
Lt Cranmore Lane
Fairwell Lane
Gason Wood
Ripley Lane
Pincott La
Overbrook
School La
Mount Pleasant
Cranmore Lane
Cranmore School
EPSOM ROAD
A246
Butlers Hill
Wix Farm
Hatchlands Park (NT)
East Clandon
Wix Hill
Jeffries Road
Shere Road
Rowbarns Way
The Warren
New Road
Blake's Lane
Blake's Lane Farm
The Sheepleas
Lark Rise
Chalk Lane
High Clandon
Hook Wood
Hillside Farm
Pebble Hill
Green Dene
Mountain Wood
Honeysuckle Bottom
Effingham Forest
Fullers Farm
Fullers Farm Road
Woodcote Lodge
Shere Road
Combe Lane
Green Dene
1 grid square represents 500 metres

Lower Farm Road
Lower Farm
Effingham Cricket Club
Hinterland House
Thornet Wood
Little Bookham
KT23
Greatlee Wood
Effingham Common Road
Preston Cross Hotel & Country Club
Water Lane
Cemetery
The Grange
Leewood Way
St Lawrence Primary School
Manor House School
Howard of Effingham School
Manorhouse Lane
Rectory Lane
Orestan Farm
Orestan Lane
Effingham
Surgery
GUILDFORD ROAD
A246
Guildford Road
St Teresas Preparatory School
Effingham Golf Club
Beech Avenue
Strathcona Avenue
Woodlands Road
Calvert Road
Chester Road
Salmons Road
Dirtham Lane
Goldstone Farm
Golf Course
High Barn Road
Warren Farm
Rowbarns
Oldlands Wood
Polesden Lacey (NT)
High Barn
Yewtree Farm
Critten Lane
Effingham Hill Farm
St Teresas School
Ranmore Common
Crocknorth
Pigden Cottage
Dogkennel Green
Works
Dunley Hill Farm
North Downs Way
Landbarn Farm
Oaken Grove
Fairfield Medical Centre
Great Bookham
Lower Road
Primary School
Infant School
Eastwick Infant School
Hawkwood Rise
Swanns Meadow
Overton Way
Beales Road
West Down
Newenham Rd
Groveside
235
254
271
H J K L M N P
11 12 13
1 2 3 4 5 6 7 8 9 10
50 51 52 53 54 55

254
236
253
272
Great Bookham
Westhumble
Ranmore Common
Denbies
Hill
Mickle
Eastwick Junior School
Eastwick Infant School
Surgery
Fairfield Medical Centre
Primary School
Infant School
South Bookham School
LEATHERHEAD ROAD
GUILDFORD RD
A246
GUILDFORD ROAD
STREET
Salvation Place
B2450
DORKING ROAD
A24
Bocketts Farm Park
River Mole
Fetcham Downs
Norbury Park
Druids Grove
Swanworth Lane
Cowslip Lane
Goldstone Farm
Polesden Road
Dorking Road
Chapel Lane
Phoenice Farm
Polesden Lacey (NT)
Crabtree Cottage
Crabtree Lane
Chapel Farm
Camilla Drive
Box Hill & Westhumble Station
Bagden Farm
Yewtree Farm
Tanner's Hatch
Ashcombe Wood
Ranmore Common Road
North Downs Way
Denbies Wine Estate
Bradley Lane
Ranmore Road
Greensand Way
ASHCOMBE ROAD
A2003
Stanway School
The Ashcombe School
Yew Tree Road
Chalkpit Lane
Keppel Road
Calvert Road
St Martins CE Primary School
Dorking West Station
Station Road
Ind Est
Ranmore Rd
Parkway
The Dorking Business Park
Dorking Mus
Rothes Road
Hart Rd
Howard Road
Dawnay Road
West Down
Dowlans Road
Oakdene Close
Crabtree Lane
Downs Way
Norbury Way
Sheridans Rd
Blackthorne Road
Hilltop Rise
Hale Pit Rd
Hales Oak
Beales Road
Church Road
1 grid square represents 500 metres

Tyrell's Wood
Tyrrells Wood Golf Club
Downside Manor
Leatherhead By-Pass Rd
Reigate Road
B2033
Thames Down Link
Clay Lane
237
Mill Way
Nower Wood
Leatherhead Downs
Givons Grove
Cherkley Court
Crabtree Drive
Downs
Mickleham Dr
Cherkley Hill
Slough Lane
Church Lane
Tumber St
Leech Lane
Headley
Crabtree Lane
Heath House
Lodgebottom Road
High Ashurst
White Hill
Headley Road
Headley Grove
Headley B2033 Road
Bottom Hl
St Michaels CE First School
School Lane
Dell Close
Mickleham Downs
Warren Farm
Juniperhill Wood
Juniper Hall
Juniper Top
Bellasis
256
Zig Zag Road
Lodge Hill
Ashurst Rough
Holly Hough
Headley Heath Approach
Ashurst Drive
Woodlands Pk
Mayburg Farm
Birchingrove Farm
Hotel
Surgery
Devonshire Av
Clump Avenue
Usherwood Close
Fort Rd
Box Hill
Box Hill Country Park
Boxhill Rd
Brockham Warren
North Downs Way
Boxhurst
Boxhill Road
Lower Boxhill Farm
A25 Reigate Road
Old Reigate Road
Betchworth
Pixham
Pixham Lane
Pixham School
Dorking Station
Dorking (Deepdene) Station
Chester Cl
Deepdene Vale
Dorking Cemetery
B2038
Brockham Lane
The Av
Hillside Gdns
Castle Gdns
Coach Rd
Dorking RFC
Kiln Lane
Hillside Cl
Betchworth Park Golf Club
Golf Course
Betchworth Park
Punchbowl Lane
The Borough
273
Brockham
Greensand Way
Nutwood Av
Mill Hl La
H
J
K
L
M
N
P
18
19
20
1
2
3
4
5
6
7
8
9
10
55
54
53
52
51
150

256
238
255
274
Walton on the Hill
Headley
Mogador
Buckland
Betchworth
KT20
RH3
M25
A25
B2032
B2033
B2220
REIGATE ROAD
DORKING ROAD
CHEQUERS LANE
WALTON ST
HEADLEY COMMON ROAD
PEBBLEHILL ROAD
STATION RD
Station Road
Boxhill Road
Slough Lane
Church Lane
LEECH LANE
Heath House
Heath Farm
Frith Park
Headley Grove
Headley Heath
Pebble Coombe
Pebble Cl
Maybury Farm
The Coombe
The Quarry
Betchworth Station
Broome Park
Wildecroft
Kemp's Farm
Rectory Lane
Tranquil Dale
Old Road
Sandy Lane
The Street
Dungates Lane
Dungate's Farm
Greensand Way
North Downs Way
Buckland Lane
Lawrence Lane
South Lane
Underhill Farm
Dowde's Farm
Clifton's Lane
Reigate Heath
Golf Course
Reigate Heath Golf Club
Flanchford Road
Wonham Manor
Wonham Lane
Trumpetshill
Sandy Lane
Bramley School
Walton on the Hill CE Junior School
Walton Heath Golf Club
Walton Heath
Banstead Heath
The Hermitage
Castle House
Holmcroft
Sturt Priory Hospital
Sturt's Lane
Love Lane
Nyefield Park
Hurst Drive
Heath Drive
Heath Drive
Egmont Road
Howard Close
Chequers Close
Nursery Road
Nursery Close
Deans Road
Breech Lane
Queens Cl
The Barnyard
Works
Surgery
Primary School
Meadow Walk
Chuck's La
Duffield Road
Russell Cl
Greenways
Wonford Cl
Surgery
Clump Avenue
Beech Cres
Barley Mow Ct
Reigate Road
Kiln Lane
Old Kiln La
Cemetery
The Walled Garden
Church St
Greensand Way
LC
PO
PH
A B C D E F G
1 2 3 4 5 6 7 8 9 10
521 22 23
55 54 53 52 51 50
1 grid square represents 500 metres

Chipstead Lane
Mugswell
Rectory Road
Millfield Lane
Beechen Lane
Green Lane
Fair Lane
Lower Kingswood
Brighton Road
Gatwick Farm
Lovelands Lane
Old Mint House
Babylon Lane
Priory Hospital Group
Kingswood Manor
Crossways Farm
Kingswood Primary School
Mogador Road
Margery
Margery Lane
Junction 8
M25
A217
REIGATE HILL
North Downs Way
Wray Lane
Reigate Hill
Gatton Bottom
Whitehall Farm
The Royal Alexandra & Albert School
Gatton Hall
Park Farm
Upper Gatton Park
GATTON PARK ROAD
Wray Common
Colesmead
Meads
CROYDON ROAD
A242
Holmesdale Road
Reigate Station
LONDON RD
WEST STREET
HIGH STREET
REIGATE
REIGATE ROAD
A25
BLACKBOROUGH ROAD
B2034
HATCHLANDS RD
STATION RD
Redhill
Reigate College
Reigate Priory Junior School
Reigate Grammar School
Reigate Parish Infant School
Wray Common Primary School
Wray Common County Middle School
Reigate Priory Park
Waterlow Road
Hockley Industrial Centre
239
258
275
H J K L M N P
25 26 27
50 51 52 53 54 55
1 2 3 4 5 6 7 8 9 10

258
240
257
276
A
B
C
D
E
F
G
1
2
3
4
5
6
7
8
9
10
528
29
30
55
54
53
52
51
50
Junction 7
Junction 7/8
M25
M23
A23 LONDON ROAD NORTH
A23
A25
B2031
Glebe Road
London Road N
Dean Lane
Alderstead Heath
ALDERSTEAD LANE
Alderstead Farm
Tollsworth Manor
Pilgrims' Way
North Downs Way
Markedge Lane
High Road
Harps Oak Lane
Harps Oak
Boars Green Farm
Beech Road
SHEPHERD'S HILL
Upper Gatton Park
Church Hill
Jolliffe Road
Gatton Bottom
Rockshaw Road
Rockshaw
Heronswood Mere
Ashcombe Road
Golf Course
Whitehall Farm
Reigate Hill Golf Club
Merstham
Merstham Stn
Quality St
Station Road North
HIGH ST
Stn Rd
Hanover Close
Grange Close
Grange Dr
SOUTH
School Hill
Primary School
Brook Road
Wood Street
Malmstone Av
Radstock Way
Laxton Gardens
Huddleston Cres
Mansfield Dr
Furzefield Primary School
Delabole Road
Chesterton Dr
Dundrey Crs
Radstock Way
Bolsover Gv
Purbeck Cl
Portland Dr
Nailsworth Cres
Avenue
Drive
Bletchingley Road
Regent Close
Surg
Worsted Green
Sutton Gdns
Weldon Wy
Paynton
St Nicholas School
Woodfield School
Gatton
The Royal Alexandra & Albert School
Gatton Hall
Rocky Lane
Bushetts Grove
Bramblewood
South Cl
London Rd
LONDON ROAD
Wells Place
The Crossways
Works
Manor Road
Albert Rd
Endsleigh Rd
Albury Road
Southcote Road
Gatton Park Business Centre
New Battlebridge Lane
Battlebridge Lane
Lane
Devon Road
Nutfield Rd
Deans Road
Melton Road
Bourne Road
Orpin Road
Wycliffe Gdns
Ash Cl
Chilberton Drive
South Merstham
The Lake
Fairhaven Road
East Surrey College
Elmwood Road
Quarryside Business Park
Ormside Way
Holmethorpe Industrial Estate
Towers Way
Holmethorpe Avenue
Holmethorpe Av
Nutfield Road
Mill Lane
Mercers Farm
Nutfield Marsh Road
Nutfield Marsh
Chilmead Farm
Chilmead Lane
Commongers Lane
PARK ROAD
Ringwood Av
Holcon Court
North Rd
Monson Road
Lyndale Road
Claremont Road
LONDON ROAD
Westway Gardens
Alpine Road
Coles Meads
Colesmead Road
South Md
Carlton Green
Carlton Road
Vandyke Close
Lawn Tennis Club
Frenches Road
Holmethorpe
St Annes Blvd
Wiggie Lane
Copley Cl
Timperley Gardens
Green Way
Colebrook Road
Hurstleigh Drive
Regent Crs
Nash Gdns
Lynwood Road
Ladbroke Rd
Brooklands Way
Woodfield Cl
Linkfield
REDHILL
St Matthews CE Primary School
Warwick Quadrant & Harlequin Theatre, Cinema & Library
Keats
Wordsworth Md
The Warwick School
Daneshill Lane
St Josephs Catholic Primary Redhill
North St
Gloucester Rd
Warwick Road
QUEENSWAY
PRINCESS WAY
Furzehill
Dome Way
Donyngs Recreation Centre
The Westway Clinic
STATION RD
Station Rd
Redhill Stn
Noke Dr
Caxton Rise
Redhill Business Cen
Sh Ctr
Cavendish Rd
LANDS RD
Charman Rd
Baxter Av
Holland Cl
Lower Bridge Rd
Chapel Rd
Oakdene Rd
HIGH ST
MARKETFIELD WAY
Fenton Close
Crosslands Road
Hillfield Road
Redstone Park
Redstone Hill
A25 REDSTONE HILL
Grovehill Road
Ridgeway Rd
Garlands Road
Hyland Business Centre
Whitepost Hill
NUTFIELD ROAD
Hotel
Fullers Wood Lane
Nutfield Cemetery
Blacklands Meadow
Doods Brow School
Shortacres
Parkwood Rd
NUTFIELD ROAD
HIGH STREET
Nutfield
Sandy Lane
Mid Street
Church Hill
Kingsfield Business Centre
Rainbow Natural Health
Rural Way
Philanthropic Road
Hogtrough Lane
Sandy Lane
Greensand Way
Kentwyns Rise
Nutfield Church CE
Hooley Lane
Redstone
Surgery
Works
1 grid square represents 500 metres

Chaldon
Rook Lane
St Peter & St Paul CE Primary School
Rook Farm
Six Brothers Field
Willey Broom La
Birchwood Lane
Common Road
Heathway
Badgers Wood
Roffes Lane
Willey Lane
Willey Farm Lane
North Downs Way
Hilltop Lane
Oakhyrst Grange School
Caterham School
Caterham Preparatory School
Harestone Valley Road
Harestone Hill
Tupwood Lane
Godstone Road
St Katharines Rd
St Johns CE Infant School
St Johns Junior School
Church Hill
Station Av
Quarry Hangers
Arthur's Seat
War Coppice Road
Whitehill Lane
Woodland Way
Weald Way
Gravelly Hill
Tupwood Scrubbs Road
Rockshaw House
Spring Bottom Lane
Warwick Wold Road
Warwick Wold
Oakwood Rd
Hextalls Lane
Roughets Lane
The Conduit
M25
Kitchen Copse
North Park Lane
North Park Farm
Place Farm
Place Farm Road
Mersham Road
The Hawthorns Pre-Prep School
Brewer Street
Pendell Road
Pendell
Sandy Lane
Big Common Lane
Ltl Common La
M23
Castle Street
High Street
A25
Bletchingley Rd
Stychens La
Stychens Cl
Castle Hill
Church Lane
Bletchingley Golf Club
Works
Cemetery
Godstone Road
White Post
Coneybury
St Catherine's Cross
Kenrick Sq
Bletchingley
Greensand Way
Outwood Lane
Sandhills
Rabies Heath Road
Coldharbour La
Bletchingley Road
Stangrave Hall
Waterhouse Lane
Water House Farm
Ivy Mill Lane
Godstone
Cooper's Hill Road
241
260
277

260
242
259
A
B
C
D
E
F
G
535
36
37
55
54
53
52
51
150
1
2
3
4
5
6
7
8
9
10
Surgery
Asprey Gv
Colliers
Greenwood Gdns
GODSTONE ROAD
B2030
Deerswood Cl
Tillingdown La
Tillingdown La
St Katharines Rd
Markville Gdns
Markfield Rd
St Johns CE Infant School
St Johns Junior School
Newstead Ri
Markfield Rd
Tupwood Lane
Hill
Upper Harestone
Road
Tupwood Scrubbs Road
GODSTONE ROAD
A22
Woldingham School
Church Road
North Downs Golf Club
Northdown Road
Southfields Road
Golf Course
Paddock Barn
North Downs Way
Quarry Road
Quarry Farm
North Downs Way
North Downs Way
Gangers Hill
Tandridgehill Lane
N Downs Way
GODSTONE HILL
Flinthall Farm
Junction 6
M25
M25
Hogtrough
Barrow Green Farm
The Priory
Fosterdown
Tyler's Green
Tylers Cl
B2235
Bakers Md
Ockleys Md
Selbourne Sq
Lindley Rd
GODSTONE HILL
Park Lane
Park
Flower Lane
A22
Rooks Nest Farm
Streete Court School
Catlin Gdns
Greenwell Cl
Clayton Md
Evelyn Gardens
A25
OXTED ROAD
Barrow Gn Rd
A25
OXTED ROAD
Godstone Road
Golf Course
Nags Hall
North Park Lane
Dumville Dr
Catlin Gdns
Salisbury Rd
Dewlands
Dewlands
Court Rd
Riders Wy
A25
HIGH ST
Godstone
Church Town
NEEDLES BANK
PO
BLETCHINGLEY ROAD
A25
Stangrave Hall
The Priory
Ivy Mill La
GODSTONE GREEN RD
The Green
Bell Meadow
Hickmans Cl
HIGH ST
Church Lane
Bullbeggars Lane
Jackass Lane
Tandridge Lane
Tandridge Court
Willow Wy
Rogers Md
Ivy Ml Cl
Ivy Mill Lane
Love La
EASTBOURNE ROAD
Leigh Pl. La
Leigh Place
Godstone Farm
Tilburstow Hill Road
B2236
Greensand Wy
Greensand Way
Greensand Way
Tandridge Lane
The Wk
Tandridge
St Peters CE Primary School
Garston Park
Entercent Road
Bone Mill La
Gibbs Brook
Tilburstowhill Common
Greensand Way
Heath Road
EASTBOURNE ROAD
Southlands
Greensand Way
Greensand Way
Orme House
South Park
Tilburstow
Tandridge Lane
Newhouse Farm
1 grid square represents 500 metres

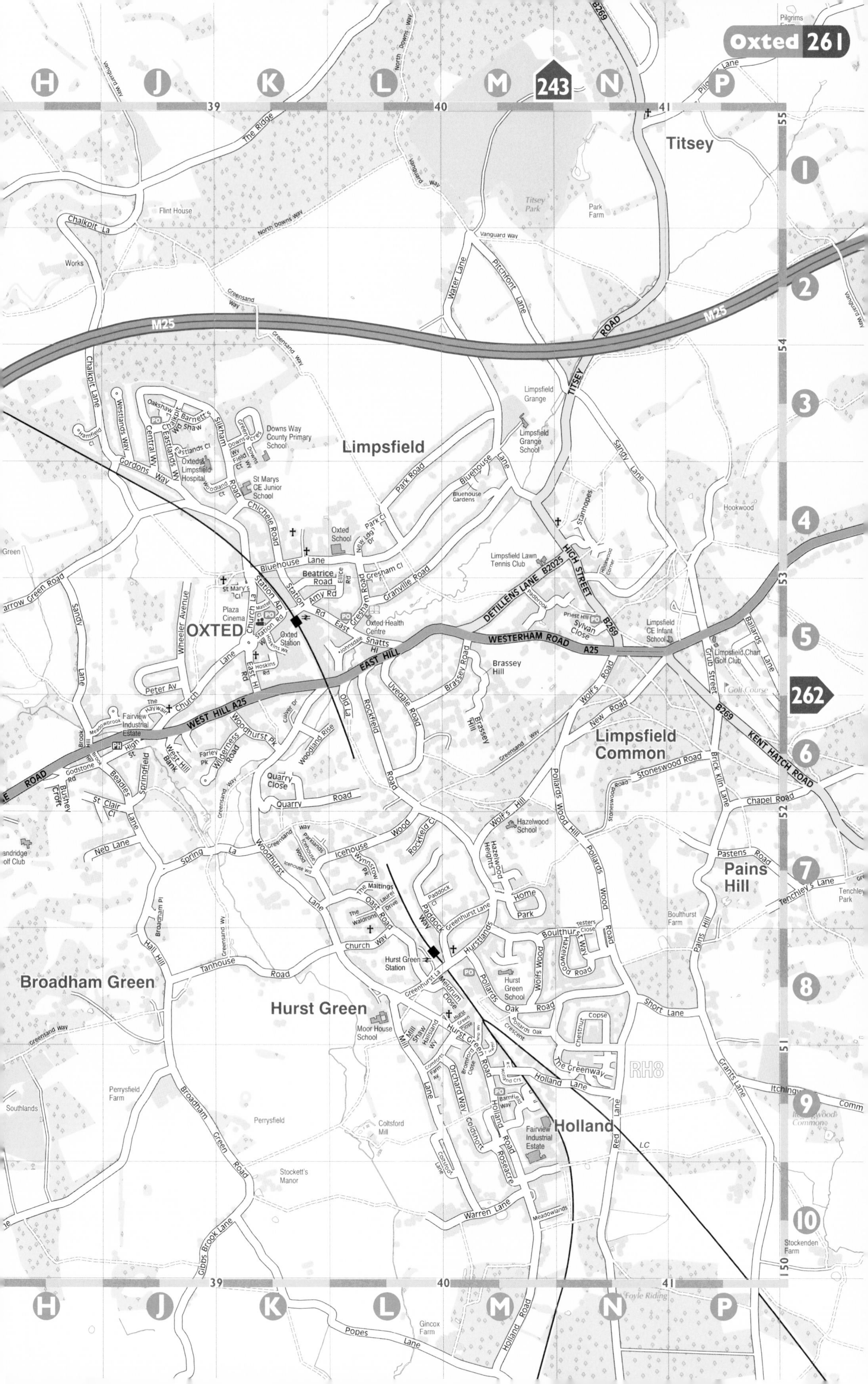
243
262
H J K L M N P
39 40 41
55 54 53 52 51 150
1 2 3 4 5 6 7 8 9 10
Titsey
Titsey Park
Park Farm
Pilgrims Farm
Flint House
Works
The Ridge
Chalkpit La
North Downs Way
Vanguard Way
Greensand Way
M25
Water Lane
Pitchfront Lane
Titsey Road
B269
Limpsfield
Limpsfield Grange
Limpsfield Grange School
Downs Way County Primary School
Oxted & Limpsfield Hospital
St Marys CE Junior School
Chalkpit Lane
Westlands Way
Central Wy
Eastlands Wy
Gordons Way
Silkham Road
Chichele Road
Bluehouse Lane
Bluehouse Gardens
Park Road
Oxted School
Beatrice Road
Amy Rd
Gresham Road
Granville Road
Sandy Lane
Stanhopes
Hookwood
Limpsfield Lawn Tennis Club
Detillens Lane B2025
High Street
Westerham Road A25
Sylvan Close
Limpsfield CE Infant School
Limpsfield Chart Golf Club
Ballards Lane
Grub Street
OXTED
Plaza Cinema
Station Ap
Station Rd
Oxted Station
Oxted Health Centre
East Hill
Snatts Hl
Church Lane
Wheeler Avenue
Peter Av
West Hill A25
Fairview Industrial Estate
Brassey Hill
Brassey Road
Uvedale Road
Rockfield Road
Old La
Woodland Rise
Wolf's Road
New Road
Limpsfield Common
Kent Hatch Road
B269
Golf Course
Stoneswood Road
Brick Kiln Lane
Chapel Road
Pastens Road
Pains Hill
Tenchley's Lane
Tenchley Park
Boulthurst Farm
Pollards Wood Road
Pollards Wood Hill
Wolf's Hill
Hazelwood School
Hazelwood Heights
Home Park
Boulthurst Way
Testers Close
Quarry Close
Quarry Road
Woodhurst Lane
Icehouse Wood
Spring La
Neb Lane
St Clair Cl
Springfield
Beadles Lane
Bushey Croft
Godstone Rd
Tandridge Golf Club
Broadham Pl
Hall Hill
Broadham Green
Tanhouse Road
Church Way
Hurst Green Station
Hurstlands
Hurst Green School
Hurst Green
Moor House School
Greenhurst La
Meldrum Close
Pollards Oak Road
Pollards Oak Crescent
Short Lane
Chestnut Copse
The Greenway
Holland Lane
RH8
Hurst Green Road
Orchard Way
Mill Lane
Colts Foot Lane
Holland Road
Fairview Industrial Estate
Holland
Red Lane
LC
Grants Lane
Itchingwood Comm
Itchingwood Common
Rosecare
Warren Lane
Meadowlands
Perrysfield Farm
Perrysfield
Coltsford Mill
Stockett's Manor
Southlands
Broadham Green Road
Gibbs Brook Lane
Popes Lane
Gincox Farm
Foyle Riding
Stockenden Farm

262
244
261
A
B
C
D
E
F
G
1
2
3
4
5
6
7
8
9
10
542
43
44
55
54
53
52
51
150
Pilgrims Farm
Pilgrims Lane
Clacket Lane
Gaysham Farm
Westerham Wood
London Road
Green
Force
M25
Clacket Lane Service Area
Hotel
Titsey Wood
Vanguard Way
Westwood Farm
Works
Broomlands Farm
Broomlands Lane
Churchill CE Primary School
Court Lodge
Croydon Road
B2024
Croft Road
Marwell
Farleycroft
Granville Road
Westways
Delagarde Road
Buckham Thorns Road
The Slip
The Paddock
Rysted Lane
South Bank
Grange Close
Westbury Terrace
Farley Nursery
Trotts Lane
New Street
Wellers Close
Black Eagle Close
Market Square
Vicarage Hill
A25
Mill Street
Surgery
Greensand Way
Farley Lane
Covers Farmhouse
High Street
Mill Lane
Westerham
Moorhouse Bank
Moorhouse
Squerryes Court Manor House & Gardens
Hookwood
Limpsfield Chart Golf Club
Grub Street
B269
Kent Hatch Road
Brick Kiln Lane
Chapel Road
Pastens Road
Pains Hill
Tenchley's Lane
Tenchleys Park
Caxton Lane
Ridlands Grove
Ridlands Lane
Ridlands Rise
Stoneleigh Road
St Andrews Way
Mill Lane
Tally Road
Moorhouse Road
Goodley Stock Road
Kent County
Surrey County
The High Chart
Goodley Stock
Limpsfield Chart
Kent Hatch
Crockhamhill Common
Trevereux Hill
Trevereux
Tenchleys Manor
Froghole
Crockham Hill
Smiths Lane
Oakdale Lane
Crockham Hill County Primary School
Deanery Road
Grants Lane
Itchingwood Common Road
Itchingwood Common
The Moat Farm
Swaynesland Road
Swaynesland
Guildables Lane
Vanguard Way
Hurst Farm
Dairy Lane
Dennettsland Road
Main Road
B2026
Spout Lane
Stockenden Farm
Crockham Grange
Redlands
Coakham Farm
1 grid square represents 500 metres

Westerham 263
Sundridge
Green
Park Farm
The Mill Works
Works
Manor Road
Woodside Road
Church Road
HIGH ST
245
Brasted
WESTERHAM ROAD
A25
A233
BRASTED ROAD
West End
Surgery
Chart Lane
Heverswood
New Road
Birchfield Farm
Sundridge and Brasted CE Primary School
St Mary's Church Road
Greystone Park
Church Road
Valence School
Westerham Golf Club
Dunsdale
Golf Course
Colinette Farm
Lodge Farm
Pipers Lane
Vines Gate
Foxwold
Brasted Chart
Piper's Green Road
Penn Lane
Penn Farm
HOSEY HILL
B2026
HOSEY COMMON ROAD
Quornden
The Phillippines
The Chart
Emmetts Road
Emmetts Garden (NT)
264
French Street
Hosey Common Lane
Horns Hill
Greensand Way
Mapleton Road
Norman Street
Scords Wood
Toy's Hill
PH
Ide Hill
Camberwell Lane
PO
Greensand Way
Scords Lane
Chartwell (NT)
Chartwell
Toy's Hill
Puddledock Lane
Bardogs Farm
Puddledock
Oakwood Lodge
HILL ROAD
B2042
Henden Manor
Tan House
Obriss Farm
Boons Park
H J K L M N P
46 47 48
1 2 3 4 5 6 7 8 9 10
55 54 53 52 51 50

264
246
263
MAIN ROAD
Sundridge
Drynill
Bessels Green
Bessels Meadow
BACK LANE
COLD
Lyndhurst
The Close
Marlborough Crescent
Brittains Lane
Kipping Cl
Redlands Rd
A
B
C
D
E
F
G
549
50
51
55
54
53
52
51
150
1
2
3
4
5
6
7
8
9
10
Sundridge and Brasted CE Primary School
St Mary's Church Road
Sundridge Place
Salters Heath
Croft Way
Greenwood Way
Downsview Road
The Middlings
Penn Lane
Back Lane
Green Lane
B2042
SEVENOAKS BY-PASS
A21(T)
TN14
Manor Farm
Lodge Barn Farm
Dibden Lane
Dibden
Penn Farm
Whitley Forest
Mill Bank Wood
Brook Place
Whitley Row
Apps Hollow
Cordons Farm
Great Norman Street Farm
Norman Street
Nightingale Lane
Goathurst Common
Rycroft Lane
White House Road
Camberwell Lane
Everlands
Bayley's Hill
Ide Hill
Ide Hill CE Aided Primary School
WHEATSHEAF HILL
Greensand Way
Yorkshill Farm
Boarhill
Hanging Bank
IDE HILL ROAD
Wickhurst Manor
Hatchlands Farm
Oakwood Lodge
Chains Farm
Bowzell Farm
Henden Manor
Old House Farm
Scollops Farm
Faulkners Hill Farm
Oak Lodge Farm
Winkhurst Green
1 grid square represents 500 metres

SEVENOAKS
Kippington
Sevenoaks Common
Hubbard's Hill
Sevenoaks Weald
Fletcher's Green
Hall's
Knole Park
Godden Green
Underriver
Oakhurst
Sevenoaks Station
TUBS HILL
B2020 ST BOTOLPH'S ROAD
A224 LONDON ROAD
HIGH ST A225
SEAL
Vine Cricket Ground
Knole Park Golf Club
Sevenoaks RFC
Lady Boswells CE Primary School
Sevenoaks Swimming Centre
Library & Museum
Stag Theatre
Superstore
Town Medical Cen
Knole (NT)
Sevenoaks School
Sevenoaks School Track
Golf Course
Blackhall
247
Stake Farm
Fawke Common
Carter's Hill
Greensand Way
St Julian's
River Hill
Riverhill House
The New School at West Heath
Weald Place
A21(T) SEVENOAKS BY-PASS
Panthurst Farm
RIVERHILL A225
TONBRIDGE ROAD
Gracious Lane
Dale Farm
Sevenoaks Weald Primary School
Elses Farm
Romshed Farm
St Margarets Old School
Bank Lane
B245 LONDON ROAD
Nizels Hotel Golf & Leisure Club
Nizels
Mansers
New House Farm
Hale Oak Rd
Scabharbour Road
Morley's Road
Egg Lane
LONDON ROAD
H J K L M N P
53 54 55
1 2 3 4 5 6 7 8 9 10

Wanborough Station
Flexford
248
Christmaspie
Wanborough
Puttenham
Compton
Shackleford
Hurtmore
Norney
Wildfield Copse
Greencut Copse
Wanborough Manor
Wanborough Wood
Flexford Ho
Hog's Back
Puttenham CE Infant School
Puttenham Golf Club
Cemetery
Puttenham Heath
Golf Course
Hurlands
Suffield Farm
Lone Barn
Prior's Wood
Priors Field School
Priors Hatch Lane
Lydling Farm
Chalk Lane
Aldro School
Hurtmore Golf Club
Queens Sports Centre
Charterhouse School St Residence
Eastbury Manor
St Mary's CE First School
Shackleford Heath
Church Croft
Mitchen Hall
Broadstreet Common
Sir Greville Sprat Stadium
West Flexford Lane
East Flexford Lane
Westwood Lane
Wanborough Hill
Puttenham Hill
Puttenham Heath Road
Hook Lane
Puttenham Lane
Lascombe Lane
Highfield Lane
Lombard Street
Summers Lane
Priorsfield Road
Hurtmore Road
Quarry Rd
Northway
Elstead Road
Peper Harow Lane
School Lane
The Street
Shackleford Road
Crenville Road
Rokers La
Eastbury Lane
Culls Road
Flexford Road
B3000
A3(T)
North Downs Way
1 grid square represents 500 metres

249
268
GU2
University of Surrey
Guildford Cathedral
Guildford Park
Onslow Village
GUILDFORD
Artington
Littleton
Broadford
Peasmarsh
Binscombe
Farncombe
Loseley Park
Loseley House
Orange Grove
Piccard's Farm
Conduit Farm
Manor Farm
Sunnydown
Polsted Manor
Compton Common
The Grange
New Pond Farm
Guildford Crematorium
Broadwater School
Godalming Leisure Centre
Broadwater Park Golf Club
Farncombe Cricket Club
Riverway Industrial Estate
The Astolat Industrial Estate
Broadford Park Business Cen
Upper Unsted Farm
Charterhouse School
Charterhouse School Students Residences
Guildford FC
Farncombe Stn
Guildford Stn
FARNHAM ROAD
A31
MIDLETON ROAD
PORTSMOUTH ROAD
OLD A3100
GUILDFORD ROAD
B3000 NEW POND ROAD
SHALFORD ROAD
QUARRY STREET
A281
YORK RD
North Downs Way
Sandy Lane
Littleton Lane
Stakescorner Road
Polsted Lane
Withies Lane
The Avenue
Guildown Avenue
Guildown Road
Woodcote
Chestnut Avenue
Mount
Beech Lane
Manor Way
Abbot's Close
Beechcroft Drive
High View Road
Egerton Road
Gill Avenue
Tilthams Corner Rd
Unstead Lane
Summers Road
Station Road
Meadrow
Peperharow Road
Summerhill
Guildford Park Rd
Madrid Rd
Poltimore Road
Onslow County Infant School
Queen Eleanor's CE Junior School
Guildford County Sch
St Nicolas CE Infant School
St Marys Tutorial College
Green Lane Infant School
Binscombe Medical Centre
Guildford Grove Primary School
The Guildford Nuffield Hospital
Guildford Hockey & Cricket Club
Riverside Business Cen
Yvonne Arnaud Theatre
Guildford Museum
Rowing Club
H J K L M N P
97 98 99
1 2 3 4 5 6 7 8 9 10
45 46 47 48 49 50

268
250
267
A
B
C
D
E
F
G
1
2
3
4
5
6
7
8
9
10
500
01
02
145
46
47
48
49
250
Higher Education
Woodbridge Road
Walnut Tree Cl
Gardner
Markenfield Road
Dapdune Rd
Drummond Rd
George Rd
Artillery Rd
Church Rd
York Rd
A246
A320
Chertsey St
London Road
Waterden Rd
Epsom Road
A25
Clandon Rd
Nightingale Road
Park Chase
Avington Close
Guildford High School
Ennismore Av
Tormead School
Cranley Road
Pitfarm Lawn Tennis Club
Hillier Rd
Pit Farm
Maori Rd
Tangier Road
St Omer Road
Rosetrees
Broadwater Rl
Warren Road
Downside Road
Little Warren Cl
One Tree Hill Road
Meads Road
Green Lane
Orchard
Daryngton Drive
Down Road
Carroll Av
Holford Road
Elles Av
High Path
Thorn Chase School
Merrow Chase
Fairway
Guildford Golf Club
Golf Course
Riverside Business Cen
Guildford Hockey & Cricket Club
Police Station
Crown Courts
Odeon Multiplex
Station Approach
Friary Centre
Onslow St
Bridge St
Royal Grammar Sch
Civic Hall
Private Medical Clinic
Surgery
High St A3100
Abbots Hosp
Surrey College
Semaphore Rd
Mount Alvernia Hospital
Pewley Bank
Pewley Down Infant School
Pewley Way
Pewley Hill
Cooper Rd
Warren Rd
Sydney Road
Cline Road
Addison Road
Holy Trinity CE Junior School
Guildford Castle
Museum
Castle Hill
Millbrook A281
Quarry Street
Yvonne Arnaud Theatre
Porridge Pot Alley
Council Building
St Nicolas CE Infant School
St Marys Tutorial College
Flower Walk
Abbot Rd
Warwicks Road
Fort Road
Warwicks Bench
Warwick's Bench Lane
Wych Elm Rise
Northdown La
Rowing Club
River Wey
Chantry Vw Rd
Chantry View Road
Echo Pit Rd
Shalford Road A281
Pilgrims' Way
North Downs Way
Tilehouse Road
Clifford Manor Road
Shepherd's Way
Pewley Down
Longdown Road
White Lane
Halfpenny Lane
South Warren Farm
Tyting Farm
Chantries
Chilworth Manor
The Street
Works
Shalford Lane
Shalford Mill(NT)
East Shalford Lane
Manor Farm
The Street A281
Tillingbourne
Wey - South Path
Dagden Rd
Dagley Lane
Orchard Rd
Shalford Infant School
Tillingbourne Road
Shalford Station
Station Road
Kings Road
Cem.
Chilworth
Blacksmith Lane
Redwood Cv
Old Mnr Gdns
Dorking Road
New Road
Bourne Cl
Hornhatch La
Nursery Gdns
Chantry Rd
Lakes Cl
Copse Close
Brook Rd
Bradstone Brook
Shalford Common
A248
Tillingbourne Junior School
Broadford Rd
Horsham Rd
Ashcroft
Chinthurst Lane
SHALFORD
Broadford Park Business Cen
Broadford
Poplar Rd
Grantley Cl
Downs Link
B2128 Kings Road
Wonersh Common
Peasmarsh
Summersbury Dr
Highfield
Horsham Rd A281
Trunley Heath Road
Riverway Industrial Estate
River Wey Navigation
Wey House School
Gosden House School
Christmas Hill
Wonersh Common Road
Blackheath Cv
Phillips Hatch
Blackheath Lane
Little Tangley
New Road
Barnett Lane
Barnett Cl
Wonersh
Barnett Hill
Cemetery
Corner
Upper Unsted Farm
Foxborough Hl Rd
Links Road
Bramley Golf Club
Gosden Cl
Drodges Cl
Eastwood Rd
Riverside Dr
The Bramley Business Cen
St Catherines School
Station Road B2128
The Street
Surgery
Cranleigh Road
Lane
Horsham Road
Clockhouse La
The Beeches
Barton Rd
Firs Rd
Linersh Dr
Rectory Close
Mill La
Greywaters
Grantley Avenue
Mellersh Hill Road
Hill Cl
Old Portsmouth Road
A3100
Downs Link
1 grid square represents 500 metres

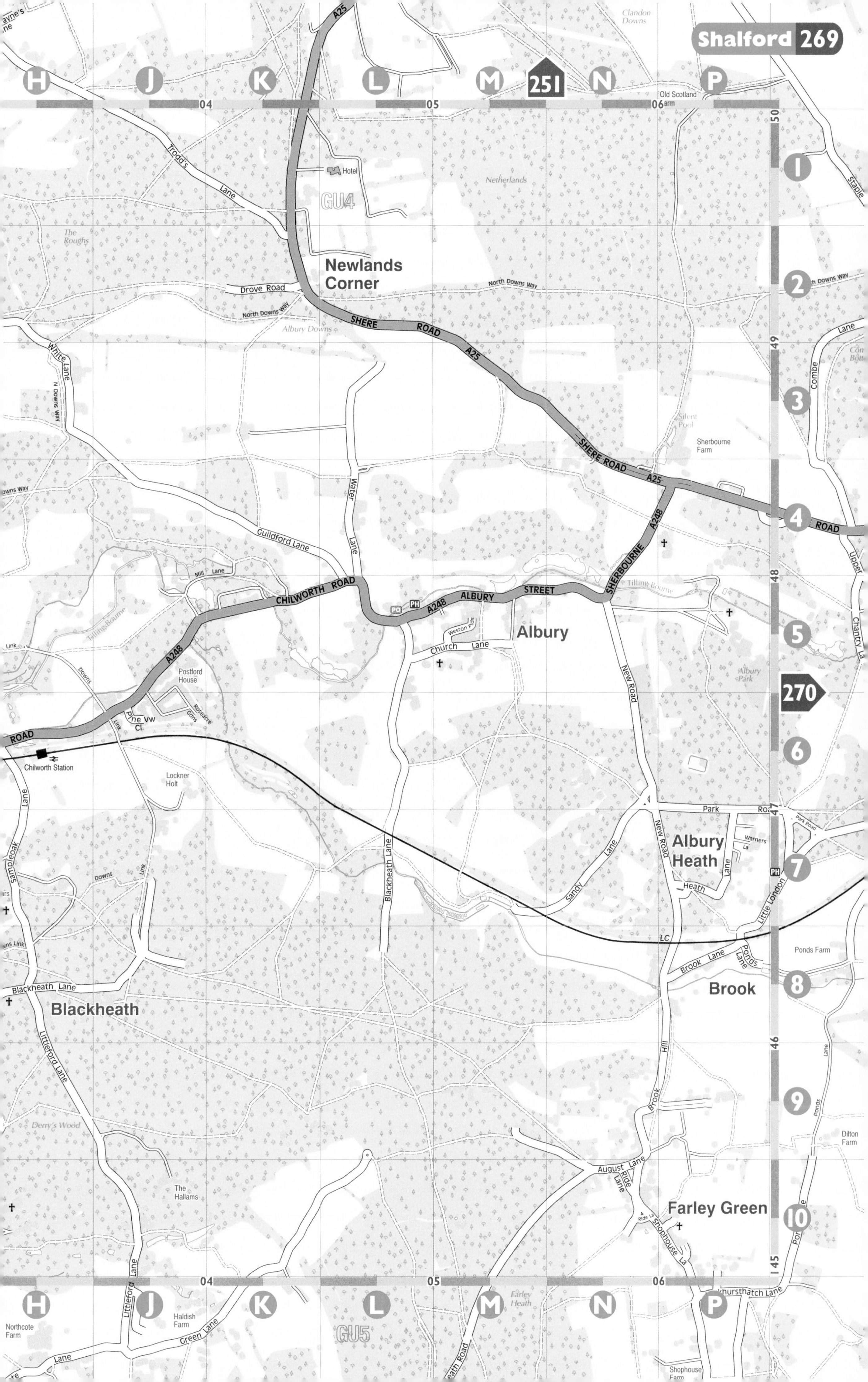

H
J
K
L
M
N
P
251
04
05
06
Clandon Downs
Old Scotland Farm
50
49
48
47
46
45
1
2
3
4
5
6
7
8
9
10
270
A25
Tradd's Lane
Hotel
GU4
Netherlands
The Roughs
Newlands Corner
Drove Road
North Downs Way
Albury Downs
SHERE ROAD A25
White Lane
N Downs Way
Silent Pool
Sherbourne Farm
Combe Lane
Staple
ROAD
Upper
Chantry La
Water Lane
Guildford Lane
Mill Lane
Tilling Bourne
CHILWORTH ROAD
A248
PO
PH
ALBURY STREET
SHERBOURNE A248
Weston Flds
Church Lane
Albury
New Road
Albury Park
Postford House
Rosacre Gdns
Pne Vw Cl
Link
Downs
ROAD
Chilworth Station
Lockner Holt
Sampleoak Lane
Downs Link
Blackheath Lane
Park Road
Albury Heath
Warners La
Heath Lane
Sandy Lane
Little London
LC
Brook Lane
Ponds Lane
Ponds Farm
Brook
Blackheath Lane
Blackheath
Littleford Lane
Derry's Wood
Brook Hill
Dilton Farm
August Lane
Ride Lane
Shophouse La
Farley Green
The Hallams
Haldish Farm
Green Lane
Farley Heath
Hurtsthatch Lane
Northcote Farm
GU5
Shophouse Farm
Heath Road
Lane

252
A
B
C
D
E
F
G
507
08
09
50
49
48
47
46
145
1
2
3
4
5
6
7
8
9
10
269
Woodcote Lodge
Shere Road
Green Dene
Combe Lane
Staple Lane
North Downs Way
Combe La
Combe Bottom
Netley Heath
Colekitchen Lane
Hollister Farm
Colekitchen Farm
Hackhurst Down
Silent Pool
Sherbourne Farm
Netley House
SHERE ROAD
A25
Shere
London La
Street
Gomshall Lane
Surgery
Shere CE Infant School
Church
Church La
Upper
Rectory La
Chantry La
Lower St
Orchard Rd
Middle St
Shere Lane
Willow Wk
Pilgrims Wy
The Spinning Wk
Pilgrims Cl
Cemetery
Pathfields
Sandy Lane
Netley Cl
Leather La
Queen Street
New Rd
Goose Gn
The Gomshall Gallery
Mill
Gomshall Station
STATION ROAD
Beggars Lane
Hackhurst Lane
LC
Hackhurst Farm
Gravel Pits La
High Vw
Heathrow
Towerhill
Tower Hill Rise
Gomshall
Wonham Way
Abinger Hammer
Abinger Hammer Village School
B2126
FELDAY ROAD
Hammerfield Dr
Burrows Lane
Works
Park Road
Little London
Hook Lane
Albury Heath
Warners La
Heath
Ponds Lane
Hound House Road
Burrows Cross
Rad Lane
Rad La
Wonham Wy
B2126 HORSHAM
Brook Lane
Ponds Farm
Burrows Lea
Lenten Cl
Pursers Lane
Broadfield Road
Crest Hl
Fulvens
Annisdowne Cl
Knobfield
Cotterell House
Lawbrook
Lawbrook Lane
Jesses Lane
Sweet La
Hoe Lane
Westfield
Sutton Pl
Sutton
Dilton Farm
Pursers Hollow
Hoe
Pursers Farm
Franksfield
Farley Green
Lane End Farm
Pond Lane
Burchets Hollow
Mackies Hill
Colmans Hl
Peaslake School
Tenningshook Wood
Hazel Hall
Lockhurstshatch Lane
Hound House
Surgery
Peaslake Lane
Plaw
Mackies Hl
Peaslake
Hotel
Walking Bottom
1 grid square represents 500 metres

H
J
K
L
M
253
N
P
11
12
13
Works
Dunley Hill Farm
High Barn Road
North Downs Way
Landbarn Farm
1
Oaken Grove
White Downs
North Downs Way
2
Rokefield
Stockman's Coomb Farm
49
Lane
3
Balchins
Deerleap Road
Sandrock Road
North Downs Way
Park Farm
Vale Farm
Coast Hill Lane
A25
COAST
HILL
Greensand Way
4
Leasers Barn
Deerleap Wood
Rookery Drive
The Rookery
Westcott Heath
48
West Lane
Westlane Barn
5
Wotton
272
A25
Sheephouse Lane
Sheephouse Green
GUILDFORD ROAD
A25
Crossways Farm
Manor Farm
Greensand Way
Wolvens Lane
6
Paddington Farm
Raikes Lane
Wotton Drive
Wotton House
Brickyard Lane
Hollow Lane
47
7
Raikes Farm
8
Raikes Lane
Abinger Lane
Abinger Common First School
PH
Sutton Abinger
Donkey Lane
46
Noons Corner Road
Abinger Common
Water Lane
Sutton Lane
Friday Street Road
9
Friday Street
PH
Glebe Lane
Broadmoo
Woodhouse Lane
Lane
Radnor
B2126
Sheephouse Lane
10
Felbury House
Pasture Wood Road
Abinger Common Road
Leith Hill Road
PO
Parkhurst
145
Shootlands
11
12
13
H
J
K
L
M
N
P
Abinger Bottom
Lemon's Farm
Sewers Farm Road
Holmbury St Mary

272
Denbies
Ranmore Road
North Downs Way
254
Greensand Way
A B C D E F G
514
15
16
St Martins CE Primary School
Dorking West Station
Station Road
Ind Est
Ranmore Rd
CHALKPIT LANE
Parkway
ASHCOMBE ROAD
Yew Tree Road
Keppel Road
Hill Rl
Limeway Ter
Landbarn Farm
LC
The Dorking Business Park
Portland Rd
Works
Dorking Mus
Curtis Rd
Beech Cl
Road
STATION RD
HIGH STREET
Shopping Centre
Mill Pond
Rothes Road
Hart Rd
Ansell Rd
Hotel
Milton Court
Miltoncourt Lane
Hanover Court
Bowling Club
Vaughan Way
WEST ST
Springfield
Rokefield
Hole Hill
RH4
Surgery
Sondes Place Dr
WESTCOTT ROAD
A25
Glebe Road
Industrial Estate
VINCENT LA
Howard Rd
Arundel Road
Vincent Rd
Norfolk Rd
Primary School
Nower Road
SOUTH STREET
Rose Hill
Upr Rose Hill
St Paul's Rd West
High Meadow Close
Marlborough Road
Chequers Pl
Cedar Cl
Springfield Road
St John's Rd
Watson Road
Bailey Road
Ashley Road
Burrell
The Chapel La
Furlong Road
Lince Lane
Lane
Westcott Street
Cradhurst Close
The Paddock
Balchins
Deerleap Road
GUILDFORD ROAD
PO
First School
School La
Milton Av
Milton Street
Broomfield Pk
Stones Lane
Pointers Hill
Parsonage La
Institute Road
Heath Rise
Sandrock Road
The Priory School
Powell Corderoy Primary School
Longfield Rd
West Bank
Vincent Drive
Falkland Rd
VINCENT DR
HORSHAM ROAD
Dorking General Hosp
Milton Heath
Hampstead Road
Greensand Way
The Nower
Nower Lodge School
Hampstead Road
Harrow Rd W
Harrow Rd East
Priory Close
Surgery
Knoll Road
Tower Hill
Tower Hill Rd
Hill Lane
A25
Greensand Way
Westcott
The Hildens
The Rookery
Rookery
Westcott Heath
Home Farm
Coldharbour Lane
Ridgeway
Ridgeway Cl
Brympton Cl
Roman Rd
Ridgeway Road
Firs Cl
Dorking Lawn Tennis & Squash Club
Ridgeway Drive
Highacre
FLINT HILL
A2003
Flint Hill Cl
Rough Rew
Bury Hill House
271
Wolvens Lane
Greensand Way
Bentsbrook Close
Bentsbrook Park
Westlees Farm
Holmwood Farm
Chadhurst Farm
Logmore Green
A24
Spook Hill
Hardy Cl
N Holm
Forge Works
Logmore Lane
Boar Hill
Squire's Farm
Redlands Farm
Redlands Lane
Swallow La
Norfolk Lane
Oaks Lane
Squire's Great Wood
Collickmoor Farm
Abinger Forest
Coldharbour Lane
Redlands Wood
Broadmoor
Sheephouse Lane
Whiteberry Road
Folly Lane
1
2
3
4
5
6
7
8
9
10
50
49
48
47
46
145
Shootlands
South Holmwood
Redlands
1 grid square represents 500 metres

H
J
K
L
M
N
P
18
19
20
255
274
REIGATE ROAD
Castle Gdns
Coach Rd
Boxhill Road
Brockham
The Av
Hillside
Links Vw
Dorking RFC
Old Kiln La
Mill Hl La
Nutwood Av
Nutwood Cl
Betchworth Park Golf Club
Golf Course
Betchworth Park
Hillside Cl
The Borough
Little Borough
Kiln Lane
Greensand Way
Mill Hill
Cemetery
RH3
Brockham
Pondtail Farm
Coach Road
Tanners Hill
Brockham School
Wheelers La
Dodds Pk
Middle Street
Wheelers Lane
Oakdene Close
Oakdene Rd
Warrenne Road
Moat House Farm
School Lane
Old Lane
Felton's Farm
Tanner's Brook
Glenfield Road
Glenfield Close
Brew House Rd
Silverdale Close
Tanners Meadow
Surgery
Boxhill Way
Ridge Cl
Tynedale Rd
The Close
Jubilee Terrace
PO
Gadbro
Tweed Lane
Parkpale Lane
Bushbury Lane
Park Cl
Middle Street
Brockham Park
Bushbury
Coleshill Farm
Roothill
Roothill Lane
Great Brockhamhurst
Brockhamhurst Road
Leigh Road
Shellwood Road
Westwood Common
Shellwood Manor
Station
Plxholme Gdns
Swan Mill Gdns
Downs Vw
Chester Cl
Vale
Leslie Road
Redcote
Dorking (Deepdene)
Dorking Cemetery
Hotel
Overdale
Punchbowl Lane
Park Rd
Ladyegate Close
Ladyegate Road
Deepdene
Deepdene Drive
DEEPDENE AVE
South Drive
Deepdene Wood
Park Copse
Park Farm
A24
Dorking Golf Club
Chart Park
Golf Course
Tilehurst Farm
Tilehurst Lane
Golden Lands Farm
Glenwood
Starhurst School
Chart Close
Chart Downs
Chart Lane
Chart Gdns
Trasher Md
Harecroft
Parris Cft
Stonebridge
South Road
Wildcroft Drive
Lake View
Larkspur Way
Magnolia Way
Dukes Ridge
Holmbury Dr
Shere Cl
Leith Vw
Abinger Close
Treelands
Shellwood Drive
Elder Wy
Road
Inholms Farm
Inholms Lane
North Holmwood Cricket Club
Blackbrook
PH
Blackbrook Road
Red Lane
Mid Holmwood Lane
wood
Holmwood Common
Brook Lodge Farm
Lodge Farm
Lodge Lane
Hawesrew Farm
Oakdale
Millbottom La
Mill Road
Henfold Lane
Wick Rd
Holmwood Park
Petersfield Farm
Ewood Farm
Ewood Lane
1
2
3
4
5
6
7
8
9
10
50
49
48
47
46
145

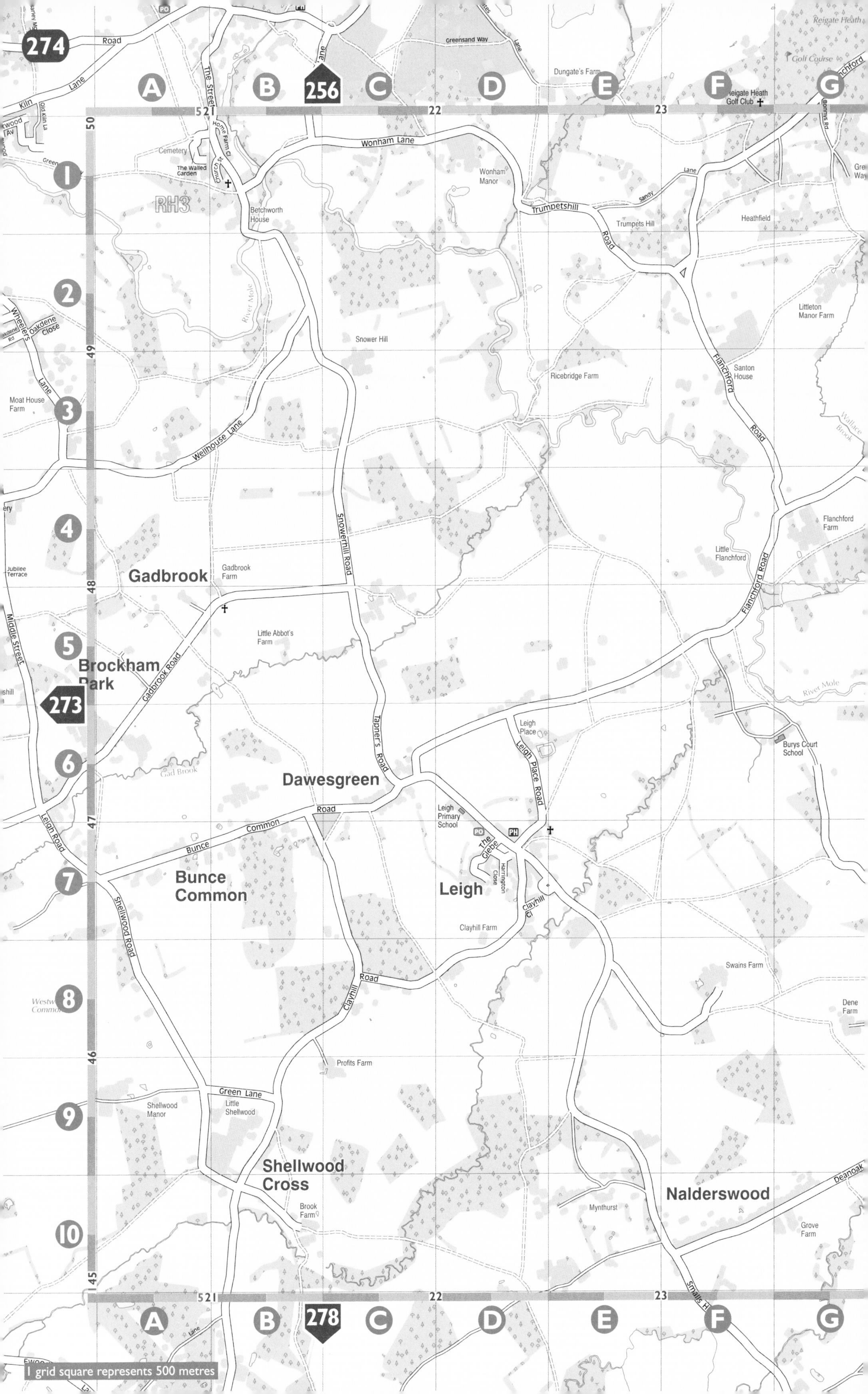

274
256
273
278
A
B
C
D
E
F
G
1
2
3
4
5
6
7
8
9
10
521
22
23
50
49
48
47
46
145
RH3
Road
Lane
Kiln
Old Kiln La
The Street
Home Farm Cl
Church St
Cemetery
The Walled Garden
Greensand Way
Wonham Lane
Wonham Manor
Dungate's Farm
Reigate Heath
Golf Course
Reigate Heath Golf Club
Flanchford
Bonnys Rd
Trumpetshill
Road
Sandy
Lane
Trumpets Hill
Heathfield
Betchworth House
River Mole
Wheelers
Oakdene Close
Lane
Moat House Farm
Snower Hill
Ricebridge Farm
Littleton Manor Farm
Santon House
Flanchford Road
Wallace Brook
Wellhouse Lane
Snowerhill Road
Gadbrook
Gadbrook Farm
Jubilee Terrace
Flanchford Farm
Little Flanchford
Middle Street
Little Abbot's Farm
Brockham Park
Gadbrook Road
Tapner's Road
Leigh Place
Leigh Place Road
River Mole
Burys Court School
Gad Brook
Dawesgreen
Road
Common
Bunce
Leigh Road
Leigh Primary School
PO
PH
The Glebe
Harrington Close
Bunce Common
Leigh
Clayhill Cl
Clayhill Farm
Shellwood Road
Swains Farm
Road
Clayhill
Dene Farm
Profits Farm
Green Lane
Shellwood Manor
Little Shellwood
Shellwood Cross
Nalderswood
Deanoak
Mynthurst
Brook Farm
Grove Farm
Smalls Hi
Lane
1 grid square represents 500 metres

REIGATE
WEST STREET
HIGH STREET
CHURCH STREET
Superstore
Cinema
Reigate Priory Junior School
Reigate Priory & Museum
Reigate Priory Park
Bancroft Court
Reigate Parish Infant School
School
REIGATE ROAD
BLACKBOROUGH ROAD
Millway
Reigate Day Hosp
Hatchlands
Hyland Business Centre
Rainbow Natural Health Centre
Hockley Industrial Centre
Surgery
Lesbourne Rd
West Rd
Blanford Road
Ringley Park Avenue
Waterlow Road
Oak Way
The Chase
Southern Clinic
High Trees Road
Dunottar School
Cockshot Lane
Smoke Lane
Furzefield Road
Belmont Rd
Cronks Hill
Dunottar Cl
Kings Avenue
St Johns Pri Sch
Pendleton Rd
Fountain Rd
Earlswood Road
Woodlands Road
Earlswood Mosque
Works
BRIGHTON ROAD
Common Rd
HORLEY ROAD
A23
A25
A217
Greensand Way
Hill House Drive
COCKSHOT HILL
Priory Drive
Randal Crs
Infant School
Park House Dr
Park
New North Road
North Rd
Smith Rd
Eastnor Road
Priory Road
Church Road
Allingham Road
Sandcross Lane
Sandcross Junior School
South Park
Clayhall Farm
Whitehall Lane
RH2
Slipshatch Road
Woodhatch
Surgery
Prices Lane
Stuart Road
Orchard Way
Kingsley Grove
Meadow Way
Dovers Garden Road
Hartswood Ave
Hitchings Way
Castle Dr
Beehive Way
Mead Vale
Blackthorn Cl
Hornbeam Road
Reigate School
Hardwick Rd
Somerset Road
Copse Rd
Arbutus Rd
Redhill & Reigate Golf Club
Pendleton Road
Earlswood Common
Golf Course
Westview Cl
Abinger Cl
Chaldon Cl
WOODHATCH ROAD
Atherfield Road
New Causeway
Tilers Way
Reeve Rd
Rushetts Road
Dovers Green School
Nuthatch Gardens
Ashdown Rd
Doversgreen
Felland Way
Kinnersley Walk
Dovers Farm
Hartswood Manor
DOVERS GREEN ROAD
Maple Road
Jason Cl
Heathfield Dr
Hampton Rd
North Road
Tollgate Avenue
South Earlswood
A2044
276
257
Brookside Farm
Sidlow
Ironsbottom
Bures Manor
Irons Bottom
Stumblehole Farm
Lonesome Lane
Lonesome Farm
Kinnersley Manor
Lodge Lane
Fontigarry Farm Business Park
Meath Green Lane
Ladyland Farm
River Mole
Wolvers
Duxhurst
Duxhurst Lane
Ridgewood Stud
REIGATE ROAD
Crutchfield Lane
279
H J K L M N P
25 26 27
50 49 48 47 46 45
1 2 3 4 5 6 7 8 9 10

276
258
275
280
Nutfield
NUTFIELD ROAD
A25
A23
A2044
A B C D E F G
1 2 3 4 5 6 7 8 9 10
528
29
30
50
49
48
47
46
145
Charman Rd
Surgery
Oakdene Rd
Grovehill Road
Whitepost Hill
Linkfield
Upper Br Road
Ridgeway Rd
Hylands Business Centre
Rainbow Natural Health Centre
Fenton Close
Fenton Road
Redstone Hill
Redstone Park
Hillfield Road
Rural Way
Kingsfield Business Centre
Palmer Cl
Chanctonbury Chase
Sylvan Way
Woodside Way
Redstone Hollow
Sandy Lane
Greensand Way
Hooley Lane
Hockley Industrial Centre
Wilton Rd
Brook Road
Sandpit Road
Victoria Rd
Redstone Rd
Earlsbrook Road
Philanthropic Road
Philanthropic Rd
Linnell Road
Redstone Cemetery
Earlswood Infant School
Hogtrough Lane
Clay Lane
Bower Hill Lane
Eastfield Rd
Eastfield Road
Hawthorn Wy
Fullers Wood Lane
Sandy Lane
Mid Street
Kentwyns Rise
Braes Md
Nutfield Church C Primary School
South Nutfield
Trindles Road
Holmesdale Road
Nutfield Station
Kings Mead
The Copse
Morris Rd
Bower Hl Cl
The Avenue
South Nutfield Cricket Club
RH1
Ridge Green
Thepps Close
Kings Cross Lane
Crab Hill Farm
Crab Hill Lane
Kings Avenue
St Johns Pri Sch
Pendleton Rd
Church Rd
Fountain
Mountview Dr
Chaldon Cl
Abinger Cl
Ifield Cl
Westview Cl
BRIGHTON ROAD
Woodlands Rd
Earlswood Road
Surgery
Works
Earlswood
St Johns
Emlyn Rd
Ifold Rd
Althorne Road
Knighton Road
Hartspiece Rd
Brambletye Junior School
Brambletye Park Road
Earlswood Mosque
Earlswood Station
Common Rd
Prince's Rd
Reed Dr
Royal Earlswood Park
HORLEY ROAD
Golf Course
Greensand Way
Canada Av
East Surrey Hospital
A&E
Three Arch Road
Canada Dr
Kings Mill Lane
Whitebushes
Redhill Aerodrome
Maple Road
Redhill FC
Jason Cl
Heston Rd
Feltham Rd
Hampton Rd
Hanworth Road
Wimborne Av
Shirley Avenue
White Bushes
Denton Cl
Edgefield Cl
Bushfield Dr
Rathgar Cl
Spencer Way
Wydene Cl
Masons Bridge Road
Green Lane
South Earlswood
Tollgate Avenue
Prince Albert Square
Horley Rd
Brookfield Cl
Hillford Place
Woodside Way
West Avenue
Copsleigh Way
Copsleigh Avenue
Salfords Prim Sch
Brookside Farm
Dean Farm
Moats Lane
South Hale Farm
Hatch Lane
Hotel
Honeycrock Lane
June Lane
Axes Lane
Axeland Park
Brownslade
Perrywood Business Park
Mead Av
Southern Av
Park Av
Park View Rd
Westmead Drive
Brighton Rd
Salfords Station
New House Lane
St George's Rd
Green Lane
Lodge Lane
Oak Lodge Dr
Horley Lodge
Horley Ldg La
Salfords Industrial Estate
SALFORDS
Picketts
Picketts Lane
Orchard Business Centre
Wood Cl
Harwood Park
Orchard Farm
Woolborough Lane
Meath Green Lane
Ladyland Farm
Salfords Industrial Est
Astra Business Centre
Heath Business Centre
Beechwood Villas
Empire Villas
Cross Oak Lane
BONEHURST ROAD
Littlelake Farm
Burstow Stream
Hathersh Farm
1 grid square represents 500 metres

Salfords 277
259
281
Bletchingley
Outwood
Wasp Green
Greensand Way
Outwood Lane
Coneybury
Rabies Heath Road
Coldharbour La
Sandhills
Coldharbour Farm
South Park Lane
Cooper's Hill Road
Lyttel Hall
M23
Sandhills Farm
Wychcroft House
Cuckseys Farm
South Park Farm
Kennels Farm
Henshaw Farm
Lamb Business Park
Lower South Park
Burstow Park Farm
Carlton Road
Lodge Farm
Prince of Wales Road
Brown's Hill
Harewood House
Outwood Common
Brickfield Road
Wasp Green Lane
Tile Barn
Dayseys Hill
Bellwether Lane
Millers Copse
Miller's Lane
Scott's Hill
Outwood Windmill
Gayhouse Lane
Hornecourt Hill
Whitewood
Whitewood Lane
Jarves Farm
Hornecourt Manor Farm
Rookery Farm
Rookery
Old Hall Farm
Wilmots Lane
Whitewood House Farm

Cross
Brook Farm
Nalderswood
Mynthurst
Grove Farm
274
A
B
C
D
E
F
G
521
22
23
45
44
43
42
41
140
1
2
3
4
5
6
7
8
9
10
Ewood Lane
Ewood Lane
Mill Lane
Broad Lane
Smalls Hill Road
Parkhouse Farm
Hammond's Copse
Deanoak Brook
Norwood Place Farm
Rose Cotta Farm
Chantersluer Farm
Becket Wood
Parkgate
PH
Partridge Lane
Hales Bridge
Cidermill Road
Rickettswood Farm
Norwood Hill
Blanks Lane
Red House
Hatchetts
Sturtwood Farm
Highworth Farm
Barn Lane
Hotel
Cudworth Lane
Cudworth
Burnt Oak Lane
Green Lane
Beggarshouse Lane
Stan Hill
The Greenings
Partridge Lane
Manor House
Beam Brook
Glover's Rd
Glover's Wood
Cidermill Farm
Home Farm
Ockley Lodge
Duke's Road
Duke's Road
Duke's Road
Russ Hill
Gatwick Zoo
Russ Hill
Duke's Rd
Boothlands Farm
Newhouse Farm
Charlwood La
Russ Hill
282
Upper Prestwood Farm
1 grid square represents 500 metres

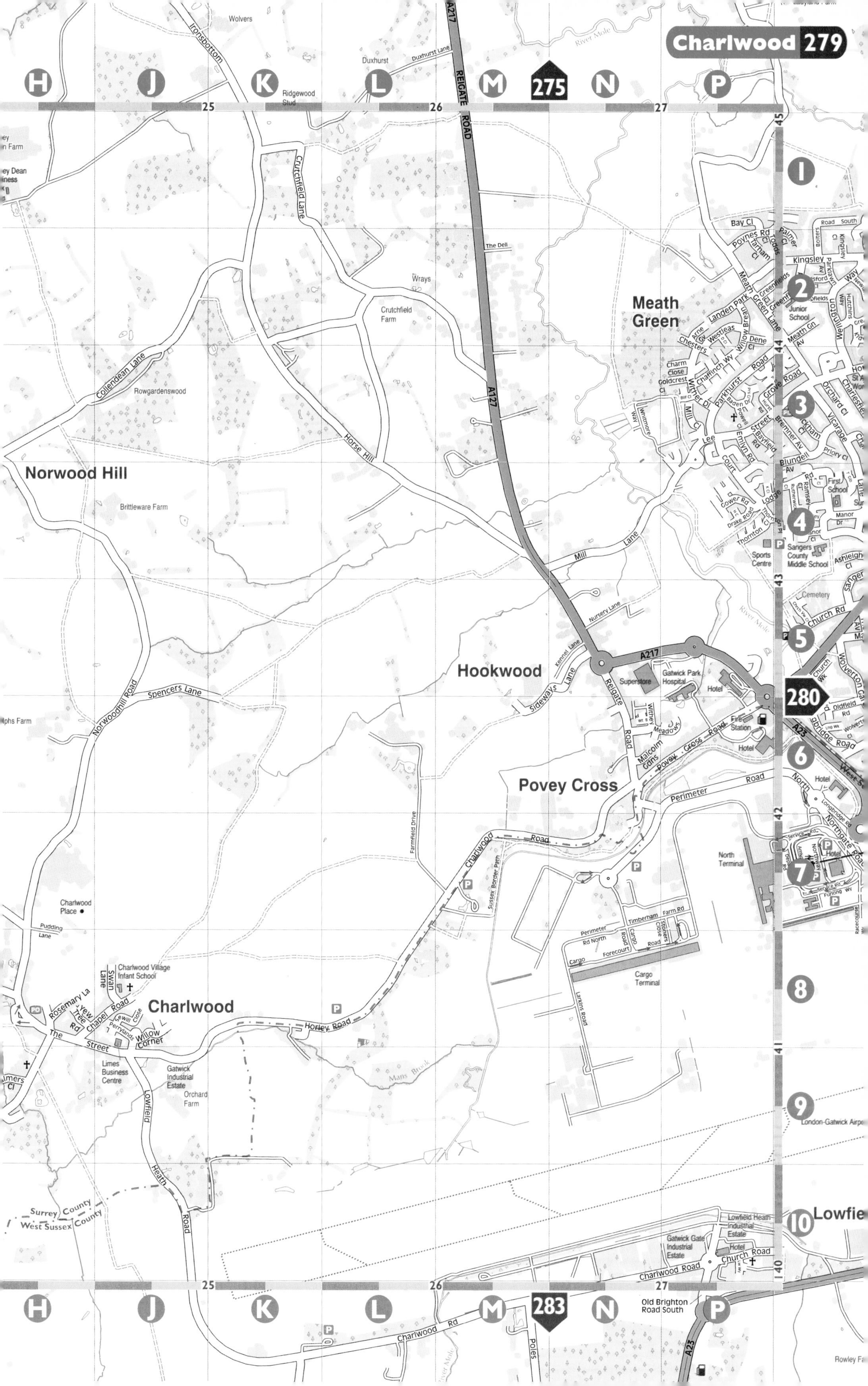

Norwood Hill
Hookwood
Meath Green
Povey Cross
Charlwood
Wolvers
Ironsbottom
Duxhurst
Duxhurst Lane
Ridgewood Stud
Crutchfield Lane
Crutchfield Farm
Wrays
The Dell
REIGATE ROAD
A217
A127
Collendean Lane
Rowgardenswood
Horse Hill
Brittleware Farm
Mill Lane
Nursery Lane
Kennel Lane
Sideways Lane
Spencers Lane
Norwoodhill Road
Superstore
Gatwick Park Hospital
Hotel
Fire Station
Reigate Road
Povey Cross Road
Malcolm Gdns
Meadows
Perimeter Road
Charlwood Road
Farmfield Drive
Sussex Border Path
North Terminal
Cargo Terminal
Larkins Road
Timberham Farm Rd
Charlwood Place
Pudding Lane
Charlwood Village Infant School
Swan Lane
Rosemary La
Yew Tree Rd
Chapel Road
The Street
Willow Corner
Horley Road
Limes Business Centre
Gatwick Industrial Estate
Orchard Farm
Lowfield Heath Road
Mans Brook
Surrey County
West Sussex County
Lowfield Heath Industrial Estate
Gatwick Gate Industrial Estate
Church Road
Old Brighton Road South
Poles
Charlwood Rd
A23
River Mole
Sports Centre
Sangers County Middle School
Junior School
First School
Cemetery
Church Rd
Longbridge Road
Northgate Road
London-Gatwick Airport
Lowfield
Rowley Fa

275
280
283

280
276
279
284
A
B
C
D
E
F
G
528
29
30
45
44
43
42
41
40
1
2
3
4
5
6
7
8
9
10
HORLEY
Fernhill
Lowfield Heath
Black Corner
Tinsley Green
Shipl
London-Gatwick Airport
London Gatwick Airport
South Terminal
North Terminal
Gatwick Airport Station
Horley Station
Junction 9a
Junction 9
M23
A23
B2036
RH6
BRIGHTON ROAD
BALCOMBE RD
BALCOMBE ROAD
LONDON ROAD
AIRPORT WAY
Cross Oak Lane
Lake Lane
Ladbroke Road
Smallfield Rd
Smallfield Road
Langshott
Haroldslea Drive
Castle Drive
Silverlea Gardens
Avenue Gardens
Balcombe Gdns
Limes Avenue
Massetts Road
Church Rd
Russells Crescent
Victoria Rd
Station Approach
Perimeter Road
Perimeter Road East
Perimeter Road South
Fernhill Road
Peeks Brook Lane
Church Lane
Antlands Lane East
Radford Road
Hathersham Lane
Burstow Stream
River Mole
Littlelake Farm
Greatlake Farm
Hathersham Farm
Harrowsley Green Farm
Burstow Hall
Burstow Lodge Business Centre
Gatwick Medical Centre
Atlas Medical Centre
Langshott County Infant School
Oakwood School
Sangers County Middle School
Yattendon School
Horley Health Centre
Police Station
Telephone Exchange
Archway Theatre
Riverside Garden Park
Sports Centre
Cemetery
Lawn Tennis Club
Bridge Industrial Estate
West Sussex County
Surrey County
Sussex Border Path
1 grid square represents 500 metres

Horley 281
Wasp Green
Miller's Copse
Miller's Lane
277
Hornecourt Manor Farm
Hornecourt Hill
Whitewood
Whitewood Lane
Jarves Farm
Rookery Farm
Rookery Hill
Old Hall Farm
Wilmot's Lane
Whitewood House Farm
Norman's Road
Horne
Church Road
Horne House Farm
Burstow Lodge
Burstow Business Centre
Hollesley Farm
Croydonbarn Lane
Weatherhill
Chapel Road
Scott's Hill
Bones Lane
Hayes Wk
The Cravens
Carey's Wood
Raleigh Drive
Tudor Close
The Woodlands
Churchill Rd
Gorse Dr
Field Wk
Meadow View
Smallfield Road
Whitehouse Farm
Weatherhill Rd
Cooper Close
Grangeway
Woodside Cres
Broadbridge La
Grange End
Works
New Road
Orchard Road
Heather Wk
Burstow Primary School
Plough Road
Wheelers Lane
The Acorns
Bridgeham Wy
Kings Md
Toronto Dr
Ontario Cl
Rough Beech
Bysshe Court
Green Farm
Smallfield
Bridgeham Grange
Broadbridge Lane
Dowlands Lane
Chithurst Lane
Geary Close
Broadbridge
Lone Oak
Redehall Road
Park Road
Chithurst Farm
Cross Lane
Dowlands Farm
Church Road
Burstow
Redeham Hall
Rede Hall
West Park
Keepers Farm
Chithurst Lane
B2037
Copthorne Bank
Effingham Road
West Park Road
Perry Farm
Baker's Wood
B2028
LANE
Dowlands Lane
East Hill Lane
Newhouse Farm
Sussex Border Path
Beechfield
Effingham Lane
Rowland Close
Heatherley
Herons Lea
Herons Close
Snow Hill
Snowhill Lane
Snowhill Business Centre
Copthorne Road
A264
Effingham Park Golf Club
Hotel
Chapel Lane
285
H J K L M N P
32 33 34
1 2 3 4 5 6 7 8 9 10
45 44 43 42 41 40

278
A
B
C
D
E
F
G
521
22
23
40
39
38
37
36
135
1
2
3
4
5
6
7
8
9
10
Hill
Duke's Road
Duke's Rd
Charlwood Rd
Russ Hill
Newhouse Farm
Boothlands Farm
Upper Prestwood Farm
Ivyhouse Farm
Sussex Border Path
Oaklands Park
Orltons
Jordans
Partridge Lane
Chaffold's Farm
Prestwood Lane
Lower Prestwood Farm
Orltons Lane
Surrey County
West Sussex County
Rusper Road
Newdigate Road
Ifieldwood
The Mount
Langhurst
Hillybarn Road
Ifield Wood
Capel Road
Highams
Langhurst Lane
Bonwycks Place
High Street
Sussex Border Path
Chowles
East Street
Burnt House Lane
Rusper Road
Rusper
PO
Rusper Primary School
Cooks Md
Normans
Pucks Croft
Steeres Hill
Ashmore La
Horsham Rd
Faygate Lane
Cobnor
Lambs Green
Lambs Green Road
Stumbleholm Farm
River Mole
Axmas Farm
Golf Course
Rusper Court House
St Andrews Road
Hoylake Close
Birkdale Drive
Fairway
Ambleside
Baldhorns Park
Wimland Road
Kilnwood End
Caryllls
Kilnwood
Coombers Farm
Kilnwood Lane
Faygate Lane
Wimlands Lane
Carylls Lea
Wimland Farm
Wimland Hill
Chetwood Road
HORSHAM
1 grid square represents 500 metres

Surrey County
West Sussex County
279
284
Gatwick Gate Industrial Estate
Charlwood Road
Charlwood Rd
Old Brighton Road South
Poles Lane
Bonnetts Lane
Amberley Farm
Langley Green
Crawley RFC
Ifield Court
Ifield Green
Ifield
Ifield Avenue
Stafford Road
Langley Lane
Rusper Road
Rectory Lane
Old Barn Theatre
Deerswood School
St Margarets CE First & Middle School
Ifield Community College
Ifield First & Middle School
Ifield Station
The Croft
Cemetery
Crawley Avenue
A23
A2011
A2220
A2219
A2004
London Road
Manor Royal
Kelvin Way
Kelvin Lane
Kelvin Business Centre
Fleming Way
Faraday Road
Industrial Estate
County Oak Way
Metcalf Way
The City Business Centre
County Oak Retail Park
Catherington Special School
Langley Green First School
Tushmore Lane
Crompton Way
Works
Hotel
Rowley Farm
West Green
Hollywood Bowl
UCG
St Georges Ct
Crawley College Annexe
West Green First School
Crawley Hosp
A&E
Northgate
Northgate First & Middle Sch
Northgate Road
High Street
The Bvd
Queens Square
Memorial Gardens
Haslett Avenue
Station Way
Crawley Station
College Road
County Mall
Library & Council Building
The Hawth Theatre & Conference
Health Centre
Swimming Pool
CRAWLEY
Gossops Green
Goffs Park
St Wilfrids RC School
Crawley Museum (Goffs Park House)
Horsham Road
Brighton Road
Southgate
Southgate First and Middle School
Southgate Av
Tilgate
St Francis of Assisi Primary School
Thomas Bennett Community College
Crawley Town FC
Broadfield East Middle School
Broadfield Health Cen
Desmond Anderson F&M School
Bewbush
Bewbush Medical Cen
Bewbush Middle School
County First School
Bewbush Leisure Centre
Waterfield First School
The Holy Trinity CE School
Broadfield

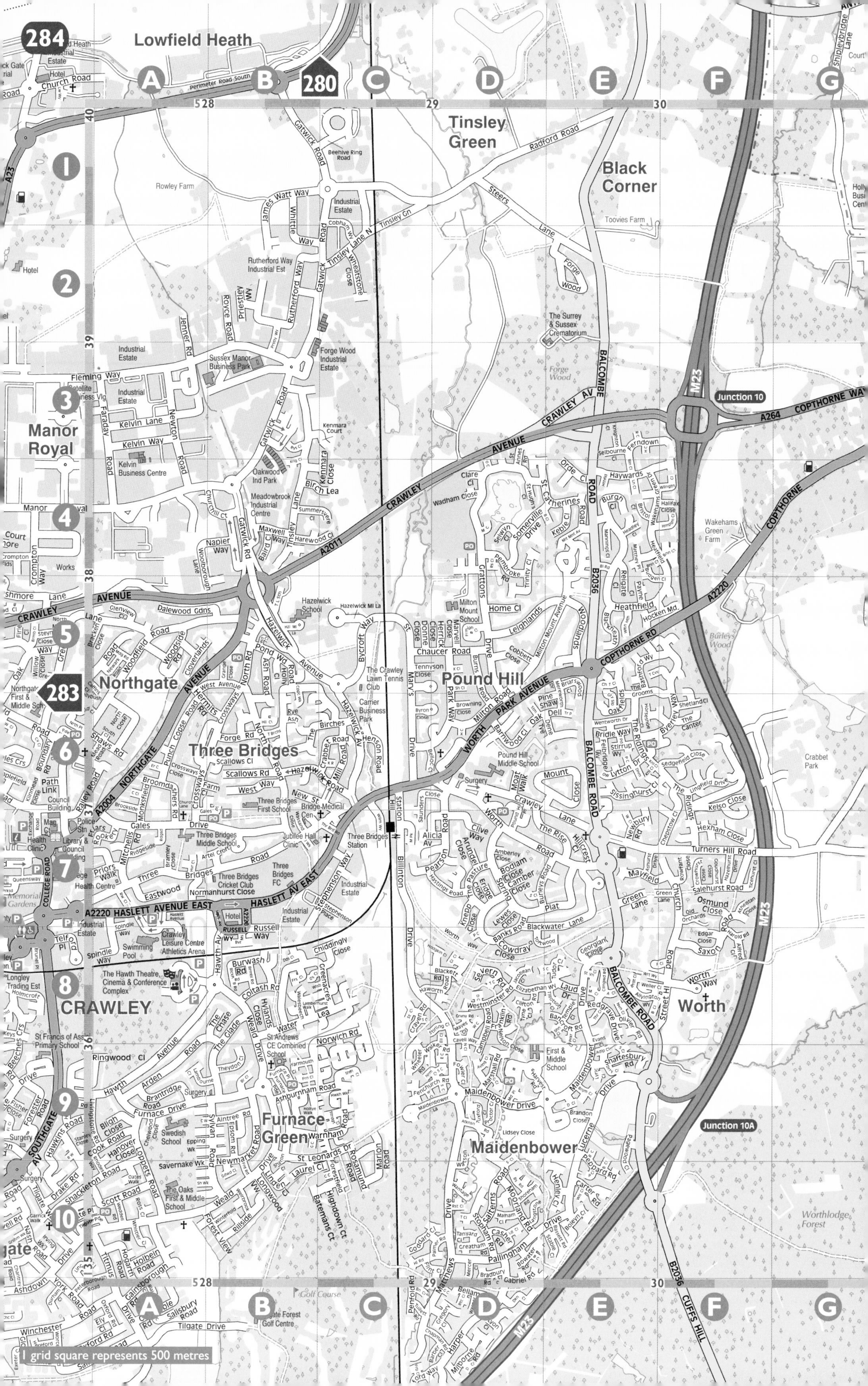
284
280
283
Lowfield Heath
Tinsley Green
Black Corner
Manor Royal
Northgate
Three Bridges
Pound Hill
CRAWLEY
Furnace Green
Maidenbower
Worth
Crabbet Park
Wakehams Green Farm
Burleys Wood
Worthlodge Forest
Forge Wood
Toovies Farm
Rowley Farm
The Surrey & Sussex Crematorium
Junction 10
Junction 10A
M23
A23
A264 COPTHORNE WAY
COPTHORNE RD
A2220
A2011
CRAWLEY AVENUE
BALCOMBE ROAD
B2036
CUFFS HILL
WORTH PARK AVENUE
A2004 NORTHGATE AVENUE
A2220 HASLETT AVENUE EAST
SOUTHGATE AV
COLLEGE ROAD
Radford Road
Steers Lane
Gatwick Road
James Watt Way
Tinsley Lane N
Fleming Way
Kelvin Lane
Kelvin Way
Faraday Road
Newton Road
Jenner Rd
Royce Road
Rutherford Way
Rutherford Way Industrial Est
Forge Wood Industrial Estate
Sussex Manor Business Park
Kelvin Business Centre
Oakwood Ind Park
Meadowbrook Industrial Centre
Hazelwick School
Milton Mount School
Three Bridges Station
Three Bridges Middle School
Three Bridges First School
Three Bridges Cricket Club
Three Bridges FC
Crawley Leisure Centre Athletics Arena
The Hawth Theatre, Cinema & Conference Complex
Pound Hill Middle School
First & Middle School
Swedish School
The Oaks First & Middle School
St Andrews CE Combined School
St Francis of Assisi Primary School
Tilgate Forest Golf Centre
Tilgate Drive
Turners Hill Road
Maidenbower Drive
528
29
30
40
39
38
37
36
35
A B C D E F G
1 2 3 4 5 6 7 8 9 10
1 grid square represents 500 metres

Newhouse Farm
Sussex Border Path
Beechfield
Effingham Lane
B2037
281
Domewood
H
J
K
L
M
N
P
32
33
34
Rowland Close
Heatherley
Snow Hill
Snowhill Lane
Herons Close
Herons Lea
Snowhill Business Centre
Golf Course
B2037
Copthorne Road
Clay Hall Lane
PH
Hotel
Effingham Park Golf Club
Chapel Lane
West Park Road
B2028
Green Lane
A264
Roffey's Close
Elger Way
Copthorne Bank
Borers
Francis Gdns
Maynard Cl
Borers Business Park
Borers Arms Road
Lashmere
Copthorne Preparatory School
Mill Lane
Great Frenches Park
Junior School
Church Road
Junior School
Meadow Rd
Business Centre
The Meadow
The Green
Knowle Drive
Knowle Close
Spring Copse
Spring Gardens
Copthorne Golf Club
The Drive
Close
Postway
Brookside
Brookview
Akehurst Close
New Town
Pinetrees Close
COPTHORNE
COMMON
ROAD
Newlands Park
South View Close
Turners Hill Road
SNOW HILL
PO
Pembley Green
Cottage Place
Lands
Calluna Drive
Kitsmead
Brookhill Road
Brookhill Close
Infant School
Lane
Bracken Close
Bramble Close
Copthorne Common Road
A264
COPTHORNE
Church
Fairway
Heather Cl
Gorse Cl
Border Chase
Erica Way
Works
Barn Court
Copthorne Common
Hotel
Copthorne Squash Club
Common
Golf Course
Sussex Border Path
Shepherd's Farm
TURNERS HILL ROAD B2028
Cuttinglye Lane
Down Park
Haven Gardens
Fermandy Lane
Sandy Lane
Hazelwood Close
Furzwood
Gardner Lane
Long Acre
Crawley Down Health Centre
Hophurst Drive
Hophurst Close
Hillside
Infant School
School
Buckley Place
Squires Close
Wyniga Close
Station Road
Sunny Avenue
Vicarage Road
Beech Gardens
Beech Holme
Brickyard Lane
Old Station Close
Kiln Road
Bricklands
Sandhill
Huntsland
Old Rowfant
Ley House
Home Farm
Rowfant
Grange Road
CRAWLEY DOWN
Worth Way
The Grange
Wallage Lane
Hayheath
Worth Way
Works
Hundred Acres
Rowfant Business Centre
Compasses Corner
TURNERS HILL ROAD
B2028
Miswells House
RH10
Worth Hall
Turners Hill Road
Medway
B2028
NORTH STREET
Hill House Close
Turners Hill
Lion Lane
Mount Lane
Standinghall Lane
Major's Hill
Tulleys Farm
PO
Willow Ridge
ROAD B2110
CHURCH
Turners Hill CE Primary School
Withypitts East
Withypitts
Rashes Farm
Standinghall Farm
B2110
The Grove
Withypitts Farm
Woodharbour
PADDOCKHURST ROAD
SELSFIELD ROAD
B2028
South Hill
Back
Standinghall
1
2
3
4
5
6
7
8
9
10
40
39
38
37
36
135

Abbey Mead 195 L6
Abbey Wood 163 L3
Abbots Langley 54 F8
Abbotswood 250 C8
Abinger Common 271 L9
Abinger Hammer 270 F6
Abridge 83 M7
Acton 135 P10
Acton Green 156 A3
Addington 224 F3
Addiscombe 203 N8
Addlestone 215 M2
Addlestonemoor 195 M9
Adeyfield 36 B6
Aimes Green 63 L4
Albury 269 M5
Albury Heath 269 P7
Aldborough Hatch 123 H2
Aldenham 73 P3
Aldersbrook 121 P6
Alperton 135 K3
Amersham 69 J4
Amersham Common 69 H5
Amersham Old Town 68 E6
Amersham on the Hill 68 G3
Amwell 21 H4
Anerley 203 P2
Anthonys 214 D8
Aperfield 244 C3
Apsley 35 N10
Ardleigh Green 125 K1
Ardley End 31 J2
Arkley 76 E9
Artington 267 N5
Asheridge 50 C2
Ashford 174 A8
Ashford Common 174 E9
Ashley Green 33 L10
Ashley Park 197 H10
Ashtead 237 K4
Austenwood 109 N1
Aveley 146 C9
Avery Hill 184 F2
Ayot Green 22 C3
Ayres End 20 E6
Badgers Mount 228 C5
Baker's Wood 111 H6
Balham 180 A3
Bandonhill 222 E2
Banstead 239 K2
Barking 142 G2
Barkingside 122 E1
Barnehurst 164 E9
Barnes 156 E7
Barnes Cray 165 J10
Barnet 77 J10
Barnet Gate 76 B10
Barnsbury 5 N3
Barwell 219 H4
Batchworth 92 A3
Batchworth Heath 92 B5
Batlers Green 74 E4
Battersea 158 A6
Bayford 42 G4
Bayley's Hill 264 F7
Bayswater 9 H7
Beaconsfield 88 B10
Bean 188 G6
Beaumont 171 N4
Beckenham 204 G3
Beckton 142 C8
Becontree 123 N10
Beddington 202 F9
Beddington Corner 202 B7
Bedford Park 156 C2
Bedmond 54 F3
Belgravia 16 C5
Bell Bar 41 K10
Bell Common 64 G8
Bellfields 249 P7
Bell Green 182 E6
Bellingdon 32 E10
Bellingham 182 F7
Belmont 94 F10
Belmont 221 K5
Belsize 53 H8
Belvedere 164 C4
Bengeo 25 J3
Benhilton 201 L10
Bennetts End 36 A9
Bentley 86 D7
Bentley Heath 77 J1
Berkhamsted 33 M5
Bermondsey 19 N2
Bernards Heath 38 C4
Berrylands 199 L6
Berry's Green 244 D2
Bessels Green 246 E10
Betchworth 255 P9
Bethnal Green 140 A5
Betsham 189 L7
Bewbush 283 J10
Bexley 163 M10
Bexleyheath 164 A10
Bickley 206 B2
Biggin 168 F5
Biggin Hill 243 N3
Binscombe 267 H9
Birch Green 24 D7
Birchwood 40 E2
Bishopsgate 171 L7
Bisley 230 G2
Blackbrook 273 K7
Black Corner 284 E1
Blackfen 185 J2
Blackheath 161 L8
Blackheath 269 H8
Blackheath Park 161 M10
Blacknest 193 H3
Blackwall 141 J9
Bletchingley 259 L10
Bloomsbury 11 K3
Bobbingworth 49 L9
Borehamwood 75 K7
The Borough 18 F2
Botany Bay 78 E2
Botley 51 M6
Bourne End 34 F8
Boveney 148 B5
Bovingdon 52 E3
Bovingdon Green 52 C5
Bovinger 48 G10
Bow 140 F4
Bow Common 140 F7
Bowes Park 98 F7
Bowmans 186 G3
Box Hill 255 M8
Boxmoor 35 L8
Brands Hill 150 E6
Brasted 245 N10
Brasted Chart 263 L4
Brays Grove 47 K2
Brentford 155 J5
Brentford End 154 G5
Brentwood 106 G3
Brewer Street 259 K7
Brickendon 43 K5
Bricket Wood 55 M7
Brick Hill 213 H1
Bridge End 234 C6
Brimsdown 80 D6
Britwell 128 E6
Brixton 159 H10
Broad Colney 57 J4
Broadford 267 P7
Broad Green 203 J7
Broadgreen Wood 43 H1
Broadham Green 261 H8
Broadley Common 46 A6
Broadmoor 272 A9
Broadoak End 24 G3
Brockham 273 M1
Brockham Park 273 P5
Brockley 182 E1
Bromley 140 G5
Bromley 205 N2
Bromley Common 206 A6
Bromley Park 205 K1
Brompton 15 N4
Brondesbury 2 A1
Brondesbury Park 136 G3
Brook 269 P8
Brook Green 156 F2
Brooklands 216 A5
Brookmans Park 59 H2
Brook Street 106 D5
Brookwood 230 F6
Broomhall 192 E7
Broom Hill 207 J7
Broxbourne 44 F6
Brunswick Park 98 B4
Buckhurst Hill 101 P4
Buckland 256 D9
Bucks Hill 53 M10
Bullen's Green 40 B8
Bulls Cross 79 P2
Bulstrode 53 H4
Bumble's Green 45 M10
Bunce Common 274 A7
Burgh Heath 238 G5
Burnham 128 B4
Burntcommon 251 J1
Burnt Oak 96 A8
Burpham 250 D6
Burrowhill 213 L5
Burrows Cross 270 C7
Burstow 281 H8
Burwood Park 217 H2
Bury Green 62 A7
Bushbury 273 M5
Bushey 94 B1
Bushey Heath 94 D1
Bushey Mead 200 G3
Bush Hill Park 79 M10
Bushy Hill 250 E8
Butlers Cross 89 L5
Byfleet 215 N9
Caldecote Hill 94 E1
Camberwell 159 N7
Camden Town 4 D4
Campions 30 A6
The Camp 38 F8
Canary Wharf 140 G10
Cannon Hill 200 G4
Canonbury 6 F3
Canons Park 95 K8
Carpenders Park 93 N3
Carshalton 221 P1
Carshalton Beeches 221 P5
Carshalton on the Hill 222 A4
Cartbridge 232 E8
Carter's Green 30 F9
Castle Green 143 M3
Castle Green 213 J9
Caterham 241 M9
Catford 183 H4
Chadwell Heath 123 N3
Chadwell St Mary 168 C2
Chafford Hundred 167 K2
Chaldon 241 J10
Chalfont Common 90 C5
Chalfont Grove 89 N7
Chalfont St Giles 89 L3
Chalfont St Peter 90 D8
Chalk 191 K4
Chalvey 149 H1
Chandler's Cross 72 A4
Charlton 162 A4
Charlton 196 D2
Charlwood 279 J8
Chartridge 50 B4
The Chart 263 L6
Chase Cross 104 F7
Chattern Hill 174 C7
Chaulden 34 G7
Cheam 221 J2
Cheapside 192 D2
Chelsea 15 M8
Chelsfield 227 P2
Chelsham 242 F3
Chenies 70 F4
Chertsey 195 K7
Chertsey Meads 195 P8
Chesham 51 H7
Chesham Bois 69 H2
Cheshunt 62 A6
Chessington 219 K3
Chessmount 51 K8
Chevening 246 A5
Chigwell 102 E3
Chigwell Row 103 L3
Childerditch 127 L2
Childsbridge 247 N5
Child's Hill 117 H7
Childwick Bury 20 B10
Childwick Green 20 A9
Chilworth 268 F6
Chingford 101 H3
Chingford Green 101 H2
Chingford Hatch 101 K5
Chipperfield 53 L7
Chipping Barnet 77 H9
Chipstead 240 B5
Chipstead 246 D8
Chislehurst 184 F10
Chislehurst West 184 D9
Chiswell Green 55 N1
Chiswick 156 C3
Chobham 213 J6
Cholesbury 32 B7
Chorleywood 70 G8
Chorleywood Bottom 70 G10
Chorleywood West 70 D9
Christmaspie 266 A1
Church End 71 J4
Church End 97 K10
Church End 136 C2
Church End 234 A7
Churchgate 62 A5
Churchgate Street 30 A7
Church Langley 47 N1
Church Town 260 B7
Cippenham 128 C10
City of London 12 D7
Clapham 158 C8
Clapham Park 180 E2
Clapton Park 120 E9
Claremont Park 217 P4
Clatterford End 67 J6
Claverhambury 63 N3
Claygate 218 E3
Clayhall 102 C10
Clay Hill 79 K3
Clement Street 187 L9
Clerkenwell 12 A1
Clewer Green 148 D9
Clewer New Town 148 F8
Clewer Village 148 F6
Clock House 222 D10
Cobham 217 H10
Cockfosters 77 P9
Codmore 51 K6
Coldblow 186 D5
Coldharbour 165 H3
Cole Green 24 B7
Coleman Green 21 M6
Cole Park 176 F2
Coleshill 68 E10
Coles Meads 258 A7
Colham Green 132 A6
Colindale 116 B1
College Park 136 D5
Collier Row 104 D9
Colliers Hatch 66 D6
Collier's Wood 179 N10
Colnbrook 150 F7
Colney Hatch 98 A7
Colney Heath 39 P8
Colney Street 56 D6
Commonwood 53 K10
Compton 266 F6
Coney Hall 225 K1
Coombe 178 B10
Coopersale Common 65 N5
Coopersale Street 65 M7
Cooper's Green 39 N1
Cooper's Hill 172 A6
Copse Hill 178 D10
Copthall Green 64 A9
Copthorne 285 J2
Corbets Tey 126 A10
Cottenham Park 200 E1
Coulsdon 240 F2
Counters End 35 K6
Cowley 131 M6
Cowley Peachy 131 M8
Coxtie Green 86 C9
Cranbourne 170 A5
Cranbrook 122 D5
Cranford 153 H6
Cranham 126 D5
Cranley Gardens 118 B2
Crawley 283 P8
Crawley Down 285 P6
Crayford 187 H1
Creekmouth 143 H7
Crews Hill 79 J1
Cricklewood 116 G9
Crockenhill 208 E7
Crockham Hill 262 F9
Crofton 206 G9
Cromer-Hyde 21 P6
Crooked Billet 178 E9
Cross Keys 264 G3
Crouch End 118 D4
Crow Green 86 F7
Croxley Green 72 B9
Croydon 203 L10
Crystal Palace 181 P8
Cubitt Town 161 H3
Cudham 244 G1
Cudworth 278 B7
Cuffley 60 G4
Cupid Green 36 C2
Curtismill Green 84 G7
Custom House 142 B9
Dagenham 144 E2
Dalston 7 M2
Dancers Hill 76 F1
Darenth 188 B8
Dartford 187 K3
Dartmouth Park 118 B7
Datchet 149 N7
Datchet Common 149 P8
Dawesgreen 274 B6
Deacons Hill 75 M10
Dean Bottom 210 G3
Debden Green 82 F4
De Beauvoir Town 7 J5
Dedworth 148 C7
Deepdene 273 J2
Denbies 254 C10
Denham 111 K7
Denham Green 111 H4
Denton 191 H3
Deptford 160 E5
Derry Downs 207 N6
Digswell Park 22 G2
Digswell Water 23 K1
Doddinghurst 86 G3
Dollis Hill 116 E8
Donkey Town 212 C9
Dorking 272 G3
Dormer's Wells 134 A9
Dorney 148 A2
Doversgreen 275 L4
Downe 226 C7
Downham 183 J8
Down Park 285 P4
Downside 235 J5
Dryhill 246 C10
Ducks Island 96 G1
Dudden Hill 116 D10
Dudswell 33 J1
Dulwich 181 N5
Dulwich Village 181 M3
Dunton Green 246 F5
Ealing 135 H9
Earl's Court 14 E6
Earlsfield 179 M4
Earlswood 276 A2
East Acton 136 B9
East Barnet 97 N1
East Bedfont 174 C3
East Burnham 128 E3
Eastbury 92 G5
East Clandon 251 P7
Eastcote 113 J5
Eastcote Village 113 J3
East Dulwich 181 P1
Eastend 28 B10
East End Green 24 D9
East Ewell 220 G6
East Finchley 117 N1
East Ham 142 B4
East Horsley 252 E3
East Molesey 198 B5
East Sheen 178 A1
East Tilbury 169 L3
Eastwick 28 E7
East Wickham 163 K7
Eden Park 204 E4
Edgware 95 N5
Edmonton 99 M5
Effingham 253 L3
Egham 172 D9
Egham Hythe 172 G9
Egham Wick 171 L10
Egypt 108 G9
Ellenbrook 40 A3
Elm Corner 234 B5
Elmers End 204 C3
Elm Park 125 J10
Elmstead 184 B8
Elstree 75 K10
Eltham 184 B2
Emerson Park 125 M4
Enfield 79 K8
Enfield Highway 80 B6
Enfield Lock 80 E3
Enfield Town 79 L7
Enfield Wash 80 D4
Englefield Green 171 N10
Epping 65 K6
Epping Green 42 E8
Epping Green 46 D10
Epping Upland 64 F2
Epsom 219 P10
Erith 164 G4
Esher 218 B1
Essendon 42 A3
Eton 149 H5
Eton Wick 148 E3
Ewell 220 E7
Eynsford 209 M9
Fair Cross 123 J10
Fairlands 249 J7
Fairlop 103 H9
Fairmile 217 N8
Falconwood 163 H10
Farleigh 224 E10
Farleigh Court 224 F10
Farley Green 269 P10
Farnborough 226 E2
Farncombe 267 J9
Farnham Common 129 J1
Farnham Park 129 H3
Farnham Royal 129 H4
Farningham 209 P7
Fawkham Green 210 G10
Felden 35 K10
Feltham 175 J5
Felthamhill 174 F8
Fernhill 280 F8
Fetcham 236 C9
Fickleshole 225 K10
Fiddlers Hamlet 65 M8
Field Common 197 N7
Fields End 34 G5
Finchley 97 K9
Finsbury 6 A9
Finsbury Park 118 G7
Flamstead End 62 A4
Flaunden 52 D8
Fleet Downs 188 A5
Fleetville 38 F6
Fletcher's Green 265 L10
Flexford 248 C10
The Folly 20 G1
Foots Cray 185 L9
Force Green 245 H10
Forestdale 224 D5
Forest Gate 121 M10
Forest Hill 182 C4
Fortis Green 118 B2
Forty Green 88 A7
Forty Hill 79 N5
Foster Street 48 A2
Foxbury 184 G8
Fox Corner 249 H1
Fox Hatch 86 E4
Fredley 254 G5
Freezy Water 80 D2
French Street 263 J6
Friday Hill 101 J4
Friday Street 271 N9
Friern Barnet 97 P5
Frithsden 34 D1
Froghole 262 G8
Frogmore 56 D4
The Frythe 22 D1
Fulham 156 G6
Fullwell Cross 102 G9
Fulmer 110 A9
Furnace Green 284 B9
Furzedown 180 C7
Gadbrook 274 A4
Gadebridge 35 J4
Gallows Corner 105 L9
Gants Hill 122 C4
Ganwick Corner 77 L1
Garston 73 K1
Gatton 258 A4
George Green 130 B8
Gerrards Cross 109 P5
Gidea Park 104 G10
Giggshill 198 F7
Gilston 28 G6
Gilston Park 28 F5
Gilwell Park 81 H7
Givons Grove 255 J1
Globe Town 140 C5
Goathurst Common 264 C6
Goddington 207 M10
Godstone 260 A7
Goff's Oak 61 K4
Golders Green 117 H4
Goldsworth Park 231 M2
Gomshall 270 D6
Goodley Stock 262 E6
Goodmayes 123 L7
Goose Green 44 C2
Gorhambury 37 K5
Gospel Oak 118 B10
Gossops Green 283 L8
Grange Hill 102 G7
Grange Park 79 H9
Gravel Hill 90 C7
Gravesend 190 E1
Grays 167 M6
Great Amwell 26 D6
Great Bookham 254 A2
Great Hivings 50 F4
Greatness 247 L6
Great Parndon 46 D3
Great Warley 106 F9
Green End 35 J7
Greenford 134 C6
Greenhill 114 E3
Greenhithe 188 G1
Greensted 67 K4
Greensted Green 67 J4
Green Street 75 M3
Green Street Green 188 F9
Green Street Green 227 H4
Greenwich 161 J4
Grovehill 35 N2
Grove Park 156 A7
Grove Park 183 P6
The Grove 72 D3
Grubb Street 210 G1
Guildford 267 N2
Guildford Park 267 M1
Hackbridge 202 C9
Hackney 140 B1
Hackney Wick 140 F1
Hacton 125 M10
Hadley 77 K7
Hadley Wood 77 N4
Haggerston 7 M7
Hailey 26 E9
Hainault 103 J8
Haldens 23 K1
Hale End 101 J7
Hall Grove 23 L7
Halls Green 45 P3
Halstead 228 B8
Ham 177 J6
Hammerfield 35 L6
Hammersmith 156 E3
Hamm Moor 215 N1
Hammond Street 61 K2
Hampstead 117 N9
Hampstead Garden Suburb 117 L3
Hampton 198 A1
Hampton Hill 176 B7
Hampton Wick 198 G1
Hamsey Green 242 B1
Handside 22 E6
Hanging Bank 264 A8
Hanwell 134 D10
Hanworth 175 L6
Harefield 91 M10
Harefield Grove 91 N8
Hare Street 46 E2
Harlesden 136 B4
Harlington 152 D5
Harlow 46 G1
Harmondsworth 151 M5
Harold Hill 105 M6
Harold Park 106 A7
Harold Wood 105 P9
Harpenden Common 20 A4
Harringay 119 H3
Harrow 114 C4
Harrow on the Hill 114 D6
Harrow Weald 94 D8
Hartham 25 K4
Hartley 211 L5
Hartley Green 211 K5
Hastingwood 48 A5
Hatch End 93 M8
Hatfield 40 C5
Hatfield Garden Village 40 B1
Hatfield Hyde 23 J8
Hatton 152 F10
Hatton Hill 212 C1
Havering-atte-Bower 104 G4
Hawk's Hill 236 E10
Hawley 187 M8
Hayes 132 D7
Hayes 205 N7
Hayes End 132 E6
Hayes Town 133 K10
Hazelwood 226 F7
Headley 255 P2
Headstone 114 A2
Heath End 32 F7
Heath Park 125 J4
Heath Side 186 G5
Hedgerley 109 J6
Hedgerley Green 109 L5
Hedgerley Hill 109 K7
Hemel Hempstead 35 P6
Hendon 116 E3
Herne Hill 181 K2
Heronsgate 90 G1
Hersham 217 K2
Hertford 25 M6
Hertford Heath 26 A8
Hertingfordbury 25 H6
Heston 153 N6
Hextable 187 H10
Higham Hill 100 D10
Highams Park 100 G8
High Barnet 76 F7
High Beach 81 N5
Highbury 119 J9
High Cross 74 C2
Higher Denham 110 F5
Highfield 35 P4
Highgate 118 A5
High Laver 49 J3
The High 28 F10
Highwood Hill 96 C3
High Wych 29 L2
Hill End 91 L7
Hillingdon 132 B3
Hillingdon Heath 132 C7
Hill Park 244 E9
Hilltop 51 J5
Hinchley Wood 198 E10
Hither Green 183 K2
Hobbs Cross 30 B10
Hobbs Cross 83 N2
Hockenden 208 C3
Hoddesdon 44 D4
Hoe 270 E9
Hogpits Bottom 52 E8
Holborn 11 N4

Holders Hill 96 G9
Holland 261 M9
Hollybush Hill 129 M1
Holmethorpe 258 C8
Holtspur 88 A10
Holyfield 63 H4
Holywell 72 F10
Homerton 140 C1
Honor Oak 182 C2
Honor Oak Park 182 D2
Hook 219 K2
Hook End 87 H1
Hook Green 186 G7
Hook Green 189 L9
Hook Heath 231 N6
Hookwood 279 M5
Hooley 240 B8
Horley 280 C2
Hornchurch 125 L7
Horne 281 N2
Hornsey 118 F2
Hornsey Vale 118 G3
Horns Green 245 H3
Horsell 232 A2
Horseman Side 85 M8
Horton 150 D9
Horton Kirby 210 C4
Hosey Hill 263 H4
Hounslow 153 P8
Hounslow West 153 L9
Housham Tye 30 E9
How Wood 56 B3
Hoxton 7 J8
Hubbard's Hill 265 J6
Hulberry 209 J9
Hunsdon 27 P2
Hunsdonbury 27 P5
Hunton Bridge 54 C9
Hurst Green 261 K8
Hurst Park 198 B2
Hurtmore 266 F10
Hutton 87 P10
Hutton Mount 107 N2
Hyde Heath 50 B10
The Hyde 116 C3
Hythe End 172 E6
Ickenham 112 B8
Ide Hill 263 P7
Ifield 283 K5
Ifield Green 283 K4
Ifieldwood 282 G4
Ilford 122 D8
Ingrave 107 P7
Irons Bottom 275 K8
Isle of Dogs 161 H3
Isleworth 154 G9
Islington 6 A5
Istead Rise 190 B10
Iver 131 J8
Iver Heath 130 G3
Ivy Chimneys 65 H8
Jack's Hatch 46 E7
Jacobs Well 249 P5
Jordans 89 L8
Joyden's Wood 186 G7
Katherines 46 B4
Kelvedon Hatch 86 C3
Kemsing 247 N3
Kenley 241 L2
Kennington 17 M10
Kensal Green 136 F5
Kensal Rise 136 G4
Kensal Town 8 A2
Kensington 14 G4
Kentish Town 4 F1
Kenton 115 H3
Keston 226 A1
Keston Mark 206 A10
Kevingtown 208 A6
Kew 155 L6
Keysers Estate 44 G7
Kidbrooke 161 P8
Kilburn 2 D6
Kingfield 232 B6
Kingsbury 115 N4
Kings Farm 190 F6
Kingsland 7 J3
Kings Langley 53 P4
Kingsmoor 46 F6
Kingston upon Thames 199 L3
Kingston Vale 178 A8
Kingswood 55 J10
Kingswood 239 J9
Kippington 265 H2
Kitt's End 77 H4
Knaphill 231 H4
Knightsbridge 15 P1
Knight's Hill 181 K4
Knockhall 188 G1
Knockholt 245 K3
Knotty Green 88 B5
Knowle Green 173 L8
Knowle Hill 193 N7
Ladywell 160 F10
Lake End 148 A1
Lakeside 166 F3
Laleham 195 M3
Lambeth 18 A3
Lambourne 83 N8
Lambourne End 103 M1
Lambs Green 282 C7
Lampton 154 A7
Lane End 188 C8
Langley 150 C2
Langleybury 54 C10
Langley Corner 130 C1
Langley Green 283 L3
Langley Vale 238 A6
Latimer 70 B3
Latton Bush 47 K5
Layters Green 89 N9
Lea Bridge 120 C8
Leasey Bridge 20 E2
Leatherhead 236 D7
Leavesden Green 54 F10
Leaves Green 226 A7
Lee 183 L2
Leigh 274 D7
Lemsford 22 C6
Lessness Heath 164 C5
Letchmore Heath 74 D5
Lett's Green 245 J2
Letty Green 24 B9
Leverstock Green 36 D7
Lewisham 161 H10
Ley Hill 51 N6
Leyton 121 J8
Leytonstone 121 L6
Lightwater 212 B7
Limehouse 140 E8
Limpsfield 261 L3
Limpsfield Chart 262 C7
Limpsfield Common 261 N6
Linford 169 J1
Lippitts Hill 81 L6
Lisson Grove 10 B3
Little Berkamstead 42 B5
Little Bookham 253 M1
Little Chalfont 69 N6
Little End 67 M10
Littlefield Common 248 G5
Little Heath 34 D4
Little Heath 59 L5
Little Heath 123 M2
Little Heath 217 N10
Little Ilford 122 D10
Little Laver 49 N1
Little Missenden 68 A3
Little Parndon 28 E10
Little Stanmore 95 L9
Little Thurrock 167 P3
Littleton 196 C3
Littleton 267 M6
Littleton Common 174 C10
Little Warley 107 L10
Littlewick 231 L2
Little Woodcote 222 B7
Littleworth Common 108 C8
Locksbottom 206 E10
Logmore Green 272 A7
London Colney 57 H2
Longcross 193 N10
Long Ditton 198 G8
Longfield 211 L3
Longford 151 M7
Longford 246 E6
Longlands 184 F6
Loudwater 71 N7
Loughton 82 C8
Love Green 130 G7
Lower Ashtead 237 H5
Lower Bobbingworth Green 49 J10
Lower Bois 51 H10
Lower Clapton 120 B9
Lower Edmonton 99 M3
Lower Feltham 174 F6
Lower Green 198 A9
Lower Halliford 196 E7
Lower Holloway 118 G10
Lower Kingswood 257 K2
Lower Nazeing 45 J9
Lower Place 135 P4
Lower Sheering 30 B2
Lower Sydenham 182 C7
Lower Woodside 41 J8
Lowfield Heath 280 A10
Low Street 169 J5
Loxford 122 F10
Loyter's Green 30 G10
Lucas End 61 K3
Lucas Green 230 C1
Luxted 226 D10
Lye Green 51 L4
Magdalen Laver 48 E4
Maida Vale 2 G9
Maidenbower 284 D9
Maitland Park 4 A1
Malden Rushett 218 G8
Manor Park 122 B9
Manor Park 129 H6
Manor Royal 283 P3
Mantles Green 68 F4
Manwood Green 31 M6
Maple Cross 90 G5
Marden Ash 67 N6
Margery 257 K5
Mark Hall North 29 K8
Mark Hall South 29 K9
Marks Gate 103 P10
Marshalswick 38 F3
Marshmoor 40 G8
Martyr's Green 234 F6
Marylebone 10 C4
Matching 31 H7
Matching Green 31 L8
Matching Tye 30 G8
Maybury 232 E3
Mayfair 10 E8
Mayford 231 P8
Maypole 186 F4
Maypole 228 A3
May's Green 234 G6
Mead Vale 275 M3
Meath Green 279 N2
Meriden 73 M2
Merrow 250 F9
Merry Hill 94 A2
Merstham 258 C4
Merton 201 K1
Merton Park 201 J2
Micklefield Green 71 K4
Mickleham 254 G4
Middle Green 130 B9
Mid Holmwood 272 G8
Mile End 140 D6
Mill End 91 J2
Mill Green 41 H1
Mill Hill 96 D6
Mill Meads 141 J4
Millwall 160 F2
Milton 190 G2
Mimbridge 213 N9
Mitcham 202 C3
Mogador 256 G5
Moneyhill 91 L2
Monken Hadley 77 H6
Monks Orchard 204 B7
Moorhouse Bank 262 D4
Moor Park 92 D5
Morden 201 K4
Morden Park 201 H6
Moreton 49 K7
Mortlake 155 P8
Motspur Park 200 D6
Mottingham 183 P5
Mount End 66 A8
Mount Hermon 232 C5
Mount Pleasant 91 L9
Muckingford 169 M4
Mugswell 257 L1
Muswell Hill 98 B10
Nalderswood 274 F10
Nash 225 N3
Nash Mills 54 B1
Nash Hyde 40 A5
Navestock Heath 85 K6
Navestock Side 86 B6
Nazeing 45 N8
Nazeing Gate 63 P1
Nazeing Long Green 63 M1
Nazeing Mead 45 J5
Neasden 116 A9
Netteswell 29 H10
New Addington 225 J4
New Ash Green 211 M9
New Barn 211 N2
New Barnet 77 L9
New Beckenham 182 D9
Newbury Park 122 G4
New Charlton 162 A3
New Cross 160 D8
New Cross Gate 160 D7
New Denham 131 K1
New Eltham 184 E5
Newgate Street 42 F10
New Greens 38 B1
New Haw 215 M4
New House 190 B5
Newington 18 B4
Newlands Corner 269 L2
New Malden 200 C3
Newman's End 30 G6
New Southgate 98 D5
Newtown 51 H5
New Town 187 N2
Newyears Green 112 B5
Nine Elms 158 E6
Noah's Arks 247 P5
Noak Hill 105 M3
Noel Park 99 J10
Nomansland 21 H5
Norbiton 199 L2
Norbury 203 J2
Normandy 248 A8
North Acton 135 P6
Northaw 60 B6
North Cheam 200 G10
Northchurch 33 J3
North Cray 186 B6
North End 117 M6
North End 164 G7
North Feltham 175 J1
North Finchley 97 M7
Northfleet 189 P1
Northfleet Green 189 P8
Northgate 284 A5
North Harrow 113 N4
North Hillingdon 132 C2
North Holmwood 272 G7
North Hyde 153 M4
North Kensington 136 G7
North Looe 220 F9
North Ockendon 126 G10
Northolt 133 P2
North Sheen 155 N8
North Stifford 147 K9
Northumberland Heath 164 D6
North Watford 73 J3
North Weald Bassett 66 A2
North Wembley 114 G6
Northwood 92 D9
Northwood Hills 92 E10
North Woolwich 162 B1
Norwood Green 153 P3
Norwood Hill 279 H4
Norwood New Town 181 L9
Notting Hill 8 B7
Nunhead 160 B10
Nuper's Hatch 104 F1
Nutfield 258 G10
Oakhurst 265 P9
Oakleigh Park 97 N3
Oakley Green 148 A8
Oakwood 78 E10
Oatlands Park 216 F1
Ockham 234 B8
Old Bexley 186 B3
Old Coulsdon 241 J6
Old Ford 140 D3
Old Harlow 29 N7
Old Hatfield 40 G3
Old Malden 200 A7
Old Oak Common 136 C6
Old Windsor 171 L3
Old Woking 232 E6
Onslow Village 267 K2
Orchard Leigh 51 N3
Orpington 207 J10
Orsett Heath 168 C1
Osidge 98 D3
Osterley 154 B6
Otford 247 H3
Ottershaw 214 F2
Otterspool 73 N3
Outwood 277 K9
Oxhey 73 L10
Oxlease 40 E5
Oxshott 218 B9
Oxted 261 J5
Pachesham Park 236 F2
Paddington 9 L4
Pains Hill 261 P7
Palmers Green 98 F4
Panshanger 23 K4
Park Barn 249 K9
Parkgate 278 A3
Park Langley 205 H6
Park Royal 135 M5
Park Street 56 B2
Parrock Farm 190 G6
Parsons Green 157 K7
Passingford Bridge 84 E5
Passmores 46 G4
Patchetts Green 74 B5
Peartree 23 H6
Peartree Green 87 J3
Peasmarsh 267 P8
Peckham 160 A8
Pedlars End 49 J7
Pednor Bottom 50 B5
Pednormead End 50 E8
Penge 182 B10
Penn Street 68 A8
Pentonville 5 P7
Perivale 135 H3
Perry Street 190 C3
Petersham 177 K4
Petts Wood 206 G4
Piccotts End 35 M2
Piercing Hill 82 G1
Pilgrims Hatch 86 G8
Pimlico 16 G7
Pimlico 36 F10
Pinnacles 46 D1
Pinner 113 L2
Pinner Green 93 K10
Pinnerwood Park 93 K8
Pirbright 230 E9
Pitch Place 249 L5
Pixham 255 H9
Plaistow 141 L5
Plaistow 183 M9
Plashet 142 A1
Plumstead 162 F4
Plumstead Common 163 J5
Ponders End 80 B9
Pond Park 50 G5
Poplar 140 F9
Potten End 34 D3
Potters Bar 59 N9
Potters Crouch 37 L10
Potter Street 47 N3
Pouchen End 34 G7
Pound Hill 284 D5
Poverest 207 K4
Povey Cross 279 M6
Poyle 151 H7
Pratt's Bottom 227 L6
Presdales 26 D4
Preston 115 J6
Prey Heath 231 N9
Primrose Hill 4 D6
Puddledock 186 E9
Puddledock 263 K9
Pudds Cross 52 B4
Purfleet 165 P5
Purley 223 H8
Putney 178 G1
Putney Heath 178 F3
Putney Vale 178 D6
Puttenham 266 A4
Pyle Hill 250 A1
Pyrford 233 J1
Pyrford Green 233 L3
Pyrford Village 233 H4
Queensbury 115 K1
Queen's Park 2 A7
Radlett 75 H1
Rainham 145 J5
Ramsden 207 M8
Ranmore Common 254 B9
Ratcliff 140 D9
Rayners Lane 113 N6
Raynes Park 200 F3
Redbridge 121 P3
Redhill 258 B8
Regent's Park 4 F8
Reigate 257 J10
Reigate Hill 257 J8
Richings Park 151 H2
Richmond 177 K1
Richmond Hill 177 K2
Rickmansworth 91 K1
Ridge 58 C10
Ridge Green 276 F3
The Ridgeway 60 C3
Ripley 233 L7
Rise Park 104 F9
The Rise 192 D6
Riverhead 246 E8
Riverview Park 191 K7
Roe Green 40 D4
Roehampton 178 C1
Roestock 40 A9
Romford 124 E3
Romney Street 229 N8
The Rookery 93 H1
Rosedale 61 N4
Rosehill 201 L8
Rose Hill 272 F2
Rosherville 190 C1
Rotherhithe 160 C2
Round Bush 74 C4
Roundshaw 222 G3
Rowley Green 76 C7
Row Town 215 J3
Roxeth 114 B7
Roydon 27 N10
Roydon Hamlet 45 P5
Rucklers Lane 53 P2
Ruislip 112 F4
Ruislip Common 112 E2
Ruislip Gardens 112 F8
Ruislip Manor 113 H7
Rush Green 26 B5
Rush Green 124 F5
Rushmore Hill 227 M9
Rusper 282 A6
Russell Hill 222 G6
Russ Hill 278 F10
Ruxley 185 P9
Rydens 197 K9
Rydeshill 249 J8
The Ryde 40 F1
Rye Meads 27 J10
Rye Park 44 G2
Sabine's Green 85 L6
St Albans 38 E4
St George in the East 13 P8
St George's Hill 216 D5
St Giles 11 K5
St Helier 201 M8
St James 11 J10
St Johns 160 F8
St Johns 231 M5
St John's 247 H8
St John's Wood 3 K6
St Julians 38 B10
St Luke's 12 F1
St Margarets 26 F7
St Margarets 177 H2
St Mary Cray 207 M5
St Pancras 5 M10
St Paul's Cray 207 K2
St Stephens 37 P8
St Vincent's Hamlet 105 P2
Salfords 276 C8
Salt Hill 129 J10
Sanderstead 223 P7
Sandridge 21 H10
Sands End 157 M8
Sandy Heath 117 M7
Sarratt 71 K1
Sarratt Bottom 71 H2
Sawbridgeworth 29 L1
Scotswood 192 C8
Seal 247 P7
Seer Green 88 G7
Seething Wells 198 G6
Selhurst 203 L5
Selsdon 224 B6
Send 232 F10
Send Grove 250 E2
Send Marsh 233 J9
Seven Kings 123 H6
Sevenoaks 247 K10
Sevenoaks Common 265 H5
Sevenoaks Weald 265 H8
Sewardstone 81 J6
Sewardstonebury 81 K9
Shackleford 266 C10
Shacklewell 119 P9
Shadwell 140 B9
Shalford 268 C7
Sheering 30 E3
Sheerwater 214 F9
Sheets Heath 230 E5
Shelley 49 P10
Shellwood Cross 274 B9
Shenfield 107 K1
Shenley 57 L10
Shenleybury 57 J7
Shepherd's Bush 136 E10
Shepperton 196 B6
Shepperton Green 196 B4
Shere 270 B4
Sherrardspark 22 E3
Shipley Bridge 280 G9
Shirley 204 B9
Shooters Hill 162 F7
Shootersway 33 K5
Shoreditch 7 H10
Shoreham 228 F7
Shorne 191 P8
Shorne Ridgeway 191 N10
Shortlands 205 K3
Shreding Green 130 E8
Shrubs Hill 193 H6
Sidcup 185 L7
Sidlow 275 L7
Silvertown 161 P1
Singlewell 190 F9
Sipson 152 A4
Slade Green 165 H8
Sleapshyde 39 P7
Slough 129 N10
Slough 149 P1
Slyfield 250 A7
Smallfield 281 H5
Smallford 39 N5
Smug Oak 56 A6
Soho 11 J6
Somers Town 5 J8
Sopwell 38 D9
Southall 133 M9
South Ascot 192 A6
South Beddington 222 E3
Southborough 206 C6
South Bromley 141 J8
South Croydon 223 K3
South Darenth 210 C1
South Earlswood 275 P5
Southend 183 H7
South Field 148 G4
Southfields 179 K4
Southfleet 189 N9
Southgate 98 F2
Southgate 283 N9
South Hackney 140 B3
South Hampstead 3 L3
South Harefield 111 N2
South Harrow 114 A8
South Hatfield 40 E7
South Hornchurch 144 E3
South Kensington 15 J6
South Lambeth 158 F6
South Merstham 258 E6
South Mimms 58 E8
South Norwood 203 L3
South Nutfield 276 F2
South Ockendon 147 H6
South Oxhey 93 J4
South Park 275 H3
South Ruislip 113 L9
South Stifford 167 J4
South Street 244 C5
South Tottenham 119 M3
South Weald 106 D3
South Wimbledon 179 M8
South Woodford 101 M10
Speed Gate 210 E9
Spital 148 G10
Spitalbrook 44 F5
Spitalfields 13 L3
Spring Grove 154 C7
Spring Park 204 F9
Staines 173 J7
Staines Green 24 D7
Stamford Hill 119 N5
Stanborough 22 C8
Stanford Rivers 67 K9
Stanmore 94 G6
Stanstead Abbots 27 K7
Stanwell 173 M2
Stanwell Moor 173 K2
Stapleford Abbotts 84 E10
Stapleford Tawney 84 D2
Stepney 140 B7
Stewards 47 H6
Steward's Green 65 L8
Stockwell 158 F9
Stoke D' Abernon 235 M1
Stoke Green 129 M6
Stoke Newington 119 N7
Stoke Poges 129 L4
Stone 188 E1
Stonebridge 273 J5
Stonehill 214 B3
Stonehill Green 186 D9
Stoneleigh 220 C2
Stonewood 189 J6
Stoughton 249 N7
Strand 11 M7
Stratford 141 H2
Stratford Marsh 140 G3
Stratford New Town 141 H1
Strawberry Hill 176 C6
Streatham 180 F8
Streatham Hill 180 F4
Streatham Park 180 C7
Streatham Vale 180 C10
Stroude 194 C2
Stroud Green 119 H4
Sudbury 114 E10
Summerstown 179 N5
Sumners 46 D5
Sunbury 197 H3
Sunbury Common 174 G10
Sundridge 183 P9
Sundridge 246 A10
Sunningdale 192 F5
Sunninghill 192 C5
Sunnymeads 150 B10
Surbiton 199 J8
Sutton 150 F4
Sutton 221 K2
Sutton Abinger 271 J9
Sutton at Hone 187 P10
Sutton Green 250 C1
Swallows Cross 87 L3

Swanley 208 F1
Swanley Bar 59 L4
Swanley Village 209 H2
Swanscombe 189 J2
The Swillett 90 F1
Tadworth 238 F8
Tandridge 260 F9
Tatling End 110 E6
Tatsfield 244 A6
Teddington 176 C9
Temple Fields 29 K7
Temple Hill 165 L10
Temple Mills 120 G10
Thames Ditton 198 F7
Thamesmead 143 J10
Theydon Bois 82 G3
Theydon Garnon 83 M2
Theydon Mount 84 B2
Thong 191 K9
Thorney 151 L1
Thornton Heath 202 F5
Thornwood Common 65 L1
Thorpe 194 F3
Thorpe Green 194 D4
Thorpe Lea 172 F10
Three Bridges 284 A6
Three Households 89 L4
Threshers Bush 48 B2
Tilbury 168 D7
Tilegate Green 48 E3
Tilgate 283 N10
Timberden Bottom 228 F6
Tinsley Green 284 D1
Titsey 261 P1
Tittenhurst 193 H3
Tokyngton 135 N1
Tolmers 60 F2
Tolworth 199 M8
Toot Hill 66 G6
Tooting Graveney 179 N8
Tottenham 99 M10
Tottenham Hale 119 N1
Totteridge 97 K2
Totteridge Green 96 F2
Tower Hill 53 J5
Tower Hill 272 G4
Townsend 38 A4
Toy's Hill 263 M8
Trumps Green 194 A6
Tufnell Park 118 D9
Tulse Hill 181 J4
Turners Hill 285 P9
Turnford 62 C1
Twickenham 176 D4
Twitton 246 F2
Two Waters 35 M9
Tye Green 46 G3
Tylers Causeway 42 C8
Tyler's Green 48 E10
Tyler's Green 260 A6
Tyler's Hill 51 M7
Tyrell's Wood 237 M10
Tyttenhanger 39 K9
Underhill 77 K10
Underriver 265 P6
Upminster 126 B7
Upper Clapton 119 P6
Upper Edmonton 99 P5
Upper Elmers End 204 E5
Upper Halliford 196 E4
Upper Holloway 118 D7
Upper Norwood 203 L1
Upper Shirley 224 B1
Upper Sydenham 181 P7
Upper Tooting 179 P6
Upper Walthamstow 121 H2
Upshire 63 P8
Upton 141 N2
Upton 149 M2
Upton Lea 129 M8
Upton Park 141 P3
Uxbridge 131 M3
Uxbridge Moor 131 L3
Vale of Health 117 N8
Valley End 212 F2
Vauxhall 17 N8
Venus Hill 52 E7
The Village 170 G6
Virginia Water 193 P3
Waddon 202 G9
Wallend 142 D3
Wallington 222 C2
Waltham Abbey 63 J8
Waltham Cross 62 B9
Walthamstow 120 F1
Walton-on-Thames 197 H8
Walton on the Hill 238 C10
Walworth 18 F8
Wanborough 266 A3
Wandle Park 203 H9
Wandsworth 157 K10
Wanstead 121 N5
Wapping 140 A10
Ware 26 E1
Warley 106 G6
Warlingham 242 C4
Warners End 35 H5
Warwick Wold 259 H5
Wasp Green 277 K10
Waterdale 55 K6
Waterend 22 A3
Water End 58 F2
Waterford 24 G1
Waterhales 85 L10
Waterside 51 J9
Watford 73 H5
Watford Heath 93 M1
Watton's Green 85 J10
Wealdstone 114 F1
Weatherhill 281 H3
Welham Green 40 E9
Well End 75 P4
Well Hill 228 C2
Welling 163 L9
The Wells 219 L10
Welsh Harp 116 A6
Welwyn Garden City 23 L3
Wembley 115 H10
Wembley Park 115 M8
Wennington 145 M9
West Acton 135 M8
West Barnes 200 F5
West Bedfont 174 A3
Westbourne Green 8 D2
West Brompton 14 G9
Westbrook Hay 34 F10
West Byfleet 215 L9
West Clandon 251 L5
Westcott 272 C4
West Court 191 H5
West Drayton 151 N2
West Dulwich 181 L5
West Ealing 134 F10
Wested 208 F7
West End 41 N4
West End 212 E10
West End 217 N2
Westerham 262 G3
West Ewell 220 B4
Westfield 232 C8
West Green 119 K1
West Green 283 M6
West Hampstead 117 K10
West Harrow 114 B5
West Heath 117 L7
West Heath 163 N5
West Hendon 116 D5
West Hill 179 H3
West Horndon 127 P4
West Horsley 252 C4
Westhumble 254 F7
West Hyde 91 H8
West Kensington 156 G4
West Kilburn 2 B9
Westminster 17 H4
West Molesey 197 N4
West Norwood 181 K7
Weston Green 198 D8
West Ruislip 112 D6
West Thurrock 166 F4
West Tilbury 169 H5
West Watford 73 H9
West Wickham 205 J8
Westwick Row 36 F7
Westwood 189 H10
West Yoke 211 J10
Wexham Street 129 P3
Weybridge 216 B1
Wheathampstead 20 G2
Whelpley Hill 52 A2
Whetstone 97 L3
Whippendell Bottom 53 M6
Whitebushes 276 C5
Whitechapel 13 M7
Whiteley Village 216 G5
White Oak 208 F2
Whitley Row 264 C5
Whitton 176 B2
Whyteleafe 241 N4
Widmore 206 A2
Wigginton Bottom 32 D1
Wildernesse 247 M8
Wildhill 41 M7
Willesden 136 D1
Willesden Green 136 E2
Willey Green 248 C7
Willowbank 111 M10
Wilmington 187 J7
Wilton Park 88 G9
Wimbledon 179 H8
Winchmore Hill 88 C1
Winchmore Hill 99 J2
Windlesham 212 A3
Windsor 149 K7
Wisley 233 P1
Woking 232 B4
Woldingham 242 F9
Woldingham Garden Village 242 E7
Wonersh 268 F10
Wooburn Common 108 A6
Woodbridge Hill 249 M8
Woodcock Hill 91 P5
Woodcote 222 F7
Woodcote 238 A2
Woodcote Green 222 C6
Wood End 132 F8
Wood End 170 B9
Wood End Green 132 F7
Woodford 101 N7
Woodford Bridge 102 C8
Woodford Green 101 M8
Woodford Wells 101 N4
Wood Green 63 P10
Wood Green 99 H9
Woodhall 23 H7
Woodham 215 K6
Woodhatch 275 K3
Woodlands 154 C9
Woodmansterne 239 N1
Woodrow 68 B8
Woodside 41 K7
Woodside 55 J8
Woodside 65 N2
Woodside 170 A7
Woodside 203 P6
Woodside Park 97 K5
Wood Street Village 248 E9
Woollensbrook 26 C10
Woolwich 162 D5
Worcester Park 200 E9
World's End 79 H8
Wormley 44 D10
Wormleybury 44 A9
Wormley West End 43 P8
Worplesdon 249 J3
Worth 284 F8
Wotton 271 M5
Wray Common 257 N8
Wraysbury 172 B3
The Wrythe 201 P9
Yeading 133 K6
Yiewsley 131 P9

USING THE STREET INDEX

Street names are listed alphabetically. Each street name is followed by its postal town or area locality, the Postcode District, the page number, and the reference to the square in which the name is found.

Standard index entries are shown as follows:

Aaron Hill Rd *EHAM* E6 ....**142** D7

Street names and selected addresses not shown on the map due to scale restrictions are shown in the index with an asterisk:

Abbeville Ms *CLAP* * SW4......................**180** E1

GENERAL ABBREVIATIONS

ACC	ACCESS
ALY	ALLEY
AP	APPROACH
AR	ARCADE
ASS	ASSOCIATION
AV	AVENUE
BCH	BEACH
BLDS	BUILDINGS
BND	BEND
BNK	BANK
BR	BRIDGE
BRK	BROOK
BTM	BOTTOM
BUS	BUSINESS
BVD	BOULEVARD
BY	BYPASS
CATH	CATHEDRAL
CEM	CEMETERY
CEN	CENTRE
CFT	CROFT
CH	CHURCH
CHA	CHASE
CHYD	CHURCHYARD
CIR	CIRCLE
CIRC	CIRCUS
CL	CLOSE
CLFS	CLIFFS
CMP	CAMP
CNR	CORNER
CO	COUNTY
COLL	COLLEGE
COM	COMMON
COMM	COMMISSION
CON	CONVENT
COT	COTTAGE
COTS	COTTAGES
CP	CAPE
CPS	COPSE
CR	CREEK
CREM	CREMATORIUM
CRS	CRESCENT
CSWY	CAUSEWAY
CT	COURT
CTRL	CENTRAL
CTS	COURTS
CTYD	COURTYARD
CUTT	CUTTINGS
CV	COVE
CYN	CANYON
DEPT	DEPARTMENT
DL	DALE
DM	DAM
DR	DRIVE
DRO	DROVE
DRY	DRIVEWAY
DWGS	DWELLINGS
E	EAST
EMB	EMBANKMENT
EMBY	EMBASSY
ESP	ESPLANADE
EST	ESTATE
EX	EXCHANGE
EXPY	EXPRESSWAY
EXT	EXTENSION
F/O	FLYOVER
FC	FOOTBALL CLUB
FK	FORK
FLD	FIELD
FLDS	FIELDS
FLS	FALLS
FLS	FLATS
FM	FARM
FT	FORT
FWY	FREEWAY
FY	FERRY
GA	GATE
GAL	GALLERY
GDN	GARDEN
GDNS	GARDENS
GLD	GLADE
GLN	GLEN
GN	GREEN
GND	GROUND
GRA	GRANGE
GRG	GARAGE
GT	GREAT
GTWY	GATEWAY
GV	GROVE
HGR	HIGHER
HL	HILL
HLS	HILLS
HO	HOUSE
HOL	HOLLOW
HOSP	HOSPITAL
HRB	HARBOUR
HTH	HEATH
HTS	HEIGHTS
HVN	HAVEN
HWY	HIGHWAY
IMP	IMPERIAL
IN	INLET
IND EST	INDUSTRIAL ESTATE
INF	INFIRMARY
INFO	INFORMATION
INT	INTERCHANGE
IS	ISLAND
JCT	JUNCTION
JTY	JETTY
KG	KING
KNL	KNOLL
L	LAKE
LA	LANE
LDG	LODGE
LGT	LIGHT
LK	LOCK
LKS	LAKES
LNDG	LANDING
LTL	LITTLE
LWR	LOWER
MAG	MAGISTRATE
MAN	MANSIONS
MD	MEAD
MDW	MEADOWS
MEM	MEMORIAL
MKT	MARKET
MKTS	MARKETS
ML	MALL
ML	MILL
MNR	MANOR
MS	MEWS
MSN	MISSION
MT	MOUNT
MTN	MOUNTAIN
MTS	MOUNTAINS
MUS	MUSEUM
MWY	MOTORWAY
N	NORTH
NE	NORTH EAST
NW	NORTH WEST
O/P	OVERPASS
OFF	OFFICE
ORCH	ORCHARD
OV	OVAL
PAL	PALACE
PAS	PASSAGE
PAV	PAVILION
PDE	PARADE
PH	PUBLIC HOUSE
PK	PARK
PKWY	PARKWAY
PL	PLACE
PLN	PLAIN
PLNS	PLAINS
PLZ	PLAZA
POL	POLICE STATION
PR	PRINCE
PREC	PRECINCT
PREP	PREPARATORY
PRIM	PRIMARY
PROM	PROMENADE
PRS	PRINCESS
PRT	PORT
PT	POINT
PTH	PATH
PZ	PIAZZA
QD	QUADRANT
QU	QUEEN
QY	QUAY
R	RIVER
RBT	ROUNDABOUT
RD	ROAD
RDG	RIDGE
REP	REPUBLIC
RES	RESERVOIR
RFC	RUGBY FOOTBALL CLUB
RI	RISE
RP	RAMP
RW	ROW
S	SOUTH
SCH	SCHOOL
SE	SOUTH EAST
SER	SERVICE AREA
SH	SHORE
SHOP	SHOPPING
SKWY	SKYWAY
SMT	SUMMIT
SOC	SOCIETY
SP	SPUR
SPR	SPRING
SQ	SQUARE
ST	STREET
STN	STATION
STR	STREAM
STRD	STRAND
SW	SOUTH WEST
TDG	TRADING
TER	TERRACE
THWY	THROUGHWAY
TNL	TUNNEL
TOLL	TOLLWAY
TPK	TURNPIKE
TR	TRACK
TRL	TRAIL
TWR	TOWER
U/P	UNDERPASS
UNI	UNIVERSITY
UPR	UPPER
V	VALE
VA	VALLEY
VIAD	VIADUCT
VIL	VILLA
VIS	VISTA
VLG	VILLAGE
VLS	VILLAS
VW	VIEW
W	WEST
WD	WOOD
WHF	WHARF
WK	WALK
WKS	WALKS
WLS	WELLS
WY	WAY
YD	YARD
YHA	YOUTH HOSTEL

POSTCODE TOWNS AND AREA ABBREVIATIONS

ABLGY	Abbots Langley
ABR/ST	Abridge/Stapleford Abbotts
ABYW	Abbey Wood
ACT	Acton
ADL/WDHM	Addlestone/Woodham
ALP/SUD	Alperton/Sudbury
AMS	Amersham
AMSS	Amersham south
ARCH	Archway
ASC	Ascot
ASHF	Ashford (Surrey)
ASHTD	Ashtead
BAGS	Bagshot
BAL	Balham
BANK	Bank
BAR	Barnet
BARB	Barbican
BARK	Barking
BARK/HLT	Barkingside/Hainault
BARN	Barnes
BAY/PAD	Bayswater/Paddington
BCTR	Becontree
BEAC	Beaconsfield
BECK	Beckenham
BELMT	Belmont
BELV	Belvedere
BERK	Berkhamsted
BERM/RHTH	Bermondsey/Rotherhithe
BETH	Bethnal Green
BF/WBF	Byfleet/West Byfleet
BFN/LL	Blackfen/Longlands
BFOR	Bracknell Forest/Windlesham
BGR/WK	Borough Green/West Kingsdown
BGVA	Belgravia
BH/WHM	Biggin Hill/Westerham
BKHH	Buckhurst Hill
BKHTH/KID	Blackheath/Kidbrooke
BLKFR	Blackfriars
BMLY	Bromley
BMSBY	Bloomsbury
BNSTD	Banstead
BORE	Borehamwood
BOW	Bow
BRKHM/BTCW	Brockham/Betchworth
BRKMPK	Brookmans Park
BRKMPK	Brookmans Park
BROCKY	Brockley
BROX	Broxbourne
BRW	Brentwood
BRWN	Brentwood north
BRXN/ST	Brixton north/Stockwell
BRXS/STRHM	Brixton south/Streatham Hill
BRYLDS	Berrylands
BTFD	Brentford
BTSEA	Battersea
BUSH	Bushey
BXLY	Bexley
BXLYHN	Bexleyheath north
BXLYHS	Bexleyheath south
CAMTN	Camden Town
CAN/RD	Canning Town/Royal Docks
CANST	Cannon Street station
CAR	Carshalton
CAT	Catford
CAVSQ/HST	Cavendish Square/Harley Street
CDALE/KGS	Colindale/Kingsbury
CDH/CHF	Chadwell St Mary/Chafford Hundred
CEND/HYS/T	Crouch End/Hornsey/Turnpike Lane
CFSP/GDCR	Chalfont St Peter/Gerrards Cross
CHARL	Charlton
CHCR	Charing Cross
CHDH	Chadwell Heath
CHEAM	Cheam
CHEL	Chelsea
CHERT	Chertsey
CHES/WCR	Cheshunt/Waltham Cross
CHESW	Cheshunt west
CHIG	Chigwell
CHING	Chingford
CHOB/PIR	Chobham/Pirbright
CHONG	Chipping Ongar
CHSGTN	Chessington
CHST	Chislehurst
CHSWK	Chiswick
CITYW	City of London west
CLAP	Clapham
CLAY	Clayhall
CLKNW	Clerkenwell
CLPT	Clapton
CMBW	Camberwell
COB	Cobham
CONDST	Conduit Street
COUL/CHIP	Coulsdon/Chipstead
COVGDN	Covent Garden
CRAWE	Crawley east
CRAWW	Crawley west
CRICK	Cricklewood
CROY/NA	Croydon/New Addington
CRW	Collier Row
CSHM	Chesham
CSTG	Chalfont St Giles
CTHM	Caterham
DAGE	Dagenham east
DAGW	Dagenham west
DART	Dartford
DEN/HRF	Denham/Harefield
DEPT	Deptford
DORK	Dorking
DTCH/LGLY	Datchet/Langley
DUL	Dulwich
E/WMO/HCT	East & West Molesey/Hampton Court
EA	Ealing
EBAR	East Barnet
EBED/NFELT	East Bedfont/North Feltham
ECT	Earl's Court
ED	Edmonton
EDEN	Edenbridge
EDGW	Edgware
EDUL	East Dulwich
EFNCH	East Finchley
EGH	Egham
EHAM	East Ham
EHSLY	East Horsley
ELTH/MOT	Eltham/Mottingham
EMB	Embankment
EMPK	Emerson Park
EN	Enfield
ENC/FH	Enfield Chase/Forty Hill
EPP	Epping

PSOM .... Epsom
RITH .... Erith
RITHM .... Erith Marshes
SH/CLAY .... Esher/Claygate
W .... Ewell
YN .... Eynsford
ARR .... Farringdon
BAR/BDGN .... Friern Barnet/Bounds Green
ELT .... Feltham
ENCHST .... Fenchurch Street
TZ .... Fitzrovia
LKWH .... Flackwell Heath
LST/FETLN .... Fleet Street/Fetter Lane
NCH .... Finchley
SBYE .... Finsbury east
SBYPK .... Finsbury Park
SBYW .... Finsbury west
STGT .... Forest Gate
STH .... Forest Hill
UL/PGN .... Fulham/Parsons Green
DMY/SEVK .... Goodmayes/Seven Kings
DST .... Godstone
FD/PVL .... Greenford/Perivale
INN .... Gray's Inn
LDGN .... Golders Green
NTH/NBYPK .... Gants Hill/Newbury Park
NWCH .... Greenwich
PK .... Gidea Park
RAYS .... Grays
RH .... Greenhithe
STN .... Garston
T/LBKH .... Great Bookham/Little Bookham
TDUN .... Great Dunmow
TPST .... Great Portland Street
U .... Guildford
UW .... Guildford west
VE .... Gravesend east
VW .... Gravesend west
WRST .... Gower Street
ACK .... Hackney
AMP .... Hampstead
ARH .... Harold Hill
ARP .... Harpenden
ART .... Hartley
AT .... Hatfield
AYES .... Hayes
BRY .... Highbury
CH .... Hornchurch
CIRC .... Holborn Circus
DN .... Hendon
DTCH .... Houndsditch
ERT/BAY .... Hertford/Bayford
ERT/WAS .... Hertford/Watton at Stone
EST .... Heston
GDN/ICK .... Hillingdon/Ickenham
GT .... Highgate
HNE .... Hemel Hempstead northeast
HOL .... High Holborn
HHS/BOV .... Hemel Hempstead south/Bovingdon
HHW .... Hemel Hempstead west
HLW .... Harlow
HLWE .... Harlow east
HLWS .... Harlow south
HLWW/ROY .... Harlow west/Roydon
HMSMTH .... Hammersmith
HNHL .... Herne Hill
HNWL .... Hanwell
HOD .... Hoddesdon
HOL/ALD .... Holborn/Aldwych
HOLWY .... Holloway
HOM .... Homerton
HOR/WEW .... Horton/West Ewell
HORL .... Horley
HORS .... Horsham
HPTN .... Hampton
HRW .... Harrow
HSLW .... Hounslow
HSLWW .... Hounslow west
HTHAIR .... Heathrow Airport
HYS/HAR .... Hayes/Harlington
IL .... Ilford
ING .... Ingatestone
IS .... Islington
ISLW .... Isleworth
IVER .... Iver
KENS .... Kensington
KGLGY .... Kings Langley
KIL/WHAMP .... Kilburn/West Hampstead
KTBR .... Knightsbridge
KTN/HRWW/WS .... Kenton/Harrow Weald/Wealdstone
KTTN .... Kentish Town
KUT .... Kingston upon Thames
KUTN/CMB .... Kingston upon Thames north/Coombe
KWD/TDW/WH .... Kingswood/Tadworth/Walton on the Hill
LBTH .... Lambeth
LEE/GVPK .... Lee/Grove Park
LEW .... Lewisham
LEY .... Leyton
LHD/OX .... Leatherhead/Oxshott
LING .... Lingfield
LINN .... Lincoln's Inn
LOTH .... Lothbury
LOU .... Loughton
LSQ/SEVD .... Leicester Square/Seven Dials
LTWR .... Lightwater
LVPST .... Liverpool Street
MANHO .... Mansion House
MBLAR .... Marble Arch
MDHD .... Maidenhead
MEO .... Meopham
MFD/CHID .... Milford/Chiddingfold
MHST .... Marylebone High Street
MLHL .... Mill Hill
MNPK .... Manor Park
MON .... Monument
MORT/ESHN .... Mortlake/East Sheen
MRDN .... Morden
MTCM .... Mitcham
MUSWH .... Muswell Hill
MV/WKIL .... Maida Vale/West Kilburn
MYFR/PICC .... Mayfair/Piccadilly
MYFR/PKLN .... Mayfair/Park Lane
NFNCH/WDSPK .... North Finchley/Woodside Park
NKENS .... North Kensington
NOXST/BSQ .... New Oxford Street/Bloomsbury Square
NRWD .... Norwood
NTGHL .... Notting Hill
NTHLT .... Northolt
NTHWD .... Northwood
NWCR .... New Cross
NWDGN .... Norwood Green
NWMAL .... New Malden
OBST .... Old Broad Street
ORP .... Orpington
OXHEY .... Oxhey
OXSTW .... Oxford Street west
OXTED .... Oxted
PECK .... Peckham
PEND .... Ponders End
PGE/AN .... Penge/Anerley
PIM .... Pimlico
PIN .... Pinner
PLMGR .... Palmers Green
PLSTW .... Plaistow
POP/IOD .... Poplar/Isle of Dogs
POTB/CUF .... Potters Bar/Cuffley
PUR .... Purfleet
PUR/KEN .... Purley/Kenley
PUT/ROE .... Putney/Roehampton
RAD .... Radlett
RAIN .... Rainham (Gt Lon)
RBRW/HUT .... Rural Brentwood/Hutton
RBSF .... Rural Bishop's Stortford
RCH/KEW .... Richmond/Kew
RCHPK/HAM .... Richmond Park/Ham
RDART .... Rural Dartford
RDKG .... Rural Dorking
REDBR .... Redbridge
REDH .... Redhill
REGST .... Regent Street
REIG .... Reigate
RGODL .... Rural Godalming
RGUE .... Rural Guildford east
RGUW .... Rural Guildford west
RKW/CH/CXG .... Rickmansworth/Chorleywood/Croxley Green
ROM .... Romford
ROMW/RG .... Romford west/Rush Green
RPLY/SEND .... Ripley/Send
RSEV .... Rural Sevenoaks
RSLP .... Ruislip
RSQ .... Russell Square
RTON .... Rural Tonbridge
RYLN/HDSTN .... Rayners Lane/Headstone
RYNPK .... Raynes Park
SBW .... Sawbridgeworth
SCUP .... Sidcup
SDTCH .... Shoreditch
SEV .... Sevenoaks
SEVS/STOTM .... Seven Sisters/South Tottenham
SHB .... Shepherd's Bush
SHGR .... Shamley Green
SHPTN .... Shepperton
SKENS .... South Kensington
SL .... Slough
SLN .... Slough north
SNWD .... South Norwood
SOCK/AV .... South Ockendon/Aveley
SOHO/CST .... Soho/Carnaby Street
SOHO/SHAV .... Soho/Shaftesbury Avenue
SRTFD .... Stratford
STA .... Staines
STAL .... St Albans
STALE/WH ... St Albans east/Wheathampstead
STALW/RED .... St Albans west/Redbourn
STAN .... Stanmore
STBT .... St Bart's
STHGT/OAK .... Southgate/Oakwood
STHL .... Southall
STHWK .... Southwark
STJS .... St James's
STJSPK .... St James's Park
STJWD .... St John's Wood
STKPK .... Stockley Park
STLK .... St Luke's
STMC/STPC .... St Mary Cray/St Paul's Cray
STNW/STAM .... Stoke Newington/Stamford Hill
STP .... St Paul's
STPAN .... St Pancras
STRHM/NOR .... Streatham/Norbury
STWL/WRAY .... Stanwell/Wraysbury
SUN .... Sunbury
SURB .... Surbiton
SUT .... Sutton
SWCM .... Swanscombe
SWFD .... South Woodford
SWLY .... Swanley
SYD .... Sydenham
TEDD .... Teddington
THDIT .... Thames Ditton
THHTH .... Thornton Heath
THMD .... Thamesmead
TIL .... Tilbury
TOOT .... Tooting
TOTM .... Tottenham
TPL/STR .... Temple/Strand
TRDG/WHET .... Totteridge/Whetstone
TRING .... Tring
TWK .... Twickenham
TWRH .... Tower Hill
UED .... Upper Edmonton
UPMR .... Upminster
UX/CGN .... Uxbridge/Colham Green
VW .... Virginia Water
VX/NE .... Vauxhall/Nine Elms
WAB .... Waltham Abbey
WALTH .... Walthamstow
WALW .... Walworth
WAN .... Wanstead
WAND/EARL .... Wandsworth/Earlsfield
WANTN .... Watford north
WAP .... Wapping
WARE .... Ware
WARL .... Warlingham
WAT .... Watford
WATW .... Watford west
WBLY .... Wembley
WBPTN .... West Brompton
WCHMH .... Winchmore Hill
WCHPL .... Whitechapel
WDGN .... Wood Green
WDR/YW .... West Drayton/Yiewsley
WDSR .... Windsor
WEA .... West Ealing
WELL .... Welling
WEST .... Westminster
WESTW .... Westminster west
WEY .... Weybridge
WFD .... Woodford
WGCE .... Welwyn Garden City east
WGCW .... Welwyn Garden City west
WHALL .... Whitehall
WHTN .... Whitton
WIM/MER .... Wimbledon/Merton
WKENS .... West Kensington
WLGTN .... Wallington
WLSDN .... Willesden
WLYN .... Welwyn
WNWD .... West Norwood
WOKN/KNAP .... Woking north/Knaphill
WOKS/MYFD .... Woking south/Mayford
WOOL/PLUM .... Woolwich/Plumstead
WOT/HER .... Walton-on-Thames/Hersham
WPK .... Worcester Park
WTHK .... West Thurrock
WWKM .... West Wickham
YEAD .... Yeading

Index - streets

1 Av WOOL/PLUM SE18 162 E2
1st Av KWD/TDW/WH KT20 257 H1
2nd Av KWD/TDW/WH KT20 257 H1
3rd Av KWD/TDW/WH KT20 257 H1
4th Av KWD/TDW/WH KT20 257 H1
5th Av KWD/TDW/WH KT20 257 H1
6th Av KWD/TDW/WH KT20 257 H1
7th Av KWD/TDW/WH KT20 257 H1
8th Av KWD/TDW/WH KT20 257 H2
9th Av KWD/TDW/WH KT20 257 H1
10th Av KWD/TDW/WH KT20 257 H2
11th Av KWD/TDW/WH KT20 257 H1
12th Av KWD/TDW/WH KT20 257 H2
13th Av KWD/TDW/WH KT20 257 H2
14th Av KWD/TDW/WH KT20 257 H2
15th Av KWD/TDW/WH KT20 257 J2
16th Av KWD/TDW/WH KT20 257 H2

A

Aaron Hill Rd EHAM E6 142 D7
Abbess Cl BRXS/STRHM SW2 181 J4
Abbeville Ms CLAP * SW4 180 E1
Abbeville Rd CEND/HSY/T N8 118 E2
CLAP SW4 180 D2
Abbey Av ALP/SUD HA0 135 K4
STALW/RED AL3 37 P9
Abbey Cha CHERT * KT16 195 L6
Abbey Cl HYS/HAR UB3 133 J10
NTHLT UB5 133 N5
PIN HA5 113 J1
ROM RM1 124 G4
SL SL1 128 D9
WOKS/MYFD GU22 233 H2
Abbey Ct CHERT * KT16 195 L7
WAB EN9 62 G10
Abbey Crs BELV DA17 164 B3
Abbey Dale Cl HLWE CM17 47 M2
Abbeydale Rd ALP/SUD HA0 135 L3
Abbey Dr ABLGY WD5 55 H8
STA TW18 195 M3
TOOT SW17 180 B8
Abbeyfield Est
BERM/RHTH SE16 160 B3
Abbeyfield Rd BERM/RHTH SE16 160 B3
Abbeyfields Cl WLSDN NW10 135 M5
Abbey Gdns BERM/RHTH SE16 19 P5
CHERT KT16 195 K6
HMSMTH W6 14 A10
STJWD NW8 3 J8
Abbey Gn CHERT * KT16 195 K6
Abbey Gv ABYW SE2 163 L3
Abbeyhill Rd BFN/LL DA15 185 M4
Abbey La BECK BR3 182 F10
SRTFD E15 141 H4
Abbey Ms STA * TW18 195 M3
STAL * AL1 38 C7
WALTH E17 120 F3
Abbey Mill End STALW/RED AL3 38 B7
Abbey Mill La STALW/RED AL3 38 B7
Abbey Mt BELV DA17 164 A4
Abbey Orchard St WEST SW1P 17 K3
Abbey Pk BECK BR3 182 F10
Abbey Park La SL SL1 108 D7
Abbey Pl CHERT * KT16 195 K3
DART * DA1 187 L1
Abbey Rd BARK IG11 142 E2
BELV DA17 163 N3
BXLYHS DA6 163 P10
CHERT KT16 195 L7
CHES/WCR EN8 62 D10
CROY/NA CR0 203 J10
EN EN1 79 M9
GNTH/NBYPK IG2 122 G3
GRH DA9 189 H1
GVE DA12 191 H4
KIL/WHAMP NW6 2 G5
SAND/SEL CR2 224 C6
SHPTN TW17 196 B8
SRTFD E15 141 J4
VW GU25 194 A5
WIM/MER SW19 179 M10
WLSDN NW10 135 N3
WOKN/KNAP GU21 231 P3
Abbey St PLSTW E13 141 M6
STHWK SE1 19 L3
Abbey Ter ABYW SE2 163 M2
Abbey Vw MLHL NW7 96 C4
RAD WD7 74 E1
Abbeyview WAB EN9 62 G9
Abbey View Rd STALW/RED AL3 38 B6
Abbey Wk E/WMO/HCT KT8 198 A3
Abbey Wd ASC SL5 192 F7
Abbey Wood La RAIN RM13 145 L4
Abbey Wood Rd ABYW SE2 163 L3
Abbot Cl BF/WBF KT14 215 N6
RSLP HA4 113 L8
STA TW18 173 N10
Abbot John Ms STALE/WH AL4 21 J2
Abbot Rd GU GU1 268 A2
Abbots Av HOR/WEW KT19 219 M7
STAL AL1 38 D9
Abbots Av West STAL AL1 38 C9
Abbotsbury Cl SRTFD E15 141 H4
WKENS W14 14 C2
Abbotsbury Gdns PIN HA5 113 K4
Abbotsbury Ms PECK SE15 160 B9
Abbotsbury Rd MRDN SM4 201 L4
NTGHL W11 14 B1
WWKM BR4 205 L9
Abbots Cl BRWN CM15 107 M2
GUW GU2 267 K3
RAIN RM13 145 K4
STMC/STPC BR5 206 F8
Abbots Dr RYLN/HDSTN HA2 113 P7
VW GU25 193 P4
Abbotsfield Rd CRAWW RH11 282 G8
Abbotsford Av SEVS/STOTM N15 119 K2
Abbotsford Cl
WOKS/MYFD GU22 232 D3
Abbotsford Gdns WFD IG8 101 M8
Abbotsford Rd GDMY/SEVK IG3 123 K7
Abbots Gdns EFNCH N2 117 N2
Abbots Gn CROY/NA CR0 224 C3
Abbotshade Rd
BERM/RHTH * SE16 140 C10
Abbotshall Av STHGT/OAK N14 98 D4
Abbotshall Rd CAT SE6 183 J4
Abbots Hl HHS/BOV * HP3 54 C1
Abbots La PUR/KEN CR8 241 K1
STHWK SE1 13 K10
Abbotsleigh Cl BELMT SM2 221 L4
Abbotsleigh Rd
STRHM/NOR SW16 180 D7
Abbots Mnr PIM SW1V 16 E7
Abbots Manor Est PIM SW1V 16 E7
Abbotsmede Cl TWK TW1 176 E5
Abbots Pk BRXS/STRHM SW2 181 H4
STAL AL1 38 E8
Abbots Pl BORE WD6 75 N4
KIL/WHAMP NW6 2 G5
Abbots Ri KGLGY WD4 54 A3
Abbots Rd ABLGY WD5 54 D7
CHEAM SM3 221 H1
EDGW HA8 96 A8
EHAM E6 142 A3
Abbots Ter CEND/HSY/T N8 118 F4
Abbotstone Rd PUT/ROE SW15 156 F9
Abbot St HACK E8 7 L1
Abbots Vw KGLGY WD4 54 A3
Abbots Wk CTHM CR3 242 A8
KENS * W8 14 G4
WDSR SL4 148 D8
Abbots Wy BECK BR3 204 D5
CHERT KT16 195 J7
GU GU1 250 G9
Abbotsweld HLWS CM18 46 G4
Abbotswell Rd BROCKY SE4 182 E1
Abbotswood GU GU1 250 C8
Abbotswood Cl BELV DA17 163 P2
GU GU1 250 C7
Abbotswood Dr WEY KT13 216 E6
Abbotswood Gdns CLAY IG5 122 C1
Abbotswood Rd EDUL SE22 159 M10
STRHM/NOR SW16 180 E6
Abbotswood Wy HYS/HAR UB3 133 J10
Abbott Av RYNPK SW20 200 G2
Abbott Cl HPTN TW12 175 M9
NTHLT UB5 133 N1
Abbott Rd POP/IOD E14 141 H7
Abbotts Cl IS * N1 6 E3
ROMW/RG RM7 124 C1
SWLY BR8 209 H4
THMD SE28 143 M9
UX/CGN UB8 131 N7
Abbotts Crs CHING E4 101 J5
ENC/FH EN2 79 J6
Abbotts Dr ALP/SUD HA0 114 G7
WAB EN9 63 M10
Abbotts Md RCHPK/HAM * TW10 177 H7
Abbotts Park Rd LEY E10 121 H5
Abbotts Ri REDH RH1 258 B8
WARE SG12 27 J7
Abbotts Rd BAR EN5 77 L8
MTCM CR4 202 D4
STHL UB1 133 M10
Abbotts Tilt WOT/HER KT12 197 M10
Abbotts V CSHM HP5 51 H4
Abbott's Wk BXLYHN DA7 163 N6
Abbotts Wy SL SL1 128 C10
WARE SG12 27 J7
Abbs Cross Gdns HCH RM12 125 K6
Abbs Cross La HCH RM12 125 K8
Abchurch La MANHO EC4N 13 H7
Abdale La BRKMPK AL9 58 E3
Abdale Rd SHB W12 136 E10
Abel Cl HHNE HP2 36 B6
Abelia Cl CHOB/PIR GU24 212 D9
Abenberg Wy RBRW/HUT CM13 107 M3
Aberavon Rd BOW E3 140 D5
Abercairn Rd STRHM/NOR SW16 180 D10
Aberconway Rd MRDN SM4 201 L3
Abercorn Cl MLHL NW7 97 H8
SAND/SEL CR2 224 C8
STJWD NW8 3 J8
Abercorn Crs RYLN/HDSTN HA2 114 A6
Abercorn Gdns CHDH RM6 123 L4
KTN/HRWW/W HA3 115 J5
Abercorn Gv RSLP HA4 112 E2
Abercorn Pl STJWD NW8 3 J9
Abercorn Rd MLHL NW7 97 H8
STAN HA7 95 H8
Abercorn Wy STHWK SE1 19 N7
WOKN/KNAP GU21 231 M4
Abercrombie Dr EN EN1 79 P5
Abercrombie St BTSEA SW11 157 P8
Abercrombie Wy
HLWW/ROY CM19 46 F3
Aberdale Gdns POTB/CUF EN6 59 J9
Aberdare Cl WWKM BR4 205 H9
Aberdare Gdns KIL/WHAMP NW6 3 H4
MLHL NW7 96 G8
Aberdare Rd PEND EN3 80 B8
Aberdeen Av SL SL1 128 F9
Aberdeen Cottages STAN * HA7 95 H8
Aberdeen La HBRY N5 119 J10
Aberdeen Pde UED * N18 100 A6
Aberdeen Pk HBRY N5 119 K9
Aberdeen Pl STJWD NW8 9 L2
Aberdeen Rd CROY/NA CR0 223 K1
HBRY N5 119 K9
KTN/HRWW/W HA3 94 E10
UED N18 99 P6
UED N18 100 A6
WLSDN NW10 116 C10
Aberdeen Ter BKHTH/KID SE3 161 J8
Aberdour Rd BCTR RM8 123 L8
Aberdour St STHWK SE1 19 J5
Aberfeldy St POP/IOD E14 141 H8
Aberford Gdns
WOOL/PLUM SE18 162 B7
Aberford Rd BORE WD6 75 M6
Aberfoyle Rd STRHM/NOR SW16 180 E9
Abergeldie Rd LEE/GVPK SE12 183 N2
Abernethy Rd LEW SE13 161 K10
Abersham Rd HACK E8 119 N10
Abery St WOOL/PLUM SE18 163 H3
Abingdon Cl CAMTN NW1 5 J2
HGDN/ICK UB10 132 A3
STHWK * SE1 19 M6
WIM/MER SW19 179 M9
WOKN/KNAP GU21 231 N4
Abingdon Pl POTB/CUF EN6 59 L8
Abingdon Rd FNCH N3 97 M10
KENS W8 14 F4
STRHM/NOR SW16 202 F1
Abingdon St WEST SW1P 17 L2
Abingdon Vls KENS W8 14 E4
Abingdon Wy ORP BR6 227 L1
Abinger Av BELMT SM2 220 F5
Abinger Cl BMLY BR1 206 B3
GDMY/SEVK IG3 123 K9
RDKG RH5 273 H6
WLGTN SM6 222 F2
Abinger Common Rd RDKG RH5 271 M10
Abinger Gdns ISLW TW7 154 D9
Abinger Gv DEPT SE8 160 E5
Abinger La RDKG RH5 271 L8
Abinger Ms MV/WKIL W9 8 E1
Abinger Rd CHSWK W4 156 C2
REDH RH1 275 P3
Abinger Wy RGUE GU4 250 E5
Ablett St BERM/RHTH SE16 160 B4
Abney Park Ter
STNW/STAM * N16 119 N7
Aboyne Dr RYNPK SW20 200 D2
Aboyne Rd TOOT SW17 179 N6
WLSDN NW10 116 B8
Abraham Ct UPMR RM14 125 P7
Abridge Cl CHES/WCR EN8 80 C1
Abridge Gdns CRW RM5 104 B7
Abridge Rd CHIG IG7 83 H10
EPP CM16 83 K3
Abridge Wy BARK IG11 143 L4
Abyssinia Cl BTSEA SW11 157 P10
Abyssinia Rd BTSEA * SW11 157 P10
Acacia Av ALP/SUD HA0 115 K10
BTFD TW8 154 G6
HCH RM12 124 G7
HYS/HAR UB3 132 G8
RSLP HA4 113 H6
SHPTN TW17 196 B5
STWL/WRAY TW19 150 B10
TOTM N17 99 L8
WDR/YW UB7 132 A9
WOKS/MYFD GU22 232 A6
Acacia Cl ADL/WDHM KT15 215 J6
CHESW EN7 61 M3
DEPT SE8 160 D3
KTN/HRWW/W HA3 94 D7
STMC/STPC BR5 206 G5
Acacia Dr ADL/WDHM KT15 215 J7
CHEAM SM3 201 J8
EW KT17 220 G10
UPMR RM14 125 P9
Acacia Gdns STJWD NW8 3 M7
UPMR RM14 126 E5
WWKM BR4 205 H9
Acacia Gv BERK HP4 33 N6
DUL SE21 181 L5
NWMAL KT3 200 B3
Acacia Ms WDR/YW UB7 151 N5
Acacia Pl STJWD NW8 3 M7
Acacia Rd ACT W3 135 P9
BECK BR3 204 E3
DART DA1 187 K4
ENC/FH EN2 79 L5
GRH DA9 188 D2
GU GU1 250 A10
HPTN TW12 175 P9
MTCM CR4 202 B2
STA TW18 173 L8
STJWD NW8 3 M7
STRHM/NOR SW16 202 F1
WALTH E17 120 D4
WAN E11 121 K7
WDGN N22 99 H9
The Acacias EBAR * EN4 77 N9
Acacia St HAT AL10 40 D7
Acacia Wk HARP AL5 20 C5
Acacia Wy BFN/LL DA15 185 J3
Academy Gdns CROY/NA CR0 203 N8
NTHLT UB5 133 L4
Academy Pl WOOL/PLUM SE18 162 C7
Academy Rd WOOL/PLUM SE18 162 C6
Acanthus Dr STHWK SE1 19 N7
Acanthus Rd BTSEA SW11 158 B9
Accommodation La
WDR/YW UB7 151 M5
Accommodation Rd CHERT KT16 194 A10
GLDGN NW11 117 J5
Ace Pde CHSGTN * KT9 199 K10
Acer Av RAIN RM13 145 L5
YEAD UB4 133 M6
Acer Dr CHOB/PIR GU24 212 E9
Acer Rd BH/WHM TN16 244 A2
Acers LCOL/BKTW AL2 56 B4
Acfold Rd FUL/PGN SW6 157 L7
Achilles Cl HHNE HP2 36 A4
STHWK SE1 19 P7
Achilles Pl WOKN/KNAP GU21 231 P3
Achilles Rd KIL/WHAMP NW6 117 K10
Achilles St NWCR SE14 160 D6
Acklam Rd NKENS W10 8 C4
Acklington Dr CDALE/KGS NW9 96 B9
Ackmar Rd FUL/PGN SW6 157 K7
Ackroyd Dr BOW E3 140 E7
Ackroyd Rd FSTH SE23 182 C3
Acland Cl WOOL/PLUM SE18 162 G6
Acland Crs CMBW SE5 159 L10
Acland Rd CRICK NW2 136 E1
Acme Rd WATN WD24 73 H4
Acock Gv NTHLT UB5 114 A9
Acol Crs RSLP HA4 113 J10
Acol Rd KIL/WHAMP NW6 2 F4
Acorn Cl CHING E4 100 G6
CHST BR7 184 F8
ENC/FH EN2 79 H5

HORL RH6 280 D3
HPTN TW12 176 A9
STAN HA7 94 G8
Acorn Gdns ACT W3 136 A7
NRWD SE19 203 N1
Acorn Gv HYS/HAR UB3 152 G6
KWD/TDW/WH KT20 239 J10
RSLP HA4 112 G9
WOKS/MYFD * GU22 232 B7
Acorn La POTB/CUF EN6 60 F5
Acorn Pde PECK * SE15 160 A6
Acorn Pl WATN WD24 73 H3
Acorn Rd DART DA1 186 G1
HHS/BOV HP3 36 B7
The Acorns HORL RH6 281 J4
SEV TN13 247 H9
STALE/WH * AL4 39 J6
Acorn St WARE SG12 28 A4
Acorns Wy ESH/CLAY KT10 218 B2
Acorn Wy FSTH SE23 182 C6
ORP BR6 226 E1
Acre Dr EDUL SE22 159 P10
Acrefield Rd CFSP/GDCR SL9 110 A2
Acre La BRXS/STRHM SW2 158 C10
CAR SM5 222 B1
Acre Pas WDSR SL4 149 J7
Acre Rd DAGE RM10 144 C2
KUTN/CMB KT2 199 K1
WIM/MER SW19 179 N9
Acres Av CHONG CM5 67 N2
Acres End AMSS HP7 69 K5
Acres Gdns KWD/TDW/WH KT20 238 F5
Acre Wy NTHWD HA6 92 G9
Acre Wd HHNE HP2 35 P6
Acrewood Wy STALE/WH AL4 39 L6
Acris St WAND/EARL SW18 179 M1
Acton Cl CHES/WCR EN8 62 D7
ED N9 99 P3
Acton Hill Ms ACT * W3 135 N10
Acton La ACT W3 155 P1
CHSWK W4 155 P3
WLSDN NW10 135 P5
Acton Ms HACK E8 7 L5
Acton St FSBYW WC1X 5 N10
Acuba Rd WAND/EARL SW18 179 L5
Acworth Pl DART * DA1 187 K2
Ada Ct MV/WKIL W9 3 K10
Ada Gdns POP/IOD E14 141 J8
SRTFD E15 141 L3
Adair Cl SNWD SE25 204 A3
Adair Rd NKENS W10 8 B2
Adam Cl SL SL1 128 F10
Adam & Eve Ms KENS W8 14 F3
Adam Rd CHING E4 100 E7
Adams Cl BRYLDS KT5 199 L6
FNCH N3 97 K8
WBLY HA9 115 N7
Adams Cft CHOB/PIR GU24 230 B6
Adamsfield CHESW EN7 61 N2
Adams House HLW CM20 28 G10
Adams Ms WDGN * N22 98 G8
Adamson Rd CAN/RD E16 141 M8
HAMP NW3 3 M3
Adams Pl HOLWY N7 118 G10
Adamsrill Rd SYD SE26 182 C7
Adams Rd BECK BR3 204 D5
TOTM N17 99 L10
Adam's Rw MYFR/PKLN W1K 10 D8
Adams Sq BXLYHS DA6 163 P9
Adam St TPL/STR WC2R 11 M8
Adams Wk KUT KT1 199 K2
Adams Wy SNWD SE25 203 N6
Adam Wk FUL/PGN * SW6 156 F6
Ada Pl BETH E2 7 P6
Adare Wk STRHM/NOR SW16 180 F5
Ada Rd ALP/SUD HA0 115 J8
CMBW SE5 159 M6
Ada St HACK E8 140 A3
Adderley Gdns ELTH/MOT SE9 184 D7
Adderley Gv BTSEA SW11 180 B1
Adderley Rd KTN/HRWW/W HA3 94 E9
Adderley St POP/IOD E14 141 H8
Addington Cl WDSR SL4 148 F9
Addington Dr NFNCH/WDSP N12 97 N7
Addington Gv SYD SE26 182 D7
Addington Rd BOW E3 140 F5
CAN/RD E16 141 K6
CROY/NA CR0 203 H8
FSBYPK N4 119 H5
SAND/SEL CR2 223 P7
WWKM BR4 205 J10
WWKM BR4 225 H1
Addington Sq CMBW SE5 159 K6
Addington Village Rd
CROY/NA CR0 224 E3
Addis Cl PEND EN3 80 C5
Addiscombe Av CROY/NA CR0 203 P7
Addiscombe Cl
KTN/HRWW/W HA3 115 H3
Addiscombe Court Rd
CROY/NA CR0 203 M8
Addiscombe Gv CROY/NA CR0 203 L9
Addiscombe Rd CROY/NA CR0 203 M9
WATW WD18 73 J8
Addison Av HSLW TW3 154 B7
NTGHL W11 8 A10
STHGT/OAK N14 78 C10
Addison Bridge Pl WKENS W14 14 C5
Addison Cl CTHM CR3 241 L8
IVER SL0 131 H9
NTHWD HA6 93 H9
STMC/STPC BR5 206 F6
Addison Crs WKENS W14 14 B3
Addison Dr LEE/GVPK SE12 183 N1
Addison Gdns BRYLDS KT5 199 L4
GRAYS RM17 167 P3
WKENS W14 156 G2
Addison Gv CHSWK W4 156 B2
Addison Pl NTGHL W11 8 A10
Addison Rd BARK/HLT IG6 102 F9
CSHM HP5 51 H5
CTHM CR3 241 L7
GU GU1 268 C2
HAYES BR2 205 A6
PEND EN3 80 B5
SNWD SE25 203 P4
TEDD TW11 176 G9
WALTH E17 120 G3
WAN E11 121 M4
WKENS W14 14 B2
Addison's Cl CROY/NA CR0 204 E9
Addison Ter CHSWK * W4 155 P3
Addison Wy GLDGN NW11 117 J2
HYS/HAR UB3 133 H8
NTHWD HA6 92 G9
Addle Hl BLKFR EC4V 12 D7
Addlestone Moor
ADL/WDHM KT15 195 M9
Addlestone Pk ADL/WDHM KT15 215 L2
Addlestone Rd ADL/WDHM KT15 215 P1
Addle St CITYW * EC2V 12 F5
Adecroft Wy E/WMO/HCT KT8 198 B3
Adela Av NWMAL KT3 200 E5
Adelaide Av BROCKY SE4 160 F10
Adelaide Cl CRAWW RH11 283 N4
EN EN1 79 M4
SL SL1 148 F1
STAN HA7 94 F5
Adelaide Ct HNWL W7 154 E1
Adelaide Gdns CHDH RM6 123 P3
Adelaide Gv SHB W12 136 D10
Adelaide Pl WEY KT13 216 E1
Adelaide Rd ASHF TW15 173 N8
CHST BR7 184 E8
HAMP NW3 3 L4
HEST TW5 153 M7
IL IG1 122 E7
LEY E10 121 H8
NWDGN UB2 153 M3
RCH/KEW TW9 155 L10
SURB KT6 199 K5
TEDD TW11 176 E9
TIL RM18 168 C7
WAND/EARL SW18 179 K1
WDSR SL4 149 L7
WEA W13 154 F1
WOT/HER KT12 197 H10
Adelaide Sq WDSR SL4 149 J8
Adelaide St CHCR * WC2N 11 L8
STALW/RED AL3 38 C5
Adelaide Ter BTFD * TW8 155 J4
Adela St NKENS W10 8 A1
Adelina Gv WCHPL E1 140 B7
Adelina Ms BAL SW12 180 E4
Adeline Pl RSQ WC1B 11 K4
Adeliza Cl BARK IG11 142 F2
Adelphi Cl CRAWE RH10 284 E9
Adelphi Crs HCH RM12 125 H7
YEAD UB4 132 F5
Adelphi Gdns SL SL1 149 K1
Adelphi Rd EW KT17 220 A9
Adelphi Ter CHCR WC2N 11 M8
Adelphi Wy YEAD UB4 132 G5
Adeney Cl HMSMTH W6 156 G5
Aden Gv STNW/STAM N16 119 L9
Adenmore Rd CAT SE6 182 F3
Aden Rd IL IG1 122 E5
PEND EN3 80 D8
Adeyfield Gdns HHNE HP2 36 A5
Adeyfield Rd HHNE HP2 36 A6
Adhara Rd NTHWD HA6 92 G6
Adie Rd HMSMTH W6 156 F2
Adine Rd PLSTW E13 141 M6
Adlers La RDKG RH5 254 F7
Adler St WCHPL E1 13 N5
Adley St CLPT E5 120 D10
Adlington Cl UED N18 99 L6
Admaston Rd WOOL/PLUM SE18 162 F6
Admiral Cl STMC/STPC BR5 207 N4
Admiral Ms NKENS W10 136 G6
Admiral Rd CRAWW RH11 283 K10
Admirals Cl STALE/WH AL4 40 B9
SWFD E18 121 N2
Admirals Ct GU GU1 250 E9
Admiral Seymour Rd
ELTH/MOT SE9 162 C10
Admiral's Ga GNWCH SE10 160 G7
Admiral Sq WBPTN * SW10 157 M7
Admiral St DEPT SE8 160 F7
HERT/BAY SG13 25 P5
Admirals Wk GRH DA9 188 G1
HAMP NW3 117 M8
HOD EN11 44 F5
STAL AL1 38 F8
Admirals Wy POP/IOD E14 160 G1
Admiralty Rd TEDD TW11 176 E10
Admiral Wk MV/WKIL W9 8 F3
Admiral Wy BERK HP4 33 L3
Adnams Wk RAIN RM13 125 H10
Adolf St CAT SE6 182 F7
Adolphus Rd FSBYPK N4 119 J7
Adolphus St DEPT SE8 160 E6
Adomar Rd BCTR RM8 123 N8
Adpar St BAY/PAD W2 9 L3
Adrian Cl DEN/HRF UB9 91 N9
Adrian Ms WBPTN SW10 15 H9
Adrian Rd ABLGY WD5 54 F7
Adrians Wk SLN SL2 129 L10
Adrienne Av STHL UB1 133 N6
Adstock Ms CFSP/GDCR * SL9 90 A9
Adstock Wy GRAYS RM17 167 L3
Advance Rd WNWD SE27 181 K7
Advent Wy UED N18 100 C6
Advice Av CDH/CHF RM16 167 M1
Adys Lawn CRICK * NW2 136 E1
Adys Rd PECK SE15 159 N9
Aerodrome Rd CDALE/KGS NW9 96 C10
Aerodrome Wy HEST TW5 153 K5
Affleck St IS * N1 5 P8
Afghan Rd BTSEA SW11 157 P8
Aftab Ter WCHPL * E1 140 A6
Afton Dr SOCK/AV RM15 146 G8
Agamemnon Rd
KIL/WHAMP NW6 117 J10
Agar Cl SURB KT6 199 L9
Agar Gv CAMTN NW1 5 K3
Agar Pl CAMTN NW1 5 H4
Agars Pl DTCH/LGLY SL3 149 M5
Agar St CHCR WC2N 11 L8
Agate Cl CAN/RD E16 142 A8
Agate Rd HMSMTH W6 156 F2
Agates La ASHTD KT21 237 J4
Agatha Cl WAP E1W 140 A10
Agaton Rd ELTH/MOT SE9 184 F5
Agave Rd CRICK NW2 116 F9
Agdon St FSBYE EC1V 12 C1
Agincourt Pl ASC SL5 192 B3
Agincourt Rd HAMP NW3 118 A9
Agister Rd CHIG IG7 103 K6
Agnes Av IL IG1 122 D9
Agnes Cl EHAM E6 142 D9
Agnesfield Cl NFNCH/WDSP N12 97 P7
Agnes Gdns BCTR RM8 123 N9
Agnes Riley Gdns CLAP * SW4 180 D3
Agnes Rd ACT W3 156 C1
Agnes Scott Ct WEY * KT13 196 C10
Agnes St POP/IOD E14 140 E8
Agnew Rd FSTH SE23 182 D3
Agraria Rd GUW GU2 267 N1
Agricola Pl EN EN1 79 N9
Aidan Cl DAGW RM9 123 P9
Ailsa Av TWK TW1 176 F1
Ailsa Cl CRAWW RH11 283 L10
Ailsa Rd TWK TW1 176 G1
Ailsa St POP/IOD E14 141 H7
Ainger Rd HAMP NW3 4 B4
Ainsdale Cl ORP BR6 206 G8
Ainsdale Crs PIN HA5 113 P1
Ainsdale Dr STHWK SE1 19 N8
Ainsdale Rd EA W5 135 J6
OXHEY WD19 93 K4
Ainsdale Wy WOKN/KNAP GU21 231 M3
Ainsley Av ROMW/RG RM7 124 D4
Ainsley Cl ED N9 99 M2
Ainsley St BETH E2 140 A5
Ainslie Wood Crs CHING E4 100 G6
Ainslie Wood Gdns CHING E4 100 G5
Ainslie Wood Rd CHING E4 100 F6
Ainsty St BERM/RHTH * SE16 160 B1
Ainsworth Cl CMBW * SE5 159 M8
CRICK NW2 116 D8
Ainsworth Rd CROY/NA CR0 203 J8
HOM E9 140 B2
Ainsworth Wy STJWD NW8 3 J5
Aintree Av EHAM E6 142 B3
Aintree Cl DTCH/LGLY SL3 151 H7
GVE DA12 190 E6
UX/CGN UB8 132 C8
Aintree Crs BARK/HLT IG6 102 F10
Aintree Gv UPMR RM14 125 N8
Aintree Rd CRAWE RH10 284 B9
GFD/PVL UB6 134 G4
Aintree St FUL/PGN SW6 157 H6
Airdrie Cl IS N1 5 N4
YEAD UB4 133 M7
Airedale HHNE HP2 35 P3
Airedale Av CHSWK W4 156 C4
Airedale Av South CHSWK * W4 156 C4
Airedale Cl RDART DA2 188 B4
Airedale Rd BAL SW12 180 A3
EA W5 155 H2
Aire Dr SOCK/AV RM15 146 G6
Airfield Wy GSTN WD25 54 G10
HCH RM12 145 J1
Airlie Gdns IL IG1 122 E6
KENS W8 8 E10
Airport Wy HORL RH6 280 B7
STWL/WRAY TW19 151 K10
Air St REGST W1B 11 H8
Aisgill Av ECT SW5 14 D8
Aisher Rd THMD SE28 143 M9
Aisher Wy SEV TN13 246 F7
Aislibie Rd LEW SE13 161 K10
Aiten Pl HMSMTH W6 156 D3
Aitken Cl HACK E8 7 N5
MTCM CR4 202 A7
Aitken Rd BAR EN5 76 F9
CAT SE6 182 G5
Aitman Dr CHSWK * W4 155 M4
Ajax Av CDALE/KGS NW9 116 B1
SL SL1 128 G9
Ajax Rd KIL/WHAMP NW6 117 J9
Akabusi Cl SNWD SE25 203 P6
Akehurst Cl CRAWE RH10 285 H2
Akehurst La BGR/WK TN15 265 K1
Akehurst St PUT/ROE SW15 178 D2
Akeman Cl STALW/RED * AL3 37 N8
Akenside Rd HAMP NW3 117 N10
Akerman Rd CMBW SE5 159 J7
SURB KT6 199 H6
Alabama St WOOL/PLUM SE18 162 G6
Alacross Rd EA W5 155 H1
Alamein Cl BROX EN10 44 C6
Alamein Gdns RDART DA2 188 C3
Alamein Rd SWCM DA10 189 J2
Alanbrooke GVE DA12 190 F3
Alanbrooke Cl
WOKN/KNAP GU21 231 H4
Alan Cl DART DA1 165 K10
Alandale Dr PIN HA5 93 J9
Alan Dr BAR EN5 77 H10
Alan Gdns ROMW/RG RM7 124 B5
Alan Hilton Ct CHERT * KT16 214 G3
Alan Hocken Wy SRTFD E15 141 K4
Alan Rd WIM/MER SW19 179 H8
Alanthus Cl LEE/GVPK SE12 183 L2
Alan Turing Rd GUW GU2 249 J10
Alan Wy DTCH/LGLY SL3 130 B8
Alaska St STHWK SE1 12 A10
Alba Cl YEAD UB4 133 L6
Albacore Crs LEW SE13 182 G2
Alba Gdns GLDGN NW11 117 H4
Albain Crs ASHF TW15 173 P5
Alban Av STALW/RED AL3 38 C4
Alban Crs BORE WD6 75 N5
EYN DA4 209 P8
Alban Pk STALE/WH * AL4 39 L6
Albans Vw GSTN WD25 55 J9
Albany MYFR/PICC W1J 10 G8
Albany Cl BUSH WD23 74 C10
BXLY DA5 185 M3
ESH/CLAY KT10 217 P5
HGDN/ICK UB10 112 B10
MORT/ESHN SW14 155 N10
SEVS/STOTM N15 119 J2
Albany Cottages HNWL * W7 134 D10
Albany Ct EPP CM16 65 J6
Albany Ctyd MYFR/PICC * W1J 11 H8
Albany Crs EDGW HA8 95 M8
ESH/CLAY KT10 218 D3
Albany Ga CSHM HP5 50 G6
Albany Ms IS N1 6 B3
KUTN/CMB * KT2 177 J9
LCOL/BKTW * AL2 55 P3
SUT SM1 221 L2
WALW SE17 18 F10
Albany Pde BTFD * TW8 155 K5
Albany Pk DTCH/LGLY SL3 150 G6
PEND * EN3 80 C4
Albany Park Av PEND EN3 80 B5
Albany Park Rd KUTN/CMB KT2 177 J9
LHD/OX KT22 236 F5
Albany Pl BTFD TW8 155 J5
EGH TW20 172 E7
HOLWY N7 119 H9
Albany Rd BELV DA17 164 A5
BRWN CM15 86 G10
BTFD TW8 155 J5
BXLY DA5 185 M3
CHDH RM6 124 A4
CHST BR7 184 E8
CMBW SE5 18 G10
CRAWW RH11 283 M7
FSBYPK N4 118 G4
HCH RM12 125 H6
LEY E10 120 F5
MNPK E12 122 A9
NWMAL KT3 200 A4
PEND EN3 80 C3
RCHPK/HAM * TW10 177 L1
TIL RM18 168 D7
UED N18 100 A6
WALTH E17 120 D4
WDSR SL4 149 H8
WDSR SL4 171 M1
WEA W13 134 G9
WGCE * AL7 23 H5
WIM/MER SW19 179 L8
WOT/HER KT12 217 L1
Albany Rw EFNCH * N2 117 P2
The Albanys REIG RH2 257 K7
REIG RH2 257 K7
Albany St CAMTN NW1 4 F9
Albany Ter RCHPK/HAM * TW10 177 L1
The Albany KUTN/CMB KT2 177 J9
Albany Vw BKHH IG9 101 M2
Alba Pl NTGHL W11 8 C5
Albatross Gdns SAND/SEL CR2 224 C7
Albatross St WOOL/PLUM SE18 163 H6
Albemarle Ap GNTH/NBYPK IG2 122 E4
Albemarle Av CHES/WCR EN8 62 B4
POTB/CUF EN6 59 L9
WHTN TW2 175 N4
Albemarle Cl GRAYS RM17 167 M1
Albemarle Gdns
GNTH/NBYPK IG2 122 E4
NWMAL KT3 200 A4
Albemarle Pk BECK * BR3 204 G1
STAN * HA7 95 H6
Albemarle Rd BECK BR3 204 G1
EBAR EN4 97 P1
Albemarle St CONDST W1S 10 G8
Albemarle Wy FARR EC1M 12 C2
Alberon Gdns GLDGN NW11 117 J2
Alberta Av SUT SM1 221 H1
Alberta Dr HORL RH6 281 H4
Alberta Est WALW SE17 18 D7
Alberta Rd BXLYHN DA7 164 D7
EN EN1 79 N10
Alberta St WALW SE17 18 D7
Albert Av CHERT KT16 195 K3
CHING E4 100 F5
VX/NE SW8 158 G6
Albert Br CHEL SW3 15 P10
DTCH/LGLY SL3 149 N9
BTSEA SW11 157 P6
Albert Bridge Ga BTSEA SW11 158 A6
Albert Carr Gdns
STRHM/NOR SW16 180 F8
Albert Cl CDH/CHF RM16 167 P2
HOM E9 140 A3
WDGN N22 98 E9
Albert Cottages WCHPL * E1 13 N3
Albert Crs CHING E4 100 F5
Albert Dr STA TW18 173 J8
WIM/MER SW19 179 H5
WOKN/KNAP GU21 214 F10
Albert Emb LBTH SE11 17 M7
Albert Gdns HLWE CM17 47 N2
WCHPL E1 140 C8
Albert Ga KTBR SW1X 16 B1
Albert Gv RYNPK SW20 200 G1
Albertine Cl EW KT17 238 E2
Albert Ms BROCKY * SE4 160 E10
FSBYPK * N4 118 G6
KENS W8 15 J3
POP/IOD * E14 140 D9
Albert Murray Cl GVE DA12 190 F3
Albert Pl FNCH N3 97 K9
KENS W8 15 H2
WDSR SL4 148 F4
Albert Rd ADL/WDHM KT15 195 N10
ASHF TW15 174 A8
ASHTD KT21 237 L4
BCTR RM8 124 A6
BELMT SM2 221 N2
BELV DA17 164 A4
BKHH IG9 102 A3
BXLY DA5 186 B2
CAN/RD E16 142 B10
CAN/RD E16 162 D1
CSHM HP5 51 H7
EA W5 134 G6
EBAR EN4 77 M8
EGH TW20 172 A9
ELTH/MOT SE9 184 B6
EW KT17 220 C9
FSBYPK N4 118 G6
HAYES BR2 206 A5
HDN NW4 116 G2
HORL RH6 280 B4
HPTN TW12 176 B8
HSLW TW3 153 P10
HYS/HAR UB3 152 F2
IL IG1 122 F8
KIL/WHAMP NW6 2 D8
KUT KT1 199 L2
MLHL NW7 96 C6
MTCM CR4 202 A3
NWDGN UB2 153 L2
NWMAL KT3 200 C4
ORP BR6 227 K2
PGE/AN SE20 182 C10
RCHPK/HAM TW10 177 K1
RDART DA2 187 K6
REDH RH1 258 D5
ROM RM1 124 G4
RYLN/HDSTN HA2 114 B1
SEVS/STOTM N15 119 M4
SNWD SE25 204 A4
STMC/STPC BR5 207 L6
SWCM DA10 189 L2
SWFD E18 121 N1
TEDD TW11 176 E9
TWK TW1 176 E4
WALTH E17 120 F3
WAN E11 121 H7
WARL CR6 242 D3
WDGN N22 98 E9
WDR/YW UB7 131 P10
WDSR SL4 149 K10
Albert Rd North REIG RH2 257 J9
WAT * WD17 73 J7
Albert Rd South WATW * WD18 73 J7
Albert Sq SRTFD E15 121 K10
VX/NE SW8 158 G6
Albert St BRW CM14 107 H6
CAMTN NW1 4 F6
NFNCH/WDSP N12 97 M6
SL SL1 149 K2
STAL AL1 38 C7
WDSR SL4 148 G7
Albert Ter CAMTN NW1 4 C5
EA * W5 134 G6
WLSDN * NW10 136 A3
Albert Terrace Ms CAMTN NW1 4 C5
Albert Wy PECK SE15 160 A6
Albion Av MUSWH N10 98 B9
VX/NE SW8 158 E8
Albion Cl BAY/PAD W2 9 P7
CRAWE RH10 284 E8
ROMW/RG RM7 124 E4
SLN SL2 129 M10
Albion Crs CSTG HP8 89 N4
Albion Dr HACK E8 7 L4
Albion Est BERM/RHTH * SE16 160 B1
Albion Gdns HMSMTH W6 156 E3
Albion Ga BAY/PAD W2 9 P7
Albion Gv STNW/STAM N16 119 M9
Albion Hl HHNE HP2 35 N7
LOU IG10 81 P
Albion Ms BAY/PAD W2 9 P
IS * N1 6 A
REIG * RH2 275 M
Albion Pde WOKN/KNAP * GU21 231 H
Albion Pk LOU IG10 82 A
Albion Pl FARR EC1M 12 C
HMSMTH W6 156 E
SNWD * SE25 203 P
WDSR SL4 148 F
Albion Rd BELMT SM2 221 N
BXLYHS DA6 164 A1
CSTG HP8 89 N
DAGE RM10 124 B1
GVE DA12 190 F
HSLW TW3 153 P1
HYS/HAR UB3 132 F
KUTN/CMB KT2 199 P
REIG RH2 275 M
STAL AL1 38 E
STNW/STAM N16 119 L1
TOTM N17 99 N1
WALTH E17 121 H
WHTN TW2 176 D
Albion Sq HACK E8 7 L
Albion St BAY/PAD W2 9 P
BERM/RHTH SE16 160 B
CROY/NA CR0 203 J
Albion Ter CHING * E4 80 G
GVE DA12 190 F
HACK E8 7 L
Albion Villas Rd FSTH SE23 182 B
Albion Wy LEW SE13 161 H10
STBT EC1A 12 E
WBLY HA9 115 M
Albion Yd IS N1 5 M
Albrighton Rd CMBW SE5 159 M
Albuhera Cl ENC/FH EN2 79 H
Albury Av BELMT SM2 220 F
BXLYHN DA7 163 P
ISLW TW7 154 E
Albury Cl CHERT KT16 193 M1
HOR/WEW KT19 219 N
HPTN TW12 175 P
Albury Dr PIN HA5 93 K
Albury Grove Rd CHES/WCR EN8 62 C
Albury Keep HORL RH6 280 C
Albury Ms MNPK E12 121 P
Albury Ride CHES/WCR EN8 62 C
Albury Rd CHSGTN KT9 219 K
GU GU1 268 C
REDH RH1 258 D
WOT/HER KT12 216 F
Albury St DEPT SE8 160 F
SHGR GU5 269 M
Albury Wk CHES/WCR EN8 62 B
Albyfield BMLY BR1 206 C
Albyn Rd DEPT SE8 160 F
Albyns La ABR/ST RM4 84 E
Alcester Crs CLPT E5 120 A
Alcester Rd WLGTN SM6 222 C
Alcock Cl WLGTN SM6 222 E
Alcock Rd HEST TW5 153 L
Alcocks Cl KWD/TDW/WH KT20 239 H
Alcocks La KWD/TDW/WH KT20 239 H
Alconbury WGCE AL7 23 P
Alconbury Rd CLPT E5 119 P
Alcorn Cl CHEAM SM3 201 K
Alcott Cl HNWL W7 134 E
Aldborough Rd DAGE RM10 144 D
UPMR RM14 125 N
Aldborough Rd North
GNTH/NBYPK IG2 123 J
Aldborough Rd South
GDMY/SEVK IG3 123 H
Aldborough Sp SL SL1 129 K
Aldbourne Rd ACT W3 136 C1
SL SL1 128 A
Aldbridge St WALW SE17 19 K
Aldburgh Ms MHST W1U 10 D
Aldbury Av WBLY HA9 135 N
Aldbury Cl GSTN WD25 73 L
STALE/WH AL4 39 H
Aldbury Gv WGCE AL7 23 L
Aldbury Ms WCHMH N21 99 L
Aldbury Rd RKW/CH/CXG WD3 91 J
Aldebert Ter VX/NE SW8 158 G
Aldeburgh Pl WFD IG8 101 M
Aldeburgh St GNWCH SE10 161 M
Alden Av SRTFD E15 141 L
Aldenham Av RAD WD7 74 F
Aldenham Dr UX/CGN UB8 132 C
Aldenham Gv RAD WD7 56 G1
Aldenham Rd GSTN WD25 74 E
OXHEY WD19 73 L1
RAD WD7 74 F
Aldenham St CAMTN NW1 5 H
Aldenholme WEY KT13 216 F
Alden Md PIN * HA5 93 P
Aldensley Rd HMSMTH W6 156 E
Alden Vw WDSR SL4 148 C
Alder Av UPMR RM14 125 N
Alderbourne La DTCH/LGLY SL3 110 A
Alderbrook Rd BAL SW12 180 C
Alderbury Rd BARN SW13 156 D
DTCH/LGLY SL3 150 C
Alderbury Rd West
DTCH/LGLY SL3 150 C
Alder Cl EGH TW20 172 B
HOD EN11 44 G
LCOL/BKTW AL2 56 A
PECK SE15 19 L1
SL SL1 128 E1
Aldercombe La CTHM CR3 259 M
Alder Dr SOCK/AV RM15 147 H
Alder Gv CRICK NW2 116 D
Alderholt Wy PECK * SE15 159 M
Alderley Ct BERK HP4 33 N
Alderman Av BARK IG11 143 K
Alderman Cl BRKMPK AL9 40 F1
Alderman Judge Ml KUT * KT1 199 K
Alderman's Hl PLMGR N13 98 F
Aldermanbury CITYW * EC2V 12 F
Aldermanbury Sq CITYW EC2V 12 F
Aldermary Rd BMLY BR1 205 M
Aldermoor Rd CAT SE6 182 E
Alderney Av HEST TW5 154 A
Alderney Gdns NTHLT UB5 133 N
Alderney Ms STHWK SE1 18 G
Alderney Rd ERITH DA8 165 H
WCHPL E1 140 C
Alderney St PIM SW1V 16 F
Alder Rd DEN/HRF UB9 131 L
IVER SL0 130 F
MORT/ESHN SW14 156 A
SCUP DA14 185 H
Alders Av WFD IG8 101 K
Aldersbrook Av EN EN1 79 M
Aldersbrook Dr KUTN/CMB KT2 177 L
Aldersbrook La MNPK E12 122 C

Aldersbrook Rd MNPK E12 ....121 P7
Alders Cl EA W5 ....155 J2
EDGW HA8 ....95 P6
WAN E11 ....121 N7
Aldersey Gdns BARK IG11 ....142 G1
Aldersey Rd GU GU1 ....250 C10
Aldersford Cl BROCKY SE4 ....160 C10
Aldersgate St STBT EC1A 12 E5
Aldersgrove E/WMO/HCT KT8 ....198 C5
Aldersgrove Av LEE/GVPK SE12 ....183 P6
Aldershot Rd CHOB/PIR GU24 ....248 D2
KIL/WHAMP NW6 ....2 D5
RGUW GU3 ....248 D6
Aldershot Ter
WOOL/PLUM * SE18 ....162 D6
Alderside Wk EGH TW20 ....172 A8
Aldersmead Av CROY/NA CR0 ....204 C6
Aldersmead Rd BECK BR3 ....182 D10
Alderson Pl STHL UB1 ....134 B10
Alderson St NKENS * W10 ....8 B1
Alders Rd EDGW HA8 ....95 P6
REIG RH2 ....257 L8
Alderstead La REDH RH1 ....258 E1
The Alders BF/WBF KT14 ....215 M8
DEN/HRF * UB9 ....131 M1
FELT TW13 ....175 M8
NWDGN UB2 ....153 N5
STRHM/NOR * SW16 ....180 D7
WCHMH N21 ....79 H10
WWKM BR4 ....204 G8
Alders Wk SBW CM21 ....29 P1
Alderton Cl BRWN CM15 ....86 G9
LOU IG10 ....82 D8
WLSDN NW10 ....116 A7
Alderton Crs HDN NW4 ....116 E3
Alderton Hall La LOU IG10 ....82 D8
Alderton Hl LOU IG10 ....82 C9
Alderton Ri LOU IG10 ....82 D8
Alderton Rd CROY/NA CR0 ....203 N7
HNHL SE24 ....159 K9
Alderton Wy HDN NW4 ....116 E3
LOU IG10 ....82 C9
Alderville Rd FUL/PGN SW6 ....157 J8
Alder Wk GSTN WD25 ....73 J1
Alder Wy SWLY BR8 ....208 E2
Alderwick Dr HSLW TW3 ....154 C9
Alderwood Cl CTHM CR3 ....259 M1
Alderwood Dr ABR/ST RM4 ....83 L7
Alderwood Rd ELTH/MOT SE9 ....184 G2
Aldford St MYFR/PKLN W1K 10 C9
Aldgate FENCHST EC3M 13 K6
Aldgate Barrs WCHPL * E1 ....13 M5
Aldgate High St TWRH EC3N 13 L6
Aldin Av North SL SL1 ....149 M1
Aldin Av South SL SL1 ....149 M1
Aldine St SHB W12 ....156 F1
Aldingbourne Cl CRAWW RH11 ....283 J6
Aldingham Gdns HCH RM12 ....125 H10
Aldington Cl CHDH RM6 ....123 M5
Aldington Rd WOOL/PLUM SE18 ....162 A2
Aldis Ms TOOT SW17 ....179 P8
Aldis St TOOT SW17 ....179 P8
Aldock WGCE AL7 ....23 K7
Aldred Rd KIL/WHAMP NW6 ....117 K10
Aldren Rd TOOT SW17 ....179 M6
Aldrich Crs CROY/NA CR0 ....225 H5
Aldriche Wy CHING E4 ....101 H7
Aldrich Gdns CHEAM SM3 ....201 J10
Aldrich Ter WAND/EARL SW18 ....179 M5
Aldridge Av EDGW HA8 ....95 N4
PEND EN3 ....80 F4
RSLP HA4 ....113 K7
STAN HA7 ....95 K9
Aldridge Ri NWMAL KT3 ....200 B7
Aldridge Rd SLN SL2 ....128 F6
Aldridge Road Vls NTGHL W11 ....8 D4
Aldridge Wk STHGT/OAK N14 ....98 F1
Aldrington Rd
STRHM/NOR SW16 ....180 D8
Aldsworth Cl MV/WKIL W9 ....8 G2
Aldwick STAL AL1 ....38 F8
Aldwickbury Crs HARP AL5 ....20 C2
Aldwick Cl CHST BR7 ....184 G6
Aldwick Rd CROY/NA CR0 ....202 G10
HARP AL5 ....20 D3
Aldworth Gv LEW SE13 ....183 H2
Aldworth Rd SRTFD E15 ....141 K2
Aldwych TPL/STR WC2R 11 N7
Aldwych Av BARK/HLT IG6 ....122 F2
Aldwych Cl HCH RM12 ....125 H7
Aldykes HAT AL10 ....40 C4
Alers Rd BXLYHS DA6 ....185 N1
Alesia Cl WDGN N22 ....98 F8
Alestan Beck Rd CAN/RD E16 ....142 A8
Alexander Av WLSDN NW10 ....136 E2
Alexander Cl BFN/LL DA15 ....185 H1
EBAR EN4 ....77 N8
HAYES BR2 ....205 M8
STHL UB1 ....134 B10
WHTN TW2 ....176 D5
Alexander Evans Ms FSTH SE23 ....182 C5
Alexander Godley Cl ASHTD KT21 ....237 L5
Alexander La BRWN CM15 ....87 M9
Alexander Ms BAY/PAD W2 ....8 G5
Alexander Pl SKENS SW7 ....15 N5
Alexander Rd ARCH N19 ....118 F8
CHST BR7 ....184 E9
COUL/CHIP CR5 ....240 C1
EGH TW20 ....172 E8
GRH DA9 ....189 H1
HERT/WAS SG14 ....25 H5
LCOL/BKTW AL2 ....57 H1
REIG RH2 ....275 K3
WELL DA16 ....163 N8
Alexander Sq CHEL SW3 ....15 N5
Alexander St BAY/PAD W2 ....8 F5
CSHM HP5 ....51 H6
Alexanders Wk CTHM CR3 ....259 N2
Alexander Ter ABYW * SE2 ....163 L4
Alexandra Av BTSEA * SW11 ....158 B7
RYLN/HDSTN HA2 ....113 N6
STHL UB1 ....133 N9
SUT SM1 ....201 K10
WARL CR6 ....242 E3
WDGN N22 ....98 E9
Alexandra Cl ASHF TW15 ....174 E10
CDH/CHF RM16 ....168 E1
RYLN/HDSTN HA2 ....113 P8
STA TW18 ....173 N9
SWLY BR8 ....208 F2
WOT/HER KT12 ....197 H9
Alexandra Cottages
NWCR * SE14 ....160 E7
Alexandra Ct ASHF TW15 ....174 E9
CRAWW * RH11 ....283 N8
Alexandra Crs BMLY BR1 ....183 L9
Alexandra Dr BRYLDS KT5 ....199 M7
NRWD SE19 ....181 M8
Alexandra Gdns CAR SM5 ....222 B5
HSLW TW3 ....154 A8
MUSWH N10 ....118 C2
WOKN/KNAP GU21 ....231 H4
Alexandra Ga SKENS SW7 ....15 L1
Alexandra Gv FSBYPK N4 ....119 J6
NFNCH/WDSP N12 ....97 L6
Alexandra Ms EFNCH N2 ....118 A1
WAT WD17 ....73 H6
Alexandra Palace Wy
CEND/HSY/T N8 ....118 D2
Alexandra Pde
RYLN/HDSTN * HA2 ....114 A9
Alexandra Park Rd MUSWH N10 ....98 C10
WDGN N22 ....98 D9
Alexandra Pl CROY/NA CR0 ....203 M8
GU GU1 ....268 C2
SNWD SE25 ....203 L5
STJWD NW8 ....3 K5
Alexandra Rd ADL/WDHM KT15 ....215 N1
ASHF TW15 ....174 E10
BH/WHM TN16 ....243 N5
BORE WD6 ....76 A4
BTFD * TW8 ....155 J5
CEND/HSY/T N8 ....119 H1
CHDH RM6 ....123 N4
CHSWK W4 ....156 A1
CROY/NA CR0 ....203 M8
ED * N9 ....100 A1
EGH TW20 ....171 P9
EHAM E6 ....142 D5
ERITH DA8 ....164 G5
EW KT17 ....220 C9
GVE DA12 ....191 H3
HDN NW4 ....116 G2
HHNE HP2 ....35 N5
HSLW TW3 ....154 A8
KGLGY WD4 ....53 K6
KGLGY WD4 ....54 B5
KUTN/CMB KT2 ....177 M10
LEY E10 ....121 H8
MORT/ESHN SW14 ....156 A9
MUSWH N10 ....98 C8
PEND EN3 ....80 C8
RAIN RM13 ....144 G3
RCH/KEW TW9 ....155 L8
RKW/CH/CXG WD3 ....71 K2
ROM RM1 ....124 G4
SEVS/STOTM N15 ....119 L3
SL SL1 ....149 J2
STAL AL1 ....38 D6
STJWD NW8 ....3 K5
SWFD E18 ....121 N1
SYD SE26 ....182 C9
THDIT KT7 ....198 E5
TIL RM18 ....168 C8
TWK TW1 ....177 H2
UX/CGN UB8 ....131 N4
WALTH E17 ....120 E4
WARL CR6 ....242 D3
WAT WD17 ....73 H6
WDSR SL4 ....149 J8
WIM/MER SW19 ....179 P10
WIM/MER SW19 ....179 K8
Alexandra Sq MRDN SM4 ....201 K5
Alexandra St CAN/RD E16 ....141 M7
NWCR SE14 ....160 D6
Alexandra Ter GU GU1 ....268 B1
Alexandra Wk EYN * DA4 ....210 C2
Alexandra Wy CHES/WCR EN8 ....62 E10
HOR/WEW KT19 ....219 M8
TIL RM18 ....169 L3
Alexandria Rd WEA W13 ....134 F9
Alexis St BERM/RHTH SE16 ....19 N5
Alfearn Rd CLPT E5 ....120 B9
Alford Gn CROY/NA CR0 ....225 J3
Alford Pl IS * N1 ....6 F8
Alford Rd ERITH DA8 ....164 D4
Alfoxton Av SEVS/STOTM N15 ....119 J2
Alfreda St BTSEA SW11 ....158 C7
Alfred Cl CHSWK W4 ....156 A3
CRAWE RH10 ....284 F8
Alfred Gdns STHL UB1 ....133 M9
Alfred Ms FITZ W1T 11 J3
Alfred Pl FITZ W1T 11 J3
GVW DA11 ....190 C4
Alfred Rd ACT W3 ....135 P10
BAY/PAD W2 ....8 F3
BELV DA17 ....164 A4
BKHH IG9 ....102 A3
BRW CM14 ....107 J3
FELT TW13 ....175 K5
FSTGT E7 ....121 L10
GVW DA11 ....190 E5
KUT KT1 ....199 K3
RDART DA2 ....187 N7
SNWD SE25 ....203 P5
SOCK/AV RM15 ....146 B10
SUT SM1 ....221 M2
Alfred's Gdns BARK IG11 ....143 H4
Alfred St BOW E3 ....140 E5
GRAYS RM17 ....167 P5
Alfred's Wy (East Ham &
Barking By-Pass) BARK IG11 ....142 G4
Alfred Vls WALTH * E17 ....121 H2
Alfreton Cl WIM/MER SW19 ....178 G6
Alfriston BRYLDS KT5 ....199 L6
Alfriston Av CROY/NA CR0 ....202 F7
RYLN/HDSTN HA2 ....113 P4
Alfriston Cl BRYLDS KT5 ....199 L6
Alfriston Rd BTSEA SW11 ....180 A1
Algar Cl STAN HA7 ....94 E6
Algar Rd ISLW TW7 ....154 F8
Algarve Rd WAND/EARL SW18 ....179 L4
Algernon Rd HDN NW4 ....116 D4
KIL/WHAMP NW6 ....2 E6
LEW SE13 ....160 G10
Algers Cl LOU IG10 ....82 A9
Algers Rd LOU IG10 ....82 B9
Alghers Md LOU IG10 ....82 A9
Algiers Rd LEW SE13 ....160 F10
Alguin Ct STAN * HA7 ....95 H7
Alibon Gdns DAGE RM10 ....124 B10
Alice La BOW E3 ....140 E3
SL SL1 ....128 A6
Alice Ms TEDD TW11 ....176 E8
Alice Ruston Pl
WOKS/MYFD GU22 ....231 P5
Alice St STHWK SE1 ....19 J4
Alice Thompson Cl
LEE/GVPK SE12 ....183 P5
Alice Walker Cl HNHL * SE24 ....159 J10
Alice Wy HSLW TW3 ....154 A10
Alicia Av CRAWE RH10 ....284 C7
KTN/HRWW/W HA3 ....114 G2
Alicia Cl KTN/HRWW/W HA3 ....114 G2
Alicia Gdns KTN/HRWW/W HA3 ....114 G2
Alie St WCHPL E1 ....13 M6
Alington Crs CDALE/KGS NW9 ....115 P6
Alington Gv WLGTN SM6 ....222 E5
Alison Cl CROY/NA CR0 ....204 C8
EHAM E6 ....142 D8
WOKN/KNAP GU21 ....232 B1
Aliwal Ms BTSEA * SW11 ....157 P10
Aliwal Rd BTSEA SW11 ....157 P10
Alkerden La GRH DA9 ....189 H2
Alkerden Rd CHSWK W4 ....156 B4
Alkham Rd STNW/STAM N16 ....119 N7
Allan Barclay Cl
STNW/STAM N16 ....119 N4
Allan Cl NWMAL KT3 ....200 A5
Allandale HHNE HP2 ....35 N4
STALW/RED AL3 ....38 A9
Allandale Av FNCH N3 ....117 H1
Allandale Crs POTB/CUF EN6 ....59 H8
Allandale Pl ORP BR6 ....207 N10
Allandale Rd EMPK RM11 ....124 G5
PEND EN3 ....80 C2
Allan Wy ACT W3 ....135 P7
Allard Cl CHESW EN7 ....61 N3
STMC/STPC BR5 ....207 M7
Allard Crs BUSH WD23 ....94 B3
Allard Wy BROX EN10 ....44 D7
Allardyce St CLAP SW4 ....158 G10
Allbrook Cl TEDD TW11 ....176 D8
Allcot Cl CRAWW RH11 ....283 H10
EBED/NFELT TW14 ....174 G4
Allcroft Rd KTTN NW5 ....4 D1
Alldicks Rd HHS/BOV HP3 ....36 A8
Allenby Av SAND/SEL CR2 ....223 K5
Allenby Cl GFD/PVL UB6 ....133 P5
Allenby Crs GRAYS RM17 ....167 N4
Allenby Dr EMPK RM11 ....125 M6
Allenby Rd BH/WHM TN16 ....244 B3
FSTH SE23 ....182 D6
GFD/PVL UB6 ....133 P8
Allen Cl MTCM CR4 ....202 C1
RAD WD7 ....57 K8
STALE/WH AL4 ....21 J4
SUN TW16 ....197 J1
Allen Ct HAT * AL10 ....40 E6
Allendale Av STHL UB1 ....133 P8
Allendale Cl CMBW SE5 ....159 L8
RDART DA2 ....188 C4
SYD SE26 ....182 C8
Allendale Rd GFD/PVL UB6 ....134 G1
Allen Edwards Dr VX/NE SW8 ....158 F7
Allen House Pk
WOKS/MYFD GU22 ....231 P6
Allen Rd BECK BR3 ....204 C2
BOW E3 ....140 E4
CROY/NA CR0 ....202 G7
GT/LBKH KT23 ....254 A2
RAIN RM13 ....145 K5
STNW/STAM N16 ....119 M9
SUN TW16 ....197 J1
Allensbury Pl HOLWY N7 ....5 K4
Allens Rd PEND EN3 ....80 B9
Allen St KENS W8 ....14 F3
Allenswood Rd ELTH/MOT SE9 ....162 B9
Allerds Rd SLN SL2 ....128 E3
Allerford Rd CAT SE6 ....182 G7
Allerton Cl BORE WD6 ....75 L4
Allerton Rd BORE WD6 ....75 K4
STNW/STAM N16 ....119 K7
Allestree Rd FUL/PGN SW6 ....157 H6
Alleyn Crs DUL SE21 ....181 L5
Alleyndale Rd BCTR RM8 ....123 M7
Alleyn Pk DUL SE21 ....181 L5
NWDGN UB2 ....153 N4
Alleyn Rd DUL SE21 ....181 L6
Allfarthing La WAND/EARL SW18 ....179 M2
Allgood Cl MRDN SM4 ....200 G6
Allgood St BETH E2 ....7 M8
All Hallows Av CHOB/PIR GU24 ....230 G8
Allhallows La CANST EC4R 12 G8
Allhallows Rd EHAM E6 ....142 B8
All Hallows Rd TOTM N17 ....99 M9
Alliance Cl ALP/SUD HA0 ....115 J9
Alliance Rd ACT W3 ....135 N6
PLSTW E13 ....141 P6
WOOL/PLUM SE18 ....163 K5
Allied Wy ACT * W3 ....156 B1
Allingham Cl HNWL W7 ....134 E9
Allingham Rd REIG RH2 ....275 K3
Allington Av SHPTN TW17 ....196 F3
TOTM N17 ....99 M7
Allington Cl GFD/PVL UB6 ....134 B2
WIM/MER SW19 ....178 G8
Allington Rd HDN NW4 ....116 E3
NKENS W10 ....2 A9
ORP BR6 ....207 H8
RYLN/HDSTN HA2 ....114 B3
Allington St WESTW SW1E 16 F4
Allison Cl GNWCH SE10 ....161 H7
WAB EN9 ....63 M9
Allison Gv DUL SE21 ....181 M4
Allison Rd ACT W3 ....135 P8
CEND/HSY/T N8 ....119 H3
Allitsen Rd STJWD NW8 ....3 N8
Allitson Rd STJWD NW8 ....3 N8
Allmains Cl WAB EN9 ....63 N1
Allnutts Rd EPP CM16 ....83 K1
Allnutt Wy CLAP SW4 ....180 E1
Alloa Rd DEPT SE8 ....160 C4
GDMY/SEVK IG3 ....123 L7
Allonby Dr RSLP HA4 ....112 C5
Allonby Gdns WBLY HA9 ....115 H6
Allotment La SEV TN13 ....247 K8
Alloway Cl WOKN/KNAP GU21 ....231 N4
Alloway Rd BOW E3 ....140 D5
Allport Ms WCHPL * E1 ....140 B7
All Saints Cl BRWN CM15 ....86 G2
CHIG IG7 ....103 L4
ED N9 ....99 N3
SWCM DA10 ....189 L1
Allsaints Crs GSTN WD25 ....55 L9
All Saints Dr BKHTH/KID SE3 ....161 L8
SAND/SEL CR2 ....223 N8
All Saints La RKW/CH/CXG WD3 ....72 B10
All Saints Ms KTN/HRWW/W HA3 ....94 D7
All Saints Pas
WAND/EARL * SW18 ....179 K1
All Saints' Rd ACT W3 ....155 P1
GVW DA11 ....190 C4
LTWR GU18 ....212 B6
NTGHL W11 ....8 C5
SUT SM1 ....201 L10
WIM/MER SW19 ....179 M10
All Saints St IS N1 ....5 N7
Allsop Pl CAMTN NW1 ....10 B2
All Souls Av CHOB/PIR GU24 ....230 G7
WLSDN NW10 ....136 E4
All Souls' Pl REGST W1B 10 F4
Allum Gv KWD/TDW/WH KT20 ....238 E7
Allum La BORE WD6 ....75 K9
Allum Wy TRDG/WHET N20 ....97 M2
Allwood Cl SYD SE26 ....182 C7
Allwood Rd CHESW EN7 ....61 N3
Allyington Wy CRAWE RH10 ....284 E8
Allyn Cl STA TW18 ....173 J9
Alma Av CHING E4 ....101 H8
HCH RM12 ....125 M8
Almack Rd CLPT E5 ....120 B9
Alma Cl MUSWH * N10 ....98 C9
WOKN/KNAP GU21 ....231 K3
Alma Ct RYLN/HDSTN * HA2 ....114 C7
Alma Crs SUT SM1 ....221 H2
Alma Cut STAL AL1 ....38 D7
Alma Gv STHWK SE1 ....19 M6
Alma Pl NRWD SE19 ....181 N10
THHTH CR7 ....203 H5
WLSDN NW10 ....136 E5
Alma Rd BERK HP4 ....33 K3
CAR SM5 ....221 P2
CSHM HP5 ....51 H5
ESH/CLAY KT10 ....198 D8
MUSWH N10 ....98 B8
PEND EN3 ....80 D9
REIG RH2 ....257 L9
SCUP DA14 ....185 K6
STAL AL1 ....38 D7
STHL UB1 ....133 M9
STMC/STPC BR5 ....207 N9
SWCM DA10 ....189 K1
WAND/EARL SW18 ....179 M1
WDSR SL4 ....148 E3
WDSR SL4 ....149 H8
Alma Rw KTN/HRWW/W * HA3 ....94 C9
Alma Sq STJWD NW8 ....3 K9
Alma St KTTN NW5 ....4 F1
SRTFD E15 ....141 J1
Alma Ter BOW E3 ....140 E3
KENS W8 ....14 F4
WAND/EARL SW18 ....179 N3
The Alma GVE * DA12 ....191 J7
Almeida St IS N1 ....6 C5
Almeric Rd BTSEA SW11 ....158 A10
Almer Rd RYNPK SW20 ....178 D10
Almington St FSBYPK * N4 ....118 F6
Almners Rd CHERT KT16 ....194 F7
Almond Av CAR SM5 ....202 A9
EA W5 ....155 K2
HGDN/ICK UB10 ....112 C8
WDR/YW UB7 ....152 B2
WOKS/MYFD GU22 ....232 A7
Almond Cl CDH/CHF RM16 ....168 D2
CRAWW RH11 ....283 K8
EGH TW20 ....171 N9
GU GU1 ....250 A6
HAYES BR2 ....206 D7
HYS/HAR UB3 ....132 F9
RSLP HA4 ....112 G8
SHPTN TW17 ....196 D2
WDSR SL4 ....148 G8
Almond Dr SWLY BR8 ....208 E3
Almond Gv BTFD TW8 ....154 G6
Almond Rd BERM/RHTH SE16 ....160 A3
HOR/WEW KT19 ....220 A7
RDART DA2 ....188 B3
SL SL1 ....128 A4
TOTM N17 ....99 P8
Almonds Av BKHH IG9 ....101 M3
The Almonds STAL AL1 ....38 G10
Almond Wy BORE WD6 ....75 N8
HAYES BR2 ....206 D7
MTCM CR4 ....202 E5
RYLN/HDSTN HA2 ....94 B10
Almons Wy SLN SL2 ....129 N7
Almorah Rd HEST TW5 ....153 L7
IS N1 ....6 G4
Almsgate RGUW GU3 ....267 H7
Alms Heath RPLY/SEND GU23 ....234 C7
Almshouse La CHSGTN KT9 ....219 H5
EN EN1 ....80 A3
Alnwick Gv MRDN SM4 ....201 L4
Alnwick Rd CAN/RD E16 ....141 P8
LEE/GVPK SE12 ....183 N3
Alperton La ALP/SUD HA0 ....135 J5
Alperton St NKENS W10 ....8 B1
Alphabet Gdns CAR SM5 ....201 N6
Alpha Cl CAMTN NW1 ....9 P1
Alpha Est HYS/HAR * UB3 ....152 F1
Alpha Gv POP/IOD E14 ....160 F1
Alpha Pl CHEL SW3 ....15 P9
KIL/WHAMP NW6 ....2 F7
MRDN * SM4 ....200 G7
Alpha Rd BRYLDS KT5 ....199 L6
CHING E4 ....100 F4
CHOB/PIR GU24 ....213 L6
CRAWW RH11 ....283 M7
CROY/NA CR0 ....203 M8
HGDN/ICK UB10 ....132 C6
HPTN TW12 ....176 C8
NWCR SE14 ....160 E7
PEND EN3 ....80 D8
UED N18 ....99 P7
WOKS/MYFD GU22 ....232 E2
Alpha St PECK SE15 ....159 P8
Alpha St North SL SL1 ....149 M1
Alpha St South SL SL1 ....149 L2
Alpha Wy EGH TW20 ....194 F1
Alphea Cl WIM/MER SW19 ....179 P10
Alpine Av BRYLDS KT5 ....199 P9
Alpine Cl CROY/NA CR0 ....203 M10
Alpine Copse BMLY BR1 ....206 D2
Alpine Gv HOM * E9 ....140 B2
Alpine Rd BERM/RHTH SE16 ....160 B3
REDH RH1 ....258 B7
WOT/HER KT12 ....197 H7
Alpine Vw SUT SM1 ....221 P2
Alpine Wk BUSH WD23 ....94 D3
Alpine Wy EHAM E6 ....142 D7
Alresford Rd GUW GU2 ....267 M1
Alric Av NWMAL KT3 ....200 B3
WLSDN NW10 ....136 A2
Alroy Rd FSBYPK N4 ....119 H5
Alsace Rd WALW SE17 ....19 J7
Alscot Rd BERM/RHTH SE16 ....19 M4
Alscot Wy STHWK SE1 ....19 L5
Alsike Rd BELV DA17 ....163 N2
Alsom Av HOR/WEW KT19 ....220 C1
Alsop Cl LCOL/BKTW AL2 ....57 K4
Alston Cl THDIT KT7 ....198 G7
Alston Rd BAR EN5 ....77 H7
HHW HP1 ....35 K7
TOOT SW17 ....179 N7
UED N18 ....100 A6
Altair Cl UED N18 ....99 N7
Altair Wy NTHWD HA6 ....92 G6
Altash Wy ELTH/MOT SE9 ....184 C5
Altenburg Av WEA W13 ....154 G2
Altenburg Gdns BTSEA SW11 ....158 A10
Alterton Cl WOKN/KNAP GU21 ....231 M3
Alt Gv WIM/MER SW19 ....179 J10
Altham Ct RYLN/HDSTN * HA2 ....94 A9
Altham Gv HLW CM20 ....29 H9
Altham Rd PIN HA5 ....93 M8
Althea St FUL/PGN SW6 ....157 L8
Althorne Gdns SWFD E18 ....121 L2
Althorne Rd REDH RH1 ....276 B2
Althorne Wy DAGE RM10 ....124 B7
Althorp Cl TRDG/WHET N20 ....96 D1
Althorpe Rd HRW * HA1 ....114 B3
Althorp Rd STAL AL1 ....38 D5
TOOT SW17 ....180 A4
Altmore Av EHAM E6 ....142 C2
Alton Av STAN HA7 ....94 E8
Altona Wy SL SL1 ....128 G8
Alton Cl BXLY DA5 ....185 P4
ISLW TW7 ....154 E8
Alton Ct STA TW18 ....195 H1
Alton Gdns BECK BR3 ....182 F10
WHTN TW2 ....176 C3
Alton Rd CROY/NA CR0 ....203 H10
PUT/ROE SW15 ....178 D4
RCH/KEW TW9 ....155 K10
TOTM N17 ....119 L1
Alton St POP/IOD E14 ....140 G7
Altwood HARP AL5 ....20 C2
Altwood Cl SL SL1 ....128 D7
Altyre Cl BECK BR3 ....204 E5
Altyre Rd CROY/NA CR0 ....203 L9
Altyre Wy BECK BR3 ....204 E5
Aluric Cl CDH/CHF RM16 ....168 E3
Alvanley Gdns KIL/WHAMP NW6 ....117 L10
Alva Wy OXHEY WD19 ....93 L3
Alverstoke Rd HARH RM3 ....105 M8
Alverstone Av EBAR EN4 ....97 N1
WAND/EARL SW18 ....179 K5
Alverstone Gdns ELTH/MOT SE9 ....184 E4
Alverstone Rd CRICK NW2 ....136 F2
MNPK E12 ....122 D9
NWMAL KT3 ....200 C4
WBLY HA9 ....115 L6
Alverston Gdns SNWD SE25 ....203 M5
Alverton STALW/RED AL3 ....38 B3
Alverton St DEPT SE8 ....160 E4
Alveston Av KTN/HRWW/W HA3 ....114 G1
Alvey St WALW SE17 ....19 J7
Alvia Gdns SUT SM1 ....221 M1
Alvington Crs HACK E8 ....119 N10
Alvista Av MDHD SL6 ....128 A8
Alway Av HOR/WEW KT19 ....219 P2
Alwen Gv SOCK/AV RM15 ....146 G7
Alwin Pl WATW WD18 ....72 F8
Alwold Crs LEE/GVPK SE12 ....183 P2
Alwyn Av CHSWK W4 ....156 A4
Alwyn Cl BORE WD6 ....75 L10
CROY/NA CR0 ....224 G4
Alwyne Av BRWN CM15 ....87 L10
Alwyne Ct WOKN/KNAP GU21 ....232 B2
Alwyne La IS N1 ....6 D3
Alwyne Pl IS N1 ....6 E3
Alwyne Rd HNWL W7 ....134 D9
IS N1 ....6 E3
WIM/MER SW19 ....179 J9
Alwyne Sq IS N1 ....6 E1
Alwyne Vls IS N1 ....6 D3
Alwyn Gdns ACT W3 ....135 N8
Alwyns Cl CHERT KT16 ....195 K6
Alwyns La CHERT KT16 ....195 J6
Alyn Bank CEND/HSY/T * N8 ....118 E4
Alyngton BERK HP4 ....33 K2
Alyth Gdns GLDGN NW11 ....117 J4
Alzey Gdns HARP AL5 ....20 C3
Amalgamated Dr BTFD TW8 ....154 F5
Amanda Cl CHIG IG7 ....102 G7
Amanda Ct DTCH/LGLY SL3 ....150 A2
Amanda Ms ROMW/RG RM7 ....124 D3
Amar Ct WOOL/PLUM SE18 ....163 J3
Amardeep Ct WOOL/PLUM SE18 ....163 J4
Amazon St WCHPL E1 ....140 A8
Ambassador Cl HSLW TW3 ....153 M8
Ambassador Gdns EHAM E6 ....142 C7
Ambassador Sq POP/IOD E14 ....160 G3
Amber Av WALTH E17 ....100 D9
Ambercroft Wy COUL/CHIP CR5 ....241 J5
Amberden Av FNCH N3 ....117 K1
Ambergate St WALW SE17 ....18 C7
Amber Gv CRICK NW2 ....116 G6
Amberley Cl CRAWE RH10 ....284 D7
HARP AL5 ....20 A1
ORP BR6 ....227 J2
PIN HA5 ....113 N1
RPLY/SEND GU23 ....251 J1
Amberley Ct CRAWW * RH11 ....283 N2
SCUP DA14 ....185 M8
Amberley Dr ADL/WDHM KT15 ....215 J6
Amberley Gdns HOR/WEW KT19 ....220 C1
Amberley Gv CROY/NA CR0 ....203 N7
SYD SE26 ....182 A7
Amberley Pl WDSR SL4 ....149 J7
Amberley Rd ABYW SE2 ....163 N5
BKHH IG9 ....101 P2
EN EN1 ....79 N10
LEY E10 ....120 F5
MV/WKIL W9 ....8 F3
PLMGR N13 ....98 G3
SLN SL2 ....128 D7
Amberley Wy HGDN/ICK UB10 ....131 P4
HSLWW TW4 ....175 K1
MRDN SM4 ....201 J7
ROMW/RG RM7 ....124 C2
Amberry Ct HLW CM20 ....28 G10
Amberside Cl ISLW TW7 ....176 C2
Amber St SRTFD * E15 ....141 J1
Amberwood Cl WLGTN SM6 ....222 F2
Amberwood Ri NWMAL KT3 ....200 B6
Amblecote COB KT11 ....217 L7
Amblecote Cl LEE/GVPK SE12 ....183 N6
Amblecote Meadow
LEE/GVPK SE12 ....183 N6
Amblecote Rd LEE/GVPK SE12 ....183 N6
Ambler Rd FSBYPK N4 ....119 J8
Ambleside BMLY BR1 ....183 J9
EPP CM16 ....65 K7
HARP * AL5 ....20 B1
Ambleside Av BECK BR3 ....204 D5
HCH RM12 ....125 J10
STRHM/NOR SW16 ....180 E7
WOT/HER KT12 ....197 K8
Ambleside Cl CRAWW RH11 ....282 G8
LEY E10 ....120 G5
REDH RH1 ....276 C5
Ambleside Crs PEND EN3 ....80 C7
Ambleside Dr EBED/NFELT TW14 ....174 G4
Ambleside Gdns BELMT SM2 ....221 M3
REDBR IG4 ....122 B2
SAND/SEL CR2 ....224 C6
WBLY HA9 ....115 J6
Ambleside Rd BXLYHN DA7 ....164 B8
WLSDN NW10 ....136 C2
Ambleside Wy EGH TW20 ....172 E10
Ambrey Wy WLGTN SM6 ....222 E5
Ambrook Rd BELV DA17 ....164 B2
Ambrosden Av WEST SW1P 17 H4
Ambrose Av GLDGN NW11 ....117 J4
Ambrose Cl DART DA1 ....164 G10
ORP BR6 ....207 J10
Ambrose St BERM/RHTH SE16 ....160 A3

Amelia St WALW SE17 18 D7
Amen Cnr STP EC4M 12 D6
Amen Ct STP EC4M 12 D6
Amerden Wy SL SL1 148 F1
America Sq TWRH * EC3N 13 L7
America St STHWK SE1 12 E10
Amerland Rd WAND/EARL SW18 179 J2
Amersham Av UED N18 99 L7
Amersham Cl HARH RM3 105 N7
Amersham Gv NWCR SE14 160 E6
Amersham Pl AMSS HP7 69 P5
Amersham Rd AMS HP6 68 G1
AMS HP6 70 A5
BEAC HP9 88 F6
CFSP/GDCR SL9 110 D5
CROY/NA CR0 203 K6
CSHM HP5 51 H10
CSTG HP8 69 N10
HARH RM3 105 M7
NWCR SE14 160 E7
RKW/CH/CXG WD3 70 E5
Amersham V NWCR SE14 160 E6
Amersham Wk HARH RM3 105 N7
Amersham Wy AMS HP6 70 B5
Amery Gdns GPK RM2 105 L10
WLSDN NW10 136 E3
Amery Rd HRW HA1 114 F7
Amesbury WAB EN9 63 M8
Amesbury Av BRXS/STRHM SW2 180 F5
Amesbury Cl WPK KT4 200 F8
Amesbury Dr CHING E4 80 G10
Amesbury Rd BMLY BR1 206 A3
DAGW RM9 143 N2
EPP CM16 65 J7
FELT TW13 175 L5
Ames Cottages POP/IOD * E14 140 D7
Ames Rd SWCM DA10 189 K2
Amethyst Rd WAN E11 121 J9
Amey Dr GT/LBKH KT23 236 B10
Amherst Av WEA W13 135 H8
Amherst Cl STMC/STPC BR5 207 K4
Amherst Dr STMC/STPC BR5 207 J4
Amherst Gdns WEA * W13 135 H8
Amherst Hl SEV TN13 246 F8
Amherst Rd SEV TN13 247 J8
WEA W13 135 H8
Amhurst Gdns ISLW TW7 154 E7
Amhurst Pde STNW/STAM * N16 119 N5
Amhurst Pk STNW/STAM N16 119 M5
Amhurst Rd STNW/STAM N16 119 N8
STNW/STAM N16 120 A10
Amhurst Ter HACK E8 119 P9
Amidas Gdns BCTR RM8 123 L9
Amiel St WCHPL E1 140 B6
Amies St BTSEA SW11 158 A9
Amina Wy BERM/RHTH SE16 19 N4
Amis Av ADL/WDHM KT15 215 K7
HOR/WEW KT19 219 M3
Amis Rd WOKN/KNAP GU21 231 K5
Amity Gv RYNPK SW20 200 F1
Amity Rd SRTFD E15 141 L2
Ammanford Gn
CDALE/KGS * NW9 116 B4
Amner Rd BTSEA SW11 180 B2
Amor Rd HMSMTH W6 156 F2
Amott Rd PECK SE15 159 P9
Ampere Wy CROY/NA CR0 202 F7
Ampleforth Cl ORP BR6 227 M1
Ampleforth Rd ABYW SE2 163 L1
Ampthill Est CAMTN NW1 4 G8
Ampthill Sq CAMTN NW1 5 H8
Ampton St FSBYW WC1X 5 N10
Amroth Cl FSTH SE23 182 A4
Amroth Gn CDALE/KGS * NW9 116 B4
Amstel Wy WOKN/KNAP GU21 231 L4
Amsterdam Rd POP/IOD E14 161 H2
Amwell Cl GSTN WD25 73 M1
WCHMH N21 79 L9
Amwell Common WGCE AL7 23 L6
Amwell Ct HOD EN11 44 F2
WAB EN9 63 K9
Amwell End WARE SG12 26 C3
Amwell Hl WARE SG12 26 E5
Amwell La STALE/WH AL4 20 G4
WARE SG12 26 F5
Amwell St CLKNW EC1R 6 A9
HOD EN11 44 F2
Amyand Cottages TWK TW1 176 G2
Amyand Park Gdns TWK TW1 176 G3
Amyand Park Rd TWK TW1 176 F3
Amy Cl WLGTN SM6 222 F4
Amy La CSHM HP5 50 G8
Amy Rd OXTED RH8 261 K5
Amyruth Rd BROCKY SE4 182 F1
Amy Warne Cl EHAM E6 142 B7
Ancaster Crs NWMAL KT3 200 D6
Ancaster Rd BECK BR3 204 C3
Ancaster St WOOL/PLUM SE18 163 H6
Anchorage Cl WIM/MER SW19 179 K8
Anchor Bvd DART * DA1 188 A2
GRH DA9 166 B10
Anchor Cl BARK IG11 143 L5
CHES/WCR EN8 62 C4
Anchor Dr RAIN RM13 145 J5
Anchor Hl WOKN/KNAP GU21 231 J3
Anchor & Hope La CHARL SE7 161 N2
Anchor La HHW HP1 35 L7
Anchor St BERM/RHTH SE16 160 A3
Anchor Ter WCHPL * E1 140 B6
Anchor Yd FSBYE * EC1V 12 F1
Ancill Cl HMSMTH W6 156 G5
Ancona Rd WLSDN NW10 136 D4
WOOL/PLUM SE18 162 G4
Andace Park Gdns BMLY * BR1 205 P1
Andalus Rd BRXN/ST SW9 158 F9
Ander Cl ALP/SUD HA0 115 J9
Andermans WDSR * SL4 148 C7
Anderson Av GUW GU2 249 N6
Anderson Cl ACT W3 136 A8
CHEAM SM3 201 K8
DEN/HRF UB9 91 K9
HOR/WEW KT19 219 N8
WCHMH N21 78 G9
Anderson Dr ASHF TW15 174 D7
Anderson Rd HOM E9 140 C1
RAD WD7 57 M9
WEY * KT13 196 E10
WFD IG8 122 A1
Anderson's Pl HSLW TW3 154 A10
Anderson Sq IS N1 6 C6
Anderson St CHEL SW3 16 A7
Anderson Wy BELV DA17 164 C1
Andover Av CAN/RD E16 142 A8
Andover Cl EBED/NFELT TW14 174 G4
GFD/PVL UB6 134 A6
HOR/WEW KT19 220 A7
UX/CGN UB8 131 L4
Andover Pl KIL/WHAMP NW6 2 G8
Andover Rd HOLWY N7 118 G7
ORP BR6 207 H8
WHTN TW2 176 C4
Andover Ter HMSMTH * W6 156 E3
Andrea Av CDH/CHF RM16 167 L1
Andre St HACK E8 119 P10
Andrew Borde St
LSQ/SEVD * WC2H 11 K5
Andrew Cl BARK/HLT IG6 102 G8
DART DA1 186 E1
RAD WD7 57 L9
Andrewes Gdns EHAM E6 142 B8
Andrew Hill La SLN SL2 109 H6
Andrew Pl VX/NE SW8 158 E7
Andrews Cl BKHH IG9 101 P3
EW KT17 220 C10
HHNE HP2 35 N4
HRW HA1 114 C5
STMC/STPC BR5 207 N3
WPK KT4 200 G9
Andrewsfield WGCE AL7 23 M5
Andrew's La CHESW EN7 61 M4
Andrews Rd HACK E8 140 A3
Andrew St POP/IOD E14 141 H8
Andrews Wk WALW SE17 18 D10
Andromeda Cl CRAWW RH11 283 H9
Andwell Cl ABYW SE2 163 L1
Anelle Ri HHS/BOV HP3 36 A10
Anerley Gv NRWD SE19 181 N10
Anerley Hl NRWD SE19 181 N9
Anerley Pk PGE/AN SE20 182 A9
Anerley Park Rd PGE/AN SE20 182 A10
Anerley Rd NRWD SE19 181 P10
PGE/AN SE20 204 A1
Anerley Station Rd PGE/AN SE20 204 A1
Anerley V NRWD SE19 181 N10
Anfield Cl BAL SW12 180 D3
Angel Cl UED N18 99 N6
Angel Corner Pde UED * N18 99 P6
Angel Ct LOTH EC2R 13 H5
Angelfield HSLW TW3 176 A1
Angel Ga GU GU1 268 A1
Angel Hl SUT SM1 201 L10
Angel Hill Dr SUT SM1 201 L10
Angelica Cl WDR/YW UB7 132 A8
Angelica Dr EHAM E6 142 D7
Angelica Gdns CROY/NA CR0 204 C8
Angelica Rd CHOB/PIR GU24 230 F1
GUW GU2 249 M6
Angel La HYS/HAR UB3 132 E7
SRTFD E15 141 J1
Angell Park Gdns BRXN/ST SW9 159 H9
Angell Rd BRXN/ST SW9 159 J9
Angell Town Est BRXN/ST * SW9 159 H8
Angel Ms WCHPL E1 140 A9
Angel Pas CANST EC4R 12 G8
Angel Pl REIG * RH2 275 L2
Angel Rd HRW HA1 114 D4
THDIT KT7 198 F8
Angel Rd (North Circular)
UED N18 99 P6
Angel Sq FSBYE * EC1V 6 C8
Angel St STBT EC1A 12 E5
Angel Wk HMSMTH W6 156 F3
Angel Wy ROM RM1 124 F3
Angerstein La BKHTH/KID SE3 161 L6
Angle Cl HGDN/ICK UB10 132 B3
Anglefield Rd BERK HP4 33 M5
Angle Rd WTHK RM20 167 J5
Anglers La KTTN NW5 4 F2
Anglers Reach SURB * KT6 199 J5
Anglesea Av WOOL/PLUM SE18 162 E3
Anglesea Pl GVE DA12 190 E2
Anglesea Rd KUT KT1 199 J4
STMC/STPC BR5 207 M6
WOOL/PLUM SE18 162 E3
Anglesey Cl ASHF TW15 174 B6
CRAWW RH11 283 M10
Anglesey Court Rd CAR SM5 222 B3
Anglesey Dr RAIN RM13 145 H6
Anglesey Gdns CAR SM5 222 B3
Anglesey Rd OXHEY WD19 93 K6
PEND EN3 80 A8
Anglesmede Crs PIN HA5 113 P1
Anglesmede Wy PIN HA5 113 N1
Angles Rd STRHM/NOR SW16 180 F7
Anglia Cl TOTM N17 100 A8
Anglian Cl WATN WD24 73 K6
Anglian Rd WAN E11 121 J8
Anglo Rd BOW E3 140 E4
Angus Cl CHSGTN KT9 219 M2
Angus Dr RSLP HA4 113 K9
Angus Gdns CDALE/KGS NW9 96 A9
Angus Rd PLSTW E13 141 P5
Angus St NWCR SE14 160 D6
Anhalt Rd BTSEA SW11 157 P6
Ankerdine Crs WOOL/PLUM SE18 162 E7
Anlaby Rd TEDD TW11 176 D8
Anley Rd HMSMTH W6 156 G1
Anmersh Gv STAN HA7 95 J9
Annabel Cl POP/IOD E14 140 G8
Anna Cl HACK E8 7 M5
Annalee Gdns SOCK/AV RM15 146 G7
Annalee Rd SOCK/AV RM15 146 G7
Annandale Gv HGDN/ICK UB10 112 D8
Annandale Rd BFN/LL DA15 185 H3
CHSWK W4 156 B3
CROY/NA CR0 203 P9
GNWCH SE10 161 L4
GUW GU2 267 N2
Anna Neagle Cl FSTGT E7 121 M9
Annan Wy ROM RM1 104 E9
Anne Boleyn's Wk BELMT SM2 220 G4
KUTN/CMB KT2 177 K8
Anne Case Ms NWMAL * KT3 200 A3
Anne of Cleves Rd DART DA1 187 L1
Anners Cl EGH TW20 194 F3
Annesley Av CDALE/KGS NW9 116 A1
Annesley Cl WLSDN NW10 116 B8
Annesley Dr CROY/NA CR0 204 E10
Annesley Rd BKHTH/KID SE3 161 N7
Anne St PLSTW E13 141 M6
Anne's Wk CTHM CR3 241 M6
Annett Cl SHPTN TW17 196 F4
Annette Cl KTN/HRWW/W HA3 94 D10
Annette Rd HOLWY N7 118 G9
Annett Rd WOT/HER KT12 197 H7
Anne Wy BARK/HLT IG6 102 F7
Annexe Market WCHPL * E1 13 L3
Annie Besant Cl BOW * E3 140 E3
Annie Brookes Cl STA TW18 172 G6
Anningsley Pk CHERT KT16 214 E6
Anning St SDTCH EC2A 13 K1
Annington Rd EFNCH N2 118 A1
Annisdowne Cl SHGR GU5 270 G8
Annis Rd HOM * E9 140 D1
Ann La WBPTN SW10 157 N6
Ann Moss Wy BERM/RHTH SE16 160 B2
Ann's Cl KTBR SW1X 16 B2
Ann St WOOL/PLUM SE18 162 G3
Annsworthy Av THHTH CR7 203 L3
Ansar Gdns WALTH E17 120 D3
Ansculf Rd SLN SL2 128 F5
Ansdell Rd PECK SE15 160 B8
Ansdell St KENS W8 15 H3
Ansdell Ter KENS W8 15 H3
Ansell Gv CAR SM5 202 A8
Ansell Rd DORK RH4 272 G1
TOOT SW17 179 P6
Anselm Cl CROY/NA CR0 203 N10
Anselm Rd FUL/PGN SW6 14 E10
PIN HA5 93 N8
Ansford Rd BMLY BR1 183 H8
Ansleigh Pl NTGHL W11 136 G9
Ansley Cl SAND/SEL CR2 224 A10
Anslow Gdns IVER SL0 130 G4
Anson Cl HHW HP1 52 C3
PUR/KEN CR8 241 L6
ROMW/RG RM7 104 C10
STAL AL1 38 G8
STALE/WH AL4 21 H10
Anson Rd CRICK NW2 116 E10
HOLWY N7 118 D9
Anson Wk NTHWD HA6 92 D5
Anstead Dr RAIN RM13 145 H4
Anstey Rd PECK SE15 159 P9
Anstice Cl CHSWK W4 156 B6
Anstridge Rd ELTH/MOT SE9 184 G2
Antelope Av CDH/CHF RM16 167 M2
Antelope Rd WOOL/PLUM SE18 162 C2
Anthony Cl OXHEY WD19 93 L2
SEV TN13 246 F7
Anthony Rd BORE WD6 75 K6
GFD/PVL UB6 134 D4
SNWD SE25 203 P6
WELL DA16 163 K7
Anthony's Cl WAP E1W 13 N9
Anthonys La SWLY BR8 209 H1
Anthony St WCHPL E1 140 A8
Anthony Wy SL SL1 128 C9
Anthorne Cl POTB/CUF EN6 59 L7
Anthus Ms NTHWD HA6 92 E8
Antill Rd BOW E3 140 D5
SEVS/STOTM N15 119 P2
Antill Ter WCHPL E1 140 C8
Antlands La HORL RH6 280 G10
Antlands La East HORL RH6 280 F10
Antlands La West HORL RH6 280 F9
Antlers Hl CHING E4 80 G9
Antoinette Ct ABLGY * WD5 54 G5
Anton Crs SUT SM1 201 K10
Antoneys Cl PIN HA5 93 L10
Antonine Ga STALW/RED AL3 37 P7
Anton Rd SOCK/AV RM15 146 G6
Anton St HACK E8 119 P10
Antrim Gv HAMP NW3 4 A1
Antrim Rd HAMP NW3 4 A1
Antrobus Cl SUT SM1 221 J2
Antrobus Rd CHSWK W4 155 P3
Anvil Cl HHS/BOV HP3 52 E4
STRHM/NOR SW16 180 D10
Anvil La COB KT11 217 H10
COB KT11 235 H1
Anvil Pl LCOL/BKTW * AL2 55 P2
Anvil Rd SUN TW16 197 H3
Anyards Rd COB KT11 217 J10
Apeldoorn Dr WLGTN SM6 222 F5
Aperdele Rd LHD/OX KT22 236 F4
Aperfield Rd BH/WHM TN16 244 B3
ERITH DA8 164 G5
Apers Av WOKS/MYFD GU22 232 C7
Apex Cl BECK BR3 204 G1
WEY KT13 196 E10
Apex Pde MLHL * NW7 96 A5
Apex Point BRKMPK * AL9 40 F8
Apley Rd REIG RH2 275 K3
Aplin Wy ISLW TW7 154 D7
Apollo Av BMLY BR1 205 N1
NTHWD HA6 93 H6
Apollo Cl HCH RM12 125 J7
Apollo Pl WAN E11 121 K8
WBPTN * SW10 157 N6
WOKN/KNAP * GU21 231 M5
Apollo Wy HHNE HP2 35 P4
WOOL/PLUM SE18 162 G2
Apothecary St BLKFR * EC4V 12 C6
Appach Rd BRXS/STRHM SW2 181 H1
Apple Blossom Ct VX/NE * SW8 158 E6
Appleby Cl CHING E4 101 H7
SEVS/STOTM N15 119 L3
WHTN TW2 176 C5
Appleby Dr HARH RM3 105 K6
Appleby Gdns
EBED/NFELT * TW14 174 G4
Appleby Rd CAN/RD E16 141 M8
HACK E8 7 P3
Appleby St BETH E2 7 L7
CHESW EN7 61 M2
Apple Cottages HHS/BOV HP3 52 D3
Applecroft BERK HP4 33 K3
LCOL/BKTW AL2 56 A4
Applecroft Rd WGCW AL8 22 E5
Appledore Av BXLYHN DA7 164 D7
RSLP HA4 113 J8
Appledore Cl EDGW HA8 95 M9
HARH RM3 105 K9
HAYES BR2 205 L5
TOOT SW17 180 A5
Appledore Crs BFN/LL DA15 185 H6
Applefield AMSS HP7 69 P5
CRAWE RH10 283 P6
Appleford Rd NKENS W10 8 B2
Appleford's Cl HOD EN11 44 E1
Apple Garth BTFD TW8 155 J3
Applegarth ESH/CLAY KT10 218 E2
Apple Garth RGODL GU7 267 H10
Applegarth Av GUW GU2 249 J10
Applegarth Dr DART DA1 187 M5
GNTH/NBYPK IG2 123 J2
Applegarth Rd THMD SE28 143 L10
WKENS * W14 156 G2
Apple Ga BRW CM14 86 E9
Apple Gv CHSGTN KT9 219 K1
EN EN1 79 M7
Apple Ldg ALP/SUD * HA0 115 H8
Apple Market KUT KT1 199 J2
Apple Orch SWLY BR8 208 E4
The Apple Orch HHNE HP2 36 A4
Apple Rd WAN E11 121 K8
Appleshaw Cl GVW DA11 190 D8
Appleton Cl AMSS HP7 69 N6
HLWW/ROY CM19 46 F2
Appleton Dr RDART DA2 187 J6
Appleton Gdns NWMAL KT3 200 D6
Appleton Rd ELTH/MOT SE9 162 B9
LOU IG10 82 E7
Appleton Wy HCH RM12 125 L6
Apple Tree Av WDR/YW UB7 132 A8
Apple Tree Cl GT/LBKH KT23 236 B10
Appletree Cl PGE/AN SE20 204 A1
Appletree Ct RGUE GU4 250 G8
Apple Tree Crs BRWN CM15 87 H4
Appletree Dell
RKW/CH/CXG * WD3 71 J8
Appletree Gdns EBAR EN4 77 P8
Appletree La DTCH/LGLY SL3 149 P2
Apple Trees Pl
WOKS/MYFD * GU22 231 P5
Appletree Wk CSHM HP5 51 J10
GSTN WD25 73 J1
Apple Tree Yd STJS * SW1Y 11 H9
Applewood Cl CRICK NW2 116 E8
TRDG/WHET N20 97 P2
Appleyard Ter PEND * EN3 80 B3
Appold St ERITH DA8 164 G5
SDTCH EC2A 13 J3
Apprentice Wy CLPT E5 120 A9
Approach La MLHL NW7 97 H6
Approach Rd ASHF TW15 174 D9
BAR EN5 77 M8
BETH E2 140 B4
E/WMO/HCT KT8 197 P5
PUR/KEN CR8 223 H8
RYNPK SW20 200 F2
STAL AL1 38 D7
WARL CR6 243 N8
The Approach ACT W3 136 A8
EN EN1 80 A6
HDN NW4 116 G3
ORP BR6 207 J9
POTB/CUF EN6 59 J8
UPMR RM14 126 A8
Appspond La LCOL/BKTW AL2 37 K10
Aprey Gdns HDN NW4 116 F2
April Cl ASHTD KT21 237 L4
FELT TW13 175 H6
HNWL W7 134 D9
ORP BR6 227 J2
April Gln FSTH SE23 182 C6
April St STNW/STAM N16 119 N9
Aprilwood Cl ADL/WDHM KT15 215 J7
Apsley Cl HRW HA1 114 B3
Apsley Rd NWMAL KT3 199 P3
SNWD SE25 204 A4
Apsley Wy CRICK NW2 116 D7
MYFR/PICC * W1J 10 E10
Aquarius TWK * TW1 176 G4
Aquarius Wy NTHWD HA6 93 H6
Aquila Cl ASHTD KT21 237 K7
Aquila St STJWD NW8 3 M7
Aquinas St STHWK SE1 12 B10
Arabella Dr PUT/ROE SW15 156 B10
Arabia Cl CHING E4 101 H1
Arabin Rd BROCKY SE4 160 D10
Araglen Av SOCK/AV RM15 146 G7
Aragon Av EW KT17 220 E5
THDIT KT7 198 E5
Aragon Cl CROY/NA CR0 225 K6
ENC/FH EN2 78 G4
HAYES BR2 206 C8
HHNE HP2 36 D1
LOU IG10 82 B10
SUN TW16 174 G10
Aragon Dr BARK/HLT IG6 102 F8
RSLP HA4 113 L6
Aragon Rd KUTN/CMB KT2 177 K8
MRDN SM4 200 G7
Aram Ct WOKS/MYFD * GU22 232 E1
Aran Cl HARP AL5 20 C5
Arandora Crs CHDH RM6 123 L5
Arbery Rd BOW E3 140 D5
Arbor Cl BECK BR3 204 G2
Arborfield Cl BRXS/STRHM SW2 180 G4
SL SL1 149 K2
Arbor Rd CHING E4 101 J4
Arbour Cl BRW CM14 107 J6
LHD/OX KT22 236 E9
Arbour Rd PEND EN3 80 C8
Arbour Sq WCHPL E1 140 B8
The Arbour HERT/BAY SG13 25 L7
Arbour Vw AMSS HP7 69 N5
Arbour Wy HCH RM12 125 J10
Arbroath Gn OXHEY WD19 93 H4
Arbroath Rd ELTH/MOT SE9 162 B9
Arbrook Cl STMC/STPC BR5 207 K3
Arbrook La ESH/CLAY KT10 218 B3
Arbuthnot La BXLY DA5 185 P2
Arbuthnot Rd NWCR SE14 160 C8
Arbutus Cl REIG RH2 275 M2
Arbutus Rd REIG RH2 275 M2
Arbutus St HACK E8 7 L5
Arcade Chambers
ELTH/MOT * SE9 184 D2
Arcade Pde CHSGTN * KT9 219 K1
Arcade Pl ROM RM1 124 F3
The Arcade BEAC * HP9 88 C8
ELTH/MOT * SE9 184 D2
LVPST * EC2M 13 J4
REDH * RH1 258 B9
WALTH * E17 120 F2
Arcadia Av FNCH N3 97 K9
Arcadia Cl CAR SM5 222 B1
Arcadian Av BXLY DA5 185 P2
Arcadian Cl BXLY DA5 185 P2
Arcadian Gdns WDGN N22 99 H8
Arcadian Rd BXLY DA5 185 P3
Arcadia St POP/IOD E14 140 F8
Arcany Rd SOCK/AV RM15 146 G6
Archangel St BERM/RHTH SE16 160 C1
Archates Av CDH/CHF RM16 167 M2
Archbishop's Pl
BRXS/STRHM SW2 180 G2
Archdale Ct SHB W12 136 E10
Archdale Pl NWMAL KT3 199 N3
Archdale Rd EDUL SE22 181 N1
Archel Rd WKENS W14 14 C9
Archer Cl KGLGY WD4 54 A5
KUTN/CMB KT2 177 K10
Archer Rd SNWD SE25 204 A4
STMC/STPC BR5 207 K6
Archers EPP CM16 46 D6
Archers Cl HERT/WAS SG14 25 K4
Archers Dr PEND EN3 80 B6
Archers Flds STAL AL1 38 E4
Archers Green La WLYN AL6 23 N3
Archer Sq DEPT SE8 160 D5
Archers Ride WGCE AL7 23 L7
Archer St SOHO/SHAV W1D 11 J7
Archer Wy SWLY BR8 208 G2
Archery Cl BAY/PAD W2 9 P6
KTN/HRWW/W HA3 114 E1
Archery Rd ELTH/MOT SE9 184 C1
The Arches CHCR * WC2N 11 M9
RYLN/HDSTN HA2 114 A7
WDSR * SL4 149 H7
Archfield WGCE AL7 23 H2
Archibald Ms MYFR/PICC W1J 10 D8
Archibald Rd HARH RM3 105 P9
HOLWY N7 118 E9
Arch Rd WOT/HER KT12 197 L10
Arch St STHWK SE1 18 E4
Archway HARH RM3 105 J7
Archway Cl ARCH * N19 118 D
NKENS W10 136 C
WIM/MER SW19 179 L
WLGTN * SM6 202 F1
Archway Ms DORK RH4 272 F
Archway Rd ARCH N19 118 D
HGT N6 118 A
Archway St BARN SW13 156 B
Arcola St HACK E8 119 N1
Arctic St KTTN NW5 118 C1
Arcturus Rd CRAWW RH11 283 H
Arcus Rd BMLY BR1 183 K
Ardbeg Rd HNHL SE24 181 L
Arden Cl BUSH WD23 94 E
HHS/BOV HP3 52 D
HRW HA1 114 C
REIG RH2 275 L
Arden Court Gdns EFNCH N2 117 N
Arden Crs DAGW RM9 143 N
POP/IOD E14 160 F
Arden Est IS N1 7 J
Arden Gv HARP AL5 20 A
ORP BR6 226 E
Arden Mhor PIN HA5 113 J
Arden Rd CRAWE RH10 284 A
FNCH N3 117 J
WEA W13 135 H
Ardens Marsh STALE/WH * AL4 39 K
Ardens Wy STALE/WH AL4 39 J
Ardent Cl SNWD SE25 203 M
Ardesley Wd WEY KT13 216 F
Ardfern Av STRHM/NOR SW16 203 H
Ardfillan Rd CAT SE6 183 J
Ardgowan Rd CAT SE6 183 K
Ardilaun Rd HBRY N5 119 K
Ardingly Cl CRAWW RH11 283 L
CROY/NA CR0 204 C1
Ardleigh Cl EMPK RM11 125 L
Ardleigh Ct BRWN CM15 107 L
Ardleigh Gdns CHEAM SM3 201 K
Ardleigh Green Rd EMPK RM11 125 L
Ardleigh Rd IS N1 7 J
WALTH E17 100 E
Ardleigh Ter WALTH E17 100 E
Ardley Cl FSTH SE23 182 D
WLSDN NW10 116 B
Ardley Crs RBSF CM22 31 J
Ardlui Rd WNWD SE27 181 K
Ardmay Gdns SURB * KT6 199 K
Ardmere Rd LEW SE13 183 J
Ardmore Av GUW GU2 249 N
Ardmore La BKHH IG9 101 N
Ardmore Pl BKHH * IG9 101 N
Ardmore Rd SOCK/AV RM15 146 G
Ardmore Wy GUW GU2 249 N
Ardoch Rd CAT SE6 183 J
Ardra Rd ED N9 100 C
Ardrossan Cl SLN SL2 129 H
Ardrossan Gdns WPK KT4 200 D1
Ardross Av NTHWD HA6 92 F
Ardshiel Cl PUT/ROE SW15 156 G
Ardshiel Dr REDH RH1 275 P
Ardwell Av BARK/HLT IG6 122 F
Ardwell Rd BRXS/STRHM SW2 180 F
Ardwick Rd CRICK NW2 117 K
Arena Est FSBYPK * N4 119 J
The Arena STKPK * UB11 132 D1
Arethusa Pl GRH * DA9 166 G1
Arethusa Wy CHOB/PIR GU24 230 E
Argall Av LEY E10 120 C
Argall Wy LEY E10 120 C
Argenta Wy WLSDN NW10 135 N
Argent Centre HYS/HAR * UB3 153 H
Argent Cl EGH TW20 172 F
Argent Ct SURB * KT6 199 M
Argent St GRAYS RM17 167 N
WTHK RM20 167 K
Argent Wy CHESW EN7 61 L
Argles Cl GRH DA9 188 F1
Argon Ms FUL/PGN SW6 157 K6
Argon Rd UED N18 100 C6
Argosy Gdns STA TW18 173 J9
Argosy La STWL/WRAY TW19 173 N3
Argus Cl ROMW/RG RM7 104 C9
Argus Wk CRAWW RH11 283 K10
Argus Wy NTHLT UB5 133 M5
Argyle Av HSLW TW3 175 P2
Argyle Cl WEA W13 134 F6
Argyle Cnr WEA * W13 134 G9
Argyle Ct WATW * WD18 72 G8
Argyle Gdns UPMR RM14 126 C8
Argyle Pl HMSMTH W6 156 E3
Argyle Rd BAR EN5 76 F8
CAN/RD E16 141 N8
GFD/PVL UB6 134 E5
HSLW TW3 176 A1
IL IG1 122 D7
NFNCH/WDSP N12 97 K6
RYLN/HDSTN HA2 114 A4
SEV TN13 265 J1
SRTFD E15 121 K9
TOTM N17 99 P9
UED N18 99 P5
WCHPL E1 140 C6
WEA W13 134 F7
Argyle Sq STPAN WC1H 5 M9
Argyle St CAMTN NW1 5 L9
Argyle Wk STPAN * WC1H 5 L10
Argyle Wy STHWK SE1 19 P8
Argyll Av SL SL1 128 F9
STHL UB1 134 A10
Argyll Cl BRXN/ST SW9 158 G9
Argyll Gdns EDGW HA8 95 N10
Argyll Rd GRAYS RM17 167 M4
HHNE HP2 35 P1
KENS W8 14 E2
WOOL/PLUM SE18 162 F2
Argyll St REGST W1B 10 G6
Arica Rd BROCKY SE4 160 D10
Ariel Cl GVE DA12 191 J7
Ariel Rd KIL/WHAMP NW6 2 E2
Ariel Wy HSLWW TW4 153 J9
SHB W12 136 F10
Arisdale Av SOCK/AV RM15 146 G5
Aristotle Rd CLAP SW4 158 E9
Ark Av CDH/CHF RM16 167 M2
Arkell Gv STRHM/NOR SW16 181 J10
Arkindale Rd CAT SE6 183 H6
Arkley Crs WALTH * E17 120 E3
Arkley Dr BAR EN5 76 D8
Arkley La BAR EN5 76 D7
Arkley Rd HHNE HP2 36 C1
WALTH E17 120 E3
Arkley Vw BAR EN5 76 E8
Arklow Rd NWCR SE14 160 E5
Arkwright Rd DTCH/LGLY SL3 151 H8
HAMP NW3 117 M10
SAND/SEL CR2 223 N6
TIL RM18 168 D8
Arkwrights HLW CM20 29 J10

Arlesford Rd BRXN/ST SW9 158 F9
Arlingford Rd BRXS/STRHM SW2 181 H2
Arlington NFNCH/WDSP N12 97 K4
Arlington Av IS N1 6 F6
Arlington Cl BFN/LL DA15 185 H3
LEW * SE13 183 J1
SUT SM1 201 K9
TWK * TW1 177 H2
Arlington Ct HYS/HAR UB3 152 E4
Arlington Crs CHES/WCR EN8 62 D10
Arlington Dr CAR SM5 202 A9
RSLP HA4 112 E4
Arlington Gdns CHSWK W4 155 P4
HARH RM3 105 M9
IL IG1 122 C5
Arlington Ldg WEY KT13 216 C1
Arlington Pde
BRXS/STRHM * SW2 158 G10
Arlington Rd ASHF TW15 174 A8
CAMTN NW1 4 F6
RCHPK/HAM TW10 177 J5
STHGT/OAK N14 98 C3
SURB KT6 199 J6
TEDD TW11 176 E7
TWK TW1 177 H2
WEA W13 134 G8
WFD IG8 101 M9
Arlington Sq IS N1 6 F6
Arlington St MYFR/PICC W1J 10 G9
Arlington Wy CLKNW EC1R 6 B9
Arliss Wy NTHLT UB5 133 K3
Arlow Rd WCHMH N21 99 H2
Armadale Cl WALTH E17 120 A2
Armadale Rd EBED/NFELT TW14 175 H1
FUL/PGN SW6 157 K6
WOKN/KNAP GU21 231 M3
Armada St DEPT SE8 160 F5
Armada Wy EHAM E6 142 F8
Armagh Rd BOW E3 140 E3
Armand Cl WAT WD17 72 G4
Armfield Cl E/WMO/HCT KT8 197 N5
Armfield Crs MTCM CR4 202 A2
Armfield Rd ENC/FH EN2 79 L5
Arminger Rd SHB W12 136 E10
Armitage Cl RKW/CH/CXG WD3 71 N8
Armitage Ct ASC SL5 192 B6
Armitage Rd GLDGN NW11 117 H6
GNWCH SE10 161 L3
Armor Rd PUR RM19 166 C3
Armour Cl HOLWY N7 5 N2
Armoury Dr GVE DA12 190 F3
Armoury Rd DEPT SE8 160 G8
Armoury Wy WAND/EARL SW18 179 K1
Armstead Wk DAGE RM10 144 B2
Armstrong Av WFD IG8 101 K7
Armstrong Cl BCTR RM8 123 N5
BMLY BR1 206 B3
EHAM E6 142 C8
LCOL/BKTW AL2 57 K3
RSEV TN14 246 C1
RSLP HA4 113 H4
WOT/HER KT12 197 H6
Armstrong Crs EBAR EN4 77 N7
Armstrong Gdns RAD WD7 57 K8
Armstrong Pl HHNE HP2 35 M4
Armstrong Rd ACT W3 136 C10
EGH TW20 171 P9
FELT TW13 175 M8
Armstrong Wy STHL UB1 154 B1
Armytage Rd HEST TW5 153 L6
Arnal Crs WAND/EARL SW18 179 H3
Arncliffe Cl FBAR/BDGN N11 98 B7
Arndale Wy EGH TW20 172 D8
Arne Cl CRAWW RH11 283 J10
Arne Gv HORL RH6 279 P2
ORP BR6 207 J10
Arne St LSQ/SEVD WC2H 11 M6
Arnett Cl RKW/CH/CXG WD3 71 K10
Arnett Sq CHING E4 100 E7
Arnett Wy RKW/CH/CXG WD3 71 K10
Arne Wk BKHTH/KID SE3 161 L10
Arneways Av CHDH RM6 123 N2
Arneway St WEST SW1P 17 K4
Arnewood Cl COB KT11 218 A10
PUT/ROE SW15 178 D4
Arney's La MTCM CR4 202 B6
Arnfield Cl CRAWW RH11 283 H8
Arngask Rd CAT SE6 183 J3
Arnheim Pl POP/IOD E14 160 F2
Arnhem Av SOCK/AV RM15 146 B10
Arnhem Dr CROY/NA CR0 225 J7
Arnison Rd E/WMO/HCT KT8 198 C4
Arnold Av East PEND EN3 80 F4
Arnold Av West PEND EN3 80 E4
Arnold Cl KTN/HRWW/W HA3 115 L5
Arnold Crs ISLW TW7 176 C1
Arnold Dr CHSGTN KT9 219 J3
Arnold Est STHWK SE1 19 M2
Arnold Gdns PLMGR N13 99 J6
Arnold Pl TIL RM18 168 F7
Arnold Rd BOW E3 140 F5
DAGW RM9 144 A2
GVE DA12 190 F5
NTHLT UB5 133 M1
STA TW18 173 M10
TOOT SW17 180 A10
TOTM N17 119 N1
WAB EN9 81 H2
WOKN/KNAP GU21 232 E2
Arnolds Av RBRW/HUT CM13 87 P9
Arnolds Cl RBRW/HUT CM13 87 P9
Arnolds La RDART DA2 187 P9
Arnold Ter STAN * HA7 94 E6
Arnos Gv STHGT/OAK N14 98 E5
Arnos Rd FBAR/BDGN N11 98 D6
Arnott Cl CHSWK W4 156 A3
THMD SE28 143 M10
Arnould Av CMBW SE5 159 L10
Arnsberg Wy BXLYHN DA7 164 B10
Arnside Gdns WBLY HA9 115 J6
Arnside Rd BXLYHN DA7 164 B7
Arnside St WALW SE17 18 F9
Arnulf St CAT SE6 182 G7
Arnull's Rd STRHM/NOR SW16 181 J9
Arodene Rd BRXS/STRHM SW2 180 G2
Arosa Rd TWK TW1 177 J2
Arragon Gdns
STRHM/NOR SW16 180 F10
WWKM BR4 204 G10
Arragon Rd EHAM E6 142 A3
TWK TW1 176 F3
WAND/EARL SW18 179 K4
Arragon Wk BF/WBF KT14 216 A9
Arran Cl CRAWW RH11 283 L10
ERITH DA8 164 E5
HHS/BOV HP3 36 D8
WLGTN SM6 222 D1
Arran Dr MNPK E12 122 A6
STAN HA7 95 H5
Arran Gn OXHEY * WD19 93 L5
Arran Ms EA W5 135 L10
Arranmore Ct BUSH * WD23 73 M8
Arran Rd CAT SE6 182 G5
Arran Wk IS N1 6 E3
Arran Wy ESH/CLAY KT10 198 A9
Arras Av MRDN SM4 201 M5
Arretine Cl STALW/RED AL3 37 N8
Arreton Md WOKN/KNAP GU21 214 B10
Arrivals Rd HORL RH6 280 A7
Arrol Rd BECK BR3 204 B3
Arrow Rd BOW E3 140 G5
Arrowsmith Rd CHIG IG7 103 J6
Arsenal Rd ELTH/MOT SE9 162 C8
Artel Cft CRAWE RH10 284 A7
Artemis Cl GVE DA12 191 H3
Arterberry Rd RYNPK SW20 178 F10
Arterial Av RAIN RM13 145 K6
Arterial Rd North Stifford
CDH/CHF RM16 167 J1
Arterial Rd Purfleet PUR RM19 166 A3
Arterial Rd West Thurrock
WTHK RM20 166 E2
Artesian Cl ROM RM1 124 G4
WLSDN NW10 136 A2
Artesian Gv BAR EN5 77 M8
Artesian Houses NTGHL * W11 8 E6
Artesian Rd NTGHL W11 8 E6
Arthingworth St SRTFD E15 141 K3
Arthurdon Rd LEW SE13 182 F1
Arthur Gv WOOL/PLUM SE18 162 F3
Arthur Rd BH/WHM TN16 243 P1
CHDH RM6 123 M5
CRAWW RH11 283 H7
ED N9 99 N3
EHAM E6 142 C4
HOLWY N7 118 G9
KUTN/CMB KT2 177 M10
NWMAL KT3 200 E5
SL SL1 149 J1
STAL AL1 38 G6
WDSR SL4 149 H7
WIM/MER SW19 179 J7
Arthur's Bridge Rd
WOKN/KNAP GU21 231 P3
Arthur St BUSH WD23 73 L7
CANST EC4R 13 H8
ERITH DA8 164 G6
GRAYS RM17 167 P5
GVW DA11 190 D3
Artichoke Dell
RKW/CH/CXG * WD3 71 H8
Artichoke Hl WAP E1W 140 A9
Artichoke Pl CMBW * SE5 159 L7
Artillery Cl GNTH/NBYPK IG2 122 F4
Artillery La LVPST EC2M 13 K4
SHB W12 136 D8
Artillery Pas WCHPL * E1 13 K4
Artillery Pl WOOL/PLUM SE18 162 C4
Artillery Rd GU GU1 268 A1
Artillery Rw GVE DA12 190 F3
Artillery Ter GU GU1 250 A10
Artington Cl ORP BR6 226 F1
Artington Wk GUW GU2 267 P3
Artisan Crs STALW/RED AL3 38 B5
Artizan St WCHPL E1 13 K5
Arun TIL RM18 169 M3
Arundel Av EW KT17 220 E6
MRDN SM4 201 J4
SAND/SEL CR2 223 M5
Arundel Cl BTSEA SW11 179 P1
BXLY DA5 186 A2
CHES/WCR EN8 62 A4
CRAWE RH10 284 D7
CROY/NA * CR0 203 J10
HHNE HP2 36 C5
HPTN TW12 176 A8
SRTFD E15 121 K9
Arundel Ct DTCH/LGLY SL3 150 A3
Arundel Dr BORE WD6 75 P8
ORP BR6 227 L2
RYLN/HDSTN HA2 113 N9
WFD IG8 101 M8
Arundel Gdns EDGW HA8 96 A8
GDMY/SEVK IG3 123 K7
NTGHL W11 8 C7
WCHMH N21 99 H2
Arundel Gv STALW/RED AL3 38 C2
STNW/STAM N16 119 M10
Arundell Rd ABLGY WD5 55 H8
Arundel Pl IS N1 6 A2
Arundel Rd BELMT SM2 221 J4
CROY/NA CR0 203 L6
DART DA1 165 K10
DORK RH4 272 F2
EBAR EN4 77 P7
HARH RM3 105 N8
HSLWW TW4 153 K9
KUT KT1 199 N2
UX/CGN UB8 131 L4
Arundel Sq HOLWY N7 6 A2
Arundel St TPL/STR WC2R 11 P7
Arundel Ter BARN SW13 156 E5
Arvon Rd HBRY N5 119 H10
Asbaston Ter IL IG1 122 F10
Ascalon St VX/NE SW8 158 D6
Ascension Rd CRW RM5 104 D7
Ascham Dr CHING E4 100 G8
Ascham End WALTH E17 100 D9
Ascham St KTTN NW5 118 D10
Aschurch Rd CROY/NA CR0 203 N7
Ascot Cl BARK/HLT IG6 103 H7
BORE WD6 75 M9
NTHLT UB5 113 P10
Ascot Ct RKW/CH/CXG * WD3 72 C10
Ascot Gdns HCH RM12 125 M9
PEND EN3 80 B3
STHL UB1 133 N7
Ascot Ga ASC * SL5 170 E10
Ascot Ms WLGTN SM6 222 D5
Ascot Pde CLAP * SW4 158 F10
Ascot Rd ASHF TW15 174 B4
EHAM E6 142 C5
GVW DA11 190 E6
SEVS/STOMT N15 119 L3
STMC/STPC BR5 207 J4
TOOT SW17 180 B9
UED N18 99 P5
WATW WD18 72 F10
Ascots La BRKMPK AL9 23 H10
Ascott Av EA W5 155 K1
Ascott Ct PIN * HA5 113 H2
Ashanti Ms HACK * E8 140 A1
Ashbeam Cl RBRW/HUT CM13 107 H7
Ashborne Sq NTHWD HA6 92 F7
Ashbourne Av BXLYHN DA7 163 P6
GLDGN NW11 117 J3
RYLN/HDSTN * HA2 114 C7
SWFD E18 121 N2
TRDG/WHET N20 98 A3
Ashbourne Cl COUL/CHIP CR5 240 D4
EA W5 135 L7
NFNCH/WDSP N12 97 L5
Ashbourne Ct STALE/WH AL4 39 H8
Ashbourne Gv CHSWK W4 156 B4
EDUL SE22 181 N1
MLHL NW7 96 A6
Ashbourne Pde EA * W5 135 L6
GLDGN * NW11 117 J2
Ashbourne Ri ORP BR6 226 G1
Ashbourne Rd BROX EN10 44 E7
EA W5 135 L6
HARH RM3 105 K5
MTCM CR4 180 B9
Ashbourne Ter WIM/MER SW19 179 K10
Ashbourne Wy GLDGN NW11 117 J3
Ashbridge Rd WAN E11 121 K5
Ashbridge St STJWD NW8 9 N2
Ashbrook EDGW * HA8 95 L7
Ashbrook Rd ARCH N19 118 E6
DAGE RM10 124 C8
WDSR SL4 171 N3
Ashburn Gdns SKENS SW7 15 J5
Ashburnham Av HRW HA1 114 E5
Ashburnham Cl EFNCH N2 117 N1
OXHEY * WD19 93 H4
Ashburnham Dr OXHEY WD19 93 H4
Ashburnham Gdns HRW HA1 114 E4
UPMR RM14 126 A6
Ashburnham Gv GNWCH SE10 160 G6
Ashburnham Pk ESH/CLAY KT10 218 B1
Ashburnham Pl GNWCH SE10 160 G6
Ashburnham Retreat
GNWCH SE10 160 G6
Ashburnham Rd BELV DA17 164 D3
CRAWE RH10 284 B9
RCHPK/HAM TW10 176 G6
WBPTN * SW10 157 M6
WLSDN NW10 136 F5
Ashburn Pl SKENS SW7 15 J5
Ashburton Av CROY/NA CR0 204 A8
GDMY/SEVK IG3 123 J9
Ashburton Cl CROY/NA CR0 203 P8
Ashburton Gdns CROY/NA CR0 203 P9
Ashburton Gv HOLWY N7 119 H9
Ashburton Rd CAN/RD E16 141 M8
CROY/NA CR0 203 P9
RSLP HA4 113 H7
Ashbury Cl HAT AL10 40 B4
Ashbury Ct BMLY BR1 183 M10
Ashbury Crs RGUE GU4 250 F8
Ashbury Dr HGDN/ICK UB10 112 C7
Ashbury Gdns CHDH RM6 123 N3
Ashbury Pl WIM/MER SW19 179 M9
Ashbury Rd BTSEA SW11 158 A9
Ashby Av CHSGTN KT9 219 M3
Ashby Cl EMPK RM11 125 P6
Ashby Gdns STAL AL1 38 C10
Ashby Gv IS * N1 6 F3
IS N1 6 F3
Ashby Ms BROCKY SE4 160 E9
Ashby Rd BERK HP4 33 J2
BROCKY SE4 160 E8
SEVS/STOMT N15 119 P3
WATN WD24 73 H4
Ashby St FSBYE EC1V 6 D10
Ashby Wk CROY/NA CR0 203 K6
Ashby Wy WDR/YW UB7 152 B6
Ashchurch Gv SHB W12 156 D1
Ashchurch Park Vls SHB W12 156 D2
Ashchurch Ter SHB W12 156 C2
Ash Cl ABLGY WD5 54 E8
BRKMPK AL9 59 K1
BRWN CM15 86 E9
CAR SM5 202 A9
DEN/HRF UB9 91 N9
DTCH/LGLY SL3 150 E2
EDGW HA8 95 P5
GSTN WD25 73 J1
KWD/TDW/WH KT20 255 P7
NWMAL KT3 200 A2
PGE/AN SE20 204 B2
REDH RH1 258 D6
ROMW/RG RM7 104 C8
SCUP DA14 185 L6
STAN HA7 94 F7
STMC/STPC BR5 206 G5
SWLY BR8 208 D2
WOKS/MYFD GU22 232 B6
WOKS/MYFD GU22 233 K1
Ashcombe WGCW AL8 23 H1
Ashcombe Av SURB KT6 199 J7
Ashcombe Gdns EDGW HA8 95 M5
Ashcombe Pde
WOKS/MYFD * GU22 232 D6
Ashcombe Pk CRICK NW2 116 B8
Ashcombe Rd CAR SM5 222 B3
DORK RH4 254 F10
REDH RH1 258 D3
WIM/MER SW19 179 K8
Ashcombe Sq NWMAL KT3 199 P3
Ashcombe St FUL/PGN * SW6 157 L8
Ashcombe Ter
KWD/TDW/WH KT20 238 E6
Ash Copse LCOL/BKTW AL2 55 N7
Ash Ct HOR/WEW KT19 219 P1
Ashcroft PIN HA5 93 P7
RGUE GU4 268 B7
Ashcroft Av BFN/LL DA15 185 K2
Ashcroft Cl HARP AL5 20 D3
Ashcroft Ct SL SL1 128 A4
Ashcroft Crs BFN/LL DA15 185 K2
Ashcroft Dr DEN/HRF UB9 111 J4
Ashcroft Pk COB KT11 217 M8
Ashcroft Ri COUL/CHIP CR5 240 F2
Ashcroft Rd BOW E3 140 D5
CHSGTN KT9 199 L10
Ashdale GT/LBKH KT23 254 B2
Ashdale Cl STWL/WRAY TW19 173 P5
WHTN TW2 176 A3
Ashdale Gv STAN HA7 94 E7
Ashdale Rd LEE/GVPK SE12 183 N4
Ashdales STAL AL1 38 C10
Ashdene PIN HA5 113 K1
Ashdene Cl ASHF * TW15 174 D10
Ashdon Cl RBRW/HUT CM13 87 P10
SOCK/AV RM15 146 G8
WFD IG8 101 N7
Ashdown WEA * W13 134 G7
Ashdown Cl BECK BR3 204 G2
BXLY DA5 186 D3
REIG RH2 275 L4
Ashdown Ct CRAWE * RH10 284 A10
Ashdown Crs CHES/WCR EN8 62 D4
KTTN * NW5 118 B10
Ashdown Dr BORE WD6 75 L6
Ashdown Gdns SAND/SEL CR2 242 A1
Ashdown Pl THDIT KT7 198 F6
Ashdown Rd BUSH WD23 73 L7
EW KT17 220 C9
HGDN/ICK UB10 132 B5
KUT KT1 199 K2
PEND EN3 80 B7
REIG RH2 275 L4
WLSDN NW10 136 B3
Ashdown Wk ROMW/RG RM7 104 C9
Ashdown Wy AMS HP6 69 J3
TOOT SW17 180 B5
Ash Dr HAT AL10 40 D7
REDH RH1 276 B2
Ashendene Rd CHESW EN7 61 J1
HERT/BAY SG13 42 G4
Ashenden Rd CLPT E5 120 D10
GUW GU2 249 L10
Ashenden Wk SLN SL2 109 J9
Ashen Dr DART DA1 187 H2
Ashen Gv WIM/MER SW19 179 K6
Ashen V SAND/SEL CR2 224 C5
Asheridge Rd CSHM HP5 50 E4
Asher Loftus Wy FBAR/BDGN N11 98 A7
Asher Wy WAP E1W 13 P9
Ashfield Av BUSH WD23 74 A10
FELT TW13 175 J4
Ashfield Cl BECK BR3 182 F10
RCHPK/HAM TW10 177 K4
Ashfield Ct EA * W5 135 K9
Ashfield La CHST BR7 184 F9
Ashfield Rd ACT W3 136 C10
CSHM HP5 51 J5
FSBYPK N4 119 K4
STHGT/OAK N14 98 D4
Ashfields GSTN WD25 72 G1
LOU IG10 82 C6
Ashfield St WCHPL E1 140 A7
Ashfield Yd WCHPL * E1 140 B7
Ashford Av ASHF TW15 174 C9
BRW CM14 106 G4
CEND/HSY/T N8 118 F2
YEAD UB4 133 L8
Ashford Cl ASHF TW15 173 P7
WALTH E17 120 E4
Ashford Crs ASHF TW15 173 P6
PEND EN3 80 B6
Ashford Gdns COB KT11 235 L2
Ashford Gn OXHEY WD19 93 L6
Ashford Rd CRICK NW2 116 G9
EHAM E6 142 C1
FELT TW13 174 E7
IVER SL0 130 F2
SHPTN TW17 174 D10
STA TW18 173 N10
SWFD E18 101 N10
Ashford St IS N1 7 J9
Ash Gn DEN/HRF UB9 131 L1
Ashgrove RSEV * TN14 245 P1
Ash Gv ALP/SUD HA0 114 F9
AMS HP6 68 F2
CRICK NW2 116 G9
DEN/HRF UB9 91 N9
EA W5 155 K1
EBED/NFELT TW14 174 F4
EN EN1 99 M1
GUW GU2 249 M10
HACK E8 140 A3
HEST TW5 153 L7
HHS/BOV HP3 36 A10
HYS/HAR UB3 132 E9
PGE/AN SE20 204 B2
PLMGR N13 99 K4
SLN SL2 129 L2
STA TW18 173 M9
STALE/WH AL4 21 H2
STHL UB1 133 P7
WDR/YW UB7 132 A9
WWKM BR4 205 H9
Ashgrove Rd ASHF TW15 174 D8
BMLY BR1 183 J9
GDMY/SEVK IG3 123 J6
SEV TN13 265 H3
Ash Groves SBW CM21 30 B1
Ash Hill Cl BUSH WD23 94 A2
Ash Hill Dr PIN HA5 113 K1
Ashingdon Cl CHING E4 101 H5
Ashington Rd FUL/PGN * SW6 157 J8
Ash Keys CRAWE RH10 283 P8
Ashlake Rd STRHM/NOR SW16 180 F7
Ashland Pl MHST W1U 10 C3
Ash La WDSR SL4 148 C8
Ashlar Pl WOOL/PLUM SE18 162 E3
Ashlea Rd CFSP/GDCR SL9 90 B10
Ashleigh Av EGH TW20 172 F10
Ashleigh Cl HORL RH6 280 A4
Ashleigh Gdns SUT SM1 201 L9
UPMR RM14 126 C8
Ashleigh Rd MORT/ESHN SW14 156 B9
PGE/AN SE20 204 A3
Ashley Av BARK/HLT IG6 102 E10
EPSOM KT18 220 A9
MRDN SM4 201 K5
Ashley Cl GT/LBKH KT23 253 N1
HDN NW4 96 F10
HHS/BOV HP3 36 A8
PIN HA5 93 J10
SEV TN13 247 J10
WEY KT13 196 F8
WGCW AL8 22 F3
Ashley Cottages ASHTD * KT21 237 L5
Ashley Ct EPSOM KT18 220 A9
WOKN/KNAP * GU21 231 L4
Ashley Crs BTSEA SW11 158 B9
WDGN N22 99 H10
Ashley Dr BNSTD SM7 221 K10
BORE WD6 75 P9
ISLW TW7 154 D5
WHTN TW2 176 A4
WOT/HER KT12 197 H10
Ashley Gdns CDH/CHF RM16 147 P10
ORP BR6 227 H2
PLMGR N13 99 K5
RCHPK/HAM TW10 177 J6
WBLY HA9 115 K7
Ashley Green Rd CSHM HP5 51 J3
Ashley La CROY/NA CR0 223 J1
HDN NW4 96 F10
MLHL NW7 96 F8
Ashley Park Av WOT/HER KT12 196 G8
Ashley Park Crs WOT/HER KT12 197 H8
Ashley Park Rd WOT/HER KT12 197 H9
Ashley Pl WEST SW1P 16 G4
Ashley Ri WOT/HER KT12 197 H10
Ashley Rd ARCH N19 118 F6
CHING E4 100 F6
DORK RH4 272 B3
EPSOM KT18 238 C3
EW KT17 220 A9
FSTGT E7 141 P2
HERT/WAS SG14 25 H6
HPTN TW12 197 P1
PEND EN3 80 B6
RCH/KEW TW9 155 K9
SEV TN13 247 J10
STAL AL1 39 H6
THDIT KT7 198 E6
THHTH CR7 202 G4
TOTM N17 119 P1
UX/CGN UB8 131 L4
WIM/MER SW19 179 L9
WOKN/KNAP GU21 231 L4
WOT/HER KT12 216 G1
Ashleys RKW/CH/CXG WD3 91 J1
Ashley Wy CHOB/PIR GU24 212 C9
Ashling Rd CROY/NA CR0 203 P8
Ashlin Rd SRTFD E15 121 J9
Ashlone Rd PUT/ROE SW15 156 F9
Ashlyn Cl BUSH WD23 73 M8
Ashlyn Gv EMPK RM11 125 L1
Ashlyns Ct BERK HP4 33 N6
Ashlyns La CHONG CM5 48 G7
Ashlyn's Pk COB KT11 217 M9
Ashlyns Rd BERK HP4 33 N6
EPP CM16 65 J6
Ashlyns Wy CHSGTN KT9 219 J3
Ashmead STHGT/OAK N14 78 D9
Ash Mead Dr DEN/HRF UB9 111 K7
Ashmead Ga BMLY BR1 205 P1
Ashmead La DEN/HRF UB9 111 K7
Ashmead Ms DEPT * SE8 160 F7
Ashmead Rd DEPT SE8 160 F8
EBED/NFELT TW14 175 H4
Ashmere Av BECK BR3 205 J2
Ashmere Cl CHEAM SM3 220 G2
Ashmere Gv BRXS/STRHM SW2 158 F10
Ash Ms EPSOM KT18 220 B10
KTTN * NW5 118 D10
Ashmill St CAMTN NW1 9 N3
Ashmole St VX/NE SW8 17 P10
Ashmore Cl PECK SE15 159 N6
Ashmore Gdns GVW DA11 190 A7
HHS/BOV HP3 36 C7
Ashmore Gv WELL DA16 162 G9
Ashmore La HAYES BR2 225 P7
Ashmore Rd MV/WKIL W9 2 C8
Ashmount Rd HGT N6 118 D5
SEVS/STOMT N15 119 N3
Ashmount Ter EA * W5 155 J3
Ashmour Gdns ROM RM1 104 E10
Ashneal Gdns RYLN/HDSTN HA2 114 C8
Ashness Gdns GFD/PVL UB6 134 G1
Ashness Rd BTSEA SW11 180 A1
Ashotts La CSHM HP5 50 A1
Ash Platt Rd BGR/WK TN15 247 M7
Ash Ride ENC/FH EN2 79 H1
Ashridge Cl HHS/BOV HP3 52 D4
KTN/HRWW/W HA3 115 H4
Ashridge Crs WOOL/PLUM SE18 162 F6
Ashridge Dr LCOL/BKTW AL2 55 M6
OXHEY WD19 93 K6
Ashridge Gdns PIN HA5 113 M2
PLMGR N13 98 F6
Ashridge La CSHM HP5 52 A7
Ashridge Ri BERK HP4 33 L4
Ashridge Wy MRDN SM4 201 J4
SUN TW16 175 H9
Ash Rd BH/WHM TN16 262 G1
CHOB/PIR GU24 248 F2
CRAWE RH10 284 B5
CROY/NA CR0 204 F9
DART DA1 187 L4
GVE DA12 190 F7
HART DA3 211 K10
MRDN SM4 201 H8
ORP BR6 227 K4
RDART DA2 187 N7
SHPTN TW17 196 B4
SRTFD E15 121 K10
WOKS/MYFD GU22 232 A6
Ash Rw HAYES BR2 206 D6
Ashstead Rd CLPT E5 119 P5
Ashtead Woods Rd ASHTD KT21 237 H3
Ashton Cl SUT SM1 221 K1
WOT/HER KT12 217 J3
Ashton Gdns CHDH RM6 123 P4
HSLWW TW4 153 N10
Ashton Rd HARH RM3 105 L8
PEND EN3 80 D2
SRTFD E15 121 J10
WOKN/KNAP GU21 231 L3
Ashton St POP/IOD E14 141 H9
Ashtree Av MTCM CR4 201 N2
Ash Tree Cl CROY/NA CR0 204 D6
Ashtree Cl ORP BR6 226 E1
Ash Tree Cl SURB KT6 199 K8
Ash Tree Dell CDALE/KGS NW9 115 P3
Ash Tree Fld HLW CM20 28 D9
Ash Tree Rd WATN WD24 73 J2
Ash Tree Wy CROY/NA CR0 204 D5
Ashtree Wy HHW HP1 35 K7
Ashurst Cl DART DA1 164 G9
NTHWD HA6 92 F8
PGE/AN SE20 204 A1
PUR/KEN CR8 241 L1
Ashurst Dr BARK/HLT IG6 122 F3
CRAWE RH10 284 E7
GNTH/NBYPK IG2 122 E4
KWD/TDW/WH KT20 255 N6
SHPTN TW17 195 P5
Ashurst Gdns
BRXS/STRHM * SW2 181 H4
Ashurst Pk ASC * SL5 192 C3
Ashurst Rd EBAR EN4 78 A9
KWD/TDW/WH KT20 238 E7
NFNCH/WDSP N12 97 P6
Ashurst Wk CROY/NA CR0 204 A9
Ash Av RKW/CH/CXG WD3 90 G6
Ashvale Dr UPMR RM14 126 D7
Ashvale Gdns CRW RM5 104 E6
UPMR RM14 126 D7
Ashvale Rd TOOT SW17 180 A8
Ashview Cl ASHF TW15 173 P9
Ashview Gdns ASHF TW15 173 P8
Ashville Rd WAN E11 121 J7
Ash Wk ALP/SUD HA0 115 H9
SOCK/AV RM15 147 J5
Ashwater Rd LEE/GVPK SE12 183 M4
Ashwell Pk HARP AL5 20 C2
Ashwells Rd BRWN CM15 86 E7
Ashwell St STALW/RED * AL3 38 C5
Ashwells Wy CSTG HP8 89 P3
Ashwin St HACK E8 7 L1
Ashwood WARL CR6 242 B6
Ashwood Av RAIN RM13 145 J5
UX/CGN UB8 132 B8
Ashwood Gdns CROY/NA CR0 224 G3
HYS/HAR UB3 152 G3
Ashwood Ms STAL AL1 38 C8
Ashwood Pk LHD/OX KT22 236 B9
WOKS/MYFD GU22 232 D4
Ashwood Rd CHING E4 101 J4
EGH TW20 171 N9
POTB/CUF EN6 59 L9

WOKS/MYFD GU22 232 C4
Ashworth Cl CMBW SE5 159 L8
Ashworth Pl GUW * GU2 249 L10
HLWE CM17 47 N1
Ashworth Rd MV/WKIL W9 3 H9
Askern Cl BXLYHS DA6 163 N10
Aske St IS N1 7 J9
Askew Crs SHB W12 156 C1
Askew Rd NTHWD HA6 92 E3
SHB W12 156 C1
Askews Farm Rd GRAYS RM17 167 K4
Askew Vls PLMGR * N13 99 J4
Askham Rd SHB W12 136 D10
Askill Dr PUT/ROE SW15 179 H1
Askwith Rd RAIN RM13 144 E4
Asland Rd SRTFD E15 141 J3
Aslett St WAND/EARL SW18 179 L3
Asmara Rd CRICK NW2 117 H10
Asmar Cl COUL/CHIP CR5 240 F1
Asmuns Hl GLDGN NW11 117 K3
Asmuns Pl GLDGN NW11 117 H3
Asolando Dr WALW SE17 18 F7
Aspasia Cl STAL AL1 38 E7
Aspdin Rd GVW DA11 190 A6
Aspen Cl COB KT11 235 M2
EA W5 155 L1
ORP BR6 227 K2
RGUE GU4 250 G7
SL SL1 128 G7
STA TW18 173 J6
SWLY BR8 208 E1
WDR/YW UB7 132 A10
Aspen Copse BMLY BR1 206 C2
Aspen Ct RBRW/HUT * CM13 107 M4
Aspen Dr ALP/SUD HA0 114 F8
Aspen Gdns MTCM CR4 202 B5
Aspen Gn ERITHM DA18 164 A2
Aspen Gv UPMR RM14 125 P9
Aspen La NTHLT UB5 133 M5
Aspenlea Rd HMSMTH W6 156 G5
Aspen Park Dr GSTN WD25 73 J1
Aspen V CTHM CR3 241 N4
Aspen Wy EW KT17 220 G10
FELT TW13 175 J6
PEND EN3 80 C1
POP/IOD E14 140 G9
WGCE AL7 23 M6
Aspern Gv HAMP NW3 117 P10
Aspfield Rw HHW HP1 35 L4
Aspinall Rd BROCKY SE4 160 C9
Aspinden Rd BERM/RHTH SE16 160 A3
Aspley Rd WAND/EARL SW18 179 L1
Asplins Rd TOTM N17 99 P9
Asplins Vls TOTM * N17 99 P9
Asprey Gv CTHM CR3 241 P10
Asquith Cl BCTR RM8 123 M6
Assam St WCHPL E1 13 N5
Assata Ms IS * N1 6 D1
Assembly Pas WCHPL E1 140 B7
Assembly Wk CAR SM5 201 P7
Assher Rd WOT/HER KT12 197 M10
Assheton Rd BEAC HP9 88 C7
Ass House La KTN/HRWW/W HA3 94 A5
Astall Cl KTN/HRWW/W HA3 94 C9
Astbury Rd PECK SE15 160 B7
Astell St CHEL SW3 15 P7
The Asters CHESW EN7 61 L4
Asteys Rw IS N1 6 C3
Astleham Wy SHPTN TW17 195 P3
Astle St BTSEA SW11 158 B8
Astley GRAYS RM17 167 L5
Astley Av CRICK NW2 116 F10
Astley Rd HHW HP1 35 M6
Aston Av KTN/HRWW/W HA3 115 H5
Aston Cl ASHTD KT21 237 H4
BUSH WD23 74 B10
SCUP DA14 185 K6
WATN WD24 74 K6
Aston Gn HEST TW5 153 K8
Aston Md WDSR SL4 148 D7
Aston Rd EA W5 135 J8
ESH/CLAY KT10 218 D2
RYNPK SW20 200 F2
Astons Rd NTHWD HA6 92 D4
Aston St WCHPL E1 140 D8
Aston Ter BAL * SW12 180 C2
Astonville St WAND/EARL SW18 179 K4
Aston Wy EPSOM KT18 238 C2
POTB/CUF EN6 59 N8
Astor Av ROMW/RG RM7 124 C4
Astor Cl ADL/WDHM KT15 215 N1
KUTN/CMB KT2 177 N9
Astoria Pde ASHF * TW15 174 B7
STRHM/NOR * SW16 180 F6
Astoria Wk BRXN/ST SW9 159 H9
Astra Cl RAIN RM13 145 J1
Astra Dr GVE DA12 191 H8
Astrop Ms HMSMTH W6 156 F2
Astrop Ter HMSMTH W6 156 F2
Astwick Av HAT AL10 40 C1
Astwood Ms SKENS SW7 15 H5
Asylum Rd PECK SE15 160 A6
Atalanta Cl PUR/KEN CR8 223 H6
Atalanta St FUL/PGN SW6 156 G7
Atbara Rd TEDD TW11 176 G9
Atcham Rd HSLW TW3 154 B10
Atcost Rd BARK IG11 143 K7
Atfield Gv BFOR GU20 212 C3
Atheldene Rd WAND/EARL SW18 179 L4
Athelney St CAT SE6 182 F6
Athelstan Cl CRAWE RH10 284 F7
HARH RM3 105 N9
Athelstane Gv BOW E3 140 E4
Athelstane Ms FSBYPK N4 119 H6
Athelstan Gdns
KIL/WHAMP * NW6 2 B4
Athelstan Rd HARH RM3 105 N9
HHS/BOV HP3 35 P9
KUT KT1 199 L4
Athelstan Wk North WGCE AL7 23 H6
Athelstan Wk South WGCE AL7 22 G6
Athelstan Wy STMC/STPC BR5 207 K1
Athelstone Rd
KTN/HRWW/W HA3 94 C10
Athena Cl KUT KT1 199 L3
RYLN/HDSTN HA2 114 C7
Athenaeum Pl MUSWH N10 118 C1
Athenaeum Rd TRDG/WHET N20 97 M2
Athena Pl NTHWD HA6 92 G9
Athenlay Rd PECK SE15 182 C1
Athens Gdns MV/WKIL * W9 8 E2
Atherden Rd CLPT E5 120 B9
Atherfield Rd REDH RH1 275 M3
Atherfold Rd BRXN/ST SW9 158 F9
Atherley Wy HSLWW TW4 175 N3
Atherstone Ms SKENS SW7 15 H5
Atherton Cl RGUE GU4 268 B6
STWL/WRAY TW19 173 N2
Atherton Dr WIM/MER SW19 178 G7
Atherton Gdns CDH/CHF RM16 168 F3
Atherton Hts ALP/SUD HA0 135 H1
Atherton Ms FSTGT E7 141 M1
Atherton Pl RYLN/HDSTN HA2 114 B1
STHL UB1 133 P9
Atherton Rd BARN SW13 156 D6
CLAY IG5 102 B10
FSTGT E7 121 L10
Atherton St BTSEA SW11 157 P8
Athlone ESH/CLAY KT10 218 D3
Athlone Cl CLPT E5 120 A10
RAD * WD7 74 G2
Athlone Ct WALTH E17 121 J1
Athlone Rd BRXS/STRHM SW2 180 G3
Athlone St KTTN NW5 4 D1
Athlon Rd ALP/SUD HA0 135 J4
Athol Cl PIN HA5 93 J9
Athole Gdns EN EN1 79 M9
Athol Gdns PIN HA5 93 J9
Atholl Rd GDMY/SEVK IG3 123 K5
Athol Rd ERITH DA8 164 D4
Athol Sq POP/IOD E14 141 H8
Athol Wy HGDN/ICK UB10 132 B5
Atkins Cl WOKN/KNAP GU21 231 M4
Atkins Dr WWKM BR4 205 J10
Atkinson Cl ORP BR6 227 K2
Atkinson Ct HORL * RH6 280 C5
Atkinson Rd CAN/RD E16 141 P7
CRAWE RH10 284 D9
Atkins Rd BAL SW12 180 D3
LEY E10 120 G4
Atlanta Bvd ROM RM1 124 F4
Atlantic Rd BRXN/ST SW9 159 H10
Atlantis Cl BARK IG11 143 L5
Atlantic Cl SWCM DA10 189 K1
Atlas Gdns CHARL SE7 161 P3
Atlas Ms HACK E8 7 M1
Atlas Rd DART DA1 165 N9
PLSTW E13 141 M4
WBLY HA9 115 P9
WLSDN NW10 136 B5
Atley Rd BOW E3 140 F3
Atlip Rd ALP/SUD HA0 135 K3
Atney Rd PUT/ROE SW15 157 H10
Atria Rd NTHWD HA6 93 H6
Attenborough Cl OXHEY WD19 93 M4
Atterbury Cl BH/WHM TN16 262 G2
Atterbury Rd FSBYPK N4 119 H4
Atterbury St WEST SW1P 17 K6
Attewood Av CRICK NW2 116 B8
Attewood Rd NTHLT UB5 133 M1
Attfield Cl TRDG/WHET N20 97 N3
Attimore Cl WGCW AL8 22 E6
Attimore Rd WGCW AL8 22 E6
Attle Cl HGDN/ICK UB10 132 B4
Attlee Cl CROY/NA CR0 203 K6
YEAD * UB4 133 J5
Attlee Ct GRAYS RM17 167 M2
Attlee Dr DART DA1 187 P1
Attlee Rd THMD SE28 143 L9
YEAD UB4 133 H5
Attlee Ter WALTH * E17 120 G1
Attneave St FSBYW WC1X 12 A1
Attwood Cl SAND/SEL CR2 224 A10
Atwell Rd PECK * SE15 159 P8
Atwood GT/LBKH KT23 235 M10
Atwood Av RCH/KEW TW9 155 M8
Atwood Rd HMSMTH W6 156 E3
Aubert Pk HBRY N5 119 H9
Aubert Rd HBRY N5 119 J9
Aubrey Av LCOL/BKTW AL2 57 H2
Aubrey Pl STJWD NW8 3 J8
Aubrey Rd CEND/HSY/T * N8 118 F3
KENS W8 8 D10
WALTH E17 120 F1
Aubreys Rd HHW HP1 35 H7
Aubrey Wk KENS W8 8 D10
Aubrietia Cl HARH RM3 105 M9
Auburn Cl NWCR SE14 160 D6
Aubyn Hl WNWD SE27 181 K7
Aubyn Sq PUT/ROE SW15 156 D10
Auckland Av RAIN RM13 144 G5
Auckland Cl CRAWW RH11 283 N4
EN EN1 80 A3
NRWD SE19 203 N1
TIL RM18 168 D8
Auckland Hl WNWD SE27 181 K7
Auckland Ri NRWD SE19 203 M1
Auckland Rd BTSEA SW11 157 P10
CTHM CR3 241 M8
IL IG1 122 E6
KUT KT1 199 L4
LEY E10 120 G8
NRWD SE19 203 N1
POTB/CUF EN6 58 G8
Aucklands Gdns NRWD SE19 203 M1
Auckland St LBTH SE11 17 N8
Aucuba Vls WELL * DA16 163 L9
Audax CDALE/KGS * NW9 96 C10
Auden Pl CAMTN NW1 4 C5
CHEAM * SM3 220 F1
Audleigh Pl CHIG IG7 102 D7
Audley Cl ADL/WDHM KT15 215 L2
BORE WD6 75 M7
MUSWH N10 98 C8
Audley Ct PIN HA5 93 K10
SWFD E18 121 L2
Audley Dr CAN/RD E16 141 N10
SAND/SEL CR2 242 B1
Audley Firs WOT/HER KT12 217 J1
Audley Gdns GDMY/SEVK IG3 123 J7
LOU IG10 82 G6
WAB EN9 63 H10
Audley Pl BELMT SM2 221 L4
Audley Rd EA W5 135 L7
ENC/FH EN2 79 J6
HDN NW4 116 D4
RCHPK/HAM TW10 177 L1
Audley Sq MYFR/PKLN * W1K 10 D9
Audrey Cl BECK BR3 204 G6
Audrey Gdns ALP/SUD HA0 114 G7
Audrey Rd IL IG1 122 E8
Audrey St BETH * E2 7 N7
Audric Cl KUTN/CMB KT2 199 M1
Audwick Cl CHES/WCR EN8 62 C4
Augur Cl STA TW18 173 J8
Augurs La PLSTW E13 141 N5
Augusta Cl E/WMO/HCT KT8 197 N3
Augusta Rd WHTN TW2 176 B5
August End DTCH/LGLY SL3 130 B8
Augustine Cl DTCH/LGLY SL3 151 H9
Augustine Ct WAB EN9 62 G9
Augustine Rd GVE DA12 190 F3
HMSMTH W6 156 G2
KTN/HRWW/W HA3 94 A9
STMC/STPC BR5 207 N3
August La SHGR GU5 269 N10
Augustus Cl BTFD TW8 155 J6
SHB W12 156 E1
STALW/RED AL3 37 P8
Augustus Rd WIM/MER SW19 179 H4
Augustus St CAMTN NW1 4 F8
Aukingford Gdns CHONG CM5 67 N2
Aukingford Gn CHONG CM5 67 N3
Aultone Wy CAR SM5 202 A10
SUT SM1 201 L9
Aulton Pl LBTH SE11 18 B8
Aurelia Gdns THHTH CR7 202 G5
Aurelia Rd CROY/NA CR0 202 F6
Auriel Av DAGE RM10 144 E1
Auriga Ms IS N1 119 L10
Auriol Cl HOR/WEW KT19 200 B10
Auriol Dr GFD/PVL UB6 134 C2
HGDN/ICK UB10 132 C1
Auriol Park Rd WPK KT4 200 B10
Auriol Rd WKENS W14 14 A6
Aurum Cl HORL RH6 280 C5
Austell Gdns MLHL NW7 96 B4
Austen Cl GRH * DA9 189 H2
LOU IG10 82 G7
THMD SE28 143 L10
TIL RM18 168 F8
Austen Rd ERITH DA8 164 C6
GU GU1 268 C1
RYLN/HDSTN HA2 114 A7
Austenway CFSP/GDCR SL9 110 A1
Austenwood Cl CFSP/GDCR SL9 89 P10
Austenwood La CFSP/GDCR SL9 90 A10
Austin Av HAYES BR2 206 B6
Austin Cl CAT SE6 182 D3
PUR/KEN CR8 241 J4
Austin Friars OBST EC2N 13 H5
Austin Friars Sq OBST * EC2N 13 H5
Austin Rd BTSEA SW11 158 B7
GVW DA11 190 C4
HYS/HAR UB3 152 G1
STMC/STPC BR5 207 K6
Austin's La HGDN/ICK UB10 112 E9
Austins Md HHS/BOV HP3 52 E4
Austins Pl HHNE HP2 35 N5
Austin St BETH E2 7 L10
Austin Vls GSTN * WD25 55 J7
Austral Cl BFN/LL DA15 185 J6
Austral Dr EMPK RM11 125 L5
Australia Rd SHB W12 136 E9
SL SL1 149 N1
Austral St LBTH SE11 18 C5
Austyn Gdns BRYLDS * KT5 199 N8
Autumn Cl EN EN1 80 A6
SL SL1 128 E10
WIM/MER SW19 179 M9
Autumn Dr BELMT SM2 221 L5
Autumn Glades HHS/BOV HP3 36 D8
Autumn Gv WGCE AL7 23 L7
Autumn St BOW E3 140 F3
Avalon Cl ENC/FH EN2 79 H6
GSTN WD25 55 M8
ORP BR6 207 N9
RYNPK SW20 201 H2
WEA W13 134 F7
Avalon Rd FUL/PGN SW6 157 L7
ORP BR6 207 M9
WEA W13 134 F6
Avard Gdns ORP BR6 226 F1
Avarn Rd TOOT SW17 180 A9
Avebury SL SL1 128 F10
Avebury Ct HHNE HP2 36 B3
Avebury Pk SURB * KT6 199 J6
Avebury Rd ORP BR6 206 G10
WAN E11 121 J6
WIM/MER SW19 201 J1
Avebury St IS N1 6 G6
Aveley By-Pass SOCK/AV RM15 146 B9
Aveley Cl ERITH DA8 164 G5
SOCK/AV RM15 146 C10
Aveley Rd UPMR RM14 146 A2
Aveline St LBTH SE11 17 P7
Aveling Cl CRAWE RH10 284 D9
PUR/KEN CR8 222 G9
Aveling Park Rd WALTH E17 100 F10
Avelon Rd CRW RM5 104 E7
RAIN RM13 145 H3
Avenell Rd FSBYPK N4 119 J8
Avening Rd WAND/EARL SW18 179 K3
Avening Ter WAND/EARL SW18 179 K2
Avenue Ap KGLGY WD4 54 B6
Avenue C ADL/WDHM KT15 195 P10
Avenue Cl HARH RM3 105 N8
HEST TW5 153 J7
KWD/TDW/WH KT20 238 E8
STHGT/OAK N14 78 D10
WDR/YW UB7 151 N2
Avenue Crs ACT W3 155 N1
HEST TW5 153 H7
Avenue De Cagny
CHOB/PIR GU24 230 E8
Avenue Dr DTCH/LGLY SL3 130 C7
Avenue Elmers SURB KT6 199 K5
Avenue Gdns ACT W3 155 N1
HEST * TW5 153 H6
HORL RH6 280 D5
MORT/ESHN SW14 156 B9
TEDD TW11 176 E10
Avenue Ldg GRAYS * RM17 167 N4
Avenue Ms MUSWH N10 118 C1
Avenue One ADL/WDHM KT15 215 P1
Avenue Pde SUN * TW16 197 J3
WCHMH * N21 99 L1
Avenue Park Rd WNWD SE27 181 J5
Avenue Ri BUSH WD23 73 P9
Avenue Rd ACT W3 155 N1
BELMT SM2 221 K6
BH/WHM TN16 244 B6
BNSTD SM7 239 L1
BRW CM14 107 H5
BTFD TW8 155 H4
BXLYHS DA6 163 P9
COB KT11 235 L2
CTHM CR3 241 L8
EPP CM16 65 J9
EPSOM KT18 220 A10
ERITH DA8 164 D6
FELT TW13 174 G6
FSTGT E7 121 N10
GDMY/SEVK IG3 123 L5
HAMP NW3 3 L3
HARH RM3 105 N8
HGT N6 118 D5
HOD EN11 45 J5
HPTN TW12 198 A1
ISLW TW7 154 D7
KUT KT1 199 K3
NFNCH/WDSP N12 97 M5
NWMAL KT3 200 B3
PGE/AN SE20 204 B1
PIN HA5 113 M1
RYNPK SW20 200 E2
SEV TN13 247 K10
SEVS/STOTM N15 119 L3
SNWD SE25 203 P2
STA TW18 172 G8
STAL AL1 38 D5
STHGT/OAK N14 78 D10
STHL UB1 133 N10
STJWD NW8 3 M4
STRHM/NOR SW16 202 E2
TEDD TW11 176 F10
WFD IG8 101 P7
WLGTN SM6 222 D4
WLSDN NW10 136 C4
Avenue South BRYLDS KT5 199 L7
Avenue Ter NWMAL KT3 199 P3
OXHEY WD19 73 M10
The Avenue ADL/WDHM KT15 215 K6
AMSS HP7 69 H4
BAR EN5 77 H7
BECK BR3 204 G1
BELMT SM2 221 J5
BH/WHM TN16 244 C8
BMLY BR1 206 A3
BRYLDS KT5 199 L6
BTSEA SW11 180 B1
BUSH WD23 73 N8
BXLY DA5 185 N3
CAR SM5 222 B4
CEND/HSY/T N8 119 H1
CHING E4 101 J7
CHOB/PIR GU24 213 L5
CHSWK W4 156 A1
CLAP SW4 158 B10
COUL/CHIP CR5 240 E1
CROY/NA CR0 203 M10
CTHM CR3 241 P5
DTCH/LGLY SL3 149 N7
EGH TW20 172 E7
ESH/CLAY KT10 218 D3
EW KT17 220 F4
FBAR/BDGN N11 98 C6
GNWCH SE10 161 J6
GVW DA11 190 D4
HCH RM12 125 L7
HERT/WAS SG14 25 J3
HEST TW5 153 H7
HGDN/ICK UB10 112 B8
HHW HP1 35 H5
HOD EN11 44 E5
HORL RH6 280 A5
HPTN TW12 175 N9
HSLW TW3 176 A1
KIL/WHAMP NW6 136 G3
KTN/HRWW/W HA3 94 E9
KWD/TDW/WH KT20 238 E8
LHD/OX KT22 218 E8
LOU IG10 82 B10
MUSWH N10 98 D10
NTHWD HA6 92 D7
ORP BR6 207 J9
PIN HA5 93 N7
PIN HA5 113 N4
POTB/CUF EN6 59 J6
RAD WD7 56 F10
RBRW/HUT CM13 107 K7
RCH/KEW TW9 155 L8
RDKG RH5 255 M10
REDH RH1 276 F3
RGUW GU3 249 K3
RGUW GU3 267 H8
ROM RM1 124 E2
SLN SL2 108 G9
STA TW18 195 L1
STMC/STPC BR5 185 L10
STWL/WRAY TW19 150 A9
SUN TW16 197 J1
TOTM N17 99 M10
TWK TW1 176 G2
UX/CGN UB8 131 N6
WAB EN9 63 P1
WAN E11 121 N4
WAT WD17 73 H6
WBLY HA9 115 L7
WDSR SL4 171 N1
WEA W13 134 G9
WPK KT4 200 C9
WWKM BR4 205 J7
Avenue Three ADL/WDHM KT15 195 P10
Avenue Two ADL/WDHM KT15 215 P1
Averil Ct SL SL1 128 B8
Averil Gv STRHM/NOR SW16 181 J9
Averill St HMSMTH W6 156 G5
Avern Gdns E/WMO/HCT KT8 198 A4
Avernons Rd PLSTW E13 141 M7
Avern Rd E/WMO/HCT KT8 198 A4
Avery Farm Rw BGVA * SW1W 16 E6
Avery Gdns GNTH/NBYPK IG2 122 C3
Avery Hill Rd ELTH/MOT SE9 184 G2
Avery Rw MYFR/PKLN W1K 10 E7
Avey La LOU IG10 81 L3
Avia Cl HHS/BOV HP3 35 N10
Aviary Cl CAN/RD E16 141 L7
Aviary Rd WOKS/MYFD GU22 233 K2
Aviemore Cl BECK BR3 204 E5
Aviemore Wy BECK BR3 204 D5
Avignon Rd BROCKY SE4 160 C9
Avington Cl GU GU1 250 B10
Avington Gv PGE/AN SE20 182 B10
Avington Wy PECK * SE15 159 N6
Avion Crs CDALE/KGS NW9 96 D10
Avior Dr NTHWD HA6 92 G5
Avis Sq WCHPL E1 140 C8
Avoca Rd TOOT SW17 180 B7
Avocet Cl STHWK SE1 19 N7
Avocet Ms THMD SE28 162 G2
Avon Cl ADL/WDHM KT15 215 K3
GSTN WD25 55 K10
GVE DA12 190 G5
SL SL1 128 D9
SUT SM1 221 M1
WPK KT4 200 D9
YEAD UB4 133 K6
Avon Ct PIN * HA5 93 P8
Avondale Av CRICK NW2 116 B8
EBAR EN4 98 A2
ESH/CLAY KT10 198 F10
NFNCH/WDSP N12 97 L6
STA TW18 173 J10
WPK KT4 200 C8
Avondale Cl HORL RH6 280 A2
LOU IG10 102 C1
WOT/HER KT12 217 K2
Avondale Ct WFD IG8 101 N9
Avondale Crs PEND EN3 80 D7
REDBR IG4 122 A3
Avondale Dr HYS/HAR UB3 133 H10
LOU IG10 82 C10
Avondale Est STHWK SE1 19 N7
Avondale Gdns HSLWW TW4 175 N1
Avondale Ms BMLY BR1 183 M9
Avondale Park Rd NTGHL W11 8 A7
Avondale Pavement STHWK SE1 19 N8
Avondale Ri PECK SE15 159 N9
Avondale Rd ASHF TW15 173 N6
BMLY BR1 183 K9
CAN/RD E16 141 K7
ELTH/MOT SE9 184 B5
FNCH N3 97 M9
KTN/HRWW/W HA3 114 E1
MORT/ESHN SW14 156 A9
PLMGR N13 99 H3
SAND/SEL CR2 223 K3
SEVS/STOTM N15 119 J3
WALTH E17 120 F5
WELL DA16 163 M8
WIM/MER SW19 179 L8
Avondale Sq STHWK SE1 19 N8
Avon Gn SOCK/AV RM15 146 G8
Avonley Rd NWCR SE14 160 B6
Avonmead WOKN/KNAP GU21 231 P4
Avonmore Av GU GU1 250 C9
Avonmore Gdns WKENS W14 14 C5
Avonmore Pl WKENS W14 14 B5
Avonmore Rd WKENS W14 14 B5
Avonmouth Rd DART DA1 187 L1
Avonmouth St STHWK SE1 18 E3
Avon Rd BROCKY SE4 160 F9
GFD/PVL UB6 133 P6
SUN TW16 174 G10
UPMR RM14 126 B4
WALTH E17 121 J1
Avon Sq HHNE HP2 36 A1
Avonstowe Cl ORP BR6 206 F10
Avontar Rd SOCK/AV RM15 146 G6
Avon Wk CRAWW RH11 283 J8
Avon Wy SWFD E18 121 M1
Avonwick Rd HSLW TW3 154 A8
Avril Wy CHING E4 101 H6
Avro Wy BF/WBF KT14 215 P6
WLGTN SM6 222 F4
Awberry Ct WATW * WD18 72 E10
Awlfield Av TOTM N17 99 L9
Awliscombe Rd WELL DA16 163 J8
Axeholm Av EDGW HA8 95 N9
Axes La REDH RH1 276 D7
Axe St BARK IG11 142 F3
Axholme Av EDGW HA8 95 M9
Axminster Crs WELL DA16 163 M7
Axminster Rd HOLWY N7 118 F8
Axtaine Rd STMC/STPC BR5 207 N7
Axtane MEO * DA13 189 L10
Axtane Cl EYN DA4 210 B2
Axwood EPSOM KT18 237 P1
Aybrook St MHST W1U 10 C4
Aycliff Ct KUT * KT1 199 M2
Aycliffe Cl BMLY BR1 206 C4
Aycliffe Dr HHNE HP2 35 P2
Aycliffe Rd BORE WD6 75 L5
SHB W12 136 C10
Ayebridges Av EGH TW20 172 F10
Ayelands HART DA3 211 K9
Ayelands La HART DA3 211 K10
Aylands Cl WBLY HA9 115 K7
Aylands Rd PEND EN3 80 C2
Aylesbury Cl FSTGT E7 141 L1
Aylesbury Crs SL SL1 129 J8
Aylesbury Est WALW SE17 19 J8
Aylesbury Rd HAYES BR2 205 M3
WALW SE17 19 H8
Aylesbury St CLKNW EC1R 12 C2
WLSDN NW10 116 A8
Aylesbury Wy BEAC HP9 88 D10
Aylesford Av BECK BR3 204 D5
Aylesford St PIM SW1V 17 J8
Aylesham Cl MLHL NW7 96 D8
Aylesham Rd ORP BR6 207 H7
Ayles Rd YEAD UB4 133 J5
Aylestone Av KIL/WHAMP NW6 136 G2
Aylesworth Av SLN SL2 128 G5
Aylesworth Sp WDSR SL4 171 N3
Aylets Fld HLWS CM18 47 H4
Aylett Rd ISLW TW7 154 D8
SNWD SE25 204 A4
UPMR RM14 126 B7
Ayley Cft EN EN1 79 P9
Ayliffe Cl KUT KT1 199 M2
Aylmer Cl STAN HA7 94 F5
Aylmer Dr STAN HA7 94 F5
Aylmer Pde EFNCH * N2 118 A3
Aylmer Rd BCTR RM8 123 P8
EFNCH N2 117 P3
SHB W12 156 B1
WAN E11 121 L5
Ayloffe Rd DAGW RM9 144 A1
Ayloffs Cl EMPK RM11 125 M2
Ayloff's Wk EMPK RM11 125 M3
Aylsham Dr HGDN/ICK UB10 112 D7
Aylsham La HARH RM3 105 K5
Aylsham Rd HOD EN11 45 H1
Aylton Est BERM/RHTH * SE16 160 B1
Aylward Gdns CSHM HP5 50 F6
Aylward Rd FSTH SE23 182 C5
RYNPK SW20 201 J2
Aylwards Ri STAN HA7 94 F5
Aylward St WCHPL * E1 140 B8
Aymer Cl STA TW18 195 H1
Aymer Dr STA TW18 195 H1
Aynhoe Rd HMSMTH * W6 156 G3
Aynho St WATW WD18 73 J9
Aynscombe Angle ORP BR6 207 K7
Aynsley Gdns HLWE CM17 47 M1
Ayot Gn WGCW AL8 22 C2
Ayot Little Green La WLYN AL6 22 C2
Ayres Cl PLSTW E13 141 M5
Ayres Crs WLSDN NW10 136 A2
Ayres End La HARP AL5 20 D5
Ayres St STHWK SE1 18 F1
Ayr Gn ROM RM1 104 F9
Ayron Rd SOCK/AV RM15 146 G6
Ayrsome Rd STNW/STAM N16 119 M8
Ayrton Rd SKENS SW7 15 L3
Ayr Wy ROM RM1 104 F9
Aysgarth Ct HARP AL5 20 A3
Aysgarth Rd DUL SE21 181 L2
Aytoun Pl BRXN/ST SW9 158 G8
Aytoun Rd BRXN/ST SW9 158 G8
Azalea Cl HNWL W7 134 E10
IL IG1 122 E10
Azalea Ct WFD * IG8 101 K8
WOKS/MYFD GU22 232 A5
Azalea Dr SWLY BR8 208 E4
Azalea Wk PIN HA5 113 J4
Azalea Wy DTCH/LGLY SL3 130 B8
Azania Ms KTTN NW5 4 E1
Azenby Rd PECK SE15 159 N8
Azof St GNWCH SE10 161 K3

B

Baalbec Rd HBRY N5 119 J10
Baas Hl BROX EN10 44 C7
Baas Hill Cl BROX EN10 44 D7

Baas La BROX EN10 44 D7
Babbacombe Cl CHSGTN KT9 219 J2
Babbacombe Gdns REDBR IG4 122 B2
Babbacombe Rd BMLY BR1 205 N1
Baber Bridge Pde
EBED/NFELT * TW14 175 K2
Baber Dr EBED/NFELT TW14 175 K2
Babington Ri WBLY HA9 135 M1
Babington Rd BCTR RM8 123 M10
HCH RM12 125 J6
HDN NW4 116 E2
STRHM/NOR SW16 180 E8
Babmaes St STJS SW1Y 11 J8
Babylon La KWD/TDW/WH KT20 257 L3
Bachelors Acre WDSR SL4 149 J7
Bachelor's La RPLY/SEND GU23 234 B10
Bache's St IS N1 7 H10
Back Church La WCHPL E1 13 N6
Back Gn WOT/HER KT12 217 K3
Back Hl CLKNW EC1R 12 B2
Back La BGR/WK TN15 247 P10
BTFD TW8 155 J6
BXLY DA5 186 B3
CDH/CHF RM16 147 H10
CEND/HSY/T N8 118 F3
CHDH RM6 123 P5
EDGW HA8 95 P9
GSTN WD25 74 D5
HAMP NW3 117 M9
PUR RM19 166 D3
RBSF CM22 30 D3
RCHPK/HAM TW10 177 H5
RGUE GU4 251 N7
RSEV TN14 264 C4
SEV TN13 246 E10
WAB EN9 45 P9
WLYN AL6 23 P1
Backley Gdns SNWD SE25 203 P6
Back Rd SCUP DA14 185 K7
TEDD TW11 176 D10
The Backs CSHM HP5 51 H7
The Back BERK HP4 34 E2
Bacon Gv STHWK SE1 19 L5
Bacon La CDALE/KGS NW9 115 N2
EDGW HA8 95 M9
Bacon Link CRW RM5 104 C7
Bacons Dr POTB/CUF EN6 60 F4
Bacon's La HGT N6 118 B6
Baconsmead DEN/HRF UB9 111 K7
Bacon St BETH E2 13 M1
Bacton St BETH E2 140 B5
Badburgham Ct WAB EN9 63 L9
Baddeley Cl PEND EN3 80 F3
Baddow Cl DAGE RM10 144 B3
WFD IG8 102 A7
Baden Cl STA TW18 173 K10
Baden Dr HORL RH6 279 P3
Baden Pl STHWK SE1 18 G1
Baden Powell Cl DAGW RM9 143 P3
SURB KT6 199 L9
Baden Powell Rd SEV TN13 246 F8
Baden Rd CEND/HSY/T N8 118 E2
GUW GU2 249 M8
IL IG1 122 E10
Bader Cl PUR/KEN CR8 241 L1
WGCE AL7 23 M5
Bader Gdns SL SL1 148 F1
Bader Wk GVW DA11 190 B6
Bader Wy RAIN RM13 145 H1
Badger Cl FELT TW13 175 J6
GUW GU2 249 N7
HSLWW TW4 153 K9
Badger Cft HHNE HP2 36 E7
Badgers Cl ASHF * TW15 174 A8
BORE * WD6 75 L6
ENC/FH EN2 79 J7
HERT/BAY SG13 26 A5
HRW HA1 114 C4
HYS/HAR UB3 132 F10
RGODL GU7 267 J9
WOKN/KNAP GU21 231 P4
Badgers Copse ORP BR6 207 J9
WPK KT4 200 C9
Badgers Ct WPK * KT4 200 C9
Badgers Cft BROX EN10 44 D7
ELTH/MOT SE9 184 D6
TRDG/WHET N20 97 H1
Badgers Hl VW GU25 193 P5
Badgers La WARL CR6 242 B5
Badgers Mt CDH/CHF RM16 168 C1
Badgers Ri RSEV TN14 228 B6
Badgers Rd RSEV TN14 228 C6
Badgers Wk CTHM CR3 241 N4
NWMAL KT3 200 B2
PUR/KEN CR8 222 D7
RKW/CH/CXG WD3 71 J8
Badgers Wd CTHM CR3 259 K1
SLN SL2 109 H10
Badger Wy HAT AL10 40 E6
Badingham Dr LHD/OX KT22 236 D10
Badlis Rd WALTH E17 100 F10
Badlow Cl ERITH DA8 164 F6
Badminton Cl BORE WD6 75 M6
HRW * HA1 114 D2
NTHLT UB5 133 P1
Badminton Ms CAN/RD E16 141 M10
Badminton Pl BROX EN10 44 D6
Badminton Rd BAL SW12 180 B2
Badsworth Rd CMBW SE5 159 K6
Bagley Cl WDR/YW UB7 151 P1
Bagley's La FUL/PGN SW6 157 L7
Bagleys Spring CHDH RM6 123 P2
Bagot Cl ASHTD KT21 237 L2
Bagshot Ct WOOL/PLUM * SE18 162 D7
Bagshot Rd ASC SL5 192 A8
CHOB/PIR GU24 212 G7
EGH TW20 171 P10
EN EN1 79 N10
WOKN/KNAP GU21 230 G5
Bagshot St WALW SE17 19 K8
Bahram Rd HOR/WEW KT19 220 A6
Baigents La BFOR GU20 212 C3
Baildon St DEPT SE8 160 E6
Bailes La RGUW GU3 248 C8
Bailey Cl PUR RM19 166 C3
WDGN N22 98 E9
WDSR SL4 148 F8
Bailey Cottages POP/IOD * E14 140 D7
Bailey Pl SYD SE26 182 B9
Bailey Rd DORK RH4 272 B3
Baillie Cl RAIN RM13 145 J6
Baillie Rd GU GU1 268 C1
Bainbridge Cl KUTN/CMB KT2 177 K8
Bainbridge Rd DAGW RM9 124 A9
Bainbridge St NOXST/BSQ WC1A 11 K5
Baines Cl SAND/SEL CR2 223 L2
Bainton Md WOKN/KNAP GU21 231 M3
Baird Av GFD/PVL UB6 134 A9
Baird Cl BUSH WD23 74 A10
CDALE/KGS NW9 115 P4
CRAWE RH10 284 B4
LEY E10 120 F6
SL SL1 148 G1
Baird Dr RGUW GU3 248 G9
Baird Gdns NRWD SE19 181 M7
Baird Rd EN EN1 80 A7
Baird St STLK EC1Y 12 F1
Bairstow Cl BORE WD6 75 K5
Baizdon Rd BKHTH/KID SE3 161 K8
Bakeham La EGH TW20 171 P10
Bakehouse Rd HORL RH6 280 A2
Baker Cl CRAWE RH10 283 N9
Baker Hill Cl GVW DA11 190 C7
Baker La MTCM CR4 202 B2
Baker Ms ORP BR6 227 J3
Baker Rd WLSDN NW10 136 B3
WOOL/PLUM SE18 162 B7
Bakers Av LEY E10 120 G4
Bakerscroft CHES/WCR * EN8 62 C4
Bakers End RYNPK SW20 201 H2
Bakers Gdns CAR SM5 201 P9
Bakers Gv WGCE AL7 23 M4
Bakers Hl BAR EN5 77 L6
CLPT E5 120 A6
Bakers La EPP CM16 65 J6
Bakers Md GDST RH9 260 B6
Bakers Meadow BRWN CM15 87 H3
Baker's Ms MHST W1U 10 C5
Bakers Rents BETH E2 7 L10
Bakers Rd CHESW EN7 62 A6
UX/CGN UB8 131 N2
Baker's Rw CLKNW EC1R 12 A2
SRTFD E15 141 K4
Baker St CAMTN NW1 10 B2
EN EN1 79 L6
HERT/BAY SG13 25 M5
MHST W1U 10 C4
POTB/CUF EN6 59 J9
WEY KT13 216 B1
Bakers Wd DEN/HRF UB9 110 G6
Baker's Yd CLKNW EC1R 12 A2
Bakery Cl BRXN/ST * SW9 158 G6
HLWW/ROY CM19 45 P1
Bakewell Dr NWMAL KT3 200 B2
Balaams La STHGT/OAK N14 98 E3
Balaam St PLSTW E13 141 M5
Balaclava Rd STHWK SE1 19 M6
SURB KT6 199 H7
Bala Gn CDALE/KGS * NW9 116 B4
Balcary Gdns BERK HP4 33 K6
Balcaskie Rd ELTH/MOT SE9 184 C1
Balchen Rd BKHTH/KID SE3 162 A8
Balchier Rd EDUL SE22 182 A2
Balchins La DORK RH4 271 P3
Balcombe Cl BXLYHS DA6 163 N10
Balcombe Gdns HORL RH6 280 D5
Balcombe Rd CRAWE RH10 284 E6
HORL RH6 280 C3
Balcombe St CAMTN NW1 10 A1
Balcon Wy BORE WD6 75 P5
Balcorne St HOM E9 140 B2
Balder Ri LEE/GVPK SE12 183 N5
Balderton St MYFR/PKLN W1K 10 D6
Baldocks Rd EPP CM16 83 H1
Baldock St BOW E3 140 G4
WARE SG12 26 C1
Baldock Wy BORE WD6 75 L5
Baldry Gdns STRHM/NOR SW16 180 F9
Baldwin Cl CRAWE * RH10 284 D10
Baldwin Crs CMBW SE5 159 K7
RGUW GU4 250 F8
Baldwin Gdns HSLW TW3 154 B7
Baldwin Rd BEAC HP9 88 G10
SL SL1 128 B5
Baldwins WGCE AL7 23 L5
Baldwin's Gdns FSBYW WC1X 12 A3
Baldwin's Hl LOU IG10 82 C5
Baldwins La RKW/CH/CXG WD3 72 B8
Baldwin's Shore WDSR SL4 149 J5
Baldwin St FSBYE EC1V 6 G10
Baldwin Ter IS N1 6 E7
Baldwyn Gdns ACT W3 135 P9
Baldwyn's Pk BXLY DA5 186 E5
Baldwyn's Rd BXLY DA5 186 E5
Bales Ter ED * N9 99 N4
Balfern Gv CHSWK W4 156 B4
Balfern St BTSEA SW11 157 P8
Balfe St IS N1 5 M8
Balfont Cl SAND/SEL CR2 223 P9
Balfour Av HNWL W7 134 E10
WOKS/MYFD GU22 232 B8
Balfour Gv TRDG/WHET N20 98 A4
Balfour Ms ED N9 99 P4
MYFR/PKLN W1K 10 D9
Balfour Pl MYFR/PKLN W1K 10 D8
Balfour Rd ACT W3 135 P7
CAR SM5 222 A4
GRAYS RM17 167 P3
HAYES BR2 206 A5
HBRY N5 119 K9
HRW HA1 114 C3
HSLW TW3 154 A9
IL IG1 122 E7
NWDGN UB2 153 L2
SNWD SE25 203 P4
WEA W13 154 G1
WEY KT13 216 A1
WIM/MER SW19 179 L10
Balfour St HERT/WAS SG14 25 K4
STHWK SE1 18 G5
Balgonie Rd CHING E4 101 J2
Balgores Crs GPK RM2 125 J1
Balgores La GPK RM2 125 J2
Balgores Sq GPK RM2 125 J2
Balgowan Cl NWMAL KT3 200 B4
Balgowan Rd BECK BR3 204 D3
Balgowan St WOOL/PLUM SE18 163 J3
Balham Gv BAL SW12 180 B3
Balham High Rd BAL SW12 180 C4
Balham Hl BAL SW12 180 C3
Balham New Rd BAL SW12 180 C3
Balham Park Rd TOOT SW17 180 A4
Balham Rd ED N9 99 P3
Balham Station Rd BAL SW12 180 B4
Balkan Wk WAP * E1W 140 A9
Balladier Wk POP/IOD E14 140 G7
Ballamore Rd BMLY BR1 183 M6
Ballance Rd HOM E9 140 C1
The Ballands North
LHD/OX KT22 236 D8
The Ballands South
LHD/OX KT22 236 D9
Ballantine St WAND/EARL SW18 157 M10
Ballantyne Dr
KWD/TDW/WH KT20 239 J7
Ballard Cl KUTN/CMB KT2 178 A10
Ballard Gn WDSR SL4 148 D6
Ballards Cl DAGE RM10 144 C3
Ballards Farm Rd SAND/SEL CR2 223 P3
Ballards Gn KWD/TDW/WH KT20 239 H5
Ballards La FNCH N3 97 L8
OXTED RH8 261 P5
Ballards Ri SAND/SEL CR2 223 P3
Ballards Rd CRICK NW2 116 D7
DAGE RM10 144 C3
Ballards Wy SAND/SEL CR2 223 P3
Ballast Quay GNWCH SE10 161 J4
Ballater Cl OXHEY WD19 93 J5
Ballater Rd CLAP SW4 158 F10
SAND/SEL CR2 223 N2
Ballencrieff Rd ASC SL5 192 E7
Ballina St FSTH SE23 182 C3
Ballingdon Rd BTSEA SW11 180 B2
Ballinger Ct BERK HP4 33 M6
Balliol Av CHING E4 101 J5
Balliol Cl CRAWE RH10 284 D4
Balliol Rd NKENS W10 136 F8
TOTM N17 99 M9
WELL DA16 163 L8
Balloch Rd CAT SE6 183 J4
Ballogie Av WLSDN NW10 116 B9
Ballow Cl CMBW * SE5 159 L6
Ball's Pond Pl IS * N1 7 H1
Ball's Pond Rd IS N1 7 H1
IS N1 7 J1
Balmain Cl EA W5 135 J10
Balmer Rd BOW E3 140 E4
Balmes Rd IS N1 7 H5
Balmoral Av BECK BR3 204 D4
FBAR/BDGN N11 98 B7
Balmoral Cl CHES/WCR EN8 62 C10
LCOL/BKTW AL2 56 B4
PUT/ROE * SW15 178 G2
SL SL1 128 D8
Balmoral Crs E/WMO/HCT KT8 197 P3
Balmoral Dr BORE WD6 76 A8
STHL UB1 133 N6
WOKS/MYFD GU22 232 F2
YEAD UB4 132 F6
Balmoral Gdns BXLY DA5 186 A3
HNWL W7 154 F2
SAND/SEL CR2 223 L6
WDSR SL4 149 J9
Balmoral Gv HOLWY N7 5 N2
Balmoral Ms SHB W12 156 C2
Balmoral Rd BRWN CM15 86 G10
CRICK NW2 136 E1
EYN DA4 187 P10
FSTGT E7 121 P9
GPK RM2 125 J2
GSTN WD25 55 H8
HCH RM12 125 L8
KUT KT1 199 L4
LEY E10 120 G7
PEND EN3 80 C2
RYLN/HDSTN HA2 113 P9
WATN WD24 73 K4
WPK KT4 200 E10
Balmoral Wy BELMT SM2 221 K6
Balmore Crs EBAR EN4 78 B9
Balmore St KTTN NW5 118 C7
Balmuir Gdns PUT/ROE SW15 156 F10
Balnacraig Av WLSDN NW10 116 B9
Balquhain Cl ASHTD KT21 237 J3
Balsams Cl HERT/BAY SG13 25 L7
Baltic Cl WIM/MER SW19 179 N10
Baltic Pl IS N1 7 K5
Baltic St East STLK EC1Y 12 F3
Baltic St West FARR EC1M 12 E2
Baltimore Pl WELL DA16 163 J8
Balvaird Pl PIM SW1V 17 K8
Balvernie Gv WAND/EARL SW18 179 J3
Bamborough Gdns SHB W12 156 F1
Bamford Av ALP/SUD HA0 135 L3
Bamford Rd BMLY BR1 183 J8
Bamford Wy CRW RM5 104 C6
Bampfylde Cl WLGTN SM6 202 D10
Bampton Dr MLHL NW7 96 D8
Bampton Rd FSTH SE23 182 D6
HARH RM3 105 M8
Bampton Wy WOKN/KNAP GU21 231 M4
Bamville Wd HARP * AL5 20 B6
Banavie Gdns BECK BR3 204 G1
Banbury Av SL SL1 128 E7
Banbury Cl ENC/FH EN2 79 J5
Banbury Ct BELMT * SM2 221 L6
COVGDN * WC2E 11 L7
Banbury Rd HOM E9 140 C2
WALTH E17 100 D8
Banbury St BTSEA * SW11 157 P8
WATW WD18 73 H9
Banbury Vls MEO DA13 189 L9
Banchory Rd BKHTH/KID SE3 161 N6
Bankside HART DA3 211 K4
Bancroft Av EFNCH N2 117 P3
Bancroft Cl ASHF * TW15 174 B8
Bancroft Ct NTHLT UB5 133 K3
REIG RH2 257 L10
Bancroft Gdns
KTN/HRWW/W HA3 94 B9
ORP BR6 207 J8
Bancroft Rd CRAWE RH10 284 E8
KTN/HRWW/W HA3 94 B10
REIG RH2 257 K10
WCHPL E1 140 C5
Banders Ri GU GU1 250 F9
Band La EGH TW20 172 C8
Bandon Ri WLGTN SM6 222 E3
Banes Down WAB EN9 45 K8
Banfield Rd PECK SE15 160 A9
Bangalore St PUT/ROE SW15 156 F9
Bangor Cl NTHLT UB5 114 A10
Bangors Cl IVER SL0 131 J8
Bangors Pk IVER * SL0 131 H6
Bangors Rd North IVER SL0 130 G3
Bangors Rd South IVER SL0 131 H6
Banim St HMSMTH W6 156 E2
Banister Rd WLSDN NW10 136 G5
Bank Av MTCM CR4 201 N2
Bank Buildings CHING * E4 101 J7
Bank End STHWK SE1 12 F9
Bankfoot GRAYS RM17 167 L3
Bankfoot Rd BMLY BR1 183 K7
Bank Gn CSHM HP5 32 B9
Bankhurst Rd CAT SE6 182 E3
Bank La BGR/WK TN15 265 P8
CRAWE RH10 283 N7
KUTN/CMB KT2 177 K10
PUT/ROE SW15 178 B1
Bank Ml BERK HP4 34 B5
Bankmill Br BERK HP4 34 C6
Bank Mill La BERK HP4 34 B6
Bank Prec CRAWE * RH10 284 B4
Banksia Rd UED N18 100 B6
Bankside ENC/FH EN2 79 J5
GVW DA11 189 P2
SAND/SEL CR2 223 N3
SEV TN13 246 E7
STHL UB1 133 L10
STHWK SE1 12 E8
WOKN/KNAP GU21 231 N4
Bankside Av NTHLT UB5 133 H4
Bankside Cl BH/WHM TN16 243 P4
CAR SM5 221 P2
ISLW TW7 154 E10
RDART DA2 186 E7
RKW/CH/CXG WD3 91 K7
Bankside Down
RKW/CH/CXG * WD3 71 N10
Bankside Dr THDIT KT7 198 G9
Bankside Rd IL IG1 122 F10
Banks La BXLYHS DA6 164 A10
EHSLY KT24 235 J8
EPP CM16 65 P8
Banks Rd BORE WD6 75 P6
CRAWE RH10 284 D8
Banks Sp SL SL1 148 G1
Bank St GVE DA12 190 E2
Banks Wy GU GU1 250 C7
Bank Ter CRAWW * RH11 283 N8
The Bank CRAWE * RH10 285 P9
HGT N6 118 C6
Bankton Rd BRXS/STRHM SW2 159 H10
Bankwell Rd LEW SE13 161 K10
Bank Willow RCHPK/HAM TW10 176 G6
Bann Cl SOCK/AV RM15 146 G9
Banner Cl PUR RM19 166 C3
Banner St STLK EC1Y 12 F2
Banning St GNWCH SE10 161 K4
Bannister Cl BRXS/STRHM SW2 181 H4
DTCH/LGLY SL3 150 B1
NTHLT UB5 114 C10
Bannister Dr RBRW/HUT CM13 87 P10
Bannister Gdns STMC/STPC BR5 207 M3
Bannister's Rd GUW GU2 267 L2
Bannockburn Rd
WOOL/PLUM SE18 163 H3
Banson's La CHONG CM5 67 P4
Bansons Wy CHONG CM5 67 P4
Banstead Gdns ED N9 99 L4
Banstead Rd BELMT SM2 221 N4
BNSTD SM7 221 H9
CAR SM5 221 P3
CTHM CR3 241 L8
EW KT17 220 E6
PUR/KEN CR8 223 H7
Banstead Rd South BELMT SM2 221 M6
Banstead St PECK SE15 160 B9
Banstead Wy WLGTN SM6 222 F2
Banstock Rd EDGW HA8 95 P7
Banting Dr WCHMH N21 78 G9
Banton Cl EN EN1 80 A6
Bantry St CMBW SE5 159 L6
Banwell Rd BXLY DA5 185 N2
Banyard Rd BERM/RHTH SE16 160 A2
Banyards EMPK RM11 125 M3
Bapchild Pl STMC/STPC BR5 207 M4
Baptist Gdns HAMP NW3 4 C1
Barandon Wk NTGHL * W11 136 G9
Barbara Cl SHPTN TW17 196 C5
Barbaraville Camp BRKMPK * AL9 41 J1
Barbauld Rd STNW/STAM N16 119 M8
Barbel Cl CHES/WCR EN8 62 F10
Barber Cl WCHMH N21 99 H1
Barberry Cl HARH RM3 105 K7
Barberry Rd HHW HP1 35 K6
Barbers Rd SRTFD E15 140 G4
Barbican BARB EC2Y 12 F3
Barbican Rd GFD/PVL UB6 134 A8
Barb Ms HMSMTH W6 156 F2
Barbon Cl BMSBY WC1N 11 M3
Barbot Cl ED N9 99 N4
Barchard St WAND/EARL SW18 179 L1
Barchester Cl HNWL W7 134 E10
Barchester Rd DTCH/LGLY SL3 150 C1
KTN/HRWW/W HA3 94 C9
Barchester St POP/IOD E14 140 G7
Barclay Cl FUL/PGN * SW6 157 K6
GT/LBKH KT23 236 A9
HERT/BAY SG13 26 A7
WATW WD18 73 H10
Barclay Ct HOD EN11 44 F4
Barclay Ov WFD IG8 101 M5
Barclay Rd CROY/NA CR0 203 L10
FUL/PGN SW6 157 K6
PLSTW E13 141 P6
UED N18 99 L7
WALTH E17 121 H3
WAN E11 121 L6
Barclay Wy WTHK RM20 166 E4
Barcombe Av BRXS/STRHM SW2 180 F5
Barcombe Cl CHST BR7 207 K3
Barden Cl DEN/HRF UB9 91 M9
Barden St WOOL/PLUM SE18 163 H6
Bardeswell Cl BRW CM14 107 H3
Bardfield Av CHDH RM6 123 N1
Bardney Rd MRDN SM4 201 L4
Bardolph Av CROY/NA CR0 224 E5
Bardolph Rd HOLWY N7 118 F9
RCH/KEW TW9 155 L10
Bardon Wk WOKN/KNAP * GU21 231 N3
Bard Rd NKENS W10 136 G9
Bards Cnr HHW HP1 35 L5
Bardsey Pl WCHPL E1 140 B7
Bardsey Wk IS N1 6 F1
Bardsley Cl CROY/NA CR0 203 N10
Bardsley La BRXS/STRHM SW2 159 H10
GNWCH SE10 161 H5
Bardwell Ct STAL * AL1 38 C7
Bardwell Rd STAL AL1 38 C7
Barfett St NKENS W10 8 C1
Barfield EYN DA4 210 A1
Barfield Av TRDG/WHET N20 98 A3
Barfield Rd BMLY BR1 206 D3
WAN * E11 121 L6
Barfields LOU IG10 82 D8
REDH RH1 259 J9
Barford Cl HDN NW4 96 D10
Barford St IS N1 6 B6
Barforth Rd PECK SE15 160 A9
Barfreston Wy PGE/AN SE20 204 A1
Bargate Cl NWMAL KT3 200 D7
WOOL/PLUM SE18 163 J4
Barge House Rd CAN/RD E16 162 E1
Barge House St STHWK SE1 12 B9
Bargery Rd CAT SE6 182 G4
Barge Wk KUT KT1 199 J2
Bargrove Av HHW HP1 35 K7
Bargrove Cl PGE/AN SE20 181 P10
Bargrove Crs CAT SE6 182 E5
Barham Av BORE WD6 75 L7
Barham Cl ALP/SUD HA0 134 G1
CHST BR7 184 E8
GVE DA12 191 J4
HAYES BR2 206 B8
ROMW/RG RM7 104 C10
WEY KT13 216 D1
Barham Ct ALP/SUD HA0 135 H1
Barham Rd CHST BR7 184 E8
CROY/NA CR0 223 K1
DART DA1 187 P3
RYNPK SW20 178 D10
Baring Cl LEE/GVPK SE12 183 M5
Baring Rd BEAC HP9 88 B8
BMLY BR1 183 N7
CROY/NA CR0 203 P8
EBAR EN4 77 N7
LEE/GVPK SE12 183 M4
Baring St IS N1 6 G6
Barington Ct RBRW/HUT CM13 87 P10
Bark Burr Rd CDH/CHF RM16 167 L1
Barker Cl KUT KT1 199 N4
Barker Dr CAMTN NW1 5 H4
Barker Rd CHERT KT16 195 H7
Barkham Rd TOTM N17 99 L8
Bark Hart Rd ORP BR6 207 L8
Barking Rd EHAM E6 142 C3
POP/IOD E14 141 K8
Bark Pl BAY/PAD W2 8 G7
Barkston Gdns ECT SW5 14 G6
Barkwood Cl ROMW/RG RM7 124 D3
Barkworth Rd BERM/RHTH SE16 160 A4
Barlborough St NWCR SE14 160 C6
Barlby Gdns NKENS W10 136 G6
Barlby Rd NKENS W10 136 F7
Barlee Crs UX/CGN UB8 131 M7
Barle Gdns SOCK/AV RM15 146 G8
Barley Cl BUSH WD23 74 A9
CRAWW RH11 283 N8
RBSF CM22 31 M1
Barleycorn Wy EMPK RM11 125 N4
Barley Cft HERT/WAS SG14 25 L3
HHNE HP2 36 D6
HLWS CM18 46 G5
Barleycroft Gn WGCW AL8 22 F5
Barleycroft Rd WGCW AL8 22 F6
Barley Fld BRWN CM15 86 E3
Barley La GDMY/SEVK IG3 123 K4
Barley Mow Cl
WOKN/KNAP GU21 231 J3
Barley Mow Ct
BRKHM/BTCW RH3 255 P10
Barley Mow La STALE/WH AL4 39 K9
WOKN/KNAP GU21 231 H2
Barley Mow Pas CHSWK W4 156 A4
Barley Mow Rd EGH TW20 171 P8
Barley Mow Wy SHPTN TW17 196 B4
Barley Ponds Cl WARE SG12 26 E2
Barley Ponds Rd WARE SG12 26 E2
Barlings Rd HARP AL5 20 A6
Barlow Cl WLGTN SM6 222 F3
Barlow Pl MYFR/PICC W1J 10 F8
Barlow Rd ACT W3 135 N10
CRAWW RH11 283 H10
CRICK NW2 2 D1
HPTN TW12 175 P10
Barlow St WALW SE17 19 H5
Barlow Wy DAGW RM9 144 E8
Barmeston Rd CAT SE6 182 G5
Barmor Cl RYLN/HDSTN HA2 94 A10
Barmouth Av GFD/PVL UB6 134 E4
Barmouth Rd CROY/NA CR0 204 C9
WAND/EARL SW18 179 M2
Barnabas Rd HOM E9 140 C1
Barnaby Cl RYLN/HDSTN HA2 114 B7
Barnaby Pl SKENS SW7 15 L6
Barnaby Wy CHIG IG7 102 D4
Barnacre Cl UX/CGN UB8 131 N8
Barnacres Rd HHS/BOV HP3 36 A10
Barnard Acres WAB EN9 45 K9
Barnard Cl CHST BR7 206 G1
SUN TW16 175 J10
WLGTN SM6 222 E4
Barnard Gdns NWMAL KT3 200 D4
YEAD UB4 133 J6
Barnard Gn WGCE AL7 23 J6
Barnard Hl MUSWH N10 98 C10
Barnard Ms BTSEA SW11 157 P10
Barnardo Dr BARK/HLT IG6 122 F2
Barnardo Gdns WCHPL * E1 140 C8
Barnardo St WCHPL E1 140 C8
Barnard Rd BTSEA SW11 157 P10
EN EN1 80 A6
MTCM CR4 202 B3
WARL CR6 242 G5
Barnards Pl SAND/SEL CR2 223 J5
Barnard Wy HHS/BOV HP3 35 P7
Barnato Cl BF/WBF KT14 215 P8
Barnby Rd WOKN/KNAP GU21 231 J3
Barnby St CAMTN NW1 5 H8
SRTFD E15 141 K3
Barn Cl ASHF TW15 174 C8
BNSTD SM7 239 N1
HHS/BOV HP3 36 A9
KTTN * NW5 118 E10
KWD/TDW/WH * KT20 255 L8
NTHLT UB5 133 K4
RAD WD7 74 F1
SLN SL2 108 G9
WGCW AL8 22 F5
Barn Ct CRAWE RH10 285 M3
Barn Crs PUR/KEN CR8 223 L9
STAN HA7 95 H7
Barncroft Cl LOU IG10 82 D9
UX/CGN UB8 132 C7
Barncroft Gn LOU IG10 82 D9
Barncroft Rd BERK HP4 33 N6
LOU IG10 82 D9
Barncroft Wy STAL AL1 38 F7
Barndicott WGCE AL7 23 M5
Barnehurst Av BXLYHN DA7 164 D7
Barnehurst Cl ERITH DA8 164 D7
Barnehurst Rd BXLYHN DA7 164 D8
Barn End Dr RDART DA2 187 K7
Barn End La SWLY BR8 187 K9
Barnes Av BARN SW13 156 D6
CSHM HP5 51 H6
NWDGN UB2 153 N3
Barnes Br CHSWK W4 156 B8
Barnes Cl MNPK E12 122 A9
Barnes Cray Rd DART DA1 165 H10
Barnesdale Crs STMC/STPC BR5 207 K6
Barnes End NWMAL KT3 200 D5
Barnes High St BARN SW13 156 C8
Barnes La KGLGY WD4 53 M4
Barnes Ri KGLGY WD4 54 A3
Barnes Rd IL IG1 122 F10
RGODL GU7 267 K9
UED N18 100 B5
Barnes St POP/IOD E14 140 D8
Barnes Ter DEPT SE8 160 E4
Barnes Wallis Dr WEY KT13 215 P7
Barnes Wy IVER SL0 131 J9
Barnet By-Pass BORE WD6 76 B9
Barnet Dr HAYES BR2 206 B9
Barnet Gate La BAR EN5 76 C10
Barnet Gv BETH E2 7 N9
Barnet Hl BAR EN5 77 J8
Barnet La BORE WD6 75 L10
TRDG/WHET N20 97 J2

Barnet Rd EBAR EN4 77 K3
LCOL/BKTW AL2 57 L4
MLHL NW7 76 B10
POTB/CUF EN6 59 M10
Barnett Cl ERITH DA8 164 G8
LHD/OX KT22 236 G5
SHGR GU5 268 F9
Barnett La SHGR GU5 268 E10
Barnett Rw RGUE GU4 250 A5
Barnetts Ct RYLN/HDSTN * HA2 114 A8
Barnett's Shaw OXTED RH8 261 J3
Barnett St WCHPL E1 140 A8
Barnett Wood La ASHTD KT21 237 H4
Barnet Wy (Barnet By-Pass)
MLHL NW7 96 A1
Barnet Wood Rd HAYES * BR2 205 N10
Barney Cl CHARL SE7 161 P4
Barn Fld BNSTD SM7 221 L10
HAMP * NW3 118 A10
Barnfield EPP CM16 65 K4
GVW DA11 190 D5
HHS/BOV HP3 36 A9
IVER SL0 131 H8
NWMAL KT3 200 B6
SL SL1 128 C10
Barnfield Av CROY/NA CR0 204 B8
KUTN/CMB KT2 177 J7
MTCM CR4 202 C4
Barnfield Cl COUL/CHIP CR5 241 K5
GRH DA9 188 E2
HOD EN11 44 F1
SWLY BR8 208 D7
WAB EN9 45 L8
Barnfield Ct HARP AL5 20 B3
Barnfield Crs RSEV TN14 247 M3
Barnfield Gdns KUTN/CMB KT2 177 K8
WOOL/PLUM * SE18 162 E5
Barnfield Rd BELV DA17 164 A5
BH/WHM TN16 244 A6
CRAWE RH10 283 N6
EA W5 135 H6
EDGW HA8 95 P9
HARP AL5 20 B3
SAND/SEL CR2 223 M5
SEV TN13 246 E9
STALE/WH AL4 39 H4
STMC/STPC BR5 207 N3
WGCE AL7 23 H7
WOOL/PLUM SE18 162 E5
Barnfield Wy OXTED RH8 261 M9
Barnfield Wood Cl BECK BR3 205 J6
Barnfield Wood Rd BECK BR3 205 J6
Barnham Rd GFD/PVL UB6 134 B5
Barnham St STHWK SE1 19 K1
Barn Hl HLWW/ROY CM19 45 N5
WBLY HA9 115 N7
Barnhill PIN HA5 113 K3
Barnhill Av HAYES BR2 205 M5
Barnhill La YEAD UB4 133 J5
Barnhill Rd WBLY HA9 115 P8
YEAD UB4 133 J6
Barnhurst Pth OXHEY WD19 93 K6
Barningham Wy
CDALE/KGS NW9 115 P4
Barn La RKW/CH/CXG WD3 91 K2
Barnlea Cl FELT TW13 175 M5
Barn Md BRWN CM15 87 H2
HLWS CM18 46 G3
Barnmead CHOB/PIR GU24 213 L6
Barnmead Gdns DAGW RM9 124 A10
Barn Meadow La GT/LBKH KT23 235 N10
Barnmead Rd BECK BR3 204 C1
DAGW RM9 124 A10
Barn Ri WBLY HA9 115 M6
Barn Rd ADL/WDHM KT15 215 L5
Barnsbury Cl NWMAL KT3 199 P4
Barnsbury Crs BRYLDS KT5 199 P8
Barnsbury Est IS N1 5 P6
Barnsbury Gv HOLWY N7 5 P3
Barnsbury La BRYLDS KT5 199 N9
Barnsbury Pk IS N1 6 A3
Barnsbury Rd IS N1 5 N6
Barnsbury Sq IS N1 6 A4
Barnsbury St IS N1 6 A4
Barnsbury Ter IS N1 5 P4
Barns Ct EPP CM16 46 E6
Barnscroft RYNPK SW20 200 E3
Barnsdale Av POP/IOD E14 160 G3
Barnsdale Cl BORE WD6 75 L5
Barnsdale Rd MV/WKIL W9 8 D1
Barnsfield Pl UX/CGN UB8 131 M2
Barnsford Crs CHOB/PIR GU24 212 F8
Barnside Ct WGCW AL8 22 F5
Barnsley Rd HARH RM3 105 N8
Barnsley St WCHPL E1 140 A6
Barnstaple La LEW SE13 161 H10
Barnstaple Rd HARH RM3 105 K6
RSLP HA4 113 K8
Barnston Wk IS * N1 6 E5
Barnston Wy RBRW/HUT CM13 87 P9
Barn St STNW/STAM N16 119 M7
Barnsway KGLGY WD4 53 P4
The Barn GRAYS * RM17 167 N3
Barnway EGH TW20 171 P8
Barn Wy WBLY HA9 115 M6
Barnwell Rd BRXS/STRHM SW2 181 H1
DART DA1 165 N9
Barnwood Cl CRAWE RH10 284 D6
MV/WKIL W9 8 G2
RGUW GU3 249 K8
RSLP HA4 112 E7
Barnwood Ct GUW GU2 249 K8
Barnwood Rd GUW GU2 249 K9
The Barnyard
KWD/TDW/WH KT20 238 D10
Baron Cl BELMT SM2 221 L6
FBAR/BDGN N11 98 B6
Baroness Rd BETH E2 7 M9
Baronet Gv TOTM N17 99 P9
Baronet Rd TOTM N17 99 P9
Baron Gdns BARK/HLT IG6 122 F1
Baron Gv MTCM CR4 201 P4
Baron Rd BCTR RM8 123 N6
Barons Cl IS * N1 6 A7
Baron's Court Rd HMSMTH W6 14 A7
Baronsfield Rd TWK * TW1 176 G2
Barons Ga EBAR EN4 77 P10
Baron's Hurst EPSOM KT18 237 P2
Barons Md HRW HA1 114 D2
Baronsmead Rd BARN SW13 156 D7
Baronsmede EA W5 155 L1
Baronsmere Ct BAR * EN5 77 H8
Baronsmere Rd EFNCH N2 117 P2
Baron's Pl STHWK SE1 18 B2
Barons Rw HARP AL5 20 C4
The Barons TWK TW1 176 G2
Baron St IS N1 6 A8
Baron's Wk CROY/NA CR0 204 D6
Barons Wy EGH TW20 172 G9
REIG RH2 275 K4
Barque Ms DEPT SE8 160 F5
Barrack La WDSR SL4 149 J7
Barrack Pth WOKN/KNAP GU21 231 L4
Barrack Rd GUW GU2 249 M8
HSLWW TW4 153 L10
Barrack Rw GVW DA11 190 E2
Barracks Hl AMSS HP7 88 E1
Barra Cl HHS/BOV HP3 36 C9
Barra Hall Rd HYS/HAR UB3 132 F9
Barrards Wy BEAC HP9 89 H7
Barrass Cl WAB EN9 80 F3
Barratt Av WDGN N22 98 C10
Barratt Wy KTN/HRWW/W HA3 114 C1
Barrenger Rd MUSWH N10 98 A9
Barrens Brae WOKS/MYFD GU22 232 D4
Barrens Cl WOKS/MYFD GU22 232 D5
Barrens Pk WOKS/MYFD GU22 232 D4
Barrett Rd GT/LBKH KT23 254 B1
WALTH E17 121 H2
Barrett's Green Rd
WLSDN NW10 135 P4
Barrett's Gv STNW/STAM N16 119 M10
Barretts Rd SEV TN13 246 E6
Barrett St MBLAR W1H 10 D6
Barrhill Rd BRXS/STRHM SW2 180 F5
Barricane WOKN/KNAP GU21 231 N5
Barrie Cl COUL/CHIP CR5 240 D2
Barriedale NWCR SE14 160 D7
Barrier Point Rd CAN/RD E16 141 P10
Barringer Sq TOOT SW17 180 B7
Barrington Cl CLAY IG5 102 C9
KTTN NW5 118 B10
Barrington Ct DORK RH4 272 F3
Barrington Dr DEN/HRF UB9 91 K8
Barrington Rd LOU IG10 82 F8
Barrington Ldg WEY KT13 216 D2
Barrington Rd BRXN/ST SW9 159 J9
CEND/HSY/T N8 118 E3
CHEAM SM3 201 K8
CRAWE RH10 283 N9
DORK * RH4 272 F3
LOU IG10 82 F8
MNPK E12 142 D1
PUR/KEN CR8 222 D8
WELL DA16 163 N8
Barrington Vls
WOOL/PLUM SE18 162 D7
Barrington Wk NRWD * SE19 181 M9
Barron's Cl CHONG CM5 67 N3
Barrow Av CAR SM5 222 A4
Barrow Cl WCHMH N21 99 J4
Barrowdene Cl PIN HA5 93 M10
Barrowell Gn WCHMH N21 99 J3
Barrowfield Cl ED N9 100 A4
Barrowgate Rd CHSWK W4 155 P4
Barrow Green Rd GDST RH9 260 F7
Barrow Hedges Cl CAR SM5 221 P4
Barrow Hedges Wy CAR SM5 221 P4
Barrow Hl WPK KT4 200 B9
Barrow Hill Cl WPK KT4 200 B9
Barrow Hill Est STJWD NW8 3 N8
Barrow Hill Rd STJWD NW8 3 N8
Barrow La CHESW EN7 61 N7
Barrow Point Av PIN HA5 93 M10
Barrow Point La PIN HA5 93 M10
Barrow Rd CROY/NA CR0 223 H2
STRHM/NOR SW16 180 E9
Barrows Rd HLWW/ROY CM19 46 C1
Barr Rd GVE DA12 191 J5
POTB/CUF EN6 59 M9
Barr's La WOKN/KNAP GU21 231 J2
Barr's Rd MDHD SL6 128 A8
WLSDN NW10 136 A2
Barry Av BXLYHN DA7 163 P6
SEVS/STOTM N15 119 N4
WDSR SL4 148 G6
Barry Cl CDH/CHF RM16 168 D2
CRAWE RH10 283 P10
LCOL/BKTW AL2 56 A1
ORP BR6 207 H10
Barry Pde EDUL * SE22 159 P10
Barry Rd EDUL SE22 181 P2
EHAM E6 142 B8
WLSDN NW10 135 P2
Barry Ter ASHF * TW15 174 A5
Barset Rd PECK SE15 160 B9
Barsons Cl PGE/AN SE20 182 B10
The Bars GU GU1 268 A1
Barston Rd WNWD SE27 181 K5
Barstow Crs BRXS/STRHM SW2 180 G4
Bartel Cl HHS/BOV HP3 36 E8
Bartelotts Rd SLN SL2 128 C6
Barter St NOXST/BSQ WC1A 11 M4
Bartholemew Ct DORK * RH4 272 F3
Bartholomew Cl STBT EC1A 12 E4
WAND/EARL SW18 157 M10
Bartholomew Dr HARH RM3 105 L10
Bartholomew La OBST EC2N 13 H6
Bartholomew Rd CAMTN NW1 4 G2
Bartholomew Sq FSBYE EC1V 12 F1
Bartholomew St STHWK SE1 19 H4
Bartholomew Vls KTTN NW5 4 G2
Bartholomew Wy SWLY BR8 208 F3
Barth Rd WOOL/PLUM SE18 163 H3
Bartle Av EHAM E6 142 B4
Bartle Rd NTGHL W11 136 G8
Bartlett Cl POP/IOD E14 140 F8
Bartlett Ct FLST/FETLN * EC4A 12 B5
Bartlett Rd BH/WHM TN16 262 F2
GVW DA11 190 D4
Bartletts Md HERT/WAS SG14 25 L2
Bartlett St SAND/SEL CR2 223 L1
Bartlow Gdns CRW RM5 104 E9
Barton Av DAGE RM10 124 D6
Barton Cl ADL/WDHM KT15 215 K3
BXLYHS DA6 185 P1
CHIG IG7 102 F3
HDN NW4 116 D3
PECK SE15 160 A9
SHPTN TW17 196 C6
Barton Gn NWMAL KT3 200 A2
Barton Mdw BARK/HLT IG6 122 E2
Barton Pl GU * GU1 250 E7
Barton Rd DTCH/LGLY SL3 150 C1
EYN DA4 210 A1
HCH RM12 125 H6
HMSMTH W6 14 A8
SCUP DA14 185 P9
SHGR GU5 268 D10
STALE/WH AL4 21 H3
The Bartons BORE * WD6 75 J10
Barton St WEST SW1P 17 L4
The Barton COB KT11 217 L8
Barton Wy BORE WD6 75 M6
RKW/CH/CXG WD3 72 C9
Bartram Cl UX/CGN UB8 132 C6
Bartram Rd BROCKY SE4 182 D1
Bartrams La EBAR EN4 77 M4
Bartrip St HOM E9 140 D1
Barts Cl BECK BR3 204 F5
Barward Cl WOOL/PLUM SE18 162 D3
Barwell Ct CHSGTN * KT9 219 H4
Barwick Rd FSTGT E7 121 N9
Barwood Av WWKM BR4 204 G8
Basden Gv FELT TW13 175 P5
Basedale Rd DAGW RM9 143 L2
Baseing Cl EHAM E6 142 D9
Basevi Wy DEPT SE8 160 F5
Basford Wy WDSR SL4 148 C9
Bashford Wy CRAWE RH10 284 E5
Bashley Rd WLSDN NW10 136 A6
Basil Av EHAM E6 142 B5
Basildene Rd HSLWW TW4 153 L9
Basildon Av CLAY IG5 102 D9
Basildon Cl BELMT SM2 221 L5
WATW WD18 72 D10
Basildon Rd ABYW SE2 163 K3
Basildon Sq HHNE HP2 36 A2
Basildon Wy CRAWW RH11 283 H10
Basil Gdns CROY/NA CR0 204 C8
WNWD SE27 181 K8
Basilon Rd BXLYHN DA7 163 P8
Basil St CHEL SW3 16 A2
Basin Ap POP/IOD E14 140 D8
Basing Cl THDIT KT7 198 F7
Basingdon Wy CMBW SE5 159 L10
Basing Dr BXLY DA5 186 A2
Basingfield Rd THDIT KT7 198 E7
Basinghall Av CITYW EC2V 12 G5
Basinghall Gdns BELMT SM2 221 L5
Basinghall St CITYW EC2V 12 G5
Basing Hl GLDGN NW11 117 J6
WBLY HA9 115 L7
Basing Pl BETH E2 7 K9
Basing Rd BNSTD SM7 221 J10
BNSTD SM7 239 J1
RKW/CH/CXG WD3 91 J2
Basing St NTGHL W11 8 C5
Basing Wy FNCH N3 117 K1
THDIT KT7 198 E7
Basire St IS N1 6 F5
Baskerville Gdns WLSDN NW10 116 B9
Baskerville Rd WAND/EARL SW18 179 P3
Basket Gdns ELTH/MOT SE9 184 B1
Baslow Cl KTN/HRWW/W HA3 94 C9
Baslow Wk CLPT E5 120 C9
Basnett Rd BTSEA * SW11 158 B9
Bassano St EDUL SE22 181 N1
Bassant Rd WOOL/PLUM SE18 163 J5
Bassein Park Rd SHB W12 156 C1
Basset Cl ADL/WDHM KT15 215 L6
Basset Dr REIG RH2 257 K9
Bassett Cl BELMT SM2 221 L5
Bassett Gdns EPP CM16 66 C2
ISLW TW7 154 B6
Bassett Rd CRAWE RH10 284 E10
NKENS W10 136 G8
UX/CGN UB8 131 M2
WOKS/MYFD GU22 232 F2
Bassetts Cl ORP BR6 226 E1
Bassett St KTTN NW5 4 C1
Bassetts Wy ORP BR6 226 E1
Bassett Wy GFD/PVL UB6 134 A8
Bassil Rd HHS/BOV HP3 35 N7
Bassingbourne Cl BROX EN10 44 E6
Bassingburn Wk WGCE AL7 23 J6
Bassingham Rd ALP/SUD HA0 135 J1
WAND/EARL SW18 179 M3
Basswood Cl PECK SE15 160 A9
Bastable Av BARK IG11 143 K4
Bastion Rd ABYW SE2 163 K4
Baston Manor Rd WWKM BR4 205 N10
Baston Rd HAYES BR2 205 N9
Bastwick St FSBYE EC1V 12 D1
Basuto Rd FUL/PGN SW6 157 K7
Bata Av TIL RM18 169 L4
Batavia Cl SUN TW16 197 J1
Batavia Rd NWCR SE14 160 D6
SUN TW16 197 J1
Batchelor St IS N1 6 B7
Batchelors Wy AMSS HP7 69 J5
CSHM HP5 50 G5
Batchwood Dr STALW/RED AL3 38 B3
Batchwood Gdns STALW/RED AL3 38 C3
Batchwood Gn STMC/STPC BR5 207 K4
Batchwood Vw STALW/RED AL3 38 B4
Batchworth Hl
RKW/CH/CXG * WD3 91 P3
Batchworth Hill London Rd
RKW/CH/CXG WD3 91 P3
Batchworth La NTHWD HA6 92 D6
Bateman Cl BARK IG11 142 F1
Bateman Ct CRAWE * RH10 284 B10
Bateman Rd CHING E4 100 F7
RKW/CH/CXG WD3 72 B10
Batemans Cnr CHSWK * W4 156 A3
Batemans Ct CRAWE RH10 284 B10
Bateman's Rw SDTCH EC2A 13 K1
Bateman St SOHO/SHAV W1D 11 J6
Bates Cl DTCH/LGLY SL3 130 B8
Bates Crs CROY/NA CR0 223 H2
STRHM/NOR SW16 180 D10
Bateson Wy WOKN/KNAP GU21 214 F10
Bates Rd HARH RM3 105 P8
Bate St POP/IOD E14 140 E9
Bates Wk ADL/WDHM KT15 215 M3
Batford Cl WGCE AL7 23 L6
Batford Ml HARP * AL5 20 C1
Bath Cl PECK SE15 160 A6
Bathgate Rd WIM/MER SW19 178 G6
Bath Gv BETH E2 7 N8
Bath House Rd CROY/NA CR0 202 F8
Bath Pas KUT KT1 199 J2
Bath Pl IS N1 7 J10
Bath Rd CHSWK W4 156 B3
DART DA1 187 J3
DTCH/LGLY SL3 151 H7
ED N9 100 A3
FSTGT E7 142 A1
SL SL1 128 F9
SL SL1 128 C9
WDR/YW UB7 151 K7
Baths Ap FUL/PGN * SW6 157 J6
Bath St FSBYE EC1V 6 F10
GVW DA11 190 E2
Bath Ter STHWK SE1 18 E4
Bathurst Av WIM/MER SW19 201 L1
Bathurst Cl IVER SL0 151 J1
Bathurst Gdns WLSDN NW10 136 E4
Bathurst Ms BAY/PAD W2 9 M7
Bathurst Rd HHNE HP2 35 N3
IL IG1 122 E6
Bathurst St BAY/PAD W2 9 M7
Bathurst Wk IVER SL0 151 H1
Bathway WOOL/PLUM SE18 162 D3
Batley Cl MTCM CR4 202 A7
Batley Pl STNW/STAM N16 119 N8
Batley Rd STNW/STAM N16 119 N8
Batman Cl SHB W12 136 E10
Baton Cl PUR RM19 166 C3
Batoum Gdns HMSMTH W6 156 F2
Batson St SHB W12 156 D1
Batsworth Rd MTCM CR4 201 N3
Batten Av WOKN/KNAP GU21 231 K5
Batten Cottages POP/IOD * E14 140 D7
Batten St BTSEA SW11 157 P9
Batterdale BRKMPK AL9 40 F3
Battersby Rd CAT SE6 183 J5
Battersea Br BTSEA SW11 157 N6
Battersea Bridge Rd
BTSEA SW11 157 P6
Battersea Church Rd
BTSEA SW11 157 N7
Battersea High St BTSEA SW11 157 N7
Battersea Park Rd BTSEA SW11 158 B7
Battersea Ri BTSEA SW11 179 P1
Battersea Sq BTSEA * SW11 157 P6
Battery Rd THMD SE28 163 H1
Battishill St IS N1 6 C4
Battlebridge La REDH RH1 258 C6
Battle Bridge La STHWK SE1 13 J10
Battle Bridge Rd CAMTN NW1 5 L8
Battle Cl WIM/MER SW19 179 M9
Battledean Rd HBRY N5 119 J10
Battlefield Rd STAL AL1 38 E4
Battle Rd ERITH DA8 164 D3
Battlers Green Dr RAD WD7 74 D3
Battleview STALE/WH AL4 21 K3
Batts Hl REDH RH1 257 N8
Batty St WCHPL E1 13 P5
Baudwin Rd CAT SE6 183 K5
Baugh Rd SCUP DA14 185 M8
The Baulk WAND/EARL SW18 179 K3
Bavant Rd STRHM/NOR SW16 202 F2
Bavaria Rd ARCH N19 118 F7
Bavent Rd CMBW SE5 159 K8
Bawdale Rd EDUL SE22 181 N1
Bawdsey Av GNTH/NBYPK IG2 123 J2
Bawtree Cl BELMT SM2 221 M6
Bawtree Rd NWCR SE14 160 D6
UX/CGN UB8 131 N1
Bawtry Rd TRDG/WHET N20 98 A4
Baxendale TRDG/WHET N20 97 M3
Baxendale St BETH E2 7 N9
Baxter Av REDH RH1 257 P10
Baxter Cl CRAWE RH10 284 C9
HGDN/ICK UB10 132 C5
NWDGN UB2 154 A2
SL SL1 149 K2
Baxter Rd CAN/RD E16 141 P8
IL IG1 122 E10
IS N1 7 H2
UED N18 100 A5
Bayards WARL CR6 242 B4
Bay Cl HORL RH6 279 P1
Bay Ct EA * W5 155 K2
Baycroft Cl PIN * HA5 113 K1
Bayeux KWD/TDW/WH KT20 238 G8
Bayfield Rd ELTH/MOT SE9 162 A10
HORL RH6 279 P3
Bayford Cl HERT/BAY SG13 25 K7
HHNE HP2 36 D1
Bayford Gn HERT/BAY SG13 43 H3
Bayford La HERT/BAY SG13 42 G1
Bayford Ms HACK * E8 140 A2
Bayford Rd WLSDN NW10 136 G5
Bayford St HACK E8 140 A2
Bayham Pl CAMTN NW1 4 G6
Bayham Rd CHSWK W4 156 A2
MRDN SM4 201 L4
SEV TN13 247 K9
WEA * W13 134 G9
Bayham St CAMTN NW1 4 G5
Bayhorne La HORL RH6 280 D6
Bayhurst Dr NTHWD HA6 92 G7
Bayleaf Cl HPTN TW12 176 C8
Bayley Md HHW * HP1 35 L8
Bayley's Hl RSEV TN14 264 F8
Bayleys Md RBRW/HUT CM13 107 P3
Bayley St FITZ W1T 11 J4
Baylie Ct HHNE HP2 35 P5
Baylie La HHNE HP2 35 P5
Baylis Pde SL SL1 129 K8
Baylis Rd SL SL1 129 J9
STHWK SE1 18 A3
Bayliss Av THMD SE28 143 N9
Bayliss Cl STHGT/OAK N14 78 F9
Bayliss Ct GU GU1 267 P1
Bayly Rd DART DA1 187 P2
Bay Manor La WTHK RM20 166 E5
Baymans Wd BRWN CM15 107 K3
Baynes Cl EN EN1 79 P5
Baynes Ms HAMP NW3 3 M1
Baynes St CAMTN NW1 5 H4
Baynham Cl BXLY DA5 186 A2
Bayonne Rd HMSMTH W6 14 A10
Bays Cl SYD SE26 182 B8
Baysfarm Ct WDR/YW UB7 151 M7
Bayston Rd STNW/STAM N16 119 N8
Bayswater Rd BAY/PAD W2 9 H8
Baythorne St BOW E3 140 E7
Baythorn La HORL RH6 280 D6
Bay Tree Av LHD/OX KT22 236 F6
Baytree Cl BFN/LL DA15 185 J4
BMLY BR1 206 A1
Bay Tree Cl CHESW * EN7 61 N3
LCOL/BKTW AL2 56 B3
Bay Tree Ct SL SL1 128 B5
Baytree Rd BRXS/STRHM SW2 158 G10
Bay Tree Wk WAT WD17 72 G4
Baywood Sq CHIG IG7 103 L5
Bazalgette Cl NWMAL KT3 199 P5
Bazalgette Gdns NWMAL KT3 199 P5
Bazely St POP/IOD E14 141 H9
Bazes Shaw HART DA3 211 L9
Bazile Rd WCHMH N21 79 H10
Beacham Cl CHARL SE7 162 A5
Beachborough Rd BMLY BR1 183 H7
Beachcroft Rd WAN E11 121 K8
Beach Gv FELT TW13 175 P6
Beachy Rd BOW E3 140 F2
Beacon Cl BNSTD SM7 238 G2
CFSP/GDCR SL9 90 B8
UX/CGN UB8 111 N10
Beacon Ct DTCH/LGLY SL3 150 F6
HERT/BAY * SG13 26 B8
Beacon Dr RDART DA2 189 H6
Beaconfield Av EPP CM16 65 J5
Beaconfield Rd EPP CM16 65 J5
Beaconfields SEV TN13 264 G2
Beaconfield Wy EPP CM16 65 J5
Beacon Hl BRW CM14 86 B3
HOLWY N7 118 F10
PUR RM19 166 A4
WOKN/KNAP GU21 231 P5
Beacon Hill Rd BRW CM14 86 A3
Beacon Pl CROY/NA CR0 202 F10
Beacon Ri SEV TN13 265 H2
Beacon Rd ERITH DA8 165 J6
HTHAIR TW6 174 B2
LEW SE13 183 J2
WARE SG12 26 F1
Beaconsfield Cl BKHTH/KID SE3 161 M5
CHSWK W4 155 P4
Beaconsfield Common La
SLN SL2 109 H5
Beaconsfield Cottages
TRDG/WHET * N20 97 K4
Beaconsfield Ct HAT * AL10 40 F2
Beaconsfield Pl EW KT17 220 B8
Beaconsfield Rd BKHTH/KID SE3 161 M5
BMLY BR1 206 A3
BRYLDS KT5 199 L7
BXLY DA5 186 F5
CAN/RD E16 141 L6
CHSWK W4 156 A2
CROY/NA CR0 203 L6
EA W5 155 H1
ED N9 99 P4
ELTH/MOT SE9 184 B6
EPSOM KT18 238 A5
ESH/CLAY KT10 218 D4
HAT AL10 40 F3
HYS/HAR UB3 133 K10
LEY * E10 121 H8
NWMAL KT3 200 A2
PEND EN3 80 C3
SEVS/STOTM N15 119 M2
SLN SL2 129 H1
STAL AL1 38 D6
TRDG/WHET N20 98 A4
TWK TW1 176 G3
WALTH E17 120 E4
WALW SE17 19 H9
WLSDN NW10 136 C1
WOKS/MYFD GU22 232 C6
Beaconsfield Wk FUL/PGN SW6 157 J7
The Beacons LOU IG10 82 D4
Beacontree Av WALTH E17 101 J9
Beacontree Rd WAN E11 121 L5
Beacon Wy BNSTD SM7 238 G2
RKW/CH/CXG WD3 91 L1
Beadles La OXTED RH8 261 J6
Beadlow Cl MRDN SM4 201 N6
Beadman Pl WNWD * SE27 181 J7
Beadman St WNWD SE27 181 J7
Beadnell Rd FSTH SE23 182 C4
Beadon Rd HAYES BR2 205 M4
HMSMTH W6 156 F3
Beads Hall La BRWN CM15 86 G8
Beaford Gv RYNPK SW20 201 H3
Beagle Cl FELT TW13 175 J7
RAD WD7 74 E3
Beagles Cl STMC/STPC BR5 207 N9
Beak St REGST W1B 10 G7
Beal Cl WELL DA16 163 K7
Beale Cl PLMGR N13 99 J6
Beale Pl BOW E3 140 E4
Beale Rd BOW E3 140 E3
Beales La WEY KT13 196 C10
Beales Rd GT/LBKH KT23 254 A2
Bealings End BEAC HP9 88 C6
Beal Rd IL IG1 122 D7
Beam Av DAGE RM10 144 C3
Beaminster Gdns BARK/HLT IG6 122 E1
Beamish Cl EPP CM16 66 D1
Beamish Dr BUSH WD23 94 B2
Beamish Rd ED N9 99 P2
STMC/STPC BR5 207 M7
Beamway DAGE RM10 144 E2
Beanacre Cl HOM * E9 140 E1
Beane River Vw HERT/WAS SG14 25 K5
Beane Rd HERT/WAS SG14 25 J5
Bean La RDART DA2 188 F5
Bean Rd BXLYHS DA6 163 N10
GRH DA9 188 G2
Beanshaw ELTH/MOT SE9 184 D7
Beansland Gv CHDH RM6 103 P10
Bear Cl ROMW/RG RM7 124 C4
Beardell St NRWD SE19 181 N9
Beardow Gv STHGT/OAK * N14 78 D10
Beard Rd RCHPK/HAM TW10 177 L8
Beardsfield PLSTW E13 141 M3
Beard's Hl HPTN TW12 197 P1
Beards Hill Cl HPTN TW12 197 P1
Beardsley Wy ACT W3 156 A1
Beards Rd ASHF TW15 174 F9
Bearfield Rd KUTN/CMB KT2 177 K10
Bear Gdns STHWK SE1 12 E9
Bearing Cl CHIG IG7 103 K5
Bearing Wy CHIG IG7 103 K5
Bear La STHWK SE1 12 D9
Bear Rd FELT TW13 175 L7
Bears Den KWD/TDW/WH KT20 239 J8
Bearstead Ri BROCKY SE4 182 E1
Bearstead Ter BECK * BR3 204 F1
Bear St LSQ/SEVD WC2H 11 K7
Bearswood End BEAC HP9 88 D7
Bearwood Cl ADL/WDHM KT15 215 K3
POTB/CUF EN6 59 N7
Beasant House WATN * WD24 73 L6
Beasley's Ait SHPTN TW17 196 G6
Beasley's Ait La SUN TW16 196 G6
Beaton Cl GRH DA9 166 C10
Beatrice Av STRHM/NOR SW16 202 G3
WBLY HA9 115 K10
Beatrice Cl PIN HA5 113 H2
PLSTW E13 141 M6
Beatrice Gdns GVW DA11 190 B5
Beatrice Pl KENS W8 14 G4
Beatrice Rd ED N9 100 B1
FSBYPK N4 119 H5
OXTED RH8 261 K4
RCHPK/HAM TW10 177 L1
STHL UB1 133 N10
STHWK SE1 19 P6
WALTH E17 120 F3
Beattie Cl EBED/NFELT TW14 174 G4
GT/LBKH KT23 235 N10
Beattock Ri MUSWH N10 118 C2
Beatty Av GU GU1 250 D9
Beatty Rd CHES/WCR EN8 62 E10
STAN HA7 95 H7
STNW/STAM N16 119 M9
Beatty St CAMTN * NW1 4 G7
Beattyville Gdns CLAY IG5 122 D1
Beauchamp Gdns
RKW/CH/CXG WD3 91 K2
Beauchamp Pl CHEL SW3 15 P3
Beauchamp Rd BTSEA SW11 157 P10
E/WMO/HCT KT8 198 A5
FSTGT E7 141 N2
SUT SM1 221 K2
THHTH CR7 203 L1
TWK TW1 176 F3
Beauchamp St HCIRC EC1N 12 A4
Beauchamp Ter PUT/ROE SW15 156 E9
Beauclare Cl ASHTD KT21 237 J7

Beauclerc Rd HMSMTH W6 156 E2
Beauclerk Cl FELT TW13 175 J4
Beaufort EHAM E6 142 D7
Beaufort Av KTN/HRWW/W HA3 114 F2
Beaufort Cl CDH/CHF RM16 167 L2
CHING E4 100 G7
EA W5 135 L7
EPP CM16 66 B3
PUT/ROE SW15 178 F4
REIG RH2 257 J9
ROMW/RG RM7 124 D2
WOKS/MYFD GU22 232 F2
Beaufort Dr GLDGN NW11 117 K2
Beaufort Gdns CHEL SW3 15 P3
HDN NW4 116 F4
HEST TW5 153 M7
IL IG1 122 D6
STRHM/NOR SW16 180 G10
Beaufort Rd EA W5 135 L7
KUT KT1 199 K4
RCHPK/HAM TW10 177 H7
REIG RH2 257 J9
RSLP * HA4 112 E7
TWK TW1 177 H3
WOKS/MYFD GU22 232 F2
Beauforts EGH TW20 171 P8
Beaufort St CHEL SW3 15 L9
Beaufort Wy EW KT17 220 D4
Beaufoy Rd TOTM N17 99 M8
Beaufoy Wk LBTH SE11 17 P6
Beaulah Pl WDSR * SL4 170 A5
Beaulieu Av CAN/RD E16 141 N10
SYD SE26 182 A7
Beaulieu Cl CDALE/KGS NW9 116 B2
DTCH/LGLY SL3 149 P8
DTCH/LGLY SL3 149 N7
HSLWW TW4 175 N1
MTCM CR4 202 B1
OXHEY WD19 93 K2
TWK TW1 177 J2
Beaulieu Dr PIN HA5 113 L4
WAB EN9 62 G9
Beaulieu Gdns WCHMH N21 99 K1
Beaulieu Pl CHSWK W4 155 P2
Beauly Wy ROM RM1 104 F9
Beaumaris Gn CDALE/KGS * NW9 116 B4
Beaumayes Cl HHW HP1 35 L7
Beaumonds STAL * AL1 38 D6
Beaumont Av ALP/SUD HA0 115 H10
RCH/KEW TW9 155 L9
RYLN/HDSTN HA2 114 A4
STAL AL1 38 G5
WKENS W14 14 C7
Beaumont Cl CRAWW RH11 283 H8
GPK RM2 105 K10
KUTN/CMB * KT2 177 M10
Beaumont Ct ALP/SUD HA0 115 H10
Beaumont Crs RAIN RM13 145 H1
WKENS W14 14 C7
Beaumont Dr ASHF TW15 174 E8
GVW DA11 190 B3
Beaumont Gdns HAMP NW3 117 K8
RBRW/HUT CM13 87 P10
Beaumont Ga RAD WD7 74 F1
Beaumont Gv WCHPL E1 140 C6
Beaumont Ms MHST * W1U 10 D3
PIN * HA5 113 M1
Beaumont Park Dr
HLWW/ROY CM19 45 N1
Beaumont Pl BAR EN5 77 J5
FITZ W1T 11 H1
ISLW TW7 176 E1
Beaumont Ri ARCH N19 118 E6
Beaumont Rd BROX EN10 43 N10
CHSWK W4 155 P2
GVW DA11 190 B3
LEY E10 120 G5
LEY E10 121 H5
NRWD SE19 181 K9
PLSTW E13 141 N5
PUR/KEN CR8 223 H9
SLN SL2 129 J7
STMC/STPC BR5 206 G6
WDSR * SL4 149 H8
WIM/MER SW19 179 H3
Beaumonts REDH RH1 276 A8
Beaumont Sq WCHPL E1 140 C7
Beaumont St MHST W1U 10 D3
Beaumont Ter LEW * SE13 183 K3
Beaumont Vw CHESW EN7 61 L2
Beaumont Wk HAMP NW3 4 B3
Beauvais Ter NTHLT UB5 133 L5
Beauval Rd EDUL SE22 181 N2
Beaverbank Rd ELTH/MOT SE9 184 G4
Beaver Cl HPTN TW12 198 A1
PGE/AN * SE20 181 P10
Beaver Rd BARK/HLT IG6 103 M6
Beavers Cl GUW GU2 249 K9
Beavers Crs HSLWW TW4 153 L10
Beavers La HSLWW TW4 153 K9
Beaverwood Rd CHST BR7 185 H8
Beavor La HMSMTH W6 156 D3
Beazley Cl WARE SG12 26 D1
Bebbington Rd
WOOL/PLUM * SE18 163 H3
Beblets Cl ORP BR6 227 J2
Beccles St POP/IOD E14 140 E8
Bec Cl RSLP HA4 113 L8
Beck Cl LEW SE13 160 G7
Beck Ct BECK BR3 204 C3
Beckenham Gdns ED N9 99 M4
Beckenham Gv HAYES BR2 205 J2
Beckenham Hill Rd BECK BR3 182 G9
Beckenham La HAYES BR2 205 K2
Beckenham Place Pk BECK BR3 182 G10
Beckenham Rd BECK BR3 204 C1
WWKM BR4 204 G7
Beckenshaw Gdns BNSTD SM7 239 P1
Becket Av EHAM E6 142 D5
Becket Cl RBRW/HUT CM13 107 H7
SNWD SE25 203 P6
WIM/MER * SW19 201 L1
Becket Fold HRW * HA1 114 E3
Becket Rd UED N18 100 B5
Beckets Sq BERK * HP4 33 M3
Becket St STHWK SE1 18 G3
Beckets Wk WARE * SG12 26 C2
Beckett Av PUR/KEN CR8 241 J1
Beckett Cl BELV DA17 163 P2
STRHM/NOR SW16 180 E5
WLSDN NW10 136 A1
Beckett La CRAWW RH11 283 N4
Becketts HERT/WAS SG14 25 H6
Beckett's Av STALW/RED AL3 38 B3
Becketts Cl EBED/NFELT TW14 175 J2
ORP BR6 207 J10
Becketts Pl KUT KT1 199 J1
Beckett Wk BECK BR3 182 D9
Beckford Cl WKENS W14 14 D6
Beckford Dr STMC/STPC BR5 206 G7
Beckford Pl WALW * SE17 18 F8
Beckford Rd CROY/NA CR0 203 N6
Beckingham Rd GUW GU2 249 M9
Beck La BECK BR3 204 C3
Beckley Cl GVE DA12 191 L5
Becklow Rd SHB W12 156 D1
Beckman Cl RSEV TN14 246 D1
Beck River Pk BECK BR3 204 E1
Beck Rd HACK E8 140 A3
Becks Rd SCUP DA14 185 K6
Beckton Rd CAN/RD E16 141 L7
Beck Wy BECK BR3 204 E3
Beckway Rd STRHM/NOR SW16 202 E2
Beckway St WALW SE17 19 H6
Beckwith Rd HNHL SE24 181 L2
Beclands Rd TOOT SW17 180 B9
Becmead Av KTN/HRWW/W HA3 114 G3
STRHM/NOR SW16 180 E7
Becondale Rd NRWD SE19 181 M8
Becontree Av BCTR RM8 123 N7
Bective Rd FSTGT E7 121 M9
PUT/ROE SW15 157 J10
Becton Pl ERITH DA8 164 C6
Bedale Cl CRAWW RH11 283 M9
Bedale Rd ENC/FH EN2 79 K4
HARH RM3 105 P6
Bedale St STHWK * SE1 12 G10
Beddington Farm Rd
CROY/NA CR0 202 F8
Beddington Gdns CAR SM5 222 B3
Beddington Gn STMC/STPC BR5 207 J1
Beddington Gv WLGTN SM6 222 E2
Beddington La CROY/NA CR0 202 F9
MTCM CR4 202 D6
Beddington Rd GDMY/SEVK IG3 123 J5
STMC/STPC BR5 207 H1
Beddington Ter CROY/NA * CR0 202 G7
Beddlestead La WARL CR6 243 L4
Bede Cl PIN HA5 93 L9
Bedens Rd SCUP DA14 185 P9
Bede Rd CHDH RM6 123 M4
Bedfont Cl EBED/NFELT TW14 174 D2
MTCM CR4 202 B2
Bedfont Ct STWL/WRAY TW19 151 K9
Bedfont Court Est
STWL/WRAY * TW19 151 L10
Bedfont Green Cl
EBED/NFELT TW14 174 D4
Bedfont La EBED/NFELT TW14 174 F3
Bedfont Rd EBED/NFELT TW14 174 D4
FELT TW13 174 G6
STWL/WRAY TW19 174 A2
Bedford Av AMS HP6 69 P5
BAR EN5 77 J9
RSQ WC1B 11 K4
SL SL1 128 F8
YEAD UB4 133 J8
Bedfordbury CHCR WC2N 11 L7
Bedford Cl CHSWK W4 156 B5
MUSWH N10 98 B8
RKW/CH/CXG WD3 70 E4
WOKN/KNAP GU21 231 P1
Bedford Cnr CHSWK * W4 156 B3
Bedford Ct CHCR WC2N 11 L8
Bedford Crs PEND EN3 80 D1
Bedford Dr SLN SL2 108 G10
Bedford Gdns HCH RM12 125 K7
KENS W8 8 E10
Bedford Hl BAL SW12 180 C5
Bedford La ASC SL5 192 G5
Bedford Pk CROY/NA CR0 203 K8
Bedford Park Rd STAL AL1 38 D6
Bedford Pl CROY/NA CR0 203 L8
RSQ WC1B 11 L3
Bedford Rd BFN/LL DA15 185 H6
CEND/HSY/T N8 118 E4
CHSWK W4 156 A2
CLAP SW4 158 F10
DART DA1 187 P3
ED N9 100 A1
EFNCH N2 117 P1
EHAM E6 142 D3
GRAYS * RM17 167 N4
GU GU1 267 P1
GVW DA11 190 C5
HRW HA1 114 B4
IL IG1 122 E8
MLHL NW7 96 B3
NTHWD HA6 92 D5
ORP BR6 207 L9
RSLP HA4 112 G9
SEVS/STOTM N15 119 L2
STAL AL1 38 D7
SWFD E18 101 M10
WALTH E17 100 F10
WDGN N22 98 F9
WEA W13 134 G9
WHTN TW2 176 C6
WPK KT4 200 F9
Bedford Rw FSBYW WC1X 11 P3
Bedford Sq RSQ WC1B 11 K4
Bedford St BERK HP4 34 A5
COVGDN WC2E 11 L7
WATN WD24 73 J5
Bedford Vls KUT * KT1 199 L2
Bedford Wy STPAN WC1H 11 K2
Bedgebury Gdns
WIM/MER SW19 179 H5
Bedgebury Rd ELTH/MOT SE9 162 A10
Bedivere Rd BMLY BR1 183 M6
Bedlow Wy CROY/NA CR0 222 G1
Bedmond La ABLGY WD5 55 H2
STALW/RED AL3 37 N8
Bedmond Rd ABLGY WD5 54 G5
HHS/BOV HP3 36 E8
Bedonwell Rd BELV DA17 163 P5
BXLYHN DA7 164 A5
Bedser Cl LBTH SE11 17 P9
THHTH CR7 203 K3
WOKN/KNAP GU21 232 D2
Bedser Dr NTHLT UB5 114 C10
Bedster Gdns E/WMO/HCT KT8 198 A2
Bedwardine Rd NRWD SE19 181 M10
Bedwell Av BRKMPK AL9 42 B4
HERT/BAY SG13 42 B2
Bedwell Cl WGCE AL7 23 H6
Bedwell Gdns HYS/HAR UB3 152 F3
Bedwell Rd BELV DA17 164 B4
TOTM N17 99 M9
Beeby Rd CAN/RD E16 141 N7
Beech Av ACT W3 136 B10
BFN/LL DA15 185 K3
BH/WHM TN16 244 A5
BKHH IG9 101 N3
BTFD TW8 154 G6
EHSLY KT24 253 L6
ENC/FH EN2 79 H1
RAD WD7 56 F9
RBRW/HUT CM13 107 L4
RSLP HA4 113 J6
SAND/SEL CR2 223 L7
SWLY BR8 208 G4
TRDG/WHET N20 97 P2
UPMR RM14 126 A8
Beech Bottom STALW/RED AL3 38 C3
Beech Cl ASHF TW15 174 E8
BF/WBF KT14 215 P8
CAR SM5 202 A9
COB KT11 217 P8
DEPT SE8 160 E5
DORK RH4 272 E1
ED N9 79 P10
EHSLY KT24 253 J5
HARP AL5 20 B6
HAT AL10 40 D5
HCH RM12 125 J8
LOU IG10 82 E7
PUT/ROE SW15 178 D3
RYNPK SW20 178 F9
STWL/WRAY TW19 173 N3
SUN TW16 197 L2
WDR/YW UB7 152 B2
WOT/HER KT12 217 K1
Beech Close Ct COB KT11 217 N7
Beech Copse BMLY BR1 206 C2
SAND/SEL CR2 223 M2
Beech Ct BERK HP4 34 A4
ELTH/MOT * SE9 184 B2
Beech Crs KWD/TDW/WH KT20 255 P6
STALE/WH AL4 21 J4
Beechcroft ASHTD KT21 237 L5
BERK HP4 33 P6
CHST BR7 184 D10
Beechcroft Av BXLYHN DA7 164 E7
GLDGN NW11 117 J5
NWMAL KT3 199 P1
PUR/KEN CR8 241 L1
RKW/CH/CXG WD3 72 D10
RYLN/HDSTN HA2 113 P5
STHL UB1 133 N10
TIL RM18 169 K3
Beechcroft Cl ASC SL5 192 C4
HEST TW5 153 M6
ORP BR6 226 G1
STRHM/NOR SW16 180 G8
Beechcroft Dr RGUW GU3 267 J3
Beechcroft Gdns WBLY HA9 115 L8
Beechcroft Mnr WEY KT13 196 E10
Beechcroft Rd BUSH WD23 73 M9
CHSGTN KT9 219 L1
CSHM HP5 50 F6
MORT/ESHN * SW14 155 P9
ORP BR6 226 G1
SWFD E18 101 N10
TOOT SW17 180 A6
Beechdale WCHMH N21 98 G3
Beechdale Rd BRXS/STRHM SW2 180 G2
Beech Dell HAYES BR2 226 C1
Beechdene KWD/TDW/WH KT20 238 E8
Beech Dr BERK HP4 34 A4
BORE WD6 75 L6
EFNCH N2 118 A1
KWD/TDW/WH KT20 239 J8
REIG RH2 257 N10
RPLY/SEND GU23 233 J10
SBW CM21 29 M3
Beechen Cliff Wy ISLW TW7 154 E7
Beechengrove PIN HA5 113 N1
Beechen Gv WAT WD17 73 J7
Beechen La KWD/TDW/WH KT20 257 J1
Beechenlea La SWLY BR8 209 H4
Beechen Pl FSTH SE23 182 B5
The Beeches Av CAR SM5 221 P4
Beeches Cl KWD/TDW/WH KT20 239 K9
PGE/AN SE20 204 B1
Beeches Crs CRAWE RH10 283 P9
Beeches Dr SLN SL2 108 G9
Beeches Pk BEAC HP9 88 C9
Beeches Rd CHEAM SM3 201 H8
SLN SL2 108 G10
TOOT SW17 179 P6
The Beeches BNSTD SM7 239 L2
BRW CM14 106 G4
CHING * E4 101 J2
HNWL * W7 154 E1
LCOL/BKTW AL2 56 C3
LHD/OX KT22 236 D10
RKW/CH/CXG WD3 71 J9
STA * TW18 173 K8
SWLY BR8 188 G10
TIL RM18 168 E8
WATW * WD18 73 J7
Beeches Wk CAR SM5 221 N5
Beeches Wy DTCH/LGLY SL3 110 B10
SL SL1 128 A5
Beeches Wd
KWD/TDW/WH KT20 239 K8
Beechey Cl CRAWE RH10 285 J2
Beechey Wy CRAWE RH10 285 J2
Beech Farm Dr STALE/WH AL4 39 L2
Beech Farm Rd WARL CR6 243 J6
Beechfield BNSTD SM7 221 L9
HOD EN11 26 F9
KGLGY WD4 54 A6
SBW CM21 30 A1
Beechfield Cl BORE WD6 75 K6
Beechfield Gdns ROMW/RG RM7 124 D5
Beechfield Rd BMLY BR1 205 P2
CAT SE6 182 E4
ERITH DA8 164 F6
FSBYPK N4 119 K4
HHW HP1 35 L7
WARE SG12 26 E1
WGCE AL7 23 H7
Beechfield Wk WAB EN9 81 J1
Beech Gdns CRAWE RH10 285 P6
DAGE RM10 144 C2
EA W5 155 K1
WOKN/KNAP GU21 232 B1
Beech Gv ADL/WDHM KT15 215 L1
AMSS HP7 69 H5
BARK/HLT IG6 103 H7
CHOB/PIR GU24 230 B6
CTHM CR3 259 L2
EPSOM KT18 238 E3
GT/LBKH KT23 253 P3
GUW GU2 249 L10
MTCM CR4 202 E5
NWMAL KT3 200 A3
SOCK/AV RM15 166 B1
Beech Hall CHERT * KT16 214 F4
Beech Hall Crs CHING E4 101 J8
Beech Hall Rd CHING E4 101 H8
Beech Hl EBAR EN4 77 N4
WOKS/MYFD GU22 232 A9
Beech Hill Av EBAR EN4 77 M5
Beech Hill Gdns WAB EN9 81 N3
Beech Hill Rd ASC SL5 192 D6
Beechhill Rd ELTH/MOT SE9 184 D1
Beech Holme CRAWE RH10 285 P5
Beech Holt LHD/OX KT22 237 H8
Beech House Rd CROY/NA CR0 203 L10
Beech Hyde La STALE/WH AL4 21 L4
Beechlands Cl HART DA3 211 M5
Beech La BEAC HP9 89 K8
GUW GU2 267 P3
Beechlawn GU GU1 268 C1
Beech Lawns NFNCH/WDSP * N12 97 N6
Beechmeads COB * KT11 217 L9
Beech Ms WARE SG12 26 C4
Beechmont Av VW GU25 194 A6
Beechmont Cl BMLY BR1 183 K8
Beechmont Rd SEV TN13 265 J5
Beechmore Gdns CHEAM SM3 200 G9
Beechmore Rd BTSEA SW11 158 A7
Beechmount Av HNWL W7 134 C7
Beecholme EW * KT17 221 H10
Beecholme Av MTCM CR4 202 C1
Beecholme Est CLPT * E5 120 B8
Beech Pk TRING * HP23 32 E4
Beechpark Wy WAT WD17 72 F3
Beech Pl EPP CM16 65 J7
STALW/RED * AL3 38 C3
Beech Rd BH/WHM TN16 243 P3
DART DA1 187 L4
DTCH/LGLY SL3 150 B1
EBED/NFELT TW14 174 F3
EPSOM KT18 238 C1
FBAR/BDGN N11 98 F7
ORP BR6 227 K4
REDH RH1 258 D2
REIG RH2 257 K7
SEV TN13 265 J1
STALW/RED AL3 38 D3
STRHM/NOR SW16 202 F2
WATN WD24 73 H3
WEY KT13 216 E1
Beechrow KUTN/CMB KT2 177 K7
Beechside CRAWE RH10 283 P8
Beech St ROMW/RG RM7 124 D2
Beech St (Below) BARB EC2Y 12 E3
Beechtree Av EGH TW20 171 N9
Beech Tree Cl CRAWE * RH10 283 N6
IS N1 6 A3
STAN HA7 95 H6
Beech Tree Gld CHING E4 101 L2
Beech Tree La STA * TW18 195 L2
Beechtree La STALW/RED AL3 37 J8
Beech Tree Pl SUT SM1 221 L2
Beech V WOKS/MYFD * GU22 232 B4
Beechvale Cl NFNCH/WDSP N12 97 P6
Beech Wk DART DA1 165 H10
EW KT17 220 D7
MLHL NW7 96 A7
Beech Wy EW KT17 238 C1
FELT TW13 175 P6
WLSDN NW10 136 A2
Beechway BXLY DA5 185 N2
GU GU1 250 E9
Beech Waye CFSP/GDCR SL9 110 C5
Beechwood
KWD/TDW/WH * KT20 255 N7
Beechwood Av AMS HP6 69 P4
COUL/CHIP CR5 240 C1
FNCH N3 117 J1
GFD/PVL UB6 134 A5
HYS/HAR UB3 132 E9
KWD/TDW/WH KT20 239 K7
ORP BR6 227 H3
POTB/CUF EN6 59 L9
RCH/KEW TW9 155 M7
RKW/CH/CXG WD3 70 E8
RSLP HA4 112 G7
RYLN/HDSTN HA2 114 A8
STA TW18 173 L9
STAL AL1 38 G4
SUN TW16 175 H9
THHTH CR7 203 J4
UX/CGN UB8 132 A8
WEY KT13 216 F1
Beechwood Cl AMS HP6 69 P5
CHESW EN7 61 M2
EFNCH * N2 118 A2
HERT/BAY SG13 25 N5
MLHL NW7 96 B6
SURB KT6 199 H7
WEY KT13 216 F1
WOKN/KNAP GU21 231 K3
Beechwood Crs BXLYHN DA7 163 N9
Beechwood Dr COB KT11 217 P7
HAYES BR2 226 A1
WFD IG8 101 L6
Beechwood Gdns CLAY IG5 122 C3
CTHM CR3 241 P8
RAIN RM13 145 J7
RYLN/HDSTN HA2 114 A8
SL SL1 149 K1
Beechwood Gv ACT W3 136 B9
Beechwood La WARL CR6 242 C5
Beechwood Mnr WEY KT13 216 F1
Beechwood Ms ED N9 99 P3
Beechwood Pk HHS/BOV HP3 35 J10
LHD/OX KT22 237 H8
RKW/CH/CXG WD3 71 J8
SWFD E18 121 M1
Beechwood Ri CHST BR7 184 E7
WATN WD24 73 J2
Beechwood Rd BEAC HP9 88 B9
CEND/HSY/T N8 118 E2
CTHM CR3 241 P8
HACK E8 7 L3
SAND/SEL CR2 223 M5
SLN SL2 129 J7
VW GU25 193 N7
WOKN/KNAP GU21 231 K4
Beechwood Vls REDH RH1 276 B10
Beechworth Cl HAMP NW3 117 L7
Beechy Lees Rd RSEV TN14 247 L3
Beecot La WOT/HER KT12 197 K9
Beecroft Rd BROCKY SE4 182 D1
Beehive Cha BRWN CM15 87 J1
Beehive Cl BORE WD6 75 J10
HACK E8 7 L3
HGDN/ICK UB10 132 A2
Beehive Gn WGCE AL7 23 K7
Beehive La REDBR IG4 122 C3
WGCE AL7 23 K8
Beehive Pl BRXN/ST SW9 159 H9
Beehive Ring Rd CRAWE RH10 284 C1
Beehive Rd CHESW EN7 61 J4
STA TW18 173 J8
Beehive Wy REIG RH2 275 L4
Beeken Dene ORP BR6 226 F1
Beel Cl AMSS HP7 69 P5
Beeleigh Rd MRDN SM4 201 L4
Beesfield La EYN DA4 209 P8
Beeston Cl HACK E8 119 P10
OXHEY WD19 93 L5
Beeston Dr CHES/WCR EN8 62 C3
Beeston Pl BGVA SW1W 16 F4
Beeston Rd EBAR EN4 77 N10
Beeston Wy EBED/NFELT TW14 175 K2
Beethoven Rd BORE WD6 95 H1
Beethoven St NKENS W10 2 B9
Beeton Cl PIN HA5 93 P8
Begbie Rd BKHTH/KID SE3 161 P7
Beggars Bush La WATW WD18 72 E9
Beggarshouse La HORL RH6 278 F7
Beggars La BH/WHM TN16 262 G1
CHOB/PIR GU24 213 H7
SHGR GU5 270 F4
Beggar's Roost La SUT SM1 221 K3
Begonia Cl EHAM E6 142 B7
Begonia Pl HPTN TW12 175 P9
Behenna Cl CRAWW RH11 283 H8
Beira St BAL SW12 180 C3
Beken Ct GSTN * WD25 73 K1
Bekesbourne St POP/IOD * E14 140 D8
Belcher Rd HOD EN11 44 F2
Belchers La WAB EN9 45 P10
Belcroft Cl BMLY BR1 183 L10
Beldam Bridge Rd
CHOB/PIR GU24 212 F10
Beldam Haw RSEV TN14 228 B7
Beldham Gdns E/WMO/HCT KT8 198 A3
Belfairs OXHEY WD19 93 L6
Belfairs Dr CHDH RM6 123 M5
Belfast Av SL SL1 129 H8
Belfast Rd SNWD SE25 204 A4
STNW/STAM N16 119 N7
Belfield Rd HOR/WEW KT19 220 A5
Belford Gv WOOL/PLUM SE18 162 D3
Belford Rd BORE WD6 75 L4
Belfort Rd PECK SE15 160 B8
Belfry Av DEN/HRF UB9 91 K9
Belfry Cl BERM/RHTH * SE16 160 A4
The Belfry REDH * RH1 258 A9
Belgrade Rd HPTN TW12 198 A1
STNW/STAM N16 119 M9
Belgrave Av GPK RM2 125 K1
Belgrave Cl ACT W3 155 P1
MLHL NW7 96 A6
STALE/WH AL4 39 H2
STHGT/OAK N14 78 D9
STMC/STPC BR5 207 M4
WOT/HER KT12 217 J1
Belgrave Crs SUN TW16 197 J1
Belgrave Gdns STHGT/OAK N14 78 E9
STJWD NW8 3 H6
Belgrave Mnr WOKS/MYFD GU22 232 B5
Belgrave Ms UX/CGN UB8 131 N6
Belgrave Ms South KTBR SW1X 16 D3
Belgrave Ms West KTBR SW1X 16 C3
Belgrave Pde SL * SL1 129 K9
Belgrave Pl KTBR SW1X 16 D4
Belgrave Rd BARN SW13 156 C6
HSLWW TW4 153 N9
IL IG1 122 D7
LEY E10 121 H6
MTCM CR4 201 N3
PIM SW1V 16 G6
PLSTW E13 141 P6
SL SL1 129 K9
SNWD SE25 203 N4
SUN TW16 197 J1
WALTH E17 120 F4
WAN E11 121 M6
Belgrave Sq KTBR SW1X 16 C3
Belgrave St WCHPL E1 140 C7
Belgrave Wk MTCM CR4 201 N3
Belgravia Cl BAR EN5 77 J7
Belgravia Gdns BMLY BR1 183 K9
Belgravia Ms KUT KT1 199 J4
Belgrove St CAMTN NW1 5 L9
Belham Rd KGLGY WD4 54 A4
Belinda Rd BRXN/ST SW9 159 J9
Belitha Vls IS N1 5 P3
Bellamy Cl ECT SW5 14 D8
EDGW HA8 95 P4
HGDN/ICK UB10 112 B8
WAT WD17 73 H5
Bellamy Dr STAN HA7 94 G9
Bellamy Rd CHES/WCR EN8 62 D5
CHING E4 100 G7
ENC/FH * EN2 79 L6
Bellamy St BAL SW12 180 C3
Bel La FELT TW13 175 M6
Bellasis Av BRXS/STRHM SW2 180 F4
Bell Av HARH RM3 105 J9
WDR/YW UB7 152 A2
Bell Bridge Rd CHERT KT16 195 J8
Bell Cl ABLGY WD5 54 G3
GRH DA9 188 E1
PIN HA5 113 K1
SLN SL2 129 N7
Bellclose Rd WDR/YW UB7 151 P1
Bell Common EPP CM16 65 H8
Bell Crs COUL/CHIP CR5 240 C7
Bell Dr WAND/EARL SW18 179 H3
Bellefield Rd STMC/STPC BR5 207 L5
Bellefields Rd BRXN/ST SW9 158 G9
Bellegrove Cl WELL DA16 163 J8
Bellegrove Rd WELL DA16 163 H8
Bellenden Rd PECK SE15 159 N8
Belle Staines Pleasaunce
CHING E4 100 F3
Belleville Rd BTSEA SW11 179 P1
Belle Vue GFD/PVL UB6 134 C3
Belle Vue Cl STA TW18 195 K1
Belle Vue La BUSH WD23 94 C2
Bellevue Pk THHTH CR7 203 K3
Belle Vue Pl SL * SL1 149 L2
Bellevue Pl WCHPL * E1 140 B6
Bellevue Rd BARN SW13 156 D8
BXLYHS DA6 186 A1
Belle Vue Rd CRW RM5 104 D7
Bellevue Rd EMPK RM11 125 N6
FBAR/BDGN N11 98 B5
KUT KT1 199 K3
Belle Vue Rd ORP BR6 226 D6
Bellevue Rd TOOT SW17 180 A3
Belle Vue Rd WALTH E17 101 J10
WARE SG12 26 D2
Bellevue Rd WEA W13 134 G6
Belle Vue Ter DEN/HRF * UB9 91 K8
Bellew St TOOT SW17 179 M6
Bell Farm Av DAGE RM10 124 D8
Bellfield CROY/NA CR0 224 E5
Bellfield Av KTN/HRWW/W HA3 94 C7
Bellfield Gdns HLWE CM17 47 M2
Bellfields Rd GU GU1 250 A8
Bell Gdns LEY * E10 120 F6
STMC/STPC BR5 207 M5
Bellgate HHNE HP2 35 P3
Bellgate Ms KTTN NW5 118 C9
Bell Gn HHS/BOV * HP3 52 E3
SYD SE26 182 D7
Bell Green La SYD SE26 182 E8
Bellhouse La BRW CM14 86 D9
Bell House Rd ROMW/RG RM7 124 D6

Bellina Ms KTTN NW5 118 C9
Bellingdon Rd CSHM HP5 50 G5
Bellingham Gn CAT SE6 182 F6
Bellingham Rd CAT SE6 183 H6
Bell La ABLGY WD5 55 H3
BERK HP4 33 K4
BRKMPK AL9 41 K10
BROX EN10 44 D7
CAN/RD E16 141 M10
HDN NW4 116 G2
HERT/WAS SG14 25 L5
HOD EN11 44 F3
LCOL/BKTW AL2 57 K5
LHD/OX KT22 236 C9
PEND EN3 80 C4
TWK TW1 176 F4
WBLY * HA9 115 J7
WCHPL E1 13 L4
WDSR SL4 148 E3
Bell Lane Cl LHD/OX KT22 236 C9
Bellman Av GVE DA12 191 H4
Bellmarsh Rd ADL/WDHM KT15 215 L1
Bell Md SBW CM21 29 P1
Bell Meadow GDST RH9 260 B8
NRWD SE19 181 M7
Bellmount Wood Av WAT WD17 72 F5
Belloc Cl CRAWE RH10 284 C6
Bello Cl BRXS/STRHM SW2 181 J4
Bellot St GNWCH SE10 161 K4
Bell Pde HSLW * TW3 154 A10
WWKM * BR4 205 H9
Bellring Cl BELV DA17 164 B5
Bell Rd E/WMO/HCT KT8 198 C5
ENC/FH EN2 79 L5
HSLW TW3 154 A10
The Bell Rbt LCOL/BKTW AL2 57 M3
Bells Hl BAR EN5 76 G9
SLN SL2 129 M3
Bells Hill Gn SLN SL2 129 M2
Bells La DTCH/LGLY SL3 150 E9
Bell St BAY/PAD W2 9 N3
REIG RH2 257 K10
SBW CM21 29 P1
WOOL/PLUM SE18 162 B7
Bellswood La IVER SL0 130 E7
Belltrees Gv STRHM/NOR SW16 180 G8
Bell Vw STALE/WH AL4 39 J6
WDSR SL4 148 E9
Bell View Cl WDSR SL4 148 E8
Bell Water Ga WOOL/PLUM SE18 162 D2
Bellwether La REDH RH1 277 J9
Bell Wharf La CANST EC4R 12 F8
Bellwood Rd PECK SE15 160 C10
Bell Yd LINN WC2A 12 A6
Belmont SLN SL2 128 F7
Belmont Av ALP/SUD HA0 135 L3
EBAR EN4 78 A9
ED N9 99 P2
GUW GU2 249 L7
NWDGN UB2 153 M2
NWMAL KT3 200 D5
PLMGR N13 98 F6
TOTM N17 119 K1
UPMR RM14 125 N7
WELL DA16 163 H8
Belmont Cir KTN/HRWW/W * HA3 94 G9
Belmont Cl CHING E4 101 J6
CLAP SW4 158 D9
EBAR EN4 78 A8
TRDG/WHET N20 97 L2
UX/CGN UB8 131 N1
WFD IG8 101 N5
Belmont Gv CHSWK W4 156 A3
LEW SE13 161 J9
Belmont Hl LEW SE13 161 J9
STAL AL1 38 C7
Belmont La CHST BR7 184 F7
STAN HA7 95 H8
Belmont Pde CHST * BR7 184 E8
GLDGN * NW11 117 J3
Belmont Pk LEW SE13 161 J10
Belmont Park Cl LEW SE13 161 K10
Belmont Park Rd LEY E10 120 G4
Belmont Ri BELMT SM2 221 J4
Belmont Rd BECK BR3 204 D2
BELMT SM2 221 K6
BUSH WD23 73 M8
CHST BR7 184 E8
CLAP SW4 158 D9
CSHM HP5 50 G5
ERITH DA8 164 B6
GRAYS RM17 167 L4
HCH RM12 125 L8
HHS/BOV HP3 35 P9
IL IG1 122 F8
KTN/HRWW/W HA3 114 E1
LHD/OX KT22 236 F8
REIG RH2 275 M1
SEVS/STOTM N15 119 K2
SNWD SE25 204 A5
UX/CGN UB8 131 N2
WHTN TW2 176 C5
WLGTN SM6 222 D2
Belmont St CAMTN NW1 4 D3
Belmont Ter CHSWK W4 156 A3
Belmor BORE WD6 75 M9
Belmore Av WOKS/MYFD GU22 232 G2
YEAD UB4 133 H8
Belmore La HOLWY * N7 118 E10
Belmore St VX/NE SW8 158 E7
Beloe Cl BARN SW13 156 D10
Belsham St HOM E9 140 B1
Belsize RKW/CH/CXG * WD3 52 G9
Belsize Av HAMP NW3 3 N1
PLMGR N13 98 G7
WEA W13 154 G2
Belsize Cl HHS/BOV HP3 36 B7
STALE/WH AL4 39 H1
Belsize Ct Garages HAMP NW3 117 N10
Belsize Crs HAMP NW3 117 N10
Belsize Gdns SUT SM1 221 L1
Belsize Gv HAMP NW3 3 P1
Belsize La HAMP NW3 3 L2
Belsize Ms HAMP NW3 3 M1
Belsize Pk HAMP NW3 3 L2
Belsize Park Gdns HAMP NW3 3 N1
Belsize Park Ms HAMP * NW3 3 M1
Belsize Pl HAMP NW3 117 N10
Belsize Rd HHS/BOV HP3 36 B7
KIL/WHAMP NW6 2 G5
KTN/HRWW/W HA3 94 C8
Belsize Sq HAMP NW3 3 M2
Belsize Ter HAMP NW3 3 M1
Belson Rd WOOL/PLUM SE18 162 C3
Belswains La HHS/BOV HP3 35 P10
Beltana Dr GVE DA12 191 H7
Beltane Dr WIM/MER SW19 178 G6
Belthorn Crs BAL SW12 180 D3
Beltinge Rd HARH RM3 125 N1
Beltona Gdns CHES/WCR EN8 62 C3
Belton Rd BERK HP4 33 M4
FSTGT E7 141 N2
SCUP DA14 185 K7
TOTM N17 119 M1
WAN E11 121 K9
WLSDN NW10 136 D1
Belton Wy BOW E3 140 F7
Beltran Rd FUL/PGN SW6 157 L8
Beltwood Rd BELV DA17 164 D3
Belvedere Av CLAY IG5 102 E10
WIM/MER SW19 179 H8
Belvedere Buildings STHWK SE1 18 D2
Belvedere Cl ESH/CLAY KT10 218 A2
GUW GU2 249 N8
GVE DA12 190 F4
TEDD TW11 176 D8
WEY KT13 216 B2
Belvedere Ct BELV DA17 164 A2
Belvedere Dr WIM/MER SW19 179 H8
Belvedere Gdns
E/WMO/HCT KT8 197 N5
LCOL/BKTW AL2 55 N3
Belvedere Gv WIM/MER SW19 179 H8
Belvedere Ms PECK SE15 160 B9
Belvedere Rd BH/WHM TN16 244 C4
BRW CM14 106 E4
BXLYHN DA7 164 A9
HNWL W7 154 D2
LEY E10 120 D6
NRWD SE19 181 N10
STHWK SE1 17 N1
THMD SE28 143 N10
Belvedere Sq WIM/MER SW19 179 H8
Belvedere Strd CDALE/KGS NW9 96 C10
The Belvedere WBPTN * SW10 157 M7
Belvedere Wy
KTN/HRWW/W HA3 115 K4
Belvoir Rd EDUL SE22 181 P3
Belvue Cl NTHLT UB5 133 P2
Belvue Rd NTHLT UB5 133 P2
Bembridge Cl KIL/WHAMP NW6 2 A3
Bembridge Gdns RSLP HA4 112 E7
Bembridge Pl GSTN * WD25 55 H9
Bemerton Est IS N1 5 N4
Bemerton St IS N1 5 N5
Bemish Rd PUT/ROE SW15 156 G9
Bempton Dr RSLP HA4 113 J7
Bemsted Rd WALTH E17 120 E1
Benares Rd WOOL/PLUM SE18 163 J3
Benbow Cl STAL AL1 38 G8
Benbow Moorings
UX/CGN * UB8 131 M7
Benbow Rd HMSMTH W6 156 E2
Benbow St DEPT SE8 160 F5
Benbow Wy UX/CGN UB8 131 M7
Benbrick Rd GUW GU2 267 M1
Benbury Cl BMLY BR1 183 H8
The Bence EGH TW20 194 E3
Bench Fld SAND/SEL CR2 223 N3
Benchleys Rd HHW HP1 35 J7
Bench Manor Crs CFSP/GDCR SL9 89 P10
The Bench RCHPK/HAM * TW10 177 H6
Bencombe Rd PUR/KEN CR8 223 H10
Bencroft CHESW EN7 61 P2
Bencroft Rd HHNE HP2 35 P6
STRHM/NOR SW16 180 D10
Bencurtis Pk WWKM BR4 205 J10
Bendall Ms CAMTN NW1 9 P3
Bendemeer Rd PUT/ROE SW15 156 G9
Bendish Rd EHAM E6 142 B2
Bendmore Av ABYW SE2 163 K4
Bendon Va WAND/EARL SW18 179 L3
Bendysh Rd BUSH WD23 73 M7
Benedict Cl ORP BR6 207 H10
Benedict Dr EBED/NFELT TW14 174 E3
Benedictine Ga CHES/WCR EN8 62 D3
Benedict Rd BRXN/ST SW9 158 G9
MTCM CR4 201 N3
Benedict Wy EFNCH * N2 117 M1
Benedict Whf MTCM CR4 201 P3
Benenden Gn HAYES BR2 205 M5
Benen-stock Rd
STWL/WRAY TW19 173 K2
Benets Rd EMPK RM11 125 P6
Benett Gdns STRHM/NOR SW16 202 F2
Benfleet Cl COB KT11 217 M8
SUT SM1 201 M10
Benfleet Wy FBAR/BDGN N11 98 B3
Benford Rd HOD EN11 44 E5
Bengal Rd IL IG1 122 E9
Bengarth Dr KTN/HRWW/W HA3 94 C10
Bengarth Rd NTHLT UB5 133 L3
Bengeo Mdw HERT/WAS * SG14 25 K2
Bengeo Ms HERT/WAS * SG14 25 K2
Bengeo St HERT/WAS SG14 25 K4
Bengeworth Rd HRW HA1 114 F7
Ben Hale Cl STAN HA7 94 F6
Benham Cl BTSEA SW11 157 N9
CHSGTN KT9 219 H3
COUL/CHIP CR5 241 J4
CSHM HP5 50 F6
Benham Gdns HSLWW TW4 175 N1
Benham Rd HNWL W7 134 D7
Benhams Dr HORL RH6 280 B2
Benhill Av SUT SM1 221 L1
Benhill Rd CMBW SE5 159 L6
SUT SM1 201 N10
Benhill Wood Rd SUT SM1 201 M10
Benhilton Gdns SUT SM1 201 L10
Benhurst Av HCH RM12 125 J9
Benhurst Cl SAND/SEL CR2 224 C6
Benhurst Gdns SAND/SEL CR2 224 B6
Benhurst La STRHM/NOR SW16 181 H8
Benin St LEW SE13 183 J3
Benjafield Cl UED N18 100 A5
Benjamin Cl CRAWE RH10 284 E9
EMPK RM11 125 H4
HACK E8 7 P6
Benjamin St FARR EC1M 12 C3
Ben Jonson Rd WCHPL E1 140 C7
Benledi St POP/IOD E14 141 J8
Bennelong Cl SHB W12 136 E9
Benner La CHOB/PIR GU24 212 E8
Bennerley Rd BTSEA SW11 179 P1
Bennet Cl KUT KT1 199 H1
Bennetsfield Rd STKPK UB11 132 C10
Bennet's Hl BLKFR * EC4V 12 D7
Bennett Cl BRKMPK AL9 23 J9
COB KT11 217 H9
NTHWD HA6 92 G8
WELL DA16 163 K8
Bennett Gv LEW SE13 160 G7
Bennett Pk BKHTH/KID SE3 161 L9
Bennett Rd CHDH RM6 123 P4
PLSTW E13 141 P6
Bennetts CSHM HP5 51 J6
Bennetts Av CROY/NA CR0 204 D9
GFD/PVL UB6 134 D3
Bennett's Castle La BCTR RM8 123 M9
Bennetts Cl MTCM CR4 202 C1
SL SL1 128 F10
STALE/WH AL4 40 A9
TOTM N17 99 N7
Bennetts Copse CHST BR7 184 B9
Bennetts End Cl HHS/BOV * HP3 36 A8
Bennetts End Rd HHS/BOV HP3 36 A7
Bennetts Farm Pl GT/LBKH KT23 253 N1
Bennett St CHSWK W4 156 B5
WHALL SW1A 10 G9
Bennetts Wy CROY/NA CR0 204 D9
Bennetts Yd UX/CGN * UB8 131 N2
Bennett Wy RDART DA2 188 C7
RGUE GU4 251 K5
Benning Cl WDSR SL4 148 C9
Benningholme Rd EDGW HA8 96 B7
Bennington Rd TOTM N17 99 M9
WFD * IG8 101 K8
Bennions Cl HCH RM12 145 L1
Bennison Dr HARH RM3 105 L10
Benn St HOM E9 140 D1
Benrek Cl BARK/HLT IG6 102 F8
Bensbury Cl PUT/ROE SW15 178 E3
Bensham Cl THHTH CR7 203 K4
Bensham Gv THHTH CR7 203 K2
Bensham La CROY/NA CR0 203 J7
Bensham Manor Rd THHTH CR7 203 K4
Benskin Rd WATW WD18 73 H9
Benskins La ABR/ST RM4 105 L2
Ben Smith Wy BERM/RHTH SE16 19 P3
Benson Av PLSTW E13 141 P4
Benson Cl HSLW TW3 153 P10
SLN SL2 129 M10
UX/CGN UB8 131 P7
Benson Quay WAP E1W 140 B9
Benson Rd CROY/NA CR0 203 H10
FSTH SE23 182 B4
GRAYS RM17 167 N5
Benthall Gdns PUR/KEN CR8 241 K2
Benthal Rd STNW/STAM N16 119 N7
Bentham Av WOKN/KNAP GU21 214 F10
Bentham Rd HOM E9 140 C1
THMD SE28 143 L10
Ben Tillet Cl BARK IG11 143 K2
CAN/RD * E16 142 C10
Bentinck Cl CFSP/GDCR SL9 110 A3
Bentinck Ms MHST W1U 10 D5
Bentinck Rd WDR/YW UB7 131 N10
Bentinck St MHST W1U 10 D5
Bentley Cl HART DA3 211 P3
Bentley Dr GNTH/NBYPK IG2 122 F4
HLWE CM17 47 M2
WEY KT13 216 B5
Bentley Heath La BAR EN5 77 H1
Bentley Ms WCHMH N21 79 L10
Bentley Pk SL SL1 128 C4
Bentley Rd HERT/WAS SG14 24 F4
IS N1 7 K2
SL SL1 128 E10
Bentley's Meadow
BGR/WK TN15 247 N6
Bentley St GVE DA12 190 F2
Bentley Wy STAN HA7 94 F6
WFD IG8 101 M4
Benton Rd IL IG1 122 G6
OXHEY WD19 93 L6
Bentons WAB * EN9 45 K8
Benton's La WNWD SE27 181 K7
Benton's Ri WNWD SE27 181 L8
Bentry Cl BCTR RM8 123 P7
Bentry Rd BCTR RM8 123 P7
Bentsbrook Cl RDKG RH5 272 G6
Bentsbrook Pk RDKG RH5 272 G6
Bentsbrook Rd RDKG RH5 272 G6
Bentsley Cl STALE/WH AL4 38 G2
Bentworth Rd SHB W12 136 E8
Benwell Ct SUN * TW16 197 H1
Ben Well Rd CHOB/PIR GU24 230 E6
Benwell Rd CHOB/PIR GU24 230 F5
HOLWY N7 119 H9
Benwick Cl BERM/RHTH SE16 160 A3
Benworth St BOW E3 140 E5
Benyon Pth SOCK/AV RM15 147 H4
Benyon Rd IS N1 7 H5
Beomonds Rw CHERT * KT16 195 K7
Berberis Cl GU GU1 249 P8
Berberis Wk WDR/YW UB7 151 P3
Berber Rd BTSEA * SW11 180 A1
Berceau Wk WAT WD17 72 F5
Bercta Rd ELTH/MOT SE9 184 F5
Berecroft HLWS CM18 46 G5
Beredens La RBRW/HUT CM13 106 E10
Berefield HHNE HP2 35 N4
Berenger Wk WBPTN * SW10 157 N6
Berens Rd STMC/STPC BR5 207 M5
WLSDN NW10 136 G5
Berens Wy CHST BR7 207 J4
Beresford Av ALP/SUD HA0 135 M3
BRYLDS KT5 199 N8
HNWL W7 134 C7
SLN SL2 129 P9
TRDG/WHET N20 98 A3
TWK TW1 177 H2
Beresford Dr BMLY BR1 206 A3
WFD IG8 101 P5
Beresford Gdns CHDH RM6 123 P3
EN EN1 79 M8
HSLWW TW4 175 N1
Beresford Rd BELMT SM2 221 J4
CEND/HSY/T N8 119 H3
CHING E4 101 K2
DORK RH4 272 G2
EFNCH N2 117 P1
GVW DA11 190 B3
HBRY N5 119 L10
HRW HA1 114 C3
KUTN/CMB KT2 199 L1
NWMAL KT3 199 P4
RKW/CH/CXG WD3 91 J2
STAL AL1 39 H7
STHL UB1 133 L10
WALTH E17 100 G9
Beresford St WOOL/PLUM SE18 162 E2
Beresford Ter HBRY N5 119 K10
Berestede Rd HMSMTH W6 156 C4
Bere St WAP E1W 140 C9
Bergenia Ct CHOB/PIR GU24 212 D9
Berger Cl STMC/STPC BR5 206 G6
Berger Rd HOM E9 140 C1
Berghem Ms WKENS W14 156 G2
Bergholt Av REDBR IG4 122 B3
Bergholt Crs STNW/STAM N16 119 M5
Bergholt Ms CAMTN NW1 5 H4
Bericot Wy WGCE AL7 23 M4
Bering Wk CAN/RD E16 142 A8
Berisford Ms WAND/EARL SW18 179 M2
Berkeley Av CLAY IG5 102 D10
CRW RM5 104 D8
CSHM HP5 50 E5
GFD/PVL UB6 134 D1
HEST TW5 153 H7
WELL DA16 163 N7
Berkeley Cl ABLGY WD5 54 G8
BORE WD6 75 M9
CSHM HP5 50 F6
KUTN/CMB KT2 177 K10
ORP BR6 207 H7
POTB/CUF EN6 59 H8
RSLP HA4 113 H8
STWL/WRAY TW19 172 G5
UPMR RM14 126 A7
WARE SG12 26 B1
Berkeley Ct RKW/CH/CXG * WD3 72 E9
WEY KT13 196 E9
WLGTN SM6 202 D10
Berkeley Crs DART DA1 187 N4
EBAR EN4 77 N9
Berkeley Dr E/WMO/HCT KT8 197 N3
EMPK RM11 125 P6
WDSR SL4 170 A4
Berkeley Gdns BF/WBF KT14 215 J10
ESH/CLAY KT10 218 F4
WCHMH N21 99 L1
WOT/HER KT12 196 G7
Berkeley Ms MBLAR W1H 10 B5
SUN TW16 197 K3
Berkeley Pl EPSOM KT18 238 A1
WIM/MER SW19 178 G9
Berkeley Rd BARN SW13 156 D7
CDALE/KGS NW9 115 M2
CEND/HSY/T N8 118 E3
HGDN/ICK UB10 132 D2
MNPK E12 122 B10
SEVS/STOTM N15 119 L4
Berkeley Sq MYFR/PICC W1J 10 F8
The Berkeleys LHD/OX KT22 236 D10
SNWD * SE25 203 P4
Berkeley St MYFR/PICC W1J 10 F8
Berkeley Ter TIL * RM18 168 D6
Berkeley Waye HEST TW5 153 M6
Berkhampstead Rd BELV DA17 164 B4
CSHM HP5 51 H6
Berkhamsted Av WBLY HA9 135 L1
Berkhamsted Rd HHW HP1 34 G4
Berkley Av CHES/WCR EN8 62 C10
Berkley Cl STALE/WH AL4 39 H2
WHTN * TW2 176 D6
Berkley Ct GU GU1 250 B10
Berkley Gv CAMTN NW1 4 C4
Berkley Pl CHES/WCR * EN8 62 C10
Berkley Rd BEAC HP9 88 C5
CAMTN NW1 4 B4
GVE DA12 190 E2
Berkley Rw GVE * DA12 190 E2
Berks Hl RKW/CH/CXG WD3 70 F9
Berkshire Av SL SL1 128 G8
Berkshire Cl CTHM CR3 241 L8
Berkshire Gdns PLMGR N13 99 H7
UED N18 100 A6
Berkshire Rd HOM E9 140 E1
Berkshire Wy EMPK RM11 125 P3
MTCM CR4 202 F4
Bermans Wy WLSDN NW10 116 B9
Bermer Rd WATN WD24 73 K5
Bermondsey St STHWK SE1 13 J10
Bermondsey Wall East
BERM/RHTH SE16 19 P2
Bermondsey Wall West
BERM/RHTH SE16 19 N1
Bermuda Rd TIL RM18 168 D8
Bernal Cl THMD SE28 143 N9
Bernard Ashley Dr CHARL SE7 161 N4
Bernard Av WEA W13 154 G2
Bernard Cassidy St
CAN/RD * E16 141 L7
Bernard Gdns WIM/MER SW19 179 J8
Bernard Gv WAB EN9 62 G9
Bernard Rd ROMW/RG RM7 124 D5
SEVS/STOTM N15 119 N3
WLGTN SM6 222 C2
Bernards Cl BARK/HLT IG6 102 F8
Bernard St BMSBY WC1N 11 L2
GVE DA12 190 E2
STALW/RED AL3 38 C5
Bernays Cl STAN HA7 95 H7
Bernay's Gv BRXN/ST SW9 158 G10
Bernel Dr CROY/NA CR0 204 E10
Berne Rd THHTH CR7 203 J5
Berners Cl SL SL1 128 D9
Berners Dr STAL AL1 38 C9
WEA W13 134 F9
Berners Ms FITZ W1T 11 H4
Berners Pl FITZ W1T 11 H5
Berners Rd IS N1 6 C6
WDGN N22 99 H9
Berners St FITZ W1T 11 H4
Berners Wy BROX EN10 44 E9
Berner Ter WCHPL * E1 13 N6
Berney Rd CROY/NA CR0 203 L7
Bernhart Cl EDGW HA8 95 P8
Bernice Cl RAIN RM13 145 K6
Bernwell Rd CHING E4 101 K4
Berridge Gn EDGW HA8 95 M8
Berridge Ms KIL/WHAMP NW6 117 K10
Berridge Rd NRWD SE19 181 L8
The Berries STALE/WH AL4 38 F2
Berriman Rd HOLWY N7 118 G8
Berrington Dr EHSLY KT24 234 G10
Berriton Road RYLN/HDSTN HA2 113 N6
Berry Av WATN WD24 73 J2
Berrybank Cl CHING E4 101 H3
Berry Cl HCH RM12 125 K10
RKW/CH/CXG WD3 91 L1
WCHMH N21 99 J2
WLSDN NW10 136 B2
Berry Cottages POP/IOD * E14 140 D8
Berrydale Rd YEAD UB4 133 M6
Berry Fld SLN SL2 129 P8
Berryfield Cl BMLY BR1 206 B1
Berry Field Cl WALTH E17 120 G2
Berry Field Pk AMS HP6 68 G3
Berryfield Rd WALW SE17 18 D7
Berry Grove La BUSH WD23 73 M4
Berrygrove La GSTN WD25 73 P5
Berryhill ELTH/MOT SE9 162 E10
Berry Hl STAN HA7 95 J5
Berryhill Gdns ELTH/MOT SE9 162 E10
Berrylands BRYLDS KT5 199 M5
HART DA3 211 M6
ORP BR6 207 M10
RYNPK SW20 200 F3
Berrylands Rd BRYLDS KT5 199 L6
Berry La DUL SE21 181 L7
RGUW GU3 231 J10
RKW/CH/CXG WD3 70 G10
RKW/CH/CXG WD3 91 L2
Berryman Cl BCTR RM8 123 M8
Berryman's La SYD SE26 182 C7
Berrymead HHNE HP2 36 A4
Berry Meade ASHTD KT21 237 L3
Berrymead Gdns ACT W3 135 P10
Berrymede Rd CHSWK W4 156 A2
Berry Pl FSBYE EC1V 6 D10
Berryscroft Rd STA TW18 173 M10
Berry's Green Rd BH/WHM TN16 244 E2
Berry's Hl BH/WHM TN16 244 E1
Berry's La BF/WBF KT14 215 N7
Berry St FSBYE EC1V 12 D2
Berry Wk ASHTD KT21 237 L5
Berry Wy EA W5 155 K2
RKW/CH/CXG WD3 91 L1
Bersham La GRAYS RM17 167 L3
Bertal Rd TOOT SW17 179 N7
Berther Rd EMPK RM11 125 M5
Berthold Ms WAB EN9 62 G9
Berthons Gdns WALTH * E17 121 J3
Berthon St DEPT SE8 160 F6
Bertie Rd SYD SE26 182 C9
WLSDN NW10 136 D1
Bertram Rd EN EN1 79 P8
HDN NW4 116 D4
KUTN/CMB KT2 177 M10
Bertram St KTTN NW5 118 C8
Bertrand St LEW SE13 160 G9
Bertrand Wy THMD SE28 143 L9
Bert Rd THHTH CR7 203 K5
Bert Wy EN EN1 79 N8
Berwick Av SL SL1 128 G9
YEAD UB4 133 L8
Berwick Cl BEAC HP9 88 G10
CHES/WCR EN8 62 F10
STAN HA7 94 E7
Berwick Crs BFN/LL DA15 185 H2
Berwick La CHONG CM5 66 F9
Berwick Pond Cl RAIN RM13 145 L4
Berwick Pond Rd RAIN RM13 145 M4
UPMR RM14 145 N1
Berwick Rd BORE WD6 75 L4
CAN/RD E16 141 N8
RAIN RM13 145 L4
WDGN N22 99 J9
WELL DA16 163 L7
Berwick St SOHO/CST W1F 11 H6
Berwick Wy RSEV TN14 247 J7
Berwyn Av HSLW TW3 154 A7
Berwyn Rd HNHL SE24 181 J4
RCHPK/HAM TW10 155 N10
Beryl Av EHAM E6 142 B7
Beryl Rd HMSMTH W6 156 G4
Berystede KUTN/CMB KT2 177 N10
Besant Cl CRICK * NW2 117 H8
Besant Rd CRICK NW2 117 H9
Besant Wy WLSDN NW10 115 P10
Besley St STRHM/NOR SW16 180 D9
Bessant Dr RCH/KEW TW9 155 N7
Bessborough Pl PIM SW1V 17 J8
Bessborough Rd HRW HA1 114 C6
PUT/ROE SW15 178 D4
Bessborough St PIM SW1V 17 J7
Bessels Green Rd SEV TN13 246 E9
Bessels Meadow SEV TN13 246 E10
Bessemer Rd CMBW SE5 159 K8
WGCE AL7 23 J3
WGCW AL8 23 H1
Bessie Lansbury Cl EHAM E6 142 D8
Bessingby Rd RSLP HA4 113 H7
Besson St NWCR SE14 160 C7
Bessy St BETH * E2 140 B5
Bestobell Rd SL SL1 129 H8
Best Ter SWLY * BR8 208 D5
Bestwood St DEPT SE8 160 C3
Beswick Ms HAMP * NW3 3 H1
KIL/WHAMP NW6 117 L10
Betam Rd HYS/HAR UB3 152 E1
Beta Rd CHOB/PIR GU24 213 L6
WOKS/MYFD GU22 232 E2
Beta Wy EGH TW20 194 F1
Betchworth Cl SUT SM1 221 N2
Betchworth Rd GDMY/SEVK IG3 123 H7
Betchworth Wy CROY/NA CR0 225 H5
Betenson Av SEV TN13 246 G8
Betham Rd GFD/PVL UB6 134 C5
Bethany Pl WOKN/KNAP * GU21 232 A4
Bethany Waye
EBED/NFELT TW14 174 F3
Bethecar Rd HRW HA1 114 D3
Bethell Av CAN/RD E16 141 L6
IL IG1 122 D5
Bethel Rd SEV TN13 247 K9
WELL DA16 163 M9
Bethersden Cl BECK BR3 182 E10
Bethnal Green Rd BETH E2 13 M1
Bethune Av FBAR/BDGN N11 98 A5
Bethune Cl CRAWE RH10 284 E8
Bethune Rd STNW/STAM N16 119 L5
WLSDN NW10 136 A6
Bethwin Rd CMBW SE5 159 J6
Betjeman Cl CHESW EN7 61 P4
COUL/CHIP CR5 240 G3
HARP * AL5 20 B2
RYLN/HDSTN HA2 113 P2
Betjeman Ct WDR/YW * UB7 131 N10
Betjeman Wy CHONG CM5 67 N2
HHW HP1 35 L4
Betley Ct WOT/HER KT12 197 J10
Betony Cl CROY/NA CR0 204 C8
Betoyne Av CHING E4 101 K5
Betsham Rd ERITH DA8 164 G6
MEO DA13 189 J8
SWCM DA10 189 K3
Betstyle Rd FBAR/BDGN N11 98 C5
Betterton Dr SCUP DA14 185 P5
Betterton Rd RAIN RM13 144 F4
Betterton St LSQ/SEVD WC2H 11 L6
Bettles Cl UX/CGN UB8 131 M4
Bettons Pk SRTFD E15 141 K3
Bettridge Rd FUL/PGN SW6 157 J8
Betts Cl BECK BR3 204 D2
Betts La WAB EN9 45 P7
Betts Rd CAN/RD E16 141 N8
Betts St WCHPL * E1 140 A9
Betts Wy CRAWE RH10 283 N3
PGE/AN SE20 204 A2
THDIT KT7 198 G8
Betula Cl PUR/KEN CR8 241 L1
Betula Ter CHES/WCR * EN8 62 D8
Between Streets COB KT11 217 J10
Beulah Av THHTH * CR7 203 K2
Beulah Cl EDGW HA8 95 N4
Beulah Crs THHTH CR7 203 K2
Beulah Gv CROY/NA CR0 203 K6
Beulah Hl NRWD SE19 181 L10
Beulah Rd EPP CM16 65 K5
HCH RM12 125 K8
SUT SM1 221 K1
THHTH CR7 203 K3
WALTH E17 120 G3
WIM/MER SW19 179 J10
Beulah Wk CTHM CR3 242 D6
Beult Rd DART DA1 165 H9
Bevan Av BARK IG11 143 K2

Bevan Cl HHS/BOV HP3 35 N8
Bevan Ct CROY/NA CR0 223 H2
Bevan Hl CSHM HP5 50 G5
Bevan House WATN WD24 73 L6
Bevan Pk EW KT17 220 C7
Bevan Pl SWLY BR8 208 G4
Bevan Rd ABYW SE2 163 L4
EBAR EN4 78 A8
Bevans Cl GRH DA9 189 H2
Bevan St IS N1 6 F6
Bevan Wy HCH RM12 125 N8
Bev Callender Cl VX/NE SW8 158 C9
Bevenden St IS N1 7 H9
Beveridge Rd WLSDN NW10 136 B2
Beverley Av BFN/LL DA15 185 J3
HSLWW TW4 153 N10
RYNPK SW20 200 C1
Beverley Cl ADL/WDHM KT15 215 N2
BARN SW13 156 D8
BTSEA SW11 157 N10
CHSGTN KT9 219 H1
EMPK RM11 125 N5
EW KT17 220 F7
WCHMH N21 99 K2
WEY KT13 196 F9
Beverley Ct BROCKY SE4 160 E9
Beverley Crs WFD IG8 101 N9
Beverley Dr EDGW HA8 115 M1
Beverley Gdns BARN SW13 156 C9
CHESW EN7 61 N7
EMPK RM11 125 M5
GLDGN NW11 117 H5
STALE/WH AL4 39 J2
STAN HA7 94 F9
WBLY HA9 115 L6
WGCE AL7 23 M5
WPK KT4 200 D8
Beverley Hts REIG RH2 257 L8
Beverley La KUTN/CMB KT2 178 B10
Beverley Ms CRAWE RH10 284 B8
Beverley Rd BARN SW13 156 C9
BXLYHN DA7 164 D8
CHING E4 101 J7
CHSWK W4 156 C4
CTHM CR3 241 M3
DAGW RM9 123 P9
EHAM E6 142 A5
HAYES BR2 206 B9
KUT KT1 199 H1
MTCM CR4 202 E4
NWDGN UB2 153 M3
NWMAL KT3 200 D4
PGE/AN SE20 204 A2
RSLP HA4 113 J7
SUN TW16 196 G1
WPK KT4 200 F9
Beverley Wy NWMAL KT3 200 C1
Beverley Wy (Kingston By-Pass)
NWMAL KT3 200 C1
Beverly Cl BROX EN10 44 D7
The Beverly MRDN SM4 200 G6
Beversbrook Rd ARCH N19 118 E8
Beverstone Rd
BRXS/STRHM SW2 180 G1
THHTH CR7 203 H4
Beverston Ms MBLAR W1H 10 A4
Bevill Cl SNWD SE25 203 P3
Bevin Cl BERM/RHTH SE16 140 D10
Bevington Rd BECK BR3 204 G2
NKENS W10 8 B3
Bevington St BERM/RHTH SE16 19 P2
Bevin Rd YEAD UB4 133 H5
Bevin Sq TOOT SW17 180 A6
Bevin Wy FSBYW WC1X 6 A8
Bevis Cl RDART DA2 188 B3
Bevis Marks HDTCH EC3A 13 K5
Bewbush Dr CRAWW RH11 283 J10
Bewcastle Gdns ENC/FH EN2 78 F8
Bewdley Cl HARP AL5 20 C5
Bewdley St IS N1 6 A3
Bewick Ms PECK SE15 160 A6
Bewick St VX/NE SW8 158 C8
Bewley Cl CHES/WCR EN8 62 C7
Bewley St WCHPL E1 140 A9
Bewlys Rd WNWD SE27 181 J8
Bexhill Cl FELT TW13 175 M5
Bexhill Dr GRAYS RM17 167 K5
Bexhill Rd BROCKY SE4 182 E2
FBAR/BDGN N11 98 E6
MORT/ESHN SW14 155 P9
Bexley Cl DART DA1 186 F1
Bexley Gdns CHDH RM6 123 L3
ED N9 99 L4
Bexley High St BXLY DA5 186 B3
Bexley La DART DA1 186 F1
SCUP DA14 185 M7
Bexley Rd ELTH/MOT SE9 184 F1
ERITH DA8 164 D6
Bexley St WDSR SL4 148 G7
Beyers Gdns HOD EN11 26 F10
Beyers Prospect HOD EN11 26 F10
Beyers Ride HOD EN11 26 F10
Beynon Rd CAR SM5 222 A2
Bianca Rd PECK SE15 19 M10
Bibsworth Rd FNCH N3 97 J10
Bibury Cl PECK SE15 19 K10
Bicester Rd RCH/KEW TW9 155 M9
Bickenhall St MHST W1U 10 B3
Bickersteth Rd TOOT SW17 180 A9
Bickerton Rd KTTN NW5 118 C7
Bickley Crs BMLY BR1 206 B4
Bickley Park Rd BMLY BR1 206 C3
Bickley Rd BMLY BR1 206 A2
LEY E10 120 G5
Bickley St TOOT SW17 179 P8
Bicknell Rd CMBW SE5 159 K9
Bickney Wy LHD/OX KT22 236 B8
Bicknoller Cl BELMT SM2 221 L6
Bicknoller Rd EN EN1 79 N5
Bicknor Rd ORP BR6 207 H7
Bidborough Cl HAYES BR2 205 L5
Bidborough St STPAN WC1H 5 L10
Biddenden Wy ELTH/MOT SE9 184 D7
Biddenham Turn GSTN WD25 73 K1
Bidder St CAN/RD E16 141 K7
Biddestone Rd HOLWY N7 118 G9
Biddles Cl SL SL1 128 D10
Biddulph Rd MV/WKIL W9 3 H10
SAND/SEL CR2 223 K5
Bideford Av GFD/PVL UB6 134 G5
Bideford Cl EDGW HA8 95 M9
FELT TW13 175 N6
HARH RM3 105 K9
Bideford Gdns EN EN1 99 M1
Bideford Rd BMLY BR1 183 L6
PEND EN3 80 E4
RSLP HA4 113 J8
WELL DA16 163 L6
Bideford Sp SLN SL2 128 G5
Bidhams Crs
KWD/TDW/WH KT20 238 F7
Bidwell Gdns FBAR/BDGN N11 98 D9
Bidwell St PECK * SE15 160 A7
The Bield REIG RH2 275 K2
Big Common La REDH RH1 259 J9
Biggerstaff Rd SRTFD E15 141 H3
Biggerstaff St FSBYPK N4 119 H7
Biggin Av MTCM CR4 202 A1
Biggin Cl CRAWW RH11 283 M9
Biggin Hl STRHM/NOR SW16 181 J10
Biggin La GRAYS RM17 168 E5
Biggin Wy NRWD SE19 181 J10
Bigginwood Rd
STRHM/NOR SW16 181 J10
Biggs Grove Rd CHESW EN7 61 M3
Bigg's Rw PUT/ROE SW15 156 G9
Bigland St WCHPL E1 140 A8
Bignell Rd WOOL/PLUM SE18 162 E4
Bignells Cnr POTB/CUF EN6 58 E10
Bignold Rd FSTGT E7 121 M9
Bigwood Rd GLDGN NW11 117 L4
Biko Cl UX/CGN UB8 131 M8
Bilberry Cl CRAWW RH11 283 L10
Billesden Rd CHOB/PIR GU24 230 B7
Billet La BERK HP4 33 M3
EMPK RM11 125 L6
IVER SL0 130 E5
Billet Rd CHDH RM6 123 M1
WALTH E17 100 C9
Billetts Hart Cl HNWL W7 154 D1
Bill Hamling Cl ELTH/MOT SE9 184 C5
Billingford Cl BROCKY SE4 160 C10
Billing Pl WBPTN * SW10 157 L6
Billing Rd WBPTN SW10 157 L6
Billings HART DA3 211 L6
Billings Cl DAGW RM9 143 M2
Billing St WBPTN * SW10 157 L6
Billington Rd NWCR SE14 160 C6
Billinton Dr CRAWE RH10 284 C7
Billiter Sq FENCHST * EC3M 13 K6
Billiter St FENCHST EC3M 13 K6
Billockby Cl CHSGTN KT9 219 L3
Billson St POP/IOD E14 161 H3
Billy Lows La POTB/CUF EN6 59 L7
Bilton Rd ERITH DA8 165 H6
GFD/PVL UB6 134 G3
Bilton Wy HYS/HAR UB3 153 J1
PEND EN3 80 E5
Bina Gdns ECT SW5 15 J6
Bincote Rd ENC/FH EN2 78 G7
Binden Rd SHB W12 156 C2
Binfield Rd BF/WBF KT14 215 P8
SAND/SEL CR2 223 N2
VX/NE SW8 158 F7
Bingfield IS N1 5 M5
Bingfield St IS N1 5 N5
Bingham Cl HHW HP1 35 J4
SOCK/AV RM15 146 G8
Bingham Ct IS * N1 6 D3
Bingham Dr STA TW18 173 N10
WOKN/KNAP GU21 231 L4
Bingham Pl MHST W1U 10 C2
Bingham Rd CROY/NA CR0 203 P8
Bingham St IS N1 6 G1
Bingley Rd CAN/RD E16 141 P8
GFD/PVL UB6 134 B6
HOD EN11 45 H3
SUN TW16 175 H10
Binney Ct CRAWE RH10 284 E4
Binney St MYFR/PKLN W1K 10 D7
Binns Rd CHSWK W4 156 B4
Binscombe RGODL GU7 267 J9
Binscombe Crs RGODL GU7 267 K10
Binscombe La RGODL GU7 267 J9
Binsey Wk ABYW SE2 163 M1
Binstead Cl CRAWW RH11 283 L5
YEAD UB4 133 M7
Binyon Crs STAN HA7 94 E6
Birbetts Rd ELTH/MOT SE9 184 C5
Birchall La HERT/WAS SG14 23 P7
Birchall Wd WGCE * AL7 23 M6
WGCE AL7 23 M6
Birchanger Rd SNWD SE25 203 P5
Birch Av CTHM CR3 241 L10
PLMGR N13 99 K4
WDR/YW UB7 132 A8
Birch Cir RGODL GU7 267 L9
Birch Cl ADL/WDHM KT15 215 N5
AMS HP6 69 K3
BKHH IG9 102 A4
BTFD TW8 154 G6
CAN/RD E16 141 K7
EYN DA4 209 L10
HART DA3 211 P2
HSLW TW3 154 C9
IVER SL0 130 G4
ROMW/RG RM7 124 C1
RPLY/SEND GU23 251 J1
SEV TN13 247 J9
SOCK/AV RM15 147 J6
TEDD TW11 176 F8
WOKN/KNAP GU21 231 P5
Birch Copse LCOL/BKTW AL2 55 M6
Birch Crs EMPK RM11 125 M2
HGDN/ICK UB10 132 A3
SOCK/AV RM15 147 J5
Birchcroft Cl CTHM CR3 259 K1
Birchdale CFSP/GDCR SL9 110 A6
Birchdale Cl BF/WBF KT14 215 M7
Birchdale Gdns CHDH RM6 123 N5
Birchdale Rd FSTGT E7 121 P10
Birchdene Dr THMD SE28 143 K10
Birch Dr HAT AL10 40 D5
RKW/CH/CXG WD3 90 G6
Birchen Cl CDALE/KGS NW9 116 A7
Birchend Cl SAND/SEL CR2 223 L3
Birchen Gv CDALE/KGS NW9 116 A7
Birchen La BANK EC3V 13 H6
Bircherley Ct HERT/WAS * SG14 25 L5
Bircherley St HERT/WAS SG14 25 L5
Birches Cl EPSOM KT18 238 B1
MTCM CR4 202 A3
PIN HA5 113 M3
The Birches BUSH WD23 74 B9
CHARL SE7 161 N5
CMBW * SE5 159 M9
CRAWE RH10 284 B6
EHSLY KT24 252 F2
EPP CM16 66 C2
HHS/BOV HP3 35 J9
HSLWW * TW4 175 N3
ORP BR6 226 D1
RBRW/HUT CM13 107 K4
STHGT/OAK N14 78 G10
SWLY BR8 208 F2
WOKS/MYFD GU22 232 C4
Birchfield Cl ADL/WDHM KT15 215 L1
COUL/CHIP CR5 240 G2
Birchfield Est HORL * RH6 282 G1
Birchfield Gv EW KT17 220 F6
Birchfield Rd CHES/WCR EN8 62 A5
Birchfield St POP/IOD E14 140 F9
Birch Gdns AMSS HP7 69 K5
DAGE RM10 124 D8
Birchgate Ms
KWD/TDW/WH * KT20 238 F7
Birch Gn HHW HP1 35 J5
STA TW18 173 J7
Birchgrove COB KT11 217 K10
Birch Gv ACT W3 135 M10
GU * GU1 249 P7
KWD/TDW/WH KT20 239 J10
LEE/GVPK SE12 183 L3
POTB/CUF EN6 59 K8
SHPTN TW17 196 F2
SL SL1 128 G7
WAN E11 121 K8
WDSR SL4 148 C7
WELL DA16 163 K10
WOKS/MYFD GU22 232 G1
Birch Hl CROY/NA CR0 224 C2
Birchin Cross Rd BGR/WK TN15 229 P10
RSEV TN14 247 M1
Birchington Cl BXLYHN DA7 164 C7
Birchington Rd BRYLDS KT5 199 L7
CEND/HSY/T N8 118 E4
KIL/WHAMP NW6 2 F5
WDSR SL4 148 F8
Birchlands Av BAL SW12 180 A3
Birch La CHOB/PIR GU24 212 C8
HHS/BOV HP3 52 E9
PUR/KEN CR8 222 F7
Birch Lea CRAWE RH10 284 B4
Birch Leys HHNE HP2 36 D1
Birch Md HAYES BR2 206 D9
Birchmead WAT WD17 72 G4
Birchmead Av PIN HA5 113 K2
Birchmead Cl STALW/RED * AL3 38 C3
Birchmore Wk HBRY N5 119 K8
Birch Pk KTN/HRWW/W HA3 94 B8
Birch Pl GRH DA9 188 D2
Birch Platt CHOB/PIR GU24 212 C9
Birch Rd BERK HP4 33 J2
BFOR GU20 212 D3
FELT TW13 175 L8
RGODL GU7 267 L9
ROMW/RG RM7 124 C1
Birch Rw HAYES BR2 206 D7
Birch Tree Av WWKM BR4 225 L2
Birch Tree Gv CSHM HP5 51 N6
Birch Tree Wk WAT WD17 72 G3
Birch Tree Wy CROY/NA CR0 204 A9
Birch V COB KT11 217 P9
Birch Wk BORE * WD6 75 M5
MTCM CR4 202 C1
Birch Wy CSHM HP5 51 J5
HARP AL5 20 B3
LCOL/BKTW AL2 57 J3
WARL CR6 242 D4
Birchway HAT AL10 40 D2
HYS/HAR UB3 133 H10
REDH RH1 276 C2
Birchwood RAD WD7 57 M10
Birchwood Av BECK BR3 204 E4
CAR SM5 202 B10
HAT AL10 40 D2
MUSWH N10 118 B1
SCUP DA14 185 L6
Birchwood Cl CRAWE RH10 284 D10
HAT AL10 40 D2
HORL RH6 280 C3
MRDN SM4 201 L4
RBRW/HUT * CM13 107 H7
Birchwood Ct EDGW HA8 95 P10
Birchwood Dr BF/WBF KT14 215 K8
HAMP NW3 117 L8
LTWR GU18 212 B6
RDART DA2 186 F7
Birchwood Gv HPTN TW12 175 P9
Birchwood La CTHM CR3 259 J1
RSEV TN14 246 A1
Birchwood Park Av SWLY BR8 208 F3
Birchwood Rd ADL/WDHM KT15 215 K8
RDART DA2 186 F7
STMC/STPC BR5 206 G4
TOOT SW17 180 C8
Birchwood Ter SWLY * BR8 208 D1
Birchwood Wy LCOL/BKTW AL2 56 A4
Birdbrook Cl DAGE RM10 144 D2
RBRW/HUT CM13 87 N10
Birdbrook Rd BKHTH/KID SE3 161 P9
Birdcage Wk STJSPK SW1H 17 H2
Birdcroft Rd WGCW AL8 22 G6
Birdham Cl BMLY BR1 206 B5
CRAWW RH11 283 L5
Bird House La ORP BR6 226 D10
Birdhurst Av SAND/SEL CR2 223 L1
Birdhurst Gdns SAND/SEL CR2 223 L1
Birdhurst Ri SAND/SEL CR2 223 M2
Birdhurst Rd SAND/SEL CR2 223 M2
WAND/EARL SW18 157 M10
WIM/MER SW19 179 P9
Birdie Wy HERT/BAY SG13 26 A4
Bird in Bush Rd PECK SE15 159 P6
Bird-in-Hand La BMLY BR1 206 A2
Bird-in-Hand Pas FSTH * SE23 182 B5
Bird La RBRW/HUT CM13 107 H10
UPMR RM14 126 C3
Birdlip Cl PECK SE15 19 J10
Birds Cl WGCE AL7 23 L7
Birds Farm Av ROMW/RG RM7 104 C9
Birdsfield La HOM E9 140 E3
Birds Gv WOKN/KNAP GU21 230 G4
Birds Hill Dr LHD/OX KT22 218 C9
Birds Hill Ri LHD/OX KT22 218 C9
Birds Hill Rd LHD/OX KT22 218 C8
Bird St MHST W1U 10 D6
Birdswood Dr WOKN/KNAP GU21 231 K5
Bird Wk WHTN TW2 175 N4
Birdwood Cl SAND/SEL CR2 224 B7
TEDD TW11 176 D7
Birkbeck Av ACT W3 135 P9
GFD/PVL UB6 134 B3
Birkbeck Gv ACT W3 136 A10
Birkbeck Hl DUL SE21 181 J5
Birkbeck Ms ACT * W3 136 A9
HACK E8 119 N10
Birkbeck Pl DUL SE21 181 J4
Birkbeck Rd ACT W3 136 A10
BECK BR3 204 C2
CEND/HSY/T N8 118 F2
EA W5 155 H3
ENC/FH EN2 79 L4
GNTH/NBYPK IG2 122 G3
HACK E8 119 N10
MLHL NW7 96 C6
NFNCH/WDSP N12 97 M6
ROMW/RG RM7 124 E6
SCUP DA14 185 K6
TOTM N17 99 N9
WIM/MER SW19 179 L8
Birkbeck St BETH E2 140 A5
Birkbeck Wy GFD/PVL UB6 134 C3
Birkdale Av HARH RM3 105 P8
PIN HA5 113 P1
Birkdale Cl BERM/RHTH * SE16 160 A4
ORP BR6 206 G7
Birkdale Dr CRAWW RH11 282 G8
Birkdale Gdns CROY/NA CR0 224 C1
OXHEY WD19 93 L4
Birkdale Rd ABYW SE2 163 K3
EA W5 135 K6
Birkenhead Av KUTN/CMB KT2 199 L2
Birkenhead St IS N1 5 M9
Birkett Wy CSTG HP8 70 A7
Birkhall Rd CAT SE6 183 J4
Birkheads Rd REIG RH2 257 K9
Birklands La STAL AL1 38 G10
Birklands Pk STAL * AL1 38 G10
Birkwood Cl BAL SW12 180 E3
Birley Rd SL SL1 129 J8
TRDG/WHET N20 97 M3
Birley St BTSEA SW11 158 B8
Birling Rd ERITH DA8 164 E6
Birnam Rd HOLWY N7 118 G7
Birnham Cl RPLY/SEND GU23 233 K10
Birse Crs WLSDN NW10 116 B9
Birstal Gn OXHEY WD19 93 L5
Birstall Rd SEVS/STOTM N15 119 M3
Biscay Rd HMSMTH W6 156 G4
Biscoe Cl HEST TW5 153 P5
Biscoe Wy LEW * SE13 161 J10
Bisenden Rd CROY/NA CR0 203 M9
Bisham Cl CRAWE RH10 284 E10
MTCM CR4 202 A7
Bisham Gdns HGT N6 118 B6
Bishop Butt Cl ORP BR6 207 J10
Bishop Cl RCHPK/HAM TW10 177 J6
Bishop Duppas Pk SHPTN TW17 196 E7
Bishop Fox Wy E/WMO/HCT KT8 197 N4
Bishop Ken Rd
KTN/HRWW/W HA3 94 E10
Bishop Kings Rd WKENS * W14 14 B5
WKENS W14 14 B5
Bishop Rd STHGT/OAK N14 98 C1
Bishops Av BMLY BR1 205 P3
BORE WD6 75 L9
CHDH RM6 123 M4
FUL/PGN SW6 156 G8
NTHWD HA6 92 F5
PLSTW E13 141 N3
The Bishops Av EFNCH N2 117 N4
Bishop's Bridge Rd BAY/PAD W2 9 H5
Bishops Cl BAR EN5 76 G10
CHSWK W4 155 P4
COUL/CHIP CR5 241 H4
ELTH/MOT SE9 184 F5
EN EN1 80 A6
HAT AL10 40 C4
HGDN/ICK UB10 132 B4
STALE/WH AL4 38 F2
SUT SM1 201 K10
WALTH E17 120 G2
Bishops Ct CHES/WCR * EN8 62 A6
GRH DA9 188 D1
STP EC4M 12 C5
Bishops Dr EBED/NFELT TW14 174 E2
NTHLT UB5 133 M3
Bishops Farm Cl WDSR SL4 148 A8
Bishopsfield HLWS CM18 47 H4
Bishopsford Rd MRDN SM4 201 M7
Bishopsgate LVPST EC2M 13 J4
Bishopsgate Ar LVPST EC2M 13 J4
Bishopsgate Rd WDSR SL4 171 M6
Bishops Gn BMLY * BR1 205 P1
Bishops Gv BFOR GU20 212 B3
EFNCH N2 117 N4
HPTN TW12 175 N7
Bishop's Hall KUT KT1 199 J2
Bishop's Hall Rd BRWN CM15 86 G10
Bishops Hl WOT/HER KT12 197 H7
Bishops Md CMBW * SE5 159 K6
HHW HP1 35 L8
Bishopsmead Cl EHSLY KT24 252 G4
HOR/WEW KT19 220 A6
Bishopsmead Dr EHSLY KT24 252 G5
Bishops Orch SLN SL2 128 G5
Bishop's Park Rd FUL/PGN SW6 156 G8
STRHM/NOR SW16 202 F1
Bishop's Pl SUT SM1 221 M2
Bishops Ri HAT AL10 40 C8
Bishop's Rd CROY/NA CR0 203 J7
FUL/PGN SW6 157 J7
HGT N6 118 B4
HNWL W7 154 D1
SL SL1 149 M1
UX/CGN UB8 132 D8
Bishops Ter LBTH * SE11 18 B5
LBTH SE11 18 B5
Bishopsthorpe Rd SYD SE26 182 B7
Bishop St IS N1 6 E5
Bishops Wk BRWN CM15 107 L3
CHST BR7 206 F1
CROY/NA CR0 224 C2
Bishop's Wy BETH E2 140 B4
EGH TW20 172 G9
Bishops Wd WOKN/KNAP GU21 231 L3
Bishopswood Rd HGT N6 118 A5
Bishop Wy WLSDN NW10 136 B2
Biskra WAT WD17 73 H5
Bisley Cl CHES/WCR EN8 62 C9
WPK KT4 200 F8
Bispham Rd WLSDN NW10 135 L5
Bisson Rd SRTFD E15 141 H4
Bistern Av WALTH E17 121 J1
Bitmead Cl CRAWW * RH11 283 H8
Bittacy Cl MLHL NW7 96 G7
Bittacy Hl MLHL NW7 96 G7
Bittacy Park Av MLHL NW7 96 G7
Bittacy Ri MLHL NW7 96 G7
Bittacy Rd MLHL NW7 96 G7
Bittams La CHERT KT16 214 G1
Bittern Cl CHESW EN7 61 J1
CRAWW RH11 282 G8
YEAD UB4 133 L7
Bitterne Dr WOKN/KNAP GU21 231 L3
Bittern Pl WDGN * N22 98 G10
Bittern St STHWK SE1 18 E2
The Bit AMSS * HP7 68 E10
Bittoms Ct KUT * KT1 199 J3
The Bittoms KUT KT1 199 J3
Bixley Cl NWDGN UB2 153 N3
Black Acre Cl AMSS HP7 69 K5
Blackacre Rd EPP CM16 83 H3
Blackall St SDTCH EC2A 13 J1
Blackberry Cl GU GU1 249 N7
SHPTN TW17 196 F4
Blackberry Farm Cl HEST TW5 153 M6
Blackberry Fld STMC/STPC BR5 207 K1
Blackbird Hl CDALE/KGS NW9 115 P7
Blackbirds La GSTN WD25 56 B10
Blackbird Yd BETH E2 7 M9
Blackborne Rd DAGE RM10 144 B1
Blackborough Cl REIG RH2 257 M10
Blackborough Rd REIG RH2 257 N10
Black Boy La SEVS/STOTM N15 119 K3
Black Boy Wd LCOL/BKTW AL2 55 P6
Blackbridge Rd
WOKS/MYFD GU22 232 A6
Blackbrook La HAYES BR2 206 D5
Blackbrook Rd RDKG RH5 273 K7
Blackburne's Ms MYFR/PKLN W1K 10 C7
Blackburn Rd KIL/WHAMP NW6 2 G2
The Blackburn GT/LBKH KT23 235 N10
Blackbury Cl POTB/CUF EN6 59 M7
Blackbush Av CHDH RM6 123 N3
Blackbush Cl BELMT SM2 221 L4
Blackbush Spring HLW CM20 29 K10
Blackcap Cl CRAWW RH11 283 M9
Black Cut STAL AL1 38 D7
Blackdale CHESW EN7 61 P3
Black Ditch Rd WAB * EN9 81 H2
Black Ditch Wy WAB EN9 80 G2
Black Dog Wk CRAWE RH10 283 P5
Blackdown Av
WOKS/MYFD GU22 233 H1
Blackdown Cl EFNCH N2 97 M10
WOKS/MYFD GU22 232 F2
Blackdown Ter
WOOL/PLUM * SE18 162 C7
Black Eagle Cl BH/WHM TN16 262 F3
Blackenham Rd TOOT SW17 180 A7
Blackett Cl EGH TW20 195 H2
Blackett Rd CRAWE RH10 284 D8
Blackett St PUT/ROE SW15 156 G9
Blacketts Wood Dr
RKW/CH/CXG WD3 70 E8
Black Fan Cl ENC/FH EN2 79 K5
Black Fan Rd WGCE AL7 23 M6
WGCE AL7 23 J4
Blackfen Pde BFN/LL * DA15 185 K2
Blackfen Rd BFN/LL DA15 185 J1
Blackfold Rd CRAWE RH10 284 B8
Blackford Cl SAND/SEL CR2 223 J5
Blackford Rd OXHEY WD19 93 L6
Blackfriars Br EMB EC4Y 12 C7
Black Friars La BLKFR EC4V 12 C6
Blackfriars Pas BLKFR EC4V 12 C7
Blackfriars Rd STHWK SE1 12 C9
Blackfriars U/P BLKFR EC4V 12 D7
Blackhall La BGR/WK TN15 247 M9
Blackheath CRAWE RH10 284 E5
Blackheath Av GNWCH SE10 161 J6
Blackheath Gv BKHTH/KID SE3 161 L8
SHGR GU5 268 E9
Blackheath Hl GNWCH SE10 161 H7
Blackheath La SHGR GU5 268 F9
SHGR GU5 269 L7
Blackheath Pk BKHTH/KID SE3 161 L9
Blackheath Ri LEW SE13 161 H8
Blackheath Rd GNWCH SE10 160 G7
Blackheath V BKHTH/KID SE3 161 K8
Blackhills ESH/CLAY KT10 217 N5
Black Horse Av CSHM HP5 51 J9
Black Horse Cl WDSR SL4 148 C8
Black Horse Ct STHWK * SE1 19 H4
Blackhorse Crs AMS HP6 69 K4
Blackhorse La CROY/NA CR0 203 P7
EPP CM16 66 E1
POTB/CUF EN6 58 A6
REIG RH2 257 L5
WALTH E17 100 C10
Black Horse Pde PIN * HA5 113 J3
Black Horse Pl UX/CGN UB8 131 L3
Black Horse Rd SCUP DA14 185 K7
Blackhorse Rd DEPT SE8 160 D5
WALTH E17 120 C2
WOKS/MYFD GU22 231 J6
Blacklands Dr YEAD UB4 132 D6
Blacklands Meadow REDH RH1 258 F9
Blacklands Rd CAT SE6 183 H7
Blacklands Ter CHEL SW3 16 A6
Blackley Cl WAT WD17 72 G3
Black Lion Ct HLWE * CM17 29 M7
Black Lion Ga KENS W8 9 H8
Black Lion Hl RAD WD7 57 K8
Black Lion La HMSMTH W6 156 D3
Blackmans Cl DART DA1 187 K4
Blackman's La WARL CR6 225 K10
Blackmans Yd BETH * E2 13 M1
Blackmead SEV TN13 246 F7
Blackmoor La WATW WD18 72 E9
Blackmore Av STHL UB1 134 C10
Blackmore Ct WAB EN9 63 M9
Blackmore Crs
WOKN/KNAP GU21 214 F10
Blackmore Rd BKHH IG9 102 B1
BRWN CM15 86 G1
GRAYS RM17 167 P4
Blackmore's Gv TEDD TW11 176 F9
Blackmore Wy UX/CGN UB8 131 N1
Blackness Cottages HAYES * BR2 226 A5
Blackness La HAYES BR2 226 A5
WOKS/MYFD GU22 232 B5
Blacknest Rd ASC SL5 193 J3
Black Park Rd DTCH/LGLY SL3 130 C4
Blackpond La SLN SL2 128 G3
Blackpool Gdns YEAD UB4 132 F6
Blackpool Rd PECK SE15 160 A8
Black Prince Cl BF/WBF KT14 216 A10
Black Prince Rd LBTH SE11 17 N6
Black Rod Cl HYS/HAR UB3 152 G2
Blackshaw Rd TOOT SW17 179 N8
Blackshots La CDH/CHF RM16 147 P9
Blacksmith Cl ASHTD KT21 237 L5
CHDH RM6 123 M4
Blacksmith La RGUE GU4 268 F5
Blacksmith Rw DTCH/LGLY SL3 150 D3
Black Smiths Cl WARE SG12 26 F4
Blacksmiths Hl SAND/SEL CR2 224 A9
Blacksmiths La CHERT KT16 195 K7
DEN/HRF UB9 110 G7
RAIN RM13 144 G3
STA TW18 195 L3
STALW/RED AL3 38 A6
STMC/STPC BR5 207 M5
Blacksmiths Wy SBW CM21 29 L2
Black's Rd HMSMTH W6 156 F4
Blackstock Rd FSBYPK N4 119 J7
Blackstone Cl REIG RH2 275 P1
Blackstone Est HACK E8 7 P3
Blackstone Hl REDH RH1 257 P10
Blackstone Rd CRICK NW2 116 F10
Blackstroud La East LTWR GU18 212 C7
Blackstroud La West LTWR GU18 212 C7
Black Swan Ct WARE * SG12 26 C2
Black Swan Yd STHWK SE1 19 J1
Blacks Yd SEV * TN13 265 J1
Blackthorn Av WDR/YW UB7 152 B3

Blackthorn Cl CRAWW RH11 283 M5
GSTN WD25 55 J8
REIG RH2 275 M2
STALE/WH AL4 39 H3
Blackthorn Ct HEST TW5 153 M6
Blackthorn Dell DTCH/LGLY SL3 149 P2
Blackthorn Dr LTWR GU18 212 A8
Blackthorne Av CROY/NA CR0 204 B8
Blackthorne Cl HAT AL10 40 C7
Blackthorne Crs DTCH/LGLY SL3 151 H8
Blackthorne Dr CHING E4 101 J5
Blackthorne Rd DTCH/LGLY SL3 151 H9
GT/LBKH KT23 254 B2
Blackthorn Gv BXLYHN DA7 163 P9
Blackthorn Pl GU * GU1 249 P7
Blackthorn Rd BH/WHM TN16 244 B2
CDH/CHF RM16 147 N10
REIG RH2 275 M2
WGCE AL7 23 K6
Blackthorn St BOW E3 140 F6
Blackthorn Wy BRW CM14 107 J6
Blacktree Ms BRXN/ST * SW9 159 H9
Blackwall La GNWCH SE10 161 K4
Blackwall Tunnel Northern Ap
BOW E3 140 G5
Blackwall Wy POP/IOD E14 141 H9
Blackwater Cl RAIN RM13 144 E7
Blackwater La CRAWE RH10 284 D8
HHS/BOV HP3 36 F9
Blackwater St EDUL SE22 181 N1
Blackwell Av GUW GU2 249 J10
Blackwell Cl CLPT E5 120 D9
KTN/HRWW/W HA3 94 C8
Blackwell Dr OXHEY WD19 73 K10
Blackwell Gdns EDGW HA8 95 M5
Blackwellhall La CSHM HP5 51 P7
Blackwell Hall La CSHM HP5 51 P9
Blackwell Rd KGLGY WD4 54 B5
Blackwood Cl BF/WBF KT14 215 M8
Blackwood St WALW SE17 18 G7
Bladen Cl WEY KT13 216 E3
Blades Cl LHD/OX KT22 237 J6
Bladindon Dr BXLY DA5 185 N3
Bladon Cl GU GU1 250 D9
Bladon Gdns RYLN/HDSTN HA2 114 A4
Blagden's La STHGT/OAK N14 98 E3
Blagdon Rd LEW SE13 182 G2
NWMAL KT3 200 C4
Blagdon Wk TEDD TW11 177 H9
Blagrove Rd NKENS W10 8 B4
Blair Av CDALE/KGS NW9 116 B5
ESH/CLAY KT10 198 B9
Blair Cl BFN/LL DA15 185 H1
HYS/HAR UB3 153 H3
IS N1 6 F1
Blairderry Rd BRXS/STRHM SW2 180 F5
Blair Dr SEV TN13 247 J9
Blairhead Dr OXHEY WD19 93 J4
Blair Rd SL SL1 129 K10
Blair St POP/IOD E14 141 H8
Blake Av BARK IG11 143 H3
Blake Cl CAR SM5 201 P8
RAIN RM13 144 G3
STAL AL1 38 F9
WELL DA16 163 H7
Blakeden Dr ESH/CLAY KT10 218 E4
Blake Gdns DART DA1 165 N10
FUL/PGN SW6 157 K7
Blakehall Rd CAR SM5 222 A3
Blake Hall Rd CHONG CM5 67 H2
WAN E11 121 M6
Blakemere Rd WGCW AL8 22 G3
Blakemore Rd
STRHM/NOR SW16 180 F6
THHTH CR7 202 G5
Blakemore Wy BELV DA17 163 P2
Blakeney Av BECK BR3 204 E1
Blakeney Cl CAMTN NW1 5 J7
HACK E8 119 P10
HOR/WEW KT19 220 A7
NTHLT/WHET N20 97 M2
Blakeney Rd BECK BR3 204 E1
Blaker Ct CHARL * SE7 161 P6
Blake Rd CAN/RD E16 141 L6
CROY/NA CR0 203 M9
FBAR/BDGN N11 98 D8
MTCM CR4 201 P3
Blaker Rd SRTFD E15 141 H3
Blakes Av NWMAL KT3 200 C5
Blakes Cl NKENS W10 136 F7
Blake's Gn WWKM BR4 205 H7
Blakes La NWMAL KT3 200 C5
RGUE GU4 252 A7
Blakesley Av EA W5 135 H8
Blake's Rd PECK SE15 159 M6
PECK * SE15 159 M6
Blakes Ter NWMAL KT3 200 D5
Blakesware Gdns WCHMH N21 99 L1
Blakewood Cl FELT TW13 175 K7
Blanchard Cl ELTH/MOT SE9 184 B6
Blanchard Gv WAB EN9 80 G4
Blanchard Ms HARH RM3 105 N8
Blanchards Hl RGUE GU4 250 B3
Blanchard Wy HACK E8 7 P2
Blanch Cl PECK SE15 160 B6
Blanchedowne CMBW SE5 159 L10
Blanche La POTB/CUF EN6 58 C10
Blanche St CAN/RD E16 141 L6
Blanchland Rd MRDN SM4 201 L5
Blanchman's Rd WARL CR6 242 D4
Blandfield Rd BAL SW12 180 B2
Blandford Av BECK BR3 204 D2
WHTN TW2 176 A4
Blandford Cl CROY/NA CR0 202 F10
DTCH/LGLY SL3 150 A2
EFNCH N2 117 M3
ROMW/RG RM7 124 C2
WOKS/MYFD GU22 232 E3
Blandford Crs CHING E4 101 H1
Blandford Rd BECK BR3 204 C2
CHSWK W4 156 B2
EA W5 155 J1
NWDGN UB2 153 P3
STAL AL1 38 F5
TEDD TW11 176 C8
Blandford Rd North
DTCH/LGLY SL3 150 A2
Blandford Rd South
DTCH/LGLY SL3 150 A2
Blandford Sq CAMTN NW1 9 P2
Blandford St MHST W1U 10 B5
Blandford Waye YEAD UB4 133 K8
Bland St ELTH/MOT SE9 162 A10
Blaney Crs EHAM E6 142 E5
Blanford Rd REIG RH2 275 M1
Blanks La HORL RH6 278 D4
Blanmerle Rd ELTH/MOT SE9 184 E4
Blann Cl ELTH/MOT SE9 184 A2
Blantyre St WBPTN SW10 157 N6
Blantyre Wk WBPTN * SW10 157 N6
Blashford St LEW SE13 183 J3
Blattner Cl BORE WD6 75 K8
Blawith Rd HRW HA1 114 D2
Blaydon Cl RSLP HA4 112 F5
TOTM * N17 100 A8
Blaydon Wk TOTM N17 100 A8
Blays Cl EGH TW20 171 P9
Blay's La EGH TW20 171 N9
Bleak Hill La WOOL/PLUM SE18 163 J5
Blean Gv PGE/AN SE20 182 B10
Bleasdale Av GFD/PVL UB6 134 F4
Blechynden St NKENS * W10 136 G9
Bledlow Cl THMD SE28 143 M9
Bledlow Ri GFD/PVL UB6 134 B4
Bleeding Heart Yd HCIRC * EC1N 12 B4
Blegborough Rd
STRHM/NOR SW16 180 D9
Blencarn Cl WOKN/KNAP GU21 231 M2
Blendon Dr BXLY DA5 185 N2
Blendon Rd BXLY DA5 185 N2
Blendon Ter WOOL/PLUM SE18 162 F4
Blendworth Wy PECK SE15 159 M6
Blenheim CDALE/KGS * NW9 96 C10
Blenheim Av GNTH/NBYPK IG2 122 D4
Blenheim Cl BF/WBF KT14 215 J9
CRAWE RH10 284 E3
DART DA1 187 K2
GFD/PVL * UB6 134 C4
OXHEY WD19 93 K1
ROMW/RG RM7 124 D2
RYNPK SW20 200 F3
SBW CM21 29 L3
UPMR RM14 126 D6
WCHMH N21 99 K2
WLGTN SM6 222 D4
Blenheim Ct BFN/LL DA15 184 G6
WFD IG8 101 N8
WGCE AL7 23 J4
Blenheim Crs NTGHL W11 8 A7
RSLP HA4 112 E7
SAND/SEL CR2 223 K4
Blenheim Dr WELL DA16 163 J7
Blenheim Gdns
BRXS/STRHM SW2 180 G2
CRICK NW2 116 F10
KUTN/CMB KT2 177 N10
SAND/SEL CR2 223 P8
SOCK/AV RM15 146 A10
WBLY HA9 115 K8
WLGTN SM6 222 D3
WOKS/MYFD GU22 231 N5
Blenheim Gv GVE DA12 190 F3
PECK SE15 159 N8
Blenheim Pde HGDN/ICK * UB10 132 C6
Blenheim Park Rd
SAND/SEL CR2 223 K5
Blenheim Pas STJWD * NW8 3 J7
Blenheim Ri SEVS/STOTM * N15 119 N2
Blenheim Rd BAR EN5 76 G7
BFN/LL DA15 185 M4
BRWN CM15 86 F10
CHSWK W4 156 B2
DART DA1 187 K2
DTCH/LGLY SL3 150 A3
EHAM E6 142 A5
FSTGT E7 121 K9
GSTN WD25 55 H9
HAYES BR2 206 B4
HOR/WEW KT19 220 A7
NTHLT UB5 134 A1
ORP BR6 207 M9
PGE/AN SE20 182 B10
RYLN/HDSTN HA2 114 A4
RYNPK SW20 200 F3
STAL AL1 38 E5
STJWD NW8 3 K7
SUT SM1 201 K10
WALTH E17 120 C1
Blenheim St MYFR/PKLN W1K 10 E6
Blenheim Ter STJWD NW8 3 J7
Blenheim Wy EPP CM16 66 B3
ISLW TW7 154 F7
Blenkarne Rd BTSEA SW11 180 A2
Blenkin Cl STALW/RED AL3 38 B2
Bleriot Rd HEST TW5 153 K6
Blessbury Rd EDGW HA8 95 P9
Blessington Rd LEW SE13 161 J10
Blessing Wy BARK IG11 143 M4
Bletchingley Cl REDH RH1 258 D5
Bletchingley Rd GDST RH9 259 P7
REDH RH1 258 D5
Bletchingly Cl THHTH CR7 203 J4
Bletchley St IS N1 6 F8
Bletchmore Cl HYS/HAR UB3 152 E4
Bletsoe Wk IS N1 6 F7
Bligh Cl CRAWE RH10 284 A9
Bligh Rd GVW DA11 190 D2
Blighs Ct SEV * TN13 265 J1
Bligh's Rd SEV TN13 265 J1
Blighs Wk SEV * TN13 265 J1
Blincoe Cl WIM/MER SW19 178 G5
Blinco La DTCH/LGLY SL3 130 B8
Blindley Rd CRAWE RH10 284 E4
Blindman's La CHES/WCR EN8 62 C6
Blissett St GNWCH SE10 161 H7
Bliss Ms NKENS * W10 2 B9
Blisworth Cl YEAD UB4 133 M6
Blithbury Rd DAGW RM9 143 L1
Blithdale Rd ABYW SE2 163 K3
Blithfield St KENS W8 14 G4
Blockhouse Rd GRAYS RM17 167 P5
Blockley Rd ALP/SUD HA0 114 G7
Bloemfontein Av SHB W12 136 E10
Bloemfontein Rd SHB W12 136 E9
Blomfield Rd BAY/PAD W2 9 H3
Blomfield St LVPST EC2M 13 H4
Blomfield Vls BAY/PAD W2 9 H4
Blomville Rd BCTR RM8 123 P7
Blondell Cl WDR/YW UB7 151 N5
Blondel St BTSEA SW11 158 B8
Blondin Av EA W5 155 H3
Blondin St BOW E3 140 F4
Bloomfield Cl WOKN/KNAP GU21 231 K4
Bloomfield Crs GNTH/NBYPK IG2 122 E4
Bloomfield Pl MYFR/PKLN W1K 10 F7
Bloomfield Rd CHESW EN7 61 K1
HAYES BR2 206 A5
HGT N6 118 B4
KUT KT1 199 K4
WOOL/PLUM SE18 162 E4
Bloomfield Ter BGVA SW1W 16 D7
Bloom Gv WNWD SE27 181 J6
Bloomhall Rd NRWD SE19 181 L8
Bloom Park Rd FUL/PGN SW6 157 J6
Bloomsbury Cl EA W5 135 L9
HOR/WEW KT19 220 A6
Bloomsbury Pl NOXST/BSQ WC1A 11 M4
Bloomsbury Sq NOXST/BSQ WC1A 11 M4
Bloomsbury St RSQ WC1B 11 K4
Bloomsbury Wy
NOXST/BSQ WC1A 11 L4
Blore Cl VX/NE SW8 158 E7
Blossom Cl DAGW RM9 143 A3
EA W5 155 K1
SAND/SEL CR2 223 N2
Blossom La ENC/FH EN2 79 K5
Blossom St WCHPL E1 13 K3
Blossom Wy HGDN/ICK UB10 132 A2
WDR/YW UB7 152 B3
Blossom Waye HEST TW5 153 M5
Blount St POP/IOD E14 140 D8
Bloxam Gdns ELTH/MOT SE9 184 B1
Bloxhall Rd LEY E10 120 E6
Bloxham Crs HPTN TW12 197 N1
Bloxworth Cl WLGTN SM6 202 D10
Blucher Rd CMBW SE5 159 K6
Blucher St CSHM HP5 50 G7
Blue Anchor La BERM/RHTH SE16 19 P5
TIL RM18 169 H3
Blue Anchor Yd WCHPL E1 13 N7
Blue Ball La EGH TW20 172 C8
Blue Ball Yd WHALL SW1A 10 G10
Blue Barn Wy WEY KT13 216 B7
Bluebell Av FSTGT E7 122 A10
MNPK E12 122 B10
Bluebell Cl CRAWW * RH11 283 L10
HERT/BAY SG13 25 P5
HHW * HP1 35 H7
HOM E9 140 B3
MTCM CR4 202 C8
ORP BR6 206 F9
ROMW/RG RM7 124 F7
SYD SE26 181 N7
Bluebell Ct WOKS/MYFD GU22 232 A5
Bluebell Dr ABLGY WD5 54 G3
CHESW EN7 61 L4
Bluebell La EHSLY KT24 252 F5
Bluebell Ri LTWR GU18 212 A7
Bluebell Wy IL IG1 142 E1
Blueberry Cl STALW/RED AL3 38 C2
WFD IG8 101 M7
Blueberry Gdns COUL/CHIP CR5 240 G2
Blueberry La RSEV TN14 245 M2
Bluebird La DAGE RM10 144 B2
Bluebird Wy LCOL/BKTW AL2 55 N6
THMD SE28 162 G1
Bluebridge Av BRKMPK AL9 59 H3
Blue Bridge Rd BRKMPK AL9 59 H3
Blue Cedars BNSTD SM7 220 G10
Blue Cedars Pl COB KT11 217 L8
Bluecoats Av HERT/WAS SG14 25 L5
Bluecoat Yd WARE SG12 26 C2
Bluefield Cl HPTN TW12 175 P8
Bluegates EW KT17 220 D4
Bluehouse Gdns OXTED RH8 261 M4
Bluehouse Hill STALW/RED AL3 37 P7
Bluehouse La OXTED RH8 261 K4
Bluehouse Rd CHING E4 101 K4
Bluemans EPP CM16 48 E10
Bluemans End EPP CM16 48 E10
Blue Riband Est CROY/NA * CR0 203 J9
Bluett Rd LCOL/BKTW AL2 57 J3
Bluewater Pkwy GRH DA9 188 E3
Blumfield Crs SL SL1 128 C6
Blundel La COB KT11 218 A10
COB KT11 235 N2
Blundell Av HORL RH6 280 A4
Blundell Cl STALW/RED AL3 38 C2
Blundell Rd EDGW * HA8 96 B8
Blundell St HOLWY N7 5 M3
Blunden Cl BCTR RM8 123 M6
Blunden Dr DTCH/LGLY SL3 150 E3
Blunesfield POTB/CUF EN6 59 N7
Blunt Rd CROY/NA CR0 223 L2
Blunts Av WDR/YW UB7 152 B6
Blunts La LCOL/BKTW AL2 37 L10
Blunts Rd ELTH/MOT SE9 184 D1
Blurton Rd CLPT E5 120 C9
Blyth Cl BORE WD6 75 L5
TWK TW1 176 E2
Blythe Cl CAT SE6 182 E3
IVER SL0 131 J8
Blythe Hl FSTH SE23 182 E3
STMC/STPC BR5 207 J1
Blythe Hill La FSTH SE23 182 E3
Blythe Hill Pl FSTH * SE23 182 D3
Blythe Ms WKENS * W14 156 G2
Blythe Rd HOD EN11 45 J5
WKENS W14 156 G2
Blythe V FSTH SE23 182 E4
Blyth Rd BMLY BR1 205 L1
HYS/HAR UB3 152 F1
THMD SE28 143 M9
WALTH E17 120 E5
Blyth's Whf POP/IOD * E14 140 D9
Blythswood Rd GDMY/SEVK IG3 123 K6
Blyth Wk UPMR RM14 126 D5
Blythway WGCE AL7 23 J2
Blythwood Rd FSBYPK N4 118 F5
PIN HA5 93 K9
Blyton Cl BEAC HP9 88 C7
Boadicea St IS N1 5 N6
Boakes Meadow RSEV TN14 228 G7
Boardman Av CHING E4 80 G9
Boardman Cl BAR EN5 77 H9
Board School Rd
WOKN/KNAP GU21 232 C2
Boardwalk Pl POP/IOD E14 141 H10
Boar Hl RDKG RH5 272 D8
Boarlands Cl SL SL1 128 E9
Boathouse Wk PECK SE15 159 N6
Boat Lifter Wy
BERM/RHTH SE16 160 D3
Bob Anker Cl PLSTW E13 141 M5
Bobbin Cl CLAP SW4 158 D9
Bobbingworth Mill CHONG CM5 49 H10
Bob Marley Wy HNHL SE24 159 H10
Bockhampton Rd
KUTN/CMB KT2 177 L10
Bocking St HACK E8 140 A3
Boddicott Cl WIM/MER SW19 179 H5
Bodell Cl CDH/CHF RM16 167 N1
Bodiam Cl CRAWE RH10 284 D7
EN EN1 79 L6
Bodiam Rd STRHM/NOR SW16 202 E1
Bodle Av SWCM DA10 189 K2
Bodley Cl EPP CM16 65 J6
NWMAL KT3 200 B5
Bodley Rd NWMAL KT3 200 B6
Bodmin Av SL SL1 128 F7
Bodmin Cl RYLN/HDSTN HA2 113 N8
STMC/STPC BR5 207 M8
Bodmin Gv MRDN SM4 201 L4
Bodmin St WAND/EARL SW18 179 K4
Bodnant Gdns RYNPK SW20 200 E3
Bodney Rd CLPT E5 120 A10
Bodwell Cl HHW HP1 35 K5
Boeing Wy NWDGN UB2 153 J2
Bognor Gdns OXHEY * WD19 93 K6
Bognor Rd WELL DA16 163 N7
Bohemia HHNE HP2 35 P5
Bohemia Pl HACK E8 140 B1
Bohun Gv EBAR EN4 77 P10
Boileau Rd BARN SW13 156 D6
EA W5 135 L8
Bois Av AMS HP6 68 G2
Bois Hall Rd ADL/WDHM KT15 215 N2
Bois Hl CSHM HP5 51 J10
Bois La AMS HP6 69 J2
Bois Ml CSHM * HP5 69 M2
Bois Moor Rd CSHM HP5 51 H10
Boissy Cl STALE/WH AL4 39 K7
Bolden St DEPT SE8 160 G8
Boldero Pl STJWD * NW8 9 N2
Bolderwood Wy WWKM BR4 204 G9
Bolding House La
CHOB/PIR GU24 212 E9
Boldmere Rd PIN HA5 113 K5
Boleyn Av EN EN1 80 A5
EW KT17 220 D6
Boleyn Cl CDH/CHF RM16 167 L2
CRAWE RH10 284 E10
HHNE HP2 36 D1
STA TW18 173 H8
Boleyn Ct BKHH IG9 101 M2
BROX EN10 44 D7
WALTH E17 120 F2
Boleyn Dr E/WMO/HCT KT8 197 N3
RSLP HA4 113 L7
STAL AL1 38 C8
Boleyn Gdns DAGE RM10 144 D2
RBRW/HUT CM13 107 M4
WWKM BR4 204 G9
Boleyn Rd EHAM E6 142 A4
FSTGT E7 141 M2
RSEV TN14 247 M3
STNW/STAM N16 119 M10
Boleyn Wk LHD/OX KT22 236 E6
Boleyn Wy BAR EN5 77 M7
BARK/HLT IG6 102 F7
SWCM DA10 189 K3
Bolina Rd BERM/RHTH SE16 160 B4
Bolingbroke Gv BTSEA SW11 179 P1
Bolingbroke Rd WKENS W14 156 G2
Bolingbroke Wk BTSEA * SW11 157 N6
Bolingbroke Wy HYS/HAR UB3 132 E10
Bolingbrook STALE/WH AL4 38 F2
Bollo Bridge Rd ACT W3 155 N2
Bollo La ACT W3 155 N2
Bolney Ct CRAWW RH11 283 J10
Bolney Ga SKENS SW7 15 N2
Bolney St VX/NE SW8 158 G6
Bolsover Gv REDH RH1 258 F5
Bolsover St GTPST W1W 10 F2
Bolstead Rd MTCM CR4 202 C1
Bolster Gv WDGN * N22 98 E9
Bolt Ct FLST/FETLN * EC4A 12 B6
Bolters La BNSTD SM7 239 J1
Bolters Rd HORL RH6 280 B2
Bolters Rd South HORL RH6 280 A2
Bolton Av WDSR SL4 149 J9
Bolton Cl CHSGTN KT9 219 J3
Bolton Crs CMBW SE5 18 B10
WDSR SL4 149 H9
Bolton Gdns BMLY BR1 183 L9
ECT SW5 15 H7
TEDD TW11 176 F9
WLSDN NW10 136 G4
Bolton Gardens Ms WBPTN SW10 15 H8
Bolton Rd CHSGTN KT9 219 J3
CHSWK W4 155 P6
FSTGT E7 141 L1
HRW HA1 114 B2
KIL/WHAMP NW6 3 H6
UED N18 99 N6
WDSR SL4 149 H9
WLSDN NW10 136 B3
Boltons Cl WOKS/MYFD GU22 233 K1
Bolton's La WDR/YW UB7 152 D6
WOKS/MYFD GU22 233 K2
The Boltons ALP/SUD HA0 114 E9
WBPTN SW10 15 J7
WFD * IG8 101 M5
Bolton St MYFR/PICC W1J 10 F9
Bombay St BERM/RHTH SE16 160 A3
Bombers La BH/WHM TN16 244 G5
Bomer Cl WDR/YW UB7 152 B6
Bomore Rd NTGHL W11 8 A7
Bonar Pl CHST BR7 184 B10
Bonar Rd PECK SE15 159 P6
Bonaventure Ct GVE DA12 191 J7
Bonchester Cl CHST BR7 184 D10
Bonchurch Cl BELMT SM2 221 L4
Bonchurch Rd NKENS W10 8 A3
WEA W13 134 G10
Bond Cl RSEV TN14 245 N1
WDR/YW UB7 132 A8
Bondfield Av YEAD UB4 133 H5
Bond Gdns WLGTN SM6 222 D1
Bond Rd MTCM CR4 202 A2
SURB KT6 199 L9
WARL CR6 242 C4
Bond's La RDKG RH5 272 G8
Bond St EA W5 135 J9
EGH TW20 171 N9
GRAYS RM17 167 P5
SRTFD E15 121 K10
Bondway VX/NE SW8 17 M10
Bonehurst Rd HORL RH6 276 B10
Bone Mill La GDST RH9 260 D10
Bones La HORL RH6 281 P3
Boneta Rd WOOL/PLUM SE18 162 C2
Bonfield Rd LEW SE13 161 H10
Bonham Gdns BCTR RM8 123 N7
Bonham Rd BCTR RM8 123 N7
BRXS/STRHM SW2 180 G1
Bonheur Rd CHSWK W4 156 A1
Bonhill St SDTCH EC2A 13 H2
Boniface Gdns
KTN/HRWW/W HA3 94 A8
Boniface Rd HGDN/ICK UB10 112 C8
Boniface Wk KTN/HRWW/W HA3 94 A8
Bonington Rd HCH RM12 125 L10
Bonita Ms PECK SE15 160 C9
Bonks Hl SBW CM21 29 N2
Bonner Hill Rd KUT KT1 199 L3
Bonner Rd BETH E2 140 B4
Bonners Cl WOKS/MYFD GU22 232 C8
Bonnersfield Cl HRW HA1 114 F4
Bonnersfield La HRW HA1 114 E4
Bonner St BETH * E2 140 B4
Bonner Wk CDH/CHF * RM16 167 L2
Bonnetts La CRAWW RH11 283 K2
Bonneville Gdns CLAP SW4 180 D2
Bonney Gv CHESW EN7 61 P6
Bonney Wy SWLY BR8 208 F2
Bonningtons RBRW/HUT CM13 107 N4
Bonnington Sq VX/NE SW8 17 N9
Bonnys Rd REIG RH2 256 C10
Bonny St CAMTN NW1 4 G4
Bonser Rd TWK TW1 176 E5
Bonsey Cl WOKS/MYFD GU22 232 B7
Bonsey La WOKS/MYFD GU22 232 B7
Bonsey's La CHOB/PIR GU24 214 B5
Bonsor Dr KWD/TDW/WH KT20 239 H8
Bonsor St CMBW SE5 159 M6
Bonville Gdns HDN NW4 116 D2
Bonville Rd BMLY BR1 183 L8
Booker Rd UED N18 99 P6
Bookham Ct GT/LBKH KT23 235 N9
Bookham Gv GT/LBKH KT23 254 A2
Bookham Rd COB KT11 235 L6
Boones Rd LEW SE13 161 K10
Boone St LEW SE13 161 K10
Boord St GNWCH SE10 161 K2
Boothby Rd ARCH N19 118 E7
Booth Cl THMD SE28 143 L9
Booth Dr STA TW18 173 N9
Booth La BLKFR EC4V 12 E7
Booth Rd CDALE/KGS NW9 96 A9
CRAWW RH11 283 H10
CROY/NA * CR0 203 J9
Booths Cl BRKMPK AL9 40 C10
Boot Pde EDGW * HA8 95 M7
Boot St IS N1 7 J10
Borage Cl CRAWW RH11 283 K10
Bordars Rd HNWL W7 134 D7
Bordars Wk HNWL W7 134 D7
Borden Av WCHMH N21 79 L10
Border Cha CRAWE RH10 285 H3
Border Crs SYD SE26 182 A8
Border Gdns CROY/NA CR0 224 G1
Border Ga MTCM CR4 201 P1
Border Rd SYD SE26 182 A8
Borderside SLN SL2 129 M8
Border's La LOU IG10 82 D8
Bordesley Rd MRDN SM4 201 L4
Bordon Wk PUT/ROE SW15 178 D3
Boreas Wk IS N1 6 D8
Boreham Av CAN/RD E16 141 M8
Boreham Rd WDGN N22 99 K9
Borers Arms Rd CRAWE RH10 285 J1
Borers Cl CRAWE * RH10 285 K2
Borgard Rd WOOL/PLUM SE18 162 C3
Borkwood Pk ORP BR6 227 J1
Borkwood Wy ORP BR6 227 H1
Borland Cl GRH DA9 188 F1
Borland Rd PECK SE15 160 B10
TEDD TW11 176 G9
Bornedene POTB/CUF EN6 59 H7
Borneo St PUT/ROE SW15 156 F9
Borough High St STHWK SE1 12 G10
Borough Hl CROY/NA CR0 203 J10
Borough Rd BH/WHM TN16 244 A7
ISLW TW7 154 D7
KUTN/CMB KT2 199 M1
MTCM CR4 201 P2
STHWK SE1 18 C3
Borough Sq STHWK SE1 18 E2
The Borough CHONG CM5 67 N5
RDKG RH5 273 M1
Borough Wy POTB/CUF EN6 59 H8
Borrell Cl BROX EN10 44 D6
Borrett Cl WALW SE17 18 E8
Borrodaile Rd WAND/EARL SW18 179 L2
Borrowdale Av
KTN/HRWW/W HA3 94 F10
Borrowdale Cl CRAWW RH11 283 L9
EGH TW20 172 E10
REDBR IG4 122 B2
SAND/SEL CR2 223 N9
Borrowdale Dr SAND/SEL CR2 223 N8
Borthwick Ms SRTFD * E15 121 K9
Borthwick Rd CDALE/KGS NW9 116 C4
SRTFD E15 121 K9
Borthwick St DEPT SE8 160 F4
Borwick Av WALTH E17 120 E1
Bosanquet Cl UX/CGN UB8 131 N7
Bosanquet Rd HOD EN11 45 H1
Bosbury Rd CAT SE6 183 H6
Boscastle Rd KTTN NW5 118 C8
Boscobel Pl BGVA SW1W 16 D5
Boscobel St BAY/PAD W2 9 M3
Boscombe Av EMPK RM11 125 L5
GRAYS RM17 168 A3
LEY E10 121 J5
Boscombe Cl CLPT E5 120 D10
EGH TW20 194 F1
Boscombe Rd SHB W12 156 D1
TOOT SW17 180 B9
WIM/MER SW19 201 K1
WPK KT4 200 F8
Bosgrove CHING E4 101 H2
Bosham Rd CRAWE RH10 284 D10
Boshers Gdns EGH TW20 172 C9
Bosman Dr BFOR GU20 192 A10
Boss St STHWK * SE1 19 L1
Bostall Heath ABYW * SE2 163 M4
Bostall Hl ABYW SE2 163 L4
Bostall La ABYW SE2 163 L3
Bostall Manorway ABYW SE2 163 L3
Bostall Park Av BXLYHN DA7 163 P6
Bostall Rd STMC/STPC BR5 185 L10
Boston Gdns BTFD TW8 154 F3
CHSWK W4 156 B5
Boston Gv RSLP HA4 112 D4
SL SL1 129 H8
Boston Manor Rd BTFD TW8 154 F3
Boston Pde HNWL * W7 154 F3
Boston Park Rd BTFD TW8 155 H4
Boston Pl CAMTN NW1 10 A2
Boston Rd CROY/NA CR0 202 G6
EDGW HA8 95 P8
EHAM E6 142 B5
HNWL W7 154 E1
Bostonthorpe Rd HNWL * W7 154 D1
Boston V HNWL W7 154 F3
Bosville Dr SEV TN13 247 H9
Bosville Rd SEV TN13 247 H9
Boswell Cl RAD WD7 57 K8
STMC/STPC BR5 207 M6
Boswell Ct BMSBY WC1N 11 M3
Boswell Rd CRAWE RH10 283 P10
THHTH CR7 203 K4
Boswell St BMSBY WC1N 11 M3
Boswick La BERK HP4 33 J1
Bosworth Cl WALTH E17 100 E9
Bosworth Crs HARH RM3 105 K7
Bosworth Rd BAR EN5 77 K7
DAGE RM10 124 B9
FBAR/BDGN N11 98 E7
NKENS W10 8 B2
Botany Bay La CHST BR7 206 F2
Botany Cl EBAR EN4 77 P8
Botany Ter PUR * RM19 165 P4
Botany Wy PUR RM19 166 A4
Boteley Cl CHING E4 101 J3
Boterys Cross REDH * RH1 259 J9
Botham Cl EDGW HA8 95 P8

Botha Rd PLSTW E13 141 N7
Bothwell Cl CAN/RD E16 141 M7
Bothwell Crs CROY/NA CR0 225 H6
Bothwell St HMSMTH W6 156 G5
Botley La CSHM HP5 51 M6
Botley Rd CSHM HP5 51 N6
HHNE HP2 36 B1
Botleys Pk CHERT * KT16 214 F2
Botolph Aly MON EC3R 13 J8
Botolph La MON EC3R 13 J8
Botsford Rd RYNPK SW20 201 H2
Bottom Harrow Rd VW GU25 194 C6
Bottom House Farm La CSTG HP8 89 J2
Bottom La KGLGY WD4 71 M1
Bottrells La CSTG HP8 89 L3
Bott Rd RDART DA2 187 N7
Bott's Ms BAY/PAD W2 8 F6
Botwell Common Rd
HYS/HAR UB3 132 E9
Botwell Crs HYS/HAR UB3 132 F8
Botwell La HYS/HAR UB3 152 G1
Boucher Cl TEDD TW11 176 E8
Boucher Dr GVW DA11 190 C6
Boughton Av HAYES BR2 205 L7
Boughton Hall Av
RPLY/SEND GU23 251 H1
Boughton Rd THMD SE28 163 H2
Boughton Wy AMS HP6 69 P5
Boulcott St WCHPL E1 140 C8
Boulevard WATW * WD18 72 E9
The Boulevard CRAWE RH10 283 N7
WATW WD18 72 E9
WFD IG8 102 D8
WGCE AL7 23 J3
Boulmer Rd UX/CGN UB8 131 M5
Boulogne Rd CROY/NA CR0 203 K6
Boulter Gdns RAIN RM13 145 H1
Boulters Cl SL SL1 148 F1
Boulthurst Wy OXTED RH8 261 M8
Boulton Rd BCTR RM8 123 P7
Boultwood Rd EHAM E6 142 C8
Bounces La ED N9 100 A3
Bounces Rd ED N9 100 A3
The Bounce HHNE HP2 35 N4
Boundaries Rd BAL SW12 180 A5
FELT TW13 175 K4
Boundary Av WALTH E17 120 E5
Boundary Cl BAR EN5 77 J5
CRAWE RH10 283 P6
GDMY/SEVK IG3 123 H9
KUT KT1 199 M3
NWDGN UB2 153 P4
Boundary Dr HERT/WAS SG14 25 L3
Boundary La PLSTW E13 142 A5
WALW SE17 18 F10
WGCE AL7 23 H9
Boundary Ms STJWD * NW8 3 K5
Boundary Pk HHNE * HP2 35 N7
Boundary Rd ASHF TW15 173 M8
BARK IG11 142 F4
BFN/LL DA15 185 H1
CFSP/GDCR SL9 90 A8
CRAWE RH10 283 P6
ED N9 80 B10
PIN HA5 113 L4
PLSTW E13 141 P4
ROM RM1 125 H4
STAL AL1 38 D4
STJWD NW8 3 J6
UPMR RM14 125 P8
WALTH E17 120 E5
WDGN N22 99 K10
WIM/MER SW19 179 N9
WLGTN SM6 222 B5
WOKN/KNAP GU21 232 D2
Boundary Rd East
ADL/WDHM KT15 215 L5
Boundary Rd North
ADL/WDHM KT15 215 L5
Boundary Rd West
ADL/WDHM KT15 215 L5
Boundary Rw STHWK SE1 18 C1
Boundary St BETH E2 7 L10
ERITH DA8 164 G6
Boundary Wy CROY/NA CR0 224 F2
GSTN WD25 55 J8
HHNE HP2 36 D3
WOKN/KNAP GU21 232 E1
Boundfield Rd CAT SE6 183 K6
Bounds Green Rd
FBAR/BDGN N11 98 E7
WDGN N22 98 F8
Bourchier Cl SEV TN13 265 J2
Bourchier St SOHO/CST W1F 11 J7
Bourdon Pl MYFR/PKLN W1K 10 F7
Bourdon Rd PGE/AN SE20 204 B2
Bourdon St MYFR/PKLN W1K 10 E8
Bourke Cl CLAP SW4 180 F2
WLSDN NW10 136 B1
Bourke Hl COUL/CHIP CR5 240 A4
Bourlet Cl FITZ W1T 10 G4
Bourn Av EBAR EN4 77 N9
SEVS/STOTM N15 119 L2
UX/CGN UB8 132 B6
Bournbrook Rd BKHTH/KID SE3 162 A9
Bourne Av CHERT KT16 195 K3
HYS/HAR UB3 152 D2
RSLP HA4 113 K10
STHGT/OAK N14 98 F3
WDSR SL4 149 H10
Bournebridge La ABR/ST RM4 104 C1
Bourne Cl BF/WBF KT14 215 L9
BROX EN10 44 E6
RGUE GU4 268 E6
WARE SG12 26 C1
Bourne Ct BF/WBF * KT14 215 P9
RSLP HA4 113 J10
Bourne Dr MTCM CR4 201 N2
Bourne End EMPK RM11 125 P5
Bourne End La HHW HP1 34 F8
Bourne End Rd NTHWD HA6 92 F5
Bourne Est HCIRC * EC1N 12 A3
Bournefield Rd CTHM CR3 241 N4
Bourne Gdns CHING E4 100 G5
Bourne Gv ASHTD KT21 237 J5
Bournehall BUSH * WD23 73 P10
Bournehall Av BUSH WD23 73 P9
Bournehall La BUSH WD23 73 P10
Bournehall Rd BUSH WD23 73 P10
Bourne Hl PLMGR N13 98 G3
Bourne Hill Cl PLMGR * N13 98 G3
Bourne La CTHM CR3 241 L7
Bourne Md BXLY DA5 186 D1
Bournemead Av NTHLT UB5 133 H4
Bournemead Cl NTHLT UB5 133 H5
Bourne Meadow EGH TW20 194 E4
Bournemouth Cl PECK SE15 159 P8
Bournemouth Rd PECK SE15 159 P8
WIM/MER SW19 201 K1
Bourne Pde BXLY * DA5 186 C3
Bourne Park Cl PUR/KEN CR8 241 M2
Bourne Rd ADL/WDHM KT15 215 L5
BERK HP4 33 L4
BUSH WD23 73 P9
BXLY DA5 186 C2
CEND/HSY/T N8 118 F4
FSTGT E7 121 L8
GVE DA12 191 J5
HAYES BR2 206 A4
REDH RH1 258 D6
RGODL GU7 267 L9
SL SL1 149 H1
VW GU25 194 A5
Bourneside VW GU25 193 M7
Bourneside Crs STHGT/OAK N14 98 E2
Bourneside Gdns CAT SE6 183 H8
Bourneside Rd ADL/WDHM KT15 215 N2
Bourne St BGVA SW1W 16 C6
CROY/NA CR0 203 J9
Bourne Ter BAY/PAD W2 8 G3
The Bourne HHW HP1 52 D3
STHGT/OAK N14 98 F2
WARE SG12 26 C1
Bourne V HAYES BR2 205 M7
Bournevale Rd
STRHM/NOR SW16 180 F7
Bourne Vw GFD/PVL UB6 134 E1
PUR/KEN CR8 241 L1
Bourne Wy ADL/WDHM KT15 215 M2
HAYES BR2 205 M9
HOR/WEW KT19 219 P1
SUT SM1 221 J2
SWLY BR8 208 D3
WOKS/MYFD GU22 232 A8
Bournewood Rd
STMC/STPC BR5 207 L7
WOOL/PLUM SE18 163 K6
Bournville Rd CAT SE6 182 F3
Bournwell Cl EBAR EN4 78 A7
Bourton Cl HYS/HAR UB3 133 H10
Bousfield Rd NWCR SE14 160 C8
Bousley Ri CHERT KT16 214 G3
Boutflower Rd BTSEA SW11 157 P10
Boutique Hall LEW * SE13 161 H10
Bouverie Gdns COUL/CHIP CR5 222 F10
KTN/HRWW/W HA3 115 J4
Bouverie Ms STNW/STAM N16 119 M7
Bouverie Pl BAY/PAD W2 9 M5
Bouverie Rd COUL/CHIP CR5 240 B4
HRW HA1 114 B4
STNW/STAM N16 119 M7
Bouverie St EMB EC4Y 12 B6
Bouverie Wy DTCH/LGLY SL3 150 B4
Bouvier Rd PEND EN3 80 B4
Boveney Cl SL SL1 148 F1
Boveney New Rd WDSR SL4 148 D3
Boveney Rd FSTH SE23 182 C3
WDSR SL4 148 B3
Boveney Wood La SL SL1 108 C8
Bovey Wy SOCK/AV RM15 146 G7
Bovill Rd FSTH SE23 182 C3
Bovingdon Av WBLY HA9 135 M1
Bovingdon Crs GSTN WD25 55 L10
Bovingdon Green La
HHS/BOV HP3 52 C4
Bovingdon La CDALE/KGS NW9 96 B9
Bovingdon Rd FUL/PGN SW6 157 L7
Bow Arrow La DART DA1 187 P2
RDART DA2 188 A2
Bowater Cl CDALE/KGS NW9 116 A3
CLAP SW4 180 F2
Bowater Pl BKHTH/KID SE3 161 N6
Bowater Rdg WEY KT13 216 E6
Bowater Rd CRAWE RH10 284 D10
WOOL/PLUM SE18 162 A2
Bow Br STALW/RED AL3 37 M3
Bow Bridge Est BOW E3 140 G5
Bow Churchyard STP * EC4M 12 F6
Bow Common La BOW E3 140 E6
Bowden Cl EBED/NFELT TW14 174 F4
Bowden Dr EMPK RM11 125 M6
Bowden Rd ASC SL5 192 B5
Bowden St LBTH SE11 18 B7
Bowditch DEPT SE8 160 E4
Bowdon Rd LEY E10 120 F5
Bowen Dr DUL SE21 181 M6
Bowen Rd HRW HA1 114 B5
Bowen St POP/IOD E14 140 G8
Bowenswood CROY/NA CR0 224 E5
Bowens Wd CROY/NA * CR0 224 E5
Bower Av GNWCH SE10 161 K7
Bower Cl CRW RM5 104 E8
NTHLT UB5 133 K4
Bower Ct WOKS/MYFD GU22 232 E2
Bowerdean St FUL/PGN SW6 157 L7
Bower Farm Rd ABR/ST RM4 104 D4
Bower Hl EPP CM16 65 K8
Bower Hill Cl REDH RH1 276 F3
Bower Hill La REDH RH1 276 E1
Bower La EYN DA4 209 M10
Bowerman Av NWCR SE14 160 D5
Bowerman Rd CDH/CHF RM16 168 D3
Bower Rd SWLY BR8 187 H10
Bowers Av GVW DA11 190 C7
Bowers Cl RGUE GU4 250 D6
Bowers Farm Dr RGUE GU4 250 D6
Bowers La RGUE GU4 250 D5
Bowers Rd RSEV TN14 228 G7
Bower St WCHPL * E1 140 C8
Bower V EPP CM16 65 K8
Bower Wy SL SL1 128 D9
Bowes Cl BFN/LL DA15 185 L2
Bowes Dr CHONG CM5 67 N3
Bowes Lyon Cl WDSR SL4 149 H7
Bowes Lyon Ms STALW/RED AL3 38 C6
Bowes Rd ACT W3 136 B9
BCTR RM8 123 M9
FBAR/BDGN N11 98 C6
STA TW18 173 H9
WOT/HER KT12 197 J9
Bowes Rd (North Circular)
PLMGR N13 98 F6
Bowes Wd HART DA3 211 L10
Bowfell Rd HMSMTH W6 156 F5
Bowford Av BXLYHN DA7 163 P7
Bowgate STAL AL1 38 D5
Bowhay RBRW/HUT CM13 107 N3
Bowhill Cl BRXN/ST SW9 159 H6
Bowie Cl CLAP SW4 180 E3
Bowland Rd CLAP SW4 158 E10
WFD IG8 101 P7
Bowland Yd KTBR * SW1X 16 B2
Bow La FNCH N3 97 M8
STP EC4M 12 F6
Bowler's Orch CSTG HP8 89 M4
Bowles Gdn EN EN1 80 A2
Bowley Cl NRWD * SE19 181 N9
Bowley La NRWD SE19 181 N8
Bowley St POP/IOD E14 140 E9
Bowling Cl HARP AL5 20 A4
Bowling Green Cl
PUT/ROE SW15 178 E3
Bowling Green Ct WBLY HA9 115 L7
Bowling Green La CLKNW EC1R 12 B2
Bowling Green Pl STHWK * SE1 18 G1
Bowling Green Rd
CHOB/PIR GU24 213 K5
Bowling Green Rw
WOOL/PLUM * SE18 162 C3
Bowling Green St LBTH SE11 18 A9
Bowling Green Wk IS N1 7 J9
Bowling Rd WARE SG12 26 D2
Bow Locks BOW * E3 141 H6
Bowls Cl STAN HA7 94 G6
Bowman Av CAN/RD E16 141 L8
Bowman Ct CRAWE * RH10 283 N6
Bowman Ms WAND/EARL SW18 179 J4
Bowmans Cl POTB/CUF EN6 59 N8
SL SL1 128 A3
WEA W13 134 G10
Bowmans Ct HHNE HP2 35 N4
Bowmans Gn GSTN WD25 73 M2
Bowmans Lea FSTH SE23 182 B3
Bowman's Meadow WLGTN SM6 202 C10
Bowman's Ms HOLWY N7 118 F8
WCHPL E1 13 N7
Bowman's Pl HOLWY N7 118 F8
Bowmans Rd DART DA1 186 G3
Bowmead ELTH/MOT SE9 184 C5
Bowmont Cl RBRW/HUT CM13 87 N10
Bowmore Wk CAMTN NW1 5 K4
Bown Cl TIL RM18 168 E8
Bowness Cl HACK E8 7 L2
Bowness Crs PUT/ROE SW15 178 B8
Bowness Dr HSLWW TW4 153 M10
Bowness Rd BXLYHN DA7 164 C8
CAT SE6 182 G3
Bowness Wy HCH RM12 125 H10
Bowood Rd BTSEA SW11 158 B10
PEND EN3 80 C6
Bowring Gn OXHEY WD19 93 K6
Bow Rd BOW E3 140 F5
Bowrons Av ALP/SUD HA0 135 J2
Bowry Dr STWL/WRAY TW19 172 C2
Bowsley Ct FELT TW13 175 H5
The Bowspirit COB KT11 235 K1
Bow St COVGDN WC2E 11 M6
SRTFD E15 121 K10
Bowyer Cl EHAM E6 142 C7
Bowyer Crs DEN/HRF UB9 111 J4
Bowyer Dr SL SL1 128 D9
Bowyer Pl CMBW SE5 159 K6
Bowyers HHNE HP2 35 N4
Bowyers Cl ASHTD KT21 237 L4
Bowyer St CMBW SE5 159 K6
Bowzell Rd RSEV TN14 264 G9
Boxall Rd DUL SE21 181 M2
Boxelder Cl EDGW * HA8 95 P6
Boxfield WGCE AL7 23 L8
Boxford Cl SAND/SEL CR2 224 C8
Boxgrove Av GU GU1 250 D8
Boxgrove La GU GU1 250 D9
Boxgrove Rd ABYW SE2 163 M2
GU GU1 250 D9
Boxhill HHNE HP2 35 N5
Boxhill Rd DORK RH4 255 K8
KWD/TDW/WH KT20 256 A6
Boxhill Wy BRKHM/BTCW RH3 273 N4
Box La BARK IG11 143 L4
HHW HP1 52 G1
HOD EN11 44 D2
Boxley Rd MRDN SM4 201 M4
Boxley St CAN/RD E16 141 N10
Boxmoor Rd CRW RM5 104 D6
KTN/HRWW/W HA3 114 G2
Boxoll Rd DAGW RM9 124 A9
Box Ridge Av PUR/KEN CR8 222 G8
Boxted Cl BKHH IG9 102 B2
Boxted Rd HHW HP1 35 J4
Box Tree Cl CSHM * HP5 51 P6
Boxtree La KTN/HRWW/W HA3 94 B9
Boxtree Rd KTN/HRWW/W HA3 94 C8
Box Tree Wk REDH RH1 275 M3
Boxwell Rd BERK HP4 33 N5
Boxwood Cl WDR/YW UB7 152 A1
Boxwood Wy WARL CR6 242 C3
Boxworth Gv IS N1 5 P5
Boyard Rd WOOL/PLUM SE18 162 E4
Boyce Cl BORE WD6 75 K5
Boyce Wy PLSTW E13 141 M6
Boycroft Av CDALE/KGS NW9 115 P4
Boyd Av STHL UB1 133 N10
Boyd Cl KUTN/CMB KT2 177 M10
Boydell Ct STJWD NW8 3 L4
Boyd Rd WIM/MER SW19 179 N9
Boyd St WCHPL E1 13 N6
Boyfield St STHWK SE1 18 D2
Boyland Rd BMLY BR1 183 L8
Boyle Av STAN HA7 94 F7
Boyle Farm Rd THDIT KT7 198 F6
Boyne Av HDN NW4 116 G2
Boyne Rd DAGE RM10 124 B8
LEW SE13 161 J9
Boyne Terrace Ms NTGHL W11 8 C9
Boyson Rd WALW SE17 18 F9
Boyton Cl CEND/HSY/T N8 118 F1
WCHPL E1 140 C6
Boyton Rd CEND/HSY/T N8 118 F1
Brabant Rd WDGN N22 98 G10
Brabazon Av WLGTN SM6 222 F5
Brabazon Rd HEST TW5 153 K6
NTHLT UB5 133 P4
Brabazon St POP/IOD E14 140 G8
Brabourne Cl NRWD SE19 181 M8
Brabourne Crs BXLYHN DA7 164 A5
Brabourne Ri BECK BR3 205 J5
Brabourn Gv PECK SE15 160 B8
Brace Cl CHESW EN7 61 J1
Bracewell Av GFD/PVL UB6 114 E10
Bracewell Rd NKENS W10 136 F7
Bracewood Gdns CROY/NA CR0 203 N10
Bracey St FSBYPK * N4 118 F7
Bracken Av BAL SW12 180 B2
CROY/NA CR0 204 F10
Brackenbridge Dr RSLP HA4 113 L8
Brackenbury Gdns HMSMTH W6 156 E2
Brackenbury Rd EFNCH N2 117 M1
HMSMTH W6 156 E2
Bracken Cl CRAWE RH10 283 P5
CRAWE RH10 285 J3
EHAM E6 142 C7
GT/LBKH KT23 235 N10
HSLWW TW4 175 P3
LOU IG10 82 E5
SLN SL2 128 J9
SUN * TW16 174 G9
WOKS/MYFD GU22 232 C4
Brackendale POTB/CUF EN6 59 K9
WCHMH N21 98 G3
Brackendale Cl HEST TW5 154 A7
Brackendale Gdns UPMR RM14 126 B9
Brackendene BXLY DA5 186 F7
LCOL/BKTW AL2 55 N6
Brackendene Cl
WOKN/KNAP GU21 232 D1
Bracken Dr CHIG IG7 102 E7
Bracken End ISLW TW7 176 C1
Brackenforde DTCH/LGLY SL3 149 P1
Bracken Gdns BARN SW13 156 D8
Bracken Hl BERK HP4 34 B4
Brackenhill COB KT11 217 P7
RSLP * HA4 113 M9
Bracken Hill Cl BMLY BR1 205 L1
Bracken Hill La BMLY BR1 205 L1
Brackenlea RGODL GU7 267 J10
Bracken Ms ROMW/RG RM7 124 B4
Bracken Pth EPSOM KT18 219 N9
Brackens Dr BRW CM14 107 J6
Brackenside HORL RH6 280 C3
The Brackens ED N9 99 M1
HHNE * HP2 35 N5
ORP BR6 227 K2
The Bracken CHING E4 101 H3
Bracken Wy CHOB/PIR GU24 213 L6
RGUW GU3 249 K8
Brackenwood SUN TW16 197 H1
Brackenwood Rd
WOKN/KNAP GU21 231 J5
Brackley WEY KT13 216 E2
Brackley Cl WLGTN SM6 222 F4
Brackley Rd BECK BR3 182 E10
CHSWK W4 156 B3
Brackley Sq WFD IG8 102 A8
Brackley St BARB EC2Y 12 F3
Brackley Ter CHSWK W4 156 B4
Bracklyn St IS N1 6 G7
Bracknell Cl WDGN N22 99 H9
Bracknell Gdns HAMP NW3 117 L10
Bracknell Pl HHNE HP2 36 A2
Bracknell Wy HAMP NW3 117 L9
Bracondale ESH/CLAY KT10 218 B2
Bracondale Rd ABYW SE2 163 K3
Bradbery RKW/CH/CXG WD3 90 G6
Bradbourne Park Rd SEV TN13 247 H9
Bradbourne Rd BXLY DA5 186 B3
GRAYS RM17 167 N5
SEV TN13 247 J8
Bradbourne St FUL/PGN SW6 157 K8
Bradbourne Vale Rd SEV TN13 246 G8
Bradbury Cl BORE WD6 75 N5
NWDGN UB2 153 N3
Bradbury Rd CRAWE RH10 284 D10
Bradbury St STNW/STAM N16 119 M10
Bradd Cl SOCK/AV RM15 147 H5
Braddock Cl ISLW TW7 154 E9
Braddon Ct BAR * EN5 77 H7
Braddon Rd RCH/KEW TW9 155 L9
Braddyll St GNWCH SE10 161 K4
Bradenham Av WELL DA16 163 K10
Bradenham Cl WALW SE17 18 G9
Bradenham Rd
KTN/HRWW/W HA3 114 G2
YEAD UB4 132 F5
Bradenhurst Cl CTHM CR3 259 N2
Braden St MV/WKIL * W9 8 G2
Bradfield Cl GU GU1 250 D7
WOKS/MYFD GU22 232 B4
Bradfield Dr BARK IG11 123 K10
Bradfield Rd CAN/RD E16 161 M1
RSLP HA4 113 M10
Bradford Cl HAYES BR2 206 C8
SYD SE26 182 A7
UED N18 99 N7
Bradford Dr HOR/WEW KT19 220 C3
Bradford Rd ACT W3 156 B1
IL IG1 122 G6
RKW/CH/CXG WD3 90 F1
SL SL1 128 F8
Bradgate POTB/CUF EN6 60 E3
Bradgate Cl POTB/CUF EN6 60 E4
Bradgate Rd CAT SE6 182 G2
Brading Crs WAN E11 121 N7
Brading Rd BRXS/STRHM SW2 180 G3
CROY/NA CR0 202 G6
Brading Ter SHB W12 156 D2
Bradiston Rd MV/WKIL W9 2 D9
Bradleigh Av GRAYS RM17 167 P3
Bradley Cl HOLWY N7 5 M2
Bradley Gdns WEA W13 134 G8
Bradley La DORK RH4 254 G8
Bradley Rd NRWD SE19 181 K9
PEND EN3 80 D4
SL SL1 129 J9
WAB EN9 81 H1
WDGN N22 98 G10
Bradley's Cl IS N1 6 A7
Bradley Stone Rd EHAM E6 142 C8
Bradman Rw EDGW * HA8 95 P8
Bradmead VX/NE * SW8 158 C7
Bradmore Gn BRKMPK AL9 59 H2
Bradmore La BRKMPK AL9 58 G2
Bradmore Park Rd HMSMTH W6 156 E2
Bradmore Wy BRKMPK AL9 59 H2
COUL/CHIP CR5 240 F4
Bradshaw Cl WDSR SL4 148 D7
WIM/MER SW19 179 K9
Bradshaw Cottages
POP/IOD * E14 140 D8
Bradshaw Rd CDH/CHF RM16 147 M10
WATN WD24 73 K5
Bradshaws HAT AL10 40 C8
Bradshaws Cl SNWD SE25 203 P3
Bradstock Rd EW KT17 220 E2
HOM E9 140 C1
Brad St STHWK SE1 12 B10
Bradwell Av DAGE RM10 124 B7
Bradwell Cl HCH RM12 145 J1
SWFD E18 121 L2
Bradwell Gn RBRW/HUT CM13 87 P10
Bradwell Ms UED N18 99 P5
Bradwell St WCHPL * E1 140 C5
Brady Av LOU IG10 82 F6
Brady St WCHPL E1 140 A6
Braemar Av ALP/SUD HA0 135 J2
BXLYHN DA7 164 D10
SAND/SEL CR2 223 K6
THHTH CR7 203 J3
WDGN N22 98 F9
WIM/MER SW19 179 K5
WLSDN NW10 116 A8
Braemar Gdns BFN/LL DA15 184 G6
CDALE/KGS NW9 96 A9
EMPK RM11 125 P4
SL SL1 148 F1
WWKM BR4 205 H8
Braemar Rd BTFD TW8 155 J5
PLSTW E13 141 M6
SEVS/STOTM N15 119 M3
WPK KT4 200 E10
Braeside ADL/WDHM KT15 215 L7
BECK BR3 182 F8
Braeside Av SEV TN13 246 G10
WIM/MER SW19 201 H1
Braeside Cl PIN HA5 93 P8
SEV TN13 246 G9
Braeside Crs BXLYHN DA7 164 D10
Braeside Rd STRHM/NOR SW16 180 D10
Braes Md REDH RH1 276 F1
Braes St IS N1 6 D4
Braesyde Cl BELV DA17 164 A3
Brafferton Rd CROY/NA CR0 223 K1
Braganza St WALW SE17 18 C8
Bragg Rd TEDD TW11 176 D10
Bragmans La RKW/CH/CXG WD3 52 G9
Braham St WCHPL E1 13 M6
Braid Av ACT W3 136 B8
Braid Cl FELT TW13 175 N5
The Braid CSHM HP5 51 K6
Braidwood Rd CAT SE6 183 J4
Brailsford Cl WIM/MER SW19 179 P10
Brailsford Rd BRXS/STRHM SW2 181 H2
Brain Cl HAT AL10 40 E8
Brainton Av EBED/NFELT TW14 175 J3
Braintree Av REDBR IG4 122 B3
Braintree Rd DAGE RM10 124 B8
RSLP HA4 113 J9
Braintree St BETH * E2 140 B5
Brair Bank CAR SM5 222 B5
Braithwaite Av ROMW/RG RM7 124 B5
Braithwaite Gdns STAN HA7 95 H9
Braithwaite Rd PEND EN3 80 E7
Brakefield Rd MEO DA13 189 N9
Brakey Hl REDH RH1 259 M10
Brakynbery BERK HP4 33 K2
Brallings La CFSP/GDCR SL9 90 D5
Bramall Cl FSTGT E7 121 L10
Bramber Cl CRAWE RH10 283 P5
Bramber Ct SL SL1 128 F10
Bramber Rd NFNCH/WDSP N12 97 P6
WKENS W14 14 C9
Bramble Acres Cl BELMT SM2 221 K4
Bramble Av RDART DA2 189 H6
Bramble Banks CAR SM5 222 B5
Bramblebury Rd
WOOL/PLUM SE18 162 G4
Bramble Cl BECK BR3 205 H5
CFSP/GDCR SL9 90 B7
CRAWE RH10 285 J2
CROY/NA CR0 224 F1
GSTN WD25 55 H10
REDH RH1 276 B2
RGUW GU3 249 K8
SEVS/STOTM N15 119 P2
SHPTN TW17 196 E4
STAN HA7 95 J8
UX/CGN UB8 132 A7
Bramble Cft ERITH DA8 164 D3
Brambledene Cl
WOKN/KNAP GU21 231 P4
Brambledown HART DA3 211 L4
STA TW18 195 L1
Brambledown Cl HAYES BR2 205 K6
Brambledown Rd CAR SM5 222 B4
SAND/SEL CR2 223 M4
Bramblefield Cl HART DA3 211 J3
Bramble Gdns SHB W12 136 C9
Bramble Hall La
KWD/TDW/WH * KT20 255 L8
Bramble La AMSS HP7 69 K7
HPTN TW12 175 N9
SEV TN13 265 J4
UPMR RM14 146 B3
Bramble Md CSTG HP8 89 M4
Bramble Ri COB KT11 217 K10
HLW CM20 28 F10
Bramble Rd HAT AL10 39 P5
Brambles Cl BTFD TW8 154 G6
CTHM CR3 241 M8
Brambles Farm Dr UX/CGN UB8 132 B5
The Brambles CHES/WCR EN8 62 C7
CHIG IG7 102 F7
RGODL GU7 267 J10
STAL AL1 38 C8
SUT * SM1 201 N9
WDR/YW UB7 151 N4
WIM/MER * SW19 179 J8
Brambletye Park Rd REDH RH1 276 A2
Brambletye Rd CRAWE RH10 284 B8
Bramble Wk EPSOM KT18 219 N10
REDH * RH1 276 B2
Bramble Wy RPLY/SEND GU23 233 J10
Bramblewood REIG RH2 258 C5
Bramblewood Cl CAR SM5 201 P8
Brambling Cl BUSH WD23 73 M8
Brambling Ri HHNE HP2 35 P3
The Bramblings CHING E4 101 J5
Bramcote Av MTCM CR4 202 A4
Bramcote Gv BERM/RHTH SE16 160 B4
Bramcote Rd PUT/ROE SW15 156 E10
Bramdean Crs LEE/GVPK SE12 183 M4
Bramdean Gdns LEE/GVPK SE12 183 M4
Bramerton Rd BECK BR3 204 E3
Bramerton St CHEL SW3 15 N9
Bramfield GSTN WD25 55 M10
Bramfield Rd BTSEA SW11 179 P2
HERT/WAS SG14 24 F3
Bramford Rd WAND/EARL SW18 157 M10
Bramham Ct NTHWD * HA6 92 F6
Bramham Gdns CHSGTN * KT9 219 J2
ECT SW5 14 G7
Bramhope La CHARL SE7 161 N5
Bramlands Cl BTSEA SW11 157 P9
Bramleas WATW WD18 72 G9
Bramley Av COUL/CHIP CR5 240 D1
SHPTN TW17 196 F3
Bramley Cl CHERT KT16 195 L8
CRAWE RH10 284 A7
HYS/HAR UB3 133 H9
MEO DA13 190 C10
ORP BR6 206 E8
REDH RH1 275 P2
RSLP HA4 112 G1
SAND/SEL CR2 223 J2
STA TW18 173 M9
STHGT/OAK N14 78 C9
SWLY BR8 208 F4
WALTH E17 100 D10
WHTN TW2 176 B2
Bramley Ct GSTN WD25 55 J8
Bramley Crs GNTH/NBYPK IG2 122 D4
VX/NE SW8 158 E6
Bramley Gdns OXHEY WD19 93 K7
Bramley Hl SAND/SEL CR2 223 K1
Bramley House Ct ENC/FH * EN2 79 L3
Bramley Hyrst SAND/SEL * CR2 223 K2
Bramley Ldg ALP/SUD HA0 115 J9
Bramley Pl DART DA1 165 H10
Bramley Rd BELMT SM2 220 G5
EA W5 155 H2

NKENS W10 136 G9
STHGT/OAK N14 78 C9
SUT SM1 221 N2
Bramley Shaw WAB EN9 63 L9
Bramley Wk HORL RH6 280 D4
Bramley Wy ASHTD KT21 237 L3
HSLWW TW4 175 N1
STALE/WH AL4 39 H7
WWKM BR4 204 G9
Brammas Cl SL SL1 149 H2
Brampton Cl CHESW EN7 61 P4
CLPT E5 120 A7
HARP AL5 20 C2
Brampton Gdns WOT/HER KT12 217 J2
Brampton Gv HDN NW4 116 E2
KTN/HRWW/W HA3 114 F2
WBLY HA9 115 M6
Brampton La HDN NW4 116 F2
Brampton Park Rd WDGN N22 119 H1
Brampton Rd BXLYHN DA7 163 N9
CDALE/KGS NW9 115 M2
CROY/NA CR0 203 N7
EHAM E6 142 A6
FSBYPK N4 119 K3
HGDN/ICK UB10 132 C4
OXHEY WD19 93 H4
STAL AL1 38 F5
Brampton Ter BORE WD6 75 M4
Bramshaw Gdns OXHEY WD19 93 L6
Bramshaw Ri NWMAL KT3 200 B6
Bramshaw Rd HOM E9 140 C1
Bramshill Gdns KTTN NW5 118 C8
Bramshill Rd WLSDN NW10 136 B4
Bramshot Av CHARL SE7 161 N5
Bramston Cl BARK/HLT IG6 103 J7
Bramston Rd WLSDN NW10 136 D4
Bramwell Cl SUN TW16 197 L2
Bramwell Ms IS N1 5 P5
Brancaster Dr MLHL NW7 96 D8
Brancaster La PUR/KEN CR8 223 K7
Brancaster Rd GNTH/NBYPK IG2 122 G4
STRHM/NOR SW16 180 F6
Brancepeth Gdns BKHH IG9 101 M3
Branch Cl HAT AL10 40 F2
Branch Hl HAMP NW3 117 M8
Branch Pl IS N1 7 H5
Branch Rd BARK/HLT IG6 103 L6
LCOL/BKTW AL2 56 C3
POP/IOD E14 140 D8
STALW/RED AL3 38 A5
Branch St CMBW SE5 159 M6
Brancker Rd KTN/HRWW/W HA3 115 J1
Brancroft Wy PEND EN3 80 D5
Brand Cl FSBYPK N4 119 J6
Brandlehow Rd PUT/ROE SW15 157 J10
Brandon Cl CHESW EN7 61 M2
CRAWE RH10 284 E9
Brandon Est WALW SE17 18 C10
Brandon Groves Av
SOCK/AV RM15 147 H5
Brandon Ms BARB * EC2Y 12 G3
Brandon Rd DART DA1 187 P3
HOLWY N7 5 L3
NWDGN UB2 153 N4
SUT SM1 221 L1
WALTH * E17 121 H2
Brandon St GVW DA11 190 E3
WALW SE17 18 F6
Brandram Ms LEW * SE13 161 K10
Brandram Rd LEW SE13 161 K9
Brandreth Ct HRW * HA1 114 E4
Brandreth Rd EHAM E6 142 C8
TOOT SW17 180 C5
The Brandries WLGTN SM6 202 E10
Brands Hatch Pk HART * DA3 210 E10
Brands Hatch Rd BGR/WK TN15 210 F10
Brandsland REIG RH2 275 L4
Brands Rd DTCH/LGLY SL3 150 E5
Brand St GNWCH SE10 161 H6
Brandville Gdns BARK/HLT IG6 122 E2
Brandville Rd WDR/YW UB7 151 P1
Brandy Wy BELMT SM2 221 K4
Branfill Rd UPMR RM14 126 A7
Brangbourne Rd BMLY BR1 183 H8
Brangton Rd LBTH SE11 17 P8
Brangwyn Crs WIM/MER SW19 201 N1
Branksea St FUL/PGN SW6 157 H6
Branksome Av UED N18 99 N7
Branksome Cl HHNE HP2 36 B5
WOT/HER KT12 197 L9
Branksome Rd
BRXS/STRHM SW2 180 F1
WIM/MER SW19 201 K1
Branksome Wy
KTN/HRWW/W HA3 115 L4
NWMAL KT3 199 P2
Bransby Rd CHSGTN KT9 219 K4
Branscombe Gdns WCHMH N21 99 H1
Branscombe St LEW SE13 160 G9
Bransdale Cl KIL/WHAMP NW6 2 F5
Bransell Cl SWLY BR8 208 D6
Bransgrove Rd EDGW HA8 95 L9
Branston Crs STMC/STPC BR5 206 G8
Branstone Rd RCH/KEW TW9 155 L7
Branton Rd GRH DA9 188 E2
Brantridge Rd CRAWE RH10 284 A9
Brants Wk HNWL W7 134 D6
Brantwood Av ERITH DA8 164 D6
ISLW TW7 154 F10
Brantwood Cl WALTH * E17 120 G1
Brantwood Dr BF/WBF KT14 215 J9
Brantwood Gdns BF/WBF KT14 215 J9
ENC/FH EN2 78 F8
REDBR IG4 122 B3
Brantwood Rd BXLYHN DA7 164 C8
HNHL SE24 181 K1
SAND/SEL CR2 223 K5
TOTM N17 99 P7
Brantwood Wy STMC/STPC BR5 207 M3
Brasenose Dr BARN SW13 156 F5
Brasher Cl NTHLT UB5 114 C10
Brassey Cl EBED/NFELT * TW14 175 H4
Brassey Hl OXTED RH8 261 M5
Brassey Rd CRICK NW2 2 D1
OXTED RH8 261 M5
Brassey Sq BTSEA SW11 158 B9
Brassie Av ACT W3 136 B8
Brasted Cl BELMT SM2 221 K6
BXLYHS DA6 185 N1
SYD SE26 182 B7
Brasted Hl RSEV TN14 245 K6
Brasted Hill Rd BH/WHM TN16 245 M8
Brasted La RSEV TN14 245 K5
Brasted Rd BH/WHM TN16 263 H2
ERITH DA8 164 F6
Brathway Rd WAND/EARL SW18 179 K3
Bratley St WCHPL E1 13 N2
Brattle Wd SEV TN13 265 K5
Braund Av GFD/PVL UB6 134 A6
Braundton Av BFN/LL DA15 185 J4
Braunston Dr YEAD UB4 133 M6
Bravington Cl SHPTN TW17 196 A5
Bravington Pl MV/WKIL * W9 8 C1
Bravington Rd MV/WKIL W9 2 C9
Braxfield Rd BROCKY SE4 160 D10
Braxted Pk STRHM/NOR SW16 180 G9
Brayard's Rd PECK SE15 160 A8
Braybourne Cl UX/CGN UB8 131 M1
Braybourne Dr ISLW TW7 154 E6
Braybrooke Gdns NRWD SE19 181 M10
Braybrook St SHB W12 136 C7
Brayburne Av VX/NE SW8 158 D8
Bray Cl BORE WD6 75 P5
CRAWE RH10 284 E9
Braycourt Av WOT/HER KT12 197 K7
Bray Crs BERM/RHTH SE16 160 C1
Braydon Rd STNW/STAM N16 119 N6
Bray Dr CAN/RD E16 141 L9
Brayfield Ter IS N1 6 A4
Brayford Sq WCHPL * E1 140 B8
Bray Gdns WOKS/MYFD GU22 233 H2
Bray Ldg CHES/WCR * EN8 62 D3
Bray Pl CHEL SW3 16 A7
Bray Rd COB KT11 235 M2
GUW GU2 267 N1
MLHL NW7 96 G7
Brays Cl AMS HP6 68 A1
Brays Green La AMS HP6 68 B1
Brays La AMS HP6 50 B10
Brays Md HLWS CM18 47 J3
Brays Meadow AMS HP6 68 B1
Brayton Gdns ENC/FH EN2 78 E8
Braywood Av EGH TW20 172 C9
Braywood Rd ELTH/MOT SE9 162 G10
Braziers End CSHM HP5 32 B7
Braziers Fld HERT/BAY SG13 25 N5
Breach Barns La WAB EN9 63 L6
Breach La DAGW RM9 144 B5
Breach Rd WTHK RM20 166 E5
Bread & Cheese La BROX EN10 61 M1
Breadcroft La HARP AL5 20 A1
Bread St STP EC4M 12 F6
Breakfield COUL/CHIP CR5 240 F2
Breakmead WGCE AL7 23 L7
Breakneck Hl GRH DA9 188 G1
Breakspear Av STAL AL1 38 E7
Breakspear Ct ABLGY WD5 54 G6
Breakspeare Cl WATN WD24 73 J4
Breakspeare Rd ABLGY WD5 54 F7
Breakspear Rd RSLP HA4 112 C4
Breakspear Rd North
DEN/HRF UB9 111 N1
Breakspear Rd South
HGDN/ICK UB10 112 A8
Breakspears Dr STMC/STPC BR5 207 K1
Breakspears Ms BROCKY SE4 160 F8
Breakspears Rd BROCKY SE4 160 E9
Breakspear Wy HHNE HP2 36 D6
Breaks Rd HAT AL10 40 E4
Bream Cl WALTH E17 120 A2
Bream Gdns EHAM E6 142 D5
Breamore Cl PUT/ROE SW15 178 D4
Breamore Rd GDMY/SEVK IG3 123 J7
Bream's Buildings LINN WC2A 12 A5
Bream St BOW E3 140 F2
Breamwater Gdns
RCHPK/HAM TW10 176 G6
Brearley Cl EDGW HA8 95 P8
HGDN/ICK UB10 131 P1
Breasley Cl PUT/ROE SW15 156 E10
Breasy Pl HDN * NW4 116 E2
Brechin Pl SKENS SW7 15 K7
Brecken Cl STALE/WH AL4 38 F2
Brecknock Rd ARCH N19 118 D9
HOLWY N7 5 K1
Brecknock Road Est ARCH * N19 118 E10
Brecon Cl MTCM CR4 202 F4
WPK KT4 200 F9
Brecon Gn CDALE/KGS * NW9 116 B4
Brecon Ms KTTN NW5 5 J1
Brecon Rd HMSMTH W6 14 A10
PEND EN3 80 B8
Brede Cl EHAM E6 142 D5
Bredgar Rd ARCH N19 118 D7
Bredhurst Cl PGE/AN SE20 182 B9
Bredon Rd CROY/NA CR0 203 N7
Bredune PUR/KEN CR8 241 L1
Bredward Cl SL SL1 128 A5
Breech La KWD/TDW/WH KT20 256 D1
Breer St FUL/PGN SW6 157 L9
Breezehurst Dr CRAWW RH11 283 J10
Breezer's Hl WAP E1W 13 P8
Brember Rd RYLN/HDSTN HA2 114 B7
Bremer Ms WALTH E17 120 G2
Bremer Rd STWL/WRAY TW19 173 K6
Bremner Av HORL RH6 280 A3
Bremner Cl SWLY BR8 209 H4
Bremner Rd SKENS SW7 15 K3
Brenchley Av GVW DA11 190 E8
Brenchley Cl CHST BR7 206 D1
HAYES BR2 205 L5
Brenchley Gdns FSTH SE23 182 B2
Brenchley Rd STMC/STPC BR5 207 H1
Brendans Cl EMPK RM11 125 M6
Brenda Rd TOOT SW17 180 A5
Brende Gdns E/WMO/HCT KT8 198 A4
Brendon SCUP * DA14 185 K7
Brendon Av WLSDN NW10 116 B9
Brendon Cl BXLYHN DA7 164 F7
ESH/CLAY KT10 218 B3
HYS/HAR UB3 152 D6
Brendon Ct RAD * WD7 56 G10
Brendon Dr ESH/CLAY KT10 218 B3
Brendon Gdns RYLN/HDSTN HA2 114 A9
Brendon Gv EFNCH N2 97 M10
Brendon Rd BCTR RM8 124 A6
CHST BR7 184 G5
Brendon St MBLAR W1H 9 P5
Brendon Vls WCHMH * N21 99 K2
Brendon Wy EN EN1 99 M1
Brenley Cl MTCM CR4 202 B3
Brenley Gdns ELTH/MOT SE9 162 A10
Brennan Rd TIL RM18 168 E8
Brent Cl BXLY DA5 185 P4
RDART DA2 188 A2
Brentcot Cl WEA W13 134 G6
Brent Crs WLSDN NW10 135 L4
Brent Cross F/O HDN NW4 116 F4
Brentfield WLSDN NW10 135 N2
Brentfield Cl WLSDN NW10 136 A1
Brentfield Gdns CRICK * NW2 116 G5
Brentfield Rd DART DA1 187 P2
WLSDN NW10 136 A1
Brentford Cl YEAD UB4 133 L6
Brent Gn HDN NW4 116 F3
Brentham Wy EA W5 135 J6
Brenthouse Rd HACK E8 140 A2
Brenthurst Rd WLSDN NW10 136 C1
Brentlands Dr DART DA1 187 P4
Brent La DART DA1 187 N3
Brent Lea BTFD TW8 155 H6
Brentmead Cl HNWL W7 134 D9
Brentmead Gdns WLSDN NW10 135 L4
Brentmoor Rd CHOB/PIR GU24 212 B9
Brenton St POP/IOD E14 140 D8
Brent Park Rd CDALE/KGS NW9 116 D6
Brent Pl BAR EN5 77 K9
Brent River Park Wk WEA W13 134 G5
Brent Rd BTFD TW8 155 H5
CAN/RD E16 141 M8
NWDGN UB2 153 K2
SAND/SEL CR2 224 A5
WOOL/PLUM SE18 162 E6
Brentside BTFD TW8 155 H5
Brentside Cl WEA W13 134 E6
Brent St HDN NW4 116 G3
Brent Ter CRICK NW2 116 F6
The Brent DART DA1 188 A3
Brentvale Av ALP/SUD HA0 135 L3
STHL UB1 134 C10
Brent View Rd CDALE/KGS NW9 116 D4
Brent Wy BTFD TW8 155 J6
DART DA1 188 A2
FNCH N3 97 K7
WBLY HA9 135 N1
Brentwick Gdns BTFD TW8 155 K3
Brentwood Cl ELTH/MOT SE9 184 F4
Brentwood Pl BRWN CM15 107 J2
Brentwood Rd CDH/CHF RM16 168 E3
CHONG CM5 67 P6
GPK RM2 125 K3
RBRW/HUT CM13 107 N6
ROM RM1 124 G4
Brereton Rd TOTM N17 99 N8
Bressenden Pl WESTW SW1E 16 F3
Bressey Av EN EN1 79 P5
Bressey Gv SWFD E18 101 L10
Bretlands Rd CHERT KT16 195 H9
Brett Cl NTHLT UB5 133 L5
STNW/STAM N16 119 M7
Brett Crs WLSDN NW10 136 A2
Brettell St WALW SE17 19 H8
Brettenham Av WALTH E17 100 F9
Brettenham Rd UED N18 99 P5
WALTH E17 100 F10
Brett Gdns DAGW RM9 143 P2
Brettgrave HOR/WEW KT19 219 P6
Brettingham Cl CRAWW * RH11 283 H10
Brett Pas HACK E8 120 A10
Brett Pl WATN WD24 73 H3
Brett Rd BAR EN5 76 F9
HACK E8 120 A10
Brett Vls ACT * W3 136 A7
Brevet Cl PUR RM19 166 C3
Brewer Rd CRAWE RH10 283 N9
Brewers Fld RDART DA2 187 K7
Brewer St REDH RH1 259 K7
REGST W1B 11 H7
Brewery Cl ALP/SUD HA0 114 F10
Brewery La BF/WBF KT14 215 P9
SEV TN13 265 J1
Brewery Rd HAYES BR2 206 B8
HOD EN11 44 F3
HOLWY N7 5 L2
WOKN/KNAP GU21 232 A3
WOOL/PLUM SE18 162 G4
Brewery Sq STHWK SE1 13 L10
Brewhouse Hl STALE/WH AL4 21 H3
Brewhouse La HERT/WAS SG14 25 K5
WAP E1W 140 A10
Brew House Rd
BRKHM/BTCW RH3 273 N4
Brewhouse Rd
WOOL/PLUM SE18 162 C3
Brewhouse St PUT/ROE SW15 157 H10
Brewhouse Wk
BERM/RHTH SE16 140 D10
Brewhouse Yd FSBYE EC1V 12 C1
GVE DA12 190 E2
Brewood Rd BCTR RM8 143 L1
Brewster Gdns NKENS W10 136 F7
Brewster Rd LEY E10 120 G6
Brian Av SAND/SEL CR2 223 M8
Brian Cl HCH RM12 125 J9
Briane Rd HOR/WEW KT19 219 P6
Brian Rd CHDH RM6 123 M3
Briants Cl PIN HA5 93 M9
Briant St NWCR SE14 160 C7
Briar Av STRHM/NOR SW16 180 G10
Briarbank Rd WEA W13 134 F8
Briarcliff HHW HP1 35 H5
Briar Cl BERK HP4 34 D2
BF/WBF KT14 215 L7
BKHH IG9 102 A3
CHES/WCR EN8 62 B5
CRAWW RH11 283 M4
EFNCH N2 97 M10
HPTN TW12 175 N8
ISLW TW7 176 E1
MDHD SL6 128 A8
PLMGR N13 99 K4
Briar Crs NTHLT UB5 134 A1
Briardale Gdns HAMP NW3 117 K8
Briarfield Av EFNCH N2 117 L1
FNCH N3 97 L10
Briar Gdns HAYES BR2 205 L8
Briar Gv SAND/SEL CR2 223 P9
Briar Hl PUR/KEN CR8 222 F7
Briar La CAR SM5 222 B5
CROY/NA CR0 224 G1
Briarleas Gdns UPMR RM14 126 D5
Briarley Cl BROX EN10 44 E8
Briar Rd BXLY DA5 186 E6
CRICK NW2 116 F9
GSTN WD25 55 H10
HARH RM3 105 K8
KTN/HRWW/W HA3 115 H3
RPLY/SEND GU23 232 E10
SHPTN TW17 196 A5
STALE/WH AL4 39 H3
STRHM/NOR SW16 202 F3
WHTN TW2 176 D4
Briars Cl HAT AL10 40 D4
Briars Ct LHD/OX KT22 218 C10
Briars La HAT AL10 40 D4
The Briars CHES/WCR EN8 62 D7
DTCH/LGLY SL3 150 C4
HERT/BAY SG13 25 P5
HLWS CM18 47 H4
RKW/CH/CXG WD3 71 K2
Briars Wk HARH RM3 105 M10
Briars Wy HART DA3 211 M5
Briars Wd HAT AL10 40 D4
HORL RH6 280 D3
Briarswood Cl CRAWE RH10 284 E5
Briarswood Wy ORP BR6 227 J2
Briar Wk BF/WBF KT14 215 K8
EDGW HA8 95 P8
NKENS W10 8 A1
PUT/ROE SW15 156 E10
Briar Wy BERK HP4 33 P6
RGUE GU4 250 E6
SLN SL2 128 G7
WDR/YW UB7 152 B1
Briarwood BRWN CM15 86 E3
Briarwood Cl CDALE/KGS * NW9 115 P4
FELT TW13 174 F6
Briarwood Ct WPK * KT4 200 D8
Briarwood Dr NTHWD HA6 93 H10
Briarwood Rd CLAP SW4 180 E1
EW KT17 220 D3
WOKN/KNAP GU21 231 J5
Briary Cl EDGW HA8 95 N10
HAMP NW3 3 N3
Briary Ct SCUP DA14 185 L8
Briary Gdns BMLY BR1 183 N8
Briary La ED N9 99 M4
Brickbarn Cl WBPTN * SW10 157 M6
Brick Ct EMB * EC4Y 12 A6
GRAYS * RM17 167 M5
Brickcroft BROX EN10 62 D2
Brickendon La HERT/BAY SG13 25 K8
Bricket Rd STAL AL1 38 D6
Brickett Cl RSLP HA4 112 D3
Brick Farm Cl RCH/KEW TW9 155 N7
Brickfield HAT AL10 40 D7
Brickfield Av HHS/BOV HP3 36 C7
Brickfield Cl BTFD TW8 155 H6
Brickfield Cottages
WOOL/PLUM SE18 163 J6
Brickfield Farm Gdns ORP BR6 226 F1
Brickfield La BAR EN5 76 C10
HYS/HAR UB3 152 E5
Brickfield Rd BOW E3 140 G6
EPP CM16 65 N5
REDH RH1 277 K9
THHTH CR7 203 J1
WIM/MER SW19 179 L7
Brickfields RYLN/HDSTN HA2 114 C7
The Brickfields WARE SG12 26 A1
Brickfields Wy WDR/YW UB7 152 A2
Brickfield Vls SUT * SM1 201 P10
Brick Kiln Cl BUSH WD23 73 M10
Brick Kiln La OXTED RH8 261 P6
Brick Knoll Pk STALE/WH AL4 39 H7
Brick La BETH E2 7 M10
EN EN1 80 A6
STAN HA7 95 J8
WCHPL E1 13 M2
Brickmakers La HHS/BOV HP3 36 C7
Brickstock Furze BRWN * CM15 107 M2
Brick St MYFR/PICC W1J 10 E10
Brickwall Cl WGCW AL8 22 D3
Brickwall La RSLP HA4 112 F6
Brickwood Cl SYD SE26 182 A6
Brickwood Rd CROY/NA CR0 203 M9
Brickyard La RDKG RH5 271 L7
Brideake Cl CRAWW RH11 283 K10
Brideale Cl PECK SE15 19 M10
Bride Ct BLKFR * EC4V 12 C6
Bride La EMB EC4Y 12 C6
Bridel Ms FSBYE EC1V 6 C8
Bride St HOLWY N7 5 P2
Bridewain St STHWK SE1 19 L3
Bridewell Pl BLKFR EC4V 12 C6
WAP E1W 140 A10
Bridford Ms REGST W1B 10 F3
Bridge Ap CAMTN NW1 4 C3
Bridge Av HMSMTH W6 156 F4
HNWL W7 134 C7
UPMR RM14 125 P8
Bridge Barn La
WOKN/KNAP GU21 231 P3
Bridge Cl BF/WBF KT14 216 A8
EN EN1 80 A6
GRH DA9 166 C9
NKENS W10 136 G8
RBRW/HUT CM13 107 K4
ROM RM1 124 F4
SL SL1 128 E9
STA TW18 173 H7
WOKN/KNAP GU21 231 P3
WOT/HER KT12 196 G7
Bridge Ct GRAYS * RM17 167 N5
RAD * WD7 74 G1
WOKN/KNAP GU21 232 A3
Bridge Dr PLMGR N13 98 G5
Bridge End WALTH E17 101 H9
Bridgefield Cl BNSTD SM7 238 F1
Bridgefield Rd SUT SM1 221 K3
Bridgefields WGCE AL7 23 J4
Bridge Foot WARE * SG12 26 C2
Bridge Gdns ASHF TW15 174 D10
E/WMO/HCT KT8 198 C4
Bridge Ga WCHMH N21 99 K1
Bridgeham Cl WEY KT13 216 B2
Bridgeham Wy HORL RH6 281 J5
Bridge Hl EPP CM16 65 J9
Bridgehill Cl GUW GU2 249 M8
Bridge House Quay
POP/IOD E14 141 H10
Bridgeland Rd CAN/RD E16 141 M9
Bridgelands CRAWE RH10 284 G2
Bridge La BTSEA SW11 157 P7
GLDGN NW11 117 H3
VW GU25 194 B6
Bridgeman Dr WDSR SL4 148 F8
Bridgeman Rd IS N1 5 P4
TEDD TW11 176 F9
Bridgeman St STJWD NW8 3 N8
Bridge Mdw NWCR SE14 160 C5
Bridge Ms WOKN/KNAP GU21 232 A3
Bridgend Rd EN EN1 80 B1
Bridgenhall Rd EN EN1 79 N5
Bridgen Rd BXLY DA5 185 P3
Bridge Pde STRHM/NOR * SW16 180 F8
WCHMH * N21 99 K1
Bridge Pk RGUE * GU4 250 F7
Bridge Pl AMS HP6 69 K4
CROY/NA CR0 203 L8
PIM SW1V 16 F5
WAT WD17 73 L9
Bridgeport Pl WAP * E1W 13 P9
Bridger Cl GSTN WD25 55 L9
Bridge Rd ASC SL5 192 C5
BECK BR3 182 E10
BELMT SM2 221 L3
BXLYHN DA7 163 P9
CHERT KT16 195 L7
CHONG CM5 49 K7
CHSGTN KT9 219 K2
COB KT11 235 J1
E/WMO/HCT KT8 198 D4
ED N9 99 P4
EHAM E6 142 C2
ERITH DA8 164 G7
EW KT17 220 C8
GRAYS RM17 167 N4
HSLW TW3 154 C9
KGLGY WD4 54 D9
LEY E10 120 E5
NWDGN UB2 153 N1
RAIN RM13 145 H6
SRTFD E15 141 J3
STMC/STPC BR5 207 L6
TWK TW1 176 G2
UX/CGN UB8 131 M4
WBLY HA9 115 M8
WDGN N22 98 F9
WEY KT13 216 A1
WGCW AL8 22 F4
WLGTN SM6 222 C2
WLSDN NW10 136 B1
Bridge Rd East WGCE AL7 23 J5
Bridge Rw CROY/NA * CR0 203 L8
Bridges Cl HORL RH6 280 E4
Bridges Ct BTSEA SW11 157 N9
HERT/WAS SG14 25 K5
Bridges Dr DART DA1 188 A1
Bridges La CROY/NA CR0 222 F1
Bridges Rd STAN HA7 94 E6
Bridge St BERK HP4 34 A5
CHSWK W4 156 A3
DTCH/LGLY SL3 150 G6
GU GU1 267 P1
HHW HP1 35 M7
LHD/OX KT22 236 F8
PIN HA5 113 L1
TWK TW1 177 J2
WEST SW1P 17 L2
WOT/HER KT12 196 G7
Bridge Ter LEW * SE13 161 J10
SRTFD E15 141 J2
The Bridge EA * W5 135 L10
KTN/HRWW/W HA3 114 E1
Bridgetown Cl NRWD SE19 181 M8
Bridge Vw ASC SL5 192 G7
Bridgeview HMSMTH W6 156 F4
Bridge Vls WIM/MER * SW19 179 K8
Bridgewater Cl CHST BR7 207 H3
Bridgewater Ct DTCH/LGLY SL3 150 D4
Bridgewater Gdns EDGW HA8 95 L10
Bridgewater Hl BERK HP4 33 L2
Bridgewater Rd ALP/SUD HA0 134 G1
BERK HP4 33 N3
RSLP HA4 113 H9
SRTFD E15 141 H3
WEY KT13 216 E3
Bridgewater Sq BARB * EC2Y 12 E3
Bridgewater St BARB EC2Y 12 E3
Bridgewater Ter WDSR SL4 149 J7
Bridgewater Wy BUSH WD23 74 A10
WDSR SL4 149 J7
Bridgeway ALP/SUD HA0 135 K2
BARK IG11 143 J2
Bridge Wy COUL/CHIP CR5 239 P5
GLDGN NW11 117 J3
HGDN/ICK UB10 112 C10
WHTN TW2 176 B3
Bridgeway St CAMTN NW1 5 H8
Bridgewood Cl PGE/AN SE20 182 A10
Bridgewood Rd
STRHM/NOR SW16 180 E10
WPK KT4 220 D1
Bridgford St WAND/EARL SW18 179 M6
Bridgman Rd CHSWK W4 155 P2
Bridgwater Rd HARH RM3 105 K6
Bridgwater Wk HARH RM3 105 L6
Bridle Cl HOD EN11 26 F9
HOR/WEW KT19 219 P1
KUT KT1 199 J4
PEND EN3 80 E3
STALW/RED AL3 38 D4
SUN TW16 197 H3
Bridle La COB KT11 236 A1
RKW/CH/CXG WD3 71 M7
SOHO/CST W1F 11 H7
TWK TW1 176 G2
Bridle Pth CROY/NA CR0 202 F10
WAT WD17 73 J6
The Bridle Pth EW KT17 220 F6
WFD IG8 101 K8
Bridlepath Wy
EBED/NFELT TW14 174 F3
Bridle Rd CROY/NA CR0 204 F10
ESH/CLAY KT10 218 G3
EW KT17 220 C9
PIN HA5 113 K4
The Bridle Rd PUR/KEN CR8 222 F6
Bridle Wy BERK HP4 33 M3
CRAWE RH10 284 E6
CROY/NA CR0 224 F2
HOD EN11 26 F10
ORP BR6 226 F1
WARE SG12 26 F5
Bridleway Cl EW KT17 220 F6
Bridle Wy (North) HOD EN11 26 F9
Bridle Wy (South) HOD EN11 26 F10
The Bridle Wy WLGTN SM6 222 D1
Bridlington Cl BH/WHM TN16 243 N5
Bridlington Rd ED N9 100 A1
OXHEY WD19 93 L4
Bridlington Sp SL SL1 148 G2
Bridport Av ROMW/RG RM7 124 C4
Bridport Pl IS N1 7 H6
Bridport Rd NTHLT UB5 134 A3
THHTH CR7 203 H3
UED N18 99 M6
Bridport Wy SLN SL2 128 G6
Bridstow Pl BAY/PAD W2 8 F5
Brief St CMBW SE5 159 J7
Brier Lea KWD/TDW/WH KT20 257 J2
Brierley Av ED N9 100 B2
Brierley Cl EMPK RM11 125 K4
SNWD SE25 203 P4
Brierley Rd BAL SW12 180 D5
WAN E11 121 J9
Brierly Cl GUW GU2 249 M8
Brierly Gdns BETH * E2 140 B4
Brier Rd KWD/TDW/WH KT20 238 E5
Briery Fld RKW/CH/CXG WD3 71 K7
Briery Wy AMS HP6 69 K3
HHNE HP2 36 B4
Brigade Cl RYLN/HDSTN HA2 114 C7
Brigade Pl CTHM CR3 241 K8
Brigade St BKHTH/KID * SE3 161 L8
Brigadier Av ENC/FH EN2 79 K5
Brigadier Hl ENC/FH EN2 79 K4
Briggeford Cl CLPT E5 119 P7
Briggs Cl MTCM CR4 202 C1
Bright Cl BELV DA17 163 N3
Brightfield Rd LEW SE13 183 K1
Bright Hl GU GU1 268 A2
Brightlands GVW DA11 190 B7
Brightlands Rd REIG RH2 257 M8
Brightling Rd BROCKY SE4 182 E2
Brightlingsea Pl POP/IOD E14 140 E9
Brightman Rd WAND/EARL SW18 179 N4
Brighton Av WALTH E17 120 E3
Brighton Cl ADL/WDHM KT15 215 M2

HGDN/ICK UB10 132 C2
Brighton Dr NTHLT UB5 133 P1
Brighton Rd ADL/WDHM KT15 215 M1
BNSTD SM7 221 J10
COUL/CHIP CR5 240 D4
CRAWW RH11 283 N10
EFNCH N2 97 M10
EHAM E6 142 D5
HORL RH6 280 A4
KWD/TDW/WH KT20 257 J2
PUR/KEN CR8 222 F10
REDH RH1 258 A10
REDH RH1 276 B8
STNW/STAM N16 119 M9
SURB KT6 199 H6
WATN WD24 73 H4
Brighton Sp SLN SL2 128 G6
Brighton Ter BRXN/ST SW9 158 G10
REDH * RH1 276 A1
Brights Av RAIN RM13 145 J6
Brightside Av STA TW18 173 M10
Brightside Rd LEW SE13 183 J2
The Brightside PEND EN3 80 C5
Bright St POP/IOD E14 140 G8
Brightview Cl LCOL/BKTW AL2 55 M5
Brightwell Cl CROY/NA CR0 203 H8
Brightwell Crs TOOT SW17 180 A8
Brightwell Rd WATW WD18 73 H9
Brig Ms DEPT SE8 160 F5
Brigstock Rd BELV DA17 164 C3
COUL/CHIP CR5 240 C1
THHTH CR7 203 J5
Brill Pl CAMTN NW1 5 K8
Brimfield Rd PUR RM19 166 C3
Brim Hl EFNCH N2 117 M2
Brimpsfield Cl ABYW SE2 163 L2
Brimsdown Av PEND EN3 80 D5
Brimshot La CHOB/PIR GU24 213 K5
Brimstone Cl ORP BR6 227 M4
Brimstone Wy BERK HP4 33 L3
Brindle Ga BFN/LL DA15 185 H4
Brindles EMPK RM11 125 M2
Brindles Cl RBRW/HUT CM13 107 P3
TIL RM18 169 K3
The Brindles BNSTD SM7 239 J3
Brindley Cl BXLYHN DA7 164 B9
GFD/PVL UB6 135 H3
Brindley St NWCR SE14 160 E7
Brindley Wy BMLY BR1 183 M8
STHL UB1 134 A9
Brindwood Rd CHING E4 100 F4
Brinkburn Cl ABYW SE2 163 K3
EDGW HA8 115 N1
Brinkburn Gdns EDGW HA8 115 M1
Brinkley Rd WPK KT4 200 E9
Brinklow Ct STAL AL1 38 A9
Brinklow Crs WOOL/PLUM SE18 162 E6
Brinkworth Rd CLAY IG5 122 B1
Brinkworth Wy HOM * E9 140 E1
Brinley Cl CHES/WCR EN8 62 C7
Brinsdale Rd HDN NW4 116 G1
Brinsley Rd KTN/HRWW/W HA3 94 C10
Brinsley St WCHPL * E1 140 A8
Brinsmead LCOL/BKTW AL2 56 C3
Brinsmead Rd HARH RM3 105 P10
Brinsworth Cl WHTN TW2 176 C4
Brinton Wk STHWK SE1 12 C10
Brion Pl POP/IOD E14 141 H7
Brisbane Av WIM/MER SW19 201 L1
Brisbane Ct CRAWW RH11 283 N4
Brisbane Rd IL IG1 122 F5
LEY E10 120 G7
Brisbane St CMBW SE5 159 L6
Briscoe Cl HOD EN11 44 E1
WAN E11 121 L7
Briscoe Rd HOD EN11 44 E1
RAIN RM13 145 K4
WIM/MER SW19 179 N9
Briset Rd ELTH/MOT SE9 162 A9
Briset St FARR EC1M 12 C3
Briset Wy HOLWY N7 118 G7
Brisson Cl ESH/CLAY KT10 217 N3
Bristol Cl CRAWE RH10 284 E4
STWL/WRAY TW19 173 P2
Bristol Gdns MV/WKIL W9 9 H2
Bristol Ms MV/WKIL W9 9 H2
Bristol Park Rd WALTH * E17 120 D2
Bristol Rd FSTGT E7 141 P1
GFD/PVL UB6 134 A3
GVE DA12 190 G6
MRDN SM4 201 M5
Bristol Wy SL SL1 129 L10
Briston Gv CEND/HSY/T N8 118 F4
Bristow Rd BXLYHN DA7 163 P7
CROY/NA CR0 222 F1
HSLW TW3 154 A9
NRWD SE19 181 M8
Britannia Cl CLAP SW4 158 E10
NTHLT UB5 133 L5
Britannia Dr GVE DA12 191 J8
Britannia Ga CAN/RD E16 141 M10
Britannia Rd BRW CM14 107 H6
BRYLDS KT5 199 L7
CHES/WCR EN8 62 E10
CSHM HP5 51 H5
FUL/PGN SW6 157 L6
IL IG1 122 E8
NFNCH/WDSP N12 97 M4
POP/IOD E14 160 F3
Britannia Rw IS N1 6 D5
Britannia St FSBYW WC1X 5 N9
Britannia Wk IS N1 6 G8
Britannia Wy FUL/PGN SW6 157 L6
STWL/WRAY TW19 173 N3
WLSDN NW10 135 N6
British Est BOW E3 140 E5
British Gv CHSWK W4 156 C4
British Grove Pas CHSWK * W4 156 C4
British Legion Rd CHING E4 101 L3
British St BOW E3 140 E5
Briton Cl SAND/SEL CR2 223 M7
Briton Crs SAND/SEL CR2 223 M7
Briton Hill Rd SAND/SEL CR2 223 M6
Brittain Rd BCTR RM8 123 P8
WOT/HER KT12 217 L2
Brittains La SEV TN13 246 G10
Britten Cl BORE WD6 75 J10
CRAWW RH11 283 J10
GLDGN NW11 117 L6
Brittenden Pde ORP * BR6 227 J3
Britten Dr STHL UB1 133 P8
Brittens Cl GUW GU2 249 M5
Britten St CHEL SW3 15 N8
Britton Av STALW/RED AL3 38 C6
Britton Cl CAT SE6 183 J3
Britton St FARR EC1M 12 C2
Britwell Dr BERK HP4 34 B3
Britwell Rd SL SL1 128 B5
Brixham Crs RSLP HA4 113 H6
Brixham Gdns GDMY/SEVK IG3 123 H10
Brixham Rd WELL DA16 163 N7
Brixham St CAN/RD E16 142 C10
Brixton Hl BRXS/STRHM SW2 180 G2
Brixton Hill Pl BRXS/STRHM SW2 180 F3
Brixton Ov BRXN/ST SW9 159 H10
Brixton Rd LBTH SE11 18 A10
WATN WD24 73 J5
Brixton Station Rd
BRXN/ST SW9 159 H9
Brixton Water La
BRXS/STRHM SW2 180 G1
Broad Acre LCOL/BKTW AL2 55 M6
Broadacre STA TW18 173 K8
Broadacre Cl HGDN/ICK UB10 112 C8
Broadacres GUW GU2 249 K8
Broad Acres HAT AL10 40 C1
RGODL GU7 267 K9
Broadbent St MYFR/PKLN * W1K 10 E7
Broad Bridge Cl BKHTH/KID SE3 161 M6
Broadbridge La HORL RH6 281 H4
Broad Cl WOT/HER KT12 197 L10
Broad Common Est
STNW/STAM * N16 119 P6
Broadcoombe SAND/SEL CR2 224 C4
Broad Ct COVGDN * WC2E 11 M6
WGCE AL7 23 H5
Broadcroft HHNE HP2 35 N4
Broadcroft Av STAN HA7 95 J10
Broadcroft Rd STMC/STPC BR5 206 G7
Broad Ditch Rd MEO DA13 189 P10
Broadeaves Cl SAND/SEL CR2 223 M2
Broadfield HLW CM20 29 H10
Broadfield Cl CRICK NW2 116 F8
KWD/TDW/WH KT20 238 F6
ROM RM1 124 G3
Broadfield Ct BUSH WD23 94 D3
Broadfield Dr CRAWW RH11 283 L10
Broadfield La HOLWY N7 5 L4
Broadfield Pde EDGW * HA8 95 N4
Broadfield Pl WGCW AL8 22 E6
Broadfield Rd CAT SE6 183 K4
HHNE HP2 36 A6
SHGR GU5 270 E8
Broadfields CHESW EN7 61 J5
E/WMO/HCT KT8 198 C6
PIN HA5 94 A10
SBW CM21 29 L2
Broadfields Av EDGW HA8 95 N5
WCHMH N21 99 H1
Broadfields Hts EDGW HA8 95 N5
Broadfields La OXHEY WD19 93 J2
Broadfield Sq EN EN1 80 A7
Broadfields Wy WLSDN NW10 116 C10
Broadford La CHOB/PIR GU24 213 K8
Broadford Pk RGUE GU4 268 A7
Broadford Rd RGUE GU4 268 A7
Broadgate WAB EN9 63 L9
Broadgates Av EBAR EN4 77 L6
Broadgates Rd
WAND/EARL SW18 179 N4
Broad Gn HERT/BAY SG13 42 G1
Broad Green Av CROY/NA CR0 203 J7
Broadgreen Rd CHESW EN7 61 L2
Broad Green Wd HERT/BAY SG13 42 G1
Broadham Green Rd OXTED RH8 261 J9
Broadham Pl OXTED RH8 261 J8
Broadhead Strd CDALE/KGS NW9 96 C10
Broadheath Dr CHST BR7 184 C8
Broad Hwy COB KT11 217 L10
Broadhinton Rd CLAP SW4 158 C9
Broadhurst ASHTD KT21 237 K2
Broadhurst Av EDGW HA8 95 N5
GDMY/SEVK IG3 123 J9
Broadhurst Cl KIL/WHAMP NW6 3 J2
Broadhurst Gdns KIL/WHAMP NW6 3 H2
KIL/WHAMP NW6 137 L1
REIG RH2 275 L3
RSLP HA4 113 K7
Broadlake Cl LCOL/BKTW AL2 57 J3
Broadlands FELT TW13 175 N6
GRAYS RM17 167 L4
HORL RH6 280 D3
Broadlands Av CSHM HP5 51 H6
PEND EN3 80 A7
SHPTN TW17 196 D6
STRHM/NOR SW16 180 F5
Broadlands Cl HGT N6 118 B5
PEND EN3 80 A7
STRHM/NOR SW16 180 F5
Broadlands Dr ASC SL5 192 B7
WARL CR6 242 B5
Broadlands Rd BMLY BR1 183 N7
HGT N6 118 A5
Broadlands Wy NWMAL KT3 200 C6
Broad La HPTN TW12 175 N10
RDART DA2 187 J7
RDKG RH5 278 A2
SEVS/STOTM N15 119 P2
Broad Lawn ELTH/MOT SE9 184 D4
Broadlawns Ct
KTN/HRWW/W HA3 94 E9
Broadleaf Gv WLYN AL6 22 E2
Broadley Gn BFOR GU20 212 C4
Broadley Rd HLWW/ROY CM19 46 C5
Broadley St STJWD NW8 9 N3
Broadley Ter CAMTN NW1 9 P2
Broadmark Rd SLN SL2 129 N9
Broadmead ASHTD KT21 237 K4
CAT SE6 182 F6
HORL RH6 280 D3
REDH * RH1 258 D4
Broadmead Av WPK KT4 200 D7
Broadmead Cl HPTN TW12 175 P9
PIN * HA5 93 M8
Broad Meadow BRWN CM15 86 E4
Broadmead Rd WFD IG8 101 M7
YEAD UB4 133 M6
Broadmeads RPLY/SEND GU23 232 E8
WARE SG12 26 C2
Broad Oak SLN SL2 129 H6
SUN TW16 174 G9
WFD IG8 101 N6
Broadoak Av PEND EN3 80 C1
Broad Oak Cl CHING E4 100 F6
STMC/STPC BR5 207 K2
Broadoak Cl RDART DA2 187 P9
Broad Oak Ct SLN SL2 129 H6
Broadoak End HERT/WAS * SG14 24 G2
Broadoak Rd ERITH DA8 164 E6
Broadoaks EPP CM16 65 J8
Broad Oaks SURB KT6 199 N8
Broadoaks Crs BF/WBF KT14 215 L10
Broad Oaks Wy HAYES BR2 205 L5
Broad Platts DTCH/LGLY SL3 150 A2
Broad Rd SWCM DA10 189 K2
Broadstone Pl MHST W1U 10 C4
Broadstone Rd HARP AL5 20 B5
HCH RM12 125 H7
Broad St CHOB/PIR GU24 212 C8
CSHM HP5 51 H6
DAGE RM10 144 B2
HHNE HP2 35 N6
RGUW GU3 249 J8
TEDD TW11 176 E9
Broad Street Av LVPST EC2M 13 J4
Broad Street Pl LVPST EC2M 13 H4
Broadstrood LOU IG10 82 D4
Broadview CDALE/KGS NW9 115 M4
Broadview Av CDH/CHF RM16 168 A1
Broadview Rd CSHM HP5 50 G3
STRHM/NOR SW16 180 E10
Broad Wk BGR/WK TN15 265 M4
BKHTH/KID SE3 161 P8
COUL/CHIP CR5 240 B8
CTHM CR3 241 N8
HEST TW5 153 L7
HLW * CM20 28 G10
KWD/TDW/WH KT20 238 F5
ORP BR6 207 N10
RCH/KEW TW9 155 L6
WCHMH N21 99 H2
Broadwalk CRAWE RH10 283 N7
RYLN/HDSTN * HA2 114 A3
SWFD E18 121 L1
Broadwalk La GLDGN NW11 117 J5
The Broad Wk North
RBRW/HUT CM13 107 M4
The Broadwalk South
RBRW/HUT CM13 107 M5
The Broad Wk KENS W8 9 H9
NTHWD HA6 92 D10
Broadwall STHWK SE1 12 B9
Broadwater BERK HP4 33 P4
POTB/CUF EN6 59 L6
Broadwater Cl
STWL/WRAY TW19 172 B3
WOKN/KNAP GU21 214 G8
WOT/HER KT12 217 H2
Broadwater Crs WGCE AL7 22 G6
Broadwater Gdns DEN/HRF UB9 111 L2
ORP BR6 226 E1
Broadwater La DEN/HRF UB9 111 L2
Broadwater Pk DEN/HRF * UB9 111 K4
Broadwater Ri GU GU1 268 D1
Broadwater Rd TOOT SW17 179 P7
TOTM N17 99 M10
WGCE AL7 23 H6
WGCW AL8 22 G6
WOOL/PLUM SE18 162 G2
Broadwater Rd North
WOT/HER KT12 216 G2
Broadwater Rd South
WOT/HER KT12 217 H2
Broadway AMSS HP7 68 G6
BARK IG11 142 F3
BXLYHS DA6 163 P10
DEN/HRF * UB9 111 K5
GPK RM2 125 H1
GRAYS RM17 167 P5
HNWL W7 134 D10
RAIN RM13 145 H6
SRTFD E15 141 J2
STA * TW18 173 L8
STJSPK SW1H 17 J2
SURB KT6 199 N8
SUT SM1 221 M1
TIL RM18 168 G8
WDSR SL4 170 A4
WOKN/KNAP GU21 230 G5
Broadway Av CROY/NA CR0 203 L5
HLWE CM17 29 L7
TWK TW1 176 G2
Broadway Cl AMSS HP7 68 G6
SAND/SEL CR2 224 A10
WFD IG8 101 N7
Broadway Ct WIM/MER * SW19 179 K9
Broadway Gdns MTCM CR4 201 P4
Broadway Market HACK E8 140 A3
Broadway Market Ms HACK E8 7 P6
Broadway Ms STNW/STAM N16 119 N5
Broadway Pde CHING * E4 101 H7
HYS/HAR * UB3 152 G1
RYLN/HDSTN * HA2 114 A3
WDR/YW * UB7 151 P1
Broadway Rd CHOB/PIR GU24 212 C5
The Broadway ACT * W3 155 M1
ADL/WDHM KT15 215 K6
BCTR RM8 124 A7
BEAC * HP9 88 C8
BEAC * HP9 88 D10
BRKMPK AL9 40 F4
CDALE/KGS NW9 116 C4
CEND/HSY/T N8 118 F4
CFSP/GDCR * SL9 90 A9
CHEAM SM3 221 H3
CRAWE RH10 283 N7
CSHM HP5 51 H7
EA W5 135 J9
FBAR/BDGN * N11 98 A6
HCH RM12 125 J9
KTN/HRWW/W HA3 94 D10
LOU IG10 82 F7
MLHL NW7 96 B6
PIN HA5 93 N8
PLSTW E13 141 M4
POTB/CUF * EN6 59 J8
RYLN/HDSTN * HA2 114 C7
STA TW18 195 M2
STAL * AL1 38 C6
STAN HA7 95 H6
THDIT KT7 198 D8
WAT WD17 73 K7
WFD IG8 101 N7
WIM/MER SW19 179 J9
WOKN/KNAP GU21 232 C3
Broadwell Pde KIL/WHAMP * NW6 3 K2
Broadwick St SOHO/CST W1F 11 H6
Broadwood GVW DA11 190 E8
Broadwood Av RSLP HA4 112 F4
Broadwood Ter WKENS W14 14 D5
Broad Yd FARR EC1M 12 C2
Brocas Cl HAMP NW3 3 P3
Brocas St WDSR SL4 149 J6
Brocas Ter WDSR SL4 149 H6
Brockdene Dr HAYES BR2 226 A1
Brockdish Av BARK IG11 123 J10
Brockenhurst E/WMO/HCT KT8 197 N5
Brockenhurst Av WPK KT4 200 B8
Brockenhurst Cl
WOKN/KNAP GU21 214 C10
Brockenhurst Gdns IL IG1 122 F10
MLHL NW7 96 B7
Brockenhurst Rd ASC SL5 192 A5
CROY/NA CR0 204 A7
Brockenhurst Wy
STRHM/NOR SW16 202 E2
Brocket Cl CHIC IG7 103 J5
Brocket Rd HOD EN11 44 F3
WGCW AL8 22 C7
Brockett Cl WGCW AL8 22 E5
Brockett Rd CDH/CHF RM16 168 D2
Brocket Vw STALE/WH AL4 21 J3
Brocket Wy CHIG IG7 103 H6
Brock Gn SOCK/AV RM15 146 G8
Brockham Cl WIM/MER SW19 179 J8
Brockham Crs CROY/NA CR0 225 J4
Brockham Dr BRXS/STRHM SW2 180 G3
GNTH/NBYPK IG2 122 F4
Brockham Hill Pk
KWD/TDW/WH KT20 255 P7
Brockhamhurst Rd
BRKHM/BTCW RH3 273 N7
Brockham La BRKHM/BTCW RH3 255 M10
Brockham St STHWK SE1 18 F3
Brockhill WOKN/KNAP * GU21 231 M3
Brockhurst Cl STAN HA7 94 E7
Brockhurst Rd CSHM HP5 51 H5
Brockill Crs BROCKY SE4 160 D10
Brocklebank Rd CHARL SE7 161 N3
WAND/EARL SW18 179 M3
Brocklehurst St NWCR SE14 160 C6
Brocklesbury Cl WATN WD24 73 K7
Brocklesby Rd SNWD SE25 204 A4
Brockles Md HLWW/ROY CM19 46 F5
Brockley Av EDGW HA8 95 K4
Brockley Cl STAN HA7 95 K5
Brockley Combe WEY KT13 216 E2
Brockley Crs CRW RM5 104 D8
Brockley Cross BROCKY SE4 160 D9
Brockley Gv BROCKY SE4 182 E1
RBRW/HUT CM13 107 M2
Brockley Hall Rd BROCKY SE4 182 D2
Brockley Hl STAN HA7 95 H3
Brockley Ms BROCKY SE4 182 D1
Brockley Pk FSTH SE23 182 D3
Brockley Ri FSTH SE23 182 D2
Brockleyside STAN * HA7 95 K5
Brockley Vw FSTH SE23 182 D3
Brockley Wy FSTH SE23 182 C1
Brockman Ri BMLY BR1 183 J7
Brock Pl BOW E3 140 G6
Brock Rd CRAWW RH11 283 L4
PLSTW E13 141 N7
Brocks Dr CHEAM SM3 201 H10
RGUW GU3 249 H6
Brockshot Cl BTFD TW8 155 J5
Brocksparkwood
RBRW/HUT CM13 107 N4
Brock St PECK * SE15 160 B9
Brockswood La WGCW AL8 22 E4
Brockton Cl ROM RM1 124 G2
Brock Wy VW GU25 193 P5
Brockway Cl GU GU1 250 E9
WAN E11 121 K7
Brockwell Cl STMC/STPC BR5 207 J5
Brockwell Park Gdns HNHL SE24 181 J3
Brockworth Cl PECK SE15 19 J10
Brodewater Rd BORE WD6 75 N6
Brodia Rd STNW/STAM N16 119 M8
Brodie Rd CHING E4 101 H2
ENC/FH EN2 79 K4
GU GU1 268 B1
Brodie St STHWK SE1 19 M7
Brodlove La WAP E1W 140 C9
Brodrick Gv ABYW SE2 163 L3
GT/LBKH KT23 253 P2
Brodrick Rd TOOT SW17 180 A4
Brograve Gdns BECK BR3 204 G2
Broke Ct RGUE GU4 250 F7
Broke Farm Dr ORP BR6 227 M5
Broken Furlong WDSR SL4 149 H4
Broken Gate La DEN/HRF UB9 110 F6
Brokes Crs REIG RH2 257 K8
Brokesley St BOW E3 140 E6
Brokes Rd REIG RH2 257 K8
Broke Wk HACK E8 7 N5
Bromar Rd CMBW SE5 159 M9
Bromborough Gn OXHEY WD19 93 K6
Bromefield STAN HA7 95 H9
Bromefield Ct WAB EN9 63 M9
Bromehead St WCHPL E1 140 B8
Bromell's Rd CLAP SW4 158 D10
Brome Rd ELTH/MOT SE9 162 C9
Bromet Cl WAT WD17 72 G4
Bromfelde Rd CLAP SW4 158 E9
Bromfield St IS N1 6 B7
Bromford Cl OXTED RH8 261 M9
Bromhall Rd DAGW RM9 143 L1
Bromhedge ELTH/MOT SE9 184 C6
Bromholm Rd ABYW SE2 163 L2
Bromleigh Cl CHES/WCR EN8 62 D4
Bromley GRAYS RM17 167 L5
Bromley Av BMLY BR1 183 K10
Bromley Common HAYES BR2 206 B7
Bromley Crs HAYES BR2 205 L3
RSLP HA4 112 G9
Bromley Gdns HAYES BR2 205 L2
Bromley Gv HAYES BR2 205 J2
Bromley Hall Rd POP/IOD E14 141 H7
Bromley High St BOW E3 140 G5
Bromley Hl BMLY BR1 183 K9
Bromley La AMS HP6 50 A10
CHST BR7 184 F10
Bromley Rd BECK BR3 204 F1
CAT SE6 182 G5
CHST BR7 206 E1
LEY E10 120 G4
TOTM N17 99 N9
UED N18 99 L5
WALTH E17 120 F1
Bromley St WCHPL E1 140 C7
Brompton Ar KTBR * SW1X 16 A2
Brompton Cl HSLWW TW4 175 N1
Brompton Dr ERITH DA8 165 J6
Brompton Gv EFNCH N2 117 P2
Brompton Park Crs FUL/PGN SW6 14 F10
Brompton Pl CHEL SW3 15 P3
Brompton Rd CHEL SW3 15 N5
Brompton Sq CHEL SW3 15 N3
Brompton Ter
WOOL/PLUM * SE18 162 D7
Bromwich Av HGT N6 118 B7
Bromyard Av ACT W3 136 B10
Bromycroft Rd SLN SL2 128 F5
Brondesbury Ms
KIL/WHAMP * NW6 2 E4
Brondesbury Pk CRICK NW2 136 G1
Brondesbury Rd KIL/WHAMP NW6 2 D7
Brondesbury Vls KIL/WHAMP NW6 2 D7
Bronhill Ter TOTM * N17 99 P9
Bronsart Rd FUL/PGN SW6 157 H6
Bronson Rd RYNPK SW20 200 G2
Bronte Cl ERITH DA8 164 C6
FSTGT * E7 121 M9
GNTH/NBYPK IG2 122 D2
TIL RM18 168 F8
Bronte Gv DART DA1 165 N10
Bronte Vw GVE DA12 190 F4
Bronti Cl WALW SE17 18 F7
Bronze Age Wy BELV DA17 164 D2
Bronze St DEPT SE8 160 F6
Brook Av DAGE RM10 144 C2
EDGW HA8 95 N7
WBLY HA9 115 M8
Brookbank Av HNWL W7 134 C7
Brookbank Rd LEW SE13 160 F9
Brook Cl ACT W3 135 M10
DORK RH4 255 H10
GPK RM2 104 G9
HOR/WEW KT19 220 B5
RSLP HA4 112 F5
RYNPK SW20 200 E3
STWL/WRAY TW19 174 A3
TOOT SW17 180 B5
Brook Ct BECK * BR3 204 E1
RAD * WD7 56 F9
Brook Crs CHING E4 100 F5
SL SL1 128 D8
UED N18 100 A5
Brookdale FBAR/BDGN N11 98 D5
Brookdale Av UPMR RM14 125 P8
Brookdale Cl UPMR RM14 126 A8
Brookdale Rd BXLY DA5 185 P2
CAT SE6 182 G3
WALTH E17 120 F1
Brookdene Av OXHEY WD19 93 J1
Brookdene Dr NTHWD HA6 92 G8
Brookdene Rd
WOOL/PLUM SE18 163 H3
Brook Dr RAD WD7 56 E9
RSLP HA4 112 F4
RYLN/HDSTN HA2 114 B2
STHWK SE1 18 B4
Brooke Av RYLN/HDSTN HA2 114 B8
Brooke Cl BUSH WD23 94 B1
Brooke Dr GVE DA12 191 L4
Brooke End OXTED * RH8 261 M9
Brooke Forest RGUW GU3 249 H6
Brookehowse Rd CAT SE6 182 G6
Brooke End SBW CM21 29 N1
Brookend Rd BFN/LL DA15 185 H4
Brooke Rd CLPT E5 119 P8
GRAYS RM17 167 M4
WALTH E17 121 H2
Brooker Rd WAB EN9 63 H10
Brookers Cl ASHTD KT21 237 H3
Brooke's Market HCIRC * EC1N 12 A3
Brooke St HCIRC EC1N 12 A4
Brooke Wy BUSH WD23 94 B1
Brook Farm Rd COB KT11 235 L1
Brookfield EPP CM16 65 M1
RGODL GU7 267 M9
RSEV TN14 247 M3
WOKN/KNAP GU21 231 N2
Brookfield Av EA W5 135 J6
MLHL NW7 96 E7
SUT SM1 201 P10
WALTH E17 121 H2
Brookfield Cl CHERT KT16 214 G3
MLHL NW7 96 E7
RBRW/HUT CM13 87 P10
REDH RH1 276 B6
Brookfield Crs
KTN/HRWW/W HA3 115 K3
MLHL NW7 96 E7
Brookfield Gdns CHES/WCR EN8 62 C3
ESH/CLAY KT10 218 E3
Brookfield La CHES/WCR EN8 62 A4
Brookfield La East
CHES/WCR EN8 62 C3
Brookfield La West
CHES/WCR EN8 62 B3
Brookfield Pk KTTN NW5 118 C8
Brookfield Pth CHING E4 101 J7
Brookfield Rd CHSWK W4 156 A1
ED N9 99 P4
HOM E9 140 D1
Brookfields CHONG CM5 67 N2
PEND EN3 80 C8
SBW CM21 29 N1
Brookfields Av MTCM CR4 201 P5
Brook Gdns BARN SW13 156 C9
CHING E4 100 G5
KUTN/CMB KT2 199 P1
Brook Ga BAY/PAD W2 10 B8
Brook Gn HMSMTH W6 156 F2
Brook Hl OXTED RH8 261 H6
SHGR GU5 269 N9
Brookhill Cl CRAWE RH10 285 H2
EBAR EN4 77 P9
Brook Hill Cl WOOL/PLUM SE18 162 E4
Brookhill Rd CRAWE RH10 285 H3
WOOL/PLUM SE18 162 E4
Brookhouse Gdns CHING E4 101 K5
Brookhurst Rd ADL/WDHM KT15 215 L3
Brooking Rd FSTGT E7 121 M10
Brookland Cl GLDGN NW11 117 K2
Brookland Garth GLDGN NW11 117 K2
Brookland Hl GLDGN NW11 117 K2
Brookland Ri GLDGN NW11 117 K2
Brooklands DART DA1 187 M4
Brooklands Ap ROMW/RG RM7 124 E2
Brooklands Av BFN/LL DA15 184 G5
WAND/EARL SW18 179 L5
Brooklands Cl COB KT11 235 M1
ROMW/RG RM7 124 E2
SUN TW16 196 F1
Brooklands Ct
KIL/WHAMP * NW6 2 C3
STAL * AL1 38 D6
WCHMH N21 79 L9
Brooklands Dr GFD/PVL UB6 135 H3
Brooklands Gdns EMPK RM11 125 K3
POTB/CUF EN6 59 H8
Brooklands La ROMW/RG RM7 124 E2
WEY KT13 216 A2
Brooklands Pk BKHTH/KID SE3 161 M9
Brooklands Rd ROMW/RG RM7 124 E2
THDIT KT7 198 E8
WEY KT13 216 C5
Brooklands Ter SUN * TW16 197 H4
The Brooklands ISLW * TW7 154 C7
Brooklands Wy REDH RH1 257 P8
Brook La BERK HP4 33 N4
BKHTH/KID SE3 161 N8
BMLY BR1 183 M9
BRWN CM15 87 H3
BXLY DA5 185 N2
CHOB/PIR GU24 213 J7
RPLY/SEND GU23 233 H8
SBW CM21 29 N1
SHGR GU5 269 P8
Brooklane Fld HLWS CM18 47 L4
Brook La North BTFD TW8 155 J4
Brooklea Cl CDALE/KGS NW9 96 B9
Brookleys CHOB/PIR GU24 213 L6
Brooklyn Av LOU IG10 82 B8
SNWD SE25 204 A4
Brooklyn Cl CAR SM5 201 P9

WOKS/MYFD GU22 232 B5
Brooklyn Gv SNWD SE25 204 A4
Brooklyn Rd HAYES BR2 206 A5
SNWD SE25 204 A4
WOKS/MYFD GU22 232 B4
Brooklyn Wy WDR/YW UB7 151 N2
Brookmans Av BRKMPK AL9 59 J2
CDH/CHF RM16 147 P10
Brookmans Cl UPMR RM14 126 D5
Brook Md HOR/WEW KT19 220 B3
Brookmead MTCM CR4 202 D6
Brookmead Av HAYES BR2 206 C5
Brookmead Cl ORP BR6 207 L6
Brook Meadow
NFNCH/WDSP N12 97 L5
Brook Meadow Cl WFD IG8 101 K7
Brookmead Rd CROY/NA CR0 202 D6
Brook Ms North BAY/PAD W2 9 K7
Brookmill Cl OXHEY * WD19 93 J1
Brookmill Rd DEPT SE8 160 F7
Brook Park Cl WCHMH N21 79 J10
Brook Pth SL SL1 128 E9
Brook Pl BAR EN5 77 K9
Brook Ri CHIG IG7 102 D4
Brook Rd BKHH IG9 101 M3
BORE WD6 75 M5
BRW CM14 106 E4
CEND/HSY/T N8 118 F2
CHES/WCR EN8 62 E10
CRICK NW2 116 D7
EPP CM16 65 K9
GNTH/NBYPK IG2 123 H4
GPK RM2 104 G10
GVW DA11 190 B4
LOU IG10 82 B9
REDH RH1 258 D4
REDH RH1 276 A1
RGUE GU4 268 F6
SBW CM21 29 N2
SURB KT6 199 K9
SWLY BR8 208 E3
THHTH CR7 203 K4
TWK TW1 176 F2
WDGN * N22 98 G10
Brook Rd South BTFD TW8 155 K5
Brooks Av EHAM E6 142 C6
Brooksbank St HOM * E9 140 C1
Brooksby Ms IS N1 6 A3
Brooksby St IS N1 6 A4
Brooksby's Wk HOM E9 120 C10
Brooks Cl WEY KT13 216 B6
Brooks Ct HERT/WAS * SG14 24 G4
Brookscroft CROY/NA CR0 224 E6
Brookscroft Rd WALTH E17 100 G9
Brooksfield WGCE AL7 23 L4
Brookshill KTN/HRWW/W HA3 94 D7
Brookshill Av KTN/HRWW/W HA3 94 C6
Brookshill Dr KTN/HRWW/W HA3 94 C6
Brookside BARK/HLT IG6 102 F7
CAR SM5 222 B2
CHERT KT16 195 H7
CRAWE RH10 284 A6
CRAWE RH10 285 H2
DTCH/LGLY SL3 150 F6
EBAR EN4 77 P10
EMPK RM11 125 M3
HAT AL10 40 A4
HERT/BAY SG13 25 M6
HGDN/ICK UB10 132 A2
HLWW/ROY CM19 46 C3
HOD EN11 44 F3
ORP BR6 207 J7
POTB/CUF EN6 58 D8
RGUE GU4 250 A5
WAB EN9 63 K8
WATN * WD24 73 L2
WCHMH N21 78 G10
Brookside Av ASHF TW15 173 M8
STWL/WRAY TW19 150 A9
Brookside Cl BAR EN5 76 G10
FELT TW13 175 H6
KTN/HRWW/W HA3 115 J3
RSLP HA4 113 M9
Brookside Crs POTB/CUF EN6 60 F5
WPK KT4 200 D8
Brookside Gdns EN EN1 80 A3
Brookside Rd ED N9 100 A5
GLDGN NW11 117 H4
MEO DA13 190 C10
OXHEY WD19 93 J1
UED N18 100 A5
YEAD UB4 133 K9
Brookside South EBAR EN4 98 B1
Brookside Wy CROY/NA CR0 204 C6
Brooks La CHSWK W4 155 M5
Brook's Ms MYFR/PKLN W1K 10 E7
Brooks Rd CHSWK W4 155 M4
PLSTW E13 141 M3
Brook St BAY/PAD W2 9 M7
BELV DA17 164 C4
BRW CM14 106 D5
KUT KT1 199 K2
MYFR/PKLN W1K 10 E7
WDSR SL4 149 J8
Brooksville Av KIL/WHAMP NW6 2 B6
Brookswood RGUE GU4 268 F7
The Brook CRAWE RH10 283 N6
Brook Va RDKG RH5 272 G8
Brookview CRAWE RH10 285 H2
Brookview Rd
STRHM/NOR SW16 180 D8
Brookville Rd FUL/PGN SW6 157 J6
Brook Wk EDGW HA8 96 A7
EFNCH * N2 97 N9
Brook Water La HDN * NW4 116 G3
Brook Wy CHIG IG7 102 D4
LHD/OX KT22 236 F4
Brookway BKHTH/KID SE3 161 M9
RAIN RM13 145 J7
Brookwood HORL RH6 280 C3
Brookwood Av BARN SW13 156 C9
Brookwood Br
WOKN/KNAP GU21 230 G6
Brookwood Cl HAYES BR2 205 L4
Brookwood Lye Rd
WOKS/MYFD GU22 230 G6
Brookwood Rd HSLW TW3 154 A8
WAND/EARL SW18 179 J4
Broom Av STMC/STPC BR5 207 L2
Broom Bank WARL CR6 243 H5
Broom Cl CHESW EN7 61 P3
ESH/CLAY KT10 218 A2
HAT AL10 40 C7
HAYES BR2 206 B6
TEDD TW11 177 J10
Broom Cnr HARP * AL5 20 B3
Broomcroft Av NTHLT UB5 133 K5
Broomcroft Dr
WOKS/MYFD GU22 232 G1
Broomdashers Rd CRAWE RH10 284 A6
Broome Cl EPSOM KT18 256 A2
Broome Pl SOCK/AV RM15 146 C10
Broome Rd HPTN TW12 197 N1
Broomer Pl CHES/WCR EN8 62 B5
Broome Wy CMBW SE5 159 L6
Broomfield GUW GU2 249 K9
HLW CM20 29 L8
LCOL/BKTW AL2 56 B3
SUN TW16 197 H1
WALTH E17 120 E5
Broomfield Av BROX EN10 62 D2
LOU IG10 82 C10
PLMGR N13 98 G5
Broomfield Cl CRW RM5 104 E7
RGUW GU3 249 K8
WOKS/MYFD GU22 232 G2
Broomfield Cottages WEA * W13 134 G10
Broomfield Ct WEY KT13 216 B3
Broomfield La PLMGR N13 98 G6
Broomfield Pk ASC SL5 192 G6
DORK RH4 272 B3
Broomfield Pl WEA W13 134 G10
Broomfield Ride LHD/OX KT22 218 C8
Broomfield Ri ABLGY WD5 54 E8
Broomfield Rd ADL/WDHM KT15 215 L7
BECK BR3 204 D4
BRYLDS KT5 199 L8
BXLYHS DA6 186 B1
CHDH RM6 123 N5
PLMGR N13 98 F6
RCH/KEW TW9 155 L7
SEV TN13 246 G8
SWCM DA10 189 K2
TEDD TW11 177 H9
WEA W13 134 G10
Broomfields ESH/CLAY KT10 218 B2
HART DA3 211 K5
Broomfield St POP/IOD E14 140 F7
Broom Gdns CROY/NA CR0 204 F10
Broom Gv WAT WD17 73 H4
Broomgrove Gdns EDGW HA8 95 M9
Broomgrove Rd BRXN/ST SW9 158 G8
Broom Hall LHD/OX KT22 218 B10
Broomhall End
WOKN/KNAP GU21 232 B2
Broomhall La ASC SL5 192 E6
WOKN/KNAP GU21 232 B2
Broomhall Rd SAND/SEL CR2 223 L5
WOKN/KNAP GU21 232 B2
Broom Hl HHW HP1 35 H7
SLN SL2 129 M2
Broomhill Ri BXLYHS DA6 186 B1
Broomhill Rd DART DA1 187 J2
GDMY/SEVK IG3 123 K7
ORP BR6 207 K7
WAND/EARL SW18 179 K1
WFD IG8 101 M7
Broomhills WGCE AL7 23 K4
Broomhouse La FUL/PGN SW6 157 K8
Broomhouse Rd FUL/PGN SW6 157 K8
Broomhurst Ct DORK RH4 272 G4
Broomlands La OXTED RH8 262 B3
Broom La CHOB/PIR GU24 213 K5
Broomleys STALE/WH AL4 39 H3
Broomloan La SUT SM1 201 K9
Broom Lock TEDD * TW11 177 H8
Broom Md BXLYHS DA6 186 B2
Broom Pk KUT KT1 177 J10
Broom Rd CROY/NA CR0 204 F10
TEDD TW11 176 G8
Brooms Cl WGCW AL8 22 G2
Broomsleigh St
KIL/WHAMP * NW6 117 K10
Broomstick Hall Rd WAB EN9 63 K9
Broomstick La CSHM HP5 51 M6
Broom Water TEDD TW11 177 H9
Broom Water West TEDD TW11 177 H8
Broom Wy WEY KT13 216 E1
Broomwood Cl BXLY DA5 186 E5
CROY/NA CR0 204 C5
Broomwood Gdns BRWN CM15 86 F10
Broomwood Rd BTSEA SW11 179 P2
STMC/STPC BR5 207 L2
Broseley Gdns HARH RM3 105 M5
Broseley Gv SYD SE26 182 D8
Broseley Rd HARH RM3 105 M5
Broster Gdns SNWD SE25 203 N3
Brougham Rd ACT W3 135 P8
HACK E8 7 P5
Brougham St BTSEA SW11 158 A8
Brough Cl KUTN/CMB * KT2 177 J8
VX/NE SW8 158 F6
Broughinge Rd BORE WD6 75 N6
Broughton Av FNCH N3 117 H1
RCHPK/HAM TW10 177 H7
Broughton Dr HNHL SE24 159 H10
Broughton Gdns HGT N6 118 D4
Broughton Rd FUL/PGN SW6 157 L8
ORP BR6 206 G9
THHTH CR7 203 H6
WEA W13 134 G9
Broughton Road Ap
FUL/PGN * SW6 157 L8
Broughton St VX/NE SW8 158 B8
Broughton Wy RKW/CH/CXG WD3 91 K1
Brouncker Rd ACT W3 155 P1
Brow Cl STMC/STPC BR5 207 N7
Brow Crs STMC/STPC BR5 207 M8
Browell's La FELT TW13 175 J5
Brown Cl WLGTN SM6 222 E4
Browne Cl BRW CM14 106 G2
Brownfields WGCE AL7 23 J4
Brownfields Ct WGCE AL7 23 J4
Brownfield St POP/IOD E14 141 H8
Browngraves Rd HYS/HAR UB3 152 D6
Brown Hart Gdns
MYFR/PKLN W1K 10 D7
Brownhill Rd CAT SE6 183 H3
Browning Av HNWL W7 134 E8
SUT SM1 221 P1
WPK KT4 200 E8
Browning Cl CRAWE RH10 284 D6
HPTN TW12 175 N7
MV/WKIL * W9 9 K2
WALTH E17 121 H2
WELL DA16 163 H7
Browning Ms CAVSQ/HST * W1G 10 D4
Browning Rd DART DA1 165 N10
ENC/FH EN2 79 L4
HARP AL5 20 B1
LHD/OX KT22 254 C1
MNPK E12 142 C1
WAN E11 121 L5
Browning St WALW SE17 18 F7
Browning Wy HEST TW5 153 L7
Brownlea Gdns GDMY/SEVK IG3 123 K7
Brownlow Ms FSBYW WC1X 11 P1
Brownlow Rd BERK HP4 33 P4
BORE WD6 75 M8
CROY/NA CR0 223 M1
FBAR/BDGN N11 98 F7
FNCH N3 97 L8
FSTGT E7 121 M9
HACK E8 7 M5
REDH RH1 257 P10
WEA * W13 134 F10
WLSDN NW10 136 B2
Brownlow St GINN WC1R 11 P4
Brownrigg Rd ASHF TW15 174 B7
Brown Rd GVE DA12 191 H5
Brown's Hl REDH RH1 277 L7
Browns La EHSLY KT24 253 L3
Brownspring Dr ELTH/MOT SE9 184 E6
Brown's Rd BRYLDS KT5 199 L7
WALTH E17 120 F1
Browns Spring BERK HP4 34 F2
Brown St MBLAR W1H 10 A5
Brownswell Rd EFNCH N2 97 N10
Brownswood Rd BEAC HP9 88 C7
FSBYPK N4 119 K7
The Brow CSTG HP8 90 A4
GSTN WD25 55 J9
REDH RH1 276 B5
Broxash Rd BTSEA SW11 180 B2
Broxbourne Av WAN E11 121 N2
Broxbourne House BOW E3 140 G6
Broxbourne Rd FSTGT E7 121 M8
ORP BR6 207 J8
Broxburn Dr SOCK/AV RM15 146 F9
Broxhill Rd ABR/ST RM4 105 H4
Broxholm Rd WNWD SE27 181 H6
Brox La ADL/WDHM KT15 214 G5
Brox Rd CHERT KT16 214 F4
Broxted Rd FSTH SE23 182 E5
Broxwood Wy STJWD NW8 3 P6
Bruce Av HCH RM12 125 K7
SHPTN TW17 196 D6
Bruce Castle Rd TOTM N17 99 N9
Bruce Cl BF/WBF KT14 215 N9
NKENS W10 136 G7
SL SL1 128 F10
WELL DA16 163 L7
Bruce Dr SAND/SEL CR2 224 C5
Bruce Gdns TRDG/WHET N20 98 A4
Bruce Gv ORP BR6 207 K8
TOTM N17 99 N10
WATN WD24 73 J4
Bruce Rd BAR * EN5 77 H7
BOW E3 140 G5
KTN/HRWW/W HA3 94 D10
MTCM CR4 180 B10
SNWD SE25 203 L4
WLSDN NW10 136 A2
Bruces Wharf Rd GRAYS RM17 167 M5
Bruce Wy CHES/WCR EN8 62 C9
Bruckner St NKENS W10 2 C10
Brudenell WDSR SL4 148 E9
Brudenell Rd TOOT SW17 180 A6
Bruffs Meadow NTHLT UB5 133 M1
Bruges Pl CAMTN NW1 5 H4
Brumana Cl WEY KT13 216 C3
Brumfield Rd HOR/WEW KT19 219 P2
Brunel Cl HEST TW5 153 J6
NRWD SE19 181 N9
NTHLT UB5 133 N5
ROM RM1 124 F2
TIL RM18 168 E8
Brunel Ct WLSDN NW10 136 D5
Brunel Est BAY/PAD W2 8 E4
Brunel Pl CRAWE RH10 283 P8
Brunel Rd ACT W3 136 B7
BERM/RHTH SE16 140 B10
WALTH E17 120 D4
WFD IG8 102 C6
Brunel St CAN/RD E16 141 L8
Brunel Wk HSLWW TW4 175 P3
Brunel Wy SL SL1 129 L10
Brune St WCHPL E1 13 L4
Brunner Cl GLDGN NW11 117 L3
Brunner Ct CHERT KT16 214 F2
Brunner Rd EA W5 135 J6
WALTH E17 120 E3
Bruno Pl WBLY HA9 115 P7
Brunswick Av FBAR/BDGN N11 98 B4
UPMR RM14 126 D5
Brunswick Cl BXLYHS DA6 163 N10
CRAWE RH10 284 B9
PIN HA5 113 M4
THDIT KT7 198 E8
WHTN TW2 176 C6
WOT/HER KT12 197 K9
Brunswick Ct STHWK SE1 19 K2
Brunswick Crs FBAR/BDGN N11 98 B4
Brunswick Dr CHOB/PIR GU24 230 C6
Brunswick Gdns BARK/HLT IG6 102 F8
EA W5 135 K5
KENS W8 8 F10
Brunswick Gv COB KT11 217 K9
FBAR/BDGN N11 98 B4
Brunswick Ms MBLAR W1H 10 B5
STRHM/NOR SW16 180 E9
Brunswick Pk CMBW SE5 159 L7
Brunswick Park Gdns
FBAR/BDGN N11 98 B3
Brunswick Park Rd
FBAR/BDGN N11 98 B3
Brunswick Pl CAMTN NW1 10 D2
IS N1 7 H10
NRWD SE19 181 P10
Brunswick Quay
BERM/RHTH SE16 160 C2
Brunswick Rd BXLYHS DA6 163 N10
CHOB/PIR GU24 230 C7
EA W5 135 J6
KUTN/CMB KT2 199 M1
LEY E10 121 H6
SEVS/STOTM N15 119 M2
SUT SM1 221 L1
WAB EN9 80 F4
Brunswick Sq BMSBY WC1N 11 M1
Brunswick St WALTH E17 121 H3
Brunswick Vls CMBW SE5 159 M7
Brunswick Wk GVE DA12 190 G2
Brunswick Wy FBAR/BDGN N11 98 C5
Brunton Pl POP/IOD E14 140 D8
Brushfield St WCHPL E1 13 K3
Brushfield Wy
WOKN/KNAP GU21 231 H4
Brushrise WATN WD24 73 H2
Brushwood Dr RKW/CH/CXG WD3 70 F8
Brushwood Rd CSHM HP5 51 J5
Brussels Rd BTSEA SW11 157 N10
Bruton Cl CHST BR7 184 C10
Bruton La MYFR/PICC W1J 10 F8
Bruton Pl MYFR/PKLN W1K 10 F8
Bruton Rd MRDN SM4 201 M4
Bruton St MYFR/PICC W1J 10 F8
Bruton Wy WEA W13 134 F7
Bryan Av WLSDN NW10 136 E2
Bryan Cl SUN TW16 175 H10
Bryan Rd BERM/RHTH SE16 160 E1
Bryanston Av WHTN TW2 176 A4
Bryanston Cl NWDGN UB2 153 N3
Bryanstone Av GUW GU2 249 L6
Bryanstone Cl GUW GU2 249 L7
Bryanstone Gv GUW GU2 249 L6
Bryanstone Rd CEND/HSY/T N8 118 E3
CHES/WCR EN8 62 E10
Bryanston Ms East MBLAR W1H 10 A4
Bryanston Ms West MBLAR W1H 10 A4
Bryanston Pl MBLAR W1H 10 A4
Bryanston Rd TIL RM18 168 F8
Bryanston Sq MBLAR W1H 10 A5
Bryanston St MBLAR W1H 10 A6
Bryant Av HARH RM3 105 L10
SLN SL2 129 J7
Bryant Cl BAR EN5 77 J9
Bryant Rd NTHLT UB5 133 K5
Bryant St SRTFD E15 141 J2
Bryantwood Rd HOLWY N7 119 H10
Brycedale Crs STHGT/OAK N14 98 E5
Bryce Rd BCTR RM8 123 M9
Bryden Cl SYD SE26 182 D8
Brydges Pl CHCR WC2N 11 L8
Brydges Rd SRTFD E15 121 J10
Brydon Wk IS N1 5 M5
Bryer Pl WDSR SL4 148 C9
Brymay Cl BOW E3 140 F4
Brympton Cl DORK RH4 272 F4
Brynford Cl WOKN/KNAP GU21 232 B1
Brynmaer Rd BTSEA SW11 158 A7
Bryn Wy STALE/WH AL4 39 J8
Bryn-y-Mawr Rd EN EN1 79 N8
Bryony Cl UX/CGN UB8 132 A7
Bryony Rd GU GU1 250 E7
SHB W12 136 D9
Bryony Wy SUN TW16 175 H9
Bubblestone Rd RSEV TN14 247 J2
Buccleuch Rd DTCH/LGLY SL3 149 M6
Buchanan Cl SOCK/AV RM15 146 B9
WCHMH N21 78 G9
Buchanan Ct BORE * WD6 75 P6
Buchanan Gdns WLSDN NW10 136 E4
Buchan Cl UX/CGN UB8 131 M5
Buchan Rd PECK SE15 160 B9
Bucharest Rd WAND/EARL SW18 179 M3
Buckden Cl LEE/GVPK SE12 183 L2
Buckettsland La BORE WD6 76 A6
Buckfast Rd MRDN SM4 201 L4
Buckfast St BETH E2 7 P10
Buckham Thorns Rd
BH/WHM TN16 262 F2
Buckhold Rd WAND/EARL SW18 179 K2
Buckhurst Av CAR SM5 201 P8
Buckhurst Cl REDH RH1 257 P8
Buckhurst La ASC SL5 192 F3
SEV TN13 265 K1
Buckhurst Rd ASC SL5 192 E2
BH/WHM TN16 244 E6
Buckhurst St WCHPL E1 140 A6
Buckhurst Wy BKHH IG9 102 A4
Buckingham Av
E/WMO/HCT KT8 198 A2
EBED/NFELT TW14 175 J2
GFD/PVL UB6 134 F3
SL SL1 128 F8
THHTH CR7 203 H1
TRDG/WHET N20 97 M1
WELL DA16 163 H10
Buckingham Av East SL SL1 129 H8
Buckingham Cl EA W5 135 H7
EMPK RM11 125 L3
EN EN1 79 M6
GU GU1 250 C9
HPTN TW12 175 N8
STMC/STPC BR5 207 H7
Buckingham Ct BELMT * SM2 221 K5
Buckingham Dr CHST BR7 184 E8
Buckingham Gdns SL SL1 149 L1
STAN HA7 95 K8
THHTH CR7 203 H2
Buckingham Ga HORL RH6 280 D7
WESTW SW1E 16 G3
Buckingham Gv HGDN/ICK UB10 132 B4
Buckingham La FSTH SE23 182 D3
Buckingham Ms WESTW * SW1E 16 G3
WLSDN NW10 136 C4
Buckingham Palace Rd
PIM SW1V 16 E5
Buckingham Pde C
FSP/GDCR * SL9 90 A9
STAN * HA7 95 H6
Buckingham Pl WESTW SW1E 16 G3
Buckingham Rd BORE WD6 76 A8
EDGW HA8 95 L8
FELT TW13 175 N7
FSTGT E7 121 L10
GVW DA11 190 A3
HRW HA1 114 C3
IL IG1 122 G7
IS N1 7 J2
KUT KT1 199 L4
LEY E10 120 G8
MTCM CR4 202 F5
RCHPK/HAM TW10 177 J5
RDKG RH5 273 H10
SWFD E18 101 L9
WAN E11 121 N2
WATN WD24 73 K3
WDGN N22 98 F9
WLSDN NW10 136 C4
Buckingham St CHCR WC2N 11 M8
Buckingham Wy WLGTN SM6 222 D5
Buckland Av DTCH/LGLY SL3 149 N2
Buckland Crs HAMP NW3 3 L3
Buckland Ga DTCH/LGLY SL3 129 N5
Buckland La BRKHM/BTCW RH3 256 D6
Buckland Ri PIN HA5 93 K9
Buckland Rd BELMT SM2 220 F6
CHSGTN KT9 219 L2
KWD/TDW/WH KT20 257 J4
LEY E10 121 H7
ORP BR6 227 H1
REIG RH2 256 G9
Bucklands OXHEY * WD19 93 L4
Bucklands Rd TEDD TW11 177 H9
Buckland St IS N1 7 H8
Bucklands Whf KUT * KT1 199 J2
Buckland Wk MRDN SM4 201 M4
Buckland Wy WPK KT4 200 F8
Buck La CDALE/KGS NW9 116 A3
Buckleigh Av RYNPK SW20 201 J3
Buckleigh Rd STRHM/NOR SW16 180 E9
Buckleigh Wy NRWD SE19 203 N1
Bucklersbury MANHO * EC4N 12 G6
Bucklers Cl BROX EN10 44 E8
Bucklers Ct BRW CM14 107 H6
Bucklers' Wy CAR SM5 202 A10
Buckles La SOCK/AV RM15 147 H7
Buckle St WCHPL E1 13 M5
Buckles Wy BNSTD SM7 239 H2
Buckley Cl DART DA1 164 G8
Buckley Pl CRAWE RH10 285 P5
Buckley Rd KIL/WHAMP NW6 2 D4
Buckmans Rd CRAWW RH11 283 N7
Buckmaster Rd BTSEA SW11 157 P10
Bucknalls Cl GSTN WD25 55 M8
Bucknalls Dr LCOL/BKTW AL2 55 N7
Bucknalls La GSTN WD25 55 M8
Bucknall St NOXST/BSQ WC1A 11 L5
Bucknall Wy BECK BR3 204 G4
Buckner Rd BRXS/STRHM SW2 158 G10
Bucknills Cl EPSOM KT18 219 P10
Buckrell Rd CHING E4 101 J3
Bucks Aly HERT/BAY SG13 42 E5
Bucks Av OXHEY WD19 93 M1
Bucks Cl BF/WBF KT14 215 L10
Bucks Cross Rd GVW DA11 190 C6
ORP BR6 227 P2
Bucks Hl KGLGY WD4 53 M8
Buckstone Cl FSTH SE23 182 B2
Buckstone Rd UED N18 99 P7
Buck St CAMTN NW1 4 F5
Buckswood Dr CRAWW RH11 283 K9
Buckters Rents
BERM/RHTH SE16 140 D10
Buckthorne Rd BROCKY SE4 182 D2
Buckton Rd BORE WD6 75 L4
Budd Cl NFNCH/WDSP N12 97 L5
Buddcroft WGCE AL7 23 L4
Buddings Cir WBLY HA9 115 P8
Budebury Rd STA TW18 173 J8
Budge La MTCM CR4 202 A7
Budgen Cl CRAWE RH10 284 E4
Budgen Dr REDH RH1 258 B7
Budge Rw MANHO EC4N 12 G7
Budgin's Hl ORP BR6 227 L8
Budleigh Crs WELL DA16 163 M7
Budoch Dr GDMY/SEVK IG3 123 K7
Buer Rd FUL/PGN SW6 157 H8
Buff Av BNSTD SM7 239 L1
Buffers La LHD/OX KT22 236 F5
Bug Hl WARL CR6 242 C6
Bugsby's Wy GNWCH SE10 161 L3
Bulbourne Cl BERK HP4 33 L3
HHW HP1 35 K7
Bulganak Rd THHTH CR7 203 K4
Bulinca St WEST * SW1P 17 L6
Bulkeley Av WDSR SL4 148 G9
Bulkeley Cl EGH TW20 171 P8
Bullace Cl HHW HP1 35 J5
Bullace Rw CMBW SE5 159 L7
Bull Aly WELL DA16 163 L9
Bullar Cl PECK SE15 159 P6
Bullard Rd TEDD * TW11 176 E9
Bullards Pl BETH E2 140 C5
Bullbaiters La AMS HP6 50 A10
Bullbanks Rd BELV DA17 164 D3
Bullbeggars La BERK HP4 34 D5
GDST RH9 260 B8
WOKN/KNAP GU21 231 N2
Bull Cl CDH/CHF RM16 167 L1
Bulleid Wy PIM SW1V 16 F6
Bullen's Green La STALE/WH AL4 40 B9
Bullen St BTSEA SW11 157 P8
Buller Rd BARK IG11 143 H2
THHTH CR7 203 L3
TOTM N17 99 P10
WDGN N22 99 H10
WLSDN NW10 136 G5
Bullers Cl SCUP DA14 185 P8
Bullers Wood Dr CHST BR7 206 B1
Bullescroft Rd EDGW HA8 95 M4
Bullfinch Cl HORL RH6 279 P3
SEV TN13 246 E8
Bullfinch Dene SEV TN13 246 E8
Bullfinch La SEV TN13 246 F8
Bullfinch Rd SAND/SEL CR2 224 C6
Bullhead Rd BORE WD6 75 P6
Bull Hl LHD/OX KT22 236 F7
Bullivant Cl GRH DA9 188 F1
Bullivant St POP/IOD E14 141 H9
Bull La CFSP/GDCR SL9 110 A2
CHST BR7 184 C10
DAGE RM10 124 C8
RGUE GU4 250 C2
STALE/WH AL4 20 F5
UED N18 99 M6
Bullock's La HERT/BAY SG13 25 K7
Bull Pln HERT/WAS SG14 25 L5
Bull Rd HARP AL5 20 A3
SRTFD E15 141 L4
Bullrush Cl CROY/NA CR0 203 M6
HAT AL10 40 E5
Bullrush Gv UX/CGN UB8 131 M6
Bulls Aly MORT/ESHN * SW14 156 A9
Bull's Br HYS/HAR UB3 153 H2
Bulls Bridge Rd NWDGN UB2 153 J2
Bullsbrook Rd HYS/HAR UB3 133 K10
Bull's Cross ENC/FH EN2 79 P2
Bulls Cross Ride CHESW EN7 61 P10
ENC/FH EN2 79 P1
Bullsland Gdns RKW/CH/CXG WD3 70 E10
Bullsland La RKW/CH/CXG WD3 70 E10
Bulls La BRKMPK AL9 41 H10
Bullsmoor Cl CHES/WCR EN8 80 B1
Bullsmoor Gdns CHES/WCR EN8 80 A1
Bullsmoor La EN EN1 80 A1
PEND EN3 80 C1
Bullsmoor Ride CHES/WCR EN8 80 B1
Bullsmoor Wy CHES/WCR EN8 80 B1
Bull Stag Gn BRKMPK AL9 40 F2
Bullswater Common Rd
CHOB/PIR GU24 248 F1
Bullwell Crs CHES/WCR EN8 62 D5
Bull Yd GVE * DA12 190 E2
PECK SE15 159 P7
Bulmer Gdns KTN/HRWW/W HA3 115 J5
Bulmer Ms NTGHL W11 8 E9
Bulstrode Av HSLW TW3 153 N9
Bulstrode Cl KGLGY WD4 53 H5
Bulstrode Gdns HSLW TW3 153 P9
Bulstrode La KGLGY WD4 53 M5
Bulstrode Pl MHST W1U 10 D4
Bulstrode Rd HSLW TW3 153 P9
Bulstrode St MHST W1U 10 D5
Bulstrode Wy CFSP/GDCR SL9 110 A3
Bulwer Court Rd WAN E11 121 J6
Bulwer Gdns BAR EN5 77 M8
Bulwer Rd BAR EN5 77 L8
UED N18 99 M5
WAN E11 121 J6
Bulwer St SHB W12 136 F10
Bumbles Green La WAB EN9 63 N1
Bunbury Wy EW KT17 238 E2
Bunby Rd SLN SL2 129 L2
Bunce Common Rd REIG RH2 274 A7
Bunce Dr CTHM CR3 241 L9

Buncefield La HHNE HP2 36 D3
Buncefield Terminal HHNE * HP2 36 E4
Bunces Cl WDSR SL4 148 G4
Bunces La WFD IG8 101 L8
Bundy's Wy STA TW18 173 J9
Bungalow Rd SNWD SE25 203 M4
The Bungalows
RYLN/HDSTN * HA2 113 N8
STRHM/NOR SW16 180 C10
WTHK * RM20 166 F5
Bunhill Rw STLK EC1Y 12 G1
Bunhouse Pl BGVA SW1W 16 C7
Bunkers Hl SCUP DA14 186 A6
Bunkers La HHS/BOV HP3 36 C10
Bunning Wy HOLWY N7 5 M3
Bunnsfield WGCE AL7 23 M4
Bunn's La MLHL NW7 96 B7
Bunny Hl GVE * DA12 191 P9
Bunsen St BOW E3 140 D4
Bunten Meade SL SL1 128 G10
Bunting Cl ED N9 100 C2
MTCM CR4 202 A5
Bunton St WOOL/PLUM SE18 162 D2
Bunyan Cl CRAWW RH11 283 H10
Bunyan Rd WALTH E17 120 D1
Bunyard Dr WOKN/KNAP GU21 214 F10
Burbage Cl CHES/WCR EN8 62 D7
HYS/HAR UB3 132 E8
STHWK SE1 18 G4
Burbage Rd HNHL SE24 181 L2
Burbeach Cl CRAWW RH11 283 L10
Burberry Cl NWMAL KT3 200 B2
Burbidge Rd SHPTN TW17 196 B4
Burbridge Wy TOTM N17 99 P10
Burcham St POP/IOD E14 140 G8
Burcharbro Rd ABYW SE2 163 N5
Burchell Ct BUSH WD23 94 B1
Burchell Rd LEY E10 120 G6
PECK SE15 160 A7
Burchets Hollow SHGR GU5 270 E10
Burchetts Wy SHPTN TW17 196 C6
Burchwall Cl CRW RM5 104 D8
Burcote Rd WAND/EARL SW18 179 N4
Burcott Gdns ADL/WDHM KT15 215 N3
Burcott Rd PUR/KEN CR8 223 H10
Burden Cl BTFD TW8 155 H4
Burdenshot Hl RGUW GU3 249 M1
Burdenshott Av
RCHPK/HAM TW10 155 N10
Burdenshott Rd RGUW GU3 249 M1
Burden Wy GUW GU2 249 N5
WAN E11 121 N7
Burder Cl IS N1 7 K1
Burder Rd IS N1 7 K1
Burdett Av GVE DA12 191 P7
RYNPK SW20 200 D1
Burdett Cl CRAWE RH10 284 E8
HNWL * W7 134 E10
SCUP DA14 185 P8
Burdett Rd BOW E3 140 E6
CROY/NA CR0 203 L6
RCH/KEW TW9 155 L8
Burdetts Rd DAGW RM9 144 A3
Burdock Cl CROY/NA CR0 204 C8
LTWR GU18 212 A7
Burdock Rd TOTM N17 119 P1
Burdon La BELMT SM2 221 J5
Burdon Pk BELMT SM2 221 J5
Bure TIL RM18 169 M2
Burfield Cl HAT AL10 40 D2
TOOT SW17 179 M7
Burfield Dr WARL CR6 242 B5
Burfield Rd RKW/CH/CXG WD3 70 E9
WDSR SL4 171 M3
Burford Cl BARK/HLT IG6 122 F2
BCTR RM8 123 M8
HGDN/ICK UB10 111 P9
Burford Gdns HOD EN11 44 G2
PLMGR N13 98 G4
SL SL1 128 B7
Burford La EW KT17 220 F7
Burford Rd BMLY BR1 206 B4
BTFD TW8 155 K4
CAT SE6 182 E5
EHAM E6 142 B5
SRTFD E15 141 J2
SUT SM1 201 K9
WPK KT4 200 D7
Burford St HOD EN11 44 F2
Burford Wk FUL/PGN * SW6 157 L6
Burford Wy CROY/NA CR0 225 H4
Burgage Ct WARE * SG12 26 C2
Burgate Cl DART DA1 164 G9
Burges Cl EMPK RM11 125 N4
Burges Gv BARN SW13 156 E6
Burges Rd EHAM E6 142 D2
STA TW18 173 K9
Burgess Av CDALE/KGS NW9 116 A4
Burgess Cl FELT TW13 175 M7
Burgess Hl CRICK NW2 117 K9
Burgess Rd SRTFD E15 121 K9
SUT SM1 221 L1
Burgess St POP/IOD E14 140 F7
Burgess Wood Rd BEAC HP9 88 A10
Burgess Wood Rd South
BEAC HP9 88 A10
Burge St STHWK SE1 19 H4
Burgett Rd SL SL1 148 G2
Burgh Cl CRAWE RH10 284 E4
Burghfield EW KT17 238 C1
Burghfield Rd MEO DA13 190 C10
Burgh Heath Rd EW KT17 238 C1
Burghill Rd SYD SE26 182 C7
Burghley Av BORE WD6 75 P9
NWMAL KT3 200 A1
Burghley Hall Cl
WIM/MER * SW19 179 H4
Burghley Pl MTCM CR4 202 A4
Burghley Rd CDH/CHF RM16 167 H2
CEND/HSY/T N8 119 H1
KTTN NW5 118 C9
WAN * E11 121 K6
WIM/MER SW19 178 G7
Burgh Mt BNSTD SM7 239 J1
Burgh St IS N1 6 D7
Burgh Wd BNSTD SM7 239 H1
Burgon St BLKFR EC4V 12 D6
Burgos Cl CROY/NA CR0 223 H3
Burgos Gv GNWCH SE10 160 G7
Burgoyne Rd BRXN/ST SW9 158 G9
FSBYPK N4 119 J4
SNWD SE25 203 N4
SUN TW16 174 G9
Burgundy Cft WGCE AL7 23 J7
Burham Cl PGE/AN SE20 182 B10
Burhill Gv PIN HA5 93 M10
Burhill Rd WOT/HER KT12 217 K3
Burke Cl PUT/ROE SW15 156 B10
Burkes Cl BEAC HP9 108 A1
Burkes Ct BEAC * HP9 88 C8
Burkes Crs BEAC HP9 88 C9
Burkes Rd BEAC HP9 88 C9
Burke St CAN/RD E16 141 L7
Burket Cl NWDGN UB2 153 M3
Burland Rd BRWN CM15 107 J2
BTSEA SW11 180 A1
CRW RM5 104 D7
Burlands CRAWW RH11 283 K4
Burlea Cl WOT/HER KT12 217 J2
Burleigh Av BFN/LL DA15 185 J1
WLGTN SM6 202 B10
Burleigh Cl ADL/WDHM KT15 215 L2
Burleigh Ct BUSH * WD23 73 M8
Burleigh Gdns ASHF TW15 174 D8
STHGT/OAK N14 98 D2
WOKN/KNAP GU21 232 C3
Burleigh Md BRKMPK AL9 40 F2
Burleigh Pde STHGT/OAK * N14 98 E2
Burleigh Pk COB KT11 217 M8
Burleigh Pl PUT/ROE SW15 178 G1
Burleigh Rd ADL/WDHM KT15 215 L1
CHEAM SM3 201 H8
CHES/WCR * EN8 62 D8
EN EN1 79 M8
HERT/BAY SG13 25 P4
HGDN/ICK UB10 132 C3
HHS/BOV HP3 36 D7
STAL AL1 38 G6
Burleigh St COVGDN WC2E 11 M7
Burleigh Wk CAT SE6 183 H4
Burleigh Wy ENC/FH EN2 79 L7
POTB/CUF EN6 60 F6
Burley Cl CHING E4 100 F6
STRHM/NOR SW16 202 E2
Burley Hl HLWE CM17 47 N2
Burley Rd CAN/RD E16 141 P8
Burleys Rd CRAWE RH10 284 E7
Burlingham Cl RGUE GU4 250 G8
Burlings La RSEV TN14 245 J3
Burlington Ar CONDST W1S 10 G8
Burlington Av RCH/KEW TW9 155 M7
ROMW/RG RM7 124 C4
SL SL1 149 K1
Burlington Cl EBED/NFELT TW14 174 E3
EHAM E6 142 B8
MV/WKIL W9 8 E1
ORP BR6 206 E9
Burlington Gdns ACT W3 135 P10
CHDH RM6 123 P5
CHSWK W4 155 P4
CONDST W1S 10 G8
Burlington La CHSWK W4 155 P6
Burlington Ms ACT W3 135 P10
Burlington Pde CRICK * NW2 116 G8
Burlington Pl FUL/PGN SW6 157 H8
PIN HA5 113 J1
REIG RH2 257 K9
WFD IG8 101 M4
Burlington Ri EBAR EN4 97 P2
Burlington Rd CHSWK * W4 155 P4
ENC/FH EN2 79 L5
FUL/PGN SW6 157 H8
ISLW TW7 154 C7
MUSWH N10 118 B1
NWMAL KT3 200 C4
SL SL1 128 A7
SL SL1 149 K1
THHTH CR7 203 K2
TOTM N17 99 P9
Burman Cl RDART DA2 188 B3
Burma Rd CHOB/PIR GU24 193 L9
STNW/STAM N16 119 L9
Burma Ter NRWD * SE19 181 M8
Burmester Rd TOOT SW17 179 M6
Burnaby Crs CHSWK W4 155 N5
Burnaby Gdns CHSWK W4 155 N5
Burnaby Rd GVW DA11 190 B3
Burnaby St WBPTN SW10 157 M6
Burnbrae Cl FNCH N3 97 L7
Burnbury Rd BAL SW12 180 D4
Burn Cl ADL/WDHM KT15 215 N1
GSTN * WD25 74 C8
LHD/OX KT22 236 B1
Burncroft Av PEND EN3 80 B7
Burndell Wy YEAD UB4 133 L7
Burnell Av RCHPK/HAM TW10 177 H8
WELL DA16 163 K8
Burnell Gdns STAN HA7 95 J10
Burnell Rd SUT SM1 221 L1
Burnell Wk RBRW/HUT CM13 107 H7
STHWK * SE1 19 M7
Burnels Av EHAM E6 142 D5
Burness Cl HOLWY N7 5 N1
UX/CGN UB8 131 N4
Burne St CAMTN NW1 9 N3
Burnet Av GU GU1 250 E7
Burnet Cl CHOB/PIR GU24 212 D9
HHS/BOV HP3 35 P7
Burnet Gv HOR/WEW KT19 219 P9
Burnett Pk HLWW/ROY CM19 46 E6
Burnett Rd ERITH DA8 165 L5
Burnett Sq HERT/WAS SG14 24 G4
Burnetts Rd WDSR SL4 148 D7
Burney Av BRYLDS KT5 199 L5
Burney Cl GT/LBKH KT23 254 B1
Burney Dr LOU IG10 82 F7
Burney Rd RDKG RH5 254 F7
Burney St GNWCH SE10 161 H6
Burnfoot Av FUL/PGN SW6 157 H7
Burnham Av BEAC HP9 108 F1
HGDN/ICK UB10 112 D9
Burnham Cl ENC/FH EN2 79 M4
KTN/HRWW/W HA3 114 F2
MLHL NW7 96 D8
STHWK SE1 19 M6
WDSR SL4 148 C8
WOKN/KNAP GU21 231 J4
Burnham Crs DART DA1 165 K10
WAN E11 121 P2
Burnham Dr REIG RH2 257 K9
WPK KT4 200 G9
Burnham Gdns CROY/NA CR0 203 N7
HEST TW5 153 J7
HYS/HAR UB3 152 E2
Burnham La SL SL1 128 C7
Burnham Rd BEAC HP9 108 D4
CHING E4 100 E6
DAGW RM9 143 L2
DART DA1 187 L1
MRDN SM4 201 L5
ROMW/RG RM7 124 D1
SCUP DA14 185 P5
STAL AL1 38 F6
WOKN/KNAP GU21 231 J4
Burnhams Rd GT/LBKH KT23 235 M10
Burnham St BETH E2 140 B5
KUTN/CMB KT2 199 M1
Burnham Ter DART * DA1 187 L1
Burnham Wy SYD SE26 182 E8
WEA W13 154 G3
Burnhill Rd BECK BR3 204 F2
Burnley Cl OXHEY WD19 93 K6
Burnley Rd BRXN/ST SW9 158 G8
WLSDN NW10 116 C10
WTHK RM20 166 E7
Burnsall Pl HARP AL5 20 B5
Burnsall St CHEL SW3 15 P7
Burns Av BFN/LL DA15 185 L2
CHDH RM6 123 M5
EBED/NFELT TW14 175 H2
STHL UB1 133 P9
Burns Cl ERITH DA8 164 G7
TOOT SW17 179 N9
WALTH E17 121 H2
WELL DA16 163 J7
YEAD UB4 133 H7
Burns Dr BNSTD SM7 221 H10
HHNE HP2 36 C1
Burnside ASHTD KT21 237 L4
HERT/WAS SG14 25 H6
HOD EN11 44 E3
SBW CM21 29 N1
STAL AL1 38 G8
Burnside Av CHING E4 100 E7
Burnside Cl BAR EN5 77 K7
BERM/RHTH SE16 140 C10
TWK TW1 176 F2
Burnside Crs ALP/SUD HA0 135 J3
Burnside Rd BCTR RM8 123 M7
Burns Pl TIL RM18 168 E7
Burns Rd ALP/SUD HA0 135 K4
BTSEA SW11 158 A8
CRAWE RH10 284 D5
WEA * W13 154 G1
WLSDN NW10 136 C3
Burns Wy HEST TW5 153 L7
Burnt Ash Hl LEE/GVPK SE12 183 L2
Burnt Ash La BMLY BR1 183 N8
Burnt Ash Rd LEE/GVPK SE12 183 L1
Burntcommon Cl
RPLY/SEND GU23 251 J1
Burntcommon La
RPLY/SEND GU23 251 K1
Burntfarm Ride CHESW EN7 61 J8
Burnt House La HORS RH12 282 C6
RDART DA2 187 M7
Burnthwaite Rd FUL/PGN SW6 157 J6
Burntmill Cl HLW CM20 28 F8
Burntmill La HLW CM20 28 F8
Burnt Oak Broadway EDGW HA8 95 N8
Burnt Oak Flds EDGW HA8 95 P9
Burnt Oak La BFN/LL DA15 185 K2
RDKG RH5 278 A7
Burnt Pollard La CHOB/PIR GU24 212 D6
Burntwood Av EMPK RM11 125 L4
Burntwood Cl CTHM CR3 241 P7
WAND/EARL * SW18 179 N4
Burntwood Grange Rd
WAND/EARL SW18 179 N4
Burntwood Gv SEV TN13 265 J3
Burntwood La CTHM CR3 241 P7
TOOT SW17 179 M6
Burntwood Rd SEV TN13 265 J4
Burntwood Vw NRWD * SE19 181 N8
Burnway EMPK RM11 125 M5
Burnwood Park Rd
WOT/HER KT12 217 J1
Buross St WCHPL E1 140 A8
Burpham Cl YEAD UB4 133 L7
Burpham La RGUE GU4 250 D5
Burrage Gv WOOL/PLUM SE18 162 E3
Burrage Pl WOOL/PLUM SE18 162 E4
Burrage Rd WOOL/PLUM SE18 162 F3
Burrard Rd CAN/RD E16 141 M8
KIL/WHAMP NW6 117 K10
Burr Bank Ter RDART * DA2 187 K7
Burr Cl BXLYHN DA7 164 A9
LCOL/BKTW AL2 57 K3
WAP E1W 13 N9
Burrell Cl CROY/NA CR0 204 D6
EDGW HA8 95 N3
Burrell Rw BECK BR3 204 F2
Burrell St STHWK SE1 12 C9
The Burrell DORK RH4 272 B3
The Burren AMS * HP6 69 J3
Burrfield Dr STMC/STPC BR5 207 N5
Burr Hill La CHOB/PIR GU24 213 K5
Burritt Rd KUT KT1 199 M2
Burroughs Cottages
POP/IOD * E14 140 D7
Burroughs Gdns HDN NW4 116 E2
The Burroughs HDN NW4 116 E2
Burroway Rd DTCH/LGLY SL3 150 E2
Burrowfield WGCE AL7 22 G7
Burrow Gn CHIG IG7 103 J6
Burrow Hill Gn CHOB/PIR GU24 213 J5
Burrow Rd CHIG IG7 103 K6
CMBW SE5 159 M10
Burrows Cl GT/LBKH KT23 235 N10
GUW GU2 249 L9
Burrows Hill Cl
STWL/WRAY TW19 151 L10
Burrows La SHGR GU5 270 D6
Burrows Ms STHWK SE1 18 C1
Burrows Rd WLSDN NW10 136 F5
Burr Rd WAND/EARL SW18 179 K4
Bursar St STHWK * SE1 13 J10
Bursdon Cl BFN/LL DA15 185 J5
Burses Wy RBRW/HUT CM13 107 N1
Bursland Rd PEND EN3 80 C8
Burslem Av BARK/HLT IG6 103 K7
Burslem St WCHPL E1 13 P6
Burstead Cl COB KT11 217 L9
Burstock Rd PUT/ROE SW15 157 H10
Burston Dr LCOL/BKTW AL2 56 B4
Burston Rd PUT/ROE SW15 178 G1
Burstow Rd RYNPK SW20 201 H1
Burtenshaw Rd THDIT KT7 198 F7
Burtley Cl FSBYPK N4 119 K6
Burton Av WATW WD18 73 H8
Burton Bank IS * N1 6 G4
Burton Cl CHSGTN KT9 219 J4
HORL RH6 280 B5
THHTH CR7 203 L3
Burton Dr WAB EN9 80 F3
Burton Gdns HEST TW5 153 N7
Burton Gv WALW SE17 18 G8
Burtonhole Cl MLHL NW7 96 G5
Burtonhole La MLHL NW7 96 G6
NFNCH/WDSP N12 97 H5
Burton La BRXN/ST * SW9 159 H8
CHESW EN7 61 M4
Burton Ms BGVA SW1W 16 D6
Burton Pl STPAN WC1H 11 K1
Burton Rd BRXN/ST SW9 159 H8
KIL/WHAMP NW6 2 D4
KUTN/CMB KT2 177 K10
LOU IG10 82 F8
SWFD E18 121 N1
Burtons Ct SRTFD E15 141 J2
Burton's La CSTG HP8 70 B8
RKW/CH/CXG WD3 70 C9
Burton's Rd HPTN TW12 176 A7
Burton St STPAN WC1H 11 K1
Burton's Wy CSTG HP8 69 P6
Burton Wy WDSR SL4 148 D9
Burt Rd CAN/RD E16 141 P10
Burtwell La WNWD SE27 181 L7
Burwash Cl STMC/STPC BR5 207 M5
Burwash Rd CRAWE RH10 284 B8
WOOL/PLUM SE18 162 G4
Burway Crs CHERT KT16 195 K4
Burwell Av GFD/PVL UB6 134 D1
Burwell Cl WCHPL * E1 140 A8
Burwell Rd LEY E10 120 D6
Burwood Av HAYES BR2 205 N9
PIN HA5 113 K3
PUR/KEN CR8 223 J10
Burwood Cl GU GU1 250 F9
REIG RH2 257 N10
SURB KT6 199 M8
WOT/HER KT12 217 K3
Burwood Gdns RAIN RM13 144 G5
Burwood Pl BAY/PAD W2 9 P5
Burwood Rd WEY KT13 216 E4
Bury Av RSLP HA4 112 D4
YEAD UB4 132 F4
Bury Cl BERM/RHTH SE16 140 C10
WOKN/KNAP GU21 232 A2
Bury Ct HDTCH EC3A 13 K5
Burycroft WGCW AL8 23 H2
Burydell La LCOL/BKTW AL2 56 C3
Bury Farm AMSS HP7 69 H6
Bury Flds GUW GU2 267 P2
Buryfield Wy WARE SG12 26 B1
Bury Gn HHW HP1 35 M5
STALE/WH AL4 21 H3
Bury Green Rd CHESW EN7 61 P7
Bury Gv MRDN SM4 201 L5
Bury Hl HHW HP1 35 M5
Bury Hill Cl HHW HP1 35 M5
Bury Holme BROX EN10 44 E9
Bury La EPP CM16 64 G6
RKW/CH/CXG WD3 91 N2
WOKN/KNAP GU21 231 P2
Bury Mdw RKW/CH/CXG WD3 91 N2
Bury Pl NOXST/BSQ WC1A 11 L4
Bury Ri HHS/BOV HP3 52 G1
Bury Rd CHING E4 81 J8
DAGE RM10 124 D10
EPP CM16 65 H7
HAT AL10 40 F3
HHW HP1 35 M5
HLWE CM17 29 M7
WDGN N22 99 H10
Bury St ED N9 99 N1
GUW GU2 267 P2
HDTCH EC3A 13 K6
RSLP HA4 112 E4
STJS SW1Y 10 G9
Bury St West ED N9 99 M1
The Bury CSHM * HP5 50 G8
Bury Wk CHEL SW3 15 N6
Burywick HARP AL5 20 A6
Busby Pl KTTN NW5 5 J1
Busch Cl ISLW TW7 154 G7
Bushbaby Cl STHWK SE1 19 J4
Bushbarns CHESW EN7 61 P5
Bushberry Rd HOM E9 140 D1
Bushbury La BRKHM/BTCW RH3 273 M5
Bushby Av BROX EN10 44 E8
Bush Cl ADL/WDHM KT15 215 M2
GNTH/NBYPK IG2 122 G3
Bush Cottages
WAND/EARL SW18 179 K1
Bushell Cl BRXS/STRHM SW2 180 G5
Bushell Gn BUSH WD23 94 C3
Bushell St WAP E1W 13 P10
Bushell Wy CHST BR7 184 D8
Bush Elms Rd EMPK RM11 125 H5
Bushetts Gv REIG RH2 258 C5
Bushey Av STMC/STPC BR5 206 G7
SWFD E18 121 L1
Bushey Cl CHING E4 101 H4
HGDN/ICK UB10 112 B7
PUR/KEN CR8 241 N2
WGCE AL7 23 L6
Bushey Cft HLWS CM18 47 H3
OXTED RH8 261 H6
Bushey Gn WGCE AL7 23 L6
Bushey Grove Rd BUSH WD23 73 L8
Bushey Hall Dr BUSH WD23 73 M8
Bushey Hall Pk BUSH * WD23 73 M8
Bushey Hall Rd BUSH WD23 73 L8
Bushey Hill Rd CMBW SE5 159 N7
Bushey La SUT SM1 201 K10
Bushey Lees BFN/LL * DA15 185 J2
Bushey Ley WGCE AL7 23 L6
Busheymill Br BUSH WD23 73 M4
Bushey Mill Crs WATN WD24 73 K3
Bushey Mill La BUSH WD23 73 N6
WATN WD24 73 K3
Bushey Rd CROY/NA CR0 204 F9
HGDN/ICK UB10 112 B7
HYS/HAR UB3 152 F3
PLSTW E13 141 P4
RYNPK SW20 200 F2
SEVS/STOTM N15 119 M4
SUT SM1 221 K1
Bushey Wy BECK BR3 205 J6
Bushfield Cl EDGW HA8 95 N3
Bushfield Crs EDGW HA8 95 N3
Bushfield Dr REDH RH1 276 B5
Bushfield Rd HHS/BOV HP3 52 F1
Bushfields LOU IG10 82 D9
Bush Gv CDALE/KGS NW9 115 P5
STAN HA7 95 J9
Bushgrove Rd BCTR RM8 123 N9
Bush Hall La BRKMPK AL9 40 G1
Bush Hl WCHMH N21 99 K1
Bush Hill Pde WCHMH * N21 99 L1
Bush Hill Rd KTN/HRWW/W HA3 115 L4
WCHMH N21 79 L10
Bush La CANST EC4R 12 G7
RPLY/SEND GU23 232 G10
Bushmead Cl SEVS/STOTM * N15 119 N2
Bushmoor Crs
WOOL/PLUM SE18 162 E6
Bushnell Rd TOOT SW17 180 C5
Bush Rd BERM/RHTH SE16 160 C3
BKHH IG9 102 A5
HACK E8 140 A3
RCH/KEW TW9 155 L5
SHPTN TW17 196 A5
WAN E11 121 L5
Bushway BCTR RM8 123 N9
Bushwood WAN E11 121 L5
Bushwood Cl BRKMPK AL9 40 E9
Bushwood Dr STHWK SE1 19 M6
Bushwood Rd RCH/KEW TW9 155 M5
Bushy Hill Dr GU GU1 250 F9
Bushy Park Gdns HPTN * TW12 176 C8
Bushy Park Rd TEDD TW11 176 G10
Bushy Rd GT/LBKH KT23 236 A8
TEDD TW11 176 D9
Bushy Shaw ASHTD KT21 237 H3
Buslins La CSHM HP5 50 D4
Butcher Rw POP/IOD E14 140 C8
Butchers La BGR/WK TN15 211 J9
Butchers Rd CAN/RD E16 141 M8
Butchers Yd ORP BR6 226 D7
Bute Av RCHPK/HAM TW10 177 K5
Bute Gdns HMSMTH W6 156 G3
RCHPK/HAM * TW10 177 K4
WLGTN SM6 222 D2
Bute Gdns West WLGTN SM6 222 D2
Bute Rd BARK/HLT IG6 122 E3
CROY/NA CR0 203 H8
WLGTN SM6 222 D1
Bute St SKENS SW7 15 L5
Bute Wk IS N1 6 G2
Butler Av HRW HA1 114 C5
Butler Rd BCTR RM8 123 L9
HRW HA1 114 B5
WLSDN NW10 136 C2
Butlers Cl AMS HP6 68 F3
WDSR SL4 148 C8
Butlers & Colonial Whf
STHWK SE1 19 M1
Butlers Court Rd BEAC HP9 88 C10
Butlers Dene Rd CTHM CR3 242 E6
Butlers Dr CHING E4 81 H4
Butlers Hl EHSLY KT24 252 C6
Butlers Pl HART * DA3 211 K10
Butler St BETH * E2 140 B5
HGDN/ICK UB10 132 C6
Buttell Cl GRAYS RM17 168 A4
Buttercross La EPP * CM16 65 K6
Buttercup Cl HARH RM3 105 L9
Buttercup Sq
STWL/WRAY * TW19 173 N4
Butterfield Cl BERM/RHTH SE16 19 P2
TOTM N17 99 K7
TWK TW1 176 E2
Butterfield La STAL AL1 38 D10
Butterfield Rd STALE/WH AL4 21 H4
Butterfields WALTH E17 121 H3
Butterfield Sq EHAM E6 142 C8
Butterfly Av DART DA1 187 N5
Butterfly La BORE WD6 74 G7
ELTH/MOT SE9 184 E2
Butterfly Wk CMBW * SE5 159 L7
WARL CR6 242 B6
Butter Hl DORK RH4 272 F2
WLGTN SM6 202 B10
Butteridges Cl DAGW RM9 144 A3
Butterly Av DART * DA1 187 N5
Buttermere Av SL SL1 128 B7
Buttermere Cl
EBED/NFELT TW14 174 G4
MRDN SM4 200 G6
STAL AL1 38 G7
STHWK SE1 19 L5
WAN E11 121 J9
Buttermere Dr PUT/ROE SW15 179 H1
Buttermere Gdns PUR/KEN CR8 223 L9
Buttermere Pl GSTN * WD25 55 H9
Buttermere Rd STMC/STPC BR5 207 N4
Buttermere Wk HACK E8 7 M2
Buttermere Wy EGH TW20 172 E10
Buttersweet Ri SBW CM21 29 P2
Butterwick GSTN WD25 73 M2
HMSMTH W6 156 F3
Butterworth Gdns WFD IG8 101 M7
Buttesland St IS N1 7 H9
Buttfield Cl DAGE RM10 144 C1
Butt Field Vw LCOL/BKTW AL2 38 B10
Buttlehide RKW/CH/CXG WD3 90 G6
Buttmarsh Cl WOOL/PLUM SE18 162 E4
Buttondene Crs BROX EN10 44 G8
Button Rd CDH/CHF RM16 167 L3
Button St SWLY BR8 209 K4
Buttsbury Rd IL IG1 122 F10
Butts Cl CRAWW RH11 283 L6
Butts Crs FELT TW13 175 P6
Butts End HHW HP1 35 K5
Butts Green Rd EMPK RM11 125 L4
Buttsmead NTHWD HA6 92 D8
Butts Piece NTHLT UB5 133 J4
Butts Rd BMLY BR1 183 K8
WOKN/KNAP GU21 232 B4
The Butts BROX EN10 44 D10
BTFD TW8 155 J5
RSEV TN14 247 J3
Buxhall Crs HOM E9 140 E1
Buxted Rd EDUL SE22 159 M10
HACK E8 7 L3
NFNCH/WDSP N12 97 P6
Buxton Av CTHM CR3 241 M7
Buxton Cl STALE/WH AL4 39 J3
WFD IG8 102 A7
Buxton Crs CHEAM SM3 221 H1
Buxton Dr NWMAL KT3 200 A2
WAN E11 121 K2
Buxton Gdns ACT W3 135 N9
Buxton La CTHM CR3 241 M7
Buxton Pth OXHEY * WD19 93 K4
Buxton Rd ARCH N19 118 E6
ASHF TW15 173 N8
CDH/CHF RM16 168 B1
CHING E4 101 J1
CRICK NW2 136 E1
EHAM E6 142 B5
EPP CM16 83 H2
ERITH DA8 164 E6
GNTH/NBYPK IG2 123 H4
MORT/ESHN SW14 156 B9
SRTFD E15 121 K10
THHTH CR7 203 J5
WAB EN9 63 M8
WALTH E17 120 D2
Buxton St WCHPL E1 13 M2
Byam St FUL/PGN SW6 157 M8
Byards Cft STRHM/NOR SW16 202 E1
Bybend Cl SLN SL2 128 G3
Bychurch End TEDD * TW11 176 E8
Bycliffe Ms GVW * DA11 190 C3
Bycliffe Ter GVW * DA11 190 C3
Bycroft Rd STHL UB1 133 P7
Bycroft St PGE/AN SE20 182 C10
Bycroft Wy CRAWE RH10 284 C5
Bycullah Av ENC/FH EN2 79 J7
Bycullah Rd ENC/FH EN2 79 J6
Byde St HERT/WAS SG14 25 K4
Byefield Cl BERM/RHTH SE16 160 D1
Byelands Cl BERM/RHTH SE16 140 C10
Byerley Wy CRAWE RH10 284 F6
Byers Cl POTB/CUF EN6 59 M10
The Bye ACT W3 136 B8
Byewaters WATW WD18 72 E10

Bye Ways *WHTN* TW2 176 A6
The Byeways *BRYLDS* KT5 199 M5
The Bye Wy *KTN/HRWW/W* HA3 94 D9
The Byeway *MORT/ESHN* SW14 155 P9
RKW/CH/CXG WD3 91 P3
Byfeld Gdns *BARN* SW13 156 D7
Byfield *WGCW* AL8 23 H2
Byfield Cl *BERM/RHTH* SE16 160 D1
Byfield Ct *RBRW/HUT* * CM13 127 P4
Byfield Rd *ISLW* TW7 154 F9
Byfleet Rd *ADL/WDHM* KT15 215 N5
COB KT11 216 C8
Byford Cl *SRTFD* E15 141 K2
Bygrove Rd *WIM/MER* SW19 179 N9
Bygrove St *POP/IOD* E14 140 G8
Byland Cl *ABYW* SE2 163 L2
WCHMH N21 98 G1
Bylands *WOKS/MYFD* GU22 232 D4
Byne Rd *CAR* SM5 201 P9
SYD SE26 182 B9
Bynes Rd *SAND/SEL* CR2 223 L4
Byng Dr *POTB/CUF* EN6 59 K7
Bynghams *HLWW/ROY* CM19 46 C3
Byng Pl *GWRST* WC1E 11 K2
Byng Rd *BAR* EN5 76 G7
Byng St *POP/IOD* E14 160 F1
Bynon Av *BXLYHN* DA7 163 P9
Byrd Rd *CRAWW* RH11 283 J10
Byrefield Rd *GUW* GU2 249 L7
Byre Rd *STHGT/OAK* N14 78 B10
Byrne Rd *BAL* SW12 180 G4
Byron Av *BORE* WD6 75 M9
CDALE/KGS NW9 115 N2
COUL/CHIP CR5 240 F1
HSLWW TW4 153 J8
MNPK E12 142 B1
NWMAL KT3 200 D5
SUT SM1 221 N1
SWFD E18 121 L1
WATN WD24 73 L5
Byron Av East *SUT* SM1 221 N1
Byron Cl *CRAWE* RH10 284 C6
HACK E8 7 N5
HPTN TW12 175 N7
PGE/AN * SE20 204 A3
SYD * SE26 182 D7
THMD SE28 143 M10
WOKN/KNAP GU21 231 K3
WOT/HER KT12 197 M8
Byron Ct *ENC/FH* EN2 79 J6
WDSR SL4 148 F9
Byron Dr *EFNCH* N2 117 N4
ERITH DA8 164 C6
Byron Gdns *SUT* SM1 221 N1
TIL RM18 168 F7
Byron Hill Rd *RYLN/HDSTN* HA2 114 C6
Byron Ms *HAMP* NW3 117 P10
Byron Pde *HGDN/ICK* * UB10 132 C6
Byron Pl *LHD/OX* KT22 236 G8
Byron Rd *ACT* W3 135 L10
ADL/WDHM KT15 215 N1
ALP/SUD HA0 115 H7
CRICK NW2 116 E7
DART DA1 166 A10
HRW HA1 114 D4
KTN/HRWW/W HA3 94 E10
LEY E10 120 G6
MLHL NW7 96 D6
SAND/SEL CR2 224 A6
WALTH E17 120 F1
Byron St *POP/IOD* E14 141 H8
Byron Ter *ED* * N9 100 B1
Byron Wy *HARH* RM3 105 K9
NTHLT UB5 133 M5
WDR/YW UB7 152 A3
YEAD UB4 132 F6
Bysouth Cl *CLAY* IG5 102 E9
By the Wood *OXHEY* WD19 93 L3
Bythorn St *BRXN/ST* SW9 158 G9
Byton Rd *TOOT* SW17 180 A9
Byttom Hl *RDKG* RH5 255 H3
Byward Av *EBED/NFELT* TW14 175 K2
Byward St *MON* EC3R 13 K8
Bywater Pl *BERM/RHTH* SE16 140 D10
Bywater St *CHEL* SW3 16 A7
Byways *BERK* HP4 34 B4
The Byways *HOR/WEW* KT19 220 C1
The Byway *BELMT* SM2 221 N5
POTB/CUF EN6 59 K9
Bywell Pl *GTPST* * W1W 10 G4
Bywood Av *CROY/NA* CR0 204 B6
Bywood Cl *PUR/KEN* CR8 241 J1

C

Cabbell Pl *ADL/WDHM* KT15 215 M1
Cabbell St *CAMTN* NW1 9 N4
Cabell Rd *GUW* GU2 249 K4
Caberfeigh Pl *REDH* * RH1 257 N10
Cabinet Wy *CHING* E4 100 E7
Cable Pl *GNWCH* SE10 161 H7
Cables Cl *BELV* DA17 164 D2
Cable St *WCHPL* E1 13 P7
Cable Trade Pk *CHARL* * SE7 161 M4
Cabot Sq *POP/IOD* E14 140 F10
Cabot Wy *EHAM* E6 142 A3
Cabrera Av *VW* GU25 194 A5
Cabrera Cl *VW* GU25 193 P6
Cabul Rd *BTSEA* SW11 157 P8
Caburn Ct *CRAWW* RH11 283 M9
Caburn Hts *CRAWW* RH11 283 M9
Cacket's La *RSEV* TN14 244 G1
The Cackstones *CRAWE* * RH10 284 E6
Cactus Cl *CMBW* * SE5 159 M8
Cadbury Cl *ISLW* TW7 154 F7
SUN TW16 174 F10
Cadbury Rd *SUN* TW16 174 F10
Cadbury Wy *BERM/RHTH* SE16 19 M4
Caddington Cl *EBAR* EN4 77 P9
Caddington Rd *CRICK* NW2 117 H8
Caddis Cl *STAN* * HA7 94 E8
Caddy Cl *EGH* TW20 172 D8
Cade La *SEV* TN13 265 K4
Cadell Cl *BETH* E2 7 M8
Cade Rd *GNWCH* SE10 161 J7
Cader Rd *WAND/EARL* SW18 179 M2
Cadet Dr *STHWK* SE1 19 M7
Cadet Pl *GNWCH* SE10 161 K5
Cadiz Rd *DAGE* RM10 144 D2
Cadiz St *WALW* SE17 18 F8
Cadlocks Hl *RSEV* TN14 228 A6
Cadman Cl *BRXN/ST* SW9 159 J6
Cadmer Cl *NWMAL* KT3 200 B4
Cadmore La *CHES/WCR* EN8 62 D4
Cadogan Av *RDART* DA2 188 C3
Cadogan Cl *HOM* * E9 140 E2
RYLN/HDSTN HA2 114 A9
TEDD TW11 176 D8
Cadogan Ct *BELMT* SM2 221 L3
Cadogan Gdns *CHEL* SW3 16 B5
FNCH * N3 97 L9
SWFD E18 121 N1
WCHMH N21 79 H9
Cadogan Ga *KTBR* SW1X 16 B5
Cadogan La *KTBR* SW1X 16 C4
Cadogan Pl *KTBR* SW1X 16 B4
Cadogan Rd *SURB* KT6 199 J5
WOOL/PLUM SE18 162 F2
Cadogan Sq *KTBR* SW1X 16 A4
Cadogan St *CHEL* SW3 16 A6
Cadogan Ter *HOM* E9 140 E1
Cadoxton Av *SEVS/STOTM* N15 119 N4
Cadwallon Rd *ELTH/MOT* SE9 184 E5
Caedmon Rd *HOLWY* N7 118 G9
Caenshill Rd *WEY* KT13 216 B4
Caenswood Hl *WEY* KT13 216 B6
Caenwood Cl *WEY* KT13 216 B3
Caen Wood Rd *ASHTD* KT21 237 H4
Caerleon Cl *ESH/CLAY* KT10 218 G4
SCUP DA14 185 M8
Caernarvon Cl *EMPK* RM11 125 P6
HHNE HP2 35 N6
MTCM CR4 202 F3
Caernarvon Dr *CLAY* IG5 102 D9
Caesars Rd *STALE/WH* AL4 21 J3
Caesars Wk *MTCM* CR4 202 A5
Caesar's Wy *SHPTN* TW17 196 E6
Caffins Cl *CRAWE* RH10 283 P5
Cage Farm Cottages
OXTED * RH8 260 G10
Cage Pond Rd *RAD* WD7 57 M9
Cages Wood Dr *SLN* SL2 108 G9
Cage Yd *REIG* * RH2 257 K10
Cahill St *STLK* * EC1Y 12 F2
Cahir St *POP/IOD* E14 160 G3
Caillard Rd *BF/WBF* KT14 215 N7
Cain's La *EBED/NFELT* TW14 174 E1
Caird St *NKENS* W10 2 B10
Cairn Av *EA* W5 135 J10
Cairndale Cl *BMLY* BR1 183 L10
Cairnfield Av *CRICK* NW2 116 B8
Cairns Av *WFD* IG8 102 C7
Cairns Cl *DART* DA1 187 L1
STALE/WH AL4 39 J7
Cairns Rd *BTSEA* SW11 179 P1
Cairn Wy *STAN* HA7 94 E7
Cairo New Rd *CROY/NA* CR0 203 J9
Cairo Rd *WALTH* * E17 120 F2
Caishowe Rd *BORE* WD6 75 N5
Caister Cl *HHS/BOV* HP3 35 P7
Caistor Park Rd *SRTFD* E15 141 L3
Caistor Rd *BAL* SW12 180 C3
Caithness Dr *EPSOM* KT18 220 A10
Caithness Gdns *BFN/LL* DA15 185 J2
Caithness Rd *HMSMTH* W6 156 G2
MTCM CR4 180 C10
Calabria Rd *HBRY* N5 6 C1
Calais Cl *CHESW* EN7 61 L2
Calais St *CMBW* SE5 159 J7
Calbourne Av *HCH* RM12 125 J10
Calbourne Rd *BAL* SW12 180 A3
Calbroke Rd *SLN* SL2 128 E6
Calbury Cl *STAL* AL1 38 G7
Calcott Cl *BRW* CM14 106 G2
Calcutta Rd *TIL* RM18 168 C8
Caldbeck *WAB* EN9 63 J10
Caldbeck Av *WPK* KT4 200 E9
Caldecot Av *CHESW* EN7 61 N5
Caldecote Gdns *BUSH* WD23 74 D10
Caldecote La *BUSH* WD23 94 E1
Caldecot Rd *CMBW* SE5 159 K8
Caldecott Wy *CLPT* E5 120 C8
Caldecot Wy *BROX* EN10 44 E8
Calder Av *BRKMPK* AL9 57 K2
GFD/PVL UB6 134 E4
Calder Ct *DTCH/LGLY* SL3 150 C4
Calderdale Cl *CRAWW* RH11 283 L9
Calder Gdns *EDGW* HA8 115 M1
Calderon Rd *WAN* E11 121 H9
Calder Rd *MRDN* SM4 201 M5
Caldervale Rd *CLAP* SW4 180 E1
Calder Wy *DTCH/LGLY* SL3 151 H9
Calderwood *GVE* DA12 191 H9
Calderwood St
WOOL/PLUM SE18 162 D3
Caldicote Gn *CDALE/KGS* * NW9 116 B4
Caldwell Rd *BFOR* GU20 212 C2
OXHEY WD19 93 L5
Caldwell St *BRXN/ST* SW9 158 G6
Caldy Rd *BELV* DA17 164 C2
Caldy Wk *IS* N1 6 F2
Caledonian Cl *GDMY/SEVK* * IG3 123 L6
Caledonian Rd *HOLWY* N7 118 G10
IS N1 5 N4
Caledonian Wy *HORL* * RH6 280 C7
Caledonian Wharf Rd
POP/IOD E14 161 J3
Caledonia Rd *STWL/WRAY* TW19 173 P4
Caledonia St *IS* N1 5 M8
Caledon Pl *GU* GU1 250 D7
Caledon Rd *BEAC* HP9 88 D8
EHAM E6 142 C3
LCOL/BKTW AL2 57 H2
WLGTN SM6 222 B1
Cale St *CHEL* SW3 15 P7
Calfstock La *EYN* DA4 209 M4
Calidore Cl *BRXS/STRHM* * SW2 180 G2
California La *BUSH* WD23 94 C2
California Rd *NWMAL* KT3 199 N4
Caling Cft *HART* DA3 211 L8
Caliph Cl *GVE* DA12 191 J6
Callaby Ter *IS* N1 6 G2
Callaghan Cottages *WCHPL* * E1 140 B7
Callander Rd *CAT* SE6 182 G5
The Callanders *BUSH* * WD23 94 D2
Callan Gv *SOCK/AV* RM15 147 H9
Callard Av *PLMGR* N13 99 J6
Callcott Rd *KIL/WHAMP* NW6 2 C4
Callcott St *KENS* W8 8 E9
Callendar Rd *SKENS* SW7 15 L3
Calley Down Crs *CROY/NA* CR0 225 J6
Callingham Cl *POP/IOD* E14 140 E7
Callis Farm Cl *STWL/WRAY* TW19 173 P2
Callis Rd *WALTH* E17 120 E4
Callisto Cl *CRAWW* RH11 283 H10
Callisto Ct *HHNE* HP2 36 A3
Callow Fld *PUR/KEN* CR8 223 H9
Callow Hl *VW* GU25 193 P2
Callowland Pl *WATN* WD24 73 J4
Callow St *CHEL* SW3 15 L9
Calluna Ct *WOKS/MYFD* GU22 232 C4
Calluna Dr *CRAWE* RH10 285 H3
Calmington Rd *CMBW* SE5 19 K8
Calmont Rd *BMLY* BR1 183 J9
Calmore Cl *HCH* RM12 125 K10
Calne Av *CLAY* IG5 102 E9
Calonne Rd *WIM/MER* SW19 178 G7
Calshot Av *CDH/CHF* RM16 167 L1
Calshot Rd *HTHAIR* TW6 152 C8
Calshot St *IS* N1 5 N7
Calshot Wy *ENC/FH* EN2 79 J7
HTHAIR TW6 152 B8
Calthorpe Gdns *EDGW* HA8 95 L6
SUT SM1 201 M10
Calthorpe St *FSBYW* WC1X 11 P1
Calton Av *DUL* SE21 181 M2
HERT/WAS SG14 24 G4
Calton Rd *BAR* EN5 77 M10
Calumet *BEAC* HP9 88 C8
Calverley Cl *BECK* BR3 182 G9
Calverley Crs *DAGE* RM10 124 B7
Calverley Gv *ARCH* N19 118 E6
Calverley Rd *EW* KT17 220 D3
Calvert Av *BETH* E2 7 K10
Calvert Cl *BELV* DA17 164 B3
SCUP DA14 185 P9
Calvert Crs *DORK* RH4 254 G10
Calverton Rd *EHAM* E6 142 D3
Calvert Rd *BAR* EN5 76 G6
DORK RH4 254 G10
EHSLY KT24 253 J4
GNWCH SE10 161 L4
Calvert St *CAMTN* NW1 4 C5
Calvin Cl *STMC/STPC* BR5 207 N3
Calvin St *WCHPL* E1 13 L2
Calydon Rd *CHARL* SE7 161 N4
Calypso Wy *BERM/RHTH* SE16 160 E2
Camac Rd *WHTN* TW2 176 C4
Camarthen Gn
CDALE/KGS * NW9 116 B4
Cambalt Rd *PUT/ROE* SW15 178 G1
Camber Cl *CRAWE* RH10 284 D7
Camberley Av *EN* EN1 79 M8
RYNPK SW20 200 E2
Camberley Cl *CHEAM* SM3 200 G10
Camberley Pl *HARP* AL5 20 C5
Camberley Rd *HTHAIR* TW6 152 B9
Cambert Wy *ELTH/MOT* SE9 161 N10
Camberwell Church St
CMBW SE5 159 L7
Camberwell Glebe *CMBW* SE5 159 L7
Camberwell Gn *CMBW* SE5 159 L7
Camberwell Gv *CMBW* SE5 159 L7
Camberwell La *RSEV* TN14 264 A7
Camberwell New Rd *CMBW* SE5 159 J6
Camberwell Rd *CMBW* SE5 18 F10
Camberwell Station Rd
CMBW SE5 159 K7
Cambeys Rd *DAGE* RM10 124 D10
Camborne Av *HARH* RM3 105 M8
WEA W13 154 G1
Camborne Cl *HTHAIR* TW6 152 B9
Camborne Crs *HTHAIR* TW6 152 B9
Camborne Dr *HHNE* HP2 35 P2
Camborne Rd *BELMT* SM2 221 K4
CROY/NA CR0 203 P7
MRDN SM4 200 G5
SCUP DA14 185 M6
WAND/EARL SW18 179 K3
WELL DA16 163 H8
Camborne Wy *HARH* RM3 105 N8
HEST TW5 153 P7
Cambourne Av *ED* N9 100 C1
Cambourne Ms *NTGHL* W11 8 A6
Cambray Rd *BAL* SW12 180 D4
ORP BR6 207 J7
Cambria Cl *BFN/LL* DA15 184 G4
HSLW TW3 153 P10
Cambria Ct *EBED/NFELT* TW14 175 J3
Cambria Crs *GVE* DA12 191 H7
Cambria Gdns *STWL/WRAY* TW19 173 P3
Cambrian Av *GNTH/NBYPK* IG2 123 H3
Cambrian Cl *WNWD* SE27 181 J6
Cambrian Gn *CDALE/KGS* * NW9 116 B3
Cambrian Gv *GVW* DA11 190 D3
Cambrian Rd *LEY* E10 120 F5
RCHPK/HAM TW10 177 L2
Cambrian Wy *HHNE* HP2 35 P3
Cambria Rd *CMBW* SE5 159 K9
Cambria St *FUL/PGN* SW6 157 L6
Cambridge Av *GFD/PVL* UB6 114 E10
GPK RM2 105 K10
KIL/WHAMP NW6 2 F7
NWMAL KT3 200 B2
SL SL1 128 A4
SL SL1 128 F8
WELL DA16 163 J10
Cambridge Barracks Rd
WOOL/PLUM SE18 162 C3
Cambridge Cl *CHES/WCR* EN8 62 B5
HSLWW TW4 153 M10
RYNPK SW20 200 E1
WALTH E17 120 E4
WDGN * N22 99 H9
WDR/YW UB7 151 N5
WLSDN NW10 115 P8
WOKN/KNAP GU21 231 L4
Cambridge Cots *BETH* E2 140 A4
TEDD * TW11 176 F8
Cambridge Dr *LEE/GVPK* SE12 183 M1
POTB/CUF EN6 59 H7
RSLP HA4 113 K7
Cambridge Gdns
CDH/CHF * RM16 168 D3
EN EN1 79 P6
KIL/WHAMP NW6 2 F7
KUT KT1 199 M2
MUSWH N10 98 B9
NKENS W10 8 B5
NKENS W10 136 G8
TOTM N17 99 L8
WCHMH N21 99 L1
Cambridge Ga *CAMTN* NW1 4 E10
Cambridge Gate Ms *CAMTN* NW1 4 F10
Cambridge Gn *ELTH/MOT* SE9 184 E4
Cambridge Gv *HMSMTH* W6 156 E3
PGE/AN * SE20 204 A1
Cambridge Grove Rd *KUT* KT1 199 M2
Cambridge Heath Rd *BETH* E2 140 A5
Cambridge Lodge Pk
HORL * RH6 280 B1
Cambridge Pde *EN* * EN1 79 P6
Cambridge Pk *TWK* TW1 177 J3
WAN E11 121 M4
Cambridge Park Rd *WAN* E11 121 L5
Cambridge Pas *HOM* E9 140 B2
Cambridge Pl *KENS* * W8 15 H2
Cambridge Rd *ASHF* TW15 174 D10
BARK IG11 142 F2
BARN SW13 156 C8
BEAC HP9 88 B9
BMLY BR1 183 M10
BTSEA SW11 158 A7
CAR SM5 221 P3
CHING E4 101 J2
E/WMO/HCT KT8 197 N4
GDMY/SEVK IG3 123 H6
HLW CM20 29 M5
HNWL W7 154 E1
HPTN TW12 175 N10
HSLWW TW4 153 M10
KIL/WHAMP NW6 2 F8
KUT KT1 199 M2
MTCM CR4 202 D3
NWMAL KT3 200 A4
RCH/KEW TW9 155 M6
RYLN/HDSTN HA2 113 P3
RYNPK SW20 200 E1
SCUP DA14 185 H7
SNWD SE25 203 P3
STAL AL1 38 G7
STHL * UB1 133 N10
TEDD TW11 176 F7
TWK TW1 177 J2
UX/CGN UB8 131 N1
WAN E11 121 M4
WATW * WD18 73 K8
WOT/HER KT12 197 J6
Cambridge Rd North *CHSWK* W4 155 N4
Cambridge Rd South *CHSWK* W4 155 N4
Cambridge Rw
WOOL/PLUM SE18 162 E4
Cambridge Sq *BAY/PAD* W2 9 N5
REDH RH1 276 B3
Cambridge St *PIM* SW1V 16 F7
Cambridge Ter *BERK* HP4 34 A5
CAMTN NW1 4 E10
ED * N9 99 N1
Cambridge Terrace Ms
CAMTN * NW1 4 F10
Cambridge Yd *HNWL* * W7 154 E1
Cambus Cl *YEAD* UB4 133 M7
Cambus Rd *CAN/RD* E16 141 M7
Camdale Rd *WOOL/PLUM* SE18 163 J6
Camden Av *FELT* TW13 175 K5
YEAD UB4 133 K9
Camden Cl *CDH/CHF* RM16 168 E3
CHST BR7 206 F1
GVW DA11 189 P4
Camden Gdns *CAMTN* NW1 4 F4
SUT SM1 221 L2
THHTH CR7 203 J3
Camden Gv *CHST* BR7 184 E9
Camden High St *CAMTN* NW1 4 F4
Camden Hill Rd *NRWD* SE19 181 M9
Camdenhurst St *POP/IOD* E14 140 D8
Camden Lock Pl *CAMTN* NW1 4 E4
Camden Ms *CAMTN* NW1 5 J3
Camden Park Rd *CHST* BR7 184 C10
HOLWY N7 5 K1
Camden Pas *IS* N1 6 C7
Camden Rd *BXLY* DA5 186 A4
CAMTN NW1 4 G4
CAR SM5 222 A1
CDH/CHF RM16 167 K2
SEV TN13 247 J8
SUT SM1 221 L2
WALTH E17 120 E4
WAN E11 121 N4
Camden Rd Permanent Wy
CAMTN * NW1 5 J6
Camden Rw *BKHTH/KID* SE3 161 K8
PIN * HA5 113 K1
Camden Sq *CAMTN* NW1 5 J2
Camden St *CAMTN* NW1 4 F4
Camden Ter *CAMTN* NW1 5 J2
Camden Wk *IS* N1 6 C6
Camden Wy *CHST* BR7 184 C10
THHTH CR7 203 J3
Camelford Wk *NTGHL* W11 8 A6
Camel Gv *KUTN/CMB* KT2 177 J8
Camellia Cl *HARH* RM3 105 M9
Camellia Ct *CHOB/PIR* GU24 212 E9
Camellia Pl *WHTN* TW2 176 A3
Camelot Cl *BH/WHM* TN16 243 P2
WIM/MER SW19 179 J7
WOOL/PLUM SE18 162 G1
Camel Rd *CAN/RD* E16 142 A10
Camera Pl *WBPTN* SW10 15 L10
Cameron Cl *BRW* CM14 107 H5
BXLY DA5 186 E6
TRDG/WHET N20 97 P3
UED N18 100 A5
Cameron Ct *WARE* SG12 26 C1
Cameron Dr *CHES/WCR* EN8 62 C10
Cameron Rd *CAT* * SE6 182 E5
CROY/NA CR0 203 J6
CSHM HP5 51 H6
GDMY/SEVK IG3 123 H6
HAYES BR2 205 M5
Cameron Ter *LEE/GVPK* * SE12 183 N6
Camerton Cl *HACK* E8 7 M2
Camfield *WGCE* AL7 23 J9
Cam Gn *SOCK/AV* RM15 146 G8
Camilla Cl *GT/LBKH* KT23 254 A1
SUN * TW16 174 F9
Camilla Dr *RDKG* RH5 254 F6
Camilla Rd *BERM/RHTH* SE16 160 A3
Camille Cl *SNWD* SE25 203 P3
Camlan Rd *BMLY* BR1 183 L7
Camlet St *BETH* E2 13 L1
Camlet Wy *EBAR* EN4 77 K6
STALW/RED AL3 38 A5
Camley St *CAMTN* NW1 5 J4
Camm Av *WDSR* SL4 148 D9
Camm Gdns *KUT* * KT1 199 L2
THDIT KT7 198 D7
Camomile Av *MTCM* CR4 202 A1
Camomile St *LVPST* EC2M 13 J5
Camomile Wy *WDR/YW* UB7 131 P8
Camomile Rd *ROMW/RG* RM7 124 E7
Campana Rd *FUL/PGN* SW6 157 K7
Campbell Av *BARK/HLT* IG6 122 F2
WOKS/MYFD GU22 232 C7
Campbell Cl *HLWE* CM17 47 L2
ROM RM1 104 F7
RSLP HA4 113 H4
STRHM/NOR * SW16 180 E8
WHTN TW2 176 C4
WOOL/PLUM SE18 162 D7
Campbell Cottages *MTCM* * CR4 202 B2
Campbell Cft *EDGW* HA8 95 M6
Campbell Gordon Wy
CRICK NW2 116 E9
Campbell Rd *BOW* E3 140 F5
CRAWE RH10 284 D9
CROY/NA CR0 203 J7
CTHM CR3 241 L7
EHAM E6 142 B3
FSTGT E7 121 K9
GVW DA11 190 C4
HNWL W7 134 D9
TOTM N17 100 B9
WALTH E17 120 E2
WEY KT13 216 B4
WHTN TW2 176 C5
Campbell Wk *IS* * N1 5 M5
Campdale Rd *ARCH* N19 118 E8
Campden Crs *ALP/SUD* HA0 114 G8
BCTR RM8 123 L9
Campden Gv *KENS* W8 14 F1
Campden Hl *KENS* W8 14 E1
Campden Hill Gdns *KENS* W8 8 E9
Campden Hill Pl *KENS* W8 8 D9
Campden Hill Rd *KENS* W8 8 E9
Campden Hill Sq *KENS* W8 8 D9
Campden House Cl *KENS* W8 14 E1
Campden House Ter *KENS* * W8 8 F10
Campden Rd *HGDN/ICK* UB10 112 A8
SAND/SEL CR2 223 M2
Campden St *KENS* W8 8 E10
Campden Ter *CHSWK* * W4 156 B4
Campen Cl *WIM/MER* SW19 179 H5
Camp End Rd *WEY* KT13 216 C8
Camperdown St *WCHPL* E1 13 M6
Campfield Rd *ELTH/MOT* SE9 184 A3
HERT/WAS SG14 25 J5
STAL AL1 38 F6
Camphill Ct *BF/WBF* KT14 215 K8
Camphill Rd *BF/WBF* KT14 215 K8
Campine Cl *CHES/WCR* EN8 62 C4
Campion Cl *DEN/HRF* UB9 111 K8
EHAM E6 142 C9
GSTN WD25 55 H9
GVW DA11 190 B7
KTN/HRWW/W HA3 115 L4
ROMW/RG RM7 124 E7
SAND/SEL CR2 223 M1
UX/CGN UB8 132 A7
Campion Ct *ALP/SUD* * HA0 135 K4
Campion Dr *KWD/TDW/WH* KT20 238 E6
Campion Gdns *WFD* IG8 101 M6
Campion Pl *THMD* SE28 143 L10
Campion Rd *HHW* HP1 35 H7
ISLW TW7 154 E7
PUT/ROE SW15 156 F10
Campions *LOU* IG10 82 D4
Campions Ct *BERK* HP4 33 M6
The Campions *BORE* WD6 75 L4
Campion Wy *EDGW* HA8 95 P5
Cample La *SOCK/AV* RM15 146 F9
Camplin Rd *KTN/HRWW/W* HA3 115 K3
Camplin St *NWCR* SE14 160 C6
Camp Rd *CFSP/GDCR* SL9 110 A5
CTHM CR3 242 D7
STAL AL1 38 E7
WIM/MER SW19 178 E8
Campsbourne Pde
CEND/HSY/T * N8 118 F2
Campsbourne Rd
CEND/HSY/T N8 118 F1
The Campsbourne
CEND/HSY/T N8 118 F2
Campsey Rd *DAGW* RM9 143 L2
Campshill Pl *LEW* SE13 183 H1
Campshill Rd *LEW* SE13 183 H1
Campus Rd *WALTH* E17 120 E4
The Campus *HHNE* * HP2 36 C4
WGCW AL8 22 G4
Camp Vw *WIM/MER* SW19 178 E8
Camp View Rd *STAL* AL1 38 G7
Cam Rd *SRTFD* E15 141 J3
Camrose Av *EDGW* HA8 95 L10
ERITH DA8 164 C5
FELT TW13 175 J7
STAN HA7 95 K10
Camrose Cl *CROY/NA* CR0 204 D7
MRDN SM4 201 K4
Camrose St *ABYW* SE2 163 K4
Canada Av *REDH* RH1 276 B4
UED N18 99 K7
Canada Crs *ACT* W3 135 P7
Canada Dr *REDH* RH1 276 B4
Canada Farm Rd *EYN* DA4 210 G5
Canada La *BROX* EN10 62 D1
Canada Park Pde *EDGW* * HA8 95 N9
Canada Rd *ACT* W3 135 P7
BF/WBF KT14 215 N7
COB KT11 217 K9
ERITH DA8 165 J6
SL SL1 149 N1
The Canadas *BROX* EN10 62 D2
Canada St *BERM/RHTH* SE16 160 C1
Canada Wy *SHB* W12 136 E9
Canadian Av *CAT* SE6 182 G4
Canal Ap *DEPT* SE8 160 D5
Canal Basin *GVE* DA12 190 G2
Canal Cl *NKENS* W10 136 G6
WCHPL E1 140 D6
Canal Est *DTCH/LGLY* * SL3 150 D1
Canal Gv *PECK* SE15 19 P9
Canal Pth *HACK* E8 7 L6
Canal Rd *GVE* DA12 190 G2
WCHPL E1 140 D6
Canal St *CMBW* SE5 18 G10
Canal Wk *CROY/NA* CR0 203 M6
IS N1 7 K5
WLSDN * NW10 135 P2
Canal Wy *DEN/HRF* UB9 91 K7
NKENS W10 136 G6
Canal Whf *DTCH/LGLY* SL3 150 D1
GFD/PVL * UB6 134 F3
Canal Yd *NWDGN* * UB2 153 J3
Canberra Cl *CRAWW* RH11 283 N4
DAGE RM10 144 E2
HCH RM12 125 K9
HDN NW4 116 D1
STALW/RED AL3 38 E2
Canberra Crs *DAGE* RM10 144 E2
Canberra Dr *NTHLT* UB5 133 K5
Canberra Rd *HTHAIR* TW6 152 B9
ABYW SE2 163 N5
CHARL SE7 161 P5
EHAM E6 142 C3
Canberra Sq *TIL* * RM18 168 D8
Canbury Av *KUTN/CMB* KT2 199 L1
Canbury Ms *SYD* SE26 181 P6
Canbury Park Rd *KUTN/CMB* KT2 199 K1
Canbury Pth *STMC/STPC* BR5 207 K4
Cancell Rd *BRXN/ST* SW9 159 H7
Candahar Rd *BTSEA* SW11 157 P8
Cander Wy *SOCK/AV* RM15 146 G9
Candlefield Rd *HHS/BOV* HP3 36 B9
Candlemas La *BEAC* HP9 88 D9
Candlemas Md *BEAC* HP9 88 D9
Candler Ms *TWK* TW1 176 F3
Candler St *SEVS/STOTM* * N15 119 L4
Candlerush Cl *WOKS/MYFD* GU22 232 E3
Candover Cl *WDR/YW* UB7 151 N6
Candover Rd *HCH* RM12 125 J6
Candover St *GTPST* * W1W 10 G4
Candy Cft *GT/LBKH* KT23 254 A2
Candy St *BOW* E3 140 E3
Cane Hl *HARH* RM3 105 L10
Canes La *HLWE* CM17 47 P4
Canewden Cl *WOKS/MYFD* GU22 232 B5
Caney Ms *CRICK* NW2 116 G7
Canfield Dr *RSLP* HA4 113 J10

Canfield Gdns KIL/WHAMP NW6 3 H3
Canfield Pl KIL/WHAMP NW6 3 J2
Canfield Rd RAIN RM13 144 G3
WFD IG8 102 B8
Canford Av NTHLT UB5 133 M3
Canford Cl ENC/FH EN2 79 H6
Canford Dr ADL/WDHM KT15 195 L9
Canford Gdns NWMAL KT3 200 B6
Canford Pl TEDD TW11 177 H9
Canford Rd BTSEA SW11 158 B10
Cangelis Cl HHW HP1 35 K8
Canham Rd CHSWK W4 156 B1
SNWD SE25 203 M3
Can Hatch KWD/TDW/WH KT20 239 H4
Canmore Gdns
STRHM/NOR SW16 180 D10
Cann Hall Rd FSTGT E7 121 L9
Canning Crs WDGN N22 98 G9
Canning Cross CMBW SE5 159 M8
Canning Pl KENS W8 15 J3
Canning Rd CROY/NA CR0 203 N9
FSBYPK N4 119 J8
KTN/HRWW/W HA3 114 D1
SRTFD E15 141 K4
WALTH E17 120 D2
Cannington Rd DAGW RM9 143 M1
Cannizaro Rd WIM/MER SW19 178 F9
Cannonbury Av PIN HA5 113 L4
Cannon Cl HPTN TW12 176 A9
RYNPK SW20 200 F3
Cannon Crs CHOB/PIR GU24 213 K7
Cannon Dr POP/IOD E14 140 F9
Cannon Gv LHD/OX KT22 236 D7
Cannon Hl KIL/WHAMP NW6 117 L10
STHGT/OAK N14 98 E4
Cannon Hill La MRDN SM4 200 G5
Cannon La HAMP NW3 117 N8
PIN HA5 113 M5
Cannon Ms WAB EN9 62 G9
Cannon Mill Av CSHM HP5 51 J9
Cannon Pl CHARL SE7 162 B4
HAMP NW3 117 M8
Cannon Rd BXLYHN DA7 163 P7
STHGT/OAK N14 98 F4
WATW WD18 73 K9
Cannon Side LHD/OX KT22 236 D8
Cannons Meadow WLYN AL6 23 P2
Cannon St STALW/RED AL3 38 C5
STP EC4M 12 E6
Cannon Street Rd WCHPL E1 140 A8
Cannon Wy E/WMO/HCT KT8 197 P4
LHD/OX KT22 236 D7
Canon Av CHDH RM6 123 M3
Canon Beck Rd
BERM/RHTH SE16 160 B1
Canonbie Rd FSTH SE23 182 B3
Canonbury Crs IS N1 6 F3
Canonbury Gv IS N1 6 E3
Canonbury La IS N1 6 C3
Canonbury Pk North IS N1 6 E2
Canonbury Pk South IS N1 6 E2
Canonbury Pl IS N1 6 D2
Canonbury Rd ENC/FH EN2 79 M5
IS N1 6 D3
Canonbury Sq IS N1 6 D3
Canonbury St IS N1 6 E3
Canonbury Vls IS N1 6 D4
Canon Mohan Cl EBAR EN4 78 B10
Canon Murnane Rd STHWK SE1 19 L4
Canon Rd BMLY BR1 205 P3
Canon Rw WHALL SW1A 17 J1
Canons Brook HLWW/ROY CM19 46 D1
Canons Cl EDGW HA8 95 L7
EFNCH N2 117 N5
RAD WD7 74 G1
REIG RH2 257 J9
Canons Cottages EDGW * HA8 95 L7
Canons Ct EDGW * HA8 95 L7
Canons Dr EDGW HA8 95 K7
Canons Fld STALE/WH AL4 21 J2
Canons Ga CHES/WCR EN8 62 E2
HLW CM20 28 D9
Canon's Hl COUL/CHIP CR5 241 H4
Canons La KWD/TDW/WH KT20 239 H5
Canonsleigh Rd DAGW RM9 143 L2
Canons Rd WARE SG12 26 B1
Canon St IS N1 6 E1
Canon's Wk CROY/NA CR0 204 C10
Canopus Wy NTHWD HA6 93 H5
STWL/WRAY TW19 173 P5
Canrobert St BETH E2 140 A4
Cantelowes Rd CAMTN NW1 5 J2
Canterbury Av BFN/LL DA15 185 M5
IL IG1 122 B5
SLN SL2 129 H6
UPMR RM14 126 E6
Canterbury Cl AMSS HP7 65 K8
BECK BR3 204 G1
CHIG IG7 103 L4
CMBW * SE5 159 K8
DART DA1 187 P3
EHAM E6 142 C8
GFD/PVL UB6 134 A7
NTHWD HA6 92 G7
Canterbury Ct DORK * RH4 272 F1
Canterbury Crs BRXN/ST SW9 159 H9
Canterbury Gv WNWD SE27 181 H6
Canterbury Pl WALW SE17 18 D6
Canterbury Rd BORE WD6 75 M6
CROY/NA CR0 202 G7
FELT TW13 175 M5
GUW GU2 249 L8
GVE DA12 190 F5
HRW HA1 114 A3
KIL/WHAMP NW6 2 E8
LEY E10 121 H5
MRDN SM4 201 M6
RYLN/HDSTN HA2 114 A3
WAT * WD17 73 J6
Canterbury Ter KIL/WHAMP NW6 2 E7
Canterbury Wy DART DA1 166 B10
RBRW/HUT CM13 107 H7
RKW/CH/CXG WD3 72 D7
WTHK RM20 166 D6
The Canter CRAWE RH10 284 F6
Cantley Gdns GNTH/NBYPK IG2 122 F4
NRWD SE19 203 N1
Cantley Rd HNWL W7 154 F2
Canton St POP/IOD E14 140 F8
Cantrell Rd BOW E3 140 E6
Cantwell Rd WOOL/PLUM SE18 162 E6
Canvey Cl CRAWW RH11 283 M10
Canvey St STHWK SE1 12 E9
Cape Cl BARK IG11 142 E2
Capel Av WLGTN SM6 222 G2
Capel Cl HAYES BR2 206 B8
TRDG/WHET N20 97 M4
Capel Gdns GDMY/SEVK IG3 123 J9
PIN HA5 113 N2
Capel La CRAWW RH11 283 J8
Capella Rd NTHWD HA6 92 G6
Capell Av RKW/CH/CXG WD3 70 F9
Capell Rd RKW/CH/CXG WD3 70 G9
Capell Wy RKW/CH/CXG WD3 70 G9
Capel Pl RDART DA2 187 K7
Capel Rd EBAR EN4 77 P10
EN EN1 80 A2
FSTGT E7 121 N9
OXHEY WD19 73 L10
Capelvere Wk WAT WD17 72 F5
Capeners Cl KTBR SW1X 16 B2
KTBR * SW1X 16 C2
Capern Rd WAND/EARL SW18 179 M4
Cape Rd SEVS/STOTM N15 119 P1
STAL AL1 38 G6
Cape Yd WAP E1W 13 P9
Capital Interchange Wy
CHSWK W4 155 M4
Capital Pl HLWW/ROY CM19 46 D2
Capitol Wy CDALE/KGS NW9 115 P1
Capland St STJWD NW8 9 M1
Caple Pde WLSDN * NW10 136 C4
Caple Rd WLSDN NW10 136 C4
Capon Cl BRW CM14 106 G2
Caponfield WGCE AL7 23 L7
Cappell La WARE SG12 27 H6
Caprea Cl YEAD UB4 133 L7
Capricorn Cl CRAWW RH11 283 H9
Capri Rd CROY/NA CR0 203 N8
Capsey Rd CRAWW RH11 283 H8
Capstan Cl CHDH RM6 123 L4
Capstan Ct GRH DA9 166 B10
Capstan Ride ENC/FH EN2 79 H6
Capstan Rd DEPT SE8 160 E3
Capstan Sq POP/IOD E14 161 H1
Capstans Whf
WOKN/KNAP GU21 231 L4
Capstan Wy BERM/RHTH SE16 140 D10
Captain Cook Cl CSTG HP8 89 M5
Captain's Cl CSHM HP5 50 F3
Captains Wk BERK HP4 34 A6
Capthorne Av RYLN/HDSTN HA2 113 M6
Capuchin Cl STAN HA7 94 G7
Capulet Ms CAN/RD E16 141 M10
Capworth St LEY E10 120 F6
Caractacus Cottage Vw
WATW WD18 93 H1
Caractacus Gn WATW WD18 72 G10
Caradoc Evans Cl
FBAR/BDGN * N11 98 C6
Caradoc St GNWCH SE10 161 K4
Caradon Cl WOKN/KNAP GU21 231 N4
Caradon Ct WAN * E11 121 K6
Caradon Wy SEVS/STOTM * N15 119 L2
Caravan La RKW/CH/CXG WD3 91 P1
The Caravan Site SOCK/AV RM15 166 C2
Caravel Cl CDH/CHF RM16 167 L2
Caravel Ms DEPT * SE8 160 F5
Caraway Cl PLSTW E13 141 N7
Caraway Pl GUW GU2 249 M5
WLGTN * SM6 202 C10
Carberry Rd NRWD SE19 181 M9
Carbery Av ACT W3 155 L1
Carbery La ASC SL5 192 A3
Carbis Cl CHING E4 101 J2
Carbis Rd POP/IOD E14 140 E8
Carbone Hl POTB/CUF EN6 60 E2
Carburton St GTPST W1W 10 F3
Carbury Cl HCH RM12 145 K1
Cardale St POP/IOD E14 161 H2
Cardamom Cl GUW GU2 249 M6
Carde Cl HERT/WAS SG14 24 G4
Carden Rd PECK SE15 160 A9
Cardiff Rd HNWL W7 154 F2
PEND EN3 80 A8
WATW WD18 73 J10
Cardiff St WOOL/PLUM SE18 163 H6
Cardiff Wy ABLGY WD5 55 H8
Cardigan Cl SL SL1 128 E9
WOKN/KNAP GU21 231 K4
Cardigan Gdns GDMY/SEVK IG3 123 K7
Cardigan Pl BKHTH/KID * SE3 161 J8
Cardigan Rd BARN SW13 156 D8
BOW E3 140 E4
RCHPK/HAM TW10 177 K2
WIM/MER SW19 179 M9
Cardigan St LBTH SE11 18 A7
Cardigan Wk IS * N1 6 F3
Cardinal Av BORE WD6 75 N7
KUTN/CMB KT2 177 K8
MRDN SM4 201 H6
Cardinal Bourne St STHWK * SE1 19 H4
Cardinal Cl CHESW EN7 61 N2
CHST BR7 206 G1
EDGW HA8 96 A8
MRDN SM4 201 H6
SAND/SEL CR2 223 P9
WPK KT4 220 D1
Cardinal Crs NWMAL KT3 199 P2
Cardinal Dr BARK/HLT IG6 102 F7
WOT/HER KT12 197 L8
Cardinal Gv STALW/RED AL3 38 A8
Cardinal Pl PUT/ROE SW15 156 G10
Cardinal Rd FELT TW13 175 J4
RSLP HA4 113 L6
Cardinal's Wk HPTN TW12 176 B10
MDHD SL6 128 B8
SUN TW16 174 F9
Cardinals Wy ARCH N19 118 E6
Cardinal Wy
KTN/HRWW/W * HA3 114 D1
RAIN RM13 145 L4
Cardine Ms PECK SE15 160 A6
Cardingham WOKN/KNAP GU21 231 M3
Cardington Sq HSLWW TW4 153 L10
Cardington St CAMTN NW1 5 H9
Cardozo Rd HOLWY N7 118 F10
Cardrew Av NFNCH/WDSP N12 97 N6
Cardross St HMSMTH W6 156 E2
Cardwell Crs ASC SL5 192 B5
Cardwell Rd HOLWY * N7 118 F9
Cardwells Keep GUW GU2 249 M7
Cardwell Ter HOLWY * N7 118 F9
Cardy Rd HHW HP1 35 L7
Carew Cl COUL/CHIP CR5 241 J5
HOLWY N7 118 G7
Carew Rd ASHF TW15 174 D9
MTCM CR4 202 B2
NTHWD HA6 92 F7
THHTH CR7 203 J3
TOTM N17 99 P10
WEA W13 155 H1
WLGTN SM6 222 D3
Carew St CMBW SE5 159 K8
Carew Wy OXHEY WD19 93 N4
Carey Cl WDSR SL4 148 G9
Carey Gdns VX/NE SW8 158 D7
Carey La CITYW EC2V 12 E5
Carey Pl WEST SW1P 17 J6
Carey Rd DAGW RM9 123 P9
Careys Copse HORL * RH6 281 J4
Careys Cft BERK HP4 33 L2
Carey's Fld SEV TN13 246 F6
Carey St LINN WC2A 11 P6
Carey's Wd HORL RH6 281 J4
Carey Wy WBLY HA9 115 N9
Carfax Pl CLAP SW4 158 E10
Carfax Rd HCH RM12 124 G9
HYS/HAR UB3 153 H4
The Carfax SYD * SE26 182 B6
Carfree Cl IS N1 6 B3
Cargill Rd WAND/EARL SW18 179 M4
Cargo Forecourt Rd HORL RH6 279 N8
Cargo Rd HORL RH6 279 N7
Cargreen Rd SNWD SE25 203 N4
Carholme Rd FSTH SE23 182 E4
Carisbrook Cl EN EN1 79 N5
Carisbrooke Av BXLY DA5 185 N4
WATN WD24 73 L5
Carisbrooke Cl EMPK RM11 125 P6
STAN HA7 95 J10
Carisbrooke Ct NTHLT * UB5 133 N3
Carisbrooke Gdns PECK * SE15 159 N6
Carisbrooke Rd BRWN CM15 86 G10
HARP AL5 20 B1
HAYES * BR2 205 P4
MTCM CR4 202 F4
WALTH * E17 120 D2
Carisbrook Rd LCOL/BKTW AL2 56 A2
Carleton Av WLGTN SM6 222 E5
Carleton Cl ESH/CLAY KT10 198 C8
Carleton Gdns ARCH * N19 118 D10
Carleton Pl EYN DA4 210 B4
Carleton Rd CHES/WCR EN8 62 C3
DART DA1 187 P3
HOLWY N7 118 E10
Carleton Vls KTTN * NW5 118 D10
Carlie Cl BOW E3 140 E4
Carlina Gdns WFD IG8 101 N6
Carlingford Rd HAMP NW3 117 N9
MRDN SM4 200 G6
SEVS/STOTM N15 119 J1
Carlisle Av ACT W3 136 B8
STALW/RED AL3 38 C4
TWRH EC3N 13 K6
Carlisle Cl KUTN/CMB KT2 199 M1
Carlisle Gdns IL IG1 122 B4
KTN/HRWW/W HA3 115 J5
Carlisle La STHWK SE1 17 P3
Carlisle Pl FBAR/BDGN N11 98 C5
WEST SW1P 16 G4
Carlisle Rd CDALE/KGS NW9 115 P1
DART DA1 187 P2
FSBYPK N4 119 H6
HPTN TW12 176 A10
KIL/WHAMP NW6 2 B5
LEY E10 120 F6
ROM RM1 124 G3
SL SL1 129 J9
SUT SM1 221 J3
Carlisle St SOHO/CST W1F 11 J6
Carlisle Wk HACK E8 7 L2
Carlisle Wy TOOT SW17 180 B8
Carlos Pl MYFR/PKLN W1K 10 D8
Carlow St CAMTN NW1 4 G7
Carlton Av EBED/NFELT TW14 175 K2
GRH DA9 188 D2
HYS/HAR UB3 152 F3
KTN/HRWW/W HA3 114 G3
SAND/SEL CR2 223 L4
STHGT/OAK N14 78 E9
Carlton Av East WBLY HA9 115 J7
Carlton Av West ALP/SUD HA0 114 G7
Carlton Bank HARP * AL5 20 A2
Carlton Cl BORE WD6 76 A8
CHSGTN KT9 219 J3
EDGW HA8 95 M6
HAMP NW3 117 K7
UPMR RM14 126 A7
WOKN/KNAP GU21 214 C10
Carlton Ct HORL * RH6 280 C2
Carlton Crs CHEAM SM3 221 H1
Carlton Dene EW * KT17 220 E2
Carlton Dr BARK/HLT IG6 122 G1
PUT/ROE SW15 178 G1
Carlton Gdns EA W5 135 H8
STJS SW1Y 11 J10
Carlton Gn REDH RH1 257 P7
SCUP * DA14 185 J7
Carlton Gv PECK SE15 160 A7
Carlton Hl STJWD NW8 3 J6
Carlton House Ter STJS SW1Y 11 J10
Carlton Ms KIL/WHAMP * NW6 117 K10
Carlton Pde SEV * TN13 247 K8
WBLY * HA9 115 K6
Carlton Park Av RYNPK SW20 200 F2
Carlton Pl WEY * KT13 216 C1
Carlton Rd CDH/CHF RM16 168 C1
CHSWK W4 156 A1
EA W5 135 H9
ERITH DA8 164 C5
FBAR/BDGN N11 98 B6
FSBYPK N4 119 H5
GPK RM2 125 H3
MNPK E12 122 A9
MORT/ESHN SW14 155 P9
NWMAL KT3 200 B2
REDH RH1 257 N8
SAND/SEL CR2 223 L4
SCUP DA14 185 J8
SLN SL2 129 N9
SUN TW16 174 G10
WALTH E17 100 D9
WAN E11 121 L6
WELL DA16 163 L9
WOKN/KNAP GU21 214 D10
WOT/HER KT12 197 J7
Carlton Sq WCHPL * E1 140 C6
Carlton St STJS SW1Y 11 J8
Carlton Ter SYD SE26 182 B6
UED * N18 99 L5
WAN * E11 121 N3
Carlton Tower Pl KTBR SW1X 16 B3
Carlton Tye HORL RH6 280 E4
Carlton V KIL/WHAMP NW6 2 E9
Carlwell St TOOT SW17 179 P8
Carlyle Av BMLY BR1 206 A3
STHL UB1 133 N9
Carlyle Cl E/WMO/HCT KT8 198 A2
EFNCH N2 117 M4
WLSDN NW10 136 A3
Carlyle Ct WBPTN * SW10 157 M7
Carlyle Gdns STHL UB1 133 N9
Carlyle Rd CROY/NA CR0 203 P9
EA W5 155 H3
MNPK E12 122 B9
STA TW18 173 J10
THMD SE28 143 L9
Carlyle Sq CHEL SW3 15 M8
Carlyon Av RYLN/HDSTN HA2 113 N9
Carlyon Cl ALP/SUD HA0 135 K3
Carlyon Rd ALP/SUD HA0 135 K4
YEAD UB4 133 K7
Carlys Cl BECK BR3 204 C2
Carmalt Gdns PUT/ROE SW15 156 F10
WOT/HER KT12 217 K2
Carmarthen Rd SL SL1 129 K9
Carmel Cl WOKS/MYFD * GU22 232 B4
Carmel Ct KENS W8 14 G1
Carmelite Rd KTN/HRWW/W HA3 94 B9
Carmelite St EMB EC4Y 12 B7
Carmelite Wy HART DA3 211 L5
Carmen St POP/IOD E14 140 G8
Carmichael Cl BTSEA * SW11 157 N9
RSLP HA4 113 H9
Carmichael Rd SNWD SE25 203 P5
Carminia Rd TOOT SW17 180 C5
Carnaby Rd BROX EN10 44 D6
Carnaby St REGST W1B 10 G7
Carnach Gn SOCK/AV RM15 146 G9
Carnac St WNWD SE27 181 L7
Carnanton Rd WALTH E17 101 J9
Carnarvon Av EN EN1 79 N6
Carnarvon Dr HYS/HAR UB3 152 D2
Carnarvon Rd BAR EN5 77 H7
LEY E10 121 H4
SRTFD E15 141 L1
SWFD E18 101 L9
Carnation Cl ROMW/RG RM7 124 F7
Carnation St ABYW SE2 163 L4
Carnbrook Rd BKHTH/KID SE3 162 A9
Carnecke Gdns ELTH/MOT SE9 184 B1
Carnegie Cl SURB KT6 199 L9
WAB EN9 80 G4
Carnegie Pl WIM/MER SW19 178 G6
Carnegie Rd STALW/RED AL3 38 C2
Carnegie St IS N1 5 N6
Carnforth Cl HOR/WEW KT19 219 N3
Carnforth Gdns HCH RM12 125 H10
Carnforth Rd STRHM/NOR SW16 180 E10
Carnoustie Dr IS N1 5 N4
Carnwath Rd FUL/PGN SW6 157 K9
Caro La HHS/BOV HP3 36 B8
Carolina Cl SRTFD E15 121 K10
Carolina Rd THHTH CR7 203 J2
Caroline Cl BAY/PAD W2 9 H8
CROY/NA CR0 223 M1
STRHM/NOR SW16 180 G7
WDR/YW UB7 151 N1
Caroline Ct ASHF TW15 174 C9
CRAWW RH11 283 N8
STAN * HA7 94 F7
Caroline Gdns BETH E2 7 K9
PECK * SE15 160 A6
Caroline Pl BAY/PAD W2 9 H7
HYS/HAR UB3 152 F6
OXHEY WD19 73 M10
VX/NE SW8 158 B8
Caroline Place Ms BAY/PAD * W2 9 H8
Caroline Rd WIM/MER SW19 179 J10
Caroline St WCHPL E1 140 C8
Caroline Ter BGVA SW1W 16 C6
Caroline Wk FUL/PGN * SW6 14 A10
Carol St CAMTN NW1 4 G5
Carolyn Cl WOKN/KNAP GU21 231 J5
Carolyn Dr ORP BR6 207 K10
Caroon Dr RKW/CH/CXG WD3 71 L2
Carpenders Av OXHEY WD19 93 M4
Carpenter Gdns WCHMH N21 99 J3
Carpenters Arms La EPP CM16 65 L1
Carpenters Cl TRDG/WHET N20 77 L10
Carpenters Ms HOLWY * N7 118 F10
Carpenter's Pl CLAP SW4 158 E10
Carpenters Rd EN EN1 80 B2
SRTFD E15 140 G2
Carpenter St MYFR/PKLN W1K 10 E8
Carpenters Wood Dr
RKW/CH/CXG WD3 70 E8
Carpenter Wy POTB/CUF EN6 59 M9
Carrara Ms HACK E8 7 N1
Carr Gv WOOL/PLUM SE18 162 B3
Carriage Dr North BTSEA SW11 158 A6
Carriage Dr South BTSEA SW11 158 A7
Carriage Dr West BTSEA SW11 158 A6
Carriage Ms IL IG1 122 F7
The Carriageway RSEV TN14 245 N10
Carrick Cl ISLW TW7 154 F9
Carrick Dr BARK/HLT IG6 102 F9
SEV TN13 247 J9
Carrick Gdns TOTM N17 99 M8
Carrick Ga ESH/CLAY KT10 198 B10
Carrick Ms DEPT SE8 160 F5
Carrill Wy BELV DA17 163 N3
Carrington Av BORE WD6 75 N9
HSLW TW3 176 A1
Carrington Cl BAR EN5 76 D9
CROY/NA CR0 204 D7
REDH RH1 258 A9
Carrington Gdns FSTGT E7 121 M9
Carrington Pl ESH/CLAY * KT10 218 A1
Carrington Rd DART DA1 187 N2
RCHPK/HAM TW10 155 M10
SL SL1 129 K9
Carrington Sq KTN/HRWW/W HA3 94 B8
Carrington St MYFR/PICC W1J 10 E10
Carrol Cl KTTN NW5 118 C9
Carroll Av GU GU1 250 E10
Carroll Cl SRTFD E15 121 L10
Carroll Hl LOU IG10 82 C7
Carronade Pl WOOL/PLUM SE18 162 G2
Carron Cl POP/IOD E14 140 G8
Carroun Rd VX/NE SW8 158 G6
Carroway La GFD/PVL UB6 134 C5
Carrow Rd DAGW RM9 143 L2
WOT/HER KT12 197 L10
Carr Rd NTHLT UB5 134 A2
WALTH E17 100 E10
Carrs La WCHMH N21 79 L9
Carr St POP/IOD E14 140 D7
Carshalton Gv SUT SM1 221 N1
Carshalton Park Rd CAR SM5 222 A2
Carshalton Pl CAR SM5 222 B1
Carshalton Rd BNSTD SM7 222 A9
MTCM CR4 202 B5
SUT SM1 221 M2
Carsington Gdns DART DA1 187 L5
Carslake Rd PUT/ROE SW15 178 F2
Carson Rd CAN/RD E16 141 M7
DUL SE21 181 K5
EBAR EN4 78 A8
Carstairs Rd CAT SE6 183 H6
Carston Cl LEE/GVPK SE12 183 L1
Carswell Cl REDBR IG4 122 A2
Carswell Rd CAT SE6 183 H3
Cartbridge Cl RPLY/SEND GU23 232 E9
Cartel Cl PUR RM19 166 C3
Carter Cl ROM RM5 104 C8
WDSR SL4 148 F8
WLGTN SM6 222 E4
Carter Dr CRW RM5 104 C5
Carteret St STJSPK SW1H 17 J2
Carteret Wy DEPT SE8 160 D3
Carterhatch La EN EN1 79 N5
PEND EN3 80 B6
Carterhatch Rd PEND EN3 80 D6
Carter La BLKFR EC4V 12 D6
Carter Pl WALW SE17 18 F8
Carter Rd CRAWE RH10 284 E10
PLSTW E13 141 N3
WIM/MER SW19 179 N9
Carters Cl KTTN * NW5 5 J1
WPK KT4 200 G9
Cartersfield Rd WAB EN9 63 H10
Carters Hill Cl ELTH/MOT SE9 183 P4
Carters La EPP CM16 46 E10
WOKS/MYFD GU22 232 F6
Carters Md HLWE CM17 47 L2
Cartersmead Cl HORL RH6 280 C3
Carter's Rd EW KT17 238 C1
Carter St WALW SE17 18 G9
Carters Yd STAL * AL1 38 C6
WAND/EARL * SW18 179 K1
Carthew Rd HMSMTH W6 156 E2
Carthew Vls HMSMTH W6 156 E2
Carthouse La WOKN/KNAP GU21 213 K10
Carthusian St FARR EC1M 12 E3
Carting La TPL/STR WC2R 11 M8
Cart La CHING E4 101 K2
Cartmel Cl REDH RH1 257 P9
TOTM N17 100 A8
Cartmel Ct NTHLT UB5 133 M1
Cartmel Gdns MRDN SM4 201 M5
Cartmel Rd BXLYHN DA7 164 B7
Cart Pth GSTN WD25 55 K9
Cartwright Gdns STPAN WC1H 5 K10
Cartwright St TWRH EC3N 13 M7
Cartwright Wy BARN SW13 156 E6
Carve Ley WGCE AL7 23 L6
Carver Rd HNHL SE24 181 K2
Carville Crs BTFD TW8 155 K3
Cary Rd WAN E11 121 K9
Carysfort Rd CEND/HSY/T N8 118 E3
STNW/STAM N16 119 L8
Cary Wk RAD WD7 56 G10
Cascade Av MUSWH N10 118 D2
Cascade Cl STMC/STPC BR5 207 M3
Cascade Rd BKHH IG9 102 A3
Cascades CROY/NA CR0 224 E6
Caselden Cl ADL/WDHM KT15 215 M2
Casella Rd NWCR SE14 160 C6
Casewick Rd WNWD SE27 181 J8
Casey Cl CAMTN NW1 9 P2
Casher Rd CRAWE RH10 284 D10
Casimir Rd CLPT E5 120 A8
Casino Av HNHL SE24 181 K1
Caspian St CMBW SE5 159 L6
Caspian Wk CAN/RD E16 142 A8
Cassandra Cl NTHLT UB5 114 C9
Cassandra Ga CHES/WCR EN8 62 E3
Casselden Rd WLSDN NW10 136 A2
Cassidy Rd FUL/PGN SW6 157 K6
Cassilda Rd ABYW SE2 163 K3
Cassilis Rd TWK TW1 176 G2
Cassiobridge Rd WATW WD18 72 F8
Cassiobridge Ter
RKW/CH/CXG * WD3 72 E9
Cassiobury Av
EBED/NFELT TW14 174 G3
Cassiobury Dr WAT WD17 72 F5
Cassiobury Park Av WATW WD18 72 F7
Cassiobury Rd WALTH E17 120 C3
Cassio Rd WATW WD18 73 J8
Cassio Whf WATW * WD18 72 E9
Cassland Rd HOM E9 140 C2
THHTH CR7 203 L4
Casslee Rd CAT SE6 182 E3
Casson St WCHPL E1 13 N4
Casstine Cl SWLY BR8 208 G1
Castellain Rd MV/WKIL W9 8 G1
Castellan Av GPK RM2 125 J1
Castellane Cl STAN HA7 94 E8
Castello Av PUT/ROE SW15 178 F1
Castell Rd LOU IG10 82 F5
Castelnau BARN SW13 156 E6
Casterbridge Rd BKHTH/KID SE3 161 M9
Casterton St HACK E8 140 A1
Castile Rd WOOL/PLUM SE18 162 D3
Castillon Rd CAT SE6 183 K5
Castlands Rd CAT SE6 182 E5
Castle Av CHING E4 101 J7
DTCH/LGLY SL3 149 M5
EW KT17 220 D5
RAIN RM13 144 F2
WDR/YW UB7 131 P9
Castlebar Hl WEA W13 134 G7
Castlebar Ms EA W5 134 G7
Castlebar Pk EA W5 134 G7
Castlebar Rd WEA W13 135 H8
Castle Baynard St BLKFR EC4V 12 D7
Castlebrook Cl LBTH SE11 18 C5
Castle Cl ACT W3 155 N1
BUSH WD23 74 A10
HARH RM3 105 K4
HAYES BR2 205 J3
HOD EN11 27 H10
REDH RH1 259 K9
REIG RH2 275 L4
WIM/MER SW19 178 G6
Castlecombe Dr WIM/MER SW19 178 G3
Castlecombe Rd ELTH/MOT SE9 184 B8
Castle Ct BANK * EC3V 13 H6
SYD SE26 182 D7
Castledine Rd PGE/AN SE20 182 A10
Castle Dr HORL RH6 280 D6
REDBR IG4 122 B4
REIG RH2 275 K6
RSEV TN14 247 M3
Castle Farm Rd RSEV TN14 228 G5
Castlefield Rd REIG RH2 257 K9
Castleford Av ELTH/MOT SE9 184 E4
Castleford Cl UED N18 99 N7
Castle Gdns DORK RH4 255 L10
Castle Ga HERT/BAY * SG13 25 K6
Castlegate RCH/KEW TW9 155 L9
Castle Gate Wy BERK HP4 33 P3
Castle Gn WEY KT13 196 F10
Castle Grove Rd CHOB/PIR GU24 213 K8
Castlehaven Rd CAMTN NW1 4 F3
Castle Hl BERK HP4 33 P3
GU GU1 268 A2
HART DA3 211 J5
WDSR SL4 149 J7
Castle Hill Av BERK HP4 33 P4
CROY/NA CR0 224 G5
Castle Hill Cl BERK HP4 33 N4
Castle Hill Pde WEA * W13 134 G9
Castle Hill Rd EGH TW20 171 N7
Castle La GVE DA12 191 L5
WESTW SW1E 16 G3

FUL/PGN SW6 157 H6
Chaldon Wy COUL/CHIP CR5 240 F3
Chale Rd BRXS/STRHM SW2 180 F2
Chalet Cl BERK HP4 33 L5
RDART DA2 186 E7
Chalet Est MLHL * NW7 96 D5
Chalfont Av AMS HP6 70 A5
WBLY HA9 135 N1
Chalfont Cl HHNE HP2 36 C1
Chalfont Gn ED N9 99 M4
Chalfont La RKW/CH/CXG WD3 70 E9
RKW/CH/CXG WD3 90 F8
Chalfont Pl STAL * AL1 38 D6
Chalfont Rd BEAC HP9 89 J6
CFSP/GDCR SL9 90 E4
ED N9 99 M4
HYS/HAR UB3 153 H1
SNWD SE25 203 N3
Chalfont Station Rd AMSS HP7 69 P6
Chalfont Wk PIN * HA5 93 K10
Chalfont Wy WEA W13 154 G2
Chalford Cl E/WMO/HCT KT8 197 P4
Chalforde Gdns GPK RM2 125 J2
Chalford Rd DUL SE21 181 L7
Chalford Wk WFD IG8 102 A9
Chalgrove WGCE AL7 23 N4
Chalgrove Av MRDN SM4 201 K5
Chalgrove Crs CLAY IG5 102 B10
Chalgrove Gdns FNCH N3 117 H1
Chalgrove Rd BELMT SM2 221 N4
HOM E9 140 B1
TOTM N17 100 A9
Chalice Cl WLGTN SM6 222 E3
Chalice Wy GRH DA9 188 D1
Chalk Ct GRAYS * RM17 167 M5
Chalk Dl WGCE AL7 23 L4
Chalkdell Flds STAL AL1 38 F3
Chalkdell Hl HHNE HP2 35 P6
Chalkenden Cl PGE/AN SE20 182 A10
Chalk Farm Pde HAMP * NW3 4 C3
Chalk Farm Rd CAMTN NW1 4 C3
Chalk Hl AMSS HP7 88 E1
CSHM HP5 50 G5
OXHEY WD19 73 M10
Chalk Hill Rd HMSMTH W6 156 G3
Chalkhill Rd WBLY HA9 115 M8
Chalklands WBLY HA9 115 P8
Chalk La ASHTD KT21 237 M5
EBAR EN4 78 A7
EHSLY KT24 252 G7
EPSOM KT18 238 A2
HLWE CM17 30 B9
MFD/CHID GU8 266 C9
Chalkley Cl MTCM CR4 202 A2
Chalk Paddock EPSOM KT18 238 A1
Chalk Pit Av STMC/STPC BR5 207 M3
Chalkpit La DORK RH4 254 F10
OXTED RH8 261 H3
Chalk Pit La SL SL1 128 A3
Chalk Pit Rd ASHTD KT21 237 P5
BNSTD SM7 239 K3
SUT SM1 221 M2
Chalkpit Ter DORK RH4 254 F10
Chalkpit Wd OXTED RH8 261 J3
Chalk Rd GVE DA12 191 K4
PLSTW E13 141 N7
Chalkstone Cl WELL DA16 163 K7
Chalkways RSEV TN14 247 M2
Chalkwell Park Av EN EN1 79 M8
Chalky Bank GVW DA11 190 D7
Chalky La CHSGTN KT9 219 J5
Challacombe Cl
RBRW/HUT CM13 107 N2
Challenge Cl GVE DA12 191 J7
WLSDN NW10 136 B3
Challenge Ct LHD/OX KT22 236 G5
Challenge Rd ASHF TW15 174 D6
Challice Wy BRXS/STRHM SW2 180 G4
Challinor HLWE CM17 47 P1
Challin St PGE/AN SE20 204 B1
Challis Rd BTFD TW8 155 J4
Challock Cl BH/WHM TN16 243 P2
Challoner Cl EFNCH N2 97 N10
Challoner Crs WKENS W14 14 C8
Challoners Cl E/WMO/HCT KT8 198 C4
Challoner St WKENS W14 14 C7
Chalmers Cl HORL RH6 279 H9
Chalmers Rd ASHF TW15 174 C7
BNSTD SM7 239 M1
Chalmers Rd East ASHF TW15 174 C7
Chalmers Wy EBED/NFELT TW14 175 J1
Chalsey Rd BROCKY SE4 160 E10
Chalton Dr EFNCH N2 117 M4
Chalton St CAMTN NW1 5 J7
Chalvey Gv SL SL1 148 G2
Chalvey Pk SL SL1 149 K1
Chalvey Rd East SL SL1 149 K1
Chalvey Rd West SL SL1 149 J1
Chamberlain Cl HLWE CM17 47 M1
WOOL/PLUM SE18 162 G2
Chamberlain Cottages
CMBW * SE5 159 L7
Chamberlain Crs WWKM BR4 204 G8
Chamberlain Gdns HSLW TW3 154 B7
Chamberlain La PIN HA5 113 H2
Chamberlain Pl WALTH * E17 120 D1
Chamberlain Rd ED N9 99 P4
EFNCH N2 97 M10
WEA W13 154 F1
Chamberlain St HAMP NW3 4 B4
Chamberlain Wy PIN HA5 113 J1
SURB KT6 199 K7
Chamberlayne Av WBLY HA9 115 K8
Chamberlayne Rd WLSDN NW10 136 F3
Chamberlens Garages
HMSMTH * W6 156 E3
Chambersbury La HHS/BOV HP3 36 C10
HHS/BOV HP3 54 B1
Chambers Cl GRH DA9 188 F1
Chambers Gdns EFNCH N2 97 N9
Chambers La WLSDN NW10 136 E2
Chambers Rd HOLWY N7 118 F9
Chambers St BERM/RHTH SE16 19 N1
HERT/WAS SG14 25 K5
Chamber St WCHPL E1 13 M7
Chambon Pl HMSMTH W6 156 D3
Chambord St BETH E2 7 M10
Champion Crs SYD SE26 182 D7
Champion Gv CMBW SE5 159 L9
Champion Hl CMBW SE5 159 L10
Champion Pk CMBW SE5 159 L9
Champion Rd SYD SE26 182 D7
UPMR RM14 126 A7
Champions Cl BORE WD6 75 N3
Champions Wy HOD EN11 26 F10
Champness Cl WNWD SE27 181 L7
Champness Rd BARK IG11 143 J2
Champney Cl DTCH/LGLY SL3 150 D9
Champneys OXHEY * WD19 93 M3
Champneys Cl BELMT SM2 221 J4
Chance Cl CDH/CHF RM16 167 L2
Chancellor Gdns SAND/SEL CR2 223 J5
Chancellor Gv DUL SE21 181 K5
Chancellor Pl CDALE/KGS NW9 96 C10
Chancellors AMSS HP7 68 A8
Chancellor's Rd HMSMTH W6 156 F4
Chancellors St HMSMTH W6 156 F4
Chancellors Whf HMSMTH * W6 156 F4
Chancelot Rd ABYW SE2 163 L3
Chancel St STHWK SE1 12 C9
Chancery Cl STALE/WH AL4 39 J1
Chancery La BECK BR3 204 G2
LINN WC2A 11 P4
Chance St BETH E2 13 L1
Chanctonbury Cha REDH RH1 276 C1
Chanctonbury Cl ELTH/MOT SE9 184 E6
Chanctonbury Dr ASC SL5 192 D7
Chanctonbury Gdns BELMT SM2 221 L4
Chanctonbury Wy CRAWW RH11 283 M9
NFNCH/WDSP N12 97 K5
Chandler Av CAN/RD E16 141 M7
Chandler Cl CRAWW RH11 283 N9
HPTN TW12 197 N1
Chandler Rd LOU IG10 82 E5
Chandlers Cl EBED/NFELT TW14 174 G3
Chandlers Ct LEE/GVPK * SE12 183 N5
Chandlers Dr ERITH DA8 164 E3
Chandler's La RKW/CH/CXG WD3 71 P3
Chandlers Ms POP/IOD E14 160 F1
Chandlers Rd STALE/WH AL4 39 H3
Chandler St WAP E1W 140 A10
Chandlers Wk BRWN CM15 86 D3
Chandlers Wy HERT/WAS SG14 25 H5
ROM RM1 124 F3
Chandler Wy PECK SE15 159 N6
Chandos Av EA W5 155 H3
STHGT/OAK N14 98 D4
TRDG/WHET N20 97 N2
WALTH * E17 100 F10
Chandos Cl AMS HP6 69 P4
BKHH IG9 101 N3
Chandos Crs EDGW HA8 95 L8
Chandos Pl CHCR WC2N 11 L8
Chandos Rd BORE WD6 75 L6
CRICK NW2 116 F10
EFNCH N2 97 N10
HRW HA1 114 B3
PIN HA5 113 K5
SRTFD E15 121 J10
STA TW18 172 G8
TOTM N17 99 M10
WLSDN NW10 136 B6
Chandos St CAVSQ/HST W1G 10 F4
Chandos Wy GLDGN NW11 117 L6
Chanlock Pth SOCK/AV RM15 146 G9
Channel Cl HEST TW5 153 P7
Channel Islands Est IS N1 6 F2
Channelsea Rd SRTFD E15 141 J3
Channing Cl EMPK RM11 125 N5
Channings WOKN/KNAP GU21 232 B1
Chanton Dr BELMT SM2 220 F6
Chantress Cl DAGE RM10 144 D3
Chantrey Cl ASHTD KT21 237 H5
SCUP DA14 185 P8
Chantrey Rd BRXN/ST SW9 158 G9
CRAWE RH10 283 P10
Chantreywood
RBRW/HUT CM13 107 M4
Chantry Av HART DA3 211 K6
Chantry Cl ENC/FH EN2 79 K4
HORL RH6 280 A3
KGLGY WD4 54 B5
KTN/HRWW/W HA3 115 L3
MLHL NW7 96 C1
MV/WKIL W9 8 D2
WDR/YW UB7 131 N9
WDSR SL4 148 F7
Chantry Hurst EPSOM KT18 238 A1
Chantry La HAT AL10 40 C5
HAYES BR2 206 A5
LCOL/BKTW AL2 57 J2
SHGR GU5 270 A5
Chantry Pl RYLN/HDSTN HA2 94 A9
Chantry Rd CHERT KT16 195 L8
CHSGTN KT9 219 L2
KTN/HRWW/W HA3 94 A9
RGUE GU4 268 E6
Chantry Sq KENS W8 14 G4
Chantry St IS N1 6 D6
The Chantry CHING * E4 101 H2
HLW CM20 29 K9
UX/CGN UB8 132 A5
Chantry View Rd GU GU1 268 A3
Chantry Wy MTCM CR4 201 N3
Chant Sq SRTFD * E15 141 J2
Chant St SRTFD E15 141 J2
Chapel Av ADL/WDHM KT15 215 L1
CHOB/PIR GU24 230 G7
Chapel Cl DART DA1 186 F1
GSTN WD25 54 G10
STAL AL1 38 C9
WTHK RM20 166 G5
Chapel Cottages HHNE HP2 35 N4
Chapel Ct DORK * RH4 272 F2
EFNCH N2 117 P1
STHWK SE1 18 G1
Chapel Cft KGLGY WD4 53 K7
Chapel Crofts BERK HP4 33 K3
Chapel End CFSP/GDCR * SL9 90 A10
HOD EN11 44 F4
Chapel Farm Rd ELTH/MOT SE9 184 C6
Chapel Flds HLWE CM17 47 M3
Chapelfields WARE SG12 27 J6
Chapel Gn PUR/KEN CR8 223 H9
Chapel Gv ADL/WDHM KT15 215 L1
KWD/TDW/WH KT20 238 F5
Chapel Hl DART DA1 164 F10
EFNCH N2 97 P10
EHSLY KT24 253 L3
Chapelhouse Cl GUW GU2 249 K10
Chapel House St POP/IOD E14 160 G4
Chapel La CHIG IG7 103 J4
CHOB/PIR GU24 230 F9
CRAWE RH10 285 N1
DORK RH4 272 B3
GT/LBKH KT23 254 B4
HERT/WAS SG14 24 C9
HLWE CM17 47 M3
PIN HA5 113 L1
SLN SL2 129 N2
UX/CGN UB8 132 B8
Chapel Market IS N1 6 A7
Chapel Park Rd
ADL/WDHM KT15 215 L1
Chapel Pl CAVSQ/HST W1G 10 E5
IS N1 6 B7
STAL * AL1 38 C9
TOTM N17 99 N8
Chapel Rd BXLYHN DA7 164 B10
EPP CM16 65 J6
HORL RH6 279 H8
HORL RH6 281 J4
HSLW TW3 154 A9
IL IG1 122 D8
KWD/TDW/WH KT20 238 F9
OXTED RH8 261 P6
REDH RH1 258 A10
TWK TW1 176 G3
WARL CR6 242 C4
WEA W13 134 G10
WNWD SE27 181 J7
Chapel Rw DEN/HRF UB9 91 M9
Chapels Cl SL SL1 128 D10
Chapel Side BAY/PAD W2 8 G7
Chapel Sq VW GU25 194 B3
Chapel St BAY/PAD W2 9 N4
BERK HP4 33 P5
ENC/FH EN2 79 K7
GU GU1 268 A2
HHNE HP2 35 N5
KTBR SW1X 16 D3
SL SL1 149 L1
WOKN/KNAP GU21 232 C3
Chapel Vw SAND/SEL CR2 224 B4
Chapel Wy ABLGY WD5 54 G3
KWD/TDW/WH KT20 238 F5
Chapel Wd HART DA3 211 K9
Chapel Wood Rd HART DA3 211 K9
Chaplaincy Gdns EMPK RM11 125 M6
Chaplemount Rd WFD * IG8 102 C7
Chaplin Cl ALP/SUD * HA0 135 J1
STHWK SE1 18 B1
Chaplin Crs SUN TW16 174 F9
Chaplin Rd ALP/SUD HA0 135 H1
CRICK NW2 136 D1
SRTFD E15 141 K4
TOTM * N17 119 N1
Chapman Cl WDR/YW UB7 152 A2
Chapman Crs
KTN/HRWW/W HA3 115 K3
Chapman Rd BELV DA17 164 B4
CROY/NA CR0 203 H8
HOM E9 140 E1
Chapmans Crs CSHM HP5 50 F5
Chapmans Gn WDGN * N22 99 H9
Chapman's La STMC/STPC BR5 207 N2
SWLY BR8 208 B2
Chapman Sq WIM/MER SW19 178 G5
Chapmans Rd RSEV TN14 245 P10
Chapman St WCHPL E1 140 A9
Chapmans Yd WAT WD17 73 K8
Chapman Ter WDGN * N22 99 J9
Chapter Cl HGDN/ICK UB10 132 A2
Chapter Ms WDSR SL4 149 J6
Chapter Rd CRICK NW2 116 D10
WALW SE17 18 D8
Chapter St WEST SW1P 17 J6
Chapter Wy HPTN TW12 175 P7
Chara Pl CHSWK W4 156 A5
Charcroft Gdns PEND EN3 80 C8
Chardia Ter CHES/WCR * EN8 62 C6
Chardin Rd CHSWK * W4 156 B3
Chardins Cl HHW HP1 35 J5
Chardmore Rd STNW/STAM N16 119 P6
Chardwell Cl EHAM E6 142 B8
Charecroft Wy WKENS W14 156 G1
Charford Rd CAN/RD E16 141 M7
Chargate Cl WOT/HER KT12 216 G3
Chargeable La PLSTW E13 141 M6
Chargeable St CAN/RD E16 141 L6
Charing Cl ORP BR6 227 J1
Charing Cross CHCR WC2N 11 K9
Charing Cross Rd
LSQ/SEVD WC2H 11 K7
Chariotts Pl WDSR * SL4 149 J7
Charlbert St STJWD NW8 3 N7
Charlbury Av STAN HA7 95 J6
Charlbury Cl HARH RM3 105 K7
Charlbury Crs HARH RM3 105 K7
Charlbury Gdns GDMY/SEVK IG3 123 J7
Charlbury Gv EA W5 135 H8
Charlbury Rd HGDN/ICK UB10 112 A9
Charldane Rd ELTH/MOT SE9 184 E6
Charlecote Gv SYD SE26 182 A6
Charlecote Rd BCTR RM8 123 P8
Charlemont Rd EHAM E6 142 C5
Charles Babbage Cl CHSGTN KT9 219 H4
Charles Barry Cl CLAP * SW4 158 D9
Charles Cl SCUP DA14 185 L7
Charles Cobb Gdns
CROY/NA CR0 223 H2
Charles Coveney Rd PECK * SE15 159 N7
Charles Crs HRW HA1 114 C5
Charles Dickens Ter
PGE/AN * SE20 182 B10
Charlesfield LEE/GVPK SE12 183 P6
Charlesfield Rd HORL RH6 280 A3
Charles Flemwell Ms
CAN/RD * E16 141 M10
Charles Gdns SLN SL2 129 M8
Charles Grinling Wk
WOOL/PLUM SE18 162 D3
Charles Ii Pl CHEL SW3 15 P8
Charles II St STJS SW1Y 11 J9
Charles La STJWD NW8 3 N8
Charles Pl CAMTN * NW1 5 H10
Charles Rd CHDH RM6 123 N5
DAGE RM10 144 E1
FSTGT E7 141 P2
RSEV TN14 228 C6
STA TW18 173 N9
WEA W13 134 F8
WIM/MER SW19 201 K1
Charles Sevright Dr MLHL NW7 96 G6
Charles Sq IS N1 7 H10
Charles Square Est IS N1 7 H10
Charles St BARN SW13 156 B9
BERK HP4 33 N5
CAN/RD E16 141 P10
CHERT KT16 195 J8
CROY/NA CR0 203 K10
EN EN1 79 N9
EPP CM16 65 K8
GRAYS RM17 167 N5
GRH DA9 188 E1
HHW HP1 35 M7
HSLW TW3 153 N8
MYFR/PICC W1J 10 E9
UX/CGN UB8 132 C6
WDSR SL4 149 H7
Charleston Cl FELT TW13 175 H6
Charleston Ct CRAWE RH10 284 C10
Charleston St WALW SE17 18 F6
Charlesworth Cl HHS/BOV HP3 35 N8
Charleville Circ SYD SE26 181 P8
Charleville Rd WKENS W14 14 B8
Charlieville Rd ERITH DA8 164 D6
Charlmont Rd TOOT SW17 179 P9
Charlock Wy GU GU1 250 E8
WATW WD18 72 G10
Charlotte Av SL SL1 129 L9
Charlotte Cl BXLYHS DA6 185 P1
STALE/WH AL4 39 K6
Charlotte Despard Av BTSEA SW11 158 C7
Charlotte Gdns CRW RM5 104 C7
Charlotte Gv HORL RH6 281 H3
Charlotte Ms ESH/CLAY * KT10 218 A1
FITZ W1T 11 H3
NKENS W10 136 G8
Charlotte Pde FSTH * SE23 182 D5
Charlotte Park Av BMLY BR1 206 B3
Charlotte Pl FITZ W1T 11 H4
WTHK RM20 166 G5
Charlotte Rd BARN SW13 156 C7
IS N1 7 J10
WLGTN SM6 222 D3
Charlotte Rw CLAP SW4 158 D9
Charlotte St FITZ W1T 11 H3
Charlotte Ter IS N1 5 P6
Charlow Cl FUL/PGN SW6 157 M8
Charlton WDSR SL4 148 B8
Charlton Av WOT/HER KT12 217 J1
Charlton Church La CHARL SE7 161 P4
Charlton Cl HGDN/ICK UB10 112 C7
HOD EN11 44 F3
SL SL1 148 G1
Charlton Crs BARK IG11 143 J4
Charlton Dene CHARL SE7 161 P6
Charlton Dr BH/WHM TN16 244 A3
Charlton Gdns COUL/CHIP CR5 240 D4
Charlton Kings WEY KT13 216 F1
Charlton King's Rd KTTN NW5 118 E10
Charlton La CHARL SE7 162 A4
SHPTN TW17 196 F4
Charlton Mead La HOD EN11 45 H4
Charlton Park La CHARL SE7 162 A6
Charlton Park Rd CHARL SE7 162 A5
Charlton Pl IS N1 6 C7
Charlton Rd BKHTH/KID SE3 161 M6
ED N9 100 C2
KTN/HRWW/W HA3 115 J2
SHPTN TW17 196 D2
WBLY HA9 115 L6
WLSDN NW10 136 B3
Charlton St WTHK RM20 167 J5
Charlton Wy BKHTH/KID SE3 161 K7
HOD EN11 44 F4
Charlwood CROY/NA CR0 224 E5
Charlwood Cl GT/LBKH KT23 236 A10
KTN/HRWW/W HA3 94 D7
Charlwood Dr LHD/OX KT22 236 C1
Charlwood La RDKG RH5 278 D10
Charlwood Pl PIM SW1V 17 H6
Charlwood Rd CRAWW RH11 283 J3
HORL RH6 279 M7
HORL RH6 279 N10
PUT/ROE SW15 156 G10
Charlwood St PIM SW1V 17 H6
Charlwood Ter PUT/ROE SW15 156 G10
Charlwood Wk CRAWW RH11 283 L4
Charman Rd REDH RH1 257 P10
Charm Cl HORL RH6 279 P3
Charmian Av STAN HA7 115 J1
Charminster Av WIM/MER SW19 201 K2
Charminster Rd LEE/GVPK SE12 184 A7
WPK KT4 200 G8
Charmouth Ct STAL AL1 38 F3
Charmouth Rd STAL AL1 38 F4
WELL DA16 163 M7
Charmwood La ORP BR6 227 L6
The Charne RSEV TN14 247 H3
Charnock SWLY BR8 208 F4
Charnock Rd CLPT E5 120 A8
Charnwood ASC SL5 192 E6
Charnwood Av WIM/MER SW19 201 K2
Charnwood Cl NWMAL KT3 200 B4
Charnwood Dr SWFD E18 121 N1
Charnwood Gdns POP/IOD E14 160 F3
Charnwood Pl TRDG/WHET N20 97 M4
Charnwood Rd EN EN1 80 A2
HGDN/ICK UB10 132 B4
SNWD SE25 203 L5
Charnwood St CLPT * E5 119 P7
Charrington Rd CROY/NA CR0 203 J9
Charrington St CAMTN NW1 5 J7
Charsley Cl AMS HP6 69 P5
Charsley Rd CAT SE6 182 G5
Charta Rd EGH TW20 172 F8
Chart Cl CROY/NA CR0 204 B6
HAYES BR2 205 K1
MTCM CR4 202 A4
RDKG RH5 273 H4
Chart Downs RDKG RH5 273 H4
Charter Av GNTH/NBYPK IG2 122 G6
Charter Cl SL SL1 149 L2
Charter Crs HSLWW TW4 153 M10
Charter Dr BXLY DA5 185 P3
Charterhouse Av ALP/SUD HA0 115 H10
Charterhouse Buildings
FARR EC1M 12 E2
Charterhouse Dr SEV TN13 247 H9
Charterhouse Ms FARR EC1M 12 D3
Charterhouse Rd HACK E8 119 P10
ORP BR6 207 K10
Charterhouse St HCIRC EC1N 12 B4
The Charterhouse FARR * EC1M 12 D2
Charteris Rd FSBYPK N4 118 G6
KIL/WHAMP NW6 2 D6
WFD IG8 101 N7
Charter Pl STA TW18 173 K9
UX/CGN UB8 131 N3
WAT * WD17 73 J8
Charter Rd KUT KT1 199 N3
SL SL1 128 D9
The Charter Rd WFD IG8 101 K7
Charters Cl NRWD SE19 181 M8
Charters Cross HLWS CM18 46 G4
Charters La ASC SL5 192 C5
Charter Sq KUT KT1 199 N2
Charters Rd ASC SL5 192 E7
Charters Wy ASC SL5 192 E7
Charter Wy GLDGN NW11 117 J2
STHGT/OAK N14 78 D10
Chartfield Av PUT/ROE SW15 178 E1
Chartfield Rd REIG RH2 275 M1
Chartfield Sq PUT/ROE * SW15 178 G1
Chart Gdns RDKG RH5 273 H5
Chartham Gv WNWD SE27 181 H6
Chartham Rd SNWD SE25 204 A3
Chart Hills Cl THMD SE28 143 P8
Chart La BH/WHM TN16 263 M1
DORK RH4 272 G2
REIG RH2 257 L10
Chart La South RDKG RH5 273 J4
Chartley Av CRICK NW2 116 B8
STAN HA7 94 E7
Chartley Pde WLSDN * NW10 116 B8
Charton Cl BELV DA17 164 A5
Chartridge OXHEY * WD19 93 L3
Chartridge Cl BAR EN5 76 D9
BUSH WD23 74 B10
Chartridge Grange Dr CSHM HP5 50 C3
Chartridge La CSHM HP5 50 C4
Chartridge Wy HHNE HP2 36 D6
Chart St IS N1 7 H9
Chart Vw BGR/WK TN15 247 P3
Chartway BGR/WK TN15 247 K10
REIG RH2 257 L10
Chartwell Cl CHST BR7 184 G5
CROY/NA CR0 203 L8
GFD/PVL UB6 134 A3
WAB EN9 63 K9
Chartwell Dr ORP BR6 226 G2
Chartwell Pl CHEAM SM3 221 H1
EPSOM KT18 220 B10
RYLN/HDSTN HA2 114 C7
Chartwell Rd NTHWD HA6 92 G7
Chartwell Wy PGE/AN SE20 204 A1
Charville La HGDN/ICK UB10 132 D5
Charville La West
HGDN/ICK UB10 132 C5
Charwood STRHM/NOR * SW16 181 H7
Charwood Cl RAD WD7 57 K9
Chasden Rd HHW HP1 35 J3
Chase Cl AMSS HP7 68 F9
Chase Ct RYNPK SW20 201 H2
Chase Court Gdns ENC/FH EN2 79 K7
Chase Cross Rd CRW RM5 104 D8
Chase End HOR/WEW KT19 220 A8
Chasefield Cl GU GU1 250 D7
Chasefield Rd TOOT SW17 180 A7
Chase Gdns CHING E4 100 F5
WHTN TW2 176 C2
Chase Gn ENC/FH EN2 79 K7
Chase Green Av ENC/FH EN2 79 J6
Chase Hl ENC/FH EN2 79 K7
Chase House Gdns EMPK RM11 125 N3
Chase La BARK/HLT IG6 122 G3
Chaseley Ct CHSWK W4 155 N4
Chaseley Dr SAND/SEL CR2 223 L6
Chaseley St POP/IOD * E14 140 D8
Chasemore Cl MTCM CR4 202 A7
Chasemore Gdns CROY/NA CR0 223 H2
Chase Ridings ENC/FH EN2 79 H6
Chase Rd ACT W3 136 A6
BRW CM14 107 H4
HOR/WEW KT19 220 A8
STHGT/OAK N14 78 D9
Chase Side ENC/FH EN2 79 K6
STHGT/OAK N14 78 B10
Chase Side Av ENC/FH EN2 79 K6
Chaseside Av RYNPK SW20 201 H1
Chaseside Cl ROM * RM1 104 F7
Chase Side Crs ENC/FH EN2 79 L5
Chaseside Gdns CHERT KT16 195 L7
Chase Sq GVE * DA12 190 E2
The Chase ASHTD KT21 237 H4
BMLY BR1 205 N3
BRW * CM14 106 G5
BRW CM14 106 G5
BRW * CM14 107 J6
BRW CM14 107 J4
BXLYHN DA7 164 C9
CHESW EN7 61 J4
CHIG IG7 102 E5
CLAP SW4 158 C9
COUL/CHIP CR5 222 D10
CRAWE RH10 284 B8
CSHM HP5 50 G5
DAGE RM10 124 G8
EDGW HA8 95 N9
EHSLY KT24 252 G2
GUW GU2 249 M10
GUW GU2 267 M1
HERT/BAY SG13 25 N6
HGDN/ICK UB10 112 B10
HHNE HP2 35 P7
KWD/TDW/WH KT20 239 M7
LHD/OX KT22 236 B1
LOU IG10 101 P1
MNPK E12 122 A9
ORP BR6 227 K7
PIN HA5 113 K4
PIN HA5 113 N2
RAD WD7 74 E1
RBRW/HUT CM13 107 P6
REIG RH2 257 N10
REIG RH2 275 N1
ROM RM1 124 F1
RSEV TN14 247 M2
STAN HA7 94 F7
STRHM/NOR SW16 180 G10
SUN TW16 197 J1
UPMR RM14 126 D8
WARE SG12 26 F5
WATW WD18 72 F8
WLGTN SM6 222 F2
WTHK RM20 167 J5
Chaseville Pde WCHMH * N21 78 G9
Chaseville Park Rd WCHMH N21 78 F9
Chase Wy STHGT/OAK N14 98 C2
Chaseways SBW CM21 29 L3
Chasewood Av ENC/FH EN2 79 J6
Chasewood Pk HRW * HA1 114 D8
Chastilian Rd DART DA1 187 H3
Chatelet Cl HORL RH6 280 C3
Chatfield SLN SL2 128 F7
Chatfield Ct CTHM CR3 241 L8
Chatfield Dr RGUE GU4 250 F8
Chatfield Rd BTSEA SW11 157 M9
CROY/NA CR0 203 J8
Chatfields CRAWW RH11 283 L9
Chatham Av HAYES BR2 205 L7
Chatham Cl CHEAM SM3 201 J7
GLDGN NW11 117 K3
Chatham Hill Rd RSEV TN14 247 K7
Chatham Pl HOM E9 140 B1
Chatham Rd BTSEA SW11 180 A2
KUTN/CMB KT2 199 M2
SWFD E18 101 L10
WALTH E17 120 D1
Chatham St WALW SE17 18 G5
WOOL/PLUM SE18 162 E2
Chatsfield EW KT17 220 D6
Chatsfield Pl EA W5 135 K8
Chatsworth Av BFN/LL DA15 185 K4
BMLY BR1 183 N8
HDN NW4 96 F10
RYNPK SW20 201 H1
WBLY HA9 115 L10
Chatsworth Cl BORE WD6 75 M7
CHSWK * W4 155 P5
HDN NW4 96 F10
WWKM BR4 205 L9
Chatsworth Crs HSLW TW3 154 C10
Chatsworth Dr EN EN1 99 P1
Chatsworth Est CLPT * E5 120 C9
Chatsworth Gdns ACT W3 135 N9
NWMAL * KT3 200 C5
RYLN/HDSTN HA2 114 A6

Chatsworth Pl LHD/OX KT22 218 C8
MTCM CR4 202 A3
TEDD TW11 176 F7
Chatsworth Ri EA W5 135 L6
Chatsworth Rd CHEAM SM3 220 G1
CHSWK W4 155 P5
CLPT E5 120 B8
CRICK NW2 136 G1
CROY/NA CR0 223 L1
DART DA1 165 K10
EA W5 135 L6
FSTGT E7 121 L10
YEAD UB4 133 J6
Chatsworth Wy WNWD SE27 181 J6
Chatteris Av HARH RM3 105 K7
Chattern Hl ASHF TW15 174 C7
Chattern Rd ASHF TW15 174 D7
Chatterton Ms FSBYPK * N4 119 J8
Chatterton Rd FSBYPK N4 119 J8
HAYES BR2 206 A5
Chatton Rw CHOB/PIR GU24 230 F3
Chatto Rd BTSEA SW11 180 A1
Chaucer Av HSLWW TW4 153 J8
RCH/KEW TW9 155 M8
WEY KT13 216 B4
YEAD UB4 133 H7
Chaucer Cl BERK HP4 33 L4
BNSTD SM7 221 H10
FBAR/BDGN N11 98 D6
TIL RM18 168 F8
WDSR SL4 149 J9
Chaucer Ct GUW GU2 267 P2
Chaucer Dr STHWK SE1 19 M6
Chaucer Gdns SUT SM1 221 K1
Chaucer Gn CROY/NA CR0 204 A7
Chaucer Pk DART DA1 187 N3
Chaucer Rd ACT W3 135 P10
ASHF TW15 173 P7
BFN/LL DA15 185 M4
CRAWE RH10 284 C5
FSTGT E7 141 M1
GVW DA11 190 A6
HARH RM3 105 J8
HNHL SE24 181 H1
SUT SM1 221 K1
WALTH E17 101 H9
WAN E11 121 M4
WELL DA16 163 J7
Chaucer Wy ADL/WDHM KT15 215 K3
DART DA1 165 P10
HOD EN11 26 F9
Chaulden House Gdns HHW HP1 35 J8
Chaulden La HHW HP1 35 H8
Chaulden Ter HHW HP1 35 J7
Chauncey Cl ED N9 99 P4
Chauncy Av POTB/CUF EN6 59 M9
Chaundrye Cl ELTH/MOT SE9 184 C2
Chauntler Rd CAN/RD E16 141 N9
Chave Cft KWD/TDW/WH * KT20 238 F5
Chavecroft Ter
KWD/TDW/WH * KT20 238 F5
Chave Rd DART DA1 187 M6
Chaworth Cl CHERT KT16 214 F3
Chaworth Rd CHERT KT16 214 F3
Cheam Cl KWD/TDW/WH KT20 238 E7
Cheam Common Rd WPK KT4 200 E9
Cheam Man CHEAM * SM3 221 H3
Cheam Park Wy CHEAM SM3 220 G3
Cheam Rd BELMT SM2 220 G5
EW KT17 220 D6
SUT SM1 221 J3
Cheam St PECK * SE15 160 A9
Cheapside CITYW EC2V 12 F6
EFNCH * N2 118 A1
PLMGR N13 99 K5
WDGN * N22 119 H1
WOKN/KNAP GU21 214 A10
Cheapside La DEN/HRF UB9 111 J7
Cheapside Rd ASC SL5 192 B3
Chedburgh WGCE AL7 23 N4
Cheddar Cl FBAR/BDGN N11 98 A7
Cheddar Waye YEAD UB4 133 J8
Cheddington Rd UED N18 99 M5
Cheelson Rd SOCK/AV RM15 147 H4
Cheeseman Cl HPTN TW12 175 M9
Cheesemans Ter WKENS W14 14 C8
Cheffins Rd HOD EN11 26 E10
Chelford Rd BMLY BR1 183 J8
Chelmer Crs BARK IG11 143 L4
Chelmer Dr SOCK/AV RM15 147 H9
Chelmer Rd CDH/CHF RM16 168 D4
HOM E9 120 C10
UPMR RM14 126 C4
Chelmsford Av CRW RM5 104 E8
Chelmsford Cl BELMT SM2 221 K5
EHAM E6 142 C8
HMSMTH W6 156 G5
Chelmsford Dr UPMR RM14 125 N8
Chelmsford Gdns IL IG1 122 B5
Chelmsford Rd BRWN CM15 87 P7
HERT/WAS SG14 25 H6
RBSF CM22 31 J1
STHGT/OAK N14 98 D1
SWFD E18 101 L9
WALTH E17 120 F4
Chelmsford Sq WLSDN NW10 136 F3
Chelsea Br CHEL SW3 16 D9
Chelsea Bridge Ga BTSEA SW11 16 E10
Chelsea Bridge Rd BGVA SW1W 16 C7
Chelsea Cl HPTN TW12 176 B9
WLSDN NW10 136 A3
WPK KT4 200 D7
Chelsea Crs CRICK * NW2 2 C1
WBPTN * SW10 157 M7
Chelsea Emb CHEL SW3 16 C9
Chelsea Flds WARE SG12 26 G9
Chelsea Gdns CHEAM SM3 221 H1
HLWE CM17 47 P2
Chelsea Harbour Dr
WBPTN SW10 157 M7
Chelsea Manor Gdns CHEL SW3 15 N9
Chelsea Manor St CHEL SW3 15 P9
Chelsea Park Gdns CHEL SW3 15 L9
Chelsea Sq CHEL SW3 15 M8
Chelsea Village FUL/PGN * SW6 157 L6
Chelsfield Av ED N9 100 C1
Chelsfield Gdns SYD SE26 182 B6
Chelsfield Hl ORP BR6 227 M5
Chelsfield La ORP BR6 227 N1
ORP BR6 228 B4
RSEV TN14 228 D5
STMC/STPC BR5 207 N7
Chelsfield Rd STMC/STPC BR5 207 M6
Chelsham Common Rd
WARL CR6 242 F2
Chelsham Court Rd WARL CR6 243 J4
Chelsham Rd CLAP SW4 158 E9
SAND/SEL CR2 223 L4
WARL CR6 242 E3
Chelsing Ri HHNE HP2 36 D7
Chelston Rd RSLP HA4 113 H7
Chelsworth Dr HARH RM3 105 M9
WOOL/PLUM SE18 162 G5
Cheltenham Av TWK TW1 176 F3
Cheltenham Cl GVE DA12 190 F8
NTHLT UB5 134 A1
NWMAL KT3 199 P3
Cheltenham Gdns EHAM E6 142 B4
LOU IG10 82 B10
Cheltenham Pl ACT W3 155 P1
KTN/HRWW/W HA3 115 K2
Cheltenham Rd LEY E10 121 H4
ORP BR6 207 K10
PECK SE15 160 B10
Cheltenham Ter CHEL SW3 16 B7
Chelverton Rd PUT/ROE SW15 156 G10
Chelveston WGCE AL7 23 N4
Chelwood Av HAT AL10 40 D2
Chelwood Cl CHING E4 80 G10
CRAWE RH10 284 A9
EW KT17 220 C8
NTHWD HA6 92 D8
Chelwood Gdns RCH/KEW TW9 155 M8
Chenappa Cl PLSTW E13 141 M5
Chenduit Wy STAN HA7 94 E6
Chene Dr STALW/RED AL3 38 C4
Cheney Rd CAMTN NW1 5 L8
Cheney Rw WALTH E17 100 E9
Cheneys Rd WAN E11 121 K8
Cheney St PIN HA5 113 K2
Chenies Av AMS HP6 70 A5
Chenies Ct HHNE HP2 36 C1
Chenies Ms GWRST WC1E 11 J2
Chenies Pde AMSS * HP7 69 P6
Chenies Pl CAMTN NW1 5 K7
Chenies Rd RKW/CH/CXG WD3 70 G6
Chenies St FITZ W1T 11 J3
The Chenies ORP BR6 207 H6
RDART DA2 186 F7
Chenies Wy WATW WD18 92 F1
Cheniston Cl BF/WBF KT14 215 K9
Cheniston Gdns KENS W8 14 F3
Chennells HAT AL10 40 C5
The Chennies HARP * AL5 20 B4
Chepstow Cl CRAWE RH10 284 F7
PUT/ROE SW15 179 H1
Chepstow Cnr BAY/PAD * W2 8 F6
Chepstow Crs GDMY/SEVK IG3 123 H4
NTGHL W11 8 E7
Chepstow Gdns STHL UB1 133 N8
Chepstow Pl BAY/PAD W2 8 F6
Chepstow Ri CROY/NA CR0 203 M10
Chepstow Rd BAY/PAD W2 8 F5
CROY/NA CR0 203 M10
HNWL W7 154 F2
Chepstow Vls NTGHL W11 8 D7
Chepstow Wy PECK SE15 159 N7
Chequers BKHH * IG9 101 N2
BKHH IG9 101 N2
BRKMPK AL9 40 G1
WGCE AL7 22 G7
Chequers Cl CDALE/KGS NW9 116 B1
HORL RH6 280 B3
KWD/TDW/WH KT20 256 D1
STMC/STPC BR5 207 J4
Chequers Dr HORL RH6 280 B3
Chequers Fld WGCE AL7 22 G8
Chequers La DAGW RM9 144 A6
GSTN WD25 55 J6
KWD/TDW/WH KT20 256 D1
Chequers Orch IVER SL0 131 J8
Chequers Pde PLMGR * N13 99 K6
Chequers Pl DORK RH4 272 G2
Chequers Rd ABR/ST RM4 105 M3
LOU IG10 82 D9
The Chequers PIN * HA5 113 L1
Chequer St STAL AL1 38 C6
STLK EC1Y 12 F2
Chequers Wy PLMGR N13 99 J6
Chequer Tree Cl
WOKN/KNAP GU21 231 K2
Cherbury Cl THMD SE28 143 N8
Cherbury St IS N1 7 H8
Cherimoya Gdns
E/WMO/HCT KT8 198 A3
Cherington Rd HNWL * W7 134 E10
Cheriton Av CLAY IG5 102 D10
HAYES BR2 205 L5
Cheriton Cl EA W5 135 H7
EBAR EN4 78 A7
STALE/WH AL4 39 J2
Cheriton Ct WOT/HER KT12 197 K8
Cheriton Dr WOOL/PLUM SE18 162 G6
Cheriton Sq TOOT SW17 180 B5
Cherkley RDKG * RH5 255 J2
Cherkley Hl RDKG RH5 255 H2
The Cherries SLN SL2 129 P8
Cherry Acre CFSP/GDCR SL9 90 A5
Cherry Av DTCH/LGLY SL3 150 A1
RBRW/HUT CM13 107 L4
STHL UB1 133 L10
SWLY BR8 208 E3
Cherry Bank HHNE * HP2 35 N4
Cherry Blossom Cl PLMGR N13 99 J6
Cherry Cl BRXS/STRHM * SW2 181 H3
CAR SM5 202 A9
EA W5 155 J2
EW KT17 220 G10
MRDN SM4 201 H4
RSLP HA4 112 G8
Cherrycot Ri ORP BR6 226 F1
Cherry Ct PIN HA5 93 L10
Cherry Crs BTFD TW8 154 G6
Cherry Cft RKW/CH/CXG * WD3 72 C10
WGCW AL8 22 G1
Cherry Croft Gdns PIN * HA5 93 N8
Cherrydale WATW WD18 72 G8
Cherrydown Av CHING E4 100 E4
Cherrydown Cl CHING E4 100 E4
Cherrydown Rd SCUP DA14 185 N5
Cherrydown Wk ROMW/RG RM7 104 C10
Cherry Dr BEAC HP9 88 A7
Cherry Gdns DAGW RM9 124 A10
NTHLT UB5 134 A2
Cherry Garden St
BERM/RHTH SE16 160 A1
Cherry Garth BTFD TW8 155 J4
Cherry Green Cl REDH RH1 276 C2
Cherry Gv HYS/HAR UB3 133 J10
UX/CGN UB8 132 D7
Cherry Hl BAR EN5 77 L10
KTN/HRWW/W HA3 94 D7
LCOL/BKTW AL2 55 P1
RKW/CH/CXG WD3 71 L7
Cherry Hill Gdns CROY/NA CR0 222 G1
Cherry Hills OXHEY WD19 93 M6
Cherry Hollow ABLGY WD5 54 G7
Cherrylands Cl
CDALE/KGS * NW9 115 P7
Cherry La AMSS HP7 68 F6
CRAWW RH11 283 M4
WDR/YW UB7 152 A3
Cherry Orch AMS HP6 69 K3
ASHTD KT21 237 N4
CHARL SE7 161 P5
HHW HP1 35 J4
SLN SL2 129 N2
STA TW18 173 K8
WDR/YW UB7 151 P1
Cherry Orchard Cl
STMC/STPC BR5 207 M5
Cherry Orchard Gdns
CROY/NA CR0 203 L8
E/WMO/HCT KT8 197 N3
Cherry Orchard Rd
CROY/NA CR0 203 L8
E/WMO/HCT KT8 197 P3
HAYES BR2 206 B9
Cherry Ri CSTG HP8 90 A3
Cherry Rd PEND EN3 80 B4
Cherry St ROMW/RG RM7 124 E3
WOKN/KNAP GU21 232 B4
Cherry Tree Av GUW GU2 249 L10
LCOL/BKTW AL2 57 J2
STA TW18 173 L9
WDR/YW UB7 132 A8
Cherry Tree Cl ALP/SUD HA0 114 F9
CRAWE RH10 284 E5
RAIN RM13 145 H4
Cherry Tree Cnr BEAC * HP9 89 K7
Cherry Tree Ct CHARL * SE7 161 P5
COUL/CHIP CR5 240 G4
Cherry Tree Dr SOCK/AV RM15 147 J6
STRHM/NOR * SW16 180 F6
Cherry Tree Gn HERT/WAS SG14 24 G3
SAND/SEL CR2 224 A10
Cherry Tree Hl EFNCH N2 117 P3
Cherry Tree La DTCH/LGLY SL3 110 C10
HHNE HP2 36 D3
RAIN RM13 144 F5
RDART DA2 186 G6
RGODL GU7 267 J9
RKW/CH/CXG WD3 90 F2
STALE/WH AL4 20 F1
Cherrytree La CFSP/GDCR SL9 90 A10
HHNE HP2 36 D1
IVER SL0 131 K3
Cherry Tree Ri BKHH IG9 102 A5
Cherry Tree Rd BEAC HP9 108 A1
EFNCH N2 118 A2
HOD EN11 44 F2
SLN SL2 128 G2
SRTFD E15 121 K10
WATN WD24 73 J2
Cherry Trees HART DA3 211 L6
Cherry Tree Wk BECK BR3 204 E4
CSHM HP5 51 J5
STLK EC1Y 12 F2
WWKM BR4 225 L1
Cherry Tree Wy STAN HA7 94 G7
Cherry Wk CDH/CHF RM16 168 D2
HAYES BR2 205 M8
RAIN RM13 144 G4
RKW/CH/CXG WD3 71 M6
Cherry Wy DTCH/LGLY SL3 150 F9
HAT AL10 40 D7
HOR/WEW KT19 220 A3
SHPTN TW17 196 E4
Cherrywood Av EGH TW20 171 N9
Cherrywood Cl BEAC HP9 89 J7
BOW E3 140 D5
KUTN/CMB KT2 177 M10
Cherrywood Dr GVW DA11 190 B7
PUT/ROE SW15 178 G1
Cherrywood La MRDN SM4 201 H4
Chertsey Bridge Rd CHERT KT16 195 N7
Chertsey Cl PUR/KEN CR8 241 J1
Chertsey Crs CROY/NA CR0 225 H6
Chertsey Dr CHEAM SM3 201 H9
Chertsey La HOR/WEW KT19 219 M8
STA TW18 173 H8
Chertsey Rd ADL/WDHM KT15 195 M10
ASHF TW15 174 E10
BF/WBF KT14 215 N7
BFOR GU20 212 D3
CHOB/PIR GU24 213 M6
IL IG1 122 G9
SHPTN TW17 195 P7
SUN TW16 174 F9
TWK TW1 176 F2
WAN E11 121 J7
WHTN TW2 176 B4
WOKN/KNAP GU21 214 D9
WOKN/KNAP GU21 232 C3
Chertsey St GU GU1 268 A1
TOOT SW17 180 B8
Chertsey Wk CHERT * KT16 195 K7
Chervil Cl FELT TW13 175 H6
Chervil Ms THMD SE28 143 L10
Cherwell Cl DTCH/LGLY SL3 150 E5
RKW/CH/CXG WD3 72 B9
Cherwell Ct HOR/WEW KT19 219 P1
Cherwell Gv SOCK/AV RM15 146 G9
Cherwell Wk CRAWW RH11 283 J8
Cherwell Wy RSLP HA4 112 D4
Cherylls Cl FUL/PGN SW6 157 L7
Cheselden Rd GU GU1 268 B1
Cheseman St SYD SE26 182 A6
Chesfield Rd KUTN/CMB KT2 177 K10
Chesham Av HAYES BR2 206 E6
Chesham Cl BELMT SM2 221 H6
KTBR * SW1X 16 C4
ROMW/RG RM7 124 E2
Chesham Crs PGE/AN SE20 204 B1
Chesham La CFSP/GDCR SL9 90 B5
Chesham Ms GU GU1 268 B1
KTBR SW1X 16 C3
Chesham Pl KTBR SW1X 16 C3
Chesham Rd AMS HP6 69 H3
BERK HP4 33 P6
CSHM HP5 32 D10
CSHM HP5 33 L9
GU GU1 268 B1
HHS/BOV HP3 52 B4
KUTN/CMB KT2 199 M1
PGE/AN SE20 204 B2
TRING HP23 32 C1
Chesham St KTBR SW1X 16 C4
WLSDN NW10 116 A8
Chesham Ter WEA W13 154 G1
Chesham Wy WATW WD18 72 F10
Cheshire Cl CHERT KT16 214 G3
EMPK RM11 125 P3
MTCM CR4 202 F3
WALTH E17 100 G9
Cheshire Gdns CHSGTN KT9 219 J3
Cheshire Rd WDGN N22 98 G8
Cheshire St BETH E2 13 N1
Chesholm Rd STNW/STAM N16 119 M8
Cheshunt Rd BELV DA17 164 B4
FSTGT E7 141 N1
Cheshunt Wash CHES/WCR EN8 62 D3
Chesilton Rd FUL/PGN SW6 157 J7
Chesil Wy YEAD UB4 132 G5
Chesley Gdns EHAM E6 142 A4
Chesney Crs CROY/NA CR0 225 H4
Chesney St BTSEA SW11 158 B7
Chesnut Av North WALTH E17 121 J2
Chesnut Gv TOTM N17 119 P1
TOTM N17 119 N1
Chesnut Rd TOTM N17 119 P1
Chesnut Rw FNCH * N3 97 K8
Chessbury Rd CSHM HP5 50 F8
Chess Cl CSHM HP5 70 A2
RKW/CH/CXG WD3 71 N8
Chessfield Pk AMS HP6 70 B5
Chess Hl RKW/CH/CXG WD3 71 N8
Chessholme Rd ASHF TW15 174 D9
Chessington Av BXLYHN DA7 163 P6
FNCH N3 117 H1
Chessington Cl HOR/WEW KT19 219 P3
Chessington Ct PIN HA5 113 N2
Chessington Hall Gdns
CHSGTN KT9 219 J4
Chessington Hill Pk CHSGTN KT9 219 M3
Chessington Pde CHSGTN * KT9 219 J2
Chessington Rd CHSGTN KT9 219 M3
Chessington Wy WWKM BR4 204 G9
Chess La RKW/CH/CXG WD3 71 N8
Chessmount Ri CSHM HP5 51 J9
Chesson Rd WKENS W14 14 C9
Chess Vale Ri RKW/CH/CXG WD3 72 A10
Chess Valley Wk CSHM HP5 69 L1
Chess Wy RKW/CH/CXG WD3 71 K7
Chesswood Ct
RKW/CH/CXG * WD3 91 N2
Chesswood Wy PIN HA5 93 L10
Chester Av RCHPK/HAM TW10 177 L2
UPMR RM14 126 D7
WHTN TW2 175 N4
Chester Cl ASHF TW15 174 E8
BARN * SW13 156 E9
DORK RH4 255 H10
GUW GU2 249 L8
KTBR SW1X 16 D2
SUT SM1 201 K9
Chester Cl North CAMTN NW1 4 F9
Chester Cl South CAMTN NW1 4 F10
Chester Crs HACK E8 119 N10
Chester Dr RYLN/HDSTN HA2 113 P4
Chesterfield Cl STMC/STPC BR5 207 N4
Chesterfield Dr DART DA1 187 J1
ESH/CLAY KT10 198 F9
SEV TN13 246 E8
Chesterfield Gdns FSBYPK N4 119 J3
GNWCH * SE10 161 J6
MYFR/PICC * W1J 10 E9
Chesterfield Gv EDUL SE22 181 N1
Chesterfield Hl MYFR/PICC W1J 10 E8
Chesterfield Rd ASHF TW15 173 P8
BAR EN5 76 G9
CHSWK W4 155 P5
FNCH N3 97 K7
HOR/WEW KT19 220 A4
LEY E10 121 H5
PEND EN3 80 D3
Chesterfield St MYFR/PICC W1J 10 E9
Chesterfield Wy HYS/HAR * UB3 153 H1
PECK SE15 160 B6
Chesterford Gdns HAMP NW3 117 L9
Chesterford Rd MNPK E12 122 C10
Chester Gdns ED N9 80 A10
MRDN SM4 201 M5
WEA * W13 134 G8
Chester Ga CAMTN NW1 4 E10
Chester Gibbons Gn
LCOL/BKTW AL2 57 J2
Chester Ms KTBR SW1X 16 E3
Chester Pl CAMTN NW1 4 E9
NTHWD * HA6 92 F8
Chester Rd BFN/LL DA15 185 H1
BORE WD6 75 P7
CAMTN NW1 4 D10
CAN/RD E16 141 K6
CHIG IG7 102 D4
ED N9 100 A2
EHSLY KT24 253 J4
FSTGT E7 142 A2
GDMY/SEVK IG3 123 J6
HSLWW TW4 153 J9
HTHAIR TW6 152 B9
KTTN NW5 118 C7
LOU IG10 82 F5
NTHWD HA6 92 G8
SL SL1 129 J8
TOTM N17 119 L1
WALTH E17 120 C3
WAN E11 121 N4
WATW WD18 73 H9
WIM/MER SW19 178 F9
Chester Rw BGVA SW1W 16 C6
Chesters HORL RH6 279 P2
Chester Sq BGVA SW1W 16 D5
Chester Square Ms BGVA * SW1W 16 E4
The Chesters NWMAL KT3 200 B1
Chester St BETH * E2 7 N6
BETH E2 13 P1
KTBR SW1X 16 D3
Chester Ter CAMTN NW1 4 E9
Chesterton Av HARP AL5 20 B2
Chesterton Cl CSHM HP5 50 G5
GFD/PVL UB6 134 A4
WAND/EARL SW18 179 K1
Chesterton Ct EA * W5 135 J8
Chesterton Dr REDH RH1 258 F4
STWL/WRAY TW19 174 A4
Chesterton Gn BEAC HP9 88 D9
Chesterton Rd NKENS W10 136 G7
PLSTW E13 141 M5
Chesterton Sq ECT SW5 14 D5
Chesterton Ter KUT KT1 199 M2
PLSTW E13 141 M5
Chester Wy LBTH SE11 18 B6
Chesthunte Rd TOTM N17 99 K9
Chestnut Aly FUL/PGN * SW6 14 D10
Chestnut Av ALP/SUD HA0 114 G10
BH/WHM TN16 244 A8
BKHH IG9 102 A4
BTFD TW8 155 J4
CDH/CHF RM16 167 N1
CEND/HSY/T N8 118 F3
CSHM HP5 51 J5
DTCH/LGLY SL3 150 B1
E/WMO/HCT KT8 198 E3
EDGW HA8 95 K7
ESH/CLAY KT10 198 C7
FSTGT E7 121 N9
GRH DA9 188 E3
GUW GU2 267 P4
HCH RM12 124 G
HOR/WEW KT19 220 B
HPTN TW12 175 P1
MORT/ESHN * SW14 156 A
NTHWD HA6 92 G1
RKW/CH/CXG WD3 71 K
TEDD TW11 176 E1
VW GU25 193 L
WDR/YW UB7 132 A
WEY KT13 216 D
WOT/HER KT12 216 F
WWKM BR4 225 K
Chestnut Av South WALTH E17 121 H
Chestnut Cl ADL/WDHM KT15 215 N
AMS HP6 69 J
ASHF TW15 174 C
BERK HP4 34 E
BFN/LL DA15 185 K
BKHH IG9 102 A
CAR SM5 202 A
CAT SE6 183 H
CFSP/GDCR SL9 90 C
EGH TW20 171 N
GVW DA11 190 C
HCH RM12 125 K
HYS/HAR UB3 132 F
KWD/TDW/WH KT20 239 K
NWCR SE14 160 E
ORP BR6 227 K
REDH RH1 276 C
RPLY/SEND GU23 233 K1
STHGT/OAK N14 78 D
STRHM/NOR SW16 181 H
SUN TW16 174 G
WARE SG12 28 A
WDR/YW UB7 152 C
Chestnut Copse OXTED RH8 261 N
Chestnut Cottages
TRDG/WHET * N20 97 H
Chestnut Dr BERK HP4 34 A
BXLYHN DA7 163 N
EGH TW20 172 A
KTN/HRWW/W HA3 94 E
PIN HA5 113 L
STAL AL1 38 G
WAN E11 121 M
WDSR SL4 148 D1
Chestnut Gln HCH RM12 124 C
Chestnut Gv ALP/SUD HA0 114 G1
BAL SW12 180 B
BARK/HLT IG6 103 H
BRW CM14 107 H
EA W5 155 J
EBAR EN4 78 A
ISLW TW7 154 F1
MTCM CR4 202 E
NWMAL KT3 200 A
RDART DA2 186 E
SAND/SEL CR2 224 A
STA TW18 173 M
WOKS/MYFD GU22 232 E
Chestnut La AMS HP6 69 K
CHOB/PIR GU24 213 H
SEV TN13 247 J1
TRDG/WHET N20 97 H
WEY KT13 216 C
Chestnut Mnr WLGTN SM6 222 C
Chestnut Manor Cl STA TW18 173 L
Chestnut Md REDH RH1 257 F
Chestnut Pl ASHTD KT21 237 K
WEY * KT13 216 C
Chestnut Ri BUSH WD23 94 A
WOOL/PLUM SE18 163 H
Chestnut Rd ASHF TW15 174 B
BEAC HP9 88 A1
DART DA1 187 L
GU GU1 250 A1
HORL RH6 280 E
KUTN/CMB KT2 177 K1
PEND EN3 80 D
RYNPK SW20 200 C
WHTN TW2 176 D
WNWD SE27 181 J
Chestnuts RBRW/HUT CM13 107 N
The Chestnuts BECK * BR3 204 C
HERT/BAY SG13 25 L
HHS/BOV HP3 35 J1
PIN * HA5 93 N
WOT/HER KT12 197 H
Chestnut Ter SUT * SM1 221 L
Chestnut Wk BGR/WK TN15 265 N
CFSP/GDCR * SL9 90 E
CRAWW RH11 283 M
EPP CM16 46 E1
SHPTN TW17 196 F
WATN WD24 73 H
Chestnut Wy FELT TW13 175 J
Cheston Av CROY/NA CR0 204 D
Chestwood Gv HGDN/ICK UB10 132 A
Cheswick Cl DART DA1 164 G1
Chesworth Cl ERITH DA8 164 F
Chettle Cl STHWK SE1 18 C
Chetwode Dr
KWD/TDW/WH KT20 238 C
Chetwode Rd
KWD/TDW/WH KT20 238 F
TOOT SW17 180 A
Chetwynd Av EBAR EN4 98 A
Chetwynd Dr HGDN/ICK UB10 132 A
Chetwynd Rd KTTN NW5 118 C
Chetwynd Vls KTTN * NW5 118 C
Chevalier Cl STAN HA7 95 J
Cheval Pl SKENS SW7 15 F
Cheval St POP/IOD E14 160 F
Cheveley Gdns SL SL1 128 E
Chevely Cl EPP CM16 65 N
Cheveney Wk HAYES BR2 205 M
Chevening La RSEV TN14 245 F
Chevening Rd GNWCH SE10 161 L
KIL/WHAMP NW6 136 C
NRWD SE19 181 L1
RSEV TN14 246 A
The Chevenings SCUP DA14 185 L
Cheverton Rd ARCH N19 118 E
Chevet St HOM E9 120 D1
Chevington CRICK * NW2 2 C
Chevington Wy HCH RM12 125 L
Cheviot Cl BELMT SM2 221 N
BNSTD SM7 239 L
BUSH WD23 74 B1
BXLYHN DA7 164 F
ENC/FH EN2 79 L
HYS/HAR UB3 152 E
Cheviot Gdns GLDGN NW11 116 C
Cheviot Rd DTCH/LGLY SL3 150 D
EMPK RM11 125 H
WNWD SE27 181 J
Cheviots HAT AL10 40 D
HHNE HP2 36 A
Cheviot Wk CRAWW * RH11 283 L

Cheviot Wy GNTH/NBYPK IG2 ......123 H3
Chevron Cl CAN/RD E16 ......141 M8
Chevy Rd STHL UB1 ......154 B1
Chewter La BFOR GU20 ......212 A1
Chewton Rd WALTH E17 ......120 D2
Cheyham Gdns BELMT SM2 ......220 G6
Cheyham Wy BELMT SM2 ......221 H6
Cheyne Av SWFD E18 ......121 L1
WHTN TW2 ......175 N4
Cheyne Cl CFSP/GDCR SL9 ......110 B6
HAYES BR2 ......206 B10
Cheyne Ct BNSTD SM7 ......239 L1
BUSH * WD23 ......73 M8
Cheyne Gdns CHEL SW3 ......15 P9
Cheyne Hl BRYLDS KT5 ......199 L4
Cheyne Ms CHEL SW3 ......15 P10
Cheyne Pth WEA W13 ......134 E7
Cheyne Pl CHEL SW3 ......16 A9
Cheyne Rd ASHF TW15 ......174 E9
Cheyne Rw CHEL SW3 ......15 N10
Cheyne Wk CROY/NA CR0 ......203 P9
CSHM HP5 ......51 J6
HDN NW4 ......116 F4
HORL RH6 ......280 A6
WCHMH N21 ......79 H9
Cheyneys Av EDGW HA8 ......95 J7
Chichele Gdns CROY/NA CR0 ......223 M1
Chichele Rd CRICK NW2 ......116 G10
OXTED RH8 ......261 K4
Chicheley Rd KTN/HRWW/W HA3 ......94 B8
Chicheley St STHWK SE1 ......17 P1
Chichester Av RSLP HA4 ......112 E7
Chichester Cl BKHTH/KID SE3 ......161 P6
DORK RH4 ......254 G10
EHAM E6 ......142 B8
HPTN TW12 ......175 N9
SOCK/AV RM15 ......146 B10
Chichester Ct EW * KT17 ......220 C5
SL SL1 ......149 N2
STAN HA7 ......115 K1
Chichester Dr PUR/KEN CR8 ......222 G8
SEV TN13 ......264 G1
Chichester Gdns IL IG1 ......122 B5
Chichester Ri GVE DA12 ......190 G7
Chichester Rd BAY/PAD W2 ......9 H3
CROY/NA CR0 ......203 M10
DORK RH4 ......254 G9
ED N9 ......99 N2
GRH DA9 ......188 E1
KIL/WHAMP NW6 ......2 E8
WAN E11 ......121 K8
Chichester St PIM SW1V 17 H8
Chichester Wy
EBED/NFELT TW14 ......175 K3
GSTN WD25 ......55 M9
POP/IOD E14 ......161 J3
Chicken La LCOL/BKTW * AL2 ......57 J3
Chicksand Est WCHPL E1 ......13 N3
Chicksand St WCHPL E1 ......13 M4
Chiddingfold NFNCH/WDSP N12 ......97 K4
Chiddingly Cl CRAWE RH10 ......284 B8
Chiddingstone Av BXLYHN DA7 ......164 A5
Chiddingstone Cl BELMT SM2 ......221 K6
Chiddingstone St FUL/PGN SW6 ......157 K8
Chieftan Dr PUR RM19 ......165 P3
Chieveley Pde BXLYHN * DA7 ......164 C9
Chieveley Rd BXLYHN DA7 ......164 C10
Chiffinch Gdns GVW DA11 ......190 B6
Chignell Pl WEA W13 ......134 F10
Chigwell Hl WAP E1W 140 A9
Chigwell La CHIG IG7 ......82 F10
LOU IG10 ......82 F8
Chigwell Park Dr CHIG IG7 ......102 D5
Chigwell Ri CHIG IG7 ......102 D3
Chigwell Rd SWFD E18 ......121 N1
Chilberton Dr REDH RH1 ......258 D6
Chilbrook Rd COB KT11 ......235 H4
Chilcote La AMSS HP7 ......69 N5
Chilcott Rd WATN WD24 ......72 F2
Childebert Rd TOOT SW17 ......180 C5
Childerditch Hall Dr
RBRW/HUT CM13 ......107 L10
Childerditch La
RBRW/HUT CM13 ......107 K8
Childerditch St RBRW/HUT CM13 ......127 M1
Childeric Rd NWCR SE14 ......160 D6
Childerley St FUL/PGN SW6 ......157 H7
Childers St DEPT SE8 ......160 D5
The Childers WFD IG8 ......102 C6
Childs Av DEN/HRF UB9 ......91 M10
Childsbridge La RSEV TN14 ......247 M4
Childsbridge Wy BGR/WK TN15 ......247 N6
Childs Cl EMPK RM11 ......125 K4
Childs Ct HYS/HAR UB3 ......133 H9
Childs Crs SWCM DA10 ......189 J2
Childs Hall Dr GT/LBKH KT23 ......253 N1
Childs Hall Rd GT/LBKH KT23 ......253 N1
Childs La NRWD * SE19 ......181 M9
Child's Pl ECT SW5 ......14 F6
Child's St ECT SW5 ......14 F5
Child's Wk ECT * SW5 ......14 F5
Childs Wy GLDGN NW11 ......117 J3
Childwick Ct HHS/BOV HP3 ......36 C9
Chilham Cl BXLY DA5 ......186 A3
GFD/PVL UB6 ......134 F4
HHS/BOV HP3 ......35 P7
Chilham Rd ELTH/MOT SE9 ......184 B7
Chilham Wy HAYES BR2 ......205 M7
Chillerton Rd TOOT SW17 ......180 B8
Chillingworth Gdns TWK * TW1 ......176 E5
Chillingworth Rd HOLWY N7 ......118 G10
Chilmans Dr GT/LBKH KT23 ......254 A1
Chilmark Gdns NWMAL KT3 ......200 C6
REDH RH1 ......258 F5
Chilmark Rd STRHM/NOR SW16 ......202 E2
Chilmead REDH * RH1 ......258 A9
Chilmead La REDH RH1 ......258 E8
Chilsey Green Rd CHERT KT16 ......195 H6
Chiltern WOKS/MYFD GU22 ......231 P8
Chiltern Av AMS HP6 ......69 J4
BUSH WD23 ......74 B10
WHTN TW2 ......175 P4
Chiltern Cl BERK HP4 ......33 L4
BORE WD6 ......75 L6
BUSH WD23 ......74 A10
BXLYHN DA7 ......164 F7
CHESW EN7 ......61 J3
CRAWW RH11 ......283 L7
CROY/NA CR0 ......203 M10
HGDN/ICK UB10 ......112 B7
STA TW18 ......173 K8
WPK KT4 ......200 F9
Chiltern Ct UX/CGN UB8 ......132 C6
Chiltern Dene ENC/FH EN2 ......78 G8
Chiltern Dr BRYLDS KT5 ......199 N5
RKW/CH/CXG WD3 ......91 J1
Chiltern Est WATN * WD24 ......73 K5
Chiltern Gdns CRICK NW2 ......116 G8
HAYES BR2 ......205 L4
HCH RM12 ......125 K8
Chiltern Hts AMSS HP7 ......69 M5
Chiltern Hl CFSP/GDCR SL9 ......90 B9
Chiltern Hills Rd BEAC HP9 ......88 B9
Chiltern Pde AMS HP6 ......69 H3
Chiltern Park Av BERK HP4 ......33 M3
Chiltern Rd BELMT SM2 ......221 M6
BOW E3 ......140 F6
GNTH/NBYPK IG2 ......123 H2
GVW DA11 ......190 B6
PIN HA5 ......113 K3
SL SL1 ......128 A7
STALE/WH AL4 ......39 H1
Chilterns HAT AL10 ......40 D7
HHNE HP2 ......35 P3
The Chilterns BELMT * SM2 ......221 L5
Chiltern St MHST W1U 10 C3
Chiltern View Rd UX/CGN UB8 ......131 M4
Chiltern Wy WFD IG8 ......101 M4
Chilthorne Cl CAT SE6 ......182 E3
Chilton Av EA W5 ......155 J3
Chilton Gn WGCE AL7 ......23 M5
Chilton Gv DEPT SE8 ......160 C3
Chilton Rd CDH/CHF RM16 ......168 D2
CSHM HP5 ......51 H5
EDGW HA8 ......95 M7
RCH/KEW TW9 ......155 M9
Chiltons Cl BNSTD SM7 ......239 L1
Chilton St BETH E2 ......13 M1
Chilvers Cl WHTN TW2 ......176 D5
Chilver St GNWCH SE10 ......161 L4
Chilwell Gdns OXHEY WD19 ......93 K5
Chilwick Rd SLN SL2 ......128 E6
Chilworth Gdns SUT SM1 ......201 M10
Chilworth Ga BROX EN10 ......44 E8
Chilworth Ms BAY/PAD W2 ......9 K6
Chilworth Rd SHGR GU5 ......269 K5
Chilworth St BAY/PAD W2 ......9 K6
Chimes Av PLMGR N13 ......99 H5
Chime Sq STALW/RED AL3 ......38 D5
Chinbrook Crs LEE/GVPK SE12 ......183 N6
Chinbrook Rd LEE/GVPK SE12 ......183 P6
Chinchilla Dr HSLWW TW4 ......153 K8
Chindit Cl BROX EN10 ......44 C6
Chindits La RBRW/HUT CM13 ......107 H6
The Chine ALP/SUD HA0 ......114 G10
DORK * RH4 ......272 G1
MUSWH N10 ......118 C2
WCHMH N21 ......79 J10
Chingdale Rd CHING E4 ......101 K4
Chingford Av CHING E4 ......100 G4
Chingford La WFD IG8 ......101 K5
Chingford Mount Rd CHING E4 ......100 F6
Chingford Rd CHING E4 ......100 F7
WALTH E17 ......100 G10
Chingley Cl BMLY BR1 ......183 K9
Ching Wy WALTH E17 ......100 E7
Chinnery Cl EN EN1 ......79 N4
Chinnor Crs GFD/PVL UB6 ......134 B4
Chinthurst La RGUE GU4 ......268 B7
Chinthurst Pk RGUE GU4 ......268 B8
Chipka St POP/IOD E14 ......161 H1
Chipley St NWCR SE14 ......160 D5
Chippendale St CLPT E5 ......120 C8
Chippendale Waye UX/CGN UB8 ......131 N2
Chippenham Cl RSLP * HA4 ......112 G2
Chippenham Gdns HARH RM3 ......105 L6
Chippenham Ms MV/WKIL W9 ......8 E2
Chippenham Rd HARH RM3 ......105 L7
MV/WKIL W9 ......8 E1
Chipperfield Cl UPMR RM14 ......126 D6
Chipperfield Rd HHS/BOV HP3 ......35 M10
KGLGY WD4 ......53 N5
STMC/STPC BR5 ......207 K2
Chipping Cl BAR EN5 ......77 H7
Chippingfield HLWE CM17 ......29 M8
Chipstead CFSP/GDCR SL9 ......89 P9
Chipstead Av THHTH CR7 ......203 J4
Chipstead Cl BELMT SM2 ......221 L5
COUL/CHIP CR5 ......240 B3
NRWD SE19 ......181 N10
REDH RH1 ......276 A1
Chipstead Ct WOKN/KNAP GU21 ......231 K3
Chipstead Gdns CRICK NW2 ......116 E7
Chipstead La COUL/CHIP CR5 ......239 L10
SEV TN13 ......246 E8
Chipstead Pk SEV TN13 ......246 E8
Chipstead Park Cl SEV TN13 ......246 E8
Chipstead Rd BNSTD SM7 ......239 J3
ERITH DA8 ......164 F6
Chipstead Station Pde
COUL/CHIP CR5 ......240 A4
Chipstead St FUL/PGN SW6 ......157 K7
Chipstead Valley Rd
COUL/CHIP CR5 ......240 C2
Chipstead Wy BNSTD SM7 ......240 A2
Chirk Cl YEAD UB4 ......133 M6
Chirton Wk WOKN/KNAP GU21 ......231 M4
Chisenhale Rd BOW E3 ......140 D4
Chisholm Rd CROY/NA CR0 ......203 M9
RCHPK/HAM TW10 ......177 L2
Chislehurst Av FNCH N3 ......97 M8
Chislehurst High St CHST BR7 ......184 E9
Chislehurst Rd BMLY BR1 ......206 B2
ORP BR6 ......207 J7
RCHPK/HAM TW10 ......177 K2
SCUP DA14 ......185 K8
STMC/STPC BR5 ......207 H4
Chislet Cl BECK BR3 ......182 F10
Chisley Rd SEVS/STOTM N15 ......119 M4
Chiswell Ct WATN WD24 ......73 K4
Chiswellgreen La LCOL/BKTW AL2 ......55 M1
Chiswell Sq BKHTH/KID SE3 ......161 N8
Chiswell St STLK EC1Y 12 G3
Chiswick Br MORT/ESHN SW14 ......155 P8
Chiswick Cl CROY/NA CR0 ......202 G10
Chiswick Common Rd
CHSWK W4 ......156 A3
Chiswick High Rd CHSWK W4 ......155 P3
Chiswick House Grounds
CHSWK * W4 ......156 A5
Chiswick La CHSWK W4 ......156 B4
Chiswick La South CHSWK W4 ......156 C5
Chiswick Ml CHSWK W4 ......156 C5
Chiswick Pk CHSWK * W4 ......155 P2
Chiswick Pier CHSWK * W4 ......156 C6
Chiswick Quay CHSWK W4 ......155 P7
Chiswick Rd CHSWK W4 ......155 P3
ED N9 ......99 P3
Chiswick Sq CHSWK W4 ......156 B5
Chiswick Staithe CHSWK W4 ......155 N7
Chiswick Village CHSWK W4 ......155 M5
Chithurst La HORL RH6 ......281 M8
Chittenden Cl HOD EN11 ......26 G10
Chitterfield Ga WDR/YW UB7 ......152 B6
Chitty's La BCTR RM8 ......123 N7
Chitty St FITZ W1T 11 H3
Chitty's Wk RGUW GU3 ......249 L6
Chivalry Rd BTSEA SW11 ......179 P1
Chivenor Gv KUTN/CMB KT2 ......177 J8
Chivers Rd BRWN CM15 ......86 E1
CHING E4 ......100 G4
Choats Rd BARK IG11 ......143 M4
Chobham Cl CHERT KT16 ......214 E3
Chobham Gdns WIM/MER SW19 ......178 G5
Chobham La CHERT KT16 ......193 M8
Chobham Park La
CHOB/PIR GU24 ......213 M6
Chobham Rd CHERT KT16 ......214 D4
CHOB/PIR GU24 ......193 H9
CHOB/PIR GU24 ......213 P9
SRTFD E15 ......121 J10
WOKN/KNAP GU21 ......213 J10
WOKN/KNAP GU21 ......230 G4
WOKN/KNAP GU21 ......232 C3
Choir Gn WOKN/KNAP GU21 ......231 K3
Cholesbury Rd TRING HP23 ......32 C5
Cholmeley Cl HGT * N6 ......118 C5
Cholmeley Crs HGT N6 ......118 C5
Cholmeley Pk HGT N6 ......118 C6
Cholmley Gdns KIL/WHAMP NW6 ......117 K10
Cholmley Rd THDIT KT7 ......198 G6
Cholmley Ter THDIT * KT7 ......198 G7
Cholmley Vls THDIT * KT7 ......198 G7
Cholmondeley Av WLSDN NW10 ......136 D4
Chopwell Cl SRTFD * E15 ......141 J2
Chorleywood Bottom
RKW/CH/CXG WD3 ......70 G9
Chorleywood Cl
RKW/CH/CXG WD3 ......91 N1
Chorleywood Crs
STMC/STPC BR5 ......207 J2
Chorleywood Rd
RKW/CH/CXG WD3 ......71 L9
Choumert Gv PECK SE15 ......159 P8
Choumert Rd PECK SE15 ......159 N9
Chow Sq HACK * E8 ......119 N10
Chrislaine Cl STWL/WRAY TW19 ......173 N2
Chrisp St POP/IOD E14 ......140 G7
Christabel Cl ISLW TW7 ......154 D9
Christ Church Av ERITH DA8 ......164 E5
Christchurch Av ALP/SUD HA0 ......135 K1
KIL/WHAMP NW6 ......2 B3
KTN/HRWW/W HA3 ......114 E2
NFNCH/WDSP N12 ......97 M7
RAIN RM13 ......144 G4
TEDD TW11 ......176 F8
Christchurch Cl ENC/FH EN2 ......79 K6
NFNCH/WDSP * N12 ......97 N8
WIM/MER SW19 ......179 N10
Christchurch Crs RAD WD7 ......74 F2
Christchurch Gdns
KTN/HRWW/W HA3 ......114 F2
Christchurch Hl HAMP NW3 ......117 N8
Christ Church La BAR EN5 ......77 H6
Christchurch Ldg EBAR * EN4 ......78 A8
Christ Church Mt
HOR/WEW KT19 ......219 N7
Christchurch Pk BELMT SM2 ......221 M4
Christchurch Pas HAMP NW3 ......117 N8
Christ Church Rd BECK * BR3 ......204 F2
BRYLDS KT5 ......199 L7
CEND/HSY/T N8 ......118 F4
EPSOM KT18 ......219 K8
GVE DA12 ......190 F4
Christchurch Rd BFN/LL DA15 ......185 J7
BRXS/STRHM SW2 ......180 G4
DART DA1 ......187 K3
HHNE HP2 ......35 N5
IL IG1 ......122 E6
MORT/ESHN SW14 ......177 N1
PUR/KEN CR8 ......223 J7
TIL RM18 ......168 D7
VW GU25 ......194 A4
WIM/MER SW19 ......179 N10
Christchurch Sq HOM E9 ......140 B3
Christchurch St CHEL SW3 ......16 A9
Christchurch Ter CHEL * SW3 ......16 A9
Christchurch Wy GNWCH SE10 ......161 K4
WOKN/KNAP GU21 ......232 C3
Christian Flds STRHM/NOR SW16 ......181 H10
Christian Fields Av GVE DA12 ......190 F7
Christian St WCHPL E1 ......13 P5
Christie Cl BROX EN10 ......44 E7
GT/LBKH KT23 ......253 N1
LTWR GU18 ......212 A6
Christie Dr SNWD SE25 ......203 P5
Christie Rd HOM E9 ......140 D1
Christies Av RSEV TN14 ......228 B6
Christina Sq FSBYPK N4 ......119 J6
Christina St SDTCH EC2A 13 J1
Christmas Hl SHGR GU5 ......268 E8
Christmas La SLN SL2 ......109 H8
Christmaspie Av RGUW GU3 ......248 A10
RGUW * GU3 ......266 A1
Christopher Av HNWL W7 ......154 F2
Christopher Cl BFN/LL DA15 ......185 J1
HCH RM12 ......125 L9
Christopher Ct WARE * SG12 ......26 C2
Christopher Gdns DAGW RM9 ......123 N10
Christopher Pl CAMTN * NW1 ......5 K9
STALW/RED * AL3 ......38 C6
Christopher Rd NWDGN UB2 ......153 J3
Christophers Ms NTGHL W11 ......8 A9
Christopher St SDTCH EC2A 13 H2
Christy Rd BH/WHM TN16 ......243 P1
Chryssell Rd BRXN/ST SW9 ......159 H6
Chrystie La GT/LBKH KT23 ......254 A2
Chubworthy St NWCR SE14 ......160 D5
Chuck's La KWD/TDW/WH KT20 ......238 E10
Chudleigh Crs GDMY/SEVK IG3 ......123 H9
Chudleigh Gdns SUT SM1 ......201 M10
Chudleigh Rd BROCKY SE4 ......182 E1
HARH RM3 ......105 M5
KIL/WHAMP NW6 ......136 F2
WHTN TW2 ......176 D2
Chudleigh St WCHPL E1 ......140 C8
Chudleigh Wy RSLP HA4 ......113 H6
Chulsa Rd SYD SE26 ......182 A8
Chumleigh St CMBW SE5 ......19 J9
Chumleigh Wk BRYLDS KT5 ......199 L4
Church Aly GVE * DA12 ......190 E2
Church Ap DUL SE21 ......181 L6
EGH TW20 ......194 F3
Church Av BECK BR3 ......204 F1
CAMTN NW1 ......4 F2
CHING E4 ......101 J7
EFNCH N2 ......97 N10
MORT/ESHN SW14 ......156 A10
NTHLT UB5 ......133 N2
NWDGN UB2 ......153 M2
PIN HA5 ......113 M4
RSLP HA4 ......112 E6
SCUP DA14 ......185 K8
Churchbury Cl EN EN1 ......79 M6
Churchbury La EN EN1 ......79 M7
Churchbury Rd ELTH/MOT SE9 ......184 A3
EN EN1 ......79 M6
Church Cl ADL/WDHM KT15 ......215 L1
BRW CM14 ......86 C3
CHOB/PIR GU24 ......230 E6
EDGW HA8 ......95 P6
EW * KT17 ......220 B9
HSLW TW3 ......153 N8
HYS/HAR UB3 ......132 E7
KWD/TDW/WH KT20 ......257 J3
LHD/OX KT22 ......236 C10
NTHWD HA6 ......92 G8
POTB/CUF EN6 ......60 F5
RAD WD7 ......74 F2
STA TW18 ......195 M3
TRDG/WHET N20 ......97 P4
UX/CGN UB8 ......131 L4
WDR/YW UB7 ......151 P2
WDSR SL4 ......149 J5
WOKN/KNAP GU21 ......232 A2
Church Ct BROX * EN10 ......44 F6
DART DA1 ......187 L6
REIG RH2 ......257 L10
Church Crs FNCH N3 ......97 J9
HOM E9 ......140 C2
MUSWH N10 ......118 C2
SOCK/AV RM15 ......147 H5
STALW/RED AL3 ......38 B5
TRDG/WHET N20 ......97 P4
Church Cft STALE/WH AL4 ......39 H8
Churchcroft Cl BAL * SW12 ......180 B3
Churchdown BMLY BR1 ......183 K7
Church Dr CDALE/KGS NW9 ......116 A6
RYLN/HDSTN HA2 ......113 P4
WWKM BR4 ......205 K10
Church Elm La DAGE RM10 ......144 B1
Church End HDN NW4 ......116 E1
HLWW/ROY CM19 ......46 D3
STALE/WH AL4 ......21 H9
WALTH * E17 ......120 G2
Church Farm EBAR * EN4 ......98 A1
Church Farm La CHEAM SM3 ......221 H3
Church Farm Wy GSTN WD25 ......74 A4
Church Fld DART DA1 ......187 L5
EPP CM16 ......65 K5
SEV TN13 ......246 G8
Churchfield HARP AL5 ......20 B3
HLW CM20 ......29 K9
Churchfield Av NFNCH/WDSP N12 ......97 M7
Churchfield Cl HYS/HAR UB3 ......132 G9
RYLN/HDSTN HA2 ......114 B2
Churchfield Ms SLN SL2 ......129 N8
Church Field Pth CHES/WCR EN8 ......62 B5
Churchfield Rd ACT W3 ......135 P10
CFSP/GDCR SL9 ......90 A9
HNWL W7 ......154 D1
REIG RH2 ......257 J9
WEA W13 ......134 G10
WELL DA16 ......163 K9
WEY KT13 ......216 B1
WLYN AL6 ......23 M2
WOT/HER KT12 ......197 H8
Church Flds RAD * WD7 ......74 F2
Churchfields BROX EN10 ......44 F6
E/WMO/HCT KT8 ......197 P3
GNWCH SE10 ......161 H5
HERT/BAY SG13 ......25 L6
LOU IG10 ......82 B8
RGUE GU4 ......250 D5
SWFD E18 ......101 M9
WOKN/KNAP GU21 ......232 A2
Churchfields Av FELT TW13 ......175 N6
WEY KT13 ......216 C1
Churchfields La BROX EN10 ......44 F6
Churchfields Rd BECK BR3 ......204 C2
Churchfield Wy
NFNCH/WDSP N12 ......97 M7
Church Gdns ALP/SUD HA0 ......114 F9
EA W5 ......155 J1
LHD/OX * KT22 ......236 G6
Church Garth ARCH * N19 ......118 E7
Churchgate CHES/WCR EN8 ......62 A6
Church Ga FUL/PGN SW6 ......157 H9
Churchgate Rd CHES/WCR EN8 ......62 A5
Churchgate St HLWE CM17 ......29 P7
Church Gn BRXN/ST * SW9 ......159 H8
HYS/HAR UB3 ......132 G8
KWD/TDW/WH * KT20 ......238 D10
WOT/HER KT12 ......217 K3
Church Gv AMS HP6 ......70 B5
DTCH/LGLY SL3 ......129 P7
KUT KT1 ......199 H1
LEW SE13 ......160 G10
Church Hl ABLGY WD5 ......54 G2
BH/WHM TN16 ......244 A8
CAR SM5 ......222 A2
CTHM CR3 ......241 N10
DART DA1 ......164 F10
DART DA1 ......187 L6
DEN/HRF UB9 ......111 M2
EPP CM16 ......65 K5
GRH DA9 ......188 D1
HERT/BAY SG13 ......26 A7
HRW HA1 ......114 D6
LOU IG10 ......82 C7
ORP BR6 ......207 K7
PUR/KEN CR8 ......222 F6
REDH RH1 ......258 C2
REDH RH1 ......258 G9
RSEV TN14 ......244 F1
SHGR GU5 ......270 B5
WALTH E17 ......120 F2
WCHMH N21 ......98 G1
WIM/MER SW19 ......179 J8
WOKN/KNAP GU21 ......232 A2
WOKS/MYFD GU22 ......233 J3
WOOL/PLUM SE18 ......162 C2
Church Hill Rd CHEAM SM3 ......220 G1
EBAR EN4 ......98 A1
SURB KT6 ......199 K5
WALTH E17 ......120 G2
Church Hill Wd STMC/STPC BR5 ......207 J5
Church Hollow PUR RM19 ......165 P4
Church Hyde WOOL/PLUM SE18 ......163 H5
Churchill Av HGDN/ICK UB10 ......132 C5
KTN/HRWW/W HA3 ......114 G4
Churchill Cl CHONG CM5 ......67 P3
DART DA1 ......188 A4
EBED/NFELT TW14 ......174 G4
LHD/OX KT22 ......236 D9
WARL CR6 ......242 B3
Churchill Ct CRAWE RH10 ......284 A4
Churchill Dr BEAC HP9 ......88 B6
WEY KT13 ......196 D10
Churchill Gdns ACT W3 ......135 M8
PIM SW1V 16 G8
Churchill Gardens Rd PIM SW1V 16 F8
Churchill Pl POP/IOD E14 ......140 G10
Churchill Rd CAN/RD E16 ......141 P8
CRICK NW2 ......136 E1
DTCH/LGLY SL3 ......150 C3
EDGW HA8 ......95 L7
EYN DA4 ......210 B4
GRAYS RM17 ......168 A5
GU GU1 ......268 B1
GVW DA11 ......190 C4
HOR/WEW KT19 ......219 M7
HORL RH6 ......281 J4
KTTN NW5 ......118 C9
SAND/SEL CR2 ......223 K5
STAL AL1 ......38 F4
Churchill Ter CHING E4 ......100 F5
Churchill Wk HOM E9 ......120 B10
Churchill Wy BH/WHM TN16 ......244 A1
BMLY BR1 ......205 M2
SUN TW16 ......175 H8
Church La ABR/ST RM4 ......83 N8
ABR/ST RM4 ......84 D8
ASC SL5 ......192 F3
ASC SL5 ......192 C4
BERK HP4 ......33 P5
BRKMPK AL9 ......40 F4
BROX EN10 ......44 C9
BRWN CM15 ......86 G3
CDALE/KGS NW9 ......115 P6
CDALE/KGS NW9 ......116 A5
CEND/HSY/T N8 ......118 G2
CFSP/GDCR SL9 ......90 A9
CHES/WCR EN8 ......62 B5
CHOB/PIR GU24 ......230 F1
CHOB/PIR GU24 ......230 C8
CHONG CM5 ......49 P10
CHSGTN KT9 ......219 L3
CHST BR7 ......206 F1
COUL/CHIP CR5 ......240 B8
CRAWE RH10 ......284 A6
CRAWE RH10 ......285 H3
CTHM CR3 ......241 H9
DAGE RM10 ......144 C1
ED * N9 ......99 P3
EFNCH N2 ......117 N1
ENC/FH EN2 ......79 L7
EPP CM16 ......66 B1
EPSOM KT18 ......255 P1
GDST RH9 ......260 C8
GSTN WD25 ......74 A4
GVE DA12 ......191 M5
HAYES BR2 ......206 B8
HHS/BOV HP3 ......52 E3
HORL RH6 ......280 F9
KGLGY WD4 ......54 B6
KTN/HRWW/W HA3 ......94 E9
LOU IG10 ......82 C7
OXTED RH8 ......261 J6
OXTED RH8 ......261 K5
PIN HA5 ......113 M1
POTB/CUF EN6 ......60 A6
PUR RM19 ......165 P4
RAIN RM13 ......145 L8
RBRW/HUT CM13 ......127 H4
RBSF CM22 ......30 E3
REDH RH1 ......259 L9
RGUW GU3 ......249 K3
RKW/CH/CXG WD3 ......71 K3
RKW/CH/CXG WD3 ......91 K2
ROM RM1 ......124 F2
RPLY/SEND GU23 ......250 E2
SHGR GU5 ......269 L5
SHGR GU5 ......270 B5
SLN SL2 ......129 N6
SLN SL2 ......129 L6
STALE/WH AL4 ......39 N8
TEDD TW11 ......176 E8
THDIT KT7 ......198 E6
TOOT SW17 ......180 A8
TOTM N17 ......99 M9
TWK TW1 ......176 F4
UPMR RM14 ......126 G10
WALTH E17 ......120 G2
WAN E11 ......121 K6
WARL CR6 ......242 C3
WARL CR6 ......243 H2
WDSR SL4 ......149 J7
WEA W13 ......155 H1
WEY KT13 ......216 B1
WIM/MER SW19 ......201 K2
WLGTN SM6 ......202 E10
Church Lane Av COUL/CHIP CR5 ......240 C8
Church Lane Dr COUL/CHIP CR5 ......240 C8
Church Langley Wy HLWE CM17 ......47 M1
Churchley Rd SYD SE26 ......182 A7
Church Leys HLWS CM18 ......47 J2
Church Manor Wy ABYW SE2 ......163 K3
Church Manorway ERITH DA8 ......164 E2
Church Md CMBW * SE5 ......159 K6
HLWW/ROY CM19 ......27 N10
Churchmead WAB * EN9 ......45 H8
Churchmead Cl EBAR EN4 ......77 P10
Church Meadow SURB KT6 ......199 H9
Churchmead Rd WLSDN NW10 ......136 D1
Church Ms ADL/WDHM KT15 ......215 M1
Churchmore Rd
STRHM/NOR SW16 ......202 D1
Church Mt EFNCH N2 ......117 N3
Church Paddock Ct WLGTN SM6 ......202 E10
Church Pde ASHF * TW15 ......174 A7
Church Pk CRAWW * RH11 ......283 K6
Church Pas BAR * EN5 ......77 J7
Church Pth CHSWK W4 ......155 P2
CROY/NA CR0 ......203 K9
GRH DA9 ......188 E2
GVW DA11 ......189 P2
MTCM CR4 ......201 P3
NFNCH/WDSP * N12 ......97 M6
RYNPK SW20 ......201 J2
WAN E11 ......121 M3
WOKN/KNAP * GU21 ......232 C3
Church Pl EA W5 ......155 J1
MTCM CR4 ......201 P3
Church Ri CHSGTN KT9 ......219 L3
FSTH SE23 ......182 C4
Church Rd ABR/ST RM4 ......85 L5
ABR/ST RM4 ......105 L2
ACT W3 ......155 P1
ADL/WDHM KT15 ......215 K2
ASC SL5 ......192 F6
ASHF TW15 ......174 A7
ASHTD KT21 ......237 J4
BARK IG11 ......142 F1
BARN SW13 ......156 D8
BEAC HP9 ......89 J7
BERK HP4 ......34 E3
BF/WBF KT14 ......215 P9
BFOR GU20 ......212 A3
BGR/WK TN15 ......247 N7
BH/WHM TN16 ......244 A3
BH/WHM TN16 ......245 L10
BRW CM14 ......86 B3
BXLYHN DA7 ......164 A8
CHEAM SM3 ......221 H3
CHOB/PIR GU24 ......212 E8
CHONG CM5 ......49 K7
CHONG CM5 ......67 L9
CRAWE RH10 ......284 F7
CRAWE RH10 ......285 J2

CRAWE RH10 285 N10
CROY/NA CR0 203 K10
CROY/NA * CR0 223 K1
CTHM CR3 241 N4
CTHM CR3 241 N9
CTHM CR3 242 C7
DEN/HRF UB9 111 M1
E/WMO/HCT KT8 198 C3
EFNCH N2 97 N9
EGH TW20 172 D8
ERITH DA8 164 D4
ESH/CLAY KT10 218 E3
EW KT17 220 B8
EYN DA4 187 P9
FELT TW13 175 K8
GNTH/NBYPK IG2 123 H4
GRH DA9 188 D1
GT/LBKH KT23 235 N9
GU GU1 268 A1
HARH RM3 105 P8
HART DA3 211 L5
HAYES BR2 205 K3
HAYES BR2 226 A4
HDN NW4 116 E2
HERT/BAY SG13 42 D5
HERT/WAS SG14 25 J4
HEST TW5 153 J4
HEST TW5 153 P6
HHS/BOV * HP3 36 D8
HLWE CM17 47 M4
HNWL W7 134 E9
HOR/WEW KT19 220 A4
HORL RH6 279 P10
HORL RH6 280 A5
HORL RH6 281 H8
HORL RH6 281 N2
HYS/HAR UB3 132 G10
ISLW TW7 154 C7
IVER SL0 130 F4
KUT KT1 199 L2
LEY E10 120 F6
LHD/OX KT22 236 G8
LOU IG10 81 M7
MEO DA13 190 F10
MEO DA13 191 H10
MNPK E12 122 C10
MTCM CR4 201 N2
NRWD SE19 181 M10
NTHLT UB5 133 N2
NTHWD HA6 92 G8
NWDGN UB2 153 N2
ORP BR6 226 F2
ORP BR6 227 N3
PEND EN3 80 B10
POTB/CUF EN6 59 L6
PUR/KEN CR8 222 F6
PUR/KEN CR8 241 L1
RCHPK/HAM TW10 177 K7
RCHPK/HAM TW10 177 K1
REDH RH1 275 P2
REIG RH2 275 K2
RSEV TN14 263 P2
RSEV TN14 265 J8
SCUP DA14 185 K7
SHPTN TW17 196 C7
SLN SL2 129 H5
STAN HA7 94 G6
SURB KT6 199 H8
SWCM DA10 189 L2
SWLY BR8 208 E7
SWLY BR8 209 L1
TEDD TW11 176 D7
TIL RM18 168 B7
TIL RM18 169 H5
TOTM N17 99 N8
UX/CGN UB8 131 N6
WALTH E17 100 D10
WARL CR6 242 C3
WAT WD17 73 H5
WDR/YW UB7 151 N1
WDSR SL4 171 N1
WELL DA16 163 L8
WGCW AL8 22 F5
WIM/MER SW19 179 H7
WLGTN SM6 202 D10
WLSDN NW10 136 B1
WOKN/KNAP GU21 231 M5
WOKN/KNAP GU21 232 A2
WPK KT4 200 B8
Church Rd South EFNCH N2 97 N10
Church Rw CHST BR7 206 F1
FUL/PGN * SW6 157 L6
HAMP NW3 117 M9
RPLY/SEND * GU23 233 M7
WAND/EARL * SW18 179 K1
Church Row Ms CHST BR7 184 F10
Church Side EPSOM KT18 219 N9
Churchside Cl BH/WHM TN16 243 P4
Church Sq SHPTN TW17 196 C7
Church St AMSS HP7 68 G6
BAY/PAD W2 9 M3
BGR/WK TN15 247 P6
BRKHM/BTCW RH3 274 B1
BRKMPK AL9 40 F3
BRKMPK AL9 41 P3
CHSWK W4 156 B5
COB KT11 235 J1
CRAWW RH11 283 M7
CROY/NA CR0 203 J10
CSHM HP5 50 G7
DAGE RM10 144 C2
DORK RH4 272 F2
ED N9 99 M2
EHSLY KT24 253 L3
ENC/FH EN2 79 K7
EPSOM KT18 220 B9
ESH/CLAY KT10 218 A1
EW KT17 220 D5
GRAYS RM17 167 P5
GVW DA11 190 E2
HERT/WAS SG14 25 L5
HHNE HP2 35 N4
HHS/BOV HP3 52 E3
HPTN TW12 198 B1
HSLW TW3 176 B1
ISLW TW7 154 G9
KUT KT1 199 J2
LHD/OX KT22 236 G8
MEO DA13 189 M8
REIG RH2 257 L10
RKW/CH/CXG WD3 91 P2
RSEV TN14 228 G7
SBW CM21 29 P1
SL SL1 128 B6
SL SL1 149 L2
SL SL1 149 H1
SRTFD E15 141 K3
STA TW18 172 G7
STALE/WH AL4 21 J3
STALW/RED AL3 38 C5
SUN TW16 197 H3
TWK TW1 176 F4
WAB EN9 63 H9
WARE SG12 26 C2
WATW * WD18 73 K8
WDSR SL4 149 J7
WEY KT13 216 B1
WOKS/MYFD GU22 232 F7
WOT/HER KT12 197 H8
Church St East
WOKN/KNAP GU21 232 C3
Church Street Est STJWD NW8 9 M2
Church St North SRTFD E15 141 K3
Church St West
WOKN/KNAP GU21 232 B3
Church Ter BGR/WK * TN15 247 N7
FUL/PGN * SW6 157 L8
HDN NW4 116 E1
LEW SE13 161 K9
RCHPK/HAM TW10 177 J1
WDSR SL4 148 D8
Church V EFNCH N2 118 A1
FSTH SE23 182 B5
Church Vw BROX EN10 44 E6
SOCK/AV RM15 166 B1
STALE/WH * AL4 21 J3
UPMR RM14 126 A7
Church View Cl HORL RH6 280 A5
Churchview Rd WHTN TW2 176 C4
Church Wk BTFD TW8 155 H5
BUSH WD23 73 P10
CDALE/KGS NW9 116 A7
CRAWE RH10 283 N7
CRICK NW2 117 J8
CTHM CR3 241 P10
DART DA1 187 L6
GVE DA12 190 G3
HORL RH6 280 A5
HYS/HAR UB3 132 F8
LHD/OX KT22 236 G8
REIG RH2 257 L10
RYNPK SW20 200 F3
SBW CM21 30 A1
STNW/STAM N16 119 L8
STRHM/NOR SW16 202 D2
WEY KT13 196 B10
WOT/HER KT12 197 H8
Churchway CAMTN NW1 5 K10
Church Wy OXTED RH8 261 L8
SAND/SEL CR2 223 N6
TRDG/WHET N20 97 P4
Churchyard Rw LBTH SE11 18 D5
Churston Av PLSTW E13 141 N3
Churston Cl BRXS/STRHM * SW2 181 J4
Churston Dr MRDN SM4 200 G5
Churston Gdns FBAR/BDGN N11 98 D7
Churton Pl CHSWK * W4 155 N5
PIM SW1V 17 H6
Churton St PIM SW1V 17 H6
Chuters Cl BF/WBF KT14 216 A8
Chuters Gv EW KT17 220 C8
The Chyne CFSP/GDCR SL9 110 C3
Chyngton Cl BFN/LL DA15 185 J6
Cibber Rd FSTH SE23 182 C5
Cicada Rd WAND/EARL SW18 179 M2
Cicely Rd PECK SE15 159 P7
Cidermill Rd RDKG RH5 278 B4
Cillocks Cl HOD EN11 44 F2
Cimba Wd GVE DA12 191 H7
Cinderford Wy BMLY BR1 183 K7
Cinder Pth WOKS/MYFD GU22 231 P5
Cinema Pde EDGW * HA8 95 M7
Cinnamon Cl CROY/NA * CR0 202 F7
Cinnamon Gdns GUW GU2 249 M5
Cinnamon St WAP E1W 140 A10
Cintra Pk NRWD SE19 181 N10
Cippenham Cl SL SL1 128 E9
Cippenham La SL SL1 128 E9
Circle POP/IOD E14 140 G10
Circle Gdns BF/WBF KT14 216 A9
WIM/MER SW19 201 K3
Circle Rd EFNCH N2 97 N10
WOT/HER KT12 216 F6
The Circle CRICK NW2 116 B8
MLHL NW7 96 A7
The Circuits PIN HA5 113 K2
Circular Rd TOTM N17 119 N1
Circular Wy WOOL/PLUM SE18 162 C5
Circus Ms MBLAR * W1H 10 A3
Circus Pl LVPST * EC2M 13 H4
Circus Rd STJWD NW8 3 L9
Circus St GNWCH SE10 161 H6
The Circus LHD/OX * KT22 236 G6
Cirencester St BAY/PAD W2 8 G3
Cirrus Crs GVE DA12 191 H8
Cissbury Hl CRAWW RH11 283 M9
Cissbury Ring North
NFNCH/WDSP N12 97 J6
Cissbury Ring South
NFNCH/WDSP N12 97 J6
Cissbury Rd SEVS/STOTM N15 119 L3
Citadel Pl LBTH SE11 17 N7
Citizen Rd HOLWY N7 119 H8
Citron Ter PECK * SE15 160 A9
City Barracks SHB * W12 136 F10
City Gdn EDGW HA8 95 M7
City Garden Rw IS N1 6 D8
City Pk WGCE * AL7 23 K4
City Rd FSBYE EC1V 6 C8
STLK EC1Y 13 H2
Civic Sq TIL RM18 168 D8
Civic Wy BARK/HLT IG6 122 F2
RSLP HA4 113 L10
Clabon Ms KTBR SW1X 16 A4
Clacket La BH/WHM TN16 244 B10
BH/WHM TN16 262 C3
Clack St BERM/RHTH SE16 160 B1
Clacton Rd TOTM * N17 99 N10
WALTH E17 120 D4
Claire Cswy GRH * DA9 166 D10
Claire Cl RBRW/HUT CM13 107 M5
Claire Ct NFNCH/WDSP N12 97 M4
Claire Gdns STAN HA7 95 H6
Claire Pl POP/IOD E14 160 F2
Clairvale EMPK RM11 125 M5
Clairvale Rd HEST TW5 153 L7
Clairview Rd TOOT SW17 180 C8
Clairville Gdns HNWL W7 134 D10
Clammas Wy UX/CGN UB8 131 M7
Clamp Hl KTN/HRWW/W HA3 94 C5
Clancarty Rd FUL/PGN SW6 157 K8
Clandon Av EGH TW20 172 F10
Clandon Cl ACT W3 155 N1
EW KT17 220 C3
Clandon Gdns FNCH N3 117 K1
Clandon Rd GDMY/SEVK IG3 123 H7
GU GU1 268 B1
RPLY/SEND GU23 251 K2
Clandon St DEPT SE8 160 F8
Clandon Ter RYNPK * SW20 200 G2
Clanricarde Gdns BAY/PAD W2 8 F8
Clapgate Rd BUSH WD23 74 A10
Clapham Common North Side
CLAP SW4 158 C10
Clapham Common South Side
CLAP SW4 180 C2
Clapham Common West Side
BTSEA SW11 180 B1
Clapham Court Ter CLAP * SW4 180 F1
Clapham Crs CLAP SW4 158 E10
Clapham High St CLAP SW4 158 E10
Clapham Manor St CLAP SW4 158 D9
Clapham Park Est CLAP * SW4 180 E3
Clapham Park Rd CLAP SW4 158 D10
Clapham Park Ter CLAP * SW4 180 F1
Clapham Rd BRXN/ST SW9 158 F8
Clappers Ga CRAWE RH10 283 N6
Clappers La CHOB/PIR GU24 213 H7
Claps Gate La EHAM E6 142 E6
Clapton Common CLPT E5 119 P5
Clapton Sq CLPT E5 120 B10
Clapton Ter STNW/STAM N16 119 P5
Clapton Wy CLPT E5 119 P9
Clara Pl WOOL/PLUM SE18 162 D3
Clare Cswy GRH DA9 166 D10
Clare Cl BF/WBF KT14 215 K9
BORE WD6 75 L10
CRAWE RH10 284 D4
EFNCH N2 117 M1
Clare Cnr ELTH/MOT SE9 184 E3
Clare Ct CTHM CR3 242 F9
NTHWD HA6 92 F6
Clare Crs LHD/OX KT22 236 F4
Claredale WOKS/MYFD GU22 232 B5
Claredale St BETH E2 7 P8
Clare Dr SLN SL2 108 G9
Clare Gdns BARK IG11 143 J1
EGH TW20 172 D8
FSTGT E7 121 M9
NTGHL W11 8 B6
Clare Hl ESH/CLAY KT10 218 A2
Clare Hl (No 2) ESH/CLAY KT10 218 A2
Clare La IS N1 6 F4
Clare Lawn Av
MORT/ESHN SW14 178 A1
Clare Ms CHONG CM5 67 P2
FUL/PGN * SW6 157 L6
Claremont CHESW EN7 61 N5
LCOL/BKTW AL2 55 P7
Claremont Av ESH/CLAY KT10 217 N3
KTN/HRWW/W HA3 115 K3
NWMAL KT3 200 E5
SUN TW16 197 J1
WOKS/MYFD GU22 232 B5
WOT/HER KT12 217 L1
Claremont Cl BRXS/STRHM SW2 180 G4
CAN/RD E16 142 D10
CDH/CHF RM16 167 P2
IS N1 6 B8
ORP BR6 226 D1
SAND/SEL CR2 224 A10
WOT/HER KT12 217 K2
Claremont Ct DORK RH4 272 G3
Claremont Crs DART DA1 164 F10
RKW/CH/CXG WD3 72 D9
Claremont Dr ESH/CLAY KT10 218 A4
SHPTN TW17 196 C6
WOKS/MYFD GU22 232 B5
Claremont End ESH/CLAY KT10 218 A3
Claremont Gdns GDMY/SEVK IG3 123 H7
SURB KT6 199 K4
UPMR RM14 126 C6
Claremont Gv CHSWK W4 156 B6
WFD IG8 101 P7
Claremont House WATW * WD18 72 E10
Claremont La ESH/CLAY KT10 218 A1
Claremont Pk FNCH N3 97 H9
Claremont Park Rd
ESH/CLAY KT10 218 A3
Claremont Rd BF/WBF KT14 215 K8
BMLY BR1 206 B4
CRICK NW2 116 F5
CROY/NA CR0 203 P8
EBAR EN4 77 M4
EMPK RM11 125 H4
ESH/CLAY KT10 218 D4
FSTGT E7 121 N10
HGT N6 118 C5
KTN/HRWW/W HA3 94 D10
MV/WKIL W9 2 B8
REDH RH1 258 B7
STA TW18 172 G8
SURB KT6 199 K5
SWLY BR8 186 F10
TEDD TW11 176 E8
TWK TW1 176 G3
WALTH E17 100 D10
WAN E11 121 J8
WDSR SL4 149 H8
WEA W13 134 F7
Claremont Sq IS N1 6 A8
Claremont St GNWCH SE10 160 G5
UED N18 99 P7
Claremont Ter THDIT * KT7 198 G7
Claremont Vls CMBW * SE5 159 L6
KUT * KT1 199 L2
Claremont Wy CRICK NW2 116 F6
Claremount Cl EPSOM KT18 238 F3
Claremount Gdns EPSOM KT18 238 F3
Clarence Av CLAP SW4 180 E3
HAYES BR2 206 B4
IL IG1 122 C4
NWMAL KT3 199 P2
UPMR RM14 125 P7
Clarence Cl BUSH WD23 94 E1
EBAR EN4 77 N9
WOT/HER KT12 217 J1
Clarence Ct HORL * RH6 280 E3
MLHL * NW7 96 C6
Clarence Crs CLAP SW4 180 E2
SCUP DA14 185 L6
WDSR SL4 149 H7
Clarence Dr EGH TW20 171 P7
Clarence Gdns CAMTN NW1 4 F10
Clarence Ga CAMTN NW1 10 B1
WFD IG8 102 D7
Clarence La PUT/ROE SW15 178 C2
Clarence Ms CLPT E5 120 A10
Clarence Pas CAMTN * NW1 5 L8
Clarence Pl CLPT E5 120 A10
GVE DA12 190 E3
Clarence Rd BERK HP4 33 P5
BH/WHM TN16 244 C4
BMLY BR1 206 B3
BRWN CM15 86 G10
BXLYHS DA6 163 P10
CAN/RD E16 141 K6
CHSWK W4 155 M4
CLPT E5 120 A9
CROY/NA CR0 203 L7
ELTH/MOT SE9 184 B5
FSTGT E7 121 P9
GRAYS RM17 167 M5
KIL/WHAMP NW6 2 C4
PEND EN3 80 B9
RCH/KEW TW9 155 L7
REDH RH1 275 N3
SCUP DA14 185 L6
SEVS/STOTM N15 119 K3
STAL AL1 38 F6
SUT SM1 221 L1
TEDD TW11 176 E9
WALTH E17 100 C10
WDGN N22 98 F8
WDSR SL4 148 G7
WIM/MER SW19 179 L9
WLGTN SM6 222 C2
WOT/HER KT12 217 J1
Clarence Rw GVE DA12 190 E3
Clarence St EGH TW20 172 C9
KUT KT1 199 J2
NWDGN UB2 153 L2
RCH/KEW TW9 155 K10
STA TW18 173 H7
Clarence Ter CAMTN NW1 10 B1
HSLW TW3 154 A10
Clarence Vls KUT * KT1 199 L2
Clarence Wk CLAP SW4 158 F8
REDH RH1 275 N3
Clarence Wy CAMTN NW1 4 E3
HORL RH6 280 E4
Clarendon Cl BAY/PAD * W2 9 N7
HHNE HP2 35 N5
STMC/STPC BR5 207 K3
Clarendon Ct SLN SL2 129 N9
Clarendon Crs WHTN TW2 176 C6
Clarendon Dr PUT/ROE SW15 156 F10
Clarendon Gdns HDN NW4 116 D1
IL IG1 122 C6
MV/WKIL W9 9 K2
RDART DA2 188 C4
WBLY HA9 115 K9
Clarendon Ga BAY/PAD W2 9 N7
CHERT KT16 214 G3
Clarendon Gn STMC/STPC BR5 207 K3
Clarendon Gv MTCM CR4 202 A3
STMC/STPC BR5 207 K4
Clarendon Ms ASHTD * KT21 237 K5
BAY/PAD W2 9 N7
BORE * WD6 75 M7
Clarendon Pth STMC/STPC BR5 207 K4
Clarendon Pl BAY/PAD W2 9 N7
RDART DA2 186 E8
SEV * TN13 265 H1
Clarendon Ri LEW SE13 161 H9
Clarendon Rd ASHF TW15 174 A7
BORE WD6 75 M7
CEND/HSY/T N8 118 G1
CHES/WCR EN8 62 C5
CROY/NA CR0 203 J9
EA W5 135 K5
GVE DA12 190 F2
HRW HA1 114 D4
HYS/HAR UB3 152 G1
LEY E10 120 G4
NTGHL W11 8 A7
REDH * RH1 258 A9
SEV TN13 247 H10
SEVS/STOTM N15 119 J2
SWFD E18 121 M1
UED N18 99 P7
WAT WD17 73 J7
WAT * WD17 73 J7
WDGN * N22 98 G10
WIM/MER SW19 179 P10
WLGTN SM6 222 D2
Clarendon St PIM SW1V 16 F7
Clarendon Ter MV/WKIL W9 9 K1
Clarendon Wk NTGHL W11 8 A6
Clarendon Wy CHST BR7 207 J3
WCHMH N21 99 K1
Clarens St CAT SE6 182 E5
Clares Pde NTHLT * UB5 134 C1
Clare Pk AMSS HP7 69 K6
Clare Rd HSLWW TW4 153 N9
MDHD SL6 128 B8
NTHLT UB5 134 C1
NWCR SE14 160 E8
STWL/WRAY TW19 173 N4
WAN E11 121 J4
WLSDN NW10 136 D2
The Clares CTHM CR3 241 P10
Clare St BETH E2 140 A4
Claret Gdns SNWD SE25 203 M4
Clareville Gv SKENS SW7 15 K6
Clareville Rd CTHM CR3 241 P10
STMC/STPC BR5 206 F9
Clareville St SKENS SW7 15 K6
Clare Wy BXLYHN DA7 163 P7
SEV TN13 265 K4
Clare Wd LHD/OX KT22 236 F4
Clarges Ms MYFR/PICC W1J 10 E9
Clarges St MYFR/PICC W1J 10 F9
Claribel Rd BRXN/ST SW9 159 J8
Clarice Wy WLGTN SM6 222 F5
Claridge Rd BCTR RM8 123 N6
Clarissa Rd CHDH RM6 123 N4
Clarissa St HACK E8 7 L5
Clarkbourne Dr GRAYS RM17 168 A5
Clark Cl ERITH DA8 165 H7
Clarke Gn GSTN WD25 73 H1
Clarkes Av WPK KT4 200 G8
Clarkes Dr WDR/YW UB7 131 P8
Clarkes Green Rd BGR/WK TN15 229 P10
Clarkes Ms CAVSQ/HST W1G 10 D3
Clarke's Rd HAT AL10 40 E2
Clarke Wy GSTN WD25 73 H1
Clarkfield RKW/CH/CXG WD3 91 K2
Clarkhill HLWS CM18 47 H5
Clarks La EPP CM16 65 J7
RSEV TN14 228 A8
WARL CR6 243 N9
Clarks Md BUSH WD23 94 B1
Clarkson Rd CAN/RD E16 141 L8
Clarkson Rw CAMTN NW1 4 F8
Clarkson St BETH * E2 140 A5
Clark's Rd IL IG1 122 G7
Clark St WCHPL E1 140 B8
Clark Wy HEST TW5 153 L6
Classon Cl WDR/YW UB7 151 P1
Claston Cl DART DA1 164 F10
Claude Rd LEY E10 121 H6
PECK SE15 160 A8
PLSTW E13 141 N3
Claude St POP/IOD E14 160 F3
Claudian Pl STALW/RED AL3 37 P7
Claudian Wy CDH/CHF RM16 168 E2
Claudia Pl WIM/MER SW19 179 H4
Claughton Rd PLSTW E13 141 P4
Clauson Av NTHLT UB5 114 A10
Clavell St GNWCH SE10 161 H5
Claverdale Rd BRXS/STRHM SW2 180 G3
Claverhambury Rd WAB EN9 63 L5
Clavering Av BARN SW13 156 E5
Clavering Cl TWK TW1 176 F7
Clavering Rd MNPK E12 122 A6
Clavering Wy RBRW/HUT CM13 87 P10
Claverley Gv FNCH N3 97 K9
Claverley Vls FNCH N3 97 L8
Claverton Cl HHS/BOV HP3 52 D4
Claverton St PIM SW1V 17 H8
Clave St WAP E1W 140 B10
Claxton Gv HMSMTH W6 156 G4
Clay Acre CSHM HP5 51 J6
Clay Av MTCM CR4 202 C2
Claybank Gv LEW SE13 160 G9
Claybridge Rd LEE/GVPK SE12 183 P7
Claybrook Cl EFNCH N2 117 N1
Claybrook Rd HMSMTH W6 156 G5
Clayburn Gdns SOCK/AV RM15 146 G10
Claybury BUSH WD23 94 A1
Claybury Rd WFD IG8 102 B8
Claycroft WGCE AL7 23 L4
Claydon Dr CROY/NA CR0 222 F1
Claydon End CFSP/GDCR SL9 110 B1
Claydon La CFSP/GDCR SL9 110 B1
Claydon Rd WOKN/KNAP GU21 231 M2
Claydown Ms WOOL/PLUM SE18 162 D4
Clayfarm Rd ELTH/MOT SE9 184 F
Claygate Cl HCH RM12 125 H
Claygate Crs CROY/NA CR0 225 H
Claygate La THDIT KT7 198 F
Claygate Lodge Cl
ESH/CLAY KT10 218 D
Claygate Rd DORK RH4 272 G
WEA W13 154 G
Clayhall Av CLAY IG5 102 C1
Clay Hall La CRAWE RH10 285 K
Clayhall La REIG RH2 275 H
WDSR SL4 171 L
Clayhanger RGUE GU4 250 F
Clay Hl ENC/FH EN2 79 K
Clayhill Cl REIG RH2 274 D
Clayhill Crs LEE/GVPK SE12 184 A
Clayhill Rd REIG RH2 274 C
Claylands Pl BRXN/ST SW9 159 H
Claylands Rd VX/NE SW8 17 P1
Clay La BUSH WD23 94 D
EPSOM KT18 237 N1
REDH RH1 276 D
RGUE GU4 250 A
Claymore HHNE HP2 35 P
Claymore Cl MRDN SM4 201 K
Claypit Hl WAB EN9 81 P
Claypole Dr HEST TW5 153 M
Claypole Rd SRTFD * E15 141 H
Claypond Av BTFD TW8 155 K
Claypond Gdns BTFD TW8 155 J
Claypond La BTFD TW8 155 K
Clayside CHIG IG7 102 G
Clay's La LOU IG10 82 D
SRTFD E15 120 G1
Clays Lane Cl SRTFD E15 120 G1
Clay St MHST W1U 10 B
Clayton Av ALP/SUD HA0 135 K
UPMR RM14 126 A1
Clayton Cl EHAM E6 142 C
Clayton Crs BTFD TW8 155 J
Clayton Croft Rd RDART DA2 187 H
Clayton Dr GUW GU2 249 L
Clayton Fld CDALE/KGS NW9 96 B
Clayton Hl CRAWW RH11 283 M
Clayton Md GDST RH9 260 A
Clayton Ms GNWCH SE10 161 J
Clayton Pde CHES/WCR * EN8 62 C
DTCH/LGLY * SL3 150 D
Clayton Rd CHSGTN KT9 219 H
EW KT17 220 B
HYS/HAR UB3 152 F
ISLW TW7 154 D
PECK SE15 159 P
ROMW/RG RM7 124 D
Clayton St LBTH SE11 18 A
Clayton Ter YEAD * UB4 133 L
Claytonville Ter BELV * DA17 164 D
Clayton Wk AMSS HP7 69 P
Clayton Wy UX/CGN UB8 131 N
Clay Tye Rd UPMR RM14 127 H
Clay Wood Cl ORP BR6 207 H
Claywood La RDART DA2 189 J
Clayworth Cl BFN/LL DA15 185 L
Cleall Av WAB EN9 63 H1
Cleanthus Cl WOOL/PLUM SE18 162 E
Cleanthus Rd WOOL/PLUM SE18 162 E
Clearbrook Wy WCHPL E1 140 B
Cleardene DORK RH4 272 G
Cleardown WOKS/MYFD GU22 232 E
Cleares Pasture SL SL1 128 A
The Clears REIG RH2 257 H
Clearwater Pl SURB KT6 199 H
Clearwater Ter WKENS W14 156 C
Clearwell Dr MV/WKIL W9 8 C
Cleave Av HYS/HAR UB3 152 F
ORP BR6 227 H
Cleaveland Rd SURB KT6 199 J
Cleave Prior COUL/CHIP CR5 239 P
Cleaverholme Cl SNWD SE25 204 A
Cleaver Sq LBTH SE11 18 B
The Cleave HARP AL5 20 C
Cleeve Hl FSTH SE23 182 A
Cleeve Park Gdns SCUP DA14 185 L
Cleeve Rd LHD/OX KT22 236 F
The Cleeve GU GU1 250 D1
Clegg St PLSTW E13 141 M
WAP E1W 140 A1
Cleland Pth LOU IG10 82 E
Clematis Cl HARH RM3 105 H
Clematis Cottages SHB * W12 136 D
Clematis Gdns WFD IG8 101 N
Clematis St SHB W12 136 C
Clem Attlee Ct FUL/PGN SW6 14 D1
Clem Attlee Pde FUL/PGN SW6 14 D
Clemence Rd DAGE RM10 144 D
Clemence St POP/IOD E14 140 D
Clement Av CLAP SW4 158 E1
Clement Cl CHSWK W4 156 A
KIL/WHAMP NW6 136 F
PUR/KEN CR8 241 J
WLSDN NW10 136 F
Clement Gdns HYS/HAR UB3 152 F
Clementhorpe Rd DAGW RM9 143 M
Clementina Rd LEY E10 120 E
Clementine Cl WEA W13 154 C
Clement Rd BECK BR3 204 C
CHES/WCR EN8 62 D
WIM/MER SW19 179 H
Clements Av CAN/RD E16 141 M
Clements Cl SL SL1 149 N
Clements Inn LINN WC2A 11 P
Clements La IL IG1 122 E

Coldstream Gdns
WAND/EARL SW18 179 J2
Cole Av CDH/CHF RM16 168 F3
Colebeck Ms IS N1 6 D2
Colebert Av WCHPL E1 140 B6
Colebrook CHERT KT16 214 G3
Colebrooke Av WEA W13 134 G8
Colebrooke Dr WAN E11 121 N5
Colebrooke Pl CHERT * KT16 214 F4
IS N1 6 D6
Colebrooke Rd REDH RH1 257 P8
Colebrooke Rw IS N1 6 C8
Colebrook Gdns LOU IG10 82 E6
Colebrook La LOU IG10 82 E6
Colebrook Ri HAYES BR2 205 K2
Colebrook Rd STRHM/NOR SW16 202 F1
Colebrook Wy FBAR/BDGN N11 98 C6
Coleby Pth CMBW * SE5 159 L6
Cole Cl THMD SE28 143 L10
Coledale Dr STAN HA7 95 H9
Coleford Rd WAND/EARL SW18 179 M1
Cole Gdns HEST TW5 153 H6
Colegrave Rd SRTFD E15 121 J10
Cole Green La WGCE AL7 23 J7
Cole Green Wy HERT/WAS SG14 25 H7
Colegrove Rd PECK SE15 19 M10
Coleherne Ms WBPTN SW10 14 G8
Coleherne Rd WBPTN SW10 14 G8
Colehill Gdns FUL/PGN * SW6 157 H7
Colehill La FUL/PGN SW6 157 H7
Colekitchen La SHGR GU5 270 D4
Coleman Cl SNWD SE25 203 P2
Coleman Flds IS N1 6 F5
Coleman Green La STALE/WH AL4 21 L6
Coleman Rd BELV DA17 164 B2
CMBW SE5 159 M6
Colemans Heath ELTH/MOT SE9 184 D6
Coleman's La WAB EN9 63 J2
Coleman St LOTH EC2R 12 G5
Colenorton Crs WDSR SL4 148 D3
Colenso Rd CLPT E5 120 B9
GNTH/NBYPK IG2 123 H6
Cole Park Gdns TWK TW1 176 F2
Cole Park Rd TWK TW1 176 F3
Colepits Wood Rd
ELTH/MOT SE9 184 G1
Coleraine Rd BKHTH/KID SE3 161 L5
CEND/HSY/T N8 119 H1
Coleridge Av MNPK E12 142 B1
SUT SM1 221 P1
Coleridge Cl CHESW EN7 61 N3
VX/NE SW8 158 C8
Coleridge Crs DTCH/LGLY SL3 151 H7
Coleridge Gdns KIL/WHAMP NW6 3 J4
Coleridge Rd ASHF TW15 173 P7
CEND/HSY/T N8 118 E4
CROY/NA CR0 204 B7
DART DA1 165 P10
FSBYPK N4 119 H7
HARH RM3 105 J8
NFNCH/WDSP N12 97 M6
TIL RM18 168 F8
WALTH E17 120 E2
Coleridge Sq WEA * W13 134 F8
Coleridge Wk GLDGN NW11 117 K2
RBRW/HUT CM13 107 P1
Coleridge Wy ORP BR6 207 K6
WDR/YW UB7 152 A3
YEAD UB4 133 H8
Cole Rd TWK TW1 176 F2
WAT WD17 73 J5
Colesburg Rd BECK BR3 204 E3
Coles Cl CHONG CM5 67 P2
Coles Crs RYLN/HDSTN HA2 114 A7
Colescroft Hl PUR/KEN CR8 241 H1
Colesdale POTB/CUF EN6 60 F6
Coles Gn BUSH WD23 94 B2
LOU IG10 82 E5
Coles Green Rd CRICK NW2 116 D6
Coles Hl HHW HP1 35 K4
Coleshill La AMSS HP7 88 C1
Coleshill Rd TEDD TW11 176 D9
Coles La BH/WHM TN16 245 M9
Colesmead Rd REDH RH1 258 A7
Colestown St BTSEA SW11 157 P8
Cole St STHWK SE1 18 F2
Coleswood Rd HARP AL5 20 B4
Colet Cl PLMGR N13 99 J7
Colet Gdns WKENS W14 156 G4
Colet Rd CRAWE RH10 283 N10
RBRW/HUT CM13 87 P9
Colets Orch RSEV TN14 247 J2
Coley Av WOKS/MYFD GU22 232 D4
Coley St FSBYW WC1X 11 P2
Colfe & Hatcliffe Glebe
LEW * SE13 182 G1
Colfe Rd FSTH SE23 182 D4
Colgate Cl CRAWW RH11 283 L5
Colgate Pl WAB * EN9 80 F3
Colgrove WGCW AL8 22 F6
Colham Av WDR/YW UB7 131 P10
Colham Green Rd UX/CGN UB8 132 B7
Colham Mill Rd WDR/YW UB7 151 N1
Colham Rd UX/CGN UB8 132 A6
Colina Ms SEVS/STOTM N15 119 J2
Colina Rd CEND/HSY/T N8 119 J3
Colin Chapman Wy HART DA3 210 E10
Colin Cl CDALE/KGS NW9 116 B2
CROY/NA CR0 204 E10
RDART DA2 188 A2
WWKM BR4 205 L10
Colin Crs CDALE/KGS NW9 116 C3
Colindale Av CDALE/KGS NW9 116 A1
STAL AL1 38 E8
Colindeep Gdns HDN NW4 116 D3
Colindeep La CDALE/KGS NW9 116 C2
Colin Dr CDALE/KGS NW9 116 C3
Colinette Rd PUT/ROE SW15 156 F10
Colin Gdns CDALE/KGS NW9 116 C3
Colin Park Rd CDALE/KGS NW9 116 B1
Colin Rd CTHM CR3 241 P9
WLSDN NW10 136 D1
Colinton Rd BCTR RM8 123 L7
Colin Wy WDSR SL4 148 G2
Coliston Rd WAND/EARL SW18 179 K3
Collamore Av WAND/EARL SW18 179 P4
Collapit Cl RYLN/HDSTN HA2 114 A4
Collard Av LOU IG10 82 F6
Collard Pl CAMTN NW1 4 E3
College Ap GNWCH SE10 161 H5
College Av EGH TW20 172 E9
EW KT17 220 C10
GRAYS RM17 167 N3
KTN/HRWW/W HA3 94 D9
SL SL1 149 K2
College Cl ADL/WDHM KT15 195 N10
KTN/HRWW/W HA3 94 D8
UED N18 99 N6
WARE SG12 26 C3
WHTN TW2 176 C4
College Ct CHES/WCR EN8 62 B6
EA * W5 135 K9
College Crs HAMP NW3 3 L2
KIL/WHAMP NW6 3 J3
REDH RH1 258 B7
WDSR SL4 148 G8
College Cross IS N1 6 B3
College Dr THDIT KT7 198 D7
College East WCHPL * E1 13 M4
College Gdns CHING E4 100 G1
ENC/FH EN2 79 L5
NWMAL KT3 200 C5
REDBR IG4 122 B3
TOOT SW17 179 P5
UED * N18 99 N6
College Gn NRWD SE19 181 M10
College Gv CAMTN NW1 5 J6
College Hl CANST * EC4R 12 F7
College Hill Rd
KTN/HRWW/W HA3 94 D8
College La HAT AL10 40 B5
WOKS/MYFD GU22 231 P5
College Ms IS N1 6 B4
WEST SW1P 17 L3
College Pde KIL/WHAMP * NW6 2 B5
College Park Cl LEW SE13 161 J10
College Pl CAMTN NW1 5 H5
STALW/RED AL3 38 B6
WALTH E17 121 K2
WBPTN * SW10 157 M6
College Rd ABLGY WD5 55 H7
BMLY BR1 183 M10
BMLY BR1 205 M1
CHES/WCR EN8 62 B6
CRAWE RH10 283 P7
CROY/NA CR0 203 L9
DUL SE21 181 M3
ENC/FH EN2 79 L6
EW KT17 220 C10
GRAYS RM17 167 P3
GU GU1 268 A1
GVW DA11 189 N1
HERT/BAY SG13 26 B9
HOD EN11 44 E1
HRW HA1 114 D4
ISLW TW7 154 E7
KTN/HRWW/W HA3 94 D9
LEY E10 121 H3
NRWD SE19 181 N8
SL SL1 128 E10
STAL AL1 38 G7
SWLY BR8 186 F10
TOTM N17 99 N7
WBLY HA9 115 J6
WCHMH N21 99 H3
WEA W13 134 G8
WIM/MER SW19 179 N9
WLSDN NW10 136 F4
WOKS/MYFD GU22 232 E2
College Sq HLW * CM20 46 G1
College St CANST * EC4R 12 F7
STALW/RED AL3 38 C6
College Ter FNCH N3 97 J9
The College EW * KT17 238 D1
College Vw ELTH/MOT SE9 184 A4
College Wy ASHF TW15 174 A7
NTHWD HA6 92 E7
WGCW AL8 22 G4
YEAD UB4 133 H8
College Yd KIL/WHAMP * NW6 2 B5
KTTN * NW5 118 C10
Collendean La HORL RH6 279 J3
Collens Fld CHOB/PIR GU24 230 D10
Collens Rd HARP AL5 20 A6
Collent St HOM E9 140 B1
Coller Crs RDART DA2 188 D8
Colless Rd SEVS/STOTM N15 119 N3
Collet Cl CHES/WCR EN8 62 C4
Collet Rd RSEV TN14 247 M3
Collett Rd BERM/RHTH SE16 19 P4
HHW HP1 35 M6
WARE SG12 26 C1
Colley Hill La SLN SL2 109 L8
Colley Land RKW/CH/CXG WD3 70 B6
Colley La REIG RH2 257 H7
Colley Manor Dr REIG RH2 256 G9
Colley Wy REIG RH2 257 H7
Collier Cl EHAM E6 142 E9
HOR/WEW KT19 219 M3
Collier Dr EDGW HA8 95 M10
Collier Rw CRAWE RH10 283 N10
Collier Row La CRW RM5 104 C9
Collier Row Rd CRW RM5 104 B9
Colliers CTHM CR3 259 P1
Colliers Cl WOKN/KNAP GU21 231 N3
Collier St IS N1 5 N8
Colliers Water La THHTH CR7 203 H5
Colliers Wd HAYES BR2 226 A2
Collier Wy RGUE GU4 250 G8
Collindale Av BFN/LL DA15 185 K4
CDALE/KGS NW9 116 A1
ERITH DA8 164 C5
Collingbourne Rd SHB W12 136 E10
Collingham Gdns ECT SW5 15 H6
Collingham Pl ECT SW5 14 G6
Collingham Rd ECT SW5 15 H5
Collingsbourne
ADL/WDHM * KT15 215 L1
Collings Cl WDGN N22 98 G7
Collington Cl GVW DA11 190 B3
Collington St GNWCH * SE10 161 J4
Collingtree Rd SYD SE26 182 B7
Collingwood Av BRYLDS KT5 199 P8
MUSWH N10 118 B1
Collingwood Cl HORL RH6 280 C3
HSLWW TW4 175 P3
Colling Wood Cl PGE/AN SE20 204 A1
Collingwood Crs GU GU1 250 D9
Collingwood Dr LCOL/BKTW AL2 57 J1
Collingwood Rd CRAWE RH10 284 E8
MTCM CR4 201 P2
RAIN RM13 144 G4
SEVS/STOTM N15 119 M2
SUT SM1 221 K1
UX/CGN UB8 132 C6
Collingwood St WCHPL E1 140 A6
Collins Av STAN HA7 95 K10
Collins Dr RSLP HA4 113 K7
Collins Meadow
HLWW/ROY CM19 46 E1
Collinson St STHWK SE1 18 E2
Collinson Wk STHWK SE1 18 E2
Collins Rd CRAWW RH11 283 H9
HBRY N5 119 K9
Collins St BKHTH/KID SE3 161 K8
Collinswood Rd SLN SL2 108 G7
Collinwood Av PEND EN3 80 B7
Collinwood Gdns
GNTH/NBYPK IG2 122 C3
Coll's Rd PECK SE15 160 B7
Collum Green Rd SLN SL2 109 K8
Collyer Av CROY/NA CR0 222 F1
Collyer Pl PECK SE15 159 P7
Collyer Rd CROY/NA CR0 222 F1
LCOL/BKTW AL2 57 J3
Colman Cl EPSOM KT18 238 F3
Colman Pde EN * EN1 79 M7
Colman Rd CAN/RD E16 141 P7
Colmans Hl SHGR GU5 270 E10
Colman Wy REDH RH1 257 P8
Colmar Cl WCHPL E1 140 C6
Colmer Pl KTN/HRWW/W HA3 94 C8
Colmer Rd STRHM/NOR SW16 180 F10
Colmore Ms PECK SE15 160 A7
Colmore Rd PEND EN3 80 B8
Colnbrook By-Pass
DTCH/LGLY SL3 150 E5
WDR/YW UB7 151 L6
Colnbrook Cl LCOL/BKTW AL2 57 K3
Colnbrook St STHWK SE1 18 C4
Colndale Rd DTCH/LGLY SL3 151 H8
Colne TIL RM18 169 M2
Colne Av OXHEY WD19 73 J10
RKW/CH/CXG WD3 91 K3
WDR/YW UB7 151 M1
Colne Bank STWL/WRAY TW19 150 F9
Colne Cl SOCK/AV RM15 147 H9
Colne Ct HOR/WEW KT19 219 P1
Colnedale Rd UX/CGN UB8 111 N10
Colne Dr HARH RM3 105 N7
WOT/HER KT12 197 L10
Colne Gdns LCOL/BKTW AL2 57 K3
Colne Ldg BUSH * WD23 73 L8
Colne Md RKW/CH/CXG WD3 91 K3
Colne Orch IVER SL0 131 J8
Colne Rd CLPT E5 120 C9
WCHMH N21 99 L1
WHTN TW2 176 D4
Colne St PLSTW E13 141 M5
Colne Va UPMR RM14 126 D4
Colne Valley Trail
HGDN/ICK UB10 111 M8
RKW/CH/CXG WD3 91 M3
Colne Valley Wy IVER SL0 131 K8
STWL/WRAY TW19 173 H4
Colne Wy HHNE HP2 36 A1
Colne Way Ct WATN * WD24 73 L3
Colney Hatch La FBAR/BDGN N11 98 A7
Colney Heath La STALE/WH AL4 39 K7
Colney Rd DART DA1 187 N2
Cologne Rd BTSEA SW11 157 N10
Colombo Rd IL IG1 122 F6
Colombo St STHWK SE1 12 C10
Colomb St GNWCH SE10 161 K4
Colonel's La CHERT KT16 195 K6
Colonels Wk ENC/FH EN2 79 J6
Colonial Av WHTN TW2 176 B2
Colonial Dr CHSWK W4 155 P3
Colonial Rd EBED/NFELT TW14 174 F3
SL SL1 149 M1
Colonial Wy WATN WD24 73 K5
Colonnade BMSBY WC1N 11 L2
The Colonnades HAT * AL10 40 F2
The Colonnade CHES/WCR EN8 62 C4
DEPT * SE8 160 E3
STALW/RED * AL3 38 A4
Colonsay HHS/BOV HP3 36 D8
Colonsay Rd CRAWW RH11 283 L10
Colosseum Ter CAMTN NW1 10 F1
Colson Pth LOU IG10 82 D8
Colson Rd CROY/NA CR0 203 L9
LOU IG10 82 E8
Colson Wy STRHM/NOR SW16 180 D7
Colsterworth Rd
SEVS/STOTM N15 119 N2
Colston Av CAR SM5 221 P1
Colston Crs CHESW EN7 61 J3
Colston Rd FSTGT E7 142 A1
MORT/ESHN SW14 155 P10
Coltash Rd CRAWE RH10 284 B8
Colt Hatch HLW CM20 28 E9
Colthurst Crs FSBYPK N4 119 J7
Colthurst Gdns HOD EN11 45 H2
Coltishall Rd HCH RM12 145 K1
Coltness Crs ABYW SE2 163 L4
Colton Gdns TOTM N17 119 K1
Colton Rd HRW HA1 114 D3
Coltsfoot WGCE AL7 23 L7
Coltsfoot Ct GRAYS RM17 168 A5
Coltsfoot Dr GU GU1 250 E7
WDR/YW UB7 131 P8
Coltsfoot La OXTED RH8 261 L9
Coltsfoot Pth HARH RM3 105 L8
The Coltsfoot HHW HP1 35 H7
Coltstead HART DA3 211 K10
Columbas Dr HAMP * NW3 117 N6
Columbia Av EDGW HA8 95 N9
RSLP HA4 113 J6
WPK KT4 200 C7
Columbia Rd BETH E2 7 L9
PLSTW * E13 141 L6
Columbia Whf PEND * EN3 80 D9
Columbia Wharf Rd
GRAYS RM17 167 M5
Columbine Av EHAM E6 142 B7
SAND/SEL CR2 223 J4
Columbine Wy HARH RM3 105 M9
LEW * SE13 161 H8
Columbus Gdns NTHWD HA6 93 H9
Colview Ct ELTH/MOT SE9 184 A5
Colvers HLWE CM17 31 K9
Colvestone Crs HACK E8 119 N10
Colville Est IS N1 7 H6
Colville Gdns LTWR GU18 212 A7
NTGHL W11 8 D6
Colville Houses NTGHL W11 8 C5
Colville Ms NTGHL W11 8 D6
Colville Pl FITZ W1T 11 H4
Colville Rd ACT W3 155 N2
ED N9 100 A2
NTGHL W11 8 D6
WALTH E17 100 D10
WAN E11 121 H8
Colville Sq NTGHL W11 8 C6
Colville Ter NTGHL W11 8 C6
Colvin Cl SYD SE26 182 B8
Colvin Gdns BARK/HLT IG6 102 F8
CHES/WCR EN8 80 C1
CHING E4 101 H4
SWFD E18 121 N2
Colvin Rd EHAM E6 142 B2
THHTH CR7 203 H5
Colwall Gdns WFD IG8 101 M6
Colwell Rd EDUL SE22 181 N1
Colwick Cl HGT N6 118 E5
Colwith Rd HMSMTH W6 156 F5
Colwood Gdns WIM/MER SW19 179 N10
Colworth Gv WALW SE17 18 F6
Colworth Rd CROY/NA CR0 203 P8
WAN E11 121 K4
Colwyn Av GFD/PVL UB6 134 E4
Colwyn Cl CRAWW RH11 283 H9
STRHM/NOR SW16 180 D8
Colwyn Crs HSLW TW3 154 B7
Colwyn Gn CDALE/KGS * NW9 116 B4
Colwyn Rd CRICK NW2 116 E8
Colyer Cl ELTH/MOT SE9 184 E5
Colyer Rd GVW DA11 190 A5
Colyers Cl ERITH DA8 164 E7
Colyers La ERITH DA8 164 D7
Colyton Cl ALP/SUD HA0 135 H1
WELL DA16 163 N7
WOKN/KNAP GU21 231 P4
Colyton Rd EDUL SE22 182 A1
Colyton Wy UED N18 99 P6
Combe Av BKHTH/KID SE3 161 L6
Combe Bank Dr RSEV TN14 245 P9
Combedale Rd GNWCH SE10 161 M4
Combe La EHSLY KT24 270 C1
SHGR GU5 270 A3
WOT/HER KT12 216 G5
Combemartin Rd
WAND/EARL SW18 179 H3
Comber Cl CRICK NW2 116 D8
Comber Gv CMBW SE5 159 K6
Combermere Cl WDSR SL4 148 G8
Combermere Rd BRXN/ST SW9 158 G9
MRDN SM4 201 L6
Combe Rd RGODL GU7 267 K9
WATW WD18 72 G10
Comberton Rd CLPT E5 120 A7
Combeside WOOL/PLUM SE18 163 J6
Combes Rd DAGW RM9 144 A2
Combe St HHW * HP1 35 M6
Combwell Crs ABYW SE2 163 K2
Comely Bank Rd WALTH E17 121 H3
Comeragh Cl WOKS/MYFD GU22 231 M5
Comeragh Ms WKENS W14 14 B8
Comeragh Rd WKENS W14 14 A8
Comerford Rd BROCKY SE4 160 D10
Comet Cl GSTN WD25 54 G10
MNPK E12 122 A9
PUR RM19 165 P3
Comet Pl DEPT SE8 160 F6
Comet Rd HAT AL10 40 C4
STWL/WRAY TW19 173 N3
Comet St DEPT SE8 160 F6
Comet Wy HAT AL10 40 D1
Comforts Farm Av OXTED RH8 261 L9
Comfrey Ct GRAYS RM17 168 A5
Commerce Rd BTFD TW8 155 H5
WDGN N22 98 G9
Commerce Wy CROY/NA CR0 202 G10
Commercial Pl GVE DA12 190 F2
Commercial Rd GU GU1 268 A1
STA TW18 173 K9
UED N18 99 M6
Commercial St WCHPL E1 13 L2
Commercial Wy PECK SE15 159 N7
WLSDN NW10 135 N4
WOKN/KNAP GU21 232 C3
Commerell Pl GNWCH SE10 161 L4
Commerell St GNWCH SE10 161 K4
Commodore Pde
STRHM/NOR * SW16 180 G10
Commodore St WCHPL E1 140 C7
Common Cl WOKN/KNAP GU21 214 A10
Commondale PUT/ROE SW15 156 F8
Commonfield Rd BNSTD SM7 221 K10
Commonfields CHOB/PIR GU24 212 E9
HLW CM20 29 H10
Common Gdns BERK HP4 34 E3
Common Gate Rd
RKW/CH/CXG WD3 70 G9
Common La ADL/WDHM KT15 215 M5
ESH/CLAY KT10 218 F4
GSTN WD25 74 D4
KGLGY WD4 54 A4
RDART DA2 187 H5
SL SL1 108 C8
WDSR SL4 149 H4
Common Rd BARN SW13 156 D9
DTCH/LGLY SL3 150 D3
ESH/CLAY KT10 218 F3
RBRW/HUT CM13 107 P6
REDH RH1 276 A2
RKW/CH/CXG WD3 70 G8
STAN HA7 94 C4
WAB EN9 46 B7
WDSR SL4 148 C3
WDSR SL4 148 F2
Common Side EPSOM KT18 237 M1
Commonside GT/LBKH KT23 235 P8
HAYES BR2 225 P1
Commonside Cl BELMT SM2 221 L7
COUL/CHIP CR5 241 J6
Commonside East MTCM CR4 202 B3
Commonside Rd HLWS CM18 47 J5
Commons La HHNE HP2 35 P5
The Commons WGCE AL7 23 K8
The Common BERK HP4 34 C3
EA W5 135 K10
HAT AL10 40 D3
KGLGY WD4 53 K8
NWDGN UB2 153 L3
RAD WD7 56 G7
RKW/CH/CXG * WD3 71 H9
STAN HA7 94 E3
Commonwealth Av
HYS/HAR UB3 132 E8
SHB W12 136 E9
Commonwealth Rd CTHM CR3 241 P9
TOTM N17 99 P8
Commonwealth Wy ABYW SE2 163 L4
Common Whf WARE SG12 26 D2
Common Wd SLN SL2 109 H9
Community Cl HEST TW5 153 J7
HGDN/ICK * UB10 112 C8
Community Rd GFD/PVL UB6 134 B3
SRTFD E15 121 J10
Como Rd FSTH SE23 182 D5
Como St ROMW/RG RM7 124 E3
Compass Hl RCHPK/HAM TW10 177 J2
Compassion Cl CRAWW RH11 283 H8
Compayne Gdns KIL/WHAMP NW6 2 G3
Comper Cl CRAWW RH11 283 H9
Comport Gn CROY/NA CR0 225 K8
Compton Av EHAM E6 142 A4
GPK RM2 125 J1
HGT N6 117 P5
IS N1 6 C2
RBRW/HUT CM13 107 P3
Compton Cl CAMTN NW1 4 F10
CRICK NW2 116 G8
EDGW HA8 95 P8
ESH/CLAY KT10 218 C3
WEA W13 134 F8
Compton Crs CHSGTN KT9 219 K3
CHSWK W4 155 P5
NTHLT UB5 133 L3
TOTM N17 99 K8
Compton Gdns LCOL/BKTW AL2 56 A
Compton Pas FSBYE EC1V 12 D
Compton Pl ERITH DA8 164 C
OXHEY WD19 93 M
STPAN WC1H 11 L
Compton Ri PIN HA5 113 M
Compton Rd CROY/NA CR0 204 A
HYS/HAR UB3 132 F
IS N1 6 D
WCHMH N21 99 J
WIM/MER SW19 179
WLSDN NW10 136 C
Compton St FSBYE EC1V 12 C
Compton Ter IS N1 6 C
WCHMH * N21 99 H
Comreddy Cl ENC/FH EN2 79
Comus Pl WALW SE17 19
Comyne Rd WATN WD24 72 C
Comyn Rd BTSEA SW11 157 P
Comyns Cl CAN/RD E16 141 L
Comyns Rd DAGW RM9 144 B
The Comyns BUSH WD23 94 B
Conant Ms WCHPL E1 13 N
Conaways Cl EW KT17 220 D
Concanon Rd BRXS/STRHM SW2 158 G
Concert Hall Ap STHWK SE1 11 P
Concord Cl NTHLT UB5 133
Concorde Cl HSLW TW3 154 A
UX/CGN UB8 131 P
Concorde Dr EHAM E6 142 C
HHNE HP2 35 N
Concorde Wy SL SL1 149 H
Concord Rd ACT W3 135 N
PEND EN3 80 B
Condell Rd VX/NE SW8 158 D
Conder St POP/IOD E14 140 D
Condor Ct GUW GU2 267 F
Condor Rd STA TW18 195 M
Condover Crs WOOL/PLUM SE18 162 E
Condray Pl BTSEA SW11 157 P
Conduit Ct COVGDN * WC2E 11 L
Conduit La DTCH/LGLY SL3 150 E
HOD EN11 44 F
SAND/SEL CR2 223 F
UED N18 100 E
Conduit La East HOD EN11 44 C
Conduit Ms BAY/PAD W2 9 L
Conduit Pas BAY/PAD W2 9 L
Conduit Pl BAY/PAD W2 9 L
Conduit Rd WOOL/PLUM SE18 162 E
SL SL1 128 E
Conduit St CONDST W1S 10 F
The Conduit REDH RH1 259
Conduit Wy WLSDN NW10 135 P
Conegar Ct SL SL1 129 K
Conewood St HBRY N5 119
Coney Acre DUL SE21 181 K
Coneyberry REDH RH1 275 M
Coney Burrows CHING E4 101 K
Coneybury REDH RH1 259 M
Coneybury Cl WARL CR6 242 A
Coney Cl CRAWW RH11 283
HAT AL10 40 E
Coneydale WGCW AL8 22 C
Coney Gv UX/CGN UB8 132 A
Coney Hall Pde WWKM * BR4 205 K
Coney Hill Rd WWKM BR4 205 M
Coney Wy VX/NE SW8 17 N
Conference Cl CHING E4 101 H
Conference Rd ABYW SE2 163 M
Conford Dr RGUE GU4 268 E
Congleton Gv WOOL/PLUM SE18 162 F
Congo Rd WOOL/PLUM SE18 162 C
Congress Rd ABYW SE2 163 M
Congreve Rd ELTH/MOT SE9 162 C
WAB EN9 63 K
Congreve St WALW SE17 19
Conical Cnr ENC/FH EN2 79 K
Coniers Wy RGUE GU4 250 E
Conifer Av CRW RM5 104 C
HART DA3 211 K
Conifer Cl CHESW EN7 61 N
ORP BR6 226 C
REIG RH2 257 K
Conifer Dr BRW CM14 107
Conifer Gdns EN EN1 79 L
STRHM/NOR SW16 180
SUT SM1 201
Conifer La EGH TW20 172 F
Conifer Pk EW KT17 220 E
Conifers WEY KT13 216 F
Conifers Cl TEDD TW11 176 G
The Conifers GSTN WD25 73 N
HHW * HP1 35
Conifer Wk WDSR * SL4 148
Conifer Wy ALP/SUD HA0 115 H
HYS/HAR UB3 133 H
SWLY BR8 208
Coniger Rd FUL/PGN SW6 157 K
Coningesby Dr WAT WD17 72 F
Coningham Ms SHB W12 136 D
Coningham Rd SHB W12 156 E
Coningsby Bank STAL AL1 38 B
Coningsby Cl BRKMPK AL9 40 F
Coningsby Cottages EA W5 155
Coningsby Ct RAD * WD7 74
Coningsby Dr POTB/CUF EN6 59 N
Coningsby Gdns CHING E4 100
Coningsby Rd EA W5 155
FSBYPK N4 119
SAND/SEL CR2 223
Conington Rd LEW SE13 160
Conisbee Ct STHGT/OAK N14 78
Conisborough Crs CAT SE6 183
Coniscliffe Cl CHST BR7 206
Coniscliffe Rd PLMGR N13 99
Conista Ct WOKN/KNAP GU21 231
Coniston Av BARK IG11 143
GFD/PVL UB6 134
UPMR RM14 125
WELL DA16 163
Coniston Cl BARN SW13 156
BXLYHN DA7 164
CHSWK W4 155
CRAWW RH11 282
DART DA1 187
ERITH DA8 164
HHS/BOV HP3 36
MRDN SM4 200
Coniston Ct BAY/PAD * W2 9
LTWR GU18 212
Coniston Crs SL SL1 128
Conistone Wy HOLWY N7 5
Coniston Gdns BELMT * SM2 221
CDALE/KGS NW9 116
ED N9 100
PIN HA5 113
REDBR IG4 122
WBLY HA9 115
Coniston Rd BMLY BR1 183
BXLYHN DA7 164

COUL/CHIP CR5 240 D2
CROY/NA CR0 203 P7
KGLGY WD4 54 A4
MUSWH N10 98 C10
TOTM N17 99 P7
WHTN TW2 176 A2
WOKS/MYFD GU22 232 E6
oniston Wy CHSGTN KT9 199 K10
EGH TW20 172 E10
HCH RM12 125 H10
REDH RH1 257 P9
onlan St NKENS W10 8 A1
onley Rd WLSDN NW10 136 B1
onley St GNWCH * SE10 161 K4
onnaught Av ASHF TW15 173 P7
CDH/CHF RM16 167 N1
CHING E4 101 J1
EBAR EN4 98 A2
EN EN1 79 M6
HSLWW TW4 175 M1
LOU IG10 82 A8
MORT/ESHN SW14 155 P9
onnaught Br CAN/RD E16 142 A10
onnaught Cl BAY/PAD W2 9 N6
EN EN1 79 M6
HHNE HP2 36 B4
LEY * E10 120 D7
SUT SM1 201 N9
UX/CGN * UB8 132 D7
onnaught Crs CHOB/PIR GU24 230 E6
onnaught Dr GLDGN NW11 117 K2
WEY KT13 216 A7
onnaught Gdns BERK HP4 33 L2
CRAWE RH10 283 N5
MRDN SM4 201 M5
MUSWH N10 118 C3
PLMGR N13 99 J5
onnaught Hl LOU IG10 82 A8
onnaught La IL IG1 122 F7
onnaught Ms FUL/PGN * SW6 157 H7
HAMP * NW3 117 P10
WOOL/PLUM SE18 162 D4
onnaught Pl BAY/PAD W2 10 A7
onnaught Rd BAR EN5 78 A10
CAN/RD E16 142 A9
CHING * E4 101 K1
CHOB/PIR GU24 230 E6
FSBYPK N4 119 H5
HARP AL5 20 A2
HCH RM12 125 L8
HPTN TW12 176 C8
IL IG1 122 G7
KTN/HRWW/W HA3 94 E9
NWMAL KT3 200 B4
RCHPK/HAM * TW10 177 L1
SL SL1 149 N1
STALW/RED AL3 38 B4
SUT SM1 201 N9
WALTH * E17 120 F3
WAN E11 121 J6
WEA W13 134 G9
WLSDN NW10 136 B4
WOOL/PLUM SE18 162 D4
onnaught Sq BAY/PAD W2 9 P6
onnaught St BAY/PAD W2 9 P6
onnaught Wy PLMGR N13 99 J5
onnell Crs EA W5 135 L6
onnemara Cl BORE * WD6 75 P10
onnington Crs CHING E4 101 J4
onnop Rd PEND EN3 80 C4
onnor Cl BARK/HLT IG6 102 F9
onnor Rd DAGW RM9 124 A9
onnor St HOM * E9 140 C3
onolly Rd HNWL W7 134 D10
onquerors Hl STALE/WH AL4 21 K3
onquest Rd ADL/WDHM KT15 215 K2
onrad Cl CDH/CHF RM16 167 N1
onrad Dr WPK KT4 200 F8
onrad Gdns CDH/CHF RM16 167 M1
onsfield Av NWMAL KT3 200 D4
onsort Cl BRW CM14 107 H6
FBAR/BDGN N11 98 A6
onsort Ms ISLW TW7 176 C2
onsort Rd PECK SE15 160 A8
onsort Wy HORL RH6 280 B4
onsort Wy East HORL RH6 280 C5
ons St STHWK * SE1 18 B1
onstable Av CAN/RD E16 141 N10
onstable Cl GLDGN NW11 117 L4
YEAD UB4 132 D4
onstable Crs SEVS/STOTM N15 119 P3
onstable Gdns EDGW HA8 95 M9
ISLW TW7 176 C1
onstable Ms BCTR RM8 123 L10
onstable Rd GVW DA11 190 B6
onstable Wk DUL SE21 181 M6
onstance Crs HAYES BR2 205 L8
onstance Rd CROY/NA CR0 203 J7
EN EN1 79 M10
SUT SM1 221 M1
WHTN TW2 176 A3
onstance St CAN/RD E16 142 B10
onstantine Rd HAMP NW3 117 P10
onstitution Hl GVE DA12 190 F4
WHALL SW1A 16 E1
WOKS/MYFD GU22 232 B4
onstitution Ri
WOOL/PLUM SE18 162 D7
onsul Gdns SWLY * BR8 187 H10
ontent St WALW SE17 18 F6
ontessa Cl ORP BR6 227 H2
ontrol Tower Rd HTHAIR TW6 152 B9
onvent Cl BECK BR3 183 H10
onvent Gdns EA W5 155 H3
NTGHL W11 8 B6
onvent Hl NRWD SE19 181 K9
onvent Rd ASHF TW15 174 C8
WDSR SL4 148 F8
onvent Wy NWDGN UB2 153 K3
onway Cl RAIN RM13 145 H2
STAN HA7 94 F7
onway Crs CHDH RM6 123 M5
GFD/PVL UB6 134 D4
onway Dr ASHF TW15 174 D9
BELMT SM2 221 L3
HYS/HAR UB3 152 D2
onway Gdns ENC/FH EN2 79 M4
GRAYS RM17 167 N6
MTCM CR4 202 E4
WBLY HA9 115 H5
nway Gv ACT W3 136 A7
nway Ms FITZ W1T 10 G3
nway Rd CRICK NW2 116 F7
FELT TW13 175 L8
HSLWW TW4 175 N3
MDHD SL6 128 A8
RYNPK SW20 200 F1
SEVS/STOTM N15 119 K3
STHGT/OAK N14 98 F4
WOOL/PLUM SE18 162 G3
Conway St FITZ W1T 10 G2
Conybeare HAMP NW3 3 P3
Conybury Cl WAB EN9 63 M8
Conyers HLW CM20 28 F9
Conyers Cl WOT/HER KT12 217 L2
Conyer's Rd STRHM/NOR SW16 180 E8
Conyer St BOW * E3 140 D4
Conyers Wy LOU IG10 82 E7
Cooden Cl BMLY BR1 183 N10
Cookes Cl WAN E11 121 L7
Cookes La CHEAM SM3 221 H3
Cookham Cl NWDGN UB2 154 A2
Cookham Dene Cl CHST BR7 206 G1
Cookham Rd SWLY BR8 208 B1
Cookhill Rd ABYW SE2 163 L1
Cook Rd CRAWE RH10 283 P9
Cook's Cl CRW RM5 104 D9
Cooks Ferry Rbt UED N18 100 D6
Cook's Hole Rd ENC/FH EN2 79 J4
Cooks Md BUSH WD23 74 A10
HORS RH12 282 A6
Cooks Meadow HORS RH12 282 A6
Cookson Gv ERITH DA8 164 C6
Cook's Rd SRTFD E15 140 G4
WALW SE17 18 C9
Cooks Spinney HLW CM20 29 K9
Cooks Vennel HHW HP1 35 K4
Cooks Wy HAT AL10 40 E6
Coolfin Rd CAN/RD E16 141 M8
Coolgardie Av CHIG IG7 102 D4
CHING E4 101 J6
Coolgardie Rd ASHF TW15 174 D8
Coolhurst Rd CEND/HSY/T N8 118 E4
Cool Oak Br CDALE/KGS NW9 116 C5
Cool Oak La CDALE/KGS NW9 116 C5
Coomassie Rd MV/WKIL W9 8 C1
Coombe Av CROY/NA CR0 223 M1
RSEV TN14 247 J6
Coombe Bank NWMAL KT3 200 B1
Coombe Cl CRAWW RH11 283 N4
EDGW HA8 95 L10
HSLW TW3 153 P10
Coombe Cnr WCHMH N21 99 J2
Coombe Crs HPTN TW12 175 M10
Coombe Dr ADL/WDHM KT15 215 J3
RSLP HA4 113 J6
Coombe End KUTN/CMB KT2 178 A10
Coombefield Cl NWMAL KT3 200 B5
Coombe Gdns BERK HP4 33 L4
NWMAL KT3 200 C4
RYNPK SW20 200 D2
Coombe Hill Ct WDSR SL4 148 C10
Coombe Hill Gld KUTN/CMB KT2 178 B10
Coombe Hill Rd KUTN/CMB KT2 178 B10
RKW/CH/CXG WD3 91 K1
Coombe House Cha NWMAL KT3 200 A1
Coombehurst Cl EBAR EN4 78 A6
Coombelands La
ADL/WDHM KT15 215 K3
Coombe La CROY/NA CR0 224 A2
RGUW GU3 249 H4
RYNPK SW20 200 C1
Coombe La West KUTN/CMB KT2 199 P1
NWMAL KT3 178 B10
Coombe Lea BMLY BR1 206 B3
Coombe Ldg CHARL SE7 161 P5
Coombe Mnr CHOB/PIR GU24 230 G1
Coombe Neville KUTN/CMB KT2 177 P10
Coombe Pk KUTN/CMB KT2 177 P8
Coombe Ridings KUTN/CMB KT2 177 P8
Coombe Ri BRWN CM15 107 L2
KUTN/CMB KT2 199 P1
Coombe Rd BUSH WD23 94 B1
CHSWK W4 156 B4
CROY/NA CR0 223 N1
GVE DA12 190 F5
HARH RM3 125 N1
HPTN TW12 175 N9
KUTN/CMB KT2 199 M1
NWMAL KT3 200 B3
RSEV TN14 247 K1
SAND/SEL CR2 223 M1
SYD SE26 182 A7
WDGN N22 99 H10
WEA W13 154 G2
WLSDN NW10 116 A8
Coomber Wy CROY/NA CR0 202 E7
Coombes Rd DAGW RM9 144 A3
LCOL/BKTW AL2 57 H2
The Coombe BRKHM/BTCW RH3 256 A7
Coombe V CFSP/GDCR SL9 110 B6
Coombe Vls WAND/EARL * SW18 179 K3
Coombe Wy BF/WBF KT14 216 A8
Coombe-Wood Dr CHDH RM6 124 A4
Coombe Wood Hl PUR/KEN CR8 223 K8
Coombe Wood Rd
KUTN/CMB KT2 177 P8
Coombfield Dr RDART DA2 188 C7
Coombs St IS N1 6 D8
Coomer Pl FUL/PGN SW6 14 D10
Cooperage Cl TOTM N17 99 N7
Cooper Av WALTH E17 100 C9
Cooper Cl GRH DA9 188 D1
HORL RH6 281 H4
STHWK SE1 18 B2
Cooper Crs CAR SM5 202 A10
Cooper Rd BFOR GU20 212 C3
CRICK NW2 116 D10
CROY/NA CR0 223 H2
GU GU1 268 B2
HDN NW4 116 G4
Cooper Rw CRAWE RH10 283 N10
Coopersale Common EPP CM16 65 N4
Coopersale La EPP CM16 83 K3
Coopersale Rd HOM E9 120 C10
Coopers Cl CHIG IG7 103 L3
DACE RM10 144 C1
EYN DA4 210 B1
STA TW18 173 H8
WCHPL E1 140 B6
Coopers Ct WARE * SG12 26 D2
Coopers Crs BORE WD6 75 P5
Coopers Green La HAT AL10 21 P10
STALE/WH AL4 39 L3
WGCW AL8 22 C9
Cooper Shaw Rd TIL RM18 168 G6
Coopers Hl CHONG CM5 67 P5
Coopers Hill Dr CHOB/PIR GU24 230 B6
Cooper's Hill La EGH TW20 171 P6
Cooper's Hill Rd REDH RH1 258 G9
Coopers La CAMTN NW1 5 K8
LEE/GVPK SE12 183 N5
LEY E10 120 G6
POTB/CUF EN6 59 P5
Coopers Lane Rd POTB/CUF EN6 60 B9
Cooper's Rd GVW DA11 190 B4
POTB/CUF EN6 59 M6
STHWK SE1 19 M8
Coopers Rw IVER SL0 130 F6
TWRH EC3N 13 L7
Cooper St CAN/RD E16 141 L7
Cooper's Yd NRWD SE19 181 M9
Cooper Wy BERK HP4 34 A5
SL SL1 148 G2
Coote Rd BCTR RM8 124 A8
BXLYHN DA7 164 A7
Copeland Rd LEY E10 120 G3
PECK SE15 159 P8
Copeman Cl SYD SE26 182 B8
Copenhagen Pl POP/IOD E14 140 E8
Copenhagen St IS N1 5 M6
Copenhagen Wy WOT/HER KT12 197 J10
Cope Pl KENS W8 14 E4
Copers Cope Rd BECK BR3 182 E10
Cope St BERM/RHTH SE16 160 C3
Copford Wk IS * N1 6 E5
Copgate Pth STRHM/NOR SW16 180 G9
Copland Av ALP/SUD HA0 115 J10
Copland Cl ALP/SUD HA0 115 H10
Copland Ms ALP/SUD HA0 135 K1
Copland Rd ALP/SUD HA0 135 K1
Copleigh Dr KWD/TDW/WH KT20 239 H6
Copleston Rd PECK SE15 159 N9
Copley Cl CMBW SE5 18 E10
HNWL * W7 134 D6
REDH RH1 257 P8
WOKN/KNAP GU21 231 K5
Copley Dene BMLY BR1 206 A1
Copley Pk STRHM/NOR SW16 180 G9
Copley Rd STAN HA7 95 H6
Copley Wy KWD/TDW/WH KT20 238 G6
Copmans Wick RKW/CH/CXG WD3 70 G9
Coppard Gdns CHSGTN KT9 219 H3
Coppelia Rd BKHTH/KID SE3 161 L10
Coppen Rd BCTR RM8 124 A5
Copperas St DEPT SE8 160 G5
Copper Beech Cl CLAY IG5 102 D9
GVE DA12 190 G3
HHW HP1 35 J9
STMC/STPC BR5 207 M5
WDSR SL4 148 C7
WOKS/MYFD GU22 231 N7
Copper Beeches HARP AL5 20 A2
Copper Beech Rd SOCK/AV RM15 147 H5
Copper Cl NRWD SE19 181 N10
Copperdale Rd HYS/HAR UB3 153 H1
Copperfield CHIG IG7 102 G7
Copperfield Av UX/CGN UB8 132 B6
Copperfield Cl GVE DA12 191 J4
PUR/KEN CR8 223 K7
Copperfield Dr SEVS/STOTM N15 119 N2
Copperfield Gdns BRW CM14 106 G2
Copperfield Ri ADL/WDHM KT15 215 J2
Copperfield Rd BOW E3 140 D6
THMD SE28 143 M8
Copperfields BEAC HP9 88 D6
BGR/WK TN15 247 N3
LHD/OX KT22 236 B8
SUN * TW16 174 G9
WGCE AL7 23 M6
Copperfield St STHWK SE1 18 D1
Copperfields Wk BGR/WK TN15 247 N3
Copperfields Wy HARH RM3 105 L9
Copperfield Wy CHST BR7 184 F9
PIN HA5 113 N2
Coppergate Cl BMLY BR1 205 N1
Copperkins Gv AMS HP6 68 G2
Coppermead Cl CRICK NW2 116 F8
Copper Mill Dr ISLW TW7 154 E8
Coppermill La RKW/CH/CXG WD3 91 J8
Copper Mill La TOOT SW17 179 M7
Coppermill La WALTH E17 120 B4
Coppermill Lock DEN/HRF * UB9 91 K8
Coppermill Rd STWL/WRAY TW19 172 E2
Copper Rdg CFSP/GDCR SL9 90 C6
Copper Rw STHWK SE1 13 L10
Copperwood HERT/BAY SG13 25 N5
Coppetts Cl NFNCH/WDSP N12 98 A8
Coppetts Rd MUSWH N10 98 A9
Coppice Cl BECK BR3 204 G4
GUW GU2 249 J9
HAT AL10 40 C8
KTN/HRWW/W HA3 94 E7
RSLP * HA4 112 D4
RYNPK SW20 200 F3
Coppice Dr PUT/ROE SW15 178 D2
STWL/WRAY TW19 172 A3
Coppice Hatch HLWS CM18 46 G3
Coppice La REIG RH2 257 J8
Coppice Pth CHIG IG7 103 L5
Coppice Rw EPP CM16 82 G2
The Coppice ASHF TW15 174 C9
BAR * EN5 77 L10
BXLY DA5 186 E6
ENC/FH EN2 79 J8
HHNE HP2 36 C5
OXHEY WD19 73 K10
WDR/YW UB7 131 P8
Coppice Wk CRAWE RH10 284 B5
TRDG/WHET N20 97 K4
Coppice Wy SLN SL2 109 J7
SWFD E18 121 L2
Coppies Gv FBAR/BDGN N11 98 C5
Copping Cl CROY/NA CR0 223 M1
The Coppings HOD EN11 26 F10
Coppins Cl BERK HP4 33 K5
Coppins La IVER SL0 131 J7
The Coppins KTN/HRWW/W HA3 94 D7
Coppock Cl BTSEA SW11 157 P8
Coppsfield E/WMO/HCT KT8 197 P3
Copse Av WWKM BR4 204 G10
Copse Bank BGR/WK TN15 247 N6
Copse Cl CHARL SE7 161 N5
NTHWD HA6 92 D9
RGUE GU4 268 F6
SL SL1 128 E10
WDR/YW UB7 151 N2
Copse Crs CRAWW RH11 283 M6
Copse Edge RGUE * GU4 250 F7
Copse Edge Av EW KT17 220 C9
Copse Gld SURB KT6 199 J8
Copse Hl BELMT SM2 221 L4
HLWW/ROY CM19 46 E4
PUR/KEN CR8 222 F9
RYNPK SW20 200 D1
Copse Hill Cl HHS/BOV HP3 52 G4
Copse La BEAC HP9 89 K8
HORL RH6 280 D3
Copsem Dr ESH/CLAY KT10 218 A3
Copsem La ESH/CLAY KT10 218 B5
LHD/OX KT22 218 B7
Copsem Wy ESH/CLAY KT10 218 B3
Copsen Wd LHD/OX KT22 218 B7
Copse Rd COB KT11 217 J9
REIG RH2 275 M2
WOKN/KNAP GU21 231 L4
Copse Side HART DA3 211 K3
RGODL GU7 267 J9
The Copse AMSS HP7 69 H4
CHING E4 101 L2
CTHM CR3 259 P2
EFNCH * N2 118 A1
GT/LBKH KT23 236 A9
HERT/BAY SG13 25 P5
HHW HP1 35 H4
REDH RH1 276 F2
WDSR * SL4 170 A4
Copse Vw SAND/SEL CR2 224 D5
Copse Wy CSHM HP5 50 F3
Copse Wd IVER SL0 130 G3
Copsewood Cl BFN/LL DA15 185 H2
Copsewood Rd WATN WD24 73 J5
Copse Wood Wy NTHWD HA6 92 D9
Copshall Cl HLWS CM18 47 H5
Copsleigh Av REDH RH1 276 B7
Copsleigh Cl REDH RH1 276 B6
Copsleigh Wy REDH RH1 276 B6
Coptefield Dr BELV DA17 163 N2
Coptfold Rd BRW CM14 107 H3
Copthall Av LOTH EC2R 13 H5
Copthall Cl CFSP/GDCR SL9 90 C8
Copthall Cnr CFSP/GDCR SL9 90 B8
Copthall Dr MLHL NW7 96 D8
Copthall Gdns MLHL NW7 96 D8
TWK * TW1 176 F4
Copthall La CFSP/GDCR SL9 90 B8
Copthall Rd East
HGDN/ICK UB10 112 B7
Copthall Rd West
HGDN/ICK UB10 112 B7
Copthall Wy ADL/WDHM KT15 215 J6
Copt Hill La KWD/TDW/WH KT20 239 H6
Copthorne Av BAL SW12 180 E3
BARK/HLT IG6 102 E7
BROX EN10 44 E6
HAYES BR2 206 C9
Copthorne Bank CRAWE RH10 285 J2
HORL RH6 281 K9
Copthorne Cl RKW/CH/CXG WD3 72 A9
SHPTN TW17 196 D6
Copthorne Common Rd
CRAWE RH10 285 J3
Copthorne Ct LHD/OX * KT22 236 F7
Copthorne Dr LTWR GU18 212 A6
Copthorne Gdns EMPK RM11 125 P3
Copthorne Ms HYS/HAR UB3 152 F3
Copthorne Ri PUR/KEN CR8 223 L9
Copthorne Rd CRAWE RH10 284 E5
LHD/OX KT22 236 G6
RKW/CH/CXG WD3 72 A10
Copthorne Wy CRAWE RH10 284 G3
Coptic St NOXST/BSQ WC1A 11 L4
Copton Cl BOW E3 140 F7
Copwood Cl NFNCH/WDSP N12 97 N5
Coral Cl CHDH RM6 123 M1
Coral Gdns HHNE HP2 36 A5
Coraline Cl STHL UB1 133 N5
Corals Md WGCE AL7 22 G6
Coral St STHWK SE1 18 B2
Coram Cl BERK HP4 33 P6
Coram St STPAN WC1H 11 L2
Coran Cl ED N9 100 C1
Corban Rd HSLW TW3 153 P9
Corbar Cl EBAR EN4 77 N4
Corbet Cl MTCM CR4 202 B8
Corbet Pl WCHPL E1 13 L3
Corbet Rd EW KT17 220 B6
Corbets Av UPMR RM14 126 A10
Corbets Tey Rd UPMR RM14 126 A5
Corbett Cl CROY/NA CR0 225 J8
Corbett Gv FBAR/BDGN N11 98 F8
Corbett Rd WALTH E17 101 J10
WAN E11 121 P4
Corbett's La BERM/RHTH SE16 160 B3
Corbicum WAN E11 121 K5
Corbin's La RYLN/HDSTN HA2 114 A8
Corbridge Crs BETH E2 140 A4
Corby Cl EGH TW20 171 P9
LCOL/BKTW AL2 55 P1
Corby Crs ENC/FH EN2 78 F8
Corby Dr EGH TW20 171 P9
Corbylands Rd BFN/LL DA15 185 H3
Corbyn St FSBYPK N4 118 F6
Corby Rd WLSDN NW10 135 P4
Corcorans BRWN CM15 86 G10
Cordelia Cl HNHL SE24 159 J10
Cordelia Gdns STWL/WRAY TW19 173 P3
Cordelia Rd STWL/WRAY TW19 173 P3
Cordelia St POP/IOD E14 140 G8
Cordell Cl CHES/WCR EN8 62 D4
Corder Cl STALW/RED AL3 37 P9
Corderoy Pl CHERT KT16 195 H6
Cordingley Rd RSLP HA4 112 E6
Cording St POP/IOD E14 140 G7
Cordova Rd BOW E3 140 D5
Cordrey Gdns COUL/CHIP CR5 240 F1
Cordwell Rd LEW SE13 183 J1
Corelli Rd BKHTH/KID SE3 162 B7
Coresbrook Wy
WOKN/KNAP GU21 230 G4
Corfe Av RYLN/HDSTN HA2 113 P9
Corfe Cl ASHTD KT21 237 H4
BORE WD6 76 A7
HHS/BOV HP3 35 P8
YEAD UB4 133 K8
Corfe Gdns SL SL1 128 F9
Corfield Rd WCHMH N21 78 G9
Corfield St BETH E2 140 A5
Corfton Rd EA W5 135 K8
Coriander Av POP/IOD E14 141 J8
Coriander Crs GUW GU2 249 M5
Cories Cl BCTR RM8 123 N7
Corinium Cl WBLY HA9 115 L9
Corinium Ga STALW/RED AL3 37 P8
Corinne Rd ARCH N19 118 D9
Corinthian Manorway
ERITH DA8 164 E3
Corinthian Rd ERITH DA8 164 E3
Corkran Rd SURB KT6 199 J7
Cork St Ms CONDST W1S 10 G8
Corkscrew Hl WWKM BR4 205 H9
Cork St CONDST W1S 10 G8
Cork Tree Wy CHING E4 100 D6
Corlett St CAMTN NW1 9 N3
Cormongers La REDH RH1 258 E9
Cormont Rd CMBW SE5 159 J7
Cormorant Cl WALTH E17 100 C9
Cormorant Rd FSTGT E7 121 L10
Cornbury Rd EDGW HA8 95 J8
Corncroft HAT AL10 40 E2
Cornelia St HOLWY N7 5 P3
Cornell Cl SCUP DA14 185 P9
Cornell Wy CRW RM5 104 C6
Corner Farm Cl
KWD/TDW/WH KT20 238 F8
Cornerfield HAT AL10 40 E1
Corner Fielde
BRXS/STRHM * SW2 180 G4
Corner Gn BKHTH/KID SE3 161 M8
Corner Hall HHS/BOV HP3 35 M8
Corner Hall Av HHS/BOV HP3 35 N8
Corner Md CDALE/KGS NW9 96 C8
Corner Meadow HLWS CM18 47 K5
Corners WGCE AL7 23 K4
Cornerside ASHF TW15 174 D10
The Corner EA * W5 135 K10
Corney Reach Wy CHSWK W4 156 B6
Corney Rd CHSWK W4 156 B5
Cornfield Cl UX/CGN UB8 131 N4
Cornfield Crs BERK HP4 33 J2
Cornfield Rd BUSH WD23 74 A8
REIG RH2 275 M1
Cornfields HHW HP1 35 L7
RGODL GU7 267 L9
Cornflower La CROY/NA CR0 204 C8
Cornflower Ter EDUL SE22 182 A2
Cornflower Wy HARH RM3 105 M9
Cornford Cl HAYES BR2 205 M5
Cornford Gv BAL SW12 180 C5
Cornhill BANK EC3V 13 H6
Cornhill Cl ADL/WDHM KT15 195 L9
Cornhill Dr PEND EN3 80 D3
Cornish Gv PGE/AN SE20 204 A1
Corn Md WGCW AL8 22 F2
Corn Mill Dr ORP BR6 207 J7
Cornmill La LEW SE13 160 G9
Cornmow Dr WLSDN NW10 116 C10
Cornshaw Rd BCTR RM8 123 N6
Cornsland BRW CM14 107 J4
Cornthwaite Rd CLPT E5 120 B8
Cornwall Av BETH E2 140 B5
BF/WBF KT14 216 A10
ESH/CLAY KT10 218 E4
FNCH N3 97 K8
SLN SL2 129 H6
STHL UB1 133 N7
WDGN N22 98 F9
WELL DA16 163 H9
Cornwall Cl BARK IG11 143 J1
CHES/WCR EN8 62 D9
EMPK RM11 125 P2
WDSR SL4 148 D4
Cornwall Crs NTGHL W11 8 A7
Cornwall Dr STMC/STPC BR5 185 M10
Cornwall Gdns SKENS SW7 15 J4
SNWD * SE25 203 N4
WLSDN NW10 136 E1
Cornwall Gv CHSWK W4 156 B4
Cornwallis Av BFN/LL DA15 184 G5
ED N9 100 A3
Cornwallis Cl CTHM CR3 241 K8
ERITH DA8 164 G5
Cornwallis Gv ED N9 100 A3
Cornwallis Rd ARCH N19 118 F7
DAGW RM9 123 P9
ED N9 100 A3
WALTH E17 120 C2
WOOL/PLUM SE18 162 E2
Cornwallis Sq ARCH N19 118 F7
Cornwallis Wk ELTH/MOT SE9 162 C9
Cornwall Ms South SKENS SW7 15 J4
Cornwall Ms West SKENS * SW7 15 H4
Cornwall Rd BELMT SM2 221 J4
BRWN CM15 86 G9
CROY/NA CR0 203 J9
DART DA1 165 N9
FSBYPK N4 119 H5
HARP AL5 20 A1
HRW HA1 114 B4
PIN HA5 93 N8
RSLP HA4 112 G7
SEVS/STOTM N15 119 L3
STAL AL1 38 D8
STHWK SE1 12 A10
TWK TW1 176 F3
UED N18 99 P6
UX/CGN UB8 131 N1
Cornwall St WCHPL * E1 140 A9
Cornwall Ter CAMTN NW1 10 B2
Cornwall Terrace Ms
CAMTN NW1 10 B2
Cornwall Wy STA TW18 173 H9
Corn Wy WAN E11 121 J8
Cornwell Av GVE DA12 190 F6
Cornwell Rd WDSR SL4 171 M2
Cornwood Cl EFNCH N2 117 N3
Cornwood Dr WCHPL E1 140 B8
Cornworthy Rd BCTR RM8 123 M10
Corona Rd LEE/GVPK SE12 183 M3
Coronation Av DTCH/LGLY SL3 130 B8
TIL RM18 169 L3
WDSR SL4 149 L8
Coronation Cl BARK/HLT IG6 122 F2
BXLY DA5 185 N2
Coronation Dr HCH RM12 125 J10
Coronation Hl EPP CM16 65 J6
Coronation Rd HYS/HAR UB3 152 G3
PLSTW E13 141 P5
WARE SG12 26 C1
WLSDN NW10 135 L5
Coronation Vls WLSDN * NW10 135 N6
Coronet Pde ALP/SUD * HA0 135 K1
Coronet St IS N1 7 J10
The Coronet HORL RH6 280 D6
Corporation Av HSLWW TW4 153 M10
Corporation Row CLKNW EC1R 12 B1
Corporation St HOLWY N7 118 F10
SRTFD E15 141 K4
Corrance Rd BRXS/STRHM SW2 158 F10
Corran Wy SOCK/AV RM15 146 G9
Corri Av STHGT/OAK N14 98 E5
Corrib Dr SUT SM1 221 P2
Corrie Gdns VW GU25 193 P7
Corrie Rd ADL/WDHM KT15 215 N1
WOKS/MYFD GU22 232 E6
Corrigan Av COUL/CHIP CR5 240 B1
Corrigan Cl HDN NW4 116 F1
Corringham Ct STAL AL1 38 E5
Corringham Rd GLDGN NW11 117 K5
WBLY HA9 115 M7
Corringway EA W5 135 L7
GLDGN NW11 117 L5
Corris Gn CDALE/KGS * NW9 116 B4
Corsair Cl STWL/WRAY TW19 173 N3
Corsair Rd STWL/WRAY TW19 173 P3
Corscombe Cl KUTN/CMB KT2 177 P8
Corsehill St STRHM/NOR SW16 180 D9
Corsham St IS N1 7 H10
Corsica St HBRY N5 6 D1
Cortayne Rd FUL/PGN * SW6 157 J8
Cortina Dr DAGW RM9 144 D5
Cortis Rd PUT/ROE SW15 178 E2
Cortis Ter PUT/ROE SW15 178 E1
Corunna Rd VX/NE SW8 158 D7
Corunna Ter VX/NE SW8 158 D7
Corve La SOCK/AV RM15 146 G9
Corwell Gdns UX/CGN UB8 132 D8
Corwell La UX/CGN UB8 132 D8
Cory Dr RBRW/HUT CM13 107 N1
Coryton Pth MV/WKIL W9 8 D1

Cory-Wright Wy STALE/WH AL4 21 K2
Cosbycote Av HNHL SE24 181 K1
Cosdach Av WLGTN SM6 222 E4
Cosedge Crs CROY/NA CR0 223 H2
Cosgrove Cl WCHMH N21 99 J3
YEAD UB4 133 L6
Cosmo Pl RSQ WC1B 11 M3
Cosmur Cl SHB W12 156 C2
Cossall Wk PECK SE15 160 A7
Cosser St STHWK SE1 18 A3
Costa St PECK SE15 159 P8
Costead Manor Rd BRW CM14 106 G2
Costells Meadow BH/WHM TN16 262 G2
Costons Av GFD/PVL UB6 134 C5
Costons La GFD/PVL UB6 134 C5
Cosway St CAMTN NW1 9 P3
Cotall St POP/IOD E14 140 F8
Coteford Cl LOU IG10 82 E6
PIN HA5 113 H3
Coteford St TOOT SW17 180 A7
Cotelands CROY/NA CR0 203 M10
Cotesbach Rd CLPT E5 120 B8
Cotesmore Gdns BCTR RM8 123 M9
Cotesmore Rd HHW HP1 35 H7
Cotford Rd THHTH CR7 203 K4
Cotham St WALW SE17 18 F6
Cotherstone HOR/WEW KT19 220 A5
Cotherstone Rd
BRXS/STRHM SW2 180 G4
Cotland Acres REDH RH1 275 N2
Cotlandswick LCOL/BKTW AL2 57 H1
Cotleigh Av BXLY DA5 185 N5
Cotleigh Rd KIL/WHAMP NW6 2 E3
ROMW/RG RM7 124 E4
Cotman Cl EFNCH N2 117 M4
Cotmandene Crs
STMC/STPC BR5 207 L2
Cotman Gdns EDGW HA8 95 M10
Cotmans Cl HYS/HAR UB3 133 H10
Coton Rd WELL DA16 163 K9
Cotsford Av NWMAL KT3 199 P5
Cotsmoor STAL * AL1 38 E6
Cotswold HHNE HP2 35 P3
Cotswold Av BUSH WD23 74 B10
Cotswold Cl BXLYHN DA7 164 F7
CRAWW RH11 283 L7
ESH/CLAY KT10 198 E9
KUTN/CMB KT2 177 P9
SL SL1 148 G2
STA TW18 173 K8
STALE/WH AL4 39 H1
UX/CGN UB8 131 M3
Cotswold Gdns CRICK NW2 116 G7
GNTH/NBYPK IG2 122 G5
Cotswold Ga CRICK NW2 117 H6
Cotswold Gn ENC/FH EN2 78 G8
Cotswold Ri ORP BR6 207 J6
Cotswold Rd BELMT SM2 221 L6
GVW DA11 190 B6
HARH RM3 105 N10
HPTN TW12 175 P9
Cotswolds HAT AL10 40 D6
Cotswold St WNWD SE27 181 J7
Cotswold Wy ENC/FH EN2 78 G7
WPK KT4 200 F9
Cottage Av HAYES BR2 206 B8
Cottage Cl CHERT KT16 214 F3
RKW/CH/CXG WD3 72 A10
RSLP HA4 112 E6
WAT WD17 72 G6
Cottage Farm Wy EGH * TW20 194 F3
Cottage Field Cl SCUP DA14 185 M4
Cottage Gdns CHES/WCR EN8 62 B5
Cottage Gn CMBW SE5 159 L6
Cottage Gv BRXN/ST SW9 158 F9
SURB KT6 199 J6
Cottage Park Rd SLN SL2 109 J7
Cottage Pl CRAWE RH10 285 M2
SKENS SW7 15 N3
Cottage Rd HOR/WEW KT19 220 A4
Cottages Crs SEV TN13 246 F6
The Cottages EDGW * HA8 95 N8
Cottage St POP/IOD E14 140 G9
Cottenham Dr CDALE/KGS NW9 116 C1
RYNPK SW20 178 E10
Cottenham Park Rd
RYNPK SW20 200 D1
Cottenham Pl RYNPK SW20 178 E10
Cottenham Rd WALTH E17 120 E2
Cotterells HHW HP1 35 M8
Cotterells Hl HHW HP1 35 M6
Cotterill Rd SURB KT6 199 L9
Cottesbrooke Cl DTCH/LGLY SL3 150 G7
Cottesbrook St NWCR SE14 160 D6
Cottesloe Cl CHOB/PIR GU24 230 E2
Cottesloe Ms STHWK SE1 18 B3
Cottesmore Av CLAY IG5 102 C10
Cottesmore Gdns KENS W8 15 H3
Cottimore Av WOT/HER KT12 197 J8
Cottimore Crs WOT/HER KT12 197 J7
Cottimore La WOT/HER KT12 197 J7
Cottimore Ter WOT/HER KT12 197 J7
Cottingham Cha RSLP HA4 113 H8
Cottingham Rd PGE/AN SE20 182 C10
VX/NE SW8 158 G6
Cottington Rd FELT TW13 175 L7
Cottington St LBTH SE11 18 B7
Cotton Av ACT W3 136 A8
Cotton Cl DAGW RM9 143 M2
Cotton Dr HERT/BAY SG13 26 A4
Cotton Fld HAT AL10 40 E2
Cotton Gardens Est LBTH SE11 18 C6
Cottongrass Cl CROY/NA CR0 204 C8
Cotton Hl BMLY BR1 183 J7
Cotton La GRH DA9 188 B1
Cottonmill Crs STAL AL1 38 C7
Cottonmill La STAL AL1 38 C8
Cotton Rd POTB/CUF EN6 59 M7
Cotton Rw BTSEA SW11 157 M9
Cottons Ap ROMW/RG RM7 124 E3
Cotton's Gdns BETH E2 7 K9
Cotton St POP/IOD E14 141 H9
Cotts Wood Dr RGUE GU4 250 D5
Couchmore Av CLAY IG5 102 C10
ESH/CLAY KT10 198 D9
Coulgate St BROCKY SE4 160 D9
Coulsdon Court Rd
COUL/CHIP CR5 240 G2
Coulsdon La COUL/CHIP CR5 240 B5
Coulsdon Pl CTHM CR3 241 L8
Coulsdon Ri COUL/CHIP CR5 240 F3
Coulsdon Rd COUL/CHIP CR5 240 G2
CTHM CR3 241 K7
Coulser Cl HHW HP1 35 K3
Coulson Cl BCTR RM8 123 M6
Coulson St CHEL SW3 16 A7
Coulson Wy SL SL1 128 A7
Coulter Cl POTB/CUF EN6 60 E3
YEAD UB4 133 M6
Coulter Rd HMSMTH W6 156 E2
Coulton Av GVW DA11 190 B3
Council Av GVW DA11 189 P2
Councillor St CMBW SE5 159 K6
Counters Cl HHW HP1 35 K6
Counter St STHWK SE1 13 J9
Countess Cl DEN/HRF UB9 91 M10
Countess Rd KTTN NW5 118 D10
Countisbury Av EN EN1 99 N1
Countisbury Gdns
ADL/WDHM KT15 215 L2
Country Wy FELT TW13 175 K8
County Ga CHST BR7 184 F6
TRDG/WHET N20 77 L10
County Gv CMBW SE5 159 K7
County Oak La CRAWE RH10 283 N2
County Oak Wy CRAWW RH11 283 N3
County Pde BTFD * TW8 155 J6
County Rd EHAM E6 142 E7
THHTH CR7 203 J2
County St STHWK SE1 18 F4
Coupland Pl WOOL/PLUM SE18 162 F4
Courage Cl EMPK RM11 125 K4
Courcy Rd CEND/HSY/T N8 119 H1
Courier Rd DAGW RM9 144 D6
Courland Gv VX/NE SW8 158 F7
Courland Rd ADL/WDHM KT15 195 L10
Courland St VX/NE SW8 158 E7
Coursers Rd STALE/WH AL4 57 M3
The Course ELTH/MOT SE9 184 D6
Courtauld Rd ARCH N19 118 E6
Courtaulds KGLGY WD4 53 L6
Courtaulds Cl THMD SE28 143 K10
Court Av BELV DA17 164 A4
COUL/CHIP CR5 241 H4
HARH RM3 105 P8
Court Bushes Rd CTHM CR3 241 P5
Court Cl FELT TW13 176 A6
HAMP * NW3 3 L4
KTN/HRWW/W HA3 115 J1
Court Close Av FELT TW13 176 A6
Court Crs CHSGTN KT9 219 J3
SL SL1 129 J8
SWLY BR8 208 F4
Court Downs Rd BECK BR3 204 G2
Court Dr CROY/NA CR0 222 G1
HGDN/ICK UB10 132 A3
STAN HA7 95 K5
SUT SM1 221 P1
Courtenay Av BELMT SM2 221 K5
HGT N6 117 P5
KTN/HRWW/W HA3 94 A8
Courtenay Dr BECK BR3 205 J2
CDH/CHF RM16 167 L2
Courtenay Gdns UPMR RM14 126 B7
Courtenay Ms WALTH E17 120 D3
WOKN/KNAP GU21 232 D2
Courtenay Rd PGE/AN SE20 182 C10
WALTH E17 120 C3
WAN * E11 121 L8
WBLY * HA9 115 J8
WOKN/KNAP GU21 232 D2
WPK KT4 200 F10
Courtenay Sq LBTH SE11 18 A8
Courtenay St LBTH SE11 17 P7
Courten Ms STAN HA7 95 H8
Court Farm Av HOR/WEW KT19 220 A2
Court Farm Gdns
HOR/WEW * KT19 220 A7
Court Farm Pk WARL * CR6 241 P2
Court Farm Rd ELTH/MOT SE9 184 A5
NTHLT UB5 133 P2
WARL CR6 241 P4
Courtfield Av HRW * HA1 114 E3
Courtfield Cl BROX * EN10 44 F6
Courtfield Crs HRW HA1 114 E3
Courtfield Gdns DEN/HRF UB9 111 K8
ECT SW5 15 H6
RSLP HA4 112 G7
WEA W13 134 F8
Courtfield Ms SKENS * SW7 15 J6
Courtfield Ri WWKM BR4 205 J10
Courtfield Rd ASHF TW15 174 C9
SKENS SW7 15 J6
Courtfields HARP AL5 20 C2
Court Gdns HOLWY N7 6 B2
Court Haw BNSTD SM7 239 P1
Court Hl COUL/CHIP CR5 239 P4
SAND/SEL CR2 223 M8
Courthill Rd LEW SE13 161 H10
Courthope Rd GFD/PVL UB6 134 C1
HAMP NW3 118 A9
WIM/MER SW19 179 H8
Courthope Vls WIM/MER SW19 179 H10
Court House Rd FNCH N3 97 L7
Courtland Av CHING E4 101 L3
IL IG1 122 C7
MLHL NW7 96 A4
STRHM/NOR SW16 180 G10
Courtland Dr CHIG IG7 102 F4
Courtland Gv THMD SE28 143 N9
Courtland Rd EHAM E6 142 B3
Courtlands RCHPK/HAM TW10 177 M1
Courtlands Av DTCH/LGLY SL3 150 A3
ESH/CLAY KT10 217 N3
HAYES BR2 205 K8
HPTN TW12 175 N9
LEE/GVPK SE12 183 N1
RCH/KEW TW9 155 N8
Courtlands Cl RSLP HA4 112 G5
SAND/SEL CR2 223 N6
WATN WD24 72 F1
Courtlands Crs BNSTD SM7 239 K2
Courtlands Dr HOR/WEW KT19 220 C3
WAT WD17 72 F2
Courtlands Rd BRYLDS KT5 199 M7
Court La DUL SE21 181 N3
HOR/WEW KT19 219 P9
IVER SL0 131 K10
SL SL1 128 C5
Court Lane Gdns DUL SE21 181 M3
Courtleas COB KT11 217 P9
Courtleet Dr BXLYHN DA7 164 C4
Courtleigh Av EBAR EN4 77 N4
Courtleigh Gdns GLDGN NW11 117 H2
Court Ldg RAD * WD7 57 M10
Court Lodge Rd HORL RH6 279 P3
Courtman Rd TOTM N17 99 K8
Court Md NTHLT UB5 133 N5
Courtmead Cl HNHL SE24 181 K2
Courtnell St BAY/PAD W2 8 E5
Courtney Cl NRWD * SE19 181 M9
Courtney Crs CAR SM5 222 A4
Courtney Pl COB KT11 217 N8
Courtney Rd CDH/CHF RM16 168 F1
CROY/NA CR0 203 H10
HOLWY N7 119 H10
HTHAIR TW6 152 B9
WIM/MER SW19 179 P10
Courtney Wy HTHAIR TW6 152 B9
Courtrai Rd BROCKY SE4 182 D2
Court Rd BNSTD SM7 239 K1
CTHM CR3 241 L9
ELTH/MOT SE9 184 C4
GDST RH9 260 B7
HGDN/ICK UB10 112 C10
NWDGN UB2 153 N3
RDART DA2 188 D8
SNWD SE25 203 N2
Court Rd (Orpington By-Pass)
ORP BR6 207 L10
Courtside CEND/HSY/T N8 118 E4
STALW/RED * AL3 38 B4
SYD * SE26 182 B6
The Courts STRHM/NOR SW16 180 F10
Court St BMLY BR1 205 M2
WCHPL E1 140 A7
The Court MUSWH * N10 118 D2
RSLP HA4 113 M9
WARL CR6 242 D4
Court Vw HGT * N6 118 C7
Court Wy ACT W3 135 P7
BARK/HLT IG6 122 F1
CDALE/KGS NW9 116 B2
HARH RM3 105 M10
WHTN TW2 176 E3
The Courtway OXHEY WD19 93 M3
Court Wood La CROY/NA CR0 224 E6
Court Yd ELTH/MOT SE9 184 B2
The Courtyards WATW * WD18 92 E1
The Courtyard BF/WBF KT14 215 K8
BH/WHM * TN16 262 G2
CRAWE * RH10 283 N8
IS N1 5 P3
STALE/WH AL4 39 L6
Cousin La CANST EC4R 12 G8
Cousins Cl WDR/YW UB7 131 P9
Couthurst Rd BKHTH/KID SE3 161 N5
Coutts Av CHSGTN KT9 219 K2
GVE DA12 191 P7
Coutts Crs KTTN * NW5 118 B8
Coval Gdns MORT/ESHN SW14 155 N10
Coval La MORT/ESHN SW14 155 N10
Coval Rd MORT/ESHN SW14 155 P10
Coveham Crs COB KT11 217 H9
Covelees Wall EHAM E6 142 D8
Covenbrook RBRW/HUT CM13 107 N4
Covent Gdn COVGDN WC2E 11 M7
Covent Garden Piazza
COVGDN WC2E 11 M7
Coventry Cl EHAM E6 142 C8
KIL/WHAMP NW6 2 F7
Coventry Cross Est BOW E3 141 H6
Coventry Rd IL IG1 122 E6
SNWD SE25 203 P4
WCHPL E1 140 A6
Coventry St MYFR/PICC W1J 11 J8
Coverack Cl CROY/NA CR0 204 D7
STHGT/OAK N14 78 D10
Coverdale HHNE HP2 35 P3
Coverdale Gdns CROY/NA CR0 203 N10
Coverdale Rd CRICK NW2 2 A2
FBAR/BDGN N11 98 B7
SHB W12 136 E10
The Coverdales BARK IG11 142 G4
Coverdale Wy SLN SL2 128 D6
Coverley Cl RBRW/HUT CM13 107 H7
WCHPL * E1 13 P3
Covert Cl BERK HP4 33 J3
CRAWE RH10 283 P6
Coverton Rd TOOT SW17 179 P7
Covert Rd BARK/HLT IG6 103 J7
BERK HP4 33 J2
Coverts Rd ESH/CLAY KT10 218 E4
The Coverts RBRW/HUT CM13 107 M2
The Covert ASC SL5 192 A7
NRWD * SE19 181 N10
NTHWD HA6 92 D9
ORP BR6 207 H6
Covert Wy EBAR EN4 77 M6
Covet Wood Cl STMC/STPC BR5 207 J6
Covey Cl WIM/MER SW19 201 L2
The Covey CRAWE RH10 284 E5
Covington Gdns
STRHM/NOR SW16 181 J10
Covington Wy
STRHM/NOR SW16 181 H10
Cowbridge HERT/WAS SG14 25 K5
Cowbridge La BARK IG11 142 E2
Cowbridge Rd
KTN/HRWW/W HA3 115 L2
Cowcross St FARR EC1M 12 C3
Cowdenbeath Pth IS N1 5 N5
Cowden Rd ORP BR6 207 J7
Cowden St CAT SE6 182 F7
Cowdray Cl CRAWE RH10 284 D8
Cowdray Rd HGDN/ICK UB10 132 D3
Cowdray Wy HCH RM12 125 H9
Cowdrey Cl EN EN1 79 M6
Cowdrey Ct DART DA1 187 J3
Cowdrey Rd WIM/MER SW19 179 L9
Cowen Av RYLN/HDSTN HA2 114 C7
Cowfold Cl CRAWW RH11 283 J10
Cowgate Rd GFD/PVL UB6 134 C5
Cowick Rd TOOT SW17 180 A7
Cowings Md NTHLT UB5 133 M2
Cowland Av PEND EN3 80 B8
Cow La BUSH * WD23 73 P9
GSTN WD25 73 K2
Cow Leaze EHAM E6 142 D8
Cowleaze Rd KUTN/CMB KT2 199 K1
Cowles CHESW EN7 61 N3
Cowley Av CHERT KT16 195 J7
GRH DA9 188 E1
Cowley Cl SAND/SEL CR2 224 B5
Cowley Crs UX/CGN UB8 131 M7
WOT/HER KT12 217 K1
Cowley Hl BORE WD6 75 M3
Cowley La CHERT KT16 195 J7
WAN * E11 121 K8
Cowley Mill Rd UX/CGN UB8 131 L4
Cowley Pl HDN NW4 116 F3
Cowley Rd ACT W3 136 C10
BRXN/ST SW9 159 H7
HARH RM3 105 J8
IL IG1 122 C5
MORT/ESHN SW14 156 B9
UX/CGN UB8 131 M5
WAN E11 121 N3
Cowley St WEST SW1P 17 L4
Cowling Cl NTGHL W11 8 A8
Cowlins HLWE CM17 29 N7
Coworth Cl ASC SL5 192 G5
Coworth Pk ASC * SL5 193 H3
Coworth Rd ASC SL5 192 F5
Cowper Av EHAM E6 142 B2
SUT SM1 221 N1
TIL RM18 168 E7
Cowper Cl CHERT KT16 195 J6
HAYES BR2 206 A4
WELL DA16 185 K1
Cowper Ct WATN WD24 73 H3
Cowper Crs HERT/WAS SG14 25 J2
Cowper Gdns STHGT/OAK N14 78 C10
WLGTN SM6 222 D3
Cowper Rd ACT W3 136 A10
BELV DA17 164 A3
BERK HP4 33 N5
CSHM HP5 50 G5
HARP AL5 20 A2
HAYES BR2 206 A4
HHW HP1 35 L7
HNWL W7 134 E9
RAIN RM13 145 H6
RCHPK/HAM TW10 177 L8
SLN SL2 128 F6
STHGT/OAK N14 98 C2
STNW/STAM N16 119 M9
UED N18 99 P6
WGCE AL7 23 J7
WIM/MER SW19 179 M9
Cowper St STLK EC1Y 13 H1
Cowper Ter NKENS * W10 136 G7
Cowshot Crs CHOB/PIR GU24 230 C6
Cowslip Cl HGDN/ICK UB10 131 P2
Cowslip La RDKG RH5 254 F4
Cowslip Rd SWFD E18 101 N10
Cowthorpe Rd VX/NE SW8 158 E7
Cox Cl RAD WD7 57 K8
Coxdean KWD/TDW/WH KT20 238 F5
Coxe Pl KTN/HRWW/W HA3 114 F2
Coxes Av SHPTN * TW17 196 F3
Coxfield Cl HHNE HP2 35 P7
Cox La HOR/WEW KT19 219 N2
Coxley Ri PUR/KEN CR8 223 K9
Coxmount Rd CHARL SE7 162 A4
Coxs Av SHPTN TW17 196 F3
Coxs Cottages WARL * CR6 225 K10
Coxson Wy STHWK SE1 19 L2
Coxtie Green Rd BRW CM14 85 P10
Coxwell Rd NRWD SE19 181 M10
WOOL/PLUM SE18 162 G4
Cozens La East BROX EN10 44 E8
Cozens La West BROX EN10 44 D8
Cozens Rd WARE SG12 26 E1
Crabbe Crs CSHM HP5 51 J5
Crabbet Rd CRAWE RH10 284 C6
Crabbs Croft Cl ORP * BR6 226 F2
Crab Hl BECK BR3 183 J10
Crab Hill La REDH RH1 276 G4
Crab La GSTN WD25 56 A10
Crabtree Av ALP/SUD HA0 135 K4
CHDH RM6 123 N2
Crabtree Cl BETH E2 7 L8
BUSH WD23 74 A9
GT/LBKH KT23 254 B2
HHS/BOV HP3 35 N8
Crabtree Dr LHD/OX KT22 237 H10
Crabtree La FUL/PGN SW6 156 G6
GT/LBKH KT23 254 B2
HARP AL5 20 B3
HHS/BOV HP3 35 N8
LHD/OX KT22 255 P2
RDKG RH5 254 E6
Crabtree Manorway North
BELV DA17 164 D1
Crabtree Manorway South
BELV DA17 164 D1
Crabtree Office Village
EGH * TW20 194 F2
Crabtree Rd CRAWW RH11 283 M6
EGH TW20 194 F2
Crabtree Wk BROX EN10 44 D5
Crackley Meadow HHNE HP2 36 C1
Craddock Rd EN EN1 79 N7
Craddocks Av ASHTD KT21 237 L2
Craddock St KTTN NW5 4 C2
Cradhurst Cl DORK RH4 272 B3
Cradley Rd ELTH/MOT SE9 184 G4
Cragg Av RAD WD7 74 E2
Cragie Lea MUSWH * N10 98 C10
Craigans CRAWW RH11 283 K7
Craigavon Rd HHNE HP2 36 A2
Craigdale Rd ROM RM1 124 G4
Craigen Av CROY/NA CR0 204 A8
Craigerne Rd BKHTH/KID SE3 161 N6
Craig Gdns SWFD E18 101 L10
Craigholm WOOL/PLUM SE18 162 D8
Craiglands STALE/WH AL4 39 J2
Craig Mt RAD WD7 74 G1
Craigmuir Pk ALP/SUD HA0 135 L3
Craignair Rd BRXS/STRHM SW2 180 G3
Craignish Av STRHM/NOR SW16 202 G2
Craig Park Rd UED N18 100 A5
Craig Rd RCHPK/HAM TW10 177 H7
UX/CGN UB8 132 C8
Craig's Ct WHALL SW1A 11 L9
Craigs Wk CHES/WCR EN8 62 C4
Craigton Rd ELTH/MOT SE9 162 C10
Craigweil Av RAD WD7 74 G1
Craigwell Cl STAN HA7 95 J6
Craigwell Dr STAN HA7 95 J6
Craigwell Av FELT TW13 175 H6
Craigwell Cl STA TW18 195 H1
Crail Rw WALW SE17 19 H6
Crakell Rd REIG RH2 275 M1
Crakers Md WATW * WD18 73 J7
Cramer St MHST W1U 10 D4
Crammavill St CDH/CHF RM16 147 M10
Crammond Cl HMSMTH * W6 14 A9
Crampshaw La ASHTD KT21 237 L6
Crampton Rd PGE/AN SE20 182 B9
Crampton's Rd RSEV TN14 247 J6
Crampton St WALW SE17 18 E7
Cranberry Cl NTHLT UB5 133 L4
Cranberry La CAN/RD E16 141 K6
Cranborne Av NWDGN UB2 153 P3
SURB KT6 199 M10
Cranborne Cl HERT/BAY SG13 25 K8
POTB/CUF EN6 59 H7
Cranborne Crs POTB/CUF EN6 59 H7
Cranborne Gdns UPMR RM14 126 A7
WGCE AL7 23 J6
Cranborne Pde POTB/CUF * EN6 58 G7
Cranborne Rd BARK IG11 142 G3
CHES/WCR EN8 62 C8
HAT AL10 40 E3
HOD EN11 44 G2
POTB/CUF EN6 59 H6
Cranborne Wk CRAWE RH10 284 A9
Cranborne Waye YEAD UB4 133 K9
Cranbourne Av WAN E11 121 N2
WDSR SL4 148 E8
Cranbourne Cl HORL * RH6 280 C2
SL SL1 129 H10
STRHM/NOR SW16 202 F3
Cranbourne Dr HARP AL5 20 B5
HOD EN11 26 G9
PIN HA5 113 L3
Cranbourne Gdns BARK/HLT IG6 122 F1
GLDGN NW11 117 J3
Cranbourne Rd MNPK E12 122 B
MUSWH N10 98 C
NTHWD HA6 112 G
SL SL1 129 H1
SRTFD E15 121 H
Cranbourn St LSQ/SEVD WC2H 11 K
Cranbrook Cl HAYES BR2 205 M
Cranbrook Dr ESH/CLAY KT10 198 B
GPK RM2 125 J
STALE/WH AL4 39 K
WHTN TW2 176 A
Cranbrook La FBAR/BDGN N11 98 C
Cranbrook Ms WALTH E17 120 E
Cranbrook Pk WDGN N22 99 H
Cranbrook Ri IL IG1 122 C
Cranbrook Rd BARK/HLT IG6 122 E
BXLYHN DA7 164 A
CHSWK W4 156 B
DEPT SE8 160 F
EBAR EN4 77 N
HSLWW TW4 153 N
IL IG1 122 D
THHTH CR7 203 K
WIM/MER SW19 179 H
Cranbrook St BETH E2 140 C
Cranbury Rd FUL/PGN SW6 157 L
Crandon Wk EYN * DA4 210 D
Crane Av ACT W3 135 P
ISLW TW7 176 F
Cranebank Ms TWK * TW1 176 C
Cranebrook WHTN TW2 176 E
Crane Cl DAGE RM10 144 E
Crane Ct FLST/FETLN EC4A 12 B
MORT/ESHN * SW14 155 P1
Cranefield Dr GSTN WD25 55 M
Craneford Cl WHTN TW2 176 E
Craneford Wy WHTN TW2 176 D
Crane Gdns HYS/HAR UB3 152 C
Crane Gv HOLWY N7 6 E
Crane Lodge Rd HEST TW5 153
Crane Md BERM/RHTH SE16 160 C
WARE SG12 26 D
Crane Park Rd WHTN TW2 176 A
Crane Rd STWL/WRAY TW19 174 B
WHTN TW2 176 C
Cranesbill Cl CDALE/KGS NW9 116 A
Cranes Dr BRYLDS KT5 199 K
Cranes Pk SURB KT6 199 K
Cranes Park Av SURB KT6 199 K
Cranes Park Crs BRYLDS KT5 199
Crane St PECK SE15 159 N
Craneswater HYS/HAR UB3 152 G
Craneswater Pk NWDGN UB2 153 N
Cranes Wy BORE WD6 75 P
Crane Wy WHTN TW2 176 B
Cranfield Crs POTB/CUF EN6 60 F
Cranfield Dr CDALE/KGS NW9 96 B
Cranfield Rd BROCKY SE4 160 F
Cranfield Rd East CAR SM5 222 B
Cranfield Rd West CAR * SM5 222 A
Cranford Av PLMGR N13 98 F
STWL/WRAY TW19 173 P
Cranford Cl PUR/KEN CR8 223 K
RYNPK * SW20 200 E
STWL/WRAY TW19 173 P
Cranford Cottages WAP * E1W 140 C
Cranford Dr HYS/HAR UB3 152 G
Cranford La HEST TW5 153 K
HTHAIR TW6 152 C
HYS/HAR UB3 152 E
Cranford Park Rd HYS/HAR UB3 152 C
Cranford Ri ESH/CLAY KT10 218 E
Cranford Rd DART DA1 187 M
Cranford St WAP E1W 140 C
Cranford Wy CEND/HSY/T N8 118 G
Cranham Gdns UPMR RM14 126 E
Cranham Rd EMPK RM11 125
Cranhurst Rd CRICK NW2 116 F1
Cranleigh Cl BXLY * DA5 186 C
CHESW EN7 61 P
ORP BR6 207 K
PGE/AN SE20 204 A
SAND/SEL CR2 223 P
Cranleigh Dr SWLY BR8 208 F
Cranleigh Gdns BARK IG11 142 C
KTN/HRWW/W HA3 115 K
KUTN/CMB KT2 177
LOU IG10 82 C1
SAND/SEL CR2 223 F
SNWD SE25 203 M
STHL UB1 133 N
SUT SM1 201
WCHMH N21 79 H
Cranleigh Ms BTSEA SW11 157 P
Cranleigh Rd ESH/CLAY KT10 198 E
FELT TW13 174 C
SEVS/STOTM N15 119 K
SHGR GU5 268 F
WIM/MER SW19 201 K
Cranleigh St CAMTN NW1 5 H
Cranley Cl GU GU1 250 D
Cranley Dr GNTH/NBYPK IG2 122 F
RSLP HA4 112 G
Cranley Gdns MUSWH N10 118 C
PLMGR N13 98 C
SKENS SW7 15 K
WLGTN SM6 222 D
Cranley Ms SKENS SW7 15 K
Cranley Pl SKENS SW7 15
WOKN/KNAP * GU21 231
Cranley Rd GNTH/NBYPK IG2 122 F
GU GU1 250 C
PLSTW E13 141 N
WOT/HER KT12 216 G
Cranley Ter HDN * NW4 96 G
Cranmer Av WEA W13 154
Cranmer Cl MRDN SM4 200 C
POTB/CUF EN6 59 M
RSLP HA4 113
STAN HA7 95 K
WARL CR6 242 D
WEY KT13 216 B
Cranmer Ct HPTN TW12 176 A
Cranmer Farm Cl MTCM CR4 202 A
Cranmer Gdns DAGE RM10 124 D
WARL CR6 242 D
Cranmer Rd BRXN/ST SW9 159 H
CROY/NA CR0 203 J
EDGW HA8 95 N
FSTGT E7 121 N
HPTN TW12 176 A
HYS/HAR UB3 132 B
KUTN/CMB KT2 177 L
MTCM CR4 202 A
SEV TN13 246 F
Cranmer Ter TOOT SW17 179 P
Cranmore La EHSLY KT24 252 C
Cranmore Rd BMLY BR1 183 L
CHST BR7 184 C
Cranmore Wy MUSWH N10 118 D

Cranston Cl HGDN/ICK UB10 112 E7
HSLW TW3 153 M8
REIG RH2 275 L1
Cranston Est IS N1 7 H7
Cranston Gdns CHING E4 100 G7
Cranston Park Av UPMR RM14 126 B9
Cranston Rd FSTH SE23 182 D4
Cranstoun Cl RGUW GU3 249 L6
Cranswick Rd BERM/RHTH SE16 160 A4
Crantock Rd CAT SE6 183 H5
Cranwell Cl BOW E3 140 G6
Cranwell Gv SHPTN TW17 196 A4
Cranwich Av WCHMH N21 99 L1
Cranwich Rd STNW/STAM N16 119 M5
Cranwood St FSBYE EC1V 7 H10
Cranworth Crs CHING E4 101 J2
Cranworth Gdns BRXN/ST SW9 159 H7
Craster Rd BRXS/STRHM SW2 180 G3
Crathie Rd LEE/GVPK SE12 183 N2
Cravan Av FELT TW13 175 H5
Cravells Rd HARP AL5 20 B5
Craven Av WEA W13 135 H9
Craven Cl CLPT * E5 119 P5
YEAD UB4 133 H8
Craven Gdns BARK IG11 143 H4
BARK/HLT IG6 102 G10
CRW RM5 104 B6
HARH RM3 106 B7
WIM/MER SW19 179 L8
Craven Hl BAY/PAD W2 9 K7
Craven Hill Gdns BAY/PAD W2 9 J7
Craven Hill Ms BAY/PAD W2 9 K7
Craven Ms BTSEA SW11 158 B9
Craven Pk WLSDN NW10 136 A2
Craven Park Ms WLSDN NW10 136 B2
Craven Park Rd
STNW/STAM N16 119 N4
WLSDN NW10 136 B3
Craven Rd BAY/PAD W2 9 K7
CRAWE RH10 284 C8
CROY/NA CR0 204 A8
KUTN/CMB KT2 199 L1
ORP BR6 207 N10
WEA W13 135 H9
WLSDN NW10 136 A3
The Cravens HORL RH6 281 H4
Craven St CHCR * WC2N 11 L9
Craven Ter BAY/PAD W2 9 K7
Craven Wk CLPT E5 119 P5
Crawford Av ALP/SUD HA0 115 J10
CDH/CHF RM16 147 N10
Crawford Cl ISLW TW7 154 D8
Crawford Gdns GFD/PVL UB6 133 N5
PLMGR N13 99 J4
Crawford Pas CLKNW EC1R 12 A2
Crawford Pl BAY/PAD W2 9 P5
Crawford Rd CMBW SE5 159 K8
HAT AL10 40 D2
Crawfords SWLY BR8 186 F10
Crawford St MBLAR W1H 10 A4
Crawley Av CRAWW RH11 283 L6
Crawley Dr HHNE HP2 36 A2
Crawley Goods Yd
CRAWE * RH10 284 C3
Crawley La CRAWE RH10 284 D6
Crawley Market CRAWE * RH10 283 N7
Crawley Rd EN EN1 99 M1
LEY E10 120 G6
WDGN N22 99 K10
Crawley's La TRING HP23 32 D2
Crawshaw Rd CHERT KT16 214 G3
Crawshay Cl SEV TN13 247 H9
Crawters Cl CRAWE RH10 284 A6
Crawthew Gv EDUL SE22 159 N10
Cray Av ASHTD KT21 237 K2
STMC/STPC BR5 207 L5
Craybrooke Rd SCUP DA14 185 L7
Crayburne MEO DA13 189 L8
Craybury End ELTH/MOT SE9 184 F5
Cray Cl DART DA1 187 H1
Craydene Rd ERITH DA8 164 G7
Crayford High St DART DA1 164 F10
Crayford Rd DART DA1 186 G1
HOLWY N7 118 F9
Crayford Wy DART DA1 165 H10
Crayke Hl CHSGTN KT9 219 K4
Craylands STMC/STPC BR5 207 M3
Craylands La SWCM DA10 189 J1
Craylands Sq SWCM DA10 189 J1
Crayleigh Ter SCUP * DA14 185 M9
Crayle St SLN SL2 128 F5
Crayonne Cl SUN TW16 196 F1
Cray Rd BELV DA17 164 B5
SCUP DA14 185 M9
SWLY BR8 208 D6
rays Pde STMC/STPC * BR5 207 M2
ray Valley Rd STMC/STPC BR5 207 K5
realock Gv WFD IG8 101 L6
realock St WAND/EARL SW18 179 L2
reasey Cl HCH RM12 125 J7
rebor St EDUL SE22 181 P2
redenhall Dr HAYES BR2 206 C8
redenhill St STRHM/NOR SW16 180 D9
rediton Hl KIL/WHAMP NW6 117 L10
rediton Rd WLSDN NW10 136 G3
rediton Wy ESH/CLAY KT10 218 F2
redon Rd BERM/RHTH SE16 160 A4
PLSTW E13 141 P4
redo Wy WTHK RM20 166 G5
reechurch La HDTCH EC3A 13 K5
reechurch Pl HDTCH * EC3A 13 K6
reed La BLKFR EC4V 12 D6
reek Cottages
E/WMO/HCT * KT8 198 D4
reek Rd BARK IG11 143 J5
DEPT SE8 160 F5
E/WMO/HCT KT8 198 D4
reekside DEPT SE8 160 F6
RAIN RM13 144 G6
he Creek GVW DA11 189 N1
SUN TW16 197 H5
reek Wy RAIN RM13 144 F7
reeland Gv CAT SE6 182 E4
ree's Meadow BFOR * GU20 212 C4
ree Wy ROM RM1 104 F8
feld Cl FUL/PGN SW6 14 A10
reffield Rd ACT W3 135 M9
reighton Av EFNCH N2 98 A10
EHAM E6 142 A4
STAL AL1 38 C10
reighton Cl SHB W12 136 E9
reighton Rd EA W5 155 J2
KIL/WHAMP NW6 136 G4
TOTM N17 99 M8
reigton Av EFNCH N2 117 P1
remer St BETH E2 7 L8
remorne Est WBPTN SW10 15 L10
remorne Gdns HOR/WEW KT19 220 A5
remorne Rd GVW DA11 190 C3
WBPTN SW10 157 M6
Crescent TWRH EC3N 13 L7
Crescent Av GRAYS RM17 168 A4
HCH RM12 124 G7
Crescent Ct GRAYS * RM17 168 A5
HORL * RH6 280 B6
Crescent Dr BRWN CM15 107 K2
STMC/STPC BR5 206 F6
Crescent East EBAR EN4 77 M4
Crescent Gdns RSLP HA4 113 J5
SWLY BR8 208 D2
WIM/MER SW19 179 K6
Crescent Gv CLAP SW4 158 D10
MTCM CR4 201 P4
Crescent La CLAP SW4 180 E1
Crescent Pde HGDN/ICK * UB10 132 B5
Crescent Pl CHEL SW3 15 N5
Crescent Ri EBAR EN4 77 P9
FNCH * N3 97 J9
WDGN N22 98 E9
Crescent Rd BECK BR3 204 G2
BFN/LL DA15 185 J6
BMLY BR1 183 M10
BRW CM14 106 G5
CEND/HSY/T N8 118 E4
CHING E4 101 K1
CTHM CR3 241 P10
DAGE RM10 124 C9
EBAR EN4 77 N8
ED N9 99 P2
ENC/FH EN2 79 J8
ERITH DA8 164 G5
FBAR/BDGN N11 98 A5
FNCH N3 97 J9
HHNE HP2 35 N6
KUTN/CMB KT2 177 M10
LEY E10 120 G7
PLSTW E13 141 M3
REDH RH1 259 K9
REIG RH2 275 K2
RYNPK SW20 200 G1
SEVS/STOTM * N15 119 J1
SHPTN TW17 196 D5
SOCK/AV RM15 166 B1
SWFD E18 101 P9
WDGN N22 98 E9
WOOL/PLUM SE18 162 E4
Crescent Rw STLK EC1Y 12 E2
Crescent St IS N1 5 P3
The Crescent ABLGY WD5 54 G6
ACT W3 136 B8
ALP/SUD HA0 114 G7
ASHF TW15 174 A8
BAR EN5 77 L7
BARN SW13 156 C8
BECK BR3 204 F1
BELMT SM2 221 K7
BXLY DA5 185 M3
CHERT KT16 195 K3
CRICK NW2 116 E8
CTHM CR3 242 F9
E/WMO/HCT KT8 197 N4
EGH TW20 172 C9
EPP CM16 65 J8
EPSOM KT18 219 M10
FBAR/BDGN N11 98 A5
GNTH/NBYPK IG2 122 D4
GRH DA9 189 H2
GSTN WD25 74 A4
GUW GU2 249 M9
GVW DA11 190 C5
HART DA3 211 K3
HLWE CM17 29 M5
HORL RH6 280 B6
HYS/HAR UB3 152 D6
LCOL/BKTW AL2 55 P6
LHD/OX KT22 236 G8
LOU IG10 82 A10
NWDGN UB2 153 M1
NWMAL KT3 199 P2
REDH * RH1 275 N3
REIG RH2 257 L10
RKW/CH/CXG WD3 72 C10
RYLN/HDSTN HA2 114 B6
SCUP DA14 185 J7
SEV TN13 247 L8
SHPTN TW17 196 G7
SL SL1 149 K1
SNWD SE25 203 L6
SURB KT6 199 K5
SUT SM1 221 N2
UPMR RM14 126 D5
WALTH E17 120 D3
WATW WD18 73 K8
WEY KT13 196 B10
WIM/MER SW19 179 K6
WWKM BR4 205 K6
Crescent Vw LOU IG10 82 A10
Crescent Wk SOCK/AV RM15 166 B1
Crescent Wy BROCKY SE4 160 F9
HORL RH6 280 B6
ORP BR6 227 H2
SOCK/AV RM15 146 C10
STRHM/NOR SW16 180 G10
Crescentway NFNCH/WDSP N12 97 P7
Crescent West EBAR EN4 77 M4
Crescent Wood Rd DUL SE21 181 P6
Cresford Rd FUL/PGN SW6 157 L7
Crespigny Rd HDN NW4 116 E4
Cressage Cl STHL UB1 133 P6
Cressall Cl LHD/OX KT22 236 G6
Cressall Md LHD/OX KT22 236 G6
Cress End RKW/CH/CXG WD3 91 K2
Cresset Cl WARE SG12 27 H8
Cresset Rd HOM E9 140 B1
Cresset St CLAP SW4 158 E9
Cressfield Cl KTTN NW5 118 B10
Cressida Rd ARCH N19 118 D6
Cressingham Gv SUT SM1 221 M1
Cressingham Rd EDGW HA8 96 A7
LEW SE13 161 H9
Cressington Cl STNW/STAM N16 119 M10
Cress Rd SL SL1 148 G1
Cresswell Gdns ECT * SW5 15 J7
Cresswell Pk BKHTH/KID SE3 161 L9
Cresswell Pl ECT SW5 15 J7
Cresswell Rd CSHM HP5 51 J10
FELT TW13 175 M6
SNWD SE25 203 P4
TWK TW1 177 J2
Cresswell Wy WCHMH N21 99 H1
Cressy Ct HMSMTH W6 156 E2
Cressy Houses WCHPL * E1 140 B7
Cressy Pl WCHPL E1 140 B7
Cressy Rd HAMP NW3 118 A9
Cressys Cnr HSLW * TW3 154 A9
Cresta Dr ADL/WDHM KT15 215 J6
Crest Av GRAYS RM17 167 N6
Crestbrook Av PLMGR N13 99 J4
Crestbrook Pl PLMGR * N13 99 H4
Crest Cl RSEV TN14 228 C7
Crest Dr PEND EN3 80 B4
Crestfield St CAMTN NW1 5 M9
Crest Gdns RSLP HA4 113 K8
Crest Hl SHGR GU5 270 F8
Cresthill Av GRAYS RM17 167 P4
Creston Av WOKN/KNAP GU21 231 K3
Creston Wy WPK KT4 200 G8
Crest Pk HHNE HP2 36 D5
Crest Rd CRICK NW2 116 D7
HAYES BR2 205 L7
SAND/SEL CR2 224 A4
The Crest BRYLDS KT5 199 M5
CHESW EN7 61 J3
HDN NW4 116 F3
KTTN * NW5 118 E10
PLMGR N13 99 H5
POTB/CUF * EN6 59 M7
SBW CM21 29 N1
Crest Vw GRH DA9 166 F10
PIN HA5 113 L2
Crest View Dr STMC/STPC BR5 206 E5
Crestway PUT/ROE SW15 178 D2
Crestwood Wy HSLWW TW4 175 N1
Creswell WOKN/KNAP * GU21 231 J3
Creswell Cnr
WOKN/KNAP * GU21 231 J3
Creswick Ct WGCE * AL7 22 G6
Creswick Rd ACT W3 135 N9
Creswick Wk GLDGN NW11 117 J2
Crete Hall Rd GVW DA11 190 A2
Crew Curve BERK HP4 33 L2
Crewdson Rd BRXN/ST SW9 158 G6
HORL RH6 280 C4
Crewe Pl WLSDN NW10 136 C5
Crewe's Av WARL CR6 242 B2
Crewe's Cl WARL CR6 242 B2
Crewe's La WARL CR6 242 C2
Crews St POP/IOD * E14 160 F3
Crewys Rd CRICK NW2 117 J7
PECK SE15 160 A8
Crib St WARE SG12 26 C1
Crichton Av WLGTN SM6 222 E2
Crichton Rd CAR SM5 222 A4
Crichton St VX/NE * SW8 158 D8
Cricketers Arms Rd ENC/FH * EN2 79 K6
Cricketers Cl CHSGTN KT9 219 J2
ERITH DA8 164 F4
STAL AL1 38 D5
STHGT/OAK N14 98 D1
Cricketers La BFOR GU20 212 C2
EGH TW20 171 P7
Cricketers Wk SYD SE26 182 B8
Cricket Field Rd UX/CGN UB8 131 N3
Cricketfield Rd CLPT E5 120 A9
WDR/YW UB7 151 M3
Cricket Gn MTCM CR4 202 A3
Cricket Ground Rd CHST BR7 206 E1
Cricket Hl REDH RH1 276 G2
Cricket La BECK BR3 182 D9
Cricket Rw EFNCH * N2 117 N1
Cricket Vw WEY KT13 216 C2
Cricket Wy WEY KT13 196 F9
Cricklade Av BRXS/STRHM SW2 180 F5
HARH RM3 105 L7
Cricklewood Broadway
CRICK NW2 116 F8
Cricklewood La CRICK NW2 117 H9
Cridland St SRTFD E15 141 L3
Crieff Rd WAND/EARL SW18 179 M2
Criffel Av BRXS/STRHM SW2 180 E5
Crimp Hl EGH TW20 171 M5
WDSR SL4 171 L3
Crimscott St STHWK SE1 19 K4
Crimsworth Rd VX/NE SW8 158 E7
Crinan St IS N1 5 M7
Cringle St VX/NE SW8 158 D6
Cripplegate St BARB * EC2Y 12 E3
Cripsey Av CHONG CM5 67 N2
Crispen Rd FELT TW13 175 M7
Crispian Cl WLSDN NW10 116 B9
Crispin Cl BEAC HP9 88 B7
Crispin Crs WLGTN SM6 202 E10
Crispin Rd EDGW HA8 95 P7
Crispin St WCHPL E1 13 L4
Crispin Wy SLN SL2 109 J9
Crisp Rd HMSMTH W6 156 F4
Criss Gv CFSP/GDCR SL9 89 P10
Criss La CFSP/GDCR SL9 89 P10
Cristowe Rd FUL/PGN * SW6 157 J8
Criterion Ms ARCH N19 118 E7
Critten La RDKG RH5 253 L8
Cricketers Ms WAND/EARL SW18 179 L1
Crockenhill Hl STMC/STPC BR5 207 N5
Crockenhill La SWLY BR8 209 H7
Crockenhill Rd STMC/STPC BR5 207 N6
Crockerton Rd TOOT SW17 180 A5
Crockford Cl ADL/WDHM KT15 215 M1
Crockford Park Rd
ADL/WDHM KT15 215 M2
Crockham Cl CRAWW RH11 283 M9
Crockham Wy ELTH/MOT SE9 184 D7
Crocknorth Rd EHSLY KT24 252 G8
Crocus Cl CROY/NA CR0 204 C8
Crocus Fld BAR EN5 77 J10
Croffets KWD/TDW/WH KT20 238 G7
Croft Av DORK RH4 254 G10
WWKM BR4 205 H8
Croft Cl BELV DA17 164 A4
CHST BR7 184 C8
HGDN/ICK UB10 132 B2
HYS/HAR UB3 152 D6
KGLGY WD4 53 K6
MLHL NW7 96 B4
Croft Ct BORE WD6 76 A7
HARP * AL5 20 A2
RSLP * HA4 112 G6
SUT * SM1 201 N9
Croftdown Rd KTTN NW5 118 B8
Croft End Rd KGLGY WD4 53 K6
Crofters WDSR SL4 171 M2
Crofters Cl ISLW TW7 176 C1
Crofters Ct DEPT SE8 160 D3
Crofters Md CROY/NA CR0 224 E5
Crofters Rd NTHWD HA6 92 F5
The Crofters WDSR * SL4 171 M2
Crofters Wy CAMTN NW1 5 J5
Croft Fld HAT AL10 40 C4
KGLGY WD4 53 K6
Croft Gdns HNWL W7 154 F1
RSLP HA4 112 F6
Crofthill Rd SLN SL2 128 G6
Croft La KGLGY WD4 53 K6
Croftleigh Av PUR/KEN CR8 241 H2
Croft Lodge Cl WFD IG8 101 N7
Croft Meadow KGLGY WD4 53 K6
Croft Ms NFNCH/WDSP N12 97 M4
Crofton ASHTD KT21 237 K4
Crofton Av BXLY DA5 185 N3
CHSWK W4 155 P6
ORP BR6 206 F9
WOT/HER KT12 197 K10
Crofton Cl CHERT KT16 214 F4
Crofton Gate Wy BROCKY SE4 182 D1
Crofton Gv CHING E4 101 J5
Crofton La STMC/STPC BR5 206 G8
Crofton Park Rd BROCKY SE4 182 E2
Crofton Rd CDH/CHF RM16 168 B1
CMBW SE5 159 M7
ORP BR6 206 D10
PLSTW E13 141 N6
Crofton Ter RCH/KEW TW9 155 L10
Crofton Wy BAR * EN5 77 L10
ENC/FH EN2 79 H6
Croft Rd BH/WHM TN16 262 E2
BMLY BR1 183 M9
CFSP/GDCR SL9 90 B10
CTHM CR3 242 E8
PEND EN3 80 D5
STRHM/NOR SW16 181 H10
SUT SM1 221 N2
WARE SG12 26 B1
WIM/MER SW19 179 M10
Crofts Pth HHS/BOV HP3 36 C8
Crofts Rd HRW HA1 114 F4
Crofts St WCHPL E1 13 N8
The Crofts HHS/BOV HP3 36 C7
SHPTN TW17 196 F4
Croft St DEPT SE8 160 D3
WCHPL E1 13 N8
The Croft ALP/SUD HA0 115 H10
BAR EN5 77 H8
BROX EN10 44 D9
CHING E4 101 K3
CRAWW RH11 283 K7
EA W5 135 K7
EDGW HA8 95 N9
HEST TW5 153 M6
LCOL/BKTW AL2 55 P1
LOU IG10 82 D6
RSLP HA4 113 K9
SWLY BR8 208 D3
WGCE AL7 23 J8
WLSDN NW10 136 C4
Croft Wy BFN/LL DA15 185 H6
RCHPK/HAM TW10 176 G6
SEV TN13 264 G1
Croftwell HARP AL5 20 E3
Crogsland Rd CAMTN NW1 4 C3
Croham Cl SAND/SEL CR2 223 M3
Croham Manor Rd
SAND/SEL CR2 223 M4
Croham Mt SAND/SEL CR2 223 M4
Croham Park Av SAND/SEL CR2 223 N2
Croham Rd SAND/SEL CR2 223 L2
Croham Valley Rd
SAND/SEL CR2 223 P3
Croindene Rd STRHM/NOR SW16 202 F1
Cromartie Rd ARCH N19 118 E5
Cromarty Rd EDGW * HA8 95 N3
Cromarty Vls BAY/PAD * W2 9 J7
Crombie Cl REDBR IG4 122 C3
Crombie Ms BTSEA * SW11 157 P8
Crombie Rd BFN/LL DA15 184 G4
Cromer Cl UX/CGN UB8 132 D8
Cromer Hyde MRDN * SM4 201 L5
Cromer Rd BAR EN5 77 M8
CHDH RM6 123 P4
EMPK RM11 125 L5
HTHAIR TW6 152 B9
LEY E10 121 J5
ROMW/RG RM7 124 D4
SNWD SE25 204 A3
TOOT SW17 180 B9
TOTM N17 99 P10
WATN WD24 73 K4
Cromer Rd West HTHAIR TW6 152 B9
Cromer St STPAN WC1H 5 M10
Cromer Ter HACK E8 119 P10
Cromer Villas Rd
WAND/EARL SW18 179 J2
Cromford Cl ORP BR6 207 H10
Cromford Rd PUT/ROE SW15 179 J1
Cromford Wy NWMAL KT3 200 A1
Cromlix Cl CHST BR7 206 E2
Crompton Flds CRAWE RH10 283 P4
Crompton Pl WAB EN9 80 F4
Crompton St BAY/PAD W2 9 L2
Crompton Wy CRAWE RH10 283 P5
Cromwell Av CHESW EN7 62 A6
HAYES BR2 205 N3
HGT N6 118 C6
HMSMTH W6 156 E4
NWMAL KT3 200 C5
Cromwell Cl CHSWK * W4 155 N4
CSTG HP8 89 P4
EFNCH N2 117 N2
STALE/WH AL4 39 J1
WOT/HER KT12 197 J8
Cromwell Ct ALP/SUD HA0 135 K4
Cromwell Crs ECT SW5 14 E5
Cromwell Dr SL SL1 129 K8
Cromwell Gv CTHM CR3 241 K7
HMSMTH W6 156 F2
Cromwell Ms SKENS * SW7 15 L5
Cromwell Pde ALP/SUD * HA0 135 K4
Cromwell Pl ACT W3 135 P10
HGT * N6 118 C6
MORT/ESHN SW14 155 P9
SKENS SW7 15 M5
Cromwell Rd ALP/SUD HA0 135 J4
ASC SL5 192 A4
BECK BR3 204 D2
BORE WD6 75 K5
BRW CM14 106 C5
BRXN/ST SW9 159 J7
CROY/NA CR0 203 L7
CTHM CR3 241 K7
FELT TW13 175 J4
FNCH N3 97 M10
FSTGT E7 141 P2
GRAYS RM17 167 M3
HERT/BAY SG13 25 N4
HSLW TW3 153 P10
HYS/HAR UB3 132 E8
KUTN/CMB KT2 199 K1
MUSWH N10 98 B8
REDH RH1 258 A10
SKENS SW7 15 L5
TEDD TW11 176 F9
WALTH E17 121 H3
WARE SG12 26 E2
WIM/MER SW19 179 K8
WPK KT4 200 A10
Cromwell St HSLW TW3 153 P10
Cromwell Ter HSLW * TW3 153 P10
Crondace Rd FUL/PGN SW6 157 K7
Crondall St IS N1 7 H8
Cronin St PECK SE15 159 N6
Cronks Hl REIG RH2 275 M1
Cronks Hill Cl REDH RH1 275 N2
Cronks Hill Rd REIG RH2 275 N2
Crooked Billet Rbt CHING E4 100 G8
Crooked La GVE DA12 190 E2
Crooked Mile WAB EN9 63 H6
Crooked Usage FNCH N3 117 H1
Crooked Wy WAB EN9 45 K8
Crooke Rd DEPT SE8 160 D4
Crookham Rd FUL/PGN SW6 157 J7
Crookhams WGCE AL7 23 K3
Crook Log BXLYHN DA7 163 N9
Crookston Rd ELTH/MOT SE9 162 D9
Croombs Rd CAN/RD E16 141 P7
Croom's Hl GNWCH SE10 161 J6
Croom's Hill Gv GNWCH SE10 161 H6
Crop Common HAT AL10 40 E2
Cropley St IS N1 6 G7
Croppath Rd DAGE RM10 124 B9
Cropthorne Ct MV/WKIL W9 3 K10
Crosby Cl BEAC HP9 108 E1
FELT TW13 175 M7
STALE/WH AL4 39 H9
Crosby Rd DAGE RM10 144 C4
FSTGT E7 141 M1
Crosby Rw STHWK SE1 18 G2
Crosby Wk HACK E8 7 L2
Crosier Cl WOOL/PLUM SE18 162 B7
Crosier Rd HGDN/ICK UB10 112 D9
Crosier Wy RSLP HA4 112 F8
Crossacres WOKS/MYFD GU22 233 H2
Crossbow Rd CHIG IG7 103 J6
Crossbrook HAT AL10 40 B5
Crossbrook Rd BKHTH/KID SE3 162 B8
Crossbrook St CHES/WCR EN8 62 C6
Cross Deep TWK TW1 176 E6
Cross Deep Gdns TWK TW1 176 E5
Crossett Gn HHS/BOV HP3 36 D8
Crossfell Rd HHS/BOV HP3 36 C8
Crossfield Cl BERK HP4 33 L5
Crossfield Est DEPT SE8 160 F6
Crossfield Pl WEY KT13 216 C4
Crossfield Rd HAMP NW3 3 M2
HOD EN11 44 G1
TOTM N17 119 K1
Crossfields STALW/RED AL3 38 A9
Crossfields Cl BERK * HP4 33 L5
Crossfield St DEPT SE8 160 F6
Crossford St BRXN/ST SW9 158 G8
Crossgate EDGW HA8 95 M4
GFD/PVL UB6 134 G1
Crossing Rd EPP CM16 65 K8
Cross Keys CRAWE RH10 283 N7
Cross Keys Cl MHST W1U 10 D4
Cross Lances Rd HSLW TW3 154 A10
Crossland Rd REDH RH1 258 B10
THHTH CR7 203 J6
Crosslands CHERT KT16 195 H10
Crosslands Av EA W5 135 L10
NWDGN UB2 153 N4
Crosslands Pde NWDGN * UB2 153 P4
Crosslands Rd HOR/WEW KT19 220 A3
Cross La BEAC HP9 108 E1
BXLY DA5 186 A3
CEND/HSY/T N8 118 G1
CHERT KT16 214 E3
HARP AL5 20 B6
HERT/WAS SG14 25 J5
HORL RH6 281 K7
Cross La East GVE DA12 190 E5
Cross La CFSP/GDCR SL9 90 C6
GU GU1 250 C10
Cross Lanes Cl CFSP/GDCR * SL9 90 C6
Cross La West GVW DA11 190 E5
Crosslet St WALW SE17 19 H5
Crosslet V GNWCH SE10 160 G7
Crossley Cl BH/WHM TN16 244 A1
Crossley St HOLWY N7 6 A1
Crossmead ELTH/MOT SE9 184 C4
OXHEY WD19 73 J10
Crossmead Av GFD/PVL UB6 133 P5
Cross Meadow CSHM HP5 50 E5
Crossness Rd BARK IG11 143 J5
Cross Oak WDSR SL4 148 F8
Cross Oak La REDH RH1 276 D10
Cross Oak Rd BERK HP4 33 M6
Crossoaks La BORE WD6 76 A1
POTB/CUF EN6 58 B10
Crosspath CRAWE * RH10 283 P6
The Crosspath RAD WD7 74 F1
Cross Rd ASC SL5 192 E8
BELMT SM2 221 K6
BUSH WD23 73 M10
CHDH RM6 123 M5
CHES/WCR EN8 62 D9
CMBW SE5 159 M8
CROY/NA CR0 203 L8
DART DA1 187 K2
EN EN1 79 M8
FBAR/BDGN N11 98 C6
FELT TW13 175 M7
GVW DA11 190 C2
HAYES BR2 206 B9
HERT/WAS SG14 25 K4
HRW HA1 114 C2
KTN/HRWW/W HA3 94 F10
KUTN/CMB KT2 177 L10
KWD/TDW/WH KT20 238 F8
PUR/KEN CR8 223 J9
RDART DA2 187 N7
ROMW/RG RM7 124 B1
RYLN/HDSTN HA2 113 P8
SCUP DA14 185 L7
STMC/STPC BR5 207 L5
SUT SM1 221 N2
WDGN N22 99 H7
WEY * KT13 196 E10
WFD IG8 102 C7
WIM/MER SW19 179 K10
Cross Roads LOU IG10 81 N6
The Crossroads EHSLY KT24 253 L4
Cross St BARN SW13 156 B8
ERITH DA8 164 F5
HPTN TW12 176 B8
IS N1 6 D5
STALW/RED AL3 38 C6
UED N18 99 P6
WARE SG12 26 D2
WAT WD17 73 K7
Crossthwaite Av HNHL SE24 159 L10
Crosswall TWRH EC3N 13 L7
Cross Wy HYS/HAR UB3 153 H1
Crossway BCTR RM8 123 M8
CDALE/KGS NW9 116 C2
CSHM HP5 51 K6
EN EN1 99 M1
NFNCH/WDSP N12 97 N7
NWMAL KT3 200 F4
PIN HA5 93 J10
RSLP HA4 113 K9
STMC/STPC BR5 206 G4
STNW/STAM N16 119 M10

THMD SE28 143 M8
WEA W13 134 F6
WGCW AL8 22 E1
WOT/HER KT12 197 J9
Crossway Pde WDGN * N22 99 J8
Crossways BEAC HP9 88 E10
BELMT SM2 221 N5
BERK HP4 33 L6
BH/WHM TN16 243 P6
BRWN CM15 87 M10
CRAWE RH10 284 A6
EGH TW20 172 G9
EHSLY KT24 253 L3
GPK RM2 125 J1
HHS/BOV HP3 36 C6
SAND/SEL CR2 224 E4
SUN TW16 196 G1
Crossways Bvd GRH DA9 188 D1
Crossways Cl CRAWE RH10 284 A6
Crossways La REIG RH2 257 M4
Crossways Rd BECK BR3 204 F4
MTCM CR4 202 C3
Crossways Ter CLPT * E5 120 B9
The Crossways BRYLDS * KT5 199 N8
COUL/CHIP CR5 240 G5
GUW GU2 267 L2
HEST TW5 153 N6
REDH RH1 258 C5
WBLY HA9 115 M7
The Crossway ELTH/MOT SE9 184 A5
The Cross Wy KTN/HRWW/W HA3 94 D10
The Crossway WDGN N22 99 J8
Crosswell Cl SHPTN TW17 196 D2
Crosthwaite Wy SL SL1 128 C7
Croston St HACK E8 7 P5
Crosts La WDGN N22 99 H8
Crothall Cl PLMGR N13 98 G4
Crouch Av BARK IG11 143 L4
Crouch Cl BECK BR3 182 F9
Crouch Cft ELTH/MOT SE9 184 D6
Crouch End Hl ARCH N19 118 E5
Crouchfield HERT/WAS SG14 25 K2
HHW HP1 35 L7
Crouch Hall Rd CEND/HSY/T N8 118 E4
Crouch Hl ARCH N19 118 F5
Crouch La CHESW EN7 61 K3
Crouchmans Cl DUL SE21 181 N6
Crouch Oak La ADL/WDHM KT15 215 M1
Crouch Rd GRAYS RM17 168 D4
WLSDN NW10 136 A2
Crouch Va UPMR RM14 126 D5
Crowborough Cl WARL CR6 242 D4
Crowborough Dr WARL CR6 242 D4
Crowborough Pth OXHEY WD19 93 L5
Crowborough Rd TOOT SW17 180 B8
Crowden Wy THMD SE28 143 M9
Crowder St WCHPL E1 140 A9
Crow Dr RSEV TN14 246 D1
Crowfoot Cl HOM E9 120 E10
Crow Gn BRWN CM15 86 F8
Crow Green La BRWN CM15 86 F9
Crow Green Rd BRWN CM15 86 E9
Crow Hl ORP * BR6 226 C6
Crowhurst Cl BRXN/ST SW9 159 H8
CRAWE RH10 284 F7
Crowhurst Md GDST RH9 260 B6
Crowhurst Wy STMC/STPC BR5 207 M5
Crowland Av HYS/HAR UB3 152 F3
Crowland Gdns STHGT/OAK N14 98 F1
Crowland Rd SEVS/STOTM N15 119 N3
THHTH * CR7 203 L4
Crowlands Av ROMW/RG RM7 124 C4
Crowland Ter IS N1 6 G3
Crowland Wk MRDN SM4 201 L6
Crow La ROMW/RG RM7 124 A5
ROMW/RG RM7 124 D5
Crowley Crs CROY/NA CR0 223 H2
Crowline Wk IS N1 6 F1
Crown Ar KUT * KT1 199 J2
Crownbourne Ct SUT * SM1 221 L1
Crown Buildings CHING * E4 101 J2
Crown Cl BOW E3 140 F3
DTCH/LGLY SL3 150 F6
HYS/HAR UB3 152 G1
KIL/WHAMP NW6 2 G1
MLHL NW7 96 C3
ORP BR6 227 K1
RBSF CM22 30 D3
WOT/HER KT12 197 K7
Crown Ct HOL/ALD WC2B 11 M6
Crown Dl NRWD SE19 181 K9
Crowndale Rd CAMTN NW1 5 H7
Crownfield BROX EN10 44 F7
Crownfield Av GNTH/NBYPK IG2 123 H3
Crownfield Rd SRTFD E15 121 J10
Crownfields SEV TN13 265 J1
Crown Ga HLW CM20 46 G1
Crown Gn GVE DA12 191 P8
Crown Hts GU GU1 268 B3
Crown Hl CROY/NA * CR0 203 K9
WAB EN9 64 C9
Crown Hill Ct ASC SL5 192 A5
Crownhill Rd WFD IG8 102 B8
WLSDN NW10 136 C3
Crown La CHST BR7 206 F1
GVE DA12 191 P7
HAYES BR2 206 A5
SLN SL2 128 G2
STHGT/OAK N14 98 D2
STRHM/NOR SW16 181 H8
VW GU25 194 A6
WIM/MER SW19 201 K3
Crown Lane Gdns WNWD * SE27 181 H8
Crown Lane Sp HAYES BR2 206 A6
Crown Meadow DTCH/LGLY SL3 150 E6
Crown Office Rw EMB EC4Y 12 A7
Crown Pde MRDN * SM4 201 L4
STHGT/OAK * N14 98 D2
Crown Pas STJS SW1Y 11 H10
Crown Pl KTTN NW5 4 F1
SDTCH EC2A 13 J2
Crown Ri CHERT KT16 195 J8
GSTN WD25 55 K10
Crown Rd BARK/HLT IG6 122 G2
BORE WD6 75 M5
BRW CM14 86 C5
EN EN1 79 P7
GRAYS RM17 167 M5
MUSWH N10 98 B8
NWMAL KT3 199 P1
ORP BR6 227 K2
RSEV TN14 228 G6
RSLP HA4 113 L10
SUT SM1 221 K1
TWK TW1 176 G2
VW GU25 193 P6
WIM/MER SW19 201 K4
Crown Sq WOKN/KNAP GU21 232 C3
Crownstone Rd
BRXS/STRHM SW2 181 H1
Crown St ACT W3 135 N10
BRW CM14 107 H3
CMBW SE5 159 K6
DAGE RM10 144 D1
EGH TW20 172 D8
RYLN/HDSTN HA2 114 C6
Crown Ter CRICK * NW2 116 G9
RCH/KEW TW9 155 L10
STHGT/OAK * N14 98 E2
Crowntree Cl ISLW TW7 154 E5
Crown Vls ACT * W3 155 P1
Crown Wk WBLY HA9 115 L8
Crown Wy WDR/YW UB7 132 A10
Crown Woods Wy
ELTH/MOT SE9 184 G1
Crown Yd HSLW TW3 154 B9
Crow Piece La SLN SL2 128 E2
Crowshott Av STAN HA7 95 H10
Crows Rd BARK IG11 142 E1
EPP CM16 65 J6
SRTFD E15 141 J5
Crowstone Rd CDH/CHF RM16 167 P1
Crowther Av BTFD TW8 155 K4
Crowther Rd SNWD SE25 203 P4
Crowthorne Cl
WAND/EARL SW18 179 J3
Crowthorne Rd NKENS W10 136 G8
Croxdale Rd BORE WD6 75 L6
Croxden Cl EDGW HA8 115 M1
Croxden Wk MRDN SM4 201 M6
Croxford Gdns WDGN N22 99 J8
Croxford Wy ROMW/RG RM7 124 E6
Croxley Cl STMC/STPC BR5 207 L2
Croxley Gn STMC/STPC BR5 207 L1
Croxley Rd MV/WKIL W9 2 D10
Croxley Vw WATW WD18 72 F10
Croxted Cl DUL SE21 181 K3
Croxted Rd DUL SE21 181 L5
Croyde Av GFD/PVL UB6 134 B5
HYS/HAR UB3 152 F3
Croyde Cl ELTH/MOT SE9 184 G3
Croydonbarn La GDST RH9 281 P3
The Croydon F/O CROY/NA CR0 223 J1
Croydon Gv CROY/NA CR0 203 J9
Croydon La BNSTD SM7 221 N9
Croydon La South BNSTD SM7 221 L10
Croydon Rd BECK BR3 204 D3
BH/WHM TN16 262 E2
CROY/NA CR0 204 C5
CROY/NA CR0 222 F1
CTHM CR3 241 P8
MTCM CR4 202 C5
PGE/AN SE20 204 A2
PLSTW E13 141 M6
REIG RH2 257 M9
WARL CR6 243 J8
WLGTN SM6 221 K1
WWKM BR4 205 K10
Croyland Rd ED N9 99 P2
Croylands Dr SURB KT6 199 K7
Croysdale Av SUN TW16 197 H3
Crozier Dr SAND/SEL CR2 224 A6
Crozier Ter HOM E9 120 C10
Crucible Cl CHDH RM6 123 L4
Crucifix La STHWK SE1 19 J1
Cruden Rd GVE DA12 191 J6
Cruden St IS N1 6 D6
Cruick Av SOCK/AV RM15 147 H8
Cruikshank St FSBYW WC1X 6 A9
Crulkshank Rd SRTFD E15 121 K9
Crummock Cl SL SL1 128 B8
Crummock Gdns
CDALE/KGS NW9 116 B3
Crumpsall St ABYW SE2 163 M3
Crundale Av CDALE/KGS NW9 115 M3
Crunden Rd SAND/SEL CR2 223 L4
Crusader Cl PUR RM19 165 P3
Crusader Gdns CROY/NA CR0 203 M10
Crusader Wy WATW WD18 72 G10
Crusoe Ms STNW/STAM N16 119 L7
Crusoe Rd ERITH DA8 165 H2
MTCM CR4 180 A10
Crutched Friars TWRH EC3N 13 K7
Crutchfield La HORL RH6 279 K1
WOT/HER KT12 197 J8
Crutchley Rd CAT SE6 183 K5
Crystal Av HCH RM12 125 M9
Crystal Palace NRWD * SE19 181 P10
Crystal Palace Pde NRWD SE19 181 N9
Crystal Palace Park Rd
NRWD SE19 181 P8
Crystal Palace Rd EDUL SE22 181 N2
Crystal Ter NRWD SE19 181 L9
Crystal Wy BCTR RM8 123 M6
HRW HA1 114 E3
Cuba Dr PEND EN3 80 B6
Cuba St POP/IOD E14 160 F1
Cubitt Sq STHL * UB1 134 B10
Cubitt St CROY/NA CR0 222 G2
FSBYW WC1X 5 P10
Cubitt Ter CLAP SW4 158 D9
Cubitt Wy WOKN/KNAP GU21 231 J4
Cublands HERT/BAY SG13 26 A5
Cuckfield Cl CRAWW RH11 283 J10
Cuckmans Dr LCOL/BKTW AL2 55 P1
Cuckmere Crs CRAWW RH11 283 J8
Cuckoo Av HNWL W7 134 C6
Cuckoo Dene HNWL W7 134 C7
Cuckoo Hall La ED N9 100 B1
Cuckoo Hl PIN HA5 113 K1
Cuckoo Hill Dr PIN HA5 113 K1
Cuckoo Hill Rd PIN HA5 113 L2
Cuckoo La CDH/CHF RM16 147 L10
CHOB/PIR GU24 212 C9
HNWL W7 134 D9
Cuckoo V CHOB/PIR GU24 212 C9
Cucumber La BRKMPK AL9 42 A7
Cuda's Cl HOR/WEW KT19 220 C1
Cuddington Av WPK KT4 200 C10
Cuddington Cl
KWD/TDW/WH KT20 238 F6
Cuddington Gld HOR/WEW KT19 219 M8
Cuddington Park Cl BNSTD SM7 221 J9
Cuddington Wy BELMT SM2 220 G8
Cudham Cl BELMT SM2 221 K6
Cudham Dr CROY/NA CR0 224 G6
Cudham La North RSEV TN14 226 F10
Cudham La South RSEV TN14 244 F1
Cudham Park Rd RSEV TN14 227 H6
Cudham Rd BH/WHM TN16 244 B5
ORP BR6 226 D7
Cudham St CAT SE6 183 H3
Cudworth Pk RDKG * RH5 278 B7
Cudworth St WCHPL E1 140 A6
Cuff Crs ELTH/MOT SE9 184 A3
Cuffley Av GSTN WD25 55 L10
Cuffley Ct HHW HP2 36 D1
Cuffley Hl CHESW EN7 61 J5
Cugley Rd RDART DA2 188 B3
Culcroft HART DA3 211 L4
Culford Gdns CHEL SW3 16 B6
Culford Gv IS N1 7 J2
Culford Ms IS N1 7 J1
Culford Rd CDH/CHF RM16 167 P1
IS N1 7 J5
Culgaith Gdns ENC/FH EN2 78 F8
Cullen Sq SOCK/AV RM15 147 H9
Cullen Wy WLSDN NW10 135 P6
Cullera Cl NTHWD HA6 92 G7
Cullerne Cl EW KT17 220 C6
Cullesden Rd PUR/KEN CR8 241 J1
Culling Rd BERM/RHTH SE16 160 B2
Cullings Ct WAB EN9 63 L9
Cullington Cl KTN/HRWW/W HA3 114 F2
Cullingworth Rd WLSDN NW10 116 D10
Culloden Cl STHWK SE1 19 P8
Culloden Rd ENC/FH EN2 79 J6
Culloden St POP/IOD E14 141 H8
Cull's Rd RGUW GU3 248 A10
Cullum St FENCHST EC3M 13 J7
Culmington Pde WEA * W13 135 H9
Culmington Rd SAND/SEL CR2 223 K4
WEA W13 135 H10
Culmore Rd PECK SE15 160 A6
Culmstock Rd BTSEA SW11 180 B1
Culpepper Cl CHIG IG7 102 E7
Culross Cl SEVS/STOTM N15 119 K2
Culross St MYFR/PKLN W1K 10 C8
Culsac Rd SURB KT6 199 K9
Culverden Rd BAL SW12 180 D6
OXHEY WD19 93 J4
Culverden Ter WEY * KT13 196 E10
Culver Dr OXTED RH8 261 K6
Culver Gv STAN HA7 95 H10
Culverhay ASHTD KT21 237 K2
Culverhouse Gdns
STRHM/NOR SW16 180 G7
Culverlands Cl STAN HA7 94 G5
Culverley Rd CAT SE6 182 G4
Culver Rd STAL AL1 38 D5
Culvers Av CAR SM5 202 A9
Culvers Cft BEAC HP9 89 H7
Culvers Retreat CAR SM5 202 A8
Culverstone Cl HAYES BR2 205 L6
Culvers Wy CAR SM5 202 A10
Culvert La UX/CGN UB8 131 L4
Culvert Pl BTSEA SW11 158 B8
Culvert Rd BTSEA SW11 158 A8
SEVS/STOTM N15 119 M3
Culvey Cl HART DA3 211 K5
Culworth St STJWD NW8 3 N8
Cumberland Av GUW GU2 249 M5
GVE DA12 190 F3
HCH RM12 125 M8
SLN SL2 129 H6
WELL DA16 163 J10
WLSDN NW10 135 N5
Cumberland Cl AMSS HP7 69 N5
BARK/HLT * IG6 102 F9
HACK E8 7 L2
HERT/WAS SG14 25 J2
HHS/BOV HP3 36 F10
HOR/WEW KT19 220 B6
RYNPK SW20 178 G10
TWK TW1 176 G2
Cumberland Dr BXLYHN DA7 163 P6
CHSGTN KT9 199 K10
DART DA1 187 N3
ESH/CLAY KT10 198 F9
Cumberland Gdns FSBYW WC1X 5 P9
HDN * NW4 96 G10
Cumberland Ga BAY/PAD W2 10 A7
CAMTN NW1 4 E9
Cumberland Market CAMTN NW1 4 E9
Cumberland Pk ACT W3 135 P9
Cumberland Pl CAMTN NW1 4 E9
CAT SE6 183 L4
SUN TW16 197 H4
Cumberland Rd ACT W3 135 P9
ASHF TW15 173 N6
BARN SW13 156 C7
ED N9 100 B2
HAYES BR2 205 K4
HNWL W7 154 E1
HRW HA1 114 A3
KTN/HRWW/W HA3 115 L1
MNPK E12 122 A9
PLSTW E13 141 N7
RCH/KEW TW9 155 M7
SNWD SE25 204 A6
WALTH E17 100 D10
WDGN N22 98 G10
Cumberlands PUR/KEN CR8 241 L1
Cumberland St PIM SW1V 16 F7
STA TW18 172 G8
Cumberland Ter CAMTN NW1 4 E8
PGE/AN * SE20 182 A10
Cumberland Terrace Ms
CAMTN NW1 4 E8
Cumberlow Av SNWD SE25 203 P3
Cumberlow Pl HHS/BOV HP3 36 D7
Cumbernauld Gdns SUN TW16 174 G8
Cumberton Rd TOTM N17 99 L9
Cumbrae Cl SLN SL2 129 M10
Cumbrae Gdns SURB KT6 199 J9
Cumbrian Av BXLYHN DA7 164 F8
Cumbrian Gdns CRICK NW2 116 G7
Cumbrian Wy UX/CGN UB8 131 N3
Cumley Rd CHONG CM5 66 F6
Cummings Hall La ABR/ST RM4 105 K4
Cumming St IS N1 5 P8
Cumnor Cl BRXN/ST * SW9 158 G8
Cumnor Gdns EW KT17 220 D3
Cumnor Ri PUR/KEN CR8 241 K3
Cumnor Rd BELMT SM2 221 M3
Cunard Crs WCHMH N21 79 L10
Cunard Rd WLSDN NW10 136 A5
Cundalls Rd WARE SG12 26 D1
Cundy Rd CAN/RD E16 141 P8
Cundy St BGVA SW1W 16 D6
Cunliffe Cl EPSOM KT18 237 N10
Cunliffe Rd HOR/WEW KT19 220 C1
Cunliffe St STRHM/NOR SW16 180 D9
Cunningham Av GU GU1 250 D9
PEND EN3 80 D2
STAL AL1 38 E8
Cunningham Cl CHDH RM6 123 M3
WWKM BR4 204 G9
Cunningham Hill Rd STAL AL1 38 E8
Cunningham Pk HRW HA1 114 C3
Cunningham Pl STJWD NW8 9 L1
Cunningham Ri EPP CM16 66 D1
Cunningham Rd BNSTD SM7 239 N1
CHES/WCR EN8 62 D3
SEVS/STOTM * N15 119 P2
Cunnington St CHSWK W4 155 P2
Cupar Rd BTSEA SW11 158 B7
Cupola Cl BMLY BR1 183 N8
Cureton St WEST SW1P 17 K7
Curfew Bell Rd CHERT KT16 195 J7
Curfew Yd WDSR * SL4 149 J7
Curlew Cl BERK HP4 33 P6
SAND/SEL CR2 224 C7
THMD SE28 143 N9
Curlew Ct BROX * EN10 44 E9
Curlew Gdns RGUE GU4 250 G8
The Curlews GVE DA12 190 G5
Curlew St STHWK SE1 19 L1
Curlew Wy YEAD UB4 133 L7
Curling Cl COUL/CHIP CR5 240 G6
Curling La GRAYS RM17 167 L4
Curling V GUW GU2 267 M2
Curnick's La WNWD SE27 181 K7
Curran Av BFN/LL DA15 185 J1
WLGTN SM6 202 B10
Curran Cl UX/CGN UB8 131 M6
Currey Rd NTHLT UB5 134 B1
Curricle St ACT W3 136 B10
Currie Hill Cl WIM/MER SW19 179 J7
Curriers La SL SL1 108 C10
Currie St HERT/BAY SG13 25 M4
Curry Ri MLHL NW7 96 G7
Cursitor St FLST/FETLN EC4A 12 A5
Curtain Pl SDTCH EC2A 13 K1
Curtain Rd SDTCH EC2A 13 J2
Curteys HLWE CM17 29 N6
Curthwaite Gdns ENC/FH EN2 78 E8
Curtis Cl RKW/CH/CXG WD3 91 K2
Curtis Dr ACT W3 136 A8
Curtis Field Rd
STRHM/NOR SW16 180 G7
Curtis La ALP/SUD HA0 135 K1
Curtismill Cl STMC/STPC BR5 207 L3
Curtis Mill La ABR/ST RM4 84 F8
Curtismill Wy STMC/STPC BR5 207 L3
Curtis Rd DORK RH4 272 E1
EMPK RM11 125 N6
HHS/BOV HP3 36 E7
HOR/WEW KT19 219 P1
HSLWW TW4 175 N3
Curtis St STHWK SE1 19 L5
Curtis Wy BERK HP4 34 A6
STHWK SE1 19 L5
Curvan Cl EW KT17 220 C6
The Curve SHB W12 136 D9
Curwen Av FSTGT E7 121 N9
Curwen Rd SHB W12 156 D1
Curzon Av BEAC HP9 88 C7
PEND EN3 80 C9
STAN HA7 94 F9
Curzon Cl ORP BR6 226 G1
WEY KT13 216 B1
Curzon Crs BARK IG11 143 J5
WLSDN NW10 136 B2
Curzon Dr GRAYS RM17 167 P6
Curzon Pl MYFR/PKLN W1K 10 D10
PIN HA5 113 K3
Curzon Rd EA W5 134 G6
MUSWH N10 98 C10
THHTH CR7 203 H6
WEY KT13 216 B1
Curzon St MYFR/PICC W1J 10 F9
Cusack Cl TWK * TW1 176 E7
Cussons Cl CHESW EN7 61 P5
Custom House Reach
BERM/RHTH * SE16 160 E2
Cutcombe Rd CMBW SE5 159 K8
Cuthberga Cl BARK IG11 142 F2
Cuthbert Cl CHESW EN7 61 N5
Cuthbert Gdns SNWD SE25 203 M3
Cuthbert Rd CROY/NA CR0 203 J9
UED N18 99 P6
WALTH E17 121 H1
Cuthbert St BAY/PAD W2 9 L3
Cutlers Gardens Ar LVPST EC2M 13 K5
Cutler St HDTCH EC3A 13 K5
Cutmore Dr STALE/WH AL4 39 N8
Cutmore St GVW DA11 190 E3
The Cut STHWK SE1 18 B1
Cuttinglye La CRAWE RH10 285 P4
Cuttsfield Ter HHW HP1 35 J7
Cutty Sark Ct GRH * DA9 188 F1
Cuxton Cl BXLYHS DA6 185 P1
Cwmbran Ct HHNE HP2 36 A2
Cyclamen Cl HPTN TW12 175 P9
Cyclamen Rd SWLY BR8 208 E4
Cyclamen Wy HOR/WEW KT19 219 P2
Cygnet Av EBED/NFELT TW14 175 K3
Cygnet Cl BORE WD6 75 P5
NTHWD HA6 92 D8
WLSDN NW10 116 A10
The Cygnets FELT TW13 175 M7
STA TW18 173 J8
Cygnet St WCHPL E1 13 M1
Cygnet Vw WTHK RM20 166 E2
Cygnet Wy YEAD UB4 133 L8
Cymbeline Ct HRW * HA1 114 E4
Cynthia St IS N1 5 P8
Cypress Av ENC/FH EN2 79 H1
WGCE AL7 23 M6
WHTN TW2 176 B3
Cypress Cl WAB * EN9 63 J10
Cypress Ct VW GU25 194 C4
Cypress Gdns BROCKY SE4 182 D1
Cypress Gv BARK/HLT IG6 103 H7
Cypress Rd GU GU1 249 P8
KTN/HRWW/W HA3 94 C10
SNWD SE25 203 M2
Cypress Tree Cl BFN/LL DA15 185 J4
Cypress Wk EGH TW20 171 N9
GSTN * WD25 73 J1
Cypress Wy EW KT17 220 G10
Cyprians Av CHOB/PIR GU24 230 G7
Cyprus Av FNCH N3 97 H10
Cyprus Cl FSBYPK N4 119 H4
Cyprus Gdns FNCH N3 97 H10
Cyprus Pl BETH E2 140 B4
EHAM E6 142 D9
Cyprus Rd ED N9 99 N3
FNCH N3 97 J10
Cyprus St BETH E2 140 B4
Cyrena Rd EDUL SE22 181 N2
Cyril Rd BXLYHN DA7 163 P8
ORP BR6 207 K7
Cyrils Wy STAL AL1 38 C9
Cyrus St FSBYE EC1V 12 D1
Czar St DEPT SE8 160 F5

D

Dabbling Cl ERITH * DA8 165 J6
Dabbs Hill La NTHLT UB5 133 N1
D'Abernon Cl ESH/CLAY KT10 217 P1
D'Abernon Dr COB KT11 235 M2
Dabin Crs GNWCH SE10 161 H7
Dacca St DEPT SE8 160 E5
Dace Rd BOW E3 140 F3
Dacorum Wy HHW HP1 35 M6
Dacre Av CLAY IG5 102 D10
SOCK/AV RM15 146 C10
Dacre Cl CHIG IG7 102 F5
GFD/PVL UB6 134 A4
Dacre Crs SOCK/AV RM15 146 C10
Dacre Gdns BORE WD6 76 A5
CHIG IG7 102 F5
LEW * SE13 161 K10
Dacre Pk LEW SE13 161 K9
Dacre Pl LEW SE13 161 K9
Dacre Rd CROY/NA CR0 202 F8
PLSTW E13 141 N3
WAN E11 121 L6
Dacres Est FSTH * SE23 182 C6
Dacres Rd FSTH SE23 182 C6
Dacre St STJSPK SW1H 17 J3
Dade Wy NWDGN UB2 153 N4
Dads Wd HLW CM20 46 F1
Daerwood Cl HAYES BR2 206 C8
Daffodil Av BRWN CM15 86 G9
Daffodil Cl CROY/NA CR0 204 C8
HPTN TW12 175 P9
Daffodil Dr CHOB/PIR GU24 230 F2
Daffodil Gdns IL IG1 122 E10
Daffodil St SHB W12 136 C9
Dafforne Rd TOOT SW17 180 A6
Dagden Rd RGUE GU4 268 B6
Dagenham Av DAGW RM9 143 P2
Dagenham Rd DAGE RM10 124 D9
LEY E10 120 E6
RAIN RM13 144 E2
ROMW/RG RM7 124 E5
Dagger La BORE WD6 74 F10
Daggs Dell Rd HHW HP1 35 H4
Dagley La RGUE GU4 268 A6
Dagmar Av WBLY HA9 115 L9
Dagmar Gdns WLSDN NW10 136 G4
Dagmar Pas IS N1 6 C3
Dagmar Rd CMBW SE5 159 M7
DAGE RM10 144 D2
FSBYPK N4 119 H5
KUTN/CMB KT2 199 L1
NWDGN UB2 153 M3
SEVS/STOTM N15 119 L1
SNWD SE25 203 M4
WDGN N22 98 E9
WDSR SL4 149 J8
Dagmar Ter IS N1 6 D4
Dagnall Crs UX/CGN UB8 131 M
Dagnall Pk SNWD SE25 203 M4
Dagnall Rd SNWD SE25 203 M4
Dagnall St BTSEA SW11 158 A7
Dagnam Park Cl HARH RM3 105 P6
Dagnam Park Dr HARH RM3 105 M6
Dagnam Park Gdns HARH RM3 105 P
Dagnam Park Sq HARH RM3 105 P
Dagnan Rd BAL SW12 180 C3
Dagonet Rd BMLY BR1 183 M6
Dagwood La BRWN CM15 86 G
Dahlia Cl CHESW EN7 61 K
Dahlia Dr SWLY BR8 208 G
Dahlia Gdns IL IG1 142 E
MTCM CR4 202 E
Dahlia Rd ABYW SE2 163 L
Dahomey Rd STRHM/NOR SW16 180 D
Daiglen Dr SOCK/AV RM15 146 F
Daimler Wy WLGTN SM6 222 F
Daines Cl MNPK E12 122 C
SOCK/AV RM15 146 F
Dainford Cl BMLY BR1 183 J
Daintry Cl KTN/HRWW/W HA3 114 F
Dairsie Rd ELTH/MOT SE9 162 D
Dairy Cl BMLY * BR1 183 N1
EYN DA4 188 A1
THHTH CR7 203 K
Dairyfields CRAWW RH11 283 K
Dairyglen Av CHES/WCR EN8 62 C
Dairy La EDEN TN8 262 E1
WOOL/PLUM SE18 162 C
Dairyman Cl CRICK * NW2 116 G
Dairymans Wk RGUE GU4 250 E
Dairy Wy ABLGY WD5 54 G
Daisy Cl CROY/NA CR0 204 C
Daisy La FUL/PGN SW6 157 K
Daisy Rd SWFD E18 101 N1
Dakota Cl CROY/NA CR0 222 G
Dakota Gdns EHAM E6 142 B
Dalberg Rd BRXS/STRHM SW2 181 H
Dalberg Wy ABYW SE2 163 N
Dalby Rd WAND/EARL SW18 157 M1
Dalbys Crs TOTM N17 99 M
Dalby St KTTN NW5 4 E
Dalcross Rd HEST TW5 153 M
Dale Av EDGW HA8 95 L
HSLWW TW4 153 M
Dalebury Rd TOOT SW17 180 A
Dale Cl ADL/WDHM KT15 215 L
ASC SL5 192 F
BAR EN5 77 L1
BKHTH/KID SE3 161 M
DART DA1 186 G
PIN HA5 93 J
SOCK/AV RM15 146 F
Dale Ct GSTN * WD25 55 H
SBW CM21 29 N
Dale Dr YEAD UB4 132 G
Dale Gdns WFD IG8 101 N
Dalegarth Gdns PUR/KEN CR8 223 L
Dale Green Rd FBAR/BDGN N11 98 C
Dale Gv NFNCH/WDSP N12 97 M
Daleham Av EGH TW20 172 D
Daleham Dr UX/CGN UB8 132 C
Daleham Gdns HAMP NW3 117 N1
Dale Lodge Rd ASC SL5 192 F
Dale Park Av CAR SM5 202 A
Dale Park Rd NRWD SE19 203 K
Dale Rd DART DA1 186 G
GFD/PVL UB6 134 A
KTTN NW5 118 B1
MEO DA13 189 M
PUR/KEN CR8 223 H
SUN * TW16 174 G1
SUT SM1 221
SWLY BR8 208 D
WALW SE17 18 D1
WOT/HER KT12 196 C
Dale Rw NTGHL * W11 8 E
Dale Side CFSP/GDCR SL9 110 E
Daleside ORP BR6 227 K
Daleside Cl ORP BR6 227 K
Daleside Dr POTB/CUF EN6 59
Daleside Gdns CHIG IG7 102 F
Daleside Rd HOR/WEW KT19 220 A
TOOT SW17 180 C
Dales Pth BORE * WD6 76 A
Dales Rd BORE WD6 76 A
Dale St CHSWK W4 156 E
The Dale HAYES BR2 226 A
WAB EN9 63 K
Dale Vw BAR * EN5 77

EPSOM KT18 237 N9
ERITH DA8 165 H8
WOKN/KNAP GU21 231 M4
Dale View Av CHING E4 101 H3
Dale View Crs CHING E4 101 H4
Dale View Gdns CHING E4 101 J4
Daleview Rd SEVS/STOTM N15 119 M4
Dalewood HARP AL5 20 C2
WGCE AL7 23 N6
Dalewood Cl EMPK RM11 125 N5
Dalewood Gdns CRAWE RH10 284 A5
WPK KT4 200 E9
Dale Wood Rd ORP BR6 207 H7
Daley St HOM E9 140 C1
Daley Thompson Wy VX/NE SW8 158 C8
Dalgarno Gdns NKENS W10 136 F7
Dalgarno Wy NKENS W10 136 F6
Dalkeith Gv STAN HA7 95 J6
Dalkeith Rd DUL SE21 181 K4
HARP AL5 20 B1
IL IG1 122 F8
Dallas Rd CHEAM SM3 221 H3
EA W5 135 L7
HDN NW4 116 D5
SYD SE26 182 A7
Dallas Ter HYS/HAR UB3 152 G2
Dallega Cl HYS/HAR UB3 132 D9
Dallinger Rd LEE/GVPK SE12 183 L2
Dalling Rd HMSMTH W6 156 E2
Dallington Cl WOT/HER KT12 217 K3
Dallington Sq FSBYE EC1V 12 D1
Dallington St FSBYE EC1V 12 D1
Dallin Rd BXLYHS DA6 163 N10
WOOL/PLUM SE18 162 E6
Dalmain Rd FSTH SE23 182 C4
Dalmally Rd CROY/NA CR0 203 N7
Dalmeny Av HOLWY N7 118 E9
STRHM/NOR SW16 203 H2
Dalmeny Cl ALP/SUD HA0 135 H1
Dalmeny Crs HSLW TW3 154 C10
Dalmeny Rd BAR EN5 77 M10
CAR SM5 222 B4
ERITH DA8 164 C7
HOLWY N7 118 E9
WPK KT4 200 E10
Dalmeyer Rd WLSDN NW10 136 C1
Dalmore Av ESH/CLAY KT10 218 E3
Dalmore Rd DUL SE21 181 K5
Dalroy Cl SOCK/AV RM15 146 F8
Dalrymple Cl STHGT/OAK N14 78 E10
Dalrymple Rd BROCKY SE4 160 D10
Dalston Gdns STAN HA7 95 K9
Dalston La HACK E8 7 L1
Dalton Av MTCM CR4 201 P2
Dalton Cl ORP BR6 207 H10
YEAD UB4 132 E6
Daltons Rd SWLY BR8 208 D9
Dalton St STALW/RED AL3 38 C5
WNWD SE27 181 J5
Dalton Wy WAT WD17 73 L9
Dalwood St CMBW SE5 159 M7
Dalyell Rd BRXN/ST SW9 158 G9
Damask Cl CHOB/PIR GU24 212 D9
Damask Crs CAN/RD E16 141 K6
Damask Gn HHW HP1 35 H7
Damer Ter WBPTN SW10 157 M6
Dames Rd FSTGT E7 121 M9
Dame St IS N1 6 E7
Damien St WCHPL E1 140 A7
Damigos Rd GVE DA12 191 J4
Damon Cl SCUP DA14 185 L6
Damsel Ct BERM/RHTH * SE16 19 P2
Damson Dr HYS/HAR UB3 133 H9
Damson Gv SL SL1 149 H1
Damson Wy STALE/WH AL4 39 H4
Damsonwood Rd NWDGN UB2 153 P2
Danbrook Rd STRHM/NOR SW16 202 F1
Danbury Cl BRW CM14 86 E9
CHDH RM6 123 N1
Danbury Crs SOCK/AV RM15 146 G8
Danbury Ms CAR SM5 222 C1
Danbury Rd LOU IG10 82 B10
RAIN RM13 144 G3
Danbury St IS N1 6 D7
Danbury Wy WFD IG8 101 P7
Danby St PECK SE15 159 N9
Dancer Rd FUL/PGN SW6 157 J7
RCH/KEW TW9 155 M9
Dancers Hill Rd BAR EN5 76 G2
Dandelion Cl ROMW/RG RM7 124 F7
Dando Crs BKHTH/KID SE3 161 N9
Dandridge Cl DTCH/LGLY SL3 150 A3
GNWCH SE10 161 L4
Danebury Av PUT/ROE SW15 178 C3
Daneby Rd CAT SE6 183 H6
Dane Cl AMSS HP7 69 L7
BXLY DA5 186 B3
ORP BR6 226 G2
Dane Ct WOKS/MYFD GU22 233 J1
Danecourt Gdns CROY/NA CR0 203 N10
Danecroft Rd HNHL SE24 181 K1
Danehurst Cl EGH TW20 172 B9
Danehurst Gdns REDBR IG4 122 B3
Danehurst St FUL/PGN SW6 157 H7
Daneland EBAR EN4 78 A10
Danemead HOD EN11 26 F10
Danemead Gv NTHLT UB5 114 A10
Danemere St PUT/ROE SW15 156 F9
Dane Pl BOW E3 140 D4
Dane Rd ASHF TW15 174 D9
IL IG1 122 F10
SEV TN13 246 F3
STHL UB1 133 M9
UED N18 100 B5
WARL CR6 242 C3
WEA W13 135 H9
WIM/MER SW19 201 M1
Danesbury Pk HERT/WAS SG14 25 L4
Danesbury Rd FELT TW13 175 J4
Danes Cl GVW DA11 189 P6
LHD/OX KT22 218 B10
Danescombe LEE/GVPK SE12 183 M4
Danescourt Crs SUT SM1 201 M9
Danescroft Av HDN * NW4 116 G3
Danescroft Gdns HDN NW4 116 G3
Danesdale Rd HOM E9 140 D1
Danesfield RPLY/SEND GU23 233 J9
Danesfield Cl WOT/HER KT12 197 J10
Danes Ga HRW HA1 114 D1
Danes Hl WOKS/MYFD GU22 232 E4
Daneshill Cl REDH RH1 257 P9
Daneshill La REDH RH1 257 P9
Danes Hill School Dr
LHD/OX * KT22 218 C10
Danesmead COB KT11 217 P7
Danes Rd ROMW/RG RM7 124 D5
The Danes LCOL/BKTW AL2 56 B4
Dane St GINN WC1R 11 N4
Danes Wy BRW CM15 86 E9
LHD/OX KT22 218 C10
Daneswood Av CAT SE6 183 H6
Daneswood Cl WEY KT13 216 C2
Danethorpe Rd ALP/SUD HA0 135 J1
Danetree Cl HOR/WEW KT19 219 P4
Danetree Rd HOR/WEW KT19 219 P4
Danette Gdns DAGE RM10 124 A7
Daneville Rd CMBW SE5 159 L7
Dangan Rd WAN E11 121 M4
Daniel Bolt Cl POP/IOD E14 140 G7
Daniel Cl CDH/CHF RM16 167 K1
CDH/CHF RM16 168 E2
HSLWW TW4 175 N3
UED N18 100 B5
WIM/MER SW19 179 P9
Daniel Gdns PECK SE15 159 N6
Daniells WGCE AL7 23 K4
Daniell Wy CROY/NA CR0 202 F8
Daniel Pl HDN NW4 116 E4
Daniel Rd ACT W3 135 L9
Daniels La WARL CR6 242 E2
Daniel's Rd PECK SE15 160 B9
Daniel Wy BNSTD SM7 221 L10
Dan Leno Wk FUL/PGN * SW6 157 L6
Danses Cl RGUE GU4 250 G8
Dansey Pl SOHO/SHAV W1D 11 J7
Dansington Rd WELL DA16 163 K10
Danson Crs WELL DA16 163 L9
Danson La WELL DA16 163 L10
Danson Md WELL DA16 163 M9
Danson Rd BXLYHS DA6 185 N1
Danson U/P BFN/LL DA15 185 M2
Dante Rd LBTH SE11 18 C5
Danube St CHEL SW3 15 P7
Danvers Rd CEND/HSY/T N8 118 E2
Danvers St CHEL SW3 15 M10
Danvers Wy CTHM CR3 241 K9
Danyon Cl RAIN RM13 145 K4
Danziger Wy BORE WD6 75 P5
Dapdune Rd GU GU1 250 A10
Daphne Gdns CHING E4 101 H4
Daphne St WAND/EARL SW18 179 M2
Daplyn St WCHPL E1 13 N3
Darblay Cl STALE/WH AL4 21 L6
D'arblay St SOHO/CST W1F 11 H6
Darby Cl CTHM CR3 241 K8
Darby Crs SUN TW16 197 K2
Darby Dr WAB EN9 63 H9
Darby Gdns SUN TW16 197 K2
Darcy Av WLGTN SM6 222 D1
Darcy Cl CHES/WCR EN8 62 D7
COUL/CHIP CR5 241 J5
RBRW/HUT CM13 107 N1
TRDG/WHET N20 97 N3
D'arcy Dr KTN/HRWW/W HA3 115 J2
D'arcy Gdns DAGW RM9 144 A3
KTN/HRWW/W HA3 115 K2
Darcy Pl ASHTD KT21 237 L3
Darcy Rd ASHTD KT21 237 L3
CHEAM SM3 220 G1
ISLW TW7 154 F7
STRHM/NOR SW16 202 D2
Darell Rd RCH/KEW TW9 155 M9
Darent Cl SEV TN13 246 D8
Darenth Dr GVE DA12 191 L4
Darenth Gdns BH/WHM TN16 262 G2
Darenth Hl RDART DA2 188 A8
Darenth La SEV TN13 246 F7
SOCK/AV RM15 146 F8
Darenth Park Av RDART DA2 188 C5
Darenth Pl RDART * DA2 188 C8
Darenth Rd DART DA1 187 P5
STNW/STAM N16 119 N5
WELL DA16 163 K7
Darenth Rd South RDART DA2 188 A7
Darenth Wy HORL RH6 280 A2
RSEV TN14 229 H7
Darenth Wood Rd RDART DA2 188 D4
Darent Md EYN DA4 210 A1
Darent Valley Pth DART DA1 165 L7
EYN DA4 210 A5
RSEV TN14 247 H1
SEV TN13 246 E7
Darfield Rd BROCKY SE4 182 E1
GU GU1 250 D7
Darfield Wy NKENS W10 136 G9
Darfur St PUT/ROE SW15 156 G9
Dargate Cl NRWD SE19 181 N10
Darien Rd BTSEA SW11 157 N9
Darkes La POTB/CUF EN6 59 K8
Dark La BRW CM14 106 F8
CHESW EN7 61 P6
HARP AL5 20 C4
RGUW GU3 266 A5
Darlands Dr BAR EN5 76 G9
Darlan Rd FUL/PGN SW6 157 J6
Darlaston Rd WIM/MER SW19 178 G10
Darley Cl ADL/WDHM KT15 215 M2
CROY/NA CR0 204 C6
Darley Cft LCOL/BKTW * AL2 56 A4
Darleydale CRAWW RH11 283 M10
Darley Dene Ct
ADL/WDHM * KT15 215 M1
Darley Dr NWMAL KT3 200 A2
Darley Rd BTSEA SW11 180 A2
ED N9 99 N2
Darling Rd BROCKY SE4 160 F9
Darling Rw WCHPL E1 140 A6
Darlington Ct BRWN CM15 86 F10
Darlington Gdns HARH RM3 105 L6
Darlington Rd WNWD SE27 181 J8
Darlton Cl DART DA1 164 G9
Darmaine Cl SAND/SEL CR2 223 K4
Darndale Cl WALTH E17 100 E10
Darnets Fld RSEV TN14 246 G3
Darnicle Hl CHESW EN7 61 H1
Darnley Pk WEY KT13 196 C10
Darnley Rd GRAYS * RM17 167 N5
GVW DA11 190 D2
HACK E8 140 A1
WFD IG8 101 M9
Darnley St GVW DA11 190 D3
Darnley Ter NTGHL W11 136 G10
Darns Hl SWLY BR8 208 D7
Darrell Cl DTCH/LGLY SL3 150 B3
Darrell Rd EDUL SE22 181 P1
Darren Cl FSBYPK N4 118 G5
Darrick Wood Rd ORP BR6 206 G9
Darrington Rd BORE WD6 75 K5
Darris Cl YEAD UB4 133 M6
Darr's La BERK HP4 33 J4
Darsley Dr VX/NE SW8 158 E7
Dart Cl DTCH/LGLY SL3 150 E5
UPMR RM14 126 C4
Dartfields HARH RM3 105 L7
Dartford Av ED N9 80 B10
Dartford Rd BXLY DA5 186 D4
DART DA1 187 H2
EYN DA4 209 N6
SEV TN13 247 K10
Dartford St WALW SE17 18 F9
Dart Gn SOCK/AV RM15 146 G8
Dartmoor Wk POP/IOD * E14 160 F3
Dartmouth Av
WOKN/KNAP GU21 214 F10
Dartmouth Cl NTGHL W11 8 D5
Dartmouth Gv GNWCH SE10 161 H7
Dartmouth Hl GNWCH SE10 161 H7
Dartmouth Park Av KTTN NW5 118 C8
Dartmouth Park Hl ARCH N19 118 C6
Dartmouth Park Rd KTTN NW5 118 C8
Dartmouth Pl CHSWK W4 156 B5
FSTH SE23 182 B5
Dartmouth Rd CRICK NW2 2 A1
HAYES BR2 205 M7
HDN NW4 116 D4
RSLP HA4 113 H8
SYD SE26 182 A6
Dartmouth Rw LEW SE13 161 H8
Dartmouth St STJSPK SW1H 17 J2
Dartmouth Ter GNWCH SE10 161 J7
Dartnell Av BF/WBF KT14 215 M8
Dartnell Cl BF/WBF KT14 215 L8
Dartnell Ct BF/WBF KT14 215 M8
Dartnell Crs BF/WBF KT14 215 L8
Dartnell Park Rd BF/WBF KT14 215 L8
Dartnell Pl BF/WBF KT14 215 L8
Dartnell Rd CROY/NA CR0 203 N7
Dartrey Wk WBPTN * SW10 157 M6
Dart St MV/WKIL W9 2 C9
The Dart HHNE HP2 36 A1
Dartview Cl GRAYS RM17 168 B3
Darvel Cl WOKN/KNAP GU21 231 M2
Darvell Dr CSHM HP5 50 F5
Darville Rd STNW/STAM N16 119 N8
Darvill's La SL SL1 149 J1
Darwell Cl EHAM E6 142 D4
Darwin Cl FBAR/BDGN N11 98 C4
ORP BR6 226 G2
STALW/RED AL3 38 D2
Darwin Dr GFD/PVL UB6 134 A8
Darwin Gdns OXHEY WD19 93 K6
Darwin Rd BTFD TW8 155 H4
DTCH/LGLY SL3 150 C1
TIL RM18 168 C7
WDGN N22 99 J9
WELL DA16 163 J9
Darwin St WALW SE17 19 H5
Darygton Dr GFD/PVL UB6 134 C4
GU GU1 250 E10
The Dashes HLW CM20 29 H10
Dashwood Cl BF/WBF KT14 215 M8
BXLYHS DA6 186 B1
DTCH/LGLY SL3 149 P3
Dashwood Lang Rd
ADL/WDHM * KT15 215 M2
Dashwood Rd CEND/HSY/T N8 118 G4
GVW DA11 190 D4
Dassett Rd WNWD SE27 181 J8
Datchelor Pl CMBW * SE5 159 L7
Datchet Cl HHNE HP2 36 C1
Datchet Pl DTCH/LGLY SL3 149 N7
Datchet Rd CAT SE6 182 E6
DTCH/LGLY SL3 150 C9
WDSR SL4 149 J6
WDSR SL4 149 M10
Datchworth Turn HHNE HP2 36 D6
Date St WALW SE17 18 G8
Daubeney Gdns TOTM N17 99 K8
Daubeney Rd CLPT E5 120 D10
TOTM N17 99 K8
Dault Rd WAND/EARL SW18 179 M2
Davenant Rd ARCH N19 118 E7
Davenant St WCHPL E1 13 P4
Davenham Av NTHWD HA6 92 G5
Davenport Cl TEDD * TW11 176 F9
Davenport Rd LEW SE13 182 G2
SCUP DA14 185 N5
Daventer Dr STAN HA7 94 E8
Daventry Av WALTH E17 120 F4
Daventry Cl DTCH/LGLY SL3 151 J7
Daventry Gdns HARH RM3 105 K6
Daventry Rd HARH RM3 105 K6
Daventry St CAMTN NW1 9 N3
Davern Cl GNWCH SE10 161 L3
Davey Cl HOLWY N7 5 P2
PLMGR N13 98 G6
Davey Rd HOM E9 140 F2
Davey St PECK SE15 19 M10
David Av GFD/PVL UB6 134 D5
David Cl HYS/HAR UB3 152 E6
David Dr HARH RM3 105 P7
Davidge St STHWK SE1 18 D2
David Ms MHST W1U 10 B3
David Rd BCTR RM8 123 P7
DTCH/LGLY SL3 151 J8
Davidson Gdns VX/NE SW8 158 F6
Davidson Rd CROY/NA CR0 203 M8
Davidson Wy ROMW/RG RM7 124 F4
David's Rd FSTH SE23 182 B4
David St SRTFD E15 141 J1
Davids Wy BARK/HLT IG6 103 H8
David Twigg Cl KUTN/CMB KT2 199 K1
Davies Cl RAIN RM13 145 K5
RGODL GU7 267 J10
SNWD SE25 203 N6
Davies La WAN E11 121 K7
Davies Ms MYFR/PKLN W1K 10 E7
Davies St HERT/BAY SG13 25 M5
MYFR/PKLN W1K 10 E7
Davies Wk ISLW TW7 154 C7
Davington Gdns BCTR RM8 123 L10
Davington Rd BCTR RM8 143 L1
Davinia Cl WFD IG8 102 C7
Davis Av GVW DA11 190 B4
Davis Cl SEV TN13 247 K8
Davis Ct STAL * AL1 38 D6
Davison Cl CHES/WCR EN8 62 C4
Davison Dr CHES/WCR EN8 62 C4
Davis Rd ACT W3 136 C10
CDH/CHF RM16 167 L2
CHSGTN KT9 219 M1
SOCK/AV RM15 146 C10
WEY KT13 216 A6
Davis St PLSTW E13 141 N4
Davisville Rd SHB W12 156 D1
Davos Cl WOKS/MYFD GU22 232 B5
Davys Cl STALE/WH AL4 21 K4
Davy's Pl GVE DA12 191 H9
Dawell Dr BH/WHM TN16 243 P3
Dawes Av HCH RM12 125 L8
ISLW TW7 176 F1
Dawes Cl CSHM HP5 50 G8
GRH DA9 188 E1
HGDN/ICK UB10 131 P4
Dawes Ct ESH/CLAY KT10 218 A1
Dawes East Rd SL SL1 128 B6
Dawes La RKW/CH/CXG WD3 71 J2
Dawes Moor Cl SLN SL2 129 P8
Dawes Rd FUL/PGN SW6 157 J6
HGDN/ICK UB10 131 P4
Dawes St WALW SE17 19 H7
Dawley WGCE AL7 23 J2
Dawley Av UX/CGN UB8 132 C7
Dawley Ct HHNE HP2 36 A2
Dawley Gn SOCK/AV RM15 146 F8
Dawley Pde UX/CGN UB8 132 D9
Dawley Ride DTCH/LGLY SL3 151 H7
Dawley Rd HYS/HAR UB3 152 F2
Dawlish Av GFD/PVL UB6 134 F4
PLMGR N13 98 F5
WAND/EARL SW18 179 L5
Dawlish Dr GDMY/SEVK IG3 123 J9
PIN HA5 113 M3
RSLP HA4 113 H7
Dawlish Rd CRICK NW2 136 G1
LEY E10 121 H7
TOTM N17 119 P1
Dawnay Gdns WAND/EARL SW18 179 N5
Dawnay Rd GT/LBKH KT23 254 A2
WAND/EARL SW18 179 M5
Dawn Cl HSLWW TW4 153 M9
Dawn Crs SRTFD E15 141 J3
Dawney Hl CHOB/PIR GU24 230 D7
Dawneys Rd CHOB/PIR GU24 230 D8
Dawn Redwood Cl
DTCH/LGLY SL3 150 D9
Dawpool Rd CRICK NW2 116 C7
Daws Hl CHING E4 81 H7
Daws La MLHL NW7 96 C6
Dawson Av BARK IG11 143 J2
STMC/STPC BR5 207 L2
Dawson Cl HYS/HAR UB3 132 E7
WDSR SL4 148 F8
WOOL/PLUM SE18 162 F3
Dawson Dr RAIN RM13 145 J2
SWLY BR8 186 F10
Dawson Gdns BARK IG11 143 J2
Dawson Pl BAY/PAD W2 8 E7
Dawson Rd BF/WBF KT14 215 N7
CRICK NW2 116 F10
KUT KT1 199 L3
Dawson St BETH E2 7 M8
Dawson Ter ED * N9 100 B1
Daybrook Rd WIM/MER SW19 201 L2
Dayemead WGCE AL7 23 L8
Daylesford Av PUT/ROE SW15 156 D10
Daylop Dr CHIG IG7 103 L4
Daymer Gdns PIN HA5 113 K2
Daymerslea Rdg LHD/OX KT22 237 H7
Day's Acre SAND/SEL CR2 223 N6
Daysbrook Rd
BRXS/STRHM SW2 180 G4
Days Cl HAT AL10 40 C4
Dayseys Hl REDH RH1 277 H9
Days La BFN/LL DA15 185 H3
BRWN CM15 86 F8
Days Md HAT AL10 40 C4
Dayspring GUW GU2 249 N6
Dayton Dr ERITH DA8 165 L5
Dayton Gv PECK SE15 160 B7
Deacon Cl COB KT11 235 J5
CTHM CR3 241 K9
PUR/KEN CR8 222 F5
STAL AL1 38 C10
The Deacon Est CHING * E4 100 E7
Deacon Fld GUW GU2 249 M9
Deacon Ms IS N1 7 H4
Deacon Rd CRICK NW2 136 D1
KUTN/CMB KT2 199 L1
Deacons Cl BORE WD6 75 M8
PIN HA5 93 J10
Deaconsfield Rd HHS/BOV HP3 55 N9
Deacons Hts BORE WD6 75 M10
Deacons Hl OXHEY WD19 73 K10
Deacon's Hill Rd BORE WD6 75 L9
Deacons Leas ORP BR6 226 G1
Deacons Ri EFNCH N2 117 N3
Deacons Ter IS * N1 6 F1
Deacons Wk HPTN TW12 175 P7
Deacon Wy WALW SE17 18 E5
WFD IG8 102 C8
Deadhearn La CSTG HP8 90 B2
Deadman's Ash La
RKW/CH/CXG WD3 71 L2
Deakin Cl WATW WD18 92 F1
Deakins Ter ORP BR6 207 K7
Deal Av SL SL1 128 E8
Deal Porters Wy
BERM/RHTH SE16 160 B2
Deal Rd TOOT SW17 180 B9
Deal St WCHPL E1 13 N3
Dealtree Cl BRWN CM15 86 G1
Dealtry Rd PUT/ROE SW15 156 F10
Deal Wk BRXN/ST SW9 159 H6
Deanacre Cl CFSP/GDCR SL9 90 B7
Dean Bradley St WEST SW1P 17 L4
Dean Cl HGDN/ICK UB10 132 A2
WDSR SL4 148 C9
WOKS/MYFD GU22 233 H2
Dean Ct ALP/SUD HA0 114 G8
GSTN * WD25 55 L9
Deancroft Rd CFSP/GDCR SL9 90 B7
Deancross St WCHPL E1 140 B8
Dean Dr STAN HA7 95 K10
Deane Av RSLP HA4 113 J10
Deane Ct NTHWD * HA6 92 F9
Deane Croft Rd PIN HA5 113 K4
Deanery Cl EFNCH N2 117 P2
Deanery Ms MYFR/PKLN * W1K 10 D9
Deanery Rd EDEN TN8 262 F10
SRTFD E15 141 K1
Deanery St MYFR/PKLN W1K 10 D9
Deane Wy RSLP HA4 113 J4
Dean Farrar St STJSPK SW1H 17 K3
Dean Fld HHS/BOV HP3 52 D3
Deanfield Gdns CROY/NA * CR0 223 L1
Dean Gdns WALTH E17 121 J2
Deanhill Ct MORT/ESHN * SW14 155 N10
Deanhill Rd MORT/ESHN SW14 155 N10
Dean La CTHM CR3 240 F10
REDH RH1 240 D10
Dean Moore Cl STAL AL1 38 C7
Deanoak La REIG RH2 274 G10
Dean Rd CRICK NW2 136 F1
CROY/NA CR0 223 L1
HPTN TW12 175 P8
HSLW TW3 176 A1
THMD SE28 143 K9
Dean Ryle St WEST SW1P 17 L5
Deansbrook Cl EDGW HA8 95 P8
Deansbrook Rd EDGW HA8 95 N8
Dean's Buildings WALW SE17 19 H6
Deans Cl ABLGY WD5 54 E8
AMS HP6 69 L3
CHSWK W4 155 N5
CROY/NA CR0 203 N10
EDGW HA8 95 P7
KWD/TDW/WH KT20 238 E10
SLN SL2 129 N3
Deans Ct BFOR GU20 212 C4
BLKFR EC4V 12 D6
Deanscroft Av CDALE/KGS NW9 115 P7
Dean's Dr MLHL NW7 96 A6
PLMGR N13 99 J7
Deansfield CTHM CR3 259 N1
Dean's Gdns STALE/WH AL4 38 F2
Deans Gate Cl FSTH SE23 182 C6
Dean's La EDGW HA8 95 P7
KWD/TDW/WH KT20 256 E1
REDH RH1 259 H9
Dean's Ms CAVSQ/HST * W1G 10 F5
Deans Rd BRW CM14 106 G4
HNWL W7 154 E1
REDH RH1 258 D6
SUT SM1 201 L10
Dean Stanley St WEST * SW1P 17 L4
Dean St FSTGT E7 121 M10
SOHO/CST W1F 11 J5
Deans Wk COUL/CHIP CR5 241 H4
Deans Wy EDGW HA8 95 P6
Deansway CSHM HP5 50 G5
ED N9 99 M4
EFNCH N2 117 N2
HHS/BOV HP3 36 A9
Deans Yd WEST SW1P 17 K3
Dean Trench St WEST * SW1P 17 L4
Dean Vls COB * KT11 217 K9
Dean Wy CSTG HP8 89 M4
Dearne Cl STAN HA7 94 F6
De'arn Gdns MTCM CR4 201 P3
Dearsley Rd EN EN1 79 P7
Deason St SRTFD * E15 141 H3
De Barowe Ms HBRY * N5 119 J9
Debden Cl KUTN/CMB KT2 177 J8
WFD IG8 102 A8
Debden La LOU IG10 82 E4
Debden Rd LOU IG10 82 E4
De Beauvoir Crs IS N1 7 J5
De Beauvoir Est IS N1 7 J5
De Beauvoir Rd IS N1 7 J3
De Beauvoir Sq IS N1 7 K4
Debenham Rd CHESW EN7 62 A3
Debnams Rd BERM/RHTH SE16 160 B3
De Bohun Av STHGT/OAK N14 78 C10
Deborah Cl ISLW TW7 154 D7
Debrabant Cl ERITH DA8 164 E5
De Broome Rd FELT TW13 175 K4
De Burgh Gdns
KWD/TDW/WH KT20 238 G5
De Burgh Pk BNSTD SM7 239 L2
Deburgh Rd WIM/MER SW19 179 M10
Decies Wy SLN SL2 129 M3
Decima St STHWK SE1 19 J3
Decimus Cl SNWD * SE25 203 L4
Deck Cl BERM/RHTH SE16 140 C10
Decoy Av GLDGN NW11 117 H3
De Crespigny Pk CMBW SE5 159 L8
Dedisham Cl CRAWE RH10 284 B8
Dedswell Dr RGUE GU4 251 K5
Dedworth Dr WDSR SL4 148 D7
Dedworth Rd WDSR SL4 148 E8
Dee Cl UPMR RM14 126 C4
Deeley Rd VX/NE SW8 158 E7
Deena Cl EA W5 135 L8
SL SL1 128 D9
Deep Acres AMS HP6 68 F2
Deepdale WIM/MER SW19 178 G7
Deepdale Av HAYES BR2 205 L4
Deepdale Cl FBAR/BDGN N11 98 B7
Deepdene POTB/CUF EN6 58 G7
Deepdene Av CROY/NA CR0 203 N10
RDKG RH5 273 H2
Deepdene Avenue Rd
DORK RH4 255 H10
Deepdene Cl WAN E11 121 M2
Deepdene Ct WCHMH N21 79 J10
Deepdene Dr RDKG RH5 273 H1
Deepdene Gdns
BRXS/STRHM SW2 180 G3
DORK RH4 272 G1
Deepdene Park Rd RDKG RH5 273 H1
Deepdene Pth LOU IG10 82 E8
Deepdene Rd HNHL SE24 159 K10
LOU IG10 82 D8
WELL DA16 163 K9
Deepdene V DORK RH4 255 H10
Deepdene Wd RDKG RH5 273 J2
Deep Fld DTCH/LGLY SL3 149 N6
Deepfields HORL RH6 280 A2
Deepfield Wy COUL/CHIP CR5 240 F2
Deep Pool La CHOB/PIR GU24 213 M9
Deeprose Cl GUW GU2 249 N6
Deepwell Cl ISLW TW7 154 F7
Deepwood La GFD/PVL UB6 134 C5
Deerbarn Rd GUW GU2 249 N9
Deerbrook Rd BRXS/STRHM SW2 181 J4
Deer Cl HERT/BAY SG13 25 N5
Deerdale Rd HNHL SE24 159 K10
Deere Av RAIN RM13 145 H1
Deerfield Cl WARE SG12 26 C1
Deerhurst Cl FELT TW13 175 H7
HART DA3 211 P3
Deerhurst Crs HPTN TW12 176 B8
Deerhurst Rd KIL/WHAMP NW6 136 G2
STRHM/NOR SW16 180 G8
Deerings Dr PIN HA5 113 H3
Deerings Rd REIG RH2 257 L10
Deerleap Gv CHING E4 80 G9
Deerleap La RSEV TN14 227 N9
Deerleap Rd DORK RH4 272 A3
Dee Rd RCH/KEW TW9 155 L10
WDSR * SL4 148 B6
Deer Pk HLWW/ROY CM19 46 D4
Deer Park Cl KUTN/CMB KT2 177 N10
Deer Park Gdns MTCM * CR4 201 N4
Deer Park Rd WIM/MER SW19 201 L2
Deer Park Wk CSHM HP5 51 K4
Deer Park Wy WWKM BR4 205 N9
Deers Farm Cl RPLY/SEND GU23 233 P2
Deerswood Av HAT AL10 40 E6
Deerswood Cl CRAWW RH11 283 L6
CTHM CR3 241 P10
Deerswood Rd CRAWW RH11 283 L6
Deeside Rd TOOT SW17 179 N6
Dee St POP/IOD E14 141 H8
The Dee HHNE HP2 36 A1
Deeves Hall La POTB/CUF EN6 58 B9
Dee Wy HOR/WEW KT19 220 B6
ROM RM1 104 F9
Defiant Wy WLGTN SM6 222 F4
Defoe Av RCH/KEW TW9 155 M6
Defoe Cl WIM/MER SW19 179 P9
Defoe Pde CDH/CHF RM16 168 E2
Defoe Rd BERM/RHTH SE16 160 E1
STNW/STAM N16 119 M7
Defoe Wy CRW RM5 104 B7
De Frene Rd SYD SE26 182 C7

Degema Rd CHST BR7 184 E8
Dehar Crs CDALE/KGS NW9 116 C5
De Havilland Cl HAT AL10 40 C3
Dehavilland Cl NTHLT UB5 133 L5
De Havilland Ct RAD * WD7 57 K8
De Havilland Dr WEY KT13 215 P7
De Havilland Rd EDGW HA8 95 N10
HEST TW5 153 K6
WLGTN SM6 222 F4
De Havilland Wy ABLGY * WD5 54 G8
ABLGY WD5 54 G8
STWL/WRAY TW19 173 N2
Deimos Dr HHNE HP2 36 B3
Dekker Rd DUL SE21 181 M2
Delabole Rd REDH RH1 258 F5
Delacourt Rd BKHTH/KID SE3 161 N6
Delafield Rd CHARL SE7 161 N4
GRAYS RM17 168 A4
Delaford Cl IVER * SL0 131 J8
Delaford Rd BERM/RHTH SE16 160 A4
Delaford St FUL/PGN SW6 157 H6
Delagarde Rd BH/WHM TN16 262 F2
Delahay Ri BERK HP4 33 N3
Delamare Crs CROY/NA CR0 204 B6
Delamare Rd CHES/WCR EN8 62 E5
Delamere Gdns MLHL NW7 96 A7
Delamere Rd BORE WD6 75 N5
EA W5 135 K10
REIG RH2 275 L4
RYNPK SW20 200 G1
YEAD UB4 133 L9
Delamere St BAY/PAD W2 9 J4
Delamere Ter BAY/PAD W2 9 H3
Delancey Pas CAMTN NW1 4 F6
Delancey St CAMTN NW1 4 F6
Delaporte Cl EW KT17 220 B8
De Lapre Cl STMC/STPC BR5 207 N7
De Lara Wy WOKN/KNAP GU21 232 A4
Delargy Cl CDH/CHF RM16 168 E2
De Laune St WALW SE17 18 C8
Delaware Rd MV/WKIL W9 8 G1
Delawyk Crs HNHL SE24 181 L2
Delcombe Av WPK KT4 200 F8
Delderfield ASHTD KT21 237 J6
Delfont Cl CRAWE RH10 284 E9
Delhi Rd EN EN1 99 N1
Delhi St IS N1 5 M6
Delia St WAND/EARL SW18 179 L3
Delisle Rd THMD SE28 163 H1
Delius Cl BORE WD6 75 H10
Dellbow Rd EBED/NFELT TW14 175 J1
Dell Cl LHD/OX KT22 236 C9
RDKG RH5 255 H3
SLN SL2 109 H10
SRTFD E15 141 J3
WFD IG8 101 N4
WLGTN SM6 222 D1
Dellcott Cl WGCW AL8 22 E4
Dellcut Rd HHNE HP2 36 B4
Dell Farm Rd RSLP HA4 112 E3
Dellfield CSHM HP5 50 F5
STAL AL1 38 E7
Dellfield Av BERK HP4 33 N3
Dellfield Cl BECK BR3 205 H1
RAD WD7 74 D1
WAT WD17 73 H6
Dellfield Crs UX/CGN UB8 131 M6
Dellfield Pde UX/CGN * UB8 131 M6
Dellfield Rd HAT AL10 40 D4
Dell La EW KT17 220 D2
Dell Lees BEAC HP9 89 H7
Dellmeadow ABLGY WD5 54 F6
Dell Meadow HHS/BOV HP3 35 P10
Dellors Cl BAR EN5 76 G9
Dellow Cl GNTH/NBYPK IG2 122 G5
Dellow St WCHPL E1 140 A9
Dell Ri LCOL/BKTW AL2 56 A2
Dell Rd BERK HP4 33 J2
EW KT17 220 D3
GRAYS RM17 167 N3
PEND EN3 80 B4
WATN WD24 73 H3
WDR/YW UB7 152 A2
Dells Cl CHING E4 100 G1
Dellside DEN/HRF UB9 111 M3
Dell Side WATN WD24 73 H3
Dell's Ms PIM * SW1V 17 H6
Dellsome La BRKMPK AL9 40 E9
STALE/WH AL4 40 B9
The Dells HHS/BOV HP3 36 C7
Dellswood Cl HERT/BAY SG13 25 M6
Dells Wood Cl HOD EN11 26 E10
The Dell ABYW SE2 163 K4
ALP/SUD HA0 114 G10
BECK * BR3 182 F10
BRW CM14 106 G7
BTFD TW8 155 H5
BXLY DA5 186 F4
CFSP/GDCR SL9 90 B7
EBED/NFELT TW14 175 J3
HERT/BAY SG13 25 K8
HORL RH6 279 M2
HORL RH6 280 C3
KWD/TDW/WH KT20 238 F7
NRWD SE19 203 N1
NTHWD HA6 92 F3
PIN HA5 93 L10
RAD WD7 74 F2
REIG * RH2 257 K9
STAL AL1 38 F4
WAB EN9 81 H2
WFD IG8 101 N4
WOKN/KNAP GU21 231 P5
Dell Wk NWMAL KT3 200 B2
Dell Wy WEA W13 135 H8
Dellwood Cl RKW/CH/CXG WD3 91 L2
Dellwood Gdns CLAY IG5 122 D1
Delmar Av HHNE HP2 36 E7
Delmeade Rd CSHM HP5 50 F8
Delme Crs BKHTH/KID SE3 161 N8
Delmey Cl CROY/NA CR0 203 N10
Deloraine St DEPT SE8 160 F7
Delorme St HMSMTH W6 156 G5
Delta Cl CHOB/PIR GU24 213 L6
WPK KT4 200 B10
Delta Dr HORL RH6 280 B6
Delta Est BETH * E2 7 N9
Delta Gain OXHEY WD19 93 L3
Delta Gv NTHLT UB5 133 L5
Delta Rd CHOB/PIR GU24 213 L6
WOKN/KNAP GU21 232 D1
WPK KT4 200 B10
Delta St BETH E2 7 N9
Delta Wy EGH TW20 194 F1
De Luci Rd ERITH DA8 164 D4
De Lucy St ABYW SE2 163 L3
Delvers Md DAGE RM10 124 D9
Delverton Rd WALW SE17 18 D7
Delves KWD/TDW/WH KT20 238 G7
Delvino Rd FUL/PGN SW6 157 K7
De Mandeville Ga EN EN1 79 P8
Demesne Rd WLGTN SM6 222 E1
Demeta Cl WBLY HA9 115 P8
De Montfort Pde
STRHM/NOR * SW16 180 F6
De Montfort Rd
STRHM/NOR SW16 180 E5
De Morgan Rd FUL/PGN SW6 157 L9
Dempster Rd WAND/EARL SW18 179 M1
Denberry Dr SCUP DA14 185 L6
Denbigh Cl CHST BR7 184 C9
EMPK RM11 125 N2
HHS/BOV HP3 35 P7
NTGHL W11 8 D7
STHL UB1 133 N8
SUT SM1 221 J2
WLSDN NW10 136 B2
Denbigh Dr WDR/YW UB7 152 D1
Denbigh Gdns
RCHPK/HAM TW10 177 L1
Denbigh Pl PIM SW1V 16 G7
Denbigh Rd EHAM E6 142 A5
HSLW TW3 154 A8
NTGHL W11 8 D7
STHL UB1 133 N8
WEA W13 134 G9
Denbigh St PIM SW1V 17 H7
Denbigh Ter NTGHL W11 8 D7
Denbridge Rd BMLY BR1 206 C2
Denby Gra HLWE CM17 47 P1
Denby Rd COB KT11 217 J9
Denchers Plat CRAWW RH11 283 N4
Dencliffe ASHF * TW15 174 B8
Den Cl BECK BR3 205 J4
Dendridge Cl EN EN1 80 A3
Dendy St BAL SW12 180 B4
Dene Av BFN/LL DA15 185 L3
HSLW TW3 153 N9
Dene Cl BROCKY SE4 160 D9
COUL/CHIP CR5 239 P5
HAYES BR2 205 L8
HORL RH6 279 P2
RDART DA2 186 F7
WPK KT4 200 C9
Denecroft Crs HGDN/ICK UB10 132 C3
Denecroft Gdns GRAYS RM17 168 A2
Dene Dr HART DA3 211 N2
ORP BR6 207 L10
Denefield Dr PUR/KEN CR8 241 L1
Dene Gdns STAN HA7 95 H6
THDIT KT7 198 F9
Dene Holm Rd GVW DA11 190 A6
Denehurst Gdns ACT W3 135 N10
HDN NW4 116 F4
RCHPK/HAM TW10 155 M10
WFD IG8 101 N5
WHTN TW2 176 C3
Dene Pth SOCK/AV RM15 146 F8
Dene Pl WOKN/KNAP GU21 231 N4
Dene Rd ASHTD KT21 237 L5
BKHH IG9 102 B2
DART DA1 187 N3
GU GU1 268 B1
NTHWD HA6 92 D7
TRDG/WHET N20 98 A2
Dene St DORK RH4 272 G2
Dene Street Gdns DORK RH4 272 G2
The Dene BELMT SM2 221 J7
CROY/NA CR0 224 C1
SEV TN13 265 J2
WBLY HA9 115 K9
WEA W13 134 G7
WOT/HER KT12 197 N5
Dene Tye CRAWE RH10 284 D6
Dene Wk HART DA3 211 K3
Denewood BAR EN5 77 M9
EW * KT17 220 B9
Denewood Cl WAT WD17 72 G3
Denewood Rd HGT N6 117 P4
Denfield DORK RH4 272 G4
Dengie Wk IS N1 6 E5
Dengil Crs KTTN NW5 118 B10
Denham Av DEN/HRF UB9 111 J7
Denham Cl DEN/HRF UB9 111 K8
HHNE HP2 36 B1
Denham Court Dr DEN/HRF UB9 111 L8
Denham Crs MTCM CR4 202 A4
Denham Dr GNTH/NBYPK IG2 122 F4
Denham Green Cl DEN/HRF UB9 111 K5
Denham Green La DEN/HRF UB9 111 H3
Denham La CFSP/GDCR SL9 90 C7
Denham Ldg DEN/HRF * UB9 131 M1
Denham Pde DEN/HRF * UB9 111 J8
Denham Pl DEN/HRF * UB9 111 K6
Denham Rd DEN/HRF UB9 111 J10
EBED/NFELT TW14 175 K3
EGH TW20 172 D7
EW KT17 220 C8
IVER SL0 130 G3
TRDG/WHET N20 98 A4
Denham Wk CFSP/GDCR SL9 90 C7
Denham Wy BARK IG11 143 H3
BORE WD6 75 P5
DEN/HRF UB9 111 K8
Denham Wy (North Orbital Rd)
RKW/CH/CXG WD3 91 H8
Denholme Rd MV/WKIL W9 2 D9
Denholme Wk RAIN RM13 144 G1
Denholm Gdns RGUE GU4 250 D7
Denison Cl EFNCH N2 117 M1
Denison Rd EA W5 135 H6
FELT TW13 174 G7
WIM/MER SW19 179 N9
Deniston Av BXLY DA5 185 N4
Denleigh Gdns THDIT * KT7 198 D6
WCHMH N21 99 H1
Denly Wy LTWR GU18 212 B6
Denman Dr ASHF TW15 174 C9
ESH/CLAY KT10 218 F2
GLDGN NW11 117 K3
Denman Dr North GLDGN NW11 117 K3
Denman Dr South GLDGN NW11 117 K3
Denman Rd PECK SE15 159 N7
Denmans CRAWE RH10 284 E6
Denman St REGST W1B 11 H8
Denmark Av WIM/MER SW19 179 H10
Denmark Ct MRDN SM4 201 K5
Denmark Gdns CAR SM5 202 A10
Denmark Gv IS N1 6 A7
Denmark Hl CMBW SE5 159 L7
HNHL SE24 159 L10
Denmark Hill Dr
CDALE/KGS NW9 116 D1
Denmark Rd BMLY BR1 205 N1
CAR SM5 202 A10
CEND/HSY/T N8 118 G2
CMBW SE5 159 K7
GU GU1 268 B1
KIL/WHAMP NW6 2 D8
KUT KT1 199 K3
SNWD SE25 203 P5
WEA W13 134 G9
WHTN TW2 176 C6
WIM/MER SW19 178 G9
Denmark St LSQ/SEVD WC2H 11 K6
PLSTW E13 141 N7
TOTM N17 100 A9
WAN E11 121 K8
WAT WD17 73 J6
Denmark Ter EFNCH * N2 118 A1
Denmead Cl CFSP/GDCR SL9 110 B5
Denmead Rd CROY/NA CR0 203 J8
Dennan Rd SURB KT6 199 L8
Denne Rd CRAWW RH11 283 N8
Denner Rd CHING E4 100 F3
Denne Ter HACK E8 7 M6
Dennett Rd CROY/NA CR0 203 H7
Dennett's Gv NWCR SE14 160 C8
Dennettsland Rd EDEN TN8 262 F10
Dennett's Rd NWCR SE14 160 B7
Denning Av CROY/NA CR0 223 H2
Denning Cl HPTN TW12 175 N9
STJWD NW8 3 K9
Denning Rd HAMP NW3 117 N9
Dennington Park Rd
KIL/WHAMP NW6 2 F1
The Denningtons WPK KT4 200 B9
Dennis Av WBLY HA9 115 L10
Dennis Cl REDH RH1 257 P8
Dennises La UPMR RM14 146 E2
Dennis Gdns STAN HA7 95 H6
Dennis La STAN HA7 94 G5
Dennis Pde STHGT/OAK * N14 98 E2
Dennis Park Crs RYNPK SW20 201 H1
Dennis Reeve Cl MTCM CR4 202 A1
Dennis Rd E/WMO/HCT KT8 198 B4
GVW DA11 190 D6
UPMR RM14 146 F3
Dennis Wy CLAP SW4 158 E9
GU GU1 250 B5
SL SL1 128 C9
Denny Av WAB EN9 63 J10
Denny Crs LBTH SE11 18 B7
Denny Ga CHES/WCR EN8 62 E3
Denny Rd DTCH/LGLY * SL3 150 C3
ED N9 100 A2
Denny's La BERK HP4 33 L7
Denny St LBTH SE11 18 B7
Den Rd HAYES BR2 205 J3
Densham Dr PUR/KEN CR8 223 H10
Densham Rd SRTFD E15 141 K3
Densley Cl WGCW AL8 22 F3
Densole Cl BECK * BR3 204 D1
Densworth Gv ED N9 100 B3
Dent Cl SOCK/AV RM15 146 F8
Denton Cl BAR EN5 76 F9
REDH RH1 276 B5
Denton Court Rd GVE DA12 191 H4
Denton Gv WOT/HER KT12 197 M9
Denton Rd BXLY DA5 186 F4
CEND/HSY/T N8 118 G3
DART DA1 186 F3
TWK TW1 177 J2
UED N18 99 M5
WELL DA16 163 M6
Denton St GVE DA12 191 H3
WAND/EARL SW18 179 L2
Denton Ter BXLY * DA5 186 F5
Denton Wy CLPT E5 120 C8
WOKN/KNAP GU21 231 M3
Denton Whf GVE * DA12 191 J2
Dents Gv KWD/TDW/WH KT20 257 J4
Dents Rd BTSEA SW11 180 A2
Denvale Wk WOKN/KNAP GU21 231 M4
Denver Cl ORP BR6 207 H6
Denver Rd DART DA1 187 H3
STNW/STAM N16 119 M5
Denyer St CHEL SW3 15 P5
Denziloe Av HGDN/ICK UB10 132 C5
Denzil Rd GUW GU2 267 N1
WLSDN NW10 116 C10
Deodar Rd PUT/ROE SW15 157 H10
Deodora Cl TRDG/WHET N20 97 P4
Departures Rd HORL RH6 280 A7
Depot Ap CRICK NW2 116 G9
Depot Rd CRAWE RH10 283 N4
EW KT17 220 B9
HSLW TW3 154 C9
Depot St CMBW SE5 18 G10
Deptford Br GNWCH SE10 160 F7
Deptford Broadway DEPT SE8 160 F7
Deptford Church St DEPT SE8 160 F6
Deptford Gn DEPT SE8 160 F5
Deptford High St DEPT SE8 160 F5
Deptford Market DEPT * SE8 160 F6
Deptford Whf DEPT SE8 160 E3
De Quincey Rd TOTM N17 99 L9
Derby Arms Rd EPSOM KT18 238 C3
Derby Av KTN/HRWW/W HA3 94 C9
NFNCH/WDSP N12 97 M6
ROMW/RG RM7 124 C4
UPMR RM14 125 N8
Derby Cl EPSOM KT18 238 E5
Derby Ga WHALL SW1A 17 L1
Derby Hl FSTH SE23 182 B5
Derby Hill Crs FSTH SE23 182 B5
Derby Rd BRYLDS KT5 199 M8
CROY/NA CR0 203 J9
FSTGT E7 142 A2
GFD/PVL UB6 134 A3
GUW GU2 249 L10
HOD EN11 45 J5
HOM E9 140 C3
HSLW TW3 154 A10
MORT/ESHN SW14 155 N10
PEND EN3 80 A9
SUT SM1 221 J3
SWFD E18 101 L9
UED N18 100 B6
UX/CGN UB8 131 M4
WAT WD17 73 K8
WIM/MER SW19 179 K10
Derby Road Br GRAYS RM17 167 N4
Derbyshire St BETH E2 7 P10
Derby Stables Rd EPSOM KT18 238 B3
Derby St MYFR/PICC W1J 10 D10
Dereham Pl CRW RM5 104 C7
SDTCH EC2A 13 K1
Dereham Rd BARK IG11 143 J1
Derek Av HOR/WEW KT19 219 M3
WBLY HA9 135 N2
WLGTN SM6 202 C10
Derek Cl HOR/WEW KT19 219 N2
Derek Walcott Cl HNHL * SE24 181 J1
Derham Gdns UPMR RM14 126 B8
Deri Av RAIN RM13 145 J6
Dericote St HACK E8 7 P5
Deri Dene Cl STWL/WRAY * TW19 173 P2
Derifall Cl EHAM E6 142 C7
Dering Pl CROY/NA CR0 223 K1
Dering Rd CROY/NA CR0 223 K1
Dering St CONDST W1S 10 E6
Dering Wy GVE DA12 191 J4
Derinton Rd TOOT SW17 180 B7
Derley Rd NWDGN UB2 153 K2
Dermody Gdns LEW * SE13 183 J1
Dermody Rd LEW SE13 183 J1
Deronda Rd BRXS/STRHM SW2 181 J4
Deroy Cl CAR SM5 222 A3
Deroy Ct CAR SM5 222 A3
Derrick Av SAND/SEL CR2 223 K6
Derrick Gdns CHARL SE7 161 P2
Derrick Rd BECK BR3 204 E3
Derry Av SOCK/AV RM15 146 F7
Derrydown WOKS/MYFD GU22 231 N7
Derry Downs STMC/STPC BR5 207 M6
Derry Rd WLGTN SM6 202 F10
Derry St KENS W8 14 G2
Dersingham Av MNPK E12 122 C9
Dersingham Rd CRICK NW2 117 H8
Derwent Av CDALE/KGS NW9 116 B3
EBAR EN4 98 A2
HGDN/ICK UB10 112 B7
MLHL NW7 96 A7
PIN HA5 93 M7
PUT/ROE SW15 178 B7
UED N18 99 L6
Derwent Cl ADL/WDHM KT15 215 N2
AMSS HP7 69 N5
CRAWW RH11 283 J8
DART DA1 187 J4
EBED/NFELT TW14 174 G4
ESH/CLAY KT10 218 D3
Derwent Crs BXLYHN DA7 164 B8
NFNCH/WDSP N12 97 M4
STAN HA7 95 H10
Derwent Dr PUR/KEN CR8 223 L10
SL SL1 128 B7
STMC/STPC BR5 206 G7
YEAD UB4 132 F7
Derwent Gdns REDBR IG4 122 B2
WBLY HA9 115 H5
Derwent Gv EDUL SE22 159 N10
Derwent Pde SOCK/AV RM15 146 F8
Derwent Ri CDALE/KGS NW9 116 B4
Derwent Rd EA W5 155 H2
EGH TW20 172 E9
HHS/BOV HP3 36 D7
LTWR GU18 212 A7
MRDN SM4 200 G6
PGE/AN SE20 203 P2
PLMGR N13 98 G5
STHL UB1 133 N8
WHTN TW2 176 A2
Derwent St GNWCH SE10 161 K4
Derwentwater Rd ACT W3 135 P10
Derwent Wy HCH RM12 125 J10
Derwent Yd EA * W5 155 H2
De Salis Rd HGDN/ICK UB10 132 D6
Desborough Cl BAY/PAD W2 9 H3
HERT/WAS SG14 25 K2
SHPTN TW17 196 B7
Desenfans Rd DUL SE21 181 M2
Deseronto Est DTCH/LGLY * SL3 150 B1
Desford Rd CAN/RD E16 141 K6
Desford Wy ASHF TW15 174 A5
Desmond Rd WATN WD24 72 G2
Desmond St NWCR SE14 160 D5
Despard Rd ARCH N19 118 D6
De Tany Ct STAL AL1 38 C7
Detillens La OXTED RH8 261 M5
Detling Cl HCH RM12 125 K10
Detling Rd BMLY BR1 183 M8
ERITH DA8 164 E6
GVW DA11 190 A4
Detmold Rd CLPT E5 120 A7
Deva Cl STALW/RED AL3 37 P8
Devalls Cl EHAM E6 142 D9
Devana End CAR SM5 202 A10
Devas Rd RYNPK SW20 200 F1
Devas St BOW E3 140 G6
Devema Cl CHST BR7 206 D1
Devenay Rd SRTFD E15 141 L2
Devenish La ASC SL5 192 C8
Devenish Rd ABYW SE2 163 K1
ASC SL5 192 C6
De Vere Gdns IL IG1 122 C7
KENS W8 15 J2
Deverell St STHWK SE1 18 G4
De Vere Ms KENS W8 15 J3
Devereux Ct TPL/STR WC2R 12 A6
Devereux Dr WAT WD17 72 F4
Devereux La BARN SW13 156 E6
Devereux Rd BTSEA SW11 180 A2
CDH/CHF RM16 167 L2
WDSR SL4 149 J8
De Vere Wk WAT WD17 72 F6
Deverills Wy DTCH/LGLY SL3 150 F3
Deveron Gdns SOCK/AV RM15 146 F7
Deveron Wy ROM RM1 104 F9
Devey Cl KUTN/CMB KT2 178 C10
Devil's La EGH TW20 172 F9
Devitt Cl ASHTD KT21 237 M2
Devizes St IS * N1 7 H6
Devoil Cl RGUE GU4 250 E6
Devoke Wy WOT/HER KT12 197 L9
Devon Av SL SL1 129 H8
WHTN TW2 176 B4
Devon Bank GUW GU2 267 P3
Devon Cl BKHH IG9 101 N3
GFD/PVL UB6 135 H3
HOR/WEW KT19 219 M8
PUR/KEN CR8 241 M2
TOTM N17 119 N1
Devon Ct STAL * AL1 38 D7
Devon Crs REIG RH2 257 N10
Devoncroft Gdns TWK TW1 176 F3
Devon Gdns FSBYPK N4 119 J4
Devonhurst Pl CHSWK * W4 156 A4
Devonia Gdns UED N18 99 K7
Devonia Rd IS N1 6 D7
Devon Man KTN/HRWW/W * HA3 115 H3
Devonport Gdns IL IG1 122 C4
Devonport Ms SHB * W12 136 E10
Devonport Rd SHB W12 136 E10
Devonport St WCHPL E1 140 B8
Devon Ri EFNCH N2 117 N2
Devon Rd BARK IG11 143 H3
BELMT SM2 221 H5
EYN DA4 210 A1
REDH RH1 258 D6
WATN WD24 73 L5
WOT/HER KT12 217 K1
Devons Est BOW E3 140 G5
Devonshire Av AMS HP6 68 G3
BELMT SM2 221 M4
DART DA1 187 J2
KWD/TDW/WH KT20 255 P7
WOKN/KNAP GU21 214 F10
Devonshire Cl CAVSQ/HST W1G 10 E3
SRTFD E15 121 K9
Devonshire Ct FELT * TW13 175 J5
Devonshire Crs MLHL NW7 96 G8
Devonshire Dr GNWCH SE10 160 G7
SURB KT6 199 J8
Devonshire Gdns CHSWK W4 155 P6
SLH/COR SS17 169 K1
TOTM N17 99 K7
WCHMH N21 99 K1
Devonshire Gn SLN SL2 128 G4
Devonshire Gv PECK SE15 160 A5
Devonshire Hill La TOTM N17 99 K7
Devonshire Ms South
CAVSQ/HST W1G 10 E3
Devonshire Ms West
CAVSQ/HST W1G 10 D2
Devonshire Pl CAVSQ/HST W1G 10 D2
CRICK NW2 117 K8
KENS * W8 14 G4
Devonshire Place Ms MHST W1U 10 D2
Devonshire Rd BELMT SM2 221 M4
BXLYHS DA6 163 P10
CAN/RD E16 141 N8
CAR SM5 222 B1
CDH/CHF RM16 167 K3
CHSWK W4 156 B4
CROY/NA CR0 203 L7
ED N9 100 B2
ELTH/MOT SE9 184 B5
FELT TW13 175 M6
FSTH SE23 182 C3
GNTH/NBYPK IG2 122 G5
GVW DA11 190 E4
HARP AL5 20 A1
HCH RM12 125 L7
HRW HA1 114 C4
MLHL NW7 96 G8
ORP BR6 207 K7
PIN HA5 93 N9
PIN HA5 113 K4
PLMGR N13 98 G5
STHL UB1 133 P7
TOTM N17 99 K7
WALTH E17 120 F4
WEA W13 155 H2
WEY * KT13 216 B1
WIM/MER SW19 179 P10
Devonshire Rw LVPST EC2M 13 K4
Devonshire Sq HAYES BR2 205 N4
LVPST EC2M 13 K5
Devonshire St CAVSQ/HST W1G 10 D3
CHSWK W4 156 B4
Devonshire Ter BAY/PAD W2 9 K6
EDUL * SE22 159 P10
Devonshire Wy CROY/NA CR0 204 E9
YEAD UB4 133 J8
Devons Rd BOW E3 140 F7
Devon St PECK SE15 160 A5
Devon Wy CHSGTN KT9 219 H1
HGDN/ICK UB10 132 A4
HOR/WEW KT19 219 N2
Devon Waye HEST TW5 153 N6
De Walden St CAVSQ/HST W1G 10 D4
Dewar Cl CRAWW * RH11 283 H8
Dewar St PECK SE15 159 P9
Dewberry Gdns EHAM E6 142 B7
Dewberry St POP/IOD E14 141 H8
Dewey Rd DAGE RM10 144 C1
IS N1 6 A7
Dewey St TOOT SW17 180 A8
Dewgrass Gv CHES/WCR EN8 80 C1
Dewhurst Rd CHES/WCR EN8 62 B5
HMSMTH W6 156 G2
Dewlands GDST RH9 260 B7
Dewlands Av RDART DA2 188 A3
Dewsbury Cl PIN HA5 113 M4
Dewsbury Gdns HARH RM3 105 L7
WPK KT4 200 D10
Dewsbury Rd HARH RM3 105 M7
WLSDN NW10 116 D10
Dexter Cl GRAYS RM17 167 M2
STAL AL1 38 F7
Dexter Rd BAR EN5 76 G10
DEN/HRF UB9 91 M10
Deyncourt Gdns UPMR RM14 126 B7
Deyncourt Rd TOTM N17 99 K9
Deynecourt Gdns WAN E11 121 P2
D'Eynsford Rd CMBW SE5 159 L7
Dharam Marg GSTN * WD25 74 D5
Diadem Ct SOHO/SHAV * W1D 11 J5
Dial Cl GRH DA9 189 H1
Diamedes Av STWL/WRAY TW19 173 N3
Diameter Rd STMC/STPC BR5 206 E7
Diamond Cl BCTR RM8 123 M6
CDH/CHF RM16 167 L2
Diamond Rd RSLP HA4 113 L9
SL SL1 149 M1
WATN WD24 73 H4
Diamond St PECK SE15 159 M6
WLSDN NW10 135 P2
Diana Cl CDH/CHF RM16 167 L2
DEPT SE8 160 E5
DTCH/LGLY SL3 130 B8
SWFD E18 101 N9
Diana Gdns SURB KT6 199 L9
Diana Pl CAMTN NW1 10 F1
Diana Rd WALTH E17 120 E1
Dianne Wy EBAR EN4 77 P8
Dianthus Cl ABYW * SE2 163 L4
CHERT KT16 195 H7
Dianthus Ct WOKS/MYFD GU22 232 A4
Diban Av HCH RM12 125 J9
Dibden La RSEV TN14 264 F3
Dibden St IS N1 6 E5
Dibdin Cl SUT SM1 201 K10
Dibdin Rd SUT SM1 201 K10
Diceland Rd BNSTD SM7 239 J2
Dicey Av CRICK NW2 116 F10
Dickens Av DART DA1 165 P10
FNCH N3 97 M9
TIL RM18 168 E7
UX/CGN UB8 132 C8
Dickens Cl ERITH DA8 164 C6
HART DA3 211 K5
HYS/HAR UB3 152 F3
RCHPK/HAM TW10 177 K5
STALW/RED AL3 38 C5
Dickens Dr ADL/WDHM KT15 215 J3
CHST BR7 184 F9
Dickens Est BERM/RHTH SE16 19 N3
Dickens La UED N18 99 M6
Dickens Ms FARR EC1M 12 C2
Dickenson Rd CEND/HSY/T N8 118 F5
FELT TW13 175 K8
Dickenson's La SNWD SE25 203 P6
Dickenson's Pl SNWD SE25 203 P6
Dickens Ri CHIG IG7 102 D4
Dickens Rd CRAWE RH10 283 N10
EHAM E6 142 A4
GVE DA12 191 H4

Dickens Sq STHWK SE1 18 F3
Dickens St VX/NE SW8 158 C8
Dickens Wy ROM RM1 124 F2
Dickerage Hl NWMAL KT3 199 P2
Dickerage La NWMAL KT3 199 P3
Dickerage Rd KUT KT1 199 P1
Dickins Cl CHESW EN7 61 P3
Dickinson Av RKW/CH/CXG WD3 72 B10
Dickinson Sq RKW/CH/CXG WD3 72 C10
Dickson CHESW EN7 61 N3
Dickson Fold PIN HA5 113 L2
Dickson Rd ELTH/MOT SE9 162 B9
Dick Turpin Wy
EBED/NFELT TW14 152 G10
Didsbury Cl EHAM E6 142 C3
Digby Crs FSBYPK N4 119 K7
Digby Gdns DAGE RM10 144 B3
Digby Pl CROY/NA CR0 203 N10
Digby Rd BARK IG11 143 J2
HOM E9 140 C1
Digby St BETH E2 140 B5
Digby Wy BF/WBF KT14 216 A8
Dig Dag Hl CHESW EN7 61 N3
Digdens Ri EPSOM KT18 237 P1
Diggon St WCHPL E1 140 C7
Dighton Rd WAND/EARL SW18 179 M1
Dignum St IS * N1 6 A7
Digswell Cl BORE WD6 75 M4
Digswell Hl WLYN AL6 22 D2
Digswell La WGCE AL7 23 J1
Digswell Ri WGCW AL8 22 G3
Digswell Rd WGCW AL8 22 G3
Digswell St HOLWY N7 6 B1
Dilhorne Cl LEE/GVPK SE12 183 N6
Dilke St CHEL SW3 16 B9
Dillwyn Cl SYD SE26 182 D7
Dilston Cl NTHLT UB5 133 F5
Dilston Rd LHD/OX KT22 236 F5
Dilton Gdns PUT/ROE SW15 178 D4
Dimes Pl HMSMTH W6 156 E3
Dimmock Dr NTHLT UB5 114 C10
Dimmocks La RKW/CH/CXG WD3 71 K2
Dimond Cl FSTGT E7 121 M9
Dimsdale Dr CDALE/KGS NW9 115 P6
EN EN1 99 P1
Dimsdale St HERT/WAS SG14 25 K5
Dimson Crs BOW E3 140 F6
Dinant Link Rd HOD EN11 44 F2
Dingle Cl BAR EN5 76 C10
CRAWW RH11 283 L6
Dingle Gdns POP/IOD * E14 140 F9
Dingle Rd ASHF TW15 174 C8
The Dingle CRAWW RH11 283 L7
HGDN/ICK UB10 132 C4
Dingley La STRHM/NOR SW16 180 E5
Dingley Pl FSBYE EC1V 6 F10
Dingley Rd FSBYE EC1V 6 E10
Dingwall Av CROY/NA CR0 203 K9
Dingwall Gdns GLDGN NW11 117 K4
Dingwall Rd CAR SM5 222 A5
CROY/NA CR0 203 L9
WAND/EARL SW18 179 M3
Dinmont Est BETH E2 7 P7
Dinmont St BETH E2 140 A4
Dinmore HHS/BOV HP3 52 C4
Dinsdale Cl WOKS/MYFD GU22 232 C4
Dinsdale Gdns BAR EN5 77 L9
SNWD SE25 203 M4
Dinsdale Rd BKHTH/KID SE3 161 L5
Dinsmore Rd BAL SW12 180 C3
Dinton Rd KUTN/CMB KT2 177 L10
WIM/MER SW19 179 N9
Diploma Av EFNCH N2 117 P2
Dippers Cl BGR/WK TN15 247 N3
Dirdene Cl EW KT17 220 C8
Dirdene Gdns EW KT17 220 C8
Dirdene Gv EW KT17 220 B8
Dirleton Rd SRTFD E15 141 L3
Dirtham La EHSLY KT24 253 J5
Disbrowe Rd HMSMTH W6 14 A10
Discovery Wk WAP E1W 140 A9
Dishforth La CDALE/KGS NW9 96 B9
Disney Pl STHWK SE1 18 F1
Disney St STHWK SE1 18 F1
Dison Cl PEND EN3 80 C5
Disraeli Cl THMD SE28 143 L10
Disraeli Ct DTCH/LGLY SL3 150 E5
Disraeli Pk BEAC HP9 88 C7
Disraeli Rd EA W5 135 J10
FSTGT E7 141 M1
PUT/ROE SW15 157 H10
WLSDN NW10 135 P4
Diss St BETH E2 7 L9
Distaff La BLKFR EC4V 12 E7
Distillery La HMSMTH W6 156 F4
Distillery Rd HMSMTH W6 156 F4
Distin St LBTH SE11 18 A6
District Rd GFD/PVL UB6 114 G10
Ditchburn St POP/IOD E14 141 H9
Ditches La COUL/CHIP CR5 240 E3
Ditchfield Rd HOD EN11 26 F10
YEAD UB4 133 M6
Ditchling Hl CRAWW RH11 283 M10
Dittisham Rd ELTH/MOT SE9 184 B7
Ditton Cl THDIT KT7 198 F7
Dittoncroft Cl SAND/SEL CR2 223 M1
Ditton Grange Cl SURB KT6 199 J8
Ditton Grange Dr SURB KT6 199 J8
Ditton Hl SURB KT6 199 H8
Ditton Hill Rd SURB KT6 199 H8
Ditton Lawn THDIT KT7 198 F8
Ditton Park Rd DTCH/LGLY SL3 150 B5
Ditton Pl PGE/AN * SE20 204 A1
Ditton Reach THDIT KT7 198 G6
Ditton Rd BXLYHS DA6 185 N1
DTCH/LGLY SL3 150 A7
NWDGN UB2 153 N4
SURB KT6 199 K8
Divot Pl HERT/BAY SG13 26 A4
Dixey Cottages EFNCH * N2 117 P3
Dixon Cl EHAM E6 142 C8
Dixon Dr WEY KT13 216 A6
Dixon Pl WWKM BR4 204 G8
Dixon Rd NWCR SE14 160 D7
SNWD SE25 203 M3
Dixons Ct WARE * SG12 26 D3
Dixons Hill Cl BRKMPK AL9 58 E1
Dixons Hill Rd BRKMPK AL9 40 F9
Dobbin Cl KTN/HRWW/W HA3 94 F10
Dobbins Pl CRAWW RH11 282 G8
Dobb's Weir Rd HOD EN11 45 J4
Dobell Rd ELTH/MOT SE9 184 C1
Dobree Av WLSDN NW10 136 E2
Dobson Cl KIL/WHAMP NW6 3 L4
Dobson Rd CRAWE RH10 283 N4
GVE DA12 191 H8
Dock Approach Rd GRAYS RM17 168 B4
Dockers Tanner Rd POP/IOD E14 160 F3
Dockett Eddy La SHPTN TW17 196 A7
Dockett Moorings CHERT * KT16 196 A8
Dockhead STHWK SE1 19 M2
Dock Hill Av BERM/RHTH SE16 160 C1
Dockland St CAN/RD E16 142 D10
Dockley Rd BERM/RHTH SE16 19 N4
Dock Rd BTFD * TW8 155 J6
CAN/RD E16 141 L9
GRAYS RM17 168 A5
Dockside Rd CAN/RD E16 142 A9
Dock St WCHPL E1 13 N7
Dockwell Cl EBED/NFELT TW14 153 H10
Doctors Cl SYD SE26 182 B8
Doctor's Commons Rd BERK HP4 33 N6
Doctors La CTHM CR3 241 H10
Dodbrooke Rd WNWD SE27 181 H6
Doddinghurst Rd BRWN CM15 87 H3
BRWN CM15 107 H1
Doddington Gv WALW SE17 18 C9
Doddington Pl WALW SE17 18 C9
Dodds Crs BF/WBF KT14 215 L10
Doddsfield Rd SLN SL2 128 F5
Dodd's La BF/WBF KT14 215 K10
CSTG HP8 89 N3
HHNE HP2 35 M1
Dodds Pk BRKHM/BTCW RH3 273 N2
Dodsley Pl ED N9 100 B4
Dodson St STHWK SE1 18 B2
Dod St POP/IOD E14 140 E8
Dodwood WGCE AL7 23 L6
Doebury Wk WOOL/PLUM SE18 163 K5
Doel Cl WIM/MER SW19 179 M10
Doggett Rd CAT SE6 182 F3
Doggetts Ct EBAR EN4 77 P9
Doggetts Farm Rd DEN/HRF UB9 110 F5
Doggetts Wy STAL AL1 38 B8
Doggetts Wood Cl CSTG HP8 69 N8
Doggetts Wood La CSTG HP8 69 N7
Doghurst Av WDR/YW UB7 152 C6
Doghurst Dr WDR/YW UB7 152 C6
Doghurst La COUL/CHIP CR5 240 A6
Dog Kennel Hl CMBW SE5 159 M9
Dog Kennel La HAT AL10 40 D3
RKW/CH/CXG WD3 71 J9
Dog La WLSDN NW10 116 B9
Dognell Gn WGCW AL8 22 E4
Dog Rose Ramble NTHLT UB5 133 H3
Dog Rose Ramble &
Hillingdon Trail
YEAD UB4 132 G3
Dogwood Cl GVW DA11 190 C7
Doherty Rd PLSTW E13 141 M6
Dolben Ct DEPT * SE8 160 E3
Dolben St STHWK * SE1 12 D10
Dolby Rd FUL/PGN SW6 157 J8
Dolby Ter HORL * RH6 279 H9
Doldens Cottages EYN * DA4 210 A4
Dolland St LBTH SE11 17 P8
Dollary Pde KUT * KT1 199 N3
Dollis Av FNCH N3 97 J9
Dollis Cl CRAWE RH10 284 D8
Dollis Crs RSLP HA4 113 K6
Dollis Hill Av CRICK NW2 116 E8
Dollis Hill Est CRICK * NW2 116 D8
Dollis Hill La CRICK NW2 116 C9
Dollis Pk FNCH N3 97 H9
Dollis Rd FNCH N3 97 J9
Dollis Valley Green Wk
GLDGN NW11 117 H2
TRDG/WHET N20 77 L10
Dollis Valley Wy BAR EN5 77 J9
Dolman Cl FNCH N3 97 M10
Dolman Rd CHSWK W4 156 A3
Dolman St CLAP SW4 158 G10
Dolphin Ap ROM RM1 124 G2
Dolphin Cl SURB KT6 199 J6
THMD SE28 143 M8
Dolphin Ct SL SL1 149 N1
STWL/WRAY TW19 173 K6
Dolphin Ct North
STWL/WRAY * TW19 173 K6
Dolphin Est SUN * TW16 196 F1
Dolphin La POP/IOD E14 140 G9
Dolphin Rd NTHLT UB5 133 N4
SL SL1 149 N1
SUN TW16 196 F1
Dolphin Rd North SUN TW16 196 E1
Dolphin Rd South SUN TW16 196 E1
Dolphin Rd West SUN TW16 196 F1
Dolphin Sq CHSWK * W4 156 B6
PIM SW1V 17 J8
Dolphin St KUT KT1 199 K2
Dolphin Wy WTHK RM20 166 D4
Dolphin Yd STAL * AL1 38 C6
WARE * SG12 26 C2
Dombey St BMSBY WC1N 11 N3
Dome Buildings
RCHPK/HAM * TW10 177 J1
Dome Hl CTHM CR3 259 M3
Dome Hill Pk SYD SE26 181 N7
Dome Hill Peak CTHM CR3 259 M2
Domett Cl CMBW SE5 159 L10
Dome Wy REDH RH1 258 A9
Domingo St FSBYE EC1V 12 E1
Dominica Cl PLSTW E13 142 A5
Dominic Ct WAB EN9 62 G9
Dominion Dr CRW RM5 104 C7
Dominion Pde HRW * HA1 114 E3
Dominion Rd CROY/NA CR0 203 N7
NWDGN UB2 153 M2
Dominion St LVPST EC2M 13 H3
Dominion Wy RAIN RM13 145 H5
Domonic Dr ELTH/MOT SE9 184 E6
Domville Cl TRDG/WHET N20 97 N3
Donald Biggs Dr GVE DA12 190 F4
Donald Dr CHDH RM6 123 M3
Donald Rd CROY/NA CR0 202 G6
PLSTW E13 141 N3
Donaldson Rd KIL/WHAMP NW6 2 D6
WOOL/PLUM SE18 162 D7
Donald Woods Gdns
BRYLDS KT5 199 N9
Doncaster Dr NTHLT UB5 113 N10
Doncaster Gdns FSBYPK * N4 119 K4
NTHLT UB5 113 N10
Doncaster Gn OXHEY WD19 93 K6
Doncaster Rd ED N9 100 A1
Doncaster Wk CRAWE * RH10 284 B9
Doncaster Wy UPMR RM14 125 N8
Donegal St IS N1 5 P8
Doneraile St FUL/PGN SW6 156 G8
Dongola Rd PLSTW E13 141 N5
TOTM N17 99 L10
Dongola Rd West PLSTW E13 141 N5
Donington Av BARK/HLT IG6 122 F5
Donkey Aly EDUL SE22 181 P3
Donkey La EN EN1 79 P6
EYN DA4 210 A9
HORL RH6 280 E8
RDKG RH5 271 L9
Donnafields CHOB/PIR GU24 230 F2
Donnay Cl CFSP/GDCR SL9 110 A4
Donne Cl CRAWE RH10 284 C5
Donnefield Av EDGW HA8 95 K7
Donne Gdns WOKS/MYFD GU22 233 H1
Donnella Cl CDH/CHF RM16 167 J2
Donne Pl CHEL SW3 15 P5
MTCM CR4 202 C4
Donne Rd BCTR RM8 123 M7
Donnington Ct CRAWW RH11 283 J10
Donnington Rd
KTN/HRWW/W HA3 115 J4
WLSDN NW10 136 E3
WPK KT4 200 D9
Donnybrook Rd
STRHM/NOR SW16 180 D10
Donoghue Cottages
POP/IOD * E14 140 D7
Donovan Av MUSWH N10 98 C10
Donovan Cl HOR/WEW KT19 220 A6
Don Phelan Cl CMBW SE5 159 L7
Don Wy ROM RM1 104 F8
Doods Park Rd REIG RH2 257 L9
Doods Pl REIG * RH2 257 M9
Doods Rd REIG RH2 257 M9
Doods Wy REIG RH2 257 N9
Doone Cl TEDD TW11 176 F9
Doon St STHWK SE1 12 A10
Dorado Gdns ORP BR6 207 N10
Doral Wy CAR SM5 222 A2
Dorando Cl SHB * W12 136 E9
Doran Dr REIG RH2 257 N10
Doran Gdns REIG * RH2 257 N10
Doran Gv WOOL/PLUM SE18 163 H6
Dora Rd WIM/MER SW19 179 K8
Dora St POP/IOD E14 140 E8
Dorchester Av BXLY DA5 185 N4
HOD EN11 44 F1
PLMGR N13 99 K5
RYLN/HDSTN HA2 114 B4
Dorchester Cl DART DA1 187 N3
NTHLT UB5 114 A10
STMC/STPC BR5 185 L10
Dorchester Ct CRICK NW2 116 G8
HNHL SE24 181 K1
RKW/CH/CXG * WD3 72 D9
STHGT/OAK N14 98 C1
WOKS/MYFD GU22 232 D2
Dorchester Dr
EBED/NFELT TW14 174 F2
HNHL SE24 181 K1
Dorchester Gdns CHING E4 100 F5
GLDGN * NW11 117 K2
Dorchester Gv CHSWK W4 156 B5
Dorchester Ms TWK TW1 177 H2
Dorchester Pde
STRHM/NOR * SW16 180 F5
Dorchester Rd GVE DA12 190 G6
MRDN SM4 201 L7
NTHLT UB5 114 A10
WEY KT13 196 C10
WPK KT4 200 F8
Dorchester Ter HDN * NW4 96 G10
Dorchester Wy
KTN/HRWW/W HA3 115 L4
Dorchester Waye YEAD UB4 133 J8
Dorcis Av BXLYHN DA7 163 P8
Dordrecht Rd ACT W3 136 B10
Dore Av MNPK E12 122 D10
Doreen Av CDALE/KGS NW9 116 A6
Dore Gdns MRDN SM4 201 L7
Dorell Cl STHL UB1 133 N7
Dorian Ct WARL * CR6 242 A5
Dorian Dr ASC SL5 192 D1
Dorian Rd HCH RM12 125 H6
Doria Rd FUL/PGN SW6 157 J8
Doric Dr KWD/TDW/WH KT20 239 J6
Doric Wy CAMTN NW1 5 J9
Dorien Rd RYNPK SW20 200 G2
Dorin Ct WARL * CR6 242 A6
WOKS/MYFD GU22 233 H1
Doris Av BXLYHN DA7 164 D7
Doris Rd ASHF TW15 174 E9
FSTGT E7 141 M2
Dorking Cl DEPT SE8 160 E5
WPK KT4 200 G9
Dorking Ri HARH RM3 105 L5
Dorking Rd EPSOM KT18 237 N1
GT/LBKH KT23 254 A3
HARH RM3 105 L5
KWD/TDW/WH KT20 256 E2
LHD/OX KT22 236 G8
RGUE GU4 268 G6
Dorking Wk HARH RM3 105 L5
Dorkins Wy UPMR RM14 126 D5
Dorlcote Rd WAND/EARL SW18 179 N3
Dorling Dr EW KT17 220 C8
Dorly Cl SHPTN TW17 196 F4
Dorman Pl ED N9 99 P3
Dormans CRAWW RH11 283 K8
Dormans Cl NTHWD HA6 92 E8
Dorman Wy STJWD NW8 3 L5
Dormay St WAND/EARL SW18 179 L1
Dormer Cl BAR EN5 76 G9
SRTFD E15 141 L1
Dormers HHS/BOV * HP3 53 H3
Dormer's Av STHL UB1 133 P8
Dormers Cl RGODL GU7 267 J10
Dormers Ri GFD/PVL UB6 134 A8
Dormer's Wells La STHL UB1 133 P8
Dormie Cl STALW/RED AL3 38 A1
Dormywood RSLP HA4 112 G3
Dornberg Cl BKHTH/KID SE3 161 M6
Dornberg Rd BKHTH/KID * SE3 161 N6
Dorncliffe Rd FUL/PGN SW6 157 H8
Dornels SLN SL2 129 P8
Dorney End CSHM HP5 50 F6
Dorney Gv WEY KT13 196 C9
Dorney Hl North BEAC HP9 108 F4
Dorney Hl South BEAC HP9 108 F5
Dorney Ri STMC/STPC BR5 207 J4
Dorney Wy HSLWW TW4 175 M1
Dorney Wood Rd SL SL1 108 B8
Dornfell St KIL/WHAMP NW6 117 J10
Dornford Gdns COUL/CHIP CR5 241 K5
Dornton Rd BAL SW12 180 C5
SAND/SEL CR2 223 M2
Dorothy Av ALP/SUD HA0 135 K2
Dorothy Evans Cl BXLYHN DA7 164 C10
Dorothy Gdns BCTR RM8 123 K9
Dorothy Rd BTSEA SW11 158 A9
Dorrien's Cft BERK HP4 33 L2
Dorrington Gdns HCH RM12 125 L6
Dorrington St HCIRC EC1N 12 A3
Dorrit Crs RGUW GU3 249 K8
Dorrit St STHWK * SE1 18 F1
Dorrit Wy CHST BR7 184 F9
Dorrofield Cl RKW/CH/CXG WD3 72 D9
Dors Cl CDALE/KGS NW9 116 A6
Dorset Av NWDGN UB2 153 P3
ROM RM1 124 E1
WELL DA16 163 J10
YEAD UB4 132 F5
Dorset Buildings EMB * EC4Y 12 C6
Dorset Cl BERK HP4 33 L4
CAMTN NW1 10 A3
YEAD * UB4 132 F5
Dorset Crs GVE DA12 191 H7
Dorset Dr EDGW HA8 95 L7
WOKS/MYFD GU22 232 E3
Dorset Gdns STRHM/NOR SW16 202 G4
Dorset Ms FNCH N3 97 K9
KTBR SW1X 16 E3
Dorset Pl SRTFD E15 141 J1
Dorset Ri EMB EC4Y 12 C6
Dorset Rd ASHF TW15 173 N6
BECK BR3 204 C3
BELMT SM2 221 K6
EA W5 155 H2
ELTH/MOT SE9 184 B5
HRW HA1 114 B4
MTCM CR4 201 P2
SEVS/STOTM N15 119 L2
VX/NE SW8 158 G6
WDGN N22 98 F9
WDSR SL4 149 H8
WIM/MER SW19 201 K1
Dorset Sq CAMTN NW1 10 A2
Dorset St MHST W1U 10 B4
Dorset Wy BF/WBF KT14 215 N7
HGDN/ICK UB10 132 A4
WHTN TW2 176 B4
Dorset Waye HEST TW5 153 N6
Dorton Cl PECK * SE15 159 M6
Dorton Dr BGR/WK TN15 247 N8
Dorton Wy RPLY/SEND GU23 233 L7
Dorville Crs HMSMTH W6 156 E2
Dorville Rd LEE/GVPK SE12 183 M1
Dothill Rd WOOL/PLUM SE18 162 F6
Douai Gv HPTN TW12 198 B1
Doubleday Rd LOU IG10 82 F7
Doughty Ms BMSBY WC1N 11 N2
Doughty St BMSBY WC1N 11 N1
Douglas Av ALP/SUD HA0 135 K2
HARH RM3 105 M10
NWMAL KT3 200 E4
WALTH E17 100 F9
WATN WD24 73 L3
Douglas Cl CDH/CHF RM16 167 K2
RGUE GU4 250 A4
STAN HA7 94 F6
WLGTN SM6 222 F3
Douglas Ct CTHM * CR3 241 K8
Douglas Crs YEAD UB4 133 K6
Douglas Dr CROY/NA CR0 204 F10
Douglas Est IS N1 6 F2
Douglas Gdns BERK HP4 33 L4
Douglas La STWL/WRAY TW19 172 C1
Douglas Ms BNSTD SM7 239 J2
CRICK NW2 117 H8
Douglas Pl POP/IOD * E14 161 H4
Douglas Rd ADL/WDHM KT15 195 L10
CAN/RD E16 141 M7
CHING E4 101 K1
ESH/CLAY KT10 198 A9
GDMY/SEVK IG3 123 K5
HSLW TW3 154 A9
IS N1 6 E3
KIL/WHAMP NW6 2 C5
KUT KT1 199 N2
REIG RH2 257 K9
ROM RM1 124 G4
SLN SL2 129 J7
STWL/WRAY TW19 173 N2
SURB KT6 199 L9
WDGN N22 99 H9
WELL DA16 163 L7
Douglas Rd North IS N1 6 F1
Douglas Rd South IS N1 6 F2
Douglas St WEST SW1P 17 J6
Douglas Ter WALTH E17 100 E9
Douglas Vls KUT * KT1 199 L2
Douglas Wy NWCR SE14 160 E6
WGCE AL7 23 M5
Doug Siddons Ct GRAYS RM17 167 P5
Doulton Cl HLWE CM17 47 P2
Doulton Ms HAMP * NW3 3 H1
The Doultons STA * TW18 173 K9
Dounesforth Gdns
WAND/EARL SW18 179 L4
Douro Pl KENS W8 15 H3
Douro St BOW E3 140 F4
Douthwaite Sq WAP E1W 13 P9
Dove Ap EHAM E6 142 B7
Dove Cl CRAWW RH11 283 N5
CROY/NA CR0 222 G4
MLHL NW7 96 D8
SAND/SEL CR2 224 C7
YEAD UB4 133 L6
Dovecot Cl PIN HA5 113 K3
Dovecote Cl WEY KT13 196 C10
Dove Ct BEAC HP9 88 C8
HAT AL10 40 D6
LOTH * EC2R 12 G6
Dovedale Av CLAY IG5 102 D10
KTN/HRWW/W HA3 115 H4
Dovedale Cl DEN/HRF UB9 91 M10
GU GU1 250 D7
WELL DA16 163 K7
Dovedale Crs CRAWW RH11 283 L9
Dovedale Ri MTCM CR4 180 A10
Dovedale Rd EDUL SE22 182 A1
RDART DA2 188 B4
Dovedon Cl STHGT/OAK N14 98 F3
Dove House Crs SLN SL2 128 D5
Dovehouse Cft HLW CM20 29 K9
Dove House Gdns CHING E4 100 F3
Dovehouse Md BARK IG11 142 G4
Dovehouse St CHEL SW3 15 N8
Dove La POTB/CUF EN6 59 L10
Dove Ms ECT SW5 15 J6
Doveney Cl STMC/STPC BR5 207 N4
Dove Pk PIN HA5 93 N8
RKW/CH/CXG WD3 70 E9
Dover Cl CRICK NW2 116 G7
ROMW/RG RM7 104 D10
Dovercourt Av THHTH CR7 203 H4
Dovercourt Est IS N1 7 H1
Dovercourt Gdns STAN HA7 95 K6
Dovercourt La SUT SM1 201 M10
Dovercourt Rd DUL SE21 181 M2
Doverfield CHESW EN7 61 K5
Doverfield Rd BRXS/STRHM SW2 180 F2
RGUE GU4 250 D7
Dover Gdns CAR SM5 202 A10
Dover House Rd PUT/ROE SW15 156 D10
Doveridge Gdns PLMGR N13 99 J5
Dove Rd IS N1 7 H1
Dove Rw BETH E2 7 N7
Dover Park Dr PUT/ROE SW15 178 E2
Dover Patrol BKHTH/KID SE3 161 N8
Dover Rd ED N9 100 B3
GVW DA11 190 A3
MNPK E12 121 P7
NRWD SE19 181 L9
SL SL1 128 E8
WOOL/PLUM SE18 162 E8
Dover Rd East GVW DA11 190 B3
Dovers Green Rd REIG RH2 275 L4
Doversmead WOKN/KNAP GU21 231 K2
Dover St MYFR/PICC W1J 10 F8
Dover Ter RCH/KEW * TW9 155 M8
Dover Wy RKW/CH/CXG WD3 72 D8
Doves Cl HAYES BR2 206 B9
Doves Yd IS N1 6 A6
Doveton Rd SAND/SEL CR2 223 L2
Doveton St WCHPL E1 140 B6
Dowanhill Rd CAT SE6 183 J4
Dowdeswell Cl PUT/ROE SW15 156 B10
Dowding Cl RAIN RM13 145 J2
Dowding Pl STAN HA7 94 F7
Dowding Rd BH/WHM TN16 244 A1
HGDN/ICK UB10 132 A2
Dowding Wy GSTN WD25 54 G10
Dower Av WLGTN SM6 222 C5
Dower Cl BEAC HP9 88 B6
Dower Pk WDSR SL4 148 D10
Dower Wk CRAWW RH11 283 K8
Dowgate Hl CANST EC4R 12 G7
Dowlands La HORL RH6 281 L5
Dowlans Cl GT/LBKH KT23 253 P3
Dowlans Rd GT/LBKH KT23 254 A3
Dowlas St CMBW SE5 159 M6
Dowlerville Rd ORP BR6 227 J3
Dowling Ct HHS/BOV HP3 35 N9
Dowman Cl WIM/MER SW19 179 L10
Downage HDN NW4 116 F1
The Downage GVW DA11 190 D5
Downalong BUSH WD23 94 C2
Downbank Av BXLYHN DA7 164 E7
Down Barns Rd RSLP HA4 113 L9
Down Cl NTHLT UB5 133 J5
Downderry Rd BMLY BR1 183 J6
Downe Av RSEV TN14 226 F8
Downe Cl HORL RH6 279 P2
WELL DA16 163 M6
Downedge STALW/RED AL3 38 A5
Downend WOOL/PLUM SE18 162 E6
Downer Dr RKW/CH/CXG WD3 71 J2
Downer Meadow RGODL GU7 267 K9
Downe Rd HAYES BR2 226 B5
MTCM CR4 202 A2
RSEV TN14 226 F10
Downer's Cottages CLAP SW4 158 D10
Downes Cl TWK TW1 176 G2
Downes Ct WCHMH N21 99 H2
Downes Rd STALE/WH AL4 38 G2
Downfield WPK KT4 200 C8
Downfield Cl HERT/BAY SG13 26 B7
MV/WKIL W9 8 G2
Downfield Rd CHES/WCR EN8 62 D7
HERT/BAY SG13 26 B7
Downfields WGCW AL8 22 E3
Down Green La STALE/WH AL4 20 G4
Down Hall Rd KUTN/CMB KT2 199 J1
Downhall Rd RBSF CM22 31 J5
Downham Cl CRW RM5 104 B8
Downham Ct WOT/HER * KT12 197 K10
Downham Rd IS N1 7 J4
Downham Wy BMLY BR1 183 K8
Downhills Av TOTM N17 119 L1
Downhills Park Rd TOTM N17 119 K1
Downhills Wy TOTM N17 119 K10
Downhurst Av MLHL NW7 96 A7
Downing Av GUW GU2 267 L1
Downing Cl RYLN/HDSTN HA2 114 B1
Downing Dr GFD/PVL UB6 134 D3
Downing Rd DAGW RM9 144 A3
Downings EHAM E6 142 D8
Downing St WHALL SW1A 17 L1
Downings Wd RKW/CH/CXG WD3 90 G6
Downland Cl COUL/CHIP CR5 222 C10
EPSOM KT18 238 E4
TRDG/WHET N20 97 M2
Downland Dr CRAWW RH11 283 M9
Downland Gdns EPSOM KT18 238 E4
Downland Pl CRAWW RH11 283 M9
Downlands WAB EN9 63 K10
Downlands Rd PUR/KEN CR8 222 F9
Downland St MV/WKIL W9 2 B9
Downland Wy EPSOM KT18 238 E4
Down La RGUW GU3 266 G4
Downleys Cl ELTH/MOT SE9 184 B5
Downman Rd ELTH/MOT SE9 162 B9
Down Pl HMSMTH W6 156 E3
Down Rd GU GU1 250 E10
TEDD TW11 176 G9
Downs Av CHST BR7 184 C8
DART DA1 187 P3
EPSOM KT18 238 C1
PIN HA5 113 N4
Downs Bridge Rd BECK BR3 205 J1
Downs Court Pde CLPT * E5 120 A10
Downs Court Rd PUR/KEN CR8 223 K9
Downsell Rd WAN E11 121 J9
Downsfield HAT AL10 40 D7
Downsfield Rd WALTH E17 120 D4
Downshall Av GDMY/SEVK IG3 123 H4
Downs Hl BECK BR3 205 J1
Downs Hill Rd EPSOM * KT18 238 B1
Downshire Hl HAMP NW3 117 N9
Downside BECK * BR3 204 F1
CHERT * KT16 195 J8
EPSOM KT18 220 B10
HHNE HP2 35 P5
SUN TW16 197 H1
TWK TW1 176 E6
Downside Bridge Rd COB KT11 217 J10
Downside Cl WIM/MER SW19 179 M9
Downside Common COB KT11 235 J4
Downside Common Rd
COB KT11 235 J4
Downside Crs HAMP NW3 117 P10
WEA W13 134 F6
Downside Orch
WOKS/MYFD GU22 232 D3
Downside Rd BELMT SM2 221 N3
COB KT11 235 J4
RGUE GU4 268 E1
Downsland Dr BRW CM14 107 H4
Downs La CLPT E5 120 A9
HAT AL10 40 D6
LHD/OX KT22 236 G9
Downs Link RGUE GU4 269 H5
SHGR GU5 268 C9
Downs Lodge Ct EPSOM * KT18 220 B10
Downs Park Rd HACK E8 119 P10
Downs Rd BECK BR3 204 G2
BELMT SM2 221 L7
CLPT E5 119 P9
CLPT E5 120 A9
COUL/CHIP CR5 240 E4

DTCH/LGLY SL3 150 A1
EN EN1 79 M8
EPSOM KT18 237 P6
EPSOM KT18 238 B1
MEO DA13 190 A7
PUR/KEN CR8 223 J7
RDKG RH5 255 H4
THHTH CR7 203 K1
Downs Side BELMT SM2 221 J7
The Downs HAT AL10 40 D6
HLW CM20 47 H1
LHD/OX KT22 254 G1
LHD/OX KT22 255 H1
RYNPK SW20 178 G10
Down St E/WMO/HCT KT8 197 P5
MYFR/PICC W1J 10 E10
Down Street Ms MYFR/PICC W1J 16 E1
Downs Va HART DA3 211 K4
Downs Vw DORK RH4 255 H10
ISLW TW7 154 E7
KWD/TDW/WH KT20 238 E7
Downsview Av
WOKS/MYFD GU22 232 C7
Downs View Cl ORP BR6 227 M6
Downsview Cl COB KT11 235 J5
SWLY BR8 208 G3
Downsview Gdns DORK RH4 272 G3
NRWD SE19 181 K10
Downs View Rd GT/LBKH KT23 254 B3
Downsview Rd NRWD SE19 181 K10
SEV TN13 264 G1
Downs Wy EPSOM KT18 238 C2
GT/LBKH KT23 254 B2
KWD/TDW/WH KT20 238 E7
OXTED RH8 261 K3
Downsway CTHM CR3 241 N2
GU GU1 250 G10
ORP BR6 227 H2
SAND/SEL CR2 223 M7
Downsway Cl
KWD/TDW/WH KT20 238 D7
The Downsway BELMT SM2 221 M5
Downs Wd EPSOM KT18 238 E3
Downswood REDH RH1 257 N8
Downton Av BRXS/STRHM SW2 180 G5
Downtown Rd
BERM/RHTH SE16 160 D1
Downway NFNCH/WDSP N12 97 P8
Down Wy NTHLT UB5 133 J5
Dowrey St IS * N1 6 A5
Dowry Wk WAT WD17 72 G4
Dowsett Rd TOTM N17 99 P10
Dowson Cl CMBW * SE5 159 L10
Doyce St STHWK * SE1 18 E1
Doyle Cl ERITH DA8 164 F7
Doyle Gdns WLSDN NW10 136 E3
Doyle Rd SNWD SE25 203 P4
D'oyley St KTBR SW1X 16 C5
Doynton St KTTN * NW5 118 C7
Draco Ga PUT/ROE * SW15 156 F9
Draco St WALW SE17 18 E9
Dragonfly Cl PLSTW E13 141 N5
Dragon La WEY KT13 216 B6
Dragon Rd PECK SE15 19 J10
Dragoon Rd DEPT SE8 160 E4
Dragor Rd WLSDN NW10 135 P5
Drake Av CTHM CR3 241 K8
DTCH/LGLY SL3 150 A3
STA TW18 173 J8
Drake Cl BERM/RHTH SE16 160 C1
BRW CM14 107 J6
Drake Crs THMD SE28 143 M8
Drakefell Rd NWCR SE14 160 C8
Drakefield Rd TOOT SW17 180 B6
Drake Ms RAIN RM13 145 H2
Drake Rd BROCKY SE4 160 F9
CDH/CHF RM16 167 K1
CHSGTN KT9 219 M2
CRAWE RH10 283 P10
CROY/NA CR0 202 G7
HORL RH6 279 P4
MTCM CR4 202 B6
RYLN/HDSTN HA2 113 N7
Drakes Cl CHES/WCR EN8 62 C4
ESH/CLAY KT10 217 P2
Drakes Ctyd KIL/WHAMP NW6 2 D5
Drakes Dr NTHWD HA6 92 C9
STAL AL1 38 G9
Drake's Rd AMSS HP7 69 J5
Drake St BMSBY WC1N 11 N4
ENC/FH EN2 79 L5
Drakes Wy HAT AL10 40 E6
WOKS/MYFD GU22 232 A8
Drakewood Rd
STRHM/NOR SW16 180 E10
Draper Cl BELV DA17 164 A3
Draper Est WALW SE17 18 D5
Draper Pl IS N1 6 D5
Drapers Rd ENC/FH EN2 79 J6
SRTFD E15 121 H9
TOTM N17 119 N1
Drappers Wy BERM/RHTH SE16 19 P5
Draven Cl HAYES BR2 205 L7
Drawell Cl WOOL/PLUM SE18 163 H4
Drax Av RYNPK SW20 178 D10
Draxmont WIM/MER SW19 179 H9
Draycot Rd SURB KT6 199 M8
WAN E11 121 N4
Draycott Av CHEL SW3 15 P6
KTN/HRWW/W HA3 114 G4
Draycott Cl CRICK NW2 116 G8
KTN/HRWW/W HA3 114 G4
Draycott Pl CHEL SW3 16 A6
Draycott Ter CHEL SW3 16 A5
Dray Ct ALP/SUD * HA0 135 H1
GUW GU2 267 N1
Drayford Cl MV/WKIL W9 8 D1
Draymans Wy ISLW TW7 154 E9
Drayson Cl WAB EN9 63 J8
Drayson Ms KENS W8 14 F2
Drayton Av LOU IG10 82 C10
ORP BR6 206 E8
POTB/CUF EN6 59 H8
WEA W13 134 F9
Drayton Bridge Rd HNWL W7 134 E9
Drayton Cl HSLWW TW4 175 N1
IL IG1 122 G6
LHD/OX KT22 236 C9
Drayton Ct WDR/YW * UB7 152 A3
Drayton Court Chambers
WEA * W13 134 G9
Drayton Gdns WBPTN SW10 15 K7
WCHMH N21 99 J1
WDR/YW UB7 151 N1
WEA W13 134 F9
Drayton Gn WEA W13 134 F9
Drayton Green Rd WEA W13 134 G9
Drayton Gv WEA W13 134 F9
Drayton Pk HBRY N5 119 H8
Drayton Park Ms HOLWY * N7 119 H10
Drayton Rd BORE WD6 75 M8
CROY/NA CR0 203 J9
TOTM N17 99 M10
WAN E11 121 J6
WEA W13 134 F8
WLSDN NW10 136 C3
Dreadnought St GNWCH SE10 161 K2
Drenon Sq HYS/HAR UB3 132 G9
Dresden Cl HAMP NW3 3 H1
Dresden Rd ARCH N19 118 D6
Dresden Wy WEY KT13 216 D2
Dressington Av BROCKY SE4 182 F2
Drew Av MLHL NW7 97 H7
Drewery Ct BKHTH/KID * SE3 161 K9
Drew Gdns GFD/PVL UB6 134 E1
Drew Meadow SLN SL2 109 H9
Drew Pl CTHM CR3 241 L9
Drew Rd CAN/RD E16 142 B10
Drews Cottages BAL * SW12 180 E5
Drews Pk BEAC HP9 88 B5
Drewstead Rd
STRHM/NOR SW16 180 E5
The Drey CFSP/GDCR SL9 90 B6
Driffield Rd BOW E3 140 D4
The Drift COB KT11 234 F10
HAYES BR2 206 A10
Drift Wy DTCH/LGLY SL3 150 F7
The Driftway BNSTD SM7 238 F1
HHNE HP2 36 A6
LHD/OX KT22 237 H9
MTCM CR4 202 B1
Driftwood Av LCOL/BKTW AL2 55 P2
Driftwood Dr PUR/KEN CR8 241 K3
Drill Hall Rd CHERT KT16 195 K7
Drinkwater Rd
RYLN/HDSTN HA2 114 A7
Drive Ct EDGW * HA8 95 M6
Drive Rd COUL/CHIP CR5 240 G6
The Drive ACT W3 135 P8
AMSS HP7 69 J4
ASHF TW15 174 E10
BAR EN5 77 M10
BAR EN5 77 H7
BARK IG11 143 J2
BECK BR3 204 F2
BELMT SM2 221 J8
BKHH IG9 101 P1
BNSTD SM7 239 H3
BRKMPK AL9 59 K1
BXLY DA5 185 N3
CFSP/GDCR SL9 90 B8
CHESW EN7 61 J4
CHESW EN7 62 A4
CHING E4 101 J1
CHST BR7 207 J1
COB KT11 217 M10
COUL/CHIP CR5 222 F10
CRAWE RH10 285 K2
CRW RM5 104 E9
DTCH/LGLY SL3 149 N7
DTCH/LGLY SL3 150 B1
EBED/NFELT TW14 175 K3
EDGW HA8 95 M6
ENC/FH EN2 79 L5
ERITH DA8 164 C6
ESH/CLAY KT10 198 B8
FBAR/BDGN N11 98 D7
FNCH N3 97 K8
GLDGN NW11 117 K5
GUW GU2 249 L10
GUW GU2 267 J2
GVE DA12 190 C7
HARH RM3 105 M9
HART DA3 211 N3
HERT/BAY * SG13 42 F10
HERT/WAS SG14 25 K3
HGDN/ICK UB10 111 P8
HGT N6 118 A3
HLW CM20 29 H10
HOD EN11 44 F1
HOLWY N7 5 N2
HOR/WEW KT19 220 C3
HORL RH6 280 C5
HSLW TW3 154 C8
IL IG1 122 B4
KUTN/CMB KT2 177 P10
KWD/TDW/WH * KT20 239 K10
LCOL/BKTW AL2 56 F1
LHD/OX KT22 236 D8
LHD/OX KT22 237 M10
LHD/OX KT22 237 K9
LOU IG10 82 B7
MRDN SM4 201 M5
NTHWD HA6 92 F9
ORP BR6 207 J9
POTB/CUF EN6 59 J9
RAD WD7 56 F10
RBRW/HUT CM13 107 H7
RGUW GU3 267 N4
RKW/CH/CXG WD3 71 L9
RYLN/HDSTN HA2 113 P5
RYNPK SW20 178 F10
SBW CM21 29 P1
SCUP DA14 185 L6
SEV TN13 247 J10
STWL/WRAY TW19 172 A1
SURB * KT6 199 K7
SWFD E18 121 M1
THHTH CR7 203 L4
WALTH E17 120 G1
WAT WD17 72 E3
WBLY HA9 115 P7
WLGTN SM6 222 D6
WOKS/MYFD GU22 231 N6
WWKM BR4 205 J7
The Driveway HHW * HP1 35 L8
POTB/CUF EN6 60 F4
Dr Johnson Av TOOT SW17 180 C6
Drodges Cl SHGR GU5 268 C9
Droitwich Cl SYD SE26 181 P6
Dromey Gdns KTN/HRWW/W HA3 94 E8
Dromore Rd PUT/ROE SW15 179 H2
Dronfield Gdns BCTR RM8 123 M10
Droop St NKENS W10 8 A1
Drop La LCOL/BKTW AL2 56 A7
Dropmore Pk SL * SL1 108 A8
Dropmore Rd SL SL1 128 B4
Drove Rd RGUE GU4 269 K2
Drovers Pl PECK SE15 160 A6
Drovers Rd SAND/SEL CR2 223 L2
Drovers Wy HAT AL10 40 E1
STALW/RED AL3 38 C6
The Drove Wy MEO DA13 190 B10
Druce Rd DUL SE21 181 M2
Drudgeon Wy RDART DA2 188 G6
Druid's Cl ASHTD KT21 237 L6
Druid St STHWK SE1 19 L1
Druids Wy HAYES BR2 205 J4
Drumaline Rdg WPK KT4 200 B9
Drummond Av ROMW/RG RM7 124 E2
Drummond Cl ERITH DA8 164 F7
Drummond Crs CAMTN NW1 5 J9
Drummond Dr
KTN/HRWW/W HA3 94 E8
Drummond Ga PIM SW1V 17 K7
Drummond Rd
BERM/RHTH SE16 160 A2
CRAWW RH11 283 H8
CROY/NA CR0 203 K9
GU GU1 250 A10
ROMW/RG RM7 124 D2
WAN E11 121 N4
Drummonds Pl RCH/KEW TW9 155 K10
The Drummonds EPP CM16 65 K6
Drummond St CAMTN NW1 10 G1
Drum St WCHPL E1 13 M5
Drury Cl CRAWE RH10 284 E9
Drury Crs CROY/NA CR0 203 H9
Drury La HOL/ALD WC2B 11 M6
WARE SG12 28 A2
Drury Rd HRW HA1 114 B5
Drury Wy WLSDN NW10 116 A10
Dryad St PUT/ROE SW15 156 G9
Dry Arch Rd ASC SL5 192 E7
Dryburgh Gdns CDALE/KGS NW9 115 M1
Dryburgh Rd PUT/ROE SW15 156 E9
Drycroft WGCE AL7 23 H9
Drydell La CSHM HP5 50 E7
Dryden Av HNWL W7 134 E8
Dryden Cl BARK/HLT IG6 103 J7
Dryden Pl TIL RM18 168 E7
Dryden Rd EN EN1 79 M10
KTN/HRWW/W HA3 94 E9
WIM/MER SW19 179 M9
WOOL/PLUM SE18 163 J7
Dryden St COVGDN WC2E 11 M6
Dryden Wy ORP BR6 207 K8
Dryfield Cl WLSDN NW10 135 P1
Dryfield Rd EDGW HA8 95 P7
Dryhill La RSEV TN14 246 C9
Dryhill Rd BELV DA17 164 A5
Dryland Av ORP BR6 227 J1
Drylands Rd CEND/HSY/T N8 118 F4
Drynham Pk WEY KT13 196 F10
Drysdale Av CHING E4 80 G10
Drysdale Cl NTHWD HA6 92 F8
Drysdale Dwellings HACK * E8 119 N10
Drysdale Pl BETH E2 7 K9
Drysdale St IS N1 7 K10
Duarte Pl CDH/CHF RM16 167 L2
Dublin Av HACK E8 7 P5
Dubrae Cl STALW/RED AL3 37 P8
Du Burstow Ter HNWL W7 154 D1
Ducal St BETH E2 7 M10
Du Cane Cl SHB * W12 136 F8
Du Cane Rd SHB W12 136 E8
Duchess Cl FBAR/BDGN N11 98 C6
SUT SM1 221 M1
Duchess Gv BKHH * IG9 101 N3
Duchess Ms CAVSQ/HST W1G 10 F4
Duchess of Bedford's Wk
KENS W8 14 D2
Duchess St REGST W1B 10 F4
SL SL1 128 D10
Duchess' Wk BGR/WK TN15 265 M1
Duchy Rd EBAR EN4 77 N4
Duchy St STHWK SE1 12 B9
Ducie St CLAP SW4 158 F10
Duckett Rd FSBYPK N4 119 J4
Ducketts Md HLWW/ROY CM19 27 N10
Ducketts Rd DART DA1 186 G1
Duckett St WCHPL E1 140 C7
Ducking Stool Ct ROM RM1 124 F2
Duck La EPP CM16 65 M2
SOHO/CST W1F 11 J6
Duck Lees La PEND EN3 80 D8
Duckling La SBW CM21 29 P1
Duck's Hill Rd NTHWD HA6 92 C8
NTHWD HA6 92 B10
Du Cros Dr STAN HA7 95 J7
Du Cros Rd ACT W3 136 B10
Dudbrook Rd BRW CM14 85 P4
Dudden Hill La WLSDN NW10 116 C9
Dudden Hill Pde WLSDN * NW10 116 C9
Duddington Cl ELTH/MOT SE9 184 A7
Dudely Rd GVW DA11 190 B3
Dudley Av CHES/WCR EN8 62 C8
KTN/HRWW/W HA3 115 H1
Dudley Cl ADL/WDHM KT15 195 L10
CDH/CHF RM16 167 K1
Dudley Dr MRDN SM4 201 H8
RSLP HA4 113 J10
Dudley Gdns RYLN/HDSTN HA2 114 C6
WEA W13 154 G1
Dudley Gv EPSOM KT18 219 P10
Dudley Rd ASHF TW15 174 A8
EBED/NFELT TW14 174 E4
FNCH N3 97 L10
HARH RM3 105 L7
IL IG1 122 E9
KIL/WHAMP NW6 2 B7
KUT KT1 199 L3
NWDGN UB2 153 L1
RCH/KEW TW9 155 L8
RYLN/HDSTN HA2 114 B7
WALTH E17 100 F10
WIM/MER SW19 179 K9
WOT/HER KT12 197 H6
Dudley St BAY/PAD * W2 9 L4
Dudley Whf IVER * SL0 130 F10
Dudlington Rd CLPT E5 120 B7
Dudmaston Ms CHEL SW3 15 M7
Dudsbury Rd DART DA1 187 J2
Dudset La HEST TW5 153 H7
Dudswell La BERK HP4 33 J1
Dudswell Ml BERK * HP4 33 H1
Dufferin Av STLK EC1Y 12 G2
Dufferin St STLK EC1Y 12 F2
Duffield Cl CDH/CHF RM16 167 L2
HRW HA1 114 E3
Duffield Dr SEVS/STOTM N15 119 N2
Duffield La SLN SL2 129 L2
Duffield Pk SLN SL2 129 L5
Duffield Rd KWD/TDW/WH KT20 238 E10
Duffins Orch CHERT KT16 214 F4
Duff St POP/IOD E14 140 G8
Dufour's Pl SOHO/CST W1F 11 H6
Dugdale Hill La POTB/CUF EN6 59 H9
Dugdales RKW/CH/CXG WD3 72 B8
Duke Humphrey Rd
BKHTH/KID SE3 161 K7
Duke of Cambridge Cl
WHTN TW2 176 C2
Duke of Edinburgh Rd SUT SM1 201 N10
Duke of Wellington Pl
WHALL SW1A 16 D2
Duke of York St STJS SW1Y 11 H9
Duke Rd BARK/HLT IG6 122 G2
CHSWK W4 156 A4
Dukes Av CDH/CHF RM16 167 M2
CHSWK W4 156 A4
EDGW HA8 95 L7
EPP CM16 83 H1
FNCH N3 97 L9
HRW HA1 114 D2
HSLWW TW4 153 M10
MUSWH N10 118 D1
NTHLT UB5 133 M2
NWMAL KT3 200 B3
PIN HA5 113 N4
RCHPK/HAM TW10 177 H7
Dukes Cl ASHF TW15 174 D7
CFSP/GDCR SL9 110 A6
EPP CM16 66 C3
HPTN TW12 175 N8
Duke's Dr RGODL GU7 266 G10
Dukes Ga CHSWK * W4 155 P3
Dukes Hl CTHM CR3 242 D6
Dukes Kiln Dr CFSP/GDCR SL9 109 P7
Duke's La ASC SL5 170 E10
KENS W8 14 G1
Duke's Ms MHST W1U 10 D5
MUSWH N10 118 C1
Dukes Orch BXLY DA5 186 D4
Duke's Pl HDTCH EC3A 13 L6
Dukes Ride CFSP/GDCR SL9 110 B6
HGDN/ICK UB10 111 P9
RDKG RH5 273 J5
Dukes Rd ACT W3 135 M6
CAMTN NW1 5 K10
EHAM E6 142 D3
RDKG RH5 278 C10
WOT/HER KT12 217 L2
Dukesthorpe Rd SYD SE26 182 C7
Duke St HOD EN11 44 F2
MBLAR W1H 10 D5
RCH/KEW TW9 155 J10
SUT SM1 221 N1
WAT WD17 73 K7
WDSR SL4 149 H7
WOKN/KNAP GU21 232 C3
Duke Street Hl STHWK SE1 13 H9
Duke Street St James's
MYFR/PICC W1J 11 H9
Dukes Va CFSP/GDCR SL9 109 N7
Dukes Wy BERK * HP4 33 M3
UX/CGN UB8 131 L3
WWKM BR4 205 K10
Dukes Wood Av CFSP/GDCR SL9 110 B5
Dukes Wood Dr CFSP/GDCR SL9 109 P6
Duke's Yd MYFR/PKLN W1K 10 D7
Dulas St FSBYPK N4 118 G6
Dulford St NTGHL W11 8 A7
Dulka Rd BTSEA SW11 180 A1
Dulverton Rd ELTH/MOT SE9 184 F5
HARH RM3 105 L7
RSLP HA4 113 H7
SAND/SEL CR2 224 B6
Dulwich Common DUL SE21 181 L4
The Dulwich Oaks DUL * SE21 181 N6
Dulwich Rd HNHL SE24 181 H1
Dulwich Village DUL SE21 181 L2
Dulwich Wy RKW/CH/CXG WD3 72 B9
Dulwich Wood Av NRWD SE19 181 M8
Dulwich Wood Pk NRWD SE19 181 M7
Dumbarton Av CHES/WCR EN8 62 C10
Dumbarton Rd
BRXS/STRHM SW2 180 F2
Dumbleton Cl KUT KT1 199 N1
Dumbreck Rd ELTH/MOT SE9 162 D10
Dumfries Cl OXHEY WD19 93 H4
Dumont Rd STNW/STAM N16 119 M8
Dumpton Pl CAMTN NW1 4 C4
Dumville Dr GDST RH9 260 A7
Dunally Pk SHPTN TW17 196 E7
Dunbar Av BECK BR3 204 D4
DAGE RM10 124 B8
STRHM/NOR SW16 203 H2
Dunbar Cl SLN SL2 129 M9
YEAD UB4 133 H7
Dunbar Ct WOT/HER KT12 197 K9
Dunbar Gdns DAGE RM10 124 B10
Dunbar Rd FSTGT E7 141 M1
NWMAL KT3 199 P4
WDGN N22 99 H9
Dunbar St WNWD SE27 181 K6
Dunblane Rd ELTH/MOT SE9 162 B9
Dunboe Pl SHPTN TW17 196 D7
Dunboyne Rd HAMP NW3 118 A10
Dunbridge St BETH E2 13 P1
Duncan Cl BAR EN5 77 M8
WGCE AL7 23 H6
Duncan Dr GU GU1 250 D9
Duncan Gdns STA TW18 173 K9
Duncan Gv ACT W3 136 B8
Duncannon Crs WDSR SL4 148 C9
Duncannon St CHCR WC2N 11 L8
Duncan Rd HACK E8 140 A3
KWD/TDW/WH KT20 239 H5
RCH/KEW TW9 155 K10
Duncan St IS N1 6 C7
Duncan Ter IS N1 6 C8
Duncan Wy BUSH WD23 73 N6
Dunch St WCHPL * E1 140 A8
Duncombe Cl AMS HP6 69 K4
HERT/WAS SG14 25 K3
Duncombe Hl FSTH SE23 182 D3
Duncombe Rd ARCH N19 118 E6
BERK HP4 33 K4
HERT/WAS SG14 25 K4
Duncrievie Rd LEW SE13 183 J2
Duncroft WDSR SL4 148 E9
WOOL/PLUM SE18 163 H6
Duncroft Cl REIG RH2 257 J10
Dundalk Rd BROCKY SE4 160 D9
Dundas Gdns E/WMO/HCT KT8 198 A3
Dundas Rd PECK SE15 160 B8
Dundee Rd PLSTW E13 141 N4
SL SL1 128 E8
SNWD SE25 204 A5
Dundee St WAP E1W 140 A10
Dundee Wy PEND EN3 80 D7
Dundela Gdns WPK KT4 220 E1
Dundonald Cl EHAM E6 142 B8
Dundonald Rd WIM/MER SW19 179 J10
WLSDN NW10 136 G3
Dundrey Crs REDH RH1 258 F5
Dunedin Dr CTHM CR3 259 M1
Dunedin Rd IL IG1 122 F6
LEY E10 120 G8
RAIN RM13 144 G5
Dunedin Wy YEAD UB4 133 K6
Dunelm Gv WNWD SE27 181 K7
Dunelm St WCHPL E1 140 C8
Dunfee Wy BF/WBF KT14 215 P8
Dunfield Rd CAT SE6 182 G8
Dunford Br WOKN/KNAP GU21 214 E7
Dunford Rd HOLWY N7 118 G9
Dungarvan Av PUT/ROE SW15 156 D10
Dungates La BRKHM/BTCW RH3 256 D9
Dunheved Cl THHTH CR7 203 H6
Dunheved Rd North THHTH CR7 203 H6
Dunheved Rd South THHTH CR7 203 H6
Dunheved Rd West THHTH CR7 203 H6
Dunholme Gn ED N9 99 N4
Dunholme La ED N9 99 N4
Dunholme Rd ED N9 99 N4
Dunkeld Rd BCTR RM8 123 L7
SNWD SE25 203 L4
Dunkellin Gv SOCK/AV RM15 146 F8
Dunkellin Wy SOCK/AV RM15 146 F8
Dunkery Rd ELTH/MOT SE9 184 A7
Dunkin Rd DART DA1 165 P10
Dunkirk Cl GVE DA12 190 F8
Dunkirk St WNWD * SE27 181 K7
Dunlace Rd CLPT E5 120 B10
Dunleary Cl HSLWW TW4 175 N3
Dunley Dr CROY/NA CR0 225 H3
Dunlin Cl REDH RH1 275 P5
Dunlin Ri RGUE GU4 250 G8
Dunlin Rd HHNE HP2 35 P1
Dunloe Av TOTM N17 119 L1
Dunloe St BETH E2 7 L8
Dunlop Pl BERM/RHTH SE16 19 M4
Dunlop Rd TIL RM18 168 C7
Dunmail Dr PUR/KEN CR8 223 M10
Dunmore GUW GU2 249 J9
Dunmore Rd KIL/WHAMP NW6 2 A6
RYNPK SW20 200 F1
Dunmow Cl CHDH RM6 123 M3
FELT * TW13 175 M7
LOU IG10 82 B10
Dunmow Dr RAIN RM13 144 G3
Dunmow Rd SRTFD E15 121 J9
Dunmow Wk IS * N1 6 E5
Dunnets WOKN/KNAP GU21 231 K3
Dunning Cl SOCK/AV RM15 146 F8
Dunningford Cl HCH RM12 124 C10
Dunnings La RBRW/HUT CM13 127 N7
Dunn Md CDALE/KGS NW9 96 C8
Dunnock Cl BORE WD6 75 M8
ED N9 100 C2
Dunnock Rd EHAM E6 142 B8
Dunn St HACK E8 119 N10
Dunny La KGLGY WD4 53 J8
Dunnymans Rd BNSTD SM7 239 J1
Dunollie Pl KTTN NW5 118 D10
Dunollie Rd KTTN NW5 118 D10
Dunoon Gdns FSTH * SE23 182 C3
Dunoon Rd FSTH SE23 182 B3
Dunottar Cl REIG RH2 275 N2
Dunraven Av REDH RH1 276 C8
Dunraven Dr ENC/FH EN2 79 H6
Dunraven Rd SHB W12 136 D10
Dunraven St MYFR/PKLN W1K 10 B7
Dunsany Rd HMSMTH W6 156 G2
Dunsbury Cl BELMT SM2 221 L5
Dunsdon Av GUW GU2 267 N1
Dunsfold Cl CRAWW RH11 283 K8
Dunsfold Ri COUL/CHIP CR5 222 E9
Dunsfold Wy CROY/NA CR0 225 H4
Dunsmore OXHEY * WD19 93 L3
Dunsmore Cl BUSH WD23 74 C10
YEAD UB4 133 L6
Dunsmore Rd WOT/HER KT12 197 J5
Dunsmore Wy BUSH WD23 74 B10
Dunsmure Rd STNW/STAM N16 119 M6
Dunspring La CLAY IG5 102 E10
Dunstable Ms CAVSQ/HST W1G 10 D3
Dunstable Rd E/WMO/HCT KT8 197 N4
HARH RM3 105 L7
RCH/KEW TW9 155 K10
Dunstall Rd RYNPK SW20 178 E9
Dunstalls HLWW/ROY CM19 46 D5
Dunstall Wy E/WMO/HCT KT8 198 A3
Dunstall Welling Est
WELL * DA16 163 L8
Dunstan Cl EFNCH * N2 117 M1
Dunstan Gld STMC/STPC * BR5 206 G6
Dunstan Houses WCHPL * E1 140 B7
Dunstan Rd COUL/CHIP CR5 240 E3
GLDGN NW11 117 J6
Dunstan's Gv EDUL SE22 182 A2
Dunstan's Rd EDUL SE22 181 P3
Dunster Av MRDN SM4 200 G8
Dunster Cl BAR EN5 76 G8
DEN/HRF UB9 91 L9
ROMW/RG RM7 104 D10
Dunster Ct BORE WD6 76 A7
FENCHST EC3M 13 J7
Dunster Crs UPMR RM14 125 P7
Dunster Dr CDALE/KGS NW9 115 P6
Dunster Gdns KIL/WHAMP NW6 2 D3
SL SL1 128 F9
Dunsters Md WGCE AL7 23 K7
Dunsterville Wy STHWK SE1 19 H2
Dunster Wy RYLN/HDSTN HA2 113 M8
Dunston Rd BTSEA SW11 158 B8
HACK E8 7 L6
Dunston St HACK E8 7 K5
Dunton Cl SURB KT6 199 K8
Dunton Rd LEY E10 120 G5
ROM RM1 124 F2
STHWK SE1 19 L6
Duntshill Rd WAND/EARL SW18 179 L4
Dunvegan Cl E/WMO/HCT KT8 198 A4
Dunvegan Rd ELTH/MOT SE9 162 C10
Dunwich Rd BXLYHN DA7 164 A7
Dunworth Ms NTGHL W11 8 C6
Duplex Ride KTBR SW1X 16 B2
Dupont Rd RYNPK SW20 200 G2
Dupont St POP/IOD E14 140 D8
Duppas Av CROY/NA CR0 223 J1
Duppas Cl SHPTN TW17 196 E5
Duppas Hill Rd CROY/NA CR0 223 H1
Duppas Hill Ter CROY/NA CR0 203 J10
Duppas Rd CROY/NA CR0 203 H10
Dupre Cl SL SL1 148 D1
Dupree Rd CHARL SE7 161 N4
Dura Den Cl BECK BR3 182 G10
Durand Gdns BRXN/ST SW9 158 G7
Durand Wy WLSDN NW10 135 P2
Durant Rd SWLY BR8 187 H9
Durants Park Av PEND EN3 80 C8
Durants Rd PEND EN3 80 B8
Durant St BETH E2 7 N9
Durban Gdns DAGE RM10 144 D2
Durban Rd BECK BR3 204 E2
GNTH/NBYPK IG2 123 H6
SRTFD E15 141 K5
TOTM N17 99 M7
WALTH E17 100 E9
WNWD SE27 181 K7
Durban Rd East WATW WD18 73 H8
Durban Rd West WATW WD18 73 H8
Durbin Rd CHSGTN KT9 219 K1
Durdans Rd STHL UB1 133 N8
Durell Gdns DAGW RM9 123 N10
Durell Rd DAGW RM9 123 N10
Durfold Dr REIG RH2 257 M10

Durford Crs PUT/ROE SW15 178 D4
Durham Av GPK RM2 125 K2
HAYES BR2 205 L4
HEST TW5 153 N5
SL SL1 128 F8
WFD IG8 102 A6
Durham Cl GUW GU2 249 L8
SBW CM21 29 M2
WARE SG12 26 G6
Durham Hl BMLY BR1 183 L7
Durham House St CHCR * WC2N 11 M8
Durham Pl CHEL SW3 16 A8
Durham Ri WOOL/PLUM SE18 162 F4
Durham Rd BORE WD6 75 P7
CAN/RD E16 141 K6
DAGE RM10 124 D10
EA W5 155 J2
EBED/NFELT TW14 175 K3
ED N9 99 P3
EFNCH N2 117 P1
HAYES BR2 205 M4
HOLWY N7 118 G7
HRW HA1 114 A3
MNPK E12 122 A9
RYNPK SW20 200 E1
SCUP DA14 185 L8
Durham Rw WCHPL E1 140 C7
Durham St LBTH SE11 17 N8
Durham Ter BAY/PAD W2 8 G5
PGE/AN * SE20 182 A10
Durham Yd BETH * E2 140 A5
Duriun Wy ERITH DA8 165 J6
Durleston Park Dr GT/LBKH KT23 254 B1
Durley Av PIN HA5 113 M4
Durley Gdns ORP BR6 227 L1
Durley Rd STNW/STAM N16 119 M5
Durlston Rd CLPT E5 119 P7
KUTN/CMB KT2 177 K9
Durndale La GVW DA11 190 B7
Durnell Wy LOU IG10 82 D7
Durnford St SEVS/STOTM N15 119 M3
Durning Rd NRWD SE19 181 L8
Durnsford Av WAND/EARL SW18 179 K5
Durnsford Rd FBAR/BDGN N11 98 E9
WAND/EARL SW18 179 K5
Durpe Crs BEAC HP9 88 G10
Durrants Cl RAIN RM13 145 K4
Durrants Dr RKW/CH/CXG WD3 72 D7
Durrants Hill Rd HHS/BOV HP3 35 N9
Durrants La BERK HP4 33 L4
Durrants Rd BERK HP4 33 L4
Durrant Wy ORP BR6 226 G2
SWCM DA10 189 K3
Durrell Rd FUL/PGN SW6 157 H7
Durrell Wy SHPTN TW17 196 E6
Durrington Av RYNPK SW20 178 F10
Durrington Park Rd
RYNPK SW20 200 F1
Durrington Rd CLPT E5 120 D9
Dursley Cl BKHTH/KID SE3 161 P8
Dursley Gdns BKHTH/KID SE3 162 A7
Dursley Rd BKHTH/KID SE3 161 P8
Durward St WCHPL E1 13 P3
Durweston Ms MHST * W1U 10 B3
Dury Falls Cl EMPK RM11 125 N6
Dury Rd BAR EN5 77 J5
Dutch Barn Cl STWL/WRAY TW19 173 N2
Dutch Gdns KUTN/CMB KT2 177 N9
Dutch Yd WAND/EARL SW18 179 K1
Duthie St POP/IOD E14 141 H9
Dutton St GNWCH SE10 161 H7
Dutton Wy IVER SL0 131 H8
Duxford Cl HCH RM12 145 J1
Duxhurst La HORL RH6 275 L10
Duxons Turn HHNE HP2 36 C5
Dwight Rd WATW WD18 92 E1
Dye House La BOW E3 140 F3
Dyer's Buildings
FLST/FETLN EC4A 12 A4
Dyer's Fld HORL RH6 281 J4
HORL * RH6 281 J4
Dyers Hall Rd WAN E11 121 K6
Dyer's La PUT/ROE SW15 156 E9
Dyers Wy HARH RM3 105 H8
Dyke Dr STMC/STPC BR5 207 M7
Dyke La STALE/WH AL4 21 K4
Dykes Pth WOKN/KNAP GU21 232 F1
Dykes Wy HAYES BR2 205 L3
Dykewood Cl BXLY DA5 186 E6
Dylan Cl BORE * WD6 95 J1
Dylan Rd BELV DA17 164 B2
Dylways CMBW SE5 159 L10
Dymchurch Cl CLAY IG5 102 D10
ORP BR6 227 H1
Dymock St FUL/PGN SW6 157 L9
Dymoke Gn STALE/WH AL4 38 F3
Dymoke Rd ROM RM1 124 G5
Dymokes Wy HOD EN11 26 F10
Dyneley Rd LEE/GVPK SE12 183 P7
Dyne Rd KIL/WHAMP NW6 2 C4
Dynes Rd RSEV TN14 247 M3
Dynevor Pl RGUW GU3 249 H6
Dynevor Rd RCHPK/HAM TW10 177 K1
STNW/STAM N16 119 M8
Dynham Rd KIL/WHAMP NW6 2 E3
Dyott St NOXST/BSQ WC1A 11 L5
Dyrham La BAR EN5 76 D2
Dysart Av KUTN/CMB KT2 177 H8
Dysart St SDTCH EC2A 13 H2
Dyson Cl WDSR SL4 148 G9
Dyson Ct ALP/SUD HA0 114 F9
DORK * RH4 272 F2
Dyson Rd FSTGT E7 141 L1
WAN E11 121 K4
Dysons Cl CHES/WCR EN8 62 C9
Dyson's Rd UED N18 100 A6
Dytchleys Rd BRW CM14 85 N8

E

Eade Rd FSBYPK N4 119 K5
Eagans Cl EFNCH * N2 117 N1
Eagle Av CHDH RM6 123 P4
Eagle Cl PEND EN3 80 B8
RAIN RM13 145 J1
WAB EN9 63 M10
WLGTN SM6 222 F3
Eagle Ct FARR EC1M 12 C3
HERT/BAY SG13 26 A4
Eagle Dr CDALE/KGS NW9 96 B10
Eagle Hl NRWD SE19 181 L9
Eagle La BRWN CM15 86 D3
WAN E11 121 M2
Eagle Ms IS N1 7 J1
Eagle Pl WBPTN SW10 15 K7
Eagle Rd ALP/SUD HA0 135 J2
GU GU1 268 A1
Eagles Dr BH/WHM TN16 244 A4
Eaglesfield Rd
WOOL/PLUM SE18 162 E7
Eagles Rd GRH DA9 166 G10
Eagle St GINN WC1R 11 N4
Eagle Ter WFD IG8 101 N8
Eagle Wy GVW DA11 189 M1
HAT AL10 40 D6
RBRW/HUT CM13 107 H7
Eagle Wharf Rd IS N1 6 F7
Ealdham Sq ELTH/MOT SE9 161 P10
Ealing Cl BORE WD6 76 A5
Ealing Gn EA W5 135 J10
Ealing Park Gdns EA W5 155 H3
Ealing Rd ALP/SUD HA0 135 K1
BTFD TW8 155 J3
NTHLT UB5 133 P2
Ealing Village EA W5 135 K8
Eamont Cl RSLP HA4 112 C5
Eamont St STJWD NW8 3 N7
Eardemont Cl DART DA1 164 G10
Eardley Crs ECT SW5 14 F7
Eardley Rd BELV DA17 164 B4
SEV TN13 247 J10
STRHM/NOR SW16 180 D9
Earl Cl FBAR/BDGN N11 98 C6
Earldom Rd PUT/ROE SW15 156 F10
Earle Gdns KUTN/CMB KT2 177 K10
Earleswood COB KT11 217 L8
Earleydene ASC SL5 192 A8
Earlham Gv FSTGT E7 121 L10
WDGN N22 98 G8
Earlham St LSQ/SEVD WC2H 11 K6
Earl Ri WOOL/PLUM SE18 162 G4
Earl Rd GVW DA11 190 B5
MORT/ESHN SW14 155 P10
Earlsbrook Rd REDH RH1 276 A2
Earls Cnr POTB/CUF * EN6 58 D9
Earl's Court Gdns ECT SW5 14 G6
Earl's Court Rd KENS W8 14 E4
Earl's Court Sq ECT SW5 14 G7
Earls Crs HRW HA1 114 D2
Earlsferry Wy IS N1 5 M4
Earlsfield Rd WAND/EARL SW18 179 M4
Earlshall Rd ELTH/MOT SE9 162 C10
Earls La POTB/CUF EN6 58 B8
SL SL1 128 E10
Earlsmead RYLN/HDSTN HA2 113 N9
Earlsmead Rd SEVS/STOTM N15 119 N3
WLSDN NW10 136 E5
Earl's Pth LOU IG10 81 P7
Earls Ter KENS W8 14 D4
Earlsthorpe Ms BAL SW12 180 B2
Earlsthorpe Rd SYD SE26 182 C7
Earlstoke Est FSBYE EC1V 6 C9
Earlstoke St FSBYE EC1V 6 C9
Earlston Gv HOM E9 140 A3
Earl St SDTCH EC2A 13 J3
WAT WD17 73 K7
Earls Wk BCTR RM8 123 L9
KENS W8 14 E4
Earlswood Av THHTH CR7 203 H5
Earlswood Gdns CLAY IG5 122 D1
Earlswood Rd REDH RH1 276 A2
Earlswood St GNWCH SE10 161 K4
Early Commons CRAWE RH10 284 A6
CRAWE * RH10 284 A6
Early Ms CAMTN NW1 4 F5
Earnshaw St NOXST/BSQ WC1A 11 K5
Easby Crs MRDN SM4 201 L6
Easebourne Rd BCTR RM8 123 M10
Easedale Dr HCH RM12 125 J10
Easington Pl GU GU1 268 C1
Easington Wy SOCK/AV RM15 146 F7
East Acton Ar ACT * W3 136 C8
East Arbour St WCHPL E1 140 C8
East Av CROY/NA CR0 222 G2
HYS/HAR UB3 152 G1
MNPK E12 142 B2
STHL UB1 133 N9
WALTH E17 120 G2
East Bank STNW/STAM N16 119 M5
Eastbank Rd HPTN TW12 176 B8
East Barnet Rd BAR EN5 77 M8
EBAR EN4 77 N9
Eastbourne Av ACT W3 136 A8
Eastbourne Gdns
MORT/ESHN SW14 155 P9
Eastbourne Ms BAY/PAD W2 9 K5
Eastbourne Rd BTFD TW8 155 J4
CHSWK W4 155 P5
EHAM E6 142 D5
FELT TW13 175 L5
GDST RH9 260 B8
SEVS/STOTM N15 119 M4
SL SL1 128 F8
SRTFD E15 141 K3
TOOT SW17 180 B9
Eastbourne Ter BAY/PAD W2 9 K5
Eastbournia Av ED N9 100 A4
Eastbridge SL SL1 149 N1
Eastbrook Av DAGE RM10 124 D9
ED N9 100 B1
Eastbrook Cl WOKN/KNAP GU21 232 D2
Eastbrook Dr DAGE RM10 124 F8
Eastbrook Rd BKHTH/KID SE3 161 N7
WAB EN9 63 K9
Eastbrook Wy HHNE HP2 35 P6
East Burnham La SLN SL2 128 F3
East Burrowfield WGCE AL7 22 G7
Eastbury Av BARK IG11 143 H3
EN EN1 79 M5
NTHWD HA6 92 F6
Eastbury Ct OXHEY * WD19 93 K1
STAL AL1 38 E5
Eastbury Gv CHSWK W4 156 B4
Eastbury La RGUW GU3 266 F6
Eastbury Rd EHAM E6 142 D6
KUTN/CMB KT2 177 K10
NTHWD HA6 92 F7
OXHEY WD19 93 K1
ROMW/RG RM7 124 E4
STMC/STPC BR5 206 G6
Eastbury Sq BARK IG11 143 J3
Eastbury Ter WCHPL E1 140 C6
Eastcastle St GTPST W1W 10 G5
Eastcheap FENCHST EC3M 13 H7
East Churchfield Rd ACT W3 136 A10
Eastchurch Rd HTHAIR TW6 152 F8
East Cl EA W5 135 M6
EBAR EN4 78 B8
GFD/PVL UB6 134 B4
LCOL/BKTW AL2 56 A1
RAIN RM13 145 J6
Eastcombe Av CHARL SE7 161 N5
East Common CFSP/GDCR SL9 110 B4
Eastcote ORP BR6 207 J8
Eastcote Av E/WMO/HCT KT8 197 N5
GFD/PVL UB6 114 F10
RYLN/HDSTN HA2 114 A7
Eastcote Dr HARP AL5 20 C5
Eastcote La NTHLT UB5 133 N1
RYLN/HDSTN HA2 113 N9
RYLN/HDSTN HA2 114 A8
Eastcote La North NTHLT UB5 133 N1
Eastcote Rd PIN HA5 113 L3
RSLP HA4 112 F5
RYLN/HDSTN HA2 114 B8
WELL DA16 162 C8
Eastcote St BRXN/ST SW9 158 F8
Eastcote Vw PIN HA5 113 K2
East Ct ALP/SUD HA0 115 H7
East Crs EN EN1 79 M9
TRDG/WHET N20 98 A5
WDSR SL4 148 E7
Eastcroft SLN SL2 128 G6
Eastcroft Rd HOR/WEW KT19 220 B4
East Cross Route HOM E9 140 E1
Eastdean Av EPSOM KT18 219 N9
East Dene Dr HARH RM3 105 L6
Eastdown Pk LEW SE13 161 J10
East Dr CAR SM5 221 P5
GSTN WD25 73 J2
LCOL/BKTW AL2 56 G3
NTHWD HA6 92 F3
SBW CM21 29 P2
STALE/WH AL4 39 K5
STMC/STPC BR5 207 L6
VW GU25 193 N6
East Duck Lees La PEND EN3 80 D8
East Dulwich Gv EDUL SE22 181 M1
East Dulwich Rd EDUL SE22 159 N10
East End Rd FNCH N3 117 L1
East End Wy PIN HA5 113 M1
East Entrance DAGE RM10 144 C4
Eastergate BEAC HP9 88 B7
Eastern Av CHDH RM6 123 N2
CHERT KT16 195 K3
CHES/WCR EN8 62 E9
CHOB/PIR GU24 230 G7
GNTH/NBYPK IG2 123 J3
PIN HA5 113 L5
SOCK/AV RM15 166 B1
WAN E11 121 P4
WTHK RM20 166 E4
Eastern Av East GPK RM2 104 G9
ROM RM1 124 E1
Eastern Av West CHDH RM6 123 P3
ROMW/RG RM7 124 D2
Eastern Perimeter Rd
HTHAIR TW6 152 G9
Eastern Rd BROCKY SE4 160 F10
EFNCH N2 118 A1
PLSTW E13 141 N4
ROM RM1 124 F3
WALTH E17 121 H3
WDGN N22 98 F9
Eastern Wy BH/WHM TN16 243 P3
Easternville Gdns
GNTH/NBYPK IG2 122 F4
Eastern Wy ERITHM DA18 164 B1
GRAYS RM17 167 M5
THMD SE28 163 K1
East Ferry Rd POP/IOD E14 160 G2
Eastfield Av WATN WD24 73 L5
Eastfield Cl SL * SL1 149 M2
Eastfield Ct STALE/WH AL4 39 J3
Eastfield Gdns DAGE RM10 124 B9
Eastfield Rd BRW CM14 107 J3
CEND/HSY/T N8 118 F1
CHES/WCR EN8 62 E8
DAGE RM10 124 B9
PEND EN3 80 C4
REDH RH1 276 C1
WALTH E17 120 F2
Eastfields PIN HA5 113 K3
Eastfields Rd ACT W3 135 P7
MTCM CR4 202 B2
East Flexford La RGUW GU3 266 E3
East Flint HHW HP1 35 H5
East Gdns WIM/MER SW19 179 P9
WOKS/MYFD GU22 232 F3
Eastgate BNSTD SM7 221 J10
East Ga HLW CM20 28 G10
Eastgate Cl THMD SE28 143 N8
Eastgate Ct GU * GU1 268 B1
Eastgate Gdns GU GU1 268 B1
Eastglade NTHWD HA6 92 F6
PIN HA5 113 N1
East Hall La RAIN RM13 145 L8
East Hall Rd STMC/STPC BR5 207 P7
Eastham Cl BAR EN5 77 J9
East Ham Crs RBRW/HUT CM13 107 M5
East Ham Manor Wy EHAM E6 142 D8
East Harding St FLST/FETLN EC4A 12 B5
East Heath Rd HAMP NW3 117 N8
East Hl BH/WHM TN16 243 N4
DART DA1 187 N3
EYN DA4 210 C1
OXTED RH8 261 L5
SAND/SEL CR2 223 M6
WAND/EARL SW18 179 M1
WBLY HA9 115 M7
WOKS/MYFD GU22 232 F2
East Hill Dr DART DA1 187 N3
East Hill La CRAWE RH10 281 L9
East Hill Rd OXTED RH8 261 K5
Eastholm GLDGN NW11 117 L2
East Holme ERITH DA8 164 E7
Eastholme HYS/HAR UB3 133 H10
East India Dock Rd POP/IOD E14 140 F8
East Kent Av GVW DA11 189 P2
Eastlake Rd CMBW SE5 159 J8
Eastlands Cl OXTED RH8 261 J3
Eastlands Crs EDUL SE22 181 N2
Eastlands Wy OXTED RH8 261 J3
East La ABLGY WD5 55 H4
ALP/SUD HA0 115 H8
EHSLY KT24 252 D2
GSTN WD25 55 J6
KUT KT1 199 J3
STALE/WH AL4 21 J2
Eastlea Av GSTN WD25 73 M3
Eastlea Ms CAN/RD E16 141 K6
Eastleigh Av RYLN/HDSTN HA2 114 A7
Eastleigh Cl BELMT SM2 221 L4
CRICK NW2 116 B8
Eastleigh Rd BXLYHN DA7 164 D8
WALTH E17 100 E10
Eastleigh Wy EBED/NFELT TW14 175 H4
East Lodge La ENC/FH EN2 78 E1
Eastman Rd ACT W3 156 A1
Eastman Wy HHNE HP2 36 B3
East Md RSLP HA4 113 L8
WGCE AL7 23 H8
Eastmead WOKN/KNAP GU21 231 N3
Eastmead Av GFD/PVL UB6 134 A5
Eastmead Cl BMLY BR1 206 B2
East Meads GUW GU2 267 L1
Eastmearn Rd DUL SE21 181 K5
East Ml GVW DA11 190 C2
East Milton Rd GVE DA12 190 G3
East Mimms HHNE HP2 35 P5
Eastmont Rd ESH/CLAY KT10 198 E9
Eastmoor Pk HARP AL5 20 B5
Eastmoor Pl WOOL/PLUM SE18 162 A2
Eastmoor St WOOL/PLUM SE18 162 A3
East Mt STALE/WH AL4 21 J2
East Mount St WCHPL * E1 140 A7
Eastney Rd CROY/NA CR0 203 J8
Eastney St GNWCH SE10 161 J4
Eastnor HHS/BOV HP3 52 D4
Eastnor Pl REIG * RH2 275 K2
Eastnor Rd ELTH/MOT SE9 184 F4
REIG RH2 275 J2
Easton Gdns BORE WD6 76 B8
Easton St FSBYW WC1X 12 A1
Eastor WGCE AL7 23 K2
East Pk CRAWW RH11 283 N8
HLWE CM17 29 M8
SBW CM21 29 P2
East Park Cl CHDH RM6 123 N3
East Parkside GNWCH SE10 161 K1
East Pl WNWD SE27 181 K7
East Pole Cottages EBAR * EN4 78 E8
East Poultry Av FARR EC1M 12 C4
East Rp HTHAIR TW6 152 C7
East Ridgeway POTB/CUF EN6 60 E4
East Rd CHDH RM6 123 P3
EBAR EN4 98 B2
EBED/NFELT TW14 174 E3
EDGW HA8 95 N9
EFNCH N2 97 P9
HLW CM20 29 L7
IS N1 6 G10
KUTN/CMB KT2 199 K1
PEND EN3 80 B4
REIG RH2 257 J9
ROMW/RG RM7 124 E5
SRTFD E15 141 M3
WDR/YW UB7 152 A3
WELL DA16 163 L8
WEY KT13 216 E4
WIM/MER SW19 179 M9
East Rochester Wy BFN/LL DA15 185 H1
DART DA1 186 E3
East Rw NKENS W10 8 B2
WAN E11 121 M4
Eastry Av HAYES BR2 205 L6
Eastry Rd ERITH DA8 164 B6
East Shalford La RGUE GU4 268 C5
East Sheen Av
MORT/ESHN SW14 178 A1
East Side SHB * W12 156 F1
Eastside Rd GLDGN NW11 117 J2
East Smithfield WAP E1W 13 M8
East Stanley Gn
DTCH/LGLY SL3 150 C3
East St BARK IG11 142 F2
BMLY BR1 205 M2
BTFD TW8 155 H6
BXLYHN DA7 164 B10
CSHM HP5 50 G8
EW KT17 220 B8
GT/LBKH KT23 254 A1
HHNE HP2 35 N6
HORS RH12 282 B6
WALW SE17 19 H7
WARE SG12 26 C2
WTHK RM20 167 K5
East Surrey Gv PECK SE15 159 N6
East Tenter St WCHPL E1 13 M6
East Ter BFN/LL * DA15 185 H4
GVE DA12 190 F2
East Thurrock Rd GRAYS RM17 167 N5
East Tilbury Rd SLH/COR SS17 169 K1
East Towers PIN HA5 113 L4
East V ACT * W3 136 C10
East Vw BAR EN5 77 J6
BRKMPK AL9 42 A3
CHING E4 101 H6
Eastview Av WOOL/PLUM SE18 163 H6
Eastville Av GLDGN NW11 117 J3
East Wk EBAR EN4 98 B2
HLW * CM20 28 G10
HYS/HAR UB3 153 H1
REIG RH2 257 L10
East Wy CROY/NA CR0 204 D9
HYS/HAR UB3 133 H10
RSLP HA4 113 H6
WAB EN9 81 J2
Eastway GUW GU2 249 L10
HAYES BR2 205 M7
HOM E9 140 D3
HOR/WEW KT19 219 P8
HORL RH6 280 C8
LEY E10 120 F9
MRDN SM4 200 G5
WAN E11 121 N3
WLGTN SM6 222 D1
Eastwell Cl BECK BR3 204 D1
Eastwick Crs RKW/CH/CXG WD3 91 J3
Eastwick Dr GT/LBKH KT23 236 A10
Eastwick Hall La HLW CM20 28 D6
Eastwick Park Av GT/LBKH KT23 236 A10
Eastwick Rd GT/LBKH KT23 254 A1
HLW CM20 28 E7
WOT/HER KT12 217 J2
Eastwick Rw HHNE HP2 36 B7
Eastwood CRAWE RH10 284 A7
Eastwood Cl SWFD E18 101 M10
TOTM * N17 100 A8
Eastwood Dr RAIN RM13 145 J8
Eastwood Ldg SHGR * GU5 268 C10
Eastwood Rd GDMY/SEVK IG3 123 K5
MUSWH N10 98 B10
SHGR GU5 268 C10
SWFD E18 101 M10
Eastwood St STRHM/NOR SW16 180 D9
Eastworth Rd CHERT KT16 195 J8
Eatington Rd LEY E10 121 J3
Eaton Cl BGVA SW1W 16 C5
STAN HA7 94 G5
Eaton Dr BRXN/ST SW9 159 J10
CRW RM5 104 C8
KUTN/CMB KT2 177 M10
Eaton Gdns DAGW RM9 143 P2
Eaton Ga BGVA SW1W 16 C5
NTHWD HA6 92 D7
Eaton La BGVA SW1W 16 F4
Eaton Ms North KTBR SW1X 16 D4
Eaton Ms South BGVA SW1W 16 D5
Eaton Ms West BGVA SW1W 16 D5
Eaton Pk COB KT11 217 M10
Eaton Park Rd COB KT11 217 M10
PLMGR N13 99 H3
Eaton Pl KTBR SW1X 16 D4
Eaton Ri EA W5 135 H7
WAN E11 121 P3
Eaton Rd BELMT SM2 221 N3
EN EN1 79 M7
HDN NW4 116 F3
HHNE HP2 36 C3
HSLW TW3 154 C10
SCUP DA14 185 N5
STAL AL1 38 G6
UPMR RM14 126 D7
Eaton Rw BGVA SW1W 16 E3
Eatons Md CHING E4 100 F3
Eaton Sq BGVA SW1W 16 D4
Eaton Ter BGVA SW1W 16 C5
BOW * E3 140 D5
Eaton Terrace Ms KTBR SW1X 16 C5
Eatonville Rd TOOT SW17 180 A5
Eatonville Vls TOOT SW17 180 A5
Ebba's Wy EPSOM KT18 237 N1
Ebberns Rd HHS/BOV HP3 35 P9
Ebbisham Dr VX/NE SW8 17 N9
Ebbisham La
KWD/TDW/WH KT20 238 C7
Ebbisham Rd EPSOM KT18 219 N10
EPSOM KT18 237 N1
WPK KT4 200 F9
Ebbsfleet Rd CRICK NW2 117 H10
Ebdon Wy BKHTH/KID SE3 161 N9
Ebenezer St IS N1 6 G9
Ebenezer Wk MTCM CR4 202 D1
Ebley Cl PECK SE15 19 L10
Ebner St WAND/EARL SW18 179 L1
Ebor St BETH E2 13 L1
Ebrington Rd
KTN/HRWW/WH HA3 115 H4
Ebsworth St FSTH SE23 182 C3
Eburne Rd HOLWY N7 118 F8
Ebury Ap RKW/CH/CXG WD3 91 N2
Ebury Bridge Rd BGVA SW1W 16 D8
Ebury Cl HAYES BR2 206 B10
NTHWD HA6 92 D6
Ebury Ms BGVA SW1W 16 D5
Ebury Ms East BGVA SW1W 16 E5
Ebury Rd RKW/CH/CXG WD3 91 N2
WAT WD17 73 L7
Ebury Sq BGVA SW1W 16 E6
Ebury St BGVA SW1W 16 D6
Ecclesbourne Cl PLMGR N13 99 H6
Ecclesbourne Gdns PLMGR N13 99 H6
Ecclesbourne Rd IS N1 6 F4
THHTH CR7 203 K5
Eccleshill RDKG RH5 273 H6
Eccles Rd BTSEA SW11 158 A10
Eccleston Cl EBAR EN4 77 P9
ORP * BR6 206 G8
Eccleston Crs CHDH RM6 123 L5
Ecclestone Ct ALP/SUD HA0 115 K10
Ecclestone Ms ALP/SUD HA0 115 K10
Ecclestone Pl WBLY HA9 115 L10
Eccleston Ms KTBR SW1X 16 D4
Eccleston Pl BGVA SW1W 16 E5
Eccleston Rd HNWL W7 134 F9
Eccleston Sq PIM SW1V 16 F6
Eccleston Square Ms PIM SW1V 16 F6
Eccleston St BGVA SW1W 16 D4
Echelforde Dr ASHF TW15 174 B7
Echo Ct GVE DA12 190 F5
Echo Hts CHING * E4 100 G2
Echo Pit Rd RGUE GU4 268 B4
Eckford St IS N1 6 A7
Eckstein Rd BTSEA SW11 157 P10
Eclipse Rd PLSTW E13 141 N7
Ecob Cl RGUW GU3 249 L6
Ecton Rd ADL/WDHM KT15 215 L1
Ector Rd CAT SE6 183 K5
Edans Ct SHB W12 156 C1
Edbrooke Rd MV/WKIL W9 8 E2
Eddiscombe Rd FUL/PGN SW6 157 J8
Eddy Cl ROMW/RG RM7 124 C4
Eddystone Rd BROCKY SE4 182 D1
Eddy St BERK HP4 33 M4
Ede Cl HSLWW TW4 153 N9
Edenbridge Cl
BERM/RHTH * SE16 160 A4
STMC/STPC BR5 207 N4
Edenbridge Rd EN EN1 79 M10
HOM * E9 140 C2
Eden Cl ADL/WDHM KT15 215 L6
ALP/SUD HA0 135 J3
BXLY DA5 186 E7
DTCH/LGLY SL3 150 D4
HAMP NW3 117 K7
KENS W8 14 F3
WAB EN9 80 F4
Edencourt Rd
STRHM/NOR SW16 180 C9
Edencroft SHGR GU5 268 D10
Edendale Rd BXLYHN DA7 164 E7
Edenfield Gdns WPK KT4 200 C10
Eden Gn SOCK/AV RM15 146 G7
Eden Gv HOLWY N7 118 G10
Eden Grove Rd BF/WBF KT14 215 P9
Edenhall Cl HHNE HP2 36 E7
Edenhall Rd HARH RM3 105 K6
Edenham Wy NKENS W10 8 C3
Edenhurst Av FUL/PGN SW6 157 J9
Eden Pde BECK * BR3 204 D4
Eden Park Av BECK BR3 204 E4
Eden Pl GVE DA12 190 E3
Eden Rd BECK BR3 204 D4
BXLY DA5 186 D7
CRAWW RH11 283 J9
CROY/NA CR0 223 L1
WALTH E17 120 G3
WNWD SE27 181 J8
Edenside Rd GT/LBKH KT23 235 N10
Edensor Rd CHSWK W4 156 B6
Eden St KUT KT1 199 J2
Edenvale Rd MTCM CR4 180 B10
Edenvale St FUL/PGN SW6 157 L8
Eden Wk KUT * KT1 199 K2
Eden Wy BECK BR3 204 F5
WARL CR6 242 D4
Ederline Av STRHM/NOR SW16 202 G3
Edes Cottages ASHTD * KT21 237 J5
Edgar Cl CRAWE RH10 284 F8
SWLY BR8 208 G3
Edgar Kail Wy CMBW SE5 159 M9
Edgarley Ter FUL/PGN * SW6 157 H7
Edgar Rd BH/WHM TN16 244 A7
BOW E3 140 G5
HSLWW TW4 175 N3
RSEV TN14 227 M3
SAND/SEL CR2 223 L6
WDR/YW UB7 131 P9
Edgars Ct WGCE * AL7 23 H6
Edgbaston Dr RAD WD7 57 K8
Edgeborough Ct GU * GU1 268 C1
Edgeborough Wy BMLY BR1 206 A1
Edgebury CHST BR7 184 E7
Edge Cl WEY KT13 216 B4
Edgecombe Cl KUTN/CMB KT2 178 A10
Edgecoombe SAND/SEL CR2 224 C5

Edgecote Cl *ACT* W3 135 P10
Edgefield Av *BARK* IG11 143 J2
Edgefield Cl *DART* DA1 188 A4
REDH RH1 276 B5
Edge Hl *WIM/MER* SW19 178 G10
WOOL/PLUM SE18 162 E5
Edge Hill Av *GLDGN* NW11 117 K2
Edgehill Ct *WOT/HER* * KT12 197 K8
Edgehill Gdns *DAGE* RM10 124 B9
Edgehill Rd *CHST* BR7 184 F6
MTCM CR4 202 C2
PUR/KEN CR8 223 H6
WEA W13 135 H8
Edgeley *GT/LBKH* KT23 235 M10
Edgeley La *CLAP* SW4 158 E9
Edgeley Rd *CLAP* SW4 158 E9
Edgell Cl *VW* GU25 194 C3
Edgell Rd *STA* TW18 173 J9
Edgel St *WAND/EARL* SW18 157 L10
Edgepoint Cl *WNWD* * SE27 181 J8
Edge St *KENS* W8 8 F9
Edgewood Dr *ORP* BR6 227 J2
Edgewood Gn *CROY/NA* CR0 204 C8
Edgeworth Av *HDN* NW4 116 D3
Edgeworth Cl *CTHM* CR3 241 P4
HDN NW4 116 D3
Edgeworth Rd *EBAR* EN4 77 P8
ELTH/MOT SE9 161 P10
Edgington Rd
STRHM/NOR SW16 180 E9
Edgington Wy *SCUP* DA14 185 M10
Edgwarebury Gdns *EDGW* HA8 95 M6
Edgwarebury La *BORE* WD6 95 L1
Edgware Rd *BAY/PAD* W2 9 L2
CDALE/KGS NW9 115 P1
Edgware Rd Burnt Oak Broadway
EDGW HA8 95 N8
Edgware Rd High St *EDGW* HA8 95 M7
Edgware Rd The Hyde
CDALE/KGS NW9 116 B2
Edgware Wy (Watford By-Pass)
EDGW HA8 95 K3
Edinburgh Av *RKW/CH/CXG* WD3 71 K10
SL SL1 128 F8
Edinburgh Cl *BETH* E2 140 B4
HGDN/ICK UB10 112 C9
PIN HA5 113 M5
Edinburgh Ct *KUT* * KT1 199 K3
Edinburgh Crs *CHES/WCR* EN8 62 D9
Edinburgh Dr *GSTN* WD25 55 H8
HGDN/ICK UB10 112 C9
STA TW18 173 N9
Edinburgh Gdns *WDSR* SL4 149 J8
Edinburgh Ga *BAY/PAD* W2 16 A1
Edinburgh Ms *TIL* RM18 168 E8
Edinburgh Pl *HLW* CM20 29 K7
Edinburgh Rd *HNWL* W7 154 E1
PLSTW E13 141 N4
SUT SM1 201 M9
UED * N18 99 P6
WALTH E17 120 F3
Edinburgh's Dr *ROMW/RG* RM7 124 D2
Edinburgh Wy *HLW* CM20 29 L7
HLWE CM17 29 M6
Edington Rd *ABYW* SE2 163 L2
PEND EN3 80 B6
Edison Av *HCH* RM12 124 G6
Edison Cl *HCH* RM12 124 G6
STALE/WH AL4 39 H7
Edison Dr *GFD/PVL* UB6 134 A8
WBLY HA9 115 K7
Edison Gv *WOOL/PLUM* SE18 163 J6
Edison Rd *CEND/HSY/T* N8 118 E4
HAYES BR2 205 M2
PEND EN3 80 E6
WELL DA16 163 J7
Edis St *CAMTN* NW1 4 C5
Edith Gdns *BRYLDS* KT5 199 N7
Edith Gv *WBPTN* SW10 15 K10
Edithna St *BRXN/ST* SW9 158 F9
Edith Rd *CHDH* RM6 123 N5
EHAM E6 142 A2
FBAR/BDGN N11 98 E8
ORP BR6 227 K2
SNWD SE25 203 L5
SRTFD E15 121 J10
WIM/MER SW19 179 L9
WKENS W14 14 B6
Edith Rw *FUL/PGN* SW6 157 L7
Edith St *BETH* E2 7 M7
Edith Ter *WBPTN* * SW10 157 M6
Edith Vls *WKENS* W14 14 C6
Edlson Cl *WALTH* E17 120 F3
Edlyn Cl *BERK* HP4 33 L4
Edmeston Cl *HOM* E9 140 D1
Edmund Beaufort Dr
STALW/RED AL3 38 C4
Edmund Gv *FELT* TW13 175 N5
Edmund Halley Wy *GNWCH* SE10 161 K1
Edmund Hurst Dr *EHAM* E6 142 E7
Edmund Rd *CDH/CHF* RM16 167 J1
MTCM CR4 201 P3
RAIN RM13 144 F5
STMC/STPC BR5 207 M6
WELL DA16 163 K9
Edmunds Av *STMC/STPC* BR5 207 N3
Edmunds Cl *YEAD* UB4 133 K7
Edmunds Rd *HERT/WAS* SG14 24 G4
Edmund St *CMBW* SE5 159 L6
Edmunds Wk *EFNCH* N2 117 P2
Edmunds Wy *SLN* SL2 129 N7
Edna Rd *RYNPK* SW20 200 G2
Edna St *BTSEA* SW11 157 P7
Edrick Rd *EDGW* HA8 95 P7
Edrick Wk *EDGW* HA8 95 P7
Edric Rd *NWCR* SE14 160 C6
Edridge Cl *BUSH* WD23 74 B9
HCH RM12 125 L10
Edridge Rd *CROY/NA* CR0 203 K10
Edulf Rd *BORE* WD6 75 N6
Edward Amey Cl *GSTN* WD25 73 K2
Edward Av *CHING* E4 100 G6
MRDN SM4 201 N5
Edward Cl *ABLGY* WD5 54 G8
CDH/CHF RM16 167 J1
ED N9 99 N1
GPK RM2 125 K1
HPTN TW12 176 B8
STAL AL1 38 E7
Edward Ct *CAN/RD* E16 141 M7
HHS/BOV HP3 35 N10
STA TW18 173 M9
WAB EN9 63 L9
Edwardes Pl *KENS* * W8 14 D4
Edwardes Sq *KENS* W8 14 D4
Edward Gv *EBAR* EN4 77 N9
Edward II Av *BF/WBF* KT14 216 A10
Edward Mann Cl East
WCHPL * E1 140 C8
Edward Mann Cl West
WCHPL * E1 140 C8
Edward Ms *CAMTN* * NW1 4 F9
Edward Pl *DEPT* SE8 160 E5
Edward Rd *BFOR* GU20 212 C3
BH/WHM TN16 244 B4
BMLY BR1 183 N10
CHDH RM6 123 P4
CHST BR7 184 E8
COUL/CHIP CR5 240 E1
CROY/NA CR0 203 M7
EBAR EN4 77 N9
EBED/NFELT TW14 174 E1
HPTN TW12 176 B8
NTHLT UB5 133 K4
PGE/AN SE20 182 C10
RYLN/HDSTN HA2 114 B1
WALTH E17 120 C2
Edwards Av *RSLP* HA4 113 K10
Edwards Cl *WPK* KT4 200 G9
Edward's Cottages *IS* N1 6 C2
Edwards Ct *EYN* DA4 209 M10
SL SL1 149 K1
Edwards Gdns *SWLY* BR8 208 E4
Edward's La *STNW/STAM* N16 119 L7
Edwards Ms *IS* N1 6 B3
MBLAR W1H 10 C6
Edwards Pl *FBAR/BDGN* N11 98 E8
Edward Sq *IS* N1 5 N6
Edwards Rd *BELV* DA17 164 B3
Edward St *CAN/RD* E16 141 M6
NWCR SE14 160 D6
Edward Temme Av *SRTFD* E15 141 L2
Edward Tyler Rd *LEE/GVPK* SE12 183 N5
Edward Wy *ASHF* TW15 174 A5
Edwina Gdns *REDBR* IG4 122 B3
Edwin Av *EHAM* E6 142 D4
Edwin Cl *BXLYHN* DA7 164 A5
EHSLY KT24 252 E1
RAIN RM13 144 G5
Edwin Petty Pl *RDART* * DA2 188 B3
Edwin Rd *EDGW* HA8 96 A7
EHSLY KT24 252 D1
RDART DA2 187 J6
WHTN TW2 176 D4
Edwin's Md *HOM* E9 120 D9
Edwin St *CAN/RD* E16 141 M7
GVE DA12 190 E3
WCHPL E1 140 B6
Edwin Ware Ct *PIN* * HA5 93 K10
Edwyn Cl *BAR* EN5 76 F9
Effie Pl *FUL/PGN* SW6 157 K6
Effie Rd *FUL/PGN* SW6 157 K6
Effingham Cl *BELMT* SM2 221 L4
Effingham Common Rd
EHSLY KT24 253 K1
Effingham Ct
WOKS/MYFD * GU22 232 B5
Effingham La *CRAWE* RH10 281 M10
Effingham Pl *EHSLY* KT24 253 L3
Effingham Rd *CEND/HSY/T* N8 119 H3
CROY/NA CR0 202 G7
HORL RH6 281 K9
LEW SE13 183 K1
REIG RH2 275 L1
SURB KT6 198 G7
Effort St *TOOT* SW17 179 P8
Effra Pde *HNHL* SE24 181 H1
Effra Rd *BRXS/STRHM* SW2 158 G10
WIM/MER SW19 179 L9
Egan Wy *HYS/HAR* UB3 132 F9
Egbert St *CAMTN* NW1 4 C5
Egerton Av *SWLY* BR8 208 G1
Egerton Cl *DART* DA1 187 J4
PIN HA5 113 H2
Egerton Crs *CHEL* SW3 15 N5
Egerton Dr *GNWCH* SE10 160 G7
Egerton Gdns *CHEL* SW3 15 N4
GDMY/SEVK IG3 123 J8
HDN NW4 116 E2
WEA W13 134 G8
WLSDN * NW10 136 F3
Egerton Gardens Ms *CHEL* SW3 15 P4
Egerton Pl *CHEL* * SW3 15 P4
WEY KT13 216 D3
Egerton Rd *ALP/SUD* HA0 135 L2
BERK HP4 33 M3
GUW GU2 267 K1
NWMAL KT3 200 C4
SLN SL2 128 D6
SNWD SE25 203 M3
STNW/STAM * N16 119 N5
WEY KT13 216 D3
WHTN TW2 176 D3
Egerton Ter *CHEL* SW3 15 P4
Egerton Wy *WDR/YW* UB7 152 C6
Egg Hall *EPP* CM16 65 K5
Egham By-Pass *EGH* TW20 172 C7
Egham Cl *CHEAM* SM3 201 H9
Egham Crs *CHEAM* SM3 200 G10
Egham Hl *EGH* TW20 172 A9
Egham Rd *PLSTW* E13 141 N7
Eghams Cl *BEAC* HP9 88 B7
Eghams Wood Rd *BEAC* HP9 88 A7
Eglantine La *EYN* DA4 210 A6
Eglantine Rd *WAND/EARL* SW18 179 M1
Egleston Rd *MRDN* SM4 201 L6
Egley Dr *WOKS/MYFD* GU22 232 A8
Egley Rd *WOKS/MYFD* GU22 232 A6
Eglington Rd *CHING* E4 101 J1
Eglinton Hl *WOOL/PLUM* SE18 162 E5
Eglinton Rd *SWCM* DA10 189 L2
WOOL/PLUM SE18 162 D5
Eglise Rd *WARL* CR6 242 D3
Egliston Ms *PUT/ROE* SW15 156 F9
Egliston Rd *PUT/ROE* SW15 156 F9
Eglon Ms *CAMTN* NW1 4 B4
Egmont Av *SURB* KT6 199 L8
Egmont Park Rd
KWD/TDW/WH KT20 256 D1
Egmont Rd *BELMT* SM2 221 M4
NWMAL KT3 200 C4
SURB KT6 199 L8
WOT/HER KT12 197 J7
Egmont St *NWCR* SE14 160 C6
Egmont Wy *KWD/TDW/WH* KT20 239 H5
Egremont Gdns *SL* SL1 128 F10
Egremont Rd *WNWD* SE27 181 H6
Egret Wy *YEAD* UB4 133 L8
Egypt La *SLN* SL2 108 G8
Eider Cl *FSTGT* E7 121 L10
Eight Acres *SL* SL1 128 A6
Eighteenth Rd *MTCM* CR4 202 F4
Eighth Av *HYS/HAR* UB3 133 H10
KWD/TDW/WH * KT20 257 J2
MNPK E12 122 C9
Eileen Rd *SNWD* SE25 203 L5
Eindoven Cl *MTCM* CR4 202 B8
Eisenhower Dr *EHAM* E6 142 B7
Elaine Gv *KTTN* NW5 118 B10
Elam Cl *CMBW* SE5 159 J8
Elam St *CMBW* SE5 159 J8
Eland Rd *BTSEA* SW11 158 A9
CROY/NA CR0 203 J10
Elan Rd *SOCK/AV* RM15 146 F7
Elba Pl *WALW* * SE17 18 F5
Elberon Av *CROY/NA* CR0 202 D6
Elbe St *FUL/PGN* SW6 157 M8
Elborough Rd *SNWD* SE25 203 P5
Elborough St *WAND/EARL* SW18 179 K4
Elbow La *HERT/BAY* SG13 26 A10
Elbow Meadow *DTCH/LGLY* * SL3 151 J7
Elbury Dr *CAN/RD* E16 141 M8
Elcho Rd *CHOB/PIR* GU24 230 B5
Elcho St *BTSEA* SW11 157 P6
Elcot Av *PECK* SE15 160 A6
Elder Av *CEND/HSY/T* N8 118 F3
Elderbeck Cl *CHESW* EN7 61 P4
Elderberry Rd *EA* W5 155 K1
Elderberry Wy *GSTN* WD25 73 J1
Elder Cl *BFN/LL* DA15 185 J4
GU GU1 250 D7
WDR/YW UB7 131 P9
Elder Ct *BUSH* WD23 94 D3
Elderfield *HLWE* CM17 29 N7
Elderfield Rd *CLPT* E5 120 C9
SLN SL2 129 L1
Elderfield Wk *WAN* E11 121 N3
Elderflower Wy *SRTFD* E15 141 K2
Elder Oak Cl *PGE/AN* SE20 204 A1
Elder Rd *CHOB/PIR* GU24 230 F1
WNWD SE27 181 K8
Eldersley Cl *REDH* RH1 258 A8
Eldersley Gdns *REDH* RH1 258 A8
Elderslie Cl *BECK* BR3 204 F6
Elderslie Rd *ELTH/MOT* SE9 184 D1
Elder St *WCHPL* E1 13 L3
Elderton Rd *SYD* SE26 182 D7
Eldertree Wy *MTCM* CR4 202 C1
Elder Wk *IS* N1 6 D5
Elder Wy *DTCH/LGLY* * SL3 150 C1
RAIN RM13 145 L5
RDKG RH5 273 H6
Eldon Av *BORE* WD6 75 M6
CROY/NA CR0 204 B9
HEST TW5 153 P6
Eldon Gv *HAMP* NW3 117 N10
Eldon Pde *WDGN* * N22 99 J9
Eldon Pk *SNWD* SE25 204 A4
Eldon Rd *CTHM* CR3 241 L7
ED N9 100 B2
HOD EN11 45 J5
KENS W8 15 H4
WALTH E17 120 E2
WDGN N22 99 J9
Eldon St *LVPST* EC2M 13 H4
Eldon Wy *WLSDN* NW10 135 N4
Eldred Dr *STMC/STPC* BR5 207 N9
Eldred Gdns *UPMR* RM14 126 D5
Eldridge Cl *EBED/NFELT* TW14 175 H4
Eleanora Ter *SUT* * SM1 221 M2
Eleanor Av *HOR/WEW* KT19 220 A6
STALW/RED AL3 38 C4
Eleanor Cl *TOTM* N17 119 N1
Eleanor Crs *MLHL* NW7 96 G5
Eleanor Cross Rd *CHES/WCR* EN8 62 D10
Eleanor Gdns *BAR* EN5 76 G9
Eleanor Gv *BARN* SW13 156 B9
HGDN/ICK UB10 112 C8
Eleanor Rd *CFSP/GDCR* SL9 89 P9
CHES/WCR EN8 62 D9
FBAR/BDGN N11 98 F7
HACK E8 140 A1
HERT/WAS SG14 25 K4
SRTFD E15 141 L1
Eleanor St *BOW* E3 140 F5
Eleanor Wy *BRW* CM14 107 J6
CHES/WCR EN8 62 E10
Electric Av *BRXN/ST* SW9 159 H10
PEND EN3 80 E2
Electric La *BRXN/ST* * SW9 159 H10
Electric Pde *SURB* KT6 199 J6
Elephant & Castle *STHWK* SE1 18 D5
Elephant La *BERM/RHTH* SE16 160 B1
Elephant Rd *WALW* SE17 18 E5
Elers Rd *HYS/HAR* UB3 152 D3
WEA W13 155 H1
Eleven Acre Ri *LOU* IG10 82 C7
Eleventh Av
KWD/TDW/WH * KT20 257 J2
Eley Rd *UED* N18 100 C6
Elfindale Rd *HNHL* SE24 181 K1
Elfin Gv *TEDD* TW11 176 E8
Elford Cl *ELTH/MOT* SE9 161 P10
Elfort Rd *HBRY* N5 119 H9
Elfrida Crs *CAT* SE6 182 F7
Elfrida Rd *WATW* WD18 73 K9
Elf Rw *WAP* E1W 140 B9
Elfwine Rd *HNWL* W7 134 D7
Elgal Cl *ORP* BR6 226 E2
Elgar Av *BRYLDS* KT5 199 N8
EA W5 155 K1
STRHM/NOR SW16 202 F3
WLSDN NW10 136 A1
Elgar Cl *BKHH* IG9 102 A3
BORE WD6 95 H1
DEPT SE8 160 E6
HGDN/ICK UB10 112 B7
PLSTW E13 141 P4
Elgar Gdns *TIL* RM18 168 D7
Elgar St *BERM/RHTH* SE16 160 D1
Elger Wy *CRAWE* RH10 285 H1
Elgin Av *ASHF* TW15 174 D9
HARH RM3 106 A8
KTN/HRWW/W HA3 94 G10
MV/WKIL W9 8 E2
SHB W12 156 D1
Elgin Crs *CTHM* CR3 241 P8
HTHAIR TW6 152 F8
NTGHL W11 8 B7
Elgin Dr *NTHWD* HA6 92 F8
Elgin Est *MV/WKIL* W9 8 E2
Elgin Gdns *GU* GU1 250 D9
Elginmeads South *MV/WKIL* W9 3 H10
Elgin Ms *NTGHL* W11 8 B6
Elgin Ms North *MV/WKIL* W9 3 H9
Elgin Pl *WEY* * KT13 216 D3
Elgin Rd *BROX* EN10 44 E10
CHES/WCR EN8 62 B6
CROY/NA CR0 203 N9
GDMY/SEVK IG3 123 H6
SUT SM1 201 M10
WDGN N22 98 D10
WEY KT13 216 B3
WLGTN SM6 222 D3
Elgiva La *CSHM* HP5 50 G7
Elgood Av *NTHWD* HA6 93 H7
Elgood Cl *NTGHL* W11 8 A8
Elham Cl *BMLY* BR1 184 A10
Elia Ms *IS* N1 6 C8
Elias Pl *LBTH* SE11 18 A10
Elia St *IS* N1 6 C8
Elibank Rd *ELTH/MOT* SE9 162 D10
Elim St *STHWK* SE1 19 H3
Elim Wy *PLSTW* E13 141 L5
Eliot Bank *FSTH* SE23 182 A5
Eliot Dr *RYLN/HDSTN* HA2 114 A7
Eliot Gdns *PUT/ROE* SW15 156 D10
Eliot Hl *BKHTH/KID* SE3 161 H8
Eliot Pk *LEW* SE13 161 H8
Eliot Pl *BKHTH/KID* SE3 161 K8
Eliot Rd *DAGW* RM9 123 N9
DART DA1 188 A1
Eliot V *BKHTH/KID* SE3 161 J8
Elizabethan Wy *CRAWE* RH10 284 D8
STWL/WRAY TW19 173 N3
Elizabeth Av *AMS* HP6 69 P5
ENC/FH EN2 79 J7
IL IG1 122 G7
IS N1 6 F4
STA TW18 173 M9
Elizabeth Barnes Ct
FUL/PGN * SW6 157 L8
Elizabeth Br *BGVA* SW1W 16 E6
Elizabeth Cl *BAR* EN5 76 G7
MV/WKIL * W9 9 K2
ROMW/RG RM7 104 C9
SUT SM1 221 J1
TIL RM18 168 E8
WAB EN9 45 J8
WGCE AL7 23 M5
Elizabeth Clyde Cl
SEVS/STOTM N15 119 M2
Elizabeth Cottages
RCH/KEW TW9 155 L7
Elizabeth Ct *HORL* * RH6 280 B4
RGODL GU7 267 K10
STALE/WH AL4 39 J3
Elizabeth Dr *EPP* CM16 83 H2
Elizabeth Gdns *ACT* W3 136 C10
ASC SL5 192 A5
STAN HA7 95 H7
SUN TW16 197 K3
Elizabeth Huggins Cottages
GVW * DA11 190 E5
Elizabeth Ms *HAMP* NW3 3 P2
Elizabeth Pl *EYN* * DA4 209 N6
SEVS/STOTM N15 119 L2
Elizabeth Ride *ED* N9 100 A1
Elizabeth Rd *BRWN* CM15 86 G10
CDH/CHF RM16 167 L2
EHAM E6 142 A3
RAIN RM13 145 J7
RGODL GU7 267 K10
SEVS/STOTM N15 119 M3
Elizabeth Sq *BERM/RHTH* SE16 140 D9
Elizabeth St *BGVA* SW1W 16 D5
GRH DA9 188 D1
Elizabeth Wy *FELT* TW13 175 K7
HLW CM20 28 D9
HLWW/ROY CM19 46 C2
NRWD SE19 181 L10
SLN SL2 129 L3
STMC/STPC BR5 207 M5
Elkington Rd *PLSTW* E13 141 N6
Elkins Gdns *RGUE* GU4 250 D7
Elkins Rd *SLN* SL2 109 K7
The Elkins *ROM* RM1 104 F10
Elkstone Rd *NKENS* W10 8 C3
Ellaline Rd *HMSMTH* W6 156 G5
Ella Ms *HAMP* NW3 118 A9
Ellanby Crs *UED* N18 100 A6
Elland Rd *PECK* SE15 160 B10
WOT/HER KT12 197 L9
Ella Rd *CEND/HSY/T* N8 118 F5
Ellement Cl *PIN* HA5 113 L3
Ellenborough Pl *PUT/ROE* SW15 156 D10
Ellenborough Rd *SCUP* DA14 185 N9
WDGN N22 99 K9
Ellenbridge Wy *SAND/SEL* CR2 223 M5
Ellenbrook Cl *WATN* * WD24 73 K5
Ellenbrook Crs *HAT* AL10 40 A4
Ellenbrook La *HAT* AL10 40 B5
Ellen Cl *BMLY* BR1 206 A3
HHNE HP2 36 A5
Ellen Ct *ED* N9 100 B3
Ellen Ms *HHNE* * HP2 36 A5
Ellen St *WCHPL* E1 13 P6
Ellen Webb Dr
KTN/HRWW/W HA3 114 D1
Elleray Rd *TEDD* TW11 176 E9
Ellerby St *FUL/PGN* SW6 156 G7
Ellerdale Rd *HAMP* NW3 117 M10
Ellerdale St *LEW* SE13 160 G10
Ellerdine Rd *HSLW* TW3 154 B10
Ellerker Gdns *RCHPK/HAM* TW10 177 K2
Ellerman Av *WHTN* TW2 175 N4
Ellerman Rd *TIL* RM18 168 C8
Ellerslie Rd *SHB* W12 136 E10
Ellerton Gdns *DAGW* RM9 143 M2
Ellerton Rd *BARN* * SW13 156 D7
DAGW RM9 143 M2
RYNPK SW20 178 D10
SURB KT6 199 L9
WAND/EARL SW18 179 N4
Ellery Rd *NRWD* SE19 181 L10
Ellery St *PECK* SE15 160 A8
Elles Av *GU* GU1 250 E10
Ellesborough Cl *OXHEY* WD19 93 K6
Ellesmere Av *BECK* BR3 204 G2
MLHL NW7 96 A4
Ellesmere Cl *RSLP* HA4 112 D5
WAN E11 121 L3
Ellesmere Dr *SAND/SEL* CR2 224 A10
Ellesmere Gdns *REDBR* IG4 122 B3
Ellesmere Gv *BAR* EN5 77 J9
Ellesmere Pl *WEY* KT13 216 F2
Ellesmere Rd *BERK* HP4 34 A5
BOW E3 140 D4
GFD/PVL UB6 134 B6
TWK TW1 177 H2
WEY KT13 216 F3
WLSDN NW10 116 D10
Ellesmere St *POP/IOD* E14 140 G8
Ellice Rd *OXTED* RH8 261 L5
Ellies Ms *ASHF* TW15 173 P5
Elliman Av *SL* SL1 129 K9
Ellingfort Rd *HACK* E8 140 A1
Ellingham Cl *HHNE* HP2 36 B4
Ellingham Rd *CHSGTN* KT9 219 J3
HHNE HP2 36 A5
SHB W12 156 D1
WAN E11 121 J9
Ellington Rd *FELT* TW13 174 G7
HSLW TW3 154 A8
MUSWH N10 118 C2
Ellington St *HOLWY* N7 6 A2
Ellington Wy *EPSOM* KT18 238 E3
Elliot Cl *CRAWE* RH10 284 D8
SRTFD E15 141 K2
WBLY HA9 115 L8
Elliot Rd *HDN* NW4 116 E4
Elliott Av *RSLP* HA4 113 J7
Elliott Cl *WGCE* AL7 22 G8
Elliott Ct *WOKN/KNAP* * GU21 232 D2
Elliott Gdns *HARH* RM3 105 J9
SHPTN TW17 196 B4
Elliott Rd *BRXN/ST* SW9 159 J6
CHSWK W4 156 B3
HAYES BR2 206 A4
STAN HA7 94 F7
THHTH CR7 203 J4
Elliotts La *BH/WHM* TN16 245 M10
Elliott's Pl *IS* N1 6 D6
Elliott Sq *HAMP* NW3 3 P4
Elliott's Rw *LBTH* SE11 18 D5
Elliott St *GVE* DA12 190 G3
Ellis Av *CFSP/GDCR* SL9 90 C9
GUW GU2 267 L2
RAIN RM13 145 H7
SL SL1 149 K1
Ellis Cl *COUL/CHIP* CR5 240 G6
CRICK NW2 136 F1
EDGW HA8 96 B7
ELTH/MOT SE9 184 F5
Elliscombe Mt *CHARL* * SE7 161 P5
Elliscombe Rd *CHARL* SE7 161 P4
Ellis Farm Cl *WOKS/MYFD* GU22 232 A8
Ellisfield Dr *PUT/ROE* SW15 178 C3
Ellison Cl *WDSR* SL4 148 E9
Ellison Gdns *NWDGN* UB2 153 N3
Ellison Rd *BARN* SW13 156 C8
BFN/LL DA15 184 G4
STRHM/NOR SW16 180 E10
Ellis Rd *COUL/CHIP* CR5 240 G6
MTCM CR4 202 A6
STHL UB1 134 B10
Ellis St *KTBR* SW1X 16 B5
Ellis Waterton Cl *SWLY* BR8 208 E4
Ellis Wy *DART* * DA1 187 N5
Elliswick Rd *HARP* AL5 20 A1
Ellman Rd *CRAWW* RH11 283 J9
Ellmore Cl *HARH* RM3 105 J9
Ellora Rd *STRHM/NOR* SW16 180 E8
Ellson Cl *CRAWE* RH10 284 D9
Ellsworth St *BETH* * E2 140 A5
Ellwood Gdns *GSTN* WD25 55 J10
Ellwood Pl *CRAWW* * RH11 283 J7
Ellwood Ri *CSTG* HP8 89 P3
Ellwood Rd *BEAC* HP9 88 A10
Elmar Gn *SLN* SL2 128 F5
Elmar Rd *SEVS/STOTM* N15 119 L2
Elm Av *EA* W5 135 K10
OXHEY WD19 93 M1
RSLP HA4 113 H6
UPMR RM14 126 A8
Elm Bank *CHOB/PIR* * GU24 213 K7
Elmbank *WCHMH* N21 98 F1
Elmbank Av *BAR* EN5 76 F8
EGH TW20 171 N10
GUW GU2 267 M1
Elmbank Dr *BMLY* BR1 206 A2
Elm Bank Gdns *BARN* SW13 156 B8
Elmbank Wy *HNWL* W7 134 C7
Elmbourne Dr *BELV* DA17 164 C3
Elmbourne Rd *TOOT* SW17 180 C6
Elmbridge *HLWE* CM17 30 A8
Elmbridge Av *BRYLDS* KT5 199 P6
Elmbridge Cl *RSLP* HA4 113 H4
Elmbridge Dr *RSLP* HA4 113 H4
Elmbridge La *WOKS/MYFD* GU22 232 C5
Elmbridge Rd *BARK/HLT* IG6 103 K7
Elmbridge Wk *HACK* * E8 7 P4
Elmbrook Cl *SUN* TW16 197 J1
Elmbrook Gdns *ELTH/MOT* SE9 162 B10
Elmbrook Rd *SUT* SM1 221 J1
Elm Cl *AMS* HP6 69 H4
BKHH IG9 102 A3
BRYLDS KT5 199 P7
CAR SM5 202 A8
DART DA1 187 K4
EPP CM16 46 E10
HDN NW4 116 G3
HYS/HAR UB3 133 H8
KWD/TDW/WH KT20 255 P6
LHD/OX KT22 236 G8
ROMW/RG RM7 104 C9
RYLN/HDSTN HA2 114 A4
RYNPK SW20 200 F4
SAND/SEL CR2 223 L3
SLN SL2 129 H1
STWL/WRAY TW19 173 N4
WAB EN9 63 J10
WAN E11 121 N4
WARL CR6 242 C3
WHTN TW2 176 A5
WOKN/KNAP GU21 232 A1
Elmcote Wy *RKW/CH/CXG* WD3 72 A10
Elm Cottages *GDST* * RH9 260 A6
MTCM * CR4 202 A2
Elm Ct *WAT* * WD17 73 J7
WOKN/KNAP GU21 231 J3
Elmcourt Rd *WNWD* SE27 181 J5
Elm Crs *EA* W5 155 K1
KUTN/CMB KT2 199 K1
Elm Cft *DTCH/LGLY* SL3 149 P7
Elmcroft *CEND/HSY/T* N8 118 G3
GT/LBKH * KT23 235 P10
Elmcroft Av *BFN/LL* DA15 185 J3
ED N9 80 A10
GLDGN NW11 117 J5
WAN E11 121 N3
Elmcroft Cl *CHSGTN* * KT9 199 K10
EA W5 135 J8
EBED/NFELT TW14 174 G2
Elmcroft Crs *GLDGN* NW11 116 G5
RYLN/HDSTN HA2 113 P1
Elmcroft Dr *ASHF* * TW15 174 B8
CHSGTN KT9 199 K10
Elmcroft Gdns *CDALE/KGS* NW9 115 M3
Elmcroft Rd *ORP* BR6 207 K7
Elmcroft St *CLPT* E5 120 B9
Elmcroft Ter *UX/CGN* * UB8 132 B8
Elmdale Rd *PLMGR* N13 98 G6
Elmdene *BRYLDS* KT5 199 P8
Elmdene Av *EMPK* RM11 125 N3
Elmdene Cl *BECK* BR3 204 E5
Elmdene Ct *WOKS/MYFD* GU22 232 B5
Elmdene Rd *WOOL/PLUM* SE18 162 E4
Elmdon Rd *HEST* TW5 153 L8
HTHAIR TW6 152 G9
SOCK/AV RM15 146 F7
Elm Dr *CHES/WCR* EN8 62 D4
CHOB/PIR GU24 213 L6
HAT AL10 40 D5
LHD/OX KT22 236 G8
RYLN/HDSTN HA2 114 A4
STALE/WH AL4 39 H6
SUN TW16 197 K2
SWLY BR8 208 E3

WDSR SL4 170 A4
Elmer Av ABR/ST RM4 104 F4
Elmer Cl ENC/FH EN2 78 G7
RAIN RM13 145 H2
Elmer Cottages LHD/OX * KT22 236 F9
Elmer Gdns EDGW HA8 95 N8
ISLW TW7 154 C9
RAIN RM13 145 H2
Elmer Ms LHD/OX KT22 236 F9
Elmer Rd CAT SE6 183 H3
Elmer's Dr TEDD TW11 176 G9
Elmers End Rd BECK BR3 204 B3
Elmerside Rd BECK BR3 204 D4
Elmers Rd CROY/NA CR0 203 P7
Elmfield GT/LBKH KT23 235 P9
Elmfield Av CEND/HSY/T N8 118 F3
MTCM CR4 202 B1
TEDD TW11 176 E8
Elmfield Cl GVW DA11 190 E4
HRW HA1 114 D7
POTB/CUF EN6 59 H9
RSEV TN14 265 J9
Elmfield Pk BMLY BR1 205 M3
Elmfield Rd BMLY BR1 205 M2
CHING E4 101 H3
EFNCH N2 117 N1
NWDGN UB2 153 M2
POTB/CUF EN6 59 H9
TOOT SW17 180 C5
WALTH E17 120 C4
Elmfield Wy MV/WKIL W9 8 D1
SAND/SEL CR2 223 N5
Elm Friars Wk HOLWY N7 5 K4
Elm Gdns EFNCH N2 117 M1
ENC/FH EN2 79 L4
EPP CM16 66 C2
ESH/CLAY KT10 218 E3
KWD/TDW/WH KT20 238 F5
MTCM CR4 202 E4
WGCW AL8 22 E5
Elmgate Av FELT TW13 175 J6
Elmgate Gdns EDGW HA8 95 P6
Elm Gn ACT W3 136 B8
HHW HP1 35 H4
Elmgreen Cl SRTFD E15 141 K3
Elm Gv BERK HP4 33 P5
CEND/HSY/T N8 118 F4
CHOB/PIR GU24 230 F2
CRICK NW2 116 G9
CTHM CR3 241 M8
EMPK RM11 125 M4
EPSOM KT18 219 P10
ERITH DA8 164 E6
KUTN/CMB KT2 199 K1
ORP BR6 207 J8
PECK SE15 159 P8
RYLN/HDSTN HA2 113 P5
SUT SM1 221 L1
WATN WD24 73 H3
WDR/YW UB7 132 A9
WIM/MER SW19 179 H10
Elmgrove Cl WOKN/KNAP GU21 231 J5
Elmgrove Crs HRW HA1 114 E3
Elmgrove Gdns HRW HA1 114 F3
Elm Grove Pde WLGTN SM6 202 B10
Elm Grove Rd BARN SW13 156 D7
COB KT11 235 L2
EA W5 155 K1
Elmgrove Rd CROY/NA CR0 204 A7
HRW HA1 114 E3
WEY KT13 216 B1
Elm Hall Gdns WAN E11 121 N4
Elm Hatch PIN HA5 93 N8
Elmhurst BELV DA17 163 P5
Elmhurst Av EFNCH * N2 117 N1
MTCM CR4 180 B10
Elmhurst Cl BUSH WD23 73 M8
Elmhurst Dr DORK RH4 272 G4
EMPK RM11 125 K5
SWFD E18 101 M10
Elmhurst Rd DTCH/LGLY SL3 150 D2
ELTH/MOT SE9 184 B5
FSTGT E7 141 N2
PEND EN3 80 B3
TOTM N17 99 M10
Elmhurst St CLAP SW4 158 E9
Elmhurst Wy LOU IG10 102 C1
Elmington Cl BXLY DA5 186 C3
Elmington Est CMBW SE5 159 K6
Elmington Rd CMBW SE5 159 L7
Elmira St LEW SE13 160 G9
Elm La CAT SE6 182 E5
RPLY/SEND GU23 234 A5
Elm Lawn Cl UX/CGN UB8 131 P2
Elmlee Cl CHST BR7 184 C9
Elmley St WOOL/PLUM SE18 162 G3
Elmore Cl ALP/SUD HA0 135 K4
Elmore Rd COUL/CHIP CR5 240 A7
LEY E10 121 H8
PEND EN3 80 C5
Elmores LOU IG10 82 D7
Elmore St IS N1 6 G3
Elm Pde SCUP * DA14 185 K7
Elm Pk ASC SL5 192 D8
BRXS/STRHM SW2 180 G2
STAN HA7 94 G6
Elm Park Av HCH RM12 125 J9
SEVS/STOTM N15 119 N3
Elm Park Gdns CHEL SW3 15 L8
HDN NW4 116 G3
Elmpark Gdns SAND/SEL CR2 224 B6
Elm Park La CHEL SW3 15 L8
Elm Park Rd CHEL SW3 15 L9
FNCH N3 97 J8
LEY E10 120 D6
PIN HA5 113 L1
SNWD SE25 203 N3
WCHMH N21 99 K1
Elm Pl SKENS SW7 15 L7
Elm Rd BAR EN5 77 J8
BECK BR3 204 E2
BH/WHM TN16 263 H1
CHSGTN KT9 219 K1
DART DA1 187 L4
EBED/NFELT TW14 174 E4
ERITH DA8 165 H7
ESH/CLAY KT10 218 E3
EW KT17 220 C3
FSTGT E7 141 L1
GRAYS RM17 167 P5
GRH DA9 188 D2
GVE DA12 190 F6
KUTN/CMB KT2 177 L10
KUTN/CMB KT2 199 L1
LHD/OX KT22 236 G8
MORT/ESHN SW14 155 P9
MTCM CR4 202 B8
NWMAL KT3 200 A3
ORP BR6 227 K4
PUR/KEN CR8 223 J9
REDH RH1 257 P10
RGODL GU7 267 L9
ROMW/RG RM7 104 C10
SCUP DA14 185 K7
SOCK/AV RM15 146 C10
THHTH CR7 203 K4
WALTH E17 121 H3
WAN E11 121 J7
WARL CR6 242 C3
WBLY HA9 115 K10
WDGN N22 99 J9
WDSR SL4 148 G9
WOKN/KNAP GU21 232 A4
Elm Rd West MRDN SM4 201 J7
Elm Rw HAMP NW3 117 M8
Elmroyd Av POTB/CUF EN6 59 J9
Elmroyd Cl POTB/CUF EN6 59 J9
Elms Av HDN NW4 116 F3
MUSWH N10 118 C1
Elmscott Gdns WCHMH N21 79 K10
Elmscott Rd BMLY BR1 183 K8
Elms Ct ALP/SUD HA0 114 E9
Elms Crs CLAP SW4 180 D2
Elmscroft Gdns POTB/CUF EN6 59 J8
Elmsdale Rd WALTH E17 120 E2
Elms Farm Rd HCH RM12 125 K10
Elms Gdns ALP/SUD HA0 114 F9
DAGW RM9 124 A9
Elmshaw Rd PUT/ROE SW15 178 D1
Elmshorn EW KT17 238 F2
Elmshott La SL SL1 128 D9
Elmshurst Crs EFNCH N2 117 N2
Elmside Rd WBLY HA9 115 M8
Elms La ALP/SUD HA0 114 F8
Elmsleigh Av KTN/HRWW/W HA3 114 G2
Elmsleigh Rd STA TW18 173 J8
WHTN TW2 176 C5
Elmslie Cl EPSOM KT18 219 P10
WFD IG8 102 C7
Elms Ms BAY/PAD W2 9 L7
Elms Park Av ALP/SUD HA0 114 F9
Elms Rd CFSP/GDCR SL9 90 B8
CLAP SW4 180 D1
KTN/HRWW/W HA3 94 D8
WARE SG12 26 F1
Elmstead Av CHST BR7 184 C8
WBLY HA9 115 K6
Elmstead Cl HOR/WEW KT19 220 B2
TRDG/WHET N20 97 K3
Elmstead Gdns WPK KT4 200 D10
Elmstead Gld CHST BR7 184 C9
Elmstead La CHST BR7 184 B10
Elmstead Rd BF/WBF KT14 215 K9
ERITH DA8 164 F7
GDMY/SEVK IG3 123 H7
Elmsted Crs WELL DA16 163 M5
The Elms BARN SW13 156 C9
BORE * WD6 75 M5
CHONG CM5 67 P6
ESH/CLAY * KT10 218 E4
HERT/BAY SG13 25 P5
LOU * IG10 81 L6
NFNCH/WDSP * N12 97 P6
TOOT * SW17 180 B6
WLGTN * SM6 222 D1
Elmstone Rd FUL/PGN SW6 157 K7
Elmstone Ter STMC/STPC * BR5 207 M4
Elm St FSBYW WC1X 11 P2
Elmsway ASHF TW15 174 A8
Elmswood GT/LBKH KT23 235 N10
Elmsworth Av HSLW TW3 154 A8
Elm Ter CRICK NW2 117 K8
ELTH/MOT SE9 184 D2
KTN/HRWW/W HA3 94 C8
WTHK RM20 166 G5
Elmton Wy STNW/STAM N16 119 P8
Elmtree Av BRWN CM15 86 E3
Elm Tree Av ESH/CLAY KT10 198 C7
Elmtree Cl BF/WBF KT14 215 P9
Elm Tree Cl ASHF TW15 174 C8
CHERT KT16 195 H9
HORL * RH6 280 B3
NTHLT UB5 133 N5
STJWD NW8 3 L9
Elm Tree Ct CHARL * SE7 161 P5
Elmtree Hl CSHM HP5 50 G6
Elm Tree Rd STJWD NW8 3 L10
Elmtree Rd TEDD TW11 176 D8
Elm Tree Wk RKW/CH/CXG * WD3 71 J8
Elm Vls HNWL * W7 134 D9
Elm Wk GPK RM2 125 H1
HAMP NW3 117 K7
ORP BR6 206 C10
RAD WD7 74 E2
RYNPK SW20 200 F4
Elmway CDH/CHF RM16 147 P9
Elm Wy BRW CM14 106 F4
FBAR/BDGN N11 98 B7
HOR/WEW KT19 220 A2
RKW/CH/CXG WD3 91 L2
WLSDN NW10 116 B9
WPK KT4 200 F10
Elmwood SBW CM21 30 A2
WGCW AL8 22 E6
Elmwood Av BORE WD6 75 N8
FELT TW13 175 J6
KTN/HRWW/W HA3 114 F3
PLMGR N13 98 F6
Elmwood Cl EW KT17 220 D4
WLGTN SM6 202 C9
Elmwood Ct ASHTD KT21 237 J3
Elmwood Crs CDALE/KGS NW9 115 P2
Elmwood Dr BXLY DA5 185 P3
EW KT17 220 D4
Elmwood Gdns HNWL W7 134 D8
Elmwood Pk CFSP/GDCR SL9 110 B6
Elmwood Rd CHSWK W4 155 P5
CROY/NA CR0 203 J7
HNHL SE24 181 L1
MTCM CR4 202 A3
REDH RH1 258 B6
SLN SL2 129 N9
WOKN/KNAP GU21 231 J5
Elmworth Gv DUL SE21 181 L5
Elnathan Ms MV/WKIL W9 9 H2
Elphinstone Rd WALTH E17 100 E10
Elphinstone St HBRY N5 119 J9
Elrick Cl ERITH DA8 164 F5
Elrington Rd HACK E8 7 N2
WFD IG8 101 M6
Elruge Cl WDR/YW UB7 151 N2
Elsa Cottages POP/IOD * E14 140 D7
Elsa Rd WELL DA16 163 M8
Elsa St WCHPL * E1 140 D7
Elsdale St HOM E9 140 B1
Elsden Ms BETH * E2 140 B4
Elsden Rd TOTM N17 99 N9
Elsdon Rd WOKN/KNAP GU21 231 M4
Elsenham Rd MNPK E12 122 C10
Elsenham St WIM/MER SW19 179 J4
Elsham Rd WAN E11 121 K8
WKENS W14 14 A2
Elsham Ter WKENS W14 14 A2
Elsiedene Rd WCHMH N21 99 K1
Elsie Lane Ct BAY/PAD W2 8 F4
Elsiemaud Rd BROCKY SE4 182 E1
Elsie Rd EDUL SE22 159 N10
Elsinge Rd EN EN1 80 A2
Elsinore Av STWL/WRAY * TW19 173 P3
Elsinore Gdns CRICK * NW2 117 H8
Elsinore Rd FSTH SE23 182 D4
Elsinore Wy RCH/KEW TW9 155 N9
Elsley Rd BTSEA SW11 158 A9
Elspeth Rd ALP/SUD HA0 115 K10
BTSEA SW11 158 A10
Elsrick Av MRDN SM4 201 K5
Elstan Wy CROY/NA CR0 204 D7
Elsted Cl CRAWW RH11 283 L5
Elsted St WALW SE17 19 H6
Elstow Cl ELTH/MOT SE9 184 C1
RSLP HA4 113 L5
Elstow Gdns DAGW RM9 143 P3
Elstow Rd DAGW RM9 143 P2
Elstree Gdns BELV DA17 163 P3
ED N9 100 A2
IL IG1 122 F10
Elstree Ga BORE * WD6 76 A6
Elstree Hl BMLY BR1 183 K10
Elstree Hl North BORE WD6 75 J9
Elstree Hl South BORE WD6 95 J1
Elstree Pk MLHL * NW7 76 A10
Elstree Rd BORE WD6 74 F10
BUSH WD23 94 C2
STAN HA7 94 E1
Elstree Wy BORE WD6 75 P6
Elswick Rd LEW SE13 160 G9
Elswick St FUL/PGN SW6 157 M8
Elsworth Cl EBED/NFELT TW14 174 F4
Elsworthy THDIT KT7 198 D6
Elsworthy Ri HAMP NW3 3 P4
Elsworthy Rd HAMP NW3 3 N5
Elsworthy Ter HAMP NW3 3 P4
Elsynge Rd WAND/EARL SW18 179 N1
Eltham Av SL SL1 128 D10
Eltham Green Rd ELTH/MOT SE9 183 P1
Eltham High St ELTH/MOT SE9 184 C2
Eltham Hl ELTH/MOT SE9 184 A1
Eltham Palace Rd
ELTH/MOT SE9 183 P2
Eltham Park Gdns
ELTH/MOT SE9 162 D10
Eltham Rd ELTH/MOT SE9 183 P1
Elthiron Rd FUL/PGN SW6 157 K7
Elthorne Av HNWL W7 154 E1
Elthorne Ct FELT TW13 175 K4
Elthorne Park Rd HNWL W7 154 E2
Elthorne Rd ARCH N19 118 E7
CDALE/KGS NW9 116 A5
UX/CGN UB8 131 N4
Elthorne Wy CDALE/KGS NW9 116 A4
Elthruda Rd LEW SE13 183 J2
Eltisley Rd IL IG1 122 E9
Elton Av ALP/SUD HA0 114 G10
BAR EN5 77 J9
GFD/PVL UB6 134 E1
Elton Cl E/WMO/HCT KT8 177 H10
Elton Pk WAT WD17 73 H6
Elton Pl STNW/STAM N16 119 M10
Elton Rd HERT/WAS SG14 25 K4
KUTN/CMB KT2 199 L1
PUR/KEN CR8 222 D8
Eltringham St WAND/EARL SW18 157 M10
Elvaston Ms SKENS SW7 15 K4
Elvaston Pl SKENS SW7 15 J4
Elveden Cl WOKS/MYFD GU22 233 L3
Elveden Pl WLSDN NW10 135 M4
WOKS/MYFD * GU22 233 L3
Elveden Rd COB KT11 217 J7
WLSDN NW10 135 M4
Elvendon Rd FBAR/BDGN N11 98 F7
Elver Gdns BETH E2 7 P9
Elverson Ms DEPT * SE8 160 E6
Elverson Rd DEPT SE8 160 G8
Elverton St WEST SW1P 17 J5
Elvet Av EMPK RM11 125 K2
Elvington Gn HAYES BR2 205 L5
Elvington La CDALE/KGS NW9 96 B9
Elvino Rd SYD SE26 182 C8
Elvis Rd CRICK NW2 136 F1
Elwell Cl EGH TW20 172 D9
Elwick Rd SOCK/AV RM15 147 H8
Elwill Wy BECK BR3 205 J4
Elwin St BETH E2 7 N9
Elwood HLWE CM17 47 P2
Elwood St HBRY N5 119 J8
Elwyn Gdns LEE/GVPK SE12 183 M3
Ely Av SL SL1 129 H7
Ely Cl AMSS HP7 69 K5
ERITH DA8 164 G8
HAT AL10 40 C3
NWMAL KT3 200 C2
Ely Cottages VX/NE * SW8 158 G6
Ely Gdns BORE WD6 76 A9
DAGE RM10 124 D8
Elyne Rd FSBYPK N4 119 H4
Ely Pl GUW * GU2 249 L8
HCIRC EC1N 12 B4
WFD IG8 102 D6
Ely Rd CROY/NA CR0 203 L5
HSLWW TW4 153 K9
HTHAIR TW6 152 G8
LEY E10 121 H4
STAL AL1 38 G7
Elysian Av STMC/STPC BR5 207 H6
Elysium Pl FUL/PGN SW6 157 J8
Elysium St FUL/PGN SW6 157 J8
Elystan Cl WLGTN SM6 222 D5
Elystan Pl CHEL SW3 15 P7
Elystan St CHEL SW3 15 N6
Elystan Wk IS N1 6 A6
Emanuel Av ACT W3 135 P8
Embankment PUT/ROE SW15 156 G9
Embankment Gdns CHEL SW3 16 B9
Embankment Pl CHCR WC2N 11 M9
The Embankment
STWL/WRAY TW19 171 P3
TWK TW1 176 F4
Embassy Ct SCUP DA14 185 L6
WLGTN * SM6 222 C3
Emba St BERM/RHTH SE16 19 P2
Ember Cl ADL/WDHM KT15 215 N2
STMC/STPC BR5 206 F7
Embercourt Rd THDIT KT7 198 D6
Ember Farm Av
E/WMO/HCT KT8 198 C6
Ember Farm Wy
E/WMO/HCT KT8 198 C5
Ember Gdns ESH/CLAY KT10 198 D7
Ember La ESH/CLAY KT10 198 C8
Ember Rd DTCH/LGLY SL3 150 E2
Emberson Vw EPP CM16 66 C2
Emberwood CRAWW * RH11 283 N5
Embleton Rd LEW SE13 160 G10
OXHEY WD19 93 H4
Embry Cl STAN HA7 94 F5
Embry Dr STAN HA7 94 F7
Embry Wy STAN HA7 94 F6
Emden Cl WDR/YW UB7 152 B1
Emden St FUL/PGN SW6 157 L7
Emerald Cl CAN/RD E16 142 B8
Emerald Ct SL SL1 149 K1
Emerald Gdns BCTR RM8 124 B6
Emerald Sq NWDGN UB2 153 L2
Emerald St BMSBY WC1N 11 N3
Emerson Dr EMPK RM11 125 L5
Emerson Gdns
KTN/HRWW/W HA3 115 L4
Emersons Av SWLY BR8 186 G10
Emerson St STHWK SE1 12 E9
Emerton Cl BXLYHS DA6 163 P10
Emerton Ct BERK HP4 33 K2
Emerton Garth BERK HP4 33 K2
Emerton Rd LHD/OX KT22 236 B6
Emery Hill St WEST SW1P 17 H4
Emery St STHWK SE1 18 B3
Emes Rd ERITH DA8 164 D6
Emilia Cl PEND EN3 80 A9
Emily Davison Dr EPSOM KT18 238 E4
Emily Pl HOLWY N7 119 H9
Emily St CAN/RD E16 141 L8
Emley Rd ADL/WDHM KT15 195 K10
Emlyn La LHD/OX KT22 236 F8
Emlyn Rd HORL RH6 279 P3
REDH RH1 276 B2
SHB W12 156 B1
Emmanuel Cl GUW GU2 249 M7
Emmanuel Rd BAL SW12 180 D4
NTHWD HA6 92 G8
Emma Rd PLSTW E13 141 L5
Emma's Crs WARE SG12 26 G7
Emma St BETH E2 140 A4
Emma Ter RYNPK * SW20 178 F10
Emmaus Wy CHIG IG7 102 D6
Emmetts Cl WOKN/KNAP GU21 232 A3
Emmetts Rd BH/WHM TN16 263 M6
Emmitt Cl RAD WD7 57 K9
Emmott Av BARK/HLT IG6 122 F3
Emmott Cl EFNCH N2 117 M4
WCHPL E1 140 D6
Emperor Cl BERK HP4 33 L2
Emperor's Ga SKENS SW7 15 J5
Empire Av UED N18 99 K7
Empire Pde UED * N18 99 L7
WBLY * HA9 115 M8
Empire Rd GFD/PVL UB6 135 H3
Empire Vls REDH RH1 276 B10
Empire Wy WBLY HA9 115 L9
Empire Wharf Rd POP/IOD E14 161 J3
Empress Av CHING E4 100 F8
IL IG1 122 C7
MNPK E12 121 P7
WFD IG8 101 L8
Empress Dr CHST BR7 184 E9
Empress Pde CHING * E4 100 F8
Empress Pl ECT SW5 14 E8
Empress Rd GVE DA12 191 H3
Empress St WALW SE17 18 F9
Empson St BOW E3 140 G6
Emsworth Cl CRAWE * RH10 284 D10
ED N9 100 B2
Emsworth Rd BARK/HLT IG6 102 E10
Emsworth St BRXS/STRHM SW2 180 G5
Emu Rd VX/NE SW8 158 C8
Ena Rd STRHM/NOR SW16 202 F3
Enborne Gn SOCK/AV RM15 146 F7
Enbrook St NKENS W10 2 B10
Enclave Ct FSBYE EC1V 12 D1
Endale Cl CAR SM5 202 A9
Endeavour Rd CHES/WCR EN8 62 D3
Endeavour Wy BARK IG11 143 K4
CROY/NA CR0 202 E7
WIM/MER SW19 179 L7
Endell St LSQ/SEVD WC2H 11 L5
Enderby St GNWCH SE10 161 K4
Enderley Rd KTN/HRWW/W HA3 94 C9
Endersby Rd BAR EN5 76 F9
Endersleigh Gdns HDN NW4 116 D2
Endlebury Rd CHING E4 101 H3
Endlesham Rd BAL SW12 180 B3
Endsleigh Cl SAND/SEL CR2 224 B6
Endsleigh Gdns IL IG1 122 C6
STPAN WC1H 11 J1
SURB KT6 199 H6
WOT/HER KT12 217 K2
Endsleigh Pl STPAN WC1H 11 K1
Endsleigh Rd HNWL W7 134 F10
NWDGN UB2 153 M3
REDH RH1 258 D5
Endsleigh St STPAN WC1H 11 K1
Endway BRYLDS KT5 199 M7
Endwell Rd BROCKY SE4 160 D8
Endymion Ct HAT AL10 40 F3
Endymion Ms HAT AL10 40 F3
Endymion Rd BRXS/STRHM SW2 180 G3
FSBYPK N4 119 J5
HAT AL10 40 F3
Energen Cl WLSDN NW10 136 B1
Enfield Cl UX/CGN UB8 131 N4
Enfield Rd ACT W3 155 N1
BTFD TW8 155 J4
EBAR EN4 78 E8
HTHAIR TW6 152 F8
IS N1 7 K4
Enford St MBLAR W1H 10 A3
Engadine Cl CROY/NA CR0 203 N10
Engadine St WAND/EARL SW18 179 J4
Engate St LEW SE13 161 H10
Engayne Gdns UPMR RM14 126 A6
Engel Pk MLHL NW7 96 F7
Engineer Cl WOOL/PLUM SE18 162 D5
Engineers Wy WBLY HA9 115 M9
England's La HAMP NW3 4 A2
LOU IG10 82 D6
England Wy NWMAL KT3 199 N4
Englefield Cl CROY/NA CR0 203 K6
EGH TW20 171 P9
EGH * TW20 171 P9
ENC/FH EN2 79 H6
STMC/STPC BR5 207 J4
Englefield Crs STMC/STPC BR5 207 K5
Englefield Pth STMC/STPC BR5 207 K4
Englefield Rd IS N1 7 H3
WOKN/KNAP * GU21 231 H3
Engleheart Dr
EBED/NFELT TW14 174 G2
Engleheart Rd CAT SE6 182 G3
Englehurst EGH TW20 171 P9
HARP AL5 20 C2
Englemere Pk COB KT11 218 A10
Englewood Rd CLAP SW4 180 C2
Engliff La WOKS/MYFD GU22 233 J2
English Gdns STWL/WRAY TW19 150 A10
English St BOW E3 140 E6
Enid Cl LCOL/BKTW AL2 55 N7
Enid St STHWK SE1 19 M3
Enmore Av SNWD SE25 203 P5
Enmore Gdns MORT/ESHN SW14 178 A1
Enmore Rd PUT/ROE SW15 156 F10
SNWD SE25 203 P5
STHL UB1 133 P6
Ennerdale Av HCH RM12 125 H10
STAN HA7 115 H1
Ennerdale Cl CRAWW RH11 283 L9
EBED/NFELT TW14 174 G4
STAL AL1 38 G8
SUT SM1 221 J1
Ennerdale Crs SL SL1 128 B7
Ennerdale Dr CDALE/KGS NW9 116 B3
Ennerdale Gdns WBLY HA9 115 H6
Ennerdale Rd BXLYHN DA7 164 B7
RCH/KEW TW9 155 L8
Ennersdale Rd LEW SE13 183 J1
Ennis Cl HARP AL5 20 C5
Ennismore Av CHSWK W4 156 C3
GFD/PVL UB6 134 D1
GU GU1 250 C10
Ennismore Gdns SKENS SW7 15 M3
THDIT KT7 198 D6
Ennismore Gardens Ms
SKENS SW7 15 M3
Ennismore Ms SKENS SW7 15 N2
Ennismore St SKENS SW7 15 N3
Ennis Rd FSBYPK N4 119 H6
WOOL/PLUM SE18 162 G5
Ensign Cl PUR/KEN CR8 223 H6
STWL/WRAY TW19 173 N4
Ensign Dr PLMGR N13 99 K4
Ensign St WCHPL E1 13 N7
Ensign Wy STWL/WRAY TW19 173 N4
Enslin Rd ELTH/MOT SE9 184 D2
Ensor Ms SKENS SW7 15 L7
Enstone Rd HGDN/ICK UB10 112 A8
PEND EN3 80 D7
Enterdent Rd GDST RH9 260 B10
Enterprise Cl CROY/NA CR0 203 H8
Enterprise Est GU * GU1 250 B6
Enterprise Rw SEVS/STOTM N15 119 N3
Enterprise Wy HHNE HP2 36 D4
TEDD TW11 176 E8
WAND/EARL SW18 157 K10
WLSDN NW10 136 C5
Enterprize Wy DEPT * SE8 160 E3
Envis Wy RGUW GU3 249 H6
Eothen Cl CTHM CR3 241 P10
Epcot Ms WLSDN * NW10 136 G5
Epirus Ms FUL/PGN SW6 157 K6
Epirus Rd FUL/PGN SW6 157 J6
Epping Cl POP/IOD E14 160 F3
ROMW/RG RM7 124 C1
Epping Gld CHING E4 81 H10
Epping Gn HHNE HP2 36 C1
Epping La ABR/ST RM4 83 L6
Epping New Rd BKHH IG9 101 N1
LOU IG10 82 A4
Epping Pl HOLWY N7 6 B2
Epping Rd CHONG CM5 48 G10
EPP CM16 46 E10
EPP CM16 65 N4
EPP CM16 66 D6
LOU IG10 82 C1
WAB EN9 46 C6
Epping Wk CRAWE RH10 284 A9
Epping Wy CHING E4 80 G10
Epple Rd FUL/PGN SW6 157 J7
Epsom Cl BXLYHN DA7 164 C9
NTHLT UB5 113 N10
Epsom College EW * KT17 220 D10
Epsom La North
KWD/TDW/WH KT20 238 E5
Epsom La South
KWD/TDW/WH KT20 238 F7
Epsom Rd ASHTD KT21 237 L4
CRAWE RH10 284 B9
CROY/NA CR0 223 H1
EHSLY KT24 252 E5
EW KT17 220 C6
GDMY/SEVK IG3 123 J4
GU GU1 268 C1
LEY E10 121 H4
LHD/OX KT22 236 G7
MRDN SM4 201 J6
RGUE GU4 250 G9
RGUE GU4 251 N7
Epsom Sq HTHAIR * TW6 152 G8
Epsom Wy HCH RM12 125 N9
Epstein Rd THMD SE28 143 L10
Epworth Rd ISLW TW7 154 G6
Epworth St SDTCH EC2A 13 H2
Equity Sq BETH E2 7 M10
Erasmus St WEST SW1P 17 K6
Erconwald St ACT W3 136 C8
Eresby Dr BECK BR3 204 F8
Eresby Pl KIL/WHAMP NW6 2 E4
Erica Cl CHOB/PIR GU24 212 D9
SL SL1 128 D9
Erica Ct WOKS/MYFD GU22 232 A4
Erica Gdns CROY/NA CR0 224 G1
Erica St SHB W12 136 D9
Erica Wy CRAWE RH10 284 G2
Eric Clarke La BARK IG11 142 E6
Ericcson Cl WAND/EARL SW18 179 K1
Eric Est BOW E3 140 E6
Eric Rd CHDH RM6 123 N5
FSTGT E7 121 M9
WLSDN NW10 136 C1
Eric St BOW E3 140 E6
Eridge Cl CRAWE RH10 284 D7
Eridge Green Cl STMC/STPC BR5 207 M8
Eridge Rd CHSWK W4 156 A2
Erin Cl BMLY BR1 183 K10
Erindale WOOL/PLUM SE18 162 G5
Erindale Ter WOOL/PLUM SE18 162 G5
Erin Ms WDGN * N22 99 J9
Eriswell Crs WOT/HER KT12 216 G3
Eriswell Rd WOT/HER KT12 216 G1
Erith Ct PUR RM19 165 P3
Erith Crs CRW RM5 104 D9
Erith High St ERITH DA8 164 F4
Erith Rd BELV DA17 164 C4
Erkenwald Cl CHERT KT16 195 H6
Erlanger Rd NWCR SE14 160 C7
Erlesmere Gdns HNWL W7 154 F2
Erlich Cottages WCHPL * E1 140 B7
Ermine Cl CHESW EN7 62 A7
HSLWW TW4 153 K8
STALW/RED AL3 37 P7
Ermine Rd LEW SE13 160 G10
SEVS/STOTM N15 119 N4
Ermine Side EN EN1 79 P9
Ermington Rd ELTH/MOT SE9 184 F5

Ermyn Cl LHD/OX KT22 237 J7
Ermyn Wy LHD/OX KT22 237 J7
Ernald Av EHAM E6 142 B4
Ernan Cl SOCK/AV RM15 146 F7
Ernan Rd SOCK/AV RM15 146 F7
Erncroft Wy TWK TW1 176 E2
Ernest Av WNWD SE27 181 J7
Ernest Cl BECK BR3 204 F5
Ernest Gdns CHSWK W4 155 N5
Ernest Gv BECK BR3 204 E5
Ernest Rd EMPK RM11 125 M4
KUT KT1 199 N2
Ernest St WCHPL E1 140 C6
Ernle Rd RYNPK SW20 178 E10
Ernshaw Pl PUT/ROE SW15 179 H1
Erpingham Rd PUT/ROE SW15 156 F9
Erridge Rd WIM/MER SW19 201 K2
Erriff Dr SOCK/AV RM15 146 F7
Errington Cl CDH/CHF RM16 168 E2
Errington Dr WDSR SL4 148 F7
Errington Rd MV/WKIL W9 8 D1
Errol Gdns NWMAL KT3 200 D4
YEAD UB4 133 J6
Erroll Rd ROM RM1 124 G2
Errol St STLK EC1Y 12 F2
Erskine Cl SUT SM1 201 P10
Erskine Crs TOTM N17 120 A2
Erskine Hl GLDGN NW11 117 K2
Erskine Ms HAMP NW3 4 B4
Erskine Rd HAMP NW3 4 B4
SUT SM1 221 N1
WALTH E17 120 E2
Erwood Rd CHARL SE7 162 B4
Esam Wy STRHM/NOR SW16 181 H8
Escombe Dr GUW GU2 249 N5
Escot Rd SUN TW16 174 F10
Escott Pl CHERT KT16 214 F3
Escot Wy BAR EN5 76 F9
Escreet Gv WOOL/PLUM SE18 162 D3
Esdaile Gdns UPMR RM14 126 C5
Esdaile La HOD EN11 44 F4
Esher Av CHEAM SM3 200 G10
ROMW/RG RM7 124 D4
WOT/HER KT12 197 H7
Esher Cl BXLY DA5 185 P4
ESH/CLAY KT10 218 A2
Esher Crs HTHAIR TW6 152 G8
Esher Gn ESH/CLAY KT10 218 A1
Esher Green Dr ESH/CLAY KT10 197 P10
Esher Ms MTCM CR4 202 B3
Esher Park Av ESH/CLAY KT10 218 B2
Esher Place Av ESH/CLAY KT10 217 P1
Esher Rd E/WMO/HCT KT8 198 C5
GDMY/SEVK IG3 123 H8
WOT/HER KT12 217 M1
Eskdale LCOL/BKTW AL2 57 L3
Eskdale Av CSHM HP5 51 J6
NTHLT UB5 133 N3
Eskdale Cl RDART DA2 188 B5
WBLY HA9 115 J7
Eskdale Gdns PUR/KEN CR8 223 L10
Eskdale Rd BXLYHN DA7 164 B8
IVER SL0 131 L4
Eskley Gdns SOCK/AV RM15 146 F7
Eskmont Rdg NRWD SE19 181 M10
Esk Rd PLSTW E13 141 N6
Esk Wy ROM RM1 104 F8
Esmar Crs CDALE/KGS NW9 116 D5
Esmeralda Rd STHWK SE1 19 P6
Esmond Cl RAIN * RM13 145 J2
Esmond Gdns CHSWK * W4 156 A3
Esmond Rd CHSWK W4 156 A2
KIL/WHAMP NW6 2 D6
Esmond St PUT/ROE SW15 157 H10
Esparto St WAND/EARL SW18 179 L3
Essendene Cl CTHM CR3 241 M9
Essendene Rd CTHM CR3 241 M9
Essenden Rd BELV DA17 164 B4
SAND/SEL CR2 223 M4
Essendine Rd MV/WKIL W9 8 F1
Essendon Gdns WGCE AL7 23 J5
Essendon Hl BRKMPK AL9 41 P3
Essex Av ISLW TW7 154 D9
SL SL1 129 H7
Essex Cl ADL/WDHM KT15 215 M1
MRDN SM4 200 G7
ROMW/RG RM7 124 C2
RSLP HA4 113 L6
WALTH E17 120 D2
Essex Ct BARN SW13 156 C8
TPL/STR * WC2R 12 A6
Essex Gdns EMPK RM11 125 P3
FSBYPK N4 119 J4
SLH/COR SS17 169 K1
Essex Gv NRWD SE19 181 L9
Essex La ABLGY WD5 54 E9
Essex Pk FNCH N3 97 L7
Essex Park Ms ACT W3 136 B10
Essex Pl CHSWK W4 155 P3
Essex Place Sq CHSWK * W4 156 A3
Essex Rd ACT W3 135 P9
BARK IG11 142 G2
BORE WD6 75 M7
CHDH RM6 123 M6
CHING E4 101 K2
CHSWK W4 156 A3
CSHM HP5 51 H5
DAGE RM10 124 D10
DART * DA1 187 L2
ENC/FH EN2 79 L8
GVW DA11 190 D4
HART DA3 211 J2
HOD EN11 44 G2
IS N1 6 E4
LEY E10 121 H4
ROMW/RG RM7 124 C2
SWFD E18 101 N10
WALTH E17 120 D4
WAT WD17 73 H6
WLSDN NW10 136 B2
WTHK RM20 166 F5
Essex Rd South WAN E11 121 J5
Essex St FSTGT E7 121 M10
STAL * AL1 38 D5
TPL/STR WC2R 12 A6
WOOL/PLUM SE18 162 F3
Essex Vls KENS W8 14 E2
Essex Wy CHONG CM5 66 G5
EPP CM16 65 K8
RBRW/HUT CM13 107 H7
Essex Whf CLPT * E5 120 F7
Essian St WCHPL E1 140 D7
Essoldo Wy EDGW HA8 115 L1
Estate Wy LEY E10 120 E6
Estcourt Rd FUL/PGN SW6 157 J6
SNWD SE25 204 A6
WAT WD17 73 K7
Estella Av NWMAL KT3 200 E4
Estelle Rd HAMP NW3 118 A9
Esterbrooke St WEST SW1P 17 J6
Este Rd BTSEA SW11 157 P9
Estfeld Cl HOD * EN11 26 G10
Esther Cl WCHMH N21 99 H1
Esther Rd WAN E11 121 K5
Estoria Cl BRXS/STRHM SW2 181 H3
Estreham Rd STRHM/NOR SW16 180 E9
Estridge Cl HSLW TW3 153 P10
Estuary Cl BARK IG11 143 L5
Eswyn Rd TOOT SW17 180 A7
Etchingham Park Rd FNCH N3 97 L8
Etchingham Rd SRTFD E15 121 H9
Etfield Gv SCUP DA14 185 L8
Ethelbert Cl HAYES BR2 205 M2
Ethelbert Gdns GNTH/NBYPK IG2 122 C3
Ethelbert Rd BMLY BR1 205 M3
ERITH DA8 164 D6
RYNPK SW20 200 G1
STMC/STPC BR5 207 N3
Ethelbert St BAL SW12 180 C4
Ethelbury Rd RDART DA2 187 M7
Ethelburga Rd HARH RM3 105 N9
Ethelburga St BTSEA * SW11 157 P7
Ethelden Av MUSWH N10 118 D2
Ethelden Rd SHB W12 136 E10
Ethelred Cl WGCE AL7 23 J6
Ethelred Est LBTH SE11 18 A6
Ethel Rd ASHF TW15 173 P8
CAN/RD E16 141 N9
Ethel St WALW * SE17 18 F6
Ethel Ter ORP * BR6 227 M5
Etheridge Rd CRICK NW2 116 F5
LOU IG10 82 F7
Etherley Rd SEVS/STOTM N15 119 K3
Etherow St EDUL SE22 181 P2
Etherstone Rd
STRHM/NOR SW16 180 G7
Ethnard Rd PECK SE15 160 A5
Ethorpe Crs CFSP/GDCR SL9 110 B3
Ethronvi Rd BXLYHN DA7 163 P9
Etloe Rd LEY E10 120 F7
Etna Rd STALW/RED AL3 38 C5
Eton Av ALP/SUD HA0 115 H9
EBAR EN4 77 P10
HAMP NW3 3 M3
HEST TW5 153 N5
NFNCH/WDSP N12 97 M8
NWMAL KT3 200 A5
Eton Cl DTCH/LGLY SL3 149 M5
WAND/EARL SW18 179 L3
Eton College Rd HAMP NW3 4 B2
Eton Ct STA TW18 173 J8
WDSR SL4 149 J6
Eton Garages HAMP NW3 3 P2
Eton Gv CDALE/KGS NW9 115 M1
LEW SE13 161 K9
Eton Pl HAMP * NW3 4 C3
Eton Ri HAMP * NW3 4 B2
Eton Rd DTCH/LGLY SL3 149 M5
HAMP NW3 4 B3
HYS/HAR UB3 152 G6
ORP BR6 227 L1
Eton Sq WDSR SL4 149 J6
Eton St RCHPK/HAM TW10 177 J1
Eton Vls HAMP NW3 4 A2
Eton Wy DART DA1 165 K10
Eton Wick Rd WDSR SL4 148 E4
Etta St DEPT SE8 160 D5
Etton Cl HCH RM12 125 M7
Etton Rd HSLW TW3 176 B1
Ettrick St POP/IOD E14 141 H8
Etwell Pl BRYLDS KT5 199 L6
Euclid Wy WTHK RM20 166 E3
Eugene Cl GPK RM2 125 K2
Eugenia Rd BERM/RHTH SE16 160 B4
Eunice Gv CSHM HP5 51 J9
Eureka Rd KUT KT1 199 M2
Europa Pk WTHK * RM20 167 H5
Europa Park Rd GU GU1 249 P9
Europa Pl FSBYE EC1V 6 E10
Europa Rd HHNE HP2 36 A3
Europe Rd WOOL/PLUM SE18 162 C2
Eustace Pl WOOL/PLUM SE18 162 C3
Eustace Rd CHDH RM6 123 N5
EHAM E6 142 B5
FUL/PGN SW6 157 K6
RGUE GU4 250 G8
Euston Av WATW WD18 72 G9
Euston Gv CAMTN NW1 10 G1
Euston Rd CAMTN NW1 10 E1
CROY/NA CR0 203 H8
Euston Sq CAMTN NW1 5 J10
Euston St CAMTN NW1 11 H1
Evandale Rd BRXN/ST SW9 159 H8
Evangelist Rd KTTN NW5 118 C9
Evans Av GSTN WD25 72 G1
Evans Cl CRAWE RH10 284 E8
GRH DA9 188 F1
HACK E8 7 M2
RKW/CH/CXG WD3 72 B9
Evansdale RAIN RM13 144 G5
Evans Gv FELT TW13 175 P5
STALE/WH AL4 39 H2
Evans Rd CAT SE6 183 K5
Evanston Av CHING E4 101 H8
Evanston Gdns REDBR IG4 122 B4
Eva Rd CHDH RM6 123 M5
Evelina Rd PECK SE15 160 B9
PGE/AN SE20 182 B10
Eveline Lowe Est
BERM/RHTH SE16 19 N4
Eveline Rd MTCM CR4 202 A1
Evelyn Av CDALE/KGS NW9 116 A2
RSLP HA4 112 G5
Evelyn Cl WHTN TW2 176 A3
WOKS/MYFD GU22 232 A6
Evelyn Crs SUN TW16 196 G1
Evelyn Denington Rd EHAM E6 142 B6
Evelyn Dr PIN HA5 93 L8
Evelyn Est DEPT SE8 160 D5
Evelyn Gdns GDST RH9 260 B6
RCH/KEW TW9 155 K10
WBPTN SW10 15 K8
Evelyn Gv EA W5 135 L10
STHL UB1 133 N8
Evelyn Rd CAN/RD E16 141 M10
CHSWK W4 156 A2
EBAR EN4 78 A8
RCH/KEW TW9 155 K9
RCHPK/HAM TW10 177 H6
RSEV TN14 247 K2
WALTH E17 121 H2
WIM/MER SW19 179 L8
Evelyns Cl UX/CGN UB8 132 B8
Evelyn Sharp Cl GPK * RM2 125 L1
Evelyn St DEPT SE8 160 E5
Evelyn Ter RCH/KEW TW9 155 K9
Evelyn Wk CRAWE RH10 283 P10
IS N1 6 G8
Evelyn Wy COB KT11 235 N2
HOR/WEW KT19 219 M7
SUN TW16 196 G1
WLGTN SM6 222 E1
Evensyde WATW WD18 72 D10
Evenwood Cl PUT/ROE * SW15 179 H1
Everard Av HAYES BR2 205 M8
SL SL1 149 K1
Everard Cl STAL AL1 38 C8
Everard Wy WBLY HA9 115 K8
Everatt Cl WAND/EARL * SW18 179 J2
Everdon Rd BARN SW13 156 D5
Everest Cl GVW DA11 190 B6
Everest Ct WOKN/KNAP GU21 231 K2
Everest Pl POP/IOD E14 141 H7
SWLY BR8 208 E4
Everest Rd ELTH/MOT SE9 184 B1
STWL/WRAY TW19 173 N3
Everest Wy HHNE HP2 36 B6
Everett Cl BUSH WD23 94 D2
CHESW EN7 61 K1
PIN HA5 112 G1
Everglade BH/WHM TN16 244 A4
Everglade Cl HART DA3 211 L4
The Everglades HSLW * TW3 154 B9
Everglade Strd CDALE/KGS NW9 96 C9
Evergreen Cl PGE/AN SE20 182 B10
Evergreen Ct
STWL/WRAY * TW19 173 N3
Evergreen Oak Av WDSR SL4 149 M9
Evergreen Sq HACK E8 7 L3
Evergreen Wk HHS/BOV HP3 35 P8
Evergreen Wy HYS/HAR UB3 132 G9
STWL/WRAY TW19 173 N3
Everilda St IS N1 5 P6
Evering Rd STNW/STAM N16 119 N8
Everington Rd MUSWH N10 98 A10
Everington St HMSMTH W6 156 G5
Everitt Rd WLSDN NW10 136 A5
Everlands Cl WOKS/MYFD GU22 232 B4
Everlasting La STALW/RED AL3 38 B4
Everleigh St FSBYPK N4 118 G6
Eve Rd ISLW TW7 154 F10
SRTFD E15 121 K9
TOTM N17 119 M1
WOKN/KNAP GU21 232 E1
Eversfield Gdns EDGW HA8 96 B8
Eversfield Rd RCH/KEW TW9 155 L8
REIG RH2 257 L10
Eversholt St CAMTN NW1 4 G7
Evershot Rd FSBYPK N4 118 G6
Eversleigh Gdns UPMR RM14 126 C6
Eversleigh Rd BAR EN5 77 M9
BTSEA SW11 158 A9
EHAM E6 142 A3
FNCH N3 97 J8
Eversley Av BXLYHN DA7 164 F8
WBLY HA9 115 M7
Eversley Cl LOU IG10 82 F7
WCHMH N21 78 G10
Eversley Crs ISLW TW7 154 C7
RSLP HA4 112 F7
WCHMH N21 78 G10
Eversley Cross BXLYHN DA7 164 F8
Eversley Mt WCHMH N21 78 G10
Eversley Pk WIM/MER SW19 178 E8
Eversley Park Rd WCHMH N21 78 G10
Eversley Rd BRYLDS KT5 199 L4
CHARL SE7 161 N5
NRWD SE19 181 L10
Eversley Wy CROY/NA CR0 204 F10
EGH TW20 194 F2
Everthorpe Rd PECK SE15 159 N9
Everton Buildings CAMTN NW1 4 G10
Everton Dr STAN HA7 115 K1
Everton Rd CROY/NA CR0 203 P8
Evesham Av WALTH E17 100 F10
Evesham Cl BELMT SM2 221 K4
GFD/PVL UB6 134 A4
REIG RH2 257 J9
Evesham Gn MRDN SM4 201 L6
Evesham Rd FBAR/BDGN N11 98 D6
GVE DA12 190 G5
MRDN SM4 201 L6
REIG RH2 257 J9
SRTFD E15 141 L2
Evesham Rd North REIG RH2 257 J9
Evesham St NTGHL W11 136 G9
Evesham Ter SURB * KT6 199 J6
Evesham Wk BRXN/ST SW9 159 H8
CMBW SE5 159 L8
Evesham Wy BTSEA SW11 158 B9
CLAY IG5 122 D1
Evreham Rd IVER SL0 131 H8
Evry Rd SCUP DA14 185 M9
Ewald Rd FUL/PGN SW6 157 J8
Ewanrigg Ter WFD IG8 101 P6
Ewan Rd HARH RM3 105 L10
Ewart Gv WDGN N22 99 H9
Ewart Pl BOW * E3 140 E4
Ewart Rd FSTH SE23 182 C3
Ewe Cl HOLWY N7 5 M1
Ewelands HORL RH6 280 D3
Ewell By-Pass EW KT17 220 D4
Ewell Court Av HOR/WEW KT19 220 B2
Ewell Downs Rd EW KT17 220 D7
Ewell House Gv EW KT17 220 C6
Ewell House Pde EW * KT17 220 C6
Ewell House Pde EW * KT17 220 C6
Ewellhurst Rd CLAY IG5 102 B10
Ewell Park Gdns EW KT17 220 D4
Ewell Park Wy EW KT17 220 D3
Ewell Rd CHEAM SM3 220 G3
SURB KT6 199 L6
THDIT KT7 198 G7
Ewelme Rd FSTH SE23 182 B4
Ewen Crs BRXS/STRHM SW2 181 H3
Ewer St STHWK SE1 12 E10
Ewhurst Av SAND/SEL CR2 223 N5
Ewhurst Cl BELMT SM2 220 F5
CRAWW RH11 283 M7
WCHPL E1 140 B7
Ewhurst Rd BROCKY SE4 182 E2
CRAWW RH11 283 L7
Ewood La RDKG RH5 278 A1
Exbury Rd CAT SE6 182 F5
Excalibur Cl CRAWW RH11 283 H7
Excel Ct LSQ/SEVD WC2H 11 K8
Excelsior Cl KUT KT1 199 M2
Exchange Ar LVPST EC2M 13 J4
Exchange Ct COVGDN * WC2E 11 M8
Exchange Rd ASC SL5 192 B5
CRAWE RH10 283 P7
WATW WD18 73 J8
Exchange Sq SDTCH * EC2A 13 K3
Exchange St ROM RM1 124 F3
Executive Pk STAL * AL1 38 G6
Exeforde Av ASHF TW15 174 B7
Exeter Cl EHAM E6 142 C8
WATN WD24 73 K6
Exeter Gdns IL IG1 122 C6
Exeter Ms FUL/PGN * SW6 157 K6
Exeter Pde CRICK * NW2 2 B1
Exeter Pl GUW * GU2 249 L8
Exeter Rd CAN/RD E16 141 M7
CRICK NW2 117 H10
CROY/NA CR0 203 M7
DAGE RM10 144 C1
ED N9 100 B3
FELT TW13 175 N6
GVE DA12 190 G6
HTHAIR TW6 152 F9
PEND EN3 80 C7
RYLN/HDSTN HA2 113 M7
STHGT/OAK N14 98 C2
WALTH E17 120 F3
WELL DA16 163 J8
Exeter St COVGDN WC2E 11 M7
Exeter Wy HTHAIR TW6 152 F8
NWCR SE14 160 E6
Exford Gdns LEE/GVPK SE12 183 N4
Exford Rd LEE/GVPK SE12 183 N5
Exhibition Rd SKENS SW7 15 M2
Exit Rd EFNCH N2 97 N10
Exmoor Cl BARK/HLT IG6 102 F9
Exmoor St NKENS W10 136 G6
Exmouth Market CLKNW EC1R 12 A1
Exmouth Ms CAMTN * NW1 5 H10
Exmouth Pl HACK E8 140 A3
Exmouth Rd GRAYS RM17 167 N5
RSLP HA4 113 K8
WALTH E17 120 E3
WELL DA16 163 M7
YEAD UB4 132 F5
Exmouth St WCHPL E1 140 B8
Exning Rd CAN/RD E16 141 L6
Exon St WALW SE17 19 J6
Explorer Av STWL/WRAY TW19 173 P4
Explorer Dr WATW WD18 72 G10
Express Dr GDMY/SEVK IG3 123 L6
Extension Rd HERT/BAY SG13 25 N5
Exton Crs WLSDN NW10 135 P2
Exton Gdns BCTR RM8 123 N10
Exton St STHWK SE1 12 A10
Eyhurst Av HCH RM12 125 H8
Eyhurst Cl CRICK NW2 116 D7
KWD/TDW/WH KT20 239 J10
Eyhurst Pk
KWD/TDW/WH * KT20 239 M9
Eyhurst Sp KWD/TDW/WH KT20 239 J10
Eylewood Rd WNWD SE27 181 K8
Eynella Rd DUL SE21 181 N3
Eynham Rd SHB W12 136 F8
Eynsford Cl STMC/STPC BR5 206 F7
Eynsford Crs SCUP DA14 185 M4
Eynsford Ri EYN DA4 229 L1
Eynsford Rd EYN DA4 209 N8
GDMY/SEVK IG3 123 H7
GRH DA9 189 H1
SWLY BR8 208 F6
Eynsford Ter WDR/YW * UB7 132 A8
Eynsham Dr ABYW SE2 163 L2
Eynswood Dr SCUP DA14 185 L8
Eyot Gdns HMSMTH W6 156 C4
Eyre Cl GPK RM2 125 J2
Eyre Street Hl CLKNW EC1R 12 A2
Eyston Dr WEY KT13 216 B6
Eythorne Rd BRXN/ST SW9 159 H7
Eywood Rd STAL AL1 38 B8
Ezra St BETH E2 7 M9

F

Faber Gdns HDN NW4 116 D3
Fabian Rd FUL/PGN SW6 157 J6
Fabian St EHAM E6 142 C6
The Facade FSTH * SE23 182 B5
REIG * RH2 257 K9
Fackenden La BGR/WK TN15 229 P9
Factory La CROY/NA CR0 203 H9
TOTM N17 99 N10
Factory Pl POP/IOD E14 161 H4
Factory Rd CAN/RD E16 142 A10
GVW DA11 189 P2
Factory Yd BEAC * HP9 88 D10
HNWL W7 134 D10
Faesten Wy BXLY DA5 186 F6
Faggots Cl RAD WD7 75 H1
Faggotters La HLWE CM17 30 F10
Faggs Rd EBED/NFELT TW14 152 G10
EBED/NFELT TW14 153 H10
Fagnall La AMSS HP7 88 B1
Fagus Av RAIN RM13 145 L5
Faints Cl CHESW EN7 61 N5
Fairacre HHS/BOV HP3 36 A10
ISLW * TW7 154 C7
NWMAL KT3 200 B3
Fairacres COB KT11 217 L8
CROY/NA CR0 224 E5
Fair Acres HAYES BR2 205 M5
Fairacres KWD/TDW/WH KT20 238 F7
RSLP HA4 112 G5
Fairacres Cl POTB/CUF EN6 59 J9
Fairbairn Cl PUR/KEN CR8 223 H9
Fairbank Av ORP BR6 206 E9
Fairbank Cl CHONG CM5 67 N5
Fairbank Est IS N1 6 G8
Fairbanks Rd TOTM N17 119 P1
Fairborne Wy GUW GU2 249 M7
Fairbourne COB KT11 217 L9
Fairbourne Cl WOKN/KNAP GU21 231 M3
Fairbourne La CTHM CR3 241 K8
Fairbourne Rd TOTM N17 119 M1
Fairbridge Rd ARCH N19 118 E7
Fairbrook Cl PLMGR N13 99 H6
Fairburn Cl BORE WD6 75 M5
Fairby Hl HART * DA3 211 K5
Fairby La HART DA3 211 K6
Fairby Rd LEE/GVPK SE12 183 N1
Fairchild Cl BTSEA SW11 157 N8
Fairchildes Av CROY/NA CR0 225 J8
Fairchildes Rd WARL CR6 243 J1
Fairchild Pl SDTCH * EC2A 13 K2
Fairchild St SDTCH EC2A 13 K2
Fair Cl BUSH WD23 94 A1
Fairclough St WCHPL E1 13 P6
Faircroft SLN SL2 128 G6
Faircross Av BARK IG11 142 F1
CRW RM5 104 E8
Faircross Wy STAL AL1 38 F4
Fairdale Gdns HYS/HAR UB3 153 H1
PUT/ROE SW15 156 E10
Fairdene Rd COUL/CHIP CR5 240 E4
Fairey CDALE/KGS * NW9 96 C10
Fairey Av HYS/HAR UB3 152 G2
Fairfax Av EW KT17 220 E5
REDH RH1 258 A9
Fairfax Cl WOT/HER KT12 197 J8
Fairfax Gdns BKHTH/KID SE3 161 P7
Fairfax Ms CEND/HSY/T * N8 119 J2
PUT/ROE SW15 156 F10
Fairfax Pl KIL/WHAMP NW6 3 K
Fairfax Rd CEND/HSY/T N8 119 H
CHSWK W4 156 B
GRAYS RM17 167 N
HERT/BAY SG13 25 N
KIL/WHAMP NW6 3 K
TEDD TW11 176 F1
TIL RM18 168 C
WOKS/MYFD GU22 232 E
Fairfax Wy MUSWH * N10 98 B
Fairfield GVE DA12 191 H
Fairfield Ap STWL/WRAY TW19 172 A
Fairfield Av CDH/CHF RM16 147 P1
DTCH/LGLY SL3 149 P
EDGW HA8 95 N
HDN NW4 116 E
HORL RH6 280 B
OXHEY WD19 93 K
RSLP HA4 112 D
STA TW18 173 J
UPMR RM14 126 B
WHTN TW2 176 A
Fairfield Cl BFN/LL DA15 185 J
BGR/WK TN15 247 P
GT/LBKH KT23 254 A
GUW GU2 249 L
HARP AL5 20 C
HCH RM12 125 H
HOR/WEW KT19 220 B
NFNCH/WDSP N12 97 M
PEND EN3 80 D
RAD * WD7 74 D
WIM/MER SW19 179 P1
Fairfield Cnr KUT * KT1 199 L
Fairfield Ct RSLP HA4 112 E
Fairfield Crs EDGW HA8 95 N
Fairfield Dr BROX EN10 44 E1
DORK RH4 254 G1
GFD/PVL UB6 135 H
RYLN/HDSTN HA2 114 B
WAND/EARL SW18 179 L
Fairfield East KUT KT1 199 K
Fairfield Gdns CEND/HSY/T N8 118 F
Fairfield Gv CHARL SE7 162 A
Fairfield La CHOB/PIR GU24 212 E
SLN SL2 128 G
Fairfield North KUT KT1 199 K
Fairfield Pk COB KT11 217 L1
Fairfield Pth CROY/NA CR0 203 L1
Fairfield Pl KUT KT1 199 K
Fairfield Ri GUW GU2 249 L
Fairfield Rd BECK BR3 204 F
BMLY BR1 183 M1
BOW E3 140 F
BRW CM14 107 H
BXLYHN DA7 164 A
CEND/HSY/T N8 118 F
CHONG CM5 67 N
CROY/NA CR0 203 L1
EPP CM16 65 L
HOD EN11 44 F
IL IG1 142 E
KUT KT1 199 K
LHD/OX KT22 236 G
SL SL1 128 B
STHL UB1 133 N
STMC/STPC BR5 206 G
STWL/WRAY TW19 172 A
UED N18 99 P
UX/CGN UB8 131 N
WALTH E17 100 D1
WDR/YW UB7 131 P1
WFD IG8 101 M
Fairfields CHERT * KT16 195 L
Fairfields Cl CDALE/KGS NW9 115 P
Fairfields Crs CDALE/KGS NW9 115 P
Fairfield South KUT KT1 199 K
Fairfield St WAND/EARL SW18 179 L
Fairfield Wy BAR EN5 77 K
COUL/CHIP CR5 222 E1
HOR/WEW KT19 220 B
Fairfield West KUT KT1 199 K
Fairfolds GSTN WD25 73 M
Fairfoot Rd BOW * E3 140 F
Fairford Av BXLYHN DA7 164 D
CROY/NA CR0 204 C
Fairford Cl BF/WBF KT14 215 J
CROY/NA CR0 204 C
HARH RM3 106 A
REIG RH2 257 M
Fairford Ct BELMT * SM2 221 L
Fairford Gdns WPK KT4 200 C1
Fairford Wy HARH RM3 106 A
Fairgreen EBAR EN4 78 A
Fairgreen Ct EBAR * EN4 78 A
Fairgreen Rd THHTH CR7 203 J
Fairham Av SOCK/AV RM15 146 F
Fairhaven EGH TW20 172 C
LCOL/BKTW * AL2 56 C
Fairhaven Av CROY/NA CR0 204 C
Fairhaven Crs OXHEY WD19 93 H
Fairhaven Rd REDH RH1 258 B
Fairhazel Gdns KIL/WHAMP NW6 3 J
Fairhill HHS/BOV HP3 36 A1
Fairholme EBED/NFELT TW14 174 E
Fairholme Av GPK RM2 125 H
Fairholme Cl HDN NW4 117 H
Fairholme Ct PIN * HA5 93 P
Fairholme Crs ASHTD KT21 237 H
YEAD UB4 132 G
Fairholme Gdns FNCH N3 117 H
UPMR RM14 126 E
Fairholme Rd ASHF TW15 173 P
CROY/NA CR0 203 H
HRW HA1 114 D
IL IG1 122 C
SUT SM1 221 J
WKENS W14 14 C
Fairholt Rd STNW/STAM N16 119 L
Fairholt St SKENS SW7 15 P
Fairkytes Av EMPK RM11 125 L
Fairland Rd SRTFD E15 141 L
Fairlands Av BKHH IG9 101 M
RGUW GU3 249 H
SUT SM1 201 K
THHTH CR7 202 G
Fairlands Rd RGUW GU3 249 H
Fair La COUL/CHIP CR5 257 M
Fairlawn CHARL SE7 161 P
GT/LBKH KT23 235 N1
WEY * KT13 216 F
Fairlawn Av CHSWK W4 155 P
EFNCH N2 117 P
WELL DA16 163 N
Fairlawn Cl ESH/CLAY KT10 218 E
FELT TW13 175 N
KUTN/CMB KT2 177 P
STHGT/OAK N14 78 E1
Fairlawn Ct CHARL * SE7 161 P
Fairlawn Dr REDH RH1 275 P

WFD IG8 101 M8
Fairlawn Gdns STHL * UB1 133 N9
Fairlawn Gv BNSTD SM7 221 N9
CHSWK W4 155 P3
Fairlawn Pk SYD SE26 182 D8
WDSR SL4 148 D10
WOKN/KNAP GU21 214 B10
Fairlawn Rd BELMT SM2 221 M7
WIM/MER SW19 179 J10
Fairlawns ADL/WDHM KT15 215 J7
HORL RH6 280 C5
SUN TW16 197 H3
TWK TW1 177 H2
WAT WD17 72 G5
Fairlawns Cl EMPK RM11 125 N5
STA TW18 173 L9
Fairlea Pl EA W5 135 H7
Fair Leas CSHM HP5 50 F5
Fairley Wy CHESW EN7 62 A4
Fairlie Gdns FSTH SE23 182 B3
Fairlie Rd SL SL1 128 F8
Fairlight Av CHING E4 101 J3
WDSR SL4 149 J8
WFD IG8 101 M7
WLSDN NW10 136 B4
Fairlight Cl CHING E4 101 J3
WPK KT4 220 F1
Fairlight Cross HART DA3 211 N3
Fairlight Dr UX/CGN UB8 131 N1
Fairlight Rd TOOT SW17 179 N7
Fairlop Cl HCH RM12 145 J1
Fairlop Gdns BARK/HLT IG6 102 F8
Fairlop Rd BARK/HLT IG6 102 F10
WAN E11 121 J5
Fairmark Dr HGDN/ICK UB10 132 B1
Fairmead BMLY BR1 206 C4
SURB KT6 199 N8
WOKN/KNAP GU21 231 P4
Fairmead Av HARP AL5 20 B3
Fairmead Cl BMLY BR1 206 C4
HEST TW5 153 L6
NWMAL KT3 200 A3
Fairmead Crs EDGW HA8 95 P5
Fairmead Gdns REDBR IG4 122 A3
Fairmead Rd CROY/NA * CR0 202 G7
HOLWY N7 118 F8
LOU IG10 81 N8
Fairmeads COB KT11 217 M9
LOU * IG10 82 E6
LOU IG10 82 E6
Fairmile Av COB KT11 217 M10
STRHM/NOR SW16 180 E8
Fairmile Ct COB KT11 217 M8
Fairmile Hts COB KT11 217 P9
Fairmile La COB KT11 217 L8
Fairmile Park Copse COB KT11 217 N8
Fairmile Park Rd COB KT11 217 N9
Fairmont Cl BELV DA17 164 A4
Fairmount Rd BRXS/STRHM SW2 180 G2
Fair Oak Cl LHD/OX KT22 218 C7
Fairoak Cl PUR/KEN CR8 241 J1
STMC/STPC BR5 206 E7
Fairoak Dr ELTH/MOT SE9 184 G1
Fairoak Gdns ROM RM1 104 F10
Fairoak La LHD/OX KT22 218 D7
Fair Oak Pl BARK/HLT IG6 102 F10
Fairoaks RGUW * GU3 248 F5
Fairoaks Gv PEND EN3 80 C3
Fairseat Cl BUSH WD23 94 D3
Fairs Rd LHD/OX KT22 236 F5
Fairstead Wk IS * N1 6 E5
Fairstone Ct HORL RH6 280 C3
Fair St HSLW TW3 154 B9
STHWK SE1 19 K1
Fairthorn Rd CHARL SE7 161 M4
Fairtrough Rd ORP BR6 227 L9
Fairview ERITH DA8 164 G6
EW KT17 220 F7
HART * DA3 210 G10
Fair Vw POTB/CUF EN6 59 L6
Fairview Av ALP/SUD HA0 135 J1
RAIN RM13 145 L4
WOKS/MYFD GU22 232 C4
Fair View Cl WALTH E17 100 D9
Fairview Cl CHIG IG7 103 H5
SYD * SE26 182 D7
WOKS/MYFD GU22 232 C4
Fairview Ct HDN * NW4 96 G10
Fairview Crs RYLN/HDSTN HA2 113 P6
Fairview Dr CHIG IG7 103 H6
ORP BR6 226 G1
SHPTN TW17 196 A5
WAT WD17 72 F2
Fairview Gdns WFD IG8 101 N9
Fairview Pl BRXS/STRHM SW2 180 G3
Fairview Rd CHIG IG7 103 H5
ENC/FH EN2 79 H5
EW KT17 220 C7
MEO DA13 190 A10
SEVS/STOTM N15 119 N4
SLN SL2 128 E6
STRHM/NOR SW16 202 G1
SUT SM1 221 N2
Fairview Vls CHING * E4 100 F8
Fairview Wy EDGW HA8 95 M5
Fairwater Av WELL DA16 163 K10
Fairwater Dr ADL/WDHM KT15 215 N5
Fairway BXLYHS DA6 185 P1
CAR SM5 221 M7
CDH/CHF RM16 147 N10
CHERT KT16 195 L8
CRAWE RH10 285 J3
CRAWW RH11 282 G8
GU GU1 250 G10
HHS/BOV HP3 36 A10
RYNPK SW20 200 F3
SBW CM21 30 A1
STMC/STPC BR5 206 G6
WARE SG12 26 B3
WFD IG8 101 P6
Fairway Av BORE WD6 75 N6
CDALE/KGS NW9 115 N1
WDR/YW UB7 131 M10
Fairway Cl CRAWE RH10 285 H3
CROY/NA CR0 204 D5
GLDGN NW11 117 M5
HOR/WEW KT19 219 P1
LCOL/BKTW AL2 56 B3
WOKS/MYFD GU22 231 N5
Fairway Ct MLHL * NW7 96 A4
Fairway Dr GFD/PVL UB6 134 A2
RDART DA2 188 A3
THMD SE28 143 N8
Fairway Gdns BECK BR3 205 J6
IL IG1 122 F10
Fairways ASHF TW15 174 B9
CHES/WCR EN8 62 C2
ISLW * TW7 154 D7
PUR/KEN CR8 241 K3
STAN HA7 95 K10
TEDD TW11 177 J10
WALTH * E17 121 H2
The Fairways REDH RH1 275 N3
The Fairway ABLGY WD5 54 E8
ACT W3 136 B8
ALP/SUD HA0 114 G7
BAR EN5 77 L10
BMLY BR1 206 C5
CHOB/PIR GU24 231 H10
E/WMO/HCT KT8 198 A3
GVW DA11 190 D5
HGDN/ICK UB10 132 A5
HLWS CM18 47 J4
HNWL * W7 134 D9
LHD/OX KT22 236 F4
MLHL NW7 96 A4
NTHLT UB5 134 B1
NTHWD HA6 92 F5
NWMAL KT3 200 A1
PLMGR N13 99 K4
RSLP HA4 113 K9
SL SL1 128 B5
STHGT/OAK N14 78 C10
UPMR RM14 126 B5
WEY KT13 216 B7
Fairweather Cl SEVS/STOTM N15 119 M2
Fairweather Rd
STNW/STAM N16 119 P4
Fairwell La EHSLY KT24 252 C4
Fairwyn Rd SYD SE26 182 D6
Faithfield BUSH * WD23 73 M10
Fakenham Cl MLHL NW7 96 D8
NTHLT UB5 133 P1
Fakruddin St WCHPL E1 13 P2
Falaise EGH TW20 172 B8
Falaize Av IL IG1 122 E9
Falcon Av BMLY BR1 206 B3
GRAYS RM17 167 N6
Falconberg Ct SOHO/SHAV * W1D 11 J5
Falcon Cl CHSWK W4 155 N5
CRAWW RH11 283 N5
DART DA1 187 N1
HAT AL10 40 D6
NTHWD HA6 92 F8
SBW CM21 29 M2
STHWK SE1 12 D9
Falcon Ct IS N1 6 D8
Falcon Crs PEND EN3 80 C9
Falcon Dr STWL/WRAY TW19 173 N2
Falconer Rd BARK/HLT IG6 103 L6
BUSH WD23 73 P10
Falconers Pk SBW CM21 29 N2
Falcon Gv BTSEA SW11 157 P9
Falconhurst LHD/OX KT22 236 C1
Falcon La BTSEA SW11 157 P9
Falcon Ms GVW DA11 190 B4
Falcon Rdg BERK HP4 33 P6
Falcon Rd BTSEA SW11 157 P9
GU GU1 250 A10
HPTN TW12 175 N10
PEND EN3 80 C9
Falcons Cl BH/WHM TN16 244 A3
Falcon St PLSTW E13 141 M6
Falcon Ter BTSEA * SW11 157 P9
Falcon Wy CDALE/KGS NW9 96 B10
GSTN WD25 55 M10
KTN/HRWW/W HA3 115 K3
SUN TW16 196 F2
WAN E11 121 M2
WGCE AL7 23 H3
Falconwood EGH TW20 172 B8
EHSLY KT24 234 G10
Falcon Wd LHD/OX KT22 236 E6
Falconwood Av WELL DA16 162 G8
Falconwood Pde WELL DA16 163 J10
Falconwood Rd CROY/NA CR0 224 E5
Falcourt Cl SUT SM1 221 L2
Falkirk Cl EMPK RM11 125 P6
Falkirk Gdns OXHEY WD19 93 L6
Falkirk St IS N1 7 K8
Falkland Av FBAR/BDGN N11 98 B5
FNCH N3 97 K8
Falkland Gv DORK RH4 272 F3
Falkland Park Av SNWD SE25 203 M3
Falkland Pl KTTN NW5 118 D10
Falkland Rd BAR EN5 77 H6
CEND/HSY/T N8 119 H2
DORK RH4 272 F3
KTTN NW5 118 D10
Falling La WDR/YW UB7 131 P9
Falloden Wy GLDGN NW11 117 K2
Fallow Cl CHIG IG7 103 J6
Fallow Court Av
NFNCH/WDSP N12 97 M7
Fallowfield RDART DA2 188 G6
STAN HA7 94 F4
WGCE AL7 23 J2
Fallowfield Cl DEN/HRF UB9 91 M9
Fallowfield Ct STAN HA7 94 F4
Fallow Flds LOU IG10 101 P1
Fallowfields Dr
NFNCH/WDSP N12 97 P7
Fallowfield Wy HORL RH6 280 C3
Fallow Ri HERT/BAY SG13 25 M5
Fallows Cl EFNCH N2 97 M10
Fallsbrook Rd
STRHM/NOR SW16 180 C9
Falman Cl ED N9 99 P2
Falmer Cl CRAWW RH11 283 N9
Falmer Rd EN EN1 79 M8
SEVS/STOTM N15 119 K3
WALTH E17 120 G1
Falmouth Av CHING E4 101 J6
Falmouth Cl LEE/GVPK SE12 183 L1
Falmouth Ct STALW/RED * AL3 38 B4
Falmouth Gdns REDBR IG4 122 A2
Falmouth Rd SL SL1 128 F8
STHWK SE1 18 F4
WOT/HER KT12 217 K1
Falmouth St SRTFD E15 121 J10
Falstaff Gdns STAL AL1 38 A9
Falstone WOKN/KNAP GU21 231 N4
Fambridge Cl SYD SE26 182 E7
Fambridge Rd BCTR RM8 124 B6
Famet Av PUR/KEN CR8 223 K9
Famet Cl PUR/KEN CR8 223 K9
Famet Wk PUR/KEN CR8 223 K9
Fane St WKENS W14 14 D9
Fanhams Rd WARE SG12 26 D1
Fanns Ri PUR RM19 165 P3
Fann St FARR EC1M 12 E2
Fanshaw Ct HERT/WAS SG14 25 J4
Fanshawe Av BARK IG11 142 F1
Fanshawe Crs DAGW RM9 123 P10
EMPK RM11 125 L4
WARE SG12 26 A1
Fanshawe Rd CDH/CHF * RM16 168 D2
RCHPK/HAM TW10 177 H7
Fanshawe St HERT/WAS SG14 25 J4
Fanshaws La HERT/BAY SG13 43 K4
Fanshaw St IS N1 7 J9
Fanthorpe St PUT/ROE SW15 156 F9
Faraday Av SCUP DA14 185 L5
Faraday Cl HOLWY N7 5 P2
SLN * SL2 128 G7
WATW WD18 72 E10
Faraday Rd ACT W3 135 P9
CRAWE RH10 284 A3
E/WMO/HCT KT8 197 P4
GFD/PVL UB6 134 A9
NKENS W10 8 A3
SLN SL2 128 G7
SRTFD E15 141 L1
WELL DA16 163 K9
WIM/MER SW19 179 L9
Faraday Wy STMC/STPC BR5 207 L4
WOOL/PLUM SE18 162 A2
Fareham Rd EBED/NFELT TW14 175 K3
Fareham St SOHO/CST * W1F 11 J5
Far End HAT AL10 40 E7
Farewell Pl MTCM CR4 201 N1
Faringdon Av HARH RM3 105 K9
HAYES BR2 206 E6
Faringford Cl POTB/CUF EN6 59 N7
Faringford Rd SRTFD E15 141 K2
Faris Barn Dr ADL/WDHM KT15 215 J8
Faris La ADL/WDHM KT15 215 J7
Farjeon Rd BKHTH/KID SE3 162 A7
Farland Rd HHNE HP2 36 B6
Farleigh Av HAYES BR2 205 L7
Farleigh Court Rd WARL CR6 224 E10
Farleigh Dean Crs CROY/NA CR0 224 G7
Farleigh Pl STNW/STAM N16 119 N9
Farleigh Rd ADL/WDHM KT15 215 K7
STNW/STAM N16 119 N9
WARL CR6 242 D3
Farleton Cl WEY KT13 216 E3
Farleycroft BH/WHM TN16 262 E2
Farley Dr GDMY/SEVK IG3 123 H6
Farley La BH/WHM TN16 262 E3
Farley Nursery BH/WHM TN16 262 F3
Farley Pk OXTED RH8 261 J6
Farley Pl SNWD SE25 203 P4
Farley Rd CAT SE6 183 H3
GVE DA12 191 J3
SAND/SEL CR2 224 A4
Farleys Cl EHSLY KT24 252 D2
Farlington Pl PUT/ROE SW15 178 E3
Farlow Cl GVW DA11 190 C6
Farlow Rd PUT/ROE SW15 156 G9
Farlton Rd WAND/EARL SW18 179 L3
Farman Ter KTN/HRWW/W * HA3 115 J2
Farm Av ALP/SUD HA0 135 H1
CRICK NW2 117 H8
RYLN/HDSTN HA2 113 P5
STRHM/NOR SW16 180 F7
SWLY BR8 208 D3
Farmborough Cl HRW HA1 114 C5
Farm Cl AMS HP6 70 A5
ASC SL5 192 B5
BAR EN5 76 E9
BELMT SM2 221 N4
BF/WBF KT14 216 A8
BKHH IG9 101 P4
BORE WD6 75 K4
CHERT KT16 194 D6
CHES/WCR EN8 62 B6
CRAWE RH10 284 A6
DAGE RM10 144 D2
EHSLY KT24 252 G4
FUL/PGN * SW6 157 K6
HERT/WAS SG14 25 H5
HGDN/ICK UB10 112 C8
LHD/OX KT22 236 C10
POTB/CUF EN6 60 F3
RBRW/HUT CM13 107 P1
RGUW GU3 249 H5
SHPTN TW17 196 B7
STA TW18 173 H8
STHL UB1 134 A9
WGCW AL8 22 F5
WLGTN SM6 222 D6
WWKM BR4 205 L10
Farmcote Rd LEE/GVPK SE12 183 M4
Farm Cottages
E/WMO/HCT * KT8 198 F4
Farm Crs SLN SL2 129 N7
Farmcroft GVW DA11 190 D5
Farmdale Rd CAR SM5 221 P4
GNWCH SE10 161 M4
Farm Dr CROY/NA CR0 204 E9
PUR/KEN CR8 222 E8
WDSR SL4 171 N2
Farm End CHING E4 81 K9
Farmer Ct WAB EN9 63 M9
Farmer Rd LEY E10 120 G6
Farmers Cl GSTN WD25 55 J9
Farmers Rd CMBW SE5 159 J6
STA TW18 173 H8
Farmer St KENS W8 8 E9
Farmfield Dr HORL RH6 279 L7
Farmfield Rd BMLY BR1 183 K8
Farm Flds SAND/SEL CR2 223 N7
Farm Gv BEAC HP9 88 B6
Farm Hill Rd WAB EN9 63 J10
Farm Holt HART DA3 211 L8
Farmhouse Cl BROX * EN10 62 E1
WOKS/MYFD GU22 232 G1
Farmhouse La HHNE HP2 36 B4
Farmhouse Rd
STRHM/NOR SW16 180 D10
Farmilo Rd WALTH E17 120 F5
Farmington Av SUT SM1 201 N10
Farmlands ENC/FH EN2 79 H5
PIN HA5 113 H2
The Farmlands NTHLT UB5 133 N1
Farmland Wk CHST BR7 184 E8
Farm La ADL/WDHM KT15 215 K3
ASHTD KT21 237 N4
BEAC HP9 89 J9
CROY/NA CR0 204 E9
EHSLY KT24 252 G4
FUL/PGN SW6 14 F10
HOD EN11 45 H1
PUR/KEN CR8 222 D6
RKW/CH/CXG WD3 71 L7
RPLY/SEND GU23 232 F9
STHGT/OAK N14 78 B10
WTHK RM20 167 K5
Farmleigh STHGT/OAK N14 98 D1
Farmleigh Cl CRAWE RH10 284 D5
Farmleigh Gv WOT/HER KT12 216 G2
Farm Pl BERK HP4 33 L4
DART DA1 165 H10
KENS W8 8 E9
Farm Rd BELMT SM2 221 N4
CDH/CHF RM16 168 C1
EDGW HA8 95 P6
ESH/CLAY KT10 197 P8
HSLWW TW4 175 M4
MRDN SM4 201 L5
NTHWD HA6 92 D6
RAIN RM13 145 K5
RKW/CH/CXG WD3 70 D8
RSEV TN14 247 K6
STA TW18 173 L9
STAL AL1 38 G5
TIL RM18 169 M3
WARL CR6 242 D5
WCHMH N21 99 K2
WLSDN NW10 136 A3
WOKS/MYFD GU22 232 E6
Farmstead Rd CAT SE6 182 G7
KTN/HRWW/W HA3 94 C9
Farm St MYFR/PICC W1J 10 E8
The Farm WIM/MER * SW19 178 G3
Farm V BXLY DA5 186 C2
Farmview COB KT11 235 L2
Farm Wk GUW GU2 267 L2
Farmway BCTR RM8 123 M9
Farm Wy BKHH IG9 101 P5
BUSH WD23 74 A8
HCH RM12 125 J9
NTHWD HA6 92 F5
STWL/WRAY TW19 173 J2
WPK KT4 200 F10
Farm Yd WDSR SL4 149 J6
Farnaby Dr SEV TN13 264 G2
Farnaby Rd BMLY BR1 205 K1
ELTH/MOT SE9 161 P10
Farnan Av WALTH E17 100 F10
Farnan Rd STRHM/NOR SW16 180 F8
Farnborough Av SAND/SEL CR2 224 D4
WALTH * E17 120 D1
Farnborough Cl WBLY HA9 115 N7
Farnborough Common
ORP BR6 206 C10
Farnborough Crs HAYES BR2 205 L8
SAND/SEL CR2 224 D5
Farnborough Hl ORP BR6 226 G2
Farnborough Wy ORP BR6 227 H3
PECK * SE15 159 M6
Farnburn Av SL SL1 128 G7
Farncombe Hl RGODL GU7 267 J10
Farncombe St BERM/RHTH SE16 19 P2
RGODL GU7 267 K10
Farndale Av PLMGR N13 99 J4
Farndale Crs GFD/PVL UB6 134 B5
Farnell Ms ECT SW5 14 G7
Farnell Rd ISLW TW7 154 C9
STA TW18 173 K6
Farnes Dr GPK RM2 105 K10
Farnham Cl HHS/BOV HP3 52 D4
SBW CM21 29 M2
TRDG/WHET N20 97 M1
Farnham Gdns RYNPK SW20 200 E2
Farnham La SLN SL2 128 E4
Farnham Park La SLN SL2 129 H3
Farnham Pl STHWK SE1 12 D10
Farnham Rd GDMY/SEVK IG3 123 J4
GUW GU2 267 J3
HARH RM3 105 L6
SL SL1 129 H10
WELL DA16 163 M8
Farnham Royal LBTH SE11 17 P8
Farningham Crs CTHM CR3 241 P9
Farningham Hill Rd SWLY BR8 209 K5
Farningham Rd CTHM CR3 241 P9
TOTM N17 99 P8
Farnley WOKN/KNAP GU21 231 L3
Farnley Rd CHING E4 101 K1
THHTH CR7 203 L4
Farnol Rd DART DA1 187 P1
Faro Cl BMLY BR1 206 D2
Faroe Rd WKENS W14 156 G2
Farorna Wk ENC/FH EN2 79 H5
Farquhar Rd NRWD SE19 181 N8
WIM/MER SW19 179 K6
Farquharson Rd CROY/NA CR0 203 K8
Farquhar St HERT/WAS SG14 25 K4
Farraline Rd WATW WD18 73 J8
Farrance Rd CHDH RM6 123 P4
Farrance St POP/IOD E14 140 F8
Farrant Av WDGN N22 99 H10
Farrant Cl ORP BR6 227 K4
Farrant Wy BORE WD6 75 K5
Farr Av BARK IG11 143 K4
Farren Rd FSTH SE23 182 D5
Farrer Ms CEND/HSY/T N8 118 D2
Farrer Rd CEND/HSY/T N8 118 D2
KTN/HRWW/W HA3 115 K3
Farriday Cl STALW/RED AL3 38 D2
Farrier Cl BMLY BR1 206 A3
UX/CGN UB8 132 B8
Farrier Rd NTHLT UB5 133 P4
Farriers WARE SG12 26 F5
Farriers Cl EW KT17 220 B8
GVE DA12 191 J4
HHS/BOV HP3 52 E4
Farriers End BROX EN10 62 E2
Farriers Rd EW KT17 220 B7
Farrier St CAMTN NW1 4 F3
Farriers Wy BORE WD6 76 A10
Farrier Wk WBPTN SW10 15 J9
Farringdon La CLKNW EC1R 12 B2
Farringdon Rd FSBYW WC1X 12 A1
Farringdon St STBT EC1A 12 C4
Farringford Cl LCOL/BKTW AL2 55 P2
Farrington Acres WEY * KT13 196 E10
Farrington Av STMC/STPC BR5 207 L3
Farrington Pl CHST BR7 184 G10
Farrins Rents BERM/RHTH SE16 140 D10
Farrow Gdns CDH/CHF RM16 147 N10
Farrow La PECK SE15 160 B6
Farrow Pl BERM/RHTH SE16 160 D2
Farr Rd ENC/FH EN2 79 L5
Farthingale La WAB EN9 63 M10
Farthing Aly STHWK SE1 19 N2
Farthing Flds WAP E1W 140 A10
Farthing Green La SLN SL2 129 M4
Farthings WOKN/KNAP GU21 231 K2
Farthings Cl CHING E4 101 K4
PIN HA5 113 J4
The Farthings HHW HP1 35 L6
KUTN/CMB KT2 199 M1
Farthing St ORP BR6 226 C4
Farwell Rd SCUP DA14 185 L7
Farwig La BMLY BR1 205 M1
Fashion St WCHPL E1 13 L4
Fashoda Rd HAYES BR2 206 A4
Fassett Rd HACK E8 7 N1
KUT KT1 199 K4
Fassett Sq HACK E8 7 N1
Fauconberg Rd CHSWK W4 155 P5
Faulkner Cl BCTR RM8 123 N5
Faulkner's Rd WOT/HER KT12 217 K2
Faulkner St NWCR SE14 160 B7
Fauna Cl CHDH RM6 123 M4
Faunce St WALW SE17 18 C8
Favart Rd FUL/PGN SW6 157 K7
Faverolle Gn CHES/WCR EN8 62 C4
Faversham Av CHING E4 101 K2
WCHMH N21 79 L10
Faversham Cl CHIG IG7 103 L3
Faversham Rd BECK BR3 204 E2
CAT SE6 182 E3
MRDN SM4 201 L6
Fawcett Cl BTSEA SW11 157 N8
STRHM/NOR SW16 181 H7
Fawcett Est CLPT * E5 119 P6
Fawcett Rd CROY/NA CR0 203 J10
WDSR SL4 148 G7
WLSDN NW10 136 C2
Fawcett St WBPTN SW10 15 J9
Fawcus Cl ESH/CLAY KT10 218 D3
Fawe Park Rd PUT/ROE SW15 157 J10
Fawe St POP/IOD E14 140 G7
Fawkes Av DART DA1 187 N5
Fawkham Av HART DA3 211 P3
Fawkham Green Rd HART DA3 210 G10
Fawkham Rd HART DA3 211 J4
Fawley Rd KIL/WHAMP NW6 117 L10
Fawnbrake Av HNHL SE24 181 J1
Fawn Ct BRKMPK AL9 40 F2
Fawn Rd CHIG IG7 103 J6
PLSTW E13 141 P4
Fawns Manor Rd
EBED/NFELT TW14 174 E4
Fawood Av WLSDN NW10 136 A2
Fawsley Cl DTCH/LGLY SL3 151 H6
Faygate Crs BXLYHS DA6 186 B1
Faygate La HORS RH12 282 B6
Faygate Rd BRXS/STRHM SW2 180 G5
Fay Gn ABLGY WD5 54 E9
Fayland Av STRHM/NOR SW16 180 D8
Faymore Gdns SOCK/AV RM15 146 F9
Feacey Down HHW HP1 35 K4
Fearn Cl EHSLY KT24 252 F5
Fearney Md RKW/CH/CXG WD3 91 K2
Fearnley Crs HPTN TW12 175 M8
HPTN TW12 175 N9
Fearnley Rd WGCW AL8 22 F6
Fearnley St WATW WD18 73 J8
Fearon St GNWCH SE10 161 M4
Featherbed La CROY/NA CR0 224 G6
HHS/BOV HP3 35 M10
Feather Dell HAT AL10 40 C4
Feathers La STWL/WRAY TW19 172 D5
Feathers Pl GNWCH SE10 161 J5
Featherstone Av FSTH SE23 182 A5
Featherstone Gdns BORE WD6 76 A8
Featherstone Rd MLHL NW7 96 E7
NWDGN UB2 153 M2
Featherstone St STLK EC1Y 12 G1
Featherstone Ter NWDGN UB2 153 M2
Featley Rd BRXN/ST SW9 159 J9
Federal Rd GFD/PVL UB6 135 H4
Federal Wy WATN WD24 73 K5
Federation Rd ABYW SE2 163 M3
Fee Farm Rd ESH/CLAY KT10 218 E4
Feenan Hwy TIL RM18 168 E6
Felbridge Av CRAWE RH10 284 E6
STAN HA7 94 F9
Felbridge Cl BELMT SM2 221 L5
STRHM/NOR SW16 181 H7
Felbrigge Rd GDMY/SEVK IG3 123 J7
Felcott Cl WOT/HER KT12 197 K10
Felcott Rd WOT/HER KT12 197 K10
Felday Rd LEW SE13 182 G2
RDKG RH5 270 G6
Felden Cl GSTN WD25 55 L10
Felden Dr HHS/BOV HP3 35 K10
Felden La HHS/BOV HP3 35 K9
Felden St FUL/PGN SW6 157 J7
Feldman Cl STNW/STAM N16 119 P6
Feldon Cl PIN HA5 93 M8
Felgate Ms HMSMTH W6 156 E3
Felhampton Rd ELTH/MOT SE9 184 E6
Felicia Wy CDH/CHF RM16 168 E3
Felipe Rd CDH/CHF RM16 167 H2
Felix Av CEND/HSY/T N8 118 F4
Felix Dr RGUE GU4 251 K4
Felix La SHPTN TW17 196 F6
Felix Rd HNWL W7 134 F9
WOT/HER KT12 197 H6
Felixstowe Rd ABYW SE2 163 L2
TOTM N17 119 N1
UED N18 99 P5
WLSDN * NW10 136 E5
Felix St BETH * E2 140 A4
Felland Wy REDH RH1 275 N4
Fellbrigg Rd EDUL SE22 181 N1
Fellbrigg St WCHPL E1 140 A6
Fellbrook RCHPK/HAM TW10 176 G6
Fellmongers Yd CROY/NA CR0 203 K10
Fellowes Cl YEAD UB4 133 L6
Fellowes La STALE/WH AL4 40 A9
Fellowes Rd CAR SM5 201 P10
Fellow Gn CHOB/PIR GU24 212 E9
Fellow Green Rd
CHOB/PIR GU24 212 E9
Fellows Rd HAMP NW3 3 M3
HAMP NW3 3 P3
Fell Pth BORE * WD6 76 A9
Fell Rd CROY/NA CR0 203 K10
Felltram Wy CHARL SE7 161 M4
Felmersham Cl CLAP SW4 158 F10
Felmingham Rd PGE/AN SE20 204 B2
Felmongers HLW CM20 29 L9
Felsberg Rd BRXS/STRHM SW2 180 F2
Fels Cl DAGE RM10 124 C8
Fels Farm Av DAGE RM10 124 D8
Felsham Rd PUT/ROE SW15 156 F9
Felspar Cl WOOL/PLUM SE18 163 J4
Felstead Av CLAY IG5 102 D9
Felstead Cl RBRW/HUT CM13 87 P10
Felstead Rd CHES/WCR EN8 62 D8
CRW RM5 104 D7
HOM E9 140 F1
HOR/WEW KT19 220 A7
LOU IG10 102 B1
ORP BR6 207 K9
WAN E11 121 M5
Felstead St HOM E9 140 E1
Felsted Rd CAN/RD E16 142 A8
Feltham Av E/WMO/HCT KT8 198 D4
Felthambrook Wy FELT TW13 175 J6
Feltham Hill Rd ASHF TW15 174 B8
ASHF TW15 174 D9
Felthamhill Rd FELT TW13 175 H7
Feltham Rd ASHF TW15 174 C7
MTCM CR4 202 A2
REDH RH1 276 A5
Felton Cl BORE * WD6 75 K4
BROX EN10 62 E1
STMC/STPC BR5 206 E6
Felton Lea SCUP DA14 185 J8
Felton Rd BARK IG11 143 H4
WEA W13 155 H1
Felton St IS N1 7 H6

Fencepiece Rd BARK/HLT IG6 102 F7
Fenchurch Av FENCHST EC3M 13 J6
Fenchurch Buildings
FENCHST EC3M 13 K6
Fenchurch Pl FENCHST * EC3M 13 K7
Fenchurch Rd CRAWE RH10 284 C9
Fenchurch St FENCHST EC3M 13 J7
Fen Cl BRWN CM15 87 P8
Fendall Rd HOR/WEW KT19 219 P2
Fendall St STHWK SE1 19 K4
Fendt Cl CAN/RD E16 141 L8
Fendyke Rd ABYW SE2 163 N3
Fenelon Pl WKENS W14 14 D6
Fengates Rd REDH RH1 257 P10
Fen Gv BFN/LL DA15 185 J2
Fenham Rd PECK SE15 159 P6
Fen La UPMR RM14 127 J10
UPMR RM14 127 N10
Fenman Ct TOTM N17 100 A9
Fenman Gdns GDMY/SEVK IG3 123 L6
Fenn Cl BMLY BR1 183 M9
Fennel Cl CAN/RD E16 141 K6
CROY/NA CR0 204 C8
GU GU1 250 E7
Fennel Crs CRAWW RH11 283 L10
Fennells HLWW/ROY CM19 46 E6
Fennells Md HOR/WEW KT19 220 C5
Fennell St WOOL/PLUM SE18 162 D5
Fenner Cl BERM/RHTH SE16 160 A3
Fenner Rd CDH/CHF RM16 167 H2
Fenner Sq BTSEA * SW11 157 N9
The Fennings AMS HP6 69 J2
Fenning St STHWK SE1 19 J1
Fennscombe Ct CHOB/PIR GU24 212 D9
Fenns La CHOB/PIR GU24 212 D9
Fenn St HOM E9 120 C10
Fenn's Wy WOKN/KNAP GU21 232 B1
Fennycroft Rd HHW HP1 35 J3
Fensomes Aly HHNE HP2 35 N5
Fensom's Cl HHNE HP2 35 N5
Fenstanton Av NFNCH/WDSP N12 97 N6
Fen St CAN/RD E16 141 L9
Fens Wy SWLY BR8 187 H9
Fentiman Rd VX/NE SW8 17 N10
Fentiman Wy EMPK RM11 125 M6
Fenton Av STA TW18 173 M9
Fenton Cl BRXN/ST * SW9 158 G8
CHST BR7 184 C8
HACK E8 7 M2
REDH RH1 258 B10
Fenton Gra HLWE CM17 47 M2
Fenton Rd REDH RH1 258 B10
TOTM N17 99 K8
Fenton's Av PLSTW E13 141 N5
Fentum Rd GUW GU2 249 M8
Fenwick Cl WOKN/KNAP GU21 231 N4
Fenwick Gv PECK SE15 159 P9
Fenwick Pl BRXN/ST SW9 158 F9
SAND/SEL CR2 223 J4
Fenwick Rd PECK SE15 159 P9
Ferdinand Pl CAMTN NW1 4 D3
Ferdinand St CAMTN NW1 4 D3
Ferguson Av BRYLDS KT5 199 L5
GPK RM2 105 K10
GVE DA12 190 F7
Ferguson Cl BECK BR3 205 H3
Ferguson Ct GPK RM2 105 L10
Ferguson Dr ACT W3 136 A8
Ferguson Gv CHES/WCR * EN8 62 C5
Ferguson's Cl POP/IOD E14 160 F3
Fergus Rd HBRY N5 119 J10
Fermandy La CRAWE RH10 285 P4
Ferme Park Rd CEND/HSY/T N8 118 F3
Fermor Rd FSTH SE23 182 D4
Fermoy Rd GFD/PVL UB6 134 A4
MV/WKIL W9 8 C2
Fern Av MTCM CR4 202 E4
Fernbank BKHH IG9 101 N2
EYN * DA4 209 N9
Fernbank Av ALP/SUD HA0 114 E9
HCH RM12 125 K9
WOT/HER KT12 197 M7
Fernbank Ms CLAP SW4 180 C2
Fernbank Rd ADL/WDHM KT15 215 K2
Fernbrook Dr RYLN/HDSTN HA2 114 A5
Fernbrook Rd LEW SE13 183 K2
Ferncliff Rd HACK E8 119 P10
Fern Cl BROX EN10 44 E9
ERITH DA8 165 J7
IS * N1 7 J7
WARL CR6 242 D4
Ferncroft Av HAMP NW3 117 K8
NFNCH/WDSP N12 97 P7
RSLP HA4 113 K7
Ferndale BMLY BR1 205 P2
GUW GU2 249 K8
Ferndale Av CHERT KT16 195 H10
HSLWW TW4 153 M9
WALTH E17 121 J3
Ferndale Cl BXLYHN DA7 163 P7
Ferndale Crs UX/CGN UB8 131 M5
Ferndale Rd ASHF TW15 173 N8
BNSTD SM7 239 J2
CLAP SW4 158 F10
CRW RM5 104 D10
FSTGT E7 141 N2
GVE DA12 190 E5
PEND EN3 80 C3
SEVS/STOTM N15 119 N4
SNWD SE25 204 A5
WAN E11 121 L7
WOKN/KNAP GU21 232 C2
Ferndale St EHAM E6 142 E9
Ferndale Ter HRW HA1 114 E3
Ferndale Wy ORP BR6 226 G2
Ferndell Av BXLY DA5 186 E6
Fern Dells HAT AL10 40 C5
Ferndene LCOL/BKTW AL2 55 N7
Ferndene Rd HNHL SE24 159 K10
Fernden Wy ROMW/RG RM7 124 C4
Ferndown CRAWE RH10 284 E3
EMPK RM11 125 P4
HORL RH6 280 B2
NTHWD HA6 93 H10
Ferndown Av ORP BR6 206 G8
Ferndown Cl BELMT SM2 221 N3
GU GU1 268 D1
PIN HA5 93 M8
Ferndown Gdns COB KT11 217 K10
Ferndown Rd ELTH/MOT SE9 184 A3
OXHEY WD19 93 K4
Fern Dr HHS/BOV HP3 35 P7
MDHD SL6 128 A8
Fernecroft STAL AL1 38 B9
The Fernery STA TW18 173 H8
Fernes Cl UX/CGN UB8 131 M3
Ferney Ct BF/WBF KT14 215 N8
Ferney Meade Wy ISLW TW7 154 F8
Ferney Rd CHESW EN7 61 L2
EBAR EN4 98 B1
Fern Gv EBED/NFELT TW14 175 J3
WGCW AL8 22 G1
Fernhall Dr REDBR IG4 122 A3
Fernhall La WAB EN9 64 A7
Fernham Rd THHTH CR7 203 K4
Fernhead Rd MV/WKIL W9 2 D9
Fernheath Wy RDART DA2 186 E8
Fernhill HLWS CM18 47 H5
LHD/OX KT22 218 C10
Fernhill Cl WOKS/MYFD GU22 231 P6
Fernhill Ct WALTH E17 101 J10
Fernhill Gdns KUTN/CMB KT2 177 J8
Fern Hill La HLWS CM18 47 J5
Fernhill La WOKS/MYFD GU22 231 P6
Fernhill Pk WOKS/MYFD GU22 231 P6
Fernhill Rd HORL RH6 280 E8
Fernhills ABLGY WD5 54 E10
Fernhill St CAN/RD E16 142 C10
Fernholme Rd PECK SE15 182 C1
Fernhurst Cl BEAC HP9 88 D9
CRAWW RH11 283 L5
Fernhurst Gdns EDGW HA8 95 M7
Fernhurst Rd ASHF TW15 174 D7
CROY/NA CR0 203 P7
FUL/PGN SW6 157 H7
Fernihough Cl WEY KT13 216 B7
Fernlands Cl CHERT KT16 195 H10
Fern La NWDGN UB2 153 N4
Fernlea GT/LBKH KT23 236 A10
Fernlea Rd BAL SW12 180 C4
MTCM CR4 202 B2
Fernleigh Cl CROY/NA CR0 223 H1
MV/WKIL * W9 8 D1
WOT/HER KT12 197 J10
Fernleigh Ct RYLN/HDSTN HA2 94 A10
WBLY HA9 115 K6
Fernleigh Rd WCHMH N21 99 H3
Fernleys STALE/WH AL4 39 H3
Fernsbury St FSBYW WC1X 6 A10
Ferns Cl PEND EN3 80 D2
SAND/SEL CR2 224 A6
Fernshaw Rd WBPTN SW10 15 J10
Fernside BKHH IG9 101 N2
Fernside Av FELT TW13 175 J7
MLHL NW7 96 A4
Fernside La SEV TN13 265 K5
Fernside Rd BAL SW12 180 A4
Fernsleigh Cl CFSP/GDCR SL9 90 B7
Ferns Rd SRTFD E15 141 K1
Fern St BOW E3 140 F6
Fernthorpe Rd
STRHM/NOR SW16 180 D9
Ferntower Rd HBRY N5 119 L10
Fern Towers CTHM CR3 259 P1
Fernville La HHNE HP2 35 N6
Fern Wk ASHF TW15 173 N8
STHWK SE1 19 P8
Fern Wy GSTN WD25 73 J1
Fernways IL IG1 122 E8
Fernwood Av ALP/SUD HA0 135 H1
STRHM/NOR SW16 180 E7
Fernwood Cl BMLY BR1 205 P2
Fernwood Crs TRDG/WHET N20 98 A4
Ferny Hl EBAR EN4 78 A4
Feroners Cl CRAWE RH10 284 B9
Ferranti Cl WOOL/PLUM SE18 162 A2
Ferraro Cl HEST TW5 153 P5
Ferrers Av WDR/YW UB7 151 N1
WLGTN SM6 222 E1
Ferrers Cl SL SL1 128 D10
Ferrers La STALE/WH AL4 21 J6
Ferrers Rd STRHM/NOR SW16 180 E8
Ferrestone Rd CEND/HSY/T N8 118 G2
Ferriby Cl IS N1 6 A3
Ferrier St WAND/EARL SW18 157 L10
Ferriers Wy KWD/TDW/WH KT20 238 F5
Ferring Cl RYLN/HDSTN HA2 114 B6
Ferrings DUL SE21 181 M5
Ferris Av CROY/NA CR0 204 E10
Ferris Rd EDUL SE22 159 P10
Ferron Rd CLPT * E5 120 A8
Ferro Rd RAIN RM13 145 H6
Ferry Av STA TW18 173 H10
Ferryhills Cl OXHEY WD19 93 K4
Ferry La BARN SW13 156 C5
BTFD TW8 155 K5
CHERT KT16 195 K6
GUW GU2 267 P4
RAIN RM13 144 F8
RCH/KEW TW9 155 L5
SHPTN TW17 196 B8
STA TW18 195 M3
STWL/WRAY TW19 172 E5
TOTM N17 120 A2
Ferrymead Av GFD/PVL UB6 133 P4
Ferrymead Dr GFD/PVL UB6 133 P5
Ferrymead Gdns GFD/PVL UB6 134 B4
Ferrymoor RCHPK/HAM TW10 176 G6
Ferry Rd BARN SW13 156 D6
E/WMO/HCT KT8 197 P3
TEDD TW11 176 G8
THDIT KT7 198 G6
TIL RM18 168 D8
TWK TW1 176 G4
Ferry Sq BTFD TW8 155 K5
Ferry St POP/IOD E14 161 H4
Feryby Rd CDH/CHF RM16 168 E2
Fesants Cft HLW CM20 29 L8
Festing Rd PUT/ROE SW15 156 G9
Festival Cl BXLY DA5 185 N4
ERITH DA8 164 G6
HGDN/ICK UB10 132 C3
Fetcham Common La
LHD/OX KT22 236 A7
Fetcham Park Dr LHD/OX KT22 236 D9
Fetherstone Cl POTB/CUF EN6 59 N8
Fetter La FLST/FETLN EC4A 12 B5
Ffinch St DEPT SE8 160 F6
Fiddicroft Av BNSTD SM7 239 L1
Fiddle Bridge La HAT AL10 40 C3
Fiddlers Cl GRH DA9 166 G10
Fidler Pl BUSH WD23 74 A10
Field Cl ABR/ST RM4 83 L7
BKHH IG9 101 P4
BMLY BR1 205 P2
CHING E4 100 G7
CHSGTN KT9 219 H2
CSHM HP5 51 K4
E/WMO/HCT KT8 198 A5
HARP AL5 20 C4
HGDN/ICK UB10 112 B7
HSLWW TW4 153 J7
HYS/HAR UB3 152 D6
RGUE GU4 250 G8
RSLP HA4 112 D6
SAND/SEL CR2 224 A10
STALE/WH AL4 38 F2
Fieldcommon La WOT/HER KT12 197 M8
Field Cottages EFNCH * N2 118 A1
FUL/PGN * SW6 157 J8
Field Ct GINN WC1R 11 P4
OXTED RH8 261 K4
Field End BAR EN5 76 E8
CHOB/PIR GU24 212 E9
COUL/CHIP CR5 222 E10
RSLP HA4 133 K1
Fieldend TEDD TW11 176 E7
Field End Cl OXHEY WD19 93 M1
Field End Rd PIN HA5 113 J3
Fieldend Rd STRHM/NOR SW16 202 D1
Fielders Cl EN EN1 79 M8
RYLN/HDSTN HA2 114 B6
Fielders Gn GU GU1 250 D10
Fielders Wy RAD WD7 57 K9
Fieldfare Rd THMD SE28 143 M9
Fieldfares LCOL/BKTW AL2 57 J3
Field Gdns CHONG CM5 67 M10
Fieldgate St WCHPL E1 13 P4
Fieldhouse Cl SWFD E18 101 N9
Fieldhouse Rd BAL SW12 180 D4
Fieldhouse Vls BNSTD * SM7 239 P1
Field Hurst DTCH/LGLY SL3 150 C3
Fieldhurst Cl ADL/WDHM KT15 215 L2
Fielding Av TIL RM18 168 E7
WHTN TW2 176 B6
Fielding Gdns DTCH/LGLY SL3 149 P1
Fielding Rd WKENS W14 156 G2
Fieldings Rd CHES/WCR EN8 62 E5
The Fieldings FSTH SE23 182 B4
HORL RH6 280 C3
WOKN/KNAP GU21 231 L2
Fielding St WALW SE17 18 E9
Fielding Ter EA * W5 135 L9
Fielding Wy RBRW/HUT CM13 87 P10
Field Kiln BRWN CM15 87 J1
Field La BTFD TW8 155 H6
RGODL GU7 267 L10
TEDD TW11 176 F8
Field Md CDALE/KGS NW9 96 B8
Field Pl NWMAL KT3 200 C6
Field Rd DEN/HRF UB9 111 H8
EBED/NFELT TW14 175 J2
FSTGT E7 121 M9
HHNE HP2 36 B7
HMSMTH W6 14 A8
OXHEY WD19 73 M10
SOCK/AV RM15 146 B10
TOTM N17 119 L1
Fields End La HHW HP1 34 G4
Fieldsend Rd CHEAM SM3 221 H2
Fields Est HACK * E8 7 P4
Fieldside Cl ORP BR6 226 F1
Fieldside Cottages
TRDG/WHET * N20 97 J1
Fields Park Crs CHDH RM6 123 N3
Field St FSBYW WC1X 5 N9
Field Vw EGH TW20 172 F8
FELT TW13 174 E7
Fieldview HORL RH6 280 C3
WAND/EARL SW18 179 N4
Fieldview Cottages
STHGT/OAK * N14 98 E3
Field View Ri LCOL/BKTW AL2 55 M5
Field View Rd POTB/CUF EN6 59 K9
Field Wk HORL RH6 281 K3
Field Wy AMSS HP7 68 G7
CFSP/GDCR SL9 90 A8
CROY/NA CR0 224 G4
GFD/PVL UB6 134 A3
HHW HP1 52 D3
HOD EN11 26 G9
RKW/CH/CXG WD3 91 L2
RPLY/SEND GU23 251 J1
RSLP HA4 112 D6
UX/CGN UB8 131 N6
WLSDN NW10 135 P2
Fieldway BCTR RM8 123 L9
BERK HP4 34 B7
CDH/CHF RM16 147 M10
STMC/STPC BR5 206 G6
WARE SG12 26 C7
Fieldway Crs HOLWY N7 119 H10
Fiennes Cl BCTR RM8 123 M6
Fiennes Wy SEV TN13 265 K3
Fiesta Dr DAGW RM9 144 D5
Fifehead Cl ASHF TW15 173 P9
Fife Rd CAN/RD E16 141 M7
KUT KT1 199 K2
MORT/ESHN SW14 177 P1
WDGN N22 99 J8
Fife Ter IS N1 5 P7
Fife Wy GT/LBKH KT23 253 P1
Fifield Pth FSTH SE23 182 C6
Fifteenth Av
KWD/TDW/WH * KT20 257 J2
Fifth Av GSTN WD25 73 L1
KWD/TDW/WH * KT20 257 J2
MNPK E12 122 C9
NKENS W10 2 A10
WTHK RM20 166 F5
Fifth Avenue Allende Av
HLW CM20 28 G10
Fifth Cross Rd WHTN TW2 176 C5
Fifth Wy WBLY HA9 115 N9
Figge's Rd MTCM CR4 180 B10
Figtree Hl HHNE HP2 35 N5
Filbert Crs CRAWW RH11 283 K7
Filborough Wy GVE DA12 191 L4
Filby Rd CHSGTN KT9 219 L3
Filey Av STNW/STAM N16 119 P6
Filey Cl BELMT SM2 221 M4
BH/WHM TN16 243 N5
CRAWW RH11 283 J9
Filey Sp SL SL1 148 G2
Filey Waye RSLP HA4 113 H7
Fillebrook Av EN EN1 79 M6
Fillebrook Rd WAN E11 121 J6
Filmer Chambers
FUL/PGN * SW6 157 J7
Filmer La RSEV TN14 247 M7
Filmer Rd FUL/PGN SW6 157 J7
WDSR SL4 148 C8
Filston La RSEV TN14 228 F9
Finborough Rd TOOT SW17 180 A10
WBPTN SW10 15 H9
Finchale Rd ABYW SE2 163 K2
Fincham Cl HGDN/ICK UB10 112 D8
Finch Av WNWD SE27 181 L7
Finch Cl BAR EN5 77 K9
HAT AL10 40 D6
WOKN/KNAP GU21 231 H3
Finchdale HHW HP1 35 K6
Finch Dr EBED/NFELT TW14 175 L3
Finches Ri GU GU1 250 E8
The Finches HERT/BAY SG13 26 A5
Finch Gdns CHING E4 100 F6
Finch Gn RKW/CH/CXG WD3 71 J8
Finchingfield Av WFD IG8 101 P8
The Finchingfields BRWN CM15 86 D3
Finch La AMSS HP7 69 M6
BANK EC3V 13 H6
BEAC HP9 88 B6
BUSH WD23 73 P8
Finchley Cl DART DA1 187 P2
Finchley La HDN NW4 116 G2
Finchley Pk NFNCH/WDSP N12 97 M5
Finchley Pl STJWD NW8 3 L7
Finchley Rd GLDGN NW11 117 J3
GRAYS RM17 167 N5
HAMP NW3 117 K7
KIL/WHAMP NW6 3 K2
STJWD NW8 3 L6
Finchley Vls NFNCH/WDSP * N12 97 N5
Finchley Wy FNCH N3 97 K7
Finch Ms PECK * SE15 159 N7
Finchmoor HLWS CM18 46 G4
Finch Rd BERK HP4 33 M5
GU * GU1 250 A10
Finden Rd FSTGT E7 121 N10
Findhorn Av YEAD UB4 133 J7
Findhorn St POP/IOD E14 141 H8
Findlay Dr RGUW GU3 249 L6
Findon Cl RYLN/HDSTN * HA2 114 A8
WAND/EARL SW18 179 K2
Findon Gdns RAIN RM13 145 H7
Findon Rd CRAWW RH11 283 L5
ED N9 100 A2
SHB W12 156 D1
Fine Bush La DEN/HRF UB9 112 C4
Fingal St GNWCH SE10 161 L4
Finglesham Cl STMC/STPC BR5 207 N8
Finians Cl HGDN/ICK UB10 132 A2
Finland Rd BROCKY SE4 160 D9
Finland St BERM/RHTH SE16 160 D2
Finlay Gdns ADL/WDHM KT15 215 M1
Finlays Cl CHSGTN KT9 219 M2
Finlay St FUL/PGN SW6 156 G7
Finnart Cl WEY KT13 216 D1
Finney Dr BFOR GU20 212 C3
Finnis St BETH E2 140 A5
Finnymore Rd DAGW RM9 143 P2
Finsbury Av LVPST * EC2M 13 H4
Finsbury Circ LVPST EC2M 13 H4
Finsbury Cottages WDGN N22 98 F8
Finsbury Est CLKNW EC1R 6 B10
Finsbury Market SDTCH EC2A 13 J2
Finsbury Park Av FSBYPK N4 119 K4
Finsbury Park Rd FSBYPK N4 119 J7
Finsbury Pavement SDTCH EC2A 13 H3
Finsbury Rd WDGN N22 98 G8
Finsbury Sq SDTCH EC2A 13 H2
Finsbury St STLK EC1Y 12 G3
Finsbury Wy BXLY DA5 186 A3
Finsen Rd HNHL SE24 159 K10
Finstock Rd NKENS W10 136 G8
Finucane Dr STMC/STPC BR5 207 M7
Finucane Gdns RAIN RM13 145 H1
Finucane Ri BUSH WD23 94 B3
Finway Ct WATW * WD18 72 G9
Finway Rd HHNE HP2 36 C2
Fiona Cl GT/LBKH KT23 235 P10
Fiona Ct ENC/FH * EN2 79 J7
Firbank WGCW * AL8 22 F5
Firbank Cl CAN/RD E16 142 A7
ENC/FH EN2 79 K8
Firbank Dr OXHEY WD19 93 M1
WOKN/KNAP GU21 231 N5
Firbank La WOKN/KNAP GU21 231 N5
Firbank Pl EGH TW20 171 N9
Firbank Rd CRW RM5 104 C6
PECK SE15 160 A8
STALW/RED AL3 38 E2
Fir Cl WOT/HER KT12 197 H7
Fircroft Cl SLN SL2 129 M1
WOKS/MYFD GU22 232 C4
Fircroft Ct WOKS/MYFD * GU22 232 C4
Fircroft Gdns HRW HA1 114 D8
Fircroft Rd CHSGTN KT9 219 L1
TOOT SW17 180 A6
Firdene BRYLDS KT5 199 P8
Fir Dene ORP BR6 206 C10
Fireball Hl ASC SL5 192 C7
Fire Bell Aly SURB KT6 199 K6
Firebell Ms SURB KT6 199 K6
Firecrest Cl HART DA3 211 N3
Firecrest Dr HAMP NW3 117 L8
Firefly Gdns EHAM E6 142 B6
Firfield Rd ADL/WDHM KT15 215 K1
Firfields WEY KT13 216 C4
Fir Grange Av WEY KT13 216 C2
Fir Gv NWMAL KT3 200 C6
Firgrove WOKN/KNAP GU21 231 M5
Firham Park Av HARH RM3 105 P8
Firhill Rd CAT SE6 182 F6
Firlands HORL RH6 280 C3
WEY KT13 216 F3
Firle Cl CRAWE RH10 283 P5
Firle Ct EW * KT17 220 C8
Firmingers Rd ORP BR6 228 C2
Firmin Rd DART DA1 187 K1
Fir Pk HLWW/ROY CM19 46 E4
Fir Rd CHEAM SM3 201 J8
FELT TW13 175 L8
Firs Av FBAR/BDGN N11 98 B7
MORT/ESHN SW14 155 P10
MUSWH N10 118 B1
WDSR SL4 148 E9
Firsby Av CROY/NA CR0 204 C8
Firsby Rd STNW/STAM N16 119 N6
Firs Cl DORK RH4 272 F4
ESH/CLAY KT10 218 D3
FSTH SE23 182 C3
HAT AL10 40 E5
IVER SL0 130 F2
MTCM CR4 202 C2
Firscroft PLMGR N13 99 K4
Firsdene Cl CHERT KT16 214 G3
Firs Dr DTCH/LGLY SL3 130 C10
HEST TW5 153 J6
LOU IG10 82 D5
Firsgrove Crs BRW CM14 106 G5
Firside Gv BFN/LL DA15 185 J4
Firs La PLMGR N13 99 K4
POTB/CUF EN6 59 L9
WCHMH N21 99 K1
Firs Park Av WCHMH N21 99 L2
Firs Park Gdns WCHMH N21 99 L2
The Firs Pk BRKMPK * AL9 41 K9
Firs Rd PUR/KEN CR8 241 J1
First Av ACT W3 136 C10
ADL/WDHM KT15 215 L5
AMSS HP7 69 H6
BXLYHN DA7 163 M6
CHDH RM6 123 M3
DAGE RM10 144 C4
E/WMO/HCT KT8 197 N4
EN EN1 79 N9
GSTN WD25 73 K1
GVW DA11 190 B4
HDN NW4 116 F2
HLW CM20 29 H
HOR/WEW KT19 220 B
HYS/HAR UB3 132 G1
KWD/TDW/WH * KT20 257 J
MNPK E12 122 B
MORT/ESHN SW14 156 B
NKENS W10 8 C
PLSTW E13 141 M
UED N18 100 B
WALTH E17 120 G
WBLY HA9 115 J
WOT/HER KT12 197 J
WTHK RM20 166 F
First Avenue Mandela Av
HLW CM20 28 G1
HLWE CM17 29 L
First Cl E/WMO/HCT KT8 198 B
First Crs SL SL1 129 H
First Cross Rd WHTN TW2 176 D
First Dr WLSDN NW10 135 P
The Firs BF/WBF * KT14 215 N
BRWN CM15 86 F1
BXLY DA5 186 E
CDH/CHF RM16 147 P1
CHESW EN7 61 M
EA W5 135 J
EBED/NFELT * TW14 174 F
EDGW * HA8 96 A
GT/LBKH * KT23 254 A
HARP * AL5 20 C
ORP * BR6 228 B
RGUW GU3 267 N
STAL AL1 38 G1
TRDG/WHET N20 97 N
WGCW AL8 22 F
First Quarter HOR/WEW * KT19 220 B
First St CHEL SW3 15 P
Firstway RYNPK SW20 200 F
First Wy WBLY HA9 115 N
Firs Wk NTHWD HA6 92 E
WFD IG8 101 M
Firsway GUW GU2 249 L
Firswood Av HOR/WEW KT19 220 B
Firth Gdns FUL/PGN SW6 157 H
Firtree Av MTCM CR4 202 B
Fir Tree Av SLN SL2 129 L
WDR/YW UB7 152 B
Fir Tree Cl CRAWW RH11 283 L
EA W5 135 K
ESH/CLAY KT10 218 B
EW KT17 238 F
HHS/BOV HP3 36 B
HOR/WEW KT19 220 C
LHD/OX KT22 237 H
ORP BR6 227 J
ROM RM1 124 E
STRHM/NOR SW16 180 D
Fir Tree Ct BORE WD6 75 L
Fir Tree Gdns CROY/NA CR0 224 F
Fir Tree Gv CAR SM5 222 A
Fir Tree Hl RKW/CH/CXG WD3 72 B
Fir Tree Pl ASHF * TW15 174 B
Fir Tree Rd BNSTD SM7 220 F1
EW KT17 238 E
GU GU1 249 P
HSLWW TW4 153 M1
LHD/OX KT22 237 H
Fir Trees ABR/ST RM4 83 L
Fir Trees Cl BERM/RHTH SE16 140 D1
Fir Tree Wk EN EN1 79 M
REIG RH2 257 N1
Fir Wk EW KT17 220 G
Firwood Av STALE/WH AL4 39 K
Firwood Cl WOKN/KNAP GU21 231 K
Firwood Rd VW GU25 193 K
Fisher Cl CRAWE RH10 283 P
CROY/NA CR0 203 N
GFD/PVL UB6 133 P
KGLGY WD4 54 B
WAB EN9 80 F
WOT/HER KT12 217 J
Fisherdene ESH/CLAY KT10 218 F
Fisherman Cl RCHPK/HAM TW10 177 H
Fishermans Dr
BERM/RHTH SE16 160 C
Fishermans Wy HOD EN11 45 J
Fishermen's Hl GVW DA11 189 N
Fisher Rd KTN/HRWW/W HA3 94 E1
Fishers Cl BUSH WD23 73 M
CHES/WCR EN8 62 F1
Fishers Ct NWCR SE14 160 C
Fishers Hatch HLW CM20 29 H1
Fisher's La CHSWK W4 156 A
Fisher St CAN/RD E16 141 M
RSQ WC1B 11 N
Fisher's Wy BELV DA17 144 D1
Fishers Wd ASC SL5 193 H
Fisherton St STJWD NW8 9 L
Fishery Rd HHW HP1 35 K
Fishguard Sp SL SL1 149 N
Fishguard Wy CAN/RD E16 142 E1
Fishponds Rd HAYES BR2 226 A
TOOT SW17 179 P
Fishpool St STALW/RED AL3 38 B
Fish Street Hl MON * EC3R 13 H
Fisons Rd CAN/RD E16 141 M1
Fitchet Cl CRAWW RH11 283 L
Fitzalan Rd ESH/CLAY KT10 218 D
FNCH N3 117 H
Fitzalan St LBTH SE11 17 P
Fitzgeorge Av NWMAL KT3 200 A1
Fitzgerald Av MORT/ESHN SW14 156 B
Fitzgerald Rd MORT/ESHN SW14 156 A
THDIT KT7 198 F
WAN E11 121 M
Fitzhardinge St MBLAR W1H 10 C
Fitzhugh Gv WAND/EARL SW18 179 N
Fitzilian Av HARH RM3 105 N
Fitzjames Av CROY/NA CR0 203 P
WKENS W14 14 B
Fitzjohn Av BAR EN5 77 H
Fitzjohn Cl RGUE GU4 250 F
Fitzjohn's Av HAMP NW3 117 N1
Fitzmaurice Pl MYFR/PICC W1J 10 F
Fitzneal St ACT W3 136 C
Fitzrobert Pl EGH TW20 172 D
Fitzroy Cl HGT N6 118 A
Fitzroy Crs CHSWK * W4 156 A
Fitzroy Gdns NRWD SE19 181 M1
Fitzroy Ms GTPST W1W 10 G
Fitzroy Pk HGT N6 118 A
Fitzroy Rd CAMTN NW1 4 C
Fitzroy Sq FITZ W1T 10 G
Fitzroy St CAMTN NW1 10 G
Fitzstephen Rd BCTR RM8 123 L1
Fitzwarren Gdns ARCH N19 118 D
Fitzwilliam Av RCH/KEW TW9 155 L
Fitzwilliam Ms CAN/RD E16 141 M1
Fitzwilliam Rd CLAP SW4 158 D
Fitzwilliams Ct HLWE CM17 29 P

itz Wygram Cl HPTN TW12 176 B8
ive Acre CDALE/KGS NW9 96 C10
iveacre Cl THHTH CR7 203 H6
ive Acres CRAWE RH10 283 P5
CSHM HP5 51 J9
HLWS CM18 47 H4
KGLGY WD4 54 A5
LCOL/BKTW AL2 57 J1
ive Acres Av LCOL/BKTW AL2 55 N5
iveash Rd GVW DA11 190 C3
ive Elms Rd DAGW RM9 124 A8
HAYES BR2 205 P10
ive Fields Cl OXHEY WD19 93 N3
ive Oaks HAT * AL10 40 E7
ive Oaks Cl WOKN/KNAP GU21 231 J5
ive Oaks La CHIG IG7 103 P7
ive Ways Jct HDN NW4 96 D9
iveways Rd BRXN/ST SW9 159 H8
ive Wents SWLY BR8 209 H2
ladbury Rd SEVS/STOTM N15 119 L4
ladgate Rd WAN E11 121 K4
lag Cl CROY/NA CR0 204 C8
lagstaff Cl WAB EN9 62 G9
lagstaff Rd WAB EN9 62 G8
he Flags HHNE HP2 36 C6
lag Wk PIN HA5 113 H4
lambard Rd HRW HA1 114 F4
lamborough Cl BH/WHM TN16 243 N5
lamborough Rd RSLP HA4 113 H8
lamborough Sp SL SL1 148 F1
lamborough St POP/IOD E14 140 D8
lamingo Wk RAIN RM13 145 H2
lamstead End Rd
CHES/WCR EN8 62 A4
lamstead Gdns DAGW RM9 143 M2
lamstead Rd DAGW RM9 143 M2
lamsted Av WBLY HA9 135 M1
lamsteed Rd CHARL SE7 162 B4
lanchford Rd REIG RH2 256 G10
SHB W12 156 C2
landers Crs TOOT SW17 180 A10
landers Rd CHSWK W4 156 B3
EHAM E6 142 C4
landers Wy HOM E9 140 C1
lank St WCHPL E1 13 N7
lash La ENC/FH EN2 79 K3
lask Wk HAMP NW3 117 M9
latfield Rd HHS/BOV HP3 36 B8
launden Bottom CSHM HP5 52 C10
launden Hl HHS/BOV HP3 52 C9
launden La HHS/BOV HP3 52 E8
RKW/CH/CXG WD3 53 H9
lavell Ms GNWCH SE10 161 K4
lavian Cl STALW/RED AL3 38 F7
laxen Cl CHING E4 100 G4
laxen Rd CHING E4 100 G4
laxley Rd MRDN SM4 201 L6
laxman Rd CMBW SE5 159 J8
laxman Ter STPAN WC1H 5 K10
laxton Rd WOOL/PLUM SE18 162 G7
lecker Cl STAN HA7 94 E6
leece Dr UED N18 99 P5
leece Rd SURB KT6 199 H8
leece Wk HOLWY N7 5 M1
leeming Cl WALTH E17 100 E10
leeming Rd WALTH E17 100 E10
leet Av RDART DA2 188 B4
UPMR RM14 126 C4
leet Cl E/WMO/HCT KT8 197 N5
RSLP HA4 112 D4
UPMR RM14 126 C4
leetdale Pde RDART * DA2 188 B4
leethall Gv CDH/CHF RM16 147 M10
leet Pl STP EC4M 12 C5
leet Rd GVW DA11 189 P6
HAMP NW3 117 P10
RDART DA2 188 B4
leetside E/WMO/HCT KT8 197 N5
leet Sq FSBYW WC1X 5 N10
leet St EMB EC4Y 12 B6
leet Street Hl BETH E2 13 N2
leet Ter CAT * SE6 183 H3
leetway EGH TW20 194 F3
Fleetwood Cl CAN/RD E16 142 A7
CHSGTN KT9 219 J4
CROY/NA CR0 203 N10
CSTG HP8 89 N3
KWD/TDW/WH KT20 238 G6
Fleetwood Ct BF/WBF KT14 215 K9
Fleetwood Rd NWMAL KT3 199 N3
SLN SL2 129 L10
WLSDN NW10 116 D10
Fleetwood Sq NWMAL KT3 199 N3
Fleetwood St STNW/STAM N16 119 M7
Fleetwood Wy OXHEY WD19 93 K5
Fleming Cl CHESW EN7 61 P2
MV/WKIL W9 8 E2
Fleming Ct CROY/NA CR0 223 H2
Fleming Crs HERT/WAS SG14 24 G5
Fleming Gdns TIL RM18 168 F7
Fleming Md WIM/MER SW19 179 P10
Fleming Rd CDH/CHF RM16 167 H3
GFD/PVL UB6 134 A8
WALW SE17 18 D9
Flemings RBRW/HUT CM13 107 H7
Fleming Wk CDALE/KGS * NW9 96 B10
Fleming Wy CRAWE RH10 283 P3
ISLW TW7 154 E9
THMD SE28 143 N9
Flemish Flds CHERT KT16 195 K7
Flemming Av RSLP HA4 113 J6
Flempton Rd LEY E10 120 D6
Fletcher Cl CHERT KT16 214 G3
CRAWE RH10 283 P9
EHAM E6 142 E9
Fletcher La LEY E10 121 H5
Fletcher Rd CHERT KT16 214 G3
CHIG IG7 103 J6
CHSWK W4 155 P2
Fletchers Cl HAYES BR2 205 N4
Fletcher St WCHPL E1 13 P7
Fletcher Wy HHNE HP2 35 M4
Fletching Rd CHARL SE7 162 A5
CLPT E5 120 B8
Fletton Rd FBAR/BDGN N11 98 F8
Fleur De Lis St WCHPL E1 13 L2
Flexford Rd RGUW GU3 266 A1
Flexley Wd WGCE AL7 23 J2
Flex Meadow HLWW/ROY CM19 46 B2
Flexmere Rd TOTM N17 99 L9
Flight Ap CDALE/KGS * NW9 96 C9
Flimwell Cl BMLY BR1 183 K8
Flinders Cl STAL AL1 38 F8
Flint Cl BNSTD SM7 221 L10
CRAWE RH10 284 C10
GT/LBKH KT23 254 B2
ORP BR6 227 J3
REDH RH1 258 A9
Flint Cottages LHD/OX * KT22 236 G7
Flint Down Cl STMC/STPC * BR5 207 K1
Flint Hl DORK RH4 272 G4
Flint Hill Cl DORK RH4 272 G5
Flintlock Cl STWL/WRAY TW19 151 K10
Flintmill Crs BKHTH/KID SE3 162 B8
Flinton St WALW SE17 19 K7
Flint St WALW SE17 19 H6
WTHK RM20 166 G5
Flint Wy STALW/RED AL3 38 B2
Flitcroft St LSQ/SEVD WC2H 11 K6
The Floats SEV TN13 246 F7
Flock Mill Pl WAND/EARL SW18 179 L4
Flockton St BERM/RHTH * SE16 19 N2
BERM/RHTH SE16 19 N1
Flodden Rd CMBW SE5 159 K7
Flood La TWK * TW1 176 F4
Flood St CHEL SW3 15 P8
Flood Wk CHEL SW3 15 P9
Flora Cl POP/IOD E14 140 G8
Flora Gdns CHDH RM6 123 M4
CROY/NA CR0 225 H7
Flora Gv STAL AL1 38 E7
Floral Dr LCOL/BKTW AL2 57 J2
Floral Pl IS N1 119 L10
Floral St COVGDN WC2E 11 M7
Flora St BELV DA17 164 A4
Florence Av ADL/WDHM KT15 215 K7
ENC/FH EN2 79 K7
MRDN SM4 201 M5
Florence Cl GSTN WD25 73 H1
HCH RM12 125 M7
HLWE CM17 47 M3
WOT/HER KT12 197 J7
WTHK RM20 167 K5
Florence Ct WAN E11 121 N2
Florence Dr ENC/FH EN2 79 K7
Florence Gdns CHSWK W4 155 P5
STA TW18 173 L10
Florence Rd ABYW SE2 163 M2
BECK BR3 204 C2
BMLY BR1 205 M1
CHSWK W4 156 A2
EA W5 135 K9
EHAM E6 141 P3
FELT TW13 175 J4
FSBYPK N4 118 G5
KUTN/CMB KT2 177 L10
NWCR SE14 160 E7
NWDGN UB2 153 L3
PLSTW E13 141 M4
SAND/SEL CR2 223 L5
WIM/MER SW19 179 L9
WOT/HER KT12 197 J7
Florence St CAN/RD E16 141 L6
HDN NW4 116 F2
IS N1 6 C4
Florence Ter NWCR SE14 160 E7
Florence Vls HGT * N6 118 C5
Florence Wy BAL SW12 180 A4
WOKN/KNAP GU21 231 H4
Florfield Rd HACK E8 140 A1
Florian Av SUT SM1 221 N1
Florian Rd PUT/ROE SW15 157 H10
Florida Cl BUSH WD23 94 C3
Florida Rd RGUE GU4 268 B6
THHTH CR7 203 J1
Florida St BETH E2 7 P10
Florin Ct UED N18 99 M5
Floriston Av HGDN/ICK UB10 132 D2
Floriston Cl STAN HA7 94 G9
Floriston Gdns STAN HA7 94 G9
Floss St PUT/ROE SW15 156 F8
Flower Crs CHERT KT16 214 E3
Flower & Dean Wk WCHPL E1 13 M4
Flowerfield RSEV TN14 246 G3
Flowerhill Wy MEO DA13 190 B10
Flower La GDST RH9 260 C5
MLHL NW7 96 C6
Flowers Cl CRICK NW2 116 D8
Flowers Ms ARCH N19 118 D7
Flower Wk GUW GU2 267 P3
Floyd Rd CHARL SE7 161 P4
Floyds La WOKS/MYFD GU22 233 K2
Fludyer St LEW SE13 161 K10
Flux's La EPP CM16 65 K9
The Flyers Wy BH/WHM TN16 262 G2
Fogerty Cl WAB EN9 80 G3
Fold Cft HLW CM20 28 D10
Foley Cl BEAC HP9 88 B7
Foley Ms ESH/CLAY KT10 218 D3
Foley Rd BH/WHM TN16 244 A4
ESH/CLAY KT10 218 D4
Foley St GTPST W1W 10 G4
Folgate St WCHPL E1 13 K3
Foliot St ACT W3 136 C8
Folkes La UPMR RM14 126 E3
Folkestone Ct DTCH/LGLY SL3 150 D4
Folkestone Rd EHAM E6 142 D4
UED N18 99 P5
WALTH E17 120 G2
Folkingham La CDALE/KGS NW9 96 A9
Folkington Cnr
NFNCH/WDSP N12 97 J6
Follet Cl WDSR SL4 171 N2
Follett Dr ABLGY WD5 54 G7
Follett St POP/IOD E14 141 H8
Folly Av STALW/RED AL3 38 B5
Folly Cl RAD WD7 74 E2
Follyfield Rd BNSTD SM7 221 K10
Folly Flds STALE/WH AL4 20 G1
Folly La RDKG RH5 272 G10
STALW/RED AL3 38 B5
WALTH E17 100 D9
Folly Pathway RAD WD7 74 E1
The Folly HERT/WAS SG14 25 L5
Folly Vw WARE SG12 26 G6
Folly Wall POP/IOD E14 161 H1
Fontaine Rd STRHM/NOR SW16 180 G9
Fontana Cl CRAWE RH10 284 E8
Fontarabia Rd BTSEA SW11 158 B10
Fontayne Av CHIG IG7 102 F5
RAIN RM13 144 F2
ROM RM1 104 F10
Fontenoy Rd TOOT SW17 180 C5
Fonteyne Gdns WFD IG8 102 A10
Fonthill Ms FSBYPK N4 118 G7
Fonthill Rd FSBYPK N4 118 G7
Font Hills EFNCH N2 97 M10
Fontley Wy PUT/ROE SW15 178 D3
Fontmell Cl ASHF TW15 174 B8
STALW/RED AL3 38 D3
Fontmell Pk ASHF TW15 174 A8
Fontwell Cl KTN/HRWW/W HA3 94 D8
NTHLT UB5 133 P1
Fontwell Dr HAYES BR2 206 E5
Fontwell Park Gdns HCH RM12 125 M9
Fontwell Rd CRAWE RH10 284 B10
Foord Cl RDART DA2 188 D5
Football La HRW HA1 114 E6
Footbury Hill Rd ORP BR6 207 K7
The Footpath PUT/ROE * SW15 178 D1
Foots Cray High St SCUP DA14 185 M9
Foots Cray La BXLY DA5 185 M4
Footscray Rd ELTH/MOT SE9 184 D2
Forbes Av POTB/CUF EN6 59 N9
Forbes Cl CRICK NW2 116 D8
HCH RM12 125 J6
Forbes St WCHPL E1 13 P6
Forbes Wy RSLP HA4 113 J7
Forburg Rd STNW/STAM N16 119 P6
Force Green La BH/WHM TN16 244 G10
Fordbridge Rd ASHF TW15 173 P9
SHPTN TW17 196 F6
SUN TW16 197 H5
Ford Cl ASHF TW15 173 P9
BUSH WD23 74 B8
HRW HA1 114 C5
RAIN RM13 144 G2
SHPTN TW17 196 B5
THHTH CR7 203 J6
Fordcroft Rd STMC/STPC BR5 207 L5
Forde Av BMLY BR1 205 P3
Fordel Rd CAT SE6 183 J4
Ford End DEN/HRF UB9 111 J7
WFD IG8 101 N7
Fordham Cl EMPK RM11 125 P5
Fordham Rd EBAR EN4 77 N7
Fordham St WCHPL E1 13 P5
Fordhook Av ACT W3 135 L9
Fordingbridge Cl CHERT * KT16 195 L8
Fordingley Rd MV/WKIL W9 2 D10
Fordington Rd HGT N6 118 A2
Ford La IVER SL0 131 K8
RAIN RM13 144 G2
Fordmill Rd CAT SE6 182 F5
Ford Rd ASHF TW15 174 A7
BOW E3 140 D4
CHERT KT16 195 L8
CHOB/PIR GU24 213 H6
CHOB/PIR GU24 230 E1
DAGE RM10 144 B2
GVW DA11 189 N1
WOKS/MYFD GU22 232 E6
Ford's Gv WCHMH N21 99 K2
Fords Park Rd CAN/RD E16 141 M8
Ford Sq WCHPL E1 140 A7
Ford St BOW E3 140 D3
CAN/RD E16 141 L8
Fordwater Rd CHERT KT16 195 L8
Fordwich Cl HERT/WAS SG14 25 H5
ORP BR6 207 J7
Fordwich Hl HERT/WAS SG14 25 H5
Fordwich Ri HERT/WAS SG14 25 H5
Fordwich Rd WGCW * AL8 22 F6
WGCW AL8 22 F6
Fordwych Rd CRICK NW2 117 H10
Fordyce Cl EMPK RM11 125 P5
Fordyce Rd LEW SE13 183 H2
Fordyke Rd BCTR RM8 123 P7
Forebury Av SBW CM21 30 A1
The Forebury SBW CM21 30 A1
Forefield LCOL/BKTW AL2 55 P3
Foreland Ct HDN NW4 97 H9
Foreland St WOOL/PLUM SE18 162 G3
Forelands Wy CSHM HP5 51 H8
Foremark Cl BARK/HLT IG6 103 J7
Foreshore DEPT SE8 160 E3
Forest Ap CHING E4 101 K1
WFD IG8 101 L8
Forest Av CHIG IG7 102 D6
CHING E4 101 K1
HHS/BOV HP3 35 N8
Forest Cl CHST BR7 206 D1
EHSLY KT24 252 G1
WAB EN9 81 N3
WAN E11 121 L3
WFD IG8 101 N5
WOKS/MYFD GU22 232 G1
Forest Ct CHING E4 101 L2
WAN E11 121 K2
Forest Crs ASHTD KT21 237 M2
Forestdale STHGT/OAK N14 98 E5
Forest Dr EPP CM16 83 H2
HAYES BR2 206 B10
KWD/TDW/WH KT20 239 K7
MNPK E12 122 A8
SUN TW16 174 G10
WFD IG8 101 J8
Forest Dr East WAN E11 121 J5
Forest Dr West WAN E11 121 H5
Forest Edge BKHH IG9 101 P4
Forester Rd CRAWE RH10 283 P9
PECK SE15 160 A10
Foresters Cl CHESW EN7 61 M3
WLGTN SM6 222 E4
WOKN/KNAP GU21 231 L4
Foresters Crs BXLYHN DA7 164 C10
Foresters Dr WALTH E17 121 J2
WLGTN SM6 222 E4
Forestfield CRAWE RH10 284 C9
Forest Gdns TOTM N17 99 N10
Forest Ga CDALE/KGS NW9 116 B2
Forest Gld CHING E4 101 K6
EPP CM16 65 M7
WAN E11 121 K4
Forest Gv HACK E8 7 L2
Forest Hill Rd EDUL SE22 182 A2
Forestholme Cl FSTH * SE23 182 B5
Forest La CHIG IG7 102 D6
EHSLY KT24 234 G10
FSTGT E7 121 M10
RAD WD7 56 G7
Forest Mount Rd WFD IG8 101 J8
Forest Pk WDSR * SL4 170 D2
Fore St BARB EC2Y 12 G4
BRKMPK AL9 40 F3
ED N9 99 P5
HERT/WAS SG14 25 L5
HLWE CM17 29 M7
PIN HA5 113 H3
Forest Rdg BECK BR3 204 F3
HAYES BR2 226 B1
Forest Ri WALTH E17 121 J1
Forest Rd BARK/HLT IG6 103 L7
CHEAM SM3 201 K8
CHES/WCR EN8 62 C5
ED N9 100 A2
EHSLY KT24 235 H9
ERITH DA8 165 H7
FELT TW13 175 K5
FSTGT E7 121 M9
GSTN WD25 55 J9
HACK E8 7 N2
LOU IG10 82 A8
PEND EN3 80 D2
RCH/KEW TW9 155 M6
ROMW/RG RM7 124 C1
WALTH E17 120 B2
WAN E11 121 J5
WDSR SL4 148 C8
WDSR SL4 170 C3
WFD IG8 101 M4
WOKS/MYFD GU22 232 G1
Forest Side BKHH IG9 101 N2
CHING E4 101 L1
EPP CM16 64 G9
FSTGT E7 121 N9
WPK KT4 200 C8
Forest St FSTGT E7 121 M10
The Forest WALTH E17 121 K2
Forest Vw CHING E4 81 J10
CRAWE RH10 284 A10
WAN E11 121 L5
Forest View Av LEY E10 121 J3
Forest View Rd MNPK E12 122 B9
WALTH E17 101 H9
Forest Wk BUSH WD23 73 N5
Forest Wy ASHTD KT21 237 M3
BFN/LL DA15 184 G3
HLWE CM17 30 C10
HLWE CM17 47 L5
LOU IG10 82 B7
STMC/STPC BR5 207 J5
WAB EN9 64 B7
WFD IG8 101 N5
Forfar Rd BTSEA SW11 158 B7
WDGN N22 99 J9
Forge Av COUL/CHIP CR5 241 H6
Forge Bridge La COUL/CHIP CR5 240 C8
Forge Cl HAYES BR2 205 M8
KGLGY WD4 53 K7
Forge Cottages EA * W5 135 J10
Forge Dr ESH/CLAY KT10 218 F4
SLN SL2 129 H1
Forge End LCOL/BKTW AL2 55 P2
WOKN/KNAP GU21 232 B3
Forgefield BH/WHM TN16 244 A2
Forge La BELMT SM2 221 H4
CRAWE * RH10 284 B6
EYN DA4 210 B4
FELT TW13 175 M8
GVE DA12 191 J5
GVE DA12 191 P8
NTHWD HA6 92 F8
SUN TW16 197 H3
Forge Ms SUN * TW16 197 H3
Forge Pl CAMTN NW1 4 D2
GVE * DA12 191 J4
Forge Rd CRAWE RH10 284 B6
The Forge RDKG * RH6 279 H8
Forge Wy RSEV TN14 228 G7
Forge Wd CRAWE RH10 284 E2
Forman Pl STNW/STAM N16 119 N9
Formby Av KTN/HRWW/W HA3 115 H1
Formby Cl DTCH/LGLY SL3 150 F3
Form Cl RAD WD7 57 K6
Formosa St MV/WKIL W9 9 H2
Formunt Cl CAN/RD E16 141 L7
Forres Cl HOD EN11 44 F1
Forres Gdns GLDGN NW11 117 K4
Forrester Pth SYD SE26 182 B7
Forresters Dr WGCE AL7 23 M6
Forrest Gdns STRHM/NOR SW16 202 G3
Forris Av HYS/HAR UB3 132 G10
Forset St MBLAR W1H 9 P5
Forstal Cl HAYES BR2 205 M3
Forster Cl CHING E4 101 J8
Forster Rd BECK BR3 204 D3
BRXS/STRHM SW2 180 F3
TOTM N17 119 N1
WALTH E17 120 D4
Forsters Cl CHDH RM6 124 A4
Forston St IS N1 6 F7
Forsyte Crs NRWD SE19 203 M1
Forsyth Gdns WALW SE17 18 D9
Forsythia Cl IL IG1 122 E10
Forsythia Pl GU * GU1 249 P8
Forsyth Pl EN EN1 79 M9
Forsyth Rd WOKN/KNAP GU21 214 F10
Forterie Gdns GDMY/SEVK IG3 123 K8
Fortescue Av WHTN TW2 176 B6
Fortescue Rd EDGW HA8 96 A9
WEY KT13 216 A1
WIM/MER SW19 179 N10
Fortess Gv KTTN NW5 118 D10
Fortess Rd KTTN NW5 118 C10
Fortess Wk KTTN NW5 118 C10
Forthbridge Rd BTSEA SW11 158 B10
Forth Rd UPMR RM14 126 C4
Fortin Cl SOCK/AV RM15 146 F9
Fortin Wy SOCK/AV RM15 146 F9
Fortis Cl CAN/RD E16 141 P8
Fortis Gn EFNCH N2 118 A1
Fortis Green Av EFNCH N2 118 B1
Fortis Green Rd MUSWH N10 118 B1
Fortismere Av MUSWH N10 118 B1
Fort La REIG RH2 257 L6
Fortnam Rd ARCH N19 118 E7
Fortnums Acre STAN HA7 94 E7
Fort Rd GU GU1 268 B3
KWD/TDW/WH KT20 255 N7
NTHLT UB5 133 P2
RSEV TN14 246 D1
STHWK SE1 19 M6
TIL RM18 168 E10
Fortrose Gdns
BRXS/STRHM SW2 180 F4
Fortrye Cl GVW DA11 190 B5
Fort St CAN/RD E16 141 N10
WCHPL * E1 13 K4
Fortuna Cl HOLWY N7 5 P1
Fortunegate Rd WLSDN NW10 136 B3
Fortune Green Rd
KIL/WHAMP NW6 117 K10
Fortune La BORE WD6 75 J10
Fortunes Md NTHLT UB5 133 M1
The Fortunes HLWS CM18 47 J3
Fortune St STLK EC1Y 12 F2
Fortune Wy WLSDN NW10 136 D5
Forty Acre La CAN/RD E16 141 M7
Forty Av WBLY HA9 115 L8
Forty Cl WBLY HA9 115 L8
Fortyfoot Rd LHD/OX KT22 237 J8
Forty Green Rd BEAC HP9 88 A7
Forty Hl EN EN1 79 N3
Forty La WBLY HA9 115 N7
Forum Magnum Sq STHWK SE1 17 N1
Forum Pl HAT * AL10 40 D3
Forumside EDGW HA8 95 M7
The Forum E/WMO/HCT KT8 198 A4
Forum Wy EDGW HA8 95 M7
Forval Cl MTCM CR4 202 A5
Forward Dr KTN/HRWW/W HA3 114 E2
Fosbury Ms BAY/PAD W2 9 H8
Foscote Ms MV/WKIL W9 8 F2
Foscote Rd HDN NW4 116 F4
Foskett Rd FUL/PGN SW6 157 J8
Foss Av CROY/NA CR0 223 H2
Fossdene Rd CHARL SE7 161 N4
Fossdyke Cl YEAD UB4 133 M7
Fosse Wy BF/WBF KT14 215 J9
WEA W13 134 F7
Fossil Rd LEW SE13 160 F9
Fossington Rd BELV DA17 163 N3
Foss Rd TOOT SW17 179 N7
Fossway BCTR RM8 123 M7
Foster Av WDSR SL4 148 D9
Foster Cl CHES/WCR EN8 62 C6
Fosterdown GDST RH9 260 A5
Foster La CITYW EC2V 12 E5
Foster Rd ACT W3 136 B9
CHSWK W4 156 A4
HHW HP1 35 L8
PLSTW E13 141 M6
Fosters Cl CHST BR7 184 C8
SWFD E18 101 N9
Fosters Gv BFOR GU20 212 A1
Fosters La WOKN/KNAP GU21 231 H3
Fosters Pth SLN SL2 128 E6
Foster St HDN NW4 116 F2
HLWE CM17 48 A3
Foster Wk HDN NW4 116 F2
Fothergill Cl PLSTW E13 141 M3
Fothergill Dr WCHMH N21 78 F9
Fotheringay Gdns SL SL1 128 F9
Fotheringham Rd EN EN1 79 N8
Fotherley Rd RKW/CH/CXG WD3 91 J3
Foulden Rd STNW/STAM N16 119 N9
Foulden Ter STNW/STAM N16 119 N9
Foulis Ter SKENS SW7 15 L6
Foulser Rd TOOT SW17 180 A6
Foulsham Rd THHTH CR7 203 K3
Founders Gdns NRWD SE19 181 K10
Founders Rd HOD EN11 26 G10
Foundry Cl BERM/RHTH SE16 140 D10
Foundry Ct CHERT KT16 195 K7
Foundry La DTCH/LGLY SL3 150 E9
Foundry Ms CAMTN NW1 11 H1
Foundry Pl WAND/EARL * SW18 179 L3
Fountain Cl UX/CGN UB8 132 D7
Fountain Dr CAR SM5 222 A4
HERT/BAY SG13 25 N4
NRWD SE19 181 N7
Fountain Farm HLWS CM18 47 J3
Fountain Gdns WDSR SL4 149 J9
Fountain Green Sq
BERM/RHTH SE16 19 P2
Fountain Ms HAMP * NW3 4 A1
Fountain Pl BRXN/ST SW9 159 H7
WAB EN9 63 H10
Fountain Rd REDH RH1 275 P2
THHTH CR7 203 K2
TOOT SW17 179 N8
Fountains Av FELT TW13 175 N6
Fountains Cl CRAWW RH11 283 K9
FELT TW13 175 N5
Fountains Crs STHGT/OAK N14 98 F1
Fountain Wk GVW DA11 190 B2
Fountayne Rd SEVS/STOTM N15 119 P2
STNW/STAM N16 119 P7
Fount St VX/NE SW8 158 E6
Four Acres COB KT11 217 M9
GU GU1 250 F8
WGCE AL7 23 H7
Fouracres PEND EN3 80 D5
Fouracres Dr HHS/BOV HP3 36 A8
The Four Acres SBW CM21 30 B1
Fouracres Wk HHS/BOV HP3 36 A8
Fourland Wk EDGW HA8 95 P7
Four Limes STALE/WH AL4 21 J3
Fournier St WCHPL E1 13 M3
Four Oaks BRW * CM14 107 K4
Four Seasons Cl BOW E3 140 F4
Four Seasons Crs CHEAM SM3 201 J9
Fourteenth Av
KWD/TDW/WH * KT20 257 J2
Fourth Av GSTN WD25 73 L1
HLW CM20 28 F10
HLWW/ROY CM19 46 D1
HYS/HAR UB3 132 G10
KWD/TDW/WH * KT20 257 J2
MNPK E12 122 C9
NKENS W10 8 A1
ROMW/RG RM7 124 D6
WTHK RM20 166 F5
Fourth Cross Rd WHTN TW2 176 C5
Fourth Dr COUL/CHIP CR5 240 E2
Fourth Wy WBLY HA9 115 N9
The Four Tubs BUSH WD23 94 C1
The Four Wents COB KT11 217 J9
The Four Wents CHING E4 101 J3
Fovant Cl HARP AL5 20 B5
Fowey Av REDBR IG4 122 A3
Fowey Cl WAP E1W 140 A10
Fowler Cl BTSEA SW11 157 N9
CRAWE RH10 284 D9
SCUP DA14 185 P8
Fowler Rd BARK/HLT IG6 103 M6
FSTGT E7 121 M9
IS N1 6 D5
Fowlers Md CHOB/PIR GU24 213 K5
Fowler's Wk EA W5 135 J6
Fowley Cl CHES/WCR EN8 62 E10
Fowley Mead Pk
CHES/WCR * EN8 62 E10
Fownes St BTSEA SW11 157 P9
Foxacre CTHM CR3 241 M8
Foxberry Rd BROCKY SE4 160 D10
Foxborough Cl DTCH/LGLY SL3 150 D4
Foxborough Gdns BROCKY SE4 182 F2
Foxborough Hill Rd SHGR GU5 268 B9
Foxbourne Rd TOOT SW17 180 B5
Fox Burrow Rd CHIG IG7 103 N5
Foxburrows Av GUW GU2 249 L10
Foxbury Av CHST BR7 184 G9
Foxbury Cl BMLY BR1 183 N9
ORP BR6 227 K2
Foxbury Dr ORP BR6 227 K3
Foxbury Rd BMLY BR1 183 N9
Fox Cl BORE WD6 75 J10
BUSH WD23 74 A9
CAN/RD E16 141 M7
CRAWW RH11 283 L5
CRW RM5 104 C6
ORP BR6 227 K2
WCHPL E1 140 B6
WEY KT13 216 E2
WOKS/MYFD GU22 232 G1
Fox Covert LHD/OX KT22 236 C10
Fox Covert Cl ASC SL5 192 B5
Foxcroft STAL AL1 38 F8
Foxcroft Rd WOOL/PLUM SE18 162 E7
Foxdell NTHWD HA6 92 E7
Foxdells HERT/WAS SG14 24 D8
Foxdell Wy CFSP/GDCR SL9 90 B6
Foxearth Cl BH/WHM TN16 244 B4
Foxearth Rd SAND/SEL CR2 224 B6
Foxearth Sp SAND/SEL CR2 224 B5
Foxenden Rd GU GU1 250 B10
Foxes Cl HERT/BAY SG13 26 A5

Foxes Dl BKHTH/KID SE3 161 M9
HAYES BR2 205 J3
Foxes Dr CHESW EN7 61 N5
Foxes Gn CDH/CHF RM16 168 D1
Foxes La POTB/CUF EN6 60 F4
Foxes Pde WAB * EN9 63 H9
Foxes Pth RGUE GU4 250 C2
Foxfield Cl NTHWD HA6 92 G7
Foxfield Rd ORP BR6 206 G9
Foxglove Cl HAT AL10 40 E5
HOD EN11 27 H10
STHL UB1 133 M9
STWL/WRAY TW19 173 N4
Foxglove Dr WAN E11 121 P2
Foxglove Gdns PUR/KEN CR8 222 F7
RGUE GU4 250 F8
Foxglove La CHSGTN KT9 219 M1
Foxglove Rd ROMW/RG RM7 124 F7
SOCK/AV RM15 147 H8
The Foxgloves HHW HP1 35 H7
Foxglove St ACT W3 136 C9
Foxglove Wy MTCM CR4 202 B7
Foxgrove STHGT/OAK N14 98 F4
Fox Gv WOT/HER KT12 197 J7
Foxgrove Av BECK BR3 182 C10
Foxgrove Dr WOKN/KNAP GU21 232 C1
Foxgrove Pth OXHEY WD19 93 L6
Foxgrove Rd BECK BR3 182 C10
Foxhall Rd UPMR RM14 126 B10
Foxham Rd ARCH N19 118 E8
Foxhanger Gdns
WOKS/MYFD GU22 232 D2
Fox Hatch BRWN CM15 86 D4
Foxherne DTCH/LGLY SL3 149 P1
Fox Hl NRWD SE19 181 N10
Foxhill WATN WD24 73 H2
Fox Hill Gdns NRWD SE19 181 N10
Foxhills WOKN/KNAP GU21 231 P4
Foxhills Cl CHERT KT16 214 E3
Fox Hills Rd CHERT KT16 214 D2
Foxhole Rd ELTH/MOT SE9 184 B1
Foxholes WEY KT13 216 E2
Foxholes Av HERT/BAY SG13 25 P5
Fox Hollow Cl WOOL/PLUM SE18 163 H4
Foxhollow Dr SLN SL2 109 H10
Fox Hollow Dr WELL DA16 163 N9
Foxhollows HAT AL10 40 E2
Foxholt Gdns WLSDN NW10 135 P2
Foxhome Cl CHST BR7 184 D9
Fox House Rd BELV DA17 164 C3
Fox & Knot St FARR * EC1M 12 D3
Foxlake Rd BF/WBF KT14 216 A8
Foxlands Cl GSTN WD25 54 C10
Foxlands Crs DAGE RM10 124 D10
Foxlands Rd DAGE RM10 124 D10
Fox La EA W5 135 K7
GT/LBKH KT23 235 N10
HAYES BR2 225 N2
PLMGR N13 98 G3
REIG RH2 257 L7
Fox La North CHERT KT16 195 J8
Fox La South CHERT * KT16 195 J8
Foxlees ALP/SUD HA0 114 F9
Foxley Cl HACK E8 119 P10
REDH RH1 276 B5
Foxley Gdns PUR/KEN CR8 223 J9
Foxley Hill Rd PUR/KEN CR8 223 H8
Foxley La PUR/KEN CR8 222 F6
Foxley Rd CMBW SE5 159 H6
PUR/KEN CR8 241 J1
THHTH CR7 203 J4
Foxleys OXHEY WD19 93 M4
Foxley Sq BRXN/ST * SW9 159 J6
Fox Manor Wy WTHK RM20 166 G5
Foxmead Cl ENC/FH EN2 78 G7
Foxmore St BTSEA SW11 158 A7
Foxoak Hl WEY KT13 216 F6
Foxon Cl CTHM CR3 241 M7
Foxon La CTHM CR3 241 L7
Foxon Lane Gdns CTHM CR3 241 M7
Fox Rd CAN/RD E16 141 L7
DTCH/LGLY SL3 150 A3
Fox's La BRKMPK AL9 41 H10
Foxton Gv MTCM CR4 201 N2
Foxton Rd HOD EN11 44 E3
WTHK RM20 167 J5
Foxwarren ESH/CLAY KT10 218 E5
Foxwell St BROCKY SE4 160 D9
Foxwood Cha WAB EN9 81 H2
Foxwood Cl FELT TW13 175 J6
MLHL NW7 96 B5
Foxwood Green Cl EN EN1 79 M10
Foxwood Gv GVW DA11 190 B4
ORP BR6 227 M6
Foxwood Rd BKHTH/KID SE3 161 L10
RDART DA2 188 G6
Foxwood Wy HART DA3 211 P2
Foyle Dr SOCK/AV RM15 146 F7
Foyle Rd BKHTH/KID SE3 161 L5
TOTM N17 99 P9
Frailey Cl WOKS/MYFD GU22 232 E2
Frailey Hl WOKS/MYFD GU22 232 E2
Framewood Rd DTCH/LGLY SL3 129 P2
Framfield Cl CRAWW RH11 283 K5
NFNCH/WDSP N12 97 K5
Framfield Rd HBRY N5 119 J10
HNWL W7 134 E8
MTCM CR4 180 B10
Framlingham Crs ELTH/MOT SE9 184 B7
Frampton Cl BELMT SM2 221 K4
Frampton Park Rd HOM E9 140 B1
Frampton Rd EPP CM16 65 K4
HSLWW TW4 175 M1
POTB/CUF EN6 59 M6
Frampton St HERT/WAS SG14 25 L5
STJWD NW8 9 M2
Francemary Rd LEW SE13 182 F1
Frances Gdns SOCK/AV RM15 146 E8
Frances Rd CHING E4 100 F7
WDSR SL4 149 H9
Frances St CSHM HP5 51 H6
WOOL/PLUM SE18 162 C3
Franche Court Rd TOOT SW17 179 M6
Franchise St CSHM HP5 51 H6
Francis Av BXLYHN DA7 164 B8
FELT TW13 175 H6
IL IG1 122 G7
STALW/RED AL3 38 C3
Francis Barber Cl
STRHM/NOR * SW16 180 G7
Franciscan Rd TOOT SW17 180 B7
Francis Chichester Cl ASC SL5 192 A5
Francis Chichester Wy
BTSEA * SW11 158 B7
Francis Cl HOR/WEW KT19 220 A1
SHPTN TW17 196 B4
Francisco Cl CDH/CHF RM16 167 H2
Francis Ct GUW * GU2 249 N8
Francis Gv WIM/MER SW19 179 J9
Francis Ms LEE/GVPK * SE12 183 L2
Francis Rd CROY/NA CR0 203 J7
CTHM CR3 241 L8
DART DA1 187 L1
EFNCH * N2 118 A2
GFD/PVL UB6 135 H4
HRW HA1 114 F3
HSLWW TW4 153 L8
LEY E10 121 H7
PIN HA5 113 K3
STMC/STPC BR5 207 N3
WARE SG12 26 C1
WATW WD18 73 J8
WLGTN SM6 222 D3
Francis St SRTFD E15 121 K10
WEST SW1P 17 H5
Francis Ter ARCH N19 118 D8
Francis Wk IS N1 5 N5
Francis Wy SL SL1 128 C9
Francklyn Gdns EDGW HA8 95 M4
Francombe Gdns ROM RM1 125 H4
Franconia Rd CLAP SW4 180 D1
Frank Burton Cl CHARL SE7 161 N4
Frank Dixon Cl DUL SE21 181 M3
Frank Dixon Wy DUL SE21 181 M4
Frankfurt Rd HNHL SE24 181 K1
Frankham St DEPT SE8 160 F6
Frankland Cl BERM/RHTH SE16 160 A2
RKW/CH/CXG WD3 92 B1
WFD IG8 101 P6
Frankland Rd CHING E4 100 F6
RKW/CH/CXG WD3 72 C10
SKENS SW7 15 L4
Franklands Dr ADL/WDHM KT15 215 J4
Franklin Av CHESW EN7 61 P6
SLN SL2 128 G7
Franklin Cl HHS/BOV * HP3 35 P9
KUT KT1 199 M3
LEW SE13 160 G7
STALE/WH AL4 40 B8
TRDG/WHET N20 97 M1
WNWD SE27 181 J6
Franklin Ct GUW GU2 249 L10
Franklin Crs MTCM CR4 202 D4
Franklin Rd BXLYHN DA7 163 P7
CRAWE RH10 284 D8
GVE DA12 190 G8
HCH RM12 145 K1
PGE/AN SE20 182 B10
WAT WD17 73 J6
WOT/HER KT12 197 H6
Franklins Ms RYLN/HDSTN HA2 114 B7
Franklin Sq WKENS W14 14 D8
Franklins Rw CHEL * SW3 16 B7
CHEL SW3 16 B7
Franklin St BOW E3 140 G5
SEVS/STOTM N15 119 M4
Franklin Wy CROY/NA CR0 202 F8
Franklyn Crs WDSR SL4 148 C9
Franklyn Gdns BARK/HLT IG6 102 G7
Franklyn Rd WLSDN NW10 136 C2
WOT/HER KT12 197 J6
Frank Martin Ct CHESW EN7 61 P6
Franks Av NWMAL KT3 199 P4
Franksfield SHGR GU5 270 F10
Franks La EYN DA4 210 A5
Franks Rd GUW GU2 249 M7
Frank Sutton Wy SL SL1 129 H9
Franks Wood Av
STMC/STPC BR5 206 E5
Frankswood Av WDR/YW UB7 132 A8
Franlaw Crs PLMGR N13 99 K5
Franmil Rd EMPK RM11 124 G5
Fransfield Gv SYD SE26 182 A6
Franshams BUSH * WD23 94 D3
Frant Cl PGE/AN SE20 182 B10
Franthorne Wy CAT SE6 182 G5
Frant Rd THHTH CR7 203 J5
Fraser Cl BXLY DA5 186 D4
Fraser Rd CHES/WCR EN8 62 D4
ED N9 100 A4
ERITH DA8 164 D4
GFD/PVL UB6 135 H3
LEY E10 120 G3
Fraser St CHSWK W4 156 B4
Frating Crs WFD IG8 101 M7
Frays Av WDR/YW UB7 151 N1
Frays Cl WDR/YW UB7 151 N2
Frayslea UX/CGN UB8 131 M4
Fray's Waye UX/CGN UB8 131 M3
Frazer Av RSLP HA4 113 K10
Frazer Cl ROMW/RG RM7 124 G5
Frean St BERM/RHTH SE16 19 N3
Freda Corbett Cl PECK SE15 159 P6
Frederica Rd CHING E4 101 J1
Frederica St HOLWY N7 5 N3
Frederick Cl BAY/PAD W2 9 P7
SUT SM1 221 J1
Frederick Crs BRXN/ST SW9 159 J6
PEND EN3 80 B6
Frederick Gdns SUT SM1 221 J2
Frederick Pl WOOL/PLUM SE18 162 E4
Frederick Rd RAIN RM13 144 E4
SUT SM1 221 J2
WALW * SE17 18 D8
Frederick Sanger Rd GUW GU2 267 J1
Frederick's Pl LOTH * EC2R 12 G6
NFNCH/WDSP N12 97 M5
Frederick Sq BERM/RHTH SE16 140 D9
Frederick's Rw FSBYE EC1V 6 C9
Frederick St FSBYW WC1X 5 N10
Frederick Ter HACK E8 7 L4
Frederic Ms KTBR * SW1X 16 C2
Frederic St WALTH E17 120 D3
Fredora Av YEAD UB4 132 G6
Freeborne Gdns RAIN RM13 145 H1
Freedom Cl WALTH E17 120 C2
Freedom St BTSEA SW11 158 A8
Freedown La BELMT SM2 221 L9
Freegrove Rd HOLWY N7 118 F10
Freeland Pk HDN NW4 97 H10
Freeland Rd EA W5 135 L9
Freelands Av SAND/SEL CR2 224 C5
Freelands Gv BMLY BR1 205 N1
Freelands Rd BMLY BR1 205 N1
COB KT11 217 J10
Freeling Wy ERITH DA8 165 H7
Freeling St IS * N1 5 M1
Freeman Cl NTHLT UB5 133 M2
SHPTN TW17 196 F4
Freeman Ct CSHM HP5 51 H6
Freeman Dr E/WMO/HCT KT8 197 N4
Freeman Rd GVE DA12 191 H6
MRDN SM4 201 N5
Freemans Cl SLN SL2 129 L1
Freemans La HYS/HAR UB3 132 F9
Freemantle Av PEND EN3 80 C9
Freemantle St WALW SE17 19 J7
Freeman Wy EMPK RM11 125 M4
Freemasons Rd CAN/RD E16 141 N8
CROY/NA CR0 203 M8
Free Prae Rd CHERT KT16 195 K8
Freesia Cl ORP BR6 227 J2
Freesia Dr CHOB/PIR GU24 230 F2
Freestone Yd DTCH/LGLY * SL3 150 G6
Freethorpe Cl NRWD SE19 203 M1
Freezeland Wy HGDN/ICK UB10 132 B1
Freightmaster Est RAIN * RM13 165 H3
Freke Rd BTSEA SW11 158 B9
Fremantle Rd BARK/HLT IG6 102 E10
BELV DA17 164 B3
Fremont St HOM E9 140 B3
Frenchaye ADL/WDHM KT15 215 M2
Frenches Rd REDH RH1 258 C7
The Frenches REDH RH1 258 B8
French Gdns COB KT11 217 K10
French Horn Ct WARE * SG12 26 C2
French Horn La HAT AL10 40 E3
Frenchlands Hatch EHSLY KT24 252 F3
French Pl SDTCH EC2A 7 K10
French's Cl WARE SG12 26 F6
French St SUN TW16 197 K2
French's Wls WOKN/KNAP GU21 231 N3
Frenchum Gdns SL SL1 128 D10
Frendsbury Rd BROCKY SE4 160 D10
Frensham CHESW EN7 61 N3
Frensham Cl STHL UB1 133 N6
Frensham Dr CROY/NA CR0 225 H4
PUT/ROE SW15 178 D6
Frensham Rd BFN/LL DA15 184 G5
PUR/KEN CR8 223 J10
Frensham St PECK SE15 19 P10
Frensham Wk SLN SL2 109 H10
Frensham Wy EW KT17 238 F2
Frere St BTSEA SW11 157 P8
Freshborough Ct GU GU1 268 C1
Freshfield Av HACK E8 7 L3
Freshfield Cl CRAWE RH10 284 B8
LEW SE13 161 J10
Freshfield Dr STHGT/OAK N14 98 C1
Freshfield Flats
KWD/TDW/WH * KT20 257 J3
Freshfields CROY/NA CR0 204 E7
Freshfields Av UPMR RM14 126 A10
Freshford St TOOT SW17 179 M6
Freshmount Gdns
HOR/WEW KT19 219 N7
Freshwater Cl TOOT SW17 180 B9
Freshwater Rd BCTR RM8 123 N6
TOOT SW17 180 B9
Freshwaters HLW CM20 29 H10
Freshwell Av CHDH RM6 123 M2
Fresh Wharf Rd BARK IG11 142 E3
Freshwood Cl BECK BR3 204 G1
Freshwood Wy WLGTN SM6 222 D5
Freston Gdns EBAR EN4 78 B9
Freston Pk FNCH N3 97 J10
Freston Rd NKENS W10 136 G9
Freta Rd BXLYHS DA6 186 A1
Fretherne Chambers WGCW * AL8 22 G5
Fretherne Rd WGCW AL8 22 G5
Frewin Rd WAND/EARL SW18 179 N4
Friar Ms WNWD SE27 181 J6
Friar Rd STMC/STPC BR5 207 K5
YEAD UB4 133 L6
Friar's Av BRWN CM15 107 M1
PUT/ROE SW15 178 C6
TRDG/WHET N20 97 P4
Friar's Cl BRWN CM15 107 M1
CHING E4 101 H4
NTHLT UB5 133 K5
STHWK * SE1 12 D9
Friarscroft BROX EN10 44 F6
Friars Cft RGUE GU4 250 F7
Friars Fld BERK HP4 33 K2
Friars Gdns ACT W3 136 A8
Friar's Ga GUW GU2 267 M2
Friars Gate Cl WFD IG8 101 M5
Friars La RBSF CM22 31 J2
RCH/KEW TW9 177 J1
Friars Md POP/IOD E14 161 H2
Friars Ms ELTH/MOT SE9 184 D1
Friars Orch LHD/OX KT22 236 C7
Friars Place La ACT W3 136 A9
Friars Ri WOKS/MYFD GU22 232 D4
Friar's Rd EHAM E6 142 A3
VW GU25 194 A4
Friars Rookery CRAWE RH10 283 P7
Friars Stile Rd
RCHPK/HAM TW10 177 K2
The Friars CHIG IG7 103 H5
HLWW/ROY CM19 46 E3
Friars Wk ABYW SE2 163 N4
STHGT/OAK N14 98 C1
Friars Wy ACT W3 136 A8
BUSH WD23 73 N5
CHERT KT16 195 K6
KGLGY WD4 54 B6
Friars Wd CROY/NA * CR0 224 D5
Friarswood CROY/NA CR0 224 D5
Friary Br GU GU1 267 P2
Friary Cl NFNCH/WDSP N12 97 P6
Friary Ct WOKN/KNAP GU21 231 L4
Friary Est PECK * SE15 159 P6
Friary La WFD IG8 101 M5
Friary Pk TRDG/WHET * N20 97 P5
Friary Park Ct ACT * W3 135 P8
Friary Pas GU GU1 267 P2
Friary Rd ACT W3 135 P8
ASC SL5 192 A6
NFNCH/WDSP N12 97 N5
PECK SE15 159 P6
STWL/WRAY TW19 171 P2
Friary St GU GU1 268 A1
The Friary CHES/WCR * EN8 62 E9
STWL/WRAY TW19 171 P2
Friary Wy CRAWE RH10 283 N8
NFNCH/WDSP N12 97 P5
Friday Hl CHING E4 101 K4
Friday Hl East CHING E4 101 K4
Friday Hl West CHING E4 101 K3
Friday Rd ERITH DA8 164 E4
MTCM CR4 180 A10
Friday St BLKFR EC4V 12 E7
Friday Street Rd RDKG RH5 271 M9
Frideswide Pl KTTN NW5 118 D10
Friendly Pl LEW SE13 160 G7
Friendly St DEPT SE8 160 F7
Friendly Street Ms DEPT SE8 160 F8
Friends Av CHES/WCR EN8 62 C8
Friends Cl CRAWW RH11 283 N4
Friends' Rd CROY/NA CR0 203 L10
PUR/KEN CR8 223 J8
Friend St FSBYE EC1V 6 C9
Friern Barnet La TRDG/WHET N20 97 N4
Friern Barnet Rd FBAR/BDGN N11 98 B6
Friern Mount Dr TRDG/WHET N20 97 M1
Friern Pk NFNCH/WDSP N12 97 N6
Friern Rd EDUL SE22 181 P2
Friern Watch Av
NFNCH/WDSP N12 97 N5
Frigate Ms DEPT SE8 160 F5
Frimley Av EMPK RM11 125 P6
WLGTN SM6 222 F2
Frimley Cl CROY/NA CR0 225 H4
WIM/MER SW19 179 H5
Frimley Ct SCUP DA14 185 M8
Frimley Crs CROY/NA CR0 225 H4
Frimley Gdns MTCM CR4 201 P3
Frimley Rd CHSGTN KT9 219 J2
GDMY/SEVK IG3 123 H8
HHW HP1 35 H5
Frimley Wy WCHPL * E1 140 C6
Fringewood Cl NTHWD HA6 92 C9
Frinstead Gv STMC/STPC BR5 207 N4
Frinsted Rd ERITH DA8 164 E6
Frinton Cl OXHEY WD19 93 J3
Frinton Dr WFD IG8 101 J8
Frinton Ms IL IG1 122 D4
Frinton Rd CRW RM5 104 B8
EHAM E6 142 A5
SCUP DA14 185 P5
SEVS/STOTM N15 119 M4
TOOT SW17 180 B9
Friston St FUL/PGN SW6 157 L8
Friston Wk CRAWW RH11 283 K6
Friswell Pl BXLYHN DA7 164 B9
Fritham Cl NWMAL KT3 200 B6
Frith Ct MLHL NW7 97 H8
The Frithe SLN SL2 129 N8
Frith Knowle WOT/HER KT12 217 J2
Frith La MLHL NW7 97 H7
Frith Manor Farm Cotts
NFNCH/WDSP * N12 97 H6
Frith Rd CROY/NA CR0 203 K9
WAN E11 121 H9
Frithsden Copse BERK HP4 34 C1
Friths Dr REIG RH2 257 L7
Frith St SOHO/SHAV W1D 11 J6
Frithville Gdns SHB W12 136 F10
Frithwald Rd CHERT KT16 195 J7
Frithwood Av NTHWD HA6 92 G7
Frizlands La DAGE RM10 124 C8
Frobisher Cl BUSH WD23 73 P10
PIN HA5 113 L5
PUR/KEN CR8 241 K3
Frobisher Crs BARB * EC2Y 12 F3
STWL/WRAY TW19 173 P3
Frobisher Gdns GU GU1 250 D9
LEY * E10 120 G4
Frobisher Rd CEND/HSY/T N8 119 H2
EHAM E6 142 C8
ERITH DA8 165 H6
STAL AL1 39 H3
Frobisher Wy GRH DA9 166 G10
GVE DA12 191 H8
HAT AL10 40 A1
Frog Grove La RGUW GU3 248 E6
Froggy La DEN/HRF UB9 110 G8
Froghole La EDEN TN8 263 H8
Frog La DAGW RM9 144 E7
RGUE GU4 250 B1
Frogley Rd EDUL SE22 159 N10
Frogmoor La RKW/CH/CXG WD3 91 N3
Frogmore LCOL/BKTW AL2 56 D3
WAND/EARL SW18 179 K1
Frogmore Av YEAD UB4 132 F6
Frogmore Cl CHEAM SM3 200 C10
SL SL1 148 F1
Frogmore Dr WDSR SL4 149 K7
Frogmore Est HBRY * N5 119 K9
Frogmore Gdns CHEAM SM3 221 H1
YEAD UB4 132 F6
Frogmore Rd HHS/BOV * HP3 35 N9
Frognal HAMP NW3 117 M9
Frognal Av HRW HA1 114 E2
SCUP DA14 185 K8
Frognal Cl HAMP NW3 117 M10
Frognal Gdns HAMP NW3 117 M9
Frognal La HAMP NW3 117 L10
Frognal Man HAMP * NW3 117 M9
Frognal Pde HAMP NW3 3 J1
Frognal Pl SCUP DA14 185 K9
Frognal Ri HAMP NW3 117 M8
Frognal Wy HAMP NW3 117 M9
Frog St BRWN CM15 86 D5
Froissart Rd ELTH/MOT SE9 184 B1
Frome TIL RM18 169 M3
Frome Rd SEVS/STOTM N15 119 J1
Frome Sq HHNE HP2 36 B1
Frome St IS N1 6 E7
Fromondes Rd CHEAM SM3 221 H2
Fromow Gdns BFOR GU20 212 C3
Fromows Cnr CHSWK * W4 155 P4
Front La UPMR RM14 126 D7
The Front BERK HP4 34 E2
Frostic Wk WCHPL E1 13 M4
Froude St VX/NE SW8 158 C8
Frowick Cl BRKMPK AL9 40 E9
Frowycke Crs POTB/CUF EN6 58 D8
Fruen Rd EBED/NFELT TW14 174 G3
Fryatt Rd TOTM N17 99 L8
Fry Cl CRW RM5 104 B6
Fryent Cl KTN/HRWW/W HA3 115 M4
Fryent Crs CDALE/KGS NW9 116 B4
Fryent Flds CDALE/KGS NW9 116 B4
Fryent Gv CDALE/KGS NW9 116 B4
Fryent Wy CDALE/KGS NW9 115 M3
Fryer Cl CSHM HP5 51 J9
Fryern Wd CTHM CR3 241 K10
Frying Pan Aly WCHPL E1 13 K4
Frymley Vw WDSR SL4 148 C7
Fry Rd EHAM E6 142 A1
WLSDN NW10 136 C3
Fryston Av COUL/CHIP CR5 222 C10
CROY/NA CR0 203 P9
Fryth Md STALW/RED AL3 38 A5
Fuchsia St ABYW SE2 163 L4
Fuchsia Wy CHOB/PIR GU24 212 D9
Fulbeck Dr CDALE/KGS NW9 96 B9
Fulbeck Wy RYLN/HDSTN HA2 94 B10
Fulbourne Cl REDH RH1 257 P8
Fulbourne Est WCHPL E1 13 P2
Fulbourne Rd WALTH E17 101 H10
Fulbourne St WCHPL E1 140 A7
Fulbrook La SOCK/AV RM15 146 E9
Fulbrook Rd ARCH N19 118 D9
Fulford Gv OXHEY WD19 93 J3
Fulford Rd CTHM CR3 241 L7
HOR/WEW KT19 220 A4
Fulford St BERM/RHTH SE16 160 A1
Fulham Broadway
FUL/PGN SW6 157 K6
Fulham Cl UX/CGN UB8 132 D6
Fulham Est FUL/PGN SW6 14 D9
Fulham High St FUL/PGN SW6 157 H8
Fulham Palace Rd FUL/PGN SW6 156 G6
Fulham Park Gdns
FUL/PGN SW6 157 J8
Fulham Park Rd FUL/PGN SW6 157 J8
Fulham Rd WBPTN SW10 15 K9
Fullarton Crs SOCK/AV RM15 146 E8
Fullbrook Av ADL/WDHM KT15 215 K7
Fullbrooks Av WPK KT4 200 C8
Fuller Cl BETH E2 13 N1
ORP BR6 227 J2
Fuller Gdns WATN WD24 73 J3
Fuller Rd BCTR RM8 123 M8
WATN WD24 73 J3
Fullers Av SURB KT6 199 L9
WFD IG8 101 L8
Fullers Cl CRW RM5 104 D8
CSHM HP5 50 G8
WAB EN9 63 L9
Fullers Farm Rd EHSLY KT24 252 C9
Fuller's Hl AMS HP6 50 E10
BH/WHM TN16 262 G2
Fullers Md HLWE CM17 47 M2
Fuller's Rd SWFD E18 101 L9
Fuller St HDN NW4 116 F2
Fullers Wy North SURB KT6 199 L10
Fullers Wy South CHSGTN KT9 219 K1
Fuller's Wd CROY/NA CR0 224 F2
Fullers Wood La REDH RH1 258 D10
Fullerton Cl BF/WBF KT14 216 A10
Fullerton Dr BF/WBF KT14 215 P10
Fullerton Rd BF/WBF KT14 215 P10
CAR SM5 221 P5
CROY/NA CR0 203 N7
WAND/EARL SW18 179 M1
Fullerton Wy BF/WBF KT14 215 P10
Fuller Wy HYS/HAR UB3 152 G4
RKW/CH/CXG WD3 72 B9
Fullmer Wy ADL/WDHM KT15 215 J6
Fullwell Av CLAY IG5 102 D9
Fullwood's Ms IS * N1 7 H9
Fulmar Cl CRAWW * RH11 282 G8
Fulmar Ct BRYLDS KT5 199 L6
Fulmar Crs HHW HP1 35 K7
Fulmar Rd RAIN RM13 145 J1
Fulmead St FUL/PGN SW6 157 L7
Fulmer Cl HPTN TW12 175 M8
Fulmer Common Rd
DTCH/LGLY SL3 130 A1
Fulmer Cnr CFSP/GDCR * SL9 110 E6
Fulmer Dr CFSP/GDCR SL9 110 B7
Fulmer La CFSP/GDCR SL9 110 C8
Fulmer Pl DTCH/LGLY * SL3 110 B9
Fulmer Rd CAN/RD E16 142 A7
DTCH/LGLY SL3 110 B9
Fulmer Wy CFSP/GDCR SL9 110 B4
WEA W13 154 G2
Fulready Rd LEY E10 121 J3
Fulstone Cl HSLWW TW4 153 N10
Fulthorp Rd BKHTH/KID SE3 161 L8
Fulton Ms BAY/PAD W2 9 J7
Fulton Rd WBLY HA9 115 M8
Fulvens SHGR GU5 270 F9
Fulwell Park Av WHTN TW2 176 B5
Fulwell Rd HPTN TW12 176 C7
Fulwich Rd DART DA1 187 N2
Fulwood Av ALP/SUD HA0 135 L4
Fulwood Gdns TWK TW1 176 E2
Fulwood Pl GINN WC1R 11 P4
Fulwood Wk WIM/MER SW19 179 H4
Furber St HMSMTH W6 156 E2
Furham Fld PIN HA5 93 P8
Furley Rd PECK SE15 159 P6
Furlong Cl MTCM CR4 202 C8
Furlong Rd DORK RH4 272 B3
HOLWY N7 6 B1
Furlongs HHW HP1 35 K5
Furlong Wy HORL RH6 280 A7
WARE SG12 26 E4
The Furlough WOKS/MYFD GU22 232 D3
Furmage St WAND/EARL SW18 179 L3
Furnace Dr CRAWE RH10 284 A9
Furnace Farm Rd CRAWE * RH10 284 B9
Furnace Pde CRAWE RH10 284 B9
Furnace Pl CRAWE RH10 284 B9
Furneaux Av WNWD SE27 181 J8
Furner Cl DART DA1 164 G9
Furness WDSR SL4 148 B8
Furness Cl CDH/CHF RM16 168 E4
Furness Rd FUL/PGN SW6 157 L8
MRDN SM4 201 L6
RYLN/HDSTN HA2 114 A5
WLSDN NW10 136 D4
Furness Wy HCH RM12 125 H10
Furnival Av SLN SL2 128 G7
Furnival Cl VW GU25 194 A6
Furnival St FLST/FETLN EC4A 12 A5
Furrow La HOM E9 120 B10
Furrows Pl CTHM CR3 241 N9
The Furrows WOT/HER KT12 197 K9
Fursby Av FNCH N3 97 K7
Furse Av STALE/WH AL4 38 F3
Further Acre CDALE/KGS NW9 96 C10
Furtherfield ABLGY WD5 54 F8
Furtherfield Cl CROY/NA CR0 203 H6
Further Green Rd CAT SE6 183 K3
Furtherground HHNE HP2 35 P7
Furzebank ASC SL5 192 C4
Furzebushes La LCOL/BKTW AL2 55 M1
Furze Cl OXHEY WD19 93 K6
REDH RH1 258 A9
Furzedown Cl EGH TW20 172 B9
Furzedown Ct HARP AL5 20 A3
Furzedown Dr TOOT SW17 180 C8
Furzedown Rd BELMT SM2 221 M7
TOOT SW17 180 C8
Furze Farm Cl CHDH RM6 103 P10
Furzefield CHESW EN7 62 A4
CRAWW RH11 283 L6
Furze Fld LHD/OX KT22 218 C9
Furzefield Cl CHST BR7 184 E9
Furzefield Ct POTB/CUF * EN6 59 H7
Furzefield Crs REIG RH2 275 M2
Furzefield Rd BEAC HP9 88 C9
BKHTH/KID SE3 161 N5
REIG RH2 275 M2
WGCE AL7 23 H6
Furzeground Wy STKPK UB11 132 D10
Furze Gv KWD/TDW/WH KT20 239 J7
Furzeham Rd WDR/YW UB7 151 P1
Furze Hl KWD/TDW/WH KT20 239 J7
PUR/KEN CR8 222 F7
Furzehill REDH RH1 257 P9
Furzehill Pde BORE * WD6 75 M8
Furzehill Rd BORE WD6 75 P9
Furzehill Sq STMC/STPC BR5 207 L4
Furze La PUR/KEN CR8 222 F7
RGODL GU7 267 L9
Furzen Cl SLN SL2 128 F5
Furzen Crs HAT AL10 40 C7
Furze Pl REDH * RH1 258 A9
Furze Rd ADL/WDHM KT15 215 J3
HHW HP1 35 H7
THHTH CR7 203 K3

Furze St BOW * E3 140 F7
Furze Vw RKW/CH/CXG WD3 70 F10
Furzewood SUN TW16 197 H1
Fusedale Wy SOCK/AV RM15 146 E9
Fuzzens Wk WDSR SL4 148 D8
Fydlers Cl ASC SL5 170 A9
Fye Foot La BLKFR * EC4V 12 E7
Fyfe Wy BMLY BR1 205 M2
Fyfield Cl BECK BR3 205 J4
Fyfield Dr SOCK/AV RM15 146 E9
Fyfield Rd BRXN/ST SW9 159 H9
CHONG CM5 49 N6
CHONG CM5 67 P2
EN EN1 79 M7
RAIN RM13 144 G3
WALTH E17 121 J1
WFD IG8 101 P8
Fynes St WEST SW1P 17 J5

G

Gabion Av PUR RM19 166 C3
Gable Cl ABLGY WD5 54 F8
DART DA1 187 H1
PIN HA5 93 P8
Gable Ct SYD SE26 182 A7
Gables Av ASHF TW15 174 A8
BORE WD6 75 L7
Gables Cl CFSP/GDCR SL9 90 B5
CMBW SE5 159 M7
DTCH/LGLY SL3 149 M5
LEE/GVPK SE12 183 M4
WOKS/MYFD GU22 232 C6
The Gables BNSTD SM7 239 J3
GRAYS * RM17 167 L3
HART DA3 211 P2
LHD/OX KT22 218 B8
NRWD * SE19 203 M1
WBLY HA9 115 L8
WEY KT13 216 D2
WOKS/MYFD * GU22 232 A5
Gabriel Cl CRW RM5 104 D8
FELT TW13 175 M7
Gabriel Gdns GVE DA12 191 H8
Gabrielle Cl WBLY HA9 115 L8
Gabrielspring Rd EYN DA4 210 C9
Gabriel Spring Rd (East)
EYN DA4 210 D9
Gabriel St FSTH SE23 182 C3
Gadbrook Rd BRKHM/BTCW RH3 274 A5
Gad Cl PLSTW E13 141 N5
Gaddesden Av WBLY HA9 135 L1
Gaddesden Crs GSTN WD25 55 L10
Gaddesden Gv WGCE AL7 23 L6
Gade Av WATW WD18 72 F8
Gade Bank RKW/CH/CXG WD3 72 E8
Gadebridge La HHW HP1 35 L4
Gadebridge Rd HHW HP1 35 L5
Gade Cl HHW HP1 35 L3
HYS/HAR UB3 133 J10
WATW WD18 72 F8
Gadesden Rd HOR/WEW KT19 219 P3
Gadeside GSTN WD25 72 F1
Gade Valley Cl KGLGY WD4 54 B4
Gade View Gdns ABLGY WD5 54 D8
Gade View Rd HHS/BOV HP3 35 M10
Gadsbury Cl CDALE/KGS NW9 116 C4
Gadsden Cl UPMR RM14 126 D4
Gadswell Cl GSTN WD25 73 M2
Gadwall Cl CAN/RD E16 141 N8
Gage Rd CAN/RD E16 141 K7
Gainford St IS N1 6 A5
Gainsboro Gdns GFD/PVL UB6 114 D10
Gainsborough Av DART DA1 187 K1
MNPK E12 122 D10
STAL AL1 38 E5
TIL RM18 168 D7
Gainsborough Cl BECK BR3 182 F10
ESH/CLAY * KT10 198 C8
Gainsborough Ct SHB W12 156 F1
WOT/HER KT12 217 H1
Gainsborough Dr GVW DA11 190 A6
SAND/SEL CR2 223 P9
Gainsborough Gdns EDGW HA8 95 L10
GLDGN NW11 117 J5
HAMP NW3 117 N8
ISLW TW7 176 C1
Gainsborough Rd BCTR RM8 123 L9
CHSWK W4 156 C3
HOR/WEW KT19 219 P6
NFNCH/WDSP N12 97 L6
NWMAL KT3 200 A6
RAIN RM13 145 H3
RCH/KEW TW9 155 L8
SRTFD E15 141 K5
WAN E11 121 K5
WFD IG8 102 B7
YEAD UB4 132 D4
Gainsborough Sq BXLYHN DA7 163 N9
Gainsborough Ter BELMT * SM2 221 J4
Gainsford Rd WALTH E17 120 E2
Gainsford St STHWK SE1 13 L10
Gainsthorpe Rd CHONG CM5 49 L9
Gainswood WGCE AL7 23 H6
Gairloch Rd CMBW SE5 159 M8
Gaisford St KTTN NW5 4 G1
Gaist Av CTHM CR3 242 A8
Gaitskell Rd ELTH/MOT SE9 184 F4
Galahad Cl SL SL1 148 F1
Galahad Rd BMLY BR1 183 M6
CRAWW RH11 283 H7
Galata Rd BARN SW13 156 D6
Galatea Sq PECK SE15 160 A9
Galbraith St POP/IOD E14 161 H2
Galdana Av BAR EN5 77 M7
Galeborough Av WFD IG8 101 J8
Gale Cl HPTN TW12 175 M9
MTCM CR4 201 N3
Gale Crs BNSTD SM7 239 K3
Galena Rd HMSMTH W6 156 E3
Galen Cl HOR/WEW KT19 219 M7
Galen Pl NOXST/BSQ WC1A 11 L4
Galesbury Rd WAND/EARL SW18 179 M2
Gales Cl RGUE * GU4 250 G7
Gales Dr CRAWE RH10 284 A7
Gales Gdns BETH E2 140 A5
Gales Pl CRAWE RH10 284 A7
Gale St BOW E3 140 F7
CHEL SW3 15 N7
DAGW RM9 143 N1
Gales Wy WFD IG8 102 B8
Galey Gn SOCK/AV RM15 146 G7
Galgate Cl WIM/MER SW19 178 G4
Gallants Farm Rd EBAR EN4 97 P1
Galleon Bvd GRH DA9 166 C10
Galleon Cl BERM/RHTH SE16 160 B1
ERITH DA8 164 E3
Galleon Rd CDH/CHF RM16 166 G3
Galleons Dr BARK IG11 143 K5
Galleons La DTCH/LGLY SL3 130 A5
The Galleons AMSS * HP7 69 H4
The Galleria HAT * AL10 40 C3
The Galleries IS * N1 6 C7
Gallery Gdns NTHLT UB5 133 L4
Gallery Rd DUL SE21 181 L4
Galley Gn HERT/BAY SG13 26 F9
Galley Hl HHW HP1 35 K4
Galley Hill Rd SWCM DA10 189 L1
Galleyhill Rd WAB EN9 63 K9
Galley La BAR EN5 76 D4
Galleymead Rd DTCH/LGLY SL3 151 J7
Galleywall Rd BERM/RHTH SE16 160 A3
Galleywood Crs CRW RM5 104 E7
Galliard Crs ED N9 99 P1
Galliard Rd ED N9 99 P1
Gallia Rd HBRY N5 119 J10
Gallions Cl BARK IG11 143 K5
Gallions Rd CAN/RD E16 142 E9
CHARL SE7 161 N3
Gallions View Rd THMD SE28 163 H1
Gallon Cl CHARL SE7 161 P3
The Gallop BELMT SM2 221 N5
SAND/SEL CR2 224 A4
Gallosson Rd WOOL/PLUM SE18 163 H3
Galloway Cha SLN SL2 129 M9
Galloway Cl BROX EN10 62 E2
Galloway Pth CROY/NA CR0 223 L1
Galloway Rd SHB W12 136 D10
Gallows Hl KGLGY WD4 54 D7
Gallows Hill La ABLGY WD5 54 D8
Gallus Cl WCHMH N21 78 G10
Gallus Sq BKHTH/KID SE3 161 N9
Gallys Rd WDSR SL4 148 C7
Galpin's Rd THHTH CR7 202 F4
Galsworthy Av CHDH RM6 123 L5
Galsworthy Cl THMD SE28 143 L10
Galsworthy Crs BKHTH/KID * SE3 161 P7
Galsworthy Rd CHERT * KT16 195 K7
CRICK NW2 117 H9
KUTN/CMB KT2 199 N1
TIL RM18 168 F7
Galton Rd ASC SL5 192 E6
Galton St NKENS W10 2 A10
Galva Cl EBAR EN4 78 B8
Galveston Rd PUT/ROE SW15 179 J1
Galvin Rd SL SL1 129 H9
Galway Cl BERM/RHTH * SE16 160 A4
Galway St FSBYE EC1V 6 F10
Gambetta St VX/NE SW8 158 C8
Gambia St STHWK SE1 12 D10
Gambles La RPLY/SEND GU23 251 M1
Gambole Rd TOOT SW17 179 P7
Games Rd EBAR EN4 77 P7
Gamlen Rd PUT/ROE SW15 156 G10
Gammon Cl HHS/BOV HP3 36 B7
Gammons La WATN WD24 73 H3
Gamuel Cl WALTH E17 120 F4
Gander Green Crs HPTN TW12 197 P1
Gander Green La CHEAM SM3 201 H9
SUT SM1 221 K3
Ganders Ash GSTN WD25 55 H9
Gandhi Cl WALTH E17 120 F4
Gandhi Ct WATN WD24 73 L6
Gangers Hl GDST RH9 260 E3
Ganghill GU GU1 250 D8
Gant Ct WAB EN9 63 L10
Ganton St SOHO/CST * W1F 11 H6
Ganton Wk OXHEY * WD19 93 M5
Gantshill Crs GNTH/NBYPK IG2 122 D3
Ganymede Pl HHNE HP2 36 A3
Gap Rd WIM/MER SW19 179 K8
Garage Rd ACT W3 135 M8
Garbrand Wk EW KT17 220 C5
Garbutt Pl MHST * W1U 10 D3
Garbutt Rd UPMR RM14 126 B7
Garden Av BXLYHN DA7 164 A9
HAT AL10 40 D7
MTCM CR4 180 C10
Garden Cl ADL/WDHM KT15 215 N1
ASHF TW15 174 D9
BAR EN5 76 F8
BNSTD SM7 239 K1
CHING E4 100 F6
HPTN TW12 175 N8
LEE/GVPK SE12 183 N6
LHD/OX KT22 237 H10
NTHLT UB5 133 M3
PUT/ROE SW15 178 E3
RSLP HA4 112 F7
STAL AL1 38 G5
WAT WD17 72 G6
WLGTN SM6 222 F2
Garden Ct SEV * TN13 247 L8
STALE/WH AL4 21 J2
TPL/STR * WC2R 12 A7
Garden End AMS HP6 69 K3
Gardeners Cl FBAR/BDGN N11 98 B3
Gardeners Rd CROY/NA CR0 203 J8
Gardener's Wk GT/LBKH KT23 254 A2
Garden Field La BERK HP4 34 C7
Garden Flats HMSMTH * W6 156 G5
Gardenia Ct CHOB/PIR GU24 212 E9
Gardenia Rd EN EN1 79 M10
Gardenia Wy WFD IG8 101 M7
Garden La BMLY BR1 183 N9
BRXS/STRHM SW2 180 G4
Garden Lodge Ct EFNCH * N2 117 N1
Garden Pl HACK E8 7 M5
RDART DA2 187 L6
Garden Reach CSTG HP8 70 A7
Garden Rd ABLGY WD5 54 F7
BMLY BR1 183 N10
PGE/AN SE20 204 B1
RCH/KEW TW9 155 M9
SEV TN13 247 L8
STJWD NW8 3 K9
WOT/HER KT12 197 J6
Garden Rw GVW DA11 190 C6
STHWK SE1 18 C4
The Gardens BECK BR3 205 H2
BRKMPK AL9 59 H3
BRWN CM15 86 G2
CEND/HSY/T * N8 118 F2
CHOB/PIR GU24 230 E8
COB * KT11 234 D5
EBED/NFELT TW14 174 E2
EDUL SE22 159 P10
ESH/CLAY KT10 217 P1
HGDN/ICK UB10 111 P7
HRW HA1 114 B4
PIN * HA5 113 N4
STNW/STAM * N16 119 N5
WAT WD17 72 G6
Garden St WCHPL E1 140 C7
Garden Studios BAY/PAD * W2 9 J4
Garden Ter PIM SW1V 17 J7
Garden Terrace Rd HLWE CM17 29 M7
Garden Vls ESH/CLAY * KT10 218 E4
Garden Wk BECK BR3 204 E1
COUL/CHIP CR5 240 C9
CRAWW RH11 283 M7
SDTCH EC2A 13 J1
Garden Wy LOU IG10 82 D4
WLSDN NW10 135 P1
Gardiner Av CRICK * NW2 116 F10
Gardiner Cl BCTR RM8 123 N9
PEND EN3 80 C10
STMC/STPC BR5 207 M2
The Gardiners HLWE CM17 47 L2
Gardner Cl WAN E11 121 N4
Gardner La CRAWE RH10 285 P5
Gardner Pl EBED/NFELT TW14 175 J2
Gardner Rd GU GU1 249 P10
PLSTW E13 141 N6
Gardners La BLKFR EC4V 12 E7
Gardnor Rd HAMP NW3 117 N9
Gard St FSBYE EC1V 6 D9
Garendon Gdns MRDN SM4 201 L7
Garendon Rd MRDN SM4 201 L7
Gareth Cl WPK KT4 200 G9
Gareth Gv BMLY BR1 183 M7
Garfield Pl WDSR * SL4 149 H8
Garfield Rd ADL/WDHM * KT15 215 M1
ADL/WDHM KT15 215 M2
BTSEA SW11 158 B9
CHING E4 101 J2
PEND EN3 80 B8
PLSTW E13 141 L6
TWK TW1 176 F4
WIM/MER SW19 179 M9
Garfield St WATN WD24 73 J4
Garford St POP/IOD E14 140 F9
Garibaldi Rd REDH RH1 276 A1
Garibaldi St WOOL/PLUM SE18 163 H3
Garland Cl CHES/WCR EN8 62 D7
HHNE * HP2 35 N5
Garland Rd STAN HA7 95 K9
WARE SG12 26 D2
WOOL/PLUM SE18 162 G6
Garlands Rd LHD/OX KT22 236 G7
REDH RH1 258 A10
Garland Wy CTHM CR3 241 L8
EMPK RM11 125 M2
Garlichill Rd EPSOM KT18 238 E3
Garlick Hl BLKFR EC4V 12 F7
Garlies Rd FSTH SE23 182 D6
Garlinge Rd KIL/WHAMP NW6 2 C2
Garman Cl UED N18 99 L6
Garman Rd TOTM N17 100 B7
Garnault Ms CLKNW EC1R 6 B10
Garnault Pl CLKNW EC1R 6 B10
Garnault Rd EN EN1 79 N4
Garner Cl BCTR RM8 123 N6
Garner Dr BROX EN10 62 D2
Garner Rd WALTH E17 101 H9
Garners Cl CFSP/GDCR SL9 90 B7
Garners End CFSP/GDCR SL9 90 B7
Garners Rd CFSP/GDCR SL9 90 B7
Garner St BETH E2 7 P8
Garnet Cl SL SL1 148 F1
Garnet Rd THHTH CR7 203 K4
WLSDN NW10 136 B1
Garnet St WAP E1W 140 B9
Garnett Cl ELTH/MOT SE9 162 C9
WATN WD24 73 L2
Garnett Dr LCOL/BKTW AL2 55 N5
Garnett Rd HAMP NW3 118 A10
Garnham St STNW/STAM N16 119 N7
Garnies Cl PECK SE15 159 N6
Garnon Md EPP CM16 65 N4
Garrad's Rd STRHM/NOR SW16 180 E6
Garrard Cl BXLYHN DA7 164 B9
CHST BR7 184 E8
Garrard Rd BNSTD SM7 239 K2
SLN SL2 128 D6
Garrard Wk WLSDN * NW10 136 B1
Garrard Wy STALE/WH AL4 21 J3
Garratt Cl CROY/NA CR0 222 F1
Garratt La WAND/EARL SW18 179 L3
Garratt Rd EDGW HA8 95 M8
Garratts La BNSTD SM7 239 J2
Garratts Rd BUSH WD23 94 B1
Garratt Ter TOOT SW17 179 P7
Garrett Cl ACT W3 136 A7
CRAWE RH10 284 D9
CSHM HP5 51 H9
Garrett St STLK EC1Y 12 E2
Garrick Av GLDGN NW11 117 H4
Garrick Cl BTSEA SW11 157 M10
EA W5 135 K6
RCH/KEW TW9 177 H1
STA TW18 173 K10
WOT/HER KT12 217 J1
Garrick Crs CROY/NA CR0 203 M9
Garrick Dr HDN NW4 96 F10
WOOL/PLUM SE18 162 G2
Garrick Gdns E/WMO/HCT KT8 197 P3
Garrick Pk HDN NW4 96 G10
Garrick Rd CDALE/KGS NW9 116 C4
GFD/PVL UB6 134 A6
RCH/KEW TW9 155 M8
Garrick St COVGDN WC2E 11 L7
GVW DA11 190 E2
Garrick Wk CRAWE RH10 283 P10
Garrick Wy HDN NW4 116 G2
Garrick Yd CHCR WC2N 11 L7
Garrison Cl HSLWW TW4 175 N1
WOOL/PLUM SE18 162 D6
Garrison La CHSGTN KT9 219 K4
Garrolds Cl SWLY BR8 208 E2
The Garrones CRAWE * RH10 284 F6
Garron La SOCK/AV RM15 146 E8
Garrow HART DA3 211 N3
Garry Cl ROM RM1 104 F8
Garry Wy ROM RM1 104 F8
Garsdale Cl FBAR/BDGN N11 98 B7
Garside Cl HPTN TW12 176 A10
WOOL/PLUM SE18 162 G2
Garsmouth Wy GSTN WD25 73 L2
Garson Gv CSHM HP5 50 F5
Garson La STWL/WRAY TW19 172 A3
Garson Rd ESH/CLAY KT10 217 N2
Garston Crs GSTN WD25 55 K10
Garston Dr GSTN WD25 55 K10
Garston La GSTN WD25 55 L10
PUR/KEN CR8 241 L1
The Garstons GT/LBKH KT23 253 N1
Garth Cl KUTN/CMB KT2 177 L8
MRDN SM4 200 G7
RSLP HA4 113 L6
Garthland Dr BAR EN5 76 E9
Garth Ms EA * W5 135 K6
Garthorne Rd FSTH SE23 182 C3
Garth Rd CHSWK W4 156 A4
CRICK NW2 117 J7
KUTN/CMB KT2 177 L8
MRDN SM4 200 G8
SEV TN13 265 K4
SOCK/AV RM15 147 H6
Garthside KUTN/CMB KT2 177 K8
The Garth ABLGY WD5 54 E9
COB KT11 217 M9
HPTN TW12 176 A9
KTN/HRWW/W HA3 115 L4
NFNCH/WDSP * N12 97 L6
Garthway NFNCH/WDSP N12 97 P7
Gartlet Rd WAT WD17 73 J7
Gartmoor Gdns WIM/MER SW19 179 J4
Gartmore Rd GDMY/SEVK IG3 123 J6
Garton Cl CRAWW RH11 283 H8
Garton Pl WAND/EARL SW18 179 M2
Gartons Cl PEND EN3 80 B9
Gartons Wy BTSEA SW11 157 M9
Garvary Rd CAN/RD E16 141 N8
Garvin Av BEAC HP9 88 D8
Garvock Dr SEV TN13 265 H2
Garway Rd BAY/PAD W2 8 G6
Gascoigne Gdns WFD IG8 101 K8
Gascoigne Pl BETH E2 7 L9
Gascoigne Rd BARK IG11 142 F3
CROY/NA CR0 225 H6
WEY KT13 196 C10
Gascon's Gv SLN SL2 128 G6
Gascony Av KIL/WHAMP NW6 2 E4
Gascoyne Cl HARH RM3 105 L9
Gascoyne Dr DART DA1 164 G9
Gascoyne Rd HOM E9 140 C2
Gascoyne Wy HERT/BAY SG13 25 L6
Gaselee St POP/IOD E14 141 H9
Gasholder Pl LBTH SE11 17 P8
Gaskarth Rd BAL SW12 180 C2
EDGW HA8 95 P9
Gaskell Rd HGT N6 118 A4
Gaskell St CLAP SW4 158 F8
Gaskin St IS N1 6 C5
Gaspar Cl ECT * SW5 15 H5
Gaspar Ms ECT SW5 15 H5
Gassiot Rd TOOT SW17 180 A7
Gassiot Wy SUT SM1 201 N10
Gasson Rd SWCM DA10 189 K2
Gasson Wood Rd CRAWW RH11 283 H9
Gastein Rd HMSMTH W6 156 G5
Gaston Bell Cl RCH/KEW TW9 155 L9
Gaston Bridge Rd SHPTN TW17 196 E5
Gaston Rd MTCM CR4 202 B3
Gaston Wy SHPTN TW17 196 E5
Gataker St BERM/RHTH SE16 160 A2
Gatcombe Ms EA W5 135 L9
Gatcombe Rd ARCH N19 118 E8
Gatcombe Wy EBAR EN4 78 A7
Gate Cl BORE WD6 75 P5
Gate Cottages EDGW * HA8 95 M3
Gatecroft HHS/BOV HP3 36 A8
Gate End NTHWD HA6 93 H8
Gateforth St STJWD NW8 9 N2
Gatehill Rd NTHWD HA6 92 G8
Gatehope Dr SOCK/AV RM15 146 E8
Gatehouse Cl KUTN/CMB KT2 177 P10
WDSR SL4 148 G9
Gatehouse Sq STHWK SE1 12 F9
Gateley Rd BRXN/ST SW9 158 G9
Gate Ms SKENS SW7 15 P2
Gater Dr ENC/FH EN2 79 L5
Gatesden Cl LHD/OX KT22 236 B9
Gatesden Rd LHD/OX KT22 236 B9
Gates Green Rd WWKM BR4 225 M1
Gateshead Rd BORE WD6 75 L6
Gateside Rd TOOT SW17 180 A6
Gatestone Rd NRWD SE19 181 M9
Gate St HHOL WC1V 11 N5
Gateway WALW SE17 18 F9
Gateway Ar IS * N1 6 C7
Gateway Cl NTHWD HA6 92 D7
Gateway Ms HACK * E8 119 N10
Gateway Pde GVE * DA12 191 J7
Gateways GU GU1 268 E1
The Gateways CHESW EN7 61 L4
RCH/KEW * TW9 155 J10
The Gateway WOKN/KNAP GU21 214 E10
Gatewick Cl SL SL1 129 K10
Gatfield Gv FELT TW13 175 P5
Gathorne Rd WDGN N22 99 H10
Gathorne St BETH E2 140 C4
Gatley Av HOR/WEW KT19 219 N2
Gatley Dr GU GU1 250 C7
Gatliff Rd BGVA SW1W 16 D8
Gatling Rd ABYW SE2 163 K4
Gatonby St PECK SE15 159 N7
Gatting Wy HGDN/ICK UB10 131 P1
Gatton Bottom REIG RH2 258 A4
Gatton Cl BELMT * SM2 221 L5
REIG RH2 257 M7
Gatton Park Rd REDH RH1 257 N7
Gatton Rd REIG RH2 257 M7
TOOT SW17 179 P7
Gattons Wy SCUP DA14 186 A7
Gatward Cl WCHMH N21 79 J10
Gatward Gn ED N9 99 M3
Gatwick Rd CRAWE RH10 284 B3
GVE DA12 190 E5
HORL RH6 284 B1
WAND/EARL SW18 179 J3
Gatwick Wy HORL RH6 280 A7
Gauden Cl CLAP SW4 158 E9
Gauden Rd CLAP SW4 158 E9
Gaumont Ap WATW WD18 73 J7
Gaumont Ter SHB * W12 156 F1
Gauntlet Cl NTHLT UB5 133 M2
Gauntlet Crs PUR/KEN CR8 241 L5
Gauntlett Ct ALP/SUD HA0 114 F10
Gauntlett Rd SUT SM1 221 N2
Gaunt St STHWK SE1 18 D3
Gautrey Rd PECK SE15 160 B8
Gavell Rd COB KT11 217 H9
Gavel St WALW * SE17 19 H5
Gavenny Pth SOCK/AV RM15 146 E8
Gaverick St POP/IOD E14 160 F3
Gaveston Cl BF/WBF KT14 216 A9
Gaveston Dr BERK HP4 33 N3
Gavestone Crs LEE/GVPK SE12 183 N3
Gavestone Rd LEE/GVPK SE12 183 N3
Gaveston Rd LHD/OX KT22 236 F6
SLN SL2 128 E5
Gavina Cl MRDN SM4 201 P5
Gaviots Cl CFSP/GDCR SL9 110 C6
Gaviots Gn CFSP/GDCR SL9 110 B6
Gaviots Wy CFSP/GDCR SL9 110 B5
Gawber St BETH E2 140 B5
Gawdrey Cl CSHM HP5 51 J9
Gawsworth Cl SRTFD E15 121 L10
Gawthorne Av MLHL NW7 97 H6
Gay Cl CRICK NW2 116 E10
Gaydon La CDALE/KGS NW9 96 B9
Gayfere Rd CLAY IG5 122 C1
EW KT17 220 D2
Gayfere St WEST SW1P 17 L4
Gayford Rd SHB W12 156 C1
Gay Gdns DAGE RM10 124 D9
Gayhouse La REDH RH1 277 M10
Gayhurst Rd HACK E8 7 N3
Gayler Cl REDH RH1 259 N10
Gaylor Rd NTHLT UB5 113 N10
TIL RM18 168 B7
Gaynes Ct UPMR RM14 126 A9
Gaynesford Rd CAR SM5 222 A4
FSTH SE23 182 C5
Gaynes Hill Rd WFD IG8 102 B8
Gaynes Park Rd UPMR RM14 125 P9
Gaynes Rd UPMR RM14 126 A7
Gay Rd SRTFD E15 141 J4
Gaysham Av GNTH/NBYPK IG2 122 D3
Gayton Cl AMS HP6 69 K1
ASHTD KT21 237 K4
Gayton Crs HAMP NW3 117 N9
Gayton Rd HAMP NW3 117 N9
HRW HA1 114 E4
Gayville Rd BTSEA SW11 180 A2
Gaywood Av CHES/WCR EN8 62 C6
Gaywood Cl BRXS/STRHM SW2 180 G4
Gaywood Rd ASHTD KT21 237 L4
WALTH E17 120 F1
Gaywood St STHWK SE1 18 D4
Gaza St WALW SE17 18 C8
Gazelle Gld GVE DA12 191 J8
Geariesville Gdns BARK/HLT IG6 122 E2
Geary Cl HORL RH6 281 J6
Geary Dr BRW CM14 107 H2
Geary Rd WLSDN NW10 116 D10
Geary St HOLWY N7 118 G10
Geddes Pl BXLYHN DA7 164 B10
Geddes Rd BUSH * WD23 74 B8
Geddings Rd HOD EN11 44 G3
Gedeney Rd TOTM N17 99 K9
Gedling Pl STHWK SE1 19 L3
Geere Rd SRTFD E15 141 L3
Gees Ct MHST W1U 10 D6
Gee St FSBYE EC1V 12 E1
Geffrye Est IS N1 7 K8
Geffrye St BETH E2 7 L7
Geisthorp Ct WAB EN9 63 M9
Geldart Rd PECK SE15 160 A6
Geldeston Rd CLPT E5 119 P7
Gellatly Rd PECK SE15 160 B8
Gelsthorpe Rd CRW RM5 104 C8
Gemini Cl CRAWW RH11 282 G9
The Generals Wk PEND EN3 80 D3
General Wolfe Rd GNWCH SE10 161 J7
Genesis Cl STWL/WRAY TW19 174 A4
Genesta Gld GVE DA12 191 K8
Genesta Rd WOOL/PLUM SE18 162 E5
Geneva Cl SHPTN TW17 196 F2
Geneva Dr HNHL SE24 159 H10
Geneva Gdns CHDH RM6 123 P3
Geneva Rd KUT KT1 199 K4
THHTH CR7 203 K5
Genever Cl CHING E4 100 F6
Genista Rd UED N18 100 A6
Genoa Av PUT/ROE SW15 178 F1
Genoa Rd PGE/AN SE20 204 B1
Genotin Rd ENC/FH EN2 79 L7
Gentleman's Rw ENC/FH EN2 79 K7
Genyn Rd GUW GU2 267 N1
Geoffrey Av HARH RM3 105 P7
Geoffrey Cl CMBW SE5 159 K8
Geoffrey Gdns EHAM E6 142 B4
Geoffrey Rd BROCKY SE4 160 E9
George Avey Cft EPP CM16 66 C2
George Beard Rd DEPT SE8 160 E3
George Crs MUSWH N10 98 B8
George Downing Est
STNW/STAM N16 119 N7
George Gange Wy
KTN/HRWW/W HA3 114 D1
George Green Dr DTCH/LGLY SL3 130 C8
George Green Rd DTCH/LGLY SL3 130 B8
George Groves Rd PGE/AN SE20 203 P1
George La HAYES BR2 205 N8
LEW SE13 183 H2
SWFD E18 121 N1
George Lovell Dr WAB EN9 80 F3
George Mathers Rd LBTH * SE11 18 C5
George Ms CAMTN NW1 4 G10
George Rd CHING E4 100 F7
GU GU1 250 A10
KUTN/CMB KT2 177 N10
NWMAL KT3 200 C4
RGODL GU7 267 K10
George Rw BERM/RHTH SE16 19 N2
Georges Dr BRWN CM15 86 E9
Georges Md BORE WD6 75 K10
George's Rd BH/WHM TN16 244 A6
HOLWY N7 5 N1
HOLWY N7 118 G10
Georges Ter CTHM CR3 241 L8
George St BARK IG11 142 F2
BERK HP4 34 A5
CAN/RD E16 141 L8
CROY/NA CR0 203 K9
CSHM HP5 51 H6
GRAYS RM17 167 M5
HERT/WAS SG14 25 K5
HHNE HP2 35 N5
HNWL W7 134 D10
HSLW TW3 153 N8
MBLAR W1H 10 B5
NWDGN UB2 153 M3
RCHPK/HAM TW10 177 J1
ROM RM1 124 G4
STA TW18 173 J7
STALW/RED AL3 38 C6
UX/CGN UB8 131 N2
WATW WD18 73 K8
George's Wood Rd BRKMPK AL9 59 K2
Georgetown Cl NRWD SE19 181 L8
Georgette Pl GNWCH SE10 161 H6
George V Av PIN HA5 113 P1
Georgeville Gdns BARK/HLT IG6 122 E2
George V Wy GFD/PVL UB6 134 G2
RKW/CH/CXG WD3 71 K2
George Wk WARE SG12 26 C2
Georgewood Rd HHS/BOV HP3 54 A1
George Wyver Cl
WIM/MER SW19 179 H3
George Yd BANK EC3V 13 H6
MYFR/PKLN W1K 10 D7
Georgiana St CAMTN NW1 4 G5
Georgian Cl CRAWE RH10 284 E8
HAYES BR2 205 N8
STA TW18 173 L7
STAN HA7 94 F8
Georgian Ct WBLY HA9 135 M1
Georgian Wy RYLN/HDSTN HA2 114 C7
Georgia Rd NWMAL KT3 199 P4
THHTH CR7 203 J1
Georgina Gdns BETH * E2 7 M9
Geraint Rd BMLY BR1 183 M6
Geraldine Rd CHSWK W4 155 M5
WAND/EARL SW18 179 M1

Geraldine St LBTH SE11 18 C4
Gerald Rd BCTR RM8 124 A7
BGVA SW1W 16 D5
CAN/RD E16 141 L6
GVE DA12 191 H3
Gerald's Gv BNSTD SM7 220 G10
Gerard Av HSLWW TW4 175 P3
Gerard Gdns RAIN RM13 144 F4
Gerard Rd BARN SW13 156 C7
HRW HA1 114 F4
Gerards Cl BERM/RHTH SE16 160 B5
Gerda Rd ELTH/MOT SE9 184 E5
Gerdview Dr RDART DA2 187 K7
Germains Cl CSHM HP5 50 G8
Germain St CSHM HP5 50 G8
Germander Dr CHOB/PIR GU24 230 F2
Germander Wy SRTFD E15 141 K5
Gernon Cl RAIN RM13 145 L4
Gernon Rd BOW E3 140 D4
Geron Wy CRICK NW2 116 F7
Gerpins La UPMR RM14 145 N4
Gerrard Crs BRW CM14 107 H4
Gerrard Gdns PIN HA5 113 H3
Gerrard Pl SOHO/SHAV * W1D 11 K7
Gerrard Rd IS N1 6 C7
Gerrards Cl STHGT/OAK N14 78 D9
Gerrards Cross Rd SLN SL2 129 M1
Gerrards Md BNSTD SM7 239 J2
Gerrard St SOHO/SHAV W1D 11 K7
Gerridge St STHWK SE1 18 B2
Gertrude Rd BELV DA17 164 B3
Gertrude St WBPTN SW10 15 K10
Gervaise Cl SL SL1 128 E10
Gervase Cl WBLY HA9 115 P8
Gervase Rd EDGW HA8 95 P9
Gervase St PECK SE15 160 A6
Gew's Cnr CHES/WCR EN8 62 C5
Ghent St CAT SE6 182 F5
Ghent Wy HACK * E8 7 M1
Ghlbert Wy BERK HP4 33 M5
Ghyll Gdns BERK * HP4 33 J2
Giant Arches Rd HNHL SE24 181 K3
Giant Tree Hl BUSH WD23 94 C3
Gibb Cft HLWS CM18 47 H5
Gibbfield Cl CHDH RM6 123 P1
Gibbins Rd SRTFD E15 141 H2
Gibbon Rd ACT W3 136 B9
KUTN/CMB KT2 199 K1
PECK SE15 160 B8
Gibbons Cl BORE WD6 75 K5
CRAWE * RH10 284 D10
STALE/WH AL4 21 H10
Gibbons Rd WLSDN NW10 136 A1
Gibbon Wk PUT/ROE * SW15 156 D10
Gibb's Acre CHOB/PIR GU24 230 E9
Gibbs Av NRWD SE19 181 L9
Gibbs Brook La OXTED RH8 261 J10
Gibbs Cl CHES/WCR EN8 62 C5
NRWD * SE19 181 L8
Gibbs Couch OXHEY WD19 93 L4
Gibbs Gn EDGW HA8 95 P5
WKENS W14 14 C7
Gibbs Rd UED N18 100 B5
Gibbs Sq NRWD * SE19 181 L8
Gibraltar Cl RBRW/HUT CM13 107 H7
Gibraltar Crs HOR/WEW KT19 220 B6
Gibraltar Wk BETH E2 7 M10
Gibson Cl CHSGTN * KT9 219 H2
EPP * CM16 66 D1
GVW DA11 190 C6
ISLW TW7 154 C9
WCHPL E1 140 B6
Gibson Ct DTCH/LGLY SL3 150 C4
Gibson Gdns STNW/STAM * N16 119 N7
Gibson Pl STWL/WRAY TW19 173 M2
Gibson Rd BCTR RM8 123 M6
HGDN/ICK UB10 112 A9
LBTH SE11 17 P6
SUT SM1 221 L2
Gibson's Hl STRHM/NOR SW16 181 H10
Gibson Sq IS N1 6 B5
Gibson St GNWCH SE10 161 K4
Gidd Hl COUL/CHIP CR5 240 B2
Gidea Av GPK RM2 125 H1
Gidea Cl GPK RM2 125 H1
Gideon Cl BELV DA17 164 C3
Gideon Ms EA * W5 155 J1
Gideon Rd BTSEA SW11 158 B9
Gidian Ct LCOL/BKTW * AL2 56 C3
Giesbach Rd ARCH N19 118 D7
Giffard Rd UED N18 99 M6
Giffard Wy GUW GU2 249 M7
Giffin St DEPT SE8 160 F6
Gifford Gdns HNWL W7 134 C7
Giffordside CDH/CHF RM16 168 E4
Gifford St IS N1 5 M4
Gift La SRTFD E15 141 K3
Giggs Hl STMC/STPC BR5 207 K2
Giggs Hill Gdns THDIT KT7 198 F8
Giggs Hill Rd THDIT KT7 198 F7
Gilbert Cl SWCM DA10 189 J2
WIM/MER * SW19 201 L1
WOOL/PLUM SE18 162 C7
Gilbert Gv EDGW HA8 95 P9
Gilbert Pl NOXST/BSQ WC1A 11 L4
Gilbert Rd BELV DA17 164 A2
BMLY BR1 183 M10
CDH/CHF RM16 167 H2
DEN/HRF UB9 91 N10
LBTH SE11 18 B5
PIN HA5 113 L2
ROM RM1 124 G2
WIM/MER SW19 179 M10
Gilbert Rw GVW * DA11 190 C5
Gilbert St HSLW TW3 154 B9
MYFR/PKLN W1K 10 D6
PEND EN3 80 B3
SRTFD E15 121 K9
Gilbey Cl HGDN/ICK UB10 112 C9
Gilbey Rd TOOT SW17 179 P7
Gilbeys Yd CAMTN NW1 4 D4
Gilbourne Rd WOOL/PLUM SE18 163 J5
Gilda Av PEND EN3 80 D9
Gilda Crs STNW/STAM N16 119 P6
Gildea Cl PIN HA5 93 P8
Gildea St REGST W1B 10 F4
Gilden Cl HLWE * CM17 29 P7
Gildenhill Rd SWLY BR8 187 K10
Gilden Wy HLWE CM17 29 N8
Gilders SBW CM21 29 N1
Gildersome St WOOL/PLUM SE18 162 D5
Gilders Rd CHSGTN KT9 219 L3
Giles Cl RAIN RM13 145 L4
STALE/WH AL4 21 H10
Giles Coppice NRWD SE19 181 N7
Giles Md EPSOM * KT18 220 B10
Giles Travers Cl EGH TW20 194 F3
Gilfrid Cl UX/CGN UB8 132 C8
Gilham's Av BNSTD SM7 220 G8
Gilhams Cottages BNSTD * SM7 221 H8
Gilkes Crs EDUL SE22 181 M2
Gilkes Pl DUL SE21 181 M2
Gillam Wy RAIN RM13 145 H1
Gillan Gn BUSH WD23 94 B3
Gillards Ms WALTH E17 120 F2
Gillards Wy WALTH E17 120 F2
Gill Av CAN/RD E16 141 M8
GUW GU2 267 K1
Gill Cl WATW WD18 72 D10
Gill Crs GVW DA11 190 C6
Gillender St BOW E3 141 H6
Gillespie Rd FSBYPK N4 119 H8
Gillett Av EHAM E6 142 B4
Gillett Pl HACK E8 119 N10
Gillett Rd THHTH CR7 203 L4
Gillett St STNW/STAM N16 119 M10
Gillham Ter TOTM N17 99 P7
Gilliam Gv PUR/KEN CR8 223 H6
Gillian Av STAL AL1 38 B10
Gillian Crs GPK RM2 105 K10
Gillian Park Rd CHEAM SM3 201 J8
Gillian St LEW SE13 182 G1
Gillian Ter BRYLDS * KT5 199 L6
Gilliat Dr RGUE GU4 250 G8
Gilliat Rd SL SL1 129 K9
Gilliat's Gn RKW/CH/CXG WD3 70 G8
Gilliatt Cl IVER SL0 131 H8
Gillingham Ms PIM SW1V 16 F5
Gillingham Rd CRICK NW2 117 H8
Gillingham Rw PIM SW1V 16 G5
Gillingham St PIM SW1V 16 F6
Gillison Wk BERM/RHTH SE16 19 P3
Gillman Dr SRTFD E15 141 K3
Gillmans Rd STMC/STPC BR5 207 L8
Gills Hl RAD WD7 74 E1
Gills Hill La RAD WD7 74 E1
Gills Hollow RAD WD7 74 E2
Gill's Rd EYN DA4 210 D1
Gill St POP/IOD E14 140 E8
Gillum Cl EBAR EN4 98 A2
Gilmais GT/LBKH KT23 254 B1
Gilman Crs WDSR SL4 148 C9
Gilmore Cl HGDN/ICK UB10 112 B8
SLN SL2 149 P1
Gilmore Crs ASHF TW15 174 B8
Gilmore Rd LEW SE13 161 J10
Gilmour Cl ENC/FH EN2 79 P1
Gilpin Av MORT/ESHN SW14 156 A10
Gilpin Cl BAY/PAD W2 9 K4
MTCM CR4 201 P2
Gilpin Crs UED N18 99 N6
WHTN TW2 176 A3
Gilpin Gn HARP AL5 20 B2
Gilpin Rd CLPT E5 120 D9
WARE SG12 26 D3
Gilpin's Gallop WARE SG12 26 G7
Gilpin's Ride BERK HP4 34 B4
Gilpin Wy HYS/HAR UB3 152 E6
Gilroy Cl RAIN RM13 144 G1
Gilroy Wy STMC/STPC BR5 207 L7
Gilsland WAB EN9 81 K1
Gilsland Rd THHTH CR7 203 L4
Gilson Ct STWL/WRAY TW19 171 P3
Gilstead Rd FUL/PGN SW6 157 L8
Gilston Pk HLW CM20 28 F4
Gilston Rd WBPTN SW10 15 K8
Gilton Rd CAT SE6 183 K6
Giltspur St STBT EC1A 12 D5
Gilwell Cl CHING E4 80 G8
Gilwell La CHING E4 81 J8
Gimcrack Hl LHD/OX KT22 236 G8
Ginhams Rd CRAWW RH11 283 L7
Gippeswyck Cl PIN HA5 93 L9
Gipsy Hl NRWD SE19 181 M8
Gipsy La BARN SW13 156 D9
GRAYS RM17 167 P5
Gipsy Rd WELL DA16 163 N8
WNWD SE27 181 L7
Gipsy Road Gdns WNWD SE27 181 K7
Giralda Cl CAN/RD E16 142 A7
Giraud St POP/IOD E14 140 G8
Girdlers Rd HMSMTH W6 156 G3
Girdwood Rd WAND/EARL SW18 179 H3
Girling Wy EBED/NFELT TW14 153 H9
Gironde Rd FUL/PGN SW6 157 J6
Girtin Rd BUSH WD23 74 A9
Girton Av CDALE/KGS NW9 115 M1
Girton Cl NTHLT UB5 134 B1
Girton Ct CHES/WCR EN8 62 D6
Girton Gdns CROY/NA CR0 204 F10
Girton Rd NTHLT UB5 134 B1
SYD SE26 182 C8
Girton Wy RKW/CH/CXG WD3 72 D9
Gisbourne Cl WLGTN SM6 202 E10
Gisburne Wy WATN WD24 73 H3
Gisburn Rd CEND/HSY/T N8 118 G2
Gissing Wk IS N1 6 B4
Gittens Cl BMLY BR1 183 L7
Glacier Wy ALP/SUD HA0 135 J4
Gladbeck Wy ENC/FH EN2 79 K8
Gladden Ct HLWS CM18 47 H5
Gladding Rd CHESW EN7 61 J1
MNPK E12 122 A9
Glade Cl SURB * KT6 199 J9
Glade Gdns CROY/NA CR0 204 D7
Glade La NWDGN UB2 154 A1
Gladeside CROY/NA CR0 204 C6
STALE/WH AL4 39 J3
WCHMH N21 98 G1
Gladesmore Rd
SEVS/STOTM N15 119 N4
Glade Sp KWD/TDW/WH KT20 239 L7
The Glades GVE DA12 190 G9
HHW HP1 35 H5
The Glade ASC SL5 192 B5
BELMT SM2 221 H5
BF/WBF KT14 215 H9
BMLY BR1 206 A2
CFSP/GDCR SL9 110 A6
CHARL SE7 161 P6
CLAY IG5 102 C10
COUL/CHIP CR5 241 H5
CRAWE RH10 284 B9
CROY/NA CR0 204 C5
ENC/FH EN2 79 H7
EW KT17 220 D3
HACK * E8 7 M2
KWD/TDW/WH KT20 239 L7
LHD/OX KT22 235 P8
LHD/OX KT22 236 A8
NFNCH/WDSP * N12 97 N5
RBRW/HUT CM13 107 M2
SEV TN13 247 J9
SHB * W12 156 E1
STA TW18 173 L10
UPMR RM14 126 B10
WCHMH N21 78 G10
WFD IG8 101 N4
WGCW AL8 22 F3
WWKM BR4 204 G10
The Gladeway WAB EN9 63 J9
Gladiator St FSTH SE23 182 D2
Glading Ter STNW/STAM N16 119 N8
Gladioli Cl HPTN TW12 175 P9
Gladsdale Dr PIN HA5 113 H2
Gladsmuir Cl WOT/HER KT12 197 K9
Gladsmuir Rd ARCH N19 118 D6
BAR EN5 77 H6
Gladstone Av EBED/NFELT TW14 175 H2
MNPK E12 142 B2
WDGN N22 99 J10
WHTN TW2 176 C3
Gladstone Gdns HSLW TW3 154 B7
Gladstone Ms KIL/WHAMP * NW6 2 C3
PGE/AN SE20 182 B10
WDGN N22 99 H10
Gladstone Pde CRICK * NW2 116 F8
Gladstone Park Gdns CRICK NW2 116 E8
Gladstone Pl BAR * EN5 76 G8
E/WMO/HCT * KT8 198 D5
Gladstone Rd ASHTD KT21 237 J4
BKHH IG9 101 P2
CHSWK * W4 156 A2
CROY/NA CR0 203 L7
CSHM HP5 51 H7
DART DA1 187 N2
HOD EN11 44 G2
KUT KT1 199 M3
NWDGN UB2 153 M1
ORP BR6 226 F2
SURB KT6 199 J9
WARE SG12 26 B1
WAT WD17 73 K7
WIM/MER SW19 179 K10
Gladstone St STHWK SE1 18 C3
Gladstone Ter VX/NE * SW8 158 C7
WNWD * SE27 181 K7
Gladstone Wy
KTN/HRWW/W HA3 114 D1
SL SL1 148 F1
Gladwell Rd BMLY BR1 183 M9
CEND/HSY/T N8 118 G4
Gladwyn Rd PUT/ROE SW15 156 G9
Gladys Rd KIL/WHAMP NW6 2 F3
Glaisher St DEPT SE8 160 G5
Glaisyer Wy IVER SL0 130 F4
Glamis Cl CHESW EN7 61 P5
Glamis Crs HYS/HAR UB3 152 D2
Glamis Dr EMPK RM11 125 M6
Glamis Pl WAP E1W 140 B9
Glamis Rd WAP E1W 140 B9
Glamis Wy NTHLT UB5 134 B1
Glamorgan Cl MTCM CR4 202 F3
Glamorgan Rd KUT KT1 177 H10
Glanfield HHNE HP2 35 P3
Glanfield Rd BECK BR3 204 E4
Glanleam Rd STAN HA7 95 J5
Glanmead BRWN CM15 107 K2
Glanmor Rd SLN SL2 129 N9
Glanthams Rd BRWN CM15 107 L3
The Glanty EGH TW20 172 F7
Glanville Dr EMPK RM11 125 N6
Glanville Rd BRXS/STRHM SW2 180 F1
HAYES BR2 205 N3
Glasbrook Av WHTN TW2 175 N4
Glasbrook Rd ELTH/MOT SE9 184 A3
Glaserton Rd STNW/STAM N16 119 M5
Glasford St TOOT SW17 180 A9
Glasgow Rd PLSTW E13 141 N4
SL SL1 128 F8
UED N18 100 A6
Glasgow Ter PIM SW1V 16 G8
Glasse Cl WEA W13 134 F9
Glasshill St STHWK SE1 18 D1
Glasshouse Flds WAP E1W 140 C9
Glasshouse St REGST W1B 11 H8
Glasshouse Wk LBTH SE11 17 M7
Glasshouse Yd STBT EC1A 12 E2
Glasslyn Rd CEND/HSY/T N8 118 E3
Glassmill La HAYES BR2 205 L2
Glass St BETH * E2 140 A6
Glass Yd WOOL/PLUM SE18 162 D2
Glastonbury Av WFD IG8 102 A8
Glastonbury Cl STMC/STPC BR5 207 M8
Glastonbury Pl WCHPL E1 140 B8
Glastonbury Rd ED N9 99 P2
MRDN SM4 201 K7
Glastonbury St KIL/WHAMP NW6 117 J10
Glaston Ct EA * W5 135 J10
Glaucus St BOW E3 140 G7
Glazbury Rd WKENS W14 14 B6
Glazebrook Cl DUL SE21 181 L5
Glazebrook Rd TEDD TW11 176 E10
Glaziers La RGUW GU3 248 A8
Gleave Cl STAL AL1 38 G5
Glebe Av ENC/FH EN2 79 J7
HGDN/ICK UB10 112 C8
KTN/HRWW/W HA3 115 K1
MTCM CR4 201 P2
RSLP HA4 133 J1
WFD IG8 101 M7
Glebe Cl BRKMPK AL9 42 A3
CFSP/GDCR SL9 90 A9
CHSWK * W4 156 B4
CRAWE RH10 283 N6
GT/LBKH KT23 253 P2
HERT/WAS SG14 25 L3
HGDN/ICK UB10 112 D9
HHS/BOV HP3 35 P9
LTWR GU18 212 B6
SAND/SEL CR2 223 N8
Glebe Cottages BRKMPK AL9 42 A3
RGUE GU4 251 L8
Glebe Ct BKHTH/KID * SE3 161 K9
EA * W5 135 J10
STAN HA7 95 H6
Glebe Crs HDN NW4 116 F2
KTN/HRWW/W HA3 115 K1
The Glebefield SEV TN13 246 G9
Glebe Gdns BF/WBF KT14 215 N10
NWMAL KT3 200 B7
Glebe House Dr HAYES BR2 205 N8
Glebe Hyrst SAND/SEL CR2 223 N8
Glebeland Gdns SHPTN TW17 196 D6
Glebelands CHIG IG7 103 L4
CRAWE RH10 285 P5
DART DA1 164 G10
E/WMO/HCT KT8 198 A5
ESH/CLAY KT10 218 E5
HLW CM20 29 J8
Glebelands Av GNTH/NBYPK IG2 122 G5
SWFD E18 101 M10
Glebelands Cl CMBW * SE5 159 M9
Glebelands Rd
EBED/NFELT TW14 175 H3
Glebe La BAR EN5 76 D10
KTN/HRWW/W HA3 115 K2
RDKG RH5 271 L9
SEV TN13 265 J2
Glebe Pth MTCM CR4 202 A3
Glebe Pl CHEL SW3 15 N9
EYN DA4 210 B4
Glebe Rd ASHTD KT21 237 J4
BARN SW13 156 D8
BELMT SM2 221 H5
BMLY BR1 205 M1
CAR SM5 222 A3
CEND/HSY/T N8 118 G2
CFSP/GDCR SL9 89 P9
CHONG CM5 67 N5
COUL/CHIP CR5 240 C10
DAGE RM10 144 C1
DORK RH4 272 E2
EGH TW20 172 F9
FNCH N3 97 M9
GVW DA11 190 C4
HACK E8 7 L3
HERT/WAS SG14 25 L3
RAIN RM13 145 J5
RSEV TN14 265 J8
STA TW18 173 L8
STAN HA7 95 H6
UX/CGN UB8 131 M4
WARL CR6 242 C3
WDSR SL4 171 N1
WLSDN NW10 136 D1
Glebe Side TWK TW1 176 E2
Glebe Sq MTCM * CR4 202 A3
Glebe St CHSWK W4 156 A4
Glebe Ter BOW E3 140 G5
The Glebe BKHTH/KID SE3 161 K9
CHST BR7 206 F1
CRAWE RH10 285 J2
GSTN WD25 55 K9
HLW CM20 29 H10
HORL RH6 280 A4
KGLGY WD4 54 B5
REIG RH2 274 D7
STRHM/NOR * SW16 180 E7
WDR/YW UB7 151 P3
WPK KT4 200 C8
Glebeway WFD IG8 101 P6
Glebe Wy AMS HP6 69 J2
EMPK RM11 125 M5
ERITH DA8 164 F5
FELT TW13 175 P6
SAND/SEL CR2 223 N8
WWKM BR4 205 H9
Gledhow Gdns ECT SW5 15 J6
Gledhow Wd
KWD/TDW/WH KT20 239 L8
Gledstanes Rd WKENS W14 14 B8
Gledwood Av YEAD UB4 133 H7
Gledwood Crs YEAD UB4 132 G7
Gledwood Dr YEAD UB4 132 G7
Gledwood Gdns YEAD UB4 133 H7
Gleed Av BUSH WD23 94 C3
Gleeson Dr ORP BR6 227 J2
Glegg Pl PUT/ROE * SW15 156 G10
Glemsford Dr HARP AL5 20 C1
Glenaffric Av POP/IOD E14 161 H3
Glen Albyn Rd WIM/MER SW19 178 G5
Glenalla Rd RSLP HA4 112 G5
Glenalmond Rd
KTN/HRWW/W HA3 115 K2
Glenalvon Wy CHARL SE7 162 B3
Glena Mt SUT SM1 221 M1
Glenarm Rd CLPT E5 120 B9
Glen Av ASHF TW15 174 B7
Glenavon Cl ESH/CLAY KT10 218 F3
Glenavon Gdns DTCH/LGLY SL3 149 P3
Glenavon Rd SRTFD E15 141 K2
Glenbarr Cl ELTH/MOT SE9 162 E9
Glenbow Rd BMLY BR1 183 K9
Glenbrook North ENC/FH EN2 78 G8
Glenbrook Rd KIL/WHAMP NW6 117 K10
Glenbrook South ENC/FH EN2 78 G8
Glenbuck Rd SURB KT6 199 J6
Glenburnie Rd TOOT SW17 180 A6
Glencairn Dr EA W5 134 G6
Glencairne Cl CAN/RD E16 142 A7
Glencairn Rd STRHM/NOR SW16 180 F10
Glen Cl KWD/TDW/WH KT20 239 H9
SHPTN TW17 196 B4
Glencoe Av GNTH/NBYPK IG2 123 H5
Glencoe Rd BUSH WD23 73 P10
DAGE RM10 124 B9
WEY KT13 196 B10
YEAD UB4 133 L6
Glencorse Gn OXHEY * WD19 93 L5
Glen Ct ADL/WDHM * KT15 215 J2
Glen Crs WFD IG8 101 N7
Glendale HHW HP1 35 L6
SWLY BR8 208 G5
Glendale Av CHDH RM6 123 M5
EDGW HA8 95 L5
WDGN N22 99 H8
Glendale Cl BRWN CM15 107 K2
ELTH/MOT SE9 162 D9
WOKN/KNAP GU21 231 P4
Glendale Dr RGUE GU4 250 F6
Glendale Gdns WBLY HA9 115 J6
Glen Dale Ms BECK BR3 204 G1
Glendale Ri PUR/KEN CR8 241 J1
Glendale Rd ERITH DA8 164 D3
GVW DA11 190 B7
Glendale Wy THMD SE28 143 M10
Glendall St CLAP SW4 158 G9
Glendarvon St PUT/ROE SW15 156 G9
Glendene Av EHSLY KT24 252 F2
Glendevon Cl EDGW HA8 95 N4
Glendish Rd TOTM N17 99 P9
Glendor Gdns MLHL NW7 96 A5
Glendower Crs ORP BR6 207 K6
Glendower Gdns
MORT/ESHN SW14 156 A9
Glendower Rd CHING E4 101 J2
MORT/ESHN SW14 156 A9
Glendown Rd ABYW SE2 163 K4
Glendun Rd ACT W3 136 B9
Gleneagle Ms STRHM/NOR SW16 180 E8
Gleneagle Rd STRHM/NOR SW16 180 E8
Gleneagles STAN HA7 94 G7
Gleneagles Cl
BERM/RHTH * SE16 160 A4
HARH RM3 105 N8
HTHAIR TW6 173 M2
ORP BR6 206 G8
OXHEY * WD19 93 L6
Gleneagles Ct CRAWE * RH10 283 N8
Gleneldon Ms STRHM/NOR SW16 180 F7
Gleneldon Rd STRHM/NOR SW16 180 F7
Glenelg Rd BRXS/STRHM SW2 180 F1
Glenesk Rd ELTH/MOT SE9 162 D10
Glenester Cl HOD EN11 26 F10
Glen Faba Rd HLWW/ROY CM19 45 L3
Glenfarg Rd CAT SE6 183 J4
Glenferrie Rd STAL AL1 38 F6
Glenfield Cl BRKHM/BTCW RH3 273 N3
Glenfield Ct HERT/WAS SG14 24 G4
Glenfield Crs RSLP HA4 112 E5
Glenfield Rd ASHF TW15 174 C9
BAL SW12 180 D4
BNSTD SM7 239 L1
BRKHM/BTCW RH3 273 N4
WEA W13 154 G1
Glenfinlas Wy CMBW SE5 159 J6
Glenforth St GNWCH SE10 161 L3
Glengall Br POP/IOD E14 160 G2
Glengall Gv POP/IOD E14 160 G2
Glengall Pl STAL * AL1 38 D9
Glengall Rd BXLYHN DA7 163 P9
EDGW HA8 95 N4
KIL/WHAMP NW6 2 D6
PECK SE15 19 M9
WFD IG8 101 M7
Glengall Ter PECK SE15 19 M9
Glen Gdns CROY/NA CR0 203 H10
Glengarnock Av POP/IOD E14 161 H3
Glengarry Rd EDUL SE22 159 M10
Glenham Dr GNTH/NBYPK IG2 122 E3
Glenhaven Av BORE WD6 75 M7
Glen Hazel BRWN CM15 87 J1
Glenhead Cl ELTH/MOT SE9 162 E9
Glenheadon Cl LHD/OX KT22 237 J9
Glenheadon Ri LHD/OX KT22 237 J9
Glenhill Cl FNCH N3 97 K10
Glenhouse Rd ELTH/MOT SE9 184 D1
Glenhurst Av BXLY DA5 186 A4
KTTN NW5 118 B9
RSLP HA4 112 D5
Glenhurst Ri NRWD SE19 181 K10
Glenhurst Rd BTFD TW8 155 H5
NFNCH/WDSP N12 97 N5
Glenilla Rd HAMP NW3 3 N1
Glenister Park Rd
STRHM/NOR SW16 180 E10
Glenister Rd CSHM HP5 51 H4
GNWCH SE10 161 L4
Glenlea Rd ELTH/MOT SE9 184 D1
Glenloch Rd HAMP NW3 3 N1
PEND EN3 80 B6
Glenluge Rd BKHTH/KID SE3 161 M5
Glenlyn Av STAL AL1 38 G7
Glenlyon Rd ELTH/MOT SE9 184 D1
Glenmere Av MLHL NW7 96 D8
Glenmore Cl ADL/WDHM KT15 195 L10
Glenmore Lawns WEA * W13 134 F8
Glenmore Pde ALP/SUD * HA0 135 K3
Glenmore Rd HAMP NW3 3 N1
WELL DA16 163 J7
Glenmore Wy BARK IG11 143 K5
Glenn Av PUR/KEN CR8 223 J7
Glennie Rd WNWD SE27 181 H6
Glenny Rd BARK IG11 142 F1
Glenorchy Cl YEAD UB4 133 M7
Glenparke Rd FSTGT E7 141 N1
Glen Ri WFD IG8 101 N7
Glen Rd CHSGTN KT9 199 K10
PLSTW E13 141 P6
WALTH E17 120 E3
WLGTN SM6 222 C5
Glenrosa Gdns GVE DA12 191 J8
Glenrosa St FUL/PGN SW6 157 M8
Glenroy St SHB W12 136 F8
Glensdale Rd BROCKY SE4 160 E9
Glenshiel Rd ELTH/MOT SE9 184 D1
Glenside CHIG IG7 102 E7
Glentanner Wy TOOT SW17 179 N6
Glen Ter POP/IOD E14 161 H1
Glentham Cottages
BARN * SW13 156 D5
Glentham Gdns BARN SW13 156 E4
Glentham Rd BARN SW13 156 D5
The Glen ADL/WDHM KT15 215 J2
ASC * SL5 192 C4
BELMT * SM2 221 M3
CROY/NA CR0 204 C10
DTCH/LGLY SL3 149 P3
ENC/FH EN2 79 J8
HAYES BR2 205 K2
HHNE HP2 36 B1
NTHWD HA6 92 E8
NWDGN UB2 153 N4
ORP BR6 206 C10
PIN HA5 113 M5
PIN HA5 113 J3
RAIN RM13 145 K6
WBLY HA9 115 J9
Glenthorne Av CROY/NA CR0 204 B8
Glenthorne Cl CHEAM SM3 201 K8
Glenthorne Gdns BARK/HLT IG6 122 D1
CHEAM SM3 201 K8
Glenthorne Rd FBAR/BDGN N11 98 A6
HMSMTH W6 156 F3
KUT KT1 199 L4
WALTH E17 120 D3
Glenthorpe Rd MRDN SM4 200 G5
Glenton Cl ROM RM1 104 F8
Glenton Rd LEW SE13 161 K10
Glenton Wy ROM RM1 104 F8
Glentrammon Av ORP BR6 227 J3
Glentrammon Cl ORP BR6 227 J3
Glentrammon Gdns ORP BR6 227 J3
Glentrammon Rd ORP BR6 227 J3
Glentworth Pl SL SL1 129 H10
Glentworth St CAMTN NW1 10 B2
Glenure Rd ELTH/MOT SE9 184 D1
Glenview ABYW SE2 163 N5
Glen Vw GVE DA12 190 F4
Glenview Cl CRAWE RH10 284 A5
Glen View Rd BMLY BR1 206 A2
Glenview Rd HHW HP1 35 L6
Glenville Av ENC/FH EN2 79 K4
Glenville Gv DEPT SE8 160 E6
Glenville Rd KUTN/CMB KT2 199 M1
Glen Wy WAT WD17 72 F4
Glenwood BROX EN10 44 E5
RDKG RH5 273 H4
WGCE AL7 23 M6
Glenwood Av CDALE/KGS NW9 116 B6
RAIN RM13 145 H6
Glenwood Cl HRW HA1 114 E3
Glenwood Dr GPK RM2 125 H3
Glenwood Gdns
GNTH/NBYPK IG2 122 D3
Glenwood Gv CDALE/KGS NW9 115 P6
Glenwood Rd CAT SE6 182 E4
EW KT17 220 D3
HSLW TW3 154 C9
MLHL NW7 96 B4
SEVS/STOTM N15 119 J3
Glenwood Rw NRWD * SE19 203 N1
Glenwood Wy CROY/NA CR0 204 C6
Glenworth Av POP/IOD E14 161 J3
Glevum Cl STALW/RED AL3 37 N8
Gliddon Rd WKENS W14 14 A7
Glimpsing Gn ERITHM DA18 163 P2
Glisson Rd HGDN/ICK UB10 132 B4
Gload Crs STMC/STPC BR5 207 N9

Globe Cl HARP AL5 20 B2
Globe Pond Rd
BERM/RHTH SE16 140 D10
Globe Rd BETH E2 140 B5
EMPK RM11 125 H4
FSTGT E7 121 L10
WFD IG8 101 P7
Globe St STHWK SE1 18 G2
Globe Ter BETH E2 140 B5
Glory Md DORK RH4 273 H5
Glossop Rd SAND/SEL CR2 225 L5
Gloster Rd NWMAL KT3 200 B4
WOKS/MYFD GU22 232 D6
Gloucester Av BFN/LL DA15 185 H5
CAMTN NW1 4 C4
CDH/CHF RM16 167 P1
CHES/WCR EN8 62 D9
EMPK RM11 125 P3
SL SL1 129 H7
TIL RM18 169 M4
WELL DA16 185 J1
Gloucester Circ GNWCH SE10 161 H6
Gloucester Cl THDIT * KT7 198 F8
WLSDN NW10 136 A2
Gloucester Ct MON EC3R 13 K8
MTCM * CR4 202 F5
RCH/KEW * TW9 155 M6
Gloucester Crs CAMTN NW1 4 E5
STA TW18 173 N9
Gloucester Dr FSBYPK N4 119 J7
GLDGN NW11 117 K2
STWL/WRAY TW19 172 F6
Gloucester Gdns BAY/PAD W2 9 H5
EBAR EN4 78 B8
GLDGN NW11 117 J5
IL IG1 122 B5
SUT SM1 201 L9
Gloucester Ga CAMTN NW1 4 D7
Gloucester Gate Ms CAMTN NW1 4 E7
Gloucester Gv EDGW HA8 96 A9
Gloucester Ms BAY/PAD W2 9 K6
Gloucester Ms West BAY/PAD W2 9 J6
Gloucester Pde BFN/LL * DA15 185 K1
HYS/HAR * UB3 152 D2
Gloucester Pl CAMTN NW1 10 A2
WDSR SL4 149 J8
Gloucester Place Ms MBLAR W1H 10 B4
Gloucester Rd ACT W3 155 P1
BAR EN5 77 L9
BELV DA17 164 A4
BRWN CM15 86 G9
CROY/NA CR0 203 L7
DART DA1 187 J2
EA W5 155 H1
ENC/FH EN2 79 K4
FELT TW13 175 K4
GUW GU2 249 L8
GVE DA12 190 F7
HPTN TW12 176 A10
HSLWW TW4 153 M10
KUT KT1 199 M2
LEY E10 120 F5
MNPK E12 122 C8
RCH/KEW TW9 155 M6
REDH RH1 258 A9
ROM RM1 124 F4
RYLN/HDSTN HA2 114 A3
SKENS SW7 15 J3
TEDD TW11 176 D8
TOTM N17 99 L10
UED N18 99 N6
WALTH E17 100 C10
WAN E11 121 N3
WHTN TW2 176 B4
Gloucester Sq BAY/PAD W2 9 M6
BETH E2 7 N6
Gloucester St PIM SW1V 16 G7
Gloucester Ter BAY/PAD W2 9 H5
STHGT/OAK * N14 98 E2
Gloucester Wk KENS W8 14 F1
Gloucester Wy CLKNW EC1R 6 B10
Glover Cl ABYW SE2 163 M3
CHESW * EN7 61 N3
Glover Dr UED N18 100 B7
Glover Rd PIN HA5 113 L4
Glovers Cl HERT/BAY SG13 25 K7
Glovers Fld BRWN CM15 86 E3
Glovers Gv RSLP HA4 112 C5
Glovers La HLWE CM17 47 P6
Glover's Rd HORL RH6 278 G8
REIG RH2 275 L1
Gloxinia Rd MEO DA13 189 N9
Glycena Rd BTSEA SW11 158 A9
Glyn Av EBAR EN4 77 N8
Glyn Cl EW KT17 220 D5
SNWD SE25 203 M2
Glyn Davies Cl SEV TN13 246 F6
Glyndebourne Pk ORP BR6 206 E10
Glynde Ms CHEL SW3 15 P4
Glynde Rd BXLYHN DA7 163 P9
Glynde St BROCKY SE4 182 E2
Glyndon Rd WOOL/PLUM SE18 162 F3
Glyn Dr SCUP DA14 185 L7
Glynfield Rd WLSDN NW10 136 B2
Glynne Rd WDGN N22 99 H10
Glyn Rd CLPT E5 120 C9
PEND EN3 80 B8
WPK KT4 200 G9
Glyn St LBTH SE11 17 N8
Glynswood CFSP/GDCR SL9 90 C8
Goat La EN EN1 79 N4
Goat Rd MTCM CR4 202 B7
Goatsfield Rd BH/WHM TN16 243 P6
Goatswood La ABR/ST RM4 105 J1
Goat Whf BTFD TW8 155 K5
Gobions Av CRW RM5 104 E8
Goblins Gn WGCE AL7 22 G6
Godalming Av WLGTN SM6 222 F2
Godalming Rd POP/IOD E14 140 G7
Godbold Rd SRTFD E15 141 K6
Goddard Cl CRAWE RH10 284 C10
SHPTN TW17 196 A3
Goddard Pl ARCH N19 118 D8
Goddard Rd BECK BR3 204 C4
CDH/CHF RM16 147 M10
Goddards Cl HERT/BAY SG13 42 D5
Goddards Wy IL IG1 122 G6
Goddington Cha ORP BR6 227 L1
Goddington La ORP BR6 207 M10
Godfrey Av NTHLT UB5 133 M3
WHTN TW2 176 C3
Godfrey Hl WOOL/PLUM SE18 162 B3
Godfrey Rd WOOL/PLUM SE18 162 C3
Godfrey St CHEL SW3 15 P7
SRTFD E15 141 H4
Godfrey Wy HSLWW TW4 175 M3
Goding St LBTH SE11 17 M8
Godley Rd BF/WBF KT14 216 A9
WAND/EARL SW18 179 N4
Godliman St BLKFR * EC4V 12 D6
Godman Rd CDH/CHF RM16 168 E2
PECK * SE15 160 A8
Godolphin Cl BELMT SM2 221 J7
PLMGR N13 99 J7
Godolphin Ct CRAWW * RH11 283 N8
Godolphin Pl ACT W3 136 A9
Godolphin Rd BEAC HP9 89 H7
SHB W12 136 E10
SL SL1 129 J9
WEY KT13 216 E3
Godric Crs CROY/NA CR0 225 J5
Godson Rd CROY/NA CR0 203 H10
Godstone Green Rd GDST RH9 260 A7
Godstone Hl GDST RH9 260 B6
Godstone Mt PUR/KEN * CR8 223 J8
Godstone Rd CTHM CR3 241 P10
GDST RH9 260 G7
OXTED RH8 261 H6
PUR/KEN CR8 223 J9
REDH RH1 259 M9
SUT SM1 221 M1
TWK TW1 176 F2
Godstow Rd ABYW SE2 163 M1
Godwin Cl CHING E4 81 H4
HOR/WEW KT19 219 P3
IS N1 6 F7
Godwin Rd FSTGT E7 121 N9
HAYES BR2 205 P3
Goffers Rd BKHTH/KID SE3 161 K7
Goffs Cl CRAWW RH11 283 M8
Goffs Crs CHESW EN7 61 K5
Goff's La CHESW EN7 61 K5
CRAWW RH11 283 L7
Goff's Oak Av CHESW EN7 61 J4
Goffs Park Rd CRAWW RH11 283 M8
Goffs Rd ASHF TW15 174 E9
Gogmore Farm Cl CHERT KT16 195 H7
Gogmore La CHERT KT16 195 K7
Goidel Cl WLGTN SM6 222 E1
Golborne Gdns NKENS W10 8 B2
Golborne Ms NKENS * W10 8 B3
Golborne Rd NKENS W10 8 B3
Goldace GRAYS RM17 167 L5
Golda Cl BAR EN5 76 G10
Goldbeaters Gv EDGW HA8 96 B7
Goldcliff Cl MRDN SM4 201 K7
Gold Cl BROX EN10 44 D6
Goldcrest Cl CAN/RD E16 142 A7
HORL RH6 279 N3
THMD SE28 143 M9
Goldcrest Ms EA * W5 135 J7
Goldcrest Wy BUSH WD23 94 B2
CROY/NA CR0 225 J5
PUR/KEN CR8 222 E6
Goldcroft HHS/BOV HP3 36 B8
Golden Crs HYS/HAR UB3 132 F10
Golden Cross Ms NTGHL W11 8 C5
Golden Dell WGCE AL7 23 J9
Golden Hind Pl DEPT * SE8 160 E3
Golden La STLK EC1Y 12 E1
Golden Lane Est STLK EC1Y 12 E1
Golden Mnr HNWL W7 134 D9
Golden Oak Cl SLN * SL2 129 H1
Golden Pde WALTH * E17 121 H1
Golden Plover Cl CAN/RD E16 141 M8
Golden Sq SOHO/CST W1F 11 H7
Golden Yd HAMP * NW3 117 M9
Golders Cl EDGW HA8 95 N6
Golders Gdns GLDGN NW11 117 H5
Golders Green Crs GLDGN NW11 117 J5
Golders Hl GLDGN * NW11 117 L7
Golderslea GLDGN * NW11 117 K6
Golders Manor Dr GLDGN NW11 116 G4
Golders Park Cl GLDGN NW11 117 K6
Golders Ri HDN NW4 116 G3
Golders Wy GLDGN NW11 117 J5
Goldfinch Cl CRAWW RH11 283 N5
ORP BR6 227 K2
Goldfinch Gdns RGUE GU4 250 G9
Goldfinch Rd SAND/SEL CR2 224 D6
THMD SE28 162 G2
Goldfinch Wy BORE WD6 75 M8
Goldhawk Ms SHB W12 156 E1
Goldhawk Rd HMSMTH W6 156 C3
SHB W12 156 E2
Goldhaze Cl WFD IG8 102 A8
Gold Hl EDGW HA8 96 A7
Gold Hl East CFSP/GDCR SL9 90 A10
Gold Hl North CFSP/GDCR SL9 89 P9
Gold Hl West CFSP/GDCR SL9 89 P9
Goldhurst Ter KIL/WHAMP NW6 3 H4
Goldings Cl CRAWE RH10 284 D8
Goldingham Av LOU IG10 82 F6
Golding Rd SEV TN13 247 K8
Goldings Crs HAT AL10 40 E3
Golding's Hl LOU IG10 82 C4
Goldings La HERT/WAS SG14 25 H2
Goldings Ri LOU IG10 82 D5
Goldings Rd LOU IG10 82 D5
The Goldings WOKN/KNAP GU21 231 L2
Golding St WCHPL E1 13 P6
Goldington Cl HOD EN11 26 E10
Goldington Crs CAMTN NW1 5 J7
Goldington St CAMTN NW1 5 J7
Gold La EDGW HA8 96 A7
Goldman Cl BETH E2 13 N1
Goldney Rd MV/WKIL W9 8 E2
Goldrill Dr FBAR/BDGN N11 98 B3
Goldrings Rd LHD/OX KT22 218 B9
Goldsboro' Rd VX/NE SW8 158 E7
Goldsborough Crs CHING E4 100 G3
Goldsdown Cl PEND EN3 80 D6
Goldsdown Rd PEND EN3 80 C6
Goldsel Rd SWLY BR8 208 F4
Goldsmid St WOOL/PLUM SE18 163 H4
Goldsmith GRAYS RM17 167 L5
Goldsmith Av ACT W3 136 A9
CDALE/KGS NW9 116 B3
MNPK E12 122 B1
ROMW/RG RM7 124 B5
Goldsmith Cl RYLN/HDSTN HA2 113 P6
Goldsmith La CDALE/KGS NW9 115 P2
Goldsmith Pl KIL/WHAMP * NW6 2 G6
Goldsmith Rd ACT W3 136 A10
FBAR/BDGN N11 98 A6
LEY E10 120 G4
PECK SE15 159 P7
WALTH E17 100 C10
Goldsmiths Cl ACT * W3 136 A10
WOKN/KNAP GU21 231 P4
Goldsmith's Rw BETH E2 7 P6
Goldsmith St CITYW EC2V 12 F5
Goldsmiths Whf GRAYS * RM17 167 M6
Goldsmith Wy STALW/RED AL3 38 B4
Goldstone Cl WARE SG12 26 C1
Goldstone Farm Vw
GT/LBKH * KT23 253 P3
Goldsworth Orch
WOKN/KNAP GU21 231 M4
Goldsworth Rd
WOKN/KNAP GU21 231 P4
Goldsworthy Gdns
BERM/RHTH SE16 160 B3
Goldsworthy Wy SL SL1 128 B8
Goldwell Rd THHTH CR7 202 G4
Goldwing Cl CAN/RD E16 141 M8
Gole Rd CHOB/PIR GU24 230 C7
Golf Cl BUSH WD23 73 L7
STAN HA7 95 H8
STRHM/NOR SW16 203 H1
WOKS/MYFD GU22 215 H10
Golf Club Dr KUTN/CMB KT2 178 A10
Golf Club Rd BRKMPK AL9 59 K2
WEY KT13 216 C6
WOKS/MYFD GU22 231 M6
Golfe Rd IL IG1 122 G8
Golf Links Av GVW DA11 190 E8
Golf Ride ENC/FH EN2 79 H1
Golf Rd BMLY BR1 206 D3
EA * W5 135 L8
PUR/KEN CR8 241 L4
Golf Side BELMT SM2 221 H7
WHTN TW2 176 C6
Golf Side Cl NWMAL KT3 200 B2
Golfside Cl TRDG/WHET N20 97 P4
Gollogly Ter CHARL SE7 161 P4
Gombards STALW/RED AL3 38 C5
Gomer Gdns TEDD TW11 176 F9
Gomer Pl TEDD TW11 176 F9
Gomm Rd BERM/RHTH SE16 160 B2
Gomms Wood Cl BEAC HP9 88 A7
Gomshall Av WLGTN SM6 222 F2
Gomshall Gdns PUR/KEN CR8 241 M1
Gomshall La SHGR GU5 270 B5
Gomshall Rd BELMT * SM2 220 F6
EW KT17 220 F6
Gondar Gdns CRICK NW2 117 J10
Gonson St DEPT SE8 160 G5
Gonston Cl WIM/MER SW19 179 H5
Gonville Av RKW/CH/CXG WD3 72 C10
Gonville Crs NTHLT UB5 134 A1
Gonville Rd THHTH CR7 202 G5
Gonville St FUL/PGN SW6 157 H9
Goodall Rd WAN E11 121 H8
Gooden Ct HRW HA1 114 D8
Goodenough Cl COUL/CHIP CR5 241 H6
Goodenough Rd
WIM/MER SW19 179 J10
Goodenough Wy
COUL/CHIP CR5 240 G6
Goodey Rd BARK IG11 143 J2
Goodge Pl FITZ W1T 11 H4
Goodge St FITZ W1T 11 H4
Goodhall St WLSDN NW10 136 C5
Goodhart Wy WWKM BR4 205 K6
Goodhew Rd SNWD SE25 203 P6
Gooding Cl NWMAL KT3 199 P4
Goodinge Cl HOLWY * N7 5 L1
Goodinge Rd HOLWY N7 5 L1
Goodlake Ct DEN/HRF UB9 111 J5
Goodley Stock Rd EDEN TN8 262 E5
Goodman Ct ALP/SUD * HA0 115 J9
Goodman Crs BRXS/STRHM SW2 180 E5
Goodman Pk SLN SL2 129 P10
Goodman Rd LEY E10 121 H5
Goodmans Ct ALP/SUD HA0 115 J9
Goodman's Stile WCHPL E1 13 N5
Goodman's Yd TWRH EC3N 13 L7
Goodmayes Av GDMY/SEVK IG3 123 K6
Goodmayes La GDMY/SEVK IG3 123 K9
Goodmayes Rd GDMY/SEVK IG3 123 K6
Goodmead Rd ORP BR6 207 K7
Goodrich Cl GSTN WD25 73 H1
Goodrich Rd EDUL SE22 181 N2
Goodson Rd WLSDN NW10 136 B2
Goods Wy CAMTN NW1 5 L7
Goodway Gdns POP/IOD E14 141 J8
Goodwin Cl BERM/RHTH SE16 19 M4
CRAWW RH11 283 H10
MTCM CR4 201 N3
Goodwin Ct CHES/WCR EN8 62 D4
Goodwin Dr SCUP DA14 185 N5
Goodwin Gdns CROY/NA CR0 223 J3
Goodwin Rd CROY/NA CR0 223 J2
ED N9 100 B2
SHB W12 156 D1
SLN SL2 128 E5
Goodwins Ct CHCR WC2N 11 L7
Goodwin St FSBYPK N4 119 H7
Goodwood Av HCH RM12 125 M8
PEND EN3 80 B3
WATN WD24 72 F1
Goodwood Cl CRAWE RH10 284 B10
HOD EN11 44 E2
MRDN SM4 201 K4
Goodwood Crs GVE DA12 190 F9
Goodwood Dr NTHLT UB5 133 P1
Goodwood Pde BECK * BR3 204 D4
Goodwood Rd NWCR SE14 160 D6
REDH RH1 258 A8
Goodwyn Av MLHL NW7 96 B6
Goodwyns Rd DORK RH4 272 G5
Goodwyn's V MUSWH N10 98 B9
Goodyers Av RAD WD7 56 E9
Goodyers Gdns HDN NW4 116 G3
Goosander Wy
WOOL/PLUM SE18 162 G2
Goose Acre CSHM HP5 51 M6
Gooseacre WGCE AL7 23 J7
Gooseacre La
KTN/HRWW/W HA3 115 J3
Goosecroft HHW HP1 35 J5
Goosefields RKW/CH/CXG WD3 71 M10
Goose Gn SHGR GU5 270 D5
SLN SL2 128 G4
Goose Green Cl STMC/STPC BR5 207 K2
Goose La WOKS/MYFD GU22 231 N8
Gooseley La EHAM E6 142 D5
Goose Rye Rd RGUW GU3 249 J2
Gooshays Dr HARH RM3 105 M7
Gooshays Gdns HARH RM3 105 M7
Goossens Cl SUT SM1 221 M2
Gophir La CANST * EC4R 12 G7
Gopsall St IS N1 7 H6
Goral Md RKW/CH/CXG WD3 91 N2
Gordon Av CHING E4 101 K7
HCH RM12 124 G7
MORT/ESHN SW14 156 B10
PUR/KEN CR8 223 K6
STAN HA7 94 E7
TWK TW1 176 F1
Gordonbrock Rd BROCKY SE4 182 F1
Gordon Cl CHERT KT16 195 H10
STA TW18 173 L9
STAL AL1 38 G7
TIL RM18 169 N6
WALTH E17 120 F4
Gordon Ct REDH * RH1 276 A2
Gordon Crs CROY/NA CR0 203 M8
HYS/HAR UB3 153 H3
Gordondale Rd WIM/MER SW19 179 K5
Gordon Dr CHERT KT16 195 H10
SHPTN TW17 196 E6
Gordon Gdns EDGW HA8 95 N10
Gordon Gv CMBW SE5 159 J8
Gordon Hl ENC/FH EN2 79 K5
Gordon House Rd KTTN NW5 118 B9
Gordon Pl GVE DA12 190 F2
KENS W8 14 F1
Gordon Prom East GVE DA12 190 G2
Gordon Rd ASHF TW15 173 P6
BARK IG11 123 H3
BECK BR3 204 E3
BELV DA17 164 D3
BFN/LL DA15 185 H1
BRWN CM15 107 M2
BRYLDS KT5 199 L7
CAR SM5 222 A3
CDH/CHF RM16 168 B1
CHDH RM6 124 A4
CHES/WCR EN8 62 F10
CHING E4 101 K1
CHSWK W4 155 N5
CSHM HP5 51 H8
CTHM CR3 241 L7
DART DA1 187 L3
EA W5 135 H9
ED N9 100 A3
ENC/FH EN2 79 L5
ESH/CLAY KT10 218 D4
FBAR/BDGN N11 98 E8
FNCH N3 97 J8
GVW DA11 190 B3
HSLW TW3 154 B10
IL IG1 122 G8
KTN/HRWW/W HA3 114 D1
KUTN/CMB KT2 199 L1
NWDGN UB2 153 M3
PECK SE15 160 A8
RCH/KEW TW9 155 L8
REDH RH1 258 B7
SEV TN13 265 J1
SHPTN TW17 196 E6
SRTFD E15 121 H9
SWFD E18 101 N9
WAN E11 121 M4
WDR/YW UB7 131 P9
WDSR SL4 148 E8
Gordon Sq STPAN WC1H 11 K1
Gordon St PLSTW E13 141 M5
STPAN WC1H 11 J1
Gordons Wk HARP AL5 20 B3
Gordons Wy OXTED RH8 261 J4
Gordon Wy BAR EN5 77 J8
BMLY BR1 205 M1
Gore Cl DEN/HRF UB9 111 L2
Gorefield Pl KIL/WHAMP NW6 2 E7
Gore Hl AMSS HP7 68 G8
Gorelands La CSTG HP8 90 B3
Gorell Rd BEAC HP9 88 G10
Gore Rd HOM E9 140 B3
RDART DA2 188 C5
RYNPK SW20 200 F2
SL SL1 128 A5
Goresbrook Rd DAGW RM9 143 M3
Gore St SKENS SW7 15 K3
Gorham Dr STAL AL1 38 D9
Gorham Pl NTGHL W11 8 A8
Goring Cl CRW RM5 104 D9
Goring Gdns BCTR RM8 123 M9
Goring Rd DAGE RM10 144 E1
FBAR/BDGN * N11 98 F7
STA TW18 172 G8
Goring St HDTCH EC3A 13 K5
Goring Wy GFD/PVL UB6 134 B4
Gorle Cl GSTN WD25 55 H10
Gorleston Rd SEVS/STOTM N15 119 L3
Gorleston St WKENS W14 14 B5
Gorling Cl CRAWW RH11 283 H8
Gorman Rd WOOL/PLUM SE18 162 C3
Gorringe Av EYN DA4 210 C2
Gorringe Park Av MTCM CR4 180 A10
Gorse Cl CRAWE RH10 285 J3
HAT AL10 40 C7
KWD/TDW/WH KT20 238 E6
Gorse Cnr HARP * AL5 20 B3
STALW/RED AL3 38 C4
Gorse Ct RGUE GU4 250 F8
Gorse Dr HORL RH6 281 J3
Gorse Hill La VW GU25 194 A4
Gorse Hill Rd VW GU25 194 A4
Gorselands HARP AL5 20 A4
Gorselands Cl BF/WBF KT14 215 M7
Gorse La CHOB/PIR GU24 213 K4
Gorse Meade SL SL1 128 G10
Gorse Ri TOOT SW17 180 B8
Gorse Rd CROY/NA CR0 204 F10
STMC/STPC BR5 208 B9
Gorse Wk WDR/YW UB7 131 P8
Gorse Wy HART DA3 211 L5
Gorseway ROMW/RG RM7 124 F7
Gorse Wood Rd HART DA3 211 L5
Gorsewood Rd
WOKN/KNAP GU21 231 J5
Gorst Rd BTSEA SW11 180 A2
WLSDN NW10 135 P6
Gorsuch Pl BETH E2 7 L9
Gorsuch St BETH E2 7 L9
Gosberton Rd BAL SW12 180 A4
Gosbury Hl CHSGTN KT9 219 K1
Gosden Cl CRAWE RH10 284 B8
SHGR GU5 268 C9
Gosden Hill Rd RGUE GU4 250 F6
Gosden Rd CHOB/PIR GU24 212 E9
Gosfield Rd BCTR RM8 124 B6
HOR/WEW KT19 220 A8
Gosfield St GTPST W1W 10 F3
Gosford Gdns REDBR IG4 122 C3
Gosforth La OXHEY WD19 93 H4
Gosforth Pth OXHEY WD19 93 H4
Goshawk Gdns YEAD UB4 132 F5
Goslar Wy WDSR SL4 148 G8
Goslett Yd SOHO/SHAV W1D 11 K5
Gosling Cl GFD/PVL UB6 133 P5
Gosling Gn DTCH/LGLY SL3 150 B2
Gosling Rd DTCH/LGLY SL3 150 B2
Gosling Wy BRXN/ST SW9 159 H7
Gospatrick Rd TOTM N17 99 K8
Gosport Dr HCH RM12 145 K1
Gosport Rd WALTH E17 120 E3
Gosport Wy PECK SE15 159 N6
Gossage Rd HGDN/ICK UB10 132 A2
WOOL/PLUM SE18 162 G4
The Gossamers GSTN WD25 73 M1
Gosselin Rd HERT/WAS SG14 25 K3
Gosset St BETH E2 7 N10
Goss Hl SWLY BR8 187 K9
Gosshill Rd CHST BR7 206 D2
Gossington Cl CHST BR7 184 E7
Gossoms Ryde BERK HP4 33 M4
Gossops Dr CRAWW RH11 283 K8
Gossops Green La CRAWW RH11 283 K8
Gosterwood St DEPT SE8 160 D5
Gostling Rd WHTN TW2 175 P4
Goston Gdns THHTH CR7 203 H3
Goswell Hl WDSR SL4 149 J7
Goswell Pl FSBYE EC1V 6 D10
Goswell Rd FSBYE EC1V 6 D9
WDSR SL4 149 J7
Gothic Cl DART DA1 187 L6
Gothic Ct HYS/HAR UB3 152 E5
Gothic Rd WHTN TW2 176 C5
Gottfried Ms KTTN NW5 118 D9
Goudhurst Cl CRAWE RH10 284 F7
Goudhurst Rd BMLY BR1 183 K8
Gouge Av GVW DA11 190 B4
Gough Rd EN EN1 80 A6
FSTGT E7 121 L9
Gough Sq FLST/FETLN EC4A 12 B5
Gough St FSBYW WC1X 11 P1
Gould Cl BRKMPK AL9 40 E10
CHONG CM5 49 K7
Gould Ct RGUE GU4 250 G8
Goulding Gdns THHTH CR7 203 K2
Gould Rd EBED/NFELT TW14 174 F3
WHTN TW2 176 D4
Gould's Gn UX/CGN UB8 132 C8
UX/CGN UB8 132 C9
Gould Ter HACK E8 120 A10
Goulston St WCHPL E1 13 L5
Goulton Rd CLPT E5 120 A10
Gourley Pl SEVS/STOTM N15 119 M3
Gourley St SEVS/STOTM N15 119 M3
Gourney Gv CDH/CHF RM16 147 N9
Gourock Rd ELTH/MOT SE9 184 D1
Govan St BETH E2 7 P6
Government Rw WAB EN9 80 F3
Govett Av SHPTN * TW17 196 D5
Govett Gv BFOR GU20 212 C2
Govier Cl SRTFD E15 141 K2
Gowan Av FUL/PGN SW6 157 H7
Gowan Rd WLSDN NW10 136 E2
Gowar Fld POTB/CUF EN6 58 D7
Gower Cl BAL SW12 180 D2
Gower Ms GWRST WC1E 11 K4
Gower Pl STPAN WC1H 11 H1
Gower Rd FSTGT E7 141 M1
HORL RH6 279 P4
ISLW TW7 154 E5
WEY KT13 216 E3
Gowers La CDH/CHF RM16 168 C1
The Gowers AMS HP6 69 K3
HLW CM20 29 K9
Gower St GWRST WC1E 11 H1
Gower's Wk WCHPL E1 13 N5
The Gower EGH TW20 194 E3
Gowings Gn SL SL1 148 D1
Gowland Pl BECK BR3 204 E2
Gowlett Rd PECK SE15 159 P9
Gowrie Pl CTHM CR3 241 K8
Gowrie Rd BTSEA SW11 158 B9
Graburn Wy E/WMO/HCT KT8 198 C3
Grace Av BXLYHN DA7 164 A8
RAD WD7 57 J9
Gracechurch St BANK EC3V 13 H7
Grace Cl BARK/HLT IG6 103 J7
BORE WD6 76 A5
EDGW HA8 95 P8
ELTH/MOT SE9 184 A6
Grace Ct SL SL1 129 H10
Gracedale Rd TOOT SW17 180 C8
Gracefield Gdns
STRHM/NOR SW16 180 F6
Grace Jones Cl HACK * E8 7 M2
Grace Pl BOW E3 140 G5
Grace Rd CROY/NA CR0 203 K6
Grace's Aly WCHPL E1 13 N7
Grace's Ms CMBW SE5 159 L8
STJWD * NW8 3 K8
Grace's Rd CMBW SE5 159 M8
Grace St BOW E3 140 G5
Gracious La SEV TN13 265 H6
Gracious Lane End RSEV TN14 264 G6
Gracious Pond Rd
CHOB/PIR GU24 213 L4
The Gradient SYD SE26 181 P7
Graeme Rd EN EN1 79 M6
Graemesdyke Av
MORT/ESHN SW14 155 N9
Graemes Dyke Rd BERK HP4 33 M6
Graffham Cl CRAWW RH11 283 L5
Grafton Cl BF/WBF KT14 215 J9
DTCH/LGLY SL3 130 B8
HSLWW TW4 175 M4
STALE/WH AL4 39 J7
WEA W13 134 F8
WPK KT4 200 B10
Grafton Crs CAMTN NW1 4 E2
Grafton Gdns BCTR RM8 123 P7
FSBYPK N4 119 K4
Grafton Ms FITZ W1T 10 G2
Grafton Park Rd WPK KT4 200 B9
Grafton Pl CAMTN NW1 5 J10
Grafton Rd ACT W3 135 P9
CROY/NA CR0 203 H8
ENC/FH EN2 78 G7
HRW HA1 114 B3
KTTN NW5 118 B10
NWMAL KT3 200 B4
WPK KT4 200 A10
Grafton Sq CLAP SW4 158 D10
Grafton St MYFR/PICC W1J 10 F8
Grafton Ter KTTN NW5 118 A10
Grafton Wy E/WMO/HCT KT8 197 N4
GTPST W1W 10 G3
Grafton Yd KTTN NW5 4 F2
Graham Av BROX EN10 44 D6
MTCM CR4 202 B1
WEA W13 154 G1
Graham Cl CROY/NA CR0 204 F9
RBRW/HUT CM13 87 P9
STAL AL1 38 C9
Grahame Park Wy MLHL NW7 96 C8
Graham Gdns SURB KT6 199 K8
Graham Rd BFOR GU20 212 B3
BXLYHN DA7 164 A10
CHSWK W4 156 A2
HACK E8 7 P1
HDN NW4 116 E4
HPTN TW12 175 P7
KTN/HRWW/W HA3 114 D1
MTCM CR4 202 B1
PLSTW E13 141 M6
PUR/KEN CR8 223 H9
SEVS/STOTM N15 119 J1
WIM/MER SW19 179 J10
Graham St IS N1 6 D8
Graham Ter BFN/LL * DA15 185 L2
BGVA SW1W 16 D6

Grainger Cl NTHLT UB5 114 B10
Grainger Rd ISLW TW7 154 E8
WDGN N22 99 K9
Grain Terminal TIL * RM18 167 P7
Gramer Cl WAN E11 121 J7
Grampian Cl BELMT SM2 221 M4
HYS/HAR UB3 152 E6
ORP BR6 207 J6
Grampian Gdns CRICK NW2 117 H6
Grampian Wy DTCH/LGLY SL3 150 D4
Granada St TOOT SW17 180 A8
Granard Av PUT/ROE SW15 178 E1
Granard Rd BAL SW12 180 A3
The Granaries WAB EN9 63 K10
Granary Cl ED N9 100 B1
HORL RH6 280 B2
STALE/WH AL4 21 J3
Granary La HARP AL5 20 A2
Granary Rd WCHPL E1 140 A6
Granary Sq IS N1 6 A2
Granary St CAMTN NW1 5 J6
The Granary HLWW/ROY CM19 27 N10
WARE SG12 27 H8
Granby Av HARP AL5 20 B1
Granby Park Rd CHESW EN7 61 N4
Granby Rd ELTH/MOT SE9 162 C8
GVW DA11 190 A2
WOOL/PLUM SE18 162 E2
Granby St BETH E2 13 M1
Granby Ter CAMTN NW1 4 G8
Grand Av BRYLDS KT5 199 N6
FARR EC1M 12 D3
MUSWH N10 118 B2
WBLY HA9 115 M10
Grand Av East WBLY HA9 115 N10
Grand Depot Rd
WOOL/PLUM SE18 162 D4
Grand Dr RYNPK SW20 200 F3
STHL UB1 154 B1
Granden Rd STRHM/NOR * SW16 202 F2
Grandfield Av WAT WD17 72 G5
Grandison Rd BTSEA SW11 180 A1
WPK KT4 200 F9
Grand Junction Whf IS * N1 6 E8
Grand Pde CRAWE * RH10 283 N7
FSBYPK * N4 119 J4
MORT/ESHN * SW14 155 P10
SURB * KT6 199 M8
WBLY * HA9 115 N7
Grand Stand Rd EPSOM KT18 238 C3
Grand Union Canal Wk
BAY/PAD W2 8 F3
BERK HP4 33 K2
DEN/HRF UB9 111 L1
DTCH/LGLY SL3 130 A10
HHW HP1 34 F8
HNWL W7 154 D2
NKENS W10 8 A1
NWDGN UB2 153 J2
RKW/CH/CXG WD3 91 K5
SLN SL2 129 N10
STHL UB1 133 N6
STKPK UB11 152 C1
WLSDN NW10 135 N4
Grand Union Cl MV/WKIL W9 8 D3
Grand Union Crs HACK E8 7 P5
Grand Union Wk CAMTN * NW1 4 F4
Grand View Av BH/WHM TN16 243 P3
Grand Wk WCHPL * E1 140 D6
Granfield St BTSEA * SW11 157 N7
Grange Av EBAR EN4 97 P2
KTN/HRWW/W HA3 94 G10
NFNCH/WDSP N12 97 M6
SNWD SE25 203 M2
TRDG/WHET N20 97 H1
WHTN TW2 176 D5
Grangecliffe Gdns SNWD SE25 203 M2
Grange Cl BFN/LL DA15 185 K6
BH/WHM TN16 262 G2
CFSP/GDCR SL9 90 B9
CRAWE RH10 284 B5
E/WMO/HCT KT8 198 A4
GUW GU2 249 N6
HERT/WAS SG14 25 J5
HHNE HP2 36 B7
HYS/HAR UB3 132 F7
LHD/OX KT22 237 J6
NWDGN UB2 153 N4
RBRW/HUT CM13 107 P6
REDH RH1 259 L9
REIG RH2 258 C4
STWL/WRAY TW19 172 B2
WAT WD17 73 H5
WFD IG8 101 M8
Grange Ct ALP/SUD * HA0 114 E8
ALP/SUD * HA0 115 H10
BELMT * SM2 221 L4
EGH * TW20 172 C8
GUW * GU2 249 N6
HERT/WAS * SG14 25 K4
NTHLT UB5 133 K4
PIN * HA5 113 M1
WAB EN9 63 H10
WLGTN * SM6 202 C10
WOT/HER KT12 197 H9
Grange Court Rd HARP AL5 20 B5
Grangecourt Rd
STNW/STAM N16 119 M6
Grange Crs CHIG IG7 102 G6
RDART DA2 188 A2
THMD SE28 143 M8
Grangedale Cl NTHWD HA6 92 F9
Grange Dr CHST BR7 184 B9
ORP BR6 227 M5
REDH RH1 258 C4
WOKN/KNAP GU21 232 B1
Grange End HORL RH6 281 H4
Grange Farm Cl
RYLN/HDSTN HA2 114 B7
Grange Flds CFSP/GDCR SL9 90 B9
Grangefields Rd RGUE GU4 250 A4
Grange Gdns BNSTD SM7 221 L9
HAMP NW3 117 L8
PIN HA5 113 N2
SLN SL2 109 J10
SNWD SE25 203 M2
STHGT/OAK N14 98 E2
WARE SG12 26 D3
Grange Gv IS N1 6 E1
Grange Hl EDGW HA8 95 P6
SNWD SE25 203 M2
Grangehill Pl ELTH/MOT SE9 162 C9
Grangehill Rd ELTH/MOT SE9 162 C10
Grange Houses HBRY * N5 119 K9
Grange La DUL SE21 181 N5
GSTN WD25 74 C5
HART DA3 211 N7
HLWW/ROY CM19 45 P1
Grange Meadow BNSTD SM7 221 L9
Grange Ms FELT * TW13 174 E6
Grangemill Rd CAT SE6 182 F6
Grangemill Wy CAT SE6 182 F5
Grangemount LHD/OX KT22 237 J6
Grange Pk EA W5 135 K10
WOKN/KNAP * GU21 214 C10
Grange Park Av WCHMH N21 79 J10
Grange Park Pl RYNPK SW20 178 E10
Grange Park Rd LEY E10 120 G6
THHTH CR7 203 L3
Grange Pl KIL/WHAMP NW6 2 E4
STA TW18 195 M2
Grange Rd ADL/WDHM KT15 215 K6
BARN SW13 156 D7
BELMT SM2 221 K4
BORE WD6 75 L9
BUSH WD23 73 M9
CFSP/GDCR SL9 90 A9
CHOB/PIR GU24 230 C8
CHSGTN KT9 219 K1
CHSWK W4 155 N4
CRAWE RH10 285 P6
CTHM CR3 259 P1
E/WMO/HCT KT8 198 A4
EA W5 135 J10
EDGW HA8 96 A7
EGH TW20 172 C8
GRAYS RM17 167 N5
GVW DA11 190 D3
HARH RM3 105 J7
HGT N6 118 B4
HRW HA1 114 F4
HYS/HAR UB3 132 F8
IL IG1 122 F9
KUT KT1 199 K3
LEY E10 120 F6
LHD/OX KT22 237 J6
ORP BR6 206 F9
PLSTW E13 141 L5
RGUW GU3 249 N5
RYLN/HDSTN HA2 114 C7
SAND/SEL CR2 223 K6
SEV TN13 265 H3
SNWD SE25 203 L3
SOCK/AV RM15 146 B10
STHL UB1 153 M1
STHWK SE1 13 K7
TOTM N17 99 P7
WALTH E17 120 D3
WLSDN NW10 136 E1
WOKN/KNAP GU21 232 B1
WOT/HER KT12 217 M1
Granger Wy EMPK RM11 125 H4
Grange St IS N1 7 H6
STALW/RED AL3 38 C5
The Grange ALP/SUD HA0 135 M2
CHOB/PIR GU24 213 K6
CROY/NA CR0 204 E9
EYN DA4 210 C1
HOD * EN11 44 F4
HOR/WEW KT19 220 A1
NWMAL * KT3 200 D5
SL * SL1 128 B5
STALE/WH * AL4 40 A9
STHWK SE1 19 L3
WDSR SL4 171 N1
WIM/MER SW19 178 G9
WOT/HER KT12 197 J9
Grange V BELMT SM2 221 L4
Grangeview Rd
TRDG/WHET N20 97 M2
Grange Wk STHWK SE1 19 K3
Grange Walk Ms STHWK SE1 19 K4
Grange Wy ERITH DA8 165 J6
HART DA3 211 L6
IVER SL0 131 J8
Grangeway HORL RH6 281 H4
KIL/WHAMP NW6 2 E4
NFNCH/WDSP N12 97 L5
WFD IG8 101 P5
Grangeway Gdns REDBR IG4 122 B3
Grangeways Cl GVW DA11 190 C7
The Grangeway WCHMH N21 79 J10
Grangewood BXLY DA5 186 A4
DTCH/LGLY SL3 129 P7
POTB/CUF EN6 59 L6
Grangewood Av CDH/CHF RM16 168 B2
RAIN RM13 146 A2
Grangewood Cl PIN HA5 113 H3
RBRW/HUT CM13 107 M4
Grangewood La BECK BR3 182 E9
Grange Yd STHWK SE1 19 L4
Granham Gdns ED N9 99 N3
Granite St WOOL/PLUM SE18 163 J4
Granleigh Rd WAN E11 121 K7
Gransden Av HACK E8 140 A2
Gransden Rd SHB W12 156 C1
Grant Av SL SL1 129 K8
Grantbridge St IS N1 6 D7
Grantchester KUT * KT1 199 M2
Grantchester Cl HRW HA1 114 E8
Grant Cl SHPTN TW17 196 C6
STHGT/OAK N14 98 D1
Grant Gdns HARP AL5 20 A1
Grantham Cl EDGW HA8 95 K4
Grantham Gdns CHDH RM6 124 A4
WARE SG12 26 D1
Grantham Gn BORE WD6 75 P9
Grantham Ms BERK HP4 34 A5
Grantham Pl MYFR/PICC W1J 10 E10
Grantham Rd BRXN/ST SW9 158 F9
CHSWK W4 156 B6
MNPK E12 122 D8
Grantham Wy CDH/CHF RM16 147 M10
Grantley Cl RGUE GU4 268 B7
Grantley Gdns GUW GU2 249 M9
Grantley Rd GUW GU2 249 M9
HSLWW TW4 153 K8
Grantley St WCHPL E1 140 C5
Grantock Rd WALTH E17 101 J9
Granton Av HCH RM12 125 N7
Granton Rd GDMY/SEVK IG3 123 K6
SCUP DA14 185 L9
STRHM/NOR SW16 202 D1
Grant Rd BTSEA SW11 157 P9
CROY/NA CR0 203 N8
KTN/HRWW/W HA3 114 D1
Grants Cl MLHL NW7 96 F8
Grants La OXTED RH8 261 P9
Grant St IS N1 6 A7
PLSTW E13 141 M5
Grant Ter CLPT * E5 119 P5
Grantully Rd MV/WKIL W9 2 G10
Grant Wk ASC SL5 192 D8
Grant Wy ISLW TW7 154 F5
Grantwood Cl REDH RH1 276 B5
Granville Ar BRXN/ST * SW9 159 H10
Granville Av ED N9 100 B4
FELT TW13 175 H5
HSLWW TW4 175 P1
SLN SL2 129 J7
Granville Cl BF/WBF KT14 216 A9
CROY/NA CR0 203 M9
WEY KT13 216 D3
Granville Dene HHS/BOV HP3 52 D3
Granville Gdns ACT W3 135 L10
HOD EN11 26 F9
STRHM/NOR SW16 202 G1
Granville Gv LEW SE13 161 H9
Granville Ms SCUP DA14 185 K7
Granville Pk LEW SE13 161 H9
Granville Pl FUL/PGN * SW6 157 L6
MBLAR W1H 10 C6
NFNCH/WDSP * N12 97 M8
PIN HA5 113 L1
Granville Rd BAR EN5 76 F8
BH/WHM TN16 262 F2
CRICK NW2 117 J7
EPP CM16 65 L5
FSBYPK N4 118 G4
GVW DA11 190 C3
HGDN/ICK UB10 132 C1
HYS/HAR UB3 152 G3
IL IG1 122 E6
KIL/WHAMP NW6 2 E8
LEY E10 120 G4
NFNCH/WDSP N12 97 M8
OXTED RH8 261 L5
PLMGR N13 98 G7
SCUP DA14 185 K7
SEV TN13 247 H10
STAL AL1 38 E6
SWFD E18 101 N10
WAND/EARL SW18 179 K3
WATW * WD18 73 K8
WDGN N22 99 J9
WELL DA16 163 M9
WEY KT13 216 D3
WIM/MER SW19 179 K10
WOKS/MYFD GU22 232 C6
Granville Sq PECK * SE15 159 M6
Granville St FSBYW WC1X 5 P10
Grape St LSQ/SEVD WC2H 11 L5
Graphite Sq LBTH SE11 17 N7
Grapsome Cl CHSGTN KT9 219 H4
Grasdene Rd WOOL/PLUM SE18 163 K6
Grasholm Wy DTCH/LGLY SL3 150 F3
Grasmere Av ACT W3 135 P9
HARP AL5 20 B1
HSLW TW3 176 A2
ORP BR6 206 E10
PUT/ROE SW15 178 A7
RSLP HA4 112 D5
SLN SL2 129 M9
WBLY HA9 115 J5
WIM/MER SW19 201 K3
Grasmere Cl EBED/NFELT TW14 174 G4
EGH TW20 172 E10
GSTN WD25 55 J8
GU GU1 250 E9
HHS/BOV HP3 36 C8
LOU IG10 82 C6
Grasmere Ct WDGN N22 98 G7
Grasmere Gdns
KTN/HRWW/W HA3 94 F10
ORP BR6 206 E10
REDBR IG4 122 B3
Grasmere Pde SLN * SL2 129 N9
Grasmere Rd BMLY BR1 205 L1
BXLYHN DA7 164 D7
LTWR GU18 212 A6
MUSWH N10 98 C9
ORP BR6 206 E10
PLSTW E13 141 M4
PUR/KEN CR8 223 J7
SNWD SE25 204 A6
STAL AL1 38 G8
STRHM/NOR SW16 180 G8
TOTM N17 99 P7
Grasmere Wy BF/WBF KT14 216 A8
Grassingham End CFSP/GDCR SL9 90 B8
Grassingham Rd CFSP/GDCR SL9 90 B8
Grassington Cl FBAR/BDGN N11 98 B6
LCOL/BKTW AL2 55 P6
Grassington Rd SCUP DA14 185 K7
Grasslands HORL RH6 281 H4
Grassmere HORL RH6 280 C3
Grassmere Rd EMPK RM11 125 N2
Grassmount FSTH SE23 182 A5
WLGTN SM6 222 D6
Grass Pk FNCH N3 97 J9
Grass Warren WLYN AL6 23 P2
Grassway WLGTN SM6 222 D1
Grassy Cl HHW HP1 35 K5
Grassy La SEV TN13 265 J3
Grasvenor Av BAR EN5 77 K10
Grately Wy PECK * SE15 159 M6
Gratton Dr WDSR SL4 148 D10
Gratton Rd WKENS W14 14 A4
Grattons Dr CRAWE RH10 284 D4
Gravel Cl CHIG IG7 103 K3
Graveley Av BORE WD6 75 P8
Graveley Dell WGCE AL7 23 L6
Gravel Hl BXLYHS DA6 186 C1
CFSP/GDCR SL9 90 A7
CROY/NA CR0 224 C3
FNCH N3 97 J10
LHD/OX KT22 236 F7
UX/CGN UB8 111 N10
Gravel Hill Cl BXLY DA5 186 C2
Gravelhill Ter HHW HP1 35 K7
Gravel La CHIG IG7 83 K10
HHW HP1 35 K6
WCHPL E1 13 L5
Gravelly Hl REDH RH1 259 N4
Gravel Pth BERK HP4 34 A5
Gravel Pits La SHGR GU5 270 D5
Gravel Pit Wy ORP BR6 207 K9
Gravel Rd EYN DA4 188 A10
HAYES BR2 206 B9
WHTN TW2 176 D4
Gravelwood Cl CHST BR7 184 F6
Gravely Ct HHNE HP2 36 D7
Gravenel Gdns TOOT * SW17 179 P8
Graveney Gv PGE/AN SE20 182 B10
Graveney Rd CRAWE RH10 284 D8
TOOT SW17 179 P7
Gravesend Rd GVE DA12 191 P7
SHB W12 136 D9
Gravetts La RGUW GU3 249 K7
Gravetye Cl CRAWE RH10 284 B9
Gray Av BCTR RM8 124 A6
Grayburn Cl CSTG HP8 89 M3
Gray Gdns RAIN RM13 145 H1
Grayham Crs NWMAL KT3 200 A4
Grayham Rd NWMAL KT3 200 A4
Grayland Cl BMLY BR1 206 A1
Graylands GRAYS * RM17 167 K5
WOKN/KNAP GU21 232 B2
Graylands Cl WOKN/KNAP GU21 232 B2
Grayling Cl CAN/RD E16 141 K6
Grayling Ct EA * W5 135 J10
Grayling Rd STNW/STAM N16 119 L7
Grayling Sq BETH E2 7 P9
The Graylings ABLGY WD5 54 F9
Gray Pl CHERT KT16 214 G3
Grays Cottages
STMC/STPC * BR5 207 M1
Grayscroft Rd
STRHM/NOR SW16 180 E10
Grays End Cl CDH/CHF RM16 167 M2
Grays Farm Rd STMC/STPC BR5 207 L1
Graysfield WGCE AL7 23 K8
Grayshott Rd BTSEA SW11 158 B9
Gray's Inn Rd FSBYW WC1X 5 M9
Gray's Inn Sq GINN WC1R 12 A3
Grays La ASHF TW15 174 C7
ASHTD KT21 237 L5
Grays Park Rd SLN SL2 129 M4
Grays Pl SLN SL2 129 L10
Grays Rd BH/WHM TN16 244 E7
HGDN/ICK UB10 131 P2
RGODL GU7 267 L10
SL SL1 129 L10
Gray St STHWK SE1 18 C1
Grays Wk CSHM HP5 50 G4
Grays Wd HORL RH6 280 D4
Grayswood Gdns RYNPK SW20 200 E2
Gray's Yd MHST * W1U 10 D6
Graywood Ct NFNCH/WDSP N12 97 M8
Grazebrook Rd STNW/STAM N16 119 L7
Grazeley Cl BXLYHS DA6 186 D1
The Grazings HHNE HP2 36 A4
Greasy Cl ABLGY WD5 54 G7
Great Benty WDR/YW UB7 151 P3
Great Braitch La HAT AL10 22 B9
Great Brays HLWS CM18 47 K2
Great Break WGCE AL7 23 L6
Great Brownings DUL SE21 181 N7
Great Bushey Dr TRDG/WHET N20 97 L2
Great Cambridge Jct PLMGR N13 99 K6
Great Cambridge Rd BROX EN10 62 D2
CHES/WCR EN8 62 B10
UED N18 99 L6
Great Castle St REGST W1B 10 G5
Great Central Av RSLP HA4 113 K10
Great Central St CAMTN NW1 10 A3
Great Central Wy WBLY HA9 115 P10
Great Chapel St SOHO/CST W1F 11 J5
Great Chertsey Rd CHSWK W4 156 A7
FELT TW13 175 N6
Great Church La HMSMTH W6 156 G4
Great College St WEST SW1P 17 L3
Great Conduit WGCE AL7 23 M4
Great Cross Av GNWCH SE10 161 K6
Great Cullings ROMW/RG RM7 124 F7
Great Cumberland Ms
MBLAR W1H 10 A6
Great Cumberland Pl MBLAR W1H 10 A5
Great Dell WGCW AL8 22 G3
Great Dover St STHWK SE1 18 G3
Greatdown Rd HNWL W7 134 E7
Great Eastern Rd BRW CM14 107 H5
SRTFD E15 141 J2
Great Eastern St SDTCH EC2A 7 J10
Great Eastern Whf
BTSEA * SW11 157 P6
Great Ellshams BNSTD SM7 239 K2
Great Elms EW * KT17 220 C7
Great Elms Rd HAYES BR2 205 P4
HHS/BOV HP3 36 A10
Great Fld CDALE/KGS NW9 96 B9
Greatfield Av EHAM E6 142 C6
Greatfield Cl LEW SE13 160 F10
Greatfields Dr UX/CGN UB8 132 B7
Greatfields Rd BARK IG11 142 G3
Greatford Dr GU GU1 250 G10
Great Fox Meadow BRWN CM15 86 E3
Great Galley Cl BARK IG11 143 L5
Great Ganett WGCE AL7 23 L7
Great Gardens Rd EMPK RM11 125 J4
Great Gatton Cl CROY/NA CR0 204 D7
Great George St STJSPK SW1H 17 K2
Great Goodwin Dr GU GU1 250 E8
Great Gregories La EPP CM16 65 H9
Great Gv BUSH WD23 74 A8
Great Groves CHESW EN7 61 M4
Great Guildford St STHWK SE1 12 E10
Greatham Rd BUSH WD23 73 L7
CRAWE RH10 284 D10
Great Harry Dr ELTH/MOT SE9 184 D6
Great Heart HHNE HP2 35 P4
Great Heath HAT AL10 40 E1
Great Hivings CSHM HP5 50 F3
Great James St BMSBY WC1N 11 N3
Greatlake Ct HORL RH6 280 C3
Great Lawn CHONG CM5 67 P3
Great Ley WGCE AL7 23 H7
Great Leylands HLWS CM18 47 K2
Great Marlborough St
SOHO/CST W1F 10 G6
Great Maze Pond STHWK SE1 13 H10
Great Meadow BROX EN10 44 F8
Great Molewood HERT/WAS SG14 25 J2
Great Nelmes Cha EMPK RM11 125 N3
Greatness La RSEV TN14 247 K7
Greatness Rd RSEV TN14 247 K7
Great New St FLST/FETLN * EC4A 12 B5
Great North Rd BRKMPK AL9 22 E10
BRKMPK AL9 40 E5
EFNCH N2 117 P2
HAT AL10 40 F1
WGCW AL8 22 E9
Great North Wy (Barnet By-Pass)
HDN NW4 116 G1
Great Oaks CHIG IG7 102 F5
RBRW/HUT CM13 87 N10
Great Oaks Pk RGUE GU4 250 E6
Greatorex St WCHPL E1 13 N3
Great Ormond St BMSBY WC1N 11 M3
Great Owl Rd CHIG IG7 102 D4
Great Palmers HHNE HP2 36 A1
Great Pk KGLGY WD4 54 B6
Great Percy St FSBYW WC1X 5 P9
Great Peter St WEST SW1P 17 J4
Great Plumtree HLW CM20 29 J9
Great Portland St GTPST * W1W 10 F2
Great Pulteney St SOHO/CST W1F 11 H7
Great Quarry GU GU1 268 A3
Great Queen St DART DA1 187 N2
HOL/ALD WC2B 11 M5
Great Rd HHNE HP2 36 A5
Great Ropers La BRW CM14 106 F7
Great Russell St FITZ W1T 11 K5
Great St Helen's HDTCH EC3A 13 J6
Great St Thomas Apostle
BLKFR EC4V 12 F7
Great Scotland Yd WHALL SW1A 11 L10
Great Slades POTB/CUF EN6 59 J9
Great Smith St WEST SW1P 17 K3
Great South-West Rd
EBED/NFELT TW14 174 D3
Great Spilmans EDUL SE22 181 M1
Great Stockwood Rd CHESW EN7 61 L2
Great Strd CDALE/KGS NW9 96 C10
Great Sturgess Rd HHW HP1 35 J6
Great Suffolk St STHWK SE1 12 D10
Great Sutton St FSBYE EC1V 12 D2
Great Swan Aly LOTH EC2R 12 G5
Great Tattenhams EPSOM KT18 238 F4
Great Thrift STMC/STPC BR5 206 F4
Great Till Cl RSEV TN14 246 F2
Great Titchfield St GTPST W1W 10 F2
Great Tower St MON EC3R 13 J7
Great Trinity La BLKFR EC4V 12 F7
Great Turnstile HHOL * WC1V 11 P4
Great Warley St
RBRW/HUT CM13 106 F5
Great Western Rd NTGHL W11 8 D4
Great West Rd CHSWK W4 155 P5
HEST TW5 153 M8
HMSMTH W6 156 E4
ISLW TW7 154 D6
Great West Rd Chiswick
CHSWK W4 156 C5
Great West Rd Ellesmere Rd
CHSWK W4 155 P5
Great West Rd Hogarth La
CHSWK W4 156 A5
Great Westwood KGLGY * WD4 71 P1
Great Whites Rd HHS/BOV HP3 36 A8
Great Winchester St OBST EC2N 13 H5
Great Windmill St
SOHO/SHAV W1D 11 J8
Greatwood CHST BR7 184 D10
Greatwood Cl CHERT KT16 214 F5
Great Woodcote Dr
PUR/KEN CR8 222 E6
Great Woodcote Pk
PUR/KEN CR8 222 F6
Greaves Cl BARK IG11 142 G2
Greaves Cottages
POP/IOD * E14 140 D7
Greaves Pl TOOT SW17 179 P7
Grebe Av YEAD UB4 133 L8
Grebe Cl FSTGT E7 121 L10
WALTH E17 100 D8
Grebe Ct SUT SM1 221 J2
Grebe Crest WTHK RM20 166 F3
Grebe Ter KUT * KT1 199 K3
Grecian Crs NRWD SE19 181 J9
Greding Wk RBRW/HUT CM13 107 N3
Greek St SOHO/SHAV W1D 11 K6
Greenacre WDSR SL4 148 D8
Greenacre Cl BAR EN5 77 J4
NTHLT UB5 113 N10
SWLY BR8 208 F4
Greenacre Ct EGH * TW20 171 P9
Greenacre Pl WLGTN SM6 202 C9
Green Acres CROY/NA CR0 203 N10
SCUP * DA14 185 J7
WGCE * AL7 23 J8
Greenacres BUSH WD23 94 C3
CRAWE RH10 284 C8
ELTH/MOT SE9 184 D2
EPP CM16 65 J4
GT/LBKH KT23 235 P10
HHS/BOV HP3 36 E8
OXTED RH8 261 K3
Greenacres Av HGDN/ICK UB10 112 A8
Greenacres Cl ORP BR6 226 F1
RAIN RM13 145 M5
Greenacres Dr STAN HA7 94 G8
Greenacre Sq
BERM/RHTH * SE16 160 C1
Greenacre Wk STHGT/OAK N14 98 E4
Greenall Cl CHES/WCR EN8 62 D6
Green Arbour Ct STP * EC4M 12 C5
Green Av MLHL NW7 96 A5
WEA W13 154 G2
Greenaway Av UED * N18 100 C6
Greenaway Gdns HAMP NW3 117 L9
Greenbank CHESW EN7 62 A4
Green Bank NFNCH/WDSP N12 97 L5
WAP E1W 140 A10
Greenbank Av ALP/SUD HA0 114 F10
Greenbank Cl CHING E4 101 H3
HARH RM3 105 L4
Greenbank Crs HDN NW4 117 H2
Greenbank Rd WAT WD17 72 E2
Greenbanks DART DA1 187 M5
STAL AL1 38 E8
UPMR RM14 126 D7
Greenbay Rd CHARL SE7 162 A6
Greenberry St STJWD NW8 3 N8
Greenbrook Av EBAR EN4 77 M5
Greenbury Cl RKW/CH/CXG WD3 70 F7
Green Chain Wk BMLY BR1 183 J10
CHARL SE7 162 A3
ELTH/MOT SE9 184 E1
SYD SE26 182 C9
THMD SE28 143 N10
Green Cl BRKMPK AL9 59 H2
CAR SM5 202 A9
CDALE/KGS NW9 115 P4
CHES/WCR EN8 62 D8
EFNCH N2 117 M5
EPP CM16 46 E10
FELT TW13 175 M8
HAYES BR2 205 K3
Greencoates HERT/BAY SG13 25 M6
Greencoat Pl WEST SW1P 17 H5
Greencoat Rw WEST SW1P 17 H4
Green Common La FLKWH HP10 108 C5
Green Court Av CROY/NA CR0 204 A9
Greencourt Av EDGW HA8 95 M9
Green Court Gdns CROY/NA CR0 204 A9
Greencourt Rd STMC/STPC BR5 207 H5
Green Court Rd SWLY BR8 208 E5
Greencroft EDGW HA8 95 P6
GU GU1 250 E10
Green Cft HAT AL10 40 D1
Greencroft Av RSLP HA4 113 K7
Greencroft Gdns EN EN1 79 M7
KIL/WHAMP NW6 3 J3
Greencroft Rd HEST TW5 153 N7
Green Curve BNSTD SM7 239 J1
Green Dl EDUL SE22 181 M1
Greendale Ms SLN SL2 129 M9
Green Dell Wy HHS/BOV HP3 36 C6
Green Dene EHSLY KT24 252 E9
Green Dragon La BTFD TW8 155 K4
WCHMH N21 78 G9
Green Dragon Yd WCHPL E1 13 N4
Green Dr RPLY/SEND GU23 233 J9
STHL UB1 133 P10
Green East Rd BEAC HP9 89 K8
Greene Fielde End STA TW18 173 N10
Greene Field Rd BERK HP4 33 P5
Green End CHSGTN KT9 219 J1

WCHMH N21 99 J3
Green End Gdns HHW HP1 35 K7
Green End La HHW HP1 35 J6
Greenend Rd CHSWK W4 156 B1
Green End Rd HHW HP1 35 K6
Greenes Ct BERK HP4 33 P4
Greene Wk BERK HP4 34 A6
Green Farm Cl ORP BR6 227 J2
Green Farm La GVE DA12 191 P6
Greenfell Man DEPT * SE8 160 E4
Greenfern Av SL SL1 128 B8
Greenfield BRKMPK AL9 40 G1
WGCW AL8 22 G2
Greenfield Av BRYLDS KT5 199 N6
OXHEY WD19 93 M3
Greenfield Dr BMLY BR1 205 P2
EFNCH N2 118 A2
Greenfield End CFSP/GDCR SL9 90 C8
Greenfield Gdns CRICK NW2 117 H7
DAGW RM9 143 M3
STMC/STPC BR5 206 F7
Greenfield Link COUL/CHIP CR5 240 F1
Greenfield Rd DAGW RM9 143 M3
RDART DA2 186 E8
SEVS/STOTM N15 119 M3
WCHPL E1 13 P4
Greenfields LOU IG10 82 D8
POTB/CUF * EN6 60 F6
STHL UB1 133 P9
Greenfields Cl HORL RH6 279 P2
Greenfields Rd HORL RH6 279 P2
Greenfield St WAB EN9 63 H10
Greenfield Wy RYLN/HDSTN HA2 114 A1
Greenfinches HART DA3 211 N3
Greenford Av HNWL W7 134 D6
STHL UB1 133 N9
Greenford Gdns GFD/PVL UB6 134 A5
Greenford Rd GFD/PVL UB6 114 D10
GFD/PVL UB6 134 B9
SUT SM1 221 L1
Green Gdns ORP BR6 226 F2
Greengate GFD/PVL UB6 134 G1
Greengate St PLSTW E13 141 N4
Green Gld EPP CM16 83 H3
Green Glades EMPK RM11 125 N4
Greenhalgh Wk EFNCH N2 117 M2
Greenham Cl STHWK SE1 18 A2
Greenham Crs CHING E4 100 E7
Greenham Rd MUSWH N10 98 B10
Greenham Wk
WOKN/KNAP GU21 231 P4
Greenhaven Dr THMD SE28 143 L8
Greenhayes Av BNSTD SM7 221 K10
Greenhayes Cl REIG RH2 257 M10
Greenhayes Gdns BNSTD SM7 239 K1
Green Heights Ct
WOKS/MYFD GU22 231 P6
Greenheys Cl NTHWD HA6 92 F9
Greenheys Dr SWFD E18 121 L1
Greenheys Pl WOKS/MYFD GU22 232 C3
Green Hl ORP BR6 226 B8
WOOL/PLUM SE18 162 C4
Greenhill BKHH IG9 101 P2
HAMP NW3 117 N9
SUT SM1 201 M9
WBLY HA9 115 N7
Greenhill Av CTHM CR3 242 A7
Greenhill Ct BAR * EN5 77 L9
Greenhill Crs WATW WD18 72 F10
Greenhill Gdns NTHLT UB5 133 N4
RGUE GU4 250 F7
Greenhill Gv MNPK E12 122 B9
Greenhill La WARL CR6 242 D3
Greenhill Pde BAR * EN5 77 L9
Greenhill Pk BAR EN5 77 L9
WLSDN NW10 136 B3
Greenhill Rd GVW DA11 190 C5
HRW HA1 114 D4
RSEV TN14 247 K1
WLSDN NW10 136 B3
Greenhills HLW CM20 47 H1
Greenhills Cl RKW/CH/CXG WD3 71 L9
Greenhill's Rents FARR * EC1M 12 C3
Greenhills Ter IS N1 7 H2
Greenhill Ter NTHLT * UB5 133 N4
Greenhill Wy HRW HA1 114 D4
WBLY HA9 115 N7
Greenhithe Cl ELTH/MOT SE9 185 H3
Greenholm Rd ELTH/MOT SE9 184 E1
Green Hundred Rd PECK SE15 19 P10
Greenhurst La OXTED RH8 261 L8
Greenhurst Rd WNWD SE27 181 H8
Greening St ABYW SE2 163 M3
Greenlake Ter STA * TW18 173 K10
Greenland Crs NWDGN UB2 153 K2
Greenland Ms DEPT SE8 160 C4
Greenland Pl CAMTN NW1 4 F5
Greenland Quay
BERM/RHTH SE16 160 C3
Greenland Rd BAR EN5 76 F10
CAMTN NW1 4 G5
Greenlands CHERT KT16 194 F10
HOR/WEW KT19 219 N2
Greenlands Rd STA TW18 173 K7
WEY KT13 196 C10
Greenland St CAMTN NW1 4 F5
Green La AMS HP6 69 J1
ASC SL5 192 D1
ASHTD KT21 237 H3
BCTR RM8 124 A7
BF/WBF KT14 216 A8
BROX EN10 44 G9
BRW CM14 86 C5
BRW CM14 106 F2
BRW CM14 106 F8
BRWN CM15 87 H10
CDH/CHF RM16 147 P7
CHERT KT16 195 H9
CHIG IG7 103 H4
CHING * E4 81 K7
CHOB/PIR GU24 213 L6
CHSGTN KT9 219 K5
COB KT11 217 M8
CRAWE RH10 283 P5
CRAWE RH10 284 E7
CRAWE RH10 285 N1
CSHM HP5 51 N9
CTHM CR3 241 K9
DTCH/LGLY SL3 149 N7
E/WMO/HCT KT8 198 A5
EDGW HA8 95 L5
EGH TW20 172 E7
EGH TW20 194 F2
EHSLY KT24 234 C10
ELTH/MOT SE9 184 D5
FELT TW13 175 M8
GU GU1 250 E10
HDN NW4 116 G3
HHNE HP2 36 E4
HHS/BOV HP3 52 D4
HLWE CM17 48 C2
HNWL W7 154 D1
HORL RH6 280 G9
HSLWW TW4 153 K10
IL IG1 122 G7
KWD/TDW/WH KT20 257 J2
LCOL/BKTW AL2 38 F10
LHD/OX KT22 237 J7
MRDN SM4 201 L7
NTHWD HA6 92 E8
NTHWD HA6 92 G8
NWMAL KT3 199 P5
OXHEY WD19 93 K2
PGE/AN SE20 182 C10
PUR/KEN CR8 222 D7
RDKG RH5 278 A7
REDH RH1 257 P8
REDH RH1 276 B5
REDH RH1 276 G8
REIG RH2 257 J10
REIG RH2 274 B9
RGODL GU7 267 K8
RGUE GU4 251 K3
RGUW GU3 248 F8
RKW/CH/CXG WD3 72 A9
SHPTN TW17 196 D5
SL SL1 128 B5
SLN SL2 128 G1
STA TW18 195 H1
STALW/RED AL3 38 B3
STAN HA7 94 G5
SUN TW16 174 G10
THHTH CR7 203 J1
UX/CGN UB8 132 D7
WAB EN9 82 A1
WDSR SL4 148 F8
WGCE AL7 23 M7
WOT/HER KT12 217 J2
WPK KT4 200 D8
Green Lane Av WOT/HER KT12 217 J2
Green Lane Cl BF/WBF KT14 216 A8
CHERT KT16 195 H9
HARP AL5 20 D3
Green Lane Cottages STAN * HA7 94 G5
Green Lane Ct SL SL1 128 B5
Green Lane Gdns THHTH CR7 203 K2
Green Lanes CEND/HSY/T N8 119 J1
FSBYPK N4 119 K6
HAT AL10 40 C1
HOR/WEW KT19 220 B5
PLMGR N13 98 G6
WCHMH N21 99 J2
WGCW AL8 22 C7
Green La West EHSLY KT24 252 B1
Greenlaw Ct EA * W5 135 J8
Greenlaw Gdns NWMAL KT3 200 C7
Green Lawns NFNCH/WDSP * N12 97 L7
RSLP * HA4 113 K6
Greenlaw St WOOL/PLUM SE18 162 D2
Green Leaf Av WLGTN SM6 222 E1
Greenleaf Cl BRXS/STRHM * SW2 181 H3
Greenleaf Ct DTCH/LGLY SL3 149 M5
Greenleafe Dr BARK/HLT IG6 122 E1
Greenleaf Rd EHAM E6 141 P3
WALTH E17 120 E1
Greenlea Pk WIM/MER * SW19 201 P1
Green Leas SUN TW16 174 G10
Green Leas Cl SUN TW16 174 G9
Greenleaves Ct ASHF * TW15 174 C9
Greenleigh Av STMC/STPC BR5 207 L4
Green Man La EBED/NFELT TW14 153 H10
WEA W13 134 F9
Greenman St IS N1 6 E4
Green Md ESH/CLAY KT10 217 N3
Greenmead Cl SNWD SE25 203 P5
Green Meadow POTB/CUF EN6 59 K6
Greenmeads WOKS/MYFD GU22 232 B8
Green Moor Link WCHMH N21 99 J1
Greenmoor Rd PEND EN3 80 B6
Green North Rd BEAC HP9 89 K7
Greenoak Pl EBAR EN4 78 A6
Greenoak Ri BH/WHM TN16 243 P4
Green Oaks NWDGN * UB2 153 L3
Greenoak Wy WIM/MER SW19 178 G7
Greenock Rd ACT W3 155 N2
SL SL1 128 F8
STRHM/NOR SW16 202 E1
Greenock Wy ROM RM1 104 F8
Greeno Crs SHPTN TW17 196 B5
Green Pde HSLW * TW3 176 A2
Green Pk STA TW18 173 H6
Green Pond Cl WALTH E17 120 D1
Green Pond Rd WALTH E17 120 D1
Green Ride LOU IG10 81 M10
Green Rd CHERT KT16 194 E4
STHGT/OAK N14 78 C10
TRDG/WHET N20 97 M4
Greensand Cl REDH RH1 258 E4
Greensand Rd REDH RH1 258 B9
Greensand Wy
BRKHM/BTCW RH3 256 D10
BRKHM/BTCW RH3 273 P1
DORK RH4 272 D3
EDEN TN8 262 F6
GDST RH9 260 C10
OXTED RH8 261 K2
OXTED RH8 262 A7
RDKG RH5 254 C10
REDH RH1 259 J10
REDH RH1 275 P3
REDH RH1 277 J2
REIG RH2 257 H8
RSEV TN14 264 E8
The Greens Cl LOU IG10 82 D6
Greens Ct NTGHL * W11 8 C10
SOHO/CST W1F 11 J7
Greens End WOOL/PLUM SE18 162 E3
Greenshank Cl WALTH E17 100 D8
Greenshaw BRW CM14 106 G2
Greenside BCTR RM8 123 M7
BORE WD6 75 M4
BXLY DA5 185 P4
RPLY/SEND * GU23 233 M7
SLN SL2 128 F7
SWLY BR8 208 E2
Greenside Cl CAT SE6 183 J5
RGUE GU4 250 F8
TRDG/WHET N20 97 N3
Greenside Rd CROY/NA CR0 203 H7
SHB W12 156 D2
Greenslade Rd BARK IG11 142 G2
Greensleeves Cl STALE/WH AL4 39 H7
Greenstead SBW CM21 29 P2
Greenstead Av WFD IG8 101 P7
Greenstead Gdns
PUT/ROE SW15 178 D1
WFD IG8 101 P7
Greensted Rd CHONG CM5 67 H4
LOU IG10 102 B1
Greenstone Ms WAN E11 121 M4
Green St FSTGT E7 121 N10
MYFR/PKLN W1K 10 B7
PEND EN3 80 C7
RAD WD7 75 M1
RKW/CH/CXG WD3 70 F6
SUN TW16 197 H1
Green Street Green Rd DART DA1 187 P4
RDART DA2 188 B6
RDART DA2 210 G1
Greenstreet Hl NWCR * SE14 160 C9
Greensward BUSH WD23 74 A10
Green Ter CLKNW EC1R 6 B10
The Green ACT W3 136 B8
ASHF * TW15 173 N8
BH/WHM * TN16 245 M10
BH/WHM TN16 262 G2
BKHH * IG9 101 N2
BXLYHN DA7 164 B7
CAR * SM5 222 B1
CHES/WCR EN8 62 B4
CRAWE RH10 285 J2
CRAWW RH11 283 M6
CROY/NA CR0 224 E5
CTHM CR3 242 F9
ED N9 99 P3
EPP CM16 82 G2
EW KT17 220 D8
FELT TW13 175 J5
GDST RH9 260 A8
HAYES BR2 205 M7
HEST TW5 153 P5
HGDN/ICK UB10 112 D7
HRW HA1 114 F7
KWD/TDW/WH KT20 238 G9
LCOL/BKTW * AL2 57 J3
LHD/OX KT22 236 C10
MRDN SM4 201 H4
NWDGN UB2 153 N1
NWMAL KT3 199 P3
ORP * BR6 227 M6
RAIN RM13 145 M9
RCH/KEW TW9 177 J1
RDART DA2 188 C5
RKW/CH/CXG WD3 72 A10
SCUP DA14 185 K8
SEV TN13 247 L8
SL SL1 149 J1
SRTFD E15 141 L1
STHGT/OAK N14 98 E3
STMC/STPC BR5 185 L10
STWL/WRAY TW19 172 B2
SUT SM1 201 L10
TOTM N17 99 K7
WAN E11 121 N4
WCHMH N21 99 H1
WDR/YW UB7 151 N2
WELL DA16 163 H10
WHTN TW2 176 D4
Green Tiles DEN/HRF * UB9 111 J5
Green Tiles La DEN/HRF UB9 111 J4
Green Trees EPP CM16 65 K7
Green V BXLYHS DA6 185 N1
EA W5 135 L8
WGCE AL7 23 K6
Greenvale Rd ELTH/MOT SE9 162 C10
WOKN/KNAP GU21 231 J5
Green Verges STAN HA7 95 J8
Green Vw CHSGTN KT9 219 L4
Greenview Av BECK BR3 204 D6
Greenview Cl ACT W3 136 B10
Green View Cl HHS/BOV HP3 52 D5
Green Wk CHONG CM5 67 N6
CRAWE RH10 283 P5
DART DA1 164 G10
HDN NW4 116 G2
NWDGN UB2 153 P4
RSLP HA4 112 G6
STHWK SE1 19 J4
WFD IG8 102 B7
The Green Wk CHING E4 101 H2
Green Wy ELTH/MOT SE9 184 A1
HART DA3 211 K5
HAYES BR2 205 B6
REDH RH1 257 P8
SL SL1 128 A4
SUN TW16 197 H4
Greenway BCTR RM8 123 M7
BERK HP4 33 M5
BH/WHM TN16 243 P6
CHST BR7 184 D8
CSHM HP5 50 G4
GT/LBKH KT23 236 A9
HARH RM3 106 A7
HARP AL5 20 C3
HHNE HP2 36 C6
HLWW/ROY CM19 46 B1
KTN/HRWW/W HA3 115 K3
PIN HA5 93 J10
RBRW/HUT CM13 107 M1
RYNPK SW20 200 F4
STHGT/OAK N14 98 F3
TRDG/WHET N20 97 K3
WLGTN SM6 222 D1
YEAD UB4 133 J6
Greenway Av WALTH E17 121 J2
Greenway Cl BF/WBF KT14 215 K9
CDALE/KGS NW9 96 A10
FBAR/BDGN N11 98 B7
FSBYPK N4 119 K7
TRDG/WHET N20 97 K3
Greenway Ct IL IG1 122 D6
Greenway Dr STA TW18 195 M1
Greenway Gdns CDALE/KGS NW9 95 P10
CROY/NA CR0 204 E10
GFD/PVL UB6 133 P5
Green Way Gdns
KTN/HRWW/W HA3 94 D10
Greenways ABLGY WD5 54 E7
BECK BR3 204 F2
CHESW EN7 61 J5
EGH TW20 172 B9
ESH/CLAY KT10 218 D1
HERT/WAS SG14 25 J5
KWD/TDW/WH KT20 256 D1
NFNCH/WDSP * N12 97 M7
Greenways Dr ASC SL5 192 D8
The Greenways TWK * TW1 176 F2
The Green Wy KTN/HRWW/W HA3 94 D9
The Greenway CDALE/KGS NW9 96 A10
CFSP/GDCR SL9 110 A1
EPSOM KT18 219 M10
HGDN/ICK UB10 112 C7
HSLWW * TW4 153 N10
OXTED RH8 261 M9
PEND EN3 80 C1
PIN HA5 113 N4
POTB/CUF EN6 59 K9
RKW/CH/CXG WD3 91 K1
SL SL1 128 C10
UX/CGN UB8 131 N4
Greenwell Cl GDST RH9 260 A6
Greenwell St GTPST W1W 10 F2
Greenwich Church St
GNWCH * SE10 161 H5
Greenwich Crs EHAM E6 142 B7
Greenwich Foot Tnl
GNWCH SE10 161 H4
Greenwich High Rd
GNWCH SE10 160 G6
Greenwich Park St
GNWCH * SE10 161 J5
Greenwich Quay DEPT * SE8 160 F5
Greenwich South St
GNWCH SE10 160 G7
Greenwich Vw POP/IOD E14 160 G2
Greenwich Wy WAB EN9 81 H2
Greenwood Av CHESW EN7 62 A7
DAGE RM10 124 C9
PEND EN3 80 D5
Greenwood Cl ADL/WDHM KT15 215 J7
AMS * HP6 69 K4
BFN/LL DA15 185 K5
CHESW EN7 62 A7
MRDN SM4 201 H4
RAD WD7 57 K8
STMC/STPC BR5 207 H6
THDIT KT7 198 F8
Greenwood Cottages ASC SL5 193 H6
Greenwood Dr CHING E4 101 H6
GSTN WD25 55 J10
REDH RH1 276 B5
Greenwood Gdns BARK/HLT IG6 102 F8
CTHM CR3 259 P1
PLMGR N13 99 J4
RAD WD7 57 K9
Greenwood La HPTN TW12 176 A8
Greenwood Pk KUTN/CMB KT2 178 B10
Greenwood Pl KTTN NW5 118 C10
Greenwood Rd BXLY DA5 186 E7
CHIG IG7 103 L5
CHOB/PIR GU24 230 A7
CROY/NA CR0 203 J7
HACK E8 7 P1
ISLW TW7 154 D9
MTCM CR4 202 E3
PLSTW E13 141 L4
THDIT KT7 198 F8
WOKN/KNAP GU21 231 K6
Greenwood Ter WLSDN * NW10 136 A3
The Greenwood GU GU1 250 D10
Greenwood Wy SEV TN13 264 G1
Green Wrythe Crs CAR SM5 201 P8
Green Wrythe La CAR SM5 201 P8
MRDN SM4 201 N6
Greenyard WAB EN9 63 H9
Greer Rd KTN/HRWW/W HA3 94 B9
Greet St STHWK SE1 12 B10
Greg Cl LEY E10 121 H4
Gregories Farm La BEAC HP9 88 C9
Gregories Rd BEAC HP9 88 B8
Gregor Ms BKHTH/KID SE3 161 M6
Gregory Av POTB/CUF EN6 59 M9
Gregory Cl WOKN/KNAP GU21 231 P3
Gregory Crs ELTH/MOT SE9 184 A3
Gregory Dr WDSR SL4 171 N2
Gregory Ms WAB EN9 62 G8
Gregory Pl KENS W8 14 G1
Gregory Rd CHDH RM6 123 N2
NWDGN UB2 153 P2
SLN SL2 109 J7
Gregson Cl BORE WD6 75 P6
Greig Cl CEND/HSY/T N8 118 F3
Greig Ter WALW SE17 18 D9
Grenaby Av CROY/NA CR0 203 L7
Grenaby Rd CROY/NA CR0 203 L7
Grenada Rd CHARL SE7 161 P6
Grenade St POP/IOD E14 140 E9
Grenadier Cl STALE/WH AL4 39 H7
Grenadier Pl CTHM CR3 241 K8
Grenadier St CAN/RD E16 142 D10
Grenadine Cl CHESW EN7 61 N3
Grena Gdns RCH/KEW TW9 155 L10
Grena Rd RCH/KEW TW9 155 L10
Grendon Cl HORL RH6 280 A2
Grendon Gdns WBLY HA9 115 M7
Grendon St STJWD NW8 9 N1
Grenfell Av EMPK RM11 124 G6
Grenfell Cl BORE WD6 75 P5
Grenfell Ct MLHL * NW7 96 E7
Grenfell Gdns
KTN/HRWW/W HA3 115 K5
Grenfell Rd BEAC HP9 88 D8
NTGHL W11 136 G9
TOOT SW17 180 A9
Grenfell Wk NTGHL W11 136 G9
Grennell Cl SUT SM1 201 N9
Grennell Rd SUT SM1 201 M9
Grenoble Gdns PLMGR N13 99 H7
Grenside Rd WEY KT13 196 C10
Grenville Av BROX EN10 44 E7
Grenville Cl BRYLDS KT5 199 P8
CHES/WCR EN8 62 C8
COB KT11 217 L9
FNCH N3 97 J9
SL SL1 128 A4
Grenville Gdns WFD IG8 101 P8
Grenville Ms HPTN TW12 176 A8
Grenville Pl MLHL NW7 96 A6
SKENS SW7 15 J5
Grenville Rd ARCH N19 118 F6
CROY/NA CR0 225 H6
MFD/CHID GU8 266 B10
WTHK RM20 166 G4
Grenville St BMSBY WC1N 11 M2
Gresford Cl STALE/WH AL4 39 J6
Gresham Av HART DA3 211 L4
TRDG/WHET N20 98 A5
WARL CR6 242 D4
Gresham Cl BXLY DA5 185 P2
ENC/FH EN2 79 K7
OXTED RH8 261 L5
Gresham Ct BERK HP4 33 N6
BRW CM14 107 H4
Gresham Dr CHDH RM6 123 L3
Gresham Gdns CRICK NW2 117 H6
Gresham Rd BECK BR3 204 D2
BRW CM14 107 H4
BRXN/ST SW9 159 H9
CAN/RD E16 141 N8
EDGW HA8 95 L7
EHAM E6 142 C4
HEST TW5 154 B7
HGDN/ICK UB10 132 B4
HPTN TW12 175 P9
OXTED RH8 261 L5
SL SL1 128 F8
SNWD * SE25 203 P4
STA TW18 173 J8
WLSDN NW10 116 A10
Gresham St CITYW EC2V 12 E5
Gresham Wk CRAWE RH10 283 P10
Gresham Wy WIM/MER SW19 179 K6
Gresley Cl SEVS/STOTM * N15 119 L2
WALTH E17 120 D4
WGCW AL8 23 H4
Gresley Rd ARCH N19 118 D6
Gressenhall Rd
WAND/EARL SW18 179 J2
Gresse St FITZ W1T 11 J4
Gresswell Cl SCUP DA14 185 K6
Greswell St FUL/PGN SW6 156 G7
Greta Bank EHSLY KT24 252 D2
Gretton Rd TOTM N17 99 M8
Greville Av SAND/SEL CR2 224 C6
Greville Cl ASHTD KT21 237 K5
BRKMPK AL9 40 E10
GUW GU2 249 K10
TWK TW1 176 G3
Greville Ct GT/LBKH KT23 254 A1
Greville Ms KIL/WHAMP NW6 2 G6
Greville Park Av ASHTD KT21 237 K4
Greville Park Rd ASHTD KT21 237 K4
Greville Rd KIL/WHAMP NW6 2 G6
RCHPK/HAM TW10 177 L2
WALTH E17 121 H2
Greville St HCIRC EC1N 12 B4
Grey Alders EW KT17 220 F10
Greycaine Rd WATN WD24 73 L3
Grey Cl EFNCH N2 117 M4
Greycoat Pl WEST SW1P 17 J4
Greycoat St WEST SW1P 17 J4
Greycot Rd BECK BR3 182 F8
Grey Eagle St WCHPL E1 13 M3
Greyfell Cl STAN HA7 94 G6
Greyfields Cl PUR/KEN CR8 223 J9
Greyfriars RBRW/HUT CM13 107 N1
Greyfriars Dr ASC SL5 192 A6
CHOB/PIR GU24 230 F1
Greyfriars Rd RPLY/SEND GU23 233 K10
Greygoose Pk HLWW/ROY CM19 46 D4
Greyhound Hl HDN NW4 116 D1
Greyhound La CDH/CHF RM16 168 D1
POTB/CUF EN6 58 D9
STRHM/NOR SW16 180 F9
Greyhound Rd HMSMTH W6 156 G5
SUT SM1 221 M2
TOTM N17 119 M1
WLSDN * NW10 136 E5
Greyhound Slip CRAWE RH10 284 E6
Greyhound Ter
STRHM/NOR SW16 202 D1
Greyhound Wy DART DA1 186 F1
Greyladies Gdns GNWCH * SE10 161 H8
Greys Park Cl HAYES BR2 225 P2
Greystead Rd FSTH SE23 182 B3
Greystoke Av PIN HA5 113 P1
Greystoke Cl BERK HP4 33 M6
Greystoke Cottages EA * W5 135 K6
Greystoke Dr RSLP HA4 112 C4
Greystoke Gdns EA W5 135 K6
ENC/FH EN2 78 E8
Greystoke Rd SL SL1 128 E7
Greystone Cl SAND/SEL CR2 224 B7
Greystone Gdns BARK/HLT IG6 102 F10
KTN/HRWW/W HA3 115 H4
Greystone Pk RSEV TN14 263 P1
Greystones Cl REIG RH2 275 N2
RSEV TN14 247 M3
Greystones Dr REIG RH2 257 M8
Greyswood Av UED * N18 100 C6
Greyswood St
STRHM/NOR SW16 180 C9
Greythorne Rd
WOKN/KNAP GU21 231 M4
Grey Towers Av EMPK RM11 125 L6
Grey Towers Gdns EMPK RM11 125 K6
Grice Av BH/WHM TN16 225 N9
Gridiron Pl UPMR RM14 126 A7
Grier Cl CRAWW RH11 283 H8
Grierson Rd FSTH SE23 182 C3
Grieves Rd GVW DA11 190 C6
Griffin Av UPMR RM14 126 D4
Griffin Cl SL SL1 149 H1
WLSDN NW10 116 E10
Griffin Ct ASHTD * KT21 237 K5
Griffin Manor Wy THMD SE28 162 G2
Griffin Rd TOTM N17 99 M10
WOOL/PLUM SE18 162 G4
The Griffins CDH/CHF RM16 167 N1
Griffin Wk GRH DA9 188 E1
Griffin Wy GT/LBKH KT23 253 P2
SUN TW16 197 H2
Griffith Cl CHDH RM6 123 M5
Griffiths Rd WIM/MER SW19 179 K10
Griffiths Wy STAL AL1 38 B8
Griffon Wy GSTN WD25 54 G10
Grifon Cl CDH/CHF RM16 167 H2
Grifon Rd CDH/CHF RM16 167 H2
Griggs Ap IL IG1 122 F7
Griggs Gdns HCH RM12 125 K10
Grigg's Pl STHWK SE1 19 K4
Griggs Rd LEY E10 121 H4
Grimsby Gv CAN/RD E16 142 E10
CAN/RD E16 162 E1
Grimsby St WCHPL E1 13 M2
Grimsdells Cnr AMS * HP6 69 J3
Grimsdell's La AMS HP6 69 J3
Grimsdyke Crs BAR EN5 76 F7
Grimsdyke Rd PIN HA5 93 M8
Grimsel Pth CMBW SE5 159 J6
Grimshaw Cl HGT * N6 118 B5
Grimshaw Wy ROM RM1 124 F3
Grimston Rd FUL/PGN SW6 157 J8
STAL AL1 38 E6
Grimthorpe Cl STALW/RED AL3 38 B3
Grimwade Av CROY/NA CR0 203 P10
Grimwood Rd TWK TW1 176 E3
Grindall Cl CROY/NA CR0 223 J1
Grindal St STHWK SE1 18 A2
Grindcobbe STAL AL1 38 C9
Grindcobbe Cl STAL AL1 38 C9
Grindleford Av FBAR/BDGN N11 98 B3
Grindley Gdns CROY/NA * CR0 203 N6
Grindstone Crs
WOKN/KNAP GU21 230 G4
Grinling Pl DEPT SE8 160 F5
Grinstead Rd DEPT SE8 160 D4
Grisedale Cl CRAWW RH11 283 M9
PUR/KEN CR8 223 M10
Grisedale Gdns PUR/KEN CR8 223 M10
Grisle Cl ED N9 100 A5
Grittleton Av WBLY HA9 135 N1
Grittleton Rd MV/WKIL W9 8 E1
Grobars Av WOKN/KNAP GU21 231 P1
Grocers' Hall Ct LOTH * EC2R 12 G6
Groombridge Cl WELL DA16 185 K1
WOT/HER KT12 217 J2
Groombridge Rd HOM E9 140 C2
Groom Cl HAYES BR2 205 N4

Groom Crs WAND/EARL SW18 179 N3
Groomfield Cl TOOT SW17 180 B7
Groom Pl KTBR SW1X 16 D3
Groom Rd BROX EN10 62 E2
Grooms Cottages CSHM HP5 51 N6
Grooms Dr RSLP HA4 113 H3
The Grooms CRAWE RH10 284 E5
Grosmont Rd WOOL/PLUM SE18 163 J4
Grosse Wy PUT/ROE SW15 178 E2
Grosvenor Av CAR SM5 222 A3
HBRY N5 119 K10
MORT/ESHN SW14 156 B9
RYLN/HDSTN HA2 114 A5
YEAD UB4 132 G4
Grosvenor Br PIM SW1V 16 F9
Grosvenor Cl LOU IG10 82 E5
Grosvenor Cottages KTBR SW1X 16 C5
Grosvenor Ct RKW/CH/CXG * WD3 72 E9
Grosvenor Crs CDALE/KGS NW9 115 M2
DART DA1 187 L1
HGDN/ICK UB10 132 C2
KTBR SW1X 16 D2
Grosvenor Crescent Ms
KTBR SW1X 16 C2
Grosvenor Dr EMPK RM11 125 K6
LOU IG10 82 E6
Grosvenor Gdns BGVA SW1W 16 E4
CRICK NW2 136 F1
EHAM E6 142 A5
GLDGN NW11 117 J4
KUTN/CMB KT2 177 J9
MORT/ESHN SW14 156 B9
MUSWH N10 118 D1
STHGT/OAK N14 78 E9
UPMR RM14 126 C7
WFD IG8 101 M7
WLGTN SM6 222 D4
Grosvenor Gardens Ms East
BGVA * SW1W 16 F3
Grosvenor Gardens Ms North
BGVA SW1W 16 E4
Grosvenor Ga BAY/PAD W2 10 B8
Grosvenor Hl MYFR/PKLN W1K 10 E7
WIM/MER SW19 179 H9
Grosvenor Ms REIG RH2 275 L3
Grosvenor Pde ACT * W3 135 M10
Grosvenor Pk CMBW SE5 18 E10
Grosvenor Park Rd WALTH E17 120 F3
Grosvenor Pl KTBR SW1X 16 D1
WEY KT13 196 E10
Grosvenor Ri East WALTH E17 120 G3
Grosvenor Rd BCTR RM8 124 A6
BELV DA17 164 A5
BORE WD6 75 M7
BROX EN10 44 E6
BTFD TW8 155 J5
BXLYHS DA6 185 N1
CHOB/PIR GU24 213 J9
CHSWK W4 155 P4
ED N9 100 A2
EHAM E6 142 A3
EPSOM KT18 238 B5
FNCH N3 97 J8
FSTGT E7 141 N1
HNWL W7 134 F10
HSLWW TW4 153 N9
IL IG1 122 F8
LEY E10 121 H6
MUSWH N10 98 C9
NTHWD HA6 92 G6
NWDGN UB2 153 N2
PIM SW1V 16 F9
RCHPK/HAM TW10 177 K1
ROMW/RG RM7 124 E5
SNWD SE25 203 P4
STA TW18 173 K10
STAL AL1 38 D7
STMC/STPC BR5 207 H6
TWK TW1 176 F3
WAN E11 121 N3
WAT WD17 73 K8
WLGTN SM6 222 C3
WWKM BR4 204 G9
Grosvenor Sq HART * DA3 211 K3
KGLGY * WD4 54 D4
MYFR/PKLN W1K 10 D7
Grosvenor St MYFR/PKLN W1K 10 D7
Grosvenor Ter CMBW SE5 18 E10
HHW HP1 35 K7
Grosvenor V RSLP HA4 112 G7
Grosvenor Wy CLPT E5 120 B7
Grosvernor Wharf Rd
POP/IOD E14 161 J3
Grote's Buildings
BKHTH/KID SE3 161 K8
Grote's Pl BKHTH/KID SE3 161 K8
Groton Rd WAND/EARL SW18 179 L5
Grotto Ct STHWK * SE1 18 E1
Grotto Pas MHST W1U 10 C3
Grotto Rd TWK TW1 176 E5
WEY KT13 216 D1
The Grotto WARE SG12 26 C3
Ground La HAT AL10 40 E2
Grove Av EW KT17 220 B9
HARP AL5 20 C4
HNWL W7 134 D8
MUSWH N10 98 D10
PIN HA5 113 M2
SUT SM1 221 K3
TWK TW1 176 E4
Grove Bank OXHEY * WD19 93 L2
Grovebury Cl ERITH DA8 164 E5
Grovebury Ct STHGT/OAK N14 98 D1
Grovebury Gdns LCOL/BKTW AL2 56 B3
Grovebury Rd THMD SE28 163 L1
Grove Cl CFSP/GDCR SL9 89 P9
FSTH SE23 182 C4
HAYES BR2 205 M9
HGDN/ICK UB10 112 B10
KUT KT1 199 K4
SL SL1 149 M2
STHGT/OAK * N14 98 C1
WDSR SL4 171 N3
Grove Cottages CHSWK * W4 156 B5
COB * KT11 235 L2
Grove Ct E/WMO/HCT KT8 198 C5
EA * W5 135 K10
EGH TW20 172 D8
WAB EN9 62 G9
Grove Crs CDALE/KGS NW9 115 P2
FELT TW13 175 M7
KUT KT1 199 K3
RKW/CH/CXG WD3 72 B8
SWFD E18 101 L10
WOT/HER KT12 197 J7
Grove Crescent Rd SRTFD E15 141 J1
Grovedale Cl CHESW EN7 61 N6
Grovedale Rd ARCH N19 118 E7
Grove Dwellings WCHPL * E1 140 B7
Grove End CFSP/GDCR SL9 89 P9
KTTN NW5 118 C9
SWFD E18 101 L10
Grove End La ESH/CLAY KT10 198 C8
Grove End Rd STJWD NW8 3 L8
Grove Farm Pk NTHWD HA6 92 E6
Grove Footpath SURB KT6 199 K4
Grove Gdns HDN * NW4 116 D3
PEND EN3 80 C5
STJWD NW8 3 P10
TEDD TW11 176 F7
Grove Green Rd LEY E10 121 H8
Grove Hall Rd BUSH WD23 73 M8
Grove Heath La
RPLY/SEND GU23 233 M10
Grove Heath North
RPLY/SEND GU23 233 L8
Groveherst Rd DART DA1 165 N9
Grove Hl CFSP/GDCR SL9 89 P8
HRW HA1 114 D5
SWFD E18 101 L10
Grove Hill Rd CMBW SE5 159 M9
HRW HA1 114 E5
Grovehill Rd REDH RH1 257 P10
Grove House Rd CEND/HSY/T N8 118 F2
Groveland Av STRHM/NOR SW16 180 C10
Groveland Ct STP EC4M 12 F6
Groveland Rd BECK BR3 204 E3
Grovelands E/WMO/HCT KT8 197 P4
HHNE HP2 36 D4
LCOL/BKTW AL2 56 A3
Grovelands Cl CMBW SE5 159 M8
RYLN/HDSTN HA2 114 A8
Grovelands Rd PLMGR N13 98 G5
PUR/KEN CR8 222 G8
SEVS/STOTM N15 119 P4
STMC/STPC BR5 185 K10
Grovelands Wy GRAYS RM17 167 L4
Groveland Wy NWMAL KT3 199 P5
Grove La CFSP/GDCR SL9 89 N9
CHIG IG7 103 J4
CMBW SE5 159 L7
COUL/CHIP CR5 240 C1
CSHM HP5 51 N3
EPP CM16 65 K6
KUT KT1 199 K4
UX/CGN UB8 132 A6
Grove Lea HAT AL10 40 D7
Groveley Rd SUN TW16 174 G8
Grove Market Pl ELTH/MOT * SE9 184 C2
Grove Md HAT AL10 40 C4
Grove Meadow WGCE AL7 23 M5
Grove Ms HMSMTH W6 156 F2
Grove Mill La RKW/CH/CXG WD3 72 D4
Grove Pk CDALE/KGS NW9 115 P2
CMBW SE5 159 M8
WAN E11 121 N3
Grove Park Av CHING E4 100 G8
Grove Park Br CHSWK W4 155 P6
Grove Park Gdns CHSWK W4 155 N6
Grove Park Rd CHSWK W4 155 N6
ELTH/MOT SE9 184 B5
RAIN RM13 145 H3
SEVS/STOTM N15 119 M2
Grove Park Ter CHSWK W4 155 N6
Grove Pl ACT W3 135 P10
BAL SW12 180 C2
BRKMPK AL9 40 F10
GSTN * WD25 74 A5
HAMP NW3 117 N8
WEY KT13 216 D2
Grover Cl HHNE HP2 35 N5
Grove Rd ACT W3 135 P10
AMS HP6 69 L3
ASHTD KT21 237 L4
BARN SW13 156 C8
BEAC HP9 88 D9
BELMT SM2 221 K3
BELV DA17 164 A5
BGR/WK TN15 247 P8
BH/WHM TN16 243 P6
BORE WD6 75 M5
BOW E3 140 D4
BTFD TW8 155 H4
BXLYHN DA7 164 D10
CHDH RM6 123 M5
CHERT KT16 195 J6
CHING E4 101 H4
CRICK NW2 136 F1
E/WMO/HCT KT8 198 C4
EA W5 135 J9
EBAR EN4 77 P7
EDGW HA8 95 M7
EPSOM KT18 220 B9
FBAR/BDGN N11 98 C6
GRAYS RM17 167 P5
GU GU1 250 F10
GVW DA11 189 N1
HARP AL5 20 C4
HHW HP1 35 K8
HOM E9 140 C3
HORL RH6 279 P3
HSLW TW3 153 P10
ISLW TW7 154 D7
LEY E10 120 G3
MTCM CR4 202 C2
NFNCH/WDSP N12 97 N6
NTHWD HA6 92 E6
PIN HA5 113 N3
RCHPK/HAM TW10 177 L2
RKW/CH/CXG WD3 91 K3
RSEV TN14 247 K7
SEVS/STOTM N15 119 M3
SHPTN TW17 196 D6
SL SL1 128 D2
STAL AL1 38 C7
SURB KT6 199 J5
SWFD E18 101 L10
THHTH CR7 203 H4
UX/CGN UB8 131 N2
WAN E11 121 L5
WARE SG12 26 E1
WDSR SL4 149 J8
WHTN TW2 176 C6
WIM/MER SW19 179 M10
WOKN/KNAP GU21 232 C2
Grove Rd West PEND EN3 80 B3
Grover Rd OXHEY WD19 73 L10
Grovers Farm Cottages
ADL/WDHM * KT15 215 H7
Groves Cl SOCK/AV RM15 146 E9
Groveside GT/LBKH KT23 253 P3
Groveside Cl ACT W3 135 M8
CAR SM5 201 P9
GT/LBKH KT23 253 P3
Groveside Rd CHING E4 101 K4
Grovestile Waye
EBED/NFELT TW14 174 E3
Grove St BERM/RHTH SE16 160 E3
UED N18 99 N7
Grove Ter KTTN NW5 118 B8
STHL * UB1 133 P9
TEDD TW11 176 F7
The Grove ADL/WDHM KT15 215 L2
AMS HP6 69 J1
BH/WHM TN16 244 A4
BRKMPK AL9 59 K3
BRW CM14 106 E5
BXLYHS DA6 163 N10
CDALE/KGS NW9 116 A3
CEND/HSY/T N8 118 E3
COUL/CHIP CR5 240 E1
CRAWW RH11 283 M7
CSHM HP5 70 A2
CTHM CR3 241 J7
EA W5 135 J10
EDGW HA8 95 N5
EGH TW20 172 D8
ENC/FH EN2 79 H6
EW KT17 220 B9
FNCH N3 97 K8
FSBYPK N4 118 G5
GFD/PVL UB6 134 B8
GLDGN NW11 117 H5
GU * GU1 268 C2
GVE DA12 190 E3
HARP * AL5 20 D4
HGDN/ICK UB10 112 B10
HGT N6 118 B6
HORL RH6 280 C5
ISLW TW7 154 D7
KGLGY * WD4 53 M6
PLMGR N13 99 H5
POTB/CUF EN6 59 M8
RAD WD7 56 F10
RKW/CH/CXG * WD3 72 B8
SCUP DA14 185 P7
SL SL1 149 M1
SRTFD E15 141 K1
SWCM DA10 189 K1
SWLY BR8 208 G3
TEDD TW11 176 F7
UPMR RM14 125 P9
WOKN/KNAP GU21 232 C2
WOT/HER KT12 197 J7
WWKM BR4 205 H10
Grove V CHST BR7 184 D9
EDUL SE22 159 M10
Grove Wk HERT/WAS SG14 25 K3
Groveway BCTR RM8 123 N9
BRXN/ST SW9 158 G7
Grove Wy ESH/CLAY KT10 198 B7
RKW/CH/CXG WD3 70 E8
UX/CGN UB8 131 N2
WBLY HA9 115 P10
Grovewood Cl RKW/CH/CXG WD3 70 E9
Grove Wood Hl COUL/CHIP CR5 222 E10
Grovewood Pl WFD IG8 102 C7
Grubbs La BRKMPK AL9 41 K8
Grub St OXTED RH8 261 P5
Grummant Rd PECK SE15 159 N7
Grundy St POP/IOD E14 140 G8
Gruneisen Rd FNCH N3 97 L8
Guardian Cl HCH RM12 125 J7
Guards Av CTHM CR3 241 K8
Guards Ct ASC SL5 192 G7
Guardsman Cl BRW CM14 107 J6
Guards Rd WDSR SL4 148 B8
Gubbins La HARH RM3 105 N9
Gubyon Av HNHL SE24 181 J1
Guernsey Cl HEST TW5 153 P7
RGUE GU4 250 D5
Guernsey Farm Dr
WOKN/KNAP * GU21 232 A1
Guernsey Gv HNHL SE24 181 K3
Guernsey Rd IS N1 6 F2
WAN E11 121 J6
Guessens Gv WGCW AL8 22 F5
Guessens Rd WGCW AL8 22 F5
Guessens Wk WGCW AL8 22 F4
Guibal Rd LEE/GVPK SE12 183 N4
Guildables La OXTED RH8 262 B10
Guildcroft GU GU1 250 D10
Guildersfield Rd
STRHM/NOR SW16 180 F10
Guildford Av FELT TW13 175 H5
Guildford Business Park Rd
GUW GU2 249 N9
Guildford Gv GNWCH SE10 160 G7
Guildford La SHGR GU5 269 K4
Guildford Park Av GUW GU2 267 N1
Guildford Park Rd GUW GU2 267 N1
Guildford Rd CHERT KT16 195 J8
CHERT KT16 214 E6
CHOB/PIR GU24 212 D8
CHOB/PIR GU24 213 J9
CHOB/PIR GU24 230 E9
CHOB/PIR GU24 230 E1
CROY/NA CR0 203 L6
DORK RH4 272 A4
EHAM E6 142 B8
GDMY/SEVK IG3 123 H7
GT/LBKH KT23 253 N3
HARH RM3 105 M7
LHD/OX KT22 236 F8
LHD/OX KT22 236 D10
LHD/OX KT22 254 C1
LTWR GU18 212 A6
RDKG RH5 271 H6
RGUE GU4 249 P1
RGUW GU3 249 H1
STAL AL1 38 G7
VX/NE SW8 158 F7
WALTH E17 101 H9
WOKS/MYFD GU22 232 A8
WOKS/MYFD GU22 232 B5
Guildford St CHERT * KT16 195 K7
STA TW18 173 K9
Guildford Wy WLGTN SM6 222 F2
Guildhall Buildings CITYW EC2V 12 F5
Guildhall Yd CITYW EC2V 12 F5
Guildhouse St PIM SW1V 16 G6
Guildown Av GUW GU2 267 N3
NFNCH/WDSP N12 97 L5
Guildown Rd GUW GU2 267 N3
Guild Rd CHARL SE7 162 A4
ERITH DA8 164 G6
Guildsway WALTH E17 100 E9
Guileshill La RPLY/SEND GU23 233 P8
Guilford Av BRYLDS KT5 199 L5
Guilford Pl BMSBY WC1N 11 N2
The Guilfords HLWE CM17 29 N6
Guilford St BMSBY WC1N 11 N2
Guillemot Pl WDGN * N22 98 G10
Guilsborough Cl WLSDN NW10 136 B2
Guinery Gv HHS/BOV HP3 36 A10
Guinevere Gdns CHES/WCR EN8 62 C6
Guinevere Rd CRAWW RH11 283 H7
Guinness Cl HOM E9 140 D2
HYS/HAR UB3 152 E2
Guinness Ct CROY/NA * CR0 203 N9
Guinness Sq STHWK SE1 19 J4
Guinness Trust
STNW/STAM * N16 119 N6
Guinness Trust Est CHEL SW3 16 A6
SRTFD * E15 141 L3
Guion Rd FUL/PGN SW6 157 J8
Gulland Cl BUSH WD23 74 B9
Gulland Wk IS N1 6 F2
Gullbrook HHW HP1 35 K6
Gull Cl WLGTN SM6 222 F4
Gullet Wood Rd GSTN WD25 73 H1
Gulliver Cl NTHLT UB5 133 N3
Gulliver Rd BFN/LL DA15 184 G5
Gulliver St BERM/RHTH SE16 160 E2
The Gulphs HERT/BAY SG13 25 L6
Gumbrells Cl RGUW GU3 249 H6
Gumleigh Rd EA W5 155 H3
Gumley Gdns ISLW TW7 154 F9
Gumley Rd WTHK RM20 167 J5
Gumping Rd STMC/STPC BR5 206 F9
Gundulph Rd HAYES BR2 205 P3
Gunfleet Cl GVE DA12 191 H3
Gun Hl TIL RM18 168 G5
Gunmakers La HOM E9 140 D3
Gunnell Cl SNWD SE25 203 N6
SYD * SE26 181 P7
Gunner Dr WAB EN9 80 F3
Gunner La WOOL/PLUM SE18 162 D4
Gunnersbury Av ACT W3 155 M2
Gunnersbury Av
(North Circular Rd)
EA W5 135 L10
Gunnersbury Cl CHSWK * W4 155 N4
Gunnersbury Crs ACT W3 155 M1
Gunnersbury Dr EA W5 155 L1
Gunnersbury Gdns ACT W3 155 M1
Gunnersbury La ACT W3 155 M1
Gunners Gv CHING E4 101 H4
Gunners Rd WAND/EARL SW18 179 N5
Gunning Cl CRAWW RH11 283 K10
Gunning Rd GRAYS RM17 167 P4
Gunning St WOOL/PLUM SE18 163 H3
Gunn Rd SWCM DA10 189 K2
Gunstor Rd STNW/STAM * N16 119 M9
Gun St WCHPL E1 13 L4
Gunter Gv EDGW HA8 96 A9
WBPTN SW10 15 J10
Gunters Md LHD/OX * KT22 218 B7
Gunterstone Rd WKENS W14 14 B7
Gunthorpe St WCHPL E1 13 M4
Gunton Rd CLPT E5 120 A8
TOOT SW17 180 B9
Gunwhale Cl BERM/RHTH SE16 140 C10
Gurdon Rd CHARL SE7 161 M4
Gurnard Cl WDR/YW UB7 131 N9
Gurnell Gv WEA W13 134 E6
Gurnells Rd BEAC HP9 89 H6
Gurney Cl BARK IG11 142 E1
BEAC HP9 88 B9
SRTFD E15 121 K10
WALTH E17 100 C9
Gurney Court Rd STAL AL1 38 E4
Gurney Crs CROY/NA CR0 202 G8
Gurney Dr EFNCH N2 117 N2
Gurney Rd CAR SM5 222 B1
FUL/PGN SW6 157 M9
NTHLT UB5 133 J5
SRTFD E15 121 K10
Gurney's Cl REDH RH1 276 A1
Guthrie St CHEL SW3 15 N7
Gutteridge La ABR/ST RM4 84 D10
Gutter La CITYW EC2V 12 E5
Guyatt Gdns MTCM CR4 202 B2
Guy Barnett Gv BKHTH/KID SE3 161 M9
Guy Rd WLGTN SM6 202 E10
Guyscliff Rd LEW SE13 183 H1
Guysfield Cl RAIN RM13 145 H3
Guysfield Dr RAIN RM13 145 H3
Guy St STHWK SE1 19 H1
Gwalior Rd PUT/ROE SW15 156 G10
Gwendolen Av PUT/ROE SW15 178 G1
Gwendoline Av PLSTW E13 141 N3
Gwendwr Rd WKENS W14 14 B7
Gweneth Cottages EDGW * HA8 95 M7
Gwent Cl GSTN WD25 55 L10
Gwillim Cl BFN/LL DA15 185 K2
Gwydor Rd BECK BR3 204 C4
Gwydyr Rd HAYES BR2 205 L3
Gwyn Cl FUL/PGN SW6 157 M6
Gwynne Av CROY/NA CR0 204 C7
Gwynne Cl WDSR SL4 148 D7
Gwynne Park Av WFD IG8 102 C7
Gwynne Rd BTSEA SW11 157 N8
CTHM CR3 241 L9
Gwynne Vaughan Av GUW GU2 249 M6
Gwynne Whf CHSWK W4 156 C5
Gwynn Rd GVW DA11 189 P5
Gwynns Wk HERT/BAY SG13 25 M5
Gylcote Cl HNHL SE24 159 L10
Gyles Pk STAN HA7 95 H9
Gyllyngdune Gdns
GDMY/SEVK IG3 123 J8
Gypsy Cl WARE SG12 26 E7
Gypsy La BRKMPK AL9 23 J10
GSTN WD25 72 E1
SLN SL2 109 K9
WARE SG12 26 E7

H

Haarlem Rd HMSMTH W6 156 G2
Haberdasher Pl IS N1 7 H9
Haberdasher St IS N1 7 H9
Habgood Rd LOU IG10 82 B7
Haccombe Rd WIM/MER SW19 179 M9
Hackbridge Park Gdns CAR SM5 202 A9
Hackbridge Rd CAR SM5 202 B9
Hacketts La WOKS/MYFD GU22 215 J10
Hackford Rd BRXN/ST SW9 158 G7
Hackford Wk BRXN/ST SW9 158 G7
Hackforth Cl BAR EN5 76 E9
Hackhurst La RDKG RH5 270 G5
Hackington Crs BECK BR3 182 F9
Hackney Cl BORE WD6 76 A9
Hackney Gv HACK E8 140 A1
Hackney Rd BETH E2 7 L9
Hacton Dr HCH RM12 125 M9
Hacton La HCH RM12 125 N7
UPMR RM14 125 N10
Haddenham Ct OXHEY * WD19 93 L4
Hadden Rd THMD SE28 163 H2
Hadden Wy NTHLT UB5 134 C1
Haddestoke Ga BROX EN10 62 E2
Haddington Rd BMLY BR1 183 J6
Haddon Cl BORE WD6 75 M6
EN EN1 79 P10
HHS/BOV HP3 36 B7
NWMAL KT3 200 C5
WEY KT13 196 E10
Haddon Gv BFN/LL DA15 185 K3
Haddon Rd RKW/CH/CXG WD3 70 F9
STMC/STPC BR5 207 M5
SUT SM1 221 L1
Haddo St GNWCH SE10 160 G5
Hadfield Cl STHL UB1 133 N5
Hadfield Rd STWL/WRAY TW19 173 N2
Hadland Cl HHW HP1 52 D2
Hadleigh Cl RYNPK SW20 201 J2
WCHPL E1 140 B6
Hadleigh Ct BROX EN10 44 E8
HARP AL5 20 D5
Hadleigh Dr BELMT SM2 221 K5
Hadleigh Rd ED N9 100 A1
Hadleigh St BETH E2 140 B6
Hadley Cl BORE WD6 75 L9
WCHMH N21 79 H10
Hadley Gdns CHSWK W4 156 A4
NWDGN UB2 153 N4
Hadley Gra HLWE CM17 47 M1
Hadley Gn BAR EN5 77 J7
Hadley Green Rd BAR EN5 77 J6
Hadley Gn West BAR EN5 77 H6
Hadley Gv BAR EN5 77 H6
Hadley Highstone BAR EN5 77 J5
Hadley Pde BAR * EN5 77 H7
Hadley Pl WEY KT13 216 B4
Hadley Rdg BAR EN5 77 J7
Hadley Rd BAR EN5 77 L7
BELV DA17 164 A3
EBAR EN4 78 B4
ENC/FH EN2 78 F4
MTCM CR4 202 E4
Hadley St KTTN NW5 4 E2
Hadley Wy WCHMH N21 79 H10
Hadley Wood Ri PUR/KEN CR8 241 J1
Hadley Wood Rd BAR EN5 77 M6
Hadlow Ct SL SL1 129 H10
Hadlow Rd SCUP DA14 185 K7
WELL DA16 163 M6
Hadlow Wy MEO DA13 190 B10
Hadrian Cl STALW/RED AL3 37 N8
STWL/WRAY TW19 173 P3
Hadrian Est BETH E2 7 P8
Hadrian's Ride EN EN1 79 N9
Hadrian St GNWCH SE10 161 K4
Hadrian Wy STWL/WRAY TW19 173 P3
Hadyn Park Rd SHB W12 156 D1
Hafer Rd BTSEA SW11 158 A10
Hafton Rd CAT SE6 183 K4
Hagden La WATW WD18 72 G8
Haggard Rd TWK TW1 176 G3
Hagger Ct WALTH * E17 121 J1
Haggerston Rd BORE WD6 75 K4
HACK E8 7 L4
Hagsdell Rd HERT/BAY SG13 25 L6
Hague St BETH E2 7 P10
Ha-ha Rd WOOL/PLUM SE18 162 C5
Haig Cl STAL AL1 38 G7
Haig Dr SL SL1 148 G1
Haig Gdns GVE DA12 190 F3
Haigh Crs REDH RH1 276 C2
Haig Rd BH/WHM TN16 244 B3
CDH/CHF RM16 168 D2
STAN HA7 95 H6
UX/CGN UB8 132 C7
Haig Rd East PLSTW E13 141 P5
Haig Rd West PLSTW E13 141 P5
Haigville Gdns BARK/HLT IG6 122 E2
Hailes Cl WIM/MER SW19 179 M9
Hailey Av HOD EN11 26 F9
Haileybury Av EN EN1 79 N10
Haileybury Rd ORP BR6 227 K1
Hailey La HOD EN11 26 C10
Hailey Rd ERITHM DA18 164 B1
Hailsham Av BRXS/STRHM SW2 180 G5
Hailsham Cl HARH RM3 105 K6
SURB KT6 199 J7
Hailsham Dr HRW HA1 114 C1
Hailsham Rd HARH RM3 105 K6
TOOT SW17 180 B9
Hailsham Ter PLMGR * N13 99 L6
Haimo Rd ELTH/MOT SE9 184 A1
Hainault Buildings LEY * E10 121 H6
Hainault Gore CHDH RM6 123 P3
Hainault Gv CHIG IG7 102 F5
Hainault Rd CHDH RM6 123 L1
CHDH RM6 124 A4
CHIG IG7 102 F5
ROMW/RG RM7 124 E1
WAN E11 121 H6
Hainault St ELTH/MOT SE9 184 E4
IL IG1 122 E7
Haines Ct WEY KT13 216 E2
Haines Wk MRDN SM4 201 L7
Haines Wy GSTN WD25 55 H10
Hainford Cl PECK SE15 160 C10
Haining Cl CHSWK W4 155 M4
Hainthorpe Rd WNWD SE27 181 J6
Hainton Cl WCHPL E1 140 A8
Halbutt St DAGW RM9 124 A9
Halcomb St IS N1 7 J6
Halcot Av BXLYHS DA6 186 C1
Halcrow St WCHPL * E1 140 A7
Halcyon Wy EMPK RM11 125 N6
Haldane Cl MUSWH N10 98 C8
WAB EN9 80 G4
Haldane Gdns GVW DA11 189 P4
Haldane Pl WAND/EARL SW18 179 L4
Haldane Rd EHAM E6 142 A5
FUL/PGN SW6 157 J6
GFD/PVL UB6 134 B9
THMD SE28 143 N9
Haldan Rd CHING E4 101 H7
Haldens WGCE AL7 23 J2
Haldon Rd WAND/EARL SW18 179 J2
Halebourne La CHOB/PIR GU24 212 F6
Hale Cl CHING E4 101 H4
EDGW HA8 95 P6
ORP BR6 226 F1
Hale Dr EDGW HA8 95 P7
MLHL NW7 96 A7
Hale End HARH RM3 105 J7
Hale End Cl RSLP HA4 113 H4
Hale End Rd WALTH E17 101 J9
Hale Ends WOKS/MYFD GU22 231 N7
Halefield Rd TOTM N17 99 P9
Hale Gdns ACT W3 135 M10
SEVS/STOTM N15 119 P1
Hale Grove Gdns MLHL NW7 96 A6
Hale La EDGW HA8 95 P6
MLHL NW7 96 A6
RSEV TN14 246 G3
Hale Oak Rd RSEV TN14 265 H10
Hale Pit Rd GT/LBKH KT23 254 B2
Hale Rd EHAM E6 142 B6
HERT/BAY SG13 25 L6
TOTM N17 119 P1
Hales Oak GT/LBKH KT23 254 B2

Halesowen Rd MRDN SM4 201 L7
Hales Pk HHNE HP2 36 D5
Hales Park Cl HHNE HP2 36 D5
Hales St DEPT SE8 160 F6
Hale St POP/IOD E14 140 G9
STA TW18 173 H7
Haleswood COB KT11 217 J10
Haleswood Rd HHNE HP2 36 B5
Halesworth Cl HARH RM3 105 M7
Halesworth Rd HARH RM3 105 M7
LEW SE13 160 G9
The Hale CHING E4 101 J8
SEVS/STOTM N15 119 P1
Haley Rd HDN NW4 116 F4
Half Acre BTFD TW8 155 J5
Halfacre Hl CFSP/GDCR SL9 90 C9
Half Acre Ms BTFD TW8 155 J6
Half Acre Rd HNWL W7 134 D10
Halfhide La CHES/WCR EN8 62 C2
Halfhides WAB EN9 63 J9
Half Moon Crs IS * N1 5 P7
Half Moon La EPP CM16 65 J7
HNHL SE24 181 K2
Half Moon Meadow HHNE HP2 36 D1
Half Moon Ms STAL AL1 38 C6
Halfmoon Pas WCHPL * E1 13 M6
Half Moon Pas WCHPL E1 13 M6
Half Moon St MYFR/PICC W1J 10 F9
Halford Cl EDGW HA8 95 N10
Halford Rd FUL/PGN SW6 14 F10
HGDN/ICK UB10 112 B10
RCHPK/HAM TW10 177 K1
WALTH E17 121 J3
Halfpenny Cl RGUE GU4 268 G6
Halfpenny La ASC SL5 192 F7
RGUE GU4 268 F3
Halfway Ct PUR RM19 165 P3
Halfway Gn WOT/HER KT12 197 J10
Halfway St BFN/LL DA15 185 H4
Haliburton Rd TWK TW1 176 F1
Haliday Wk IS * N1 7 H1
Halidon Ri HARH RM3 106 A7
Halifax Cl CRAWE RH10 284 F4
TEDD TW11 176 D9
Halifax Rd ENC/FH EN2 79 K6
GFD/PVL UB6 134 A3
RKW/CH/CXG WD3 90 F1
Halifax St SYD SE26 182 A6
Halifax Wy WGCE AL7 23 P5
Halifield Dr BELV DA17 163 P2
Haling Gv SAND/SEL CR2 223 K4
Haling Park Gdns SAND/SEL CR2 223 J3
Haling Park Rd SAND/SEL CR2 223 J3
Haling Rd SAND/SEL CR2 223 L3
Halings La DEN/HRF UB9 110 C2
Halkin Ar KTBR SW1X 16 C3
Halkingcroft DTCH/LGLY SL3 149 P1
Halkin Ms KTBR * SW1X 16 C3
Halkin Pl KTBR SW1X 16 C3
Halkin St KTBR SW1X 16 D2
Hallam Cl BRWN CM15 86 G3
CHST BR7 184 C8
WATN WD24 73 K6
Hallam Gdns PIN HA5 93 M8
Hallam Ms REGST W1B 10 F3
Hallam Rd SEVS/STOTM N15 119 J2
Hallam St GTPST W1W 10 F3
Halland Cl CRAWE RH10 284 B6
Halland Wy NTHWD HA6 92 E7
Hall Av SOCK/AV RM15 146 B10
Hall Cl EA W5 135 K7
RGODL GU7 267 K10
RKW/CH/CXG WD3 91 K2
Hall Ct DTCH/LGLY SL3 149 N6
TEDD TW11 176 E8
Hall Crs SOCK/AV RM15 166 B1
Hall Dene Cl GU GU1 250 F9
Hall Dr DEN/HRF UB9 91 M9
SYD SE26 182 B8
Halley Rd FSTGT E7 141 P1
Halley's Ap WOKN/KNAP GU21 231 M4
Halley's Ct WOKN/KNAP * GU21 231 M4
Halleys Rdg HERT/WAS SG14 25 H6
Halley St POP/IOD E14 140 D7
Halley's Wk ADL/WDHM KT15 215 M4
Hall Farm Cl STAN HA7 94 G5
Hall Farm Dr WHTN TW2 176 C3
Hallfield Est BAY/PAD W2 9 H6
Hallford Wy DART DA1 187 K2
Hall Gdns CHING E4 100 E5
STALE/WH AL4 40 A9
Hall Ga STJWD NW8 3 K10
Hall Gv WGCE AL7 23 L7
Hall Heath Cl STAL AL1 38 G4
Hall Hl OXTED RH8 261 J8
The Halliards WOT/HER KT12 197 H6
Halliday Cl RAD WD7 57 K8
Halliday Sq STHL UB1 134 C10
Halliford Cl SHPTN TW17 196 F3
Halliford Rd SHPTN TW17 196 F5
SUN TW16 197 H4
Halliford St IS N1 6 F3
Halling Hl HLW CM20 29 J9
Hallington Cl WOKN/KNAP GU21 231 N3
Halliwell Rd BRXS/STRHM SW2 180 G2
Halliwick Court Pde
FBAR/BDGN * N11 98 A6
Halliwick Rd MUSWH N10 98 B9
Hall La BRWN CM15 87 L10
CHING E4 100 E6
HARH RM3 106 B10
HDN NW4 96 D10
HYS/HAR UB3 152 E6
UPMR RM14 126 B3
UPMR RM14 126 B6
Hall Meadow SL SL1 128 B4
Hallmead Rd SUT SM1 201 L10
Hallmores BROX EN10 44 F5
Hall Oak Wk KIL/WHAMP NW6 2 D1
Hallowell Av CROY/NA CR0 222 F1
Hallowell Cl MTCM CR4 202 B3
Hallowell Rd NTHWD HA6 92 F8
Hallowes Crs OXHEY WD19 93 H4
Hallowfield Wy MTCM CR4 201 N3
Hall Pk BERK HP4 34 B6
Hall Park Ga BERK HP4 34 B7
Hall Park Hl BERK HP4 34 B7
Hall Park Rd UPMR RM14 126 B10
Hall Pl BAY/PAD W2 9 L2
STAL * AL1 38 D5
WOKN/KNAP GU21 232 D2
Hall Place Cl STAL AL1 38 D5
Hall Place Crs BXLY DA5 186 D1
Hall Place Dr WEY KT13 216 F2
Hall Place Gdns STAL AL1 38 D5
Hall Rd CHDH RM6 123 M4
DART DA1 165 N10
EHAM E6 142 C3
GPK RM2 125 J1
GVW DA11 189 P6
HHNE HP2 36 C4
ISLW TW7 176 C1
MV/WKIL W9 3 K10
SHGR GU5 268 C10
SOCK/AV RM15 166 B1
WAN E11 121 J9
WLGTN SM6 222 C5
Halls Farm Cl WOKN/KNAP GU21 231 J3
Hallside Rd EN EN1 79 N4
Hallsland Wy OXTED RH8 261 L9
Halls Ter HGDN/ICK * UB10 132 C6
Hall St FSBYE EC1V 6 D9
NFNCH/WDSP N12 97 M6
Hallsville Rd CAN/RD E16 141 L8
Hallswelle Pde GLDGN * NW11 117 J3
Hallswelle Rd GLDGN NW11 117 J3
Hall Ter SOCK/AV RM15 166 C1
The Hall BKHTH/KID SE3 161 M9
Hall Vw ELTH/MOT SE9 184 A5
The Hall Wk BERK * HP4 34 A5
Hallwood Crs BRWN CM15 107 K1
Hallywell Crs EHAM E6 142 C7
Halnaker Wk CRAWW * RH11 283 J10
Halons Rd ELTH/MOT SE9 184 D3
Halpin Pl WALW SE17 19 H6
Halsbrook Rd BKHTH/KID SE3 161 P9
Halsbury Cl STAN HA7 94 G6
Halsbury Rd SHB W12 136 E10
Halsbury Rd East NTHLT UB5 114 B9
Halsbury Rd West NTHLT UB5 114 A10
Halsend HYS/HAR * UB3 133 J10
Halsey Dr HHW HP1 35 J4
Halsey Pk LCOL/BKTW AL2 57 L3
Halsey Pl WATN * WD24 73 J4
Halsey Rd WATW WD18 73 J7
Halsey St CHEL SW3 16 A5
Halsham Crs BARK IG11 143 J1
Halsmere Rd CMBW SE5 159 J7
Halstead Cl CROY/NA CR0 203 K10
Halstead Gdns WCHMH N21 99 L2
Halstead Hl CHESW EN7 61 M6
Halstead La RSEV TN14 245 P1
Halstead Rd EN EN1 79 M8
ERITH DA8 164 F7
WAN E11 121 N3
WCHMH N21 99 L2
Halstead Wy RBRW/HUT CM13 87 N10
Halstow Rd GNWCH SE10 161 M4
WLSDN NW10 136 G5
Halsway HYS/HAR UB3 133 H10
Halt Dr TIL RM18 169 K3
Halter Cl BORE WD6 76 A9
Halton Cl FBAR/BDGN N11 98 A7
Halton Cross St IS * N1 6 D5
Halton Pl IS * N1 6 E5
Halton Rd CDH/CHF RM16 168 E2
IS N1 6 D4
Halt Pde CDALE/KGS * NW9 116 A2
Halt Robin Rd BELV DA17 164 B3
Haltside HAT AL10 40 A5
Halwick Cl HHW HP1 35 L7
Hambalt Rd CLAP SW4 180 D1
Hamberlins La BERK HP4 32 G2
Hamble Cl RSLP HA4 112 F7
WOKN/KNAP GU21 231 M3
Hambledon Cl UX/CGN UB8 132 C7
Hambledon Ct EA * W5 135 K9
Hambledon Gdns SNWD SE25 203 N3
Hambledon Hl EPSOM KT18 237 P2
Hambledon Pl DUL SE21 181 N4
GT/LBKH KT23 235 P9
Hambledon Rd CTHM CR3 241 L9
WAND/EARL SW18 179 J3
Hambledon V EPSOM KT18 237 P2
Hambledown Rd
ELTH/MOT * SE9 184 G3
Hamble La SOCK/AV RM15 146 E7
Hamble St FUL/PGN SW6 157 L9
Hambleton STWL/WRAY * TW19 171 P4
Hambleton Cl WPK KT4 200 F9
Hambleton Hl CRAWW RH11 283 M9
Hamblings Cl RAD WD7 57 J9
Hambro Av HAYES BR2 205 M8
Hambrook Rd SNWD SE25 204 A3
Hambro Rd BRW CM14 107 J3
STRHM/NOR SW16 180 E9
Hambrough Rd STHL UB1 133 M10
Hamburgh Ct CHES/WCR EN8 62 C4
Ham Common
RCHPK/HAM TW10 177 J6
Hamden Crs DAGE RM10 124 C8
Hamel Cl KTN/HRWW/W HA3 115 J2
Hamels Dr HERT/BAY SG13 26 A4
Hamer Cl HHS/BOV HP3 52 D4
Hamerton Rd GVW DA11 189 N1
Hameway EHAM E6 142 D6
Ham Farm Rd RCHPK/HAM TW10 177 J7
Hamfield Cl OXTED RH8 261 H3
Hamfrith Rd SRTFD E15 141 L1
Ham Gate Av RCHPK/HAM TW10 177 K7
Hamilton Av BARK/HLT IG6 122 E2
CHEAM SM3 201 H9
COB KT11 217 H9
ED N9 99 P1
HOD EN11 44 F1
ROM RM1 104 E10
SURB KT6 199 M9
WOKS/MYFD GU22 233 H2
Hamilton Cl BERM/RHTH SE16 160 D1
CHERT KT16 195 J8
EBAR EN4 77 P8
FELT TW13 174 G8
GUW * GU2 249 M5
HOR/WEW KT19 219 P8
LCOL/BKTW AL2 55 P6
POTB/CUF EN6 58 D9
PUR/KEN CR8 223 J8
STJWD NW8 3 L10
TOTM N17 119 N1
Hamilton Ct EA W5 135 L9
HAT * AL10 40 E6
Hamilton Crs BRW CM14 107 H6
HSLW TW3 176 A1
PLMGR N13 99 H5
RYLN/HDSTN HA2 113 N8
Hamilton Dr ASC SL5 192 D7
EMPK RM11 105 M10
GUW GU2 249 M5
Hamilton Gdns SL SL1 128 A5
STJWD NW8 3 K9
Hamilton Gordon Ct GU GU1 249 P9
Hamilton Md HHS/BOV * HP3 52 D3
Hamilton Ms WEY * KT13 216 B1
Hamilton Pde FELT * TW13 175 H7
Hamilton Pk HBRY N5 119 J9
Hamilton Pk West HBRY N5 119 J9
Hamilton Pl GUW GU2 249 M5
KWD/TDW/WH KT20 239 J9
MYFR/PKLN W1K 10 D10
SUN TW16 175 J10
Hamilton Rd BERK HP4 33 N5
BFN/LL DA15 185 K7
BTFD TW8 155 J5
BXLYHN DA7 163 P8
CHSWK W4 156 B2
EA W5 135 K9
EBAR EN4 77 P8
ED N9 99 P1
EFNCH N2 117 M1
FELT TW13 174 F8
GLDGN NW11 116 G5
GPK RM2 125 J3
HRW HA1 114 D3
HYS/HAR UB3 133 J9
IL IG1 122 E9
KGLGY WD4 54 D9
OXHEY WD19 93 J4
SL SL1 128 F8
SRTFD E15 141 K5
STAL AL1 38 F5
STHL UB1 133 N10
THHTH CR7 203 L3
UX/CGN UB8 131 N6
WALTH E17 100 D10
WHTN * TW2 176 D4
WIM/MER SW19 179 L10
WLSDN NW10 116 D10
WNWD SE27 181 L7
Hamilton Road Ms
WIM/MER SW19 179 L10
Hamilton Sq NFNCH/WDSP * N12 97 M7
Hamilton St DEPT SE8 160 F5
WATW WD18 73 K9
Hamilton Ter STJWD NW8 3 J8
Hamilton Wy FNCH N3 97 K7
PLMGR N13 99 J5
WLGTN SM6 222 E5
Ham La EGH TW20 171 N7
WDSR SL4 149 P10
Hamlea Cl BKHTH/KID SE3 183 M1
Hamlet Cl CRW RM5 104 B8
LCOL/BKTW AL2 55 N6
LEW SE13 161 K10
Hamlet Gdns HMSMTH W6 156 D3
Hamlet Hl HLWW/ROY CM19 45 P5
Hamlet Rd CRW RM5 104 B8
NRWD SE19 181 N10
Hamlet Sq CRICK NW2 117 H8
Hamlets Wy BOW E3 140 E6
The Hamlet BERK HP4 34 D2
CMBW * SE5 159 L9
Hamlet Wy STHWK SE1 19 H2
Hamlin Crs PIN HA5 113 K3
Hamlin Rd SEV TN13 246 F7
Hamlyn Cl EDGW HA8 95 K4
Hamlyn Gdns NRWD SE19 181 M10
Hammarskjold Rd HLW CM20 28 F10
Hammelton Rd BMLY BR1 205 M1
Hammerfield Dr RDKG RH5 270 G7
Hammer La HHNE HP2 36 A5
Hammer Pde GSTN * WD25 55 H9
Hammers Ga LCOL/BKTW AL2 55 P2
Hammers La MLHL NW7 96 D5
Hammersmith Br HMSMTH W6 156 E4
Hammersmith Bridge Rd
BARN SW13 156 E5
Hammersmith Broadway
HMSMTH W6 156 F3
Hammersmith Emb
BARN * SW13 156 F4
Hammersmith F/O HMSMTH W6 156 F4
Hammersmith Gv HMSMTH W6 156 F2
Hammersmith Rd HMSMTH W6 156 G3
Hammersmith Ter
HMSMTH * W6 156 D4
Hammer Yd CRAWW * RH11 283 N8
Hammet Cl YEAD UB4 133 L7
Hammett St TWRH EC3N 13 L7
Hamm Moor La
ADL/WDHM KT15 215 P2
Hammond Av MTCM CR4 202 C2
Hammond Cl CHESW EN7 61 N2
HPTN TW12 197 P1
NTHLT UB5 114 C10
WOKN/KNAP GU21 231 P1
Hammond End SLN SL2 108 G9
Hammond Rd EN EN1 80 A7
NWDGN UB2 153 M2
WOKN/KNAP GU21 231 P1
Hammonds Cl BCTR RM8 123 M8
Hammonds La HAT AL10 21 N8
RBRW/HUT CM13 106 G7
STALE/WH AL4 21 M8
Hammond St KTTN NW5 4 G1
Hammondstreet Rd CHESW EN7 61 M1
Hammond Wy LTWR GU18 212 A6
Hamond Cl SAND/SEL CR2 223 J5
Hamonde Cl EDGW HA8 95 N3
Hamond Sq IS N1 7 J7
Ham Park Rd FSTGT E7 141 M2
Hampden Av BECK BR3 204 D2
CSHM HP5 50 F6
Hampden Cl CAMTN NW1 5 K8
CRAWE RH10 284 F4
EPP CM16 66 B3
SLN SL2 129 M5
Hampden Crs BRW CM14 107 H6
CHESW EN7 62 A7
Hampden Gurney St
MBLAR W1H 10 A6
Hampden Hl BEAC HP9 88 A9
WARE SG12 26 E2
Hampden Hill Cl WARE SG12 26 E1
Hampden La TOTM N17 99 N9
Hampden Pl LCOL/BKTW AL2 56 D5
Hampden Rd ARCH N19 118 E7
BECK BR3 204 D2
CEND/HSY/T N8 119 H2
CFSP/GDCR SL9 90 A9
DTCH/LGLY SL3 150 C2
GRAYS RM17 167 N4
KTN/HRWW/W HA3 94 B9
KUT KT1 199 M3
MUSWH N10 98 B8
TOTM N17 99 P9
WCHPL E1 140 B7
Hampden Wy STHGT/OAK N14 98 C2
WAT WD17 72 F2
Hampermill La OXHEY WD19 93 K2
Hampshire Av SL SL1 129 H7
Hampshire Cl UED N18 100 A6
Hampshire Hog La
HMSMTH * W6 156 E3
Hampshire Rd EMPK RM11 125 P2
WDGN N22 98 G8
Hampshire St KTTN NW5 5 J1
Hampson Wy VX/NE SW8 158 G7
Hampstead Cl THMD SE28 143 L10
Hampstead Gdns GLDGN NW11 117 K4
Hampstead Ga HAMP NW3 117 M10
Hampstead Gn HAMP NW3 117 P10
Hampstead Gv HAMP NW3 117 M9
Hampstead Hill Gdns
HAMP NW3 117 P9
Hampstead La DORK RH4 272 E3
HGT N6 118 A5
Hampstead Rd CAMTN NW1 4 G8
DORK RH4 272 F3
Hampstead Sq HAMP NW3 117 M8
Hampstead Wy GLDGN NW11 117 K3
Hampton Cl FBAR/BDGN N11 98 B6
KIL/WHAMP NW6 2 E10
RYNPK * SW20 178 F10
Hampton Ct IS N1 6 C2
Hampton Court Av
E/WMO/HCT KT8 198 C6
Hampton Court Crs
E/WMO/HCT * KT8 198 C3
Hampton Court Est THDIT * KT7 198 D5
Hampton Court Rd
E/WMO/HCT KT8 198 F3
HPTN TW12 198 C2
Hampton Court Wy
E/WMO/HCT KT8 198 D4
ESH/CLAY KT10 198 D9
THDIT KT7 198 D7
Hampton Crs GVE DA12 191 H5
Hampton Gdns SBW CM21 29 L4
Hampton Gv EW KT17 220 C7
Hampton La FELT TW13 175 M7
Hampton Ri KTN/HRWW/W HA3 115 K4
Hampton Rd CHING E4 100 E6
CROY/NA CR0 203 K6
FSTGT E7 121 N10
HPTN TW12 176 C8
IL IG1 122 F9
REDH RH1 276 A5
WAN E11 121 J6
WHTN TW2 176 C6
WPK KT4 200 D9
Hampton Rd East FELT TW13 175 N6
Hampton Rd West FELT TW13 175 M5
Hampton St WALW SE17 18 D6
Ham Ridings RCHPK/HAM TW10 177 L8
Hamsey Green Gdns WARL CR6 242 A2
Hamsey Wy SAND/SEL CR2 242 A1
Ham Shades Cl BFN/LL DA15 185 J6
Hamstel Rd HLW CM20 28 E9
Ham St RCHPK/HAM TW10 177 H5
The Ham BTFD TW8 155 H6
Ham Vw CROY/NA CR0 204 D6
Ham Yd SOHO/SHAV * W1D 11 J7
Hanameel St CAN/RD E16 141 N10
Hanbury Cl CHES/WCR EN8 62 C6
HDN NW4 116 F1
WARE SG12 26 C2
Hanbury Ct HRW * HA1 114 E4
Hanbury Dr BH/WHM TN16 225 N9
WCHMH N21 78 G8
Hanbury Rd ACT W3 155 N1
CRAWW RH11 283 H8
TOTM N17 100 A10
Hanbury St WCHPL E1 13 N3
Hancock Ct BORE WD6 75 P5
Hancock Rd BOW E3 141 H5
NRWD SE19 181 L9
Hancocks Mt ASC SL5 192 C6
Hancroft Rd HHS/BOV HP3 36 A8
Handa Cl HHS/BOV HP3 36 C9
Handa Wk IS N1 6 F1
Hand Ct HHOL WC1V 11 P4
Handcroft Rd CROY/NA CR0 203 J7
Handel Cl EDGW HA8 95 L7
Handel Crs TIL RM18 168 D6
Handel Pde EDGW * HA8 95 M7
Handel Pl WLSDN NW10 136 A1
Handel St BMSBY WC1N 11 L1
Handel Wy EDGW HA8 95 M8
Handen Rd LEW SE13 183 K1
Handforth Rd BRXN/ST SW9 159 H6
IL IG1 122 E8
Hand La SBW CM21 29 M2
Handley Gv CRICK NW2 116 G8
Handley Page Rd WLGTN SM6 222 G4
Handley Rd HOM E9 140 B2
Handowe Cl HDN NW4 116 D2
Handside Cl WGCW AL8 22 F5
WPK KT4 200 G8
Handside Gn WGCW AL8 22 F4
Handside La WGCW AL8 22 E6
Handsworth Av CHING E4 101 J7
Handsworth Cl OXHEY WD19 93 H4
Handsworth Rd TOTM N17 119 L1
Handtrough Wy BARK IG11 142 E4
Hanford Cl WAND/EARL SW18 179 K4
Hanford Rd SOCK/AV RM15 146 B10
Hangar Rd DEN/HRF UB9 111 H2
Hangar Ruding OXHEY WD19 93 N4
Hangar View Wy ACT W3 135 M8
Hanger Cl HHW HP1 35 L7
Hanger Gn EA W5 135 M6
Hanger Hl WEY KT13 216 C2
Hanger La EA W5 135 L9
Hanger La (North Circular Rd)
EA W5 135 K5
Hanger Vale La EA W5 135 L8
Hang Grove Hl ORP BR6 226 E9
Hanging Hill La
RBRW/HUT CM13 107 N4
Haning Hill La RBRW/HUT CM13 87 P10
Hankey Pl STHWK SE1 19 H2
Hankins La MLHL NW7 96 B3
Hanley Cl WDSR SL4 148 C7
Hanley Gdns FSBYPK N4 118 G6
Hanley Pl BECK BR3 182 F10
Hanley Rd FSBYPK N4 118 F6
Hannah Cl BECK BR3 204 G3
WLSDN * NW10 115 P9
Hannah Mary Wy STHWK SE1 19 P6
Hannan Cl WLSDN NW10 115 P9
Hannards Wy CHIG IG7 103 L6
Hannay La ARCH N19 118 E5
Hannell Rd FUL/PGN SW6 157 H6
Hannen Rd WNWD * SE27 181 J6
Hannibal Rd STWL/WRAY TW19 173 P3
WCHPL E1 140 B7
Hannibal Wy CROY/NA CR0 222 G2
Hannington Rd CLAP SW4 158 C9
Hanover Av CAN/RD E16 141 M10
FELT TW13 175 H4
Hanover Cir HYS/HAR UB3 132 D8
Hanover Cl CHEAM SM3 221 H1
CRAWE RH10 284 A9
EGH TW20 171 N9
RCH/KEW TW9 155 M6
REDH RH1 258 D4
SL SL1 149 M2
WDSR SL4 148 E7
Hanover Ct DORK RH4 272 E2
WOKS/MYFD * GU22 232 A5
Hanover Dr CHST BR7 184 F7
Hanover Gdns ABLGY * WD5 54 G6
BARK/HLT IG6 102 F8
LBTH SE11 18 A10
Hanover Gn HHW HP1 35 K8
Hanover Pk PECK SE15 159 P7
Hanover Pl COVGDN WC2E 11 M6
Hanover Rd SEVS/STOTM N15 119 N2
WIM/MER SW19 179 M10
WLSDN NW10 136 F2
Hanover Sq CONDST W1S 10 F6
Hanover Steps BAY/PAD * W2 9 P6
Hanover St CONDST W1S 10 F6
CROY/NA CR0 203 J10
Hanover Ter CAMTN NW1 3 P10
Hanover Terrace Ms CAMTN NW1 3 P10
Hanover Wk HAT AL10 40 C7
WEY KT13 196 E10
Hanover Wy BXLYHN DA7 163 N9
WDSR SL4 148 E8
Hanover Yd IS * N1 6 D7
Hansard Ms WKENS W14 156 G1
Hansart Wy ENC/FH EN2 79 H5
Hans Crs CHEL SW3 16 A3
Hanselin Cl STAN HA7 94 E6
Hansells Md HLWW/ROY CM19 45 M1
Hansen Dr WCHMH N21 78 G9
Hanshaw Dr EDGW HA8 96 A9
Hansler Gv E/WMO/HCT KT8 198 C5
Hansler Rd EDUL SE22 181 N1
Hansol Rd BXLYHS DA6 185 P1
Hansom Ter BMLY * BR1 205 N1
Hanson Cl BAL SW12 180 C3
BECK * BR3 182 G9
GU GU1 250 C7
MORT/ESHN SW14 155 P9
WDR/YW UB7 152 A2
Hanson Dr LOU IG10 82 F6
Hanson Gdns STHL UB1 153 M1
Hanson St GTPST W1W 10 G3
Hans Pl KTBR SW1X 16 A3
Hans Rd CHEL SW3 16 A3
Hans St KTBR SW1X 16 B4
Hanway Pl FITZ W1T 11 J5
Hanway Rd HNWL W7 134 C8
Hanway St FITZ W1T 11 J5
Hanworth La CHERT KT16 195 J8
Hanworth Rd FELT TW13 175 J4
HPTN TW12 175 N7
HSLW TW3 154 A10
HSLWW TW4 175 N3
REDH RH1 276 A5
SUN TW16 175 H10
Hanworth Ter HSLW TW3 154 A10
Hanyards La POTB/CUF EN6 60 E4
Hapgood Cl NTHLT UB5 114 C10
Harben Pde KIL/WHAMP * NW6 3 L3
Harben Rd KIL/WHAMP NW6 3 K3
Harberson Rd BAL SW12 180 C4
SRTFD E15 141 L3
Harbert Gdns LCOL/BKTW AL2 56 A5
Harberton Rd ARCH N19 118 D6
Harberts Rd HLWW/ROY CM19 46 E2
Harbet Rd BAY/PAD W2 9 M4
UED N18 100 C6
Harbex Cl BXLY DA5 186 C3
Harbinger Rd POP/IOD E14 160 G3
Harbledown Pl STMC/STPC BR5 207 M4
Harbledown Rd FUL/PGN SW6 157 K7
SAND/SEL CR2 223 P7
Harbord Cl CMBW SE5 159 L8
Harbord St FUL/PGN SW6 156 G7
Harborne Cl OXHEY WD19 93 K6
Harborough Av BFN/LL DA15 185 H3
Harborough Rd
STRHM/NOR SW16 180 G7
Harbour Av WBPTN SW10 157 M7
Harbourer Rd BARK/HLT IG6 103 L6
Harbourfield Rd BNSTD SM7 239 L1
Harbour Rd CMBW SE5 159 K9
Harbour Yd WBPTN * SW10 157 M7
Harbridge Av PUT/ROE SW15 178 C3
Harbury Rd CAR SM5 221 P5
Harbut Rd BTSEA SW11 157 N10
Harcamlow Wy WARE SG12 27 M3
Harcastle Cl YEAD UB4 133 M6
Harcombe Rd STNW/STAM N16 119 M8
Harcourt STWL/WRAY TW19 172 B2
Harcourt Av BFN/LL DA15 185 M2
EDGW HA8 95 P4
MNPK E12 122 C9
WLGTN SM6 222 C1
Harcourt Buildings EMB * EC4Y 12 A7
Harcourt Cl EGH TW20 172 F9
ISLW TW7 154 F9
Harcourt Fld WLGTN SM6 222 C1
Harcourt Ms ROM RM1 124 G3
Harcourt Rd BROCKY SE4 160 E10
BUSH WD23 74 B9
BXLYHS DA6 163 P10
SRTFD E15 141 L4
THHTH CR7 202 G6
WDGN N22 98 E9
WDSR SL4 148 D7
WIM/MER SW19 179 K10
WLGTN SM6 222 C1
Harcourt St CAMTN NW1 9 P4
Harcourt Ter WBPTN SW10 15 H8
Hardcastle Cl SNWD SE25 203 P6
Hardcourts Cl WWKM BR4 224 G1
Hardell Cl EGH TW20 172 D8
Hardel Wk BRXS/STRHM SW2 181 H3
Harden Rd GVW DA11 190 C5
Hardens Manorway
WOOL/PLUM SE18 162 A2
Harders Rd PECK SE15 160 A8
Hardess St HNHL SE24 159 K9
Hardham Cl CRAWW RH11 283 K5
Hardie Cl WLSDN NW10 116 A10
Hardie Rd DAGE RM10 124 D8
Harding Cl CROY/NA CR0 203 N10
GSTN WD25 55 K9
KUTN/CMB KT2 199 L1
WALW SE17 18 E9
Hardinge Rd UED N18 99 M6
WLSDN NW10 136 F3
Hardinge St WCHPL E1 140 B8
WOOL/PLUM SE18 162 E2
Harding Pde HARP * AL5 20 A2
Harding Rd BXLYHN DA7 164 A8
CDH/CHF RM16 168 D2
CSHM HP5 51 J6
EPSOM KT18 238 B5
Hardings WGCE AL7 23 M4
Hardings La PGE/AN SE20 182 C9
Hardings Rw IVER SL0 130 F5
Hardley Crs EMPK RM11 125 L2
Hardman Rd CHARL SE7 161 N4
KUTN/CMB KT2 199 K2
Hardres Ter STMC/STPC * BR5 207 N9
Hardwick Cl LHD/OX KT22 236 B1

STAN HA7 95 H6
Hardwicke Crs DART DA1 188 A2
Hardwicke Av HEST * TW5 153 P7
Hardwicke Gdns AMS HP6 69 K4
Hardwicke Ms FSBYW * WC1X 5 P10
Hardwicke Pl LCOL/BKTW AL2 57 J3
Hardwicke Rd CHSWK W4 155 P3
PLMGR N13 98 F6
RCHPK/HAM TW10 177 H7
REIG RH2 257 K9
Hardwicke St BARK IG11 142 F3
Hardwick Gn WEA W13 134 G7
Hardwick La CHERT KT16 194 F7
Hardwick Rd REDH RH1 275 N2
Hardwick St CLKNW EC1R 6 B10
Hardwick's Wy
WAND/EARL SW18 179 K1
Hardwidge St STHWK SE1 19 J1
Hardy Av CAN/RD E16 141 M10
GVW DA11 190 B5
RSLP HA4 113 J10
Hardy Cl BAR EN5 77 H9
BERM/RHTH SE16 160 C1
CRAWE RH10 284 D6
HORL RH6 279 P4
PIN HA5 113 L5
RDKG RH5 272 G6
Hardy Cottages GNWCH * SE10 161 J5
Hardy Gv DART DA1 165 P10
Hardy Pas WDGN N22 98 G9
Hardy Rd BKHTH/KID SE3 161 L5
CHING E4 100 E7
HHNE HP2 36 A5
WIM/MER SW19 179 L10
Hardy Wy ENC/FH EN2 79 H5
Hare And Billet Rd
BKHTH/KID SE3 161 J7
Harebell WGCE AL7 23 H9
Harebell Cl HERT/BAY SG13 26 A5
Harebell Dr EHAM E6 142 D7
Harebell Hl COB KT11 217 L10
Harebell Wy HARH RM3 105 L8
The Harebreaks WATN WD24 73 J3
Hare Ct EMB * EC4Y 12 A6
Harecourt Rd IS N1 6 E1
Hare Crs GSTN WD25 55 H8
Harecroft DORK RH4 273 H5
GT/LBKH KT23 236 A9
Haredale Rd HNHL SE24 159 K10
Haredon Cl FSTH SE23 182 B3
Harefield ESH/CLAY KT10 198 D10
HLW CM20 29 K10
Harefield Av BELMT SM2 221 H5
Harefield Cl ENC/FH EN2 79 H5
Harefield Ms BROCKY SE4 160 E9
Harefield Pl STALE/WH AL4 39 J3
Harefield Rd BROCKY SE4 160 E9
CEND/HSY/T N8 118 E3
RKW/CH/CXG WD3 91 N3
SCUP DA14 185 N5
STRHM/NOR SW16 180 G10
UX/CGN UB8 131 N1
Hare Hall La GPK RM2 125 J2
Harehatch La SLN SL2 108 F6
Hare Hl ADL/WDHM KT15 215 J3
Hare Hill Cl WOKS/MYFD GU22 233 K1
Harelands Cl WOKN/KNAP GU21 231 P3
Hare La CRAWW RH11 283 L4
ESH/CLAY KT10 218 C3
HAT AL10 40 E6
Hare Marsh BETH * E2 13 N1
Harendon KWD/TDW/WH KT20 238 F7
Harepark Cl HHW HP1 35 J5
Hare Rw BETH E2 140 A4
Hares Bank CROY/NA CR0 225 J6
Haresfield Rd DAGE RM10 144 B1
Harestone Dr CTHM CR3 241 N10
Harestone Hl CTHM CR3 259 N2
Harestone La CTHM CR3 259 M1
Harestone Valley Rd CTHM CR3 259 N1
Hare St HLWW/ROY CM19 46 E1
WOOL/PLUM SE18 162 D2
Hare St Springs
HLWW/ROY CM19 46 E1
Hare Ter WTHK * RM20 167 J4
Hare Wk IS N1 7 K8
Harewood RKW/CH/CXG WD3 71 M9
Harewood Av CAMTN NW1 9 P1
NTHLT UB5 133 M2
Harewood Cl CRAWE RH10 284 B4
NTHLT UB5 133 N2
REIG RH2 257 M8
Harewood Dr CLAY IG5 102 C10
Harewood Gdns SAND/SEL CR2 242 A1
Harewood Hl EPP CM16 83 H1
Harewood Pl CONDST W1S 10 F6
SL SL1 149 M2
Harewood Rd BRWN CM15 86 G10
ISLW TW7 154 E6
OXHEY WD19 93 J3
RGUE GU4 250 F7
SAND/SEL CR2 223 M3
WIM/MER SW19 179 P9
Harewood Rw CAMTN NW1 9 P3
Harewood Ter NWDGN UB2 153 N3
Harfield Gdns CMBW * SE5 159 M9
Harfield Rd SUN TW16 197 L2
Harford Cl CHING E4 100 G1
Harford Dr WAT WD17 72 F4
Harforde Ct HERT/BAY * SG13 25 P5
Harford Rd CHING E4 100 G1
Harford St WCHPL E1 140 D6
Harford Wk EFNCH N2 117 N2
Harfst Wy SWLY BR8 208 D1
Harglaze Ter CDALE/KGS * NW9 116 B1
Hargood Cl KTN/HRWW/W HA3 115 M4
Hargood Rd BKHTH/KID SE3 161 P7
Hargrave Pk KTTN NW5 118 D7
Hargrave Rd ARCH N19 118 D7
Hargreaves Av CHESW EN7 62 A7
Hargreaves Cl CHESW EN7 62 A7
Hargwyne St BRXN/ST SW9 158 G9
Haringey Pk CEND/HSY/T N8 118 F4
Haringey Rd CEND/HSY/T N8 118 F2
Harington Pl REIG RH2 257 K8
Harington Ter UED * N18 99 L5
Harkett Cl KTN/HRWW/W HA3 94 E10
Harkness CHESW EN7 62 A5
Harkness Cl EW KT17 238 F2
HARH RM3 105 N6
Harkness Rd SL SL1 128 A7
Harland Av BFN/LL DA15 184 G6
CROY/NA CR0 203 N10
Harland Cl WIM/MER SW19 201 L3
Harland Rd LEE/GVPK SE12 183 M4
Harlands Gv ORP BR6 226 E1
Harlech Gdns HEST TW5 153 K5
Harlech Rd ABLGY WD5 55 H7
STHGT/OAK N14 98 F4
Harlequin Av BTFD TW8 154 F5
Harlequin Cl ISLW TW7 176 D1
YEAD UB4 133 L7
Harlequin Ct WEA * W13 135 H9
Harlequin Rd TEDD * TW11 176 G10
The Harlequin WAT * WD17 73 K8
Harlescott Rd PECK SE15 160 C10
Harlesden Cl HARH RM3 105 N8
Harlesden Gdns WLSDN NW10 136 C3
Harlesden Rd HARH RM3 105 N7
STAL AL1 38 F6
WLSDN NW10 136 D2
Harley Cl ALP/SUD * HA0 135 J1
Harley Ct STALE/WH * AL4 39 J2
Harley Crs HRW HA1 114 C2
Harleyford BMLY BR1 205 N1
Harleyford Rd LBTH SE11 17 N9
Harleyford St LBTH SE11 18 A10
Harley Gdns ORP BR6 227 H1
WBPTN SW10 15 K8
Harley Gv BOW E3 140 E5
Harley Pl CAVSQ/HST W1G 10 E4
Harley Rd HAMP NW3 3 M4
HRW HA1 114 C2
WLSDN NW10 136 B4
Harley St CAVSQ/HST W1G 10 E2
Harley Vls WLSDN * NW10 136 B4
Harlinger St WOOL/PLUM SE18 162 B2
The Harlings HERT/BAY SG13 26 B9
Harlington Cl HYS/HAR UB3 152 D6
Harlington High St
HYS/HAR UB3 152 E6
Harlington Rd BXLYHN DA7 163 P9
UX/CGN UB8 132 C7
Harlington Rd East
EBED/NFELT TW14 175 J3
Harlington Rd West
EBED/NFELT TW14 175 J2
Harlow Common HLWE CM17 47 N4
Harlow Ct HHNE HP2 36 A2
Harlow Gdns CRW RM5 104 D7
Harlow Rd CHONG CM5 49 K6
HLWE CM17 30 C4
HLWE CM17 30 D8
HLWW/ROY CM19 27 P10
PLMGR N13 99 L4
RAIN RM13 144 G3
SBW CM21 29 M3
Harlyn Dr PIN HA5 113 J1
Harman Av GVW DA11 190 E8
WFD IG8 101 L8
Harman Cl CHING E4 101 J5
CRICK NW2 117 H8
Harman Dr BFN/LL DA15 185 J2
CRICK NW2 117 H8
Harman Pl PUR/KEN CR8 223 J7
Harman Rd EN EN1 79 N9
Harmer Rd SWCM DA10 189 L2
Harmer St GVE DA12 190 F2
Harmondsworth La
WDR/YW UB7 151 P5
Harmondsworth Rd
WDR/YW UB7 151 P2
Harmony Cl CRAWW RH11 283 H9
GLDGN NW11 117 H3
HAT AL10 40 D2
WLGTN SM6 222 F5
Harmony Wy HAYES BR2 205 M2
HDN NW4 116 F2
Harmood Gv CAMTN * NW1 4 E3
Harmood St CAMTN NW1 4 E2
Harms Gv RGUE GU4 250 F7
Harmsworth Ms STHWK SE1 18 B4
Harmsworth St WALW SE17 18 C8
Harmsworth Wy
TRDG/WHET N20 97 J2
Harness Rd THMD SE28 163 K1
Harness Wy STALE/WH AL4 39 J3
Harnetts Cl SWLY * BR8 208 E7
Harold Av BELV DA17 164 A4
HYS/HAR UB3 152 G2
Harold Cl HLWW/ROY CM19 46 C2
Harold Court Rd HARH RM3 106 A7
Harold Crs WAB EN9 63 H8
Harold Rd CEND/HSY/T N8 118 G3
CHING E4 101 H4
CRAWE RH10 284 F8
NRWD SE19 181 L10
PLSTW E13 141 N3
RDART DA2 187 N7
SEVS/STOTM N15 119 N3
SUT SM1 221 N1
WAN E11 121 K6
WFD IG8 101 M9
WLSDN NW10 136 A5
Haroldslea HORL RH6 280 F5
Haroldslea Cl HORL RH6 280 D6
Haroldslea Dr HORL RH6 280 D6
Harolds Rd HLWW/ROY CM19 46 C2
Haroldstone Rd WALTH E17 120 C3
Harold Vw HARH RM3 105 N10
Harp Cross La MON EC3R 13 J8
Harpenden Rd HARP AL5 20 A4
MNPK E12 121 P7
STALE/WH AL4 20 G3
STALW/RED AL3 38 C1
WNWD SE27 181 J5
Harper Cl STHGT/OAK N14 78 D9
Harper La RAD WD7 56 F7
Harper Rd EHAM E6 142 C8
STHWK SE1 18 F3
Harpers La BRWN CM15 87 J3
Harpers Yd ISLW * TW7 154 E8
Harpesford Av VW GU25 193 P5
Harp Island Cl WLSDN NW10 116 A7
Harpley Sq WCHPL E1 140 B6
Harpour Rd BARK IG11 142 F1
Harp Rd HNWL W7 134 E6
Harpsden St BTSEA SW11 158 B7
Harpsfield Broadway HAT AL10 40 C3
Harps Oak La REDH RH1 258 A1
Harptree Wy STAL AL1 38 E4
Harpurs KWD/TDW/WH KT20 238 G7
Harpur St BMSBY WC1N 11 N3
Harraden Rd BKHTH/KID SE3 161 P7
Harrap Cha GRAYS RM17 167 L4
Harrier Cl RAIN RM13 145 J1
Harrier Ms THMD SE28 162 G1
Harriers Cl EA W5 135 K9
Harrier Wy EHAM E6 142 C7
WAB EN9 63 M10
Harries Cl CSHM HP5 50 G5
Harriescourt WAB EN9 63 M8
Harries Rd YEAD UB4 133 K6
Harriet Cl BRXS/STRHM SW2 181 H3
HACK E8 7 N5
Harriet Gdns CROY/NA CR0 203 P9
Harriet St KTBR SW1X 16 B2
Harriet Wk KTBR SW1X 16 B2
Harriet Walker Wy
RKW/CH/CXG WD3 91 J1
Harriet Wy BUSH WD23 94 C1
Harringay Gdns CEND/HSY/T N8 119 J2
Harringay Rd CEND/HSY/T N8 119 J3
Harrington Cl CROY/NA CR0 202 F9
REIG RH2 274 D7
WDSR SL4 148 E10
WLSDN NW10 116 A8
Harrington Ct MV/WKIL W9 2 C9
Harrington Gdns SKENS SW7 15 J6
Harrington Hl CLPT E5 120 A6
Harrington Rd SKENS SW7 15 L5
SNWD SE25 203 P4
WAN E11 121 K6
Harrington Sq CAMTN NW1 4 G7
Harrington St CAMTN NW1 4 G8
Harrington Wy
WOOL/PLUM SE18 162 A2
Harriott Cl GNWCH SE10 161 L3
Harriotts Cl ASHTD KT21 237 J6
Harriotts La ASHTD KT21 237 H5
Harris Cl CRAWW RH11 283 L10
ENC/FH EN2 79 J5
GVW DA11 190 B6
HARH RM3 105 M8
HEST TW5 153 P7
Harris La RAD WD7 57 M10
Harrison Cl NTHWD HA6 92 D7
REIG RH2 275 L1
TRDG/WHET N20 97 P2
Harrison Ct SHPTN TW17 196 C5
SHPTN * TW17 196 C5
Harrison Dr EPP CM16 66 C2
Harrison Rd DAGE RM10 144 C1
Harrison's Ri CROY/NA CR0 203 J10
Harrison St STPAN WC1H 5 M10
Harrisons Whf PUR RM19 165 P4
Harrison Wk CHES/WCR EN8 62 C6
Harrison Wy SEV TN13 247 H8
SL SL1 128 C10
Harris Pth CRAWW RH11 283 L10
Harris Rd BXLYHN DA7 163 P7
DAGW RM9 124 A10
GSTN WD25 73 H1
Harris's La WARE SG12 26 B2
Harris St CMBW SE5 159 L6
WALTH E17 120 E5
Harris Wy SUN TW16 196 F1
Harrods Gn EDGW * HA8 95 M6
Harrogate Ct DTCH/LGLY SL3 150 D4
Harrogate Rd OXHEY WD19 93 K4
Harrold Rd BCTR RM8 123 L10
Harrow Av EN EN1 79 N10
Harroway Rd BTSEA SW11 157 N8
Harrowby Gdns GVW DA11 190 B5
Harrowby St MBLAR W1H 9 P5
Harrow Cl ADL/WDHM KT15 195 L9
CHSGTN KT9 219 J4
DORK RH4 272 F3
Harrow Crs HARH RM3 105 J8
Harrowdene Cl ALP/SUD HA0 115 J9
Harrowdene Gdns TEDD TW11 176 F10
Harrowdene Rd ALP/SUD HA0 115 J9
Harrow Dr ED N9 99 N2
EMPK RM11 125 K5
Harrowes Meade EDGW HA8 95 M4
Harrow Fields Gdns HRW HA1 114 D8
Harrow Gdns ORP BR6 227 L1
WARL CR6 242 E2
Harrowgate Rd HOM E9 140 D1
Harrow Gn WAN E11 121 K8
Harrowlands Pk DORK RH4 272 G3
Harrow La POP/IOD E14 141 H9
RGODL GU7 267 K10
Harrow Manor Wy ABYW SE2 163 M2
THMD SE28 143 M10
Harrow Pk HRW HA1 114 D7
Harrow Pl WCHPL E1 13 K5
Harrow Rd ALP/SUD HA0 114 F9
ALP/SUD HA0 135 H1
ASHF TW15 174 B4
CAR SM5 221 P3
DTCH/LGLY SL3 150 C2
IL IG1 122 F9
RSEV TN14 245 P1
WAN E11 121 L8
WARL CR6 242 E1
WLSDN NW10 136 E5
Harrow Rd East DORK RH4 272 G4
Harrow Road F/O BAY/PAD W2 9 M4
Harrow Rd West DORK RH4 272 F4
Harrowsley Ct HORL RH6 280 C3
Harrow St CAMTN * NW1 9 P3
Harrow Vw HGDN/ICK UB10 132 D5
HYS/HAR UB3 133 H9
RYLN/HDSTN HA2 114 C1
Harrow View Rd EA W5 134 G6
Harrow Wy OXHEY WD19 93 M4
SHPTN TW17 196 D2
Harrow Weald Pk
KTN/HRWW/W HA3 94 C7
Harston Dr PEND EN3 80 F4
Hartcliff Ct HNWL * W7 154 E1
Hart Cl REDH RH1 259 N9
Hart Cnr WTHK * RM20 167 J4
Hart Crs CHIG IG7 103 J6
Hart Dyke Rd STMC/STPC BR5 207 M9
SWLY BR8 208 E3
Harte Rd HSLW TW3 153 N8
Hartfield Av BORE WD6 75 M8
NTHLT UB5 133 J4
Hartfield Cl BORE WD6 75 M9
Hartfield Crs WIM/MER SW19 179 J10
WWKM BR4 205 M10
Hartfield Gv PGE/AN SE20 204 A1
Hartfield Pl GVW DA11 190 A3
Hartfield Rd CHSGTN KT9 219 J2
WIM/MER SW19 179 J10
WWKM BR4 225 M1
Hartfield Ter BOW E3 140 F4
Hartford Av
KTN/HRWW/W HA3 114 F1
Hartforde Rd BORE WD6 75 M6
Hartford Rd BXLY DA5 186 B2
HOR/WEW KT19 219 M3
Hart Gdns DORK RH4 272 G1
Hart Gv ACT W3 135 N10
STHL UB1 133 P7
Harthall La KGLGY WD4 54 C4
Hartham Cl HOLWY N7 118 F10
ISLW TW7 154 F7
Hartham Common
HERT/WAS * SG14 25 L4
Hartham La HERT/WAS SG14 25 K5
Hartham Rd HOLWY N7 118 F10
ISLW TW7 154 E7
TOTM N17 99 N10
Harting Ct CRAWW RH11 283 J10
Harting Rd ELTH/MOT SE9 184 B7
Hartington Cl HRW HA1 114 D9
ORP BR6 226 F2
Hartington Pl REIG * RH2 257 K8
Hartington Rd CAN/RD E16 141 N8
CHSWK W4 155 N6
NWDGN * UB2 153 N2
TWK TW1 176 G3
VX/NE SW8 158 F7
WALTH E17 120 D4
WEA W13 134 G9
Hartismere Rd FUL/PGN SW6 157 J6
Hartlake Rd HOM E9 140 C1
Hartland Cl ADL/WDHM KT15 215 M6
EDGW HA8 95 M3
SL SL1 129 J10
WCHMH N21 79 K10
Hartland Dr EDGW HA8 95 M3
RSLP HA4 113 J8
Hartland Rd ADL/WDHM KT15 215 K4
CAMTN NW1 4 E3
CHES/WCR EN8 62 C6
EPP CM16 65 K7
FBAR/BDGN N11 98 A6
HCH RM12 125 H7
HPTN TW12 176 A7
ISLW TW7 154 F9
KIL/WHAMP NW6 2 C7
MRDN SM4 201 K7
SRTFD E15 141 L2
Hartland Rd Arches
CAMTN * NW1 4 D3
Hartlands Cl BXLY DA5 186 A2
The Hartlands HEST TW5 153 J5
Hartland Wy CROY/NA CR0 204 D9
MRDN SM4 201 J7
Hartley Av EHAM E6 142 P5
MLHL NW7 96 C6
Hartley Bottom Rd HART DA3 211 N8
Hartley Cl BMLY BR1 206 C2
DTCH/LGLY SL3 129 P3
MLHL NW7 96 C6
Hartley Copse WDSR SL4 171 M2
Hartley Down COUL/CHIP CR5 240 G1
Hartley Farm PUR/KEN CR8 240 G1
Hartley Hl HART DA3 211 M8
PUR/KEN CR8 240 G1
Hartley Old Rd PUR/KEN CR8 240 G1
Hartley Rd BH/WHM TN16 262 G1
CROY/NA CR0 203 K7
HART DA3 211 K2
WAN E11 121 L6
WELL DA16 163 M6
Hartley St BETH E2 140 B5
Hartley Wy PUR/KEN CR8 240 G1
Hartmann Rd CAN/RD E16 142 A10
Hartmoor Ms PEND EN3 80 C3
Hartnoll St HOLWY N7 118 G10
Harton Cl BMLY BR1 206 A1
Harton Rd ED N9 100 A3
Harton St DEPT SE8 160 F7
Hart Rd BF/WBF KT14 215 P9
DORK RH4 272 G1
HLWE CM17 29 M6
STAL AL1 38 C7
Hartsbourne Av BUSH WD23 94 B3
Hartsbourne Cl BUSH WD23 94 C3
Hartsbourne Rd BUSH WD23 94 C3
Hartsbourne Wy HHNE HP2 36 D7
Harts Cl BUSH WD23 73 P6
Hartscroft CROY/NA CR0 224 D5
Harts Gdns GUW GU2 249 N7
Harts Gv WFD IG8 101 M6
Hart Shaw HART DA3 211 N2
Hartshill GUW GU2 249 J9
Hartshill Cl HGDN/ICK UB10 132 B1
Hartshill Rd GVW DA11 190 C5
Hartshorn Gdns EHAM E6 142 D6
Hartsland Rd SEV TN13 247 K9
Harts La BARK IG11 142 E1
NWCR SE14 160 D6
Hartslock Dr ABYW SE2 163 N1
Hartsmead Rd ELTH/MOT SE9 184 C5
Hartspiece Rd REDH RH1 276 B2
Hartspring La GSTN WD25 74 A5
Hart Sq MRDN * SM4 201 L5
Hart St BRW CM14 107 H3
MON EC3R 13 K7
Hartsway PEND EN3 80 A8
Hartswood RDKG RH5 273 J5
Hartswood Av REIG RH2 275 K4
Hartswood Cl BRW CM14 107 K5
Hartswood Gdns SHB * W12 156 C2
Hartswood Gn BUSH WD23 94 C3
Hartswood Rd BRW CM14 107 K5
SHB W12 156 C1
Hartsworth Cl PLSTW E13 141 L4
Hartville Rd WOOL/PLUM SE18 163 H3
Hartwell Dr BEAC HP9 88 C8
CHING E4 101 H7
Hartwell St HACK * E8 7 L1
Harty Cl CDH/CHF RM16 147 N10
Harvard Hl CHSWK W4 155 N4
Harvard Rd CHSWK W4 155 N4
ISLW TW7 154 D7
LEW SE13 183 H1
Harvel Cl CHST BR7 207 K3
Harvel Crs ABYW SE2 163 N4
Harvest Bank AMS HP6 50 B10
Harvest Bank Rd WWKM BR4 205 M10
Harvest Ct STALE/WH AL4 39 H2
Harvest End GSTN WD25 74 F3
Harvester Rd HOR/WEW KT19 220 A6
Harvesters Cl ISLW TW7 176 C1
Harvesters Ms STALE/WH * AL4 39 J2
Harvest La LOU IG10 102 A1
THDIT KT7 198 F6
Harvest Md HAT AL10 40 E3
Harvest Rd BUSH WD23 74 A8
CRAWE RH10 284 D9
EGH TW20 172 A8
FELT TW13 175 H7
Harvestside HORL RH6 280 D3
Harvest Wy SWLY BR8 208 D7
Harvey CDH/CHF RM16 167 N1
Harvey Dr HPTN TW12 198 A1
Harveyfields WAB EN9 63 H10
Harvey Gdns CHARL SE7 161 P4
GU * GU1 268 B1
LOU IG10 82 E7
Harvey Rd CEND/HSY/T N8 118 G3
CMBW SE5 159 L7
DTCH/LGLY SL3 150 E2
GU GU1 268 B2
HGDN/ICK UB10 132 B4
HSLWW TW4 175 N3
IL IG1 122 E10
LCOL/BKTW AL2 57 H2
NTHLT UB5 133 K2
RKW/CH/CXG WD3 72 B10
WAN E11 121 K6
WOT/HER KT12 197 H7
Harvey's La ROMW/RG RM7 124 E7
Harvey St IS N1 7 H6
Harvill Rd SCUP DA14 185 N8
Harvil Rd DEN/HRF UB9 111 M2
Harvington Wk HACK * E8 7 P4
Harwater Dr LOU IG10 82 C6
Harwell Cl RSLP HA4 112 E6
Harwich Rd SL SL1 128 F8
Harwood Av BMLY BR1 205 N2
EMPK RM11 125 M1
MTCM CR4 201 P3
Harwood Cl ALP/SUD HA0 115 J9
NFNCH/WDSP N12 97 P7
WGCW AL8 23 H1
WLYN AL6 23 P1
Harwood Dr HGDN/ICK UB10 132 A3
Harwood Gdns WDSR SL4 171 N3
Harwood Hall La UPMR RM14 146 A1
Harwood Hl WGCW AL8 23 H2
Harwood Ms FUL/PGN * SW6 157 L6
Harwood Pk REDH RH1 276 B9
Harwood Rd FUL/PGN SW6 157 K6
Harwoods Rd WATW WD18 73 H8
Harwood Ter FUL/PGN SW6 157 L7
Hascombe Ter CMBW * SE5 159 L8
Hasedines Rd HHW HP1 35 K5
Haselbury Rd UED N18 99 M5
Haseldine Mdw HAT AL10 40 C5
Haseldine Rd LCOL/BKTW AL2 57 J2
Haseley End FSTH * SE23 182 B3
Haselrigge Rd CLAP SW4 158 E10
Haseltine Rd SYD SE26 182 E7
Haselwood Dr ENC/FH EN2 79 J8
Haskard Rd DAGW RM9 123 N9
Hasker St CHEL SW3 15 P5
Haslam Av CHEAM SM3 201 H8
Haslam Cl HGDN/ICK UB10 112 D7
IS N1 6 B3
Haslam St PECK SE15 159 N7
Haslemere Av EBAR EN4 98 A2
HDN NW4 116 G4
HEST TW5 153 K8
HNWL W7 154 F2
MTCM CR4 201 N2
WAND/EARL SW18 179 L5
Haslemere Cl HPTN TW12 175 N8
WLGTN SM6 222 F2
Haslemere Gdns FNCH N3 117 J1
Haslemere Heathrow Est
HSLWW * TW4 153 J8
Haslemere Rd BXLYHN DA7 164 A8
CEND/HSY/T N8 118 F5
GDMY/SEVK IG3 123 J7
THHTH CR7 203 J5
WCHMH N21 99 J3
WDSR SL4 148 F7
Hasler Cl THMD SE28 143 L9
Haslett Av CRAWE RH10 284 A7
Haslett Av East CRAWE RH10 284 A7
Haslett Av West CRAWE RH10 283 N7
Haslett Rd SHPTN TW17 196 F2
Haslewood Av HOD EN11 44 F2
Hasluck Gdns BAR EN5 77 M10
Hassard St BETH E2 7 M8
Hassendean Rd BKHTH/KID SE3 161 N5
Hassett Rd HOM E9 140 C1
Hassocks Cl SYD SE26 182 A6
Hassocks Ct CRAWW RH11 283 J10
Hassocks Rd STRHM/NOR SW16 202 E1
Hassock Wd HAYES BR2 226 A1
Hassop Rd CRICK NW2 116 G9
Hasted Cl GRH DA9 189 H2
Hasted Rd CHARL SE7 162 A4
Hastings Av BARK/HLT IG6 122 F2
Hastings Cl BAR EN5 77 M8
PECK * SE15 159 P6
WTHK RM20 167 K5
Hastings Dr SURB KT6 199 H6
Hastings Meadow SLN * SL2 129 M3
Hastings Rd CRAWE RH10 284 C7
CROY/NA CR0 203 N8
FBAR/BDGN N11 98 D6
GPK RM2 125 J3
HAYES BR2 206 B8
TOTM * N17 119 L1
WEA W13 134 G9
Hastings St STPAN WC1H 5 L10
Hastings Ter SEVS/STOTM * N15 119 K3
Hastings Wy BUSH WD23 73 M8
RKW/CH/CXG WD3 72 C8
Hastingwood Rd HLWE CM17 47 P6
Hastoe Cl YEAD UB4 133 M6
Hatcham Park Ms NWCR SE14 160 C7
Hatcham Park Rd NWCR SE14 160 C7
Hatcham Rd PECK SE15 160 B5
Hatchard Rd ARCH N19 118 E7
Hatch Cl ADL/WDHM KT15 195 L10
Hatchcroft HDN NW4 116 E1
Hatch End BFOR GU20 212 B3
Hatchett Rd EBED/NFELT TW14 174 D4
Hatch Gdns KWD/TDW/WH KT20 238 G6
Hatchgate HORL RH6 280 A5
Hatchgate Gdns SL SL1 128 C5
Hatch Gv CHDH RM6 123 P2
Hatchlands Rd REDH RH1 257 P10
Hatch La CHING E4 101 J5
REDH RH1 276 G7
RPLY/SEND GU23 234 C5
WDR/YW UB7 151 N6
WDSR SL4 148 F9
Hatch Pl RCHPK/HAM TW10 177 L8
Hatch Rd BRWN CM15 86 F9
STRHM/NOR SW16 202 F2
Hatch Side CHIG IG7 102 D6
The Hatch PEND EN3 80 C5
WDSR SL4 148 B6
Hatchwoods WFD IG8 101 L5
Hatcliffe Cl BKHTH/KID SE3 161 L9
Hatcliffe St GNWCH SE10 161 L4
Hatfield Av HAT AL10 40 C1
Hatfield Cl BARK/HLT IG6 122 E1
BELMT SM2 221 K5
BF/WBF * KT14 215 L8
HCH RM12 125 L10
MTCM * CR4 201 N4
Hatfield Ct BKHTH/KID * SE3 161 M6
Hatfield Crs HHNE HP2 36 A2
Hatfield Rd ASHTD KT21 237 L5
BRKMPK AL9 23 P10
CHSWK W4 156 A1
HNWL W7 134 F10
POTB/CUF EN6 59 M7
SL SL1 149 M1
SRTFD E15 121 K10
STAL AL1 38 G6
WATN WD24 73 J5
Hatfields LOU IG10 82 E7
STHWK SE1 12 B9
Hathaway Cl HAYES BR2 206 C8
RSLP HA4 112 G9
STAN HA7 94 F6

Hathaway Ct STALE/WH AL4 39 K6
Hathaway Crs MNPK E12 142 C1
Hathaway Gdns CHDH RM6 123 N3
WEA W13 134 E7
Hathaway Rd CROY/NA CR0 203 J7
GRAYS RM17 167 N2
Hatherleigh Cl CHSGTN KT9 219 J2
MRDN SM4 201 K4
Hatherleigh Gdns POTB/CUF EN6 59 N8
Hatherleigh Rd RSLP HA4 113 H7
Hatherleigh Wy HARH RM3 105 L9
Hatherley Crs SCUP DA14 185 K5
Hatherley Gdns CEND/HSY/T N8 118 F4
EHAM E6 142 A5
Hatherley Gv BAY/PAD W2 8 G5
Hatherley Rd RCH/KEW TW9 155 L7
SCUP DA14 185 K6
WALTH E17 120 E2
Hatherley St WEST SW1P 17 H6
Hathern Gdns ELTH/MOT SE9 184 D7
Hatherop Rd HPTN TW12 175 N10
Hathersham Cl HORL RH6 281 H3
Hathersham La HORL RH6 280 G1
Hatherwood ASHTD KT21 237 J6
Hathorne Cl PECK SE15 160 A8
Hathorne Ter ARCH * N19 118 E6
Hathway St PECK SE15 160 B8
Hatley Av BARK/HLT IG6 122 F2
Hatley Cl FBAR/BDGN N11 98 A6
Hatley Rd HOLWY N7 118 G7
Hat & Mitre Ct FARR EC1M 12 D2
Hatteraick St BERM/RHTH SE16 160 B1
Hattersfield Cl BELV DA17 164 A3
Hatters La WATW WD18 72 F9
Hatton Av SLN SL2 129 J5
Hatton Cl CDH/CHF RM16 167 J2
GVW DA11 190 B6
WOOL/PLUM SE18 162 G6
Hatton Ct WDSR SL4 149 H8
Hatton Cross Est HTHAIR * TW6 152 G10
Hatton Gdn CLKNW EC1R 12 B2
Hatton Gdns MTCM CR4 202 A5
Hatton Gn EBED/NFELT TW14 153 H10
Hatton Gv WDR/YW * UB7 151 N1
Hatton Hl BFOR GU20 212 B2
Hatton Pl HCIRC EC1N 12 B2
Hatton Rd CHES/WCR EN8 62 C5
CROY/NA CR0 203 H8
EBED/NFELT TW14 174 D3
HTHAIR TW6 152 G10
Hatton Rd North HTHAIR TW6 152 E7
Hatton Rw STJWD * NW8 9 M2
Hatton St STJWD NW8 9 M2
Hatton Wall HCIRC EC1N 12 A3
Haunch of Venison Yd
MYFR/PKLN W1K 10 E6
Havana Cl ROM RM1 124 F4
Havana Rd WIM/MER SW19 179 K5
Havannah St POP/IOD E14 160 F1
Havant Rd WALTH E17 121 H1
Havelock Cl SHB * W12 136 E9
Havelock Pl HRW HA1 114 D4
Havelock Rd BELV * DA17 164 A3
CROY/NA CR0 203 N9
DART DA1 187 J3
GVW DA11 190 C4
HAYES BR2 205 P4
KGLGY WD4 54 A4
KTN/HRWW/W HA3 114 D1
NWDGN UB2 153 M2
TOTM N17 99 P10
WIM/MER SW19 179 M8
Havelock St IL IG1 122 E7
IS N1 5 M5
Havelock Ter VX/NE SW8 158 C6
Havelock Wk FSTH SE23 182 B4
Haven Cl ELTH/MOT SE9 184 C6
HAT AL10 40 C3
SCUP DA14 185 M9
SWLY BR8 208 G2
WIM/MER SW19 178 G6
YEAD UB4 132 F7
Haven Ct BRYLDS * KT5 199 L6
Havenfield KGLGY WD4 53 L7
Haven Gdns CRAWE RH10 285 P4
Havengore Av GVE DA12 191 H3
Haven Gn EA W5 135 J8
Havenhurst Ri ENC/FH EN2 79 H6
Haven La EA W5 135 K8
Haven Pl CDH/CHF RM16 167 P1
Haven Rd ASHF TW15 174 C7
Haven St CAMTN * NW1 4 E4
The Haven GRAYS RM17 168 C3
RCH/KEW TW9 155 M9
SUN TW16 175 H10
Havenwood WBLY HA9 115 N8
Havercroft Cl STAL AL1 38 B8
Haverfield Gdns RCH/KEW TW9 155 M6
Haverfield Rd BOW E3 140 C5
Haverford Wy EDGW HA8 95 L9
Havergal Vls CEND/HSY/T * N8 119 J2
Haverhill Rd BAL SW12 180 D4
CHING E4 101 H2
Havering Dr ROM RM1 124 F2
Havering Gdns CHDH RM6 123 M3
Havering Rd ROM RM1 104 E6
Havering St WCHPL E1 140 C8
Havering Wy BARK IG11 143 L5
Havers Av WOT/HER KT12 217 L2
Haversham Cl CRAWE RH10 284 A7
TWK TW1 177 J3
Haverstock Hl HAMP NW3 3 P1
Haverstock Pl IS * N1 6 B8
Haverstock Rd KTTN NW5 118 B10
Haverstock St IS N1 6 D8
Haverthwaite Rd ORP BR6 206 G10
Havil St CMBW SE5 159 M7
Havisham Pl STRHM/NOR SW16 181 J9
Havisham Rd GVE DA12 191 K4
Hawarden Gv HNHL SE24 181 K3
Hawarden Hl CRICK NW2 116 D8
Hawarden Rd CTHM CR3 241 K7
WALTH E17 120 C2
Haward Rd HOD EN11 45 H1
Hawbridge Rd WAN E11 121 J6
Hawes Cl NTHWD HA6 92 G8
Hawes La WAB EN9 81 H4
WWKM BR4 205 H8
Hawes Rd BMLY BR1 205 N1
KWD/TDW/WH KT20 238 G6
UED N18 100 A7
Hawes St IS N1 6 D4
Haweswater Dr GSTN WD25 55 K9
Hawfield Bank ORP BR6 207 N10
Hawfield Gdns LCOL/BKTW AL2 56 C2
Hawgood St BOW E3 140 F7
Hawk Cl WAB EN9 63 M10
Hawk Cnr WTHK * RM20 167 J4
Hawkdene CHING E4 80 G10
Hawkenbury HLWW/ROY CM19 46 D3
Hawke Park Rd WDGN N22 119 J1
Hawke Pl BERM/RHTH * SE16 160 C1
Hawke Rd NRWD SE19 181 L9
Hawkesbury Rd PUT/ROE SW15 178 E1
Hawkes Cl GRAYS RM17 167 N5
Hawkesfield Rd FSTH SE23 182 D5
Hawkes Leap BFOR GU20 212 A1
Hawkesley Cl TWK TW1 176 F7
Hawkesmoor Rd CRAWW RH11 283 H9
Hawkes Pl SEV TN13 265 H3
Hawkes Rd EBED/NFELT TW14 175 H3
MTCM CR4 201 P1
Hawkesworth Cl NTHWD HA6 92 F8
Hawkewood Rd SUN TW16 197 J3
Hawkhirst Rd PUR/KEN CR8 241 L2
Hawkhurst COB KT11 217 P10
Hawkhurst Gdns CRW RM5 104 E7
Hawkhurst Rd
STRHM/NOR SW16 180 E10
Hawkhurst Wk CRAWE RH10 284 C9
Hawkhurst Wy NWMAL KT3 200 A5
WWKM BR4 204 G9
Hawkinge Wy HCH RM12 145 K1
Hawkings Wy HHW HP1 52 D2
Hawkins Av GVE DA12 190 F7
Hawkins Cl BORE WD6 75 P6
EDGW HA8 96 A6
HRW HA1 114 C5
Hawkins Dr CDH/CHF RM16 167 J1
Hawkins Rd CRAWE RH10 283 P9
TEDD TW11 176 G9
Hawkins Wy CAT SE6 182 F8
Hawkley Gdns WNWD SE27 181 J5
Hawkridge Cl CHDH RM6 123 M4
Hawkridge Dr GRAYS RM17 168 A4
Hawksbrook La BECK BR3 204 G6
Hawkshead Cl BMLY BR1 183 K10
Hawkshead La BRKMPK AL9 59 H4
Hawkshead Rd CHSWK W4 156 B2
POTB/CUF EN6 59 L5
WLSDN * NW10 136 C2
Hawks Hl EPP CM16 66 B3
LHD/OX KT22 236 E9
Hawkshill STAL * AL1 38 F7
Hawkshill Cl ESH/CLAY KT10 217 P3
Hawks Hill Cl LHD/OX KT22 236 E9
Hawks Hill Ct LHD/OX KT22 236 E9
Hawkshill Dr HHW HP1 35 H9
Hawkshill Pl ESH/CLAY * KT10 217 P3
Hawkshill Rd SLN SL2 128 F5
Hawkshill Wy ESH/CLAY KT10 217 N3
Hawkslade Rd PECK SE15 182 C1
Hawksley Rd STNW/STAM N16 119 L8
Hawksmead Cl PEND * EN3 80 C1
Hawks Ms GNWCH * SE10 161 H6
Hawksmoor RAD WD7 57 M9
Hawksmoor Cl EHAM E6 142 B8
WOOL/PLUM SE18 163 H4
Hawksmoor Ms WCHPL E1 140 A9
Hawksmoor St HMSMTH W6 156 G5
Hawksmouth CHING E4 100 G1
Hawks Rd KUT KT1 199 L2
Hawkstone Rd
BERM/RHTH SE16 160 B3
Hawksview COB KT11 217 N9
Hawksway STA TW18 173 J6
Hawkswell Cl WOKN/KNAP GU21 231 L3
Hawkswood La DTCH/LGLY SL3 110 C10
Hawkwell Wk IS * N1 6 F5
Hawkwood Crs CHING E4 80 G10
Hawkwood Dell GT/LBKH KT23 253 P2
Hawkwood La CHST BR7 206 F1
Hawkwood Mt CLPT E5 120 A6
Hawkwood Ri GT/LBKH KT23 253 P2
Hawlands Dr PIN HA5 113 M5
Hawley Cl HPTN TW12 175 N9
Hawley Crs CAMTN NW1 4 F4
Hawley Rd CAMTN NW1 4 E3
DART DA1 187 M5
UED N18 100 C6
Hawley St CAMTN NW1 4 E4
Hawley Ter RDART * DA2 187 P7
Hawley V RDART * DA2 187 P8
Hawley Wy ASHF TW15 174 B8
Haworth Rd CRAWE RH10 284 C8
Hawridge La CSHM HP5 32 D9
Hawridge V CSHM HP5 32 E8
Hawstead La ORP BR6 228 A2
Hawstead Rd LEW SE13 182 G2
Hawsted BKHH IG9 101 N1
Hawth Av CRAWE RH10 284 B7
Hawth Cl CRAWE RH10 283 P9
Hawthorn Av PLMGR N13 98 F6
RAIN RM13 145 J6
RBRW/HUT CM13 107 L4
THHTH CR7 203 J1
Hawthorn Cl ABLGY WD5 54 G8
BNSTD SM7 221 H10
CRAWW RH11 283 M4
GVE DA12 190 E7
HARP AL5 20 C4
HERT/WAS SG14 25 H4
HEST TW5 153 J6
HPTN TW12 175 P8
IVER SL0 130 F5
REDH RH1 276 B5
STMC/STPC BR5 206 G6
WAT WD17 72 G4
WOKS/MYFD GU22 232 B6
Hawthorn Crs SAND/SEL CR2 224 B7
Hawthornden Cl
NFNCH/WDSP N12 97 P7
Hawthorndene Cl HAYES * BR2 205 L9
Hawthorndene Rd HAYES BR2 205 M9
Hawthorn Dr DEN/HRF UB9 131 M1
RYLN/HDSTN HA2 113 P4
WWKM BR4 225 K1
Hawthorne Av BH/WHM TN16 244 A1
CAR SM5 222 B4
CHESW EN7 62 A6
HRW HA1 114 F4
MTCM CR4 201 N2
RSLP HA4 113 J4
WDSR SL4 170 A5
Hawthorne Cl BMLY BR1 206 C3
CHESW EN7 62 A7
IS N1 7 J1
Hawthorne Ct
STWL/WRAY * TW19 173 N3
Hawthorne Crs SL SL1 129 K8
WDR/YW UB7 152 A1
Hawthorne Dr WDSR * SL4 170 A4
Hawthorne Gv CDALE/KGS NW9 115 P5
PGE/AN SE20 204 A1
Hawthorne Pl EW KT17 220 B8
Hawthorne Rd BMLY BR1 206 C3
EGH TW20 172 F8
RAD WD7 56 F10
UED N18 99 N7
WALTH E17 120 F1
Hawthornes HAT AL10 40 C6
Hawthorne Wy ED N9 99 N3
RGUE GU4 250 E6
Hawthorn Farm Av NTHLT UB5 133 M3
Hawthorn Gdns EA W5 155 J2
Hawthorn Gv ENC/FH EN2 79 L4
Hawthorn Hatch BTFD TW8 154 G6
Hawthorn La HHW HP1 35 J5
SLN SL2 128 E2
Hawthorn Ms HDN NW4 97 H9
Hawthorn Pl ERITH DA8 164 D4
HYS/HAR * UB3 132 G9
RGUE * GU4 250 A5
Hawthorn Rd BKHH IG9 101 P5
BTFD TW8 154 G6
BXLYHS * DA6 164 A10
CEND/HSY/T N8 118 E1
DART DA1 187 L5
HOD EN11 44 G1
RPLY/SEND GU23 233 J10
SUT SM1 223 N2
WLGTN SM6 222 C4
WLSDN NW10 136 D2
WOKS/MYFD GU22 232 A6
Hawthorns HART DA3 211 L4
HLWS CM18 47 J5
WFD IG8 101 M4
WGCW AL8 22 G3
The Hawthorns BERK HP4 33 M4
CSTG HP8 69 P6
DTCH/LGLY SL3 151 J7
EW KT17 220 C3
HHS/BOV HP3 35 J10
OXTED RH8 261 M9
RKW/CH/CXG WD3 90 G6
Hawthorn Ter BFN/LL DA15 185 J2
WEY * KT13 216 B7
Hawthorn Wk NKENS W10 8 A1
Hawthorn Wy ADL/WDHM KT15 215 L6
CHOB/PIR GU24 230 F2
CSHM HP5 51 J5
LCOL/BKTW AL2 37 P10
REDH RH1 276 C2
SHPTN TW17 196 E4
Hawtrees RAD WD7 74 E1
Hawtrey Av NTHLT UB5 133 L4
Hawtrey Cl SL SL1 149 N1
Hawtrey Dr RSLP HA4 113 H5
Hawtrey Rd HAMP NW3 3 N4
WDSR SL4 149 H8
Haxted Rd BMLY BR1 205 N1
Haybourn Md HHW HP1 35 L7
Hayburn Wy HCH RM12 124 G6
Hay Cl BORE WD6 75 P6
SRTFD E15 141 K2
Haycroft Cl PUR/KEN CR8 241 J5
Haycroft Gdns WLSDN NW10 136 D3
Haycroft Rd BRXS/STRHM SW2 180 F1
SURB KT6 199 J9
Hay Currie St POP/IOD E14 140 G8
Hayday Rd CAN/RD E16 141 M6
Hayden Ct ADL/WDHM KT15 215 L6
Hayden Rd WAB EN9 81 H1
Haydens Cl STMC/STPC BR5 207 M7
Hayden's Pl NTGHL W11 8 C5
Haydens Rd HLWW/ROY CM19 46 F1
Hayden Wy CRW RM5 104 D10
Haydn Av PUR/KEN CR8 241 H1
Haydock Av NTHLT UB5 133 P1
Haydock Cl HCH RM12 125 N9
Haydock Gn NTHLT UB5 133 P1
Haydon Cl CDALE/KGS NW9 115 P2
EN EN1 79 M10
Haydon Dell Farm BUSH * WD23 93 N1
Haydon Dr PIN HA5 113 K2
Haydon Park Rd
WIM/MER SW19 179 K8
Haydon Pl GU GU1 268 A1
Haydon Rd BCTR RM8 123 M7
OXHEY WD19 73 M10
Haydon's Rd WIM/MER SW19 179 M9
Haydon St TWRH EC3N 13 L7
Haydon Wk WCHPL E1 13 L6
Haydon Wy BTSEA SW11 157 M10
Hayes Barton WOKS/MYFD GU22 232 F2
Hayes Cha WWKM BR4 205 J6
Hayes Cl HAYES BR2 205 M9
WTHK RM20 167 H5
Hayes Crs CHEAM SM3 220 G1
GLDGN NW11 117 J3
Hayes Dr RAIN RM13 145 J2
Hayes End Dr YEAD UB4 132 B7
Hayes End Rd YEAD UB4 132 E6
Hayesford Park Dr HAYES BR2 205 L5
Hayes Gdn HAYES BR2 205 M9
Hayes Hl HAYES BR2 205 K8
Hayes Hill Rd HAYES BR2 205 L8
Hayes La BECK BR3 205 J3
HAYES BR2 205 N4
PUR/KEN CR8 241 J2
Hayes Mead Rd HAYES BR2 205 K8
Hayes Pl CAMTN NW1 9 P2
Hayes Rd HAYES BR2 205 M4
NWDGN UB2 153 K3
RDART DA2 188 D3
Hayes St HAYES BR2 205 N8
Hayes Ter GVE * DA12 191 P8
The Hayes EPSOM KT18 238 B5
Hayes Wk HORL RH6 281 H3
Hayes Wy BECK BR3 205 H4
Hayes Wood Av HAYES BR2 205 N8
Hayfield Cl BUSH WD23 74 A8
Hayfield Pas WCHPL E1 140 B7
Hayfield Rd STMC/STPC BR5 207 K5
Hayfields HORL RH6 280 D3
Haygarth Pl WIM/MER SW19 178 G8
Haygreen Cl KUTN/CMB KT2 177 N9
Hay Green La BRWN CM15 87 J1
Hay Hl MYFR/PICC W1J 10 F8
Hayland Cl CDALE/KGS NW9 116 A2
Hay La CDALE/KGS NW9 116 A2
DTCH/LGLY SL3 110 A9
Hayle TIL RM18 169 M2
Hayles St LBTH SE11 18 C5
Haylett Gdns KUT * KT1 199 J4
Hayling Av FELT TW13 175 H6
Hayling Cl STNW/STAM N16 119 M10
Hayling Rd OXHEY WD19 92 G4
Hayman Crs YEAD UB4 132 B4
Haymarket STJS SW1Y 11 J8
Haymeads WGCW AL8 23 H2
Haymeads Dr ESH/CLAY KT10 218 B3
Haymer Gdns WPK KT4 200 D10
Haymerle Rd PECK SE15 15 N10
Haymill Cl GFD/PVL UB6 134 E5
Haymill Rd SL SL1 128 C6
Hayne Rd BECK BR3 204 E1
Haynes Cl BKHTH/KID SE3 161 K9
DTCH/LGLY SL3 130 E10
FBAR/BDGN N11 98 B4
RPLY/SEND GU23 233 L8
TOTM N17 100 A8
WGCE AL7 23 K6
Haynes La NRWD SE19 181 M9
Haynes Md BERK HP4 33 M3
Haynes Rd ALP/SUD HA0 135 K2
EMPK RM11 125 L3
GVW DA11 190 C6
Hayne St STBT EC1A 12 D3
Haynt Wk RYNPK SW20 201 H3
Hay Pl SWLY * BR8 208 D6
Hayse Hl WDSR SL4 148 C7
Hays La STHWK SE1 13 J9
Haysleigh Gdns PGE/AN SE20 203 P2
Hay's Ms MYFR/PICC W1J 10 E8
Haysoms Cl ROM RM1 124 F2
Haystall Cl YEAD UB4 132 F4
Hay St BETH E2 7 P6
Hays Wk BELMT SM2 220 G6
Hayter Rd BRXS/STRHM SW2 180 F1
Hayton Cl HACK E8 7 M2
The Haywain OXTED RH8 261 J6
Hayward Cl DART DA1 186 E1
WIM/MER SW19 179 L10
Hayward Dr DART * DA1 187 N6
Hayward Gdns PUT/ROE SW15 178 F2
Hayward Rd THDIT KT7 198 E8
TRDG/WHET N20 97 M3
Haywards CRAWE RH10 284 E4
Haywards Cl CHDH RM6 123 M3
Haywards Md WDSR SL4 148 E4
Hayward's Pl CLKNW * EC1R 12 C2
Haywood Cl PIN HA5 93 L10
Haywood Dr RKW/CH/CXG * WD3 71 J9
Haywood Pk RKW/CH/CXG WD3 71 J9
Haywood Pl CDH/CHF * RM16 168 F1
Haywood Ri ORP BR6 227 H2
Haywood Rd HAYES BR2 206 A4
Haywoods Dr HHW HP1 35 J9
Hayword Ct WAB EN9 63 L10
Hazel Av GU GU1 249 P6
WDR/YW UB7 152 B2
Hazel Bank BRYLDS KT5 199 P8
Hazelbank Rd CAT SE6 183 J5
CHERT KT16 195 M7
Hazelbourne Rd BAL SW12 180 C2
Hazelbrouck Gdns BARK/HLT IG6 102 G8
Hazelbury Av ABLGY WD5 54 D8
Hazelbury Cl WIM/MER SW19 201 K2
Hazelbury Gn UED N18 99 M4
Hazelbury La ED N9 99 M4
Hazel Cl BTFD * TW8 154 G6
CDALE/KGS NW9 96 C10
CHESW EN7 61 M2
CRAWW RH11 283 M4
CROY/NA CR0 204 C7
EGH TW20 171 N9
HCH RM12 125 J8
MTCM CR4 202 E4
PLMGR N13 99 L4
REIG RH2 275 M2
WHTN TW2 176 B3
Hazel Ct RKW/CH/CXG * WD3 91 H5
Hazelcroft PIN HA5 93 P7
Hazelcroft Cl HGDN/ICK UB10 132 A2
Hazeldean Rd WLSDN NW10 136 A2
Hazeldell Link HHW * HP1 35 H7
Hazeldell Rd HHW HP1 35 H7
Hazeldene ADL/WDHM KT15 215 M2
CHES/WCR EN8 62 D8
Hazeldene Ct PUR/KEN CR8 241 L1
Hazeldene Dr PIN HA5 113 K1
Hazeldene Gdns HGDN/ICK UB10 132 D3
Hazeldene Rd BCTR RM8 123 L7
WELL DA16 163 M8
Hazeldon Rd BROCKY SE4 182 D1
Hazel Dr ERITH DA8 165 H7
RPLY/SEND GU23 251 J1
SOCK/AV RM15 147 H5
Hazeleigh RBRW/HUT CM13 107 N4
Hazeleigh Gdns WFD IG8 102 B6
Hazel End SWLY BR8 208 F5
Hazel Gdns CDH/CHF RM16 168 B2
EDGW HA8 95 N5
Hazelgreen Cl WCHMH N21 99 J2
Hazel Gv ALP/SUD HA0 135 K3
CHDH RM6 123 P1
EN * EN1 79 P10
GSTN WD25 73 J1
HAT AL10 40 C7
ORP BR6 206 E9
STA TW18 173 L9
SYD SE26 182 C7
WGCE AL7 23 L4
Hazelhurst BECK BR3 205 J1
HORL RH6 280 D3
Hazelhurst Cl RGUE GU4 250 E5
Hazelhurst Dr CRAWE RH10 284 F7
Hazelhurst Rd SL SL1 128 B4
TOOT SW17 179 M7
Hazell Crs ROMW/RG RM7 104 C9
Hazell Pk AMSS HP7 69 H5
Hazellville Rd ARCH N19 118 E5
Hazell Wy SLN SL2 129 L1
Hazel Md BAR EN5 76 E9
EW KT17 220 D6
Hazelmere Cl EBED/NFELT TW14 174 E2
LHD/OX KT22 236 G5
NTHLT UB5 134 A4
Hazelmere Dr NTHLT UB5 133 N4
Hazelmere Gdns EMPK RM11 125 J3
Hazelmere Rd KIL/WHAMP NW6 2 D5
NTHLT UB5 133 N4
STALE/WH AL4 39 H3
STMC/STPC BR5 206 F4
Hazelmere Wk NTHLT UB5 133 N4
Hazelmere Wy HAYES BR2 205 M6
Hazel Pde LHD/OX * KT22 236 B8
Hazel Ri EMPK RM11 125 K4
Hazel Rd BERK HP4 34 A6
BF/WBF KT14 215 K10
DART DA1 187 L5
ERITH DA8 165 H7
LCOL/BKTW AL2 56 A4
REIG RH2 275 M2
SRTFD * E15 121 K10
WLSDN NW10 136 E5
Hazel Rw NFNCH/WDSP * N12 97 N6
The Hazels WLYN * AL6 23 P1
Hazeltree La NTHLT UB5 133 M5
Hazel Tree Rd WATN WD24 73 J3
Hazel Wk HAYES BR2 206 D6
Hazel Wy CHING E4 100 E7
COUL/CHIP CR5 240 A5
LHD/OX KT22 236 B8
STHWK SE1 19 L5
Hazelwick Av CRAWE RH10 284 B5
Hazelwick Mill La CRAWE RH10 284 B5
Hazelwick Rd CRAWE RH10 284 B6
Hazelwood CRAWW RH11 283 K7
DORK * RH4 272 G3
TIL RM18 169 K3
Hazelwood Av MRDN SM4 201 L4
Hazelwood Cl CLPT E5 120 D8
CRAWE RH10 285 N5
CSHM HP5 51 J5
EA W5 155 K1
RYLN/HDSTN HA2 114 A2
Hazelwood Ct SURB KT6 199 K6
Hazelwood Crs PLMGR N13 99 H5
Hazelwood Dr PIN HA5 93 J10
STALE/WH AL4 39 H4
Hazelwood Gdns BRWN CM15 86 F9
Hazelwood Gv SAND/SEL CR2 224 A10
Hazelwood Hts OXTED RH8 261 M7
Hazelwood La ABLGY WD5 54 E8
COUL/CHIP CR5 240 A5
PLMGR N13 99 H5
Hazelwood Park Cl
BARK/HLT IG6 103 H6
Hazelwood Rd EN EN1 79 N10
OXTED RH8 261 N8
RKW/CH/CXG WD3 72 D10
RSEV TN14 226 G8
WALTH E17 120 D3
WOKN/KNAP GU21 231 K4
Hazlebury Rd FUL/PGN SW6 157 L8
Hazledean Rd CROY/NA CR0 203 L9
Hazledene Rd CHSWK W4 155 P5
Hazlemere Gdns WPK KT4 200 D8
Hazlemere Rd SLN SL2 129 N10
Hazlewell Rd PUT/ROE SW15 178 F1
Hazlewood Crs NKENS W10 8 B2
Hazlitt Cl FELT TW13 175 M7
Hazlitt Ms WKENS W14 14 A4
Hazlitt Rd WKENS W14 14 A4
Hazon Wy HOR/WEW KT19 220 A8
Heacham Av HGDN/ICK UB10 112 D8
Headcorn Rd BMLY BR1 183 L8
THHTH CR7 202 G4
TOTM N17 99 N8
Headfort Pl KTBR SW1X 16 D2
Headingley Cl CHESW EN7 61 N2
RAD WD7 57 K8
Headington Rd
WAND/EARL SW18 179 M4
Headlam Rd CLAP SW4 180 E2
Headlam St WCHPL E1 140 A6
Headley Ap IL IG1 122 D3
Headley Av WLGTN SM6 222 G2
Headley Cha BRW CM14 107 H5
Headley Cl CHSGTN KT9 219 M3
CRAWE RH10 284 E4
Headley Common Rd
EPSOM KT18 256 A3
Headley Dr CROY/NA CR0 225 H4
GNTH/NBYPK IG2 122 E4
KWD/TDW/WH KT20 238 E5
Headley Gv KWD/TDW/WH KT20 238 E6
KWD/TDW/WH KT20 256 A4
Headley Heath Ap
KWD/TDW/WH KT20 255 N6
Headley Pde EPSOM * KT18 238 A5
Headley Rd ASHTD KT21 237 P4
EPSOM KT18 237 P6
LHD/OX KT22 237 H8
RDKG RH5 255 H5
Headstone Dr HRW HA1 114 C2
Headstone Gdns
RYLN/HDSTN HA2 114 B2
Headstone La KTN/HRWW/W HA3 94 A9
Headstone Pde HRW * HA1 114 C2
Headstone Rd HRW HA1 114 D3
Head St WCHPL E1 140 C8
Headway Cl RCHPK/HAM TW10 177 H7
The Headway EW KT17 220 C5
Heald St NWCR SE14 160 E7
Healey Rd WATW WD18 72 G10
Healey St CAMTN NW1 4 E2
Healy Dr ORP BR6 207 J10
Heard's La BRWN CM15 87 L7
Hearne Rd CHSWK W4 155 M4
Hearnes Cl BEAC HP9 89 J6
Hearn Ri NTHLT UB5 133 L3
Hearn Rd ROM RM1 124 G4
Hearn's Buildings WALW SE17 19 H6
Hearns Cl STMC/STPC BR5 207 M4
Hearns Rd STMC/STPC BR5 207 M4
Hearn St SDTCH EC2A 13 K2
Hearnville Rd BAL SW12 180 B4
Heatham Pk WHTN TW2 176 E3
Heath Av BXLYHN DA7 163 N5
STALW/RED AL3 38 C4
Heathbourne Rd BUSH WD23 94 E2
STAN HA7 94 D3
Heathbridge WEY * KT13 216 B3
Heath Brow HAMP NW3 117 M8
HHW HP1 35 M8
Heath Cl BNSTD SM7 221 L10
EA W5 135 L6
GLDGN NW11 117 L5
GPK RM2 125 H1
HARP AL5 20 A4
HHW HP1 35 M7
HYS/HAR UB3 152 E6
POTB/CUF EN6 59 L6
SAND/SEL CR2 223 J3
STMC/STPC BR5 207 M6
STWL/WRAY TW19 173 M2
SWLY BR8 208 F2
VW GU25 194 A4
Heathclose Av DART DA1 187 J3
Heathclose Rd DART DA1 187 H4
Heathcote KWD/TDW/WH KT20 238 G7
Heathcote Av CLAY IG5 102 C10
HAT AL10 40 D2
Heathcote Gdns HLWE CM17 47 P1
Heathcote Gv CHING E4 101 H4
Heathcote Rd EPSOM KT18 220 A10
TWK TW1 176 G2
Heathcote St BMSBY WC1N 11 N1
Heathcote Wy WDR/YW UB7 131 N10
Heathcroft EA W5 135 L6
WGCE AL7 23 M4
Heathcroft Av SUN TW16 174 G10
Heathcroft Gdns WALTH E17 101 J9
Heathdale Av HSLWW TW4 153 M9
Heathdene KWD/TDW/WH KT20 239 H5
Heathdene Dr BELV DA17 164 C3
Heathdene Mnr WAT * WD17 72 G5
Heathdene Rd
STRHM/NOR SW16 180 G10
WLGTN SM6 222 C4
Heathdown Rd
WOKS/MYFD GU22 232 G1
Heath Dr BELMT SM2 221 M5
CHOB/PIR GU24 230 F6
EPP CM16 83 H1
GPK RM2 105 H9
HAMP NW3 117 L9

KWD/TDW/WH KT20 ....256 D1
POTB/CUF EN6 ....59 K6
RPLY/SEND GU23 ....232 E9
RYNPK SW20 ....200 F4
Heathedge SYD * SE26 ....182 A5
Heathend Rd BXLY DA5 ....186 F4
Heather Av ROM RM1 ....104 E10
Heatherbank CHST BR7 ....206 D2
ELTH/MOT SE9 ....162 C8
Heatherbank Cl DART DA1 ....186 F2
Heather Cl ABLGY WD5 ....55 H8
ADL/WDHM KT15 ....215 L6
BRWN CM15 ....86 G9
CRAWE RH10 ....285 J3
EHAM E6 ....142 D8
GUW GU2 ....249 N8
HPTN TW12 ....197 N1
ISLW TW7 ....176 C1
KWD/TDW/WH KT20 ....239 H8
LEW SE13 ....183 J3
REDH RH1 ....258 C7
ROM RM1 ....104 E9
UX/CGN UB8 ....132 A7
VX/NE SW8 ....158 C9
WOKN/KNAP GU21 ....231 P1
Heatherdale Cl KUTN/CMB KT2 ....177 M9
Heatherdeane EHSLY KT24 ....252 E1
Heatherdene Cl FNCH N3 ....97 M8
MTCM CR4 ....201 N4
Heatherden Gn IVER SL0 ....130 F3
Heather Dr ASC SL5 ....192 G7
DART DA1 ....187 H3
ENC/FH EN2 ....79 J6
ROM RM1 ....104 E10
Heather End SWLY BR8 ....208 E5
Heatherfold Wy PIN HA5 ....112 G1
Heather Gdns BELMT SM2 ....221 K3
GLDGN NW11 ....117 H4
ROM RM1 ....104 E10
Heather Gln ROM RM1 ....104 E10
Heatherlands HORL * RH6 ....280 D3
SUN TW16 ....175 H9
Heather La WDR/YW UB7 ....131 P8
Heatherley Dr CLAY IG5 ....122 C1
Heather Park Dr ALP/SUD HA0 ....135 M2
Heather Park Pde
ALP/SUD * HA0 ....135 L2
Heather Pl ESH/CLAY KT10 ....218 A1
Heather Ri BUSH WD23 ....73 N6
Heather Rd CHING E4 ....100 E7
CRICK NW2 ....116 C7
LEE/GVPK SE12 ....183 M5
WGCW AL8 ....22 F7
Heatherset Cl ESH/CLAY KT10 ....218 B2
Heatherset Gdns
STRHM/NOR SW16 ....180 G10
Heatherside Cl GT/LBKH * KT23 ....253 N1
Heatherside Dr VW GU25 ....193 M6
Heatherside Gdns SLN SL2 ....109 J8
Heatherside Rd HOR/WEW KT19 ....220 A4
SCUP DA14 ....185 M6
Heathers Land RDKG RH5 ....273 H5
The Heathers STWL/WRAY TW19 ....174 A3
Heatherton Pk AMS HP6 ....68 G2
Heathervale Rd
ADL/WDHM KT15 ....215 L6
Heather Wk CHOB/PIR GU24 ....230 C7
EDGW HA8 ....95 N6
HORL RH6 ....281 K4
NKENS W10 ....8 B1
Heather Wy CHOB/PIR GU24 ....213 K4
HHNE HP2 ....35 N5
POTB/CUF EN6 ....59 J8
ROM RM1 ....104 E9
SAND/SEL CR2 ....224 C5
STAN HA7 ....94 E7
Heatherwood Cl MNPK E12 ....121 N7
Heatherwood Dr YEAD UB4 ....132 E4
Heath Farm La STALW/RED AL3 ....38 D4
Heathfield CHING E4 ....101 H4
CHST BR7 ....184 F9
COB KT11 ....217 P10
CRAWE RH10 ....284 E4
HRW * HA1 ....114 E5
Heathfield Av ASC SL5 ....192 D5
WAND/EARL SW18 ....179 N3
Heathfield Cl CAN/RD E16 ....142 A7
HAYES BR2 ....225 P2
POTB/CUF EN6 ....59 L6
WOKS/MYFD GU22 ....232 D4
Heathfield Cottages
GRAYS * RM17 ....167 K5
Heathfield Dr MTCM CR4 ....201 P1
REDH RH1 ....275 P5
WIM/MER SW19 ....179 P10
Heathfield Gdns CHSWK W4 ....155 P4
CROY/NA * CR0 ....223 K1
GLDGN NW11 ....116 G4
WAND/EARL SW18 ....179 N2
Heathfield La CHST BR7 ....184 F9
Heathfield North WHTN TW2 ....176 D3
Heathfield Pk CRICK NW2 ....136 F1
Heathfield Park Dr CHDH RM6 ....123 L3
Heathfield Ri RSLP HA4 ....112 D5
Heathfield Rd ACT W3 ....155 N1
BMLY BR1 ....183 L10
BUSH WD23 ....73 M8
BXLYHS DA6 ....164 A10
CROY/NA CR0 ....223 L2
HAYES BR2 ....225 P2
SEV TN13 ....246 G8
WAND/EARL SW18 ....179 M2
WOKS/MYFD GU22 ....232 D4
WOT/HER KT12 ....217 M1
Heathfield South WHTN TW2 ....176 E3
Heathfield Sq WAND/EARL SW18 ....179 N3
Heathfield Ter CHSWK W4 ....155 P4
SWLY * BR8 ....208 E2
WOOL/PLUM SE18 ....163 H5
Heathfield V SAND/SEL CR2 ....224 C5
Heath Gdns DART * DA1 ....187 K4
TWK TW1 ....176 E4
Heathgate GLDGN NW11 ....117 L4
HERT/BAY SG13 ....26 A8
Heathgate Pl HAMP NW3 ....118 A10
Heath Gv PGE/AN SE20 ....182 B10
SUN TW16 ....174 G10
Heath Hl DORK RH4 ....272 G2
Heathhurst Rd SAND/SEL CR2 ....223 M5
Heathland Rd STNW/STAM N16 ....119 M6
Heathlands KWD/TDW/WH KT20 ....238 G8
Heathlands Cl SUN TW16 ....197 H2
TWK TW1 ....176 E5
WOKN/KNAP GU21 ....214 B10
Heathlands Ct HSLWW TW4 ....175 M1
Heathlands Dr STALW/RED AL3 ....38 D4
Heathlands Ri DART DA1 ....187 J3
Heathlands Wy HSLWW TW4 ....175 M1
Heath La BKHTH/KID SE3 ....161 J8
DART DA1 ....187 J4
HERT/BAY SG13 ....26 B9
HHW HP1 ....35 M8
SHGR GU5 ....269 P7
Heathlee Rd BKHTH/KID SE3 ....161 L10
DART DA1 ....186 F2
Heathley End CHST BR7 ....184 F9
Heath Ldg BUSH * WD23 ....94 C2
Heathman's Rd FUL/PGN * SW6 ....157 J7
Heath Md WIM/MER SW19 ....178 G6
Heath Mill La RGUW GU3 ....249 H1
Heathpark Dr BFOR GU20 ....212 D3
Heath Park Dr BMLY BR1 ....206 B3
Heath Park Rd GPK RM2 ....125 H3
Heath Ridge Gn COB KT11 ....217 P9
Heath Ri DORK RH4 ....272 B4
HAYES BR2 ....205 M6
PUT/ROE SW15 ....178 G2
Heathrise RPLY/SEND GU23 ....233 L9
Heath Ri VW GU25 ....194 A4
Heath Rd AMS HP6 ....50 B10
BXLY DA5 ....186 D4
CDH/CHF RM16 ....168 C1
CHDH RM6 ....123 N5
CTHM CR3 ....241 L9
DART DA1 ....186 G2
HGDN/ICK UB10 ....132 D6
HRW HA1 ....114 B5
HSLW TW3 ....154 B10
LHD/OX KT22 ....218 B8
OXHEY WD19 ....93 L1
POTB/CUF EN6 ....59 L6
STAL AL1 ....38 D5
THHTH CR7 ....203 K3
TWK TW1 ....176 E4
VX/NE SW8 ....158 C8
WEY KT13 ....216 B2
WOKN/KNAP GU21 ....232 C1
Heathrow SHGR GU5 ....270 D5
Heathrow Cl WDR/YW UB7 ....151 L7
Heath's Cl EN EN1 ....79 L6
Heath Side STMC/STPC BR5 ....206 F8
Heathside ESH/CLAY KT10 ....198 D10
HAMP NW3 ....117 N9
HSLWW TW4 ....175 N3
STALE/WH AL4 ....39 N9
STALW/RED AL3 ....38 D4
WEY KT13 ....216 C2
Heathside Av BXLYHN DA7 ....163 P8
Heathside Cl ESH/CLAY KT10 ....198 D10
GNTH/NBYPK IG2 ....122 G3
NTHWD HA6 ....92 E6
Heathside Ct
KWD/TDW/WH KT20 ....238 E9
Heathside Crs
WOKS/MYFD GU22 ....232 C3
Heathside Gdns
WOKS/MYFD GU22 ....232 D3
Heathside Park Rd
WOKS/MYFD GU22 ....232 C4
Heathside Pl
KWD/TDW/WH KT20 ....238 G4
Heathside Rd NTHWD HA6 ....92 E5
WOKS/MYFD GU22 ....232 C4
Heathstan Rd SHB W12 ....136 D8
Heath St DART DA1 ....187 L3
HAMP NW3 ....117 M8
The Heath CTHM CR3 ....241 K10
HNWL * W7 ....154 D1
RAD WD7 ....56 F9
Heath Vw EFNCH N2 ....117 M2
EHSLY KT24 ....252 G1
Heathview Av DART DA1 ....186 F2
Heath View Cl EFNCH N2 ....117 M2
Heath View Crs DART DA1 ....187 H3
Heath View Dr ABYW SE2 ....163 N5
Heath View Gdns
CDH/CHF RM16 ....167 P1
Heathview Gdns PUT/ROE SW15 ....178 F3
Heath View Rd CDH/CHF RM16 ....167 P1
Heathview Rd THHTH CR7 ....203 H4
Heath Vls WAND/EARL * SW18 ....179 M4
WOOL/PLUM SE18 ....163 J4
Heathville Rd ARCH N19 ....118 F5
Heathwall St BTSEA SW11 ....158 A9
Heath Wy ERITH DA8 ....164 D7
IVER SL0 ....130 G4
RAD WD7 ....57 H6
Heathway BKHTH/KID SE3 ....161 M6
CROY/NA CR0 ....204 E10
CTHM CR3 ....259 K1
DAGW RM9 ....124 A9
EHSLY KT24 ....234 G10
NWDGN * UB2 ....153 L3
WFD IG8 ....101 P5
Heathwood Gdns CHARL SE7 ....162 B3
SWLY BR8 ....208 D2
Heathwood Pde SWLY * BR8 ....208 D2
Heathwood Wk BXLY DA5 ....186 F4
Heaton Av HARH RM3 ....105 J8
Heaton Cl CHING E4 ....101 H4
HARH RM3 ....105 K8
Heaton Grange Rd GPK RM2 ....104 G9
Heaton Rd MTCM CR4 ....180 B10
PECK SE15 ....160 A9
Heaton Wy HARH RM3 ....105 K8
Heaver Rd BTSEA * SW11 ....157 N9
Heavitree Cl WOOL/PLUM SE18 ....162 G4
Heavitree Rd WOOL/PLUM SE18 ....162 G4
Heay Flds WGCE AL7 ....23 M4
Hebden Ter TOTM N17 ....99 M7
Hebdon Rd TOOT SW17 ....179 P6
Heber Rd CRICK NW2 ....116 G10
EDUL SE22 ....181 N2
Hebron Rd HMSMTH W6 ....156 E2
Hecham Cl WALTH E17 ....100 D10
Heckfield Pl FUL/PGN SW6 ....157 K6
Heckford Cl WATW WD18 ....72 D10
Heckford St WAP E1W 140 C9
Hector St WOOL/PLUM * SE18 ....163 H3
Heddington Gv HOLWY N7 ....118 G10
Heddon Cl ISLW TW7 ....154 F10
Heddon Court Av EBAR EN4 ....78 A9
Heddon Court Pde EBAR * EN4 ....78 B9
Heddon Rd EBAR EN4 ....78 A9
Heddon St CONDST W1S 10 G8
Hedgebrooms WGCE AL7 ....23 M4
Hedge Hl ENC/FH EN2 ....79 J5
Hedge La PLMGR N13 ....99 K5
Hedgeley REDBR IG4 ....122 C2
Hedgemans Rd DAGW RM9 ....143 N2
Hedgemans Wy DAGW RM9 ....143 P1
Hedge Place Rd GRH DA9 ....188 D2
Hedgerley Ct WOKN/KNAP GU21 ....231 P3
Hedgerley Gdns GFD/PVL UB6 ....134 B4
Hedgerley Hl SLN SL2 ....109 J8
Hedgerley La BEAC HP9 ....108 E1
SLN SL2 ....109 K4
Hedgerow CFSP/GDCR SL9 ....90 B7
Hedge Rw HHW HP1 ....35 K4
Hedgerow La BAR EN5 ....76 E9
Hedgerows SBW CM21 ....30 A1
The Hedgerows GVW DA11 ....190 B5
Hedger's Gv HOM * E9 ....140 D1
Hedger St LBTH SE11 ....18 C7
Hedges Cl HAT AL10 ....40 E3
Hedgeside BERK HP4 ....34 D2
Hedgeway GUW GU2 ....267 M2
Hedgewood Gdns CLAY IG5 ....122 D2
Hedgley St LEE/GVPK SE12 ....183 L1
Hedingham Cl HORL RH6 ....280 D3
IS N1 ....6 E4
Hedingham Rd BCTR RM8 ....123 L10
EMPK RM11 ....125 P6
WTHK RM20 ....167 H4
Hedley Av WTHK RM20 ....167 H6
Hedley Rd HSLWW TW4 ....175 P3
STAL AL1 ....38 G6
Hedley Rw HBRY N5 ....119 L10
Hedworth Av CHES/WCR EN8 ....62 C9
Heenan Cl BARK IG11 ....142 F1
Heene Rd ENC/FH EN2 ....79 L6
Heidegger Crs BARN SW13 ....156 E6
Heigham Rd EHAM E6 ....142 A2
Heighams HLWW/ROY CM19 ....46 C4
Heighton Gdns CROY/NA CR0 ....223 J2
Heights Cl BNSTD SM7 ....239 H2
RYNPK SW20 ....178 E10
The Heights BECK * BR3 ....183 H10
CHARL SE7 ....161 P4
LOU IG10 ....82 C6
NTHLT UB5 ....113 P10
SEV * TN13 ....246 F8
WAB EN9 ....63 N1
WEY * KT13 ....216 B6
Heiron St WALW SE17 ....18 D10
Helby Rd CLAP SW4 ....180 E2
Helder Gv LEE/GVPK SE12 ....183 L3
Helder St SAND/SEL CR2 ....223 L5
Heldmann Cl ISLW TW7 ....154 C10
Helena Cl EBAR EN4 ....77 N3
Helena Pl HOM E9 ....140 A3
Helena Rd EA W5 ....135 J7
PLSTW E13 ....141 L4
WALTH E17 ....120 F3
WDSR SL4 ....149 J8
WLSDN NW10 ....116 E10
Helena Sq BERM/RHTH SE16 ....140 D9
Helen Av EBED/NFELT TW14 ....175 J3
Helen Cl DART DA1 ....187 J3
E/WMO/HCT KT8 ....198 A4
EFNCH N2 ....117 M1
Helen Rd EMPK RM11 ....125 L1
Helens Ga CHES/WCR EN8 ....62 E2
Helenslea Av GLDGN NW11 ....117 J6
Helen's Pl BETH E2 ....140 B5
Helen St WOOL/PLUM * SE18 ....162 E3
Helford Cl RSLP HA4 ....112 F7
Helford Wk WOKN/KNAP GU21 ....231 M4
Helford Wy UPMR RM14 ....126 C4
Helgiford Gdns SUN TW16 ....174 F10
Heligan Cl ORP BR6 ....227 J1
Helions Rd HLWW/ROY CM19 ....46 E1
Helix Gdns BRXS/STRHM SW2 ....180 G2
Helix Rd BRXS/STRHM SW2 ....180 G2
Helleborine GRAYS RM17 ....167 L4
Hellings St WAP E1W 13 P10
Helm Cl HOR/WEW KT19 ....219 M8
Helme Cl WIM/MER SW19 ....179 J8
Helmet Rw FSBYE EC1V 12 F1
Helmore Rd BARK IG11 ....143 H2
Helmsdale WOKN/KNAP GU21 ....231 N4
Helmsdale Cl ROM RM1 ....104 F8
YEAD * UB4 ....133 M6
Helmsdale Rd ROM RM1 ....104 F8
STRHM/NOR SW16 ....202 D1
Helmsley Pl HACK E8 ....140 A2
Helmsley St HACK E8 ....140 A2
Helsinki Sq BERM/RHTH SE16 ....160 E2
Helston Cl PIN * HA5 ....93 N8
PIN HA5 ....93 N8
Helston Gv HHNE * HP2 ....35 N1
Helston La WDSR SL4 ....148 G7
Helston Pl ABLGY WD5 ....54 G8
Helvellyn Cl EGH TW20 ....172 E10
Helvetia St CAT SE6 ....182 E5
Hemans St VX/NE SW8 ....158 E6
Hemel Hempstead Rd
HHS/BOV HP3 ....36 F8
STALW/RED AL3 ....37 P6
Hemery Rd NTHLT UB5 ....114 C10
Hemingford Rd CHEAM SM3 ....220 F1
IS N1 ....5 P5
WAT WD17 ....72 F2
Heming Rd EDGW HA8 ....95 N7
Hemington Av FBAR/BDGN N11 ....98 A6
Hemlock Cl KWD/TDW/WH KT20 ....239 H9
Hemlock Rd SHB W12 ....136 C9
Hemmen La HYS/HAR UB3 ....132 G9
Hemming Cl HPTN TW12 ....197 P1
Hemmings Cl SCUP DA14 ....185 L5
The Hemmings BERK HP4 ....33 L6
Hemming St WCHPL E1 ....13 P2
Hemming Wy GSTN WD25 ....73 H2
SLN SL2 ....128 G5
Hemmingway Cl KTTN NW5 ....118 B9
Hemnall St EPP CM16 ....65 J7
Hempshaw Av BNSTD SM7 ....240 A2
Hempson Av DTCH/LGLY SL3 ....149 P2
Hempstall WGCE AL7 ....23 L7
Hempstead Cl BKHH IG9 ....101 M3
Hempstead La BERK HP4 ....34 F3
Hempstead Rd HHS/BOV HP3 ....54 E2
KGLGY WD4 ....54 A3
WALTH E17 ....121 J1
WAT WD17 ....72 E2
Hemp Wk WALW SE17 ....19 H5
Hemsby Rd CHSGTN KT9 ....219 L3
Hemstal Rd KIL/WHAMP NW6 ....2 E3
Hemsted Rd ERITH DA8 ....164 F7
Hemswell Dr CDALE/KGS NW9 ....96 B9
Hemsworth St IS N1 ....7 J8
Hemwood Rd WDSR SL4 ....148 C9
Henbit Cl KWD/TDW/WH KT20 ....238 E5
Henbury Wy OXHEY WD19 ....93 L4
Henchley Dene RGUE GU4 ....250 G7
Henchman St SHB W12 ....136 C8
Hencroft St North SL SL1 ....149 L1
Hencroft St South SL SL1 ....149 L1
Hendale Av HDN NW4 ....116 D1
Henderson Av GUW GU2 ....249 N5
Henderson Cl STALW/RED AL3 ....38 B2
WLSDN NW10 ....135 P1
Henderson Dr DART DA1 ....165 P10
STJWD NW8 ....3 P10
Henderson Pl ABLGY WD5 ....54 G3
Henderson Rd BH/WHM TN16 ....225 P8
CROY/NA CR0 ....203 L6
ED N9 ....100 A2
FSTGT E7 ....141 P1
WAND/EARL SW18 ....179 P3
YEAD UB4 ....133 H5
Hendersons Cl HCH RM12 ....125 J7
Hendham Rd TOOT SW17 ....179 P5
Hendon Av FNCH N3 ....97 H9
Hendon Gdns CRW RM5 ....104 D7
Hendon Gv HOR/WEW KT19 ....219 M5
Hendon Hall Ct HDN * NW4 ....116 G1
Hendon La FNCH N3 ....117 H1
Hendon Park Rw GLDGN * NW11 ....117 J4
Hendon Rd ED N9 ....99 P3
Hendon Ter ASHF * TW15 ....174 E9
Hendon Wy CRICK NW2 ....117 H6
STWL/WRAY TW19 ....173 N1
Hendon Wood La MLHL NW7 ....96 D1
Hendren Cl NTHLT UB5 ....114 C10
Hendre Rd STHWK SE1 ....19 K6
Hendrick Av BAL SW12 ....180 A2
Heneage Crs CROY/NA CR0 ....225 H6
Heneage La HDTCH EC3A 13 K6
Heneage St WCHPL E1 ....13 M4
Henfield Cl ARCH N19 ....118 D6
BXLY DA5 ....186 B2
Henfield Rd WIM/MER SW19 ....201 J1
Henfold La RDKG RH5 ....273 K10
Hengelo Gdns MTCM CR4 ....201 N4
Hengist Rd ERITH DA8 ....164 D6
LEE/GVPK SE12 ....183 N3
Hengist Wy HAYES BR2 ....205 J4
Hengrave Rd FSTH SE23 ....182 B3
Hengrove Ct BXLY DA5 ....185 P4
Hengrove Crs ASHF TW15 ....173 N6
Henhurst Rd MEO DA13 ....191 H10
Henley Av CHEAM SM3 ....201 H10
Henley Bank GUW GU2 ....267 M2
Henley Cl BERM/RHTH * SE16 ....160 B1
CRAWE RH10 ....284 E10
GFD/PVL * UB6 ....134 B4
ISLW TW7 ....154 E7
Henley Ct WOKS/MYFD GU22 ....232 D6
Henley Deane GVW DA11 ....190 B7
Henley Dr BERM/RHTH SE16 ....19 M5
KUTN/CMB KT2 ....178 C10
Henley Gdns CHDH RM6 ....123 P3
PIN HA5 ....113 J1
Henley Ga CHOB/PIR GU24 ....248 B3
Henley Pk RGUW * GU3 ....248 C5
Henley Rd CAN/RD E16 ....162 C1
IL IG1 ....122 F9
SL SL1 ....128 D8
UED N18 ....99 M5
WLSDN NW10 ....136 F3
Henley St BTSEA SW11 ....158 B8
Henley Wy FELT TW13 ....175 L8
Hennel Cl FSTH SE23 ....182 B6
Hennessy Ct WOKN/KNAP GU21 ....214 F9
Hennessy Rd ED N9 ....100 B3
Henniker Gdns EHAM E6 ....142 A5
Henniker Ms CHEL SW3 ....15 L9
Henniker Rd SRTFD E15 ....121 J10
Henningham Rd TOTM N17 ....99 L9
Henning St BTSEA SW11 ....157 P7
Henrietta Cl DEPT SE8 ....160 F5
Henrietta Ms BMSBY WC1N 11 M1
Henrietta Pl CAVSQ/HST W1G 10 E5
Henrietta St COVGDN WC2E 11 M7
SRTFD E15 ....121 H10
Henriques St WCHPL E1 ....13 P5
Henry Addlington Cl EHAM E6 ....142 E7
Henry Cl ENC/FH EN2 ....79 M4
Henry Cooper Wy
LEE/GVPK SE12 ....184 A6
Henry Darlot Dr MLHL NW7 ....97 H6
Henry Dickens Ct NTGHL W11 ....136 G9
Henry Doulton Dr TOOT SW17 ....180 B7
Henry Jackson Rd
PUT/ROE SW15 ....156 G9
Henry Macaulay Av
KUTN/CMB KT2 ....199 J1
Henry Peters Dr TEDD TW11 ....176 D8
Henry Rd EBAR EN4 ....77 N9
EHAM E6 ....142 B4
FSBYPK N4 ....119 K6
SL SL1 ....149 J1
Henry's Av WFD IG8 ....101 L6
Henrys Grant STAL AL1 ....38 D7
STAL * AL1 ....38 D7
Henryson Rd BROCKY SE4 ....182 F1
Henry St BMLY BR1 ....205 N1
GRAYS RM17 ....167 P5
HHS/BOV HP3 ....35 N10
Henry Wells Sq HHNE * HP2 ....36 A2
Hensford Gdns SYD SE26 ....182 A7
Henshall St IS N1 ....7 H2
Henshaw Cl CRAWW RH11 ....283 J9
Henshawe Rd BCTR RM8 ....123 N8
Henshaw St WALW SE17 ....18 G5
Henslowe Rd EDUL SE22 ....181 P1
Henslow Wy WOKN/KNAP GU21 ....214 C10
Henson Av CRICK NW2 ....116 F10
Henson Cl ORP BR6 ....206 E9
Henson Pl NTHLT UB5 ....133 K3
Henstead Rd CRAWE RH10 ....284 C6
Henstridge Pl STJWD NW8 ....3 N7
Hensworth Rd ASHF TW15 ....173 N9
Henty Cl BTSEA SW11 ....157 P6
CRAWW RH11 ....283 H10
Henty Wk PUT/ROE SW15 ....178 E1
Henville Rd BMLY BR1 ....205 N1
Henwick Rd ELTH/MOT SE9 ....162 A9
Henwood Side WFD IG8 ....102 C7
Hepburn Gdns HAYES BR2 ....205 L8
Hepple Cl ISLW TW7 ....154 G8
Hepscott Rd HOM E9 ....140 F1
Hepworth Gdns BARK IG11 ....123 K10
Hepworth Rd STRHM/NOR SW16 ....180 F10
Hepworth Wy WOT/HER KT12 ....196 G8
Herald Gdns WLGTN SM6 ....202 C10
Heralds Pl LBTH SE11 ....18 C5
Herald St BETH E2 ....140 A6
Herbal Hl CLKNW EC1R 12 B2
Herbert Crs KTBR SW1X 16 B3
WOKN/KNAP GU21 ....231 K4
Herbert Gdns CHDH RM6 ....123 N5
CHSWK W4 ....155 N5
WLSDN NW10 ....136 E4
Herbert Pl WOOL/PLUM SE18 ....162 G5
Herbert Rd BXLYHN DA7 ....163 P8
CDALE/KGS NW9 ....116 D4
EMPK RM11 ....125 M5
FBAR/BDGN N11 ....98 F8
GDMY/SEVK IG3 ....123 H7
HAYES BR2 ....206 A5
KUT KT1 ....199 L3
MNPK E12 ....122 B9
SEVS/STOTM N15 ....119 N3
STHL UB1 ....133 N10
SWCM DA10 ....189 L2
SWLY BR8 ....208 G3
WALTH E17 ....120 E5
WIM/MER SW19 ....179 J10
WOOL/PLUM SE18 ....162 E6
Herbert St HHNE HP2 ....35 N5
KTTN NW5 ....4 C1
PLSTW E13 ....141 M4
Herbrand St BMSBY WC1N 11 L1
Hercies Rd HGDN/ICK UB10 ....132 A1
Hercules Pl HOLWY N7 ....118 F8
Hercules Rd STHWK SE1 ....17 P4
Hercules St HOLWY N7 ....118 F8
Hereford Av EBAR EN4 ....98 A2
Hereford Cl EPSOM KT18 ....220 A9
GUW GU2 ....249 L8
STA TW18 ....195 L1
Hereford Copse
WOKS/MYFD GU22 ....231 N5
Hereford Gdns IL IG1 ....122 B5
PIN HA5 ....113 M3
WHTN * TW2 ....176 B4
Hereford Ms BAY/PAD W2 ....8 F5
Hereford Pl NWCR * SE14 ....160 E6
Hereford Retreat PECK SE15 ....159 P6
Hereford Rd ACT W3 ....135 P9
BAY/PAD W2 ....8 F6
EA W5 ....155 H2
FELT TW13 ....175 K6
WAN E11 ....121 N3
Hereford Sq SKENS SW7 ....15 K6
Hereford St BETH E2 ....13 N1
Hereford Wy CHSGTN KT9 ....219 H2
Herent Dr CLAY IG5 ....122 C1
Hereward Av PUR/KEN CR8 ....223 H6
Hereward Cl WAB EN9 ....63 H8
Hereward Gdns PLMGR N13 ....99 H6
Hereward Gn LOU IG10 ....82 F5
Hereward Rd TOOT SW17 ....179 P7
Herga Ct WAT WD17 ....73 H6
Herga Rd KTN/HRWW/W HA3 ....114 E2
Herington Gv RBRW/HUT CM13 ....107 M1
Heriot Av CHING E4 ....100 F3
Heriot Rd CHERT KT16 ....195 K7
HDN NW4 ....116 F3
Heriots Cl STAN HA7 ....94 F5
Heritage Cl STAL * AL1 ....38 C6
UX/CGN UB8 ....131 M6
Heritage Hl HAYES BR2 ....225 P2
Heritage Lawn HORL RH6 ....280 D3
Heritage Pl WAND/EARL * SW18 ....179 N2
Heritage Vw HRW HA1 ....114 E8
Heritage Wk RKW/CH/CXG * WD3 ....71 H7
Herkomer Cl BUSH WD23 ....74 A10
Herkomer Rd BUSH WD23 ....73 P9
Herlwyn Av RSLP HA4 ....112 F8
Herlwyn Gdns TOOT SW17 ....180 A7
Herm Cl ISLW TW7 ....154 B6
Hermes Cl MV/WKIL W9 ....8 E2
Hermes St IS N1 ....6 A8
Hermes Wy WLGTN SM6 ....222 E4
Hermiston Av CEND/HSY/T N8 ....118 F3
Hermitage Cl DTCH/LGLY SL3 ....149 P2
ENC/FH EN2 ....79 J6
ESH/CLAY KT10 ....218 F3
RCHPK/HAM * TW10 ....177 J1
SHPTN TW17 ....196 B4
SWFD E18 ....121 L2
Hermitage Cottages STAN * HA7 ....94 D6
Hermitage Ct POTB/CUF EN6 ....59 M9
Hermitage Gdns HAMP NW3 ....117 K8
NRWD SE19 ....181 K10
Hermitage La CRICK NW2 ....117 K8
CROY/NA CR0 ....203 N7
STRHM/NOR SW16 ....180 G10
WDSR SL4 ....148 F9
Hermitage Rd FSBYPK N4 ....119 K5
NRWD SE19 ....181 L9
PUR/KEN CR8 ....241 K2
WOKN/KNAP GU21 ....231 J5
Hermitage Rw HACK * E8 ....119 P10
Hermitage St BAY/PAD W2 ....9 L4
The Hermitage BARN * SW13 ....156 C7
FELT * TW13 ....174 G6
FSTH SE23 ....182 B4
KUT * KT1 ....199 J4
LEW * SE13 ....161 H8
RCHPK/HAM TW10 ....177 K1
UX/CGN * UB8 ....131 N1
Hermitage Wk SWFD E18 ....121 L2
Hermitage Wall WAP E1W 13 P10
Hermitage Wy STAN HA7 ....94 F9
Hermitage Woods Crs
WOKN/KNAP GU21 ....231 J6
Hermit Rd CAN/RD E16 ....141 L6
Hermits Rd CRAWE RH10 ....284 A5
Hermit St FSBYE EC1V 6 C9
Hermon Gv HYS/HAR UB3 ....133 H10
Hermon Hl WAN E11 ....121 M2
Herndon Cl EGH TW20 ....172 D7
Herndon Rd WAND/EARL SW18 ....179 M1
Herne Cl WLSDN NW10 ....116 A10
Herne Ct BUSH * WD23 ....94 B2
Herne Hl HNHL SE24 ....181 K1
Herne Hill Rd HNHL SE24 ....159 K9
Herne Ms UED N18 ....99 P5
Herne Pl HNHL SE24 ....181 J2
Herne Rd BUSH WD23 ....74 A10
SURB KT6 ....199 J9
Herneshaw HAT AL10 ....40 C6
Herns La WGCE AL7 ....23 L5
Herns Wy WGCE AL7 ....23 K3
Heron Cl BKHH IG9 ....101 M2
CRAWW RH11 ....283 M5
GUW GU2 ....249 N7
HHS/BOV HP3 ....54 A1
RKW/CH/CXG WD3 ....91 N3
SBW CM21 ....29 N2
UX/CGN UB8 ....131 N1
WALTH E17 ....100 E10
WLSDN NW10 ....136 B1
Heron Ct DORK * RH4 ....272 F1
HAYES BR2 ....205 P4
KUT * KT1 ....199 K3
Heron Crs SCUP DA14 ....185 H7
Heron Dl ADL/WDHM KT15 ....215 N2
Herondale SAND/SEL CR2 ....224 C5
Herondale Av WAND/EARL SW18 ....179 N4
Heron Dr DTCH/LGLY SL3 ....150 E3
FSBYPK N4 ....119 K7
WARE SG12 ....27 H8
Heronfield EGH TW20 ....171 N9
POTB/CUF EN6 ....59 M6
Heron Flight Av RAIN RM13 ....145 H2
Herongate Rd CHES/WCR EN8 ....62 C3
MNPK E12 ....121 P7
SWLY BR8 ....186 F9
Heron Hl BELV DA17 ....164 A3
Heron Md PEND EN3 ....80 F4
Heron Ms IL IG1 ....122 E7
Heron Pl RKW/CH/CXG WD3 ....91 K7
Heron Quays POP/IOD E14 ....140 F10
Heron Rd CROY/NA * CR0 ....203 M8
HNHL SE24 ....159 K10

TWK TW1 154 F10
The Heronry WOT/HER KT12 217 H3
Herons Cl CRAWE RH10 281 P10
Heronscourt LTWR GU18 212 B7
Heronscroft LTWR GU18 212 B7
Herons Cft WEY KT13 216 D3
Herons Elm BERK HP4 33 K2
Heronsforde WEA W13 135 H8
Heronsgate EDGW HA8 95 M6
Heronsgate Rd
RKW/CH/CXG WD3 70 E10
Herons Lea CRAWE RH10 281 P10
Heronslea GSTN WD25 73 K2
Herons Lea HGT * N6 118 A4
Heronslea Dr STAN HA7 95 K6
Herons Pl ISLW TW7 154 G9
Herons Ri EBAR EN4 77 P8
Herons Wy CHOB/PIR GU24 230 C7
Herons Wd HLW CM20 28 E9
Herons Wood Ct HORL * RH6 280 C3
Heronswood Pl WGCE AL7 23 K6
Heronswood Rd WGCE AL7 23 J5
Heron Wk NTHWD HA6 92 F5
Heron Wy HAT AL10 40 D6
UPMR RM14 126 D6
WTHK RM20 166 G4
Heronway RBRW/HUT CM13 107 N2
Herrick Cl CRAWE RH10 284 D5
Herrick Rd FSBYPK N4 119 K8
Herrick St WEST SW1P 17 K6
Herries St NKENS W10 2 B8
Herringham Rd CHARL SE7 161 P2
Herrings La BFOR GU20 212 C3
Herrongate Cl EN EN1 79 M6
Hersant Cl WLSDN NW10 136 D3
Herschell Rd FSTH SE23 182 C3
Herschel Park Dr SL SL1 149 L1
Herschel St SL SL1 149 L1
Hersham Centre
WOT/HER * KT12 217 L2
Hersham Cl PUT/ROE SW15 178 D3
Hersham Gdns WOT/HER KT12 217 J1
Hersham Pl WOT/HER * KT12 217 L2
Hersham Rd WOT/HER KT12 217 K1
Hershell Ct MORT/ESHN * SW14 155 N10
Hertford Av MORT/ESHN SW14 178 A1
Hertford Cl EBAR EN4 77 N7
Hertford Ct STAN * HA7 95 J8
Hertford End Ct NTHWD * HA6 92 F6
Hertford Rd BARK IG11 142 E2
BRKMPK AL9 23 L10
EBAR EN4 77 M7
ED N9 100 A2
EFNCH N2 117 P1
GNTH/NBYPK IG2 123 H4
HOD EN11 44 D1
IS N1 7 K5
PEND EN3 80 B4
WARE SG12 26 E7
WARE SG12 26 C3
WGCE AL7 23 K2
WLYN AL6 24 A1
Hertford Road High St PEND EN3 80 B10
Hertfordshire Wy
HERT/WAS SG14 25 H1
Hertford St MYFR/PKLN W1K 10 E10
Hertford Wy MTCM CR4 202 F4
Hertingfordbury Rd
HERT/WAS SG14 24 F7
HERT/WAS SG14 24 G6
Hertslet Rd HOLWY N7 118 G8
Hertsmere Rd POP/IOD E14 140 F10
Hertswood Ct BAR * EN5 77 H8
Hervey Cl FNCH N3 97 K9
Hervey Park Rd WALTH E17 120 D2
Hervines Ct AMS HP6 69 H3
Hervines Rd AMS HP6 68 G3
Hesa Rd HYS/HAR UB3 133 H8
Hesewall Cl VX/NE SW8 158 D8
Hesiers Hl WARL CR6 243 K3
Hesiers Rd WARL CR6 243 K2
Hesketh Av RDART DA2 188 A4
Hesketh Pl NTGHL W11 8 A8
Hesketh Rd FSTGT E7 121 M8
Heslop Rd BAL SW12 180 A4
Hesper Ms ECT SW5 14 G7
Hesperus Crs POP/IOD E14 160 G3
Hessel Rd WEA W13 154 F1
Hessel St WCHPL E1 140 A8
Hesselyn Dr RAIN RM13 145 J2
Hessle Gv EW KT17 220 C7
Hestercombe Av FUL/PGN SW6 157 H8
Hesterman Wy CROY/NA CR0 202 F8
Hester Rd BTSEA SW11 157 P6
UED N18 99 P6
Hester Ter RCH/KEW TW9 155 M9
Heston Av HEST TW5 153 M6
Heston Grange La HEST TW5 153 N5
Heston Rd HEST TW5 153 P6
REDH RH1 276 A5
Heston St DEPT SE8 160 E7
Heswell Gn OXHEY * WD19 93 H4
Hetchleys HHW HP1 35 K3
Hetherington Cl SLN SL2 128 E5
Hetherington Rd CLAP SW4 158 F10
SHPTN TW17 196 D2
Hetherington Wy
HGDN/ICK UB10 111 P9
Hethersett Cl REIG RH2 257 M7
Hetley Rd SHB W12 136 E10
Heton Gdns HDN NW4 116 D2
Heusden Wy CFSP/GDCR SL9 110 C6
Hevelius Cl GNWCH SE10 161 L4
Hever Court Rd GVE DA12 190 F9
Hever Cft ELTH/MOT SE9 184 D7
Hever Gdns BMLY BR1 206 D2
Heverham Rd WOOL/PLUM SE18 163 H3
Hevers Av HORL RH6 280 A3
Heversham Rd BXLYHN DA7 164 B8
Hewens Rd HGDN/ICK UB10 132 D5
Hewer St NKENS W10 136 G7
Hewers Wy KWD/TDW/WH KT20 238 E6
Hewett Cl STAN HA7 94 G5
Hewett Pl SWLY BR8 208 E4
Hewett St SDTCH EC2A 13 K2
Hewish Rd UED N18 99 M5
Hewison St BOW E3 140 E4
Hewitt Av WDGN N22 99 J10
Hewitt Cl CROY/NA CR0 204 F10
STALE/WH AL4 21 J4
Hewitt Rd CEND/HSY/T N8 119 H3
Hewitts Rd ORP BR6 228 A4
Hewlett Rd BOW E3 140 D4
The Hexagon HGT N6 118 A6
Hexal Rd CAT SE6 183 K6
Hexham Cl CRAWE RH10 284 F7
Hexham Gdns ISLW TW7 154 F6
Hexham Rd BAR EN5 77 L8
MRDN SM4 201 L8
WNWD SE27 181 K5
Hextalls La REDH RH1 259 L4
Heybourne Rd TOTM N17 100 A8
Heybridge Av STRHM/NOR SW16 180 G9
Heybridge Ct HERT/WAS SG14 24 G4
Heybridge Dr BARK/HLT IG6 122 G1
Heybridge Wy LEY E10 120 D5
Heydons Cl STALW/RED AL3 38 C4
Heyford Av RYNPK SW20 201 J3
VX/NE SW8 158 F6
Heyford End LCOL/BKTW * AL2 56 C3
Heyford Rd MTCM CR4 201 P2
RAD WD7 74 E3
Heyford Ter VX/NE SW8 158 F6
Heyford Wy HAT AL10 40 F2
Heygate Est WALW SE17 18 F5
Heygate St WALW SE17 18 E6
Heymede LHD/OX KT22 237 H9
Heynes Rd BCTR RM8 123 M9
Heysham Dr OXHEY WD19 93 K6
Heysham La HAMP NW3 117 L8
Heysham Rd SEVS/STOTM N15 119 L4
Heythorpe Cl WOKN/KNAP GU21 231 L3
Heythorp St WAND/EARL SW18 179 J4
Heythrop Dr HGDN/ICK UB10 112 A9
Heywood Av CDALE/KGS NW9 96 B9
Heyworth Rd CLPT E5 120 A9
FSTGT E7 121 L10
Hibbert Av WATN WD24 73 L4
Hibbert Rd KTN/HRWW/W HA3 94 E10
WALTH E17 120 E5
Hibbert St BTSEA SW11 157 M9
Hibberts Wy CFSP/GDCR SL9 110 B1
Hibbs Cl SWLY BR8 208 E2
Hibernia Dr GVE DA12 191 J6
Hibernia Gdns HSLW TW3 175 P1
Hibernia Rd HSLW TW3 153 P10
Hichisson Rd PECK SE15 182 B1
Hickin Cl CHARL SE7 162 A3
Hickin St POP/IOD E14 161 H2
Hickling Rd IL IG1 122 E10
Hickman Av CHING E4 101 H7
Hickman Cl BROX EN10 44 D6
CAN/RD E16 142 A7
Hickman Rd CHDH RM6 123 M5
Hickmans Cl GDST RH9 260 B8
Hicks Av GFD/PVL UB6 134 C5
Hicks Cl BTSEA SW11 157 P9
Hicks St DEPT SE8 160 D4
Hidalgo Ct HHNE HP2 36 A4
Hidcote Cl WOKS/MYFD GU22 232 E2
Hidcote Gdns RYNPK SW20 200 E3
The Hideaway ABLGY WD5 54 G7
Hide Pl WEST SW1P 17 J6
Hide Rd HRW HA1 114 C2
The Hides HLW CM20 28 G10
Higgins Rd CHESW EN7 61 L3
Highacre DORK RH4 272 G5
High Acres ABLGY WD5 54 E8
Higham Hill Rd WALTH E17 120 D1
Higham Md CSHM HP5 51 H6
Higham Pl WALTH E17 120 D1
Higham Rd CSHM HP5 51 H6
TOTM N17 119 L1
WFD IG8 101 M7
Highams Hl CRAWW RH11 283 J8
Highams Hill Cottages
HAYES * BR2 225 M8
Highams La CHOB/PIR GU24 212 F3
Higham Station Av CHING E4 100 G7
The Highams WALTH * E17 101 H9
Higham St WALTH E17 120 D1
Higham Vw EPP CM16 66 C2
High Ash Cl TIL RM18 169 K2
High Ash Rd STALE/WH AL4 21 H4
Highbank Pl WAND/EARL * SW18 179 L3
Highbanks Cl WELL DA16 163 K6
Highbanks Rd PIN HA5 94 A7
Highbank Wy CEND/HSY/T N8 119 H4
High Barn Rd EHSLY KT24 253 L5
Highbarns HHS/BOV HP3 54 B1
Highbarrow Rd CROY/NA CR0 203 N8
High Beech SAND/SEL CR2 223 M4
High Beeches CFSP/GDCR SL9 110 A6
EW KT17 220 G10
ORP BR6 227 K3
SCUP DA14 185 P8
High Beeches Cl PUR/KEN CR8 222 E6
High Beech Rd LOU IG10 82 B8
High Bois La AMS HP6 69 J1
Highbridge Rd BARK IG11 142 E3
Highbridge St WAB EN9 62 G9
Highbrook Rd BKHTH/KID SE3 162 A9
High Broom Crs WWKM BR4 204 G7
Highbury Av HOD EN11 44 F1
THHTH CR7 203 H2
Highbury Cl NWMAL KT3 199 P4
WWKM BR4 204 G9
Highbury Cnr HBRY N5 6 C1
Highbury Crs HBRY N5 119 J10
Highbury Est HBRY N5 119 K10
Highbury Gdns IL IG1 123 H7
Highbury Gra HBRY N5 119 J9
Highbury Gv HBRY N5 119 J10
Highbury Hl HBRY N5 6 D1
Highbury New Pk HBRY N5 6 D1
Highbury Pk HBRY N5 119 J9
Highbury Pl HBRY N5 6 C1
Highbury Qd HBRY N5 119 K8
Highbury Rd WIM/MER SW19 179 H8
Highbury Station Pde IS * N1 6 C2
Highbury Station Rd IS N1 6 B2
Highbury Ter HBRY N5 119 J10
Highbury Terrace Ms HBRY N5 119 J10
High Canons BORE WD6 75 P3
High Cedar Dr RYNPK SW20 178 E10
Highclere ASC SL5 192 C5
GU GU1 250 D7
Highclere Cl PUR/KEN CR8 241 K1
Highclere Ct WOKN/KNAP GU21 231 H3
Highclere Dr HHS/BOV HP3 36 C10
Highclere Gdns
WOKN/KNAP GU21 231 H3
Highclere Rd NWMAL KT3 200 A3
WOKN/KNAP GU21 231 H3
Highclere St SYD SE26 182 D7
Highcliffe Dr PUT/ROE SW15 178 C2
Highcliffe Gdns REDBR IG4 122 B3
High Cl RKW/CH/CXG WD3 71 M9
Highcombe CHARL SE7 161 N5
Highcombe Cl ELTH/MOT SE9 184 A4
High Coombe Pl KUTN/CMB KT2 178 A10
High Coppice AMSS HP7 69 H5
Highcotts La RGUE GU4 251 K2
Highcroft CDALE/KGS NW9 116 B3
Highcroft Av ALP/SUD HA0 135 L2
Highcroft Ct GT/LBKH KT23 235 P9
Highcroft Gdns GLDGN NW11 117 J4
Highcroft Rd ARCH N19 118 F5
HHS/BOV HP3 53 K1
Highcroft Trailer Gdns
HHS/BOV * HP3 52 E2
High Cross GSTN WD25 74 C3
Highcross Rd MEO DA13 189 J9
High Cross Rd SEVS/STOTM N15 119 P1
Highdaun Dr STRHM/NOR SW16 202 G4
High Dells HAT AL10 40 C5
Highdown WPK KT4 200 B9
Highdown Ct CRAWE RH10 284 C10
High Down Rd BELMT SM2 221 L7
Highdown Rd PUT/ROE SW15 178 E2
High Dr CTHM CR3 242 E8
LHD/OX KT22 218 C10
NWMAL KT3 199 P1
High Elms CHIG IG7 103 H5
UPMR RM14 126 D6
WFD IG8 101 M6
High Elms Cl NTHWD HA6 92 D7
High Elms La GSTN WD25 55 J2
High Elms Rd ORP BR6 226 F5
Higher Dr BNSTD SM7 220 G9
EHSLY KT24 252 F3
PUR/KEN CR8 223 H9
Higher Gn EW KT17 220 D9
Highfield BNSTD SM7 239 P5
CSTG HP8 90 A3
HLWS CM18 47 K2
KGLGY WD4 53 P4
OXHEY WD19 93 N4
RGUE GU4 268 C8
Highfield Av CDALE/KGS NW9 115 P3
ERITH DA8 164 C5
GFD/PVL UB6 114 D10
GLDGN NW11 116 G5
HARP AL5 20 F5
ORP BR6 227 J3
PIN HA5 113 N3
WBLY HA9 115 K8
Highfield Cl AMS HP6 69 J3
CDALE/KGS NW9 115 P3
CRW RM5 104 D7
LEW SE13 183 J2
LHD/OX KT22 218 C7
NTHWD HA6 92 F9
SURB KT6 199 H8
WDGN N22 99 H9
Highfield Cottages SWLY * BR8 187 J9
Highfield Ct EGH TW20 171 P9
STHGT/OAK N14 78 D10
Highfield Crs HCH RM12 125 N7
NTHWD HA6 92 F9
Highfield Dr BROX EN10 44 D7
HAYES BR2 205 K4
HGDN/ICK UB10 111 P8
HOR/WEW KT19 220 C4
WWKM BR4 204 G10
Highfield Gdns CDH/CHF RM16 168 A1
EPP CM16 65 H7
GLDGN NW11 117 H4
Highfield Hl NRWD SE19 181 L10
Highfield La HHNE HP2 36 A4
STALE/WH AL4 39 H8
Highfield Link CRW RM5 104 D7
Highfield Pl EPP CM16 65 H7
Highfield Rd ACT W3 135 N7
BERK HP4 34 A6
BF/WBF KT14 215 K9
BH/WHM TN16 243 P3
BMLY BR1 206 C4
BRYLDS KT5 199 P7
BUSH WD23 73 M9
BXLYHS DA6 186 A1
CHERT KT16 195 K8
CHESW EN7 61 M2
CRW RM5 104 D7
CSHM HP5 50 G5
CTHM CR3 241 P8
DART DA1 187 L3
EGH TW20 172 A9
FELT TW13 175 H4
GLDGN * NW11 117 H4
HCH RM12 125 N7
HERT/BAY SG13 25 L7
ISLW TW7 154 E7
NTHWD HA6 92 F9
PUR/KEN CR8 222 G6
RSEV TN14 247 M2
STALE/WH AL4 20 G10
STMC/STPC BR5 207 J3
SUN TW16 196 G4
SUT SM1 221 P2
WCHMH N21 99 J3
WDSR SL4 148 E9
WFD IG8 102 B8
WOT/HER KT12 197 H8
Highfield Rd South DART DA1 187 L3
High Flds ASC SL5 192 E5
Highfields ASHTD KT21 237 J5
EHSLY KT24 252 G4
KGLGY * WD4 53 P4
LHD/OX KT22 236 C10
POTB/CUF EN6 60 F4
RAD WD7 74 E1
Highfields Gv HGT N6 118 B6
Highfield Wy POTB/CUF EN6 59 L7
RKW/CH/CXG WD3 71 L10
RKW/CH/CXG WD3 91 M1
High Firs RAD WD7 74 E1
SWLY BR8 208 F4
High Firs Crs HARP AL5 20 C3
High Foleys ESH/CLAY KT10 218 G4
High Garth ESH/CLAY KT10 218 B3
Highgate Av HGT N6 118 C5
Highgate Cl HGT N6 118 B5
Highgate Edge EFNCH * N2 117 P3
Highgate Gv SBW CM21 29 N1
Highgate High St HGT N6 118 B6
Highgate Hl ARCH N19 118 C6
Highgate Rd KTTN NW5 118 B8
Highgate Spinney
CEND/HSY/T * N8 118 E4
Highgate West Hl HGT N6 118 B7
High Gv BMLY BR1 205 P1
STALW/RED AL3 38 C4
WGCW AL8 22 E4
WOOL/PLUM SE18 162 G6
Highgrove Cl CHST BR7 206 B1
FBAR/BDGN N11 98 B6
Highgrove Ms CAR SM5 201 P10
Highgrove Rd BCTR RM8 123 M10
Highgrove Wy RSLP HA4 113 H4
High Hill Ferry CLPT E5 120 A6
High Holborn HHOL WC1V 11 M5
High House La CDH/CHF RM16 168 G2
Highland Av BRW CM14 107 H2
DAGE RM10 124 D8
HNWL W7 134 D8
LOU IG10 82 C10
Highland Cottages WLGTN * SM6 222 C1
Highland Cft BECK BR3 182 G8
Highland Dr BUSH WD23 94 A1
HHS/BOV HP3 36 C6
Highland Pk FELT TW13 174 G7
Highland Rd AMSS HP7 69 J5
BMLY BR1 205 L1
BXLYHS DA6 164 B10
NRWD SE19 181 M9
NTHWD HA6 93 H10
PUR/KEN CR8 223 H10
RSEV TN14 228 C7
WAB EN9 45 K8
Highlands BRKMPK AL9 40 F1
OXHEY WD19 93 K2
Highlands Av ACT W3 135 P9
LHD/OX KT22 237 H8
WCHMH N21 78 G9
Highlands Cl CFSP/GDCR SL9 90 C8
HSLW TW3 154 A7
LHD/OX KT22 236 G8
Highlands End CFSP/GDCR SL9 90 C8
Highlands Gdns IL IG1 122 C6
Highlands Hl SWLY BR8 209 H2
Highlands La CFSP/GDCR SL9 90 C7
WOKS/MYFD GU22 232 B7
Highlands Pk BGR/WK TN15 247 M7
LHD/OX KT22 237 J9
Highlands Rd BAR EN5 77 K8
BEAC HP9 89 H6
LHD/OX KT22 237 H8
REDH RH1 257 N9
STMC/STPC BR5 207 L7
The Highlands BAR * EN5 77 L8
EDGW HA8 95 N10
EHSLY KT24 252 F1
POTB/CUF EN6 59 M7
RKW/CH/CXG WD3 91 L1
SLN SL2 109 H9
Highland Ter LEW * SE13 160 G9
High La CTHM CR3 242 E5
HNWL W7 134 C8
RBSF CM22 30 F5
WARL CR6 242 E4
Highlea Cl CDALE/KGS NW9 96 B9
High Level Dr SYD SE26 181 P7
Highlever Rd NKENS W10 136 F7
High Limes NRWD * SE19 181 M9
High Md CHIG IG7 102 F3
HRW HA1 114 D3
Highmead WOOL/PLUM SE18 163 J6
High Md WWKM BR4 205 J9
Highmead Crs ALP/SUD HA0 135 L2
High Meadow Cl DORK RH4 272 G3
PIN HA5 113 J2
High Meadow Crs
CDALE/KGS NW9 116 A3
High Meadow Pl CHERT KT16 195 J6
High Mdw CHIG IG7 102 G6
High Meads STALE/WH AL4 21 H3
High Meads Rd CAN/RD E16 142 A8
Highmoor AMSS HP7 69 J5
Highmore Rd BKHTH/KID SE3 161 K6
High Mt HDN * NW4 116 D4
High Oak Rd WARE SG12 26 C1
High Oaks CRAWW RH11 283 L9
ENC/FH EN2 78 G4
STALW/RED AL3 38 B1
High Oaks Rd WGCW AL8 22 E4
Highover Pk AMSS HP7 69 H6
The High Pde
STRHM/NOR * SW16 180 F6
High Park Av EHSLY KT24 252 G2
High Park Rd RCH/KEW TW9 155 M7
High Pastures RBSF CM22 30 D3
High Pth WIM/MER SW19 201 L1
High Path Rd GU GU1 250 F10
High Pewley GU GU1 268 B2
High Pine Cl WEY KT13 216 D2
High Pines WARL CR6 242 B5
High Point ELTH/MOT SE9 184 E6
Highpoint WEY KT13 216 B2
High Rdg MUSWH * N10 98 C9
POTB/CUF EN6 60 F3
Highridge Cl EPSOM * KT18 238 B1
High Ridge Cl HHS/BOV HP3 53 N1
Highridge Pl ENC/FH * EN2 78 G4
High Ridge Rd HHS/BOV HP3 53 N1
High Rd BF/WBF KT14 215 P8
BKHH IG9 101 N2
BRKMPK AL9 41 P4
BROX EN10 44 E8
BUSH WD23 94 C2
CDH/CHF RM16 147 K10
CHDH RM6 124 A4
CHIG IG7 102 E4
COUL/CHIP CR5 239 P10
EPP CM16 47 L10
EPP CM16 48 E10
EPP CM16 64 F9
EPP CM16 66 C3
FBAR/BDGN N11 98 C6
GSTN WD25 54 G10
IL IG1 122 E8
KTN/HRWW/W HA3 94 D8
LEY E10 120 G4
NFNCH/WDSP N12 97 M4
RDART DA2 187 J6
TOTM N17 99 N10
TRDG/WHET N20 97 M1
UX/CGN UB8 131 M7
WBLY HA9 115 K10
WDGN N22 99 H10
WLSDN NW10 136 B1
High Road Broxbourne
BROX EN10 44 E7
High Road Eastcote PIN HA5 113 K2
High Road Great North Rd
EFNCH N2 97 N10
High Road Ickenham
HGDN/ICK UB10 112 D8
High Road Leyton LEY E10 120 G7
High Road Leytonstone
WAN E11 121 K8
High Road Turnford BROX EN10 62 D1
High Road Woodford Gn
WFD IG8 101 M4
High Road Wormley
BROX EN10 44 E10
Highshore Rd PECK SE15 159 N8
High Silver LOU IG10 82 A8
High Standing CTHM CR3 259 K1
Highstead Crs ERITH DA8 164 F7
Highstone Av WAN E11 121 M4
High St ABLGY WD5 54 G6
ABLGY WD5 54 G3
ACT W3 135 P10
ADL/WDHM KT15 215 L1
AMSS HP7 68 F5
ASC SL5 192 F5
ASC SL5 192 C5
BAR EN5 77 J8
BARK/HLT IG6 102 F10
BECK BR3 204 F1
BELMT SM2 221 L3
BERK HP4 35 J5
BGR/WK TN15 247 P3
BGR/WK TN15 245 N7
BH/WHM TN16 245 M10
BH/WHM TN16 262 F3
BMLY BR1 205 M2
BNSTD SM7 239 K1
BORE WD6 75 J10
BRW CM14 107 H3
BTFD TW8 155 J5
BUSH WD23 73 P10
CAR SM5 222 A2
CEND/HSY/T N8 118 F2
CFSP/GDCR SL9 90 B9
CHEAM SM3 221 H3
CHES/WCR EN8 62 C4
CHES/WCR EN8 62 C8
CHES/WCR EN8 62 D10
CHOB/PIR GU24 212 D8
CHOB/PIR GU24 213 K7
CHONG CM5 67 P5
COB KT11 217 J10
CRAWE RH10 283 N7
CROY/NA CR0 203 K10
CSHM HP5 50 G7
CTHM CR3 241 M9
DART DA1 187 M2
DEN/HRF UB9 91 M10
DORK RH4 272 G2
DTCH/LGLY SL3 149 N7
DTCH/LGLY SL3 150 D3
DTCH/LGLY SL3 150 F6
E/WMO/HCT KT8 197 P4
EA W5 135 J10
EGH TW20 172 C8
EMPK RM11 125 L6
EPP CM16 65 J7
ESH/CLAY KT10 218 E3
ESH/CLAY KT10 218 A1
EW KT17 220 C5
EW KT17 220 A9
EYN DA4 209 N6
EYN DA4 209 M9
FELT TW13 174 G6
GDST RH9 260 B7
GRAYS RM17 167 M4
GRH DA9 166 G10
GT/LBKH KT23 254 A1
GUW GU2 267 P2
GVE DA12 190 E2
GVW DA11 189 N2
HEST TW5 153 J6
HHNE HP2 35 M5
HHS/BOV HP3 52 D3
HLWE CM17 29 M7
HLWW/ROY CM19 27 N10
HOD EN11 44 F3
HORL RH6 280 C4
HPTN TW12 176 B9
HPTN TW12 198 A1
HRW HA1 114 D7
HSLW TW3 154 A9
HYS/HAR UB3 152 E5
IVER SL0 131 J8
KGLGY WD4 54 B5
KTN/HRWW/W HA3 94 D10
KTN/HRWW/W HA3 114 D1
KUT KT1 199 H1
KUT KT1 199 J3
KWD/TDW/WH KT20 238 F9
LCOL/BKTW AL2 57 H1
LHD/OX KT22 218 C9
LHD/OX KT22 236 G8
MLHL NW7 96 E6
NTHWD HA6 92 G9
NWMAL KT3 200 B4
ORP BR6 207 K8
ORP BR6 226 D7
ORP BR6 226 F2
OXTED RH8 261 J6
OXTED RH8 261 N4
PGE/AN SE20 182 B10
PIN HA5 113 M1
POTB/CUF EN6 59 L9
PUR/KEN CR8 223 H7
RDART DA2 188 G6
REDH RH1 258 A10
REDH RH1 258 C4
REDH RH1 258 G10
REDH RH1 259 L9
REIG RH2 257 K10
RKW/CH/CXG WD3 91 N2
ROM RM1 124 F3
RPLY/SEND GU23 233 M7
RSEV TN14 228 G6
RSEV TN14 247 H2
RSLP HA4 112 F5
SCUP DA14 185 K7
SEV TN13 246 D8
SEV TN13 265 K1
SHPTN TW17 196 C6
SL SL1 128 B5
SL SL1 149 J2
SNWD SE25 203 N4
SOCK/AV RM15 146 B10
SRTFD E15 141 J2
STA TW18 173 J7
STAL AL1 38 C6
STALE/WH AL4 20 G10
STALE/WH AL4 21 J2
STALE/WH AL4 39 N8
STHGT/OAK N14 98 E2
STMC/STPC BR5 207 M6
STWL/WRAY TW19 172 B2
STWL/WRAY TW19 173 N2
SUT SM1 221 L1
SWCM DA10 189 L1
SWLY BR8 208 F3
TEDD TW11 176 F8
THDIT KT7 198 F6
THHTH CR7 203 K4
UX/CGN UB8 131 M7
UX/CGN UB8 131 M2
WALTH E17 120 E2
WAN E11 121 N4
WARE SG12 26 C2
WARE SG12 27 H7
WARE SG12 28 A2
WAT WD17 73 J8
WBLY HA9 115 L9
WDR/YW UB7 131 P10
WDR/YW UB7 151 N5
WDSR SL4 149 J5
WEY KT13 216 B1
WHTN TW2 176 B3
WIM/MER SW19 178 G8
WOKN/KNAP GU21 231 H4

WOKN/KNAP GU21 231 P2
WOKN/KNAP GU21 232 C3
WOKS/MYFD GU22 232 D7
WOT/HER KT12 197 H8
WWKM BR4 204 G8
High Street Collier's Wd
WIM/MER SW19 179 N10
High Street Gn HHNE HP2 36 B3
High Street Harlesden
WLSDN NW10 136 C4
High Street Ms WIM/MER SW19 179 H8
High St North MNPK E12 142 B1
High St South EHAM E6 142 C4
The High HLW * CM20 28 F10
High Timber St BLKFR EC4V 12 E7
High Tor Cl BMLY BR1 183 N10
High Tree Cl ADL/WDHM KT15 215 K2
High Trees BRXS/STRHM SW2 181 H4
CROY/NA CR0 204 D8
EBAR EN4 77 P9
High Trees Cl CTHM CR3 241 N8
High Trees Rd REIG RH2 275 N1
High Vw BELMT SM2 221 J7
CSTG HP8 90 A3
HAT AL10 40 C6
PIN HA5 113 K2
RKW/CH/CXG WD3 71 K8
SHGR GU5 270 D5
WATW WD18 72 G10
Highview CTHM CR3 241 M10
WOKN/KNAP * GU21 231 K3
Highview Av EDGW HA8 95 P5
High View Av GRAYS RM17 167 P4
WLGTN SM6 222 G4
High View Cl LOU IG10 81 P9
Highview Cl POTB/CUF EN6 59 M9
High View Cl SNWD SE25 203 N2
High View Ct REIG * RH2 257 N10
Highview Crs RBRW/HUT CM13 87 P10
High View Gdns GRAYS RM17 167 P4
Highview Gdns EDGW HA8 95 P6
FBAR/BDGN N11 98 D6
FNCH N3 117 H1
POTB/CUF EN6 59 M9
STALE/WH AL4 39 H1
UPMR RM14 126 A7
High View Rd GUW GU2 267 J3
NRWD SE19 181 L9
SWFD E18 101 L10
Highview Rd SCUP DA14 185 L7
WEA W13 134 F8
Highview Ter DART * DA1 187 L1
Highwayman's Rdg BFOR GU20 212 A1
The Highway BELMT SM2 221 M5
ORP BR6 227 L2
STAN HA7 94 E9
WAP E1W 140 B9
High Wickfield WGCE AL7 23 M6
Highwold COUL/CHIP CR5 240 B4
Highwood Av BUSH WD23 73 N5
NFNCH/WDSP N12 97 M5
Highwood Cl BRW CM14 106 G1
ORP BR6 206 F9
PUR/KEN CR8 241 K3
Highwood Dr ORP BR6 206 F9
Highwood Gdns CLAY IG5 122 C3
Highwood Gv MLHL NW7 96 A6
Highwoodhall La HHS/BOV HP3 36 E10
HHS/BOV HP3 54 B1
Highwood Hl MLHL NW7 96 C3
Highwood La LOU IG10 82 D10
Highwood Rd ARCH N19 118 F8
High Wood Rd HOD EN11 26 E10
Highwoods CTHM CR3 259 M1
LHD/OX KT22 237 H7
High Worple RYLN/HDSTN HA2 113 M5
Highworth Rd FBAR/BDGN N11 98 E7
Highworth St CAMTN * NW1 9 P3
High Wych La SBW CM21 29 K1
High Wych Rd HLW CM20 29 H5
SBW * CM21 29 N2
Hilary Av MTCM CR4 202 B3
Hilary Cl FUL/PGN * SW6 157 L6
HCH RM12 125 L10
Hilary Rd ACT W3 136 C9
Hilberry Ct BUSH * WD23 94 A1
Hilbert Rd CHEAM SM3 220 G1
Hilborough Cl WIM/MER SW19 179 M10
Hilborough Rd HACK * E8 7 M4
Hilborough Wy ORP BR6 226 G2
Hilbury HAT AL10 40 C5
Hilda May Av SWLY BR8 208 F3
Hilda Rd CAN/RD E16 141 K6
EHAM E6 142 A2
Hilda Ter BRXN/ST * SW9 159 H8
Hilda Vale Rd ORP BR6 226 D1
Hildenborough Gdns BMLY BR1 183 K9
Hilden Dr ERITH DA8 165 J6
Hildenlea Pl HAYES BR2 205 K2
Hildenley Cl REDH RH1 258 E4
The Hildens DORK RH4 272 B4
The Hilders ASHTD KT21 237 N3
Hildreth St BAL SW12 180 C4
Hildyard Rd FUL/PGN SW6 14 F9
Hiley Rd WLSDN NW10 136 F5
Hilfield La GSTN WD25 74 A5
Hilgay GU GU1 250 C10
Hilgay Cl GU GU1 250 C10
Hilgrove Rd KIL/WHAMP NW6 3 K4
Hiliary Gdns STAN HA7 95 H10
Hiljon Crs CFSP/GDCR SL9 90 B9
Hillars Heath Rd COUL/CHIP CR5 240 F1
Hillary Av GVW DA11 190 B6
Hillary Crs WOT/HER KT12 197 K8
Hillary Dr ISLW TW7 154 E10
Hillary Ri BAR EN5 77 K8
Hillary Rd DTCH/LGLY SL3 150 B2
HHNE HP2 36 B5
NWDGN UB2 153 P2
Hill Av AMS HP6 69 H4
Hillbarn SAND/SEL CR2 223 M7
Hillbeck Cl PECK SE15 160 B6
Hillbeck Wy GFD/PVL UB6 134 C3
Hillborne Cl HYS/HAR UB3 153 H4
Hillborough Cl WIM/MER * SW19 179 M10
Hillbrook Gdns WEY KT13 216 B4
Hillbrook Rd TOOT SW17 180 A6
Hill Brow BMLY BR1 206 A1
DART DA1 186 G2
Hillbrow NWMAL KT3 200 C3
Hillbrow Cl BXLY DA5 186 E7
RGUW GU3 248 G9
Hillbrow Rd BMLY BR1 183 K10
ESH/CLAY KT10 218 B1
Hill Bunker's BELV DA17 164 B3
Hillbury Av KTN/HRWW/W HA3 114 G3
Hillbury Cl AMS HP6 69 H4
WARL CR6 242 A4
Hillbury Gdns WARL CR6 242 B4
Hillbury Rd TOOT SW17 180 C6
WARL CR6 241 P3
Hill Cl BAR EN5 76 F9
CHST BR7 184 E8
COB KT11 217 P8
CRICK NW2 116 E8
GLDGN NW11 117 K4
HRW HA1 114 D8
MEO DA13 190 B10
PUR/KEN CR8 223 K8
STAN HA7 94 G5
WOKN/KNAP GU21 232 A2
Hill Common HHS/BOV HP3 36 B10
Hillcote Av STRHM/NOR SW16 181 H10
Hill Ct BERK HP4 34 A4
Hillcourt Av NFNCH/WDSP N12 97 L7
Hillcourt Rd EDUL SE22 182 A2
Hill Crs BRYLDS KT5 199 L5
BXLY DA5 186 D4
EMPK RM11 125 K4
HRW HA1 114 F3
TRDG/WHET N20 97 L3
WPK KT4 200 F9
Hill Crest BFN/LL DA15 185 K3
POTB/CUF EN6 59 M10
SEV TN13 247 H8
SURB * KT6 199 K7
Hillcrest HAT AL10 40 D5
HGT N6 118 B5
HNHL * SE24 159 L10
KWD/TDW/WH * KT20 255 N7
STALW/RED * AL3 38 A8
WCHMH N21 99 J1
WEY KT13 216 C1
Hillcrest Av CHERT KT16 195 H10
EDGW HA8 95 N5
GLDGN NW11 117 H3
PIN HA5 113 L2
WTHK RM20 166 F5
Hillcrest Cl BECK BR3 204 E6
CRAWE RH10 284 E7
EPSOM KT18 238 C1
SYD SE26 181 P7
Hillcrest Dr GRH DA9 188 F1
Hill Crest Gdns CRICK NW2 116 D8
Hillcrest Gdns ESH/CLAY KT10 198 E10
HDN NW4 117 H2
Hill Crest Rd CHONG CM5 66 F6
Hillcrest Rd ACT W3 135 M10
BH/WHM TN16 244 A2
BMLY BR1 183 M7
CTHM CR3 241 N3
DART DA1 186 F3
EA W5 135 K7
EMPK RM11 125 H5
GUW GU2 249 L9
LOU IG10 82 A10
ORP BR6 207 K9
PUR/KEN CR8 222 G6
RAD WD7 57 M9
WALTH E17 101 J10
Hillcrest Vw BECK BR3 204 E6
Hillcrest Wy EPP CM16 65 K7
Hillcroft LOU IG10 82 D6
Hillcroft Av PIN HA5 113 N4
PUR/KEN CR8 222 D9
Hillcroft Crs EA W5 135 J8
OXHEY WD19 93 J2
RSLP HA4 113 L8
WBLY HA9 115 L9
Hillcroft Rd CSHM HP5 51 J5
EHAM E6 142 E7
Hillcroome Rd BELMT SM2 221 N3
Hillcross Av MRDN SM4 201 H6
Hilldale Rd SUT SM1 221 J1
Hilldeane Rd PUR/KEN CR8 223 H6
Hilldene Av HARH RM3 105 K7
Hilldene Cl HARH RM3 105 L6
Hilldown Rd HAYES BR2 205 K8
HHW HP1 35 K4
STRHM/NOR SW16 180 F10
Hill Dr CDALE/KGS NW9 115 P6
STRHM/NOR SW16 202 G3
Hilldrop Crs HOLWY N7 118 E10
Hilldrop Est HOLWY N7 118 E10
Hilldrop La HOLWY N7 118 E10
Hilldrop Rd BMLY BR1 183 N9
HOLWY N7 118 E10
Hill Dyke Rd STALE/WH AL4 21 J4
Hill End ORP BR6 207 J9
WOOL/PLUM SE18 162 D7
Hill End La STAL AL1 38 G9
STALE/WH AL4 39 H9
Hill End Rd DEN/HRF UB9 91 L7
Hillersdon SLN SL2 129 N7
Hillersdon Av BARN SW13 156 D8
EDGW HA8 95 L6
Hillery Cl WALW SE17 19 H6
Hilley Field La LHD/OX KT22 236 B8
Hill Farm Av GSTN WD25 55 H9
Hill Farm La CSTG HP8 89 L2
Hill Farm Rd CFSP/GDCR SL9 90 B8
CSHM HP5 51 J10
NKENS W10 136 F7
Hillfield HAT AL10 40 E1
Hillfield Av ALP/SUD HA0 135 K2
CDALE/KGS NW9 116 B3
CEND/HSY/T N8 118 G2
MRDN SM4 201 P6
Hillfield Cl GU GU1 250 F8
REDH RH1 258 B10
RYLN/HDSTN HA2 114 B2
Hillfield Ct HHNE HP2 35 P6
Hillfield La South BUSH WD23 74 D10
Hillfield Pde MRDN * SM4 201 N6
Hillfield Pk MUSWH N10 118 C1
WCHMH N21 99 H3
Hillfield Park Ms MUSWH N10 118 C2
Hill Field Rd HPTN TW12 175 N10
Hillfield Rd CFSP/GDCR SL9 90 B8
HHNE HP2 35 N6
KIL/WHAMP NW6 2 G1
REDH RH1 258 B10
SEV TN13 246 F6
Hillfield Sq CFSP/GDCR SL9 90 B8
Hillfoot Av CRW RM5 104 D9
Hillfoot Rd CRW RM5 104 D9
Hillford Pl REDH RH1 276 B6
Hill Gardens Cravan
BAY/PAD * W2 9 J7
Hillgate Pl BAL SW12 180 C2
KENS W8 8 E9
Hillgate St KENS W8 8 E9
Hill Gv FELT TW13 175 N5
ROM RM1 124 F1
Hillhampton ASC SL5 192 E7
Hillhouse WAB EN9 63 L9
Hill House Av STAN HA7 94 E8
Hill House Cl CRAWE RH10 285 P9
WCHMH N21 99 H1
Hill House Dr CDH/CHF RM16 168 F4
REIG RH2 275 L2
WEY KT13 216 B7
Hill House Drive HPTN TW12 197 P1
Hill House Rd RDART DA2 188 B3
STRHM/NOR SW16 180 G8
Hillhurst Gdns CTHM CR3 241 M6
Hilliard Rd NTHWD HA6 92 G9
Hilliard's Ct WAP E1W 140 B10
Hilliards Rd UX/CGN UB8 131 N8
Hillier Cl BAR EN5 77 L10
Hillier Gdns CROY/NA CR0 223 H2
Hillier Pl CHSGTN KT9 219 J3
Hillier Rd BTSEA SW11 180 A2
GU GU1 250 D10
Hilliers Av UX/CGN UB8 132 B5
Hillier's La CROY/NA CR0 202 F10
Hillingdale BH/WHM TN16 243 N4
Hillingdon Av SEV TN13 247 K7
STWL/WRAY TW19 173 P4
Hillingdon Hl HGDN/ICK UB10 131 P5
UX/CGN UB8 132 A5
Hillingdon Pde UX/CGN * UB8 132 C6
Hillingdon Ri SEV TN13 247 L8
Hillingdon Rd BXLYHN DA7 164 D9
GSTN WD25 55 H10
GVW DA11 190 E5
HGDN/ICK UB10 131 P3
Hillingdon St WALW SE17 18 D10
Hillingdon Trail DEN/HRF UB9 111 N1
HYS/HAR UB3 153 H4
Hill La KWD/TDW/WH KT20 239 H7
RSLP HA4 112 D6
Hill Ley HAT AL10 40 C4
Hill Leys POTB/CUF EN6 60 F4
Hillman Cl EMPK RM11 125 L1
Hillman St HACK E8 140 A1
Hillmarton Rd HOLWY N7 118 F10
Hillmarton Ter HOLWY * N7 118 F10
Hill Md BERK HP4 33 M6
Hillmead CRAWW RH11 283 J7
Hillmead Dr BRXN/ST SW9 159 J10
Hillmont Rd ESH/CLAY KT10 198 D10
Hillmore Gv SYD SE26 182 C8
Hillmount WOKS/MYFD * GU22 232 B4
Hill Pk LHD/OX * KT22 236 F5
Hill Park Ct LHD/OX * KT22 236 E5
Hill Pl CRAWW RH11 283 M8
SLN SL2 128 G2
Hillpoint RKW/CH/CXG WD3 71 M9
Hillreach WOOL/PLUM SE18 162 C4
Hillrise DTCH/LGLY SL3 150 D5
Hill Ri CFSP/GDCR SL9 90 A10
DORK RH4 254 F10
ED N9 80 A10
ESH/CLAY KT10 198 G9
GFD/PVL UB6 134 B3
GLDGN NW11 117 L2
POTB/CUF EN6 59 M10
POTB/CUF EN6 60 A9
RCHPK/HAM TW10 177 J1
RDART DA2 188 C8
RKW/CH/CXG WD3 91 L1
RSLP HA4 112 D6
UPMR RM14 125 P7
Hillrise Av WATN WD24 73 L4
Hill Rise Crs CFSP/GDCR SL9 90 B10
Hillrise Rd ARCH N19 118 F5
CRW RM5 104 D7
Hill Rd BRW CM14 106 F4
CAR SM5 221 P3
DART DA1 187 M5
EPP CM16 83 H3
GT/LBKH KT23 236 A8
HRW HA1 114 F3
HRW HA1 114 G8
MTCM CR4 202 C1
MUSWH N10 98 A9
NTHWD HA6 92 E7
PIN HA5 113 M4
PUR/KEN CR8 222 G8
STJWD NW8 3 K8
SUT SM1 221 L2
Hillsboro Rd EDUL SE22 181 M1
Hillsborough Gn OXHEY * WD19 93 H4
Hill's Chace BRW CM14 107 H5
Hillsgrove Cl WELL DA16 163 M6
Hill Shaw HART DA3 211 L6
Hill Side BAR EN5 77 M9
Hillside AMSS HP7 69 K6
ASC * SL5 192 B5
BAR * EN5 76 D9
BNSTD SM7 239 H1
CDALE/KGS NW9 116 A2
CSHM HP5 50 F4
DEN/HRF UB9 111 M3
ESH/CLAY * KT10 218 A2
EYN DA4 209 N7
GRAYS RM17 168 A3
HAT AL10 40 D4
HLWE CM17 47 M3
HOD EN11 44 E2
RDART DA2 188 D4
SL SL1 149 K1
VW GU25 193 P6
WARE SG12 26 C3
WGCE AL7 23 L8
WIM/MER SW19 178 G9
WLSDN NW10 136 A3
WOKS/MYFD GU22 232 A6
Hillside Av BORE WD6 75 P7
CHES/WCR EN8 62 C7
FBAR/BDGN N11 98 A7
GVE DA12 190 G5
PUR/KEN CR8 223 J9
WBLY HA9 115 L9
WFD IG8 101 P6
Hillside Cl ABLGY WD5 54 F8
BNSTD SM7 239 H2
CFSP/GDCR SL9 90 B7
CRAWW RH11 283 L9
CSTG HP8 89 N4
MRDN SM4 201 H4
MV/WKIL W9 2 G10
RDKG RH5 273 M1
WFD IG8 101 P6
WOKN/KNAP GU21 231 K3
Hillside Cottages BNSTD * SM7 222 A9
Hillside Ct SWLY BR8 209 H4
Hillside Crs CHES/WCR EN8 62 C7
ENC/FH EN2 79 L4
NTHWD HA6 93 H9
OXHEY WD19 73 L10
RYLN/HDSTN HA2 114 B7
WARE SG12 26 G7
Hillside Dr EDGW HA8 95 M7
GVE DA12 190 G5
Hillside Gdns ADL/WDHM KT15 215 J2
BAR EN5 77 H8
BERK HP4 34 A6
BRKHM/BTCW RH3 255 M10
BRXS/STRHM * SW2 181 H5
EDGW HA8 95 L5
FBAR/BDGN * N11 98 D7
HGT N6 118 B4
KTN/HRWW/W HA3 115 K5
NTHWD HA6 93 H8
WLGTN SM6 222 D4
Hillside Gv MLHL NW7 96 D8
STHGT/OAK N14 98 E1
Hillside La HAYES BR2 205 M9
WARE SG12 26 F6
Hillside Pk ASC SL5 192 E8
Hillside Ri NTHWD HA6 93 H8
Hillside Rd ASHTD KT21 237 L3
BELMT SM2 221 J4
BH/WHM TN16 244 B5
BRXS/STRHM SW2 180 G5
BUSH WD23 73 M9
COUL/CHIP CR5 240 F4
CROY/NA CR0 223 J2
CTHM CR3 241 P4
DART DA1 187 H2
EA W5 135 K7
EW KT17 220 F6
HAYES BR2 205 L3
NTHWD HA6 93 H8
PIN HA5 93 J8
RAD WD7 74 G1
RKW/CH/CXG WD3 70 F9
RSEV TN14 247 N3
SEV TN13 247 L9
SEVS/STOTM N15 119 M4
STAL AL1 38 D5
STHL UB1 133 P6
STNW/STAM N16 119 M5
Hillside Ter GVE * DA12 190 E4
HERT/BAY SG13 25 K7
The Hillside ORP BR6 227 L5
Hillside Wk BRW CM14 106 F4
Hillside Wy RGODL GU7 267 J10
Hills La NTHWD HA6 92 F9
Hillsleigh Rd KENS W8 8 D9
Hillsmead Wy SAND/SEL CR2 223 P10
Hills Ms EA * W5 135 K9
Hills Pl SOHO/CST W1F 11 L5
Hillspur Cl GUW GU2 249 L9
Hillspur Rd GUW GU2 249 L9
Hill's Rd BKHH IG9 101 N2
Hillstowe St CLPT E5 120 B7
Hill St MYFR/PICC W1J 10 E9
STALW/RED AL3 38 B6
Hillswood Dr CHERT KT16 214 F1
The Hill AMSS HP7 68 B10
CTHM CR3 241 N10
GVW DA11 189 P2
HLWE CM17 29 M7
STALE/WH AL4 21 J3
Hill Top GLDGN NW11 117 L2
LOU IG10 82 D7
MRDN SM4 201 J7
Hilltop WALTH * E17 120 G1
Hill Top Cl LOU IG10 82 D7
Hilltop Cl ASC SL5 192 D2
CHESW EN7 61 N2
LHD/OX KT22 237 H9
RGUW GU3 249 L6
Hilltop Cottages SYD * SE26 182 A7
Hilltop Gdns DART DA1 187 N1
ORP BR6 207 H9
Hilltop La CTHM CR3 259 H2
Hilltop Ri GT/LBKH KT23 254 B2
Hilltop Rd BERK HP4 33 P6
CTHM CR3 241 M3
KGLGY WD4 54 E3
KIL/WHAMP NW6 2 F3
REIG RH2 275 L2
WTHK RM20 166 F5
Hill Top Vw WFD * IG8 102 C7
Hilltop Wk CTHM CR3 242 D6
Hilltop Wy STAN HA7 94 F4
Hill Tree Cl SBW CM21 29 N2
Hill Vw BERK HP4 33 M3
CHOB/PIR * GU24 213 H1
Hillview CTHM CR3 241 N3
RYNPK SW20 178 E10
Hillview Av EMPK RM11 125 K4
KTN/HRWW/W HA3 115 K3
Hill View Cl KWD/TDW/WH KT20 238 F7
PUR/KEN CR8 223 J7
Hillview Cl PIN HA5 93 N7
Hillview Ct WOKS/MYFD GU22 232 B4
Hill View Crs GUW GU2 249 L8
IL IG1 122 C4
Hillview Crs ORP BR6 207 H8
Hillview Dr REDH RH1 276 B1
Hill View Dr WELL DA16 163 H8
Hill View Gdns CDALE/KGS NW9 116 A3
Hillview Gdns CHES/WCR EN8 62 D3
HDN NW4 116 G2
PIN HA5 113 P1
Hill View Rd ESH/CLAY KT10 218 F4
HART DA3 211 N3
ORP BR6 207 J8
STWL/WRAY TW19 172 A2
TWK TW1 176 F2
WOKS/MYFD GU22 232 C4
Hillview Rd CHST BR7 184 D8
MLHL NW7 96 G5
PIN HA5 93 N8
SUT SM1 201 M10
Hill Wy AMSS HP7 68 G7
Hillway CDALE/KGS NW9 116 B6
HGT N6 118 B7
Hill Waye CFSP/GDCR SL9 110 C4
Hillwood Cl RBRW/HUT CM13 107 N2
Hillwood Gv RBRW/HUT CM13 107 N2
Hillworth BECK * BR3 204 G2
Hillworth Rd BRXS/STRHM SW2 181 H3
Hillyard Rd HNWL W7 134 D7
Hillyard St BRXN/ST SW9 159 H7
Hillybarn Rd CRAWW RH11 282 F4
Hillydeal Rd RSEV TN14 247 K1
Hilly Fld HLWS CM18 47 J5
Hillyfield WALTH E17 100 D10
Hillyfield Cl HOM E9 120 D10
Hilly Flds BROCKY * SE4 160 F10
WGCE AL7 23 M4
Hillyfields LOU IG10 82 D6
Hilly Fields Crs BROCKY SE4 160 F10
Hilmay Dr HHW HP1 35 L7
Hilperton Rd SL SL1 149 K1
Hilsea St CLPT E5 120 B9
Hilton Av NFNCH/WDSP N12 97 N6
Hilton Cl UX/CGN UB8 131 L4
Hilton Wy SAND/SEL CR2 242 A1
Himalayan Wy WATW WD18 72 G10
Himley Rd TOOT SW17 179 P8
Hinchley Cl ESH/CLAY KT10 198 E10
Hinchley Dr ESH/CLAY KT10 198 E10
Hinchley Wy ESH/CLAY KT10 198 F10
Hinckley Rd EDUL SE22 159 P10
Hind Cl CHIG IG7 103 J6
Hind Ct FLST/FETLN * EC4A 12 B6
Hind Crs ERITH DA8 164 D6
Hinde Ms MHST * W1U 10 D5
Hindes Rd HRW HA1 114 D3
Hinde St MHST W1U 10 D5
Hind Gv POP/IOD E14 140 F8
Hindhead Cl CRAWW RH11 283 M9
UX/CGN UB8 132 C7
Hindhead Gdns NTHLT UB5 133 M3
Hindhead Gn OXHEY WD19 93 K6
Hindhead Wy WLGTN SM6 222 F2
Hindmans Rd EDUL SE22 181 P1
Hindmans Wy DAGW RM9 144 A5
Hindmarsh Cl WCHPL E1 13 P7
Hindrey Rd CLPT E5 120 A10
Hindsley's Pl FSTH SE23 182 B5
Hind Ter WTHK * RM20 167 J5
Hinkler Rd KTN/HRWW/W HA3 115 J1
Hinkley Cl DEN/HRF UB9 111 M2
Hinksey Cl DTCH/LGLY SL3 150 E2
Hinstock Rd WOOL/PLUM SE18 162 F6
Hinton Av HSLWW TW4 153 L10
Hinton Cl ELTH/MOT SE9 184 B4
Hinton Rd BRXN/ST SW9 159 J9
SL SL1 128 D9
UED N18 99 M5
UX/CGN UB8 131 M3
WLGTN SM6 222 D3
Hipkins Pl BROX EN10 44 D6
Hipley St WOKS/MYFD GU22 232 E6
Hippodrome Pl NTGHL W11 8 A8
Hitcham Rd LEY E10 120 E5
Hitchcock Cl SHPTN TW17 196 A3
Hitchen Hatch La SEV TN13 247 H9
Hitchens Cl HHW HP1 35 J5
Hitches Yd WARE * SG12 26 C2
Hitchin Cl HARH RM3 105 K5
Hitchings Wy REIG RH2 275 K4
Hitherbaulk WGCE AL7 22 G7
Hitherbroom Rd HYS/HAR UB3 133 H10
Hitherbury Cl GUW GU2 267 P3
Hither Farm Rd BKHTH/KID SE3 161 P9
Hitherfield Rd BCTR RM8 123 P7
STRHM/NOR SW16 180 G5
Hither Green La LEW SE13 183 H1
Hither Meadow CFSP/GDCR * SL9 90 B9
Hithermoor Rd
STWL/WRAY TW19 173 K2
Hitherway WGCW AL8 22 G1
Hitherwell Dr KTN/HRWW/W HA3 94 C9
Hitherwood Cl HCH RM12 125 L9
REDH RH1 257 N8
Hitherwood Dr DUL SE21 181 N7
Hive La GVW DA11 189 N1
Hive Rd BUSH WD23 94 C3
Hiving's Hl CSHM HP5 50 F4
Hivings Pk CSHM HP5 50 G4
Hoadly Rd STRHM/NOR SW16 180 E6
Hobart Cl TRDG/WHET N20 97 P3
YEAD UB4 133 L6
Hobart Dr YEAD UB4 133 L6
Hobart Gdns THHTH CR7 203 L3
Hobart La YEAD UB4 133 L6
Hobart Pl BGVA SW1W 16 E4
RCHPK/HAM TW10 177 L3
Hobart Rd BARK/HLT IG6 102 F10
DAGW RM9 123 N9
TIL RM18 168 D7
WPK KT4 200 E10
YEAD UB4 133 L6
Hobart Wk STALW/RED AL3 38 E2
Hobbayne Rd HNWL W7 134 C8
Hobbes Wk PUT/ROE SW15 178 E1
Hobbs Cl BF/WBF KT14 215 L9
CHES/WCR EN8 62 C5
STALE/WH AL4 39 K7
Hobbs Cross Rd EPP CM16 65 M10
HLWE CM17 30 A8
Hobbs Gn EFNCH N2 117 M1
Hobbs Hill Rd HHS/BOV HP3 35 P10
Hobbs Pl IS N1 7 J6
Hobbs Place Est IS N1 7 J7
Hobbs Rd WNWD SE27 181 K7
Hobbs Wy WGCW AL8 22 F6
Hobby Horse Cl CHESW EN7 61 L2
Hobday St POP/IOD E14 140 G8
Hoblands End CHST BR7 185 H9
Hobletts Rd HHNE HP2 36 A5
Hobsons Cl HOD EN11 26 E10
Hobsons Pl WCHPL E1 13 N3
Hobtoe Rd HLW CM20 28 D10
Hobury St WBPTN SW10 15 K10
Hockenden La SWLY BR8 208 B3
Hocken Md CRAWE RH10 284 E5
Hockering Gdns
WOKS/MYFD GU22 232 E4
Hockering Rd WOKS/MYFD GU22 232 D4
Hocker St BETH * E2 7 L10
Hockford Cl RGUW GU3 248 G2
Hocklands WGCE AL7 23 M4
Hockley Av EHAM E6 142 B4
Hockley Dr GPK RM2 105 J10
Hockley La SLN SL2 129 N2
Hockley Ms BARK IG11 143 H4
Hocroft Av CRICK NW2 117 J8
Hocroft Rd CRICK NW2 117 J9
Hocroft Wk CRICK NW2 117 J8
Hodder Dr GFD/PVL UB6 134 E4
Hoddesdon Rd BELV DA17 164 B4
WARE SG12 27 H7
Hodds Wood Rd CSHM HP5 51 H9
Hodford Rd GLDGN NW11 117 J6
Hodge La WDSR * SL4 149 H10
Hodgemoor Vw CSTG HP8 89 L4
Hodges Wy WATW WD18 73 H10
Hodgkin Cl CRAWE RH10 284 C8
Hodgkins Cl THMD SE28 143 N9
Hodgson Gdns GU GU1 250 D7
Hodings Rd HLW CM20 28 E10
Hodister Cl CMBW SE5 159 K6
Hodson Cl RYLN/HDSTN HA2 113 N8
Hodson Crs STMC/STPC BR5 207 N6
Hodson Pl WAB * EN9 80 F4
Hoebrook Cl WOKS/MYFD GU22 232 A7
Hoecroft WAB EN9 45 L8
Hoe La ABR/ST RM4 83 L7
EN EN1 80 A4
SHGR GU5 270 F9
WAB EN9 45 L8
WARE SG12 26 C5
Hoe Meadow BEAC HP9 88 B7
Hoestock Rd SBW CM21 29 N1
Hoe St WALTH E17 120 F2
The Hoe OXHEY WD19 93 L3
Hoffman Sq IS * N1 7 H9
Hogan Ms BAY/PAD W2 9 L3
Hogarth Av ASHF TW15 174 D9
BRW CM14 107 K4

Hogarth Cl CAN/RD E16 142 A7
EA W5 135 K7
SL SL1 128 D9
Hogarth Crs CROY/NA CR0 203 K7
WIM/MER SW19 201 N1
Hogarth Gdns HEST TW5 153 P6
Hogarth Hl GLDGN NW11 117 J2
Hogarth Pl ECT * SW5 14 G6
Hogarth Reach LOU IG10 82 C9
Hogarth Rd BCTR RM8 123 L10
CDH/CHF RM16 147 M10
CRAWE RH10 284 A10
ECT SW5 14 G6
EDGW HA8 95 M10
Hogarth Ter CHSWK * W4 156 B5
Hogarth Wy HPTN TW12 198 B1
Hogback Wood Rd BEAC HP9 88 A7
Hogfair La SL SL1 128 B6
Hogg End La STALW/RED AL3 37 H4
Hogg La BORE WD6 74 F8
CDH/CHF RM16 167 M2
Hog Hill Rd CRW RM5 104 A8
Hog La CSHM HP5 32 G8
Hogpits Bottom HHS/BOV HP3 52 D8
Hogscross La COUL/CHIP CR5 240 A8
Hogsdell La HERT/BAY SG13 26 A7
Hogshead Pas WAP * E1W 140 A9
Hogshill La COB KT11 217 K10
Hogsmill Wy HOR/WEW KT19 219 P2
Hogtrough Hl BH/WHM TN16 245 K8
Hogtrough La OXTED RH8 260 G4
REDH RH1 276 E1
Holbeach Gdns BFN/LL DA15 185 H2
Holbeach Rd CAT SE6 182 F3
Holbeck La CHESW EN7 61 N2
Holbeck Rw PECK SE15 159 P6
Holbein Ga NTHWD HA6 92 F6
Holbein Ms BGVA SW1W 16 C7
Holbein Pl BGVA SW1W 16 C6
Holbein Rd CRAWE RH10 284 A10
Holberton Gdns WLSDN NW10 136 E5
Holborn HCIRC EC1N 12 A4
Holborn Circ HCIRC EC1N 12 B4
Holborn Cl STALE/WH AL4 39 J1
Holborn Pl HHOL WC1V 11 N4
Holborn Rd PLSTW E13 141 N7
Holborn Viad STBT EC1A 12 C5
Holborn Wy MTCM CR4 202 A2
Holbreck Pl WOKS/MYFD GU22 232 C4
Holbrook Cl EN EN1 79 N5
Holbrooke Ct HOLWY N7 118 F8
Holbrook La CHST BR7 184 G10
Holbrook Meadow EGH TW20 172 F9
Holbrook Rd SRTFD E15 141 L4
Holbrook Wy HAYES BR2 206 C6
Holburne Cl BKHTH/KID SE3 161 P7
Holburne Gdns BKHTH/KID SE3 162 A7
Holburne Rd BKHTH/KID SE3 161 P7
Holcombe Cl BH/WHM TN16 262 G2
Holcombe Hl MLHL NW7 96 D4
Holcombe Rd TOTM N17 119 N1
Holcombe St HMSMTH W6 156 E4
Holcon Ct REDH RH1 258 B7
Holcote Cl BELV DA17 163 P2
Holcroft Rd HOM E9 140 B2
Holdbrook Wy HARH RM3 105 N10
Holden Av CDALE/KGS NW9 115 P6
NFNCH/WDSP N12 97 L6
Holdenby Rd BROCKY SE4 182 D1
Holden Cl BCTR RM8 123 L8
HERT/BAY SG13 25 M4
Holden Gdns BRW CM14 107 J6
Holdenhurst Av FNCH N3 97 L8
Holden Rd NFNCH/WDSP N12 97 L5
Holden St BTSEA SW11 158 B8
Holden Wy UPMR RM14 126 C6
Holdernesse Rd ISLW TW7 154 F7
TOOT SW17 180 A6
Holderness Wy WNWD SE27 181 J8
Holder Rd CRAWE RH10 284 C10
Holders Hill Av HDN NW4 96 G10
Holders Hill Crs HDN NW4 116 G1
Holders Hill Dr HDN NW4 96 G10
Holders Hill Gdns HDN NW4 96 G10
Holders Hill Pde HDN * NW4 97 H9
Holders Hill Rd HDN NW4 96 G10
The Holdings BRKMPK AL9 40 G2
Holecroft WAB EN9 63 K10
Hole Hl DORK RH4 272 A2
Holford Ms FSBYW * WC1X 5 N9
Holford Rd GU GU1 250 F10
HAMP NW3 117 M8
TIL RM18 168 G3
Holford St FSBYW WC1X 6 A9
Holford Yd FSBYW * WC1X 6 A8
Holgate Av BTSEA SW11 157 N9
Holgate Rd DAGE RM10 124 B10
Holgate St CHARL SE7 162 A2
Holland Av BELMT SM2 221 K4
RYNPK SW20 200 C1
Holland Cl BAR EN5 97 N1
HAYES BR2 205 L9
REDH RH1 258 A10
ROMW/RG RM7 124 D3
STAN HA7 94 G6
Holland Crs OXTED RH8 261 M9
Holland Dr FSTH SE23 182 D6
Holland Gdns EGH TW20 195 J2
GSTN WD25 73 K1
WKENS W14 14 B3
Holland Gv BRXN/ST SW9 159 H6
Holland La OXTED RH8 261 M9
Holland Pk NTGHL W11 8 B10
Holland Park Av GDMY/SEVK IG3 123 H4
NTGHL W11 14 A1
Holland Park Gdns WKENS W14 8 A10
Holland Park Ms NTGHL W11 8 C10
Holland Park Rd WKENS W14 14 C4
Holland Park Ter NTGHL * W11 8 B10
Holland Pas IS N1 6 E5
Holland Pl KENS * W8 14 G1
Holland Rd ALP/SUD HA0 135 J1
EHAM E6 142 C3
OXTED RH8 261 M9
SNWD SE25 203 P5
SRTFD E15 141 K5
WKENS W14 14 C4
WLSDN NW10 136 D3
Hollands Cl GVE DA12 191 P8
Holland's Cft WARE SG12 28 A2
The Hollands WOKS/MYFD GU22 232 B4
WPK KT4 200 C8
Holland St KENS W8 14 F2
STHWK SE1 12 D9
Holland Villas Rd WKENS W14 14 A1
Holland Wk STAN HA7 94 F6
Holland Wy HAYES BR2 205 L9
Hollar Rd STNW/STAM N16 119 N8
Hollen St SOHO/CST W1F 11 H6
Holles Cl HPTN TW12 175 P9
Holles St CAVSQ/HST W1G 10 F5
Holley Rd ACT W3 156 B1
Hollickwood Av
NFNCH/WDSP N12 98 A7
Holliday Sq BTSEA SW11 157 N9
Holliday St BERK HP4 34 A5
Hollidge Wy DAGE RM10 144 C1
Holliers Wy HAT AL10 40 D4
Hollies Av BF/WBF KT14 215 J9
BFN/LL DA15 185 J5
Hollies Cl STRHM/NOR SW16 181 H9
TWK TW1 176 E5
Hollies Ct ADL/WDHM KT15 215 M2
Hollies End MLHL NW7 96 E6
Hollies Rd EA W5 155 H3
The Hollies ADL/WDHM * KT15 215 M2
BAR * EN5 76 D9
GVE DA12 190 G9
HART DA3 211 P3
HHS/BOV HP3 52 D5
KTN/HRWW/W HA3 114 F2
RKW/CH/CXG WD3 90 F1
STAL * AL1 38 D5
WOKN/KNAP * GU21 231 J3
Hollies Wy BAL * SW12 180 B3
POTB/CUF EN6 59 M7
Holligrave Rd BMLY BR1 205 M1
Hollin Ct CRAWE RH10 283 P4
Hollingbourne Av BXLYHN DA7 164 A7
Hollingbourne Gdns WEA W13 134 G7
Hollingbourne Rd HNHL SE24 181 K1
Hollingsworth Rd SAND/SEL CR2 224 A3
Hollington Crs NWMAL KT3 200 C6
Hollington Rd EHAM E6 142 C5
TOTM N17 99 P10
Hollingworth Cl
E/WMO/HCT KT8 197 N4
Hollingworth Rd
STMC/STPC BR5 206 E7
Hollingworth Wy BH/WHM TN16 262 G2
Hollis Pl GRAYS RM17 167 M2
Hollis Rw REDH * RH1 276 A2
Hollman Gdns
STRHM/NOR SW16 181 J9
Holloway Cl WDR/YW UB7 151 P4
Holloway Dr VW GU25 194 B4
Holloway Hl CHERT KT16 194 F10
Holloway La RKW/CH/CXG WD3 70 E4
WDR/YW UB7 152 B3
Holloway Rd ARCH N19 118 E7
EHAM E6 142 C5
WAN E11 121 J8
Holloways La BRKMPK AL9 40 G9
Holloway St HSLW TW3 154 A9
Hollow Cl GUW GU2 267 N1
Hollowfield Av GRAYS RM17 168 A3
Hollow Hill La IVER SL0 130 E9
Hollow La RDKG RH5 271 L7
VW GU25 193 P3
The Hollow CRAWW RH11 283 J8
WFD IG8 101 L5
Hollow Wy CSHM HP5 50 D6
Hollow Way La AMS HP6 69 K1
Holly Av ADL/WDHM KT15 215 K6
STAN HA7 95 K10
WOT/HER KT12 197 L8
Hollybank CHOB/PIR GU24 212 E9
Holly Bank MUSWH * N10 118 D2
Hollybank Cl HPTN TW12 175 P8
Hollybank Rd BF/WBF KT14 215 K10
Holly Bank Rd
WOKS/MYFD GU22 231 N7
Hollybrake Cl CHST BR7 184 G10
Hollybush Av LCOL/BKTW AL2 37 P10
Hollybush Cl BERK HP4 34 G2
CRAWE RH10 283 P6
OXHEY WD19 93 K1
SEV TN13 247 K10
WAN E11 121 M3
Hollybush Gdns BETH E2 140 A5
Hollybush Hl SLN SL2 129 N2
WAN E11 121 L4
Holly Bush La HPTN TW12 175 N10
SEV TN13 247 K10
Hollybush La AMS HP6 69 J3
BRKMPK AL9 23 J9
DEN/HRF UB9 110 F6
HHW HP1 35 J5
IVER SL0 130 E8
ORP BR6 228 B3
WGCE AL7 23 H8
Hollybush Pl BETH E2 140 A5
Hollybush Rd CRAWE RH10 283 P6
CSHM HP5 50 F3
GVE DA12 190 F5
KUTN/CMB KT2 177 K8
Hollybush Rw TRING * HP23 32 C1
Hollybush St PLSTW E13 141 N5
Hollybush Ter NRWD * SE19 181 M9
Holly Bush V HAMP * NW3 117 M9
Hollybush Wy CHESW EN7 61 P4
Holly Cl BECK BR3 205 H4
BKHH IG9 102 A4
CHERT KT16 193 M10
CRAWE RH10 284 B5
EGH TW20 171 N9
FELT TW13 175 M8
HAT AL10 40 C5
SLN SL2 109 H9
WLSDN NW10 136 B2
WOKN/KNAP GU21 231 N5
Hollycombe EGH TW20 172 A7
Holly Crs BECK BR3 204 E5
WDSR SL4 148 C8
WFD IG8 101 J8
Holly Cft HERT/WAS SG14 24 G4
Hollycroft Av HAMP NW3 117 K8
WBLY HA9 115 K7
Hollycroft Cl SAND/SEL CR2 223 M2
WDR/YW UB7 152 B5
Hollycroft Gdns WDR/YW UB7 152 B5
Hollycross Rd WARE SG12 26 E3
Hollydale Cl NTHLT UB5 114 A10
Hollydale Dr HAYES BR2 206 C10
Hollydale Rd PECK SE15 160 B8
Holly Dell HERT/BAY SG13 25 K7
Hollydown Wy WAN E11 121 J8
Holly Dr BERK HP4 34 A6
CHING E4 100 G1
POTB/CUF EN6 59 L9
SOCK/AV RM15 147 J6
WDSR SL4 171 K1
Holly Farm Rd NWDGN UB2 153 M4
Hollyfield HAT AL10 40 D7
Holly Fld HLWW/ROY CM19 46 F4
Hollyfield Av FBAR/BDGN N11 98 A6
Hollyfield Rd BRYLDS KT5 199 L7
Hollyfields BROX EN10 62 D2
Holly Gdns WDR/YW UB7 152 A1
Hollygrove BUSH WD23 94 C1
Holly Gv CDALE/KGS NW9 115 P5
PECK SE15 159 N8
PIN HA5 93 M9
Hollygrove Cl HSLWW TW4 153 N10
Holly Hedge Rd COB KT11 217 J10
Holly Hedges La HHS/BOV HP3 52 F6
Holly Hedge Ter LEW SE13 183 H1
Holly Hl HAMP NW3 117 M9
WCHMH N21 78 G10
Holly Hill Dr BNSTD SM7 239 K3
Holly Hill Rd BELV DA17 164 C4
Holly Hock CHOB/PIR GU24 230 F1
Holly Hough
KWD/TDW/WH KT20 255 N6
Holly La BNSTD SM7 239 N4
RGUW GU3 249 J5
Holly La East BNSTD SM7 239 L2
Holly La West BNSTD SM7 239 L3
Holly Lea RGUE GU4 250 A4
Holly Ldg WOKN/KNAP * GU21 231 K3
Holly Lodge Gdns HGT N6 118 B7
Hollymead CAR SM5 202 A10
Hollymead Rd COUL/CHIP CR5 240 B4
Holly Ms WBPTN SW10 15 K8
Hollymoor La HOR/WEW KT19 220 A6
Holly Mt HAMP * NW3 117 M9
Hollymount Cl GNWCH SE10 161 H7
Holly Pde COB * KT11 217 J10
Holly Pk FNCH N3 117 J1
FSBYPK N4 118 F5
Holly Park Gdns FNCH N3 117 K1
Holly Park Rd FBAR/BDGN N11 98 B6
HNWL W7 134 E10
Holly Rd CHSWK * W4 156 A3
DART DA1 187 L4
HPTN TW12 176 B9
HSLW TW3 154 A10
ORP BR6 227 K4
PEND EN3 80 C2
REIG RH2 275 L2
TWK TW1 176 F4
Holly St HACK E8 7 M2
Hollytree Av SWLY BR8 208 F2
Hollytree Cl CFSP/GDCR SL9 90 B6
CSHM HP5 51 N7
WIM/MER SW19 178 G4
Holly Tree Cl HHNE HP2 36 C6
Hollytree Pde SCUP * DA14 185 M8
Holly Tree Rd CTHM CR3 241 M8
Hollyview Cl HDN NW4 116 D4
Holly Vls HMSMTH * W6 156 E2
Holly Wk HAMP NW3 117 M9
HARP AL5 20 C2
WDSR SL4 170 D7
WGCW AL8 22 F1
Holly Wy MTCM CR4 202 E4
Hollywood Gdns YEAD UB4 133 J8
Hollywood Ms WBPTN SW10 15 J9
Hollywood Rd CHING E4 100 D6
WBPTN SW10 15 J9
Hollywoods CROY/NA CR0 224 E5
Hollywood Wy ERITH DA8 165 J7
WFD IG8 101 J8
Holman Ct EW * KT17 220 D5
Holman Rd BTSEA SW11 157 N8
HOR/WEW KT19 219 P2
Holmbank Dr SHPTN TW17 196 F4
Holmbridge Gdns PEND EN3 80 C8
Holmbrook Dr HDN NW4 116 G3
Holmbury Cl BUSH WD23 94 D3
CRAWW RH11 283 M9
Holmbury Ct WIM/MER SW19 179 P10
Holmbury Dr RDKG RH5 273 H5
Holmbury Gdns HYS/HAR UB3 132 G10
Holmbury Gv CROY/NA CR0 224 E4
Holmbury Mnr SCUP * DA14 185 K7
Holmbury Pk CHST BR7 184 B10
Holmbury Vw CLPT E5 120 A6
Holmbush Rd PUT/ROE SW15 179 H2
Holm Cl ADL/WDHM KT15 215 H8
Holmcote Gdns HBRY N5 119 K10
Holmcroft CRAWE RH10 283 P8
KWD/TDW/WH KT20 256 E1
Holmcroft Wy HAYES BR2 206 C5
Holmdale SLN SL2 129 P9
Holmdale Cl BORE WD6 75 L6
Holmdale Gdns HDN NW4 116 G3
Holmdale Rd CHST BR7 184 F8
KIL/WHAMP NW6 117 K10
Holmdale Ter SEVS/STOTM N15 119 M4
Holmdene Av HNHL SE24 181 K1
MLHL NW7 96 D7
RYLN/HDSTN HA2 114 A1
Holmdene Cl BECK BR3 205 H2
Holmdene Ct BMLY BR1 206 B3
Holmead Rd FUL/PGN SW6 157 L6
Holmebury Cl BUSH * WD23 94 D3
Holme Cl CHES/WCR EN8 62 D7
HAT AL10 40 C7
Holme Lacey Rd LEE/GVPK SE12 183 L2
Holme Lea GSTN WD25 55 K10
Holme Pk BORE WD6 75 L6
Holme Pl HHNE HP2 36 D5
Holme Rd EHAM E6 142 B3
EMPK RM11 125 P6
HAT AL10 40 C1
Holmes Av MLHL NW7 97 H6
WALTH E17 120 E1
Holmes Cl ASC SL5 192 B6
WOKS/MYFD GU22 232 B7
Holmesdale CHES/WCR EN8 80 B1
Holmesdale Av
MORT/ESHN SW14 155 N9
Holmesdale Cl GU GU1 250 E9
SNWD SE25 203 N3
Holmesdale Hl EYN DA4 210 C1
Holmesdale Pk REDH * RH1 258 G10
Holmesdale Rd CROY/NA CR0 203 L5
EYN DA4 210 C1
HGT N6 118 C5
RCH/KEW TW9 155 L7
RDKG RH5 272 G6
REDH RH1 276 G2
REIG RH2 257 L9
SNWD SE25 203 M4
TEDD TW11 177 H10
WELL DA16 163 N8
Holmesdale Ter RDKG * RH5 272 G6
Holmesley Rd BROCKY SE4 182 D2
Holmes Meadow EPP CM16 46 E7
Holmes Rd KTTN NW5 4 E1
TWK TW1 176 E5
WIM/MER SW19 179 M10
Holmes Ter STHWK SE1 12 A10
Holmethorpe Av REDH RH1 258 C7
Holme Wy STAN HA7 94 E7
Holmewood Gdns
BRXS/STRHM SW2 180 G3
Holmewood Rd
BRXS/STRHM SW2 180 F3
SNWD SE25 203 M3
Holmfield Av HDN NW4 116 G3
Holm Gv HGDN/ICK UB10 132 B2
Holmhurst Rd BELV DA17 164 C4
Holmlea Rd DTCH/LGLY SL3 150 A7
Holmlea Wk DTCH/LGLY SL3 149 P7
Holmleigh Av DART DA1 165 K10
Holmleigh Rd STNW/STAM N16 119 M6
Holm Oak Cl WAND/EARL SW18 179 J2
Holm Oak Pk WATW * WD18 73 H9
Holmsdale Cl IVER SL0 131 J8
Holmsdale Gv BXLYHN DA7 164 F8
Holmshaw Cl SYD SE26 182 D7
Holmshill La BORE WD6 76 C3
Holmside Ri OXHEY WD19 93 J4
Holmside Rd BAL SW12 180 B2
Holmsley Cl NWMAL KT3 200 C6
Holmstall Av EDGW HA8 95 P10
Holmstall Pde EDGW * HA8 95 P10
Holmwood Av BRWN CM15 87 M9
SAND/SEL CR2 223 N9
Holmwood Cl ADL/WDHM KT15 215 K2
BELMT SM2 220 G5
EHSLY KT24 252 F4
NTHLT UB5 134 A1
RYLN/HDSTN HA2 114 B1
Holmwood Gdns FNCH N3 97 K10
WLGTN SM6 222 C3
Holmwood Gv MLHL NW7 96 A6
Holmwood Rd BELMT SM2 220 F5
CHSGTN KT9 219 K2
GDMY/SEVK IG3 123 H7
PEND EN3 80 C2
Holmwood View Rd RDKG RH5 272 G8
Holne Cha EFNCH N2 117 M4
MRDN SM4 201 K6
Holness Rd SRTFD E15 141 L1
Holroyd Rd ESH/CLAY KT10 218 E5
PUT/ROE SW15 156 F10
Holsart Cl KWD/TDW/WH KT20 238 E8
Holstein Av WEY KT13 216 B1
Holstock Rd IL IG1 122 F7
Holsworth Cl RYLN/HDSTN HA2 114 B3
Holsworthy Sq FSBYW WC1X 11 P2
Holsworthy Wy CHSGTN KT9 219 H2
Holt Cl BORE WD6 75 L8
CHIG IG7 103 J6
MUSWH N10 118 B2
THMD SE28 143 L9
Holton St WCHPL E1 140 C6
Holt Rd ALP/SUD HA0 114 G8
CAN/RD E16 142 B10
HARH RM3 105 M8
Holtsmere Cl GSTN WD25 73 K1
The Holt BARK/HLT IG6 102 F7
HHNE HP2 35 P7
MRDN * SM4 201 K4
WGCE AL7 23 N6
WLGTN SM6 222 D1
Holt Wy CHIG IG7 103 J6
Holtwhite Av ENC/FH EN2 79 K6
Holtwhite's Hl ENC/FH EN2 79 J5
Holtwood Rd LHD/OX KT22 218 B9
Holtye Wk CRAWE RH10 284 B9
Holwell Hyde WGCE AL7 23 M7
Holwell Hyde La BRKMPK AL9 23 M9
Holwell La BRKMPK AL9 23 P10
Holwell Pl PIN HA5 113 M2
Holwell Rd WGCE AL7 23 H6
Holwood Cl WOT/HER KT12 197 K9
Holwood Park Av ORP BR6 226 C1
Holwood Pl CLAP SW4 158 E10
Holybourne Av PUT/ROE SW15 178 D3
Holy Cross Hl BROX EN10 43 P9
Holyfield Rd WAB EN9 63 H5
Holyhead Cl BOW E3 140 F5
Holyoake Av WOKN/KNAP GU21 231 P3
Holyoake Ct BERM/RHTH SE16 160 D1
Holyoake Crs WOKN/KNAP GU21 231 P3
Holyoake Ter SEV TN13 247 H10
Holyoake Wk EA W5 135 H6
EFNCH N2 117 M1
Holyoak Rd LBTH SE11 18 C5
Holyport Rd FUL/PGN SW6 156 F6
Holyrood Av RYLN/HDSTN HA2 113 M9
Holyrood Crs STAL AL1 38 C10
Holyrood Gdns CDH/CHF RM16 168 F3
EDGW HA8 95 N10
Holyrood Rd BAR EN5 77 M10
Holyrood St STHWK SE1 13 J10
Holywell Cl BERM/RHTH * SE16 160 A4
BKHTH/KID SE3 161 M5
STWL/WRAY TW19 173 P4
Holywell Hl STAL AL1 38 C7
Holywell La SDTCH EC2A 13 K1
Holywell Rd WATW WD18 73 H9
Holywell Rw SDTCH EC2A 13 J2
Holywell Wy STWL/WRAY TW19 173 P4
Home Cl BROX EN10 44 E10
CAR SM5 202 A9
CRAWE RH10 284 D5
HLW CM20 47 J1
LHD/OX KT22 236 C7
NTHLT UB5 133 N5
VW GU25 194 A6
Home Ct FELT * TW13 175 H4
SURB * KT6 199 J5
Homecroft Gdns LOU IG10 82 E8
Homecroft Rd SYD SE26 182 B8
WDGN N22 99 J9
Homedean Rd SEV TN13 246 D8
Home Farm Cl
BRKHM/BTCW RH3 274 B1
CHERT KT16 214 D4
EPSOM KT18 238 G3
ESH/CLAY KT10 218 A3
SHPTN TW17 196 F4
THDIT KT7 198 E7
Home Farm Ct CSTG * HP8 89 M4
Home Farm Gdns
WOT/HER KT12 197 K9
Home Farm Rd BERK HP4 33 J2
RBRW/HUT CM13 107 K9
RKW/CH/CXG WD3 92 B5
Homefarm Rd HNWL W7 134 D8
Home Farm Wy DTCH/LGLY SL3 129 P3
Homefield BERK HP4 34 E2
HHS/BOV HP3 52 E4
WAB EN9 63 M8
Homefield Av GNTH/NBYPK IG2 123 H3
Homefield Cl ADL/WDHM KT15 215 H8
EPP CM16 65 K5
HORL RH6 280 C3
LHD/OX KT22 237 H7
STMC/STPC BR5 207 L4
SWLY BR8 208 G3
WLSDN NW10 135 P1
YEAD UB4 133 L6
Homefield Gdns EFNCH N2 117 N1
KWD/TDW/WH KT20 238 F6
WIM/MER SW19 201 M2
Homefield Ms BECK * BR3 204 F1
Homefield Pk SUT SM1 221 L3
Homefield Ri ORP BR6 207 K8
Homefield Rd ALP/SUD HA0 114 F9
BMLY BR1 205 P1
BUSH WD23 73 P9
CHSWK W4 156 C3
COUL/CHIP CR5 241 J6
EDGW HA8 96 A7
HHNE HP2 36 B6
RAD WD7 74 E3
RKW/CH/CXG WD3 70 G8
SEV TN13 246 F8
WARE SG12 26 D1
WARL CR6 242 B5
WIM/MER SW19 179 H9
WOT/HER KT12 197 N7
Homefield St IS * N1 7 J8
The Homefield MRDN * SM4 201 K4
Home Gdns DAGE RM10 124 D8
DART DA1 187 M2
Home Hl SWLY BR8 186 G10
Homeland Dr BELMT SM2 221 L5
Homelands LHD/OX KT22 237 H7
Homelands Dr NRWD SE19 181 M10
Home Lea ORP BR6 227 J2
Homeleigh Ct CHES/WCR EN8 62 A6
Homeleigh Rd PECK SE15 182 C1
Home Ley WGCE AL7 23 H5
Home Md STAN HA7 95 H9
Home Mead Cl GVE DA12 190 E3
Home Meadow BNSTD SM7 239 K2
SLN SL2 129 H4
WGCE AL7 23 H5
Homemead Rd CROY/NA CR0 202 D6
HAYES BR2 206 C5
Home Pk OXTED RH8 261 M7
Home Park Ct KUT * KT1 199 J4
Home Park Mill Link Rd
KGLGY WD4 54 C7
Home Park Rd WIM/MER SW19 179 J7
Home Park Wk SURB KT6 199 J4
Homer Cl BXLYHN DA7 164 D7
Homer Dr POP/IOD E14 160 F3
Homerfield WGCW AL8 22 F5
Home Rd BTSEA SW11 157 P8
Homer Rd CROY/NA CR0 204 C6
HOM E9 140 D1
Homer Rw CAMTN NW1 9 P4
Homersham Rd KUT KT1 199 M2
Homers Rd WDSR SL4 148 C7
Homer St CAMTN NW1 9 P4
Homerswood La WLYN AL6 22 D1
Homerton Gv HOM E9 120 C10
Homerton High St HOM E9 120 C10
Homerton Rd HOM E9 120 E10
Homerton Rw HOM E9 120 B10
Homerton Ter HOM E9 140 B1
Homesdale Cl WAN E11 121 M3
Homesdale Rd CTHM CR3 241 L9
HAYES BR2 205 P4
ORP BR6 207 H7
Homesfield GLDGN NW11 117 K3
Homestall GUW GU2 249 J10
Homestall Rd EDUL SE22 182 B1
Homestead Cl LCOL/BKTW AL2 56 B3
Homestead Gdns ESH/CLAY KT10 218 D2
Homestead La WGCE AL7 23 J8
Homestead Paddock
STHGT/OAK N14 78 C9
Homestead Pk CRICK NW2 116 C8
Homestead Rd BCTR RM8 124 A7
CTHM CR3 241 L9
FUL/PGN SW6 157 J6
HAT AL10 40 E2
ORP BR6 227 L4
RKW/CH/CXG WD3 91 N1
STA TW18 173 L9
The Homestead DART DA1 187 K2
Homestead Wy CROY/NA CR0 225 H7
Homewaters Av SUN TW16 196 G1
Homeway HARH RM3 106 A7
Home Wy RKW/CH/CXG WD3 91 J2
Homewillow Cl WCHMH N21 79 J10
Homewood DTCH/LGLY SL3 130 A8
Homewood Av POTB/CUF EN6 60 F3
Homewood Cl HPTN TW12 175 N9
Homewood Crs CHST BR7 185 H9
Homewood Gdns SNWD * SE25 203 M5
Homewood La POTB/CUF EN6 60 D3
Homewood Rd STAL AL1 38 G3
Honduras St FSBYE EC1V 12 E1
Honeybourne Rd
KIL/WHAMP NW6 117 L10
Honeybourne Wy
STMC/STPC BR5 206 F8
Honey Brook WAB EN9 63 K9
Honeybrook Rd BAL SW12 180 D3
Honey Cl BRWN CM15 87 J1
DAGE RM10 144 D1
Honeycrock La REDH RH1 276 B7
Honeycroft LOU IG10 82 D8
WGCW AL8 22 F6
Honeycroft Dr STALE/WH AL4 39 H9
Honeycroft Hl HGDN/ICK UB10 131 P2
Honeycross Rd HHW HP1 35 H7
Honeyden Rd SCUP DA14 185 P9
Honey Hl HGDN/ICK UB10 132 A2
Honey La CHES/WCR EN8 62 E10
WAB EN9 63 L10
Honeyman Cl CRICK NW2 136 G2
Honeymeade HLW CM20 29 M4
Honeypot Cl KTN/HRWW/W HA3 115 L2
Honeypot La BRW CM14 106 F7
STAN HA7 95 J9
Honeypots Rd
WOKS/MYFD GU22 232 A8
Honeysett Rd TOTM N17 99 N10
Honeysuckle Bottom
EHSLY KT24 252 F10
Honeysuckle Cl BRWN CM15 86 G9
HARH RM3 105 K7
HERT/BAY SG13 25 P5
HORL RH6 280 D3
IVER SL0 130 F8
STHL UB1 133 M9
Honeysuckle Fld CSHM HP5 51 H5
Honeysuckle Gdns
CROY/NA CR0 204 C7
HAT AL10 40 E5
Honeysuckle La CRAWW RH11 283 M4
Honeywell Rd BTSEA SW11 179 P2
Honeywood Cl POTB/CUF EN6 59 N9
Honeywood Rd ISLW * TW7 154 F10
WLSDN NW10 136 C4
Honeywood Wk CAR SM5 222 A1
Honister Cl STAN HA7 94 G9
Honister Gdns STAN HA7 94 C8
Honister Hts PUR/KEN CR8 223 L10

Honister Pl STAN HA7 94 G9
Honiton Gdns PECK * SE15 160 B8
Honiton Rd KIL/WHAMP NW6 2 C7
ROMW/RG RM7 124 E4
WELL DA16 163 J8
Honley Rd CAT SE6 182 G3
Honnor Gdns ISLW TW7 154 C8
Honnor Rd STA TW18 173 N10
Honor Oak Pk FSTH SE23 182 B3
Honor Oak Ri FSTH SE23 182 B2
Honor Oak Rd FSTH SE23 182 B4
Honours Md HHW * HP1 52 D3
Hood Av MORT/ESHN SW14 177 P1
STHGT/OAK N14 78 C10
STMC/STPC BR5 207 L5
Hood Cl CROY/NA CR0 203 J8
Hoodcote Gdns WCHMH N21 99 J1
Hood Rd RAIN RM13 144 F3
RYNPK SW20 178 C10
Hood Wk ROMW/RG RM7 104 C9
Hook End Rd BRWN CM15 86 G1
Hooke Rd EHSLY KT24 252 G1
Hooker's Rd WALTH E17 120 C1
Hook Farm Rd HAYES BR2 206 A5
Hook Fld HLWS CM18 47 H3
Hookfield HOR/WEW KT19 219 P9
Hookfields GVW DA11 190 B6
Hook Ga EN EN1 80 A3
Hook Green La RDART DA2 186 G6
Hook Green Rd MEO DA13 189 J10
Hook Heath Av
WOKS/MYFD GU22 231 N5
Hook Heath Gdns
WOKS/MYFD GU22 231 L7
Hook Heath Rd
WOKS/MYFD GU22 231 P7
Hook Hl SAND/SEL CR2 223 M6
Hook Hill La WOKS/MYFD GU22 231 N7
Hook Hill Pk WOKS/MYFD GU22 231 N7
Hooking Gn RYLN/HDSTN HA2 114 A3
Hook La ABR/ST RM4 84 A10
CHOB/PIR GU24 212 B9
POTB/CUF EN6 60 A8
RGUW GU3 266 C7
SHGR GU5 270 C7
WELL DA16 163 J10
Hook Mill La CHOB/PIR GU24 212 C5
Hook Ri North SURB KT6 199 L10
Hook Ri South CHSGTN KT9 199 L10
Hook Rd CHSGTN KT9 219 J2
HOR/WEW KT19 219 P6
SURB KT6 199 K9
Hooks Hall Dr DAGE RM10 124 D3
Hookstone La CHOB/PIR GU24 212 E7
Hookstone Wy WFD IG8 102 A8
The Hook BAR EN5 77 N10
Hook Underpass
(Kingston By-Pass)
SURB KT6 199 J10
Hook Wk EDGW HA8 95 P7
Hookwood Cnr OXTED RH8 261 N4
Hookwood Rd ORP BR6 227 M7
Hooley La REDH RH1 276 A1
Hooper Rd CAN/RD E16 141 M8
Hooper's Ms ACT W3 135 P10
Hooper St WCHPL E1 13 N6
Hoop La GLDGN NW11 117 J5
The Hoo HLWE CM17 29 M6
Hop Ct ALP/SUD * HA0 135 H1
Hope Cl BTFD TW8 155 K4
CHDH RM6 123 N2
IS N1 6 F1
LEE/GVPK SE12 183 N6
SUT SM1 221 M2
Hopedale Rd CHARL SE7 161 N5
Hopefield Av KIL/WHAMP NW6 2 B7
Hope Gn GSTN WD25 55 H9
Hope Pk BMLY BR1 183 L10
Hope Rd SWCM DA10 189 L2
Hopes Cl HEST TW5 153 P5
Hope St BTSEA SW11 157 N9
Hope Ter WTHK * RM20 167 J4
Hopetown St WCHPL * E1 13 M4
Hopewell Dr GVE DA12 191 J8
Hopewell St CMBW SE5 159 L6
Hopfield Av BF/WBF KT14 215 P8
Hopgarden La SEV TN13 265 H4
Hop Gdns CHCR WC2N 11 L8
Hopgood St SHB W12 136 F10
Hopground Cl STAL AL1 38 F8
Hopkins Cl GPK RM2 125 K1
MUSWH N10 98 B8
Hopkins Crs STALE/WH AL4 20 G10
Hopkinsons Pl CAMTN NW1 4 B5
Hopkins St SOHO/CST W1F 11 H6
Hopkins Yd STAL AL1 38 D7
Hoppers Rd WCHMH N21 99 H3
Hoppett Rd CHING E4 101 K4
The Hoppety
KWD/TDW/WH KT20 238 G8
Hopping La IS N1 6 D2
Hoppingwood Av NWMAL KT3 200 B3
The Hoppitt CHONG CM5 49 K6
Hoppner Rd YEAD UB4 132 E4
Hopton Gdns NWMAL KT3 200 D6
Hopton Pde STRHM/NOR * SW16 180 F8
Hopton Rd STRHM/NOR SW16 180 F8
WOOL/PLUM SE18 162 E2
Hoptons Gdns STHWK * SE1 12 D9
Hopton St STHWK SE1 12 D9
Hopwood Cl TOOT SW17 179 M6
Hopwood Rd WALW SE17 19 H9
Hopwood Wk HACK * E8 7 H4
Horace Av ROMW/RG RM7 124 E6
Horace Rd BARK/HLT IG6 122 F1
FSTGT E7 121 N9
KUT KT1 199 L3
Horatio Pl POP/IOD E14 161 H1
Horatio St BETH E2 7 M8
Horatius Wy CROY/NA CR0 222 G3
Horbeam Cl BORE WD6 75 M5
Horbury Crs NTGHL W11 8 E8
Horbury Ms NTGHL W11 8 D8
Horder Rd FUL/PGN SW6 157 H7
Hordle Gdns STAL AL1 38 E7
Hordle Prom East PECK SE15 159 N6
Hordle Prom North PECK * SE15 159 N6
Hordle Prom West PECK SE15 159 M6
Horksley Gdns RBRW/HUT CM13 87 P10
Horley Cl BXLYHS DA6 186 B1
Horley Lodge La REDH RH1 276 A9
Horley Rd ELTH/MOT SE9 184 B7
HORL RH6 279 K8
REDH RH1 276 A5
Horley Rw HORL RH6 280 A3
Hormead Rd NKENS W10 8 C2
Hornbeam Av UPMR RM14 125 P9
Hornbeam Cha SOCK/AV RM15 147 J5
Hornbeam Cl EPP CM16 83 H3
IL IG1 122 C10
LBTH SE11 18 A5
MLHL NW7 96 C4
NTHLT UB5 113 N10
RBRW/HUT CM13 107 N4
Hornbeam Crs BTFD TW8 154 G6
Hornbeam Gdns DTCH/LGLY SL3 149 M2
Hornbeam Gv CHING E4 101 K4
Hornbeam La BRKMPK AL9 41 P7
CHING E4 81 K9
Hornbeam Rd BKHH IG9 102 A4
EPP CM16 82 G3
GU GU1 249 P7
REIG RH2 275 M3
YEAD UB4 133 K7
Hornbeams HLW CM20 28 F9
LCOL/BKTW AL2 55 N6
WGCE * AL7 23 L6
Hornbeams Av EN EN1 80 B1
Hornbeams Ri FBAR/BDGN N11 98 B7
The Hornbeams HLW CM20 28 F9
Hornbeam Wy CHESW EN7 61 N5
HAYES BR2 206 D6
Hornbill Cl UX/CGN UB8 131 N8
Hornbuckle Cl RYLN/HDSTN HA2 114 C7
Hornby Cl HAMP NW3 3 M3
Horncastle Cl LEE/GVPK SE12 183 M3
Horncastle Rd LEE/GVPK SE12 183 M3
Hornchurch Cl KUTN/CMB KT2 177 J8
Hornchurch Hl CTHM CR3 241 N3
Hornchurch Rd EMPK RM11 125 J6
HCH RM12 125 H6
Horndean Cl CRAWE RH10 284 E3
PUT/ROE SW15 178 D4
Horndon Cl CRW RM5 104 D9
Horndon Gn CRW RM5 104 D9
Horndon Rd CRW RM5 104 D9
Hornecourt Hl GDST RH9 277 N10
Horner La MTCM CR4 201 N2
Horne Rd SHPTN TW17 196 A4
The Hornets WATW WD18 73 J8
Horne Wy PUT/ROE SW15 156 F8
Hornfair Rd CHARL SE7 162 A5
Hornford Wy ROMW/RG RM7 124 F5
Hornhatch RGUE GU4 268 E7
Hornhatch Cl RGUE GU4 268 E6
Hornhatch La RGUE GU4 268 D6
Hornhill Rd RKW/CH/CXG WD3 90 F6
Horniman Dr FSTH SE23 182 A4
Horniman Gdns FSTH * SE23 182 A4
Horning Cl ELTH/MOT SE9 184 B7
Horn La ACT W3 135 P10
GNWCH SE10 161 M3
WFD IG8 101 M7
Horn Link Wy GNWCH SE10 161 M3
Hornminster Gln EMPK RM11 125 P7
Horn Park Cl LEE/GVPK SE12 183 N1
Horn Park La LEE/GVPK SE12 183 N1
Horns Cl HERT/BAY SG13 25 K7
Horns End Pl PIN HA5 113 K2
Hornsey Chambers CLPT * E5 120 A7
Hornsey La ARCH N19 118 D5
Hornsey Lane Est ARCH * N19 118 E5
Hornsey Lane Gdns HGT N6 118 D5
Hornsey Park Rd
CEND/HSY/T N8 118 G1
Hornsey Ri ARCH N19 118 E5
Hornsey Rise Gdns ARCH N19 118 E5
Hornsey Rd ARCH N19 118 F6
Hornsey St HOLWY N7 118 G10
Hornsfield WGCE AL7 23 M4
Hornshay St PECK SE15 160 B5
Horns Mill Rd HERT/BAY SG13 25 J8
Horns Rd BARK/HLT IG6 122 F3
HERT/BAY SG13 25 K6
Hornton Pl KENS W8 14 F2
Hornton St KENS W8 14 F1
Horsa Rd ERITH DA8 164 D6
LEE/GVPK SE12 183 P3
Horsebridges Cl DAGW RM9 143 P3
Horsecroft BNSTD SM7 239 J3
Horsecroft Cl ORP BR6 207 L8
Horsecroft Mdw BNSTD * SM7 239 K2
Horsecroft Rd EDGW HA8 96 A8
HHW HP1 35 K8
HLWW/ROY CM19 46 B2
Horse Fair KUT KT1 199 J2
Horseferry Pl GNWCH SE10 161 H5
Horseferry Rd POP/IOD E14 140 D9
WEST SW1P 17 J4
Horse Guards Av WHALL SW1A 11 L10
Horse Guards Rd WHALL SW1A 11 K10
Horse Hl CSHM HP5 52 A8
HORL RH6 279 L3
Horse Leaze EHAM E6 142 E8
Horselers HHS/BOV HP3 36 B9
Horsell Birch WOKN/KNAP GU21 231 M1
Horsell Common Rd
WOKN/KNAP GU21 213 P10
Horsell Ct CHERT KT16 195 L7
Horsell Moor WOKN/KNAP GU21 232 A3
Horsell Pk WOKN/KNAP GU21 232 A2
Horsell Park Cl
WOKN/KNAP GU21 232 A3
Horsell Ri WOKN/KNAP GU21 232 A1
Horsell Rise Cl
WOKN/KNAP GU21 232 A1
Horsell Rd HBRY N5 119 H10
STMC/STPC BR5 207 K1
Horsell V WOKN/KNAP GU21 232 B1
Horsell Wy WOKN/KNAP GU21 231 P2
Horselydown La STHWK SE1 19 L1
Horsemans Dr LCOL/BKTW AL2 55 P2
Horseman Side BRW CM14 85 L10
Horsemoor Cl DTCH/LGLY SL3 150 D3
Horsemoor La AMSS HP7 68 A10
Horsenden Av GFD/PVL UB6 114 D10
Horsenden Crs GFD/PVL UB6 114 E10
Horsenden La North
GFD/PVL UB6 134 D1
Horsenden La South
GFD/PVL UB6 134 F3
Horseshoe Cl CRAWE RH10 284 E6
CRICK NW2 116 E7
POP/IOD E14 161 H4
Horse Shoe Crs NTHLT UB5 133 P4
Horseshoe Dr UX/CGN UB8 132 B8
Horseshoe Hl SL SL1 108 B9
WAB EN9 63 P9
Horseshoe La ENC/FH EN2 79 K7
GSTN WD25 55 J8
TRDG/WHET N20 96 G2
Horseshoe La East GU GU1 250 E9
Horseshoe La West GU GU1 250 E9
Horseshoe Rdg WEY KT13 216 D7
The Horseshoe BNSTD SM7 239 J1
COUL/CHIP CR5 222 E9
HHS/BOV HP3 36 D8
Horse Yd IS N1 6 D5
Horsfeld Gdns ELTH/MOT SE9 184 B1
Horsfeld Rd ELTH/MOT SE9 184 A1
Horsfield Cl RDART DA2 188 B3
Horsford Rd BRXS/STRHM SW2 180 G1
Horsham Av NFNCH/WDSP N12 97 P6
Horsham Rd BXLYHS DA6 186 A2
CRAWW RH11 283 M8
DORK RH4 272 F3
EBED/NFELT TW14 174 D2
SHGR GU5 268 B8
SHGR GU5 270 G8
Horshoe La East GU GU1 250 E9
Horsley Cl HOR/WEW KT19 220 A9
Horsley Dr CROY/NA CR0 225 H4
KUTN/CMB KT2 177 J8
Horsley Rd BMLY BR1 205 N1
CHING E4 101 H3
COB KT11 235 J5
Horsleys RKW/CH/CXG WD3 90 G6
Horsley St WALW SE17 18 G9
Horsmans Pl DART * DA1 187 M3
Horsman St CMBW SE5 18 F10
Horsmonden Cl ORP BR6 207 H7
Horsmonden Rd BROCKY SE4 182 E1
Horticultural Pl CHSWK W4 156 A4
Horton Av CRICK NW2 117 H9
Horton Bridge Rd WDR/YW UB7 132 A10
Horton Cl WDR/YW UB7 132 A10
Horton Gdns DTCH/LGLY * SL3 150 C9
HOR/WEW KT19 219 P7
Horton Hl HOR/WEW KT19 219 P7
Horton La HOR/WEW KT19 219 M7
Horton Pde WDR/YW * UB7 131 P10
Horton Pl BH/WHM TN16 262 G2
Horton Rd DTCH/LGLY SL3 149 P7
DTCH/LGLY SL3 150 E7
DTCH/LGLY SL3 151 H9
EYN DA4 210 B3
HACK E8 140 A1
STWL/WRAY TW19 151 K10
WDR/YW UB7 131 P10
Horton St LEW SE13 160 G9
Hortons Wy BH/WHM TN16 262 G2
Horton Wy CROY/NA CR0 204 C5
EYN DA4 209 N7
Hortus Rd NWDGN UB2 153 N1
Horvath Cl WEY KT13 216 E1
Hosack Rd BAL SW12 180 A5
Hoselands Vw HART DA3 211 K4
Hoser Av LEE/GVPK SE12 183 M5
Hosey Common La
BH/WHM TN16 263 H6
Hosey Common Rd
BH/WHM TN16 263 H5
Hosey Hl BH/WHM TN16 263 H3
Hosier La STBT EC1A 12 C4
Hoskin's Cl CAN/RD E16 141 P8
HYS/HAR UB3 152 G4
Hoskins Rd OXTED RH8 261 K5
Hoskins St GNWCH SE10 161 J4
Hoskins Wk OXTED RH8 261 K5
Hospital Bridge Rd WHTN TW2 176 A4
Hospital Hl CSHM HP5 51 H8
Hospital Rd HSLW TW3 153 P9
SEV TN13 247 K7
Hospital Wy LEW SE13 183 J2
Hotham Cl E/WMO/HCT KT8 197 P3
EYN DA4 187 P10
SWLY BR8 209 J1
Hotham Rd PUT/ROE SW15 156 F9
WIM/MER SW19 179 M10
Hotham St SRTFD E15 141 K3
Hothfield Pl BERM/RHTH SE16 160 B2
Hotspur Rd NTHLT UB5 133 P4
Hotspur St LBTH SE11 18 A7
Hottsfield HART DA3 211 K3
Houblon Rd RCHPK/HAM TW10 177 K1
Houblons Hl EPP CM16 65 N7
Houghton Cl HACK E8 7 M2
HPTN TW12 175 M9
Houghton Rd CRAWE * RH10 284 D10
SEVS/STOTM N15 119 N2
Houghton St HOL/ALD * WC2B 11 P6
Houlder Crs CROY/NA CR0 223 J3
Hound House Rd SHGR GU5 270 B7
Houndsden Rd WCHMH N21 78 G10
Houndsditch HDTCH EC3A 13 K5
Houndsfield Rd ED N9 100 A1
Hounslow Av HSLW TW3 176 A1
Hounslow Gdns HSLW TW3 176 A1
Hounslow Rd EBED/NFELT TW14 175 J3
FELT TW13 175 L6
HSLW TW3 176 A2
Housden Cl STALE/WH AL4 21 K4
Housefield Wy STALE/WH AL4 39 H9
House La STALE/WH AL4 21 H10
Houseman Wy CMBW SE5 159 L6
Housewood End HHW HP1 35 L3
Houston Rd FSTH SE23 182 D5
SURB KT6 198 G6
Hove Av WALTH E17 120 E3
Hove Cl GRAYS RM17 167 M5
RBRW/HUT CM13 107 P3
Hoveden Rd CRICK NW2 116 G10
Hove Gdns SUT SM1 201 L8
Hoveton Rd THMD SE28 143 M8
Hoveton Wy WFD IG8 102 E9
Howard Agne Cl HHW HP1 52 D3
Howard Av BXLY DA5 185 M4
EW KT17 220 D6
SLN SL2 129 J7
Howard Cl ACT W3 135 N8
ASHTD KT21 237 L4
BUSH WD23 94 D1
CRICK * NW2 117 H9
EHSLY KT24 252 E1
FBAR/BDGN N11 98 B3
HPTN TW12 176 B10
KWD/TDW/WH KT20 256 C1
LHD/OX KT22 237 H9
LOU IG10 82 B10
STALE/WH AL4 39 H9
SUN TW16 174 G9
WAB EN9 63 J10
WATN WD24 72 G2
Howard Dr BORE WD6 76 A8
Howard Gdns GU GU1 250 D9
Howard Pl REIG RH2 257 K8
Howard Rdg RGUE GU4 250 D6
Howard Rd BARK IG11 142 G3
BEAC HP9 89 E9
BMLY BR1 183 M10
BRYLDS KT5 199 L6
CDH/CHF RM16 167 H2
COUL/CHIP CR5 240 D1
CRICK NW2 116 G9
CSHM HP5 50 G4
DART DA1 187 P2
DORK RH4 272 F2
EHAM E6 142 C4
EHSLY KT24 235 H8
GFD/PVL UB6 134 A8
GT/LBKH KT23 254 A3
IL IG1 122 E9
ISLW TW7 154 E9
NWMAL KT3 200 B3
PGE/AN SE20 204 B1
RDKG * RH5 273 H6
REIG RH2 275 L1
SEVS/STOTM N15 119 M4
SNWD SE25 203 P5
STNW/STAM N16 119 L9
UPMR RM14 126 B7
WALTH E17 120 F1
WAN E11 121 K8
Howards Cl PIN * HA5 93 J10
WOKS/MYFD GU22 232 D6
Howards Crest Cl BECK BR3 205 H2
Howards Dr HHW HP1 35 J3
Howardsgate WGCW AL8 22 G5
Howards La ADL/WDHM KT15 215 H3
PUT/ROE SW15 156 F10
Howard's Rd PLSTW E13 141 M5
WOKS/MYFD GU22 232 C6
Howards Thicket
CFSP/GDCR SL9 109 P7
Howard St THDIT KT7 198 G7
Howards Wood Dr
CFSP/GDCR SL9 110 A7
Howard Wk EFNCH N2 117 M2
Howard Wy BAR EN5 76 G9
HLW CM20 29 J8
Howarth Rd ABYW SE2 163 K4
Howberry Cl EDGW HA8 95 J7
Howberry Rd EDGW HA8 95 J7
THHTH CR7 203 L1
Howbury La ERITH DA8 165 H8
Howbury Rd DART DA1 165 H8
PECK SE15 160 B9
Howcroft Crs FNCH N3 97 K8
Howcroft La GFD/PVL UB6 134 C5
Howden Cl THMD SE28 143 M9
Howden Rd SNWD SE25 203 N2
Howden St PECK SE15 159 P9
Howe Cl RAD WD7 57 K8
ROMW/RG RM7 104 B9
Howe Dell HAT AL10 40 E4
Howe Dr BEAC HP9 88 D6
CTHM CR3 241 L8
Howell Cl CHDH RM6 123 N3
Howell Hl BELMT * SM2 220 F6
Howell Hill Cl EW KT17 220 F7
Howell Hill Gv EW KT17 220 F7
Howell Wk WALW SE17 18 D6
Howe Rd HHS/BOV HP3 36 B8
Howfield Gn HOD EN11 26 E10
Howfield Pl TOTM * N17 119 M1
Howgate Rd MORT/ESHN SW14 156 A9
Howick Pl WEST SW1P 17 H4
Howicks Gn WGCE AL7 23 K8
Howie St BTSEA SW11 157 P6
Howitt Cl HAMP NW3 3 N1
Howitt Rd HAMP NW3 3 P1
Howitts Cl ESH/CLAY KT10 217 P3
Howland Ct PIN * HA5 93 P7
Howland Garth STAL AL1 38 B10
Howland Ms East FITZ W1T 11 H3
Howlands WGCE AL7 23 K8
Howland St FITZ W1T 11 H3
Howland Wy BERM/RHTH SE16 160 D1
How La COUL/CHIP CR5 240 B4
Howletts La RSLP HA4 112 D4
Howletts Rd HNHL SE24 181 K2
Howley Pl BAY/PAD W2 9 K3
Howley Rd CROY/NA CR0 203 J10
Howsman Rd BARN SW13 156 D5
Hows Md EPP CM16 48 E10
Howson Rd BROCKY SE4 160 D10
Howson Ter RCHPK/HAM * TW10 177 K2
How's Rd UX/CGN UB8 131 M3
How's St BETH E2 7 L7
Howton Pl BUSH WD23 94 C2
How Wd LCOL/BKTW AL2 56 A4
Hoxton Market IS N1 7 J10
Hoxton Sq IS N1 7 J10
Hoxton St IS N1 7 J6
Hoylake Cl CRAWW RH11 282 G8
Hoylake Crs HGDN/ICK UB10 112 B6
Hoylake Gdns HARH RM3 105 P9
MTCM CR4 202 D3
OXHEY WD19 93 L5
RSLP HA4 113 J6
Hoylake Rd ACT W3 136 B8
Hoyland Cl PECK * SE15 160 A6
Hoyle Rd TOOT SW17 179 P8
Hoy St CAN/RD E16 141 L8
Hoy Ter WTHK * RM20 167 J4
Hubbard Cl UX/CGN UB8 132 C8
Hubbard Dr CHSGTN KT9 219 H3
Hubbard Rd WNWD SE27 181 K7
Hubbards Cha EMPK RM11 125 P3
Hubbards Cl EMPK RM11 125 P3
Hubbard's Hl SEV TN13 265 J7
Hubbards Rd RKW/CH/CXG WD3 70 G9
Hubbard St SRTFD E15 141 K3
Hubert Cl WIM/MER * SW19 201 M1
Hubert Day Cl BEAC HP9 88 C8
Hubert Gv BRXN/ST SW9 158 F9
Hubert Rd BRW CM14 106 G4
DTCH/LGLY SL3 150 A2
EHAM E6 142 A5
RAIN RM13 144 G5
Hucknall Cl HARH RM3 105 N7
Huddart St BOW E3 140 E7
Huddleston Cl BETH * E2 140 B4
Huddlestone Crs REDH RH1 258 E1
Huddlestone Rd CRICK NW2 136 E1
FSTGT E7 121 L9
Huddleston Rd ARCH N19 118 D8
Hudson Cl SHB * W12 136 E9
STAL AL1 38 B9
WATN WD24 72 G2
Hudson Ct GUW GU2 249 L10
Hudson Pl WOOL/PLUM SE18 162 F4
Hudson Rd BXLYHN DA7 164 A8
CRAWE RH10 283 P9
HYS/HAR UB3 152 E5
Hudsons KWD/TDW/WH KT20 238 G7
Huggens College GVW * DA11 189 N1
Huggin Hl BLKFR EC4V 12 F7
Huggins La BRKMPK AL9 40 E9
Huggins Pl BRXS/STRHM SW2 180 G4
Hughan Rd SRTFD E15 121 J10
Hugh Dalton Av FUL/PGN SW6 14 C10
Hughenden Av
KTN/HRWW/W HA3 114 G3
Hughenden Gdns NTHLT UB5 133 K5
Hughenden Rd SL SL1 129 J8
STALE/WH AL4 38 G3
WPK KT4 200 D7
Hughes Rd ASHF TW15 174 D10
CDH/CHF RM16 168 D2
HYS/HAR UB3 133 J9
Hughes Ter CAN/RD * E16 141 L7
Hughes Wk CROY/NA CR0 203 K7
Hugh Gaitskell Cl FUL/PGN SW6 14 C10
Hugh Ms PIM SW1V 16 F6
Hugh Pl WEST SW1P 17 J5
Hugh St PIM SW1V 16 F6
Hugo Gdns RAIN RM13 144 G1
Hugon Rd FUL/PGN SW6 157 L9
Hugo Rd ARCH N19 118 D9
Huguenot Pl WAND/EARL SW18 179 M1
WCHPL E1 13 M3
Hullbridge Ms IS N1 6 G5
Hull Cl BERM/RHTH * SE16 140 C10
CHESW EN7 61 L2
SL SL1 149 H1
Hullett's La BRWN CM15 86 E8
Hull Gn HLWE CM17 31 L9
Hull Gv HLWW/ROY CM19 46 D6
Hull St FSBYE EC1V 6 E10
Hulme Pl STHWK SE1 18 F2
Hulse Av BARK IG11 142 G1
ROMW/RG RM7 104 C9
Hulsewood Cl RDART DA2 187 J6
Hulton Cl LHD/OX KT22 237 H9
Hulverston Cl BELMT SM2 221 L6
Humber Av SOCK/AV RM15 146 E8
Humber Dr NKENS W10 136 G6
UPMR RM14 126 C4
Humber Rd BKHTH/KID SE3 161 M5
CRICK NW2 116 E7
DART DA1 187 L1
Humberstone Rd PLSTW E13 141 P5
Humber Wy DTCH/LGLY SL3 150 D3
Humbolt Cl GUW GU2 249 K10
Humbolt Rd HMSMTH W6 14 A10
Hume Av TIL RM18 168 E9
Hume Cl TIL RM18 168 D9
Humes Av HNWL W7 154 E2
Hume Wy RSLP HA4 113 H4
Hummer Rd EGH TW20 172 D7
Humphrey Cl CLAY * IG5 102 C9
LHD/OX KT22 236 B8
Humphrey St STHWK SE1 19 L7
Humphries Cl DAGW RM9 124 A9
Hundred Acre CDALE/KGS NW9 96 C10
Hundred Acre CHES/WCR * EN8 62 F10
Hundred Acres La AMSS HP7 69 J6
Hungerdown CHING E4 101 H2
Hungerford Av SLN SL2 129 K7
Hungerford Br STHWK SE1 11 N9
Hungerford Rd HOLWY N7 118 F10
Hungerford St WCHPL * E1 140 A8
Hungry Hill La RPLY/SEND GU23 251 M2
Hunsdon WGCE AL7 23 N5
Hunsdon Cl DAGW RM9 143 P1
Hunsdon Dr SEV TN13 247 J9
Hunsdon Rd NWCR SE14 160 C6
WARE SG12 27 K7
Hunslett St BETH * E2 140 B4
Hunstanton Cl CRAWW RH11 282 G8
DTCH/LGLY SL3 150 F6
Hunston Rd MRDN SM4 201 L8
Hunt Cl BKHTH/KID * SE3 161 M8
STALE/WH AL4 39 J3
Hunter Av BRWN CM15 87 M10
Hunter Cl BAL SW12 180 B4
BORE WD6 75 P9
POTB/CUF EN6 59 L9
STHWK SE1 19 H4
Huntercombe Cl MDHD SL6 128 A8
Huntercombe La North SL SL1 128 B7
Huntercombe La South
MDHD SL6 128 A10
Hunter Ct CMBW * SE5 159 L10
Huntercrombe Gdns
OXHEY WD19 93 K6
Hunter Dr HCH RM12 125 K9
Hunter Rd CRAWW RH11 283 N10
GU GU1 268 B1
RYNPK SW20 200 F1
THHTH CR7 203 L3
Hunters Cl BXLY DA5 186 F6
CSHM HP5 50 F6
HHS/BOV HP3 52 F5
HOR/WEW KT19 219 P9
Hunters Ct RCH/KEW TW9 177 J1
Huntersfield Cl REIG RH2 257 M7
Hunter's Gv CRW RM5 104 C6
HYS/HAR UB3 133 H10
KTN/HRWW/W HA3 115 H2
ORP BR6 226 F1
Hunters Hall Rd DAGE RM10 124 B9
Hunters Hl RSLP HA4 113 K8
Hunter's La GSTN WD25 54 G10
Hunters Md CHONG CM5 67 P6
Hunters Meadow NRWD SE19 181 M7
Hunters Oak HHNE HP2 36 C1
Hunters Pk BERK HP4 34 B4
Hunters Reach CHESW EN7 61 N5
Hunters Ride LCOL/BKTW AL2 55 P7
Hunters Rd CHSGTN KT9 199 K10
IL IG1 122 E10
Hunters Sq DAGE RM10 124 B9
Hunter St BMSBY WC1N 11 M1
Hunters Wk RSEV TN14 227 P10
Hunters Wy CROY/NA CR0 223 M1
ENC/FH EN2 79 H5
SL SL1 148 D1
WGCE AL7 23 J8
Hunting Cl ESH/CLAY KT10 217 P1
Huntingdon Cl BROX EN10 44 D10
MTCM CR4 202 F4
Huntingdon Gdns CHSWK * W4 155 P6
WPK KT4 200 F10
Huntingdon Rd ED N9 100 B2
EFNCH N2 117 P1
REDH * RH1 258 A10
WOKN/KNAP GU21 231 K3
Huntingdon St CAN/RD E16 141 L8
IS N1 5 P3
Huntingfield CROY/NA CR0 224 E4
Huntingfield Rd PUT/ROE SW15 178 D2
Huntingfield Wy EGH TW20 172 G10
Hunting Ga HHNE HP2 35 P2
Hunting Gate Cl ENC/FH EN2 79 H7
Hunting Gate Dr CHSGTN KT9 219 K4
Hunting Gate Ms WHTN * TW2 176 D4
Huntings Rd DAGE RM10 144 B1
Huntington Pl DTCH/LGLY SL3 150 E2
Huntland Cl RAIN RM13 145 J7
Huntley Av GVW DA11 189 N2
Huntley St GWRST WC1E 11 H2
Huntley Wy RYNPK * SW20 200 D2
Huntly Dr FNCH N3 97 K7
Huntly Rd SNWD SE25 203 M4
Hunton Bridge Hl KGLGY WD4 54 D9
Hunton St WCHPL E1 13 N3
Hunt Rd GVW DA11 190 B6
NWDGN UB2 153 P2
Hunts Cl GUW GU2 249 J9

Hunt's La SRTFD E15 141 H4
Huntsman Cl FELT TW13 175 J7
Huntsman Rd BARK/HLT IG6 103 L7
Huntsmans Cl WARL CR6 242 B5
Huntsmans Dr UPMR RM14 126 B10
Huntsman St WALW SE17 19 J6
Hunts Md PEND EN3 80 C7
Hunts Mede Cl CHST BR7 184 C10
Huntsmill Rd HHW HP1 35 H7
Huntsmoor Rd HOR/WEW KT19 220 A2
Huntspill St TOOT SW17 179 M6
Hunts Slip Rd DUL SE21 181 M6
Huntsworth Ms CAMTN NW1 10 A1
Hurdwick Pl CAMTN * NW1 4 G7
Hurley Cl WOT/HER KT12 197 J9
Hurley Gdns RGUE GU4 250 D7
Hurley Rd GFD/PVL UB6 134 A7
Hurlfield RDART DA2 187 K6
Hurlford WOKN/KNAP GU21 231 M3
Hurlingham Gdns FUL/PGN SW6 157 J9
Hurlingham Pk FUL/PGN * SW6 157 J9
Hurlingham Rd BXLYHN DA7 164 A6
FUL/PGN SW6 157 J8
Hurlingham Sq FUL/PGN * SW6 157 K9
Hurlock St FSBYPK N4 119 J8
Hurlstone Rd SNWD SE25 203 L5
Hurn Court Rd HEST TW5 153 L8
Hurnford Cl SAND/SEL CR2 223 M6
Huron Cl ORP BR6 227 J3
Huron Rd TOOT SW17 180 B5
Hurren Cl BKHTH/KID SE3 161 K9
Hurricane Wy EPP CM16 66 A3
GSTN WD25 55 H9
Hurry Cl SRTFD E15 141 K2
Hursley Rd CHIG IG7 103 J6
Hurst Av CHING E4 100 F4
HGT N6 118 D4
Hurstbourne Gdns BARK IG11 142 G1
Hurstbourne Rd FSTH SE23 182 D4
Hurst Cl CHING E4 100 F4
CHSGTN KT9 219 M2
CRAWW RH11 283 J9
EPSOM KT18 237 P10
GLDGN NW11 117 L4
HAYES BR2 205 L8
NTHLT UB5 133 N1
WGCE AL7 23 M6
WOKS/MYFD GU22 231 P6
Hurstcourt Rd CHEAM SM3 201 L8
Hurst Cft GU GU1 268 B3
Hurstdene Av HAYES BR2 205 L8
STA TW18 173 L9
Hurstdene Gdns
SEVS/STOTM N15 119 M5
Hurst Dr CHES/WCR EN8 62 C10
KWD/TDW/WH KT20 256 D2
Hurst Farm Rd RSEV TN14 265 J8
Hurstfield HAYES BR2 205 M5
Hurstfield Crs YEAD UB4 132 F7
Hurstfield Dr MDHD SL6 128 A8
Hurstfield Rd E/WMO/HCT KT8 197 P3
Hurst Green Cl OXTED RH8 261 M8
Hurst Green Rd OXTED RH8 261 M8
Hurst Gv WOT/HER KT12 196 G8
Hurstlands OXTED RH8 261 M8
Hurstlands Cl EMPK RM11 125 K5
Hurst La ABYW SE2 163 N4
E/WMO/HCT KT8 198 B4
EGH TW20 194 C3
EPSOM KT18 238 A8
RSEV TN14 265 J9
Hurstleigh Cl REDH RH1 258 A8
Hurstleigh Dr REDH RH1 258 A8
Hurstleigh Gdns CLAY IG5 102 C9
Hurstlings WGCE AL7 23 L7
Hurst Park Av HCH RM12 125 M9
Hurst Pl DART * DA1 187 K2
NTHWD HA6 92 C9
Hurst Ri BAR EN5 77 K7
Hurst Rd BFN/LL DA15 185 L5
BKHH IG9 102 A2
CROY/NA CR0 223 L2
E/WMO/HCT KT8 198 B3
EPSOM KT18 238 B9
ERITH DA8 164 D6
HOR/WEW KT19 220 A7
HORL RH6 279 P3
SL SL1 128 C7
WALTH E17 120 G1
WCHMH N21 99 H2
WOT/HER KT12 197 L4
Hurst Springs BXLY DA5 185 P4
Hurst St HNHL SE24 181 J2
Hurst View Rd SAND/SEL CR2 223 M4
Hurst Wy SAND/SEL CR2 223 M3
SEV TN13 265 K3
WOKS/MYFD GU22 215 H10
Hurstway Wk NKENS * W10 136 G9
Hurstwood Av BRWN CM15 106 G1
BXLY DA5 185 P4
BXLYHN DA7 164 F7
SWFD E18 121 N2
Hurstwood Dr BMLY BR1 206 C3
Hurstwood Rd GLDGN NW11 117 H2
Hurtmore Cha RGODL GU7 266 G9
Hurtmore Rd RGODL GU7 266 E10
Hurtwood Rd WOT/HER KT12 197 N7
Hurworth Av DTCH/LGLY SL3 149 P2
Huson Cl HAMP NW3 3 N3
Hussain Cl ALP/SUD HA0 114 E9
Hussars Cl HSLWW TW4 153 M9
Husseywell Crs HAYES BR2 205 M8
Hutchingson's Rd CROY/NA CR0 225 H7
Hutching's St POP/IOD E14 160 F1
Hutchings Wk GLDGN NW11 117 L2
Hutchins Cl HCH RM12 125 M8
SRTFD E15 141 H2
Hutchinson Ter WBLY HA9 115 J8
Hutchins Rd THMD SE28 143 K9
Hutchins Wy HORL RH6 280 A2
Hutton Cl BFOR GU20 212 C4
HERT/WAS SG14 25 H5
NTHLT UB5 114 C10
WFD IG8 101 N7
Hutton Ga RBRW/HUT CM13 107 N1
Hutton Gv NFNCH/WDSP N12 97 L6
Hutton La KTN/HRWW/W HA3 94 B8
Hutton Rd BRWN CM15 107 L1
Hutton Rw EDGW HA8 95 P8
Hutton St EMB EC4Y 12 B6
Hutton Wk KTN/HRWW/W HA3 94 B8
Huxbear St BROCKY SE4 182 E1
Huxley UED * N18 99 L6
Huxley Cl NTHLT UB5 133 M4
RGODL GU7 267 J10
Huxley Dr CHDH RM6 123 L5
Huxley Gdns WLSDN NW10 135 L5
Huxley Pde UED * N18 99 L6
Huxley Pl PLMGR N13 99 J5
Huxley Rd GUW GU2 267 J1
LEY E10 121 H7
UED N18 99 L5
WELL DA16 163 J9
Huxley Sayze UED * N18 99 L6
Huxley St NKENS W10 2 A10
Hyacinth Cl HPTN TW12 175 P9
Hyacinth Dr HGDN/ICK UB10 131 P2
Hyacinth Rd PUT/ROE SW15 178 D4
Hyatts Yd CSHM * HP5 36 C7
Hyburn Cl HHS/BOV HP3 50 G8
LCOL/BKTW AL2 55 N6
Hycliffe Gdns CHIG IG7 102 F5
Hyde Av POTB/CUF EN6 59 L9
Hyde Cl BAR EN5 77 J7
PLSTW E13 141 M4
Hyde Crs CDALE/KGS NW9 116 B3
Hyde Dr CRAWW RH11 283 H8
STMC/STPC BR5 207 L4
Hyde Estate Rd CDALE/KGS NW9 116 C3
Hydefield Cl ED N9 99 L2
Hydefield Ct ED N9 99 M3
Hyde Gn BEAC HP9 88 E8
Hyde La BTSEA SW11 157 P7
HHS/BOV HP3 52 D3
KGLGY WD4 54 C3
LCOL/BKTW AL2 56 D4
Hyde Md WAB EN9 45 K9
Hyde Mdw HHS/BOV HP3 52 D4
Hyde Park Av WCHMH N21 99 K3
Hyde Park Cnr MYFR/PICC W1J 16 D1
Hyde Park Crs BAY/PAD W2 9 N6
Hyde Park Gdns BAY/PAD W2 9 M7
WCHMH N21 99 K2
Hyde Park Gardens Ms
BAY/PAD W2 9 M7
Hyde Park Ga KENS W8 15 J2
Hyde Park Gate Ms SKENS * SW7 15 K2
Hyde Park Pl BAY/PAD W2 9 P7
Hyde Park Sq BAY/PAD W2 9 N6
Hyde Park St BAY/PAD W2 9 N7
Hyderabad Wy SRTFD E15 141 K2
Hyde Rd BXLYHN DA7 164 A8
IS N1 7 H6
RCHPK/HAM TW10 177 L1
SAND/SEL CR2 223 M9
WAT * WD17 73 H7
Hyder Rd CDH/CHF RM16 168 F2
Hydeside Gdns ED N9 99 N3
Hyde's Pl IS N1 6 C3
Hyde St DEPT SE8 160 F5
Hyde Ter SUN TW16 174 F9
The Hyde CDALE/KGS NW9 116 A1
WARE SG12 26 A1
Hydethorpe Av ED N9 99 N3
Hydethorpe Rd BAL SW12 180 D4
Hyde V GNWCH SE10 161 H6
Hyde Va WGCE AL7 23 L5
Hyde Wk MRDN SM4 201 K7
Hyde Wy ED N9 99 N3
HYS/HAR UB3 152 G3
WGCE AL7 23 H5
Hyland Cl EMPK RM11 125 J5
Hylands Cl CRAWE RH10 284 B8
Hylands Ms EPSOM KT18 237 P1
Hylands Rd EPSOM KT18 237 P1
WALTH E17 101 J10
Hyland Wy EMPK RM11 125 J5
Hylle Cl WDSR SL4 148 D7
Hylton St WOOL/PLUM SE18 163 J3
Hyndewood FSTH * SE23 182 C6
Hyndman St PECK SE15 160 A5
Hynton Rd BCTR RM8 123 M7
Hyperion Ct CRAWW RH11 283 H9
HHNE HP2 36 A3
Hyperion Pl HOR/WEW KT19 220 A5
Hyrons Cl AMS HP6 69 K4
Hyrons La AMS HP6 69 J4
Hyson Rd BERM/RHTH SE16 160 A4
Hythe Av BXLYHN DA7 163 P6
Hythe Cl STMC/STPC BR5 207 M4
UED N18 99 P5
Hythe End Rd STWL/WRAY TW19 172 D5
Hythe Field Av EGH TW20 172 G9
Hythe Park Rd EGH TW20 172 F8
Hythe Rd STA TW18 172 G8
THHTH CR7 203 L2
WLSDN NW10 136 C5
Hythe St DART DA1 187 M1
The Hythe STA TW18 173 H8
Hyver Hl MLHL NW7 76 A10

I

Ibbetson Pth LOU IG10 82 E7
Ibbotson Av CAN/RD E16 141 L8
Ibbott St WCHPL E1 140 B6
Iberian Av WLGTN SM6 222 E1
Ibis La CHSWK W4 155 P7
Ibis Wy YEAD UB4 133 L8
Ibscott Cl DAGE RM10 144 D1
Ibsley Gdns PUT/ROE SW15 178 D4
Ibsley Wy EBAR EN4 77 P9
Icehouse Wd OXTED RH8 261 K7
Iceland Rd BOW E3 140 F3
Ickburgh Est CLPT * E5 120 A7
Ickburgh Rd CLPT E5 120 A8
Ickenham Cl RSLP HA4 112 E7
Ickenham Rd RSLP HA4 112 E6
Ickleton Rd ELTH/MOT SE9 184 B7
Icklingham Rd COB KT11 217 K8
Icknield Cl STALW/RED AL3 37 N8
Icknield Dr GNTH/NBYPK IG2 122 E3
Ickworth Park Rd WALTH E17 120 D2
Ida Rd SEVS/STOTM N15 119 L3
Ida St POP/IOD E14 141 H8
Ide Hill Rd RSEV TN14 264 A8
Iden Cl HAYES BR2 205 L6
Idlecombe Rd TOOT SW17 180 B9
Idleigh Court Rd HART DA3 211 N9
Idmiston Rd FSTGT E7 121 L10
WNWD SE27 181 K6
WPK KT4 200 C7
Idmiston Sq WPK KT4 200 C7
Idol La MON EC3R 13 J8
Idonia St DEPT SE8 160 E5
Iffley Cl UX/CGN UB8 131 E2
Iffley Rd HMSMTH W6 156 E2
Ifield Av CRAWW RH11 283 M6
Ifield Cl REDH RH1 275 P3
Ifield Dr CRAWW RH11 283 K3
Ifield Gn CRAWW RH11 283 K4
Ifield Pk CRAWW * RH11 283 J7
Ifield Rd CRAWW RH11 283 L6
HORL RH6 279 H10
WBPTN SW10 15 H9
Ifield St CRAWW RH11 283 J5
Ifield Wy GVE DA12 190 G9
Ifield Wd CRAWW RH11 282 G4
Ifold Rd REDH RH1 276 B2
Ightham Rd ERITH DA8 164 B6
Ikona Ct WEY * KT13 216 D2
Ilbert St NKENS W10 2 A10
Ilchester Gdns BAY/PAD W2 8 G7
Ilchester Pl WKENS W14 14 D3
Ilchester Rd BCTR RM8 123 L10
Ildersly Gv DUL SE21 181 L5
Ilderton Rd BERM/RHTH SE16 160 B5
Ilex Cl EGH TW20 171 N10
SUN TW16 197 K2
Ilex Rd WLSDN NW10 136 C1
Ilex Wy STRHM/NOR SW16 181 H8
Ilford Hl IL IG1 122 D8
Ilford La IL IG1 122 E9
Ilfracombe Crs HCH RM12 125 K9
Ilfracombe Gdns CHDH RM6 123 L5
Ilfracombe Rd BMLY BR1 183 L6
Iliffe St WALW SE17 18 D7
Iliffe Yd WALW SE17 18 D7
Ilkley Cl NRWD * SE19 181 L9
Ilkley Rd CAN/RD E16 141 P7
OXHEY WD19 93 L6
Illingworth WDSR SL4 148 D9
Illingworth Cl MTCM CR4 201 N3
Illingworth Wy EN EN1 79 M9
Ilmington Rd
KTN/HRWW/W HA3 115 J4
Ilminster Gdns BTSEA SW11 157 P10
Imber Cl STHGT/OAK N14 98 D1
Imber Cross THDIT * KT7 198 E7
Imber Gv ESH/CLAY KT10 198 C7
Imber Park Rd ESH/CLAY KT10 198 C8
Imber St IS N1 6 G6
Imperial Av STNW/STAM * N16 119 M9
Imperial Cl RYLN/HDSTN HA2 113 P4
Imperial College Rd SKENS SW7 15 L4
Imperial Ct WDSR SL4 148 F9
Imperial Dr GVE DA12 191 J8
RYLN/HDSTN HA2 113 P6
Imperial Gdns MTCM CR4 202 C3
Imperial Pk LHD/OX * KT22 236 F6
Imperial Pl BORE * WD6 75 N7
CHST BR7 206 D1
Imperial Rd EBED/NFELT TW14 174 F3
FUL/PGN SW6 157 L7
WDGN N22 98 F8
WDSR SL4 148 F9
Imperial Sq FUL/PGN SW6 157 L7
Imperial St BOW E3 141 H5
Imperial Wy CHST BR7 184 F6
CROY/NA CR0 222 G3
KTN/HRWW/W HA3 115 K4
WATN WD24 73 K5
Imre Cl SHB W12 136 E10
Inca Dr ELTH/MOT SE9 184 E3
Ince Rd WOT/HER KT12 216 F2
Inchmery Rd CAT SE6 182 G5
Inchwood CROY/NA CR0 224 G5
Indells HAT AL10 40 C5
Independent Pl HACK E8 119 N10
Independents Rd
BKHTH/KID SE3 161 L9
Inderwick Rd CEND/HSY/T N8 118 G4
Indescon Ct POP/IOD E14 160 F1
India Rd SL SL1 149 N1
India St TWRH EC3N 13 L6
India Wy SHB W12 136 E9
Indigo Ms POP/IOD * E14 141 H9
STNW/STAM N16 119 L8
Indus Rd CHARL SE7 161 P6
Ingal Rd PLSTW E13 141 M6
Ingate Pl VX/NE SW8 158 C7
Ingatestone Rd MNPK E12 121 P6
SNWD SE25 204 A5
WFD IG8 101 N8
Ingelow St VX/NE SW8 158 C8
Ingels Md EPP CM16 65 J5
Ingersoll Rd PEND EN3 80 B4
SHB W12 136 E10
Ingestre Pl SOHO/CST W1F 11 H6
Ingestre Rd FSTGT E7 121 M9
KTTN NW5 118 C9
Ingham Cl SAND/SEL CR2 224 C5
Ingham Rd KIL/WHAMP NW6 117 K9
SAND/SEL CR2 224 B5
Inglebert St CLKNW EC1R 6 A9
Ingleboro Dr PUR/KEN CR8 223 L9
Ingleborough St BRXN/ST SW9 159 H8
Ingleby Dr HRW HA1 114 C8
Ingleby Gdns CHIG IG7 103 J4
Ingleby Rd CDH/CHF RM16 168 E2
DAGE RM10 144 C1
HOLWY N7 118 F8
IL IG1 122 E6
Ingleby Wy CHST BR7 184 D8
WLGTN SM6 222 E5
Ingle Cl PIN HA5 113 N1
Ingledew Rd WOOL/PLUM SE18 162 G4
Inglefield POTB/CUF EN6 59 K6
Inglefield Sq WAP * E1W 140 A10
Ingleglen EMPK RM11 125 P5
SLN SL2 108 G10
Inglehurst ADL/WDHM KT15 215 L6
Inglehurst Gdns REDBR IG4 122 C3
Inglemere Rd FSTH SE23 182 C6
TOOT SW17 180 A10
Ingles WGCW AL8 23 H2
Ingleside DTCH/LGLY SL3 151 H7
Ingleside Cl BECK BR3 182 F10
Ingleside Gv BKHTH/KID SE3 161 L5
Inglethorpe St FUL/PGN SW6 156 G7
Ingleton Av WELL DA16 185 K1
Ingleton Rd CAR SM5 221 P5
UED N18 99 P7
Ingleton St BRXN/ST SW9 159 H8
Ingleway NFNCH/WDSP N12 97 N7
Inglewood CHERT KT16 195 J10
CROY/NA CR0 224 D5
SWLY * BR8 208 F2
WOKN/KNAP GU21 231 J4
Inglewood Cl BARK/HLT IG6 103 J7
HCH RM12 125 L9
POP/IOD E14 160 F3
Inglewood Copse BMLY BR1 206 B2
Inglewood Rd BXLYHN DA7 164 E10
KIL/WHAMP NW6 117 K10
Inglis Rd CROY/NA CR0 203 N8
EA W5 135 K9
Inglis St CMBW SE5 159 J7
Ingoldsby Rd GVE DA12 191 H4
Ingram Av EFNCH N2 117 M5
Ingram Cl LBTH SE11 17 P5
STAN HA7 95 H6
Ingram Rd DART DA1 187 M4
EFNCH N2 117 P4
GRAYS RM17 167 P3
THHTH CR7 203 K1
Ingrams Cl WOT/HER KT12 217 K2
Ingram Wy GFD/PVL UB6 134 C3
Ingrave Rd BRW CM14 107 K4
ROM RM1 124 E2
Ingrave St BTSEA SW11 157 N9
Ingrebourne Gdns UPMR RM14 126 B6
Ingrebourne Rd RAIN RM13 145 J6
Ingress St CHSWK W4 156 B4
Ingress Ter MEO * DA13 189 L7
Ingreway HARH RM3 106 A7
Inholms La RDKG RH5 273 H6
Inigo Jones Rd CHARL SE7 162 A6
Inkerman Pde
WOKN/KNAP * GU21 231 K4
Inkerman Rd KTTN NW5 4 E1
STAL AL1 38 D7
WDSR SL4 148 E3
WOKN/KNAP GU21 231 K4
Inkerman Ter CSHM HP5 51 H9
Inkerman Wy WOKN/KNAP GU21 231 K4
Inks Gn CHING E4 101 H6
Inkwell Cl NFNCH/WDSP N12 97 M4
Inman Rd WAND/EARL SW18 179 M3
WLSDN NW10 136 B3
Inmans Rw WFD IG8 101 M5
Inner Cir CAMTN NW1 4 C10
Inner Park Rd WIM/MER SW19 178 G5
Inner Ring East HTHAIR TW6 152 C9
Innes Cl RYNPK SW20 201 H2
Innes Ct HHS/BOV HP3 35 N8
Innes Gdns PUT/ROE SW15 178 E2
Innes Yd CROY/NA CR0 203 K10
Inniskilling Rd PLSTW E13 141 P4
Innovation Cl ALP/SUD HA0 135 K3
Innova Wy PEND EN3 80 E2
Inskip Cl LEY E10 120 G7
Inskip Dr EMPK RM11 125 M6
Inskip Rd BCTR RM8 123 N6
Institute Pl HACK E8 120 A10
Institute Rd DORK RH4 272 B3
EPP CM16 65 N5
Instone Rd DART DA1 187 L3
Integer Gdns WAN * E11 121 J5
International Av HEST TW5 153 K4
Inver Ct BAY/PAD W2 9 H6
Inveresk Gdns WPK KT4 200 C10
Inverforth Cl HAMP NW3 117 M7
Inverforth Rd FBAR/BDGN N11 98 C6
Inverine Rd CHARL SE7 161 N4
Invermore Pl WOOL/PLUM SE18 162 F3
Inverness Av EN EN1 79 M5
Inverness Dr BARK/HLT IG6 103 H7
Inverness Gdns KENS W8 8 G10
Inverness Ms BAY/PAD W2 9 H7
Inverness Pl BAY/PAD W2 9 H7
Inverness Rd HSLW TW3 153 N10
NWDGN UB2 153 M3
UED N18 100 A6
WPK KT4 200 G8
Inverness St CAMTN NW1 4 E5
Inverness Ter BAY/PAD W2 9 H6
WDGN * N22 99 J9
Inverton Rd PECK SE15 160 C10
Invicta Cl CHST BR7 184 D8
EBED/NFELT TW14 174 G4
Invicta Gv NTHLT UB5 133 N5
Invicta Pde SCUP * DA14 185 L7
Invicta Plaza STHWK SE1 12 C9
Invicta Rd BKHTH/KID SE3 161 M6
RDART DA2 188 A2
Inville Rd WALW SE17 19 H8
Inwood Av COUL/CHIP CR5 241 H6
HSLW TW3 154 B9
Inwood Cl CROY/NA CR0 204 D9
Inwood Rd HSLW TW3 154 B10
Inworth St BTSEA SW11 157 P8
Inworth Wk IS * N1 6 E5
Iona Cl CAT SE6 182 F3
CRAWW RH11 283 L10
MRDN SM4 201 L7
Iona Crs SL SL1 128 D8
Ion Sq BETH * E2 7 N8
Ipswich Rd SL SL1 128 E8
TOOT SW17 180 B9
Ireland Cl EHAM E6 142 C7
Ireland Pl WDGN N22 98 F8
Irene Ms HNWL * W7 134 E10
Irene Rd COB KT11 218 A10
FUL/PGN SW6 157 K7
ORP BR6 207 J7
Ireton Av WEY KT13 196 G9
Ireton Cl MUSWH N10 98 B8
Ireton Pl GRAYS RM17 167 M3
Ireton St BOW E3 140 F6
Iris Av BXLY DA5 185 P2
Iris Cl BRWN CM15 86 G9
CROY/NA CR0 204 C8
EHAM E6 142 B7
SURB * KT6 199 L7
Iris Crs BXLYHN DA7 164 A5
Iris Rd CHOB/PIR GU24 230 F1
HOR/WEW KT19 219 N2
Iris Wy CHING E4 100 E7
Irkdale Av EN EN1 79 N5
Iron Bridge Cl STHL UB1 134 B10
WLSDN NW10 116 B10
Iron Bridge Rd WDR/YW * UB7 132 C10
Ironbridge Rd WDR/YW * UB7 132 B10
Iron Bridge Rd North
WDR/YW UB7 132 B10
Iron Bridge Rd South
WDR/YW UB7 152 B1
Iron Dr HERT/BAY SG13 26 A4
Iron Mill La DART DA1 164 G10
Iron Mill Pl DART DA1 164 G10
WAND/EARL * SW18 179 L2
Iron Mill Rd WAND/EARL SW18 179 L2
Ironmonger La CITYW EC2V 12 G6
Ironmonger Rw FSBYE EC1V 6 F10
Ironsbottom REIG RH2 275 J10
Ironside Cl BERM/RHTH SE16 160 C1
Irons Wy CRW RM5 104 D8
Irvine Av KTN/HRWW/W HA3 114 F1
Irvine Cl TRDG/WHET N20 97 P3
Irvine Gdns SOCK/AV RM15 146 E8
Irvine Pl VW GU25 194 B5
Irvine Wy ORP BR6 207 J7
Irving Av NTHLT UB5 133 L3
Irving Gv BRXN/ST SW9 158 G8
Irving Ms IS N1 6 E2
Irving Rd WKENS W14 156 G2
Irving St LSQ/SEVD WC2H 11 K8
Irving Wk CRAWE RH10 283 P10
Irving Wy SWLY BR8 208 E2
Irwell Est BERM/RHTH * SE16 160 B1
Irwin Av WOOL/PLUM SE18 163 H6
Irwin Cl HGDN/ICK UB10 112 B8
Irwin Gdns WLSDN NW10 136 E3
Irwin Rd GUW GU2 267 M1
Isabel Ga CHES/WCR EN8 62 E2
Isabella Cl STHGT/OAK N14 98 D1
Isabella Ct RCHPK/HAM * TW10 177 L2
Isabella Dr ORP BR6 226 F1
Isabella Rd HOM * E9 120 B10
Isabella St STHWK SE1 12 C10
Isabelle Cl CHESW EN7 61 K5
Isabel St BRXN/ST SW9 158 G7
Isambard Ms POP/IOD E14 161 H2
Isambard Pl BERM/RHTH SE16 140 B10
Isbells Dr REIG RH2 275 L2
Isenburg Wy HHNE HP2 35 N1
Isham Rd STRHM/NOR SW16 202 F2
Isis Cl RSLP HA4 112 D4
Isis Dr UPMR RM14 126 D4
Isis St WAND/EARL SW18 179 M5
Island Cl STA TW18 173 H7
Island Farm Av E/WMO/HCT KT8 197 N5
Island Farm Rd E/WMO/HCT KT8 197 N5
Island Rd MTCM CR4 180 A10
Island Rw POP/IOD E14 140 E8
Isla Rd WOOL/PLUM SE18 162 F5
Islay Gdns HSLWW TW4 175 L1
Islay Wy IS * N1 6 F2
Islay Whf POP/IOD * E14 141 H7
Isledon Rd HOLWY N7 119 H8
Islehurst Cl CHST BR7 206 D1
Islington Gn IS N1 6 C6
Islington High St IS N1 6 C7
Islington Park Ms IS N1 6 C3
Islington Park St IS N1 6 B3
Islip Gdns EDGW HA8 96 A7
NTHLT UB5 133 M2
Islip Manor Rd NTHLT UB5 133 M2
Islip St KTTN NW5 118 D10
Ismailia Rd FSTGT E7 141 N2
Ismay Cl SL * SL1 129 K8
Isom Cl PLSTW E13 141 N5
Istead Ri MEO DA13 190 C10
Itchingwood Common Rd
OXTED RH8 261 P9
Ivanhoe Cl CRAWW RH11 283 N4
UX/CGN UB8 131 N7
Ivanhoe Dr KTN/HRWW/W HA3 94 G10
Ivanhoe Rd CMBW SE5 159 N9
HSLWW TW4 153 L9
Ivatt Pl WKENS W14 14 D8
Ivatt Wy SEVS/STOTM N15 119 J1
Iveagh Av WLSDN NW10 135 M4
Iveagh Cl HOM E9 140 C3
NTHWD HA6 92 C9
WLSDN NW10 135 M4
Iveagh Rd GUW GU2 267 N1
Ivedon Rd WELL DA16 163 M8
Ive Farm Cl LEY E10 120 F7
Ive Farm La LEY E10 120 F7
Iveley Rd CLAP SW4 158 D8
Iverdale Cl IVER SL0 130 F9
Ivere Dr BAR EN5 77 L10
Iverhurst Cl BXLYHS DA6 185 N1
Iver La IVER SL0 131 L7
Iver Ldg IVER SL0 131 J7
Iverna Ct KENS W8 14 F3
Iverna Gdns EBED/NFELT TW14 174 E1
KENS W8 14 F3
Iverson Rd KIL/WHAMP NW6 2 D2
Ivers Wy CROY/NA CR0 224 G4
Ives Gdns ROM RM1 124 G2
Ives Rd CAN/RD E16 141 K7
DTCH/LGLY SL3 150 D2
HERT/WAS SG14 25 J4
Ives St CHEL SW3 15 P5
Ivimey St BETH E2 7 P9
Ivinghoe Cl EN EN1 79 M6
GSTN WD25 73 L1
STALE/WH AL4 39 H1
Ivinghoe Rd BCTR RM8 123 L10
BUSH WD23 74 C10
RKW/CH/CXG WD3 91 J1
Ivor Cl GU GU1 268 C1
Ivor Gv ELTH/MOT SE9 184 E4
Ivor Pl CAMTN NW1 10 A2
Ivor St CAMTN NW1 4 G4
Ivory Cl STALE/WH AL4 39 H8
Ivory Ct FELT TW13 175 H5
HHS/BOV HP3 35 P9
Ivorydown BMLY BR1 183 M7
Ivory Wk CRAWW RH11 283 H10
Ivy Bower Cl GRH DA9 188 G1
Ivybridge BROX EN10 44 F5
Ivybridge Cl TWK TW1 176 F2
Ivy Bridge Cl UX/CGN UB8 131 P5
Ivy Chimneys Rd EPP CM16 65 H8
Ivychurch Cl PGE/AN SE20 182 A10
Ivy Church La STHWK * SE1 19 L7
Ivy Cl DART DA1 187 P2
GVE DA12 190 F7
PIN HA5 113 K5
RYLN/HDSTN HA2 113 N9
SUN TW16 197 K2
Ivy Cottages UX/CGN * UB8 132 B5
Ivy Crs CHSWK W4 155 P3
SL SL1 128 E9
Ivydale Rd CAR SM5 202 A9
PECK SE15 160 C9
Ivyday Gv STRHM/NOR SW16 180 G6
Ivydene WOKN/KNAP GU21 230 G4
WOT/HER KT12 197 N5
Ivydene Cl REDH RH1 276 C5
SUT SM1 221 M1
Ivy Gdns CEND/HSY/T N8 118 F4
MTCM CR4 202 E3
Ivy House La BERK HP4 34 B5
SEV TN13 246 E3
Ivyhouse Rd DAGW RM9 143 N1
HGDN/ICK UB10 112 C8
Ivy La HSLWW TW4 153 N10
RSEV TN14 245 P2
WOKS/MYFD GU22 232 E4
Ivy Lea RKW/CH/CXG * WD3 91 K2
Ivy Lodge La HARH RM3 106 B10
Ivy Mill Cl GDST RH9 260 A8
Ivy Mill La REDH RH1 259 P8
Ivymount Rd WNWD SE27 181 H6
Ivy Rd BROCKY SE4 160 E10
CAN/RD E16 141 M8
CRICK NW2 116 F9
HSLW TW3 154 A10
LEY E10 120 F4
STHGT/OAK N14 98 D1
SURB * KT6 199 M9
TOOT SW17 179 P8
Ivy St IS N1 7 J7
Ivy Ter HOD EN11 45 H1
Ivy Wk DAGW RM9 143 P1
NTHWD * HA6 92 F9
Ixworth Pl CHEL SW3 15 N6
Izane Rd BXLYHS DA6 164 A10

J

Jacaranda Cl NWMAL KT3 200 B3
Jacaranda Gv HACK E8 7 M4
Jackass La GDST RH9 260 E7
HAYES BR2 225 N3
Jack Clow Rd SRTFD E15 141 K4
Jack Cornwell St MNPK E12 122 D9
Jackdaw Cl CRAWW RH11 283 M5
Jackdaws WGCE AL7 23 M5
Jackets La DEN/HRF UB9 92 A8
Jacketts Fld ABLGY WD5 54 G6
Jack Evans Ct SOCK/AV RM15 146 F8
Jackman Ms WLSDN NW10 116 B8
Jackman's La WOKN/KNAP GU21 231 M5
Jackman St HACK E8 140 A3
Jacks La DEN/HRF UB9 91 K9
Jackson Cl EMPK RM11 125 N2
EPSOM KT18 220 A10
GRH DA9 188 E1
HOM E9 140 C2
Jackson Rd BARK IG11 142 G3
EBAR EN4 77 P10
HAYES BR2 206 C8
HGDN/ICK UB10 131 P2
HOLWY N7 118 G9
Jacksons Cl CHONG * CM5 67 P5
Jacksons Dr CHESW EN7 61 P4
Jackson's La HGT N6 118 B5
Jackson's Pl CROY/NA CR0 203 L8
Jackson St WOOL/PLUM SE18 162 D5
Jackson's Wy CROY/NA CR0 204 F10
Jack Stevens Cl HLWE * CM17 47 M3
Jack Walker Ct HBRY N5 119 J9
Jacob Cl WDSR SL4 148 D7
Jacobean Cl CRAWE RH10 284 D8
Jacobs Av HARH RM3 105 M10
Jacobs Cl DAGE RM10 124 C9
Jacob St STHWK SE1 19 M1
Jacob's Well Ms MHST W1U 10 D5
Jacobs Well Rd RGUE GU4 250 A5
Jacqueline Cl NTHLT UB5 133 M3
Jacqueline Creft Ter HGT * N6 118 B4
Jacqueline Vls WALTH * E17 121 H3
Jade Cl BCTR RM8 123 M6
CAN/RD E16 142 A8
CRICK NW2 116 G5
Jade Ter KIL/WHAMP * NW6 3 K3
Jaffe Rd IL IG1 122 F6
Jaffray Rd HAYES BR2 206 A4
Jaggard Wy BAL SW12 180 A3
Jagger Cl RDART DA2 188 B3
Jago Cl WOOL/PLUM SE18 162 F5
Jago Wk CMBW SE5 159 L6
Jail La BH/WHM TN16 244 A1
Jamaica Rd BERM/RHTH SE16 160 A2
STHWK SE1 19 L2
THHTH CR7 203 J6
Jamaica St WCHPL E1 140 B7
James Av BCTR RM8 124 A6
CRICK NW2 116 F10
James Cl BUSH WD23 73 M9
GLDGN * NW11 117 H4
GPK RM2 125 H3
PLSTW E13 141 M4
James Collins Cl NKENS W10 8 C2
James Gdns WDGN N22 99 K8
James Joyes Wk HNHL * SE24 159 J10
James La WAN E11 121 H5
James Lee Sq PEND EN3 80 F4
James Martin Cl DEN/HRF UB9 111 K4
Jameson St KENS W8 8 F9
James Pl TOTM N17 99 N8
James Rd DART DA1 187 H3
RGUW GU3 267 P8
James St BARK IG11 142 F2
COVGDN WC2E 11 M7
EN EN1 79 N9
EPP CM16 65 J4
HSLW TW3 154 C9
MHST W1U 10 D6
WDSR SL4 149 J7
Jamestown Rd CAMTN NW1 4 E5
Jamestown Wy POP/IOD E14 141 J9
James Watt Wy CRAWE RH10 284 B1
ERITH DA8 164 F5
James Yd CHING * E4 101 J7
Jamnagar Cl STA TW18 173 J9
Jane Cl HHNE HP2 36 C1
Jane St WCHPL E1 140 A8
Janet St POP/IOD E14 160 F2
Janeway Pl BERM/RHTH SE16 160 A1
Janeway St BERM/RHTH SE16 19 P2
Janmead RBRW/HUT CM13 107 N1
Janoway Hill La
WOKN/KNAP GU21 231 P5
Janson Cl SRTFD E15 121 K10
WLSDN NW10 116 A8
Janson Rd SRTFD E15 121 K10
Jansons Rd SEVS/STOTM N15 119 M1
Japan Crs FSBYPK N4 118 G6
Japan Rd CHDH RM6 123 N4
Japonica Cl WOKN/KNAP GU21 231 P4
Jardine Rd WAP E1W 140 C9
Jarman Cl HHS/BOV HP3 35 P8
Jarrah Cottages PUR * RM19 166 C5
Jarrett Cl BRXS/STRHM SW2 181 J4
Jarrow Cl MRDN SM4 201 L5
Jarrow Rd BERM/RHTH SE16 160 B3
CHDH RM6 123 M4
TOTM N17 120 A2
Jarrow Wy HOM E9 120 D9
Jarvis Cleys CHESW EN7 61 N2
Jarvis Cl BAR EN5 76 G9
Jarvis Rd EDUL SE22 159 M10
SAND/SEL CR2 223 L3
Jarvis Wy HARH RM3 105 M10
Jasmin Cl NTHWD HA6 92 G9
Jasmine Cl HAYES BR2 206 E9
IL IG1 122 E10
REDH RH1 276 B5
STHL UB1 133 M9
WOKN/KNAP GU21 231 L2
Jasmine Ct LEE/GVPK SE12 183 M2
Jasmine Dr HERT/BAY SG13 25 P5
Jasmine Gdns CROY/NA CR0 204 G10
HAT AL10 40 C2
RYLN/HDSTN HA2 113 P7
Jasmine Gv PGE/AN SE20 204 A1
Jasmine Rd ROMW/RG RM7 124 F7
Jasmine Ter WDR/YW UB7 152 B1
Jasmin Rd HOR/WEW KT19 219 N3
Jasmin Wy HHW HP1 35 H5
Jason Cl REDH RH1 275 P5
WEY KT13 216 D2
Jasons Cl BRW CM14 106 E5
Jasons Dr RGUE GU4 250 F7
Jasons Hl CSHM HP5 51 N5
Jason Wk ELTH/MOT SE9 184 D7
Jasper Cl PEND EN3 80 B4
Jasper Rd CAN/RD E16 142 A8
NRWD SE19 181 N9
Javelin Wy NTHLT UB5 133 L5
Jay Av ADL/WDHM * KT15 195 P10
Jaycroft ENC/FH EN2 79 H5
Jay Gdns CHST BR7 184 C7
Jay Ms SKENS SW7 15 K2
Jean Batten Cl CROY/NA CR0 222 G4
Jebb Av BRXS/STRHM SW2 180 F2
Jebb St BOW E3 140 F4
Jedburgh Rd PLSTW E13 141 P5
Jedburgh St BTSEA SW11 158 B10
Jeddo Ms SHB * W12 156 C1
Jeddo Rd SHB W12 156 C1
Jefferson Cl DTCH/LGLY SL3 150 D3
GNTH/NBYPK IG2 122 E3
WEA W13 154 G2
Jeffrey's Pl CAMTN NW1 4 G3
Jeffrey's Rd CLAP SW4 158 F8
PEND EN3 80 E8
Jeffrey's St CAMTN NW1 4 F3
Jeffries Pas GU * GU1 268 A1
Jeffries Rd EHSLY KT24 252 C7
Jeffs Cl HPTN * TW12 176 A9
Jeffs Rd SUT SM1 221 J1
Jeger Av BETH E2 7 L6
Jeken Rd ELTH/MOT SE9 161 P10
Jelf Rd BRXS/STRHM SW2 181 H1
Jellicoe Av GVE DA12 190 F6
Jellicoe Cl SL SL1 148 G1
Jellicoe Gdns STAN HA7 94 E7
Jellicoe Rd TOTM N17 99 L8
WATW WD18 73 H10
Jemmett Cl KUTN/CMB KT2 199 N1
Jem Paterson Ct HRW * HA1 114 D9
Jengar Cl SUT SM1 221 L1
Jenkins Av LCOL/BKTW AL2 55 M6
Jenkins La BARK IG11 142 E4
Jenkins Rd PLSTW E13 141 N6
Jenner Av ACT W3 136 A7
Jenner Dr CHOB/PIR GU24 212 F9
Jenner Rd CRAWE RH10 284 A2
GU GU1 268 B1
STNW/STAM N16 119 N7
Jennery La SL SL1 128 B5
Jennett Rd CROY/NA CR0 203 H10
Jennifer Rd BMLY BR1 183 L6
Jenningham Dr CDH/CHF RM16 147 M10
Jennings Cl ADL/WDHM KT15 215 M5
SURB KT6 199 H7
Jennings Rd EDUL SE22 181 N2
STAL AL1 38 E5
Jennings Wy BAR EN5 76 F7
HHS/BOV HP3 35 P8
HORL RH6 280 E4
Jenningtree Rd ERITH DA8 165 J6
Jenningtree Wy BELV DA17 164 D1
Jenny Hammond Cl WAN E11 121 L8
Jenson Wy NRWD SE19 181 N10
Jenton Av BXLYHN DA7 163 P7
Jephson Rd FSTGT E7 141 P2
Jephson St CMBW SE5 159 L7
Jephtha Rd WAND/EARL SW18 179 K2
Jeppo's La MTCM CR4 202 A4
Jepps Cl CHESW EN7 61 M3
Jerdan Pl FUL/PGN SW6 157 K6
Jeremiah St POP/IOD E14 140 G8
Jeremy's Gn UED N18 100 A5
Jermyn St STJS SW1Y 10 G9
Jerningham Av CLAY IG5 102 E10
Jerningham Rd NWCR SE14 160 D8
Jerome Crs STJWD NW8 9 N1
Jerome Dr STALW/RED AL3 37 P8
Jerome St WCHPL E1 13 L3
Jerounds HLWW/ROY CM19 46 E3
Jerrard St LEW SE13 160 G9
Jerrold St IS * N1 7 K8
Jersey Av KTN/HRWW/W HA3 94 G10
Jersey Cl CHERT KT16 195 J10
HOD EN11 44 F2
RGUE GU4 250 E5
Jersey Dr STMC/STPC BR5 206 G6
Jersey La STAL AL1 38 G4
STALE/WH AL4 21 H10
Jersey Rd CAN/RD E16 141 P7
HEST TW5 154 A7
HNWL W7 154 F1
IL IG1 122 E9
IS N1 6 F2
RAIN RM13 145 H2
TOOT SW17 180 C10
WAN E11 121 J6
Jersey St BETH E2 140 A5
Jersey Vls HNWL * W7 154 D1
Jerusalem Pas CLKNW EC1R 12 C2
Jervis Av PEND EN3 80 D1
Jerviston Gdns
STRHM/NOR SW16 181 H9
Jesmond Av WBLY HA9 135 L1
Jesmond Cl MTCM CR4 202 C3
Jesmond Dene HAMP * NW3 3 J1
Jesmond Rd CROY/NA CR0 203 N7
Jesmond Wy STAN HA7 95 K6
Jessam Av STNW/STAM N16 120 A6
Jessamine Pl RDART DA2 188 B3
Jessamine Rd HNWL W7 134 D10
Jessamine Ter SWLY * BR8 208 D1
Jessamy Rd WEY KT13 196 B9
Jessel Dr LOU IG10 82 F6
Jesse Rd LEY E10 121 H6
Jesses La SHGR GU5 270 D9
Jessett Cl ERITH DA8 164 E3
Jessica Rd WAND/EARL SW18 179 M2
Jessiman Ter SHPTN TW17 196 B5
Jessop Av NWDGN UB2 153 N3
Jessops Wy MTCM CR4 202 D6
Jessup Cl WOOL/PLUM SE18 162 F3
Jetstar Wy NTHLT UB5 133 M5
Jetty Wk GRAYS RM17 167 M5
Jevington Wy LEE/GVPK SE12 183 N4
Jewel Rd WALTH E17 120 F1
Jewels Hl WARL CR6 225 M8
Jewry St TWRH EC3N 13 L6
Jews Rw WAND/EARL SW18 157 L10
Jews Wk SYD SE26 182 A7
Jeymer Av CRICK NW2 116 E10
Jeymer Dr GFD/PVL UB6 134 B3
Jeypore Rd WAND/EARL SW18 179 M3
Jillian Cl HPTN TW12 175 P10
Jim Bradley Cl WOOL/PLUM SE18 162 D3
The Jinnings WGCE AL7 23 L8
Joan Crs ELTH/MOT SE9 184 A3
Joan Gdns BCTR RM8 123 P7
Joan Rd BCTR RM8 123 P7
Joan St STHWK SE1 12 C10
Jocelyn Rd RCH/KEW TW9 155 K9
Jocelyns HLWE CM17 29 M7
Jocelyn St PECK SE15 159 P7
Jocketts Hl HHW HP1 35 J6
Jocketts Rd HHW HP1 35 J7
Jockey's Flds FSBYW WC1X 11 P3
Jodane Rd DEPT SE8 160 E3
Jodrell Cl ISLW TW7 154 F7
Jodrell Rd HOM E9 140 E3
Jodrell Wy WTHK RM20 166 E4
Joel St NTHWD HA6 93 H10
PIN HA5 113 H1
Johanna St STHWK * SE1 18 A2
John Adam St CHCR WC2N 11 M9
John Aird Ct BAY/PAD W2 9 K3
John Archer Wy
WAND/EARL SW18 179 N2
John Ashby Cl BRXS/STRHM SW2 180 F2
John Austin Cl KUTN/CMB KT2 199 K1
John Bradshaw Rd
STHGT/OAK N14 98 E2
John Burns Dr BARK IG11 143 H3
Johnby Cl PEND EN3 80 D3
John Campbell Rd
STNW/STAM N16 119 M10
John Carpenter St EMB EC4Y 12 C7
John Cobb Rd WEY KT13 216 B4
John Eliot Cl WAB EN9 45 K8
John Felton Rd BERM/RHTH SE16 19 N2
John Fisher St WCHPL E1 13 N7
John Gooch Dr ENC/FH EN2 79 J5
John Goodchild Wy KUT KT1 199 N3
John Harrison Wy GNWCH SE10 161 L2
John Islip St WEST SW1P 17 L6
John Lamb Ct KTN/HRWW/W HA3 94 D9
John Maurice Cl WALW SE17 18 G5
John McKenna Wk
BERM/RHTH SE16 19 P3
John Parker Sq BTSEA * SW11 157 N9
John Penn St LEW SE13 160 G7
John Perrin Pl
KTN/HRWW/W HA3 115 K5
John Prince's St CAVSQ/HST W1G 10 F5
John Rennie Wk WAP E1W 140 A9
John Roll Wy BERM/RHTH SE16 19 P3
John Ruskin St CMBW SE5 159 J6
John Russell Cl GUW GU2 249 M7
John's Av HDN NW4 116 F2
John's Cl ASHF TW15 174 D7
HART DA3 211 L5
Johnsdale OXTED RH8 261 L5
John Silkin La DEPT SE8 160 C4
Johns La CSHM HP5 33 J8
MRDN SM4 201 M5
John's Ms BMSBY WC1N 11 P2
John Smith Av FUL/PGN SW6 157 J6
Johnson Cl GVW DA11 190 A6
HACK E8 7 N5
Johnson Ct HHS/BOV HP3 35 P8
Johnson Rd CROY/NA CR0 203 L7
HAYES BR2 206 A5
HEST TW5 153 K6
WLSDN NW10 136 A3
Johnsons Av RSEV TN14 228 C6
Johnson's Cl CAR SM5 202 A10
Johnsons Dr HPTN TW12 198 B1
Johnson's Pl PIM SW1V 17 H8
Johnson St NWDGN UB2 153 K2
WCHPL E1 140 B8
Johnsons Wy GRH DA9 189 H2
WLSDN NW10 135 N6
Johnsons Whf GRH * DA9 166 F10
Johnson Wk CRAWE RH10 283 N10
John Spencer Sq IS N1 6 D2
Johns Pl WCHPL E1 140 A8
John's Rd BH/WHM TN16 244 A6
John's Ter CROY/NA CR0 203 M8
The Johns CHONG CM5 67 P3
Johnston Cl BRXN/ST SW9 158 G7
Johnstone Rd EHAM E6 142 C5
Johnston Rd WFD IG8 101 M6
Johnston Wk GUW GU2 249 M6
John St BMSBY WC1N 11 P2
EN EN1 79 N9
GRAYS RM17 167 P5
HSLW TW3 153 M8
SNWD SE25 203 P4
SRTFD E15 141 L3
Johns Wk CTHM CR3 241 P5
John Tate Rd HERT/BAY SG13 25 N6
John Taylor Ct SL SL1 129 H10
John Trundle Highwalk
BARB * EC2Y 12 E3
John Williams Cl PECK SE15 160 C5
John Wilson St
WOOL/PLUM SE18 162 D3
John Wooley Cl LEW * SE13 161 K10
Joiners Arms Yd CMBW * SE5 159 L7
Joiner's Cl CFSP/GDCR SL9 90 C8
Joiners La CFSP/GDCR SL9 90 B9
Joiner St STHWK SE1 12 G10
Joiners Wy CFSP/GDCR SL9 90 B8
Joint Rd EFNCH N2 97 P9
Joinville Pl ADL/WDHM KT15 215 N1
Jolesfield CRAWW RH11 283 J10
Jolive Ct GU * GU1 268 D1
Jolliffe Rd REDH RH1 258 D2
Jollys La YEAD UB4 133 L7
Jonathan St LBTH SE11 17 N7
Jones Rd CHESW EN7 61 J6
PLSTW E13 141 N6
Jones Wy SLN SL2 109 J7
Jonquil Cl WGCE AL7 23 L7
Jonson Cl MTCM CR4 202 C4
YEAD UB4 133 H7
Jordan Cl GSTN WD25 72 G1
RYLN/HDSTN HA2 113 N8
SAND/SEL CR2 223 N7
Jordan Rd GFD/PVL UB6 134 G3
Jordans Cl CRAWW RH11 283 N5
DAGE RM10 124 C9
GU GU1 250 D9
REDH RH1 276 B5
STWL/WRAY TW19 173 M3
Jordans Crs CRAWW RH11 283 N4
Jordans La BEAC HP9 89 K8
Jordans Ms WHTN TW2 176 D5
Jordans Rd RKW/CH/CXG WD3 91 K1
Jordans Wy BEAC HP9 89 L7
LCOL/BKTW AL2 55 M6
RAIN RM13 145 L4
Joseph Av ACT W3 136 A8
Josephine Av BRXS/STRHM SW2 180 G1
KWD/TDW/WH KT20 257 J3
Josephine Cl
KWD/TDW/WH KT20 257 J3
Joseph Locke Wy
ESH/CLAY KT10 197 P9
Joseph Powell Cl BAL SW12 180 D2
Joseph Ray Rd WAN E11 121 K7
Joseph's Rd GU GU1 250 A9
Joseph St BOW E3 140 E7
Joseph Trotter Cl CLKNW EC1R 6 B10
Joshua St POP/IOD E14 141 H8
Josling Cl GRAYS RM17 167 L5
Joslings Cl SHB W12 136 D9
Joslin Rd PUR RM19 166 B4
Joslyn Cl PEND EN3 80 F4
Joubert St BTSEA SW11 158 A8
Journeys End SLN SL2 129 K7
Jowett St PECK SE15 159 N6
Joyce Av UED N18 99 N6
Joyce Ct WAB EN9 63 J10
Joyce Green La DART DA1 165 L7
Joyden's Wood Rd BXLY DA5 186 E7
Joydon Dr CHDH RM6 123 L4
Joyners Cl DAGW RM9 124 A9
Joyners Fld HLWS CM18 46 F5
Joy Rd GVE DA12 190 F4
Jubilee Arch WDSR * SL4 149 J7
Jubilee Av CHING E4 101 H7
LCOL/BKTW AL2 57 J2
ROMW/RG RM7 124 D3
WARE SG12 26 E1
WHTN TW2 176 B4
Jubilee Br STHWK SE1 12 F8
Jubilee Cl CDALE/KGS NW9 116 A4
GRH DA9 189 H2
KUT KT1 199 H1
PIN HA5 93 K10
ROMW/RG RM7 124 C3
STWL/WRAY TW19 173 M3
Jubilee Crs ADL/WDHM KT15 215 N2
ED N9 99 P2
GVE DA12 191 H5
Jubilee Dr RSLP HA4 113 L9
Jubilee Gdns STHL UB1 133 P7
STHWK * SE1 11 P10
Jubilee Market COVGDN * WC2E 11 M7
Jubilee Pl CHEL SW3 15 P7
Jubilee Ri BGR/WK TN15 247 N7
Jubilee Rd CHEAM SM3 220 G4
GFD/PVL UB6 134 G3
ORP BR6 228 B3
WATN WD24 73 H4
WTHK RM20 166 G5
Jubilee St WCHPL E1 140 B8
Jubilee Ter BRKHM/BTCW RH3 273 P4
DORK RH4 272 G1
FUL/PGN * SW6 157 H8
The Jubilee GNWCH * SE10 160 G6
Jubilee Vls ESH/CLAY * KT10 198 D8
Jubilee Wk CRAWE RH10 284 B7
Jubilee Wy CHSGTN KT9 199 N10
EBED/NFELT TW14 175 H4
SCUP DA14 185 K5
WIM/MER SW19 201 L1
Judd St STPAN WC1H 5 L10
Jude St CAN/RD E16 141 L8
Judeth Gdns GVE DA12 191 H8
Judge Heath La UX/CGN UB8 132 D8
Judge's Hl POTB/CUF EN6 60 A5
Judge St WATN WD24 73 J4
Judges' Wk HAMP NW3 117 M8
Judge Wk ESH/CLAY KT10 218 D3
Judith Av CRW RM5 104 C7
Juer St BTSEA SW11 157 P6
Juglans Rd ORP BR6 207 K8
Jules Thorn Av EN EN1 79 P7
Julia Gdns BARK IG11 143 N4
Juliana Cl EFNCH N2 117 M1
Julian Av ACT W3 135 N9
Julian Cl BAR EN5 77 L7
WOKN/KNAP GU21 231 P4
Julian Hl HRW HA1 114 D7
WEY KT13 216 B4
Julian Pl POP/IOD E14 160 G4
Julian Rd ORP BR6 227 K3
Julians Cl SEV TN13 265 H3
Julians Wy SEV TN13 265 H3
Julian Tayler Pth SYD * SE26 182 A5
Julien Rd COUL/CHIP CR5 240 D1
EA W5 155 H2
Juliette Rd PLSTW E13 141 M4
Juliette Wy PUR RM19 165 N1
Julius Nyerere Cl IS N1 5 P6
Junction Ap BTSEA SW11 157 P9
LEW SE13 161 H9
Junction Ms BAY/PAD W2 9 N5
Junction Pl BAY/PAD * W2 9 M5
Junction Rd ARCH N19 118 D8
ASHF TW15 174 D8
BRW CM14 107 H5
DART DA1 187 L2
DORK RH4 272 F2
EA W5 155 H3
ED N9 99 P2
HRW HA1 114 C4
LTWR GU18 212 A6
PLSTW E13 141 N3
ROM RM1 124 G2
SAND/SEL CR2 223 L3
TOTM N17 119 P1
Junction Rd East CHDH RM6 123 P5
Junction Rd West CHDH RM6 123 N5
June Cl COUL/CHIP CR5 222 C10
June La REDH RH1 276 C7
Junewood Cl ADL/WDHM KT15 215 J7
Juniper Av LCOL/BKTW AL2 55 P7
Juniper Cl BAR EN5 76 G9
BH/WHM TN16 244 B3
BROX EN10 62 E1
CHSGTN KT9 219 L3
GU GU1 249 N5
REIG RH2 275 M2
Juniper Ct CHDH RM6 123 L4
KTN/HRWW/W * HA3 94 E9
NTHWD * HA6 93 H9
RBRW/HUT * CM13 107 L4
Juniper Crs CAMTN NW1 4 D4
Juniper Dr CHOB/PIR GU24 230 F1
CHOB/PIR GU24 230 F1
SOCK/AV RM15 147 K5
Juniper Gdns MTCM CR4 202 D1
RAD WD7 57 K9
SUN TW16 174 G9
Juniper Ga RKW/CH/CXG WD3 91 N3
Juniper Gn HHW HP1 35 H6
Juniper Gv WAT WD17 73 H4
Juniper La EHAM E6 142 B7
Juniper Rd CRAWW RH11 283 M4
IL IG1 122 D9
REIG RH2 275 M2
Juniper St WCHPL * E1 140 B9
Juniper Wy HARH RM3 105 M9
HYS/HAR UB3 132 E9
Juno Wy NWCR SE14 160 C5
Jupiter Dr HHNE HP2 36 A4
Jupiter Wy HOLWY N7 5 P1
Jupp Rd SRTFD E15 141 J2
Jupp Rd West SRTFD E15 141 H3
Jura Cl CRAWW RH11 283 L10
Jurgens Rd PUR * RM19 166 B3
Jury St GVE DA12 190 E2
Justice Wk CHEL SW3 15 N10
Justin Cl BTFD TW8 155 J6
Justin Rd CHING E4 100 E7
Jute La PEND EN3 80 D6
Jutland Pl EGH TW20 172 F8
Jutland Rd CAT SE6 183 H3
PLSTW E13 141 M6
Jutsums Av ROMW/RG RM7 124 C4
Jutsums La ROMW/RG RM7 124 C4
Juxon Cl CRAWW RH11 283 J9
RYLN/HDSTN HA2 94 A9
Juxon St LBTH SE11 17 P5

K

Kaduna Cl PIN HA5 113 J3
Kale Rd ERITHM DA18 163 N1
Kambala Rd BTSEA SW11 157 N8
Kandlewood RBRW/HUT CM13 107 N1
Kangley Bridge Rd SYD SE26 182 E8
Kaplan Dr WCHMH N21 78 G9
Karen Cl BRWN CM15 107 H1
RAIN RM13 144 F4
Karen Ct BMLY BR1 205 L1
Karenza Ct WBLY * HA9 115 H5
Karina Cl CHIG IG7 103 H6
Kashgar Rd WOOL/PLUM SE18 163 J4
Kashmir Cl ADL/WDHM KT15 215 N5
Kashmir Rd CHARL SE7 162 A6
Kassala Rd BTSEA SW11 158 A7
Katescroft WGCE AL7 23 H9
Katharine St CROY/NA CR0 203 K10
Katherine Cl ADL/WDHM KT15 215 K3
BERM/RHTH SE16 140 C10
Katherine Gdns BARK/HLT IG6 102 F8
ELTH/MOT SE9 162 A10
Katherine Pl ABLGY WD5 55 H8
Katherine Rd EHAM E6 142 A2
Katherine Sq NTGHL W11 8 A9
Katherine's Wy HLWW/ROY CM19 46 D4
Kathleen Av ACT W3 135 P7
ALP/SUD HA0 135 K2
Kathleen Rd BTSEA SW11 158 A9
Katrine Sq HHNE HP2 35 N2
Kavanaghs Rd BRW CM14 106 F4
Kavanaghs Ter BRW CM14 106 G4
Kay Av ADL/WDHM KT15 195 P10
Kaye Don Wy WEY KT13 216 B6
Kayemoor Rd BELMT SM2 221 P4
Kay Rd BRXN/ST SW9 158 F8
Kays Ter SWFD * E18 101 L10
Kay St BETH E2 7 P7
SRTFD * E15 141 J2
WELL DA16 163 L7
Kay Wk STALE/WH AL4 39 J5
Kaywood Cl DTCH/LGLY SL3 149 P2
Kean St HOL/ALD WC2B 11 N6
Kearton Cl PUR/KEN CR8 241 K3
Keary Rd SWCM DA10 189 L3
Keatley Gn CHING E4 100 E7
Keats Av CAN/RD E16 141 N10
HARH RM3 105 J8
REDH RH1 258 B8
Keats Cl CHIG IG7 102 F7
PEND EN3 80 C9
STHWK SE1 19 L6
TOOT SW17 179 N9
WAN E11 121 N3
YEAD UB4 133 H7
Keats Est STNW/STAM * N16 119 N7
Keats Gdns TIL RM18 168 E8
Keats Gv HAMP NW3 117 P9
Keats La WDSR SL4 149 J5
Keats Pde ED * N9 99 P3
Keats Rd BELV DA17 164 D2
WELL DA16 163 H7
Keats Wy CROY/NA CR0 204 B6
GFD/PVL UB6 134 A7
WDR/YW UB7 152 A3
Keble Cl CRAWE RH10 284 E4
NTHLT UB5 114 B10
WPK KT4 200 C8
Keble Pl BARN SW13 156 E5
Keble St TOOT SW17 179 M7
Keble Ter ABLGY WD5 54 G8
Kechill Gdns HAYES BR2 205 M7
Kedleston Dr STMC/STPC BR5 207 J6
Kedleston Wk BETH E2 140 A5
Keeble Cl WOOL/PLUM * SE18 162 E5
Keedonwood Rd BMLY BR1 183 K7
Keel Cl BARK IG11 143 M4
BERM/RHTH SE16 140 C10
Keel Dr SL SL1 128 G10
Keele Cl WATN WD24 73 K6
Keeler Cl WDSR SL4 148 D9
Keeley Rd CROY/NA CR0 203 K9
Keeley St HOL/ALD WC2B 11 N6
Keeling Rd ELTH/MOT SE9 184 A1
Keely Cl EBAR EN4 77 P9
Keemor Cl WOOL/PLUM * SE18 162 D6
Keensacre IVER SL0 130 G4
Keens Cl STRHM/NOR SW16 180 E8
Keens La RGUW GU3 249 L6
Keens Park Rd RGUW GU3 249 L6
Keen's Rd CROY/NA CR0 223 K1
Keen's Yd IS N1 6 D2
Keepers Cl RGUE GU4 250 G7
Keepers Farm Cl WDSR SL4 148 D8
Keepers Ms TEDD TW11 177 H9
Keepers Wk VW GU25 194 A5
The Keep BKHTH/KID SE3 161 M8
KUTN/CMB KT2 177 L9
Keesey St WALW SE17 18 G9
Keetons Rd BERM/RHTH * SE16 160 A2
BERM/RHTH SE16 160 A2
Keevil Dr WIM/MER SW19 178 G3
Keighley Cl HOLWY N7 118 F9
Keightley Dr ELTH/MOT SE9 184 F4
Keilder Cl HGDN/ICK UB10 132 B4
Keildon Rd BTSEA SW11 158 A10
Keir Hardie Est CLPT * E5 120 A6
Keir Hardie Wy BARK IG11 143 K2
YEAD * UB4 133 H5
Keith Av EYN DA4 188 A9
Keith Connor Cl VX/NE SW8 158 C9
Keith Gv SHB W12 156 D1
Keith Park Crs BH/WHM TN16 225 P8
Keith Park Rd HGDN/ICK UB10 132 A2
Keith Rd BARK IG11 142 G4
HYS/HAR UB3 152 F2
WALTH E17 100 E9
Keiths Rd HHS/BOV HP3 36 B7
Keith Wy EMPK RM11 125 M5
Kelbrook Rd BKHTH/KID SE3 162 B8
Kelburn Wy RAIN RM13 145 H5
Kelbys WGCE AL7 23 M4
Kelceda Cl CRICK NW2 116 D7

Kelf Gv HYS/HAR UB3 132 G8
Kelfield Gdns NKENS W10 136 G8
Kelfield Ms NKENS W10 136 G7
Kelland Cl CEND/HSY/T * N8 118 E3
Kelland Rd PLSTW E13 141 M6
Kellaway Rd BKHTH/KID SE3 161 P8
Keller Cresent MNPK E12 122 A9
Kellerton Rd LEW SE13 183 K1
Kellett Rd BRXS/STRHM SW2 159 H10
Kelling Gdns CROY/NA CR0 203 J7
Kellino St TOOT SW17 180 A7
Kellner Rd THMD SE28 163 J2
Kell St STHWK SE1 18 D3
Kelly Av PECK SE15 159 N7
Kelly Cl BORE WD6 76 A6
SHPTN TW17 196 F2
WLSDN NW10 116 A8
Kelly Ms MV/WKIL W9 8 D2
Kelly Rd MLHL NW7 97 H7
Kelly St CAMTN NW1 4 F2
Kelly Wy CHDH RM6 123 P3
Kelman Cl CHES/WCR EN8 62 C7
CLAP SW4 158 E8
Kelmore Gv EDUL SE22 159 P10
Kelmscott Cl WALTH E17 100 E9
WATW WD18 73 H10
Kelmscott Crs WATW WD18 73 H9
Kelmscott Gdns SHB W12 156 D2
Kelmscott Rd BTSEA SW11 179 P1
Kelpatrick Rd SL SL1 128 C8
Kelross Rd HBRY N5 119 J9
Kelsall Cl BKHTH/KID SE3 161 N8
Kelsey Cl HORL RH6 280 A4
Kelsey La BECK BR3 204 F3
Kelsey Park Av BECK BR3 204 G3
Kelsey Park Rd BECK BR3 204 F2
Kelsey Rd STMC/STPC BR5 207 L2
Kelsey Sq BECK BR3 204 F2
Kelsey St BETH E2 13 P1
Kelsey Wy BECK BR3 204 F3
Kelshall GSTN WD25 73 M2
Kelsie Wy BARK/HLT IG6 103 H7
Kelso Cl CRAWE RH10 284 F6
Kelso Dr GVE DA12 191 J7
Kelso Pl KENS W8 14 G3
Kelso Rd CAR SM5 201 M7
Kelston Rd BARK/HLT IG6 102 E10
Kelton Vls KUT * KT1 199 L2
Kelvedon Av WOT/HER KT12 216 F4
Kelvedon Cl KUTN/CMB KT2 177 M9
Kelvedon Gn BRWN CM15 86 E3
Kelvedon Hall La BRW CM14 86 A2
Kelvedon Rd FUL/PGN SW6 157 J6
Kelvedon Wy WFD IG8 102 C7
Kelvin Av LHD/OX KT22 236 E6
PLMGR N13 98 G7
Kelvinbrook E/WMO/HCT KT8 198 A3
Kelvin Cl HOR/WEW KT19 219 M3
Kelvin Crs KTN/HRWW/W HA3 94 D8
Kelvin Dr TWK TW1 176 G2
Kelvin Gdns CROY/NA CR0 202 F7
STHL UB1 133 P8
Kelvin Gv SURB KT6 199 K10
SYD SE26 182 A6
Kelvington Cl CROY/NA CR0 204 D7
Kelvington Rd PECK SE15 182 C1
Kelvin La CRAWE RH10 284 A3
Kelvin Pde ORP BR6 207 H8
Kelvin Rd HBRY N5 119 J9
TIL RM18 168 D8
WELL DA16 163 K9
Kelvin Wy CRAWE RH10 284 A3
Kember St IS * N1 5 N4
Kemble Cl POTB/CUF EN6 59 N9
WEY KT13 216 E1
Kemble Dr HAYES BR2 206 B10
Kemble Pde POTB/CUF * EN6 59 M8
Kemble Rd CROY/NA CR0 203 J10
FSTH SE23 182 C4
TOTM N17 99 P9
Kembleside Rd BH/WHM TN16 243 P4
Kemble St HOL/ALD WC2B 11 N6
Kemerton Rd BECK BR3 204 G2
CMBW SE5 159 K9
CROY/NA CR0 203 N7
Kemey's St HOM E9 120 D10
Kemishford WOKS/MYFD GU22 231 M9
Kemnal Rd CHST BR7 184 F9
Kempe Cl DTCH/LGLY SL3 150 F3
STAL AL1 38 B10
Kempe Rd EN EN1 80 A2
KIL/WHAMP NW6 136 G4
Kemp Gdns CROY/NA CR0 203 K6
Kemplay Rd HAMP NW3 117 N9
Kemp Pl BUSH WD23 73 P10
Kemprow GSTN WD25 74 C1
Kemps Dr NTHWD HA6 92 G8
POP/IOD E14 140 F9
Kempsford Gdns ECT SW5 14 F8
Kempsford Rd LBTH SE11 18 B6
Kempshott Rd
STRHM/NOR SW16 180 F10
Kempson Rd FUL/PGN SW6 157 K7
Kempthorne Rd DEPT SE8 160 D3
Kempthorne St GVW * DA11 190 E2
Kempton Av HCH RM12 125 N9
NTHLT UB5 133 P1
SUN TW16 197 J1
Kempton Cl ERITH DA8 164 D5
HGDN/ICK UB10 112 D9
Kempton Ct SUN TW16 197 J1
Kempton Pk SUN * TW16 197 K1
Kempton Rd EHAM E6 142 C3
HPTN TW12 197 N2
Kempton Wk CROY/NA CR0 204 D6
Kempt St WOOL/PLUM SE18 162 D5
Kemsing Cl BXLY DA5 185 P3
THHTH * CR7 203 K4
Kemsing Rd GNWCH SE10 161 M4
Kemsley Cha SLN SL2 129 H3
Kemsley Cl GRH DA9 188 G2
GVW DA11 190 C7
Kemsley Rd BH/WHM TN16 244 A5
Kenbury Cl HGDN/ICK UB10 112 B8
Kenbury St CMBW SE5 159 K8
Kenchester Cl VX/NE SW8 158 F6
Kendal Av ACT W3 135 M7
BARK IG11 143 H3
EPP CM16 65 K6
UED N18 99 L5
Kendal Cl CMBW SE5 159 J6
EBED/NFELT TW14 174 G4
REDH RH1 257 N9
SLN SL2 129 M9
WFD IG8 101 L3
YEAD UB4 132 F4
Kendal Ct ACT W3 135 M7
Kendal Cft HCH RM12 125 H10
Kendal Dr SLN SL2 129 M9
Kendale CDH/CHF RM16 168 E2
HHS/BOV HP3 36 C7
Kendale Rd BMLY BR1 183 K8
Kendal Gdns SUT SM1 201 M9
UED N18 99 L5
Kendall Av BECK BR3 204 D2
SAND/SEL CR2 223 L5
Kendall Av South SAND/SEL CR2 223 K6
Kendall Cl WGCE AL7 23 J9
Kendall Pl MHST W1U 10 C4
Kendall Rd BECK BR3 204 D2
ISLW TW7 154 F8
WOOL/PLUM SE18 162 B7
Kendalmere Cl MUSWH N10 98 C9
Kendal Pde UED * N18 99 L5
Kendal Pl PUT/ROE SW15 179 J1
Kendal Rd WLSDN NW10 116 D9
Kendals Cl RAD WD7 74 D2
Kendal Steps BAY/PAD * W2 9 P6
Kendal St BAY/PAD W2 9 P6
Kender St NWCR SE14 160 B6
Kendoa Rd CLAP SW4 158 E10
Kendon Cl WAN E11 121 N3
Kendor Av HOR/WEW KT19 219 P7
Kendra Hall Rd SAND/SEL CR2 223 J4
Kendrey Gdns WHTN TW2 176 D2
Kendrick Ms SKENS SW7 15 L5
Kendrick Pl SKENS * SW7 15 L6
Kendrick Rd DTCH/LGLY SL3 149 N2
Kenelm Cl HRW HA1 114 F8
Kenerne Dr BAR EN5 77 H9
Kenford Cl GSTN WD25 55 J8
Kenilford Rd BAL SW12 180 C3
Kenilworth Av COB KT11 218 A10
HARH RM3 106 A6
RYLN/HDSTN HA2 113 N9
WALTH E17 100 F10
WIM/MER SW19 179 K8
Kenilworth Cl BNSTD SM7 239 L2
HHS/BOV HP3 35 P7
SL SL1 149 L2
Kenilworth Ct WAT WD17 73 H5
Kenilworth Crs EN EN1 79 M5
Kenilworth Dr BORE WD6 75 P7
RKW/CH/CXG WD3 72 C8
WOT/HER KT12 197 L10
Kenilworth Gdns
GDMY/SEVK IG3 123 J7
HCH RM12 125 K8
LOU IG10 82 C10
OXHEY WD19 93 K6
STA TW18 173 M8
STHL * UB1 133 N5
WOOL/PLUM SE18 162 E8
YEAD UB4 132 G7
Kenilworth Rd ASHF TW15 173 N6
BOW E3 140 D4
EA W5 135 K10
EDGW HA8 95 P3
EW KT17 220 D3
KIL/WHAMP NW6 2 D5
PGE/AN SE20 204 C1
STMC/STPC BR5 206 F6
Kenilworth Ter BELMT * SM2 221 K4
Kenley Av CDALE/KGS NW9 96 B9
Kenley Cl BXLY DA5 186 B3
CHST BR7 207 H3
EBAR EN4 77 P8
Kenley Gdns HCH RM12 125 N7
THHTH CR7 203 J4
Kenley La PUR/KEN CR8 223 K10
Kenley Rd KUT KT1 199 N2
TWK TW1 176 F2
WIM/MER SW19 201 K2
Kenley Wk CHEAM SM3 220 G1
NTGHL W11 8 A8
Kenlor Rd TOOT SW17 179 N8
Kenmara Cl CRAWE RH10 284 C4
Kenmara Ct CRAWE RH10 284 C3
Kenmare Dr MTCM CR4 180 A10
Kenmare Gdns PLMGR N13 99 K5
Kenmare Rd THHTH CR7 203 H6
Kenmere Gdns ALP/SUD HA0 135 M3
Kenmere Rd WELL DA16 163 M8
Kenmont Gdns WLSDN NW10 136 E5
Kenmore Av KTN/HRWW/W HA3 114 F2
Kenmore Crs YEAD UB4 132 G5
Kenmore Gdns EDGW HA8 95 N10
Kenmore Rd KTN/HRWW/W HA3 115 J1
PUR/KEN CR8 223 J10
Kenmure Rd HACK * E8 120 A10
Kenmure Yd HACK * E8 120 A10
Kennard Rd FBAR/BDGN N11 98 A6
SRTFD E15 141 J2
Kennard St BTSEA SW11 158 B7
CAN/RD E16 142 C10
Kenneally WDSR SL4 148 B8
Kennedy Av HOD EN11 44 E3
PEND EN3 80 B10
Kennedy Cl CHES/WCR EN8 62 D4
MTCM CR4 202 B2
PIN HA5 93 N7
PLSTW E13 141 M4
SLN SL2 129 H1
STMC/STPC BR5 206 G8
Kennedy Gdns SEV TN13 247 K9
Kennedy Rd BARK IG11 143 H3
HNWL W7 134 D7
Kennedy Wk WALW SE17 19 H6
Kennel Cl GT/LBKH KT23 236 B10
Kennel La BFOR GU20 216 A2
HORL RH6 279 N5
LHD/OX KT22 236 B9
Kennel Wood Crs CROY/NA CR0 225 J7
Kennelwood La HAT AL10 40 E3
Kennet Cl BTSEA SW11 157 N10
CRAWW RH11 283 J8
UPMR RM14 126 D4
Kennet Dr YEAD UB4 133 M7
Kenneth Av IL IG1 122 E9
Kenneth Crs CRICK NW2 116 E10
Kenneth Gdns STAN HA7 94 F7
Kenneth Moor Rd IL * IG1 122 E9
Kenneth Rd BNSTD SM7 239 N1
CHDH RM6 123 P5
Kennet Rd DART DA1 165 H9
ISLW TW7 154 F9
MV/WKIL W9 8 D1
Kennet St WAP E1W 13 P9
Kennett Rd DTCH/LGLY SL3 150 E2
Kennett Wharf La BLKFR EC4V 12 F7
Kenninghall Rd CLPT E5 120 A8
UED N18 100 A6
Kenning Rd HOD EN11 44 F1
Kenning St BERM/RHTH SE16 160 B1
Kennings Wy LBTH SE11 18 B7
Kennington Gdns KUT KT1 199 J3
Kennington Gv LBTH SE11 17 P9
Kennington La LBTH SE11 17 P8
Kennington Ov LBTH SE11 17 P9
Kennington Park Gdns LBTH SE11 18 C9
Kennington Park Pl WALW SE17 18 B9
Kennington Park Rd LBTH SE11 18 A10
Kennington Rd LBTH SE11 18 A4
Kenny Dr CAR SM5 222 B5
Kennylands Rd BARK/HLT IG6 103 K8
Kenny Rd MLHL NW7 97 H7
Kenrick Pl MHST W1U 10 C3
Kenrick Sq REDH RH1 259 M10
Kensal Whf NKENS * W10 8 A1
Kensington Av MNPK E12 142 B1
THHTH CR7 203 H1
WATW WD18 72 G8
Kensington Church Ct KENS W8 14 G2
Kensington Church St KENS W8 8 F9
Kensington Church Wk
KENS * W8 14 G1
Kensington Cl FBAR/BDGN * N11 98 B6
STAL AL1 38 F8
Kensington Ct GRAYS * RM17 167 P5
KENS W8 15 H2
Kensington Court Gdns
KENS * W8 15 H3
Kensington Court Ms KENS * W8 15 H3
Kensington Court Pl KENS W8 15 H3
Kensington Dr WFD IG8 102 A10
Kensington Gdns IL IG1 122 C6
Kensington Gardens Sq
BAY/PAD W2 8 G6
Kensington Ga SKENS SW7 15 J3
Kensington Gore SKENS SW7 15 K2
Kensington High St KENS W8 14 E3
Kensington Palace KENS * W8 9 H10
Kensington Palace Gdns KENS W8 8 G9
Kensington Park Gdns NTGHL W11 8 C8
Kensington Park Ms NTGHL * W11 8 C6
Kensington Park Rd NTGHL W11 8 C6
Kensington Pl KENS W8 8 E10
Kensington Rd BRWN CM15 86 F10
KENS W8 15 H2
NTHLT UB5 133 P4
ROMW/RG RM7 124 D4
SKENS SW7 15 N2
Kensington Sq KENS W8 14 G2
Kensington Ter SAND/SEL CR2 223 L4
Kensington Wy BORE WD6 76 A7
Kent Av DAGW RM9 144 B5
SL SL1 129 H7
WEA W13 134 G7
WELL DA16 185 J1
Kent Cl BORE WD6 76 A4
ORP BR6 227 H3
STA TW18 173 N9
STRHM/NOR SW16 202 F4
UX/CGN UB8 131 M1
Kent Ct CDALE/KGS * NW9 96 B10
Kent Dr EBAR EN4 78 B8
HCH RM12 125 L9
TEDD TW11 176 D8
Kentford Wy NTHLT UB5 133 M3
Kent Gdns RSLP HA4 113 H4
WEA W13 134 G7
Kent Gate Wy CROY/NA CR0 224 E3
Kent Hatch Rd OXTED RH8 261 P6
Kent House La BECK BR3 182 D9
Kent House Rd BECK BR3 182 C10
Kentish La BRKMPK AL9 41 M10
Kentish Rd BELV DA17 164 B3
Kentish Town Rd KTTN NW5 4 F2
Kentish Wy BMLY BR1 205 N2
Kentlea Rd THMD SE28 163 H1
Kentmere Rd WOOL/PLUM SE18 163 H3
Kenton Av HRW HA1 114 E5
STHL UB1 133 P9
SUN TW16 197 L2
Kenton Gdns KTN/HRWW/W HA3 115 H3
STAL AL1 38 E7
Kenton La KTN/HRWW/W HA3 94 F9
Kenton Park Av
KTN/HRWW/W HA3 115 J2
Kenton Park Cl
KTN/HRWW/W HA3 115 H2
Kenton Park Crs
KTN/HRWW/W HA3 115 J2
Kenton Park Pde
KTN/HRWW/W * HA3 115 H3
Kenton Park Rd
KTN/HRWW/W HA3 115 H2
Kenton Rd HOM E9 140 C1
HRW HA1 114 E5
KTN/HRWW/W HA3 115 K3
Kentons La WDSR SL4 148 D8
Kenton St STPAN WC1H 11 L1
Kenton Wy WOKN/KNAP GU21 231 K3
YEAD UB4 132 F5
Kent Rd BFOR GU20 212 C2
CHSWK W4 155 P2
DAGE RM10 124 C10
DART DA1 187 M2
E/WMO/HCT KT8 198 B4
GRAYS RM17 167 P5
GVW DA11 190 D4
HART DA3 211 J2
KUT KT1 199 J3
RCH/KEW TW9 155 M6
STMC/STPC BR5 207 L6
WCHMH N21 99 L2
WOKS/MYFD GU22 232 E2
WWKM BR4 204 G8
Kents Av HHS/BOV HP3 35 N10
Kents La EPP CM16 48 E7
Kent St BETH E2 7 M7
PLSTW E13 141 N5
Kent Ter CAMTN NW1 3 P10
Kent Vw SOCK/AV RM15 166 B1
Kent View Gdns GDMY/SEVK IG3 123 H8
Kent Wy SURB KT6 199 K10
Kentwell Cl BROCKY * SE4 160 D10
Kentwode Gn BARN SW13 156 D6
Kentwyns Ri REDH RH1 276 G1
Kent Yd SKENS SW7 15 P2
Kenver Av NFNCH/WDSP N12 97 P7
Kenward Rd ELTH/MOT SE9 183 P1
Kenway RAIN RM13 145 K4
ROMW/RG RM7 104 D10
Ken Wy WBLY HA9 115 P7
Kenway Cl RAIN RM13 145 K5
Kenway Dr AMSS HP7 69 N5
Kenway Rd ECT SW5 14 G6
Kenway Wk RAIN RM13 145 L5
Kenwood Av HART DA3 211 P3
Kenwood Cl GLDGN NW11 117 N6
WDR/YW UB7 152 B5
Kenwood Dr BECK BR3 205 H3
RKW/CH/CXG WD3 91 J3
WOT/HER KT12 217 J3
Kenwood Gdns CLAY IG5 122 D2
SWFD E18 121 N1
Kenwood Pk WEY KT13 216 E3
Kenwood Rdg PUR/KEN CR8 241 J3
Kenwood Rd ED N9 99 P3
HGT N6 118 A4
Kenworth Cl CHES/WCR EN8 62 C9
Kenworthy Rd HOM E9 120 D10
Kenwyn Dr CRICK NW2 116 B8
Kenwyn Rd CLAP SW4 158 E10
DART DA1 187 L1
RYNPK SW20 200 F1
Kenya Ct HORL * RH6 280 A3
Kenya Rd CHARL SE7 162 A6
Kenyngton Dr SUN TW16 175 H8
Kenyngton Pl
KTN/HRWW/W HA3 115 H3
Kenyons EHSLY KT24 252 C4
Kenyon St FUL/PGN SW6 156 G7
Keogh Rd SRTFD E15 141 K1
Kepler Rd CLAP SW4 158 F10
Keppel Rd DAGW RM9 123 P9
DORK RH4 254 G10
EHAM E6 142 C2
Keppel Sp WDSR SL4 171 N3
Keppel St GWRST WC1E 11 K3
WDSR SL4 149 J8
Kerbela St BETH E2 13 N1
Kerbey St POP/IOD E14 140 G8
Kerdistone Cl POTB/CUF EN6 59 L6
Kerfield Crs CMBW SE5 159 L7
Kerfield Pl CMBW SE5 159 L7
Kernel Ct GU * GU1 249 P10
Kerria Wy CHOB/PIR GU24 212 D9
Kerri Cl BAR EN5 76 F8
Kerril Cft HLW CM20 28 D10
Kerrill Av COUL/CHIP CR5 241 H5
Kerrison Pl EA W5 135 J10
Kerrison Rd BTSEA SW11 157 P9
EA W5 135 J10
SRTFD E15 141 J3
Kerry Av PUR RM19 165 N1
STAN HA7 95 H5
Kerry Cl CAN/RD E16 141 N8
PLMGR N13 98 G3
UPMR RM14 126 E5
Kerry Ct STAN HA7 95 J5
Kerry Dr UPMR RM14 126 E5
Kerry Pth NWCR SE14 160 E5
Kerry Rd NWCR SE14 160 E5
Kerry Ter WOKN/KNAP GU21 232 E2
Kersey Dr SAND/SEL CR2 224 B8
Kersey Gdns HARH RM3 105 M8
Kersfield Rd PUT/ROE SW15 178 G2
Kershaw Cl CDH/CHF RM16 167 H2
EMPK RM11 125 L5
Kershaw Rd DAGE RM10 124 B8
Kersley Ms BTSEA SW11 158 A7
Kersley Rd STNW/STAM N16 119 M8
Kersley St BTSEA SW11 158 A8
Kerstin Cl HYS/HAR UB3 132 G9
Kerswell Cl SEVS/STOTM N15 119 M3
Kerwick Cl HOLWY N7 5 M3
Keslake Rd KIL/WHAMP NW6 136 G4
Kessock Cl WALTH E17 120 A3
Kesters Rd CSHM HP5 51 J8
Kesteven Cl BARK/HLT IG6 103 J7
Keston Av ADL/WDHM KT15 215 K7
COUL/CHIP CR5 241 H5
HAYES BR2 225 P2
Keston Cl UED N18 99 L4
WELL DA16 163 M6
Keston Gdns HAYES BR2 225 P1
Keston Ms WAT WD17 73 J6
Keston Park Cl HAYES BR2 226 C1
Keston Rd PECK SE15 159 P9
THHTH CR7 202 G6
TOTM N17 119 L1
Kestrel Av EHAM E6 142 B7
HNHL SE24 181 J1
STA TW18 173 J6
Kestrel Cl BARK/HLT IG6 103 L5
BERK HP4 33 P6
CDALE/KGS NW9 96 B10
CRAWW RH11 283 M5
GSTN WD25 55 M10
HOR/WEW KT19 219 M7
KUTN/CMB KT2 177 J7
RAIN RM13 145 J2
RGUE GU4 250 G8
WLSDN NW10 116 A10
Kestrel Gn HAT AL10 40 D5
Kestrel Pl NWCR * SE14 160 D5
Kestrel Rd WAB EN9 63 M10
The Kestrels LCOL/BKTW AL2 55 M7
Kestrel Wy CROY/NA CR0 225 J5
HYS/HAR UB3 152 E1
WGCE AL7 23 J3
WOKN/KNAP GU21 231 N1
Keswick Av EMPK RM11 125 L6
KUTN/CMB KT2 178 B8
SHPTN TW17 196 F3
WIM/MER SW19 201 K2
Keswick Cl CRAWW RH11 282 G9
STAL AL1 38 G7
SUT SM1 221 M1
Keswick Ct SLN SL2 129 L9
Keswick Dr LTWR GU18 212 A7
PEND EN3 80 B2
Keswick Gdns REDBR IG4 122 B3
RSLP HA4 112 E4
WBLY HA9 115 K10
Keswick Ms EA W5 135 K10
Keswick Rd BXLYHN DA7 164 B8
EGH TW20 172 E10
GT/LBKH KT23 254 B1
ORP BR6 207 J8
PUT/ROE SW15 179 H1
WHTN TW2 176 B2
WWKM BR4 205 K9
Kettering Rd HARH RM3 105 M8
PEND EN3 80 C3
Kettering St STRHM/NOR SW16 180 C9
Kettlebaston Rd LEY E10 120 E6
Kettlebury Wy CHONG CM5 67 N6
Kettlewell Cl FBAR/BDGN N11 98 B7
WOKN/KNAP GU21 232 B1
Kettlewell Ct SWLY BR8 208 G2
Kettlewell Hl WOKN/KNAP GU21 232 B1
Kevan Dr RPLY/SEND GU23 251 H1
Kevelioc Rd TOTM N17 99 K9
Kevin Cl HSLWW TW4 153 L8
Kevington Cl STMC/STPC BR5 207 J4
Kevington Dr CHST BR7 207 J4
Kew Br RCH/KEW TW9 155 M5
Kew Bridge Arches CHSWK * W4 155 M5
Kew Bridge Rd BTFD TW8 155 L5
Kew Crs CHEAM SM3 201 J10
Kewferry Dr NTHWD HA6 92 C6
Kewferry Rd NTHWD HA6 92 D7
Kew Foot Rd RCH/KEW TW9 155 K10
Kew Gardens Rd RCH/KEW TW9 155 L6
Kew Gn RCH/KEW TW9 155 L5
Kew Meadow Pth
RCH/KEW TW9 155 N7
Kew Rd RCH/KEW TW9 155 K10
Key Cl WCHPL E1 140 A6
Keyes Rd CRICK NW2 116 G10
DART DA1 165 P10
Keyfield STAL * AL1 38 C7
Keyfield Ter STAL AL1 38 C7
Keymer Cl BH/WHM TN16 243 P2
Keymer Rd BRXS/STRHM SW2 180 G5
CRAWW RH11 283 N9
Keynes Cl EFNCH N2 118 A1
Keynsham Av WFD IG8 101 K5
Keynsham Gdns ELTH/MOT SE9 184 B1
Keynsham Rd ELTH/MOT SE9 184 A1
MRDN SM4 201 L8
Keynton Cl HERT/WAS SG14 24 G4
Keyse Rd STHWK SE1 19 L4
Keysers Rd BROX EN10 44 F8
Keysham Av HEST TW5 153 H7
Keystone Crs IS N1 5 M8
Keywood Dr SUN TW16 175 H9
Keyworth Cl CLPT E5 120 D9
Keyworth St STHWK SE1 18 D3
Kezia St DEPT SE8 160 D4
Khama Rd TOOT SW17 179 P7
Khartoum Pl GVE DA12 190 F2
Khartoum Rd IL IG1 122 E10
PLSTW E13 141 N5
TOOT SW17 179 N7
Khyber Rd BTSEA SW11 157 P8
Kibes La WARE SG12 26 C2
Kibworth St VX/NE SW8 158 G6
Kidborough Down
GT/LBKH KT23 253 P3
Kidborough Rd CRAWW RH11 283 J9
Kidbrooke Gdns BKHTH/KID SE3 161 M8
Kidbrooke Gv BKHTH/KID SE3 161 M7
Kidbrooke La ELTH/MOT SE9 162 B10
Kidbrooke Park Cl
BKHTH/KID SE3 161 N7
Kidbrooke Park Rd
BKHTH/KID SE3 161 N7
Kidbrooke Wy BKHTH/KID SE3 161 N8
Kidderminster Rd CROY/NA CR0 203 J8
SLN SL2 128 F5
Kidderpore Av HAMP NW3 117 K9
Kidderpore Gdns HAMP NW3 117 K9
Kidd Pl CHARL SE7 162 B4
Kidlington Wy CDALE/KGS NW9 96 B10
Kidworth Cl HORL RH6 280 A2
Kielder Cl BARK/HLT IG6 103 J7
Kier Pk ASC SL5 192 B3
Kilberry Cl ISLW TW7 154 C7
Kilbride Ct HHNE HP2 36 A2
Kilburn Br KIL/WHAMP NW6 2 F6
Kilburn High Rd KIL/WHAMP NW6 2 C2
Kilburn La NKENS W10 2 A9
Kilburn Park Rd KIL/WHAMP NW6 2 E10
Kilburn Pl KIL/WHAMP NW6 2 F6
Kilburn Priory KIL/WHAMP NW6 2 G6
Kilburn Sq KIL/WHAMP NW6 2 E6
Kilburn V KIL/WHAMP NW6 2 F6
Kilby Cl GSTN WD25 73 L1
Kilcorral Cl EW KT17 220 D10
Kildare Cl RSLP HA4 113 K6
Kildare Gdns BAY/PAD W2 8 F5
Kildare Rd CAN/RD E16 141 M7
Kildare Ter BAY/PAD W2 8 F5
Kildoran Rd CLAP SW4 180 F1
Kildowan Rd GDMY/SEVK IG3 123 K6
Kilfillan Gdns BERK HP4 33 M6
Kilgour Rd FSTH SE23 182 D2
Kilkie St FUL/PGN SW6 157 M8
Killarney Rd WAND/EARL SW18 179 M2
Killburns Mill Cl WLGTN SM6 202 C9
Killearn Rd CAT SE6 183 J4
Killester Gdns EW KT17 220 E1
Killewarren Wy STMC/STPC BR5 207 M7
Killick Cl SEV TN13 246 F7
Killick St IS N1 5 N7
Killieser Av BRXS/STRHM SW2 180 F5
Killip Cl CAN/RD E16 141 L8
Killowen Av NTHLT UB5 114 B10
Killowen Rd HOM * E9 140 C1
Killyon Rd VX/NE SW8 158 D8
Kilmaine Rd FUL/PGN SW6 157 H6
Kilmarnock Gdns BCTR RM8 123 M8
Kilmarnock Pk REIG RH2 257 L9
Kilmarnock Rd OXHEY WD19 93 L5
Kilmarsh Rd HMSMTH W6 156 F3
Kilmartin Av STRHM/NOR SW16 203 H3
Kilmartin Rd GDMY/SEVK IG3 123 K7
Kilmartin Wy HCH RM12 125 J10
Kilmington Cl RBRW/HUT CM13 107 N3
Kilmington Rd BARN SW13 156 D5
Kilmiston Av SHPTN TW17 196 D6
Kilmorey Gdns TWK TW1 176 G1
Kilmorey Rd TWK TW1 154 G10
Kilmorie Rd FSTH SE23 182 D4
Kiln Av AMS HP6 69 P4
Kiln Cl HYS/HAR UB3 152 E5
Kilncroft HHS/BOV HP3 36 C8
Kilndown GVE DA12 190 F9
Kilner St POP/IOD E14 140 F7
Kilnfield CHONG CM5 67 N5
WGCE AL7 23 J2
Kiln Gnd HHS/BOV HP3 36 B8
Kiln Ground Cl WARE SG12 26 D1
Kiln La ASC SL5 170 A9
ASC SL5 192 F5
BRKHM/BTCW RH3 255 P10
CSHM HP5 51 M7
EW KT17 220 B7
HLWE CM17 47 M2
HORL RH6 280 A2
RPLY/SEND GU23 233 L10
SLN SL2 109 H6
Kilnmead CRAWE RH10 283 P6
Kilnmead Cl CRAWE RH10 283 P6
Kiln Ms TOOT SW17 179 N8
Kiln Pl KTTN NW5 118 B9
Kiln Rd EPP CM16 66 B3
Kilnside ESH/CLAY KT10 218 F4
Kiln Wy GRAYS RM17 167 L4
NTHWD HA6 92 F7
Kilnwood RSEV TN14 228 A9
Kiln Wood La CRW RM5 104 E6
Kilnwood La HORS RH12 282 D10
Kilpatrick Wy YEAD UB4 133 M7
Kilravock St NKENS W10 2 A10
Kilross Rd EBED/NFELT TW14 174 E4
Kilrue La WOT/HER KT12 216 G1
Kilrush Ter WOKN/KNAP GU21 232 D2
Kilsha Rd WOT/HER KT12 197 J6
Kilsmore La CHES/WCR EN8 62 C4
Kilvinton Dr ENC/FH EN2 79 L4
Kilworth Av BRWN CM15 87 M10
Kimbell Gdns FUL/PGN SW6 157 H7
Kimbell Pl ELTH/MOT SE9 161 P10
Kimbell Cl WGCE AL7 23 L7

Kimber Cl WDSR SL4 148 F9
Kimber Ct RGUE * GU4 250 G8
Kimberley Av EHAM E6 142 B4
GNTH/NBYPK IG2 122 G5
PECK SE15 160 A8
ROMW/RG RM7 124 C4
Kimberley Cl DTCH/LGLY SL3 150 C3
HORL RH6 279 P4
Kimberley Dr SCUP DA14 185 N5
Kimberley Gdns EN EN1 79 N7
FSBYPK N4 119 J3
Kimberley Pl PUR/KEN CR8 223 H7
Kimberley Ride COB KT11 218 A9
Kimberley Rd BECK BR3 204 C2
BRXN/ST SW9 158 F8
CAN/RD E16 141 L6
CHING E4 101 K2
CRAWE RH10 284 C6
CROY/NA CR0 203 J6
KIL/WHAMP NW6 2 B5
STALW/RED AL3 38 B5
TOTM N17 99 P10
UED N18 100 A7
WALTH E17 100 D9
WAN E11 121 J7
Kimberley Wy CHING E4 101 K2
Kimber Rd WAND/EARL SW18 179 L3
Kimbers Dr SL SL1 128 C5
Kimble Cl WATW * WD18 72 F10
Kimble Crs BUSH WD23 94 B1
Kimble Rd TOOT SW17 179 N9
Kimbolton Cl LEE/GVPK SE12 183 L2
Kimbolton Gn BORE WD6 75 P8
Kimmeridge Gdns
ELTH/MOT SE9 184 B7
Kimmeridge Rd ELTH/MOT SE9 184 B7
Kimps Wy HHS/BOV HP3 36 B9
Kimpton Av BRWN CM15 106 G1
Kimpton Cl HHNE HP2 36 C1
Kimpton Pl GSTN WD25 55 L10
Kimpton Rd CHEAM SM3 201 J10
CMBW SE5 159 L7
Kimpton's Cl CHONG CM5 67 N2
POTB/CUF EN6 58 G9
Kimptons Md POTB/CUF EN6 58 G9
Kinburn Dr EGH TW20 172 B8
Kinburn St BERM/RHTH * SE16 160 C1
Kincaid Rd PECK SE15 160 A6
Kincardine Gdns MV/WKIL * W9 8 E2
Kinch Gv WBLY HA9 115 L5
Kincraig Dr SEV TN13 247 H9
Kinder Cl THMD SE28 143 M9
Kinderscout HHS/BOV HP3 36 B8
Kindersley Wy ABLGY WD5 54 D7
Kinder St WCHPL E1 140 A8
Kinfauns Av EMPK RM11 125 K4
Kinfauns Rd BRXS/STRHM SW2 181 H5
GDMY/SEVK IG3 123 L6
Kingaby Gdns RAIN RM13 145 H2
King Alfred Av CAT SE6 182 F6
King Alfred Rd HARH RM3 105 N10
King Arthur Cl PECK SE15 160 B6
King Arthur Ct CHES/WCR EN8 62 D7
King Charles Crs BRYLDS KT5 199 L7
King Charles' Rd BRYLDS KT5 199 L6
RAD WD7 57 K8
King Charles St WHALL SW1A 17 K1
King Charles Ter WAP * E1W 140 A9
King Charles Wk
WIM/MER * SW19 179 H4
King Croft Rd HARP AL5 20 C4
Kingcup Cl CROY/NA CR0 204 C8
Kingcup Dr CHOB/PIR GU24 230 F1
King David La WCHPL E1 140 B9
Kingdon Rd KIL/WHAMP NW6 2 F1
King Edward Av DART DA1 187 L2
RAIN RM13 145 L4
King Edward Dr CDH/CHF RM16 168 B2
SURB KT6 199 K10
King Edward Rd BAR EN5 77 K8
BRW CM14 107 H4
CHES/WCR EN8 62 D9
GRH DA9 166 F10
LEY E10 121 H6
OXHEY WD19 73 M10
RAD WD7 57 L9
ROM RM1 124 G4
WALTH E17 120 D1
King Edward's Gdns ACT W3 135 M10
King Edward's Gv TEDD TW11 176 G9
King Edward's Rd BARK IG11 142 G3
ED N9 100 A1
HACK E8 140 A3
PEND EN3 80 C8
RSLP HA4 112 E6
WARE SG12 26 D1
King Edward St HHS/BOV HP3 35 N10
SL SL1 149 J1
STBT EC1A 12 E5
King Edward The Third Ms
BERM/RHTH SE16 160 A1
King Edward VII Av WDSR SL4 149 K6
King Edward Wk STHWK SE1 18 B4
Kingfield Cl WOKS/MYFD GU22 232 C6
Kingfield Dr WOKS/MYFD GU22 232 C6
Kingfield Gdns
WOKS/MYFD GU22 232 C6
Kingfield Rd EA W5 135 J6
WOKS/MYFD GU22 232 C6
Kingfield St POP/IOD E14 161 H3
Kingfisher Cl CRAWE RH10 284 B4
NTHWD HA6 92 C9
RBRW/HUT CM13 107 M1
STALE/WH AL4 21 J2
STMC/STPC BR5 207 N4
THMD SE28 143 M9
WARE SG12 27 H8
WOT/HER KT12 217 M2
Kingfisher Ct DORK * RH4 272 F1
Kingfisher Dr HHS/BOV HP3 54 A1
RCHPK/HAM TW10 177 H7
REDH RH1 258 B7
RGUE GU4 250 F8
STA TW18 173 J7
Kingfisher Gdns SAND/SEL CR2 224 C6
Kingfisher Lure KGLGY * WD4 54 C5
RKW/CH/CXG WD3 71 L8
Kingfisher Pl WDGN * N22 98 G10
Kingfisher Rd UPMR RM14 126 E6
Kingfisher St EHAM E6 142 B7
Kingfisher Wy CROY/NA CR0 204 C5
WLSDN * NW10 136 A1
King Gdns CROY/NA CR0 223 J2
King Garth Ms FSTH SE23 182 B5
King George Av BUSH WD23 74 A10
CAN/RD E16 142 A8
GNTH/NBYPK IG2 122 G4
WOT/HER KT12 197 L8
King George Cl ROMW/RG RM7 124 D1
SUN * TW16 174 F8
King George Rd WAB * EN9 63 H10
WARE SG12 26 D1
King Georges Av WATW WD18 72 F9
King George's Dr
ADL/WDHM KT15 215 K6
King George Sq
RCHPK/HAM TW10 177 L2
King George's Rd BRWN CM15 86 G10
King George St GNWCH SE10 161 H6
King George VI Av MTCM CR4 202 A4
TIL RM18 169 L3
Kingham Cl WAND/EARL SW18 179 M3
King Harolds Wy BXLYHN DA7 163 N6
King Harry La STALW/RED AL3 37 P7
King Harry St HHNE HP2 35 N6
King Henry Ct WAB * EN9 81 H2
King Henry Ms ORP BR6 227 J2
King Henry's Dr CROY/NA CR0 225 H5
King Henry's Ms PEND EN3 80 F3
King Henry's Rd HAMP NW3 3 N4
KUT KT1 199 N3
King Henry St STNW/STAM N16 119 M10
King Henry's Wk IS N1 7 J1
King Henry Ter WAP * E1W 140 A9
Kinghorn St STBT * EC1A 12 E4
King James Av POTB/CUF EN6 60 F5
King James St STHWK SE1 18 D2
King John Ct SDTCH EC2A 13 K1
King John's Cl STWL/WRAY TW19 171 P2
King John St WCHPL E1 140 C7
King John's Wk ELTH/MOT SE9 184 B3
Kinglake Est WALW * SE17 19 J7
Kinglake St WALW SE17 19 J8
Kingly Ct REGST * W1B 11 H7
Kingly St REGST W1B 10 G6
Kingpost Pde RGUE * GU4 250 E6
King & Queen Cl ELTH/MOT SE9 184 B7
King & Queen St WALW SE17 18 F7
King & Queen Whf
BERM/RHTH * SE16 140 C10
Kingsand Rd LEE/GVPK SE12 183 M5
Kings Arbour NWDGN UB2 153 M4
King's Arms Yd LOTH EC2R 12 G5
Kingsash Dr YEAD UB4 133 M6
Kings Av BAL SW12 180 E4
BF/WBF KT14 215 N8
BMLY BR1 183 M9
CAR SM5 221 P4
CHDH RM6 124 A4
CHOB/PIR GU24 230 C5
CLAP SW4 180 F2
EA W5 135 J8
GFD/PVL UB6 134 A8
HEST TW5 154 A7
HHS/BOV HP3 36 A10
MUSWH N10 118 B1
NWMAL KT3 200 C4
REDH RH1 275 P2
SUN TW16 174 G8
WATW WD18 73 H8
WCHMH N21 99 J2
WFD IG8 101 P6
King's Bench St STHWK SE1 18 D1
King's Bench Wk EMB * EC4Y 12 B7
Kingsbridge Av EA W5 155 L1
Kingsbridge Ct POP/IOD E14 160 F3
Kingsbridge Rd BARK IG11 142 G4
HARH RM3 105 M7
MRDN SM4 200 G7
NKENS W10 136 F8
NWDGN UB2 153 N3
WOT/HER KT12 197 J7
Kingsbrook LHD/OX KT22 236 F4
Kingsbury Av STALW/RED AL3 38 A5
Kingsbury Crs STA TW18 172 G7
Kingsbury Dr WDSR SL4 171 M3
Kingsbury Rd CDALE/KGS NW9 115 M3
IS N1 7 K1
Kingsbury Ter IS N1 7 K1
King's Cha BRW CM14 107 H4
E/WMO/HCT KT8 198 B3
Kingsclere Cl PUT/ROE SW15 178 D3
Kingsclere Pl ENC/FH EN2 79 K6
Kingscliffe Gdns
WIM/MER SW19 179 J4
Kings Cl CSTG HP8 90 A3
DART DA1 164 F10
HDN NW4 116 G2
KGLGY WD4 53 L7
LEY E10 120 G5
NTHWD HA6 92 G7
STA TW18 173 N10
THDIT KT7 198 F6
WATW WD18 73 K8
WOT/HER * KT12 197 J8
King's College Rd HAMP NW3 3 N3
RSLP HA4 112 G4
Kingscote Hl CRAWW RH11 283 L9
Kingscote Rd CHSWK W4 156 A2
CROY/NA CR0 204 A7
NWMAL KT3 200 A3
Kingscote St EMB EC4Y 12 C7
Kings Ct KWD/TDW/WH KT20 238 F8
PLSTW E13 141 N3
STHWK * SE1 18 D1
Kingscourt Rd
STRHM/NOR SW16 180 E6
King's Crs FSBYPK N4 119 K8
Kingscroft WGCE AL7 23 L4
Kingscroft Rd BNSTD SM7 239 N1
CRICK NW2 2 C1
LHD/OX KT22 236 G6
King's Cross Br FSBYW * WC1X 5 M9
Kings Cross La REDH RH1 276 G3
King's Cross Rd FSBYW WC1X 5 P9
Kingsdale Gdns NTGHL W11 136 G10
Kingsdale Rd BERK HP4 33 M6
PGE/AN SE20 204 C1
WOOL/PLUM SE18 163 J5
Kingsdene KWD/TDW/WH KT20 238 E7
Kingsdon La HLWE CM17 47 M2
Kingsdown Av ACT W3 136 B9
SAND/SEL CR2 223 K5
WEA W13 154 G1
Kingsdown Cl
BERM/RHTH * SE16 160 A4
GVE DA12 191 J4
NTGHL W11 136 G8
Kingsdowne Ct EA * W5 135 K9
Kingsdowne Rd SURB KT6 199 K7
Kingsdown Rd ARCH N19 118 F8
CHEAM SM3 221 H2
EW KT17 220 D9
WAN E11 121 K8
Kingsdown Wy HAYES BR2 205 M6
Kings Dr BRYLDS KT5 199 M7
EDGW HA8 95 L5
GVE DA12 190 E6
THDIT KT7 198 G6
WBLY HA9 115 N7
The Kings Dr WOT/HER KT12 216 G5
Kingsend RSLP HA4 112 F6
Kingsend Ct RSLP * HA4 112 F6
Kings Farm WALTH * E17 100 G9
Kings Farm Av
RCHPK/HAM TW10 155 M10
Kings Farm Rd RKW/CH/CXG WD3 70 G10
Kingsfield HOD EN11 44 F1
WDSR SL4 148 C7
Kingsfield Av RYLN/HDSTN HA2 114 A3
Kingsfield Ct OXHEY WD19 73 L10
Kingsfield Dr PEND EN3 80 C1
Kingsfield Rd HRW * HA1 114 C5
OXHEY WD19 93 L1
Kingsfield Ter DART * DA1 187 L2
Kingsfield Wy PEND EN3 80 C1
Kingsford Av WLGTN SM6 222 F4
Kingsford St KTTN NW5 118 A10
Kingsford Wy EHAM E6 142 C7
Kings Gdns IL IG1 122 G6
KIL/WHAMP NW6 2 F4
UPMR RM14 126 D5
Kingsgate CRAWE * RH10 283 P7
STALW/RED AL3 38 A8
WBLY HA9 115 P8
Kingsgate Av FNCH N3 117 K1
Kingsgate Cl BXLYHN DA7 163 P7
STMC/STPC BR5 207 M2
Kingsgate Est IS * N1 7 K2
Kingsgate Pl KIL/WHAMP NW6 2 E4
Kingsgate Rd KIL/WHAMP NW6 2 E3
KUT KT1 199 K1
King's Gn LOU IG10 82 B7
Kingsground ELTH/MOT SE9 184 A3
King's Gv PECK SE15 160 A7
ROM RM1 125 H3
Kings Hall Ms LEW * SE13 161 H9
Kings Hall Rd BECK BR3 182 C10
Kings Head Hl CHING E4 100 G1
King's Head La BF/WBF KT14 215 N7
King's Hwy WOOL/PLUM SE18 163 H5
Kingshill Av CRW RM5 104 D7
KTN/HRWW/W HA3 114 G2
STALE/WH AL4 38 G3
WPK KT4 200 D7
YEAD UB4 132 F5
Kingshill Ct BAR * EN5 77 H8
Kingshill Dr KTN/HRWW/W HA3 94 G10
Kingshill Wy BERK HP4 33 M7
Kingshold Rd HOM E9 140 B2
Kingsholm Gdns ELTH/MOT SE9 162 A10
Kingshurst Rd LEE/GVPK SE12 183 M3
Kings Keep HAYES * BR2 205 K3
SURB * KT6 199 K4
Kingsland HLWS CM18 46 F3
Kingsland Ct CRAWE * RH10 284 B7
Kingsland Gn STNW/STAM N16 7 K1
Kingsland Pas HACK * E8 7 L1
Kingsland Rd BETH E2 7 K8
HACK E8 7 L4
HHW HP1 35 K8
PLSTW E13 141 P5
Kings La BFOR GU20 212 D2
EGH TW20 171 M8
KGLGY WD4 53 K7
SUT SM1 221 N2
Kingslawn Cl PUT/ROE SW15 178 E1
Kingslea LHD/OX KT22 236 F6
Kingsleigh Pl MTCM CR4 202 A3
Kingsleigh Wk HAYES BR2 205 L4
Kingsley Av BNSTD SM7 239 K1
BORE WD6 75 L6
CHES/WCR EN8 62 A5
DART DA1 187 P1
EGH TW20 171 N9
HSLW TW3 154 B8
STHL UB1 133 P9
SUT SM1 221 N1
WEA W13 134 F8
Kingsley Cl DAGE RM10 124 C9
GLDGN NW11 117 M3
HORL RH6 280 A2
Kingsley Ct BRKMPK AL9 23 J9
EDGW * HA8 95 N3
GPK RM2 125 J4
Kingsley Dr WPK KT4 200 C9
Kingsley Gdns CHING E4 100 F6
EMPK RM11 125 L2
Kingsley Gv REIG RH2 275 K3
Kingsley Ms CHST BR7 184 E9
KENS * W8 15 H4
WAP * E1W 140 A9
Kingsley Pl HGT N6 118 B5
Kingsley Rd BARK/HLT IG6 102 F9
CRAWW RH11 283 K10
CROY/NA CR0 203 H8
FSTGT E7 141 M2
HORL RH6 280 A2
HSLW TW3 154 B8
KIL/WHAMP NW6 2 D5
LOU IG10 82 G7
ORP BR6 227 J3
PIN HA5 113 N2
PLMGR N13 99 H5
RYLN/HDSTN HA2 114 B9
WALTH E17 101 H10
WIM/MER SW19 179 L8
Kingsley St BTSEA SW11 158 A9
Kingsley Wk CDH/CHF RM16 168 D3
Kingsley Wy EFNCH N2 117 M4
Kingsley Wood Dr
ELTH/MOT SE9 184 C6
Kingslyn Crs NRWD SE19 203 M1
Kings Lynn Dr HARH RM3 105 L7
Kings Ml HMSMTH * W6 156 F3
Kingsman Dr CDH/CHF RM16 147 N9
Kingsman St WOOL/PLUM SE18 162 C3
Kings Md HORL RH6 281 J4
REDH RH1 276 F2
Kingsmead BAR EN5 77 K8
BH/WHM TN16 244 A2
CHES/WCR EN8 62 C4
POTB/CUF EN6 60 F4
RCHPK/HAM TW10 177 L2
SBW CM21 29 P2
STALE/WH AL4 39 J3
WAB * EN9 45 H8
WOKN/KNAP GU21 232 D2
Kingsmead Av CDALE/KGS NW9 116 A5
ED N9 100 A2
MTCM CR4 202 D3
ROM RM1 124 F4
SUN TW16 197 K3
SURB KT6 199 M9
WPK KT4 200 E10
Kingsmead Cl BFN/LL DA15 185 K5
HLWW/ROY CM19 45 N2
HOR/WEW KT19 220 A4
TEDD TW11 176 G9
Kingsmead Dr NTHLT UB5 133 N2
Kings Meadow KGLGY WD4 54 B4
Kingsmead Pde NTHLT * UB5 133 N2
Kings Mead Pk ESH/CLAY KT10 218 D4
Kingsmead Rd
BRXS/STRHM SW2 181 H5
Kingsmead Wy HOM E9 120 D9
Kingsmere Cl PUT/ROE SW15 156 G9
Kingsmere Pk CDALE/KGS NW9 115 P6
Kingsmere Pl STNW/STAM * N16 119 L6
Kingsmere Rd WIM/MER SW19 178 G5
King's Ms BMSBY WC1N 11 P2
CHIG * IG7 102 F3
HHNE * HP2 35 N5
Kingsmill Ct HAT AL10 40 E6
Kingsmill Gdns DAGW RM9 124 A10
Kings Mill La REDH RH1 276 E4
Kingsmill Rd DAGW RM9 124 A10
Kingsmill Ter STJWD NW8 3 M7
Kingsmoor Rd HLWW/ROY CM19 46 E4
Kingsnympton Pk
KUTN/CMB KT2 177 N10
Kings Oak ROMW/RG RM7 124 B1
King's Orch ELTH/MOT SE9 184 B2
King's Paddock HPTN TW12 198 B1
Kings Pde CAR * SM5 201 P10
SHB * W12 156 D2
TOTM * N17 119 N1
WLSDN * NW10 136 F3
Kingspark Ct SWFD E18 121 M1
Kings Pas WAN * E11 121 K5
Kings Pl CHSWK W4 155 P4
LOU IG10 102 A1
STHWK SE1 18 E2
King Sq FSBYE EC1V 6 E10
King's Quay WBPTN * SW10 157 M7
Kings Reach EMB * EC4Y 12 B7
Kingsridge Gdns DART DA1 187 L2
Kings Rd ADL/WDHM KT15 215 L6
ASC SL5 192 C5
BAR EN5 76 F7
BARK IG11 142 F2
BELMT SM2 221 K6
BERK HP4 33 N6
BGVA SW1W 16 D5
BH/WHM TN16 243 P3
BRW CM14 107 H3
CHES/WCR EN8 62 D10
CHING E4 101 J2
CHOB/PIR GU24 212 F10
CSTG HP8 90 A3
EA W5 135 J7
EGH TW20 172 D7
EHAM E6 141 P3
FELT TW13 175 K4
FUL/PGN SW6 157 L7
HERT/BAY SG13 25 P4
HORL RH6 280 B4
KUTN/CMB KT2 177 L10
LCOL/BKTW AL2 57 H2
MORT/ESHN SW14 156 A9
MTCM CR4 202 B3
ORP BR6 227 J1
RCHPK/HAM TW10 177 L1
RGUE GU4 268 B6
ROM RM1 125 H3
RYLN/HDSTN HA2 113 N7
SL SL1 149 K2
SNWD SE25 203 P3
STALW/RED AL3 38 A5
SURB KT6 199 H8
TEDD TW11 176 C8
TOTM N17 99 N9
TWK TW1 176 G2
UED * N18 99 P6
UX/CGN UB8 131 N4
WAN E11 121 K5
WBPTN SW10 15 L10
WDGN N22 98 G9
WDR/YW UB7 152 A1
WDSR SL4 149 J10
WIM/MER SW19 179 K9
WOKN/KNAP GU21 232 D2
WOT/HER KT12 197 J9
King's Scholars' Pas WEST SW1P 16 G4
Kings Shade Wk EPSOM * KT18 220 A9
Kings Sq HAT * AL10 40 A1
Kings's Rd GU GU1 250 A10
King Stable St WDSR SL4 149 J6
King Stairs Cl BERM/RHTH SE16 160 A1
King's Ter CAMTN NW1 4 G6
Kingsthorpe Rd SYD SE26 182 C7
Kingston Av CHEAM SM3 201 H10
EBED/NFELT TW14 174 F2
EHSLY KT24 252 F2
LHD/OX KT22 236 G7
WDR/YW UB7 132 A9
Kingston By-Pass
ESH/CLAY KT10 198 D10
Kingston Cl CHDH RM6 123 P1
NTHLT UB5 133 N2
TEDD TW11 176 G9
Kingston Ct GVW DA11 189 N2
Kingston Crs ASHF TW15 173 M8
BECK BR3 204 E1
Kingston Gdns CROY/NA CR0 202 F10
Kingston Hall Rd KUT KT1 199 J3
Kingston Hl KUTN/CMB KT2 199 M1
Kingston Hill Av CHDH RM6 123 P1
Kingston Hill Pl KUTN/CMB KT2 177 P7
Kingston House Est SURB * KT6 198 G6
Kingston House Gdns
LHD/OX * KT22 236 G7
Kingston La EHSLY KT24 252 B3
TEDD TW11 176 G9
UX/CGN UB8 131 P5
WDR/YW UB7 152 A1
Kingston Ldg NWMAL KT3 200 B4
Kingston Pde GRAYS * RM17 167 N3
Kingston Ri ADL/WDHM KT15 215 K6
Kingston Rd ASHF TW15 173 P9
BRYLDS KT5 199 N9
EBAR EN4 77 N9
ED N9 99 P3
EW KT17 220 C4
HOR/WEW KT19 220 B2
IL IG1 122 F9
LHD/OX KT22 236 G2
NWDGN UB2 153 N1
NWMAL KT3 200 A4
PUT/ROE SW15 178 E4
ROM RM1 124 G2
RYNPK SW20 201 H2
SHPTN TW17 174 A9
STA TW18 173 K7
TEDD TW11 176 G9
Kingston Sq NRWD SE19 181 L8
Kingston V PUT/ROE SW15 178 A7
Kingstown St CAMTN NW1 4 C5
King St CHERT KT16 195 K8
CITYW EC2V 12 F6
COVGDN WC2E 11 L7
CSHM HP5 50 G8
EFNCH * N2 97 N10
GVE DA12 190 E2
HMSMTH W6 156 C3
NWDGN UB2 153 M2
PLSTW E13 141 M6
RCH/KEW TW9 177 J1
STJS SW1Y 11 H10
TOTM N17 99 N9
TWK TW1 176 F4
WATW WD18 73 K8
King St Cloisters HMSMTH * W6 156 E3
King Street Pde TWK * TW1 176 F4
Kings Wk SAND/SEL CR2 224 A10
Kings Warren LHD/OX KT22 218 C7
Kingswater Pl BTSEA * SW11 157 P6
Kings Wy CROY/NA CR0 222 G2
HRW HA1 114 D2
Kingsway CFSP/GDCR SL9 110 B1
HOL/ALD WC2B 11 N5
HYS/HAR UB3 132 D7
MORT/ESHN SW14 155 N9
NWMAL KT3 200 F4
PEND EN3 80 A9
POTB/CUF EN6 60 F6
SLN SL2 128 G1
STMC/STPC BR5 206 G5
STWL/WRAY TW19 173 N4
WBLY HA9 115 K9
WOKN/KNAP GU21 232 A4
WWKM BR4 205 L10
Kingsway Av SAND/SEL CR2 224 B5
WOKN/KNAP GU21 232 A4
Kingsway Crs RYLN/HDSTN HA2 114 B2
Kingsway North Orbital Rd
GSTN WD25 55 H10
Kingsway Pde
STNW/STAM * N16 119 L8
Kingsway Pl CLKNW EC1R 12 B1
Kingsway Rd CHEAM SM3 221 H4
Kingsway Ter WEY KT13 216 B4
The Kingsway EW KT17 220 C6
Kingswear Rd KTTN NW5 118 C8
RSLP HA4 113 H7
Kingswell Ride POTB/CUF EN6 60 F6
Kingswick Cl ASC SL5 192 D4
Kingswick Dr ASC SL5 192 C4
Kingswood Av BELV DA17 164 A3
HAYES BR2 205 K3
HEST TW5 153 N8
HPTN TW12 176 A9
KIL/WHAMP NW6 2 A6
SAND/SEL CR2 242 A1
SWLY BR8 208 G3
THHTH CR7 203 H5
Kingswood Cl DART DA1 187 K2
EGH TW20 172 A7
EN EN1 79 N8
GU GU1 250 F9
NWMAL KT3 200 C6
ORP BR6 206 G7
SURB KT6 199 K7
TRDG/WHET N20 77 M10
VX/NE SW8 158 F6
WEY KT13 216 C4
Kingswood Creek
STWL/WRAY TW19 172 A1
Kingswood Dr BELMT SM2 221 L5
CAR SM5 202 A8
NRWD SE19 181 M7
Kingswood La WARL CR6 242 B1
Kingswood Pk FNCH N3 97 J10
Kingswood Pl LEW SE13 161 K10
Kingswood Ri EGH TW20 172 A8
Kingswood Rd
BRXS/STRHM SW2 180 F2
CHSWK W4 155 P2
GDMY/SEVK IG3 123 K6
GSTN WD25 55 J10
HAYES BR2 205 K3
KWD/TDW/WH KT20 238 E7
PGE/AN SE20 182 B9
SEV TN13 246 F7
WAN E11 121 K5
WIM/MER SW19 201 J1
Kingswood Ter CHSWK W4 155 P2
Kingswood Wy SAND/SEL CR2 224 C8
WLGTN SM6 222 F2
Kingsworth Cl BECK BR3 204 D5
Kingsworthy Cl KUT KT1 199 L2
Kings Yd PUT/ROE * SW15 156 G9
RKW/CH/CXG * WD3 91 P2
SRTFD * E15 140 F1
Kingthorpe Rd WLSDN NW10 136 A2
Kingthorpe Ter WLSDN * NW10 136 A2
Kingwell Rd EBAR EN4 77 N4
King William Ct WAB * EN9 81 H1
King William La GNWCH SE10 161 K4
King William St MANHO EC4N 13 H7
King William Wk GNWCH SE10 161 H5
Kingwood Rd FUL/PGN SW6 157 H6
Kinlet Rd WOOL/PLUM SE18 162 F6
Kinloch Dr CDALE/KGS NW9 116 B5
Kinloch St HOLWY N7 118 G8
Kinloss Gdns FNCH N3 117 J1
Kinloss Rd CAR SM5 201 M7
Kinnaird Av BMLY BR1 183 L9
CHSWK W4 155 P6
Kinnaird Cl BMLY BR1 183 L9
SL SL1 128 B8
Kinnaird Wy WFD IG8 102 C7
Kinnear Rd SHB W12 156 C1
Kinnersley Mnr REIG * RH2 275 M8
Kinnersley Wk REIG RH2 275 K5
Kinnerton Pl North KTBR * SW1X 16 B2
Kinnerton Pl South KTBR * SW1X 16 B2
Kinnerton St KTBR SW1X 16 C2
Kinnerton Yd KTBR * SW1X 16 C2
Kinnoul Rd HMSMTH W6 14 A9
Kinross Av WPK KT4 200 D9
Kinross Cl KTN/HRWW/W HA3 115 L3
SUN TW16 174 G8
Kinross Dr SUN TW16 174 G8
Kinross Ter WALTH E17 100 E10
Kinsale Rd PECK SE15 159 P9
Kintyre Cl STRHM/NOR SW16 202 G2
Kinveachy Gdns CHARL SE7 162 B4
Kinver Rd SYD SE26 182 B7
Kipings KWD/TDW/WH KT20 238 G8
Kipling Av TIL RM18 168 E7
Kipling Cl CRAWE RH10 284 D5
Kipling Dr TOOT SW17 179 N9
Kipling Est STHWK SE1 19 H2
Kipling Rd BXLYHN DA7 163 P7
DART DA1 188 A1
Kipling St STHWK SE1 19 H2
Kipling Ter ED * N9 99 L4
Kipling Wy HARP AL5 20 A2
Kippington Cl SEV TN13 246 G10

ippington Dr ELTH/MOT SE9 184 A4
ippington Rd SEV TN13 265 H1
irby Cl BARK/HLT IG6 103 H7
HARH RM3 105 P6
HOR/WEW KT19 220 C2
LOU IG10 102 B1
NTHWD HA6 92 G7
irby Est BERM/RHTH * SE16 160 A2
WDR/YW * UB7 131 N9
irby Gv STHWK SE1 19 J1
irby Rd RDART DA2 188 B3
WOKN/KNAP GU21 231 P2
irby St HCIRC EC1N 12 B3
irchen Rd WEA W13 134 G9
irdford Cl CRAWW RH11 283 K5
irkcaldy Gn OXHEY WD19 93 K4
irkdale SYD SE26 182 A5
irkdale Cnr SYD * SE26 182 B7
irkdale Rd WAN E11 121 K6
irkefields GUW GU2 249 M7
irkfield Cl WEA W13 134 G10
irkham Rd EHAM E6 142 B8
irkham St WOOL/PLUM SE18 163 H5
irkland Av CLAY IG5 102 D10
WOKN/KNAP GU21 231 K2
irkland Cl BFN/LL DA15 185 H2
irklands WGCW AL8 23 H1
irkland Wk HACK E8 7 L2
irk La WOOL/PLUM SE18 162 F5
irkleas Rd SURB KT6 199 K8
irklees Rd BCTR RM8 123 M10
THHTH CR7 203 H5
irkley Rd WIM/MER SW19 201 K1
irkly Cl SAND/SEL CR2 223 M5
irkmichael Rd POP/IOD E14 141 H8
irk Rd WALTH E17 120 E4
irkside Rd BKHTH/KID SE3 161 M5
irk's Pl POP/IOD E14 140 E7
irkstall Av TOTM N17 119 L2
irkstall Gdns BRXS/STRHM SW2 180 E4
irkstall Rd BRXS/STRHM SW2 180 F4
irksted Rd MRDN SM4 201 L8
irkstone Wy BMLY BR1 183 K10
irkton Rd SEVS/STOTM N15 119 M2
irkwall Pl BETH * E2 140 B5
irkwall Sp SL SL1 129 K7
irkwood Rd PECK SE15 160 A8
irn Rd WEA W13 134 G9
irrane Cl NWMAL KT3 200 C5
irtle Rd CSHM HP5 51 H7
irtley Rd SYD SE26 182 D7
irtling St VX/NE SW8 158 D6
irton Cl CHSWK W4 156 A3
HCH RM12 145 K1
rton Gdns BETH E2 7 M10
irton Ldg WAND/EARL * SW18 179 L2
irton Rd PLSTW E13 141 P4
rton Wk EDGW HA8 95 P8
rwyn Wy CMBW SE5 159 J6
tcat Ter BOW E3 140 F5
tchener Av GVE DA12 190 F7
tchener Cl STAL AL1 38 F7
tchener Rd EFNCH N2 117 P1
FSTGT E7 141 N1
THHTH CR7 203 L3
TOTM N17 119 M1
WALTH E17 100 G9
te Fld BERK HP4 33 K2
te Pl BETH E2 7 P9
ites Cl CRAWW RH11 283 K7
ite Yd BTSEA * SW11 158 A7
ithurst Cl CRAWW RH11 283 M9
itley Gdns NRWD SE19 203 N1
itsbury Rd BERK HP4 33 N5
itsbury Ter BERK HP4 33 N5
itsmead CRAWE RH10 285 H3
itsmead La CHERT KT16 193 P8
itson Rd BARN SW13 156 D7
CMBW SE5 159 K6
itson Wy HLW CM20 28 F10
itswell Wy RAD WD7 56 E9
ittiwake Cl CRAWW RH11 282 G9
SAND/SEL CR2 224 D6
ittiwake Pl NTHLT UB5 133 L5
ittiwake Wy YEAD UB4 133 L7
itto Rd NWCR SE14 160 C8
itt's End Rd BAR EN5 77 H3
iver Rd ARCH N19 118 F7
lea Av BAL SW12 180 D2
napdale Cl FSTH SE23 182 A5
napmill Rd CAT SE6 182 F5
napmill Wy CAT SE6 182 F5
napp Cl WLSDN NW10 136 B1
napp Rd ASHF TW15 174 A7
BOW E3 140 F6
napton Ms TOOT SW17 180 B9
naresborough Dr
WAND/EARL SW18 179 L4
naresborough Pl ECT SW5 14 G5
natchbull Rd CMBW SE5 159 J7
WLSDN NW10 136 A3
nave Wood Rd RSEV TN14 247 M3
nebworth Av WALTH E17 100 F9
nebworth Pth BORE WD6 76 A8
nebworth Rd
STNW/STAM * N16 119 M9
nee Hl ABYW SE2 163 M3
nee Hill Crs ABYW SE2 163 M3
nella Gn WGCE AL7 23 K5
nella Rd WGCE AL7 23 J6
neller Gdns ISLW TW7 176 C2
neller Rd BROCKY SE4 160 D10
NWMAL KT3 200 B7
WHTN TW2 176 B2
nepp Cl CRAWE RH10 284 D7
nifton Ct POTB/CUF * EN6 58 G7
night Cl BCTR RM8 123 M9
nighten St WAP E1W 140 A10
nighthead Point
POP/IOD * E14 160 F1
nightland Rd CLPT E5 120 A7
nighton Cl CRAWE RH10 284 E3
ROMW/RG RM7 124 E4
SAND/SEL CR2 223 J5
WFD IG8 101 N5
nighton Dr WFD IG8 101 N5
nighton La BKHH IG9 101 N3
nighton Park Rd SYD SE26 182 C8
nighton Rd FSTGT E7 121 M8
REDH RH1 276 B2
ROMW/RG RM7 124 D4
RSEV TN14 246 G3
nighton-Way La DEN/HRF UB9 111 L10
nightrider Ct BLKFR * EC4V 12 D6
nightrider St BLKFR EC4V 12 D7
night's Av EA W5 155 K1
nightsbridge SKENS SW7 15 P2
nightsbridge Crs STA TW18 173 L9
nightsbridge Gdns
ROMW/RG RM7 124 E3
Knightsbridge Gn KTBR * SW1X 16 A2
Knightsbridge Wy HHNE HP2 35 P5
Knights Chambers ED * N9 99 P4
Knights Cl EGH * TW20 172 G9
WDSR SL4 148 C7
Knights Cft HART DA3 211 L10
Knightsfield WGCW AL8 22 G1
Knight's Hl WNWD SE27 181 J8
Knight's Hill Sq WNWD SE27 181 J7
Knight's La ED N9 99 P4
Knights Manor Wy DART DA1 187 N2
Knights Orch HHW HP1 35 J4
STALW/RED AL3 38 B6
Knight's Pk KUT KT1 199 K3
Knights Pl REDH RH1 258 B9
WDSR SL4 149 H9
Knights Rdg ORP BR6 227 L2
Knights Rd CAN/RD E16 141 M10
STAN HA7 95 H5
Knight St SBW CM21 29 H2
Knights Wk ABR/ST RM4 83 L7
LBTH SE11 18 C6
Knights Wy BARK/HLT IG6 102 F7
RBRW/HUT CM13 107 M4
Knightswood WOKN/KNAP GU21 231 L3
Knightswood Cl EDGW HA8 95 P3
Knightswood Rd RAIN RM13 144 G4
Knightwood Cl REIG RH2 275 K2
Knightwood Crs NWMAL KT3 200 B6
Knipp Hl COB KT11 217 N9
Knivet Rd FUL/PGN SW6 14 E10
Knobfield SHGR GU5 270 G9
Knobs Hill Rd SRTFD E15 140 G3
Knockhall Cha GRH DA9 189 H1
Knockhall Rd GRH DA9 189 H2
Knockholt Rd ELTH/MOT SE9 184 A1
RSEV TN14 228 A10
Knole Cl CRAWE RH10 284 E6
CROY/NA * CR0 204 B6
Knole La BGR/WK TN15 265 K2
Knole Rd DART DA1 187 H3
SEV TN13 247 L9
The Knole ELTH/MOT SE9 184 D7
MEO DA13 190 B10
Knole Wy BGR/WK TN15 265 K1
Knole Wd ASC * SL5 192 D8
Knoll Crs NTHWD HA6 92 F10
Knoll Dr STHGT/OAK N14 98 B1
Knolles Crs BRKMPK AL9 40 E10
Knoll Gn HHNE * HP2 35 P4
Knollmead BRYLDS KT5 199 P8
Knoll Park Rd CHERT KT16 195 J8
Knoll Ri ORP BR6 207 J8
Knoll Rd BXLY DA5 186 B3
DORK RH4 272 F4
SCUP DA14 185 L8
WAND/EARL SW18 179 M1
Knolls Cl WPK KT4 200 E10
The Knolls EW KT17 238 F2
The Knoll BECK BR3 204 G1
CHERT KT16 195 J8
COB KT11 217 P9
HAYES BR2 205 M9
HERT/BAY SG13 26 A4
LHD/OX KT22 237 H7
PIN * HA5 93 L10
WEA W13 135 H7
Knolly's Cl STRHM/NOR SW16 181 H6
WNWD * SE27 181 J6
Knolly's Rd STRHM/NOR SW16 181 H6
Knolton Wy SLN SL2 129 N8
Knottisford St BETH E2 140 C5
Knottocks Cl BEAC HP9 88 C6
Knottocks Dr BEAC HP9 88 C6
Knottocks End BEAC HP9 88 C6
Knotts Green Rd LEY E10 121 H4
Knotts Pl SEV TN13 247 H10
Knowle Av BXLYHN DA7 163 P6
Knowle Cl BRXN/ST SW9 159 H9
CRAWE RH10 285 K2
Knowle Dr CRAWE RH10 285 J2
HARP AL5 20 C4
Knowle Gdns BF/WBF KT14 215 J9
Knowle Gn STA TW18 173 K8
Knowle Gv VW GU25 193 P7
Knowle Grove Cl VW GU25 193 P7
Knowle Hl VW GU25 193 N7
Knowle Pk COB KT11 235 M1
Knowle Park Av STA TW18 173 L9
Knowle Rd HAYES BR2 206 B9
WHTN TW2 176 D4
Knowles Cl WDR/YW UB7 131 P10
Knowles Ct HRW HA1 114 E4
Knowles Hill Crs LEW SE13 183 J1
The Knowle HOD EN11 44 F4
KWD/TDW/WH * KT20 238 E7
Knowl Hl WOKS/MYFD GU22 232 E5
Knowlton Gn HAYES BR2 205 L5
Knowl Wy BORE WD6 75 K9
Knowsley Av STHL UB1 134 A10
Knowsley Rd BTSEA SW11 158 A8
Knox Rd FSTGT E7 141 M1
GUW GU2 249 N6
Knox St MBLAR W1H 10 A3
Knoyle St NWCR SE14 160 D5
Knutsford Av WATN WD24 73 L4
Kohat Rd WIM/MER SW19 179 L8
Koh-i-Noor Av BUSH WD23 73 P10
Koonowla Cl BH/WHM TN16 244 A1
Kooringa WARL CR6 242 A3
Korda Cl SHPTN TW17 196 A3
Korea Cottages COB * KT11 235 L2
Kossuth St GNWCH SE10 161 K4
Kramer Ms ECT SW5 14 G8
Kreedman Wk HACK * E8 119 P10
Kuala Gdns STRHM/NOR SW16 202 G1
Kydbrook Cl STMC/STPC BR5 206 F7
Kylemore Cl EHAM E6 142 A4
Kylemore Rd KIL/WHAMP NW6 2 E3
Kymberley Rd HRW * HA1 114 D4
Kyme Rd ROM RM1 124 G4
Kynance Cl HARH RM3 105 K4
Kynance Gdns STAN HA7 95 H9
Kynance Ms KENS W8 15 H4
Kynance Pl KENS W8 15 J4
Kynaston Av THHTH CR7 203 K5
Kynaston Cl KTN/HRWW/W HA3 94 C8
Kynaston Ct CTHM CR3 259 M1
Kynaston Crs THHTH CR7 203 K5
Kynaston Rd BMLY BR1 183 M8
ENC/FH EN2 79 L5
STMC/STPC BR5 207 L7
STNW/STAM N16 119 M8
THHTH CR7 203 K5
Kynaston Wd KTN/HRWW/W HA3 94 C8
Kynersley Cl CAR SM5 202 A10
Kynoch Rd UED N18 100 C5
Kyrle Rd BTSEA SW11 180 B2
Kytes Dr GSTN WD25 55 L9
Kyverdale Rd STNW/STAM N16 119 N5

L

Laburnham Cl UPMR RM14 126 F5
Laburnham Gdns UPMR RM14 126 E5
Laburnum Av DART DA1 187 K4
ED N9 99 M3
HCH RM12 125 H7
SUT SM1 201 P10
SWLY BR8 208 E3
TOTM N17 99 L8
WDR/YW UB7 132 A9
Laburnum Cl CHES/WCR EN8 62 C7
CHING E4 100 E7
GU GU1 249 P7
Laburnum Ct STAN HA7 95 H5
Laburnum Crs SUN TW16 197 J1
Laburnum Gdns CROY/NA CR0 204 C7
Laburnum Gv CDALE/KGS NW9 115 P5
DTCH/LGLY SL3 150 D5
GVW DA11 190 A3
HSLW TW3 153 N10
LCOL/BKTW AL2 55 P1
NWMAL KT3 200 A2
SOCK/AV RM15 147 J6
STHL UB1 133 N6
WCHMH N21 99 K3
Laburnum Pl EGH TW20 171 N9
ELTH/MOT * SE9 184 D1
Laburnum Rd CHERT KT16 195 K8
CHERT * KT16 195 K8
EPP CM16 65 M5
EPSOM KT18 220 B9
HOD EN11 44 G1
HYS/HAR UB3 152 G3
MTCM CR4 202 B2
WIM/MER SW19 179 M10
WOKS/MYFD GU22 232 A6
Laburnum St BETH E2 7 L6
Laburnum Wk HCH RM12 125 K10
Laburnum Wy HAYES BR2 206 D7
STWL/WRAY TW19 174 A4
Lacebark Cl BFN/LL DA15 185 J3
Lacemaker Ct AMSS * HP7 69 H6
Lacey Av COUL/CHIP CR5 241 H6
Lacey Cl ED N9 99 P3
EGH TW20 172 G10
Lacey Dr BCTR RM8 123 M8
COUL/CHIP CR5 241 H6
EDGW HA8 95 K5
HPTN TW12 197 N1
Laceys Yd CSHM * HP5 50 G7
Lackford Rd COUL/CHIP CR5 240 A4
Lackington St SDTCH EC2A 13 H3
Lackmore Rd EN EN1 80 B1
Lacock Cl WIM/MER SW19 179 M9
Lacon Rd EDUL SE22 159 P10
Lacrosse Wy STRHM/NOR SW16 202 E1
Lacy Gn COUL/CHIP CR5 241 H6
Lacy Rd PUT/ROE SW15 156 G10
Ladas Rd WNWD SE27 181 K8
Ladbroke Crs NTGHL W11 8 B6
Ladbroke Gdns NTGHL W11 8 C7
Ladbroke Gv NKENS W10 8 A4
REDH RH1 258 B9
Ladbroke Ms NTGHL W11 8 B9
Ladbroke Rd EN EN1 79 N10
EPSOM KT18 220 A10
HORL RH6 280 B2
NTGHL W11 8 D9
REDH RH1 258 B8
Ladbroke Sq NTGHL W11 8 D8
Ladbroke Ter NTGHL W11 8 D8
Ladbroke Wk NTGHL W11 8 D9
Ladbrook Cl PIN HA5 113 N3
Ladbrooke Cl POTB/CUF EN6 59 K8
Ladbrooke Crs SCUP DA14 185 N6
Ladbrooke Dr POTB/CUF EN6 59 K8
Ladbrooke Rd SL SL1 149 H2
Ladbrook Rd SNWD SE25 203 L3
Ladderstile Ride
RCHPK/HAM TW10 177 N8
Ladderswood Wy
FBAR/BDGN N11 98 D6
Ladds Wy SWLY BR8 208 E4
Ladies Gv STALW/RED AL3 38 A4
Lady Booth Rd KUT KT1 199 K2
Ladycroft Gdns ORP BR6 226 F2
Ladycroft Rd LEW SE13 160 G9
Ladycroft Wk STAN HA7 95 J9
Ladycroft Wy ORP BR6 226 F2
Ladyday Pl SL SL1 129 H10
Ladyegate Cl RDKG RH5 273 J1
Ladyegate Rd RDKG RH5 273 H2
Ladyfields GVW DA11 190 C7
LOU IG10 82 E8
Lady Forsdyke Wy
HOR/WEW KT19 219 M5
Ladygate La RSLP HA4 112 D4
Ladygrove CROY/NA CR0 224 D5
Lady Gv WGCE AL7 23 H9
Ladygrove Dr RGUE GU4 250 E5
Lady Harewood Wy
HOR/WEW KT19 219 M5
Lady Hay WPK KT4 200 C9
Lady Margaret Rd ARCH N19 118 D9
ASC SL5 192 E8
CRAWW RH11 283 K6
STHL UB1 133 N6
Ladymead GU GU1 249 P9
Ladymead Cl CRAWE RH10 284 D10
Ladymeadow HHS/BOV HP3 53 N3
Ladymount WLGTN SM6 222 E1
Lady St John Sq
HERT/WAS * SG14 25 H5
Lady's Cl WATW WD18 73 K8
Ladyship Ter EDUL * SE22 182 A3
Ladyshot HLW CM20 29 K10
Ladysmith Av EHAM E6 142 B4
GNTH/NBYPK IG2 122 G5
Ladysmith Rd CAN/RD E16 141 L5
ELTH/MOT SE9 184 D2
EN EN1 79 N6
KTN/HRWW/W HA3 94 D10
STALW/RED AL3 38 C5
TOTM N17 99 P10
UED N18 100 A6
Lady Somerset Rd KTTN NW5 118 C9
Ladythorpe Cl ADL/WDHM KT15 215 L1
Ladywalk RKW/CH/CXG WD3 91 H6
Ladywell Prospect SBW CM21 30 A2
Ladywell Rd LEW SE13 182 F1
Ladywell St SRTFD E15 141 L3
Ladywood Av STMC/STPC BR5 207 H5
Ladywood Cl RKW/CH/CXG WD3 71 L7
Ladywood Rd HERT/WAS SG14 24 G5
RDART DA2 188 D8
SURB KT6 199 M9
Lafone Av FELT TW13 175 K5
Lafone St STHWK SE1 19 L1
Lagado Ms BERM/RHTH SE16 140 C10
Lagger Cl CSTG HP8 89 N4
The Lagger CSTG HP8 89 N4
Laglands Cl REIG RH2 257 M8
Lagley Meadow BERK * HP4 33 M4
Lagonda Av BARK/HLT IG6 103 J7
Lagonda Wy DART DA1 165 K10
Lagoon Rd STMC/STPC BR5 207 L5
Laidlaw Dr WCHMH N21 78 G9
Laidon Sq HHNE HP2 35 N2
Laing Cl CHIG IG7 102 G7
Laing Dean NTHLT UB5 133 K3
Laings Av MTCM CR4 202 A2
Lainlock Pl HSLW TW3 154 A7
Lainson St WAND/EARL SW18 179 K3
Lairdale Cl DUL SE21 181 K4
Laird Av CDH/CHF RM16 168 A1
Lairs Cl HOLWY N7 5 M1
Laitwood Rd BAL SW12 180 C4
Lake Av BMLY BR1 183 M9
RAIN RM13 145 L4
SL SL1 129 J9
Lake Cl BF/WBF KT14 215 N8
Lakedale Rd WOOL/PLUM SE18 163 H4
Lake Dr BUSH WD23 94 B3
Lake End Ct MDHD * SL6 128 A8
Lake End Rd MDHD SL6 128 A9
WDSR SL4 148 A1
Lakefield Rd WDGN N22 99 J10
Lakefields Cl RAIN RM13 145 L4
Lake Gdns DAGE RM10 124 B10
RCHPK/HAM TW10 176 G6
WLGTN SM6 202 C10
Lakehall Gdns THHTH CR7 203 J5
Lakehall Rd THHTH CR7 203 J5
Lake House Rd WAN E11 121 M8
Lakehurst Rd HOR/WEW KT19 220 B2
Lakeland Cl CHIG IG7 103 L5
KTN/HRWW/W HA3 94 C7
Lake La HORL RH6 280 D2
Lakenheath STHGT/OAK N14 78 E9
Lake Ri ROM RM1 124 G1
WTHK RM20 166 F3
Lake Rd CHDH RM6 123 N2
CROY/NA CR0 204 E9
DAGW RM9 144 C5
VW GU25 193 N4
WAB EN9 45 K7
WIM/MER SW19 179 J8
Lakers Ri BNSTD SM7 239 P2
Lakes Cl RGUE GU4 268 E6
Lakeside BECK BR3 204 G3
ENC/FH EN2 78 E8
HOR/WEW KT19 220 B3
RAIN RM13 145 M4
REDH RH1 258 B8
WEA W13 135 H8
WEY KT13 196 F9
WLGTN SM6 222 C1
WOKN/KNAP GU21 231 K5
Lakeside Av REDBR IG4 122 A2
THMD SE28 143 K10
Lakeside Cl BFN/LL DA15 185 M1
CHIG IG7 103 J5
RSLP HA4 112 D2
SNWD SE25 203 P2
WOKN/KNAP GU21 231 K5
Lakeside Crs BRW CM14 107 J4
EBAR EN4 78 A10
Lakeside Dr ESH/CLAY KT10 218 B3
HAYES BR2 206 B10
SLN SL2 129 K3
Lakeside Gra WEY KT13 196 D10
Lakeside Pl LCOL/BKTW AL2 57 J4
Lakeside Rd CHES/WCR EN8 62 B4
DTCH/LGLY SL3 151 J6
PLMGR N13 98 G5
WKENS W14 156 G2
Lakeside Wy WBLY HA9 115 M9
Lakes La BEAC HP9 108 E1
Lakes Rd HAYES BR2 225 P2
Lakeswood Rd STMC/STPC BR5 206 E6
The Lake BUSH WD23 94 C2
Lake Vw EDGW HA8 95 L6
KGLGY * WD4 54 C4
POTB/CUF EN6 59 M9
RDKG RH5 273 H5
Lake View Est BOW * E3 140 C4
Lake View Rd SEV TN13 247 H9
Lakeview Rd WELL DA16 163 L10
WNWD SE27 181 H8
Lake View Ter UED * N18 99 N5
Lakis Cl HAMP NW3 117 M9
Laleham Abbey STA * TW18 195 M4
Laleham Av MLHL NW7 96 A4
Laleham Cl STA TW18 195 L1
Laleham Ct SUT * SM1 221 M2
WOKN/KNAP * GU21 232 B2
Laleham Reach CHERT KT16 195 L2
Laleham Rd CAT SE6 183 H3
SHPTN TW17 195 P4
STA TW18 173 J9
Lalor St FUL/PGN SW6 157 H8
Lambarde Av ELTH/MOT SE9 184 D7
Lambarde Dr SEV TN13 247 H9
Lambarde Rd SEV TN13 247 H8
Lambardes HART DA3 211 L10
Lambardes Cl ORP BR6 227 M7
Lamb Cl GSTN WD25 55 K10
HAT AL10 40 E5
TIL RM18 168 F8
Lamb Ct STALE/WH * AL4 21 K4
Lamberhurst Cl STMC/STPC BR5 207 N8
Lamberhurst Rd BCTR RM8 123 P6
WNWD SE27 181 H7
Lamberhurst Wk CRAWE RH10 284 B8
Lambert Av DTCH/LGLY SL3 150 B2
RCH/KEW TW9 155 M9
Lambert Cl BH/WHM TN16 244 A2
Lambert Ct BUSH WD23 73 L8
Lambert Jones Ms BARB * EC2Y 12 E3
Lambert Rd BNSTD SM7 221 K10
BRXS/STRHM SW2 180 F1
CAN/RD E16 141 N8
NFNCH/WDSP N12 97 N6
Lambert's Pl CROY/NA CR0 203 L8
Lambert's Rd SURB KT6 199 K5
Lambert St IS N1 6 A4
Lambert Wy NFNCH/WDSP N12 97 M6
Lambeth Br WEST SW1P 17 M5
Lambeth High St STHWK SE1 17 N6
Lambeth Hl BLKFR * EC4V 12 E7
Lambeth Palace Rd STHWK SE1 17 N4
Lambeth Rd CROY/NA CR0 203 H8
STHWK SE1 18 A4
Lambeth Wk LBTH SE11 17 P5
Lamb La HACK E8 140 A2
Lamble St KTTN NW5 118 B9
Lambley Rd DAGW RM9 143 L1
Lambly Hl VW GU25 194 B3
Lambolle Pl HAMP NW3 3 P2
Lambolle Rd HAMP NW3 3 N2
Lambourn Cha RAD WD7 74 D2
Lambourn Cl HNWL W7 154 E1
KTTN * NW5 118 D9
Lambourne Av WIM/MER SW19 179 J7
Lambourne Cl CHIG IG7 103 L4
CRAWE RH10 284 A9
Lambourne Ct UX/CGN UB8 131 L3
Lambourne Crs CHIG IG7 103 L3
WOKN/KNAP GU21 214 G9
Lambourne Dr COB KT11 235 K1
Lambourne Gdns BARK IG11 143 J2
CHING E4 100 F3
EN EN1 79 N6
HCH RM12 125 L7
Lambourne Gv KUT KT1 199 N2
Lambourne Pl BKHTH/KID SE3 161 N7
Lambourne Rd BARK IG11 143 H2
CHIG IG7 103 J5
GDMY/SEVK IG3 123 H7
WAN E11 121 H5
Lambourn Rd CLAP SW4 158 C9
Lambrook Ter FUL/PGN SW6 157 H7
Lambs Cl ED * N9 99 P3
POTB/CUF EN6 60 G5
Lamb's Conduit Pas FSBYW WC1X 11 N3
Lamb's Conduit St BMSBY WC1N 11 N2
Lambscroft Av LEE/GVPK SE12 183 P6
Lambscroft Wy CFSP/GDCR SL9 90 B10
Lambs Green Rd HORS RH12 282 C8
Lamb's La North RAIN RM13 145 L6
Lamb's La South RAIN RM13 145 K7
Lambs Meadow WFD IG8 102 A10
Lambs Ms IS N1 6 C6
Lamb's Pas STLK EC1Y 12 G2
Lambs Ter ED * N9 99 L3
Lamb St WCHPL E1 13 L3
Lambs Wk ENC/FH EN2 79 K6
Lambton Av CHES/WCR EN8 62 C9
Lambton Pl NTGHL W11 8 D7
Lambton Rd ARCH N19 118 F6
RYNPK SW20 200 F1
Lamb Wk STHWK SE1 19 J2
Lambyn Cft HORL RH6 280 D3
Lamerock Rd BMLY BR1 183 L7
Lamerton Rd BARK/HLT IG6 102 E10
Lamerton St DEPT SE8 160 F5
Lamford Cl TOTM N17 99 L8
Lamington St HMSMTH W6 156 E3
Lamlash St LBTH SE11 18 C5
Lammas Av MTCM CR4 202 B2
Lammas Cl STA TW18 173 H6
Lammas Ct WDSR SL4 149 H8
Lammas Dr STA TW18 172 G7
Lammas La ESH/CLAY KT10 217 P1
Lammasmead BROX EN10 44 E9
Lammas Park Gdns EA W5 135 H10
Lammas Rd HOM E9 140 C2
LEY E10 120 D7
RCHPK/HAM TW10 177 H7
SL SL1 128 C7
WATW WD18 73 K9
Lammermoor Rd BAL * SW12 180 C3
Lamont Rd WBPTN SW10 15 K10
Lamont Road Pas WBPTN SW10 15 L10
Lamorbey Cl BFN/LL DA15 185 J5
Lamorbey Pk BFN/LL * DA15 185 L4
Lamorna WOKS/MYFD * GU22 232 B4
Lamorna Av GVE DA12 190 G5
Lamorna Cl ORP BR6 207 K7
RAD WD7 56 G10
WALTH E17 101 H10
Lamorna Gv STAN HA7 95 J9
Lampard Gv STNW/STAM N16 119 N6
Lampern Sq BETH E2 7 P9
Lampeter Cl WOKS/MYFD GU22 232 B4
Lampeter Sq HMSMTH W6 14 A10
Lampits HOD EN11 44 G3
Lamplighter Cl WCHPL E1 140 B6
Lamplighters Cl DART DA1 187 N2
WAB EN9 63 M10
Lampmead Rd LEW SE13 183 K1
Lamport Cl WOOL/PLUM SE18 162 C3
Lampton Av HEST TW5 153 P7
Lampton House Cl
WIM/MER SW19 178 G7
Lampton Park Rd HSLW TW3 154 A8
Lampton Rd HSLW TW3 154 A8
Lamsey Rd HHS/BOV HP3 35 N8
Lamson Rd RAIN RM13 144 G6
Lanacre Av CDALE/KGS NW9 96 B9
Lanark Cl EA W5 135 H7
Lanark Pl MV/WKIL W9 9 K1
Lanark Rd MV/WKIL W9 3 H8
Lanbury Rd PECK SE15 160 C10
Lancashire Ct MYFR/PKLN W1K 10 E7
Lancaster Av BARK IG11 143 H2
EBAR EN4 77 N4
GU GU1 268 C2
MTCM CR4 202 F5
SLN SL2 129 H6
WAN E11 121 N2
WIM/MER SW19 178 G8
WNWD SE27 181 J5
Lancaster Cl BRWN CM15 86 F9
CDALE/KGS NW9 96 C8
CRAWE RH10 284 E4
EGH TW20 172 A8
HAYES BR2 205 L4
IS N1 7 K4
STWL/WRAY TW19 173 P2
TOTM * N17 99 P8
WOKN/KNAP GU21 232 D2
Lancaster Ct BAY/PAD W2 9 K7
WOT/HER KT12 197 H7
Lancaster Dr HAMP NW3 3 N2
HCH RM12 125 J10
HHW HP1 52 C3
LOU IG10 82 B9
POP/IOD E14 141 H10
Lancaster Gdn KUTN/CMB KT2 177 J8
Lancaster Gdns WIM/MER SW19 179 H8
Lancaster Ga BAY/PAD W2 9 K8
Lancaster Gv HAMP NW3 3 M2
Lancaster Ms BAY/PAD W2 9 K7
RCHPK/HAM TW10 177 K2
WAND/EARL * SW18 179 L1
Lancaster Pk RCHPK/HAM TW10 177 K1
Lancaster Pl TWK TW1 176 F3
WIM/MER SW19 178 G8
Lancaster Rd UX/CGN UB8 131 N1
EBAR EN4 77 N8
ENC/FH EN2 79 L5
EPP CM16 66 B2
FBAR/BDGN N11 98 E7
FSBYPK N4 119 H5
FSTGT E7 141 M2
NTGHL W11 8 A6

NTHLT UB5 134 B1
RYLN/HDSTN HA2 113 P3
SNWD SE25 203 N2
STAL AL1 38 E4
STHL UB1 133 M9
UED N18 99 N6
WALTH E17 100 C10
WAN E11 121 K7
WIM/MER SW19 178 G8
WLSDN NW10 116 C10
WTHK RM20 167 J3
Lancaster Stables HAMP NW3 3 P2
Lancaster St STHWK SE1 18 C2
Lancaster Ter BAY/PAD W2 9 L7
Lancaster Wk HYS/HAR UB3 132 D8
Lancaster Wy ABLGY WD5 54 G7
Lancaster West NTGHL W11 8 A7
Lancastrian Rd WLGTN SM6 222 F4
Lancefield St MV/WKIL W9 2 C10
Lancell St STNW/STAM N16 119 M7
Lancelot Av ALP/SUD HA0 115 J9
Lancelot Cl CRAWW RH11 283 H7
SL SL1 148 F1
Lancelot Crs ALP/SUD HA0 115 J9
Lancelot Gdns EBAR EN4 98 B1
Lancelot Pde ALP/SUD * HA0 115 K10
Lancelot Pl SKENS SW7 16 A2
Lancelot Rd ALP/SUD HA0 115 J9
BARK/HLT IG6 103 H7
WELL DA16 163 K10
Lance Rd HRW HA1 114 B5
Lancer Sq KENS W8 14 G1
Lancey Cl CHARL SE7 162 A3
Lanchester Rd HGT N6 118 A3
Lancing Cl CRAWW RH11 283 K6
Lancing Gdns ED N9 99 N2
Lancing Rd CROY/NA CR0 202 G6
FELT TW13 174 G5
GNTH/NBYPK IG2 122 G4
HARH RM3 105 M8
ORP BR6 207 L9
WEA W13 134 G9
Lancing St CAMTN NW1 5 J10
Lancing Wy RKW/CH/CXG WD3 72 C9
Lancresse Cl UX/CGN UB8 131 N1
Landale Gdns DART DA1 187 K4
Landau Wy BROX EN10 62 E2
ERITH DA8 165 L4
Landcroft Rd EDUL SE22 181 N2
Landells Rd EDUL SE22 181 N2
Landen Pk HORL RH6 279 P2
Lander Rd GRAYS RM17 168 A4
Landford Cl RKW/CH/CXG WD3 91 P3
Landford Rd PUT/ROE SW15 156 F9
Landgrove Rd WIM/MER SW19 179 K8
Landleys Flds KTTN * NW5 118 E10
Landmann Wy NWCR SE14 160 C5
Landmead Rd CHES/WCR EN8 62 D5
Landon Pl KTBR SW1X 16 A3
Landons Cl POP/IOD E14 141 H10
Landon Wy ASHF * TW15 174 C9
Landor Rd BRXN/ST SW9 158 F9
Landor Wk SHB W12 156 D1
Landra Gdns WCHMH N21 79 J10
Landridge Dr EN EN1 80 A4
Landridge Rd FUL/PGN SW6 157 H8
Landrock Rd CEND/HSY/T N8 118 F4
Landscape Rd WARL CR6 242 A5
WFD IG8 101 N8
Landseer Av GVW DA11 190 A6
MNPK E12 122 D10
Landseer Cl EDGW HA8 95 M10
HCH RM12 125 J6
WIM/MER SW19 201 M1
Landseer Rd ARCH N19 118 F8
EN EN1 79 P9
NWMAL KT3 200 A7
SUT SM1 221 K3
Lands' End BORE WD6 75 J10
Landstead Rd WOOL/PLUM SE18 162 G6
Landview Gdns CHONG CM5 67 N6
Landway BGR/WK TN15 247 N6
The Landway BGR/WK TN15 247 P3
STMC/STPC BR5 207 M3
Lane Ap MLHL * NW7 97 H6
Lane Av GRH DA9 189 H2
Lane Cl ADL/WDHM KT15 215 K2
CRICK NW2 116 E8
Lane End BERK HP4 33 L5
BXLYHN DA7 164 C9
EPSOM KT18 219 N10
HAT AL10 40 C7
HLWE CM17 47 P2
Lane End Dr WOKN/KNAP GU21 231 H3
Lanefield Wk WGCW AL8 22 F5
Lane Gdns BUSH WD23 94 D2
Lanercost Gdns STHGT/OAK N14 78 F10
Lanercost Rd BRXS/STRHM SW2 181 H5
CRAWW RH11 283 M8
Lanes Av GVW DA11 190 C6
Laneside CHST BR7 184 E8
EDGW HA8 95 P6
Laneside Av BCTR RM8 124 A5
The Lane BKHTH/KID SE3 161 M9
CHERT KT16 195 K3
STJWD NW8 3 J8
VW GU25 194 B3
Laneway PUT/ROE SW15 178 E1
Lanfranc Rd BOW E3 140 D4
Lanfrey Pl WKENS W14 14 C8
Langafel Cl HART DA3 211 K2
Langaller La LHD/OX KT22 236 A7
Langbourne Av HGT N6 118 B7
Langbourne Wy ESH/CLAY KT10 218 E3
Langbrook Rd BKHTH/KID SE3 162 A9
Lang Cl GT/LBKH KT23 236 A9
Langcroft Cl CAR SM5 202 A10
Langdale Av HARP AL5 20 C1
MTCM CR4 202 A3
Langdale Cl BCTR RM8 123 M6
MORT/ESHN SW14 155 N10
ORP BR6 206 E10
WALW SE17 18 E9
WOKN/KNAP GU21 231 P2
Langdale Crs BXLYHN DA7 164 B7
Langdale Dr YEAD UB4 132 F4
Langdale Gdns HCH RM12 125 H10
PEND EN3 80 C1
Langdale Pde MTCM * CR4 202 A2
Langdale Rd CRAWW RH11 282 G9
GNWCH SE10 161 H6
THHTH CR7 203 H4
Langdale St WCHPL * E1 140 A8
Langdale Ter BORE * WD6 76 A7
Langdon Ct WLSDN NW10 136 B3
Langdon Crs EHAM E6 142 D4
Langdon Dr CDALE/KGS NW9 115 P6
Langdon Park Rd HGT N6 118 C5
Langdon Pl MORT/ESHN SW14 155 P9
Langdon Rd HAYES BR2 205 N3
MRDN SM4 201 M5
Langdon Shaw SCUP DA14 185 J8
Langdon Wk MRDN SM4 201 M5
Langdon Wy STHWK SE1 19 P6
Langfield Cl WAB EN9 45 K8
Langford Cl HACK E8 119 P10
SEVS/STOTM N15 119 M4
Langford Crs EBAR EN4 78 A8
Langford Gn RBRW/HUT CM13 87 P10
Langford Pl SCUP DA14 185 K6
STJWD NW8 3 K8
Langford Rd EBAR EN4 78 A8
FUL/PGN SW6 157 L8
WFD IG8 101 P7
Langfords BKHH IG9 102 A3
Langham Cl STALE/WH AL4 39 H1
Langham Ct EMPK RM11 125 L5
RSLP * HA4 113 J10
Langham Dene PUR/KEN CR8 241 J1
Langham Dr GDMY/SEVK IG3 123 L4
Langham Gdns ALP/SUD HA0 115 H7
EDGW HA8 95 P8
RCHPK/HAM TW10 177 H7
WCHMH N21 79 H9
WEA W13 134 G9
Langham House Cl
RCHPK/HAM TW10 177 J7
Langham Pde
SEVS/STOTM * N15 119 J1
Langham Park Pl HAYES BR2 205 L4
Langham Pl CAVSQ/HST W1G 10 F4
CHSWK W4 156 B5
EGH TW20 172 C8
SEVS/STOTM N15 119 J1
Langham Rd EDGW HA8 95 P7
RYNPK SW20 200 F1
SEVS/STOTM N15 119 K2
TEDD TW11 176 G8
Langham St GTPST W1W 10 G4
Langhedge Cl UED N18 99 N7
Langhedge La UED N18 99 N6
Langholm Cl BAL SW12 180 E3
Langholme BUSH WD23 94 B2
Langhorn Dr WHTN TW2 176 D3
Langhorne Rd DAGE RM10 144 B2
Langhurst La HORS RH12 282 D5
Langland Ct NTHWD HA6 92 D8
Langland Crs STAN HA7 95 J10
Langland Dr PIN HA5 93 M8
Langland Gdns CROY/NA CR0 204 E9
HAMP NW3 117 L10
Langlands Dr RDART DA2 188 D8
Langlands Ri HOR/WEW KT19 219 P9
Langler Rd WLSDN NW10 136 F4
Langley Av HHS/BOV HP3 35 P9
RSLP HA4 113 J7
SURB KT6 199 J8
WPK KT4 200 G9
Langley Broom DTCH/LGLY SL3 150 C4
Langleybury La KGLGY WD4 54 C10
Langley Cl EPSOM KT18 238 A5
GU GU1 249 P9
HARH RM3 105 P8
Langley Ct BECK * BR3 204 G4
CHESW * EN7 61 K4
COVGDN WC2E 11 L7
Langley Crs DAGW RM9 143 M2
EDGW HA8 95 P4
HYS/HAR UB3 152 G6
KGLGY WD4 54 B6
STALW/RED AL3 38 B4
WAN E11 121 N5
Langley Dr ACT W3 155 N1
BRW CM14 106 F4
CRAWW RH11 283 M5
WAN E11 121 N5
Langley Gdns DAGW RM9 143 N2
STMC/STPC BR5 206 E6
Langley Gn WAB * EN9 45 J8
Langley Gv NWMAL KT3 200 A2
STALE/WH AL4 21 H9
Langley Hl KGLGY WD4 54 A5
Langley Hill Cl KGLGY WD4 54 B5
Langley La ABLGY WD5 54 G6
CRAWW RH11 283 K5
VX/NE SW8 17 M9
Langley Lodge La KGLGY WD4 53 P7
Langley Oaks Av SAND/SEL CR2 223 P6
Langley Pde CRAWW RH11 283 M4
Langley Pk DTCH/LGLY * SL3 130 D7
EDGW HA8 96 B7
Langley Park Rd BELMT SM2 221 M3
IVER SL0 130 G8
Langley Pl CRAWW RH11 283 M4
Langley Quay DTCH/LGLY * SL3 150 D1
Langley Rd ABLGY WD5 54 F7
BECK BR3 204 C4
DTCH/LGLY SL3 149 P2
ISLW TW7 154 E8
KGLGY WD4 53 L6
SAND/SEL CR2 224 C5
STA TW18 173 J9
SURB KT6 199 K7
WAT WD17 72 G5
WELL DA16 163 M5
WIM/MER SW19 201 J1
Langley Rw BAR EN5 77 J5
Langley St LSQ/SEVD WC2H 11 L6
Langley Vale Rd EPSOM KT18 238 A4
Langley Wk CRAWW RH11 283 L4
Langley Wy WAT WD17 72 G5
WWKM BR4 205 J8
Langley Whf KGLGY * WD4 54 B3
Langley Wd BECK * BR3 205 K5
Langmans Wy
WOKN/KNAP GU21 231 K2
Langmead Dr BUSH WD23 94 C2
Langmead St WNWD SE27 181 J7
Langport Ct WOT/HER KT12 197 K8
Langridge Ms HPTN TW12 175 N9
Langroyd Rd TOOT SW17 180 A5
Langshott HORL RH6 280 E2
Langshott Cl ADL/WDHM KT15 215 H7
Langshott La HORL RH6 280 D3
Langside Av PUT/ROE SW15 156 D10
Langside Crs STHGT/OAK N14 98 E4
Langstone Cl CRAWE RH10 284 D10
Langston Hughes Cl
HNHL * SE24 159 J10
Langston Rd LOU IG10 82 G8
Lang St WCHPL E1 140 B6
Langthorn Ct LOTH * EC2R 13 H5
Langthorne Crs GRAYS RM17 167 P3
Langthorne Rd WAN E11 121 J8
Langthorne St FUL/PGN SW6 156 G7
Langton Av EHAM E6 142 D5
EW KT17 220 C7
TRDG/WHET N20 97 M1
Langton Cl ADL/WDHM KT15 195 L10
FSBYW WC1X 5 P10
SL SL1 128 C10
WOKN/KNAP GU21 231 L3
Langton Gv NTHWD HA6 92 D6
Langton Ri EDUL SE22 182 A3
Langton Rd BRXN/ST SW9 159 J6
CRICK NW2 116 F8
E/WMO/HCT KT8 198 B5
HOD EN11 44 E3
KTN/HRWW/W HA3 94 B8
Langton's Meadow SLN SL2 129 H1
Langton St WBPTN SW10 15 K10
Langton Vls TOTM * N17 99 P9
Langton Wy BKHTH/KID SE3 161 M6
CDH/CHF RM16 168 F3
CROY/NA CR0 223 M1
EGH TW20 172 F9
Langtry Pl FUL/PGN SW6 14 F9
NTHLT UB5 133 L4
Langtry Rd KIL/WHAMP NW6 2 G6
Langtry Wk KIL/WHAMP NW6 3 K3
Langwood Cha TEDD TW11 177 H9
Langwood Cl ASHTD KT21 237 M3
Langwood Gdns WAT WD17 73 H5
Langworth Cl RDART DA2 187 L6
Langworth Dr YEAD UB4 133 J8
Lanhill Rd MV/WKIL W9 8 E1
Lanier Rd LEW SE13 183 H2
Lanigan Dr HSLW TW3 176 A1
Lankaster Gdns EFNCH N2 97 N9
Lankers Dr RYLN/HDSTN HA2 113 N4
Lankton Cl BECK BR3 205 H1
Lannock Rd HYS/HAR UB3 132 G10
Lannoy Rd ELTH/MOT SE9 184 F4
Lanrick Copse BERK HP4 34 B4
Lanrick Rd POP/IOD E14 141 J8
Lanridge Rd ABYW SE2 163 N2
Lansbury Av BARK IG11 143 K2
CHDH RM6 123 P3
EBED/NFELT TW14 175 J2
UED N18 99 L6
Lansbury Cl WLSDN NW10 115 P10
Lansbury Crs DART DA1 187 P1
Lansbury Dr YEAD UB4 132 G5
Lansbury Gdns POP/IOD * E14 141 J8
Lansbury Rd PEND EN3 80 C5
Lansbury Wy UED N18 99 M6
Lanscombe Wk VX/NE * SW8 158 F6
Lansdell Rd MTCM CR4 202 B2
Lansdown GU GU1 250 D10
Lansdown Cl WOKN/KNAP GU21 231 L5
WOT/HER KT12 197 K6
Lansdowne Av BXLYHN DA7 163 M6
ORP BR6 206 E8
SL SL1 129 K10
Lansdowne Cl BRYLDS KT5 199 N9
RYNPK SW20 178 G10
TWK TW1 176 E4
Lansdowne Copse WPK * KT4 200 D9
Lansdowne Ct BROX * EN10 44 F6
SL SL1 129 K10
WPK KT4 200 D9
Lansdowne Crs NTGHL W11 8 B8
Lansdowne Dr HACK E8 7 P2
Lansdowne Gdns VX/NE SW8 158 F7
Lansdowne Gn VX/NE SW8 158 F6
Lansdowne Gv WLSDN NW10 116 B9
Lansdowne Hl WNWD SE27 181 J6
Lansdowne La CHARL SE7 162 A4
Lansdowne Ms CHARL SE7 162 A4
NTGHL W11 8 C10
Lansdowne Pl NRWD SE19 181 N10
STHWK * SE1 19 H3
Lansdowne Ri NTGHL W11 8 B8
Lansdowne Rd BMLY BR1 183 M10
CHING E4 100 F3
CROY/NA CR0 203 K9
CSHM HP5 51 H5
FNCH N3 97 J8
GDMY/SEVK IG3 123 J6
HOR/WEW KT19 219 P4
HSLW TW3 154 A9
MUSWH N10 98 D10
NTGHL W11 8 B8
PUR/KEN CR8 223 H8
RYNPK SW20 178 F10
SEV TN13 247 L9
STA TW18 173 L10
STAN HA7 95 H7
SWFD E18 121 M1
TOTM N17 99 P9
UX/CGN UB8 132 C8
WALTH E17 120 F4
WAN E11 121 L7
Lansdowne Sq GVW DA11 190 C2
Lansdowne Ter BMSBY WC1N 11 M2
Lansdowne Wk NTGHL W11 8 B9
Lansdowne Wy VX/NE SW8 158 F7
Lansdowne Wood Cl
WNWD SE27 181 J6
Lansdown Pl GVW DA11 190 C4
Lansdown Rd CFSP/GDCR SL9 90 A9
FSTGT E7 141 P2
SCUP DA14 185 L6
TIL RM18 168 C8
Lansfield Av UED N18 99 P5
Lantern Cl ALP/SUD HA0 115 J10
PUT/ROE SW15 156 D10
Lanterns Ct POP/IOD E14 160 F2
Lantern Wy WDR/YW UB7 151 P1
Lant St STHWK SE1 18 E1
Lanvanor Rd PECK SE15 160 B8
Lapford Cl MV/WKIL W9 8 D1
Lapis Cl GVE DA12 191 L4
La Plata Gv BRW CM14 106 G4
Lapse Wood Wk DUL SE21 182 A4
Lapstone Gdns
KTN/HRWW/W HA3 115 H4
Lapwing Cl CROY/NA CR0 224 D6
ERITH * DA8 165 J6
HHNE HP2 35 P2
Lapwing Gv RGUE GU4 250 G8
Lapwing Pl GSTN * WD25 55 K8
Lapwings HART DA3 211 N3
Lapwing Wy ABLGY WD5 55 H7
YEAD UB4 133 L8
Lapworth Cl ORP BR6 207 M9
Lapworth Ct BAY/PAD W2 9 H3
Lara Cl CHSGTN KT9 219 K4
LEW SE13 183 H2
Larbert Rd STRHM/NOR SW16 202 D1
Larby Pl EW KT17 220 B6
Larch Av ACT W3 136 B10
ASC SL5 192 D5
GU GU1 249 P8
LCOL/BKTW AL2 55 M6
Larch Cl BAL SW12 180 C5
CHESW EN7 61 M3
DEPT SE8 160 E5
FBAR/BDGN N11 98 B7
KWD/TDW/WH KT20 239 M7
REIG RH2 275 M2
SLN SL2 128 G7
WARL CR6 242 D5
Larch Crs HOR/WEW KT19 219 N3
YEAD UB4 133 K6
Larch Dene ORP BR6 206 D9
Larch Dr CHSWK * W4 155 M4
Larches Av EN EN1 80 B1
MORT/ESHN SW14 156 A10
The Larches BERK HP4 33 J4
BUSH WD23 73 M9
HGDN/ICK UB10 132 C4
PLMGR N13 99 K4
STALE/WH AL4 39 J2
WOKN/KNAP GU21 232 B2
Larch Gv BFN/LL DA15 185 J4
Larchmoor Pk SLN * SL2 109 M10
Larch Ri BERK HP4 33 M4
Larch Rd CRICK NW2 116 F9
DART DA1 187 L4
LEY E10 120 F7
Larch Tree Wy CROY/NA CR0 204 F10
Larch Wy HAYES BR2 206 D7
Larchwood Av CRW RM5 104 C7
Larchwood Cl BNSTD SM7 239 H2
CRW RM5 104 D7
Larchwood Dr EGH TW20 171 N9
Larchwood Gdns BRWN CM15 86 F10
Larchwood Rd ELTH/MOT SE9 184 E5
HHNE HP2 36 A4
WOKN/KNAP GU21 231 J6
Larcombe Cl CROY/NA CR0 223 N1
Larcom St WALW SE17 18 F6
Larden Rd ACT W3 156 B1
Largewood Av SURB KT6 199 M9
Larissa St WALW * SE17 19 H6
Lark Av STA TW18 173 J6
Larkbere Rd SYD SE26 182 D7
Larken Cl BUSH WD23 94 B2
Larken Dr BUSH WD23 94 B2
Larkfield COB KT11 217 H9
Larkfield Av KTN/HRWW/W HA3 114 G1
Larkfield Ct HORL RH6 281 H4
Larkfield Rd RCH/KEW TW9 155 K10
SCUP DA14 185 J6
SEV TN13 246 D9
Larkfields GVW DA11 190 B6
Larkhall Cl WOT/HER KT12 217 K3
Larkhall La CLAP SW4 158 E8
Larkhall Ri CLAP SW4 158 D9
Larkham Cl FELT TW13 174 F6
Larkhill Ter WOOL/PLUM * SE18 162 D6
Larkin Cl COUL/CHIP CR5 240 G3
RBRW/HUT CM13 107 P1
Larkings La DTCH/LGLY SL3 129 N3
Larkins Rd HORL RH6 279 N8
Lark Ri CRAWW RH11 283 M5
EHSLY KT24 252 F7
HAT AL10 40 D6
Lark Rw BETH E2 140 B3
Larksfield EGH TW20 171 N10
Larks Fld HART DA3 211 L4
Larksfield HORL RH6 280 C3
Larkshall Crs CHING E4 101 H5
Larkshall Rd CHING E4 101 J7
Larkspur Cl CDALE/KGS NW9 115 N3
HHW HP1 35 H5
ORP BR6 207 M9
RSLP HA4 112 C5
SOCK/AV RM15 147 H5
TOTM N17 99 L8
Larkspur Gv EDGW HA8 95 P5
Larkspur Wy HOR/WEW KT19 219 P2
RDKG RH5 273 J5
Larks Rdg LCOL/BKTW AL2 55 P2
Larks Ri CSHM HP5 51 J9
Larks Wy WOKN/KNAP GU21 231 H2
Larkswood HLWE CM17 47 L3
Larkswood Cl ERITH DA8 165 H7
Larkswood Ri PIN HA5 113 K2
STALE/WH AL4 39 H1
Larkswood Rd CHING E4 100 F5
Lark Wy CAR SM5 201 P7
Larkway Cl CDALE/KGS NW9 116 A2
Larkwell La HART DA3 211 L4
Larmans Rd PEND EN3 80 B2
Larnach Rd HMSMTH W6 156 G5
Larne Rd RSLP HA4 112 G5
Larner Rd ERITH DA8 164 F6
La Roche Cl DTCH/LGLY SL3 149 P2
Larpent Av PUT/ROE SW15 178 F1
Larsen Dr WAB EN9 63 J10
Larwood Cl NTHLT UB5 114 C10
Lascelles Av HRW HA1 114 C5
Lascelles Cl BRWN CM15 86 G9
WAN E11 121 J7
Lascelles Rd DTCH/LGLY SL3 149 N2
Lascott's Rd WDGN N22 98 G7
Lashmere CRAWE RH10 285 L2
Lassa Rd ELTH/MOT SE9 184 B1
Lassell St GNWCH SE10 161 J4
Lasswade Rd CHERT KT16 195 J7
Latchett Rd SWFD E18 101 N9
Latchford Ms STALE/WH AL4 21 J2
Latchford Pl CHIG IG7 103 L5
Latchingdon Gdns WFD IG8 102 B7
Latchmere Cl RCHPK/HAM TW10 177 K8
Latchmere La KUTN/CMB KT2 177 L9
Latchmere Rd BTSEA SW11 158 A8
KUTN/CMB KT2 177 K9
Latchmere St BTSEA SW11 158 A8
Latchmoor Av CFSP/GDCR SL9 110 A2
Latchmoor Gv CFSP/GDCR SL9 110 A2
Latchmoor Wy CFSP/GDCR SL9 110 A2
Lateward Rd BTFD TW8 155 J5
Latham Cl BH/WHM TN16 243 P2
EHAM E6 142 B8
RDART DA2 188 D5
Latham Rd BXLYHS DA6 186 B1
TWK TW1 176 E3
Latham's Wy CROY/NA CR0 202 G8
Lathkill Cl EN EN1 99 P1
Lathom Rd EHAM E6 142 C2
Latimer Av EHAM E6 142 C3
Latimer Cl AMS HP6 69 P5
CRAWW RH11 283 N4
HHNE HP2 36 C1
PIN HA5 93 K9
WATW WD18 92 F1
WOKS/MYFD GU22 232 E2
WPK KT4 220 E1
Latimer Dr HCH RM12 125 L8
Latimer Gdns PIN HA5 93 K9
WGCE AL7 23 L5
Latimer Pl NKENS W10 136 F8
Latimer Rd AMS HP6 70 C4
BAR EN5 77 L7
CROY/NA * CR0 203 J10
CSHM HP5 51 K10
CSHM HP5 69 M2
FSTGT E7 121 N
NKENS W10 136 F
SEVS/STOTM N15 119 M
TEDD TW11 176 E
WIM/MER SW19 179 L
Latimer Wy BEAC HP9 88 B
Latium Cl STAL AL1 38 C
Latona Dr GVE DA12 191 J
Latona Rd PECK SE15 19 N1
La Tourne Gdns ORP BR6 206 F1
Lattimer Pl CHSWK W4 156 B
Lattimore Rd STAL AL1 38 D
STALE/WH AL4 21 H
Latton Cl ESH/CLAY KT10 218 A
WOT/HER KT12 197 N
Latton Gn HLWS CM18 47 J
Latton Hall Cl HLW CM20 29 K1
Latton House HLWS CM18 47 L
Latton St HLW CM20 47 L
Latymer Cl WEY KT13 216 D
Latymer Gdns FNCH * N3 97 H1
Latymer Rd ED N9 99 N
Latymer Wy ED N9 99 L
Laud Dr CRAWE RH10 284 E
Lauder Cl NTHLT UB5 133 L
Lauderdale Dr
RCHPK/HAM TW10 177 J
Lauderdale Pde MV/WKIL * W9 2 G1
Lauderdale Pl BARB * EC2Y 12 F
Lauderdale Rd ABLGY WD5 54 D
MV/WKIL W9 3 H1
Laud St CROY/NA CR0 203 K1
LBTH SE11 17 N
Laughton Rd NTHLT UB5 133 L
Launcelot Rd BMLY BR1 183 M
Launcelot St STHWK SE1 18 A
Launceston Cl HARH RM3 105 K
Launceston Gdns GFD/PVL UB6 135 H
Launceston Pl KENS W8 15 J
Launceston Rd GFD/PVL UB6 135 H
Launch St POP/IOD E14 161 H
Launders Ga ACT * W3 155 N
Launder's La RAIN RM13 145 M
Laundress La CLPT * E5 119 P
Laundry La WAB EN9 63 L
Laundry Rd GU GU1 267 P
HMSMTH W6 14 A1
Laura Cl EN EN1 79 M
WAN E11 121 P
Lauradale Rd EFNCH N2 118 A
Laura Dr SWLY BR8 187 H1
Laura Pl CLPT E5 120 B
Laura Ter FSBYPK * N4 119 J
Laureate Wy HHW HP1 35 L
Laurel Av DTCH/LGLY SL3 150 B
EGH TW20 171 N
GVE DA12 190 F
POTB/CUF EN6 59 J
TWK TW1 176 E
Laurel Bank CHOB/PIR * GU24 213 K
HHS/BOV HP3 35 J
NFNCH/WDSP * N12 97 M
Laurel Bank Gdns FUL/PGN SW6 157 J
Laurel Bank Rd ENC/FH EN2 79 K
Laurel Cl BARK/HLT IG6 102 F
CRAWE RH10 284 B1
DART DA1 187 K
DTCH/LGLY SL3 151 H
HHNE HP2 36 A
RBRW/HUT CM13 87 N
SCUP DA14 185 K
TOOT SW17 179 P
Laurel Ct AMS HP6 69 H
IVER * SL0 130 G
RBRW/HUT * CM13 87 P1
Laurel Crs CROY/NA CR0 204 F1
ROMW/RG RM7 124 F
WOKN/KNAP GU21 214 F
Laureldene RGUW GU3 248 A1
Laurel Dr OXTED RH8 261 L
SOCK/AV RM15 147 J
WCHMH N21 99 H
Laurel Flds POTB/CUF EN6 59 J
Laurel Gdns CHING E4 100 G
HNWL W7 134 D1
HSLWW TW4 153 M1
MLHL NW7 96 A
Laurel Gv PGE/AN SE20 182 A1
SYD SE26 182 C
Laurel La WDR/YW UB7 151 P
Laurel Pk KTN/HRWW/W HA3 94 E
Laurel Rd BARN SW13 156 D
CFSP/GDCR SL9 90 A
HPTN TW12 176 C
RYNPK SW20 200 E
STAL AL1 38 E
Laurels Cl STALW/RED AL3 38 A
Laurels Rd IVER SL0 130 G
The Laurels BERK HP4 34 E
BNSTD SM7 239 J
BORE * WD6 75 M
BUSH * WD23 94 D
CHESW EN7 61 M
CMBW * SE5 159 J
COB KT11 235 M
CRAWE * RH10 284 B
HART DA3 211 P
RDART * DA2 187 K
Laurel St HACK E8 7 M
Laurel Vw NFNCH/WDSP N12 97 L
Laurel Vls HNWL * W7 154 D
Laurel Wy NFNCH/WDSP N12 97 K
SWFD E18 121 L
Laurence Ms SHB W12 156 D
Laurence Pountney Hl
CANST * EC4R 12 G
Laurence Pountney La
CANST EC4R 12 G
Laurie Gv NWCR SE14 160 D
Laurie Rd HNWL W7 134 D
Laurier Rd CROY/NA CR0 203 N
KTTN NW5 118 C
Lauries Cl HHW HP1 34 E
Laurimel Cl STAN HA7 94 G
Laurino Pl BUSH WD23 94 B
Lauriston Cl WOKN/KNAP GU21 231 J
Lauriston Rd HOM E9 140 C
WIM/MER SW19 178 G
Lausanne Rd CEND/HSY/T N8 119 H
PECK SE15 160 B
Lauser Rd STWL/WRAY TW19 173 M
Laustan Cl GU GU1 250 F1
Lavant Cl CRAWW RH11 283 J
Lavender Av BRWN CM15 86 G
CDALE/KGS NW9 115 P
MTCM CR4 201 P1
WPK KT4 200 F1
Lavender Cl CAR SM5 222 B1
CHEL SW3 15 M1
CHESW EN7 61 N

COUL/CHIP * CR5 240 D5
CTHM CR3 259 K1
HARH RM3 105 L8
HAYES BR2 206 B6
HLW CM20 29 H10
REDH RH1 276 C5
SOCK/AV RM15 147 K5
Lavender Cottages
LHD/OX * KT22 237 H8
Lavender Ct E/WMO/HCT KT8 198 A3
Lavender Gdns BTSEA SW11 158 A10
ENC/FH EN2 79 J4
KTN/HRWW/W HA3 94 D7
Lavender Gv HACK E8 7 N4
MTCM CR4 201 P1
Lavender Hl BTSEA SW11 158 A9
ENC/FH EN2 79 K5
SWLY BR8 208 E3
Lavender Park Rd
BF/WBF * KT14 215 K9
Lavender Pl IL IG1 122 E10
Lavender Ri WDR/YW UB7 152 B1
Lavender Rd BERM/RHTH SE16 140 D10
BTSEA SW11 157 N9
CAR SM5 222 B2
CROY/NA CR0 202 G6
ENC/FH EN2 79 L5
HOR/WEW KT19 219 N2
SUT SM1 221 N1
UX/CGN UB8 132 A7
WOKS/MYFD GU22 232 E2
Lavender St SRTFD E15 141 K1
Lavender Sweep BTSEA SW11 158 A10
Lavender Ter BTSEA * SW11 157 P9
Lavender V WLGTN SM6 222 E3
Lavender Wk HHNE HP2 35 N4
Lavender Wy CROY/NA CR0 204 C6
Lavengro Rd WNWD SE27 181 K5
Lavenham Rd WAND/EARL SW18 179 J5
Lavernock Rd BXLYHN DA7 164 B8
Lavers Rd STNW/STAM N16 119 M8
Laverstoke Gdns PUT/ROE SW15 178 C3
Laverton Ms ECT * SW5 15 H6
Laverton Pl ECT SW5 15 H6
Lavidge Rd ELTH/MOT SE9 184 B5
Lavina Gv IS N1 5 N7
Lavington Cl CRAWW RH11 283 J6
Lavington Rd CROY/NA CR0 202 G10
WEA W13 134 G10
Lavington St STHWK SE1 12 D10
Lavinia Av GSTN WD25 55 K10
Lavinia Rd DART DA1 187 N2
Lavrock La RKW/CH/CXG WD3 92 A1
Lawbrook La SHGR GU5 270 D9
Lawdon Gdns CROY/NA CR0 223 J1
Lawford Av RKW/CH/CXG WD3 70 F10
Lawford Cl HCH RM12 125 K9
RKW/CH/CXG WD3 70 F10
WLGTN SM6 222 F5
Lawford Gdns DART DA1 187 K1
PUR/KEN CR8 241 K2
Lawford Rd CHSWK W4 155 P6
IS N1 7 J4
KTTN NW5 4 G2
Lawford's Hill Rd RGUW GU3 231 H10
Lawkland SLN SL2 129 H5
Lawless St POP/IOD * E14 140 G9
Lawley Rd STHGT/OAK N14 98 C1
Lawley St CLPT E5 120 B9
Lawn Av WDR/YW UB7 151 M1
Lawn Cl BMLY BR1 183 N10
DTCH/LGLY SL3 149 P6
EN EN1 99 N1
NWMAL KT3 200 B2
RSLP HA4 112 G8
SWLY BR8 208 D2
Lawn Crs RCH/KEW TW9 155 M8
Lawn Farm Gv CHDH RM6 123 P2
Lawn Gdns HNWL W7 134 D10
Lawn House Cl POP/IOD E14 161 H1
Lawn La HHS/BOV HP3 35 M8
VX/NE SW8 17 M9
Lawn Pk SEV TN13 265 J3
Lawn Rd BECK BR3 182 E10
GUW GU2 267 P3
GVW DA11 189 P1
HAMP NW3 118 A10
UX/CGN UB8 131 M2
Lawns Ct WBLY * HA9 115 M7
Lawns Crs GRAYS RM17 168 A5
The Lawns Dr BROX EN10 44 E8
Lawnsmead SHGR GU5 268 E10
Lawns Pl GRAYS * RM17 168 A5
The Lawns BELMT SM2 221 H4
BKHTH/KID * SE3 161 L9
BRW * CM14 107 K6
CHING E4 100 F6
DTCH/LGLY * SL3 151 H7
HHW HP1 35 H5
NRWD SE19 203 L1
PIN HA5 94 A8
RAD WD7 57 K9
SCUP DA14 185 L7
STALW/RED AL3 38 B5
WGCW AL8 22 G2
Lawns Wy CRW RM5 104 D8
Lawnswood BAR * EN5 77 H9
Lawn Ter BKHTH/KID SE3 161 L9
The Lawn DTCH/LGLY * SL3 149 P7
NWDGN UB2 153 P4
Lawn V PIN HA5 93 L10
Lawrance Gdns CHES/WCR EN8 62 C4
Lawrance Rd STALW/RED AL3 38 B2
Lawrance Sq GVW * DA11 190 C6
Lawrence Av MLHL NW7 96 B5
MNPK E12 122 D9
NWMAL KT3 200 A6
PLMGR N13 99 J5
WALTH E17 100 C9
WARE SG12 27 H7
Lawrence Cl HERT/WAS SG14 24 F4
RGUE GU4 250 E5
SEVS/STOTM N15 119 M2
SHB * W12 136 E9
Lawrence Ct MLHL NW7 96 B6
OXHEY * WD19 93 L4
Lawrence Crs BFOR GU20 212 C3
DAGE RM10 124 D8
EDGW HA8 95 M10
Lawrence Dr HGDN/ICK UB10 112 D9
Lawrence Gdns MLHL NW7 96 C4
TIL RM18 168 E6
Lawrence Hl CHING E4 100 F3
Lawrence Hill Gdns DART DA1 187 K2
Lawrence Hill Rd DART DA1 187 K2
Lawrence La BRKHM/BTCW RH3 256 E8
CITYW EC2V 12 F6
Lawrence Moorings SBW CM21 30 A2
Lawrence Pde ISLW * TW7 154 G9
Lawrence Pl IS N1 5 M5
Lawrence Rd EA W5 155 H3
EHAM E6 142 B3
ERITH DA8 164 C6
GPK RM2 125 J3
HPTN TW12 175 N10
HSLWW TW4 153 K10
PIN HA5 113 L3
PLSTW E13 141 N3
RCHPK/HAM TW10 177 H7
SEVS/STOTM N15 119 M1
SNWD SE25 203 N4
UED N18 100 A5
WWKM BR4 225 M1
YEAD UB4 132 D4
Lawrence St CAN/RD E16 141 L7
CHEL SW3 15 N10
MLHL NW7 96 C5
Lawrence Wy SL SL1 128 B7
WLSDN NW10 115 P8
Lawrence Yd SEVS/STOTM N15 119 M2
Lawrie Park Av SYD SE26 182 A8
Lawrie Park Crs SYD SE26 182 A8
Lawrie Park Gdns SYD SE26 182 A8
Lawrie Park Rd SYD SE26 182 B9
Laws Cl CRAWW RH11 283 H8
Lawson Cl CAN/RD E16 141 P7
WIM/MER SW19 178 G6
Lawson Gdns DART DA1 187 L1
PIN HA5 113 J1
Lawson Rd DART DA1 165 L10
PEND EN3 80 B5
STHL UB1 133 N6
Lawson Ter SHGR * GU5 268 E10
Lawson Wk CAR SM5 222 A6
Lawson Wy ASC SL5 192 G6
Law St STHWK SE1 19 H3
Lawton Rd BOW E3 140 D5
EBAR EN4 77 N7
LEY E10 121 H6
LOU IG10 82 E7
Laxcon Cl WLSDN NW10 116 A10
Laxey Rd ORP BR6 227 J3
Laxley Cl CMBW SE5 159 J6
Laxton Gdns REDH RH1 258 E4
Laxton Pl CAMTN NW1 10 F1
Layard Rd BERM/RHTH SE16 160 A3
EN EN1 79 N5
THHTH CR7 203 L2
Layard Sq BERM/RHTH SE16 160 A3
Lay Brook STALE/WH AL4 38 F2
Layburn Crs DTCH/LGLY SL3 150 E5
Laycock St IS N1 6 B2
Layer Gdns ACT W3 135 M9
Layfield Cl HDN NW4 116 E5
Layfield Crs HDN NW4 116 E5
Layfield Rd HDN NW4 116 E5
Layhams Rd HAYES BR2 225 M4
WWKM BR4 225 K1
Layhill HHNE HP2 35 N4
Laymarsh Cl BELV DA17 164 A2
Laymead Cl NTHLT UB5 133 M1
Laystall St FSBYW WC1X 12 A2
Layter's Av CFSP/GDCR SL9 89 P10
Layter's Av South CFSP/GDCR SL9 89 P10
Layter's Cl CFSP/GDCR SL9 89 P10
Layter's End CFSP/GDCR SL9 89 P10
Layter's Green La CFSP/GDCR SL9 89 M10
Layters Wy CFSP/GDCR SL9 110 A3
Layton Ct WEY KT13 216 C1
Layton Crs CROY/NA CR0 223 H2
Layton Pl RCH/KEW TW9 155 M7
Layton Rd BTFD TW8 155 J4
HSLW TW3 154 A10
Layton's La SUN TW16 196 G2
Layzell Wk ELTH/MOT SE9 184 A4
Lazenby Ct COVGDN * WC2E 11 L7
Leabank Cl HRW HA1 114 D8
Leabank Sq HOM E9 140 F1
Leabank Vw SEVS/STOTM N15 119 P4
Leabourne Rd STNW/STAM N16 119 P4
Lea Bridge Rd CLPT E5 120 C7
Lea Bushes GSTN WD25 73 M1
Leachcroft CFSP/GDCR SL9 89 N8
Leach Gv LHD/OX KT22 237 H8
Lea Cl BUSH WD23 74 A9
CRAWW RH11 283 J8
Lea Cottages MTCM * CR4 202 B2
Lea Crs RSLP HA4 112 G9
Leacroft ASC SL5 192 F5
STA TW18 173 L8
Leacroft Av BAL SW12 180 A3
Leacroft Cl PUR/KEN CR8 241 K2
STA TW18 173 L7
WCHMH N21 99 J3
WDR/YW UB7 131 P9
Leacroft Rd IVER SL0 130 G9
Leadale Av CHING E4 100 F3
Leadale Rd STNW/STAM N16 119 P4
Leadbeaters Cl FBAR/BDGN N11 98 A6
Leadenhall Pl FENCHST EC3M 13 J6
Leadenhall St BANK EC3V 13 J6
Leader Av MNPK E12 122 D10
The Leadings WBLY HA9 115 P8
Leaf Cl NTHWD HA6 92 E8
THDIT KT7 198 D5
Leaf Gv STRHM/NOR SW16 181 H8
Leafield Cl STRHM/NOR SW16 181 J9
WOKN/KNAP GU21 231 N4
Leafield La SCUP DA14 186 A7
Leafield Rd RYNPK SW20 201 J3
SUT SM1 201 K9
Leaford Crs WATN WD24 72 G3
Leaforis Rd CHESW EN7 61 P4
Leafy Gv HAYES BR2 225 P2
Leafy Oak Rd LEE/GVPK SE12 183 P7
Leafy Wy CROY/NA CR0 203 N9
Lea Gdns WBLY HA9 115 L10
Leagrave St CLPT E5 120 B8
Lea Gn BRKMPK * AL9 41 H1
Lea Hall Gdns LEY * E10 120 F6
Lea Hall Rd LEY E10 120 F6
Leaholme Gdns SL SL1 128 B7
Leaholme Waye RSLP HA4 112 C4
Leahurst Rd LEW SE13 183 J1
Leake St STHWK SE1 17 P1
Lealand Rd SEVS/STOTM N15 119 N4
Leamington Av BMLY BR1 183 P8
MRDN SM4 201 J4
ORP BR6 227 H1
WALTH E17 120 F3
Leamington Cl BMLY BR1 183 P7
HSLW TW3 176 B1
Leamington Crs
RYLN/HDSTN HA2 113 M8
Leamington Gdns
GDMY/SEVK IG3 123 J7
Leamington Pk ACT W3 136 A7
Leamington Pl YEAD UB4 132 G6
Leamington Rd HARH RM3 105 P6
NWDGN UB2 153 L3
Leamington Road Vls NTGHL W11 8 D4
Leamore St HMSMTH W6 156 E3
Lea Mt CHESW EN7 61 M4
Leamouth Rd EHAM E6 142 B8
POP/IOD E14 141 J8
Leander Dr GVE DA12 191 J7
Leander Gdns GSTN * WD25 73 M3
Leander Rd BRXS/STRHM SW2 180 G2
NTHLT UB5 133 P4
THHTH CR7 202 G4
Leapale La GU GU1 268 A1
Leapale Rd GU GU1 268 A1
Learner Dr RYLN/HDSTN HA2 113 P7
Lea Rd BECK BR3 204 F2
CDH/CHF RM16 168 D4
ENC/FH EN2 79 L5
HOD EN11 45 H1
NWDGN UB2 153 M3
SEV TN13 265 K3
WAB EN9 62 F10
WATN * WD24 73 J4
Learoyd Gdns EHAM E6 142 D9
Leas Cl CHSGTN KT9 219 L4
Leas Dl ELTH/MOT SE9 184 D6
Leas Dr IVER SL0 131 H8
Leasey Bridge La STALE/WH AL4 20 E2
Leasey Dell Dr STALE/WH AL4 20 F1
Leas Gn CHST BR7 185 J9
Leaside GT/LBKH KT23 235 P9
HHNE HP2 36 D7
Leaside Av MUSWH N10 118 B1
Leaside Ct HGDN/ICK UB10 132 C5
Leaside Rd CLPT E5 120 B6
Leas La WARL CR6 242 C4
Leasowes Rd LEY E10 120 F6
Leas Rd GU GU1 267 P1
WARL CR6 242 C4
The Leas BUSH WD23 73 N6
HHS/BOV HP3 36 B10
STA * TW18 173 K7
UPMR RM14 126 C5
Leasway BRW CM14 107 J4
CDH/CHF RM16 147 P10
UPMR RM14 126 B8
Leathart Cl HCH RM12 145 J2
The Lea EGH TW20 172 E10
Leatherbottle Gn ERITHM DA18 164 A2
Leather Cl MTCM CR4 202 B2
Leatherdale St WCHPL * E1 140 C5
Leather Gdns SRTFD E15 141 K3
Leatherhead By-Pass Rd
LHD/OX KT22 237 J8
Leatherhead Cl
STNW/STAM N16 119 M6
Leatherhead Rd ASHTD KT21 237 J6
CHSGTN KT9 218 G10
GT/LBKH KT23 254 B2
LHD/OX KT22 218 C10
LHD/OX KT22 236 C1
Leather La EMPK RM11 125 L6
HCIRC EC1N 12 A3
SHGR GU5 270 D5
Leathermarket Ct STHWK SE1 19 J2
Leathermarket St STHWK SE1 19 J2
Leathersellers Cl BAR * EN5 77 H7
Leathsale Rd RYLN/HDSTN HA2 114 A8
Leathwaite Rd BTSEA SW11 158 A10
Leathwell Rd DEPT SE8 160 G8
Lea V DART DA1 164 E10
Lea Valley Rd CHING E4 80 E10
Lea Valley Wk BRKMPK AL9 22 F9
BRKMPK AL9 24 A10
BRKMPK AL9 41 H1
CLPT E5 120 A5
HERT/BAY SG13 25 M4
HERT/WAS SG14 24 D8
TOTM N17 100 A10
WAB EN9 62 F2
WARE SG12 26 F5
WGCW AL8 22 C5
Leaveland Cl BECK BR3 204 F4
Leaver Gdns GFD/PVL UB6 134 C4
Leavesden Rd STAN HA7 94 F7
WATN WD24 73 J4
WEY KT13 216 C2
Leaves Green Crs HAYES BR2 225 P7
Leaves Green Rd HAYES BR2 226 A7
Leaview WAB EN9 62 G9
Leaway CLPT * E5 120 B6
Leazes Av CTHM CR3 241 H9
Lebanon Av FELT TW13 175 L8
Lebanon Cl WAT WD17 72 E2
Lebanon Dr COB KT11 217 P9
Lebanon Gdns BH/WHM TN16 244 A3
WAND/EARL SW18 179 K2
Lebanon Pk TWK TW1 176 G3
Lebanon Rd CROY/NA CR0 203 M8
WAND/EARL SW18 179 K1
Lebrun Sq BKHTH/KID SE3 161 N10
Lechford Rd HORL RH6 280 A6
Lechmere Ap WFD IG8 102 A10
Lechmere Av CHIG IG7 102 F5
Lechmere Rd CRICK NW2 136 E1
Leckford Rd WAND/EARL SW18 179 M5
Leckwith Av ABYW SE2 163 P5
Lecky St SKENS SW7 15 L7
Leconfield Av BARN SW13 156 C9
Leconfield Rd HBRY N5 119 L9
Le Corte Cl KGLGY WD4 54 A5
Lectern La STAL AL1 38 D10
Leda Av PEND EN3 80 C5
Leda Rd WOOL/PLUM SE18 162 C2
Ledborough Ga BEAC HP9 88 E8
Ledborough La BEAC HP9 88 D7
Ledborough Wd BEAC HP9 88 D7
Ledbury Ms North NTGHL W11 8 E7
Ledbury Ms West NTGHL * W11 8 E7
Ledbury Rd CROY/NA CR0 223 K1
NTGHL W11 8 D5
REIG RH2 257 K10
Ledbury St PECK SE15 159 P6
Ledger Cl GU GU1 250 E8
Ledger Dr ADL/WDHM KT15 215 J3
Ledger's Rd SL SL1 149 J1
WARL CR6 242 G5
Ledrington Rd NRWD SE19 181 N9
Ledway Dr WBLY HA9 115 L5
Lee Acre DORK * RH4 273 H5
Lee Av CHDH RM6 123 P4
Leechcroft Av BFN/LL DA15 185 J1
SWLY BR8 208 G3
Leechcroft Rd WLGTN SM6 202 B10
Leech La LHD/OX KT22 255 P2
Lee Church St LEW SE13 161 K10
Lee Cl HERT/BAY SG13 25 K7
WALTH E17 100 C9
WARE SG12 27 H7
Lee Conservancy Rd HOM E9 120 E10
Leecroft Rd BAR EN5 77 H8
Leeds Cl ORP BR6 207 N9
Leeds Rd IL IG1 122 G6
SL SL1 129 K9
Leeds St UED N18 99 P6
Lee Farm Cl CSHM HP5 51 L6
Leefe Wy POTB/CUF EN6 60 E4
Lee Gardens Av EMPK RM11 125 P6
Lee Gn STMC/STPC BR5 207 K5
Lee Gv CHIG IG7 102 E3
Lee High Rd LEW SE13 161 J10
Leeke St FSBYW WC1X 5 N9
Leeland Rd WEA W13 134 F10
Leeland Ter WEA W13 134 F10
Leeland Wy WLSDN NW10 116 B9
Leeming Rd BORE WD6 75 L5
Leemount Cl HDN * NW4 116 G2
Lee Pk BKHTH/KID SE3 161 L10
Lee Park Wy UED N18 100 C6
Lee Rd BKHTH/KID SE3 161 L9
EN EN1 79 P10
GFD/PVL UB6 135 H3
MLHL NW7 96 G8
WIM/MER SW19 201 L1
Lees Av NTHWD HA6 92 G9
Leeside BAR EN5 77 H10
POTB/CUF EN6 59 N8
Leeside Crs GLDGN NW11 117 H4
Leeside Rd TOTM N17 100 A7
Leeson Gdns WDSR SL4 148 D3
Leeson Rd HNHL * SE24 181 H1
Leesons Hl CHST BR7 207 H3
Leesons Wy STMC/STPC BR5 207 J2
Lees Pde UX/CGN * UB8 132 C6
Lees Pl MYFR/PKLN W1K 10 C7
Lees Rd UX/CGN UB8 132 C6
The Lees CROY/NA CR0 204 E9
Lee St HACK E8 7 L5
HORL RH6 279 P3
Lee Ter BKHTH/KID SE3 161 K9
Lee Vw ENC/FH EN2 79 J5
Leeward Gdns WIM/MER SW19 179 H9
Leeway DEPT SE8 160 E4
The Leeways CHEAM * SM3 221 H3
Leewood Cl LEE/GVPK * SE12 183 L2
Leewood Pl SWLY BR8 208 E4
Leewood Wy EHSLY KT24 253 K3
Lefevre Wk BOW E3 140 E3
Leffern Rd SHB W12 156 D1
Lefroy Rd SHB W12 156 C1
Left Side STHGT/OAK * N14 98 E2
Legard Rd HBRY N5 119 J8
Legatt Rd ELTH/MOT SE9 184 A1
Leggatt Rd SRTFD E15 141 H4
Leggatts Cl WATN WD24 72 G2
Leggatts Ri GSTN WD25 73 H1
Leggatts Wy WATN WD24 73 H2
Leggatts Wood Av
WATN WD24 73 J2
Legge St LEW SE13 183 H1
Leggfield Ter HHW HP1 35 J6
Leghorn Rd WLSDN NW10 136 D4
WOOL/PLUM SE18 162 G4
Legion Cl IS N1 6 B2
Legion Ter BOW E3 140 F3
Legion Wy NFNCH/WDSP N12 97 P8
Legon Av ROMW/RG RM7 124 D6
Legra Av HOD EN11 44 F3
Legrace Av HSLWW TW4 153 L8
Leicester Av MTCM CR4 202 F4
Leicester Cl WPK KT4 220 F1
Leicester Gdns GDMY/SEVK IG3 123 H5
Leicester Pl LSQ/SEVD * WC2H 11 K7
Leicester Rd BAR EN5 77 L9
CROY/NA CR0 203 M7
EFNCH N2 117 P1
TIL RM18 168 C7
WAN E11 121 N3
WLSDN NW10 136 A2
Leicester Sq LSQ/SEVD WC2H 11 K8
Leicester St SOHO/SHAV W1D 11 K7
Leigham Av STRHM/NOR SW16 180 F6
Leigham Court Rd
STRHM/NOR SW16 180 G6
Leigham Dr ISLW TW7 154 D6
Leigham Hall Pde
STRHM/NOR * SW16 180 F6
Leigham V STRHM/NOR SW16 181 H6
Leigh Av REDBR IG4 122 A2
Leigh Cl ADL/WDHM KT15 215 J4
NWMAL KT3 200 A4
Leigh Common WGCE AL7 23 H7
Leigh Ct BORE * WD6 76 A6
RYLN/HDSTN * HA2 114 D6
Leigh Court Cl COB KT11 217 K10
Leigh Crs CROY/NA CR0 224 G4
Leigh Dr HARH RM3 105 L5
Leigh Gdns WLSDN NW10 136 F4
Leigh Hill Rd COB KT11 217 K10
Leigh Hunt Dr STHGT/OAK N14 98 E2
Leighlands CRAWE RH10 284 D5
Leigh Orchard Cl
STRHM/NOR SW16 180 G6
Leigh Pk DTCH/LGLY * SL3 149 P6
Leigh Pl COB KT11 217 K10
COB KT11 235 K1
RDART * DA2 187 P8
WELL DA16 163 K8
Leigh Place La GDST RH9 260 C8
Leigh Place Rd REIG RH2 274 D6
Leigh Rd BRKHM/BTCW RH3 273 P6
COB KT11 217 J9
EHAM E6 142 D2
GVW DA11 190 E5
HBRY N5 119 J9
HSLW TW3 154 C10
LEY E10 121 H5
SL SL1 128 G9
Leigh Rodd OXHEY WD19 93 M4
Leigh Sq WDSR SL4 148 C8
Leigh St STPAN WC1H 11 L1
Leigh Ter STMC/STPC * BR5 207 L3
Leighton Av MNPK E12 122 D10
PIN HA5 113 M1
Leighton Buzzard Rd HHW HP1 35 M4
Leighton Cl EDGW HA8 95 M10
Leighton Crs KTTN NW5 118 D10
Leighton Gdns SAND/SEL CR2 224 A9
TIL RM18 168 D6
WLSDN NW10 136 F4
Leighton Gv KTTN NW5 118 D10
Leighton Pl KTTN NW5 118 D10
Leighton Rd EN EN1 79 N9
KTN/HRWW/W HA3 94 C10
KTTN NW5 118 D10
WEA W13 154 F1
Leighton St CROY/NA CR0 203 J8
Leighton Wy EPSOM KT18 220 A10
Leila Parnell Pl CHARL SE7 161 P5
Leinster Av MORT/ESHN SW14 155 P9
Leinster Gdns BAY/PAD W2 9 J6
Leinster Ms BAY/PAD W2 9 J8
Leinster Pl BAY/PAD W2 9 J6
Leinster Rd MUSWH N10 118 C2
Leinster Sq BAY/PAD W2 8 F7
Leinster Ter BAY/PAD W2 9 J7
Leiston Sp SL SL1 129 K8
Leisure La BF/WBF * KT14 215 L8
Leisure Wy NFNCH/WDSP N12 97 N8
Leith Cl CDALE/KGS NW9 116 A6
SL SL1 129 M10
Leithcote Gdns
STRHM/NOR SW16 180 G7
Leithcote Pth STRHM/NOR SW16 180 G6
Leith Hl STMC/STPC BR5 207 K1
Leith Hill Rd RDKG RH5 271 M10
Leith Park Rd GVW DA11 190 E4
Leith Rd EW KT17 220 B8
WDGN N22 99 J9
Leith Towers BELMT * SM2 221 L4
Leith Vw RDKG RH5 273 H6
Leith Yd KIL/WHAMP * NW6 2 F5
Lela Av HSLWW TW4 153 K8
Lelitia Cl HACK E8 7 N6
Leman St WCHPL E1 13 M6
Lemark Cl STAN HA7 95 H7
Le May Av LEE/GVPK SE12 183 N6
Le May Cl HORL RH6 280 B3
Lemmon Rd GNWCH SE10 161 K5
Lemna Rd WAN E11 121 K5
Lemon Field Dr GSTN WD25 55 M8
Lemonwell Dr ELTH/MOT SE9 184 E1
Lemsford Cl SEVS/STOTM N15 119 P4
Lemsford Ct BORE WD6 75 P8
Lemsford La WGCW AL8 22 E6
Lemsford Rd HAT AL10 40 D2
STAL AL1 38 E6
Lemsford Village WGCW AL8 22 C6
Lena Crs ED N9 100 B3
Lena Gdns HMSMTH W6 156 F2
Lena Kennedy Cl CHING E4 101 H7
Lendal Ter CLAP * SW4 158 E9
Lenelby Rd SURB KT6 199 M8
Len Freeman Pl FUL/PGN SW6 14 C10
Lenham Rd BXLYHN DA7 164 A5
LEW SE13 161 L10
SUT SM1 221 L1
THHTH CR7 203 L2
Lenmore Av GRAYS RM17 167 P2
Lennard Av WWKM BR4 205 K9
Lennard Cl WWKM BR4 205 K9
Lennard Rd CROY/NA CR0 203 K8
HAYES BR2 206 C8
SEV TN13 246 F6
SYD SE26 182 B9
Lennard Rw SOCK/AV RM15 146 C10
Lennard Ter PGE/AN * SE20 182 C9
Lennon Rd CRICK NW2 116 F10
Lennox Av GVW DA11 190 D2
Lennox Cl ROM RM1 124 G4
Lennox Gdns CROY/NA CR0 223 J1
IL IG1 122 C6
KTBR SW1X 16 A4
WLSDN NW10 116 C9
Lennox Gardens Ms CHEL SW3 16 A5
Lennox Rd FSBYPK N4 118 G7
GVW DA11 190 C2
WALTH E17 120 E4
Lennox Rd East GVW DA11 190 D3
Lenor Cl BXLYHS DA6 163 P10
Lensbury Cl CHES/WCR EN8 62 D4
Lensbury Wy ABYW SE2 163 N2
Lens Rd FSTGT E7 141 P2
Lenten Cl SHGR GU5 270 E8
Lent Green La SL SL1 128 A6
Lenthall Av GRAYS RM17 167 M1
Lenthall Rd HACK E8 7 M3
LOU IG10 82 G8
Lenthorp Rd GNWCH SE10 161 L3
Lentmead Rd BMLY BR1 183 L6
Lenton Ri RCH/KEW TW9 155 K9
Lenton St WOOL/PLUM SE18 162 G3
Lenton Ter FSBYPK * N4 119 H7
Lent Rise Rd MDHD SL6 128 A8
Leof Crs CAT SE6 182 G8
Leominster Rd MRDN SM4 201 M6
Leominster Wk MRDN SM4 201 M6
Leonard Av MRDN SM4 201 M5
ROMW/RG RM7 124 E6
RSEV TN14 247 J1
SWCM DA10 189 K3
Leonard Ct KENS * W8 14 E3
Leonard Pl HAYES * BR2 206 B10
STNW/STAM * N16 119 M9
Leonard Rd CHING E4 100 F7
ED * N9 99 N4
FSTGT E7 121 M9
MTCM CR4 202 D1
NWDGN UB2 153 L2
Leonardslee Ct CRAWE * RH10 284 C10
Leonard St CAN/RD E16 142 B10
SDTCH EC2A 13 H1
Leonard Wy BRW CM14 106 D5
Leontine Cl PECK SE15 159 P6
Leopold Av WIM/MER SW19 179 J8
Leopold Ms HOM E9 140 B3
Leopold Rd CRAWW RH11 283 M7
EA W5 135 L10
EFNCH N2 117 N1
WALTH E17 120 F3
WIM/MER SW19 179 J7
WLSDN NW10 136 B2
Leopold St BOW E3 140 E7
Leo St PECK SE15 160 A6
Le Personne Rd CTHM CR3 241 L8
Leppoc Rd CLAP SW4 180 E1
Leret Wy LHD/OX KT22 236 F7
Leroy St STHWK SE1 19 J5
Lerry Cl WKENS W14 14 D9
Lerwick Dr SL SL1 129 K7
Lesbourne Rd REIG RH2 275 L1
Lescombe Cl FSTH SE23 182 D6
Lescombe Rd FSTH SE23 182 D6
Lesley Cl BXLY DA5 186 C3
SWLY BR8 208 E3
Leslie Gdns BELMT SM2 221 K4
Leslie Gv CROY/NA CR0 203 L8
Leslie Grove Pl CROY/NA * CR0 203 M8
Leslie Park Rd CROY/NA CR0 203 M8
Leslie Rd CAN/RD E16 141 N8
CHOB/PIR GU24 213 J6
DORK RH4 255 J10
EFNCH N2 117 N1
WAN E11 121 J9
Lesney Pk ERITH DA8 164 E5
Lesney Park Rd ERITH DA8 164 E5
Lessar Av CLAP SW4 180 D1
Lessingham Av TOOT SW17 180 A7
Lessing St FSTH SE23 182 D3
Lessington Av ROMW/RG RM7 124 D4
Lessness Av BXLYHN DA7 163 N6
Lessness Pk BELV DA17 164 A4

Lessness Rd MRDN SM4 201 M6
Lester Av SRTFD E15 141 K6
Leston Cl RAIN RM13 145 J5
Leswin Pl STNW/STAM N16 119 N8
Leswin Rd STNW/STAM N16 119 N8
Letchfield CSHM HP5 51 N7
Letchford Gdns WLSDN NW10 136 D5
Letchford Ms WLSDN * NW10 136 D5
Letchford Ter
KTN/HRWW/W * HA3 94 A9
Letchmore Rd RAD WD7 74 F2
Letchworth Av
EBED/NFELT TW14 174 G3
Letchworth Cl HAYES BR2 205 M5
OXHEY WD19 93 L6
Letchworth Dr HAYES BR2 205 M5
Letchworth St TOOT SW17 180 A7
Letter Box La SEV TN13 265 K5
Letterstone Rd FUL/PGN SW6 157 J6
Lettice St FUL/PGN SW6 157 J8
Lett Rd SRTFD E15 141 J2
Leucha Rd WALTH E17 120 D3
Levana Cl WIM/MER SW19 179 H4
Levehurst Wy CLAP SW4 158 F8
Leven Cl CHES/WCR * EN8 62 C9
OXHEY * WD19 93 L6
Levendale Rd FSTH SE23 182 D5
Leven Dr CHES/WCR EN8 62 C9
Leven Rd POP/IOD E14 141 H7
Leven Wy HHNE HP2 35 N2
HYS/HAR UB3 132 F8
Leveret Cl CROY/NA CR0 225 J7
GSTN WD25 55 H10
Leveret La CRAWW RH11 283 L5
Leverett St CHEL SW3 15 P5
Leverholme Gdns ELTH/MOT SE9 184 D7
Leverson St STRHM/NOR SW16 180 D9
Lever Sq CDH/CHF RM16 168 D3
Leverstock Green Rd HHNE HP2 36 B5
Lever St FSBYE EC1V 6 E10
Leverton Pl KTTN NW5 118 D10
Leverton St KTTN NW5 118 D10
Leverton Wy WAB EN9 63 H9
Leveson Rd CDH/CHF RM16 168 E2
Levett Gdns GDMY/SEVK IG3 123 J9
Levett Rd BARK IG11 143 H1
LHD/OX KT22 236 G6
Levine Gdns BARK IG11 143 N4
Levylsdene GU GU1 250 G10
Lewes Cl CRAWE RH10 284 D7
GRAYS RM17 167 M5
NTHLT UB5 133 P1
Lewes Ct SL SL1 149 H1
Lewesdon Cl WIM/MER SW19 178 G4
Lewes Rd BMLY BR1 206 A2
HARH RM3 105 L5
NFNCH/WDSP N12 97 P6
Leweston Pl STNW/STAM N16 119 N5
Lewes Wy RKW/CH/CXG WD3 72 C8
Lewgars Av CDALE/KGS NW9 115 P4
Lewing Cl ORP BR6 207 H8
Lewin Rd BXLYHS DA6 163 P10
MORT/ESHN SW14 156 A9
STRHM/NOR SW16 180 E9
Lewins Rd CFSP/GDCR SL9 110 A1
EPSOM KT18 219 N10
Lewins Wy SL SL1 128 E9
Lewis Av WALTH E17 100 F9
Lewis Cl ADL/WDHM KT15 215 M1
BRWN CM15 107 L1
DEN/HRF UB9 91 M10
STHGT/OAK N14 98 D1
Lewis Crs WLSDN NW10 116 A10
Lewis Gdns EFNCH N2 97 N10
Lewis Gv LEW SE13 161 H10
Lewisham High St LEW SE13 182 G2
Lewisham Hl LEW SE13 161 H8
Lewisham Pk LEW SE13 182 G2
Lewisham Rd LEW SE13 161 H8
Lewisham Wy BROCKY SE4 160 E8
Lewis La CFSP/GDCR SL9 90 B9
Lewis Pl HACK E8 119 P10
Lewis Rd EMPK RM11 125 K4
MTCM CR4 201 P2
RCHPK/HAM * TW10 177 J1
SCUP DA14 185 M6
STHL UB1 153 M1
SUT SM1 221 L1
SWCM DA10 189 K2
WELL DA16 163 M9
Lewis St CAMTN NW1 4 F3
Lewis Wy DAGE RM10 144 C1
Lexden Dr CHDH RM6 123 L4
Lexden Rd ACT W3 135 N9
MTCM CR4 202 E4
Lexden Ter WAB * EN9 63 H10
Lexham Gdns AMS HP6 69 H3
KENS W8 14 F5
Lexham Ms KENS W8 14 F5
Lexington Cl BORE WD6 75 L7
Lexington Ct POTB/CUF * EN6 58 G7
PUR/KEN CR8 223 K6
Lexington St SOHO/CST W1F 11 H6
Lexington Wy BAR EN5 76 G8
UPMR RM14 126 D4
Lexton Gdns BAL SW12 180 E4
Leyborne Av WEA W13 155 H1
Leyborne Pk RCH/KEW TW9 155 M7
Leybourne Av BF/WBF KT14 216 A9
Leybourne Cl BF/WBF KT14 216 A9
HAYES BR2 205 M5
Leybourne Rd CAMTN NW1 4 F4
CDALE/KGS NW9 115 M3
HGDN/ICK UB10 132 D3
WAN E11 121 L6
Leybourne St CAMTN NW1 4 E4
Leyburn Cl WALTH E17 121 H2
Leyburn Crs HARH RM3 105 M8
Leyburn Gdns CROY/NA CR0 203 M9
Leyburn Gv UED N18 99 P7
Leyburn Rd HARH RM3 105 M8
UED N18 99 P7
Leycester Cl BFOR GU20 212 A1
Leycroft Gdns ERITH DA8 165 J7
Leycroft Wy HARP AL5 20 D4
Leydenhatch La SWLY BR8 208 E1
Leyden St WCHPL E1 13 L4
Leyes Rd CAN/RD E16 141 P9
Leyfield WPK KT4 200 B9
Leyhill Cl SWLY BR8 208 F5
Leyland Av PEND EN3 80 D6
STAL AL1 38 C8
Leyland Cl CHES/WCR EN8 62 B5
Leyland Rd LEE/GVPK SE12 183 L1
Leylands La STWL/WRAY TW19 151 J10
Leylang Rd NWCR SE14 160 C6
Leys Av DAGE RM10 144 D3
Leys Cl DAGE RM10 144 D2
DEN/HRF UB9 91 N9
HRW HA1 114 C2
Leysdown WGCE AL7 23 N5
Leysdown Av BXLYHN DA7 164 D10
Leysdown Rd ELTH/MOT SE9 184 B5
Leysfield Rd SHB W12 156 D1
Leys Gdns EBAR EN4 78 B9
Leyspring Rd WAN E11 121 L6
Leys Rd HHS/BOV HP3 36 A8
LHD/OX KT22 218 C8
Leys Rd East PEND EN3 80 D5
The Leys AMS HP6 68 G1
Leys The EFNCH N2 117 M2
The Leys KTN/HRWW/W HA3 115 L4
STALE/WH AL4 39 J3
WOT/HER * KT12 217 M1
Ley St IL IG1 122 E7
Leyswood Dr GNTH/NBYPK IG2 123 H3
Leythe Rd ACT W3 155 P1
Leyton Cross Rd RDART DA2 186 G6
Leyton Gra LEY E10 120 F7
Leyton Green Rd LEY E10 121 H4
Leyton Park Rd LEY E10 121 H7
Leyton Rd SRTFD E15 121 H10
WIM/MER SW19 179 M10
Leytonstone Rd SRTFD E15 121 K10
Leywick St SRTFD E15 141 K4
Leywood Cl AMSS HP7 69 J5
Lezayre Rd ORP BR6 227 J3
Liardet St NWCR SE14 160 D5
Liberia Rd HBRY N5 6 D1
Liberty Av WIM/MER SW19 201 N1
Liberty Cl HERT/BAY SG13 25 K7
Liberty Hall Rd ADL/WDHM KT15 215 K2
Liberty La ADL/WDHM KT15 215 L2
Liberty Ms WDGN * N22 99 J9
Liberty Ri ADL/WDHM KT15 215 K3
Liberty St BRXN/ST SW9 158 G7
Liberty Wk STAL * AL1 38 G7
Libra Rd BOW E3 140 E3
PLSTW E13 141 M4
Library Pde WLSDN * NW10 136 B3
Library St STHWK SE1 18 D2
Lichfield Cl EBAR EN4 78 A7
Lichfield Gdns RCH/KEW * TW9 177 K1
Lichfield Gv FNCH N3 97 K9
Lichfield Pl STAL * AL1 38 E5
Lichfield Rd BCTR RM8 123 L9
BOW E3 140 D5
CRICK NW2 117 H9
ED N9 99 P3
EHAM E6 142 A5
HSLWW TW4 153 K9
NTHWD HA6 113 H2
RCH/KEW TW9 155 L7
WFD IG8 101 K5
Lichfield Ter RCHPK/HAM * TW10 177 K1
UPMR RM14 126 D7
Lichfield Wy BROX EN10 44 E8
SAND/SEL CR2 224 C6
Lidbury Rd MLHL NW7 97 H7
Lidcote Gdns BRXN/ST * SW9 159 H8
Liddall Wy WDR/YW UB7 132 A10
Liddell WDSR SL4 148 B9
Liddell Cl KTN/HRWW/W HA3 115 J1
Liddell Gdns WLSDN NW10 136 F4
Liddell Rd KIL/WHAMP NW6 2 E1
Lidding Rd KTN/HRWW/W HA3 115 J3
Liddington Hall Dr RGUW GU3 249 K7
Liddington New Rd RGUW GU3 249 K7
Liddington Rd SRTFD E15 141 L3
Liddon Rd BMLY BR1 205 P3
PLSTW E13 141 N5
Liden Cl LEY E10 120 E5
Lidfield Rd STNW/STAM N16 119 L9
Lidgate Rd PECK * SE15 159 N6
Lidiard Rd WAND/EARL SW18 179 M5
Lido Rd GU GU1 250 A9
Lido Sq TOTM N17 99 L9
Lidsey Cl CRAWE RH10 284 D9
Lidstone Cl WOKN/KNAP GU21 231 N3
Lidyard Rd ARCH N19 118 D6
Lieutenant Ellis Wy CHESW EN7 61 N7
Liffler Rd WOOL/PLUM SE18 163 H4
Lifford St PUT/ROE SW15 156 G10
Lightcliffe Rd PLMGR N13 99 H5
Lighterman Ms WCHPL E1 140 C8
Lighterman's Rd POP/IOD E14 160 F1
Lightfoot Rd CEND/HSY/T N8 118 F3
Lightswood Cl CHESW EN7 61 L5
Lightwater Meadow LTWR GU18 212 A7
Lightwater Rd LTWR GU18 212 A7
Ligonier St BETH E2 13 L1
Lilac Av EN EN1 80 B2
WOKS/MYFD GU22 232 A6
Lilac Cl BRWN CM15 86 G9
CHESW EN7 62 A7
CHING E4 100 E7
GU GU1 249 P6
Lilac Gdns CROY/NA CR0 204 F10
EA W5 155 J2
HYS/HAR UB3 132 F8
ROMW/RG RM7 124 F6
SWLY BR8 208 E3
Lilac Pl LBTH SE11 17 N6
WDR/YW UB7 132 A9
Lilac Rd HOD EN11 44 G1
Lilac St SHB W12 136 D9
Lilac Wy HARP AL5 20 C5
Lila Pl SWLY BR8 208 F4
Lilburne Gdns ELTH/MOT SE9 184 B1
Lilburne Rd ELTH/MOT SE9 184 B1
Lile Crs HNWL W7 134 D7
Lilestone St CAMTN NW1 9 N1
Lilford Rd BRXN/ST SW9 159 J8
Lilian Barker Cl LEE/GVPK SE12 183 M1
Lilian Board Wy NTHLT UB5 114 C10
Lilian Crs RBRW/HUT CM13 107 P3
Lilian Gdns WFD IG8 101 N9
Lilian Rd MTCM CR4 202 D1
Lillechurch Rd BCTR RM8 143 L1
Lilleshall Rd MRDN SM4 202 A5
Lilley Cl BRW CM14 106 E5
WAP E1W 13 P10
Lilley Dr KWD/TDW/WH KT20 239 L8
Lilley La MLHL * NW7 96 B6
Lilley Wy SL SL1 128 D10
Lillian Av ACT W3 155 M1
Lillian Rd BARN SW13 156 D5
Lilliard Cl HOD EN11 26 G9
Lillie Rd BH/WHM TN16 244 A4
FUL/PGN SW6 156 G5
Lillieshall Rd CLAP SW4 158 C9
Lillie Yd FUL/PGN SW6 14 E9
Lillington Gardens Est PIM SW1V 17 H6
Lilliput Av NTHLT UB5 133 M3
Lilliput Rd ROMW/RG RM7 124 E5
Lily Cl WKENS W14 14 A6
Lily Dr WDR/YW UB7 151 N3
Lily Gdns ALP/SUD HA0 135 H4
Lily Pl HCIRC EC1N 12 B3
Lily Rd LEY E10 120 F4
Lilyville Rd FUL/PGN SW6 157 J7
Limbourne Av BCTR RM8 124 A5
Limbrick Rd HARP AL5 20 A5
Limburg Rd BTSEA SW11 157 P10
Lime Av GVW DA11 190 A3
RBRW/HUT CM13 107 L4
UPMR RM14 125 P9
WDR/YW UB7 132 A9
WDSR SL4 149 L6
WDSR SL4 170 E6
Limeburner La STP EC4M 12 C5
Limebush Cl ADL/WDHM KT15 215 M5
Lime Cl BKHH IG9 102 A3
BMLY BR1 206 B4
CRAWE RH10 285 J2
CRAWW RH11 283 M4
KTN/HRWW/W HA3 94 F10
OXHEY WD19 93 L1
REIG RH2 275 L3
RGUE GU4 251 L4
ROMW/RG RM7 124 D3
RSLP HA4 112 G1
SOCK/AV RM15 147 H5
WAP E1W 13 P9
WARE SG12 26 D1
Lime Crs SUN TW16 197 K2
Limecroft Cl HOR/WEW KT19 220 A4
Limecroft Rd WOKN/KNAP GU21 230 G3
Limedene Cl PIN HA5 93 L9
Lime Gv ADL/WDHM KT15 215 K1
BARK/HLT IG6 103 J7
BFN/LL DA15 185 J2
BRWN CM15 87 H4
GU GU1 249 N6
HYS/HAR UB3 132 E9
NWMAL KT3 200 A3
ORP BR6 206 E9
RGUE GU4 251 L4
RSLP HA4 113 J4
SHB W12 156 F1
TRDG/WHET N20 97 H2
TWK TW1 176 E2
WARL CR6 242 D5
WOKS/MYFD GU22 232 B7
Limeharbour POP/IOD E14 160 G2
Limehouse POP/IOD * E14 140 F9
Limehouse Cswy POP/IOD E14 140 E9
Limehouse Link POP/IOD E14 140 D9
Lime Kiln Dr CHARL SE7 161 N5
Lime Meadow Av SAND/SEL CR2 223 P9
Lime Pit La RSEV TN14 246 D3
Limerick Cl BAL SW12 180 D3
Limerick Gdns UPMR RM14 126 E5
Lime Rd SWLY BR8 208 E3
Limerston St WBPTN SW10 15 K9
Limes Av BARN SW13 156 C8
CAR SM5 202 A8
CHIG IG7 102 F6
CROY/NA CR0 202 G10
GLDGN NW11 117 H5
HORL RH6 280 C6
MLHL NW7 96 B7
NFNCH/WDSP N12 97 M5
PGE/AN SE20 182 A10
WAN E11 121 N2
The Limes Av FBAR/BDGN N11 98 C6
Limes Cl ASHF TW15 174 B8
CAR SM5 202 A9
FBAR/BDGN * N11 98 D6
Limes Ct HOD * EN11 44 F3
Limesdale Gdns EDGW HA8 95 P10
Limes Field Rd BARN SW13 156 B9
Limesford Rd PECK SE15 160 C10
Limes Gdns WAND/EARL SW18 179 K2
Limes Gv LEW SE13 161 H10
Limes Rd BECK BR3 204 G2
CHES/WCR EN8 62 C8
CROY/NA CR0 203 L6
EGH TW20 172 C8
WEY KT13 216 B1
Limes Rw ORP BR6 226 E2
The Limes AMS HP6 68 G1
CMBW * SE5 159 M9
EMPK RM11 125 L1
EYN * DA4 209 N7
LHD/OX KT22 236 G9
PUR RM19 165 P4
RBRW/HUT CM13 107 L4
RKW/CH/CXG * WD3 91 M2
STALW/RED AL3 38 D4
WAND/EARL * SW18 179 K2
WDSR SL4 148 B8
WGCE AL7 23 K7
WOKN/KNAP GU21 232 A1
WOKN/KNAP * GU21 232 D2
Lime St FENCHST EC3M 13 J7
WALTH E17 120 D2
Lime Street Pas BANK * EC3V 13 J6
Limes Wk EA W5 155 J1
PECK * SE15 160 B10
Lime Tree Av GRH DA9 188 F4
THDIT KT7 198 D8
Limetree Cl BRXS/STRHM SW2 180 G4
Lime Tree Cl GT/LBKH KT23 235 P10
Lime Tree Ct PIN * HA5 93 P8
Lime Tree Gv CROY/NA CR0 204 E10
Limetree Pl MTCM CR4 202 C1
Lime Tree Pl STAL AL1 38 D7
Lime Tree Rd HEST TW5 154 A7
Lime Tree Ter FSTH * SE23 182 E4
Lime Tree Wk AMSS HP7 69 L5
BUSH WD23 94 D2
ENC/FH EN2 79 K4
RKW/CH/CXG WD3 71 L9
SEV TN13 265 J1
VW GU25 194 B4
WWKM BR4 225 L1
Lime Wk DEN/HRF UB9 111 M10
HHS/BOV HP3 36 A8
SRTFD * E15 141 K3
Lime Wy RAD WD7 57 H7
Limeway Ter DORK RH4 254 F10
Limewood Cl WALTH E17 120 E2
WEA W13 134 G8
WOKN/KNAP GU21 231 J6
Limewood Rd ERITH DA8 164 D6
Limpsfield Av THHTH CR7 202 G5
WIM/MER SW19 178 G5
Limpsfield Rd SAND/SEL CR2 223 P8
WARL CR6 242 B2
Linacre Rd CRICK NW2 136 E1
Lince La DORK RH4 272 C2
Linces Wy WGCE AL7 23 L7
Linchfield Rd DTCH/LGLY SL3 149 P7
Linchmere Pl CRAWW RH11 283 K6
Linchmere Rd LEE/GVPK SE12 183 M3
Linclon Cl ERITH DA8 164 G8
Lincoln Av ROMW/RG RM7 124 E6
STHGT/OAK N14 98 D4
WHTN TW2 176 B5
WIM/MER SW19 178 G6
Lincoln Cl CRAWE RH10 283 P10
EMPK RM11 125 P3
GFD/PVL UB6 134 B3
RYLN/HDSTN HA2 113 N3
WGCE AL7 23 M4
Lincoln Ct BERK HP4 33 N5
BORE WD6 76 A9
Lincoln Crs EN EN1 79 M8
Lincoln Dr OXHEY WD19 93 K4
RKW/CH/CXG WD3 72 C8
WOKS/MYFD GU22 233 H1
Lincoln Est BOW E3 140 F6
Lincoln Gdns IL IG1 122 B5
Lincoln Green Rd
STMC/STPC BR5 207 J5
Lincoln Hatch La SL SL1 128 B6
Lincoln Ms KIL/WHAMP NW6 2 C5
Lincoln Pde EFNCH * N2 117 P1
Lincoln Pk AMSS HP7 69 K5
Lincoln Rd ALP/SUD HA0 135 J1
CFSP/GDCR SL9 90 B9
DORK RH4 255 H10
EFNCH N2 117 P1
EN EN1 79 M8
ERITH DA8 164 G8
FELT TW13 175 N6
GUW GU2 249 L8
MTCM CR4 202 F5
NTHWD HA6 112 G1
NWMAL KT3 199 P3
PLSTW E13 141 N6
RYLN/HDSTN HA2 113 N3
SCUP DA14 185 L8
SNWD SE25 204 A3
SWFD E18 101 L9
WPK KT4 200 E8
Lincoln's Cl STALE/WH AL4 39 H1
Lincolns Fld EPP CM16 65 J5
Lincoln's Inn Flds LINN WC2A 11 N5
Lincolns La BRW CM14 86 B10
The Lincolns MLHL NW7 96 C4
Lincoln St CHEL SW3 16 A6
WAN E11 121 K7
Lincoln Ter BELMT * SM2 221 K4
Lincoln Wy EN EN1 80 A9
RKW/CH/CXG WD3 72 C8
SL SL1 128 C9
SUN TW16 196 F1
Lincombe Rd BMLY BR1 183 L6
Lindal Crs STHGT/OAK N14 78 F9
Lindale Cl VW GU25 193 L4
The Lindales TOTM N17 99 P7
Lindal Rd BROCKY SE4 182 E1
Lindbergh WGCE AL7 23 M5
Lindbergh Rd WLGTN SM6 222 F5
Linden Av COUL/CHIP CR5 240 C2
DART DA1 187 K4
EN EN1 79 P5
HSLW TW3 176 A1
RSLP HA4 113 H6
THHTH CR7 203 J4
WBLY HA9 115 L10
WLSDN NW10 136 G4
Linden Chase Rd SEV TN13 247 J8
Linden Cl ADL/WDHM KT15 215 K7
CHESW EN7 62 A6
CRAWE RH10 284 B10
KWD/TDW/WH KT20 238 G6
ORP BR6 227 K2
PUR RM19 166 B5
RSLP HA4 113 H6
STAN HA7 94 G6
STHGT/OAK N14 78 D10
THDIT KT7 198 F7
Linden Cottages
WIM/MER * SW19 179 H9
Linden Ct EGH TW20 171 N9
HARP AL5 20 A3
LHD/OX KT22 236 G7
Linden Crs GFD/PVL UB6 134 E1
KUT KT1 199 L2
STAL AL1 39 H6
WFD IG8 101 N7
Linden Dr CFSP/GDCR SL9 90 B9
CTHM CR3 241 K10
SLN SL2 129 H3
Lindenfield CHST BR7 206 E2
Linden Gdns BAY/PAD W2 8 F8
CHSWK W4 156 A4
EN EN1 79 P5
LHD/OX KT22 237 H7
Linden Gld HHW HP1 35 L7
Linden Gv NWMAL KT3 200 B3
PECK SE15 160 A9
PGE/AN SE20 182 B9
WARL CR6 242 D4
WOT/HER KT12 196 G9
Linden Lea DORK * RH4 273 H4
EFNCH N2 117 M3
GSTN WD25 55 H9
PIN * HA5 93 N8
Linden Leas WWKM BR4 205 J9
Linden Ms BAY/PAD W2 8 F8
IS N1 119 L10
Linden Pit Pth LHD/OX KT22 236 G7
Linden Pl EHSLY * KT24 252 F2
EW KT17 220 B8
MTCM CR4 201 P4
Linden Ri BRW CM14 107 J6
Linden Rd FBAR/BDGN N11 98 A3
GU GU1 250 A10
HPTN TW12 197 P1
LHD/OX KT22 236 G7
MUSWH N10 118 C2
SEVS/STOTM N15 119 K2
WEY KT13 216 D5
Lindens Cl EHSLY KT24 253 M4
Linden Sq DEN/HRF UB9 91 K7
SEV TN13 246 F8
The Lindens CHSWK W4 155 P7
CRAWE RH10 285 J2
HAT * AL10 40 C3
HHS/BOV HP3 35 J9
LOU IG10 82 C9
NFNCH/WDSP * N12 97 N6
WAB * EN9 81 P1
WALTH * E17 120 G2
Linden St ROMW/RG RM7 124 E2
Linden Ter UX/CGN * UB8 131 N8
Linden Wy RPLY/SEND GU23 251 J1
SHPTN TW17 196 D5
STHGT/OAK N14 78 D10
WLGTN SM6 222 D6
WOKS/MYFD GU22 232 C7
Lindfield Gdns GU GU1 250 C9
HAMP NW3 117 M10
Lindfield Rd CROY/NA CR0 203 N6
EA W5 135 H6
HARH RM3 105 M6
Lindfield St POP/IOD E14 140 F8
Lindfield Ter WOKN/KNAP * GU21 231 P2
Lindhill Cl PEND EN3 80 C6
Lindisfarne Cl GVE DA12 191 H5
Lindisfarne Md HOM E9 120 D9
Lindisfarne Rd BCTR RM8 123 M8
RYNPK SW20 178 D10
Lindiswara Ct
RKW/CH/CXG * WD3 72 B10
Lindley Est PECK * SE15 159 P6
Lindley Pl RCH/KEW TW9 155 M7
Lindley Rd GDST RH9 260 B6
LEY E10 121 H7
WOT/HER KT12 197 M10
Lindley St WCHPL E1 140 B7
Lindlings HHW HP1 35 H7
Lindo Cl CSHM HP5 50 G6
Lindore Rd BTSEA SW11 158 A10
Lindores Rd CAR SM5 201 M7
Lindo St PECK SE15 160 B8
Lind Rd SUT SM1 221 M2
Lindrop St FUL/PGN SW6 157 M8
Lindsay Cl CHSGTN KT9 219 K4
HOR/WEW KT19 219 P9
STWL/WRAY TW19 173 N2
Lindsay Dr KTN/HRWW/W HA3 115 K4
SHPTN TW17 196 E6
Lindsay Pl CHESW EN7 62 A6
Lindsay Rd ADL/WDHM KT15 215 K7
HPTN TW12 176 A7
WPK KT4 200 E9
Lindsay Sq PIM SW1V 17 K7
Lindsell St GNWCH SE10 161 H7
Lindsey Cl BMLY BR1 206 A3
BRW CM14 106 F5
MTCM CR4 202 F4
Lindsey Gdns
EBED/NFELT * TW14 174 E3
Lindsey Ms IS N1 6 F3
Lindsey Rd BCTR RM8 123 M8
DEN/HRF UB9 111 K8
Lindsey St EPP CM16 65 K5
STBT EC1A 12 D3
Lindsey Wy EMPK RM11 125 K3
Lind St DEPT SE8 160 G8
Lindum Pl STALW/RED AL3 37 N8
Lindum Rd TEDD TW11 177 H10
Lindway WNWD SE27 181 J8
Linfield Cl HDN NW4 116 F1
WOT/HER * KT12 217 J2
Linfields AMSS HP7 69 P6
Linford Cl HLWW/ROY CM19 46 F3
Linford End HLWW/ROY CM19 46 F3
Linford Rd CDH/CHF RM16 168 E4
WALTH E17 121 H1
Linford St VX/NE SW8 158 D7
Lingards Rd LEW SE13 161 H10
Lingey Cl BFN/LL DA15 185 J5
Lingfield Av BRYLDS KT5 199 K4
RDART DA2 188 A3
UPMR RM14 125 N8
Lingfield Cl EN EN1 79 M10
NTHWD HA6 92 F8
Lingfield Ct NTHLT * UB5 133 P4
Lingfield Crs ELTH/MOT SE9 162 G10
Lingfield Dr CRAWE RH10 284 F6
Lingfield Gdns COUL/CHIP CR5 241 J5
ED N9 100 A1
Lingfield Rd GVE DA12 190 E5
WIM/MER SW19 178 G9
WPK KT4 200 F10
Lingfield Wy WAT WD17 72 G4
Lingham St BRXN/ST SW9 158 F8
Lingholm Wy BAR EN5 76 G9
Lingmere Cl CHIG IG7 102 F3
Lingmoor Dr GSTN WD25 55 K10
Ling Rd CAN/RD E16 141 M7
ERITH DA8 164 D5
Lingwell Rd TOOT SW17 179 P6
Lingwood Gdns ISLW TW7 154 D6
Lingwood Rd CLPT E5 119 P5
Linhope St CAMTN NW1 10 A1
Linington Av CSHM HP5 51 M6
Link Cl HAT AL10 40 E4
Link Dr HAT AL10 40 E4
Linkfield E/WMO/HCT KT8 197 P3
Link Fld HAYES BR2 205 M6
Linkfield WGCE AL7 23 H9
Linkfield Gdns REDH RH1 257 P10
Linkfield La REDH RH1 258 A9
Linkfield Rd ISLW TW7 154 E8
Linkfield St REDH RH1 257 P10
Link La WLGTN SM6 222 E3
Linklea Cl CDALE/KGS NW9 96 B8
Link Rd ADL/WDHM KT15 215 P1
DAGW RM9 144 C4
DTCH/LGLY SL3 149 P6
EBED/NFELT TW14 174 G3
FBAR/BDGN N11 98 B5
HHW HP1 35 M3
MTCM CR4 202 B8
WATN WD24 73 L6
Links Av GPK RM2 105 J10
HERT/BAY SG13 26 A4
MRDN SM4 201 K4
Links Brow LHD/OX KT22 236 D9
Links Cl ASHTD KT21 237 H3
Linkscroft Av ASHF TW15 174 C9
Links Dr BORE WD6 75 L7
RAD WD7 56 E9
TRDG/WHET N20 97 K2
Links Gdns STRHM/NOR SW16 181 H10
Links Green Wy COB KT11 217 P10
Linkside CHIG IG7 102 F6
NFNCH/WDSP N12 97 K7
NWMAL KT3 200 B2
Linkside Cl ENC/FH EN2 78 G7
Linkside Gdns ENC/FH EN2 78 G7
Links Pl ASHTD KT21 237 J3
Links Rd ACT W3 135 M8
ASHF TW15 173 P8
ASHTD KT21 237 H3
CRICK NW2 116 C7
EW KT17 220 D9
SHGR GU5 268 B10
TOOT SW17 180 B9
WFD IG8 101 M6
WWKM BR4 205 H8
Links Side ENC/FH EN2 78 G7
The Links CHES/WCR EN8 62 C2
WALTH E17 120 D2
WOT/HER KT12 197 H9
Link St HOM E9 140 B1
Links Vw DART DA1 187 K4
FNCH N3 97 J8
STALW/RED AL3 38 A4
Links View Av RDKG RH5 255 M10
Links View Cl STAN HA7 94 F2

Linksview Ct HPTN * TW12 176 C7
Links View Rd CROY/NA CR0 204 F10
HPTN TW12 176 B8
Links Wy BECK BR3 204 F6
EHSLY KT24 253 M4
NTHWD HA6 92 D9
RKW/CH/CXG WD3 72 D7
Linksway HDN NW4 96 G10
NTHWD HA6 92 E9
Linkswood Rd SL SL1 128 B4
Links Yd WCHPL E1 13 M3
The Link ACT W3 135 N8
ALP/SUD HA0 115 H6
CRAWW RH11 283 N6
NTHLT * UB5 113 N10
PEND EN3 80 D5
PIN HA5 113 K4
SLN SL2 129 N8
TEDD TW11 176 E9
Link Wy DEN/HRF UB9 111 K4
EMPK RM11 125 M6
HAYES BR2 206 B7
RCHPK/HAM TW10 176 G5
STA TW18 173 L9
Linkway BCTR RM8 123 M9
FSBYPK N4 119 K5
GUW GU2 249 L10
HORL RH6 280 D8
PIN HA5 93 L9
RYNPK SW20 200 E3
WOKS/MYFD GU22 232 F3
Linkway Rd BRW CM14 106 E4
The Linkway BAR EN5 77 K10
BELMT SM2 221 M5
Linkwood Wk CAMTN NW1 5 K3
Linley Cl TIL RM18 169 N6
Linley Crs ROMW/RG RM7 124 C1
Linley Rd TOTM N17 99 M10
Linnell Cl GLDGN NW11 117 L4
Linnell Dr GLDGN NW11 117 L4
Linnell Rd CMBW SE5 159 M8
REDH RH1 276 B1
UED N18 99 P6
Linnet Cl BUSH WD23 94 B2
ED N9 100 C2
SAND/SEL CR2 224 C6
THMD SE28 143 M9
Linnet Gv RGUE GU4 250 G8
Linnet Ms BAL SW12 180 B3
Linnet Rd ABLGY WD5 55 H7
Linnett Cl CHING E4 101 H5
Linnet Wy PUR RM19 166 A4
Linom Rd CLAP SW4 158 F10
Linscott Rd CLPT E5 120 B9
Linsdell Rd BARK IG11 142 F3
Linsey Cl HHS/BOV HP3 36 B10
Linsey St BERM/RHTH SE16 19 P4
Linslade Cl HSLWW TW4 175 M1
PIN HA5 113 J1
Linslade Rd ORP BR6 227 K3
Linstead St KIL/WHAMP NW6 2 E1
Linstead Wy WAND/EARL SW18 179 H3
Linster Gv BORE WD6 75 P9
Linthorpe Av ALP/SUD HA0 135 H1
Linthorpe Rd EBAR EN4 77 P7
STNW/STAM N16 119 M5
Linton Av BORE WD6 75 L6
Linton Cl CAR SM5 202 A7
CHARL SE7 161 P4
WELL DA16 163 K7
Linton Ct ROM RM1 104 F10
Linton Gdns EHAM E6 142 B8
Linton Gld CROY/NA CR0 224 D6
Linton Gv WNWD SE27 181 J8
Linton Rd BARK IG11 142 F2
Linton's La EW KT17 220 B8
Linton St IS N1 6 F6
Lintott Ct STWL/WRAY TW19 173 N2
Linver Rd FUL/PGN SW6 157 J8
Linwood SBW * CM21 29 P1
Linwood Cl CMBW SE5 159 N8
Linwood Crs EN EN1 79 P5
Linwood Wy HARP AL5 20 B4
Linzee Rd CEND/HSY/T N8 118 F2
Lion Av TWK TW1 176 E4
Lion Cl SHPTN TW17 195 P3
Lion Ct BORE WD6 75 P5
Lionel Gdns ELTH/MOT SE9 184 A1
Lionel Ms NKENS W10 8 A3
Lionel Rd ELTH/MOT SE9 184 A1
Lionel Rd North BTFD TW8 155 K2
Lionel Rd South BTFD TW8 155 L4
Lion Gate Gdns RCH/KEW TW9 155 L9
Lion Green Rd COUL/CHIP CR5 240 E1
Lion La CRAWE RH10 285 P9
Lion Mills BETH * E2 7 P8
Lion Park Av CHSGTN KT9 219 M1
Lion Rd BXLYHS DA6 163 P10
CROY/NA CR0 203 K5
ED N9 100 P3
EHAM E6 142 C7
WHTN TW2 176 E4
Lions Cl LEE/GVPK SE12 183 P6
Lion Wy BTFD TW8 155 J6
Lion Wharf Rd ISLW TW7 154 G9
Liphook Cl HCH RM12 124 G9
Liphook Crs FSTH SE23 182 B3
Liphook Rd OXHEY WD19 93 L5
Lippitts Hl LOU IG10 81 K6
Lipsham Cl BNSTD SM7 221 N9
Lisbon Av WHTN TW2 176 B5
Lisbon Cl WALTH E17 100 E10
Lisburne Rd HAMP NW3 118 A9
Lisford St PECK SE15 159 N7
Lisgar Ter WKENS W14 14 C5
Liskeard Gdns BKHTH/KID SE3 161 M7
Lisle Cl GVE DA12 191 L5
TOOT SW17 180 C7
Lisle Pl GRAYS RM17 167 M2
Lisle St SOHO/SHAV W1D 11 K7
Lismore HHS/BOV HP3 36 D8
WIM/MER * SW19 179 J8
Lismore Circ HAMP NW3 118 A10
Lismore Cl ISLW TW7 154 F8
Lismore Crs CRAWW RH11 283 L10
Lismore Pk SLN SL2 129 L8
Lismore Rd SAND/SEL CR2 223 M3
TOTM N17 119 L1
Lismore Wk IS N1 6 F1
Lissant Cl SURB KT6 199 H7
Lissenden Gdns KTTN NW5 118 B9
Lissoms Rd COUL/CHIP CR5 240 B4
Lisson Gv CAMTN NW1 9 K1
Lisson St CAMTN NW1 9 N3
Lister Av HARH RM3 105 L10
Lister Cl ACT W3 136 A7
WIM/MER SW19 201 P1
Lister Gdns UED N18 99 K6
Lister Ms HOLWY N7 118 G9
Lister Rd TIL RM18 168 D8
WAN E11 121 K6
Liston Rd CLAP SW4 158 D9
TOTM N17 99 P9
Listowel Cl BRXN/ST SW9 159 H6
Listowel Rd DAGE RM10 124 B8
Listria Pk STNW/STAM N16 119 M7
Litcham Sp SL SL1 129 J8
Litchfield Av MRDN SM4 201 J7
SRTFD * E15 141 K1
Litchfield Gdns WLSDN NW10 136 D1
Litchfield Rd SUT SM1 221 M1
Litchfield Wy GLDGN NW11 117 M3
GUW GU2 267 L2
Lithgow's Rd HTHAIR TW6 152 F10
Lithos Rd HAMP NW3 3 H1
Little Acre BECK BR3 204 F3
STALW/RED AL3 38 C3
Little Acres WARE SG12 26 C3
Little Albany St CAMTN NW1 10 F1
Little Argyll St CONDST * W1S 10 G6
Little Aston Rd HARH RM3 105 N8
Little Belhus Cl SOCK/AV RM15 146 F6
Little Benty WDR/YW UB7 151 N4
Little Berkhamstead La
BRKMPK AL9 42 A6
Little Birch Cl ADL/WDHM KT15 215 N5
Little Birches BFN/LL DA15 185 H5
The Little Boltons WBPTN SW10 15 H7
Little Bookham St GT/LBKH KT23 253 N2
Little Bornes DUL SE21 181 M7
Little Borough
BRKHM/BTCW RH3 273 M1
Little Brays HLWS CM18 47 K2
Little Bridge Rd BERK * HP4 34 A5
Little Britain STBT EC1A 12 E4
Littlebrook Av SL SL1 128 D7
Littlebrook Cl CROY/NA CR0 204 C6
Littlebrook Gdns CHES/WCR EN8 62 C6
Littlebrook Manor Wy DART DA1 187 P1
Little Brook Rd HLWW/ROY CM19 45 P1
Little Buntings WDSR SL4 148 E9
Little Burrow WGCE AL7 22 G7
Littlebury Ct BRWN CM15 86 E3
Littlebury Rd CLAP * SW4 158 E9
Little Bury St ED N9 99 M1
Little Bushey La BUSH WD23 73 P7
Little Catherells HHW HP1 35 H4
Little Cattins HLWW/ROY CM19 46 C5
Little Cedars NFNCH/WDSP N12 97 M5
Little Chesters
KWD/TDW/WH * KT20 256 D1
Little Chester St KTBR SW1X 16 E3
Little Cloisters WEST SW1P 17 L3
Little Collins REDH * RH1 277 J10
Littlecombe Cl PUT/ROE * SW15 178 G2
Little Common La REDH RH1 259 J8
Littlecote Cl WIM/MER SW19 178 G3
Littlecote Pl PIN HA5 93 N9
Little Ct WWKM BR4 205 K9
Littlecourt Rd SEV TN13 247 H10
Little Crabtree CRAWW RH11 283 M6
Little Cranmore La EHSLY KT24 252 C4
Littlecroft ELTH/MOT SE9 162 D9
MEO DA13 190 B10
Littlecroft Rd EGH TW20 172 C8
Littledale ABYW SE2 163 K5
Little Deans Yd WEST SW1P 17 L3
Little Dell WGCW AL8 22 G3
Little Dimocks BAL SW12 180 C5
Little Dorrit Ct STHWK SE1 18 F1
Littledown Rd SL SL1 129 L10
Little Dragons LOU IG10 82 A8
Little Ealing La EA W5 155 H3
Little Edward St CAMTN * NW1 4 F9
Little Elms HYS/HAR UB3 152 E6
Little Essex St TPL/STR * WC2R 12 A7
Little Ferry Rd TWK * TW1 176 G4
Littlefield Cl ARCH N19 118 D9
KUT KT1 199 K2
RGUW GU3 249 J6
Littlefield Rd EDGW HA8 95 P8
Littlefield Wy RGUW GU3 249 H6
Littleford La RGUE GU4 269 H8
Little Foxes HERT/BAY * SG13 44 B3
Little Friday Rd CHING E4 101 K3
Little Ganett WGCE AL7 23 L7
Little Gaynes Gdns UPMR RM14 126 A9
Little Gaynes La UPMR RM14 125 P9
Little Gearies BARK/HLT IG6 122 E2
Little George St WEST SW1P 17 L2
Little Gerpins Rd UPMR RM14 145 N3
Little Graylings ABLGY WD5 54 F9
Little Greencroft CSHM HP5 50 F3
Little Green La CHERT KT16 195 H10
RKW/CH/CXG WD3 72 E9
Little Green St KTTN * NW5 118 C9
Little Gregories La EPP CM16 82 G1
Little Gv BUSH WD23 74 A8
DORK * RH4 273 H4
Littlegrove EBAR EN4 77 P10
Little Grove Av CHESW EN7 61 M3
Little Grove Fld
HLWW/ROY CM19 46 F1
Little Hardings WGCE AL7 23 M4
Little Hayes KGLGY WD4 54 B5
Little Heath CHARL SE7 162 B5
CHDH RM6 123 L2
Little Heath La BERK HP4 34 E7
Littleheath La COB KT11 217 P10
Little Heath Rd BXLYHN DA7 164 A7
CHOB/PIR GU24 213 K5
Littleheath Rd SAND/SEL CR2 224 A5
Little Hide GU GU1 250 E8
Little Hl RKW/CH/CXG WD3 70 F10
Little Hivings CSHM HP5 50 F3
Little How Cft ABLGY WD5 54 D7
Little Ilford La MNPK E12 122 C9
Littlejohn Rd HNWL W7 134 E8
STMC/STPC BR5 207 K6
Little Julians Hl SEV TN13 265 H3
Little Kiln RGODL GU7 267 K9
Little Lake WGCE AL7 23 L8
Little La HARP AL5 20 B5
Little Laver Rd CHONG CM5 49 N6
HLWE CM17 31 M9
Little Ley WGCE AL7 23 L8
Little London SHGR GU5 269 P7
Little Marlborough St
REGST * W1B 10 G6
Little Martins BUSH WD23 74 A9
Littlemead ESH/CLAY KT10 218 C1
Little Md HAT AL10 40 E1
WOKN/KNAP GU21 231 L3
Littlemede ELTH/MOT SE9 184 C6
Little Mimms HHNE HP2 35 N5
Littlemoor Rd IL IG1 122 G8
Littlemore Rd ABYW SE2 163 K1
Little Moreton Cl BF/WBF * KT14 215 L8
Little Moss La PIN HA5 93 M10
Little Mundells WGCE AL7 23 J4
Little Newport St
LSQ/SEVD WC2H 11 K7
Little New St FLST/FETLN EC4A 12 B5
Little Orch ADL/WDHM KT15 215 K7
HHNE HP2 36 B4
WOKN/KNAP GU21 214 D10
Little Orchard Cl ABLGY WD5 54 E7
PIN * HA5 93 M10
Little Orchards EPSOM KT18 220 B10
Little Orchard Wy RGUE GU4 268 B8
Little Oxhey La OXHEY WD19 93 M6
Little Pk HHS/BOV HP3 52 D4
Little Park Dr FELT TW13 175 L5
Little Park Gdns ENC/FH EN2 79 K7
Little Piper's Cl CHESW EN7 61 J5
Little Platt GUW GU2 249 J9
Little Pluckett's Wy BKHH IG9 102 A2
Little Portland St REGST W1B 10 F5
Littleport Sp SL SL1 129 K8
Little Potters BUSH WD23 94 C1
Little Pynchons HLWS CM18 47 J4
Little Queens Rd TEDD TW11 176 E9
Little Queen St DART DA1 187 N3
Little Redlands BMLY BR1 206 B2
Little Reeves Av AMSS HP7 69 L5
Little Rdg WGCE AL7 23 K5
Little Riding WOKS/MYFD GU22 232 E2
Little Rivers WGCE AL7 23 K4
Little Rd HHNE HP2 35 P5
HYS/HAR UB3 152 G1
SL SL1 108 B8
Little Roke Av PUR/KEN CR8 223 J10
Little Roke Rd PUR/KEN CR8 223 K10
Little Rownings FSTH SE23 182 A5
Littlers Cl WIM/MER SW19 201 N1
Little Russell St NOXST/BSQ WC1A 11 L4
Little St James's St WHALL SW1A 10 G10
Little St Leonards
MORT/ESHN SW14 155 P9
Little Shardeloes AMSS HP7 68 F6
Little Smith St WEST SW1P 17 K3
Little Spring CSHM HP5 50 G4
Little Stock Rd CHESW EN7 61 L2
Littlestone Cl BECK BR3 182 F9
Little Strd CDALE/KGS NW9 96 C10
Little Stream Cl NTHWD HA6 92 F6
Little St GUW GU2 249 N6
WAB EN9 81 H2
Little Sutton La DTCH/LGLY SL3 150 E5
Little Thistle WGCE AL7 23 M7
Little Thrift STMC/STPC BR5 206 F4
Little Titchfield St GTPST W1W 10 G4
Littleton Av CHING E4 101 L2
Littleton Crs HRW HA1 114 E7
Littleton La REIG RH2 275 H2
RGUW GU3 267 M6
STA TW18 195 P5
Littleton Rd ASHF TW15 174 D10
HRW HA1 114 E7
Littleton St WAND/EARL SW18 179 M5
Little Trinity La BLKFR EC4V 12 F7
Little Tumners Ct RGODL GU7 267 K10
Little Turnstile LINN WC2A 11 N4
Little Wade WGCE AL7 23 J8
Little Wk HLW * CM20 28 G10
Little Warley Hall La
RBRW/HUT CM13 107 K10
Little Warren Cl RGUE GU4 268 E2
Littlewick Rd WOKN/KNAP GU21 231 J2
Little Widbury WARE SG12 26 E2
Little Widbury La WARE SG12 26 E2
Little Windmill Hl KGLGY WD4 53 H8
Littlewood LEW SE13 183 H1
Little Wd SEV TN13 247 K8
Little Wood Cl STMC/STPC BR5 207 K1
Littlewood Cl WEA W13 154 G2
Little Woodcote Est
WLGTN * SM6 222 C6
Little Woodcote La CAR SM5 222 C8
Little Woodlands WDSR SL4 148 E9
Littleworth Av ESH/CLAY KT10 218 C2
Littleworth Common Rd
ESH/CLAY KT10 198 C10
Littleworth La ESH/CLAY KT10 218 C1
Littleworth Pl ESH/CLAY KT10 218 C1
Littleworth Rd ESH/CLAY KT10 218 C2
Little Youngs WGCW AL8 22 F5
Littlt Halliards WOT/HER * KT12 197 H6
Livermere Rd HACK E8 7 L5
Liverpool Gv WALW SE17 18 G8
Liverpool Rd CAN/RD E16 141 K7
EA W5 155 J1
HOLWY N7 6 A1
KUTN/CMB KT2 177 M10
LEY E10 121 H4
SL SL1 128 G8
STAL AL1 38 D6
THHTH CR7 203 K3
WATW WD18 73 J9
Liverpool St LVPST EC2M 13 J4
Livesey Cl KUT KT1 199 L3
Livesey Pl PECK SE15 19 P9
Livingstone Gdns GVE DA12 190 G8
Livingstone Rd BTSEA SW11 157 N9
CRAWE RH10 283 P9
CTHM CR3 241 L8
GVE DA12 190 G8
HSLW TW3 154 B10
LEY E10 120 G4
PLMGR N13 98 F7
SRTFD E15 141 H3
STHL UB1 133 L9
THHTH CR7 203 L2
Livingstone Wk HHNE HP2 36 A2
Lizard St FSBYE EC1V 6 F10
Lizban St BKHTH/KID SE3 161 N6
Llanbury Cl CFSP/GDCR SL9 90 B8
Llanelly Rd CRICK NW2 117 J7
Llanover Rd WBLY HA9 115 J8
WOOL/PLUM SE18 162 D6
Llanthony Rd MRDN SM4 201 N6
Llanvanor Rd CRICK NW2 117 J7
Llewellyn St BERM/RHTH SE16 19 P2
Lloyd Av COUL/CHIP CR5 222 B10
STRHM/NOR SW16 202 F1
Lloyd Baker St FSBYW WC1X 6 A10
Lloyd Ct PIN HA5 113 L3
Lloyd Ms PEND EN3 80 F4
Lloyd Park Av CROY/NA CR0 223 N1
Lloyd Rd DAGW RM9 144 A1
EHAM E6 142 C3
WALTH E17 120 C2
WPK KT4 200 F10
Lloyd's Av TWRH EC3N 13 K6
Lloyds Ct CRAWE * RH10 283 P4
Lloyd's Pl BKHTH/KID * SE3 161 K8
Lloyd Sq FSBYW WC1X 6 A9
Lloyd's Rw CLKNW EC1R 6 B10
Lloyd St FSBYW WC1X 6 A9
Lloyds Wy BECK BR3 204 D5
Lloyd Thomas Ct WDGN * N22 98 G8
Lloyd Vls BROCKY SE4 160 F8
Loampit Hl LEW SE13 160 F8
Loampit V LEW SE13 160 G9
Loanda Cl HACK E8 7 L5
Loates La WAT WD17 73 K7
Loats Rd CLAP SW4 180 F2
Lobelia Rd CHOB/PIR GU24 230 F1
Local Board Rd WAT WD17 73 L9
Locarno Rd ACT W3 135 P10
GFD/PVL UB6 134 B6
Lochaber Rd LEW SE13 161 K10
Lochaline St HMSMTH W6 156 F5
Lochan Cl YEAD UB4 133 M6
Lochinvar Cl SL SL1 148 G1
Lochinvar St BAL SW12 180 C3
Lochmere Cl ERITH DA8 164 C5
Lochnagar St POP/IOD E14 141 H7
Lochnell Rd BERK HP4 33 L3
Lock Cha LEW SE13 161 K9
Lock Cl STHL * UB1 154 B1
WOKN/KNAP GU21 215 H8
Locke Cl RAIN RM13 144 G1
Locke Gdns SLN SL2 149 P1
Locke-King Cl WEY KT13 216 B4
Locke King Rd WEY KT13 216 B4
Lockers Park La HHW HP1 35 L5
Lockesley Dr STMC/STPC BR5 207 J6
Lockesley Sq SURB * KT6 199 J6
Locket Rd KTN/HRWW/W HA3 94 E10
Lockets Cl WDSR SL4 148 C7
Locke Wy WOKN/KNAP GU21 232 C3
Lockfield Av PEND EN3 80 D6
Lockfield Dr WOKN/KNAP GU21 231 K3
Lockgate Cl HOM E9 120 E10
Lockhart Cl HOLWY N7 5 N1
Lockhart Rd COB KT11 217 K9
Lockhart St BOW E3 140 E6
Lockhurst St CLPT E5 120 C9
Lockington Rd VX/NE SW8 158 C7
Lock Keepers Cottages
TOTM * N17 120 A2
Lock La WOKS/MYFD GU22 233 L2
Lockley Crs HAT AL10 40 E2
Lockmead Rd LEW SE13 161 H9
SEVS/STOTM N15 119 P4
Lock Pth WDSR SL4 148 C5
Lock Rd GU GU1 250 A6
RCHPK/HAM TW10 177 H7
Lock's La MTCM CR4 202 B1
Locksley Dr WOKN/KNAP GU21 231 L3
Locksley Est POP/IOD E14 140 E8
Locksley St POP/IOD E14 140 E7
Locksmeade Rd
RCHPK/HAM TW10 176 G7
Lockswood CHOB/PIR GU24 230 G6
Locks Yd BGR/WK * TN15 265 K1
Lockwood Cl SYD SE26 182 C7
Lockwood Ct CRAWE * RH10 284 A5
Lockwood Pth
WOKN/KNAP GU21 214 G9
Lockwood Sq BERM/RHTH SE16 160 A2
Lockwood Wy CHSGTN KT9 219 M2
WALTH E17 100 C10
Lockyer Pl BH/WHM * TN16 262 G2
Lockyer Rd PUR RM19 166 B4
Lockyer St STHWK SE1 19 H2
Locomotive Dr
EBED/NFELT TW14 175 H4
Locton Gn BOW * E3 140 E3
Loddiges Rd HOM E9 140 B2
Loddon Sp SL SL1 129 K9
Loder Cl WOKN/KNAP GU21 214 G9
Loder St PECK SE15 160 B6
Lodge Av BCTR RM8 123 L10
BORE WD6 75 L9
CROY/NA CR0 202 G10
DAGW RM9 143 L3
DART DA1 187 K2
GPK RM2 125 H3
KTN/HRWW/W HA3 115 K2
Lodgebottom Rd RDKG RH5 255 M3
Lodge Cl CHIG IG7 103 K4
COB KT11 235 K2
CRAWW RH11 283 M7
EDGW * HA8 95 L7
EGH TW20 172 A8
EW KT17 220 F6
HERT/WAS SG14 25 K3
ISLW TW7 154 G7
LHD/OX KT22 236 C8
MTCM CR4 202 B8
ORP BR6 207 L8
RDKG RH5 273 H6
SL SL1 149 H1
UED N18 99 K6
UX/CGN UB8 131 M6
Lodge Ct ALP/SUD * HA0 115 K10
GVE DA12 191 P9
Lodge Crs CHES/WCR EN8 62 C10
ORP BR6 207 L8
Lodge Dr BRKMPK AL9 40 G1
PLMGR N13 99 H5
RKW/CH/CXG WD3 71 M8
Lodge End RAD WD7 56 G10
RKW/CH/CXG WD3 72 B8
Lodge Fld WGCE AL7 23 H2
Lodge Gdns BECK BR3 204 E5
Lodge Hall HLWS CM18 47 H5
Lodge Hl PUR/KEN CR8 241 H1
WELL DA16 163 L6
Lodgehill Park Cl
RYLN/HDSTN HA2 114 A7
Lodge La BH/WHM TN16 262 F3
BXLY DA5 185 N2
CDH/CHF RM16 167 M1
CROY/NA CR0 224 G4
CRW RM5 104 B7
CSTG HP8 69 K9
NFNCH/WDSP N12 97 M6
RDKG RH5 273 L10
REDH RH1 275 P8
WAB EN9 81 J1
Lodge Mansions Pde
PLMGR * N13 99 H5
Lodge Ms HBRY * N5 119 K9
Lodge Pl SUT SM1 221 L2
Lodge Rd BMLY BR1 183 P10
CROY/NA CR0 203 J6
EPP CM16 64 D10
HDN NW4 116 F2
LHD/OX KT22 236 B8
RKW/CH/CXG WD3 72 E8
STJWD NW8 3 M10
SUT SM1 221 L2
WLGTN SM6 222 C2
The Lodge SHB * W12 156 G1
Lodge Vls WFD IG8 101 L8
Lodge Wy ASHF TW15 173 P5
SHPTN TW17 196 D2
WDSR SL4 148 D9
Lodore Gdns CDALE/KGS NW9 116 B3
Lodore Gn HGDN/ICK UB10 111 P8
Lodore St POP/IOD E14 141 H8
Loewen Rd CDH/CHF RM16 168 D2
Lofthouse Pl CHSGTN KT9 219 H3
Loftie St BERM/RHTH SE16 19 P2
Lofting Rd IS N1 6 A4
Loftus Rd SHB W12 136 E10
Loftus Vls SHB * W12 136 E10
Logan Cl HSLWW TW4 153 N9
PEND EN3 80 C5
Logan Ms KENS W8 14 E5
ROM RM1 124 F3
Logan Pl KENS W8 14 E5
Logan Rd ED N9 100 A3
WBLY HA9 115 K7
The Logans BAR * EN5 76 G7
Logmore La DORK RH4 272 D7
Logs Hl CHST BR7 184 B10
Logs Hill Cl CHST BR7 206 B1
Lois Dr SHPTN TW17 196 C5
Lolesworth Cl WCHPL * E1 13 M4
Lollards Cl AMS HP6 69 H3
Lollard St LBTH SE11 17 P5
Lollesworth La EHSLY KT24 252 D2
Loman Pth SOCK/AV RM15 146 E8
Loman St STHWK SE1 18 D1
Lomas Cl CROY/NA CR0 225 H4
Lomas St WCHPL E1 13 P3
Lombard Av GDMY/SEVK IG3 123 H6
PEND EN3 80 B5
Lombard Rd BTSEA SW11 157 N8
FBAR/BDGN N11 98 C6
WIM/MER SW19 201 L2
The Lombards EMPK RM11 125 N5
Lombard St BANK EC3V 13 H6
EYN DA4 210 B4
MFD/CHID GU8 266 A10
Lombard Vls FBAR/BDGN * N11 98 C6
Lombard Wall CHARL SE7 161 N2
Lombardy Cl HHNE HP2 36 E7
WOKN/KNAP GU21 231 L3
WOKN/KNAP * GU21 231 L3
Lombardy Dr BERK HP4 34 A6
Lombardy Pl BAY/PAD W2 8 G8
Lombardy Wy BORE WD6 75 K5
Lomond Cl ALP/SUD HA0 135 L2
SEVS/STOTM N15 119 M2
Lomond Gdns SAND/SEL CR2 224 D4
Lomond Gv CMBW SE5 159 L6
Lomond Rd HHNE HP2 35 N2
Loncin Mead Av
ADL/WDHM KT15 215 M5
Loncroft Rd CMBW SE5 19 K9
Londesborough Rd
STNW/STAM N16 119 M9
London Br CANST EC4R 13 H8
London Bridge Wk STHWK * SE1 13 H9
Londonderry Pde ERITH * DA8 164 E6
London Flds HACK * E8 140 A2
London Fields East Side
HACK E8 140 A2
London Fields West Side
HACK E8 7 P3
London La BMLY BR1 183 L10
HACK E8 140 A2
SHGR GU5 270 B5
London Loop BNSTD SM7 221 J9
BORE WD6 75 N10
COUL/CHIP CR5 240 F5
CROY/NA CR0 204 C10
ENC/FH EN2 78 F3
MLHL NW7 95 P1
PUR/KEN CR8 241 M1
SAND/SEL CR2 224 C5
WWKM BR4 205 J10
London Ms BAY/PAD W2 9 M6
London Rd ABR/ST RM4 83 K7
ABR/ST RM4 84 E5
ASC SL5 192 B3
BARK IG11 142 E2
BEAC HP9 88 E10
BERK HP4 34 A5
BFOR GU20 192 B10
BGR/WK TN15 265 N9
BH/WHM TN16 244 F9
BMLY BR1 183 L10
BRW CM14 106 F4
BUSH WD23 73 M10
CHDH RM6 124 B4
CHONG CM5 67 L10
CRAWE RH10 283 N6
CROY/NA CR0 203 J8
CSTG HP8 89 P3
CTHM CR3 241 L9
DART DA1 186 E1
DORK RH4 255 H8
DTCH/LGLY SL3 149 P6
DTCH/LGLY SL3 149 P2
EGH TW20 171 P10
ENC/FH EN2 79 L9
EPP CM16 47 L8
EW KT17 220 C5
EYN DA4 209 L6
FSTH SE23 182 B4
GRAYS RM17 167 K5
GRH DA9 188 D2
GU GU1 250 D7
GU GU1 268 B1
GVW DA11 190 A2
HERT/BAY SG13 25 P7
HHS/BOV HP3 35 N9
HHW HP1 34 E8
HLWE CM17 29 M8
HLWE CM17 47 M5
HORL RH6 280 B7
ISLW TW7 154 D8
KUT KT1 199 K2
MRDN SM4 201 P5
MRDN SM4 201 K5
MTCM CR4 202 B7
PLSTW E13 141 M4
PUR RM19 166 A2
RAD WD7 57 L9
RDART DA2 188 B3
REDH RH1 258 B9
REIG RH2 257 K10
RKW/CH/CXG WD3 91 P2
ROMW/RG RM7 124 D4
RPLY/SEND GU23 251 H2
RSEV TN14 228 A5
RSEV TN14 228 D9
RYLN/HDSTN HA2 114 D7
SBW CM21 29 P1
SEV TN13 246 E4
SOCK/AV RM15 165 N1
STA TW18 173 J7
STAL AL1 38 F9
STAN HA7 95 H6

STHWK SE1 18 C3
STRHM/NOR SW16 202 G2
STWL/WRAY TW19 173 N5
SWCM DA10 189 K1
SWLY BR8 208 D2
THHTH CR7 203 H6
TIL RM18 168 E8
TWK TW1 176 F3
WARE SG12 26 C3
WBLY HA9 115 K10
WLGTN SM6 202 C9
WTHK RM20 167 J5
London Rd East AMSS HP7 69 K7
CSTG HP8 69 L8
London Rd North
COUL/CHIP CR5 240 C10
REDH RH1 258 C2
London Rd Purfleet PUR RM19 166 A5
London Rd South REDH RH1 258 C5
London Rd West AMSS HP7 69 H6
London Rd West Thurrock
WTHK RM20 166 E5
Londons Cl UPMR RM14 126 B10
London Sq GU * GU1 250 B10
London Stile CHSWK W4 155 M4
London St BAY/PAD W2 9 L6
CHERT KT16 195 K7
FENCHST * EC3M 13 K7
London Ter BETH * E2 7 N8
London Wall BARB EC2Y 12 F4
London Wall Buildings
LVPST EC2M 13 H4
Loneacre BFOR * GU20 212 D3
Lone Oak HORL RH6 281 J6
Lonesome La REIG RH2 275 M4
Lonesome Wy MTCM CR4 202 C1
Long Acre COVGDN WC2E 11 L6
CRAWE RH10 285 P5
HLWE CM17 29 L7
STMC/STPC BR5 207 N9
Long Acre Ct WEA * W13 134 F7
Longacre Pl CAR * SM5 222 B3
Longacre Rd WALTH E17 101 J9
Longacres STALE/WH AL4 39 J6
Longaford Wy RBRW/HUT CM13 107 P2
Long Arrotts HHW HP1 35 L4
Long Av CHOB/PIR GU24 230 F7
Long Banks HLWS CM18 46 G4
Long Barn Cl GSTN WD25 58 H8
Long Barn Rd RSEV TN14 265 J9
Longbeach Rd BTSEA SW11 158 A9
Longboat Rw STHL UB1 133 N8
Longbottom La BEAC HP9 88 F7
Longbourne Wy CHERT KT16 195 J6
Longboyds COB KT11 235 J1
Longbridge Rd BARK IG11 142 G1
BCTR RM8 123 K9
HORL RH6 280 A6
Longbridge Wk HORL RH6 280 A6
Longbridge Wy LEW SE13 183 H1
UX/CGN UB8 131 L4
Long Buftlers HARP AL5 20 E3
Longbury Cl STMC/STPC BR5 207 L3
Longbury Dr STMC/STPC BR5 207 L3
Longchamp Cl HORL RH6 280 D4
Long Chaulden HHW HP1 35 H7
Longcliffe Pth OXHEY WD19 93 H4
Long Cl SLN SL2 128 G2
Long Copse Cl GT/LBKH KT23 236 A9
Long Ct PUR RM19 165 P3
Longcroft ELTH/MOT SE9 184 D6
Long Cft OXHEY WD19 93 J1
Longcroft Av BNSTD SM7 221 M10
Long Croft Dr CHES/WCR EN8 62 E10
Longcrofte Rd EDGW HA8 95 J8
Longcroft Gdns WGCW AL8 22 G6
Longcroft Gn WGCW AL8 22 G7
Longcroft La HHS/BOV HP3 52 F4
WGCW AL8 22 G6
Longcroft Ri LOU IG10 82 E9
Long Croft Rd RKW/CH/CXG WD3 90 G6
Longcross Rd CHERT KT16 193 N10
Long Deacon Rd CHING E4 101 K2
Longdean Pk HHS/BOV HP3 36 B10
Longdon Wd HAYES BR2 226 B1
Longdown La North EW KT17 220 D9
Longdown La South EW KT17 238 D1
Longdown Rd CAT SE6 182 F7
EW KT17 220 D10
RGUE GU4 268 E3
Long Dr ACT W3 136 B8
GFD/PVL UB6 134 A3
RSLP HA4 113 K9
SL SL1 128 B5
WDR/YW * UB7 151 P1
Long Dyke GU GU1 250 E8
Long Elmes KTN/HRWW/W HA3 94 A9
Long Elms ABLGY WD5 54 E9
Long Elms Cl ABLGY WD5 54 E9
Long Fallow LCOL/BKTW AL2 55 P3
Longfellow Dr RBRW/HUT CM13 107 P1
Longfellow Rd BOW * E3 140 D5
WALTH * E17 120 E4
WPK KT4 200 D8
Longfellow Wy STHWK * SE1 19 M6
Long Fld CDALE/KGS NW9 96 B8
Longfield BMLY BR1 205 L1
HHS/BOV HP3 36 C8
HLWS CM18 47 K3
LOU IG10 81 P9
SLN SL2 109 J8
Longfield Av EA W5 135 H9
EMPK RM11 124 G5
HART DA3 211 P2
MLHL NW7 96 D8
PEND EN3 80 B3
WALTH E17 120 D2
WBLY HA9 115 K6
WLGTN SM6 202 B8
Longfield Crs
KWD/TDW/WH KT20 238 F6
SYD SE26 182 B6
Longfield Dr AMS HP6 68 G4
MORT/ESHN SW14 177 N1
WIM/MER SW19 201 P1
Longfield Est STHWK SE1 19 M5
Longfield La CHESW EN7 61 N3
Longfield Rd CSHM HP5 50 E5
DORK RH4 272 E3
EA W5 135 H8
HARP AL5 20 B4
Long Flds CHONG CM5 67 P6
Longfield St WAND/EARL SW18 179 K3
Longford Av EBED/NFELT TW14 174 F2
STHL UB1 133 P9
STWL/WRAY TW19 173 P4
Longford Cl HPTN TW12 175 P7
YEAD UB4 133 L9
Longford Ct HOR/WEW KT19 219 P1
Longford Gdns SUT SM1 201 M10
YEAD UB4 133 L9
Longford Rd WHTN TW2 175 P4
Longford St CAMTN NW1 10 F1
Longford Wy STWL/WRAY TW19 173 P5
Long Furlong Dr SLN SL2 128 D6
Long Gore RGODL GU7 267 K9
Long Gn CHIG IG7 103 H5
Long Gv BEAC HP9 89 H7
HARH RM3 105 M10
Long Grove Rd HOR/WEW KT19 219 N6
Longhayes Av CHDH RM6 123 N1
Longheath Dr GT/LBKH KT23 235 M10
Longheath Gdns CROY/NA CR0 204 B5
Longhedge St BTSEA SW11 158 B8
Long Hl CTHM CR3 242 D7
Longhill Rd CAT SE6 183 J5
Longhook Gdns NTHLT UB5 133 H4
Longhope Cl PECK SE15 19 K10
Longhouse Rd CDH/CHF RM16 168 E2
Longhurst Rd CROY/NA CR0 204 A6
EHSLY KT24 252 F5
LEW SE13 183 K1
Long John HHS/BOV HP3 36 A8
Longland Dr TRDG/WHET N20 97 L4
Longlands HHNE HP2 36 A5
Longlands Av COUL/CHIP CR5 222 C10
Longlands Cl CHES/WCR EN8 62 C8
Longlands Park Crs
BFN/LL DA15 185 H6
Longlands Rd BFN/LL DA15 185 H6
WGCE AL7 23 J7
Long La BXLYHN DA7 164 A8
CDH/CHF RM16 167 M1
CROY/NA CR0 204 B6
FNCH N3 97 M10
HGDN/ICK UB10 112 C8
HHS/BOV HP3 52 C7
RKW/CH/CXG WD3 70 F10
STBT EC1A 12 D3
STHWK SE1 19 H2
STWL/WRAY TW19 174 A3
Longleat Rd EN EN1 79 M9
Longleat Wy EBED/NFELT TW14 174 D3
Longleigh La ABYW SE2 163 M5
Long Ley HLW CM20 47 J1
WGCE AL7 23 M5
Longley Av ALP/SUD HA0 135 L3
Longley Rd CROY/NA CR0 203 J7
HRW HA1 114 C3
TOOT SW17 179 P9
Long Leys CHING E4 100 G7
Longley St STHWK SE1 19 N6
Longley Wy CRICK NW2 116 F8
Long Lodge Dr WOT/HER KT12 197 K10
Long Mark Rd CAN/RD E16 142 A8
Longmarsh Vw EYN DA4 210 A1
Long Md CDALE/KGS NW9 96 C9
Longmead CHST BR7 206 D2
GU GU1 250 F10
HAT AL10 40 E1
WDSR SL4 148 D7
Longmead Cl BRWN CM15 107 K2
CTHM CR3 241 M7
Longmead Dr SCUP DA14 185 N5
Longmead La SL SL1 128 C2
Long Meadow CSHM HP5 51 H4
KTTN * NW5 5 J1
RBRW/HUT CM13 107 P3
Longmeadow GT/LBKH KT23 253 N1
SEV TN13 246 E7
Long Meadow Cl BECK BR3 205 H7
Longmeadow Rd BFN/LL DA15 185 H4
Longmeadow Vls HORL * RH6 279 H10
Longmead Rd HOR/WEW KT19 220 B6
HYS/HAR UB3 132 G9
THDIT KT7 198 D7
TOOT SW17 180 A8
Longmere Gdns
KWD/TDW/WH KT20 238 F5
Longmere Rd CRAWE RH10 283 N5
Long Mimms HHNE HP2 35 P5
Long Moor CHES/WCR EN8 62 D5
Longmoore St PIM SW1V 16 G6
Longmore Av BAR EN5 77 M10
Longmore Cl RKW/CH/CXG WD3 91 J5
Longmore Gdns WGCE AL7 23 J5
Longmore Rd WOT/HER KT12 217 M1
Longnor Rd WCHPL E1 140 C5
Long Pk AMS HP6 69 H2
Long Park Cl AMS HP6 69 H2
Long Park Wy AMS HP6 69 H1
Long Pond Rd BKHTH/KID SE3 161 K7
Longport Cl BARK/HLT IG6 103 K7
Long Reach EHSLY KT24 234 C10
Long Reach Rd BARK IG11 143 J6
Longreach Rd ERITH DA8 165 J6
Long Readings La SLN SL2 128 G5
Longridge Gv WOKS/MYFD GU22 215 H10
Longridge La GFD/PVL UB6 134 A9
Longridge Rd ECT SW5 14 E6
Long Ridings Av
RBRW/HUT CM13 87 N9
Long Rd CLAP SW4 158 D10
Longs Cl WOKS/MYFD GU22 233 K2
Longsdon Wy CTHM CR3 241 P10
Long Shaw LHD/OX KT22 236 F5
Longshaw Rd CHING E4 101 J4
Longshore DEPT SE8 160 E3
Longside Cl EGH TW20 194 F1
Long Spring STALW/RED AL3 38 E2
Longspring WATN WD24 73 J3
Longstaff Crs WAND/EARL SW18 179 K2
Longstaff Rd WAND/EARL SW18 179 K2
Longstone Av WLSDN NW10 136 C2
Longstone Rd IVER SL0 130 F4
TOOT SW17 180 C8
Long St BETH E2 7 L8
WAB EN9 64 B6
Longthornton Rd
STRHM/NOR SW16 202 D2
Longton Av SYD SE26 181 P7
Longton Gv SYD SE26 182 A7
Longtown Rd HARH RM3 105 K6
Long Vw BERK HP4 33 M3
Longview Wy CRW RM5 104 E9
Longville Rd LBTH SE11 18 C5
Long Wk CSTG HP8 70 B7
KWD/TDW/WH KT20 238 F5
NWMAL KT3 199 P3
STHWK SE1 19 K3
WDSR * SL4 171 J1
Longwalk Rd STKPK UB11 132 C10
The Long Wk WDSR SL4 171 J4
Long Wd HLWS CM18 46 G6
Longwood Cl UPMR RM14 126 B10
Longwood Ct WPK KT4 200 D9
Long Wood Dr BEAC HP9 89 L7
Longwood Dr PUT/ROE SW15 178 D2
Longwood Gdns CLAY IG5 122 C2
Longwood La AMSS HP7 69 J5
Longwood Rd HERT/WAS SG14 24 G4
PUR/KEN CR8 241 L2
Longwood Vw CRAWE RH10 284 B10
Longworth Cl THMD SE28 143 N8
Long Yd BMSBY WC1N 11 N2
The Loning CDALE/KGS NW9 116 C2
PEND EN3 80 B4
Lonsdale HHNE HP2 35 P3
Lonsdale Av EHAM E6 142 A6
ROMW/RG RM7 124 D4
WBLY HA9 115 K10
Lonsdale Cl EHAM E6 142 B6
LEE/GVPK SE12 184 A6
UX/CGN UB8 132 D8
Lonsdale Crs GNTH/NBYPK IG2 122 E4
RDART DA2 188 B5
Lonsdale Dr ENC/FH EN2 78 E8
STHGT/OAK N14 78 F9
Lonsdale Dr North ENC/FH EN2 78 F9
Lonsdale Gdns
STRHM/NOR SW16 202 G4
Lonsdale Ms RCH/KEW * TW9 155 M7
Lonsdale Pl IS N1 6 B4
Lonsdale Rd BARN SW13 156 C6
BXLYHN DA7 164 A8
CHSWK W4 156 C3
DORK RH4 272 G1
KIL/WHAMP NW6 2 C7
NTGHL W11 8 C6
NWDGN UB2 153 L2
SNWD SE25 204 A4
WAN E11 121 L5
WEY KT13 216 B4
Lonsdale Sq IS N1 6 B4
Loobert Rd SEVS/STOTM N15 119 M1
Looe Gdns BARK/HLT IG6 122 E1
Loom La RAD WD7 74 E3
Loom Pl RAD WD7 74 F2
Loop Rd CHST BR7 184 F9
EPSOM KT18 237 P2
WAB EN9 62 G8
WOKS/MYFD GU22 232 C6
Lopen Rd UED N18 99 M5
Loppets Rd CRAWE RH10 284 A9
Loraine Cl PEND EN3 80 B9
Loraine Cottages HOLWY * N7 118 G9
Loraine Gdns ASHTD KT21 237 K3
Loraine Rd CHSWK W4 155 N5
HOLWY N7 118 G9
Lord Av CLAY IG5 122 C2
Lord Chancellor Wk
KUTN/CMB KT2 199 P1
Lord Chatham's Ride RSEV TN14 245 N3
Lorden Wk BETH E2 7 N10
Lord Gdns CLAY IG5 122 B2
Lord Hills Rd BAY/PAD W2 9 H3
Lord Holland La BRXN/ST * SW9 159 H8
Lord Knyvett Cl
STWL/WRAY TW19 173 N2
Lord Knyvetts Ct
STWL/WRAY * TW19 173 P2
Lord Mayors Dr SLN SL2 128 E1
Lord Napier Pl HMSMTH W6 156 D4
Lord North St WEST SW1P 17 L4
Lord Roberts Ms FUL/PGN * SW6 157 L6
Lordsbury Fld WLGTN SM6 222 D6
Lords Cl DUL SE21 181 K5
FELT TW13 175 M5
RAD WD7 57 K8
Lordsgrove Cl
KWD/TDW/WH KT20 238 E6
Lordship Gv STNW/STAM N16 119 L7
Lordship La DUL SE21 181 P4
EDUL SE22 181 N2
TOTM N17 99 K9
Lordship Pk STNW/STAM N16 119 L7
Lordship Park Ms
STNW/STAM N16 119 K7
Lordship Pl CHEL SW3 15 N10
Lordship Rd CHESW EN7 62 A6
NTHLT UB5 133 M2
STNW/STAM N16 119 L6
Lordship Ter STNW/STAM N16 119 L7
Lordsmead Rd TOTM N17 99 M9
Lord St CAN/RD E16 142 B10
GVE DA12 190 E3
HOD EN11 44 D3
WAT WD17 73 K7
Lords Vw STJWD NW8 3 N10
Lords Wd WGCE AL7 23 M5
Lordswood Cl RDART DA2 188 D7
Lord Warwick St
WOOL/PLUM SE18 162 C2
Lorenzo St FSBYW WC1X 5 N9
Loretto Gdns
KTN/HRWW/W HA3 115 K2
Lorian Cl NFNCH/WDSP N12 97 L5
Lorian Dr REIG RH2 257 M9
Loriners CRAWE RH10 283 N10
Loriners Cl COB KT11 217 H10
Loring Rd BERK HP4 33 P6
ISLW TW7 154 E8
TRDG/WHET N20 97 P3
WDSR SL4 148 E7
Loris Rd HMSMTH W6 156 F2
Lorn Ct BRXN/ST SW9 159 H8
Lorne Av CROY/NA CR0 204 C7
Lorne Cl STJWD NW8 3 P10
WDSR SL4 148 G2
Lorne Gdns CROY/NA CR0 204 C7
WAN E11 121 P2
WKENS W14 156 G1
WOKN/KNAP GU21 231 J5
Lorne Rd BRW CM14 107 H5
FSBYPK N4 118 G6
FSTGT E7 121 N9
KTN/HRWW/W HA3 94 E10
RCHPK/HAM TW10 177 L1
WALTH E17 120 F3
Lorne Ter FNCH * N3 97 J10
The Lorne GT/LBKH KT23 253 P2
Lorn Rd BRXN/ST SW9 158 G8
Lorraine Pk KTN/HRWW/W HA3 94 D8
Lorrimore Rd WALW SE17 18 D10
Lorrimore Sq WALW SE17 18 D9
Lorton Cl GVE DA12 191 H5
Loseberry Rd ESH/CLAY KT10 218 C2
Loseley Rd RGODL GU7 267 K9
Losfield Rd WDSR SL4 148 D7
Lossie Dr IVER SL0 130 E9
Lothair Rd EA W5 155 J1
Lothair Rd North FSBYPK N4 119 J4
Lothair Rd South FSBYPK N4 119 H5
Lothbury LOTH EC2R 12 G5
Lothian Av YEAD UB4 133 J7
Lothian Cl ALP/SUD HA0 114 F9
Lothian Rd BRXN/ST SW9 159 J7
Lothian Wd KWD/TDW/WH KT20 238 E8
Lothrop St NKENS W10 2 A10
Lots Rd WBPTN SW10 157 M6
Lotus Rd BH/WHM TN16 244 C4
Loubet St TOOT SW17 180 A9
Loudhams Rd AMSS HP7 69 P5
Loudhams Wood La CSTG HP8 70 A6
Loudoun Av GNTH/NBYPK IG2 122 E3
Loudoun Rd STJWD NW8 3 K6
Loudwater Cl SUN TW16 197 H4
Loudwater Dr RKW/CH/CXG WD3 71 M8
Loudwater Hts
RKW/CH/CXG WD3 71 L7
Loudwater La RKW/CH/CXG WD3 71 M9
Loudwater Rdg
RKW/CH/CXG WD3 71 M8
Loughborough Pk HNHL SE24 159 J10
Loughborough Rd BRXN/ST SW9 159 H8
Loughborough St LBTH SE11 17 P7
Lough Rd HOLWY N7 5 P1
HOLWY N7 118 G10
Loughton La EPP CM16 82 G3
Loughton Wy BKHH IG9 102 A2
Louisa Cl HOM E9 140 B2
Louisa St WCHPL E1 140 C7
Louise Bennett Cl HNHL * SE24 159 J10
Louise Gdns RAIN RM13 144 F5
Louise Rd SRTFD E15 141 K1
Louise Wk HHS/BOV HP3 52 D4
Louis Flds RGUW GU3 249 H6
Louisville Rd TOOT SW17 180 B6
Louvaine Rd BTSEA SW11 157 N10
Louvain Rd RDART DA2 188 D3
Louvain Wy GSTN WD25 55 J8
Lovage Ap EHAM E6 142 B7
Lovat Cl CRICK NW2 116 C8
Lovat La FENCHST EC3M 13 J7
Lovatt Cl EDGW HA8 95 N7
Lovatts RKW/CH/CXG WD3 72 B8
Loveday Rd WEA W13 134 G10
Love Green La IVER SL0 130 G7
Lovegrove St STHWK SE1 19 P8
Lovegrove Wk POP/IOD E14 141 H10
Love Hill La DTCH/LGLY SL3 130 D9
Lovejoy La WDSR SL4 148 C8
Lovekyn Cl KUTN/CMB KT2 199 K2
Lovelace Av HAYES BR2 206 D6
Lovelace Cl EHSLY KT24 235 H9
Lovelace Dr WOKS/MYFD GU22 233 H2
Lovelace Gdns BARK IG11 123 K9
SURB KT6 199 J7
WOT/HER KT12 217 K2
Lovelace Gn ELTH/MOT SE9 162 C9
Lovelace Rd DUL SE21 181 K5
EBAR EN4 97 P1
SURB KT6 198 H7
Lovelace Vls THDIT * KT7 198 G7
Lovelands La CHOB/PIR GU24 213 H9
KWD/TDW/WH KT20 257 L3
Love La ABLGY WD5 54 G6
BXLY DA5 186 B2
CHEAM SM3 221 H3
CHONG CM5 67 P4
CITYW EC2V 12 F5
GDST RH9 260 B8
IVER SL0 130 G8
KGLGY WD4 53 P5
KWD/TDW/WH KT20 256 D2
MRDN SM4 201 K7
MTCM CR4 201 P3
PIN HA5 113 M1
SNWD SE25 204 A3
SOCK/AV RM15 166 B1
SURB KT6 199 J9
TIL RM18 169 M5
TOTM N17 99 N8
WFD IG8 102 C7
WOOL/PLUM SE18 162 D3
Lovel Av WELL DA16 163 K8
Lovel Cl HHW HP1 35 K6
Lovel End CFSP/GDCR SL9 89 P8
Loveletts CRAWW RH11 283 K8
Lovel Hl ASC * SL5 170 A8
Lovelinch Cl PECK SE15 160 B5
Lovel La ASC SL5 170 A8
Lovell Pl BERM/RHTH SE16 160 D2
Lovell Rd EN EN1 80 A1
GFD/PVL UB6 134 A8
RCHPK/HAM TW10 177 H6
Lovells Cl LTWR GU18 212 A6
Lovell Wk RAIN RM13 145 H1
Lovel Md CFSP/GDCR SL9 89 P8
Lovelock Cl PUR/KEN CR8 241 K3
Lovel Rd CFSP/GDCR SL9 89 P8
Loveridge Ms KIL/WHAMP NW6 2 C2
Loveridge Rd KIL/WHAMP NW6 2 D2
Lovering Rd CHESW EN7 61 K1
Lover's La GRH DA9 167 J10
Lovet Rd HLWW/ROY CM19 46 D2
Lovett Dr CAR SM5 201 M7
Lovett Rd DEN/HRF UB9 111 M1
EGH TW20 172 E7
Lovett Wy WLSDN NW10 115 P10
Love Wk CMBW SE5 159 L8
Lovibonds Av ORP BR6 206 E10
WDR/YW UB7 132 A8
Lowbell La LCOL/BKTW AL2 57 K3
Lowbrook Rd IL IG1 122 E9
Lowburys DORK RH4 272 F5
Low Cl GRH DA9 188 F1
Lowdell Cl WDR/YW UB7 131 P8
Lowden Rd ED N9 100 A2
HNHL SE24 159 J10
STHL UB1 133 M9
Lowe Av CAN/RD E16 141 M7
Lowe Cl CHIG IG7 103 K6
Lowell St POP/IOD E14 140 D8
Lowen Rd RAIN RM13 144 E4
Lower Addiscombe Rd
CROY/NA CR0 203 L8
Lower Addison Gdns WKENS W14 14 A2
Lower Adeyfield Rd HHNE HP2 35 N5
Lower Barn HHS/BOV HP3 36 A9
Lower Barn Rd PUR/KEN CR8 223 K8
Lower Bedfords Rd ROM RM1 105 H7
Lower Belgrave St BGVA SW1W 16 E4
Lower Boston Rd HNWL W7 134 D10
Lower Bridge Rd REDH RH1 258 A10
Lower Britwell Rd SL SL1 128 C6
Lower Broad St DAGE RM10 144 B3
Lower Bury La EPP CM16 65 H7
Lower Camden CHST BR7 206 C1
Lower Church St CROY/NA * CR0 203 J9
Lower Cippenham La SL SL1 128 E10
Lower Clabdens WARE SG12 26 E2
Lower Clapton Rd CLPT E5 120 A9
Lower Clarendon Wk NTGHL W11 8 A6
Lower Common South
PUT/ROE SW15 156 E9
Lower Coombe St CROY/NA CR0 223 K1
Lower Ct HOR/WEW KT19 220 A7
Lower Court Rd HOR/WEW KT19 219 P7
Lower Crs SLH/COR SS17 169 K2
Lower Cft SWLY BR8 208 G4
Lower Dagnall St STALW/RED AL3 38 B6
Lower Derby Rd WAT WD17 73 K8
Lower Downs Rd RYNPK SW20 200 G1
Lower Dr BEAC HP9 88 C6
Lower Dunnymans BNSTD SM7 221 J10
Lower Edgeborough Rd GU GU1 268 C1
Lower Emms HHNE HP2 36 D1
Lower Farm Rd EHSLY KT24 235 J10
Lowerfield WGCE AL7 23 K6
Lower Forecourt HORL RH6 280 C8
Lower Gravel Rd HAYES BR2 206 B8
Lower Green Gdns WPK KT4 200 D8
Lower Green Rd ESH/CLAY KT10 198 A9
Lower Gn West MTCM CR4 201 P3
Lower Grosvenor Pl KTBR SW1X 16 E3
Lower Grove Rd
RCHPK/HAM TW10 177 L2
Lower Guildford Rd
WOKN/KNAP GU21 231 J3
Lower Hall La CHING E4 100 D6
Lower Hampton Rd SUN TW16 197 L2
Lower Ham Rd KUTN/CMB KT2 177 J9
Lower Hatfield Rd
HERT/BAY SG13 24 G10
Lower Higham Rd GVE DA12 191 J4
Lower High St WAT WD17 73 L9
Lower Hill Rd HOR/WEW KT19 219 N8
Lower Island Wy WAB EN9 80 G1
Lower James St SOHO/CST * W1F 11 H7
Lower John St SOHO/CST W1F 11 H7
Lower Kenwood Av
STHGT/OAK N14 78 F9
Lower Kings Rd BERK HP4 33 P4
Lower Lea Crossing
POP/IOD E14 141 K9
Lower Lees Rd SLN SL2 128 F5
Lower Luton Rd STALE/WH AL4 20 E1
Lower Maidstone Rd
FBAR/BDGN N11 98 D7
Lower Mardyke Av RAIN RM13 144 D4
Lower Marsh STHWK SE1 18 A2
Lower Marsh La KUT KT1 199 M4
Lower Md IVER SL0 130 G5
Lower Meadow CHES/WCR EN8 62 C3
HLWS CM18 47 H5
Lower Merton Ri HAMP NW3 3 N4
Lower Morden La MRDN SM4 201 H6
Lower Mortlake Rd
RCH/KEW TW9 155 K10
Lower Noke Cl BRW CM14 105 M3
Lower Northfield BNSTD SM7 221 J10
Lower Paddock Rd OXHEY WD19 73 M10
Lower Park Rd BELV DA17 164 B2
BNSTD SM7 239 P4
FBAR/BDGN N11 98 D6
LOU IG10 82 A9
Lower Paxton Rd STAL AL1 38 D7
Lower Peryers EHSLY KT24 252 F4
Lower Pillory Down CAR SM5 222 B9
Lower Plantation
RKW/CH/CXG WD3 71 M7
Lower Queen's Rd BKHH IG9 102 B3
Lower Range Rd GVE DA12 191 H3
Lower Richmond Rd
PUT/ROE SW15 156 F9
Lower Rd BELV DA17 164 C2
BERM/RHTH SE16 160 B1
CFSP/GDCR SL9 90 B9
DEN/HRF UB9 110 F5
ERITH DA8 164 E3
GT/LBKH KT23 253 N2
GVE DA12 191 P5
GVW DA11 167 M10
HHS/BOV HP3 54 B2
LHD/OX KT22 236 C9
LOU IG10 82 D5
PUR/KEN CR8 223 J9
REIG RH2 275 N2
RKW/CH/CXG WD3 70 G8
RYLN/HDSTN HA2 114 C7
STMC/STPC BR5 207 L6
SUT SM1 221 N2
SWLY BR8 187 J10
TIL RM18 168 D10
WARE SG12 26 E5
Lower Sales HHW HP1 35 J7
Lower Sandfields
RPLY/SEND GU23 232 G9
Lower Sand Hills SURB KT6 199 H7
Lower Sawleywood BNSTD SM7 221 J10
Lower Shott GT/LBKH KT23 254 A2
Lower Sloane St BGVA SW1W 16 B6
Lower Station Rd DART DA1 186 F2
Lower Strd CDALE/KGS NW9 96 C10
Lower St SHGR GU5 270 B5
Lower Sunbury Rd HPTN TW12 197 N2
Lower Swaines EPP CM16 65 H6
Lower Tail OXHEY WD19 93 M4
Lower Teddington Rd KUT KT1 199 J1
Lower Ter HAMP NW3 117 M8
Lower Thames St MON EC3R 13 J8
Lower Tub BUSH WD23 94 C1
Lower Village Rd ASC SL5 192 B8
Lower Wood Rd ESH/CLAY KT10 218 F2
Lower Yott HHNE HP2 35 P2
Lowestoft Dr SL SL1 128 B8
Lowestoft Rd WATN WD24 73 J3
Loweswater Cl GSTN WD25 55 K6
WBLY HA9 115 J7
The Lowe CHIG IG7 103 K3
Lowfield SBW CM21 29 P2
Lowfield Heath Rd HORL RH6 279 J7
Lowfield La HOD EN11 44 F4
Lowfield Rd ACT W3 135 P7
KIL/WHAMP NW6 2 E3
Lowfield St DART DA1 187 M3
Lowfield Wy HORL RH6 279 P10
Low Hall Cl CHING E4 100 F1
Low Hall La WALTH E17 120 D4
Low Hill Rd HLWW/ROY CM19 45 L4
Lowick Rd HRW HA1 114 D2
Lowland Gdns ROMW/RG RM7 124 C5
Lowlands BRKMPK AL9 40 F1
Lowlands Rd HRW HA1 114 D9
PIN HA5 113 K8
SOCK/AV RM15 146 B10
STWL/WRAY TW19 173 N3
Lowman Rd HOLWY N7 118 G9
Lowndes Av CSHM HP5 50 G6
Lowndes Cl KTBR SW1X 16 D4
Lowndes Ct REGST W1B 10 C6
Lowndes Pl KTBR * SW1X 16 C5
Lowndes Sq KTBR SW1X 16 B3
Lowndes St KTBR SW1X 16 B4
Lowood St WCHPL E1 140 A8
Low Rd BRKMPK AL9 42 A4
Lowry Crs MTCM CR4 201 P2
Lowry Rd BCTR RM8 123 L1
Lowshoe La ROMW/RG RM7 104 C5

Lowson Gv OXHEY WD19 93 M1
Low Street La TIL RM18 169 J4
Lowswood Cl NTHWD HA6 92 D9
Lowther Cl BORE WD6 75 L9
Lowther Dr ENC/FH EN2 78 F8
Lowther Hl FSTH SE23 182 D3
Lowther Man BARN * SW13 156 D7
Lowther Rd BARN SW13 156 C7
HOLWY * N7 119 H10
KUTN/CMB KT2 199 L1
STAN HA7 115 L1
WALTH E17 100 D10
Lowth Rd CMBW SE5 159 K8
Loxford Av EHAM E6 142 A4
Loxford La IL IG1 122 F10
Loxford Rd BARK IG11 142 E1
CTHM CR3 259 N1
Loxford Wy CTHM CR3 259 N1
Loxham Rd CHING E4 100 G8
Loxham St STPAN * WC1H 5 M10
Loxley Cl SYD SE26 182 C8
Loxley Ct WARE * SG12 26 D2
Loxley Rd BERK HP4 33 K3
HPTN TW12 175 N7
WAND/EARL SW18 179 N4
Loxton Rd FSTH SE23 182 C4
Loxwood Cl EBED/NFELT TW14 174 E4
STMC/STPC BR5 207 N9
Loxwood Rd TOTM N17 119 M1
Loxwood Wk CRAWW RH11 283 J5
Lubbock Rd CHST BR7 184 C10
Lubbock St NWCR SE14 160 B6
Lucan Dr STA TW18 173 N10
Lucan Pl CHEL SW3 15 N6
Lucan Rd BAR EN5 77 H7
Lucas Av PLSTW E13 141 N3
RYLN/HDSTN HA2 113 P7
Lucas Gdns EFNCH N2 97 M10
Lucas Green Rd CHOB/PIR GU24 230 C1
Lucas Rd GRAYS RM17 167 M2
PGE/AN SE20 182 B9
Lucas Sq GLDGN NW11 117 K4
Lucas St DEPT SE8 160 F8
Lucern Cl CHESW * EN7 61 M3
Lucerne Cl PLMGR N13 98 F4
WOKS/MYFD GU22 232 B5
Lucerne Dr CRAWE RH10 284 E9
Lucerne Gv WALTH E17 121 J2
Lucerne Ms KENS * W8 8 F9
Lucerne Rd HBRY N5 119 J9
ORP BR6 207 J8
THHTH CR7 203 J5
Lucerne Wy HARH RM3 105 L7
Lucey Rd BERM/RHTH SE16 19 N4
Lucey Wy BERM/RHTH SE16 19 P5
Lucie Av ASHF TW15 174 C9
Lucien Rd TOOT SW17 180 B7
WAND/EARL SW18 179 L5
Lucknow St WOOL/PLUM SE18 163 H6
Lucks Hl HHW HP1 35 H6
Lucorn Cl LEE/GVPK SE12 183 L2
Luctons Av BKHH IG9 101 P2
Luddesdon Rd ERITH DA8 164 B6
Luddington Av EGH TW20 194 C2
Ludford Cl CDALE/KGS NW9 96 B10
CROY/NA CR0 223 J1
Ludgate Broadway BLKFR * EC4V 12 D6
Ludgate Circ STP * EC4M 12 C6
Ludgate Hl STP EC4M 12 C6
Ludgate Sq BLKFR * EC4V 12 D6
Ludham Cl THMD SE28 143 M8
Ludlow Cl HAYES BR2 205 M3
RYLN/HDSTN HA2 113 N9
Ludlow Md OXHEY WD19 93 J4
Ludlow Pl GRAYS RM17 167 N2
Ludlow Rd EA W5 135 H6
FELT TW13 175 H6
Ludlow St FSBYE * EC1V 12 E1
Ludlow Wy EFNCH N2 117 M2
RKW/CH/CXG WD3 72 D8
Ludovick Wk PUT/ROE SW15 156 B10
Ludwick Cl WGCE * AL7 23 J7
Ludwick Gn WGCE * AL7 23 J6
Ludwick Wy WGCE AL7 23 J5
Luff Cl WDSR SL4 148 D9
Luffield Rd ABYW SE2 163 L2
Luffman Rd LEE/GVPK SE12 183 N6
Lugard Rd PECK SE15 160 A8
Lugg Ap MNPK E12 122 D8
Luke St SDTCH EC2A 13 J1
Lukin Crs CHING E4 101 J4
Lukin St WCHPL E1 140 B9
Lullarook Cl BH/WHM TN16 243 P2
Lullingstone Av SWLY BR8 208 G3
Lullingstone Cl STMC/STPC BR5 185 L10
Lullingstone Crs STMC/STPC BR5 185 K10
Lullingstone La EYN DA4 209 K10
LEW SE13 183 J2
Lullingstone Rd BELV DA17 164 A5
Lullington Garth BMLY * BR1 183 K10
BORE * WD6 75 P9
MLHL NW7 97 J6
Lullington Rd DAGW RM9 143 P2
PGE/AN SE20 181 P10
Lulworth Av CHESW EN7 61 J5
HEST TW5 154 A7
WBLY HA9 115 H5
Lulworth Cl CRAWW RH11 283 K10
RYLN/HDSTN HA2 113 N8
Lulworth Crs MTCM CR4 201 P2
Lulworth Dr CRW RM5 104 C6
PIN HA5 113 L5
Lulworth Gdns
RYLN/HDSTN HA2 113 M7
Lulworth Rd ELTH/MOT SE9 184 B5
PECK * SE15 160 A8
WELL DA16 163 J8
Lulworth Waye YEAD UB4 133 J8
Lumbards WGCE AL7 23 K2
Lumen Rd WBLY * HA9 115 J7
Lumley Cl BELV DA17 164 B5
Lumley Gdns CHEAM SM3 221 H2
Lumley Rd CHEAM SM3 221 H3
HORL RH6 280 B4
Lumley St MYFR/PKLN W1K 10 D6
Lunar Cl BH/WHM TN16 244 A2
Luna Rd THHTH CR7 203 K3
Lundin Wk OXHEY * WD19 93 L5
Lundy Cl CRAWW RH11 283 M10
Lundy Dr HYS/HAR UB3 152 F3
Lundy Wk IS N1 6 F2
Lunedale Rd RDART DA2 188 B4
Lunghurst Rd CTHM CR3 242 F7
Lunham Rd NRWD SE19 181 M9
Lupin Cl BRXS/STRHM SW2 181 J5
CROY/NA CR0 204 C8
ROMW/RG RM7 124 E7
WDR/YW UB7 151 N4
Luppits Cl RBRW/HUT CM13 107 M2
Lupton Cl LEE/GVPK SE12 183 N7
Lupton St KTTN NW5 118 D9
Lupus St PIM SW1V 17 J7
Lurgan Av HMSMTH W6 156 G5
Lurline Gdns BTSEA SW11 158 B7
Luscombe Wy VX/NE SW8 158 F6
Lushes Ct LOU IG10 82 E9
Lushes Rd LOU IG10 82 E9
Lushington Dr COB KT11 217 J10
Lushington Rd CAT SE6 182 G8
WLSDN NW10 136 E4
Lushington Ter HACK E8 119 P10
Lusted Hall La BH/WHM TN16 243 P6
Lusteds Cl DORK RH4 273 H5
Luther Cl EDGW HA8 95 P3
Luther King Cl WALTH E17 120 D4
Luther King Rd HLW CM20 46 F1
Luthers Cl BRWN CM15 86 D3
Luton Pl GNWCH SE10 161 H6
Luton Rd PLSTW E13 141 M6
SCUP DA14 185 M6
WALTH E17 120 D1
Luton St STJWD NW8 9 M2
Luttrell Av PUT/ROE SW15 178 E1
Lutwyche Rd FSTH SE23 182 E5
Lutyens Cl CRAWW RH11 283 H9
Luxborough La CHIG IG7 102 C5
Luxborough St MHST W1U 10 C2
Luxemburg Gdns HMSMTH W6 156 G3
Luxfield Rd ELTH/MOT SE9 184 B4
Luxford Pl SBW CM21 30 A2
Luxford St BERM/RHTH SE16 160 C3
Luxmore St BROCKY SE4 160 E7
Luxor St CMBW SE5 159 J8
Luxted Rd ORP BR6 226 D8
Lyall Av DUL SE21 181 M7
Lyall Ms KTBR SW1X 16 C4
Lyall Ms West KTBR * SW1X 16 C4
Lyall St KTBR SW1X 16 C4
Lyal Rd BOW E3 140 D4
Lycaste Cl STAL AL1 38 E7
Lycett Pl SHB W12 156 D1
Lych Ga GSTN WD25 55 L9
Lych Gate Rd ORP BR6 207 K8
Lych Gate Wk HYS/HAR UB3 132 G9
Lych Wy WOKN/KNAP GU21 232 A2
Lyconby Gdns CROY/NA CR0 204 D7
Lycrome La CSHM HP5 51 J4
Lycrome Rd CSHM HP5 51 K4
Lydd Cl BFN/LL DA15 185 H6
Lydden Ct WAND/EARL SW18 179 L3
Lydden Gv WAND/EARL SW18 179 L3
Lydd Rd BXLYHN DA7 164 A6
Lydeard Rd EHAM E6 142 C2
Lydele Cl WOKN/KNAP GU21 232 C1
Lydford Av SLN SL2 129 J7
Lydford Cl STNW/STAM N16 119 M10
Lydford Rd CRICK NW2 136 G1
MV/WKIL W9 8 D1
SEVS/STOTM N15 119 L3
Lydhurst Av BRXS/STRHM SW2 180 G5
Lydia Ms BRKMPK AL9 40 F10
Lydia Rd ERITH DA8 164 G5
Lydney Cl PECK SE15 159 M6
WIM/MER SW19 179 H5
Lydon Rd CLAP SW4 158 D9
Lydsey Cl SLN SL2 128 F5
Lydstep Rd CHST BR7 184 D7
Lye Green Rd CSHM HP5 51 K6
Lye La LCOL/BKTW AL2 55 P4
Lyell Rd WDSR SL4 148 B9
The Lye KWD/TDW/WH KT20 238 F8
Lyfield COB KT11 218 A10
Lyford Rd WAND/EARL SW18 179 N3
Lyford St CHARL SE7 162 B3
Lygean Av WARE SG12 26 D2
Lygon Pl BGVA * SW1W 16 E4
Lyham Cl CLAP SW4 180 F2
Lyham Rd BRXS/STRHM SW2 180 F1
Lyle Cl MTCM CR4 202 B7
Lyle Pk SEV TN13 247 J9
Lyles La WGCW AL8 23 H3
Lymbourne Cl BELMT SM2 221 K6
Lymden Gdns REIG RH2 275 L2
Lyme Av BERK HP4 33 J2
Lyme Farm Rd LEE/GVPK SE12 161 M10
Lyme Gv HOM E9 140 B2
Lymer Av NRWD SE19 181 N8
Lyme Regis Rd BNSTD SM7 239 J3
Lyme Rd WELL DA16 163 J7
Lymescote Gdns SUT SM1 201 K9
Lyme St CAMTN NW1 4 G4
Lyme Ter CAMTN NW1 4 G4
Lyminge Cl SCUP DA14 185 J7
Lyminge Gdns WAND/EARL SW18 179 P4
Lymington Av WDGN N22 99 H10
Lymington Cl STRHM/NOR SW16 202 E2
Lymington Ct GSTN * WD25 55 H10
Lymington Dr RSLP HA4 112 E7
Lymington Gdns
HOR/WEW KT19 220 C2
Lymington Rd BCTR RM8 123 N6
KIL/WHAMP NW6 2 G1
Lympstone Gdns PECK SE15 159 P6
Lynbridge Gdns PLMGR N13 99 J5
Lynbrook Cl PECK SE15 159 M6
RAIN RM13 144 E4
Lynceley Gra EPP CM16 65 K5
Lynchen Cl HEST TW5 153 H7
Lynch Cl UX/CGN UB8 131 M2
Lynchen Cl HEST TW5 153 H7
Lynch Hill La SLN SL2 128 D6
The Lynch HOD EN11 44 G3
UX/CGN UB8 131 M2
Lyncourt BKHTH/KID * SE3 161 J8
Lyncroft Av PIN HA5 113 J3
Lyncroft Gdns EW KT17 220 C5
HSLW TW3 176 B1
KIL/WHAMP NW6 117 K10
WEA W13 155 H1
Lyndale BRWN CM15 86 E3
Lyndale Av CRICK NW2 117 J8
ESH/CLAY * KT10 198 D7
Lyndale Av CRICK NW2 117 J8
Lyndale Cl BKHTH/KID SE3 161 L5
Lyndale Hampton Court Wy
ESH/CLAY KT10 198 D7
Lyndale Rd REDH RH1 258 A7
Lynden Wy SWLY BR8 208 D3
Lyndhurst Av BRYLDS KT5 199 N8
MLHL NW7 96 B7
NFNCH/WDSP N12 98 A7
PIN HA5 93 H10
STHL UB1 134 A10
STRHM/NOR SW16 202 E2
SUN TW16 197 H3
WHTN TW2 175 N4
Lyndhurst Cl BXLYHN DA7 164 C9
CRAWW RH11 283 N8
CROY/NA CR0 203 N10
HARP AL5 20 B1
ORP BR6 226 E1
WLSDN NW10 116 A8
WOKN/KNAP GU21 232 A1
Lyndhurst Ct BELMT * SM2 221 K4
Lyndhurst Dr EMPK RM11 125 K6
HARP AL5 20 B1
NWMAL KT3 200 B6
SEV TN13 246 F10
WAN E11 121 H5
Lyndhurst Gdns BARK IG11 143 H1
EN EN1 79 M8
FNCH N3 97 H9
GNTH/NBYPK IG2 122 G4
HAMP NW3 117 N10
PIN HA5 93 J9
Lyndhurst Gv CMBW SE5 159 M8
Lyndhurst Leys HAYES * BR2 205 J2
Lyndhurst Prior SNWD * SE25 203 M3
Lyndhurst Ri CHIG IG7 102 D5
Lyndhurst Rd BXLYHN DA7 164 C9
CHING E4 101 H8
COUL/CHIP CR5 240 B2
CSHM HP5 50 G4
GFD/PVL UB6 134 A6
HAMP NW3 117 N10
REIG RH2 275 K3
THHTH CR7 203 H4
UED N18 99 P5
WDGN N22 99 H7
Lyndhurst Sq PECK SE15 159 N7
Lyndhurst Ter HAMP NW3 117 N10
Lyndhurst Wy BELMT SM2 221 K5
CHERT KT16 195 H10
PECK SE15 159 N7
RBRW/HUT CM13 107 P2
Lyndon Av BFN/LL DA15 185 J1
PIN HA5 93 M7
WLGTN SM6 202 B10
Lyndon Md STALE/WH AL4 21 H9
Lyndon Rd BELV DA17 164 B3
Lyndon Yd TOOT SW17 179 L7
Lyndsey Pl CHESW * EN7 62 A6
Lyndwood Dr WDSR SL4 171 M2
Lyndwood Pde WDSR * SL4 171 M2
Lyne Cl VW GU25 194 C6
Lyne Crs WALTH E17 100 E9
Lyne Crossing Rd CHERT KT16 194 D6
Lynegrove Av ASHF TW15 174 D8
Lyneham Wk CLPT * E5 120 D10
Lyne La CHERT KT16 194 D8
Lyne Rd VW GU25 194 A6
Lynette Av CLAP SW4 180 C2
Lyne Wy HHW HP1 35 J4
Lynford Cl EDGW HA8 95 P9
Lynford Gdns EDGW HA8 95 N4
GDMY/SEVK IG3 123 J7
Lynford Ter ED * N9 99 N2
Lynhurst Crs HGDN/ICK UB10 132 D2
Lynhurst Rd HGDN/ICK UB10 132 D2
Lynmere Rd WELL DA16 163 L8
Lyn Ms STNW/STAM * N16 119 N9
Lynmouth Av EN EN1 79 N10
MRDN SM4 200 G7
Lynmouth Dr RSLP HA4 113 J7
Lynmouth Gdns GFD/PVL UB6 134 G3
HEST TW5 153 L7
Lynmouth Ri STMC/STPC BR5 207 L4
Lynmouth Rd EFNCH N2 118 A1
GFD/PVL UB6 134 G3
STNW/STAM N16 119 N6
WALTH E17 120 D4
WGCE AL7 23 J5
Lynn Cl ASHF TW15 174 E8
KTN/HRWW/W HA3 94 C10
Lynne Cl ORP * BR6 227 J3
SAND/SEL CR2 224 B7
Lynnett Rd BCTR RM8 123 N7
Lynne Wk ESH/CLAY KT10 218 B2
Lynne Wy NTHLT UB5 133 L4
WLSDN NW10 136 B1
Lynn Ms WAN E11 121 K7
Lynn Rd BAL SW12 180 C3
GNTH/NBYPK IG2 122 G5
WAN E11 121 K7
Lynn St ENC/FH EN2 79 L5
Lynn Wk REIG RH2 275 L4
Lynross Cl HARH RM3 105 M10
Lynscott Wy SAND/SEL CR2 223 J5
Lynstead Cl BMLY BR1 205 P2
Lynsted Cl BXLYHS DA6 186 C1
Lynsted Ct BECK BR3 204 D2
Lynsted Gdns ELTH/MOT SE9 162 A10
Lynton Av ACT W3 135 P8
CDALE/KGS NW9 116 C2
NFNCH/WDSP N12 97 N5
ROMW/RG RM7 104 C9
STAL AL1 39 H8
STMC/STPC BR5 207 L4
WEA W13 134 F8
Lynton Cl CHSGTN KT9 219 K1
ISLW TW7 154 E10
WLSDN NW10 116 B10
Lynton Crs GNTH/NBYPK IG2 122 E4
Lynton Est STHWK SE1 19 M6
Lynton Gdns EN EN1 99 M1
FBAR/BDGN N11 98 E7
Lynton Md TRDG/WHET N20 97 K4
Lynton Pde CHES/WCR * EN8 62 C6
Lynton Rd ACT W3 135 M9
CEND/HSY/T N8 118 E3
CHING E4 100 G6
CROY/NA CR0 203 H6
CSHM HP5 50 G4
GVW DA11 190 D4
KIL/WHAMP NW6 2 D6
NWMAL KT3 200 A5
RYLN/HDSTN HA2 113 M7
STHWK SE1 19 M6
Lynton Rd South GVW DA11 190 D4
Lynton Ter ACT * W3 135 P8
Lynwood GUW GU2 267 N1
Lynwood Av COUL/CHIP CR5 240 C1
DTCH/LGLY SL3 150 A2
EGH TW20 172 B9
EW KT17 220 C10
Lynwood Cl RYLN/HDSTN HA2 113 M8
SWFD E18 101 P9
WOKN/KNAP GU21 214 G9
Lynwood Crs ASC SL5 192 D6
Lynwood Dr CRW RM5 104 C8
NTHWD HA6 92 F9
WPK KT4 200 D9
Lynwood Gdns CROY/NA CR0 222 G1
STHL UB1 133 N8
Lynwood Gv ORP BR6 207 H7
WCHMH N21 99 H2
Lynwood Hts RKW/CH/CXG WD3 71 L9
Lynwood Rd EA W5 135 J5
ESH/CLAY KT10 198 E9
EW KT17 220 C10
REDH RH1 258 B8
THDIT KT7 198 E9
TOOT SW17 180 A6
Lynwood Ter WIM/MER * SW19 201 J1
Lynx Hl EHSLY KT24 252 G3
Lyon Meade STAN HA7 95 H9
Lyon Park Av ALP/SUD HA0 135 K1
Lyon Rd HRW HA1 114 E4
ROM RM1 124 G5
WIM/MER SW19 201 M1
WOT/HER KT12 197 M9
Lyons Ct DORK RH4 272 G2
Lyonsdene KWD/TDW/WH KT20 257 J3
Lyonsdown Av BAR EN5 77 M10
Lyonsdown Rd BAR EN5 77 M10
Lyons Dr GUW GU2 249 M5
Lyons Pl STJWD NW8 9 L2
Lyon St IS N1 5 N4
Lyons Wk WKENS W14 14 A5
Lyon Wy GFD/PVL UB6 134 D3
STALE/WH AL4 39 M6
Lyoth Rd STMC/STPC BR5 206 F9
Lyrical Wy HHW HP1 35 L4
Lyric Cl CRAWE RH10 284 E9
Lyric Dr GFD/PVL UB6 134 A6
Lyric Ms SYD SE26 182 B7
Lyric Rd BARN SW13 156 C7
Lysander CDALE/KGS * NW9 96 C9
Lysander Cl HHW HP1 52 C3
Lysander Gdns SURB KT6 199 L6
Lysander Gv ARCH N19 118 E6
Lysander Ms ARCH * N19 118 F6
Lysander Rd CROY/NA CR0 222 G3
RSLP HA4 112 E7
Lysander Wy ABLGY WD5 55 H8
ORP BR6 206 F10
WGCE AL7 23 N4
Lys Hill Gdns HERT/WAS SG14 25 J3
Lysias Rd BAL SW12 180 B2
Lysia St FUL/PGN SW6 156 G6
Lysons Wk PUT/ROE * SW15 178 D1
Lyster Ms COB KT11 217 K9
Lytchet Rd BMLY BR1 183 M10
Lytchet Wy PEND EN3 80 B5
Lytchgate Cl SAND/SEL CR2 223 M4
Lytcott Dr E/WMO/HCT KT8 197 N3
Lytcott Gv EDUL SE22 181 N1
Lytham Av OXHEY WD19 93 L6
Lytham Cl THMD SE28 143 P8
Lytham Gv EA W5 135 K5
Lytham St WALW SE17 18 G8
Lyttelton Rd LEY E10 120 G8
Lyttleton Cl HAMP NW3 3 N4
Lyttleton Rd CEND/HSY/T * N8 119 H1
Lytton Av PEND EN3 80 D4
PLMGR N13 99 H3
Lytton Cl EFNCH N2 117 N3
NTHLT UB5 133 N2
Lytton Dr CRAWE RH10 284 E6
Lytton Gdns WGCW AL8 22 G5
WLGTN SM6 222 E1
Lytton Gv PUT/ROE SW15 178 G1
Lytton Rd BAR EN5 77 M8
CDH/CHF RM16 168 D3
GPK RM2 125 J3
PIN HA5 93 M8
WAN E11 121 K5
WOKS/MYFD GU22 232 E2
Lyttons Wy HOD EN11 26 F10
Lyveden Rd BKHTH/KID SE3 161 N6
WIM/MER SW19 179 P9
Lywood Cl KWD/TDW/WH KT20 238 F8

M

Mabbotts KWD/TDW/WH KT20 238 G7
Mabbutt Cl LCOL/BKTW AL2 55 M6
Mabel Rd SWLY BR8 187 H9
Mabel St WOKN/KNAP GU21 232 A4
Maberley Crs NRWD SE19 181 P10
Maberley Rd BECK BR3 204 C3
NRWD SE19 203 N1
Mabey's Wk SBW CM21 29 L2
Mabledon Pl CAMTN NW1 5 K10
Mablethorpe Rd FUL/PGN SW6 157 H6
Mabley St HOM E9 120 D10
Macaret Cl TRDG/WHET N20 97 L1
Macarthur Cl FSTGT E7 141 M1
Macarthur Ter CHARL * SE7 162 A5
Macaulay Av ESH/CLAY KT10 198 D9
Macaulay Rd CLAP SW4 158 C9
CTHM CR3 241 M8
EHAM E6 142 A4
Macbean St WOOL/PLUM SE18 162 D2
Macbeth St HMSMTH W6 156 E4
Macclesfield Br STJWD NW8 3 P7
Macclesfield Rd FSBYE EC1V 6 E9
SNWD SE25 204 A5
Macclesfield St SOHO/SHAV W1D 11 K7
Macdonald Av DAGE RM10 124 C8
EMPK RM11 125 M2
Macdonald Cl AMS HP6 69 H1
Macdonald Rd ARCH N19 118 D7
FBAR/BDGN N11 98 A6
FSTGT E7 121 M9
WALTH E17 101 H10
Macdonald Wy EMPK RM11 125 M2
Macdonnell Gdns GSTN WD25 72 G1
Macduff Rd BTSEA SW11 158 B7
Mace Cl WAP E1W 140 A10
Mace Gtwy CAN/RD E16 141 M9
Mace La RSEV TN14 226 G9
Macer's La BROX EN10 44 E10
Mace St BETH E2 140 C4
Macfarlane La ISLW TW7 154 E5
Macfarlane Rd SHB W12 136 F10
Mac Farren Pl CAMTN NW1 10 D2
Macgregor Rd CAN/RD E16 141 P7
Machell Rd PECK SE15 160 B9
Macintosh Cl CHESW EN7 61 L2
Mackay Rd CLAP SW4 158 C9
Mackennal St STJWD NW8 3 P8
Mackenzie Cl SHB * W12 136 E9
Mackenzie Rd BECK BR3 204 D1
HOLWY N7 5 N1
Mackenzie St SL SL1 149 L1
Mackenzie Wy GVE DA12 190 G9
Mackeson Rd HAMP * NW3 118 A9
Mackie Rd BRXS/STRHM SW2 181 H3
Mackies Hl SHGR GU5 270 E10
Mackintosh La HOM E9 120 C10
Macklin St HOL/ALD * WC2B 11 M5
Macks Rd BERM/RHTH SE16 19 P5
Mackworth St CAMTN NW1 4 G9
Maclean Rd FSTH SE23 182 D2
Maclean Ter GVE * DA12 191 J5
Maclennan Av RAIN RM13 145 L5
Macleod Cl GRAYS RM17 168 A3
Macleod Rd STHGT/OAK N14 78 F9
Macleod St WALW SE17 18 F8
Maclise Rd WKENS W14 14 A4
Macoma Rd WOOL/PLUM SE18 162 G5
Macoma Ter WOOL/PLUM SE18 162 G5
Maconochies Rd POP/IOD * E14 160 G4
Macon Wy UPMR RM14 126 E4
Macquarie Wy POP/IOD E14 160 G3
Macroom Rd MV/WKIL W9 2 D9
Madan Rd BH/WHM TN16 262 G1
Mada Rd ORP BR6 206 E10
Maddams St BOW E3 140 G6
Madden Cl SWCM DA10 189 K2
Maddesfield Ct RAD WD7 57 K9
Maddison Cl TEDD TW11 176 E9
Maddocks Cl SCUP DA14 185 N9
Maddock Wy WALW SE17 18 C10
Maddox La GT/LBKH KT23 235 M10
Maddox Pk GT/LBKH KT23 235 M9
Maddox Rd HHNE HP2 36 C6
HLW CM20 29 H10
Maddox St MYFR/PKLN W1K 10 F7
Madehurst Ct CRAWW RH11 283 J10
Madeira Av BMLY BR1 205 K1
Madeira Crs BF/WBF KT14 215 J9
Madeira Gv WFD IG8 101 P7
Madeira Rd BF/WBF KT14 215 J9
MTCM CR4 202 A4
PLMGR N13 99 J5
STRHM/NOR SW16 180 F8
WAN E11 121 J6
Madeira Wk EPSOM KT18 220 A10
REIG RH2 257 N9
WDSR SL4 149 J7
Madeley Rd EA W5 135 K8
Madeline Gv IL IG1 122 G10
Madeline Rd PGE/AN SE20 181 P10
Madells EPP CM16 65 J7
Madge Gill Wy EHAM E6 142 B3
Madge Hl HNWL * W7 134 D9
Madgeways Cl WARE * SG12 26 E6
Madgeways La WARE SG12 26 E6
Madinah Rd HACK E8 7 N1
Madison Crs WELL DA16 163 M6
Madison Gdns BXLYHN DA7 163 M6
Madison Wy SEV TN13 246 G9
Madras Pl HOLWY N7 6 A1
Madras Rd IL IG1 122 E9
Madrid Rd BARN SW13 156 D7
GUW GU2 267 N1
Madron St STHWK SE1 19 K7
Maesmaur Rd BH/WHM TN16 244 A7
Mafeking Av BTFD TW8 155 K5
EHAM E6 142 A4
GNTH/NBYPK IG2 122 G5
Mafeking Rd CAN/RD E16 141 L6
EN EN1 79 N7
STWL/WRAY TW19 172 E5
TOTM N17 99 P10
Magazine Ga BAY/PAD * W2 9 P9
Magazine Pl LHD/OX KT22 236 G8
Magazine Rd CTHM CR3 241 J8
Magdala Av KTTN NW5 118 D7
Magdala Rd ISLW TW7 154 F9
SAND/SEL CR2 223 L4
Magdalen Cl BF/WBF KT14 215 P10
Magdalen Crs BF/WBF KT14 215 P10
Magdalene Cl CRAWE RH10 284 D4
Magdalene Gdns EHAM E6 142 D6
Magdalene Rd SHPTN TW17 196 A4
Magdalen Rd WAND/EARL SW18 179 M4
Magdalen St STHWK SE1 13 J10
Magdelan Gv ORP BR6 227 L1
Magee St LBTH SE11 18 A9
Magellan Ter CRAWE * RH10 284 B3
Magna Carta La
STWL/WRAY TW19 172 A4
Magna Cl HARP AL5 20 C5
Magna Rd EGH TW20 171 N9
Magnaville Rd BUSH WD23 94 D1
Magnet Rd WBLY * HA9 115 J7
WTHK RM20 167 H5
Magnin Cl HACK * E8 7 P5
Magnolia Av ABLGY WD5 54 G8
Magnolia Cl HERT/BAY SG13 25 P5
KUTN/CMB KT2 177 N9
LCOL/BKTW AL2 56 C2
LEY E10 120 F7
SOCK/AV RM15 147 K6
Magnolia Ct HGDN/ICK * UB10 132 C1
HORL * RH6 280 B4
KTN/HRWW/W HA3 115 L5
Magnolia Dr BH/WHM TN16 244 A2
Magnolia Gdns DTCH/LGLY SL3 149 N2
EDGW HA8 95 P5
Magnolia Pl CLAP * SW4 180 F1
EA * W5 135 J7
GU * GU1 249 P7
Magnolia Rd CHSWK W4 155 N5
Magnolia St WDR/YW UB7 151 N3
Magnolia Wy BRWN CM15 86 G9
HOR/WEW KT19 219 P2
RDKG RH5 273 J5
Magnolia Whf CHSWK * W4 155 N5
Magnum Cl RAIN RM13 145 K6
Magpie Cl CDALE/KGS NW9 96 B10
COUL/CHIP CR5 240 D4
EN EN1 79 P5
FSTGT E7 121 L10
Magpie Hall Cl HAYES BR2 206 B6
Magpie Hall La HAYES BR2 206 B7
HAYES BR2 206 C5
Magpie Hall Rd BUSH WD23 94 D3
Magpie La AMSS HP7 88 F2
RBRW/HUT CM13 107 J10
Magpie Pl GSTN * WD25 55 K8
NWCR * SE14 160 D5
Magpies EPP CM16 46 D10
Magri Wk WCHPL E1 140 B7
Maguire Dr RCHPK/HAM TW10 177 H7
Maguire St STHWK SE1 19 M1
Mahlon Av RSLP HA4 113 J10
Mahogany Cl BERM/RHTH SE16 140 D10
Mahon Cl EN EN1 79 N5
Mahonia Cl CHOB/PIR * GU24 212 E9
Maida Av BAY/PAD W2 9 K3
CHING E4 100 G1
Maida Rd BELV DA17 164 B2
Maida V KIL/WHAMP NW6 3 H8
Maida Vale Rd DART DA1 187 H2
Maida Wy CHING E4 100 G1
Maidenbower Dr CRAWE RH10 284 D9
Maidenbower La CRAWE RH10 284 C9
Maidenbower Pl CRAWE RH10 284 D9
Maiden Erlegh Av BXLY DA5 185 P4
Maidenhead Rd WDSR SL4 148 D6
Maidenhead St HERT/WAS SG14 25 L5
Maidenhead Yd HERT/WAS SG14 25 L5
Maiden La CAMTN NW1 5 K3
CRAWW RH11 283 M5
DART DA1 165 H10

STHWK SE1 12 F10
Maiden Rd SRTFD E15 141 K2
Maidens Br ENC/FH * EN2 79 P3
Maidenshaw Rd
HOR/WEW KT19 220 A8
Maidenstone Hl GNWCH SE10 161 H7
Maidstone Av CRW RM5 104 D10
Maidstone Buildings Ms
STHWK SE1 12 F10
Maidstone Rd FBAR/BDGN N11 98 E7
GRAYS RM17 167 M5
SCUP DA14 186 A10
Main Av EN EN1 79 N9
NTHWD HA6 92 D4
Main Barracks
WOOL/PLUM * SE18 162 C4
Main Dr CFSP/GDCR SL9 109 P3
GFD/PVL * UB6 134 F5
IVER SL0 151 H2
WBLY * HA9 115 J8
Main Ga TIL * RM18 168 C8
Mainridge Rd CHST BR7 184 D7
Main Rd BFN/LL DA15 185 H6
BH/WHM TN16 225 P9
BH/WHM TN16 244 A2
EDEN TN8 262 F10
EYN DA4 188 A9
EYN DA4 209 M6
GPK RM2 105 K10
HART DA3 211 K2
ORP * BR6 227 M5
RDART DA2 211 H1
ROM RM1 124 G2
RSEV TN14 245 K4
RSEV TN14 245 P10
STMC/STPC BR5 207 M3
SWLY BR8 208 D6
SWLY BR8 208 G1
WDSR * SL4 148 B6
Main Road Gorse Hl EYN DA4 210 A8
Mainstone Crs CHOB/PIR GU24 230 C7
Mainstone Rd CHOB/PIR GU24 230 E2
Main St ADL/WDHM KT15 195 P10
FELT TW13 175 L8
Maise Webster Cl
STWL/WRAY * TW19 173 N3
Maismore St PECK SE15 19 N10
The Maisonettes SUT * SM1 221 J2
Maitland Cl BF/WBF KT14 215 K9
GNWCH SE10 160 G6
HSLWW TW4 153 N9
WOT/HER KT12 197 M9
Maitland Park Rd HAMP NW3 4 B2
Maitland Park Vls HAMP NW3 4 B1
Maitland Rd SRTFD * E15 141 L1
SYD SE26 182 C9
Maizecroft HORL RH6 280 D3
Maizey Ct BRWN CM15 86 F9
Majendie Rd WOOL/PLUM SE18 162 G4
Major Rd BERM/RHTH SE16 19 P3
SRTFD E15 121 H10
Major's Farm Rd DTCH/LGLY SL3 150 A6
Major's Hl CRAWE RH10 285 L9
Makepeace Av HGT N6 118 B7
Makepeace Rd NTHLT UB5 133 M4
WAN E11 121 M2
Makins St CHEL SW3 15 P6
Malabar St POP/IOD E14 160 F1
Malacca Farm RGUE GU4 251 L4
Malam Gdns POP/IOD E14 140 G9
Malan Cl BH/WHM TN16 244 B3
Malan Sq RAIN RM13 145 J1
Malborough Rd WATW WD18 73 J8
Malbrook Rd PUT/ROE SW15 156 E10
Malcolm Cl PGE/AN * SE20 182 B10
Malcolm Ct STAN HA7 95 H6
Malcolm Crs HDN NW4 116 D3
Malcolm Dr SURB KT6 199 J8
Malcolm Gdns HORL RH6 279 N6
Malcolm Gavin Cl TOOT SW17 179 P5
Malcolm Pl BETH E2 140 B6
Malcolm Rd COUL/CHIP CR5 240 E1
HGDN/ICK UB10 112 A9
PGE/AN SE20 182 B10
SNWD SE25 203 P6
WCHPL E1 140 B6
WIM/MER SW19 179 H9
Malcolm Wy WAN E11 121 M3
Malden Av NTHLT UB5 134 D1
SNWD SE25 204 A4
Malden Crs KTTN NW5 4 D2
Malden Flds BUSH WD23 73 L9
Malden Green Av WPK KT4 200 C8
Malden Hl NWMAL KT3 200 C4
Malden Hill Gdns NWMAL KT3 200 C3
Malden Pk NWMAL KT3 200 C6
Malden Pl KTTN NW5 118 B10
Malden Rd BORE WD6 75 M7
CHEAM SM3 220 G1
KTTN NW5 118 A10
WAT * WD17 73 J6
WPK KT4 200 C7
Malden Wy NWMAL KT3 200 C5
Malden Wy (Kingston By-Pass)
NWMAL KT3 200 B6
Maldon Cl CMBW * SE5 159 M9
IS N1 6 E5
Maldon Ct HARP AL5 20 A1
Maldon Rd ACT W3 135 P9
ED N9 99 N4
ROMW/RG RM7 124 D5
WLGTN SM6 222 C2
Maldon Wk WFD IG8 101 P7
Malet Cl EGH * TW20 172 G9
Malet St GWRST WC1E 11 J2
Maley Av WNWD SE27 181 J5
Malford Gv SWFD E18 121 M1
Malfort Rd CMBW SE5 159 M9
Malham Cl CRAWE RH10 284 D10
FBAR/BDGN N11 98 B7
Malham Rd FSTH SE23 182 C4
Malham Ter UED * N18 100 A7
Malins Cl BAR * EN5 76 E9
Malkin Dr BEAC HP9 88 B8
HLWE CM17 47 P2
Mallams Ms BRXN/ST SW9 159 H9
Mallard Cl BAR * EN5 77 N10
DART DA1 187 N1
HORL RH6 280 B2
HSLWW TW4 175 P3
KIL/WHAMP NW6 2 F6
REDH RH1 258 B7
UPMR RM14 126 E5
Mallard Ct DORK * RH4 272 F1
WALTH * E17 121 J1
Mallard Dr SL SL1 128 E9
Mallard Pl TWK TW1 176 F6
WDGN * N22 98 G10
Mallard Rd ABLGY WD5 55 H7
SAND/SEL CR2 224 C6
Mallards Ct OXHEY * WD19 93 N4
Mallard's Reach WEY KT13 196 E9
Mallards Ri HLWE CM17 47 M1
Mallards Rd WFD IG8 101 N8
The Mallards HHS/BOV HP3 54 A1
STA TW18 195 L2
Mallard Wk CROY/NA CR0 204 C5
Mallard Wy CDALE/KGS NW9 115 P5
GSTN WD25 73 M2
NTHWD HA6 92 D8
RBRW/HUT CM13 107 M1
WLGTN SM6 222 D5
Mall Chambers KENS * W8 8 F9
Mallet Dr NTHLT UB5 113 N10
Mallet Rd LEW SE13 183 J2
Malling Cl CROY/NA * CR0 204 B6
Malling Gdns MRDN SM4 201 M6
Malling Wy HAYES BR2 205 L7
Mallinson Cl HCH RM12 125 K10
Mallinson Rd BTSEA SW11 179 P1
WLGTN SM6 202 E10
Mallion Ct WAB EN9 63 L9
Mallord St CHEL SW3 15 M9
Mallory Cl BROCKY SE4 160 D10
Mallory Gdns EBAR EN4 98 B1
Mallory St CAMTN NW1 9 P2
Mallow Cl CROY/NA CR0 204 C8
GVW DA11 190 B7
KWD/TDW/WH KT20 238 E5
Mallow Ct GRAYS RM17 168 A5
Mallow Crs RGUE GU4 250 E7
Mallow Md MLHL NW7 97 H8
Mallows Gn HLWW/ROY CM19 46 D5
The Mallows HGDN/ICK UB10 112 C8
Mallow St FSBYE EC1V 12 G1
Mallow Wk CHESW * EN7 61 L4
Mall Rd HMSMTH W6 156 E4
The Mall BTFD * TW8 155 J5
BXLYHS * DA6 164 B10
EA W5 135 K9
HCH RM12 125 J6
KTN/HRWW/W HA3 115 L4
LCOL/BKTW AL2 56 B3
MORT/ESHN SW14 177 P1
SRTFD * E15 141 J2
STHGT/OAK N14 98 F4
SURB KT6 199 J5
WHALL SW1A 16 G1
Mall Vls HMSMTH * W6 156 E4
Mallys Pl EYN DA4 210 B1
Malmains Cl BECK BR3 205 J5
Malmains Wy BECK BR3 205 H4
Malm Cl RKW/CH/CXG WD3 91 N3
Malmesbury Cl PIN HA5 113 H2
Malmesbury Rd BOW E3 140 E4
CAN/RD E16 141 K7
MRDN SM4 201 M7
SWFD E18 101 L9
Malmesbury Ter CAN/RD E16 141 L7
Malmesbury West Est BOW E3 140 E5
Malmes Cft HHS/BOV HP3 36 D8
Malmsdale WGCW AL8 22 G1
Malmstone Av REDH RH1 258 D4
Malory Cl BECK BR3 204 C1
Malpas Dr PIN HA5 113 L3
Malpas Rd BROCKY SE4 160 E8
CDH/CHF RM16 168 F2
DAGW RM9 143 N1
HACK E8 140 A1
SLN SL2 129 N9
Malta Rd LEY E10 120 F6
TIL RM18 168 C8
Malta St FSBYE EC1V 12 C1
Maltby Cl ORP BR6 207 K8
Maltby Dr EN EN1 80 A4
Maltby Rd CHSGTN KT9 219 M3
Maltby St STHWK SE1 19 L2
Malt Hl EGH TW20 172 B8
Malt House Cl WDSR SL4 171 N3
Malthouse Ct CHOB/PIR * GU24 212 E8
RGUE * GU4 268 B5
Malthouse Dr FELT TW13 175 L8
Malthouse La CHOB/PIR GU24 212 E8
GVE DA12 191 P8
RGUW GU3 231 H10
Malthouse Ms DEN/HRF * UB9 91 M9
Malthouse Rd CRAWE RH10 283 N8
Malthouse Sq BEAC HP9 108 E1
The Malthouse HERT/WAS * SG14 25 L5
Malting Md HAT * AL10 40 F3
Maltings Ms HERT/BAY * SG13 25 K6
Maltings Dr STALE/WH AL4 21 H4
Maltings Hl CHONG CM5 49 L6
Maltings La EPP CM16 65 K5
Maltings Pl FUL/PGN SW6 157 L7
The Maltings AMSS * HP7 68 G5
BF/WBF KT14 215 P9
HERT/BAY * SG13 25 M5
HHNE * HP2 35 N4
KGLGY WD4 54 D9
ORP BR6 207 J8
OXTED RH8 261 L7
ROM RM1 124 G5
SHGR * GU5 270 D5
SNWD * SE25 203 M3
STA TW18 173 H7
Malting Wy ISLW TW7 154 E9
Maltmans La CFSP/GDCR SL9 109 P1
Malton Av SL SL1 128 G8
Malton Ms NKENS * W10 8 A5
WOOL/PLUM SE18 163 H5
Malton Rd NKENS W10 8 A5
Malton St WOOL/PLUM SE18 163 H5
Maltravers St TPL/STR WC2R 11 P7
Malt St STHWK SE1 19 N9
Malus Cl ADL/WDHM KT15 215 J4
HHNE HP2 36 B6
Malus Dr ADL/WDHM KT15 215 J4
Malva Cl WAND/EARL SW18 179 L1
Malvern Av BXLYHN DA7 163 P6
CHING E4 101 J8
RYLN/HDSTN HA2 113 M8
Malvern Cl CHERT KT16 214 F3
HGDN/ICK UB10 112 B7
MTCM CR4 202 D3
NKENS W10 8 C4
STALE/WH AL4 22 E10
SURB KT6 199 K8
Malvern Dr FELT TW13 175 L8
GDMY/SEVK IG3 123 J9
WFD IG8 101 P6
Malvern Gdns CRICK NW2 117 H7
KTN/HRWW/W HA3 115 K2
LOU IG10 82 C10
Malvern Ms KIL/WHAMP NW6 2 E10
Malvern Pl MV/WKIL W9 2 D9
Malvern Rd CEND/HSY/T N8 118 G1
CRAWW RH11 283 M9
EHAM E6 142 B3
EMPK RM11 125 H4
GRAYS RM17 168 B3
HACK E8 7 N4
HPTN TW12 197 P1
HYS/HAR UB3 152 F6
KIL/WHAMP * NW6 2 D8
ORP BR6 227 L1
PEND EN3 80 D3
SURB KT6 199 K9
THHTH CR7 203 H4
TOTM N17 119 P1
WAN E11 121 K7
Malvern Ter ED N9 99 N2
IS N1 6 A5
Malvern Wy HHNE HP2 35 P4
RKW/CH/CXG WD3 72 C9
WEA W13 134 G7
Malvina Av GVE DA12 190 E5
Malwood Rd BAL SW12 180 C2
Malyons Rd LEW SE13 182 G1
SWLY BR8 186 G10
Malyons Ter BROCKY SE4 182 G1
The Malyons SHPTN * TW17 196 E6
Managers St POP/IOD * E14 141 H10
Manan Cl HHS/BOV HP3 36 D8
Manaton Cl PECK SE15 160 A9
Manaton Crs STHL UB1 133 P8
Manbey Gv SRTFD E15 141 K1
Manbey Park Rd SRTFD E15 141 K1
Manbey Rd SRTFD * E15 141 K1
Manbey St SRTFD E15 141 K1
Manbre Rd HMSMTH W6 156 F5
Manbrough Av EHAM E6 142 C5
Manchester Dr NKENS W10 8 A2
Manchester Gv POP/IOD E14 161 H4
Manchester Ms MHST W1U 10 C4
Manchester Rd POP/IOD E14 161 H4
SEVS/STOTM N15 119 L4
THHTH CR7 203 K3
Manchester Sq MBLAR W1H 10 D5
Manchester St MHST W1U 10 C4
Manchester Wy DAGE * RM10 124 C9
Manchuria Rd BTSEA SW11 180 B2
Manciple St STHWK SE1 19 H2
Mandalay Rd CLAP SW4 180 D1
Mandarin Wy YEAD UB4 133 L8
Mandela Cl WLSDN NW10 135 P2
Mandela Pl WATN WD24 73 L6
Mandela Rd CAN/RD E16 141 M8
Mandela St BRXN/ST SW9 159 H6
CAMTN NW1 5 H5
Mandela Wy STHWK SE1 19 K5
Mandelyns BERK HP4 33 K2
Mandeville Cl BROX EN10 44 E6
GUW GU2 249 M7
HERT/BAY SG13 25 K8
WAT WD17 72 G4
WIM/MER SW19 179 H10
Mandeville Dr STAL AL1 38 C9
SURB KT6 199 J8
Mandeville Pl MHST W1U 10 D5
Mandeville Ri WGCW AL8 22 G3
Mandeville Rd HERT/BAY SG13 25 K8
ISLW TW7 154 F8
NTHLT UB5 133 P1
PEND EN3 80 D3
POTB/CUF EN6 59 M8
SHPTN TW17 196 B5
STHGT/OAK N14 98 C3
Mandeville St CLPT E5 120 D8
Mandrake Rd TOOT SW17 180 A6
Mandrake Wy SRTFD * E15 141 K2
Mandrell Rd BRXS/STRHM SW2 180 F1
Manette St SOHO/SHAV W1D 11 K6
Manfield Cl SLN SL2 128 F5
Manford Cl CHIG IG7 103 L5
Manford Cross CHIG IG7 103 K6
Manford Wy CHIG IG7 103 K6
Manfred Rd PUT/ROE SW15 179 J1
Manger Rd HOLWY N7 5 M1
Mangles Rd GU GU1 250 A8
Mangrove Dr HERT/BAY SG13 25 M7
Mangrove La HERT/BAY SG13 25 M8
Mangrove Rd HERT/BAY SG13 25 M6
Manilla St POP/IOD E14 160 F1
Manister Rd ABYW SE2 163 K2
Manland Av HARP AL5 20 B1
Manland Wy HARP AL5 20 B1
Manley Ct STNW/STAM N16 119 N8
Manley Rd HHNE HP2 35 P5
Manley St CAMTN NW1 4 C5
Manly Dixon Dr PEND EN3 80 D3
Mannamead EPSOM KT18 238 B5
Mannamead Cl EPSOM KT18 238 B5
Mann Cl CROY/NA CR0 203 K10
Mannicotts WGCW AL8 22 E5
Manningford Cl FSBYE * EC1V 6 C9
Manning Gdns
KTN/HRWW/W HA3 115 J5
Manning Pl RCHPK/HAM TW10 177 L2
Manning Rd DAGE RM10 144 B2
STMC/STPC BR5 207 N5
WALTH E17 120 D2
Mannings Cl CRAWE RH10 284 E4
Manning St SOCK/AV RM15 146 B10
Manningtree Cl WIM/MER SW19 179 H4
Manningtree Rd RSLP HA4 113 J9
Manningtree St WCHPL E1 13 N5
Mannin Rd CHDH RM6 123 L5
Mannock Dr LOU IG10 82 F6
Mannock Rd DART DA1 165 N9
WDGN N22 119 J1
Mann's Cl ISLW TW7 176 E1
Manns Rd EDGW HA8 95 M7
Manoel Rd WHTN TW2 176 B5
Manor Av BROCKY SE4 160 E8
CTHM CR3 241 M10
EMPK RM11 125 K3
HHS/BOV HP3 35 N9
HSLWW TW4 153 L9
NTHLT UB5 133 N2
Manorbrook BKHTH/KID SE3 161 M10
Manor Cha WEY KT13 216 C2
Manor Cl BAR EN5 77 H8
BERK * HP4 33 P5
CDALE/KGS NW9 115 N2
DAGE RM10 144 E1
DART DA1 164 E10
EHSLY KT24 252 F4
GVE DA12 191 L5
HAT AL10 40 C1
HERT/WAS SG14 25 L3
HORL RH6 280 A4
MLHL * NW7 96 A6
RDART DA2 187 H6
ROM RM1 125 H3
RSLP HA4 112 G6
SOCK/AV RM15 146 B10
THMD SE28 143 M8
WARL CR6 242 D3
WOKS/MYFD GU22 233 J2
WPK KT4 200 B8
Manor Cottages NTHWD HA6 92 G9
Manor Cottages Ap EFNCH N2 97 M10
Manor Ct ACT * W3 155 M3
ALP/SUD * HA0 115 K10
CHES/WCR * EN8 62 C7
DEN/HRF UB9 91 M10
E/WMO/HCT * KT8 197 P4
EN EN1 80 A2
HRW * HA1 114 E4
KUTN/CMB * KT2 199 M1
POTB/CUF * EN6 59 J8
RAD WD7 74 E3
SL SL1 128 E10
WEY KT13 216 C1
Manor Court Rd HNWL W7 134 D9
Manor Crs BEAC HP9 89 J6
BF/WBF KT14 216 A9
BRYLDS KT5 199 M6
CHOB/PIR GU24 230 C6
EMPK RM11 125 K3
GUW GU2 249 N8
HOR/WEW KT19 219 M8
Manor Cft EDGW * HA8 95 M7
Manor Croft Pde
CHES/WCR * EN8 62 C6
Manorcrofts Rd EGH TW20 172 D9
Manordene Cl THDIT KT7 198 F8
Manordene Rd THMD SE28 143 M8
Manor Dr ADL/WDHM KT15 215 K6
AMS HP6 68 G2
BRYLDS KT5 199 M6
ESH/CLAY KT10 198 E10
FELT TW13 175 L8
HART DA3 211 M6
HOR/WEW KT19 220 B3
HORL RH6 280 A4
LCOL/BKTW AL2 55 P3
MLHL NW7 96 A6
STHGT/OAK N14 98 C1
SUN TW16 197 H2
TRDG/WHET N20 97 P4
WBLY HA9 115 L9
Manor Dr North NWMAL KT3 200 A7
WPK KT4 200 B8
The Manor Dr WPK KT4 200 B8
Manor Est BERM/RHTH SE16 160 A3
Manor Farm Av SHPTN TW17 196 C6
Manor Farm Cl WDSR SL4 148 E9
Manor Farm Cottages WDSR SL4 171 M1
Manor Farm Ct EGH * TW20 172 D8
Manor Farm Dr CHING E4 101 K4
Manor Farm La EGH TW20 172 D8
Manor Farm Rd ALP/SUD HA0 135 J4
EN EN1 80 A1
STRHM/NOR SW16 203 H2
Manor Fld GVE DA12 191 P8
Manorfields Cl CHST BR7 207 J3
Manor Forstal HART DA3 211 L10
Manor Gdns ACT W3 155 M3
EHSLY KT24 253 L4
GUW GU2 249 N8
HOLWY N7 118 F8
HPTN TW12 176 A10
RCH/KEW TW9 155 L10
RGODL GU7 267 K10
RSLP HA4 113 K10
RYNPK SW20 201 J2
SAND/SEL CR2 223 N3
SUN TW16 197 H1
VX/NE * SW8 158 D8
Manor Ga NTHLT UB5 133 M2
Manorgate Rd KUTN/CMB KT2 199 M1
Manor Green Rd HOR/WEW KT19 219 P8
Manor Gv BECK BR3 204 G2
PECK SE15 160 B5
RCH/KEW TW9 155 M10
Manor Hall Av HDN NW4 96 F10
Manor Hall Dr HDN NW4 96 G10
Manor Hall Gdns LEY E10 120 F6
Manor Hatch HLWS CM18 47 K2
Manor Hatch Cl HLWS CM18 47 L2
Manor Hl BNSTD SM7 240 A1
Manor House Ct EPSOM * KT18 219 P9
SHPTN * TW17 196 C7
Manor House Dr
KIL/WHAMP NW6 136 G2
NTHWD HA6 92 C8
Manor House Gdns ABLGY WD5 54 E7
Manor House La DTCH/LGLY SL3 149 N7
Manorhouse La GT/LBKH KT23 253 M2
Manor House Wy ISLW TW7 154 G9
Manor La CFSP/GDCR SL9 110 A5
FELT TW13 175 H5
HART DA3 211 H7
HART DA3 211 M6
HYS/HAR UB3 152 E5
KWD/TDW/WH KT20 257 K5
LEW SE13 183 K1
SUN TW16 197 H2
SUT SM1 221 M2
Manor Lane Ter LEW SE13 161 K10
Manor Leaze EGH TW20 172 E8
Manor Ldg GUW * GU2 249 N8
Manor Ms KIL/WHAMP NW6 2 F7
Manor Mt FSTH SE23 182 B4
Manor Pde HAT AL10 40 C1
HRW * HA1 114 E4
STNW/STAM * N16 119 N7
Manor Pk CHST BR7 206 G2
LEW SE13 183 J1
RCH/KEW TW9 155 L10
STA TW18 172 G6
Manor Park Cl WWKM BR4 204 G8
Manor Park Crs EDGW HA8 95 M7
Manor Park Dr RYLN/HDSTN HA2 114 A1
Manor Park Gdns EDGW HA8 95 M6
Manor Park Rd CHST BR7 206 F1
EFNCH N2 117 M1
MNPK E12 122 A9
SUT SM1 221 M2
WLSDN NW10 136 B3
WWKM BR4 204 G8
Manor Pl BORE * WD6 75 P7
CHST BR7 206 G2
EBED/NFELT TW14 175 H4
GT/LBKH KT23 253 P2
MTCM CR4 202 D3
STA TW18 173 L8
SUT SM1 221 L2
WALW SE17 18 D8
Manor Rd AB/ST RM4 103 N2
ASHF TW15 174 A8
BAR EN5 77 H8
BEAC HP9 89 J6
BECK BR3 204 F2
BELMT SM2 221 J4
BFN/LL DA15 185 J6
BH/WHM TN16 224 B6
BXLY DA5 186 C4
CAN/RD E16 141 K7
CHDH RM6 123 N4
CHIG IG7 102 D7
CSHM HP5 50 G5
DAGE RM10 144 D1
DART DA1 164 F10
E/WMO/HCT KT8 198 C4
ENC/FH EN2 79 L6
ERITH DA8 164 G5
GRAYS RM17 167 P5
GUW GU2 249 N8
GVE * DA12 190 E2
HART DA3 211 P5
HAT AL10 40 C1
HLWE CM17 29 M6
HOD EN11 44 F1
HRW HA1 114 F4
HYS/HAR UB3 133 H8
LCOL/BKTW AL2 57 H2
LEY E10 120 F5
LOU IG10 81 N4
LOU IG10 81 N10
MTCM CR4 202 D3
POTB/CUF EN6 59 J7
RCH/KEW TW9 155 L9
REDH RH1 258 D5
REIG RH2 257 J8
ROM RM1 125 H3
RPLY/SEND GU23 233 J9
RSEV TN14 245 N10
RSLP HA4 112 E6
RYNPK SW20 201 J2
SNWD SE25 203 P3
STAL AL1 38 D5
STALE/WH AL4 20 E1
STNW/STAM N16 119 M6
SWCM DA10 189 J2
TEDD TW11 176 F8
TIL RM18 168 D8
TOTM N17 99 P9
WAB EN9 63 J9
WALTH E17 100 D10
WAT WD17 73 J5
WDGN N22 98 F7
WDSR SL4 148 D8
WEA W13 134 F9
WHTN TW2 176 B5
WLGTN SM6 222 C2
WOKN/KNAP GU21 231 P2
WOT/HER KT12 196 G7
WTHK RM20 167 H5
WWKM BR4 204 G9
Manor Rd North ESH/CLAY KT10 198 E10
WLGTN SM6 222 C1
Manor Rd South ESH/CLAY KT10 218 D1
Manor Royal CRAWE RH10 283 P4
Manorside BAR EN5 77 H8
Manor Sq BCTR RM8 123 M7
Manor St BERK HP4 34 A5
Manor V BTFD TW8 155 H4
Manor Vw FNCH N3 97 L10
HART * DA3 211 M6
Manorville Rd HHS/BOV HP3 35 M10
Manor Wk WEY KT13 216 C2
Manorway EN EN1 99 M1
WFD IG8 101 P6
Manor Wy BECK BR3 204 F3
BKHTH/KID SE3 161 M10
BNSTD SM7 240 A2
BORE WD6 75 P7
BRW CM14 106 F4
BXLY DA5 186 B4
BXLYHN DA7 164 E9
CDALE/KGS NW9 116 B2
CHING E4 101 J5
CSHM HP5 51 J6
EGH TW20 172 C9
GRAYS RM17 167 P6
GUW GU2 267 K3
GVW DA11 167 M9
HAYES BR2 206 B6
LHD/OX KT22 236 B2
MTCM CR4 202 D3
NWDGN UB2 153 L3
POTB/CUF EN6 59 K6
PUR/KEN CR8 222 F8
RAIN RM13 144 F6
RKW/CH/CXG WD3 72 B8
RSLP HA4 112 F5
RYLN/HDSTN HA2 114 A2
SAND/SEL CR2 223 M3
STMC/STPC BR5 206 F4
SWCM DA10 167 K10
WOKS/MYFD GU22 232 E6
WPK KT4 200 B8
Manor Waye UX/CGN UB8 131 N4
The Manor Wy WLGTN SM6 222 C1
Manor Wood Rd PUR/KEN CR8 222 F9
Manresa Rd CHEL SW3 15 M8
Mansard Beeches TOOT SW17 180 B8
Mansard Cl HCH RM12 125 H7
PIN HA5 113 L1
Manscroft Rd HHW HP1 35 L4
Manse Cl HYS/HAR UB3 152 E5
Mansefield Cl CSHM HP5 50 G4
Mansel Cl GUW GU2 249 N5
SLN SL2 129 N7
Mansel Gv WALTH E17 100 F9
Mansell Cl WDSR SL4 148 D8
Mansell Rd ACT W3 136 A10
GFD/PVL UB6 134 A7
Mansell St WCHPL E1 13 M6
Mansell Wy CTHM CR3 241 L8
Mansel Rd WIM/MER SW19 179 H9
Mansergh Cl WOOL/PLUM SE18 162 B6
Manse Rd STNW/STAM N16 119 N8
Manser Rd RAIN RM13 144 F5
Manse Wy SWLY BR8 209 H4
Mansfield SBW CM21 29 K2
Mansfield Av EBAR EN4 78 A10
RSLP HA4 113 J6
SEVS/STOTM N15 119 L2
Mansfield Cl ED N9 79 P10
STMC/STPC BR5 207 N7
Mansfield Dr REDH RH1 258 E4
YEAD UB4 132 F6
Mansfield Gdns HCH RM12 125 L7
HERT/WAS SG14 25 K3
Mansfield Hl CHING E4 100 G2
Mansfield Ms CAVSQ/HST W1G 10 E4
Mansfield Rd ACT W3 135 N6
CHSGTN KT9 219 H2
HAMP NW3 118 A10
IL IG1 122 D7
SAND/SEL CR2 223 L3
SWLY BR8 186 F9
WALTH E17 120 E2
WAN E11 121 N4
Mansfield St CAVSQ/HST W1G 10 E4
Mansford St BETH E2 7 P8
Manship Rd MTCM CR4 202 B1

Mansion House Pl MANHO * EC4N 12 G6
Mansion La IVER SL0 130 F10
Manson Ms SKENS SW7 15 K6
Manson Pl SKENS SW7 15 L6
Manstead Gdns CHDH RM6 123 M5
RAIN RM13 145 J8
Manston Av NWDGN UB2 153 P3
Manston Cl CHES/WCR EN8 62 B6
PGE/AN SE20 204 B1
Manstone Rd CRICK NW2 117 H10
Manston Gv KUTN/CMB KT2 177 J8
Manston Rd HLW CM20 47 H1
RGUE GU4 250 D6
Manston Wy HCH RM12 145 J1
STALE/WH AL4 39 J7
Manthorpe Rd
WOOL/PLUM SE18 162 F4
Mantilla Rd TOOT SW17 180 B7
Mantle Rd BROCKY SE4 160 D9
Mantlet Cl STRHM/NOR SW16 180 D10
Mantle Wy SRTFD E15 141 K2
Manton Av HNWL W7 154 E1
Manton Cl HYS/HAR UB3 132 F9
Manton Rd ABYW SE2 163 K3
WAB EN9 80 F3
Manton Ter ADL/WDHM * KT15 215 M1
Mantua St BTSEA SW11 157 N9
Mantus Cl WCHPL E1 140 B6
Mantus Rd WCHPL E1 140 B6
Manus Wy TRDG/WHET N20 97 M3
Manville Gdns TOOT SW17 180 C6
Manville Rd TOOT SW17 180 B5
Manwood Rd BROCKY SE4 182 E2
Manwood St CAN/RD E16 142 C10
Manygate La SHPTN TW17 196 D6
Many Gates BAL SW12 180 C5
Maori Rd GU GU1 268 C1
Mapesbury Rd CRICK NW2 2 A2
Mapeshill Pl CRICK NW2 136 F1
Mape St BETH E2 140 A6
Maple Av ACT W3 136 B10
CHING E4 100 E7
RYLN/HDSTN HA2 114 A7
STALW/RED AL3 38 B2
UPMR RM14 126 A8
WDR/YW UB7 131 P9
Maple Cl BARK/HLT IG6 103 H7
BKHH IG9 102 A4
BUSH WD23 73 M6
CLAP SW4 180 E2
CRAWW RH11 283 M4
CTHM CR3 241 N3
FNCH N3 97 K7
HAT AL10 40 D5
HCH RM12 125 J8
HPTN TW12 175 N9
MTCM CR4 202 C1
RBRW/HUT CM13 107 L4
RSLP HA4 113 J4
STMC/STPC BR5 206 G5
STNW/STAM N16 119 P4
SWLY BR8 208 F2
YEAD UB4 133 L5
Maple Ct EGH TW20 171 N9
NWMAL KT3 200 A3
Maple Crs BFN/LL DA15 185 K2
SLN SL2 129 N9
Maplecroft Cl EHAM E6 142 A8
Maplecroft La WAB EN9 45 K7
Mapledale Av CROY/NA CR0 204 A10
Mapledene Est HACK * E8 7 N3
Mapledene Rd HACK E8 7 M3
Maple Dr SOCK/AV RM15 147 J6
Maplefield LCOL/BKTW AL2 56 A5
Maplefield La CSTG HP8 69 N7
Maple Gdns ASHF TW15 173 P5
EDGW HA8 96 B8
Maple Ga LOU IG10 82 D6
Maple Gn HHW HP1 35 H4
Maple Gv BTFD TW8 154 G6
CDALE/KGS NW9 115 P5
EA W5 155 J2
GU GU1 250 A8
STHL UB1 133 N7
WAT WD17 73 H5
WGCE AL7 23 J2
WOKS/MYFD GU22 232 B7
Maplehurst LHD/OX KT22 236 C9
Maplehurst Cl KUT KT1 199 K4
Maple Leaf Cl ABLGY WD5 55 H8
Maple Leaf Dr BFN/LL DA15 185 J4
Mapleleafe Gdns BARK/HLT IG6 122 E1
Maple Leaf Sq
BERM/RHTH * SE16 160 C1
Maple Lodge Cl
RKW/CH/CXG WD3 91 H5
Maple Ms KIL/WHAMP * NW6 2 G7
STRHM/NOR SW16 180 G8
Maple Pl EW KT17 220 G10
FITZ W1T 11 H3
WDR/YW UB7 131 P10
Maple Rd ASHTD KT21 237 J5
CTHM CR3 241 N3
DART DA1 187 K4
GRAYS RM17 167 P5
GVE DA12 190 F7
PGE/AN SE20 204 A1
REDH RH1 276 A4
RPLY/SEND GU23 233 K10
SURB KT6 199 J5
WAN E11 121 K4
YEAD UB4 133 K5
Maplescombe La EYN DA4 209 P10
Maples Pl WCHPL * E1 140 A7
Maple Springs WAB EN9 63 M9
Maplestead Rd
BRXS/STRHM SW2 180 G3
DAGW RM9 143 L3
The Maples BNSTD SM7 221 L9
CHERT KT16 214 E3
CHESW EN7 61 M4
E/WMO/HCT * KT8 177 H10
ESH/CLAY * KT10 218 F4
HART DA3 211 N3
HLWW/ROY CM19 46 E6
Maple St FITZ W1T 10 G3
ROMW/RG RM7 124 D2
Maplethorpe Rd THHTH CR7 203 H4
Mapleton Cl HAYES BR2 205 M5
Mapleton Crs PEND EN3 80 B4
WAND/EARL SW18 179 L2
Mapleton Rd BH/WHM TN16 263 H6
CHING E4 101 H4
EN EN1 80 A6
WAND/EARL SW18 179 K2
Maple Wk NKENS * W10 136 G6
Maple Wy COUL/CHIP CR5 240 C7
FELT TW13 175 H6
Maplewood Gdns BEAC HP9 88 A10
Maplin Cl WCHMH N21 78 G10
Maplin Pk DTCH/LGLY SL3 150 E1
Maplin Rd CAN/RD E16 141 M8
Maplin St BOW E3 140 E5
Mapperley Dr WFD IG8 101 K8
Maran Wy ERITHM DA18 163 N2
Marban Rd MV/WKIL W9 2 C9
Marbeck Cl WDSR SL4 148 C7
Marble Cl ACT W3 135 N10
Marble Dr CRICK NW2 116 G6
Marble Hill Cl TWK TW1 176 G3
Marble Hill Gdns TWK TW1 176 G3
Marble Quay WAP E1W 13 M9
Marbles Wy KWD/TDW/WH KT20 238 G5
Marbrook Ct LEE/GVPK SE12 183 P6
Marcellina Wy ORP BR6 207 H10
Marcet Rd DART DA1 187 K1
Marchant Rd WAN E11 121 J7
Marchant St NWCR SE14 160 D5
Marchbank Rd WKENS * W14 14 D8
Marchmant Cl HCH RM12 125 K8
Marchmont Gn HHNE HP2 35 N4
Marchmont Rd
RCHPK/HAM TW10 177 L1
WLGTN SM6 222 D5
Marchmont St BMSBY WC1N 11 L1
March Rd TWK TW1 176 E3
WEY KT13 216 B2
Marchside Cl HEST TW5 153 L7
Marchwood Cl CMBW SE5 159 M6
Marchwood Crs EA W5 135 H8
Marcia Ct SL SL1 128 E10
Marcia Rd STHWK SE1 19 K6
Marcilly Rd WAND/EARL SW18 179 N1
Marconi Rd GVW DA11 190 A6
LEY E10 120 F6
Marconi Wy GFD/PVL UB6 134 A8
STALE/WH AL4 39 J6
Marcon Pl HACK E8 7 P1
Marco Rd HMSMTH W6 156 E2
Marcus Ct WOKS/MYFD GU22 232 C4
Marcuse Rd CTHM CR3 241 K9
Marcus Garvey Ms EDUL SE22 182 A2
Marcus Garvey Wy HNHL SE24 159 H10
Marcus Rd DART DA1 187 H3
Marcus St SRTFD E15 141 K3
WAND/EARL SW18 179 L2
Marcus Ter WAND/EARL SW18 179 L2
Mardale Dr CDALE/KGS NW9 116 A3
Mardell Rd CROY/NA CR0 204 C5
Marden Av HAYES BR2 205 M6
Marden Crs BXLY DA5 186 D1
CROY/NA CR0 202 G6
Marden Rd CROY/NA CR0 202 G6
ROM RM1 124 F4
TOTM N17 99 M10
Marden Sq BERM/RHTH SE16 160 A2
The Mardens CRAWW RH11 283 L6
Marder Rd WEA W13 154 F1
Mardyke Rd HLW CM20 29 K9
Mardyke Vw SOCK/AV * RM15 166 D2
Marechal Niel Av BFN/LL DA15 184 G6
Marechal Niel Pde BFN/LL * DA15 184 G6
Mareschal Rd GUW GU2 267 P2
Marescroft Rd SLN SL2 128 D6
Maresfield CROY/NA CR0 203 M10
Maresfield Gdns HAMP NW3 117 M10
Mare St HACK E8 140 A2
Marfleet Cl CAR SM5 201 P9
Marford Rd STALE/WH AL4 21 M3
WGCW AL8 22 C6
Margaret Av BRWN * CM15 107 M1
CHING E4 80 G10
STALW/RED AL3 38 C4
Margaret Bondfield Av
BARK IG11 143 K2
Margaret Cl ABLGY WD5 54 G8
GPK RM2 125 J3
POTB/CUF EN6 59 M9
STA TW18 173 N10
WAB EN9 63 J9
Margaret Dr EMPK RM11 125 N6
Margaret Gardner Dr
ELTH/MOT SE9 184 C5
Margaret Ingram Cl
FUL/PGN * SW6 14 C10
Margaret Lockwood Cl
KUT * KT1 199 L4
Margaret Rd BXLY DA5 185 N2
EBAR EN4 77 N8
EPP CM16 65 K5
GPK RM2 125 J3
GU GU1 267 P1
STNW/STAM * N16 119 N6
Margaret St GTPST W1W 10 G5
Margaretta Ter CHEL SW3 15 N9
Margaretting Rd MNPK E12 121 P7
Margaret Wy PUR/KEN CR8 241 J5
REDBR IG4 122 B4
Margate Rd CLAP SW4 180 F1
Margeholes OXHEY WD19 93 M3
Margery Gv KWD/TDW/WH KT20 257 H5
Margery La KWD/TDW/WH KT20 257 J5
Margery Rd BCTR RM8 123 N8
Margery St FSBYW WC1X 6 A10
Margery Wd WGCE AL7 23 K1
Margherita Pl WAB EN9 63 L10
Margin Dr WIM/MER SW19 178 G8
Margravine Gdns HMSMTH W6 156 G4
Margravine Rd HMSMTH W6 156 G5
Marguerite Vls RYNPK * SW20 178 E10
Marham Gdns MRDN SM4 201 M6
WAND/EARL SW18 179 P4
Maria Cl BERM/RHTH SE16 19 P5
Mariam Gdns HCH RM12 125 N7
Marian Cl CDH/CHF RM16 147 K10
YEAD UB4 133 L6
Marian Gdns GSTN WD25 55 J9
Marian Pl BETH E2 140 A4
Marian Rd STRHM/NOR SW16 202 D1
Marian Sq BETH E2 7 P7
Marian St BETH * E2 140 A4
Marian Wy WLSDN NW10 136 C2
Maria Ter WCHPL E1 140 C7
Maria Theresa Cl NWMAL KT3 200 A5
Maricas Av KTN/HRWW/W HA3 94 C9
Marie Curie CMBW * SE5 159 M7
Marie Lloyd Wk HACK * E8 7 N2
Marie Manor Wy RDART * DA2 188 B6
Mariette Wy WLGTN SM6 222 F5
Marigold Aly STHWK SE1 12 C8
Marigold Cl STHL UB1 133 M9
Marigold Ct GU GU1 250 B7
Marigold Dr CHOB/PIR GU24 230 F1
Marigold Pl HLWE * CM17 29 L7
Marigold St BERM/RHTH SE16 160 A1
Marigold Wy CROY/NA CR0 204 C8
Marina Ap YEAD UB4 133 M7
Marina Av NWMAL KT3 200 E6
Marina Cl CHERT KT16 195 L8
Marina Dr DART DA1 187 P4
GVW DA11 190 C3
WELL DA16 163 H8
Marina Gdns CHES/WCR EN8 62 B6
ROMW/RG RM7 124 C3
Marina Pde STA * TW18 195 L1
Marina Wy IVER SL0 131 J9
SL SL1 128 C9
TEDD TW11 177 J10
Marine Ct PUR RM19 165 N3
Marine Dr BARK IG11 143 L5
WOOL/PLUM SE18 162 C3
Marinefield Rd FUL/PGN SW6 157 L8
Mariner Gdns RCHPK/HAM TW10 176 G6
Mariner Rd MNPK E12 122 D9
Mariners Dr RGUW GU3 248 A8
Mariners Ms POP/IOD E14 161 J3
Mariner Wy HHNE HP2 36 B7
Marine St BERM/RHTH SE16 19 N3
Marion Av SHPTN TW17 196 C5
Marion Cl BARK/HLT IG6 102 G8
BUSH WD23 73 N5
Marion Crs STMC/STPC BR5 207 L5
Marion Gv WFD IG8 101 K6
Marion Rd CRAWE RH10 284 C10
CROY/NA CR0 203 K5
MLHL NW7 96 D6
Marion Wk HHNE * HP2 36 A1
Marischal Rd LEW SE13 161 J9
Marisco Cl CDH/CHF RM16 168 E3
Marish La DEN/HRF UB9 110 F2
Marish Whf DTCH/LGLY * SL3 150 B1
Maritime Cl GRH DA9 188 G1
Maritime Quay POP/IOD E14 160 F4
Maritime St BOW E3 140 E6
Marius Rd TOOT SW17 180 B5
Marjoram Cl GUW GU2 249 M6
Marjorams Av LOU IG10 82 D6
Marjorie Gv BTSEA SW11 158 A10
Mark Av CHING E4 80 G10
Mark Cl BXLYHN DA7 163 P7
HAYES BR2 226 B1
STHL UB1 133 P10
Mark Dr CFSP/GDCR SL9 90 A5
Markedge La COUL/CHIP CR5 240 A10
REIG RH2 258 A3
Markenfield Rd GU GU1 250 A10
Markenhorn RGODL GU7 267 J10
Markeston Gn OXHEY WD19 93 L5
Market Chambers ENC/FH * EN2 79 L5
Market Est HOLWY N7 5 L1
Market Field Rd REDH RH1 258 A9
Marketfield Wy REDH RH1 258 A10
Market La DTCH/LGLY SL3 150 F2
EDGW HA8 95 P9
Market Link ROM RM1 124 F2
Market Meadow
STMC/STPC BR5 207 M4
Market Ms MYFR/PICC W1J 10 E10
Market Oak La HHS/BOV HP3 36 B10
Market Pde BMLY * BR1 205 M1
ED * N9 99 P3
EW * KT17 220 C5
FELT * TW13 175 M5
LEY * E10 120 G4
SCUP * DA14 185 K7
SNWD * SE25 203 P4
STNW/STAM * N16 119 P6
WALTH * E17 120 E1
Market Pl ABR/ST RM4 83 L7
ACT W3 135 P10
BERM/RHTH SE16 19 P5
BTFD TW8 155 H6
CFSP/GDCR SL9 90 A9
DART DA1 187 M3
DTCH/LGLY * SL3 150 F6
EFNCH N2 117 N1
HAT AL10 40 E3
HERT/WAS * SG14 25 L5
KUT * KT1 199 J2
ROM RM1 124 F3
SOHO/SHAV W1D 10 G5
STAL AL1 38 C6
TIL * RM18 168 D8
WAT WD17 73 K6
Market Rd HOLWY N7 5 L2
RCH/KEW TW9 155 M9
Market Sq BH/WHM TN16 262 F3
BMLY BR1 205 L1
ED N9 100 A3
Market St DART DA1 187 M3
EHAM E6 142 C4
GU GU1 268 A1
HERT/WAS SG14 25 L5
HLWE CM17 29 M7
WATW WD18 73 J8
WOOL/PLUM SE18 162 D3
Market Ter BTFD * TW8 155 K5
The Market CAR * SM5 201 M8
COVGDN * WC2E 11 M7
HNWL * W7 154 E1
PECK * SE15 159 P8
RCH/KEW * TW9 177 J1
SUT * SM1 201 M8
Market Wk AMSS * HP7 68 G6
Market Wy BH/WHM TN16 262 G2
Markfield CROY/NA CR0 224 E7
Markfield Gdns CHING E4 100 G1
Markfield Rd CTHM CR3 260 A1
SEVS/STOTM N15 119 P2
Mark Hall Moors HLW CM20 29 L8
Markham Pl CHEL * SW3 16 A7
Markham Rd CHESW EN7 61 K2
Markham Sq CHEL SW3 16 A7
Markham St CHEL SW3 15 P7
Markhole Cl HPTN TW12 175 N10
Markhouse Av WALTH E17 120 D4
Markhouse Rd WALTH E17 120 E4
Mark La GVE DA12 191 H2
MON EC3R 13 K7
Markmanor Av WALTH E17 120 D5
Mark Oak La LHD/OX KT22 235 P7
Mark Rd HHNE HP2 36 B4
WDGN N22 99 J10
Mark's Av CHONG CM5 67 N3
Marksbury Av RCH/KEW TW9 155 M9
Marks Rd ROMW/RG RM7 124 D3
WARL CR6 242 D4
Marks Sq GVW DA11 190 C7
Markstone Ter ORP * BR6 207 K7
Mark St REIG RH2 257 L9
SDTCH EC2A 13 J1
SRTFD E15 141 K2
Mark Ter RYNPK * SW20 178 F10
Markville Gdns CTHM CR3 259 P1
Mark Wy RGODL GU7 266 G9
SWLY BR8 209 H5
The Markway SUN TW16 197 K2
Markwell Cl SYD SE26 182 A7
Markwell Wd EPP CM16 46 E7
Markyate Rd BCTR RM8 123 L10
Marlands Rd CLAY IG5 122 B1
Marlborogh Rd ISLW TW7 154 G6
Marlborough Av EDGW HA8 95 N4
HACK E8 7 N5
RSLP HA4 112 D4
STHGT/OAK N14 98 D4
Marlborough Cl CDH/CHF RM16 167 P1
ORP BR6 207 J7
TRDG/WHET N20 98 A4
UPMR RM14 126 D6
WALW SE17 18 D6
WIM/MER SW19 179 P9
WOT/HER KT12 197 L10
Marlborough Ct REGST W1B 10 G6
Marlborough Crs CHSWK W4 156 A2
SEV TN13 246 F10
Marlborough Dr CLAY IG5 122 B1
WEY KT13 196 D10
Marlborough Gdns
TRDG/WHET N20 98 A4
UPMR RM14 126 D6
Marlborough Ga BAY/PAD W2 9 L8
STAL AL1 38 D6
Marlborough Gv STHWK SE1 19 N8
Marlborough Hl HRW HA1 114 D2
STJWD NW8 3 K6
Marlborough La CHARL SE7 161 P5
Marlborough Ms
BRXS/STRHM SW2 158 G10
Marlborough Pde FSBYPK * N4 119 K6
HGDN/ICK * UB10 132 C6
Marlborough Park Av
BFN/LL DA15 185 K4
Marlborough Pl STJWD NW8 3 J8
Marlborough Ri HHNE HP2 35 P3
Marlborough Rd ARCH N19 118 F7
ASHF TW15 173 P8
BCTR RM8 123 M9
BRWN CM15 86 F10
CHING E4 100 G7
CHSWK W4 155 P4
DART DA1 187 K2
DORK RH4 272 G2
DTCH/LGLY SL3 150 A3
EA W5 155 J1
ED N9 99 N2
FELT TW13 175 L5
FSTGT E7 141 P2
HAYES BR2 205 P4
HGDN/ICK UB10 132 C6
HPTN TW12 175 P9
NWDGN UB2 153 K2
RCHPK/HAM TW10 177 K2
ROMW/RG RM7 124 B2
SAND/SEL CR2 223 K4
SRTFD * E15 121 K9
STAL AL1 38 D6
SUT SM1 201 K10
SWFD E18 121 M1
WDGN N22 98 G8
WELL DA16 163 N9
WHALL SW1A 11 H10
WIM/MER SW19 179 P9
WOKN/KNAP GU21 232 D2
WOOL/PLUM SE18 162 E2
Marlborough St CHEL SW3 15 N6
Marlborough Yd ARCH N19 118 E7
The Marld ASHTD KT21 237 L4
Marle Gdns WAB EN9 63 H8
Marler Rd FSTH SE23 182 E4
Marlescroft Wy LOU IG10 82 E9
Marley Av BXLYHN DA7 163 N5
Marley Cl ADL/WDHM KT15 215 J3
GFD/PVL UB6 133 P5
SEVS/STOTM N15 119 J2
Marley Ri DORK RH4 272 F5
Marley Rd WGCE AL7 23 K7
Marlin Cl BERK HP4 33 L4
SUN TW16 174 F9
Marlin Copse BERK HP4 33 M6
Marlingdene Cl HPTN TW12 175 P9
Marlings Cl CHST BR7 207 H4
CTHM CR3 241 M3
Marlings Park Av CHST BR7 207 H4
Marling Wy GVE DA12 191 H8
Marlins Cl RKW/CH/CXG WD3 71 H6
SUT * SM1 221 M2
Marlins End BERK HP4 33 L6
Marlins Meadow WATW WD18 72 E10
Marlin Sq ABLGY WD5 54 G7
The Marlins NTHWD HA6 92 G7
Marlins Turn HHW HP1 35 L3
Marloes Cl ALP/SUD HA0 115 J9
Marloes Rd KENS W8 14 G3
Marlow Av PUR RM19 165 P3
Marlow Cl PGE/AN SE20 204 A3
Marlow Ct CDALE/KGS NW9 116 C1
CRAWE RH10 283 N6
Marlow Crs TWK TW1 176 E2
Marlow Dr CHEAM SM3 200 G10
Marlowe Cl BARK/HLT IG6 102 F9
CHST BR7 184 G9
Marlowe Rd WALTH E17 121 H2
Marlowes HHNE HP2 35 N6
The Marlowes DART DA1 164 E10
STJWD NW8 3 L6
Marlowe Wy CROY/NA CR0 202 F9
Marlow Gdns HYS/HAR UB3 152 E2
Marlow Rd EHAM E6 142 C5
NWDGN UB2 153 N2
PGE/AN SE20 204 A3
Marlow Wy BERM/RHTH SE16 160 C1
Marlpit Av COUL/CHIP CR5 240 F3
Marlpit La COUL/CHIP CR5 240 E2
Marl Rd WAND/EARL SW18 157 L10
Marlton St GNWCH SE10 161 L4
Marlwood Cl BFN/LL DA15 185 H5
Marlyns Cl RGUE GU4 250 D6
Marlyns Dr RGUE GU4 250 D7
Marlyon Rd BARK/HLT IG6 103 L6
Marmadon Rd
WOOL/PLUM SE18 163 J3
Marmion Ap CHING E4 100 F5
Marmion Av CHING E4 100 E5
Marmion Cl CHING E4 100 E5
Marmion Ms BTSEA * SW11 158 B9
Marmion Rd BTSEA SW11 158 B10
Marmont Rd PECK SE15 159 P7
Marmora Rd EDUL SE22 182 B2
Marmot Rd HSLWW TW4 153 L9
Marne Av FBAR/BDGN N11 98 C5
WELL DA16 163 K9
Marnell Wy HSLWW TW4 153 L9
Marne St NKENS W10 2 A9
Marney Rd BTSEA SW11 158 B10
Marneys Cl EPSOM KT18 237 M1
Marnfield Crs BRXS/STRHM SW2 180 G4
Marnham Av CRICK NW2 117 H9
Marnham Crs GFD/PVL UB6 134 A5
Marnham Pl ADL/WDHM KT15 215 M1
Marnham Ri HHW HP1 35 K4
Marnock Rd BROCKY SE4 182 E1
Maroon St POP/IOD E14 140 D7
Maroons Wy CAT SE6 182 F8
Marquess Rd IS N1 6 G1
Marquess Rd North IS N1 6 G2
Marquess Rd South IS N1 6 F2
Marquis Cl ALP/SUD HA0 135 L2
HARP AL5 20 C1
Marquis La HARP AL5 20 C1
Marquis Rd CAMTN NW1 5 K2
FSBYPK N4 118 G6
WDGN N22 98 G7
Marrabon Cl BFN/LL DA15 185 K4
Marrick Cl PUT/ROE SW15 156 D10
Marrilyne Av PEND EN3 80 E4
Marriner Ct HYS/HAR * UB3 132 F9
Marriot Rd MUSWH N10 98 A9
Marriott Cl EBED/NFELT TW14 174 E2
Marriott Lodge Cl
ADL/WDHM KT15 215 M1
Marriott Rd BAR EN5 76 G7
DART DA1 187 P3
FSBYPK N4 118 G6
SRTFD E15 141 K3
Marriotts Cl CDALE/KGS NW9 116 C4
Marriotts Wy HHS/BOV HP3 35 N8
Marriotts Yd BAR * EN5 76 G7
Marriott Ter RKW/CH/CXG WD3 71 J8
Mar Rd SOCK/AV RM15 147 H6
Marrod's Bottom AMSS HP7 88 B3
Marrowells WEY KT13 196 F10
Marryat Pl WIM/MER SW19 179 H7
Marryat Rd EN EN1 80 A1
WIM/MER SW19 178 G8
Marryat Sq FUL/PGN * SW6 157 H7
Marsala Rd LEW SE13 160 G10
Marsden Cl WGCW AL8 22 E7
Marsden Gn WGCW AL8 22 E6
Marsden Rd ED N9 100 A3
PECK SE15 159 N9
WGCW AL8 22 E6
Marsden St KTTN NW5 4 C2
Marsden Wy ORP BR6 227 J1
Marshall Av STALW/RED AL3 38 D3
Marshall Cl FBAR/BDGN N11 98 C5
HRW HA1 114 C5
HSLWW TW4 175 N1
SAND/SEL CR2 223 P9
WAND/EARL SW18 179 M2
Marshall Dr YEAD UB4 132 G7
Marshall Est MLHL * NW7 96 D5
Marshall Pde
WOKS/MYFD * GU22 233 J1
Marshall Pl ADL/WDHM KT15 215 M5
Marshall Rd CRAWE RH10 284 D9
TOTM N17 99 L9
Marshalls Cl HOR/WEW KT19 219 P9
Marshalls Dr ROM RM1 124 F1
Marshalls Gv WOOL/PLUM SE18 162 B3
Marshalls Rd ROMW/RG RM7 124 E2
SUT SM1 221 L1
Marshall St SOHO/CST W1F 11 H6
Marshalls Wy STALE/WH AL4 20 E1
Marshal's Dr STAL AL1 38 F3
Marshalsea Rd STHWK SE1 18 F1
Marshalswick La STAL AL1 38 F3
Marsham Cl CHST * BR7 184 E8
Marsham La CFSP/GDCR SL9 110 C3
Marsham Ldg CFSP/GDCR SL9 110 B4
Marsham St WEST SW1P 17 K5
Marsham Wy CFSP/GDCR SL9 110 B3
Marsh Av HOR/WEW KT19 220 B6
MTCM CR4 202 A2
Marshbrook Cl BKHTH/KID SE3 162 A9
Marsh Cl CHES/WCR EN8 62 E9
MLHL NW7 96 C4
Marshcroft Dr CHES/WCR EN8 62 D6
Marsh Dr CDALE/KGS NW9 116 C4
Marshe Cl POTB/CUF EN6 59 N8
Marsh Farm Rd WHTN TW2 176 E4
Marshfield DTCH/LGLY SL3 149 P7
Marshfield St POP/IOD E14 161 H2
Marshfoot Rd GRAYS RM17 168 C4
Marshgate Dr HERT/BAY SG13 25 M4
Marshgate La SRTFD E15 140 G2
Marsh Green Rd DAGE RM10 144 B3
Marsh Hl HOM E9 120 D10
WAB EN9 63 K3
Marsh La ADL/WDHM KT15 215 L1
HLWE CM17 29 P6
LEY E10 120 E7
MLHL NW7 96 B4
STAN HA7 95 H6
TOTM N17 100 A8
WARE SG12 26 D3
WARE SG12 27 J8
Marshmoor Crs BRKMPK AL9 40 G8
Marshmoor La BRKMPK AL9 40 F8
Marsh Rd ALP/SUD HA0 135 J5
PIN HA5 113 M2
Marshside Cl ED N9 100 B2
Marsh St DART DA1 165 P8
POP/IOD * E14 160 G3
Marsh Ter STMC/STPC * BR5 207 N4
Marsh Wall POP/IOD E14 160 F1
Marsh Wy DAGW RM9 144 E5
Marshwood Rd LTWR GU18 212 C7
Marsland Cl WALW SE17 18 D8
Marston HOR/WEW KT19 219 P7
Marston Av CHSGTN KT9 219 K3
DAGE RM10 124 B8
Marston Cl CSHM HP5 50 F3
DAGE RM10 124 B8
HHS/BOV HP3 36 B7
KIL/WHAMP NW6 3 K3
Marston Ct WOT/HER * KT12 197 K8
Marston Dr WARL CR6 242 D4
Marston Rd CLAY IG5 102 B10
HOD EN11 44 G2
TEDD TW11 176 G8
WOKN/KNAP GU21 231 N3
Marston Wy NRWD SE19 181 J10
Marsworth Av PIN HA5 93 L9
Marsworth Cl WATW * WD18 72 F10
YEAD UB4 133 M7
Martaban Rd STNW/STAM N16 119 M7
Martello St HACK E8 140 A2
Martell Rd DUL SE21 181 L6
Martel Pl HACK E8 7 M1
Marten Ga STALE/WH AL4 38 F2
Marten Rd WALTH E17 100 F10
Martens Av BXLYHN DA7 164 D10
Martens Cl BXLYHN DA7 164 D10
Martham Cl THMD SE28 143 N9
Martha Rd SRTFD E15 141 K1
Martha's Buildings FSBYE EC1V 12 G1
Martha St WCHPL E1 140 B8
Marthorne Crs
KTN/HRWW/W HA3 94 C10

Martian Av HHNE HP2 36 A3
Martin Bowes Rd ELTH/MOT SE9 162 C9
Martin Cl CRAWW RH11 283 N5
ED N9 100 C2
HAT AL10 40 D6
HGDN/ICK UB10 131 P4
SAND/SEL CR2 224 C7
WARL CR6 242 A2
WDSR SL4 148 B7
Martin Crs CROY/NA CR0 202 G8
Martindale IVER SL0 130 F6
MORT/ESHN SW14 177 P1
Martindale Av CAN/RD E16 141 M9
ORP BR6 227 K2
Martindale Cl RGUE GU4 250 G8
Martindale Rd BAL SW12 180 C3
HHW HP1 35 J5
HSLWW TW4 153 M10
WOKN/KNAP GU21 231 L4
Martin Dene BXLYHS DA6 186 A1
Martin Dr NTHLT UB5 113 N10
RAIN RM13 145 J6
Martineau Cl ESH/CLAY KT10 218 C1
Martineau Dr DORK RH4 272 G4
Martineau Rd HBRY N5 119 J9
Martineau St WCHPL E1 140 B9
Martinfield WGCE AL7 23 J4
Martingale Cl SUN TW16 197 H4
Martingales Cl
RCHPK/HAM TW10 177 J6
Martin Gdns BCTR RM8 123 M9
Martin Gv WIM/MER SW19 201 K3
Martini Dr WAB EN9 80 F3
Martin La CANST EC4R 13 H7
Martin Ri BXLYHS DA6 186 A1
Martin Rd BCTR RM8 123 M9
GUW GU2 249 M8
RDART DA2 187 K6
SL SL1 149 K2
SOCK/AV RM15 146 C10
Martins Cl GU GU1 250 F9
RAD WD7 74 D2
STMC/STPC BR5 207 N3
WWKM BR4 205 J9
Martins Dr CHES/WCR EN8 62 D4
HERT/BAY SG13 26 A5
Martins Mt BAR EN5 77 K8
Martin's Pln SLN SL2 129 L5
Martin's Rd HAYES BR2 205 K2
Martin's Shaw SEV TN13 246 D8
The Martins SYD SE26 182 A8
WBLY * HA9 115 L8
Martin St THMD SE28 143 H10
Martins Wk MUSWH * N10 98 B9
Martinsyde WOKS/MYFD GU22 232 F3
Martin Wy RYNPK SW20 201 H3
WOKN/KNAP GU21 231 M4
Martlesham WGCE AL7 23 P5
Martlesham Cl HCH RM12 125 K10
Martlet Gv NTHLT UB5 133 L5
The Martlets CRAWE RH10 283 P7
Martlett Ct HOL/ALD WC2B 11 M6
Martley Dr IL IG1 122 E3
Martock Cl KTN/HRWW/W HA3 114 F2
Marton Cl CAT SE6 182 F6
Marton Rd STNW/STAM * N16 119 M7
Martyr Cl STAL AL1 38 C10
Martyr Rd GU GU1 268 A1
Martyrs Av CRAWW RH11 283 M4
Martyrs La WOKN/KNAP GU21 214 E8
Martys Yd HAMP * NW3 117 N9
Marunden Gn SLN SL2 128 E5
Marvell Av YEAD UB4 133 H7
Marvell Cl CRAWE RH10 284 D5
Marvels Cl LEE/GVPK SE12 183 N5
Marvels La LEE/GVPK SE12 183 N5
Marville Rd FUL/PGN SW6 157 J6
Marvin St HACK * E8 140 A1
Marwell BH/WHM TN16 262 E2
Marwell Cl ROM RM1 125 H4
WWKM BR4 205 L9
Marwood Cl KGLGY WD4 54 A5
WELL DA16 163 L9
Mary Adelaide Cl PUT/ROE SW15 178 B6
Mary Ann Buildings DEPT SE8 160 F5
Maryatt Av RYLN/HDSTN HA2 114 A7
Marybank WOOL/PLUM SE18 162 C3
Mary Cl KTN/HRWW/W HA3 115 L2
Mary Datchelor Cl CMBW SE5 159 L7
Maryfield Cl BXLY DA5 186 F6
Marygold Wk AMS HP6 69 P5
Mary Gn STJWD * NW8 3 H5
Maryhill Cl PUR/KEN CR8 241 K3
Maryland HAT AL10 40 C4
Maryland Pk SRTFD E15 121 K10
Maryland Rd MV/WKIL W9 8 F2
SRTFD E15 121 J10
THHTH CR7 203 J1
WDGN N22 99 H7
Maryland Sq SRTFD E15 121 K10
Marylands Rd MV/WKIL W9 8 F2
Maryland St SRTFD E15 121 J10
Maryland Wk IS * N1 6 E5
Maryland Wy SUN TW16 197 H2
Mary Lawrencson Pl
BKHTH/KID SE3 161 L6
Marylebone High St MHST W1U 10 D3
Marylebone La MHST W1U 10 D5
Marylebone Ms CAVSQ/HST W1G 10 D4
Marylebone Pas GTPST W1W 11 H5
Marylebone Rd CAMTN NW1 9 P3
Marylebone St MHST W1U 10 D4
Marylee Wy LBTH SE11 17 P6
Maryon Gv CHARL SE7 162 B3
Maryon Ms HAMP NW3 117 P9
Maryon Rd CHARL SE7 162 B3
Mary Peters Dr NTHLT UB5 114 C10
Mary Pl NTGHL W11 8 A8
Mary Rd GU GU1 267 P1
Mary Rose Cl HPTN TW12 197 P1
WTHK RM20 167 H3
Maryrose Wy TRDG/WHET N20 97 N2
Mary Seacole Cl HACK * E8 7 L5
Mary Secole Cl HACK E8 7 L5
Maryside DTCH/LGLY SL3 150 B1
Mary's Ter TWK TW1 176 F3
Mary St CAN/RD E16 141 L7
IS N1 6 F6
Mary Ter CAMTN NW1 4 F6
Masbro' Rd WKENS W14 156 G2
Mascalls Gdns BRW CM14 106 E5
Mascalls La BRW CM14 106 E5
Mascalls Rd CHARL SE7 161 P5
Mascotts Cl CRICK NW2 116 E8
Masefield Av BORE WD6 75 N9
STAN HA7 94 E6
STHL UB1 133 P9
Masefield Cl ERITH DA8 164 G7
HARH RM3 105 J9
Masefield Crs GPK RM2 105 K9
STHGT/OAK N14 78 D9
Masefield Dr UPMR RM14 126 B5
Masefield Gdns EHAM E6 142 D6
Masefield La YEAD UB4 133 J6
Masefield Rd CDH/CHF RM16 168 B1
CRAWW RH11 283 H10
DART DA1 188 A1
FELT TW13 175 N7
GVW DA11 190 A6
Masefield Vw ORP BR6 206 F10
Masefield Wy STWL/WRAY TW19 174 A4
Mashie Rd ACT W3 136 B8
Mashiters Hl CRW RM5 104 E9
Mashiters Wk ROM RM1 124 F1
Maskall Cl BRXS/STRHM * SW2 181 H4
Maskell Rd TOOT SW17 179 M6
Maskelyne Cl BTSEA SW11 157 P7
Mason Cl BERM/RHTH SE16 19 P7
BORE WD6 76 A6
BXLYHN DA7 164 C9
HPTN TW12 197 N1
RYNPK SW20 200 G1
Mason Ct WBLY * HA9 115 M7
Mason Dr HARH RM3 105 M10
Masonic Hall Rd CHERT KT16 195 J6
Mason Rd CRAWE RH10 283 P9
WFD IG8 101 K5
Mason's Arms Ms CONDST * W1S 10 F6
Mason's Av CITYW EC2V 12 G5
CROY/NA CR0 203 K10
KTN/HRWW/W HA3 114 E2
Mason's Bridge Rd REDH RH1 276 C5
Masons Ct EW * KT17 220 D5
Masons Hl HAYES BR2 205 M3
WOOL/PLUM SE18 162 E3
Masons Paddock DORK RH4 254 F10
Masons Pde CHESW * EN7 61 K4
Mason's Pl FSBYE EC1V 6 D9
MTCM CR4 202 A1
Masons Rd EN EN1 80 A2
HHNE HP2 36 C5
SL SL1 128 D9
Mason St WALW SE17 19 H5
Masons Yd FSBYE EC1V 12 E1
STJS SW1Y 11 H9
Mason Wy WAB EN9 63 K9
Massetts Rd HORL RH6 280 A5
Massey Cl FBAR/BDGN N11 98 C6
Massie Rd HACK E8 7 N2
Massingberd Wy TOOT SW17 180 C7
Massinger St WALW SE17 19 J6
Massingham St WCHPL E1 140 C6
Masson Av RSLP HA4 133 K1
Master Cl OXTED RH8 261 K5
Masterman Rd EHAM E6 142 B5
Masters Dr BERM/RHTH SE16 160 A4
Master's St WCHPL E1 140 C7
Masthead Cl GRH DA9 166 B10
Mast House Ter POP/IOD * E14 160 F3
Masthouse Ter POP/IOD E14 160 F3
Mastmaker Rd POP/IOD E14 160 F1
Maswell Park Crs HSLW TW3 176 B1
Maswell Park Rd HSLW TW3 176 A1
Matcham Rd WAN E11 121 K8
Matching Fld BRWN CM15 86 E3
Matching Rd HLWE CM17 30 C7
RBSF CM22 31 J2
Matchless Dr WOOL/PLUM SE18 162 D6
Matfield Cl HAYES BR2 205 M5
Matfield Rd BELV DA17 164 B5
Matham Gv EDUL SE22 159 N10
Matham Rd E/WMO/HCT KT8 198 C5
Matheson Rd WKENS W14 14 C6
Mathews Av EHAM E6 142 D4
Mathews Park Av SRTFD E15 141 L1
Mathews Yd LSQ/SEVD * WC2H 11 L6
Mathias Cl EPSOM KT18 219 P9
Mathieson Ct STHWK SE1 18 D2
Mathisen Wy DTCH/LGLY SL3 151 H7
Matilda Cl NRWD SE19 181 L10
Matilda St IS N1 5 P6
Matlock Cl BAR EN5 76 G9
Matlock Crs CHEAM SM3 221 H1
OXHEY WD19 93 K4
Matlock Gdns CHEAM SM3 221 H1
HCH RM12 125 M8
Matlock Pl CHEAM SM3 221 H1
Matlock Rd CTHM CR3 241 M8
LEY E10 121 H4
Matlock St WCHPL E1 140 D8
Matlock Wy NWMAL KT3 200 A1
Matthew Arnold Cl COB KT11 217 H10
STA TW18 173 M9
Matthew Cl NKENS * W10 136 G6
Matthew Ct MTCM CR4 202 E5
Matthew's Gdns CROY/NA CR0 225 J7
Matthews La STA TW18 173 J7
Matthews Rd NTHLT UB5 114 C10
Matthews St BTSEA * SW11 158 A8
REIG RH2 275 K4
Matthey Pl CRAWE RH10 284 E4
Matthias Rd STNW/STAM N16 119 L10
Mattingly Wy PECK SE15 159 N6
Mattison Rd FSBYPK N4 119 H4
Mattock La WEA W13 135 H10
Maud Cashmore Wy
WOOL/PLUM SE18 162 C2
Maude Cl BEAC HP9 88 F10
Maude Crs WATN WD24 73 J3
Maude Rd BEAC HP9 88 F10
CMBW SE5 159 M8
SWLY BR8 187 H9
WALTH E17 120 D3
Maudesville Cottages HNWL W7 134 D10
Maude Ter WALTH E17 120 D2
Maud Gdns BARK IG11 143 J4
PLSTW E13 141 L4
Maud Rd LEY E10 121 H8
PLSTW E13 141 L3
Maudslay Rd ELTH/MOT SE9 162 C9
Maud St CAN/RD E16 141 L7
Maud Wilkes Cl KTTN NW5 118 D10
Mauleverer Rd
BRXS/STRHM SW2 180 F1
Maundeby Wk WLSDN * NW10 116 B10
Maunder Rd HNWL W7 134 D10
Maunds Hatch HLWS CM18 46 G5
Maunsell Pk CRAWE RH10 284 C7
Maunsel St WEST SW1P 17 J5
Maurice Av CTHM CR3 241 L8
WDGN N22 99 J10
Maurice Brown Cl MLHL * NW7 96 G6
Maurice St SHB W12 136 E8
Maurice Wk GLDGN NW11 117 M2
Maurier Cl NTHLT UB5 133 K3
Mauritius Rd GNWCH SE10 161 K3
Maury Rd STNW/STAM N16 119 P7
Mavelstone Rd BMLY BR1 206 A1
Maverton Rd BOW * E3 140 F3
Mavis Av HOR/WEW KT19 220 B2
Mavis Cl HOR/WEW KT19 220 B2
Mavis Gv HCH RM12 125 M7
Mawbey Est STHWK SE1 19 N8
Mawbey Pl STHWK SE1 19 M8
Mawbey Rd CHERT KT16 214 G3
STHWK SE1 19 M8
Mawbey St VX/NE SW8 158 F6
Mawney Cl ROMW/RG RM7 104 C10
Mawney Rd ROMW/RG RM7 104 C10
Mawson Cl RYNPK SW20 201 H2
Mawson La CHSWK W4 156 C5
Maxey Gdns DAGW RM9 123 P9
Maxey Rd DAGW RM9 123 P9
WOOL/PLUM SE18 162 F3
Maxfield Cl TRDG/WHET N20 97 M1
Maximfeldt Rd ERITH DA8 164 F4
Maxim Rd DART DA1 186 F1
ERITH DA8 164 F4
WCHMH N21 79 H10
Maxted Cl HHNE HP2 36 D4
Maxted Cnr HHNE * HP2 36 C3
Maxted Pk HRW HA1 114 D5
Maxted Rd HHNE HP2 36 C4
PECK SE15 159 N9
Maxwell Cl CROY/NA CR0 202 F8
HYS/HAR UB3 133 H9
RKW/CH/CXG WD3 91 K3
Maxwell Dr BF/WBF KT14 215 M7
Maxwell Gdns ORP BR6 207 J10
Maxwell Ri OXHEY WD19 93 M1
Maxwell Rd ASHF TW15 174 D9
BEAC HP9 88 C8
BORE WD6 75 N7
FUL/PGN SW6 157 L6
NTHWD HA6 92 E8
STAL AL1 38 G7
WDR/YW UB7 151 P3
WELL DA16 163 K10
Maxwell Wy CRAWE RH10 284 B4
Maxwelton Av MLHL NW7 96 A6
Maxwelton Cl MLHL NW7 96 A6
Mayall Rd HNHL SE24 181 J1
Maya Rd EFNCH N2 117 M2
May Av GVW DA11 190 C4
STMC/STPC BR5 207 L5
Maybank Av ALP/SUD HA0 114 F9
HCH RM12 125 J10
SWFD E18 101 N10
Maybank Gdns PIN HA5 113 H3
Maybank Rd SWFD E18 101 P9
May Bate Av KUTN/CMB KT2 199 J1
Mayberry Pl BRYLDS KT5 199 L7
Maybourne Cl SYD * SE26 182 A9
Maybourne Ri
WOKS/MYFD GU22 232 A10
Maybrick Rd EMPK RM11 125 K3
Maybury Av CHES/WCR EN8 62 A4
RDART DA2 188 A4
Maybury Cl EN EN1 80 A4
KWD/TDW/WH KT20 239 H5
SL SL1 128 C7
STMC/STPC BR5 206 E5
Maybury Gdns WLSDN NW10 136 D2
Maybury Hl WOKS/MYFD GU22 232 E3
Maybury Rd BARK IG11 143 K4
PLSTW E13 141 P6
WOKN/KNAP GU21 232 D2
Maybury St TOOT SW17 179 P8
Maybush Rd EMPK RM11 125 M5
Maychurch Cl STAN HA7 95 J9
May Cl CHSGTN KT9 219 L3
STALW/RED AL3 38 C4
Maycock Gv NTHWD HA6 92 G7
Maycroft PIN HA5 93 J10
Maycroft Av GRAYS RM17 168 A4
Maycroft Gdns GRAYS RM17 168 A4
Maycroft Rd CHESW EN7 61 M2
Maycross Av MRDN SM4 201 J4
Mayday Gdns BKHTH/KID SE3 162 B8
Mayday Rd THHTH CR7 203 J6
Maydwell Ldg BORE WD6 75 L6
Mayefield Rd THHTH CR7 202 G4
Mayell Cl LHD/OX KT22 237 H9
Mayerne Rd ELTH/MOT SE9 184 A1
Mayesbrook Rd BARK IG11 143 J3
GDMY/SEVK IG3 123 K8
Mayes Cl CRAWE RH10 284 D8
SWLY BR8 209 H4
WARL CR6 242 C4
Mayesford Rd CHDH RM6 123 M5
Mayes Rd WDGN N22 98 G10
Mayeswood Rd LEE/GVPK SE12 183 P7
Mayfair Av CHDH RM6 123 N4
IL IG1 122 C7
WELL DA16 163 N7
WHTN TW2 176 B3
WPK KT4 200 D8
Mayfair Cl BECK BR3 204 G1
STALE/WH AL4 39 H1
SURB KT6 199 K8
Mayfair Gdns TOTM N17 99 K7
WFD IG8 101 M8
Mayfair Ms HAMP * NW3 4 B4
Mayfair Pl MYFR/PICC W1J 10 F9
Mayfair Rd DART DA1 187 L1
Mayfair Ter STHGT/OAK N14 98 E1
Mayfare RKW/CH/CXG WD3 72 E9
Mayfield BXLYHN DA7 164 A9
CRAWE RH10 284 E7
LHD/OX KT22 237 H7
SWCM DA10 189 K2
WGCW AL8 22 F1
Mayfield Av ADL/WDHM KT15 215 L6
CHSWK W4 156 B3
KTN/HRWW/W HA3 114 G3
NFNCH/WDSP N12 97 M5
ORP BR6 207 J8
STHGT/OAK N14 98 D3
WEA W13 154 C2
WFD IG8 101 M7
Mayfield Cl ADL/WDHM KT15 215 M6
ASHF TW15 174 C9
CLAP SW4 180 E1
HACK E8 7 L2
HGDN/ICK UB10 132 C5
HLWE CM17 30 A7
PGE/AN * SE20 204 A1
REDH RH1 276 B6
THDIT KT7 198 G8
WOT/HER KT12 217 H1
Mayfield Crs ED N9 80 A10
THHTH CR7 202 G4
Mayfield Dr PIN HA5 113 N2
Mayfield Gdns BRW CM14 106 G2
BRW CM14 107 H2
HDN NW4 116 G4
HNWL W7 134 C8
STA TW18 173 J10
WOT/HER KT12 217 H1
Mayfield Gn GT/LBKH KT23 253 P3
Mayfield Rd ACT W3 135 N9
BCTR RM8 123 M6
BELMT SM2 221 N3
BELV DA17 164 D3
BMLY BR1 206 B5
CEND/HSY/T N8 118 G4
CHING E4 101 J3
GVW DA11 190 C4
HACK E8 7 L4
PEND EN3 80 C6
PLSTW E13 141 L6
SAND/SEL CR2 223 L5
SHB W12 156 B1
WALTH E17 100 D10
WEY KT13 216 A2
WIM/MER SW19 201 J1
WOT/HER KT12 217 H1
Mayfields CDH/CHF RM16 167 P1
WBLY HA9 115 M7
Mayfields Cl WBLY HA9 115 M7
Mayfield Vls SCUP * DA14 185 M9
Mayflower Av HHNE HP2 35 N6
Mayflower Cl BERM/RHTH SE16 160 C3
CRAWE RH10 284 E8
HERT/WAS SG14 24 F7
RSLP HA4 112 D4
SOCK/AV RM15 147 H6
WAB EN9 45 K9
Mayflower Rd BRXN/ST SW9 158 F9
LCOL/BKTW AL2 56 A3
WTHK RM20 167 H4
Mayflower St BERM/RHTH SE16 160 B1
Mayflower Wy CHONG CM5 67 P3
SLN SL2 109 H10
Mayfly Cl PIN HA5 113 K5
STMC/STPC BR5 207 N4
Mayford Cl BAL SW12 180 A3
BECK BR3 204 C3
WOKS/MYFD GU22 232 A8
Mayford Rd BAL SW12 180 A3
May Gdns BORE WD6 75 J10
GFD/PVL UB6 135 H4
Maygoods UX/CGN UB8 131 N7
Maygoods Cl UX/CGN UB8 131 N7
Maygoods Gn UX/CGN UB8 131 N7
Maygood St IS N1 5 P7
Maygoods Vw UX/CGN * UB8 131 M7
Maygreen Crs EMPK RM11 125 H5
Maygrove Rd KIL/WHAMP NW6 2 D2
Mayhall La AMS HP6 68 G1
Mayhew Cl CHING E4 100 F4
Mayhill Rd BAR EN5 77 H10
CHARL SE7 161 N5
Mayhurst Av WOKS/MYFD GU22 232 F2
Mayhurst Crs WOKS/MYFD GU22 232 F2
Maylands Av HCH RM12 125 J9
HHNE HP2 36 C4
Maylands Dr SCUP DA14 185 N6
UX/CGN UB8 131 N1
Maylands Rd OXHEY WD19 93 K5
Maylands Wy HARH RM3 106 B7
Maylins Dr SBW CM21 29 N1
Maynard Cl CRAWE RH10 285 K1
ERITH DA8 164 G6
FUL/PGN SW6 157 L6
SEVS/STOTM N15 119 M3
Maynard Dr STAL AL1 38 C9
Maynard Pl POTB/CUF EN6 60 F5
Maynard Rd HHNE HP2 35 N7
WALTH E17 121 H3
Maynards EMPK RM11 125 M5
Maynards Quay WAP * E1W 140 B9
Mayne Av STALW/RED AL3 37 N8
Maynooth Gdns MTCM CR4 202 A7
Mayo Cl CHES/WCR EN8 62 B4
Mayo Gdns HHW HP1 35 L7
Mayola Rd CLPT E5 120 B9
Mayo Rd CROY/NA CR0 203 L5
WLSDN NW10 136 B1
WOT/HER KT12 197 H7
Mayow Rd SYD SE26 182 C7
Mayplace Av DART DA1 165 H10
Mayplace Cl BXLYHN DA7 164 C9
Mayplace La WOOL/PLUM SE18 162 E5
Mayplace Rd BXLYHN DA7 164 D9
Mayplace Rd East BXLYHN DA7 164 C9
Mayplace Rd West BXLYHN DA7 164 B10
Maypole Crs BARK/HLT IG6 102 G8
ERITH DA8 165 L5
Maypole Dr CHIG IG7 103 K4
Maypole Rd GVE DA12 191 J4
ORP BR6 228 A3
May Rd CHING E4 100 F7
PLSTW E13 141 M4
RDART DA2 187 N7
WHTN TW2 176 D4
Mayroyd Av SURB KT6 199 M9
May's Buildings Ms GNWCH SE10 161 J6
Mays Cl WEY KT13 216 A6
Mays Ct CHCR WC2N 11 L8
Maysfield Rd RPLY/SEND GU23 232 G9
Mays Gn COB * KT11 234 G6
Mays Gv RPLY/SEND GU23 232 G9
May's Hill Rd HAYES BR2 205 K2
Mays La BAR EN5 96 E1
Maysoule Rd BTSEA SW11 157 N10
Mays Rd HPTN TW12 176 C8
May St WKENS W14 14 C8
Mayswood Gdns DAGE RM10 144 D1
Maythorne Cl WATW WD18 72 F8
Maythorne Cottages LEW SE13 183 J2
Mayton St HOLWY N7 118 G8
Maytree Cl EDGW HA8 95 P4
GU GU1 249 N7
RAIN RM13 144 F4
Maytree Ct MTCM CR4 202 B3
Maytree Crs WATN WD24 72 G2
Maytree La STAN HA7 94 E7
Maytrees RAD WD7 74 F3
WOKN/KNAP GU21 231 H3
Maytree Wk BRXS/STRHM * SW2 181 H5
Mayville Est STNW/STAM * N16 119 M10
Mayville Rd IL IG1 122 E10
WAN E11 121 K7
Maywater Cl SAND/SEL CR2 223 L7
Maywin Dr EMPK RM11 125 N6
Maywood Cl BECK * BR3 182 G10
Maze Hl GNWCH SE10 161 K5
Mazenod Av KIL/WHAMP NW6 2 F4
Maze Rd RCH/KEW TW9 155 M6
McAdam Cl HOD EN11 44 F1
McAdam Dr ENC/FH EN2 79 J6
McAlmont Rdg RGODL GU7 267 J10
McAuley Cl ELTH/MOT SE9 184 D1
STHWK SE1 18 A3
McCall Cl CLAP SW4 158 F8
McCall Crs CHARL SE7 162 B4
McCarthy Rd FELT TW13 175 L8
McClintock Pl WAB EN9 80 G4
McCoid Wy STHWK SE1 18 E2
McCrone Ms HAMP * NW3 3 M1
McCudden Rd DART DA1 165 N9
McCullum Rd BOW E3 140 E3
McDermott Cl BTSEA SW11 157 P8
McDermott Rd PECK SE15 159 P9
McDonald Ct HAT AL10 40 D6
McDonough Cl CHSGTN KT9 219 K1
McDougall Ct RCH/KEW TW9 155 M8
McDougall Rd BERK HP4 34 A5
McDowall Cl CAN/RD E16 141 M7
McEntee Av WALTH E17 100 D9
McEwan Wy SRTFD * E15 141 J3
McGrath Rd FSTGT E7 121 L10
McGregor Rd NTGHL W11 8 C5
McIntosh Cl ROM RM1 124 F1
WLGTN SM6 222 F4
McIntosh Rd ROM RM1 124 F1
McKay Rd RYNPK SW20 178 E10
McKellar Cl BUSH WD23 94 B3
McKenzie Rd BROX EN10 44 F6
Mckenzie Wy HOR/WEW KT19 219 M6
Mckerrell Rd PECK SE15 159 P7
Mckillop Wy SCUP DA14 185 M10
McLeod Rd ABYW SE2 163 M3
McLeod's Ms SKENS SW7 15 H4
McMillan Cl GVE DA12 190 F7
McMillan St DEPT * SE8 160 F5
McNair Rd NWDGN UB2 153 P2
McNeil Rd CMBW SE5 159 M8
McNicol Dr WLSDN NW10 135 P4
McRae La MTCM CR4 202 A7
Mead Av DTCH/LGLY SL3 150 E1
REDH RH1 276 B8
Mead Barn EPP CM16 83 H2
Mead Cl CAMTN * NW1 4 D3
CDH/CHF RM16 167 N1
DEN/HRF UB9 111 K7
DTCH/LGLY SL3 150 E1
EGH TW20 172 E9
GPK RM2 105 H10
KTN/HRWW/W HA3 94 C9
LOU IG10 82 E6
REDH RH1 258 B7
STWL/WRAY TW19 172 A4
SWLY BR8 209 H5
Mead Ct CDALE/KGS NW9 115 P3
EGH TW20 172 F9
WAB EN9 62 G10
WOKN/KNAP GU21 231 K2
Mead Crs CHING E4 101 H5
DART DA1 187 L4
GT/LBKH KT23 253 P1
SUT SM1 221 P1
Meadcroft Rd LBTH SE11 18 C10
Mead Dr COUL/CHIP CR5 222 F10
Meade Cl CHSWK W4 155 M5
Mead End ASHTD KT21 237 L3
Meades La CSHM HP5 50 G8
The Meades WEY * KT13 216 E3
Meadfield EDGW HA8 95 N3
Mead Fld RYLN/HDSTN * HA2 113 N8
Meadfield Av DTCH/LGLY SL3 150 D2
Meadfield Rd DTCH/LGLY SL3 150 E2
Meadfoot Rd STRHM/NOR SW16 202 D1
Meadgate Av WFD IG8 102 B6
Meadgate Rd HOD EN11 45 J6
Mead Gv CHDH RM6 123 N1
Mead House La YEAD UB4 132 E6
Meadhurst Pk SUN TW16 174 F9
Meadhurst Rd CHERT * KT16 195 L8
Meadlands Dr
RCHPK/HAM TW10 177 J5
Mead La CHERT KT16 195 L8
HERT/BAY SG13 25 M4
Meadow Ap CRAWE RH10 285 H2
Meadow Av CROY/NA CR0 204 C6
RAD WD7 57 H7
Meadow Bank EHSLY KT24 252 G3
Meadowbank BKHTH/KID SE3 161 L9
BRYLDS KT5 199 L6
HAMP NW3 4 A4
KGLGY WD4 54 B6
OXHEY WD19 93 K1
WCHMH N21 78 G10
Meadowbank Cl FUL/PGN SW6 156 F6
Meadowbank Gdns HSLWW TW4 153 H7
Meadowbank Rd
CDALE/KGS NW9 116 A5
LTWR GU18 212 B6
Meadowbanks BAR EN5 76 D9
Meadowbrook OXTED RH8 261 H6
Meadowbrook Cl DTCH/LGLY SL3 151 H8
Meadowbrook Rd DORK RH4 272 F1
Meadow Cl BAR EN5 77 J10
BRKMPK AL9 40 G10
BXLYHS DA6 186 A1
CAT SE6 182 F8
CHING E4 100 G2
CHST BR7 184 E8
CRAWE RH10 285 H2
CSHM * HP5 50 F3
ESH/CLAY KT10 198 E10
HERT/BAY SG13 25 N4
HOM E9 120 E10
HSLWW TW4 175 P2
LCOL/BKTW * AL2 55 P6
LCOL/BKTW AL2 57 J3
NTHLT UB5 133 P4
PEND EN3 80 D5
PUR/KEN CR8 222 E9
RAD WD7 57 H6
RCHPK/HAM TW10 177 K4
RGODL GU7 267 K10
RSLP HA4 112 G4
RYNPK SW20 200 F4
SEV TN13 247 H9
SLH/COR SS17 169 K2
STALE/WH AL4 39 H3
WDSR SL4 171 N2
WOT/HER KT12 217 N1
Meadow Cott La AMSS HP7 68 E10
Meadow Ct EPSOM KT18 219 P9
STA TW18 173 H6
Meadowcourt Rd
BKHTH/KID SE3 161 L10
Meadow Cft BMLY BR1 206 C3
HAT AL10 40 C4
Meadowcroft BERK HP4 33 J2
BUSH * WD23 74 A10
CFSP/GDCR SL9 90 A10
STAL AL1 38 F10
Meadow Croft Cl HORL RH6 280 D7
Meadowcroft Cl CRAWW RH11 283 J8
PLMGR * N13 99 J3
Meadowcroft Farm
RDART * DA2 188 G10
Meadowcroft Rd PLMGR N13 99 H3
Meadowcross WAB EN9 63 K10
Meadow Dell HAT AL10 40 C4
Meadow Dr AMS HP6 69 K3

HDN NW4 96 F10
MUSWH N10 118 B1
RPLY/SEND GU23 233 J9
Meadow Gdns EDGW HA8 95 N7
STA TW18 172 G8
Meadow Garth WLSDN NW10 135 P1
Meadow Gn WGCW AL8 22 F5
Meadow Hl AMSS HP7 68 E9
COUL/CHIP CR5 222 D9
NWMAL KT3 200 B6
Meadowlands BAR EN5 76 C9
BGR/WK TN15 247 N6
COB KT11 217 H9
CRAWW RH11 283 M7
EMPK RM11 125 M5
OXTED RH8 261 M10
RGUE GU4 251 L6
Meadow La BEAC HP9 88 E9
LEE/GVPK * SE12 183 P6
LHD/OX KT22 236 B8
WDSR SL4 148 G5
Meadowlea Cl WDR/YW UB7 151 N5
Meadow Ms VX/NE SW8 17 N10
Meadow Pl CHSWK * W4 156 B6
VX/NE SW8 158 F6
Meadow Ri COUL/CHIP CR5 222 E9
WOKN/KNAP GU21 231 H3
Meadow Rd ASHF TW15 174 E8
ASHTD KT21 237 K3
BARK IG11 143 J2
BERK HP4 33 N3
BORE WD6 75 N6
BUSH WD23 74 A9
CDH/CHF RM16 147 P10
DAGW RM9 144 A1
DTCH/LGLY SL3 150 B2
EPP CM16 65 J5
ESH/CLAY KT10 218 D2
FELT TW13 175 M5
GSTN WD25 55 H10
GVW DA11 189 P4
GVW DA11 190 D5
HAYES BR2 205 K1
HHS/BOV HP3 54 B1
LOU IG10 82 B9
PIN HA5 113 L2
RGUE GU4 250 D6
ROMW/RG RM7 124 D6
STHL UB1 133 N9
SUT SM1 221 P1
VW GU25 193 K5
VX/NE SW8 17 N10
WIM/MER SW19 179 M10
Meadow Road Cl BERK HP4 33 M3
Meadow Rw STHWK SE1 18 E4
Meadows Cl LEY E10 120 F7
RBRW/HUT CM13 107 P7
Meadows End SUN TW16 197 H1
Meadowside BEAC HP9 89 L8
DART DA1 187 M4
ELTH/MOT SE9 161 P10
GT/LBKH KT23 235 P9
HORL RH6 280 C3
TWK TW1 177 J3
WOT/HER KT12 197 K9
Meadowside Rd BELMT SM2 221 H5
UPMR RM14 126 B10
Meadows Leigh Cl WEY KT13 196 D10
The Meadows AMSS HP7 69 K5
GUW GU2 267 P3
ORP BR6 227 M3
RBRW/HUT CM13 107 P7
RSEV TN14 228 A9
SBW CM21 30 B1
WARL CR6 242 C3
Meadow Stile CROY/NA CR0 203 K10
Meadowsweet Cl CAN/RD E16 142 A7
NWMAL KT3 200 F5
The Meadow CHST BR7 184 F9
CRAWE RH10 285 H2
HERT/BAY SG13 26 D9
WGCE AL7 23 M5
Meadow Vw BFN/LL DA15 185 L2
CSTG HP8 89 M4
EPP CM16 65 K5
HORL RH6 281 K4
HRW HA1 114 D6
STWL/WRAY TW19 173 J1
SWLY * BR8 208 E6
UX/CGN * UB8 131 M7
Meadowview Rd BXLY DA5 185 P2
CAT SE6 182 F7
HOR/WEW KT19 220 B5
Meadow View Rd THHTH CR7 203 J5
YEAD UB4 132 E6
Meadow Wk DAGW RM9 144 A1
EW KT17 220 C4
HARP AL5 20 B3
HOR/WEW KT19 220 B3
KWD/TDW/WH KT20 238 E10
RDART DA2 187 K7
SWFD E18 121 M2
WLGTN SM6 202 C10
Meadow Wy ABLGY WD5 54 G3
ADL/WDHM KT15 215 L1
AMS HP6 68 B1
CDALE/KGS NW9 116 A3
CHIG IG7 102 F3
CHOB/PIR GU24 212 E9
CHSGTN KT9 219 K2
EHSLY KT24 252 E1
GT/LBKH KT23 236 A9
HHS/BOV HP3 35 J9
KGLGY WD4 54 B6
KWD/TDW/WH KT20 239 H3
ORP BR6 206 D10
POTB/CUF EN6 59 K10
RDART DA2 188 B3
REIG RH2 275 L4
RKW/CH/CXG WD3 91 M1
RSLP HA4 113 J4
SBW CM21 30 B2
UPMR RM14 126 B8
WBLY HA9 115 J9
WDSR SL4 171 N2
Meadow Waye HEST TW5 153 M6
The Meadow Wy
KTN/HRWW/W HA3 94 D9
Mead Pth TOOT SW17 179 N9
Mead Pl CROY/NA CR0 203 J8
HOM E9 140 B1
RKW/CH/CXG WD3 91 L2
Mead Plat WLSDN NW10 135 P1
Mead Rd CHST BR7 184 F9
CRAWE RH10 284 A6
CTHM CR3 241 N9
DART DA1 187 L4
EDGW HA8 95 M7
GVW DA11 190 E5
RAD WD7 57 M9
RCHPK/HAM TW10 177 H6
UX/CGN UB8 131 N1
WOT/HER KT12 217 M1
Mead Rw STHWK SE1 18 A3
Meadside Cl BECK BR3 204 D1
Meads La GDMY/SEVK IG3 123 J5
STALE/WH AL4 21 J2
Meads Rd GU GU1 250 E10
PEND EN3 80 D5
WDGN N22 99 J10
The Meads BERK HP4 33 L3
CHEAM SM3 200 C10
EDGW HA8 96 A7
LCOL/BKTW AL2 55 N5
MTCM * CR4 201 P5
UPMR RM14 126 D7
UX/CGN UB8 131 P6
WEY KT13 216 D3
Meadsway RBRW/HUT CM13 106 G7
Mead Temple HHNE HP2 35 N4
The Mead ABR/ST RM4 83 L7
ASHTD KT21 237 K5
BEAC * HP9 88 D9
BECK BR3 205 H2
BROX * EN10 44 G7
CHES/WCR EN8 62 B5
DORK * RH4 273 H5
EFNCH N2 97 M10
HART DA3 211 K9
HGDN/ICK UB10 112 B7
OXHEY WD19 93 M4
WEA W13 134 G7
WLGTN SM6 222 E3
WWKM BR4 205 J8
Meadvale Rd CROY/NA CR0 203 N7
EA W5 134 G6
Meadview Rd WARE SG12 26 B3
Mead Wk CHONG CM5 67 N6
DTCH/LGLY SL3 150 E1
Mead Wy BUSH WD23 73 M6
COUL/CHIP CR5 240 F4
CROY/NA CR0 204 D9
HAYES BR2 205 L6
RGUE GU4 250 F5
RSLP HA4 112 E4
SL SL1 128 C7
Meadway ASHF TW15 174 B7
BAR EN5 77 K8
BECK BR3 205 H1
BERK HP4 34 B4
BRYLDS KT5 199 P8
EHSLY KT24 253 M4
ESH/CLAY KT10 218 A5
GDMY/SEVK IG3 123 H9
GLDGN NW11 117 L4
GPK RM2 105 H10
GRAYS RM17 168 A3
HARP AL5 20 D4
HOD EN11 44 F5
HOR/WEW KT19 219 P8
LHD/OX KT22 218 C10
PEND EN3 80 C2
RSEV TN14 228 A9
RYNPK SW20 200 F4
STA TW18 173 K10
STALE/WH AL4 40 A9
STHGT/OAK N14 98 E3
WARL CR6 242 B2
WFD IG8 101 P6
WGCE AL7 23 J7
WHTN TW2 176 C4
Meadway Cl BAR EN5 77 K7
GLDGN NW11 117 L4
PIN HA5 94 A7
STA TW18 173 J10
Meadway Ct EA * W5 135 L7
Meadway Dr ADL/WDHM KT15 215 M4
WOKN/KNAP GU21 231 P2
Meadway Gdns RSLP HA4 112 E4
Meadway Pk CFSP/GDCR SL9 110 A6
The Meadway BKHH IG9 102 A2
BKHTH/KID SE3 161 J8
HORL RH6 280 D4
ORP BR6 227 L2
POTB/CUF EN6 60 G4
SEV TN13 246 G8
Meaford Wy PGE/AN SE20 182 A10
Meanley Rd MNPK E12 122 B10
Meard St SOHO/CST W1F 11 J6
Meare Cl KWD/TDW/WH KT20 238 F9
Meath Cl STMC/STPC BR5 207 L5
Meath Green Av HORL RH6 280 A2
Meath Green La REDH RH1 275 P9
Meath Rd IL IG1 122 F8
SRTFD E15 141 L4
Meath St BTSEA SW11 158 C7
Meautys STALW/RED AL3 37 N8
Mecklenburgh Pl BMSBY WC1N 11 N1
Mecklenburgh Sq BMSBY WC1N 11 N1
Mecklenburgh St BMSBY WC1N 11 N1
Medawar Rd GUW GU2 267 J1
Medburn St CAMTN NW1 5 J7
Medbury Rd GVE DA12 191 J4
Medcalf Rd PEND EN3 80 E3
Medcroft Gdns
MORT/ESHN SW14 155 P10
Medebourne Cl BKHTH/KID SE3 161 M9
Medebridge Rd CDH/CHF RM16 147 L8
Mede Fld LHD/OX KT22 236 C10
Medesenge Wy PLMGR N13 99 J7
Medfield St PUT/ROE SW15 178 D3
Medhurst Cl BOW E3 140 D4
CHOB/PIR GU24 213 L5
Medhurst Crs GVE DA12 191 J6
Medhurst Gdns GVE DA12 191 J6
Median Rd CLPT E5 120 B10
Medick Ct GRAYS RM17 168 B5
Medina Av ESH/CLAY KT10 198 D10
Medina Rd GRAYS RM17 168 A4
HOLWY N7 119 H8
Medlake Rd EGH TW20 172 F9
Medland Cl MTCM CR4 202 B8
Medlar Cl CRAWW RH11 283 M4
GU GU1 249 P8
NTHLT UB5 133 L4
Medlar Dr SOCK/AV RM15 147 K6
Medlar Rd GRAYS RM17 168 A5
Medlar St CMBW SE5 159 K7
Medley Rd KIL/WHAMP NW6 2 E2
Medman Cl UX/CGN UB8 131 M4
Medora Rd BRXS/STRHM SW2 180 G2
ROMW/RG RM7 124 E2
Medow Md RAD WD7 56 E9
Medusa Rd LEW SE13 182 G2
Medway CRAWE RH10 285 P8
Medway Cl CROY/NA CR0 204 B6
GSTN WD25 55 K10
IL IG1 122 F10
Medway Dr GFD/PVL UB6 134 E4
Medway Gdns ALP/SUD HA0 114 F9
Medway Pde GFD/PVL * UB6 134 E4
Medway Rd BOW E3 140 D4
CRAWW RH11 283 J8
DART DA1 165 H9
HHNE HP2 36 A1
Medway St WEST SW1P 17 J4
Medwick Ms HHNE HP2 36 C1
Medwin St BRXS/STRHM SW2 158 G10
Meerbrook Rd ELTH/MOT SE9 161 P9
Meeson Rd SRTFD E15 141 L2
Meesons La GRAYS RM17 167 L3
Meeson St CLPT E5 120 D9
Meesons Whf SRTFD * E15 141 H4
Meeting Aly WAT * WD17 73 K8
Meeting Field Pth HOM * E9 140 B1
Meeting House Aly WAP * E1W 140 A10
Meeting House La PECK SE15 160 A7
Megg La KGLGY WD4 53 L5
Mehetabel Rd HACK E8 140 B1
Meister Cl IL IG1 122 G6
Melanda Cl CHST BR7 184 C8
Melanie Cl BXLYHN DA7 163 P7
Melaris Ms KIL/WHAMP NW6 117 K10
Melba Gdns TIL RM18 168 D6
Melbourne Av PLMGR N13 98 G7
RYLN/HDSTN HA2 114 A1
SL SL1 129 H8
WEA W13 134 F10
Melbourne Cl ORP BR6 207 H7
STALW/RED AL3 38 E2
WLGTN SM6 222 D2
Melbourne Ct WGCW AL8 22 E6
Melbourne Gdns CHDH RM6 123 P3
Melbourne Gv EDUL SE22 159 N10
Melbourne Ms BRXN/ST SW9 159 H7
CAT SE6 183 H3
Melbourne Pl HOL/ALD WC2B 11 P6
Melbourne Rd BUSH WD23 74 A9
EHAM E6 142 C4
IL IG1 122 E6
LEY E10 120 G5
TEDD TW11 177 H9
TIL RM18 168 B7
WALTH E17 120 D2
WIM/MER SW19 201 K1
WLGTN SM6 222 C2
Melbourne Sq BRXN/ST SW9 159 H7
Melbourne Ter EDUL * SE22 159 M10
FUL/PGN * SW6 157 L6
Melbourne Wy EN EN1 79 N10
Melbury Av NWDGN UB2 154 A2
Melbury Cl BF/WBF KT14 215 K10
CHERT KT16 195 K7
CHST BR7 184 C9
ESH/CLAY KT10 218 G3
Melbury Ct WKENS W14 14 D3
Melbury Dr CMBW SE5 159 M6
Melbury Gdns RYNPK SW20 200 E1
Melbury Rd KTN/HRWW/W HA3 115 L3
WKENS W14 14 C3
Melbury Ter CAMTN NW1 9 P2
Melcombe Gdns
KTN/HRWW/W HA3 115 L4
Melcombe Pl CAMTN NW1 10 A3
Melcombe St CAMTN NW1 10 B2
Meldon Cl FUL/PGN * SW6 157 L7
Meldone Cl BRYLDS KT5 199 N6
Meldrum Cl OXTED RH8 261 L8
STMC/STPC BR5 207 M6
Meldrum Rd GDMY/SEVK IG3 123 K7
Melfield Gdns CAT SE6 182 G7
Melfont Av THHTH CR7 203 J3
Melford Av BARK IG11 143 H1
Melford Cl CHSGTN KT9 219 L2
Melford Rd DUL SE21 181 P4
EHAM E6 142 C6
IL IG1 122 G7
WALTH E17 120 D2
WAN E11 121 K7
Melfort Rd THHTH CR7 203 J3
Melgund Rd HBRY N5 119 H10
Melina Cl HYS/HAR UB3 132 E7
Melina Pl STJWD NW8 3 L10
Melina Rd SHB W12 156 E1
The Melings HHNE HP2 36 C1
Melior Pl STHWK * SE1 19 J1
Melior St STHWK SE1 19 H1
Meliot Rd CAT SE6 183 J5
Melksham Cl HARH RM3 105 N8
Melksham Gdns HARH RM3 105 M8
Melksham Gn HARH RM3 105 M8
Meller Cl WLGTN SM6 202 F10
Melling Dr EN EN1 79 P5
Melling St WOOL/PLUM SE18 163 H5
Mellish Gdns WFD IG8 101 M6
Mellish St POP/IOD E14 160 E2
Mellish Wy EMPK RM11 125 K3
Mellison Rd TOOT SW17 179 P8
Mellitus St SHB W12 136 C8
Mellor Cl WOT/HER KT12 197 N7
Mellow Cl BNSTD SM7 221 L10
Mellow La East YEAD UB4 132 D6
Mellows Rd CLAY IG5 122 C1
WLGTN SM6 222 E2
Mells Crs ELTH/MOT SE9 184 C7
Mell St GNWCH SE10 161 K4
Melody Rd BH/WHM TN16 243 P4
WAND/EARL SW18 179 M1
Melon Pl KENS * W8 14 F1
Melon Rd PECK SE15 159 P7
WAN E11 121 K8
Melrose Av BORE WD6 75 N9
CRICK NW2 116 F10
GFD/PVL UB6 134 A4
MTCM CR4 180 C10
POTB/CUF EN6 59 L9
STRHM/NOR SW16 202 G3
WDGN N22 99 J9
WHTN TW2 176 A3
WIM/MER SW19 179 J5
Melrose Cl GFD/PVL UB6 134 A4
LEE/GVPK SE12 183 M4
YEAD UB4 133 H7
Melrose Crs ORP BR6 226 G1
Melrose Dr STHL UB1 133 P10
Melrose Gdns EDGW HA8 115 N1
HMSMTH W6 156 F2
NWMAL KT3 200 A3
WOT/HER KT12 217 K2
Melrose Pl WAT WD17 72 G4
Melrose Rd BARN SW13 156 C8
BH/WHM TN16 243 P2
COUL/CHIP CR5 240 C1
RYLN/HDSTN HA2 113 N2
WAND/EARL SW18 179 J2
WEY KT13 216 B2
WIM/MER SW19 201 K2
Melrose Ter HMSMTH W6 156 F1
Melrose Vls BECK * BR3 204 F2
Melsa Rd MRDN SM4 201 M6
Melsted Rd HHW HP1 35 L6
Melstock Av UPMR RM14 126 B9
Melthorne Dr RSLP HA4 113 K8
Melthorpe Gdns
WOOL/PLUM SE18 162 A7
Melton Cl RSLP HA4 113 K6
Melton Flds HOR/WEW KT19 220 A5
Melton Gdns ROM RM1 124 G5
Melton Pl HOR/WEW KT19 220 A5
Melton Rd REDH RH1 258 D6
Melton St CAMTN NW1 5 H10
Melville Av GFD/PVL UB6 114 E10
RYNPK SW20 178 D10
SAND/SEL CR2 223 N2
Melville Cl HGDN/ICK UB10 112 F8
Melville Ct DEPT SE8 160 C3
Melville Gdns PLMGR N13 99 H6
Melville Pl IS N1 6 E4
Melville Rd BARN SW13 156 D7
RAIN RM13 145 H6
ROMW/RG RM7 104 C8
SCUP DA14 185 M5
WALTH E17 120 E2
WLSDN NW10 136 A2
Melville Villas Rd ACT * W3 136 A10
Melvin Rd PGE/AN SE20 204 B1
Melvinshaw LHD/OX KT22 237 H7
Melvyn Cl CHESW EN7 61 J4
Memel St STLK EC1Y 12 E2
Memorial Av SRTFD E15 141 K5
Memorial Cl HEST TW5 153 N5
Memorial Wy WAT WD17 73 H7
Mendip Cl DTCH/LGLY SL3 150 D4
HYS/HAR UB3 152 E6
STALE/WH AL4 39 H1
SYD SE26 182 B7
WPK KT4 200 F9
Mendip Dr GLDGN NW11 117 H7
Mendip Houses BETH * E2 140 B5
Mendip Rd BTSEA SW11 157 M9
BUSH WD23 74 B10
BXLYHN DA7 164 F7
EMPK RM11 125 H5
GNTH/NBYPK IG2 123 H3
Mendip Wk CRAWW RH11 283 L7
Mendip Wy HHNE HP2 35 P3
Mendlesham WGCE AL7 23 P5
Mendora Rd FUL/PGN SW6 157 H6
Mendoza Cl EMPK RM11 125 M3
Menelik Rd CRICK NW2 117 H9
Menlo Gdns NRWD SE19 181 L10
Menotti St BETH E2 13 P1
Mentmore Cl
KTN/HRWW/W HA3 115 H4
Mentmore Rd STAL AL1 38 C8
Mentmore Ter HACK E8 140 A2
Meon Cl KWD/TDW/WH KT20 238 E8
Meon Rd ACT W3 155 P1
Meopham Rd MTCM CR4 202 D1
Mepham Crs KTN/HRWW/W HA3 94 B8
Mepham Gdns
KTN/HRWW/W HA3 94 B8
Mepham St STHWK SE1 12 A10
Mera Dr BXLYHN DA7 164 B10
Merantum Wy WIM/MER SW19 201 L1
Merbury Cl LEW SE13 183 H1
Merbury Rd THMD SE28 142 G10
Merbury St WOOL/PLUM SE18 162 E2
Mercator Pl POP/IOD E14 160 F4
Mercator Rd LEW SE13 161 J10
Mercer Cl CRAWE RH10 284 D10
THDIT KT7 198 E7
Merceron Houses BETH * E2 140 B5
Merceron St WCHPL E1 140 A6
Mercer Pl PIN HA5 93 K10
Mercers HHNE HP2 35 P4
HLWW/ROY CM19 46 D4
Mercers Cl GNWCH SE10 161 L3
Mercers Cottages WCHPL * E1 140 D8
Mercers Pl HMSMTH W6 156 F3
Mercers Rd ARCH N19 118 E8
Mercers Rw STAL AL1 38 B8
Mercer St LSQ/SEVD WC2H 11 L6
Merchant Dr HERT/BAY SG13 25 N4
Merchant St BOW * E3 140 E5
Merchiston Rd CAT SE6 183 J5
Merchland Rd ELTH/MOT SE9 184 F4
Mercia Gv LEW SE13 161 H9
Mercian Wy SL SL1 128 D10
Mercier Rd PUT/ROE SW15 179 H1
Mercury Cl CRAWW RH11 283 H10
Mercury Gdns ROM RM1 124 G3
Mercury House HYS/HAR * UB3 152 G1
Mercury Rd BTFD TW8 155 H4
Mercury Wk HHNE HP2 36 A3
Mercury Wy NWCR SE14 160 C5
Mercy Ter LEW SE13 182 G1
Merebank La WLGTN SM6 222 G2
Mere Cl ORP BR6 206 E9
WIM/MER SW19 178 G3
Meredith Av CRICK NW2 116 F10
Meredith Cl PIN HA5 93 L8
Meredith Ms BROCKY * SE4 160 E10
Meredith Rd CDH/CHF RM16 168 D3
Meredith St CLKNW EC1R 6 C10
PLSTW E13 141 M5
Meredyth Rd BARN SW13 156 D8
Mere End CROY/NA CR0 204 C7
Merefield SBW CM21 29 P2
Merefield Gdns
KWD/TDW/WH KT20 238 G5
Mere Rd KWD/TDW/WH KT20 238 E10
SHPTN * TW17 196 C6
SL SL1 149 L2
WEY KT13 196 E10
Mereside ORP BR6 206 D9
Mereside Pk ASHF * TW15 174 D7
Meretone Cl BROCKY SE4 160 D10
Merevale Crs MRDN SM4 201 M6
Mereway Rd WHTN TW2 176 C4
Merewood Cl BMLY BR1 206 D2
Merewood Rd BXLYHN DA7 164 D8
Mereworth Cl HAYES BR2 205 L5
Mereworth Dr CRAWE RH10 284 E5
WOOL/PLUM SE18 162 E6
Meriden Cl BARK/HLT IG6 102 F9
BMLY BR1 184 A10
Meriden Wy GSTN WD25 73 M3
Meridian Gv HORL RH6 280 D3
Meridian Rd CHARL SE7 162 A6
Meridian Sq SRTFD E15 141 J2
Meridian Wy ED N9 100 B4
WARE SG12 26 G6
Merifield Rd ELTH/MOT SE9 161 P10
Merino Cl WAN E11 121 P2
Merivale Rd HRW HA1 114 B5
PUT/ROE SW15 157 H10
Merland Cl KWD/TDW/WH KT20 238 F6
Merland Gn KWD/TDW/WH KT20 238 F6
Merland Ri KWD/TDW/WH KT20 238 F5
Merle Av DEN/HRF UB9 91 M10
Merlewood Cl CTHM CR3 241 L6
Merlewood Dr CHST BR7 206 C1
Merley Ct CDALE/KGS NW9 115 P6
Merlin Cl CRAWW RH11 283 H7
CROY/NA CR0 222 G3
CROY/NA CR0 223 M1
CRW RM5 104 E7
DTCH/LGLY * SL3 150 E5
MTCM CR4 201 P3
NTHLT UB5 133 K5
WAB EN9 63 M10
Merlin Crs EDGW HA8 95 L9
Merlin Gdns CRW RM5 104 E7
Merling Cft BERK HP4 33 K3
Merlin Gv BARK/HLT IG6 102 E8
BECK BR3 204 E4
Merlin Rd CRW RM5 104 E7
MNPK E12 122 A7
WELL DA16 163 K10
Merlin Rd North WELL DA16 163 K10
Merlins Av RYLN/HDSTN HA2 113 N6
Merlin St FSBYW WC1X 6 A10
Merlin Wy EPP CM16 66 B1
GSTN WD25 54 G10
Mermagen Dr RAIN RM13 145 J2
Mermaid Ct STHWK SE1 18 G1
Mermerus Gdns GVE DA12 191 J7
Merredene St BRXS/STRHM SW2 180 G2
Merriam Cl CHING E4 101 H6
Merrick Rd NWDGN UB2 153 N3
Merrick Sq STHWK SE1 18 G3
Merridene WCHMH N21 79 J10
Merrielands Crs DAGW RM9 144 A4
Merrilands Rd WPK KT4 200 F8
Merrilees Rd BFN/LL DA15 185 H3
Merrilyn Cl ESH/CLAY KT10 218 F3
Merriman Rd BKHTH/KID SE3 161 P7
Merrington Rd FUL/PGN SW6 14 F9
Merrion Av STAN HA7 95 J6
Merritt Gdns CHSGTN KT9 219 H3
Merritt Rd BROCKY SE4 182 E1
Merritt Wk BRKMPK AL9 40 E10
Merrivale STHGT/OAK N14 78 E10
Merrivale Av REDBR IG4 122 A2
Merrivale Gdns
WOKN/KNAP GU21 231 P3
Merrivale Ms WDR/YW * UB7 131 N10
Merrow Cha GU GU1 250 F10
Merrow Common Rd RGUE GU4 250 G7
Merrow Copse GU GU1 250 E9
Merrow Ct GU * GU1 250 G10
Merrow Cft GU GU1 250 F9
Merrow Dr HHW HP1 35 H5
Merrow La RGUE GU4 250 F5
Merrow Rd BELMT SM2 220 G5
Merrow St RGUE GU4 250 G8
WALW SE17 18 G8
Merrow Wk WALW SE17 19 H7
Merrow Wy CROY/NA CR0 225 H3
GU * GU1 250 G9
Merrow Woods GU GU1 250 E8
Merrydown Wy CHST BR7 206 B1
Merryfield BKHTH/KID SE3 161 L8
Merryfield Cl BORE WD6 75 L6
Merryfield Gdns STAN HA7 95 H6
Merryfields STALE/WH AL4 39 K6
UX/CGN UB8 131 N4
Merryfields Cl HART DA3 211 L4
Merryhill Cl CHING E4 100 G1
Merry Hill Mt BUSH WD23 94 A2
Merry Hill Rd BUSH WD23 93 P1
Merryhills Cl BH/WHM TN16 244 A2
Merryhills Dr ENC/FH EN2 78 F8
Merrylands CHERT KT16 195 H10
Merrylands Farm GT/LBKH KT23 235 N10
Merrylands Rd GT/LBKH KT23 235 N9
Merrymeet BNSTD SM7 222 A10
Merryweather Cl DART DA1 187 N2
Merryweather Ct NWMAL * KT3 200 B5
Merrywood Gv
KWD/TDW/WH KT20 256 G6
Merrywood Pk REIG RH2 257 L8
Mersey Av UPMR RM14 126 C4
Mersey Pl HHNE HP2 36 A1
Mersey Rd WALTH E17 120 E1
Mersham Dr CDALE/KGS NW9 115 M3
Mersham Pl PGE/AN SE20 204 A1
THHTH CR7 203 L2
Mersham Rd THHTH CR7 203 L3
Merstham Rd REDH RH1 259 H6
Merten Rd CHDH RM6 123 P5
Merthyr Ter BARN SW13 156 E5
Merton Av CHSWK W4 156 C3
HART DA3 211 K4
HGDN/ICK UB10 132 C2
NTHLT UB5 114 B10
Merton Gdns
KWD/TDW/WH KT20 238 G6
STMC/STPC BR5 206 E5
Merton Hall Gdns RYNPK SW20 201 H1
Merton Hall Rd WIM/MER SW19 201 H1
Merton High St WIM/MER SW19 179 M10
Merton La HGT N6 118 A7
Merton Pl CDH/CHF RM16 168 D3
WIM/MER * SW19 201 M1
Merton Ri HAMP NW3 3 N3
Merton Rd BARK IG11 143 J2
ENC/FH EN2 79 L4
GDMY/SEVK IG3 123 J5
LEY E10 121 H3
RYLN/HDSTN HA2 114 B6
SL SL1 149 M2
SNWD SE25 203 N5
WAND/EARL SW18 179 K3
WATW WD18 73 J8
WIM/MER SW19 179 L10
Merton Wy E/WMO/HCT KT8 198 B4
HGDN/ICK UB10 132 C2
LHD/OX KT22 236 F5
Mertoun Ter MBLAR * W1H 10 A5
Merttins Rd PECK SE15 160 C10
Meru Cl KTTN NW5 118 B10
Mervan Rd BRXS/STRHM SW2 159 H10
Mervyn Av ELTH/MOT SE9 184 F6
Mervyn Rd SHPTN TW17 196 D7
WEA W13 154 F2
Merwin Wy WDSR * SL4 148 C9
Mesne Wy RSEV TN14 228 G8
Messaline Av ACT W3 135 P8
Messant Cl GPK RM2 105 L10
Messent Rd ELTH/MOT SE9 183 P1
Messeter Pl ELTH/MOT SE9 184 D2
Messina Av KIL/WHAMP NW6 2 E4
Metcalf Rd ASHF TW15 174 C8
Metcalf Wy CRAWW RH11 283 N3
Meteor St BTSEA SW11 158 B10
Meteor Wy WLGTN SM6 222 F4
Metford Crs WAB EN9 80 F4

Metheringham Wy
CDALE/KGS NW9 96 B10
Methley St LBTH SE11 18 B8
Methuen Cl EDGW HA8 95 M8
Methuen Pk MUSWH N10 98 C10
Methuen Rd BELV DA17 164 C3
BXLYHS DA6 164 A10
EDGW HA8 95 M8
Methwold Rd NKENS W10 136 G7
Metro Centre STALW/RED * AL3 38 E2
STMC/STPC * BR5 207 L6
Metropolitan Cl POP/IOD E14 140 F7
Metropolitan Station Ap
WATW WD18 72 G7
Metropolitan Whf WAP * E1W 140 B10
Meux Cl CHESW EN7 61 P7
Mews Clare FUL/PGN SW6 157 L6
Mewsend BH/WHM TN16 244 A4
Mews North BGVA SW1W 16 E4
Mews Pl WFD IG8 101 M5
Mews South PIM SW1V 17 H7
Mews St WAP E1W 13 M9
The Mews BECK * BR3 204 F1
CEND/HSY/T N8 119 H2
GU * GU1 250 G10
HARP * AL5 20 A2
NFNCH/WDSP * N12 97 L6
REDBR IG4 122 A3
REIG * RH2 257 L9
ROM RM1 124 F2
SEV * TN13 247 H10
STRHM/NOR * SW16 202 G1
TWK * TW1 176 G2
WATW * WD18 73 K8
Mexfield Rd PUT/ROE SW15 179 J1
Meyer Gn EN EN1 79 P4
Meyer Rd ERITH DA8 164 D5
Meymott St STHWK SE1 12 C10
Meynell Crs HOM E9 140 C2
Meynell Gdns HOM E9 140 C2
Meynell Rd HARH RM3 105 J7
HOM E9 140 C2
Meyrick Cl WOKN/KNAP GU21 231 K2
Meyrick Rd BTSEA SW11 157 N9
WLSDN NW10 136 D1
Mezen Cl NTHWD HA6 92 E6
Miah Ter WAP * E1W 13 P10
Micawber Av UX/CGN UB8 132 B6
Micawber St IS N1 6 E9
Michael Crs HORL RH6 280 B6
Michael Gdns EMPK RM11 125 L2
GVE DA12 191 H9
Michael Gaynor Cl HNWL W7 134 E10
Michaelmas Cl RYNPK SW20 200 F3
Michael Rd FUL/PGN SW6 157 L7
SNWD SE25 203 M3
WAN E11 121 K6
Michaels Cl LEW SE13 161 K9
Michaels La HART DA3 210 G9
Micheldever Rd LEW SE13 183 K2
Michelet Cl LTWR GU18 212 A6
Michelham Gdns
KWD/TDW/WH * KT20 238 F6
TWK TW1 176 E6
Michigan Av MNPK E12 122 B9
Michleham Down
NFNCH/WDSP N12 97 J5
Micholls Av CFSP/GDCR SL9 90 B6
Micklefield Rd HHNE HP2 36 D6
Micklefield Wy BORE WD6 75 K6
Mickleham Cl STMC/STPC BR5 207 J2
Mickleham Dr LHD/OX KT22 255 H2
Mickleham Gdns CHEAM SM3 221 H3
Mickleham Rd STMC/STPC BR5 207 J1
Mickleham Wy CROY/NA CR0 225 J4
Micklem Dr HHW HP1 35 J5
Micklethwaite Rd FUL/PGN SW6 14 F10
Midcot Wy BERK HP4 33 L3
Midcroft RSLP HA4 112 F6
SLN SL2 128 G6
Mid Cross La CFSP/GDCR SL9 90 C6
Middle Boy ABR/ST RM4 83 L7
Middle Cl COUL/CHIP CR5 241 H6
EW KT17 220 B8
Middle Dartrey Wk
WBPTN * SW10 157 M6
Middle Dene MLHL NW7 96 A4
Middle Dr BEAC HP9 88 C6
Middle Farm Pl EHSLY KT24 253 L3
Middlefield HAT AL10 40 D3
HORL RH6 280 D3
STJWD NW8 3 L5
WGCE AL7 23 H9
Middlefield Av HOD EN11 44 F1
Middlefield Cl HOD EN11 44 F1
STALE/WH AL4 39 H3
Middlefield Rd HOD EN11 44 F1
Middlefields CROY/NA CR0 224 D5
WEA W13 134 G7
Middle Furlong BUSH WD23 74 A8
Middle Gn BRWN CM15 87 H3
DTCH/LGLY SL3 130 B9
Middle Green Cl BRYLDS KT5 199 L6
Middlegreen Rd DTCH/LGLY SL3 130 A10
Middleham Gdns UED N18 99 P7
Middleham Rd UED N18 99 P7
Middle Hl EGH TW20 171 P8
Middlehill HHW HP1 35 H6
Middleknights Hl HHW HP1 35 K4
Middle La BGR/WK TN15 247 N7
CEND/HSY/T N8 118 F3
EW KT17 220 B8
HHS/BOV HP3 52 D5
TEDD TW11 176 E9
Middle Lane Ms CEND/HSY/T N8 118 F3
Middlemead Cl GT/LBKH KT23 253 P1
Middle Meadow CSTG HP8 89 N4
Middlemead Rd GT/LBKH KT23 253 N1
Middle Ope WATN WD24 73 J3
Middle Park Av ELTH/MOT SE9 184 A2
Middle Rd BERK HP4 33 N5
DEN/HRF UB9 110 F5
EBAR EN4 77 P10
LHD/OX KT22 236 G7
PLSTW E13 141 M4
RBRW/HUT CM13 107 P5
RYLN/HDSTN HA2 114 C7
STRHM/NOR SW16 202 D2
WAB EN9 62 G8
Middle Rw NKENS W10 8 A2
Middlesborough Rd UED N18 99 P7
Middlesex Pl HOM E9 140 B1
Middlesex Rd MTCM CR4 202 F5
Middlesex St WCHPL E1 13 K4
Middle St BRKHM/BTCW RH3 273 N2
CROY/NA CR0 203 K9
SHGR GU5 270 B5
STBT EC1A 12 E3
WAB EN9 45 L9
Middle Temple La TPL/STR WC2R 12 A6
Middleton Av CHING E4 100 E5
GFD/PVL UB6 134 C4
SCUP DA14 185 M9
Middleton Buildings GTPST W1W 10 G4
Middleton Cl CHING E4 100 E4
Middleton Dr BERM/RHTH SE16 160 C1
PIN HA5 113 H1
Middleton Gdns
GNTH/NBYPK IG2 122 E4
Middleton Gv HOLWY N7 118 F10
Middleton Hall La BRWN CM15 107 K3
Middleton Pl GTPST W1W 10 G4
Middleton Rd BRWN CM15 107 K2
CAR SM5 201 N7
COB KT11 235 J5
GLDGN NW11 117 K5
HACK E8 7 L4
HOR/WEW * KT19 220 A6
HYS/HAR UB3 132 E7
NWMAL KT3 199 P3
RKW/CH/CXG WD3 91 K2
Middleton St BETH E2 140 A5
Middleton Wy CRAWW RH11 283 H8
LEW SE13 161 J10
Middle Wk SL SL1 128 A5
WOKN/KNAP * GU21 232 B3
Middleway GLDGN NW11 117 L3
Middle Wy STRHM/NOR SW16 202 E2
WATN WD24 73 J3
The Middle Wy
KTN/HRWW/W HA3 94 E10
Middle Yd STHWK SE1 13 H9
The Middlings SEV TN13 264 G2
Middlings Wd SEV TN13 264 G1
Midfield Av BXLYHN DA7 164 D9
SWLY BR8 187 H9
Midfield Wy STMC/STPC BR5 207 L1
Midford Pl FITZ * W1T 11 H2
Midgley Rd CRAWE RH10 284 A5
Midholm GLDGN NW11 117 L2
WBLY HA9 115 M6
Midholm Cl GLDGN * NW11 117 L2
Midholm Rd CROY/NA CR0 204 D10
Mid Holmwood La RDKG RH5 272 G8
Midhope Cl WOKS/MYFD GU22 232 B5
Midhope Gdns
WOKS/MYFD GU22 232 B5
Midhope Rd WOKS/MYFD GU22 232 A5
Midhope St STPAN WC1H 5 M10
Midhurst Av CROY/NA CR0 203 H7
MUSWH N10 118 B1
Midhurst Cl CRAWW RH11 283 K6
HCH RM12 125 H9
Midhurst Gdns HGDN/ICK UB10 132 D2
Midhurst Hl BXLYHS DA6 186 B1
Midhurst Pde MUSWH * N10 118 B1
Midhurst Rd HNWL W7 154 F1
Midland Arches CRICK * NW2 116 E7
Midland Crs HAMP NW3 3 J1
Midland Rd CAMTN NW1 5 K8
HHNE HP2 35 N6
LEY E10 121 H5
Midland Ter WLSDN NW10 136 B6
Midleton Industrial Estate Rd
GUW GU2 249 N9
Midleton Rd GUW GU2 249 L10
Midlothian Rd BOW E3 140 E6
Midmoor Rd BAL SW12 180 D4
WIM/MER SW19 200 G1
Midship Cl BERM/RHTH * SE16 140 C10
Midship Point POP/IOD * E14 160 F1
Midstrath Rd WLSDN NW10 116 B9
Mid St REDH RH1 258 G10
Midsummer Av HSLWW TW4 153 N10
Midsummer Wk
WOKN/KNAP GU21 232 A2
Midway CHEAM SM3 201 J7
STALW/RED AL3 38 A9
WOT/HER KT12 197 J9
Midway Av CHERT KT16 195 K3
EGH TW20 194 E3
Midway Cl STA TW18 173 L6
Midwinter Cl WELL DA16 163 K9
Miena Wy ASHTD KT21 237 J3
Mighell Av REDBR IG4 122 A3
Milan Rd STHL UB1 153 N1
Milborne Gv WBPTN SW10 15 K8
Milborne St HOM E9 140 B1
Milborough Crs LEE/GVPK SE12 183 K2
Milbourne La ESH/CLAY KT10 218 B3
Milbrook ESH/CLAY KT10 218 B3
Milburn Dr WDR/YW UB7 131 P9
Milburn Wk EPSOM KT18 238 B1
Milcote St STHWK SE1 18 C2
Mildenhall Rd CLPT E5 120 B9
SL SL1 129 K8
Mildmay Av IS N1 7 H1
Mildmay Gv North IS N1 119 L10
Mildmay Gv South IS N1 119 L10
Mildmay Pk IS N1 119 L10
Mildmay Pl RSEV TN14 228 G7
STNW/STAM * N16 119 M10
Mildmay Rd IL IG1 122 E8
IS N1 119 L10
ROMW/RG RM7 124 D3
Mildmay St IS N1 7 H1
Mildred Av BORE WD6 75 M8
HYS/HAR UB3 152 E3
NTHLT UB5 114 A10
WATW WD18 73 H8
Mildred Cl DART DA1 187 P2
Mildred Rd ERITH DA8 164 F4
Mile Cl WAB EN9 63 H9
Mile End Pl WCHPL E1 140 C6
Mile End Rd WCHPL E1 140 B7
The Mile End WALTH E17 100 C9
Mile House Cl STAL AL1 38 F9
Mile House La STAL AL1 38 E10
Mile Pth WOKS/MYFD GU22 231 N6
Mile Rd WLGTN SM6 202 B8
Miles Cl HLWW/ROY CM19 46 E2
Miles Dr THMD SE28 143 H10
Miles La COB KT11 217 M9
Milespit Hl MLHL NW7 96 E6
Miles Pl BRYLDS * KT5 199 L4
Miles Rd CEND/HSY/T N8 118 F1
HOR/WEW KT19 220 A8
MTCM CR4 201 P3
Miles St VX/NE SW8 17 L10
Milestone Cl BELMT SM2 221 N3
ED N9 99 P3
RPLY/SEND GU23 233 K8
Milestone Rd NRWD SE19 181 N9
Mile Stone Rd RDART DA2 188 A2
Miles Wy TRDG/WHET N20 97 P3
Milfoil St SHB W12 136 D9
Milford Cl ABYW SE2 163 P5
STALE/WH AL4 39 J2
Milford Ct SL SL1 149 M1
Milford Gdns ALP/SUD HA0 115 J10
EDGW HA8 95 M8
Milford Gv SUT SM1 221 M1
Milford La TPL/STR WC2R 12 A7
Milford Ms STRHM/NOR SW16 180 G6
Milford Rd STHL UB1 133 P9
WEA W13 134 G10
Milkhouse Ga GU * GU1 268 A2
Milking La ORP BR6 226 B8
Milk St BMLY BR1 183 N8
CAN/RD E16 142 E10
CITYW EC2V 12 F5
Milkwell Gdns WFD IG8 101 N8
Milkwell Yd CMBW SE5 159 K7
Milkwood RGUE * GU4 268 C7
Milkwood Rd HNHL SE24 181 J1
Milk Yd WAP E1W 140 B9
Millacres WARE * SG12 26 D2
Millais Av MNPK E12 122 D10
Millais Gdns EDGW HA8 95 M10
Millais Pl TIL RM18 168 D6
Millais Rd EN EN1 79 N9
NWMAL KT3 200 B7
WAN E11 121 H9
Millais Wy HOR/WEW KT19 219 P1
Millan Cl ADL/WDHM KT15 215 L6
Milland Ct BORE WD6 76 A5
Millard Cl STNW/STAM N16 119 M10
Mill Av UX/CGN UB8 131 M4
Millbank HHS/BOV HP3 35 N10
WEST SW1P 17 L5
Millbank Av CHONG CM5 67 N5
Millbank Est WEST SW1P 17 K6
The Millbank CRAWW RH11 283 J7
Millbank Wy LEE/GVPK SE12 183 M1
Millbottom La RDKG RH5 273 J10
Millbourne Rd FELT TW13 175 M7
Mill Br BAR * EN5 77 J9
HERT/WAS SG14 25 K5
Mill Bridge Pl UX/CGN UB8 131 L4
Millbro SWLY BR8 209 H1
Millbrook GUW GU2 268 A2
WEY KT13 216 F1
Millbrook Av WELL DA16 162 G10
Millbrook Gdns CHDH RM6 123 P4
GPK RM2 104 F10
Millbrook Rd BRXN/ST SW9 159 J9
BUSH WD23 73 N5
ED N9 100 A2
Mill Brook Rd STMC/STPC BR5 207 M4
Millbrook Wy DTCH/LGLY SL3 151 H8
Mill Cl CAR * SM5 202 B9
CSHM HP5 51 K10
GT/LBKH KT23 235 P10
HHS/BOV HP3 54 B1
HHW HP1 35 L2
HORL RH6 279 P3
WARE SG12 26 C2
WDR/YW UB7 151 N2
WGCW AL8 22 D6
Millcombe Cl WOKN/KNAP GU21 231 N4
Mill Cnr BAR EN5 77 J5
Millcrest Rd CHESW EN7 61 J4
Millennium Br STHWK SE1 12 E8
Millennium Cl CAN/RD E16 141 M8
UX/CGN UB8 131 L4
Millennium Dr POP/IOD E14 161 J2
Millennium Pl BETH * E2 140 A4
Millennium Sq STHWK SE1 19 L1
Millennium Wy GNWCH SE10 161 K1
Millennium Whf POP/IOD E14 161 J3
RKW/CH/CXG * WD3 91 P2
Miller Av PEND * EN3 80 F4
Miller Cl MTCM CR4 202 A7
Miller Pl CFSP/GDCR SL9 90 A5
Miller Rd CROY/NA CR0 202 G8
GVE DA12 191 K5
RGUE GU4 250 F7
WIM/MER SW19 179 N9
Miller's Av HACK E8 119 N10
Millers Cl CHIG IG7 103 L5
MLHL NW7 96 D5
STA TW18 173 L8
Millers Copse EPSOM KT18 238 A5
REDH RH1 277 J10
Miller's Ct CHSWK W4 156 C4
Millersdale HLWW/ROY CM19 46 E5
Millers Green Cl ENC/FH EN2 79 J7
Miller's La CHIG IG7 103 L2
REDH RH1 277 J10
WARE SG12 27 H7
Millers Ri STAL AL1 38 D7
Miller's Ter HACK E8 119 N10
Miller St CAMTN NW1 4 G7
Miller's Wy HMSMTH W6 156 F1
Millers Yd FNCH N3 97 L9
HERT/WAS SG14 25 L5
Miller Wk STHWK SE1 12 B10
Millet Rd GFD/PVL UB6 134 A5
Mill Farm Av SUN TW16 174 F10
Mill Farm Cl PIN HA5 93 K10
Mill Farm Crs HSLWW TW4 175 M4
Mill Fld HLWE CM17 29 M7
Millfield BERK HP4 34 A4
HART DA3 211 K9
SUN TW16 196 E1
WGCE AL7 23 M4
Millfield Av WALTH E17 100 D9
Millfield Dr GVW DA11 190 B5
Millfield La HART DA3 211 K9
HGT N6 118 A7
KWD/TDW/WH KT20 257 K1
Millfield Rd EDGW HA8 95 P10
HSLWW TW4 175 M4
Millfields CSHM HP5 51 H9
Millfields Cl STMC/STPC BR5 207 L4
Millfields Rd CLPT E5 120 B9
Millfield Wk HHS/BOV HP3 36 B9
Millford WOKN/KNAP GU21 231 N3
Mill Gdns SYD SE26 182 A7
Mill Gn MTCM * CR4 202 B7
Mill Green La BRKMPK AL9 23 H10
Mill Green Rd MTCM CR4 202 B7
WGCE AL7 23 H6
Millgrove St BTSEA SW11 158 B7
Millharbour POP/IOD E14 160 G2
Millhaven Cl CHDH RM6 123 L4
Millhedge Cl COB KT11 235 M2
Mill Hl BARN SW13 156 D9
BRKHM/BTCW RH3 273 N1
BRWN CM15 107 K1
Mill Hill Gv ACT * W3 135 N10
Mill Hill La BRKHM/BTCW RH3 255 N10
GVE DA12 191 N8
Mill Hill Rd ACT W3 155 N1
BARN SW13 156 E9
Mill Hill Ter ACT W3 135 N10
Millhouse La ABLGY WD5 55 H3
Mill House La CHERT KT16 194 E4
Millhouse Pl WNWD SE27 181 J7
Millhurst Ms HLWE CM17 29 P7
Millicent Rd LEY * E10 120 E6
Milligan St POP/IOD E14 140 E9
Milliners Ct STAL * AL1 38 D6
Milling Rd EDGW HA8 96 A8
Millington Rd HYS/HAR UB3 152 F2
Mill La ABR/ST RM4 85 K6
AMSS HP7 68 F5
ASC SL5 192 G2
BF/WBF KT14 216 A9
BH/WHM TN16 262 F3
BROX EN10 44 E7
BRWN CM15 86 D3
BRWN CM15 87 J1
CAR SM5 222 B1
CFSP/GDCR SL9 110 C3
CHDH RM6 123 P4
CHES/WCR EN8 62 D4
CHING E4 80 G7
CHOB/PIR GU24 230 C10
CHONG CM5 49 K4
CHONG CM5 66 F5
CRAWE RH10 285 M2
CRAWW RH11 283 K5
CRICK NW2 117 H10
CROY/NA CR0 203 H10
CSTG HP8 89 M3
DORK RH4 272 G1
DTCH/LGLY SL3 150 E9
EGH TW20 194 F4
EW KT17 220 C5
EYN DA4 209 M8
GUW GU2 268 A2
HLWE CM17 29 P7
HORL RH6 279 N4
KGLGY WD4 54 B5
LHD/OX KT22 236 F8
ORP BR6 226 D6
OXTED RH8 261 L8
OXTED RH8 262 C7
RDKG RH5 278 A2
REDH RH1 258 D7
RGUE GU4 269 J5
RGUW GU3 267 P8
RPLY/SEND GU23 233 N5
RSEV TN14 228 G6
RSEV TN14 247 K7
WDSR SL4 148 F6
WFD IG8 101 L6
WOOL/PLUM SE18 162 D4
WTHK RM20 167 J4
Mill Lane Cl BROX EN10 44 E7
Millman Ms BMSBY * WC1N 11 N2
Millman Pl BMSBY WC1N 11 N2
Millman St BMSBY WC1N 11 N2
Millmark Gv NWCR SE14 160 D8
Millmarsh La PEND EN3 80 D6
Millmead BF/WBF KT14 216 A8
GUW GU2 267 P2
Mill Md STA TW18 173 J7
Mill Mead Rd TOTM N17 120 A1
Millmead Ter GUW GU2 267 P2
Millmead Wy HERT/WAS SG14 25 J4
Mill Park Av HCH RM12 125 M7
Mill Pl CHST BR7 206 D1
DART DA1 165 H10
DTCH/LGLY SL3 150 A8
KUT KT1 199 L3
POP/IOD E14 140 D8
Mill Plat ISLW TW7 154 F8
Mill Plat Av ISLW TW7 154 F8
Mill Pond Cl SEV TN13 247 L7
Millpond Ct ADL/WDHM KT15 215 P2
Millpond Est BERM/RHTH * SE16 160 A1
Mill Pond Rd BFOR GU20 212 A1
DART DA1 187 M2
Mill Race WARE SG12 27 J7
Mill Rdg EDGW HA8 95 L6
Mill Rd CAN/RD E16 141 N10
COB KT11 235 K1
CRAWE RH10 284 C6
ERITH DA8 164 D6
ESH/CLAY KT10 197 P9
EW KT17 220 C8
GVW DA11 190 B3
HERT/BAY SG13 25 L4
IL IG1 122 D8
KWD/TDW/WH KT20 238 G9
PUR RM19 166 A5
RDART DA2 187 N7
RDKG RH5 273 H10
SEV TN13 246 F6
SOCK/AV RM15 146 B9
WDR/YW UB7 151 N2
WHTN TW2 176 B5
WIM/MER SW19 179 M10
Mill Rw BXLY * DA5 186 C3
IS N1 7 K6
Mills Cl HGDN/ICK UB10 132 B4
Mills Crs BGR/WK TN15 247 N6
Mills Gv HDN NW4 116 G1
POP/IOD E14 141 H7
Mill Shaw OXTED RH8 261 L8
Millshot Cl FUL/PGN SW6 156 F7
Millside CAR SM5 202 A9
Millside Ct GT/LBKH * KT23 253 P1
Millside Pk WDSR * SL4 148 C8
Millside Pl ISLW TW7 154 G8
Millsmead Wy LOU IG10 82 C6
Millson Cl TRDG/WHET N20 97 N3
Mills Rd WOT/HER KT12 217 K2
Mills Rw CHSWK W4 156 A3
Mills Sp WDSR SL4 171 N3
Millstead Cl
KWD/TDW/WH KT20 238 E9
Mill Stone Cl EYN DA4 210 B2
Millstone Ms EYN DA4 210 B1
Millstream Cl HERT/WAS * SG14 25 J5
PLMGR N13 99 H6
Millstream La SL SL1 128 D10
Millstream Rd STHWK SE1 19 L2
Mill St BERK HP4 33 P5
BH/WHM TN16 262 G3
CONDST W1S 10 F7
DTCH/LGLY SL3 150 G6
HHS/BOV HP3 35 N10
HLWE CM17 47 P4
KUT KT1 199 K3
REDH RH1 275 P1
SLN SL2 129 L10
STHWK SE1 19 M2
Mills Wy RBRW/HUT CM13 107 P2
Millthorne Cl RKW/CH/CXG WD3 72 A9
Mill V HAYES BR2 205 M3
Mill View Cl EW KT17 220 C4
Millview Cl REDH RH1 257 N8
Mill View Gdns CROY/NA CR0 204 C10
Millwall Dock Rd POP/IOD E14 160 F2
Millwards HAT AL10 40 E7
Millway REIG RH2 257 N10
Mill Wy BUSH WD23 73 M6
EBED/NFELT TW14 175 J1
LHD/OX KT22 255 L1
MLHL NW7 96 B6
RKW/CH/CXG WD3 91 J2
Millway Gdns NTHLT UB5 133 N1
Millwell Crs CHIG IG7 102 G6
Millwood Rd HSLW TW3 176 B1
STMC/STPC BR5 207 M3
Milman Cl PIN HA5 113 L1
Milman Rd KIL/WHAMP NW6 136 G4
Milman's St WBPTN SW10 15 L10
Milne Cl CRAWW RH11 283 H10
Milne Fld PIN HA5 93 P8
Milne Gdns ELTH/MOT SE9 184 B1
Milne Pk East CROY/NA CR0 225 J7
Milne Pk West CROY/NA CR0 225 J7
Milner Ap CTHM CR3 241 P7
Milner Cl CTHM CR3 241 P8
GSTN WD25 55 J10
Milner Ct BUSH WD23 74 A10
Milner Dr COB KT11 217 N8
WHTN TW2 176 C3
Milner Pl IS N1 6 B5
Milner Rd BCTR RM8 123 M7
CTHM CR3 241 P8
KUT KT1 199 J3
MRDN SM4 201 N5
SRTFD E15 141 K5
THHTH CR7 203 L3
WIM/MER SW19 201 L1
Milner Sq IS N1 6 B4
Milner St CHEL SW3 16 A5
Milneway DEN/HRF UB9 91 L9
Milnthorpe Rd CHSWK W4 156 A5
Milo Rd EDUL SE22 181 N2
Milroy Av GVW DA11 190 B5
Milroy Wk STHWK SE1 12 B9
Milton Av BAR EN5 77 J9
CDALE/KGS NW9 115 N1
CFSP/GDCR SL9 110 A2
CROY/NA CR0 203 L7
DORK RH4 272 C3
EHAM E6 142 A2
GVE DA12 190 G4
HCH RM12 124 G7
HGT N6 118 D5
RSEV TN14 228 C6
SUT SM1 201 N10
WLSDN NW10 136 A3
Milton Cl DTCH/LGLY SL3 150 D9
EFNCH N2 117 M4
STHWK SE1 19 L6
SUT SM1 201 N10
YEAD UB4 133 H8
Milton Ct BARB EC2Y 12 G3
HGDN/ICK UB10 112 C8
WAB EN9 63 H10
Miltoncourt La DORK RH4 272 D2
Milton Court Rd NWCR SE14 160 D5
Milton Crs CHONG CM5 67 N2
GNTH/NBYPK IG2 122 F5
Milton Dene HHNE HP2 36 C1
Milton Dr BORE WD6 75 N8
SHPTN TW17 195 P4
Milton Flds CSTG HP8 89 N4
Milton Gdns EPSOM KT18 220 B10
STWL/WRAY TW19 174 A4
TIL RM18 168 E7
Milton Gv FBAR/BDGN N11 98 D6
STNW/STAM N16 119 L9
Milton Hall Rd GVE DA12 190 G4
Milton Hl CSTG HP8 89 N4
Milton Lawns AMS HP6 69 J2
Milton Mount Av CRAWE RH10 284 D5
Milton Pk EGH * TW20 172 D10
HGT N6 118 D5
Milton Pl GVE DA12 190 F2
Milton Rd ACT W3 136 A10
ADL/WDHM KT15 215 K3
BELV DA17 164 B3
BRW CM14 106 G4
CDALE/KGS * NW9 116 D5
CRAWE RH10 284 D6
CROY/NA CR0 203 L7
CSHM HP5 50 G5
CTHM CR3 241 L7
EGH TW20 172 C8
GRAYS RM17 167 N3
GVE DA12 190 E2
HARP AL5 20 A2
HGDN/ICK UB10 112 C9
HGT N6 118 D5
HNHL SE24 181 J1
HNWL W7 134 E9
HPTN TW12 175 P10
HRW HA1 114 D2
MLHL NW7 96 D6
MORT/ESHN SW14 156 A9
MTCM CR4 180 B10
ROM RM1 125 H4
SEV TN13 246 F7
SEVS/STOTM N15 119 J1
SLN SL2 129 J6
SUT SM1 201 K10
SWCM DA10 189 K2
WALTH E17 120 F2
WARE SG12 26 C1
WELL DA16 163 J7
WIM/MER SW19 179 M9
WLGTN SM6 222 D3
WOT/HER KT12 197 L10
Milton St BARB EC2Y 12 G3
DORK RH4 272 C3
SWCM DA10 189 J2
WATN WD24 73 J5
Milton Wy GT/LBKH KT23 254 B1
WDR/YW UB7 152 A3
Milverton Dr HGDN/ICK UB10 112 D9
Milverton Gdns GDMY/SEVK IG3 123 J7
Milverton Rd KIL/WHAMP NW6 136 F2
Milverton St LBTH SE11 18 B8
Milverton Wy ELTH/MOT SE9 184 D7
Milwards HLWW/ROY CM19 46 D5
Milward St WCHPL E1 140 A7
Mimms Hall Rd POTB/CUF EN6 58 G7
Mimms La BORE WD6 58 A9
RAD WD7 57 M9
Mimosa Cl BRWN CM15 86 G9
HARH RM3 105 K8
ORP BR6 207 M10
Mimosa Rd YEAD UB4 133 K7
Mimosa St FUL/PGN SW6 157 J7
Mimram Rd HERT/WAS SG14 25 J6
Mina Av DTCH/LGLY SL3 150 A1
Minard Rd CAT SE6 183 K3
Mina Rd WALW SE17 19 K8
WIM/MER SW19 201 K1
Minchenden Crs STHGT/OAK N14 98 E4
Minchen Rd HLW CM20 29 K10
Minchin Cl LHD/OX KT22 236 F8

Mincing La CHOB/PIR GU24 213 L5
MON EC3R 13 J7
Minden Rd CHEAM SM3 201 H9
PGE/AN SE20 204 A1
Minehead Rd RYLN/HDSTN HA2 113 P8
STRHM/NOR SW16 180 G8
Mineral La CSHM HP5 51 H8
Mineral St WOOL/PLUM SE18 163 H3
Minera Ms BGVA SW1W 16 D5
Minerva Cl BRXN/ST SW9 159 H6
SCUP DA14 185 H7
STWL/WRAY * TW19 173 K1
Minerva Dr WAT WD17 72 F2
Minerva Rd CHING E4 100 G8
KUT KT1 199 L2
WLSDN NW10 135 P6
Minerva St BETH E2 140 A4
Minerva Wy BEAC HP9 88 F10
Minet Av WLSDN NW10 136 B4
Minet Dr HYS/HAR UB3 133 H10
Minet Gdns HYS/HAR UB3 133 J10
WLSDN NW10 136 B4
Minet Rd CMBW SE5 159 J8
Minford Gdns WKENS W14 156 G1
Ming St POP/IOD E14 140 F9
Minimax Cl EBED/NFELT TW14 175 H2
The Minims HAT AL10 40 D3
Minister Ct LCOL/BKTW AL2 56 D4
Ministry Wy ELTH/MOT SE9 184 C5
Mink Ct HSLWW TW4 153 K8
Minniecroft Rd SL SL1 128 A5
Minniedale BRYLDS KT5 199 L5
Minnow Wk WALW SE17 19 K6
Minorca Rd WEY KT13 216 B1
Minories TWRH EC3N 13 L6
Minshull Pl BECK * BR3 182 F10
Minshull St VX/NE * SW8 158 E7
Minson Rd HOM E9 140 C3
Minstead Gdns PUT/ROE SW15 178 C3
Minstead Wy NWMAL KT3 200 B6
Minster Av SUT SM1 201 K9
Minster Cl HAT AL10 40 D6
Minster Ct MON * EC3R 13 J7
Minster Dr CROY/NA CR0 223 M1
Minster Gdns E/WMO/HCT KT8 197 N4
Minsterley Av SHPTN TW17 196 F4
Minster Rd BMLY BR1 183 N10
CRICK NW2 117 H10
Minster Wy DTCH/LGLY SL3 150 C1
EMPK RM11 125 N6
Minstrel Cl HHW HP1 35 L5
Minstrel Gdns BRYLDS KT5 199 L4
Mint Cl HGDN/ICK UB10 132 C5
Mintern Cl PLMGR N13 99 J4
Minterne Av NWDGN UB2 153 P3
Minterne Rd KTN/HRWW/W HA3 115 L3
Minterne Waye YEAD UB4 133 K8
Mintern St IS N1 7 H7
Mint Gdns DORK RH4 272 F1
Mint La KWD/TDW/WH KT20 257 K5
Minton La HLWE CM17 47 M1
Minton Ms HAMP * NW3 3 H1
Minton Ri MDHD SL6 128 A8
Mint Rd BNSTD SM7 239 M2
WLGTN SM6 222 C2
Mint St STHWK SE1 18 E1
Mint Wk CROY/NA CR0 223 K10
WARL CR6 242 C3
WOKN/KNAP GU21 231 K3
Mirabel Rd FUL/PGN SW6 157 J6
Mirador Crs SLN SL2 129 N9
Miramar Wy HCH RM12 125 L10
Miranda Cl WCHPL E1 140 B7
Miranda Rd ARCH N19 118 D6
Mirfield St CHARL SE7 162 A2
Miriam Rd WOOL/PLUM SE18 163 H4
Mirren Cl RYLN/HDSTN HA2 113 N9
Mirrie La DEN/HRF UB9 110 F3
Misbourne Av CFSP/GDCR SL9 90 B6
Misbourne Cl CFSP/GDCR SL9 90 B6
Misbourne Ct AMSS * HP7 68 G6
Misbourne Mdw DEN/HRF UB9 110 F6
Misbourne Rd HGDN/ICK UB10 132 B4
Miskin Rd DART DA1 187 K3
Miskin Wy GVE DA12 190 G9
Missden Dr HHS/BOV HP3 36 D8
Missenden Cl EBED/NFELT TW14 174 G4
Missenden Gdns MRDN SM4 201 M6
SL SL1 128 A8
Missenden Rd CSHM HP5 50 E8
Mission Gv WALTH E17 120 E3
Mission Pl PECK SE15 159 P7
Mistletoe Cl CROY/NA CR0 204 C8
Mistley Rd HLW CM20 29 K9
Misty's Fld WOT/HER KT12 197 K8
Mitali Pas WCHPL E1 13 N6
Mitcham La STRHM/NOR SW16 180 D8
Mitcham Pk MTCM CR4 201 P4
Mitcham Rd CROY/NA CR0 202 E6
EHAM E6 142 B5
GDMY/SEVK IG3 123 J5
TOOT SW17 180 A8
Mitchell Av GVW DA11 190 A5
Mitchellbrook Wy WLSDN NW10 136 A1
Mitchell Cl ABLGY WD5 55 H8
ABYW SE2 163 M4
BELV DA17 164 D2
DART DA1 187 M5
HHW HP1 52 C3
RAIN RM13 145 K4
SL SL1 148 F1
STAL AL1 38 C10
WGCE AL7 23 M5
Mitchell Rd ORP BR6 227 J1
PLMGR N13 99 J6
Mitchells Cl RGUE GU4 268 B6
Mitchells Rd CRAWE RH10 284 A7
Mitchell St FSBYE EC1V 12 E1
Mitchell Wk AMS HP6 69 K4
Mitchell Wy BMLY BR1 205 M1
WLSDN NW10 135 P1
Mitchison Rd IS N1 6 G2
Mitchley Av PUR/KEN CR8 223 L9
Mitchley Gv SAND/SEL CR2 223 P9
Mitchley Hl SAND/SEL CR2 223 N9
Mitchley Rd TOTM N17 119 P1
Mitchley Vw SAND/SEL CR2 223 P9
Mitford Rd ARCH N19 118 F7
Mitre Cl BELMT SM2 221 M4
HAYES BR2 205 L2
SHPTN TW17 196 E6
Mitre Ct HERT/WAS * SG14 25 L5
Mitre Rd SRTFD E15 141 K4
STHWK SE1 18 B1
Mitre Sq HDTCH EC3A 13 K6
Mitre St HDTCH EC3A 13 K6
The Mitre POP/IOD E14 140 E9
Mitre Wy WLSDN NW10 136 E7
Mixbury Gv WEY KT13 216 E3
Mixnams La CHERT KT16 195 K3
Mizen Cl COB KT11 217 L10
Mizen Wy COB KT11 235 K1
Moat Cl BUSH WD23 74 A9
ORP BR6 227 J3
Moat Ct ASHTD KT21 237 K3
ELTH/MOT * SE9 184 C2
Moat Crs EFNCH N2 117 L1
Moat Cft WELL DA16 163 M9
Moat Dr HRW HA1 114 B2
RSLP HA4 112 F5
SLN SL2 129 P7
Moated Farm Dr
ADL/WDHM KT15 215 M4
Moat Farm Rd NTHLT UB5 133 N1
Moatfield Rd BUSH WD23 74 A9
Moat La ERITH DA8 165 H7
Moat Pl ACT W3 135 N8
BRXN/ST SW9 158 G9
DEN/HRF UB9 111 L9
Moat Side FELT TW13 175 K7
PEND EN3 80 B8
Moats La REDH RH1 276 F6
The Moat NWMAL KT3 200 B1
Moat Wk CRAWE RH10 284 D6
Moatwood Gn WGCE AL7 23 H6
Moberly Rd CLAP SW4 180 E3
Modbury Gdns HAMP NW3 4 B2
Model Cottages WEA * W13 154 G1
Model Farm Cl ELTH/MOT SE9 184 B6
Moelyn Ms HRW HA1 114 F3
Moffat Rd PLMGR N13 98 F7
THHTH CR7 203 K2
TOOT SW17 179 P7
Moffats Cl BRKMPK AL9 59 K2
Moffats La BRKMPK AL9 59 H3
Mogador Rd
KWD/TDW/WH KT20 257 H4
Mogden La ISLW TW7 176 E1
Mohammad Khan Rd WAN * E11 121 L6
Moiety Rd POP/IOD E14 160 F1
Moira Cl TOTM N17 99 M10
Moira Rd ELTH/MOT SE9 162 C10
Moir Cl SAND/SEL CR2 223 P5
Molash Rd STMC/STPC BR5 207 N4
Mole Abbey Gdns
E/WMO/HCT KT8 197 P3
Mole Cl CRAWW RH11 283 L5
Mole Ct HOR/WEW KT19 219 P1
Molember Rd E/WMO/HCT KT8 198 D5
Mole Rd LHD/OX KT22 236 C7
WOT/HER KT12 217 L2
Molescroft ELTH/MOT SE9 184 F6
Molesey Av E/WMO/HCT KT8 197 N4
Molesey Cl WOT/HER KT12 217 L1
Molesey Dr CHEAM SM3 201 H9
Molesey Park Av
E/WMO/HCT KT8 198 A5
Molesey Park Cl
E/WMO/HCT KT8 198 B5
Molesey Park Rd
E/WMO/HCT KT8 198 C5
Molesey Rd WOT/HER KT12 197 M5
WOT/HER KT12 217 L1
Molesford Rd FUL/PGN * SW6 157 K7
Molesham Cl E/WMO/HCT KT8 198 A3
Molesham Wy E/WMO/HCT KT8 198 A4
Moles Hl LHD/OX KT22 218 C7
Molesworth HOD EN11 26 F9
Molesworth St LEW SE13 161 H9
Mole Valley Pl ASHTD KT21 237 J5
Molewood Rd HERT/WAS SG14 25 J4
Mollands Ct SOCK/AV RM15 147 K6
Mollands La SOCK/AV RM15 147 H6
Mollison Av PEND EN3 80 D1
Mollison Dr WLGTN SM6 222 F4
Mollison Ri GVE DA12 190 G9
Mollison Wy EDGW HA8 95 L10
Molly Huggins Cl BAL SW12 180 D3
Molteno Rd WAT WD17 73 H5
Molyneux Dr TOOT SW17 180 C7
Molyneux Rd BFOR GU20 212 B3
RGODL GU7 267 L10
WEY KT13 216 B1
Molyneux St MBLAR W1H 9 P4
Molyns Ms SL SL1 128 D10
Momples Rd HLW CM20 29 K10
Monahan Av PUR/KEN CR8 222 G8
Monarch Cl CRAWW RH11 283 K10
EBED/NFELT TW14 174 F5
RAIN RM13 145 H4
TIL RM18 168 E8
WWKM BR4 225 L1
Monarch Dr CAN/RD E16 142 A7
Monarch Ms WNWD SE27 181 H8
Monarch Pde MTCM * CR4 202 A2
Monarch Pl BKHH IG9 101 P3
Monarch Rd BELV DA17 164 B2
Monarch's Wy CHES/WCR EN8 62 D9
RSLP * HA4 112 E6
Monarch Wk RAD * WD7 57 L9
Mona Rd PECK SE15 160 B8
Monastery Cl STALW/RED * AL3 38 B6
Monastery Gdns
DTCH/LGLY * SL3 149 N9
ENC/FH EN2 79 L6
Mona St CAN/RD E16 141 L7
Monaveen Gdns
E/WMO/HCT KT8 198 A3
Monck's Rw WAND/EARL * SW18 179 J2
Monck St WEST SW1P 17 K4
Monclar Rd CMBW SE5 159 L10
Moncorvo Cl SKENS SW7 15 N2
Moncrieff St PECK SE15 159 P8
Mondial Wy WDR/YW UB7 152 D6
Monega Rd FSTGT E7 141 P1
Money Av CTHM CR3 241 L8
Moneyhill Ct RKW/CH/CXG * WD3 91 L2
Money Hill Rd RKW/CH/CXG WD3 91 M2
Money Hole La WLYN AL6 23 P4
Money La WDR/YW UB7 151 N2
Money Rd CTHM CR3 241 L8
Mongers La EW KT17 220 D6
Monica Cl WATN WD24 73 L6
Monier Rd BOW E3 140 F2
Monivea Rd BECK BR3 182 E10
Monkchester Cl LOU IG10 82 D5
Monk Dr CAN/RD E16 141 M9
Monkfrith Av STHGT/OAK N14 78 C10
Monkfrith Wy STHGT/OAK N14 98 C1
Monkham's Av WFD IG8 101 N6
Monkham's Dr WFD IG8 101 N6
Monkham's La WFD IG8 101 N5
Monkleigh Rd MRDN SM4 201 H3
Monks Av BAR EN5 77 M10
E/WMO/HCT KT8 197 N5
Monksbury HLWS CM18 47 K4
Monks Cha RBRW/HUT CM13 107 P6
Monks Cl ABYW SE2 163 N3
ASC SL5 192 A6
BROX EN10 44 F6
ENC/FH EN2 79 K6
RSLP HA4 113 L9
STAL AL1 38 D8
Monks Crs ADL/WDHM KT15 215 L2
WOT/HER KT12 197 J8
Monksdene Gdns SUT SM1 201 L10
Monks Dr ACT W3 135 M7
ASC SL5 192 A6
Monksfield CRAWE RH10 284 A7
Monksfield Wy SLN SL2 128 F6
Monks Gn LHD/OX KT22 236 B7
Monksgrove LOU IG10 82 D9
Monks Horton Wy STAL AL1 38 F4
Monksmead BORE WD6 75 P8
Monks Orch DART DA1 187 K5
Monks Orchard Rd BECK BR3 204 F8
Monks Pk WBLY HA9 135 P1
Monks Park Gdns WBLY HA9 135 N1
Monks Ri WGCW AL8 22 G8
Monks Rd BNSTD SM7 239 K3
ENC/FH EN2 79 J6
VW GU25 194 A4
WDSR SL4 148 C8
Monks Rw WARE SG12 26 C1
Monk St WOOL/PLUM SE18 162 D3
Monks Wk ASC SL5 192 A6
MEO DA13 189 M9
REIG RH2 257 L10
Monks Wy BECK BR3 204 F6
GLDGN NW11 117 J2
STA TW18 173 N10
STMC/STPC BR5 206 F8
Monkswell La COUL/CHIP CR5 239 L10
Monkswick Rd HLW CM20 29 J9
Monkswood WGCW AL8 22 F1
Monkswood Av WAB EN9 63 J9
Monkswood Gdns BORE WD6 76 A9
CLAY IG5 122 D1
Monkton Rd WELL DA16 163 J8
Monkton St LBTH SE11 18 B5
Monkville Av GLDGN NW11 117 J2
Monkville Pde GLDGN * NW11 117 J2
Monkwell Sq BARB EC2Y 12 F4
Monkwood Cl ROM RM1 125 H3
Monmouth Av KUT KT1 177 H10
SWFD E18 121 N2
Monmouth Cl CHSWK W4 156 A2
MTCM CR4 202 F4
WELL DA16 163 K10
Monmouth Gv BTFD TW8 155 K3
Monmouth Pl BAY/PAD W2 8 F6
Monmouth Rd BAY/PAD W2 8 F6
DAGW RM9 124 A10
ED N9 100 A3
EHAM E6 142 C5
HYS/HAR UB3 152 F3
WAT WD17 73 J7
Monmouth St LSQ/SEVD WC2H 11 L6
Monnery Rd ARCH N19 118 D8
Monnow Rd SOCK/AV RM15 146 B9
STHWK SE1 19 N6
Monoux Gv WALTH E17 100 F9
Monro Dr GUW GU2 249 N7
Monroe Crs EN EN1 80 A5
Monroe Dr MORT/ESHN SW14 177 N1
Monro Gdns KTN/HRWW/W HA3 94 D8
Monro Pl HOR/WEW KT19 219 M5
Mons Cl HARP AL5 20 C5
Monsell Rd FSBYPK N4 119 J8
Monson Rd BROX EN10 44 E6
NWCR SE14 160 C6
REDH RH1 258 A7
WLSDN NW10 136 D4
Mons Wk EGH TW20 172 F8
Mons Wy HAYES BR2 206 B6
Montacute Rd BUSH WD23 94 D1
CAT SE6 182 E3
CROY/NA CR0 225 H5
MRDN SM4 201 N6
Montagu Crs UED N18 100 A5
Montague Av BROCKY SE4 160 E10
HNWL W7 134 E10
SAND/SEL CR2 223 M8
Montague Cl STHWK SE1 12 G9
SWLY BR8 208 G4
WOT/HER KT12 197 H7
Montague Dr CTHM CR3 241 K8
Montague Gdns ACT W3 135 M9
Montague Hall Pl BUSH WD23 73 P10
Montague Pl GWRST WC1E 11 K3
SWLY * BR8 208 G4
Montague Rd BERK HP4 33 N5
CEND/HSY/T N8 118 G3
CROY/NA CR0 203 J8
HACK E8 119 P10
HNWL W7 154 E1
HSLW TW3 154 A9
NWDGN UB2 153 M3
RCHPK/HAM TW10 177 K2
SEVS/STOTM * N15 119 P2
SL SL1 129 L9
UX/CGN UB8 131 N2
WAN E11 121 L7
WEA W13 134 G8
WIM/MER SW19 179 L10
Montague Sq NWCR SE14 160 B6
Montague St RSQ WC1B 11 L3
STBT EC1A 12 E4
Montague Ter HAYES * BR2 205 L4
Montagu Gdns UED N18 100 A4
WLGTN SM6 222 D1
Montagu Man MHST W1U 10 A4
Montagu Ms North MBLAR W1H 10 B4
Montagu Ms South MBLAR W1H 10 B5
Montagu Ms West MBLAR W1H 10 B5
Montagu Pl MBLAR W1H 10 A4
Montagu Rd DTCH/LGLY SL3 149 N7
HDN NW4 116 D4
UED N18 100 B5
Montagu Rw MHST W1U 10 B4
Montagu Sq MBLAR W1H 10 B4
Montagu St MBLAR W1H 10 B5
Montalt Rd WFD IG8 101 L6
Montana Cl SAND/SEL CR2 223 L6
Montana Gdns CAT SE6 182 E8
SUT SM1 221 M2
Montana Rd RYNPK SW20 200 F1
TOOT SW17 180 B6
Montayne Rd CHES/WCR EN8 62 C8
Montbelle Rd ELTH/MOT SE9 184 E6
Montbretia Cl STMC/STPC BR5 207 M4
Montcalm Cl HAYES BR2 205 M6
YEAD UB4 133 J5
Montcalm Rd CHARL SE7 162 A6
Montclare St BETH E2 7 L10
Monteagle Av BARK IG11 142 F1
Monteagle Wy PECK SE15 160 A9
Montefiore St VX/NE SW8 158 C8
Monteith Rd BOW E3 140 E3
Montem La SL SL1 149 J1
Montem Rd FSTH SE23 182 E3
NWMAL KT3 200 B4
Montem St FSBYPK N4 118 G6
Montenotte Rd CEND/HSY/T N8 118 D3
Monterey Cl BXLY DA5 186 D5
Montesquieu Ter CAN/RD * E16 141 L8
Montford Pl LBTH SE11 18 A9
Montford Rd SUN TW16 197 H4
Montfort Gdns BARK/HLT IG6 102 F7
Montfort Pl WIM/MER SW19 178 G4
Montfort Ri REDH RH1 276 A8
Montford Rd RSEV TN14 247 M3
Montgomerie Cl BERK HP4 33 M5
Montgomerie Dr GUW GU2 249 M5
Montgomery Av ESH/CLAY KT10 198 D9
HHNE HP2 36 B5
Montgomery Cl BFN/LL DA15 185 H1
MTCM * CR4 202 F4
Montgomery Crs HARH RM3 105 L6
Montgomery Dr CHES/WCR EN8 62 D4
Montgomery Pl SLN SL2 129 P8
Montgomery Rd CHSWK W4 155 P3
EDGW HA8 95 L7
EYN DA4 210 C1
WOKS/MYFD GU22 232 B4
Montholme Rd BTSEA SW11 180 A2
Monthope Rd WCHPL E1 13 N4
Montolieu Gdns PUT/ROE SW15 178 E1
Montpelier Av BXLY DA5 185 N3
EA W5 135 H7
Montpelier Cl HGDN/ICK UB10 132 B3
Montpelier Gdns CHDH RM6 123 M5
EHAM E6 142 A5
Montpelier Gv KTTN NW5 118 D10
Montpelier Ms SKENS SW7 15 P3
Montpelier Pl SKENS SW7 15 P3
WCHPL E1 140 B8
Montpelier Ri GLDGN NW11 117 H5
WBLY HA9 115 J6
Montpelier Rd EA W5 135 J7
FNCH N3 97 M9
PECK SE15 160 A7
PUR/KEN CR8 223 J6
SUT SM1 221 M1
Montpelier Rw BKHTH/KID SE3 161 L8
TWK TW1 176 G3
Montpelier Sq SKENS SW7 15 P3
Montpelier St SKENS SW7 15 P2
Montpelier Ter SKENS SW7 15 P2
Montpelier V BKHTH/KID * SE3 161 L8
Montpelier Wk SKENS SW7 15 P2
Montpelier Wy GLDGN NW11 117 H5
Montpellier Ct WDSR SL4 149 H8
Montrave Rd PGE/AN SE20 182 B9
Montreal Pl HOL/ALD WC2B 11 N7
Montreal Rd IL IG1 122 F5
SEV TN13 246 F9
TIL RM18 168 D9
Montrell Rd BRXS/STRHM SW2 180 F4
Montrose Av BFN/LL DA15 185 K3
DTCH/LGLY SL3 149 P6
EDGW HA8 96 A10
GPK RM2 105 K10
KIL/WHAMP NW6 2 B7
SL SL1 128 G8
WELL DA16 162 G9
WHTN TW2 176 A3
Montrose Cl ASHF TW15 174 D9
WELL DA16 163 J9
WFD IG8 101 M5
Montrose Crs ALP/SUD HA0 135 K1
NFNCH/WDSP N12 97 L7
Montrose Gdns LHD/OX KT22 218 C8
MTCM CR4 202 A3
SUT SM1 201 L9
Montrose Pl KTBR SW1X 16 D2
Montrose Rd EBED/NFELT TW14 174 E2
KTN/HRWW/W HA3 94 D10
Montrose Vls HMSMTH * W6 156 D4
Montrose Wk WEY KT13 196 C10
Montrose Wy DTCH/LGLY SL3 150 A7
FSTH SE23 182 C4
Montrouge Crs EW KT17 238 F2
Montserrat Av WFD IG8 101 J8
Montserrat Cl NRWD SE19 181 L8
Montserrat Rd PUT/ROE SW15 157 H10
Monument Hl WEY KT13 216 C1
Monument La CFSP/GDCR SL9 90 B7
Monument Rd WEY KT13 216 C1
WOKN/KNAP GU21 232 E1
Monument St MON EC3R 13 H8
Monument Wy
SEVS/STOTM N15 119 N1
Monument Wy East
WOKN/KNAP GU21 232 E1
Monument Wy West
WOKN/KNAP GU21 232 D1
Monza St WAP E1W 140 B9
Moodkee St BERM/RHTH SE16 160 B2
Moody St WCHPL E1 140 C5
Moon Ct LEE/GVPK * SE12 161 M10
Moon La BAR EN5 77 J7
Moon St IS N1 6 C5
Moorcroft EDGW * HA8 95 N9
Moorcroft Cl CRAWW RH11 283 L6
Moorcroft Gdns HAYES BR2 206 B5
Moorcroft La UX/CGN UB8 132 B7
Moorcroft Rd STRHM/NOR SW16 180 F6
Moorcroft Wy PIN HA5 113 M3
Moordown WOOL/PLUM SE18 162 D7
Moore Av TIL RM18 168 E8
WTHK RM20 167 K4
Moore Cl ADL/WDHM KT15 215 L2
MORT/ESHN SW14 155 P9
MTCM * CR4 202 C2
SL SL1 148 G1
WLGTN SM6 222 F4
Moore Crs DAGW RM9 143 L3
Moorefield Rd TOTM N17 119 N1
Moore Grove Crs EGH TW20 172 B10
Mooreland Rd BMLY BR1 183 L10
Moorend WGCE AL7 23 K8
Moor End Rd HHW HP1 35 M7
Moore Park Rd FUL/PGN SW6 157 L6
Moore Rd BERK HP4 33 L3
CHOB/PIR GU24 230 A7
NRWD SE19 181 K9
SWCM DA10 189 K2
Moorescroft BRWN CM15 86 D3
Moores La WDSR SL4 148 E3
Moore's Rd DORK RH4 272 G1
Moore St CHEL SW3 16 A5
Moore Wy BELMT SM2 221 K5
Moorey Cl SRTFD E15 141 L3
Moorfield RDKG * RH5 273 J10
Moorfield Av EA W5 135 J6
Moorfield Rd CHSGTN KT9 219 K2
DEN/HRF UB9 111 K4
GU GU1 250 A6
ORP BR6 207 K7
PEND EN3 80 B5
UX/CGN UB8 131 N8
Moorfields HLWS CM18 46 F6
LVPST EC2M 12 G4
Moorfields Cl STA TW18 195 H1
Moorfields Highwalk BARB EC2Y 12 G4
Moor Furlong SL SL1 128 D10
Moorgate LOTH EC2R 12 G5
Moorgate Pl LOTH * EC2R 12 G5
Moorhall Rd DEN/HRF UB9 111 L3
Moor Hall Rd HLWE CM17 30 A7
Moorhayes Dr STA TW18 195 M3
Moorhead Wy BKHTH/KID SE3 161 N10
Moorhen Cl ERITH DA8 165 J6
Moorholme WOKS/MYFD GU22 232 B5
Moorhouse Rd BAY/PAD W2 8 E5
KTN/HRWW/W HA3 115 J1
OXTED RH8 262 C6
Moorhurst Av CHESW EN7 61 J5
The Moorings BF/WBF KT14 215 M8
CHSWK * W4 155 M5
GT/LBKH KT23 253 P1
STWL/WRAY TW19 171 P3
WDSR * SL4 148 C6
Moorland Cl HSLWW TW4 175 P3
ROMW/RG RM7 104 C9
Moorland Rd BRXN/ST SW9 159 J10
CRAWE RH10 284 D10
HHW HP1 35 J8
WDR/YW UB7 151 M6
Moorlands LCOL/BKTW * AL2 56 D4
WGCE AL7 23 K8
Moorlands Av MLHL NW7 96 E7
The Moorlands
WOKS/MYFD GU22 232 C7
Moor La BARB EC2Y 12 G4
CHSGTN KT9 219 L2
RKW/CH/CXG WD3 71 H2
RKW/CH/CXG WD3 91 P3
STWL/WRAY TW19 172 F4
UPMR RM14 126 E6
WDR/YW UB7 151 M5
WOKS/MYFD GU22 232 B8
Moor La Crossing WATW WD18 92 D1
Moormead Dr HOR/WEW KT19 220 B2
Moor Mead Rd TWK TW1 176 F2
Moormede Crs STA TW18 173 J7
Moor Mill La LCOL/BKTW AL2 56 D5
Moor Pk HORL * RH6 280 C5
Moor Park Crs CRAWW RH11 282 G8
Moor Park Gdns KUTN/CMB KT2 178 B10
NTHWD * HA6 92 D3
Moor Park Rd NTHWD HA6 92 E7
Moor Pl BFOR GU20 212 A2
Moor Rd CSHM HP5 51 H9
The Moor Rd RSEV TN14 247 J6
Moorside WGCE AL7 23 K8
Moorside Rd BMLY BR1 183 K7
Moorsom Wy COUL/CHIP CR5 240 E3
The Moors WGCE AL7 23 K4
Moorstown Ct SL SL1 149 K1
Moor St SOHO/SHAV W1D 11 K6
Moors Wk WGCE AL7 23 M5
Moortown Rd OXHEY WD19 93 K5
Moor Vw WATW WD18 93 H1
Morant Gdns CRW RM5 104 C6
Morant Rd CDH/CHF RM16 168 E2
Morants Court Rd RSEV TN14 246 D4
Morant St POP/IOD E14 140 F9
Mora Rd CRICK NW2 116 F9
Mora St FSBYE EC1V 6 F10
Morat St BRXN/ST SW9 158 G7
Moravian Pl WBPTN SW10 15 M10
Moravian St BETH E2 140 B4
Moray Av HYS/HAR UB3 132 G10
Moray Cl EDGW * HA8 95 N3
ROM RM1 104 F8
Moray Dr SLN SL2 129 M8
Moray Ms HOLWY N7 118 G7
Moray Rd HOLWY N7 118 G7
Moray Wy ROM RM1 104 E8
Mordaunt Gdns DAGW RM9 143 P2
Mordaunt Rd WLSDN NW10 136 A3
Mordaunt St BRXN/ST SW9 158 G9
Morden Cl KWD/TDW/WH KT20 238 G6
Morden Ct MRDN SM4 201 L4
Morden Court Pde
WIM/MER * SW19 201 L3
Morden Gdns GFD/PVL UB6 114 E10
MTCM CR4 201 N4
Morden Hall Rd MRDN SM4 201 L3
Morden Hl LEW SE13 161 H8
Morden La LEW SE13 161 H8
Morden Rd BKHTH/KID SE3 161 M8
CHDH RM6 123 P5
WIM/MER SW19 201 L2
Morden Road Ms
BKHTH/KID SE3 161 M8
Morden St LEW SE13 160 G7
Morden Wy CHEAM SM3 201 K7
Morden Wharf Rd GNWCH SE10 161 K2
Mordon Rd GDMY/SEVK IG3 123 J5
Mordred Rd CAT SE6 183 K5
Moreau Wk DTCH/LGLY SL3 130 B8
Morecambe Cl CRAWW RH11 283 J9
HCH RM12 125 J10
WCHPL * E1 140 C7
Morecambe Gdns STAN HA7 95 J5
Morecambe St WALW SE17 18 F6
Morecambe Ter UED * N18 99 L5
More Cir RGODL GU7 267 K10
More Cl CAN/RD E16 141 L8
PUR/KEN CR8 222 G7
WKENS W14 156 G3
Morecoombe Cl KUTN/CMB KT2 177 N10
Morecote Cl RGUE GU4 268 B7
Moree Wy UED N18 99 P5
Moreland Cl DTCH/LGLY SL3 150 F6
Moreland Cottages BOW * E3 140 F4
Moreland Dr CFSP/GDCR SL9 110 C4
Morelands Av CDH/CHF RM16 167 P1
Moreland St FSBYE EC1V 6 D9
Moreland Wy CHING E4 100 G4
More La ESH/CLAY KT10 198 A10
Morel Ct SEV TN13 247 J8
Morella Cl VW GU25 193 P4
Morella Rd BAL SW12 180 A3
Morello Av UX/CGN UB8 132 C7
Morello Cl SWLY BR8 208 E4
Morello Dr DTCH/LGLY SL3 130 C10
Moremead WAB EN9 63 J9
Moremead Rd CAT SE6 182 E7
Morena St CAT SE6 182 G3
More Rd RGODL GU7 267 K10
Moresby Av BRYLDS KT5 199 N7
Moresby Rd CLPT E5 120 A6
Mores La BRW CM14 86 C7
Moretaine Rd ASHF TW15 173 N6
Moreton Av ISLW TW7 154 C7
Moreton Br CHONG CM5 49 K7

Moreton Cl CHESW EN7 62 A3
CLPT E5 120 B7
MLHL NW7 96 F7
SEVS/STOTM N15 119 L4
Moreton Ct DART DA1 164 F9
Moreton Gdns WFD IG8 102 B6
Moreton Pl PIM SW1V 17 H7
Moreton Rd CHONG CM5 49 H9
SAND/SEL CR2 223 L2
SEVS/STOTM N15 119 L4
WPK KT4 200 D9
Moreton St PIM SW1V 17 H7
Moreton Ter PIM SW1V 17 H7
Moreton Terrace Ms South
PIM SW1V 17 H7
Moreton Wy SL SL1 128 C10
Morewood Cl SEV TN13 246 G9
Morford Cl RSLP HA4 113 J5
Morford Wy RSLP HA4 113 J5
Morgan Av WALTH E17 121 J2
Morgan Cl DAGE RM10 144 B2
NTHWD HA6 92 G6
Morgan Crs EPP CM16 83 H2
Morgan Dr RDART DA2 188 D3
Morgan Gdns GSTN WD25 74 A4
Morgan Rd BMLY BR1 183 M10
HOLWY N7 119 H10
NKENS W10 8 C3
Morgans Cl HERT/BAY SG13 25 L7
Morgan's La HYS/HAR UB3 132 E7
STHWK SE1 13 J10
Morgan's Rd HERT/BAY SG13 25 L7
Morgan St BOW E3 140 D5
CAN/RD E16 141 L7
Morgan's Wk HERT/BAY SG13 25 L8
Morgan Wy RAIN RM13 145 K5
WFD IG8 102 B7
Moriatry Cl HOLWY N7 118 F9
Morice Rd HOD EN11 44 E1
Morie St WAND/EARL SW18 157 L10
Morieux Rd LEY E10 120 E6
Moring Rd TOOT SW17 180 B7
Morkyns Wk DUL * SE21 181 M6
Morland Av CROY/NA CR0 203 M8
DART DA1 187 J1
Morland Cl GLDGN NW11 117 L6
HPTN TW12 175 N8
MTCM CR4 201 P3
Morland Est HACK * E8 7 P3
Morland Gdns STHL UB1 134 A10
WLSDN NW10 136 A2
Morland Ms IS N1 6 B4
Morland Rd CROY/NA CR0 203 N7
DAGE RM10 144 B2
IL IG1 122 E7
KTN/HRWW/W HA3 115 K3
PGE/AN SE20 182 C10
SUT SM1 221 M2
WALTH E17 120 C3
Morland Wy CHES/WCR EN8 62 D4
Morley Av CHING E4 101 J8
UED N18 99 P5
WDGN N22 99 H10
Morley Cl DTCH/LGLY SL3 150 C1
ORP BR6 206 E9
Morley Crs EDGW HA8 95 P3
RSLP HA4 113 K7
Morley Crs East STAN HA7 115 H1
Morley Crs West STAN HA7 115 H1
Morley Gv HLW CM20 28 F10
Morley Hl ENC/FH EN2 79 L4
Morley Rd BARK IG11 142 G3
CHDH RM6 123 P3
CHEAM SM3 201 J8
CHST BR7 206 F1
LEW SE13 161 H10
LEY E10 121 H6
SAND/SEL CR2 223 N6
SRTFD E15 141 L4
TWK TW1 177 J2
Morley Sq CDH/CHF RM16 168 D3
Morley's Rd RSEV TN14 265 L9
Morley St STHWK SE1 18 B2
Morna Rd CMBW SE5 159 K8
Morning La HOM E9 140 B1
Morningside Rd WPK KT4 200 E9
Mornington Av BMLY BR1 205 P3
IL IG1 122 D5
WKENS W14 14 C6
Mornington Ct BXLY DA5 186 E4
Mornington Crs CAMTN NW1 4 G7
HEST TW5 153 J7
Mornington Gv BOW E3 140 F5
Mornington Ms CMBW SE5 159 K7
Mornington Pl CAMTN NW1 4 F7
Mornington Rd ASHF TW15 174 D8
CHING E4 101 J1
DEPT SE8 160 E6
GFD/PVL UB6 134 A7
RAD WD7 56 F10
WAN E11 121 L6
WFD IG8 101 L5
Morningtons HLWW/ROY CM19 46 E5
Mornington St CAMTN NW1 4 F7
Mornington Ter CAMTN NW1 4 F6
Mornington Wk
RCHPK/HAM TW10 177 H7
Morocco St STHWK SE1 19 J2
Morpeth Av BORE WD6 75 L4
Morpeth Cl HHS/BOV HP3 35 P7
Morpeth Gv HOM E9 140 C3
Morpeth Rd HOM E9 140 B3
Morpeth St BETH E2 140 C5
Morpeth Ter WEST SW1P 16 G4
Morpeth Wk TOTM * N17 100 A8
Morrab Gdns GDMY/SEVK IG3 123 J8
Morrel Cl BAR EN5 77 M7
Morrell Ct WGCE * AL7 23 J4
Morrice Cl DTCH/LGLY SL3 150 C3
Morris Av MNPK E12 122 C10
Morris Bishop Ter HGT * N6 118 B4
Morris Cl CFSP/GDCR SL9 90 C9
CROY/NA CR0 204 D6
ORP BR6 207 H10
Morris Ct CHING E4 100 G4
WAB EN9 63 L10
Morris Gdns DART DA1 187 P1
WAND/EARL SW18 179 K3
Morrish Rd BRXS/STRHM SW2 180 F3
Morrison Av TOTM N17 119 M1
Morrison Rd BARK IG11 143 P4
YEAD UB4 133 J5
Morrison St BTSEA SW11 158 B9
Morris Pl FSBYPK N4 119 H7
Morris Rd BCTR RM8 124 A7
HARH RM3 105 J8
ISLW TW7 154 E9
POP/IOD E14 140 G7
REDH RH1 276 F2
WAN E11 121 K9
Morris St WCHPL E1 140 A8
Morriston Cl OXHEY WD19 93 K6
Morris Wy LCOL/BKTW AL2 57 J2
Morse Cl DEN/HRF UB9 91 M10
PLSTW E13 141 M5
Morshead Rd MV/WKIL W9 2 F10
Morson Rd PEND EN3 80 D10
Morston Cl KWD/TDW/WH KT20 238 E6
Mortain Dr BERK HP4 33 L3
Morten Gdns DEN/HRF UB9 111 K5
Mortens Wd AMSS HP7 69 J6
Morteyne Rd TOTM N17 99 L9
Mortham St SRTFD E15 141 K3
Mortimer Cl BAL SW12 180 E5
BUSH WD23 74 A10
CRICK NW2 117 J8
Mortimer Crs STJWD NW8 2 G6
WPK KT4 200 A10
Mortimer Dr WCHMH N21 79 L9
Mortimer Ga CHES/WCR EN8 62 E3
Mortimer Pl KIL/WHAMP NW6 2 G6
Mortimer Rd BH/WHM TN16 225 P8
DTCH/LGLY SL3 150 A2
EHAM E6 142 C5
ERITH DA8 164 E5
IS N1 7 K3
MTCM CR4 202 A1
ORP BR6 207 K9
WEA W13 135 H8
WLSDN NW10 136 F5
Mortimer Sq NTGHL W11 136 G9
Mortimer St REGST W1B 10 F5
Mortimer Ter KTTN * NW5 118 C9
Mortlake Cl CROY/NA CR0 202 G10
Mortlake Dr MTCM CR4 201 P1
Mortlake High St
MORT/ESHN SW14 156 A9
Mortlake Rd CAN/RD E16 141 N8
IL IG1 122 F9
MORT/ESHN SW14 155 N9
Morton KWD/TDW/WH KT20 238 G7
Morton Cl CROY/NA CR0 222 G4
WOKN/KNAP GU21 231 P1
Morton Crs FBAR/BDGN N11 98 E5
Morton Gdns WLGTN SM6 222 D2
Morton Ms ECT * SW5 14 G6
Morton Pl STHWK SE1 18 A4
Morton Rd IS N1 6 F4
MRDN SM4 201 N5
SRTFD E15 141 L2
WOKN/KNAP GU21 231 P1
Morton Wy STHGT/OAK N14 98 D4
Morvale Cl BELV DA17 164 A3
Morval Rd BRXS/STRHM SW2 181 H1
Morven Cl POTB/CUF EN6 59 M7
Morven Rd TOOT SW17 180 A6
Morville St BOW E3 140 F4
Morwell St FITZ W1T 11 J4
Mosbach Gdns
RBRW/HUT CM13 107 N3
Moscow Pl BAY/PAD W2 8 G7
Moscow Rd BAY/PAD W2 8 G7
Moselle Av WDGN N22 99 H10
Moselle Cl CEND/HSY/T N8 118 G1
Moselle Rd BH/WHM TN16 244 B4
Moselle St TOTM N17 99 N8
Mosford Cl HORL RH6 280 A2
Mospey Crs EW KT17 238 C1
Moss Bank GRAYS RM17 167 L3
Mossborough Cl
NFNCH/WDSP N12 97 L7
Mossbury Rd BTSEA SW11 157 P9
Moss Cl PIN HA5 93 N10
RKW/CH/CXG WD3 91 N3
WCHPL E1 13 P3
Mossdown Cl BELV DA17 164 B3
Mossendew Cl DEN/HRF UB9 91 N9
Mossfield COB KT11 217 H9
Mossford Gn BARK/HLT IG6 122 E1
Mossford La BARK/HLT IG6 102 F10
Mossford St BOW E3 140 E6
Moss Gdns SAND/SEL CR2 224 C4
Moss Gn WGCE AL7 23 H7
Moss Hall Crs NFNCH/WDSP N12 97 L7
Moss Hall Gv FNCH N3 97 L7
Moss La PIN HA5 113 N1
ROM RM1 124 G4
Mosslea Rd CTHM CR3 241 N2
HAYES BR2 206 A5
ORP BR6 206 F10
PGE/AN SE20 182 B10
Mossop St CHEL SW3 15 P5
Moss Rd DAGE RM10 144 B2
GSTN WD25 55 J10
SOCK/AV RM15 147 H7
Moss Side LCOL/BKTW AL2 55 N6
Mossville Gdns MRDN SM4 201 J3
Moss Wy RDART DA2 188 C7
Moston Cl HYS/HAR UB3 152 G4
Mostyn Av WBLY HA9 115 L10
Mostyn Gdns WLSDN NW10 136 G5
Mostyn Gv BOW E3 140 E4
Mostyn Rd BRXN/ST SW9 159 H7
BUSH WD23 74 B9
EDGW HA8 96 A8
WIM/MER SW19 201 J2
Mostyn Ter REDH RH1 276 B1
Mosul Wy HAYES BR2 206 B6
Mosyer Dr STMC/STPC BR5 207 N9
Motcomb St KTBR SW1X 16 C3
Moth Cl WLGTN SM6 222 F4
The Mothers Sq CLPT * E5 120 A9
Motherwell Wy WTHK RM20 166 F4
Motley St VX/NE SW8 158 D8
Motspur Pk NWMAL KT3 200 C6
Mottingham Gdns
ELTH/MOT SE9 184 A4
Mottingham La ELTH/MOT SE9 183 P4
Mottingham Rd ED N9 80 C10
ELTH/MOT SE9 184 B6
Mottisfont Rd ABYW SE2 163 K2
Motts Hill La
KWD/TDW/WH KT20 238 D9
Mott St CHING E4 81 K5
Mouchotte Cl BH/WHM TN16 225 N8
Moulins Rd HOM E9 140 B2
Moultain Hl SWLY BR8 209 H4
Moulton Av HEST TW5 153 M8
Moultrie Wy UPMR RM14 126 D5
Moundfield Rd
STNW/STAM N16 119 P4
Mountacre Cl SYD SE26 181 N7
Mount Adon Pk DUL SE21 181 P3
Mountague Pl POP/IOD E14 141 H9
Mount Angelus Rd
PUT/ROE SW15 178 C3
Mount Ararat Rd
RCHPK/HAM TW10 177 K1
Mount Ash Rd SYD SE26 182 A6
Mount Av CHING E4 100 F4
CTHM CR3 241 K10
EA W5 135 J7
HARH RM3 106 B7
RBRW/HUT CM13 107 N1
STHL UB1 133 P8
Mountbatten Cl NRWD SE19 181 M8
SL SL1 149 M2
STAL AL1 38 G9
WOOL/PLUM SE18 163 H5
Mountbatten Ct BKHH IG9 102 A3
Mountbatten Sq WDSR SL4 149 H7
Mountbel Rd
KTN/HRWW/W * HA3 94 F10
Mount Cl BMLY BR1 206 B1
CAR SM5 222 B5
CRAWE RH10 284 D6
EA * W5 135 H7
EBAR EN4 78 B8
HHW HP1 35 J6
LHD/OX KT22 236 E9
PUR/KEN CR8 241 K2
SEV TN13 246 G9
SLN SL2 109 H9
WOKS/MYFD GU22 231 N7
The Mount Cl VW GU25 194 A6
Mountcombe Cl SURB KT6 199 K7
Mount Cottages BXLYHS * DA6 163 P10
Mount Ct WWKM BR4 205 K9
Mount Crs BRW CM14 107 J5
Mount Culver Av SCUP DA14 185 N9
Mount Dr LCOL/BKTW AL2 56 C1
RYLN/HDSTN HA2 113 N3
WBLY HA9 115 P7
The Mount Dr REIG RH2 257 M8
Mountearl Gdns
STRHM/NOR SW16 180 G6
Mount Echo Av CHING E4 100 G2
Mount Echo Dr CHING E4 100 G2
Mount Ephraim La
STRHM/NOR SW16 180 E6
Mount Ephraim Rd
STRHM/NOR SW16 180 E6
Mount Felix WOT/HER KT12 196 G8
Mountfield Cl LEW SE13 183 J3
Mountfield Rd EA W5 135 J8
EHAM E6 142 C4
FNCH N3 117 K1
HHNE HP2 35 P6
Mountfield Wy STMC/STPC BR5 207 M4
Mountford St WCHPL * E1 13 N5
Mountfort Ter IS N1 6 A4
Mount Gdns SYD SE26 182 A6
Mount Grace Rd POTB/CUF EN6 59 K7
Mount Gv EDGW HA8 95 P4
Mountgrove Rd FSBYPK N4 119 K8
Mount Harry Rd SEV TN13 247 J9
Mount Hermon Rd
WOKS/MYFD GU22 232 A5
Mount Hill La CFSP/GDCR SL9 109 N6
Mounthurst Rd HAYES BR2 205 M7
Mountington Park Cl
KTN/HRWW/W HA3 115 J4
Mountjoy Cl THMD SE28 163 L1
Mount La CRAWE RH10 285 P9
DEN/HRF UB9 110 G7
Mount Lee EGH TW20 172 B8
Mount Mills FSBYE EC1V 6 D10
Mountnessing La BRWN CM15 87 K4
Mountnessing Rd BRWN CM15 87 M2
Mount Nod Rd
STRHM/NOR SW16 180 G6
Mount Nugent CSHM HP5 50 F3
Mount Pde EBAR * EN4 77 P8
Mount Pk CAR SM5 222 B5
Mount Park Av
RYLN/HDSTN HA2 114 C7
SAND/SEL CR2 223 J5
Mount Park Crs EA W5 135 J8
Mount Park Rd EA W5 135 J7
PIN HA5 113 H3
RYLN/HDSTN HA2 114 C7
Mount Pl ACT W3 135 N10
Mount Pleasant ALP/SUD HA0 135 K3
BH/WHM TN16 244 A3
DEN/HRF UB9 91 K9
EBAR EN4 78 A8
EHSLY KT24 252 C5
EHSLY KT24 253 M4
EW KT17 220 C6
FSBYW WC1X 11 P3
GUW GU2 267 P2
RDKG * RH5 270 G6
RSLP HA4 113 K8
RYLN/HDSTN * HA2 114 D7
STALW/RED AL3 38 B5
WEY KT13 196 B10
WNWD SE27 181 K7
Mount Pleasant Cl BRKMPK AL9 40 F1
Mount Pleasant Cottages
EGH * TW20 172 A9
Mount Pleasant Crs
FSBYPK * N4 118 G5
Mount Pleasant Hl CLPT E5 120 A7
Mount Pleasant La BRKMPK AL9 40 F1
CLPT E5 120 A6
LCOL/BKTW AL2 55 M6
Mount Pleasant Pl
WOOL/PLUM SE18 162 G3
Mount Pleasant Rd CHIG IG7 102 G5
CRW RM5 104 E7
CTHM CR3 241 P9
DART DA1 187 N2
EA W5 135 H6
LEW SE13 183 H2
NWMAL KT3 199 P3
RSEV TN14 265 J9
TOTM N17 99 M10
WALTH E17 100 D10
WLSDN NW10 136 F2
Mount Pleasant Vls FSBYPK N4 118 G5
Mount Ri FSTH SE23 182 B5
REDH RH1 275 N2
Mount Rd BCTR RM8 124 A6
BXLYHS DA6 185 P1
CHOB/PIR GU24 213 N8
CHSGTN KT9 219 L1
CRICK NW2 116 E8
DART DA1 186 G2
EBAR EN4 77 P9
EPP CM16 65 P8
FELT TW13 175 M6
HDN NW4 116 D4
HERT/WAS SG14 25 H6
HYS/HAR UB3 153 H1
IL IG1 122 E10
MTCM CR4 201 N2
NRWD * SE19 181 L9
NWMAL KT3 200 A3
STALE/WH AL4 21 J2
WAND/EARL SW18 179 K5
WOKS/MYFD GU22 231 N7
Mount Rw MYFR/PKLN W1K 10 E8
Mountsfield Cl
STWL/WRAY TW19 173 K1
Mounts Hl ASC SL5 170 B8
WDSR SL4 170 B5
Mountside GUW GU2 267 N3
KTN/HRWW/W HA3 94 E9
Mountsorrel HERT/BAY SG13 25 N5
Mounts Pond Rd BKHTH/KID SE3 161 J8
The Mount Sq HAMP * NW3 117 M8
Mounts Rd GRH DA9 188 G2
Mount Stewart Av
KTN/HRWW/W HA3 115 J4
Mount St DORK RH4 272 F2
MYFR/PKLN W1K 10 C8
Mount Ter WCHPL E1 140 A7
The Mount BMLY * BR1 206 B1
BRW CM14 107 H4
BXLYHS * DA6 186 C1
CHESW EN7 61 L2
CLPT * E5 120 A7
COUL/CHIP CR5 240 B1
ESH/CLAY KT10 217 P3
EW KT17 220 C6
GUW GU2 267 N3
HAMP NW3 117 M9
HARH RM3 105 K4
HORS RH12 282 E4
KWD/TDW/WH KT20 257 J2
LHD/OX KT22 236 D9
NTHLT * UB5 114 A10
NWMAL KT3 200 C3
POTB/CUF EN6 59 L6
RKW/CH/CXG WD3 71 M10
TRDG/WHET N20 97 M3
VW GU25 194 A6
WARL CR6 241 P5
WBLY HA9 115 N7
WEY KT13 196 F9
WOKN/KNAP GU21 232 A4
WPK KT4 220 E1
Mount Vw ENC/FH EN2 78 G4
LCOL/BKTW AL2 57 K3
NWDGN * UB2 153 L3
RKW/CH/CXG WD3 91 L2
Mountview MLHL NW7 96 A4
NTHWD HA6 93 H7
Mountview Cl REDH RH1 275 P2
Mountview Dr REDH RH1 275 P2
Mount View Rd CDALE/KGS NW9 116 A2
CHING E4 101 H1
ESH/CLAY KT10 218 G4
FSBYPK N4 118 G5
Mountview Rd CHESW EN7 61 M2
ORP BR6 207 K7
Mount Vls WNWD SE27 181 J6
Mount Wy CAR SM5 222 B5
Mountway POTB/CUF EN6 59 K6
Mount Wy WGCE AL7 23 J8
Mountway Cl WGCE AL7 23 J8
Mountwood E/WMO/HCT KT8 198 A3
Mountwood Cl SAND/SEL CR2 224 A6
Movers La BARK IG11 142 G3
Mowatt Cl ARCH N19 118 E6
Mowbray Av BF/WBF KT14 215 P9
Mowbray Crs EGH TW20 172 D8
Mowbray Dr CRAWW RH11 283 J9
Mowbray Gdns DORK RH4 254 G10
NTHLT * UB5 133 P3
Mowbray Rd BAR EN5 77 M8
EDGW HA8 95 M5
HLW CM20 29 J9
KIL/WHAMP NW6 2 A3
NRWD SE19 203 N1
RCHPK/HAM TW10 177 H6
Mowbrays Cl CRW RM5 104 D9
Mowbrays Rd CRW RM5 104 D10
Mowbrey Gdns LOU IG10 82 F5
Mowlem St BETH E2 140 A4
Mowll St BRXN/ST SW9 159 H6
Moxom Av CHES/WCR EN8 62 D6
Moxon Cl PLSTW E13 141 L4
Moxon St BAR EN5 77 J7
MHST W1U 10 C4
Moye Cl BETH E2 7 P7
Moyers Rd WAN E11 121 H6
Moylan Rd HMSMTH W6 14 B10
Moyne Pl WLSDN NW10 135 M5
Moynihan Dr STHGT/OAK N14 78 F9
Moys Cl CROY/NA CR0 202 F6
Moyser Rd TOOT SW17 180 C8
Mozart Est MV/WKIL W9 2 C9
Mozart St MV/WKIL W9 2 C10
Muchelney Rd MRDN SM4 201 M6
Muckhatch La EGH TW20 194 E3
Muckingford Rd TIL RM18 169 J3
Muggeridge Cl SAND/SEL CR2 223 L2
Muggeridge Rd DAGE RM10 124 C9
Muir Cl WAND/EARL SW18 179 P2
Muirdown Av MORT/ESHN SW14 155 P10
Muirfield ACT W3 136 B8
Muirfield Cl BERM/RHTH * SE16 160 A4
CRAWW RH11 282 G8
OXHEY * WD19 93 K6
Muirfield Crs POP/IOD E14 160 G2
Muirfield Gn OXHEY WD19 93 K5
Muirfield Rd OXHEY WD19 93 J5
WOKN/KNAP GU21 231 M4
Muirkirk Rd CAT SE6 183 H4
Muir Rd CLPT E5 119 P9
Muir St CAN/RD E16 142 C10
Mulberry Av STWL/WRAY TW19 173 P4
WDSR SL4 149 L9
Mulberry Cl BROX EN10 44 E10
CHING E4 100 F3
EBAR EN4 77 N8
GPK RM2 125 J2
HDN NW4 116 F1
LCOL/BKTW AL2 56 A4
NTHLT UB5 133 M4
STRHM/NOR SW16 180 D7
WAT WD17 72 F2
WEY KT13 196 C10
WOKN/KNAP GU21 214 B10
Mulberry Crs BTFD TW8 154 G6
WDR/YW UB7 152 B1
Mulberry Dr DTCH/LGLY SL3 150 B4
PUR RM19 165 N3
Mulberry Gdns RAD WD7 57 K9
Mulberry Gn HLWE CM17 29 N7
Mulberry Hl BRWN CM15 107 L1
Mulberry La CROY/NA CR0 203 N8
Mulberry Ms NWCR SE14 160 E7
Mulberry Pde WDR/YW UB7 152 B2
Mulberry Pl HMSMTH W6 156 D4
Mulberry Rd CRAWW RH11 283 L4
GVW DA11 190 B7
HACK E8 7 L4
Mulberry St WCHPL E1 13 N5
Mulberry Trees SHPTN TW17 196 E7
Mulberry Wk CHEL SW3 15 M9
Mulberry Wy BARK/HLT IG6 122 F2
BELV DA17 164 D1
SWFD E18 101 N10
Mulgrave Rd BELMT SM2 221 J4
CROY/NA CR0 203 L10
EA W5 135 J5
HRW HA1 114 F7
WKENS W14 14 C9
WLSDN NW10 116 C9
WOOL/PLUM SE18 162 C3
Mulgrave Wy WOKN/KNAP GU21 231 K4
Mulholland Cl MTCM CR4 202 C2
Mulkern Rd ARCH N19 118 E6
Mullards Cl MTCM CR4 202 A8
Mullein Ct GRAYS RM17 168 A5
Mullens Rd EGH TW20 172 F8
Mullet Gdns BETH E2 7 P9
Mullins Pth MORT/ESHN SW14 156 A9
Mullion Cl KTN/HRWW/W HA3 94 A9
Mullion Wk OXHEY WD19 93 L5
Mull Wk IS * N1 6 F2
Mulready St STJWD NW8 9 N2
Multi Wy ACT W3 156 B1
Multon Rd WAND/EARL SW18 179 N3
Mumford Ct CITYW EC2V 12 F5
Mumford Rd HNHL SE24 181 J1
Mumfords La CFSP/GDCR SL9 109 M1
Muncaster Cl ASHF TW15 174 B7
Muncaster Rd ASHF TW15 174 C8
BTSEA SW11 158 A10
Muncies Ms CAT SE6 183 H5
Mundania Rd EDUL SE22 182 A2
Munday Rd CAN/RD E16 141 M8
Munday's Boro Rd RGUW GU3 266 A5
Mundells CHESW EN7 61 P3
WGCE AL7 23 J4
Munden Gv WATN WD24 73 K4
Munden St WKENS W14 14 A5
Mundesley Sp SL SL1 129 K8
Mundesly Cl OXHEY WD19 93 K5
Mundford Rd CLPT E5 120 B7
Mundon Gdns IL IG1 122 G6
Mund St WKENS W14 14 D8
Mundy St IS N1 7 J9
Munford Dr SWCM DA10 189 L3
Mungo-Park Cl BUSH * WD23 94 B3
Mungo Park Rd GVE DA12 190 G8
RAIN RM13 145 H1
Mungo Park Wy STMC/STPC BR5 207 M7
Munnery Wy ORP BR6 206 D10
Munnings Gdns ISLW TW7 176 C1
Munro Dr FBAR/BDGN * N11 98 D7
Munro Ms NKENS W10 8 B3
Munro Rd BUSH WD23 74 A9
Munslow Gdns SUT SM1 221 M1
Munstead Vw RGUW GU3 267 N5
Munster Av HSLWW TW4 153 M10
Munster Gdns PLMGR N13 99 K5
Munster Ms FUL/PGN * SW6 157 J6
Munster Rd FUL/PGN SW6 157 H6
TEDD TW11 177 H9
Munster Sq CAMTN NW1 4 F10
Munton Rd WALW SE17 18 F5
Murchison Av BXLY DA5 185 N4
Murchison Rd HOD EN11 44 G1
LEY E10 121 H7
Murdoch Cl STA TW18 173 K8
Murdock Cl CAN/RD E16 141 L8
Murdock St PECK SE15 160 A5
Murfett Cl WIM/MER SW19 179 H5
Murfitt Wy UPMR RM14 125 P9
Muriel Av WATW WD18 73 K9
Muriel St IS N1 5 P6
Murillo Rd LEW SE13 161 J10
Murphy St STHWK SE1 18 A2
Murray Av BMLY BR1 205 N3
HSLW TW3 176 A1
Murray Ct ASC SL5 192 B6
Murray Crs PIN HA5 93 L9
Murray Gv IS N1 6 G8
Murray Ms CAMTN NW1 5 J3
Murray Rd BERK HP4 33 P4
CHERT KT16 214 G3
EA W5 155 H3
NTHWD HA6 92 F9
RCHPK/HAM TW10 176 G5
STMC/STPC BR5 207 L3
WIM/MER SW19 178 G9
Murray's La BF/WBF KT14 215 N10
Murray Sq CAN/RD E16 141 M8
Murray St CAMTN NW1 5 H3
Murray Ter HAMP NW3 117 M9
Murrells Wk GT/LBKH KT23 235 P9
The Murreys ASHTD KT21 237 J4
Murthering La ABR/ST RM4 85 H8
Murton Ct STAL AL1 38 D5
Murtwell Dr CHIG IG7 102 F7
Musard Rd HMSMTH W6 14 B9
Musbury St WCHPL E1 140 B8
Muscatel Pl CMBW SE5 159 M7
Muschamp Rd CAR SM5 201 P9
PECK SE15 159 N9
Muscovy St TWRH EC3N 13 K8
Museum St NOXST/BSQ WC1A 11 L4
Musgrave Cl CHESW EN7 61 N3
EBAR EN4 77 M5
Musgrave Crs FUL/PGN SW6 157 K6
Musgrave Rd ISLW TW7 154 E7
Musgrove Rd NWCR SE14 160 C7
Musjid Rd BTSEA SW11 157 N8
Muskalls Cl CHESW EN7 61 P3
Muskham Rd HLW CM20 29 K8
Musk Hl HHW HP1 35 H7
Musleigh Mnr WARE SG12 26 E2
Musley Hl WARE SG12 26 D1
Musley La WARE SG12 26 D1
Musquash Wy HSLWW TW4 153 K8
Mussenden Ct WATN * WD24 73 J5
Mussenden La EYN DA4 210 C6
Mustard Mill Rd STA TW18 173 J7
Muston Rd CLPT E5 120 A7
Muswell Av MUSWH N10 98 C10
Muswell Hl MUSWH N10 118 C1
Muswell Hill Broadway
MUSWH N10 118 C1
Muswell Hill Pl MUSWH N10 118 C2
Muswell Hill Rd HGT N6 118 B4
MUSWH N10 118 B2
Muswell Ms MUSWH N10 118 C1
Muswell Rd MUSWH N10 98 C10
Mutchetts Cl GSTN WD25 55 M9
Mutrix Rd KIL/WHAMP NW6 2 F5
Mutton La POTB/CUF EN6 58 G7
Mutton Pl CAMTN NW1 4 D2
Mutton Rw CHONG CM5 67 K6
Muybridge Rd NWMAL KT3 199 P2
Myatt Rd BRXN/ST SW9 159 J7
Mycenae Rd BKHTH/KID SE3 161 M5

Myddelton Av EN EN1 79 M4
Myddelton Gdns WCHMH N21 99 K1
Myddelton Pk TRDG/WHET N20 97 N4
Myddelton Pas CLKNW EC1R 6 B9
Myddelton Rd CEND/HSY/T N8 118 F1
Myddelton Sq CLKNW EC1R 6 B9
Myddelton St CLKNW EC1R 6 B10
Myddleton Av FSBYPK N4 119 J7
Myddleton Rd UX/CGN UB8 131 M3
WARE SG12 26 C3
WDGN N22 98 F8
Myers Cl RAD WD7 57 K8
Myers La NWCR SE14 160 C5
Mygrove Cl RAIN RM13 145 L4
Mygrove Gdns RAIN RM13 145 L4
Mygrove Rd RAIN RM13 145 L4
Myles Ct CHESW EN7 61 K5
Mylis Cl SYD SE26 182 A7
Mylne Cl CHES/WCR EN8 62 B3
HMSMTH * W6 156 D4
Mylne St CLKNW EC1R 6 A8
Mylor Cl WOKN/KNAP GU21 214 B10
Mymms Dr BRKMPK AL9 59 K3
Mynchen End BEAC HP9 88 C5
Mynchen Rd BEAC HP9 88 B6
Mynn's Cl EPSOM KT18 219 N10
Myra St ABYW SE2 163 K4
Myrdle St WCHPL E1 13 P4
The Myrke DTCH/LGLY SL3 149 L3
Myrna Cl WIM/MER SW19 179 P10
Myron Pl LEW SE13 161 H9
Myrtle Aly WOOL/PLUM SE18 162 D2
Myrtle Av EBED/NFELT TW14 152 F10
RSLP HA4 113 H5
Myrtleberry Cl HACK E8 7 L2
Myrtle Cl DTCH/LGLY SL3 151 H7
EBAR EN4 98 A2
ERITH DA8 164 F6
LTWR GU18 212 A7
UX/CGN UB8 132 A7
WDR/YW UB7 152 A3
Myrtle Cottages DORK * RH4 272 G5
Myrtle Crs SLN SL2 129 L9
Myrtledene Rd ABYW SE2 163 K4
Myrtle Gdns HNWL W7 134 D10
Myrtle Gv ENC/FH EN2 79 L4
NWMAL KT3 199 P2
SOCK/AV RM15 166 B1
Myrtle Pl RDART DA2 188 C4
Myrtle Rd ACT W3 135 P10
BRW CM14 107 H5
CROY/NA CR0 204 F10
DART DA1 187 L5
DORK RH4 272 F1
EHAM E6 142 B3
HARH RM3 105 K7
HPTN TW12 176 B9
HSLW TW3 154 B8
PLMGR N13 99 K4
SUT SM1 221 M2
WALTH E17 120 D4
Myrtleside Cl NTHWD HA6 92 E8
Myrtle St IS N1 7 J8
Myrtle Wk IS N1 7 J8
Mysore Rd BTSEA SW11 158 A10
Myton Rd DUL SE21 181 L6

N

Nadine St CHARL SE7 161 P4
Naffenton Ri LOU IG10 82 A9
Nagle Cl WALTH E17 101 J10
Nag's Head La UPMR RM14 106 B9
WELL DA16 163 L9
Nags Head Rd PEND EN3 80 B8
Nailsworth Crs REDH RH1 258 E5
Nailzee Cl CFSP/GDCR SL9 110 B5
Nairn Cl HARP AL5 20 C5
Nairn Ct TIL * RM18 168 C8
Nairne Gv HNHL SE24 181 L1
Nairn Gn OXHEY WD19 93 H4
Nairn Rd RSLP HA4 133 K1
Nairn St POP/IOD E14 141 H7
Nalders Rd CSHM HP5 51 J5
Nallhead Rd FELT TW13 175 K8
Namba Roy Cl
STRHM/NOR SW16 180 G7
Namton Dr STRHM/NOR SW16 202 G4
Nan Clark's La MLHL NW7 96 C3
Nancy Downs OXHEY WD19 93 K1
Nankin St POP/IOD E14 140 F8
Nansen Rd BTSEA SW11 158 B10
GVE DA12 190 G7
Nansen Village
NFNCH/WDSP * N12 97 L5
Nantes Cl WAND/EARL SW18 157 M10
Nant Rd CRICK NW2 117 J7
Nant St BETH E2 140 A5
Naoroji St FSBYW WC1X 6 A10
Napier Av FUL/PGN SW6 157 J9
POP/IOD E14 160 F4
Napier Cl DEPT SE8 160 E6
HCH RM12 125 J6
LCOL/BKTW AL2 57 J1
WDR/YW UB7 152 A2
WKENS W14 14 C3
Napier Ct CTHM CR3 241 M8
LEE/GVPK SE12 183 N5
Napier Dr BUSH WD23 73 M8
Napier Gdns GU GU1 250 E9
Napier Gv IS N1 6 F8
Napier Pl WKENS W14 14 C4
Napier Rd ALP/SUD HA0 115 J10
ASHF TW15 174 E10
BELV DA17 164 A3
EHAM E6 142 D3
GVW DA11 190 C4
HAYES BR2 205 N3
ISLW TW7 154 F10
PEND EN3 80 C9
SAND/SEL CR2 223 L4
SNWD SE25 204 A4
SRTFD E15 141 K4
TOTM N17 119 M1
WAN E11 121 K8
WDR/YW UB7 151 N7
WKENS W14 14 B4
WLSDN NW10 136 E5
Napier Ter IS N1 6 C4
Napier Wk ASHF TW15 174 E10
Napier Wy CRAWE RH10 284 A4
Napoleon Rd CLPT E5 120 A8
TWK * TW1 176 G3
Napsbury Av LCOL/BKTW AL2 57 H2
Napsbury La LCOL/BKTW AL2 56 F1
STAL AL1 38 F9
The Nap KGLGY WD4 54 B5
Napton Cl YEAD UB4 133 M6
Narbonne Av CLAP SW4 180 D2
Narboro Ct ROM RM1 125 H4
Narborough Cl HGDN/ICK UB10 112 D7
Narborough St FUL/PGN SW6 157 L8
Narcissus Rd KIL/WHAMP NW6 117 K10
Narcot La CSTG HP8 89 N8
Narcot Rd CSTG HP8 89 M6
Narcot Wy CSTG HP8 89 M5
Nare Rd SOCK/AV RM15 146 B9
Narford Rd CLPT E5 119 P8
Narrow Boat Cl THMD SE28 162 G1
Narrow La WARL CR6 242 A5
Narrow St ACT W3 135 N10
POP/IOD E14 140 D9
Narrow Wy HAYES BR2 206 B6
Nascot Pl WAT WD17 73 J6
Nascot Rd WAT WD17 73 J6
Nascot St SHB W12 136 F8
WAT WD17 73 J6
Nascot Wood Rd WAT WD17 72 G3
Naseby Cl ISLW TW7 154 D7
KIL/WHAMP NW6 3 K4
Naseby Ct WOT/HER * KT12 197 K9
Naseby Rd CLAY IG5 102 C9
DAGE RM10 124 B8
NRWD SE19 181 L9
Nash Cl BORE WD6 75 L8
BRKMPK AL9 40 G9
SUT SM1 201 N10
Nash Cft MEO DA13 190 B7
Nash Gdns REDH RH1 258 A8
Nash Gn BMLY BR1 183 M10
Nash La HAYES BR2 225 M3
Nashleigh Hl CSHM HP5 51 J5
Nash Mills La HHS/BOV HP3 54 A2
Nash Rd BROCKY SE4 160 D10
CHDH RM6 123 N2
CRAWE RH10 283 P10
DTCH/LGLY SL3 150 C4
ED N9 100 B3
Nash St CAMTN NW1 4 F9
Nash Wy KTN/HRWW/W HA3 114 G4
Nasmyth St HMSMTH W6 156 E2
Nassau Rd BARN SW13 156 C7
Nassau St GTPST W1W 10 G4
Nassington Rd HAMP NW3 117 P9
Nasturtium Dr CHOB/PIR GU24 230 F1
Natalie Cl EBED/NFELT TW14 174 E3
Natal Rd FBAR/BDGN N11 98 F6
IL IG1 122 E9
STRHM/NOR SW16 180 E9
THHTH CR7 203 L3
Nathan Cl UPMR RM14 126 D6
Nathaniel Cl WCHPL E1 13 M4
Nathans Rd ALP/SUD HA0 115 H7
Nathan Wy THMD SE28 163 J2
National Ter BERM/RHTH * SE16 160 A1
Nation Wy CHING E4 101 H2
Natwoke Cl BEAC HP9 88 C6
Naunton Wy HCH RM12 125 L8
Naval Rw POP/IOD E14 141 H9
Navarino Gv HACK E8 7 N1
Navarino Rd HACK E8 7 P1
Navarre Gdns CRW RM5 104 C7
Navarre Rd EHAM E6 142 B4
Navarre St BETH E2 13 L1
Navestock Cl CHING * E4 101 H4
Navestock Crs WFD IG8 101 P9
Navestock Side BRW CM14 86 B6
Navestock Ter WFD IG8 101 P8
Navigator Dr STHL UB1 154 B1
Navy St CLAP SW4 158 E9
Nayim Pl HACK E8 140 A1
Naylor Gv PEND EN3 80 C9
Naylor Rd PECK SE15 160 A6
TRDG/WHET N20 97 M3
Nazareth Cl PECK SE15 160 A8
Nazeingbury Cl WAB EN9 45 J8
Nazeingbury Pde WAB * EN9 45 J8
Nazeing Common WAB EN9 45 P9
Neal Av STHL UB1 133 N6
Neal Cl CFSP/GDCR SL9 110 E6
NTHWD HA6 93 H9
Neal Ct HERT/WAS SG14 25 K5
Nealden St BRXN/ST SW9 158 G9
Neale Cl EFNCH N2 117 M1
Neal St LSQ/SEVD WC2H 11 L6
WATW WD18 73 K9
Neal Ter FSTH * SE23 182 C4
Neal Yd LSQ/SEVD WC2H 11 L6
Neaole Cl BORE WD6 75 P5
Near Acre CDALE/KGS NW9 96 C9
Neasden Cl WLSDN NW10 116 B10
Neasden La WLSDN NW10 116 A8
Neasden La North WLSDN NW10 116 B8
Neasham Rd BCTR RM8 123 L10
Neate St CMBW SE5 19 J10
Neath Gdns MRDN SM4 201 M6
Neathouse Pl PIM SW1V 16 G5
Neats Acre RSLP HA4 112 E5
Neatscourt Rd EHAM E6 142 A7
Neave Crs HARH RM3 105 K9
Neb La OXTED RH8 261 H7
Nebraska St STHWK SE1 18 G2
Neckinger STHWK SE1 19 M3
Neckinger Est BERM/RHTH SE16 19 M3
Neckinger St STHWK SE1 19 M2
Nectarine Wy LEW SE13 160 G8
Necton Rd STALE/WH AL4 21 K3
Needham Cl WDSR SL4 148 D7
Needham Rd NTGHL W11 8 E6
Needleman St BERM/RHTH SE16 160 C1
Needles Bank GDST RH9 260 A7
Neela Cl HGDN/ICK UB10 112 C9
Neeld Crs HDN NW4 116 E3
WBLY HA9 115 M10
Neil Cl ASHF TW15 174 D8
Neild Wy RKW/CH/CXG WD3 91 J1
Neils Yd LSQ/SEVD * WC2H 11 L6
Nelgarde Rd CAT SE6 182 F3
Nella Rd HMSMTH W6 156 G5
Nelldale Rd BERM/RHTH SE16 160 A3
Nellgrove Rd UX/CGN UB8 132 C6
Nell Gwynn Av SHPTN TW17 196 E6
Nell Gwynn Cl RAD WD7 57 K8
Nell Gwynne Av ASC SL5 192 C4
Nell Gwynne Cl HOR/WEW KT19 219 M7
Nello James Gdns WNWD SE27 181 L7
Nelmes Cl EMPK RM11 125 N3
Nelmes Crs EMPK RM11 125 M3
Nelmes Rd EMPK RM11 125 M5
Nelmes Wy EMPK RM11 125 M2
Nelson Av STAL AL1 38 G9
Nelson Cl AMSS HP7 68 B10
BH/WHM TN16 244 B3
BRW CM14 107 J6
CRAWE RH10 284 D8
CROY/NA CR0 203 J8
DTCH/LGLY SL3 150 A3
EBED/NFELT * TW14 174 G4
HGDN/ICK UB10 132 C5
KIL/WHAMP NW6 2 E9
ROMW/RG RM7 104 C9
WOT/HER KT12 197 J8
Nelson Gdns BETH E2 7 P9
GU GU1 250 D9
HSLWW TW4 175 P2
Nelson Grove Rd
WIM/MER SW19 201 L1
Nelson La HGDN/ICK UB10 132 C6
Nelson Mandela Cl
MUSWH N10 98 A10
Nelson Mandela Rd
BKHTH/KID SE3 161 P9
Nelson Pl IS N1 6 D8
SCUP DA14 185 K7
Nelson Rd ASHF TW15 173 P8
BELV DA17 164 A4
CEND/HSY/T N8 118 G3
CHING E4 100 G7
CTHM CR3 241 L9
DART DA1 187 K2
ED N9 100 A4
GNWCH SE10 161 H5
GVW DA11 190 C5
HAYES BR2 205 P4
HGDN/ICK UB10 132 C5
HSLWW TW4 175 P2
NWMAL KT3 200 A5
PEND EN3 80 C10
RAIN RM13 144 G4
RYLN/HDSTN HA2 114 C6
SCUP DA14 185 K7
SEVS/STOTM N15 119 M2
SOCK/AV RM15 147 H4
STAN HA7 95 H7
WAN E11 121 M2
WDR/YW UB7 152 A7
WDSR SL4 148 E9
WHTN TW2 176 B2
WIM/MER SW19 179 L10
Nelsons Sq STHWK SE1 18 C1
Nelsons Rw CLAP SW4 158 E10
Nelson St CAN/RD E16 141 L9
EHAM E6 142 C4
HERT/WAS SG14 25 J4
WCHPL E1 140 A8
Nelsons Yd CAMTN NW1 4 G7
Nelson Ter FSBYE EC1V 6 D8
Nelson Wk HOR/WEW KT19 219 M5
Nelwyn Av EMPK RM11 125 N3
Nemoure Rd ACT W3 135 P9
Nene Gdns FELT TW13 175 N5
Nene Rd HTHAIR TW6 152 C7
Nepaul Rd BTSEA SW11 157 P8
Nepean St PUT/ROE SW15 178 D2
Neptune Cl CRAWW RH11 283 H9
RAIN RM13 144 G4
Neptune Ct BORE * WD6 75 M7
Neptune Dr HHNE HP2 35 P4
Neptune Rd HRW HA1 114 C4
HTHAIR * TW6 152 D7
Neptune St BERM/RHTH SE16 160 B2
Nesbit Cl BKHTH/KID SE3 161 K9
Nesbit Rd ELTH/MOT SE9 162 A10
Nesbitts Aly BAR * EN5 77 J7
Nesbitt Sq NRWD * SE19 181 M10
Nesham St WAP E1W 13 N9
Ness Rd ERITH DA8 165 L5
Ness St BERM/RHTH SE16 19 N3
Nesta Rd WFD IG8 101 L7
Nestle's Av HYS/HAR UB3 152 G2
Neston Rd WATN WD24 73 K3
Nestor Av WCHMH N21 79 J10
Nethan Dr SOCK/AV RM15 146 B9
Netheravon Rd CHSWK W4 156 C4
HNWL W7 134 E10
Netheravon Rd South
CHSWK W4 156 C5
Netherbury Rd EA W5 155 J2
Netherby Gdns ENC/FH EN2 78 F8
Netherby Pk WEY KT13 216 F2
Netherby Rd FSTH SE23 182 B3
Nether Cl FNCH N3 97 K8
Nethercote Av
WOKN/KNAP GU21 231 L3
Nether Ct MLHL * NW7 97 J7
Nethercourt Av FNCH N3 97 K7
Netherfield Gdns BARK IG11 142 G1
Netherfield La WARE SG12 27 J8
Netherfield Rd HARP AL5 20 A7
NFNCH/WDSP N12 97 L6
TOOT SW17 180 B6
Netherford Rd CLAP SW4 158 D8
Netherhall Rd HLWW/ROY CM19 45 L3
Netherhall Wy HAMP NW3 3 J1
HAMP NW3 117 M10
Netherlands Rd BAR EN5 77 N10
The Netherlands COUL/CHIP CR5 240 D5
Netherleigh Cl ARCH * N19 118 C6
Netherleigh Pk REDH RH1 276 F3
Nether Mt GUW GU2 267 N2
Nethern Court Rd CTHM CR3 242 F9
Netherne La COUL/CHIP CR5 240 D8
Netherpark Dr GPK RM2 104 G10
Nether St FNCH N3 97 K9
Netherton Gv WBPTN SW10 15 J10
Netherton Rd SEVS/STOTM N15 119 L4
TWK TW1 176 F1
Netherway STALW/RED AL3 37 P9
Netherwood CRAWW RH11 283 K10
Netherwood Pl HMSMTH * W6 156 G2
Netherwood Rd BEAC HP9 88 C6
HMSMTH W6 156 G2
Netherwood St
KIL/WHAMP NW6 2 D3
Netley Cl CHEAM SM3 220 G2
CROY/NA CR0 225 H4
SHGR GU5 270 D4
Netley Dr WOT/HER KT12 197 N7
Netley Gdns MRDN SM4 201 M7
Netley Rd BTFD TW8 155 K5
GNTH/NBYPK IG2 122 G3
MRDN SM4 201 M7
WALTH E17 120 E3
Netley St CAMTN NW1 4 G10
Netteswellbury Farm
HLWS CM18 47 J2
Netteswell Orch HLW CM20 28 G10
Netteswell Rd HLW CM20 29 H9
Nettlecombe Cl BELMT SM2 221 L5
Nettlecroft HHW HP1 35 L7
WGCE AL7 23 L4
Nettleden Av WBLY HA9 135 M1
Nettleden Rd BERK HP4 34 D2
Nettlefold Pl WNWD SE27 181 K5
Nettlestead Cl BECK BR3 182 E10
Nettles Ter GU GU1 250 A10
Nettleton Rd HGDN/ICK UB10 112 A9
HTHAIR TW6 152 C7
NWCR SE14 160 C6
Nettlewood Rd
STRHM/NOR SW16 180 E10
Neuchatel Rd CAT SE6 182 E5
Nevada Cl NWMAL KT3 199 P4
Nevada St GNWCH SE10 161 H6
Nevell Rd CDH/CHF RM16 168 E2
Nevern Pl ECT SW5 14 F6
Nevern Rd ECT SW5 14 E6
Nevern Sq ECT SW5 14 F7
Nevil Cl NTHWD HA6 92 E6
Nevile Cl CRAWW RH11 283 K10
Neville Av NWMAL KT3 200 A1
Neville Cl ACT W3 155 P1
BFN/LL DA15 185 J7
BNSTD SM7 221 L10
ESH/CLAY KT10 217 N3
HSLW TW3 153 P8
KIL/WHAMP NW6 2 D8
PECK SE15 159 P6
POTB/CUF EN6 59 J7
SLN SL2 129 L1
WAN E11 121 L8
Neville Dr EFNCH N2 117 M4
Neville Gdns BCTR RM8 123 N8
Neville Gill Cl WAND/EARL SW18 179 K2
Neville Pl WDGN N22 98 G9
Neville Rd BARK/HLT IG6 102 F9
BCTR RM8 123 N7
CROY/NA CR0 203 L7
EA W5 135 J6
FSTGT E7 141 M2
KIL/WHAMP NW6 2 D8
KUT KT1 199 M2
RCHPK/HAM TW10 177 H6
Neville St SKENS SW7 15 L7
Neville Ter SKENS * SW7 15 L7
Neville Wk CAR SM5 201 P7
Nevill Gv WATN WD24 73 J5
Nevill Rd STNW/STAM N16 119 M9
Nevill Wy LOU IG10 82 B10
Nevil Wk CAR * SM5 201 P7
Nevin Dr CHING E4 100 G2
Nevinson Cl WAND/EARL SW18 179 N2
Nevis Cl ROM RM1 104 F7
Nevis Rd TOOT SW17 180 B5
New Acres Rd THMD SE28 143 H10
Newall Rd HTHAIR TW6 152 D7
New Ar UX/CGN * UB8 131 N3
The New Ar HERT/WAS * SG14 25 L5
Newark Cl RGUE GU4 250 E5
RPLY/SEND GU23 233 J7
Newark Ct WOT/HER KT12 197 K8
Newark Crs WLSDN NW10 136 A5
Newark Gn BORE WD6 76 A7
Newark Knok EHAM E6 142 D8
Newark La RPLY/SEND GU23 233 J6
Newark Rd BFOR GU20 212 A1
CRAWE RH10 284 A5
SAND/SEL CR2 223 L3
Newark St WCHPL E1 140 A7
Newark Wy HDN NW4 116 D2
New Ash Cl EFNCH N2 117 N1
New Barn Cl CROY/NA CR0 222 G3
New Barnes Av STAL AL1 38 F9
New Barn La CTHM CR3 241 M3
Newbarn La BEAC HP9 89 K5
RSEV TN14 244 G2
New Barn Rd HART DA3 211 N3
MEO DA13 189 P8
SWLY BR8 208 F1
New Barns Av MTCM CR4 202 E4
New Barn St PLSTW E13 141 M6
New Barns Wy CHIG IG7 102 E4
New Battlebridge La REDH RH1 258 C6
Newberries Av RAD WD7 74 G1
Newberry Crs WDSR SL4 148 B7
New Berry La WOT/HER KT12 217 L2
Newbery Rd ERITH DA8 164 G7
Newbery Wy SLN SL1 149 J1
Newbiggin Pth OXHEY WD19 93 K5
Newbold Cottages WCHPL * E1 140 B8
Newbolt Av CHEAM SM3 220 F2
Newbolt Rd STAN HA7 94 E7
New Bond St MYFR/PKLN W1K 10 F6
Newborough Gn NWMAL KT3 200 A4
New Brent St HDN NW4 116 F3
New Bridge St STP EC4M 12 C6
New Broad St LVPST EC2M 13 H4
New Broadway EA W5 135 J9
HGDN/ICK * UB10 132 C6
Newburgh Rd ACT W3 135 P10
GRAYS RM17 168 A4
Newburgh St SOHO/CST W1F 10 G6
New Burlington Ms CONDST W1S 10 G7
New Burlington Pl CONDST W1S 10 G7
New Burlington St CONDST W1S 10 G7
Newburn St LBTH SE11 17 P7
Newbury Av PEND EN3 80 E3
Newbury Cl HARH RM3 105 K7
NTHLT UB5 133 N1
Newbury Gdns HARH RM3 105 L7
HOR/WEW KT19 220 C1
UPMR RM14 125 N8
Newbury Ms KTTN NW5 4 D2
Newbury Rd CHING E4 101 H7
CRAWE RH10 284 E7
GNTH/NBYPK IG2 122 G4
HARH RM3 105 K6
HAYES BR2 205 M3
WDR/YW UB7 152 A7
Newbury St STBT EC1A 12 E4
Newbury Wk HARH RM3 105 L6
Newbury Wy NTHLT UB5 133 M1
New Butt La DEPT * SE8 160 F6
Newby Cl EN EN1 79 M6
Newby Pl POP/IOD E14 141 H9
Newby St VX/NE SW8 158 C9
Newcastle Av BARK/HLT IG6 103 K7
Newcastle Cl STP EC4M 12 C5
Newcastle Pl BAY/PAD W2 9 M4
Newcastle Rw CLKNW EC1R 12 B1
New Cswy REIG RH2 275 L3
New Cavendish St MHST W1U 10 D4
New Change STP EC4M 12 E6
New Charles St FSBYE EC1V 6 D9
New Chiltern AMSS * HP7 69 K5
New Church Rd CMBW SE5 159 K6
Newchurch Rd SL SL1 128 E7
New City Rd PLSTW E13 141 P5
New Cl FELT TW13 175 M8
WIM/MER SW19 201 M3
New College Ms IS * N1 6 B3
New College Pde HAMP NW3 3 L2
Newcombe Pk ALP/SUD HA0 135 L3
MLHL NW7 96 B6
Newcombe Ri WDR/YW UB7 131 P8
Newcombe St KENS * W8 8 F9
Newcome Gdns
STRHM/NOR SW16 180 F7
Newcomen Rd BTSEA SW11 157 N9
WAN * E11 121 L8
Newcomen St STHWK SE1 18 G1
Newcome Rd RAD WD7 57 M10
New Compton St
LSQ/SEVD * WC2H 11 K6
New Coppice WOKN/KNAP GU21 231 K5
New Cottages BRKMPK AL9 58 G4
DORK * RH4 272 E3
REIG * RH2 256 G8
New Ct NTHLT UB5 114 A10
TPL/STR * WC2R 12 A7
Newcourt UX/CGN UB8 131 M7
Newcourt St STJWD NW8 3 N8
New Covent Garden Market
VX/NE SW8 17 K9
New Crane Pl WAP * E1W 140 B10
New Crescent Yd
WLSDN * NW10 136 C4
Newcroft Cl UX/CGN UB8 132 A7
New Cross Rd GUW GU2 249 M8
NWCR SE14 160 B6
Newdales Cl ED N9 99 P3
Newdene Av NTHLT UB5 133 L4
Newdigate STRHM/NOR * SW16 181 H7
Newdigate Gn DEN/HRF UB9 91 N9
Newdigate Rd DEN/HRF UB9 91 M9
HORS RH12 282 A5
Newdigate Rd East
DEN/HRF UB9 91 N9
Newell Ri HHS/BOV HP3 35 P9
Newell Rd HHS/BOV HP3 35 P9
Newell St POP/IOD E14 140 E9
New End HAMP NW3 117 M9
New End Sq HAMP NW3 117 N9
New England St STALW/RED AL3 38 B6
Newenham Rd GT/LBKH KT23 253 P2
Newent Cl CAR SM5 202 A8
PECK SE15 159 M6
New Era Est IS N1 7 J6
New Farm Av HAYES BR2 205 M4
New Farm Dr ABR/ST RM4 83 M7
New Farm La NTHWD HA6 92 F9
New Ferry Ap WOOL/PLUM SE18 162 D2
New Fetter La FLST/FETLN EC4A 12 B5
Newfield Cl HPTN TW12 197 P1
Newfield La HHNE HP2 36 A6
Newfield Ri CRICK NW2 116 D8
Newfields WGCW AL8 22 E6
Newfield Wy STALE/WH AL4 39 J8
Newford Cl HHNE HP2 36 C5
New Ford Rd CHES/WCR EN8 62 E10
New Forest La CHIG IG7 102 D7
Newgale Gdns EDGW HA8 95 L9
New Garden Dr WDR/YW UB7 151 P1
Newgate CROY/NA CR0 203 K8
Newgate Cl FELT TW13 175 M5
STALE/WH AL4 39 J3
Newgate St CHING E4 101 K4
STBT EC1A 12 D5
Newgatestreet Rd CHESW EN7 61 J2
Newgate Street Village
HERT/BAY SG13 60 F1
New Globe Wk STHWK SE1 12 E9
New Goulston St WCHPL E1 13 L5
New Green Pl NRWD SE19 181 M9
New Greens Av STALW/RED AL3 38 C1
Newhall Cl HHS/BOV * HP3 52 D3
New Hall Dr HARH RM3 105 M9
Newhall Gdns WOT/HER KT12 197 K9
Newham's Rw STHWK SE1 19 K2
Newham Wy CAN/RD E16 141 L7
Newhaven Cl HYS/HAR UB3 152 G3
Newhaven Crs ASHF TW15 174 E8
Newhaven Gdns ELTH/MOT SE9 162 A10
Newhaven La PLSTW E13 141 L7
Newhaven Rd SNWD SE25 203 L5
Newhaven Sp SLN * SL2 128 G6
New Haw Rd ADL/WDHM KT15 215 M2
New Heston Rd HEST TW5 153 N6
Newhouse Av CHDH RM6 123 N1
Newhouse Cl NWMAL KT3 200 B7
Newhouse Crs GSTN WD25 55 J9
New House Farm La RGUW GU3 249 H9
Newhouse La CHONG CM5 49 K8
New House La GVW DA11 190 C6
REDH RH1 276 E8
New House Pk STAL AL1 38 F9
Newhouse Rd HHW HP1 52 D2
Newhouse Wk MRDN SM4 201 M7
Newick Cl BXLY DA5 186 C2
Newick Rd CLPT E5 120 A8
Newing Gn BMLY BR1 184 A10
Newington Barrow Wy
HOLWY N7 118 G8
Newington Butts LBTH SE11 18 D6
Newington Cswy STHWK SE1 18 E3
Newington Gn STNW/STAM N16 119 L10
Newington Green Rd IS N1 6 G1
New Inn Broadway
SDTCH * EC2A 13 K1
New Inn La RGUE GU4 250 E7
New Inn Sq SDTCH * EC2A 13 K1
New Inn St SDTCH * EC2A 13 K1
New Inn Yd SDTCH EC2A 13 K1
New Kelvin Av TEDD TW11 176 D9
New Kent Rd STAL AL1 38 C6
STHWK SE1 18 E5
New King's Rd FUL/PGN SW6 157 K8
FUL/PGN SW6 157 J8
New King St DEPT SE8 160 F5
Newland Cl PIN HA5 93 M7
STAL AL1 38 F9
Newland Dr EN EN1 80 A5
Newland Gdns HNWL W7 154 F1
Newland Rd CEND/HSY/T N8 118 F1
Newlands Av RAD WD7 56 E10
THDIT KT7 198 D8
WOKS/MYFD GU22 232 C7
Newlands Cl ALP/SUD HA0 135 H1
EDGW HA8 95 K4
HORL RH6 280 A2
NWDGN UB2 153 M4
WOT/HER KT12 217 M1
Newlands Ct WBLY HA9 115 M7
Newlands Crs GU GU1 268 C2
Newlands Dr DTCH/LGLY SL3 151 H9
Newlands Pk ABLGY * WD5 54 G2
CRAWE RH10 285 M2
SYD SE26 182 B9
Newlands Pl BAR EN5 76 G9
Newlands Quay WAP E1W 140 B9
Newlands Rd CRAWW RH11 283 M8
HHW HP1 35 H5
STRHM/NOR SW16 202 F2
WFD IG8 101 L3
The Newlands WLGTN SM6 222 D4
Newland St CAN/RD E16 142 B10
Newlands Wk GSTN WD25 55 L9
Newlands Wy CHSGTN KT9 219 H2

POTB/CUF EN6 59 L6
Newlands Wd CROY/NA CR0 224 E5
Newlands Woods
CROY/NA * CR0 224 E5
New La RGUE GU4 232 C10
Newling Cl EHAM E6 142 C8
Newling Est BETH E2 7 M10
New Lodge Dr OXTED RH8 261 L4
New London St MON * EC3R 13 K7
New Lydenburg St CHARL SE7 161 P2
Newlyn Cl LCOL/BKTW AL2 55 M6
UX/CGN UB8 132 B7
Newlyn Gdns RYLN/HDSTN HA2 113 N5
Newlyn Rd BAR EN5 77 J8
TOTM N17 99 N9
WELL DA16 163 J8
Newman Cl CRAWE RH10 284 D8
EMPK RM11 125 M3
Newman Rd BMLY BR1 205 M1
CROY/NA CR0 202 G7
HYS/HAR UB3 133 J9
PLSTW E13 141 N5
WALTH E17 120 C3
Newmans Dr RBRW/HUT CM13 107 P1
Newmans La LOU IG10 82 D7
Newmans Pl ASC SL5 192 G7
Newman's Rd GVW DA11 190 C5
Newman's Rw LINN WC2A 11 P4
Newman St FITZ W1T 11 H4
Newman's Wy EBAR EN4 77 M6
Newmarket Av NTHLT UB5 113 P10
Newmarket Ct STALW/RED AL3 38 B5
Newmarket Rd CRAWE RH10 284 B10
Newmarket Wy HCH RM12 125 M9
New Mile Rd ASC SL5 192 A2
New Mill Rd STMC/STPC BR5 207 M1
Newminster Ct ENC/FH * EN2 79 J6
Newminster Rd MRDN SM4 201 M6
New Mount St SRTFD * E15 141 J3
Newnham Av RSLP HA4 113 K6
Newnham Cl LOU IG10 82 A10
NTHLT UB5 134 B1
THHTH CR7 203 K2
Newnham Gdns NTHLT UB5 134 B1
Newnham Gn WDGN * N22 99 H9
Newnham Pde CHES/WCR * EN8 62 C6
Newnham Pl CDH/CHF RM16 168 D3
Newnham Rd WDGN N22 98 G9
Newnhams Cl BMLY BR1 206 C3
Newnham Ter STHWK SE1 18 A3
Newnham Wy
KTN/HRWW/W HA3 115 H4
New North Pl SDTCH EC2A 13 J1
New North Rd BARK/HLT IG6 102 G8
IS N1 7 H8
REIG RH2 275 J3
New North St BMSBY WC1N 11 N3
Newnton Cl FSBYPK N4 119 L5
New Oak Rd EFNCH N2 97 M10
New Oxford St NOXST/BSQ WC1A 11 L5
New Pde ASHF * TW15 174 A7
DORK * RH4 272 G1
GT/LBKH * KT23 254 B2
RKW/CH/CXG * WD3 72 A10
WDR/YW * UB7 131 P10
New Park Av PLMGR N13 99 K4
New Park Cl NTHLT UB5 133 M1
New Park Dr HHNE HP2 36 C5
New Park Est UED N18 100 B6
New Park Rd ASHF TW15 174 D8
BAL SW12 180 F4
DEN/HRF UB9 91 M9
HERT/BAY SG13 42 D10
New Peachey La UX/CGN UB8 131 N8
Newpiece LOU IG10 82 E7
New Pl BFOR * GU20 192 D9
New Place Gdns UPMR RM14 126 C7
New Place Sq
BERM/RHTH * SE16 160 A2
New Plaistow Rd SRTFD E15 141 K3
New Pond Pde RSLP * HA4 113 H8
New Pond Rd RGUW GU3 267 K8
RGUW GU3 267 N9
Newport Av POP/IOD E14 141 J9
Newport Cl PEND EN3 80 D3
Newport Ct SOHO/SHAV W1D 11 K7
Newport Md OXHEY * WD19 93 L5
Newport Pl SOHO/SHAV * W1D 11 K7
Newport Rd BARN SW13 156 D7
HTHAIR TW6 152 B7
SLN SL2 128 D6
WALTH * E17 120 D2
WAN E11 121 J7
YEAD UB4 132 E7
Newports SBW CM21 29 M2
SWLY BR8 208 E7
Newport St LBTH SE11 17 N6
Newquay Crs RYLN/HDSTN HA2 113 M7
Newquay Gdns OXHEY WD19 93 J3
Newquay Rd CAT SE6 182 G5
New Quebec St MBLAR W1H 10 D6
New River Av WARE SG12 26 G7
New River Cl HOD EN11 44 G2
New River Crs PLMGR N13 99 J5
New River Wy FSBYPK N4 119 L5
New Rd ABR/ST RM4 83 N10
ABYW SE2 163 N3
ALP/SUD HA0 114 E9
AMS HP6 69 K3
AMSS HP7 68 E8
BERK HP4 33 L2
BERK HP4 34 A4
BROX EN10 44 E5
BRW CM14 107 J3
BTFD * TW8 155 J5
CEND/HSY/T N8 118 E3
CHING E4 100 G5
CSTG HP8 70 B7
DAGW RM9 143 M2
DTCH/LGLY SL3 150 A7
DTCH/LGLY SL3 150 D2
E/WMO/HCT KT8 197 P3
EBED/NFELT TW14 174 E2
EBED/NFELT TW14 175 J4
ED N9 99 P4
ESH/CLAY KT10 218 B1
EYN DA4 210 B2
FELT TW13 175 M8
GDMY/SEVK IG3 123 H7
GRAYS RM17 167 M5
GSTN WD25 74 D5
GVW DA11 190 D2
HERT/WAS SG14 25 L3
HLWE CM17 29 N7
HORL RH6 281 J4
HSLW TW3 154 A10
HYS/HAR UB3 152 D6
KGLGY WD4 53 J6
KUTN/CMB KT2 177 M10
KWD/TDW/WH KT20 238 F9
MLHL NW7 97 H8
MTCM CR4 202 B8
ORP BR6 207 K7
OXTED RH8 261 N6
POTB/CUF EN6 58 D9
RAD WD7 57 M10
RAD WD7 74 D2
RCHPK/HAM TW10 177 H7
RGUE GU4 251 P7
RGUE GU4 268 E7
RKW/CH/CXG WD3 71 J5
RKW/CH/CXG WD3 72 A9
RSEV TN14 245 N10
SHGR GU5 268 E9
SHGR GU5 269 N5
SHGR GU5 270 D5
SHPTN TW17 196 B3
STA TW18 172 F8
SWLY BR8 208 G3
UX/CGN UB8 132 D6
WARE SG12 26 D2
WAT WD17 73 K8
WCHPL E1 140 A7
WDGN N22 99 K8
WELL DA16 163 L8
WEY KT13 216 D2
WGCW AL8 22 D8
New Road Hl HAYES BR2 226 B5
New Rw CHCR WC2N 11 L7
Newry Rd TWK TW1 154 F10
Newsam Av SEVS/STOTM N15 119 L3
Newsham Rd WOKN/KNAP GU21 231 L3
Newsholme Dr WCHMH N21 78 G9
New Site ADL/WDHM * KT15 215 P1
New Spring Gardens Wk
LBTH * SE11 17 M8
New Sq LINN WC2A 11 P5
SL SL1 149 L1
Newstead HAT AL10 40 C7
Newstead Av ORP BR6 206 G10
Newstead Cl NFNCH/WDSP N12 97 P7
Newstead Ct NTHLT * UB5 133 M5
Newstead Hall HORL RH6 280 E5
Newstead Ri CTHM CR3 260 A2
Newstead Rd LEE/GVPK SE12 183 L3
Newstead Wk MRDN SM4 201 M7
Newstead Wy WIM/MER SW19 178 G7
New St BERK HP4 34 A5
BH/WHM TN16 262 F3
CRAWE RH10 284 B6
LVPST EC2M 13 K4
STA TW18 173 K7
WATW * WD18 73 K8
New Street Hl BMLY BR1 183 N8
New Street Rd BGR/WK TN15 211 P10
New Street Sq FLST/FETLN EC4A 12 B5
New Swan Yd GVE * DA12 190 E2
Newteswell Dr WAB EN9 63 J8
Newton Abbot Rd GVW DA11 190 C5
Newton Av ACT W3 155 P1
MUSWH N10 98 B9
Newton Cl DTCH/LGLY SL3 150 C1
HARP AL5 20 C5
HOD EN11 26 G9
RYLN/HDSTN HA2 113 P7
WALTH E17 120 D4
Newton Ct WDSR SL4 171 M2
Newton Crs BORE WD6 75 P8
Newton Dr SBW CM21 29 N2
Newton Gv CHSWK W4 156 B2
Newton La WDSR SL4 171 N2
Newton Rd ALP/SUD HA0 135 L2
BAY/PAD W2 8 F6
CRAWE RH10 284 A3
CRICK NW2 116 F9
ISLW TW7 154 E8
KTN/HRWW/W HA3 94 D9
PUR/KEN CR8 222 D8
SEVS/STOTM N15 119 N3
SRTFD * E15 121 J10
TIL RM18 168 D8
WDR/YW UB7 151 P7
WELL DA16 163 K9
WIM/MER SW19 179 H10
Newtons Cl RAIN RM13 144 F2
Newton's Ct GRH DA9 166 C10
Newtonside Orch WDSR * SL4 171 M2
Newton St HOL/ALD WC2B 11 M5
Newton's Yd WAND/EARL SW18 179 K1
Newton Ter HAYES BR2 206 A6
Newton Wk EDGW HA8 95 N9
Newton Wy UED N18 99 K6
Newton Wood Rd ASHTD KT21 237 L2
New Tower Buildings
WAP * E1W 140 A10
New Town CRAWE RH10 285 J2
Newtown Rd DEN/HRF UB9 131 L1
Newtown St BTSEA * SW11 158 C7
New Trinity Rd EFNCH N2 117 N1
New Union Cl POP/IOD E14 161 H2
New Union St BARB EC2Y 12 G4
New Vls TOTM * N17 99 P9
New Wanstead WAN E11 121 M4
New Way La HLWE CM17 30 E10
New Way Rd CDALE/KGS NW9 116 B2
New Wharf Rd IS N1 5 M7
New Wickham La EGH TW20 172 D10
New Wd WGCE AL7 23 M4
Newyears Green La
DEN/HRF UB9 112 A4
New Years La RSEV TN14 227 K10
New Zealand Av WOT/HER KT12 196 G8
WOT/HER KT12 197 H8
New Zealand Wy RAIN RM13 144 G5
Niagara Av EA W5 155 H3
Niagara Cl CHES/WCR EN8 62 C5
IS N1 6 F7
Nibthwaite Rd HRW HA1 114 D3
Nicholas Cl GFD/PVL UB6 134 A4
SOCK/AV RM15 147 H5
STALW/RED AL3 38 C3
WATN WD24 73 J3
Nicholas Gdns EA W5 135 J10
SL SL1 128 D10
WOKS/MYFD GU22 233 H2
Nicholas La HERT/WAS SG14 25 L5
MANHO EC4N 13 H7
Nicholas Rd BCTR RM8 124 A7
BORE WD6 75 L10
CROY/NA CR0 222 F1
WCHPL E1 140 B6
Nicholas Wy HHNE HP2 36 A4
NTHWD HA6 92 D9
Nicholay Rd ARCH N19 118 E6
Nicholes Rd HSLW TW3 153 P10
Nichol La BMLY BR1 183 M10
Nicholl Rd EPP CM16 65 J7
Nicholls WDSR SL4 148 B9
Nicholls Av UX/CGN UB8 132 B6
Nicholls Fld HLWS CM18 47 L2
Nichollsfield Wk HOLWY N7 118 F10
Nicholl St BETH E2 7 N6
Nichols Cl FSBYPK * N4 119 H6
Nichols Gn EA W5 135 K7
Nicholson Dr BUSH WD23 94 B2
Nicholson Ms EGH * TW20 172 D8
KUT KT1 199 K4
Nicholson Rd CROY/NA CR0 203 N8
Nicholson St STHWK SE1 12 C10
Nicholson Wk EGH TW20 172 D8
Nickelby Cl THMD SE28 143 M8
Nickleby Cl UX/CGN UB8 132 C8
Nickleby Rd GVE DA12 191 K4
Nicky Line HHNE HP2 35 P6
Nicola Cl KTN/HRWW/W HA3 94 C10
SAND/SEL CR2 223 K3
Nicola Ms BARK/HLT IG6 102 E8
Nicol Cl CFSP/GDCR SL9 89 P9
Nicol End CFSP/GDCR SL9 89 P9
Nicoll Pl HDN NW4 116 E4
Nicoll Rd WLSDN NW10 136 B3
Nicoll Wy BORE WD6 76 A9
Nicol Rd CFSP/GDCR SL9 89 P9
Nicolson Rd STMC/STPC BR5 207 M7
Nicosia Rd WAND/EARL SW18 179 P3
Nidderdale HHNE HP2 36 A3
Niederwald Rd SYD SE26 182 D7
Nield Rd HYS/HAR UB3 152 G1
Nigel Cl NTHLT UB5 133 M3
Nigel Fisher Wy CHSGTN KT9 219 H4
Nigel Ms IL IG1 122 E9
Nigel Playfair Av HMSMTH W6 156 E4
Nigel Rd FSTGT E7 121 P10
PECK SE15 159 P9
Nigeria Rd CHARL SE7 161 P6
Nightingale Av CHING E4 101 K6
EHSLY KT24 252 E1
UPMR RM14 126 E6
Nightingale Cl ABLGY WD5 55 H7
BH/WHM TN16 243 P1
CAR SM5 202 B9
CHING E4 101 K5
CHSWK W4 155 P5
COB KT11 217 L7
CRAWW RH11 283 M5
GVW DA11 190 B7
HOR/WEW KT19 219 M8
PIN HA5 113 K3
RAD WD7 74 E2
Nightingale Cnr
STMC/STPC * BR5 207 N4
Nightingale Crs EHSLY KT24 252 E1
Nightingale Dr HOR/WEW KT19 219 N3
Nightingale Gv LEW SE13 183 J1
Nightingale La BAL SW12 180 A3
BMLY BR1 205 P2
CEND/HSY/T N8 118 F2
RCHPK/HAM TW10 177 K3
RSEV TN14 264 C6
STAL AL1 39 H10
WAN E11 121 N3
Nightingale Ms KUT * KT1 199 J3
LBTH SE11 18 B5
Nightingale Pk SLN SL2 128 E2
Nightingale Pl RKW/CH/CXG WD3 91 N1
WBPTN SW10 15 K9
WOOL/PLUM SE18 162 D5
Nightingale Rd BUSH WD23 73 P9
CAR SM5 202 A10
CHESW EN7 61 K1
CLPT E5 120 A8
CSHM * HP5 50 G5
E/WMO/HCT KT8 198 A5
ED N9 100 B1
EHSLY KT24 252 G1
ESH/CLAY KT10 217 N2
GU GU1 250 A10
HNWL W7 134 E10
HPTN TW12 175 P9
RKW/CH/CXG WD3 91 M1
RSEV TN14 247 L3
SAND/SEL CR2 224 C7
STMC/STPC BR5 206 F6
WDGN N22 98 F9
WLSDN NW10 136 C4
WOT/HER * KT12 197 K7
Nightingale Shott EGH TW20 172 C9
Nightingales La CSTG HP8 70 A9
Nightingale Sq BAL SW12 180 B3
The Nightingales
STWL/WRAY TW19 174 A4
Nightingale V WOOL/PLUM SE18 162 D5
Nightingale Wk BAL SW12 180 C2
WDSR SL4 149 H9
Nightingale Wy DEN/HRF UB9 111 J4
EHAM E6 142 B7
REDH RH1 259 M10
SWLY BR8 208 F3
Nile Cl STNW/STAM N16 119 N8
Nile Dr ED N9 100 B3
Nile Rd PLSTW E13 141 P4
Nile St IS N1 6 G9
Nile Ter PECK SE15 19 M8
Nimbus Rd HOR/WEW KT19 220 A6
Nimrod Cl NTHLT UB5 133 L5
STALE/WH AL4 39 H4
Nimrod Pas HACK * E8 7 K2
Nimrod Rd STRHM/NOR SW16 180 C9
Nina Mackay Cl SRTFD * E15 141 K3
Nine Acres SL SL1 128 E10
Nine Acres Cl MNPK E12 122 B10
Nineacres Wy COUL/CHIP CR5 240 F2
Nine Elms Cl EBED/NFELT TW14 174 G4
UX/CGN UB8 131 N7
Nine Elms Gv GVW DA11 190 D3
Nine Elms La VX/NE SW8 17 J10
Ninefields WAB EN9 63 L9
Ninehams Cl CTHM CR3 241 L6
Ninehams Gdns CTHM CR3 241 L6
Ninehams Rd BH/WHM TN16 244 A7
CTHM CR3 241 L7
Nine Stiles Cl DEN/HRF UB9 131 L1
Nineteenth Rd MTCM CR4 202 F4
Ninhams Wd ORP BR6 226 D1
Ninian Rd HHNE HP2 35 P1
Ninnings Rd CFSP/GDCR SL9 90 C8
Ninnings Wy CFSP/GDCR SL9 90 C8
Ninth Av HYS/HAR UB3 133 H9
KWD/TDW/WH * KT20 257 J2
Nita Rd BRW CM14 107 H6
Nithdale Rd WOOL/PLUM SE18 162 E6
Nithsdale Gv HGDN/ICK UB10 112 D8
Niton Cl BAR EN5 76 G10
Niton Rd RCH/KEW * TW9 155 M9
Niton St FUL/PGN SW6 156 G6
Niven Cl BORE WD6 75 P5
CRAWE RH10 284 E8
Nixey Cl SL SL1 149 M1
Nizels La RTON TN11 265 N10
No 1 St WOOL/PLUM SE18 162 E2
No 2 St WOOL/PLUM SE18 162 E2
Noahs Ct CRAWE * RH10 285 P9
Noak Hill Rd HARH RM3 105 L4
Nobel Dr HYS/HAR UB3 152 F6
Nobel Rd UED N18 100 B5
Noble Cnr HEST * TW5 153 P7
Noble St CITYW EC2V 12 E5
Nobles Wy EGH TW20 172 B10
Noel Rd ACT W3 135 M8
EHAM E6 142 B6
IS N1 6 C7
Noel St SOHO/CST * W1F 11 H6
Noke Dr REDH RH1 258 B9
Noke La LCOL/BKTW AL2 55 M2
Noke Side LCOL/BKTW AL2 55 P3
The Nokes HHW HP1 35 K4
Nolan Wy CLPT E5 119 P9
Nolton Pl EDGW HA8 95 L9
Nonsuch Cl BARK/HLT IG6 102 E7
Nonsuch Court Av EW KT17 220 E6
Nonsuch Pl CHEAM * SM3 220 G4
Nonsuch Wk BELMT SM2 220 G6
The Nook WARE SG12 26 G7
Noons Corner Rd RDKG RH5 271 N9
Norbiton Av KUT KT1 199 M2
Norbiton Common Rd
NWMAL KT3 199 N3
Norbiton Rd POP/IOD E14 140 E8
Norbroke St ACT W3 136 C9
Norburn St NKENS W10 8 A4
Norbury Av HSLW TW3 176 C1
STRHM/NOR SW16 202 G1
WATN WD24 73 K5
Norbury Cl STRHM/NOR SW16 203 H1
Norbury Court Rd
STRHM/NOR SW16 202 F2
Norbury Crs STRHM/NOR SW16 203 H2
Norbury Cross
STRHM/NOR SW16 202 F3
Norbury Gdns CHDH RM6 123 N3
Norbury Gv MLHL NW7 96 B4
Norbury Hl STRHM/NOR SW16 181 H10
Norbury Ri STRHM/NOR SW16 202 F3
Norbury Rd CHING E4 100 F6
REIG RH2 257 J10
THHTH CR7 203 K2
Norbury Vls KUT * KT1 199 L2
Norbury Wy GT/LBKH KT23 254 B1
Norcombe Gdns
KTN/HRWW/W HA3 115 H4
Norcott Cl YEAD UB4 133 K6
Norcott Rd STNW/STAM N16 119 P7
Norcroft Gdns EDUL SE22 181 P3
Norcutt Rd WHTN TW2 176 D4
Nordenfeldt Rd ERITH DA8 164 E4
Nordmann Pl SOCK/AV RM15 147 J6
Norelands Dr SL SL1 128 B4
Norfield Rd RDART DA2 186 D7
Norfolk Av PLMGR N13 99 J7
SAND/SEL CR2 223 P6
SEVS/STOTM N15 119 N4
SL SL1 129 H7
WATN WD24 73 K4
Norfolk Cl DART DA1 187 P2
EBAR EN4 78 B8
EFNCH N2 117 P1
HORL RH6 280 B5
PLMGR N13 99 J7
TWK * TW1 176 G2
Norfolk Ct BAR * EN5 77 H8
Norfolk Crs BAY/PAD W2 9 N5
BFN/LL DA15 185 H3
Norfolk Farm Cl
WOKS/MYFD GU22 232 F1
Norfolk Farm Rd
WOKS/MYFD GU22 232 G1
Norfolk Gdns BORE WD6 76 A8
BXLYHN DA7 164 A7
WOKN/KNAP * GU21 231 L5
Norfolk House
RKW/CH/CXG * WD3 91 P2
Norfolk House Rd
STRHM/NOR SW16 180 E6
Norfolk La RDKG RH5 272 G8
Norfolk Ms NKENS W10 8 B4
Norfolk Pl BAY/PAD W2 9 M5
WELL DA16 163 K8
Norfolk Rd BAR EN5 77 K7
BARK IG11 143 H2
DAGE RM10 124 C10
DORK RH4 272 F2
EHAM E6 142 C3
ESH/CLAY KT10 218 D2
FELT TW13 175 K4
GDMY/SEVK IG3 123 H6
GVE DA12 190 G2
HRW HA1 114 A3
PEND EN3 80 A10
RKW/CH/CXG WD3 91 P2
ROMW/RG RM7 124 D4
STJWD NW8 3 M6
THHTH CR7 203 K3
UPMR RM14 125 P8
UX/CGN UB8 131 N1
WALTH E17 100 D9
WIM/MER SW19 179 P10
WLSDN NW10 136 B2
Norfolk Rw STHWK SE1 17 N5
Norfolk Sq BAY/PAD W2 9 M6
Norfolk Square Ms BAY/PAD W2 9 M6
Norfolk St FSTGT E7 121 M10
Norgrove Pk CFSP/GDCR SL9 110 B2
Norgrove St BAL SW12 180 B4
Norheads La BH/WHM TN16 243 P2
Norhyrst Av SNWD SE25 203 N3
Nork Gdns BNSTD SM7 221 H10
Nork Ri BNSTD SM7 238 G2
Nork Wy BNSTD SM7 238 G1
Norland Pl NTGHL W11 8 B10
Norland Rd NTGHL W11 136 G10
Norlands Crs CHST BR7 206 E1
Norlands Ga CHST * BR7 206 E1
Norlands La EGH TW20 195 H2
Norland Sq NTGHL W11 8 A10
Norley V PUT/ROE SW15 178 D4
Norlington Rd LEY E10 121 H6
Norman Av EW KT17 220 C8
FELT TW13 175 M5
SAND/SEL CR2 223 K6
STHL UB1 133 M9
TWK TW1 176 G3
WDGN N22 99 K9
Normanby Cl PUT/ROE SW15 179 J1
Normanby Rd WLSDN NW10 116 C10
Norman Cl KWD/TDW/WH KT20 238 E5
ORP BR6 206 F10
ROMW/RG RM7 104 C10
RSEV TN14 247 L3
WAB EN9 63 J9
Norman Colyer Ct
HOR/WEW * KT19 220 A6
Norman Ct POTB/CUF EN6 59 M6
Norman Crs HEST TW5 153 L6
PIN HA5 93 K9
RBRW/HUT CM13 107 M4
Normand Ms WKENS W14 14 B9
Normand Rd WKENS W14 14 C9
Normandy Av BAR EN5 77 J9
Normandy Cl CRAWE RH10 284 C9
SYD SE26 182 D6
Normandy Ct HHNE HP2 35 N5
Normandy Dr BERK HP4 33 M4
HYS/HAR UB3 132 D8
Normandy Rd BRXN/ST SW9 159 H7
STALW/RED AL3 38 C5
Normandy Ter CAN/RD E16 141 N8
Normandy Wk EGH * TW20 172 F8
Normandy Wy ERITH DA8 164 F7
HOD EN11 45 J1
Norman Gv BOW E3 140 D4
Normanhurst RBRW/HUT CM13 87 P10
Normanhurst Av WELL DA16 163 N7
Normanhurst Cl CRAWE RH10 284 A7
Normanhurst Dr TWK TW1 176 G1
Normanhurst Rd
BRXS/STRHM SW2 180 G5
STMC/STPC BR5 207 L2
WOT/HER KT12 197 L9
Norman Pde SCUP * DA14 185 P6
Norman Rd ASHF TW15 174 E9
BELV DA17 144 C10
DART DA1 187 M4
EHAM E6 142 C6
EMPK RM11 125 H5
GNWCH SE10 160 G6
IL IG1 122 E10
SEVS/STOTM N15 119 N3
SUT SM1 221 K2
THHTH CR7 203 J5
WAN E11 121 K7
WIM/MER SW19 179 M10
Normans Cl GVW DA11 190 D3
UX/CGN UB8 131 P7
WDGN * N22 99 K9
WLSDN NW10 136 A1
Normansfield Av
E/WMO/HCT KT8 177 H10
Normansfield Cl BUSH WD23 94 A1
Normanshire Dr CHING E4 100 F5
Normans Md WLSDN NW10 136 A1
Norman's Rd HORL RH6 281 K2
The Normans SLN SL2 129 N8
Norman St FSBYE EC1V 6 E10
RSEV TN14 263 P6
Norman Ter KIL/WHAMP * NW6 117 J10
Normanton Av WIM/MER SW19 179 K5
Normanton Pk CHING E4 101 K4
Normanton Rd SAND/SEL CR2 223 M3
Normanton St FSTH SE23 182 C5
Norman Wy ACT W3 135 N7
STHGT/OAK N14 98 F3
Normington Cl
STRHM/NOR SW16 181 H8
Norrels Dr EHSLY KT24 252 G2
Norrels Ride EHSLY KT24 252 G2
Norrice Lea EFNCH N2 117 N3
Norris Gv BROX EN10 44 D6
Norris La HOD EN11 44 F2
Norris Ri HOD EN11 44 E2
Norris Rd HOD EN11 44 F3
STA TW18 173 J7
Norris St STJS SW1Y 11 J8
Norris Wy DART DA1 164 G9
Norroy Rd PUT/ROE SW15 156 G10
Norrys Cl EBAR EN4 78 A9
Norrys Rd EBAR EN4 78 A8
Norseman Cl GDMY/SEVK IG3 123 L6
Norseman Wy GFD/PVL UB6 134 A3
Norstead Pl PUT/ROE SW15 178 D5
Norsted La ORP BR6 227 L7
North Access Rd WALTH E17 120 C4
North Acre BNSTD SM7 239 J2
CDALE/KGS NW9 96 B9
North Acton Rd WLSDN NW10 136 A4
Northallerton Wy HARH RM3 105 L6
Northall Rd BXLYHN DA7 164 D8
Northampton Av SL SL1 129 H8
Northampton Gv IS N1 119 K10
Northampton Pk IS N1 6 F1
Northampton Rd CLKNW EC1R 12 B1
CROY/NA CR0 203 P9
PEND EN3 80 D8
Northampton Rw CLKNW EC1R 12 B1
Northampton Sq FSBYE EC1V 6 C10
Northampton St IS N1 6 E3
Northanger Rd
STRHM/NOR SW16 180 F9
North Ap GSTN WD25 55 H10
RKW/CH/CXG WD3 92 D3
North Ash Rd HART DA3 211 L10
North Audley St MYFR/PKLN W1K 10 C6
North Av CAR SM5 222 B4
HYS/HAR UB3 133 H9
RAD WD7 57 K8
RCH/KEW TW9 155 M7
RYLN/HDSTN HA2 114 A4
STHL UB1 133 N9
UED N18 99 P5
WEA W13 134 G8
WOT/HER KT12 216 F5
Northaw Cl HHNE HP2 36 C1
Northaw Pl POTB/CUF * EN6 59 P6
Northaw Rd West POTB/CUF EN6 60 B6
North Bank STJWD NW8 3 N10
Northbank Rd WALTH E17 101 H10
North Barn BROX EN10 44 G8
North Birkbeck Rd WAN E11 121 J8
Northborough Rd SLN SL2 128 F6
STRHM/NOR SW16 202 F2
Northbourne HAYES BR2 205 M7
RGODL GU7 267 L9
Northbourne Rd CLAP SW4 158 E10
North Bridge Rd BERK HP4 33 L3
Northbrook Dr NTHWD HA6 92 B10
Northbrook Rd BAR EN5 77 H10
CROY/NA CR0 203 L5
IL IG1 122 D7
LEW SE13 183 J1
WDGN N22 98 F7
Northbrooks HLWW/ROY CM19 46 E2
Northburgh St FSBYE EC1V 12 D2
North Burnham Cl SL SL1 128 A4
North Carriage Dr BAY/PAD W2 9 P7
Northchurch La CSHM HP5 33 H7
Northchurch Rd IS N1 6 G3
WBLY HA9 135 M1
Northchurch Ter IS N1 7 J4
North Circular Rd CHING * E4 100 D7
EFNCH N2 97 M10

GLDGN NW11 117 H2
SWFD E18 121 P1
WLSDN NW10 116 A10
Northcliffe Cl WPK KT4 200 B10
Northcliffe Dr TRDG/WHET N20 97 J2
North Cl BAR EN5 76 F9
BXLYHS DA6 163 N10
CHIG IG7 103 K6
CRAWE RH10 284 A6
DAGE RM10 144 B3
EBED/NFELT TW14 174 E2
LCOL/BKTW AL2 56 A1
MRDN SM4 201 H4
RDKG RH5 273 H6
WDSR SL4 148 E7
North Colonnade POP/IOD E14 140 F10
North Common WEY * KT13 216 D1
North Common Rd EA W5 135 K9
UX/CGN UB8 111 N10
Northcote ADL/WDHM KT15 215 N1
Northcote Av BRYLDS KT5 199 M7
EA W5 135 K9
ISLW TW7 176 F1
STHL UB1 133 M9
Northcote Crs EHSLY KT24 252 D1
Northcote Rd BTSEA SW11 157 P10
CROY/NA CR0 203 L6
EHSLY KT24 252 D1
GVW DA11 190 C4
NWMAL KT3 199 P3
SCUP DA14 185 H7
TWK TW1 176 F1
WALTH E17 120 D2
WLSDN NW10 136 B2
Northcott Av WDGN N22 98 F9
North Countess Rd WALTH E17 100 E10
Northcourt RKW/CH/CXG * WD3 91 K2
North Cray Rd BXLY DA5 186 B5
North Crs CAN/RD E16 141 J6
FITZ W1T 11 J3
FNCH N3 97 J10
Northcroft SLN SL2 128 G6
Northcroft Cl EGH TW20 171 N8
Northcroft Gdns EGH TW20 171 N8
Northcroft Rd EGH TW20 171 N8
HOR/WEW KT19 220 B4
WEA W13 154 G1
Northcroft Vls EGH TW20 171 N8
North Cross Rd BARK/HLT IG6 122 F2
EDUL SE22 181 N1
Northdene CHIG IG7 102 G6
North Dene HEST TW5 154 A7
MLHL NW7 96 A4
Northdene Gdns
SEVS/STOTM N15 119 N4
North Down SAND/SEL CR2 223 M7
Northdown Cl RSLP HA4 112 G8
Northdown Gdns
GNTH/NBYPK IG2 123 H3
Northdown La GU GU1 268 B3
Northdown Rd BELMT SM2 221 K6
CFSP/GDCR SL9 90 B7
EMPK RM11 125 J5
GDST RH9 260 F1
HART DA3 211 K2
HAT AL10 40 D7
RSEV TN14 247 M3
WELL DA16 163 L8
North Downs Crs CROY/NA CR0 224 G6
North Downs Rd CROY/NA CR0 224 G6
North Downs St IS N1 5 N8
North Downs Wy
BRKHM/BTCW RH3 256 B6
OXTED RH8 243 M9
RDKG RH5 253 P10
REDH RH1 258 F2
RGUE GU4 268 D4
SEV TN13 246 E4
North Dr CHOB/PIR GU24 230 B7
GPK RM2 125 K1
HSLW TW3 154 B8
ORP BR6 227 H1
RSLP HA4 112 F5
STALE/WH AL4 39 K4
STRHM/NOR SW16 180 D7
VW GU25 193 K5
North End BKHH IG9 101 P1
CROY/NA CR0 203 K8
GLDGN NW11 117 M7
Northend HHS/BOV HP3 36 C8
RBRW/HUT CM13 107 H6
North End Av HAMP NW3 117 M7
North End Crs WKENS W14 14 C6
North End La ASC SL5 192 F7
ORP BR6 226 E5
Northend Rd ERITH DA8 164 G7
North End Rd FUL/PGN SW6 157 K6
GLDGN NW11 117 K6
WBLY HA9 115 M8
WKENS W14 14 C8
North End Wy HAMP NW3 117 M7
Northern Av ED N9 99 N3
Northernhay Wk MRDN SM4 201 H4
Northern Perimeter Rd
HTHAIR TW6 152 D7
Northern Perimeter Rd (West)
HTHAIR TW6 151 M7
Northern Relief Rd BARK IG11 142 F2
Northern Rd SLN SL2 129 J6
Northey Av BELMT SM2 220 G6
North Eyot Gdns HMSMTH * W6 156 C4
Northey St POP/IOD E14 140 D9
North Farm LOU IG10 81 P10
Northfield HART DA3 211 L3
LTWR GU18 212 A7
RGUE GU4 268 B8
Northfield Av PIN HA5 113 L2
STMC/STPC BR5 207 M6
WEA W13 134 G10
Northfield Cl BMLY BR1 206 B1
HYS/HAR UB3 152 G2
Northfield Ct STA TW18 195 L1
Northfield Crs CHEAM SM3 221 H1
Northfield Gdns WATN WD24 73 K3
Northfield Pde HYS/HAR * UB3 152 G2
Northfield Pk HYS/HAR UB3 152 F2
Northfield Pl WEY KT13 216 C4
North Field Rd HEST TW5 153 L5
Northfield Rd BORE WD6 75 N5
CHES/WCR EN8 62 D8
COB KT11 217 H9
DAGW RM9 124 A9
EBAR EN4 77 P7
EHAM E6 142 C1
PEND EN3 80 A10
STA TW18 195 L1
STNW/STAM N16 119 M5
WDSR SL4 148 E3
WEA W13 154 G1
Northfields ASHTD KT21 237 K5
EW KT17 220 B7
GRAYS RM17 167 P3
WAND/EARL SW18 157 K10
Northfields Rd ACT W3 135 P7
North Gdns WIM/MER SW19 179 N10
North Ga HLW CM20 28 F10
Northgate NTHWD HA6 92 D8
Northgate Av CRAWE RH10 284 A6
Northgate Dr CDALE/KGS NW9 116 B4
Northgate Pth BORE WD6 75 L4
Northgate Pl CRAWE RH10 283 P6
Northgate Rd CRAWE RH10 283 N7
HORL RH6 280 A7
North Gower St CAMTN NW1 4 G10
North Gn SL SL1 129 K9
North Gv CHERT KT16 195 J6
HGT N6 118 B5
HLWS CM18 47 K2
SEVS/STOTM N15 119 L3
North Hl HGT N6 118 A4
RKW/CH/CXG WD3 71 H6
North Hill Av HGT N6 118 A4
North Hill Dr HARH RM3 105 L5
North Hyde Gdns HYS/HAR UB3 153 H2
North Hyde La NWDGN UB2 153 M4
North Hyde Rd HYS/HAR UB3 152 F2
North Hyde Whf NWDGN * UB2 153 K3
Northiam NFNCH/WDSP N12 97 K5
Northiam St HACK E8 140 A3
Northington St BMSBY WC1N 11 N3
North Kent Av GVW DA11 189 P2
Northlands POTB/CUF EN6 59 N7
Northlands Av ORP BR6 227 H1
Northlands St CMBW SE5 159 K8
North La TEDD TW11 176 E9
North Lodge Cl PUT/ROE * SW15 178 G1
North Looe EW * KT17 220 F9
North Md CRAWE RH10 283 P5
REDH RH1 258 A7
Northmead Rd SLN SL2 128 E6
North Ms BMSBY WC1N 11 P2
North Moors GU GU1 250 B6
North Mt TRDG/WHET * N20 97 M3
Northolm EDGW HA8 96 A5
Northolme Cl CDH/CHF * RM16 167 P2
Northolme Gdns EDGW HA8 95 M9
Northolme Ri ORP BR6 207 H9
Northolme Rd HBRY N5 119 J9
Northolt Av RSLP HA4 113 J10
Northolt Gdns GFD/PVL UB6 114 E10
Northolt Rd RYLN/HDSTN HA2 114 A9
WDR/YW UB7 151 N7
Northolt Wy HCH RM12 125 K10
North Orbital Rd DEN/HRF UB9 111 J2
LCOL/BKTW AL2 55 N4
STALE/WH AL4 39 P7
North Orbital Rd (St Albans Rd)
GSTN WD25 55 L9
Northover BMLY BR1 183 L6
North Pde CHSGTN KT9 219 L2
EDGW * HA8 95 M10
STHL * UB1 133 P8
North Pk CFSP/GDCR SL9 110 B1
ELTH/MOT SE9 184 C2
IVER SL0 151 H2
North Park La REDH RH1 259 P5
North Pas WAND/EARL SW18 179 K1
North Pl HLW CM20 29 K6
TEDD TW11 176 E9
WAB EN9 62 G9
WIM/MER SW19 180 A10
North Pole La HAYES BR2 225 M3
North Pole Rd SHB W12 136 F8
Northport St IS N1 7 H6
Northridge Rd GVE DA12 190 F6
Northridge Wy HHW HP1 35 J7
North Riding LCOL/BKTW AL2 55 P6
North Ri BAY/PAD * W2 9 P6
North Rd ABR/ST RM4 104 F3
AMS HP6 69 H2
BELV DA17 164 C2
BERK HP4 33 N5
BMLY BR1 205 N1
BRW CM14 107 H2
BTFD TW8 155 K5
CHDH RM6 123 P3
CHES/WCR EN8 62 D9
CRAWE RH10 284 B6
DART DA1 186 G2
EA W5 155 J2
EBED/NFELT TW14 174 E2
ED N9 100 A2
EDGW HA8 95 N9
EFNCH N2 97 P9
GDMY/SEVK IG3 123 H7
GUW GU2 249 N7
HERT/WAS SG14 25 J5
HEST TW5 153 K5
HGT N6 118 B5
HOD EN11 44 F2
HOLWY N7 5 L1
HYS/HAR UB3 132 E7
PUR RM19 166 B3
RCH/KEW TW9 155 M8
REIG RH2 275 J3
RKW/CH/CXG WD3 70 G9
SOCK/AV RM15 147 J2
STHL UB1 133 P9
SURB KT6 199 J6
TOOT SW17 179 N9
WDR/YW UB7 152 A2
WIM/MER SW19 179 M9
WOKN/KNAP GU21 232 D2
WOOL/PLUM SE18 163 H3
WOT/HER KT12 217 K2
WWKM BR4 204 G8
North Road Av BRW CM14 107 H2
HERT/WAS SG14 25 J4
North Road Gdns
HERT/WAS SG14 25 J5
Northrop Rd HTHAIR TW6 152 F7
North Rw DTCH/LGLY * SL3 110 B9
MYFR/PKLN W1K 10 C7
North Service Rd BRW CM14 107 H3
North Several BKHTH/KID * SE3 161 J8
Northside Rd BMLY BR1 205 M1
North Side Wandsworth Common
WAND/EARL SW18 179 M1
Northspur Rd SUT SM1 201 K10
North Sq ED N9 100 A3
GLDGN NW11 117 K3
North Station Ap REDH * RH1 276 G2
Northstead Rd
BRXS/STRHM SW2 181 H5
North St BARK IG11 142 E2
BMLY BR1 205 M1
BXLYHN DA7 164 B10
CAR SM5 222 A1
CRAWE RH10 285 P9
DART DA1 187 L3
DORK RH4 272 F2
EGH TW20 172 C8
EMPK RM11 125 L5
GVE DA12 190 E3
HDN NW4 116 F3
ISLW TW7 154 F9
LHD/OX KT22 236 F8
PLSTW E13 141 N4
REDH RH1 258 A9
RGODL GU7 267 K10
ROMW/RG RM7 124 E2
VX/NE SW8 158 C9
WAB EN9 45 K8
North Tenter St WCHPL E1 13 M6
North Ter CHEL SW3 15 N5
Northumberland Aly
TWRH * EC3N 13 K6
Northumberland Av CHCR WC2N 11 L9
EMPK RM11 125 K3
EN EN1 80 A4
ISLW TW7 154 E7
MNPK E12 121 P6
WELL DA16 163 H10
Northumberland Cl ERITH DA8 164 D6
STWL/WRAY TW19 173 P2
Northumberland Crs
EBED/NFELT TW14 174 F2
Northumberland Gdns
BMLY BR1 206 D4
ED N9 99 N4
MTCM CR4 202 F5
Northumberland Gv TOTM N17 100 A8
Northumberland Pk ERITH DA8 164 D6
TOTM N17 99 P8
Northumberland Pl BAY/PAD W2 8 E5
Northumberland Rd BAR EN5 77 M10
EHAM E6 142 B8
MEO DA13 190 C10
RYLN/HDSTN HA2 113 N3
SLH/COR SS17 169 J1
WALTH E17 120 F5
Northumberland Wy
BXLYHN DA7 164 D7
Northumbria St POP/IOD E14 140 F8
North Verbena Gdns
HMSMTH * W6 156 D4
North Vw EA W5 135 H6
PIN HA5 113 K5
WIM/MER SW19 178 E8
Northview SWLY BR8 208 F2
North View Av TIL RM18 168 D2
North View Crs EPSOM KT18 238 F3
North View Crs WLSDN NW10 116 C9
Northview Dr WFD IG8 102 A10
Northview Pde HOLWY * N7 118 F8
North View Rd CEND/HSY/T N8 118 E1
SEV TN13 247 K7
North Vls CAMTN NW1 5 J2
North Wy CDALE/KGS NW9 115 N1
ED N9 100 B3
FBAR/BDGN N11 98 D7
HGDN/ICK UB10 131 P2
PIN HA5 113 K4
Northway GLDGN NW11 117 L3
GUW GU2 249 M8
HORL RH6 280 A7
RGODL GU7 266 G10
RKW/CH/CXG WD3 91 N1
RYNPK SW20 201 H3
WGCE AL7 23 J6
WLGTN SM6 222 D1
Northway Crs MLHL NW7 96 B5
Northway Rd CMBW SE5 159 K9
CROY/NA CR0 203 N6
Northways Pde HAMP NW3 3 L3
North Weald La KUTN/CMB KT2 177 H8
North Western Av GSTN WD25 73 P8
WATN WD24 72 G1
North Western Av Colne Wy
WATN WD24 73 K2
North Western Av Elton Wy
GSTN WD25 74 A6
North Western Av Gade Side
KGLGY WD4 72 D1
North Western Av Otterspool
Wy GSTN WD25 73 N4
North Western Av Tylers Way
BUSH WD23 74 B8
North Western Av
Watford By-Pass
STAN HA7 74 F10
North Wharf Rd BAY/PAD W2 9 L4
Northwick Av HRW HA1 114 F4
Northwick Cir
KTN/HRWW/W HA3 115 H4
Northwick Cl STJWD NW8 9 L1
Northwick Park Rd HRW HA1 114 E4
Northwick Rd ALP/SUD HA0 135 J3
OXHEY WD19 93 K5
Northwick Ter STJWD NW8 9 L1
Northwold Dr PIN HA5 113 K1
Northwold Rd STNW/STAM N16 119 N7
Northwood CDH/CHF RM16 168 E1
WGCE AL7 23 N5
Northwood Av HCH RM12 125 H9
PUR/KEN CR8 223 H9
WOKN/KNAP GU21 231 J4
Northwood Cl CHESW EN7 61 N3
Northwood Gdns CLAY IG5 122 D2
GFD/PVL UB6 114 E10
NFNCH/WDSP N12 97 N6
Northwood Pk CRAWE * RH10 284 B3
Northwood Pl ERITH DA18 164 A2
Northwood Rd CAR SM5 222 B3
DEN/HRF UB9 91 P9
FSTH SE23 182 E4
HGT N6 118 C5
HTHAIR TW6 151 N7
THHTH CR7 203 K2
Northwood Wy DEN/HRF UB9 111 N9
NTHWD HA6 93 H8
North Woolwich Rd CAN/RD E16 141 N10
North Worple Wy
MORT/ESHN SW14 156 A9
Nortoft Rd CFSP/GDCR SL9 90 C7
Norton Av BRYLDS KT5 199 N7
Norton Cl BORE WD6 75 M5
CHING E4 100 F6
RGUW GU3 249 J2
Norton Folgate WCHPL E1 13 K2
Norton Gdns STRHM/NOR SW16 202 F2
Norton Pk ASC SL5 192 B5
Norton Rd ALP/SUD HA0 135 J1
DAGE RM10 144 E1
LEY E10 120 E6
UX/CGN UB8 131 N5
Norval Gn BRXN/ST * SW9 159 H8
Norval Rd ALP/SUD HA0 114 G7
Norway Dr SLN SL2 129 N7
Norway Ga BERM/RHTH SE16 160 D2
Norway Pl POP/IOD E14 140 E8
Norway St GNWCH SE10 160 G5
Norwich Pl BXLYHS DA6 164 B10
Norwich Rd CRAWE RH10 284 B9
FSTGT E7 121 M10
GFD/PVL UB6 134 A3
PIN HA5 112 G1
THHTH CR7 203 K3
Norwich St FLST/FETLN EC4A 12 A5
Norwich Wk EDGW HA8 95 P8
Norwich Wy RKW/CH/CXG WD3 72 C7
Norwood Av ALP/SUD HA0 135 L3
ROMW/RG RM7 124 E5
Norwood Cl EHSLY KT24 253 M4
HERT/WAS SG14 24 G4
NWDGN UB2 153 P3
WHTN TW2 176 C5
Norwood Ct AMSS * HP7 68 G6
Norwood Crs HTHAIR TW6 152 D7
Norwood Dr RYLN/HDSTN HA2 113 N4
Norwood Farm La COB KT11 217 H7
Norwood Gdns NWDGN UB2 153 N3
YEAD UB4 133 K6
Norwood Green Rd NWDGN UB2 153 P5
Norwood High St WNWD SE27 181 J6
Norwood Hl HORL RH6 278 G4
Norwoodhill Rd HORL RH6 279 J6
Norwood La IVER SL0 130 G6
Norwood Park Rd WNWD SE27 181 K8
Norwood Rd CHES/WCR EN8 62 D6
EHSLY KT24 253 M4
HNHL SE24 181 J4
NWDGN UB2 153 M2
Notley End EGH * TW20 171 P10
Notley St CMBW SE5 159 L6
Notson Rd SNWD SE25 204 A4
Notting Barn Rd NKENS W10 136 G6
Nottingdale Sq NTGHL W11 8 A9
Nottingham Av CAN/RD E16 141 P7
Nottingham Cl GSTN WD25 55 H10
WOKN/KNAP GU21 231 L4
Nottingham Ct LSQ/SEVD * WC2H 11 L6
Nottingham Pl MHST W1U 10 C2
Nottingham Rd ISLW TW7 154 E8
LEY E10 121 H4
RKW/CH/CXG WD3 90 F2
SAND/SEL CR2 223 K1
TOOT SW17 180 A4
Nottingham St MHST W1U 10 C3
Nottingham Ter CAMTN NW1 10 C2
Notting Hill Ga KENS W8 8 D9
Nova Ms MRDN SM4 201 H7
Novar Cl ORP BR6 207 J7
Nova Rd CROY/NA CR0 203 J8
Novar Rd ELTH/MOT SE9 184 F4
Novello St FUL/PGN SW6 157 K7
Novello Wy BORE WD6 76 A5
Nowell Rd BARN SW13 156 D5
Nower Hl PIN HA5 113 N2
Nower Rd DORK RH4 272 F2
The Nower RSEV TN14 245 J6
RSEV TN14 245 N2
Noyna Rd TOOT SW17 180 A6
Nuding Cl LEW SE13 160 F9
Nuffield Rd SWLY BR8 187 H9
Nugent Rd ARCH N19 118 F6
GUW GU2 267 J1
SNWD SE25 203 N3
Nugents Ct PIN * HA5 93 M9
Nugent's Pk PIN HA5 93 M9
Nugent Ter STJWD NW8 3 K8
Numbers Farm KGLGY * WD4 54 D5
Nunappleton Wy OXTED RH8 261 M8
Nuneaton Rd DAGW RM9 143 N2
Nunhead Gv PECK SE15 160 A9
Nunhead La PECK SE15 160 A9
Nunnery Cl STAL AL1 38 D8
Nunnery Stables STAL AL1 38 C8
Nunnington Cl ELTH/MOT SE9 184 B6
Nunn's Rd ENC/FH EN2 79 K6
Nunns Wy GRAYS RM17 168 A3
Nunsbury Dr BROX EN10 62 D1
Nuns La STAL AL1 38 D10
Nuns Wk VW GU25 194 A5
Nupton Dr BAR EN5 76 F10
Nurse Cl EDGW HA8 95 P9
Nurseries Rd STALE/WH AL4 21 K4
Nursery Av BXLYHN DA7 164 A9
CROY/NA CR0 204 C9
FNCH N3 97 L10
Nursery Cl ADL/WDHM KT15 215 J6
AMSS HP7 69 K5
BROCKY SE4 160 E8
CHDH RM6 123 N4
CROY/NA CR0 204 C9
EBED/NFELT TW14 175 J3
EW KT17 220 B6
KWD/TDW/WH KT20 256 E1
ORP BR6 207 J7
PEND EN3 80 C5
RDART DA2 188 B3
SEV TN13 247 K8
SOCK/AV RM15 147 H6
SWLY BR8 208 D2
WFD IG8 101 N6
WOKN/KNAP GU21 231 P2
Nursery Flds SBW CM21 29 N1
Nursery Gdns CHEAM SM3 201 K8
CHESW EN7 61 L4
CHST BR7 184 E9
HSLWW TW4 175 N1
PEND EN3 80 C5
RGUE GU4 268 E6
STA TW18 173 L10
SUN TW16 196 G2
WGCE AL7 23 H2
Nursery Hl WGCE AL7 23 H2
Nurserylands CRAWW RH11 283 K7
Nursery La BETH E2 7 L6
DTCH/LGLY SL3 129 P10
FSTGT E7 141 M1
HORL RH6 279 N5
NKENS W10 136 F7
Nurserymans Rd FBAR/BDGN N11 98 B3
Nursery Pl SEV TN13 246 E8
Nursery Rd BROX * EN10 62 D1
BRXN/ST SW9 158 G10
EFNCH N2 97 N9
HACK E8 140 B1
HOD EN11 26 G10
KWD/TDW/WH KT20 256 E1
LOU IG10 82 A8
MDHD SL6 128 A8
MTCM CR4 201 P4
PIN HA5 113 K1
RGODL GU7 267 L10
STHGT/OAK N14 98 D1
SUN TW16 196 F2
SUT SM1 221 M1
THHTH CR7 203 L4
WAB EN9 45 J8
WIM/MER SW19 179 H10
WIM/MER SW19 201 L2
WOKN/KNAP GU21 231 J3
Nursery Rw BAR * EN5 77 H7
WALW SE17 18 G6
Nursery St TOTM N17 99 N8
The Nursery ERITH DA8 164 G6
Nursery Wk HDN NW4 116 E1
Nursery Wy OXTED * RH8 261 K5
STWL/WRAY TW19 172 A2
Nursery Waye UX/CGN UB8 131 N3
Nurstead Rd ERITH DA8 164 B6
Nutberry Av CDH/CHF RM16 167 M1
Nutberry Cl CDH/CHF RM16 167 M1
Nutbourne St NKENS W10 2 A9
Nutbrook St PECK SE15 159 N9
Nutbrowne Rd DAGW RM9 144 A3
Nutcombe La DORK RH4 272 E1
Nutcroft Gv LHD/OX KT22 236 D8
Nutcroft Rd PECK SE15 160 A6
Nutfield WGCE AL7 23 K2
Nutfield Cl CAR SM5 201 P10
UED N18 99 P7
Nutfield Gdns GDMY/SEVK IG3 123 J7
NTHLT UB5 133 K4
Nutfield Marsh Rd REDH RH1 258 E7
Nutfield Rd COUL/CHIP CR5 240 B2
CRICK NW2 116 D7
EDUL SE22 181 N1
REDH RH1 258 D6
REDH RH1 258 C10
SRTFD E15 121 H9
THHTH CR7 203 J4
Nutfield Wy ORP BR6 206 D9
Nutford Pl BAY/PAD W2 9 P5
Nut Gv WGCW AL8 22 G2
Nuthatch HART DA3 211 N3
Nuthatch Gdns REIG RH2 275 M4
THMD SE28 162 G1
Nuthurst Av BRXS/STRHM SW2 180 G5
Nuthurst Cl CRAWW RH11 283 K6
Nutkins Wy CSHM HP5 51 H5
Nutley Cl SWLY BR8 208 G1
Nutley La REIG RH2 257 J9
Nutley Ter HAMP NW3 3 K1
Nutmead Cl BXLY DA5 186 D4
Nutmeg Cl CAN/RD E16 141 K6
Nutmeg La POP/IOD E14 141 J8
Nuttall St IS N1 7 K7
Nutter La WAN E11 121 P3
Nuttfield Cl RKW/CH/CXG * WD3 72 C10
Nutt Gv EDGW HA8 95 J3
Nut Tree Cl ORP BR6 207 N10
Nutt St PECK SE15 159 N6
Nutty La SHPTN TW17 196 D4
Nutwell St TOOT SW17 179 P8
Nutwood Av BRKHM/BTCW RH3 273 P1
Nutwood Cl BRKHM/BTCW RH3 273 P1
Nutwood Gdns CHESW EN7 61 M2
Nuxley Rd BELV DA17 164 A5
Nyanza St WOOL/PLUM SE18 162 G5
Nyefield Pk KWD/TDW/WH KT20 256 D2
Nye Wy HHS/BOV HP3 52 D4
Nylands Av RCH/KEW TW9 155 M8
Nymans Ct CRAWE * RH10 284 C10
Nymans Gdns RYNPK SW20 200 E3
Nynehead St NWCR SE14 160 D6
Nyon Gv FSTH SE23 182 E5
Nyssa Cl WFD IG8 102 C7
Nyth Cl UPMR RM14 126 C4

O

Oakapple Cl SAND/SEL CR2 224 A10
Oak Av CEND/HSY/T N8 118 F2
CHOB/PIR GU24 230 F7
CROY/NA CR0 204 F9
EGH TW20 172 F10
ENC/FH EN2 78 G5
HEST TW5 153 L6
HGDN/ICK UB10 112 C7
HPTN TW12 175 M8
LCOL/BKTW AL2 55 P6
MUSWH N10 98 C8
SEV TN13 265 J4
TOTM N17 99 L8
UPMR RM14 126 A8
WDR/YW UB7 152 B2
Oakbank LHD/OX KT22 236 B9
WOKS/MYFD GU22 232 B5
Oakbank Av WOT/HER KT12 197 N7
Oakbank Gv HNHL SE24 159 K10
Oakbrook Cl BMLY BR1 183 N7
Oakbury Rd FUL/PGN SW6 157 L8
Oak Cl CRAWE RH10 284 G2
DART DA1 164 F10
HHS/BOV HP3 36 A10
KWD/TDW/WH KT20 255 N6
RGODL GU7 267 K9
STHGT/OAK N14 98 C1
WAB EN9 63 J10
Oakcombe Cl NWMAL KT3 200 B1
Oak Cottage Cl CAT SE6 183 K4
RGUW GU3 249 H9
Oak Cottages HNWL * W7 154 D1
ORP * BR6 228 C2
Oak Ct CRAWE * RH10 283 N3
Oak Crs CAN/RD E16 141 K7
Oakcroft Cl BF/WBF KT14 215 J10
PIN HA5 93 J10
Oakcroft Rd BF/WBF KT14 215 J10
BKHTH/KID SE3 161 J8
CHSGTN KT9 219 L1
Oakcroft Vls CHSGTN KT9 219 L1
Oakdale STHGT/OAK N14 98 C2
WGCW AL8 22 G2
Oakdale Av KTN/HRWW/W HA3 115 K3
NTHWD HA6 93 H10
Oakdale Cl OXHEY WD19 93 K5
Oakdale Gdns CHING E4 101 H6
Oakdale La EDEN TN8 262 F9
Oakdale Rd FSBYPK N4 119 K4
FSTGT E7 141 N2
HOR/WEW KT19 220 A5
OXHEY WD19 93 K4
PECK SE15 160 B9
STRHM/NOR SW16 180 F8
SWFD E18 101 N10
WAN E11 121 J7
WEY KT13 196 B10
Oakdale Wy MTCM CR4 202 B7
Oak Dell CRAWE RH10 284 D6
Oakdene ASC SL5 192 E6
BEAC HP9 88 D8
CHES/WCR EN8 62 D6
CHOB/PIR GU24 213 L6
KWD/TDW/WH KT20 239 H6

Oakdene Av CHST BR7 184 D8
ERITH DA8 164 D5
THDIT KT7 198 F8
Oakdene Cl BRKHM/BTCW RH3 273 P2
GT/LBKH KT23 254 B3
PIN HA5 93 N8
Oak Dene Cl ROM RM1 125 J4
Oakdene Dr BRYLDS KT5 199 P8
Oakdene Ms CHEAM SM3 201 J8
Oakdene Pk FNCH N3 97 J8
Oakdene Rd BRKHM/BTCW RH3 273 N2
COB KT11 217 J10
GT/LBKH KT23 235 N10
HGDN/ICK UB10 132 C4
HHS/BOV HP3 36 A10
REDH RH1 258 A10
RGUW GU3 267 P8
SEV TN13 247 H8
STMC/STPC BR5 207 K6
WATN WD24 73 J2
Oakdene Wy STAL AL1 39 H6
Oakden St LBTH SE11 18 B5
Oak Dr BERK HP4 34 A6
KWD/TDW/WH KT20 255 N6
SBW CM21 29 M3
Oaken Coppice ASHTD KT21 237 M5
Oak End HLWS * CM18 47 J3
Oak End Dr IVER SL0 130 F4
Oaken Dr ESH/CLAY KT10 218 E3
Oak End Wy ADL/WDHM KT15 215 H8
CFSP/GDCR SL9 110 C3
Oaken Gv WGCE AL7 23 H8
Oaken La ESH/CLAY KT10 218 D1
Oakenshaw Cl SURB KT6 199 K7
Oakeshott Av HGT N6 118 B7
Oakey La STHWK SE1 18 A3
Oak Farm BORE WD6 75 P9
Oak Fld CSHM HP5 50 G6
Oakfield CHING E4 100 G6
RKW/CH/CXG WD3 91 K1
WOKN/KNAP GU21 231 K2
Oakfield Av KTN/HRWW/W HA3 114 G1
SL SL1 128 G10
Oakfield Cl NWMAL KT3 200 C5
POTB/CUF EN6 59 J7
WEY KT13 216 D1
Oakfield Ct BORE * WD6 75 N8
Oakfield Dr REIG RH2 257 K8
Oakfield Gdns BECK BR3 204 F5
CAR SM5 201 P8
GFD/PVL UB6 134 C6
UED N18 99 M5
Oakfield Gld WEY KT13 216 D1
Oakfield La HAYES BR2 225 P1
RDART DA2 187 H5
Oakfield Park Rd DART DA1 187 L5
Oakfield Pl DART DA1 187 L5
Oakfield Rd ASHF TW15 174 C8
ASHTD KT21 237 K4
COB KT11 217 J9
CROY/NA CR0 203 K8
EHAM E6 142 B3
FNCH N3 97 L9
FSBYPK N4 119 H4
IL IG1 122 E8
PGE/AN SE20 182 A10
STHGT/OAK N14 98 F3
WALTH E17 100 D10
WIM/MER SW19 178 G6
Oakfields BF/WBF KT14 215 L10
CRAWE RH10 284 E6
GUW GU2 249 K8
SEV TN13 265 J2
WOT/HER KT12 197 H8
Oakfields Rd GLDGN NW11 117 H4
Oakfield St WBPTN SW10 15 J9
Oakford Rd KTTN NW5 118 D9
Oak Gdns CROY/NA CR0 204 F9
EDGW HA8 95 P10
Oak Gld EPP CM16 65 N5
NTHWD HA6 92 C9
Oak Gln EMPK RM11 125 M1
Oak Grange Rd RGUE GU4 251 L5
Oak Gn ABLGY WD5 54 F8
Oak Gv CRICK NW2 116 G9
HAT AL10 40 C4
HERT/BAY SG13 25 M7
RSLP HA4 113 J6
SUN TW16 175 J10
WWKM BR4 205 H9
Oak Grove Rd PGE/AN SE20 204 B1
Oakhall Dr SUN TW16 174 G8
Oak Hall Rd WAN E11 121 N4
Oakham Cl CAT * SE6 182 E5
Oakham Dr HAYES BR2 205 M4
Oakhampton Rd MLHL NW7 96 G9
Oakhaven CRAWE RH10 283 N9
Oak Hl EPSOM KT18 238 A2
RGUE GU4 250 F6
RGUW GU3 248 F8
SURB KT6 199 K7
WFD IG8 101 J8
Oakhill ESH/CLAY KT10 218 F3
Oakhill Av HAMP NW3 117 L9
PIN HA5 93 M10
Oakhill Cl ASHTD KT21 237 H4
RKW/CH/CXG WD3 91 H5
Oak Hill Crs SURB KT6 199 K7
WFD IG8 101 K8
Oak Hill Gdns WALTH E17 101 K9
Oakhill Gdns WEY KT13 196 F9
Oak Hill Gv SURB KT6 199 K6
Oak Hill Pk HAMP NW3 117 L9
Oak Hill Park Ms HAMP NW3 117 M9
Oakhill Pl PUT/ROE SW15 179 K1
Oak Hill Rd ABR/ST RM4 104 E1
SEV TN13 265 H1
SURB * KT6 199 K6
Oakhill Rd ADL/WDHM KT15 215 J3
ASHTD KT21 237 H4
BECK BR3 205 H2
ORP BR6 207 J9
PUR RM19 166 A4
PUT/ROE SW15 179 J1
REIG RH2 275 L1
RKW/CH/CXG WD3 90 G5
STRHM/NOR SW16 202 F1
SUT SM1 201 L10
Oak Hill Wy HAMP NW3 117 L9
Oakhouse Rd BXLYHS DA6 186 B1
Oakhurst CHOB/PIR GU24 213 K5
Oakhurst Av BXLYHN DA7 163 P6
EBAR EN4 97 P1
Oakhurst Cl BARK/HLT IG6 102 F9
CHST BR7 206 C1
TEDD TW11 176 D8
WALTH E17 121 K2
Oakhurst Gdns BXLYHN DA7 163 P6
CHING E4 101 L2
WALTH E17 121 K2
Oakhurst Gv EDUL SE22 159 P10
Oakhurst Pl WATW * WD18 72 G8
Oakhurst Ri CAR SM5 221 P6
Oakhurst Rd HOR/WEW KT19 219 P3
PEND EN3 80 C2
Oakington WGCE AL7 23 N5
Oakington Av AMS HP6 70 B5
HYS/HAR UB3 152 E3
RYLN/HDSTN HA2 113 P5
WBLY HA9 115 L8
Oakington Dr SUN TW16 197 K2
Oakington Manor Dr WBLY HA9 115 M10
Oakington Rd MV/WKIL W9 8 F1
Oakington Wy CEND/HSY/T N8 118 F4
Oakland Gdns RBRW/HUT CM13 87 P9
Oakland Pl BKHH IG9 101 M3
Oakland Rd SRTFD E15 121 K9
Oaklands BERK HP4 33 M5
HORL RH6 280 D4
LHD/OX KT22 236 C10
PLMGR N13 98 G3
PUR/KEN CR8 223 K10
Oaklands Av BFN/LL DA15 185 J3
BRKMPK AL9 59 H3
ED N9 80 A10
ESH/CLAY KT10 198 C8
ISLW TW7 154 E5
OXHEY WD19 93 J2
ROM RM1 124 F1
THHTH CR7 203 H4
WWKM BR4 204 G10
Oaklands Cl ALP/SUD HA0 115 J10
BXLYHS DA6 186 A1
CHSGTN KT9 219 H1
RGUE GU4 268 B8
STMC/STPC BR5 207 H6
Oaklands Ct ADL/WDHM KT15 195 L10
WAT WD17 73 H5
Oaklands Dr HLWE CM17 47 M2
REDH RH1 276 C2
SOCK/AV RM15 147 H7
Oaklands Gdns PUR/KEN CR8 223 K10
Oaklands Ga NTHWD HA6 92 F7
Oaklands Gv BROX EN10 44 D10
SHB W12 136 D10
Oaklands La BAR EN5 76 E8
BH/WHM TN16 243 P1
STALE/WH AL4 39 L4
Oaklands Ms CRICK NW2 116 G9
Oaklands Park Av IL IG1 122 F7
Oaklands Pl CLAP SW4 158 D10
Oaklands Rd BMLY BR1 183 K10
BXLYHS DA6 164 A10
CHESW EN7 61 M2
CRICK NW2 116 G9
GVW DA11 190 C7
HNWL W7 156 E1
MORT/ESHN SW14 156 A9
RDART DA2 188 A4
TRDG/WHET N20 97 J1
Oaklands Wy
KWD/TDW/WH KT20 238 F8
WLGTN SM6 222 D4
Oakland Wy HOR/WEW KT19 220 A3
Oak La EFNCH N2 97 N10
EGH TW20 171 P6
FBAR/BDGN N11 98 E7
ISLW TW7 154 D10
POP/IOD E14 140 E9
POTB/CUF EN6 60 G4
SEV TN13 264 G5
TWK TW1 176 F3
WDSR SL4 148 F7
WFD IG8 101 L5
WOKS/MYFD GU22 232 E2
Oaklawn Rd LHD/OX KT22 236 E2
Oak Leaf Cl HOR/WEW * KT19 219 P8
Oakleafe Gdns CLAY IG5 122 E1
Oakleigh Av EDGW HA8 95 N10
SURB KT6 199 M8
TRDG/WHET N20 97 N2
Oakleigh Cl SWLY BR8 208 F3
TRDG/WHET N20 98 A4
Oakleigh Ct EDGW * HA8 95 P10
OXTED * RH8 261 K5
Oakleigh Crs TRDG/WHET N20 97 P4
Oakleigh Dr RKW/CH/CXG WD3 72 D10
Oakleigh Gdns EDGW HA8 95 L6
ORP BR6 227 H1
TRDG/WHET N20 97 M2
Oakleigh Ms TRDG/WHET * N20 97 M3
Oakleigh Park Av CHST BR7 206 D2
Oakleigh Pk North
TRDG/WHET N20 97 N2
Oakleigh Pk South
TRDG/WHET N20 97 P2
Oakleigh Rd HGDN/ICK UB10 132 D2
PIN HA5 93 N7
Oakleigh Rd North
TRDG/WHET N20 97 N3
Oakleigh Rd South
FBAR/BDGN N11 98 B5
Oakleigh Wy MTCM CR4 202 C1
SURB KT6 199 M8
Oakley Av ACT W3 135 M9
BARK IG11 143 J1
CROY/NA CR0 222 F1
Oakley Cl ADL/WDHM KT15 215 N1
CHING E4 101 H4
HNWL W7 134 D9
ISLW TW7 154 C7
WTHK RM20 167 H5
Oakley Crs FSBYE * EC1V 6 D8
SL SL1 129 K9
Oakley Dell RGUE GU4 250 F8
Oakley Dr BFN/LL DA15 184 G4
HARH RM3 105 P6
HAYES BR2 206 B10
LEW SE13 183 J2
Oakley Gdns BNSTD SM7 239 L1
CEND/HSY/T N8 118 G3
CHEL SW3 15 P9
Oakley Green Rd WDSR SL4 148 A6
Oakley Pk BFN/LL DA15 185 M3
Oakley Pl STHWK SE1 19 L8
Oakley Rd HARP AL5 20 C4
HAYES BR2 206 B10
HRW HA1 114 D4
IS N1 6 G3
SNWD SE25 204 A5
WARL CR6 241 P4
Oakley Sq CAMTN NW1 5 H7
Oakley St CHEL SW3 15 N9
Oakley Yd BETH * E2 13 M1
Oak Lodge Av CHIG IG7 102 G6
Oak Lodge Cl STAN HA7 95 H6
WOT/HER KT12 217 K2
Oak Lodge Dr REDH RH1 276 B8
WWKM BR4 204 G7
Oak Lodge La BH/WHM TN16 262 G1
Oak Md RGODL GU7 267 J9
Oakmead Av HAYES BR2 205 M6
Oakmeade PIN HA5 93 P7
Oakmead Gdns EDGW HA8 96 A5
Oakmead Gn EPSOM KT18 237 P1
Oakmead Pl MTCM CR4 201 P1
Oakmead Rd BAL SW12 180 C4
CROY/NA CR0 202 E6
Oakmere Av POTB/CUF EN6 59 M9
Oakmere Cl POTB/CUF EN6 59 N7
Oakmere La POTB/CUF EN6 59 M8
Oakmere Rd ABYW SE2 163 K5
Oakmoor Wy CHIG IG7 103 H6
Oakmore Gdns STMC/STPC BR5 207 M4
Oak Pk BF/WBF KT14 215 H9
Oak Park Gdns WIM/MER SW19 178 G4
Oak Piece EPP CM16 66 D1
Oakridge CHOB/PIR GU24 212 E9
Oak Rdg DORK RH4 272 G5
Oakridge LCOL/BKTW AL2 55 N5
Oakridge Av RAD WD7 56 E9
Oakridge Dr EFNCH N2 117 N1
Oakridge La GSTN WD25 56 D10
Oakridge Rd BMLY BR1 183 K7
Oak Ri BKHH IG9 102 A4
Oak Rd BH/WHM TN16 262 G1
COB KT11 235 L1
CRAWW RH11 283 M8
CTHM CR3 241 M8
EA W5 135 J9
EPP CM16 65 J6
ERITH DA8 164 D6
ERITH DA8 165 H7
GRAYS RM17 167 P5
GRH DA9 188 D2
GVE DA12 190 E6
HARH RM3 105 N9
LHD/OX KT22 236 F5
NWMAL KT3 200 A2
ORP BR6 227 K4
REIG RH2 257 L9
Oak Rw MTCM CR4 202 D2
Oakroyd Av POTB/CUF EN6 59 J9
Oakroyd Cl POTB/CUF EN6 59 J10
Oaks Av CRW RM5 104 D10
FELT TW13 175 M5
NRWD SE19 181 M8
WPK KT4 220 E1
Oaks Cl LHD/OX KT22 236 F7
RAD WD7 74 E1
Oaksford Av SYD SE26 182 A6
Oaks Gv CHING E4 101 K3
Oakshade Rd BMLY BR1 183 J7
LHD/OX KT22 218 B10
Oakshaw OXTED RH8 261 J3
Oakshaw Rd WAND/EARL SW18 179 L3
Oakside DEN/HRF UB9 131 L1
Oakside Ct HORL RH6 280 D3
Oakside La HORL RH6 280 D3
Oaks La CROY/NA CR0 204 B10
GNTH/NBYPK IG2 123 H2
RDKG RH5 272 G8
Oaks Pk BNSTD * SM7 222 A8
Oaks Rd CROY/NA CR0 224 A2
PUR/KEN CR8 223 J10
REIG RH2 257 N9
STWL/WRAY TW19 173 N1
WOKN/KNAP GU21 232 B3
The Oaks BERK HP4 33 M5
BF/WBF KT14 215 K10
BORE * WD6 75 M5
DORK * RH4 272 G5
EPSOM KT18 220 B10
FELT * TW13 175 M5
HAYES * BR2 206 D6
MRDN * SM4 201 H4
NFNCH/WDSP N12 97 L5
OXHEY WD19 93 K2
RSLP HA4 112 E5
STA * TW18 173 J7
SURB KT6 199 H10
SWLY BR8 208 F2
WFD IG8 101 K8
WOKN/KNAP * GU21 232 B3
WOOL/PLUM SE18 162 F4
YEAD UB4 132 D4
Oaks Tr CAR SM5 222 B6
Oak St HHS/BOV HP3 36 A10
ROMW/RG RM7 124 D3
Oaks Wy CAR SM5 222 A4
EPSOM KT18 238 E5
PUR/KEN CR8 223 K10
SURB KT6 199 J9
Oakthorpe Rd PLMGR N13 99 H6
Oak Tree Av GRH DA9 188 E3
Oaktree Av PLMGR N13 99 H4
Oaktree Cl RBRW/HUT CM13 107 L4
Oak Tree Cl ABLGY WD5 54 E8
HAT AL10 40 D3
HERT/BAY SG13 25 P5
LOU IG10 82 F5
RGUE GU4 249 P4
RGUE GU4 250 F5
STAN HA7 95 H8
VW GU25 194 A6
WEA * W13 135 H8
WOKN/KNAP GU21 230 G4
Oak Tree Ct BORE * WD6 75 J10
Oak Tree Dell CDALE/KGS NW9 115 P3
Oak Tree Dr EGH TW20 171 P8
GU GU1 249 P6
TRDG/WHET N20 97 L2
Oak Tree Gdns BMLY BR1 183 N8
Oaktree Garth WGCE AL7 23 K6
Oaktree Gv IL IG1 122 G10
Oak Tree Rd STJWD NW8 3 M10
WOKN/KNAP GU21 230 G4
Oakview Cl CHESW EN7 62 A4
Oakview Gdns EFNCH N2 117 N2
Oakview Gv CROY/NA CR0 204 D8
Oakview Rd CAT SE6 182 G8
Oak Village HAMP NW3 118 B9
Oak Vls GLDGN * NW11 117 J4
Oak Wy ACT W3 136 B10
ASHTD KT21 237 M2
CRAWE RH10 283 P5
CROY/NA CR0 204 C6
EBED/NFELT TW14 174 F4
REIG RH2 275 N1
STHGT/OAK N14 98 B1
Oakway AMS HP6 68 G1
CDH/CHF RM16 147 N10
HAYES BR2 205 J2
RYNPK SW20 200 F4
WOKN/KNAP GU21 231 K5
Oakway Cl BXLY DA5 185 P2
Oakways ELTH/MOT SE9 184 E2
Oakwell Dr POTB/CUF EN6 60 C9
Oak Wd BERK HP4 53 L6
Oakwood GUW GU2 249 M5
WLGTN SM6 222 C5
Oakwood Av BECK BR3 205 H2
BORE WD6 75 N3
HAYES BR2 205 N3
HOR/WEW KT19 219 M5
MTCM CR4 201 N2
PUR/KEN CR8 223 J8
STHGT/OAK N14 98 E1
STHL UB1 133 P9
Oakwood Cha EMPK RM11 125 N5
Oakwood Cl CHST BR7 184 C9
DART DA1 188 A4
EHSLY KT24 252 F3
REDH RH1 258 B10
REDH * RH1 276 G2
STHGT/OAK N14 78 D10
WFD IG8 102 B7
Oakwood Ct CHOB/PIR GU24 230 F2
WKENS W14 14 C3
Oakwood Crs GFD/PVL UB6 134 F1
WCHMH N21 78 F10
Oakwood Dr BXLYHN DA7 164 D10
EDGW HA8 95 P7
EHSLY KT24 252 F3
NRWD SE19 181 L9
STALE/WH AL4 39 H5
Oakwood Gdns GDMY/SEVK IG3 123 J7
ORP BR6 206 F9
SUT SM1 201 K9
WOKN/KNAP GU21 230 F4
Oakwood Hl LOU IG10 82 D10
Oakwood La WKENS W14 14 C3
Oakwood Pde EBAR * EN4 78 D9
Oakwood Park Cottages
STHGT/OAK * N14 78 G10
Oakwood Park Rd
STHGT/OAK N14 78 F10
Oakwood Pl CROY/NA CR0 203 H6
Oakwood Ri CTHM CR3 259 M1
HART DA3 211 K3
Oakwood Rd BFOR GU20 212 D3
CROY/NA CR0 203 H6
GLDGN NW11 117 K3
HORL RH6 280 B3
LCOL/BKTW AL2 55 N5
ORP BR6 206 F9
PIN HA5 93 J10
REDH RH1 259 H5
RYNPK SW20 200 D1
VW GU25 193 P5
WOKN/KNAP GU21 231 K5
Oakworth Rd NKENS W10 136 F7
Oak Yd WAT * WD17 73 K8
Oarsman Pl E/WMO/HCT KT8 198 D4
Oast House Cl STWL/WRAY TW19 172 B3
Oast House Wy STMC/STPC BR5 207 L4
Oast Rd OXTED RH8 261 L7
Oast Wy HART DA3 211 K6
Oates Cl HAYES BR2 205 J3
Oates Rd CRW RM5 104 C6
Oates Wk CRAWE RH10 284 A10
Oatfield Rd KWD/TDW/WH KT20 238 E7
ORP BR6 207 J8
Oatland Ri WALTH E17 100 D10
Oatlands CRAWW RH11 283 K8
HORL RH6 280 C3
Oatlands Av WEY KT13 216 E2
Oatlands Cha WEY KT13 196 F10
Oatlands Cl WEY KT13 216 D1
Oatlands Dr SL SL1 129 J8
WEY KT13 196 E10
Oatlands Gn WEY KT13 196 E10
Oatlands Mere WEY KT13 196 E10
Oatlands Rd KWD/TDW/WH KT20 239 H5
PEND EN3 80 B5
Oat La CITYW EC2V 12 E5
Oban Cl PLSTW E13 141 P6
Oban Ct SL SL1 149 J1
Oban Rd PLSTW E13 141 P5
SNWD SE25 203 L4
Oban St POP/IOD E14 141 J8
Oberon Cl BORE WD6 75 P5
Oberon Wy CRAWW RH11 283 H10
SHPTN TW17 195 P3
Oberstein Rd BTSEA SW11 157 N10
Oborne Cl HNHL SE24 181 J1
Observatory Gdns KENS W8 14 E1
Observatory Rd
MORT/ESHN SW14 155 P10
SKENS SW7 15 M3
The Observatory SL * SL1 149 M1
Occam Rd GUW GU2 249 J10
Occupation La EA W5 155 J3
WOOL/PLUM SE18 162 E7
Occupation Rd WALW SE17 18 E7
WATW WD18 73 J9
WEA W13 154 G1
Ocean Est WCHPL E1 140 C6
Ocean St WCHPL E1 140 C7
Ockenden Cl WOKS/MYFD GU22 232 C4
Ockenden Gdns
WOKS/MYFD GU22 232 C5
Ockenden Rd WOKS/MYFD GU22 232 C4
Ockendon Ms IS * N1 7 H2
Ockendon Rd IS N1 6 G2
UPMR RM14 146 C1
Ockham Dr EHSLY KT24 234 E10
STMC/STPC BR5 185 K10
Ockham La COB KT11 235 H4
RPLY/SEND GU23 234 D6
Ockham Rd North
RPLY/SEND GU23 234 C8
Ockham Rd South EHSLY KT24 252 F5
Ockley Ct RGUE GU4 250 E5
Ockley Rd CROY/NA CR0 202 G7
STRHM/NOR SW16 180 F6
Ockleys Md GDST RH9 260 B5
Octagon Ar LVPST * EC2M 13 J4
Octagon Rd WOT/HER KT12 216 F6
Octavia Cl MTCM CR4 201 P5
Octavia Ct WATN WD24 73 K6
Octavia Ms CRICK * NW2 136 F1
Octavia Rd ISLW TW7 154 E9
Octavia St BTSEA SW11 157 P7
Octavia Wy STA TW18 173 K9
Octavius St DEPT SE8 160 F6
October Pl HDN * NW4 116 G1
Odard Rd E/WMO/HCT KT8 197 P4
Odds Farm Est FLKWH * HP10 108 A5
Odencroft Rd SLN SL2 128 F5
Odeon Pde ELTH/MOT * SE9 162 B10
GFD/PVL * UB6 134 G1
HOLWY * N7 118 F8
ISLW * TW7 154 D8
RKW/CH/CXG * WD3 91 P2
Odessa Rd FSTGT E7 121 L9
WLSDN NW10 136 D4
Odessa St BERM/RHTH SE16 160 E2
Odessey Rd BORE WD6 75 N5
Odger St BTSEA SW11 158 A8
Odhams Wk LSQ/SEVD WC2H 11 L6
Odsey Vls FSBYPK * N4 119 H4
Offa Rd STALW/RED AL3 38 B6
Offa's Md HOM E9 120 D9
Offas Wy STALE/WH AL4 21 J3
Offenham Rd ELTH/MOT SE9 184 C7
Offerton Rd CLAP SW4 158 D9
Offham Slope NFNCH/WDSP N12 97 J6
Offley Rd BRXN/ST SW9 159 H6
Offord Cl TOTM N17 99 P8
Offord Rd IS N1 5 P3
Offord St HOLWY N7 5 N3
Off Upper Manor Rd RGODL GU7 267 K10
Ogard Rd HOD EN11 45 H1
Ogilby St WOOL/PLUM SE18 162 C3
Oglander Rd PECK SE15 159 N10
Ogle St GTPST W1W 10 G3
Oglethorpe Rd DAGE RM10 124 A8
Ohio Rd PLSTW E13 141 L6
Oil Mill La HMSMTH W6 156 D4
Okeburn Rd TOOT SW17 180 B8
Okehampton Crs WELL DA16 163 L7
Okehampton Rd WLSDN NW10 136 F3
Okehampton Sq HARH * RM3 105 K7
Olaf St NTGHL W11 136 G9
Old Acre BF/WBF KT14 215 K10
Oldacre CHOB/PIR GU24 212 E8
Old Amersham Rd
CFSP/GDCR SL9 110 E6
Old Av BF/WBF KT14 215 H10
WEY KT13 216 D4
Old Avenue Cl WOKN/KNAP GU21 215 H9
Old Bailey STP EC4M 12 D6
Old Barn Cl BELMT SM2 221 H4
BGR/WK TN15 247 P3
Old Barn La CTHM CR3 241 N2
RKW/CH/CXG WD3 72 A9
Old Barn Rd EPSOM KT18 237 P3
Old Barn Wy BXLYHN DA7 164 E10
Old Barrack Yd KTBR SW1X 16 C1
Oldberry Rd EDGW HA8 96 A7
Old Bethnal Green Rd BETH E2 7 P9
Old Bexley La BXLY DA5 186 E5
Old Bond St CONDST W1S 10 G8
Oldborough Rd ALP/SUD HA0 115 H7
Old Brewery Ms HAMP NW3 117 N9
Old Bridge Cl NTHLT UB5 133 P4
Old Bridge St KUT KT1 199 J2
Old Brighton Rd South
CRAWW RH11 283 N1
Old Broad St LVPST EC2M 13 J5
Old Bromley Rd BMLY BR1 183 J8
Old Brompton Rd ECT SW5 14 F8
Old Buildings LINN WC2A 12 A5
Old Burlington St CONDST W1S 10 G7
Oldbury Cl STMC/STPC BR5 207 N4
Oldbury Gv BEAC HP9 88 C6
Oldbury Pl MHST W1U 10 D3
Oldbury Rd CHERT KT16 195 H7
EN EN1 79 P6
The Old Carriageway SEV TN13 246 D9
Old Castle St WCHPL E1 13 L5
Old Cavendish St CAVSQ/HST W1G 10 E5
Old Chapel Rd SWLY BR8 208 D7
Old Charlton Rd SHPTN TW17 196 D5
Old Chertsey Rd CHOB/PIR GU24 213 N6
Old Chestnut Av ESH/CLAY KT10 217 P3
Old Church La CDALE/KGS NW9 115 P7
GFD/PVL UB6 134 F5
STAN HA7 94 G7
Old Church Pth ESH/CLAY KT10 218 A1
Oldchurch Ri ROMW/RG RM7 124 F4
Old Church Rd CHING E4 100 F4
WCHPL * E1 140 C8
Oldchurch Rd ROMW/RG RM7 124 F4
Old Church St CHEL SW3 15 M9
Old Claygate La ESH/CLAY KT10 218 F3
The Old Coach Rd
HERT/WAS SG14 24 A8
Old Common COB * KT11 217 J8
Old Common Rd COB KT11 217 J8
Old Compton St SOHO/SHAV W1D 11 J7
Old Cote Dr HEST TW5 153 P5
Old Ct ASHTD KT21 237 K5
Old Court Pl KENS W8 14 G1
Old Court Rd GUW GU2 267 M1
The Old Ctyd BMLY BR1 205 N1
Old Crabtree La HHS/BOV HP3 35 P7
Old Cross HERT/WAS * SG14 25 K5
HERT/WAS SG14 25 K5
Old Crown SL * SL1 149 L1
Old Crown La BRW CM14 86 C6
Old Dairy Ms BAL SW12 180 B4
KTTN * NW5 4 F1
Old Dartford Rd EYN DA4 209 N6
Old Dean HHS/BOV HP3 52 D3
Old Deer Pk RCH/KEW * TW9 155 L9
Old Deer Park Gdns
RCH/KEW TW9 155 K9
Old Devonshire Rd BAL SW12 180 C3
Old Dock Cl RCH/KEW TW9 155 M5
Old Dover Rd BKHTH/KID SE3 161 M6
Old Downs HART DA3 211 K5
Old Dr SHGR * GU5 270 D4
The Old Dr WGCW AL8 22 E6
Olden La PUR/KEN CR8 223 H8
Old Esher Cl WOT/HER * KT12 217 L2
Old Esher Rd WOT/HER KT12 217 L2
Old Farleigh Rd SAND/SEL CR2 224 B6
WARL CR6 242 E1
Old Farm Av BFN/LL DA15 184 G4
STHGT/OAK N14 98 D1
Old Farm Cl BEAC HP9 88 B6
HSLWW TW4 153 N10
Old Farm Gdns SWLY BR8 208 G3
Old Farmhouse Dr LHD/OX KT22 236 C1
Old Farm Rd EFNCH N2 97 N9
GU GU1 250 A7
HPTN TW12 175 N9
WDR/YW UB7 151 N1
Old Farm Rd East BFN/LL DA15 185 K5
Old Farm Rd West BFN/LL DA15 185 J5
Old Ferry Dr STWL/WRAY TW19 171 P2
Old Field Cl AMS HP6 70 B5
Oldfield Cl BMLY BR1 206 C4
NTHLT UB5 114 D10
STAN HA7 94 F6
Oldfield Farm Gdns
GFD/PVL UB6 134 C3
Oldfield Gdns ASHTD KT21 237 J5
Oldfield Gv DEPT SE8 160 C3
Oldfield La North GFD/PVL UB6 134 C1
Oldfield La South GFD/PVL UB6 134 B5
Oldfield Ms HGT N6 118 D5
Oldfield Rd ACT W3 156 C1
BMLY BR1 206 C4
BXLYHN DA7 163 P8
HHW HP1 35 H7
HORL RH6 280 A6
HPTN TW12 197 P1

LCOL/BKTW AL2 57 J1
STNW/STAM N16 119 M8
WIM/MER SW19 179 H9
WLSDN NW10 136 C2
Oldfields Circ NTHLT UB5 134 B1
Oldfields Rd CHEAM SM3 201 K9
Oldfieldwood WOKS/MYFD GU22 232 E3
Old Fishery La HHW HP1 35 J8
Old Fish Street Hl BLKFR * EC4V 12 E7
Old Fives Ct SL SL1 128 B5
Old Fleet La STP EC4M 12 C5
Old Fold Cl BAR * EN5 77 J5
Old Fold La BAR EN5 77 J5
Old Fold Vw BAR EN5 76 F7
Old Ford Lock BOW * E3 140 F2
Old Ford Rd BETH E2 140 B4
BOW E3 140 E3
Old Forge Cl GSTN WD25 55 H9
STAN HA7 94 F5
WGCE AL7 23 J1
Old Forge Crs SHPTN TW17 196 C6
Old Forge Rd EN EN1 79 N4
Old Forge Rw HERT/BAY * SG13 26 A8
Old Forge Wy SCUP DA14 185 L7
Old Fox Cl CTHM CR3 241 J7
Old French Horn La HAT AL10 40 E3
Old Gannon Cl NTHWD HA6 92 D5
Old Garden Ct STALW/RED AL3 38 B6
The Old Gdn SEV TN13 246 E9
Old Gloucester St BMSBY WC1N 11 M3
Old Grove Cl CHESW EN7 61 L2
Old Hall Cl PIN HA5 93 M9
Old Hall Dr PIN HA5 93 M9
Old Hall Ri HLWE CM17 47 P1
Oldhall St HERT/WAS SG14 25 L5
Oldham Ter ACT W3 135 P10
Old Harpenden Rd
STALW/RED AL3 38 D2
Old Herns La WGCE AL7 23 M3
Old Hertford Rd BRKMPK AL9 40 F2
Old Hwy HOD EN11 44 G1
Old Hl CHST BR7 206 D1
ORP BR6 227 H3
WOKS/MYFD GU22 232 A6
Oldhill St STNW/STAM N16 119 P6
Old Hollow CRAWE RH10 284 G5
Old Homesdale Rd HAYES BR2 205 P4
Old Horsham Rd CRAWW RH11 283 L9
Old Hospital Cl TOOT * SW17 180 A4
Old House Cl EW KT17 220 C6
WIM/MER SW19 179 H8
Old House Ct DTCH/LGLY * SL3 130 A8
Oldhouse Ct HHNE HP2 36 A6
Oldhouse Cft HLW CM20 29 H9
Old House Gdns TWK * TW1 177 H2
Oldhouse La CHOB/PIR GU24 212 F10
CHOB/PIR GU24 212 B5
Old House La HLWW/ROY CM19 46 A4
KGLGY WD4 72 B1
Old House Rd HHNE HP2 36 A6
Old Howlett's La RSLP * HA4 112 E4
Oldings Cnr HAT AL10 22 E10
Old Jamaica Rd BERM/RHTH SE16 19 N3
Old James St PECK SE15 160 A9
Old Jewry LOTH * EC2R 12 G6
Old Kenton La CDALE/KGS NW9 115 N3
Old Kent Rd PECK SE15 160 A5
STHWK SE1 19 P9
Old Kiln La BRKHM/BTCW RH3 255 P10
Old Kingston Rd WPK KT4 199 P10
Old La BH/WHM TN16 244 A7
COB KT11 234 E5
OXTED RH8 261 L6
Old Lane Gdns COB KT11 234 G8
Old Leys HAT AL10 40 D8
Old Lodge Dr BEAC HP9 88 C10
Old Lodge La PUR/KEN CR8 222 G9
Old Lodge Wy STAN HA7 94 F6
Old London Rd EPSOM KT18 238 D4
HERT/BAY SG13 25 M5
KUTN/CMB KT2 199 L2
RDKG RH5 255 H4
RSEV TN14 228 B6
RSEV TN14 245 P1
STAL AL1 38 D7
Old Maidstone Rd SCUP DA14 186 A10
Old Malden La WPK KT4 200 B9
The Old Maltings
HERT/BAY * SG13 25 K6
Old Malt Wy WOKN/KNAP GU21 232 A3
Old Manor Cl CRAWW RH11 283 K5
Old Manor Dr ISLW TW7 176 B2
Old Manor Gdns RGUE GU4 268 F6
Old Manor Wy BXLYHN DA7 164 E8
ELTH/MOT SE9 184 C8
Old Manor Yd ECT SW5 14 G6
Old Market Sq BETH E2 7 L9
Old Martyrs CRAWW RH11 283 N4
Old Marylebone Rd CAMTN NW1 9 P4
Old Md CFSP/GDCR SL9 90 B7
Old Meadow Cl BERK HP4 33 M7
Old Merrow St RGUE GU4 250 F7
Old Mill Cl EYN DA4 209 M8
Old Mill Ct SWFD E18 121 P1
Old Mill Gdns BERK HP4 34 A5
Old Mill La REDH RH1 258 C4
UX/CGN UB8 131 L7
Old Mill Rd DEN/HRF UB9 111 K8
KGLGY WD4 54 D10
KUT KT1 199 L3
WOOL/PLUM SE18 162 G5
Old Mitre Ct EMB * EC4Y 12 B6
Old Montague St WCHPL E1 13 N4
Old Nazeing Rd BROX EN10 44 F7
WAB EN9 45 H8
Old Nichol St BETH E2 13 L1
Old North St FSBYW * WC1X 11 N3
Old Nursery Ct SLN SL2 109 H7
Old Nursery Pl ASHF TW15 174 C8
Old Oak STAL AL1 38 D9
Old Oak Av COUL/CHIP CR5 239 P5
Old Oak Cl COB KT11 217 J9
Old Oak Common La
WLSDN NW10 136 B6
Old Oak Gdns BERK * HP4 33 K2
Old Oak La WLSDN NW10 136 C5
Old Oak Rd ACT W3 136 C9
Old Oaks WAB EN9 63 K8
Old Orch BF/WBF KT14 216 A8
HLWS CM18 46 G3
LCOL/BKTW AL2 56 C2
SUN TW16 197 K2
Old Orchard Cl UX/CGN UB8 132 B8
Old Orchard Ms BERK HP4 33 P6
Old Orchards CRAWE RH10 284 F7
The Old Orch HAMP * NW3 118 A9
Old Otford Rd RSEV TN14 247 J4
Old Palace Rd CROY/NA CR0 203 K10
GUW GU2 267 M1
WEY KT13 196 C10
Old Palace Yd RCH/KEW TW9 177 H1
Old Paradise St LBTH SE11 17 N5
Old Park Av BAL SW12 180 B2
ENC/FH EN2 79 K8
Old Parkbury La LCOL/BKTW AL2 56 E5
Old Park Gv WCHMH N21 79 K8
Old Park La MYFR/PICC W1J 10 D10
Old Park Ms HEST TW5 153 N6
Oldpark Ride CHESW EN7 61 L8
Old Park Ridings WCHMH N21 79 J10
Old Park Rd ABYW SE2 163 K4
ENC/FH EN2 79 J7
PLMGR N13 98 G4
Old Park Rd South ENC/FH EN2 79 J8
Old Park Vw ENC/FH EN2 79 H7
Old Parvis Rd BF/WBF KT14 215 M8
Old Perry St CHST BR7 185 H10
GVW DA11 190 B5
Old Portsmouth Rd RGUW GU3 267 P6
Old Pottery Cl REIG RH2 275 L2
Old Pound Cl ISLW TW7 154 F7
Old Priory DEN/HRF UB9 112 C5
Old Pye St WEST SW1P 17 J3
Old Quebec St MBLAR W1H 10 B6
Old Queen St STJSPK SW1H 17 K2
Old Rectory Cl
KWD/TDW/WH KT20 238 D10
Old Rectory Dr HAT AL10 40 E4
Old Rectory Gdns EDGW HA8 95 M7
STALE/WH AL4 21 J2
Old Rectory La DEN/HRF UB9 111 H5
EHSLY KT24 252 F2
Old Rectory Rd CHONG CM5 67 J9
Old Redding KTN/HRWW/W HA3 94 A6
Old Redstone Dr REDH RH1 276 B1
Old Reigate Rd
BRKHM/BTCW RH3 255 P10
DORK RH4 255 K10
Oldridge Rd BAL SW12 180 B3
Old Rd ABR/ST RM4 85 L6
ADL/WDHM KT15 215 J4
BRKHM/BTCW RH3 256 C9
DART DA1 164 E10
HLWE CM17 29 M5
LEW SE13 161 K10
PEND EN3 80 B5
Old Rd East GVE DA12 190 G4
Old Rd West GVW DA11 190 C4
Old Royal Free Sq IS N1 6 B6
Old Ruislip Rd NTHLT UB5 133 K4
Old's Ap WATW WD18 92 D2
Old Sax La CSHM HP5 50 C3
Old School Cl BECK BR3 204 C2
Old School Ct STWL/WRAY TW19 172 B3
SWLY * BR8 208 F2
Old School Crs FSTGT E7 141 M1
Old School La BRKHM/BTCW RH3 273 M3
Old School Ms WEY KT13 216 E1
Old School Pl WOKS/MYFD GU22 232 B7
Old School Rd UX/CGN UB8 132 A6
Old Schools La EW KT17 220 C5
Old School Sq THDIT KT7 198 E6
Old School Ter CHEAM * SM3 220 G4
Old's Cl WATW WD18 92 C2
Old Seacoal La STP * EC4M 12 C6
Old Shire La CFSP/GDCR SL9 90 E4
RKW/CH/CXG WD3 70 D10
WAB EN9 63 M10
Old Shire Lane Circular Wk
RKW/CH/CXG WD3 90 F1
Old Slade La DTCH/LGLY SL3 151 J4
Old Sopwell Gdns STAL AL1 38 D8
Old South Cl PIN HA5 93 L9
Old South Lambeth Rd
VX/NE * SW8 158 F6
Old Sq LINN WC2A 11 P5
Old Stable Ms FSBYPK * N4 119 K8
Old Station Ap LHD/OX KT22 236 F7
Old Station Gdns TEDD * TW11 176 F9
Old Station La STWL/WRAY TW19 172 C2
Old Station Rd HYS/HAR * UB3 152 F2
LOU IG10 82 B9
Oldstead Rd BMLY BR1 183 J7
Old St FSBYE EC1V 12 E1
PLSTW E13 141 N4
The Old Surrey Ms GDST * RH9 260 B6
Old Swan Yd CAR SM5 222 A1
Old Town CLAP SW4 158 D10
CROY/NA CR0 203 H10
Old Tramyard WOOL/PLUM SE18 163 H3
Old Tye Av BH/WHM TN16 244 B1
Old Uxbridge Rd
RKW/CH/CXG WD3 91 J10
The Old Wk RSEV TN14 247 J3
Old Watford Rd LCOL/BKTW AL2 55 M6
Old Westhall Cl WARL CR6 242 B5
Old Woking Rd BF/WBF KT14 215 K9
WOKS/MYFD GU22 215 J10
WOKS/MYFD GU22 232 E4
Old Woolwich Rd GNWCH SE10 161 J5
The Old Yews HART DA3 211 N3
Old York Rd WAND/EARL SW18 179 L1
Oleander Cl ORP BR6 226 G2
O'Leary Sq WCHPL E1 140 A3
Olga St BOW E3 140 D4
Olinda Rd STNW/STAM N16 119 N4
Oliphant St NKENS W10 2 A9
Oliver Av SNWD SE25 203 N3
Oliver Cl ADL/WDHM KT15 215 L1
CHSWK W4 155 N5
HHS/BOV HP3 35 P10
LCOL/BKTW AL2 56 C3
WTHK RM20 166 E6
Oliver Crs EYN DA4 209 N7
Oliver Gdns EHAM E6 142 B7
Oliver Gv SNWD SE25 203 N4
Olive Rd CRICK NW2 116 F9
DART DA1 187 L4
EA W5 155 J2
PLSTW E13 141 P5
WIM/MER * SW19 179 M10
Oliver Ri HHS/BOV HP3 35 P10
Oliver Rd ASC SL5 192 A4
BRWN CM15 87 M9
HHS/BOV HP3 36 A10
LEY E10 120 G7
NWMAL KT3 199 P2
RAIN RM13 144 G3
SUT SM1 221 N1
SWLY BR8 208 E3
WALTH E17 121 H3
WTHK RM20 166 E7
Olivers Cl BERK HP4 34 F2
Oliver's Yd STLK EC1Y 13 H1
Olive St ROMW/RG RM7 124 E3
Olivia Gdns DEN/HRF UB9 91 M9
Olivier Rd CRAWE RH10 284 E8
Ollard's Gv LOU IG10 82 A8
Olleberrie La RKW/CH/CXG WD3 53 H8
Ollerton Gn BOW E3 140 E3
Ollerton Rd FBAR/BDGN N11 98 E6
Olley Cl WLGTN SM6 222 F4
Ollgar Cl ACT W3 136 C10
Olliffe St POP/IOD E14 161 H2
Olmar St STHWK SE1 19 N9
Olney Rd WALW SE17 18 D10
Olron Crs BXLYHS DA6 185 N1
Olven Rd WOOL/PLUM SE18 162 F6
Olveston Wk MRDN SM4 201 N6
Olwen Ms PIN HA5 93 L10
Olyffe Av WELL DA16 163 K8
Olyffe Dr BECK BR3 205 H1
Olympia Wy WKENS W14 14 B4
Olympic Wy GFD/PVL UB6 134 A3
WBLY HA9 115 M9
Oman Av CRICK NW2 116 F10
O'Meara St STHWK SE1 12 F10
Omega Ct WARE * SG12 26 C1
Omega Maltings WARE * SG12 26 D2
Omega Pl IS N1 5 M8
Omega Rd WOKN/KNAP GU21 232 D1
Omega St NWCR SE14 160 E7
Omega Wy EGH TW20 194 F1
Ommaney Rd NWCR SE14 160 C7
Omnibus Wy WALTH E17 100 F10
Ondine Rd EDUL SE22 159 N10
Onega Ga BERM/RHTH SE16 160 D2
One Pin La SLN SL2 109 H9
One Tree Cl FSTH SE23 182 B2
One Tree Hill Rd RGUE GU4 268 E2
One Tree La BEAC HP9 88 D8
One Tree Pl AMS * HP6 69 H4
Ongar Cl ADL/WDHM KT15 215 J3
CHDH RM6 123 M3
Ongar Hl ADL/WDHM KT15 215 K3
Ongar Pl ADL/WDHM KT15 215 K3
BRW CM14 107 J3
Ongar Rd ABR/ST RM4 83 M6
ADL/WDHM KT15 215 K2
BRWN CM15 86 F10
FUL/PGN SW6 14 F9
Ongar Wy RAIN RM13 144 F3
Onra Rd LEY E10 120 F5
Onslow Av BELMT SM2 221 J6
RCHPK/HAM TW10 177 K1
Onslow Cl CHING E4 101 J3
HAT AL10 40 E4
Onslow Crs CHST BR7 206 E1
WOKS/MYFD GU22 232 D3
Onslow Dr SCUP DA14 185 N6
Onslow Gdns CHONG CM5 67 P3
MUSWH N10 118 C3
SAND/SEL CR2 223 P8
SKENS SW7 15 L6
SWFD E18 121 N1
THDIT KT7 198 D8
WCHMH N21 79 H9
WLGTN SM6 222 D4
Onslow Ms CHERT KT16 195 J6
Onslow Ms East SKENS SW7 15 L6
Onslow Ms West SKENS SW7 15 L6
Onslow Pde STHGT/OAK * N14 98 C2
Onslow Rd ASC SL5 192 G7
CROY/NA CR0 203 H7
GU GU1 250 A10
NWMAL KT3 200 D4
RCHPK/HAM TW10 177 K1
WOT/HER KT12 217 H1
Onslow Sq SKENS SW7 15 L6
Onslow St FARR EC1M 12 B2
GU GU1 267 P1
Onslow Wy THDIT KT7 198 D8
WOKS/MYFD GU22 233 J1
Ontario Cl HORL RH6 281 H5
Ontario St STHWK SE1 18 D4
Ontario Wy POP/IOD E14 140 F9
On the Hl OXHEY WD19 93 M3
Opal Cl CAN/RD E16 142 A5
Opal Ct DTCH/LGLY SL3 129 P6
Opal St LBTH SE11 18 C7
Opendale Rd SL SL1 128 A7
Openshaw Rd ABYW SE2 163 L4
Openview WAND/EARL SW18 179 M4
Ophir Ter PECK SE15 159 P7
Opossum Wy HSLWW TW4 153 K9
Oppenheim Rd LEW SE13 161 H8
Oppidans Rd HAMP NW3 4 A4
Optima Pk DART * DA1 165 H9
Opus Pk GU * GU1 250 A6
Oram Pl HHS/BOV HP3 35 N9
Orange Court La ORP BR6 226 D5
Orange Gv CHIG IG7 102 F7
WAN E11 121 K8
Orange Hill Rd EDGW HA8 95 P8
Orange Pl BERM/RHTH SE16 160 B2
Orangery La ELTH/MOT SE9 184 C1
The Orangery RCHPK/HAM TW10 177 H5
Orange St LSQ/SEVD WC2H 11 K8
Orange Tree Hl ROM RM1 104 E6
Oratory La CHEL * SW3 15 M7
Orbain Rd FUL/PGN SW6 157 H6
Orbel St BTSEA SW11 157 P7
Orbital Crs GSTN WD25 72 G1
Orbital One DART * DA1 188 A5
Orb St WALW SE17 18 G6
Orchard BUSH WD23 94 C2
Orchard Av ADL/WDHM KT15 215 K1
ASHF TW15 174 D9
BELV DA17 163 P5
BERK HP4 33 M5
CROY/NA CR0 204 D9
DART DA1 187 J3
EBED/NFELT TW14 174 E1
FNCH N3 117 K1
GSTN WD25 55 J7
GVW DA11 190 E8
HEST TW5 153 M6
MTCM CR4 202 B8
NWMAL KT3 200 B2
RAIN RM13 145 K6
RBRW/HUT CM13 107 L4
SL SL1 128 C7
STHGT/OAK N14 78 D10
STHL UB1 133 M10
THDIT KT7 198 F8
TRDG/WHET N20 97 N3
WDSR SL4 148 F7
Orchard Cl ALP/SUD HA0 135 K3
ASHF TW15 174 D9
ASHTD KT21 237 J6
BNSTD SM7 221 L10
BORE WD6 75 L8
BXLYHN DA7 163 P7
CHING E4 101 J5
CHOB/PIR GU24 212 C9
CRICK NW2 116 D9
DEN/HRF UB9 131 L1
EDGW HA8 95 K7
EHSLY KT24 234 G10
FSTH SE23 182 B2
GU GU1 250 E10
HART DA3 211 N2
HHNE HP2 36 A4
HOR/WEW * KT19 219 N3
HORL RH6 280 A3
LHD/OX KT22 236 C8
NKENS W10 8 B3
POTB/CUF EN6 60 F4
RAD WD7 74 D3
RBSF CM22 30 D3
RGUW GU3 248 A10
RKW/CH/CXG WD3 70 G7
RSEV TN14 247 K7
RSLP HA4 112 D5
RYNPK SW20 200 F4
SOCK/AV RM15 147 H6
STAL AL1 38 E7
WARE SG12 26 C1
WARE SG12 27 H7
WAT WD17 72 G6
WOKS/MYFD GU22 232 E2
WOT/HER KT12 197 J7
Orchard Cottages
HYS/HAR * UB3 152 F1
KUTN/CMB * KT2 199 M1
Orchard Ct WLGTN * SM6 222 C2
WPK * KT4 200 D8
Orchard Crs EDGW HA8 95 P6
EN EN1 79 N5
Orchard Cft HLW CM20 29 K9
Orchard Dr BKHTH/KID SE3 161 K8
EDGW HA8 95 L6
EPP CM16 83 H2
GRAYS RM17 167 M1
LCOL/BKTW AL2 56 A2
RKW/CH/CXG WD3 70 F7
SHPTN TW17 196 F3
UX/CGN UB8 131 N6
WAT WD17 72 G5
WOKN/KNAP GU21 232 B1
Orchard End CTHM CR3 241 M8
GT/LBKH KT23 236 B10
WEY KT13 196 F9
Orchard End Av AMSS HP7 69 L5
Orchardfield Rd RGODL GU7 267 L10
Orchard Gdns CHSGTN KT9 219 K1
EHSLY KT24 253 M4
EPSOM KT18 237 P1
WAB EN9 62 C10
Orchard Ga CDALE/KGS NW9 116 B2
ESH/CLAY KT10 198 C8
GFD/PVL UB6 134 G1
SLN SL2 109 H10
Orchard Gn ORP BR6 207 H9
Orchard Gv CFSP/GDCR SL9 89 P9
CROY/NA CR0 204 D7
EDGW HA8 95 M9
KTN/HRWW/W HA3 115 L3
ORP BR6 207 J9
PGE/AN SE20 181 P10
Orchard Hl BFOR GU20 212 C4
DART DA1 186 F1
LEW SE13 160 G8
Orchard House La STAL AL1 38 C7
Orchard La AMS HP6 69 J4
BRWN CM15 86 E9
E/WMO/HCT KT8 198 C6
RYNPK SW20 200 E1
WFD IG8 101 P5
Orchard Lea MEO * DA13 189 L7
Orchard Lea Cl
WOKS/MYFD GU22 233 H1
Orchardleigh LHD/OX KT22 236 G8
Orchardleigh Av PEND EN3 80 B6
Orchard Mains
WOKS/MYFD GU22 231 P6
Orchard Md HAT AL10 40 C4
Orchardmede WCHMH N21 79 L10
Orchard Ms IS N1 7 H4
The Orchard on the Gn
RKW/CH/CXG WD3 72 A9
Orchard Pde POTB/CUF * EN6 58 G7
Orchard Pl CHES/WCR * EN8 62 C6
POP/IOD E14 141 K9
STMC/STPC * BR5 207 M3
TOTM N17 99 N8
UX/CGN * UB8 131 M7
Orchard Ri CROY/NA CR0 204 D8
KUTN/CMB KT2 199 P1
RCHPK/HAM TW10 155 N10
RSLP HA4 112 G1
Orchard Ri East BFN/LL DA15 185 H1
Orchard Ri West BFN/LL DA15 185 H1
Orchard Rd BAR EN5 77 H8
BEAC HP9 88 E10
BEAC HP9 89 H6
BELV DA17 164 B3
BMLY BR1 205 P1
BTFD TW8 155 H5
CHSGTN KT9 219 K1
CSTG HP8 89 P3
DAGE RM10 144 B3
DORK RH4 272 G3
GUW GU2 267 L2
GVW DA11 189 P5
HGT N6 118 C5
HORL RH6 281 J4
HPTN TW12 175 N10
HSLWW TW4 175 N1
HYS/HAR UB3 133 H9
KUT KT1 199 K2
ORP BR6 226 E2
ORP BR6 227 M5
PEND EN3 80 B9
RCH/KEW TW9 155 M9
REIG RH2 257 L10
RGUE GU4 250 E6
RGUE GU4 268 B6
ROMW/RG RM7 104 C10
RSEV TN14 246 G2
SAND/SEL CR2 224 A10
SCUP DA14 185 H7
SEV TN13 246 F8
SHGR GU5 270 B5
SOCK/AV RM15 147 H7
SUN TW16 175 H10
SUT SM1 221 K2
SWCM DA10 189 K1
TWK TW1 176 F1
WDSR SL4 171 N3
WELL DA16 163 L9
Orchards Cl BF/WBF KT14 215 K10
Orchardson St STJWD NW8 9 L2
Orchard Sq BROX EN10 44 F10
WKENS W14 14 C8
The Orchards CRAWW RH11 282 G8
EPP CM16 65 K8
Orchard St CRAWE RH10 283 N7
DART DA1 187 M2
HHS/BOV HP3 35 N10
MBLAR W1H 10 C6
STALW/RED AL3 38 B7
THDIT KT7 198 G8
WALTH E17 120 D2
Orchard Ter EN * EN1 79 P10
GRH * DA9 188 D1
WLSDN * NW10 116 C9
The Orchard BKHTH/KID SE3 161 J8
BROX * EN10 44 F6
CHSWK W4 156 A3
EW KT17 220 C4
GLDGN NW11 117 K3
HERT/WAS SG14 25 J2
HORL * RH6 280 B4
KGLGY WD4 54 B5
LTWR GU18 212 A7
RDKG RH5 273 H6
SEV TN13 246 F7
SWLY BR8 208 E2
VW GU25 194 B5
WCHMH N21 79 L10
WGCW AL8 22 G3
WOKN/KNAP GU21 231 N2
WOKS/MYFD GU22 232 B8
Orchard Vls SCUP * DA14 185 M9
Orchardville SL SL1 128 A6
Orchard Wy ADL/WDHM KT15 215 L2
ASHF TW15 174 A5
BGR/WK TN15 247 P3
CHESW EN7 61 J3
CHIG IG7 103 K4
CROY/NA CR0 204 D7
DORK RH4 272 G3
DTCH/LGLY SL3 130 B10
EN EN1 79 M7
ESH/CLAY KT10 218 B3
HHS/BOV HP3 52 D4
KWD/TDW/WH KT20 257 H2
OXTED RH8 261 M9
POTB/CUF EN6 59 L4
RDART DA2 187 L6
REIG RH2 275 L3
RGUW * GU3 231 J10
RGUW GU3 248 A10
RKW/CH/CXG WD3 91 K1
RPLY/SEND GU23 250 F1
SUT SM1 221 N1
Orchard Waye UX/CGN UB8 131 N4
Orchehill Av CFSP/GDCR SL9 110 A2
Orchehill Ri CFSP/GDCR SL9 110 B3
Orchid Cl CHSGTN KT9 219 H4
STHL UB1 133 M8
Orchid Ct EGH * TW20 172 E7
Orchid Dr CHOB/PIR GU24 230 F1
Orchid Rd STHGT/OAK N14 98 D1
Orchid St SHB W12 136 D9
Orchis Gv GRAYS RM17 167 L3
Orchis Wy HARH RM3 105 N7
Orde Cl CRAWE RH10 284 E4
Orde Hall St BMSBY * WC1N 11 N3
Ordell Rd BOW E3 140 E4
Ordnance Cl FELT TW13 175 H5
Ordnance Crs GNWCH SE10 161 K1
Ordnance Hl STJWD NW8 3 M6
Ordnance Ms STJWD NW8 3 M7
Ordnance Rd CAN/RD E16 141 L7
GVE DA12 190 F2
PEND EN3 80 C3
WOOL/PLUM SE18 162 D5
Oregano Cl WDR/YW UB7 132 A9
Oregano Wy GUW GU2 249 M5
Oregon Av MNPK E12 122 C9
Oregon Cl NWMAL KT3 199 P4
Oregon Sq ORP BR6 206 G8
Orestan La EHSLY KT24 253 K3
Orestes Ms KIL/WHAMP * NW6 117 K10
Oreston Rd RAIN RM13 145 L5
Orford Gdns TWK TW1 176 E5
Orford Rd CAT SE6 182 G6
SWFD E18 121 N1
WALTH E17 120 F3
Organ Hall Rd BORE WD6 75 K5
Oriel Cl CRAWE RH10 284 D4
MTCM CR4 202 E4
Oriel Ct HAMP NW3 117 M9
Oriel Dr BARN SW13 156 F5
Oriel Gdns CLAY IG5 122 C1
Oriel Rd HOM E9 140 C1
Oriel Wy NTHLT UB5 134 A2
Oriental Cl WOKN/KNAP GU21 232 C3
Oriental Rd ASC SL5 192 C4
CAN/RD E16 142 A10
WOKS/MYFD GU22 232 E2
Orient Cl STAL AL1 38 D8
Orient St LBTH SE11 18 C5
Orient Wy CLPT E5 120 C8
LEY E10 120 F8
Oriole Cl ABLGY WD5 55 H7
Oriole Wy THMD SE28 143 L9
Orion Rd MUSWH N10 98 B7
Orion Wy NTHWD HA6 92 G5
Orissa Rd WOOL/PLUM SE18 163 H4
Orkney St BTSEA SW11 158 B8
Orlando Gdns HOR/WEW KT19 220 A6
Orlando Rd CLAP SW4 158 D9
Orleans Rd NRWD SE19 181 L9
TWK TW1 176 G3
Orlestone Gdns ORP BR6 227 P2
Orleston Ms HOLWY N7 6 B1
Orleston Rd HOLWY N7 6 B1
Orley Farm Rd HRW HA1 114 D8
Orlick Rd GVE DA12 191 L5
Orltons La HORS RH12 282 C3
Ormanton Rd SYD SE26 181 P7
Orme Ct BAY/PAD W2 8 G8
Orme Court Ms BAY/PAD * W2 9 H8
Orme La BAY/PAD W2 8 G8
Ormeley Rd BAL SW12 180 C3
Orme Rd KUT KT1 199 N2
Ormerod Gdns MTCM CR4 202 B2
Ormesby Cl THMD SE28 143 N9
Ormesby Dr POTB/CUF EN6 58 G8
Ormesby Wy KTN/HRWW/W HA3 115 L4
Orme Sq BAY/PAD W2 8 G8
Orme Square Ga KENS W8 8 G8
Ormiston Gv SHB W12 136 E10
Ormiston Rd GNWCH SE10 161 M4
Ormond Av HPTN TW12 198 A1
ORP BR6 206 F9
Ormond Cl BMSBY WC1N 11 M3
Ormond Crs HPTN TW12 176 A10
Ormond Dr HPTN TW12 176 A10
Ormonde Av HOR/WEW KT19 220 A5
Ormonde Ct STJWD * NW8 4 A6
Ormonde Ga CHEL SW3 16 A8
Ormonde Pl BGVA * SW1W 16 D7
WEY * KT13 216 E3
Ormonde Ri BKHH IG9 101 P2
Ormonde Rd MORT/ESHN SW14 155 N9

NTHWD HA6 92 E5
WOKN/KNAP GU21 231 P2
Ormonde Ter STJWD NW8 4 A6
Ormond Rd ARCH N19 118 F6
RCHPK/HAM TW10 177 J1
Ormond Yd STJS SW1Y 11 H9
Ormsby BELMT * SM2 221 L4
Ormsby Gdns GFD/PVL UB6 134 B4
Ormsby Pl STNW/STAM N16 119 N8
Ormsby St BETH E2 7 L7
Ormside St PECK SE15 160 B5
Ormside Wy REDH RH1 258 C6
Ormskirk Rd OXHEY WD19 93 L5
Ornan Rd HAMP NW3 117 P10
Oronsay HHS/BOV HP3 36 C8
Oronsay Wk IS N1 6 F2
Orphanage Rd WAT WD17 73 K6
Orpheus St CMBW SE5 159 L7
Orpington By-Pass RSEV TN14 228 B5
Orpington Gdns UED N18 99 M4
Orpington Rd CHST BR7 207 H3
WCHMH N21 99 H2
Orpin Rd REDH RH1 258 D6
Orpwood Cl HPTN TW12 175 N9
Orsett Heath Crs CDH/CHF RM16 168 D2
Orsett Ms BAY/PAD W2 9 J5
Orsett Rd GRAYS RM17 167 N4
Orsett St LBTH SE11 17 P7
Orsett Ter BAY/PAD W2 9 J5
WFD IG8 101 P9
Orsman Rd IS N1 7 J6
Orton Cl STALE/WH AL4 38 F2
Orton St WAP E1W 13 N10
Orville Rd BTSEA SW11 157 N8
Orwell Cl HYS/HAR UB3 132 F9
WDSR SL4 149 J9
Orwell Ct WATN * WD24 73 L6
Orwell Gdns REIG RH2 275 L2
Orwell Rd PLSTW E13 141 P4
Osbaldeston Rd
STNW/STAM N16 119 P7
Osberton Rd LEE/GVPK SE12 183 M1
Osbert St WEST SW1P 17 J6
Osborn Cl HACK E8 7 N5
Osborne Av STWL/WRAY TW19 173 P4
Osborne Cl BECK BR3 204 D4
EBAR EN4 78 A7
EMPK RM11 125 J4
FELT TW13 175 L8
Osborne Ct EA * W5 135 K7
WDSR SL4 149 H8
Osborne Gdns POTB/CUF EN6 59 L6
THHTH CR7 203 K2
Osborne Gv WALTH E17 120 E2
Osborne Ms WDSR * SL4 149 H8
Osborne Rd ACT W3 155 N1
BELV DA17 164 A4
BKHH IG9 101 N2
BROX EN10 44 F5
BRWN CM15 86 G10
CHES/WCR EN8 62 D3
CRICK NW2 136 E1
EGH TW20 172 C9
EMPK RM11 125 J4
FSBYPK N4 119 H6
FSTGT E7 121 N10
GFD/PVL UB6 134 B8
HOM E9 140 E1
HSLWW TW4 153 N9
KUTN/CMB KT2 177 K10
LEY E10 120 G8
PEND EN3 80 D6
PLMGR N13 99 H4
POTB/CUF EN6 59 L6
REDH RH1 258 B7
THHTH CR7 203 K2
WATN WD24 73 K4
WDSR SL4 149 J9
WOT/HER KT12 197 H8
Osborne Sq DAGW RM9 124 A9
Osborne St SL SL1 149 L1
Osborne Ter TOOT * SW17 180 B8
Osborn Gdns MLHL NW7 96 G8
Osborn La FSTH SE23 182 D3
Osborn Rd UX/CGN * UB8 131 M2
Osborn St WCHPL E1 13 M4
Osborn Ter BKHTH/KID SE3 161 L10
Osborn Wy WGCW AL8 22 G4
Osbourne Av KGLGY WD4 54 A4
Osbourne Ct RYLN/HDSTN * HA2 114 A2
Osbourne Rd RDART DA2 188 A2
Oscar Faber Pl IS * N1 7 K4
Oscar St DEPT SE8 160 F7
Oseney Crs KTTN NW5 5 H1
Osgood Av ORP BR6 227 J2
Osgood Gdns ORP BR6 227 J2
O'shea Gv BOW E3 140 E3
Osidge La STHGT/OAK N14 98 B2
Osier Crs MUSWH N10 98 A9
Osier Pl EGH TW20 172 F9
Osiers Rd WAND/EARL SW18 157 K10
Osier St WCHPL E1 140 B6
Osier Wy BNSTD SM7 221 H10
LEY E10 120 G8
MTCM CR4 201 P5
Oslac Rd CAT SE6 182 G8
Osman Rd ED N9 99 P4
HMSMTH * W6 156 F2
Osmond Cl RYLN/HDSTN HA2 114 B7
Osmond Gdns WLGTN SM6 222 D2
Osmund Cl CRAWE RH10 284 F7
Osmund St SHB W12 136 C8
Osnaburgh St CAMTN NW1 10 F2
Osnaburgh Ter CAMTN NW1 10 F1
Osney Cl CRAWW RH11 283 M8
Osney Wk MRDN SM4 201 N6
Osney Wy GVE DA12 191 J5
Osprey Cl EHAM E6 142 B7
GSTN * WD25 55 M10
SWFD E18 121 M2
WALTH E17 100 D8
WDR/YW UB7 151 N1
Osprey Est BERM/RHTH SE16 160 C3
Osprey Gdns SAND/SEL CR2 224 C6
Osprey Ms PEND EN3 80 A9
Osprey Rd WAB EN9 63 M10
Ospringe Cl PGE/AN SE20 182 B10
Ospringe Rd KTTN NW5 118 D9
Osram Rd WBLY * HA9 115 J8
Ossian Rd FSBYPK N4 118 G5
Ossington Buildings MHST * W1U 10 C3
Ossington Cl BAY/PAD * W2 8 F8
Ossington St BAY/PAD W2 8 F7
Ossory Rd STHWK SE1 19 N9
Ossulston St CAMTN NW1 5 K8
Ossulton Pl EFNCH * N2 117 M1
Ossulton Wy EFNCH N2 117 M2
Ostade Rd BRXS/STRHM SW2 180 G3
Ostell Crs WAB EN9 80 F4
Osten Ms SKENS SW7 15 H4
Osterberg Rd DART DA1 165 N10
Osterley Av ISLW TW7 154 C6
Osterley Crs ISLW TW7 154 D7
Osterley Gdns THHTH CR7 203 K2
Osterley La NWDGN UB2 154 A4
Osterley Park Rd NWDGN * UB2 153 N2
Osterley Park View Rd
HNWL W7 154 D1
Osterley Rd ISLW TW7 154 D6
STNW/STAM N16 119 M9
Oster St STALW/RED AL3 38 B5
Ostliffe Rd PLMGR N13 99 J6
Oswald Cl LHD/OX KT22 236 B8
Oswald Rd LHD/OX KT22 236 B8
STAL AL1 38 D7
STHL UB1 133 M10
Oswald's Md CLPT E5 120 D9
Oswald St CLPT E5 120 C8
Oswald Ter CRICK * NW2 116 F8
Osward CROY/NA * CR0 224 E5
Osward Pl ED N9 99 P3
Osward Rd BAL SW12 180 A5
Oswin St LBTH SE11 18 D5
Oswyth Rd CMBW SE5 159 M8
Otford Cl BMLY BR1 206 D3
BXLY DA5 186 C2
PGE/AN SE20 204 B1
Otford Crs BROCKY SE4 182 E2
Otford La RSEV TN14 228 A9
Otford Rd RSEV TN14 247 J4
Othello Cl LBTH SE11 18 C7
Otis St BOW E3 141 H5
Otley Dr GNTH/NBYPK IG2 122 E4
Otley Rd CAN/RD E16 141 P8
Otley Ter CLPT E5 120 B7
Otley Wy OXHEY WD19 93 K4
Otlinge Rd STMC/STPC BR5 207 N4
Ottawa Gdns DAGE RM10 144 E2
Ottawa Rd TIL RM18 168 D8
Ottaway St CLPT E5 119 P8
Otterbourne Rd CHING E4 101 J4
CROY/NA CR0 203 K9
Otterburn Gdns ISLW TW7 154 F6
Otterburn St TOOT SW17 180 A9
Otter Cl CHERT KT16 214 E3
Otterden Cl ORP BR6 227 H1
Otterden St CAT SE6 182 F7
Otterfield Rd WDR/YW UB7 131 P9
Otter Gdns HAT AL10 40 E5
Ottermead La CHERT KT16 214 F3
Otter Rd GFD/PVL UB6 134 B6
Otters Cl STMC/STPC BR5 207 N4
Otterspool La GSTN WD25 73 M4
Otterspool Wy GSTN WD25 73 N5
Otto Cl SYD * SE26 182 A5
Ottoman Ter WAT WD17 73 K7
Otto St WALW SE17 18 C10
Ottways Av ASHTD KT21 237 J5
Ottways La ASHTD KT21 237 K5
Otway Cl CRAWW RH11 283 J9
Otway Gdns BUSH WD23 94 D1
Otways Cl POTB/CUF EN6 59 L9
Oulton Crs BARK IG11 143 J1
POTB/CUF EN6 58 G8
Oulton Rd SEVS/STOTM N15 119 L3
Oulton Wy OXHEY WD19 93 N5
Oundle Av BUSH WD23 74 B10
Ousden Cl CHES/WCR EN8 62 D6
Ousden Dr CHES/WCR EN8 62 D6
Ouseley Rd BAL SW12 180 A4
STWL/WRAY TW19 171 P3
Outdowns EHSLY KT24 253 J6
Outer Cir CAMTN NW1 4 B7
Outfield Rd CFSP/GDCR SL9 90 A8
Outgate Rd WLSDN NW10 136 C2
Outing's La BRWN CM15 86 G2
Outlook Dr CSTG HP8 90 A4
Outram Pl IS N1 5 M5
WEY KT13 216 D2
Outram Rd CROY/NA CR0 203 N9
EHAM E6 142 B3
WDGN N22 98 E9
Outwich St HDTCH * EC3A 13 K5
Outwood La
KWD/TDW/WH KT20 239 L8
REDH RH1 259 L10
REDH RH1 277 L9
Oval Ct EDGW * HA8 95 P8
Oval Gdns GRAYS RM17 167 P2
Oval Pl VX/NE SW8 158 G6
Oval Rd CAMTN NW1 4 E5
CROY/NA CR0 203 L9
Oval Rd North DAGE RM10 144 C3
Oval Rd South DAGE RM10 144 C4
The Oval BETH E2 140 A4
BFN/LL DA15 185 K3
BNSTD SM7 221 K10
BROX EN10 62 D1
GUW GU2 267 M1
HART DA3 211 P3
RGODL GU7 267 L10
RGUW GU3 248 G9
Oval Wy CFSP/GDCR SL9 110 B2
LBTH SE11 17 P8
Ovenden Rd RSEV TN14 245 N6
Overbrae BECK BR3 182 F9
Overbrook EHSLY KT24 252 C5
Overbrook Wk EDGW HA8 95 M8
Overbury Av BECK BR3 204 G3
Overbury Crs CROY/NA CR0 225 H6
Overbury Rd FSBYPK N4 119 L4
Overbury St CLPT E5 120 C9
Overcliffe GVW DA11 190 D2
Overcliff Rd GRAYS RM17 168 A4
LEW SE13 160 F9
Overcourt Cl BFN/LL DA15 185 L2
Overdale ASHTD KT21 237 K2
RDKG RH5 273 H1
REDH RH1 259 K9
RSEV TN14 265 J9
Overdale Av NWMAL KT3 199 P2
Overdale Rd CSHM HP5 50 G4
EA W5 155 H2
Overdene Dr CRAWW RH11 283 K7
Overdown Rd CAT SE6 182 F7
Overhill WARL CR6 242 B5
Overhill Cottages MTCM * CR4 202 B2
Overhill Rd EDUL SE22 181 P3
PUR/KEN CR8 223 H5
Overhill Wy BECK BR3 205 J5
Overlea Rd CLPT E5 119 P5
Overlord Cl BROX EN10 44 D6
Overmead ELTH/MOT SE9 184 G3
SWLY BR8 208 F5
Over Minnis HART DA3 211 L10
Overstand Cl BECK BR3 204 F5
Overstone Gdns CROY/NA CR0 204 E7
Overstone Rd HARP AL5 20 B2
HMSMTH W6 156 F3
Overstream RKW/CH/CXG WD3 71 L8
Over the Misbourne
CFSP/GDCR SL9 110 D4
Over the Misbourne Rd
DEN/HRF UB9 110 F4
Overthorpe Cl
WOKN/KNAP GU21 231 K3
Overton Cl ISLW TW7 154 E7
WLSDN NW10 135 P1
Overton Dr CHDH RM6 123 M5
WAN E11 121 N5
Overton Rd ABYW SE2 163 M2
BELMT SM2 221 K3
BRXN/ST SW9 159 H8
LEY E10 120 D6
STHGT/OAK N14 78 F9
Overton's Yd CROY/NA CR0 203 K10
Overy Liberty DART DA1 187 M3
Overy St DART DA1 187 N2
Ovesdon Av RYLN/HDSTN HA2 113 N6
Oveton Wy GT/LBKH KT23 253 P2
Ovett Cl NRWD SE19 181 M9
Ovex Cl POP/IOD E14 161 H2
Ovington Ct WOKN/KNAP GU21 231 L2
Ovington Gdns CHEL SW3 15 P4
Ovington Ms CHEL SW3 15 P4
Ovington Sq CHEL SW3 15 P4
Ovington St CHEL SW3 15 P4
Owen Cl CROY/NA CR0 203 L6
CRW RM5 104 B7
THMD SE28 143 M10
YEAD * UB4 133 J5
Owen Gdns WFD IG8 102 B7
Owenite St ABYW SE2 163 L3
Owen Pl LHD/OX * KT22 236 G8
Owen Rd BFOR GU20 212 C2
PLMGR N13 99 K6
YEAD UB4 133 J5
Owen's Ct FSBYE EC1V 6 C9
Owen's Rw FSBYE EC1V 6 C9
Owen St FSBYE EC1V 6 C8
Owens Wy FSTH SE23 182 D3
RKW/CH/CXG WD3 72 B9
Owen Wy WLSDN NW10 135 P1
Owgan Cl CMBW SE5 159 L6
Owl Cl SAND/SEL CR2 224 C6
Owlets Hall Cl HARH RM3 125 N1
Owletts CRAWE RH10 284 E6
Owl Pk LOU * IG10 81 L6
Owlsears Cl BEAC HP9 88 C7
Ownstead Gdns SAND/SEL CR2 223 N7
Ownsted Hl CROY/NA CR0 225 H6
Oxberry Av FUL/PGN SW6 157 H8
Oxdowne Cl COB KT11 218 A10
Oxenden Wood Rd ORP BR6 227 L3
Oxendon Dr HOD EN11 44 F4
Oxendon St SOHO/SHAV * W1D 11 J8
Oxenford St PECK SE15 159 N9
Oxenhill Rd RSEV TN14 247 M3
Oxenpark Av WBLY HA9 115 K5
Oxestalls Rd DEPT SE8 160 D4
Oxfield Cl BERK HP4 33 M6
Oxford Av CDH/CHF RM16 168 D3
EMPK RM11 125 P2
HEST TW5 153 P4
HYS/HAR UB3 152 G6
RYNPK SW20 201 H2
SL SL1 128 E7
STAL AL1 39 H7
Oxford Cl ASHF TW15 174 D10
CHES/WCR EN8 62 B5
ED N9 100 A3
GVE DA12 191 J5
MTCM CR4 202 D3
NTHWD HA6 92 D5
Oxford Ct BRW CM14 107 J5
MANHO EC4N 12 G7
Oxford Crs NWMAL KT3 200 A6
Oxford Dr RSLP HA4 113 K7
Oxford Gdns CHSWK W4 155 M4
DEN/HRF UB9 111 K8
NKENS W10 136 G8
TRDG/WHET N20 97 N2
WCHMH N21 99 K1
Oxford Ga HMSMTH * W6 156 G3
Oxford Ms BXLY DA5 186 B4
Oxford Rd CAR SM5 221 P3
CFSP/GDCR SL9 109 M2
DEN/HRF UB9 111 L10
EA W5 135 J9
ED N9 100 A3
FSBYPK N4 119 H6
GU GU1 268 A2
HARH RM3 105 N7
HPTN TW12 176 C8
HRW HA1 114 B4
IL IG1 122 F9
KIL/WHAMP NW6 2 F7
KTN/HRWW/W HA3 114 E1
NRWD SE19 181 L9
PEND EN3 80 A9
PUT/ROE SW15 157 H10
REDH RH1 257 P9
SCUP DA14 185 L8
SRTFD E15 141 J1
WDSR SL4 149 H7
WFD IG8 102 A6
WLGTN * SM6 222 D2
Oxford Rd East WDSR SL4 149 H7
Oxford Rd North CHSWK W4 155 N4
Oxford Rd South CHSWK W4 155 M4
Oxford Rw SUN * TW16 197 K3
Oxford Sq BAY/PAD W2 9 N6
Oxford St MYFR/PKLN W1K 10 C6
WATW WD18 73 J9
Oxford Ter GU GU1 268 A2
Oxford Wk STHL UB1 133 N10
Oxford Wy FELT TW13 175 L7
Oxgate Court Pde CRICK * NW2 116 E7
Oxgate Gdns CRICK NW2 116 E8
Oxgate La CRICK NW2 116 E7
Oxhawth Crs HAYES BR2 206 D5
Oxhey Av OXHEY WD19 93 L1
Oxhey Dr OXHEY WD19 93 J5
Oxhey La OXHEY WD19 93 L1
Oxhey Ridge Cl OXHEY WD19 93 H6
Oxhey Rd OXHEY WD19 93 K1
Oxleas EHAM E6 142 E8
Oxleas Cl WELL DA16 162 G8
Oxlease Dr HAT AL10 40 E5
Oxleay Rd RYLN/HDSTN HA2 113 P6
Oxleigh Cl NWMAL KT3 200 B5
Oxley Cl GPK RM2 105 K10
STHWK SE1 19 M7
Oxleys Rd CRICK NW2 116 E8
WAB EN9 63 M9
The Oxleys HLWE CM17 29 N7
Oxlow La DAGE RM10 124 B9
Oxonian St EDUL SE22 159 N10
Oxshott Ri COB KT11 217 M10
Oxshott Rd LHD/OX KT22 236 F4
Oxshott Wy COB KT11 235 M1
Oxted Cl MTCM CR4 201 N3
Oxted Rd GDST RH9 260 E7
Oxtoby Wy STRHM/NOR SW16 202 E1
Oyster Catchers Cl CAN/RD E16 141 N8
Oysterfields STALW/RED AL3 38 A5
Oyster La BF/WBF KT14 215 P8
Oyster Rw WCHPL E1 140 B8
Ozolins Wy CAN/RD E16 141 L8

P

Paceheath Cl CRW RM5 104 E7
Pace Pl WCHPL E1 140 A8
Pacific Cl EBED/NFELT TW14 174 G4
SWCM DA10 189 K1
Pacific Rd CAN/RD E16 141 M8
Packet Boat La UX/CGN UB8 131 L8
Packham Rd GVW DA11 190 C6
Packhorse Cl STALE/WH AL4 39 H3
Packhorse La RAD WD7 58 A7
Packhorse Rd CFSP/GDCR SL9 110 B4
SEV TN13 246 D9
Packington Sq IS N1 6 E6
Packington St IS N1 6 D6
Packmores Rd ELTH/MOT SE9 184 G1
Padbrook OXTED RH8 261 M5
Padbury Cl EBED/NFELT TW14 174 E4
Padbury Ct BETH E2 7 M10
Padcroft Rd WDR/YW UB7 131 N10
Paddenswick Rd HMSMTH W6 156 D2
Paddick Cl HOD EN11 44 E2
Paddington Cl YEAD UB4 133 L6
Paddington Gn BAY/PAD W2 9 L4
Paddington St MHST W1U 10 C3
Paddock Cl BKHTH/KID SE3 161 M9
EYN DA4 210 B1
NTHLT UB5 133 P4
ORP BR6 226 E1
OXHEY WD19 73 M10
OXTED RH8 261 L7
SYD SE26 182 C7
WARE SG12 28 A2
WPK KT4 200 B8
Paddock Gdns NRWD SE19 181 M9
Paddockhurst Rd CRAWW RH11 283 K8
Paddock La BAR EN5 76 B8
Paddock Md HLWS CM18 46 F6
Paddock Rd BXLYHS DA6 163 P10
CRICK NW2 116 D8
RSLP HA4 113 L8
Paddocks Cl COB KT11 217 K10
RYLN/HDSTN HA2 114 A9
STMC/STPC BR5 207 N9
Paddocks Md WOKN/KNAP GU21 231 K2
Paddocks Rd RGUE GU4 250 D6
The Paddocks ABR/ST RM4 84 G10
EA * W5 155 J2
EBAR EN4 78 A7
GT/LBKH KT23 254 A2
HERT/BAY SG13 26 A8
MLHL * NW7 97 J7
RGUW GU3 248 B10
RKW/CH/CXG WD3 71 J8
STALE/WH * AL4 39 N8
WBLY HA9 115 N7
WEY KT13 196 F10
WEY * KT13 215 P7
WGCE AL7 23 L4
Paddocks Wy ASHTD KT21 237 K4
CHERT KT16 195 L8
The Paddock BH/WHM TN16 262 F2
BROX EN10 44 F6
CFSP/GDCR SL9 90 B6
CRAWE RH10 284 E6
DORK RH4 272 A3
DTCH/LGLY SL3 149 N7
GU GU1 250 G9
HAT AL10 40 D3
HGDN/ICK UB10 112 C9
VW * GU25 194 B6
WDSR * SL4 148 B6
WDSR * SL4 170 A4
Paddock Wk WARL CR6 242 A5
Paddock Wy CHST BR7 184 G10
OXTED RH8 261 L7
WOKN/KNAP GU21 214 E10
Paddock Wd HARP AL5 20 D4
Padfield Rd CMBW SE5 159 K9
Padnall Rd CHDH RM6 123 P2
Padstow Cl DTCH/LGLY * SL3 150 B2
Padstow Rd ENC/FH EN2 79 J6
Padstow Wk EBED/NFELT TW14 174 G5
Padua Rd PGE/AN SE20 204 B1
Pagden St VX/NE SW8 158 C7
Pageant Cl TIL RM18 168 F7
Pageant Crs POP/IOD E14 140 E10
Pageant Rd STAL AL1 38 C7
Pageant Wk CROY/NA CR0 203 M10
Page Cl DAGW RM9 123 P10
FELT TW13 175 M9
KTN/HRWW/W HA3 115 L4
RDART DA2 189 H6
Page Crs CROY/NA CR0 223 J2
ERITH DA8 164 G6
Page Green Rd
SEVS/STOTM * N15 119 P3
Page Heath La BMLY BR1 206 A3
Page Heath Vls BMLY BR1 206 A3
Page Hl WARE SG12 26 A1
Pagehurst Rd CROY/NA CR0 203 P7
Page Meadow MLHL NW7 96 D8
Page Rd EBED/NFELT TW14 174 E2
HERT/BAY SG13 25 P5
Pages Cft BERK HP4 33 M3
Page's Hl MUSWH N10 98 B10
Page's La MUSWH N10 98 B10
UX/CGN UB8 131 M1
Page St MLHL NW7 96 D9
WEST SW1P 17 K5
Page's Wk STHWK SE1 19 J5
Pages Yd CHSWK * W4 156 B5
Paget Av SUT SM1 201 N10
Paget Cl HPTN TW12 176 C7
Paget Gdns CHST BR7 206 E1
Paget La ISLW TW7 154 C9
Paget Pl KUTN/CMB * KT2 177 P9
THDIT KT7 198 E8
Paget Ri WOOL/PLUM SE18 162 D6
Paget Rd DTCH/LGLY SL3 150 C3
HGDN/ICK UB10 132 D6
IL IG1 122 E9
STNW/STAM N16 119 L6
Paget St FSBYE EC1V 6 C9
Paget Ter WOOL/PLUM SE18 162 E5
Pagette Wy GRAYS RM17 167 M4
Pagewood Cl CRAWE RH10 284 E9
Pagitts Gv EBAR EN4 77 L5
Paglesfield RBRW/HUT CM13 87 P10
Pagnell St NWCR SE14 160 E6
Pagoda Av RCH/KEW TW9 155 L9
Pagoda Gdns BKHTH/KID SE3 161 J8
Paiges Farm Cl RSEV TN14 265 K9
Paignton Rd RSLP HA4 113 H8
SEVS/STOTM N15 119 M4
Paines Brook Wy HARH RM3 105 N7
Paines Cl PIN HA5 113 M1
Paine's La PIN HA5 93 M10
Pain's Cl MTCM CR4 202 C2
Pains Hl COB * KT11 216 G10
OXTED RH8 261 P8
Pains Hill Pk COB * KT11 216 G9
Painsthorpe Rd
STNW/STAM N16 119 M8
Painters Ash La GVW DA11 190 A6
Painters La PEND EN3 80 D1
Painters Rd GNTH/NBYPK IG2 123 K1
Paisley Rd CAR SM5 201 N8
WDGN N22 99 J9
Pakeman St HOLWY N7 118 G8
Pakenham Cl BAL SW12 180 B4
Pakenham St FSBYW WC1X 5 P10
Pakes Wy EPP CM16 83 H3
Palace Av KENS W8 9 H10
Palace Cl KGLGY WD4 54 A6
SL SL1 128 E10
Palace Ct BAY/PAD W2 8 G7
KTN/HRWW/W HA3 115 K4
Palace Court Gdns MUSWH N10 118 D1
Palace Dr WEY KT13 196 C10
Palace Garden Ms KENS W8 8 F9
Palace Gdns BKHH IG9 102 A2
Palace Gardens Ter KENS W8 8 F9
Palace Gdns West WEY KT13 196 C10
Palace Ga KENS W8 15 J2
Palace Gates Rd WDGN N22 98 F9
Palace Gn CROY/NA CR0 224 E4
KENS W8 15 H1
Palace Gv BMLY BR1 205 N1
NRWD SE19 181 N10
Palace Ms FUL/PGN * SW6 157 J6
Palace Pde WALTH * E17 120 E2
Palace Pl WESTW SW1E 16 G3
Palace Rd ADL/WDHM KT15 215 L5
BH/WHM TN16 244 D7
BMLY BR1 205 N1
BRXS/STRHM SW2 180 G4
CEND/HSY/T N8 118 E3
E/WMO/HCT KT8 198 B3
FBAR/BDGN N11 98 F8
KUT KT1 199 J4
NRWD SE19 181 N10
RSLP HA4 113 M9
Palace Sq NRWD SE19 181 N10
Palace St WESTW SW1E 16 G3
Palace Vw BMLY BR1 205 N3
CROY/NA CR0 224 E1
LEE/GVPK SE12 183 M5
Palace View Rd CHING E4 100 G6
Palamos Rd LEY E10 120 F6
Palatine Av STNW/STAM N16 119 M9
Palatine Rd STNW/STAM N16 119 M9
Palemead Cl FUL/PGN SW6 156 G7
Palermo Rd WLSDN NW10 136 D4
Palestine Gv WIM/MER SW19 201 N1
Palewell Cl STMC/STPC BR5 207 L2
Palewell Common Dr
MORT/ESHN SW14 178 A1
Palewell Pk MORT/ESHN SW14 178 A1
Paley Gdns LOU IG10 82 E7
Palfrey Cl STALW/RED AL3 38 C4
Palfrey Pl BRXN/ST SW9 158 G6
Palgrave Av STHL UB1 133 P9
Palgrave Gdns CAMTN NW1 9 P1
Palgrave Rd SHB W12 156 C2
Palins Wy CDH/CHF RM16 147 M10
Palissy St BETH E2 7 L10
Pallant Wy ORP BR6 206 D10
Pallas Rd HHNE HP2 36 A4
Pallett Ct HOD * EN11 44 G5
Pallet Wy WOOL/PLUM SE18 162 B7
Pallingham Dr CRAWE RH10 284 D10
Palliser Dr RAIN RM13 145 H7
Palliser Rd CSTG HP8 89 M4
HMSMTH W6 14 A7
Pall Ml STJS SW1Y 11 J10
Pall Ml East STJS SW1Y 11 J9
Pall Mall Pl STJS SW1Y 11 H10
Palmar Crs BXLYHN DA7 164 B9
Palmar Rd BXLYHN DA7 164 B8
Palmarsh Rd STMC/STPC BR5 207 N4
Palm Av SCUP DA14 185 N9
Palm Cl LEY E10 120 G8
Palmeira Rd WELL DA16 163 N9
Palmer Av BUSH WD23 74 A10
CHEAM SM3 220 F1
GVE DA12 190 G7
Palmer Cl HERT/WAS SG14 25 K3
HEST TW5 153 P7
HORL RH6 280 A2
REDH RH1 276 B1
WWKM BR4 205 J9
Palmer Crs CHERT KT16 214 G3
KUT KT1 199 K3
Palmer Gdns BAR EN5 76 G9
Palmer Pl HOLWY N7 119 H10
Palmer Rd BCTR RM8 123 N6
CRAWE RH10 284 D10
HERT/WAS SG14 25 L3
PLSTW E13 141 N6
Palmer's Av GRAYS RM17 167 P4
Palmers Dr GRAYS RM17 167 P3
Palmers Gv E/WMO/HCT KT8 197 P4
WAB EN9 45 L8
Palmers Hl EPP CM16 65 K5
Palmers La PEND EN3 80 B5
Palmer's Moor La IVER SL0 131 K6
Palmers Orch RSEV TN14 228 G7
Palmers Rd BETH E2 140 C4
BORE WD6 75 P5
FBAR/BDGN N11 98 D6
MORT/ESHN SW14 155 P9
STRHM/NOR SW16 202 G2
Palmerston Av DTCH/LGLY SL3 149 N2
Palmerston Cl WGCW AL8 22 F5
WOKN/KNAP GU21 214 D10
Palmerston Crs PLMGR N13 98 G6
WOOL/PLUM SE18 162 F5
Palmerstone Rd RAIN RM13 145 K4
Palmerston Gdns WTHK RM20 167 J4
Palmerston Gv WIM/MER SW19 179 K10
Palmerston Rd ACT W3 155 P2
BKHH IG9 101 P3
CAR SM5 222 A1
CROY/NA CR0 203 L5
FSTGT E7 121 N10
HSLW TW3 154 B7
KIL/WHAMP NW6 2 D3

KTN/HRWW/W * HA3 114 D1
MORT/ESHN SW14 155 P10
ORP BR6 226 F1
SUT SM1 221 M2
WALTH E17 120 E2
WDGN N22 98 G8
WHTN TW2 176 D2
WIM/MER SW19 179 K10
WTHK RM20 167 J4
Palmerston Wy VX/NE * SW8 158 C6
Palmer St STJSPK SW1H 17 J3
Palmers Wy CHES/WCR EN8 62 D5
Palmers Whf KUT * KT1 199 J2
Palm Gv EA W5 155 K2
GU GU1 249 P5
Palm Rd ROMW/RG RM7 124 D3
Pamela Av HHS/BOV HP3 36 A9
Pamela Ct FNCH * N3 97 L7
Pamela Gdns PIN HA5 113 J3
Pampisford Rd PUR/KEN CR8 223 H7
Pams Wy HOR/WEW KT19 220 A2
Pancake La HHS/BOV HP3 36 E7
Pancras La MANHO EC4N 12 F6
Pancras Rd CAMTN NW1 5 J7
Pancroft ABR/ST RM4 83 L7
Pandora Rd KIL/WHAMP NW6 2 E1
Panfield Ms GNTH/NBYPK IG2 122 D4
Panfield Rd ABYW SE2 163 K1
Pangbourne Av NKENS * W10 136 F7
Pangbourne Dr STAN HA7 95 J6
Panhard Pl GFD/PVL UB6 134 A9
Pank Av BAR EN5 77 N9
Pankhurst Cl ISLW TW7 154 E9
Pankhurst Pl WATN WD24 73 K7
Pankhurst Rd WOT/HER KT12 197 K7
Pankridge OXHEY * WD19 93 L3
Panmuir Rd RYNPK SW20 200 E1
Panmure Cl HBRY N5 119 J9
Panmure Rd SYD SE26 182 A6
Pannells Cl CHERT KT16 195 J8
Pannells Ct GU GU1 268 A1
Panshanger Dr WGCE AL7 23 L5
Pansy Gdns SHB W12 136 D9
Panter's SWLY BR8 186 G10
Panther Dr WLSDN NW10 116 A10
Pantile Rd WEY KT13 216 E1
Pantile Rw DTCH/LGLY SL3 150 D3
Pantiles Cl PLMGR N13 99 J6
WOKN/KNAP GU21 231 N4
The Pantiles BMLY BR1 206 B3
BUSH WD23 94 C1
BXLYHN DA7 164 A6
Panton Cl CROY/NA * CR0 203 J8
Panton St LSQ/SEVD WC2H 11 K8
Panxworth Rd HHS/BOV HP3 35 N8
Paper Buildings EMB * EC4Y 12 B7
Papercourt La RPLY/SEND GU23 233 J8
Paper Ms DORK RH4 272 G1
Papermill Cl CAR SM5 222 B1
Papillons Wk BKHTH/KID SE3 161 M8
Papworth Gdns HOLWY N7 118 G10
Papworth Wy BRXS/STRHM SW2 181 H3
Parade Cl RPLY/SEND GU23 232 F9
Parade Ct EHSLY * KT24 252 F2
Parade Ms BRXS/STRHM SW2 181 J5
Parade Ter CDALE/KGS * NW9 116 D4
The Parade BH/WHM * TN16 243 P7
BROCKY * SE4 160 E7
BRW CM14 107 H4
BTSEA * SW11 157 N10
CAR * SM5 222 A2
CMBW * SE5 159 M9
CRAWE RH10 283 P6
CROY/NA * CR0 202 F6
CROY/NA * CR0 222 G2
DART * DA1 186 G1
EA * W5 135 J8
EPSOM KT18 220 A9
ESH/CLAY KT10 218 D3
FSBYPK * N4 119 H7
GFD/PVL * UB6 134 G1
GUW * GU2 249 N5
GVE * DA12 190 G5
HARH * RM3 106 A7
HART * DA3 211 K5
HAT * AL10 40 F2
KUT * KT1 199 K2
KWD/TDW/WH * KT20 239 H5
LHD/OX * KT22 236 G6
OXHEY * WD19 93 L4
PGE/AN * SE20 204 B1
RCH/KEW * TW9 155 M9
SOCK/AV * RM15 166 B1
STA * TW18 172 G8
SUN TW16 174 G10
SUT * SM1 201 J10
SWCM * DA10 189 L1
SYD * SE26 182 A7
UX/CGN * UB8 131 M7
VW * GU25 194 A6
WATW WD18 73 J7
WOKN/KNAP * GU21 232 B3
Paradise HHNE HP2 35 N7
Paradise Cl CHESW EN7 62 A4
Paradise Pas HOLWY N7 119 H10
Paradise Rd CLAP SW4 158 F8
RCHPK/HAM TW10 177 K1
WAB EN9 63 H10
Paradise Rw BETH * E2 140 A5
Paradise St BERM/RHTH SE16 160 A1
Paradise Wk CHEL SW3 16 A9
Paragon Cl CAN/RD E16 141 M8
Paragon Gv BRYLDS KT5 199 L6
Paragon Ms WALW SE17 19 H5
Paragon Pl BKHTH/KID SE3 161 L8
Paragon Rd HACK E8 140 A1
The Paragon BKHTH/KID SE3 161 M8
Parbury Ri CHSGTN KT9 219 K3
Parbury Rd FSTH SE23 182 D2
Parchment Cl AMS HP6 69 K3
Parchmore Rd THHTH CR7 203 J2
Parchmore Wy THHTH CR7 203 J2
Pardoner St STHWK SE1 19 H3
Pardon St FSBYE EC1V 12 D1
Pares Cl WOKN/KNAP GU21 232 A2
Parfett St WCHPL E1 13 P4
Parfour Dr PUR/KEN CR8 241 K2
Parfrey St HMSMTH W6 156 F5
Parham Dr GNTH/NBYPK IG2 122 E4
Parham Rd CRAWW RH11 283 J6
Paringdon Rd HLWW/ROY CM19 46 E5
Paris Gdn STHWK SE1 12 C9
Parish Cl GSTN WD25 55 K10
HCH RM12 125 J7
Parish Gate Dr BFN/LL DA15 185 H2
Parish La PGE/AN SE20 182 C10
SLN SL2 109 H8
Parish Whf WOOL/PLUM SE18 162 B3
Park Ap BERM/RHTH * SE16 160 B2
WELL DA16 163 L10
Park Av BARK IG11 142 F1
BMLY BR1 183 M9
BUSH WD23 73 L6
CAR SM5 222 B3
CRICK NW2 136 F1
CTHM CR3 241 M10
EGH TW20 172 F10
EHAM E6 142 D3
EN EN1 79 M10
FNCH N3 97 L9
GLDGN NW11 117 L6
GVE DA12 190 F4
GVW DA11 190 B4
HLWE CM17 47 M4
HSLW TW3 176 A2
IL IG1 122 D7
MORT/ESHN SW14 156 A10
MTCM CR4 180 C10
ORP BR6 206 C9
ORP BR6 207 K10
PLMGR N13 99 H4
POTB/CUF EN6 59 M9
RAD WD7 56 G9
RBRW/HUT CM13 107 P2
REDH RH1 276 A8
RKW/CH/CXG WD3 71 K9
RSLP HA4 112 F4
SHPTN TW17 196 F3
STA TW18 173 J9
STAL AL1 38 F5
STHL UB1 153 N1
STWL/WRAY TW19 172 A1
UED N18 99 P5
UPMR RM14 126 D5
WATW WD18 73 H7
WCHMH N21 79 L9
WDGN N22 98 F10
WFD IG8 101 N6
WLSDN NW10 135 L5
WTHK RM20 166 F5
WWKM BR4 205 H9
Park Av East EW KT17 220 D3
Park Av North CEND/HSY/T N8 118 E2
WLSDN NW10 116 E10
Park Avenue Rd TOTM N17 100 A8
Park Av South CEND/HSY/T N8 118 E2
Park Av West EW KT17 220 D3
Park Barn Dr GUW GU2 249 K9
Park Barn East GUW GU2 249 L9
Park Barn Pde GUW * GU2 249 K10
Park Bvd GPK RM2 104 G9
Park Cha GU GU1 250 B10
WBLY HA9 115 L9
Park Cl ADL/WDHM KT15 215 L6
BRKHM/BTCW RH3 273 N5
BRKMPK AL9 40 F3
BRKMPK AL9 59 J2
BUSH WD23 73 L7
CAR SM5 222 A3
CRICK NW2 116 D8
EGH * TW20 171 L8
EPP CM16 66 B3
ESH/CLAY KT10 217 N3
HOM E9 140 B3
HPTN TW12 198 B1
HSLW TW3 176 B1
KTN/HRWW/W HA3 94 D10
KUTN/CMB KT2 199 M1
LHD/OX KT22 236 C10
OXTED RH8 261 L4
RKW/CH/CXG WD3 92 C5
SKENS * SW7 16 A2
TRDG/WHET * N20 97 N5
WDSR SL4 149 J8
WEY KT13 196 G10
WKENS W14 14 D3
WLSDN NW10 135 L5
Park Copse RDKG RH5 273 J2
Park Cnr WDSR SL4 148 D9
Park Corner Dr EHSLY KT24 252 F4
Park Corner Rd MEO DA13 189 L7
Park Cottages FNCH * N3 97 J10
Park Ct BF/WBF * KT14 215 K9
DUL * SE21 181 L6
HLW CM20 28 G10
NWMAL KT3 200 A4
SYD * SE26 182 A9
WBLY HA9 115 K10
WOKS/MYFD GU22 232 C4
Park Crs ASC SL5 192 E5
BORE WD6 75 L7
EMPK RM11 125 H5
ENC/FH EN2 79 L8
ERITH DA8 164 D5
FNCH N3 97 L8
KTN/HRWW/W HA3 94 D9
REGST W1B 10 E2
WHTN TW2 176 C4
Park Crescent Ms East
REGST W1B 10 F2
Park Crescent Ms West
CAVSQ/HST W1G 10 E2
Park Cft EDGW HA8 95 P9
Parkcroft Rd LEE/GVPK SE12 183 L3
Parkdale Crs WPK KT4 200 A10
Parkdale Rd WOOL/PLUM SE18 163 H4
Park Dr ACT W3 155 M2
ASC SL5 192 E6
CHARL SE7 162 B4
DAGE RM10 124 D8
GLDGN NW11 117 L6
HART DA3 211 K3
KTN/HRWW/W HA3 94 C7
MORT/ESHN SW14 178 A1
POTB/CUF EN6 59 L7
RBSF CM22 31 J1
ROM RM1 124 E2
RYLN/HDSTN HA2 113 P5
UPMR RM14 126 B9
WCHMH N21 79 K10
WEY KT13 216 C2
WOKS/MYFD GU22 232 C4
Park End BMLY BR1 205 L1
HAMP NW3 117 P9
Park End Rd ROM RM1 124 F2
Parker Av HERT/WAS SG14 25 L3
TIL RM18 168 F7
Parker Cl CAN/RD E16 142 B10
CRAWE RH10 284 E8
Parker Ms HOL/ALD * WC2B 11 M5
Parke Rd BARN SW13 156 D7
SUN TW16 197 H4
Parker Rd CROY/NA CR0 223 K1
GRAYS RM17 167 L4
Parker's Cl ASHTD KT21 237 K5
Parker's Hl ASHTD KT21 237 K5
Parker's La ASHTD KT21 237 L5
Parkers Rw STHWK SE1 19 N2
STHWK SE1 19 M2
Parker St CAN/RD E16 142 B10
HOL/ALD WC2B 11 M5
WATN WD24 73 J5
Parkes Rd CHIG IG7 103 J6
Park Farm Cl EFNCH N2 117 M1
Park Farm Rd BMLY BR1 206 A1
KUTN/CMB KT2 177 K10
UPMR RM14 125 N10
Parkfield BGR/WK TN15 247 N9
RKW/CH/CXG WD3 71 J8
Parkfield Av AMS HP6 69 J3
FELT TW13 175 H6
HGDN/ICK UB10 132 C5
MORT/ESHN SW14 156 B10
NTHLT UB5 133 L4
RYLN/HDSTN HA2 94 B10
Parkfield Cl CRAWW RH11 283 J7
EDGW HA8 95 N7
NTHLT UB5 133 M4
Parkfield Crs FELT TW13 175 H6
RSLP HA4 113 M7
RYLN/HDSTN HA2 94 B10
Parkfield Dr NTHLT UB5 133 L4
Parkfield Gdns
RYLN/HDSTN HA2 114 A1
Parkfield Pde FELT * TW13 175 H6
Parkfield Rd FELT TW13 175 H6
HGDN/ICK UB10 112 C7
NTHLT UB5 133 M4
NWCR SE14 160 E7
RYLN/HDSTN HA2 114 B8
WLSDN NW10 136 D2
Park Flds HLWW/ROY CM19 45 M1
Parkfields CROY/NA CR0 204 E8
LHD/OX KT22 218 C7
PUT/ROE SW15 156 F10
WGCW AL8 22 G5
Parkfields Av CDALE/KGS NW9 116 A6
RYNPK SW20 200 E1
Parkfields Cl CAR SM5 222 B1
Parkfields Rd KUTN/CMB KT2 177 L8
Parkfield St IS N1 6 B7
Parkfield Wy HAYES BR2 206 C6
Park Gdns CDALE/KGS NW9 115 N1
ERITH DA8 164 E3
KUTN/CMB KT2 177 L8
Park Ga EA W5 135 J7
EA * W5 135 J7
EFNCH N2 117 N1
WCHMH N21 98 G1
Parkgate BKHTH/KID SE3 161 L9
SL SL1 128 B6
Parkgate Av EBAR EN4 77 M5
Parkgate Cl KUTN/CMB KT2 177 N9
Park Gate Ct HPTN * TW12 176 B8
WOKS/MYFD * GU22 232 B4
Parkgate Crs EBAR EN4 77 M5
Parkgate Gdns
MORT/ESHN SW14 178 A1
Parkgate Rd BTSEA SW11 157 P6
CAR SM5 222 B2
ORP BR6 228 D1
REIG RH2 275 L1
WATN WD24 73 K3
Park Gates RYLN/HDSTN * HA2 113 P9
Park Gn GT/LBKH KT23 235 P10
Park Gv BMLY BR1 205 N1
BXLYHN DA7 164 D10
CSTG HP8 70 A7
EDGW HA8 95 L6
FBAR/BDGN N11 98 E8
SRTFD E15 141 M3
Park Grove Rd WAN E11 121 K7
Park Hall Rd DUL SE21 181 L5
EFNCH N2 117 P2
REIG RH2 257 K8
Parkham St BTSEA SW11 157 N7
Park Hl BMLY BR1 206 B4
CAR SM5 222 A3
CLAP SW4 180 E1
EA W5 135 J7
FSTH SE23 182 A5
HLWE CM17 29 L8
LOU IG10 82 A9
RCHPK/HAM TW10 177 L2
Park Hill Cl CAR SM5 221 P2
Parkhill Cl HCH RM12 125 K7
Park Hill Ri CROY/NA CR0 203 M9
Park Hill Rd CROY/NA CR0 203 M9
CROY/NA CR0 223 M1
EW KT17 220 C7
HAYES BR2 205 K2
HHW HP1 35 L6
RSEV TN14 247 M3
WLGTN SM6 222 C4
Parkhill Rd BFN/LL DA15 185 H6
BXLY DA5 186 A3
CHING E4 101 H1
HAMP NW3 118 A10
Parkhill Wk HAMP NW3 118 A10
Parkholme Rd HACK E8 7 N2
Park Horsley EHSLY KT24 253 H5
Park House Dr REIG RH2 275 J2
Park House Gdns TWK TW1 177 H1
Parkhouse St CMBW SE5 159 L6
Parkhurst HOR/WEW KT19 219 P6
Parkhurst Gdns BXLY DA5 186 B3
Parkhurst Gv HORL RH6 279 P3
Parkhurst Rd BXLY DA5 186 B3
FBAR/BDGN N11 98 B5
GUW GU2 249 M9
HERT/WAS SG14 25 J4
HOLWY N7 118 F9
HORL RH6 279 P3
MNPK E12 122 D9
SUT SM1 221 N1
TOTM N17 99 P10
WALTH * E17 120 D2
WDGN N22 98 G8
Parkinson St STALE/WH AL4 21 J3
Parkland Av DTCH/LGLY SL3 150 A4
ROM RM1 104 F10
UPMR RM14 126 A10
Parkland Cl HOD EN11 26 G10
SEV TN13 265 K5
Parkland Gv ASHF TW15 174 B7
Parkland Rd ASHF TW15 174 B7
WDGN N22 98 G10
WFD IG8 101 N8
Parklands ADL/WDHM KT15 215 M2
BRYLDS KT5 199 L5
BUSH * WD23 74 B10
CHIG IG7 102 F4
GT/LBKH KT23 235 P9
HGT N6 118 C5
HHW HP1 35 J4
OXTED RH8 261 K7
RDKG RH5 272 G6
WAB EN9 63 K8
Parklands Cl EBAR EN4 77 N4
MORT/ESHN SW14 177 P1
Parklands Dr FNCH N3 117 H1
STALW/RED AL3 37 P7
Parklands Pde HEST * TW5 153 L8
Parklands Pl GU GU1 250 E10
Parklands Rd TOOT SW17 180 C8
Parklands Wy WPK KT4 200 B9
Parkland Wy CHONG CM5 67 N6
Park La ASHTD KT21 237 L4
BEAC HP9 88 E10
BGR/WK TN15 247 P9
BGR/WK TN15 247 P4
BROX EN10 44 D5
CAR SM5 222 B1
CHDH RM6 123 N4
CHEAM SM3 221 H3
CHES/WCR EN8 62 C9
CHESW EN7 61 P3
COUL/CHIP CR5 240 E7
CROY/NA CR0 203 L10
DEN/HRF UB9 91 K9
DTCH/LGLY SL3 149 N2
DTCH/LGLY SL3 150 D9
EMPK RM11 125 H5
HHNE HP2 35 N7
HLW CM20 28 G9
HYS/HAR UB3 153 H6
MBLAR W1H 10 B7
RAIN RM13 145 J1
RCH/KEW * TW9 155 J10
REIG RH2 257 J10
RGUE GU4 250 G7
RYLN/HDSTN HA2 114 A8
SEV TN13 247 K10
SL SL1 108 D10
SOCK/AV RM15 146 C10
SRTFD * E15 141 H3
STALE/WH AL4 39 P9
STAN HA7 94 F4
SWLY BR8 209 K2
TEDD TW11 176 E9
TOTM N17 99 N8
UED N18 99 N4
WBLY HA9 115 L9
WDSR SL4 170 A4
YEAD UB4 132 F6
Park Lane Cl TOTM N17 99 P8
Park La East REIG RH2 275 J3
Park La Paradise BROX EN10 43 P10
Parklawn Av EPSOM KT18 219 N9
HORL RH6 280 A2
Park Lawn Rd WEY KT13 216 D1
Parklea Cl CDALE/KGS NW9 96 B9
Parkleigh Rd WIM/MER SW19 201 L2
Park Ley Rd CTHM CR3 242 C6
Parkleys KUTN/CMB KT2 177 J7
Parkleys Pde KUTN/CMB * KT2 177 J7
Park Md BFN/LL DA15 185 K1
HLW CM20 28 E10
RYLN/HDSTN HA2 114 A8
Parkmead LOU IG10 82 D9
PUT/ROE SW15 178 E2
Parkmead Gdns MLHL NW7 96 C7
Park Meadow BRKMPK AL9 40 F3
BRWN CM15 87 J4
Park Ms BRKMPK * AL9 40 F3
CHST BR7 184 E9
NKENS W10 2 B8
STWL/WRAY TW19 174 A3
Park Nook Gdns ENC/FH EN2 79 L3
Parkpale La BRKHM/BTCW RH3 273 M5
Park Pde ACT * W3 155 M2
HYS/HAR * UB3 132 F8
WLSDN NW10 136 C4
Park Pl ACT W3 155 M3
AMS HP6 69 K4
BEAC HP9 89 J6
BMLY * BR1 205 N1
DEN/HRF * UB9 91 M9
EA W5 135 J10
GVE DA12 190 F2
HPTN TW12 176 B9
LCOL/BKTW AL2 56 C3
POP/IOD E14 140 F10
SEV TN13 246 E9
WBLY HA9 115 L9
WHALL SW1A 10 G10
WOKS/MYFD * GU22 232 C4
Park Place Vls BAY/PAD W2 9 K3
Park Ridings CEND/HSY/T N8 119 H1
Park Ri BERK HP4 33 K3
KTN/HRWW/W HA3 94 D9
LHD/OX KT22 236 F7
Park Rise Cl LHD/OX KT22 236 G7
Park Rise Rd FSTH SE23 182 D4
Park Rd ALP/SUD HA0 135 K1
AMS HP6 69 L3
ASHF TW15 174 C8
ASHTD KT21 237 K4
BAR EN5 77 J8
BECK BR3 182 E10
BMLY BR1 205 N1
BNSTD SM7 239 M2
BRW CM14 106 G2
BRYLDS KT5 199 L6
BUSH WD23 73 P10
CAMTN NW1 10 B2
CDALE/KGS NW9 116 D5
CDALE/KGS NW9 116 A5
CEND/HSY/T N8 118 E3
CEND/HSY/T N8 119 J2
CHEAM SM3 221 H3
CHES/WCR EN8 62 C9
CHST BR7 184 E9
CHSWK W4 156 A5
CSHM HP5 50 G7
CTHM CR3 241 M9
DART DA1 187 P3
E/WMO/HCT KT8 198 B4
E/WMO/HCT KT8 199 H1
EBAR EN4 77 N8
EFNCH N2 117 N1
EGH TW20 172 D7
EHAM E6 141 P3
ESH/CLAY KT10 218 A1
FBAR/BDGN N11 98 E8
FELT TW13 175 L7
GU GU1 250 A10
GVW DA11 190 E5
HERT/BAY SG13 25 M5
HGDN/ICK UB10 131 P1
HHW HP1 35 M8
HNWL W7 134 E9
HOD EN11 44 F3
HORL RH6 281 K6
HPTN TW12 176 B8
HSLW TW3 176 B1
IL IG1 122 G8
ISLW TW7 154 G7
KUT KT1 199 H1
KUTN/CMB KT2 177 L8
LEY E10 120 F6
MNPK E12 122 A9
NWMAL KT3 200 A4
OXTED RH8 261 L4
PEND EN3 80 D2
POTB/CUF EN6 60 B6
PUR/KEN CR8 241 K1
RAD WD7 74 F1
RCHPK/HAM TW10 177 L2
REDH RH1 258 A8
RKW/CH/CXG WD3 91 P1
SHGR GU5 269 P7
SHPTN TW17 196 B8
SLN SL2 129 J4
SNWD SE25 203 M4
SRTFD E15 141 M3
STHGT/OAK N14 98 E1
STJWD NW8 3 P10
STMC/STPC BR5 207 M6
STWL/WRAY TW19 173 L2
SUN TW16 175 J10
SWCM DA10 189 K2
SWLY BR8 208 G4
TEDD TW11 176 E10
TWK TW1 177 H2
UED N18 99 N5
UPMR RM14 125 P9
UX/CGN UB8 131 N2
WALTH E17 120 E3
WAN E11 121 N6
WARE SG12 26 A2
WARL CR6 225 K10
WAT WD17 73 H5
WIM/MER SW19 179 N10
WLGTN SM6 202 C9
WLGTN SM6 222 C2
WLSDN * NW10 136 B3
WOKS/MYFD GU22 232 E3
WOKS/MYFD GU22 232 C3
YEAD UB4 132 F7
Park Rd East ACT W3 155 P1
UX/CGN UB8 131 N4
Park Rd North ACT W3 155 N1
CHSWK W4 156 A5
Park Rw GNWCH SE10 161 J5
Park Royal Rd WLSDN NW10 135 P5
Parkshot RCH/KEW TW9 155 J10
Park Side ADL/WDHM KT15 215 L6
BKHH IG9 101 N3
CRICK NW2 116 D8
HYS/HAR * UB3 132 F9
Parkside BECK * BR3 204 G2
BKHTH/KID * SE3 161 L6
CDH/CHF RM16 168 A2
CFSP/GDCR SL9 110 C3
CHEAM SM3 221 H3
CHES/WCR EN8 62 D10
CRAWE RH10 283 P7
FNCH N3 97 L9
HPTN TW12 176 C8
KGLGY * WD4 54 B3
MLHL NW7 96 D7
OXHEY * WD19 73 K10
RSEV TN14 227 P9
SCUP DA14 185 L5
WIM/MER SW19 178 G7
Parkside Av BMLY BR1 206 B4
BXLYHN DA7 164 E8
ROM RM1 104 E10
TIL RM18 168 E8
WIM/MER SW19 178 G8
Parkside Cl EHSLY KT24 252 G1
PGE/AN SE20 182 B10
Parkside Crs BRYLDS KT5 199 P6
HOLWY N7 119 H8
Parkside Cross BXLYHN DA7 164 F8
Parkside Dr EDGW HA8 95 M4
WAT WD17 72 F6
Parkside Est HOM * E9 140 C3
Parkside Gdns COUL/CHIP CR5 240 C3
EBAR EN4 98 A2
WIM/MER SW19 178 G7
Parkside Pde DART * DA1 164 G8
Parkside Pl EHSLY KT24 252 F1
Parkside Rd ASC SL5 192 F6
BELV DA17 164 C3
HSLW TW3 176 A1
NTHWD HA6 92 G6
Parkside St BTSEA SW11 158 B7
Parkside Ter ORP * BR6 207 K8
UED * N18 99 L5
Parkside Wk SL SL1 149 M2
Parkside Wy RYLN/HDSTN HA2 114 A2
Park Sq WDSR * SL4 170 A4
Park Sq East CAMTN NW1 10 E1
Park Square Ms CAMTN NW1 10 E2
Park Sq West CAMTN NW1 10 E1
Parkstead Rd PUT/ROE SW15 178 D1
Park Steps BAY/PAD * W2 9 P7
Parkstone Av EMPK RM11 125 M4
UED N18 99 N6
Parkstone Rd PECK * SE15 159 P8
Park St BERK HP4 33 N4
BRKMPK AL9 40 F3
CROY/NA CR0 203 K10
DTCH/LGLY SL3 150 G7
GU GU1 267 P2
LCOL/BKTW AL2 56 C3
MYFR/PKLN W1K 10 C8
SL SL1 149 L2
STHWK SE1 12 E9
TEDD TW11 176 D9
WDSR SL4 149 J7
Park Street La LCOL/BKTW AL2 56 A5
Park Ter CAR * SM5 201 P10
GRH DA9 189 H1
GSTN * WD25 55 L9
PEND * EN3 80 D4
RSEV * TN14 245 N10
WPK KT4 200 D8
The Park CAR SM5 222 A2
EA W5 135 J10
GLDGN NW11 117 L6
GT/LBKH KT23 235 P10
HGT N6 118 B5
SCUP DA14 185 J8
STAL AL1 38 F4
Parkthorne Cl
RYLN/HDSTN * HA2 114 A4
Parkthorne Dr RYLN/HDSTN HA2 113 P4
Parkthorne Rd BAL SW12 180 E3
Park Vw ACT W3 135 P7
ADL/WDHM * KT15 215 M2
BRKMPK AL9 40 F2
CRAWW RH11 283 M8
EW * KT17 220 C9
GT/LBKH KT23 253 P1
HOD EN11 44 F4
HORL RH6 280 B4
NWMAL KT3 200 C3

PIN HA5 93 N9
POTB/CUF EN6 59 M9
SOCK/AV RM15 146 C10
WBLY HA9 115 N10
WCHMH N21 98 G1
Parkview WDR/YW * UB7 131 P9
Parkview Cha SL SL1 128 D8
Park View Cl STAL AL1 38 F7
Park View Ct NFNCH/WDSP * N12 97 P5
WOKS/MYFD * GU22 232 C5
Park View Crs FBAR/BDGN N11 98 C5
Park View Dr MTCM CR4 201 N2
Park View Est HBRY * N5 119 K9
Park View Gdns GRAYS RM17 167 N4
HDN NW4 116 F3
WDGN * N22 99 H9
REDBR IG4 122 C2
Parkview Rd CROY/NA CR0 203 P8
Park View Rd BERK HP4 33 N5
CRICK NW2 116 C9
CTHM CR3 242 D8
EA W5 135 K7
ELTH/MOT SE9 184 E4
FNCH N3 97 L9
PIN HA5 93 J7
REDH RH1 276 B7
STHL UB1 133 P10
TOTM N17 119 P1
UX/CGN UB8 132 B8
WELL DA16 163 M9
Parkview V RGUE GU4 250 F7
Park Village East CAMTN NW1 4 E7
Park Village West CAMTN NW1 4 E7
Park Vls TOOT * SW17 179 P8
Parkville Rd FUL/PGN SW6 157 J6
Park Vis GNWCH SE10 161 J5
Park Wk WBPTN SW10 15 K9
Park Wallis GVW DA11 189 N1
Park Wy BRWN CM15 107 L2
BXLY DA5 186 G6
CRAWE RH10 284 D5
E/WMO/HCT KT8 198 A3
EBED/NFELT TW14 175 J3
EDGW HA8 95 N9
ENC/FH EN2 79 H6
GLDGN NW11 117 H3
GT/LBKH KT23 235 P9
RKW/CH/CXG WD3 91 M2
RSLP HA4 113 H6
TRDG/WHET N20 98 A5
Parkway CAMTN NW1 4 F5
CROY/NA CR0 225 H5
DORK RH4 272 F1
ERITHM DA18 163 P2
GDMY/SEVK IG3 123 J8
GPK RM2 104 G10
GU GU1 250 B9
HGDN/ICK UB10 132 B2
HLWW/ROY CM19 46 B1
RAIN RM13 145 H6
RAIN * RM13 145 H6
RYNPK SW20 200 G4
SBW CM21 29 P2
STHGT/OAK N14 98 F3
WEY KT13 216 E1
WFD IG8 101 P6
WGCW AL8 22 G5
Parkway Cl WGCW AL8 22 F5
Parkway Ct STAL AL1 38 G9
Parkway Gdns WGCW AL8 22 F6
The Parkway HEST TW5 153 J3
IVER SL0 130 F3
NTHLT UB5 133 L5
Park West BAY/PAD W2 9 P5
Park West Pl BAY/PAD W2 9 P5
Parkwood BECK BR3 182 F10
Parkwood Av ESH/CLAY KT10 198 B8
Park Wood Cl BNSTD SM7 238 G1
Parkwood Cl HOD EN11 44 D5
Parkwood Dr HHW HP1 35 J6
Parkwood Gv SUN TW16 197 H3
Parkwood Ms HGT N6 118 C4
Parkwood Rd BH/WHM TN16 244 B7
Park Wood Rd BNSTD SM7 238 G1
Parkwood Rd BXLY DA5 186 A3
ISLW TW7 154 E7
REDH RH1 258 F9
WIM/MER SW19 179 J8
Park Wood Vw BNSTD SM7 238 F2
Park Works Rd REDH RH1 258 G9
Parlaunt Rd DTCH/LGLY SL3 150 E3
Parley Dr WOKN/KNAP GU21 231 P4
Parliament Ct WCHPL * E1 13 K4
Parliament Hl HAMP NW3 117 P9
Parliament Hill Flds KTTN * NW5 118 B8
Parliament Sq WEST SW1P 17 L2
HERT/WAS SG14 25 L5
Parliament St WHALL SW1A 17 L1
Parma Crs BTSEA SW11 158 A10
Parmiter St BETH E2 140 A4
Parnall Rd HLWS CM18 46 G5
Parndon Mill La HLW CM20 28 E8
Parndon Wood Rd
HLWW/ROY CM19 46 F6
Parnell Cl ABLGY WD5 54 G6
EDGW HA8 95 N5
SHB W12 156 E2
WTHK RM20 167 H4
Parnell Gdns WEY KT13 216 A7
Parnell Rd BOW E3 140 E3
Parnel Rd WARE SG12 26 E1
Parnham Av LTWR GU18 212 C7
Parnham St POP/IOD * E14 140 D8
Parolles Rd ARCH N19 118 D6
Paroma Rd BELV DA17 164 B2
Parpins KGLGY * WD4 53 P4
Parr Av EW KT17 220 E5
Parr Cl ED N9 100 A5
LHD/OX KT22 236 E6
WTHK RM20 167 H3
Parr Crs HHNE HP2 36 C1
Parris Cft RDKG RH5 273 H5
Parrock Av GVE DA12 190 F4
Parrock Rd GVE DA12 190 F3
Parrock St GVE DA12 190 E2
Parrotts Cl RKW/CH/CXG WD3 72 B8
Parrotts Fld HOD EN11 44 G2
Parrott's La TRING HP23 32 A6
Parr Rd EHAM E6 142 A3
STAN HA7 95 J9
Parrs Cl SAND/SEL CR2 223 L5
Parr's Pl HPTN TW12 175 P10
Parr St IS N1 6 G7
Parry Av EHAM E6 142 C8
Parry Cl EW KT17 220 D4
Parry Dr WEY KT13 216 B6
Parry Gn North DTCH/LGLY SL3 150 C3
Parry Gn South DTCH/LGLY SL3 150 D3
Parry Pl WOOL/PLUM SE18 162 E3
Parry Rd NKENS W10 2 B9
SNWD SE25 203 M3
Parry St VX/NE SW8 17 L9
Parsifal Rd KIL/WHAMP NW6 117 K10
Parsloe Rd EPP CM16 46 D7
Parsloes Av DAGW RM9 123 P10
Parsonage Cl ABLGY WD5 54 F6
HYS/HAR UB3 132 G8
WARL CR6 242 D2
Parsonage Fld BRWN CM15 87 J3
Parsonage Gdns ENC/FH EN2 79 K6
Parsonage La BRKMPK AL9 40 E9
DORK RH4 272 B3
ENC/FH EN2 79 L6
EYN DA4 188 A9
SCUP DA14 186 A7
SLN SL2 129 H1
WDSR SL4 148 F7
Parsonage Leys HLW CM20 47 J1
Parsonage Manorway
ERITH DA8 164 B5
Parsonage Pl AMSS * HP7 69 H5
Parsonage Rd BRKMPK AL9 40 E9
CSTG HP8 89 N4
EGH TW20 172 A8
RAIN RM13 145 K4
RKW/CH/CXG WD3 91 N1
WTHK RM20 167 H5
Parsonage Sq DORK RH4 272 F1
Parsonage St POP/IOD E14 161 H3
Parsons Cl HORL RH6 279 P3
Parsonsfield Cl BNSTD SM7 238 G1
Parsonsfield Rd BNSTD SM7 238 G2
Parsons Gn FUL/PGN SW6 157 K7
GU GU1 250 A8
Parsons Green La FUL/PGN SW6 157 K7
Parsons Gv EDGW HA8 95 M4
Parsons La RDART DA2 187 J6
Parson's Md CROY/NA CR0 203 J8
E/WMO/HCT KT8 198 B3
Parsons Rd EDGW HA8 95 M4
PLSTW E13 141 P4
Parson St HDN NW4 116 F1
Parson's Wood La SLN SL2 129 J2
Parthenia Rd FUL/PGN SW6 157 K7
Parthia Cl KWD/TDW/WH KT20 238 E5
Partingdale La MLHL NW7 96 G6
Partridge Cl BAR EN5 76 F10
BUSH * WD23 94 B2
CAN/RD E16 142 A7
CSHM HP5 51 K4
STAN HA7 95 K5
Partridge Ct HLWS CM18 47 H3
Partridge Dr ORP BR6 206 F10
Partridge Gn ELTH/MOT SE9 184 D6
Partridge Knoll PUR/KEN CR8 223 J8
Partridge La HORS RH12 282 B3
RDKG RH5 278 A3
Partridge Md BNSTD SM7 238 F1
Partridge Rd HLWS CM18 46 G3
HPTN TW12 175 N9
SCUP DA14 185 H6
STALW/RED AL3 38 C2
Partridge Wy RGUE GU4 250 G8
WDGN N22 98 F9
Parva Cl HARP AL5 20 C5
Parvills WAB EN9 63 J8
Parvis Rd BF/WBF KT14 215 P8
Pasadena Cl HYS/HAR UB3 153 H1
Pascal St VX/NE SW8 158 E6
Pascoe Rd LEW SE13 183 J1
Pasfield WAB EN9 63 J9
Pasley Cl WALW SE17 18 D8
Pasquier Rd WALTH E17 120 D1
Passey Pl ELTH/MOT SE9 184 C2
Passfield Dr POP/IOD E14 140 G7
Passmore Gdns FBAR/BDGN N11 98 E7
Passmore St BGVA SW1W 16 C6
Pastens Rd OXTED RH8 261 P7
Pasteur Cl CDALE/KGS NW9 96 B10
Pasteur Dr HARH RM3 105 L10
Pasteur Gdns UED N18 99 K6
Paston Cl WLGTN SM6 202 D10
Paston Crs LEE/GVPK SE12 183 N3
Paston Rd HHNE HP2 35 N4
Pastor St LBTH SE11 18 D5
Pasture Cl ALP/SUD HA0 114 G8
BUSH WD23 94 B1
Pasture Rd ALP/SUD HA0 114 G7
CAT SE6 183 K4
DAGW RM9 124 A10
Pastures Md HGDN/ICK UB10 132 B1
The Pastures HAT AL10 40 E5
HHW HP1 35 H5
LCOL/BKTW AL2 37 P10
OXHEY WD19 93 J1
TRDG/WHET N20 97 J2
WGCE AL7 23 K7
The Pasture CRAWE RH10 284 D7
Patcham Ter VX/NE SW8 158 C7
Patching Cl CRAWW RH11 283 J6
Patching Wy YEAD UB4 133 M7
The Patch SEV TN13 246 F8
Paternoster Cl WAB EN9 63 L9
Paternoster Hl WAB EN9 63 L8
Paternoster Rw ABR/ST RM4 105 K2
STP EC4M 12 D6
Pater St KENS W8 14 E4
Pates Manor Dr
EBED/NFELT TW14 174 E3
Pathfield Rd STRHM/NOR SW16 180 E9
Pathfields SHGR GU5 270 B6
Path Link CRAWE RH10 283 P6
Path Stort Valley Wy
HERT/BAY SG13 43 J8
The Path WIM/MER SW19 201 L1
The Pathway OXHEY WD19 93 L2
RAD WD7 74 E2
RPLY/SEND GU23 251 J1
Patience Rd BTSEA SW11 157 P8
Patio Cl CLAP SW4 180 E2
Patmore La WOT/HER KT12 216 G3
Patmore Link Rd HHNE HP2 36 D6
Patmore Rd WAB EN9 63 K10
Patmore St VX/NE SW8 158 D7
Patmore Wy CRW RM5 104 C6
Patmos Rd BRXN/ST SW9 159 J6
Paton Cl BOW E3 140 F5
Patricia Cl SL SL1 128 D9
Patricia Ct WELL DA16 163 L6
Patricia Dr EMPK RM11 125 M6
Patricia Vls TOTM * N17 100 A9
Patrick Gv WAB EN9 62 G9
Patrick Rd PLSTW E13 141 P5
Patrington Cl CRAWW RH11 283 K10
UX/CGN UB8 131 M5
Patriot Sq BETH E2 140 A4
Patrol Pl CAT SE6 182 G2
Patshull Pl KTTN NW5 4 G2
Patshull Rd KTTN NW5 4 G1
Pattenden Rd FSTH SE23 182 E4
Patten Rd WAND/EARL SW18 179 P3
Patterdale Cl BMLY BR1 183 K9
CRAWW RH11 283 M10
Patterdale Rd PECK SE15 160 B6
RDART DA2 188 B4
Patterson Rd CSHM HP5 50 G4
NRWD SE19 181 N9
Pattina Wk BERM/RHTH SE16 140 D10
Pattison Rd CRICK NW2 117 K8
Paul Cl SRTFD E15 141 K2
Paulet Rd CMBW SE5 159 J8
Paul Gdns CROY/NA CR0 203 N9
Paulhan Rd KTN/HRWW/W HA3 115 J2
Paulin Dr WCHMH N21 99 H1
Pauline Crs WHTN TW2 176 B4
Paulinus Cl STMC/STPC BR5 207 M2
Paul Julius Cl POP/IOD E14 141 J9
Paul Robeson Cl EHAM E6 142 D5
Pauls Ct HOD * EN11 44 F3
Pauls La HOD EN11 44 F3
Paul's Pl ASHTD KT21 237 N5
Paul St SDTCH EC2A 13 J1
SRTFD E15 141 K3
Paultons Sq CHEL SW3 15 M9
Paultons St CHEL SW3 15 M10
Pauntley St ARCH N19 118 D6
Paveley Dr BTSEA SW11 157 P6
Paveley St CAMTN NW1 9 P1
The Pavement CLAP SW4 158 D10
EA * W5 155 K2
REDH * RH1 258 A10
TEDD * TW11 176 G10
WAN * E11 121 H6
WIM/MER * SW19 179 J9
WNWD * SE27 181 K7
Pavet Cl DAGE RM10 144 C1
Pavilion Gdns STA TW18 173 L10
Pavilion Ldg RYLN/HDSTN * HA2 114 C6
Pavilion Pde SHB * W12 136 F8
Pavilion Rd IL IG1 122 C5
KTBR SW1X 16 B2
The Pavilions EPP CM16 66 D1
Pavilion St KTBR SW1X 16 B4
The Pavilion CHES/WCR * EN8 62 D10
VX/NE * SW8 158 E6
Pavilion Wy AMS HP6 69 P5
EDGW HA8 95 P8
RSLP HA4 113 K7
Pavillion Ter SHB * W12 136 F8
Pawleyne Cl PGE/AN SE20 182 B10
Pawsey Cl PLSTW E13 141 M3
Pawson's Rd CROY/NA CR0 203 K6
Pax Cl CRAWW RH11 283 H9
Paxford Rd ALP/SUD HA0 114 G7
Paxton Av SL SL1 149 H2
Paxton Cl RCH/KEW TW9 155 L8
WOT/HER * KT12 197 K7
Paxton Gdns WOKN/KNAP GU21 215 H9
Paxton Pl WNWD SE27 181 M7
Paxton Rd BERK * HP4 34 B5
BMLY BR1 183 M10
CHSWK W4 156 B5
FSTH SE23 182 D6
STAL AL1 38 D7
TOTM N17 99 P8
Paxton Ter PIM SW1V 16 F9
Paycock Rd HLWW/ROY CM19 46 D3
Payne Cl BARK IG11 143 H2
CRAWE RH10 284 E5
Paynell Ct BKHTH/KID SE3 161 K9
Payne Rd BOW E3 140 G4
Paynesfield Av
MORT/ESHN SW14 156 A9
Paynes Field Cl BERK HP4 33 J3
Paynesfield Rd BH/WHM TN16 243 P6
BUSH WD23 94 E1
Paynes La WAB EN9 45 H10
Payne St DEPT SE8 160 E5
Paynes Wk HMSMTH W6 14 A10
Payzes Gdns WFD * IG8 101 L7
Peabody Av PIM SW1V 16 F8
Peabody Cl CROY/NA CR0 204 B8
GNWCH * SE10 160 G7
PIM SW1V 16 F8
Peabody Cottages HNHL * SE24 181 K3
Peabody Est BTSEA * SW11 157 P10
CLKNW * EC1R 12 B2
CMBW * SE5 159 L7
HMSMTH * W6 156 F4
HNHL SE24 181 J3
NKENS * W10 136 F7
STHWK * SE1 12 B9
STHWK * SE1 12 E9
STLK * EC1Y 12 F2
TOTM * N17 99 M9
Peabody Hl DUL SE21 181 J4
Peabody Sq IS * N1 6 E5
Peabody Ter CLKNW * EC1R 12 B2
Peace Cl GFD/PVL UB6 134 C3
SNWD SE25 203 M4
STHGT/OAK N14 78 C9
Peace Gv WBLY HA9 115 N8
Peacemaker Cl CRAWW RH11 283 H9
Peace Prospect WAT WD17 73 H7
Peace Rd DTCH/LGLY SL3 130 D5
Peace St WOOL/PLUM SE18 162 D5
Peach Cft GVW DA11 190 B6
Peaches Cl BELMT SM2 221 H4
Peachey Cl UX/CGN UB8 131 N8
Peachey La UX/CGN UB8 131 N7
Peach Rd NKENS W10 136 G5
Peachum Rd BKHTH/KID SE3 161 L5
Peacock Av EBED/NFELT TW14 174 E4
Peacock Cl EMPK RM11 125 M2
Peacock Gdns CROY/NA CR0 224 D6
Peacocks HLWW/ROY CM19 46 C3
Peacocks Cl BERK HP4 33 L3
Peacock St GVE DA12 190 F3
WALW SE17 18 D6
Peacock Yd WALW SE17 18 D6
Peakes La CHESW EN7 61 N3
Peakes Pl STAL * AL1 38 E6
Peakes Wy CHESW EN7 61 N3
Peaketon Av REDBR IG4 122 A3
Peak Hl SYD SE26 182 B7
Peak Hill Av SYD SE26 182 B7
Peak Hill Gdns SYD SE26 182 B7
Peak Rd GUW GU2 249 M7
Peaks Hl PUR/KEN CR8 222 F6
Peaks Hill Ri PUR/KEN CR8 222 F6
The Peak SYD SE26 182 B6
Pea La BERK HP4 33 J3
UPMR RM14 146 F1
Peal Gdns WEA W13 134 F5
Peall Rd CROY/NA CR0 202 G6
Pear Av SHPTN TW17 196 F3
Pearce Cl MTCM CR4 202 B2
Pearcefield Av FSTH SE23 182 B4
Pearce Rd CSHM HP5 50 G5
Pearces Wk STAL * AL1 38 C7
Pear Cl CDALE/KGS NW9 116 A2
NWCR SE14 160 D6
Pearcroft Rd WAN E11 121 J7
Pearcy Cl HARH RM3 105 M8
Peardon St VX/NE SW8 158 C8
Peareswood Gdns STAN HA7 95 J9
Peareswood Rd ERITH DA8 164 G7
Pearfield Rd FSTH SE23 182 D6
Pear Gv WAN E11 121 J8
Pearl Cl CRICK NW2 116 G5
EHAM E6 142 D8
Pearl Ct WOKN/KNAP GU21 231 K2
Pearl Gdns SL SL1 128 G10
Pearl Rd WALTH E17 120 F1
Pearl St WAP E1W 140 A10
Pearmain Cl SHPTN TW17 196 C5
Pearman St STHWK SE1 18 B3
Pear Pl STHWK SE1 18 A1
Pears Av SHPTN * TW17 196 F3
Pearscroft Ct FUL/PGN SW6 157 L7
Pearscroft Rd FUL/PGN SW6 157 L8
Pearson Av HERT/BAY SG13 25 K7
Pearson Rd CRAWE RH10 284 C7
Pearson's Av NWCR SE14 160 F7
Pearsons Cl HERT/BAY SG13 25 K7
Pearson St BETH E2 7 L7
Pearson Wy DART DA1 187 N5
Pears Rd HSLW TW3 154 B9
Pear Tree Av WDR/YW UB7 132 A8
Pear Tree Cl ADL/WDHM KT15 215 K2
AMSS HP7 69 L5
BEAC HP9 89 H7
BETH E2 7 L6
BXLYHN DA7 164 E7
MTCM CR4 201 P2
SWLY BR8 208 E2
Peartree Cl BRWN CM15 87 J4
HHW HP1 35 K5
SAND/SEL CR2 224 A10
SL SL1 128 E10
SOCK/AV RM15 147 H4
WGCE AL7 23 H5
Pear Tree Ct CLKNW EC1R 12 B2
Peartree Ct WGCE AL7 23 H6
Peartree Gdns BCTR RM8 123 L10
ROMW/RG RM7 104 C10
Pear Tree Hl REDH * RH1 276 B9
Peartree La BRWN CM15 87 H3
WAP * E1W 140 B9
WGCE AL7 23 H6
Pear Tree Md HLWS CM18 47 K3
Pear Tree Rd ADL/WDHM KT15 215 K2
ASHF TW15 174 D8
Peartree Rd EN EN1 79 M7
HHW HP1 35 K5
Peartrees RBRW/HUT CM13 107 P7
The Pear Trees WDR/YW * UB7 131 N9
Peartree St FSBYE EC1V 12 D1
Pear Tree Wk CHESW EN7 61 L2
Peartree Wy GNWCH SE10 161 M3
Pearwood Cottages STAN * HA7 95 H3
Peary Pl BETH E2 140 B5
Peascod St WDSR SL4 149 J7
Peascroft Rd HHS/BOV HP3 36 B9
Pease Cl HCH RM12 145 J2
Peasmead Ter CHING * E4 101 H5
Peatfield Cl BFN/LL DA15 185 H6
Peatmore Av WOKS/MYFD GU22 233 K2
Peatmore Cl WOKS/MYFD GU22 233 K2
Peatmore Dr CHOB/PIR GU24 230 B7
Pebble Cl KWD/TDW/WH KT20 256 B4
Pebble Hl EHSLY KT24 252 D9
Pebblehill Rd BRKHM/BTCW RH3 256 B6
Pebble La EPSOM KT18 237 M8
Pebworth Rd HRW HA1 114 F7
Peckarmans Wd DUL SE21 181 P6
Peckett Sq HBRY * N5 119 K9
Peckford Pl BRXN/ST SW9 159 H8
Peckham Gv PECK SE15 159 M6
Peckham High St PECK SE15 159 P7
Peckham Hill St PECK SE15 159 P6
Peckham Park Rd PECK SE15 159 P6
Peckham Rd CMBW SE5 159 M7
Peckham Rye EDUL SE22 159 P10
Peck's Hl WAB EN9 45 K7
Pecks Yd WCHPL * E1 13 L3
Peckwater St KTTN NW5 118 D10
Pedlars End CHONG CM5 49 J7
Pedlars Wk HOLWY * N7 118 F10
Pedley Rd BCTR RM8 123 M6
Pedley St WCHPL E1 13 M2
Pednor Bottom CSHM HP5 50 A4
Pednormead End CSHM HP5 50 G8
Pednor Rd CSHM HP5 50 D5
Pedro St CLPT E5 120 C8
Peek Crs WIM/MER SW19 178 G8
Peeks Brook La HORL RH6 280 G5
Peel Cl CHING E4 100 G3
ED N9 99 P4
WDSR SL4 148 G9
Peel Ct SL SL1 128 G7
Peel Crs HERT/WAS SG14 25 J2
Peel Dr CDALE/KGS NW9 116 C1
CLAY IG5 122 B1
Peel Gv BETH E2 140 B4
Peel Pas KENS * W8 8 E10
Peel Pl CLAY IG5 102 B10
Peel Prec KIL/WHAMP NW6 2 D8
Peel Rd ALP/SUD HA0 115 H8
KIL/WHAMP NW6 2 D9
KTN/HRWW/W HA3 114 D1
ORP BR6 226 F1
SWFD E18 101 L9
Peel St KENS W8 8 E10
Peel Wy HARH RM3 105 N10
UX/CGN UB8 131 P7
Peerage Wy EMPK RM11 125 M5
Peerglow Est PEND * EN3 80 B9
Peerless Dr DEN/HRF UB9 111 L2
Peerless St FSBYE EC1V 6 G10
Pegamoid Rd UED N18 100 B4
Pegasus Cl STNW/STAM * N16 119 L9
Pegasus Ct BTFD TW8 155 L4
GVE DA12 190 F6
Pegasus Pl FUL/PGN * SW6 157 K7
LBTH SE11 18 A9
Pegasus Rd CROY/NA CR0 223 H3
Pegasus Wy FBAR/BDGN N11 98 C7
Pegelm Gdns EMPK RM11 125 N5
Peggotty Wy UX/CGN UB8 132 C8
Pegg Rd HEST TW5 153 L6
Pegler Wy CRAWE RH10 283 N7
Pegley Gdns LEE/GVPK SE12 183 M5
Pegmire La GSTN WD25 74 B5
Pegrams Rd HLWS CM18 46 F4
Peg's La HERT/BAY SG13 25 L6
Pegwell Cl CRAWW RH11 283 J9
Pegwell St WOOL/PLUM SE18 163 H6
Peket Cl STA TW18 195 H1
Pekin St POP/IOD E14 140 F8
Peldon Rd HLWW/ROY CM19 46 D
Peldon Wk IS * N1 6 D
Pelham Av BARK IG11 143 J
Pelham Cl CMBW SE5 159 M
Pelham Cottages BXLY * DA5 186 C
Pelham Ct HHNE HP2 36 D
WGCE AL7 23 M
Pelham Crs SKENS SW7 15 N
Pelham Pl SKENS SW7 15 N
Pelham Rd BXLYHN DA7 164 B
GVW DA11 190 C
IL IG1 122 G
PGE/AN SE20 204 B
SEVS/STOTM N15 119 N
SWFD E18 121 N
WDGN N22 99 H1
WIM/MER SW19 179 K1
Pelham Rd South GVW DA11 190 C
Pelhams Cl ESH/CLAY KT10 217 P
The Pelhams GSTN WD25 73 L
Pelham St SKENS SW7 15 M
Pelhams Wk ESH/CLAY KT10 197 P1
Pelham Wy GT/LBKH KT23 254 A
Pelier St WALW SE17 18 F
Pelinore Rd CAT SE6 183 K
Pellant Rd FUL/PGN SW6 14 B1
Pellatt Gv WDGN N22 99 H
Pellatt Rd EDUL SE22 181 N
WBLY HA9 115 J
Pellerin Rd STNW/STAM N16 119 M10
Pelling Hl WDSR SL4 171 N
Pelling St POP/IOD E14 140 E
Pellipar Cl PLMGR N13 99 H
Pellipar Rd WOOL/PLUM SE18 162 C
Pelly Ct EPP CM16 65 J
Pelly Rd PLSTW E13 141 M3
Pelter St BETH E2 7 L
Pelton Av BELMT SM2 221 L
Pelton Rd GNWCH SE10 161 K
Pembar Av WALTH * E17 120 D
Pemberley Cha HOR/WEW KT19 219 N
Pemberley Cl HOR/WEW KT19 219 N
Pember Rd WLSDN NW10 136 G5
Pemberton Av GPK RM2 125 J
Pemberton Cl STAL AL1 38 C
Pemberton Gdns ARCH N19 118 D8
CHDH RM6 123 P3
SWLY BR8 208 F3
Pemberton Pl ESH/CLAY KT10 198 B10
HACK E8 140 A
Pemberton Rd E/WMO/HCT KT8 198 B4
FSBYPK N4 119 H3
SLN SL2 128 D6
Pemberton Rw FLST/FETLN EC4A 12 B5
Pemberton Ter ARCH N19 118 D8
Pembley Gn CRAWE RH10 285 M2
Pembrey Wy HCH RM12 145 K
Pembridge Av HSLWW TW4 175 N4
Pembridge Cl HHS/BOV HP3 52 C4
Pembridge Crs NTGHL W11 8 D7
Pembridge Gdns BAY/PAD W2 8 E8
Pembridge La BROX EN10 43 N7
Pembridge Ms NTGHL W11 8 E
Pembridge Pl BAY/PAD W2 8 F
Pembridge Rd HHS/BOV HP3 52 D4
NTGHL W11 8 E8
Pembridge Sq BAY/PAD W2 8 E8
Pembridge Vls NTGHL W11 8 E7
Pembroke Av BRYLDS KT5 199 N5
EN EN1 80 A5
KTN/HRWW/W HA3 114 F1
RSLP HA4 113 L6
WOT/HER KT12 217 L1
Pembroke Cl ASC SL5 192 C5
BNSTD SM7 239 L3
BROX EN10 44 D10
EMPK RM11 125 P2
ERITH DA8 164 D3
KTBR SW1X 16 D2
Pembroke Dr CHESW EN7 61 J5
Pembroke Gdns DAGE RM10 124 C8
KENS W8 14 D5
WOKS/MYFD GU22 232 D4
Pembroke Gardens Cl KENS W8 14 D4
Pembroke Ldg STAN * HA7 95 H7
Pembroke Ms KENS * W8 14 E4
MUSWH N10 98 B9
SEV * TN13 265 K1
Pembroke Pde ERITH * DA8 164 D4
Pembroke Pl EDGW HA8 95 M8
EYN DA4 210 A1
ISLW TW7 154 D8
KENS * W8 14 E4
Pembroke Rd BMLY BR1 205 P2
CEND/HSY/T N8 118 F2
CRAWE RH10 284 D4
ECT SW5 14 E5
EHAM E6 142 C7
ERITH DA8 164 D4
GDMY/SEVK IG3 123 J6
GFD/PVL UB6 134 A6
MTCM CR4 202 B2
MUSWH N10 98 B9
NTHWD HA6 92 D4
PLMGR N13 99 K4
RSLP HA4 112 F6
SEV TN13 265 J1
SEVS/STOTM N15 119 N3
SNWD SE25 203 M4
WALTH E17 120 G3
WBLY HA9 115 J8
WKENS W14 14 D5
WOKS/MYFD GU22 232 D3
Pembroke Sq KENS W8 14 E4
Pembroke St IS N1 5 M4
Pembroke Ter STJWD * NW8 3 L6
Pembroke Vls KENS W8 14 E4
Pembroke Wk KENS W8 14 E5
Pembrook Ms BTSEA * SW11 157 N10
Pembury Av WPK KT4 200 D7
Pembury Cl CLPT * E5 120 A10
COUL/CHIP CR5 222 B10
HAYES BR2 205 L7
Pembury Ct HYS/HAR UB3 152 E5
Pembury Crs SCUP DA14 185 P5
Pembury Rd BXLYHN DA7 163 P6
CLPT E5 120 A10
SNWD SE25 203 P4
TOTM N17 99 N9
Pemdevon Rd CROY/NA CR0 203 H7
Pemell Cl WCHPL E1 140 B6
Pemerich Cl HYS/HAR * UB3 152 G4
Pempath Pl WBLY HA9 115 J7
Pemsel Ct HHS/BOV HP3 35 P8
Penally Pl IS N1 7 H5
Penang St WAP E1W 140 A10
Penard Rd NWDGN UB2 153 P2
Penarth St PECK SE15 160 B5
Penates ESH/CLAY KT10 218 C1
Penberth Rd CAT SE6 183 H5

Penbury Rd NWDGN UB2 153 N4
Pencombe Ms NTGHL W11 8 D7
Pencraig Wy PECK * SE15 160 A5
Pencroft Dr DART DA1 187 K3
Pendall Cl EBAR EN4 77 P8
Penda Rd ERITH DA8 164 C6
Pendarves Rd RYNPK SW20 200 F1
Penda's Md HOM E9 120 D9
Pendell Av HYS/HAR UB3 152 G6
Pendell Ms REDH * RH1 276 A1
Pendell Rd REDH RH1 259 J7
Pendennis Cl BF/WBF KT14 215 K10
Pendennis Ct HARP AL5 20 C4
Pendennis Rd ORP BR6 207 M9
SEV TN13 247 J9
STRHM/NOR SW16 180 F7
TOTM N17 119 L1
Penderel Rd HSLW TW3 175 P1
Penderry Ri CAT SE6 183 J5
Penderyn Wy HOLWY N7 118 E9
Pendle Ct HGDN/ICK * UB10 132 C3
Pendle Rd STRHM/NOR SW16 180 C9
Pendlestone Rd LEY E10 120 G3
Pendleton Cl REDH RH1 276 A2
Pendleton Rd REDH RH1 275 N3
Pendragon Rd BMLY BR1 183 M6
Pendrell Rd BROCKY SE4 160 D9
Pendrell St WOOL/PLUM SE18 162 G5
Pendula Dr YEAD UB4 133 L6
Pendulum Ms HACK * E8 119 N10
Penenden HART DA3 211 L9
Penerley Rd CAT SE6 182 G4
RAIN RM13 145 J7
Penfold Cl CROY/NA CR0 203 H10
Penfold Pl BAY/PAD W2 9 N3
Penfold Rd ED N9 100 C2
Penfold St STJWD NW8 9 M2
Penford Gdns ELTH/MOT SE9 162 A10
Penford St CMBW SE5 159 J8
Pengarth Rd BXLY DA5 185 N1
Penge La PGE/AN SE20 182 B10
Pengelly Cl CHESW EN7 62 A6
Penge Rd PLSTW E13 141 P2
SNWD SE25 203 P3
Penhall Rd CHARL SE7 162 A3
Penhill Rd BXLY DA5 185 M3
Penhurst WOKN/KNAP GU21 214 C10
Penhurst Rd BARK/HLT IG6 102 E8
Penifather La GFD/PVL UB6 134 C5
Penington Rd BEAC HP9 108 A1
Peninsular Cl EBED/NFELT TW14 174 E2
Peninsular Park Rd CHARL SE7 161 M4
Penistone Rd STRHM/NOR SW16 180 F10
Penlow Rd HLWS CM18 46 F4
Penman Cl LCOL/BKTW AL2 55 P3
Penmon Rd ABYW SE2 163 K2
Pennack Rd PECK SE15 19 M10
Pennant Ms KENS W8 14 G5
Pennant Ter WALTH E17 100 E10
Pennard Rd SHB W12 156 F1
The Pennards SUN TW16 197 K3
Penn Av CSHM HP5 50 F6
Penn Cl CRAWW RH11 283 N4
GFD/PVL UB6 134 A4
KTN/HRWW/W HA3 115 H2
RKW/CH/CXG WD3 70 G10
UX/CGN UB8 131 N6
Penn Ct CRAWW * RH11 283 J7
Penn Dr DEN/HRF UB9 111 J4
Penne Cl RAD WD7 56 F10
Penner Cl WIM/MER SW19 179 H5
Penners Gdns SURB KT6 199 K7
Pennethorne Cl HOM E9 140 B3
Pennethorne Rd PECK SE15 160 A6
Penney Cl DART DA1 187 L3
Penn Gdns CHST BR7 206 E2
CRW RM5 104 B8
Penn Gaskell La CFSP/GDCR SL9 90 C6
Pennine Cl CRAWW RH11 283 L7
Pennine Dr CRICK NW2 116 G7
Pennine La CRICK NW2 117 H7
Pennine Pde CRICK * NW2 117 H7
Pennine Rd SLN SL2 128 F7
Pennine Wy BXLYHN DA7 164 F7
GVW DA11 190 B6
HHNE HP2 36 A3
HYS/HAR UB3 152 E6
Pennings Av GUW GU2 249 L7
Pennington Cl CRW RM5 104 B7
Pennington Dr STHGT/OAK N14 78 F9
WEY KT13 196 F10
Pennington Rd CFSP/GDCR SL9 90 A8
The Penningtons AMS HP6 69 K3
Pennington St WAP E1W 140 A9
Pennington Wy LEE/GVPK SE12 183 N5
Penniston Cl WDGN N22 99 K10
Penn La BXLY DA5 185 N2
RSEV TN14 263 P3
Penn Meadow SLN SL2 129 L3
Penn Rd BEAC HP9 88 B6
DTCH/LGLY SL3 150 A7
HOLWY N7 118 F10
LCOL/BKTW AL2 56 B3
RKW/CH/CXG WD3 91 J2
SLN SL2 129 J6
Penn St IS N1 7 H6
Penn Wy RKW/CH/CXG WD3 70 G10
Penny Cl RAIN RM13 145 J5
Pennycroft SAND/SEL CR2 224 D5
Penny Dr RGUW GU3 248 G9
Pennyfield COB KT11 217 H9
Penny Flds BRW CM14 107 H5
Pennyfields POP/IOD E14 140 F9
Penny La SHPTN TW17 196 F7
Pennylets Gn SLN SL2 129 L2
Pennymead HLW CM20 47 K1
Pennymead Dr EHSLY KT24 252 G3
Pennymoor Wk MV/WKIL * W9 8 D1
Pennypot La CHOB/PIR GU24 212 G9
Pennyroyal Av EHAM E6 142 D8
Penpoll Rd HACK E8 140 A1
Penpool La WELL DA16 163 L9
Penrhyn Av WALTH E17 100 F9
Penrhyn Crs MORT/ESHN * SW14 155 P10
WALTH E17 100 F9
Penrhyn Gdns KUT * KT1 199 J4
Penrhyn Gv WALTH E17 100 F9
Penrhyn Rd KUT KT1 199 K4
Penrith Cl BECK BR3 204 G1
PUT/ROE SW15 179 H1
REDH RH1 257 P9
Penrith Crs RAIN RM13 125 H10
Penrith Pl STRHM/NOR SW16 181 J5
Penrith Rd BARK/HLT IG6 103 J7
HARH RM3 105 P7
NWMAL KT3 200 A4
SEVS/STOTM N15 119 L3
THHTH CR7 203 K2
Penrith St STRHM/NOR SW16 180 D9
Penrose Av OXHEY WD19 93 M3
Penrose Ct EGH TW20 171 P9
HHNE HP2 35 P2
Penrose Gv WALW SE17 18 E8
Penrose Rd LHD/OX KT22 236 B8
Penrose St WALW SE17 18 E8
Penryn St CAMTN NW1 5 J7
Penry St STHWK SE1 19 K6
Pensbury Pl VX/NE SW8 158 D8
Pensbury St VX/NE SW8 158 D8
Penscroft Gdns BORE WD6 76 A8
Pensford Av RCH/KEW TW9 155 M8
Penshurst HLWE CM17 29 L8
Penshurst Av BFN/LL DA15 185 K2
Penshurst Cl CFSP/GDCR SL9 90 A10
CRAWE RH10 284 E6
Penshurst Gdns EDGW HA8 95 N6
Penshurst Gn HAYES BR2 205 L5
Penshurst Rd BXLYHN DA7 164 A7
HOM E9 140 C2
POTB/CUF EN6 59 N7
THHTH CR7 203 J5
TOTM N17 99 N8
Penshurst Wy BELMT SM2 221 K4
STMC/STPC BR5 207 M4
Pensilver Cl EBAR * EN4 77 P8
Penson's La CHONG CM5 67 H4
Penstemon Cl FNCH N3 97 K7
Penta Ct BORE * WD6 75 M8
Pentelow Gdns
EBED/NFELT TW14 175 H2
Pentire Cl UPMR RM14 126 D4
Pentire Rd WALTH E17 101 J9
Pentland HHNE HP2 36 A3
Pentland Av EDGW HA8 95 N3
SHPTN TW17 196 B5
Pentland Cl CRICK NW2 117 H7
ED N9 100 B3
Pentland Pl NTHLT UB5 133 M3
Pentland Rd BUSH WD23 74 B10
SLN SL2 128 F7
Pentlands Cl MTCM CR4 202 C3
Pentland St WAND/EARL SW18 179 M2
Pentland Wy HGDN/ICK UB10 112 D8
Pentley Pk WGCW AL8 22 G2
Pentlow St PUT/ROE SW15 156 F8
Pentlow Wy BKHH IG9 102 B1
Pentney Rd BAL SW12 180 D4
CHING E4 101 J2
RYNPK SW20 201 H1
Penton Av STA TW18 173 J10
Penton Dr CHES/WCR EN8 62 C5
Penton Gv IS N1 6 A8
Penton Hall Dr STA TW18 195 K1
Penton Hook Rd STA TW18 173 K10
Penton Pl WALW SE17 18 E7
Penton Ri FSBYW WC1X 5 P9
Penton Rd STA TW18 173 J10
Penton St IS N1 6 A7
Pentonville Rd IS N1 5 N8
Pentreath Av GUW GU2 267 L1
Pentrich Av EN EN1 79 P4
Pentridge St PECK SE15 159 N6
Pentstemon Dr SWCM DA10 189 K1
Pentyre Av UED N18 99 L6
Penventon Ct TIL * RM18 168 D8
Penwerris Av ISLW TW7 154 B6
Penwith Rd WAND/EARL SW18 179 L5
Penwith Wk WOKS/MYFD GU22 232 A5
Penwood End
WOKS/MYFD GU22 231 N7
Penwortham Rd SAND/SEL CR2 223 L6
STRHM/NOR SW16 180 C9
Penylan Pl EDGW * HA8 95 M9
Penywern Rd ECT SW5 14 F7
Penzance Cl DEN/HRF * UB9 91 N9
Penzance Gdns HARH RM3 105 P7
Penzance Pl NTGHL W11 8 A9
Penzance Rd HARH RM3 105 P7
Penzance Sp SLN SL2 128 G6
Penzance St NTGHL W11 8 A9
Peony Gdns SHB W12 136 D9
Peplins Cl BRKMPK AL9 59 H2
Peplins Wy BRKMPK AL9 59 H1
Peploe Rd KIL/WHAMP NW6 136 G4
Peplow Cl WDR/YW UB7 131 N10
Peppard Rd CRAWE RH10 284 E9
Pepper Cl CTHM CR3 259 M1
EHAM E6 142 C7
Pepper Hl GVW DA11 189 P6
WARE SG12 26 E6
Peppermead Sq BROCKY * SE4 182 F1
Peppermint Cl CROY/NA CR0 202 F7
Peppermint Pl WAN E11 121 K8
Pepper St POP/IOD E14 160 G2
STHWK SE1 18 E1
Peppett's Gn CSHM HP5 32 C9
Peppie Cl STNW/STAM N16 119 M7
Pepys Cl ASHTD KT21 237 M3
DTCH/LGLY SL3 150 E5
GVW DA11 190 A6
HGDN/ICK UB10 112 C9
TIL RM18 168 F7
Pepys Crs BAR EN5 76 F9
Pepys Est DEPT SE8 160 E4
Pepys Park Est DEPT SE8 160 E3
Pepys Ri ORP BR6 207 J8
Pepys Rd NWCR SE14 160 C7
RYNPK SW20 200 F1
Pepys St TWRH EC3N 13 K7
Perceval Av HAMP NW3 117 P10
Percheron Dr WOKN/KNAP GU21 230 G5
Percheron Rd BORE WD6 76 A10
Perch St HACK E8 119 N9
Percival Ct TOTM N17 99 N8
Percival Gdns CHDH RM6 123 M4
Percival Rd EMPK RM11 125 K4
EN EN1 79 N8
FELT TW13 174 G5
MORT/ESHN SW14 177 P1
ORP BR6 206 E9
Percival St FSBYE EC1V 12 C1
Percival Wy HOR/WEW KT19 219 P1
Percy Av ASHF TW15 174 B8
Percy Bryant Rd SUN TW16 174 F10
Percy Bush Rd WDR/YW UB7 152 A2
Percy Gdns PEND EN3 80 C9
WPK KT4 200 A8
YEAD UB4 132 F5
Percy Ms FITZ W1T 11 J4
Percy Rd BXLYHN DA7 163 P8
CAN/RD E16 141 K7
GDMY/SEVK IG3 123 K5
GUW GU2 249 N8
HPTN TW12 175 P10
ISLW TW7 154 F10
MTCM CR4 202 B7
NFNCH/WDSP N12 97 M6
PGE/AN SE20 204 C1
ROMW/RG RM7 124 D1
SHB W12 156 D1
SNWD SE25 203 N5
WAN E11 121 K5
WATW WD18 73 M10
WCHMH N21 99 K1
WHTN TW2 176 A4
Percy St FITZ W1T 11 J4
GRAYS RM17 167 P5
Percy Ter CSTG HP8 89 M4
Percy Wy WHTN TW2 176 B4
Peregrine Cl GSTN WD25 55 M10
WLSDN NW10 116 A10
Peregrine Ct WELL DA16 163 J7
Peregrine Gdns CROY/NA CR0 204 D9
Peregrine Rd BARK/HLT IG6 103 L6
SUN TW16 196 F2
Peregrine Wy WIM/MER SW19 178 F10
Peregrin Rd WAB EN9 63 M10
Perham Rd WKENS W14 14 C8
Perham Wy LCOL/BKTW AL2 57 J2
Peridot St EHAM E6 142 B7
Perifield DUL SE21 181 K4
Perimeade Rd GFD/PVL UB6 135 H4
Perimeter Rd East HORL RH6 280 C8
Perimeter Rd North HORL RH6 279 N8
Perimeter Rd South HORL RH6 280 A10
Periton Rd ELTH/MOT SE9 162 A10
Perivale Gdns GSTN WD25 55 J10
WEA W13 134 G6
Perivale La GFD/PVL UB6 134 F5
Perivale Village GFD/PVL * UB6 135 H5
Perkin Cl ALP/SUD HA0 114 G10
Perkins Cl GRH DA9 188 E1
Perkin's Rents WEST SW1P 17 J3
Perkins Rd BARK/HLT IG6 123 J2
Perkins Sq STHWK SE1 12 F9
Perks Cl BKHTH/KID SE3 161 K8
Perleybrooke La
WOKN/KNAP GU21 231 M3
Permain Cl RAD WD7 57 K9
Perpins Rd ELTH/MOT SE9 185 H2
Perram Cl BROX EN10 62 D2
Perran Cl HART DA3 211 L4
Perran Rd BRXS/STRHM SW2 181 J5
Perren St KTTN * NW5 4 E1
Perrers Rd HMSMTH W6 156 E2
Perrin Cl ASHF TW15 174 A8
Perrin Ct WOKN/KNAP GU21 232 E1
Perrin Rd ALP/SUD HA0 114 F9
Perrin's Ct HAMP * NW3 117 M9
Perrin's Wk HAMP NW3 117 M9
Perrior Rd RGODL GU7 267 K10
Perriors Cl CHESW EN7 61 P3
Perry Av ACT W3 136 A8
Perry Cl RAIN RM13 144 E4
UX/CGN UB8 132 C8
Perry Ct SEVS/STOTM * N15 119 M4
Perrycroft WDSR SL4 148 E9
Perryfield HLWE CM17 31 K9
Perryfield Rd CRAWW RH11 283 N8
Perryfields Wy SL SL1 128 A6
Perryfield Wy CDALE/KGS NW9 116 C4
RCHPK/HAM TW10 176 G5
Perry Gdns ED N9 99 M4
Perry Garth NTHLT UB5 133 K3
Perry Gv DART DA1 165 P10
Perry Hall Cl ORP BR6 207 K7
Perry Hall Rd ORP BR6 207 J6
Perry Hl CAT SE6 182 E5
WAB EN9 45 L8
Perry How WPK KT4 200 C8
Perrylands HORL RH6 279 J8
Perrylands La HORL RH6 280 G5
Perry Mnr CHST BR7 185 H9
Perrymans Farm Rd
GNTH/NBYPK IG2 122 G4
Perryman Wy SLN SL2 128 E5
Perry Md BUSH WD23 74 B10
ENC/FH EN2 79 J6
Perrymead St FUL/PGN SW6 157 K7
Perryn Rd ACT W3 136 A9
BERM/RHTH SE16 160 A2
Perry Oak Dr HTHAIR TW6 151 N8
Perry Oaks Dr WDR/YW UB7 151 H8
Perry Ri FSTH SE23 182 D6
Perry Rd HLWS CM18 46 F2
Perrysfield Rd CHES/WCR EN8 62 C4
Perrys La ORP BR6 227 L9
Perry Spring HLWE CM17 47 M3
Perry St CHST BR7 185 H9
DART DA1 164 F9
GVW DA11 190 B4
Perry V FSTH SE23 182 B5
Perry Wy SOCK/AV RM15 146 B9
Perrywood WGCW * AL8 22 G3
Persant Rd CAT SE6 183 K6
Perseverance Pl BRXN/ST * SW9 159 H6
Persfield Ms EW * KT17 220 C6
Persfield Rd EW KT17 220 D6
Pershore Cl GNTH/NBYPK IG2 122 E3
Pershore Gv CAR SM5 201 N6
Pert Cl MUSWH N10 98 C8
Perth Av CDALE/KGS NW9 116 A5
SL SL1 128 G8
YEAD UB4 133 K6
Perth Cl CRAWW RH11 283 N4
RYNPK SW20 200 C2
Perth Rd BARK IG11 142 G4
BECK BR3 205 H2
FSBYPK N4 119 H6
GNTH/NBYPK IG2 122 E4
LEY E10 120 D6
PLSTW E13 141 N4
WDGN N22 99 J9
Perth Ter GNTH/NBYPK IG2 122 F5
Perwell Av RYLN/HDSTN HA2 113 N6
Pescot Av HART DA3 211 M3
Pescot Hl HHW HP1 35 L4
Petauel Rd TEDD TW11 176 D8
Petavel Rd TEDD TW11 176 D9
Peter Av OXTED RH8 261 J5
WLSDN NW10 136 E2
Peterboat Cl GNWCH SE10 161 K3
Peterborough Av UPMR RM14 126 D6
Peterborough Ms FUL/PGN SW6 157 K8
Peterborough Rd CAR SM5 201 P6
FUL/PGN SW6 157 K8
GUW GU2 249 L8
HRW HA1 114 D6
LEY E10 121 H3
Peterborough Vls FUL/PGN SW6 157 L7
Petergate BTSEA SW11 157 M10
Peterhead Ms DTCH/LGLY SL3 150 D4
Peterhill Cl CFSP/GDCR SL9 90 B6
Peterlee Ct HHNE HP2 36 A2
Peters Av LCOL/BKTW AL2 57 H2
Peters Cl BCTR RM8 123 N6
EDGW HA8 95 J7
WELL DA16 163 H8
Petersfield STALW/RED AL3 38 D2
Petersfield Av HARH RM3 105 M7
SLN SL2 129 M10
STA TW18 173 M8
Petersfield Cl HARH RM3 105 P7
UED N18 99 K6
Petersfield Crs COUL/CHIP CR5 240 F1
Petersfield Ri PUT/ROE SW15 178 E4
Petersfield Rd ACT W3 155 P1
STA TW18 173 M8
Petersham Av BF/WBF KT14 215 P8
Petersham Cl BF/WBF KT14 215 P8
RCHPK/HAM TW10 177 J5
SUT SM1 221 J2
Petersham Dr STMC/STPC BR5 207 J2
Petersham Gdns
STMC/STPC BR5 207 J2
Petersham La SKENS SW7 15 J3
Petersham Ms SKENS SW7 15 J4
Petersham Pl SKENS SW7 15 J4
Petersham Rd
RCHPK/HAM TW10 177 K2
Petersham Ter CROY/NA * CR0 202 F10
Peter's Hl BLKFR EC4V 12 E7
Petersmead Cl
KWD/TDW/WH KT20 238 F9
Peter's Pl BERK HP4 33 K3
Peterstone Rd ABYW SE2 163 L1
Peterstow Cl WIM/MER SW19 179 H5
Peter St SOHO/CST W1F 11 J7
Peterswood HLWS CM18 46 G5
Peters Wood Hl WARE SG12 26 C4
Peterwood Wy CROY/NA CR0 202 G9
Petherton Rd HBRY N5 119 K10
Petiver Cl HOM * E9 140 B2
Petley Rd HMSMTH W6 156 F5
Peto Pl CAMTN NW1 10 F1
Petre Cl RBRW/HUT CM13 127 P4
Petresfield Wy RBRW/HUT CM13 127 P4
Petridge Rd REDH RH1 276 A5
Petrie Cl CRICK * NW2 2 B1
Petros Gdns HAMP NW3 3 H1
Pett Cl EMPK RM12 125 J7
Petten Cl STMC/STPC BR5 207 N8
Petten Gv STMC/STPC BR5 207 M8
Petters Rd ASHTD KT21 237 L2
Petticoat Sq WCHPL E1 13 L5
Petticoat Tower WCHPL * E1 13 L5
Pettits Bvd GPK RM2 104 F10
Pettits Cl ROM RM1 104 F10
Pettits La BRWN CM15 87 K3
ROM RM1 124 F1
Pettits La North ROM RM1 104 E9
Pettit's Pl DAGE RM10 124 B10
Pettit's Rd DAGE RM10 124 B10
Pettiward Cl PUT/ROE SW15 156 F10
Pettley Gdns ROMW/RG RM7 124 E3
Pettman Crs THMD SE28 162 G2
Pettsgrove Av ALP/SUD HA0 115 H10
Pett's Hl RYLN/HDSTN HA2 114 A9
Petts La SHPTN TW17 196 B4
Pett St CHARL SE7 162 B3
Petts Wood Rd STMC/STPC BR5 206 G5
Petty France STJSPK SW1H 17 H3
Pettys Cl CHES/WCR EN8 62 C4
Petworth Cl COUL/CHIP CR5 240 D5
NTHLT UB5 133 N2
Petworth Ct CRAWW RH11 283 J10
Petworth Gdns HGDN/ICK UB10 132 D3
RYNPK SW20 200 E3
Petworth Rd BXLYHS DA6 186 B1
NFNCH/WDSP N12 97 P6
Petworth St BTSEA SW11 157 P7
Petworth Wy HCH RM12 124 G9
Petyt Pl CHEL SW3 15 N10
Petyward CHEL SW3 15 P6
Pevensey Av EN EN1 79 L6
FBAR/BDGN N11 98 E6
Pevensey Cl CRAWE RH10 284 D8
ISLW TW7 154 B6
Pevensey Rd FELT TW13 175 M4
FSTGT E7 121 M9
SLN SL2 128 F7
TOOT SW17 179 N7
Peverel Rd CRAWW RH11 283 H8
Peveret Cl FBAR/BDGN * N11 98 C6
Peveril Dr TEDD TW11 176 C8
Pewley Bank GU GU1 268 B2
Pewley Hl GU GU1 268 A2
Pewley Point GU GU1 268 B2
Pewley Wy GU GU1 268 B2
Pewsey Cl CHING E4 100 F6
Peyton Pl GNWCH SE10 161 H6
Pharaoh Cl MTCM CR4 202 A7
Pheasant Cl BERK HP4 33 P6
CAN/RD E16 141 N8
PUR/KEN CR8 223 J9
Pheasant Hl CSTG HP8 89 P3
Pheasant Ri CSHM HP5 51 J9
Pheasants Wy RKW/CH/CXG WD3 91 L1
Pheasant Wk CFSP/GDCR SL9 90 A5
Phelips Rd EPP CM16 46 D6
Phelp St WALW SE17 18 G8
Phelps Wy HYS/HAR UB3 152 G3
Phene St CHEL SW3 15 P9
Philanthropic Rd REDH RH1 276 B1
Philan Wy CRW RM5 104 E7
Philbeach Gdns ECT SW5 14 D6
Philbye Ms SL SL1 148 E1
Philchurch Pl WCHPL E1 13 P6
Philip Av ROMW/RG RM7 124 E6
Philip Cl BRWN CM15 86 G10
Philip Gdns CROY/NA CR0 204 E9
Philip La SEVS/STOTM N15 119 L2
Philippa Gdns ELTH/MOT SE9 184 A1
Philip Rd PECK SE15 159 P9
RAIN RM13 144 F5
STA TW18 173 N9
Philips Cl MTCM CR4 202 B8
Philip St PLSTW E13 141 M6
Philip Sydney Rd WTHK RM20 167 J4
Phillida Rd HARH RM3 105 P10
Phillimore Ct RAD * WD7 74 D2
Phillimore Gdns KENS W8 14 E2
WLSDN NW10 136 F3
Phillimore Gardens Cl KENS * W8 14 E3
Phillimore Pl KENS W8 14 E2
RAD WD7 74 D2
Phillimore Wk KENS W8 14 E3
Phillip Av SWLY BR8 208 E4
Phillipers GSTN WD25 73 M1
Phillipp St IS N1 7 K6
Phillips Cl DART DA1 187 J2
Phillips Hatch SHGR GU5 268 F9
Philpot La CHOB/PIR GU24 213 P8
FENCHST EC3M 13 J7
Philpots Cl WDR/YW UB7 131 N9
Philpot St WCHPL * E1 140 A8
Phineas Pett Road Rd
ELTH/MOT SE9 162 B9
Phipp's Bridge Rd
WIM/MER SW19 201 M2
Phipps Hatch La ENC/FH EN2 79 K4
Phipps Rd SL SL1 128 C7
Phipp St SDTCH EC2A 13 J1
Phoebeth Rd LEW SE13 182 F1
Phoenix Cl HACK * E8 7 L5
NTHWD HA6 92 G5
WWKM BR4 205 J9
Phoenix Ct BTFD TW8 155 K4
GU * GU1 268 A2
Phoenix Dr HAYES BR2 226 A1
Phoenix Pk BTFD * TW8 155 J4
Phoenix Pl DART DA1 187 L3
FSBYW WC1X 11 P1
Phoenix Rd CAMTN NW1 5 J9
PGE/AN SE20 182 B9
Phoenix St LSQ/SEVD WC2H 11 K6
Phoenix Wy HEST TW5 153 L5
Phoenix Wharf Rd STHWK SE1 19 M2
The Phygtle CFSP/GDCR SL9 90 B7
Phyllis Av NWMAL KT3 200 E5
The Piazza COVGDN WC2E 11 M7
Picardy Manorway BELV DA17 164 C1
Picardy Rd BELV DA17 164 B4
Picardy St BELV DA17 164 B2
Piccadilly MYFR/PICC W1J 10 E10
Piccadilly Ar MYFR/PICC W1J 10 G9
Piccadilly Circ MYFR/PICC W1J 11 J8
Piccotts End HHW HP1 35 M4
Piccotts End La HHNE HP2 35 M3
Piccotts End Rd HHW HP1 35 L2
Pickard St FSBYE EC1V 6 D9
Pickering Av EHAM E6 142 D4
Pickering Gdns FBAR/BDGN N11 98 B7
SNWD SE25 203 N6
Pickering Pl STJS * SW1Y 11 H10
Pickering St IS N1 6 D5
Pickets Cl BUSH WD23 94 C2
Pickets St BAL SW12 180 B3
Pickett Cft STAN HA7 95 J9
Picketts WGCW AL8 22 G2
Picketts La REDH RH1 276 D9
Pickett's Lock La ED N9 100 C3
Pickford Cl BXLYHN DA7 163 P8
Pickford Dr DTCH/LGLY SL3 130 B10
Pickford La BXLYHN DA7 163 P8
Pickford Rd BXLYHN DA7 163 P8
Pickfords Gdns SL SL1 129 K10
Pickfords Whf IS * N1 6 E8
Pick Hl WAB EN9 63 M8
Pickhurst Gn HAYES BR2 205 L7
Pickhurst La HAYES BR2 205 K5
Pickhurst Md HAYES BR2 205 L7
Pickhurst Pk HAYES BR2 205 K5
Pickhurst Ri WWKM BR4 205 J8
Pickins Piece DTCH/LGLY SL3 150 D8
Pickwick Cl HSLWW TW4 175 M1
Pickwick Gdns GVW DA11 190 A6
Pickwick Ms UED N18 99 M6
Pickwick Pl HRW HA1 114 D5
Pickwick Rd DUL SE21 181 L3
Pickwick St STHWK SE1 18 E2
Pickwick Wy CHST BR7 184 F9
Pickworth Cl VX/NE * SW8 158 F6
Picquets Wy BNSTD SM7 239 H2
Picton Pl MBLAR W1H 10 D6
Picton St CMBW SE5 159 L6
Piedmont Rd WOOL/PLUM SE18 162 G4
Pield Heath Av UX/CGN UB8 132 B6
Pield Heath Rd UX/CGN UB8 132 B7
Piercing Hl EPP CM16 82 G1
Pier Head WAP * E1W 140 A10
Pierian Spring HHW HP1 35 L4
Piermont Pl BMLY BR1 206 A2
Piermont Rd EDUL SE22 182 A1
Pierrepoint Ar IS * N1 6 C7
Pierrepoint Rd ACT W3 135 N9
Pierrepoint Rw IS N1 6 C7
Pier Rd CAN/RD E16 162 C1
EBED/NFELT TW14 175 J1
ERITH DA8 164 F5
GRH DA9 166 G10
GVW DA11 190 C2
Pierson Rd WDSR SL4 148 C8
Pier St POP/IOD E14 161 H3
Pier Ter WAND/EARL SW18 157 L10
Pier Wy WOOL/PLUM SE18 162 G2
Pier Whf GRAYS * RM17 167 M6
Pigeonhouse La COUL/CHIP CR5 257 M1
Pigeon La HPTN TW12 175 P7
Piggottshill La HARP AL5 20 B4
Piggotts Orch AMSS HP7 68 G6
Piggs Cnr GRAYS * RM17 167 P2
Pigott St POP/IOD E14 140 F8
Pike Cl BMLY BR1 183 N8
Pike La UPMR RM14 126 E10
Pike Rd MLHL NW7 96 A5
Pike's End PIN HA5 113 J2
Pikes Hl EW KT17 220 B9
Pikestone Cl YEAD * UB4 133 M6
Pike Wy EPP CM16 66 B3
Pilgrimage St STHWK SE1 18 G2
Pilgrim Cl GSTN WD25 55 L9
LCOL/BKTW AL2 56 B3
MRDN SM4 201 L7
Pilgrim Hl WNWD SE27 181 K7
Pilgrims Cl BRWN CM15 86 E9
NTHLT UB5 114 B10
PLMGR N13 98 G5
RDKG RH5 254 F8
SHGR GU5 270 B5
Pilgrims Ct DART DA1 187 P1
Pilgrim's La BRW CM14 86 C8
CDH/CHF RM16 147 H10
CDH/CHF RM16 167 J3
CTHM CR3 258 G2
HAMP NW3 117 N9
OXTED RH8 243 P10
Pilgrims Ms POP/IOD E14 141 J9
Pilgrims Pl ASHF * TW15 174 A7
REIG RH2 257 K8
Pilgrim's Ri EBAR EN4 77 P9
Pilgrims' Rd SWCM DA10 167 K10
Pilgrim St BLKFR * EC4V 12 C6
Pilgrims Vw GRH DA9 189 H2
Pilgrims Wy ARCH N19 118 E6
CHOB/PIR GU24 230 F2
DART DA1 188 A4
RDKG RH5 254 G7
REIG RH2 257 J8
RGUE GU4 268 B4
RSEV TN14 247 M2
SAND/SEL CR2 223 N3
SAND/SEL * CR2 223 N2
SHGR GU5 270 B5
SWLY HA9 115 N6
Pilgrims Wy East RSEV TN14 247 K2
Pilgrims Wy West RSEV TN14 246 G2
Pilkington Rd ORP BR6 206 F10

PECK SE15 160 A8
Pilkingtons HLWE CM17 47 N1
Pilot Cl DEPT SE8 160 E5
Pilots Pl GVE DA12 190 F2
Pilsden Cl WIM/MER * SW19 178 G4
Piltdown Rd OXHEY WD19 93 L5
Pilton Pl WALW SE17 18 F7
Pimlico Rd BGVA SW1W 16 C7
Pimms Cl RGUE GU4 250 D6
Pinceybrook Rd HLWS CM18 46 F5
Pinchbeck Rd ORP BR6 227 J3
Pinchfield RKW/CH/CXG WD3 90 G6
Pinchin & Johnsons Yd WCHPL E1 13 P7
Pinchin St WCHPL E1 13 P7
Pincott La EHSLY KT24 252 C5
Pincott Pl BROCKY SE4 160 C9
Pincott Rd BXLYHS DA6 186 B1
WIM/MER SW19 179 M10
Pincroft Wd HART DA3 211 P4
Pindar Rd HOD EN11 45 H2
Pindar St SDTCH EC2A 13 J3
Pindock Ms MV/WKIL W9 9 H2
Pine Apple Ct WESTW * SW1E 16 G3
Pineapple Rd AMSS HP7 69 L5
Pine Av CHOB/PIR GU24 230 E7
GVE DA12 190 G4
SRTFD E15 121 J10
WWKM BR4 204 G8
Pine Cl ADL/WDHM KT15 215 L7
BERK HP4 33 N5
CHES/WCR EN8 62 B4
CRAWW RH11 283 M4
LEY E10 120 F7
NTHWD HA6 92 F7
PGE/AN SE20 204 B1
PUR/KEN CR8 241 K3
STAN HA7 94 G5
STHGT/OAK N14 98 D1
SWLY BR8 208 G4
WOKN/KNAP GU21 231 P3
Pine Coombe CROY/NA CR0 224 C1
Pinecote Dr ASC SL5 192 E7
Pine Ct UPMR RM14 125 P9
Pine Crs CAR SM5 221 N7
Pinecrest Gdns ORP BR6 226 E1
Pinecroft GPK RM2 125 K2
HHS/BOV HP3 36 A10
KTN/HRWW/W HA3 115 L3
RBRW/HUT CM13 107 N1
WELL DA16 163 K6
Pinecroft Crs BAR EN5 77 H8
Pine Dean GT/LBKH KT23 254 A1
Pinefield Cl POP/IOD * E14 140 F9
Pinefields ADL/WDHM * KT15 215 L1
Pine Gdns BRYLDS KT5 199 M6
HORL RH6 280 B5
RSLP HA4 113 J6
Pine Gld ORP BR6 226 C1
Pine Gv BFOR GU20 212 C3
BRKMPK AL9 59 L1
BUSH WD23 73 N5
FSBYPK N4 118 F7
LCOL/BKTW AL2 55 N6
TRDG/WHET N20 97 J2
WEY KT13 216 C2
WIM/MER SW19 179 J8
Pine Grove Ms WEY * KT13 216 D2
Pine Hl EPSOM KT18 238 A2
Pinehurst ASC SL5 192 C5
RSEV TN14 247 M7
Pinehurst Cl ABLGY WD5 54 F8
KWD/TDW/WH KT20 239 K8
Pinelands Cl BKHTH/KID * SE3 161 L6
Pinel Cl VW GU25 194 B4
Pinelees Ct MORT/ESHN * SW14 155 P10
Pinemartin Cl CRICK NW2 116 F8
Pineneedle La SEV TN13 247 J9
Pine Pk RGUW * GU3 248 F5
Pine Pl EW KT17 220 G10
Pine Rdg CAR SM5 222 B5
STAL * AL1 38 F9
Pine Rd CRICK NW2 116 F9
FBAR/BDGN N11 98 B3
WOKS/MYFD GU22 231 P6
Pines Av EN EN1 80 B2
Pines Cl AMS HP6 68 G5
Pine Shaw CRAWE RH10 284 D6
Pines Rd BMLY BR1 206 B2
The Pines BORE WD6 75 L6
CDH/CHF RM16 147 N10
HHW HP1 35 J10
NRWD * SE19 181 J9
PUR/KEN CR8 223 J9
SUN TW16 197 H3
WFD IG8 101 L4
WOKN/KNAP GU21 214 C10
Pine St CLKNW EC1R 12 A1
Pinetree Cl CFSP/GDCR SL9 89 P8
Pine Tree Cl HEST TW5 153 J7
HHNE HP2 35 N5
Pine Tree Hl WOKS/MYFD GU22 232 G2
Pine Trees STA * TW18 173 H8
Pinetrees Cl CRAWE RH10 285 J2
Pine Trees Dr HGDN/ICK UB10 111 P9
Pine View Cl RGUE GU4 269 J6
Pine Wk BELMT SM2 221 N6
BERK HP4 33 J2
BNSTD SM7 240 A2
BRYLDS KT5 199 M6
CAR SM5 221 N6
COB KT11 217 L10
CTHM CR3 241 M8
EHSLY KT24 252 G4
GT/LBKH KT23 254 A1
Pine Wy EGH TW20 171 N9
Pine Wd SUN TW16 197 H1
Pinewood WGCE AL7 23 H7
Pinewood Av ADL/WDHM KT15 215 M5
BFN/LL DA15 185 H4
PIN HA5 94 A7
RAIN RM13 145 J6
SEV TN13 247 L7
UX/CGN UB8 132 A8
Pinewood Cl BORE WD6 76 A5
CFSP/GDCR SL9 110 E4
CROY/NA CR0 204 D10
HLWE CM17 47 M3
IVER SL0 130 F2
ORP BR6 206 G8
PIN HA5 94 A7
STAL AL1 39 H6
TIL RM18 169 L2
WAT WD17 73 H5
WOKN/KNAP GU21 232 D1
Pinewood Dr ORP BR6 227 H2
POTB/CUF EN6 59 J7
STA * TW18 173 K8
Pinewood Gdns HHS/BOV HP3 35 P8
HHW HP1 35 L6
Pinewood Gn IVER SL0 130 F2
Pinewood Gv ADL/WDHM KT15 215 L6
WEA W13 135 H8
Pinewood Ldg BUSH * WD23 94 C2
Pinewood Ms STWL/WRAY TW19 173 N2
Pinewood Pk ADL/WDHM KT15 215 L7
Pinewood Rd ABR/ST RM4 104 D5
ABYW SE2 163 N5
FELT TW13 175 J6
HAYES BR2 205 M4
IVER SL0 130 E3
VW GU25 193 L4
Pinfold Rd BUSH WD23 73 N6
STRHM/NOR SW16 180 F7
Pinglestone Cl WDR/YW UB7 151 P6
Pinkcoat Cl FELT TW13 175 J6
Pinkham Wy North Circular Rd
MUSWH N10 98 A8
Pink La SL SL1 128 A4
Pinks Hl SWLY BR8 208 F5
Pinkwell Av HYS/HAR UB3 152 E3
Pinkwell La HYS/HAR UB3 152 D3
Pinley Gdns DAGW RM9 143 L3
Pinnacle Hl BXLYHN DA7 164 C10
Pinnacle Hl North BXLYHN DA7 164 C9
Pinnacles WAB EN9 63 K10
Pinnate Pl WGCE AL7 23 H9
Pinn Cl UX/CGN UB8 131 N8
Pinnell Rd ELTH/MOT SE9 162 A10
Pinner Ct PIN HA5 113 P2
Pinner Gn PIN HA5 93 K10
Pinner Gv PIN HA5 113 M2
Pinner Hl PIN HA5 93 J8
Pinner Hill Rd PIN HA5 93 K9
Pinner Park Av
RYLN/HDSTN HA2 94 B10
Pinner Park Gdns
RYLN/HDSTN HA2 94 B10
Pinner Rd HRW HA1 114 A3
NTHWD HA6 92 G9
OXHEY WD19 73 L10
PIN HA5 113 N2
Pinner Vw RYLN/HDSTN HA2 114 B2
Pinnock's Av GVW DA11 190 B1
Pinn Wy RSLP HA4 112 E5
Pinstone Wy CFSP/GDCR SL9 110 B7
Pintail Cl EHAM E6 142 B7
Pintail Rd WFD IG8 101 N8
Pintail Wy YEAD UB4 133 L7
Pinto Cl BORE * WD6 76 A10
Pinto Wy BKHTH/KID SE3 161 N10
Pioneer Cl SHB W12 136 E8
Pioneer St PECK SE15 159 P7
Pioneer Wy SHB W12 136 F8
SWLY BR8 208 F3
WATW WD18 72 G10
Piper Cl HOLWY N7 118 G10
Piper Rd KUT KT1 199 M3
Pipers Av HARP AL5 20 C4
Pipers Cl COB KT11 235 L1
SL SL1 128 B5
Piper's End VW GU25 194 A3
Pipers Gdns CROY/NA CR0 204 D7
Pipers Gn CDALE/KGS NW9 115 P3
Pipers Green La EDGW HA8 95 K4
Piper's Green Rd BH/WHM TN16 263 K4
Pipers La BH/WHM TN16 263 L3
HARP AL5 20 D4
Pipewell Rd CAR SM5 201 P6
Pippbrook Gdns DORK RH4 272 G1
Pippens WGCW AL8 23 H2
Pippin Cl CRICK NW2 116 D8
CROY/NA CR0 204 E8
RAD WD7 57 K9
Pippins Cl WDR/YW UB7 151 N2
Pippins Ct ASHF TW15 174 C9
The Pippins DTCH/LGLY SL3 130 C10
Piquet Rd PGE/AN SE20 204 B2
Pirbright Crs CROY/NA CR0 225 H3
Pirbright Rd RGUW GU3 248 B5
WAND/EARL SW18 179 J4
Pirbright Ter CHOB/PIR * GU24 230 E9
Pirie St CAN/RD E16 141 N10
Pirrip Cl GVE DA12 191 J4
Pirton Cl STALE/WH AL4 39 H1
Pishiobury Dr SBW CM21 29 N3
Pitcairn Cl ROMW/RG RM7 124 B2
Pitcairn Rd MTCM CR4 180 A10
Pitchfont La OXTED RH8 261 M2
Pitchford St SRTFD E15 141 J2
Pitch Pond Cl BEAC HP9 88 A6
Pit Farm Rd GU GU1 250 D10
Pitfield HART DA3 211 L4
Pitfield Crs THMD SE28 143 K10
Pitfield St IS N1 7 J8
Pitfield Wy PEND * EN3 80 B5
WLSDN NW10 135 P1
Pitfold Rd LEE/GVPK SE12 183 M3
Pitlake CROY/NA CR0 203 J9
Pitman St CMBW SE5 159 K6
Pitsea Pl WCHPL E1 140 C8
Pitsea St WCHPL E1 140 C8
Pitsfield WGCW AL8 22 G2
Pitshanger La EA W5 134 G6
Pitshanger Pk WEA W13 134 G5
Pitson Cl ADL/WDHM KT15 215 N1
Pitstone Cl STALE/WH AL4 39 H1
Pitt Crs WIM/MER SW19 179 L7
Pitt Dr STALE/WH AL4 39 H9
Pittman Cl RBRW/HUT CM13 107 P6
Pittman Gdns IL IG1 122 F10
Pittman's Fld HLW CM20 29 J10
Pitt Pl EW * KT17 220 B10
Pitt Rd EW KT17 220 B10
ORP BR6 226 F1
RYLN/HDSTN HA2 114 B7
THHTH CR7 203 K5
Pitt's Head Ms MYFR/PKLN W1K 10 D10
Pittsmead Av HAYES BR2 205 M7
Pitts Rd SL SL1 129 H10
Pitt St KENS W8 14 F1
Pittville Gdns SNWD SE25 203 P3
Pit Wood Gn
KWD/TDW/WH KT20 238 F6
Pix Farm La HHW HP1 34 E7
Pixham La DORK RH4 255 H9
Pixholme Gv DORK RH4 255 H10
Pixies Hill Crs HHW HP1 35 J8
Pixies Hill Rd HHW HP1 35 J7
Pixley St POP/IOD E14 140 E8
Pixton Wy CROY/NA CR0 224 D5
Place Farm Av ORP BR6 206 G8
Place Farm La BRWN CM15 86 F3
Place Farm Rd REDH RH1 259 L6
Placehouse La COUL/CHIP CR5 240 G5
Plackett Wy SL SL1 128 C10
Plaines Cl SL SL1 128 E10
The Plain EPP CM16 65 L5
Plaistow Gv BMLY BR1 183 N10
SRTFD E15 141 L3
Plaistow La BMLY BR1 183 M10
Plaistow Park Rd PLSTW E13 141 N4
Plaistow Rd PLSTW E13 141 M4
SRTFD E15 141 L3
Plaitford Cl RKW/CH/CXG WD3 91 P3
Plane Av GVW DA11 190 A3
The Planes CHERT KT16 195 M7
Plane St SYD SE26 182 A6
Plane Tree Crs FELT TW13 175 J6
Plantaganet Pl WAB EN9 62 G9
Plantagenet Cl HOR/WEW KT19 220 A1
Plantagenet Gdns CHDH RM6 123 N5
Plantagenet Pl CHDH RM6 123 N5
Plantagenet Rd BAR EN5 77 M8
Plantain Gdns WAN * E11 121 J8
Plantain Pl STHWK SE1 18 G1
Plantation Cl GRH DA9 188 E2
Plantation Dr STMC/STPC BR5 207 N8
Plantation La WARL CR6 242 D5
Plantation Rd AMS HP6 69 K3
ERITH DA8 165 H7
SWLY BR8 187 H10
The Plantation BKHTH/KID SE3 161 M8
Plantation Wk HHW HP1 35 K3
Plantation Wy AMS HP6 69 K3
Plashet Gdns RBRW/HUT CM13 107 M5
Plashet Gv EHAM E6 141 P3
Plashet Rd PLSTW E13 141 M3
Plashets RBSF CM22 30 D2
Plassy Rd CAT SE6 182 G3
Platford Gn EMPK RM11 125 M2
Platina St SDTCH EC2A 13 H1
Plato Rd CLAP SW4 158 F10
Platt Meadow RGUE GU4 250 G7
Platt's La HAMP NW3 117 K8
Platts Rd PEND EN3 80 B5
Platt St CAMTN NW1 5 J7
The Platt AMSS HP7 68 G6
Plawsfield Rd BECK BR3 204 C1
Plaxtol Cl BMLY BR1 205 P1
Plaxtol Rd ERITH DA8 164 B6
Playfair St HMSMTH * W6 156 F4
Playfield Av CRW RM5 104 D9
Playfield Crs EDUL SE22 181 M1
Playfield Rd EDGW HA8 95 P10
Playford Rd FSBYPK N4 118 G7
Playgreen Wy CAT SE6 182 F7
Playground Cl BECK BR3 204 C2
Playhouse Sq HLW CM20 46 F1
Playhouse Yd BLKFR EC4V 12 C6
Plaza Pde ALP/SUD * HA0 135 K1
Pleasance Rd PUT/ROE SW15 178 E1
STMC/STPC BR5 207 L2
The Pleasance PUT/ROE SW15 156 E10
Pleasant Gv CROY/NA CR0 204 E10
Pleasant Mt HERT/BAY SG13 26 B7
Pleasant Pl IS N1 6 D4
RKW/CH/CXG * WD3 91 H8
WOT/HER KT12 217 L3
Pleasant Ri BRKMPK AL9 40 F1
Pleasant Vw ERITH DA8 164 F4
ORP BR6 226 F2
Pleasant Wy ALP/SUD HA0 135 H4
Pleasure Pit Rd ASHTD KT21 237 N4
Plender St CAMTN NW1 4 G6
Pleshey Rd HOLWY N7 118 E9
Plesman Wy WLGTN * SM6 222 F5
Plevna Crs SEVS/STOTM N15 119 M4
Plevna Rd ED N9 99 P4
HPTN TW12 198 A1
Plevna St POP/IOD E14 161 H2
Pleydell Av HMSMTH W6 156 C2
NRWD SE19 181 N10
Pleydell Est FSBYE * EC1V 6 F10
Pleydell Gdns NRWD * SE19 181 N9
Pleydell St EMB EC4Y 12 B6
Plimsoll Cl POP/IOD E14 140 G8
Plimsoll Rd FSBYPK N4 119 J8
Plough Cl CRAWW RH11 283 J5
Plough Farm Cl RSLP HA4 112 E4
Plough Hl POTB/CUF EN6 60 F5
Plough La BERK HP4 34 E2
COB KT11 235 H2
CROY/NA CR0 222 F1
DEN/HRF UB9 91 M7
EDUL SE22 181 N2
PUR/KEN CR8 222 G6
RKW/CH/CXG WD3 53 J9
SLN SL2 129 N3
TEDD * TW11 176 F8
WIM/MER SW19 179 L8
WLGTN SM6 222 F5
Plough Lane Cl WLGTN SM6 222 F2
Ploughlees La SL SL1 129 K9
Ploughmans Cl CAMTN NW1 5 J5
Ploughmans End ISLW TW7 176 C1
WGCE AL7 23 M6
Plough Pl FLST/FETLN * EC4A 12 B5
Plough Ri UPMR RM14 126 D5
Plough Rd BTSEA SW11 157 N9
HOR/WEW KT19 220 A4
HORL RH6 281 K4
Plough St WCHPL * E1 13 N5
Plough Ter BTSEA SW11 157 N10
Plough Wy BERM/RHTH SE16 160 C3
Plough Yd SDTCH EC2A 13 K2
Plover Cl BERK HP4 33 P6
CRAWW RH11 283 M5
STA TW18 173 J6
Plover Gdns UPMR RM14 126 E6
Plovers Md BRWN CM15 87 J1
Plovers Ri CHOB/PIR GU24 230 D6
Plover Wy BERM/RHTH SE16 160 D2
YEAD UB4 133 L8
Plowden Buildings EMB * EC4Y 12 A7
Plowman Cl UED N18 99 L6
Plowman Wy BCTR RM8 123 M6
Ployters Rd HLWW/ROY CM19 46 F5
Plumbers Rw WCHPL E1 13 N4
Plumbridge St GNWCH * SE10 161 H7
Plum Garth BTFD TW8 155 J3
Plum La WOOL/PLUM SE18 162 E6
Plummer La MTCM CR4 202 A1
Plummer Rd CLAP SW4 180 D2
Plumpton Av HCH RM12 125 N8
Plumpton Cl NTHLT UB5 133 P1
Plumpton Rd HOD EN11 45 H1
Plumpton Wy CAR SM5 201 P10
Plumstead Common Rd
WOOL/PLUM SE18 162 F5
Plumstead High St
WOOL/PLUM SE18 162 G3
Plumstead Rd WOOL/PLUM SE18 162 F3
Plumtree Cl DAGE RM10 144 C1
Plumtree Ct FLST/FETLN EC4A 12 B5
Pluto Ri HHNE HP2 35 P4
Plymouth Dr BGR/WK TN15 247 K10
Plymouth Pk BGR/WK TN15 247 K10
Plymouth Rd BMLY BR1 205 N1
CAN/RD E16 141 M7
SL SL1 128 D8
WTHK RM20 167 H4
Plymouth Whf POP/IOD E14 161 J3
Plympton Av KIL/WHAMP NW6 2 C4
Plympton Cl BELV DA17 163 P2
Plympton Pl STJWD * NW8 9 N2
Plympton Rd KIL/WHAMP NW6 2 C4
Plympton St STJWD NW8 9 N2
Plymstock Rd WELL DA16 163 M6
Pocklington Cl CDALE/KGS NW9 96 B10
Pocock Av WDR/YW UB7 152 A2
Pococks La WDSR SL4 149 K4
Pocock St STHWK SE1 18 C1
Podmore Rd WAND/EARL SW18 157 M10
Poets Cha HHW HP1 35 L4
Poets Cl HHW HP1 35 L5
Poets Ct HARP AL5 20 A2
Poets Ga CHESW EN7 61 L4
Poet's Rd HBRY N5 119 L10
Poets Wy HRW HA1 114 D2
Pointalls Cl FNCH N3 97 M10
Point Cl GNWCH SE10 161 H7
Pointer Cl THMD SE28 143 N8
Pointers Cl POP/IOD E14 160 G4
Pointers Hl DORK RH4 272 B4
Pointers Rd COB KT11 234 E3
The Pointers ASHTD KT21 237 K6
Point Hl GNWCH SE10 161 H7
Point Pl WBLY HA9 135 N2
Point Pleasant
WAND/EARL SW18 157 K10
Poland St SOHO/CST W1F 11 H5
Polayn Garth WGCW AL8 22 F4
Polebrook Rd BKHTH/KID SE3 161 P9
Polecroft La CAT SE6 182 E5
Polegate Cottages
WTHK * RM20 167 K5
Polehanger La HHW HP1 35 H4
Pole Hill Rd CHING E4 101 H1
HGDN/ICK UB10 132 C6
Polesden Gdns RYNPK SW20 200 E3
Polesden La RPLY/SEND GU23 233 J8
Polesden Rd GT/LBKH KT23 254 A5
Polesden Vw GT/LBKH KT23 254 A3
Poles Hl CSHM HP5 50 F5
RKW/CH/CXG WD3 53 H9
Poles La CRAWW RH11 283 M1
Polesteeple Hl BH/WHM TN16 244 A3
Polesworth Rd DAGW RM9 144 A4
Polhill RSEV TN14 246 D1
Police Station Rd
WOT/HER KT12 217 K3
Pollard Av DEN/HRF UB9 111 J4
Pollard Cl CAN/RD E16 141 M9
CHIG IG7 103 K6
HOLWY N7 118 G10
WDSR SL4 171 N1
Pollard Hatch HLWW/ROY CM19 46 E4
Pollard Rd MRDN SM4 201 N5
TRDG/WHET N20 97 P3
WOKS/MYFD GU22 232 E2
Pollard Rw BETH E2 7 P9
Pollards CRAWW RH11 283 K8
RKW/CH/CXG WD3 90 G6
Pollards Cl CHESW EN7 61 K5
LOU IG10 81 P9
Pollards Crs
STRHM/NOR SW16 202 F3
Pollards Hl East
STRHM/NOR SW16 202 G3
Pollards Hl North
STRHM/NOR SW16 202 G3
Pollards Hl South
STRHM/NOR SW16 202 F3
Pollards Hl West
STRHM/NOR SW16 202 F3
Pollards Oak Crs OXTED RH8 261 M8
Pollards Oak Rd OXTED RH8 261 M8
Pollard St BETH E2 7 P9
Pollards Wood Hl OXTED RH8 261 M6
Pollards Wood Rd OXTED RH8 261 N7
STRHM/NOR SW16 202 F2
Pollen St CONDST W1S 10 F6
Pollitt Dr STJWD NW8 9 L1
Pollyhaugh EYN DA4 209 M10
Polperro Cl ORP BR6 207 J6
Polperro Ms LBTH SE11 18 C5
Polsted La RGUW GU3 267 J6
Polsted Rd CAT SE6 182 E3
Polthorne Gv WOOL/PLUM SE18 162 F3
Poltimore Rd GUW GU2 267 M2
Polworth Rd STRHM/NOR SW16 180 F8
Polygon Rd CAMTN NW1 5 J9
The Polygon CLAP * SW4 158 D10
Polytechnic St
WOOL/PLUM SE18 162 D3
Pomell Wy WCHPL E1 13 M5
Pomeroy Cl AMSS HP7 69 J6
Pomeroy Crs WATN WD24 73 J2
Pomeroy St NWCR SE14 160 B6
Pomfret Rd CMBW SE5 159 J9
Pomoja La ARCH N19 118 F7
Pompadour Cl BRW CM14 107 H6
Pond Cl AMSS HP7 68 B10
BKHTH/KID SE3 161 M8
DEN/HRF UB9 91 M10
NFNCH/WDSP N12 97 P7
WOT/HER KT12 217 H3
Pond Cottage La BECK BR3 204 F8
Pond Cft HAT AL10 40 C3
WGCE AL7 23 H6
Ponder St HOLWY * N7 5 N3
Pond Farm Cl
KWD/TDW/WH KT20 238 E10
Pond Farm Est CLPT * E5 120 B8
Pondfield Crs STALE/WH AL4 38 G3
Pondfield La GVE DA12 191 P10
RBRW/HUT CM13 107 M5
Pondfield Rd DAGE RM10 124 C10
HAYES BR2 205 K8
ORP BR6 206 E10
PUR/KEN CR8 241 J2
Pond Gn RSLP HA4 112 F7
Pond Hill Gdns CHEAM * SM3 221 H3
Pond La CFSP/GDCR SL9 89 N9
SHGR GU5 270 D10
Pond Md DUL SE21 181 L2
Pond Meadow GUW GU2 249 K10
Pond Park Rd CSHM HP5 50 G5
Pond Piece LHD/OX KT22 218 A10
Pond Pl CHEL SW3 15 N6
Pond Rd BKHTH/KID SE3 161 L9
EGH TW20 172 F9
HHS/BOV HP3 54 B1
SRTFD E15 141 K4
WOKS/MYFD GU22 231 M6
Pondside Cl HYS/HAR UB3 152 E6
Ponds La SHGR GU5 269 P8
The Ponds WEY KT13 216 E3
Pond St HAMP NW3 117 P10
Pond Wk UPMR RM14 126 D7
Pond Wy TEDD TW11 177 H9
Pondwicks AMSS HP7 68 G5
Pondwicks Cl STALW/RED AL3 38 B7
Pondwood Ri ORP BR6 207 H7
Pond Wood Rd CRAWE RH10 284 B5
Ponler St WCHPL E1 140 A8
Ponsard Rd WLSDN NW10 136 E5
Ponsford St HOM E9 120 B10
Ponsonby Pl WEST SW1P 17 K7
Ponsonby Rd PUT/ROE SW15 178 E3
Ponsonby Ter WEST SW1P 17 K7
Pontefract Rd BMLY BR1 183 M8
Ponton Rd VX/NE SW8 158 E6
Pont St KTBR SW1X 16 A4
Pont Street Ms CHEL SW3 16 A4
Pony Cha COB KT11 217 N9
Pool Cl BECK BR3 182 F8
E/WMO/HCT KT8 197 N5
Pool Ct CAT SE6 182 F5
Poole Cl RSLP HA4 112 F7
Poole Court Rd HEST TW5 153 M8
Pool End Cl SHPTN TW17 196 B5
Poole Rd EMPK RM11 125 N5
HOM E9 140 C1
HOR/WEW KT19 220 A3
WOKN/KNAP GU21 232 B4
Pooles Buildings FSBYW WC1X 12 A2
Pooles La WBPTN * SW10 157 M6
Pooles Pk FSBYPK N4 119 H7
Poole St IS N1 6 G6
Poole Wy YEAD * UB4 132 F5
Pooley Av EGH TW20 172 E8
Pooley Green Rd EGH TW20 172 E8
Pooleys La BRKMPK AL9 40 E9
Pool La SL SL1 129 K9
Poolmans Rd WDSR SL4 148 C9
Poolmans St BERM/RHTH SE16 160 C1
Pool Rd E/WMO/HCT KT8 197 N5
HRW HA1 114 C5
Poolsford Rd CDALE/KGS NW9 116 B2
Poonah St WCHPL E1 140 B8
Pope Cl EBED/NFELT TW14 174 G4
WIM/MER * SW19 179 N9
Pope Rd HAYES BR2 206 A5
Pope's Av WHTN TW2 176 D5
Popes Cl DTCH/LGLY SL3 150 F6
Popes Dr FNCH N3 97 K9
Popes Gv CROY/NA CR0 204 E10
WHTN TW2 176 D5
Pope's La EA W5 155 J2
WATN WD24 73 J3
Pope's Rd ABLGY WD5 54 F7
BRXN/ST * SW9 159 H10
Pope St STHWK SE1 19 K2
Popham Cl FELT TW13 175 M6
Popham Gdns RCH/KEW * TW9 155 N9
Popham Rd IS N1 6 E5
Popham St IS N1 6 E5
Popinjays Rw CHEAM * SM3 220 G2
Popis Gdns WARE SG12 26 D1
Poplar Av AMSS HP7 69 L5
GVE DA12 190 F7
HAT AL10 40 A4
LHD/OX KT22 236 G8
MTCM CR4 202 A1
NWDGN UB2 154 A2
ORP BR6 206 E9
WDR/YW UB7 132 A9
Poplar Bath St POP/IOD E14 140 G9
Poplar Cl CRAWW RH11 283 M4
CSHM HP5 51 H4
DTCH/LGLY SL3 151 H7
HOM E9 120 E10
PIN HA5 93 L9
SOCK/AV RM15 147 J6
Poplar Court Pde TWK * TW1 177 H2
Poplar Crs HMSMTH W6 156 F1
HOR/WEW KT19 219 P3
Poplar Dr EW KT17 220 G10
RBRW/HUT CM13 87 P10
Poplar Farm Cl HOR/WEW KT19 219 P3
Poplar Gdns NWMAL KT3 200 A2
Poplar Gn WOKS/MYFD GU22 232 B5
Poplar Gv FBAR/BDGN N11 98 B7
NWMAL KT3 200 A3
WBLY HA9 115 P8
Poplar High St POP/IOD E14 140 G9
Poplar Ms SHB W12 136 F10
Poplar Mt BELV DA17 164 C3
Poplar Pl BAY/PAD W2 8 G7
HYS/HAR UB3 133 H9
THMD SE28 143 M9
Poplar Rd ASHF TW15 174 D8
CHEAM SM3 201 J8
DEN/HRF UB9 131 M1
HNHL SE24 159 K10
LHD/OX KT22 236 G8
RGUE GU4 268 B7
WIM/MER SW19 201 K2
Poplar Rd South
WIM/MER SW19 201 K3
Poplar Rw EPP CM16 83 H3
Poplars WGCE AL7 23 L4
Poplars Cl GSTN WD25 55 J8
HART DA3 211 P3
HAT AL10 40 A4
RSLP HA4 112 F6
Poplar Shaw WAB EN9 63 L9
Poplars Rd LEY E10 120 G4
The Poplars ABR/ST RM4 83 L7
BORE * WD6 75 M5
CHESW EN7 61 M2
DEN/HRF * UB9 91 M9
HHW HP1 35 L7
STAL AL1 38 G10
Poplar St ROMW/RG RM7 124 D2
Poplar Vw WBLY * HA9 115 J7
Poplar Wk CROY/NA CR0 203 K9
CTHM CR3 241 M9
HNHL SE24 159 K10
Poplar Wy BARK/HLT IG6 122 F2
FELT TW13 175 J6
Poppins Ct FLST/FETLN EC4A 12 C6
Poppleton Rd WAN E11 121 K4
Poppy Cl HHW HP1 35 H5
MTCM CR4 202 B8
Poppyfields WGCE AL7 23 M5
Poppy La CROY/NA CR0 204 B7
Poppy Wk CHESW EN7 61 L6
Porchester Cl EMPK RM11 125 M4
HART DA3 211 L4
Porchester Garden Ms
BAY/PAD * W2 9 H6
Porchester Gdns BAY/PAD W2 9 H7
Porchester Ga BAY/PAD * W2 9 J8
Porchester Md BECK BR3 182 G9
Porchester Pl BAY/PAD W2 9 P6
Porchester Rd BAY/PAD W2 9 H5
KUT KT1 199 N2
Porchester Sq BAY/PAD W2 9 H5

Porchester Square Ms
BAY/PAD W2 9 H5
Porchester Ter BAY/PAD W2 9 J6
Porchester Ter North
BAY/PAD W2 9 H5
Porchfield Cl BELMT SM2 221 L6
GVE DA12 190 F5
Porch Wy TRDG/WHET N20 98 A4
Porcupine Cl ELTH/MOT SE9 184 B5
Porden Rd BRXN/ST SW9 158 G10
Porlock Av RYLN/HDSTN HA2 114 B6
Porlock Rd EN EN1 99 N1
Porlock St STHWK SE1 19 H1
Porridge Pot Aly GUW GU2 268 A2
Porrington Cl CHST BR7 206 C1
Portal Cl RSLP HA4 113 H9
WNWD SE27 181 H6
Port Av GRH DA9 188 G2
Portbury Cl PECK SE15 159 P7
Portchester Cl CMBW SE5 159 K10
Portchester Ga BAY/PAD W2 9 J8
Portcullis Lodge Rd ENC/FH EN2 79 L7
Portelet Rd WCHPL E1 140 C5
Porten Rd WKENS W14 14 A4
Porter Cl WTHK RM20 167 H5
Porter Rd EHAM E6 142 C8
Porters Av DAGW RM9 143 L1
Porters Cl BRW CM14 106 F2
Porters Park Dr RAD WD7 57 K8
Porter St MHST W1U 10 B3
STHWK SE1 12 F9
Porters Wk WAP * E1W 140 A9
Porters Wy WDR/YW UB7 152 A2
Porters Wd STALW/RED AL3 38 E2
Porteus Rd BAY/PAD W2 9 K4
Portgate Cl MV/WKIL W9 8 D1
Porthcawe Rd SYD SE26 182 D7
Port Hl HERT/WAS SG14 25 K5
ORP BR6 227 L8
Porthkerry Av WELL DA16 163 K10
Portia Wy BOW E3 140 E6
Portinscale Rd PUT/ROE SW15 179 H1
Portland Av BFN/LL DA15 185 K2
GVE DA12 190 E5
NWMAL KT3 200 C7
STNW/STAM N16 119 N6
Portland Cl CHDH RM6 123 P3
SL SL1 128 C6
Portland Cottages
CROY/NA * CR0 202 E7
Portland Crs ASHF TW15 174 E7
ELTH/MOT SE9 184 B5
GFD/PVL UB6 134 A6
STAN HA7 95 J10
Portland Crs West STAN HA7 115 J1
Portland Dr CHESW EN7 61 P7
ENC/FH EN2 79 M4
REDH RH1 258 D5
Portland Gdns CHDH RM6 123 N3
FSBYPK N4 119 J4
Portland Gv VX/NE SW8 158 G7
Portland Ms SOHO/CST W1F 11 H6
Portland Pl CAVSQ/HST W1G 10 E2
EW KT17 220 B8
HART * DA3 211 K3
HERT/BAY SG13 26 B7
SNWD SE25 203 P4
Portland Pl Flats EW * KT17 220 B8
Portland Ri FSBYPK N4 119 J6
Portland Rd ASHF TW15 173 P6
BMLY BR1 183 P7
DORK RH4 272 F1
ELTH/MOT SE9 184 B5
GVW DA11 190 A2
GVW DA11 190 E4
KUT KT1 199 K3
MTCM CR4 201 P2
NTGHL W11 8 A8
NWDGN UB2 153 N2
SEVS/STOTM N15 119 M2
SNWD SE25 204 A4
YEAD UB4 132 F5
Portland Sq WAP E1W 140 A10
Portland St STALW/RED AL3 38 B6
WALW SE17 18 G8
Portland Ter GU * GU1 268 B1
RCH/KEW * TW9 155 J10
Portley La CTHM CR3 241 M7
Portley Wood Rd CTHM CR3 241 N7
Portman Av MORT/ESHN SW14 156 A9
Portman Cl BXLY DA5 186 F4
BXLYHN DA7 163 N9
MBLAR W1H 10 C5
STALE/WH AL4 39 H1
Portman Dr WFD IG8 102 A10
Portman Gdns CDALE/KGS NW9 116 A1
HGDN/ICK UB10 132 B2
Portman Ga CAMTN NW1 9 P2
Portman Ms South MBLAR W1H 10 C6
Portman Pl BETH E2 140 B5
Portman Rd KUT KT1 199 L2
Portman Sq MBLAR W1H 10 B5
Portman St MBLAR W1H 10 C6
Portman Towers MBLAR W1H 10 B5
Portmeers Cl WALTH * E17 120 E4
Portmore Gdns CRW RM5 104 B6
Portmore Park Rd WEY * KT13 216 A1
Portmore Quays WEY KT13 216 A1
Portmore Wy WEY * KT13 196 B10
Portnall Dr VW GU25 193 K6
Portnall Ri VW GU25 193 L5
Portnall Rd MV/WKIL W9 2 C9
VW GU25 193 L5
Portnalls Cl COUL/CHIP CR5 240 C2
Portnalls Ri COUL/CHIP CR5 240 D2
Portnalls Rd COUL/CHIP CR5 240 C3
Portnoi Cl ROM RM1 104 E10
Portobello Cl CSHM HP5 50 F5
Portobello Ct NTGHL * W11 8 D7
Portobello Ms NTGHL * W11 8 E8
Portobello Rd NKENS W10 8 A3
Portpool La FSBYW WC1X 12 A3
Portree St POP/IOD E14 141 J8
Portsdown Av GLDGN NW11 117 J4
Portsdown Ms GLDGN NW11 117 J4
Portsea Ms BAY/PAD W2 9 P6
Portsea Pl BAY/PAD W2 9 P6
Portsea Rd TIL RM18 168 F7
Portslade Rd VX/NE SW8 158 D8
Portsmouth Av THDIT KT7 198 F7
Portsmouth Rd COB KT11 216 G9
COB KT11 216 E10
ESH/CLAY KT10 217 P3
KUT KT1 199 J3
PUT/ROE SW15 178 E3
RPLY/SEND GU23 233 K10
Portsmouth St LINN WC2A 11 N5
Portsoken St TWRH EC3N 13 L7
Portugal Gdns WHTN * TW2 176 B5
Portugal Rd WOKN/KNAP GU21 232 C2
Portugal St LINN WC2A 11 P6
Port V HERT/WAS SG14 25 J4
Port Wy CHOB/PIR GU24 230 F3
Portway EW KT17 220 D6
SRTFD E15 141 L3
Portway Crs EW KT17 220 D5
Portway Gdns
WOOL/PLUM SE18 162 A7
Postboys Rw COB * KT11 217 H10
Postern Gn ENC/FH EN2 79 H6
The Postern BARB * EC2Y 12 F4
Postfield WGCE AL7 23 K2
Post House La GT/LBKH KT23 253 P1
Post La WHTN TW2 176 C4
Post Meadow IVER SL0 130 G5
Postmill Cl CROY/NA CR0 204 B10
Post Office Ap FSTGT E7 121 N10
Post Office La DTCH/LGLY SL3 130 A8
Post Office Rd HLW CM20 28 F10
Post Office Wk HERT/WAS * SG14 25 L5
Post Rd NWDGN UB2 154 A2
Postway Ms IL IG1 122 E8
Postwood Gn HERT/BAY SG13 26 B8
Post Wood Rd WARE SG12 26 D4
Potash Rd HLWE CM17 31 L8
Potier St STHWK SE1 19 H4
Potkiln La BEAC HP9 109 H1
Potten End Hl HHW HP1 35 H1
Potter Cl MTCM * CR4 202 C2
Potterells BRKMPK * AL9 58 G1
The Potteries BAR * EN5 77 K9
CHERT KT16 215 H3
Potterne Cl WIM/MER SW19 178 G3
Potters Bar Station Yd
POTB/CUF * EN6 59 K7
Potters Cl CROY/NA CR0 204 D8
LOU IG10 82 B6
Potters Cross IVER SL0 131 H5
Potterscrouch La
LCOL/BKTW AL2 37 L10
Potters Fld EN * EN1 79 M8
HLWE CM17 47 N3
STALW/RED AL3 38 D2
Potters Flds STHWK SE1 13 K10
Potters Gv NWMAL KT3 199 P4
Potters Heights Cl PIN HA5 93 J8
Potter's La BAR EN5 77 K8
BORE WD6 75 P5
RPLY/SEND GU23 250 E1
STRHM/NOR * SW16 180 E9
Potter's Rd BAR EN5 77 L8
FUL/PGN SW6 157 M8
Potter St HLWE CM17 47 M2
NTHWD HA6 93 H9
Potter Street Hl NTHWD HA6 93 J7
Potters Wy REIG RH2 275 M4
Pottery La NTGHL W11 8 A8
Pottery Rd BTFD TW8 155 K5
BXLY DA5 186 D5
Pottery St BERM/RHTH * SE16 160 A1
Pott St BETH E2 140 A5
Pouchen End La HHW HP1 34 G7
Poulcott STWL/WRAY TW19 172 B2
Poulett Gdns TWK TW1 176 E5
Poulett Rd EHAM E6 142 C4
Poulter Pk MTCM * CR4 201 P6
Poulters Wd HAYES BR2 226 A2
Poultney Cl RAD WD7 57 K8
Poulton Av SUT SM1 201 N10
Poulton Cl HACK E8 140 A1
Poultry LOTH EC2R 12 G6
Pound Cl ORP BR6 206 G9
STALE/WH * AL4 21 H9
SURB KT6 199 H8
WAB EN9 45 K9
Pound Ct ASHTD KT21 237 L4
RGUW GU3 248 G8
Pound Court Dr ORP BR6 206 G9
Pound Crs LHD/OX KT22 236 C7
Pound Fld GSTN WD25 72 G1
GU GU1 250 A9
Poundfield Gdns
WOKS/MYFD GU22 232 F6
Poundfield Rd LOU IG10 82 D9
Pound Hl RGUW GU3 248 G9
Pound Hill Pl CRAWE RH10 284 D7
Pound La BFOR GU20 212 B3
HOR/WEW KT19 220 A7
RAD WD7 57 L9
RGUW GU3 248 G9
RSEV TN14 245 N1
SEV TN13 247 K10
WLSDN NW10 136 D1
Pound Park Rd CHARL SE7 162 A3
Pound Pl ELTH/MOT SE9 184 D2
RGUE GU4 268 C7
Pound Place Cl RGUE GU4 268 C6
Pound Rd BNSTD SM7 239 K3
CHERT KT16 195 L7
Pound St CAR SM5 222 A2
Poundwell WGCE AL7 23 K6
Pounsley Rd SEV TN13 246 F7
Pountney Rd BTSEA SW11 158 B9
Poverest Rd STMC/STPC BR5 207 J5
Povey Cross Rd HORL RH6 279 P6
Powderham Ct
WOKN/KNAP GU21 231 J4
Powder Mill La DART DA1 187 M5
WHTN TW2 175 N4
Powdermill La WAB EN9 62 G9
Powdermill Ms WAB EN9 62 G9
Powdermill Wy WAB EN9 62 G8
Powell Av RDART DA2 188 D5
Powell Cl EDGW HA8 95 L7
GUW GU2 267 L2
HORL RH6 279 P3
Powell Gdns DAGE RM10 124 B9
Powell Rd BKHH IG9 101 P1
CLPT E5 120 A8
Power Dr PEND EN3 80 E2
Power Rd CHSWK W4 155 M3
Powers Ct TWK TW1 177 J3
Powerscroft Rd CLPT E5 120 B9
SCUP DA14 185 M9
Powis Ct BUSH * WD23 94 C2
POTB/CUF EN6 59 M10
Powis Gdns GLDGN NW11 117 J5
NTGHL W11 8 D5
Powis Ms NTGHL W11 8 D5
Powis Pl BMSBY WC1N 11 M2
Powis Rd BOW E3 140 G5
Powis Sq NTGHL W11 8 D6
Powis St WOOL/PLUM SE18 162 D2
Powis Ter NTGHL W11 8 D5
Powlett Pl CAMTN NW1 4 D3
Pownall Gdns HSLW TW3 154 A10
Pownall Rd HACK E8 7 N6
HSLW TW3 154 A10
Pownsett Ter IL IG1 122 F10
Powster Rd BMLY BR1 183 M8
Powys Cl BXLYHN DA7 163 N5
Powys Ct BORE WD6 76 A7
Powys La PLMGR N13 98 F5
Poyle La SL SL1 128 A3
Poyle Pk DTCH/LGLY * SL3 151 H9
Poyle Rd DTCH/LGLY SL3 151 H8
GU GU1 268 B2
Poynder Rd TIL RM18 168 E7
Poynders Hl HHNE HP2 36 D7
Poynders Rd CLAP SW4 180 D3
Poynes Rd HORL RH6 279 P2
Poynings Cl HARP AL5 20 E3
ORP BR6 207 M9
Poynings Rd ARCH N19 118 D8
CRAWW RH11 282 G8
The Poynings IVER SL0 151 J3
Poynings Wy HARH RM3 105 M9
NFNCH/WDSP N12 97 K6
Poyntell Crs CHST BR7 206 G1
Poynter Rd EN EN1 79 N9
Poynton Rd TOTM N17 99 P10
Poyntz Rd BTSEA SW11 158 A8
Poyser St BETH E2 140 A5
Prae Cl STALW/RED AL3 38 A5
Praed Ms BAY/PAD W2 9 M5
Praed St BAY/PAD W2 9 M5
Praetorian Ct STAL AL1 38 B9
Pragel St PLSTW E13 141 N4
Pragnell Rd LEE/GVPK SE12 183 N5
Prague Pl BRXS/STRHM SW2 180 F1
Prah Rd FSBYPK N4 119 H7
Prairie Cl ADL/WDHM KT15 195 L10
Prairie Rd ADL/WDHM KT15 195 L10
Prairie St VX/NE SW8 158 B8
Pratt Ms CAMTN NW1 4 G6
Pratts La WOT/HER KT12 217 L1
Pratt St CAMTN NW1 5 H5
Pratt Wk LBTH SE11 17 P5
Prayle Gv CRICK NW2 116 G6
Prebend Gdns CHSWK W4 156 C3
Prebend St IS N1 6 E6
Precinct Rd HYS/HAR UB3 133 H9
The Precincts SL SL1 128 A6
The Precinct BROX * EN10 44 E6
Premier Av CDH/CHF RM16 167 P1
Premier Pl POP/IOD E14 140 F9
Premier Pde HORL * RH6 280 C4
Premier Park Rd WLSDN NW10 135 N4
Prentis Rd STRHM/NOR SW16 180 E7
Prentiss Ct CHARL SE7 162 A3
Presburg Rd NWMAL KT3 200 B5
Prescelly Pl EDGW HA8 95 L9
Prescot St WCHPL E1 13 M7
Prescott Av STMC/STPC BR5 206 E6
Prescott Cl HCH RM12 125 J6
Prescott Gn LOU IG10 82 F7
Prescott Pl CLAP SW4 158 E9
Prescott Rd CHES/WCR EN8 62 D3
DTCH/LGLY SL3 151 H8
Presdales Dr WARE SG12 26 C3
Presentation Ms
BRXS/STRHM SW2 180 G5
Presidents Dr WAP E1W 140 A10
President St FSBYE * EC1V 6 E8
Press Rd UX/CGN UB8 131 N2
WLSDN NW10 116 A8
Prestage Wy POP/IOD E14 141 H9
Prestbury Crs BNSTD SM7 240 A2
Prestbury Rd FSTGT E7 141 P2
Prestbury Sq ELTH/MOT SE9 184 C7
Prested Rd BTSEA SW11 157 P10
Preston Av CHING E4 101 J7
Preston Cl STHWK * SE1 19 J5
WHTN TW2 176 D6
Preston Ct WOT/HER KT12 197 K8
Preston Dr HOR/WEW KT19 220 B3
WAN E11 121 P3
WELL DA16 163 N7
Preston Gdns IL IG1 122 B4
PEND EN3 80 D3
WLSDN * NW10 136 B1
Preston Gv ASHTD KT21 237 H3
Preston Hl CSHM HP5 51 J5
KTN/HRWW/W HA3 115 K5
Preston La KWD/TDW/WH KT20 238 F6
Preston Pl RCHPK/HAM TW10 177 K1
WLSDN NW10 136 D1
Preston Rd GVW DA11 190 B4
HARH RM3 105 L5
KTN/HRWW/W HA3 115 K5
NRWD SE19 181 J9
RYNPK SW20 178 D10
SHPTN TW17 196 B5
SLN SL2 129 P9
WAN E11 121 K4
WBLY HA9 115 K7
Prestons Rd HAYES BR2 205 M10
POP/IOD E14 141 H10
Preston Vls KUT * KT1 199 L2
Preston Waye WBLY HA9 115 K6
Prestwich Ter CLAP * SW4 180 E1
Prestwick Cl CRAWW RH11 282 G8
NWDGN UB2 153 M4
Prestwick Rd OXHEY WD19 93 L3
Prestwood OXHEY * WD19 93 M3
SLN SL2 129 N8
Prestwood Av
KTN/HRWW/W HA3 114 G2
Prestwood Cl CRAWW RH11 283 L4
KTN/HRWW/W HA3 114 G2
WOOL/PLUM SE18 163 K6
Prestwood Dr CRW RM5 104 D6
Prestwood Gdns CROY/NA CR0 203 K7
Prestwood La CRAWW RH11 282 F3
Prestwood St IS * N1 6 F8
Pretoria Av WALTH E17 120 C3
Pretoria Crs CHING E4 101 H2
Pretoria Pde LEW * SE13 160 F8
Pretoria Rd CAN/RD E16 141 L5
CHERT KT16 195 J8
CHING E4 101 H2
IL IG1 122 E9
ROMW/RG RM7 124 D2
STRHM/NOR SW16 180 C9
TOTM N17 99 N7
WAN E11 121 J6
WATW WD18 73 H8
Pretoria Rd North UED N18 99 N7
Pretty La COUL/CHIP CR5 240 C7
Prevost Rd FBAR/BDGN N11 98 B3
Prey Heath Cl WOKS/MYFD GU22 231 P10
Prey Heath Rd
WOKS/MYFD GU22 231 N10
Price Cl MLHL NW7 97 H7
TOOT SW17 180 A6
Price Rd CROY/NA CR0 223 J2
Prices La REIG RH2 275 K3
Price's St STHWK SE1 12 D10
Pricklers Hl BAR EN5 77 L9
Prickley Wd HAYES BR2 205 L8
Prideaux Pl ACT W3 136 A9
FSBYW WC1X 5 P9
Prideaux Rd BRXN/ST SW9 158 F9
Pridham Rd THHTH CR7 203 L4
Priest Croft Cl CRAWW RH11 283 K7
Priestfield Rd FSTH SE23 182 D6
Priest Hl EGH TW20 171 P5
OXTED RH8 261 N5
Priestlands Park Rd
BFN/LL DA15 185 J6
Priest La CHOB/PIR GU24 212 B10
Priestley Cl STNW/STAM * N16 119 N5
Priestley Gdns CHDH RM6 123 L4
WOKS/MYFD GU22 232 D6
Priestley Rd GUW GU2 267 J1
MTCM CR4 202 B2
Priestley Wy CRAWE RH10 284 B2
CRICK NW2 116 D6
WALTH E17 120 C1
Priest Park Av RYLN/HDSTN HA2 113 P7
Priests Av ROM RM1 104 E10
Priests Br MORT/ESHN SW14 156 B9
Priests Fld RBRW/HUT CM13 107 P6
Priest's La BRWN CM15 107 K3
Prima Rd BRXN/ST SW9 159 H6
Primley La RBSF CM22 30 D2
Primrose Av ENC/FH EN2 79 L5
GDMY/SEVK IG3 123 K5
HORL RH6 280 C6
Primrose Cl CAT SE6 183 H8
CRAWW RH11 283 L10
HAT AL10 40 E5
MTCM CR4 202 C8
RYLN/HDSTN HA2 113 N8
Primrose Dr CHOB/PIR GU24 230 F1
HERT/BAY SG13 26 A5
WDR/YW UB7 151 N3
Primrose Fld HLWS CM18 47 J4
Primrose Gdns BUSH WD23 94 A1
HAMP NW3 3 P1
RSLP HA4 113 K10
Primrose Gln EMPK RM11 125 M2
Primrose Hl BRW CM14 107 H4
EMB EC4Y 12 B6
KGLGY WD4 54 C4
Primrose Hill Rd HAMP NW3 4 A4
Primrose Hill Studios
CAMTN NW1 4 C5
Primrose La CROY/NA CR0 204 B8
Primrose Ms CAMTN * NW1 4 B4
Primrose Pth CHESW EN7 61 P7
Primrose Rd LEY E10 120 G6
SWFD E18 101 N10
WOT/HER KT12 217 K2
Primrose Sq HOM E9 140 B2
Primrose St SDTCH EC2A 13 J3
Primrose Ter GVE * DA12 190 F4
Primrose Wk EW KT17 220 C4
NWCR SE14 160 D6
Primrose Wy ALP/SUD HA0 135 J4
Primula St SHB W12 136 D9
Prince Albert STJWD NW8 3 P7
Prince Albert Rd STJWD NW8 3 N9
Prince Albert Sq REDH RH1 276 A5
Prince Arthur Rd HAMP NW3 117 M10
Prince Charles Av EYN DA4 210 C2
Prince Charles Dr HDN NW4 116 F5
Prince Charles Rd
BKHTH/KID SE3 161 L7
Prince Charles Wy WLGTN SM6 202 C10
Prince Consort Cottages
WDSR SL4 149 J8
Prince Consort Dr CHST BR7 206 G1
Prince Consort Rd SKENS SW7 15 L3
Prince Consort's Dr WDSR SL4 170 E2
Princedale Rd NTGHL W11 8 B9
Prince Edward Rd HOM E9 140 E1
Prince Edward St BERK HP4 33 P5
Prince George Av
STHGT/OAK N14 78 D9
Prince George Rd
STNW/STAM N16 119 M9
Prince George's Av
RYNPK SW20 200 F2
Prince Georges Rd
WIM/MER SW19 201 N1
Prince Henry Rd CHARL SE7 162 A6
Prince Imperial Rd CHST BR7 184 E10
WOOL/PLUM SE18 162 C7
Prince John Rd ELTH/MOT SE9 184 B1
Princelet St WCHPL E1 13 M3
Prince of Orange La
GNWCH * SE10 161 H6
Prince of Wales Cl HDN NW4 116 E2
Prince of Wales Dr BTSEA SW11 158 A7
Prince of Wales Ga SKENS SW7 15 N1
Prince of Wales Pas CAMTN * NW1 4 G10
Prince of Wales Rd
BKHTH/KID SE3 161 L7
CAN/RD E16 141 P8
KTTN NW5 4 C2
REDH RH1 277 H8
SUT SM1 201 N9
Prince of Wales Ter CHSWK W4 156 B4
KENS W8 15 H2
Prince Pk HHW HP1 35 K7
Prince Philip Av CDH/CHF RM16 147 M10
Prince Regent La PLSTW E13 141 P6
Prince Regent Ms CAMTN NW1 4 G10
Prince Regent Rd HSLW TW3 154 B9
Prince Rd SNWD SE25 203 M5
Prince Rupert Rd ELTH/MOT SE9 162 C10
Princes Ar MYFR/PICC W1J 11 H9
Princes Av ACT W3 155 M2
CAR SM5 222 A4
CDALE/KGS NW9 115 M2
FNCH N3 97 L9
MUSWH N10 118 B1
PEND EN3 80 D2
PLMGR N13 99 H6
RDART DA2 188 A4
RGODL GU7 267 H10
SAND/SEL CR2 242 A1
STMC/STPC BR5 207 H5
SURB KT6 199 M9
WATW WD18 73 H9
WDGN N22 98 E9
WFD IG8 101 N5
Princes Cl BERK HP4 33 M3
CDALE/KGS NW9 115 M2
EDGW HA8 95 M6
EPP CM16 66 D1
HPTN TW12 176 C7
SAND/SEL CR2 242 A1
SCUP DA14 185 N6
WDSR SL4 148 E4
Princes Ct WBLY HA9 115 K10
Princes Dr HRW HA1 114 D1
LHD/OX KT22 218 D8
Princesfield Rd WAB EN9 63 N9
Princes Gdns ACT W3 135 M7
EA W5 135 H6
RGUW * GU3 249 K3
SKENS SW7 15 M3
Princes Ga SKENS SW7 15 M3
SKENS SW7 15 N2
Princes Gate Ct SKENS SW7 15 L2
Princes Gate Ms SKENS SW7 15 M3
Princes La MUSWH N10 118 B1
Prince's Ms BAY/PAD W2 8 F7
HMSMTH * W6 156 E4
Princes Pde GLDGN * NW11 117 H4
POTB/CUF * EN6 59 L9
Princes Pk RAIN RM13 145 H2
Princes Park Av GLDGN NW11 117 H4
HYS/HAR UB3 132 E9
Princes Park Cir HYS/HAR UB3 132 E9
Princes Park Cl HYS/HAR UB3 132 E9
Princes Park La HYS/HAR UB3 132 E9
Princes Park Pde HYS/HAR UB3 132 E9
Princes Pl NTGHL W11 8 A9
Prince's Pln HAYES BR2 206 B7
Princes Ri LEW SE13 161 H8
Princes Riverside Rd
BERM/RHTH SE16 140 C10
Princes Rd ASHF TW15 174 A8
BARK/HLT IG6 122 G2
BKHH IG9 101 P3
BRW CM14 85 P6
DART DA1 187 J3
EGH TW20 172 C9
FELT TW13 174 G6
GVE DA12 190 F7
HPTN TW12 176 C7
KUTN/CMB KT2 199 M1
MORT/ESHN SW14 156 A9
PGE/AN SE20 182 C9
RCH/KEW TW9 155 L7
RCHPK/HAM TW10 177 L1
RDART DA2 188 B4
REDH RH1 276 A2
ROM RM1 125 H3
SWLY BR8 187 H9
UED N18 100 B5
WEA W13 134 G10
WEY KT13 216 C2
WIM/MER SW19 179 K9
Princess Alice Wy THMD SE28 162 G1
Princess Av TIL RM18 169 M3
WBLY HA9 115 K7
WDSR SL4 148 G9
Princess Crs FSBYPK N4 119 J7
Princess Diana Dr STALE/WH AL4 39 H7
Princesses Pde DART * DA1 186 G1
Princess Gdns
WOKS/MYFD GU22 232 E2
Princess La RSLP HA4 112 F6
Princess Louise Cl BAY/PAD W2 9 M3
Princess Margaret Rd TIL RM18 169 L3
Princess Mary's Rd
ADL/WDHM KT15 215 M1
Princess May Rd
STNW/STAM N16 119 M9
Princess Ms HAMP NW3 3 M1
Princess Pde ORP * BR6 206 D10
Prince's Sq BAY/PAD W2 8 F7
Princess Rd CAMTN NW1 4 C5
CRAWW RH11 283 M7
CROY/NA CR0 203 K6
KIL/WHAMP NW6 2 E8
WOKS/MYFD GU22 232 E2
Princess St BXLYHN DA7 164 A9
STHWK SE1 18 D4
Princes St CONDST W1S 10 F6
GVW DA11 190 E2
LOTH EC2R 12 G6
RCH/KEW TW9 177 K1
SL SL1 149 N1
SUT SM1 221 N1
TOTM N17 99 M7
WARE SG12 26 C1
Princess Wy REDH RH1 258 B9
Prince's Ter PLSTW E13 141 N3
Prince St DEPT SE8 160 E5
WAT WD17 73 K7
Princes Vw DART DA1 187 P4
Princes Wy BKHH IG9 101 P3
CROY/NA CR0 222 G2
RBRW/HUT CM13 107 M3
RSLP HA4 113 M9
WIM/MER SW19 178 G3
WWKM BR4 225 L1
Prince's Yd NTGHL * W11 8 B10
Princethorpe Rd SYD SE26 182 C7
Princeton St GINN WC1R 11 N4
Pringle Gdns PUR/KEN CR8 222 G6
STRHM/NOR SW16 180 D7
Printers Inn Ct FLST/FETLN EC4A 12 A5
Printers Wy HLW CM20 29 K6
Printinghouse La HYS/HAR UB3 152 F1
Printing House Yd BETH * E2 7 K10
Priolo Rd CHARL SE7 161 P4
Prior Av BELMT SM2 221 P4
Prior Bolton St IS N1 6 D2
Prior Cha GRAYS RM17 167 L3
Prioress Rd WNWD SE27 181 J6
Prioress St STHWK SE1 19 H4
Prior Gv CSHM HP5 51 H6
Prior Rd IL IG1 122 D8
Priors Cl HERT/BAY SG13 26 A8
SL SL1 149 M2
Priors Ct WOKN/KNAP GU21 231 M4
Priors Cft WALTH E17 100 D10
WOKS/MYFD GU22 232 D6
Priors Fld NTHLT UB5 133 M1
Priorsfield Rd RGODL GU7 266 F9
Priorsford Av STMC/STPC BR5 207 K4
Priors Gdns RSLP HA4 113 K10
Priors Hatch La RGODL GU7 266 E8
Priors Md EN EN1 79 M5
GT/LBKH KT23 254 B1
Priors Pk HCH RM12 125 K8
Priors Rd WDSR SL4 148 C9
The Priors ASHTD KT21 237 J5
Prior St GNWCH SE10 161 H6
Priors Wk CRAWE RH10 284 A7
Priorswood RGUW GU3 266 E7
Priors Wood Rd HERT/BAY SG13 26 B8
Priory Av ALP/SUD HA0 114 E9
CEND/HSY/T N8 118 E2
CHEAM SM3 220 G1
CHING E4 100 E4
CHSWK W4 156 B2
HLWE CM17 29 M6
STMC/STPC BR5 206 G6
WALTH E17 120 F3
Priory Cl ALP/SUD HA0 114 E9
ASC SL5 192 F7

BECK BR3 204 D3
BMLY BR1 206 C1
BROX EN10 44 D10
BRWN CM15 86 F9
CHING E4 100 E4
DART DA1 187 K1
DEN/HRF UB9 111 K8
DEN/HRF UB9 111 L2
DORK RH4 272 F4
HOD EN11 44 F4
HORL RH6 280 A3
HPTN TW12 197 N1
HYS/HAR UB3 133 J9
RSLP HA4 112 G6
STAN HA7 94 E4
STHGT/OAK N14 78 C9
SUN TW16 175 H10
SWFD E18 101 M9
TRDG/WHET N20 97 J1
WIM/MER * SW19 201 L1
WOKN/KNAP GU21 214 G9
WOT/HER KT12 197 H10
Priory Cottages EA * W5 135 L7
Priory Ct BLKFR * EC4V 12 D6
DORK * RH4 272 G4
HLWS CM18 47 L4
VX/NE SW8 158 E7
WALTH E17 120 E1
Priory Crs ALP/SUD HA0 114 F8
CHEAM SM3 220 G1
NRWD SE19 181 K10
Priory Dr ABYW SE2 163 N4
REIG RH2 275 K2
STAN HA7 94 E4
Priory Field Dr EDGW HA8 95 N5
Priory Flds EYN DA4 209 N9
Priory Gdns ALP/SUD HA0 114 F9
ASHF TW15 174 E8
BARN SW13 156 C9
BERK HP4 33 P5
CHSWK * W4 156 B3
DART DA1 187 L1
DEN/HRF UB9 111 M2
HGT N6 118 C4
HPTN TW12 175 N10
SNWD SE25 203 K4
Priory Ga CHES/WCR EN8 62 E3
Priory Gn STA TW18 173 L8
Priory Green Est IS N1 5 N7
Priory Gv CLAP SW4 158 F7
HARH RM3 105 M5
Priory Hl ALP/SUD HA0 114 F9
DART DA1 187 L2
Priory La E/WMO/HCT KT8 197 P4
EYN DA4 209 N8
PUT/ROE SW15 178 C1
Priory Leas ELTH/MOT * SE9 184 B4
Priory Market Pl DART * DA1 187 M3
Priory Md BRWN CM15 87 H2
Priory Ms HCH RM12 125 J6
STA TW18 173 L8
Priory Pk BKHTH/KID SE3 161 L9
Priory Park Rd ALP/SUD HA0 114 F9
KIL/WHAMP NW6 2 D4
Priory Pth HARH RM3 105 M4
Priory Pl DART DA1 187 L2
Priory Rd ASC SL5 192 F7
BARK IG11 142 G2
CEND/HSY/T N8 118 E2
CFSP/GDCR SL9 109 H2
CHEAM SM3 220 G1
CHSGTN KT9 199 K10
CHSWK W4 156 A2
CROY/NA CR0 203 H7
DART DA1 165 L10
EHAM E6 142 A3
HARH RM3 105 M4
HPTN TW12 175 N10
HSLW TW3 176 B1
KIL/WHAMP NW6 2 G4
LOU IG10 82 B8
MUSWH N10 118 D2
RCH/KEW TW9 155 M5
REIG RH2 275 K2
SL SL1 128 B7
WIM/MER SW19 179 N10
Priory St BOW E3 140 G5
HERT/WAS SG14 25 L5
WARE SG12 26 B2
Priory Ter KIL/WHAMP NW6 2 G5
The Priory BKHTH/KID SE3 161 L9
CROY/NA * CR0 203 H10
GDST RH9 260 A7
ORP * BR6 207 L7
Priory Vw BUSH WD23 94 D1
Priory Vls FBAR/BDGN * N11 98 A7
Priory Wk STAL AL1 38 D9
WBPTN SW10 15 K8
Priory Wy CFSP/GDCR SL9 110 A1
DTCH/LGLY SL3 149 N6
NWDGN UB2 153 L2
RYLN/HDSTN HA2 114 A2
WDR/YW UB7 151 P5
Pritchard's Rd BETH E2 7 P7
Priter Rd BERM/RHTH SE16 19 P4
Private Rd EN EN1 79 L9
Probert Rd BRXS/STRHM SW2 181 H1
Probyn Rd BRXS/STRHM SW2 181 J5
Procter St GINN WC1R 11 N4
Proctor Cl CRAWE RH10 284 D9
MTCM CR4 202 B1
Proctor Gdns GT/LBKH KT23 254 A1
Proctors Cl EBED/NFELT TW14 175 H4
Profumo Rd WOT/HER KT12 217 L2
Progress Wy CROY/NA CR0 202 G9
EN EN1 79 P9
WDGN N22 99 H9
Promenade Approach Rd
CHSWK W4 156 B6
Promenade De Verdun
PUR/KEN CR8 222 E7
The Promenade CHSWK W4 156 B7
EDGW * HA8 95 M6
Prospect Cl BELV DA17 164 B3
HEST TW5 153 N7
RSLP HA4 113 L5
SYD SE26 182 A7
Prospect Cottages
WAND/EARL SW18 157 K10
Prospect Crs WHTN TW2 176 B2
Prospect Gv GVE DA12 190 G3
Prospect Hl WALTH E17 120 G2
Prospect La EGH TW20 171 M8
Prospect Pl CHSWK W4 156 A4
CRAWW RH11 283 M7
CRICK NW2 117 J8
DART DA1 187 M2
EFNCH N2 117 N2
EW KT17 220 B9
GRAYS * RM17 167 N5
GVE DA12 190 G3
HAYES BR2 205 N3
ROMW/RG RM7 104 D10
RYNPK SW20 178 E10
STA TW18 173 J8
WAP E1W 140 B10
Prospect Rd BAR EN5 77 K8
CHES/WCR EN8 62 B5
CRICK NW2 117 J8
EMPK RM11 125 N1
SEV TN13 247 K9
STAL AL1 38 C8
SURB KT6 199 H6
WFD IG8 101 P6
Prospect St BERM/RHTH SE16 160 A1
Prospect V CHARL SE7 162 B3
Prospero Rd ARCH N19 118 E6
Prossers KWD/TDW/WH KT20 238 G7
Prothero Gdns HDN NW4 116 E3
Prothero Rd FUL/PGN SW6 157 H6
Prout Gv WLSDN NW10 116 B9
Prout Rd CLPT E5 120 A8
Providence Cl HOM * E9 140 C3
Providence Ct MYFR/PKLN W1K 10 D7
Providence La HYS/HAR UB3 152 E6
Providence Pl BF/WBF * KT14 215 K10
IS N1 6 C6
ROMW/RG RM7 104 A9
Providence Rd WDR/YW UB7 131 P10
Providence Row Cl BETH E2 140 A5
Providence Sq STHWK SE1 19 J1
Providence St GRH DA9 188 F1
Providence Ter CRAWE * RH10 285 P9
Providence Yd BETH * E2 7 N9
Provincial Ter PGE/AN * SE20 182 C10
Provost Est IS N1 6 G9
Provost Rd HAMP NW3 4 B3
Provost St IS N1 6 G8
Prowse Av BUSH WD23 94 B3
Prowse Pl CAMTN NW1 4 G3
Pruden Cl STHGT/OAK * N14 98 D3
Prune Hl EGH TW20 172 A10
Prunus Cl CHOB/PIR GU24 212 D9
Prusom St WAP E1W 140 A10
Pryor Cl ABLGY WD5 54 G8
Puckshill WOKN/KNAP GU21 231 J3
Pudding La CHIG IG7 83 H10
HHW HP1 35 K4
HORL RH6 279 H7
MON EC3R 13 H7
Pudding Mill La SRTFD E15 140 G3
Puddingstone Dr STALE/WH AL4 39 H8
Puddle Dock BLKFR EC4V 12 D7
Puddledock La BH/WHM TN16 263 K8
RDART DA2 186 F8
Puers La BEAC HP9 89 K7
Puffin Cl BARK IG11 143 L5
CROY/NA CR0 204 C5
Puffin Rd CRAWW * RH11 282 G8
Pulborough Rd
WAND/EARL SW18 179 J3
Pulborough Wy HSLWW TW4 153 K10
Pulford Rd SEVS/STOTM N15 119 L4
Pulham Av BROX EN10 44 D6
EFNCH N2 117 M2
Puller Rd BAR EN5 76 G6
HHW HP1 35 K7
Pulleys Av EHAM E6 142 B5
Pulleys Cl HHW HP1 35 J5
Pulleys La HHW HP1 35 J5
Pullfields CSHM HP5 50 F6
Pullman Cl STAL AL1 38 D8
Pullman Gdns PUT/ROE SW15 178 F2
Pullman Ms LEE/GVPK SE12 183 N6
Pullman Pl ELTH/MOT SE9 184 B1
Pullmans Pl STA TW18 173 K8
Pulpit Cl CSHM HP5 50 F5
Pulross Rd BRXN/ST SW9 158 G9
Pulteney Cl BOW E3 140 E3
Pulteney Rd SWFD E18 121 N1
Pulton Pl FUL/PGN SW6 157 K6
Puma Ct WCHPL E1 13 L3
Pump Aly BTFD TW8 155 J6
Pump Cl NTHLT UB5 133 P4
Pump Ct EMB * EC4Y 12 A6
Pump Hl LOU IG10 82 C6
Pump House Cl HAYES BR2 205 L2
Pumping Station Rd CHSWK W4 156 B6
Pumpkin Hl SL SL1 128 D1
Pump La ASC SL5 192 D1
CSHM HP5 51 K9
EPP CM16 46 E10
HYS/HAR UB3 153 H1
NWCR SE14 160 B6
Punch Bowl La CSHM HP5 51 H8
HHNE HP2 36 E3
Punchbowl La RDKG RH5 273 J1
Punch Bowl La STALW/RED AL3 37 H2
Punchbowl Pk HHNE * HP2 36 E3
Punch Copse Rd CRAWE RH10 284 A6
Punch Cft HART DA3 211 K10
Punderson's Gdns BETH E2 140 A5
Purbeck Av NWMAL KT3 200 C6
Purbeck Cl REDH RH1 258 D5
Purbeck Dr CRICK NW2 116 G7
WOKN/KNAP GU21 214 C10
Purbeck Rd EMPK RM11 125 H5
Purberry Gv EW KT17 220 C6
Purberry Shot EW * KT17 220 C6
Purbrock Av GSTN WD25 73 K2
Purbrook St STHWK SE1 19 K3
Purcell Cl BORE WD6 75 J5
PUR/KEN CR8 223 K10
Purcell Crs FUL/PGN * SW6 156 G5
Purcell Ms WLSDN * NW10 136 B2
Purcell Rd CRAWW RH11 283 J10
GFD/PVL UB6 134 A7
Purcells Av EDGW HA8 95 M6
Purcell St IS N1 7 J7
Purchese St CAMTN NW1 5 J7
Purdy St BOW E3 140 G6
Purelake Ms LEW * SE13 161 J9
Purfleet By-Pass PUR RM19 166 B4
Purfleet Deep Whf PUR * RM19 166 B5
Purfleet Rd SOCK/AV RM15 146 A10
Purford Gn HLWS CM18 47 K2
Purkiss Rd HERT/BAY SG13 25 K8
Purland Cl BCTR RM8 124 A6
Purland Rd THMD SE28 163 J1
Purleigh Av WFD IG8 102 B7
Purley Av CRICK NW2 117 H7
Purley Bury Av PUR/KEN CR8 223 K7
Purley Bury Cl PUR/KEN CR8 223 K7
Purley Cl CLAY IG5 102 D10
CRAWE RH10 284 E10
Purley Downs Rd PUR/KEN CR8 223 K6
Purley Hl PUR/KEN CR8 223 J8
Purley Knoll PUR/KEN CR8 222 G7
Purley Oaks Rd SAND/SEL CR2 223 L6
Purley Pde PUR/KEN * CR8 223 H7
Purley Park Rd PUR/KEN CR8 223 J6
Purley Pl IS N1 6 C3
Purley Ri PUR/KEN CR8 222 G8
Purley Rd ED N9 99 L4
SAND/SEL CR2 223 L4
Purley V PUR/KEN CR8 223 J9
Purley Wy PUR/KEN CR8 223 H7
Purlieu Wy EPP CM16 83 H1
Purlings Rd BUSH WD23 74 A9
Purneys Rd ELTH/MOT SE9 162 A10
Purrett Rd WOOL/PLUM SE18 163 J4
Pursers Cross Rd
FUL/PGN * SW6 157 J7
Pursers Hollow SHGR GU5 270 E10
Pursers La SHGR GU5 270 E8
Pursewardens Cl WEA W13 135 H10
Pursley Gdns BORE WD6 75 M4
Pursley Rd MLHL NW7 96 E8
Purton Ct SLN SL2 129 H2
Purton La SLN SL2 129 H2
Purves Rd WLSDN NW10 136 E5
Putney Br PUT/ROE SW15 157 H9
Putney Bridge Ap
PUT/ROE SW15 157 H9
Putney Bridge Rd
PUT/ROE SW15 157 H10
Putney Common
PUT/ROE SW15 156 F9
Putney Ex PUT/ROE * SW15 156 G10
Putney Heath PUT/ROE SW15 178 E2
Putney Heath La PUT/ROE SW15 178 G2
Putney High St PUT/ROE SW15 157 H10
Putney Hl PUT/ROE SW15 178 G2
Putney Park Av PUT/ROE SW15 156 D10
Putney Park La PUT/ROE SW15 156 E10
Putney Rd PEND EN3 80 C2
Puttenham Cl OXHEY WD19 93 K4
Puttenham Heath Rd
RGUW GU3 266 C5
Puttenham Hl RGUW GU3 266 B4
Puttenham La MFD/CHID GU8 266 B8
Putters Cft HHNE HP2 36 A1
Puttocks Cl BRKMPK AL9 40 F9
Puttocks Dr BRKMPK AL9 40 F9
Pycombe Cnr NFNCH/WDSP N12 97 J5
Pycroft Wy UED N18 99 P5
Pyebush La BEAC HP9 108 F2
Pye Cl CTHM CR3 241 L9
Pyecombe Ct CRAWW RH11 283 J10
Pyenest Rd HLWW/ROY CM19 46 E4
Pylbrook Rd SUT SM1 201 K10
Pyle Hl WOKS/MYFD GU22 232 A10
WOKS/MYFD GU22 250 B1
Pym Cl EBAR EN4 77 N9
Pymers Md DUL SE21 181 K4
Pymmes Brook Trail EBAR EN4 77 P9
Pymmes Cl EBAR EN4 98 A1
PLMGR N13 98 F5
Pymmes Cl PLMGR N13 98 G6
TOTM N17 100 A9
Pymmes Gdns North ED N9 99 N4
Pymmes Gdns South ED N9 99 N4
Pymmes Green Rd
FBAR/BDGN N11 98 C5
Pymmes Rd PLMGR N13 98 F7
Pymms Brook Dr EBAR EN4 77 P8
Pym Pl GRAYS RM17 167 M3
Pynchester Cl HGDN/ICK UB10 112 B7
Pyne Rd SURB KT6 199 M8
Pynest Green La WAB EN9 81 M3
Pynham Cl ABYW SE2 163 K2
Pynnacles Cl STAN HA7 94 G6
Pyrcroft La WEY KT13 216 C2
Pyrcroft Rd CHERT KT16 195 J7
Pyrford Common Rd
WOKS/MYFD GU22 233 H2
Pyrford Heath
WOKS/MYFD GU22 233 J2
Pyrford Rd BF/WBF KT14 215 K10
WOKS/MYFD GU22 233 L2
Pyrford Woods Cl
WOKS/MYFD GU22 233 J1
Pyrford Woods Rd
WOKS/MYFD GU22 233 J1
Pyrland Rd HBRY N5 119 L10
RCHPK/HAM TW10 177 L2
Pyrles Gn LOU IG10 82 E6
Pyrles La LOU IG10 82 E6
Pyrmont Gv WNWD SE27 181 J6
Pyrmont Rd CHSWK W4 155 M5
Pytchley Crs NRWD SE19 181 K9
Pytchley Rd CMBW SE5 159 M9
Pytt Fld HLWE CM17 47 L2

Q

The Quadrangle BAY/PAD W2 9 N5
GUW GU2 267 M1
HNHL * SE24 181 K1
WBPTN * SW10 157 M7
WGCW AL8 22 F4
Quadrant Ar REGST W1B 11 H8
Quadrant Cl HDN * NW4 116 E3
Quadrant Gv HAMP NW3 118 A10
Quadrant Rd RCH/KEW TW9 155 J10
THHTH CR7 203 J4
The Quadrant BELMT SM2 221 M3
BXLYHN DA7 163 N6
EDGW * HA8 95 M7
NKENS * W10 136 G5
PUR RM19 166 B3
RCH/KEW TW9 155 K10
RYLN/HDSTN * HA2 114 C1
RYNPK SW20 201 H1
STALE/WH AL4 38 G3
Quadrant Wy WEY KT13 216 A1
Quad Rd WBLY * HA9 115 J8
Quaggy Wk BKHTH/KID SE3 161 M10
Quail Gdns CROY/NA CR0 224 D6
Quainton St WLSDN NW10 116 A8
Quaker Cl SEV TN13 247 L9
Quaker La NWDGN UB2 153 P2
WAB EN9 63 H10
Quakers Cl HART DA3 211 L3
Quakers Course CDALE/KGS NW9 96 C9
Quaker's Hall La SEV TN13 247 K8
Quakers La POTB/CUF EN6 59 L6
Quakers Pl FSTGT E7 122 A10
Quaker St WCHPL E1 13 L2
Quakers Wk WCHMH N21 79 L10
Quakers Wy RGUW GU3 249 H6
Quality Ct LINN WC2A 12 A5
Quality St REDH RH1 258 C4
Quantock Cl CRAWW RH11 283 L7
DTCH/LGLY SL3 150 D4
HYS/HAR UB3 152 E6
STALE/WH AL4 39 H2
Quantock Gdns CRICK * NW2 116 G7
Quantock Rd BXLYHN DA7 164 F8
Quantocks HHNE HP2 36 A3
Quarles Cl CRW RM5 104 B8
Quarley Wy PECK SE15 159 N6
Quarrendon Rd AMSS HP7 69 J6
Quarrendon St FUL/PGN SW6 157 K7
Quarr Rd CAR SM5 201 N6
Quarry Cl LHD/OX KT22 237 J7
OXTED RH8 261 K6
Quarry Gdns LHD/OX KT22 237 J7
Quarry Hl BGR/WK TN15 247 L9
GRAYS RM17 167 M4
Quarry Hill Pk REIG RH2 257 M7
Quarry Ms PUR RM19 165 P3
Quarry Park Rd SUT SM1 221 J3
Quarry Ri SUT SM1 221 J3
Quarry Rd GDST RH9 260 B4
OXTED RH8 261 K6
RGODL GU7 266 F10
WAND/EARL SW18 179 M2
Quarry Springs HLW CM20 47 K1
Quarry St GU GU1 268 A2
The Quarry BRKHM/BTCW RH3 256 A8
Quarry Wy WTHK RM20 166 E5
Quartermaine Av
WOKS/MYFD GU22 232 C8
Quartermass Cl HHW HP1 35 K5
Quartermass Rd HHW HP1 35 K5
Quartermile La LEY E10 120 G9
Quatre Ports CHING * E4 101 J6
Quaves Rd DTCH/LGLY SL3 149 N2
Quay House PUP/IOD * E14 160 F1
Quay La GRH DA9 166 G10
Quebec Av BH/WHM TN16 262 G2
Quebec Cl HORL RH6 281 H4
Quebec Ms MBLAR W1H 10 B6
Quebec Rd GNTH/NBYPK IG2 122 F5
TIL RM18 168 D8
YEAD UB4 133 K9
Quebec Sq BH/WHM TN16 262 G2
Quebec Wy BERM/RHTH SE16 160 C1
Queen Adelaide Rd
PGE/AN SE20 182 B9
Queen Anne Av HAYES BR2 205 M3
Queen Anne Dr ESH/CLAY KT10 218 D4
Queen Anne Ga BXLYHN DA7 163 N9
Queen Anne Ms CAVSQ/HST W1G 10 F4
Queen Anne Rd HOM E9 140 C1
Queen Anne's Cl WDSR SL4 170 G6
WHTN TW2 176 C6
Queen Anne's Gdns CHSWK W4 156 B2
EA W5 155 K1
EN EN1 79 M10
MTCM * CR4 202 A3
Queen Anne's Ga STJSPK SW1H 17 J2
Queen Anne's Gv CHSWK W4 156 B2
EA W5 155 K1
ED N9 99 L1
EN EN1 79 M10
Queen Annes Ms LHD/OX * KT22 236 G7
Queen Anne's Pl EN EN1 79 M10
Queen Annes Ride WDSR * SL4 170 G6
WDSR SL4 171 H3
Queen Anne's Rd WDSR SL4 149 H10
Queen Anne's Ter
LHD/OX * KT22 236 G7
Queen Anne St CAVSQ/HST W1G 10 E4
Queen Anne Ter WAP * E1W 140 A9
Queenborough Gdns CHST BR7 184 G9
GNTH/NBYPK IG2 122 D2
Queen Caroline Est HMSMTH W6 156 F4
Queen Caroline St HMSMTH W6 156 F4
Queendale Ct WOKN/KNAP GU21 231 L2
Queen Eleanor's Rd GUW GU2 267 L1
Queen Elizabeth Av TIL RM18 169 M3
Queen Elizabeth Buildings
EMB * EC4Y 12 A7
Queen Elizabeth Ct WAB * EN9 81 J1
Queen Elizabeth Gdns
MRDN SM4 201 K4
Queen Elizabeth Ii Br GRH DA9 166 D8
Queen Elizabeth Rd
KUTN/CMB * KT2 199 L1
WALTH E17 120 D1
Queen Elizabeth's Cl
STNW/STAM N16 119 L7
Queen Elizabeth's Dr
CROY/NA CR0 225 J6
STHGT/OAK N14 98 F2
Queen Elizabeth St STHWK SE1 19 K1
Queen Elizabeth's Wk
STNW/STAM N16 119 L6
WDSR SL4 149 L8
WLGTN SM6 222 E1
Queen Elizabeth Wk
BARN SW13 156 D7
Queen Elizabeth Wy
WOKS/MYFD GU22 232 C5
Queenhill Rd SAND/SEL CR2 224 A6
Queenhithe BLKFR EC4V 12 F8
Queenhythe Rd RGUE GU4 250 A4
Queen Margaret's Gv IS N1 119 M10
Queen Mary Av MRDN SM4 200 G5
TIL RM18 169 M3
Queen Mary Cl CHSGTN KT9 199 M10
ROM RM1 124 G4
WOKS/MYFD * GU22 232 F2
Queen Mary Rd NRWD SE19 181 J9
SHPTN TW17 196 D2
Queen Mary's Av CAR SM5 222 A4
WATW WD18 72 F8
Queen Marys Ct WAB * EN9 81 H1
Queen Mary's Dr
ADL/WDHM KT15 215 J6
Queen Mother Ga BAY/PAD W2 10 D10
Queens Acre CHEAM SM3 220 G4
WDSR SL4 149 J10
Queens Av BF/WBF KT14 215 N8
FELT TW13 175 K7
FNCH N3 97 M8
GFD/PVL UB6 134 A8
KTN/HRWW/W HA3 114 G1
MUSWH N10 118 B1
TRDG/WHET N20 97 N3
WATW WD18 72 G8
WCHMH N21 99 J2
WFD IG8 101 N6
Queensberry Ms West
SKENS * SW7 15 L5
Queensberry Pl SKENS SW7 15 L5
Queensberry Wy SKENS * SW7 15 L5
Queensborough Ms BAY/PAD * W2 9 J7
Queensborough Pas BAY/PAD W2 9 J7
Queensborough Studios
BAY/PAD W2 9 J7
Queensborough Ter BAY/PAD W2 9 H7
Queensbridge Pk ISLW TW7 176 C2
Queensbridge Rd HACK E8 7 M4
Queensbury Rd CDALE/KGS NW9 116 A5
WLSDN NW10 135 L4
Queensbury Station Pde
EDGW HA8 115 L1
Queensbury St IS N1 6 F4
Queens Circ VX/NE SW8 158 C6
Queens Cl CHOB/PIR GU24 230 F3
EDGW HA8 95 M6
ESH/CLAY * KT10 218 A1
KWD/TDW/WH KT20 238 D10
WDSR SL4 171 M1
WLGTN SM6 222 C2
Queen's Club Gdns WKENS W14 14 B9
Queens Ct BELMT * SM2 221 K7
SL * SL1 129 L9
WEY KT13 216 F2
WOKS/MYFD * GU22 232 C4
Queenscourt WBLY HA9 115 K9
Queens Court Ride COB KT11 217 H9
Queens Crs DORK * RH4 272 F3
KTTN NW5 4 C2
RCHPK/HAM TW10 177 L1
STALE/WH AL4 38 G3
Queenscroft Rd ELTH/MOT SE9 184 A1
Queensdale Crs NTGHL W11 136 G10
Queensdale Rd NTGHL W11 8 A10
Queensdale Wk NTGHL W11 8 A10
Queens Down Rd CLPT E5 120 A9
Queens Dr ABLGY WD5 54 G8
BRYLDS KT5 199 M7
CHES/WCR EN8 62 F10
DTCH/LGLY SL3 130 C3
EA W5 135 L8
FSBYPK N4 119 J7
GUW GU2 249 M7
LEY E10 120 F5
LHD/OX KT22 218 B7
RGODL GU7 266 G10
RSEV TN14 247 K6
THDIT KT7 198 F6
The Queen's Dr
RKW/CH/CXG WD3 71 J10
Queen's Elm Sq CHEL SW3 15 L8
Queen's Farm Rd GVE DA12 191 P5
Queen's Gdns BAY/PAD W2 9 J7
EA W5 135 H7
HDN NW4 116 F3
HEST TW5 153 M7
RAIN RM13 144 E4
RDART DA2 188 A4
UPMR RM14 126 E4
Queens Garth FSTH * SE23 182 B5
Queensgate COB KT11 217 L8
Queens Ga HORL RH6 280 B7
SKENS SW7 15 K2
Queens Gate Gdns CHST BR7 206 G1
Queensgate Gdns
PUT/ROE SW15 156 E10
Queen's Gate Gdns SKENS SW7 15 J4
Queen's Gate Ms SKENS SW7 15 J3
Queensgate Pl KIL/WHAMP NW6 2 E4
Queen's Gate Pl SKENS SW7 15 K4
Queen's Gate Place Ms
SKENS SW7 15 K4
Queen's Gate Ter SKENS SW7 15 J3
Queen's Gv STJWD NW8 3 L6
Queen's Grove Rd CHING E4 101 J2
Queen's Head St IS N1 6 D6
Queenshill Ldg ASC SL5 192 A3
Queens Hill Ri ASC SL5 192 B3
Queens Keep TWK * TW1 177 H2
Queensland Av UED N18 99 K7
WIM/MER SW19 201 L1
Queensland Pl HOLWY N7 119 H9
Queensland Rd HOLWY N7 119 H9
Queens La MUSWH N10 118 C1
Queensmead DTCH/LGLY SL3 149 N7
LHD/OX * KT22 218 B7
STJWD NW8 3 M5
Queensmead Av EW KT17 220 E6
Queen's Mead Rd HAYES BR2 205 L2
Queensmere Cl WIM/MER SW19 178 G5
Queensmere Rd SL SL1 149 L1
WIM/MER SW19 178 G5
Queen's Ms BAY/PAD W2 9 H7
Queensmill Rd FUL/PGN SW6 156 G6
Queens Pde CEND/HSY/T * N8 119 J2
CRICK * NW2 136 F1
EA * W5 135 L8
FBAR/BDGN * N11 98 A6
FBAR/BDGN * N11 98 F8
HDN * NW4 116 E3
Queens Parade Cl
FBAR/BDGN N11 98 A6
Queens Park Gdns FELT * TW13 174 G6
Queen's Park Rd CTHM CR3 241 M9
HARH RM3 105 N9
Queen's Pl MRDN SM4 201 K4
WAT WD17 73 K7
WOT/HER KT12 216 F2
Queen Sq BMSBY WC1N 11 M2
Queen's Ride BARN SW13 156 D9
Queen's Ri RCHPK/HAM TW10 177 L2
Queen's Rd ASC SL5 192 C5
BAR EN5 76 G7
BARK IG11 142 F2
BECK BR3 204 D2
BELMT SM2 221 K6
BERK HP4 33 M4
BKHH IG9 101 N3
BMLY BR1 205 M2
BRW CM14 107 H4
CHES/WCR EN8 62 D10
CHOB/PIR GU24 230 D6
CHST BR7 184 E9
CROY/NA CR0 203 J6
CSHM * HP5 51 H6
DTCH/LGLY SL3 149 N7
EA W5 135 K8
ED N9 100 A3
EGH TW20 172 C9
EN EN1 79 M8
EPP CM16 66 D1
ERITH DA8 164 F5
FBAR/BDGN N11 98 F8
FELT TW13 175 J4
FNCH N3 97 M9
GU GU1 250 A10
GVE DA12 190 F6
HARP AL5 20 A4
HDN NW4 116 F3
HERT/BAY SG13 25 L6
HORL RH6 280 B4
HPTN TW12 176 A7
HSLW TW3 154 A9
HYS/HAR UB3 132 F8
KUTN/CMB KT2 177 M10
LOU IG10 82 C7
MORT/ESHN SW14 156 A9
MRDN SM4 201 K4
MTCM CR4 201 N3
NWDGN UB2 153 L1

NWMAL KT3 200 C4
PECK SE15 160 B7
PLSTW E13 141 N3
RCHPK/HAM TW10 177 L2
SL SL1 129 L9
TEDD TW11 176 E9
THDIT KT7 198 E5
TWK TW1 176 E4
UX/CGN UB8 131 M5
WALTH E17 120 E4
WAN E11 121 K5
WARE SG12 26 E1
WAT WD17 73 K8
WDR/YW UB7 152 A1
WDSR SL4 148 D4
WDSR SL4 149 H8
WELL DA16 163 L8
WEY KT13 216 E2
WIM/MER SW19 179 L8
WLGTN SM6 222 C2
WOKN/KNAP GU21 231 H4
WOT/HER KT12 216 F2
Queen's Rd West PLSTW E13 141 M4
Queens Rw WALW * SE17 18 G9
WALW SE17 18 G9
Queens Sq CRAWE RH10 283 N7
The Queen's Sq HHNE HP2 36 A6
Queen's Ter ISLW TW7 154 F10
PLSTW E13 141 N3
STJWD NW8 3 L6
THDIT * KT7 198 F6
WCHPL * E1 140 B6
Queens Terrace Cottages
HNWL * W7 154 D1
Queensthorpe Ms SYD * SE26 182 C7
Queensthorpe Rd SYD SE26 182 C7
Queens Town Gdns RAIN RM13 144 G5
Queenstown Rd VX/NE SW8 16 E10
Queen St BRW CM14 107 H6
BXLYHN DA7 164 A9
CHERT KT16 195 K8
CROY/NA CR0 223 K1
ERITH * DA8 164 F5
GVE DA12 190 E2
KGLGY WD4 53 K7
MYFR/PICC W1J 10 E9
ROMW/RG RM7 124 E4
SHGR GU5 270 D5
STALW/RED AL3 38 B6
TOTM N17 99 M7
Queen Street Pl CANST EC4R 12 F8
Queensville Rd CLAP SW4 180 E3
Queens Wk ASHF TW15 173 N7
CDALE/KGS NW9 115 P7
CHING E4 101 J2
EA W5 135 H6
HRW HA1 114 D2
RSLP HA4 113 K8
Queens Walk Ter RSLP * HA4 113 K8
Queens Wy CHES/WCR EN8 62 E10
FELT TW13 175 K7
HDN NW4 116 F3
RAD WD7 57 K7
Queensway BAY/PAD W2 9 H5
CHONG CM5 67 N2
CRAWE RH10 283 P7
CROY/NA CR0 222 G2
HAT AL10 40 D4
HHW HP1 35 M5
PEND EN3 80 B8
REDH RH1 258 A9
STMC/STPC BR5 206 F5
SUN TW16 197 J2
WOT/HER KT12 217 K2
WWKM BR4 225 M1
Queensway North
WOT/HER KT12 217 K1
Queensway South
WOT/HER KT12 217 K1
The Queensway
CFSP/GDCR SL9 110 A2
Queens Well Av
TRDG/WHET N20 97 P5
Queenswood Av HEST TW5 153 N8
HPTN TW12 176 A9
THHTH CR7 203 H5
WALTH E17 101 H9
WLGTN SM6 222 E1
Queenswood Crs GSTN WD25 55 H9
Queenswood Gdns WAN E11 121 M6
Queenswood Pk FNCH N3 97 H10
Queenswood Rd BFN/LL DA15 185 J1
FSTH SE23 182 D6
Queen's Wood Rd HGT N6 118 C4
Queenswood Rd
WOKN/KNAP GU21 231 J5
Queen's Yd FITZ W1T 11 H2
Queen Victoria Av ALP/SUD HA0 135 J2
Queen Victoria St BLKFR EC4V 12 E7
Queen Victoria's Wk WDSR SL4 149 H6
Queen Victoria Ter WAP * E1W 140 A9
Quemerford Rd HOLWY N7 118 G10
Quendell Wk HHNE HP2 35 P6
Quendon Dr WAB EN9 63 J9
Quennell Cl ASHTD KT21 237 L5
Quennell Wy RBRW/HUT CM13 107 P1
Quentin Pl LEW SE13 161 K9
Quentin Rd BKHTH/KID SE3 161 K9
Quentins Dr BH/WHM TN16 244 E2
Quentins Wk BH/WHM * TN16 244 E2
Quentin Wy VW GU25 193 N4
Quernmore Cl BMLY BR1 183 M8
Quernmore Rd BMLY BR1 183 M9
FSBYPK N4 119 H4
Querrin St FUL/PGN SW6 157 M8
Questor DART * DA1 187 N5
Quex Ms KIL/WHAMP NW6 2 F5
Quex Rd KIL/WHAMP NW6 2 F5
Quickbeams WGCE AL7 23 K2
Quickberry Pl AMSS * HP7 69 H5
Quickley Brow
RKW/CH/CXG * WD3 70 E10
Quickley La RKW/CH/CXG WD3 70 F10
Quickley Ri RKW/CH/CXG WD3 70 F10
Quickly Brow RKW/CH/CXG WD3 70 E10
Quickmoor La KGLGY WD4 53 L9
Quick Rd CHSWK W4 156 B4
Quicks Rd WIM/MER SW19 179 L10
Quick St IS N1 6 D8
Quickswood HAMP NW3 3 P3
Quickwood Cl RKW/CH/CXG WD3 71 J10
Quiet Cl ADL/WDHM KT15 215 K1
Quiet Nook HAYES BR2 206 A10
Quill Hall La AMS HP6 69 L3
The Quillot WOT/HER KT12 216 G2
Quill St EA W5 135 K5
FSBYPK N4 119 H8
Quilp St STHWK SE1 18 E1
Quilter Rd STMC/STPC BR5 207 M8
Quilter St BETH E2 7 N9
WOOL/PLUM SE18 163 J4
Quinbrookes SLN SL2 129 P8
Quince Cl ASC SL5 192 C4
Quince Dr CHOB/PIR GU24 230 G1
Quinces Cft HHW HP1 35 K4
Quince Tree Cl SOCK/AV RM15 147 H6
Quincy Rd EGH TW20 172 D8
Quinta Dr BAR EN5 76 E9
Quintin Av RYNPK SW20 201 H1
Quinton Cl BECK BR3 205 H3
HEST TW5 153 J6
WLGTN SM6 222 C1
Quinton Rd THDIT KT7 198 F8
Quinton St WAND/EARL SW18 179 M5
Quinton Wy WAB EN9 81 H1
Quintrell Cl WOKN/KNAP GU21 231 N3
Quixley St POP/IOD E14 141 J9
Quorn Rd EDUL SE22 159 M10

R

Raans Rd AMS HP6 69 L4
Rabbit Rw KENS * W8 8 F9
Rabbits Rd EYN DA4 210 E2
MNPK E12 122 B9
Rabies Heath Rd REDH RH1 259 P10
Rablus Pl EYN * DA4 209 N6
Rabournmead Dr RSLP HA4 113 M10
Raby Rd NWMAL KT3 200 A4
Raby St POP/IOD * E14 140 D8
Raccoon Wy HSLWW TW4 153 K8
Racecourse Wy HORL RH6 280 A8
Racefield Cl GVE DA12 191 P9
Rachel Cl BARK/HLT IG6 122 G1
Rackham Cl CRAWW RH11 283 N9
WELL DA16 163 L8
Rackham Ms STRHM/NOR SW16 180 D9
Racton Rd FUL/PGN SW6 14 E10
Radbourne Av EA W5 155 H3
Radbourne Cl CLPT E5 120 C9
Radbourne Ct
KTN/HRWW/W * HA3 114 G4
Radbourne Crs WALTH E17 121 J1
Radbourne Rd BAL SW12 180 D3
Radburn Cl HLWS CM18 47 K5
Radcliffe Av ENC/FH EN2 79 K5
WLSDN NW10 136 D4
Radcliffe Gdns CAR SM5 221 P4
Radcliffe Rd CROY/NA CR0 203 N9
KTN/HRWW/W HA3 94 F10
STHWK SE1 19 K3
WCHMH N21 99 J2
Radcliffe Wy NTHLT UB5 133 L5
Radcot Av DTCH/LGLY SL3 150 E2
Radcot St LBTH SE11 18 B8
Raddington Rd NKENS W10 8 B4
Radfield Wy ELTH/MOT SE9 184 G3
Radford Est WLSDN * NW10 136 B5
Radford Rd CRAWE RH10 284 D1
LEW SE13 183 H2
Radford Wy BARK IG11 143 J5
Radipole Rd FUL/PGN SW6 157 J7
Radius Pk EBED/NFELT * TW14 152 G10
Radland Rd CAN/RD E16 141 M8
Rad La SHGR GU5 270 E8
Radlet Av FSTH SE23 182 A6
Radlett Cl FSTGT E7 141 L1
Radlett La RAD WD7 57 J10
Radlett Park Rd RAD WD7 56 G10
Radlett Pl STJWD NW8 3 N6
Radlett Rd GSTN WD25 74 B4
LCOL/BKTW AL2 56 D5
WATN WD24 73 L6
Radley Av GDMY/SEVK IG3 123 J9
Radley Cl EBED/NFELT TW14 174 G4
Radley Ct BERM/RHTH SE16 160 C1
Radley Gdns KTN/HRWW/W HA3 115 K2
Radley Ms KENS W8 14 F4
Radley Rd TOTM N17 99 M10
Radley's La SWFD E18 101 M10
Radleys Md DAGE RM10 144 C1
Radley Sq CLPT * E5 120 B7
Radley Ter CAN/RD * E16 141 L7
Radlix Rd LEY E10 120 F6
Radnor Av HRW HA1 114 D3
WELL DA16 185 L1
Radnor Cl CHST BR7 185 H9
MTCM CR4 202 F5
Radnor Crs REDBR IG4 122 C3
WOOL/PLUM SE18 163 K6
Radnor Gdns EN EN1 79 M5
TWK TW1 176 E5
Radnor Hall BORE * WD6 75 K9
Radnor La SHGR GU5 271 H10
Radnor Ms BAY/PAD W2 9 M6
Radnor Pl BAY/PAD W2 9 N6
Radnor Rd HRW HA1 114 C3
KIL/WHAMP NW6 2 A7
PECK SE15 159 P6
TWK TW1 176 E4
WEY KT13 196 B10
Radnor St FSBYE EC1V 6 F10
Radnor Ter WKENS W14 14 C5
Radnor Wk CHEL SW3 15 P8
CROY/NA CR0 204 D7
Radnor Wy DTCH/LGLY SL3 150 B3
WLSDN NW10 135 N6
Radolphs KWD/TDW/WH KT20 238 G8
Radstock Av KTN/HRWW/W HA3 114 F1
Radstock Cl FBAR/BDGN N11 98 B6
Radstock St BTSEA * SW11 157 P6
Radstock Wy REDH RH1 258 E4
Radstone Ct WOKS/MYFD GU22 232 C4
Raebarn Gdns BAR EN5 76 E9
Raeburn Av BRYLDS KT5 199 N6
DART DA1 187 J1
Raeburn Cl EFNCH N2 117 M4
KUT KT1 177 J10
Raeburn Ct WOKN/KNAP * GU21 231 M5
Raeburn Rd BFN/LL DA15 185 H2
EDGW HA8 95 M10
YEAD UB4 132 E4
Raeburn St BRXS/STRHM SW2 158 F10
Raeside Cl BEAC HP9 89 H7
Rafford Wy BMLY BR1 205 N2
Ragged Hall La LCOL/BKTW AL2 37 L10
Ragge Wy BGR/WK TN15 247 N6
Raggleswood CHST BR7 206 D1
Rag Hill Rd BH/WHM TN16 244 A7
Raglan Av CHES/WCR EN8 62 C10
Raglan Cl HSLWW TW4 175 M1
REIG RH2 257 M8
Raglan Ct CROY/NA CR0 223 J2
Raglan Gdns OXHEY WD19 93 J2
Raglan Rd BELV DA17 164 A3
EN EN1 99 M1
HAYES BR2 205 P4
REIG RH2 257 L8
WALTH E17 121 H3
WOKN/KNAP GU21 231 K4
WOOL/PLUM SE18 162 F4
Raglan St KTTN NW5 4 F1
Raglan Ter RYLN/HDSTN * HA2 114 A9
Raglan Vls WALTH * E17 121 H3
Raglan Wy NTHLT UB5 134 B1
Ragley Cl ACT W3 155 P1
Rags La CHESW EN7 61 M3
Rahn Rd EPP CM16 65 K7
Raider Cl ROMW/RG RM7 104 C9
Raikes La RDKG RH5 271 J8
Railey Ms KTTN NW5 118 D10
Railey Rd CRAWE RH10 283 P7
Railshead Rd ISLW TW7 154 G10
Railton Rd GUW GU2 249 N6
HNHL SE24 181 H1
Railway Ap CHERT * KT16 195 J8
KTN/HRWW/W HA3 114 E2
STHWK SE1 13 H9
TWK TW1 176 F3
WLGTN * SM6 222 C3
Railway Ar BRXN/ST * SW9 159 H10
Railway Av BERM/RHTH SE16 160 B1
Railway Cottages BNSTD * SM7 221 J10
OXTED * RH8 261 M9
SHB * W12 156 F1
SRTFD * E15 141 K4
WIM/MER * SW19 179 L7
Railway Gv NWCR SE14 160 E6
Railway Pl BELV DA17 164 B2
HERT/BAY SG13 25 M5
Railway Ri EDUL SE22 159 M10
Railway Rd CHES/WCR EN8 62 E9
TEDD TW11 176 D7
Railway Side BARN SW13 156 B9
Railway Station Whf LEY * E10 120 D6
Railway St BCTR RM8 123 M6
GVW DA11 189 M1
HERT/WAS SG14 25 L5
IS N1 5 M8
Railway Ter BH/WHM TN16 262 G1
FELT TW13 175 H4
KGLGY WD4 54 B3
LEW SE13 182 G1
SL SL1 129 L10
STA TW18 172 G8
WALTH E17 101 H9
Railway Vw DTCH/LGLY * SL3 150 C9
Rainborough Cl WBLY HA9 135 P1
Rainbow Av POP/IOD E14 160 G4
Rainbow Ct OXHEY WD19 73 K10
WOKN/KNAP GU21 231 K2
Rainbow Rd CDH/CHF RM16 167 H3
HLWE CM17 30 F8
Rainbow St CMBW SE5 159 M6
Rainer Cl CHES/WCR EN8 62 C5
Raine St WAP E1W 140 A10
Rainham Cl BTSEA SW11 179 P2
ELTH/MOT SE9 185 H2
Rainham Rd RAIN RM13 144 G2
WLSDN NW10 136 F5
Rainham Rd North DAGE RM10 124 C7
Rainham Rd South DAGE RM10 124 C9
DAGE RM10 144 D1
Rainhill Wy BOW E3 140 F5
Rainsborough Av DEPT SE8 160 D3
Rainsford Rd WLSDN NW10 135 N5
Rainsford St BAY/PAD W2 9 N5
Rainton Rd CHARL SE7 161 M4
Rainville Rd HMSMTH W6 156 F5
Raisins Hl PIN HA5 113 J1
Raith Av STHGT/OAK N14 98 E4
Raleigh Av WLGTN SM6 222 E1
YEAD UB4 133 J7
Raleigh Cl ERITH DA8 164 G5
HDN NW4 116 F3
PIN HA5 113 L5
RSLP HA4 112 G7
SL SL1 128 F10
Raleigh Ct CRAWE * RH10 284 B2
STA TW18 173 K7
Raleigh Dr BRYLDS KT5 199 P8
ESH/CLAY KT10 218 C2
HORL RH6 281 H4
TRDG/WHET N20 97 P4
Raleigh Gdns MTCM CR4 202 A2
Raleigh Ms IS N1 6 D6
ORP BR6 227 J2
Raleigh Rd CEND/HSY/T N8 119 H2
ENC/FH EN2 79 L8
FELT TW13 174 G5
MUSWH N10 97 P9
NWDGN UB2 153 M4
PGE/AN SE20 182 C10
RCH/KEW TW9 155 L9
Raleigh St IS N1 6 D6
Raleigh Wk CRAWE RH10 283 P9
Raleigh Wy FELT TW13 175 K8
STHGT/OAK N14 98 E2
Ralliwood Rd ASHTD KT21 237 M5
Ralph Perring Ct BECK BR3 204 F4
Ralphs Cross GT/LBKH * KT23 254 B2
Ralston St CHEL SW3 16 A8
Ralston Wy OXHEY WD19 93 L3
Rama Cl STRHM/NOR SW16 180 F10
Ramac Wy CHARL SE7 161 N3
Rambler Cl MDHD SL6 128 A8
STRHM/NOR SW16 180 D7
Rambler La DTCH/LGLY SL3 149 P2
Ramblers Wy WGCE AL7 23 L6
Rambling Wy BERK HP4 34 E3
Rame Cl TOOT SW17 180 B8
Ram Gorse HLW CM20 28 E9
Ramilles Cl BRXS/STRHM SW2 180 F2
Ramillies Pl SOHO/CST W1F 10 G6
Ramillies Rd BFN/LL DA15 185 L2
CHSWK W4 156 A2
MLHL NW7 96 B3
Ramillies St SOHO/CST W1F 10 G6
Ramney Dr PEND EN3 80 D2
Ramones Ter MTCM * CR4 202 D4
Ramornie Cl WOT/HER KT12 217 N1
The Ramparts STALW/RED AL3 38 A8
Rampart St WCHPL E1 140 A8
Ram Pas KUT KT1 199 J2
Rampayne St PIM SW1V 17 J7
Rampton Cl CHING E4 100 F4
Ramsay Cl BROX EN10 44 D7
Ramsay Gdns GPK RM2 105 J9
Ramsay Rd ACT W3 155 P2
BFOR GU20 212 D2
FSTGT E7 121 L9
Ramsbury Rd STAL AL1 38 D7
Ramscote La CSHM HP5 50 E1
Ramscroft Cl ED N9 99 M1
Ramsdale Rd TOOT SW17 180 B8
Ramsden Cl STMC/STPC BR5 207 M8
Ramsden Dr CRW RM5 104 B8
Ramsden Ga BAL * SW12 180 C3
Ramsden Rd BAL SW12 180 B3
ERITH DA8 164 E6
FBAR/BDGN N11 98 A6
ORP BR6 207 L7
STMC/STPC BR5 207 M8
Ramsey Cl BRKMPK AL9 59 N3
CDALE/KGS NW9 116 C4
HORL RH6 280 A4
NTHLT UB5 114 C10
STAL AL1 38 F8
Ramsey Ct SLN SL2 128 C6
Ramsey Lodge Ct STAL AL1 38 D5
Ramsey Pl CTHM CR3 241 K8
Ramsey Rd THHTH CR7 202 G6
Ramsey St BETH E2 13 P1
Ramsey Wk IS N1 6 G1
Ramsey Wy STHGT/OAK N14 98 D1
Ramsgate St HACK E8 7 M1
Ramsgill Ap GNTH/NBYPK IG2 123 J2
Ramsgill Dr GNTH/NBYPK IG2 123 J3
Rams Gv CHDH RM6 123 P2
Ramson Ri HHW HP1 35 H7
Ram St WAND/EARL SW18 179 L1
Ramulis Dr YEAD UB4 133 M6
Ramus Wood Av ORP BR6 227 H2
Rancliffe Gdns ELTH/MOT SE9 162 B10
Rancliffe Rd EHAM E6 142 B4
Randal Crs REIG RH2 275 K2
Randall Av CRICK NW2 116 E8
Randall Cl BTSEA SW11 157 P7
DTCH/LGLY SL3 150 C4
ERITH DA8 164 D5
Randall Dr HCH RM12 125 K9
Randall Pl GNWCH SE10 161 H6
Randall Rd LBTH SE11 17 N7
Randall Rw LBTH SE11 17 N6
Randalls Crs LHD/OX KT22 236 F6
Randalls Park Av LHD/OX KT22 236 F6
Randalls Park Dr LHD/OX KT22 236 F7
Randalls Ride HHNE HP2 35 P4
Randalls Rd LHD/OX KT22 236 D6
Randalls Wy LHD/OX KT22 236 F7
Randell's Rd IS N1 5 M5
Randisbourne Gdns CAT * SE6 182 G6
Randle Rd RCHPK/HAM TW10 177 H7
Randlesdown Rd CAT SE6 182 F7
Randle's La ORP BR6 227 N10
Randolph Ap CAN/RD E16 141 P8
Randolph Av KIL/WHAMP NW6 2 G8
Randolph Cl BXLYHN DA7 164 D9
COB KT11 235 P1
KUTN/CMB * KT2 177 P8
WOKN/KNAP GU21 231 K3
Randolph Crs MV/WKIL W9 9 J2
Randolph Gdns KIL/WHAMP NW6 2 G8
Randolph Ms MV/WKIL W9 9 K2
Randolph Rd DTCH/LGLY SL3 150 B2
EW KT17 220 C10
HAYES BR2 206 C8
MV/WKIL W9 9 J2
STHL * UB1 153 N1
WALTH * E17 120 G3
Randolph St CAMTN NW1 4 G4
Randon Cl PIN HA5 94 A10
Ranelagh WDSR * SL4 170 A4
Ranelagh Av BARN SW13 156 D8
FUL/PGN SW6 157 J9
Ranelagh Cl EDGW HA8 95 M5
Ranelagh Dr EDGW HA8 95 M5
TWK TW1 154 G10
Ranelagh Gdns CHSWK W4 155 P6
FUL/PGN SW6 157 H9
GVW DA11 190 C3
IL IG1 122 D6
WAN E11 121 P3
Ranelagh Gv BGVA SW1W 16 D7
Ranelagh Pl NWMAL KT3 200 B5
Ranelagh Rd ALP/SUD HA0 115 J10
EA W5 155 J1
EHAM E6 142 D3
HHNE HP2 35 L6
PIM SW1V 17 H8
REDH RH1 257 P10
SRTFD E15 141 K3
STHL UB1 133 L10
TOTM N17 119 M1
WAN E11 121 K9
WDGN N22 98 G9
WLSDN NW10 136 C4
Ranfurly Rd SUT SM1 201 K9
Rangefield Rd BMLY BR1 183 M9
Rangemoor Rd
SEVS/STOTM N15 119 N3
Range Rd GVE DA12 190 G3
Rangers Rd LOU IG10 81 N10
Range Wy SHPTN TW17 196 B7
Rangeworth Pl BFN/LL DA15 185 J6
Rangoon St TWRH * EC3N 13 L6
Rankin Cl CDALE/KGS NW9 116 B1
Ranleigh Gdns BXLYHN DA7 164 A6
Ranleigh Wk HARP AL5 20 C5
Ranmere St BAL SW12 180 C4
Ranmoor Gdns HRW HA1 114 C2
Ranmore Av CROY/NA CR0 203 N10
Ranmore Cl REDH RH1 258 B7
Ranmore Common Rd
RDKG RH5 254 C9
Ranmore Pth STMC/STPC BR5 207 K4
Ranmore Pl WEY * KT13 216 D2
Ranmore Rd BELMT SM2 220 G5
DORK RH4 272 F1
RDKG RH5 254 D10
Rannoch Cl EDGW HA8 95 N3
Rannoch Rd HMSMTH W6 156 F5
Rannoch Wk HHNE HP2 35 N2
Rannock Av CDALE/KGS NW9 116 A5
Ranskill Rd BORE WD6 75 M5
Ransom Cl OXHEY WD19 93 K1
Ransome Cl CRAWW RH11 282 G10
Ransom Rd CHARL * SE7 161 P4
Ranston St CAMTN NW1 9 N3
Rant Meadow HHS/BOV HP3 36 B7
Ranulf Cl HLWE CM17 29 M5
Ranulf Rd CRICK NW2 117 J9
Ranwell Cl BOW * E3 140 E3
Ranworth Av HOD EN11 26 G9
Ranworth Cl ERITH DA8 164 F8
HHS/BOV HP3 35 N8
Ranworth Gdns POTB/CUF EN6 58 G7
Ranworth Rd ED N9 100 B3
Ranyard Cl CHSGTN KT9 199 L10
Raphael Av ROM RM1 124 G1
TIL RM18 168 D7
Raphael Cl RAD WD7 57 K8
Raphael Dr THDIT KT7 198 E7
WATN WD24 73 L6
Raphael Rd GVE DA12 190 G3
Raphael St SKENS SW7 16 A2
Rapier Cl PUR RM19 165 N3
Rapley's Fld CHOB/PIR GU24 230 D9
Rapsley La WOKN/KNAP GU21 230 G4
Rasehill Cl RKW/CH/CXG WD3 71 M9
Rashleigh Wy EYN DA4 210 B4
Rasper Rd TRDG/WHET N20 97 M3
Rastell Av BAL SW12 180 E5
Ratcliffe Cl LEE/GVPK SE12 183 M3
UX/CGN UB8 131 N5
Ratcliffe Cross St WCHPL * E1 140 C8
Ratcliffe La POP/IOD E14 140 D8
Ratcliff Rd FSTGT E7 121 P10
Rathbone Market CAN/RD * E16 141 L7
Rathbone Pl FITZ W1T 11 J4
Rathbone Sq CROY/NA * CR0 223 K1
Rathbone St CAN/RD E16 141 L7
FITZ W1T 11 H4
Rathcoole Av CEND/HSY/T N8 118 G3
Rathcoole Gdns CEND/HSY/T N8 118 G3
Rathfern Rd FSTH SE23 182 E4
Rathgar Av WEA W13 134 G10
Rathgar Cl FNCH N3 97 J10
REDH RH1 276 B5
Rathgar Rd BRXN/ST SW9 159 J9
Rathlin HHS/BOV HP3 36 C8
Rathlin Rd CRAWW RH11 283 L10
Rathmell Dr CLAP SW4 180 E2
Rathmore Rd CHARL SE7 161 N4
GVW DA11 190 D3
Rat's La LOU IG10 81 N4
Rattray Rd BRXS/STRHM SW2 159 H10
Ratty's La HOD EN11 45 J3
Raul Rd PECK SE15 159 P8
Raveley St KTTN NW5 118 D9
Ravel Gdns SOCK/AV RM15 146 B8
Ravel Rd SOCK/AV RM15 146 C8
Raven Cl CDALE/KGS NW9 96 C10
RKW/CH/CXG WD3 91 M1
Raven Ct HAT AL10 40 D6
Ravencroft CDH/CHF RM16 168 E1
Ravencroft Crs ELTH/MOT SE9 184 C6
Ravendale Rd SUN TW16 196 G2
Ravenet St BTSEA SW11 158 C7
Ravenfield Rd TOOT SW17 180 A6
Ravenhill Rd PLSTW E13 141 P3
Raven La CRAWW RH11 283 M5
Ravenna Rd PUT/ROE SW15 178 G1
Ravenoak Wy CHIG IG7 103 H6
Ravenor Park Rd GFD/PVL UB6 134 A5
Raven Rd SWFD E18 101 P10
Raven Rw WCHPL E1 140 A7
Ravens Ait SURB * KT6 199 J5
Ravensbourne Av HAYES BR2 205 J1
STWL/WRAY TW19 173 P4
Ravensbourne Crs HARH RM3 125 N1
Ravensbourne Gdns CLAY IG5 102 D9
WEA W13 134 G7
Ravensbourne Pk BROCKY SE4 182 F3
Ravensbourne Park Crs CAT SE6 182 E3
Ravensbourne Pl DEPT SE8 160 G8
Ravensbourne Rd BMLY BR1 205 M3
DART DA1 165 H9
FSTH SE23 182 E3
TWK TW1 177 H2
Ravensbury Av MRDN SM4 201 M5
Ravensbury Gv MTCM CR4 201 N4
Ravensbury La MTCM CR4 201 N4
Ravensbury Rd STMC/STPC BR5 207 J4
WAND/EARL SW18 179 L5
Ravensbury Ter
WAND/EARL SW18 179 L5
Ravenscar Rd BMLY BR1 183 K7
SURB KT6 199 L9
Ravens Cl CDALE/KGS NW9 96 B10
EN EN1 79 M6
HAYES BR2 205 L2
REDH RH1 258 A9
WOKN/KNAP GU21 231 H2
Ravenscourt SUN TW16 196 G1
Ravenscourt Av HMSMTH W6 156 D3
Ravenscourt Cl HCH RM12 125 M8
RSLP HA4 112 D5
Ravenscourt Dr HCH RM12 125 M8
Ravenscourt Gdns HMSMTH W6 156 C3
Ravenscourt Gv HCH RM12 125 M7
Ravenscourt Pk HMSMTH W6 156 D3
Ravenscourt Pl HMSMTH W6 156 E3
Ravenscourt Rd HMSMTH W6 156 E3
STMC/STPC BR5 207 K3
Ravenscourt Sq HMSMTH W6 156 D2
Ravenscraig Rd FBAR/BDGN N11 98 C5
Ravenscroft BROX * EN10 44 E6
GSTN WD25 73 M1
HARP AL5 20 C5
Ravenscroft Av GLDGN NW11 117 J5
WBLY HA9 115 K6
Ravenscroft Cl CAN/RD E16 141 M7
Ravenscroft Cottages BAR * EN5 77 K10
BAR * EN5 77 K8
Ravenscroft Pk BAR EN5 76 G7
Ravenscroft Rd BECK BR3 204 B2
CAN/RD E16 141 M7
CHSWK W4 155 P3
WEY KT13 216 D7
Ravenscroft St BETH E2 7 M8
Ravensdale Av NFNCH/WDSP N12 97 M5
Ravensdale Gdns NRWD SE19 181 L10
Ravensdale Ms STA TW18 173 L9
Ravensdale Rd HSLWW TW4 153 M9
STNW/STAM N16 119 N5
Ravensdell HHW HP1 35 J5
Ravensdon St LBTH SE11 18 B8
Ravensfield DAGW RM9 123 N9
Ravens Fld DTCH/LGLY SL3 150 A1
Ravensfield EGH TW20 171 N9
Ravensfield Gdns
HOR/WEW KT19 220 B2
Ravenshaw St KIL/WHAMP NW6 117 J10
Ravenshead Cl SAND/SEL CR2 224 B7
Ravenshill CHST BR7 206 E1
Ravenshurst Av HDN NW4 116 F2
Ravenside Cl UED N18 100 C6
Ravens La BERK HP4 34 A5
Ravenslea Rd BAL SW12 180 A3
Ravensmead CFSP/GDCR SL9 90 C6
Ravensmead Rd HAYES BR2 183 J10
Ravensmede Wy CHSWK W4 156 C3
Ravensmere EPP CM16 65 K6
Ravens Ms BKHTH/KID * SE3 183 M1
Ravenstone Rd
CDALE/KGS * NW9 116 C4
CEND/HSY/T N8 118 G1
Ravenstone St BAL SW12 180 B4
Ravens Wy LEE/GVPK SE12 183 M1
Ravens Wold PUR/KEN CR8 241 K1
Ravenswood BXLY DA5 185 P4
Ravenswood Av SURB KT6 199 L9
WWKM BR4 205 H8
Ravenswood Cl COB KT11 235 L1
CRW RM5 104 C6

Ravenswood Ct
KUTN/CMB * KT2 177 N9
WOKS/MYFD GU22 232 C4
Ravenswood Crs
RYLN/HDSTN HA2 113 N7
WWKM BR4 205 H8
Ravenswood Gdns ISLW TW7 154 D7
Ravenswood Pk NTHWD HA6 93 H7
Ravenswood Rd BAL SW12 180 C3
CROY/NA CR0 203 J10
WALTH E17 121 H2
Ravensworth Rd
ELTH/MOT SE9 184 C7
SLN SL2 128 F5
WLSDN * NW10 136 E5
Ravent Rd LBTH SE11 17 P6
Ravey St SDTCH EC2A 13 J1
Ravine Gv WOOL/PLUM SE18 163 H5
Rav Pinter Cl STNW/STAM N16 119 M5
Rawdon Dr HOD EN11 44 F4
Rawlings Cl ORP BR6 227 J2
Rawlings La BEAC HP9 89 J4
Rawlings St CHEL SW3 16 A5
Rawlins Cl FNCH N3 117 H1
SAND/SEL CR2 224 E4
Rawnsley Av MTCM CR4 201 N5
Raworth Cl CRAWE * RH10 284 D9
Rawreth Wk IS N1 6 F5
Rawson St BTSEA SW11 158 B7
Rawsthorne Cl CAN/RD E16 142 C10
Rawstorne Pl FSBYE * EC1V 6 C9
Rawstorne St FSBYE EC1V 6 C9
Ray Bell Ct BROCKY * SE4 160 E8
Rayburn Rd EMPK RM11 125 P5
HHW HP1 35 K4
Raydean Rd BAR EN5 77 K9
Raydons Gdns DAGW RM9 123 P9
Raydons Rd DAGW RM9 123 P10
Raydon St KTTN NW5 118 C7
Rayfield EPP CM16 65 J6
WGCW AL8 22 C2
Rayfield Cl HAYES BR2 206 B6
Rayford Av LEE/GVPK SE12 183 L3
Rayford Cl DART DA1 187 K1
Ray Gdns BARK IG11 143 K4
STAN HA7 94 G6
Ray Lamb Wy ERITH DA8 165 J5
Raylands Md CFSP/GDCR SL9 109 P3
Rayleas Cl WOOL/PLUM SE18 162 E7
Rayleigh Av TEDD TW11 176 D9
Rayleigh Cl PLMGR N13 99 L4
RBRW/HUT CM13 107 P1
Rayleigh Ct KUT KT1 199 M2
Rayleigh Pde RBRW/HUT * CM13 87 P10
Rayleigh Ri SAND/SEL CR2 223 M3
Rayleigh Rd CAN/RD E16 141 N10
PLMGR N13 99 K4
RBRW/HUT CM13 87 P10
WFD IG8 101 P8
WIM/MER SW19 201 J1
Rayley La EPP CM16 48 B10
Ray Lodge Rd WFD IG8 101 P7
Raymead Av THHTH CR7 203 H5
Raymead Cl LHD/OX KT22 236 D8
Raymead Wy LHD/OX KT22 236 D8
Raymer Cl STAL AL1 38 D5
Raymere Gdns
WOOL/PLUM SE18 162 G6
Raymer Wk HORL RH6 280 D3
Raymond Av HNWL W7 154 F2
SWFD E18 121 L1
Raymond Buildings GINN * WC1R 11 P3
Raymond Cl ABLGY WD5 54 E8
DTCH/LGLY SL3 151 H7
SYD SE26 182 B8
Raymond Crs GUW GU2 267 L1
Raymond Gdns CHIG IG7 103 L4
Raymond Rd BECK BR3 204 D4
DTCH/LGLY SL3 150 D3
GNTH/NBYPK IG2 122 D5
PLSTW E13 141 P2
WIM/MER SW19 179 J9
Raymonds Cl WGCE * AL7 23 H7
Raymonds Pln WGCE AL7 23 H7
Raymond Wy ESH/CLAY * KT10 218 F3
Raymouth Rd BERM/RHTH SE16 160 A3
Rayne Ct SWFD E18 121 L2
Rayners Cl ALP/SUD HA0 115 J10
DTCH/LGLY SL3 150 F6
Rayners Gdns NTHLT UB5 133 J5
Rayners La PIN HA5 113 N3
Rayner's Rd PUT/ROE SW15 179 H1
Raynes Av WAN E11 121 P5
Raynham Av UED N18 99 P7
Raynham Rd HMSMTH W6 156 E3
UED N18 99 P6
Raynham St HERT/BAY SG13 25 M4
Raynham Ter UED N18 99 P6
Raynor Cl STHL UB1 133 N10
Raynor Pl IS N1 6 F5
Raynsford Rd WARE SG12 26 D2
Raynton Cl RYLN/HDSTN HA2 113 M6
YEAD UB4 132 G6
Raynton Dr YEAD UB4 132 G5
Raynton Rd PEND EN3 80 C3
Ray Rd CRW RM5 104 C6
E/WMO/HCT KT8 198 A5
Rays Av UED N18 100 B5
WDSR SL4 148 E6
Ray's Hl CSHM HP5 32 B7
EYN DA4 210 B4
Rays Rd UED N18 100 B5
WWKM BR4 205 H7
Ray St CLKNW EC1R 12 B2
Ray Street Br CLKNW * EC1R 12 B2
Raywood Cl WDR/YW UB7 152 D6
Reachview Cl CAMTN NW1 5 H4
Read Ct WAB EN9 63 M9
The Readens BNSTD SM7 239 P2
Reading Arch Rd REDH RH1 258 A10
Reading La HACK E8 140 A1
Reading Rd NTHLT UB5 114 A10
SUT SM1 221 M2
The Readings HLWS CM18 47 J4
RKW/CH/CXG WD3 71 J7
Reading Wy MLHL NW7 96 G6
Read Rd ASHTD KT21 237 J3
Reads Cl IL IG1 122 E8
Reads Rest La
KWD/TDW/WH KT20 239 J5
Read Wy GVE DA12 190 G8
Reapers Cl CAMTN NW1 5 J5
Reapers Wy ISLW TW7 176 C1
Reardon Pth WAP E1W 140 A10
Reardon St WAP E1W 140 A10
Reaston St NWCR SE14 160 B6
Reckitt Rd CHSWK W4 156 B4
Record St PECK SE15 160 B5
Recovery St TOOT SW17 179 P8
Recreation Av HARH RM3 105 N10
ROMW/RG RM7 124 D3
Recreation Rd GU GU1 249 P10
HAYES BR2 205 L2
NWDGN UB2 153 M3
SYD SE26 182 C7
Recreation Wy MTCM CR4 202 F3
Rector St IS N1 6 E6
Rectory Cha BRWN CM15 87 H3
RBRW/HUT CM13 127 K2
Rectory Cl ASHTD KT21 237 L5
BF/WBF KT14 215 P9
BRKMPK AL9 41 P3
CHING E4 100 F4
DART DA1 164 F10
FNCH N3 97 J9
RGUE GU4 250 G8
RYNPK SW20 200 F2
SCUP DA14 185 L7
SHPTN TW17 196 B3
SLN SL2 129 H5
STAN HA7 94 G7
SURB KT6 199 H8
WARE SG12 28 A3
WDSR SL4 148 F7
Rectory Fld HLWW/ROY CM19 46 E3
Rectory Field Crs CHARL SE7 161 P6
Rectory Gdns BECK * BR3 204 F1
CEND/HSY/T N8 118 F2
CHST * BR7 206 F1
HAT AL10 40 E4
NTHLT UB5 133 N3
UPMR RM14 126 C7
Rectory Gn BECK BR3 204 E1
Rectory Gv CLAP SW4 158 D9
CROY/NA CR0 203 J9
FELT TW13 175 N7
Rectory Hl AMSS HP7 69 H5
Rectory La AMSS HP7 68 G5
ASHTD KT21 237 L4
BERK HP4 33 P5
BF/WBF KT14 215 P9
BFOR GU20 212 B4
BH/WHM TN16 244 B9
BH/WHM TN16 245 M10
BNSTD SM7 240 A1
BRKHM/BTCW RH3 256 C8
CRAWW RH11 283 J5
EDGW HA8 95 M7
GT/LBKH KT23 253 N2
HLWW/ROY CM19 46 E3
HORL RH6 278 G8
KGLGY WD4 54 B4
LOU IG10 82 D6
RAD WD7 57 L9
RAD WD7 57 P7
RKW/CH/CXG WD3 91 N2
SCUP DA14 185 L7
SEV TN13 265 J2
SHGR GU5 270 A5
STAN HA7 94 G6
SURB KT6 199 H8
TOOT SW17 180 B8
WLGTN SM6 222 D1
Rectory Meadow MEO DA13 189 M9
Rectory Orch WIM/MER SW19 179 H7
Rectory Pk SAND/SEL CR2 223 M9
Rectory Park Av NTHLT UB5 133 N5
Rectory Pl CHST * BR7 206 F1
WOOL/PLUM SE18 162 D3
Rectory Rd ACT W3 135 N10
BARN SW13 156 D8
BECK BR3 204 F1
COUL/CHIP CR5 257 N1
DAGE RM10 144 B1
GRAYS RM17 168 A2
HAYES BR2 226 A4
HEST TW5 153 J8
HYS/HAR UB3 133 H8
MNPK E12 122 C10
NWDGN UB2 153 N2
RKW/CH/CXG WD3 91 N1
STNW/STAM N16 119 N7
SUT SM1 201 K10
SWCM DA10 189 K3
TIL RM18 168 G5
WALTH E17 120 G2
WGCW AL8 22 E2
Rectory Sq WCHPL E1 140 C7
Rectory Wy HGDN/ICK UB10 112 C7
Rectory Wd HLW CM20 28 F10
Reculver Ms UED N18 99 P5
Reculver Rd BERM/RHTH SE16 160 B4
Red Anchor Cl CHEL * SW3 15 M10
Redan Pl BAY/PAD W2 8 G6
Redan St WKENS W14 156 G2
Redan Ter CMBW SE5 159 J8
Redbarn Cl PUR/KEN CR8 223 J7
Red Barracks Rd
WOOL/PLUM SE18 162 C3
Redberry Gv SYD SE26 182 B6
Redbourne Av FNCH N3 97 K9
Redbourn Rd HHNE HP2 36 C1
STALW/RED AL3 37 M2
Redbridge Gdns CMBW SE5 159 M6
Redbridge La East REDBR IG4 122 A4
Redbridge La West WAN E11 121 N4
Redburn St CHEL SW3 16 A9
Redbury Cl RAIN RM13 145 J6
Redcar Cl NTHLT UB5 114 A10
Redcar Rd HARH RM3 105 N6
Redcar St CMBW * SE5 159 K6
Redcastle Cl WCHPL E1 140 B9
Red Cedars Rd ORP BR6 207 H7
Redchurch St BETH E2 13 L1
Redcliffe Cl ECT SW5 14 G8
Redcliffe Gdns IL IG1 122 D6
WBPTN SW10 15 H8
Redcliffe Ms WBPTN SW10 15 H8
Redcliffe Pl WBPTN SW10 15 J10
Redcliffe Rd WBPTN SW10 15 J8
Redcliffe Sq WBPTN SW10 15 H8
Redcliffe St WBPTN SW10 15 H9
Redclose Av MRDN SM4 201 K5
Redclyffe Rd EHAM E6 141 P3
Redcote Pl DORK RH4 255 J10
Red Cottage Ms DTCH/LGLY SL3 149 P2
Red Ct SL SL1 129 K10
Redcourt WOKS/MYFD GU22 232 G1
Redcroft Rd GFD/PVL UB6 134 B9
Redcross Wy STHWK SE1 18 F1
Redden Court Rd HARH RM3 125 M1
Redding Cl RDART DA2 188 D5
Redding Dr AMS HP6 68 G3
Reddings HHS/BOV HP3 36 A8
WGCW AL8 22 F4
Reddings Av BUSH WD23 74 A9
Reddings Cl MLHL NW7 96 C5
The Reddings BORE WD6 75 L7
MLHL NW7 96 C4
Reddington Cl SAND/SEL CR2 223 L5
Reddington Dr DTCH/LGLY SL3 150 C3
Redding Wy WOKN/KNAP GU21 231 J4
Reddins Rd PECK SE15 159 P6
Reddons Rd BECK BR3 182 D10
Reddown Rd COUL/CHIP CR5 240 E4
Reddy Rd ERITH DA8 164 G5
Rede Ct WEY * KT13 196 C10
Redehall Rd HORL RH6 281 J6
Rede Pl BAY/PAD W2 8 F6
Redesdale Gdns ISLW TW7 154 F6
Redesdale St CHEL SW3 16 A9
Redfern Av HSLWW TW4 175 P3
Redfern Cl UX/CGN UB8 131 M3
Redfern Gdns GPK RM2 105 L10
Redfern Rd CAT SE6 183 H3
WLSDN NW10 136 B2
Redfield La ECT SW5 14 G5
Redford Av COUL/CHIP CR5 240 C1
THHTH CR7 202 G4
WLGTN SM6 222 F3
Redford Cl FELT TW13 174 G5
Redford Rd WDSR SL4 148 C7
Redford Wk IS * N1 6 D5
Redford Wy UX/CGN UB8 131 M2
Redgate Dr HAYES BR2 205 N9
Redgate Ter PUT/ROE SW15 178 G2
Redgrave Cl SNWD SE25 203 N6
Redgrave Dr CRAWE RH10 284 E8
Redgrave Rd PUT/ROE SW15 156 G10
Redgrave Ter BETH * E2 7 P10
Redhall Cl HAT AL10 40 C7
Redhall Dr HAT AL10 40 C7
Redhall La RKW/CH/CXG WD3 71 P5
Redhall Ter ACT * W3 135 M9
Redheath Cl GSTN WD25 72 G1
Red Hl CHST BR7 184 D8
Redhill Dr EDGW HA8 95 P10
Redhill Rd COB KT11 216 C9
Redhill St CAMTN NW1 4 F8
Red House Cl BEAC HP9 88 A7
WARE SG12 26 D4
Red House La BXLYHS DA6 163 N10
WOT/HER KT12 197 H9
Redhouse Rd BH/WHM TN16 243 P7
Red House Rd CROY/NA CR0 202 E6
Red House Sq IS * N1 6 F3
Redington Gdns HAMP NW3 117 L9
Redington Rd HAMP NW3 117 L8
Redland Gdns E/WMO/HCT * KT8 197 N4
Redlands COUL/CHIP CR5 240 F2
Redlands La RDKG RH5 272 F8
Redlands Rd PEND EN3 80 D5
SEV TN13 246 G10
Redlands Wy BRXS/STRHM SW2 180 F3
Red La ESH/CLAY KT10 218 F3
OXTED RH8 261 N9
RDKG RH5 273 M7
Redleaf Cl BELV DA17 164 B5
Redleaves Av ASHF TW15 174 C9
Redlees Cl ISLW TW7 154 F10
Red Lion Cl GSTN WD25 74 A3
STMC/STPC BR5 207 M6
WALW SE17 18 G9
Red Lion Ct FLST/FETLN EC4A 12 B6
HSLW * TW3 154 A9
Red Lion Crs HLWE CM17 47 M3
Red Lion Hl EFNCH N2 97 N10
Red Lion La CHOB/PIR GU24 213 K5
HHS/BOV HP3 54 A2
HLWE CM17 47 M3
RKW/CH/CXG WD3 71 K1
WOOL/PLUM SE18 162 D7
Red Lion Pde PIN * HA5 113 M1
Red Lion Pl WOOL/PLUM * SE18 162 D7
Red Lion Rd CHOB/PIR GU24 213 K5
SURB KT6 199 L9
Red Lion Rw WALW SE17 18 F10
Red Lion Sq BMSBY WC1N 11 N4
WAND/EARL * SW18 179 K1
Red Lion St CSHM HP5 50 G8
GINN WC1R 11 N4
RCHPK/HAM TW10 177 J1
Red Lion Yd MYFR/PKLN * W1K 10 D9
Red Lodge Crs BXLY DA5 186 E6
Red Lodge Gdns BERK HP4 33 M6
Red Lodge Rd BXLY DA5 186 E6
WWKM BR4 205 H8
Redman Cl NTHLT UB5 133 K4
Redmans La RSEV TN14 228 G3
Redman's Rd WCHPL E1 140 B7
Redmead La WAP * E1W 13 N10
Redmead Rd HYS/HAR UB3 152 F3
Redmore Rd HMSMTH * W6 156 E3
Red Oak Cl ORP BR6 206 E10
Red Pl MYFR/PKLN W1K 10 C7
Red Post Hl HNHL SE24 181 L1
Redricks La HLW CM20 29 J5
Redriffe Rd PLSTW E13 141 L4
Redriff Rd BERM/RHTH SE16 160 D2
ROMW/RG RM7 104 C10
Red Rd BORE WD6 75 L7
BRW CM14 106 G5
Redroofs Cl BECK BR3 204 G1
Redruth Cl WDGN N22 98 G8
Redruth Rd HARH RM3 105 N6
HOM E9 140 B3
Redstart Cl CROY/NA CR0 225 J6
EHAM E6 142 B7
NWCR * SE14 160 D6
Redstone Hl REDH RH1 258 B10
Redstone Hollow REDH RH1 276 B1
Redstone Mnr REDH RH1 258 B10
Redstone Pk REDH RH1 258 B10
Redstone Rd REDH RH1 276 B1
Redston Rd CEND/HSY/T N8 118 E2
Red St MEO DA13 189 N9
Redvers Rd WARL CR6 242 C4
WDGN N22 99 H10
Redvers St IS N1 7 K9
Redwald Rd CLPT E5 120 C9
Redway Dr WHTN TW2 176 B3
Red Willow HLWW/ROY CM19 46 C4
Redwing Av RGODL GU7 267 J8
Redwing Cl SAND/SEL CR2 224 C7
Redwing Gdns BF/WBF KT14 215 L8
Redwing Gv ABLGY WD5 55 H7
Redwing Ri RGUE GU4 250 G8
Redwing Rd WLGTN SM6 222 F3
Redwood EGH TW20 195 H2
Redwood Cha SOCK/AV RM15 147 H6
Redwood Cl BERM/RHTH SE16 140 D10
BFN/LL DA15 185 K4
CRAWE RH10 283 P5
HGDN/ICK UB10 132 C4
OXHEY WD19 93 K5
PUR/KEN CR8 223 K10
STHGT/OAK N14 98 E1
Redwood Dr ASC SL5 192 G6
HHS/BOV HP3 35 P8
Redwood Gdns CHING * E4 100 G1
SL SL1 129 J9
Redwood Gv RGUE GU4 268 F6
Redwood Ms ASHF * TW15 174 E10
Redwood Mt REIG RH2 257 K7
Redwood Ri BORE WD6 75 M3
Redwoods ADL/WDHM KT15 215 K3
HERT/WAS SG14 25 K4
The Redwoods WDSR SL4 149 J9
Redwood Wy BAR EN5 76 G9
Reece Ms SKENS SW7 15 L5
Reed Av ORP BR6 207 H10
Reed Cl CAN/RD E16 141 M7
IVER SL0 131 H8
LCOL/BKTW AL2 57 J3
LEE/GVPK SE12 183 M1
Reed Dr REDH RH1 276 B3
Reede Rd DAGE RM10 144 B1
Reede Wy DAGE RM10 144 C1
Reedham Cl LCOL/BKTW AL2 55 P5
TOTM N17 120 A2
Reedham Dr PUR/KEN CR8 222 G9
Reedham Park Av PUR/KEN CR8 241 H2
Reedham St PECK * SE15 159 P8
Reedholm Vls STNW/STAM N16 119 L9
Reedings CRAWW RH11 282 G9
Reed Pl WOKN/KNAP GU21 215 H9
Reed Pond Wk GPK RM2 104 G10
Reed Rd TOTM N17 99 N10
Reeds Crs WATN WD24 73 K6
Reedsfield Cl ASHF TW15 174 C6
Reedsfield Rd ASHF TW15 174 B7
Reed's Pl CAMTN NW1 4 G3
The Reeds WGCE AL7 22 G6
Reedworth St LBTH SE11 18 B6
Reenglass Rd STAN * HA7 95 J5
Rees Dr STAN HA7 95 K5
Rees Gdns CROY/NA CR0 203 N6
Reesland Cl MNPK E12 142 D1
Rees St IS N1 6 F6
Reets Farm Cl CDALE/KGS NW9 116 B4
Reeve Rd REDH RH1 275 M4
Reeves Av CDALE/KGS NW9 116 A5
Reeves Cnr CROY/NA CR0 203 J9
Reeves Crs SWLY BR8 208 E3
Reeves La HLWW/ROY CM19 45 P5
Reeves Ms MYFR/PKLN W1K 10 C8
Reeves Rd BOW E3 140 G6
WOOL/PLUM SE18 162 E5
Reform Rw TOTM N17 99 N10
Reform St BTSEA SW11 158 A8
Regal Cl EA W5 135 J7
WCHPL E1 13 P3
Regal Ct MTCM CR4 202 A3
UED N18 99 N6
Regal Crs WLGTN SM6 202 C10
Regal Dr FBAR/BDGN N11 98 C6
Regalfield Cl GUW GU2 249 M6
Regal La CAMTN NW1 4 D6
Regal Wy KTN/HRWW/W HA3 115 K4
WATN WD24 73 K4
Regan Cl GUW GU2 249 N5
Regan Wy IS N1 7 J8
Regarder Rd CHIG IG7 103 L6
Regarth Av ROM RM1 124 F4
Regency Cl CHIG IG7 102 F6
EA W5 135 K8
HPTN TW12 175 N8
Regency Ct ADL/WDHM * KT15 215 N1
BRW CM14 107 H3
EN EN1 79 L9
HLWS CM18 47 K4
Regency Dr BF/WBF KT14 215 J9
RSLP HA4 112 F6
Regency Gdns EMPK RM11 125 K5
WOT/HER * KT12 197 K8
Regency Lawn KTTN * NW5 118 C8
Regency Ms BECK BR3 205 H1
WLSDN NW10 136 D1
Regency Pde HAMP * NW3 3 L4
Regency Pl WEST * SW1P 17 J5
Regency St WEST SW1P 17 K6
Regency Ter HGT * N6 118 A4
SKENS * SW7 15 L7
Regency Wk CROY/NA CR0 204 D6
Regency Wy BXLYHN DA7 163 N9
Regent Av HGDN/ICK UB10 132 C2
Regent Cl ADL/WDHM KT15 215 M5
CDH/CHF RM16 167 P1
HEST TW5 153 J7
KGLGY WD4 54 B5
KTN/HRWW/W HA3 115 K4
NFNCH/WDSP N12 97 M6
REDH RH1 258 D5
STALE/WH AL4 39 H2
WGCE AL7 23 H6
Regent Ct GUW * GU2 249 N8
Regent Crs REDH RH1 258 A8
Regent Gdns GDMY/SEVK IG3 123 K4
Regent Pde BELMT * SM2 221 M3
STNW/STAM * N16 119 N5
Regent Pk LHD/OX * KT22 236 F6
Regent Pl WIM/MER SW19 179 M8
Regent Rd BRYLDS KT5 199 L5
EPP CM16 65 J6
HNHL SE24 181 J2
Regents Av PLMGR N13 99 H6
Regents Cl CTHM CR3 241 M4
RAD WD7 56 F10
SAND/SEL CR2 223 M3
YEAD UB4 132 F7
Regents Dr HAYES BR2 226 A2
Regents Ms HORL RH6 280 B4
STJWD NW8 3 K7
Regents Pk CAMTN NW1 4 D9
Regent's Park Rd CAMTN NW1 4 B5
FNCH N3 117 J1
Regent's Park Ter CAMTN NW1 4 E5
Regents Pl LOU IG10 102 A1
Regents Plaza KIL/WHAMP * NW6 2 G7
Regent Sq BELV DA17 164 C3
STPAN WC1H 5 M10
Regent's Rw HACK E8 7 N6
Regent St CHSWK W4 155 M4
CONDST W1S 10 G6
WATN WD24 73 J4
WLSDN NW10 136 G5
Regents Wk ASC SL5 192 B6
Regents Whf IS * N1 5 N7
Regent Whf IS * N1 5 N7
Reginald Rd DEPT SE8 160 F6
FSTGT E7 141 M2
HARH RM3 105 P9
NTHWD HA6 92 G9
Reginald Sq DEPT SE8 160 F6
Regina Rd FSBYPK N4 118 G6
NWDGN UB2 153 M3
SNWD SE25 203 P4
WEA W13 134 F10
Regina Ter WEA W13 134 F10
Regis Rd KTTN NW5 118 C10
Regnart Buildings CAMTN NW1 5 H10
Reid Av CTHM CR3 241 L7
Reid Cl COUL/CHIP CR5 240 C2
PIN HA5 113 H1
Reidhaven Rd WOOL/PLUM SE18 163 H3
Reigate Av MRDN SM4 201 L8
Reigate Cl CRAWE RH10 284 E4
Reigate Hl REIG RH2 257 L8
Reigate Hill Cl REIG RH2 257 K7
Reigate Rd BMLY BR1 183 M5
DORK RH4 255 K10
EPSOM KT18 238 G3
EW KT17 220 C6
GDMY/SEVK IG3 123 J7
HORL RH6 275 M10
HORL RH6 279 N5
LHD/OX KT22 237 H9
LHD/OX KT22 237 K10
REIG RH2 257 M10
Reigate Wy WLGTN SM6 222 F2
Reighton Rd CLPT E5 119 P8
Reindorp Cl GUW GU2 267 M1
Relay Rd SHB W12 136 F9
Relf Rd PECK SE15 159 P9
Reliance Ar BRXN/ST * SW9 159 H10
Relton Ms SKENS SW7 15 P3
Rembrandt Cl BGVA * SW1W 16 C7
POP/IOD E14 161 J2
Rembrandt Ct HOR/WEW KT19 220 C3
Rembrandt Dr GVW DA11 190 A6
Rembrandt Rd EDGW * HA8 95 M10
LEW SE13 161 K10
Remington Rd EHAM E6 142 B8
SEVS/STOTM N15 119 L4
Remington St IS N1 6 D8
Remnant St HOL/ALD WC2B 11 N5
Remus Rd BOW E3 140 F2
Rendle Cl CROY/NA CR0 203 N5
Rendlesham Av RAD WD7 74 E3
Rendlesham Cl WARE SG12 26 A1
Rendlesham Rd CLPT E5 119 P9
ENC/FH EN2 79 J5
Rendlesham Wy
RKW/CH/CXG WD3 70 F10
Renforth St BERM/RHTH SE16 160 B1
Renfree Wy SHPTN TW17 196 B7
Renfrew Cl EHAM E6 142 D9
Renfrew Rd HEST TW5 153 L8
KUTN/CMB KT2 177 P10
LBTH SE11 18 C5
The Renmans ASHTD KT21 237 L2
Renmuir St TOOT SW17 180 A9
Rennell St LEW SE13 161 H9
Renness Rd WALTH E17 120 D1
Rennets Cl ELTH/MOT SE9 184 G1
Rennets Wood Rd
ELTH/MOT SE9 184 G1
Rennie Cl ASHF TW15 173 N6
Rennie Est BERM/RHTH SE16 160 A3
Rennie St STHWK SE1 12 C9
Rennie Ter REDH RH1 276 B1
Rennison Cl CHESW EN7 61 N3
Renown Cl CROY/NA CR0 203 J8
ROMW/RG RM7 104 B9
Rensburg Rd WALTH E17 120 C3
Rensburg Vls WALTH * E17 120 C3
Renshaw Cl BELV DA17 164 A5
Renters Av HDN NW4 116 F4
Renton Cl BRXS/STRHM * SW2 180 G2
Renton Dr STMC/STPC BR5 207 N7
Renwick Rd BARK IG11 143 L6
Repens Wy YEAD UB4 133 L6
Rephidim St STHWK SE1 19 H4
Replingham Rd
WAND/EARL SW18 179 J4
Reporton Rd FUL/PGN SW6 157 H7
Repository Rd
WOOL/PLUM SE18 162 C5
Repton Av ALP/SUD HA0 115 H9
GPK RM2 125 H1
HYS/HAR UB3 152 E3
Repton Cl SUT SM1 221 P2
Repton Ct BECK BR3 204 G1
Repton Dr GPK RM2 125 H2
Repton Gdns GPK RM2 125 H1
Repton Gn STALW/RED AL3 38 C3
Repton Gv CLAY IG5 102 C9
Repton Pl AMSS * HP7 69 M5
Repton Rd KTN/HRWW/W HA3 115 L2
ORP BR6 227 K1
Repton St POP/IOD E14 140 D8
Repton Wy RKW/CH/CXG WD3 72 B9
Repulse Cl ROMW/RG RM7 104 C9
Reservoir Cl THHTH CR7 203 L3
Reservoir Rd BROCKY SE4 160 D8
RSLP HA4 112 D3
STHGT/OAK N14 78 D9
Reson Wy HHW HP1 35 L7
Restell Cl BKHTH/KID SE3 161 K5
Restmor Wy WLGTN SM6 202 B9
Reston Cl BORE WD6 75 M4
Reston Pl SKENS SW7 15 J2
Restons Crs ELTH/MOT SE9 184 G2
Retford Cl BORE WD6 75 M4
HARH RM3 105 P7
Retford Pth HARH RM3 105 P7
Retford Rd HARH RM3 105 P8
Retford St BETH * E2 7 K8
Retingham Wy CHING E4 100 G3
Retreat Cl KTN/HRWW/W HA3 115 H3
Retreat Pl HOM E9 140 B1
Retreat Rd RCH/KEW TW9 177 J1
The Retreat AMS HP6 70 B5
BARN SW13 156 B9
BRW CM14 106 G2
BRYLDS KT5 199 L6
CDALE/KGS NW9 116 A3
EGH TW20 172 A9
GRAYS RM17 167 N5
ORP BR6 227 L3
RBRW/HUT CM13 87 N10
RYLN/HDSTN HA2 113 P5
SEV * TN13 247 K10
THHTH CR7 203 L4
WPK KT4 200 E10
Retreat Wy CHIG IG7 103 L4
Reubens Rd RBRW/HUT CM13 87 N10
Reunion Rw WAP * E1W 140 A9
Reveley Sq BERM/RHTH SE16 160 D1
Revell Cl LHD/OX KT22 236 A8
Revell Dr LHD/OX KT22 236 A8
Revell Ri WOOL/PLUM SE18 163 J5
Revell Rd KUT KT1 199 N2
SUT SM1 221 J3
Revelon Rd BROCKY SE4 160 D10
Revels Cl HERT/WAS SG14 25 L3
Revels Rd HERT/WAS SG14 25 L3
Revelstoke Rd WIM/MER SW19 179 K5
Reventlow Rd ELTH/MOT SE9 184 F4
Reverdy Rd STHWK SE1 19 N6

Reverend Cl RYLN/HDSTN HA2 114 A8
Revesby Cl CHOB/PIR GU24 212 C9
Revesby Rd CAR SM5 201 P6
Review Rd CRICK NW2 116 C7
DAGE RM10 144 C4
Rewell St FUL/PGN * SW6 157 M6
Rewley Rd CAR SM5 201 N6
Rex Av ASHF TW15 174 B9
Rex Pl MYFR/PKLN W1K 10 D9
Reydon Av WAN E11 121 P4
Reynard Cl BMLY BR1 206 C3
Reynard Dr NRWD SE19 181 N10
Reynard Pl NWCR * SE14 160 D5
Reynardson Rd TOTM N17 99 K8
Reynard's Wy LCOL/BKTW AL2 55 N5
Reynard Wy HERT/BAY SG13 25 P5
Reynolds Av CHDH RM6 123 M5
CHSGTN KT9 219 K4
MNPK E12 122 D10
Reynolds Cl CAR SM5 202 A8
GLDGN NW11 117 L5
HHW HP1 35 K5
WIM/MER SW19 201 N1
Reynolds Crs STALE/WH AL4 38 G1
Reynolds Dr EDGW HA8 115 L1
Reynolds Pl BKHTH/KID SE3 161 N6
CRAWW RH11 283 M6
RCHPK/HAM TW10 177 L2
Reynolds Rd BEAC HP9 88 B8
CHSWK W4 155 P2
CRAWW RH11 283 M6
NWMAL KT3 200 A7
PECK SE15 182 B1
YEAD UB4 133 K6
Reynolds Wy CROY/NA CR0 223 M1
Reynolds Yd CSHM * HP5 50 G8
Rheidol Ms IS N1 6 E7
Rheidol Ter IS N1 6 D7
Rheingold Wy WLGTN SM6 222 F5
Rheola Cl TOTM N17 99 N9
Rhoda St BETH E2 13 M1
Rhodes Av WDGN N22 98 D9
Rhodes Cl EGH TW20 172 F8
Rhodes Ct EGH * TW20 172 F8
Rhodesia Rd BRXN/ST SW9 158 F8
WAN E11 121 J7
Rhodes St HOLWY N7 118 G10
Rhodes Wy CRAWE RH10 284 A9
WATN WD24 73 L6
Rhodeswell Rd BOW E3 140 D7
Rhododendron Ride EGH TW20 171 L8
Rhodrons Av CHSGTN KT9 219 K2
Rhondda Gv BOW E3 140 D5
Rhyl Rd GFD/PVL UB6 134 E4
Rhyl St KTTN NW5 4 D1
Rhymes HHW HP1 35 L4
Rhys Av FBAR/BDGN N11 98 E8
Rialto Rd MTCM CR4 202 B2
Ribble Cl WFD IG8 101 P7
Ribbledale LCOL/BKTW AL2 57 L3
Ribblesdale HHNE HP2 35 P3
Ribblesdale Av FBAR/BDGN N11 98 A7
NTHLT UB5 134 A1
Ribblesdale Rd CEND/HSY/T N8 118 G2
RDART DA2 188 B4
STRHM/NOR SW16 180 C8
Ribbon Dance Ms CMBW SE5 159 L7
Ribchester Av GFD/PVL UB6 134 E5
Ribston Cl HAYES BR2 206 C8
RAD WD7 57 J9
Rib V HERT/WAS SG14 25 L2
Ricardo Rd WDSR SL4 171 N2
Ricardo St POP/IOD E14 140 G8
Ricards Rd WIM/MER SW19 179 J8
Rice Cl HHNE HP2 36 A5
Rice Pde STMC/STPC * BR5 206 G5
Richard Cl WOOL/PLUM SE18 162 B3
Richard House Dr CAN/RD E16 142 A8
Richards Av ROMW/RG RM7 124 D3
Richards Cl BUSH WD23 94 C1
HGDN/ICK UB10 132 B3
HRW HA1 114 F3
HYS/HAR UB3 152 E5
Richards Cottages CAR * SM5 222 A2
Richards Fld HOR/WEW KT19 220 A5
Richardson Cl GRH DA9 188 E1
HACK * E8 7 L5
LCOL/BKTW AL2 57 K3
Richardson Crs CHESW EN7 61 J1
Richardson Pl STALE/WH AL4 39 N8
Richardson Rd SRTFD * E15 141 K4
Richardson's Ms FITZ W1T 10 G2
Richard's Pl CHEL SW3 15 P6
WALTH E17 120 F1
Richards Rd COB KT11 218 A10
Richard Stagg Cl STAL AL1 38 G4
Richard St WCHPL E1 140 A8
Richards Wy SL SL1 128 F10
Richbell Cl ASHTD KT21 237 J4
Richbell Pl BMSBY WC1N 11 N3
Richborne Ter VX/NE SW8 158 G6
Richborough Cl STMC/STPC BR5 207 N4
Richborough Ct CRAWW * RH11 283 M8
Richborough Rd CRICK NW2 116 G9
Richens Cl HSLW TW3 154 C8
Riches Rd IL IG1 122 F7
Richfield Rd BUSH * WD23 94 C2
Richford Ga HMSMTH * W6 156 F2
Richford Rd SRTFD E15 141 L3
Richford St HMSMTH W6 156 F1
Richings Wy IVER SL0 151 J2
Richland Av COUL/CHIP CR5 240 B1
Richlands Av EW KT17 220 D1
Richmer Rd ERITH DA8 165 H6
Richmond Av CHING E4 101 J6
EBED/NFELT TW14 174 F2
HGDN/ICK UB10 132 C1
IS N1 6 A5
RYNPK SW20 201 H1
WLSDN NW10 136 E1
Richmond Buildings
SOHO/CST W1F 11 J6
Richmond Cl BH/WHM TN16 243 N5
EPSOM KT18 220 B10
GT/LBKH KT23 236 B10
WALTH E17 120 E4
Richmond Ct BROX EN10 44 E6
CRAWE RH10 283 P8
POTB/CUF * EN6 59 M7
Richmond Crs CHING E4 101 J6
ED N9 99 P2
IS N1 5 P5
SL SL1 149 M1
STA * TW18 173 J8
Richmond Dr SHPTN TW17 196 D6
WAT WD17 72 F6
Richmond Gdns HDN NW4 116 D3
KTN/HRWW/W HA3 94 E8
Richmond Gn CROY/NA CR0 202 F10
Richmond Gv IS N1 6 C4
Richmond Hl RCHPK/HAM TW10 177 K2
Richmond Ms SOHO/CST W1F 11 J6
Richmond Pde TWK * TW1 177 H2
Richmond Park Rd
KUTN/CMB KT2 177 K10
MORT/ESHN SW14 177 P1
Richmond Pl WOOL/PLUM SE18 162 F3
Richmond Rd BAR EN5 77 L9
CHING * E4 101 J2
COUL/CHIP CR5 240 C1
CROY/NA CR0 202 F10
EA W5 155 K1
EFNCH * N2 97 M10
FBAR/BDGN N11 98 F7
FSTGT E7 121 N10
GRAYS RM17 167 P5
HACK E8 7 L3
IL IG1 122 F8
ISLW TW7 154 F10
KUTN/CMB KT2 199 K1
POTB/CUF EN6 59 M7
ROM RM1 124 G4
RYNPK SW20 200 E1
SEVS/STOTM N15 119 M4
STA TW18 173 J8
THHTH CR7 203 J4
TWK TW1 176 G3
WAN E11 121 J7
Richmond St PLSTW E13 141 M4
Richmond Ter WHALL SW1A 17 L1
Richmond Vls WALTH * E17 100 G9
Richmond Wy GT/LBKH KT23 236 A10
RKW/CH/CXG WD3 72 D8
SHB W12 156 G1
WAN E11 121 M7
Richmondwood ASC SL5 192 G8
Richmount Gdns BKHTH/KID SE3 161 M9
Rich St POP/IOD E14 140 E9
Rickard Cl BRXS/STRHM SW2 181 H4
HDN NW4 116 D2
WDR/YW UB7 151 N2
Rickards Cl SURB KT6 199 K9
Ricketts Hill Rd BH/WHM TN16 244 A4
Rickett St FUL/PGN SW6 14 F9
Rickfield CRAWW RH11 283 K8
Rickfield Cl HAT AL10 40 D6
Rickford Hl RGUW GU3 249 J2
Rickman Crs ADL/WDHM KT15 195 L10
Rickman Hl COUL/CHIP CR5 240 C3
Rickman Hill Rd COUL/CHIP CR5 240 C4
Rickman's La SLN SL2 129 K1
Rickman St WCHPL E1 140 B6
Rickmansworth La
CFSP/GDCR SL9 90 C6
Rickmansworth Rd AMS HP6 69 K4
DEN/HRF UB9 91 M9
NTHWD HA6 92 C7
PIN HA5 93 J10
RKW/CH/CXG WD3 71 H7
WATW WD18 72 F8
Rick Roberts Wy SRTFD E15 141 J3
Ricksons La EHSLY KT24 252 C3
Rickthorne Rd ARCH N19 118 F7
Rickwood HORL RH6 280 C3
Rickyard GUW GU2 249 J10
Ridding La GFD/PVL UB6 114 E10
Riddings La HLWS CM18 47 K5
The Riddings CTHM CR3 259 N1
Riddlesdown Av PUR/KEN CR8 223 K8
Riddlesdown Rd PUR/KEN CR8 223 K6
Riddons Rd LEE/GVPK SE12 183 P6
Ride La SHGR GU5 269 N10
Rideout St WOOL/PLUM SE18 162 C3
Rider Cl BFN/LL DA15 185 H2
Riders Wy GDST RH9 260 B7
The Ride BTFD TW8 154 G4
PEND EN3 80 B7
Ridgdale St BOW E3 140 F4
Ridge Av DART DA1 186 G2
WCHMH N21 99 K1
Ridgebank SL SL1 128 E9
Ridgebrook Rd ELTH/MOT SE9 161 P10
Ridge Cl BRKHM/BTCW RH3 273 N4
CDALE/KGS NW9 116 A2
HDN NW4 96 G10
THMD SE28 162 G1
WOKS/MYFD GU22 231 N7
Ridge Crest ENC/FH EN2 78 G5
Ridgecroft Cl BXLY DA5 186 D4
Ridgefield WAT WD17 72 F3
Ridgegate Cl REIG RH2 257 N8
Ridge Gn REDH RH1 276 F3
Ridge Green Cl REDH RH1 276 F3
Ridge Hl GLDGN NW11 117 H6
Ridgehurst Av GSTN WD25 54 G9
Ridgelands LHD/OX KT22 236 C10
Ridge La WAT WD17 72 F2
Ridge Langley SAND/SEL CR2 223 P6
Ridge Lea HHW HP1 35 J7
Ridgemead Cl STHGT/OAK N14 98 F3
Ridgemead Rd EGH TW20 171 N6
Ridgemont Gdns EDGW HA8 95 P5
Ridgemount GUW GU2 267 N1
WEY KT13 196 F9
Ridgemount Av COUL/CHIP CR5 240 C3
CROY/NA CR0 204 C9
Ridgemount End CFSP/GDCR SL9 90 B6
Ridgemount Gdns ENC/FH EN2 79 J7
Ridge Mount Rd ASC SL5 192 F8
Ridgemount Wy REDH RH1 275 N2
Ridge Pk WLGTN SM6 222 E6
Ridge Rd CEND/HSY/T N8 118 G4
CHEAM SM3 201 J8
CRICK NW2 117 J8
MTCM CR4 180 C10
WCHMH N21 99 L2
Ridgeside CRAWE RH10 284 A7
The Ridges RGUW GU3 267 P5
Ridge St WATN WD24 73 J4
Ridge Ter WCHMH * N21 99 K1
The Ridge ASC * SL5 192 F7
BAR * EN5 77 J9
BRYLDS KT5 199 M5
BXLY DA5 186 A3
COUL/CHIP CR5 222 F10
CTHM CR3 261 K1
EPSOM KT18 237 P4
LHD/OX KT22 236 C10
ORP BR6 206 G9
PUR/KEN CR8 222 E6
WHTN TW2 176 C3
WOKS/MYFD GU22 232 E3
Ridgeview LCOL/BKTW AL2 57 L4
Ridgeview Cl BAR EN5 76 G10
Ridgeview Rd NFNCH/WDSP N12 97 L4
Ridge Wy DART DA1 186 G2
FELT TW13 175 M6
IVER SL0 131 H9
RKW/CH/CXG WD3 91 L1
VW GU25 194 B5
Ridgeway BERK HP4 33 L5
GRAYS RM17 168 B3
HAYES BR2 205 M9
HOR/WEW KT19 219 P8
RAD WD7 56 H7
RBRW/HUT CM13 107 N2
RDART DA2 188 D8
TRING HP23 32 A1
WFD IG8 101 P5
WGCE AL7 23 L6
WOT/HER KT12 196 G8
Ridgeway Av EBAR EN4 78 A10
GVE DA12 190 E6
Ridgeway Cl CSHM HP5 50 G4
DORK RH4 272 F4
HHS/BOV HP3 54 A1
WOKN/KNAP GU21 232 A2
Ridgeway Ct REDH * RH1 275 P1
Ridgeway Crs ORP BR6 207 H10
Ridgeway Crescent Gdns
ORP BR6 207 H9
Ridgeway Dr BMLY BR1 183 N7
DORK RH4 272 F5
Ridgeway East BFN/LL DA15 185 J1
Ridgeway Gdns REDBR IG4 122 B3
WOKN/KNAP GU21 232 A1
Ridgeway Rd CSHM HP5 50 G4
DORK RH4 272 F4
ISLW TW7 154 D6
REDH RH1 258 A10
Ridgeway Rd North ISLW TW7 154 D6
Ridgeways HLWE CM17 47 P1
The Ridge Wy SAND/SEL CR2 223 M6
The Ridgeway ACT W3 155 M2
AMSS HP7 69 K6
CDALE/KGS NW9 116 A2
CHING E4 101 H2
CHOB/PIR GU24 230 E6
CROY/NA CR0 202 G10
ENC/FH EN2 78 D2
FBAR/BDGN N11 98 A5
FNCH N3 97 L8
GLDGN NW11 117 J6
GPK RM2 125 H2
GVE DA12 191 P10
HARH RM3 105 M9
HERT/WAS SG14 24 G4
HORL RH6 280 B6
KTN/HRWW/W HA3 115 H4
LHD/OX KT22 218 B10
LHD/OX KT22 236 C9
LTWR GU18 212 A6
MLHL NW7 96 E5
POTB/CUF EN6 60 B3
POTB/CUF EN6 78 A1
RAD WD7 74 E3
RSLP HA4 113 H5
RYLN/HDSTN HA2 113 N3
STALE/WH AL4 38 F2
STAN HA7 95 H7
STHGT/OAK N14 98 F3
WAT WD17 72 F3
Ridgeway West BFN/LL DA15 185 H1
Ridgewell Cl DAGE RM10 144 C3
IS N1 6 F5
SYD SE26 182 E7
Ridgewood MEO DA13 211 P1
Ridgmont Rd STAL AL1 38 D7
Ridgmount Gdns GWRST WC1E 11 J3
Ridgmount Rd
WAND/EARL SW18 179 L1
Ridgmount St GWRST WC1E 11 J3
Ridgway RCHPK/HAM * TW10 177 K2
WIM/MER SW19 178 F10
WOKS/MYFD GU22 233 J1
Ridgway Gdns WIM/MER SW19 178 G10
Ridgway Pl WIM/MER SW19 179 H9
Ridgway Rd BRXN/ST SW9 159 J9
WOKS/MYFD GU22 233 J1
The Ridgway BELMT SM2 221 N4
Ridgwell Rd CAN/RD E16 141 P7
Riding Court Rd DTCH/LGLY SL3 149 P5
Riding Hl SAND/SEL CR2 223 P9
Riding House St GTPST W1W 10 G4
Ridings Av WCHMH N21 79 J8
The Ridings ADL/WDHM KT15 215 H3
AMS HP6 69 J1
ASHTD KT21 237 J3
BH/WHM TN16 244 B3
BRYLDS KT5 199 M5
COB KT11 217 P8
CRAWE RH10 284 E6
CSHM HP5 70 A2
EA W5 135 L6
EBAR * EN4 97 P1
EHSLY KT24 252 F1
EPSOM KT18 238 B1
EW KT17 220 C5
HERT/WAS SG14 25 H6
IVER SL0 151 J3
KWD/TDW/WH KT20 239 J6
REDH RH1 257 N8
RPLY/SEND GU23 233 K9
SUN TW16 197 H1
WDSR * SL4 148 B6
The Riding GLDGN NW11 117 J5
WOKN/KNAP GU21 214 E10
Ridlands Gv OXTED RH8 262 B6
Ridlands La OXTED RH8 262 B6
Ridlands Ri OXTED RH8 262 B6
Ridler Rd EN EN1 79 M4
Ridley Av WEA W13 154 G2
Ridley Cl HARH RM3 105 J9
Ridley Rd FSTGT E7 121 P9
HACK E8 119 N10
HAYES BR2 205 L3
WARL CR6 242 B4
WELL DA16 163 L7
WIM/MER SW19 179 L10
WLSDN NW10 136 D4
Ridsdale Rd PGE/AN SE20 204 A1
WOKN/KNAP GU21 231 N3
Riefield Rd ELTH/MOT SE9 162 F10
Riesco Dr CROY/NA CR0 224 B3
Riffel Rd CRICK NW2 116 F10
Riffhams RBRW/HUT CM13 107 N4
Rifle Pl NTGHL W11 136 G10
Rifle Range La HRW HA1 114 E6
Rifle St POP/IOD E14 140 G7
Rigault Rd FUL/PGN SW6 157 H8
Rigby Cl CROY/NA CR0 203 H10
Rigby Gdns CDH/CHF RM16 168 E3
Rigby La HYS/HAR UB3 152 E1
Rigby Ms IL IG1 122 D7
Rigby Pl WAB EN9 80 F3
Rigden St POP/IOD E14 140 G8
Rigeley Rd WLSDN NW10 136 D5
Rigg Ap LEY E10 120 C6
Rigge Pl CLAP SW4 158 E10
Riggindale Rd
STRHM/NOR SW16 180 E8
Right Side STHGT/OAK * N14 98 E2
Riley Rd PEND EN3 80 B4
STHWK SE1 19 L3
Riley St WBPTN SW10 15 L10
Rillside CRAWE RH10 284 B10
Rinaldo Rd BAL SW12 180 C3
Ring Cl BMLY BR1 183 N10
Ringcroft St HOLWY N7 119 H10
Ringer's Rd BMLY BR1 205 M3
Ringford Rd WAND/EARL SW18 179 J1
Ringlet Cl CAN/RD E16 141 N7
Ringley Av HORL RH6 280 B5
Ringley Park Av REIG RH2 275 N1
Ringley Park Rd REIG RH2 257 M10
Ringmer Av FUL/PGN SW6 157 H7
Ringmer Pl WCHMH N21 79 L9
Ringmer Wy BMLY BR1 206 C5
Ringmore Dr RGUE GU4 250 F7
Ringmore Ri FSTH SE23 182 A3
Ringmore Rd WOT/HER KT12 197 K10
Ring Rd North HORL RH6 280 C7
Ring Rd South HORL RH6 280 D8
Ringshall Rd CHST BR7 207 K3
Ringslade Rd WDGN N22 98 G10
Ringstead Rd CAT SE6 182 G3
SUT SM1 221 N1
Ring Wy FBAR/BDGN N11 98 D7
Ringway NWDGN UB2 153 M5
Ringway Rd LCOL/BKTW AL2 56 A3
Ringwold Cl BECK BR3 182 D10
Ringwood Av CROY/NA CR0 202 F7
EFNCH N2 118 A1
HCH RM12 125 L7
ORP BR6 227 M6
REDH RH1 258 A7
Ringwood Cl CRAWE RH10 283 P9
PIN * HA5 113 K1
Ringwood Gdns PUT/ROE SW15 178 D5
Ringwood Rd WALTH E17 120 E4
Ringwood Wy HPTN TW12 175 P7
WCHMH N21 99 J1
Ripley Av EGH TW20 172 B9
Ripley Cl BMLY BR1 206 C5
CROY/NA CR0 225 H3
DTCH/LGLY SL3 150 B3
Ripley Gdns MORT/ESHN SW14 156 A9
Ripley La RPLY/SEND GU23 234 A10
Ripley Ms WAN * E11 121 K4
Ripley Rd BELV DA17 164 B3
CAN/RD E16 141 P8
ENC/FH EN2 79 K5
GDMY/SEVK IG3 123 J7
HPTN TW12 175 P10
RGUE GU4 251 N4
Ripleys Market DART * DA1 187 M3
Ripley Vw LOU IG10 82 E4
Ripley Vls WEA * W13 135 H8
Ripley Wy CHESW EN7 62 A6
HHW HP1 35 H5
HOR/WEW KT19 219 M7
Ripon Cl GUW GU2 249 L7
NTHLT UB5 113 P10
Ripon Gdns CHSGTN KT9 219 J2
IL IG1 122 B4
Ripon Rd ED N9 100 A1
TOTM N17 119 L1
WOOL/PLUM SE18 162 E5
Ripon Wy BORE WD6 75 P9
STALE/WH AL4 39 J2
Rippersley Rd WELL DA16 163 K7
Ripple Rd BARK IG11 142 F2
Ripplevale Gv IS N1 5 P4
Rippolson Rd WOOL/PLUM SE18 163 J4
Ripston Rd ASHF TW15 174 E8
Risborough Cl MUSWH * N10 118 C1
Risborough Dr WPK KT4 200 D7
Risborough St STHWK SE1 18 D1
Risdens HLWS CM18 46 F5
Risdon St BERM/RHTH SE16 160 B1
Risebridge Cha ROM RM1 104 C10
Risebridge Rd GPK RM2 104 G10
Risedale Cl HHS/BOV HP3 35 P9
Risedale Hl HHS/BOV HP3 35 P9
Risedale Rd BXLYHN DA7 164 C9
HHS/BOV HP3 35 P9
Riseldine Rd FSTH SE23 182 D2
Rise Park Bvd GPK RM2 104 G9
Rise Park Pde ROM RM1 104 F10
Rise Rd ASC SL5 192 D6
The Rise AMSS HP7 69 H5
BKHH IG9 102 A2
BORE WD6 75 L9
BXLY DA5 185 M3
CRAWE RH10 284 D7
DART DA1 164 G10
EDGW HA8 95 N6
EHSLY KT24 252 F2
EW KT17 220 C6
GFD/PVL UB6 114 F10
GVE DA12 191 H7
HGDN/ICK UB10 132 A4
KWD/TDW/WH KT20 238 F7
LCOL/BKTW AL2 56 C1
MLHL NW7 96 C7
PLMGR N13 99 H5
SAND/SEL CR2 224 B5
SEV TN13 265 K4
WAN E11 121 M3
WLSDN NW10 116 A8
Riseway BRWN CM15 107 K4
Rising Hill Cl NTHWD * HA6 92 D7
Risinghill St IS N1 6 A7
Risingholme Cl BUSH WD23 94 A1
KTN/HRWW/W HA3 94 D9
Risingholme Rd
KTN/HRWW/W HA3 94 D10
The Risings WALTH E17 121 J2
Risley Av TOTM N17 99 M9
Rita Rd VX/NE SW8 158 F6
Ritches Rd SEVS/STOTM N15 119 K3
Ritchie Rd CROY/NA CR0 204 A6
Ritchie St IS N1 6 B7
Ritchings Av WALTH E17 120 D2
Ritcroft Cl HHS/BOV HP3 36 C7
Ritcroft Dr HHS/BOV HP3 36 C7
Ritcroft St HHS/BOV HP3 36 C7
Ritherdon Rd TOOT SW17 180 B5
Ritson Rd HACK E8 7 M1
Ritter St WOOL/PLUM SE18 162 D5
Ritz Ct POTB/CUF EN6 59 K7
Rivaz Pl HOM E9 140 B1
Rivenhall End WGCE AL7 23 M5
Rivenhall Gdns SWFD E18 121 L2
River Av HOD EN11 44 G2
PLMGR N13 99 J4
THDIT KT7 198 F7
Riverbank DORK * RH4 272 A2
E/WMO/HCT KT8 198 D3
HHW HP1 35 L2
River Bank THDIT KT7 198 E5
WCHMH N21 99 K1
Riverbank Rd BMLY BR1 183 M6
The Riverbank WDSR SL4 148 G6
Riverbank Wy BTFD TW8 155 H5
River Barge Cl POP/IOD E14 161 H1
River Cl CHES/WCR EN8 62 F10
RAIN RM13 145 J7
RSLP HA4 112 G4
STHL UB1 154 B1
WAN E11 121 P4
River Ct WOKN/KNAP GU21 214 F10
Rivercourt Rd HMSMTH W6 156 E3
Riverdale Dr WAND/EARL SW18 179 L4
WOKS/MYFD GU22 232 C7
Riverdale Gdns TWK TW1 177 H1
Riverdale Rd BXLY DA5 186 A3
ERITH DA8 164 C4
FELT TW13 175 M7
TWK TW1 177 H2
WOOL/PLUM SE18 163 J4
Riverdene EDGW HA8 95 P5
Riverdene Rd IL IG1 122 D8
River Dr UPMR RM14 126 B4
Riverfield Rd STA TW18 173 J9
River Front EN EN1 79 L7
River Gdns CAR SM5 202 B9
EBED/NFELT TW14 175 J1
River Grove Pk BECK BR3 204 E1
Riverhead Cl WALTH E17 100 C10
Riverhead Dr BELMT SM2 221 L6
River Hl COB KT11 235 J1
Riverhill SEV TN13 265 M7
Riverholme Dr HOR/WEW KT19 220 A5
River La COB KT11 235 M2
LHD/OX KT22 236 C6
RCHPK/HAM TW10 177 J4
River Md CRAWW RH11 283 K4
Rivermead BF/WBF KT14 216 A9
E/WMO/HCT KT8 198 B3
SURB * KT6 199 J5
Rivermead Cl ADL/WDHM * KT15 215 M4
TEDD TW11 176 G8
Rivermead Rd UED * N18 100 C6
River Meads WARE SG12 27 H6
River Meads Av WHTN TW2 176 A6
Rivermill HLW CM20 28 F9
River Mt WOT/HER KT12 196 G7
River Mount Gdns GUW GU2 267 P3
Rivernook Cl WOT/HER KT12 197 K5
River Pde SEV * TN13 246 F8
River Pk HHW HP1 35 K8
River Park Av STA TW18 172 G7
Riverpark Gdns HAYES BR2 183 J10
River Park Rd WDGN N22 98 G10
River Park Vw ORP BR6 207 L7
River Pl IS N1 6 E4
River Reach TEDD TW11 177 H9
River Rd BARK IG11 143 H4
BKHH IG9 102 B2
BRW CM14 106 D5
STA TW18 195 J1
WDSR * SL4 148 B6
Riversdale GVW DA11 190 B5
Riversdale Rd CRW RM5 104 C8
HBRY N5 119 J8
THDIT KT7 198 F5
Riversdell Cl CHERT KT16 195 J7
Riversend Rd HHS/BOV HP3 35 M9
Riversfield Rd EN EN1 79 M7
Riverside CHARL SE7 161 N2
CHERT * KT16 195 K2
DORK RH4 255 J10
EYN DA4 209 L9
GU GU1 250 A8
HDN NW4 116 E5
HORL RH6 280 B6
LCOL/BKTW AL2 57 K3
RCH/KEW * TW9 155 M5
SHPTN TW17 196 F7
STWL/WRAY TW19 171 P3
SUN * TW16 197 L2
TWK TW1 176 G4
Riverside Av BROX EN10 44 F8
E/WMO/HCT KT8 198 C5
LTWR GU18 212 B7
Riverside Cl CHOB/PIR GU24 230 E6
CLPT E5 120 B6
HNWL W7 134 D6
KGLGY WD4 54 C8
KUT KT1 199 J4
STAL AL1 38 D8
STMC/STPC BR5 207 M2
WLGTN SM6 202 C10
Riverside Ct CHING * E4 80 G10
CSHM * HP5 51 H9
HLW CM20 29 M5
Riverside Dr CHSWK W4 156 A6
ESH/CLAY KT10 217 P1
GLDGN * NW11 117 H4
MTCM CR4 201 P5
RCHPK/HAM TW10 176 G6
RKW/CH/CXG WD3 91 N2
SHGR GU5 268 D10
STA TW18 195 J1
Riverside Gdns ALP/SUD HA0 135 K4
BERK HP4 33 M4
ENC/FH EN2 79 K6
HMSMTH W6 156 E4
WOKS/MYFD GU22 232 E7
Riverside Ms BROX * EN10 44 D9
CROY/NA * CR0 202 F10
WARE * SG12 26 C2
Riverside Pl FBAR/BDGN * N11 98 D4
STWL/WRAY TW19 173 N2
Riverside Rd IL IG1 122 E8
OXHEY WD19 73 J10
SCUP DA14 185 P6
SEVS/STOTM N15 119 P4
SRTFD E15 141 H4
STA TW18 173 J10
STAL AL1 38 D7
STWL/WRAY TW19 173 N1
TOOT SW17 179 L7
WOT/HER KT12 217 L1
The Riverside E/WMO/HCT * KT8 198 C3
Riverside Vls SURB * KT6 199 H6
Riverside Wk ISLW TW7 154 D9
KUT KT1 199 J2
WDSR SL4 149 J6
Riverside Wy DART DA1 187 M1
UX/CGN UB8 131 L3
Riversmead HOD EN11 44 F4
Riversmeet HERT/WAS SG14 25 J6
River St CLKNW EC1R 6 A9
WARE SG12 26 D2
WDSR SL4 149 J6
River Ter HMSMTH W6 156 F4
Riverton Cl MV/WKIL W9 2 D10

River Vw ADL/WDHM * KT15 ....215 M2
CDH/CHF RM16 ....168 D4
Riverview GU * GU1 ....249 P10
River Vw WGCE AL7 ....23 H1
Riverview Gdns BARN SW13 ....156 E5
COB KT11 ....217 H9
River View Gdns TWK TW1 ....176 E5
Riverview Pk CAT SE6 ....182 F5
Riverview Rd CHSWK W4 ....155 N6
GRH * DA9 ....188 F1
HOR/WEW KT19 ....220 A2
Riverview Ter PUR * RM19 ....166 A4
River Wk DEN/HRF UB9 ....111 M10
SUN TW16 ....197 L2
WOT/HER KT12 ....197 H6
River Wy FELT TW13 ....176 A5
GNWCH SE10 ....161 L2
HLW CM20 ....29 K6
HOR/WEW KT19 ....220 A2
LOU IG10 ....82 D10
Riverway PLMGR N13 ....99 H6
STA TW18 ....195 L1
River Whf BELV * DA17 ....164 E1
Riverwood La CHST BR7 ....206 G2
Rivett-Drake Rd GUW GU2 ....249 M6
Rivey Cl BF/WBF KT14 ....215 J10
Rivington Av WFD IG8 ....102 A10
Rivington Crs CDALE/KGS NW9 ....96 B8
Rivington Pl SDTCH EC2A 7 K10
Rivington St SDTCH EC2A 7 K10
Rivington Wk HACK E8 ....7 N5
Rivulet Rd TOTM N17 ....99 K8
Rixon Cl DTCH/LGLY SL3 ....130 B8
Rixon St HOLWY N7 ....119 H8
Rixsen Rd MNPK E12 ....122 B10
Roach Rd HOM E9 ....140 F2
Road House Est
WOKS/MYFD * GU22 ....232 D6
Roads Pl ARCH N19 ....118 F7
Roakes Av ADL/WDHM KT15 ....195 L9
Roan St GNWCH SE10 ....161 H5
Robarts Cl PIN HA5 ....113 J3
Robb Rd STAN HA7 ....94 F7
Robbs Cl HHW HP1 ....35 K4
Robe End HHW HP1 ....35 J4
Robert Adam St MBLAR W1H 10 C5
Roberta St BETH E2 ....7 N9
Robert Av LCOL/BKTW AL2 ....38 B10
Robert Cl CHIG IG7 ....103 J6
MV/WKIL W9 ....9 K2
POTB/CUF EN6 ....59 H9
WOT/HER KT12 ....217 J2
Robert Keen Cl PECK SE15 ....159 P7
Robert Lowe Cl NWCR SE14 ....160 C6
Roberton Dr BMLY BR1 ....205 P2
Robert Rd SLN SL2 ....109 J7
Robertsbridge Rd CAR SM5 ....201 M7
Roberts Cl CHEAM SM3 ....220 G4
CHES/WCR EN8 ....62 D6
ELTH/MOT SE9 ....184 G4
HARH RM3 ....105 J9
STMC/STPC BR5 ....207 M5
STWL/WRAY TW19 ....173 M2
WDR/YW UB7 ....131 P10
Roberts Ct CHSGTN * KT9 ....219 J2
WLSDN NW10 ....136 B1
Roberts La CFSP/GDCR SL9 ....90 D6
Roberts Ms KTBR * SW1X 16 C4
Robertson Cl BROX EN10 ....62 D2
Robertson Rd BERK HP4 ....34 A5
SRTFD E15 ....141 H3
Robertson St VX/NE SW8 ....158 C9
Robert's Pl CLKNW * EC1R 12 B1
Roberts Rd BELV DA17 ....164 B4
MLHL NW7 ....97 H6
WALTH E17 ....100 G9
WATW WD18 ....73 K9
Robert St CAMTN NW1 ....4 F10
CHCR WC2N 11 M8
CROY/NA CR0 ....203 K10
WOOL/PLUM SE18 ....162 G3
Roberts Wy EGH TW20 ....171 P10
HAT AL10 ....40 C6
Roberts Wood Dr CFSP/GDCR SL9 ....90 D6
Robeson St BOW E3 ....140 E7
Robeson Wy BORE WD6 ....75 P5
Robina Cl BXLYHS DA6 ....163 N10
NTHWD HA6 ....92 G10
Robin Cl ADL/WDHM KT15 ....215 N2
CRAWW RH11 ....283 M5
CRW RM5 ....104 E8
HPTN TW12 ....175 M8
MLHL NW7 ....96 B4
WARE SG12 ....27 H8
Robin Gdns REDH RH1 ....258 B8
Robin Gv BTFD TW8 ....155 H5
HGT N6 ....118 B7
KTN/HRWW/W HA3 ....115 L4
Robin Hl BERK HP4 ....33 P6
RGODL GU7 ....267 J10
Robin Hill Dr CHST BR7 ....184 B9
Robinhood Cl MTCM CR4 ....202 D4
Robin Hood Cl SL SL1 ....128 D10
WOKN/KNAP GU21 ....231 L4
Robin Hood Crs
WOKN/KNAP GU21 ....231 K3
Robin Hood Dr BUSH WD23 ....73 N5
KTN/HRWW/W HA3 ....94 E8
Robin Hood Gdns POP/IOD * E14 ....141 H9
Robin Hood Gn STMC/STPC BR5 ....207 K5
Robin Hood La BXLYHS DA6 ....185 P1
HAT AL10 ....40 D3
Robinhood La MTCM CR4 ....202 D5
Robin Hood La POP/IOD E14 ....141 H9
PUT/ROE SW15 ....178 B6
RGUE GU4 ....232 C10
SUT SM1 ....221 K2
Robin Hood Meadow HHNE HP2 ....36 A1
Robin Hood Rd BRWN CM15 ....106 G1
PUT/ROE SW15 ....178 B7
WOKN/KNAP GU21 ....231 L4
Robin Hood Wy GFD/PVL UB6 ....134 E1
Robin Hood Wy
(Kingston By-Pass)
PUT/ROE SW15 ....178 B7
Robinia Av GVW DA11 ....190 A3
Robinia Cl BARK/HLT IG6 ....103 H7
PGE/AN SE20 ....203 P1
Robinia Crs LEY E10 ....120 G7
Robin Md WGCE AL7 ....23 K2
Robin Pl GSTN * WD25 ....55 J8
Robins Cl LCOL/BKTW AL2 ....57 K3
UX/CGN UB8 ....131 M7
Robins Dl WOKN/KNAP GU21 ....231 H3
Robinsfield HHW HP1 ....35 M6
Robins Gv WWKM BR4 ....205 M10
Robins Nest Hl HERT/BAY SG13 ....42 D4
Robinson Av CHESW EN7 ....61 J4
Robinson Cl HCH RM12 ....145 J2
Robinson Crs BUSH WD23 ....94 B2
Robinson Rd BETH E2 ....140 B4
CRAWW RH11 ....283 N8
DAGE RM10 ....124 B9
WIM/MER SW19 ....179 P9
Robinson's Cl WEA W13 ....134 F7
Robinson St CHEL SW3 ....16 A9
Robins Orch CFSP/GDCR SL9 ....90 B7
Robins Rd HHS/BOV HP3 ....36 B8
The Robins BRWN CM15 ....87 J1
Robins Wy HAT AL10 ....40 C7
Robinsway WOT/HER KT12 ....217 K1
Robinswood Cl BEAC HP9 ....88 B6
Robin Wy GUW GU2 ....249 N6
POTB/CUF EN6 ....60 F4
STA TW18 ....173 J6
STMC/STPC BR5 ....207 L3
Robin Willis Wy WDSR SL4 ....171 M2
Robinwood Gv UX/CGN UB8 ....132 A6
Robinwood Pl
RCHPK/HAM TW10 ....178 A7
Robsart St BRXN/ST SW9 ....158 G8
Robson Av WLSDN NW10 ....136 D3
Robson Cl CFSP/GDCR SL9 ....90 B6
EHAM E6 ....142 B8
ENC/FH EN2 ....79 J6
Robson Rd WNWD SE27 ....181 J6
Robsons Cl CHES/WCR EN8 ....62 B5
Robyns Cft GVW DA11 ....190 B6
Robyns Wy SEV TN13 ....246 G8
Roch Av EDGW HA8 ....95 L10
Rochdale Rd ABYW SE2 ....163 L4
Rochdale Wy DEPT SE8 ....160 F6
Rochelle Cl BTSEA SW11 ....157 N10
Rochelle St BETH E2 ....7 L10
Rochemont Wk HACK * E8 ....7 M6
Roche Rd STRHM/NOR SW16 ....202 F1
Rochester Av BMLY BR1 ....205 N2
FELT TW13 ....174 G5
PLSTW E13 ....141 P3
Rochester Cl BFN/LL DA15 ....185 L2
EN EN1 ....79 M5
STRHM/NOR * SW16 ....180 F10
Rochester Dr BXLY DA5 ....186 B2
GSTN * WD25 ....73 K1
PIN HA5 ....113 L3
Rochester Gdns CROY/NA CR0 ....203 M10
CTHM CR3 ....241 M8
IL IG1 ....122 C5
Rochester Ms CAMTN NW1 ....5 H3
EA * W5 ....155 H3
Rochester Pde FELT * TW13 ....175 H6
Rochester Pl CAMTN NW1 ....4 G2
Rochester Rd CAMTN NW1 ....4 G2
CAR SM5 ....222 A1
DART DA1 ....187 P3
EGH TW20 ....172 G8
GVE DA12 ....191 J5
NTHWD HA6 ....112 G1
Rochester Rw WEST SW1P 17 H5
Rochester Sq CAMTN NW1 ....5 H3
Rochester St WEST SW1P 17 J4
Rochester Ter CAMTN NW1 ....4 G2
Rochester Wk STHWK * SE1 ....12 G9
Rochester Wy BKHTH/KID SE3 ....161 N7
DART DA1 ....186 F3
ELTH/MOT SE9 ....162 C9
RKW/CH/CXG WD3 ....72 C8
Rochester Wy Relief Rd
ELTH/MOT SE9 ....184 B1
Roche Wk MRDN SM4 ....201 N6
Rochford Av BRWN CM15 ....87 M9
CHDH RM6 ....123 M3
WAB EN9 ....63 J10
Rochford Cl BROX EN10 ....62 D2
EHAM E6 ....142 A4
HCH RM12 ....145 J1
Rochford Gn LOU IG10 ....82 F7
Rochfords Gdns SLN SL2 ....129 P10
Rochford Wk HACK * E8 ....7 P4
Rochford Wy CROY/NA CR0 ....202 F6
Rockall Ct DTCH/LGLY SL3 ....150 E2
Rock Av MORT/ESHN SW14 ....156 A9
Rockbourne Rd FSTH SE23 ....182 C4
Rockchase Gdns EMPK RM11 ....125 M4
Rockcliffe Av KGLGY WD4 ....54 C6
Rock Cl MTCM CR4 ....201 N2
Rockdale Gdns SEV * TN13 ....265 J1
Rockdale Pleasance SEV * TN13 ....265 K1
Rockell's Pl EDUL SE22 ....182 A2
Rockfield Cl OXTED RH8 ....261 L7
Rockfield Rd OXTED RH8 ....261 L6
Rockford Av GFD/PVL UB6 ....134 G4
Rock Grove Wy BERM/RHTH SE16 ....19 P5
Rockhall Rd CRICK NW2 ....116 G9
Rockhampton Rd SAND/SEL CR2 ....223 M3
STRHM/NOR SW16 ....181 H7
Rock Hl NRWD SE19 ....181 N7
ORP BR6 ....228 C3
Rockingham Av EMPK RM11 ....125 J4
Rockingham Cl PUT/ROE SW15 ....156 C10
UX/CGN * UB8 ....131 M3
Rockingham Ga BUSH WD23 ....74 B10
Rockingham Pde UX/CGN UB8 ....131 M2
Rockingham Rd UX/CGN UB8 ....131 L3
Rockingham St STHWK SE1 ....18 E4
Rockland Rd PUT/ROE SW15 ....157 H10
Rocklands Dr KTN/HRWW/W HA3 ....94 G10
Rockleigh HERT/WAS SG14 ....25 J5
Rockleigh Ct BRWN CM15 ....107 M1
Rockley Rd SHB W12 ....156 G1
Rockmount Rd NRWD SE19 ....181 L9
WOOL/PLUM SE18 ....163 J4
Rockshaw Rd REDH RH1 ....258 D3
Rocks La BARN SW13 ....156 D9
Rock St FSBYPK N4 ....119 H7
Rockware Av GFD/PVL UB6 ....134 D3
Rockways BAR EN5 ....76 C10
Rockwell Gdns NRWD SE19 ....181 M7
Rockwell Rd DAGE RM10 ....124 C10
Rockwood Gdns LOU IG10 ....82 F7
Rocky La REIG RH2 ....258 B5
Rocliffe St IS N1 ....6 D8
Rocombe Crs FSTH * SE23 ....182 B3
Rocque La BKHTH/KID SE3 ....161 L9
Rodborough Rd GLDGN NW11 ....117 K6
Roden Cl HLWE CM17 ....30 A7
Roden Gdns CROY/NA CR0 ....203 M6
Rodenhurst Rd CLAP SW4 ....180 D3
Roden St HOLWY N7 ....118 G8
IL IG1 ....122 D8
Rodeo Cl ERITH DA8 ....165 J7
Roderick Rd HAMP NW3 ....118 A9
Rodgers Cl BORE WD6 ....75 J10
Roding Dr BRWN CM15 ....86 E3
Roding Gdns LOU IG10 ....82 B10
Roding La BKHH IG9 ....102 B2
Roding La North WFD IG8 ....102 B10
Roding La South REDBR IG4 ....122 A3
Roding Ms WAP E1W 13 P9
Roding Rd CLPT E5 ....120 C9
EHAM E6 ....142 E7
LOU IG10 ....82 C9
Rodings Rw BAR * EN5 ....77 H8
The Rodings UPMR RM14 ....126 C4
Roding Vw BKHH IG9 ....102 A2
Roding Wy RAIN RM13 ....145 L4
Rodmarton St MHST W1U 10 B4
Rodmell Cl YEAD UB4 ....133 M6
Rodmell Slope NFNCH/WDSP N12 ....97 J6
Rodmere St GNWCH SE10 ....161 K4
Rodmill La BRXS/STRHM SW2 ....180 F3
Rodney Av STAL AL1 ....38 F8
Rodney Cl CROY/NA CR0 ....203 J8
NWMAL KT3 ....200 B5
PIN HA5 ....113 M5
WOT/HER * KT12 ....197 K8
Rodney Crs HOD EN11 ....44 F1
Rodney Gdns PIN HA5 ....113 J3
WWKM BR4 ....225 M1
Rodney Pl STHWK SE1 ....18 F5
WALTH E17 ....100 D10
WIM/MER SW19 ....201 M1
Rodney Rd CHONG CM5 ....67 N5
HSLWW TW4 ....175 P2
MTCM CR4 ....201 P2
NWMAL KT3 ....200 B5
WALW SE17 ....18 F6
WAN E11 ....121 N2
WOT/HER KT12 ....197 J9
Rodney St IS N1 ....5 P7
Rodney Wy DTCH/LGLY SL3 ....151 H7
GU GU1 ....250 D9
ROMW/RG RM7 ....104 C9
Rodona Rd WEY KT13 ....216 E7
Rodway Rd BMLY BR1 ....205 N1
PUT/ROE SW15 ....178 D3
Rodwell Cl RSLP * HA4 ....113 K6
Rodwell Rd EDUL SE22 ....181 N2
Roebuck Cl ASHTD KT21 ....237 K6
FELT TW13 ....175 J7
HERT/BAY SG13 ....25 P5
REIG RH2 ....257 K10
Roebuck Gn SL SL1 ....128 D10
Roebuck La BKHH IG9 ....101 P2
Roebuck Rd BARK/HLT IG6 ....103 L7
CHSGTN KT9 ....219 M2
Roedean Av PEND EN3 ....80 B5
Roedean Cl ORP BR6 ....227 L1
PEND EN3 ....80 B5
Roedean Crs PUT/ROE SW15 ....178 B2
Roe End CDALE/KGS NW9 ....115 P2
Roefields Cl HHS/BOV HP3 ....35 K10
Roe Gn CDALE/KGS NW9 ....115 P3
Roe Green Cl HAT AL10 ....40 B5
Roe Green La HAT AL10 ....40 C4
Roehampton Cl GVE DA12 ....191 H3
PUT/ROE SW15 ....156 D10
Roehampton Dr CHST BR7 ....184 F9
Roehampton Ga PUT/ROE SW15 ....178 B2
Roehampton High St
PUT/ROE SW15 ....178 D3
Roehampton La PUT/ROE SW15 ....178 D1
Roehampton V PUT/ROE SW15 ....178 C6
Roe Hill Cl HAT AL10 ....40 C5
Roehyde Wy HAT AL10 ....40 B6
Roe La CDALE/KGS NW9 ....115 N2
Roestock Gdns STALE/WH AL4 ....40 B8
Roestock La STALE/WH AL4 ....40 A9
Roe Wy WLGTN SM6 ....222 F4
Rofant Rd NTHWD HA6 ....92 F7
Roffes La CTHM CR3 ....259 L1
Roffey Cl HORL RH6 ....280 A4
PUR/KEN CR8 ....241 J2
Roffey's Cl CRAWE RH10 ....285 H1
Roffey St POP/IOD E14 ....161 H1
Roffords WOKN/KNAP GU21 ....231 N3
Rogers Cl CHESW EN7 ....61 L3
COUL/CHIP CR5 ....241 J4
Rogers Ct SWLY BR8 ....209 H4
Rogers Gdns DAGE RM10 ....124 B10
Rogers La SLN SL2 ....129 L3
WARL CR6 ....242 E4
Rogers Md GDST RH9 ....260 A8
Rogers Rd CAN/RD E16 ....141 L8
DAGE RM10 ....124 B10
GRAYS RM17 ....167 P3
TOOT SW17 ....179 N7
Rogers Ruff NTHWD HA6 ....92 D9
Roger St BMSBY WC1N 11 P2
Rojack Rd FSTH SE23 ....182 C4
Rokeby Gdns WFD IG8 ....101 M9
Rokeby Pl RYNPK SW20 ....178 E10
Rokeby Rd BROCKY * SE4 ....160 E8
Rokeby St SRTFD E15 ....141 K3
Roke Cl PUR/KEN CR8 ....223 K10
Roke Lodge Rd PUR/KEN CR8 ....223 J9
Roke Rd PUR/KEN CR8 ....241 K1
Roker Park Av HGDN/ICK UB10 ....111 P9
Rokers La MFD/CHID GU8 ....266 C10
Rokesby Cl WELL DA16 ....162 G8
Rokesby Pl ALP/SUD HA0 ....115 J10
Rokesly Rd SLN SL2 ....128 E5
Rokesly Av CEND/HSY/T N8 ....118 F3
Roland Gdns SKENS SW7 ....15 K7
Roland Ms WCHPL * E1 ....140 C7
Roland Rd WALTH E17 ....121 J2
Roland St STAL AL1 ....38 F6
Roland Wy WALW SE17 ....19 H8
WBPTN SW10 ....15 K7
WPK KT4 ....200 C9
Roles Gv CHDH RM6 ....123 N2
Rolfe Cl BECK HP9 ....88 D10
EBAR EN4 ....77 P8
Rolinsden Wy HAYES BR2 ....226 A1
Rollesby Rd CHSGTN KT9 ....219 M3
Rollesby Wy THMD SE28 ....143 M9
Rolleston Av STMC/STPC BR5 ....206 E6
Rolleston Cl STMC/STPC BR5 ....206 E7
Rolleston Rd SAND/SEL CR2 ....223 L4
Roll Gdns GNTH/NBYPK IG2 ....122 D3
Rollins St PECK SE15 ....160 B5
Rollit Crs HSLW TW3 ....175 P1
Rollit St HOLWY N7 ....119 H10
Rollo Rd SWLY BR8 ....186 C10
Rolls Buildings FLST/FETLN EC4A 12 A5
Rollscourt Av HNHL SE24 ....181 K1
Rolls Park Av CHING E4 ....100 F7
Rolls Park Rd CHING E4 ....100 G6
Rolls Rd STHWK SE1 ....19 M7
Rollswood WGCE AL7 ....23 H8
Rolt St DEPT SE8 ....160 D5
Rolvenden Gdns BMLY BR1 ....206 A1
Rolvenden Pl TOTM N17 ....99 P9
Romana Ct STA * TW18 ....173 K7
Roman Cl ACT W3 ....155 N1
EBED/NFELT TW14 ....175 K1
RAIN RM13 ....144 E4
Roman Farm Wy GUW GU2 ....249 J8
Romanfield Rd
BRXS/STRHM SW2 ....180 G3
Roman Gdns KGLGY WD4 ....54 C6
Romanhurst Av HAYES BR2 ....205 K4
Romanhurst Gdns BECK BR3 ....205 K4
Roman Ri NRWD SE19 ....181 L9
SBW CM21 ....29 N1
Roman Rd BETH E2 ....140 C4
CHSWK W4 ....156 B3
DORK RH4 ....272 F4
EHAM E6 ....142 B6
GVW DA11 ....189 P6
IL IG1 ....142 E1
MUSWH N10 ....98 C8
RAD WD7 ....74 F1
RDART DA2 ....188 G5
Roman Sq THMD SE28 ....143 K10
Roman St HOD EN11 ....44 F2
Romans Wy WOKS/MYFD GU22 ....233 K1
Roman V HLWE CM17 ....29 M6
Roman Villa Rd EYN DA4 ....188 B9
Roman Wk RAD * WD7 ....74 E2
Roman Wy CROY/NA CR0 ....203 J9
DART DA1 ....186 F1
EN EN1 ....79 N9
HOLWY N7 ....5 N1
Romany Ct HHNE HP2 ....36 D5
Romany Gdns CHEAM SM3 ....201 K7
Romany Ri STMC/STPC BR5 ....206 F8
Roma Rd WALTH E17 ....120 D1
Romberg Rd TOOT SW17 ....180 B6
Romborough Gdns LEW SE13 ....183 H1
Romborough Wy LEW SE13 ....183 H1
Rom Crs ROMW/RG RM7 ....124 F5
Romeland BORE WD6 ....75 J10
STALW/RED AL3 ....38 B6
WAB EN9 ....63 H9
Romeland Hl STALW/RED AL3 ....38 B6
Romero Sq ELTH/MOT SE9 ....161 P10
Romeyn Rd STRHM/NOR SW16 ....180 G6
Romford Rd CHIG IG7 ....103 L5
CHONG CM5 ....67 M9
MNPK E12 ....122 D8
SOCK/AV RM15 ....146 B5
SRTFD E15 ....141 K2
Romford St WCHPL E1 ....13 P4
Romilly Dr OXHEY WD19 ....93 M5
Romilly Rd FSBYPK N4 ....119 J7
Romilly St SOHO/SHAV W1D 11 K7
Rommany Rd WNWD SE27 ....181 L7
Romney Cha EMPK RM11 ....125 N4
Romney Cl ASHF TW15 ....174 D8
CHSGTN KT9 ....219 K1
GLDGN NW11 ....117 L6
RYLN/HDSTN HA2 ....113 P5
TOTM N17 ....100 A9
Romney Dr BMLY BR1 ....184 A10
RYLN/HDSTN HA2 ....113 P5
Romney Gdns BXLYHN DA7 ....164 A7
Romney Lock Rd WDSR SL4 ....149 J6
Romney Rd GNWCH SE10 ....161 H5
GVW DA11 ....190 B6
NWMAL KT3 ....200 A6
WOOL/PLUM SE18 ....162 E2
YEAD UB4 ....132 E4
Romney Rw CRICK * NW2 ....116 G7
Romola Rd BRXS/STRHM SW2 ....181 J4
Romsey Cl DTCH/LGLY SL3 ....150 C2
ORP BR6 ....226 F1
Romsey Dr SLN SL2 ....109 J8
Romsey Rd DAGW RM9 ....143 N3
WEA * W13 ....134 F9
Rom Valley Wy ROMW/RG RM7 ....124 F4
Rona Cl CRAWW RH11 ....283 L10
Ronald Av SRTFD E15 ....141 K5
Ronald Cl BECK BR3 ....204 E5
Ronald Rd BEAC HP9 ....88 E9
HARH RM3 ....105 P9
Ronaldsay Sp SL SL1 ....129 K7
Ronalds Rd BMLY BR1 ....205 M1
HBRY N5 ....119 H10
Ronaldstone Rd BFN/LL DA15 ....185 H2
Ronald St WCHPL E1 ....140 B8
Rona Rd HAMP NW3 ....118 B9
Ronart St KTN/HRWW/W HA3 ....114 E1
Rona Wk IS * N1 ....6 G2
Rondu Rd CRICK NW2 ....117 H10
Ronelean Rd SURB KT6 ....199 L10
Roneo Cnr ROMW/RG RM7 ....124 G6
Roneo Link HCH RM12 ....124 G6
Ronfearn Av STMC/STPC BR5 ....207 N5
Ron Green Ct ERITH DA8 ....164 E4
Ron Leighton Wy EHAM E6 ....142 B3
Ronneby Cl WEY KT13 ....196 F10
Ronsons Wy STALW/RED AL3 ....38 E2
Ronson Wy LHD/OX KT22 ....236 F7
Ronver Rd LEE/GVPK SE12 ....183 M4
Rood La FENCHST EC3M 13 J7
Rookby Ct WCHMH N21 ....99 J3
Rook Cl WBLY HA9 ....115 N8
Rookeries Cl FELT TW13 ....175 J6
Rookery Cl LHD/OX KT22 ....236 D10
Rookery Ct WTHK * RM20 ....166 F5
Rookery Dr CHST BR7 ....206 D1
DORK RH4 ....271 P4
Rookery Gdns STMC/STPC BR5 ....207 M5
Rookery Hl ASHTD KT21 ....237 M4
REDH RH1 ....281 J1
Rookery La HAYES BR2 ....206 A6
Rookery Rd CLAP SW4 ....158 D10
ORP BR6 ....226 C6
STA TW18 ....173 L8
The Rookery
STRHM/NOR * SW16 ....180 G9
WTHK RM20 ....166 F5
Rookery Vw GRAYS RM17 ....168 A4
Rookery Wy CDALE/KGS NW9 ....116 C3
KWD/TDW/WH KT20 ....257 J3
Rookesley Rd STMC/STPC BR5 ....207 N7
Rookfield Av MUSWH N10 ....118 D2
Rookfield Cl MUSWH N10 ....118 D2
Rook La CTHM CR3 ....241 H10
Rookley Cl BELMT SM2 ....221 M6
Rooks Cl WGCW * AL8 ....22 G6
Rooks Hl RKW/CH/CXG WD3 ....71 M8
WGCW AL8 ....22 F6
Rooksmead Rd SUN TW16 ....196 G2
Rooks Ter WDR/YW * UB7 ....151 P1
Rookstone Rd TOOT SW17 ....180 B8
Rookwood Av LOU IG10 ....82 F7
NWMAL KT3 ....200 D4
WLGTN SM6 ....222 E1
Rookwood Cl GRAYS RM17 ....167 N3
REDH RH1 ....258 C5
Rookwood Ct GUW GU2 ....267 P3
Rookwood Gdns CHING * E4 ....101 L3
Rookwood Rd STNW/STAM N16 ....119 N4
Roosevelt Wy DAGE RM10 ....144 E1
Rootes Dr NKENS W10 ....136 G6
Roothill La BRKHM/BTCW RH3 ....273 M6
Ropemaker Rd
BERM/RHTH SE16 ....160 D1
Ropemaker's Flds
POP/IOD * E14 ....140 E9
Ropemaker St BARB EC2Y 12 G3
Roper La STHWK SE1 ....19 K2
Ropers Av CHING E4 ....101 H6
Roper St ELTH/MOT SE9 ....184 C1
Roper Wy MTCM CR4 ....202 B2
Ropery St BOW E3 ....140 E6
Rope St BERM/RHTH SE16 ....160 D2
Ropewalk Gdns WCHPL * E1 ....13 P5
Ropewalk Ms HACK * E8 ....7 L4
Rope Yard Rails
WOOL/PLUM SE18 ....162 E2
Ropley St BETH E2 ....7 N8
Rosa Alba Ms HBRY N5 ....119 K9
Rosa Av ASHF TW15 ....174 B7
Rosalind Franklin Cl GUW GU2 ....267 K1
Rosaline Rd FUL/PGN SW6 ....157 H6
Rosaline Ter FUL/PGN * SW6 ....157 H6
Rosamond St SYD SE26 ....182 A6
Rosamond Vls
MORT/ESHN * SW14 ....156 A10
Rosamund Cl SAND/SEL CR2 ....223 L1
Rosamund Rd CRAWE RH10 ....284 C9
Rosary Cl HSLW TW3 ....153 M8
Rosary Ct POTB/CUF EN6 ....59 L6
Rosary Gdns ASHF TW15 ....174 C7
BUSH WD23 ....94 D1
SKENS SW7 ....15 K6
Rosaville Rd FUL/PGN SW6 ....157 J6
Roscoe St STLK EC1Y 12 F2
Roscoff Cl EDGW HA8 ....95 N9
Roseacre OXTED RH8 ....261 M9
Roseacre Cl EMPK RM11 ....125 N6
SHPTN TW17 ....196 B5
WEA W13 ....134 G7
Roseacre Gdns RGUE GU4 ....269 J6
WGCE AL7 ....23 M5
Roseacre Rd WELL DA16 ....163 L9
Rose Aly STHWK SE1 ....12 F9
Roseary Cl WDR/YW UB7 ....151 N3
Rose Av GVE DA12 ....191 H4
MRDN SM4 ....201 M5
MTCM CR4 ....202 A1
SWFD E18 ....101 N10
Rose Bank BRW CM14 ....107 J4
Rosebank EPSOM KT18 ....219 P10
PGE/AN SE20 ....182 A10
WAB EN9 ....63 K10
Rosebank Av ALP/SUD HA0 ....114 E9
HCH RM12 ....125 K10
Rose Bank Cl NFNCH/WDSP N12 ....97 P6
Rosebank Cl TEDD TW11 ....176 F9
Rosebank Cottages REIG * RH2 ....275 L2
Rosebank Est BOW E3 ....140 E4
Rosebank Gdns ACT * W3 ....136 A8
BOW * E3 ....140 D4
GVW DA11 ....190 B4
Rosebank Gv WALTH E17 ....120 E1
Rosebank Rd HNWL W7 ....154 D1
LEY E10 ....120 F4
Rosebank Wk CAMTN NW1 ....5 K4
Rosebank Wy ACT W3 ....136 A8
Rose Bates Dr CDALE/KGS NW9 ....115 M2
Roseberry Cl UPMR RM14 ....126 E4
Roseberry Ct WAT WD17 ....73 H5
Roseberry Gdns DART DA1 ....187 K3
FSBYPK N4 ....119 J4
ORP BR6 ....207 H10
UPMR RM14 ....126 E5
Roseberry Pl HACK E8 ....7 L2
Roseberry Rd EPSOM KT18 ....238 B5
Roseberry St BERM/RHTH SE16 ....160 A3
Rosebery Av BFN/LL DA15 ....185 H3
CLKNW EC1R 12 A1
EW KT17 ....220 B10
MNPK E12 ....142 B1
NWMAL KT3 ....200 C2
RYLN/HDSTN HA2 ....113 M9
THHTH CR7 ....203 K2
TOTM N17 ....99 P10
Rosebery Cl MRDN SM4 ....200 G6
Rosebery Ct CLKNW EC1R 12 A1
GVW DA11 ....190 C6
Rosebery Crs WOKS/MYFD GU22 ....232 C6
Rosebery Gdns
CEND/HSY/T * N8 ....118 F3
SUT SM1 ....221 L1
WEA W13 ....134 F8
Rosebery Ms MUSWH N10 ....98 D10
Rosebery Pde EW * KT17 ....220 C4
Rosebery Rd BUSH WD23 ....94 A2
CLAP SW4 ....180 F2
ED N9 ....99 P4
GRAYS RM17 ....167 K5
ISLW TW7 ....176 B1
KUT KT1 ....199 N2
MUSWH N10 ....98 D10
SUT SM1 ....221 J3
Rosebine Av WHTN TW2 ....176 C3
Rosebriar Cl WOKS/MYFD GU22 ....233 K2
Rosebriars CTHM CR3 ....241 M6
ESH/CLAY KT10 ....218 B2
Rosebriar Wk WATN WD24 ....72 G2
Rosebury Dr CHOB/PIR GU24 ....230 F1
Rosebury Rd FUL/PGN SW6 ....157 L8
Rosebury Sq WFD IG8 ....102 D8
Rosebury V RSLP HA4 ....113 H7
Rose Bushes EW KT17 ....238 F2
Rose Cottages HAYES * BR2 ....225 P7
Rose Ct CHESW EN7 ....61 P3
WCHPL E1 ....13 L4
Rosecourt Rd CROY/NA CR0 ....202 G6
Rosecroft Av HAMP NW3 ....117 K8
Rosecroft Cl BH/WHM TN16 ....244 C4
STMC/STPC BR5 ....207 M6
Rosecroft Ct NTHWD * HA6 ....92 D7
Rosecroft Dr WAT WD17 ....72 F3
Rose Croft Gdns CRICK NW2 ....116 D8
Rosecroft Gdns WHTN TW2 ....176 C4
Rosecroft Rd STHL UB1 ....133 P6
Rosecroft Wk ALP/SUD HA0 ....115 J10
PIN HA5 ....113 L3
Rose & Crown Yd STJS * SW1Y 11 H10
Rosedale ASHTD KT21 ....237 H4
Rose Dl ORP BR6 ....206 E9
Rosedale WGCE AL7 ....23 J1
Rosedale Av CHESW EN7 ....61 N5
HYS/HAR UB3 ....132 E7
Rosedale Cl ABYW SE2 ....163 L2
CRAWW RH11 ....283 K9
HNWL W7 ....154 E1
LCOL/BKTW AL2 ....55 M6
RDART DA2 ....188 A3
STAN HA7 ....94 G7
Rosedale Gdns DAGW RM9 ....143 L2
Rosedale Rd CRW RM5 ....124 D1
DAGW RM9 ....143 L2
EW KT17 ....220 D2
FSTGT E7 ....121 P10

GRAYS RM17 168 A4
RCH/KEW TW9 155 K10
Rosedale Wy CHESW EN7 61 P4
Rosedene Av CROY/NA CR0 202 F2
GFD/PVL UB6 133 P5
MRDN SM4 201 K5
STRHM/NOR SW16 180 G6
Rosedene Cl DART DA1 187 K3
Rosedene Gdns
GNTH/NBYPK IG2 122 D2
Rosedene Ter LEY E10 120 G7
Rosedew Rd HMSMTH W6 156 G5
Rose Dr CSHM HP5 51 J8
Rose End WPK KT4 200 C8
Rosefield POP/IOD E14 140 F9
SEV TN13 247 H10
Rosefield Cl CAR SM5 221 P2
Rosefield Gdns CHERT KT16 214 C3
POP/IOD E14 140 F9
Rosefield Rd STA TW18 173 K7
Rose Garden Cl EDGW HA8 95 K7
Rose Gdns EA W5 155 J2
FELT TW13 175 H5
STHL UB1 133 P6
STWL/WRAY TW19 173 N3
WATW WD18 73 H9
Rose Gln CDALE/KGS NW9 116 A2
ROMW/RG RM7 124 F6
Rosehart Ms NTGHL * W11 8 E6
Rosehatch Av CHDH RM6 123 N1
Roseheath HHW HP1 35 H5
Roseheath Rd HSLWW TW4 175 N1
Rosehill BERK HP4 33 N5
Rose Hl DORK RH4 272 F2
Rosehill ESH/CLAY KT10 218 F3
HPTN TW12 197 P1
Rose Hl SUT SM1 201 L9
Rose Hill Arch Ms DORK * RH4 272 F2
Rosehill Av SUT SM1 201 M8
WOKN/KNAP GU21 231 P2
Rosehill Cl HOD EN11 44 E3
Rosehill Court Pde
MRDN * SM4 201 M7
Rosehill Farm Meadow
BNSTD SM7 239 L1
Rosehill Gdns ABLGY WD5 54 D8
GFD/PVL UB6 114 E10
SUT SM1 201 L9
Rose Hill Pk West SUT SM1 201 M8
Rosehill Rd BH/WHM TN16 243 P3
WAND/EARL SW18 179 M2
Roseland Cl TOTM N17 99 L8
Roselands Av HOD EN11 44 E1
Rose La CHDH RM6 123 P2
RPLY/SEND GU23 233 N8
STALE/WH AL4 21 H1
Roselare Cl BH/WHM TN16 262 G1
Rose Lawn BUSH WD23 94 B2
Roseleigh Av HBRY N5 119 J9
Roseleigh Cl TWK TW1 177 J2
Rosemary Av E/WMO/HCT KT8 197 P3
ED N9 100 A2
ENC/FH EN2 79 L5
FNCH N3 97 L10
HSLWW TW4 153 L8
ROM RM1 124 G1
Rosemary Cl CROY/NA CR0 202 F7
OXTED RH8 261 M9
SOCK/AV RM15 147 H5
UX/CGN * UB8 132 B7
Rosemary Ct HORL * RH6 279 P3
Rosemary Crs RGUW GU3 249 L6
Rosemary Dr POP/IOD E14 141 J8
REDBR IG4 122 A3
Rosemary Gdns BCTR RM8 124 A6
CHSGTN KT9 219 K1
Rosemary La EGH TW20 194 E3
HORL RH6 279 H8
HORL RH6 280 C5
MORT/ESHN SW14 155 P9
Rosemary Rd PECK SE15 159 N6
TOOT SW17 179 L6
WELL DA16 163 J7
Rosemary St IS N1 6 C5
Rosemead CDALE/KGS NW9 116 C5
CHERT KT16 195 L7
Rose Md POTB/CUF EN6 59 M6
Rosemead Av FELT TW13 174 G5
MTCM CR4 202 D3
WBLY HA9 115 K10
Rosemead Cl REDH RH1 275 N2
Rosemont Av NFNCH/WDSP N12 97 M7
Rosemont Rd ACT W3 135 N9
ALP/SUD HA0 135 K3
HAMP NW3 3 J1
NWMAL KT3 199 P3
RCHPK/HAM TW10 177 K2
Rosemoor St CHEL SW3 16 A6
Rosemount HLWW/ROY CM19 46 E4
Rosemount Av BF/WBF KT14 215 K9
Rosemount Cl WFD IG8 102 C7
Rosemount Dr BMLY BR1 206 C4
Rosemount Rd WEA W13 134 F8
Rosenau Crs BTSEA SW11 158 A7
Rosenau Rd BTSEA SW11 157 P7
Rosendale Rd DUL SE21 181 K4
Roseneath Av WCHMH N21 99 J2
Roseneath Ct CTHM * CR3 259 P1
Roseneath Rd BTSEA SW11 180 D2
Roseneath Wk EN EN1 79 M8
Rosenheath Cl ORP BR6 227 L4
Rosens Wk EDGW HA8 95 N4
Rosenthal Rd CAT SE6 182 C2
Rosenthorpe Rd PECK SE15 182 D1
Rose Park Cl YEAD UB4 133 K6
Roserton St POP/IOD E14 161 H1
Rosery Ga BTSEA SW11 158 C6
The Rosery CROY/NA CR0 204 C6
Roses Cottages DORK * RH4 272 F2
Roses La WDSR SL4 148 C8
The Roses WFD * IG8 101 L8
Rose St COVGDN WC2E 11 L7
GVW DA11 189 N2
Rosethorn Cl BAL SW12 180 D3
Rosetrees GU GU1 268 D1
Rosetta Cl VX/NE SW8 158 F6
Rose V HOD EN11 44 F3
Rose Va BRW CM14 107 H4
Roseveare Rd LEE/GVPK SE12 183 P7
Rose Vw ADL/WDHM * KT15 215 M2
Roseville Av HSLWW TW4 175 P1
Roseville Rd HYS/HAR UB3 153 H4
Rosevine Rd RYNPK SW20 200 F1
Rose Wk BRYLDS KT5 199 N5
CRAWW * RH11 283 L9
PUR/KEN CR8 222 E7
SL SL1 128 G7
STALE/WH AL4 38 G4
WWKM BR4 205 J9
The Rose Wk RAD WD7 74 C2
Rosewarne Cl WOKN/KNAP GU21 231 M4
Roseway DUL SE21 181 L2
EDGW HA8 95 P5
Rose Wy LEE/GVPK SE12 183 M1
Rosewell Cl PGE/AN SE20 182 A10
Rosewood RDART DA2 186 F7
Rose Wd WOKS/MYFD GU22 232 D5
Rosewood Av GFD/PVL UB6 114 F10
HCH RM12 125 H10
Rosewood Cl SCUP DA14 185 M6
SOCK/AV RM15 147 K5
Rosewood Ct HHW * HP1 35 H5
KUTN/CMB KT2 177 M10
Rosewood Dr ENC/FH EN2 79 H1
SHPTN TW17 196 A5
Rosewood Gv SUT SM1 201 M9
Rosewood Ter PGE/AN * SE20 182 B10
Rosewood Wy CHOB/PIR GU24 212 D9
SLN SL2 109 H10
Rosher Cl SRTFD E15 141 J2
Rosherville Wy GVW DA11 190 B2
Rosina St HOM E9 120 C10
Roskell Rd PUT/ROE SW15 156 G9
Rosken Gv SLN SL2 128 G4
Roslin Rd ACT W3 155 N2
Roslin Wy BMLY BR1 183 M8
Roslyn Cl BROX EN10 44 D7
MTCM CR4 201 N2
Roslyn Gdns GPK RM2 104 G10
Roslyn Ms SEVS/STOTM * N15 119 M3
Roslyn Rd SEVS/STOTM N15 119 L3
Rosmead Rd NTGHL W11 8 B7
Rosoman Pl CLKNW EC1R 12 B1
Rosoman St CLKNW EC1R 6 B10
Rossall Cl EMPK RM11 125 H4
Rossall Crs WLSDN NW10 135 L5
Ross Av BCTR RM8 124 A7
MLHL NW7 97 H6
Ross Cl CRAWE RH10 284 A10
HYS/HAR UB3 152 E3
KTN/HRWW/W HA3 94 B8
Ross Crs GSTN WD25 73 H1
Rossdale SUT SM1 221 P2
Rossdale Dr CDALE/KGS NW9 115 P6
ED N9 80 B10
Rossdale Rd PUT/ROE SW15 156 F10
Rossell Rd TIL RM18 168 C8
Rosse Ms BKHTH/KID SE3 161 N7
Rossendale St CLPT E5 120 A7
Rossendale Wy CAMTN NW1 5 H4
Rossetti Gdns COUL/CHIP CR5 240 G3
Rossetti Rd BERM/RHTH SE16 160 A4
Rossignol Gdns CAR SM5 202 B9
Rossindel Rd HSLW TW3 175 P1
Rossington Av BORE WD6 75 K4
Rossington Cl EN EN1 80 A4
Rossington St CLPT * E5 120 A7
Rossiter Cl DTCH/LGLY SL3 150 B3
Rossiter Flds BAR EN5 77 H10
Rossiter Ldg GU * GU1 268 D1
Rossiter Rd BAL SW12 180 C4
Rossland Cl BXLYHS DA6 186 B1
Rosslyn Av BARN SW13 156 B9
BCTR RM8 124 A5
CHING E4 101 L3
EBAR EN4 77 P10
EBED/NFELT TW14 175 H2
HARH RM3 105 M10
Rosslyn Cl HYS/HAR UB3 132 E7
SUN TW16 174 F9
WWKM BR4 205 L10
Rosslyn Crs HRW HA1 114 E2
WBLY HA9 115 K8
Rosslyn Hl HAMP NW3 117 N10
Rosslyn Pk WEY KT13 216 E1
Rosslyn Park Ms HAMP NW3 117 N10
Rosslyn Rd BARK IG11 142 G2
TWK TW1 177 H2
WALTH * E17 121 H2
WATW WD18 73 J7
Rossmore Cl CAMTN * NW1 9 P2
CRAWE RH10 284 E3
Rossmore Rd CAMTN NW1 9 P1
Ross Pde WLGTN SM6 222 C3
Ross Rd COB KT11 217 K9
DART DA1 187 H2
SNWD SE25 203 M3
WHTN TW2 176 B4
WLGTN SM6 222 D3
Ross Wy ELTH/MOT SE9 162 B9
NTHWD HA6 92 G5
Rossway Dr BUSH WD23 74 B9
Rossway La TRING HP23 32 F1
Rosswood Gdns WLGTN SM6 222 C3
Rostella Rd TOOT SW17 179 N7
Rostrever Gdns HYS/HAR UB3 132 F10
Rostrevor Av SEVS/STOTM N15 119 N4
Rostrevor Gdns IVER SL0 130 G4
NWDGN UB2 153 M4
Rostrevor Rd FUL/PGN SW6 157 J7
WIM/MER SW19 179 K8
Roswell Cl CHES/WCR EN8 62 D6
Rotary St STHWK SE1 18 C3
Rothbury Av RAIN RM13 145 J7
Rothbury Gdns ISLW TW7 154 F6
Rothbury Rd HOM E9 140 E2
Roth Dr RBRW/HUT CM13 107 N3
Rother Cl GSTN WD25 55 K10
Rother Crs CRAWW RH11 283 H9
Rotherfield Rd CAR SM5 222 B1
PEND EN3 80 C3
Rotherfield St IS N1 6 F4
Rotherham Wk STHWK * SE1 12 D10
Rotherhill Av STRHM/NOR SW16 180 E9
Rotherhithe New Rd
BERM/RHTH SE16 160 A4
Rotherhithe Old Rd
BERM/RHTH SE16 160 C3
Rotherhithe St
BERM/RHTH SE16 160 A1
Rotherhithe Tnl
BERM/RHTH SE16 160 B1
Rothermere Rd CROY/NA CR0 222 G2
Rothervale HORL RH6 280 A2
Rotherwick Hl EA W5 135 L6
Rotherwick Rd GLDGN NW11 117 K5
Rotherwood Cl RYNPK SW20 201 H1
Rotherwood Rd PUT/ROE SW15 156 G9
Rothery St IS * N1 6 D5
Rothery Ter BRXN/ST * SW9 159 J6
Rothesay Av NTHLT UB5 134 C1
RCHPK/HAM TW10 155 N10
RYNPK SW20 201 H2
Rothesay Rd SNWD SE25 203 L4
Rothes Rd DORK RH4 272 G1
Rothsay Rd FSTGT E7 141 P2
Rothsay St STHWK SE1 19 J3
Rothschild Rd CHSWK W4 155 P3
Rothschild St WNWD SE27 181 J7
Rothwell Gdns DAGW RM9 143 M2
Rothwell Rd DAGW RM9 143 M3
Rothwell St CAMTN NW1 4 B5
Rotterdam Dr POP/IOD E14 161 H2
Rouel Rd BERM/RHTH SE16 19 N5
Rouge La GVE DA12 190 E4
Rougemont Av MRDN SM4 201 K6
Roughdown Av HHS/BOV HP3 35 K9
Roughdown Rd HHS/BOV HP3 35 L9
Roughdown Villas Rd
HHS/BOV HP3 35 K9
Roughets La REDH RH1 259 M5
Roughlands WOKS/MYFD GU22 233 H1
Rough Rew RDKG RH5 272 G5
Rough Rd WOKS/MYFD GU22 231 H8
The Roughs NTHWD HA6 92 F4
Roughtallys EPP CM16 66 A3
Roughwood Cl WAT WD17 72 F4
Roughwood La CSTG HP8 70 B10
Rounce La CHOB/PIR GU24 212 C9
Round Ash Wy HART DA3 211 K6
Roundaway Rd CLAY IG5 102 C10
Roundcroft CHESW EN7 61 N2
Roundel Cl BROCKY SE4 160 E10
Round Gv CROY/NA CR0 204 C7
Roundhay Cl FSTH SE23 182 C5
Roundheads End BEAC HP9 88 A7
Roundhedge Wy ENC/FH EN2 78 G4
Round Hl FSTH SE23 182 A5
Roundhill WOKS/MYFD GU22 232 E5
Roundhill Dr ENC/FH EN2 78 G8
WOKS/MYFD GU22 232 E4
Roundhills WAB EN9 63 K10
Roundhill Wy COB KT11 218 A7
GUW GU2 249 L10
The Roundings HERT/BAY SG13 26 B9
Roundlyn Gdns STMC/STPC BR5 207 L4
Roundmead Av LOU IG10 82 D7
Roundmead Cl LOU IG10 82 D7
Roundmoor Dr CHES/WCR EN8 62 D5
Round Oak Rd WEY KT13 216 A1
Roundtable Rd BMLY BR1 183 L6
Roundthorn Wy
WOKN/KNAP GU21 231 L2
Roundtree Rd ALP/SUD HA0 114 G10
Roundway EGH TW20 172 F8
Roundways RSLP HA4 112 G8
The Roundway ESH/CLAY KT10 218 E3
TOTM N17 99 K9
WATW WD18 72 G10
Roundwood CHST BR7 206 E2
HHS/BOV HP3 53 P3
Roundwood Av
RBRW/HUT CM13 107 M2
STKPK UB11 132 D10
Roundwood Cl RSLP * HA4 112 E5
Roundwood Dr WGCW AL8 22 F4
Roundwood Gv
RBRW/HUT CM13 107 N1
Roundwood Pk WLSDN * NW10 136 D3
Round Wood Rd AMS HP6 69 L3
Roundwood Rd WLSDN NW10 136 B1
Roundwood Vw BNSTD SM7 238 G1
Roundwood Wy BNSTD SM7 238 G1
Rounton Rd BOW E3 140 F6
WAB EN9 63 K9
Roupell Rd BRXS/STRHM SW2 180 G4
Roupell St STHWK SE1 12 B10
Rousden St CAMTN NW1 4 G4
Rousebarn La RKW/CH/CXG WD3 72 A4
Rouse Ct CFSP/GDCR * SL9 90 C8
CFSP/GDCR SL9 110 C3
Rouse Gdns DUL SE21 181 M7
Rous Rd BKHH IG9 102 B1
Routemaster Cl PLSTW E13 141 N5
Routh Rd WAND/EARL SW18 179 P3
Routh St EHAM E6 142 C7
Rover Av BARK/HLT IG6 103 J7
Rowallan Rd FUL/PGN SW6 157 H6
Rowan Av CHING E4 100 E7
EGH TW20 172 F8
Rowan Cl ALP/SUD HA0 114 F8
CRAWE RH10 284 A7
EA W5 155 K1
GU GU1 249 N7
IL IG1 122 G10
KTN/HRWW/W HA3 94 E7
LCOL/BKTW AL2 55 P7
NWMAL KT3 200 B2
REIG RH2 275 M2
STALE/WH AL4 39 K6
STRHM/NOR SW16 202 D1
Rowan Crs DART DA1 187 K4
STRHM/NOR SW16 202 D1
Rowan Dr BROX EN10 44 E10
CDALE/KGS NW9 116 D1
Rowan Gdns CROY/NA CR0 203 N10
IVER SL0 130 F4
Rowan Gn East
RBRW/HUT CM13 107 L5
Rowan Gn West
RBRW/HUT CM13 107 L5
Rowan Gv COUL/CHIP CR5 240 C7
SOCK/AV RM15 146 B9
Rowanhurst Dr SLN SL2 109 H10
Rowan Md KWD/TDW/WH KT20 238 E5
Rowan Pl AMS HP6 69 L4
HYS/HAR UB3 132 G9
Rowan Rd BTFD TW8 154 G6
BXLYHN DA7 163 P9
HMSMTH W6 156 G3
STRHM/NOR SW16 202 D2
SWLY BR8 208 E3
WDR/YW UB7 151 N3
Rowans WGCE AL7 23 J2
Rowans Cl HART DA3 211 J2
The Rowans BROX EN10 44 D5
CFSP/GDCR SL9 109 P1
HHW HP1 35 K6
PLMGR N13 99 K4
SOCK/AV RM15 146 B10
SUN TW16 174 G8
WOKS/MYFD GU22 232 B4
Rowans Wy LOU IG10 82 C8
Rowan Ter PGE/AN * SE20 203 P1
WIM/MER * SW19 179 H10
Rowantree Cl WCHMH N21 99 L2
Rowantree Rd ENC/FH EN2 79 J6
WCHMH N21 99 L2
Rowan Wk EFNCH N2 117 M4
EMPK RM11 125 L2
HAYES BR2 206 C10
NKENS * W10 8 A1
SBW CM21 29 P1
Rowan Wy CHDH RM6 123 M1
HARP AL5 20 B3
SL SL1 128 G7
SOCK/AV RM15 147 J6
Rowanwood Av BFN/LL DA15 185 K4
Rowbarns Wy EHSLY KT24 252 G6
Rowben Cl TRDG/WHET N20 97 L2
Rowberry Cl FUL/PGN SW6 156 G6
Rowbury RGODL GU7 267 L9
Rowcroft HHW HP1 35 H7
Rowcross St STHWK SE1 19 L7
Rowdell Rd NTHLT UB5 133 P3
Rowden Pde CHING * E4 100 F7
Rowden Rd BECK BR3 204 D1
CHING E4 100 G7
HOR/WEW KT19 219 P1
Rowditch La BTSEA SW11 158 B8
Rowdon Av WLSDN NW10 136 E2
Rowdow La RSEV TN14 247 L2
Rowdown Crs CROY/NA CR0 225 J5
Rowdowns Rd DAGW RM9 144 A3
Rowe Gdns BARK IG11 143 J4
Rowe La CHOB/PIR GU24 230 F10
HOM E9 120 B10
Rowena Crs BTSEA SW11 157 P8
Rowe Wk RYLN/HDSTN HA2 113 P8
Rowfant Cl CRAWE RH10 284 F7
Rowfant Rd TOOT SW17 180 B5
Rowhedge RBRW/HUT CM13 107 M4
Row Hl ADL/WDHM KT15 215 J3
Rowhill Rd CLPT E5 120 A9
RDART DA2 187 H8
Rowhurst Av ADL/WDHM KT15 215 L3
Rowington Cl BAY/PAD W2 8 G3
Rowland Av KTN/HRWW/W HA3 115 H1
Rowland Cl CRAWE RH10 281 M10
WDSR SL4 148 C9
Rowland Crs CHIG IG7 103 H5
Rowland Gv SYD SE26 182 A6
Rowland Hill Av TOTM N17 99 K8
Rowland Hill St HAMP NW3 117 P10
Rowland Pl NTHWD * HA6 92 F8
Rowlands Av PIN HA5 93 P7
Rowlands Cl CHES/WCR EN8 62 C6
HGT * N6 118 B4
MLHL NW7 96 D8
Rowlandsfields
CHES/WCR * EN8 62 C6
Rowlands Rd BCTR RM8 124 A7
Rowland Wy ASHF TW15 174 D10
WIM/MER SW19 201 L1
Rowlatt Cl RDART DA2 187 K7
Rowlatt Dr STALW/RED AL3 37 P8
Rowley Av BFN/LL DA15 185 L3
Rowley Cl ALP/SUD HA0 135 L2
OXHEY WD19 73 M10
WOKS/MYFD GU22 233 K2
Rowley Ct CTHM CR3 241 K8
Rowley Gdns FSBYPK N4 119 K5
Rowley Green Rd BAR EN5 76 D9
Rowley La BAR EN5 76 B8
BORE WD6 76 A5
DTCH/LGLY SL3 130 B4
Rowley Md EPP CM16 65 M1
Rowley Rd SEVS/STOTM N15 119 K3
Rowley's Rd HERT/BAY SG13 25 N4
Rowley Wk HNHE HP2 36 D1
Rowley Wy STJWD NW8 3 K4
Rowlheys Pl WDR/YW UB7 151 P2
Rowlls Rd KUT KT1 199 L3
Rowmarsh Cl GVW DA11 190 A6
Rowney Gdns DAGW RM9 143 M1
SBW CM21 29 M3
Rowney Rd DAGW RM9 143 L1
Rowney Wd SBW CM21 29 M2
Rowntree Cl KIL/WHAMP NW6 2 F2
PLSTW E13 141 N6
Rowntree Rd WHTN TW2 176 D4
Rowse Cl SRTFD E15 140 G3
Rowsley Av HDN NW4 116 F1
The Rows HLW * CM20 28 F10
Rowstock Gdns HOLWY N7 118 E10
The Row AMSS * HP7 68 B10
Rowton Rd WOOL/PLUM SE18 162 F6
Row Town ADL/WDHM KT15 215 J4
Rowzill Rd SWLY BR8 186 G9
Roxborough Av HRW HA1 114 D5
ISLW TW7 154 E6
Roxborough Pk HRW HA1 114 D5
Roxborough Rd HRW HA1 114 C3
Roxbourne Cl NTHLT UB5 133 L1
Roxburgh Av UPMR RM14 126 B8
Roxburgh Rd WNWD SE27 181 J8
Roxburn Wy RSLP HA4 112 G8
Roxby Pl FUL/PGN SW6 14 F9
Roxeth Green Av
RYLN/HDSTN HA2 114 A8
Roxeth Gv RYLN/HDSTN HA2 114 A9
Roxeth Hl RYLN/HDSTN HA2 114 C7
Roxford Cl SHPTN TW17 196 F5
Roxley Rd LEW SE13 183 H2
Roxton Gdns CROY/NA CR0 224 E3
Roxwell Cl SL SL1 128 D10
Roxwell Gdns RBRW/HUT CM13 87 P9
Roxwell Rd BARK IG11 143 K4
SHB W12 156 D1
Roxwell Wy WFD IG8 101 P8
Roxy Av CHDH RM6 123 M5
Royal Albert Rd EHAM E6 142 D9
Royal Albert Wy CAN/RD E16 142 A9
Royal Ar CONDST W1S 10 G8
Royal Arsenal West
WOOL/PLUM * SE18 162 D4
Royal Av CHEL SW3 16 C9
CHES/WCR EN8 62 D9
WPK KT4 200 B9
Royal Circ WNWD SE27 181 H6
Royal Cl DEPT SE8 160 E5
GDMY/SEVK IG3 123 M6
STNW/STAM * N16 119 M6
WDR/YW UB7 132 A8
WPK KT4 200 B9
Royal College St CAMTN NW1 5 H4
Royal Ct BANK EC3V 13 H6
ELTH/MOT * SE9 184 C4
EN * EN1 79 M10
HHS/BOV HP3 35 P9
Royal Crs NTGHL W11 156 G1
RSLP HA4 113 M9
Royal Crescent Ms NTGHL W11 156 G1
Royal Docks Rd EHAM E6 142 E7
Royal Dr EPSOM KT18 238 E4
Royal Earlswood Pk REDH RH1 276 B4
Royal Herbert Pavilions
WOOL/PLUM * SE18 162 C7
Royal Hl GNWCH SE10 161 H6
Royal Hospital Rd CHEL SW3 16 A9
Royal La WDR/YW UB7 132 A8
Royal Ms BAL SW12 180 C3
The Royal Ms WHALL SW1A 16 F3
Royal Mint Pl WCHPL E1 13 M7
Royal Mint St TWRH EC3N 13 M7
Royal Naval Pl NWCR SE14 160 E6
Royal Oak Centre
PUR/KEN * CR8 223 K6
Royal Oak Pl EDUL SE22 182 A2
Royal Oak Rd BXLYHS DA6 186 A1
HACK E8 140 A1
WOKN/KNAP GU21 231 P4
Royal Opera Ar STJS * SW1Y 11 J9
Royal Orchard Cl
WAND/EARL SW18 179 H3
Royal Pde BKHTH/KID SE3 161 L8
CHST BR7 184 F10
FUL/PGN * SW6 157 H6
Royal Pier Rd GVE DA12 190 E2
Royal Pl GNWCH SE10 161 H6
Royal Rd CAN/RD E16 141 P8
RDART DA2 187 P8
SCUP DA14 185 N6
STAL AL1 38 G6
TEDD TW11 176 C8
WALW SE17 18 C9
Royal Route WBLY HA9 115 L9
Royal St STHWK SE1 17 P3
Royal Terrace Pier GVE * DA12 190 F2
Royal Victor Pl BOW E3 140 C4
Royce Cl BROX EN10 44 E7
Royce Gv GSTN WD25 54 G10
Royce Rd CRAWE RH10 284 B2
Roycraft Av BARK IG11 143 J4
Roycroft Cl BRXS/STRHM * SW2 181 H4
SWFD E18 101 N9
Roydene Rd WOOL/PLUM SE18 163 H5
Roydon Cl LOU IG10 102 B1
Roydon Ct WOT/HER KT12 217 H1
Roydon Rd HLWW/ROY CM19 28 B10
WARE SG12 27 J7
Roy Gdns GNTH/NBYPK IG2 123 H2
Roy Gv HPTN TW12 176 A9
Royle Cl CFSP/GDCR SL9 90 C8
GPK RM2 125 J3
Royle Crs WEA W13 134 F6
Roy Rd NTHWD HA6 92 G8
Royston Av BF/WBF KT14 215 P8
CHING E4 100 F6
SUT SM1 201 N10
WLGTN SM6 222 E1
Royston Cl CRAWE RH10 284 B3
HERT/WAS SG14 25 J5
HEST TW5 153 J7
WOT/HER KT12 197 H8
Royston Gdns IL IG1 122 A4
Royston Gv PIN HA5 93 N7
Royston Park Rd PIN HA5 93 N7
Royston Rd BF/WBF KT14 215 P8
DART DA1 186 G2
HARH RM3 105 P8
PGE/AN SE20 204 C1
RCHPK/HAM TW10 177 K1
STAL AL1 38 G7
The Roystons BRYLDS KT5 199 N5
Royston St BETH E2 140 B4
Royston Wy SL SL1 128 C7
Rozel Rd CLAP SW4 158 D8
Rubastic Rd NWDGN UB2 153 K2
Rubens Pl NTHLT UB5 133 K4
Rubens St CAT SE6 182 E5
Rubin Cl CHOB/PIR GU24 212 D9
Ruby Cl SL SL1 148 F1
Ruby Ms WALTH * E17 120 F1
Ruby Rd WALTH E17 120 F1
Ruby St PECK SE15 160 A5
Ruby Triangle PECK * SE15 160 A5
Ruckholt Cl LEY E10 120 G8
Ruckholt Rd LEY E10 121 H8
Rucklers La KGLGY WD4 53 K4
Ruckles Wy AMSS HP7 69 H6
Rucklidge Av WLSDN NW10 136 C4
Rudall Crs HAMP NW3 117 N9
Ruddlesway WDSR SL4 148 C7
Ruddington Cl CLPT E5 120 D9
Ruddock Cl EDGW HA8 95 P8
Ruddstreet Cl WOOL/PLUM SE18 162 E3
Ruden Wy EW KT17 238 E1
Rudge Ri ADL/WDHM KT15 215 J2
Rudgwick Rd CRAWW RH11 283 J6
Rudgwick Ter STJWD * NW8 3 P6
Rudland Rd BXLYHN DA7 164 C9
Rudloe Rd BAL SW12 180 D3
Rudolf Pl VX/NE SW8 17 M10
Rudolph Rd BUSH WD23 73 P10
KIL/WHAMP NW6 2 F8
PLSTW E13 141 L4
Rudsworth Cl DTCH/LGLY SL3 150 G7
Rudyard Gv EDGW HA8 95 P7
Rue De St Lawrence WAB EN9 63 H10
Ruffetts Cl SAND/SEL CR2 224 A4
The Ruffetts SAND/SEL CR2 224 A4
Ruffetts Wy KWD/TDW/WH KT20 239 H4
Ruffle Cl WDR/YW UB7 151 P1
Rufford Cl HRW HA1 114 F4
WAT WD17 72 G3
Rufford St IS N1 5 M5
Rufus Cl RSLP HA4 113 L8
Rufus St IS N1 7 J10
Rufwood CRAWE RH10 285 N5
Rugby Av ALP/SUD HA0 115 H9
ED N9 99 N2
NTHLT UB5 134 C1
Rugby Cl HRW HA1 114 D2
Rugby Gdns DAGW RM9 143 M1
Rugby La BELMT SM2 220 G5
Rugby Rd CDALE/KGS NW9 115 M2
CHSWK W4 156 B1
DAGW RM9 143 L2
WHTN TW2 176 D2
Rugby St BMSBY WC1N 11 N2
Rugby Wy RKW/CH/CXG WD3 72 C9
Ruggles-Brise Rd ASHF TW15 173 N8
Rugg St POP/IOD E14 140 F9
Rugosa Rd CHOB/PIR GU24 212 D9
Ruislip Cl GFD/PVL UB6 134 A6
Ruislip Ct RSLP * HA4 112 G7
Ruislip Rd NTHLT UB5 133 K3
Ruislip Rd East GFD/PVL UB6 134 B6
Ruislip St TOOT SW17 180 A7
Rumballs Rd HHS/BOV HP3 36 B9
Rumbold Rd FUL/PGN SW6 157 L6
HOD EN11 45 H1
Rum Cl WAP E1W 140 A9
Rumsey Cl HPTN TW12 175 N9
Rumsey Rd BRXN/ST SW9 158 G9
Rumsley CHESW EN7 61 P5
Runbury Cir CDALE/KGS NW9 116 A7
Runcie Cl STALE/WH AL4 38 F2
Runciman Cl ORP BR6 227 M6
Runcorn Cl WALTH E17 120 A2
Runcorn Crs HHNE HP2 36 A2
Runcorn Pl NTGHL W11 8 A8
Rundell Crs HDN NW4 116 E3
Rundells HLWS CM18 47 K5
Runes Cl MTCM CR4 201 N4
Runham Rd HHS/BOV HP3 35 P8
Runnelfield HRW HA1 114 D8
Runnemede Rd EGH TW20 172 D8

Running Waters
RBRW/HUT CM13 107 M5
Runnymede WIM/MER SW19 201 N1
Runnymede Cl WHTN TW2 176 A2
Runnymede Ct EGH TW20 172 D7
Runnymede Crs
STRHM/NOR SW16 202 E1
Runnymede Gdns
GFD/PVL UB6 134 C4
WHTN TW2 176 A2
Runnymede Rd WHTN TW2 176 A2
Runrig Hl AMS HP6 69 K1
Runsley WGCE AL7 23 K2
Runtley Wood La RGUE GU4 250 C1
The Runway RSLP HA4 113 J10
Rupack St BERM/RHTH * SE16 160 B1
Rupert Av WBLY HA9 115 K10
Rupert Ct E/WMO/HCT * KT8 197 P4
SOHO/SHAV W1D 11 J7
Rupert Gdns BRXN/ST SW9 159 J8
Rupert Rd ARCH N19 118 E8
CHSWK W4 156 B2
GUW GU2 267 N1
KIL/WHAMP NW6 2 D8
Rupert St SOHO/SHAV * W1D 11 J7
Rural Cl HCH RM12 125 J6
Rural V GVW DA11 190 B3
Rural Wy REDH RH1 258 B10
STRHM/NOR SW16 180 C10
Rusbridge Cl HACK E8 119 P10
Ruscoe Dr WOKS/MYFD GU22 232 D3
Ruscoe Rd CAN/RD E16 141 L8
Ruscombe Dr LCOL/BKTW AL2 56 A2
Ruscombe Gdns DTCH/LGLY SL3 149 M6
Ruscombe Wy
EBED/NFELT TW14 174 G3
Rusham Park Av EGH TW20 172 C9
Rusham Rd BAL SW12 180 A2
EGH TW20 172 C9
Rushbrook Crs WALTH E17 100 E9
Rushbrook Rd ELTH/MOT SE9 184 F5
Rush Cl WARE SG12 27 H7
Rush Cft RGODL GU7 267 M9
Rushcroft Rd BRXS/STRHM SW2 159 H10
CHING E4 100 G8
Rushden Cl NRWD SE19 181 L10
Rushdene ABYW SE2 163 M2
Rushdene Av EBAR EN4 97 P1
Rushdene Cl NTHLT UB5 133 K4
Rushdene Crs NTHLT UB5 133 J4
Rushdene Rd BRWN CM15 107 H1
PIN HA5 113 K4
Rushdene Wk BH/WHM TN16 244 A3
Rushden Gdns CLAY IG5 122 D1
MLHL NW7 96 F7
Rushdon Cl CDH/CHF RM16 167 M2
ROM RM1 125 H3
Rush Dr WAB EN9 81 H2
Rushen Dr HERT/BAY SG13 26 B8
Rushes Md HLWS CM18 47 H3
UX/CGN UB8 131 M3
Rushet Rd STMC/STPC BR5 207 K2
Rushett Cl THDIT KT7 198 G8
Rushett Dr DORK RH4 272 G5
Rushett La CHSGTN KT9 219 J8
Rushett Rd THDIT KT7 198 G7
Rushetts Pl CRAWW RH11 283 M4
Rushetts Rd CRAWW RH11 283 L4
REIG RH2 275 M4
Rushey Cl NWMAL KT3 200 A4
Rushey Gn CAT SE6 182 G3
Rushey Hl ENC/FH EN2 78 G8
Rushey Md BROCKY SE4 182 F1
Rushfield POTB/CUF EN6 58 G9
SBW CM21 29 P1
Rushford Rd BROCKY SE4 182 E2
Rush Green Gdns
ROMW/RG RM7 124 D6
Rush Green Rd ROMW/RG RM7 124 D6
Rushgrove Av CDALE/KGS NW9 116 C2
Rushgrove Pde
CDALE/KGS * NW9 116 C3
Rushgrove St WOOL/PLUM SE18 162 C3
Rush Hill Ms BTSEA SW11 158 B9
Rush Hill Rd BTSEA SW11 158 B9
Rushleigh Av CHES/WCR EN8 62 C6
Rushley Cl HAYES BR2 226 A1
Rushmead BETH E2 140 A5
RCHPK/HAM TW10 176 G6
Rushmead Cl CROY/NA CR0 223 N1
Rushmere Av UPMR RM14 126 B8
Rushmere Ct WPK KT4 200 D9
Rushmere La CSHM HP5 51 M4
Rushmere Pl EGH TW20 172 B8
WIM/MER SW19 178 G8
Rushmon Pl CHEAM * SM3 221 H3
Rushmon Vls NWMAL * KT3 200 C4
Rushmoor Cl GUW GU2 249 L7
PIN HA5 113 J2
RKW/CH/CXG WD3 91 N3
Rushmore Cl BMLY BR1 206 B3
Rushmore Ct WATW * WD18 72 E10
Rushmore Hl ORP BR6 227 M6
RSEV TN14 227 N10
Rushmore Rd CLPT E5 120 B9
Rusholme Av DAGE RM10 124 B8
Rusholme Gv NRWD SE19 181 M8
Rusholme Rd PUT/ROE SW15 178 G2
Rushout Av KTN/HRWW/W HA3 114 G4
Rushton Av GSTN WD25 73 H1
Rushton Gv HLWE CM17 47 N1
Rushton St IS N1 7 H7
Rushworth Rd REIG RH2 257 K9
Rushworth St STHWK SE1 18 D1
Rushymead BGR/WK TN15 247 P4
Rushy Meadow La CAR SM5 201 P9
Ruskin Av EBED/NFELT TW14 174 G3
MNPK E12 142 B1
RCH/KEW TW9 155 M6
UPMR RM14 126 B5
WAB EN9 63 K10
WELL DA16 163 K9
Ruskin Cl CHESW EN7 61 M2
CRAWE RH10 284 D4
GLDGN NW11 117 L4
Ruskin Dr ORP BR6 207 H10
WELL DA16 163 K9
WPK KT4 200 E9
Ruskin Gdns EA W5 135 J6
HARH RM3 105 J9
KTN/HRWW/W HA3 115 L3
Ruskin Gv DART DA1 187 P1
WELL DA16 163 K8
Ruskin Rd BELV DA17 164 B3
CAR SM5 222 B2
CDH/CHF RM16 168 D3
CROY/NA CR0 203 J9
ISLW TW7 154 E9
STA TW18 173 J9
STHL UB1 133 M9
TOTM N17 99 N9
Ruskin Wk ED N9 99 P3
HAYES BR2 206 B6
HNHL SE24 181 K1
Ruskin Wy WIM/MER SW19 201 N2
Rusland Av ORP BR6 206 G10
Rusland Park Rd HRW HA1 114 D2
Rusper Cl CRICK NW2 116 F8
STAN HA7 95 H5
Rusper Rd CRAWW RH11 283 J7
DAGW RM9 143 M1
HORS RH12 282 A4
WDGN N22 99 J10
Ruspers Keep CRAWW RH11 283 J6
Russel Cl BECK BR3 204 G3
Russell Av STALW/RED AL3 38 C6
WDGN N22 99 J10
Russell Cl AMS HP6 70 A5
BRWN CM15 106 G1
BXLYHN DA7 164 B10
CHARL SE7 161 P6
DART DA1 165 H9
KWD/TDW/WH KT20 256 D1
NTHWD HA6 92 D6
RSLP HA4 113 K7
WLSDN NW10 135 P2
WOKN/KNAP GU21 231 P1
Russell Ct BAR * EN5 77 M8
CSHM HP5 51 H5
LCOL/BKTW AL2 55 P6
LHD/OX KT22 236 G8
WHALL SW1A 11 H10
Russell Crs GSTN WD25 72 G1
Russellcroft Rd WGCW AL8 22 F4
Russell Dr STWL/WRAY TW19 173 N2
Russell Gdns GLDGN NW11 117 H4
RCHPK/HAM TW10 177 H5
TRDG/WHET N20 97 P3
WDR/YW UB7 152 B4
WKENS W14 14 A3
Russell Gardens Ms WKENS W14 14 A3
Russell Green Cl PUR/KEN CR8 223 H6
Russell Gv BRXN/ST SW9 159 H7
MLHL NW7 96 B6
Russell Hl PUR/KEN CR8 222 G6
Russell Hill Pl PUR/KEN CR8 223 H7
Russell Hill Rd PUR/KEN CR8 223 H6
Russell Kerr Cl CHSWK * W4 155 P6
Russell La TRDG/WHET N20 98 A3
WAT WD17 72 E2
Russell Pde GLDGN * NW11 117 H4
Russell Pl EYN DA4 209 P1
HAMP NW3 117 P10
HHS/BOV HP3 35 L9
Russell Rd BKHH IG9 101 P2
CAN/RD E16 141 M8
CDALE/KGS NW9 116 C4
CEND/HSY/T N8 118 E4
CHING E4 100 E5
EN EN1 79 N4
GVE DA12 190 G2
LEY E10 120 G4
MTCM CR4 201 P3
NTHLT UB5 114 B10
NTHWD HA6 92 D4
SEVS/STOTM N15 119 M3
SHPTN TW17 196 D7
TIL RM18 168 B7
TRDG/WHET N20 97 P3
WALTH E17 120 E1
WDGN N22 118 G1
WHTN TW2 176 C5
WIM/MER SW19 179 K10
WKENS W14 14 B3
WOKN/KNAP GU21 231 P1
WOT/HER KT12 197 H6
Russells KWD/TDW/WH KT20 238 G8
Russells Crs HORL RH6 280 B5
Russell's Dr CHES/WCR * EN8 62 D7
Russell Sq GWRST WC1E 11 K3
Russell's Ride CHES/WCR EN8 62 C7
Russell St HERT/WAS SG14 25 K5
HOL/ALD WC2B 11 N6
WDSR SL4 149 J7
Russell Ter EYN * DA4 210 B4
Russell Wy CRAWE RH10 284 B8
OXHEY WD19 93 J1
SUT SM1 221 L2
Russel Rd GRAYS RM17 167 M3
Russet Av SUN TW16 196 F3
Russet Cl CHESW * EN7 61 M2
HORL RH6 280 D4
STWL/WRAY TW19 173 J2
UX/CGN UB8 132 D6
WOT/HER KT12 197 L10
Russet Crs HOLWY * N7 118 G10
Russet Dr CROY/NA CR0 204 D8
RAD WD7 57 K8
STALE/WH AL4 39 H7
Russets EMPK RM11 125 M2
Russets Cl CHING E4 101 J5
The Russets CFSP/GDCR SL9 90 A10
Russett Cl ORP BR6 227 L2
Russett Hl CFSP/GDCR SL9 110 B1
Russetts Cl WOKN/KNAP GU21 232 C1
Russett Wy SWLY BR8 208 E2
Russett Wd WGCE AL7 23 N6
Russet Wy RDKG RH5 273 J5
Russ Hl HORL RH6 278 F9
RDKG RH5 282 D1
Russia Dock Rd
BERM/RHTH * SE16 140 D10
Russia La BETH E2 140 B4
Russia Rw CITYW EC2V 12 F6
Russington Rd SHPTN TW17 196 E6
Rusthall Av CHSWK W4 156 A2
Rusthall Cl CROY/NA CR0 204 B6
Rustic Av STRHM/NOR SW16 180 C10
Rustic Cl UPMR RM14 126 D6
Rustic Pl ALP/SUD HA0 115 J9
Rustington Wk MRDN SM4 201 J7
Ruston Av BRYLDS KT5 199 N7
Ruston Cl CRAWE RH10 284 D10
Ruston Ms NTGHL W11 8 A6
Ruston Rd WOOL/PLUM SE18 162 B2
Ruston St BOW E3 140 E3
Rust Sq CMBW SE5 159 L6
Rutford Rd STRHM/NOR SW16 180 F8
Ruth Cl KTN/HRWW/W HA3 115 L2
Ruthen Cl EPSOM KT18 219 N10
Rutherford Cl BELMT SM2 221 N3
BORE WD6 75 P6
UX/CGN UB8 132 A6
WDSR SL4 148 E7
Rutherford St WEST SW1P 17 J5
Rutherford Wy BUSH WD23 94 C2
CRAWE RH10 284 B2
WBLY HA9 115 M8
Rutherglen Rd ABYW SE2 163 K5
Rutherwick Cl HORL RH6 280 A4
Rutherwick Ri COUL/CHIP CR5 240 F3
Rutherwyke Cl EW KT17 220 D3
Rutherwyk Rd CHERT KT16 195 H7
Ruthin Cl CDALE/KGS NW9 116 B4
Ruthin Rd BKHTH/KID SE3 161 M5
Ruthven Av CHES/WCR EN8 62 C9
Ruthven St HOM E9 140 C3
Rutland Ap EMPK RM11 125 P3
Rutland Av BFN/LL DA15 185 K3
SL SL1 129 H7
Rutland Cl ASHTD KT21 237 K3
BXLY DA5 185 N4
DART DA1 187 L3
HOR/WEW KT19 220 A6
MORT/ESHN SW14 155 N9
REDH RH1 258 A9
Rutland Ct CHST BR7 206 D1
SKENS SW7 15 N2
Rutland Dr EMPK RM11 125 P3
MRDN SM4 201 K7
RCHPK/HAM TW10 177 J4
Rutland Gdns BCTR RM8 123 M10
CROY/NA CR0 223 M1
FSBYPK N4 119 J4
HHNE HP2 36 A5
SKENS SW7 15 P2
WEA * W13 134 F7
Rutland Ga BELV DA17 164 C4
HAYES BR2 205 L4
SKENS SW7 15 N2
Rutland Gate Ms SKENS * SW7 15 N2
Rutland Gv HMSMTH W6 156 E4
Rutland Ms STJWD NW8 3 H6
Rutland Ms South SKENS * SW7 15 N3
Rutland Pk CAT SE6 182 E5
CRICK NW2 136 F1
Rutland Pl BUSH * WD23 94 C2
FARR * EC1M 12 D3
Rutland Rd FSTGT E7 142 A2
HOM E9 140 C3
HRW HA1 114 B4
HYS/HAR UB3 152 A7
IL IG1 122 E9
STHL UB1 133 P6
WALTH E17 120 F4
WAN E11 121 N3
WHTN TW2 176 C5
WIM/MER SW19 179 P10
Rutland St SKENS SW7 15 P3
Rutland Wk CAT SE6 182 E5
Rutland Wy STMC/STPC BR5 207 M6
Rutley Cl WALW SE17 18 C9
Rutlish Rd WIM/MER SW19 201 K1
Rutson Rd BF/WBF KT14 216 A10
Rutter Gdns MTCM CR4 201 N4
Rutters Cl WDR/YW UB7 152 B1
Rutt's Ter NWCR SE14 160 C7
The Rutts BUSH WD23 94 C2
Ruvigny Gdns PUT/ROE SW15 156 G9
Ruxbury Rd CHERT KT16 194 G6
Ruxley Cl HOR/WEW KT19 219 N2
SCUP DA14 185 N9
Ruxley Crs ESH/CLAY KT10 218 G4
Ruxley La HOR/WEW KT19 219 N3
HOR/WEW KT19 219 P2
Ruxley Ms HOR/WEW KT19 219 N2
Ruxley Rdg ESH/CLAY KT10 218 F4
Ruxley Towers ESH/CLAY * KT10 218 F4
Ruxton Cl SWLY BR8 208 F3
Ruxton Ct SWLY BR8 208 F3
Ryall Cl LCOL/BKTW AL2 55 M5
Ryan Cl ELTH/MOT SE9 161 N10
RSLP HA4 113 J6
Ryan Ct OXHEY * WD19 93 M1
Ryan Dr BTFD TW8 154 F5
Ryan Wy WATN WD24 73 K5
Ryarsh Crs ORP BR6 227 H1
Rycroft WDSR SL4 148 E9
Rycroft La RSEV TN14 264 F6
Rycroft Wy TOTM * N17 119 N1
Ryculff Sq BKHTH/KID SE3 161 L8
Rydal Cl CRAWW RH11 282 G9
HDN NW4 97 H9
PUR/KEN CR8 223 K9
Rydal Crs GFD/PVL UB6 134 G5
Rydal Dr BXLYHN DA7 164 B7
WWKM BR4 205 K9
Rydal Gdns CDALE/KGS NW9 116 B3
HSLW TW3 176 A2
PUT/ROE SW15 178 B8
WBLY HA9 115 H6
Rydal Mt HAYES * BR2 205 L4
POTB/CUF * EN6 59 H9
Rydal Pl LTWR GU18 212 A7
Rydal Rd STRHM/NOR SW16 180 E8
Rydal Wy EGH TW20 172 E10
PEND EN3 80 B10
RSLP HA4 113 K9
Ryde Cl RPLY/SEND GU23 233 M7
Ryde Heron WOKN/KNAP GU21 231 K6
Rydens Av WOT/HER KT12 197 K9
Rydens Cl WOT/HER KT12 197 K9
Rydens Gv WOT/HER KT12 217 L1
Rydens Pde WOKS/MYFD * GU22 232 E6
Rydens Pk WOT/HER KT12 197 L9
Rydens Rd WOT/HER KT12 197 J10
Rydens Wy WOKS/MYFD GU22 232 D6
Ryde Pl TWK TW1 177 H2
Ryder Cl BUSH WD23 74 A10
HERT/BAY SG13 26 A4
HHS/BOV HP3 52 D4
Ryder Dr BERM/RHTH SE16 160 A4
Ryder Gdns RAIN RM13 144 G1
Ryders Av STALE/WH AL4 40 B6
Ryder Seed Ms STAL * AL1 38 C7
Ryder's Ter STJWD NW8 3 J7
Ryder St STJS SW1Y 10 G9
Rydes Av GUW GU2 249 L7
Ryde's Hill Crs RGUW GU3 249 L6
Ryde's Hill Rd GUW GU2 249 L6
The Ryde BRKMPK AL9 40 F1
STA TW18 195 L1
Ryde Vale Rd BAL SW12 180 C5
Rydings WDSR SL4 148 E9
Rydon's La COUL/CHIP CR5 241 K6
Rydon St IS N1 6 F6
Rydon's Wood Cl
COUL/CHIP CR5 241 K6
Rydston Cl HOLWY N7 5 M3
Rye Ash CRAWE RH10 284 B6
Rye Brook Rd LHD/OX KT22 236 F4
Rye Cl BXLY DA5 186 C2
GUW GU2 249 K9
HCH RM12 144 D1
Ryecotes Md DUL SE21 181 M4
Rye Ct SL * SL1 149 M2
Rye Crs STMC/STPC BR5 207 M8
Ryecroft GVE DA12 191 H8
HAT AL10 40 C6
HLWW/ROY CM19 46 E1
Ryecroft Av CLAY IG5 102 E10
WHTN TW2 176 A4
Ryecroft Cl HHNE HP2 36 D7
Ryecroft Crs BAR EN5 76 E9
Ryecroft Rd CSHM HP5 50 F9
LEW SE13 183 H1
RSEV TN14 247 H3
STMC/STPC BR5 206 G6
STRHM/NOR SW16 181 H9
Ryecroft St FUL/PGN SW6 157 L7
Ryedale EDUL SE22 182 A2
Ryedale Ct SEV TN13 246 F7
Ryefeld Cl HOD EN11 26 G9
Ryefield Av HGDN/ICK UB10 132 D3
Ryefield Crs PIN * HA5 93 H10
Ryefield Pde NTHWD * HA6 93 H10
Ryefield Rd NRWD SE19 181 K9
Rye Gv CHOB/PIR GU24 212 D6
Rye Hill Pk PECK SE15 160 B10
Rye Hill Rd HLWS CM18 46 G6
Ryeland Cl WDR/YW UB7 131 P8
Ryelands CRAWW RH11 283 K8
HORL * RH6 280 D3
WGCE AL7 23 J8
Ryelands Cl CTHM CR3 241 M7
Ryelands Ct LHD/OX KT22 236 F4
Ryelands Crs LEE/GVPK SE12 183 P2
Ryelands Pl WEY KT13 196 F10
Rye La PECK SE15 159 P7
RSEV TN14 246 G5
Rye Rd HOD EN11 27 J10
HOD EN11 44 G2
PECK SE15 160 C10
The Rye STHGT/OAK N14 98 D1
Rye Wk PUT/ROE SW15 178 G1
Rye Wy EDGW HA8 95 L7
Ryfold Rd WIM/MER SW19 179 K6
Rykhill CDH/CHF RM16 168 E2
Ryland Cl FELT TW13 174 G7
Rylandes Rd CRICK NW2 116 D8
SAND/SEL CR2 224 A5
Ryland Rd KTTN NW5 4 E1
Rylett Crs SHB W12 156 C2
Rylett Rd SHB W12 156 C1
Rylston Rd FUL/PGN SW6 14 C10
PLMGR N13 99 L4
Rymer Rd CROY/NA CR0 203 M7
Rymer St HNHL SE24 181 J2
Rymill Cl HHS/BOV HP3 52 D4
Rymill St CAN/RD E16 142 D10
Rysbrack St CHEL SW3 16 A3
Rysted La BH/WHM TN16 262 F2
Rythe Ct THDIT KT7 198 F7
Rythe Rd ESH/CLAY KT10 218 C2
The Rythe LHD/OX KT22 218 A6
Ryvers End DTCH/LGLY SL3 150 C2
Ryvers Rd DTCH/LGLY SL3 150 C2
Ryves Cottages MTCM * CR4 202 B2

S

Sabbarton St CAN/RD E16 141 L8
Sabina Rd CDH/CHF RM16 168 F3
Sabine Rd BTSEA SW11 158 A9
Sabines Rd ABR/ST RM4 85 N7
Sable Cl HSLWW TW4 153 K9
Sable St IS N1 6 D3
Sach Rd CLPT E5 120 A7
Sackville Av HAYES BR2 205 M8
Sackville Cl HRW HA1 114 C8
SEV TN13 247 J8
Sackville Crs HARH RM3 105 M9
Sackville Est STRHM/NOR SW16 180 F6
Sackville Gdns IL IG1 122 C6
Sackville Rd BELMT SM2 221 K4
DART DA1 187 L5
Sackville St MYFR/PICC W1J 11 H8
Sacombe Rd HERT/WAS SG14 25 K2
HHW HP1 35 J4
Saddington St GVE DA12 190 E3
Saddlebrook Pk SUN TW16 174 F10
Saddler Rw CRAWE RH10 283 N10
Saddlers Cl BORE * WD6 76 A9
PIN HA5 93 P6
Saddlers Hall EYN * DA4 209 L10
Saddlers Ms KUT * KT1 199 H1
Saddler's Pk EYN DA4 209 L10
Saddlers Wk KGLGY * WD4 54 B5
Saddlers Wy EPSOM KT18 238 A5
Saddlescombe Wy
NFNCH/WDSP N12 97 K6
Sadleir Rd STAL AL1 38 D8
Sadler Cl CHESW EN7 61 K1
MTCM CR4 202 A2
Sadlers Cl RGUE GU4 250 G9
Sadlers Md HLWS CM18 47 K2
Sadlers Ride E/WMO/HCT KT8 198 B2
Sadlers Wy HERT/WAS SG14 25 H5
Saffron Av POP/IOD E14 141 J9
Saffron Cl CRAWW RH11 283 K10
CROY/NA CR0 202 F6
DTCH/LGLY SL3 149 N7
HOD EN11 44 E2
Saffron Hl HCIRC EC1N 12 B3
Saffron La HHW HP1 35 K5
Saffron Platt GUW GU2 249 M6
Saffron Rd CDH/CHF RM16 167 H3
CRW RM5 104 E10
Saffron St FARR EC1M 12 B3
Saffron Wy SURB KT6 199 J8
Sage Cl EHAM E6 142 C7
Sage St WCHPL E1 140 B9
Sage Wy FSBYW WC1X 5 N10
Sage Yd SURB * KT6 199 L8
Saigasso Cl CAN/RD E16 142 A8
Sail St LBTH SE11 17 P5
Sainfoin End HHNE HP2 36 B4
Sainfoin Rd TOOT SW17 180 B5
Sainsbury Rd NRWD SE19 181 M8
St Agatha's Dr KUTN/CMB KT2 177 L9
St Agatha's Gv CAR SM5 202 A8
St Agnells Ct HHNE HP2 36 B2
St Agnells La HHNE HP2 36 A1
St Agnes Cl HOM * E9 140 B3
St Agnes Pl CMBW SE5 18 B10
St Agnes Well STLK EC1Y 13 H1
St Aidan's Rd EDUL SE22 182 A3
WEA W13 154 G1
St Aidan's Wy GVE DA12 191 H6
St Albans Av CHSWK W4 156 A2
EHAM E6 142 C5
FELT TW13 175 L8
UPMR RM14 126 D6
WEY KT13 196 B10
St Alban's Cl GVE DA12 190 G6
RGUW GU3 248 G9
WDSR * SL4 149 J7
St Albans Crs WDGN N22 99 H9
St Albans Farm HSLWW * TW4 175 K1
St Alban's Gdns GVE DA12 190 G6
TEDD TW11 176 F8
St Alban's Gv CAR SM5 201 P7
KENS W8 15 H3
KENS W8 15 H3
St Albans Hl HHS/BOV HP3 35 P9
St Albans La ABLGY WD5 54 G2
GLDGN NW11 117 K6
St Alban's Ms BAY/PAD W2 9 M3
St Alban's Pl IS N1 6 C6
St Albans Rd BAR EN5 77 H5
DART DA1 187 N2
EPP CM16 65 N5
GDMY/SEVK IG3 123 J6
GSTN WD25 55 L10
HARP AL5 20 A5
HHS/BOV HP3 35 N7
KTTN NW5 118 B8
KUTN/CMB KT2 177 K9
POTB/CUF EN6 58 D8
REIG RH2 257 K8
STALE/WH AL4 38 F2
SUT SM1 221 J1
WAT WD17 73 J6
WFD IG8 101 M8
WLSDN NW10 136 B3
St Albans Rd East HAT AL10 40 E3
St Albans Rd West HAT AL10 39 P4
St Alban's St STJS SW1Y 11 J8
WDSR SL4 149 J7
St Albans Ter HMSMTH W6 14 A9
St Alfege Rd CHARL SE7 162 A5
St Alphage Gdn BARB EC2Y 12 F4
St Alphage Gdns BARB * EC2Y 12 F4
St Alphage Highwalk BARB EC2Y 12 F4
St Alphage Wk EDGW * HA8 95 P10
St Alphege Rd ED N9 100 B1
St Alphonsus Rd CLAP SW4 158 D10
St Amunds Cl CAT SE6 182 F7
St Andrew Av CHOB/PIR GU24 230 G7
St Andrew Ms HERT/WAS * SG14 25 K5
St Andrews HORL * RH6 280 C5
St Andrews Av ALP/SUD HA0 114 F9
HCH RM12 124 G10
St Andrews Cl
BERM/RHTH * SE16 160 A4
CRICK * NW2 116 E8
EPP CM16 48 D10
NFNCH/WDSP * N12 97 M5
REIG RH2 275 L1
RSLP HA4 113 L7
SHPTN TW17 196 E4
STAN * HA7 95 H10
STWL/WRAY TW19 172 B2
THDIT KT7 198 G8
WDSR SL4 171 M2
WOKN/KNAP GU21 231 P3
St Andrew's Ct
WAND/EARL SW18 179 M5
WAT * WD17 73 J5
St Andrew's Crs WDSR SL4 148 E8
St Andrews Dr ORP BR6 207 L6
STAN HA7 95 H9
St Andrews Gdns COB KT11 217 K9
St Andrews Ga
WOKS/MYFD * GU22 232 C4
St Andrew's Gv STNW/STAM N16 119 L6
St Andrew's Hl BLKFR EC4V 12 D7
St Andrews Meadow
HLWS CM18 47 J2
St Andrew's Ms
STNW/STAM * N16 119 M5
St Andrews Pl BRWN CM15 107 L3
CAMTN NW1 10 E1
St Andrew's Rd ACT W3 136 B8
CAR SM5 201 P10
CDALE/KGS NW9 116 A6
COUL/CHIP CR5 240 C2
CRAWW RH11 282 G8
CROY/NA CR0 223 K1
ED N9 100 B1
EN EN1 79 L7
GLDGN NW11 117 J4
GVE * DA12 190 E3
HGDN/ICK UB10 131 P3
HHS/BOV HP3 35 M10
HNWL W7 154 D1
IL IG1 122 C5
PLSTW E13 141 N5
ROMW/RG RM7 124 E4
SCUP DA14 185 N6
SURB KT6 199 J6
TIL RM18 168 B8
WALTH E17 100 C10
WAN E11 121 K4
WKENS W14 14 B9
WLSDN NW10 136 E1
St Andrew's Sq NTGHL * W11 8 A6
SURB KT6 199 J6
St Andrews Ter OXHEY * WD19 93 K6
St Andrew St HCIRC EC1N 12 B4
HERT/WAS SG14 25 K5
St Andrew's Wk COB KT11 235 J1
St Andrews Wy BOW E3 140 G6
OXTED RH8 262 B7
SL SL1 128 C9
St Anna Rd BAR * EN5 76 G9
St Anne's Av STWL/WRAY TW19 173 N3
St Annes Bvd REDH RH1 258 B8
St Annes Cl CDH/CHF * RM16 147 N10
CHESW * EN7 61 P4
HGT N6 118 B8
OXHEY WD19 93 K5
St Annes Ct SOHO/CST W1F 11 J6
St Anne's Dr REDH RH1 258 B9
St Annes Gdns WLSDN NW10 135 L5
St Annes Mt REDH * RH1 258 B9
St Anne's Pk BROX EN10 44 F6
St Anne's Pas POP/IOD * E14 140 E8
St Annes Ri REDH RH1 258 B9
St Annes Rd ALP/SUD HA0 115 J10
BRWN CM15 87 P5
CRAWE RH10 284 D3
DEN/HRF UB9 111 M1
LCOL/BKTW AL2 57 J3
WAN E11 121 J7
St Anne's Rw POP/IOD E14 140 E8
St Anne St POP/IOD E14 140 E8
St Annes Wy REDH * RH1 258 B9
St Ann's BARK IG11 142 F3
WOKS/MYFD * GU22 232 B4
St Ann's Cl CHERT KT16 195 J5
St Anns Ct HDN * NW4 116 E1
St Ann's Crs WAND/EARL SW18 179 L2
St Ann's Gdns HAMP NW3 4 B1
St Ann's Hl WAND/EARL SW18 179 L1
St Ann's Hill Rd CHERT KT16 194 F6
St Ann's Park Rd
WAND/EARL SW18 179 M2
St Ann's Rd BARK IG11 142 F3

BARN * SW13 156 C8
CHERT KT16 195 J6
ED N9 99 N3
HRW HA1 114 D4
NTGHL W11 136 G9
SEVS/STOTM N15 119 L3
St Ann's St WEST SW1P 17 K3
St Ann's Ter STJWD NW8 3 M7
St Ann's Vls NTGHL W11 136 G10
St Anns Wy BH/WHM * TN16 244 E2
CROY/NA CR0 223 J3
St Anselm's Pl MYFR/PKLN W1K 10 E7
St Anselms Rd HYS/HAR UB3 152 G1
St Anthonys Av HHS/BOV HP3 36 C8
WFD IG8 101 P7
St Anthonys Cl TOOT SW17 179 P5
WAP E1W 13 N9
St Anthony's Ct HAYES BR2 206 E8
St Anthony's Wy
EBED/NFELT TW14 152 G10
St Antony's Rd FSTGT E7 141 N2
St Arvans Cl CROY/NA CR0 203 M10
St Asaph Rd PECK SE15 160 C9
St Aubyns DORK * RH4 272 G4
St Aubyn's Av HSLWW TW4 175 P1
WIM/MER SW19 179 J8
St Aubyns Cl ORP BR6 207 J10
St Aubyns Gdns ORP BR6 207 J9
St Aubyn's Rd NRWD SE19 181 N9
St Audrey Av BXLYHN DA7 164 B8
St Audreys Cl HAT AL10 40 E7
St Audreys Gn WGCE AL7 23 J6
St Augusta Ct STALW/RED AL3 38 C4
St Augustine Rd CDH/CHF RM16 168 E3
St Augustine's Av BMLY BR1 206 B5
EA W5 135 K4
SAND/SEL CR2 223 K4
WBLY HA9 115 K8
St Augustines Cl BROX EN10 44 E6
St Augustines Dr BROX EN10 44 E6
St Augustine's Rd BELV DA17 164 A3
CAMTN NW1 5 J3
St Austell Cl EDGW HA8 95 L10
St Austell Rd LEW SE13 161 H8
St Awdry's Rd BARK IG11 142 G2
St Barnabas Av CHOB/PIR GU24 230 F8
St Barnabas Cl BECK BR3 205 H2
St Barnabas Gdns
E/WMO/HCT KT8 197 P5
St Barnabas Rd MTCM CR4 180 B10
SUT SM1 221 N2
SWFD E18 101 N9
Saint Barnabas Rd WALTH E17 120 F4
St Barnabas St BGVA * SW1W 16 D7
St Barnabas Ter HOM E9 120 C10
St Barnabas Vls VX/NE SW8 158 F7
St Barnabus St BGVA SW1W 16 D7
St Bartholomew's Cl SYD SE26 182 B7
St Bartholomew's Ct GU GU1 268 C2
St Bartholomew's Rd EHAM E6 142 B3
St Benedict's Av GVE DA12 191 H6
St Benets Cl TOOT * SW17 179 P5
St Benet's Gv MRDN SM4 201 M7
St Benjamins Dr ORP BR6 227 M5
St Bernards CROY/NA CR0 203 M10
St Bernards Cl WNWD SE27 181 L7
St Bernards Rd DTCH/LGLY SL3 149 P2
EHAM E6 142 A3
STALW/RED AL3 38 C5
St Blaise Av BMLY BR1 205 N2
St Botolph Rd GVW DA11 190 A6
St Botolph's Av SEV TN13 247 H10
St Botolph's Rd SEV TN13 247 J10
St Botolph St HDTCH EC3A 13 L5
St Brelades Cl DORK RH4 272 F4
St Bride's Av EDGW HA8 95 L9
St Brides Cl ERITHM DA18 163 N1
St Bride St FLST/FETLN EC4A 12 C5
St Catharine's Rd BROX EN10 44 F5
St Catherines WEY * KT13 196 C10
WOKS/MYFD GU22 231 P5
St Catherines Cl CHSGTN KT9 219 J3
TOOT * SW17 179 P5
St Catherines Ct FELT TW13 175 H4
St Catherine's Cross REDH RH1 259 M10
St Catherine's Dr GUW GU2 267 N4
NWCR SE14 160 C8
St Catherine's Hl GUW GU2 267 P4
St Catherines Ms CHEL SW3 16 A5
St Catherine's Pk GU GU1 268 C2
St Catherines Rd CHING E4 100 F3
CRAWE RH10 284 D4
St Cecilia Rd CDH/CHF RM16 168 E3
St Chad Av WOKS/MYFD GU22 231 H8
St Chads Cl SURB KT6 199 H7
St Chad's Dr GVE DA12 191 H6
St Chad's Gdns CHDH RM6 123 P5
St Chad's Pl FSBYW WC1X 5 M9
St Chad's Rd CHDH RM6 123 P4
TIL RM18 168 D7
St Chad's St STPAN WC1H 5 M9
St Charles Pl NKENS W10 8 A4
WEY KT13 216 B2
St Charles Rd BRW CM14 106 G3
St Charles Sq NKENS W10 8 A3
St Christopher Rd UX/CGN UB8 131 N8
St Christopher's Cl ISLW TW7 154 D7
St Christophers Ct
RKW/CH/CXG * WD3 70 G8
St Christophers Dr HYS/HAR UB3 133 J9
St Christopher's Ms WLGTN SM6 222 D2
St Christopher's Pl MHST W1U 10 D6
St Clair Cl CLAY IG5 102 C10
OXTED RH8 261 H6
REIG RH2 257 M10
St Clair Dr WPK KT4 200 E10
St Clair Rd PLSTW E13 141 N4
St Clair's Rd CROY/NA CR0 203 M9
St Clare St TWRH EC3N 13 L6
St Clement Cl UX/CGN UB8 131 N8
St Clement's Av WTHK RM20 166 F5
St Clements Cl GVW * DA11 190 C6
St Clements Ct PUR RM19 165 P3
St Clement's La LINN WC2A 11 P6
St Clement's Rd WTHK RM20 167 H6
St Clements St HOLWY N7 6 A3
St Clements Yd EDUL * SE22 181 N1
St Cloud Rd WNWD SE27 181 K7
St Columba's Cl GVE DA12 191 H6
St Crispins Cl HAMP NW3 117 P9
STHL UB1 133 N8
St Crispins Wy CHERT KT16 214 F5
St Cross Ct HOD EN11 44 F5
St Cross St HCIRC EC1N 12 B3
St Cuthbert's Cl EGH TW20 172 A9
St Cuthberts Gdns PIN * HA5 93 N8
St Cuthbert's Rd CRICK NW2 2 C1
HOD EN11 27 H10
PLMGR N13 99 H7
St Cyprian's St TOOT SW17 180 A7
St David Cl UX/CGN UB8 131 N7
St David's COUL/CHIP CR5 240 G3
St Davids Cl BERM/RHTH * SE16 160 A4
HHS/BOV HP3 36 E8
IVER SL0 130 G3
REIG RH2 257 M9
WBLY HA9 115 P8
WWKM BR4 204 G7
St David's Crs GVE DA12 190 G7
St David's Dr BROX EN10 44 E5
EDGW HA8 95 L9
EGH TW20 171 P10
St Davids Ms BOW * E3 140 D5
St David's Pl HDN NW4 116 E5
St David's Rd SWLY BR8 186 G9
St Davids Sq POP/IOD E14 160 G4
St Denis Rd WNWD SE27 181 L7
St Deny's Cl WOKN/KNAP * GU21 231 J4
St Dionis Rd FUL/PGN SW6 157 J8
St Donatt's Rd NWCR SE14 160 E7
St Dunstan's Av ACT W3 136 A9
St Dunstans Cl HYS/HAR UB3 152 G3
St Dunstan's Dr GVE DA12 191 H6
St Dunstan's Gdns ACT W3 136 A9
St Dunstan's Hl MON * EC3R 13 J8
SUT SM1 221 H1
St Dunstan's La BECK BR3 205 H6
MON * EC3R 13 J8
St Dunstan's Rd FELT TW13 174 G6
FSTGT E7 141 N1
HEST * TW5 153 K8
HMSMTH W6 156 G4
HNWL W7 154 D1
HSLWW TW4 153 J8
SNWD SE25 203 N4
WARE SG12 28 A3
St Edith's Rd BGR/WK TN15 247 P4
St Edmunds BERK HP4 33 P6
St Edmunds Av RSLP HA4 112 E4
St Edmunds Cl ABYW SE2 163 N1
CRAWW RH11 283 N4
STJWD NW8 4 A6
TOOT SW17 179 P5
St Edmunds Dr STAN HA7 94 F9
St Edmund's La WHTN TW2 176 A3
St Edmunds Rd DART DA1 165 N10
ED N9 99 P1
IL IG1 122 C4
St Edmunds Sq BARN SW13 156 F5
St Edmund's Ter STJWD NW8 3 P6
St Edmunds Wk STALE/WH AL4 39 J7
St Edmund's Wy HLWE CM17 29 M7
St Edwards Cl CROY/NA CR0 225 J7
GLDGN NW11 117 K4
St Edwards Wy ROM RM1 124 F2
St Egberts Wy CHING E4 101 H2
St Elizabeth Dr EPSOM KT18 219 P10
St Elmo Cl SLN SL2 129 J6
St Elmo Crs SLN SL2 129 J6
St Elmo Rd ACT W3 156 C1
St Elmos Rd BERM/RHTH SE16 160 D1
St Erkenwald Ms BARK IG11 142 G3
St Erkenwald Rd BARK IG11 142 G3
St Ervans Rd NKENS W10 8 B3
St Etheldreda's Dr HAT AL10 40 F4
St Evroul Ct WARE SG12 26 C1
St Faith's Cl ENC/FH EN2 79 K5
St Faith's Rd HNHL SE24 181 J4
St Fidelis' Rd ERITH DA8 164 E3
St Fillans WOKS/MYFD * GU22 232 E2
St Fillans Rd CAT SE6 183 H4
St Francis Av GVE DA12 191 H7
St Francis Cl ORP BR6 207 H6
OXHEY WD19 93 J2
POTB/CUF EN6 59 M9
St Francis Gdns CRAWE RH10 285 K1
St Francis Rd DEN/HRF UB9 111 J4
EDUL SE22 159 M10
St Francis Wy CDH/CHF RM16 168 F3
IL IG1 122 G9
St Gabriel's Cl WAN E11 121 N6
St Gabriel's Rd CRICK NW2 116 G10
St George Av CHOB/PIR GU24 230 G8
St Georges HORL * RH6 280 C5
St George's Av CDALE/KGS NW9 115 P2
EA W5 155 J1
EMPK RM11 125 N5
FSTGT E7 141 N2
GRAYS RM17 167 P3
HOLWY N7 118 E9
STHL UB1 133 N9
WEY KT13 216 D3
St George's Circ STHWK SE1 18 C2
St Georges Cl ALP/SUD HA0 114 F8
BRWN CM15 86 G1
GLDGN * NW11 117 J4
HORL RH6 280 C4
THMD SE28 143 N8
WDSR SL4 148 D7
WEY KT13 216 D2
St Georges Ct CRAWE RH10 283 N6
St George's Crs GVE DA12 190 G7
SL SL1 128 C9
St George's Dr HGDN/ICK UB10 112 A8
OXHEY WD19 93 M4
PIM SW1V 16 F7
PIM SW1V 16 G7
St George's Est WCHPL E1 13 P7
St Georges Flds BAY/PAD W2 9 P6
St George's Gdns EW KT17 220 C10
SURB KT6 199 N9
St George's Gv TOOT SW17 179 N6
St George's La ASC SL5 192 A3
MON * EC3R 13 H7
St Georges Ms CHSWK * W4 155 P5
HAMP NW3 4 B4
St Georges Pde CAT * SE6 182 E5
St Georges Rd ADL/WDHM KT15 215 M1
BECK BR3 204 G1
BMLY BR1 206 C2
CHSWK W4 156 A1
DAGW RM9 123 P10
ED N9 99 P4
EN EN1 79 N4
FELT TW13 175 L7
FSTGT E7 141 N2
HHS/BOV HP3 35 M10
HNWL W7 134 E10
IL IG1 122 C5
KUTN/CMB KT2 177 M10
LEY E10 121 H8
MTCM CR4 202 C3
PLMGR N13 98 G4
RCH/KEW TW9 155 L9
REDH RH1 276 E8
SCUP DA14 185 N9
SEV TN13 247 J8
STHWK SE1 18 C4
STMC/STPC BR5 206 G6
SWLY BR8 208 G4
TWK TW1 176 G1
WATN WD24 73 J4
WEY KT13 216 E3
WIM/MER SW19 179 J9
WLGTN SM6 222 C2
St Georges Rd West BMLY BR1 206 B2
St Georges's Ct STP * EC4M 12 C5
St George's Sq FSTGT E7 141 N2
GVW * DA11 190 E2
NWMAL * KT3 200 B3
PIM SW1V 17 J7
St George's Square Ms PIM SW1V 17 J8
St George's Ter HAMP NW3 4 B4
PECK * SE15 159 P6
St George St CONDST W1S 10 F7
St George's Wk CROY/NA CR0 203 K9
St Georges Wy PECK * SE15 19 K10
PECK SE15 19 K10
St Gerards Cl CLAP SW4 180 D1
St German's Pl BKHTH/KID SE3 161 M7
St German's Rd FSTH SE23 182 D4
St Giles Av DAGE RM10 144 C2
HGDN/ICK UB10 112 D9
POTB/CUF EN6 58 D9
St Giles Churchyard BARB * EC2Y 12 F4
St Giles Cl DAGE RM10 144 C2
ORP BR6 226 G2
St Giles High St LSQ/SEVD WC2H 11 K5
St Giles Rd CMBW SE5 159 M7
St Gothard Rd WNWD SE27 181 L6
St Gregory Cl RSLP HA4 113 K9
St Gregory's Crs GVE DA12 191 H5
St Helena Rd BERM/RHTH SE16 160 C3
St Helena St FSBYW * WC1X 6 A10
St Helena Ter RCH/KEW * TW9 177 J1
St Helen Cl UX/CGN UB8 131 N8
St Helens THDIT * KT7 198 D7
St Helen's Cl STALE/WH AL4 21 J3
St Helen's Crs STRHM/NOR SW16 202 G1
St Helen's Gdns NKENS W10 136 G8
St Helen's Pl OBST EC2N 13 J5
St Helens Rd ERITHM DA18 163 N1
IL IG1 122 C4
STRHM/NOR SW16 202 G2
WEA W13 134 G10
St Helier Av MRDN SM4 201 M7
St Heliers Av HSLWW TW4 175 P1
St Helier's Rd LEY E10 120 G4
STALE/WH AL4 38 G1
St Hilda's Av ASHF TW15 173 P8
St Hilda's Cl CRAWE * RH10 284 D4
HORL RH6 280 C4
KIL/WHAMP * NW6 136 G3
TOOT SW17 179 P5
WOKN/KNAP GU21 231 J3
St Hilda's Rd BARN SW13 156 E5
St Hilda's Wy GVE DA12 190 G7
St Huberts Cl CFSP/GDCR SL9 110 B7
St Huberts La CFSP/GDCR SL9 110 C7
St Hughes Cl TOOT * SW17 179 P5
St Hugh's Cl CRAWE RH10 284 D4
St Hugh's Rd PGE/AN * SE20 182 A10
St Ives CRAWE * RH10 284 D6
St Ives Cl HARH RM3 105 N8
St Ivians Dr GPK RM2 125 H1
St James' Av CHONG CM5 67 N6
EW KT17 220 C7
SUT SM1 221 K2
TRDG/WHET N20 97 P4
WEA W13 134 F10
St James Cl EPSOM KT18 220 B10
NWMAL KT3 200 C5
RSLP HA4 113 K7
STJWD NW8 4 A7
TRDG/WHET N20 97 P4
WOKN/KNAP GU21 231 M4
St James' Ct WESTW * SW1E 17 H3
St James' Gdns ALP/SUD HA0 135 J2
St James Ga CTHM * CR3 241 P8
St James' La RDART DA2 188 D3
St James Ms POP/IOD * E14 161 H2
WEY KT13 216 C1
St James Oaks GVW * DA11 190 D3
St James Pl DART DA1 187 L2
SL * SL1 128 B8
St James Rd CAR SM5 201 P10
EBAR EN4 77 N7
ED N9 100 A3
FSTGT E7 121 L10
MTCM CR4 180 B10
PUR/KEN CR8 223 J9
SURB KT6 199 J6
SUT SM1 221 K2
WATW WD18 73 J9
St James's NWCR SE14 160 D7
St James's Av BECK BR3 204 D3
BETH E2 140 B4
GVW DA11 190 D3
HPTN TW12 176 B8
St James's Chambers
STJS * SW1Y 11 H9
St James's Cl TOOT * SW17 180 B8
TOOT * SW17 180 A5
WOOL/PLUM SE18 162 F4
St James's Cottages
RCHPK/HAM * TW10 177 J1
St James's Ct KUT * KT1 199 K3
WESTW SW1E 17 H3
St James's Crs BRXN/ST SW9 159 H9
St James's Dr BAL SW12 180 A4
St James's Gdns CAMTN * NW1 4 G10
NTGHL W11 8 A9
St James's Gv BTSEA * SW11 158 A8
St James's La MUSWH N10 118 C2
St James's Market STJS * SW1Y 11 J8
St James's Ms WALTH E17 120 D3
St James's Pk CROY/NA CR0 203 K7
St James's Pl WHALL SW1A 10 G10
St James Sq HART * DA3 211 K3
SURB KT6 199 H7
St James's Rd BERM/RHTH SE16 19 P3
BRW CM14 107 H4
CHESW EN7 61 K4
CROY/NA CR0 203 K7
GVW DA11 190 D3
HPTN TW12 176 A8
KUT KT1 199 J2
SEV TN13 247 J8
STHWK SE1 19 P8
St James's Rw CHSGTN * KT9 219 J3
St James's Sq STJS SW1Y 11 J9
St James's St GVW DA11 190 D2
WALTH E17 120 D3
WHALL SW1A 10 G9
St James's Ter STJWD NW8 4 A6
St James's Terrace Ms
STJWD NW8 4 A6
St James St HMSMTH W6 156 F4
St James Ter BAL * SW12 180 B4
ORP * BR6 227 M5
St James Wk CLKNW EC1R 12 C1
IVER SL0 151 H1
St James Wy SCUP DA14 185 P8
St Jerome's Gv UX/CGN UB8 132 D8
St Joan Cl CRAWW RH11 283 N4
St Joan's Rd ED N9 99 N3
St John Cl FUL/PGN * SW6 157 K6
St John's RDKG RH5 273 H6
St John's Av BRW CM14 107 J5
EW KT17 220 C8
FBAR/BDGN N11 98 A6
HLWE CM17 29 M7
LHD/OX KT22 236 G7
PUT/ROE SW15 178 G1
WLSDN NW10 136 C3
St John's Church Rd HACK * E8 120 B10
St Johns Cl BH/WHM * TN16 244 E2
FUL/PGN * SW6 157 K6
LHD/OX KT22 237 H7
POTB/CUF EN6 59 M9
RAIN RM13 145 H2
STHGT/OAK * N14 78 D10
TRDG/WHET * N20 97 M3
UX/CGN * UB8 131 L3
WBLY HA9 115 K10
St Johns Cottages
PGE/AN * SE20 182 B10
St Johns Ct BKHH * IG9 101 N2
BKHH IG9 101 N2
EGH TW20 172 D8
HARP * AL5 20 B4
ISLW TW7 154 E8
LCOL/BKTW AL2 57 H2
STAL AL1 38 G5
St John's Crs BRXN/ST SW9 159 H9
St John's Dr WAND/EARL SW18 179 L4
WDSR SL4 148 E8
WOT/HER KT12 197 K8
St John's Est IS N1 7 H8
STHWK SE1 19 L1
St John's Gdns NTGHL W11 8 C8
St John's Gv ARCH N19 118 D7
BARN * SW13 156 C8
RCH/KEW * TW9 155 K10
St John's Hl BTSEA SW11 157 P10
PUR/KEN CR8 241 H3
SEV TN13 247 K9
St John's Hill Gv BTSEA SW11 157 N10
St John's Hill Rd
WOKN/KNAP GU21 231 M5
St John's La FARR EC1M 12 C2
HART DA3 211 L6
WARE SG12 26 F5
St John's Lye (Festival Path)
WOKN/KNAP GU21 231 L5
St Johns Ms WOKN/KNAP GU21 231 M4
St Johns Pde SCUP * DA14 185 L7
WEA * W13 134 G10
St John's Pk BKHTH/KID SE3 161 M6
St John's Pl FARR EC1M 12 C2
St Johns Ri BH/WHM * TN16 244 E2
WOKN/KNAP GU21 231 N5
St John's Rd BARK IG11 143 H3
BTSEA SW11 157 P10
CAN/RD E16 141 M8
CAR SM5 201 P10
CDH/CHF RM16 168 E4
CHING E4 100 G4
CRAWW RH11 283 M7
CRAWW * RH11 283 M7
CROY/NA CR0 203 J10
CRW RM5 104 D6
DORK RH4 272 B3
E/WMO/HCT KT8 198 C4
EHAM E6 142 B3
EPP CM16 65 J6
ERITH DA8 164 E4
FELT TW13 175 N7
GLDGN NW11 117 J4
GNTH/NBYPK IG2 123 H5
GUW GU2 267 L1
GVE DA12 190 G3
HARP AL5 20 B4
HHW HP1 35 L8
HRW HA1 114 E4
ISLW TW7 154 E8
KUT KT1 199 H2
LHD/OX KT22 237 H7
LOU IG10 82 C6
NWDGN UB2 153 M2
NWMAL KT3 199 P3
PGE/AN SE20 182 B10
RCH/KEW TW9 155 K10
RDART DA2 188 B3
REDH RH1 276 A2
SCUP DA14 185 L7
SEV TN13 247 J8
SEVS/STOTM N15 119 M4
SLN SL2 129 M9
STMC/STPC BR5 206 G6
SUT SM1 201 K9
UX/CGN UB8 131 L4
WALTH E17 100 G10
WAT WD17 73 J6
WBLY HA9 115 J9
WDSR SL4 148 F8
WELL DA16 163 L9
WIM/MER SW19 179 H10
WOKN/KNAP GU21 231 M5
St John's Sq FARR EC1M 12 C2
St John's St HERT/WAS SG14 25 L5
St John's Ter ENC/FH EN2 79 L3
FSTGT E7 141 N1
NKENS W10 136 G6
WOOL/PLUM SE18 162 F5
St John's Terrace Rd REDH RH1 276 A2
St John St FSBYE EC1V 6 B8
St John's V BROCKY SE4 160 F8
St John's Vls ARCH N19 118 E7
KENS W8 15 H4
KENS * W8 15 H4
St Johns Wk HLWE CM17 29 M7
St John's Wy ADL/WDHM KT15 195 K9
ARCH N19 118 D7
St John's Well Ct BERK HP4 33 N4
St John's Well La BERK HP4 33 N4
St John's Wood High St
STJWD NW8 3 M8
St John's Wood Pk STJWD NW8 3 L6
St John's Wood Rd STJWD NW8 9 L1
St John's Wood Ter STJWD NW8 3 N7
St Josephs Cl NKENS W10 8 B4
ORP BR6 227 J1
St Joseph's Dr STHL UB1 133 M10
St Josephs Gv HDN NW4 116 E2
St Joseph's Rd ED N9 100 A1
St Joseph's St VX/NE * SW8 158 C7
St Joseph's V BKHTH/KID SE3 161 J8
St Jude's Cl EGH TW20 171 P8
St Jude's Rd BETH E2 140 A4
EGH TW20 171 P7
St Jude St STNW/STAM N16 119 M10
St Julian's Cl
STRHM/NOR * SW16 181 H7
St Julian's Farm Rd WNWD SE27 181 H7
St Julian's Rd KIL/WHAMP NW6 2 D4
STAL AL1 38 C8
St Justin Cl STMC/STPC BR5 207 N3
St Katharine's Prec
CAMTN * NW1 4 E7
St Katharines Rd CTHM CR3 259 P1
St Katharine's Wy TWRH EC3N 13 M9
St Katherines Rd ERITHM DA18 163 N1
St Katherines Wk NTGHL * W11 136 G9
St Katherine's Wy BERK HP4 33 L2
St Keverne Rd ELTH/MOT SE9 184 B7
St Kilda Rd ORP BR6 207 J8
WEA W13 154 F1
St Kilda's Rd BRWN CM15 106 G1
HRW HA1 114 D4
STNW/STAM N16 119 L6
St Kitts Ter NRWD SE19 181 M8
St Laurence Cl STMC/STPC BR5 207 N3
UX/CGN UB8 131 M7
St Laurence Dr BROX EN10 44 D9
St Laurence's Cl
KIL/WHAMP NW6 136 G3
St Laurence Wy SL SL1 149 M2
St Lawrence Cl ABLGY WD5 54 F6
EDGW HA8 95 L8
HHS/BOV HP3 52 D3
St Lawrence Cottages
POP/IOD * E14 141 H10
St Lawrence Dr PIN HA5 113 J3
St Lawrence Rd UPMR RM14 126 B7
St Lawrence St POP/IOD E14 141 H10
St Lawrence Ter NKENS W10 8 A4
St Lawrence Wy BRXN/ST * SW9 159 H8
CTHM CR3 241 L9
LCOL/BKTW AL2 55 N6
St Leonard's Av CHING E4 101 J7
KTN/HRWW/W HA3 115 H3
WDSR SL4 149 H8
St Leonards Cl BUSH WD23 73 M8
GRAYS RM17 167 L5
HERT/WAS SG14 25 M3
WELL DA16 163 K9
St Leonard's Ct STALE/WH AL4 21 H10
St Leonards Crs STALE/WH AL4 21 H10
St Leonards Dr CRAWE RH10 284 B10
St Leonard's Gdns HEST TW5 153 M6
IL IG1 122 F10
St Leonard's Hl WDSR SL4 148 C10
St Leonards Ri ORP BR6 227 H1
St Leonards Rd AMS HP6 69 K2
CROY/NA CR0 203 J10
ESH/CLAY KT10 218 E3
HERT/WAS SG14 25 L3
KWD/TDW/WH KT20 238 F5
MORT/ESHN SW14 155 P9
POP/IOD E14 141 H7
SURB KT6 199 J5
THDIT KT7 198 F6
WAB EN9 45 J10
WDSR SL4 148 G10
WDSR SL4 170 C2
WEA W13 135 H9
WLSDN NW10 136 A6
St Leonards Sq KTTN NW5 4 D2
St Leonard's St BOW E3 140 G5
St Leonards Ter CHEL * SW3 16 A7
CHEL SW3 16 A8
St Leonards Wk IVER SL0 151 J2
STRHM/NOR SW16 180 G10
St Leonards Wy HCH RM12 125 J6
St Loo Av CHEL SW3 15 P9
St Louis Rd WNWD SE27 181 K7
St Loy's Rd TOTM N17 99 M10
St Lucia Dr SRTFD E15 141 L3
St Luke Cl UX/CGN UB8 131 N8
St Luke's Av CLAP SW4 158 E10
ENC/FH EN2 79 L4
IL IG1 122 E10
St Lukes Cl RDART DA2 188 D8
SNWD SE25 204 A6
SWLY BR8 208 E2
St Lukes Ct WOKN/KNAP * GU21 214 F10
St Luke's Est FSBYE * EC1V 6 G10
St Luke's Ms NTGHL W11 8 D5
St Lukes Pl STAL * AL1 38 G7
St Luke's Rd CTHM CR3 241 N4
HGDN/ICK * UB10 131 P2
NTGHL W11 8 D4
WDSR SL4 171 M2
St Lukes's Cl FSBYE EC1V 12 F1
St Luke's Sq CAN/RD E16 141 L8
GU GU1 268 C1
St Luke's St CHEL SW3 15 N7
St Lukes Yd MV/WKIL * W9 2 C8
St Magnus Ct HHS/BOV * HP3 36 D8
St Malo Av ED N9 100 B4
St Margarets BARK IG11 142 G3
GU GU1 250 C9
RCHPK/HAM * TW10 177 P8
St Margarets Av ASHF TW15 174 C8
BFN/LL DA15 184 G6
BH/WHM * TN16 244 E2
CHEAM SM3 201 H10
RYLN/HDSTN HA2 114 B8
SEVS/STOTM N15 119 J2
TRDG/WHET N20 97 M2
UX/CGN UB8 132 B6
St Margaret's Cl BERK HP4 34 A6
IVER SL0 130 G4
ORP BR6 227 L1
RDART DA2 188 C5
St Margarets Ct
PUT/ROE * SW15 156 E10
St Margaret's Crs GVE DA12 191 H6
PUT/ROE * SW15 178 E1
St Margarets Dr EPSOM KT18 220 A10
TWK TW1 176 G1
St Margaret's Gv TWK TW1 176 F2
WAN E11 121 L8
WOOL/PLUM SE18 162 F5
St Margarets La KENS W8 14 G4
St Margarets Ms
RCHPK/HAM * TW10 177 P8
St Margaret's Rd BROCKY SE4 160 E10
COUL/CHIP CR5 240 C7
EDGW HA8 95 N6
EYN DA4 188 D10
HNWL W7 154 D1
MNPK E12 121 P7
RSLP HA4 112 E4
TOTM N17 119 M1
TWK TW1 154 G10
WARE SG12 26 F9
WLSDN NW10 136 F5

St Margaret's Ter
WOOL/PLUM SE18 162 F4
St Margaret St WEST SW1P 17 L2
St Margarets Wy HHNE HP2 36 E6
St Mark Av CHOB/PIR GU24 230 G9
St Mark's Av GVW DA11 190 B3
St Mark's Cl BAR EN5 77 L7
FUL/PGN SW6 157 K7
STALE/WH AL4 39 N8
St Mark's Crs CAMTN NW1 4 D5
St Marks Ga HOM E9 140 D2
St Mark's Gv WBPTN * SW10 157 L6
St Mark's Hl SURB KT6 199 K6
St Mark's Pl NTGHL W11 8 B6
WDSR SL4 149 H8
WIM/MER * SW19 179 J9
St Mark's Ri HACK E8 119 N10
St Mark's Rd EA W5 135 K10
EN EN1 79 N10
EPSOM KT18 238 F4
HAYES BR2 205 N3
HNWL W7 154 D1
MTCM CR4 202 A2
NKENS W10 136 G7
NTGHL W11 8 A6
SNWD SE25 203 P4
TEDD TW11 176 G10
WDSR SL4 149 H8
St Mark's Sq CAMTN NW1 4 C5
St Mark St WCHPL E1 13 M6
St Marks Vls HOLWY * N7 118 G7
St Martha's Av
WOKS/MYFD GU22 232 C7
St Marthas Ct RGUE * GU4 268 E6
St Martin Cl UX/CGN UB8 131 N8
St Martin's Ap RSLP HA4 112 F5
St Martin's Av EHAM E6 142 A4
EPSOM KT18 220 B10
St Martin's Cl CAMTN NW1 4 G5
EHSLY KT24 252 F5
EN EN1 80 A5
ERITHM DA18 163 N1
EW * KT17 220 C9
OXHEY WD19 93 K5
RBRW/HUT * CM13 107 P2
WDR/YW UB7 151 M2
St Martin's Ct ASHF TW15 173 M8
LSQ/SEVD * WC2H 11 L7
LSQ/SEVD * WC2H 11 L7
St Martins Dr EYN DA4 209 L10
WOT/HER KT12 197 K10
St Martin's La CHCR WC2N 11 L7
St Martin's Le Grand STBT EC1A 12 E5
St Martins Meadow
BH/WHM TN16 245 M9
St Martins Ms DORK RH4 272 F2
WOKS/MYFD GU22 233 K2
St Martin's Pl CHCR WC2N 11 L8
St Martin's Rd BRXN/ST SW9 158 G8
DART DA1 187 N2
ED N9 100 A3
St Martin's St LSQ/SEVD * WC2H 11 K8
St Martin's Wy TOOT SW17 179 M6
St Mary Abbots Pl KENS * W8 14 D4
KENS W8 14 D4
St Mary Abbots Ter WKENS W14 14 C4
St Mary At Hl MON EC3R 13 J8
St Mary Av WLGTN SM6 202 B10
St Mary Axe HDTCH EC3A 13 J6
St Marychurch St
BERM/RHTH SE16 160 B1
St Mary Graces Ct TWRH * EC3N 13 M8
St Mary Rd WALTH E17 120 F2
St Marys BARK IG11 142 G4
WEY * KT13 196 E10
St Mary's Ap MNPK E12 122 C10
St Mary's Av BERK HP4 33 J3
BRWN CM15 87 M9
FNCH N3 97 H10
HAYES BR2 205 K3
NTHWD HA6 92 F6
NWDGN UB2 154 A3
STWL/WRAY TW19 173 N3
TEDD * TW11 176 E9
WAN E11 121 N4
St Mary's Church Rd RSEV TN14 263 P1
St Mary's Cl CHSGTN KT9 219 L4
DEN/HRF UB9 111 L1
EW KT17 220 C4
GRAYS * RM17 168 A5
GVE DA12 190 F5
LHD/OX KT22 236 C9
OXTED RH8 261 K5
STMC/STPC BR5 207 L2
SUN TW16 197 H4
TOTM * N17 99 N10
WATW * WD18 73 K8
St Mary's Ct BH/WHM TN16 262 G2
POTB/CUF EN6 59 L8
SHB * W12 156 C2
St Marys Ctyd WARE * SG12 26 C2
St Mary's Crs HDN NW4 116 E1
HYS/HAR UB3 132 G9
ISLW TW7 154 C6
STWL/WRAY TW19 173 N3
St Mary's Dr CRAWE RH10 284 C5
EBED/NFELT TW14 174 D3
SEV TN13 246 F9
St Marys Est BERM/RHTH * SE16 160 B1
St Marys Gdns LBTH * SE11 18 B5
LBTH SE11 18 B5
St Mary's Ga KENS W8 14 G4
KENS * W8 14 G4
St Mary's Gn BH/WHM TN16 243 P4
EFNCH N2 117 M1
St Mary's Gv BARN SW13 156 E9
BH/WHM TN16 243 P4
CHSWK W4 155 N5
IS N1 6 D2
RCH/KEW TW9 155 L10
St Mary's Hl ASC SL5 192 B6
St Mary's La HERT/WAS SG14 24 G7
UPMR RM14 125 P7
UPMR RM14 126 F7
UPMR RM14 127 K6
St Mary's Man BAY/PAD W2 9 K3
St Mary's Ms KIL/WHAMP NW6 2 G4
St Mary's Mt CTHM CR3 241 N10
St Mary's Pth IS N1 6 D5
St Mary's Pl EA W5 155 J1
KENS W8 14 G4
KENS * W8 15 H4
St Mary's Rd ASC SL5 192 A7
BXLY DA5 186 D4
CDH/CHF RM16 168 E3
CEND/HSY/T * N8 118 F2
CHES/WCR EN8 62 B5
DEN/HRF UB9 111 J4
DEN/HRF UB9 111 L1
DTCH/LGLY SL3 150 B1
E/WMO/HCT KT8 198 C5
EA W5 155 J1
EBAR EN4 98 A1
ED N9 100 B2
GLDGN NW11 117 H5
GRH DA9 188 D1
HHNE HP2 35 N5
HYS/HAR UB3 132 G9
IL IG1 122 F7
LEY E10 121 H8
LHD/OX KT22 236 G8
PECK SE15 160 B7
PLSTW E13 141 N4
REIG RH2 275 L1
SAND/SEL CR2 223 L6
SNWD SE25 203 M3
SURB KT6 199 H7
SWLY BR8 208 E4
WATW WD18 73 J8
WEY KT13 216 E1
WIM/MER SW19 179 H8
WLSDN NW10 136 B3
WOKN/KNAP GU21 231 P3
WPK KT4 200 B9
St Mary's Sq BAY/PAD W2 9 L3
EA * W5 155 J1
St Mary's Ter BAY/PAD W2 9 L3
BORE * WD6 75 J10
St Mary St WOOL/PLUM SE18 162 C3
St Marys Vw KTN/HRWW/W HA3 115 H3
WATW * WD18 73 K8
St Mary's Wk HYS/HAR UB3 132 G9
LBTH * SE11 18 B5
LBTH SE11 18 B5
STALE/WH AL4 38 G2
St Mary's Wy CFSP/GDCR SL9 90 A10
CHIG IG7 102 D6
CSHM HP5 50 G7
HART DA3 211 K3
St Matthew Cl UX/CGN UB8 131 N8
St Matthews Av SURB KT6 199 K8
St Matthews Cl OXHEY WD19 73 L10
RAIN RM13 145 H2
St Matthews Dr BMLY BR1 206 C3
St Matthew's Rd
BRXS/STRHM SW2 180 G1
EA W5 135 K10
REDH RH1 258 A9
St Matthew St WEST SW1P 17 J3
St Matthias Cl CDALE/KGS NW9 116 C3
St Maur Rd FUL/PGN SW6 157 J7
St Meddens CHST * BR7 184 G10
St Merryn Cl WOOL/PLUM SE18 162 G6
St Michael's Aly BANK EC3V 13 H6
St Michaels Av ED N9 100 B1
HHS/BOV HP3 36 C8
HHS/BOV HP3 36 C7
RGUW GU3 249 H5
WBLY HA9 135 M1
St Michaels Cl BMLY BR1 206 B3
CAN/RD E16 142 A7
ERITHM * DA18 163 N1
FNCH N3 97 J10
HLW CM20 29 H10
HLW CM20 29 H10
NFNCH/WDSP N12 97 P6
SOCK/AV RM15 146 B9
WOT/HER KT12 197 K9
WPK KT4 200 C9
St Michaels Ct GLDGN * NW11 117 J5
SLN * SL2 128 C6
St Michael's Crs PIN HA5 113 M4
St Michaels Dr GSTN WD25 55 J9
RSEV TN14 247 L2
St Michael's Gdns NKENS W10 8 A4
St Michael's Gn BEAC HP9 88 D8
St Michaels Ri WELL * DA16 163 L7
St Michaels Rd ASHF TW15 174 B8
BROX EN10 44 E6
BRXN/ST SW9 158 G8
CDH/CHF RM16 168 E4
CRICK NW2 116 F9
CROY/NA * CR0 203 K8
CTHM CR3 241 L8
WELL DA16 163 L9
WLGTN SM6 222 D3
WOKN/KNAP GU21 214 G10
St Michael's St BAY/PAD W2 9 M5
STALW/RED AL3 38 A6
St Michaels Ter HGT * N6 118 B6
WDGN N22 98 F10
St Michaels Wy POTB/CUF EN6 59 L6
St Mildred's Ct LOTH * EC2R 12 G6
St Mildreds Rd CAT SE6 183 K3
GU GU1 250 C9
St Monica's Rd
KWD/TDW/WH KT20 239 J7
St Nazaire Cl EGH * TW20 172 F8
St Neots Cl BORE WD6 75 M4
St Neot's Rd HARH RM3 105 N8
St Nicholas Av GT/LBKH KT23 254 A1
HCH RM12 125 H8
St Nicholas Cl AMSS HP7 69 N5
BORE WD6 75 J10
UX/CGN UB8 131 N8
St Nicholas Crs
WOKS/MYFD GU22 233 K2
St Nicholas Dr SHPTN TW17 196 B7
St Nicholas Glebe TOOT SW17 180 B9
St Nicholas Gv RBRW/HUT CM13 107 P6
St Nicholas Hl LHD/OX KT22 236 G8
St Nicholas Mt HHW HP1 35 J6
St Nicholas Rd SUT SM1 221 L2
THDIT KT7 198 E6
WOOL/PLUM SE18 163 J4
St Nicholas St DEPT SE8 160 E7
St Nicholas Wy SUT SM1 221 L1
St Nicolas La CHST BR7 206 B1
St Ninian's Ct TRDG/WHET N20 98 A8
St Norbert Rd BROCKY SE4 160 D10
St Normans Wy EW KT17 220 D6
St Olaf's Rd FUL/PGN SW6 157 H6
St Olave's Cl STA TW18 173 J10
St Olave's Rd EHAM E6 142 D3
St Olave's Wk STRHM/NOR SW16 202 D2
St Omer Rdg GU GU1 268 D1
St Omer Rd GU GU1 268 D1
St Onge Pde EN * EN1 79 L7
St Oswald's Pl LBTH SE11 17 N7
St Oswald's Rd
STRHM/NOR SW16 203 J1
St Oswulf St WEST * SW1P 17 K6
St Pancras Gdns CAMTN * NW1 5 J7
St Pancras Wy CAMTN NW1 5 H3
St Patrick's Gdns GVE DA12 190 G7
St Patrick's Pl CDH/CHF RM16 168 E3
St Paul Cl UX/CGN UB8 131 N7
St Paul's Av BERM/RHTH * SE16 140 C10
CRICK NW2 136 E1
KTN/HRWW/W HA3 115 L3
SLN SL2 129 L9
St Paul's Church Yd
BLKFR * EC4V 12 D6
St Paul's Cl ADL/WDHM KT15 215 K1
ASHF TW15 174 D8
CAR SM5 201 P7
CHARL SE7 162 A4
CHSGTN KT9 219 J1
EA W5 155 L1
EA W5 155 L1
HSLW TW3 153 M8
HYS/HAR UB3 152 E4
SOCK/AV RM15 146 B9
SWCM DA10 189 K3
St Paul's Cray Rd CHST BR7 206 G1
St Pauls Crs CAMTN NW1 5 K3
CAMTN NW1 5 K3
St Paul's Dr SRTFD E15 121 J10
St Pauls Ms CAMTN NW1 5 K3
St Paul's Pl IS N1 6 G1
SOCK/AV RM15 146 B9
STAL AL1 38 F6
St Pauls Ri PLMGR N13 99 J7
St Pauls Rd BARK IG11 142 F3
BTFD TW8 155 M9
ERITH DA8 164 D6
HHNE HP2 35 P5
IS N1 6 F1
RCH/KEW TW9 155 L9
STA TW18 172 G8
THHTH CR7 203 K3
TOTM N17 99 P8
WOKS/MYFD GU22 232 D3
St Paul's Rd East DORK RH4 272 G3
St Paul's Rd West DORK RH4 272 F3
St Pauls Ter WALW SE17 18 D9
St Paul St IS N1 6 E6
St Paul's Wy FNCH N3 97 L8
POP/IOD E14 140 E7
WAB * EN9 63 J9
WATN WD24 73 K6
St Paul's Wood Hl
STMC/STPC BR5 207 H2
St Peters CHERT * KT16 194 F10
St Peters Av BH/WHM * TN16 244 E2
CHONG CM5 67 N2
UED N18 99 P5
St Petersburgh Ms BAY/PAD W2 8 G7
St Petersburgh Pl BAY/PAD * W2 8 G8
St Peter's Cl BAR EN5 76 E9
BETH E2 7 P8
BUSH WD23 94 C2
CHST BR7 184 G10
GNTH/NBYPK IG2 123 H2
HAT AL10 40 D3
RKW/CH/CXG WD3 91 L3
RSLP HA4 113 L7
SL SL1 128 A6
STA TW18 173 J9
STALW/RED AL3 38 C5
SWCM DA10 189 L3
TOOT SW17 179 P5
WDSR SL4 171 M1
WOKS/MYFD GU22 232 F6
St Peters Ct CFSP/GDCR * SL9 90 B9
E/WMO/HCT KT8 197 P4
HDN * NW4 116 F3
LEE/GVPK * SE12 183 L1
St Peter's Gdns WNWD * SE27 181 H6
St Peter's Gv HMSMTH W6 156 D3
St Peter's Pth WALTH E17 121 K2
St Peters Pl MV/WKIL W9 8 G2
St Peter's Rd BRW CM14 106 G5
CDH/CHF RM16 168 E3
CRAWW RH11 283 M7
CROY/NA CR0 223 L1
E/WMO/HCT KT8 197 P4
ED N9 100 A2
HMSMTH * W6 156 D4
KUT KT1 199 M2
STAL AL1 38 D6
STHL UB1 133 P7
TWK TW1 176 G1
UX/CGN UB8 131 N7
WOKS/MYFD GU22 232 E7
St Peter's Sq BETH E2 7 P8
HMSMTH W6 156 D3
St Peter's St IS N1 6 D6
SAND/SEL CR2 223 L2
STAL AL1 38 C5
St Peter's Ter FUL/PGN SW6 157 H6
St Peter's Vls HMSMTH W6 156 D3
St Peter's Wy CHERT KT16 215 H1
EA W5 135 J7
HYS/HAR UB3 152 E2
IS N1 7 K4
RKW/CH/CXG WD3 70 E8
St Philip's Av WPK KT4 200 E9
St Philip Sq VX/NE * SW8 158 C8
St Philip's Rd HACK E8 7 N2
SURB KT6 199 J6
St Philip St VX/NE SW8 158 C8
St Philip's Wy IS N1 6 F6
St Pinnock Av STA TW18 195 K1
St Quentin Rd WELL DA16 163 J9
St Quintin Av NKENS W10 136 F7
St Quintin Rd PLSTW E13 141 N5
St Raphael's Wy WLSDN NW10 115 P10
St Regis Cl MUSWH N10 98 C10
St Richards Ms CRAWE * RH10 284 A7
St Ronans Cl EBAR EN4 77 N4
St Ronans Crs WFD IG8 101 M8
St Rule St VX/NE SW8 158 D8
St Saviour Av CHOB/PIR GU24 230 G7
St Saviour's Est STHWK SE1 19 L3
St Saviours Pl GU * GU1 249 P10
St Saviour's Rd
BRXS/STRHM SW2 180 G1
CROY/NA CR0 203 K6
Saints Cl WNWD SE27 181 J7
Saints Dr FSTGT E7 122 A10
St Silas Pl KTTN NW5 4 C2
St Simon's Av PUT/ROE SW15 178 F1
St Stephens Av ASHTD KT21 237 K3
SHB W12 136 E10
STALW/RED AL3 38 A8
WALTH E17 121 H3
WEA W13 134 G8
St Stephens Cl KTTN * NW5 118 A10
STALW/RED AL3 38 A9
STHL UB1 133 P7
WALTH E17 120 G3
St Stephen's Crs BAY/PAD * W2 8 F5
RBRW/HUT CM13 107 M5
THHTH CR7 203 H3
St Stephen's Garden Est
BAY/PAD W2 8 D5
St Stephen's Gdns BAY/PAD W2 8 F5
TWK TW1 177 H2
St Stephen's Gv LEW SE13 161 H9
St Stephen's Hl STAL AL1 38 B8
St Stephen's Ms BAY/PAD W2 8 F4
St Stephens Pde WHALL SW1A 17 L1
St Stephens Rd BAR EN5 76 G9
BOW E3 140 D3
EHAM E6 141 P2
HSLW TW3 175 P2
PEND EN3 80 C3
WALTH E17 120 G3
WDR/YW UB7 131 N10
WEA W13 134 G8
St Stephens Ter VX/NE * SW8 158 F6
VX/NE SW8 158 G6
St Stephen's Wk SKENS SW7 15 J5
Saint's Wk CDH/CHF RM16 168 F3
St Swithin's La MANHO EC4N 12 G7
St Swithun's Rd LEW * SE13 183 J1
St Teresa Wk CDH/CHF RM16 168 E3
St Theresa Cl EPSOM KT18 219 P10
St Theresa's Rd
EBED/NFELT TW14 152 G10
St Thomas Cl SURB KT6 199 L8
WOKN/KNAP GU21 231 P3
St Thomas Ct BXLY DA5 186 B3
St Thomas' Dr PIN HA5 93 M9
STMC/STPC BR5 206 F8
St Thomas Gdns IL IG1 142 F1
St Thomas Pl STALE/WH AL4 21 J3
St Thomas Rd BELV DA17 164 D1
BRW CM14 107 J3
CAN/RD E16 141 M8
CHSWK W4 155 P6
GVW * DA11 190 B4
STHGT/OAK N14 98 E1
St Thomas's Av GVW DA11 190 E5
St Thomas's Cl WAB EN9 63 N9
St Thomas's Dr RGUE * GU4 251 P7
St Thomas's Gdns HAMP NW3 4 C1
St Thomas's Ms GU GU1 268 C2
St Thomas's Pl GRAYS RM17 167 P5
HOM * E9 140 B2
St Thomas's Rd FSBYPK N4 119 H7
WLSDN NW10 136 B3
St Thomas's Sq HACK E8 140 A2
St Thomas St STHWK SE1 13 H10
St Thomas's Wy FUL/PGN SW6 157 J6
St Thomas Wk DTCH/LGLY SL3 150 G6
St Ursula Gv PIN HA5 113 L3
St Ursula Rd STHL UB1 133 P8
St Vincent Cl CRAWE RH10 284 E8
WNWD SE27 181 J8
St Vincent Dr STAL AL1 38 F8
St Vincent Rd WHTN TW2 176 B2
WOT/HER KT12 197 J10
St Vincents Cottages
WATW * WD18 73 J8
St Vincents Rd DART DA1 187 P2
St Vincent St MHST W1U 10 D4
St Vincent's Wy POTB/CUF EN6 59 M10
St Wilfrid's Cl EBAR * EN4 77 P9
St Wilfrid's Rd EBAR EN4 77 N9
St Winefride's Av MNPK E12 122 C10
St Winifred's Cl CHIG IG7 102 F6
St Winifred's Rd BH/WHM TN16 244 C4
TEDD TW11 176 G9
St Yon Ct STALE/WH AL4 39 J6
Sakins Cft HLWS CM18 47 J4
Saladin Dr PUR RM19 165 P3
Salamanca Pl LBTH SE11 17 N6
Salamanca St LBTH SE11 17 N6
Salamander Cl KUTN/CMB KT2 177 H8
Salamander Quay KUT * KT1 199 J1
Salamons Wy RAIN RM13 144 F8
Salbrook Rd REDH RH1 276 B8
Salcombe Dr CHDH RM6 124 A4
MRDN SM4 200 G8
Salcombe Gdns MLHL NW7 96 F7
Salcombe Rd ASHF TW15 173 P7
STNW/STAM N16 119 N10
WALTH E17 120 E5
Salcombe Wy RSLP HA4 113 H7
Salcot Crs CROY/NA CR0 225 H6
Salcote Rd GVE DA12 191 H8
Salcott Rd BTSEA SW11 179 P1
CROY/NA CR0 202 F10
Salehurst Cl KTN/HRWW/W HA3 115 K3
Salehurst Rd BROCKY SE4 182 E2
CRAWE RH10 284 F7
Salem Pl CROY/NA CR0 203 K10
GVW DA11 190 A3
Salem Rd BAY/PAD W2 9 H7
Sale Pl BAY/PAD W2 9 N5
Sale St BETH E2 7 P10
Salford Rd BAL SW12 180 E4
Salisbury Av BARK IG11 142 G2
BELMT SM2 221 J3
FNCH N3 97 J10
SLN SL2 129 H6
STAL AL1 38 G5
SWLY BR8 209 H4
Salisbury Cl AMSS HP7 69 K5
POTB/CUF EN6 59 M8
WALW SE17 18 G5
WPK KT4 200 C10
Salisbury Ct EMB EC4Y 12 B6
Salisbury Crs CHES/WCR EN8 62 C5
Salisbury Gdns WGCE AL7 23 J6
WIM/MER * SW19 179 H10
Salisbury Pavement
FUL/PGN * SW6 157 K6
Salisbury Pl BF/WBF KT14 215 M7
BRXN/ST SW9 158 G7
MBLAR W1H 10 A3
Salisbury Prom
CEND/HSY/T * N8 119 J3
Salisbury Rd BAR EN5 77 H7
BNSTD SM7 239 L1
BXLY DA5 186 B4
CAR SM5 222 A3
CHING E4 100 F4
CROY/NA CR0 203 P6
DAGE RM10 144 C1
ED N9 99 P4
FELT TW13 175 K4
FSBYPK N4 119 J3
FSTGT E7 141 M1
GDMY/SEVK IG3 123 H7
GDST RH9 260 B7
GPK RM2 125 J3
GRAYS RM17 167 P5
GVW DA11 190 C4
HAYES BR2 206 B5
HOD EN11 45 H2
HOR/WEW KT19 220 A1
HRW HA1 114 C3
HSLWW TW4 153 K9
LEY E10 121 H7
MNPK E12 122 A10
NWDGN * UB2 153 M3
NWMAL KT3 200 A3
PEND EN3 80 E3
PIN HA5 113 H2
RCH/KEW TW9 155 K10
RDART DA2 188 B4
UX/CGN UB8 131 L4
WALTH E17 121 H3
WATN WD24 73 J4
WDGN N22 99 J10
WEA W13 154 G1
WGCE AL7 23 J6
WIM/MER SW19 179 H10
WOKS/MYFD GU22 232 B5
Salisbury Sq EMB * EC4Y 12 B6
HERT/WAS * SG14 25 L5
Salisbury St ACT W3 155 P1
STJWD NW8 9 M2
Salisbury Ter PECK SE15 160 B9
Salix Cl SUN TW16 175 J10
Salix Rd GRAYS RM17 168 A5
Sally Murray Cl MNPK E12 122 D9
Salmen Rd PLSTW E13 141 L4
Salmon Cl WGCE AL7 23 K2
Salmond's Gv RBRW/HUT CM13 107 P6
Salmon La POP/IOD E14 140 D8
Salmon Ms KIL/WHAMP * NW6 117 K10
Salmon Rd BELV DA17 164 B4
DART DA1 165 N9
Salmons La CTHM CR3 241 M6
Salmons La West CTHM CR3 241 M6
Salmons Rd CHSGTN KT9 219 K3
ED N9 99 P2
EHSLY KT24 253 K5
Salmon St POP/IOD * E14 140 E8
WBLY HA9 115 P7
Salomons Rd PLSTW E13 141 P7
Salop Rd WALTH E17 120 C4
Saltash Cl SUT SM1 221 J1
Saltash Rd BARK/HLT IG6 102 G8
WELL DA16 163 M7
Saltbox Hl BH/WHM TN16 225 N9
Salt Box Rd RGUW GU3 249 M5
Saltcoats Rd CHSWK W4 156 B1
Saltcroft Cl WBLY HA9 115 N6
Saltdean Cl CRAWW RH11 283 N10
Salter Cl RYLN/HDSTN HA2 113 N8
Salterford Rd TOOT SW17 180 B9
Salterns Rd CRAWE RH10 284 D10
Salter Rd BERM/RHTH SE16 140 C10
Salter's Cl BERK HP4 33 L3
RKW/CH/CXG WD3 91 P2
Salters Gdns WAT * WD17 73 H5
Salters' Hall Ct MANHO * EC4N 12 G7
Salter's Hl NRWD SE19 181 L8
Salters Rd NKENS W10 136 G6
WALTH E17 121 J2
Salters Rw IS * N1 6 G2
Salter St POP/IOD E14 140 F9
WLSDN NW10 136 D5
Salterton Rd HOLWY N7 118 F8
Saltford Cl ERITH DA8 164 F4
Salt Hill Av SL SL1 129 H10
Salt Hill Cl UX/CGN UB8 111 N10
Salt Hill Dr SL SL1 129 H10
Salt Hill Wy SL SL1 129 H10
Saltley Cl EHAM E6 142 B8
Saltram Crs MV/WKIL W9 2 D9
Saltwell St POP/IOD E14 140 F9
Saltwood Cl ORP BR6 227 M1
Saltwood Gv WALW SE17 18 G8
Salusbury Rd KIL/WHAMP NW6 2 B5
Salvador TOOT SW17 179 P8
Salvation Pl LHD/OX KT22 236 F10
Salvia Gdns GFD/PVL UB6 134 F4
Salvington Rd CRAWW RH11 283 J10
Salvin Rd PUT/ROE SW15 156 G9
Salway Cl WFD IG8 101 M8
Salway Pl SRTFD E15 141 J1
Salway Rd SRTFD E15 141 J1
Salwey Crs BROX EN10 44 F6
Samantha Cl WALTH E17 120 E5
Samaritan Cl CRAWW RH11 283 H9
Sam Bartram Cl CHARL SE7 161 P4
Samels Ct HMSMTH W6 156 D4
Samford St STJWD NW8 9 N2
Samian Ga STALW/RED AL3 37 N8
Samos Rd PGE/AN SE20 204 A2
Samphire Cl CRAWW RH11 283 K10
Samphire Ct GRAYS RM17 168 B5
Sampleoak La RGUE GU4 269 H7
Sampson Av BAR EN5 76 G9
Sampson Cl BELV DA17 163 N2
Sampsons Gn SLN SL2 128 E5
Sampsons Hl AMSS HP7 88 D1
Sampson St WAP E1W 13 P10
Samson St PLSTW E13 141 P4
Samuel Cl HACK E8 7 M5
NWCR SE14 160 C5
WOOL/PLUM SE18 162 B3
Samuel Gray Gdns
KUTN/CMB KT2 199 J1
Samuel Sq STAL * AL1 38 C7
Samuel St WOOL/PLUM SE18 162 C3
Sancroft Cl CRICK NW2 116 E8
Sancroft Rd KTN/HRWW/W HA3 94 E10
Sancroft St LBTH SE11 17 P7
Sanctuary Cl DART DA1 187 K2
DEN/HRF UB9 91 M8
Sanctuary Rd STWL/WRAY TW19 174 B2
Sanctuary St STHWK SE1 18 F2
The Sanctuary BXLY DA5 185 N2
WEST SW1P 17 K3
Sandall Cl EA W5 135 K6
Sandall Rd EA W5 135 K6
KTTN NW5 4 E2
Sandalls Spring HHW HP1 35 J4
Sandal Rd NWMAL KT3 200 B4
UED N18 99 P6
Sandal St SRTFD E15 141 K3
Sandalwood GUW GU2 267 N1
Sandalwood Av CHERT KT16 194 G10
Sandalwood Cl WCHPL E1 140 D6
Sandalwood Dr RSLP HA4 112 D5
Sandalwood Rd FELT TW13 175 J6
Sanday Cl HHS/BOV HP3 36 C8
Sandbach Pl WOOL/PLUM SE18 162 F4
Sandbanks Hl RDART DA2 189 H9
Sandbourne Av WIM/MER SW19 201 L3
Sandbourne Rd BROCKY SE4 160 D8
Sandbrook Cl MLHL NW7 96 A7
Sandbrook Rd STNW/STAM N16 119 M8
Sandby Gn ELTH/MOT SE9 162 B9
Sandcliff Rd ERITH DA8 164 E3
Sandcroft Cl PLMGR N13 99 J7
Sandcross La REIG RH2 275 J3
Sandell's Av ASHF TW15 174 D7
Sandell St STHWK SE1 18 A1
Sandelswood End BEAC HP9 88 C6
Sandelwood Wy BEAC HP9 88 C7
Sanders Cl HPTN TW12 176 B8
LCOL/BKTW AL2 57 J3

Sanders Cnr ENC/FH * EN2 79 J1
Sandersfield Rd BNSTD SM7 239 K1
Sanders La MLHL NW7 96 F8
Sanderson Cl KTTN * NW5 118 C9
RBRW/HUT * CM13 127 P4
Sanderson Rd UX/CGN UB8 131 M1
Sandersons Av RSEV TN14 228 B6
Sanders Pde
STRHM/NOR * SW16 180 F9
Sanders Rd HHS/BOV HP3 36 A9
Sanderstead Av CRICK NW2 117 H7
Sanderstead Cl BAL SW12 180 D3
Sanderstead Court Av
SAND/SEL CR2 223 P9
Sanderstead Hl SAND/SEL CR2 223 M7
Sanderstead Rd LEY E10 120 D6
SAND/SEL CR2 223 L4
STMC/STPC BR5 207 L6
Sandes Pl LHD/OX KT22 236 F4
Sandfield Gdns THHTH CR7 203 J3
Sandfield Pl THHTH CR7 203 K3
Sandfield Rd STAL AL1 38 F6
THHTH CR7 203 J3
Sandfields RPLY/SEND GU23 232 G10
Sandfield Ter GU GU1 268 A1
Sandford Av LOU IG10 82 F7
WDGN N22 99 J9
Sandford Rd BXLYHS DA6 163 P10
EHAM E6 142 C5
HAYES BR2 205 M4
Sandford Rw WALW SE17 18 G7
Sandford St FUL/PGN SW6 157 L6
Sandgate Cl ROMW/RG RM7 124 D5
Sandgate La WAND/EARL SW18 179 P4
Sandgate Rd WELL DA16 163 M6
Sandgate St PECK SE15 160 A5
Sandhills WLGTN SM6 222 E1
Sandhills Ct VW GU25 194 B5
Sandhills La VW GU25 194 B5
Sandhills Rd REIG RH2 275 K2
Sandhurst Av BRYLDS KT5 199 N7
RYLN/HDSTN HA2 114 A4
Sandhurst Cl CDALE/KGS NW9 115 M1
SAND/SEL CR2 223 M5
Sandhurst Ct HARP AL5 20 C5
Sandhurst Dr GDMY/SEVK IG3 123 J9
Sandhurst Pde CAT * SE6 183 H4
Sandhurst Rd BFN/LL DA15 185 J6
BXLY DA5 185 N1
CAT SE6 183 J4
CDALE/KGS NW9 115 M1
ED N9 80 B10
ORP BR6 207 K10
TIL RM18 168 F8
Sandhurst Wy SAND/SEL CR2 223 M4
Sandifer Dr CRICK NW2 116 G8
Sandifield HAT AL10 40 E7
Sandiford Rd CHEAM SM3 201 J9
Sandiland Crs HAYES BR2 205 L9
Sandilands CROY/NA CR0 203 P10
SEV TN13 246 E8
Sandilands Rd FUL/PGN SW6 157 L7
Sandison St PECK SE15 159 N9
Sandlands Gv
KWD/TDW/WH KT20 238 D9
Sandlands Rd
KWD/TDW/WH KT20 238 D9
Sandland St GINN WC1R 11 P4
Sandlers End SLN SL2 128 G6
Sandling Ri ELTH/MOT SE9 184 D6
Sandlings Cl PECK SE15 160 A8
Sandmere Cl HHNE HP2 36 B7
Sandmere Rd CLAP SW4 158 F10
Sandon Cl ESH/CLAY KT10 198 C7
Sandon Pl CHONG CM5 67 P6
Sandon Rd CHES/WCR EN8 62 B6
Sandow Crs HYS/HAR UB3 152 G2
Sandown Av DAGE RM10 144 D1
ESH/CLAY KT10 218 B2
HCH RM12 125 L7
Sandown Cl HEST TW5 153 H7
Sandown Ct BELMT * SM2 221 L4
DAGE RM10 144 D1
SYD * SE26 182 A6
Sandown Dr CAR SM5 222 B5
Sandown Ga ESH/CLAY KT10 198 C9
Sandown Rd COUL/CHIP CR5 240 B2
ESH/CLAY KT10 218 B1
GVE DA12 190 F9
SL SL1 128 E7
SNWD SE25 204 A5
WATN WD24 73 K4
Sandown Wy NTHLT UB5 133 M1
Sandpiper Cl BERM/RHTH SE16 160 E1
CRAWW RH11 282 G9
WALTH E17 100 C8
Sandpiper Dr ERITH DA8 165 J6
Sandpiper Rd SAND/SEL CR2 224 C7
SUT SM1 221 J2
The Sandpipers GVE DA12 190 G5
Sandpiper Ter CLAY * IG5 122 E1
Sandpiper Wy STMC/STPC BR5 207 N4
Sandpit Hall Rd CHOB/PIR GU24 213 M8
Sandpit Heath RGUW GU3 249 J6
Sandpit La BRW CM14 86 E10
STAL AL1 38 E5
Sandpit Pl CHARL SE7 162 B4
Sandpit Rd BMLY BR1 183 K8
DART DA1 165 K10
REDH RH1 275 P1
WGCE AL7 23 H7
Sandpits Rd CROY/NA CR0 224 C1
RCHPK/HAM TW10 177 J5
Sandra Cl HSLW TW3 176 A1
WDGN N22 99 K9
Sandridgebury La
STALW/RED AL3 20 G9
STALW/RED AL3 38 D2
Sandridge Cl HRW HA1 114 D2
Sandridge Pk STALW/RED * AL3 38 E1
Sandridge Rd STAL AL1 38 D4
Sandridge St ARCH N19 118 D7
Sandringham Av
HLWW/ROY CM19 46 B1
RYNPK SW20 201 H1
Sandringham Cl EN EN1 79 M6
WIM/MER * SW19 178 G4
WOKS/MYFD GU22 233 K2
Sandringham Ct SL SL1 128 C8
Sandringham Crs
RYLN/HDSTN HA2 113 P8
STALE/WH AL4 38 G1
Sandringham Dr ASHF TW15 173 N7
WELL DA16 163 H8
Sandringham Gdns
BARK/HLT IG6 122 F1
CEND/HSY/T N8 118 F4
HEST TW5 153 H7
NFNCH/WDSP N12 97 N7
Sandringham Pk COB KT11 217 N8
Sandringham Rd BARK IG11 143 J1
BMLY BR1 183 M8
BRWN CM15 86 G9
CRICK NW2 116 E10
CROY/NA CR0 203 K5
FSTGT E7 121 P10
GLDGN NW11 117 H5
HACK E8 119 N10
LEY E10 121 J5
NTHLT UB5 133 P2
POTB/CUF EN6 59 L6
STWL/WRAY TW19 173 P1
WATN WD24 73 J3
WDGN N22 119 K1
WPK KT4 200 D10
Sandringham Wy CHES/WCR EN8 62 B10
Sandrock Pl CROY/NA CR0 224 C1
Sandrock Rd DORK RH4 272 A4
LEW SE13 160 F9
Sandroyd Wy COB KT11 217 P9
Sands End La FUL/PGN SW6 157 L7
Sands Farm Dr SL SL1 128 B6
Sandstone Rd LEE/GVPK SE12 183 N5
Sands Wy WFD IG8 102 C7
Sandtoft Rd CHARL SE7 161 N5
Sandway Rd STMC/STPC BR5 207 M4
Sandwell Crs KIL/WHAMP NW6 2 F1
Sandwich St STPAN WC1H 5 L10
Sandwick Cl MLHL NW7 96 D8
Sandy Bank Rd GVE DA12 190 E4
Sandy Bury ORP BR6 206 G10
Sandy Cl HERT/WAS SG14 25 J5
WOKS/MYFD GU22 232 F3
Sandycombe Rd
EBED/NFELT TW14 175 H4
RCH/KEW TW9 155 M8
Sandycoombe Rd TWK TW1 177 H2
Sandy Ct COB KT11 217 N9
Sandycroft ABYW SE2 163 K5
Sandy Cft EW KT17 220 F6
Sandycroft Rd AMS HP6 69 N5
Sandy Dr COB KT11 217 P7
EBED/NFELT TW14 174 F4
Sandy Hill Av WOOL/PLUM SE18 162 E4
Sandy Hill La WOOL/PLUM SE18 162 E3
Sandyhill Rd IL IG1 122 E9
Sandy Hill Rd WLGTN SM6 222 D5
WOOL/PLUM SE18 162 E4
Sandy Holt COB KT11 217 N9
Sandy La ASC SL5 192 F5
BELMT SM2 221 H4
BH/WHM TN16 262 G1
BRKHM/BTCW RH3 256 B10
BUSH WD23 74 B7
CDH/CHF RM16 168 E5
CHOB/PIR GU24 213 K5
COB KT11 217 N8
CRAWE RH10 285 P5
E/WMO/HCT KT8 198 G1
KTN/HRWW/W HA3 115 L4
KWD/TDW/WH KT20 239 J10
MEO DA13 189 K7
MTCM CR4 202 B1
NTHWD HA6 92 G3
ORP BR6 207 K7
OXTED RH8 261 H5
OXTED RH8 261 N3
RCHPK/HAM TW10 177 H5
RDART DA2 189 J6
REDH RH1 258 F10
REDH RH1 259 J8
REIG RH2 274 E1
RGUW GU3 248 C7
RGUW GU3 267 M5
RPLY/SEND GU23 232 F9
SEV TN13 247 K9
SHGR GU5 269 N7
SHGR GU5 270 B6
SOCK/AV RM15 145 P9
STMC/STPC BR5 185 N10
TEDD TW11 176 F10
VW GU25 194 B5
WOKS/MYFD GU22 232 E4
WOKS/MYFD GU22 233 K2
WOT/HER KT12 197 J6
WTHK RM20 166 G5
Sandy La North WLGTN SM6 222 E2
Sandy La South WLGTN SM6 222 D5
Sandy Ldg PIN * HA5 93 P7
Sandy Lodge Ct NTHWD * HA6 92 F6
Sandy Lodge La NTHWD HA6 92 E3
Sandy Lodge Rd
RKW/CH/CXG WD3 92 C3
Sandy Lodge Wy NTHWD HA6 92 F6
Sandy Md HOR/WEW KT19 219 M6
Sandymount Av STAN HA7 95 H6
Sandy Rdg CHST BR7 184 D9
Sandy Ri CFSP/GDCR SL9 90 B9
Sandy Rd ADL/WDHM KT15 215 K3
GLDGN NW11 117 L7
Sandy's Rw WCHPL E1 13 K4
Sandy Wy COB KT11 217 P8
CROY/NA CR0 204 E10
WOKS/MYFD GU22 232 F3
WOT/HER KT12 196 G8
Sanford La STNW/STAM N16 119 N7
Sanford St NWCR SE14 160 D5
Sanford Ter STNW/STAM N16 119 N8
Sanger Av CHSGTN KT9 219 L2
Sanger Dr RPLY/SEND GU23 232 F8
Sangers Dr HORL RH6 280 A5
Sangley Rd CAT SE6 182 G3
SNWD SE25 203 M4
Sangora Rd BTSEA SW11 157 N10
Sansom Rd WAN * E11 121 L7
Sansom St CMBW SE5 159 L6
Sans Wk CLKNW EC1R 12 C1
Santers La POTB/CUF EN6 59 H9
Santley St BRXS/STRHM SW2 158 F10
Santos Rd PUT/ROE SW15 179 K1
Sanway Cl BF/WBF KT14 215 P10
Sanway Rd BF/WBF KT14 215 P10
Saperton Wk LBTH SE11 17 P5
Sapho Pk GVE DA12 191 J7
Saphora Cl ORP BR6 226 G2
Sappers Cl SBW CM21 30 A1
Sapphire Cl BCTR RM8 123 M6
Sapphire Rd DEPT SE8 160 D3
Sappho Ct WOKN/KNAP GU21 231 K2
Saracen Cl CROY/NA CR0 203 L6
Saracens Head HHNE HP2 36 B5
Saracen St POP/IOD E14 140 F8
Sara Crs GRH DA9 166 F10
Sarah St BETH E2 7 K9
Sara Pk GVE DA12 191 H7
Saratoga Rd CLPT E5 120 B9
Sardinia St HOL/ALD WC2B 11 N6
Sarel Wy HORL RH6 280 C2
Sargeant Cl UX/CGN UB8 131 N5
Sarita Cl KTN/HRWW/W HA3 94 C10
Sark Cl HEST TW5 153 P6
Sarnesfield Rd ENC/FH * EN2 79 L8
Sarratt Av HHNE HP2 36 B1
Sarratt La RKW/CH/CXG WD3 71 L6
Sarratt Rd RKW/CH/CXG WD3 71 L3
Sarre Av HCH RM12 145 K1
Sarre Rd CRICK NW2 117 J10
Sarsby Dr STWL/WRAY TW19 172 D5
Sarsen Av HSLW TW3 153 N8
Sarsfeld Rd BAL SW12 180 A4
Sarsfield Rd GFD/PVL UB6 134 G4
Sartor Rd PECK SE15 160 C10
Sarum Complex UX/CGN * UB8 131 L4
Sarum Gn WEY KT13 196 F10
Sarum Pl HHNE HP2 35 P2
Sarum Ter BOW * E3 140 E6
Satanita Cl CAN/RD E16 142 A8
Satchell Md CDALE/KGS NW9 96 C9
Satchwell Rd BETH * E2 7 N10
Satinwood Ct HHS/BOV HP3 35 P8
Sattar Ms STNW/STAM * N16 119 L8
Saturn Cl CRAWW RH11 283 H9
Saturn Wy HHNE HP2 36 A3
Sauls Gn WAN E11 121 K8
Sauncey Av HARP AL5 20 A1
Saunders Cl CHES/WCR EN8 62 B4
CRAWE RH10 284 C7
GVW DA11 190 B5
POP/IOD * E14 140 E9
Saunders Copse
WOKS/MYFD GU22 231 N8
Saunders End AMS HP6 50 B10
Saunders La WOKS/MYFD GU22 231 L8
Saunders Ness Rd POP/IOD E14 161 J3
Saunders Rd HGDN/ICK UB10 132 A2
WOOL/PLUM SE18 163 J4
Saunders St LBTH SE11 18 A5
Saunders Wy DART DA1 187 N5
THMD SE28 143 L9
Saunderton Rd ALP/SUD HA0 114 G10
Saunton Av HYS/HAR UB3 152 G6
Saunton Rd HCH RM12 125 H7
Savage Gdns EHAM E6 142 C8
TWRH EC3N 13 K7
Savay Cl DEN/HRF UB9 111 K5
Savay La DEN/HRF UB9 111 K5
Savernake Ct STAN * HA7 94 G7
Savernake Rd ED N9 79 P10
HAMP NW3 118 A9
Savernake Wk CRAWE RH10 284 A10
Savery Dr SURB KT6 198 G7
Savile Cl NWMAL KT3 200 B5
THDIT KT7 198 E8
Savile Gdns CROY/NA CR0 203 N9
Savile Rw CONDST W1S 10 G7
Savill Cl CHESW * EN7 61 K1
Saville Crs ASHF TW15 174 E9
Saville Rd CAN/RD E16 142 B10
CHDH RM6 124 A4
CHSWK W4 156 A2
TWK TW1 176 E4
Saville Rw HAYES BR2 205 L8
Savill Gdns RYNPK SW20 200 D3
Savill Rw WFD IG8 101 L7
Savona Cl WIM/MER SW19 178 G10
Savona St VX/NE SW8 158 D6
Savoy Av HYS/HAR UB3 152 F4
Savoy Cl DEN/HRF UB9 91 N10
EDGW HA8 95 M6
SRTFD E15 141 K3
Savoy Ct TPL/STR * WC2R 11 M8
Savoy Hl TPL/STR WC2R 11 N8
Savoy Pde EN * EN1 79 M7
Savoy Pl CHCR WC2N 11 M8
Savoy Rd DART DA1 187 K1
Savoy Rw TPL/STR WC2R 11 N7
Savoy Steps TPL/STR * WC2R 11 N8
Savoy St TPL/STR WC2R 11 N7
Savoy Wy TPL/STR WC2R 11 N8
Savoy Wd EPP CM16 46 D7
Sawbill Cl YEAD UB4 133 L7
Sawells BROX EN10 44 E7
Sawkins Cl WIM/MER SW19 178 G5
Sawley Rd SHB W12 136 D10
Sawtry Cl CAR SM5 201 N7
Sawtry Wy BORE WD6 75 M4
Sawyer Cl ED N9 99 P3
Sawyer's Cl WDSR SL4 148 D6
Sawyer's Hall La BRWN CM15 107 H1
Sawyer's Hl RCHPK/HAM TW10 177 L3
Sawyers La POTB/CUF EN6 58 G10
Sawyers Lawn WEA W13 134 E8
Sawyer St STHWK SE1 18 E1
Sawyers Wy HHNE HP2 36 A6
Saxby Rd BRXS/STRHM SW2 180 F3
Saxham Rd BARK IG11 143 H3
Saxley HORL RH6 280 D3
Saxlingham Rd CHING E4 101 J4
Saxon Av FELT TW13 175 M5
Saxonbury Av SUN TW16 197 J3
Saxonbury Cl MTCM CR4 201 N3
Saxonbury Gdns SURB KT6 199 H8
Saxon Cl AMS HP6 69 J4
DTCH/LGLY SL3 150 C1
GVW DA11 189 P6
HARH RM3 105 N10
RBRW/HUT CM13 107 M4
RSEV TN14 246 G3
SURB KT6 199 J6
UX/CGN UB8 131 P7
WALTH E17 120 F5
Saxon Ct BORE WD6 75 K5
Saxon Dr ACT W3 135 N8
Saxonfield Cl BRXS/STRHM SW2 180 G3
Saxon Hl BH/WHM * TN16 262 G2
Saxon Pl EYN DA4 210 B5
Saxon Rd ASHF TW15 174 E9
BMLY BR1 183 L10
BOW E3 140 E4
CRAWE RH10 284 F8
CROY/NA CR0 203 L5
EHAM E6 142 C6
IL IG1 142 E1
RDART DA2 187 M7
STALE/WH AL4 21 J4
STHL UB1 133 M9
WBLY HA9 115 P8
WDGN N22 99 J9
WOT/HER KT12 197 L10
Saxons KWD/TDW/WH KT20 238 G7
Saxon Shore Wy GVE DA12 190 F2
Saxon Wy REIG RH2 257 J9
STHGT/OAK N14 78 E10
WDR/YW UB7 151 M5
WDSR SL4 171 N2
Saxony Pde HYS/HAR UB3 132 D7
Saxton Cl LEW SE13 161 J9
Saxton Ms WAT * WD17 73 H5
Saxville Rd STMC/STPC BR5 207 L3
Sayer Cl GRH DA9 188 F1
Sayers Cl LHD/OX KT22 236 B10
Sayers Gdns BERK HP4 33 M2
Sayesbury La UED N18 99 P6
Sayesbury Rd SBW CM21 29 P1
Sayes Ct ADL/WDHM KT15 215 L2
Sayes Court Farm Dr
ADL/WDHM KT15 215 L2
Sayes Court Rd STMC/STPC BR5 207 K3
Sayes Court St DEPT SE8 160 E4
Sayes Gdns SBW CM21 30 A1
Sayward Cl CSHM HP5 51 J5
Scabharbour Rd RSEV TN14 265 K9
Scadbury Gdns STMC/STPC BR5 207 K2
Scads Hill Cl ORP BR6 207 J6
Scafell Rd SL SL1 128 E7
Scala St FITZ W1T 11 H3
Scales Rd TOTM N17 119 N1
Scallows Cl CRAWE RH10 284 B6
Scallows Rd CRAWE RH10 284 B6
Scammell Wy WATW WD18 72 G10
Scampston Ms NKENS W10 136 G8
Scampton Rd HTHAIR TW6 174 A2
Scandrett St WAP * E1W 140 A10
Scarba Wk IS N1 6 G2
Scarborough Cl BELMT SM2 221 J6
BH/WHM TN16 243 P4
Scarborough Rd ED N9 100 B1
FSBYPK N4 119 H5
HTHAIR TW6 174 D2
WAN E11 121 J6
Scarborough St WCHPL E1 13 M6
Scarborough Wy SL SL1 148 G1
Scarbrook Rd CROY/NA CR0 203 K10
Scarle Rd ALP/SUD HA0 135 J1
Scarlet Cl STMC/STPC BR5 207 L4
Scarlet Rd CAT SE6 183 K6
Scarlett Cl WOKN/KNAP GU21 231 L4
Scarsbrook Rd BKHTH/KID SE3 162 A9
Scarsdale Pl KENS * W8 14 G3
Scarsdale Rd RYLN/HDSTN HA2 114 B8
Scarsdale Vls KENS W8 14 F4
Scarth Rd BARN SW13 156 C9
Scatterdells La KGLGY WD4 53 J6
Scatterdells Pk KGLGY * WD4 53 K6
Scawen Cl CAR SM5 222 B1
Scawen Rd DEPT SE8 160 D4
Scawfell St BETH E2 7 M8
Scaynes Link NFNCH/WDSP N12 97 K5
Sceptre Rd BETH E2 140 B5
Scholars Ms WGCW AL8 22 G3
Scholars Rd BAL SW12 180 D4
CHING E4 101 H2
Scholars Wk CFSP/GDCR SL9 90 B7
GUW GU2 267 N1
Scholars Wy AMS HP6 69 L4
Scholefield Rd ARCH N19 118 E6
Schonfeld Sq STNW/STAM N16 119 L7
School Cl BRKMPK AL9 42 A3
CHOB/PIR GU24 230 E1
DART DA1 164 G10
GU GU1 250 A8
Schoolfield Rd WTHK RM20 166 F5
School Green La EPP CM16 66 D1
School Hl REDH RH1 258 D4
School House La TEDD TW11 176 G10
Schoolhouse La WAP * E1W 140 C9
School La ADL/WDHM KT15 215 K1
AMSS HP7 68 F5
AMSS HP7 68 A8
BEAC HP9 89 J7
BFOR GU20 212 C3
BGR/WK TN15 247 N7
BRKMPK AL9 42 A3
BUSH WD23 94 A1
CFSP/GDCR SL9 90 A10
CHIG IG7 103 J5
CHOB/PIR GU24 230 D8
CHONG CM5 48 E3
DORK RH4 272 C3
EGH TW20 172 D8
EHSLY KT24 252 C5
EYN DA4 210 E6
HAT AL10 40 E3
HLW CM20 29 H8
KUT KT1 199 H1
LCOL/BKTW AL2 55 N10
LHD/OX KT22 236 C8
PIN * HA5 113 M2
RBRW/HUT CM13 107 P7
RDART DA2 189 H6
RDKG RH5 255 H3
RGUE GU4 251 P7
RGUW GU3 266 B5
RPLY/SEND GU23 234 C8
SHPTN TW17 196 C6
SLN SL2 129 L9
SLN SL2 129 N2
SURB KT6 199 L8
SWLY BR8 187 J10
WELL DA16 163 L9
WLYN AL6 23 P2
School Md ABLGY WD5 54 E8
School Pde DEN/HRF * UB9 91 M10
School Pas KUT KT1 199 L2
STHL UB1 133 N10
School Rd ASC SL5 192 C5
ASHF TW15 174 C9
BRWN CM15 86 D3
CHONG CM5 66 G6
CHST BR7 206 F1
DAGE RM10 144 B3
E/WMO/HCT KT8 198 C4
GVE DA12 190 F6
HPTN TW12 176 B9
HSLW TW3 154 B9
KUT * KT1 199 H1
POTB/CUF EN6 59 M6
WDR/YW UB7 151 N5
WLSDN NW10 136 A6
School Road Av HPTN TW12 176 B9
School Rw HHW HP1 35 J7
School Wy BCTR RM8 123 L8
Schoolway NFNCH/WDSP N12 97 N7
Schooner Cl BARK IG11 143 L5
POP/IOD E14 161 J2
POP/IOD * E14 161 J2
Schooner Ct GRH DA9 166 B10
Schroder Ct EGH TW20 171 N8
Schubert Rd BORE WD6 75 J10
PUT/ROE SW15 179 J1
Scillonian Rd GUW GU2 267 M1
Sclater St WCHPL E1 13 L1
Scoles Crs BRXS/STRHM SW2 181 H4
Scope Wy KUT KT1 199 K4
Scords La BH/WHM TN16 263 M8
Scoresby St STHWK SE1 12 C10
Scorton Av GFD/PVL UB6 134 F4
Scory Cl CRAWW RH11 283 K10
Scotch Common WEA W13 134 F7
Scot Gv PIN HA5 93 L8
Scotia Rd BRXS/STRHM SW2 181 H3
Scotland Bridge Rd
ADL/WDHM KT15 215 K7
Scotland Gn TOTM N17 99 N10
Scotland Green Rd PEND EN3 80 C9
Scotland Green Rd North
PEND EN3 80 C8
Scotland Rd BKHH IG9 101 P2
Scotlands Dr SLN SL2 128 G2
Scotney Cl ORP BR6 226 D1
Scots Cl STWL/WRAY TW19 173 N4
Scotscraig RAD WD7 74 E1
Scotsdale Cl BELMT SM2 221 H4
CHST BR7 207 H4
Scotsdale Rd LEE/GVPK SE12 183 N1
Scotshall La WARL CR6 243 H1
Scots Hl RKW/CH/CXG WD3 72 A10
Scots Hill Cl RKW/CH/CXG WD3 72 A10
Scots Mill La RKW/CH/CXG WD3 72 A10
Scotswood Cl BEAC HP9 88 C6
Scotswood St CLKNW * EC1R 12 B1
Scotswood Wk TOTM * N17 100 A8
Scott Av WARE SG12 26 G7
Scott Cl GUW GU2 249 M8
HOR/WEW KT19 219 P2
SLN SL2 109 H10
STRHM/NOR SW16 202 G1
WDR/YW UB7 152 A3
Scott Crs ERITH DA8 164 G7
RYLN/HDSTN HA2 114 A6
Scott Ellis Gdns STJWD NW8 3 L10
Scottes La BCTR RM8 123 N6
Scott Farm Cl THDIT KT7 198 G8
Scott Gdns HEST TW5 153 L6
Scott Lidgett Crs
BERM/RHTH SE16 19 N2
Scott Rd CDH/CHF RM16 168 D3
CRAWE RH10 284 A10
GVE DA12 190 G8
Scotts Av HAYES BR2 205 J2
SUN TW16 174 F10
Scotts Cl HCH RM12 125 K10
WARE SG12 26 C3
Scotts Dr HPTN TW12 176 A10
Scotts Farm Rd HOR/WEW KT19 219 P3
Scott's Grove Cl CHOB/PIR GU24 213 J9
Scott's Grove Rd
CHOB/PIR GU24 212 G10
Scott's Hl HORL RH6 281 L3
Scott's La HAYES BR2 205 J3
Scotts Pas WOOL/PLUM * SE18 162 E3
Scotts Rd BMLY BR1 183 M10
LEY E10 121 H6
NWDGN UB2 153 K2
SHB W12 156 E1
WARE SG12 26 C3
Scott St WCHPL E1 140 A6
Scotts Vw WGCW AL8 22 F6
Scotts Wy SEV TN13 246 F8
SUN TW16 174 F10
Scottswood Cl BUSH WD23 73 M6
Scottswood Rd BUSH WD23 73 M6
Scott Trimmer Wy HEST TW5 153 M8
Scottwell Dr CDALE/KGS NW9 116 C3
Scoulding Rd CAN/RD E16 141 L8
Scouler St POP/IOD E14 141 J9
Scout La CLAP SW4 158 D9
Scout Wy MLHL NW7 96 A5
Scovell Crs STHWK * SE1 18 E2
Scovell Rd STHWK SE1 18 E2
Scratchers La EYN DA4 210 C10
Scrattons Ter BARK IG11 143 N4
Scriveners Cl HHNE HP2 35 P6
Scriven St HACK E8 7 M5
Scrooby St CAT SE6 182 G2
Scrubbits Sq RAD WD7 74 F1
Scrubbitts Park Rd RAD WD7 74 F1
Scrubs La WLSDN NW10 136 D5
Scrutton St SDTCH EC2A 13 J2
Scudders Hl HART DA3 211 H6
Scutari Rd EDUL SE22 182 A1
Scylla Crs HTHAIR TW6 174 C3
Scylla Pl WOKN/KNAP * GU21 231 M5
Scylla Rd HTHAIR TW6 174 C2
PECK SE15 160 A9
Seaborough Rd CDH/CHF RM16 168 F2
Seabright St BETH E2 140 A5
Seabrook Dr WWKM BR4 205 K9
Seabrook Gdns ROMW/RG RM7 124 B5
Seabrook Rd BCTR RM8 123 N8
KGLGY WD4 54 E4
Seaburn Cl RAIN RM13 144 F5
Seacole Cl ACT W3 136 A8
Seacourt Rd ABYW SE2 163 N1
DTCH/LGLY SL3 150 E3
Seacroft Gdns OXHEY WD19 93 L4
Seafield Rd FBAR/BDGN N11 98 E5
Seaford Cl RSLP HA4 112 E7
Seaford Rd EN EN1 79 M8
HTHAIR TW6 173 N1
SEVS/STOTM N15 119 L3
WALTH E17 120 G1
WEA W13 134 G10
Seaford St STPAN WC1H 5 M10
Seaforth Av NWMAL KT3 200 E5
Seaforth Cl ROM RM1 104 F8
Seaforth Crs HBRY N5 119 K10
Seaforth Dr CHES/WCR EN8 62 C10
Seaforth Gdns HOR/WEW KT19 220 C1
WCHMH N21 98 G1
WFD IG8 101 P6
Seager Buildings DEPT * SE8 160 F7
Seager Pl BOW E3 140 E7
Seagrave Cl WCHPL * E1 140 C7
Seagrave Rd FUL/PGN SW6 14 F9
Seagry Rd WAN E11 121 M4
Sealand Rd HTHAIR TW6 174 B2
Seal Dr BGR/WK TN15 247 N7
Seal Hollow Rd SEV TN13 247 K10
Seal Rd SEV TN13 247 L7
Seal St HACK E8 119 N9
Seaman Cl LCOL/BKTW AL2 56 C1
Searches La ABLGY WD5 55 J3
Searchwood Rd WARL CR6 242 A4
Searle Hl REIG RH2 275 K2
Searles Cl BTSEA SW11 157 P6
Searles Dr EHAM E6 142 E7
Searles Rd STHWK SE1 19 H5
Sears St CMBW SE5 159 L6
Seasprite Cl NTHLT UB5 133 L5
Seaton Av GDMY/SEVK IG3 123 H10
Seaton Cl LBTH SE11 18 B7
PLSTW E13 141 M6
PUT/ROE SW15 178 E3
WHTN TW2 176 C2
Seaton Dr ASHF TW15 173 P5
Seaton Gdns RSLP HA4 113 H8
Seaton Rd ALP/SUD * HA0 135 K4
DART DA1 187 H3
HHS/BOV HP3 35 N9

HYS/HAR UB3 152 E3
LCOL/BKTW AL2 57 J3
MTCM CR4 201 P2
WELL DA16 163 M6
WHTN TW2 176 B2
Seaton St UED N18 99 P6
Sebastian Av BRWN CM15 87 M10
Sebastian St FSBYE EC1V 6 D10
Sebastopol Rd ED N9 99 P5
Sebbon St IS N1 6 D4
Sebergham Gv MLHL NW7 96 D8
Sebert Rd FSTGT E7 121 N10
Sebright Rd BAR EN5 76 G6
HHW HP1 35 K8
Secker Crs KTN/HRWW/W HA3 94 B9
Secker St STHWK SE1 12 A10
Second Av ACT W3 136 C10
ADL/WDHM KT15 215 L5
CHDH RM6 123 M3
DAGE RM10 144 C4
EN EN1 79 N9
GSTN WD25 73 L1
HDN NW4 116 G2
HLWS CM18 47 J1
HYS/HAR UB3 132 C10
KWD/TDW/WH * KT20 257 J2
MNPK E12 122 B9
MORT/ESHN SW14 156 B9
NKENS W10 8 B1
PLSTW E13 141 M5
UED N18 100 B5
WALTH E17 120 F3
WBLY HA9 115 J7
WOT/HER KT12 197 J6
WTHK RM20 166 F5
Second Cl E/WMO/HCT KT8 198 A4
Second Crs SL SL1 129 H7
Second Cross Rd WHTN TW2 176 C5
Second Wy WBLY HA9 115 N9
Sedan Wy WALW SE17 19 J7
Sedcombe Cl SCUP DA14 185 L7
Sedcote Rd PEND EN3 80 B9
Sedding St KTBR SW1X 16 C5
Seddon Rd MRDN SM4 201 N5
Seddon St FSBYW WC1X 5 N10
Sedgebrook Rd BKHTH/KID SE3 162 A8
Sedgecombe Av
KTN/HRWW/W HA3 115 H3
Sedgefield Cl CRAWE RH10 284 F6
HARH RM3 105 N5
Sedgefield Crs HARH RM3 105 N6
Sedgeford Rd SHB W12 136 C10
Sedge Gn HLWW/ROY CM19 45 L5
WAB EN9 45 K6
Sedgehill Rd CAT SE6 182 F8
Sedgemere Av EFNCH N2 117 M1
Sedgemere Rd ABYW SE2 163 M2
Sedgemoor Dr DAGE RM10 124 B9
Sedge Rd TOTM N17 100 B8
Sedgeway CAT SE6 183 L4
Sedgewick Cl CRAWE RH10 284 D7
Sedgewood Cl HAYES BR2 205 L7
Sedgmoor Pl CMBW SE5 159 M6
Sedgwick Av HGDN/ICK UB10 132 C2
Sedgwick Rd LEY E10 121 H7
Sedgwick St HOM E9 120 C10
Sedleigh Rd WAND/EARL SW18 179 J2
Sedlescombe Rd FUL/PGN SW6 14 E10
Sedley MEO DA13 189 M8
Sedley Cl EN EN1 80 A4
Sedley Gv DEN/HRF UB9 111 M2
Sedley Pl MYFR/PKLN W1K 10 E6
Sedley Ri LOU IG10 82 C6
Sedum Cl CDALE/KGS NW9 115 N3
Seeley Dr DUL SE21 181 M7
Seeleys HLWE CM17 29 M7
Seeleys Ct BEAC * HP9 88 C8
Seeleys Rd BEAC HP9 88 B7
Seelig Av CDALE/KGS NW9 116 D5
Seely Rd TOOT SW17 180 B9
Seer Green La BEAC HP9 89 J6
Seer Md BEAC HP9 89 J7
Seething La TWRH EC3N 13 K7
Seething Wells La SURB KT6 199 H6
Sefton Av KTN/HRWW/W HA3 94 C10
MLHL NW7 96 A6
Sefton Cl CHOB/PIR GU24 212 E9
SLN SL2 129 L3
STAL AL1 38 E5
STMC/STPC BR5 207 J4
Sefton Ct ENC/FH * EN2 79 J6
Sefton Paddock SLN SL2 129 M2
Sefton Pk SLN * SL2 129 M2
Sefton Rd CROY/NA CR0 203 P8
HOR/WEW KT19 220 A6
STMC/STPC BR5 207 J4
Sefton St PUT/ROE SW15 156 F8
Sefton Wy UX/CGN UB8 131 M8
Segrave Cl WEY KT13 216 B4
Sekforde St CLKNW EC1R 12 C2
Sekhon Ter FELT TW13 175 P6
Selah Dr SWLY BR8 208 D1
Selan Gdns YEAD UB4 133 J7
Selbie Av WLSDN NW10 116 C10
Selborne Av BXLY DA5 185 P4
MNPK E12 122 D9
Selborne Gdns GFD/PVL UB6 134 F4
HDN NW4 116 D2
Selborne Rd CMBW SE5 159 L8
CROY/NA CR0 203 M10
IL IG1 122 D7
NWMAL KT3 200 B2
SCUP DA14 185 L7
STHGT/OAK N14 98 F4
WALTH E17 120 E3
WDGN N22 98 G9
Selbourne Av ADL/WDHM KT15 215 L6
SURB KT6 199 L9
Selbourne Cl ADL/WDHM KT15 215 L6
CRAWE RH10 284 E3
Selbourne Rd GU GU1 250 D7
Selbourne Sq GDST RH9 260 B6
Selby Av STALW/RED * AL3 38 C6
Selby Cha RSLP HA4 113 J7
Selby Cl CHSGTN KT9 219 K4
CHST BR7 184 D9
Selby Gdns STHL UB1 133 P6
Selby Gn CAR SM5 201 P7
Selby Rd ASHF TW15 174 D9
CAR SM5 201 P7
EA W5 134 G6
PGE/AN SE20 203 P2
PLSTW E13 141 N7
TOTM N17 99 M7
WAN E11 121 K8
Selby St WCHPL E1 13 P2
Selby Wk WOKN/KNAP GU21 231 N4
Selcroft Rd PUR/KEN CR8 223 J8
Selden Hl HHNE HP2 35 N7
Selden Rd PECK SE15 160 B8
Sele Ml HERT/WAS SG14 25 J5
Sele Rd HERT/WAS SG14 25 J5
Selham Cl CRAWW RH11 283 K6
Selhurst Cl WIM/MER SW19 178 G4
WOKN/KNAP GU21 232 C1
Selhurst New Rd SNWD SE25 203 M6
Selhurst Pl CROY/NA CR0 203 M6
Selhurst Rd ED N9 99 L4
SNWD SE25 203 M5
Selinas La BCTR RM8 123 P5
Selkirk Dr ERITH DA8 164 F7
Selkirk Rd TOOT SW17 179 P7
WHTN TW2 176 B5
Sellar's Hl RGODL GU7 267 J10
Sell Cl CHESW EN7 61 J1
Sellers Hall Cl FNCH N3 97 K8
Sellincourt Rd TOOT SW17 179 P8
Sellindge Cl BECK BR3 182 E10
Sellons Av WLSDN NW10 136 C3
Sells Rd WARE SG12 26 E1
The Sells GU GU1 268 D2
Sellwood Dr BAR EN5 76 G9
Selsdon Av SAND/SEL CR2 223 L3
Selsdon Cl CRW RM5 104 D9
SURB KT6 199 K5
Selsdon Crs SAND/SEL CR2 224 B6
Selsdon Park Rd SAND/SEL CR2 224 D5
Selsdon Rd ADL/WDHM KT15 215 K7
CRICK NW2 116 C7
PLSTW E13 141 P3
SAND/SEL CR2 223 M4
WAN E11 121 M5
WNWD SE27 181 J6
Selsdon Wy POP/IOD E14 160 G2
Selsea Pl STNW/STAM N16 119 M10
Selsey Crs WELL DA16 163 N7
Selsey St POP/IOD E14 140 F7
Selsfield Rd CRAWE RH10 285 P10
Selvage La MLHL NW7 96 A6
Selway Cl PIN HA5 113 J2
Selwood Cl STWL/WRAY * TW19 173 M2
Selwood Gdns
STWL/WRAY TW19 173 M2
Selwood Pl SKENS SW7 15 L7
Selwood Rd BRW CM14 106 E4
CHEAM SM3 201 J8
CHSGTN KT9 219 J1
CROY/NA CR0 204 A9
WOKS/MYFD GU22 232 E6
Selwood Ter SKENS SW7 15 L7
Selworthy Cl WAN E11 121 M3
Selworthy Rd CAT SE6 182 E6
Selwyn Av CHING E4 101 H7
GDMY/SEVK IG3 123 J4
HAT AL10 40 A5
RCH/KEW TW9 155 L9
Selwyn Cl CRAWE RH10 284 D4
HSLWW TW4 153 M10
WDSR SL4 148 C8
Selwyn Ct EDGW HA8 95 N8
Selwyn Crs HAT AL10 40 B4
WELL DA16 163 L10
Selwyn Dr HAT AL10 40 B4
Selwyn Rd BOW E3 140 E4
NWMAL KT3 200 A5
PLSTW E13 141 N3
TIL RM18 168 C8
WLSDN NW10 136 B2
Semaphore Rd GU GU1 268 B2
Semley Pl BGVA SW1W 16 D6
Semley Rd STRHM/NOR SW16 202 F2
Semper Cl WOKN/KNAP GU21 231 K3
Semper Rd CDH/CHF RM16 168 F1
Sempill Rd HHS/BOV HP3 35 P9
Senate St PECK SE15 160 B8
Send Barns La RPLY/SEND GU23 233 H10
Send Cl RPLY/SEND GU23 232 F9
Send Hl RPLY/SEND GU23 250 F1
Send Marsh Rd RPLY/SEND GU23 233 H9
Send Parade Cl
RPLY/SEND * GU23 232 F9
Send Rd RPLY/SEND GU23 232 F9
Seneca Rd THHTH CR7 203 K4
Senga Rd MTCM CR4 202 B8
Senhouse Rd CHEAM SM3 200 G10
Senior St BAY/PAD W2 8 G3
Senlac Rd LEE/GVPK SE12 183 N4
Sennen Rd EN EN1 99 N1
Senrab St WCHPL E1 140 C8
Sentinel Cl YEAD UB4 133 M6
September Wy STAN HA7 94 G7
Sequoia Cl BUSH WD23 94 C2
Sequoia Gdns ORP BR6 207 J7
Sequoia Pk CRAWW RH11 283 N9
PIN HA5 94 A7
Serbin Cl WAN E11 121 H5
Sergehill La ABLGY WD5 55 H2
Serjeant's Inn EMB * EC4Y 12 B6
Serle St LINN WC2A 11 P5
Sermon Dr SWLY BR8 208 D3
Sermon La BLKFR EC4V 12 E6
Serpentine Rd BAY/PAD W2 9 P10
SEV TN13 247 K9
Service Rd HORL RH6 280 A7
The Service Rd POTB/CUF EN6 59 K8
Service Route No 1 SRTFD E15 141 J2
Service Route No 2 SRTFD E15 141 J2
Service Route No 3 SRTFD E15 141 J1
Servicen Dr BMLY BR1 206 A1
Setchell Est STHWK SE1 19 L5
Setchell Rd STHWK SE1 19 L5
Setchell Wy STHWK SE1 19 L5
Seton Gdns DAGW RM9 143 M2
Settle Rd HARH RM3 105 P5
Settles St WCHPL E1 13 P4
Settrington Rd FUL/PGN SW6 157 L8
Seven Acres CAR SM5 201 P9
NTHWD HA6 93 H7
SWLY BR8 208 E6
Seven Arches Ap WEY KT13 216 A4
Seven Arches Rd BRW CM14 107 K4
Sevenex Pde WBLY * HA9 115 K10
Seven Hills Cl WEY KT13 216 F5
Sevenhills Rd IVER SL0 110 E10
Seven Hills Rd WOT/HER KT12 216 F4
Seven Hills Rd (South) COB KT11 216 F9
Seven Kings Rd GDMY/SEVK IG3 123 H6
Sevenoaks By-Pass SEV TN13 264 F2
Sevenoaks Cl BELMT SM2 221 K6
HARH RM3 105 K5
Sevenoaks Rd BROCKY SE4 182 E2
ORP BR6 227 J5
ORP BR6 227 J1
RSEV TN14 247 J2
Sevenoaks Wy STMC/STPC BR5 207 M2
Seven Sisters Rd HOLWY N7 118 G8
Seventh Av HYS/HAR UB3 133 H10
KWD/TDW/WH * KT20 257 J2
MNPK E12 122 C9
Severalls Av CSHM HP5 51 H6
Severn TIL RM18 169 L2
Severnake Cl POP/IOD E14 160 F3
Severn Av GPK RM2 125 J1
NKENS W10 2 B10
Severn Crs DTCH/LGLY SL3 150 E4
Severn Dr EN EN1 79 P4
ESH/CLAY KT10 198 F9
UPMR RM14 126 C4
WOT/HER KT12 197 L9
Severnmead HHNE HP2 35 P3
Severn Rd CRAWE RH10 284 D8
SOCK/AV RM15 146 B8
Severns Fld EPP CM16 65 K5
Severnvale LCOL/BKTW * AL2 56 D2
Severn Wy GSTN WD25 55 K10
WLSDN NW10 116 C10
Severus Rd BTSEA SW11 157 P10
Seville Ms IS N1 7 J4
Seville St KTBR SW1X 16 B2
Sevington Rd HDN NW4 116 E4
Sevington St MV/WKIL W9 8 G2
Seward Rd BECK BR3 204 C2
HNWL W7 154 F1
Sewardstone Rd BETH E2 140 B4
CHING E4 80 G8
WAB EN9 63 H10
Sewardstone St WAB EN9 63 H10
Sewardstone Wy WAB EN9 81 H2
Seward St FSBYE EC1V 12 D1
Sewdley St CLPT E5 120 C8
Sewell Cl STALE/WH AL4 39 K6
Sewell Harris Cl HLW CM20 29 J10
Sewell Rd ABYW SE2 163 K1
Sewells WGCW AL8 23 H2
Sewell St PLSTW E13 141 M5
Sewill Cl HORL RH6 279 J8
Sextant Av POP/IOD E14 161 J3
Sexton Cl CHESW EN7 61 J1
RAIN RM13 144 G3
Sexton Rd TIL RM18 168 C7
Seymer Rd ROM RM1 124 E1
Seymour Av CTHM CR3 241 K9
EW KT17 220 E5
MRDN SM4 200 G7
TOTM N17 99 P10
Seymour Cl E/WMO/HCT KT8 198 B5
LOU IG10 82 B10
PIN HA5 93 N9
Seymour Ct COB * KT11 216 G9
Seymour Crs HHNE HP2 35 P6
Seymour Dr HAYES BR2 206 C8
Seymour Gdns BROCKY SE4 160 C9
BRYLDS KT5 199 L5
FELT TW13 175 J7
IL IG1 122 C6
RSLP HA4 113 L6
TWK TW1 176 G3
Seymour Ms EW KT17 220 D6
MBLAR W1H 10 C5
Seymour Pl MBLAR W1H 9 P4
SNWD SE25 204 A4
WOKS/MYFD GU22 231 N6
Seymour Rd BERK HP4 33 K3
CAR SM5 222 B2
CDH/CHF RM16 167 H2
CEND/HSY/T N8 119 J3
CHING E4 100 G2
CHSWK W4 155 P3
CSTG HP8 89 P5
E/WMO/HCT KT8 198 B5
ED N9 100 A3
EHAM E6 142 A3
FNCH N3 97 L8
GVW DA11 190 A4
HPTN TW12 176 B8
KUT KT1 199 J1
LEY E10 120 F6
MTCM CR4 202 B7
SL SL1 149 H1
STALW/RED AL3 38 D3
TIL RM18 168 C7
WAND/EARL SW18 179 J3
WIM/MER SW19 178 G6
Seymours HLWW/ROY CM19 46 C4
Seymour St BAY/PAD W2 10 A6
WOOL/PLUM SE18 162 F3
Seymour Ter PGE/AN SE20 204 A1
Seymour Vls PGE/AN SE20 204 A1
Seymour Wk SWCM DA10 189 K3
WBPTN SW10 15 J9
Seymour Wy SUN TW16 174 F9
Seyssel St POP/IOD E14 161 H3
Shaa Rd ACT W3 136 A9
Shabden Cottages
COUL/CHIP * CR5 240 A7
Shacklands Rd RSEV TN14 228 D7
Shackleford Rd MFD/CHID GU8 266 C10
WOKS/MYFD GU22 232 D6
Shacklegate La TEDD TW11 176 D7
Shackleton Cl FSTH SE23 182 A5
Shackleton Rd CRAWE RH10 283 P10
SL SL1 129 L9
STHL UB1 133 N9
Shackleton Wy ABLGY * WD5 55 H8
WGCE AL7 23 N5
Shacklewell La HACK E8 119 N9
Shacklewell Rd STNW/STAM N16 119 N9
Shacklewell Rw HACK E8 119 N9
Shacklewell St BETH E2 13 M1
Shadbolt Cl WPK KT4 200 C9
Shad Thames STHWK SE1 13 L10
Shadwell Dr NTHLT UB5 133 N5
Shadwell Gdns WCHPL * E1 140 B9
Shadwell Pierhead WAP E1W 140 B9
Shady Bush Cl BUSH WD23 94 B1
Shady La WAT WD17 73 J6
Shaef Wy TEDD TW11 176 F10
Shafter Rd DAGE RM10 144 D1
Shaftesbury LOU IG10 82 A7
Shaftesbury Av BAR EN5 77 M8
EBED/NFELT TW14 175 H2
KTN/HRWW/W HA3 115 J4
MYFR/PICC W1J 11 H7
NWDGN UB2 153 P3
PEND EN3 80 C6
RYLN/HDSTN HA2 114 A6
Shaftesbury Cir
RYLN/HDSTN * HA2 114 B6
Shaftesbury Ct
RKW/CH/CXG * WD3 72 D9
Shaftesbury Crs STA TW18 173 N10
Shaftesbury Gdns WLSDN NW10 136 B6
Shaftesbury La DART DA1 166 A10
Shaftesbury Ms KENS * W8 14 F4
Shaftesbury Pde
RYLN/HDSTN * HA2 114 B6
Shaftesbury Pl BARB * EC2Y 12 E4
Shaftesbury Rd ARCH N19 118 F6
BECK BR3 204 E2
CAR SM5 201 N7
CHING E4 101 J2
CHOB/PIR GU24 230 E2
CRAWE RH10 284 E9
EPP CM16 65 J5
FSTGT E7 141 P2
LEY E10 120 G3
RCH/KEW TW9 155 K9
ROM RM1 124 G4
UED N18 99 M7
WAT WD17 73 K7
WOKS/MYFD GU22 232 E3
The Shaftesburys BARK IG11 142 F4
Shaftesbury St IS N1 6 F8
Shaftesbury Ter HMSMTH * W6 156 C3
Shaftesbury Wy WHTN TW2 176 C6
Shaftesbury Waye YEAD UB4 133 J7
Shafto Ms KTBR SW1X 16 A4
Shafton Ms HOM * E9 140 C3
Shafton Rd HOM E9 140 C3
Shaggy Calf La SLN SL2 129 M9
Shakespeare Av
EBED/NFELT TW14 175 H2
FBAR/BDGN N11 98 D6
TIL RM18 168 E8
WLSDN NW10 135 P3
YEAD UB4 133 J6
Shakespeare Crs MNPK E12 142 C2
WLSDN NW10 136 A3
Shakespeare Dr
KTN/HRWW/W HA3 115 L4
Shakespeare Gdns EFNCH N2 118 A2
Shakespeare Rd ACT W3 135 P10
ADL/WDHM KT15 215 N1
BXLYHN DA7 163 P7
DART DA1 165 P10
FNCH * N3 97 K9
HARP AL5 20 A2
HNHL SE24 181 J1
HNWL W7 134 E9
MLHL NW7 96 D5
ROM RM1 124 G4
WALTH E17 100 C10
Shakespeare Sq BARK/HLT IG6 102 E7
Shakespeare St WATN WD24 73 J4
Shakespeare Ter
RCH/KEW * TW9 155 M9
Shakespeare Wy FELT TW13 175 K7
Shakletons CHONG CM5 67 P4
Shakspeare Ms STNW/STAM N16 119 M9
Shakspeare Wk
STNW/STAM N16 119 M9
Shalcomb St WBPTN SW10 15 K10
Shalcross Dr CHES/WCR EN8 62 E6
Shaldon Dr MRDN SM4 201 H5
RSLP HA4 113 K8
Shaldon Rd EDGW HA8 95 L10
Shaldon Wy WOT/HER KT12 197 K10
Shalfleet Dr NKENS W10 136 G9
Shalford Cl ORP BR6 226 F1
Shalford Ct IS * N1 6 C7
Shalford La RGUE GU4 268 B5
Shalford Rd GU GU1 268 A3
Shalimar Gdns ACT W3 135 P9
Shalimar Rd ACT W3 135 P9
Shallcross Crs HAT AL10 40 C7
Shallons Rd ELTH/MOT SE9 184 E7
Shalstone Rd MORT/ESHN SW14 155 N9
Shalston Vls SURB KT6 199 L6
The Shambles GU GU1 268 A2
Shambrook Rd CHESW EN7 61 J1
Shamrock Cl LHD/OX KT22 236 C7
Shamrock Rd CROY/NA CR0 202 G6
GVE DA12 191 H3
Shamrock St CLAP SW4 158 E9
Shamrock Wy STHGT/OAK N14 98 C2
Shandon Rd CLAP SW4 180 D2
Shand St STHWK SE1 19 K1
Shandy St WCHPL E1 140 C7
Shanklin Cl CHESW EN7 61 N5
Shanklin Gdns OXHEY WD19 93 K5
Shanklin Rd CEND/HSY/T N8 118 E3
SEVS/STOTM N15 119 P2
Shannon Cl CRICK NW2 116 G8
HEST TW5 153 L4
Shannon Gv BRXN/ST SW9 158 G10
Shannon Pl STJWD NW8 3 P7
Shannon Wy BECK BR3 182 G9
SOCK/AV RM15 146 B8
Shantock Hall La HHS/BOV HP3 52 B5
Shantock La HHS/BOV HP3 52 B6
Shantung Pl CSHM * HP5 51 H9
Shap Crs CAR SM5 202 A8
Shapland Wy PLMGR N13 98 D6
Shapwick Cl FBAR/BDGN N11 98 A6
Shardcroft Av HNHL SE24 181 J1
Shardeloes Rd BROCKY SE4 160 E8
Shard's Sq PECK SE15 19 P10
Sharland Cl THHTH CR7 203 H6
Sharland Rd GVE DA12 190 F5
Sharman Ct SCUP DA14 185 K7
Sharnbrooke Cl WELL DA16 163 M9
Sharney Av DTCH/LGLY SL3 150 E2
Sharon Cl CRAWE RH10 284 B10
GT/LBKH KT23 235 P10
HOR/WEW KT19 219 P9
SURB KT6 199 H8
Sharon Gdns HOM E9 140 B3
Sharon Rd CHSWK W4 156 A4
PEND EN3 80 D6
Sharpcroft HHNE HP2 35 N4
Sharpecroft HLWW/ROY CM19 46 F1
Sharpes La HHW HP1 34 E7
Sharples Hall St CAMTN NW1 4 B4
Sharps La RSLP HA4 112 E5
Sharpthorne Cl CRAWW RH11 283 J7
Sharp Wy DART DA1 165 N9
Sharratt St PECK SE15 160 B5
Sharsted St WALW SE17 18 C8
Sharvel La NTHLT UB5 133 H3
Shavers Pl MYFR/PICC W1J 11 J8
Shaw Av BARK IG11 143 P4
Shawbridge HLWW/ROY CM19 46 F4
Shawbrooke Rd ELTH/MOT SE9 162 A10
Shawbury Rd EDUL SE22 181 N1
Shaw Cl BUSH WD23 94 D3
CHERT KT16 214 F3
CHES/WCR EN8 62 B5
EW KT17 220 C7
HCH RM12 125 J6
SAND/SEL CR2 223 N8
THMD SE28 143 L10
Shaw Crs SAND/SEL CR2 223 M8
TIL RM18 168 E7
Shaw Dr WOT/HER KT12 197 K7
Shawfield Pk BMLY BR1 206 A2
Shawfield St CHEL SW3 15 P8
Shawford Rd HOR/WEW KT19 220 A3
Shaw Gdns BARK IG11 143 P4
Shaw Gv KWD/TDW/WH KT20 239 H10
Shawley Crs EPSOM KT18 238 F4
Shawley Wy EPSOM KT18 238 F4
Shaw Rd BH/WHM TN16 243 P6
BMLY BR1 183 L6
EDUL SE22 159 M10
PEND EN3 80 C5
Shaw's Cottages FSTH SE23 182 D6
Shaw Sq WALTH E17 100 D9
Shaws Rd CRAWE RH10 283 P6
The Shaws WGCE AL7 23 M6
The Shaw CHST * BR7 184 F10
Shaw Wy WLGTN SM6 222 F4
Shaxton Crs CROY/NA CR0 225 H5
Sheaf Cottages THDIT * KT7 198 D8
Sheares Hoppit WARE SG12 28 A1
Shearing Dr MRDN SM4 201 M7
Shearling Wy HOLWY N7 5 M1
Shearman Rd BKHTH/KID SE3 161 L10
Shearwater HART DA3 211 N3
Shearwater Rd SUT SM1 221 J2
Shearwater Wy YEAD UB4 133 L8
Shearwood Crs DART DA1 164 G9
Sheath La LHD/OX KT22 218 A9
Sheaths Cottages THDIT * KT7 198 G7
Sheaveshill Av CDALE/KGS NW9 116 B1
Sheaveshill Pde
CDALE/KGS * NW9 116 B2
Sheehy Wy SLN SL2 129 N9
Sheen Common Dr
RCHPK/HAM TW10 155 M10
Sheen Court Rd
RCHPK/HAM TW10 155 M10
Sheendale Rd RCH/KEW TW9 155 L10
Sheenewood SYD SE26 182 A8
Sheen Gate Gdns
MORT/ESHN SW14 155 P10
Sheen Gv IS N1 6 A5
Sheen La MORT/ESHN SW14 155 P10
Sheen Pk RCH/KEW TW9 155 K10
Sheen Rd RCHPK/HAM TW10 155 K10
STMC/STPC BR5 207 J4
Sheen Wy WLGTN SM6 222 G2
Sheen Wd MORT/ESHN SW14 177 P1
Sheepbarn La WARL CR6 225 M8
Sheepcot Dr GSTN WD25 55 K10
Sheepcote WGCE AL7 23 K8
Sheepcote Cl BEAC HP9 88 B7
HEST TW5 153 H6
Sheepcote Gdns DEN/HRF UB9 111 K4
Sheepcote La BTSEA SW11 158 A8
STALE/WH AL4 21 K3
STMC/STPC BR5 208 B4
Sheepcote Rd HHNE HP2 36 A6
HRW HA1 114 E4
WDSR SL4 148 D8
Sheepcotes Rd CHDH RM6 123 N2
Sheepcot La GSTN WD25 55 J9
Sheepfield La AMSS HP7 69 J5
Sheepfold Rd GUW GU2 249 L7
Sheephouse Gn RDKG RH5 271 N5
Sheephouse La RDKG RH5 271 P10
RDKG RH5 271 N5
Sheephouse Rd HHS/BOV HP3 36 A8
Sheephouse Wy NWMAL KT3 200 A8
Sheeplands Av GU GU1 250 F8
Sheep La HACK E8 140 A3
Sheep Wk REIG RH2 257 J7
Sheepwalk SHPTN TW17 196 A6
Sheep Walk Ms WIM/MER SW19 178 G9
Sheering Dr HLWE CM17 29 P8
Sheering Lower Rd SBW CM21 30 A3
Sheering Mill La SBW CM21 30 A1
Sheering Rd HLWE CM17 29 P7
Sheerwater Av ADL/WDHM KT15 215 H8
Sheerwater Rd ADL/WDHM KT15 215 H8
CAN/RD E16 142 A7
WOKN/KNAP GU21 215 H8
Sheethanger La HHS/BOV HP3 35 K10
Sheet's Heath La
CHOB/PIR GU24 230 F5
Sheet St WDSR SL4 149 J8
Sheet Street Rd WDSR SL4 170 E5
Sheffield Cl CRAWE RH10 284 C9
Sheffield Dr HARH RM3 105 P6
Sheffield Rd EBED/NFELT TW14 174 D2
SL SL1 129 H8
Sheffield St LINN * WC2A 11 N6
Sheffield Ter KENS W8 14 E1
Sheffield Wy HTHAIR TW6 174 E1
Shefton Ri NTHWD HA6 93 H8
Sheila Rd CRW RM5 104 C8
The Sheilings BGR/WK TN15 247 N6
EMPK RM11 125 N3
Shelbourne Cl PIN HA5 113 N1
Shelbourne Rd TOTM N17 100 A9
Shelburne Dr HSLWW TW4 175 P2
Shelburne Rd HOLWY N7 118 G9
Shelbury Cl SCUP DA14 185 K6
Shelbury Rd EDUL SE22 182 A1
Sheldon Av CLAY IG5 102 E10
HGT N6 118 A5
Sheldon Cl CHESW EN7 61 L2
CRAWE RH10 284 E8
HLWE CM17 47 P1
LEE/GVPK SE12 183 N1
PGE/AN SE20 204 A1
REIG RH2 275 L1
Sheldon Ct GU GU1 268 C1
Sheldon Rd BXLYHN DA7 164 A7
CRICK NW2 116 G9
DAGW RM9 143 P2
UED N18 99 M5
Sheldon St CROY/NA CR0 203 K10
Sheldrake Cl CAN/RD E16 142 C10
Sheldrake Pl KENS W8 14 D1
Sheldrick Cl MTCM CR4 201 N2
Shelduck Cl FSTGT E7 121 L10
Sheldwich Ter HAYES * BR2 206 B6
Shelford Pl STNW/STAM N16 119 L8
Shelford Ri NRWD SE19 181 M10
Shelford Rd BAR EN5 76 F10
Shelgate Rd BTSEA SW11 180 A1
Shellbank La RDART DA2 188 G8
Shell Cl HAYES BR2 206 B6
Shellduck Cl CDALE/KGS NW9 96 B10
Shelley Av GFD/PVL UB6 134 C5
HCH RM12 124 G7
MNPK E12 142 B1
Shelley Cl CHONG CM5 67 N2
COUL/CHIP CR5 240 G3
CRAWE RH10 284 D5
DTCH/LGLY SL3 150 D4
EDGW HA8 95 M5
GFD/PVL UB6 134 C5
NTHWD HA6 92 G6
ORP BR6 207 H10
YEAD UB4 133 H7
Shelley Crs HEST TW5 153 L7
STHL UB1 133 N8
Shelley Dr WELL DA16 163 H7
Shelley Gdns ALP/SUD HA0 115 H7

Shelley Gv LOU IG10 ....82 C8
Shelley La DEN/HRF UB9 ....91 K8
Shelley Ms HHS/BOV * HP3 ....35 N9
Shelley Pl TIL RM18 ....168 E7
Shelley Rd CSHM HP5 ....50 G5
WLSDN NW10 ....136 A3
Shelleys La RSEV TN14 ....245 K2
Shelley Wy TOOT SW17 ....179 N9
Shellfield Cl STWL/WRAY TW19 ....173 K1
Shellgrove Rd
STNW/STAM * N16 ....119 M10
Shellness Rd CLPT E5 ....120 A10
Shell Rd LEW SE13 ....160 G9
Shellwood Dr RDKG RH5 ....273 H6
Shellwood Rd BTSEA SW11 ....158 A8
REIG RH2 ....274 A7
Shelly Cl BNSTD SM7 ....238 G1
Shelmerdine Cl BOW E3 ....140 F7
Shelson Av FELT TW13 ....174 G6
Shelson Pde FELT * TW13 ....174 G6
Shelton Av WARL CR6 ....242 B3
Shelton Cl GUW GU2 ....249 M5
WARL CR6 ....242 B3
Shelton Rd WIM/MER SW19 ....201 K1
Shelton St LSQ/SEVD * WC2H 11 L6
Shelvers Gn KWD/TDW/WH KT20 ....238 F7
Shelvers Hl KWD/TDW/WH KT20 ....238 F7
Shelvers Sp KWD/TDW/WH KT20 ....238 F7
Shelvers Wy
KWD/TDW/WH KT20 ....238 F7
Shenden Cl SEV TN13 ....265 K4
Shenden Wy SEV TN13 ....265 K4
Shenfield Cl COUL/CHIP CR5 ....240 C5
Shenfield Ct HLWS CM18 ....46 F4
Shenfield Crs BRWN CM15 ....107 K3
Shenfield Gdns RBRW/HUT CM13 ....87 N10
Shenfield Gn BRWN CM15 ....107 M1
Shenfield Pl BRWN CM15 ....107 K1
Shenfield Rd BRWN CM15 ....107 K2
WFD IG8 ....101 N8
Shenfield St IS N1 ....7 K8
Shenley Av RSLP HA4 ....112 G7
Shenleybury RAD WD7 ....57 K6
Shenleybury Cottages RAD WD7 ....57 K7
Shenley Hl RAD WD7 ....56 G10
Shenley La LCOL/BKTW AL2 ....56 G1
Shenley Rd BORE WD6 ....75 M7
CMBW SE5 ....159 M7
DART DA1 ....187 P2
HEST TW5 ....153 M7
HHNE HP2 ....36 C1
RAD WD7 ....75 J1
Shenstone Dr SL SL1 ....128 C6
Shenstone Gdns HARH RM3 ....105 K9
Shenstone Hl BERK HP4 ....34 B4
Shenstone Pk ASC SL5 ....192 D4
Shenwood Ct BORE WD6 ....75 M3
Shepherd Cl CRAWE RH10 ....283 N10
Shepherdess Pl FSBYE EC1V 6 F9
Shepherdess Wk IS N1 ....6 F7
Shepherd Market
MYFR/PICC * W1J 10 E10
Shepherd's Bush Gn SHB W12 ....156 F1
Shepherd's Bush Market
SHB W12 ....156 F1
Shepherd's Bush Pl SHB * W12 ....156 G1
Shepherd's Bush Rd
HMSMTH W6 ....156 F2
Shepherds Cl CHDH RM6 ....123 N3
HGT N6 ....118 C4
ORP BR6 ....207 J10
SHPTN TW17 ....196 C6
UX/CGN * UB8 ....131 M6
Shepherds Ct HERT/WAS SG14 ....25 K2
Shepherds Gn CHST BR7 ....184 G10
HHW HP1 ....35 H7
Shepherd's Hl GUW GU2 ....249 M8
HARH RM3 ....105 P10
HGT N6 ....118 C4
REDH RH1 ....258 D2
Shepherds La BEAC HP9 ....88 E10
BFOR GU20 ....212 F2
DART DA1 ....187 H4
GUW GU2 ....249 L7
HOM * E9 ....120 C10
RKW/CH/CXG WD3 ....70 G10
Shepherd's Leas
ELTH/MOT * SE9 ....162 G10
Shepherds Pl MYFR/PKLN W1K 10 C7
Shepherds Rd WATW WD18 ....72 G7
Shepherd St GVW DA11 ....190 A3
MYFR/PICC W1J 10 E10
Shepherds Wk BUSH WD23 ....94 C3
CRICK NW2 ....116 D7
EPSOM KT18 ....237 N7
HAMP NW3 ....117 N10
Shepherds Wy BRKMPK AL9 ....59 M3
CSHM HP5 ....51 J9
RGUE GU4 ....268 B4
RKW/CH/CXG WD3 ....91 L1
SAND/SEL CR2 ....224 C4
Shepiston La WDR/YW UB7 ....152 C3
Shepley Cl CAR SM5 ....202 B10
HCH RM12 ....125 L10
Shepley Dr ASC SL5 ....193 J6
Shepley End ASC SL5 ....193 H5
Shepley Ms PEND EN3 ....80 F4
Sheppard Cl EN EN1 ....80 A4
SURB KT6 ....199 K4
Sheppard Dr BERM/RHTH SE16 ....160 A4
Sheppards HLWW/ROY CM19 ....46 C4
Sheppards Cl STALW/RED AL3 ....38 D3
Sheppard St CAN/RD E16 ....141 L6
Shepperton Cl BORE WD6 ....76 A5
Shepperton Court Dr
SHPTN TW17 ....196 C5
Shepperton Marina
SHPTN * TW17 ....196 F6
Shepperton Rd IS N1 ....6 F5
STA TW18 ....195 N4
STMC/STPC BR5 ....206 F6
Shepperton Studios
SHPTN * TW17 ....196 A3
Sheppey Cl CRAWW RH11 ....283 L10
ERITH DA8 ....165 J6
Sheppey Gdns DAGW RM9 ....143 M2
Sheppey Rd DAGW RM9 ....143 L2
Sheppey's La KGLGY WD4 ....54 F4
Sheppey Wk IS N1 ....6 F3
Sheppy Pl GVE DA12 ....190 E3
Shepton Houses BETH * E2 ....140 B5
Sherard Rd ELTH/MOT SE9 ....184 B1
Sherards Orch HLWW/ROY CM19 ....46 E3
Sheraton Cl BORE WD6 ....75 L9
Sheraton Dr HOR/WEW KT19 ....219 P9
Sheraton Ms WATW * WD18 ....72 F8
Sherborne Av NWDGN UB2 ....153 P3
PEND EN3 ....80 B6
Sherborne Cl DTCH/LGLY SL3 ....151 H7
EPSOM KT18 ....238 F3
YEAD UB4 ....133 K8
Sherborne Crs CAR SM5 ....201 P7
Sherborne Gdns
CDALE/KGS NW9 ....115 M1
WEA W13 ....134 G8
Sherborne La MANHO EC4N 12 G7
Sherborne Pl NTHWD HA6 ....92 E7
Sherborne Rd CHEAM SM3 ....201 K9
CHSGTN KT9 ....219 K2
EBED/NFELT TW14 ....174 E3
STMC/STPC BR5 ....207 J5
Sherborne St IS N1 ....6 G5
Sherborne Vls WEA * W13 ....134 G7
Sherborne Wy RKW/CH/CXG WD3 ....72 C8
Sherboro Rd SEVS/STOTM N15 ....119 N4
Sherbourne SHGR GU5 ....269 N5
Sherbourne Cl HHS/BOV HP3 ....35 P7
Sherbourne Dr VW GU25 ....193 J5
WDSR SL4 ....148 E10
Sherbourne Gdns SHPTN TW17 ....196 F7
Sherbourne Wk SLN SL2 ....109 H9
Sherbrooke Cl BXLYHN DA7 ....164 B10
Sherbrooke Rd FUL/PGN SW6 ....157 H6
Sherbrooke Ter FUL/PGN * SW6 ....157 H6
Sherbrook Gdns WCHMH N21 ....99 J1
Shere Av BELMT SM2 ....220 F6
Shere Cl CHSGTN KT9 ....219 J2
RDKG RH5 ....273 H6
Sheredan Rd CHING E4 ....101 J6
Sheredes Dr HOD EN11 ....44 E5
Shere La SHGR GU5 ....270 B5
Shere Rd EHSLY KT24 ....252 D6
GNTH/NBYPK IG2 ....122 D3
RGUE GU4 ....269 L2
SHGR GU5 ....270 A4
Sherfield Av RKW/CH/CXG WD3 ....91 N4
Sherfield Cl KUT KT1 ....199 N4
Sherfield Gdns PUT/ROE SW15 ....178 C2
Sherfield Rd GRAYS RM17 ....167 N5
Sheridan Cl HARH RM3 ....105 J8
HGDN/ICK UB10 ....132 C6
HHW HP1 ....35 L7
Sheridan Ct DART DA1 ....165 P10
HSLWW TW4 ....175 M1
Sheridan Crs CHST BR7 ....206 E2
Sheridan Dr REIG RH2 ....257 L8
Sheridan Gdns
KTN/HRWW/W HA3 ....115 J4
Sheridan Gra ASC SL5 ....192 F6
Sheridan Pl HPTN TW12 ....198 A1
Sheridan Rd BELV DA17 ....164 B3
BXLYHN DA7 ....163 P9
FSTGT E7 ....121 L8
MNPK E12 ....122 B10
OXHEY WD19 ....93 L1
RCHPK/HAM TW10 ....177 H6
WIM/MER SW19 ....201 J1
Sheridans Rd GT/LBKH KT23 ....254 B2
Sheridan St WCHPL E1 ....140 A8
Sheridan Ter NTHLT * UB5 ....114 A10
Sheridan Wk CAR SM5 ....222 A2
GLDGN NW11 ....117 K4
Sheridan Wy BECK BR3 ....204 E1
Sheriden Wk BROX EN10 ....44 D6
Sheriff Wy GSTN WD25 ....55 H9
Sheringham Av MNPK E12 ....122 C9
ROMW/RG RM7 ....124 D4
STHGT/OAK N14 ....78 E10
WHTN TW2 ....175 N4
Sheringham Dr BARK IG11 ....123 J10
Sheringham Rd HOLWY N7 ....5 P1
PGE/AN SE20 ....204 A2
Sherington Av PIN HA5 ....93 P8
Sherington Rd CHARL SE7 ....161 N5
Sherland Ct RAD * WD7 ....74 F1
Sherland Rd TWK TW1 ....176 E4
Sherlies Av ORP BR6 ....207 H9
Sherlock Ms MHST W1U 10 C3
Sherman Rd BMLY BR1 ....205 M1
SL SL1 ....129 K7
Shernbroke Rd WAB EN9 ....63 L10
Shernhall St LEY E10 ....121 H3
Sherrard Rd FSTGT E7 ....141 P1
Sherrardspark Rd WGCW AL8 ....22 F3
Sherrards Wy BAR EN5 ....77 K9
Sherrick Green Rd WLSDN NW10 ....116 E10
Sherriff Rd KIL/WHAMP NW6 ....2 F2
Sherringham Av FELT TW13 ....175 H6
TOTM N17 ....99 P10
Sherrock Gdns HDN NW4 ....116 D2
Sherry Ms BARK IG11 ....142 G2
Sherwin Rd NWCR SE14 ....160 C7
Sherwood CDH/CHF RM16 ....147 K10
SURB KT6 ....199 J9
Sherwood Av GFD/PVL UB6 ....134 D1
POTB/CUF EN6 ....59 H8
RSLP HA4 ....112 F4
STALE/WH AL4 ....38 G3
STRHM/NOR SW16 ....202 F1
SWFD E18 ....121 N1
YEAD UB4 ....133 J6
Sherwood Cl BXLY DA5 ....185 M2
DTCH/LGLY SL3 ....150 B2
LHD/OX KT22 ....236 B9
WEA W13 ....134 G10
WOKN/KNAP GU21 ....231 K3
Sherwood Ct MBLAR W1H 10 A4
Sherwood Crs REIG RH2 ....275 L4
Sherwood Gdns BARK IG11 ....142 G2
BERM/RHTH SE16 ....19 P8
POP/IOD E14 ....160 F3
Sherwood House
RYLN/HDSTN * HA2 ....114 B8
Sherwood Park Av BFN/LL DA15 ....185 K3
Sherwood Park Rd MTCM CR4 ....202 D4
SUT SM1 ....221 K2
Sherwood Pl HHNE HP2 ....36 A2
Sherwood Rd BARK/HLT IG6 ....122 G2
COUL/CHIP CR5 ....240 D2
CROY/NA CR0 ....204 A7
HDN NW4 ....96 F10
HPTN TW12 ....176 B8
RYLN/HDSTN HA2 ....114 B7
WELL DA16 ....163 H9
WIM/MER SW19 ....179 J10
Sherwoods Ri HARP AL5 ....20 C3
Sherwoods Rd OXHEY WD19 ....93 M1
Sherwood St SOHO/SHAV W1D 11 H7
TRDG/WHET N20 ....97 N4
Sherwood Ter TRDG/WHET N20 ....97 N4
Sherwood Wk CRAWE RH10 ....284 A10
Sherwood Wy WWKM BR4 ....205 H9
Shetland Cl BORE WD6 ....76 A10
CRAWE RH10 ....284 F6
RGUE GU4 ....250 E5
Shetland Rd BOW E3 ....140 E4
Shevon Wy BRW CM14 ....106 E5
Shewens Rd WEY KT13 ....216 E1
Shey Copse WOKS/MYFD GU22 ....232 F3
Shield Dr BTFD TW8 ....154 G5
Shieldhall St ABYW SE2 ....163 M3
Shield Rd ASHF TW15 ....174 D7
Shifford Pth FSTH * SE23 ....182 C6
Shilburn Wy WOKN/KNAP GU21 ....231 M4
Shillibeer Pl MBLAR W1H 9 P4
Shillibeer Wk CHIG IG7 ....103 J4
Shillingford St IS * N1 ....6 D5
Shilling Pl HNWL * W7 ....134 F10
Shillitoe Av POTB/CUF EN6 ....58 G8
The Shimmings GU GU1 ....250 D9
Shinfield St SHB W12 ....136 F8
Shingle Ct WAB EN9 ....63 M9
Shinglewell Rd ERITH DA8 ....164 B6
Shinners Cl SNWD SE25 ....203 P5
Ship Field Cl BH/WHM TN16 ....243 P7
Ship Hl BH/WHM TN16 ....244 A7
SL SL1 ....108 D6
Shipka Rd BAL SW12 ....180 C4
Ship La EYN DA4 ....209 M1
MORT/ESHN SW14 ....155 P9
SOCK/AV RM15 ....166 C1
SWLY BR8 ....209 L1
Shipleybridge La HORL RH6 ....280 G10
Shipley Rd CRAWW RH11 ....283 K7
Shipman Rd CAN/RD E16 ....141 N8
FSTH SE23 ....182 C5
Ship & Mermaid Rw STHWK * SE1 ....19 H1
Ship St DEPT SE8 ....160 F7
Ship Tavern Pas BANK EC3V 13 J7
Shipton Cl BCTR RM8 ....123 N8
Shipton Rd HGDN/ICK UB10 ....112 A9
Shipton St BETH E2 ....7 M9
Shipwright Rd
BERM/RHTH SE16 ....160 D1
Shipwright Yd STHWK * SE1 ....13 J10
Ship Yd WEY KT13 ....196 B10
Shirburn Cl FSTH SE23 ....182 B3
Shirbutt St POP/IOD E14 ....140 F9
Shirebrook Rd BKHTH/KID SE3 ....162 A8
Shire Cl BROX * EN10 ....62 E2
Shire Ct EW KT17 ....220 C4
Shirehall Cl HDN NW4 ....116 G4
Shirehall Gdns HDN NW4 ....116 G4
Shirehall La HDN NW4 ....116 G4
Shirehall Pk HDN NW4 ....116 G4
Shirehall Rd RDART DA2 ....187 L8
Shire Horse Wy ISLW TW7 ....154 E9
Shire La CFSP/GDCR SL9 ....90 E6
ORP BR6 ....226 E4
ORP BR6 ....227 H2
RKW/CH/CXG WD3 ....70 E9
Shiremeade BORE WD6 ....75 L9
Shire Pde CRAWE * RH10 ....284 E6
Shire Pl CRAWE * RH10 ....284 E6
REDH RH1 ....276 A2
Shires Pk WGCE * AL7 ....23 H3
WGCE * AL7 ....23 L4
The Shires RCHPK/HAM TW10 ....177 K7
Shirland Ms MV/WKIL W9 ....2 D10
Shirland Rd MV/WKIL W9 ....2 D10
Shirley Av BELMT SM2 ....221 J6
BXLY DA5 ....185 N3
COUL/CHIP CR5 ....241 J5
CROY/NA CR0 ....204 B8
REDH RH1 ....276 A5
SUT SM1 ....221 P1
WDSR SL4 ....148 E7
Shirley Church Rd
CROY/NA CR0 ....204 C10
Shirley Cl BROX EN10 ....44 E10
CHES/WCR EN8 ....62 B5
DART DA1 ....165 K10
GVE DA12 ....191 L5
HSLW TW3 ....176 B1
WALTH * E17 ....120 G3
Shirley Crs BECK BR3 ....204 D4
Shirley Dr HSLW TW3 ....176 B2
Shirley Gdns BARK IG11 ....143 H1
HCH RM12 ....125 K7
HNWL W7 ....134 E10
Shirley Gv BTSEA SW11 ....158 B9
ED N9 ....100 B1
Shirley Hills Rd CROY/NA CR0 ....224 C2
Shirley Oaks Rd CROY/NA CR0 ....204 C8
Shirley Park Rd CROY/NA CR0 ....204 A8
Shirley Pl WOKN/KNAP GU21 ....231 H3
Shirley Rd ABLGY WD5 ....54 G8
BFN/LL DA15 ....185 H6
CHSWK W4 ....156 A1
CROY/NA CR0 ....204 A8
ENC/FH EN2 ....79 K7
SRTFD E15 ....141 K2
STAL AL1 ....38 E7
WLGTN SM6 ....222 D5
Shirley Rw SNWD * SE25 ....203 P2
Shirley St CAN/RD E16 ....141 L8
Shirley Wy CROY/NA CR0 ....204 E10
Shirlock Rd HAMP NW3 ....118 A9
Shobden Rd TOTM N17 ....99 L9
Shobroke Cl CRICK NW2 ....116 F8
Shoebury Rd EHAM E6 ....142 C2
Shoe La FLST/FETLN EC4A 12 B5
Sholden Gdns STMC/STPC BR5 ....207 M5
Shonks Mill Rd ABR/ST RM4 ....85 J4
Shooters Av KTN/HRWW/W HA3 ....115 H2
Shooters Dr WAB EN9 ....45 K8
Shooters Hl WOOL/PLUM SE18 ....162 C7
Shooters Hill Rd BKHTH/KID SE3 ....161 K7
Shooters Rd ENC/FH EN2 ....79 H4
Shootersway BERK HP4 ....32 G3
Shootersway La BERK HP4 ....33 L6
Shootersway Pk BERK HP4 ....33 L5
Shoot-Up Hl CRICK NW2 ....2 C1
Shophouse La SHGR GU5 ....269 N10
Shoplands WGCW AL8 ....22 G2
Shop Rd WDSR * SL4 ....148 B6
Shord Hl PUR/KEN CR8 ....241 L2
Shore Cl EBED/NFELT TW14 ....175 H3
HPTN TW12 ....175 M8
Shorediche Cl HGDN/ICK UB10 ....112 A8
Shoreditch High St WCHPL E1 ....13 K3
Shore Gv FELT TW13 ....175 P5
Shoreham Cl CROY/NA CR0 ....204 B6
WAND/EARL SW18 ....179 L1
Shoreham La ORP BR6 ....228 B3
RSEV TN14 ....228 B8
SEV TN13 ....246 G8
Shoreham Pl RSEV TN14 ....229 H8
Shoreham Ri SLN SL2 ....128 C6
Shoreham Rd CRAWE RH10 ....284 D10
RSEV TN14 ....247 J1
STMC/STPC BR5 ....207 L1
Shoreham Rd (East)
HTHAIR TW6 ....173 P1
Shoreham Rd (West)
HTHAIR TW6 ....173 P1
Shoreham Wy HAYES BR2 ....205 M6
Shorehill La BGR/WK TN15 ....247 P1
Shore Pl HOM E9 ....140 B2
Shore Rd HOM E9 ....140 B2
Shore's Rd WOKN/KNAP GU21 ....214 C10
The Shore GVW DA11 ....189 P1
Shorncliffe Rd CMBW SE5 ....19 L8
Shorndean St CAT SE6 ....183 H4
Shorne Cl BFN/LL DA15 ....185 L2
STMC/STPC BR5 ....207 N4
Shornefield Cl BMLY BR1 ....206 D3
Shorne Ifield Rd GVE DA12 ....191 L9
Shorrolds Rd FUL/PGN SW6 ....157 K6
Shortacres REDH RH1 ....258 G9
Short Cl CRAWW RH11 ....283 N5
Short Cft BRWN CM15 ....86 E3
Shortcroft Rd EW KT17 ....220 C4
Shorter Av BRWN CM15 ....87 L10
Shorter St WCHPL E1 ....13 L7
Shortfern SLN SL2 ....129 P8
Short Gallop CRAWE * RH10 ....284 E6
Shortgate NFNCH/WDSP N12 ....97 J5
Shortlands HMSMTH W6 ....156 G3
HYS/HAR UB3 ....152 E5
Shortlands Av CHONG CM5 ....67 N2
Shortlands Cl BELV DA17 ....164 A2
UED N18 ....99 L4
Shortlands Gdns HAYES BR2 ....205 K2
Shortlands Gv HAYES BR2 ....205 J3
Shortlands Rd HAYES BR2 ....205 J3
KUTN/CMB KT2 ....177 L10
LEY E10 ....120 G5
Short La LCOL/BKTW AL2 ....55 M5
OXTED RH8 ....261 N8
STWL/WRAY TW19 ....174 A3
Shortmead Dr CHES/WCR EN8 ....62 D7
Short Rd CHSWK W4 ....156 B5
STWL/WRAY TW19 ....173 P2
WAN E11 ....121 K7
Shorts Cft CDALE/KGS NW9 ....115 N2
Shorts Gdns LSQ/SEVD * WC2H 11 L6
Shorts Rd CAR SM5 ....221 P1
Short St STHWK SE1 ....18 B1
Shortway CSHM HP5 ....50 G5
ELTH/MOT SE9 ....162 B9
Short Wy NFNCH/WDSP N12 ....97 P7
WHTN TW2 ....176 B3
Shortwood Av STA TW18 ....173 L6
Shotfield WLGTN SM6 ....222 C3
Shothanger Wy HHS/BOV HP3 ....52 G1
Shott Cl SUT SM1 ....221 M2
Shottendane Rd FUL/PGN * SW6 ....157 K7
Shottery Cl ELTH/MOT SE9 ....184 B6
Shottfield Av MORT/ESHN SW14 ....156 B10
Shottfield Cl STALE/WH AL4 ....21 H9
Shott Lower CHESW EN7 ....61 N2
Shoulder of Mutton Aly
POP/IOD E14 ....140 D9
Shouldham St MBLAR W1H 9 P4
Showers Wy HYS/HAR UB3 ....133 H10
Shrapnel Cl WOOL/PLUM SE18 ....162 B6
Shrapnel Rd ELTH/MOT SE9 ....162 C9
Shrewsbury Av
KTN/HRWW/W HA3 ....115 K2
MORT/ESHN SW14 ....155 P10
Shrewsbury Cl SURB KT6 ....199 K9
Shrewsbury Crs WLSDN NW10 ....136 A3
Shrewsbury La
WOOL/PLUM SE18 ....162 E7
Shrewsbury Ms BAY/PAD W2 ....8 E5
Shrewsbury Rd BAY/PAD W2 ....8 E4
BECK BR3 ....204 D3
CAR SM5 ....201 P7
EBED/NFELT TW14 ....174 D2
FBAR/BDGN N11 ....98 E7
MNPK E12 ....142 A1
REDH RH1 ....257 P10
Shrewsbury St NKENS W10 ....136 F6
Shrewton Rd TOOT * SW17 ....180 A10
Shrimpton Cl BEAC HP9 ....88 C5
Shrimpton Rd BEAC HP9 ....88 C5
Shroffold Rd BMLY BR1 ....183 K7
Shropshire Cl MTCM CR4 ....202 F4
Shropshire Rd WDGN N22 ....98 G8
Shroton St CAMTN NW1 ....9 N3
The Shrubberies CHIG IG7 ....102 F6
STAL * AL1 ....38 C8
SWFD E18 ....101 M10
Shrubbery Gdns WCHMH N21 ....99 J1
Shrubbery Rd EYN DA4 ....210 C1
GVE DA12 ....190 E4
STHL UB1 ....133 N10
STRHM/NOR SW16 ....180 F7
The Shrubbery HHW HP1 ....35 H5
SURB * KT6 ....199 K8
UPMR RM14 ....126 B8
Shrubbs Hl CHOB/PIR GU24 ....213 H5
Shrubbs Hill La ASC SL5 ....193 H6
Shrub Hill Rd HHW HP1 ....35 J7
Shrubland Cl TRDG/WHET * N20 ....97 N3
Shrubland Gv WPK KT4 ....200 F10
Shrubland Rd BNSTD SM7 ....239 J2
HACK E8 ....7 N5
LEY E10 ....120 F5
WALTH E17 ....120 F3
Shrublands BRKMPK AL9 ....59 L2
Shrublands Av BERK HP4 ....33 M5
CROY/NA CR0 ....224 F1
Shrublands Cl CHIG IG7 ....102 F7
SYD SE26 ....182 B6
Shrublands Dr LTWR GU18 ....212 A7
Shrublands Rd BERK HP4 ....33 M4
The Shrublands POTB/CUF EN6 ....59 H9
Shrubsall Cl ELTH/MOT SE9 ....184 B4
Shuna Wk IS N1 ....6 G1
Shurland Av EBAR EN4 ....77 N10
Shurland Gdns PECK * SE15 ....159 N6
Shurlock Av SWLY BR8 ....208 E2
Shurlock Dr ORP BR6 ....226 F1
Shuters Sq WKENS W14 ....14 C8
Shuttle Cl BFN/LL DA15 ....185 J3
Shuttlemead BXLY DA5 ....186 A3
Shuttle Rd DART DA1 ....165 H9
Shuttle St WCHPL E1 ....13 N2
Shuttleworth Rd BTSEA SW11 ....157 N8
Sibella Rd CLAP SW4 ....158 E8
Sibley Av HARP AL5 ....20 C4
Sibley Cl BXLYHS DA6 ....185 P1
Sibley Ct UX/CGN UB8 ....132 D7
Sibley Gv MNPK E12 ....142 B2
Sibneys Gn HLWS CM18 ....47 H5
Sibthorpe Rd BRKMPK AL9 ....40 G10
LEE/GVPK SE12 ....183 N3
Sibthorp Rd MTCM * CR4 ....202 A2
Sibton Rd CAR SM5 ....201 P7
Sicilian Av NOXST/BSQ * WC1A 11 M4
Sicilion Av NOXST/BSQ WC1A 11 M4
Sicklefield Cl CHESW EN7 ....61 N2
Sidbury Cl ASC SL5 ....192 F5
Sidbury St FUL/PGN SW6 ....157 H7
Sidcup By-Pass Rd SCUP DA14 ....185 H7
Sidcup Hl SCUP DA14 ....185 L8
Sidcup Hill Gdns SCUP * DA14 ....185 M8
Sidcup Pl SCUP DA14 ....185 K8
Sidcup Rd LEE/GVPK SE12 ....183 N1
Siddeley Dr HSLWW TW4 ....153 M9
Siddons La CAMTN NW1 ....10 B2
Siddons Rd CROY/NA CR0 ....203 H10
FSTH SE23 ....182 D5
TOTM N17 ....99 P9
Side Rd DEN/HRF UB9 ....110 G5
WALTH E17 ....120 E3
Sideways La HORL RH6 ....279 M6
Sidewood Rd ELTH/MOT SE9 ....184 G4
Sidford Cl HHW HP1 ....35 J6
Sidford Pl STHWK SE1 ....17 P4
The Sidings BROX EN10 ....44 E8
HAT AL10 ....40 B5
HHNE HP2 ....35 N6
LOU IG10 ....82 B10
STA TW18 ....173 L7
WAN E11 ....121 H6
Sidmouth Av ISLW TW7 ....154 D8
Sidmouth Cl OXHEY WD19 ....93 J3
Sidmouth Dr RSLP HA4 ....113 H8
Sidmouth Pde CRICK * NW2 ....136 F2
Sidmouth Rd LEY E10 ....121 H8
PECK SE15 ....159 N7
STMC/STPC BR5 ....207 L4
WELL DA16 ....163 M6
WLSDN NW10 ....136 F2
Sidmouth St STPAN WC1H 5 M10
Sidney Av PLMGR N13 ....98 G6
Sidney Cl UX/CGN UB8 ....131 M2
Sidney Elson Wy EHAM E6 ....142 D4
Sidney Gdns BTFD TW8 ....155 J5
RSEV TN14 ....247 K2
Sidney Gv FSBYE EC1V 6 C8
Sidney Rd BECK BR3 ....204 D2
BRXN/ST SW9 ....158 G8
EPP CM16 ....82 G2
FSTGT E7 ....121 M8
RYLN/HDSTN HA2 ....114 B1
SNWD SE25 ....203 P5
STA TW18 ....173 K7
TWK TW1 ....176 F2
WDGN N22 ....98 G8
WDSR SL4 ....148 B9
WOT/HER KT12 ....197 J10
Sidney Sq WCHPL * E1 ....140 B7
Sidney St WCHPL E1 ....140 B8
Sidworth St HACK E8 ....140 A2
Siebert Rd BKHTH/KID SE3 ....161 M5
Siemens Rd WOOL/PLUM SE18 ....162 A2
Sienna Ter CRICK * NW2 ....116 D7
Sierra Dr DAGW RM9 ....144 C4
Sigdon Rd HACK E8 ....119 P10
The Sigers RSLP HA4 ....113 J4
Signmakers Yd CAMTN * NW1 ....4 F6
Sigrist Sq KUTN/CMB KT2 ....199 K1
Silbury Av MTCM CR4 ....201 P1
Silbury St IS * N1 ....6 G9
Silchester Dr CRAWW RH11 ....283 K10
Silchester Rd NKENS W10 ....136 G8
Silecroft Rd BXLYHN DA7 ....164 B7
Silesia Buildings HACK E8 ....140 A2
Silex St STHWK SE1 ....18 D2
Silistria Cl WOKN/KNAP GU21 ....231 H4
Silk Cl LEE/GVPK SE12 ....183 M1
Silkfield Rd CDALE/KGS NW9 ....116 B3
Silkham Rd OXTED RH8 ....261 J3
Silk Mill Rd OXHEY WD19 ....93 J1
Silk Mills Cl RSEV TN14 ....247 K7
Silk Mills Pth LEW SE13 ....161 H9
Silkmore La EHSLY KT24 ....252 C3
RPLY/SEND GU23 ....252 A2
Silkstream Pde EDGW * HA8 ....95 P9
Silkstream Rd EDGW HA8 ....95 P9
Silk St BARB EC2Y 12 F3
Silo Cl RGODL GU7 ....267 L9
Silo Dr RGODL GU7 ....267 L9
Silo Rd RGODL GU7 ....267 L9
Silsoe Rd WDGN N22 ....118 G1
Silver Birch Av CHING E4 ....100 E6
EPP CM16 ....65 P3
Silver Birch Cl ADL/WDHM KT15 ....215 H8
FBAR/BDGN N11 ....98 B7
HGDN/ICK UB10 ....111 P9
RDART DA2 ....186 F7
THMD SE28 ....143 K10
Silver Birches RBRW/HUT CM13 ....107 M2
Silver Birch Ms BARK/HLT IG6 ....102 F7
Silverbirch Wk HAMP * NW3 ....4 B2
Silvercliffe Gdns EBAR EN4 ....77 P8
Silver Cl KTN/HRWW/W HA3 ....94 C8
KWD/TDW/WH KT20 ....239 H10
NWCR * SE14 ....160 D6
Silver Ct WGCE * AL7 ....23 K4
Silver Crs CHSWK W4 ....155 N3
Silverdale CAMTN NW1 ....4 G8
ENC/FH EN2 ....78 F8
HART DA3 ....211 L4
SYD SE26 ....182 B7
Silverdale Av LHD/OX KT22 ....218 B10
WEY KT13 ....196 G9
Silverdale Cl BRKHM/BTCW RH3 ....273 N4
HNWL W7 ....134 D10
NTHLT UB5 ....113 N10
SUT SM1 ....221 J1
Silverdale Ct STA * TW18 ....173 L8
Silverdale Dr ELTH/MOT SE9 ....184 B5
HCH RM12 ....125 J10
SUN TW16 ....197 J2
Silverdale Gdns HYS/HAR UB3 ....153 H1
Silverdale Rd BUSH WD23 ....73 M9
BXLYHN DA7 ....164 C8
CHING E4 ....101 J7
HYS/HAR UB3 ....153 H1
STMC/STPC BR5 ....206 F4
STMC/STPC BR5 ....207 K3
Silver Dell WATN WD24 ....72 G1
Silverdene NFNCH/WDSP * N12 ....97 L7
Silver Dene PUT/ROE * SW15 ....178 F1
Silverfield BROX EN10 ....44 E8
Silverglade CHSGTN KT9 ....219 H8
Silverhall St ISLW TW7 ....154 F9
Silver Hl BORE WD6 ....75 P2
CSTG HP8 ....89 N3
Silverholme Cl
KTN/HRWW/W HA3 ....115 K5
Silverlands Cl CHERT * KT16 ....194 G10
Silver La PUR/KEN CR8 ....222 E8
WWKM BR4 ....205 J9
Silverlea Gdns HORL RH6 ....280 D5
Silverleigh Rd THHTH CR7 ....202 G4
Silverlocke Rd GRAYS RM17 ....168 A5
Silvermere Av CRW RM5 ....104 C7
Silvermere Dr UED * N18 ....100 C6
Silvermere Rd LEW SE13 ....182 F2
Silvermere Rw SNWD * SE25 ....203 P2
Silver Rd GVE DA12 ....191 H5
SHB W12 ....136 G9

Silversmiths Wy
WOKN/KNAP GU21 231 P4
Silver Spring Cl ERITH DA8 164 C5
Silversted La BH/WHM TN16 244 G7
Silverstone Cl REDH RH1 258 A8
Silverston Wy STAN HA7 95 H7
Silver St ABR/ST RM4 83 L7
CHESW EN7 61 L6
ENC/FH EN2 79 L7
UED N18 99 L5
WAB EN9 63 H10
Silverthorn Dr HHS/BOV HP3 36 C10
Silverthorne Rd VX/NE SW8 158 C8
Silverthorn Gdns CHING E4 100 F3
Silverton Rd HMSMTH W6 156 G6
Silvertown Wy CAN/RD E16 141 L8
Silver Tree Cl WOT/HER KT12 217 H1
Silvertree La GFD/PVL UB6 134 C5
Silver Trees LCOL/BKTW AL2 55 N6
Silver Wk BERM/RHTH SE16 140 E10
Silver Wy HGDN/ICK UB10 132 C4
ROMW/RG RM7 124 C1
Silverwood CRAWE * RH10 285 N2
Silverwood Cl BECK BR3 182 F10
CDH/CHF RM16 147 M9
CROY/NA CR0 224 E5
NTHWD HA6 92 D9
Silvester Rd EDUL SE22 181 N1
Silvesters HLWW/ROY CM19 46 C3
Silvester St STHWK SE1 18 G2
Silwood Cl ASC SL5 192 C2
Silwood Pk ASC * SL5 192 C2
Silwood Rd ASC SL5 192 E4
Silwood St BERM/RHTH SE16 160 C4
Simmil Rd ESH/CLAY KT10 218 D2
Simmonds Ri HHS/BOV HP3 35 N8
Simmons Cl DTCH/LGLY * SL3 150 D3
TRDG/WHET N20 97 P2
Simmons La CHING E4 101 J3
Simmons Pl CDH/CHF RM16 147 M10
STA TW18 173 H8
Simmons Rd WOOL/PLUM SE18 162 E4
Simmons' Wy TRDG/WHET N20 97 P3
Simms Cl CAR SM5 201 P9
Simms Gdns EFNCH N2 97 M10
Simms Rd STHWK SE1 19 P6
Simnel Rd LEE/GVPK SE12 183 N3
Simon Cl NTGHL W11 8 D7
Simon Dean HHS/BOV HP3 52 D3
Simonds Rd LEY E10 120 F7
Simone Cl BMLY BR1 206 A1
Simone Dr PUR/KEN CR8 241 K2
Simons Cl CHERT KT16 214 F3
Simons Wk EGH TW20 171 P10
SRTFD E15 121 J10
Simplemarsh Rd
ADL/WDHM KT15 215 K1
Simpson Cl WCHMH N21 78 G9
Simpson Dr ACT W3 136 A8
Simpson Rd HSLWW TW4 175 N2
RAIN RM13 144 G1
RCHPK/HAM TW10 177 H7
Simpson's Rd HAYES BR2 205 M3
POP/IOD E14 140 G9
Simpson St BTSEA SW11 157 P8
Simpson Wy SURB KT6 199 H6
Sims Cl ROM RM1 124 G2
Sinclair Cl CRAWE RH10 284 D9
Sinclair Dr BELMT SM2 221 L5
Sinclair Gdns WKENS W14 156 G1
Sinclair Gv GLDGN NW11 116 G4
Sinclair Rd CHING E4 100 E6
WKENS W14 14 A5
Sinclair Wy RDART DA2 188 C7
Sinclare Cl EN EN1 79 N5
Sincots Rd REDH RH1 258 A10
Sinderby Cl BORE WD6 75 K5
Singapore Rd HNWL W7 134 F10
Singer St FSBYE EC1V 7 H10
Singles Cross RSEV * TN14 245 N1
Single's Cross La RSEV TN14 245 M1
Single St BH/WHM TN16 244 E5
Singleton Cl CROY/NA CR0 203 K7
HCH RM12 124 G9
WIM/MER SW19 180 A10
Singleton Rd DAGW RM9 124 A10
Singleton Scarp
NFNCH/WDSP N12 97 K6
Singlewell Rd GVW DA11 190 E6
Singret Pl UX/CGN * UB8 131 M6
Sinnott Rd WALTH E17 100 C9
Sion Rd TWK TW1 176 G4
Sipson Cl WDR/YW UB7 152 B5
Sipson La HYS/HAR UB3 152 D5
Sipson Rd WDR/YW UB7 152 A2
Sipson Wy WDR/YW UB7 152 B6
Sir Abraham Dawes Cottages
PUT/ROE * SW15 157 H10
Sir Alexander Cl ACT W3 136 C10
Sir Cyril Black Wy
WIM/MER SW19 179 J10
Sirdar Rd MTCM CR4 180 B9
NTGHL W11 136 G9
WDGN N22 119 J1
Sirdar Strd GVE DA12 191 J8
Sir Francis Wy BRW CM14 106 G3
Sir Henry Peakes Dr SLN SL2 128 F1
Sir Thomas Moore Est CHEL SW3 15 M10
Sirus Rd NTHWD HA6 93 H6
Sise La MANHO * EC4N 12 G5
Siskin Cl BORE WD6 75 M8
BUSH WD23 73 M8
Sisley Rd BARK IG11 143 H3
Sispara Gdns WAND/EARL SW18 179 J2
Sissinghurst Cl CRAWE RH10 284 E6
Sissinghurst Rd CROY/NA CR0 203 P7
Sister Mabel's Wy PECK * SE15 159 P6
Sisters Av BTSEA SW11 158 A10
Sistova Rd BAL SW12 180 C4
Sisulu Pl BRXN/ST SW9 159 H9
Sittingbourne Av WCHMH N21 79 L10
Sitwell Gv STAN HA7 94 E6
Siverst Cl NTHLT UB5 134 A1
Siviter Wy DAGE RM10 144 C2
Siward Rd HAYES BR2 205 N3
TOOT SW17 179 M6
TOTM N17 99 L9
Six Acres HHS/BOV HP3 36 B9
Sixteenth Av
KWD/TDW/WH * KT20 257 J2
Sixth Av GSTN WD25 73 L1
HYS/HAR UB3 132 G10
KWD/TDW/WH * KT20 257 J2
MNPK E12 122 C9
NKENS W10 2 A10
Sixth Cross Rd WHTN TW2 176 B6
Skardu Rd CRICK NW2 117 H10
Skarnings Ct WAB EN9 63 M9
Skeena Hl WIM/MER SW19 179 H3
Skeet Hill La STMC/STPC BR5 208 A9
Skeffington Rd EHAM E6 142 C3
Skelbrook St WAND/EARL SW18 179 L5
Skelgill Rd PUT/ROE SW15 157 J10
Skelley Rd SRTFD E15 141 L2
Skelton Cl HACK E8 7 M2
Skelton Rd FSTGT E7 141 M1
Skelton's La LEY E10 120 G5
Skelwith Rd HMSMTH W6 156 F5
Skerne Rd KUTN/CMB KT2 199 J1
Sketchley Gdns
BERM/RHTH SE16 160 C4
Sketty Rd EN EN1 79 N7
Skibbs La ORP BR6 207 P10
Skid Hill La WARL CR6 243 L1
Skidmore Wy RKW/CH/CXG WD3 91 P2
Skiers St SRTFD E15 141 K3
Skiffington Cl BRXS/STRHM SW2 181 H4
Skimpans Cl BRKMPK AL9 40 G10
Skinner Pl BGVA * SW1W 16 C6
Skinners La ASHTD KT21 237 J4
BLKFR EC4V 12 F7
HEST TW5 154 A7
Skinner St CLKNW EC1R 6 B10
Skinney La EYN DA4 210 C3
Skippers Cl GRH DA9 188 G1
Skipsey Av EHAM E6 142 C5
Skipton Cl FBAR/BDGN N11 98 B7
Skipton Dr HYS/HAR UB3 152 D2
Skipton Wy HORL RH6 280 C2
Skipworth Rd HOM E9 140 B3
Skyes Dr STA TW18 173 L8
Skylark Rd DEN/HRF UB9 110 F6
Skylines Village POP/IOD * E14 161 H1
Sky Peals Rd WFD IG8 101 J9
Skyport Dr WDR/YW UB7 151 N6
Skys Wood Rd STALE/WH AL4 38 G2
Slacksbury Hatch
HLWW/ROY CM19 46 E1
Sladebrook Rd BKHTH/KID SE3 162 A9
Slade Ct CHERT KT16 214 G3
RAD WD7 74 G2
Sladedale Rd WOOL/PLUM SE18 163 H4
Slade End EPP CM16 83 H2
Slade Gdns ERITH DA8 164 G7
Slade Green Rd ERITH DA8 164 G7
Sladen Pl CLPT E5 120 A9
Slade Oak La DEN/HRF UB9 110 F4
Slade Rd CHERT KT16 214 G3
CHOB/PIR GU24 230 C6
Slades Cl ENC/FH EN2 79 H7
Slades Dr CHST BR7 184 F6
Slades Gdns ENC/FH EN2 79 H6
Slades Hl ENC/FH EN2 79 H7
Slades Ri ENC/FH EN2 79 H7
The Slade WOOL/PLUM SE18 163 H5
Slade Wk WALW SE17 18 D10
Slagrove Pl BROCKY SE4 182 F1
Slaidburn St WBPTN SW10 15 K10
Slaithwaite Rd LEW SE13 161 H10
Slaney Pl HOLWY N7 119 H10
Slaney Rd ROM RM1 124 F3
Slattery Rd FELT TW13 175 K4
Slaugham Ct CRAWW RH11 283 J10
Sleaford Gn OXHEY WD19 93 L4
Sleaford St VX/NE SW8 158 D6
Sleapcross Gdns STALE/WH AL4 39 P7
Sleapshyde La STALE/WH AL4 39 P8
Sleddale HHNE HP2 35 P3
Sleepers Farm Rd
CDH/CHF RM16 168 E1
Sleets End HHW HP1 35 L4
Slewins Cl EMPK RM11 125 K3
Slewins La EMPK RM11 125 K3
Slievemore Cl CLAP SW4 158 E9
Slimmons Dr STALE/WH AL4 38 F2
Slines New Rd CTHM CR3 242 C6
Slines Oak Rd CTHM CR3 242 F9
Slinfold Wk CRAWW RH11 283 K6
Slingsby Pl COVGDN WC2E 11 N6
Slipe La BROX EN10 44 E10
Slippers Hl HHNE HP2 35 N5
Slippers Pl BERM/RHTH SE16 160 A2
Slipshatch Rd REIG RH2 275 J4
Slipshoe St REIG RH2 257 J10
The Slip BH/WHM TN16 262 F2
Sloane Av CHEL SW3 15 P6
Sloane Ct East CHEL SW3 16 C7
Sloane Ct West CHEL SW3 16 C7
Sloane Gdns BGVA SW1W 16 C6
ORP BR6 206 F10
Sloane Sq BGVA SW1W 16 B6
HART * DA3 211 K3
Sloane St KTBR SW1X 16 B4
Sloane Ter KTBR SW1X 16 B5
Sloane Wk CROY/NA CR0 204 E6
Sloansway WGCE AL7 23 J2
Slocock Hl WOKN/KNAP GU21 231 P3
Slocum Cl THMD SE28 143 M9
Slough La BRKHM/BTCW RH3 256 D9
CDALE/KGS NW9 115 P3
EPSOM KT18 255 P1
Slough Rd IVER SL0 130 G5
WDSR SL4 149 J4
Slyfield Gn GU GU1 250 B6
Sly St WCHPL * E1 140 A8
Smaldon Cl WDR/YW UB7 152 B2
Smallberry Av ISLW TW7 154 E8
Smallbrook Ms BAY/PAD W2 9 L6
Smallcroft WGCE AL7 23 L4
Smalley Cl STNW/STAM N16 119 N8
Smallfield Rd HORL RH6 280 C4
HORL RH6 281 M4
Smallford La STALE/WH AL4 39 N7
Small Grains HART DA3 210 G10
Smallmead HORL RH6 280 C4
Smalls Hill Rd REIG RH2 274 F10
Smalls Md CRAWW RH11 283 M7
Smallwood Cl STALE/WH AL4 21 K4
Smallwood Rd TOOT SW17 179 N7
Smarden Cl BELV DA17 164 B4
Smart Cl HARH RM3 105 J9
Smarts Gn CHESW EN7 61 N2
Smart's Heath La
WOKS/MYFD GU22 231 M9
Smart's Heath Rd
WOKS/MYFD GU22 231 M9
Smart's La LOU IG10 82 B8
Smart's Pl HHOL WC1V 11 M5
UED N18 99 P6
Smarts Rd GVE DA12 190 E6
Smart St BETH E2 140 C5
Smeaton Cl WAB EN9 63 K9
Smeaton Rd WAB EN9 80 F3
WAND/EARL SW18 179 K3
WFD IG8 102 C6
Smeaton St WAP E1W 140 A10
Smedley St VX/NE SW8 158 E8
Smeed Rd BOW E3 140 F2
Smiles Pl LEW SE13 161 H8
Smitham Bottom La
PUR/KEN CR8 222 E8
Smitham Downs Rd
COUL/CHIP CR5 222 F9
Smithbarn Cl HORL RH6 280 C3
Smith Cl BERM/RHTH SE16 140 C10
CRAWE RH10 283 N10
The Smithers BRKHM/BTCW RH3 273 N2
Smithfield HHNE HP2 35 N4
Smithfields HHNE HP2 35 N4
Smithfield St STBT EC1A 12 C4
Smithies Rd ABYW SE2 163 L3
Smith Rd REIG RH2 275 J3
Smith's Ct SOHO/SHAV * W1D 11 J7
Smiths La CHESW EN7 61 L2
EDEN TN8 262 F9
WDSR SL4 148 D8
Smithson Rd TOTM N17 99 L9
Smith St BRYLDS KT5 199 L6
CHEL SW3 16 A7
WATW WD18 73 K8
Smith Ter CHEL SW3 16 A8
Smithwood Cl WIM/MER SW19 179 H4
Smithy Cl KWD/TDW/WH KT20 257 J2
Smithy La KWD/TDW/WH KT20 257 J2
Smithy's Gn BFOR GU20 212 C3
Smithy St WCHPL E1 140 B7
Smoke La REIG RH2 275 L2
Smugglers Wy
WAND/EARL SW18 157 L10
Smugglers Whf GRH DA9 188 G1
Smug Oak La LCOL/BKTW AL2 56 A6
Smyrks Rd WALW * SE17 19 K8
WALW SE17 19 K8
Smyrna Rd KIL/WHAMP NW6 2 E4
Smythe Rd EYN DA4 209 P1
Smythe St POP/IOD E14 140 G9
Snag La RSEV TN14 226 G8
Snakes Hl BRW CM14 86 B7
Snakes La EBAR EN4 78 C7
Snakes La East WFD IG8 101 P7
Snakes La West WFD IG8 101 M7
Snape Sp SL SL1 129 K8
Snaresbrook Dr STAN HA7 95 J5
Snaresbrook Rd WAN E11 121 K2
Snarsgate St NKENS W10 136 F7
Snatts Hl OXTED RH8 261 L5
Sneath Av GLDGN NW11 117 J5
Snell Hatch CRAWW RH11 283 L7
Snelling Av GVW DA11 190 C5
Snellings Rd WOT/HER KT12 217 K2
Snells La AMSS HP7 69 N6
Snell's Pk UED N18 99 N7
Snells Wood Ct AMSS HP7 69 P6
Sneyd Rd CRICK NW2 116 F10
Snipe Cl ERITH DA8 165 J6
Snowbury Rd FUL/PGN SW6 157 L8
Snowcrete DTCH/LGLY * SL3 129 P4
Snowden Av HGDN/ICK UB10 132 C4
Snowden Cl WDSR SL4 148 C10
Snowden Dr CDALE/KGS NW9 116 B4
Snowden St SDTCH EC2A 13 J2
Snowdon Crs HYS/HAR UB3 152 D2
Snowdon Rd West HTHAIR TW6 174 D2
Snowdown Cl PGE/AN SE20 204 B1
Snowdrop Cl HPTN TW12 175 P9
Snowdrop Wy CHOB/PIR GU24 230 F3
Snowerhill Rd
BRKHM/BTCW RH3 274 C4
Snow Hl CRAWE RH10 281 N10
STBT EC1A 12 C4
Snowhill Cottages CSHM HP5 33 L10
Snowhill La CRAWE RH10 281 N10
Snowsfields STHWK SE1 19 H1
Snowshill Rd MNPK E12 122 B10
Snows Paddock BFOR GU20 192 A10
Snows Ride BFOR GU20 212 A1
Snowy Fielder Waye ISLW TW7 154 G8
Soames St PECK SE15 159 N9
Soames Wk NWMAL KT3 200 B1
Soane Cl CRAWW RH11 283 H9
Soham Rd PEND EN3 80 E3
Soho Sq SOHO/SHAV W1D 11 J5
Soho St SOHO/SHAV W1D 11 J5
Sojourner Truth Cl HACK * E8 140 A1
Solander Gdns WCHPL E1 140 A9
Solar Ct WATW * WD18 72 G9
Solar Wy PEND EN3 80 E1
Solebay St WCHPL E1 140 D6
Solecote GT/LBKH KT23 253 P1
Sole Farm Av GT/LBKH KT23 253 N1
Sole Farm Cl GT/LBKH KT23 235 N10
Sole Farm Rd GT/LBKH KT23 253 N1
Solefields Rd SEV TN13 265 J4
Solent Ri PLSTW E13 141 M5
Solent Rd KIL/WHAMP NW6 117 K10
Soleoak Dr SEV TN13 265 J3
Solesbridge Cl RKW/CH/CXG WD3 71 J7
Solesbridge La RKW/CH/CXG WD3 71 J7
Solid La BRWN CM15 86 E5
Solna Av PUT/ROE SW15 178 F1
Solna Rd WCHMH N21 99 L2
Solomon Av UED N18 99 P5
Solomons Court Rd BNSTD SM7 239 N3
Solomon's Hl RKW/CH/CXG WD3 91 N1
Solomon's Pas PECK SE15 160 A10
Solon New Rd CLAP SW4 158 F10
Solon Rd CLAP SW4 158 F10
Solway HHNE HP2 36 A4
TIL RM18 169 M2
Solway Cl HACK E8 7 M2
HSLWW TW4 153 M9
Solway Rd EDUL SE22 159 P10
WDGN N22 99 J9
Somaford Gv EBAR EN4 77 N10
Somali Rd CRICK NW2 117 J9
Somerby Cl BROX EN10 44 F7
Somerby Rd BARK IG11 142 G2
Somercoates Cl EBAR EN4 77 P7
Somerden Rd STMC/STPC BR5 207 N7
Somerfield Cl
KWD/TDW/WH KT20 239 H5
Somerfield Rd FSBYPK N4 119 J7
Somerford Cl PIN HA5 113 H2
Somerford Gv STNW/STAM N16 119 N9
TOTM N17 99 P8
Somerford Pl BEAC HP9 88 C8
Somerford St WCHPL * E1 140 A6
Somerford Wy
BERM/RHTH SE16 160 D1
Somerhill Av BFN/LL DA15 185 L3
Somerhill Rd WELL DA16 163 L8
Someries Rd HHW HP1 35 J4
Somerleyton Rd BRXN/ST SW9 159 H10
Somersby Gdns REDBR IG4 122 C3
Somers Cl CAMTN * NW1 5 J7
REIG RH2 257 K9
Somers Crs BAY/PAD W2 9 N6
Somerset Av CHSGTN KT9 219 J1
RYNPK SW20 200 E2
WELL DA16 185 J1
Somerset Cl HOR/WEW KT19 220 B6
NWMAL KT3 200 B6
TOTM N17 99 L10
WFD IG8 101 M9
Somerset Gdns EMPK RM11 125 P6
HGT N6 118 B5
LEW SE13 160 G8
STRHM/NOR SW16 202 G3
TEDD TW11 176 D8
TOTM * N17 99 M8
Somerset Rd BAR EN5 77 L9
BTFD TW8 155 H5
CHSWK W4 156 A2
DART DA1 187 J2
HDN NW4 116 F2
HRW HA1 114 B4
KUT KT1 199 L2
ORP BR6 207 K7
PEND EN3 80 F4
REIG RH2 275 N2
SLH/COR SS17 169 K1
STHL UB1 133 P7
TEDD TW11 176 D8
TOTM N17 119 N1
UED N18 99 N6
WALTH E17 120 F3
WEA W13 134 G10
WIM/MER SW19 178 G6
Somerset Sq WKENS W14 14 B2
Somerset St Little TWRH EC3N 13 L6
Somerset Wy IVER SL0 151 J1
Somerset Waye HEST TW5 153 M5
Somersham WGCE AL7 23 N5
Somersham Rd BXLYHN DA7 163 P8
Somers Pl BRXS/STRHM SW2 180 G3
Somers Rd BRKMPK AL9 40 F10
BRXS/STRHM SW2 180 G2
REIG RH2 257 K9
WALTH E17 120 E2
Somers Sq BRKMPK AL9 40 F9
Somers Wy BUSH WD23 94 B1
Somerswey RGUE GU4 268 B8
Somerton Av RCH/KEW TW9 155 N9
Somerton Cl PUR/KEN CR8 241 H2
Somerton Rd CRICK NW2 116 G8
PECK SE15 160 A10
Somertons Cl GUW GU2 249 M6
Somertrees Av LEE/GVPK SE12 183 N5
Somervell Rd RYLN/HDSTN HA2 113 N10
Somerville Av BARN SW13 156 F5
Somerville Dr CRAWE RH10 284 D4
Somerville Rd CHDH RM6 123 M3
COB KT11 217 P10
DART DA1 187 N2
PGE/AN SE20 182 C10
WDSR SL4 149 H4
Sommers Ct WARE * SG12 26 D3
Sonderburg Rd HOLWY N7 118 G7
Sondes Farm DORK * RH4 272 E2
Sondes Place Cottages
DORK * RH4 272 E2
Sondes Place Dr DORK RH4 272 E2
Sondes St WALW SE17 18 G9
Sonia Cl OXHEY WD19 93 K1
Sonia Gdns CRICK NW2 116 C9
HEST TW5 153 P6
NFNCH/WDSP N12 97 M5
Sonning Gdns HPTN TW12 175 M9
Sonning Rd CROY/NA CR0 203 P6
Soothouse Spring
STALW/RED AL3 38 E2
Soper Cl CHING E4 100 E6
FSTH SE23 182 C4
Soper Dr CTHM CR3 241 L9
Soper Ms PEND EN3 80 F4
Sopers Rd POTB/CUF EN6 60 G5
Sophia Cl HOLWY N7 5 N1
Sophia Rd CAN/RD E16 141 N8
LEY E10 120 G6
Sophia Sq BERM/RHTH SE16 140 D9
Sopwell La STAL AL1 38 C7
Sopwith Av CHSGTN KT9 219 K2
Sopwith Cl BH/WHM TN16 244 A2
RCHPK/HAM TW10 177 L8
Sopwith Dr WEY KT13 215 P7
Sopwith Rd HEST TW5 153 K6
Sopwith Wy KUTN/CMB KT2 199 K1
VX/NE SW8 158 C6
Sorbie Cl WEY KT13 216 D3
Sorrel Bank CROY/NA CR0 224 D5
Sorrel Cl THMD SE28 143 K10
Sorrel Gdns EHAM E6 142 B7
Sorrel La POP/IOD E14 141 J8
Sorrell Cl BRXN/ST * SW9 159 H8
NWCR SE14 160 D6
Sorrell Wy GVW DA11 190 B7
Sorrel Wk ROM RM1 124 G1
Sorrento Rd SUT SM1 201 L10
Sospel Ct SLN SL2 129 H4
Sotheby Rd HBRY N5 119 K9
Sotheran Cl HACK E8 7 P5
Sotheron Rd WAT WD17 73 K6
Soudan Rd BTSEA SW11 158 A7
Souldern Rd WKENS * W14 156 G2
Souldern St WATW WD18 73 J9
Sounds Ldg SWLY BR8 208 D6
South Access Rd WALTH E17 120 D5
South Acre CDALE/KGS NW9 96 C10
Southacre Wy PIN HA5 93 K9
South Africa Rd SHB W12 136 E9
South Albert Rd REIG RH2 257 J9
Southall Cl WARE SG12 26 C1
Southall Ct STHL * UB1 133 N9
Southall La HEST TW5 153 J4
Southall Pl STHWK SE1 18 G2
Southall Wy BRW CM14 106 E5
Southampton Buildings
LINN * WC2A 12 A4
Southampton Gdns MTCM CR4 202 F5
Southampton Pl
NOXST/BSQ WC1A 11 M4
Southampton Rd HAMP NW3 118 A10
HTHAIR TW6 174 A2
Southampton Rw RSQ WC1B 11 M3
Southampton St COVGDN WC2E 11 M7
Southampton Wy CMBW SE5 159 L6
Southam St NKENS W10 8 B2
South Ap NTHWD HA6 92 E4
South Audley St MYFR/PKLN W1K 10 D8
South Av CAR SM5 222 B4
CHING E4 100 G1
EGH TW20 172 F9
RCH/KEW * TW9 155 M8
STHL UB1 133 N9
WOT/HER KT12 216 F6
South Avenue Gdns STHL UB1 133 N9
South Bank BH/WHM TN16 262 G2
STHWK SE1 12 B8
SURB KT6 199 K6
Southbank THDIT KT7 198 G7
South Bank Rd BERK HP4 33 L3
South Bank Ter SURB * KT6 199 K6
South Birkbeck Rd WAN E11 121 J8
South Black Lion La
HMSMTH W6 156 D4
South Bolton Gdns
WBPTN SW10 15 H7
The South Border PUR/KEN CR8 222 E7
Southborough Cl SURB KT6 199 J8
Southborough La HAYES BR2 206 B5
Southborough Rd BMLY BR1 206 B3
HOM E9 140 B3
SURB KT6 199 K8
Southborough Rd (The Lane)
SURB * KT6 199 K8
Southbourne HAYES BR2 205 M7
Southbourne Av
CDALE/KGS NW9 95 P10
Southbourne Cl PIN HA5 113 M5
Southbourne Crs HDN NW4 117 H2
Southbourne Gdns IL IG1 122 F10
LEE/GVPK SE12 183 N1
RSLP HA4 113 J6
Southbridge Pl CROY/NA CR0 223 K1
Southbridge Rd CROY/NA CR0 223 K1
Southbridge Wy NWDGN UB2 153 M1
Southbrook SBW CM21 29 P2
Southbrook Dr CHES/WCR EN8 62 C4
Southbrook Rd LEW SE13 183 K2
STRHM/NOR SW16 202 F1
South Bucks Wy CFSP/GDCR SL9 90 D10
DEN/HRF UB9 111 K6
Southbury Av EN EN1 79 P8
Southbury Cl HCH RM12 125 L10
Southbury Rd EN EN1 79 N8
South Carriage Dr KTBR SW1X 16 B1
SKENS SW7 15 N2
South Charlton Mead La
HOD EN11 45 H4
Southchurch Ct PLMGR N13 98 G6
Southchurch Rd EHAM E6 142 C4
Southcliffe Dr CFSP/GDCR SL9 90 B6
South Cl BAR EN5 77 J7
BXLYHS DA6 163 N10
CRAWE RH10 284 A6
DAGE RM10 144 B3
FELT TW13 175 P6
HGT N6 118 C4
LCOL/BKTW AL2 56 A1
PIN HA5 113 N5
SL SL1 128 C9
WDR/YW UB7 152 A2
WOKN/KNAP GU21 231 P2
South Close Gn REIG RH2 258 C5
South Colonnade POP/IOD E14 140 F10
Southcombe St WKENS W14 14 A5
Southcote WOKN/KNAP GU21 232 A2
Southcote Av BRYLDS KT5 199 N7
FELT TW13 175 H5
Southcote Ri RSLP HA4 112 E5
Southcote Rd ARCH N19 118 D9
REDH RH1 258 D6
SAND/SEL CR2 223 M6
SNWD SE25 204 A5
WALTH E17 120 C3
South Cottage Dr
RKW/CH/CXG WD3 71 J9
South Cottage Gdns
RKW/CH/CXG WD3 71 J9
South Countess Rd WALTH E17 120 E1
South Crs CAN/RD E16 141 J6
Southcroft EGH TW20 171 N8
SLN SL2 128 G6
Southcroft Av WELL DA16 163 H9
WWKM BR4 205 M9
Southcroft Rd ORP BR6 207 H10
STRHM/NOR SW16 180 C9
South Cross Rd BARK/HLT IG6 122 F3
South Croxted Rd DUL SE21 181 L6
Southdale CHIG IG7 102 G7
Southdean Gdns
WIM/MER SW19 179 J5
South Dene MLHL NW7 96 A4
Southdene RSEV TN14 228 A9
Southdown Av HNWL W7 154 F2
Southdown Ct HAT AL10 40 D7
Southdown Crs
GNTH/NBYPK IG2 123 H3
RYLN/HDSTN HA2 114 B6
Southdown Dr RYNPK SW20 178 G10
Southdown Rd CAR SM5 222 B5
CTHM CR3 242 E8
EMPK RM11 125 J5
HARP AL5 20 A3
HAT AL10 40 D7
RYNPK SW20 200 G1
WOT/HER KT12 217 M1
South Downs Wy
BRKHM/BTCW RH3 255 C6
DORK RH4 255 H8
KWD/TDW/WH KT20 255 L8
Southdown Vls
SEVS/STOTM * N15 119 J3
South Dr BEAC HP9 108 A1
BELMT SM2 221 H6
BNSTD SM7 221 P9
BRW CM14 107 J5
CHOB/PIR GU24 230 B7
COUL/CHIP CR5 240 E1
GPK RM2 125 K1
ORP BR6 227 H2
POTB/CUF EN6 60 F6
RDKG RH5 273 H2
RSLP HA4 112 F6
STALE/WH AL4 39 K5
VW GU25 193 M7
South Ealing Rd EA W5 155 J1
South Eastern Av ED N9 99 N4
South Eaton Pl BGVA SW1W 16 D5
South Eden Park Rd BECK BR3 204 G6
South Edwardes Sq KENS W8 14 D4
South End CROY/NA CR0 223 K1
GT/LBKH KT23 254 A2
KENS W8 15 H3
Southend Arterial Rd
EMPK RM11 125 M1
RBRW/HUT CM13 126 G3
RBRW/HUT CM13 127 M3
Southend Cl ELTH/MOT SE9 184 E2
Southend Crs ELTH/MOT SE9 184 D2
Southend La CAT SE6 182 E7
WAB EN9 63 N10
Southend Rd BECK BR3 182 F10
GRAYS RM17 167 P3
South End Rd HAMP NW3 117 P9
RAIN RM13 145 H3
Southend Rd REDBR IG4 122 B1
Southend Rd (North Circular)
WALTH E17 101 J9

South End Rw KENS W8 15 H3
Southerland Cl WEY KT13 216 D1
Southern Av EBED/NFELT TW14 175 H4
REDH RH1 276 B7
SNWD SE25 203 N3
Southern Down FELT * TW13 175 K4
Southern Dr LOU IG10 82 C10
Southerngate Wy NWCR SE14 160 D6
Southern Gv BOW E3 140 E5
Southernhay LOU IG10 82 A9
Southern Perimeter Rd
HTHAIR TW6 174 C2
Southern Pl SWLY BR8 208 E4
Southern Rd EFNCH N2 118 A2
PLSTW E13 141 N4
Southern Rw NKENS W10 8 A2
Southerns La COUL/CHIP CR5 239 M10
Southern St IS N1 5 N7
Southern Ter HOD * EN11 26 G10
Southern Wy CHDH RM6 124 B4
HLWW/ROY CM19 46 D4
Southernwood Cl HHNE HP2 36 B5
Southerton Rd HMSMTH * W6 156 F3
Southerton Wy RAD WD7 57 K9
South Esk Rd FSTGT E7 141 P1
Southey Rd BRXN/ST SW9 159 H7
SEVS/STOTM N15 119 M3
WIM/MER SW19 179 K10
Southey St PGE/AN SE20 182 C10
Southey Wk TIL RM18 168 E7
Southfield BAR EN5 76 G10
WGCE AL7 22 G7
Southfield Av WATN WD24 73 K4
Southfield Cl UX/CGN UB8 132 B6
South Field Cl WDSR SL4 148 B2
Southfield Gdns SL SL1 128 A7
TWK TW1 176 E7
Southfield Pk RYLN/HDSTN HA2 114 A2
Southfield Pl WEY KT13 216 C4
Southfield Rd CHES/WCR EN8 62 D8
CHST BR7 207 J3
CHSWK W4 156 A1
HOD EN11 44 F1
PEND EN3 80 A10
Southfields E/WMO/HCT KT8 198 D6
HDN NW4 116 E1
Southfields Av ASHF TW15 174 C9
Southfields Ms
WAND/EARL * SW18 179 K2
Southfields Rd CTHM CR3 242 G9
GDST RH9 260 G1
WAND/EARL SW18 179 K2
Southfield Wy STALE/WH AL4 39 J3
Southfleet Av HART DA3 211 N2
Southfleet Rd GVW DA11 190 C4
ORP BR6 207 H10
RDART DA2 189 H7
SWCM DA10 189 M3
South Gdns WBLY * HA9 115 M7
WIM/MER SW19 179 N10
South Ga HLW CM20 46 G1
PUR RM19 166 B3
Southgate Av CRAWE RH10 283 N10
South Gate Av FELT TW13 174 E7
Southgate Dr CRAWE RH10 283 N9
Southgate Gv IS N1 7 H4
Southgate Pde CRAWE * RH10 283 N9
Southgate Rd CRAWW RH11 283 N9
IS N1 7 H4
POTB/CUF EN6 59 M9
South Gipsy Rd WELL DA16 163 N9
South Gn SL SL1 129 K9
South Gv CHERT KT16 195 J6
HGT N6 118 B6
SEVS/STOTM N15 119 L3
WALTH E17 120 E3
South Hall Cl EYN DA4 209 N7
South Hall Dr RAIN RM13 145 J7
South Hl CHST BR7 184 C9
GU GU1 268 A2
NTHWD * HA6 92 F9
South Hill Av HRW HA1 114 C8
South Hill Gv HRW HA1 114 D9
South Hill Pk HAMP NW3 117 P9
South Hill Park Gdns HAMP NW3 117 P9
South Hill Rd GVE DA12 190 E4
HAYES BR2 205 K3
HHW HP1 35 M6
Southholme Cl NRWD SE19 203 M1
Southill La PIN HA5 113 H2
Southill Rd CHST BR7 184 B10
Southill St POP/IOD E14 140 G8
South Island Pl BRXN/ST SW9 158 G6
South Kensington Station Ar
SKENS SW7 15 M5
South Kent Av GVW DA11 189 P2
South Lambeth Pl VX/NE SW8 17 M9
South Lambeth Rd VX/NE SW8 17 M10
Southland Rd WOOL/PLUM SE18 163 J6
Southlands Av HORL RH6 280 B3
ORP BR6 227 H1
Southlands Cl COUL/CHIP CR5 240 G3
Southlands Dr WIM/MER SW19 178 G5
Southlands Gv BMLY BR1 206 B3
Southlands La OXTED RH8 260 G10
Southlands Rd DEN/HRF UB9 111 J8
HAYES BR2 206 A4
IVER SL0 131 H1
Southland Ter PUR * RM19 166 A4
Southland Wy ISLW TW7 176 C1
South La KUT KT1 199 J3
NWMAL KT3 200 A4
South La West NWMAL KT3 200 A4
Southlea Rd WDSR SL4 149 M9
South Ley WGCE AL7 23 H8
South Lodge Av MTCM CR4 202 F4
South Lodge Crs ENC/FH EN2 78 E8
South Lodge Dr STHGT/OAK N14 78 F9
South Lodge Rd WOT/HER KT12 217 H5
South Md CDALE/KGS NW9 96 C9
HOR/WEW KT19 220 C4
REDH RH1 258 A7
Southmead Crs CHES/WCR EN8 62 D6
South Meadow La WDSR SL4 149 H6
Southmead Rd WIM/MER SW19 179 H4
South Molton La
MYFR/PKLN W1K 10 E6
South Molton Rd CAN/RD E16 141 M8
South Molton St MYFR/PKLN W1K 10 E6
Southmont Rd ESH/CLAY KT10 198 D9
Southmoor Wy HOM E9 140 E1
South Mt TRDG/WHET * N20 97 M3
South Norwood Hl SNWD SE25 203 M2
South Oak Rd STRHM/NOR SW16 180 G7
Southold Ri ELTH/MOT SE9 184 C6
Southolm St VX/NE SW8 158 C7
South Ordnance Rd PEND EN3 80 F3
Southover BMLY BR1 183 M8
NFNCH/WDSP N12 97 K4
South Pde CHEL SW3 15 M7
CHSWK W4 156 A3
EDGW * HA8 95 M10
HORL * RH6 280 A3
REDH * RH1 258 D4
WLGTN * SM6 222 D3
South Pk CFSP/GDCR SL9 110 C3
SEV TN13 265 J1
South Park Av RKW/CH/CXG WD3 71 J9
South Park Crs CAT SE6 183 K4
CFSP/GDCR SL9 110 C3
IL IG1 122 G8
South Park Dr CFSP/GDCR SL9 110 B2
IL IG1 123 H8
South Park Gdns BERK HP4 33 N4
South Park Gv NWMAL KT3 199 P4
South Park Hill Rd
SAND/SEL CR2 223 L2
South Park La REDH RH1 277 P3
South Park Ms FUL/PGN SW6 157 L9
South Park Rd IL IG1 122 G8
WIM/MER SW19 179 K9
South Park Ter IL IG1 122 G8
South Park Vw CFSP/GDCR SL9 110 C2
South Park Wy RSLP HA4 133 K1
South Pier Rd HORL RH6 280 B8
South Pl BRYLDS KT5 199 L7
HLW CM20 29 K8
LVPST EC2M 13 H4
PEND EN3 80 B9
South Place Ms LVPST EC2M 13 H4
Southport Rd WOOL/PLUM SE18 162 G3
South Rdg WEY KT13 216 C6
Southridge Pl RYNPK SW20 178 G10
South Riding LCOL/BKTW AL2 55 P6
South Ri BAY/PAD * W2 9 P7
CAR SM5 221 P5
South Rd AMS HP6 69 H2
CHDH RM6 123 M3
CHOB/PIR GU24 230 E2
EA W5 155 J3
ED N9 99 P2
EDGW HA8 95 N9
EGH TW20 171 P9
ERITH DA8 164 G5
FELT TW13 175 L8
FSTH SE23 182 C5
GUW GU2 249 N8
HLW CM20 29 K8
HPTN TW12 175 M9
REIG RH2 275 L1
RKW/CH/CXG WD3 70 F9
SOCK/AV RM15 147 H5
STHL UB1 133 N10
WDR/YW UB7 152 B2
WEY KT13 216 C6
WEY KT13 216 D2
WHTN TW2 176 C6
WIM/MER SW19 179 N9
WOKN/KNAP GU21 214 A10
WOKN/KNAP GU21 231 P1
South Rw BKHTH/KID SE3 161 M8
DTCH/LGLY * SL3 110 A9
Southsea Av WATW WD18 73 H8
Southsea Rd KUT KT1 199 K4
South Sea St BERM/RHTH SE16 160 E2
South Side CFSP/GDCR SL9 110 A1
HMSMTH W6 156 C2
SEVS/STOTM * N15 119 N2
Southside Common
WIM/MER SW19 178 G9
Southspring ELTH/MOT SE9 184 G3
South Sq GINN WC1R 12 A4
GLDGN NW11 117 K4
South Station Ap REDH RH1 276 G2
South St BMLY BR1 205 M2
BRW CM14 107 H3
DORK RH4 272 F3
EPSOM KT18 220 A9
GVE DA12 190 E3
HERT/WAS SG14 25 L5
ISLW TW7 154 F9
MYFR/PKLN W1K 10 D9
PEND EN3 80 C9
RAIN RM13 144 D4
ROM RM1 124 F3
STA TW18 173 J8
WARE SG12 27 H7
South Tenter St WCHPL E1 13 M7
South Ter DORK RH4 272 G3
EYN * DA4 209 N7
SKENS SW7 15 N5
SURB KT6 199 K6
WDGN N22 98 F10
South V HRW HA1 114 D9
NRWD SE19 181 M9
Southvale Rd BKHTH/KID SE3 161 K8
South Vale Rd SURB KT6 199 K9
South Vw BMLY BR1 205 P2
WDSR * SL4 149 H4
South View Av TIL RM18 168 D7
Southview Av WLSDN NW10 116 C10
South View Cl BXLY DA5 186 A2
CRAWE RH10 285 M2
Southview Cl CHESW EN7 61 M2
SWLY BR8 209 H4
TOOT SW17 180 B8
South View Ct NRWD * SE19 181 K10
WOKS/MYFD GU22 232 B4
South View Crs GNTH/NBYPK IG2 122 E4
Southview Dr SWFD E18 121 N1
South View Dr UPMR RM14 125 P8
Southview Gdns WLGTN SM6 222 D4
South View Hts WTHK * RM20 167 H5
South View Rd ASHTD KT21 237 J5
CEND/HSY/T N8 118 E1
CFSP/GDCR SL9 110 A2
LOU IG10 82 C10
PIN HA5 93 J7
RDART DA2 187 L6
WTHK RM20 167 H5
Southview Rd BMLY BR1 183 J7
CTHM CR3 242 G10
WARL CR6 241 P5
Southviews SAND/SEL CR2 224 C5
South Vls CAMTN NW1 5 K2
Southville VX/NE SW8 158 E7
Southville Cl EBED/NFELT TW14 174 F3
HOR/WEW KT19 220 A5
Southville Crs EBED/NFELT TW14 174 F4
Southville Rd EBED/NFELT TW14 174 F4
THDIT KT7 198 F7
South Wk REIG * RH2 257 L10
WWKM BR4 205 K10
Southwark Br CANST EC4R 12 F8
Southwark Bridge Rd STHWK SE1 12 F9
Southwark Park Est
BERM/RHTH * SE16 160 A3
Southwark Park Rd
BERM/RHTH SE16 19 M5
Southwark Pl BMLY BR1 206 C3
Southwark St STHWK SE1 12 D9
Southwater Cl BECK BR3 182 G10
CRAWW RH11 283 K7
South Wy ABLGY WD5 54 E9
CAR SM5 221 N6
CROY/NA CR0 204 D10
FBAR/BDGN N11 98 D7
HAT AL10 40 D8
PUR RM19 166 D2
RYLN/HDSTN HA2 113 P2
WAB EN9 80 G3
WBLY HA9 115 M10
Southway GLDGN NW11 117 L4
GUW GU2 249 K10
HAYES BR2 205 M7
RYNPK SW20 200 G4
TRDG/WHET N20 97 K3
WLGTN SM6 222 D1
Southway Pk GUW * GU2 249 M8
Southways Pk CRAWE * RH10 283 N2
South Weald Dr WAB EN9 63 J9
South Weald Rd BRW CM14 106 F4
Southwell Av NTHLT UB5 133 P1
Southwell Gdns SKENS SW7 15 J5
Southwell Grove Rd WAN E11 121 K7
Southwell Rd CMBW SE5 159 K9
CROY/NA CR0 203 H6
KTN/HRWW/W HA3 115 J4
South Western Rd TWK TW1 176 F2
Southwest Rd WAN E11 121 J6
South Wharf Rd BAY/PAD W2 9 L5
GRAYS RM17 167 L5
Southwick Ms BAY/PAD W2 9 M5
Southwick Pl BAY/PAD W2 9 N6
Southwick St BAY/PAD W2 9 N5
Southwick Yd BAY/PAD * W2 9 P6
Southwold Dr BARK IG11 123 K10
Southwold Rd BXLY DA5 186 C2
CLPT E5 120 A7
WATN WD24 73 K3
Southwood Sp DTCH/LGLY SL3 150 F1
Southwood Av CHERT KT16 214 F4
COUL/CHIP CR5 240 D1
HGT N6 118 C5
KUTN/CMB KT2 199 P1
WOKN/KNAP GU21 231 J4
Southwood Cl BMLY BR1 206 C4
WPK KT4 200 G8
Southwood Dr BRYLDS KT5 199 P7
Southwood Gdns BARK/HLT IG6 122 E2
ESH/CLAY KT10 198 F10
Southwood La HGT N6 118 B5
Southwood Lawn Rd HGT N6 118 B5
Southwood Pk HGT * N6 118 C5
Southwood Rd ELTH/MOT SE9 184 E5
THMD SE28 143 L10
South Worple Wy
MORT/ESHN SW14 156 A9
Sovereign Cl EA W5 135 H7
PUR/KEN CR8 222 G6
RSLP HA4 112 F6
WAP E1W 140 A9
Sovereign Ct E/WMO/HCT KT8 197 N4
Sovereign Crs BERM/RHTH SE16 140 D9
Sovereign Gv ALP/SUD HA0 115 J9
Sovereign Ms BETH * E2 7 L7
Sovereign Pk HHNE * HP2 36 C4
WLSDN * NW10 136 A3
Sovereign Rd BARK IG11 143 M5
Sowerby Cl ELTH/MOT SE9 184 C1
Sowrey Av RAIN RM13 144 G1
Space Waye EBED/NFELT TW14 175 H1
Spackmans Wy WDSR SL4 149 H2
Spa Cl NRWD SE19 203 M1
Spa Dr EPSOM KT18 219 M10
Spafield St CLKNW * EC1R 12 A1
Spa Green Est CLKNW * EC1R 6 B9
Spa Hl THHTH CR7 203 L1
Spalding Cl EDGW HA8 96 B8
Spalding Rd HDN NW4 116 E3
TOOT SW17 180 C8
Spalt Cl RBRW/HUT CM13 107 M3
Spanby Rd BOW E3 140 F6
Spaniards Cl GLDGN NW11 117 M6
Spaniards End GLDGN NW11 117 M6
Spaniards Rd HAMP NW3 117 M7
Spanish Pl MHST * W1U 10 D5
Spanish Rd WAND/EARL SW18 179 M1
Spareleaze Hl LOU IG10 82 C8
Sparepenny La EYN DA4 209 M7
Sparkbridge Rd HRW HA1 114 D6
Sparke Ter CAN/RD * E16 141 L8
Sparkford Gdns
FBAR/BDGN N11 98 B6
Sparks Cl ACT W3 136 A8
BCTR RM8 123 N7
HPTN TW12 175 M9
Spa Rd BERM/RHTH SE16 19 L4
Sparrow Cl HPTN TW12 175 M9
Sparrow Dr STMC/STPC BR5 206 F8
Sparrow Farm Dr
EBED/NFELT TW14 175 K3
Sparrow Farm Rd EW KT17 220 D1
Sparrow Gn DAGE RM10 124 C8
Sparrow Rw CHOB/PIR GU24 212 G3
Sparrows Herne BUSH WD23 94 A1
Sparrows La ELTH/MOT SE9 184 F3
HLWE CM17 31 M6
RBSF CM22 31 M4
Sparrows Md REDH RH1 258 B7
Sparrows Wy BUSH * WD23 94 B1
Sparrows Wick BUSH * WD23 94 B2
Sparrowswick Ride
STALW/RED AL3 38 B1
Sparsholt Rd ARCH N19 118 G6
BARK IG11 143 H3
Sparta St LEW SE13 161 H7
Sparvell Rd WOKN/KNAP GU21 230 G5
Speakers Ct CROY/NA * CR0 203 L8
Spearman St
WOOL/PLUM * SE18 162 D5
Spear Ms ECT SW5 14 F6
Spears Rd ARCH N19 118 F6
Speart La HEST TW5 153 M6
Spedan Cl HAMP NW3 117 L8
Speedbird Wy WDR/YW UB7 151 L6
Speedgate Hl HART DA3 210 F9
Speedwell Cl RGUE GU4 250 F7
Speedwell St DEPT SE8 160 F6
Speer Rd THDIT KT7 198 E6
Speirs Cl NWMAL KT3 200 C6
Spekehill ELTH/MOT SE9 184 C6
Speke Rd THHTH CR7 203 L2
Speldhurst Cl HAYES BR2 205 L5
Speldhurst Rd CHSWK W4 156 A2
HOM E9 140 C2
Spellbrook Wk IS * N1 6 F5
Spelman St WCHPL E1 13 N3
Spelthorne Gv SUN TW16 174 G10
Spelthorne La ASHF TW15 174 D10
Spence Av BF/WBF KT14 215 P10
Spence Cl BERM/RHTH SE16 160 E1
Spencer Av CHESW EN7 61 M2
PLMGR N13 98 G7
YEAD UB4 133 H7
Spencer Cl EPSOM KT18 238 B5
FNCH N3 97 J10
ORP BR6 207 H9
UX/CGN UB8 131 M5
WFD IG8 101 P6
WLSDN NW10 135 L5
WOKN/KNAP GU21 214 F10
Spencer Dr EFNCH N2 117 M4
Spencer Gdns EGH TW20 172 A8
MORT/ESHN SW14 177 P1
Spencer Ga STAL AL1 38 D4
Spencer Hl WIM/MER SW19 179 H9
Spencer Hill Rd WIM/MER SW19 179 H10
Spencer House SURB * KT6 199 K5
Spencer Ms HMSMTH W6 14 A9
STAL AL1 38 D5
Spencer Pk WAND/EARL SW18 179 N1
Spencer Pl CROY/NA CR0 203 L7
IS N1 6 C3
STALE/WH AL4 21 H9
WEST SW1P 17 H4
Spencer Ri KTTN NW5 118 C9
Spencer Rd ACT W3 135 P10
ALP/SUD HA0 115 H7
BMLY BR1 183 L10
BTSEA SW11 157 N10
CEND/HSY/T N8 118 G3
CHSWK W4 155 P6
COB KT11 235 J1
CTHM CR3 241 L7
DTCH/LGLY SL3 150 C2
E/WMO/HCT KT8 198 B4
EHAM E6 142 A3
FBAR/BDGN N11 98 C5
GDMY/SEVK IG3 123 J6
ISLW TW7 154 C7
KTN/HRWW/W HA3 94 D10
MTCM CR4 202 A7
MTCM CR4 202 B3
RAIN RM13 144 E5
RYNPK SW20 200 E1
SAND/SEL CR2 223 M2
TOTM N17 99 P9
WALTH E17 101 H10
WHTN TW2 176 D6
Spencers Cft HLWS CM18 47 K3
Spencers La HORL RH6 279 J6
Spencers Rd CRAWW RH11 283 M8
Spencer St FSBYE EC1V 6 C10
GVW DA11 190 D3
HERT/BAY SG13 25 M4
NWDGN UB2 153 L2
STALW/RED AL3 38 C6
Spencer Wk PUT/ROE SW15 156 G10
RKW/CH/CXG WD3 71 M9
TIL RM18 168 D8
Spencer Wy HHW HP1 35 K3
REDH RH1 276 B5
Spenser Av WEY KT13 216 B5
Spenser Crs UPMR RM14 126 B5
Spenser Gv STNW/STAM N16 119 M9
Spenser Ms DUL SE21 181 L4
Spenser Rd HARP AL5 20 B2
HNHL SE24 181 J1
Spenser St WESTW SW1E 17 H3
Spensley Wk STNW/STAM N16 119 L8
Speranza St WOOL/PLUM SE18 163 J4
Sperling Rd TOTM N17 99 N10
Spert St POP/IOD E14 140 D9
Speyhawk Pl POTB/CUF EN6 59 L6
Speyside STHGT/OAK N14 78 D10
Spey St POP/IOD E14 141 H7
Spey Wy ROM RM1 104 F8
Spezia Rd WLSDN NW10 136 D4
Spiceall RGUW GU3 266 G6
Spicer Cl CMBW SE5 159 J8
WOT/HER KT12 197 K6
Spicersfield CHESW EN7 61 P3
Spicers Fld LHD/OX KT22 218 C9
Spicer St STALW/RED AL3 38 B6
Spices Yd CROY/NA CR0 223 K1
Spielman Rd DART DA1 165 N10
Spiers Wy HORL RH6 280 C6
Spigurnell Rd TOTM N17 99 L9
Spikes Bridge Rd STHL UB1 133 M8
Spillbutters BRWN CM15 86 G2
Spilsby Cl CDALE/KGS NW9 96 B10
Spilsby Rd HARH RM3 105 M8
Spindle Cl WOOL/PLUM SE18 162 B2
Spindles TIL RM18 168 D6
Spindle Wy CRAWE RH10 283 P8
Spindlewood Gdns
CROY/NA CR0 223 L1
Spindlewoods
KWD/TDW/WH KT20 238 E8
Spindrift Av POP/IOD E14 160 G3
Spinel Cl WOOL/PLUM SE18 163 J4
Spingate Cl HCH RM12 125 K10
Spinnaker Cl BARK IG11 143 L5
Spinnells Rd RYLN/HDSTN HA2 113 N6
Spinners Wk WDSR SL4 149 H7
Spinney SL SL1 128 G10
Spinney Cl BECK BR3 204 G4
COB KT11 217 P7
NWMAL KT3 200 B5
RAIN RM13 144 F4
WDR/YW UB7 131 P9
WPK KT4 200 C10
Spinneycroft LHD/OX KT22 236 C1
Spinney Dr EBED/NFELT TW14 174 D3
Spinney Gdns DAGW RM9 123 P10
NRWD SE19 181 N8
Spinney Hl ADL/WDHM KT15 215 J2
Spinney La WDSR SL4 170 A4
Spinney Oak BMLY BR1 206 B2
CHERT KT16 214 G3
Spinney Pl AMSS * HP7 69 H5
Spinneys Dr STALW/RED * AL3 38 A8
The Spinneys BMLY BR1 206 C2
Spinney St HERT/BAY SG13 25 P5
The Spinney ALP/SUD HA0 114 F8
ASC SL5 192 D5
BARN * SW13 156 E5
BEAC HP9 88 D10
BERK HP4 33 L6
CHEAM SM3 220 F1
CHONG CM5 67 N6
CRAWW RH11 283 L9
CSHM HP5 51 J5
EPSOM KT18 238 E5
GT/LBKH KT23 236 A10
HERT/BAY SG13 25 P5
HLW CM20 29 K10
HOD EN11 44 E5
HORL RH6 280 B2
LHD/OX KT22 218 B8
NFNCH/WDSP * N12 97 M8
POTB/CUF EN6 59 N7
PUR/KEN CR8 223 J7
RBRW/HUT CM13 87 P10
RPLY/SEND GU23 251 M3
SCUP DA14 185 P8
STAN HA7 95 K5
STRHM/NOR SW16 180 D6
SUN TW16 197 H1
SWLY BR8 208 F2
WAT WD17 73 H5
WCHMH N21 99 H1
WGCE AL7 23 H6
Spinney Wy RSEV TN14 226 G7
The Spinning Wk SHGR GU5 270 B5
Spinning Wheel Md HLWS CM18 47 K4
Spire Cl GVE DA12 190 E4
The Spires DART DA1 187 L5
Spirit Quay WAP E1W 13 P9
Spital Heath RDKG RH5 273 H1
Spital La BRW CM14 106 E4
Spital Sq WCHPL E1 13 K3
Spital St DART DA1 187 L2
WCHPL E1 13 N3
Spital Yd WCHPL * E1 13 K3
Spitfire Est HEST * TW5 153 K4
Spitfire Wy HEST TW5 153 K4
Spode Wk KIL/WHAMP * NW6 117 L10
Spondon Rd SEVS/STOTM N15 119 P2
Spook Hl RDKG RH5 272 G7
Spoonbill Cl YEAD UB4 133 L7
Spooners Dr LCOL/BKTW AL2 56 B3
Spooner Wk WLGTN SM6 222 E2
Sportsbank St CAT SE6 183 H3
Spottons Gv TOTM N17 99 K9
Spout Hl CROY/NA CR0 224 F2
Spout La EDEN TN8 262 F10
STWL/WRAY TW19 173 K1
Spout La North
STWL/WRAY TW19 151 L10
Spratt Hall Rd WAN E11 121 M4
Spratts La ADL/WDHM KT15 215 H3
Spray St WOOL/PLUM SE18 162 E3
Spreighton Rd E/WMO/HCT KT8 198 A4
Sprimont Pl CHEL SW3 16 A7
Springall St PECK SE15 160 A6
Springate Fld DTCH/LGLY SL3 150 B1
Spring Av EGH TW20 172 B9
Springbank WCHMH N21 78 G10
Springbank Av HCH RM12 125 K10
Springbank Rd LEW SE13 183 K2
Springbank Wk CAMTN NW1 5 J4
Spring Bottom La REDH RH1 259 K3
Springbourne Ct BECK BR3 205 H1
Spring Bridge Rd EA W5 135 J9
Spring Cl BAR EN5 76 G9
BCTR RM8 123 N6
BORE WD6 75 M6
CSHM HP5 70 A2
DEN/HRF UB9 91 N9
Springclose La CHEAM SM3 221 H3
Spring Copse CRAWE RH10 285 K2
Springcopse Rd REIG RH2 275 M1
Spring Cnr FELT * TW13 175 H6
Spring Cottages SURB * KT6 199 J5
Spring Court Rd ENC/FH EN2 79 H4
Springcroft HART DA3 211 M6
Springcroft Av EFNCH N2 118 A1
Spring Crofts BUSH WD23 73 P9
Spring Cross HART DA3 211 M10
Springdale Rd STNW/STAM N16 119 L9
Spring Dr PIN HA5 113 H4
Springett Pl AMS HP6 69 L3
Springfarm Cl RAIN RM13 145 L5
Springfield BUSH WD23 94 C2
CLPT E5 120 A6
EPP CM16 65 J8
LTWR GU18 212 B7
OXTED RH8 261 J6
Springfield Av HPTN TW12 176 A9
MUSWH N10 118 D1
RYNPK SW20 201 J3
SWLY BR8 208 G4
Springfield Cl CHONG CM5 67 N2
CSHM HP5 51 H9
NFNCH/WDSP N12 97 L6
POTB/CUF EN6 59 N7
RKW/CH/CXG WD3 72 C9
STAN HA7 94 F4
WDSR SL4 148 G8
WOKN/KNAP GU21 231 J4
Springfield Dr GNTH/NBYPK IG2 122 F3
Springfield Gdns BMLY BR1 206 C4
CDALE/KGS NW9 116 A3
CLPT E5 120 A6
RSLP HA4 113 J6
UPMR RM14 126 B8
WFD IG8 101 P8
WWKM BR4 204 G9
Springfield Gv CHARL SE7 161 P5
SUN TW16 197 H1
Springfield La KIL/WHAMP NW6 2 G6
WEY KT13 216 C1
Springfield Mdw WEY KT13 216 C1
Springfield Mt CDALE/KGS NW9 116 B3
Springfield Pl NWMAL KT3 199 P4
Springfield Ri SYD SE26 182 A7
Springfield Rd ASHF TW15 174 A8
Spring Field Rd BERK HP4 33 L2
Springfield Rd BMLY BR1 206 C4
BXLYHN DA7 164 C9
CDH/CHF RM16 168 B1
CHES/WCR EN8 62 D8
CHING E4 101 K2
CRAWW RH11 283 M8
CSHM HP5 51 H8
DORK RH4 272 A3
DTCH/LGLY SL3 150 E6
EHAM E6 142 C2
EW KT17 220 F6
FBAR/BDGN N11 98 D6
GSTN WD25 55 J9
GU GU1 268 B1
HHNE HP2 36 A5
HNWL W7 134 D10
HRW HA1 114 D4
HYS/HAR UB3 133 K10
KUT KT1 199 K4
SEVS/STOTM N15 119 P2
SRTFD * E15 141 K5
STAL AL1 38 F7
STALE/WH AL4 39 N6
STJWD NW8 3 J6
SYD SE26 182 A8
TEDD TW11 176 F8
THHTH CR7 203 K1
WALTH E17 120 E4
WDSR SL4 148 G8
WELL DA16 163 L9

WHTN TW2 175 P4
WIM/MER SW19 179 J8
WLGTN SM6 222 C2
Springfields AMS HP6 69 H3
BROX EN10 44 E5
WGCW AL8 22 E7
Springfields Cl CHERT KT16 195 L8
Springfield Wk KIL/WHAMP NW6 2 G6
Springfield Wy STMC/STPC BR5 207 M3
Spring Gdns ASC SL5 192 A4
BH/WHM TN16 243 P4
CRAWE RH10 285 K2
E/WMO/HCT KT8 198 B5
GSTN WD25 73 K1
HBRY N5 119 K10
HCH RM12 125 J9
ORP BR6 227 L3
ROMW/RG RM7 124 D3
WFD IG8 101 P8
WHALL SW1A 11 L9
WLGTN SM6 222 D2
Spring Gln HAT AL10 40 C5
Spring Gv CHSWK W4 155 M4
GT/LBKH KT23 236 A9
GVE DA12 190 E4
HPTN TW12 198 A1
LOU IG10 82 A10
MTCM CR4 202 B1
RGODL GU7 267 K9
Spring Grove Crs HEST TW5 154 B7
Spring Grove Rd HSLW TW3 154 B7
RCHPK/HAM TW10 177 L1
Springhall La SBW CM21 29 P2
Springhall Rd SBW CM21 29 P1
Springhaven Cl GU GU1 250 D10
Spring Head Rd BGR/WK TN15 247 N3
Springhead Rd ERITH DA8 164 G5
GVW DA11 189 P3
Spring Hl CLPT E5 119 P5
SYD SE26 182 B7
Spring Hills HLW CM20 28 D10
Springholm Cl BH/WHM TN16 243 P4
Springhurst Cl CROY/NA CR0 224 E1
Spring Lake STAN HA7 94 G5
Spring La CLPT E5 120 A6
HHW HP1 35 K5
MUSWH N10 118 B1
OXTED RH8 261 J7
SL SL1 128 E10
SLN SL2 128 G2
SNWD SE25 204 A6
Springle La HERT/BAY SG13 26 E8
Spring Ms MHST * W1U 10 B3
Spring Park Av CROY/NA CR0 204 C9
Springpark Dr BECK BR3 205 H3
FSBYPK N4 119 K6
Spring Park Rd CROY/NA CR0 204 C9
Spring Pl FNCH N3 97 K10
KTTN NW5 118 B10
Spring Plat CRAWE RH10 284 D7
Spring Plat Ct CRAWE * RH10 284 D7
Springpond Rd DAGW RM9 123 P10
Springrice Rd LEW SE13 183 H2
Spring Ri EGH TW20 172 B9
Spring Rd FELT TW13 174 G6
Spring Shaw Rd STMC/STPC BR5 207 K1
The Springs BROX EN10 44 E10
HERT/BAY * SG13 25 N4
Spring St BAY/PAD W2 9 L6
EW KT17 220 C5
Spring Tide Cl PECK * SE15 159 P7
Spring V BXLYHN DA7 164 C10
GRH DA9 189 H2
Springvale Av BTFD TW8 155 J4
Spring Vale Cl SWLY BR8 186 G10
Springvale Ct GVW * DA11 189 P5
Spring V North DART DA1 187 L3
Spring V South DART * DA1 187 L3
Springvale Ter WKENS W14 156 G2
Spring View Rd WARE SG12 26 B3
Spring Villa Rd EDGW HA8 95 M8
Spring Vls WEA * W13 134 G10
Spring Wk BROX EN10 44 B7
WCHPL E1 13 N3
Springwater Cl
WOOL/PLUM * SE18 162 D7
Spring Wy HHNE HP2 36 C4
Springwell Av RKW/CH/CXG WD3 91 K3
WLSDN NW10 136 C3
Springwell Ct
RKW/CH/CXG * WD3 91 K3
WARE * SG12 27 H7
Springwell La RKW/CH/CXG WD3 91 K4
Springwell Rd HEST TW5 153 L7
STRHM/NOR SW16 181 H7
Springwood CHESW EN7 61 N2
Springwood Cl DEN/HRF UB9 91 N9
Springwood Crs EDGW HA8 95 P3
Spring Woods VW GU25 193 N4
Springwood Wk STALE/WH AL4 39 H3
Springwood Wy ROM RM1 125 H3
Sprowston Ms FSTGT E7 141 M1
Sprowston Rd FSTGT E7 121 M10
Sprucedale Cl SWLY BR8 208 F2
Sprucedale Gdns CROY/NA CR0 224 C1
PUR/KEN CR8 222 F5
Spruce Hl HLWS CM18 47 H5
Spruce Hills Rd WALTH E17 101 H10
Spruce Rd BH/WHM TN16 244 A2
Spruce Wy LCOL/BKTW AL2 56 A3
Sprules Rd BROCKY SE4 160 D8
Spur Cl ABLGY WD5 54 E9
ABR/ST RM4 83 L7
Spur Dr KWD/TDW/WH KT20 239 L7
Spurfield E/WMO/HCT KT8 198 A3
Spurgate RBRW/HUT CM13 107 M3
Spurgeon Av NRWD SE19 203 L1
Spurgeon Cl CRAWW * RH11 283 M6
Spurgeon Rd NRWD SE19 181 L10
Spurgeon St STHWK SE1 18 G4
Spurling Rd DAGW RM9 144 A1
EDUL * SE22 159 N10
Spurrell Av RDART DA2 186 E7
Spur Rd BARK IG11 142 F5
EBED/NFELT TW14 175 J1
ISLW TW7 154 F6
ORP BR6 207 K9
SEVS/STOTM * N15 119 L2
STAN HA7 95 K5
STHWK SE1 18 A2
WHALL SW1A 16 G2
Spurstowe Rd HACK E8 140 A1
Spurstowe Ter HACK E8 119 P10
The Spur CHES/WCR * EN8 62 C4
SL SL1 128 C7
WOKN/KNAP GU21 230 G4
Squadrons Ap HCH RM12 145 K1
The Square BH/WHM TN16 243 P6
BROX EN10 44 D9
CAR SM5 222 B2
CRAWE RH10 283 N7
GUW GU2 267 L2
HHW * HP1 35 N6
HMSMTH W6 156 F4
RCHPK/HAM TW10 177 K1
SBW CM21 29 P1
SEV TN13 246 F8
STKPK UB11 132 E10
SWLY * BR8 208 E3
WATN WD24 73 J3
WDR/YW UB7 151 L7
WFD IG8 101 M6
Squarey St TOOT SW17 179 M6
Squerryes Mede
BH/WHM * TN16 262 F3
Squire Gdns STJWD NW8 3 L10
Squire's Bridge Rd SHPTN TW17 196 A4
Squires Ct CRAWE RH10 285 P5
Squires Ct WIM/MER SW19 179 K7
Squires Fld SWLY BR8 209 H1
Squires La FNCH N3 97 L10
Squire's Mt HAMP NW3 117 N8
Squire's Rd SHPTN TW17 196 A4
Squires Wk ASHF TW15 174 E10
Squires Wy RDART DA2 186 F7
Squires Wood Dr CHST * BR7 184 C10
Squirrel Cha HHW HP1 35 H5
Squirrel Cl CRAWW RH11 283 L4
HSLWW TW4 153 K9
Squirrel Dr WDSR SL4 170 A4
Squirrel Ms HNWL * W7 134 F9
Squirrel's Cha CDH/CHF RM16 168 D1
Squirrels Cl HGDN/ICK UB10 132 B2
NFNCH/WDSP N12 97 M5
RGODL GU7 267 J8
Squirrels Gn GT/LBKH KT23 235 P9
WPK KT4 200 C9
Squirrel's Heath Av GPK RM2 125 J1
Squirrels Heath La EMPK RM11 125 K2
Squirrels Heath Rd HARH RM3 105 M10
The Squirrels BUSH WD23 74 C10
HERT/BAY SG13 25 P5
LEW SE13 161 J9
PIN HA5 113 N1
Squirrel's Wy EPSOM KT18 238 A1
Squirrel Wd BF/WBF KT14 215 L8
Squirries St BETH E2 7 P9
Stable Cl CRAWE RH10 284 E10
NTHLT UB5 133 P4
Stable La BEAC HP9 89 H7
Stable Ms REIG RH2 257 K10
WNWD SE27 181 K8
Stables End ORP BR6 206 F10
Stables Ms POTB/CUF * EN6 59 N4
The Stables COB KT11 217 N10
Stables Wy LBTH SE11 18 A7
Stable Wk EFNCH * N2 97 N9
Stable Wy NKENS W10 136 F8
Stable Yard Rd WHALL SW1A 11 H10
Stacey Av UED N18 100 B5
Stacey Cl GVE DA12 191 H8
LEY E10 121 J3
Stacey St HOLWY N7 119 H8
LSQ/SEVD WC2H 11 K6
Stackfield HLW CM20 29 H8
Stackfield Rd CRAWW RH11 283 H8
Stackhouse St KTBR SW1X 16 A3
Stacklands WGCW AL8 22 E7
Stack La HART DA3 211 L5
Stack Rd EYN DA4 210 C4
Stacy Pth CMBW * SE5 159 M6
Stadium Rd WOOL/PLUM SE18 162 C6
Stadium St WBPTN SW10 157 M6
Stadium Wy DART DA1 186 F2
HLWW/ROY CM19 28 C10
WBLY HA9 115 L9
Staffa Rd LEY E10 120 D6
Stafford Av EMPK RM11 125 L1
SLN SL2 129 H6
Stafford Cl CDH/CHF RM16 167 H3
CHEAM SM3 221 H3
CHES/WCR EN8 62 A5
CTHM CR3 241 N9
GRH DA9 188 E1
KIL/WHAMP NW6 2 E10
MDHD SL6 128 A8
SLH/COR SS17 169 K2
STHGT/OAK N14 78 D9
WALTH E17 120 E4
Stafford Dr BROX EN10 44 F6
Stafford Gdns CROY/NA CR0 222 G2
Stafford Lake CHOB/PIR GU24 230 F4
Stafford Pl RCHPK/HAM TW10 177 L3
WESTW SW1E 16 G3
Stafford Rd BOW E3 140 E4
CRAWW RH11 283 K4
CROY/NA CR0 223 H1
CTHM CR3 241 N9
FSTGT E7 141 P2
KIL/WHAMP NW6 2 E9
KTN/HRWW/W HA3 94 B8
NWMAL KT3 199 P3
RSLP HA4 112 G9
SCUP DA14 185 H7
WLGTN SM6 222 D3
Staffords HLWE CM17 29 P7
Staffordshire St PECK SE15 159 P7
Staffords Pl HORL RH6 280 C5
Stafford Ter KENS W8 14 E3
Stafford Wy SEV TN13 265 K3
Stagbury Av COUL/CHIP CR5 239 P4
Stagbury Cl COUL/CHIP CR5 239 P5
Stag Cl EDGW HA8 95 N10
Stagelands CRAWW RH11 283 L5
Staggart Gn BARK/HLT IG6 103 J6
Stagg Hl POTB/CUF EN6 77 N1
Stag Green Av BRKMPK AL9 40 F2
Stag Hl GUW GU2 267 M1
Stag La BERK HP4 33 M4
BKHH IG9 101 N3
CDALE/KGS NW9 115 P2
EDGW HA8 95 N10
PUT/ROE SW15 178 C6
RKW/CH/CXG WD3 70 F10
Stag Leys ASHTD KT21 237 K6
Stag Leys Cl BNSTD SM7 239 P1
Stag Pl WESTW SW1E 16 G3
Stags Wy ISLW TW7 154 E5
Stainash Crs STA TW18 173 L8
Stainash Pde STA * TW18 173 L8
Stainbank Rd MTCM CR4 202 C3
Stainby Cl WDR/YW UB7 151 P2
Stainby Rd SEVS/STOTM N15 119 N1
Stainer Rd BORE WD6 75 J5
Stainer St STHWK SE1 13 H10
Staines Av CHEAM SM3 200 G9
Staines By-pass
STWL/WRAY TW19 173 H6
Staines La CHERT KT16 195 J6
Staines Lane Cl CHERT KT16 195 J5
Staines Rd CHERT KT16 195 K4
EBED/NFELT TW14 174 E3
HSLWW TW4 175 L1
IL IG1 122 G9
STA TW18 195 L1
STWL/WRAY TW19 172 C4
WHTN TW2 176 B6
Staines Rd East SUN TW16 197 K1
Staines Rd West ASHF TW15 174 D10
Stainford Cl ASHF TW15 174 E8
Stainforth Rd GNTH/NBYPK IG2 122 G5
WALTH E17 120 F2
Staining La CITYW EC2V 12 F5
Stainmore Cl CHST BR7 206 G1
Stainsbury St BETH E2 140 B4
Stainsby Pl POP/IOD * E14 140 F8
Stainsby Rd POP/IOD E14 140 F8
Stains Cl CHES/WCR EN8 62 D4
Stainton Rd LEW SE13 183 J3
PEND EN3 80 B5
Stainton Wk WOKN/KNAP GU21 231 P4
Stairfoot La SEV TN13 246 D8
Staiths Wy KWD/TDW/WH KT20 238 E6
Stakers Ct HARP AL5 20 A2
Stakescorner Rd RGUW GU3 267 M8
Stalbridge St CAMTN NW1 9 P3
Stalham St BERM/RHTH SE16 160 A2
Stalham Wy WFD IG8 102 E9
Stambourne Wy NRWD SE19 181 M10
WWKM BR4 205 H10
Stamford Brook Av
HMSMTH W6 156 C2
Stamford Brook Gdns
HMSMTH W6 156 C2
Stamford Brook Rd
HMSMTH W6 156 C2
Stamford Cl KTN/HRWW/W HA3 94 D8
POTB/CUF EN6 59 N8
SEVS/STOTM N15 119 P2
STHL UB1 133 P9
Stamford Cottages
FUL/PGN * SW6 157 L6
Stamford Dr HAYES BR2 205 L4
Stamford Gdns DAGW RM9 143 M2
Stamford Green Rd EPSOM KT18 219 N9
Stamford Gv East
STNW/STAM N16 119 P6
Stamford Gv West
STNW/STAM N16 119 P6
Stamford Hl STNW/STAM N16 119 N6
Stamford Rd DAGW RM9 143 L2
EHAM E6 142 B3
IS N1 7 K3
SEVS/STOTM N15 119 P3
WAT WD17 73 J6
WOT/HER KT12 197 L10
Stamford St STHWK SE1 12 A10
Stamp Pl BETH E2 7 L9
Stanborough HACK * E8 7 L1
Stanborough Av BORE WD6 75 M4
Stanborough Cl HPTN TW12 175 N9
WGCW AL8 22 F6
Stanborough Gn WGCW AL8 22 F7
Stanborough La WGCW AL8 22 F7
Stanborough Ms WGCW * AL8 22 G5
Stanborough Rd HSLW TW3 154 C9
WGCW AL8 22 E8
Stanbridge Cl CRAWW RH11 283 H8
Stanbridge Pl WCHMH N21 99 J3
Stanbridge Rd PUT/ROE SW15 156 F9
Stanbrook Rd ABYW SE2 163 L1
GVW DA11 190 C4
Stanbury Av WAT WD17 72 F3
Stanbury Ct HAMP NW3 4 A2
Stanbury Rd PECK SE15 160 A7
Stancroft CDALE/KGS NW9 116 B2
Standale Gv RSLP HA4 112 D3
Standard Pl SDTCH EC2A 7 K10
Standard Rd BELV DA17 164 B4
BXLYHS DA6 163 P10
HSLWW TW4 153 M9
ORP BR6 226 D6
PEND EN3 80 D4
WLSDN NW10 135 P6
Standen Av HCH RM12 125 L8
Standen Rd WAND/EARL SW18 179 K3
Standfield ABLGY WD5 54 F7
Standfield Rd DAGE RM10 124 B10
Standingford EPP CM16 46 E6
Standinghall La CRAWE RH10 285 H9
Standish Rd HMSMTH W6 156 D3
Standring Ri HHS/BOV HP3 35 L9
Stane Cl WIM/MER SW19 179 L10
Stane Wy EW KT17 220 D6
WOOL/PLUM SE18 162 A6
Stanfield Rd BOW E3 140 D4
Stanfields Ct HLW CM20 29 H10
Stanford Cl HPTN TW12 175 N9
ROMW/RG RM7 124 C4
RSLP HA4 112 D4
WFD IG8 102 B6
Stanford Ct WAB EN9 63 M9
Stanford Gdns SOCK/AV RM15 146 D10
Stanford Pl STHWK SE1 19 J6
Stanford Rivers Rd CHONG CM5 67 P7
Stanford Rd CDH/CHF RM16 168 B1
FBAR/BDGN N11 98 A6
KENS W8 15 H4
STRHM/NOR SW16 202 F2
The Stanfords EW KT17 220 C8
Stanford St WEST SW1P 17 J6
Stanford Wy STRHM/NOR SW16 202 E2
Stangate Crs BORE WD6 76 B9
Stangate Gdns STAN HA7 94 G5
Stanger Rd SNWD SE25 203 P4
Stanham Pl DART DA1 165 H10
Stanham Rd DART DA1 187 K1
Stan Hl HORL RH6 278 F7
Stanhope Av FNCH N3 117 J1
HAYES BR2 205 M8
KTN/HRWW/W HA3 94 C9
Stanhope Cl BERM/RHTH * SE16 160 C1
Stanhope Gdns FSBYPK N4 119 J4
HGT N6 118 C4
IL IG1 122 C6
MLHL NW7 96 C6
SKENS SW7 15 K5
Stanhope Ga BAY/PAD W2 10 A7
MYFR/PKLN W1K 10 D10
Stanhope Gv BECK BR3 204 E5
Stanhope Heath
STWL/WRAY TW19 173 M2
Stanhope Ms East SKENS SW7 15 K5
Stanhope Ms South SKENS SW7 15 K6
Stanhope Ms West SKENS SW7 15 K5
Stanhope Pde CAMTN NW1 4 F9
Stanhope Park Rd GFD/PVL UB6 134 B6
Stanhope Pl BAY/PAD W2 10 A6
Stanhope Rd BAR EN5 76 G10
BCTR RM8 124 A7
BFN/LL DA15 185 K7
BXLYHN DA7 163 P8
CAR SM5 222 B4
CHES/WCR EN8 62 D9
CROY/NA CR0 203 M10
GFD/PVL UB6 134 B7
HGT N6 118 D4
NFNCH/WDSP N12 97 M6
RAIN RM13 145 H4
SL SL1 128 C8
STAL AL1 38 E7
SWCM DA10 189 L1
WALTH E17 120 G3
Stanhope Rw MYFR/PICC * W1J 10 E10
Stanhopes OXTED RH8 261 N4
Stanhope St CAMTN NW1 4 G9
Stanhope Ter BAY/PAD W2 9 M7
TWK * TW1 176 E3
Stanhope Wy SEV TN13 246 E8
STWL/WRAY TW19 173 M2
Stanier Cl CRAWE RH10 284 C8
ECT SW5 14 D8
Stanier Ri BERK HP4 33 L2
Staniland Dr WEY KT13 216 A7
Stanlake Rd SHB W12 136 F10
Stanlake Vls SHB W12 136 F10
Stanley Av ALP/SUD HA0 135 K2
BARK IG11 143 J5
BCTR RM8 124 A6
BECK BR3 205 H3
CSHM HP5 50 G7
GFD/PVL UB6 134 B3
GPK RM2 125 H2
LCOL/BKTW AL2 55 P1
NWMAL KT3 200 D5
Stanley Cl ALP/SUD HA0 135 K2
COUL/CHIP CR5 240 G3
CRAWE RH10 283 P9
GPK RM2 125 H2
GRH DA9 188 D1
HCH RM12 125 K7
UX/CGN UB8 131 N4
Stanley Cottages SLN SL2 129 L10
Stanley Crs GVE DA12 190 G8
NTGHL W11 8 C7
Stanleycroft Cl ISLW TW7 154 D7
Stanley Dr HAT AL10 40 E6
Stanley Gdns ACT W3 156 B1
BORE WD6 75 K5
CRICK NW2 116 F10
MTCM * CR4 180 B9
NTGHL W11 8 C7
SAND/SEL CR2 223 P8
WLGTN SM6 222 D3
WOT/HER KT12 217 K2
Stanley Gardens Rd TEDD TW11 176 D8
Stanley Gn West DTCH/LGLY SL3 150 C3
Stanley Gv THHTH CR7 203 H6
VX/NE SW8 158 B8
Stanley Hl AMSS HP7 69 K6
CHOB/PIR GU24 230 B8
Stanley Hill Av AMSS HP7 69 J5
Stanley Park Dr ALP/SUD HA0 135 L2
Stanley Park Rd CAR SM5 222 A4
Stanley Pas CAMTN NW1 5 L8
Stanley Pl CHONG CM5 67 P5
Stanley Rd ACT W3 155 N2
ASHF TW15 173 P8
BELMT SM2 221 L3
CAR SM5 222 B4
CHING E4 101 J2
CROY/NA CR0 203 H7
ED N9 99 N2
EFNCH N2 117 N2
EN EN1 79 M7
FBAR/BDGN N11 98 E7
GRAYS RM17 167 N4
HAYES BR2 205 P3
HCH RM12 125 K7
HERT/BAY SG13 25 M6
HSLW TW3 154 B10
IL IG1 122 G7
LEY E10 120 G4
MNPK E12 122 B10
MORT/ESHN SW14 155 N10
MRDN SM4 201 K4
MTCM CR4 180 B10
MUSWH N10 98 C8
NTHWD HA6 93 H9
ORP BR6 207 J8
RYLN/HDSTN HA2 114 B7
SCUP DA14 185 K6
SEVS/STOTM N15 119 J2
SRTFD E15 141 J3
STHL UB1 133 M9
SWCM DA10 189 L2
SWFD E18 101 L9
TEDD TW11 176 D8
WAT WD17 73 K7
WBLY HA9 135 L1
WHTN TW2 176 C6
WIM/MER SW19 179 K10
WOKN/KNAP GU21 232 C3
Stanley Rd North RAIN RM13 144 F3
Stanley Rd South RAIN RM13 144 G4
Stanley Sq CAR SM5 222 A5
Stanley St CTHM CR3 241 K8
DEPT SE8 160 E6
Stanley Ter ARCH * N19 118 F7
BXLYHS * DA6 164 B10
Stanley Wy STMC/STPC BR5 207 L5
Stanmer St BTSEA SW11 157 P7
Stanmore Cha STALE/WH AL4 39 J7
Stanmore Gdns RCH/KEW TW9 155 L9
SUT SM1 201 M10
Stanmore Hl STAN HA7 94 G5
Stanmore Rd BELV DA17 164 D3
RCH/KEW TW9 155 L9
SEVS/STOTM N15 119 J2
WAN E11 121 L6
WATN WD24 73 J5
Stanmore St IS N1 5 N5
Stanmore Ter BECK BR3 204 F2
Stanmore Wy LOU IG10 82 D5
Stanmount Rd LCOL/BKTW * AL2 55 P1
Stannard Ms HACK * E8 7 N1
Stannard Rd HACK E8 7 N1
Stannary St LBTH SE11 18 B9
Stannet Wy WLGTN SM6 222 D1
Stansfeld Rd CAN/RD E16 142 A8
Stansfield Rd BRXN/ST SW9 158 G9
HSLWW TW4 153 J8
Stansgate Rd DAGE RM10 124 B7
Stanstead Cl HAYES BR2 205 L5
Stanstead Dr HOD EN11 44 G1
Stanstead Gv FSTH SE23 182 E4
Stanstead Mnr AMSS * HP7 69 H5
Stanstead Rd CTHM CR3 241 M10
FSTH SE23 182 C4
HERT/BAY SG13 25 P4
HOD EN11 26 G10
WAN E11 121 N3
WARE SG12 26 C6
Stansted Cl HCH RM12 145 J1
Stansted Crs BXLY DA5 185 N4
Stansted Rd HTHAIR TW6 174 A2
Stanswood Gdns CMBW SE5 159 M6
Stanthorpe Cl
STRHM/NOR * SW16 180 F8
Stanthorpe Rd
STRHM/NOR SW16 180 F8
Stanton Av TEDD TW11 176 D9
Stanton Cl HOR/WEW KT19 219 N2
STALE/WH AL4 39 J2
STMC/STPC BR5 207 M7
WPK KT4 200 G8
Stanton Rd BARN SW13 156 C8
CROY/NA CR0 203 K7
RYNPK SW20 200 G2
Stanton St PECK * SE15 159 P7
Stantons Whf SHGR GU5 268 D10
Stanton Wy DTCH/LGLY SL3 150 B3
SYD SE26 182 E7
Stanway Cl CHIG IG7 103 H6
Stanway Cottages CHERT * KT16 195 K7
Stanway Gdns ACT W3 135 M10
EDGW HA8 95 P7
Stanway Rd WAB EN9 63 M9
Stanway St IS N1 7 K7
Stanwell Cl STWL/WRAY TW19 173 N2
Stanwell Gdns
STWL/WRAY TW19 173 N2
Stanwell Moor Rd
STWL/WRAY TW19 173 L5
WDR/YW UB7 151 L7
Stanwell New Rd STA TW18 173 L7
Stanwell Pl STWL/WRAY * TW19 173 M2
Stanwell Rd ASHF TW15 173 P6
DTCH/LGLY SL3 150 E9
EBED/NFELT TW14 174 C3
Stanwick Rd WKENS W14 14 C6
Stanworth St STHWK SE1 19 L2
Stanwyck Gdns HARH RM3 105 J6
Stapenhill Rd ALP/SUD HA0 114 G8
Staple Cl BXLY DA5 186 E6
Staplefield Cl
BRXS/STRHM * SW2 180 F4
PIN HA5 93 M8
Stapleford WGCE AL7 23 M5
Stapleford Av GNTH/NBYPK IG2 123 H3
Stapleford Cl CHING E4 101 H4
KUT KT1 199 M2
WIM/MER SW19 179 H3
Stapleford Gdns CRW RM5 104 B7
Stapleford Rd ABR/ST RM4 84 C8
ALP/SUD HA0 135 J2
Stapleford Wy BARK IG11 143 L5
Staple Hl CHOB/PIR GU24 213 J3
Staplehurst Cl REDH RH1 275 M4
Staplehurst Rd CAR SM5 221 P4
LEW SE13 183 J1
REDH RH1 275 M4
Staple Inn HHOL WC1V 12 A4
Staple La RGUE GU4 251 N8
Staples Cl BERM/RHTH SE16 140 D10
Staples Rd LOU IG10 82 B7
Staple St STHWK SE1 19 H2
Stapleton Cl POTB/CUF EN6 59 N7
Stapleton Crs RAIN RM13 145 H1
Stapleton Gdns CROY/NA CR0 223 H2
Stapleton Hall Rd FSBYPK N4 118 G5
Stapleton Rd BORE WD6 75 M4
BXLYHN DA7 164 A6
ORP BR6 207 J10
TOOT SW17 180 B6
Stapleton Vls
STNW/STAM * N16 119 M9
Stapley Rd BELV DA17 164 B4
STALW/RED AL3 38 C5
Staplyton Rd BAR EN5 77 H7
Starboard Av GRH DA9 188 G2
Starboard Wy POP/IOD E14 160 F2
Starch House La BARK/HLT IG6 102 G10
Starcross St CAMTN NW1 5 H10
Starfield Rd SHB W12 156 D1
Star & Garter Hl
RCHPK/HAM TW10 177 K4
Star Hl DART DA1 186 F1
WOKS/MYFD GU22 231 P5
Star Hill Rd RSEV TN14 246 A2
Star Holme Ct WARE SG12 26 D2
Starkey Cl CHESW EN7 61 K1
Star La CAN/RD E16 141 K6
COUL/CHIP CR5 240 B7
EPP CM16 65 K6
STMC/STPC BR5 207 N4
Starlight Wy STALE/WH AL4 39 H8
Starling Cl BKHH IG9 101 M2
HART DA3 211 N3
PIN HA5 113 K1
Starling La POTB/CUF EN6 60 G4
Starling Pl GSTN * WD25 55 K8
Starmans Cl DAGW RM9 143 P3
Star Pl WAP E1W 13 N8
Star Rd HGDN/ICK UB10 132 D6
ISLW TW7 154 C8
WKENS W14 14 C9
Starrock La COUL/CHIP CR5 240 B6
Starrock Rd COUL/CHIP CR5 240 C5
Star St BAY/PAD W2 9 M5
WARE SG12 26 D2
Starts Cl ORP BR6 206 D10
Starts Hill Av ORP BR6 226 E2
Starts Hill Rd ORP BR6 206 E10
Starveall Cl WDR/YW UB7 152 A2
Starwood Cl BF/WBF KT14 215 M7
Starwood Ct DTCH/LGLY SL3 149 P2
Star Yd LINN WC2A 12 A5
State Farm Av ORP BR6 226 E1
Staten Gdns TWK TW1 176 E4
Statham Gv STNW/STAM N16 119 L8
UED N18 99 M6
Station Ap ALP/SUD HA0 134 G1
BAR EN5 77 M8
BECK BR3 182 D10
BELMT SM2 221 H4
BELMT SM2 221 L6
BF/WBF KT14 215 K8
BKHH * IG9 102 A5
BKHTH/KID SE3 161 N9
BXLYHN DA7 163 P8
BXLYHN DA7 164 D8
CAMTN * NW1 10 C2
CAT SE6 182 E8
CFSP/GDCR SL9 110 B3
CHES/WCR * EN8 62 D10
CHING * E4 101 K1
CHING * E4 101 J7
CHST BR7 184 B9
CHST BR7 206 D1

COUL/CHIP CR5 240 A4
COUL/CHIP CR5 240 E2
CROY/NA * CR0 203 L9
CTHM CR3 241 P3
DART DA1 187 M2
DEN/HRF UB9 110 G5
DORK RH4 255 H10
EHSLY KT24 252 F2
ESH/CLAY KT10 198 E10
EW KT17 220 E6
FBAR/BDGN N11 98 C6
FSTGT * E7 121 N9
FUL/PGN * SW6 157 H9
GFD/PVL UB6 134 B2
GLDGN * NW11 116 G5
GU GU1 267 P1
HARP AL5 20 A2
HAYES BR2 205 M8
HOR/WEW KT19 220 A9
HOR/WEW KT19 220 C2
HORL RH6 280 C4
HPTN TW12 197 P1
HYS/HAR UB3 152 G2
KUTN/CMB KT2 199 M1
LHD/OX KT22 236 F7
NTHWD HA6 92 F8
ORP BR6 207 J9
ORP BR6 227 L2
OXHEY WD19 93 L4
OXTED RH8 261 K5
PIN HA5 113 M1
PUR/KEN * CR8 223 H7
RAD WD7 74 F1
RCH/KEW TW9 155 M7
RKW/CH/CXG WD3 70 F8
RSEV TN14 247 K2
RSLP HA4 112 F6
RSLP HA4 113 J10
SAND/SEL CR2 223 L5
SHPTN * TW17 196 D6
STA TW18 173 K8
STMC/STPC BR5 207 L4
STRHM/NOR SW16 180 E8
SUN TW16 197 H1
SWFD * E18 101 N10
SWLY BR8 208 F4
VW GU25 194 A4
WALTH * E17 120 F3
WAN * E11 121 K9
WAN E11 121 M3
WATW * WD18 72 G8
WDR/YW UB7 131 P10
WELL DA16 163 J8
WEY KT13 216 B3
WFD * IG8 101 P7
WLSDN NW10 136 C5
WOKS/MYFD GU22 232 C3
Station Ap East REDH RH1 276 A2
Station Approach Rd
CHSWK W4 155 P6
COUL/CHIP CR5 240 E1
HORL * RH6 280 C7
KWD/TDW/WH KT20 238 F8
TIL RM18 168 D10
Station Ap West REDH RH1 276 A2
Station Ar GTPST * W1W 10 F2
Station Av CTHM CR3 241 P10
HOR/WEW KT19 220 B5
NWMAL KT3 200 B3
WOT/HER KT12 216 G1
Station Buildings HAYES * BR2 205 M8
Station Chambers EA * W5 135 M6
Station Cl BRKMPK AL9 59 H2
HPTN TW12 198 A1
POTB/CUF EN6 59 J7
Station Cottages WDGN * N22 98 F10
Station Ct AMSS * HP7 69 H4
Station Crs ALP/SUD HA0 134 G1
ASHF TW15 173 N7
BKHTH/KID SE3 161 M4
SEVS/STOTM N15 119 L2
Stationers Hall Ct STP * EC4M 12 D6
Station Est BECK BR3 204 C4
Station Estate Rd
EBED/NFELT TW14 175 J4
Station Footpath KGLGY WD4 54 C6
Station Garage Ms
STRHM/NOR * SW16 180 E9
Station Gdns CHSWK W4 155 P6
Station Gv ALP/SUD HA0 135 K1
Station Hl CRAWE RH10 284 C6
HAYES BR2 205 M9
Station House Ms UED N18 99 P5
Station La HCH RM12 125 M7
Station Ms POTB/CUF * EN6 59 K7
Station Pde ACT * W3 135 L10
BAL * SW12 180 B4
BARK IG11 142 F2
BECK * BR3 204 C4
BELMT * SM2 221 M3
BMLY * BR1 205 M1
BXLYHN * DA7 163 P8
CHSWK * W4 155 P3
CHSWK * W4 155 P6
CLPT * E5 120 A8
CRICK NW2 136 F1
DEN/HRF UB9 111 K5
EBAR * EN4 78 B8
EBED/NFELT * TW14 175 J3
EDGW * HA8 95 K8
EHAM * E6 141 P3
EHAM * E6 142 B2
EHSLY * KT24 252 F2
HCH RM12 125 J9
KTN/HRWW/W * HA3 94 G10
NTHLT * UB5 114 A10
NTHLT * UB5 133 P2
RCH/KEW TW9 155 M7
ROM * RM1 124 F4
RSLP * HA4 112 D7
RYLN/HDSTN * HA2 114 A9
SEV * TN13 247 H10
STHGT/OAK N14 98 E2
VW GU25 194 A4
Station Pas PECK SE15 160 B7
SWFD E18 101 N10
Station Pl FSBYPK N4 119 H7
Station Ri WNWD SE27 181 J5
Station Rd ADL/WDHM KT15 215 M1
AMSS HP7 69 H5
ARCH N19 118 D8
ASC SL5 192 F6
ASHF TW15 174 A7
BAR EN5 77 L9
BARK/HLT IG6 122 G1
BARN SW13 156 C8
BCTR RM8 123 N6
BEAC HP9 88 D9
BELMT SM2 221 K6
BELV DA17 164 B2
BERK HP4 34 A4
BF/WBF KT14 215 K8
BFN/LL DA15 185 K5
BH/WHM TN16 245 L9
BMLY BR1 205 M1
BORE WD6 75 M8
BRKHM/BTCW RH3 256 B7
BRKMPK AL9 58 G1
BROX EN10 44 E6
BXLYHN DA7 163 P9
CAR SM5 222 A1
CFSP/GDCR SL9 110 B3
CHERT KT16 195 J8
CHES/WCR EN8 62 F10
CHIG IG7 102 E4
CHING E4 101 J2
CHOB/PIR GU24 213 L8
CHSGTN KT9 219 K2
COB KT11 235 M3
CRAWE RH10 283 N8
CROY/NA CR0 203 K8
CSHM * HP5 50 G7
CTHM CR3 241 N4
CTHM CR3 242 D8
DART DA1 186 G2
DORK RH4 272 E1
DTCH/LGLY SL3 150 D1
EA W5 135 L8
EDGW HA8 95 M7
EGH TW20 172 D8
EPP CM16 65 K7
EPP CM16 66 C3
ESH/CLAY KT10 198 C8
ESH/CLAY KT10 218 C2
EYN DA4 209 L10
EYN DA4 210 A2
FBAR/BDGN N11 98 C6
FNCH N3 97 K9
GPK RM2 125 J2
GRH DA9 188 F1
GVW DA11 189 N2
HARH RM3 105 N9
HARP AL5 20 A2
HART DA3 211 K2
HAYES BR2 205 K2
HDN NW4 116 D4
HERT/WAS SG14 24 B8
HHS/BOV HP3 35 L8
HLWE CM17 29 M7
HNWL W7 134 D10
HOLWY N7 118 D8
HORL RH6 280 C4
HPTN TW12 198 A1
HRW HA1 114 E4
HSLW TW3 154 A10
HYS/HAR UB3 152 F3
IL IG1 122 E8
KGLGY WD4 54 C5
KUT KT1 199 J1
KUTN/CMB KT2 199 M1
LCOL/BKTW AL2 55 P7
LEW SE13 161 H9
LHD/OX KT22 236 F7
LOU IG10 82 B9
MEO DA13 189 L7
MLHL NW7 96 B7
MNPK E12 122 A9
NRWD SE19 181 P9
NWMAL KT3 200 E5
ORP BR6 207 J9
PGE/AN SE20 182 B9
POTB/CUF EN6 60 G5
PUR/KEN CR8 223 K10
RAD WD7 74 F1
REDH RH1 257 P9
REDH RH1 258 A9
REDH RH1 258 D4
RGODL GU7 267 L10
RGUE GU4 268 B6
RKW/CH/CXG WD3 91 N1
RSEV TN14 228 A7
RSEV TN14 229 H7
RSEV TN14 247 J2
RYLN/HDSTN HA2 114 A3
SCUP DA14 185 K6
SEV TN13 246 F6
SEVS/STOTM N15 119 P1
SHGR GU5 268 C10
SHGR GU5 270 E5
SHPTN TW17 196 D5
SL SL1 128 D8
SNWD SE25 203 N4
STALE/WH AL4 21 J2
STALE/WH AL4 39 N5
STMC/STPC BR5 207 M4
STWL/WRAY TW19 172 C2
SUN TW16 175 H10
SWLY BR8 208 F4
TEDD TW11 176 F9
THDIT KT7 198 E7
TIL RM18 169 L6
TWK TW1 176 E4
UPMR RM14 126 B7
UX/CGN UB8 131 M6
WAB EN9 63 K3
WALTH E17 120 D4
WARE SG12 26 C2
WARE SG12 27 H7
WAT WD17 73 J6
WCHMH N21 99 J2
WDGN N22 98 F10
WDR/YW UB7 151 P1
WIM/MER SW19 201 M1
WLSDN NW10 136 C4
WWKM BR4 205 H8
Station Rd East OXTED RH8 261 K5
Station Rd North BELV DA17 164 C2
REDH RH1 258 D4
Station Rd South REDH RH1 258 D4
Station Rd West OXTED RH8 261 K5
Station Rw RGUE GU4 268 B6
Station Sq STMC/STPC BR5 206 F5
Station St SRTFD E15 141 J2
Station Ter CMBW SE5 159 K7
WLSDN NW10 136 G4
Station Vw GFD/PVL UB6 134 C3
GU GU1 267 P1
Station Wy BKHH IG9 153 P9
CHEAM SM3 221 H3
CRAWE RH10 283 N8
STAL AL1 38 E6
Station Yd ASHF * TW15 174 A7
KWD/TDW/WH * KT20 239 J7
PUR/KEN * CR8 223 J7
RSLP * HA4 112 E6
STHL * UB1 153 N1
TWK TW1 176 F3
Staunton Rd KUTN/CMB KT2 177 L10
SLN SL2 129 J7
Staunton St DEPT SE8 160 E5
Staveley Cl HOLWY * N7 118 F9
PECK SE15 160 B7
Staveley Gdns CHSWK W4 156 A7
Staveley Rd ASHF TW15 174 E9
CHSWK W4 155 P5
Staveley Wy WOKN/KNAP GU21 231 K3
Staverton Rd CRICK NW2 136 F2
EMPK RM11 125 L4
Stave Yard Rd BERM/RHTH SE16 140 D10
Stavordale Rd CAR SM5 201 M7
HBRY N5 119 H9
Stayne End VW GU25 193 M4
Stayner's Rd WCHPL E1 140 C6
Stayton Rd SUT SM1 201 K10
St Catherines Rd RSLP HA4 112 D3
Steadfast Rd KUT KT1 199 J1
Stead St WALW SE17 18 G6
Steam Farm La
EBED/NFELT TW14 152 G10
Stean St HACK E8 7 L5
Stebbing Wy BARK IG11 143 K4
Stebondale St POP/IOD E14 161 H4
Stedly SCUP * DA14 185 K7
Stedman Cl BXLY DA5 186 F6
HGDN/ICK UB10 112 B8
Steed Cl HCH RM12 125 J7
Steedman St WALW SE17 18 E6
Steeds Rd MUSWH N10 98 A9
Steeds Wy LOU IG10 82 B7
Steel Ap BARK IG11 143 L4
Steele Av GRH DA9 188 F1
Steele Rd CHSWK W4 155 P2
ISLW TW7 154 F10
TOTM N17 119 M1
WAN E11 121 K9
WLSDN NW10 135 P4
Steele's Ms South HAMP NW3 4 B2
Steele's Rd HAMP NW3 4 A2
Steeles Studios HAMP * NW3 4 A2
Steel's La LHD/OX KT22 218 A10
WCHPL E1 140 B8
Steelyard Pas CANST EC4R 12 G8
Steep Cl ORP BR6 227 J3
Steep Hl CHOB/PIR GU24 213 H4
CROY/NA CR0 223 M1
STRHM/NOR SW16 180 E6
Steeplands BUSH WD23 94 A1
Steeple Cl FUL/PGN SW6 157 H9
WIM/MER SW19 179 H7
Steeple Heights Dr
BH/WHM TN16 244 A3
Steeple Point ASC SL5 192 A3
Steeplestone Cl UED N18 99 K6
Steeple Wk IS N1 6 F5
Steeple Wy BRWN CM15 86 G2
Steerforth St WAND/EARL SW18 179 L5
Steers La CRAWE RH10 284 D1
Steers Md MTCM CR4 202 A1
Steers Wy BERM/RHTH SE16 160 D1
Stella Rd TOOT SW17 180 A9
Stelling Rd ERITH DA8 164 E6
Stellman Cl CLPT E5 119 P8
Stembridge Rd PGE/AN SE20 204 A2
Sten Cl WAB EN9 80 F3
Stenning Av TIL RM18 169 L3
Stepbridge Pth
WOKN/KNAP * GU21 232 A3
Stepgates CHERT KT16 195 L7
Stepgates Cl CHERT * KT16 195 L7
Stephan Cl HACK E8 7 P5
Stephen Av RAIN RM13 145 H1
Stephen Cl CRAWW RH11 283 N4
EGH TW20 172 F9
ORP BR6 207 J10
Stephendale Rd FUL/PGN SW6 157 L8
Stephen Ms FITZ W1T 11 J4
Stephen Pl CLAP SW4 158 D9
Stephen Rd BXLYHN DA7 164 D9
Stephens Cl HARH RM3 105 K6
Stephenson Av TIL RM18 168 D7
Stephenson Ct SL SL1 149 L1
Stephenson Dr WDSR SL4 148 G7
Stephenson Pl CRAWE RH10 284 C7
Stephenson Rd HNWL W7 134 E8
HSLWW TW4 175 P3
WALTH * E17 120 D3
Stephenson St CAN/RD E16 141 K7
WLSDN NW10 136 B5
Stephenson Wy BUSH WD23 73 L5
CAMTN NW1 11 H1
CRAWE RH10 284 C7
Stephen's Rd SRTFD E15 141 K3
Stephen St FITZ W1T 11 J5
Stephyns Chambers HHW * HP1 35 M7
Stepney Cswy WCHPL E1 140 C8
Stepney Cl CRAWE RH10 284 D9
Stepney Gn WCHPL E1 140 B7
Stepney High St WCHPL E1 140 C7
Stepney Wy WCHPL E1 140 A7
The Steps EHSLY * KT24 253 L3
Sterling Av CHES/WCR EN8 62 C10
EDGW HA8 95 L5
SHPTN TW17 196 F3
Sterling Cl WLSDN NW10 136 D2
Sterling Gdns NWCR SE14 160 D5
Sterling Pk CRAWE * RH10 284 C2
Sterling Pl BTFD TW8 155 K3
Sterling Rd ENC/FH EN2 79 L5
Sterling St SKENS SW7 15 P2
Sterling Wy (North Circular)
UED N18 99 L6
Stern Cl BARK IG11 143 M4
Sterndale Rd DART DA1 187 N3
WKENS * W14 156 G2
Sterne St SHB W12 156 G1
Sternhall La PECK SE15 159 P9
Sternhold Av BRXS/STRHM SW2 180 E5
Sterry Crs DAGE RM10 124 B10
Sterry Dr HOR/WEW KT19 220 B1
THDIT KT7 198 D6
Sterry Gdns DAGE RM10 144 B1
Sterry Rd BARK IG11 143 J3
DAGE RM10 124 B9
Sterry St STHWK SE1 18 G2
Steucers La FSTH SE23 182 D4
Steve Biko La CAT SE6 182 F7
Steve Biko Rd HOLWY N7 119 H8
Steve Biko Wy HSLW TW3 153 P9
Stevedale Rd WELL DA16 163 M8
Stevedore St WAP E1W 140 A10
Stevenage Crs BORE WD6 75 K5
Stevenage Ri HHNE HP2 36 A2
Stevenage Rd EHAM E6 142 D1
FUL/PGN SW6 156 G7
Stevens Av HOM E9 140 B1
Stevens Cl BECK BR3 182 F9
BXLY DA5 186 E7
EW KT17 220 E8
HPTN TW12 175 N9
PIN HA5 113 K3
RDART DA2 188 D8
Stevens Gn BUSH WD23 94 B2
Stevens' La ESH/CLAY KT10 218 F4
Stevenson Cl BAR EN5 77 N10
ERITH DA8 165 J6
Stevenson Crs BERM/RHTH SE16 19 P7
Stevenson Rd SLN SL2 109 J7
Stevens Pl PUR/KEN CR8 223 J9
Stevens Rd BCTR RM8 123 L7
Stevens St STHWK SE1 19 K3
Steventon Rd SHB W12 136 C9
Steward Cl CHES/WCR EN8 62 D6
Stewards Cl EPP CM16 65 K9
Stewards Green Rd EPP CM16 65 L8
Steward St WCHPL E1 13 K3
Stewart KWD/TDW/WH KT20 238 G7
Stewart Av SHPTN TW17 196 B3
SL SL1 129 L7
UPMR RM14 126 A8
Stewart Cl ABLGY WD5 55 H8
CDALE/KGS * NW9 115 P4
CHST BR7 184 E8
HPTN TW12 175 M9
WOKN/KNAP GU21 231 L3
Stewart Rd HARP AL5 20 A1
WAN E11 121 J9
Stewartsby Cl UED N18 99 K6
Stewarts Dr SLN SL2 108 G10
Stewarts Gv CHEL * SW3 15 M7
CHEL SW3 15 M7
Stewart's La VX/NE SW8 158 C6
Stewarts Rd VX/NE SW8 158 D6
VX/NE SW8 158 D7
Stewart St POP/IOD E14 161 H1
Stew La BLKFR EC4V 12 E7
Steyne Rd ACT W3 135 N10
Steyning Cl CRAWE RH10 283 P5
PUR/KEN CR8 241 J2
Steyning Gv ELTH/MOT SE9 184 C7
Steynings Wy NFNCH/WDSP N12 97 K6
Steyning Wy HSLWW TW4 153 K10
Steynton Av BXLY DA5 185 P5
Stickland Rd BELV DA17 164 B3
Stickleton Cl GFD/PVL UB6 134 A5
Stifford Clays Rd CDH/CHF RM16 147 L10
Stifford Hl CDH/CHF RM16 147 J10
SOCK/AV RM15 147 H9
Stifford Rd SOCK/AV RM15 146 E9
Stile Cft HLWS CM18 47 K3
Stilecroft Gdns ALP/SUD HA0 114 G8
Stile Hall Gdns CHSWK W4 155 M4
Stile Pth SUN TW16 197 H3
Stile Rd DTCH/LGLY SL3 150 A3
Stiles Cl ERITH DA8 164 C4
HAYES BR2 206 C6
Stillingfleet Rd BARN SW13 156 D6
Stillington St WEST SW1P 17 H5
Stillness Rd FSTH SE23 182 D2
Stilton Pth BORE WD6 75 M4
Stilwell Dr UX/CGN UB8 132 A6
Stipularis Dr YEAD UB4 133 L6
Stirling Av PIN HA5 113 L5
SHPTN * TW17 196 F3
Stirling Cl BNSTD SM7 239 J3
CRAWE RH10 284 C8
RAIN RM13 145 J5
STRHM/NOR SW16 202 D1
UX/CGN UB8 131 M5
WDSR SL4 148 C8
Stirling Dr ORP BR6 227 L2
Stirling Gv HSLW TW3 154 B8
Stirling Rd ACT W3 155 N2
BRXN/ST SW9 158 F8
GUW GU2 249 J10
HYS/HAR UB3 153 J9
KTN/HRWW/W HA3 114 E1
PLSTW E13 141 N4
SL SL1 128 F7
TOTM N17 99 P9
WALTH E17 120 D1
WDGN N22 99 J9
WHTN TW2 175 P3
Stirling Wk BRYLDS KT5 199 N6
Stirling Wy ABLGY WD5 55 H8
BORE WD6 76 A10
WGCE AL7 23 P5
Stirrup Wy CRAWE RH10 284 E6
Stites Hill Rd CTHM CR3 241 J6
Stiven Crs RYLN/HDSTN HA2 113 N8
Stoat Cl HERT/BAY SG13 25 P5
Stoats Nest Rd COUL/CHIP CR5 240 F1
Stockbreach Cl HAT AL10 40 D3
Stockbreach Rd HAT AL10 40 D3
Stockbury Rd CROY/NA CR0 204 B6
Stockdale Rd BCTR RM8 124 A7
Stockdales Rd WDSR SL4 148 E3
Stockdove Wy GFD/PVL UB6 134 E5
Stocker Gdns DAGW RM9 143 M2
Stockers Farm Rd
RKW/CH/CXG WD3 91 M4
Stockers La WOKS/MYFD GU22 232 C6
Stockfield HORL * RH6 280 C3
Stockfield Av HOD EN11 44 F1
Stockfield Rd ESH/CLAY KT10 218 D2
STRHM/NOR SW16 180 E6
Stockhams Cl SAND/SEL CR2 223 L6
Stock Hl BH/WHM TN16 244 A2
Stockholm Rd BERM/RHTH SE16 160 B4
Stockholm Wy WAP E1W 13 N9
Stockhurst Cl PUT/ROE SW15 156 F8
Stockings La HERT/BAY SG13 42 E4
Stockingswater La PEND EN3 80 D7
Stockland Rd ROMW/RG RM7 124 E4
Stock La RDART DA2 187 K7
Stockley Cl WDR/YW UB7 152 C1
Stockley Farm Rd WDR/YW UB7 152 C2
Stockley Rd UX/CGN UB8 132 B8
WDR/YW UB7 152 C2
Stock Orchard Crs HOLWY * N7 118 G9
Stock Orchard St HOLWY N7 118 G10
Stockport Rd RKW/CH/CXG WD3 90 F1
STRHM/NOR SW16 202 E1
Stocks Cl HORL RH6 280 C5
Stocksfield BRWN CM15 86 E3
Stocksfield Rd WALTH * E17 121 H1
Stocks La BRWN CM15 86 E3
Stocks Meadow HHNE HP2 36 B5
Stocks Pl HGDN/ICK UB10 132 B3
POP/IOD E14 140 E9
Stock St PLSTW E13 141 M4
Stockton Cl BAR EN5 77 M8
Stockton Gdns MLHL NW7 96 A4
TOTM N17 99 K8
Stockton Rd REIG RH2 275 K3
TOTM N17 99 K8
UED N18 99 P7
Stockwell Av BRXN/ST SW9 158 G9
Stockwell Cl BMLY BR1 205 N2
CHESW EN7 61 P4
Stockwell Gdns BRXN/ST SW9 158 G7
Stockwell Gn BRXN/ST SW9 158 G8
Stockwell La BRXN/ST SW9 158 G8
Stockwell Park Crs
BRXN/ST SW9 158 G8
Stockwell Park Rd
BRXN/ST SW9 158 G7
Stockwell Park Wk
BRXN/ST SW9 158 G9
Stockwell Rd BRXN/ST SW9 158 G8
Stockwell St GNWCH SE10 161 H5
Stockwell Ter BRXN/ST SW9 158 G7
Stocton Cl GU GU1 249 P9
Stocton Rd GU GU1 249 P9
Stodart Rd PGE/AN SE20 204 B1
Stoford Cl WIM/MER SW19 179 H4
Stoke Av BARK/HLT IG6 103 K7
Stoke Cl COB KT11 235 N2
Stoke Common Rd SLN SL2 109 M9
Stoke Cottages LHD/OX * KT22 236 C7
Stoke Court Dr SLN SL2 129 K3
Stoke Flds GU GU1 250 A10
Stoke Gdns SL SL1 129 K10
Stoke Gn SLN SL2 129 M6
Stoke Gv GU GU1 250 A10
Stoke Ms GU GU1 268 A1
Stokenchurch St FUL/PGN SW6 157 L7
Stoke Newington Church St
STNW/STAM N16 119 L8
Stoke Newington Common
STNW/STAM N16 119 N8
Stoke Newington High St
STNW/STAM N16 119 N8
Stoke Newington Rd
STNW/STAM N16 119 N10
Stoke Park Av SLN SL2 129 H5
Stoke Park Ct GU * GU1 250 A10
Stoke Pl WLSDN NW10 136 C5
Stoke Poges La SL SL1 129 K10
Stoke Ridings
KWD/TDW/WH * KT20 238 G9
Stoke Rd COB KT11 235 M2
GU GU1 250 A9
KUTN/CMB KT2 177 P10
RAIN RM13 145 L4
SLN SL2 129 M7
WOT/HER KT12 197 K10
Stokesay SLN SL2 129 L9
Stokesby Rd CHSGTN KT9 219 L3
Stokes Cl CRAWE RH10 284 D10
Stokesheath Rd LHD/OX KT22 218 B7
Stokesley St SHB W12 136 C8
Stokes Ridings
KWD/TDW/WH KT20 238 G9
Stokes Rd CROY/NA CR0 204 C6
EHAM E6 142 B6
Stoll Cl CRICK NW2 116 F8
Stompond La WOT/HER KT12 197 H9
Stomp Rd SL SL1 128 A7
Stonard Rd BCTR RM8 123 L10
PLMGR N13 99 H4
Stonards Hl EPP CM16 65 M7
LOU IG10 82 C10
Stondon Pk FSTH SE23 182 D3
Stonebanks WOT/HER KT12 197 H7
Stonebridge Fld WDSR SL4 148 G4
Stonebridge Flds RGUE GU4 268 A7
Stonebridge Pk WLSDN NW10 136 A2
Stonebridge Rd GVW DA11 189 M1
SEVS/STOTM N15 119 M3
Stonebridge Wy WBLY HA9 135 N1
Stonebridge Whf RGUE GU4 268 A7
Stone Buildings LINN WC2A 11 P4
Stone Cl BCTR RM8 124 A7
CLAP SW4 158 D8
WDR/YW UB7 132 A10
Stonecot Cl MRDN SM4 201 H8
Stonecot Hl MRDN SM4 201 H8
Stonecourt Cl HORL RH6 280 D4
Stone Crs EBED/NFELT TW14 174 G3
Stonecroft AMS HP6 68 B1
Stonecroft Av IVER SL0 131 H8
Stonecroft Cl BAR EN5 76 E8
Stonecroft Rd ERITH DA8 164 D6
Stonecroft Wy CROY/NA CR0 202 F7
Stonecrop Cl CRAWW RH11 283 K10
Stonecrop Rd GU GU1 250 F8
Stonecross STAL AL1 38 D5
Stonecross Rd HAT AL10 40 E2
Stonecutter St FLST/FETLN EC4A 12 C5
Stonefield Cl BXLYHN DA7 164 B9
CRAWE RH10 283 N8
RSLP HA4 113 M10
Stonefield St IS N1 6 B5
Stonefield Wy CHARL SE7 162 A6
RSLP HA4 113 L10
Stonegate Cl STMC/STPC BR5 207 M3
Stone Gv STAN HA7 95 K5
Stonegrove Gdns EDGW HA8 95 L6
Stonehall Av IL IG1 122 B4
Stone Hall Gdns KENS * W8 14 G4
Stone Hall Pl KENS * W8 14 G4
Stone Hall Rd WCHMH N21 98 G1
Stoneham Rd FBAR/BDGN N11 98 D6
Stonehill Cl GT/LBKH KT23 253 P1
MORT/ESHN SW14 178 A1
Stonehill Crs CHERT KT16 214 B3
Stonehill Ga ASC * SL5 192 C6
Stonehill Rd CHERT KT16 214 B3
CHOB/PIR GU24 214 A4
CHSWK W4 155 M4
MORT/ESHN SW14 177 P1
Stonehills WGCW AL8 22 G5
Stonehills Ct DUL SE21 181 M6
Stonehill Woods Pk
RDART * DA2 186 C9
Stonehorse Rd PEND EN3 80 B9
Stone House Ct HDTCH EC3A 13 K5
Stone House Gdns CTHM CR3 259 M1
Stonehouse La ORP BR6 227 N5
PUR RM19 166 D4
Stonehouse Rd ORP BR6 227 N5
Stoneings La RSEV TN14 245 J4
Stonelea Rd HHS/BOV HP3 36 A9
Stoneleigh Av EN EN1 80 A4
WPK KT4 200 D10
Stoneleigh Broadway EW KT17 220 D2
Stoneleigh Cl CHES/WCR EN8 62 C9
Stoneleigh Crs HOR/WEW KT19 220 D2
Stoneleigh Dr HOD EN11 26 G10
Stoneleigh Pk WEY KT13 216 D3
Stoneleigh Park Av
CROY/NA CR0 204 C6
Stoneleigh Park Rd
HOR/WEW KT19 220 C3
Stoneleigh Pl NTGHL W11 136 G9
Stoneleigh Rd CAR SM5 201 P7
CLAY IG5 122 B1
OXTED RH8 262 B6
TOTM N17 99 N10
Stoneleigh St NTGHL W11 136 G9

Stonemasons Cl
SEVS/STOTM * N15 119 L2
Stoneness Rd WTHK RM20 166 G5
Stonenest St FSBYPK N4 118 G6
Stone Park Av BECK BR3 204 F4
Stone Pl WPK KT4 200 D9
Stone Place Rd GRH DA9 188 D1
Stone Rd HAYES BR2 205 L5
Stoners Cl HORL RH6 279 N7
Stones Cross Rd SWLY BR8 208 D5
Stones End St STHWK SE1 18 E2
Stones La DORK RH4 272 B3
Stone's Rd EW KT17 220 B7
Stone St CROY/NA CR0 223 H2
GVE DA12 190 E2
Stoneswood Rd OXTED RH8 261 N6
Stonewall EHAM E6 142 D7
Stonewood RDART DA2 189 H6
Stonewood Rd ERITH DA8 164 F4
Stoney Aly WOOL/PLUM SE18 162 D8
Stoneyard La POP/IOD E14 140 G9
Stoney Brook GUW GU2 249 K9
Stoney Cl BERK HP4 33 L3
Stoney Cft COUL/CHIP CR5 240 D8
Stoneycroft WGCE AL7 23 K4
Stoneycroft Cl LEE/GVPK SE12 183 L3
Stoneycroft Rd WFD IG8 102 B7
Stoneydown WALTH E17 120 D2
Stoneydown Av WALTH E17 120 D2
Stoneyfield Rd COUL/CHIP CR5 240 G3
Stoneyfields Gdns EDGW HA8 95 P5
Stoneyfields La EDGW HA8 95 P6
Stoney Gv CSHM HP5 51 J6
Stoneyland Ct EGH TW20 172 C8
Stoneylands Rd EGH TW20 172 C8
Stoney La HDTCH EC3A 13 K5
HHS/BOV HP3 52 E3
HHW HP1 34 E9
KGLGY WD4 53 H6
NRWD SE19 181 N9
SLN SL2 128 F3
Stoney Meade SL SL1 128 G10
Stoney St STHWK SE1 12 G9
Stonhouse St CLAP SW4 158 D9
Stonnell's Rd BTSEA SW11 180 A1
Stonny Cft ASHTD KT21 237 L3
Stonor Rd WKENS W14 14 C6
Stonycroft Cl PEND EN3 80 D6
Stony Hl ESH/CLAY KT10 217 N4
Stony La CHONG CM5 49 J9
CSHM HP5 70 B3
Stony Pth LOU IG10 82 C5
Stonyshotts WAB EN9 63 K10
Stony Wd HLWS CM18 46 G2
Stopes St PECK SE15 159 N6
Stopford Rd PLSTW E13 141 M3
WALW * SE17 18 D8
Stopham Rd CRAWE RH10 284 D10
Store Rd CAN/RD E16 162 D1
Storers Quay POP/IOD E14 161 J3
Store St GWRST WC1E 11 J4
SRTFD E15 121 J10
Storey Rd HGT N6 118 A4
WALTH E17 120 E2
Storeys Ga STJSPK * SW1H 17 K2
WEST SW1P 17 K2
Storey St HHS/BOV HP3 35 N10
Stories Ms CMBW * SE5 159 M8
Stories Rd CMBW SE5 159 M9
Stork Rd FSTGT E7 141 L1
Storksmead Rd EDGW HA8 96 B8
Storks Rd BERM/RHTH SE16 19 P4
Stormont Rd BTSEA SW11 158 B10
HGT N6 118 A5
Stormont Wy CHSGTN KT9 219 H2
Stormount Dr HYS/HAR UB3 152 D1
Stornaway Rd DTCH/LGLY SL3 150 F3
Stornaway Strd GVE DA12 191 J7
Stornoway HHS/BOV HP3 36 C8
Storrington Rd CROY/NA CR0 203 N8
Storr's La RGUW GU3 231 H10
Stortford Rd HOD EN11 44 G2
Stort Ml HLW CM20 29 L5
Stort Valley Wy HLW CM20 29 N4
HLWE CM17 30 F9
HLWE CM17 48 D8
HLWW/ROY CM19 45 L1
SBW CM21 30 D1
Story St IS N1 5 N4
Stothard St WCHPL E1 140 B6
Stott Cl WAND/EARL SW18 179 N2
Stoughton Av CHEAM SM3 220 G2
Stoughton Cl PUT/ROE SW15 178 D4
Stoughton Rd GUW GU2 249 M7
Stour Av NWDGN UB2 153 P2
Stourcliffe St BAY/PAD W2 10 A6
Stour Cl HAYES BR2 225 P1
WDSR SL4 148 G2
Stourhead Cl WIM/MER SW19 178 G3
Stourhead Gdns RYNPK SW20 200 D3
Stour Rd BOW E3 140 F2
CDH/CHF RM16 168 D4
DAGE RM10 124 B7
DART DA1 165 H9
Stourton Av FELT TW13 175 N7
Stour Wy UPMR RM14 126 D4
Stovell Rd WDSR SL4 148 G6
Stowage DEPT SE8 160 F5
Stow Crs WALTH E17 100 D9
Stowe Crs RSLP HA4 112 C4
Stowe Gdns ED N9 99 N2
Stowell Av CROY/NA CR0 225 J6
Stowe Pl SEVS/STOTM N15 119 M1
Stowe Rd ORP BR6 227 L1
SHB W12 156 E1
SL SL1 128 D9
The Stow HLW CM20 29 J9
Stowting Rd ORP BR6 227 H1
Stox Md KTN/HRWW/WH HA3 94 C9
Stracey Rd WLSDN NW10 136 A3
Strachan Pl RYNPK SW20 178 F9
Stradbroke Dr CHIG IG7 102 E7
Stradbroke Gv BKHH IG9 102 A2
CLAY IG5 122 B1
Stradbroke Pk CHIG IG7 102 E7
Stradbroke Rd HBRY N5 119 K9
Stradbrook Cl RYLN/HDSTN HA2 113 N8
Stradella Rd HNHL SE24 181 K2
Strafford Av CLAY IG5 102 D10
Strafford Cl POTB/CUF EN6 59 K8
Strafford Ga POTB/CUF EN6 59 K8
Strafford Rd ACT W3 155 P1
BAR EN5 77 H7
HSLW TW3 153 N9
TWK TW1 176 F3
Strafford St POP/IOD E14 160 F1
Strahan Rd BOW E3 140 D5
Straight Rd HARH RM3 105 J6
WDSR SL4 171 N2
Straightsmouth GNWCH SE10 161 H6
The Straight NWDGN UB2 153 L1
Strait Rd EHAM E6 142 B9
The Straits WAB EN9 62 G8
Straker's Rd EDUL SE22 160 A10
Strand CHCR WC2N 11 L9
Strandburgh Pl HHS/BOV * HP3 36 C8
Strand Cl CRAWE RH10 284 E9
EPSOM KT18 238 A5
Strandfield Cl WOOL/PLUM SE18 163 H4
Strand-on-the-Green CHSWK W4 155 M5
Strand Pl UED N18 99 M5
Strangeways WAT WD17 72 F2
Strangways Ter WKENS W14 14 C3
Stranraer Gdns SL SL1 129 K10
Stranraer Wy IS N1 5 N4
Strasburg Rd BTSEA SW11 158 B7
Stratfield Dr BROX EN10 44 D5
Stratfield Park Cl WCHMH N21 99 J1
Stratfield Rd BORE WD6 75 L7
SL SL1 149 M1
Stratford Av HGDN/ICK UB10 132 A4
Stratford Cl BARK IG11 143 K2
DAGE RM10 144 D2
SLN SL2 128 C6
Stratford Ct NWMAL KT3 200 A4
Stratford Gv PUT/ROE SW15 156 G10
Stratford House Av BMLY BR1 206 B3
Stratford Pl MHST W1U 10 D6
Stratford Rd HTHAIR TW6 174 C2
KENS W8 14 F4
NWDGN UB2 153 M3
PLSTW E13 141 M3
THHTH CR7 203 H4
WAT WD17 73 H6
YEAD UB4 133 J6
Stratford Vls CAMTN NW1 5 H3
Stratford Wy HHS/BOV HP3 35 L9
LCOL/BKTW AL2 55 N5
WAT WD17 72 G6
Strathan Cl WAND/EARL SW18 179 H2
Strathaven Rd LEE/GVPK SE12 183 N2
Strathblaine Rd BTSEA SW11 179 N1
Strathbrook Rd
STRHM/NOR SW16 180 G10
Strathcona Av EHSLY KT24 253 M4
Strathcona Gdns
WOKN/KNAP GU21 231 J5
Strathcona Rd WBLY HA9 115 J7
Strathdale STRHM/NOR SW16 180 G8
Strathdon Dr TOOT SW17 179 N6
Strathearn Av HYS/HAR UB3 152 G6
WHTN TW2 176 B4
Strathearn Cottages
TRDG/WHET * N20 97 K4
Strathearn Pl BAY/PAD W2 9 N7
Strathearn Rd SUT SM1 221 K2
WIM/MER SW19 179 K8
Stratheden Rd BKHTH/KID SE3 161 M7
Strathfield Gdns BARK IG11 142 G1
Strathleven Rd
BRXS/STRHM SW2 180 F1
Strathmore TIL RM18 169 M3
Strathmore Cl CTHM CR3 241 M7
Strathmore Gdns EDGW HA8 95 N10
FNCH N3 97 L9
HCH RM12 124 G6
Strathmore Rd CRAWW RH11 283 K4
CROY/NA CR0 203 K7
TEDD TW11 176 D7
WIM/MER SW19 179 K6
Strathnairn St STHWK SE1 19 P6
Strathray Gdns HAMP NW3 3 N2
Strath Ter BTSEA SW11 157 P10
Strathville Rd WAND/EARL SW18 179 K5
Strathyre Av STRHM/NOR SW16 203 H3
Stratton Av ENC/FH EN2 79 L3
WLGTN SM6 222 E5
Stratton Chase Dr CSTG HP8 89 M3
Stratton Cl BXLYHN DA7 163 P9
EDGW HA8 95 L7
HEST TW5 153 N7
WIM/MER SW19 201 J2
WOT/HER * KT12 197 K8
Strattondale St POP/IOD E14 161 H2
Stratton Dr BARK IG11 123 H10
Stratton Gdns STHL UB1 133 N8
Stratton Pl AMSS * HP7 69 L5
Stratton Rd BXLYHN DA7 163 P9
HARH RM3 105 P6
SUN TW16 196 G2
WIM/MER SW19 201 K2
Stratton St MYFR/PICC W1J 10 F9
Stratton Ter BH/WHM TN16 262 F5
Stratton Wk HARH RM3 105 P6
Strauss Rd CHSWK * W4 156 A1
Strawberry Cl CHOB/PIR GU24 230 C7
Strawberry Flds CHOB/PIR GU24 230 F1
SWLY BR8 208 F2
WARE SG12 26 A1
Strawberry Hill Rd TWK TW1 176 E6
Strawberry La CAR SM5 202 A10
Strawberry Ri CHOB/PIR GU24 230 F1
Strawberry Ter MUSWH * N10 98 A9
Strawberry V EFNCH N2 97 N9
TWK TW1 176 E6
Straw Cl CTHM CR3 241 K9
Strawfields WGCE AL7 23 L4
Strawmead HAT AL10 40 E2
Strayfield Rd ENC/FH EN2 79 H2
Streakes Field Rd CRICK NW2 116 D7
Stream Cl BF/WBF KT14 215 P8
Streamdale ABYW SE2 163 L5
Streamside SL SL1 128 E10
Streamside Cl ED N9 99 N2
HAYES BR2 205 M4
Stream Wy BELV DA17 164 B5
Streatfeild Av EHAM E6 142 C3
Streatfield Rd
KTN/HRWW/WH HA3 115 H1
Streatham Cl
STRHM/NOR * SW16 180 F5
Streatham Common
STRHM/NOR * SW16 180 E10
Streatham Common North
STRHM/NOR SW16 180 G8
Streatham Common South
STRHM/NOR SW16 180 F9
Streatham Ct
STRHM/NOR SW16 180 F6
Streatham Gn
STRHM/NOR * SW16 180 F7
Streatham High Rd
STRHM/NOR SW16 180 F7
Streatham Hl BRXS/STRHM SW2 180 F4
Streatham Pl BRXS/STRHM SW2 180 E3
Streatham Rd MTCM CR4 202 B1
Streatham St NOXST/BSQ WC1A 11 L5
Streatham V STRHM/NOR SW16 180 D10
Streathbourne Rd TOOT SW17 180 B5
Streatleigh Pde
STRHM/NOR * SW16 180 F5
Streatley Pl HAMP NW3 117 N9
Streatley Rd KIL/WHAMP NW6 2 C4
Streeters La WLGTN SM6 202 E10
Streetfield Ms BKHTH/KID SE3 161 M8
Street Hl CRAWE RH10 284 F8
Streets Heath CHOB/PIR GU24 212 E7
The Street ASHTD KT21 237 L4
BRKHM/BTCW RH3 256 A10
EHSLY KT24 252 C4
EHSLY KT24 253 L4
EYN DA4 210 A4
GVE DA12 191 P8
HORL RH6 279 H8
KGLGY WD4 53 K7
LHD/OX KT22 236 C8
MFD/CHID GU8 266 C10
RBSF CM22 30 E3
RGUE GU4 251 K6
RGUE GU4 251 N7
RGUE GU4 268 A5
RGUW GU3 266 A5
RGUW GU3 266 G7
SHGR GU5 268 D10
Streimer Rd SRTFD E15 141 H4
Strelley Wy ACT W3 136 B9
Stretton Rd CROY/NA CR0 203 M7
RCHPK/HAM TW10 177 H5
Stretton Wy BORE WD6 75 K4
Strickland Av DART DA1 165 N10
Strickland Cl CRAWW RH11 283 H8
Strickland Rw WAND/EARL SW18 179 N3
Strickland St DEPT SE8 160 F8
Strickland Wy ORP BR6 227 J1
Stride Rd PLSTW E13 141 L4
Strimon Cl ED N9 100 B3
Stringer's Av RGUE GU4 250 A4
Stringhams Copse
RPLY/SEND GU23 233 J10
Stripling Wy WATW WD18 73 H10
Strode Cl MUSWH N10 98 B8
Strode Rd FSTGT E7 121 M9
FUL/PGN SW6 156 G6
TOTM N17 99 M10
WLSDN NW10 136 D1
Strodes College La EGH TW20 172 C8
Strode St EGH TW20 172 D7
Stroma Cl HHS/BOV HP3 36 D8
Stroma Ct SL SL1 128 C9
Strone Rd FSTGT E7 141 P1
Strone Wy YEAD UB4 133 M6
Strongbow Crs ELTH/MOT SE9 184 C1
Strongbow Rd ELTH/MOT SE9 184 C1
Strongbridge Cl
RYLN/HDSTN HA2 113 P6
Stronsa Rd SHB W12 156 C1
Stronsay HHS/BOV HP3 36 D8
Strood Av ROMW/RG RM7 124 E6
Strood La ASC SL5 170 B9
Stroud Cl WDSR SL4 148 C9
Stroud Crs PUT/ROE SW15 178 C6
Stroude Rd EGH TW20 172 D10
VW GU25 194 B3
Stroudes Cl WPK KT4 200 C7
Stroud Fld NTHLT UB5 133 M1
Stroud Ga RYLN/HDSTN HA2 114 A9
Stroud Green Rd FSBYPK N4 118 G6
Stroud Green Wy CROY/NA CR0 204 B6
Stroudley Cl CRAWE RH10 284 C8
Stroud Rd SNWD SE25 203 P6
WIM/MER SW19 179 K6
Strouds Cl CHDH RM6 123 L3
Stroudwater Pk WEY KT13 216 C3
Stroud Wy ASHF TW15 174 C9
Stroughton Cl LBTH SE11 17 P6
Strout's Pl BETH E2 7 N6
Strudgate Cl CRAWE RH10 284 C9
Strutton Gnd WEST SW1P 17 J3
Struttons Av GVW DA11 190 C5
Strype St WCHPL E1 13 L4
Stuart Av CDALE/KGS NW9 116 D5
EA W5 155 L1
HAYES BR2 205 M8
RYLN/HDSTN HA2 113 N8
WOT/HER KT12 197 K8
Stuart Cl BRWN CM15 86 G9
CRAWE RH10 284 D8
HGDN/ICK UB10 132 B1
SWLY BR8 186 G10
WDSR SL4 148 E8
Stuart Ct AMS * HP6 69 J4
BORE WD6 75 J10
Stuart Crs CROY/NA CR0 204 E10
HYS/HAR UB3 132 D8
REIG RH2 275 K3
WDGN N22 98 G9
Stuart Evans Cl WELL DA16 163 M9
Stuart Gv TEDD TW11 176 D8
Stuart Mantle Wy ERITH DA8 164 E6
Stuart Pl MTCM CR4 202 A1
Stuart Rd ACT W3 135 P10
BARK IG11 143 J3
EBAR EN4 97 P1
GRAYS RM17 167 N4
GVW DA11 190 D2
KIL/WHAMP NW6 2 E10
KTN/HRWW/WH HA3 114 E1
PECK SE15 160 B10
RCHPK/HAM TW10 176 G5
REIG RH2 275 K3
THHTH CR7 203 K4
WARL CR6 242 A6
WELL DA16 163 L7
WIM/MER SW19 179 K6
Stuarts Cl HHS/BOV HP3 35 N8
Stuart Wy CHESW EN7 62 A7
STA TW18 173 L9
VW GU25 193 M4
WDSR SL4 148 D8
Stubbers La UPMR RM14 146 D1
Stubbs Cl CDALE/KGS NW9 115 P3
Stubbs Dr BERM/RHTH SE16 160 A4
Stubbs End Cl AMS HP6 69 K3
Stubbs Hl ORP BR6 227 M9
Stubbs La KWD/TDW/WH KT20 257 J4
Stubbs Wy WIM/MER SW19 201 N1
Stubbs Wd AMS HP6 69 K2
Stubs Cl DORK RH4 273 H4
Stubs Hl DORK RH4 273 H4
Stucley Pl CAMTN NW1 4 F4
Stucley Rd ISLW TW7 154 B6
Studdridge St FUL/PGN SW6 157 K8
Studd St IS N1 6 C5
Stud Gn GSTN WD25 55 H8
Studholme Ct
KIL/WHAMP * NW6 117 K9
Studholme St PECK SE15 160 A6
Studio Pl KTBR * SW1X 16 B2
Studios Rd SHPTN TW17 196 A3
The Studios BUSH WD23 73 P10
Studio Wy BORE WD6 75 P5
Studland Cl BFN/LL DA15 185 J6
Studland Rd BF/WBF KT14 216 A9
HNWL W7 134 C8
KUTN/CMB KT2 177 K9
SYD SE26 182 C8
Studland St HMSMTH W6 156 E3
Studley Av CHING E4 101 J8
Studley Cl CLPT E5 120 D10
Studley Ct SCUP DA14 185 L8
Studley Crs HART DA3 211 P2
Studley Dr REDBR IG4 122 A4
Studley Grange Rd HNWL W7 154 D2
Studley Rd CLAP SW4 158 F7
DAGW RM9 143 N2
FSTGT E7 141 N1
Stukeley Rd FSTGT E7 141 N2
Stukeley St HOL/ALD WC2B 11 M5
Stumblets CRAWE RH10 284 D6
Stumps Hill La BECK BR3 182 F9
Sturdy Rd PECK SE15 160 A8
Sturge Av WALTH E17 100 G9
Sturgeon Rd WALW SE17 18 E8
Sturges Fld CHST BR7 184 G10
Sturgess Av HDN NW4 116 E5
Sturge St STHWK SE1 18 E2
Sturlas Wy CHES/WCR EN8 62 C9
Sturmer Cl STALE/WH AL4 39 H7
Sturmer Wy HOLWY N7 118 G10
Sturminster Cl YEAD UB4 133 K8
Sturrock Cl SEVS/STOTM N15 119 L2
Sturry St POP/IOD E14 140 G8
Sturt Ct GU GU1 250 E8
Sturt's La KWD/TDW/WH KT20 256 C3
Sturt St IS N1 6 F8
Stutfield St WCHPL E1 13 P6
Stychens Cl REDH RH1 259 K9
Stychens La REDH RH1 259 K9
Stylecroft Rd CSTG HP8 90 A4
Styles End GT/LBKH KT23 254 A3
Styles Gdns BRXN/ST SW9 159 J9
Styles Wy BECK BR3 205 H4
Styventon Pl CHERT KT16 195 J7
Subrosa Dr REDH RH1 258 C6
Subrosa Pk REDH * RH1 258 C6
Succomb's Hl CTHM CR3 242 A6
Succombs Pl WARL CR6 242 A5
Sudbourne Rd
BRXS/STRHM SW2 180 F1
Sudbrooke Rd BAL SW12 180 A2
Sudbrook Gdns
RCHPK/HAM TW10 177 K6
Sudbrook La RCHPK/HAM TW10 177 K4
Sudbury EHAM E6 142 D8
Sudbury Av ALP/SUD HA0 115 H8
Sudbury Court Dr HRW HA1 114 F8
Sudbury Court Rd ALP/SUD HA0 114 F8
Sudbury Crs ALP/SUD HA0 114 G10
BMLY BR1 183 M8
Sudbury Cft ALP/SUD HA0 114 E9
Sudbury Gdns CROY/NA CR0 223 M1
Sudbury Heights Av
GFD/PVL UB6 114 E10
Sudbury Hl HRW HA1 114 D8
Sudbury Hl Cl ALP/SUD HA0 114 E9
Sudbury Rd BARK IG11 123 J10
Sudeley St IS N1 6 D8
Sudicamps Ct WAB EN9 63 M9
Sudlow Rd WAND/EARL SW18 157 K10
Sudrey St STHWK SE1 18 E2
Suez Av GFD/PVL UB6 134 E4
Suez Rd PEND EN3 80 D8
Suffield Cl SAND/SEL CR2 224 C8
Suffield Rd CHING E4 100 G4
PGE/AN SE20 204 B2
SEVS/STOTM * N15 119 N3
Suffolk Cl BORE WD6 76 A9
HORL RH6 280 B5
LCOL/BKTW AL2 57 H1
SL SL1 128 C8
Suffolk Dr RGUE GU4 250 E5
Suffolk La CANST EC4R 12 G7
Suffolk Park Rd WALTH E17 120 D2
Suffolk Rd BARK IG11 142 G2
BARN SW13 156 C6
DAGE RM10 124 C10
DART DA1 187 M2
GDMY/SEVK IG3 123 H4
GVE DA12 190 G2
PEND EN3 80 A9
PLSTW E13 141 L5
POTB/CUF EN6 59 H8
RYLN/HDSTN HA2 113 N4
SCUP DA14 185 M9
SEVS/STOTM N15 119 L4
SNWD SE25 203 N4
WLSDN NW10 136 B2
WPK KT4 200 C9
Suffolk St FSTGT E7 121 M10
STJS SW1Y 11 K9
Suffolk Vls WAND/EARL * SW18 179 K3
Suffolk Wy BGR/WK TN15 265 K1
EMPK RM11 125 P2
Sugar House La SRTFD E15 141 H4
Sugar La HHW HP1 34 E8
Sugar Loaf Wk BETH * E2 140 B5
Sugden Rd BTSEA SW11 158 B9
THDIT KT7 198 F8
Sugden Wy BARK IG11 143 J4
Sulgrave Gdns SHB W12 156 F1
Sulgrave Rd HMSMTH W6 156 F1
Sulina Rd BRXS/STRHM SW2 180 F3
Sulivan Ct FUL/PGN SW6 157 K8
Sulivan Rd FUL/PGN SW6 157 K9
Sullington Hl CRAWW RH11 283 N9
Sullivan Av CAN/RD E16 142 A7
Sullivan Cl BTSEA SW11 157 P9
DART DA1 187 J2
E/WMO/HCT KT8 198 A3
Sullivan Crs DEN/HRF UB9 91 N10
Sullivan Dr CRAWW RH11 283 H10
Sullivan Rd LBTH SE11 18 B5
TIL RM18 168 D7
Sullivans Reach WOT/HER KT12 196 G7
WOT/HER KT12 197 H7
Sullivan Wy BORE WD6 75 H10
Sultan Rd WAN E11 121 N2
Sultan St BECK BR3 204 C2
CMBW SE5 159 K6
Sumatra Rd KIL/WHAMP NW6 2 E1
Sumburgh Rd BAL SW12 180 B2
Sumburgh Wy SL SL1 129 J7
Summer Av E/WMO/HCT KT8 198 D5
Summer Cl HHNE HP2 35 N4
Summercourt Rd WCHPL E1 140 B8
Summer Dl WGCW AL8 22 G1
Summerene Cl
STRHM/NOR SW16 180 D10
Summerfield ASHTD KT21 237 J5
HAT AL10 40 D7
Summerfield Av KIL/WHAMP NW6 2 B7
NFNCH/WDSP N12 97 P7
Summerfield Cl LCOL/BKTW AL2 57 H2
Summerfield La SURB KT6 199 J9
Summerfield Pl CHERT * KT16 214 G3
Summerfield Rd GSTN WD25 73 H1
LOU IG10 82 A10
WEA W13 134 G6
Summerfields Cl
ADL/WDHM KT15 215 K2
Summerfield St LEE/GVPK SE12 183 L3
Summer Gdns E/WMO/HCT KT8 198 D5
Summer Gv BORE WD6 75 J10
Summerhayes Cl
WOKN/KNAP GU21 214 B10
Summerhays COB KT11 217 L9
Summer Hl BORE WD6 75 M9
CHST BR7 206 D2
Summerhill Cl ORP BR6 227 H1
Summerhill Ct STAL * AL1 38 E5
Summerhill Gv EN EN1 79 M10
Summerhill Rd DART DA1 187 L3
SEVS/STOTM N15 119 L2
Summerhill Wy MTCM CR4 202 B1
Summerhouse Av HEST TW5 153 M7
Summerhouse Dr RDART DA2 186 E8
Summerhouse La DEN/HRF UB9 91 K8
GSTN WD25 74 B5
WDR/YW UB7 151 N5
Summerhouse Rd
STNW/STAM N16 119 M7
Summerhouse Wy ABLGY WD5 54 G6
Summerland Gdns MUSWH N10 118 C1
Summerlands Av ACT W3 135 P9
Summerlay Cl
KWD/TDW/WH KT20 239 H7
Summerlea SL SL1 128 G10
Summerlee Av EFNCH N2 118 A2
Summerlee Gdns EFNCH N2 118 A2
Summerleigh WEY * KT13 216 E3
Summerley St WAND/EARL SW18 179 L5
Summerly Av REIG RH2 257 K9
Summer Pl WATW * WD18 72 G10
Summer Rd E/WMO/HCT KT8 198 C5
Summersbury Dr RGUE GU4 268 B8
Summersby Rd HGT N6 118 C4
Summers Cl BELMT SM2 221 K4
WBLY HA9 115 N6
WEY KT13 216 B7
Summersland Rd STALE/WH AL4 39 H2
Summers La NFNCH/WDSP N12 97 N8
RGODL GU7 266 F9
Summer's Rd RGODL GU7 267 L10
SL SL1 128 B5
Summers Rw NFNCH/WDSP N12 97 P7
Summers St CLKNW EC1R 12 A2
Summerstown TOOT SW17 179 M6
Summersvere Cl CRAWE RH10 284 B4
Summers Wy LCOL/BKTW * AL2 57 K3
Summers Wd BORE * WD6 75 N8
Summerswood Cl PUR/KEN CR8 241 L2
Summerswood La BORE WD6 76 B1
Summerton Wy THMD SE28 143 N9
Summer Trees SUN TW16 197 J1
Summerville Gdns SUT SM1 221 J3
Summerwood Rd TWK TW1 176 E2
Summit Av CDALE/KGS NW9 116 A3
Summit Centre POTB/CUF * EN6 59 H6
WDR/YW * UB7 151 N6
Summit Cl CDALE/KGS NW9 116 A2
EDGW HA8 95 M8
STHGT/OAK N14 98 D3
Summit Dr WFD IG8 102 A10
Summit Est STNW/STAM * N16 119 P5
Summit Rd NTHLT UB5 133 P2
POTB/CUF EN6 59 H6
WALTH E17 120 G2
The Summit LOU IG10 82 C5
Summit Wy NRWD SE19 181 M10
STHGT/OAK N14 98 C3
Sumner Av PECK SE15 159 N7
Sumner Cl LHD/OX KT22 236 C10
ORP BR6 226 F1
Sumner Gdns CROY/NA CR0 203 H8
Sumner Pl ADL/WDHM KT15 215 K2
SKENS SW7 15 M6
Sumner Place Ms SKENS SW7 15 M6
Sumner Rd CROY/NA CR0 203 J8
HRW HA1 114 B5
PECK SE15 19 M10
Sumner Rd South
CROY/NA CR0 203 H8
Sumners Farm Cl EPP CM16 46 D6
Sumner St STHWK SE1 12 E9
Sumnmit Pl WEY KT13 216 B4
Sumpter Cl HAMP NW3 3 K2
Sumpter Yd STAL AL1 38 C7
Sunbeam Crs NKENS W10 136 F6
Sunbeam Rd WLSDN NW10 135 P6
Sunbury Av MLHL NW7 96 A6
MORT/ESHN SW14 156 A10
Sunbury Ct BAR * EN5 77 H8
SUN TW16 197 L2
Sunbury Court Rd SUN TW16 197 K2
Sunbury Gdns MLHL NW7 96 A6
Sunbury La BTSEA SW11 157 N7
WOT/HER KT12 197 H6
Sunbury Rd CHEAM SM3 200 G10
FELT TW13 174 G6
WDSR SL4 149 J5
Sunbury St WOOL/PLUM SE18 162 C2
Sunbury Wy FELT TW13 175 K8
Sun Cl WDSR SL4 149 J5
Sun Ct ERITH DA8 164 G8
Suncroft Pl SYD SE26 182 B6
Sundale Av SAND/SEL CR2 224 B6
Sunderland Av STAL AL1 38 F5
Sunderland Gv GSTN WD25 54 G10
Sunderland Mt FSTH * SE23 182 C5
Sunderland Rd EA W5 155 J2
FSTH SE23 182 C4
Sunderland Ter BAY/PAD W2 8 G5
Sunderland Wy MNPK E12 122 A7
Sundew Av SHB W12 136 D9
Sundew Cl LTWR GU18 212 C7
Sundew Ct ALP/SUD * HA0 135 K4
Sundew Rd HHW HP1 35 H8
Sundial Av SNWD SE25 203 N2
Sundon Crs VW GU25 193 N5
Sundorne Rd CHARL SE7 161 N4
Sundown Av SAND/SEL CR2 223 N7
Sundown Rd ASHF TW15 174 D8
Sundridge Av BMLY BR1 184 A10
WELL DA16 162 G8
Sundridge Cl DART DA1 187 P2
Sundridge Hl RSEV TN14 245 M4
Sundridge La RSEV TN14 245 L3
Sundridge Pde BMLY * BR1 183 N10
Sundridge Rd CROY/NA CR0 203 N8

RSEV TN14 246 B6
WOKS/MYFD GU22 232 D5
Sunfields Pl BKHTH/KID SE3 161 N6
Sunflower Wy HARH RM3 105 L9
Sun Hl HART DA3 210 F9
WOKS/MYFD GU22 231 N7
Sun in Sands Rbt
BKHTH/KID SE3 161 N6
Sunken Rd CROY/NA CR0 224 B2
Sunkist Wy WLGTN SM6 222 F5
Sunland Av BXLYHS DA6 163 P10
Sun La BKHTH/KID SE3 161 N6
GVE DA12 190 F5
Sunleigh Rd ALP/SUD HA0 135 K3
Sunley Gdns GFD/PVL UB6 134 F4
Sunlight Cl WIM/MER * SW19 179 M9
Sunlight Sq BETH E2 140 A5
Sunmead Cl LHD/OX KT22 236 E8
Sunmead Pde LHD/OX * KT22 236 F8
Sunmead Rd HHNE HP2 35 N4
SUN TW16 197 H3
Sunna Gdns SUN TW16 197 J2
Sunning Av ASC SL5 192 D7
Sunningdale STHGT/OAK N14 98 E6
Sunningdale Av ACT W3 136 B9
BARK IG11 142 G3
FELT TW13 175 M5
RAIN RM13 145 J6
RSLP HA4 113 K6
Sunningdale Cl
BERM/RHTH * SE16 160 A4
STAN HA7 94 F8
SURB KT6 199 K9
THMD SE28 143 P8
Sunningdale Ct CRAWW RH11 283 N9
Sunningdale Gdns
CDALE/KGS NW9 115 P3
KENS W8 14 F4
Sunningdale Ldg EDGW * HA8 95 L6
Sunningdale Ms WGCE * AL7 23 J1
Sunningdale Pk ASC * SL5 192 E5
Sunningdale Rd HAYES BR2 206 B4
RAIN RM13 145 H2
SUT SM1 201 J10
Sunningfield Rd HDN NW4 116 E1
Sunningfields Crs HDN NW4 96 E10
Sunninghill GVW DA11 190 B5
Sunninghill Cl ASC SL5 192 C4
Sunninghill Ct ACT * W3 155 P1
Sunninghill Pk ASC * SL5 170 D9
ASC * SL5 192 C2
Sunninghill Rd ASC SL5 170 C8
ASC SL5 192 C5
LEW SE13 160 G8
Sunnings La UPMR RM14 146 C1
Sunningvale Av BH/WHM TN16 243 P3
Sunningvale Cl BH/WHM TN16 244 A2
Sunny Av CRAWE RH10 285 P5
Sunny Bank EPSOM KT18 237 P2
SNWD SE25 203 P3
WARL CR6 242 D3
Sunnybank Rd POTB/CUF EN6 59 K9
Sunny Crs WLSDN NW10 135 P2
Sunny Cft HLWS CM18 47 J4
Sunnycroft Gdns UPMR RM14 126 E5
Sunnycroft Rd HSLW TW3 154 A8
SNWD SE25 203 P3
STHL UB1 133 P7
Sunnydale ORP BR6 206 D9
Sunnydale Gdns MLHL NW7 96 A7
Sunnydale Rd LEE/GVPK SE12 183 N1
Sunnydell LCOL/BKTW AL2 56 A2
Sunnydene Av CHING E4 101 J6
RSLP HA4 113 H6
Sunnydene Cl HARH RM3 105 N8
Sunnydene Gdns ALP/SUD HA0 135 H1
Sunnydene Rd PUR/KEN CR8 223 J9
Sunnydene St SYD SE26 182 D7
Sunnyfield BRKMPK AL9 40 G1
MLHL NW7 96 C5
Sunny Gardens Rd HDN NW4 96 F10
Sunny Hl HDN NW4 116 E1
Sunnyhill Cl CLPT E5 120 D9
CRAWE RH10 285 P5
Sunnyhill Rd HHW HP1 35 L6
RKW/CH/CXG WD3 90 G7
STRHM/NOR SW16 180 F7
Sunnyhurst Cl SUT SM1 201 K10
Sunnymead CRAWW RH11 283 N7
Sunnymead Av MTCM CR4 202 E3
Sunnymead Rd CDALE/KGS NW9 116 A5
PUT/ROE SW15 178 E1
Sunnymede CHIG IG7 103 L4
Sunnymede Av CAR SM5 221 N7
CSHM HP5 51 K4
HOR/WEW KT19 220 B5
Sunnymede Dr BARK/HLT IG6 122 E2
Sunny Nook Gdns
SAND/SEL CR2 223 L3
Sunny Pl HDN NW4 116 F2
Sunny Ri CTHM CR3 241 L10
The Sunny Rd PEND EN3 80 C5
Sunnyside CRICK NW2 117 J8
FSTH * SE23 182 E3
WAB EN9 45 L8
WIM/MER SW19 179 H9
WOKN/KNAP * GU21 230 G5
WOT/HER KT12 197 K5
Sunnyside Dr CHING E4 101 H1
Sunnyside Gdns UPMR RM14 126 B8
Sunnyside Rd ARCH N19 118 E5
CSHM HP5 50 G6
EA W5 135 J10
EPP CM16 65 J8
IL IG1 122 F8
LEY E10 120 F6
TEDD TW11 176 C7
Sunnyside Rd East ED N9 99 P4
Sunnyside Rd North ED * N9 99 N4
Sunnyside Rd South ED * N9 99 N4
Sunny Vw CDALE/KGS NW9 116 A3
Sunny Wy NFNCH/WDSP N12 97 P8
Sun Pas BERM/RHTH SE16 19 N3
Sunray Av BRYLDS KT5 199 N9
CMBW SE5 159 L10
HAYES BR2 206 B6
HNHL SE24 159 L10
WDR/YW UB7 151 N1
Sunrise Av HCH RM12 125 K8
Sunrise Cl FELT TW13 175 N6
Sunrise Crs HHS/BOV HP3 35 P9
Sun Rd SWCM DA10 189 L2
WKENS W14 14 C8
Sunset Av CHING E4 100 G2
WFD IG8 101 M6
Sunset Cl ERITH DA8 165 J6
Sunset Gdns SNWD SE25 203 M2
Sunset Rd CMBW SE5 159 K10
THMD SE28 143 K10
WIM/MER SW19 178 E8
Sunset Vw BAR EN5 77 H6
Sunshine Wy MTCM CR4 202 A2
Sun Sq HHNE HP2 35 N5
Sun St SBW CM21 30 C10
SDTCH EC2A 13 H3
WAB EN9 63 H9
Superior Dr ORP BR6 227 J3
Surbiton Ct SURB KT6 199 H6
Surbiton Crs SURB KT6 199 K4
Surbiton Hall Cl KUT KT1 199 K4
Surbiton Hill Pk BRYLDS KT5 199 L5
Surbiton Hill Rd SURB KT6 199 K4
Surbiton Rd KUT KT1 199 J4
Surlingham Cl THMD SE28 143 N9
Surly Hall Wk WDSR SL4 148 E7
Surma Cl WCHPL E1 13 P2
Surman Crs RBRW/HUT CM13 107 P1
Surmans Cl DAGW RM9 143 M3
Surrendale Pl MV/WKIL W9 8 F2
Surrey Av SLN SL2 129 H7
Surrey Canal Rd
BERM/RHTH SE16 160 B5
Surrey Crs CHSWK W4 155 M4
Surrey Dr EMPK RM11 125 P3
Surrey Gdns COB KT11 234 G9
FSBYPK N4 119 K4
Surrey Gv SUT SM1 201 N10
WALW SE17 19 J8
Surrey Hills Av
KWD/TDW/WH KT20 255 P7
Surrey Hills Wy
KWD/TDW/WH KT20 255 P6
Surrey La BTSEA SW11 157 P7
Surrey Ms WNWD SE27 181 M7
Surrey Quays Rd
BERM/RHTH SE16 160 B2
Surrey Rd BARK IG11 143 H2
DAGE RM10 124 C10
DAGE RM10 124 D10
HRW HA1 114 B4
PECK SE15 182 C1
WWKM BR4 204 G8
Surrey Rw STHWK SE1 18 C1
Surrey Sq WALW SE17 19 J7
Surrey St CROY/NA CR0 203 K10
PLSTW E13 141 N5
TPL/STR WC2R 11 P7
Surrey Ter WALW SE17 19 K6
Surrey Water Rd
BERM/RHTH SE16 140 C10
Surridge Cl RAIN RM13 145 K5
Surridge Gdns NRWD SE19 181 L9
Surr St HOLWY N7 118 F10
Susan Cl ROMW/RG RM7 124 D1
Susannah St POP/IOD E14 140 G8
Susan Rd BKHTH/KID SE3 161 N8
Susan Wd CHST BR7 206 D1
Sussex Av HARH RM3 105 N8
ISLW TW7 154 D9
Sussex Border Pth
CRAWE RH10 285 L3
HORL RH6 279 M7
Sussex Cl ARCH * N19 118 F7
CSTG HP8 89 N3
HOD EN11 44 F2
NWMAL KT3 200 B4
REDBR IG4 122 C4
REIG RH2 275 N1
SL SL1 149 N1
TWK TW1 176 G2
WOKN/KNAP GU21 231 H4
Sussex Ct WOKN/KNAP GU21 231 H3
Sussex Crs NTHLT UB5 133 P1
Sussex Gdns BAY/PAD W2 9 M6
CHSGTN KT9 219 J3
EFNCH N2 118 A3
FSBYPK N4 119 K3
Sussex Ga EFNCH * N2 118 A3
Sussex Keep SL * SL1 149 N1
Sussex Ms East BAY/PAD * W2 9 M7
Sussex Ms West BAY/PAD W2 9 M7
Sussex Pl BAY/PAD W2 9 M6
CAMTN NW1 10 A1
CFSP/GDCR * SL9 90 B7
DTCH/LGLY SL3 149 N1
HMSMTH W6 156 F4
NWMAL KT3 200 B4
SL SL1 149 M1
Sussex Rd BRW CM14 106 G5
CAR SM5 222 A3
DART DA1 187 P3
EHAM E6 142 D4
ERITH DA8 164 C6
HGDN/ICK UB10 112 D9
HRW HA1 114 B3
MTCM * CR4 202 F5
NWDGN UB2 153 L2
NWMAL KT3 200 B4
SAND/SEL CR2 223 L3
SCUP DA14 185 L8
STMC/STPC BR5 207 M6
WATN WD24 73 H4
WOKN/KNAP GU21 231 H4
WWKM BR4 204 G8
Sussex Sq BAY/PAD W2 9 M7
Sussex St PIM SW1V 16 F8
PLSTW E13 141 N5
Sussex Ter PGE/AN * SE20 182 B10
PUR * RM19 166 A4
Sussex Wy ARCH N19 118 E6
EBAR EN4 78 C9
Sutcliffe Cl BUSH WD23 74 B8
GLDGN NW11 117 L3
Sutcliffe Rd WELL DA16 163 M8
WOOL/PLUM SE18 163 H5
Sutherland Av BH/WHM TN16 244 A3
HYS/HAR UB3 152 B3
MV/WKIL W9 8 F2
POTB/CUF EN6 60 E4
RGUE GU4 250 B4
STMC/STPC BR5 207 J6
SUN TW16 196 G2
WEA W13 134 E10
WELL DA16 162 G10
Sutherland Cl BAR EN5 77 H8
GVE DA12 191 L5
Sutherland Ct CDALE/KGS NW9 115 N2
WGCE AL7 23 J4
Sutherland Dr GU GU1 250 D7
WIM/MER SW19 201 N1
Sutherland Gdns
MORT/ESHN SW14 156 B9
SUN TW16 196 G2
WPK KT4 200 E8
Sutherland Gv TEDD TW11 176 D8
WAND/EARL SW18 179 J3
Sutherland House WALTH * E17 120 D1
Sutherland Pl BAY/PAD W2 8 E5
Sutherland Rd BELV DA17 164 B2
BOW E3 140 E4
CHSWK W4 156 A5
CROY/NA CR0 203 H7
ED N9 99 P2
PEND EN3 80 A2
STHL UB1 133 N8
TOTM N17 99 P8
WALTH E17 120 D1
WEA W13 134 F8
Sutherland Rw PIM SW1V 16 F7
Sutherland Sq WALW SE17 18 E8
Sutherland St PIM SW1V 16 F7
Sutherland Vls WEA * W13 134 F9
Sutherland Wk WALW SE17 18 F8
Sutherland Wy POTB/CUF EN6 60 E4
Sutlej Rd CHARL SE7 161 P6
Sutterton St HOLWY N7 5 N2
Sutton Av DTCH/LGLY SL3 149 P1
WOKN/KNAP GU21 231 K5
Sutton Cl BECK BR3 204 G1
BROX EN10 44 D6
CHSWK * W4 155 P5
LOU IG10 102 B1
PIN HA5 113 H3
Sutton Common Rd CHEAM SM3 201 J7
Sutton Ct BELMT SM2 222 A1
CHSWK * W4 155 P5
EA * W5 135 K10
WARE * SG12 26 D3
Sutton Court Rd BELMT SM2 221 M3
CHSWK W4 155 P5
HGDN/ICK UB10 132 C3
PLSTW E13 141 P5
SUT SM1 221 M3
Sutton Crs BAR EN5 76 G9
Sutton Dene HSLW TW3 154 A7
Sutton Est IS * N1 6 C3
The Sutton Est IS N1 6 C3
Sutton Gdns CROY/NA CR0 203 N5
REDH RH1 258 E5
Sutton Green Rd RGUE GU4 250 B2
Sutton Gv SUT SM1 221 N2
Sutton Hall HEST TW5 153 P6
Sutton La BELMT SM2 221 L8
BNSTD SM7 239 L1
CHSWK W4 155 P4
DTCH/LGLY SL3 150 E5
HSLW TW3 153 N8
RDKG RH5 271 J9
Sutton La South CHSWK W4 155 P5
Sutton Park Rd SUT SM1 221 L3
Sutton Pl DTCH/LGLY SL3 150 E5
HOM E9 120 B10
SHGR GU5 270 G9
Sutton Rd BARK IG11 143 H4
HEST TW5 153 P7
MUSWH N10 98 B9
PLSTW E13 141 L6
STAL AL1 38 G7
WALTH E17 100 C9
WAT WD17 73 K7
Sutton Rw SOHO/SHAV W1D 11 J5
Suttons Av HCH RM12 125 K8
Suttons Gdns HCH RM12 125 L8
Suttons La HCH RM12 125 L10
Sutton Sq HEST TW5 153 N7
HOM * E9 120 B10
Sutton St WCHPL E1 140 B8
Sutton Wy HEST TW5 153 N7
NKENS W10 136 F7
Swabey Rd DTCH/LGLY SL3 150 D3
Swaby Rd WAND/EARL SW18 179 M5
Swaffield Rd SEV TN13 247 K8
WAND/EARL SW18 179 M3
Swain Cl TOOT SW17 180 C9
Swain Rd THHTH CR7 203 K5
Swains Cl WDR/YW UB7 151 P1
Swain's La KTTN NW5 118 B8
Swainson Rd ACT W3 156 C1
Swains Rd MTCM CR4 180 A10
Swain St STJWD NW8 9 M2
Swaisland Rd DART DA1 187 J1
Swaislands Dr DART DA1 186 G1
Swakeleys Dr HGDN/ICK UB10 112 B9
Swakeleys Rd HGDN/ICK UB10 111 P9
Swale Cl SOCK/AV RM15 146 B8
Swaledale Cl CRAWW RH11 283 M10
FBAR/BDGN N11 98 B7
Swaledale Rd RDART DA2 188 B4
Swale Rd DART DA1 165 H9
Swallands Rd CAT SE6 182 F6
Swallow Cl BUSH WD23 94 A2
BXLYHN DA7 164 F7
CDH/CHF RM16 167 H3
GRH DA9 188 E1
NWCR SE14 160 B7
RKW/CH/CXG WD3 91 M1
STA TW18 173 J7
Swallow Ct RSLP * HA4 113 K6
WGCE * AL7 23 J5
Swallowdale IVER SL0 130 G5
SAND/SEL CR2 224 C5
Swallowdale La HHNE HP2 36 B3
Swallow Dr NTHLT UB5 133 P4
WLSDN NW10 136 A1
Swallow End WGCE AL7 23 J5
Swallowfield EGH TW20 171 N9
Swallowfield Rd CHARL SE7 161 N4
Swallowfields WGCE AL7 23 J5
Swallowfield Wy HYS/HAR UB3 152 E1
Swallow Gdns HAT AL10 40 D6
STRHM/NOR SW16 180 E8
Swallow La RDKG RH5 272 G8
STAL AL1 38 G9
Swallow Oaks ABLGY WD5 54 G7
Swallow Pk HHNE * HP2 36 C2
Swallow Pl REGST W1B 10 F6
Swallow Ri WOKN/KNAP GU21 231 H3
Swallow Rd CRAWW RH11 283 M5
Swallows HLWE CM17 29 M7
The Swallows WGCE AL7 23 J1
Swallow St CONDST W1S 11 H8
EHAM E6 142 B7
IVER SL0 130 G5
Swallowtail Cl STMC/STPC BR5 207 N4
Swanage Rd CHING E4 101 H8
WAND/EARL SW18 179 M2
Swanage Waye YEAD UB4 133 K8
Swan Ap EHAM E6 142 B7
Swan Av UPMR RM14 126 E6
Swanbourne Dr HCH RM12 125 L9
Swanbridge Rd BXLYHN DA7 164 B7
Swan Cl CROY/NA * CR0 203 M7
CSHM HP5 50 G3
FELT TW13 175 M7
RKW/CH/CXG WD3 91 N1
STMC/STPC BR5 207 K3
WALTH E17 100 D9
Swan Ct GU GU1 250 A8
HHW * HP1 35 M6
Swandon Wy WAND/EARL SW18 157 L10
Swan Dr CDALE/KGS NW9 96 B10
Swanfield Rd CHES/WCR EN8 62 D9
Swanfield St BETH E2 7 L10
Swanhill WGCE AL7 23 K2
Swan Island TWK * TW1 176 F6
Swanland Rd BRKMPK AL9 58 E3
POTB/CUF EN6 58 E10
Swan La BRWN CM15 86 D3
CANST EC4R 13 H8
DART DA1 186 G3
GU GU1 268 A1
HORL RH6 279 J8
LOU IG10 101 P1
TRDG/WHET N20 97 M4
Swanley Bar La POTB/CUF EN6 59 L4
Swanley Crs POTB/CUF EN6 59 L5
Swanley La SWLY BR8 208 G3
Swanley Rd WELL DA16 163 M7
Swanley Village Rd SWLY BR8 209 J1
Swan Md HHS/BOV HP3 54 A1
STHWK SE1 19 J4
Swan Ms BRXN/ST SW9 158 G8
Swan Mill Gdns DORK RH4 255 H10
Swanns Meadow GT/LBKH KT23 253 P2
Swan Pas WCHPL E1 13 M8
Swan & Pike Rd PEND EN3 80 F4
Swan Pl BARN SW13 156 C8
Swan Rd BERM/RHTH SE16 160 B1
FELT TW13 175 M7
GFD/PVL UB6 134 A8
IVER SL0 131 J7
WDR/YW UB7 151 N1
Swans Cl STALE/WH AL4 39 K7
Swanscombe Rd CHSWK W4 156 B4
NTGHL W11 136 G10
Swanscombe St SWCM DA10 189 L2
Swansea Rd HTHAIR TW6 174 D2
PEND EN3 80 B8
Swanshope LOU IG10 82 E6
Swans Rd CHES/WCR EN8 62 C10
Swanston Pth OXHEY WD19 93 K4
Swan St ISLW TW7 154 G9
STHWK SE1 18 F2
The Swansway WEY * KT13 196 B10
Swanton Gdns WIM/MER SW19 178 G4
Swanton Rd ERITH DA8 164 B6
Swan Wk CHEL SW3 16 A9
SHPTN TW17 196 F7
Swan Wy PEND EN3 80 C6
Swanwick Cl PUT/ROE SW15 178 C3
Swanworth La RDKG RH5 254 G4
Swan Yd IS N1 6 C2
Swanzy Rd RSEV TN14 247 K6
Sward Rd STMC/STPC BR5 207 K6
Swaton Rd BOW E3 140 F6
Swaylands Rd BELV DA17 164 B5
Swaynesland Rd OXTED RH8 262 C10
Swayne's La GU GU1 251 H10
Swaythling Cl UED N18 100 A5
Sweden Ga BERM/RHTH SE16 160 D3
Sweeney Crs STHWK SE1 19 M2
Sweeps Ditch Cl STA TW18 195 K1
Sweeps La EGH TW20 172 C8
STMC/STPC BR5 207 N5
Sweet Briar WGCE AL7 23 K7
Sweetbriar Cl HHW HP1 35 K3
Sweet Briar Gn UED N18 99 N4
Sweet Briar Gv ED N9 99 N4
Sweet Briar Wk UED N18 99 N5
Sweetcroft La HGDN/ICK UB10 132 A2
Sweet La SHGR GU5 270 E9
Sweetmans Av PIN HA5 113 L1
Sweets Wy TRDG/WHET N20 97 N3
Swete St PLSTW E13 141 M4
Sweyne HLWE CM17 47 M4
Sweyne Rd SWCM DA10 189 K2
Sweyn Pl BKHTH/KID SE3 161 M8
Swievelands Rd BH/WHM TN16 243 N5
Swift Cl HYS/HAR UB3 132 G8
RYLN/HDSTN HA2 114 A7
UPMR RM14 126 D6
WALTH E17 100 D8
WARE SG12 27 H8
Swiftfields WGCE AL7 23 J4
Swift La CRAWW RH11 283 N5
Swift Rd FELT TW13 175 L7
NWDGN UB2 153 N2
Swiftsden Wy BMLY BR1 183 K9
Swift St FUL/PGN SW6 157 H7
Swiftsure Rd CDH/CHF RM16 167 H3
Swiller's La GVE DA12 191 P8
Swinbrook Rd NKENS W10 8 B3
Swinburne Crs CROY/NA CR0 204 B6
Swinburne Gdns TIL RM18 168 E8
Swinburne Rd PUT/ROE SW15 156 D10
Swinderby Rd ALP/SUD HA0 135 K1
Swindon Cl GDMY/SEVK IG3 123 H7
Swindon Gdns HARH RM3 105 N6
Swindon La HARH RM3 105 N6
Swindon Rd HTHAIR TW6 174 D1
Swindon St SHB * W12 136 E10
Swinfield Cl FELT TW13 175 M7
Swinford Gdns BRXN/ST SW9 159 J9
Swingate La WOOL/PLUM SE18 163 H6
Swing Gate La BERK HP4 34 A6
Swinnerton St HOM E9 120 D10
Swinton Cl WBLY HA9 115 N6
Swinton Pl FSBYW WC1X 5 N9
Swinton St FSBYW WC1X 5 N9
Swires Shaw HAYES BR2 226 A1
Swiss Av WATW WD18 72 F8
Swiss Cl WATW WD18 72 F7
Swithland Gdns ELTH/MOT SE9 184 C7
Swyncombe Av BTFD TW8 154 G3
Swynford Gdns HDN NW4 116 D2
Sybil Phoenix Cl DEPT SE8 160 C4
Sybourn St WALTH E17 120 E5
Sycamore Ap RKW/CH/CXG WD3 72 D9
Sycamore Av BFN/LL DA15 185 J2
BOW E3 140 E3
EA W5 155 J2
HAT AL10 40 D5
HYS/HAR UB3 132 F9
UPMR RM14 125 P8
Sycamore Cl ACT W3 136 B10
AMS HP6 69 J3
BUSH WD23 73 M6
CAN/RD E16 141 K6
CAR SM5 222 A1
CHESW EN7 61 N3
CRAWW RH11 283 M4
EBAR EN4 77 N10
FELT TW13 175 H6
GSTN WD25 73 J1
GVE DA12 190 G3
LHD/OX KT22 236 E8
NTHLT UB5 133 M3
TIL RM18 168 C7
UED N18 99 P5
WDR/YW UB7 132 A9
Sycamore Ct WEY KT13 196 C10
Sycamore Dene CSHM HP5 51 J4
Sycamore Dr BRW CM14 107 H2
LCOL/BKTW AL2 56 C3
SWLY BR8 208 F3
Sycamore Fld HLWW/ROY CM19 46 D5
Sycamore Gdns MTCM CR4 201 N2
SHB W12 156 E1
Sycamore Gv CAT SE6 183 H2
CDALE/KGS NW9 115 P5
NWMAL KT3 200 B3
PGE/AN SE20 203 P1
Sycamore Hl FBAR/BDGN N11 98 B7
Sycamore Ms CLAP SW4 158 D9
ERITH * DA8 164 E4
Sycamore Pl AMS * HP6 69 H4
Sycamore Ri BERK HP4 34 A6
CSTG HP8 89 M4
EW KT17 220 G10
Sycamore Rd AMS HP6 69 J3
CSTG HP8 89 M4
DART DA1 187 L3
GU GU1 250 A10
RKW/CH/CXG WD3 72 D9
WIM/MER SW19 178 F9
The Sycamores HHS/BOV HP3 35 J9
RAD WD7 56 G10
Sycamore St FSBYE EC1V 12 E2
Sycamore Wk DTCH/LGLY SL3 130 B8
EGH TW20 171 N9
NKENS W10 8 A1
REIG RH2 275 M3
Sycamore Wy SOCK/AV RM15 147 J6
TEDD TW11 177 H9
Sydcote DUL * SE21 181 K5
Sydenham Av SYD SE26 182 A8
WCHMH N21 78 G9
Sydenham Cl ROM RM1 124 G2
Sydenham Cottages
LEE/GVPK * SE12 183 P5
Sydenham Hl SYD SE26 181 P6
Sydenham Pk SYD SE26 182 B6
Sydenham Park Rd SYD SE26 182 B6
Sydenham Ri FSTH SE23 182 A5
Sydenham Rd CROY/NA CR0 203 K9
GU GU1 268 A2
SYD SE26 182 C8
Sydenham Station Ap SYD SE26 182 B7
Sydmons Ct FSTH * SE23 182 B3
Sydner Rd STNW/STAM N16 119 N9
Sydney Av PUR/KEN CR8 222 G8
Sydney Cl SKENS SW7 15 M6
Sydney Crs ASHF TW15 174 C9
Sydney Gv HDN NW4 116 F3
SL SL1 129 H8
Sydney Ms SKENS SW7 15 M6
Sydney Pl GU GU1 268 C1
SKENS SW7 15 M6
Sydney Rd ABYW SE2 163 N2
BARK/HLT IG6 102 F10
BXLYHS DA6 163 N10
CEND/HSY/T N8 119 H2
EBED/NFELT TW14 175 H4
ENC/FH EN2 79 L7
GU GU1 268 C1
MUSWH N10 98 C9
RCH/KEW TW9 155 K10
RYNPK SW20 200 G2
SCUP DA14 185 H7
SUT SM1 221 K1
TEDD TW11 176 E8
TIL RM18 168 D8
WAN E11 121 N4
WATW WD18 72 F9
WEA W13 134 F10
Sydney St CHEL SW3 15 N7
Sydney Ter ESH/CLAY * KT10 218 E3
Syke Cluan IVER SL0 151 H1
Syke Ings IVER SL0 151 H2
Sykes Rd SL SL1 128 G8
Sylvana Cl HGDN/ICK UB10 132 A3
Sylvan Av CHDH RM6 124 A4
EMPK RM11 125 N4
MLHL NW7 96 B7
WDGN N22 99 H8
Sylvan Cl CDH/CHF RM16 167 K3
HHS/BOV HP3 36 B7
OXTED RH8 261 N5
SAND/SEL CR2 224 A6
WOKS/MYFD GU22 232 E4
Sylvandale WGCE AL7 23 M6
Sylvan Gdns SURB KT6 199 J7
Sylvan Gv CRICK NW2 116 G9
PECK SE15 160 A6
Sylvan Hl NRWD SE19 203 M1
Sylvan Rd CRAWE RH10 284 B9
FSTGT E7 141 M1
IL IG1 122 F7
NRWD SE19 203 N1
WALTH * E17 120 F3
WAN E11 121 M3
Sylvan Ter PECK * SE15 160 A6
Sylvan Wy BCTR RM8 123 L8
CHIG IG7 103 L4
REDH RH1 276 B1
WGCE AL7 23 N5
WWKM BR4 225 K1
Sylverdale Rd CROY/NA CR0 203 J10
PUR/KEN CR8 223 J9
Sylvester Av CHST BR7 184 C9
Sylvester Pth HACK * E8 140 A1
Sylvester Rd ALP/SUD HA0 115 H10
EFNCH N2 97 M10
HACK * E8 140 A1
WALTH * E17 120 E5
Sylvesters HLWW/ROY CM19 46 C3
Sylvia Av PIN HA5 93 N7
RBRW/HUT CM13 107 P3
Sylvia Cl CHOB/PIR GU24 230 F1
Sylvia Gdns WBLY HA9 135 N2
Symes Ms CAMTN NW1 4 G7
Symington Ms HOM * E9 120 C10
Symister Ms IS * N1 7 J10
Symonds Ct CHES/WCR EN8 62 C4
Symons St CHEL SW3 16 B6
Symphony Ms NKENS * W10 2 B9
Syon Gate Wy BTFD TW8 154 F6
Syon La ISLW TW7 154 E5
Syon Pk ISLW * TW7 154 G9
Syon Park Gdns ISLW TW7 154 E6
Syracuse Av RAIN RM13 145 L5
Sythwood WOKN/KNAP GU21 231 N3
Szabo Crs RGUW GU3 248 A10

T

Tabard Garden Est STHWK SE1 18 G1
Tabard St STHWK SE1 18 G3

Tabarin Wy EW KT17 238 F2
Tabernacle Av PLSTW E13 141 M6
Tabernacle St SDTCH EC2A 13 H2
Tableer Av CLAP SW4 180 D1
Tabley Rd HOLWY N7 118 F9
Tabor Gdns CHEAM SM3 221 H3
Tabor Gv WIM/MER SW19 179 H10
Tabor Rd HMSMTH W6 156 E2
Tabrums Wy UPMR RM14 126 D5
Tachbrook Rd
EBED/NFELT TW14 174 G3
NWDGN UB2 153 L3
UX/CGN UB8 131 M4
Tachbrook St PIM SW1V 17 H6
Tack Ms BROCKY SE4 160 F9
Tadema Rd WBPTN SW10 157 M6
Tadlows Cl UPMR RM14 126 A10
Tadmor Cl SUN TW16 196 G4
Tadmor St SHB W12 136 G10
Tadorne Rd KWD/TDW/WH KT20 238 F7
Tadworth Av NWMAL KT3 200 C4
Tadworth Cl KWD/TDW/WH KT20 238 G8
Tadworth Pde HCH RM12 125 J9
Tadworth Rd CRICK NW2 116 D7
Tadworth St
KWD/TDW/WH KT20 238 F9
Taeping St POP/IOD E14 160 G3
Taffy's How MTCM CR4 201 P3
Tait Rd CROY/NA CR0 203 M7
Takeley Cl CRW RM5 104 E10
WAB EN9 63 J9
Talacre Rd KTTN NW5 4 D1
Talbot Av DTCH/LGLY SL3 150 C2
EFNCH N2 117 N1
OXHEY WD19 93 M1
Talbot Cl REIG RH2 275 L1
SEVS/STOTM N15 119 N2
Talbot Ct BANK EC3V 13 H7
HHS/BOV * HP3 35 N8
Talbot Crs HDN NW4 116 D3
Talbot Gdns GDMY/SEVK IG3 123 K7
Talbot Pl BKHTH/KID SE3 161 K8
DTCH/LGLY SL3 149 P7
Talbot Rd ALP/SUD HA0 115 J10
ASHF TW15 173 N8
CAR SM5 222 B2
DAGW RM9 144 A2
EDUL SE22 159 M10
EHAM E6 142 C4
FSTGT E7 121 M9
HAT AL10 40 D1
HGT N6 118 B4
ISLW TW7 154 F10
KTN/HRWW/W HA3 94 E10
NTGHL W11 8 C6
NWDGN UB2 153 M3
RKW/CH/CXG WD3 91 P2
SEVS/STOTM N15 119 N2
THHTH CR7 203 L4
WDGN N22 98 D10
WEA * W13 134 F9
WHTN TW2 176 D4
Talbot Sq BAY/PAD W2 9 L6
Talbot St HERT/BAY SG13 25 M5
Talbot Wk NTGHL * W11 8 A6
WLSDN * NW10 136 B1
Talbot Yd STHWK SE1 12 G10
Talbrook BRW CM14 106 E4
Talcott Pth BRXS/STRHM * SW2 181 H4
Taleworth Cl ASHTD KT21 237 J6
Taleworth Pk ASHTD KT21 237 J6
Taleworth Rd ASHTD KT21 237 J5
Talfourd Pl PECK SE15 159 N7
Talfourd Rd PECK SE15 159 N7
Talgarth Rd HMSMTH W6 14 A7
Talisman Cl GDMY/SEVK IG3 123 L6
Talisman Sq SYD SE26 181 P7
Talisman Wy EW KT17 238 F2
WBLY HA9 115 L8
Tallack Rd LEY E10 120 E6
Tall Elms Cl HAYES BR2 205 L5
Tallents Cl EYN DA4 188 A10
Tallis Cl CAN/RD E16 141 N8
CRAWW RH11 283 J10
Tallis Gv CHARL SE7 161 N5
Tallis St EMB EC4Y 12 B7
Tallis Vw WLSDN NW10 136 A1
Tallis Wy BORE WD6 75 J5
Tall Oaks AMS HP6 69 J3
Tall Trees DTCH/LGLY SL3 151 H7
STRHM/NOR SW16 202 G3
Tall Trees Cl EMPK RM11 125 L4
Tally Rd OXTED RH8 262 B7
Talma Gdns WHTN TW2 176 D3
Talmage Cl FSTH SE23 182 B3
Talman Cl CRAWW * RH11 283 H8
Talman Gv STAN HA7 95 J7
Talma Rd BRXS/STRHM SW2 159 H10
Talus Cl PUR RM19 166 C3
Talwin St BOW E3 140 G5
Tamar Cl BOW * E3 140 E3
CRAWE RH10 284 D8
UPMR RM14 126 D4
Tamar Dr SOCK/AV RM15 146 B8
Tamar Gn HHNE HP2 36 A1
Tamarind Cl GUW GU2 249 M5
Tamarind Yd WAP E1W 13 P9
Tamarisk Cl STALW/RED AL3 38 C2
Tamarisk Rd SOCK/AV RM15 147 H5
Tamarisk Sq SHB W12 136 C9
Tamarisk Wy SL SL1 128 F10
Tamar St CHARL SE7 162 B3
Tamar Wy DTCH/LGLY SL3 150 E4
Tamerton Sq WOKS/MYFD GU22 232 B5
Tamesis Gdns WPK KT4 200 B9
Tamesis Strd GVE DA12 191 H8
Tamian Wy HSLWW TW4 153 K10
Tamworth Av WFD IG8 101 K7
Tamworth La MTCM CR4 202 C3
Tamworth Pk MTCM CR4 202 C4
Tamworth Pl CROY/NA * CR0 203 K9
Tamworth Rd CROY/NA CR0 203 K9
HERT/BAY SG13 25 N4
Tamworth St FUL/PGN SW6 14 E9
Tancred Rd FSBYPK N4 119 J4
Tandridge Dr ORP BR6 206 G8
Tandridge Gdns SAND/SEL CR2 223 N9
Tandridgehill La GDST RH9 260 E4
Tandridge La OXTED RH8 260 F9
Tandridge Rd WARL CR6 242 C5
Tanfield Av CRICK NW2 116 C9
Tanfield Cl CHESW EN7 61 P3
Tanfield Rd CROY/NA CR0 223 K1
Tangent Link HARH RM3 105 L9
Tangent Rd HARH RM3 105 L9
Tangier La WDSR SL4 149 J5
Tangier Rd GU GU1 268 D1
RCHPK/HAM TW10 155 N9
Tangier Wy KWD/TDW/WH KT20 239 H3
Tangier Wd KWD/TDW/WH KT20 239 H4
Tangleberry Cl BMLY BR1 206 C4
Tangle Tree Cl EFNCH N2 97 L10
Tanglewood Cl CHERT KT16 193 N10
CROY/NA CR0 204 B10
STAN HA7 94 D3
WOKS/MYFD GU22 232 G2
Tanglewood Ride
CHOB/PIR GU24 212 C8
Tanglewood Wy FELT TW13 175 J6
Tangley Gv PUT/ROE SW15 178 C3
Tangley La RGUW GU3 249 L6
Tangley Park Rd HPTN * TW12 175 N8
Tanglyn Av SHPTN TW17 196 B5
Tangmere Crs HCH RM12 145 J1
Tangmere Gdns NTHLT UB5 133 K4
Tangmere Gv KUTN/CMB KT2 177 J8
Tangmere Rd CRAWW RH11 283 J7
Tangmere Wy CDALE/KGS NW9 96 B10
Tanhouse Fld KTTN * NW5 118 E10
Tan House La BRW CM14 85 P7
Tanhouse Rd OXTED RH8 261 J8
Tankerton Houses STPAN * WC1H 5 M10
Tankerton Rd SURB KT6 199 L9
Tankerton St STPAN WC1H 5 M10
Tankerton Ter CROY/NA * CR0 202 G7
Tankerville Rd
STRHM/NOR SW16 180 E10
Tank Hill Rd PUR RM19 165 P3
Tank La PUR RM19 165 P3
Tankridge Rd CRICK NW2 116 E7
The Tanneries WCHPL * E1 140 B6
Tanners Cl STALW/RED AL3 38 B5
WOT/HER KT12 197 J6
Tanners Crs HERT/BAY SG13 25 K7
Tanners Dean LHD/OX KT22 237 J8
Tanners End La UED N18 99 M5
Tannersfield SHGR GU5 268 B8
Tanners Hl ABLGY WD5 54 G7
BRKHM/BTCW RH3 273 N2
DEPT SE8 160 F7
Tanners La BARK/HLT IG6 122 F1
Tanners Meadow
BRKHM/BTCW RH3 273 N4
Tanner St BARK IG11 142 F1
STHWK SE1 19 K2
Tanners Wy WARE SG12 27 P2
Tanners Wood La ABLGY WD5 54 F8
Tannery Cl CROY/NA CR0 204 C5
DAGE RM10 124 C8
Tannery La RPLY/SEND GU23 233 H8
SHGR * GU5 268 C9
The Tannery REDH RH1 257 P10
Tannington Ter FSBYPK * N4 119 H8
Tannsfeld Rd SYD SE26 182 C8
Tannsfield Dr HHNE HP2 36 A4
Tannsmore Cl HHNE HP2 36 A4
Tansley Cl HOLWY * N7 118 E10
Tanswell St STHWK * SE1 18 A2
Tansy Cl EHAM E6 142 D8
HARH RM3 105 M7
RGUE GU4 250 F8
Tansycroft WGCE AL7 23 L4
Tantallon Rd BAL SW12 180 B4
Tant Av CAN/RD E16 141 L8
Tanza Rd HAMP NW3 118 A9
Tapestry Cl BELMT SM2 221 L4
Taplow Ct MTCM CR4 201 P4
Taplow St IS N1 6 F8
Tapner's Rd REIG RH2 274 C6
Tappesfield Rd PECK SE15 160 B9
Tapping Cl KUTN/CMB * KT2 177 M10
Tapp St BETH * E2 140 A6
Tapster St BAR EN5 77 J7
Taransay HHS/BOV HP3 36 C8
Tara Pk COUL/CHIP CR5 240 A6
Tara Ter BROCKY * SE4 160 D9
Tarbay La WDSR SL4 148 A8
Tarbert Rd EDUL SE22 181 M1
Tarbert Wk WCHPL E1 140 B9
Target Cl EBED/NFELT TW14 174 F2
Tarham Cl HORL RH6 279 P2
Tariff Rd UED N18 99 P7
Tarleton Gdns FSTH SE23 182 A4
Tarling Cl SCUP DA14 185 L8
Tarling Rd CAN/RD E16 141 L8
EFNCH N2 97 M10
Tarling St WCHPL E1 140 A8
Tarmac Wy WDR/YW UB7 151 L6
Tarnbank STHGT/OAK N14 78 F9
Tarn St STHWK SE1 18 E4
Tarnwood Pk ELTH/MOT SE9 184 C4
Tarnworth Rd HARH RM3 105 P6
Tarpan Wy BROX EN10 62 E2
Tarragon Cl NWCR * SE14 160 D6
Tarragon Dr GUW GU2 249 M5
Tarragon Gv SYD SE26 182 C9
Tarrant Dr HARP AL5 20 B4
Tarrant Pl BF/WBF * KT14 215 J9
MBLAR W1H 10 A4
Tarriff Crs DEPT SE8 160 E4
Tarrington Cl
STRHM/NOR * SW16 180 E7
Tartar Hl COB KT11 217 J9
Tartar Rd COB KT11 217 K9
Tarver Rd WALW SE17 18 D8
Tarves Wy GNWCH SE10 160 G6
Tash Pl FBAR/BDGN * N11 98 C6
Tasker Cl HYS/HAR UB3 152 D6
Tasker Rd CDH/CHF RM16 168 E2
HAMP NW3 118 A10
Tasmania Ter UED N18 99 K7
Tasman Rd BRXN/ST SW9 158 F9
Tasso Rd HMSMTH W6 14 A9
Tate Cl LHD/OX KT22 237 H9
Tate Gdns BUSH WD23 94 D1
Tate Rd CAN/RD E16 142 C10
CFSP/GDCR SL9 90 C6
SUT SM1 221 K2
Tates Orch HART DA3 211 L6
Tatnell Rd FSTH SE23 182 D2
Tatsfield Av WAB EN9 45 J9
Tatsfield La BH/WHM TN16 244 C7
Tattenham Corner Rd
EPSOM KT18 238 D4
Tattenham Crs EPSOM KT18 238 D4
Tattenham Gv EPSOM KT18 238 E4
Tattenham Wy
KWD/TDW/WH KT20 239 H3
Tattersall Cl ELTH/MOT SE9 184 B1
Tattle Hl HERT/WAS SG14 24 F1
Tatton Crs CLPT E5 119 N5
Tatum Rd WLSDN NW10 135 P2
Tatum St WALW SE17 19 H6
Tauber Cl BORE WD6 75 L8
Tauheed Cl FSBYPK N4 119 K7
Taunton Av CTHM CR3 241 N9
HSLW TW3 154 B8
RYNPK SW20 200 E2
Taunton Cl BARK/HLT IG6 103 J7
BXLYHN DA7 164 E9
CHEAM SM3 201 K8
Taunton Dr EFNCH N2 97 M10
ENC/FH EN2 79 H7
Taunton La COUL/CHIP CR5 241 H5
Taunton Ms CAMTN NW1 10 A2
Taunton Pl CAMTN NW1 10 A1
Taunton Rd GFD/PVL UB6 134 A3
GVW DA11 189 M1
HARH RM3 105 K5
LEW SE13 183 K1
Taunton V GVE DA12 190 G6
Taunton Wy STAN HA7 115 K1
Tavern Cl CAR SM5 201 P7
Taverners HHNE HP2 35 P4
Taverners Cl NTGHL * W11 8 A10
Taverner Sq HBRY * N5 119 K9
Taverners Wy CHING E4 101 K2
HOD EN11 44 F3
Tavistock Av GFD/PVL UB6 134 F4
STAL AL1 38 B9
WALTH E17 120 C1
Tavistock Cl HARH RM3 105 L9
POTB/CUF EN6 59 N7
STA TW18 173 N10
STAL AL1 38 C9
STNW/STAM * N16 119 M10
Tavistock Ct COVGDN * WC2E 11 M7
Tavistock Crs MTCM CR4 202 F4
NTGHL W11 8 D4
Tavistock Gdns GDMY/SEVK IG3 123 H9
Tavistock Gv CROY/NA CR0 203 L7
Tavistock Ms NTGHL * W11 8 C5
Tavistock Pl STHGT/OAK * N14 78 C10
STPAN WC1H 11 K1
Tavistock Rd CAR SM5 201 N8
CROY/NA CR0 203 L8
EDGW HA8 95 L9
FSBYPK N4 119 L4
FSTGT E7 121 L9
HAYES BR2 205 M4
HGDN/ICK UB10 112 E10
NTGHL W11 8 C4
SRTFD E15 141 L1
SWFD E18 121 M1
WATN WD24 73 L5
WDR/YW UB7 131 N10
WELL DA16 163 M7
WLSDN NW10 136 C4
Tavistock Sq STPAN WC1H 11 K1
Tavistock St COVGDN WC2E 11 M7
Tavistock Ter ARCH N19 118 E8
Taviton St STPAN WC1H 11 J1
Tavy Cl LBTH SE11 18 B7
Tawney Common EPP CM16 66 B8
Tawney La ABR/ST RM4 84 D5
EPP CM16 66 D8
Tawney Rd THMD SE28 143 L9
Tawneys Rd HLWS CM18 47 J3
Tawny Av UPMR RM14 126 A10
Tawny Cl FELT TW13 175 H6
WEA W13 134 G10
Tawny Wy BERM/RHTH SE16 160 C3
Tayben Av WHTN TW2 176 D2
Taybridge Rd BTSEA SW11 158 B9
Tayburn Cl POP/IOD E14 141 H8
Tayfield Cl HGDN/ICK UB10 112 D8
Tayles Hill Dr EW KT17 220 C6
Taylifers HLWW/ROY CM19 46 D6
Taylor Av RCH/KEW TW9 155 N8
Taylor Cl CRW RM5 104 B8
HOR/WEW KT19 219 M7
HPTN TW12 176 B8
HSLW TW3 154 B7
ORP BR6 227 J1
STALE/WH AL4 38 F2
TOTM N17 99 P8
Taylor Rd ASHTD KT21 237 J3
WIM/MER SW19 179 P10
WLGTN SM6 222 C2
Taylor Rw RDART DA2 187 K6
Taylors Av HOD EN11 44 F4
Taylor's Buildings
WOOL/PLUM SE18 162 E3
Taylors Cl SCUP DA14 185 J7
Taylors Ct FELT TW13 175 H5
Taylor's Gn ACT * W3 136 B8
Taylor's La BAR EN5 77 J5
SYD SE26 182 A7
WLSDN NW10 136 B1
Taylors Md MLHL * NW7 96 D6
Taylors Rd CSHM HP5 51 J5
Taylor Wk CRAWW RH11 283 M7
Taymount Ri FSTH SE23 182 B5
Taynton Dr REDH RH1 258 E6
Tayport Cl IS N1 5 N4
Tayside Dr EDGW HA8 95 N4
Tay Wy ROM RM1 104 G9
Taywood Rd NTHLT UB5 133 N5
Teak Cl BERM/RHTH SE16 140 D10
Teal Av STMC/STPC BR5 207 N4
Teal Cl CAN/RD E16 142 A7
SAND/SEL CR2 224 C7
Teal Ct DORK * RH4 272 F1
Teal Dr NTHWD HA6 92 D8
Teale St BETH E2 7 P7
Tealing Dr HOR/WEW KT19 220 A1
Teal Wy HHS/BOV HP3 54 A1
Teasel Cl CRAWW RH11 283 L10
CROY/NA CR0 204 C8
Teasel Wy SRTFD E15 141 K5
Teazlewood Pk LHD/OX KT22 236 F3
Tebworth Rd TOTM N17 99 N8
Technology Pk
CDALE/KGS * NW9 116 A1
Teck Cl ISLW TW7 154 F8
Tedder Cl CHSGTN KT9 219 H2
HGDN/ICK UB10 132 A2
RSLP HA4 112 B5
Tedder Rd HHNE HP2 36 B5
SAND/SEL CR2 224 C4
Teddington Cl HOR/WEW KT19 220 A6
Teddington Pk TEDD TW11 176 E8
Teddington Park Rd TEDD TW11 176 E7
Tedworth Gdns CHEL SW3 16 A8
Tedworth Sq CHEL SW3 16 A8
Tees Av GFD/PVL UB6 134 D4
Tees Cl UPMR RM14 126 C5
Teesdale CRAWW RH11 283 M10
HHNE HP2 35 P3
Teesdale Av ISLW TW7 154 F7
Teesdale Cl BETH E2 7 P8
Teesdale Gdns ISLW TW7 154 F7
SNWD SE25 203 M2
Teesdale Rd RDART DA2 188 B4
SL SL1 128 E7
WAN E11 121 L4
Teesdale St BETH E2 140 A4
Teesdale Yd BETH * E2 140 A4
Tees Dr HARH RM3 105 L4
Tee Side HERT/BAY SG13 26 A4
The Tee ACT W3 136 B8
Teevan Cl CROY/NA CR0 203 P7
Teevan Rd CROY/NA CR0 203 P7
Tegg's La WOKS/MYFD GU22 233 J2
Teignmouth Cl CLAP SW4 158 E10
EDGW HA8 95 L10
Teignmouth Rd CRICK NW2 116 G10
WELL DA16 163 M8
Telcote Wy RSLP * HA4 113 K5
Telegraph Hl HAMP NW3 117 L8
Telegraph La ESH/CLAY KT10 218 E1
Telegraph Pl POP/IOD E14 160 G3
Telegraph Rd PUT/ROE SW15 178 F3
Telegraph St LOTH EC2R 12 G5
Telegraph Tr WLGTN SM6 222 B7
Telephone Pl FUL/PGN SW6 14 D9
Telferscot Rd BAL SW12 180 E4
Telford Av BAL SW12 180 E4
Telford Cl GSTN WD25 73 L1
NRWD SE19 181 N9
WALTH E17 120 D5
Telford Ct GU GU1 268 C1
Telford Dr SL SL1 128 F10
WOT/HER KT12 197 K7
Telford Pl CRAWE RH10 283 P8
Telford Rd CDALE/KGS NW9 116 C4
CHST BR7 184 G5
GFD/PVL UB6 134 A9
HSLWW TW4 175 P3
LCOL/BKTW AL2 57 H3
NKENS W10 8 A3
Telford Rd North Circular Rd
FBAR/BDGN N11 98 D7
Telfords Yd WAP E1W 13 P8
Telford Ter PIM SW1V 16 G9
Telford Wy ACT W3 136 B7
YEAD UB4 133 M7
Telham Ct CRAWW * RH11 283 J10
Telham Rd EHAM E6 142 D4
Tell Gv EDUL SE22 159 N10
Tellisford ESH/CLAY KT10 218 A1
Tellson Av WOOL/PLUM SE18 162 B7
Telscombe Cl ORP BR6 207 H9
Telston La RSEV TN14 246 G3
Temeraire St BERM/RHTH SE16 160 B1
Tempelhof Av HDN NW4 116 F5
Temperance St STALW/RED AL3 38 B6
Temperley Rd BAL SW12 180 B3
Tempest Av POTB/CUF EN6 59 M8
Tempest Md EPP CM16 66 C3
Tempest Rd EGH TW20 172 F9
Tempest Wy RAIN RM13 145 H1
Templar Dr GVW DA11 190 D8
THMD SE28 143 N8
Templar Pl HPTN TW12 175 P10
Templars Av GLDGN NW11 117 J4
Templars Ct DART * DA1 187 P1
Templars Crs FNCH N3 97 K10
Templars Dr
KTN/HRWW/W * HA3 94 C7
Templar St CMBW SE5 159 J8
Temple Av BCTR RM8 124 B6
CROY/NA CR0 204 E10
EMB EC4Y 12 B7
TRDG/WHET N20 97 N1
Temple Bank HLW CM20 29 L6
Temple Bar Rd
WOKN/KNAP GU21 231 L5
Temple Cl CHESW EN7 61 P7
CRAWE RH10 284 E8
FNCH N3 97 J10
WAN E11 121 K5
WAT WD17 72 G6
WOOL/PLUM SE18 162 F2
Templecombe Ms
WOKS/MYFD * GU22 232 E2
Templecombe Rd HOM E9 140 B3
Templecombe Wy MRDN SM4 201 H5
Templecroft ASHF TW15 174 E9
Templedene Av STA TW18 173 L10
Temple Dwellings BETH * E2 140 A4
Temple Field Cl ADL/WDHM KT15 215 L3
Temple Flds HERT/WAS SG14 25 K2
Temple Fortune Hl GLDGN NW11 117 K3
Temple Fortune La GLDGN NW11 117 J4
Temple Gdns BCTR RM8 123 N8
EMB * EC4Y 12 A7
GLDGN NW11 117 J4
RKW/CH/CXG WD3 92 C4
STA TW18 195 J1
WCHMH * N21 99 J3
Temple Gv ENC/FH EN2 79 J7
GLDGN NW11 117 K4
Temple Hl DART DA1 187 N1
Temple Hill Sq DART DA1 187 N1
Temple La EMB EC4Y 12 B6
Templeman Cl PUR/KEN CR8 241 H2
Templeman Rd HNWL W7 134 E7
Temple Md HHNE HP2 35 N4
HLWW/ROY CM19 45 N1
Templemead Cl ACT W3 136 B8
Temple Mead Cl STAN HA7 94 G7
Temple Mills La LEY E10 120 G9
Templepan La RKW/CH/CXG WD3 71 P3
Temple Pde BAR * EN5 97 N1
Temple Pk UX/CGN UB8 132 B5
Temple Pl TPL/STR WC2R 11 P7
Templer Av CDH/CHF RM16 168 D3
Temple Rd CEND/HSY/T N8 118 G2
CHSWK W4 155 P2
CRICK NW2 116 F9
CROY/NA CR0 223 L1
EA W5 155 J2
EHAM E6 142 B3
HOR/WEW KT19 220 A8
HSLW TW3 154 A10
RCH/KEW TW9 155 L8
WDSR SL4 149 H8
Temple Sheen Rd
MORT/ESHN SW14 155 P10
Temple St BETH E2 140 A4
Temple Ter WDGN * N22 99 H10
Templeton Av CHING E4 100 F5
Templeton Cl STNW/STAM * N16 119 M10
THHTH CR7 203 L1
Templeton Pl ECT SW5 14 F6
Templeton Rd SEVS/STOTM N15 119 L4
Temple Vw STALW/RED AL3 38 A4
Temple Wy SLN SL2 109 H10
SUT SM1 201 N10
Templewood WEA W13 134 G7
WGCW AL8 22 G2
Templewood Av HAMP NW3 117 L8
Temple Wood Dr REDH * RH1 258 A7
Templewood Gdns HAMP NW3 117 L8
Templewood La SLN SL2 109 H10
Temple Yd BETH E2 7 P10
Tempsford WGCE * AL7 23 N5
WGCE AL7 23 N5
Tempsford Av BORE WD6 76 A8
Tempsford Cl ENC/FH EN2 79 K7
Temsford Cl RYLN/HDSTN HA2 94 B10
Ten Acre WOKN/KNAP GU21 231 M4
Ten Acre La EGH TW20 194 F2
Ten Acres Cl LHD/OX KT22 236 C10
Tenbury Cl FSTGT E7 122 A10
Tenbury Ct BAL SW12 180 E4
Tenby Av KTN/HRWW/W HA3 94 G10
Tenby Cl CHDH RM6 123 P4
Tenby Dr ASC SL5 192 C5
Tenby Gdns NTHLT UB5 133 P1
Tenby Rd CHDH RM6 123 P4
EDGW HA8 95 L10
PEND EN3 80 B7
WALTH E17 120 D3
WELL DA16 163 N7
Tenchley's La OXTED RH8 262 A7
Tench St WAP * E1W 140 A10
Tenda Rd BERM/RHTH SE16 160 A3
Tendring Rd HLWS CM18 46 F3
Tendring Wy CHDH RM6 123 M3
Tenham Av BRXS/STRHM SW2 180 E5
Tennand Cl CHESW EN7 61 N2
Tennants Rw TIL * RM18 168 B8
Tenniel Cl BAY/PAD W2 9 J6
GUW GU2 249 N8
Tennison Av BORE WD6 75 N9
Tennison Cl COUL/CHIP CR5 241 J6
Tennison Rd SNWD SE25 203 N4
Tennis St STHWK SE1 18 G1
Tenniswood Rd EN EN1 79 M5
Tennyson Av CDALE/KGS NW9 115 P1
GRAYS RM17 167 N2
MNPK E12 142 B2
NWMAL KT3 200 E5
TWK TW1 176 E4
WAB EN9 63 K10
WAN E11 121 M5
Tennyson Cl CRAWE RH10 284 C5
EBED/NFELT TW14 175 H2
PEND EN3 80 C9
WELL DA16 163 H7
Tennyson Rd ADL/WDHM KT15 215 P1
ASHF TW15 173 P8
DART DA1 187 P1
HARH RM3 105 K8
HNWL W7 134 E9
HSLW TW3 154 B8
KIL/WHAMP NW6 2 C5
LCOL/BKTW AL2 55 P2
MLHL NW7 96 E5
PGE/AN SE20 182 C10
RBRW/HUT CM13 107 P1
SRTFD E15 141 K2
WALTH E17 120 E4
WIM/MER SW19 179 M9
Tennyson St VX/NE SW8 158 C8
Tennyson Wk GVW DA11 190 A6
TIL RM18 168 E8
Tennyson Wy HCH RM12 124 G6
SLN SL2 128 D6
Tensing Av GVW * DA11 190 B6
Tensing Rd NWDGN UB2 153 P2
Tentelow La NWDGN UB2 154 A2
Tenterden Cl ELTH/MOT SE9 184 C7
HDN NW4 116 G1
Tenterden Dr HDN NW4 116 G1
Tenterden Gdns CROY/NA CR0 203 P7
HDN NW4 116 G1
Tenterden Gv HDN NW4 116 F2
Tenterden Rd BCTR RM8 124 A7
CROY/NA CR0 203 P7
TOTM N17 99 N8
Tenterden St CONDST W1S 10 F6
Tenter Gnd WCHPL * E1 13 L4
Tenth Av KWD/TDW/WH * KT20 257 J2
Tent St WCHPL E1 140 A6
Tenzing Rd HHNE HP2 36 B6
Tercel Pth CHIG IG7 103 L5
Terence Cl GVE DA12 191 J5
Teresa Gdns CHES/WCR EN8 62 B10
Terling Cl WAN E11 121 L8
Terling Rd BCTR RM8 124 B7
The Terlings BRW CM14 106 F4
Terling Wk IS * N1 6 E5
Terminus Pl PIM SW1V 16 F4
Terminus St HLW CM20 28 G10
Tern Gdns UPMR RM14 126 D6
Tern Rd CRAWW RH11 282 G8
Tern Wy BRW CM14 106 D5
Terrace Gdns BARN SW13 156 C8
WAT WD17 73 J6
Terrace La RCHPK/HAM TW10 177 K2
Terrace Rd HOM E9 140 C2
PLSTW E13 141 M3
WOT/HER KT12 197 J6
The Terraces RDART DA2 188 B3
Terrace St GVE DA12 190 E2
The Terrace ADL/WDHM KT15 215 P2
ASC SL5 192 C5
BARN SW13 156 B8
BETH * E2 140 B5
CHING * E4 101 K4
DEPT * SE8 160 E3
EFNCH * N2 116 B2
FNCH * N3 97 J10
FSTH * SE23 182 D3
GVE DA12 190 E2
KIL/WHAMP NW6 2 E5
SEV TN13 246 E8
WOKS/MYFD * GU22 232 D7
Terrace Vls HMSMTH * W6 156 D4
Terrace Wk DAGW RM9 123 P10
Terrac St RCH/KEW TW9 155 L10
Terrapin Rd TOOT SW17 180 C6
Terretts Pl IS N1 6 C4
Terrick Rd WDGN N22 98 F9
Terrick St SHB W12 136 E8
Terrilands PIN HA5 113 N1
Terront Rd SEVS/STOTM N15 119 K3
Terry Pl UX/CGN * UB8 131 M7
Tessa Sanderson Wy NTHLT UB5 114 C10
Testard Rd GUW GU2 267 P2
Testers Cl OXTED RH8 261 N7
Testerton Wk NTGHL * W11 136 G9
Testwood Rd WDSR SL4 148 C7
Tetcott Rd WBPTN SW10 157 M6
Tetherdown MUSWH N10 118 B1
Tethys Rd HHNE HP2 36 A3
Tetty Wy HAYES BR2 205 M2

Teversham La VX/NE SW8 158 F7
Teviot Av SOCK/AV RM15 146 B8
Teviot Cl GUW GU2 249 M7
WELL DA16 163 L7
Teviot St POP/IOD E14 141 H7
Tewin Cl STALE/WH AL4 39 H2
Tewin Ct WGCE AL7 23 J4
Tewin Rd HHNE HP2 36 D6
WGCE AL7 23 J4
Tewkesbury Av FSTH SE23 182 A4
PIN HA5 113 M3
Tewkesbury Cl BF/WBF KT14 215 N7
LOU IG10 82 B10
Tewkesbury Gdns
CDALE/KGS NW9 115 N1
Tewkesbury Rd CAR SM5 201 N8
FSBYPK N4 119 L5
WEA W13 134 F10
Tewkesbury Ter FBAR/BDGN N11 98 D7
Tewson Rd WOOL/PLUM SE18 163 H4
Teynham Av WCHMH N21 79 L10
Teynham Gn HAYES BR2 205 M5
Teynton Ter TOTM N17 99 K9
Thackeray Av TIL RM18 168 E7
TOTM N17 99 P10
Thackeray Cl ISLW TW7 154 F8
RYLN/HDSTN HA2 113 P6
UX/CGN UB8 132 C8
WIM/MER SW19 178 G10
Thackeray Dr CHDH RM6 123 K5
Thackeray Ms HACK * E8 7 N2
Thackeray Rd EHAM E6 142 A4
VX/NE SW8 158 C8
Thackeray St KENS W8 15 H3
Thakeham Cl SYD SE26 182 A8
Thalia Cl GNWCH SE10 161 J5
Thal Massing Cl
RBRW/HUT CM13 107 N3
Thame Rd BERM/RHTH SE16 160 C1
Thames Av CHERT KT16 195 K3
DAGW RM9 144 D5
GFD/PVL UB6 134 E4
HHNE HP2 36 A1
WBPTN SW10 157 M7
Thames Bank MORT/ESHN SW14 155 P8
Thamesbank Pl THMD SE28 143 M8
Thames Cir POP/IOD E14 160 F3
Thames Cl CHERT KT16 195 L7
HPTN TW12 198 A2
RAIN RM13 145 J8
Thamesdale LCOL/BKTW AL2 57 L3
Thames Down Link ASHTD KT21 237 M2
CHSGTN KT9 219 P1
EPSOM KT18 219 L10
WPK KT4 200 A10
Thames Dr CDH/CHF RM16 168 D4
RSLP HA4 112 D4
Thames Eyot TWK * TW1 176 F5
Thamesfield Ct SHPTN TW17 196 D7
Thamesfield Ms SHPTN * TW17 196 D7
Thames Ga DART DA1 187 P1
Thamesgate STA TW18 195 L2
Thamesgate Cl
RCHPK/HAM TW10 176 G7
Thameside TEDD TW11 177 J10
Thames Lock SHPTN * TW17 196 B9
Thames Md WDSR SL4 148 D7
WOT/HER KT12 197 H7
Thames Meadow
E/WMO/HCT KT8 197 P3
WOT/HER KT12 196 E8
Thamesmere Dr THMD SE28 143 K9
Thames Pth BERM/RHTH SE16 160 E2
BOW E3 141 H4
BTSEA SW11 16 D10
CHSWK W4 156 C7
CLPT E5 120 C8
EGH TW20 172 B5
GNWCH SE10 161 M2
RCH/KEW TW9 155 H8
STA TW18 173 J10
VX/NE SW8 17 J10
WEY KT13 196 C9
WOT/HER KT12 197 K3
Thames Pl PUT/ROE SW15 156 G9
Thamespoint TEDD * TW11 177 J10
Thames Quay WBPTN * SW10 157 M7
Thames Reach KUT * KT1 199 J1
Thames Rd BARK IG11 143 K5
CAN/RD E16 142 A10
CHSWK W4 155 N5
DART DA1 165 H9
DTCH/LGLY SL3 150 E3
GRAYS RM17 167 N6
WDSR * SL4 148 B6
Thames Side KUTN/CMB KT2 199 J1
STA TW18 195 M5
THDIT KT7 198 G6
WDSR SL4 149 J6
Thames St GNWCH SE10 161 H5
HPTN TW12 198 A2
KUT KT1 199 J2
STA TW18 173 J8
SUN TW16 197 J3
WDSR SL4 149 J7
WEY KT13 196 C9
WOT/HER KT12 196 G7
Thamesvale Cl HSLW TW3 153 P8
Thames Vw GRAYS RM17 168 D4
Thames Village CHSWK W4 155 P7
Thames Wy GVW DA11 190 A4
Thamley PUR RM19 165 P3
Thanescroft Gdns CROY/NA CR0 203 M10
Thanet Dr HAYES BR2 206 A10
Thanet Pl CROY/NA CR0 223 K1
Thanet Rd BXLY DA5 186 B3
ERITH DA8 164 F6
Thanet St STPAN WC1H 5 L10
Thane Vls HOLWY N7 118 G8
Thant Cl LEY E10 120 G9
Tharp Rd WLGTN SM6 222 E2
Thatcham Gdns TRDG/WHET N20 97 M1
Thatcher Cl CRAWE RH10 283 N10
Thatchers Cl HORL RH6 280 C2
LOU IG10 82 F6
Thatchers Cft HHNE HP2 35 P2
Thatchers La RGUW GU3 249 J3
Thatchers Wy ISLW TW7 176 C1
Thatches Gv CHDH RM6 123 P2
Thaxted Gn RBRW/HUT CM13 87 P9
Thaxted Pl RYNPK SW20 178 G10
Thaxted Rd BKHH IG9 102 B1
ELTH/MOT SE9 184 F5
Thaxted Wy WAB EN9 63 J9
Thaxton Rd WKENS W14 14 D9
Thayers Farm Rd BECK BR3 204 D1
Thayer St MHST W1U 10 D4
Thaynesfield POTB/CUF EN6 59 N7
Theatre St BTSEA SW11 158 A9
Theberton St IS N1 6 B5
The Beverly MRDN SM4 200 G6
Theed St STHWK SE1 12 A10
Thele Av WARE SG12 27 J7
Theleway Cl HOD EN11 26 G10
Thellusson Wy RKW/CH/CXG WD3 91 J1
Thelma Cl GVE DA12 191 J8
Thelma Gv TEDD TW11 176 F9
Thelusson Ct RAD * WD7 74 F1
Theobald Crs KTN/HRWW/W HA3 94 A9
Theobald Rd CROY/NA CR0 203 J9
WALTH E17 120 E5
Theobalds Av GRAYS RM17 167 P4
Theobald's Cl POTB/CUF EN6 60 G6
Theobald's Gv CHES/WCR * EN8 62 C8
Theobald's La CHES/WCR EN8 62 A8
Theobalds Park Rd ENC/FH EN2 79 J1
Theobald's Rd FSBYW WC1X 11 N3
POTB/CUF EN6 60 F6
Theobald St RAD WD7 74 G2
STHWK SE1 18 G4
Theodora Wy PIN HA5 112 G1
Theodore Rd LEW SE13 183 J2
Thepps Cl REDH RH1 276 G3
Therapia La CROY/NA CR0 202 E7
Therapia Rd EDUL SE22 182 B2
Theresa Rd HMSMTH W6 156 D3
Theresa's Wk SAND/SEL CR2 223 L5
Therfield Rd STALW/RED AL3 38 C3
Thermopylae Ga POP/IOD E14 160 G3
Theseus Wk IS N1 6 D8
Thesiger Rd PGE/AN SE20 182 C10
Thessaly Rd VX/NE SW8 158 E7
Thetford Cl PLMGR N13 99 J7
Thetford Rd ASHF TW15 173 P7
DAGW RM9 143 N2
NWMAL KT3 200 A6
Theydon Cl CRAWE RH10 284 B9
Theydon Ct WAB EN9 63 N9
Theydon Gdns RAIN RM13 144 F2
Theydon Ga EPP * CM16 83 H2
Theydon Gv EPP CM16 65 K6
WFD IG8 101 P7
Theydon Park Rd EPP CM16 83 H5
Theydon Pl EPP CM16 65 J7
Theydon Rd CLPT E5 120 B7
EPP CM16 64 G10
Theydon St WALTH E17 120 E5
Thicket Crs SUT SM1 221 M1
Thicket Gv DAGW RM9 143 M1
PGE/AN SE20 181 P10
Thicket Rd PGE/AN SE20 182 A10
SUT SM1 221 M1
Thicket Ter PGE/AN * SE20 181 P10
The Thicket WDR/YW UB7 131 P8
Thickthorne La STA TW18 173 M10
Thieves La HERT/WAS SG14 24 G5
HERT/WAS SG14 24 G4
Third Av ACT W3 136 C10
CHDH RM6 123 M4
DAGE RM10 144 C3
EN EN1 79 N9
GSTN WD25 73 L1
GVW * DA11 190 C4
HLWS CM18 46 G1
HLWW/ROY CM19 46 E2
HYS/HAR UB3 132 G10
KWD/TDW/WH * KT20 257 J2
MNPK E12 122 B9
NKENS W10 8 B1
PLSTW E13 141 M5
WALTH E17 120 F3
WBLY HA9 115 J7
WTHK RM20 166 F5
Third Cl E/WMO/HCT KT8 198 A4
Third Crs SL SL1 129 H7
Third Cross Rd WHTN TW2 176 C5
Third Wy WBLY HA9 115 N9
Thirkleby Cl SL SL1 129 H10
Thirleby Rd EDGW HA8 96 A9
WEST SW1P 17 H4
Thirlestane STAL AL1 38 D5
Thirlmere Av GFD/PVL UB6 135 H5
SL SL1 128 B7
Thirlmere Cl EGH TW20 172 E10
Thirlmere Dr STAL AL1 38 G8
Thirlmere Gdns NTHWD HA6 92 C6
WBLY HA9 115 H6
Thirlmere Ri BMLY BR1 183 L9
Thirlmere Rd BXLYHN DA7 164 D8
CRAWW RH11 282 G9
MUSWH N10 98 C9
STRHM/NOR SW16 180 E7
Thirsk Cl NTHLT UB5 133 P1
Thirsk Rd BORE WD6 75 M4
BTSEA SW11 158 B9
MTCM CR4 180 B10
SNWD SE25 203 L4
Thirteenth Av
KWD/TDW/WH * KT20 257 J2
Thirza Rd DART DA1 187 N2
Thistlebrook ABYW SE2 163 M2
Thistle Cl HHW HP1 35 H7
Thistlecroft HHW HP1 35 L7
Thistlecroft Gdns STAN HA7 95 J9
Thistlecroft Rd WOT/HER KT12 217 K1
Thistledene BF/WBF KT14 215 J9
THDIT KT7 198 D6
Thistledene Av CRW RM5 104 C6
RYLN/HDSTN HA2 113 M8
Thistle Gv WBPTN SW10 15 K8
WGCE AL7 23 M8
Thistlemead CHST BR7 206 E2
Thistle Md LOU IG10 82 D7
Thistle Rd GVE DA12 191 H3
The Thistles HHW HP1 35 L5
Thistlewaite Rd CLPT E5 120 A8
Thistle Wy HORL RH6 281 K3
Thistlewood Cl HOLWY N7 118 G7
Thistlewood Crs CROY/NA CR0 225 J8
Thistleworth Cl ISLW TW7 154 C6
Thistley Cl NFNCH/WDSP N12 97 P7
Thoby La BRWN CM15 87 M3
Thomas A'Beckett Cl
ALP/SUD HA0 114 E9
Thomas Av CTHM CR3 241 K7
Thomas Baines Rd BTSEA SW11 157 N9
Thomas Bata Av TIL RM18 169 L3
Thomas Cl BRWN CM15 107 K3
Thomas Cribb Ms EHAM E6 142 C8
Thomas Dean Rd SYD * SE26 182 E7
Thomas Dinwiddy Rd
LEE/GVPK SE12 183 N5
Thomas Doyle St STHWK SE1 18 C3
Thomas Dr GVE DA12 190 G5
Thomas' La CAT SE6 182 G3
Thomas Moore Sq WAP E1W 13 N8
Thomas Moore Wy EFNCH N2 117 M1
Thomas More St WAP E1W 13 N8
Thomas North Ter CAN/RD * E16 141 L7
Thomas Pl KENS W8 14 G4
Thomas Rd POP/IOD E14 140 E8
Thomas Rochford Wy
CHES/WCR EN8 62 E3
Thomas St WOOL/PLUM SE18 162 D3
Thomas Wall Cl SUT SM1 221 L2
Thompkins La SLN SL2 128 E2
Thompson Av RCH/KEW TW9 155 N9
Thompson Cl DTCH/LGLY SL3 150 D3
IL IG1 122 F7
Thompson Rd DAGW RM9 124 A8
EDUL SE22 181 N2
HGDN/ICK UB10 131 P2
HSLW TW3 154 A10
Thompson's Av CMBW * SE5 159 K6
CMBW SE5 159 K6
Thompsons Cl CHESW EN7 61 N5
CHOB/PIR GU24 230 C9
Thompson's La CHOB/PIR GU24 213 J5
Thompson Wy
RKW/CH/CXG WD3 91 K1
Thomson Crs CROY/NA CR0 203 H8
Thomson Rd KTN/HRWW/W HA3 114 D1
Thong La GVE DA12 191 K9
Thorburn Sq STHWK SE1 19 N6
Thorburn Wy WIM/MER * SW19 201 N1
Thoresby St IS N1 6 F9
Thorkhill Gdns THDIT KT7 198 F8
Thorkhill Rd THDIT KT7 198 G8
Thorley Cl BF/WBF KT14 215 K10
Thorley Gdns BF/WBF KT14 215 K10
Thorley Rd CDH/CHF RM16 147 M10
Thornaby Gdns UED N18 99 P7
Thornash Cl WOKN/KNAP GU21 231 P1
Thornash Rd WOKN/KNAP GU21 231 P2
Thornash Wy WOKN/KNAP GU21 231 P1
Thorn Av BUSH WD23 94 B2
Thorn Bank GUW GU2 267 M2
Thornbridge Rd IVER SL0 130 F3
Thornbury HARP AL5 20 C2
Thornbury Av ISLW TW7 154 C6
Thornbury Cl HOD EN11 26 G9
STNW/STAM N16 119 M10
Thornbury Gdns BORE WD6 75 P8
Thornbury Rd CLAP SW4 180 F2
ISLW TW7 154 C6
Thornby Rd CLPT E5 120 B8
Thorncliffe Rd CLAP SW4 180 E2
NWDGN UB2 153 N4
Thorn Cl HAYES BR2 206 D6
NTHLT UB5 133 N5
Thorncombe Rd EDUL SE22 181 M1
Thorn Ct BELMT * SM2 221 L4
Thorncroft EGH TW20 171 P10
EMPK RM11 125 J4
HHS/BOV HP3 36 C8
Thorncroft Cl COUL/CHIP CR5 241 H5
Thorncroft Rd SUT SM1 221 L1
Thorncroft St VX/NE SW8 158 F6
Thorndales BRW CM14 107 J5
Thorndean St WAND/EARL SW18 179 M5
Thorndene Av TRDG/WHET N20 98 B2
Thorndike SLN SL2 128 F7
Thorndike Av NTHLT UB5 133 L3
Thorndike Cl WBPTN SW10 157 M6
Thorndike St PIM * SW1V 17 J6
Thorndon Ap RBRW/HUT CM13 107 P8
Thorndon Av RBRW/HUT CM13 127 P3
Thorndon Cl STMC/STPC BR5 207 J2
Thorndon Gdns HOR/WEW KT19 220 B1
Thorndon Ga RBRW/HUT CM13 107 N7
Thorndon Rd STMC/STPC BR5 207 J2
Thorndown La BFOR GU20 212 C4
Thorn Dr DTCH/LGLY SL3 130 B8
Thorndyke Cl CRAWE RH10 284 E8
Thorndyke Ct PIN * HA5 93 N8
Thorne Cl ASHF TW15 174 D10
CAN/RD E16 141 M8
ERITH DA8 164 C5
HHW HP1 35 L8
WAN * E11 121 K9
Thorneloe Gdns CROY/NA CR0 223 J2
Thorne Rd VX/NE SW8 158 F6
Thorne's Cl BECK BR3 205 H3
Thorne St BARN SW13 156 B9
Thornet Wood Rd BMLY BR1 206 D3
Thorney Crs BTSEA * SW11 157 N6
Thorneycroft Cl WOT/HER KT12 197 K6
Thorneycroft Dr WAB EN9 80 F4
Thorney Hedge Rd CHSWK W4 155 N3
Thorney La North IVER SL0 131 J8
Thorney La South IVER SL0 151 J1
Thorney Mill Rd IVER SL0 151 K2
Thorney St WEST SW1P 17 L5
Thornfield Av MLHL NW7 97 H9
Thornfield Pde MLHL * NW7 97 H8
Thornfield Rd SHB W12 156 E1
Thornford Rd LEW SE13 183 H1
Thorngate Rd MV/WKIL W9 8 F1
Thorngrove Rd PLSTW E13 141 N3
Thornham Gv SRTFD E15 121 J10
Thornham St GNWCH SE10 160 G5
Thornhaugh St STPAN WC1H 11 K2
Thornhill EPP CM16 66 D2
Thornhill Av SURB KT6 199 K9
WOOL/PLUM SE18 163 H6
Thornhill Bridge Whf IS N1 5 N6
Thornhill Crs IS N1 5 P4
Thornhill Gdns BARK IG11 143 H2
LEY E10 120 G7
Thornhill Gv IS N1 6 A4
Thornhill Rd CROY/NA CR0 203 K7
HGDN/ICK UB10 112 B9
IS N1 6 A3
LEY E10 120 G7
NTHWD HA6 92 D5
SURB KT6 199 K9
Thornhill Sq IS N1 5 P4
Thornhill Wy SHPTN TW17 196 B5
Thorn La RAIN RM13 145 L4
Thornlaw Rd WNWD SE27 181 H7
Thornleas Pl EHSLY KT24 252 F2
Thornley Cl TOTM N17 99 P8
Thornley Dr RYLN/HDSTN HA2 114 A7
Thornridge BRW CM14 106 G1
Thornsbeach Rd CAT SE6 183 H4
Thornsett Pl PGE/AN SE20 204 A2
Thornsett Rd PGE/AN SE20 204 A2
WAND/EARL SW18 179 L5
Thornsett Ter PGE/AN * SE20 204 A2
Thorn's Meadow BH/WHM TN16 245 M9
Thornton Av BAL SW12 180 E4
CHSWK W4 156 B3
CROY/NA CR0 202 G6
WDR/YW UB7 152 A2
Thornton Cl GUW GU2 249 M7
HORL RH6 279 P4
WDR/YW UB7 152 A2
Thornton Crs COUL/CHIP CR5 241 H5
Thornton Dene BECK BR3 204 F2
Thornton Gdns BAL SW12 180 E4
Thornton Gv PIN HA5 93 P7
Thornton Hl WIM/MER SW19 179 H10
Thornton Pl HORL RH6 279 P4
MBLAR W1H 10 A3
Thornton Rd BAL SW12 180 E3
BAR EN5 77 H7
BELV * DA17 164 C3
BMLY BR1 183 M8
CAR SM5 201 P7
IL IG1 122 E9
MORT/ESHN SW14 156 A9
POTB/CUF EN6 59 M6
THHTH CR7 203 H5
UED N18 100 B4
WAN E11 121 J7
WIM/MER SW19 178 G9
Thornton Rw THHTH CR7 203 H5
Thorntons Farm Av
ROMW/RG RM7 124 D7
Thornton St BRXN/ST SW9 159 H8
HERT/WAS SG14 25 L5
STALW/RED AL3 38 B5
Thornton Wy GLDGN NW11 117 L3
Thorntree Rd CHARL SE7 162 A4
Thornville Gv MTCM CR4 201 M2
Thornville St DEPT SE8 160 F7
Thornwood Cl SWFD E18 101 N10
Thornwood Rd EPP CM16 65 L4
LEW SE13 183 K1
Thorogood Gdns SRTFD E15 121 K10
Thorogood Wy RAIN RM13 144 F3
Thorold Cl SAND/SEL CR2 224 C6
Thorold Rd IL IG1 122 E7
WDGN N22 98 F8
Thorparch Rd VX/NE SW8 158 E7
Thorpebank Rd SHB W12 136 D10
Thorpe By-pass EGH TW20 194 E3
Thorpe Cl CROY/NA CR0 225 H7
NKENS W10 8 B5
ORP BR6 207 H9
SYD * SE26 182 C7
Thorpe Crs OXHEY WD19 93 J1
WALTH E17 100 E10
Thorpedale Gdns
GNTH/NBYPK IG2 122 D2
Thorpedale Rd FSBYPK N4 118 F6
Thorpefield Cl STALE/WH AL4 39 J3
Thorpe Hall Rd WALTH E17 101 H9
Thorpe Lea Rd EGH TW20 172 E10
Thorpe Pk CHERT * KT16 195 J3
Thorpe Rd BARK IG11 142 G2
CHERT KT16 194 G5
EGH TW20 172 G9
EHAM E6 142 C3
FSTGT E7 121 M8
KUTN/CMB KT2 177 K10
SEVS/STOTM N15 119 M4
STAL AL1 38 C7
WALTH E17 101 H10
Thorpes Cl GUW GU2 249 M7
Thorpeside Cl EGH TW20 195 H2
Thorpewood Av FSTH SE23 182 A5
Thorpland Av HGDN/ICK UB10 112 D8
Thorsden Cl WOKS/MYFD GU22 232 B5
Thorsden Ct
WOKS/MYFD * GU22 232 B4
Thorsden Wy NRWD * SE19 181 M8
Thorverton Rd CRICK NW2 117 H8
Thoydon Rd BOW E3 140 D4
Thrale Rd STRHM/NOR SW16 180 D8
Thrale St STHWK SE1 12 F10
Thrasher Cl HACK * E8 7 L5
Thrawl St WCHPL E1 13 M4
Threadneedle St LOTH EC2R 13 H6
Three Arches Pk REDH * RH1 276 A4
Three Arch Rd REDH RH1 276 B6
Three Bridges Rd CRAWE RH10 284 A7
Three Castles Pth ASC SL5 170 D10
WDSR SL4 149 N10
Three Cherrytrees La HHNE HP2 36 C2
Three Close La BERK HP4 33 P6
Three Colts La BETH E2 140 A6
Three Colt St POP/IOD * E14 140 E9
Three Corners BXLYHN DA7 164 C8
HHS/BOV * HP3 36 B8
Three Forests Wy ABR/ST RM4 84 E3
HLWW/ROY CM19 45 L1
LOU IG10 82 A5
SBW CM21 29 P2
WAB EN9 46 A7
Three Gates GU GU1 250 F9
Three Gates Rd HART DA3 210 F7
Three Horseshoes Rd
HLWW/ROY CM19 46 E3
Three Households CSTG HP8 89 L5
Three Kings Yd MYFR/PKLN W1K 10 E7
Three Mill La SRTFD E15 141 H5
Three Oak La STHWK SE1 19 L1
Three Oaks Cl HGDN/ICK UB10 112 A8
Three Pears Rd GU GU1 250 G10
Three Valleys Wy BUSH WD23 73 L9
Threshers Pl NTGHL W11 8 A7
Thriffwood FSTH SE23 182 B6
Thrift Farm La BORE WD6 75 P6
Thriftfield HHNE HP2 35 N4
Thrift La BH/WHM * TN16 245 H3
Thrifts Md EPP CM16 83 H3
The Thrift RDART DA2 189 H6
Thrift V RGUE GU4 250 G7
Thrigby Rd CHSGTN KT9 219 L3
Throckmorten Rd CAN/RD E16 141 N8
Throgmorton Av OBST EC2N 13 H5
Throgmorton St LOTH EC2R 13 H6
Throstle Pl GSTN * WD25 55 K8
Throwley Cl ABYW SE2 163 M2
Throwley Rd SUT SM1 221 L2
Throwley Wy SUT SM1 221 L1
Thrums WATN WD24 73 J3
Thrupp Cl MTCM CR4 202 C2
Thrupps Av WOT/HER KT12 217 L2
Thrupps La WOT/HER KT12 217 L2
Thrush Av HAT AL10 40 D6
Thrush Gn RKW/CH/CXG WD3 91 M1
RYLN/HDSTN HA2 113 P2
Thrush La POTB/CUF EN6 60 F4
Thrush St WALW SE17 18 E7
Thumbswood WGCE AL7 23 K8
Thumpers HHNE HP2 35 P4
Thundercourt WARE SG12 26 C1
Thunderer Rd DAGW RM9 143 P6
Thundridge Cl WGCE AL7 23 L6
Thurbarn Rd CAT SE6 182 G8
Thurgood Rd HOD EN11 44 F1
Thurland Rd BERM/RHTH SE16 19 N3
Thurlby Cl WFD IG8 102 C7
Thurlby Rd ALP/SUD HA0 135 J1
WNWD SE27 181 H7
Thurleigh Av BAL SW12 180 B2
Thurleigh Rd BAL SW12 180 A2
Thurleston Av MRDN SM4 201 H5
Thurlestone Av GDMY/SEVK IG3 123 J9
NFNCH/WDSP N12 98 A7
Thurlestone Cl SHPTN * TW17 196 D6
Thurlestone Pde SHPTN * TW17 196 D6
Thurlestone Rd WNWD SE27 181 H6
Thurloe Cl SKENS SW7 15 N5
Thurloe Gdns ROM RM1 124 F4
Thurloe Pl SKENS SW7 15 M5
Thurloe Place Ms SKENS * SW7 15 M5
Thurloe Sq SKENS SW7 15 M5
Thurloe St SKENS SW7 15 M5
Thurloe Wk GRAYS RM17 167 M2
Thurlow Cl CHING E4 100 G7
Thurlow Gdns ALP/SUD * HA0 115 J10
CHIG IG7 102 G7
Thurlow Hl DUL SE21 181 K4
Thurlow Park Rd DUL SE21 181 J5
Thurlow Rd HAMP NW3 117 N10
HNWL W7 154 F1
Thurlow St WALW SE17 19 J8
Thurlow Ter KTTN NW5 118 A10
Thurlow Wk WALW SE17 19 J7
Thurlston Rd RSLP HA4 113 H8
Thurlton Ct WOKN/KNAP GU21 232 B2
Thurnham Wy
KWD/TDW/WH KT20 238 G6
Thurrock Park Wy GRAYS RM17 168 A6
Thursby Rd WOKN/KNAP GU21 231 M4
Thursland Rd SCUP DA14 185 P8
Thursley Crs CROY/NA CR0 225 J4
Thursley Gdns WIM/MER SW19 178 G5
Thursley Rd ELTH/MOT SE9 184 C6
Thurso Cl HARH RM3 106 A7
Thurso St TOOT SW17 179 N7
Thurstan Rd RYNPK SW20 178 E10
Thurstans HLWW/ROY CM19 46 E6
Thurston Rd DEPT SE8 160 G8
SL SL1 129 J8
STHL UB1 133 N8
Thurtle Rd BETH E2 7 M7
Thwaite Cl ERITH DA8 164 D5
Thyer Cl ORP BR6 226 F1
Thyme Ct GU GU1 250 E7
Thyra Gv NFNCH/WDSP N12 97 L7
Tibbatt's Rd BOW E3 140 G6
Tibbenham Pl CAT * SE6 182 G4
Tibberton Sq IS N1 6 E4
Tibbets Cl WIM/MER SW19 178 G4
Tibbet's Ride PUT/ROE SW15 178 G3
Tibbles Cl GSTN WD25 73 M1
Tibbs Hill Rd ABLGY WD5 54 G6
Tiber Gdns IS N1 5 M6
Ticehurst Cl CRAWE RH10 284 F7
STMC/STPC BR5 185 K10
Ticehurst Rd FSTH SE23 182 D5
Tichborne RKW/CH/CXG WD3 90 G6
Tichmarsh HOR/WEW KT19 219 P6
Tickenhall Dr HLWE CM17 47 N1
Tickford Cl ABYW SE2 163 M1
Tidal Basin Rd CAN/RD E16 141 L9
Tidenham Gdns CROY/NA CR0 203 M10
Tideswell Rd CROY/NA CR0 204 F10
PUT/ROE SW15 156 F10
Tideway Cl RCHPK/HAM TW10 176 G7
Tidey St BOW E3 140 F7
Tidford Rd WELL DA16 163 J8
Tidworth Rd BOW E3 140 F6
Tidy's La EPP CM16 65 K5
Tiepigs La WWKM BR4 205 K9
Tierney Rd BRXS/STRHM SW2 180 F4
Tierney Ter BRXS/STRHM * SW2 180 F4
Tiger La HAYES BR2 205 N4
Tiger Wy CLPT E5 120 A9
Tigres Cl ED N9 100 B3
Tilbrook Rd BKHTH/KID SE3 161 P9
Tilburstow Hill Rd GDST RH9 260 B8
Tilbury Cl PECK SE15 159 N6
STMC/STPC BR5 207 L2
Tilbury Gdns TIL RM18 168 D10
Tilbury Md HLWS CM18 47 K2
Tilbury Rd EHAM E6 142 C4
LEY E10 121 H5
Tilbury Wk DTCH/LGLY SL3 150 E2
Tildesley Rd PUT/ROE SW15 178 F2
Tilecroft WGCW AL8 22 G2
Tile Farm Rd ORP BR6 206 G10
Tilegate Rd CHONG CM5 48 D5
HLWS CM18 47 J3
Tilehouse Cl BORE WD6 75 L7
Tilehouse La DEN/HRF UB9 111 H3
RKW/CH/CXG WD3 91 H9
Tilehouse Rd RGUE GU4 268 B4
Tilehouse Wy DEN/HRF UB9 111 J5
Tilehurst La RDKG RH5 273 K3
Tilehurst Rd CHEAM SM3 221 H2
WAND/EARL SW18 179 N4
Tile Kiln Cl HHS/BOV HP3 36 C7
Tile Kiln Crs HHS/BOV HP3 36 C7
Tile Kiln La BXLY DA5 186 E5
DEN/HRF UB9 112 C5
HGT N6 118 C6
HHS/BOV HP3 36 B7
PLMGR N13 99 K6
Tiler's Wy REDH RH1 275 M4
Tileyard Rd HOLWY N7 5 L3
Tilford Av CROY/NA CR0 225 H4
Tilford Gdns WIM/MER SW19 178 G4
Tilgate Common REDH RH1 259 K9
Tilgate Pde CRAWE RH10 283 P10
Tilgate Pl CRAWE RH10 283 P10
Tilgate Wy CRAWE RH10 283 P10
Tilia Rd CLPT E5 120 A9
Till Av EYN DA4 209 N7
Tiller Rd POP/IOD E14 160 F2
Tillett Cl WLSDN NW10 135 P1
Tillett Wy BETH E2 7 N9
Tillet Wy BETH E2 7 N9
Tilley La EPSOM KT18 237 P9
Tillingbourne Gdns FNCH N3 117 J1
Tillingbourne Gn
STMC/STPC BR5 207 K4
Tillingbourne Rd RGUE GU4 268 B6
Tillingbourne Wy GLDGN NW11 117 J2
Tillingdown Hl CTHM CR3 242 A8
Tillingdown La CTHM CR3 242 A10
CTHM CR3 260 A1
Tillingham Ct WAB EN9 63 M9
Tillingham Wy NFNCH/WDSP N12 97 K5
Tilling Rd CRICK NW2 116 E6
Tilling Wy WBLY * HA9 115 J8
Tillman St WCHPL E1 140 A8
Tilloch St IS * N1 5 N4
Tillotson Cl CRAWE RH10 284 E8
Tillotson Rd ED N9 99 N3
IL IG1 122 D5
KTN/HRWW/W HA3 94 A8
Tillwicks Rd HLWS CM18 47 J2
Tilmans Md EYN DA4 209 N7
Tilney Gdns IS N1 6 G2
Tilney Rd DAGW RM9 144 A1

NWDGN UB2 153 K3
Tilney St MYFR/PKLN W1K 10 D9
Tilson Cl CMBW * SE5 159 M6
Tilson Gdns CLAP SW4 180 F3
Tilson Rd TOTM N17 99 P9
Tilston Cl WAN E11 121 L8
Tilstone Av WDSR SL4 148 D4
Tilstone Cl WDSR SL4 148 D3
Tilsworth Rd BEAC HP9 108 B1
Tilsworth Wk STALE/WH AL4 39 H1
Tilt Cl COB KT11 235 M2
Tilthams Corner Rd RGODL GU7 267 N9
Tilthams Gn RGODL GU7 267 N10
Tilt Meadow COB KT11 235 M2
Tilton St FUL/PGN SW6 14 B10
Tilt Rd COB KT11 235 L2
Tilt Vw COB * KT11 235 K1
The Tiltwood ACT W3 135 P9
Tilt Yard Ap ELTH/MOT SE9 184 C2
Timber Cl CHST BR7 206 D2
GT/LBKH KT23 254 B3
WOKS/MYFD GU22 233 J1
Timbercroft HOR/WEW KT19 220 B1
WGCE AL7 23 J2
Timbercroft La
WOOL/PLUM SE18 163 H5
Timberdene Av BARK/HLT IG6 102 F9
Timberham Farm Rd HORL RH6 279 N7
Timber Hl ASHTD KT21 237 K5
Timber Hill Rd CTHM CR3 241 P10
Timberland Cl PECK * SE15 159 P6
Timberland Rd WCHPL * E1 140 A8
Timberling Gdns SAND/SEL CR2 223 L6
Timber Mill Wy CLAP SW4 158 E9
Timber Orch HERT/WAS SG14 25 H1
Timber Pond Rd
BERM/RHTH SE16 160 C1
Timber Rdg RKW/CH/CXG WD3 71 M8
Timberslip Dr WLGTN SM6 222 E5
The Timbers CHEAM * SM3 221 H3
Timber St FSBYE * EC1V 12 E1
Timbertop Rd BH/WHM TN16 243 P4
Timberwharf Rd
SEVS/STOTM N15 119 P4
Time Sq HACK * E8 119 N10
Times Sq SUT * SM1 221 L2
Timothy Cl BXLYHS DA6 185 P1
Timothy Rd POP/IOD E14 140 E7
Timperley Gdns REDH RH1 257 P8
Timplings Rw HHW HP1 35 L4
Timsway STA TW18 173 J8
Tindale Cl SAND/SEL CR2 223 L7
Tindall Cl HARH RM3 105 N10
Tindal St BRXN/ST SW9 159 J7
Tine Rd CHIG IG7 103 H6
Tinkers La TRING HP23 32 F3
WDSR SL4 148 C8
Tinmans Rw COB * KT11 235 K4
Tinniswood Cl HOLWY * N7 119 H10
Tinsey Cl EGH TW20 172 E8
Tinsley Gn CRAWE RH10 284 C2
Tinsley La CRAWE RH10 284 B4
Tinsley La North CRAWE RH10 284 C2
Tinsley La South CRAWE RH10 284 B5
Tinsley Rd WCHPL E1 140 B7
Tintagel Cl EW KT17 220 C10
HHNE HP2 35 N1
Tintagel Crs EDUL SE22 159 N10
Tintagel Dr STAN HA7 95 J6
Tintagel Rd STMC/STPC BR5 207 M9
Tintagel Wy WOKS/MYFD GU22 232 D2
Tintells La EHSLY KT24 252 C4
Tintern Av CDALE/KGS NW9 115 N1
Tintern Cl PUT/ROE SW15 179 H1
SL SL1 149 H2
WIM/MER SW19 179 M10
Tintern Gdns WCHMH N21 98 F1
Tintern Rd CAR SM5 201 N8
CRAWW RH11 283 K9
WDGN N22 99 K9
Tintern St CLAP SW4 158 F10
Tintern Wy RYLN/HDSTN HA2 114 A6
Tinto Rd CAN/RD E16 141 M7
Tinwell Ms BORE WD6 76 A9
Tinworth St LBTH SE11 17 M7
Tippendell La LCOL/BKTW AL2 55 P1
Tippetts Cl ENC/FH EN2 79 K5
Tips Cross Md BRWN CM15 86 G1
Tipthorpe Rd BTSEA SW11 158 B9
Tipton Dr CROY/NA CR0 223 M1
Tiptree Cl CHING E4 101 H4
EMPK RM11 125 P6
Tiptree Crs CLAY IG5 102 D10
Tiptree Dr ENC/FH EN2 79 L8
Tiptree Rd RSLP HA4 113 J9
Tirlemont Rd SAND/SEL CR2 223 K4
Tirrell Rd CROY/NA CR0 203 K6
Tisbury Rd STRHM/NOR SW16 202 F2
Tisdall Pl WALW SE17 19 H6
Titan Ct BTFD TW8 155 L4
Titan Rd GRAYS RM17 167 M4
HHNE HP2 36 A3
Titchborne Rw BAY/PAD W2 9 P6
Titchfield Rd CAR SM5 201 N8
PEND EN3 80 D3
STJWD NW8 3 P6
Titchfield Wk CAR SM5 201 N7
Titchwell Rd WAND/EARL SW18 179 N3
Tite Hl EGH TW20 172 A8
Tite St CHEL SW3 16 A9
Tithe Barn Cl KUTN/CMB KT2 199 L1
STAL AL1 38 B9
Tithe Barn Ct ABLGY * WD5 54 G5
Tithe Barn Wy NTHLT UB5 133 J4
Tithe Cl MLHL NW7 96 D9
VW GU25 194 A6
WOT/HER KT12 197 J6
YEAD UB4 132 G7
Tithe Ct DTCH/LGLY SL3 150 D3
HDN * NW4 96 D9
Tithe Farm Av RYLN/HDSTN HA2 113 P8
Tithe Farm Cl RYLN/HDSTN HA2 113 P8
Tithelands HLWW/ROY CM19 46 C4
Tithe La STWL/WRAY TW19 172 C2
Tithepit Shaw La SAND/SEL CR2 242 A1
WARL CR6 242 A3
Tithe Wk MLHL NW7 96 D9
Titian Av BUSH WD23 94 D1
Titlarks Hill Rd ASC SL5 192 G8
Titley Cl CHING E4 100 F6
Titmus Cl UX/CGN UB8 132 D8
Titmus Dr CRAWE RH10 284 A10
Titmuss Av THMD SE28 143 L9
Titmuss St SHB * W12 156 E1
Titness Pk ASC * SL5 192 F3
Titsey Hl OXTED RH8 243 N10
WARL CR6 243 L10
Titsey Rd OXTED RH8 261 N3
Tiverton Av CLAY IG5 122 D1
Tiverton Ct HARP * AL5 20 D5
Tiverton Dr ELTH/MOT SE9 184 F4
Tiverton Gv HARH RM3 105 P6
Tiverton Rd ALP/SUD HA0 135 K4
EDGW HA8 95 L10
HSLW TW3 154 A8
POTB/CUF EN6 59 N7
RSLP HA4 113 H8
SEVS/STOTM N15 119 M2
UED N18 99 M6
WLSDN NW10 136 G3
Tiverton St STHWK SE1 18 E3
Tiverton Wy CHSGTN KT9 219 H2
Tivoli Gdns CHARL SE7 162 B3
Tivoli Rd CEND/HSY/T N8 118 E3
HSLWW TW4 153 M10
WNWD SE27 181 K8
Toad La HSLWW TW4 153 N10
Tobago St POP/IOD * E14 160 F1
Tobin Cl HAMP NW3 3 P3
Toby Wy SURB KT6 219 N9
Tockley Rd SL SL1 128 A5
Toddbrook HLWW/ROY CM19 46 E2
Todd Cl RAIN RM13 145 L6
Todds Cl HORL RH6 279 P2
Toft Av GRAYS RM17 168 A3
Toftwood Cl CRAWE RH10 284 D8
Tokenhouse Yd LOTH EC2R 12 G5
Tokyngton Av WBLY HA9 135 M1
Toland Sq PUT/ROE SW15 178 D1
Tolcarne Dr PIN HA5 93 H10
Toley Av WBLY HA9 115 K5
Tollbridge Cl NKENS W10 8 C1
Tolldene Cl WOKN/KNAP GU21 231 K3
Tollers La COUL/CHIP CR5 240 G5
Tollesbury Gdns BARK/HLT IG6 102 G10
Tollet St WCHPL E1 140 C6
Tollgate GU GU1 250 G9
Tollgate Av REDH RH1 276 A5
Tollgate Cl RKW/CH/CXG WD3 71 J8
Tollgate Dr DUL SE21 181 M5
YEAD UB4 133 L9
Tollgate Gdns KIL/WHAMP NW6 2 G7
Tollgate Rd BRKMPK AL9 58 D1
CHES/WCR EN8 80 C1
DORK RH4 272 G5
EHAM E6 142 B7
RDART DA2 188 C3
STALE/WH AL4 40 B10
Tollhouse La WLGTN SM6 222 D5
Tollhouse Wy ARCH N19 118 D7
Tollington Pk HOLWY N7 118 G7
Tollington Pl FSBYPK N4 118 G7
Tollington Rd HOLWY N7 118 G9
Tollington Wy HOLWY N7 118 F8
Tollpit End HHW HP1 35 K3
Tolmers Av POTB/CUF EN6 60 F4
Tolmers Gdns POTB/CUF EN6 60 F5
Tolmers Rd POTB/CUF EN6 60 F3
Tolmer's Sq CAMTN NW1 11 H1
Tolpits Cl WATW WD18 72 G9
Tolpits La WATW WD18 72 G10
Tolpuddle Av PLSTW E13 141 P3
Tolpuddle St IS N1 6 A7
Tolsford Rd CLPT E5 120 A10
Tolson Rd ISLW TW7 154 F9
Tolvaddon WOKN/KNAP GU21 231 M3
Tolverne Rd RYNPK SW20 200 F1
Tolworth Cl SURB KT6 199 N8
Tolworth Gdns CHDH RM6 123 N3
Tolworth Park Rd SURB KT6 199 L9
Tolworth Ri North BRYLDS KT5 199 P7
Tolworth Ri South BRYLDS KT5 199 P8
Tolworth Rd SURB KT6 199 K9
Tom Cribb Rd WOOL/PLUM SE18 162 F2
Tom Jenkinson Rd CAN/RD E16 141 M10
Tomkins Cl BORE WD6 75 K5
Tomkyns La UPMR RM14 126 C2
Tomlin Cl HOR/WEW KT19 220 A7
Tomlin Rd SLN SL2 128 D6
Tomlin's Gv BOW E3 140 F5
Tomlinson Cl BETH E2 7 M10
CHSWK W4 155 N4
Tomlins Orch BARK IG11 142 F3
Tomlin's Ter POP/IOD E14 140 D8
Tom Mann Cl BARK IG11 143 H3
Tom Nolan Cl SRTFD E15 141 K4
Tompion St FSBYE EC1V 6 C10
Toms Cft HHNE HP2 35 P7
Toms Fld HAT AL10 40 B5
Tom's Hl KGLGY WD4 71 P2
Tom's La KGLGY WD4 54 D4
Tom Smith Cl GNWCH SE10 161 K5
Tomswood Hl BARK/HLT IG6 102 E8
Tomswood Rd CHIG IG7 102 D7
Tonbridge By-Pass RSEV TN14 265 M9
Tonbridge Cl BNSTD SM7 222 A10
Tonbridge Crs
KTN/HRWW/W HA3 115 K2
Tonbridge Rd HARH RM3 105 L8
SEV TN13 265 K3
WOT/HER KT12 197 M4
Tonbridge St STPAN WC1H 5 L10
Tonfield Rd CHEAM SM3 201 J8
Tonsley Hl WAND/EARL SW18 179 L1
Tonsley Pl WAND/EARL SW18 179 L1
Tonsley Rd WAND/EARL SW18 179 L1
Tonsley St WAND/EARL SW18 179 L1
Tonstall Rd HOR/WEW KT19 220 A6
MTCM CR4 202 B2
Tooke Cl PIN HA5 93 M9
Took's Ct FLST/FETLN EC4A 12 A5
Tooley St GVW DA11 190 A3
STHWK SE1 13 H9
Toorack Rd KTN/HRWW/W HA3 94 C10
Toot Hill Rd CHONG CM5 66 G5
Tooting Bec Gdns
STRHM/NOR SW16 180 E7
Tooting Bec Rd TOOT SW17 180 B6
Tooting Gv TOOT SW17 179 P8
Tooting High St TOOT SW17 179 P7
Tootswood Rd HAYES BR2 205 K5
Tooveys Mill Cl KGLGY WD4 54 B5
Topaz Ct SL SL1 128 G10
Topcliffe Dr ORP BR6 226 G1
Top Dartford Rd SWLY BR8 187 H9
Topham Sq TOTM N17 99 K9
Topham St CLKNW * EC1R 12 A1
Top House Ri CHING E4 101 H1
Topiary Sq RCH/KEW TW9 155 L9
The Topiary ASHTD KT21 237 K6
Topland Rd CFSP/GDCR SL9 90 A8
Toplands Av SOCK/AV RM15 146 A10
Topley St ELTH/MOT SE9 161 P10
Topmast Point POP/IOD * E14 160 F1
Top Pk BECK BR3 205 K5
CFSP/GDCR SL9 109 P4
Topping La UX/CGN UB8 131 N5
Topsfield Pde CEND/HSY/T * N8 118 F3
Topsfield Rd CEND/HSY/T N8 118 F3
Topsham Rd TOOT SW17 180 A6
Topstreet Wy HARP AL5 20 B3
Torbay Rd KIL/WHAMP NW6 2 C4
RYLN/HDSTN HA2 113 M7
Torbay St CAMTN NW1 4 F3
Torbridge Cl EDGW HA8 95 K8
Torcross Dr FSTH SE23 182 B5
Torcross Rd RSLP HA4 113 J8
Tor Gdns KENS W8 14 E1
Torin Ct EGH TW20 171 P8
Torland Dr LHD/OX KT22 218 C10
Tor La WEY KT13 216 E7
Tormead Cl SUT SM1 221 K3
Tormead Rd GU GU1 250 C10
Tormount Rd WOOL/PLUM SE18 163 H5
Toronto Av MNPK E12 122 C9
Toronto Dr HORL RH6 281 H5
Toronto Rd IL IG1 122 E6
TIL RM18 168 D8
Torquay Gdns REDBR IG4 122 A2
Torquay Sp SLN SL2 128 G5
Torquay St BAY/PAD W2 8 G4
Torrance Cl HCH RM12 125 K6
Torrens Rd BRXS/STRHM SW2 180 G1
Torrens Sq SRTFD E15 141 L1
Torrens St FSBYE EC1V 6 C8
Torrens Wk GVE DA12 191 H8
Torriano Av KTTN NW5 118 E10
Torriano Ms KTTN NW5 118 D10
Torridge Gdns PECK SE15 160 B10
Torridge Rd DTCH/LGLY SL3 150 E5
THHTH CR7 203 J5
Torridon Cl WOKN/KNAP GU21 231 N3
Torridon Rd CAT SE6 183 J4
Torrington Av NFNCH/WDSP N12 97 N6
Torrington Cl ESH/CLAY KT10 218 D3
Torrington Dr LOU IG10 82 F8
POTB/CUF EN6 59 N8
RYLN/HDSTN HA2 114 A9
Torrington Gdns FBAR/BDGN N11 98 D7
GFD/PVL UB6 135 H3
LOU IG10 82 F8
Torrington Gv NFNCH/WDSP N12 97 P6
Torrington Pk NFNCH/WDSP N12 97 N5
Torrington Pl FITZ W1T 11 H3
WAP E1W 13 P10
Torrington Rd BCTR RM8 124 A6
BERK HP4 33 N5
ESH/CLAY KT10 218 D3
GFD/PVL UB6 135 H3
RSLP HA4 113 H8
Torrington Sq CROY/NA * CR0 203 L7
GWRST WC1E 11 K2
Torrington Wy MRDN SM4 201 K7
Tor Rd WELL DA16 163 M7
Torr Rd PGE/AN SE20 182 C10
Tortoiseshell Wy BERK HP4 33 L3
Torver Rd HRW HA1 114 D2
Torver Wy ORP BR6 206 G10
Torwood Cl BERK HP4 33 L5
Torwood La CTHM CR3 241 N6
Torwood Rd PUT/ROE SW15 178 D1
Torworth Rd BORE WD6 75 L5
Tothill St STJSPK SW1H 17 J2
Totnes Rd WELL DA16 163 L6
Totnes Vls FBAR/BDGN * N11 98 D6
Totnes Wk EFNCH N2 117 N2
Tottan Ter WCHPL * E1 140 C8
Tottenhall Rd PLMGR N13 99 H7
Tottenham Court Rd FITZ W1T 11 H2
Tottenham Gn East
SEVS/STOTM N15 119 N2
Tottenham La CEND/HSY/T N8 118 F3
Tottenham Ms FITZ * W1T 11 H3
Tottenham Rd IS N1 7 J2
Tottenham South Side
SEVS/STOTM N15 119 N2
Tottenham St GTPST W1W 11 H4
Totterdown St TOOT SW17 180 A7
Totteridge Common
TRDG/WHET N20 96 D3
Totteridge La TRDG/WHET N20 97 K3
Totteridge Rd PEND EN3 80 C3
Totteridge Village
TRDG/WHET N20 97 J2
Totternhoe Cl
KTN/HRWW/W HA3 115 H3
Totton Rd THHTH CR7 203 H3
Toulmin Dr STALW/RED AL3 38 B2
Toulmin St STHWK SE1 18 E2
Toulon St CMBW SE5 159 K6
Tournay Rd FUL/PGN SW6 157 J6
Toussaint Wk BERM/RHTH SE16 19 P3
Tovey Av HOD EN11 44 F1
Tovey Cl LCOL/BKTW AL2 57 J2
WAB EN9 45 K9
Tovil Cl PGE/AN SE20 203 P2
Towcester Rd BOW E3 140 G6
Tower Br TWRH EC3N 13 L9
Tower Bridge Ap TWRH EC3N 13 L9
Tower Bridge Rd STHWK SE1 19 J5
Tower Buildings WAP * E1W 140 A10
Tower Cl BERK HP4 33 M6
CHIG IG7 102 E7
EPP CM16 48 E10
GVE DA12 191 H8
HAMP NW3 117 N10
HORL RH6 280 A4
ORP BR6 207 J9
PGE/AN SE20 182 A10
WOKN/KNAP GU21 232 A3
Tower Ct BRW CM14 106 G3
LSQ/SEVD * WC2H 11 L6
Tower Cft EYN DA4 209 M9
Tower Gdns ESH/CLAY KT10 218 G4
Tower Gardens Rd TOTM N17 99 K9
Towergate Cl UX/CGN UB8 111 P10
Tower Gv WEY KT13 196 F9
Tower Hamlets Rd FSTGT E7 121 L10
WALTH E17 120 F1
Tower Hl BRW CM14 107 H3
DORK RH4 272 G4
KGLGY WD4 53 H5
Towerhill SHGR GU5 270 D6
Tower Hl TWRH EC3N 13 K8
Tower Hill La STALE/WH AL4 21 L6
Tower Hill Ri SHGR GU5 270 D6
Tower Hill Rd DORK RH4 272 G4
Tower Hill Ter MON EC3R 13 K8
Tower La WBLY * HA9 115 J8
Tower Ms CLPT * E5 120 D10
Tower Mill Rd PECK * SE15 159 M6
Tower Park Rd DART DA1 186 G1
Tower Pl MON EC3R 13 K8
Tower Ri RCH/KEW TW9 155 K9
Tower Rd AMSS HP7 68 F9
BELV DA17 164 D3
BXLYHN DA7 164 C10
DART DA1 187 K3
EPP CM16 65 H6
KWD/TDW/WH KT20 238 F9
ORP BR6 207 J9
WARE SG12 26 D1
WHTN TW2 176 D6
WLSDN NW10 136 D2
Tower Royal MANHO * EC4N 12 F7
Towers Av HGDN/ICK UB10 132 D5
Towers Ct HGDN/ICK * UB10 132 D5
Towers Pl RCHPK/HAM TW10 177 K1
Towers Rd GRAYS RM17 167 P4
HHNE HP2 35 P5
PIN HA5 93 M9
STHL UB1 133 P6
The Towers PUR/KEN CR8 241 K1
Tower St HERT/WAS SG14 25 K3
LSQ/SEVD * WC2H 11 K6
Towers Wk WEY KT13 216 C3
Towers Wd EYN DA4 210 C1
Tower Ter WDGN N22 98 G10
Tower Vw CROY/NA CR0 204 D8
Tower Whf GVW * DA11 167 N10
Towfield Rd FELT TW13 175 N5
Town Barn Rd CRAWW RH11 283 M7
Town Bridge Ct CSHM HP5 50 G8
Towncourt Crs STMC/STPC BR5 206 F5
Towncourt La STMC/STPC BR5 206 G6
Towncourt Pth FSBYPK N4 119 K6
Townend CTHM CR3 241 M8
Town End Cl CTHM CR3 241 M8
Town End Pde KUT * KT1 199 J3
Towney Md NTHLT UB5 133 N4
Town Farm Wy
STWL/WRAY * TW19 173 N3
Townfield CSHM HP5 50 G8
RKW/CH/CXG WD3 91 M1
Townfield Cnr GVE DA12 190 F4
Townfield Rd DORK RH4 272 F3
HYS/HAR UB3 132 G10
Town Flds HAT AL10 40 D3
Townfield Sq HYS/HAR UB3 132 G10
Town Field Wy ISLW TW7 154 F8
Towngate COB KT11 235 M1
Town Hall Approach Rd
SEVS/STOTM N15 119 N2
Town Hall Ar BERK * HP4 33 P5
Townhall Av CHSWK W4 156 A4
Town Hall Pde
BRXS/STRHM * SW2 158 G10
Town Hall Rd BTSEA SW11 158 A9
Townholm Crs HNWL W7 154 E2
Town La STWL/WRAY TW19 173 N2
Townley Ct SRTFD E15 141 L1
Townley Rd BXLYHS DA6 186 A1
DUL SE21 181 M1
Townley St WALW SE17 18 G7
Town Md CRAWW RH11 283 N6
REDH RH1 259 L9
Town Meadow BTFD TW8 155 J6
Townmead Rd FUL/PGN SW6 157 M8
RCH/KEW TW9 155 N8
Town Mead Rd WAB EN9 63 H10
Town Quay BARK IG11 142 E3
STA * TW18 195 M3
Town Rd ED N9 100 A3
Townsend HHNE HP2 35 N4
Townsend Av STAL AL1 38 D5
STHGT/OAK N14 98 E5
Townsend Dr STALW/RED AL3 38 C3
Townsend La CDALE/KGS NW9 116 A5
WOKS/MYFD GU22 232 E7
Townsend Rd ASHF TW15 173 P8
CSHM HP5 50 G6
SEVS/STOTM N15 119 N3
STHL UB1 133 M10
WOOL/PLUM SE18 162 E2
Townsend St WALW SE17 19 H6
Townsend Wy NTHWD HA6 92 G8
Townsend Yd HGT N6 118 C6
Townshead Cl SCUP DA14 185 L9
Townshend Est STJWD NW8 3 N7
Townshend Rd CHST BR7 184 E8
RCH/KEW TW9 155 L10
STJWD NW8 3 N6
Townshend St HERT/WAS SG14 25 M5
Townshend Ter RCH/KEW TW9 155 L10
Townshott Cl GT/LBKH KT23 253 P2
Townson Av NTHLT UB5 133 J4
Townson Wy NTHLT UB5 133 H4
Town Square Crs GRH DA9 188 E3
Town Tree Rd ASHF TW15 174 B8
Town Whf ISLW * TW7 154 G9
Towpath SHPTN TW17 196 A8
WOT/HER * KT12 197 J4
Towpath Rd UED * N18 100 C6
Towpath Wy CROY/NA CR0 203 N6
Towton Rd WNWD SE27 181 K5
Toynbec Cl CHST BR7 184 E7
Toynbee Rd RYNPK SW20 201 H1
Toynbee St WCHPL E1 13 L4
Toyne Wy HGT N6 118 A4
Toy's Hl BH/WHM TN16 263 M7
The Tracery BNSTD SM7 239 L1
Tracey Av CRICK * NW2 116 F10
Tracious Cl WOKN/KNAP GU21 231 N2
Tracyes Rd HLWS CM18 47 L3
Trade Cl PLMGR N13 99 H5
Trader Rd EHAM E6 142 E8
Tradescant Rd VX/NE SW8 158 F6
Trading Estate Rd
WLSDN * NW10 135 P6
Trafalgar Av BROX EN10 44 E7
PECK SE15 159 N7
STHWK SE1 19 M8
TOTM N17 99 M7
WPK KT4 200 G8
Trafalgar Ct COB KT11 217 H9
Trafalgar Dr WOT/HER KT12 197 J10
Trafalgar Gdns WCHPL E1 140 C7
Trafalgar Gv GNWCH SE10 161 J5
Trafalgar Pl UED N18 99 P6
WAN E11 121 M2
Trafalgar Rd DART DA1 187 M5
GNWCH SE10 161 K4
GVW DA11 190 D3
RAIN RM13 144 G4
WHTN TW2 176 C5
WIM/MER SW19 179 L10
Trafalgar Sq CHCR WC2N 11 K9
Trafalgar St WALW SE17 18 G7
Trafalgar Wy CROY/NA CR0 202 G9
POP/IOD E14 141 H10
Trafford Cl RAD WD7 57 K8
SRTFD E15 120 G10
Trafford Rd THHTH CR7 202 G5
Tramway Av ED N9 100 A1
SRTFD E15 141 J2
Tramway Pth MTCM CR4 201 P4
Tranley Ms HAMP * NW3 117 P9
Tranmere Rd ED N9 99 N1
WAND/EARL SW18 179 M5
WHTN TW2 176 A3
Tranquil Dl BRKHM/BTCW RH3 256 C8
Tranquil Ri ERITH DA8 164 F4
Tranquil V BKHTH/KID SE3 161 L8
Transept St CAMTN NW1 9 P4
Transmere Rd STMC/STPC BR5 206 F6
Transom Sq POP/IOD E14 160 G4
Transport Av BTFD TW8 154 G5
Tranton Rd BERM/RHTH SE16 160 A2
Trapp's La CSHM HP5 51 H9
Trap's Hl LOU IG10 82 C8
Traps La NWMAL KT3 200 B2
Trapstyle Rd WARE SG12 25 P1
Trasher Md RDKG RH5 273 H5
Travellers Cl BRKMPK AL9 40 F9
Travellers La HAT AL10 40 D6
Travellers Site WALTH * E17 100 E8
Travellers Wy HEST TW5 153 K8
Travers Cl WALTH E17 100 C9
Travers Rd HOLWY N7 119 H8
Travic Rd SLN SL2 128 E5
Travis Ct SLN SL2 128 G5
Treacher's Cl CSHM HP5 50 G7
Treacy Cl BUSH WD23 94 B3
Treadgold St NTGHL W11 136 G9
Treadway St BETH E2 140 A4
Treadwell Rd EPSOM KT18 238 C1
Treaty St IS N1 5 N6
Trebble Rd SWCM DA10 189 K2
Trebeck St MYFR/PICC W1J 10 E9
Trebellan Dr HHNE HP2 36 A5
Trebovir Rd ECT SW5 14 F7
Treby St BOW E3 140 E6
Trecastle Wy HOLWY * N7 118 E9
Tredegar Rd BOW E3 140 E4
FBAR/BDGN N11 98 E8
RDART DA2 187 H6
Tredegar Sq BOW E3 140 E5
Trederwen Rd HACK E8 7 P5
Tredown Rd SYD SE26 182 B8
Tredwell Cl HAYES BR2 206 A4
Tredwell Rd WNWD SE27 181 J7
Treebourne Rd BH/WHM TN16 243 P3
Treebys Av RGUE GU4 250 A4
Tree Cl HHS/BOV HP3 36 C8
RCHPK/HAM TW10 177 J4
Treelands RDKG RH5 273 H5
Treen Av BARN SW13 156 B9
Tree Rd CAN/RD E16 141 P8
Treeside Cl WDR/YW UB7 151 N3
Treetops BGR/WK TN15 247 P3
Tree Tops BRWN CM15 107 H2
Treetops GVE DA12 190 E8
Tree Tops WARL CR6 241 P4
Treetops Cl ABYW SE2 163 P4
NTHWD HA6 92 E6
Treetops Vw LOU IG10 82 A10
Tree View Cl NRWD SE19 203 M1
Tree View Ct REIG * RH2 257 N10
Treewall Gdns BMLY BR1 183 N7
Treeway REIG RH2 257 L7
Trefgarne Rd DAGE RM10 124 F7
Trefoil Rd WAND/EARL SW18 179 M1
Trefusis Wk WAT WD17 72 F5
Tregaron Av CEND/HSY/T N8 118 F5
Tregaron Gdns NWMAL KT3 200 B4
Tregarthen Pl LHD/OX KT22 237 H7
Tregarth Pl WOKN/KNAP GU21 231 L3
Tregarvon Rd BTSEA SW11 158 B10
Tregelles Rd HOD EN11 44 F1
Tregenna Av RYLN/HDSTN HA2 113 P9
Tregenna Cl STHGT/OAK N14 78 D9
Tregony Rd ORP BR6 227 J1
Trego Rd HOM E9 140 F2
Tregothnan Rd BRXN/ST SW9 158 F9
Tregunter Rd WBPTN SW10 15 J9
Trehaven Pde REIG RH2 275 L3
Trehearn Rd BARK/HLT IG6 102 G8
Treherne Ct BRXN/ST * SW9 159 J7
Trehern Rd MORT/ESHN SW14 156 A9
Trehurst St CLPT E5 120 D10
Trelawn Cl CHERT KT16 214 F4
Trelawney Av DTCH/LGLY SL3 150 A2
Trelawney Est HOM * E9 140 B1
Trelawney Gv WEY KT13 216 B3
Trelawney Rd BARK/HLT IG6 102 G8
Trelawn Rd BRXS/STRHM SW2 181 H1
LEY E10 121 H8
Trelawny Cl WALTH E17 120 G2
Treloar Gdns NRWD SE19 181 L9
Tremadoc Rd CLAP SW4 158 E10
Tremaine Gv HHNE HP2 35 P2
Tremaine Rd PGE/AN SE20 204 A2
Tremlett Gv ARCH N19 118 D8
Tremlett Ms ARCH * N19 118 D8
Trenance WOKN/KNAP GU21 231 M3
Trenance Gdns GDMY/SEVK IG3 123 K8
Trenchard Av RSLP HA4 113 J10
Trenchard Cl CDALE/KGS NW9 96 B9
STAN HA7 94 G7
WOT/HER KT12 217 K2
Trenchard St GNWCH SE10 161 J4
Trenches La DTCH/LGLY SL3 130 D10
Trenham Dr WARL CR6 242 B2
Trenholme Rd PGE/AN SE20 182 A10
Trenholme Ter PGE/AN SE20 182 A10
Trenmar Gdns WLSDN NW10 136 E5
Trent TIL RM18 169 M3
Trent Av EA W5 155 H2
UPMR RM14 126 C4
Trentbridge Cl BARK/HLT IG6 103 J7
Trent Cl CRAWW RH11 283 J9
RAD WD7 57 K8
Trent Ct WAN E11 121 M3
Trent Gdns STHGT/OAK N14 78 C10
Trentham Crs WOKS/MYFD GU22 232 D7
Trentham Dr STMC/STPC BR5 207 K4
Trentham Rd REDH RH1 276 A2
Trentham St WAND/EARL SW18 179 K4
Trent Pk EBAR * EN4 78 D6
Trent Rd BKHH IG9 101 N2
BRXS/STRHM SW2 180 G1
DTCH/LGLY SL3 150 E5
Trent Wy WPK KT4 200 F10
YEAD UB4 132 F5
Trentwood Side ENC/FH EN2 78 G7
Treport St WAND/EARL SW18 179 L3
Tresco Cl BMLY BR1 183 K9
Trescoe Gdns CRW RM5 104 D6
PIN HA5 113 M5
Tresco Gdns GDMY/SEVK IG3 123 J7
Tresco Rd BERK HP4 33 L4
PECK SE15 160 A10
Tresham Crs STJWD NW8 9 N1
Tresham Rd BARK IG11 143 J2
Tresilian Av WCHMH N21 78 G9
Tresillian Wy WOKN/KNAP GU21 231 M3
Tressell Cl IS N1 6 D4
Tressillian Crs BROCKY SE4 160 F9
Tressillian Rd BROCKY SE4 160 F9
Tresta Wk WOKN/KNAP GU21 231 M1

Trestis Cl YEAD UB4 133 L6
Treswell Rd DAGW RM9 143 P3
Tretawn Gdns MLHL NW7 96 B5
Tretawn Pk MLHL NW7 96 B5
Trevalga Wy HHNE HP2 35 N1
Trevanion Rd WKENS W14 14 B7
Trevanne Plat CRAWE RH10 284 E6
Treve Av HRW HA1 114 B5
Trevellance Wy GSTN WD25 55 K9
Trevelyan Av MNPK E12 122 C9
Trevelyan Cl DART DA1 165 N10
Trevelyan Crs
KTN/HRWW/W HA3 115 J5
Trevelyan Gdns WLSDN * NW10 136 F3
Trevelyan Rd FSTGT E7 121 K9
TOOT SW17 179 P9
Trevelyan Wy BERK HP4 33 N3
Trevera Ct CHES/WCR * EN8 62 D9
HOD * EN11 44 F2
Trevereux Hl OXTED RH8 262 D8
Treveris St STHWK SE1 12 D10
Treverton St NKENS W10 136 G6
Treves Cl WCHMH N21 78 G9
Treville St PUT/ROE SW15 178 E3
Treviso Rd FSTH SE23 182 C5
Trevithick Cl EBED/NFELT TW14 174 G4
Trevithick Dr DART DA1 165 N10
Trevithick St DEPT SE8 160 F5
Trevone Gdns PIN HA5 113 M4
Trevor Cl EBAR EN4 77 N10
HAYES BR2 205 L7
ISLW TW7 176 E1
KTN/HRWW/W HA3 94 E8
NTHLT UB5 133 K4
Trevor Crs RSLP HA4 112 G9
Trevor Gdns EDGW HA8 96 A9
Trevor Pl SKENS SW7 15 P2
Trevor Rd EDGW HA8 96 A9
HYS/HAR UB3 152 F1
WFD IG8 101 M8
WIM/MER SW19 179 H10
Trevor Sq SKENS SW7 15 P2
Trevor St SKENS SW7 15 P2
Trevose Av BF/WBF KT14 215 J10
Trevose Rd WALTH E17 101 J9
Trevose Wy OXHEY WD19 93 K4
Trewarden Av IVER SL0 130 G4
Trewenna Dr CHSGTN KT9 219 J2
POTB/CUF EN6 59 N8
Trewince Rd RYNPK SW20 200 F1
Trewint St WAND/EARL SW18 179 M5
Trewsbury Rd SYD SE26 182 C8
Treyford Cl CRAWW RH11 283 J7
Triandra Wy YEAD UB4 133 L7
Triangle Pas BAR * EN5 77 M8
Triangle Pl CLAP SW4 158 E10
Triangle Rd HACK E8 140 A3
The Triangle BFN/LL * DA15 185 K3
NWMAL KT3 199 P2
WOKN/KNAP GU21 231 P4
Trident Av HAT * AL10 40 B3
Trident Rd GSTN WD25 54 G10
Trident St BERM/RHTH SE16 160 C3
Trident Wy NWDGN UB2 153 J2
Trigg's Cl WOKS/MYFD GU22 232 A5
Trigg's La WOKN/KNAP GU21 231 P5
Trig La BLKFR EC4V 12 E7
Trigon Rd VX/NE SW8 158 G6
Trilby Rd FSTH SE23 182 C5
Trim St NWCR SE14 160 E5
Trinder Rd ARCH N19 118 F6
BAR EN5 76 F9
Trindles Rd REDH RH1 276 G2
Tring Av EA W5 135 L10
STHL UB1 133 N8
WBLY HA9 135 M1
Tring Cl BARK/HLT IG6 122 F3
HARH RM3 105 N5
Tring Gdns HARH RM3 105 M5
Tringham Cl CHERT KT16 214 E2
Tring Rd BERK HP4 33 H2
Trinidad Gdns DAGE RM10 144 E2
Trinidad St POP/IOD E14 140 E9
Trinity Av EFNCH N2 117 N1
EN EN1 79 N10
Trinity Buoy Whf POP/IOD * E14 141 J7
Trinity Church Rd BARN SW13 156 E5
Trinity Church Sq STHWK SE1 18 F3
Trinity Churchyard GU * GU1 268 A2
Trinity Cl CLAP * SW4 158 D10
CRAWE RH10 284 D5
HACK E8 7 M1
HAYES BR2 206 B8
HSLWW TW4 153 M9
LEW SE13 161 J10
NTHWD HA6 92 F7
SAND/SEL CR2 223 M5
STWL/WRAY TW19 173 M2
WAN E11 121 K7
Trinity Ct ELTH/MOT SE9 184 E2
RKW/CH/CXG * WD3 91 P3
Trinity Crs ASC SL5 192 F5
TOOT SW17 180 A5
Trinity Gdns BRXN/ST SW9 158 G10
CAN/RD E16 141 L7
DART DA1 187 L2
Trinity Gn WCHPL * E1 140 B7
Trinity Gv GNWCH SE10 161 H7
HERT/WAS SG14 25 K4
Trinity Hall Cl WATN WD24 73 K7
Trinity La CHES/WCR EN8 62 D8
Trinity Ms HHS/BOV HP3 36 E7
PGE/AN * SE20 204 B1
Trinity Pde HSLW * TW3 154 A9
Trinity Pk CHING * E4 100 E7
Trinity Pl BXLYHS DA6 164 A10
WDSR * SL4 149 H8
Trinity Ri HNHL SE24 181 J3
Trinity Rd BARK/HLT IG6 122 F1
EFNCH N2 117 N1
GVE DA12 190 F3
HERT/BAY SG13 26 B8
RCH/KEW * TW9 155 L9
STHL UB1 133 M10
TOOT SW17 180 A5
WAND/EARL SW18 179 N2
WARE SG12 26 D1
WDGN N22 98 G9
WIM/MER SW19 179 K9
WOKN/KNAP GU21 230 G4
Trinity Sq TWRH EC3N 13 K8
Trinity St CAN/RD E16 141 L7
ENC/FH EN2 79 K6
STHWK SE1 18 F2
Trinity Wk HERT/BAY SG13 26 B8
Trinity Wy ACT W3 136 B9
CHING E4 100 E7
Trio Pl STHWK SE1 18 F2
Tripton Rd HLWS CM18 47 H2
Tristan Ldg BUSH * WD23 73 M8
Tristan Sq BKHTH/KID SE3 161 K9
Tristram Cl WALTH E17 121 J1
Tristram Rd BMLY BR1 183 L7
Triton Sq CAMTN NW1 10 G1
Triton Wy HHNE HP2 36 A4
Tritton Av CROY/NA CR0 222 F1
Tritton Rd WNWD SE27 181 L6
Trittons KWD/TDW/WH KT20 238 F7
Triumph Cl HYS/HAR UB3 152 D7
Triumph Rd EHAM E6 142 C8
Trivett Cl GRH DA9 188 F1
Triumph Cl CDH/CHF RM16 167 H3
Trodd's La RGUE GU4 269 J1
Trojan Wy CROY/NA CR0 202 G10
Trolling Down Hl RDART DA2 188 A5
Troon Cl BERM/RHTH * SE16 160 A4
CRAWW RH11 282 G8
Troon St WCHPL E1 140 D8
Troopers Dr HARH RM3 105 L5
Trosley Av GVW DA11 190 E5
Trosley Rd BELV DA17 164 B5
Trossachs Rd EDUL SE22 181 M1
Trothy Rd STHWK SE1 19 P6
Trotsworth Av VW GU25 194 A4
Trotters Bottom BAR EN5 76 D3
Trotter's Gap WARE SG12 27 K7
Trotters La CHOB/PIR GU24 213 N8
Trotters Rd HLWS CM18 47 K4
Trotter Wy HOR/WEW KT19 219 M8
Trotton Cl CRAWE RH10 284 D10
Trott Rd MUSWH N10 98 B8
Trotts La BH/WHM TN16 262 F3
Trott St BTSEA SW11 157 N7
Trotwood CHIG IG7 102 G6
Troughton Rd CHARL SE7 161 N4
Troutbeck Cl SLN SL2 129 M9
Troutbeck Rd NWCR SE14 160 D7
Trout La WDR/YW UB7 131 M9
Trout Ri RKW/CH/CXG WD3 71 L7
Trout Rd WDR/YW UB7 131 N10
Troutstream Wy
RKW/CH/CXG WD3 71 L8
Trouvere Pk HHW HP1 35 L4
Trouville Rd BAL SW12 180 D2
Trowbridge Rd HARH RM3 105 L7
HOM E9 140 E1
Trowers Wy REDH RH1 258 C7
Trowley Ri ABLGY WD5 54 F7
Trowlock Av TEDD TW11 177 H9
Trowlock Island TEDD TW11 177 J9
Trowlock Wy TEDD TW11 177 H9
Troy Ct KENS W8 14 E3
Troy Rd NRWD SE19 181 L9
Troy Town PECK SE15 159 P9
Trubshaw Rd NWDGN UB2 153 P2
Trueman Cl EDGW * HA8 95 N8
Truesdale Dr DEN/HRF UB9 111 M2
Trulock Rd TOTM N17 99 P8
Truman's Rd STNW/STAM N16 119 M10
Trumpers Wy HNWL W7 154 E2
Trumper Wy SL * SL1 128 E10
Trumpetshill Rd REIG RH2 274 D1
Trumpington Dr STAL AL1 38 C9
Trumpington Rd FSTGT E7 121 L9
Trumpsgreen Av VW GU25 194 A6
Trumps Green Cl VW GU25 194 B5
Trumpsgreen Rd VW GU25 193 P8
Trumps Mill La VW GU25 194 C6
Trump St CITYW EC2V 12 F6
Trundlers Wy BUSH WD23 94 D2
Trundle St STHWK SE1 18 E1
Trundleys Rd DEPT SE8 160 D5
DEPT SE8 160 C4
Trundley's Ter DEPT SE8 160 C3
Trunley Heath Rd SHGR GU5 267 P9
Truro Gdns IL IG1 122 B5
Truro Rd GVE DA12 190 G6
WALTH E17 120 E2
WDGN N22 98 F8
Truro St KTTN NW5 4 C2
Truro Wy YEAD UB4 132 F5
Trusedale Rd EHAM E6 142 C8
Truslove Rd WNWD SE27 181 H8
Truss Hill Rd ASC SL5 192 B5
Trussley Rd HMSMTH W6 156 F2
Trustons Gdns EMPK RM11 125 H5
Trust Rd CHES/WCR EN8 62 D10
Tryfan Cl REDBR IG4 122 A3
Tryon Crs HOM E9 140 B3
Tryon St CHEL SW3 16 A7
Trys Hill Longcross Rd
CHERT KT16 194 B10
Trystings Cl ESH/CLAY KT10 218 F3
Tuam Rd WOOL/PLUM SE18 162 G5
Tubbenden Cl ORP BR6 207 H9
Tubbenden Dr ORP BR6 226 G1
Tubbenden La ORP BR6 226 G1
Tubbenden La South ORP BR6 226 G2
Tubbs Rd WLSDN NW10 136 C4
Tubs Hl SEV TN13 247 H10
Tubs Hill Pde SEV * TN13 247 H10
Tubwell Rd SLN SL2 129 N3
Tucker Rd CHERT KT16 214 G3
Tucker St WATW WD18 73 K9
Tuckey Gv RPLY/SEND GU23 233 J10
Tuck Rd RAIN RM13 145 H1
Tudor Av CHESW EN7 62 A7
GPK RM2 125 H1
HPTN TW12 175 P9
WATN WD24 73 L3
WPK KT4 200 E10
Tudor Cir RGODL GU7 267 K10
Tudor Cl ASHF TW15 173 P7
BNSTD SM7 239 H1
BRWN CM15 87 L10
BRXS/STRHM * SW2 180 G2
CDALE/KGS NW9 115 P7
CHEAM SM3 220 G2
CHESW EN7 62 A7
CHIG IG7 102 D5
CHSGTN KT9 219 K2
CHST BR7 206 C1
COB KT11 217 N9
COUL/CHIP CR5 241 H4
CRAWE RH10 284 E8
DART DA1 187 J2
GT/LBKH KT23 235 N10
GVW DA11 190 B4
HAMP NW3 3 N1
HAT AL10 40 B7
HGT N6 118 D5
HORL RH6 281 J4
HPTN TW12 176 B8
MLHL NW7 96 D7
PIN HA5 113 H3
SAND/SEL CR2 242 A1
WARE SG12 28 A3
WFD IG8 101 N6
WLGTN SM6 222 D4
WOKS/MYFD GU22 232 D3
Tudor Ct AMS * HP6 69 J4
BORE WD6 75 K6
ELTH/MOT * SE9 162 B10
SWLY BR8 208 D7
WALTH E17 120 E5
Tudor Ct North WBLY HA9 115 M10
Tudor Ct South WBLY HA9 115 M10
Tudor Crs BARK/HLT IG6 102 F7
ENC/FH EN2 79 K5
RSEV TN14 247 K3
Tudor Dr GPK RM2 125 H2
KUTN/CMB KT2 177 K8
MRDN SM4 200 G6
RSEV TN14 247 K2
WATN WD24 73 L4
WOT/HER KT12 197 L8
Tudor Est WLSDN * NW10 135 N4
Tudor Gdns ACT W3 135 M8
BARN SW13 156 B9
CDALE/KGS NW9 115 P7
GPK RM2 125 H2
SL SL1 128 B7
TWK TW1 176 E4
UPMR RM14 126 B7
WWKM BR4 225 H10
Tudor Gv HOM E9 140 B2
Tudor La WDSR SL4 171 P3
Tudor Manor Gdns GSTN WD25 55 L8
Tudor Orch BERK * HP4 33 K3
Tudor Pde ELTH/MOT * SE9 162 B10
Tudor Pk AMS HP6 69 H3
Tudor Pl NRWD * SE19 181 N10
WIM/MER SW19 179 P10
Tudor Ri BROX EN10 44 D7
Tudor Rd ASHF TW15 174 E9
BAR EN5 77 K7
BARK IG11 143 J2
BECK BR3 205 H3
CHING E4 100 G7
ED N9 100 A1
EHAM E6 141 P3
HACK E8 140 A3
HPTN TW12 175 P10
HSLW TW3 154 C10
HYS/HAR UB3 132 E8
KTN/HRWW/W HA3 94 C10
KUTN/CMB KT2 177 M10
NRWD SE19 181 N10
PIN HA5 93 K10
RGODL GU7 267 K10
SNWD SE25 204 A5
STALE/WH AL4 21 K3
STALW/RED AL3 38 D2
STHL UB1 133 M9
Tudor Sq HYS/HAR UB3 132 E7
WARE * SG12 26 C2
The Tudors REIG * RH2 257 M7
Tudor St EMB EC4Y 12 B7
Tudor Vls CHESW * EN7 61 M5
Tudor Wk LHD/OX KT22 236 F6
WARE * SG12 26 C1
WATN WD24 73 L3
Tudor Wy ACT W3 155 M1
HERT/WAS SG14 25 H5
HGDN/ICK UB10 132 B1
RKW/CH/CXG WD3 91 K2
STHGT/OAK N14 98 E2
STMC/STPC BR5 206 G6
WAB EN9 63 J9
WDSR SL4 148 D7
Tudor Well Cl STAN HA7 94 G6
Tudway Rd ELTH/MOT SE9 161 P10
Tufnail Rd DART DA1 187 N2
Tufnell Park Rd HOLWY N7 118 E9
Tufter Rd CHIG IG7 103 J6
Tufton Gdns E/WMO/HCT KT8 198 A2
Tufton Rd CHING E4 100 F5
Tufton St WEST SW1P 17 L4
Tugboat St THMD SE28 163 H1
Tugela Rd CROY/NA CR0 203 L6
Tugela St CAT SE6 182 E5
Tugmutton Cl ORP BR6 226 E1
Tulip Cl BRWN CM15 86 G9
CROY/NA CR0 204 C8
EHAM E6 142 C7
HARH RM3 105 K7
HPTN TW12 175 N9
STHL UB1 154 B1
Tulip Gdns CHING * E4 101 J4
IL IG1 142 E1
Tulip Wy WDR/YW UB7 151 N3
Tull St MTCM CR4 202 A7
Tulse Cl BECK BR3 205 H3
Tulse Hl BRXS/STRHM SW2 180 G2
Tulsemere Rd WNWD SE27 181 K5
Tulyar Cl KWD/TDW/WH KT20 238 E5
Tumber St EPSOM KT18 255 P1
Tumbler Rd HLWS CM18 47 K2
Tumblewood Rd BNSTD SM7 239 H2
Tumbling Bay WOT/HER KT12 197 H6
Tumbling Bay Weir WARE * SG12 26 E1
Tummons Gdns SNWD SE25 203 M2
Tuncombe Rd UED N18 99 M5
Tunfield Rd HOD EN11 26 G10
Tunis Rd SHB W12 136 F10
Tunley Rd BAL SW12 180 B5
WLSDN NW10 136 B3
Tunmarsh La PLSTW E13 141 P5
Tunmers End CFSP/GDCR SL9 89 P9
Tunnan Leys EHAM E6 142 D8
Tunnel Av GNWCH SE10 161 J1
Tunnel Gdns FBAR/BDGN N11 98 D8
Tunnel Link Rd HTHAIR TW6 174 B1
Tunnel Rd BERM/RHTH SE16 160 B1
Tunnel Rd East WDR/YW UB7 152 C6
Tunnel Rd West WDR/YW UB7 152 B7
Tunnel Wood Cl WAT WD17 72 G3
Tunnel Wood Rd WAT WD17 72 G3
Tunnmeade CRAWW RH11 283 H8
HLW CM20 29 K10
Tunsgate GU GU1 268 A2
Tunsgate Sq GU * GU1 268 A2
Tuns La SL SL1 149 H2
Tunstall Av BARK/HLT IG6 103 K7
Tunstall Cl ORP BR6 227 H1
Tunstall Rd BRXN/ST SW9 158 G10
CROY/NA CR0 203 M8
Tunstock Wy BELV DA17 163 P2
Tunworth Cl CDALE/KGS NW9 115 P4
Tunworth Crs PUT/ROE SW15 178 C2
Tupelo Rd LEY E10 120 G7
Tupwood La CTHM CR3 259 P2
Tupwood Scrubbs Rd
CTHM * CR3 241 P6
GDST RH9 259 P4
Turene Cl BTSEA SW11 157 M10
Turfhouse La CHOB/PIR GU24 213 K5
Turin Rd ED N9 100 B1
Turin St BETH E2 7 N10
Turkey Oak Cl NRWD SE19 203 M1
Turkey St EN EN1 79 P2
Turks Cl UX/CGN UB8 132 B5
Turks Rw CHEL SW3 16 B7
Turle Rd FSBYPK * N4 118 G7
STRHM/NOR SW16 202 F2
Turlewray Cl FSBYPK N4 118 G6
Turley Cl SRTFD E15 141 K3
Turmore Dl WGCW AL8 22 D5
Turnagain La STP * EC4M 12 C5
Turnage Rd BCTR RM8 123 P6
Turnant Rd TOTM N17 99 K9
Turnberry Cl BERM/RHTH * SE16 160 A4
Turnberry Ct OXHEY * WD19 93 K4
Turnberry Dr LCOL/BKTW AL2 55 M6
Turnberry Wy ORP BR6 206 G8
Turnbull Cl RDART DA2 188 D3
Turnbury Cl THMD SE28 143 N8
Turner Av MTCM CR4 202 A1
SEVS/STOTM N15 119 M2
WHTN TW2 176 B6
Turner Cl ALP/SUD HA0 115 J10
CMBW SE5 159 J7
GLDGN NW11 117 L4
GU GU1 250 C7
HYS/HAR UB3 132 B4
Turner Ct CMBW * SE5 159 L10
DART DA1 187 K1
Turner Dr GLDGN NW11 117 L4
Turner Rd BH/WHM TN16 225 P8
BUSH WD23 74 B8
DTCH/LGLY SL3 149 P1
EDGW HA8 95 K10
NWMAL KT3 200 A7
RDART DA2 188 G6
WALTH E17 121 H2
Turners Cl CHONG CM5 67 N5
STA TW18 173 L8
Turners Gdns SEV TN13 265 K4
Turner's Hl CHES/WCR EN8 62 C6
HHNE HP2 35 P7
Turners Hill Rd CRAWE RH10 284 F7
CRAWE RH10 285 N2
Turners La WOT/HER KT12 217 J3
Turners Meadow Wy BECK BR3 204 E1
Turner's Oak Shaw HART DA3 211 K9
Turners Pl EYN * DA4 210 B1
Turners Rd POP/IOD E14 140 E7
Turner St CAN/RD E16 141 L8
WCHPL E1 140 A7
Turners Wk CSHM HP5 51 H6
Turners Wy CROY/NA CR0 203 H9
Turner's Wd GLDGN NW11 117 M6
Turners Wood Dr CSTG HP8 90 A4
Turneville Rd WKENS W14 14 C9
Turney Rd DUL SE21 181 K3
Turneys Orch RKW/CH/CXG WD3 70 G9
Turnford Pl BROX * EN10 62 D2
Turnford Vls BROX * EN10 62 E2
Turnham Cl GUW GU2 267 P4
Turnham Green Ter CHSWK W4 156 B3
Turnham Rd BROCKY SE4 182 D1
Turnmill St FARR EC1M 12 B2
Turnoak Av WOKS/MYFD GU22 232 B6
Turnoak La WOKS/MYFD GU22 232 B6
Turnoak Pk WDSR SL4 148 D10
Turnors HLWW/ROY CM19 46 F1
Turnpike Cl DEPT SE8 160 E6
Turnpike Dr ORP BR6 227 M5
Turnpike Gn HHNE HP2 36 A2
Turnpike La CDH/CHF RM16 168 G4
CEND/HSY/T N8 119 H2
SUT SM1 221 M2
UX/CGN UB8 131 P5
Turnpike Link CROY/NA CR0 203 M9
Turnpike Ms CEND/HSY/T * N8 119 H2
Turnpike Pde CEND/HSY/T * N8 119 J1
Turnpike Pl CRAWW RH11 283 N5
Turnpike Wy ISLW TW7 154 F7
Turnstone HART DA3 211 M3
Turnstone Cl CDALE/KGS * NW9 96 B10
HGDN/ICK UB10 112 C10
PLSTW E13 141 M5
SAND/SEL CR2 224 D6
The Turnstones GSTN WD25 73 M2
GVE DA12 190 G5
Turnstone Ter WEA * W13 134 E6
Turp Av CDH/CHF RM16 167 P1
Turpentine La PIM SW1V 16 F7
Turpin Av CRW RM5 104 B8
Turpin Cl PEND EN3 80 F3
Turpington Cl HAYES BR2 206 B6
Turpington La HAYES BR2 206 B5
Turpin La ERITH DA8 165 H5
Turpin Rd EBED/NFELT TW14 174 G2
Turpins Cl HERT/WAS SG14 24 G5
Turpin's La WFD IG8 102 C6
Turpins Ri BFOR GU20 212 A1
Turpins Yd CRICK * NW2 116 E7
Turpin Wy WLGTN SM6 222 C4
Turquand St WALW SE17 18 F6
Turret Gv CLAP SW4 158 D9
Turton Rd ALP/SUD HA0 115 K10
Turton Wy SL SL1 149 J2
Turville St BETH * E2 13 L1
Tuscan Rd WOOL/PLUM SE18 162 G4
Tuscany Gdns CRAWE RH10 283 P5
Tushmore Av CRAWE RH10 283 P4
Tushmore Ct CRAWE * RH10 283 P5
Tushmore Crs CRAWE RH10 283 P4
Tushmore La CRAWE RH10 283 P5
Tuskar St GNWCH SE10 161 K4
Tussauds Cl RKW/CH/CXG WD3 72 B9
Tussock Cl CRAWW RH11 283 K9
Tuxford Cl BORE * WD6 75 K4
CRAWE RH10 284 D9
Tweed TIL RM18 169 M3
Tweed Cl BERK HP4 33 N4
Tweeddale Gv HGDN/ICK UB10 112 D8
Tweeddale Rd CAR SM5 201 N8
Tweed La BRKHM/BTCW RH3 273 N4
CRAWW RH11 283 J4
Tweedmouth Rd PLSTW E13 141 N4
Tweed Rd DTCH/LGLY SL3 150 E5
Tweed Wy ROM RM1 104 E8
Tweedy Rd BMLY BR1 205 M1
Tweenways CSHM HP5 51 J6
Twelve Acre Cl GT/LBKH KT23 235 N10
Twelve Acres WGCE AL7 23 H7
Twelve Av KWD/TDW/WH * KT20 257 J2
Twelvetrees Crs BOW E3 141 H6
Twentyman Cl WFD IG8 101 M6
Twickenham Br TWK TW1 177 H1
Twickenham Cl CROY/NA CR0 202 G10
Twickenham Gdns GFD/PVL UB6 114 F10
KTN/HRWW/W HA3 94 D8
Twickenham Rd FELT TW13 175 N6
ISLW TW7 154 F10
RCH/KEW TW9 177 H1
TEDD TW11 176 F7
WAN E11 121 J7
Twig Folly Cl BOW E3 140 C4
Twig Folly Whf BETH * E2 140 C4
Twigg Cl ERITH DA8 164 F6
Twilley St WAND/EARL SW18 179 L3
Twinches La SL SL1 128 G10
Twine Cl BARK IG11 143 L5
Twine Ct WCHPL E1 140 B9
Twineham Gn NFNCH/WDSP N12 97 K5
Twine Ter BOW * E3 140 E6
Twining Av WHTN TW2 176 B6
Twinn Rd MLHL NW7 97 H7
Twinoaks COB KT11 217 P9
Twisden Rd KTTN NW5 118 C9
Twisleton Ct DART DA1 187 L2
The Twitten CRAWW RH11 283 M7
Twitton La RSEV TN14 246 F2
Twitton Mdw RSEV TN14 246 F2
Two Acres WGCE AL7 23 J8
Two Beeches HHNE * HP2 36 A1
Two Dells La CSHM HP5 33 L10
Two Gates La CSHM HP5 32 D10
Two Mile Dr SL SL1 128 D10
Two Waters Rd HHS/BOV HP3 35 M9
Twybridge Wy WLSDN NW10 135 P2
Twycross Rd RGODL GU7 267 J10
Twyford Abbey Rd WLSDN NW10 135 L5
Twyford Av ACT W3 135 M9
EFNCH N2 118 A1
Twyford Crs ACT W3 135 M10
Twyford Rd CAR SM5 201 N8
IL IG1 122 F10
RYLN/HDSTN HA2 114 A5
STALE/WH AL4 39 H2
Twyford St IS N1 5 N5
Twyne Cl CRAWW RH11 283 J9
Twyner Cl HORL RH6 280 D3
Twynersh Av CHERT KT16 195 J6
Tyas Rd CAN/RD E16 141 L6
Tybenham Rd WIM/MER SW19 201 K3
Tyberry Rd EN EN1 80 A7
Tyburn La HRW HA1 114 D5
The Tyburns RBRW/HUT CM13 107 P3
Tyburn Wy MBLAR W1H 10 B7
Tycehurst Hl LOU IG10 82 C8
Tychbourne Dr RGUE GU4 250 F7
Tydcombe Rd WARL CR6 242 B5
Tye Green Village HLWS * CM18 47 J4
Tye La ORP BR6 226 F2
Tyers Ga STHWK SE1 19 J2
Tyers St LBTH SE11 17 N7
Tyers Ter LBTH SE11 17 N8
Tyeshurst Cl ABYW SE2 163 P4
Tyfield Cl CHES/WCR EN8 62 B6
Tylecroft Rd STRHM/NOR SW16 202 F2
Tyle Gn EMPK RM11 125 M3
Tylehost GUW GU2 249 M6
Tylehurst Gdns IL IG1 122 F10
Tyle Pl WDSR SL4 171 M1
Tyler Cl BETH E2 7 L7
Tyler Gdns ADL/WDHM KT15 215 M1
Tyler Rd CRAWE RH10 283 N10
Tylers HARP AL5 20 C2
Tylers Cswy HERT/BAY SG13 42 D8
Tylers Cl GDST RH9 260 A6
KGLGY WD4 54 A5
Tylers Crs HCH RM12 125 K10
Tylersfield ABLGY WD5 54 G7
Tylers Ga KTN/HRWW/W HA3 115 K4
Tylers Green Rd SWLY BR8 208 D6
Tylers Hill Rd CSHM HP5 51 L6
Tylers Rd HLWW/ROY CM19 46 E6
Tyler St GNWCH SE10 161 K4
Tyler Wy BRW CM14 106 G2
Tylney Av NRWD SE19 181 N8
Tylney Cft HLWW/ROY CM19 46 E3
Tylney Rd BMLY BR1 206 A2
FSTGT E7 121 P9
Tynan Cl EBED/NFELT TW14 175 H4
Tyndale La IS N1 6 C3
Tyndale Ter IS N1 6 C3
Tyndall Rd LEY E10 121 H7
WELL DA16 163 J9
Tyne Cl CRAWE RH10 284 D8
UPMR RM14 126 C4
Tynedale LCOL/BKTW AL2 57 L3
Tynedale Cl RDART DA2 188 C4
Tynedale Rd BRKHM/BTCW RH3 273 N4
Tyne Gdns SOCK/AV RM15 146 B9
Tyneham Cl BTSEA * SW11 158 B9
Tyneham Rd BTSEA SW11 158 B8
Tynemouth Cl EHAM E6 142 E8
Tynemouth Dr EN EN1 79 P4
Tynemouth Rd MTCM CR4 180 B10
SEVS/STOTM N15 119 N2
WOOL/PLUM SE18 163 H4
Tynemouth St FUL/PGN SW6 157 M8
Tynemouth Ter
SEVS/STOTM * N15 119 N2
Tyne St WCHPL E1 13 M5
Tynley Gv RGUE GU4 250 A4
Type St BETH E2 140 C4
Typleden Cl HHNE HP2 35 N4
Tyrawley Rd FUL/PGN SW6 157 L7
Tyre La CDALE/KGS * NW9 116 B2
Tyrell Cl HRW HA1 114 D9
Tyrell Gdns WDSR SL4 148 E9
Tyrell Pl BRWN * CM15 107 L2
Tyrells Cl UPMR RM14 126 A7
Tyrone Rd EHAM E6 142 C4
Tyron Wy SCUP DA14 185 H7
Tyrrell Av WELL DA16 185 K1
Tyrrell Rd EDUL SE22 159 P10
Tyrrells Hall Cl GRAYS RM17 168 A5
Tyrrel Wy CDALE/KGS NW9 116 C5
Tyrwhitt Av GUW GU2 249 N6
Tyrwhitt Rd BROCKY SE4 160 F9
Tysea Cl HLWS CM18 47 J4
Tysea Hl ABR/ST RM4 104 G2
Tysea Rd HLWS CM18 47 J4
Tysoe Av PEND EN3 80 E2
Tysoe St CLKNW EC1R 6 A10
Tyson Gdns FSTH * SE23 182 B3
Tyson Rd FSTH SE23 182 B3
Tyssen Pl SOCK/AV RM15 147 H4
Tyssen Rd STNW/STAM * N16 119 N8
Tyssen St HACK E8 7 M1
Tythebarn Cl RGUE GU4 250 E5
Tythebarns La RPLY/SEND GU23 251 K2
Tytherton Rd ARCH N19 118 E8
Tyttenhanger Gn STALE/WH AL4 39 J9

U

Uamvar St POP/IOD E14 140 G7
Uckfield Gv MTCM CR4 202 B1
Uckfield Rd PEND EN3 80 C3
Udall Gdns CRW RM5 104 B7
Udall St WEST SW1P 17 H6
Udney Park Rd TEDD TW11 176 F8

Uffington Rd WLSDN NW10 136 D3
WNWD SE27 181 H7
Ufford Cl KTN/HRWW/W HA3 94 A8
Ufford Rd KTN/HRWW/W HA3 94 A8
Ufford St STHWK SE1 18 B1
Ufton Gv IS N1 7 J3
Ufton Rd IS N1 7 J4
Uhura Sq STNW/STAM * N16 119 M8
Ullathorne Rd
STRHM/NOR SW16 180 D7
Ulleswater Rd PLMGR N13 98 F5
Ulleswater Vls PLMGR * N13 98 F5
Ullin St POP/IOD E14 141 H7
Ullswater Cl BMLY BR1 183 K9
KUTN/CMB * KT2 178 A7
LTWR GU18 212 A6
SL SL1 128 B7
YEAD UB4 132 F4
Ullswater Ct RYLN/HDSTN * HA2 113 P5
Ullswater Crs COUL/CHIP CR5 240 F2
PUT/ROE SW15 178 A7
Ullswater Rd BARN SW13 156 D6
HHS/BOV HP3 36 D8
LTWR GU18 212 A6
WNWD SE27 181 J6
Ullswater Wy HCH RM12 125 H10
Ulstan Cl CTHM CR3 242 F9
Ulster Gdns PLMGR N13 99 K5
Ulster Pl CAMTN NW1 10 E2
Ulundi Rd BKHTH/KID SE3 161 K5
Ulva Rd PUT/ROE SW15 156 G10
Ulverscroft Rd EDUL SE22 181 P1
Ulverston Cl STAL * AL1 38 G6
Ulverston Rd WALTH E17 101 J10
Ulwyn Av BF/WBF KT14 215 P9
Ulysses Rd KIL/WHAMP NW6 117 J10
Umberville Wy SLN SL2 128 E6
Umbria St PUT/ROE SW15 178 D2
Umfreville Rd FSBYPK N4 119 J4
Underacres Cl HHNE HP2 36 B5
Undercliff Rd LEW SE13 160 F9
Underhill BAR EN5 77 K9
Underhill Ct BAR * EN5 77 K9
Underhill Park Rd REIG RH2 257 K7
Underhill Rd EDUL SE22 181 P1
Underhill St CAMTN NW1 4 F6
Underne Av STHGT/OAK N14 98 C3
Undershaft HDTCH EC3A 13 J6
Undershaw Rd BMLY BR1 183 K6
Underwood Ct CTHM CR3 241 N10
Underwood Rd CHING E4 100 G6
CTHM CR3 259 M1
WCHPL E1 13 N2
WFD IG8 102 A8
Underwood Rw IS N1 6 F9
Underwood St IS N1 6 F9
The Underwood ELTH/MOT SE9 184 C5
Undine Rd POP/IOD E14 160 G3
Undine St TOOT SW17 180 A8
Uneeda Dr GFD/PVL UB6 134 C3
Unicorn Wk GRH DA9 188 E1
Union Cl WAN E11 121 J9
Union Ct CLAP SW4 158 F8
Union Dr WCHPL * E1 140 D6
Union Gn HHNE HP2 35 N5
Union Gv VX/NE SW8 158 E8
Union Rd ALP/SUD HA0 135 K1
CLAP SW4 158 E8
CROY/NA CR0 203 K7
FBAR/BDGN N11 98 E7
HAYES BR2 206 A5
NTHLT UB5 133 P4
Union Sq IS N1 6 E6
Union St BAR EN5 77 H8
KUT KT1 199 J2
SRTFD E15 141 J3
STHWK SE1 12 D10
Union Wk BETH E2 7 L9
Unity Cl CROY/NA CR0 224 G5
WLSDN NW10 136 D1
WNWD SE27 181 K8
Unity Ms CAMTN NW1 5 J7
Unity Rd PEND EN3 80 B3
Unity Wy WOOL/PLUM SE18 162 A2
University Campus GUW GU2 249 N10
University Cl BUSH WD23 73 N8
CDALE/KGS NW9 96 C8
University Gdns BXLY DA5 186 A3
University Rd WIM/MER SW19 179 N9
University St FITZ W1T 11 H2
University Wy DART DA1 165 L9
EHAM E6 142 D9
Unstead La SHGR GU5 267 P10
Unwin Av EBED/NFELT TW14 174 E1
Unwin Cl PECK SE15 19 N10
Unwin Rd ISLW TW7 154 D9
SKENS SW7 15 M3
Upbrook Ms BAY/PAD W2 9 K6
Upcerne Rd WBPTN SW10 157 M6
Upcroft WDSR SL4 148 G9
Upcroft Av EDGW HA8 95 P6
Updale Cl POTB/CUF EN6 59 H9
Updale Rd SCUP DA14 185 J7
Updown Hl BFOR GU20 212 C3
Upfield CROY/NA CR0 204 A9
HORL RH6 280 B5
Upfield Cl HORL RH6 280 B6
Upfield Rd HNWL W7 134 E6
Upfolds Gn RGUE GU4 250 F6
Uphall Rd IL IG1 122 E10
Upham Park Rd CHSWK W4 156 B3
Uphill Dr CDALE/KGS NW9 115 P3
MLHL NW7 96 B6
Uphill Gv MLHL NW7 96 B5
Uphill Rd MLHL NW7 96 B5
Upland Av CSHM HP5 50 G4
Upland Court Rd HARH RM3 105 N10
Upland Dr BRKMPK AL9 59 L1
Upland Rd BELMT SM2 221 N4
BXLYHN DA7 164 A9
CTHM CR3 242 F6
EDUL SE22 181 P3
EPP CM16 64 G1
PLSTW E13 141 M6
SAND/SEL CR2 223 L2
Uplands ASHTD KT21 237 J6
BECK BR3 204 F2
RKW/CH/CXG WD3 72 A10
WARE SG12 26 E1
WGCW AL8 22 F1
Uplands Av WALTH E17 120 C1
Uplands Cl CFSP/GDCR SL9 110 B6
MORT/ESHN SW14 177 N1
Uplands Dr LHD/OX KT22 218 C10
Uplands Park Rd ENC/FH EN2 79 H6
Uplands Rd CEND/HSY/T N8 118 G3
CHDH RM6 123 N1
EBAR EN4 98 B2
ORP BR6 207 L8
PUR/KEN CR8 241 K3
WFD IG8 102 B8
The Uplands CFSP/GDCR SL9 110 B6
LCOL/BKTW AL2 55 M6
LOU IG10 82 C7
RSLP HA4 113 H6
Uplands Wy SEV TN13 246 G9
WCHMH N21 79 H9
Upland Wy EPSOM KT18 238 F4
Upminster Rd HCH RM12 125 N7
Upminster Rd North RAIN RM13 145 K5
Upminster Rd South RAIN RM13 145 H6
Upney Cl HCH RM12 125 K10
Upney La BARK IG11 143 J2
Upnor Wy WALW SE17 19 K7
Uppark Dr GNTH/NBYPK IG2 122 F4
Upper Abbey Rd BELV DA17 164 A3
Upper Addison Gdns WKENS W14 14 A1
Upper Ashlyns Rd BERK HP4 33 N6
Upper Austin Lodge Rd EYN DA4 229 L2
Upper Bardsey Wk IS N1 6 F1
Upper Barn HHS/BOV HP3 36 A9
Upper Belgrave St KTBR SW1X 16 D3
Upper Belmont Rd CSHM HP5 50 G4
Upper Berenger Wk
WBPTN * SW10 157 N6
Upper Berkeley St BAY/PAD W2 10 A6
Upper Beulah Hl NRWD SE19 203 M1
Upper Blantyre Wk
WBPTN * SW10 157 N6
Upper Bourne End La HHW HP1 34 E10
Upper Brentwood Rd GPK RM2 125 K2
Upper Bridge Rd REDH RH1 257 P10
Upper Brighton Rd SURB KT6 199 J6
Upper Brockley Rd BROCKY SE4 160 E8
Upper Brook St MYFR/PKLN W1K 10 C7
Upper Butts BTFD TW8 155 H5
Upper Caldy Wk IS N1 6 F2
Upper Camelford Wk
NTGHL * W11 8 A6
Upper Cheyne Rw CHEL SW3 15 N10
Upper Clabdens WARE SG12 26 E2
Upper Clapton Rd CLPT E5 120 A7
Upper Clarendon Wk
NTGHL * W11 8 A6
Upper Cornsland BRW CM14 107 J4
Upper Court Rd CTHM CR3 242 F9
HOR/WEW KT19 219 P7
Upper Culver Rd STAL AL1 38 D4
Upper Dagnall St
STALW/RED * AL3 38 C6
Upper Dartrey Wk
WBPTN * SW10 157 M6
Upper Dengie Wk IS * N1 6 E5
Upper Dr BEAC HP9 88 C6
BH/WHM TN16 243 P4
Upper Dunnymans BNSTD SM7 221 J10
Upper Edgeborough Rd GU GU1 268 C1
Upper Elmers End Rd BECK BR3 204 D4
Upper Fairfield Rd LHD/OX KT22 236 G7
Upper Farm Rd E/WMO/HCT KT8 197 N4
Upperfield Rd WGCE AL7 23 J6
Upper Forecourt HORL RH6 280 C8
Upper George St CSHM HP5 51 H6
Upper Gladstone Rd CSHM * HP5 51 H6
Upper Gn East MTCM CR4 202 A2
Upper Gn West MTCM CR4 202 A2
Upper Grosvenor St
MYFR/PKLN W1K 10 C8
Upper Grotto Rd TWK TW1 176 E5
Upper Gnd STHWK SE1 12 A9
Upper Gv SNWD SE25 203 M4
Upper Grove Rd BELV DA17 164 A5
Upper Guildown Rd GUW GU2 267 N3
Upper Gulland Wk IS * N1 6 F3
Upper Halliford Rd SHPTN TW17 196 F2
Upper Hall Pk BERK HP4 34 B7
Upper Ham Rd
RCHPK/HAM TW10 177 J7
Upper Handa Wk IS N1 6 G1
Upper Harestone CTHM CR3 259 P3
Upper Harley St CAMTN NW1 10 D2
Upper Hawkwell Wk IS * N1 6 F5
Upper Heath Rd STAL AL1 38 E4
Upper High St EW KT17 220 B9
Upper Hwy ABLGY WD5 54 D8
Upper Hill Ri RKW/CH/CXG WD3 71 L10
Upper Hitch OXHEY WD19 93 M2
Upper Holly Hill Rd BELV DA17 164 C4
Upper Hook HLWS CM18 47 J3
Upper John St REGST W1B 11 H7
Upper Kiln DORK * RH4 273 H4
Upper Lattimore Rd STAL AL1 38 D6
Upper Lees Rd SLN SL2 128 F5
Upper Lismore Wk IS N1 6 F2
Upper Ldg KENS * W8 9 H10
Upper Ml HMSMTH W6 156 E4
Upper Manor Rd RGODL GU7 267 K10
Upper Marlborough Rd STAL AL1 38 D6
Upper Marsh STHWK SE1 17 P3
Upper Marsh La HOD EN11 44 F4
Upper Meadow CSHM HP5 50 G6
Upper Mealines HLWS CM18 47 K4
Upper Montagu St MBLAR W1H 10 B4
Upper Mulgrave Rd BELMT SM2 221 H4
Upper North St POP/IOD E14 140 F7
Upper Paddock Rd OXHEY WD19 73 M10
Upper Pk HLW CM20 28 E10
LOU IG10 82 A9
Upper Park Rd BELV DA17 164 C3
BMLY BR1 205 N1
FBAR/BDGN N11 98 C6
HAMP NW3 4 A1
KUTN/CMB KT2 177 M9
Upper Pth DORK * RH4 273 H4
Upper Phillimore Gdns KENS W8 14 E2
Upper Pillory Down CAR SM5 222 B9
Upper Pines BNSTD SM7 240 A3
Upper Rainham Rd HCH RM12 124 G9
Upper Ramsey Wk IS N1 6 G2
Upper Rawreth Wk IS * N1 6 F5
Upper Richmond Rd
PUT/ROE SW15 156 E10
Upper Richmond Rd West
RCHPK/HAM TW10 155 M10
Upper Rd DEN/HRF UB9 110 G5
PLSTW E13 141 M5
WLGTN SM6 222 E2
Upper Rose Hl DORK RH4 272 G3
Upper Ryle BRW CM14 106 G1
Upper St Martin's La
LSQ/SEVD WC2H 11 L6
Upper Sales HHW HP1 35 J7
Upper Sawleywood
BNSTD SM7 221 J10
Upper Selsdon Rd
SAND/SEL CR2 223 N5
Upper Sheppey Wk IS N1 6 F2
Upper Sheridan Rd BELV DA17 164 B3
Upper Shirley Rd CROY/NA CR0 204 B10
Upper Shot WGCE AL7 23 K4
Upper Shott CHESW EN7 61 N2
Upper Sq ISLW TW7 154 F9
Upper Stanford Rd
CHOB/PIR GU24 248 E1
Upper Station Rd RAD WD7 74 F1
Upper Stonyfield
HLWW/ROY CM19 46 E1
Upper St IS N1 6 B7
SHGR GU5 270 A4
Upper Sunbury Rd HPTN TW12 197 N1
Upper Sutton La HEST TW5 153 P7
Upper Swaines EPP CM16 65 J6
Upper Tachbrook St PIM SW1V 17 H5
Upper Tail OXHEY WD19 93 M4
Upper Talbot Wk NTGHL W11 8 A6
Upper Teddington Rd KUT KT1 199 H1
Upper Ter HAMP NW3 117 M8
Upper Thames St BLKFR EC4V 12 E7
Upper Tollington Pk FSBYPK N4 119 H6
Upperton Rd GUW GU2 267 P1
SCUP DA14 185 J8
Upperton Rd East PLSTW E13 141 P5
Upperton Rd West PLSTW E13 141 P5
Upper Tooting Pk TOOT SW17 180 A5
Upper Tooting Rd TOOT SW17 180 A7
Upper Town Rd GFD/PVL UB6 134 A6
Upper Tulse Hl
BRXS/STRHM SW2 180 G3
Upper Vernon Rd SUT SM1 221 N2
Upper Village Rd ASC SL5 192 B5
Upper Wk VW GU25 194 B4
Upper Walthamstow Rd
WALTH E17 121 J2
Upper West St REIG RH2 257 J10
Upper Whistler Wk
WBPTN * SW10 157 M6
Upper Wickham La WELL DA16 163 L8
Upper Wimpole St
CAVSQ/HST W1G 10 D3
Upper Woburn Pl CAMTN NW1 5 K10
Upper Woodcote Village
PUR/KEN CR8 222 E9
Uppingham Av STAN HA7 115 H1
Upsdell Av PLMGR N13 99 H7
Upshire Rd WAB EN9 63 L8
Upshott La WOKS/MYFD GU22 233 J3
Upstall St CMBW SE5 159 J7
Upton WOKN/KNAP GU21 231 N3
Upton Av FSTGT E7 141 M2
STALW/RED AL3 38 C5
Upton Cl BXLY DA5 186 A2
LCOL/BKTW AL2 56 C1
SL SL1 149 L2
Upton Court Rd DTCH/LGLY SL3 149 M2
Upton Dene BELMT SM2 221 L4
Upton Gdns KTN/HRWW/W HA3 115 H4
Upton La FSTGT E7 141 N1
Upton Lea Pde SLN * SL2 129 N9
Upton Lodge Cl BUSH WD23 94 B1
Upton Pk SL SL1 149 K2
Upton Park Rd FSTGT E7 141 N2
Upton Rd BXLYHS DA6 163 P10
DTCH/LGLY SL3 149 M2
HSLW TW3 153 P9
THHTH CR7 203 L2
UED N18 99 P6
WATW WD18 73 J8
WOOL/PLUM SE18 162 F5
Upton Rd South BXLY DA5 186 A2
Upway CFSP/GDCR SL9 90 C9
NFNCH/WDSP N12 97 P8
Upwood Rd LEE/GVPK SE12 183 M2
STRHM/NOR SW16 202 F1
Uranus Rd HHNE HP2 35 P4
Urban Av HCH RM12 125 K8
Urlwin St CMBW SE5 18 E10
Urlwin Wk BRXN/ST SW9 159 H7
Urmston Dr WIM/MER SW19 179 H4
Ursula Ms FSBYPK N4 119 J6
Ursula St BTSEA SW11 157 P7
Urswick Rd CLPT E5 120 B10
DAGW RM9 143 P2
Usborne Ms VX/NE SW8 158 G6
Usher Rd BOW E3 140 E3
Usherwood Cl
KWD/TDW/WH KT20 255 P7
Usk Rd BTSEA SW11 157 M10
SOCK/AV RM15 146 B8
Usk St BETH E2 140 C5
Uvedale Cl CROY/NA CR0 225 J7
Uvedale Crs CROY/NA CR0 225 J7
Uvedale Rd DAGE RM10 124 B8
ENC/FH EN2 79 L9
OXTED RH8 261 L5
Uverdale Rd WBPTN SW10 157 M6
Uxbridge Rd DTCH/LGLY SL3 130 B7
EA W5 135 K9
FELT TW13 175 L5
HGDN/ICK UB10 132 C6
HPTN TW12 175 P7
RKW/CH/CXG WD3 91 L2
SL SL1 149 M1
SLN SL2 129 P9
SURB KT6 199 J4
YEAD UB4 133 H8
Uxbridge Rd (Harrow Weald)
KTN/HRWW/W HA3 94 A8
Uxbridge Rd (Hatch End) PIN HA5 93 M9
Uxbridge Rd (High St)
STHL UB1 133 N10
Uxbridge Rd (Pinner)
PIN HA5 93 L10
Uxbridge Rd (Stanmore)
STAN HA7 94 E7
Uxbridge Rd (The Broadway)
YEAD UB4 133 L9
Uxbridge St KENS W8 8 E9
Uxendon Crs WBLY HA9 115 K6
Uxendon Hl WBLY HA9 115 L6

V

Vache La CSTG HP8 89 P3
Vache Ms CSTG * HP8 90 A1
Vaillant Rd WEY KT13 216 D1
Valance Av CHING E4 101 L2
Valan Leas HAYES BR2 205 K3
Vale Av BORE WD6 75 N9
Vale Cl BRWN CM15 86 E9
CFSP/GDCR SL9 90 A9
COUL/CHIP CR5 222 F10
EFNCH N2 118 A1
MV/WKIL W9 3 J10
ORP BR6 226 D1
TWK * TW1 176 F6
WEY KT13 196 E10
WOKN/KNAP GU21 232 B2
Vale Cottages PUT/ROE * SW15 178 B6
Vale Ct ACT * W3 136 C10
STALE/WH AL4 21 J4
WEY KT13 196 E10
Vale Crs PUT/ROE SW15 178 B7
Vale Cft ESH/CLAY KT10 218 E4
PIN HA5 113 M3
Vale Dr BAR EN5 77 J8
Vale End EDUL SE22 159 N10
Vale Farm Rd WOKN/KNAP GU21 232 A3
Vale Gv ACT W3 136 A10
FSBYPK N4 119 K5
SL SL1 149 K2
Vale La ACT W3 135 M7
Valence Av BCTR RM8 123 N6
Valence Circ BCTR RM8 123 N8
Valence Dr CHESW EN7 61 P4
Valence Rd ERITH DA8 164 E6
Valence Wood Rd BCTR RM8 123 N8
Valencia Rd STAN HA7 95 H5
Valency Cl NTHWD HA6 92 G5
Valentia Pl BRXN/ST SW9 159 H10
Valentine Av BXLY DA5 185 P5
Valentine Pl STHWK SE1 18 C1
Valentine Rd HOM * E9 140 C1
RYLN/HDSTN HA2 114 A8
Valentines Rd IL IG1 122 E6
Valentines Wy DAGE RM10 124 F7
Valentine Wy CSTG HP8 90 A4
Valentyne Cl CROY/NA CR0 225 K7
Vale of Health HAMP NW3 117 M8
Valerian Wy SRTFD E15 141 K5
Valerie Cl STAL AL1 38 G6
Vale Ri CSHM HP5 51 H4
GLDGN NW11 117 J6
Vale Rd BMLY BR1 206 D2
BUSH WD23 73 M9
CSHM HP5 51 H3
DART DA1 187 J4
ESH/CLAY KT10 218 D5
FSBYPK N4 119 K5
FSTGT E7 141 N1
GVW DA11 190 B4
HOR/WEW KT19 220 C1
MTCM CR4 202 E3
SUT SM1 221 L1
WDSR SL4 148 F3
WEY KT13 196 E10
WPK KT4 200 C10
Vale Rd North SURB KT6 199 K9
Vale Royal HOLWY N7 5 L4
Valeside HERT/WAS SG14 25 H6
Valeswood Rd BMLY BR1 183 L8
Vale Ter FSBYPK N4 119 K4
The Vale ACT W3 136 A10
BRW CM14 107 H2
CFSP/GDCR SL9 90 A9
CHEL SW3 15 L9
COUL/CHIP CR5 222 F10
CRICK NW2 116 G8
CROY/NA CR0 204 C9
EBED/NFELT TW14 175 J2
HEST TW5 153 M5
MUSWH N10 98 B9
RSLP HA4 113 K9
STHGT/OAK N14 98 F1
SUN * TW16 175 H9
WFD IG8 101 M8
Valetta Gv PLSTW E13 141 M4
Valetta Rd ACT W3 156 B1
Valette St HACK * E8 140 A1
Valiant Cl NTHLT UB5 133 L5
ROMW/RG RM7 104 B10
Valiant Wy EHAM E6 142 C7
Vallance Pl HARP AL5 20 B4
Vallance Rd BETH E2 7 P10
WDGN N22 98 D10
Vallentin Rd WALTH E17 121 H2
Valley Av NFNCH/WDSP N12 97 N5
Valley Cl DART DA1 186 G2
HERT/BAY SG13 25 L6
LOU IG10 82 C10
PIN HA5 93 J10
WAB EN9 63 H8
WARE SG12 26 A1
Valley Dr CDALE/KGS NW9 115 N3
GVE DA12 190 G6
SEV TN13 265 J1
Valley End DTCH/LGLY SL3 129 P6
Valley End Rd CHOB/PIR GU24 212 G3
Valleyfield Rd STRHM/NOR SW16 180 G8
Valley Fields Crs ENC/FH EN2 79 H6
Valley Gdns ALP/SUD HA0 135 L2
GRH DA9 188 G2
WIM/MER SW19 179 N10
The Valley Gn WGCW AL8 22 F4
Valley Gv CHARL SE7 161 P4
Valley Hl LOU IG10 82 C10
LOU IG10 102 B1
Valley Pk WATW * WD18 92 D1
Valley Ri GSTN WD25 55 J9
STALE/WH AL4 20 E1
Valley Rd BERK HP4 33 L3
DART DA1 186 G2
ERITH DA8 164 D3
HART DA3 210 G8
HAYES BR2 205 K2
HGDN/ICK UB10 131 P4
PUR/KEN CR8 241 L1
RKW/CH/CXG WD3 71 K9
STALW/RED AL3 38 D2
STMC/STPC BR5 207 L1
STRHM/NOR SW16 180 G7
WGCW AL8 22 E5
Valley Side CHING E4 100 F2
Valleyside HHW HP1 35 J6
Valley Vw BAR EN5 77 H10
BH/WHM TN16 243 P4
CHESW EN7 61 K4
CSHM HP5 50 F5
GRH DA9 188 G2
Valley View Gdns PUR/KEN CR8 241 M1
Valley View Ter EYN * DA4 209 N8
Valley Wk CROY/NA CR0 204 B9
RKW/CH/CXG WD3 72 D9
Valley Wy CFSP/GDCR SL9 109 P4
Valliere Rd WLSDN NW10 136 D5
Valliers Wood Rd BFN/LL DA15 184 G4
Vallis Wy CHSGTN KT9 219 J1
WEA W13 134 F7
Valmar Rd CMBW SE5 159 K7
Valnay St TOOT SW17 180 A8
Valognes Av WALTH E17 100 D9
Valonia Gdns WAND/EARL SW18 179 J2
Vambery Rd WOOL/PLUM SE18 162 F5
Vanbrough Crs NTHLT UB5 133 K4
Vanbrugh Cl CRAWW RH11 283 H10
Vanbrugh Dr WOT/HER KT12 197 K7
Vanbrugh Flds BKHTH/KID SE3 161 L5
Vanbrugh Hl GNWCH SE10 161 K4
Vanbrugh Pk BKHTH/KID SE3 161 L6
Vanbrugh Park Rd
BKHTH/KID SE3 161 L6
Vanbrugh Park Rd West
BKHTH/KID SE3 161 L6
Vanbrugh Rd CHSWK W4 156 A2
Vanbrugh Ter BKHTH/KID SE3 161 L7
Vanburgh Cl CAN/RD E16 142 A7
ORP BR6 207 H8
Vancouver Cl HOR/WEW KT19 219 P7
Vancouver Ct HORL RH6 281 H4
Vancouver Dr CRAWW RH11 283 N4
Vancouver Man EDGW * HA8 95 N9
Vancouver Rd EDGW HA8 95 N9
FSTH SE23 182 D5
RCHPK/HAM TW10 177 H7
YEAD UB4 133 J6
Vanda Crs STAL AL1 38 E7
Vanderbilt Rd WAND/EARL SW18 179 L4
Vanderbilt Vls SHB * W12 156 G1
Vandome Cl CAN/RD E16 141 N8
Vandon St STJSPK SW1H 17 H3
Van Dyck Av NWMAL KT3 200 A7
Vandyke Cl PUT/ROE SW15 178 G2
REDH RH1 258 A8
Vandyke Cross ELTH/MOT SE9 184 B1
Vandy St SDTCH EC2A 13 J2
Vane Cl HAMP NW3 117 N10
KTN/HRWW/W HA3 115 L4
Vanessa Cl BELV DA17 164 B4
Vanessa Wk GVE DA12 191 J8
Vanessa Wy BXLY DA5 186 E6
Vanguard CDALE/KGS * NW9 96 B8
Vanguard Cl CAN/RD E16 141 M7
CROY/NA CR0 203 J8
ROMW/RG RM7 104 C10
Vanguard St DEPT SE8 160 F7
Vanguard Wy CROY/NA CR0 223 N1
EDEN TN8 262 D10
HTHAIR TW6 152 F8
OXTED RH8 261 L1
OXTED RH8 262 A2
WARL CR6 224 E9
WLGTN SM6 222 F4
Vanneck Sq PUT/ROE * SW15 178 D1
Vanners CRAWE RH10 283 P6
Vanners Pde BF/WBF * KT14 215 P9
Vanoc Gdns BMLY BR1 183 M7
Vanquisher Wk GVE DA12 191 J6
Vansittart Est WDSR SL4 149 H7
Vansittart Rd FSTGT E7 121 M9
WDSR SL4 148 G7
Vansittart St NWCR SE14 160 D6
Vanston Pl FUL/PGN SW6 157 K6
Vantorts Cl SBW CM21 29 P1
Vantorts Rd SBW CM21 29 P2
Vant Rd TOOT SW17 180 A8
Vapery La CHOB/PIR GU24 230 C7
Varcoe Rd BERM/RHTH SE16 160 A4
Vardens Rd BTSEA SW11 157 N10
Varden St WCHPL E1 140 A8
Varley Rd CAN/RD E16 141 N8
Varley Wy MTCM CR4 201 N2
Varna Rd FUL/PGN SW6 157 H6
HPTN * TW12 198 A1
Varndell St CAMTN NW1 4 G9
Varney Cl CHESW EN7 61 P3
HHW HP1 35 J6
Varney Rd HHW HP1 35 J6
Varsity Dr ISLW * TW7 176 E1
Varsity Rw MORT/ESHN SW14 155 P8
Vartry Rd SEVS/STOTM N15 119 M4
Vassall Rd BRXN/ST SW9 159 H6
Vauban Est BERM/RHTH SE16 19 M4
Vauban St BERM/RHTH SE16 19 M4
Vaughan Av HCH RM12 125 L9
HDN NW4 116 D3
HMSMTH W6 156 C3
Vaughan Est BETH * E2 7 L9
Vaughan Gdns IL IG1 122 C5
WDSR SL4 148 E3
Vaughan Rd CMBW SE5 159 K8
HARP AL5 20 A2
HRW HA1 114 B5
SRTFD E15 141 L1
THDIT KT7 198 G7
WELL DA16 163 J8
Vaughan St BERM/RHTH SE16 160 E1
Vaughan Wy DORK RH4 272 F2
SLN SL2 128 D6
WAP E1W 13 P8
Vaughan Williams Cl DEPT SE8 160 F6
Vaux Crs WOT/HER KT12 217 J3
Vauxhall Br LBTH SE11 17 L8
Vauxhall Bridge Rd PIM SW1V 16 G4
Vauxhall Cl GVW DA11 190 C3
Vauxhall Gdns SAND/SEL CR2 223 K3
Vauxhall Gv VX/NE SW8 17 M9
Vauxhall Pl DART DA1 187 M3
Vauxhall Rd HHNE HP2 36 B6
Vauxhall St LBTH SE11 17 P7
Vauxhall Wk LBTH SE11 17 N7
Vawdrey Cl WCHPL E1 140 B6
Veals Md MTCM CR4 201 P1
Vectis Gdns TOOT SW17 180 C9
Vectis Rd TOOT SW17 180 C9
Veda Rd LEW SE13 160 F10
Vega Crs NTHWD HA6 92 G6
Vegal Crs EGH TW20 171 P8
Vega Rd BUSH WD23 94 B1
Veldene Wy RYLN/HDSTN HA2 113 N8
Velizy Av HLW CM20 28 G10
Vellum Dr CAR SM5 202 B10
Venables Cl DAGE RM10 124 C9
Venables St STJWD NW8 9 M2
Vencourt Pl HMSMTH W6 156 D4
Venetian Rd CMBW SE5 159 K8
Venetia Rd EA W5 155 J1
FSBYPK N4 119 J4
Venette Cl RAIN RM13 145 J7
Venner Rd SYD SE26 182 B9
Venners Cl BXLYHN DA7 164 F8
Venn St CLAP SW4 158 D10
Ventnor Av STAN HA7 94 G9
Ventnor Dr NFNCH/WDSP N12 97 L4
Ventnor Gdns BARK IG11 143 H1
Ventnor Rd BELMT SM2 221 L4
NWCR SE14 160 C6
Ventnor Ter SEVS/STOTM * N15 119 P2
Venton Cl WOKN/KNAP GU21 231 N3
Ventura Pk LCOL/BKTW AL2 56 E5
Venture Cl BXLY DA5 185 P3
Venue St POP/IOD E14 140 G7
Venus Hl HHS/BOV HP3 52 D7
Venus Rd WOOL/PLUM SE18 162 C2
Veny Crs HCH RM12 125 L10
Vera Av WCHMH N21 79 H9
Vera Ct OXHEY WD19 93 L1
Vera Lynn Cl FSTGT E7 121 M9
Vera Rd FUL/PGN SW6 157 H7
Verbena Cl CAN/RD E16 141 K6

SOCK/AV RM15 147 H8
WDR/YW UB7 151 N4
Verbena Gdns HMSMTH W6 156 D4
Ver-Colne Valley Wk BUSH WD23 73 L7
HHS/BOV HP3 52 A4
STAL AL1 38 D7
Verdant La CAT SE6 183 K4
Verdayne Av CROY/NA CR0 204 C8
Verdayne Gdns WARL CR6 242 B2
Verderers Rd CHIG IG7 103 K6
Verdun Rd BARN SW13 156 D6
WOOL/PLUM SE18 163 K5
Verdure Cl GSTN WD25 55 M8
Vereker Dr SUN TW16 197 H3
Vereker Rd WKENS W14 14 B8
Vere Rd LOU IG10 82 F8
Vere St MHST W1U 10 E6
Verity Cl NTGHL W11 8 A7
Veritys HAT AL10 40 D4
Verlum Cl WGCE AL7 23 J5
Vermont Cl ENC/FH EN2 79 J8
Vermont Rd NRWD SE19 181 L9
SLN SL2 128 D6
SUT SM1 201 L10
WAND/EARL SW18 179 L2
Verney Cl BERK HP4 33 L4
Verney Gdns DAGW RM9 123 P9
Verney Rd BERM/RHTH SE16 160 A4
DAGW RM9 123 P10
DTCH/LGLY SL3 150 D3
Verney St WLSDN NW10 116 A8
Verney Wy BERM/RHTH SE16 160 A4
Vernham Rd WOOL/PLUM SE18 162 F5
Vernon Av MNPK E12 122 C9
PEND EN3 80 D2
RYNPK SW20 200 C2
WFD IG8 101 N7
Vernon Cl CHERT KT16 214 G3
HOR/WEW KT19 219 P3
STMC/STPC BR5 207 L3
Vernon Crs EBAR EN4 78 B9
RBRW/HUT CM13 107 M4
Vernon Dr CTHM CR3 241 K8
DEN/HRF UB9 91 M9
STAN HA7 94 F9
Vernon Pl BMSBY WC1N 11 M4
Vernon Ri FSBYW WC1X 5 P9
NTHLT UB5 114 C10
Vernon Rd BOW E3 140 E4
BUSH WD23 73 M9
CEND/HSY/T * N8 119 H1
CRW RM5 104 D6
FELT TW13 174 G5
GDMY/SEVK IG3 123 J6
MORT/ESHN SW14 156 A9
SRTFD E15 141 K2
SUT SM1 221 M2
SWCM DA10 189 L2
WALTH E17 120 E2
WAN E11 121 K6
Vernon's Cl STAL AL1 38 D7
Vernon Sq FSBYW * WC1X 5 P9
Vernon St WKENS W14 14 A6
Vernon Wk KWD/TDW/WH KT20 238 G6
Vernon Wy GUW GU2 249 L9
Vernon Yd NTGHL W11 8 C7
Veroan Rd BXLYHN DA7 163 P8
Verona Cl UX/CGN UB8 131 M8
Verona Dr SURB KT6 199 K9
Verona Gdns GVE DA12 191 H7
Veronica Cl HARH RM3 105 K8
Veronica Gdns MTCM CR4 202 D1
Veronica Rd TOOT SW17 180 C6
Veronique Gdns
GNTH/NBYPK IG2 122 F3
Verralls WOKS/MYFD GU22 232 E3
Verran Rd BAL * SW12 180 C3
Ver Rd STALW/RED AL3 38 B6
Versailles Rd PGE/AN SE20 181 P10
Verulam Av PUR/KEN CR8 222 D8
WALTH E17 120 E5
Verulam Ct CDALE/KGS * NW9 116 D5
Verulam Rd GFD/PVL UB6 133 P6
STALW/RED AL3 38 A5
Verulam St FSBYW WC1X 12 A3
Verwood Dr EBAR EN4 78 A7
Verwood Rd RYLN/HDSTN HA2 94 B10
Veryan WOKN/KNAP GU21 231 M3
Veryan Cl STMC/STPC BR5 207 M4
Vespan Rd SHB W12 156 D1
Vesta Av STAL AL1 38 B9
Vesta Rd BROCKY SE4 160 D8
Vestris Rd FSTH SE23 182 C5
Vestry Rd CMBW SE5 159 M7
RSEV TN14 247 J5
WALTH E17 120 G3
Vestry St IS N1 6 G9
Vevers Rd REIG RH2 275 L3
Vevey St FSTH SE23 182 E5
Vexil Cl PUR RM19 166 C3
Veysey Cl HHW HP1 35 L8
Viaduct Pl BETH E2 140 A5
Viaduct Rd EFNCH N2 97 N10
WARE SG12 26 D3
Viaduct St BETH E2 140 A5
Viaduct Ter EYN * DA4 210 B2
The Viaduct MUSWH * N10 118 C2
SWFD E18 101 M10
Viaduct Wy WGCE AL7 23 J2
Vian Av PEND EN3 80 D1
Vian St LEW SE13 160 G9
Via Romana GVE DA12 191 L4
Vibart Gdns BRXS/STRHM SW2 180 G3
Vibart Wk IS N1 5 M5
Vibia Cl STWL/WRAY TW19 173 N3
Viburnum Ct CHOB/PIR GU24 212 D9
Vicarage Av EGH TW20 172 E9
Vicarage Cswy HERT/BAY SG13 26 A7
Vicarage Cl BEAC HP9 89 H7
BRW CM14 106 D5
ERITH DA8 164 D5
GT/LBKH KT23 253 P1
HHW HP1 35 M8
KWD/TDW/WH KT20 239 H10
NTHLT UB5 133 N3
POTB/CUF EN6 60 A6
RSLP HA4 112 E5
STAL AL1 38 B9
WPK KT4 200 B8
Vicarage Ct BECK * BR3 204 D3
EGH TW20 172 E9
Vicarage Crs BTSEA SW11 157 N7
EGH TW20 172 E8
Vicarage Dr BARK IG11 142 F2
BECK BR3 204 F1
GVW DA11 189 P2
MORT/ESHN SW14 178 A1
Vicarage Farm Rd HEST TW5 153 M7
Vicarage Flds WOT/HER KT12 197 K6
Vicarage Gdns BERK HP4 34 E2
KENS * W8 14 F1
MTCM CR4 201 P3
Vicarage Ga GUW GU2 267 M2
KENS W8 8 G10
Vicarage Gate Ms
KWD/TDW/WH * KT20 239 H10
Vicarage Gv CMBW SE5 159 L7
Vicarage Hl BH/WHM TN16 262 G2
Vicarage La CHIG IG7 102 G4
EHAM E6 142 C5
EPP CM16 48 C10
GVE DA12 191 K5
HHS/BOV HP3 52 E2
HORL RH6 280 A3
IL IG1 122 G6
KGLGY WD4 54 A5
LHD/OX KT22 236 G8
RPLY/SEND GU23 250 F2
SRTFD E15 141 K1
STA TW18 195 L3
STWL/WRAY TW19 172 B4
Vicarage Ms CHSWK * W4 156 B5
Vicarage Pde SEVS/STOTM * N15 119 K2
Vicarage Pk WOOL/PLUM SE18 162 F4
Vicarage Rd BERK HP4 34 D2
BXLY DA5 186 C4
CHOB/PIR GU24 213 J7
CRAWE RH10 285 P6
CROY/NA CR0 203 H10
DAGE RM10 144 C2
E/WMO/HCT KT8 199 H1
EGH TW20 172 E8
EPP CM16 65 M5
HCH RM12 125 H6
HDN NW4 116 D4
LEY E10 120 G5
MORT/ESHN SW14 177 P1
SRTFD E15 141 L2
STA TW18 173 H6
SUN TW16 174 G8
SUT SM1 221 K1
TEDD TW11 176 F8
TOTM N17 99 P8
WARE SG12 26 D2
WATW WD18 73 J8
WFD IG8 102 B8
WHTN TW2 176 D5
WHTN TW2 176 B2
WOKS/MYFD GU22 232 C7
WOOL/PLUM SE18 162 F4
Vicarage Sq GRAYS RM17 167 M5
Vicarage Wk BTSEA * SW11 157 N7
Vicarage Wy CFSP/GDCR SL9 110 C4
DTCH/LGLY SL3 150 G6
RYLN/HDSTN HA2 113 P5
WLSDN NW10 116 A8
Vicarage Wd HLW CM20 29 J10
Vicars Bridge Cl ALP/SUD HA0 135 K4
Vicar's Cl EN EN1 79 M6
HACK E8 140 B3
SRTFD E15 141 M3
Vicars Hl LEW SE13 160 G10
Vicar's Moor La WCHMH N21 99 H1
Vicars Oak Rd NRWD SE19 181 M9
Vicar's Rd KTTN NW5 118 B10
Viceroy Cl EFNCH * N2 117 P2
Viceroy Pde EFNCH * N2 117 P1
Viceroy Rd VX/NE SW8 158 F7
Vickers Cl CROY/NA CR0 222 G4
Vickers Dr (North) WEY KT13 215 P6
Vickers Dr North WEY KT13 215 P6
Vickers Dr South WEY KT13 215 P7
Vickers Rd ERITH DA8 164 E4
Victor Ap HCH RM12 125 L6
Victor Cl HCH RM12 125 L6
Victor Gdns HCH RM12 125 L6
Victor Gv ALP/SUD HA0 135 K2
Victoria Ar PIM SW1V 16 F4
Victoria Av CAR SM5 202 B10
CDH/CHF RM16 167 P1
CRW RM5 104 C7
E/WMO/HCT KT8 198 A3
EHAM E6 142 A3
FNCH N3 97 J9
HGDN/ICK UB10 132 C2
HSLWW TW4 175 P1
SAND/SEL CR2 223 K6
SURB KT6 199 J6
WBLY HA9 135 N1
Victoria Cl CDH/CHF RM16 167 P1
E/WMO/HCT KT8 197 P3
EBAR EN4 77 N8
HORL RH6 280 B4
HRW * HA1 114 E4
HYS/HAR UB3 132 E8
RKW/CH/CXG WD3 91 N1
WEY KT13 196 E10
Victoria Cottages RCH/KEW TW9 155 L7
WCHPL * E1 13 N3
Victoria Ct RGUE * GU4 268 B6
WBLY HA9 135 M1
Victoria Crs IVER SL0 131 J2
NRWD SE19 181 M9
SEVS/STOTM N15 119 M3
WIM/MER * SW19 179 J10
Victoria Dock Rd CAN/RD E16 141 L8
Victoria Dr EYN DA4 210 G2
WIM/MER SW19 178 G3
Victoria Emb TPL/STR WC2R 11 N8
WHALL SW1A 17 M2
Victoria Gdns BH/WHM TN16 243 P1
HEST TW5 153 M7
NTGHL W11 8 D9
Victoria Ga BAY/PAD W2 9 M7
HLWE CM17 47 L1
Victoria Gv KENS W8 15 J3
NFNCH/WDSP N12 97 N6
Victoria Grove Ms NTGHL * W11 8 E8
Victoria Hill Rd SWLY BR8 208 G1
Victoria La HYS/HAR UB3 152 E4
Victoria Ms KIL/WHAMP NW6 2 E6
WAND/EARL SW18 179 M4
Victorian Gv STNW/STAM N16 119 M8
Victorian Rd STNW/STAM N16 119 M8
Victoria Pde RCH/KEW * TW9 155 M7
Victoria Park Rd HOM E9 140 C3
Victoria Park Sq BETH E2 140 B5
Victoria Park Studios HOM * E9 140 B1
Victoria Pl EW KT17 220 B8
RCHPK/HAM TW10 177 J2
Victoria Ri CLAP SW4 158 C9
Victoria Rd ACT W3 136 A7
ADL/WDHM KT15 215 N1
ASC SL5 192 A5
BARK IG11 142 E1
BERK HP4 33 P6
BFN/LL DA15 185 J6
BKHH IG9 101 J3
BRW CM14 107 H5
BUSH WD23 94 A2
BXLYHS DA6 186 B1
CHING E4 101 K2
CHST BR7 184 D8
COUL/CHIP CR5 240 E1
CRAWW RH11 283 M7
CSHM HP5 51 H7
DAGE RM10 124 D10
DART DA1 187 L1
EBAR EN4 77 N8
ERITH DA8 164 F5
FELT TW13 175 J4
FSBYPK N4 118 G5
GVW DA11 190 C4
HARP AL5 20 A2
HAYES BR2 206 A5
HDN NW4 116 F2
HORL RH6 280 B4
KENS W8 15 J4
KIL/WHAMP NW6 2 C7
KUT KT1 199 L2
MLHL NW7 96 C6
MORT/ESHN SW14 156 A9
MTCM CR4 179 P10
NWDGN UB2 153 N2
PLSTW E13 141 M4
REDH RH1 276 B1
ROM RM1 124 G3
RSLP HA4 113 H6
SEVS/STOTM * N15 119 P2
SLN SL2 129 H1
SLN SL2 129 N10
STA TW18 173 H6
SURB KT6 199 J6
SUT SM1 221 N2
SWFD E18 121 N1
TEDD TW11 176 F9
TWK TW1 176 G3
UED N18 99 N5
UX/CGN UB8 131 M2
WAB EN9 63 H10
WALTH E17 101 H10
WAN E11 121 J9
WATN WD24 73 J4
WDGN N22 98 E9
WDSR SL4 148 E4
WEA W13 134 G7
WEY KT13 196 E10
WOKN/KNAP GU21 231 J3
Victoria Sq BGVA SW1W 16 F3
Victoria St BELV DA17 164 A4
EGH TW20 171 P9
PIM SW1V 16 F4
SL SL1 149 L1
SRTFD E15 141 K2
STAL AL1 38 D6
WDSR SL4 149 J7
Victoria Ter DORK * RH4 272 F2
EA * W5 135 J10
FSBYPK N4 119 H6
RYLN/HDSTN HA2 114 D6
Victoria Vls RCH/KEW TW9 155 L9
Victoria Wy CHARL SE7 161 N4
WEY KT13 196 E10
WOKN/KNAP GU21 232 B3
Victoria Yd WCHPL * E1 13 P6
Victor Rd PGE/AN SE20 182 C10
RYLN/HDSTN HA2 114 B1
TEDD TW11 176 D8
WDSR SL4 149 H9
WLSDN NW10 136 E5
Victor's Crs RBRW/HUT CM13 107 N3
Victors Dr HPTN * TW12 175 M9
Victor Smith Ct
LCOL/BKTW * AL2 55 P7
Victors Wy BAR EN5 77 J7
Victor Vls UED * N18 99 L4
Victory Av MRDN SM4 201 M5
Victory Cl CDH/CHF RM16 167 H3
Victory Pk WBLY * HA9 115 J8
Victory Park Rd
ADL/WDHM KT15 195 M10
Victory Pl NRWD * SE19 181 M9
WALW SE17 18 F5
Victory Rd BERK HP4 33 M4
CHERT KT16 195 K8
RAIN RM13 145 H4
WAN E11 121 N2
WIM/MER SW19 179 M10
Victory Wy BERM/RHTH SE16 160 D1
GRH DA9 166 B10
HEST TW5 153 K4
RDART * DA2 188 B3
ROMW/RG RM7 104 C10
Vienna Cl CLAY IG5 102 A10
View Cl BH/WHM TN16 243 P2
CHIG IG7 102 G6
HGT N6 118 A5
HRW HA1 114 C2
View Crs CEND/HSY/T N8 118 E3
Viewfield Cl KTN/HRWW/W HA3 115 K5
Viewfield Rd BFN/LL DA15 185 M4
WAND/EARL SW18 179 J2
Viewland Rd WOOL/PLUM SE18 163 J4
Viewlands Av BH/WHM TN16 245 H6
View Rd HGT N6 118 A5
POTB/CUF EN6 59 M8
The View ABYW SE2 163 P4
Viga Rd WCHMH N21 79 H10
Vigerons Wy CDH/CHF RM16 168 E3
Viggory La WOKN/KNAP GU21 231 N1
Vigilant Cl SYD SE26 181 P7
Vigilant Wy GVE DA12 191 J8
Vignoles Rd ROMW/RG RM7 124 B5
Vigors Cft HAT AL10 40 C5
Vigo St MYFR/PICC W1J 10 G8
Viking Gdns EHAM E6 142 B7
Viking Pl LEY E10 120 E6
Viking Rd GVW DA11 189 P6
STHL UB1 133 M9
Viking Wy BELV DA17 164 D2
BRWN CM15 86 G10
Villa Cl GVE DA12 191 L5
Villacourt Rd WOOL/PLUM SE18 163 K6
Village Ar CHING * E4 101 J2
Village Cl CHING E4 101 H6
HAMP * NW3 117 N10
HOD EN11 45 J1
WEY KT13 196 E10
Village Gdns EW KT17 220 C6
Village Green Av BH/WHM TN16 244 B3
Village Green Rd DART DA1 165 H10
Village Green Wy BH/WHM TN16 244 B3
Village La SLN SL2 109 J6
Village Ms CDALE/KGS * NW9 116 A7
Village Mt HAMP * NW3 117 M9
Village Park Cl EN EN1 79 M10
Village Rd AMSS HP7 68 E10
DEN/HRF UB9 111 K6
EGH TW20 194 F3
EN EN1 79 L10
FNCH N3 97 H10
WDSR SL4 148 A2
Village Rw BELMT SM2 221 K4
The Village CHARL SE7 161 P5
GLDGN * NW11 117 M7
WDSR * SL4 170 G5
Village Wy AMSS HP7 70 A6
ASHF TW15 174 A7
BECK BR3 204 F3
HNHL SE24 181 L2
PIN HA5 113 M5
SAND/SEL CR2 223 P9
WLSDN NW10 116 A9
Village Wy East
RYLN/HDSTN HA2 113 N5
Villa Rd BRXN/ST SW9 159 H9
Villas Rd WOOL/PLUM SE18 162 F3
Villa St WALW SE17 19 H8
Villiers Av BRYLDS KT5 199 L5
WHTN TW2 175 N4
Villiers Cl BRYLDS KT5 199 L4
Villiers Crs STALE/WH AL4 39 J3
Villiers Gv BELMT SM2 220 G5
Villiers Rd BECK BR3 204 C2
CRICK NW2 136 D1
ISLW TW7 154 D8
KUT KT1 199 L3
OXHEY WD19 73 M10
SLN SL2 129 J7
STHL UB1 133 N10
Villiers St CHCR WC2N 11 M9
HERT/WAS SG14 25 M5
The Villiers WEY * KT13 216 E3
Villier St UX/CGN UB8 131 N5
Vincam Cl WHTN TW2 175 P3
Vincennes Est WNWD * SE27 181 L7
Vincent Av BRYLDS KT5 199 N8
CAR SM5 221 N7
Vincent Cl BAR EN5 77 K7
BARK/HLT IG6 102 F7
BFN/LL DA15 185 H4
CHERT KT16 195 H7
CHES/WCR EN8 62 D4
ESH/CLAY KT10 198 A10
GT/LBKH KT23 236 A9
HAYES BR2 205 N4
WDR/YW UB7 152 B5
Vincent Dr DORK RH4 272 F3
SHPTN TW17 196 F3
Vincent Gdns CRICK NW2 116 C8
Vincent La DORK RH4 272 F2
Vincent Pde ARCH * N19 118 F6
Vincent Rd ACT W3 155 P2
ALP/SUD HA0 135 L2
CHERT KT16 195 H7
CHING E4 101 J7
COB KT11 235 M2
COUL/CHIP CR5 240 D2
CROY/NA CR0 203 M7
DAGW RM9 143 P2
DORK RH4 272 F2
HSLWW TW4 153 L9
ISLW TW7 154 C7
KUT KT1 199 M3
RAIN RM13 145 K6
SEVS/STOTM N15 119 K2
WDGN N22 99 H10
WOOL/PLUM * SE18 162 E3
Vincent Rw HPTN TW12 176 B9
Vincents Cl BERM/RHTH SE16 160 D1
COUL/CHIP CR5 240 A6
Vincent Sq BH/WHM TN16 225 P9
WDGN * N22 99 H10
WEST SW1P 17 H5
Vincent St CAN/RD E16 141 M7
WEST SW1P 17 J5
Vincent Ter IS N1 6 C7
Vincent Vls SEVS/STOTM * N15 119 K2
Vincent Wk DORK * RH4 272 F2
Vincenzo Cl BRKMPK AL9 40 F9
Vince St FSBYE EC1V 7 H10
Vine Av SEV TN13 247 J10
Vine Cl BRYLDS KT5 199 L6
RGUW GU3 249 J2
STWL/WRAY TW19 173 K1
SUT SM1 201 M10
WDR/YW UB7 152 B3
WGCW AL8 23 H3
Vine Cottages HNWL * W7 134 D10
WCHPL * E1 140 B8
Vine Ct KTN/HRWW/W HA3 115 K4
WCHPL E1 13 P4
Vine Court Rd SEV TN13 247 K10
Vine Gdns IL IG1 122 F10
Vinegar St WAP E1W 140 A10
Vinegar Yd STHWK SE1 19 J1
Vine Gv HGDN/ICK UB10 132 A2
HLW CM20 28 G6
Vine Hl CLKNW EC1R 12 A2
Vine La HGDN/ICK UB10 132 A3
STHWK SE1 13 K10
Vine Pl HSLW TW3 154 A10
Viners Cl WOT/HER KT12 197 K6
Vines Av FNCH N3 97 L9
Vine Sq WKENS W14 14 C8
Vine St CONDST W1S 11 H8
HGDN/ICK UB10 132 A4
ROMW/RG RM7 124 D3
TWRH EC3N 13 L6
UX/CGN UB8 131 N3
Vine Street Br FARR EC1M 12 B2
Vine Street Crs TWRH * EC3N 13 L7
The Vine SEV TN13 247 K10
Vineway BRW CM14 107 H2
Vine Yd STHWK SE1 18 F1
Vineyard Av MLHL NW7 97 H8
Vineyard Cl CAT SE6 182 F4
KUT KT1 199 L3
Vineyard Gv FNCH N3 97 L9
Vineyard Hill Rd WIM/MER SW19 179 K7
Vineyard Ms CLKNW * EC1R 12 A1
Vineyard Pth MORT/ESHN SW14 156 A9
Vineyard Rd FELT TW13 175 H6
Vineyard Rw E/WMO/HCT KT8 199 H1
Vineyards Rd POTB/CUF EN6 60 C5
The Vineyard RCHPK/HAM TW10 177 J1
SUN * TW16 197 H3
WARE SG12 26 E1
WGCW * AL8 22 G3
Vineyard Wk CLKNW EC1R 12 A1
Viney Bank CROY/NA CR0 224 E5
Viney Rd LEW SE13 160 G9
Vining St BRXN/ST SW9 159 H10
Vinlake Av HGDN/ICK UB10 112 A8
Vinson Cl ORP BR6 207 K8
Vintry Ms WALTH E17 120 F2
Viola Av ABYW SE2 163 L3
EBED/NFELT TW14 175 K2
STWL/WRAY TW19 173 P4
Viola Cl SOCK/AV RM15 147 H5
Viola Sq SHB W12 136 C9
Violet Av ENC/FH EN2 79 L4
UX/CGN UB8 132 A7
Violet Cl CAN/RD E16 141 K6
DEPT SE8 160 E5
MTCM CR4 202 B8
Violet Gdns CROY/NA CR0 223 J2
Violet Hl STJWD NW8 3 J8
Violet La CROY/NA CR0 223 J2
Violet Rd BOW E3 140 G6
LEY E10 120 F4
SWFD E18 101 N10
Violet St BETH E2 140 A6
Violet Ter UX/CGN * UB8 132 B7
Violet Wy RKW/CH/CXG WD3 71 M8
Virgil Dr BROX EN10 44 E9
Virgil St STHWK SE1 17 P3
Virginia Av VW GU25 193 P5
Virginia Cl ASHTD KT21 237 J4
CRW RM5 104 D8
NWMAL KT3 199 P4
STA TW18 195 M3
WEY KT13 216 D3
Virginia Dr VW GU25 193 P4
Virginia Gdns BARK/HLT IG6 102 G10
Virginia Pk VW * GU25 194 B4
Virginia Pl COB KT11 217 H10
Virginia Rd BETH E2 7 L10
THHTH CR7 203 J1
Virginia St WAP E1W 13 P8
Viscount Cl FBAR/BDGN N11 98 B6
Viscount Dr EHAM E6 142 C7
Viscount Gdns BF/WBF KT14 215 P8
Viscount Gv YEAD UB4 133 L5
Viscount Rd STWL/WRAY TW19 173 N3
Viscount St STLK EC1Y 12 E2
Viscount Wy HTHAIR TW6 152 F10
Vista Av PEND EN3 80 C6
Vista Dr REDBR IG4 122 A3
The Vista ELTH/MOT SE9 184 A2
Vista Wy KTN/HRWW/W HA3 115 K4
Viveash Cl HYS/HAR UB3 152 G2
Vivian Av HDN NW4 116 E3
WBLY HA9 115 M1
Vivian Cl OXHEY WD19 93 H3
Vivian Gdns OXHEY WD19 93 H2
WBLY HA9 115 M10
Vivian Rd BOW E3 140 D4
Vivian Sq PECK SE15 160 A9
Vivian Wy EFNCH N2 117 N3
Vivien Cl CHSGTN KT9 219 K4
Vivienne Cl CRAWW RH11 283 N4
TWK TW1 177 J2
Vixen Dr HERT/BAY SG13 25 P5
Vixen Ms HACK * E8 7 L5
Voce Rd WOOL/PLUM SE18 162 G6
Voewood Cl NWMAL KT3 200 C6
Vogan Cl REIG RH2 275 L3
Volante Wy GVE DA12 191 H7
Voltaire Rd CLAP SW4 158 E9
Volt Av WLSDN NW10 136 A5
Volta Wy CROY/NA CR0 202 G8
Voluntary Pl WAN E11 121 M4
Vorley Rd ARCH N19 118 D7
Voss Ct STRHM/NOR SW16 180 F9
Voss St BETH E2 7 P10
Voyagers Cl THMD SE28 143 M8
Vulcan Cl EHAM E6 142 D8
Vulcan Ga ENC/FH EN2 79 H6
Vulcan Rd BROCKY SE4 160 E8
Vulcan Ter BROCKY SE4 160 E8
Vulcan Wy CROY/NA CR0 225 K6
HOLWY N7 5 P1
Vyner Rd ACT W3 136 A9
Vyner St BETH E2 140 A4
Vyners Wy HGDN/ICK UB10 112 B10
The Vyne BXLYHN DA7 164 C9
Vyse Cl BAR EN5 76 F8

W

Wacketts CHESW EN7 61 P3
Wadard Ter SWLY * BR8 209 K5
Wadding St WALW SE17 18 G6
Waddington Av COUL/CHIP CR5 241 H5
Waddington Cl COUL/CHIP CR5 241 J5
CRAWW RH11 283 K10
EN EN1 79 M8
Waddington Rd SRTFD E15 121 J10
STALW/RED AL3 38 C6
Waddington St SRTFD E15 141 J1
Waddington Wy NRWD SE19 203 K1
Waddon Cl CROY/NA CR0 203 H10
Waddon Court Rd CROY/NA CR0 223 H1
Waddon Marsh Wy
CROY/NA CR0 202 G8
Waddon New Rd CROY/NA CR0 203 J10
Waddon Park Av CROY/NA CR0 223 H1
Waddon Rd CROY/NA CR0 203 J10
Waddon Wy CROY/NA CR0 223 H3
Wade Av STMC/STPC BR5 207 N7
Wade Dr SL SL1 128 F10
Wade Rd CAN/RD E16 141 P8
Wade's Gv WCHMH N21 99 H1
Wade's Hl WCHMH N21 79 H10
Wade's La TEDD TW11 176 F8
Wadesmill Rd HERT/WAS SG14 25 L2
Wadeson St BETH E2 140 A4
Wade's Pl POP/IOD E14 140 G9
The Wades HAT AL10 40 D7
The Wade WGCE AL7 23 J8
Wadeville Av CHDH RM6 123 P4
Wadeville Cl BELV DA17 164 B4
Wadham Av CHING E4 100 G8
Wadham Cl CRAWE RH10 284 D4
SHPTN TW17 196 D7
Wadham Gdns HAMP NW3 3 N4
NTHLT UB5 134 C1
Wadham Rd ABLGY WD5 54 G7
CHING E4 100 G8
PUT/ROE SW15 157 H10
Wadhurst Cl PGE/AN SE20 204 A2
Wadhurst Rd CHSWK W4 156 A2
Wadley Cl HHNE HP2 36 A7
Wadley Rd WAN E11 121 K5
Wadsworth Cl GFD/PVL UB6 135 H4
PEND EN3 80 C9

Wadsworth Rd GFD/PVL UB6 134 G4
Wager St BOW E3 140 E6
Waggon Cl GUW GU2 249 K9
Waggoners Yd WARE SG12 26 C1
Waghorn Rd KTN/HRWW/W HA3 115 J1
PLSTW E13 141 P3
Waghorn St PECK SE15 159 P9
Wagner St PECK SE15 160 B6
Wagon Rd BAR EN5 77 K1
Wagon Wy RKW/CH/CXG WD3 71 M7
Wagstaff Gdns DAGW RM9 143 M2
Wagtail Cl CDALE/KGS NW9 96 B10
Wagtail Gdns SAND/SEL CR2 224 C6
Wagtail Wk BECK BR3 205 H5
Wagtail Wy STMC/STPC BR5 207 N4
Waid Cl DART DA1 187 N2
Waights Ct KUTN/CMB KT2 199 K1
Wain Cl POTB/CUF EN6 59 L5
Wainfleet Av CRW RM5 104 D10
Wainford Cl WIM/MER SW19 178 G4
Wainwright Gv ISLW TW7 154 C10
Wainwrights CRAWW RH11 283 N10
Waite Davies Rd LEE/GVPK SE12 183 L3
Waite St PECK SE15 19 L9
Wakefield Cl BF/WBF KT14 215 P8
Wakefield Crs SLN SL2 129 L2
Wakefield Gdns IL IG1 122 B4
NRWD SE19 181 M10
Wakefield Ms STPAN WC1H 5 M10
Wakefield Rd FBAR/BDGN N11 98 E6
GRH DA9 189 H1
RCHPK/HAM TW10 177 J1
SEVS/STOTM N15 119 N3
Wakefield St BMSBY WC1N 11 M1
EHAM E6 142 B3
GVW * DA11 190 E2
UED N18 99 P6
Wakefields Wk CHES/WCR * EN8 62 D7
Wakehams Green Dr
CRAWE RH10 284 E4
Wakehams Hl PIN HA5 113 N1
Wakeham St IS N1 6 G2
Wakehurst Dr CRAWE RH10 283 N10
Wakehurst Rd BTSEA SW11 179 P1
Wakeling Rd HNWL W7 134 E7
Wakeling St WCHPL * E1 140 D8
Wakelin Rd SRTFD E15 141 K4
Wakely Cl BH/WHM TN16 243 P4
Wakeman Rd WLSDN NW10 136 F5
Wakemans Hill Av
CDALE/KGS NW9 116 A3
Wakerfield Cl EMPK RM11 125 N3
Wakering Rd BARK IG11 142 F2
Wakerly Cl EHAM E6 142 C8
Wakley St FSBYE EC1V 6 C9
Walberswick St VX/NE SW8 158 F6
Walbrook MANHO EC4N 12 G7
Walburgh St WCHPL E1 140 A8
Walburton Rd PUR/KEN CR8 222 D9
Walcorde Av WALW SE17 18 F6
Walcot Rd PEND EN3 80 E6
Walcot Sq LBTH SE11 18 B5
Walcott St WEST * SW1P 17 H5
Waldeck Gv WNWD SE27 181 J6
Waldeck Rd CHSWK W4 155 M5
DART DA1 187 N3
MORT/ESHN SW14 155 P9
SEVS/STOTM N15 119 J1
WEA W13 134 G8
Waldegrave Gdns TWK TW1 176 E5
UPMR RM14 126 A7
Waldegrave Pk HARP AL5 20 C2
TWK TW1 176 E7
Waldegrave Rd BCTR RM8 123 M7
BMLY BR1 206 B5
CEND/HSY/T * N8 119 H1
EA W5 135 L9
NRWD SE19 181 N10
TWK TW1 176 E7
Waldegrove CROY/NA CR0 203 N10
Waldemar Av FUL/PGN SW6 157 H7
WEA W13 135 H10
Waldemar Rd WIM/MER SW19 179 K8
Walden Av CHST BR7 184 C7
PLMGR N13 99 K5
RAIN RM13 144 E4
Walden Cl BELV DA17 164 A4
Walden Gdns THHTH CR7 202 G4
Waldenhurst Rd STMC/STPC BR5 207 N7
Walden Pde CHST * BR7 184 C9
Walden Pl WGCW AL8 22 G3
Walden Rd CHST BR7 184 C9
EMPK RM11 125 L4
TOTM N17 99 L9
WGCW AL8 22 G3
Waldens Cl STMC/STPC BR5 207 N7
Waldenshaw Rd FSTH SE23 182 B4
Waldens Park Rd
WOKN/KNAP GU21 231 P3
Waldens Rd STMC/STPC BR5 207 P6
WOKN/KNAP GU21 232 A3
Walden St WCHPL * E1 140 A8
Walden Wy BARK/HLT IG6 103 H8
EMPK RM11 125 L4
MLHL NW7 96 G7
Waldo Cl CLAP SW4 180 D1
Waldon TIL RM18 169 L3
Waldo Pl WIM/MER SW19 179 P10
Waldorf Cl SAND/SEL CR2 223 J5
Waldo Rd BMLY BR1 205 P3
WLSDN NW10 136 D5
Waldram Crs FSTH SE23 182 B4
Waldram Park Rd FSTH SE23 182 C4
Waldrist Wy ERITHM DA18 164 A1
Waldron Gdns HAYES BR2 205 J3
Waldronhyrst CROY/NA CR0 223 J1
Waldron Ms CHEL SW3 15 M9
Waldron Rd RYLN/HDSTN HA2 114 D6
WAND/EARL SW18 179 M6
The Waldrons CROY/NA CR0 223 K1
OXTED RH8 261 L7
Waldron's Yd RYLN/HDSTN HA2 114 C7
Waldstock Rd THMD SE28 143 K9
Waleran Cl STAN HA7 94 E7
Walerand Rd LEW SE13 161 H8
Wales Av CAR SM5 222 A2
Walesbeech CRAWE RH10 284 B8
Wales Farm Rd ACT W3 136 A7
Waleton Acres WLGTN * SM6 222 D3
Waley St WCHPL * E1 140 C7
Walfield Av TRDG/WHET N20 97 L1
Walford Rd RDKG RH5 272 G6
STNW/STAM N16 119 M9
UX/CGN UB8 131 M4
Walfords Cl HLWE CM17 29 M8
Walfrey Gdns DAGW RM9 143 P2
Walham Green Ct
FUL/PGN * SW6 157 L6
Walham Gv FUL/PGN SW6 157 K6
Walham Ri WIM/MER SW19 179 H9
Walham Yd FUL/PGN SW6 157 K6
Walkden Rd CHST BR7 184 D7
Walker Cl DART DA1 164 G9
EBED/NFELT TW14 174 G3
FBAR/BDGN N11 98 D5
HNWL W7 134 D10
HPTN TW12 175 N9
WOOL/PLUM SE18 162 F3
Walker Rd CRAWE RH10 284 C9
Walkers Cl HARP AL5 20 B4
Walker's Ct SOHO/CST W1F 11 J7
Walkerscroft Md DUL SE21 181 K4
Walker's Pl PUT/ROE * SW15 157 H10
Walkers Rd HARP AL5 20 A4
Walkfield Dr EPSOM KT18 238 E3
Walkley Rd DART DA1 187 J1
The Walks EFNCH N2 117 N1
The Walk EMPK RM11 125 N7
OXTED RH8 260 F9
PLMGR * N13 99 H4
POTB/CUF EN6 59 K8
Walk Wood Ri BEAC HP9 108 B1
Wallace Cl HGDN/ICK UB10 131 P4
RGUW GU3 249 H6
SHPTN TW17 196 F4
THMD SE28 143 N9
Wallace Crs CAR SM5 222 A2
Wallace Flds EW KT17 220 C8
Wallace Gdns SWCM DA10 189 K2
Wallace Rd GRAYS RM17 167 M3
IS N1 6 F1
Wallace Wk ADL/WDHM KT15 215 M1
DTCH/LGLY SL3 149 L4
Wallage La CRAWE RH10 285 L7
Wallasey Crs HGDN/ICK UB10 112 B7
Wallbutton Rd BROCKY SE4 160 D8
Wallcote Av CRICK NW2 116 G6
The Walled Gdn
BRKHM/BTCW RH3 274 A1
WLYN * AL6 23 K1
Wall End Rd EHAM E6 142 D2
Wallenger Av GPK RM2 125 J1
Waller Dr NTHWD * HA6 93 H10
NTHWD HA6 93 H10
Waller La CTHM CR3 241 N9
Waller Rd BEAC HP9 88 E9
NWCR SE14 160 C7
Wallers Cl DAGW RM9 143 P3
WFD IG8 102 C7
Waller's Hoppet LOU IG10 82 C6
Wallers Wy HOD EN11 26 G10
Wallflower St SHB W12 136 C9
Wallgrave Rd ECT SW5 14 G5
Wallhouse Rd ERITH DA8 165 K6
Wallingford Av NKENS W10 136 G7
Wallingford Rd UX/CGN UB8 131 L4
Wallingford Wk STAL AL1 38 C9
Wallington Cl RSLP HA4 112 D4
Wallington Rd CSHM HP5 50 G6
GDMY/SEVK IG3 123 J5
Wallis Cl BTSEA SW11 157 N9
HCH RM12 125 J6
RDART DA2 187 H6
Wallis Ct CRAWE * RH10 284 A3
Wallis Ms LHD/OX * KT22 236 F8
Wallis Rd GFD/PVL UB6 134 A8
HOM E9 140 E1
Wallorton Gdns
MORT/ESHN SW14 156 A10
Wallside BARB * EC2Y 12 F4
Wall St IS N1 7 H2
Wallwood Rd WAN E11 121 J5
Wallwood St POP/IOD E14 140 E7
Walmar Cl EBAR EN4 77 N5
Walmer Cl CHING E4 100 G3
ORP BR6 226 G1
ROMW/RG RM7 104 C10
Walmer Gdns HNWL W7 154 F1
Walmer Rd NTGHL W11 8 A8
Walmer Ter WOOL/PLUM SE18 162 F3
Walmgate Rd GFD/PVL UB6 134 G3
Walmington Fold
NFNCH/WDSP N12 97 K7
Walm La CRICK NW2 116 G10
Walney Wk IS N1 6 F1
Walnut Av WDR/YW UB7 152 B2
Walnut Cl BARK/HLT IG6 122 F2
CAR SM5 222 A2
DEPT SE8 160 E5
EPSOM KT18 238 C1
HYS/HAR UB3 132 F9
LCOL/BKTW AL2 56 A3
Walnut Ct EA * W5 155 K1
WGCE AL7 23 H8
Walnut Dr KWD/TDW/WH KT20 239 H10
Walnut Gdns SRTFD E15 121 K10
Walnut Gn BUSH WD23 73 N6
Walnut Gv BNSTD SM7 220 G10
HHNE HP2 35 N6
WCHMH N21 79 L9
WGCE AL7 23 H8
Walnut La CRAWW RH11 283 L4
Walnut Ms BELMT SM2 221 M4
Walnut Rd LEY E10 120 F7
Walnuts Rd ORP BR6 207 K8
Walnut Tree Av DART DA1 187 M5
MTCM * CR4 201 P3
Walnut Tree Cl BARN SW13 156 C7
BNSTD SM7 221 H8
CHES/WCR EN8 62 C7
CHST BR7 206 F1
GU GU1 249 P10
HOD EN11 44 F3
Walnut Tree Gdns RGODL GU7 267 K10
Walnut Tree La BF/WBF KT14 215 N8
Walnut Tree Pk GU * GU1 249 P10
Walnut Tree Rd BCTR RM8 123 N7
BTFD TW8 155 K5
ERITH DA8 164 F4
GNWCH * SE10 161 K4
HEST * TW5 153 N5
SHPTN TW17 196 D3
Walnut Tree Wk LBTH SE11 18 A6
WARE SG12 26 C5
Walnut Wk HERT/BAY SG13 25 M5
Walnut Wy AMS HP6 68 B1
BKHH IG9 102 A4
RSLP HA4 133 K1
SWLY BR8 208 E2
Walpole Av COUL/CHIP CR5 240 A5
RCH/KEW TW9 155 L8
Walpole Cl GRAYS RM17 167 P3
PIN HA5 93 P8
WEA W13 155 H1
Walpole Crs TEDD TW11 176 E8
Walpole Gdns CHSWK W4 155 P4
WHTN TW2 176 C5
Walpole Ms STJWD NW8 3 L6
Walpole Pl TEDD TW11 176 E8
Walpole Rd CROY/NA CR0 203 L9
EHAM E6 141 P2
HAYES BR2 206 A5
SL SL1 128 C8
SURB KT6 199 K7
SWFD E18 101 L9
TEDD TW11 176 E8
TOTM N17 99 K10
WALTH E17 120 D2
WDSR SL4 171 N3
WHTN TW2 176 D5
WIM/MER SW19 179 N9
Walpole St CHEL SW3 16 A7
Walrond Av WBLY HA9 115 K10
Walsham Cl STNW/STAM N16 119 P6
THMD SE28 143 N9
Walsham Rd EBED/NFELT TW14 175 J3
NWCR SE14 160 C8
Walsh Crs CROY/NA CR0 225 K8
Walshford Wy BORE WD6 75 M4
Walsingham Cl HAT AL10 40 C3
Walsingham Gdns
HOR/WEW KT19 220 B1
Walsingham Pk CHST BR7 206 G2
Walsingham Rd BTSEA SW11 180 B2
CLPT E5 119 P8
CROY/NA CR0 225 H6
ENC/FH EN2 79 L8
MTCM CR4 202 A5
STMC/STPC BR5 207 L1
WEA * W13 134 F10
Walsingham Wk BELV DA17 164 B5
Walsingham Wy LCOL/BKTW AL2 57 H3
Walter's Md ASHTD KT21 237 K3
Walters Rd PEND EN3 80 B9
SNWD SE25 203 M4
Walter St BETH E2 140 C5
KUTN/CMB * KT2 199 K1
Walters Wy FSTH SE23 182 C2
Walters Yd BMLY BR1 205 M2
Walter Ter WCHPL E1 140 C8
Walterton Rd MV/WKIL W9 8 D2
Walter Wk EDGW HA8 95 P7
Waltham Av CDALE/KGS NW9 115 M4
GUW GU2 249 N7
HYS/HAR UB3 152 D2
Waltham Cl DART DA1 187 H2
RBRW/HUT CM13 87 P10
STMC/STPC BR5 207 N8
Waltham Dr EDGW HA8 95 M10
Waltham Gdns PEND EN3 80 B2
Waltham Ga CHES/WCR EN8 62 D2
Waltham Pk WALTH E17 100 F8
Waltham Rd CAR SM5 201 N8
CTHM CR3 242 A8
NWDGN UB2 153 M2
WAB EN9 63 K2
WFD IG8 102 B7
Walthamstow Av CHING E4 100 F8
Walthamstow Av (North Circular)
CHING E4 100 D6
Waltham Wy CHING E4 100 E4
Waltheof Av TOTM N17 99 L9
Waltheof Gdns TOTM N17 99 L9
Walton Av CHEAM SM3 201 J10
NWMAL KT3 200 C4
RYLN/HDSTN HA2 113 N10
Walton Bridge Rd SHPTN TW17 196 F7
Walton Cl CRICK NW2 116 E7
HRW HA1 114 C2
VX/NE SW8 158 F6
Walton Ct WOKN/KNAP GU21 232 D1
Walton Dr HRW HA1 114 C2
WLSDN NW10 136 A1
Walton Gdns ACT W3 135 N7
FELT TW13 174 G7
RBRW/HUT CM13 87 P9
WAB EN9 62 G9
WBLY HA9 115 K7
Walton Gn CROY/NA CR0 224 G5
Walton Heath CRAWE RH10 284 E5
Walton La SHPTN TW17 196 E7
SLN SL2 128 E4
WEY KT13 196 D9
Walton Pk WOT/HER KT12 197 L9
Walton Park La WOT/HER KT12 197 L9
Walton Pl CHEL SW3 16 A3
Walton Rd BUSH WD23 73 L8
CRW RM5 104 A8
EPSOM KT18 237 P7
HOD EN11 44 G1
HRW HA1 114 C2
MNPK E12 122 D9
PLSTW E13 141 P4
SCUP DA14 185 L6
SEVS/STOTM * N15 119 N2
WARE SG12 26 C3
WOKN/KNAP GU21 232 D2
WOT/HER KT12 197 L5
Walton's Hall Rd SLH/COR SS17 169 K1
Walton St CHEL SW3 15 P5
ENC/FH EN2 79 L5
KWD/TDW/WH KT20 238 D10
STAL AL1 38 E5
Walton Ter WOKN/KNAP GU21 232 E1
Walton Vls IS * N1 7 K4
Walton Wy ACT W3 135 N7
MTCM CR4 202 D4
Walt Whitman Cl HNHL * SE24 159 J10
Walverns Cl OXHEY WD19 73 K10
Walworth Pl WALW SE17 18 F8
Walworth Rd WALW SE17 18 E5
Walwyn Av BMLY BR1 206 A3
Wambrook Cl RBRW/HUT CM13 107 P3
Wanborough Dr PUT/ROE SW15 178 E4
Wanborough Hl RGUW GU3 266 B3
Wanderer Dr BARK IG11 143 L5
Wandle Bank CROY/NA CR0 202 F10
WIM/MER SW19 179 N9
Wandle Cl CRAWE RH10 284 D8
Wandle Ct HOR/WEW KT19 219 P1
Wandle Court Gdns
CROY/NA CR0 202 F10
Wandle Rd CROY/NA CR0 202 F10
CROY/NA CR0 203 K10
MRDN SM4 201 N5
TOOT SW17 179 P5
WLGTN SM6 202 C9
Wandle Side CROY/NA CR0 202 G10
WLGTN SM6 202 C10
Wandle Wy MTCM CR4 202 A5
WAND/EARL SW18 179 L4
Wandon Rd FUL/PGN SW6 157 L6
Wandsworth Br
WAND/EARL SW18 157 M9
Wandsworth Bridge Rd
FUL/PGN SW6 157 L7
Wandsworth Common West Side
WAND/EARL SW18 179 M1
Wandsworth High St
WAND/EARL SW18 179 K1
Wandsworth Rd CLAP SW4 158 C9
VX/NE SW8 17 L9
Wangey Rd CHDH RM6 123 N5
Wanless Rd HNHL SE24 159 K9
Wanley Rd CMBW SE5 159 L10
Wanlip Rd PLSTW E13 141 N6
Wanmer Ct REIG * RH2 257 K9
Wannions Cl CSHM HP5 51 M6
Wannock Gdns BARK/HLT IG6 102 E8
Wansbeck Rd HOM E9 140 E2
Wansbury Wy SWLY BR8 209 H5
Wansdown Pl FUL/PGN SW6 157 L6
Wansey St WALW SE17 18 F6
Wansford Cl BRW CM14 106 E4
Wansford Gn WOKN/KNAP GU21 231 L3
Wansford Pk BORE WD6 76 A8
Wansford Rd WFD IG8 101 P9
Wanstead Cl BMLY BR1 205 P2
Wanstead La IL IG1 122 B4
Wanstead Park Av MNPK E12 122 A7
Wanstead Park Rd IL IG1 122 B6
Wanstead Pl WAN E11 121 M4
Wanstead Rd BMLY BR1 205 P2
Wansunt Rd BXLY DA5 186 D4
Wantage Cl CRAWE RH10 284 D10
Wantage Rd LEE/GVPK SE12 183 L1
Wantz La RAIN RM13 145 J6
Wantz Rd DAGE RM10 124 C9
The Waplings
KWD/TDW/WH * KT20 238 E10
Wapping Dock St WAP * E1W 140 A10
Wapping High St WAP E1W 13 P10
Wapping La WAP E1W 140 A9
Wapping Wall WAP E1W 140 B10
Wapseys La SLN SL2 109 K4
Wapseys Wd CFSP/GDCR * SL9 109 K3
Wapshott Rd STA TW18 173 H9
Warbank Cl CROY/NA CR0 225 K6
Warbank Crs CROY/NA CR0 225 K6
Warbank La KUTN/CMB KT2 178 C10
Warbeck Rd SHB W12 136 E10
Warberry Rd WDGN N22 98 G10
Warblers Gn COB KT11 217 N10
Warboys Ap KUTN/CMB KT2 177 N9
Warboys Crs CHING E4 101 H6
Warboys Rd KUTN/CMB KT2 177 N9
Warburton Cl IS N1 7 J1
KTN/HRWW/W HA3 94 C7
Warburton Rd HACK E8 140 A3
WHTN TW2 176 A4
Warburton St HACK E8 140 A3
Warburton Ter WALTH E17 100 G10
Warbury La WOKN/KNAP GU21 231 H2
War Coppice Rd REDH RH1 259 L3
Wardalls Gv NWCR * SE14 160 B6
Ward Av GRAYS RM17 167 N3
Ward Cl CHESW * EN7 61 P3
ERITH DA8 164 E5
IVER SL0 131 J9
SAND/SEL CR2 223 M2
WARE SG12 26 B1
Wardell Cl CDALE/KGS NW9 96 B8
Warden Av CRW RM5 104 D6
RYLN/HDSTN HA2 113 M6
Warden Rd KTTN NW5 4 D1
Wardens Gv STHWK SE1 12 E10
Ward Gdns SL SL1 128 D9
Ward Hatch HLW CM20 29 L6
Ward La WARL CR6 242 B2
Wardle St HOM E9 120 C10
Wardley St WAND/EARL SW18 179 L3
Wardo Av FUL/PGN SW6 157 H7
Wardour Ms SOHO/CST W1F 11 H6
Wardour St SOHO/CST W1F 11 H5
Ward Pl AMSS * HP7 68 G6
Ward Rd ARCH N19 118 D9
SRTFD * E15 141 J3
Wardrobe Pl BLKFR * EC4V 12 D6
The Wardrobe RCH/KEW * TW9 177 J1
Ward Royal WDSR SL4 149 H7
Ward Royal Pde WDSR * SL4 149 H7
Wards Pl EGH TW20 172 F9
Wards Rd GNTH/NBYPK IG2 122 G5
Ward St GU GU1 268 A1
Wareham Cl HSLW TW3 154 A10
Waremead Rd GNTH/NBYPK IG2 122 E3
Warenford Wy BORE WD6 75 M5
Warenne Hts REDH RH1 275 N2
Warenne Rd LHD/OX KT22 236 B8
Ware Park Rd HERT/WAS SG14 25 L3
Warepoint Dr THMD SE28 162 G1
Ware Rd HERT/BAY SG13 25 P4
HOD EN11 44 F1
WARE SG12 26 F8
Warescot Cl BRWN CM15 106 G1
Warescot Rd BRWN CM15 106 G1
Wareside Cl WGCE AL7 23 L6
Warfield Rd EBED/NFELT TW14 174 F3
HPTN TW12 198 A1
WLSDN NW10 136 G5
Warfield Yd WLSDN * NW10 136 G5
Wargrave Av SEVS/STOTM N15 119 P4
Wargrave Rd RYLN/HDSTN HA2 114 B8
Warham Rd FSBYPK N4 119 H6
KTN/HRWW/W HA3 94 E10
RSEV TN14 247 J2
SAND/SEL CR2 223 K2
Warham St CMBW SE5 159 J6
Waring Cl ORP BR6 227 J3
Waring Dr ORP BR6 227 J3
Waring Rd SCUP DA14 185 M9
Waring St WNWD SE27 181 K7
Warkworth Gdns ISLW TW7 154 F6
Warkworth Rd TOTM N17 99 L8
Warland Rd WOOL/PLUM SE18 162 G6
Warley Av ROMW/RG RM7 124 A5
YEAD UB4 133 H8
Warley Gap RBRW/HUT CM13 106 G8
Warley Hl RBRW/HUT CM13 107 H6
Warley Mt BRW CM14 107 H5
Warley Rd CLAY IG5 102 D9
ED N9 100 B3
RBRW/HUT CM13 106 D10
WFD IG8 101 N8
YEAD UB4 133 H8
Warley St BETH E2 140 C5
UPMR RM14 127 J5
Warlingham Rd THHTH CR7 203 J4
Warlock Rd MV/WKIL W9 8 D1
Warlow Cl WAB EN9 80 F3
Warlters Cl HOLWY * N7 118 F9
Warlters Rd HOLWY N7 118 F9
Warltersville Rd ARCH N19 118 F5
Warltersville Wy HORL RH6 280 D6
Warmark Rd HHW HP1 35 H4
Warming Cl CLPT E5 120 C8
Warmington Rd HNHL SE24 181 K2
Warmington St PLSTW E13 141 M6
Warminster Rd SNWD SE25 203 P2
Warminster Sq SNWD SE25 203 P2
Warminster Wy MTCM CR4 202 C1
Warndon St BERM/RHTH SE16 160 B3
Warneford Pl OXHEY WD19 73 M10
Warneford Rd
KTN/HRWW/W HA3 115 J1
Warneford St HOM E9 140 A3
Warne Pl BFN/LL DA15 185 L2
Warner Av CHEAM SM3 201 H9
Warner Cl CDALE/KGS NW9 116 C5
HPTN TW12 175 N8
HYS/HAR UB3 152 E6
SL SL1 128 D10
SRTFD E15 121 K10
Warner Pl BETH E2 7 P8
Warner Rd BMLY BR1 183 L10
CEND/HSY/T N8 118 E2
CMBW SE5 159 K7
WALTH E17 120 D2
WARE SG12 26 C3
Warners Av HOD EN11 44 E5
Warners End Rd HHW HP1 35 K6
Warners La SHGR GU5 269 P7
Warner St CLKNW EC1R 12 A2
Warner Ter POP/IOD * E14 140 F7
Warner Yd CLKNW EC1R 12 A2
Warnford Rd ORP BR6 227 J2
Warnham Court Rd CAR SM5 222 A4
Warnham Rd CRAWE RH10 284 B9
NFNCH/WDSP N12 97 N6
Warple Ms ACT * W3 156 B1
Warple Wy ACT W3 156 B1
Warpole Pk WEY KT13 216 B4
Warren Av BELMT SM2 221 J6
BMLY BR1 183 K10
ORP BR6 227 J2
RCHPK/HAM TW10 155 N10
SAND/SEL CR2 224 C4
WAN * E11 121 J8
Warren Cl BXLYHS DA6 186 B1
DTCH/LGLY SL3 150 B2
ED N9 100 C1
ESH/CLAY KT10 218 A1
HAT AL10 40 E1
WBLY HA9 115 J7
YEAD UB4 133 K7
Warren Ct BGR/WK TN15 265 K1
CHIG IG7 102 G5
Warren Crs ED N9 99 N1
Warren Cutting KUTN/CMB KT2 178 A10
Warren Dl WGCW AL8 22 G2
Warrender Rd ARCH N19 118 D8
CSHM HP5 51 K5
Warrender Wy RSLP HA4 113 H5
Warren Dr CRAWW RH11 283 K6
GFD/PVL UB6 134 A6
HCH RM12 125 H8
KWD/TDW/WH KT20 239 J8
ORP BR6 227 L2
RSLP HA4 113 L5
Warren Dr North BRYLDS KT5 199 N8
Warren Dr South BRYLDS KT5 199 P8
The Warren Dr WAN E11 121 P5
Warreners La WEY KT13 216 E5
Warren Fld EPP CM16 65 K8
IVER SL0 130 F4
Warrenfield Cl CHESW EN7 61 P7
Warren Flds STAN * HA7 95 H5
Warren Gdns ORP BR6 227 K2
Warrengate La POTB/CUF EN6 58 F7
Warrengate Rd BRKMPK AL9 58 F4
Warren Gn HAT AL10 40 E1
Warren Gv BORE WD6 76 A8
Warren Hl EPSOM KT18 238 A2
LOU IG10 81 P9
Warren La BRWN CM15 86 D5
CDH/CHF RM16 167 J3
LHD/OX KT22 218 B8
OXTED RH8 261 M10
STAN HA7 94 F3
WOKS/MYFD GU22 233 K4
WOOL/PLUM SE18 162 E2
Warren Lodge Dr
KWD/TDW/WH KT20 239 H10
Warren Md BNSTD SM7 238 F1
Warren Ms GTPST W1W 10 G2
Warrenne Rd BRKHM/BTCW RH3 273 P3
Warrenne Wy REIG RH2 257 K10
Warren Pde SLN * SL2 129 P10
Warren Pk KUTN/CMB KT2 177 P9
KWD/TDW/WH * KT20 255 P7
WARL CR6 242 C4
Warren Park Rd HERT/WAS SG14 25 K4
SUT SM1 221 N3
Warren Pl HERT/WAS * SG14 25 L5
Warren Pond Rd CHING E4 101 L1
Warren Ri NWMAL KT3 200 A1
Warren Rd ADL/WDHM KT15 215 K6
ASHF TW15 174 F10
BARK/HLT IG6 122 G3
BNSTD SM7 238 G1
BUSH WD23 94 B2
BXLYHS DA6 186 B1
CHING E4 101 H3
CRICK NW2 116 C7
CROY/NA CR0 203 M8
DART DA1 187 M6
GU GU1 268 C1
HAYES BR2 205 M9
HGDN/ICK UB10 111 P9
KUTN/CMB KT2 177 P9
LCOL/BKTW AL2 38 B10
LEY E10 121 H8
MEO DA13 189 N8
ORP BR6 227 J2
PUR/KEN CR8 223 J8
REIG RH2 257 L9
RGODL GU7 267 K10
SCUP DA14 185 M6
WAN E11 121 H8
WAN E11 121 P4
WHTN TW2 176 C2
WIM/MER SW19 179 P9
Warrens Shawe La EDGW HA8 95 N3
The Warrens HART DA3 211 L6
Warren St FITZ W1T 10 G2
Warren Ter CDH/CHF * RM16 167 J1
HERT/WAS SG14 25 L3
The Warren ASHTD KT21 237 L6
CAR SM5 221 N5
CFSP/GDCR SL9 90 C8
CSHM HP5 50 D4
EHSLY KT24 252 G6
GVE DA12 190 G7
HEST TW5 153 N6
HOR/WEW KT19 220 A1
KGLGY WD4 54 A5
KWD/TDW/WH KT20 239 H9
LHD/OX KT22 218 B8
MNPK E12 122 B9
RAD WD7 56 H9

YEAD UB4 ....133 H8
Warren Vw GVE DA12 ....191 P8
Warren Wy MLHL NW7 ....97 H7
WEY KT13 ....216 D3
Warren Wood Cl HAYES BR2 ....205 M9
Warriner Av HCH RM12 ....125 L7
Warriner Dr ED N9 ....99 P4
Warriner Gdns BTSEA SW11 ....158 A7
Warrington Av SL SL1 ....129 H8
Warrington Crs MV/WKIL W9 ....9 J2
Warrington Gdns EMPK RM11 ....125 K4
MV/WKIL W9 ....9 J2
Warrington Pl POP/IOD * E14 ....141 H10
Warrington Rd BCTR RM8 ....123 N7
CROY/NA CR0 ....203 J10
HRW HA1 ....114 D3
RCHPK/HAM TW10 ....177 J1
Warrington Sp WDSR SL4 ....171 N3
Warrington Sq BCTR RM8 ....123 N7
Warrior Av GVE DA12 ....190 F7
Warrior Sq MNPK E12 ....122 D9
Warsaw Cl RSLP HA4 ....133 J1
Warspite Rd WOOL/PLUM SE18 ....162 B2
Warton Rd SRTFD E15 ....141 H3
Warwall EHAM E6 ....142 E8
Warwick Av EDGW HA8 ....95 N4
EGH TW20 ....194 F1
MV/WKIL W9 ....9 H2
POTB/CUF EN6 ....60 E3
RYLN/HDSTN HA2 ....113 N9
SLN SL2 ....129 H6
STA TW18 ....173 M9
Warwick Cl BUSH WD23 ....94 D1
BXLY DA5 ....186 A3
EBAR EN4 ....77 N9
HERT/BAY SG13 ....25 K7
HPTN TW12 ....176 B10
ORP BR6 ....207 K10
POTB/CUF EN6 ....60 E3
RDKG RH5 ....272 G10
Warwick Ct HHOL WC1V 11 P4
RKW/CH/CXG WD3 ....71 J7
Warwick Crs BAY/PAD W2 ....9 J3
YEAD UB4 ....132 G6
Warwick Deeping CHERT KT16 ....214 F2
Warwick Dene EA W5 ....135 K10
Warwick Dr BARN SW13 ....156 E9
CHES/WCR EN8 ....62 C4
Warwick Gdns ASHTD KT21 ....237 H3
FSBYPK N4 ....119 K3
GPK RM2 ....125 K1
IL IG1 ....122 E6
THDIT KT7 ....198 E5
THHTH * CR7 ....203 H4
WKENS W14 ....14 D5
Warwick Gv BRYLDS KT5 ....199 L7
CLPT E5 ....120 A6
Warwick House St STJS SW1Y 11 K9
Warwick La RAIN RM13 ....145 N4
STP EC4M 12 D5
WOKN/KNAP GU21 ....231 M5
Warwick Pde
KTN/HRWW/W * HA3 ....94 G10
Warwick Pl BORE * WD6 ....76 A7
BRW CM14 ....86 B8
EA W5 ....155 J1
GVW DA11 ....189 N1
MV/WKIL W9 ....9 J3
THDIT * KT7 ....198 F6
UX/CGN UB8 ....131 M2
Warwick Pl North PIM * SW1V 16 G6
Warwick Rd ASHF TW15 ....173 P8
BAR EN5 ....77 L8
BEAC HP9 ....88 C8
BORE WD6 ....76 A7
CHING E4 ....100 F6
COUL/CHIP CR5 ....222 D10
EA W5 ....135 K10
FBAR/BDGN N11 ....98 E7
FSTGT E7 ....141 L1
HSLWW TW4 ....153 J9
KUT KT1 ....199 H1
MNPK E12 ....122 B10
NWDGN UB2 ....153 N2
NWMAL KT3 ....199 P3
PEND EN3 ....80 E3
PGE/AN SE20 ....204 A3
RAIN RM13 ....145 K6
REDH RH1 ....258 A9
SCUP DA14 ....185 L8
STAL AL1 ....38 E4
SUT SM1 ....221 M2
THDIT KT7 ....198 E5
THHTH CR7 ....203 H3
UED N18 ....99 M5
WALTH E17 ....100 E9
WAN E11 ....121 N3
WDR/YW UB7 ....131 P10
WELL DA16 ....163 M9
WHTN TW2 ....176 D4
WKENS W14 ....14 D6
Warwick Rw WESTW SW1E 16 G3
Warwicks Bench GU GU1 ....268 B3
Warwick's Bench La GU GU1 ....268 B3
Warwick Sq PIM SW1V 16 G7
STP * EC4M 12 D5
Warwick Square Ms PIM SW1V 16 G6
Warwicks Rd GU GU1 ....268 A2
Warwick St REGST W1B 11 H7
Warwick Ter LEY * E10 ....121 J3
WOOL/PLUM SE18 ....162 G5
Warwick Vls EGH * TW20 ....194 F1
Warwick Wy PIM SW1V 16 F6
RKW/CH/CXG WD3 ....72 D8
Warwick Wold Rd REDH RH1 ....259 H5
Warwick Yd STLK * EC1Y 12 F1
Washington Av HHNE HP2 ....35 P1
MNPK E12 ....122 B9
Washington Cl BOW E3 ....140 G5
REIG RH2 ....257 K8
Washington Dr SL SL1 ....128 C9
WDSR SL4 ....148 D9
Washington Rd BARN SW13 ....156 D6
CRAWW RH11 ....283 H10
EHAM E6 ....141 P2
KUT KT1 ....199 M2
SWFD E18 ....101 L10
WPK KT4 ....200 E9
Wash La BAR EN5 ....76 F1
POTB/CUF EN6 ....58 F9
Washneys Rd ORP BR6 ....227 K9
Washpond La WARL CR6 ....243 H4
Washponds Cottages
WARL * CR6 ....243 H4
The Wash HERT/WAS SG14 ....25 L5
Wasp Green La REDH RH1 ....277 J9
Wassand Cl CRAWE RH10 ....284 B7
Wastdale Rd FSTH SE23 ....182 C4
Watchfield Ct CHSWK * W4 ....155 P4
Watchlytes WGCE AL7 ....23 M5
Watchmead WGCE AL7 ....23 K5
The Watch NFNCH/WDSP * N12 ....97 M5
Watcombe Rd SNWD SE25 ....204 A5
Waterbank Rd CAT SE6 ....182 G6
Waterbeach WGCE AL7 ....23 N5
Waterbeach Cl SL SL1 ....129 J8
Waterbeach Rd DAGW RM9 ....143 M1
SL SL1 ....129 J8
Water Brook La HDN * NW4 ....116 F3
Watercress Dr RSEV TN14 ....247 K6
Watercress Pl IS N1 ....7 K4
Watercress Rd CHESW EN7 ....61 L2
Watercress Wy
WOKN/KNAP GU21 ....231 N3
Watercroft Rd RSEV TN14 ....228 A6
Waterdale HERT/BAY SG13 ....25 K7
Waterdale Rd ABYW SE2 ....163 K5
Waterdales GVW DA11 ....190 A4
Waterden Cl GU * GU1 ....268 C1
Waterden Rd GU GU1 ....268 B1
SRTFD E15 ....120 F10
Waterend La STALE/WH AL4 ....21 P3
Water End Rd BERK HP4 ....34 E3
Waterer Gdns
KWD/TDW/WH KT20 ....239 H4
Waterer Ri WLGTN SM6 ....222 E3
Waterers Ri WOKN/KNAP GU21 ....231 J3
Waterfall Cl VW GU25 ....193 L3
Waterfall Cottages
WIM/MER SW19 ....179 N9
Waterfall Rd STHGT/OAK N14 ....98 D4
WIM/MER SW19 ....179 N9
Waterfall Ter TOOT SW17 ....179 P9
Waterfield KWD/TDW/WH KT20 ....238 E5
WGCE AL7 ....23 L4
Waterfield Cl BELV DA17 ....164 B2
THMD SE28 ....143 L10
Waterfield Cottages
MORT/ESHN * SW14 ....155 N10
Waterfield Dr WARL CR6 ....242 A5
Waterfield Gdns CRAWW RH11 ....283 H9
SNWD SE25 ....203 M4
Waterfield Gn
KWD/TDW/WH KT20 ....238 E6
Waterfields LHD/OX KT22 ....236 G5
Waterfields Wy WAT WD17 ....73 L8
Waterford Cl COB KT11 ....217 M7
Waterford Common
HERT/WAS SG14 ....25 J1
Waterford Gn WGCE AL7 ....23 L5
Waterford Rd FUL/PGN SW6 ....157 L6
Waterfront WTHK * RM20 ....166 F2
The Waterfront BORE * WD6 ....74 G10
Water Gdns STAN HA7 ....94 G7
The Water Gdns BAY/PAD W2 ....9 N5
Watergate St DEPT SE8 ....160 F5
The Watergate OXHEY WD19 ....93 L3
Waterhall Av CHING E4 ....101 K5
Waterhall Cl WALTH E17 ....100 C9
Waterhead Cl ERITH DA8 ....164 F6
Waterhoose Moor HLWS CM18 ....47 H2
Waterhouse Cl HAMP NW3 ....117 N10
Waterhouse La
KWD/TDW/WH KT20 ....239 J7
PUR/KEN CR8 ....241 K5
REDH RH1 ....259 N8
Waterhouse St HHW HP1 ....35 M6
Wateringbury Cl
STMC/STPC BR5 ....207 L3
Water La BERK HP4 ....33 P5
CAMTN NW1 ....4 F4
CHOB/PIR GU24 ....230 D5
COB KT11 ....217 N10
ED N9 ....100 A2
GDMY/SEVK IG3 ....123 J8
GT/LBKH KT23 ....253 M2
HHS/BOV HP3 ....52 E5
HLWW/ROY CM19 ....46 B5
KGLGY WD4 ....54 C5
KUT KT1 ....199 J1
OXTED RH8 ....261 M2
PECK SE15 ....160 B6
PUR RM19 ....165 P3
RCH/KEW TW9 ....177 J1
RDKG RH5 ....271 J9
RSEV TN14 ....228 G8
SCUP DA14 ....186 A5
SHGR GU5 ....269 L4
SRTFD E15 ....141 K1
TWK TW1 ....176 F4
WAT WD17 ....73 K8
Water Lea CRAWE RH10 ....284 B8
Water Lily Cl STHL UB1 ....154 B1
Waterloo Br TPL/STR WC2R 11 N8
Waterloo Cl EBED/NFELT TW14 ....174 G4
Waterloo Gdns BETH E2 ....140 B4
ROMW/RG RM7 ....124 E4
Waterloo Pl CAR * SM5 ....202 A10
RCH/KEW TW9 ....155 M5
STJS SW1Y 11 J9
Waterloo Rd BARK/HLT IG6 ....102 F10
BRW CM14 ....107 H2
CRICK NW2 ....116 D7
EHAM E6 ....141 P2
FSTGT E7 ....121 L10
HOR/WEW KT19 ....220 A8
LEY E10 ....120 F5
ROMW/RG RM7 ....124 E3
STHWK SE1 ....11 P9
SUT SM1 ....221 N2
UX/CGN UB8 ....131 M3
Waterloo St GVE DA12 ....190 F3
Waterloo Ter IS N1 ....6 C4
WEY * KT13 ....216 B1
Waterlow Rd ARCH N19 ....118 D6
REIG RH2 ....275 M1
Waterman Cl OXHEY WD19 ....73 J10
Waterman Ct SL SL1 ....128 D10
Watermans Cl KUTN/CMB * KT2 ....177 K10
Watermans Ms EA * W5 ....135 K9
Waterman St PUT/ROE SW15 ....156 G9
Watermans Wy EPP CM16 ....66 B3
Waterman Wy WAP E1W 140 A10
Watermark Wy HERT/BAY SG13 ....25 N5
Watermead EBED/NFELT TW14 ....174 F4
KWD/TDW/WH KT20 ....238 E7
WOKN/KNAP GU21 ....231 L2
Watermead La MTCM CR4 ....202 A6
Water Meadow CSHM HP5 ....50 G8
Watermeadow Cl ERITH DA8 ....165 J6
Watermeadow La FUL/PGN SW6 ....157 M8
Watermead Rd CAT SE6 ....183 H7
Watermead Wy TOTM N17 ....100 B8
Watermens Sq PGE/AN * SE20 ....182 B10
Water Ms PECK SE15 ....160 B10
Watermill Cl RCHPK/HAM TW10 ....177 H6
Watermill La HERT/WAS SG14 ....25 L2
UED N18 ....99 M6
Water Mill Wy EYN DA4 ....210 A2
FELT TW13 ....175 N5
Watermill Wy WIM/MER SW19 ....201 M1
Watermint Cl STMC/STPC BR5 ....207 N4
Watermint Quay CLPT E5 ....119 P5
Waterperry La CHOB/PIR GU24 ....213 L6
Water Rd ALP/SUD HA0 ....135 L3
Water Rw WARE * SG12 ....26 C2
Waters Dr RKW/CH/CXG WD3 ....91 P2
STA TW18 ....173 J7
Water's Edge FUL/PGN * SW6 ....156 G7
Watersedge HOR/WEW KT19 ....219 P1
Watersfield Wy EDGW HA8 ....95 J8
Waterside CSHM HP5 ....51 H8
DART DA1 ....186 F1
HORL RH6 ....280 B2
KGLGY WD4 ....54 B5
LCOL/BKTW AL2 ....57 K3
RAD WD7 ....56 G10
UX/CGN UB8 ....131 M7
WALTH E17 ....120 B4
WGCE AL7 ....23 K3
Waterside Cl BARK IG11 ....123 K9
BERM/RHTH * SE16 ....19 P2
CRAWW RH11 ....283 H9
HARH * RM3 ....105 P8
HARH RM3 ....105 P8
HOM E9 ....140 E3
NTHLT UB5 ....133 N5
SURB KT6 ....199 K9
Waterside Ct KGLGY WD4 ....54 C5
LEW * SE13 ....161 J10
Waterside Dr DTCH/LGLY SL3 ....150 C1
WOT/HER KT12 ....197 J5
Waterside Ms GU GU1 ....249 P8
RKW/CH/CXG WD3 ....91 K7
Waterside Pl CAMTN NW1 ....4 D5
Waterside Rd GU GU1 ....250 A7
NWDGN UB2 ....153 P2
Waterside Wy TOOT SW17 ....179 M7
WOKN/KNAP GU21 ....231 N4
Waterslade REDH RH1 ....257 P10
Watersmeet HLWW/ROY CM19 ....46 E5
Watersmeet Cl RGUE GU4 ....250 D5
Watersmeet Wy THMD SE28 ....143 N8
Waterson Rd CDH/CHF RM16 ....168 E3
Waterson St BETH E2 ....7 K9
Watersplash Cl KUT KT1 ....199 K3
Watersplash Ct LCOL/BKTW * AL2 ....57 L3
Water Splash La ASC SL5 ....192 D1
Watersplash La HEST TW5 ....153 J4
HYS/HAR UB3 ....153 H3
Watersplash Rd SHPTN TW17 ....196 B4
Waters Rd CAT SE6 ....183 K6
KUT KT1 ....199 N2
Waters Sq KUT KT1 ....199 N3
Water St TPL/STR WC2R 12 A7
Waterton Av GVE DA12 ....191 H3
Water Tower Cl UX/CGN UB8 ....111 P10
Water Tower Hl CROY/NA CR0 ....223 L1
Water Tower Pl IS N1 ....6 B6
Waterway Rd LHD/OX KT22 ....236 F8
Waterworks La CLPT E5 ....120 C7
Waterworks Rd
BRXS/STRHM SW2 ....180 F2
Watery La CHOB/PIR GU24 ....213 J6
CHONG CM5 ....49 L1
HAT AL10 ....40 B5
HYS/HAR UB3 ....152 E4
NTHLT UB5 ....133 K4
RYNPK SW20 ....201 J2
SCUP DA14 ....185 L9
Wates Wy BRWN CM15 ....107 J2
MTCM CR4 ....202 A6
Wateville Rd TOTM N17 ....99 K9
Watford Cl BTSEA SW11 ....157 P7
GU GU1 ....250 C10
Watford Field Rd WATW WD18 ....73 K9
Watford Heath OXHEY WD19 ....93 L1
Watford Heath Farm
OXHEY * WD19 ....93 L1
Watford Int WATN * WD24 ....73 K5
Watford Rd BORE WD6 ....75 H10
CAN/RD E16 ....141 M7
HRW HA1 ....114 F7
KGLGY WD4 ....54 B6
LCOL/BKTW AL2 ....55 P2
NTHWD HA6 ....92 G8
RAD WD7 ....74 D2
RKW/CH/CXG WD3 ....72 B10
STAL AL1 ....38 A9
Watford Wy HDN NW4 ....116 D2
Watford Wy (Barnet By-Pass)
MLHL NW7 ....96 B5
Wathen Rd DORK RH4 ....272 G1
Watkin Rd WBLY HA9 ....115 N8
Watkinson Rd HOLWY N7 ....5 N1
Watling Av EDGW HA8 ....96 P9
Watling Cl HHNE HP2 ....35 P3
Watling Ct STP EC4M 12 F6
Watling Knoll RAD WD7 ....56 E9
Watlings Cl CROY/NA CR0 ....204 D6
Watling St BXLYHS DA6 ....164 C10
DART DA1 ....188 A3
GVW DA11 ....190 E8
LCOL/BKTW AL2 ....56 C1
MEO DA13 ....189 N6
STAL AL1 ....38 B9
STP EC4M 12 E6
Watlington Gv SYD SE26 ....182 D8
Watlington Rd HLWE CM17 ....29 N7
Watling Vw STAL AL1 ....38 B9
Watney Market WCHPL E1 ....140 A8
Watney Rd MORT/ESHN SW14 ....155 P9
Watneys Rd MTCM CR4 ....202 E5
Watney St WCHPL E1 ....140 A8
Watson Av CHEAM SM3 ....201 H9
EHAM E6 ....142 D2
STALW/RED AL3 ....38 E3
Watson Cl CRAWE RH10 ....284 D10
STNW/STAM N16 ....119 L10
WIM/MER SW19 ....179 P9
WTHK RM20 ....166 F7
Watson Rd DORK RH4 ....272 B3
Watson's Ms CAMTN NW1 ....9 P4
Watsons Rd WDGN N22 ....98 G9
Watson's St DEPT SE8 ....160 F6
Watson's Wk STAL AL1 ....38 D7
Wattendon Rd PUR/KEN CR8 ....241 J2
Wattisfield Rd CLPT E5 ....120 B8
Wattleton Rd BEAC HP9 ....88 C10
Watton Rd WARE SG12 ....26 B1
Watts Cl KWD/TDW/WH * KT20 ....238 G8
SEVS/STOTM N15 ....119 M3
Watts Crs PUR RM19 ....166 B3
Watts Gv BOW E3 ....140 F7
Watt's La CHST BR7 ....206 E1
KWD/TDW/WH KT20 ....238 G8
TEDD TW11 ....176 F8
Watts Lea WOKN/KNAP GU21 ....231 M2
Watt's Md KWD/TDW/WH KT20 ....238 G8
Watts Rd THDIT KT7 ....198 F7
Watts St WAP E1W 140 A10
Wat Tyler Rd BKHTH/KID SE3 ....161 H8
Wauthier Cl PLMGR N13 ....99 J6
Wavell Cl CHES/WCR EN8 ....62 D3
Wavell Dr BFN/LL DA15 ....185 H2
Wavell Gdns SLN SL2 ....128 E5
Wavell Rd BEAC HP9 ....88 G10
Wavel Ms KIL/WHAMP NW6 ....2 G4
Wavel Pl NRWD SE19 ....181 N7
Wavendene Av EGH TW20 ....172 F10
Wavendon Av CHSWK W4 ....156 A4
Waveney HHNE HP2 ....36 A1
Waveney Av PECK SE15 ....160 A10
Waveney Cl WAP E1W 13 P9
Waverley Av BRYLDS KT5 ....199 N6
CHING E4 ....100 E5
PUR/KEN CR8 ....241 M2
SUT SM1 ....201 L9
WALTH E17 ....121 J1
WBLY HA9 ....115 L10
WHTN TW2 ....175 N4
Waverley Cl E/WMO/HCT KT8 ....197 P5
HAYES BR2 ....206 A5
HYS/HAR UB3 ....152 E3
Waverley Ct WOKS/MYFD GU22 ....232 B4
Waverley Crs HARH RM3 ....105 K7
WOOL/PLUM SE18 ....162 G5
Waverley Dr CHERT KT16 ....194 G10
VW GU25 ....193 M4
Waverley Gdns BARK IG11 ....143 H4
BARK/HLT IG6 ....102 F10
CDH/CHF RM16 ....167 M1
EHAM E6 ....142 B7
NTHWD HA6 ....93 H9
Waverley Gv HDN NW4 ....116 G1
Waverley Pl FSBYPK * N4 ....119 J6
LHD/OX * KT22 ....236 G8
STJWD NW8 ....3 L7
Waverley Rd CEND/HSY/T N8 ....118 E4
COB KT11 ....218 A10
ENC/FH EN2 ....79 J8
EW KT17 ....220 E2
RAIN RM13 ....145 J5
RYLN/HDSTN HA2 ....113 M7
SL SL1 ....129 H7
SNWD SE25 ....204 A4
STALW/RED AL3 ....38 B4
STHL UB1 ....133 P9
SWFD E18 ....101 P9
TOTM N17 ....100 A8
WALTH E17 ....121 H1
WEY KT13 ....216 B2
WOOL/PLUM SE18 ....162 F4
Waverley Wy CAR SM5 ....221 P3
Waverton Rd WAND/EARL SW18 ....179 M3
Waverton St MYFR/PICC W1J 10 D9
Wavertree Rd BRXS/STRHM SW2 ....180 F3
SWFD E18 ....101 M10
Waxlow Crs STHL UB1 ....133 P8
Waxlow Rd WLSDN NW10 ....135 P4
Waxwell La PIN HA5 ....93 L10
Wayborne Gv RSLP HA4 ....112 D4
Waycross Rd UPMR RM14 ....126 D4
Waye Av HEST TW5 ....153 H7
Wayfarer Rd NTHLT UB5 ....133 M5
Wayfarers Pk BERK * HP4 ....33 L5
Wayfaring Gn GRAYS RM17 ....167 L4
Wayford St BTSEA SW11 ....157 P8
Wayland Av HACK E8 ....119 P10
Waylands HYS/HAR UB3 ....132 E7
STWL/WRAY TW19 ....172 B2
SWLY BR8 ....208 G4
Waylands Cl RSEV TN14 ....245 P1
Waylett Pl ALP/SUD * HA0 ....115 J9
WNWD SE27 ....181 J6
Wayne Cl ORP BR6 ....207 J10
Wayneflete Tower Av
ESH/CLAY KT10 ....197 P10
Waynflete Av CROY/NA CR0 ....203 J10
Waynflete Sq NKENS W10 ....136 G9
Waynflete St WAND/EARL SW18 ....179 M5
Wayre St HLWE CM17 ....29 M7
Wayside CRAWW RH11 ....283 H9
CRICK NW2 ....117 H6
CROY/NA * CR0 ....224 G3
KGLGY WD4 ....53 L6
MORT/ESHN SW14 ....155 P10
POTB/CUF EN6 ....59 N8
RAD WD7 ....57 J9
Wayside Av BUSH WD23 ....74 C10
HCH RM12 ....125 L7
Wayside Cl ROM RM1 ....124 G1
STHGT/OAK N14 ....78 D10
Wayside Ct TWK TW1 ....177 H2
Wayside Gdns CFSP/GDCR SL9 ....110 A5
DAGE RM10 ....124 B10
Wayside Gv CHST BR7 ....184 C7
Wayside Ms GNTH/NBYPK IG2 ....122 D4
The Wayside HHS/BOV HP3 ....36 D7
The Way REIG RH2 ....257 N9
Wayville Rd DART DA1 ....188 A3
Weald Br EPP CM16 ....48 F8
Weald Bridge Rd EPP CM16 ....48 F8
Weald Cl BERM/RHTH SE16 ....160 A4
BRW CM14 ....106 F4
HAYES BR2 ....206 B9
MEO DA13 ....190 B10
RGUE GU4 ....268 B6
RSEV TN14 ....265 J9
Weald Dr CRAWE RH10 ....284 B10
Weald Hall La EPP CM16 ....65 M1
Weald La KTN/HRWW/W HA3 ....94 C10
Weald Park Wy BRW CM14 ....106 D4
Weald Ri KTN/HRWW/W HA3 ....94 D8
Weald Rd BRW CM14 ....105 P2
HGDN/ICK UB10 ....132 B4
SEV TN13 ....265 J4
Weald Sq CLPT * E5 ....120 A7
Wealdstone Rd CHEAM SM3 ....201 J9
The Weald CHST BR7 ....184 C9
Wealdway MEO DA13 ....190 E9
Weald Wy REDH RH1 ....259 M4
REIG RH2 ....275 M4
ROMW/RG RM7 ....124 C4
YEAD UB4 ....132 F5
Wealdwood Gdns PIN HA5 ....94 A7
Weale Rd CHING E4 ....101 J4
Weall Gn GSTN WD25 ....55 J6
Weardale Av RDART DA2 ....188 B5
Weardale Gdns ENC/FH EN2 ....79 K5
Weardale Rd LEW SE13 ....183 J1
Wear Pl BETH E2 ....140 A5
Wearside Rd LEW SE13 ....160 G10
Weasdale Ct WOKN/KNAP GU21 ....231 L2
Weatherall Cl ADL/WDHM KT15 ....215 L2
Weatherhill Cl HORL RH6 ....280 G4
Weatherhill Rd HORL RH6 ....281 H4
Weaver Cl CRAWW * RH11 ....283 H8
EHAM E6 ....142 E9
Weavers Cl GVW DA11 ....190 D4
ISLW TW7 ....154 E10
Weavers La RSEV TN14 ....247 K7
STHWK SE1 ....13 K10
Weaver St WCHPL E1 ....13 N2
Weavers Wy CAMTN NW1 ....5 J5
Weaver Wk WNWD SE27 ....181 J7
Webb Cl CSHM HP5 ....50 G6
DTCH/LGLY SL3 ....150 A3
NKENS W10 ....136 F6
Webber Cl BORE WD6 ....75 J10
ERITH DA8 ....165 J6
Webber Rw STHWK SE1 ....18 B2
Webber St STHWK SE1 ....18 B1
Webb Est CLPT * E5 ....119 P5
Webb Pl WLSDN NW10 ....136 C5
Webb Rd BKHTH/KID SE3 ....161 L5
Webbscroft Rd DAGE RM10 ....124 C9
Webbs Meadow BGR/WK TN15 ....265 K1
Webb's Rd BTSEA SW11 ....180 A1
YEAD UB4 ....133 H5
Webb St STHWK SE1 ....19 J4
Webster Cl COB KT11 ....218 A10
HCH * RM12 ....125 L8
WAB EN9 ....63 M9
Webster Gdns EA W5 ....135 J10
Webster Rd BERM/RHTH SE16 ....19 P4
LEY E10 ....121 H8
Websters Cl WOKS/MYFD GU22 ....231 M6
Weddell Rd CRAWE RH10 ....284 A10
Wedderburn Rd BARK IG11 ....142 G3
HAMP NW3 ....117 N10
Wedgewood Cl EPP CM16 ....65 K6
NTHWD * HA6 ....92 D8
Wedgewood Dr HLWE CM17 ....47 N2
Wedgwoods BH/WHM * TN16 ....243 P7
Wedgwood Wk
KIL/WHAMP * NW6 ....117 L10
Wedgwood Wy NRWD SE19 ....181 K10
Wedhey HLWW/ROY CM19 ....46 F1
Wedlake Cl EMPK RM11 ....125 M6
Wedlake St NKENS * W10 ....8 B1
Wedmore Av CLAY IG5 ....102 D9
Wedmore Gdns ARCH N19 ....118 F7
Wedmore Rd GFD/PVL UB6 ....134 C5
Wedmore St ARCH N19 ....118 E8
Wednesbury Gdns HARH RM3 ....105 N8
Wednesbury Gn HARH RM3 ....105 N8
Wednesbury Rd HARH RM3 ....105 N8
Weech Rd KIL/WHAMP NW6 ....117 K9
Weedington Rd KTTN NW5 ....118 B10
Weedon Cl CFSP/GDCR SL9 ....89 N9
Weedon Hl AMS HP6 ....68 C1
Weedon La AMS HP6 ....68 F2
Weekes Dr SL SL1 ....128 G10
Weekley Sq BTSEA * SW11 ....157 N9
Weigall Rd LEE/GVPK SE12 ....161 M10
Weighbridge Rd
ADL/WDHM KT15 ....215 L5
Weighhouse St MYFR/PKLN W1K 10 D7
Weighton Rd
KTN/HRWW/W HA3 ....94 C9
PGE/AN SE20 ....204 A2
Weihurst Gdns SUT SM1 ....221 N2
Weimar St PUT/ROE SW15 ....157 H9
Weirbrook CRAWE RH10 ....284 B10
Weirdale Av TRDG/WHET N20 ....98 A3
Weird Wd HART DA3 ....211 P3
Weir Hall Av UED N18 ....99 L7
Weir Hall Gdns UED N18 ....99 L6
Weir Hall Rd UED N18 ....99 L6
Weir Pl STA TW18 ....195 H1
Weir Rd BAL SW12 ....180 D4
BXLY DA5 ....186 C3
CHERT KT16 ....195 L7
WIM/MER SW19 ....179 L6
WOT/HER KT12 ....197 H6
Weirside Gdns WDR/YW UB7 ....131 N10
Weirs Pas CAMTN NW1 ....5 K9
Weiss Rd PUT/ROE SW15 ....156 G9
Welbeck Av BFN/LL DA15 ....185 K4
BMLY BR1 ....183 M7
YEAD UB4 ....133 J6
Welbeck Cl BORE WD6 ....75 M7
EW KT17 ....220 D4
NWMAL KT3 ....200 C5
Welbeck Ri HARP AL5 ....20 C5
Welbeck Rd CAR SM5 ....201 P7
EBAR EN4 ....77 N10
EHAM E6 ....142 A5
RYLN/HDSTN HA2 ....114 A6
SUT SM1 ....201 N9
Welbeck St MHST W1U 10 D4
Welbeck Vls WCHMH * N21 ....99 K2
Welbeck Wy MHST W1U 10 E5
Welby St CMBW SE5 ....159 J7
Welch Pl PIN * HA5 ....93 K9
Welclose St STALW/RED AL3 ....38 B6
Welcomes Cottages CTHM * CR3 ....242 F9
Welcomes Rd PUR/KEN CR8 ....241 K1
Welden SLN SL2 ....129 P8
Weldon Cl RSLP HA4 ....133 J1
Weldon Dr E/WMO/HCT KT8 ....197 N4
Weldon Wy REDH RH1 ....258 E5
Weld Pl FBAR/BDGN N11 ....98 C6
Welfare Rd SRTFD E15 ....141 K2
Welford Cl CLPT E5 ....120 C8
Welford Pl WIM/MER SW19 ....179 K7
Welham Cl BRKMPK AL9 ....40 F10
Welham Mnr BRKMPK AL9 ....40 F10
Welham Rd TOOT SW17 ....180 B8
Welhouse Rd CAR SM5 ....201 P8
Welkin Gn HHNE HP2 ....36 D5
Wellacre Rd KTN/HRWW/W HA3 ....114 G4
Wellan Cl BFN/LL DA15 ....185 L1
Welland Cl DTCH/LGLY SL3 ....150 D5
Welland Gdns GFD/PVL UB6 ....134 E4
Welland Ms WAP E1W 13 P9
Wellands HAT AL10 ....40 D2
Wellands Cl BMLY BR1 ....206 C2
Welland St GNWCH SE10 ....161 H5
Well Ap BAR EN5 ....76 F9
Wellbrook Rd ORP BR6 ....226 D1
Wellbury Ter HHNE HP2 ....36 D6
Well Cl RSLP HA4 ....113 M8
STRHM/NOR SW16 ....180 G7
WOKN/KNAP GU21 ....231 P3
Wellclose Sq WAP E1W 13 P7
Wellclose St WAP E1W 13 P8
Wellcome Av DART DA1 ....165 M10
Well Cottage Cl WAN E11 ....121 P5
Well Ct MANHO EC4N 12 F6
Well Cft HHW HP1 ....35 L5
Wellcroft Cl WGCE AL7 ....23 K7
Wellcroft Rd SL SL1 ....128 G10
WGCE AL7 ....23 K6
Welldon Crs HRW HA1 ....114 D4
Well End Rd BORE WD6 ....75 P3
Wellen Ri HHS/BOV HP3 ....35 P9
Weller Cl AMS HP6 ....69 K3
CRAWE RH10 ....284 E8

Weller Pl ORP * BR6 226 D7
Weller Rd AMS HP6 69 K3
Wellers Cl BH/WHM TN16 262 F3
Wellers Ct CAMTN NW1 5 L8
Wellers Gv CHESW EN7 61 P4
Weller St STHWK SE1 18 E1
Wellesford Cl BNSTD SM7 239 J3
Wellesley EPP CM16 46 D6
Wellesley Av HMSMTH W6 156 E2
IVER SL0 151 J2
NTHWD HA6 92 G6
Wellesley Cl CHARL * SE7 161 P4
Wellesley Ct MV/WKIL W9 3 J9
Wellesley Court Rd
CROY/NA * CR0 203 L9
Wellesley Crs POTB/CUF EN6 59 H9
WHTN TW2 176 D5
Wellesley Gv CROY/NA CR0 203 L9
Wellesley Pde WHTN * TW2 176 D6
Wellesley Park Ms ENC/FH EN2 79 J6
Wellesley Pth SL SL1 149 M1
Wellesley Pl CAMTN * NW1 5 J10
KTTN NW5 118 B10
Wellesley Rd BELMT SM2 221 M3
BRW CM14 107 H2
CHSWK W4 155 M4
CROY/NA CR0 203 K8
HRW HA1 114 D3
IL IG1 122 E7
KTTN NW5 118 B10
SL SL1 149 M1
WALTH E17 120 F4
WAN E11 121 M3
WHTN TW2 176 C6
Wellesley St WCHPL E1 140 C7
Wellesley Ter IS N1 6 F9
Welley Av STWL/WRAY TW19 150 B10
Welley Rd STWL/WRAY TW19 172 B1
Well Farm Rd CTHM CR3 241 P5
Well Fld HART DA3 211 L4
Wellfield Av MUSWH N10 118 C1
Wellfield Cl HAT AL10 40 D3
Wellfield Gdns CAR SM5 221 P5
Wellfield Rd HAT AL10 40 E3
STRHM/NOR SW16 180 F7
Wellfields LOU IG10 82 D7
Wellfit St HNHL SE24 159 J9
Wellgarth GFD/PVL UB6 134 G1
Well Garth WGCE AL7 23 H6
Wellgarth Rd GLDGN NW11 117 L6
Well Gv TRDG/WHET N20 97 M2
Well Hall Pde ELTH/MOT SE9 162 C10
Well Hall Rd ELTH/MOT SE9 162 C10
Well Hl ORP BR6 228 C2
Well Hill La ORP BR6 228 C4
Wellhouse La BAR EN5 76 F8
BRKHM/BTCW RH3 274 A3
Wellhouse Rd BECK BR3 204 E4
Welling High St WELL DA16 163 L9
Wellington Av BFN/LL DA15 185 K2
CHING E4 100 F3
ED N9 100 A4
HSLWW TW4 175 P1
PIN HA5 93 N9
SEVS/STOTM N15 119 P4
VW GU25 193 N6
WOOL/PLUM SE18 162 F2
WPK KT4 200 F10
Wellington Cl CRAWE RH10 284 F4
DAGE RM10 144 D2
NTGHL W11 8 E6
NWCR SE14 160 C7
OXHEY WD19 93 M4
WOT/HER KT12 196 G8
Wellington Crs NWMAL KT3 199 P3
Wellington Dr DAGE RM10 144 D2
PUR/KEN CR8 222 G6
WGCE AL7 23 M5
Wellington Gdns CHARL SE7 161 P4
HPTN TW12 176 C7
Wellington Gv GNWCH SE10 161 J6
Wellington Hl LOU IG10 81 N4
Wellingtonia Av ABR/ST RM4 104 F4
Wellington Ms HOLWY N7 5 N2
Wellington Pde BFN/LL * DA15 185 K1
Wellington Park Est
CRICK * NW2 116 D7
Wellington Pl BROX * EN10 44 B9
BRW CM14 107 H6
COB KT11 217 P8
EFNCH * N2 117 P3
RGODL * GU7 267 K10
STJWD NW8 3 M9
Wellington Rd ASHF TW15 173 P8
BELV DA17 164 A4
BXLY DA5 185 N2
CROY/NA CR0 203 J7
CTHM CR3 241 K8
DART DA1 187 K2
EA W5 155 H3
EBED/NFELT TW14 174 F1
EHAM E6 142 C3
EN EN1 79 M9
EPP CM16 66 B3
FSTGT E7 121 M10
HAYES BR2 205 P4
HPTN TW12 176 C7
KTN/HRWW/W HA3 114 D1
LCOL/BKTW AL2 57 J2
LEY E10 120 D6
PIN HA5 93 N9
STAL AL1 38 G7
STJWD NW8 3 M8
STMC/STPC BR5 207 L6
TIL RM18 168 D8
UX/CGN UB8 131 M3
WALTH E17 120 D1
WAN E11 121 M3
WAT WD17 73 J6
WIM/MER SW19 179 K5
WLSDN * NW10 136 G5
Wellington Rd North
HSLWW TW4 153 N9
Wellington Rd South
HSLWW TW4 153 N10
Wellington Rw BETH E2 7 M9
Wellington Sq CHEL SW3 16 A7
Wellington St COVGDN WC2E 11 M7
GVE DA12 190 F3
HERT/WAS SG14 25 J4
SL SL1 149 K1
WOOL/PLUM SE18 162 D3
Wellington Ter CEND/HSY/T * N8 119 H1
NTGHL W11 8 F8
RYLN/HDSTN HA2 114 C6
WAP * E1W 140 A10
WOKN/KNAP * GU21 231 K4
Wellington Wy BOW E3 140 F5
HORL RH6 280 A2
WEY KT13 216 A6
Welling Wy ELTH/MOT SE9 162 G9
Well La BRWN CM15 86 E7
CDH/CHF RM16 147 K10
HLW CM20 46 D1
HLWW/ROY CM19 28 D10
MORT/ESHN SW14 177 P1
WOKN/KNAP GU21 231 P3
Wellmeade Dr SEV TN13 265 J3
Wellmeadow Rd HNWL W7 154 F3
LEW SE13 183 K2
Well Pth WOKN/KNAP GU21 231 P3
Well Rd BAR EN5 76 F9
HAMP NW3 117 N8
POTB/CUF EN6 59 P5
RSEV TN14 247 K3
Well-Row HERT/BAY SG13 42 G3
Wells Cl GT/LBKH KT23 236 A10
NTHLT UB5 133 K5
SAND/SEL CR2 223 M2
STALW/RED AL3 38 B5
WDSR SL4 148 F6
Wells Dr CDALE/KGS NW9 116 A6
Wells Gdns IL IG1 122 B5
RAIN RM13 144 G1
Wells House Rd WLSDN NW10 136 B7
Wellside Cl BAR EN5 76 F8
Wellside Gdns MORT/ESHN SW14 155 P10
Wells La ASC SL5 192 A3
RGUW GU3 248 B7
Wells Ms FITZ * W1T 11 H4
Wellsmoor Gdns BMLY BR1 206 D3
Wells Park Rd SYD SE26 181 P6
Wells Pl CMBW SE5 159 M6
REDH RH1 258 C6
Wellsprings Crs WBLY HA9 115 N8
Wells Ri STJWD NW8 4 A6
Wells Rd BMLY BR1 206 C2
EPSOM KT18 237 N1
HMSMTH W6 156 F1
RGUE GU4 250 F7
Wells Sq FSBYW WC1X 5 N10
Wells St GTPST W1W 10 G4
Wellstead Av ED N9 100 B1
Wellstead Rd EHAM E6 142 D4
Wells Ter FSBYPK N4 119 H7
The Wells STHGT/OAK N14 98 E2
Wellstones WAT * WD17 73 J8
Well St HOM E9 140 B2
SRTFD E15 141 K1
Wells Wy CMBW SE5 19 H10
SKENS SW7 15 L3
Wellswood Cl HHNE HP2 36 C5
Wells Yd WARE * SG12 26 C2
Well Wk HAMP NW3 117 N8
Well Wy EPSOM KT18 219 M10
Wellwood Cl COUL/CHIP CR5 222 F10
Wellwood Rd GDMY/SEVK IG3 123 K6
Welsford St STHWK SE1 19 N7
Welsh Cl PLSTW E13 141 M5
Welshpool St HACK * E8 7 P5
Welshside CDALE/KGS * NW9 116 B3
Welstead Wy CHSWK W4 156 C2
Welsummer Wy CHES/WCR EN8 62 C3
Weltje Rd HMSMTH W6 156 D4
Welton Rd WOOL/PLUM SE18 163 H6
Welwyn Av EBED/NFELT TW14 174 G2
Welwyn Cl CRAWW RH11 283 H10
Welwyn Ct HHNE HP2 36 A2
Welwyn Rd HERT/WAS SG14 24 F4
Welwyn St BETH E2 140 B5
Welwyn Wy YEAD UB4 132 F6
Wembley Hill Rd WBLY HA9 115 L10
Wembley Park Dr WBLY HA9 115 L9
Wembley Rd HPTN TW12 197 P1
Wembley Wy WBLY HA9 135 N1
Wemborough Rd STAN HA7 94 G9
Wembury Rd HGT N6 118 C5
Wemyss Rd BKHTH/KID SE3 161 L8
Wendela Cl WOKS/MYFD GU22 232 C4
Wendela Ct HRW HA1 114 D8
Wendell Rd SHB W12 156 C1
Wendley Dr ADL/WDHM KT15 215 J6
Wendling Rd CAR SM5 201 N8
Wendon St BOW E3 140 E3
Wendover Cl HARP AL5 20 C2
STALE/WH AL4 39 H1
YEAD UB4 133 L6
Wendover Dr NWMAL KT3 200 C6
Wendover Gdns
RBRW/HUT CM13 107 N3
Wendover Pl STA TW18 172 G8
Wendover Rd ELTH/MOT SE9 162 A9
HAYES BR2 205 N4
SL SL1 128 A7
STA TW18 172 G8
WLSDN NW10 136 C4
Wendover Wy BUSH WD23 74 B10
HCH RM12 125 K10
ORP BR6 207 K6
WELL DA16 185 K1
Wendron Cl WOKN/KNAP GU21 231 M4
The Wend COUL/CHIP CR5 222 E10
Wendy Cl EN EN1 79 N10
Wendy Crs GUW GU2 249 M8
Wendy Wy ALP/SUD HA0 135 K3
Wengeo La WARE SG12 26 A1
Wenlak Cl DEN/HRF UB9 111 K8
Wenlock Cl CRAWW RH11 283 K9
Wenlock Edge DORK * RH4 273 H4
Wenlock Gdns HDN * NW4 116 D2
Wenlock Rd EDGW HA8 95 N7
IS N1 6 E8
Wenlock St IS N1 6 F8
Wennington Rd BOW E3 140 C4
RAIN RM13 145 J7
Wensley Av WFD IG8 101 M8
Wensley Cl CRW RM5 104 B6
ELTH/MOT SE9 184 C2
HARP AL5 20 C5
Wensleydale CRAWW RH11 283 M10
HHNE HP2 35 P3
Wensleydale Av CLAY IG5 102 B10
Wensleydale Gdns HPTN TW12 176 A10
Wensleydale Rd HPTN TW12 175 P10
Wensley Rd UED N18 100 A7
Wensum Wy RKW/CH/CXG WD3 91 N2
Wentbridge Pth BORE WD6 75 M4
Wentland Cl CAT SE6 183 J5
Wentland Rd CAT SE6 183 J5
Wentworth Av BORE WD6 75 L9
FNCH N3 97 K8
SLN SL2 128 F5
Wentworth Cl ASHF TW15 174 C7
FNCH N3 97 L8
GVW DA11 190 D8
HAYES * BR2 205 M9
MRDN SM4 201 K7
ORP BR6 227 H2
POTB/CUF EN6 59 K7
RPLY/SEND GU23 233 L7
SURB KT6 199 J9
THMD SE28 143 N8
WAT WD17 72 G4
Wentworth Crs HYS/HAR UB3 152 E2
PECK SE15 159 P6
Wentworth Dr CRAWE RH10 284 E6
DART DA1 187 H3
PIN HA5 113 H3
VW GU25 193 L4
Wentworth Gdns PLMGR N13 99 J4
Wentworth Hl WBLY HA9 115 L6
Wentworth Ms BOW E3 140 D6
Wentworth Pk FNCH N3 97 L8
Wentworth Pl CDH/CHF RM16 168 A2
CSHM * HP5 51 H8
STAN * HA7 94 G7
Wentworth Rd BAR EN5 76 G6
CROY/NA CR0 203 H7
GLDGN NW11 117 J4
HERT/BAY SG13 25 K8
MNPK E12 122 A9
NWDGN UB2 153 K3
Wentworth St WCHPL E1 13 L5
Wentworth Wy PIN HA5 113 L2
RAIN RM13 145 J5
SAND/SEL CR2 241 P1
Wenvoe Av BXLYHN DA7 164 C8
Wepham Cl YEAD UB4 133 L7
Wernbrook St WOOL/PLUM SE18 162 F5
Werndee Rd SNWD SE25 203 P4
Werneth Hall Rd CLAY IG5 122 C1
Werrington St CAMTN NW1 5 H8
Werter Rd PUT/ROE SW15 157 H10
Wescott Wy UX/CGN UB8 131 M4
Wesleyan Pl KTTN NW5 118 C9
Wesley Av CAN/RD E16 141 M10
HSLW TW3 153 M8
WLSDN NW10 136 A5
Wesley Cl CHESW EN7 61 K4
CRAWW RH11 283 H10
HOLWY N7 118 G7
HORL RH6 280 B2
REIG RH2 275 J1
RYLN/HDSTN HA2 114 B7
STMC/STPC BR5 207 M3
WALW SE17 18 D6
Wesley Dr EGH TW20 172 D9
Wesley Hl CSHM HP5 50 G6
Wesley Pl WDSR * SL4 170 A5
Wesley Rd EFNCH N2 97 P10
HYS/HAR UB3 133 H9
LEY E10 121 H5
WLSDN NW10 135 P3
Wesley Sq NTGHL W11 136 G8
Wesley St CAVSQ/HST W1G 10 D4
Wessels KWD/TDW/WH KT20 238 G7
Wessex Av WIM/MER SW19 201 K2
Wessex Cl GDMY/SEVK IG3 123 H4
KUTN/CMB KT2 199 N1
Wessex Ct BECK * BR3 204 D1
Wessex Dr ERITH DA8 164 F8
PIN HA5 93 M8
Wessex Gdns CRICK NW2 117 H6
Wessex La GFD/PVL UB6 134 C4
Wessex Rd HTHAIR TW6 151 M10
Wessex St BETH E2 140 B5
Wessex Ter MTCM * CR4 201 P5
Wessex Wy GLDGN NW11 117 H5
Wesson Md CMBW * SE5 159 K6
Westacott YEAD UB4 132 F7
West Acres AMSS HP7 69 J6
Westacres ESH/CLAY KT10 217 N4
Westall Cl HERT/WAS SG14 25 K6
Westall Rd LOU IG10 82 E7
Westanley Av AMSS HP7 69 J5
West Ap STMC/STPC BR5 206 F5
West Arbour St WCHPL E1 140 C8
West Av CRAWE RH10 284 A5
FNCH N3 97 K7
HDN NW4 116 G3
HYS/HAR UB3 132 G9
LCOL/BKTW AL2 56 A1
PIN HA5 113 N4
REDH RH1 276 A6
STHL UB1 133 N9
WALTH E17 120 G3
WLGTN SM6 222 F2
WOT/HER KT12 216 F6
West Avenue Rd WALTH E17 120 F2
West Bank BARK IG11 142 E3
DORK RH4 272 E3
ENC/FH EN2 79 K7
STNW/STAM N16 119 M5
Westbank Rd HPTN TW12 176 B9
West Barnes La NWMAL KT3 200 D5
Westbeech Rd WDGN N22 119 H1
Westbere Dr STAN HA7 95 J6
Westbere Rd CRICK NW2 117 H9
Westbourne Av ACT W3 136 A8
CHEAM SM3 201 H9
Westbourne Cl YEAD UB4 133 K6
Westbourne Crs BAY/PAD W2 9 L7
Westbourne Crescent Ms
BAY/PAD W2 9 L7
Westbourne Dr BRW CM14 106 E5
FSTH SE23 182 C4
Westbourne Gdns BAY/PAD W2 8 G5
Westbourne Ga BAY/PAD W2 9 M8
Westbourne Gv NTGHL W11 8 C7
Westbourne Grove Ms
NTGHL * W11 8 E6
Westbourne Grove Ter
BAY/PAD W2 8 G5
Westbourne Pde
HGDN/ICK * UB10 132 C6
Westbourne Park Rd NTGHL W11 8 C5
Westbourne Park Vls
BAY/PAD W2 8 F4
Westbourne Pl ED N9 100 A4
Westbourne Rd BXLYHN DA7 163 N6
CROY/NA CR0 203 N6
FELT TW13 174 G6
HOLWY N7 5 P1
STA TW18 173 L10
SYD SE26 182 C9
UX/CGN UB8 132 C6
Westbourne St BAY/PAD W2 9 L7
Westbourne Ter BAY/PAD W2 9 J4
Westbourne Terrace Ms
BAY/PAD W2 9 J5
Westbourne Terrace Rd
BAY/PAD W2 9 J4
Westbridge Cl SHB W12 136 D10
Westbridge Rd BTSEA SW11 157 N7
Westbrook Av HPTN TW12 175 N10
Westbrook Cl EBAR EN4 77 N7
Westbrook Crs EBAR EN4 77 N7
Westbrook Dr STMC/STPC BR5 207 N8
Westbrooke Crs WELL DA16 163 M9
Westbrooke Rd BFN/LL DA15 184 G5
WELL DA16 163 M9
Westbrook Rd BKHTH/KID SE3 161 M7
HEST TW5 153 N6
STA TW18 173 J8
THHTH CR7 203 L1
West Burrowfield WGCE AL7 22 G7
Westbury CHES/WCR * EN8 62 C6
Westbury Ar WDGN * N22 119 J1
Westbury Av ALP/SUD HA0 135 K2
ESH/CLAY KT10 218 E3
STHL UB1 133 P6
WDGN N22 99 J10
Westbury Cl CTHM * CR3 241 N4
RSLP HA4 113 H5
SHPTN * TW17 196 C6
Westbury Dr BRW CM14 106 G4
Westbury Gv FNCH N3 97 K7
Westbury La BKHH IG9 101 P3
Westbury Lodge Cl PIN HA5 113 L1
Westbury Pl BTFD TW8 155 J5
Westbury Ri HLWE CM17 47 N2
Westbury Rd ALP/SUD HA0 135 K2
BARK IG11 142 G3
BECK BR3 204 D3
BKHH IG9 101 P2
BMLY BR1 206 A1
BRW CM14 107 H3
CROY/NA CR0 203 L6
EA W5 135 K8
FBAR/BDGN N11 98 F7
FELT TW13 175 L4
FSTGT E7 121 N10
NFNCH/WDSP N12 97 K7
NTHWD HA6 92 F5
NWMAL KT3 200 A4
PGE/AN SE20 204 C1
WALTH E17 120 F2
WATW WD18 73 J9
Westbury Ter BH/WHM TN16 262 F2
FSTGT E7 141 N1
UPMR RM14 126 D7
Westbush Cl HOD EN11 26 E10
Westcar La WOT/HER KT12 217 J3
West Carriage Dr BAY/PAD W2 15 M1
West Central St
NOXST/BSQ WC1A 11 L5
West Chantry RYLN/HDSTN HA2 94 A9
Westchester Dr HDN NW4 116 G1
Westcliffe Vls KUT * KT1 199 L2
West Cl ASHF TW15 173 P7
BAR EN5 76 E9
EBAR EN4 78 B8
ED N9 99 N4
GFD/PVL UB6 134 B4
HOD EN11 44 F1
RAIN RM13 145 J6
WBLY HA9 115 L6
Westcombe Av CROY/NA CR0 202 F6
Westcombe Dr BAR EN5 77 K9
Westcombe Hl BKHTH/KID SE3 161 M5
Westcombe Park Rd
BKHTH/KID SE3 161 M6
West Common CFSP/GDCR SL9 110 A3
HARP AL5 20 A4
West Common Cl HARP AL5 20 A5
West Common Gv HARP AL5 20 A5
West Common Rd HAYES BR2 205 M9
UX/CGN UB8 111 N10
Westcoombe Av RYNPK SW20 200 C1
Westcote Ri RSLP HA4 112 D5
Westcote Rd STRHM/NOR SW16 180 D8
Westcott WGCE AL7 23 N4
Westcott Av GVW DA11 190 D6
Westcott Cl BMLY BR1 206 B5
CROY/NA CR0 224 G5
SEVS/STOTM N15 119 N4
Westcott Crs HNWL W7 134 D7
Westcott House POP/IOD * E14 140 F9
Westcott Rd DORK RH4 272 E2
WALW SE17 18 D9
Westcott St DORK RH4 272 A3
Westcott Wy BELMT SM2 220 F6
West Ct ALP/SUD HA0 115 H7
Westcourt Pde GVE * DA12 191 J6
West Crs WDSR SL4 148 E7
West Crescent Rd GVE DA12 190 E2
Westcroft SLN SL2 128 G6
Westcroft Cl CRICK NW2 117 H9
PEND EN3 80 B4
Westcroft Ct BROX EN10 44 F5
Westcroft Gdns MRDN SM4 201 J3
Westcroft Ms HMSMTH * W6 156 D3
Westcroft Rd CAR SM5 222 B1
Westcroft Sq HMSMTH W6 156 D3
Westcroft Wy CRICK NW2 117 H9
West Cromwell Rd WKENS W14 14 D7
West Cross Route NTGHL W11 136 G9
West Cross Wy BTFD TW8 154 G5
Westdale Rd WOOL/PLUM SE18 162 E5
Westdean Av LEE/GVPK SE12 183 N4
Westdean Cl WAND/EARL SW18 179 L2
Westdean La CSHM HP5 50 B4
West Dene Dr HARH RM3 105 L6
Westdene Wy WEY KT13 196 F10
West Down GT/LBKH KT23 254 A3
Westdown Rd CAT SE6 182 F3
SRTFD E15 121 H9
West Drayton Park Av
WDR/YW UB7 151 P2
West Drayton Rd UX/CGN UB8 132 D7
West Dr ADL/WDHM * KT15 215 L6
ASC SL5 193 J5
BELMT SM2 220 G5
CAR SM5 221 N6
GSTN WD25 73 J2
KTN/HRWW/W HA3 94 C7
KWD/TDW/WH KT20 238 G4
TOOT SW17 180 C7
West Drive Gdns
KTN/HRWW/W HA3 94 C7
West Eaton Pl KTBR SW1X 16 C5
West Eaton Place Ms
KTBR * SW1X 16 C5
Wested La SWLY BR8 209 H7
West Ella Rd WLSDN NW10 136 B2
West End BGR/WK TN15 247 N3
BH/WHM TN16 263 L1
West End Av LEY E10 121 H3
PIN HA5 113 L2
West End Cl WLSDN NW10 135 P2
West End Ct PIN * HA5 113 L2
West End Gdns ESH/CLAY KT10 217 N2
NTHLT UB5 133 K4
West End La BAR EN5 76 G8
BRKMPK AL9 41 M4
ESH/CLAY KT10 217 N4
HYS/HAR UB3 152 D6
KIL/WHAMP NW6 2 F3
PIN HA5 113 L1
SLN SL2 129 K3
West End Rd BROX EN10 43 N9
NTHLT UB5 133 K2
RSLP HA4 113 J10
STHL UB1 133 M10
Westerdale HHNE HP2 35 P3
Westerdale Rd GNWCH SE10 161 M4
Westerfield Rd
SEVS/STOTM * N15 119 N3
Westerfolds Cl
WOKS/MYFD GU22 232 F3
Westergate Rd ABYW SE2 163 P5
Westerham Av UED N18 99 L4
Westerham Cl ADL/WDHM KT15 215 M3
BELMT * SM2 221 K6
Westerham Dr BFN/LL DA15 185 M2
Westerham Hl BH/WHM TN16 244 E8
Westerham Rd BH/WHM TN16 263 K1
HAYES BR2 226 A3
LEY E10 120 G4
OXTED RH8 261 M5
RSEV TN14 246 B9
SEV TN13 246 D9
Westerley Crs SYD * SE26 182 E8
Westermain ADL/WDHM KT15 215 M6
Western Av ACT W3 135 P6
BRW CM14 107 H2
CHERT KT16 195 K3
CHOB/PIR GU24 230 F7
DAGE RM10 144 D1
DEN/HRF UB9 111 M9
EA W5 135 K5
EGH TW20 194 E3
EPP CM16 65 J8
GLDGN NW11 116 G4
GPK RM2 105 K10
HGDN/ICK UB10 132 B1
WTHK * RM20 166 E3
Western Cl CHERT * KT16 195 K3
Western Ct FNCH * N3 97 K7
Western Cross Cl GRH DA9 189 H2
Western Dr SHPTN TW17 196 E5
Western Gdns ACT W3 135 M9
Western Gtwy CAN/RD E16 141 N9
Western La BAL SW12 180 B3
Western Man BAR * EN5 77 L9
Western Ms MV/WKIL W9 8 D2
Western Pde BAR EN5 77 K9
HGDN/ICK * UB10 132 C1
Western Perimeter Rd
STWL/WRAY TW19 151 L10
Western Pl DORK * RH4 272 F2
Western Rd BRW CM14 107 H3
BRXN/ST SW9 159 H9
EA W5 135 J9
EFNCH N2 118 A1
MTCM CR4 201 P1
NWDGN UB2 153 K3
PLSTW E13 141 N3
ROM RM1 124 F3
SUT SM1 221 K2
WAB EN9 45 K8
WALTH E17 121 H3
WDGN N22 98 G10
WLSDN NW10 135 P6
Western Ter HMSMTH * W6 156 D4
HOD * EN11 26 G10
Western Vw HYS/HAR UB3 152 G1
Westernville Gdns
GNTH/NBYPK IG2 122 F5
Western Wy BAR EN5 77 K10
THMD SE28 163 J1
West Farm Av ASHTD KT21 237 H4
West Farm Cl ASHTD KT21 237 H5
West Farm Dr ASHTD KT21 237 J5
Westferry Circ POP/IOD E14 140 F10
Westferry Rd POP/IOD E14 140 E9
Westfield AMS HP6 68 B1
BRKMPK AL9 41 K9
HLWS CM18 47 H2
REIG RH2 257 L7
SEV TN13 247 K8
SHGR GU5 270 F9
WGCE AL7 23 K4
Westfield Av SAND/SEL CR2 223 L9
WATN WD24 73 L4
WOKS/MYFD GU22 232 B7
Westfield Cl CDALE/KGS NW9 115 P1
CHES/WCR EN8 62 E7
FUL/PGN * SW6 157 M6
GVE DA12 190 F9
PEND EN3 80 D7
SUT SM1 221 J1
Westfield Common
WOKS/MYFD GU22 232 B8
Westfield Ct STALE/WH AL4 39 J3
Westfield Dr GT/LBKH KT23 236 A8
KTN/HRWW/W HA3 115 J3
Westfield Gdns
KTN/HRWW/W HA3 115 J2
Westfield Gv WOKS/MYFD GU22 232 B6
Westfield La KTN/HRWW/W HA3 115 J2
Westfield Pde
ADL/WDHM * KT15 215 N6
Westfield Pk PIN HA5 93 N8
Westfield Park Dr WFD IG8 102 B7
Westfield Rd BEAC HP9 88 B10
BECK BR3 204 E2
BERK HP4 33 K3
BXLYHN DA7 164 D9
CRAWW RH11 283 L7
CROY/NA CR0 203 J9
DAGW RM9 123 P9
GU GU1 250 B6
HERT/WAS SG14 25 K3
HOD EN11 44 E2
MLHL NW7 96 A4
MTCM CR4 201 P2
SLN SL2 128 G6
SURB KT6 199 J5
SUT SM1 221 J1
WEA W13 154 G1
WOKS/MYFD GU22 232 A9
WOT/HER KT12 197 M7
Westfields BARN SW13 156 C9
STALW/RED AL3 37 P8
Westfields Av BARN SW13 156 B9
Westfields Rd ACT W3 135 N7
Westfield St WOOL/PLUM SE18 162 A2
Westfield Wy RSLP HA4 112 F8
WCHPL E1 140 D5
WOKS/MYFD GU22 232 B8
West Flexford La RGUW GU3 266 D1
West Gdns EW KT17 220 B6
WAP E1W 140 A9
WIM/MER SW19 179 P9
West Ga EA W5 135 K5
HLW CM20 46 F1
Westgate Crs SL SL1 128 E9
Westgate Est
EBED/NFELT * TW14 174 C4

Westgate Rd BECK BR3 205 H1
DART DA1 187 L2
SNWD SE25 204 A4
Westgate St HACK E8 140 A3
Westgate Ter WBPTN SW10 15 H8
Westglade Ct
KTN/HRWW/W HA3 115 J3
West Green Dr CRAWW RH11 283 M7
West Green Pl GFD/PVL UB6 134 C3
West Green Rd
SEVS/STOTM N15 119 L2
West Gv GNWCH SE10 161 H7
WFD IG8 101 P7
WOT/HER KT12 217 J1
Westgrove La GNWCH SE10 161 H7
West Halkin St KTBR SW1X 16 C3
West Hall BF/WBF * KT14 215 M10
West Hallowes ELTH/MOT SE9 184 A4
Westhall Pk WARL CR6 242 B5
West Hall Rd RCH/KEW TW9 155 N7
Westhall Rd WARL CR6 241 P4
West Ham La SRTFD E15 141 J2
West Hampstead Ms
KIL/WHAMP NW6 2 G2
West Harding St
FLST/FETLN * EC4A 12 B5
Westharold SWLY BR8 208 E3
West Hatch Mnr RSLP HA4 112 G6
Westhay Gdns
MORT/ESHN SW14 177 N1
West Heath CHOB/PIR GU24 230 C9
West Heath Av GLDGN NW11 117 K6
West Heath Cl DART * DA1 186 G2
HAMP NW3 117 K8
West Heath Dr GLDGN NW11 117 K6
West Heath Gdns HAMP NW3 117 K7
West Heath La SEV TN13 265 J4
West Heath Rd BXLYHN DA7 163 N5
DART DA1 186 G2
HAMP NW3 117 K8
West Hl DART DA1 187 L2
HGT N6 118 B6
HOR/WEW KT19 219 P9
ORP BR6 226 C8
OXTED RH8 261 J6
PUT/ROE SW15 178 G3
RYLN/HDSTN HA2 114 D7
SAND/SEL CR2 223 M5
WBLY HA9 115 L6
West Hill Av HOR/WEW KT19 219 P8
West Hill Bank OXTED RH8 261 J6
West Hill Cl CHOB/PIR GU24 230 D8
Westhill Cl GVE DA12 190 E4
West Hill Dr DART DA1 187 K2
Westhill Pk HGT N6 118 A7
West Hill Ri DART DA1 187 L2
West Hill Rd HOD EN11 44 E1
WAND/EARL SW18 179 J2
WOKS/MYFD GU22 232 A5
West Hill Wy TRDG/WHET N20 97 L2
Westholm GLDGN NW11 117 L2
West Holme ERITH DA8 164 D7
Westholme ORP BR6 207 H7
Westholme Gdns RSLP HA4 113 H6
Westhorne Av ELTH/MOT SE9 183 P2
Westhorpe Gdns HDN NW4 116 F1
Westhorpe Rd PUT/ROE SW15 156 F9
West House Cl WIM/MER SW19 179 H4
Westhumble St RDKG RH5 254 G7
Westhurst Dr CHST BR7 184 E8
West Hyde La CFSP/GDCR SL9 90 C8
West India Av POP/IOD E14 140 F10
West India Dock Rd
POP/IOD E14 140 E8
West Kent Av GVW DA11 189 P2
Westlake Cl PLMGR N13 99 H4
YEAD UB4 133 M6
Westland Av EMPK RM11 125 M6
Westland Cl STWL/WRAY * TW19 173 P2
Westland Dr BRKMPK AL9 59 H3
HAYES BR2 205 L9
Westland Pl FSBYE EC1V 6 G10
Westland Rd WAT * WD17 73 J6
Westlands Av SL SL1 128 B8
Westlands Cl HYS/HAR UB3 153 H3
SL SL1 128 B8
Westlands Ct EPSOM KT18 237 P1
Westlands Ter BAL SW12 180 D2
Westlands Wy OXTED RH8 261 J3
Westland Vw CDH/CHF RM16 147 M10
West La BERM/RHTH SE16 160 A1
RDKG RH5 271 L5
Westlea Av GSTN WD25 73 M3
Westlea Cl BROX EN10 44 E10
Westlea Rd BROX EN10 44 E9
HNWL W7 154 F2
Westleas HORL RH6 279 P2
Westlees Cl RDKG RH5 273 H5
Westleigh Av COUL/CHIP CR5 240 B2
PUT/ROE SW15 178 F1
Westleigh Dr BMLY BR1 206 B2
Westleigh Gdns EDGW HA8 95 M9
West Links ALP/SUD HA0 135 J5
Westlinton Cl MLHL NW7 97 H7
West Lodge Av ACT W3 135 M10
West Lodge Ct ACT * W3 135 M10
Westlyn Cl RAIN RM13 145 K5
Westly Wd WGCE AL7 23 K4
Westmacott Dr
EBED/NFELT TW14 175 H4
West Malling Wy HCH RM12 125 J10
West Md HOR/WEW KT19 220 B3
HORL RH6 280 D4
RSLP HA4 113 K9
WGCE AL7 23 L8
Westmead PUT/ROE SW15 178 E3
WDSR SL4 148 G9
WOKN/KNAP GU21 231 N4
Westmead Dr REDH RH1 276 B8
Westmeade Cl CHESW EN7 62 A5
Westmead Rd SUT SM1 221 N1
West Meads GUW GU2 267 L1
Westmede BARK/HLT IG6 102 F7
Westmere Dr MLHL NW7 96 A4
West Ms PIM SW1V 16 F9
TOTM * N17 100 A8
West Ml GVW DA11 190 C2
Westminster Av THHTH CR7 203 J2
Westminster Br WEST SW1P 17 M2
Westminster Bridge Rd
STHWK SE1 17 N2
Westminster Cl
EBED/NFELT TW14 175 H4
TEDD TW11 176 F8
Westminster Ct HARP * AL5 20 B4
STALW/RED AL3 38 B8
WOKS/MYFD * GU22 232 E7
Westminster Dr PLMGR N13 98 F6
Westminster Gdns BARK IG11 143 H4
BARK/HLT IG6 102 G10
CHING E4 101 K2
Westminster Ldg
STALW/RED * AL3 38 B8
Westminster Rd CRAWE RH10 284 D8
ED N9 100 A2
HNWL W7 134 D10
SUT SM1 201 N9
Westmoat Cl BECK BR3 183 H10
Westmont Rd ESH/CLAY KT10 198 D9
Westmoor Gdns PEND EN3 80 C6
Westmoor Rd PEND EN3 80 C6
Westmoor St CHARL SE7 162 A3
Westmoreland Av EMPK RM11 125 K3
WELL DA16 163 H9
Westmoreland Dr BELMT SM2 221 L5
Westmoreland Pl EA * W5 135 J7
HAYES * BR2 205 M3
PIM SW1V 16 F8
Westmoreland Rd BARN SW13 156 C7
CDALE/KGS NW9 115 L2
HAYES BR2 205 K5
WALW SE17 18 G9
Westmoreland St
CAVSQ/HST W1G 10 D4
Westmoreland Ter
PGE/AN * SE20 182 A10
PIM SW1V 16 F7
Westmore Rd BH/WHM TN16 243 P6
Westmorland Cl HOR/WEW KT19 220 B6
MNPK E12 122 A7
TWK TW1 176 G2
Westmorland Rd HRW HA1 114 A3
LEY E10 120 F4
Westmorland Wy MTCM CR4 202 E4
Westmount Centre YEAD * UB4 133 L9
Westmount Ct EA * W5 135 L7
Westmount Rd ELTH/MOT SE9 162 C8
West Oak BECK BR3 205 J1
Westoe Rd ED N9 100 A3
Weston Av ADL/WDHM KT15 215 K1
E/WMO/HCT KT8 197 M4
ESH/CLAY KT10 198 D7
WTHK RM20 166 E3
Weston Cl COUL/CHIP CR5 240 G6
POTB/CUF EN6 59 J8
RBRW/HUT CM13 107 P1
Weston Dr KTN/HRWW/W HA3 94 G9
Weston Flds SHGR GU5 269 M5
Weston Gdns ISLW TW7 154 C7
WOKS/MYFD GU22 233 H2
Weston Gn DAGW RM9 123 P9
THDIT KT7 198 D8
Weston Green Rd
ESH/CLAY KT10 198 C8
Weston Gv BMLY BR1 205 L1
Weston Lea EHSLY KT24 252 E1
Weston Pk CEND/HSY/T N8 118 F4
KUT KT1 199 K2
THDIT KT7 198 D8
Weston Park Cl THDIT * KT7 198 D8
Weston Ri FSBYW WC1X 5 P9
Weston Rd BMLY BR1 205 L1
CHSWK W4 155 P2
DAGW RM9 123 P9
ENC/FH EN2 79 L6
EW KT17 220 B7
GUW GU2 249 M9
SL SL1 128 E7
THDIT KT7 198 D8
Weston St STHWK SE1 19 H3
Weston Wk HACK E8 140 A2
Weston Wy WOKS/MYFD GU22 233 H2
Westover Cl BELMT SM2 221 L5
Westover Hl HAMP NW3 117 K7
Westover Rd WAND/EARL SW18 179 M2
Westow Hl NRWD SE19 181 M9
Westow St NRWD SE19 181 M9
West Pk ELTH/MOT SE9 184 B5
West Park Av RCH/KEW TW9 155 M7
West Park Cl CHDH RM6 123 N3
HEST TW5 153 N5
West Park Hl BRW CM14 106 F4
West Park Rd CRAWE RH10 285 N2
HOR/WEW KT19 219 L8
LING RH7 281 P9
RCH/KEW TW9 155 M7
STHL UB1 134 B10
West Parkside GNWCH SE10 161 K1
West Pl NWDGN * UB2 154 A3
WIM/MER SW19 178 F8
West Point WDSR SL4 128 C10
Westpole Av EBAR EN4 78 C8
Westport Rd PLSTW E13 141 N6
Westport St WCHPL E1 140 C8
West Poultry Av FARR EC1M 12 C4
West Quarters SHB W12 136 D8
West Quay Dr YEAD UB4 133 M7
West Rp HTHAIR TW6 152 B7
Westray HHS/BOV HP3 36 D8
Westridge Cl HHW HP1 35 J6
West Ridge Gdns GFD/PVL UB6 134 B4
West Riding LCOL/BKTW AL2 55 N6
West Ri BAY/PAD * W2 9 P7
West Rd BERK HP4 33 M4
CHDH RM6 123 P4
CHEL SW3 16 B9
CHSGTN KT9 219 H7
CLAP SW4 180 E1
EA W5 135 K7
EBAR EN4 98 B2
EBED/NFELT TW14 174 E3
EFNCH N2 97 N10
GU GU1 268 B1
HLW CM20 29 K7
KUTN/CMB KT2 199 P1
REIG RH2 275 L1
ROMW/RG RM7 124 E5
SOCK/AV RM15 146 G5
SRTFD E15 141 L3
TOTM N17 100 A7
WDR/YW UB7 152 A2
WEY KT13 216 C4
Westrow Dr BARK IG11 143 J1
Westrow Gdns GDMY/SEVK IG3 123 J7
West Shaw HART DA3 211 J2
West Sheen V RCH/KEW TW9 155 L10
West Side BROX EN10 62 D1
Westside HDN NW4 96 E10
West Side Common
WIM/MER SW19 178 F8
Westside Ct CHOB/PIR * GU24 212 D9
West Smithfield STBT EC1A 12 C4
West Sq HLW * CM20 28 F10
LBTH SE11 18 C4
West St BETH E2 140 A4
BMLY BR1 205 M1
BXLYHN DA7 164 A10
CAR SM5 202 A10
CRAWW RH11 283 N8
CROY/NA CR0 223 K1
DORK RH4 272 F2
EPSOM KT18 219 P9
ERITH DA8 164 E3
EW KT17 220 B6
GRAYS RM17 167 M5
GVW DA11 190 D2
HERT/BAY SG13 25 K6
HOR/WEW KT19 219 P9
REIG RH2 257 J10
RYLN/HDSTN HA2 114 C6
SUT SM1 221 L2
WALTH E17 120 G3
WAN E11 121 K8
WARE SG12 26 C2
WAT WD17 73 J6
WOKN/KNAP GU21 232 C3
West Street La CAR SM5 222 A1
West Street Pl CROY/NA * CR0 223 K1
West Temple Sheen
MORT/ESHN SW14 177 N1
West Tenter St WCHPL E1 13 M6
West Ter BFN/LL * DA15 185 H4
West Thurrock Wy WTHK RM20 166 F3
West Towers PIN HA5 113 L4
West Valley Rd HHS/BOV HP3 35 M10
West Vw CSHM HP5 51 J5
EBED/NFELT TW14 174 D4
HAT AL10 40 D2
LOU IG10 82 C7
Westview HNWL W7 134 D8
West View Av CTHM CR3 241 N4
West View Cl RAIN RM13 145 K5
Westview Cl NKENS W10 136 F8
RAIN * RM13 145 K5
REDH RH1 275 P3
WLSDN NW10 116 C10
Westview Ct BORE WD6 75 J10
Westview Crs ED N9 99 M1
Westview Dr WFD IG8 102 A10
West View Gdns BORE WD6 75 J10
Westview Ri HHNE HP2 35 N5
West View Rd DART DA1 187 N2
STALW/RED AL3 38 C5
SWLY BR8 208 E6
WARL CR6 242 A5
Westville Rd SHB W12 156 D1
THDIT KT7 198 F7
West Wk EBAR EN4 98 B2
HYS/HAR UB3 133 H10
Westward Ho GU GU1 250 C8
Westward Rd CHING E4 100 E6
Westward Wy
KTN/HRWW/W HA3 115 K4
West Warwick Pl PIM * SW1V 16 G6
West Wy BRW CM14 106 F4
CAR SM5 221 N6
CRAWE RH10 284 B6
CROY/NA CR0 204 D9
EDGW HA8 95 N7
HARP AL5 20 B1
HEST TW5 153 N7
PIN HA5 113 L2
RKW/CH/CXG WD3 91 L2
RSLP HA4 112 G6
SHPTN TW17 196 E6
STMC/STPC BR5 206 G5
UED N18 99 L5
WAB EN9 80 G3
WLSDN NW10 116 A9
WWKM BR4 205 J6
Westway CRAWE RH10 285 H2
CTHM CR3 241 L8
GUW GU2 249 L8
HORL RH6 280 C8
RYNPK SW20 200 E4
SHB W12 136 D9
Westway Cl RYNPK SW20 200 E3
West Way Gdns CROY/NA CR0 204 C9
Westway Gdns REDH RH1 258 B7
Westways BH/WHM TN16 262 F2
HOR/WEW KT19 220 C1
Westwell Cl STMC/STPC BR5 207 N8
Westwell Rd STRHM/NOR SW16 180 F9
Westwell Road Ap
STRHM/NOR SW16 180 F9
Westwick Cl HHNE HP2 36 E7
Westwick Gdns HEST TW5 153 J8
HMSMTH W6 156 G1
Westwick Pl GSTN WD25 55 K10
Westwick Rw HHNE HP2 36 E7
Westwood Av ADL/WDHM KT15 215 J8
BRW CM14 106 F5
NRWD SE19 203 K1
RYLN/HDSTN HA2 114 A9
Westwood Cl AMS HP6 70 A5
BMLY BR1 206 A3
ESH/CLAY KT10 198 B10
POTB/CUF EN6 59 K6
RSLP HA4 112 C4
Westwood Dr AMS HP6 70 A5
Westwood Gdns BARN SW13 156 C9
Westwood Hl SYD SE26 181 P8
Westwood La RGUW GU3 266 A2
WELL DA16 163 K10
Westwood Pk FSTH SE23 182 A3
Westwood Pl SYD * SE26 181 P8
Westwood Rd BARN SW13 156 C9
BFOR GU20 212 C2
CAN/RD E16 141 N10
COUL/CHIP CR5 240 E4
GDMY/SEVK IG3 123 J6
MEO DA13 189 K8
West Woodside BXLY DA5 185 P4
Wetheral Dr STAN HA7 94 G9
Wetherby Cl NTHLT UB5 134 A1
Wetherby Gdns ECT SW5 15 J6
Wetherby Ms ECT SW5 15 H7
Wetherby Pl ECT SW5 15 J6
Wetherby Rd BORE WD6 75 K5
ENC/FH EN2 79 K5
Wetherby Wy CHSGTN KT9 219 K4
Wetherden St WALTH E17 120 E5
Wethered Rd SL SL1 128 A8
Wetherell Rd HOM E9 140 C3
Wetherill Rd MUSWH N10 98 B9
Wetherly Cl HLWE CM17 29 M8
Wettern Cl SAND/SEL CR2 223 M6
Wetton Pl EGH TW20 172 C8
Wexfenne Gdns
WOKS/MYFD GU22 233 L2
Wexford Rd BAL SW12 180 A3
Wexham Park La DTCH/LGLY SL3 129 P6
Wexham Pl DTCH/LGLY * SL3 130 A1
Wexham Rd SL SL1 149 M1
SLN SL2 129 N7
Wexham St SLN SL2 129 N5
Wexham Woods DTCH/LGLY SL3 129 P7
Wey Av CHERT KT16 195 K3
Weybank RPLY/SEND GU23 233 P2
Weybarton BF/WBF KT14 216 A9
Weybourne Cl HARP AL5 20 C1
Weybourne Pl SAND/SEL CR2 223 L6
Weybourne St
WAND/EARL SW18 179 M5
Weybridge Ct STHWK * SE1 160 A4
Weybridge Pk WEY KT13 216 B2
Weybridge Rd ADL/WDHM KT15 215 P1
THHTH CR7 203 H4
Weybrook Dr RGUE GU4 250 E5
Wey Cl BF/WBF KT14 215 L9
Wey Ct ADL/WDHM KT15 215 N5
HOR/WEW KT19 219 P1
Weydown Cl GUW GU2 249 L5
WIM/MER SW19 179 H4
Weydown La GUW GU2 249 M5
Weyhill Rd WCHPL E1 13 P5
Weylands Pk WEY KT13 216 E3
Wey La CSHM HP5 50 G8
Weylea Av RGUE GU4 250 D7
Weylond Rd BCTR RM8 124 A8
Wey Manor Rd ADL/WDHM KT15 215 N5
Weyman Rd BKHTH/KID SE3 161 P7
Weymead Cl CHERT KT16 195 M8
Weymouth Av EA W5 155 H2
MLHL NW7 96 B6
Weymouth Cl EHAM E6 142 E8
Weymouth Ct BELMT * SM2 221 L4
Weymouth Ms CAVSQ/HST W1G 10 E3
Weymouth Rd YEAD UB4 132 F5
Weymouth St CAVSQ/HST W1G 10 D3
HHS/BOV HP3 35 N10
Weymouth Ter BETH E2 7 M7
Weymouth Vls HOLWY * N7 118 G7
Weymouth Wk STAN HA7 94 F7
Wey Rd WEY KT13 196 A10
Weyside Cl BF/WBF KT14 216 A8
Weyside Gdns GU GU1 249 N8
Weyside Rd GU GU1 249 N9
Wey - South Pth GUW GU2 267 P2
Weyview Cl GU GU1 249 P8
Wey View Ct GU * GU1 267 P1
Whadcoat St FSBYPK N4 119 H7
Whalebone Av CHDH RM6 124 A4
Whalebone Gv CHDH RM6 124 A4
Whalebone La North CHDH RM6 123 P2
Whalebone La South BCTR RM8 124 A5
Whales Yd SRTFD * E15 141 K2
Whaley Rd POTB/CUF EN6 59 M9
Wharf Bridge Rd ISLW TW7 154 G9
Wharfdale Cl FBAR/BDGN N11 98 B7
Wharfdale Rd IS N1 5 M7
Wharfedale HHNE HP2 35 P3
Wharfedale Gdns
STRHM/NOR SW16 202 G4
Wharfedale Rd RDART DA2 188 B4
Wharfedale St WBPTN SW10 14 G8
Wharf La RKW/CH/CXG WD3 91 P1
RPLY/SEND GU23 232 F9
TWK TW1 176 F4
Wharf Pl BETH E2 7 P6
Wharf Rd BROX EN10 44 E10
BRW CM14 107 H4
GRAYS RM17 167 L5
GU GU1 249 P10
GVE DA12 191 H2
HHW HP1 35 L8
IS N1 6 E8
PEND EN3 80 D10
SRTFD E15 141 J3
STWL/WRAY TW19 171 P3
Wharfside Rd CAN/RD E16 141 K8
Wharf St CAN/RD E16 141 K7
The Wharf GRH * DA9 166 G10
Wharley Hook HLWS CM18 47 J4
Wharncliffe Dr STHL UB1 134 C10
Wharncliffe Gdns SNWD SE25 203 M2
Wharncliffe Rd SNWD SE25 203 L2
Wharton Cl WLSDN NW10 136 B1
Wharton Cottages
FSBYW * WC1X 5 P10
Wharton Rd BMLY BR1 205 N1
Wharton St FSBYW WC1X 5 P10
Whateley Rd EDUL SE22 181 N1
GUW GU2 249 M5
PGE/AN SE20 182 C10
Whatley Av RYNPK SW20 200 G3
Whatman Rd FSTH SE23 182 C3
Whatmore Cl STWL/WRAY TW19 173 K2
Wheastone Rd NKENS * W10 8 B3
Wheatash Rd ADL/WDHM KT15 195 L9
Wheatbarn WGCE AL7 23 L4
The Wheatbutts WDSR SL4 148 E4
Wheat Cl STALE/WH AL4 38 F2
Wheatfield HAT AL10 40 E3
HHNE HP2 35 N4
Wheatfields HLWE CM17 29 N5
PEND EN3 80 D5
Wheatfield Wy HORL RH6 280 C3
KUT KT1 199 K3
Wheathampstead Rd HARP AL5 20 C3
Wheathill Rd PGE/AN SE20 204 A2
Wheat Knoll PUR/KEN CR8 241 K2
Wheatlands HEST TW5 153 P5
Wheatlands Rd DTCH/LGLY SL3 149 N2
TOOT SW17 180 B6
Wheatley Cl EMPK RM11 125 L3
GRH DA9 188 F1
HDN NW4 96 D10
SBW CM21 29 M2
WGCE AL7 23 K7
Wheatley Gdns ED N9 99 M3
Wheatley Rd ISLW TW7 154 E9
WGCE AL7 23 J6
Wheatleys STALE/WH AL4 39 H4
Wheatley St CAVSQ/HST W1G 10 D4
Wheatley Terrace Rd ERITH DA8 164 G5
Wheatley Wy CFSP/GDCR SL9 90 B7
Wheatly Crs HYS/HAR UB3 133 H9
Wheatsheaf Cl CHERT KT16 214 G3
Wheat Sheaf Cl POP/IOD E14 160 F3
Wheatsheaf Cl
WOKN/KNAP GU21 232 C1
Wheatsheaf Hl RSEV TN14 228 A5
RSEV TN14 264 A7
Wheatsheaf La FUL/PGN SW6 156 F6
STA TW18 173 J10
VX/NE SW8 158 F6
Wheatsheaf Pde WDSR * SL4 171 M1
Wheatsheaf Rd ROM RM1 124 G4
WARE SG12 28 A1
Wheatsheaf Ter FUL/PGN * SW6 157 J6
Wheatstone Cl CRAWE RH10 284 C2
WIM/MER SW19 201 N1
Wheeler Av OXTED RH8 261 J5
Wheeler Gdns IS N1 5 M5
Wheeler La WCHPL E1 13 L3
Wheeler Rd CRAWE RH10 284 C9
Wheelers EPP CM16 65 J5
Wheelers Cl WAB EN9 45 K8
Wheelers Cross BARK IG11 142 G4
Wheelers Dr RSLP HA4 112 D4
Wheelers Farm Gdns EPP CM16 66 C2
Wheelers Gn WAB * EN9 45 L8
Wheelers La BRKHM/BTCW RH3 273 N2
BRW CM14 86 A8
EPSOM KT18 219 P10
HHS/BOV HP3 35 P8
HORL RH6 281 H5
Wheelers Orch CFSP/GDCR SL9 90 B7
Wheel Farm Dr DAGE RM10 124 D8
Wheelock Cl ERITH DA8 164 C6
Wheelright Cl BUSH WD23 74 A10
Wheelwrights Pl
DTCH/LGLY * SL3 150 F6
Wheelwright St HOLWY N7 5 N3
Whelan Wy WLGTN SM6 202 E10
Wheler St WCHPL E1 13 L2
Whellock Rd CHSWK W4 156 B2
Whenman Av BXLY DA5 186 D5
Wherwell Rd GUW GU2 267 P2
Whetstone Cl TRDG/WHET N20 97 N3
Whetstone Pk LINN WC2A 11 N5
Whetstone Rd BKHTH/KID SE3 161 P8
Whewell Rd ARCH N19 118 F7
Whichcote St STHWK * SE1 12 A10
Whidborne Cl DEPT SE8 160 F8
Whidborne St STPAN WC1H 5 M10
Whielden La AMSS HP7 68 C9
Whielden St AMSS HP7 68 G7
Whimbrel Cl PUR/KEN CR8 223 L7
Whimbrel Wy YEAD UB4 133 L8
Whinchat Rd THMD SE28 162 G2
Whinfell Cl STRHM/NOR SW16 180 E8
Whinfell Wy GVE DA12 191 J7
Whinshill Ct ASC SL5 192 F8
Whinyates Rd ELTH/MOT SE9 162 B9
Whipley Cl RGUE GU4 250 E5
Whippendell Cl STMC/STPC BR5 207 L1
Whippendell Hl KGLGY WD4 53 M6
Whippendell Rd WATW WD18 72 F9
Whippendell Wy
STMC/STPC BR5 207 L1
Whipps Cross Rd WAN E11 121 K3
Whiskin St CLKNW EC1R 6 C10
Whisper Wd RKW/CH/CXG WD3 71 L7
Whistler Cl CRAWE RH10 284 A10
Whistler Gdns EDGW HA8 95 L10
Whistlers Av BTSEA * SW11 157 N6
Whistler St HBRY N5 119 J9
Whistler Wk WBPTN * SW10 157 M6
Whiston Rd BETH E2 7 L7
Whitakers Wy LOU IG10 82 C5
Whitbread Cl TOTM N17 99 P9
Whitbread Rd BROCKY SE4 160 D10
Whitburn Rd LEW SE13 182 G1
Whitby Av WLSDN NW10 135 N5
Whitby Cl BH/WHM TN16 243 N5
GRH DA9 188 F1
Whitby Gdns CDALE/KGS NW9 115 M1
SUT SM1 201 N9
Whitby Pde RSLP * HA4 113 K7
Whitby Rd RSLP HA4 113 J8
RYLN/HDSTN HA2 114 B8
SL SL1 129 H9
SUT SM1 201 N9
WOOL/PLUM SE18 162 C3
Whitby St WCHPL E1 13 L1
Whitcher Cl NWCR SE14 160 D5
Whitcher Pl CAMTN NW1 4 G2
Whitchurch Av EDGW HA8 95 L8
Whitchurch Cl EDGW HA8 95 L7
Whitchurch Gdns EDGW HA8 95 L7
Whitchurch La EDGW HA8 95 K8
Whitchurch Pde EDGW * HA8 95 M8
Whitchurch Rd HARH RM3 105 M5
NKENS W10 136 G9
Whitcomb St SOHO/SHAV W1D 11 J7
Whitear Wk SRTFD E15 141 J1
White Av GVW DA11 190 C6
Whitebarn La DAGE RM10 144 B4
Whitebeam Av HAYES BR2 206 D7
Whitebeam Cl BRXN/ST * SW9 158 G6
CHESW EN7 61 M2
Whitebeam Dr REIG RH2 275 M3
SOCK/AV RM15 147 H5
Whitebeams HAT AL10 40 D7
LCOL/BKTW AL2 56 A4
White Beam Wy
KWD/TDW/WH KT20 238 D7
White Bear Pl HAMP * NW3 117 N9
White Bear Yd CLKNW * EC1R 12 A2
Whiteberry Rd RDKG RH5 272 A10
White Bridge Av MTCM CR4 201 N4
White Bridge Cl
EBED/NFELT TW14 174 G2
Whitebroom Rd HHW HP1 35 H4
White Bushes REDH RH1 276 B4
White Butts Rd RSLP HA4 113 L8
Whitechapel High St WCHPL E1 13 M5
Whitechapel Rd WCHPL E1 13 N4
White Church La WCHPL E1 13 N5
White City Cl SHB W12 136 F9
White City Rd SHB W12 136 E9
White Cl SL SL1 129 J10
White Conduit St IS N1 6 B7
Whitecote Rd GFD/PVL UB6 134 A8
White Craig Cl PIN HA5 93 P6
Whitecroft STAL AL1 38 G9
SWLY BR8 208 F2
Whitecroft Cl BECK BR3 205 J4
Whitecroft Wy BECK BR3 205 H4
Whitecross St STLK EC1Y 12 F1
Whitefield Av CRICK NW2 116 F5
PUR/KEN CR8 241 H2
Whitefield Cl STMC/STPC BR5 207 M3
WAND/EARL SW18 179 H2
Whitefields Rd CHES/WCR EN8 62 B4
Whitefoot La CAT SE6 183 J7
Whitefoot Ter BMLY BR1 183 L6
Whiteford Rd SLN SL2 129 K7
White Friars SEV TN13 265 H3
Whitefriars Dr
KTN/HRWW/W HA3 94 D10
Whitefriars St EMB EC4Y 12 B6
White Gate Gdns
KTN/HRWW/W HA3 94 D8
White Gates HCH RM12 125 K7
Whitegates WOKS/MYFD GU22 232 C6
Whitegates Cl RKW/CH/CXG WD3 72 B8
Whitegate Wy
KWD/TDW/WH KT20 238 E6
Whitehall WHALL SW1A 11 L10
Whitehall Cl CHIG IG7 103 K4
WAB EN9 45 L8
Whitehall Ct WHALL SW1A 11 L10
Whitehall Crs CHSGTN KT9 219 J2
Whitehall Dr CRAWW RH11 283 H7
Whitehall Farm La VW GU25 194 B3
Whitehall Gdns ACT W3 135 M10
CHING E4 101 J2

CHSWK W4 155 N5
WHALL SW1A 11 L10
Whitehall La BKHH IG9 101 M3
EGH TW20 172 C10
ERITH DA8 164 G8
GRAYS RM17 167 P5
REIG RH2 275 J4
STWL/WRAY TW19 172 D2
Whitehall Pk ARCH N19 118 D6
Whitehall Park Rd CHSWK W4 155 N5
Whitehall Pl CAR SM5 222 C1
WHALL SW1A 11 L10
Whitehall Rd CHING E4 101 K3
GRAYS RM17 167 P3
HAYES BR2 206 A5
HNWL W7 154 F1
HRW HA1 114 D5
THHTH CR7 203 H5
UX/CGN UB8 131 N3
Whitehall St TOTM N17 99 N8
Whitehands Cl HOD EN11 44 E3
White Hart Cl CSTG HP8 89 M4
SEV TN13 265 K4
White Hart Dr HHNE HP2 36 A7
White Hart La BARN SW13 156 B8
RGUW GU3 248 F9
ROMW/RG RM7 104 B9
WDGN N22 99 H9
White Hart Meadow BEAC HP9 88 D10
White Hart Mdw
RPLY/SEND GU23 233 M7
White Hart Pde SEV * TN13 246 F8
The White Hart Pde SEV * TN13 246 F8
White Hart Rd HHNE HP2 36 B7
ORP BR6 207 K7
WDSR SL4 149 J2
WOOL/PLUM SE18 163 H3
White Hart Rw CHERT * KT16 195 K7
White Hart St LBTH SE11 18 B7
White Hart Ter TOTM * N17 99 N8
White Hart Wd SEV TN13 265 K5
White Hart Yd GVE * DA12 190 F2
STHWK SE1 12 G10
Whitehaven CHESW * EN7 61 M4
SL SL1 129 L9
Whitehaven Cl HAYES BR2 205 M4
Whitehaven St STJWD NW8 9 N2
Whitehead Cl RDART DA2 187 K6
UED N18 99 L6
WAND/EARL SW18 179 M3
Whiteheads Gv CHEL SW3 15 P6
CHEL SW3 15 P7
White Heart Av UX/CGN UB8 132 D7
Whiteheath Av RSLP HA4 112 D5
White Hedge Dr STALW/RED AL3 38 B4
White Hermitage
STWL/WRAY * TW19 171 P1
White Heron Ms TEDD * TW11 176 E9
White Hl BERK HP4 33 P10
Whitehill BERK HP4 34 A4
White Hl BFOR GU20 212 A1
COUL/CHIP CR5 239 N9
CSHM HP5 51 H7
HHW HP1 35 J7
NTHWD HA6 92 B7
SAND/SEL CR2 223 L6
WLYN AL6 22 D1
White Hill Cl CSHM HP5 51 H6
Whitehill Ct BERK HP4 34 A4
Whitehill La GVE DA12 190 G6
REDH RH1 259 L3
RPLY/SEND GU23 234 D9
Whitehill Pde GVE DA12 190 F6
Whitehill Pl VW GU25 194 B5
Whitehill Rd DART DA1 187 H1
GVE DA12 190 F5
HART DA3 211 J2
MEO DA13 189 J10
Whitehills Rd LOU IG10 82 D7
Whitehorn Pl WDR/YW UB7 132 A10
White Horse Dr EPSOM KT18 219 P10
White Horse Hl CHST BR7 184 D7
White Horse La LCOL/BKTW AL2 57 J2
RPLY/SEND GU23 233 M7
WCHPL E1 140 C6
Whitehorse La SNWD SE25 203 M4
White Horse Rd EHAM E6 142 C5
WDSR SL4 148 C8
Whitehorse Rd CROY/NA CR0 203 K7
WCHPL E1 140 D7
White Horse St MYFR/PICC W1J 10 F10
Whitehouse Av BORE WD6 75 N8
White House Cl CFSP/GDCR SL9 90 B8
Whitehouse Dr GU GU1 250 E10
White House Dr STAN HA7 95 H5
Whitehouse La ABLGY WD5 55 J2
White House La ENC/FH EN2 79 K5
RGUE GU4 250 A5
White House Rd RSEV TN14 264 D6
Whitehouse Wy IVER SL0 130 G5
STHGT/OAK N14 98 C3
Whitehurst Dr UED * N18 100 C6
White Kennett St WCHPL E1 13 K5
White Knights Rd WEY KT13 216 D4
White Knobs Wy CTHM CR3 259 P1
Whitelands BRWN CM15 87 J1
Whitelands Av RKW/CH/CXG WD3 70 E7
Whitelands Wy HARH RM3 105 L9
White La BH/WHM TN16 243 N9
RGUE GU4 268 F2
Whiteleaf Rd HHS/BOV HP3 35 M9
White Ledges WEA W13 135 H8
Whitelegg Rd PLSTW E13 141 L4
Whiteley WDSR SL4 148 D6
Whiteley Rd NRWD SE19 181 L8
Whiteleys Pde HGDN/ICK * UB10 132 C6
Whiteleys Wy FELT TW13 175 P6
White Lilies Island WDSR SL4 148 F6
White Lion Ct BANK EC3V 13 J6
PECK * SE15 160 B5
White Lion Hl BLKFR EC4V 12 D7
White Lion Rd AMSS HP7 69 M5
White Lion Sq HAT AL10 40 D3
White Lion St HHS/BOV HP3 35 N10
IS N1 6 A8
White Lion Wk GU * GU1 268 A1
White Lion Yd CSHM * HP5 51 H8
White Ldg NRWD SE19 181 J10
White Lodge Cl BELMT SM2 221 M4
EFNCH N2 117 N4
SEV TN13 247 J9
White Lodge Gdns REDH RH1 276 B8
The White Ldg BAR * EN5 77 H7
White Lyon Ct BARB EC2Y 12 E3
White Lyons Rd BRW CM14 107 H4
Whitemore Rd GU GU1 250 A6
White Oak Dr BECK BR3 205 H2
White Oak Gdns BFN/LL DA15 185 J3
Whiteoaks BNSTD SM7 221 L9
Whiteoaks La GFD/PVL UB6 134 C4
White Oak Sq SWLY * BR8 208 F3
White Orchards STAN HA7 94 F6
TRDG/WHET N20 97 J1
White Pillars
WOKS/MYFD * GU22 231 P6
White Post Fld SBW CM21 29 N1
White Post Hl EYN DA4 209 P7
Whitepost Hl REDH RH1 257 P10
White Post La HOM E9 140 E2
White Post St PECK SE15 160 B6
White Rd SRTFD E15 141 K2
White Rose La
WOKS/MYFD GU22 232 C3
Whites Av GNTH/NBYPK IG2 123 H4
Whites Cl GRH DA9 189 H2
White's Grounds STHWK SE1 19 K1
Whites Grounds Est STHWK SE1 19 K1
White Shack La
RKW/CH/CXG WD3 72 A3
Whites La DTCH/LGLY SL3 149 N5
Whites Meadow BMLY * BR1 206 D4
White's Rw WCHPL E1 13 L4
White's Sq CLAP SW4 158 E10
Whitestile Rd BTFD TW8 155 H4
Whitestone La HAMP NW3 117 M8
Whitestone Wk HAMP NW3 117 M8
HHW HP1 35 K3
White St NWDGN UB2 153 L1
White Stubbs La BROX EN10 43 N7
Whitethorn WGCE AL7 23 K6
Whitethorn Av COUL/CHIP CR5 240 B1
WDR/YW UB7 131 P9
Whitethorn Gdns CROY/NA CR0 204 A9
EMPK RM11 125 K4
ENC/FH EN2 79 L9
Whitethorn St BOW E3 140 F6
Whitewaits HLW CM20 29 H10
White Wy GT/LBKH KT23 254 A2
Whitewebbs La ENC/FH EN2 79 N1
Whitewebbs Pk ENC/FH * EN2 79 M1
Whitewebbs Rd ENC/FH EN2 79 J1
Whitewebbs Wy
STMC/STPC BR5 207 J1
Whitewood Cottages
BH/WHM TN16 243 P6
Whitewood Rd BERK HP4 33 M5
Whitfield Cl GUW GU2 249 M7
Whitfield Pl FITZ W1T 10 G2
Whitfield Rd BXLYHN DA7 164 A6
EHAM E6 141 P2
GNWCH SE10 161 J7
Whitfield St FITZ W1T 11 H3
Whitfield Wy RKW/CH/CXG WD3 91 J2
Whitford Gdns MTCM CR4 202 A3
Whitgift Av SAND/SEL CR2 223 K2
Whitgift St CROY/NA CR0 203 K10
LBTH SE11 17 N5
Whit Hern Ct CHES/WCR EN8 62 B6
Whitings Rd BAR EN5 76 F9
Whitings Wy EHAM E6 142 D7
Whitland Rd CAR SM5 201 N8
Whitlars Dr KGLGY WD4 54 A4
Whitley Cl ABLGY WD5 55 H8
STWL/WRAY TW19 173 P2
Whitley Rd HOD EN11 44 G1
TOTM N17 99 M10
Whitlock Dr WIM/MER SW19 179 H3
Whitman Rd BOW E3 140 D6
Whitmead Cl SAND/SEL CR2 223 L3
Whitmoor La RGUE GU4 250 A2
Whitmore Av CDH/CHF RM16 147 N9
HARH RM3 105 M10
Whitmore Cl FBAR/BDGN N11 98 C6
Whitmore Est IS N1 7 K6
Whitmore Gdns WLSDN NW10 136 F4
Whitmore La ASC SL5 192 F5
Whitmore Rd BECK BR3 204 E3
HRW HA1 114 B5
IS N1 7 J6
Whitmores Cl EPSOM * KT18 237 P1
Whitmores Wd HHNE HP2 36 C5
Whitmore Wy HORL RH6 279 N3
Whitnell Wy PUT/ROE * SW15 178 F1
Whitney Av REDBR IG4 122 A2
Whitney Rd LEY E10 120 F5
Whitney Wk SCUP DA14 185 P9
Whitstable Cl BECK BR3 204 E1
Whitstable Pl CROY/NA CR0 223 K1
Whittaker Av RCH/KEW * TW9 177 J1
Whittaker Rd CHEAM SM3 201 J10
EHAM E6 141 P2
SLN SL2 128 D6
Whittaker St BGVA SW1W 16 C6
Whittaker Wy YEAD UB4 133 L8
Whitta Rd MNPK E12 122 A9
Whittell Gdns SYD SE26 182 B6
Whittenham Cl SLN SL2 129 M10
Whittingstall Rd FUL/PGN SW6 157 J7
HOD EN11 44 G1
Whittington Av BANK EC3V 13 J6
YEAD UB4 132 G7
Whittington Ms
NFNCH/WDSP N12 97 M5
Whittington Rd CRAWE RH10 283 N10
WDGN N22 98 G7
Whittington Wy PIN HA5 113 M3
Whittlebury Cl CAR SM5 222 A4
Whittle Cl GFD/PVL UB6 134 A8
WALTH E17 120 D4
Whittle Pkwy SL SL1 128 C8
Whittle Rd HEST TW5 153 K6
NWDGN UB2 154 A1
Whittlesea Rd KTN/HRWW/W HA3 94 B8
Whittlesey St STHWK SE1 12 B10
Whittle Wy CRAWE RH10 284 B1
Whitton Av East GFD/PVL UB6 114 E10
Whitton Av West NTHLT UB5 114 A10
Whitton Cl GFD/PVL UB6 134 G1
Whitton Dene HSLW TW3 176 A1
Whitton Dr GFD/PVL UB6 134 F1
Whitton Manor Rd ISLW TW7 176 B2
Whitton Rd HSLW TW3 154 A10
WHTN TW2 176 D2
Whitton Waye HSLW TW3 175 P2
Whitwell Rd GSTN WD25 73 L1
PLSTW E13 141 M5
Whitworth Rd CRAWW RH11 283 N2
SNWD SE25 203 M3
WOOL/PLUM SE18 162 D6
Whitworth St GNWCH SE10 161 K4
Whopshott Av
WOKN/KNAP GU21 231 P2
Whopshott Cl
WOKN/KNAP GU21 231 N2
Whopshott Dr
WOKN/KNAP GU21 231 P2
Whorlton Rd PECK SE15 159 P9
Whybridge Cl RAIN RM13 144 F3
Whybrow Gdns BERK HP4 34 B3
Whymark Av WDGN N22 119 H1
Whytebeam Vw CTHM CR3 241 N4
Whytecliffe Rd North
PUR/KEN CR8 223 J7
Whytecliffe Rd South
PUR/KEN CR8 223 H8
Whytecroft HEST TW5 153 L6
Whyteleafe Hl CTHM CR3 241 M5
Whyteleafe Rd CTHM CR3 241 M7
Whyteville Rd FSTGT E7 141 N1
Wichling Cl STMC/STPC BR5 207 N8
Wick Av STALE/WH AL4 21 J3
Wickenden Rd SEV TN13 247 K8
Wickens Meadow RSEV * TN14 246 G5
Wickersley Rd BTSEA SW11 158 B8
Wickers Oake NRWD * SE19 181 N7
Wicker St WCHPL E1 13 P6
Wicket Rd GFD/PVL UB6 134 F5
The Wickets ASHF TW15 173 P7
Wickets Wy BARK/HLT IG6 103 J7
The Wicket CROY/NA CR0 224 F2
Wickford Dr HARH RM3 105 N6
Wickford St WCHPL E1 140 B6
Wickford Wy WALTH E17 120 C2
Wickham Av CHEAM SM3 220 F2
CROY/NA CR0 204 D9
Wickham Cha WWKM BR4 205 J7
Wickham Cl DEN/HRF UB9 91 N9
EN EN1 80 A7
HORL RH6 280 A3
NWMAL KT3 200 C5
Wickham Ct WWKM * BR4 225 J1
Wickham Court Rd WWKM BR4 205 H9
Wickham Crs WWKM BR4 205 H9
Wickham Fld RSEV * TN14 246 G2
Wickham Gdns BROCKY SE4 160 E9
Wickham La ABYW SE2 163 K5
EGH TW20 172 D10
Wickham Rd BECK BR3 204 G2
BROCKY SE4 160 E9
CDH/CHF RM16 168 F1
CHING E4 101 H8
CROY/NA CR0 204 B9
KTN/HRWW/W HA3 94 C10
Wickham St LBTH SE11 17 N7
WELL DA16 163 H8
Wickhams Wy HART DA3 211 L5
Wickhams Whf WARE * SG12 26 D2
Wickham Wy BECK BR3 205 H4
Wickhurst Rd RSEV TN14 264 G8
Wicklands Rd WARE SG12 28 A3
Wick La BOW E3 140 F3
EGH TW20 171 L9
Wickliffe Av FNCH N3 97 H10
Wickliffe Gdns WBLY HA9 115 M7
Wicklow St FSBYW WC1X 5 N9
Wick Rd EGH TW20 171 N10
HOM E9 140 C1
TEDD TW11 176 G10
TRING HP23 32 B1
Wicks Cl LEE/GVPK SE12 184 A7
Wicksteed Cl BXLY DA5 186 E6
The Wick HERT/WAS SG14 25 J2
Wickwood St CMBW SE5 159 J8
Wildbrook BRWN CM15 87 H2
Widbury Gdns WARE SG12 26 E2
Widbury Hl WARE SG12 26 F2
Widdenham Rd HOLWY N7 118 G9
Widdicombe Av
RYLN/HDSTN HA2 113 M7
Widdin St SRTFD E15 141 K2
Widecombe Cl HARH RM3 105 L9
Widecombe Gdns REDBR IG4 122 B2
Widecombe Rd ELTH/MOT SE9 184 B6
Widecombe Wy EFNCH N2 117 N3
Widecroft Rd IVER SL0 131 H8
Widegate St WCHPL E1 13 K4
Widenham Cl PIN HA5 113 K3
Widewater Pl DEN/HRF * UB9 111 M3
Wide Wy STRHM/NOR SW16 202 E3
Widford Rd WARE SG12 28 A1
WGCE AL7 23 L5
Widgeon Cl CAN/RD E16 141 N8
Widgeon Rd ERITH DA8 165 J6
Widgeon Wy GSTN WD25 73 M2
Widley Rd MV/WKIL W9 2 F10
Widmore Cl CSHM HP5 50 D2
Widmore Dr HHNE HP2 36 B4
Widmore Lodge Rd BMLY BR1 206 A2
Widmore Rd BMLY BR1 205 N2
UX/CGN UB8 132 C6
Widworthy Hayes
RBRW/HUT CM13 107 N2
Wieland Rd NTHWD HA6 93 H8
Wigeon Wy YEAD UB4 133 L8
Wiggenhall Rd WATW WD18 73 J9
Wiggie La REDH RH1 258 B8
Wiggington Bottom TRING HP23 32 C1
Wiggins Md CDALE/KGS NW9 96 C8
Wigginton Av WBLY HA9 135 M1
Wightman Rd CEND/HSY/T N8 119 H2
Wigley Bush La BRW CM14 106 D3
Wigley Rd FELT TW13 175 L4
Wigmore Pl CAVSQ/HST * W1G 10 E5
Wigmore Rd CAR SM5 201 N9
Wigmores North WGCW AL8 22 G4
Wigmore St MBLAR W1H 10 D5
Wigram Rd WAN E11 121 P4
Wigram Sq WALTH E17 121 H1
Wigston Cl UED N18 99 M6
Wigston Rd PLSTW E13 141 N6
Wigton Gdns STAN HA7 95 K9
Wigton Pl LBTH * SE11 18 B8
Wigton Rd HARH RM3 105 M5
WALTH E17 100 E9
Wigton Wy HARH RM3 105 M5
Wilberforce Rd CDALE/KGS NW9 116 C3
FSBYPK N4 119 J7
Wilberforce Wy GVE DA12 190 G8
WIM/MER SW19 178 G9
Wilbraham Pl KTBR SW1X 16 B5
Wilbury Av BELMT SM2 221 J6
Wilbury Wy UED N18 99 L6
Wilby Ms NTGHL W11 8 D8
Wilcon Wy GSTN WD25 55 L10
Wilcot Av OXHEY WD19 93 M1
Wilcot Cl CHOB/PIR GU24 230 F2
OXHEY WD19 93 M1
Wilcot Gdns CHOB/PIR GU24 230 E2
Wilcox Cl BORE WD6 75 P5
VX/NE SW8 158 F6
Wilcox Gdns SHPTN TW17 195 P3
Wilcox Rd SUT * SM1 221 L1
TEDD TW11 176 C7
VX/NE SW8 158 F6
Wild Acres BF/WBF KT14 215 M7
Wild Ct HOL/ALD WC2B 11 N5
Wildcroft Dr RDKG RH5 273 J5
Wildcroft Gdns STAN HA7 95 J7
Wildcroft Rd PUT/ROE SW15 178 F3
Wilde Cl HACK E8 7 N5
TIL RM18 168 F8
Wilde Pl PLMGR N13 99 J7
Wilder Cl RSLP HA4 113 J6
Wildernesse Av BGR/WK TN15 247 M8
Wildernesse Mt SEV TN13 247 L8
Wilderness Rd CHST BR7 184 E10
GUW GU2 267 L1
OXTED RH8 261 K6
The Wilderness BERK HP4 33 P5
E/WMO/HCT KT8 198 B5
HPTN * TW12 176 A7
Wilde Rd ERITH DA8 164 C6
Wilders Cl WOKN/KNAP GU21 231 P4
Wilderton Rd STNW/STAM N16 119 M5
Wildfell Rd CAT SE6 182 G3
Wildfield Cl RGUW GU3 248 G9
Wild Goose Dr PECK SE15 160 B7
Wildgreen North DTCH/LGLY SL3 150 D3
Wildgreen South DTCH/LGLY SL3 150 D3
Wild Hatch GLDGN NW11 117 K4
Wildhill Rd BRKMPK AL9 41 J7
Wild Oaks Cl NTHWD HA6 92 G7
Wild's Rents STHWK SE1 19 J3
Wild St HOL/ALD WC2B 11 M6
Wildwood NTHWD HA6 92 E7
Wildwood Av LCOL/BKTW AL2 55 N6
Wildwood Cl EHSLY KT24 252 G1
LEE/GVPK SE12 183 L3
WOKS/MYFD GU22 233 J1
Wildwood Ct PUR/KEN CR8 241 L1
Wildwood Gv GLDGN NW11 117 M6
Wildwood Ri GLDGN NW11 117 M6
Wildwood Rd GLDGN NW11 117 M5
Wilford Cl ENC/FH * EN2 79 L7
NTHWD HA6 92 E8
Wilford Rd CROY/NA CR0 203 K6
DTCH/LGLY SL3 150 B3
Wilfred Av RAIN RM13 145 H7
Wilfred St GVE DA12 190 E2
WESTW SW1E 16 G3
WOKN/KNAP GU21 232 A3
Wilfrid Gdns ACT W3 135 P7
Wilhelmina Av COUL/CHIP CR5 240 D5
Wilkes Rd BTFD TW8 155 K5
Wilkes St WCHPL E1 13 M3
Wilkins Cl HYS/HAR UB3 152 G4
MTCM CR4 201 P1
Wilkin's Green La HAT AL10 39 P5
Wilkins Green Ter
STALE/WH * AL4 39 N6
Wilkins Gv WGCW AL8 22 G6
Wilkinson Cl CHESW EN7 61 K2
HGDN/ICK UB10 132 C3
Wilkinson Rd CAN/RD E16 141 P8
Wilkinson St VX/NE SW8 158 G6
Wilkinson Wy CHSWK W4 156 A1
HHS/BOV HP3 36 A10
Wilkin St KTTN NW5 4 D1
Wilkin Street Ms KTTN * NW5 4 E1
Wilks Av DART DA1 187 N5
Wilks Gdns CROY/NA CR0 204 D8
Wilks Pl IS N1 7 K8
Willan Rd TOTM N17 99 L10
Willan Wall CAN/RD E16 141 L9
Willard St VX/NE SW8 158 C9
Willats Cl CHERT * KT16 195 J6
Willcocks Cl CHSGTN KT9 199 K10
Willcott Rd ACT W3 135 N10
Will Crooks Gdns ELTH/MOT SE9 162 A10
Willenhall Av BAR EN5 77 M10
Willenhall Dr HYS/HAR UB3 132 F9
Willenhall Rd WOOL/PLUM SE18 162 E4
Willerfield Rd WLSDN NW10 135 P5
Willersley Av BFN/LL DA15 185 J4
ORP BR6 206 G10
Willersley Cl BFN/LL DA15 185 J4
Willesden La KIL/WHAMP NW6 136 G2
Willes Rd KTTN NW5 4 E1
Willett Cl NTHLT UB5 133 K5
Willett Cl STMC/STPC BR5 207 H6
Willett Rd THHTH CR7 203 H5
Willetts La DEN/HRF UB9 111 J9
Willett Wy STMC/STPC BR5 206 G5
Willey Broom La CTHM CR3 259 H1
Willey Farm La CTHM CR3 259 K2
Willey La CTHM CR3 259 L1
William Barefoot Dr
ELTH/MOT SE9 184 D7
William Booth Rd PGE/AN SE20 203 P1
William Carey Wy HRW HA1 114 D4
William Cl CRW RM5 104 D9
EFNCH N2 97 N10
LEW SE13 161 H9
STHL UB1 154 B1
William Ct HHS/BOV HP3 35 N10
William Covell Cl ENC/FH * EN2 78 G4
William Ellis Cl WDSR SL4 171 M1
William Ellis Wy
BERM/RHTH * SE16 19 P4
William Evans Rd
HOR/WEW KT19 219 M7
William Evelyn Ct RDKG * RH5 271 N5
William Gdns PUT/ROE SW15 178 E1
William Guy Gdns BOW E3 140 G5
William Hartley Yd SLN * SL2 129 N6
William IV St CHCR WC2N 11 L8
William Margrie Cl PECK * SE15 159 P8
William Ms KTBR SW1X 16 B2
William Morley Cl EHAM E6 142 A3
William Morris Cl WALTH E17 121 J2
William Morris Wy FUL/PGN SW6 157 M9
William Moulder Ct CSHM HP5 50 G4
William Rd CAMTN NW1 4 G10
CTHM CR3 241 L8
GU GU1 249 P10
SUT SM1 221 M2
WIM/MER SW19 179 H10
Williams Av WALTH E17 100 D10
William's Buildings BETH * E2 140 B6
Williams Cl CEND/HSY/T * N8 118 E4
FUL/PGN SW6 157 H6
Williams Gv SURB KT6 199 H6
WDGN N22 99 H9
Williams La MORT/ESHN SW14 155 P9
MRDN SM4 201 M6
Williamson Cl GNWCH SE10 161 L4
Williamson Rd FSBYPK N4 119 J4
Williamson St HOLWY * N7 118 F9
Williamson Wy MLHL NW7 97 H7
RKW/CH/CXG WD3 91 K2
William Sq BERM/RHTH SE16 140 D10
Williams Rd NWDGN UB2 153 M3
WEA * W13 134 F10
Williams Ter CROY/NA CR0 223 H3
William St BARK IG11 142 F2
BERK HP4 34 A5
BUSH WD23 73 L7
CAR SM5 201 P10
GRAYS RM17 167 P5
GVE DA12 190 E3
KTBR SW1X 16 B2
LEY E10 121 H4
SL SL1 129 L10
SL SL1 149 L1
TOTM N17 99 N8
WDSR SL4 149 J7
Williams Wy CRAWE RH10 284 C7
RAD WD7 75 H1
Willifield Wy GLDGN NW11 117 K3
Willingale Rd LOU IG10 82 F5
Willingdon Rd WDGN N22 99 J10
Willinghall Cl WAB EN9 63 J8
Willingham Cl KTTN NW5 118 D10
Willingham Ter KTTN * NW5 118 D10
Willingham Wy KUT KT1 199 M2
Willington Rd BRXN/ST SW9 158 F9
Willis Av BELMT SM2 221 P3
Willis Cl EPSOM KT18 219 N9
Willis Rd CROY/NA CR0 203 K7
ERITH DA8 164 D3
SRTFD E15 141 L4
Willis St POP/IOD E14 140 G8
Willmore End WIM/MER SW19 201 L1
Willoners SLN SL2 128 F7
Willoughby Av CROY/NA CR0 222 G1
Willoughby Cl BROX EN10 44 D7
Willoughby Dr RAIN RM13 144 F2
Willoughby Gv TOTM N17 100 A8
Willoughby La TOTM N17 100 A8
Willoughby Ms TOTM N17 100 A8
Willoughby Park Rd TOTM N17 100 A8
Willoughby Rd CEND/HSY/T N8 119 H1
DTCH/LGLY SL3 150 E2
HAMP NW3 117 N9
KUTN/CMB KT2 199 L1
TWK TW1 177 H1
Willoughby Wy CHARL SE7 161 N3
Willow Av BARN SW13 156 C8
BFN/LL DA15 185 K2
DEN/HRF UB9 131 M1
SWLY BR8 208 G4
WDR/YW UB7 132 A9
Willow Bank WOKS/MYFD GU22 232 B8
Willowbank Gdns
KWD/TDW/WH KT20 238 E8
Willow Brean HORL RH6 279 P3
Willow Bridge Rd IS N1 6 E2
Willowbrook HPTN * TW12 176 A8
WDSR SL4 149 J3
Willowbrook Est PECK * SE15 159 N6
Willowbrook Rd NWDGN UB2 153 N2
PECK SE15 19 M10
STWL/WRAY TW19 173 P4
Willowby Ct LCOL/BKTW AL2 57 J2
Willow Cl ADL/WDHM KT15 215 J7
BKHH IG9 102 A4
BRWN CM15 87 J4
BTFD TW8 155 H5
BXLY DA5 186 A2
CHESW EN7 61 M2
CRAWE RH10 283 P5
DTCH/LGLY SL3 150 F6
HAYES BR2 206 C5
HCH RM12 125 J8
RBRW/HUT CM13 87 N10
STMC/STPC BR5 207 L6
Willow Cnr HORL RH6 279 J8
Willow Ct HORL * RH6 280 C1
STAN * HA7 95 J8
Willowcourt Av
KTN/HRWW/W HA3 114 G3
Willow Crs STAL AL1 39 H6
Willow Crs East DEN/HRF UB9 111 M10
Willow Crs West DEN/HRF UB9 111 M10
Willow Dean PIN * HA5 93 L10
Willowdene BRWN CM15 86 E9
Willow Dene BUSH WD23 94 D1
Willowdene CHES/WCR EN8 62 D3
HGT * N6 118 A5
Willow Dene PIN HA5 93 L10
Willowdene Cl WHTN TW2 176 B3
Willowdene Ct BRW CM14 107 H5
Willow Dr BAR EN5 77 H8
RGUW GU3 248 B10
RPLY/SEND GU23 233 K10
Willow Edge KGLGY WD4 54 B5
Willow End NTHWD HA6 93 H7
TRDG/WHET N20 97 K3
Willowfield HLWS CM18 46 G2
Willow Gdns HEST * TW5 153 P7
RSLP HA4 112 G7
Willow Gn CHOB/PIR GU24 212 F9
Willow Gv CHST BR7 184 D9
RSLP HA4 112 G7
WDSR SL4 148 F9
Willowhayne Dr WOT/HER KT12 197 J7
Willowhayne Gdns WPK KT4 220 F1
Willow La AMSS HP7 69 L7
GU GU1 250 D9
MTCM CR4 202 A5
WATW WD18 73 H9
WOOL/PLUM SE18 162 C3
Willowmead CHIG IG7 103 K4
Willow Md DORK RH4 272 F1
Willowmead HERT/WAS SG14 25 H6
Willow Md SBW CM21 29 P2
Willowmead STA TW18 195 L1
Willowmead Cl EA W5 135 J7
WOKN/KNAP GU21 231 M2
Willowmere ESH/CLAY KT10 218 B1
Willow Mt CROY/NA CR0 223 M1
Willow Pk RSEV TN14 246 G3
SLN SL2 129 M2
Willow Pl HLWE CM17 48 A5
WDSR SL4 149 H5
WEST SW1P 17 H5
Willow Rdg CRAWE RH10 285 P10
Willow Rd CHDH RM6 123 P4
DART DA1 187 K4
DTCH/LGLY SL3 151 H8
EA W5 155 K1
EN EN1 79 M6
ERITH DA8 165 H7
HAMP NW3 117 N9
NWMAL KT3 199 P4
REDH RH1 275 M3
RGODL GU7 267 L9
WLGTN SM6 222 C4
Willows Av MRDN SM4 201 L5
Willows Cl PIN HA5 93 K10
Willowside LCOL/BKTW AL2 57 K3
Willows Pth EPSOM KT18 219 N10
Willows Ter WLSDN * NW10 136 C4
The Willows AMS HP6 68 G1
BECK * BR3 204 F1
BF/WBF KT14 215 P9
BORE * WD6 75 M5
EBAR * EN4 77 P10
ESH/CLAY KT10 218 D3
GRAYS RM17 168 A5
GUW * GU2 249 L5

LTWR GU18 212 B7
OXHEY WD19 93 J1
RGUE * GU4 250 G8
RKW/CH/CXG WD3 91 K3
STAL AL1 38 G10
WARE * SG12 26 G7
WEY KT13 196 B10
Willow St CHING E4 101 J1
ROMW/RG RM7 124 D2
SDTCH EC2A 13 J1
Willow Ter EYN * DA4 209 M9
PGE/AN * SE20 204 A1
Willowtree Cl HGDN/ICK UB10 112 D8
Willow Tree Cl HOM E9 140 D3
WAND/EARL SW18 179 L4
YEAD UB4 133 K6
Willow Tree La YEAD UB4 133 K6
Willow Tree Wk BMLY BR1 205 N1
Willowtree Wy
STRHM/NOR SW16 203 H1
Willow V CHST BR7 184 D9
GT/LBKH KT23 236 A9
SHB W12 136 D10
Willow Vw WARE * SG12 26 D3
WIM/MER SW19 201 N1
Willow Wk CHEAM SM3 201 J10
DART * DA1 187 M1
EGH TW20 171 P8
KWD/TDW/WH KT20 255 N6
ORP BR6 206 E10
REDH RH1 276 C2
SEVS/STOTM N15 119 J2
SHGR GU5 270 B5
STHWK SE1 19 K5
UPMR RM14 126 D6
WALTH E17 120 E3
WCHMH N21 78 G10
Willow Wy ALP/SUD * HA0 114 F8
BF/WBF KT14 215 M7
FNCH N3 97 L8
GDST RH9 260 A8
GU GU1 249 N6
HARH RM3 106 A7
HAT AL10 40 C7
HHW HP1 35 L4
HOR/WEW KT19 220 A3
LCOL/BKTW AL2 55 P3
NTGHL W11 136 G9
POTB/CUF EN6 59 L9
RAD WD7 74 D2
SUN TW16 197 H4
SYD SE26 182 A6
WHTN TW2 176 A5
WOKS/MYFD GU22 232 B6
Willow Wood Cl SL SL1 128 A4
Willow Wood Crs SNWD SE25 203 M6
Willow Wren Whf NWDGN * UB2 153 J3
Willrose Crs ABYW SE2 163 L4
Wills Crs HSLW TW3 176 A2
Wills Gv MLHL NW7 96 D6
Willshaw St NWCR SE14 160 F7
Willson Rd EGH TW20 171 N8
Wilman Gv HACK E8 7 P3
Wilmar Cl UX/CGN UB8 131 N2
YEAD UB4 132 E6
Wilmar Gdns WWKM BR4 204 G8
Wilmar Wy BGR/WK TN15 247 N6
Wilmer Cl RCHPK/HAM TW10 177 L8
Wilmer Crs RCHPK/HAM TW10 177 L8
Wilmer Gdns IS N1 7 J6
Wilmerhatch La EPSOM KT18 237 N3
Wilmer Lea Cl SRTFD E15 141 H2
Wilmer Pl STNW/STAM N16 119 N7
Wilmer Wy STHGT/OAK N14 98 E6
Wilmington Av CHSWK W4 156 A6
ORP BR6 207 M9
Wilmington Court Rd
RDART DA2 187 H6
Wilmington Gdns BARK IG11 142 G2
Wilmington Sq FSBYW WC1X 6 A10
Wilmington St FSBYW WC1X 6 A10
Wilmot Cl PECK * SE15 159 P6
Wilmot Cottages BNSTD * SM7 239 L1
Wilmot Gn RBRW/HUT CM13 107 H7
Wilmot Pl CAMTN NW1 4 G3
HNWL W7 134 D10
Wilmot Rd CAR * SM5 222 A2
DART DA1 187 J1
LEY E10 120 G7
PUR/KEN CR8 223 H8
SL SL1 128 A5
TOTM N17 119 L1
Wilmots Cl REIG RH2 257 M9
Wilmot's La HORL RH6 281 M3
REDH RH1 277 L10
Wilmot St BETH E2 140 A6
Wilmot Wy BNSTD SM7 221 K10
Wilmount St WOOL/PLUM SE18 162 E3
Wilna Rd WAND/EARL SW18 179 M3
Wilsham St NTGHL W11 136 G10
Wilshere Av STAL AL1 38 B9
Wilsman Rd SOCK/AV RM15 147 H4
Wilsmere Dr KTN/HRWW/W HA3 94 D8
NTHLT UB5 133 M1
Wilson Av MTCM CR4 179 P10
Wilson Cl CRAWE RH10 284 E10
SAND/SEL CR2 223 L2
WBLY HA9 115 L5
Wilson Dr CHERT KT16 214 E2
WBLY HA9 115 L5
Wilson Gdns HRW HA1 114 B5
Wilson Gv BERM/RHTH SE16 160 A1
Wilson La EYN DA4 210 E2
Wilson Rd CHSGTN KT9 219 L3
CMBW SE5 159 L7
IL IG1 122 C5
PLSTW E13 142 A5
Wilsons KWD/TDW/WH KT20 238 G7
Wilson's Av TOTM N17 99 N10
Wilson's Pl POP/IOD E14 140 E8
Wilson's Rd HMSMTH W6 156 G4
Wilson St SDTCH EC2A 13 H3
WALTH E17 121 H3
WCHMH N21 99 H1
Wilson Wk HMSMTH * W6 156 C3
Wilson Wy WOKN/KNAP GU21 232 A2
Wilstone Cl YEAD UB4 133 M6
Wilstone Dr STALE/WH AL4 39 H1
Wilthorne Gdns DAGE RM10 144 C2
Wilton Av CHSWK W4 156 B4
Wilton Cl WDR/YW UB7 151 N5
Wilton Crs BEAC HP9 88 D8
HERT/BAY SG13 25 K8
KTBR SW1X 16 C2
WDSR SL4 148 C10
WIM/MER SW19 201 J1
Wilton Dr CRW RM5 104 D8
Wilton Est HACK * E8 7 P2
Wilton Gdns E/WMO/HCT KT8 197 P3
WOT/HER KT12 197 L8
Wilton Gv NWMAL KT3 200 C6
WIM/MER SW19 179 J10
Wilton La BEAC HP9 89 J8
Wilton Ms HACK * E8 140 A1
KTBR SW1X 16 D3
Wilton Pl ADL/WDHM KT15 215 N5
KTBR SW1X 16 C1
Wilton Rd ABYW SE2 163 M2
BEAC HP9 88 D7
EBAR EN4 78 A8
HSLWW TW4 153 L9
MUSWH N10 98 B10
PIM SW1V 16 G4
REDH RH1 276 A1
WIM/MER SW19 179 P10
Wilton Rw KTBR SW1X 16 C2
Wilton Sq IS N1 6 G5
Wilton St KTBR SW1X 16 E3
Wilton Ter KTBR SW1X 16 C3
Wilton Vls IS N1 6 G6
Wilton Wk FELT * TW13 175 J5
Wilton Wy HACK E8 7 N2
HERT/BAY SG13 25 K7
Wiltshire Av EMPK RM11 125 N2
SLN SL2 129 H6
Wiltshire Cl CHEL SW3 15 P6
MLHL * NW7 96 C6
RDART DA2 188 C3
Wiltshire Gdns FSBYPK N4 119 K4
WHTN TW2 176 B4
Wiltshire La PIN HA5 113 H2
RSLP HA4 112 G1
Wiltshire Rd BRXN/ST SW9 159 H9
ORP BR6 207 K7
THHTH CR7 203 H3
Wiltshire Rw IS N1 6 G6
Wilverley Crs NWMAL KT3 200 B6
Wimbart Rd BRXS/STRHM * SW2 180 G3
Wimbledon Br WIM/MER SW19 179 J9
Wimbledon Hill Rd
WIM/MER SW19 179 H9
Wimbledon Park Rd
WIM/MER SW19 179 H6
Wimbledon Park Side
WIM/MER SW19 178 G5
Wimbledon Rd TOOT SW17 179 M7
Wimbolt St BETH E2 7 N9
Wimborne Av NWDGN UB2 153 P3
REDH RH1 276 A5
STMC/STPC BR5 207 J3
YEAD UB4 133 J8
Wimborne Cl BKHH IG9 101 P3
EW KT17 220 B9
LEE/GVPK SE12 183 L1
SBW CM21 29 N1
WPK KT4 200 F8
Wimborne Dr CDALE/KGS NW9 115 M1
PIN HA5 113 L5
Wimborne Gdns WEA W13 134 G8
Wimborne Gv WAT WD17 72 F3
Wimborne Rd ED N9 99 P3
TOTM N17 99 M10
Wimborne Wy BECK BR3 204 C3
Wimbourne St IS N1 6 G7
Wimlands La HORS RH12 282 A10
Wimpole Cl HAYES BR2 205 P4
KUT KT1 199 L2
Wimpole Ms CAVSQ/HST W1G 10 E3
Wimpole Rd WDR/YW UB7 131 N10
Wimpole St CAVSQ/HST W1G 10 E5
Wimshurst Cl CROY/NA CR0 202 F8
Winans Wk BRXN/ST SW9 159 H8
Wincanton Cl CRAWE RH10 284 E7
Wincanton Crs NTHLT UB5 113 P10
Wincanton Gdns BARK/HLT IG6 122 E1
Wincanton Rd HARH RM3 105 L4
WAND/EARL SW18 179 J3
Winchcombe Rd CAR SM5 201 N7
Winchcomb Gdns
ELTH/MOT SE9 162 A9
Winchdells HHS/BOV HP3 36 B9
Winchelsea Av BXLYHN DA7 164 A6
Winchelsea Cl PUT/ROE SW15 178 G1
Winchelsea Rd TOTM N17 119 M1
WLSDN NW10 136 A3
Winchelsey Ri SAND/SEL CR2 223 N3
Winchendon Rd FUL/PGN SW6 157 J6
TEDD TW11 176 C7
Winchester Av CDALE/KGS NW9 115 L1
HEST TW5 153 N5
KIL/WHAMP NW6 2 B5
UPMR RM14 126 E6
Winchester Cl AMSS HP7 69 K5
DTCH/LGLY SL3 151 H7
EN * EN1 79 M9
ESH/CLAY KT10 217 P1
HAYES BR2 205 L3
KUTN/CMB KT2 177 N10
LBTH * SE11 18 D6
Winchester Crs GVE DA12 190 C6
Winchester Dr PIN HA5 113 L3
Winchester Pk HAYES BR2 205 L3
Winchester Pl HACK E8 119 N10
HGT N6 118 C6
Winchester Rd CHING E4 101 H8
ED N9 99 N2
FELT TW13 175 N6
HAMP NW3 3 M3
HAYES BR2 205 L3
HGT N6 118 C6
HYS/HAR UB3 152 F6
IL IG1 122 G8
KTN/HRWW/W HA3 115 K2
ORP BR6 227 M1
TWK TW1 176 G2
WELL DA16 163 N8
WOT/HER KT12 197 H8
Winchester Sq STHWK SE1 12 G9
Winchester St ACT W3 135 P10
PIM SW1V 16 F7
Winchester Wk STHWK SE1 12 G9
Winchester Wy
RKW/CH/CXG WD3 72 C9
Winchfield Cl
KTN/HRWW/W HA3 115 H4
Winchfield Rd SYD SE26 182 D8
Winchfield Wy RKW/CH/CXG WD3 91 M1
Winchilsea Crs E/WMO/HCT KT8 198 B2
Winchmore Hill Rd
STHGT/OAK N14 98 F1
Winchmore Vls WCHMH * N21 98 G1
Winchstone Cl SHPTN TW17 196 A4
Winch Vw EPP CM16 65 L5
Winckley Cl KTN/HRWW/W HA3 115 L3
Wincott St LBTH SE11 18 B5
Wincrofts Dr ELTH/MOT SE9 162 G10
Windall Cl NRWD SE19 203 P1
Windborough Rd CAR SM5 222 B4
Windermere Av FNCH N3 97 K10
HCH RM12 125 H10
KIL/WHAMP NW6 2 B6
RSLP HA4 113 K5
STAL AL1 38 G8
WBLY HA9 115 H6
WIM/MER SW19 201 L3
Windermere Cl DART DA1 187 J4
EBED/NFELT TW14 174 F4
EGH TW20 172 E10
HHS/BOV HP3 36 D7
ORP BR6 206 E10
RKW/CH/CXG WD3 70 G9
STWL/WRAY TW19 173 N5
Windermere Gdns REDBR IG4 122 B3
Windermere Gv WBLY HA9 115 H6
Windermere Hall EDGW * HA8 95 L6
Windermere Rd ARCH * N19 118 D7
BXLYHN DA7 164 D8
COUL/CHIP CR5 240 F1
CROY/NA CR0 203 N8
EA W5 155 H2
LTWR GU18 212 A6
MUSWH N10 98 C9
PUT/ROE SW15 178 B7
STHL UB1 133 N7
STRHM/NOR SW16 202 D1
WWKM BR4 205 K9
Windermere Wy REDH RH1 257 P9
SL SL1 128 B7
WDR/YW UB7 131 P10
Winders Rd BTSEA * SW11 157 P8
Windfield Cl SYD SE26 182 C7
Windgates RGUE GU4 250 F7
Windham Av CROY/NA CR0 225 J6
Windham Rd RCH/KEW TW9 155 L9
Wind Hl CHONG CM5 49 H5
Windhill WGCE AL7 23 K4
Windhover Wy GVE DA12 191 H7
Winding Shot HHW HP1 35 K5
The Windings SAND/SEL CR2 223 N7
Winding Wy BCTR RM8 123 M8
Windlass Pl DEPT SE8 160 D3
Windle Cl BFOR GU20 212 C3
Windlesham Ct BFOR GU20 212 B1
Windlesham Gv WIM/MER SW19 178 G4
Windlesham Rd CHOB/PIR GU24 212 D7
Windley Cl FSTH SE23 182 B5
Windmill Av EW KT17 220 C7
STALE/WH AL4 39 H2
Windmill Cl CTHM CR3 241 K7
EW KT17 220 C8
HORL RH6 280 C4
LEW * SE13 161 H8
STHWK SE1 19 P6
SUN TW16 174 F10
SURB KT6 199 H8
UPMR RM14 125 P7
WAB EN9 63 K10
WDSR SL4 148 C8
Windmill Ct CRAWE RH10 283 N5
Windmill Dr CLAP SW4 180 C1
HAYES BR2 225 P1
LHD/OX KT22 236 G9
REDH RH1 257 N8
RKW/CH/CXG WD3 72 A10
Windmill End EW KT17 220 C8
Windmill Fld BFOR GU20 212 C3
WARE SG12 26 C3
Windmill Flds HLWE CM17 30 A7
Windmill Gdns ENC/FH EN2 79 H6
Windmill Gv CROY/NA CR0 203 K7
Windmill Hl AMSS HP7 88 E1
ENC/FH EN2 79 J7
HAMP * NW3 117 M8
KGLGY WD4 53 J8
RSLP HA4 112 G5
Windmill La BAR EN5 76 C10
BUSH WD23 94 D2
CHES/WCR EN8 62 D6
EW KT17 220 C7
GFD/PVL UB6 134 B7
NWDGN UB2 154 C2
SRTFD E15 141 J1
STHL UB1 134 B10
THDIT KT7 198 G7
WARE SG12 26 C3
Windmill Pas CHSWK * W4 156 B3
Windmill Ri KUTN/CMB KT2 177 N10
Windmill Rd CFSP/GDCR SL9 90 A8
CHSWK W4 156 B3
CROY/NA CR0 203 K7
DTCH/LGLY SL3 110 A10
EA W5 155 H3
HHNE HP2 35 P6
HPTN TW12 176 A8
MTCM CR4 202 D5
SEV TN13 265 J6
SL SL1 129 J10
SUN TW16 196 F1
UED N18 99 L5
WAND/EARL SW18 179 N2
WIM/MER SW19 178 E8
Windmill Rd West SUN TW16 196 F1
Windmill Rw LBTH SE11 18 A8
Windmill Shott EGH TW20 172 C9
Windmill St BUSH WD23 94 D2
FITZ W1T 11 J4
GVE DA12 190 E2
Windmill Ter SHPTN * TW17 196 F7
Windmill Wk STHWK * SE1 12 B10
Windmill Wy BRWN CM15 86 D3
REDH RH1 257 N8
RSLP HA4 112 G6
Windmill Wd AMS HP6 68 F3
Windmore Av POTB/CUF EN6 58 F7
Windridge Cl STALW/RED AL3 37 P8
Windrose Cl BERM/RHTH SE16 160 C1
Windrush NWMAL KT3 199 N4
Windrush Av DTCH/LGLY SL3 150 E2
Windrush Cl BTSEA * SW11 157 N10
CHSWK * W4 155 P6
CRAWW RH11 283 J9
HGDN/ICK UB10 112 A9
Windrush La FSTH SE23 182 C6
Windrush Rd WLSDN NW10 136 A3
Winds End Cl HHNE * HP2 36 B4
Windsor Av CDH/CHF RM16 167 N1
CHEAM SM3 201 H10
E/WMO/HCT KT8 197 P3
EDGW HA8 95 N5
HGDN/ICK UB10 132 C2
NWMAL KT3 199 P5
WALTH E17 100 D10
WIM/MER SW19 201 M1
Windsor Br WDSR SL4 149 J6
Windsor Cl CHESW EN7 61 P6
CHST BR7 184 E8
FNCH N3 97 H10
GUW GU2 267 L2
HHS/BOV HP3 35 P8
HHS/BOV HP3 52 D4
NTHWD HA6 93 H10
RYLN/HDSTN HA2 113 P8
SL * SL1 128 B6
WNWD SE27 181 K7
Windsor Ct AMS * HP6 69 J4
PIN * HA5 113 L1
STHGT/OAK N14 98 D1
Windsor Court Rd
CHOB/PIR GU24 213 K5
Windsor Crs RYLN/HDSTN HA2 113 P8
WBLY HA9 115 M8
Windsor Dr ASHF TW15 173 N7
DART DA1 187 H2
EBAR EN4 78 A10
HERT/WAS SG14 24 G4
ORP BR6 227 K3
Windsor End BEAC HP9 108 E1
Windsor Gdns CROY/NA CR0 202 F10
HYS/HAR UB3 152 E2
MV/WKIL * W9 8 E2
Windsor Great Pk ASC * SL5 170 E10
Windsor Gv WNWD SE27 181 K7
Windsor La SL SL1 128 B6
Windsor Ms CAT SE6 183 H4
Windsor Park Rd HYS/HAR UB3 152 G6
Windsor Pl CHERT * KT16 195 K6
Windsor Rd ASC SL5 170 A10
BAR EN5 76 G10
BCTR RM8 123 P8
BRWN CM15 86 G10
BXLYHS DA6 163 P10
CFSP/GDCR SL9 109 P6
CHING E4 100 G5
CHOB/PIR GU24 213 K5
CRICK NW2 136 E1
CSHM HP5 50 G4
DTCH/LGLY SL3 149 M6
EA W5 135 J9
EGH TW20 172 C6
EMPK RM11 125 K5
FNCH N3 97 H10
FSTGT E7 121 N10
GVE DA12 190 E7
HOLWY N7 118 F8
HSLWW TW4 153 J8
IL IG1 122 F9
KTN/HRWW/W HA3 94 B9
KUTN/CMB KT2 177 K10
LEY E10 120 G7
NWDGN UB2 153 N2
PEND EN3 80 C2
PLMGR N13 99 H4
RCH/KEW TW9 155 L8
SL SL1 149 K1
STWL/WRAY TW19 172 A4
SUN TW16 175 H10
TEDD TW11 176 C8
THHTH CR7 203 J2
TOTM N17 99 P10
WAN E11 121 M6
WATN WD24 73 K4
WDSR SL4 171 P3
WPK KT4 200 D9
The Windsors BKHH IG9 102 B3
Windsor St CHERT KT16 195 K6
IS N1 6 D6
UX/CGN UB8 131 M3
Windsor Ter IS N1 6 F9
Windsor Wk CMBW SE5 159 L8
WEY KT13 216 C2
Windsor Wy HMSMTH W6 156 G3
RKW/CH/CXG WD3 91 K2
WOKS/MYFD GU22 232 F2
Windsor Wd WAB EN9 63 K9
Winds Rdg RPLY/SEND GU23 250 F1
Windus Rd STNW/STAM N16 119 N6
Windward Cl PEND EN3 80 C1
Windycroft Cl PUR/KEN CR8 222 E9
Windy Hl RBRW/HUT CM13 107 P2
Windy Rdg BMLY BR1 206 B1
Windyridge CRAWW RH11 283 K8
Windy Ridge Cl WIM/MER SW19 178 G8
Wine Cl WAP E1W 140 B9
Winern Glebe BF/WBF KT14 215 N9
Winery La KUT KT1 199 L3
Winey Cl CHSGTN KT9 219 H4
Winford Dr BROX EN10 44 E8
Winforton St GNWCH SE10 161 H7
Winfrith Rd WAND/EARL SW18 179 M3
Wingate Crs CROY/NA CR0 202 F6
Wingate Rd HMSMTH W6 156 E2
IL IG1 122 E10
SCUP DA14 185 M8
Wingate Wy STAL AL1 38 F7
Wingfield GRAYS RM17 167 L4
Wingfield Cl ADL/WDHM KT15 215 L6
RBRW/HUT CM13 107 M4
Wingfield Ct WATW * WD18 72 E10
Wingfield Gdns UPMR RM14 126 D4
Wingfield Ms PECK * SE15 159 P9
Wingfield Rd GVW DA11 190 E3
KUTN/CMB KT2 177 L9
SRTFD E15 121 K10
WALTH E17 120 G3
Wingfield St PECK SE15 159 P9
Wingfield Wy RSLP HA4 133 J1
Wingford Rd CLAP SW4 180 F2
Wingletye La EMPK RM11 125 N2
Wingmore Rd HNHL SE24 159 K9
Wingrave Crs BRW CM14 106 D5
Wingrave Rd HMSMTH W6 156 F5
Wingrove Rd CAT SE6 183 K5
Wings Cl SUT SM1 221 K1
Wingway BRW CM14 107 H2
Winifred Av HCH RM12 125 L9
Winifred Pl NFNCH/WDSPP N12 97 M6
Winifred Rd BCTR RM8 123 P7
COUL/CHIP CR5 240 B2
DART DA1 187 J1
ERITH DA8 164 F4
HHS/BOV HP3 35 N10
HPTN TW12 175 P7
WIM/MER SW19 201 K1
Winifred St CAN/RD E16 142 C10
Winifred Ter EN EN1 99 N1
Winkers Cl CFSP/GDCR SL9 90 C9
Winkers La CFSP/GDCR SL9 90 C9
Winkfield Pln WDSR SL4 170 A3
Winkfield Rd WDGN N22 99 H9
WDSR SL4 170 B3
Winkley St BETH E2 140 A4
Winkworth Cottages
WCHPL * E1 140 B6
Winkworth Rd BNSTD SM7 221 K10
Winlaton Rd BMLY BR1 183 J7
Winmill Rd BCTR RM8 124 A8
Winn Bridge Cl WFD IG8 102 A9
Winn Common Rd
WOOL/PLUM SE18 163 H5
Winnett St SOHO/SHAV W1D 11 J7
Winnington Cl EFNCH N2 117 N4
Winnington Rd EFNCH N2 117 N4
PEND EN3 80 B4
Winnington Wy
WOKN/KNAP GU21 231 N4
Winnipeg Dr ORP BR6 227 J3
Winnock Rd WDR/YW UB7 131 N10
Winn Rd LEE/GVPK SE12 183 M4
Winns Av WALTH E17 100 E10
Winns Ms SEVS/STOTM N15 119 M2
Winns Ter WALTH E17 100 F10
Winsbeach WALTH E17 121 J1
Winscombe Crs EA W5 135 J6
Winscombe St KTTN NW5 118 C8
Winscombe Wy STAN HA7 94 F6
Winsford Rd CAT SE6 182 E6
Winsford Ter UED * N18 99 L6
Winsham Gv BTSEA SW11 180 B1
Winslade Rd BRXS/STRHM SW2 180 F1
Winsland Ms BAY/PAD W2 9 L5
Winsland St BAY/PAD W2 9 L5
Winsley St GTPST W1W 10 G5
Winslow Cl PIN HA5 113 J4
WLSDN NW10 116 B8
Winslow Gv CHING E4 101 K3
Winslow Rd HMSMTH W6 156 F5
Winslow Wy FELT TW13 175 L6
WOT/HER KT12 197 K10
Winsor Ter EHAM E6 142 D7
Winstane Cl AMS HP6 50 G10
Winstanley Cl COB KT11 217 J10
Winstanley Rd BTSEA SW11 157 N9
Winstead Gdns DAGE RM10 124 D10
Winston Av CDALE/KGS NW9 116 B5
Winston Churchill Wy
CHES/WCR EN8 62 B9
Winston Cl GRH DA9 188 E2
KTN/HRWW/W HA3 94 E7
ROMW/RG RM7 124 C2
Winston Ct PIN HA5 94 A8
Winston Dr COB KT11 235 M2
Winston Gdns BERK HP4 33 L5
Winston House SURB * KT6 199 K5
Winston Rd STNW/STAM N16 119 L9
Winston Wy IL IG1 122 E8
POTB/CUF EN6 59 K9
WOKS/MYFD GU22 232 E6
Winstre Rd BORE WD6 75 M5
Winter Av EHAM E6 142 B3
Winterborne Av ORP BR6 206 G10
Winterbourne Gv WEY KT13 216 D3
Winterbourne Rd BCTR RM8 123 M7
FSTH SE23 182 E4
THHTH CR7 203 H4
Winter Box Wk
RCHPK/HAM TW10 177 L1
Winterbrook Rd HNHL SE24 181 K2
Winterburn Cl FBAR/BDGN N11 98 B7
Winterdown Gdns
ESH/CLAY KT10 217 N3
Winterdown Rd ESH/CLAY KT10 217 M3
Winterfold CRAWE * RH10 284 B10
CRAWE RH10 284 B10
Winterfold Cl WIM/MER SW19 179 H5
Winterhill Wy RGUE GU4 250 E6
Winterscroft Rd HOD * EN11 44 E2
Wintersells Rd BF/WBF KT14 215 N6
Winters Rd THDIT KT7 198 G7
Winterstoke Rd FSTH SE23 182 E4
Winters Wy WAB EN9 63 M9
Winterton Pl WBPTN SW10 15 K9
Winterwell Rd
BRXS/STRHM SW2 180 F1
Winthorpe Rd PUT/ROE SW15 157 H10
Winthorpe St WCHPL E1 140 A7
Winthrop St WCHPL * E1 140 A7
Winton Ap RKW/CH/CXG WD3 72 D9
Winton Av FBAR/BDGN N11 98 D8
Winton Cl ED N9 100 C1
Winton Crs RKW/CH/CXG WD3 72 C9
Winton Dr CHES/WCR EN8 62 D5
RKW/CH/CXG WD3 72 D9
Winton Gdns EDGW HA8 95 L8
Winton Rd ORP BR6 226 E1
WARE SG12 26 E2
The Wintons BUSH * WD23 94 C2
Winton Ter STAL * AL1 38 D7
Winton Wy STRHM/NOR SW16 181 H8
Winvale SL SL1 149 K2
Winwood SLN SL2 129 P8
Wireless Rd BH/WHM TN16 244 A1
Wirral Wood Cl CHST BR7 184 D9
Wisbeach Rd CROY/NA CR0 203 L5
Wisborough Cl CRAWW RH11 283 J10
Wisborough Rd SAND/SEL CR2 223 N5
Wisdons Cl DAGE RM10 124 C6
Wise La MLHL NW7 96 D7
WDR/YW UB7 151 N3
Wiseman Rd LEY * E10 120 F7
Wisemans Gdns SBW CM21 29 M2
Wise Rd SRTFD E15 141 H3
Wiseton Rd TOOT SW17 179 P4
Wishart Rd BKHTH/KID SE3 162 A7
Wishbone Wy
WOKN/KNAP GU21 231 L2
Wisley La RPLY/SEND GU23 233 P2
Wisley Rd BTSEA SW11 180 A1
STMC/STPC BR5 185 K10
Wistaria Cl BRWN CM15 86 G9
ORP BR6 206 E9
Wisteria Cl IL IG1 122 E10
Wisteria Gdns SWLY BR8 208 E2
Wisteria Rd LEW SE13 161 J10
Wistlea Crs STALE/WH AL4 39 N8
Witan Ct CRAWW RH11 283 J10
Witan St BETH E2 140 A5
Witches La SEV TN13 246 E9
Witchford WGCE AL7 23 N5
Witham Cl LOU IG10 82 B10
Witham Rd DAGE RM10 124 B10
GPK RM2 125 J3
ISLW TW7 154 C7
PGE/AN SE20 204 B3
WEA W13 134 F10
Withens Cl STMC/STPC * BR5 207 M4
Witherby Cl SAND/SEL CR2 223 M2
Wither Dl HORL RH6 279 P3
The Witherings EMPK RM11 125 M3
Witherington Rd HBRY * N5 119 H10
Withers Md CDALE/KGS NW9 96 C9
Witherston Wy ELTH/MOT SE9 184 D5
Withey Brook HORL RH6 279 N6
Withey Cl WDSR SL4 148 D7
Witheygate Av STA TW18 173 L9
Withey Mdw HORL RH6 279 N6
Withies La RGUW GU3 267 H7
The Withies LHD/OX KT22 236 G6
WOKN/KNAP GU21 231 K3
Withybed Cnr
KWD/TDW/WH KT20 238 E9
Withy Cl LTWR GU18 212 B6

Withy Cft DTCH/LGLY SL3 130 B8
Withy La RSLP HA4 112 D3
Withy Md CHING E4 101 J4
Withypitts CRAWE RH10 285 P10
Withypitts East CRAWE RH10 285 P10
Withy Pl LCOL/BKTW AL2 56 B4
Witley Crs CROY/NA CR0 225 H3
Witley Gdns NWDGN UB2 153 N3
Witley Rd ARCH N19 118 D7
Witney Cl HGDN/ICK UB10 112 A9
PIN HA5 93 N7
Witney Pth FSTH * SE23 182 C6
Wittenham Wy CHING E4 101 J4
Wittering Cl KUTN/CMB KT2 177 J8
Wittersham Rd BMLY BR1 183 L8
Wivenhoe Cl PECK SE15 159 P9
Wivenhoe Ct HSLWW TW4 153 N10
Wivenhoe Rd BARK IG11 143 K4
Wiverton Rd SYD SE26 182 B9
Wix Hl EHSLY KT24 252 C6
Wix Rd DAGW RM9 143 N3
Wix's La BTSEA SW11 158 C10
Woburn WEA * W13 134 G7
Woburn Av EPP CM16 83 H3
HCH RM12 125 H9
PUR/KEN CR8 223 H7
Woburn Cl BUSH WD23 74 B10
WIM/MER SW19 179 M9
Woburn Hl ADL/WDHM KT15 195 M9
Woburn Pk ADL/WDHM * KT15 195 N9
Woburn Pl STPAN WC1H 11 K1
Woburn Rd CAR SM5 201 P8
CRAWW RH11 283 K9
CROY/NA CR0 203 K8
Woburn Sq STPAN WC1H 11 K2
Woburn Wk STPAN WC1H 5 K10
Wodehouse Av PECK SE15 159 N7
Wodehouse Rd DART DA1 165 P10
Wodeland Av GUW GU2 267 N2
Woffington Cl E/WMO/HCT KT8 199 H1
Wokindon Rd CDH/CHF RM16 168 E2
Woking Cl PUT/ROE SW15 156 C10
Woking Rd RGUE GU4 249 P3
Wold Cl CRAWW RH11 283 J9
Woldham Pl HAYES BR2 205 P4
Woldham Rd HAYES BR2 205 P4
Woldhurstlea Cl CRAWW RH11 283 K9
Woldingham Rd CTHM CR3 242 A6
Wolds Dr ORP BR6 226 D1
The Wold CTHM CR3 242 F8
Wolfe Cl HAYES BR2 205 M6
YEAD UB4 133 J5
Wolfe Crs CHARL SE7 162 A4
Wolferton Rd MNPK E12 122 C9
Wolfington Rd WNWD SE27 181 J7
Wolf La WDSR SL4 148 C9
Wolfram Cl LEW SE13 183 K1
Wolf's Hl OXTED RH8 261 M7
Wolf's Rd OXTED RH8 261 N6
Wolfs Wd OXTED RH8 261 M8
Wolftencroft Cl BTSEA SW11 157 P9
Wollaston Cl WALW SE17 18 D6
Wolmer Cl EDGW HA8 95 M5
Wolmer Gdns EDGW HA8 95 M4
Wolseley Av WAND/EARL SW18 179 K5
Wolseley Gdns CHSWK W4 155 N5
Wolseley Rd CEND/HSY/T N8 118 E4
CHSWK W4 155 P3
FSTGT E7 141 N2
KTN/HRWW/W HA3 114 D1
MTCM CR4 202 B7
ROMW/RG RM7 124 E5
WDGN N22 98 G9
Wolseley St STHWK SE1 19 M2
Wolsey Av CHESW EN7 61 N5
EHAM E6 142 D5
WALTH E17 120 E1
Wolsey Cl HSLW TW3 154 B10
KUTN/CMB KT2 199 N1
NWDGN UB2 154 B2
RYNPK SW20 178 E10
WPK KT4 220 D1
Wolsey Ct ELTH/MOT * SE9 184 C2
Wolsey Crs CROY/NA CR0 225 H5
MRDN SM4 201 J7
Wolsey Dr KUTN/CMB KT2 177 K8
WOT/HER KT12 197 L8
Wolsey Gdns BARK/HLT IG6 102 E7
Wolsey Gv EDGW HA8 96 A8
ESH/CLAY KT10 218 A1
Wolsey Ms KTTN NW5 4 G1
ORP BR6 227 J2
Wolsey Rd ASHF TW15 173 P7
E/WMO/HCT KT8 198 C4
EN EN1 80 A6
ESH/CLAY KT10 218 A1
HHNE HP2 35 N7
HPTN TW12 176 A9
IS N1 119 L10
RKW/CH/CXG WD3 92 D3
SUN TW16 174 G10
Wolsey St WCHPL E1 140 B7
Wolsey Wk WOKN/KNAP GU21 232 B3
Wolsey Wy CHSGTN KT9 219 M2
Wolsley Cl DART DA1 186 F1
Wolstan Cl DEN/HRF UB9 111 K8
Wolstonbury NFNCH/WDSP N12 97 K6
Wolstonbury Cl CRAWW RH11 283 M9
Wolvens La DORK RH4 271 P6
Wolvercote Rd ABYW SE2 163 N1
Wolverley St BETH * E2 140 A5
Wolverton Av KUTN/CMB KT2 199 M1
Wolverton Cl HORL RH6 280 A6
Wolverton Gdns EA W5 135 L9
HMSMTH W6 156 G3
HORL RH6 280 A5
Wolverton Rd STAN HA7 94 G7
Wolverton Wy STHGT/OAK N14 78 D9
Wolves La WDGN N22 99 H8
Wombwell Gdns GVW DA11 190 A5
Womersley Rd CEND/HSY/T N8 118 G4
Wonersh Common Rd
SHGR GU5 268 E10
Wonersh Wy BELMT SM2 220 G5
Wonford Cl KWD/TDW/WH KT20 256 D2
NWMAL KT3 200 B1
Wonham La BRKHM/BTCW RH3 274 C5
Wonham Wy SHGR GU5 270 E8
Wontford Rd PUR/KEN CR8 241 H1
Wontner Cl IS N1 6 E4
Wontner Rd BAL SW12 180 A5
Wooburn Cl UX/CGN UB8 132 C6
Wooburn Common Rd
FLKWH HP10 108 A7
Woodall Cl CHSGTN KT9 219 J3
Woodall Rd PEND EN3 80 C10
Wood Av PUR RM19 166 B3
Woodbank Av CFSP/GDCR SL9 110 A4
Woodbank Dr CSTG HP8 90 A4
Woodbank Rd BMLY BR1 183 L6
Woodbastwick Rd SYD SE26 182 C9
Woodberry Av RYLN/HDSTN HA2 114 B2
WCHMH N21 99 H3
Woodberry Cl SUN TW16 175 H9
Woodberry Crs MUSWH N10 118 C1
Woodberry Down EPP CM16 65 K5
FSBYPK N4 119 K6
Woodberry Gdns
NFNCH/WDSP N12 97 M7
Woodberry Gv BXLY DA5 186 E6
FSBYPK N4 119 K5
NFNCH/WDSP N12 97 M7
Woodberry Wy CHING E4 101 H1
NFNCH/WDSP N12 97 M7
Woodbine Cl HLWW/ROY CM19 46 F3
WHTN TW2 176 C5
Woodbine Gv ENC/FH EN2 79 L4
PGE/AN SE20 182 A10
Woodbine La WPK KT4 200 E10
Woodbine Pl WAN E11 121 M4
Woodbine Rd BFN/LL DA15 185 H4
Woodbines Av KUT KT1 199 J3
Woodbine Ter HOM E9 140 B1
Woodborough Rd
PUT/ROE SW15 156 E10
Woodbourne Av
STRHM/NOR SW16 180 E6
Woodbourne Dr ESH/CLAY KT10 218 E3
Woodbourne Gdns WLGTN SM6 222 C4
Woodbridge Av LHD/OX KT22 236 F4
Woodbridge Cl HARH RM3 105 L4
HOLWY N7 118 G7
Woodbridge Gv LHD/OX KT22 236 F4
Woodbridge Hl GUW GU2 249 N9
Woodbridge Hill Gdns
GUW * GU2 249 M9
Woodbridge La HARH RM3 105 L4
Woodbridge Mdw GU GU1 249 P9
Woodbridge Rd BARK IG11 123 J10
GU GU1 268 A1
Woodbridge St CLKNW EC1R 12 C1
Woodbrook Gdns WAB EN9 63 K9
Woodbrook Rd ABYW SE2 163 K5
Woodburn Cl HDN NW4 116 G3
Woodbury Cl BH/WHM TN16 244 C4
CROY/NA CR0 203 N9
WAN E11 121 N2
Woodbury Dr BELMT SM2 221 M6
Woodbury Hl LOU IG10 82 B6
Woodbury Park Rd WEA W13 134 G6
Woodbury Rd WALTH E17 120 G2
Woodbury St TOOT SW17 179 P8
Woodby Dr ASC SL5 192 E7
Woodchester Pk BEAC HP9 88 B5
Woodchester Sq BAY/PAD W2 8 G3
Woodchurch Cl BFN/LL DA15 184 G6
Woodchurch Dr BMLY BR1 184 A10
Woodchurch Rd
KIL/WHAMP NW6 2 F4
Wood Cl BETH E2 13 N1
BXLY DA5 186 F6
CDALE/KGS NW9 116 A5
HAT AL10 40 E4
HRW HA1 114 C5
REDH RH1 276 B9
WDSR SL4 149 H10
Woodclyffe Dr CHST BR7 206 D2
Woodcock Ct
KTN/HRWW/W HA3 115 K5
Woodcock Dell Av
KTN/HRWW/W HA3 115 H5
Woodcock Dr CHOB/PIR GU24 213 H4
Woodcock Hl
KTN/HRWW/W HA3 115 H3
RKW/CH/CXG WD3 91 P6
Woodcockhill STALE/WH AL4 21 J10
Woodcock La CHOB/PIR GU24 212 G4
Woodcocks CAN/RD E16 141 P7
Woodcombe Crs FSTH SE23 182 B4
Wood Common HAT AL10 40 E1
Woodcot Cl ED N9 80 B10
Woodcote HORL RH6 280 C3
RGUW GU3 267 N4
Woodcote Av HCH RM12 125 H9
MLHL NW7 96 F7
THHTH CR7 203 J4
WLGTN SM6 222 C5
Woodcote Cl CHES/WCR EN8 62 B6
EPSOM KT18 220 A10
KUTN/CMB KT2 177 L8
Woodcote Dr ORP BR6 206 G7
Woodcote End EPSOM KT18 238 A1
Woodcote Gn WLGTN SM6 222 D5
Woodcote Green Rd
EPSOM KT18 237 P2
Woodcote Grove Rd
COUL/CHIP CR5 240 E1
Woodcote House Ct
EPSOM * KT18 238 A1
Woodcote Hurst EPSOM KT18 237 P2
Woodcote La PUR/KEN CR8 222 E7
Woodcote Ms LOU IG10 102 A1
WLGTN SM6 222 C3
Woodcote Pk COUL/CHIP * CR5 222 C9
Woodcote Park Av
PUR/KEN CR8 222 D7
Woodcote Park Rd EPSOM KT18 237 P2
Woodcote Pl WNWD * SE27 181 J8
Woodcote Rd WAN E11 121 M5
WLGTN SM6 222 C3
Woodcote Side EPSOM KT18 237 N1
Woodcote Valley Rd
PUR/KEN CR8 222 E9
Wood Crs HHS/BOV HP3 35 N7
Wood Crest BELMT * SM2 221 M4
Woodcrest Rd PUR/KEN CR8 222 F9
Woodcrest Wk REDH RH1 257 P8
Woodcroft ELTH/MOT SE9 184 C6
GFD/PVL UB6 134 F1
HLWS CM18 46 F3
WCHMH N21 98 G2
Woodcroft Av MLHL NW7 96 B8
STAN HA7 94 F9
WARE SG12 27 J7
Woodcroft Crs HGDN/ICK UB10 132 C3
Woodcroft Ms DEPT SE8 160 D3
Woodcroft Rd CRAWW RH11 282 G9
CSHM HP5 51 J4
THHTH CR7 203 J5
Woodcutters Av CDH/CHF RM16 167 P1
Wood Dene PECK * SE15 160 A7
Wood Dr CHST BR7 184 B9
SEV TN13 264 G2
Woodedge Cl CHING E4 101 L2
Wooden Bridge Ter
WNWD * SE27 181 J6
Wood End HYS/HAR UB3 132 F8
LCOL/BKTW AL2 56 B4
SWLY BR8 208 D4
Woodend ESH/CLAY KT10 198 B9
LHD/OX KT22 255 H1
NRWD SE19 181 K9
SUT SM1 201 M9
Wood End Av RYLN/HDSTN HA2 114 A9
Woodend Cl CRAWE RH10 284 B5
Wood End Cl HHNE HP2 36 D5
NTHLT UB5 114 C10
SLN SL2 109 J8
Woodend Cl WOKN/KNAP GU21 231 M5
Wood End Cl WOKS/MYFD GU22 233 J2
Woodend Dr ASC SL5 192 A5
Woodend Gdns ENC/FH EN2 78 F8
Wood End Gdns NTHLT UB5 114 B10
Wood End Gn YEAD UB4 132 G7
Wood End Green Rd
HYS/HAR UB3 132 E7
Wood End La NTHLT UB5 134 A1
Woodend Pk COB KT11 235 L1
Wood End Rd NTHLT UB5 114 C9
Woodend Rd WALTH E17 101 H10
The Wood End WLGTN SM6 222 C5
Wood End Wy NTHLT UB5 114 B10
Wooder Gdns FSTGT E7 121 L9
Wooderson Cl SNWD SE25 203 M4
Woodfall Av BAR EN5 77 J9
Woodfall Dr DART DA1 164 G10
Woodfall Rd FSBYPK N4 119 H6
Woodfall St CHEL SW3 16 A8
Wood Farm Rd HHNE HP2 35 P6
Woodfarrs CMBW SE5 159 L10
Woodfield ASHTD KT21 237 J3
Wood Fld HAMP * NW3 118 A10
Woodfield Av ALP/SUD HA0 115 H8
CAR SM5 222 B3
CDALE/KGS NW9 116 B2
EA W5 135 H6
GVW DA11 190 E4
NTHWD HA6 92 F5
STRHM/NOR SW16 180 E6
Woodfield Cl ASHTD KT21 237 J3
COUL/CHIP CR5 240 D5
CRAWE RH10 283 P6
EN EN1 79 M8
NRWD SE19 181 K10
REDH RH1 257 P9
Woodfield Crs EA W5 135 J6
Woodfield Dr EBAR EN4 98 B2
GPK RM2 125 H2
HHS/BOV HP3 36 E8
Woodfield Gdns HHS/BOV HP3 36 D8
NWMAL KT3 200 C5
Woodfield Gv STRHM/NOR SW16 180 E6
Woodfield Hl COUL/CHIP CR5 240 C5
Woodfield La ASHTD KT21 237 K2
BRKMPK AL9 41 P9
Woodfield Pk AMS HP6 68 G3
Woodfield Ri BUSH WD23 94 C1
Woodfield Rd ASHTD KT21 237 J3
CRAWE RH10 284 A5
EA W5 135 H6
ESH/CLAY * KT10 198 E9
ESH/CLAY KT10 198 E9
HSLWW TW4 153 J8
MV/WKIL W9 8 D3
RAD WD7 74 F2
WGCE AL7 23 J5
Woodfields SEV TN13 246 E9
WATW * WD18 73 K8
The Woodfields SAND/SEL CR2 223 N7
Woodfield Wy FBAR/BDGN N11 98 E8
HCH RM12 125 L6
REDH RH1 257 P9
STALE/WH AL4 39 H3
The Woodfines EMPK RM11 125 L4
Woodford Av GNTH/NBYPK IG2 122 C3
Woodford Bridge Rd REDBR IG4 122 A1
Woodford Ct WAB EN9 63 M9
Woodford Crs PIN HA5 93 J10
Woodford New Rd WALTH E17 121 K1
WFD IG8 101 L8
Woodford Pl WBLY HA9 115 K6
Woodford Rd FSTGT E7 121 N9
SWFD E18 121 M2
WAT WD17 73 J6
Woodford Wy SLN SL2 128 F5
Woodgate GSTN WD25 55 J9
Woodgate Av CHSGTN KT9 219 J2
POTB/CUF EN6 60 C9
Woodgate Crs NTHWD HA6 93 H7
Woodgate Dr
STRHM/NOR SW16 180 E10
Woodgavil BNSTD SM7 239 J2
Woodger Cl GU GU1 250 F8
Woodger Rd SHB W12 156 F1
Woodgers Gv SWLY BR8 208 G2
Woodget Cl EHAM E6 142 B8
Woodgrange Av ACT W3 135 L10
EN EN1 79 P10
KTN/HRWW/W HA3 115 H3
NFNCH/WDSP N12 97 N7
Woodgrange Cl
KTN/HRWW/W HA3 115 J3
Woodgrange Gdns EN EN1 79 P10
Woodgrange Ter EN * EN1 79 P10
Woodgreen Rd WAB EN9 63 P9
Woodhall Av DUL SE21 181 N6
PIN HA5 93 M9
Woodhall Cl HERT/WAS SG14 25 K3
UX/CGN UB8 111 N10
Woodhall Ct WGCE AL7 23 H6
Woodhall Crs EMPK RM11 125 N5
Woodhall Dr DUL SE21 181 N6
PIN HA5 93 L9
Woodhall Ga PIN HA5 93 L8
Woodhall La BFOR GU20 192 D9
HHNE HP2 35 P5
OXHEY WD19 93 L4
RAD WD7 57 M10
WGCE AL7 23 H7
Woodham Ct SWFD E18 121 L2
Woodham La ADL/WDHM KT15 215 L6
ADL/WDHM KT15 215 H8
WOKN/KNAP GU21 214 E9
Woodham Park Rd
ADL/WDHM KT15 215 J6
Woodham Park Wy
ADL/WDHM KT15 215 J7
Woodham Ri WOKN/KNAP GU21 232 D1
Woodham Rd CAT SE6 183 H6
WOKN/KNAP GU21 214 C10
Woodham Wy WARE SG12 27 H7
Woodham Waye
WOKN/KNAP GU21 214 E9
Woodhatch Cl EHAM E6 142 B7
Woodhatch Rd REDH RH1 275 N4
Woodhatch Spinney
COUL/CHIP CR5 240 F2
Woodhaven Gdns BARK/HLT IG6 122 F2
Woodhaven Ms WOT/HER * KT12 217 H1
Woodhaw EGH TW20 172 E7
Woodhayes HORL RH6 280 C3
Woodhayes Rd RYNPK SW20 178 F10
Woodhead Dr ORP BR6 207 H10
Woodheyes Rd WLSDN NW10 116 B10
Woodhill CHARL SE7 162 B3
HLWS CM18 47 H4
RPLY/SEND GU23 250 G1
Woodhill Av CFSP/GDCR SL9 110 C4
Woodhill Ct RPLY/SEND GU23 250 G1
Woodhill Crs KTN/HRWW/W HA3 115 J4
Woodhouse Av GFD/PVL UB6 134 E4
Woodhouse Cl GFD/PVL UB6 134 E4
HYS/HAR UB3 152 F2
Woodhouse Eaves NTHWD HA6 93 H6
Woodhouse Gv MNPK E12 142 B1
Wood House La BROX EN10 43 N7
Woodhouse La SHGR GU5 271 H9
Woodhouse Rd
NFNCH/WDSP N12 97 P7
WAN E11 121 L8
Woodhurst Av GSTN WD25 73 L1
STMC/STPC BR5 206 F6
Woodhurst Dr DEN/HRF UB9 111 J3
Woodhurst La OXTED RH8 261 K7
Woodhurst Pk OXTED RH8 261 K6
Woodhurst Rd ABYW SE2 163 K4
ACT W3 135 P10
Woodhyrst Gdns PUR/KEN CR8 241 J1
Wooding Gv HLWW/ROY CM19 46 E1
Woodington Cl ELTH/MOT SE9 184 D2
Woodison St BOW E3 140 D6
Woodknoll Dr CHST BR7 206 C1
Woodland Ap GFD/PVL UB6 134 F1
Woodland Av HART DA3 211 L5
HHW HP1 35 L7
RBRW/HUT CM13 87 P9
SL SL1 129 J9
WDSR SL4 148 E10
Woodland Cl CDALE/KGS NW9 115 P4
EHSLY KT24 252 G3
HART DA3 211 P3
HGDN/ICK UB10 112 C7
HHW HP1 35 L7
HOR/WEW * KT19 220 B3
NRWD SE19 181 M9
RBRW/HUT CM13 87 P9
WFD IG8 101 N4
Woodland Ct GLDGN * NW11 117 H3
OXTED RH8 261 J4
STALW/RED * AL3 38 E2
Woodland Crs GNWCH SE10 161 K5
Woodland Dr EHSLY KT24 252 G3
STALE/WH AL4 39 H5
WAT WD17 72 G5
Woodland Gdns ISLW TW7 154 D9
MUSWH N10 118 C3
SAND/SEL CR2 224 B7
Woodland Gld SLN SL2 109 J8
Woodland Gv WEY KT13 216 E1
Woodland Hl NRWD SE19 181 M9
Woodland La RKW/CH/CXG WD3 70 G7
Woodland Mt HERT/BAY SG13 25 N5
Woodland Pl HHW HP1 35 L7
Woodland Ri BGR/WK TN15 247 N8
GFD/PVL UB6 134 F1
MUSWH N10 118 C2
OXTED RH8 261 K6
WGCW AL8 22 F3
Woodland Rd CHING E4 101 H2
FBAR/BDGN N11 98 C6
HERT/BAY SG13 26 B8
LOU IG10 82 B7
NRWD SE19 181 M8
RKW/CH/CXG WD3 90 G6
THHTH CR7 203 H4
Woodlands ADL/WDHM KT15 195 P10
ASHTD * KT21 237 L4
BRKMPK AL9 59 L3
CFSP/GDCR SL9 110 C4
CRAWE RH10 284 E5
GLDGN NW11 117 H3
LCOL/BKTW AL2 56 B3
RAD WD7 56 F10
RPLY/SEND GU23 251 J1
RYLN/HDSTN HA2 113 P2
RYNPK SW20 200 F4
WOKS/MYFD GU22 232 B4
Woodlands Av ACT W3 135 N10
BERK HP4 34 A6
BF/WBF KT14 215 J9
BFN/LL DA15 185 H4
CHDH RM6 123 P4
EMPK RM11 125 L3
FNCH N3 97 M8
NWMAL KT3 200 A1
REDH RH1 276 A1
RSLP HA4 113 K6
WAN E11 121 N6
WPK KT4 200 C9
Woodlands Cl BMLY BR1 206 C2
BORE WD6 75 N8
CDH/CHF RM16 168 B2
CFSP/GDCR SL9 110 D4
CHERT KT16 214 E6
ESH/CLAY KT10 218 E4
GLDGN NW11 117 H3
HOD * EN11 44 F4
SWLY BR8 208 G2
Woodlands Copse ASHTD KT21 237 J2
Woodlands Ct REDH * RH1 276 A2
WOKS/MYFD GU22 232 B5
Woodlands Dr BEAC HP9 88 B7
HOD EN11 44 F5
STAN HA7 94 E7
SUN TW16 197 K2
Woodlands Gdns EPSOM KT18 238 F3
WALTH * E17 121 K2
Woodlands Gld BEAC HP9 88 B7
Woodlands Gv COUL/CHIP CR5 240 C3
GNWCH SE10 161 K4
ISLW TW7 154 D8
Woodlands Hl BEAC HP9 108 D4
Woodlands La CHOB/PIR GU24 212 E4
COB KT11 235 P3
GVE DA12 191 N10
Woodlands Pde ASHF TW15 174 D9
Woodlands Pk ADL/WDHM KT15 215 J2
BXLY DA5 186 D7
GU GU1 250 E9
KWD/TDW/WH KT20 255 N7
WOKN/KNAP GU21 214 F9
Woodlands Park Rd
BKHTH/KID SE3 161 K5
SEVS/STOTM N15 119 K3
Woodlands Ri SWLY BR8 208 G2
Woodlands Rd BARN SW13 156 C9
BF/WBF KT14 215 J10
BMLY BR1 206 C2
BUSH WD23 73 M8
BXLYHN DA7 163 P9
ED N9 100 B2
EHSLY KT24 253 N4
ENC/FH EN2 79 L4
EPSOM KT18 237 M1
GU GU1 250 A6
HARH RM3 105 P9
HERT/BAY SG13 25 N5
HRW HA1 114 E3
IL IG1 122 F8
ISLW TW7 154 D9
KGLGY WD4 54 B3
LHD/OX KT22 236 C4
ORP BR6 227 K3
REDH RH1 276 A2
ROM RM1 124 G1
STHL UB1 133 L10
SURB KT6 199 J7
VW GU25 193 P4
WALTH E17 121 H1
WAN * E11 121 K7
Woodlands Rd East VW GU25 193 P4
Woodlands Rd West VW GU25 193 P3
Woodlands St LEW SE13 183 J3
Woodlands Ter SWLY * BR8 208 D6
The Woodlands AMS HP6 69 H1
CMBW * SE5 159 J6
ESH/CLAY KT10 198 B9
HORL RH6 281 J4
HRW * HA1 114 D7
ISLW TW7 154 E8
LEW SE13 183 J3
NRWD SE19 181 K10
ORP BR6 227 L3
STAN * HA7 94 G6
STHGT/OAK N14 98 C2
WLGTN SM6 222 C5
Woodland St HACK * E8 7 L1
Woodlands Wy ASHTD KT21 237 M2
KWD/TDW/WH KT20 255 P6
PUT/ROE SW15 179 J1
Woodland Ter CHARL SE7 162 B3
Woodland Vw CSHM HP5 51 J9
RGODL GU7 267 K8
Woodland Wk HAMP NW3 117 P10
HOR/WEW KT19 219 M3
Woodland Wy ABLGY WD5 54 G3
ABYW SE2 163 N3
BRYLDS KT5 199 N9
CHESW EN7 61 J4
CHONG CM5 67 N6
CROY/NA CR0 204 D8
EPP CM16 83 H1
GRH DA9 188 F1
KWD/TDW/WH KT20 239 H8
MLHL NW7 96 B7
MRDN SM4 201 J4
MTCM CR4 180 B10
PUR/KEN CR8 223 H9
REDH RH1 259 M4
STMC/STPC BR5 206 F4
WCHMH N21 99 H3
WEY KT13 216 E2
WFD IG8 101 N4
Wood La CDALE/KGS NW9 116 A5
CTHM CR3 241 L10
DAGE RM10 124 B7
HCH RM12 125 H10
HGT N6 118 C4
HHNE HP2 35 N7
ISLW TW7 154 D5
IVER SL0 130 F6
KWD/TDW/WH KT20 239 J3
RDART DA2 188 E6
RSLP HA4 112 E7
SHB W12 136 F8
SL SL1 148 E2
STAN HA7 94 G4
WEY KT13 216 D5
WFD IG8 101 L6
WOKN/KNAP GU21 231 J4
Wood Lane End HHNE HP2 36 C5
Woodlawn Cl PUT/ROE SW15 179 J1
Woodlawn Crs WHTN TW2 176 A5
Woodlawn Dr FELT TW13 175 L5
Woodlawn Gv
WOKN/KNAP GU21 232 C1
Woodlawn Rd FUL/PGN SW6 156 G6
Woodlea HART DA3 211 P3
LCOL/BKTW AL2 55 P1
Woodlea Dr HAYES BR2 205 K5
Woodlea Gv NTHWD HA6 92 D7
Woodlea Rd STNW/STAM N16 119 M8
Woodleigh Av NFNCH/WDSP N12 97 P7
Woodleigh Gdns
STRHM/NOR SW16 180 F6
Woodley Cl TOOT SW17 180 A10
Woodley Ct AMSS * HP7 69 J5
Woodley Hl CSHM HP5 51 J10
Woodley La SUT SM1 201 P10
Woodley Rd ORP BR6 207 M9
WARE SG12 26 E1
Wood Lodge Gdns BMLY BR1 184 B10
Wood Lodge Gra SEV * TN13 247 K8
Wood Lodge La WWKM BR4 205 H10
Woodmancote Gdns
BF/WBF KT14 215 K9
Woodmancourt RGODL GU7 267 H9
Woodman La CHING E4 81 J9
Woodman Pth BARK/HLT IG6 103 H6
Woodman Rd BRW CM14 107 H6
COUL/CHIP CR5 240 D1
HHS/BOV HP3 35 P8
Woodmans Gv WLSDN NW10 116 C10
Woodmansterne La BNSTD SM7 239 L1
CAR SM5 222 A8
WLGTN SM6 222 C7
Woodmansterne Rd CAR SM5 221 P6
COUL/CHIP CR5 240 D1
STRHM/NOR SW16 202 F1
Woodmansterne St BNSTD SM7 239 P1
Woodman St CAN/RD E16 142 D10
Woodmans Yd WAT WD17 73 K8
Wood Md TOTM * N17 99 P7
Wood Meads EPP CM16 65 K5
Woodmere ELTH/MOT SE9 184 C3
Woodmere Av CROY/NA CR0 204 C7
WATN WD24 73 L4
Woodmere Cl BTSEA SW11 158 B9
CROY/NA CR0 204 C7
Woodmere Gdns CROY/NA CR0 204 C7
Woodmere Wy BECK BR3 205 J5
Woodmill Ms HOD * EN11 44 G1
Woodmount SWLY BR8 208 E7
Woodnook Rd
STRHM/NOR SW16 180 C8
Woodpecker Cl BUSH WD23 94 B2
COB KT11 217 M8
ED N9 80 B9
HAT * AL10 40 C7

KTN/HRWW/W HA3 94 E9
Woodpecker Mt CROY/NA CR0 224 D5
Woodpecker Rd THMD SE28 143 M9
Woodpecker Wy
WOKS/MYFD GU22 232 A9
Woodplace Cl COUL/CHIP CR5 240 D5
Woodplace La COUL/CHIP CR5 240 D6
Wood Pond Cl BEAC HP9 89 H7
Woodquest Av HNHL SE24 181 J1
Woodredon Cl HLWW/ROY CM19 45 N2
Woodridden Hl WAB EN9 82 A1
Wood Ride EBAR EN4 77 N5
STMC/STPC BR5 206 G4
Woodridge Cl ENC/FH * EN2 79 H5
Woodridge Wy NTHWD HA6 92 F7
Wood Riding WOKS/MYFD GU22 233 H1
Wood Ridings WEY * KT13 216 B3
Woodridings Av PIN HA5 93 N9
Woodridings Cl PIN HA5 93 N8
Woodriffe Rd WAN E11 121 J5
Wood Ri GUW GU2 249 K8
PIN HA5 113 H3
Wood Rd BH/WHM TN16 243 P4
RGODL GU7 267 L10
SHPTN TW17 196 B4
Woodrow WOOL/PLUM SE18 162 B3
Woodrow Av YEAD UB4 132 G7
Woodrow Cl GFD/PVL UB6 134 G2
Woodrow Ct TOTM N17 100 A8
Woodroyd Av HORL RH6 280 A5
Woodroyd Gdns HORL RH6 280 A6
Woodruff Av GU GU1 250 D7
Woodrush Cl NWCR SE14 160 D6
Woodrush Wy CHDH RM6 123 N2
Woods Av HAT AL10 40 D5
Woodseer St WCHPL E1 13 M3
Woodsford Sq WKENS W14 14 B1
Woodshire Rd DAGE RM10 124 C8
Woodshore Cl VW GU25 193 N6
Woodshots Meadow WATW WD18 72 E9
Woodside BKHH IG9 101 P3
BORE WD6 75 L8
CHESW EN7 61 P7
EHSLY KT24 252 D2
EPP CM16 65 N3
GLDGN NW11 117 K3
HERT/BAY SG13 26 B8
KWD/TDW/WH KT20 257 J4
LHD/OX KT22 236 A8
ORP BR6 227 K2
WATN WD24 73 H3
WIM/MER SW19 179 J8
WOT/HER KT12 197 H8
Woodside Av ALP/SUD HA0 135 K3
AMS HP6 69 J2
BEAC HP9 88 B8
CHST BR7 184 F8
ESH/CLAY KT10 198 D7
HGT N6 118 A3
NFNCH/WDSP N12 97 M5
SNWD SE25 204 A6
WOT/HER KT12 217 J1
Woodside Cl ALP/SUD HA0 135 K3
BEAC HP9 88 B8
BRYLDS KT5 199 P7
BXLYHN DA7 164 E10
CFSP/GDCR SL9 90 B10
CTHM CR3 241 M10
RAIN RM13 145 K6
RSLP HA4 112 E4
STAN HA7 94 F6
WOKN/KNAP GU21 231 J3
Woodside Ct EA * W5 135 K10
Woodside Court Rd
CROY/NA CR0 203 P7
Woodside Crs BFN/LL DA15 185 H6
HORL RH6 281 H4
Woodside Dr RDART DA2 186 F7
Woodside End ALP/SUD HA0 135 K3
Woodside Gdns CHING E4 100 G6
TOTM N17 99 N10
Woodside Grange Rd
NFNCH/WDSP N12 97 L5
Woodside Gn CROY/NA CR0 203 P7
Woodside Gv NFNCH/WDSP N12 97 M4
Woodside Hl CFSP/GDCR SL9 90 B10
Woodside La ASC SL5 170 B8
BRKMPK AL9 41 K8
BXLY DA5 185 N2
NFNCH/WDSP N12 97 L4
WDSR SL4 170 B7
Woodside Pde BFN/LL * DA15 185 H6
Woodside Pk SNWD SE25 203 P6
Woodside Park Av WALTH E17 121 J2
Woodside Park Rd
NFNCH/WDSP N12 97 L5
Woodside Pl ALP/SUD HA0 135 K3
Woodside Rd AMS HP6 69 J3
ASC SL5 170 A8
BEAC HP9 88 B8
BFN/LL DA15 185 H6
BMLY BR1 206 B5
BXLYHN DA7 164 E10
COB KT11 217 P9
CRAWE RH10 284 A5
GSTN WD25 55 J7
GUW GU2 249 L6
KUTN/CMB KT2 177 K10
LCOL/BKTW AL2 55 N6
NTHWD HA6 92 G8
NWMAL KT3 200 A2
PLSTW E13 141 P6
PUR/KEN CR8 222 F9
RSEV TN14 245 N10
SEV TN13 247 J9
SNWD SE25 204 A6
SUT SM1 201 M10
WDGN N22 99 H8
WFD IG8 101 M5
Woodside Wk AMS * HP6 69 J3
Woodside Wy CROY/NA CR0 204 B6
MTCM CR4 202 C1
REDH RH1 276 B6
REDH RH1 276 B1
VW GU25 193 N3
Woodslands HORL RH6 280 E3
Wood's Ms MYFR/PKLN W1K 10 B7
Woodsome Rd KTTN NW5 118 B8
Wood's Pl STHWK SE1 19 K4
Woodspring Rd WIM/MER SW19 179 H5
Wood's Rd PECK SE15 160 A7
Woodstead Gv EDGW HA8 95 K7
The Woods HGDN/ICK UB10 112 C9
NTHWD HA6 93 H6
RAD WD7 56 G10
Woodstock RGUE GU4 251 L4
Woodstock Av CHEAM SM3 201 J7
DTCH/LGLY SL3 150 A3
GLDGN NW11 117 H5
HARH RM3 106 A6
HNWL W7 154 F2
ISLW TW7 176 F1
STHL UB1 133 N5
Woodstock Cl BXLY DA5 186 A4
HERT/BAY SG13 26 A7
STAN HA7 95 K10
WOKN/KNAP GU21 232 B2
Woodstock Crs ED N9 80 A10
Woodstock Dr HGDN/ICK UB10 111 P9
Woodstock Gdns BECK BR3 204 G1
GDMY/SEVK IG3 123 K7
YEAD UB4 132 G7
Woodstock Gra EA * W5 135 K10
Woodstock Gv RGODL GU7 267 K10
SHB W12 156 G1
Woodstock La North SURB KT6 199 H9
Woodstock La South
ESH/CLAY KT10 218 G2
Woodstock Ms CAVSQ/HST W1G 10 D4
Woodstock Ri CHEAM SM3 201 J8
Woodstock Rd ALP/SUD HA0 135 L2
BROX EN10 44 D5
BUSH WD23 94 D1
CAR SM5 222 B2
CHSWK W4 156 B3
COUL/CHIP CR5 240 C1
CROY/NA CR0 203 L10
FSBYPK N4 119 H6
FSTGT E7 141 P2
GLDGN NW11 117 J5
WALTH E17 101 J10
Woodstock Rd North STAL AL1 38 G4
Woodstock Rd South STAL AL1 38 G6
Woodstock St CAN/RD E16 141 L8
MYFR/PKLN W1K 10 E6
Woodstock Ter POP/IOD E14 140 G9
Woodstock Wy MTCM CR4 202 D2
Wood Stoke SLN SL2 109 L9
Woodstone Av EW KT17 220 D2
Wood St BAR EN5 76 F8
BARB EC2Y 12 F4
CAN/RD E16 141 N9
CHSWK W4 156 B4
GRAYS RM17 167 P5
KUT KT1 199 J1
MTCM CR4 202 B7
REDH RH1 258 D5
SWLY BR8 209 K1
WALTH E17 121 H1
Woodsway LHD/OX KT22 218 D10
Woodsyre NRWD SE19 181 N7
Wood Ter CRICK * NW2 116 C7
Woodthorpe Rd ASHF TW15 173 N8
PUT/ROE SW15 156 E10
Woodtree Cl HDN NW4 96 F10
Wood V EDUL SE22 182 A4
HAT AL10 40 E4
MUSWH N10 118 D3
Woodvale Av SNWD SE25 203 N3
Woodvale Pk STAL * AL1 38 G6
Woodvale Wy CRICK NW2 116 G8
Wood Vw GRAYS RM17 168 B3
HHW HP1 35 L4
POTB/CUF EN6 60 F3
Woodview CHSGTN KT9 219 H8
RDART * DA2 188 F9
SLN * SL2 128 E2
Woodview Av CHING E4 101 H5
Woodview Cl KUTN/CMB KT2 178 A7
SAND/SEL CR2 224 A10
Woodview Rd SWLY BR8 208 D2
Woodville Cl LEE/GVPK SE12 183 M1
TEDD TW11 176 F7
Woodville Cottages GVE * DA12 191 H2
Woodville Court Ms WAT * WD17 73 H6
Woodville Gdns BARK/HLT IG6 122 E1
EA W5 135 K8
RSLP HA4 112 D5
SURB * KT6 199 J7
Woodville Gv WELL * DA16 163 K9
Woodville Pl GVE DA12 190 E3
Woodville Rd BAR EN5 77 L7
EA W5 135 K8
GLDGN NW11 117 H5
KIL/WHAMP NW6 2 D7
LHD/OX KT22 236 G6
MRDN SM4 201 K4
RCHPK/HAM TW10 176 G6
STNW/STAM N16 119 M10
SWFD E18 101 N10
THHTH CR7 203 K4
WALTH E17 120 D2
WAN E11 121 L6
Woodville St CHARL SE7 162 B3
Woodward Av HDN NW4 116 D3
Woodward Cl ESH/CLAY KT10 218 E3
GRAYS RM17 167 N3
Woodwarde Rd EDUL SE22 181 M2
Woodward Gdns DAGW RM9 143 M2
STAN HA7 94 E8
Woodward Hts GRAYS RM17 167 N3
Woodward Rd DAGW RM9 143 L2
Woodwards HLWW/ROY CM19 46 F3
Woodward Ter GRH DA9 188 D2
Wood Wy ORP BR6 206 D9
Woodway GU GU1 250 E9
RBRW/HUT CM13 107 M2
Woodway Crs HRW HA1 114 F4
Woodwaye OXHEY WD19 93 K1
Woodwell St WAND/EARL SW18 179 M1
Wood Whf GNWCH SE10 160 G5
Woodwicks RKW/CH/CXG WD3 90 G6
Woodyard Cl KTTN NW5 118 B10
Woodyard La DUL SE21 181 M3
Woodyates Rd LEE/GVPK SE12 183 M2
Woodyers Cl SHGR GU5 268 E10
Woolacombe Rd BKHTH/KID SE3 161 P8
Woolacombe Wy HYS/HAR UB3 152 F3
Woolands Rd WAN E11 121 K7
Woolborough Cl CRAWE RH10 283 P6
Woolborough La CRAWE RH10 284 A4
REDH RH1 276 G9
Woolborough Rd CRAWE RH10 283 N6
Wooler St WALW SE17 18 G8
Woolf Cl THMD SE28 143 L10
Woolf Ms STPAN WC1H 11 L1
Woolhampton Wy CHIG IG7 103 L4
Woolhams CTHM CR3 259 N2
Woollam Crs STALW/RED AL3 38 B2
Woollard St WAB EN9 63 H10
Woollaston Rd FSBYPK N4 119 J4
Woollett Cl DART DA1 165 H10
Woolmans Cl BROX EN10 44 E8
Woolmead Av CDALE/KGS NW9 116 D5
Woolmer Cl BORE WD6 75 M4
Woolmerdine Ct BUSH WD23 73 L7
Woolmer Dr HHNE HP2 36 D6
Woolmer Gdns UED N18 99 P7
Woolmer Rd UED N18 99 P6
Woolmers La HERT/WAS SG14 24 C9
Woolmore St POP/IOD E14 141 H9
Woolneigh St FUL/PGN SW6 157 L9
Woolridge Wy HOM * E9 140 B2
Wool Rd RYNPK SW20 178 E9
Woolstaplers Wy
BERM/RHTH SE16 19 N4
Woolston Cl WALTH E17 100 C10
Woolstone Rd FSTH SE23 182 D5
Woolwich Church St
CHARL SE7 162 A3
Woolwich Common
WOOL/PLUM SE18 162 D5
Woolwich High St
WOOL/PLUM SE18 162 D2
Woolwich Manor Wy EHAM E6 142 C6
Woolwich New Rd
WOOL/PLUM SE18 162 D4
Woolwich Rd ABYW SE2 163 N5
BXLYHN DA7 164 B9
GNWCH SE10 161 M4
Wooster Gdns POP/IOD E14 141 J8
Wooster Rd BEAC HP9 88 B7
Wootton Cl EMPK RM11 125 L3
EPSOM KT18 238 B2
Wootton Dr HHNE HP2 36 A1
Wootton Gv FNCH N3 97 K9
Wootton St STHWK SE1 18 B1
Worbeck Rd PGE/AN SE20 204 A2
Worcester Av TOTM N17 99 P8
UPMR RM14 126 E6
Worcester Cl CRICK NW2 116 D8
CROY/NA CR0 204 E9
GRH DA9 188 G1
MEO DA13 190 C10
MTCM CR4 202 B2
Worcester Ct WOT/HER KT12 197 K9
Worcester Crs MLHL NW7 96 B4
WFD IG8 101 N6
Worcester Dr ASHF TW15 174 C9
CHSWK W4 156 B2
Worcester Gdns IL IG1 122 B5
NTHLT UB5 134 B1
SL SL1 149 J1
WPK KT4 200 B10
Worcester Ms HAMP * NW3 3 H1
Worcester Park Rd WPK KT4 199 P10
Worcester Rd BELMT SM2 221 K4
GUW GU2 249 L8
HAT AL10 40 C3
MNPK E12 122 C8
REIG RH2 257 K9
UX/CGN UB8 131 M7
WALTH E17 100 C10
WIM/MER SW19 179 J8
Worcesters Av EN EN1 79 P4
Wordsworth Av GFD/PVL UB6 134 C4
MNPK E12 142 B2
PUR/KEN CR8 241 L1
SWFD E18 121 L1
Wordsworth Cl CRAWE * RH10 284 C5
HARH RM3 105 K9
TIL RM18 168 F8
Wordsworth Ct HAT * AL10 40 D3
Wordsworth Dr CHEAM SM3 220 F1
Wordsworth Md REDH RH1 258 C8
Wordsworth Pde
CEND/HSY/T * N8 119 J2
Wordsworth Pl HAMP NW3 118 A10
Wordsworth Rd
ADL/WDHM KT15 215 N1
FELT TW13 175 N7
PGE/AN SE20 182 C10
SLN SL2 128 C6
STHWK SE1 19 L6
STNW/STAM N16 119 M9
WELL DA16 163 H7
WLGTN SM6 222 D3
Wordsworth Wk GLDGN NW11 117 J2
Wordsworth Wy DART DA1 165 P10
WDR/YW UB7 151 P3
Worfield St BTSEA SW11 157 P6
Worgan St BERM/RHTH SE16 160 C2
LBTH SE11 17 N7
Works Rd ADL/WDHM KT15 215 L5
Worland Rd SRTFD E15 141 K2
World's End COB KT11 217 H10
EPSOM * KT18 238 A2
Worlds End Est WBPTN * SW10 157 N6
Worlds End La ORP BR6 227 K4
WCHMH N21 78 G9
Worlds End Pas WBPTN * SW10 157 N6
Worley Rd STALW/RED AL3 38 B5
Worlidge St HMSMTH W6 156 F4
Worlingham Rd EDUL SE22 159 N10
Wormholt Rd SHB W12 136 D10
Wormholt Ter SHB * W12 136 D10
Wormley Ct WAB EN9 63 M9
Wormley Lodge Cl BROX EN10 44 E9
Wormwood St LVPST EC2M 13 J5
Wormyngford Ct WAB EN9 63 M9
Wornington Green Est
NKENS W10 8 A3
Wornington Rd NKENS W10 8 A2
Woronzow Rd STJWD NW8 3 M6
Worple Av ISLW TW7 176 F1
STA TW18 173 L9
WIM/MER SW19 179 G10
Worple Cl RYLN/HDSTN HA2 113 N6
Worple Rd EPSOM KT18 238 A1
ISLW TW7 154 F10
LHD/OX KT22 236 G9
RYNPK SW20 200 G1
STA TW18 173 L10
Worple Road Ms
WIM/MER SW19 179 J9
Worplesdon Hill Heath House Rd
WOKS/MYFD GU22 231 H8
Worplesdon Rd RGUW GU3 249 L5
Worple St MORT/ESHN SW14 156 A9
The Worple STWL/WRAY TW19 172 C2
Worple Wy RCHPK/HAM TW10 177 K1
RYLN/HDSTN HA2 113 N6
Worrin Cl BRWN CM15 107 L2
Worrin Rd BRWN CM15 107 L3
Worsfold Cl RPLY/SEND GU23 232 E9
Worships Hl SEV TN13 246 F9
Worship St SDTCH EC2A 13 H2
Worslade Rd TOOT SW17 179 N7
Worsley Bridge Rd CAT SE6 182 E8
Worsley Rd WAN E11 121 K9
Worsopp Dr CLAP SW4 180 D1
Worsted Gn REDH RH1 258 E5
Worth Cl ORP BR6 227 H1
Worthfield Cl HOR/WEW KT19 220 A4
Worth Gv WALW SE17 18 G8
Worthing Cl SRTFD E15 141 K3
Worthing Rd HEST TW5 153 N5
Worthington Cl MTCM CR4 202 C4
Worthington Rd SURB KT6 199 L8
Worth Park Av CRAWE RH10 284 D6
Worth Rd CRAWE RH10 284 D7
Worth Wy CRAWE RH10 284 D8
Wortley Rd CROY/NA CR0 203 H7
EHAM E6 142 A2
Worton Gdns ISLW TW7 154 C8
Worton Rd ISLW TW7 154 E9
Worton Wy ISLW TW7 154 C8
Wotton Dr RDKG RH5 271 M6
Wotton Gn STMC/STPC BR5 207 N4
Wotton Rd CRICK NW2 116 F9
Wotton Wy BELMT SM2 220 F6
Wouldham Rd CAN/RD E16 141 L8
WTHK RM20 167 K5
Wouldham Ter STMC/STPC * BR5 207 L3
Wrabness Wy STA TW18 195 L1
Wragby Rd WAN * E11 121 K8
Wrampling Pl ED N9 99 P3
Wrangley Ct WAB EN9 63 M9
Wray Av CLAY IG5 122 D1
Wray Cl EMPK RM11 125 L5
Wray Common Rd REIG RH2 257 M9
Wray Crs FSBYPK N4 118 F7
Wrayfield Av REIG RH2 257 M9
Wrayfield Rd CHEAM SM3 200 G10
Wraylands Dr REIG RH2 257 N8
Wray La REIG RH2 257 M6
Wraymead Pl REIG * RH2 257 L9
Wray Mill Pk REDH RH1 257 N8
Wray Park Rd REIG RH2 257 L9
Wray Rd BELMT SM2 221 J5
Wraysbury Cl HSLWW TW4 175 M1
Wraysbury Rd
STWL/WRAY TW19 172 F6
Wrays Wy YEAD UB4 132 F7
Wrekin Rd WOOL/PLUM SE18 162 F6
Wren Av CRICK NW2 116 F9
NWDGN UB2 153 N3
Wren Cl CAN/RD E16 141 L8
ED N9 100 C2
SAND/SEL CR2 224 C6
STMC/STPC BR5 207 N3
Wren Ct CRAWE * RH10 283 P10
Wren Crs ADL/WDHM KT15 215 N2
BUSH WD23 94 B2
Wren Dr WAB EN9 63 M10
WDR/YW UB7 151 N1
Wren Gdns DAGW RM9 123 N10
HCH RM12 124 G6
Wren Ms LEW * SE13 161 K10
Wren Pl BRW CM14 107 J4
Wren Rd CMBW SE5 159 L7
DAGW RM9 123 N10
SCUP DA14 185 M6
Wren's Av ASHF TW15 174 D8
Wrens Cft GVW DA11 190 B7
Wrensfield HHW HP1 35 K6
Wren's Hl LHD/OX KT22 236 B1
The Wrens HLWW/ROY CM19 46 E1
Wren St FSBYW WC1X 11 P1
Wren Ter LOU IG10 82 E5
Wrentham Av WLSDN NW10 136 G4
Wrenthorpe Rd BMLY BR1 183 K7
Wren Wk TIL RM18 168 E6
Wren Wd WGCE AL7 23 L4
Wrenwood Wy PIN HA5 113 J2
Wrexham Rd BOW E3 140 F4
HARH RM3 105 L5
Wricklemarsh Rd
BKHTH/KID SE3 161 N8
Wrigglesworth St NWCR SE14 160 C6
Wright WDSR SL4 148 D9
Wright Cl LEW SE13 161 J10
STALE/WH AL4 21 J4
Wright Gdns SHPTN TW17 196 B5
Wright Rd HEST TW5 153 K6
Wrightsbridge Rd BRW CM14 105 N2
Wrights Cl DAGE RM10 124 C9
Wrights La BRWN CM15 87 J2
KENS * W8 14 F3
KENS W8 14 G3
Wrights Pl WLSDN * NW10 135 P1
Wright's Rd BOW E3 140 E4
SNWD SE25 203 M3
Wright's Rw CAR SM5 222 C1
Wrigley Cl CHING * E4 101 J6
Wrotham Rd BAR EN5 77 H6
CAMTN NW1 5 H4
GVW DA11 190 D6
WEA W13 135 H10
WELL DA16 163 M7
Wroths Pth LOU IG10 82 C5
Wrottesley Rd WLSDN NW10 136 D4
WOOL/PLUM SE18 162 F5
Wroughton Rd BTSEA SW11 180 A2
Wroughton Ter HDN * NW4 116 E2
Wroxall Rd DAGW RM9 143 M1
Wroxham Av HHS/BOV HP3 35 N8
Wroxham Gdns ENC/FH EN2 79 H1
FBAR/BDGN N11 98 D8
POTB/CUF EN6 58 G7
Wroxham Rd THMD SE28 143 N9
Wroxton Rd PECK SE15 160 A8
Wrythe Gn CAR SM5 202 A10
Wrythe Green Rd CAR SM5 202 A10
Wrythe La CAR SM5 201 N8
Wulfstan St SHB W12 136 C8
Wulstan Pk POTB/CUF EN6 59 N8
Wyatt Cl BUSH WD23 94 D1
FELT TW13 175 L4
YEAD UB4 133 H7
Wyatt Dr BARN SW13 156 E5
Wyatt Park Rd
BRXS/STRHM SW2 180 G5
Wyatt Rd DART DA1 164 G9
FSBYPK N4 119 K8
FSTGT E7 141 M1
STA TW18 173 K8
WDSR SL4 148 C9
Wyatt's Cl RKW/CH/CXG WD3 71 K7
Wyatts Green La BRWN CM15 87 J2
Wyatt's Green Rd BRWN CM15 87 J2
Wyatt's La WALTH E17 121 H1
Wyatt's Rd RKW/CH/CXG WD3 71 J8
Wybert St CAMTN NW1 10 F1
Wyborne Wy WLSDN NW10 135 P2
Wyburn Av BAR EN5 77 J7
Wychcombe Studios
HAMP * NW3 4 A2
Wyche Gv SAND/SEL CR2 223 M5
Wych Elm HLW CM20 28 F10
Wych Elm Cl EMPK RM11 125 P4
Wych Elm Ri GU GU1 268 B3
Wych Elm Rd EMPK RM11 125 P3
Wychelm Rd LTWR GU18 212 B7
Wych Elms LCOL/BKTW AL2 56 A4
Wycherley Cl BKHTH/KID SE3 161 L6
Wycherley Crs BAR EN5 77 L10
Wychford Dr SBW CM21 29 M2
Wych Hl WOKS/MYFD GU22 231 P5
Wych Hill La WOKS/MYFD GU22 232 A5
Wych Hill Pk WOKS/MYFD GU22 232 A5
Wych Hill Ri WOKS/MYFD GU22 231 P5
Wychwood Av EDGW HA8 95 J7
THHTH CR7 203 J3
Wychwood Cl EDGW HA8 95 J7
SUN TW16 175 H9
Wychwood End HGT N6 118 D5
Wychwood Gdns CLAY IG5 122 C2
Wychwood Wy NTHWD HA6 92 G8
Wycliffe Cl WELL DA16 163 J7
Wycliffe Rd BTSEA SW11 158 B8
WIM/MER SW19 179 L9
Wycliffe Rw GVW DA11 190 C4
Wyclif St FSBYE EC1V 6 C10
Wycombe End BEAC HP9 108 C1
Wycombe Gdns CRICK NW2 117 J7
Wycombe Pl STAL AL1 38 G3
WAND/EARL * SW18 179 M2
Wycombe Rd ALP/SUD HA0 135 M3
GNTH/NBYPK IG2 122 C3
TOTM N17 99 P9
Wycombe Wy STALE/WH AL4 38 G3
Wyddial Gn WGCE AL7 23 L5
Wydell Cl MRDN SM4 200 F6
Wydenhurst Rd CROY/NA CR0 203 P7
Wydeville Manor Rd
LEE/GVPK SE12 183 N7
Wyecliffe Gdns REDH RH1 258 D6
Wye Cl ASHF TW15 174 C7
ORP BR6 207 J7
RSLP HA4 112 D4
Wyedale LCOL/BKTW AL2 57 L3
Wyemead Crs CHING E4 101 K3
Wye Rd GVE DA12 190 G5
Wye St BTSEA SW11 157 N9
Wyeths Ms EW * KT17 220 C9
Wyeth's Rd EW KT17 220 C9
Wyevale Cl PIN HA5 113 H1
Wyfields CLAY IG5 102 E9
Wyfold Rd FUL/PGN SW6 157 H7
Wyke Cl ISLW TW7 154 E5
Wyke Gdns HNWL W7 154 E2
Wykeham Av DAGW RM9 143 M1
EMPK RM11 125 L4
Wykeham Cl GVE DA12 191 H9
WDR/YW UB7 152 B5
Wykeham Gn DAGW RM9 143 M1
Wykeham Hl WBLY HA9 115 L6
Wykeham Ri TRDG/WHET N20 97 H2
Wykeham Rd GU GU1 250 G9
HDN NW4 116 F3
KTN/HRWW/W HA3 114 G2
Wykeridge Cl CSHM HP5 50 G3
Wyke Rd BOW E3 140 F2
RYNPK SW20 200 F2
Wylands Rd DTCH/LGLY SL3 150 D4
Wylchin Cl PIN HA5 112 G2
Wyldes Cl GLDGN NW11 117 M6
Wyldewood ASC SL5 192 C6
Wyldfield Gdns ED N9 99 N3
Wyld Wy WBLY HA9 135 N1
Wyldwood Cl HLWE CM17 29 M5
Wyleu St FSTH SE23 182 D3
Wylie Rd NWDGN UB2 153 P2
Wyllen Cl WCHPL E1 140 B6
Wyllyotts Pl POTB/CUF EN6 59 J8
Wylo Dr BAR EN5 76 D10
Wymark Cl RAIN RM13 144 G4
Wymering Rd MV/WKIL W9 2 F10
Wymers Cl SL SL1 128 A4
Wymond St PUT/ROE SW15 156 F9
Wynan Rd POP/IOD E14 160 G4
Wynaud Ct WDGN N22 98 G7
Wyncham Av BFN/LL DA15 185 H4
Wynches Farm Dr STALE/WH AL4 39 J5
Wynchgate KTN/HRWW/W HA3 94 D8
STHGT/OAK N14 98 F1
Wynchlands Crs STALE/WH AL4 39 J6
Wyncote Wy SAND/SEL CR2 224 C5
Wyncroft Cl BMLY BR1 206 C3
Wyndale Av CDALE/KGS NW9 115 M4
Wyndcliff Rd CHARL SE7 161 N5
Wyndcroft Cl ENC/FH EN2 79 J7
Wyndham Av COB KT11 217 H9
Wyndham Cl BELMT SM2 221 K4
ORP BR6 206 F8
Wyndham Crs HSLWW TW4 175 N2
KTTN NW5 118 D8
SL SL1 128 A4
Wyndham Est CMBW SE5 159 K6
Wyndham Ms MBLAR W1H 10 A4
Wyndham Pl MBLAR W1H 10 A4
Wyndham Rd CMBW SE5 159 K6
EBAR EN4 98 A2
EHAM E6 142 A2
KUTN/CMB KT2 177 L10
WEA W13 154 G2
WOKN/KNAP GU21 231 N4
Wyndhams End BRKMPK AL9 23 J9
Wyndham St MBLAR W1H 10 A3
Wyndham Yd HNHL SE24 181 L1
Wynell Rd FSTH SE23 182 C6
Wynford Gv STMC/STPC BR5 207 L3
Wynford Pl BELV DA17 164 B5
Wynford Rd IS N1 5 N7
Wynford Wy ELTH/MOT SE9 184 C6
Wyngrave Pl BEAC HP9 88 A6
Wynlea Cl CRAWE RH10 285 P5
Wynlie Gdns PIN HA5 93 J10
Wynndale Rd SWFD E18 101 N9
Wynne Rd BRXN/ST SW9 159 H8
Wynn's Av BFN/LL DA15 185 K1
Wynnstay Gdns KENS W8 14 F3
Wynnstow Pk OXTED RH8 261 L7
Wynnswick Rd BEAC HP9 89 H6
Wynsham Wy BFOR GU20 212 A2
Wynter St BTSEA SW11 157 M10
Wynton Gdns SNWD SE25 203 M5
Wynton Gv WOT/HER KT12 197 H10
Wynton Pl ACT W3 135 N8
Wynyard Ter LBTH SE11 17 P8
Wynyatt St FSBYE EC1V 6 C9
Wyre Gv EDGW HA8 95 P4
HYS/HAR UB3 153 H3
Wyresdale Crs GFD/PVL UB6 134 E5
Wysemead HORL RH6 280 D3
Wyteleaf Cl RSLP HA4 112 D4
Wythburn Pl MBLAR W1H 10 A6
Wythenshawe Rd DAGE RM10 124 B8
Wythes Cl BMLY BR1 206 C2
Wythes Rd CAN/RD E16 142 B10
Wythfield Rd ELTH/MOT SE9 184 C2
Wyton WGCE AL7 23 N5
Wyvenhoe Rd RYLN/HDSTN HA2 114 B8
Wyvern Cl DART DA1 187 K3
ORP BR6 207 L10
Wyvern Est NWMAL * KT3 200 D3
Wyvern Pl ADL/WDHM * KT15 215 L1
Wyvern Rd PUR/KEN CR8 223 H6
Wyvern Wy UX/CGN UB8 131 L2

Wyvil Rd VX/NE SW8 158 F6
Wyvis St POP/IOD E14 140 G7

Y

Yabsley St POP/IOD E14 141 H10
Yaffle Rd WEY KT13 216 D6
Yalding Gv STMC/STPC BR5 207 N4
Yalding Rd BERM/RHTH SE16 19 N4
Yale Cl HSLWW TW4 175 N1
Yale Wy HCH RM12 125 H9
Yarborough Rd WIM/MER SW19 201 N1
Yarbridge Cl BELMT * SM2 221 L6
Yardley Cl CHING E4 80 G9
REIG RH2 257 L8
Yardley La CHING E4 80 G10
Yardley St FSBYW WC1X 6 A10
FSBYW WC1X 12 A1
Yard Md EGH TW20 172 D6
Yarm Cl LHD/OX KT22 237 H9
Yarm Court Rd LHD/OX KT22 237 H9
Yarmouth Crs CRAWE RH10 284 B9
Yarmouth Crs WALTH E17 120 A3
Yarmouth Pl MYFR/PICC W1J 10 E10
Yarmouth Rd SL SL1 129 H8
WATN WD24 73 J4
Yarm Wy LHD/OX KT22 237 H9
Yarnton Wy ERITHM DA18 163 P1
Yarrow Crs EHAM E6 142 B7
Yarrowside AMSS HP7 69 N6
Yateley St WOOL/PLUM SE18 162 A2
Yattendon Rd HORL RH6 280 C4
Yeading Av RSLP HA4 113 M7
Yeading Fk YEAD UB4 133 K7
Yeading Gdns YEAD UB4 133 J7
Yeading La YEAD UB4 133 J8
Yeames Cl WEA W13 134 F8
Yearling Cl WARE SG12 26 E4
Yeate St IS N1 6 E10
Yeatman Rd HGT N6 118 A4
Yeats Cl BKHTH/KID * SE3 161 J8
REDH RH1 275 M3
WLSDN NW10 136 B1
Ye Cnr BUSH WD23 73 L10
Yeend Cl E/WMO/HCT KT8 197 P4
Yeldham Rd HMSMTH W6 156 G4
Yeldham Vls HMSMTH * W6 156 G4
Yellowcress Dr CHOB/PIR GU24 230 F2
Yellowpine Wy CHIG IG7 103 L5
Yelverton Cl HARH RM3 105 K9
Yelverton Rd BTSEA SW11 157 N8
Yenston Cl MRDN SM4 201 K6
Yeoman Cl EHAM E6 142 E9
Yeoman Rd NTHLT UB5 133 M2
Yeomanry Cl EW KT17 220 C8
Yeomans Acre RSLP HA4 113 H4
Yeoman's Mdw SEV TN13 265 H2
Yeoman's Rw CHEL SW3 15 P4
Yeomans Ter
WOKN/KNAP * GU21 231 J3
Yeoman St BERM/RHTH SE16 160 D3
Yeomans Wy EN * EN1 80 A6
Yeoman Wy REDH RH1 276 C5
Yeomen Wy BARK/HLT IG6 102 F7
Yeo St BOW E3 140 G7
Yeoveney Cl STWL/WRAY TW19 172 G5
Yeovil Cl ORP BR6 207 H9
Yeovil Rd SL SL1 128 D7
Yeovilton Pl KUTN/CMB KT2 177 J8
Yerbury Rd ARCH N19 118 E8
Yester Dr CHST BR7 184 B10
Yester Pk CHST BR7 184 C10
Yester Rd CHST BR7 184 C10
Yevele Wy EMPK RM11 125 M5
Yew Av WDR/YW UB7 131 P9
Yewbank Cl PUR/KEN CR8 241 L1
Yew Cl BKHH IG9 102 A3
CHESW * EN7 61 M3
Yewdale Cl BMLY BR1 183 K9
Yewfield Rd WLSDN NW10 136 C2
Yew Gv CRICK NW2 116 G9
WCCE AL7 23 M6
Yewlands HOD EN11 44 F4
SBW CM21 29 P2
Yewlands Cl BNSTD SM7 239 L1
Yewlands Dr HOD EN11 44 F4
Yew Pl WEY * KT13 196 G10
Yews Av EN EN1 80 A2
The Yews ASHF * TW15 174 C7
BF/WBF * KT14 215 P8
GVE DA12 190 C5
Yew Tree Bottom Rd EW KT17 238 E3
Yewtree Cl RYLN/HDSTN HA2 114 A2
Yew Tree Cl BEAC HP9 88 E10
COUL/CHIP CR5 240 A5
CSHM HP5 51 M6
HORL RH6 280 B2
RBRW/HUT CM13 87 N10
SEV TN13 246 E9
WCHMH N21 99 H1
WELL DA16 163 K7
WPK KT4 200 B8
Yew Tree Ct BORE WD6 75 J10
Yew Tree Dr CTHM CR3 259 N1
GU GU1 249 N5
HHS/BOV HP3 52 E4
Yewtree End LCOL/BKTW AL2 56 A3
Yew Tree Gdns CHDH RM6 123 P3
EPSOM KT18 237 P1
ROMW/RG * RM7 124 E3
ROMW/RG RM7 124 E3
Yew Tree La REIG RH2 257 L7
Yewtree Rd BECK BR3 204 E3
Yew Tree Rd DORK RH4 254 F10
HGDN/ICK UB10 132 A3
HORL RH6 279 H8
SHB W12 136 C9
SL SL1 149 M2
Yewtrees EGH TW20 194 F3
Yew Trees SHPTN * TW17 196 A4
Yew Tree Wk EHSLY KT24 253 L3
HSLWW TW4 175 N1
PUR/KEN CR8 223 K6
Yew Wk HOD EN11 44 F4
HRW HA1 114 D6
Yoakley Rd STNW/STAM N16 119 M7
Yoke Cl HOLWY N7 5 M1
Yolande Gdns ELTH/MOT SE9 184 B1
Yonge Pk HOLWY N7 119 H8
York Av BFN/LL DA15 185 H5
HNWL W7 134 D10
KTN/HRWW/W HA3 94 G9
MORT/ESHN SW14 177 P1
SL SL1 129 J8
UX/CGN UB8 132 D8
WDSR SL4 148 G8
York Br CAMTN NW1 10 C1
York Buildings CHCR WC2N 11 M8
York Cl BF/WBF KT14 215 P8
BRWN CM15 107 L1
CMBW * SE5 159 K8
EHAM E6 142 C8
HNWL W7 134 D10
KGLGY WD4 54 B5
MRDN SM4 201 L4
York Crs BORE WD6 76 A6
LOU IG10 82 B7
Yorke Gdns REIG RH2 257 K9
Yorke Ga WAT WD17 73 H6
Yorke Gate Rd CTHM CR3 241 L8
Yorke Rd REIG RH2 257 K9
RKW/CH/CXG WD3 72 B10
Yorkes HLWS CM18 47 J3
York Gdns WOT/HER KT12 197 L9
York Ga CAMTN NW1 10 D2
STHGT/OAK N14 98 F1
York Gv PECK SE15 160 B7
York Hl LOU IG10 82 B7
STRHM/NOR SW16 181 J6
York House Pl KENS W8 14 G1
Yorkland Av WELL DA16 163 J10
York Ms IL IG1 122 D7
KTTN NW5 118 C10
York Pde BTFD * TW8 155 J4
CDALE/KGS * NW9 116 D4
York Pl BTSEA SW11 157 M9
GRAYS RM17 167 M5
IL IG1 122 D7
York Ri KTTN NW5 118 C8
ORP BR6 207 H8
York Rd ACT W3 135 P8
BAR EN5 77 M9
BELMT SM2 221 K3
BF/WBF KT14 215 N8
BH/WHM TN16 243 N5
BRWN CM15 107 L1
BTFD TW8 155 J4
BTSEA SW11 157 M10
CHES/WCR EN8 62 D10
CHING E4 100 F6
CROY/NA CR0 203 H7
DART DA1 187 N3
EA W5 155 H2
EPP CM16 66 B3
FBAR/BDGN N11 98 E7
FSTGT E7 141 M1
GU GU1 268 A1
GVE DA12 190 F6
GVW DA11 190 A3
HSLW TW3 154 A9
IL IG1 122 D8
KUTN/CMB KT2 177 L10
LEY E10 121 H8
NTHWD HA6 93 H10
RAIN RM13 144 E2
RCHPK/HAM TW10 177 L1
SAND/SEL CR2 224 C6
STAL AL1 38 E5
STHWK SE1 17 P1
TEDD TW11 176 D7
UED N18 100 A6
UX/CGN UB8 131 N2
WALTH E17 120 C3
WATW WD18 73 K9
WCHMH N21 99 L1
WDSR SL4 148 G8
WEY KT13 216 D2
WIM/MER SW19 179 L9
WOKS/MYFD GU22 232 A5
Yorkshire Cl STNW/STAM N16 119 M8
Yorkshire Gdns UED N18 100 A6
Yorkshire Grey Yd HHOL * WC1V 11 N4
Yorkshire Rd MTCM CR4 202 F5
POP/IOD E14 140 D8
York Sq POP/IOD * E14 140 D8
York St BARK IG11 142 E3
MBLAR W1H 10 A4
MHST W1U 10 B3
MTCM CR4 202 B7
TWK TW1 176 F4
York St Chambers MHST * W1U 10 B3
York Ter ENC/FH EN2 79 K4
ERITH DA8 164 D7
York Ter East CAMTN NW1 10 D2
York Ter West CAMTN NW1 10 C2
Yorkton St BETH E2 7 N7
York Wy CHSGTN KT9 219 J4
FELT TW13 175 N6
GSTN WD25 73 L2
HHS/BOV HP3 35 P7
HOLWY N7 5 L2
IS N1 5 M7
TRDG/WHET N20 98 A4
York Way Ct IS N1 5 M6
York Way Est HOLWY N7 5 L2
Youngfield Rd HHW HP1 35 J5
Youngmans Cl ENC/FH EN2 79 K5
Young Rd CAN/RD E16 141 P8
Youngs Ri WGCW AL8 22 E5
Youngs Rd GNTH/NBYPK IG2 122 G3
Young St KENS W8 14 G2
LHD/OX KT22 236 E10
Youngstroat La CHOB/PIR GU24 214 B6
Yoxley Ap GNTH/NBYPK IG2 122 F4
Yoxley Dr GNTH/NBYPK IG2 122 F4
Yukon Rd BAL SW12 180 C3
Yule Cl LCOL/BKTW AL2 55 N6
Yuletide Cl WLSDN NW10 136 B1
Yunus Khan Cl WALTH E17 120 F3

Z

Zambra Wy BGR/WK TN15 247 N6
Zampa Rd BERM/RHTH SE16 160 B4
Zander Ct BETH E2 7 P9
Zangwill Rd BKHTH/KID SE3 162 A7
Zealand Av WDR/YW UB7 151 N6
Zealand Rd BOW E3 140 D4
Zelah Rd STMC/STPC BR5 207 L7
Zennor Rd BAL SW12 180 D4
Zenoria St EDUL SE22 159 N10
Zermatt Rd THHTH CR7 203 K4
Zetland St POP/IOD E14 141 H7
Zig Zag Rd PUR/KEN CR8 241 K2
RDKG RH5 255 H6
Zinnia Dr CHOB/PIR GU24 230 F2
Zion Pl GVW DA11 190 E3
THHTH CR7 203 L4
Zion Rd THHTH CR7 203 L4
Zoar St STHWK SE1 12 E9
Zoffany St ARCH N19 118 E7

Index - featured places

AAIS
DART DA1 187 M3
Aarotya Medical Centre
TOTM N17 119 K2
Abbey Business Centre
VX/NE SW8 158 D7
The Abbey Clinic
BELV DA17 164 A4
Abbey Gateway
STALW/RED AL3 38 B6
Abbey Industrial Estate
ALP/SUD HA0 135 L3
MTCM CR4 202 A5
Abbeylands School
ADL/WDHM KT15 215 K2
Abbey Mead Industrial Park
WAB EN9 62 G10
Abbey Medical Centre
STJWD NW8 3 H6
Abbey Mills
WIM/MER SW19 201 M1
Abbey Park Industrial Estate
BARK IG11 142 E4
Abbey Primary School
ABYW SE2 163 M2
STALW/RED AL3 38 B7
Abbey (rems of)
ABYW SE2 163 L5
Abbey Road Health Centre
SRTFD E15 141 K3
Abbey School for the
English Language
STJWD NW8 3 K8
Abbey Trading Estate
SYD SE26 182 D8
Abbey Tutorial College
BAY/PAD W2 8 F6
Abbey Wharf Industrial Estate
BARK IG11 142 G5
Abbey Wood School
ABYW SE2 163 K2
Abbotsbury First School
MRDN SM4 201 L5
Abbotsfield School
HGDN/ICK UB10 132 C4
Abbot's Hill School
HHS/BOV HP3 54 C1
Abbots Hospital
GU GU1 268 A1
Abbots Langley Primary School
ABLGY WD5 54 F5
Abbotsweld Primary School
HLWS CM18 46 G3
Abbotswood Medical Centre
ABLGY WD5 55 H8
ABC Cinema
CAT SE6 182 G4
ESH/CLAY KT10 218 A1
GVE DA12 190 E2
HAMP NW3 117 P10
PUT/ROE SW15 157 H9
STA TW18 173 H7
STRHM/NOR SW16 180 F5
Abercorn Place School
STJWD NW8 3 K8
Abercorn Trading Estate
ALP/SUD HA0 135 J3
Aberdeen Wharf
WAP E1W 140 A10
Aberdour School
KWD/TDW/WH KT20 239 J4
Aberglen Industrial Estate
HYS/HAR UB3 152 E1
Abinger Common First School
RDKG RH5 271 L8
Abinger Hammer Village School
RDKG RH5 270 G5
Abney Park Cemetery
STNW/STAM N16 119 M7
Aboyne Lodge Primary School
STALW/RED AL3 38 C5
Abridge Golf & Country Club
EPP CM16 84 A3
Acacia Business Centre
WAN E11 121 K8
Acland Burghley School
KTTN NW5 118 C9
Acorn Industrial Park
DART DA1 186 G2
Acorn Medical Centre
HGDN/ICK UB10 132 B3
Acorn Trading Centre
WTHK RM20 167 J5
Acre Road Health Clinic
KUTN/CMB KT2 177 L10
Activity World
HAT AL10 40 E1
Acton Business Centre
WLSDN NW10 136 A6
Acton Central Industrial Estate
ACT W3 135 N9
Acton Health Centre
ACT W3 135 P10
Acton High School
ACT W3 155 M1
Acton Hospital
ACT W3 155 M1
Acton Lane Medical Centre
CHSWK W4 156 A1
Acton Park Industrial Estate
ACT W3 136 C10
CHSWK W4 156 A1
Acton Superbowl
ACT W3 135 M6
Acton Swimming Baths
ACT W3 135 P10
Acumen (Anglo School)
NRWD SE19 181 M10
Adams Bridge Business Centre
WBLY HA9 115 N10
Adamsrill Primary School
SYD SE26 182 D6
Adath Yisroel Cemetery
EN EN1 79 N5
Addey & Stanhope School
NWCR SE14 160 E7
Addington Business Centre
CROY/NA CR0 225 K6
The Addington Golf Club
CROY/NA CR0 224 E5
Addington Palace Golf Club
CROY/NA CR0 224 D3
Addiscombe Cricket Club
CROY/NA CR0 203 N10
Addison Primary School
WKENS W14 156 G2
Addlestone Cemetery
ADL/WDHM KT15 195 K10
Adelphi Theatre
COVGDN WC2E 11 M8
Adeyfield School
HHNE HP2 36 B6
Adler Industrial Estate
HYS/HAR UB3 152 E1
Admiral Hyson Industrial Estate
BERM/RHTH SE16 160 A3
Admiralty Arch
STJS SW1Y 11 K9
ADT Technology College
PUT/ROE SW15 179 J1
The Adult College of Barking &
Dagenham
BARK IG11 143 H1
Adult Education Centre
DART DA1 187 N3
POP/IOD E14 161 H2
Africa Centre
COVGDN WC2E 11 M7
Agora Shopping Centre
PECK SE15 159 P8
Ainslie Wood Primary School
CHING E4 100 G6
Airbase Unity
Elementary School
HGDN/ICK UB10 112 D7
Airbus Coach Station
HTHAIR TW6 152 A9
Air Call Business Centre
CDALE/KGS NW9 116 A1
Airedale Physiotherapy Clinic
CHSWK W4 156 C4
Airlinks Golf Club
NWDGN UB2 153 K3
Air Links Industrial Estate
HEST TW5 153 K4
Airport Gate Business Centre
WDR/YW UB7 152 A6
Airport Industrial Estate
BH/WHM TN16 244 A1
AIU London
MHST W1U 10 D4
Aksaray Sports Club
STNW/STAM N16 119 L9
Alban Arena Cinema
STAL AL1 38 C6
Alban Wood Infant School
GSTN WD25 55 J9
Alban Wood Junior School
GSTN WD25 55 J9
Albany Centre & Theatre
DEPT SE8 160 E6
Albany Clinic
BFN/LL DA15 185 K7
WIM/MER SW19 179 L10
The Albany College
HDN NW4 116 E3
Albany School Grant Maintained
PEND EN3 80 C4
The Albany School
HCH RM12 125 J7
Albemarle Independant College
BAY/PAD W2 9 H7
Albemarle Primary School
WIM/MER SW19 179 H5
Albert Memorial
SKENS SW7 15 L1
Albery Theatre
CHCR WC2N 11 L7
Albion Health Centre
WCHPL E1 140 A7
Albion Junior & Infant School
BERM/RHTH SE16 160 B1
Albion Street Health Centre
BERM/RHTH SE16 160 B1
Albright Industrial Estate
RAIN RM13 144 G7
The Alchemy Gallery
CLKNW EC1R 12 A1
Aldenham Country Park
BORE WD6 74 G9
Aldenham Golf & Country Club
GSTN WD25 74 A4
Aldenham School
BORE WD6 74 E6
Alderbrook Primary School
BAL SW12 180 C3
Aldersbrook County
Secondary School
MNPK E12 121 P6
Aldersbrook Primary School
WAN E11 121 P6
The Alderton Primary School
LOU IG10 82 D9
Alderwood Primary School
ELTH/MOT SE9 184 G2
Aldro School
MFD/CHID GU8 266 B10
Aldwickbury Park Golf Club
HARP AL5 20 D2
Aldwych Theatre
HOL/ALD WC2B 11 N6
Alexander Barracks
CHOB/PIR GU24 230 A7
Alexander First School
WDSR SL4 148 B8
Alexander Mcleod
Primary School
ABYW SE2 163 L4
Alexandra Avenue Clinic
RYLN/HDSTN HA2 113 N7
Alexandra Business Centre
PEND EN3 80 C8
Alexandra Infant School
KUTN/CMB KT2 177 M10
PGE/AN SE20 182 C10
Alexandra Junior School
HSLW TW3 154 A8
SYD SE26 182 C9
Alexandra Palace
WDGN N22 118 E1
Alexandra Palace Ice Rink
WDGN N22 98 E10
Alexandra Primary School
WDGN N22 98 G10
Alexandra School
RYLN/HDSTN HA2 113 N7
Alfred Mizen First School
MTCM CR4 202 E3
Alfred Salter Primary School
BERM/RHTH SE16 160 C1
Alfreds Way Industrial Estate
BARK IG11 143 K3
Alfriston Special School
BEAC HP9 88 B5
Allegery Clinic
CAVSQ/HST W1G 10 E5
Allenby Infant School
GFD/PVL UB6 133 P8
Allen Edwards Primary School
CLAP SW4 158 F7
The All England Lawn Tennis &
Croquet Club
WIM/MER SW19 178 G6
Alleyns School
EDUL SE22 181 M1
Allfarthing JMI School
WAND/EARL SW18 179 M2
All Nations Christian College
WARE SG12 26 G3
All Saints Benhilton School
SUT SM1 201 L10
All Saints Catholic School
BCTR RM8 124 B6
All Saints CE First School
WIM/MER SW19 179 M10
All Saints CE Infant School
LHD/OX KT22 236 F5
All Saints CE Junior School
NRWD SE19 203 M1
All Saints CE Primary School
BKHTH/KID SE3 161 K8
CRICK NW2 117 J8
FUL/PGN SW6 157 H8
PUT/ROE SW15 156 F9
TRDG/WHET N20 97 N3
All Souls CE Primary School
GTPST W1W 10 G4
Allum Medical Centre
WAN E11 121 J5
Alma Junior & Infant School
BERM/RHTH SE16 19 N5
Alma Primary School
PEND EN3 80 D9
Almeida Theatre
IS N1 6 C4
Al Muntada Islamic School
FUL/PGN SW6 157 J7
Alperton Cemetery
ALP/SUD HA0 135 J3
Alperton Community School
ALP/SUD HA0 135 K2
Alperton High School
ALP/SUD HA0 135 J3
Alperton Sports Ground
ALP/SUD HA0 135 J4
Alpha Business Centre
WALTH E17 120 E3
Alpha Business Park
BRKMPK AL9 40 F9
Alpine Business Centre
EHAM E6 142 D7
Alscot Road Industrial Estate
STHWK SE1 19 M5
Altmore Infant School
EHAM E6 142 C2
The Alton School
PUT/ROE SW15 178 C3
Ambler Primary School
FSBYPK N4 119 J8
Ambleside Junior School
WOT/HER KT12 197 K8
Ambresbury Banks Fort
EPP CM16 64 E10
Amc Business Centre
WLSDN NW10 135 N5
American Community School
EGH TW20 193 P1
HGDN/ICK UB10 132 A3
The American
Community School
COB KT11 217 L6
American Golf at Sunbury
SHPTN TW17 196 D4
Amersham & Chiltern RFC
AMS HP6 68 F2
Amersham Hill Cricket Club
AMS HP6 69 K4
The Amersham School
AMSS HP7 69 K6
Amersham Town FC
AMSS HP7 68 F5
Amersham & Wycombe College
AMSS HP7 69 L5
AMF Bowling
CRAWW RH11 283 N7
HHNE HP2 36 C4
LEW SE13 161 H9
Amherst Primary School
HACK E8 119 P10
Amherst School
SEV TN13 246 E9
Ampthill Square Medical Centre
CAMTN NW1 4 G8
Amwell View School (Special)
WARE SG12 26 G7
Amy Johnson Primary School
WLGTN SM6 222 F4
Anchorage Point
Industrial Estate
CHARL SE7 161 P2
Anchor Bay Industrial Estate
ERITH DA8 164 G6
Anchor Retail Park
WCHPL E1 140 B6
Andover Medical Centre
HOLWY N7 118 G8
The Andrew Ewing
Primary School
HEST TW5 153 N6

Andrews Lane Junior & Infant School CHESW EN7 61 P4
Anerley Primary School PGE/AN SE20 203 P1
Anerley School PGE/AN SE20 203 P1
Angel Centre DART DA1 187 M2
Angerstein Business Park GNWCH SE10 161 M3
Anglesea Centre GVW DA11 190 E2
Anglian Industrial Estate BARK IG11 143 J6
Anglia Polytechnic University BRWN CM15 107 J2
Animal Cemetery REDBR IG4 122 A1
Annandale Primary School GNWCH SE10 161 L4
Annemount School EFNCH N2 117 M4
Annunciation RC Infant School EDGW HA8 96 A9
The Annunciation RC Junior School EDGW HA8 96 A7
Anson Primary School CRICK NW2 116 G10
Ante Natal Clinic MUSWH N10 118 B1
Anthony Roper Primary School EYN DA4 209 M9
Apex Industrial Estate WLSDN NW10 136 C6
Apex Retail Park FELT TW13 175 N6
Apollo Theatre SOHO/SHAV W1D 11 J7
Apollo Victoria Theatre PIM SW1V 16 G4
Apostolic Nuncio WIM/MER SW19 178 F6
Applecroft Junior Middle & Infant School WGCW AL8 22 E5
Applegarth Primary School CROY/NA CR0 224 G3
Apsley House, The Wellington Museum BAY/PAD W2 16 C1
Apsley Mills Retail Park HHS/BOV HP3 35 P10
Aquarius Business Park CRICK NW2 116 D6
Aquarius Golf Club EDUL SE22 182 B1
Arbour Vale Special School SLN SL2 129 M8
Arcadia Shopping Centre EA W5 135 J9
The Archbishop Lanfranc School CROY/NA CR0 202 F6
Archbishop Michael Ramsey Technology College CMBW SE5 159 J6
Archbishop Sumners CE Primary School LBTH SE11 18 B6
Archbishop Tenisons CE School CROY/NA CR0 203 N10
Archbishop Tenison's School VX/NE SW8 17 P10
Archdale Business Centre RYLN/HDSTN HA2 114 B7
Archdeacon Cambridge's CE Primary School WHTN TW2 176 D5
Arches Business Centre NWDGN UB2 153 N1
Arches Leisure Centre GNWCH SE10 161 J5
Archgate Business Centre NFNCH/WDSP N12 97 M6
Archway Business Centre ARCH N19 118 E8
Archway Theatre HORL RH6 280 B5
Ardleigh Green Primary School EMPK RM11 125 L1
Arena Estate FSBYPK N4 119 J4
Argyle Primary School STPAN WC1H 5 L9
Arkley Golf Club BAR EN5 76 C9
Arklow Trading Estate NWCR SE14 160 D5
Armchair Theatre LBTH SE11 18 A9
Armourers & Braziers' Hall LOTH EC2R 12 G4
Army Training Regiment CHOB/PIR GU24 230 B7
Arndale Health Centre WAND/EARL SW18 179 K2
Arnett Hills Primary School RKW/CH/CXG WD3 71 K10
Arnhem Wharf Primary School POP/IOD E14 160 E2
Arnold House School STJWD NW8 3 L7
Arnot Abbey FARR EC1M 12 C3
Arsenal FC (Highbury) HBRY N5 119 H8
Art College LBTH SE11 18 C8
Arts Centre
BMLY BR1 206 A1
GVE DA12 190 E2
HAMP NW3 117 L10
WDSR SL4 149 H8
Arts Centre & Staines Theatre STA TW18 173 H7
Art School BECK BR3 204 D5
Arts Theatre
LSQ/SEVD WC2H 11 K7
PUT/ROE SW15 156 G10
Ashbourne Independent Sixth Form College KENS W8 15 H1
Ashburnham Primary School WBPTN SW10 157 N6
Ashburton High School CROY/NA CR0 204 A7
Ashburton Primary School CROY/NA CR0 204 A6
Ashby Mill School CLAP SW4 180 F1
The Ashcombe School DORK RH4 254 G10
Asheridge Road Industrial Estate CSHM HP5 50 F5
Ashfield Junior School BUSH WD23 94 A1
Ashford CE Primary School ASHF TW15 174 C9
Ashford Clinic ASHF TW15 173 P6
Ashford High School ASHF TW15 173 P6
Ashford Hospital A & E STWL/WRAY TW19 173 P5
Ashford Industrial Estate ASHF TW15 174 D7
Ashford Manor Golf Club ASHF TW15 174 A9
Ashford Park Primary School ASHF TW15 173 N7
The Ashford & St Peters Hospital CHERT KT16 194 G10
Ashford Sports Club
ASHF TW15 173 N7
STWL/WRAY TW19 174 A4
Ashgrove College WALTH E17 120 F1
Ashgrove Estate BMLY BR1 183 J9
Ashgrove School BMLY BR1 205 N2
Ash Industrial Estate HLWW/ROY CM19 46 C2
Ashleigh Commercial Estate CHARL SE7 161 P3
Ashley Centre Shopping Precinct EPSOM KT18 220 A9
Ashley Primary School WOT/HER KT12 197 H8
Ashlyns School BERK HP4 33 P7
Ashmead Primary School BROCKY SE4 160 F8
Ashmole Primary School VX/NE SW8 17 P10
Ashmole School STHGT/OAK N14 98 D2
Ashmount Primary School ARCH N19 118 D5
Ashtead Clinic ASHTD KT21 237 K3
Ashtead Cricket Club ASHTD KT21 237 K3
Ashtead Hospital ASHTD KT21 237 K6
Ashton House School ISLW TW7 154 C7
Ashton Playing Fields Track WFD IG8 102 B7
Aspen House School CMBW SE5 18 C10
Aspen House Secondary & Primary School BRXS/STRHM SW2 180 F3
Asquith Court School KTN/HRWW/W HA3 114 G4
Asquith School PEND EN3 80 B8
Assembly Rooms KUT KT1 199 K4
Associated Newspapers BERM/RHTH SE16 160 C2
Astley Cooper School HHNE HP2 36 B1
The Astolat Industrial Estate RGUW GU3 267 P8
Aston Clinic NWMAL KT3 200 B4
Aston House School EA W5 135 J8
Astra Business Centre REDH RH1 276 B10
Asylum Medical Centre CEND/HSY/T N8 119 H1
Athelney Primary School CAT SE6 182 F6
Athelstan House School HPTN TW12 197 P1
Athena Medical Centre CLPT E5 120 B9
Atherton Leisure Centre FSTGT E7 141 L1
Athlone House Hospital HGT N6 118 A6
Athlon Industrial Estate ALP/SUD HA0 135 J4
Atkinson Morley Hospital RYNPK SW20 178 E10
Atlas Business Centre CRICK NW2 116 E7
Atlas Medical Centre HORL RH6 280 B8
Atlas Transport Estate BTSEA SW11 157 M8
Atwood Primary School SAND/SEL CR2 223 P10
Audley Primary School CTHM CR3 241 M7
Auriol Junior School HOR/WEW KT19 220 C1
Austin Lodge Golf Club EYN DA4 229 M5
Australia House HOL/ALD WC2B 11 P6
Aveley FC SOCK/AV RM15 146 B9
Aveley Medical Centre SOCK/AV RM15 147 H6
Aveley Primary School SOCK/AV RM15 146 D10
The Aveley School SOCK/AV RM15 146 C9
Aveling Park School WALTH E17 100 F10
Avenue Industrial Estate
CHING E4 100 E7
GPK RM2 105 L10
Avenue Medical Centre SLN SL2 128 F5
Avenue Primary School
KIL/WHAMP NW6 2 A4
MNPK E12 122 B9
The Avenue Primary School BELMT SM2 221 K6
Avigdor Primary School STNW/STAM N16 119 L7
Avondale Park Primary School NTGHL W11 8 A8
Avon House School WFD IG8 101 M5
Avon Trading Estate WKENS W14 14 D6
Axis Business Centre SRTFD E15 140 G3
Axton Chase School HART DA3 211 L3
Aycliffe Drive Primary School HHNE HP2 35 P2
Aylands School PEND EN3 80 B2
The Aylesham Centre PECK SE15 159 P7
Ayloff Primary School HCH RM12 125 J9
Aylward First & Middle Schools STAN HA7 95 J6
Aylward School UED N18 99 L5
Aylwin Girls School BERM/RHTH SE16 19 M5
Aysgarth Medical Centre IVER SL0 130 G4
BAA Heathrow Visitor Centre HTHAIR TW6 152 D7
Babington House School CHST BR7 184 C9
Back Care Clinic WPK KT4 200 D8
Bacons City Technology College BERM/RHTH SE16 160 C1
Bacon's College BERM/RHTH SE16 140 D10
Baden Powell House SKENS SW7 15 K5
Baden Powell Primary School CLPT E5 120 A8
Bakers Hall MON EC3R 13 K8
Balaam Leisure Centre PLSTW E13 141 M6
Bales College NKENS W10 136 G5
Balfour Business Centre NWDGN UB2 153 L2
Balfour Medical Centre GRAYS RM17 167 P3
Balgowan Primary School BECK BR3 204 D2
Balham Health Centre BAL SW12 180 C5
Balmoral Trading BARK IG11 143 J7
Baltic Exchange HDTCH EC3A 13 K5
Bancrofts School WFD IG8 101 M4
Bandon Hill Cemetery WLGTN SM6 222 E2
Bandon Hill Primary School WLGTN SM6 222 E3
Bangabandhu Primary School BETH E2 140 B5
Bank of England (& Museum) LOTH EC2R 12 G6
Bank of England Extension STP EC4M 12 E6
Bankside Jetty STHWK SE1 12 E8
Bankside Park Industrial Estate BARK IG11 143 K5
Bannister Stadium KTN/HRWW/W HA3 94 B7
Bannockburn Primary School WOOL/PLUM SE18 163 J3
Banqueting House WHALL SW1A 11 L10
Banstead Athletic FC KWD/TDW/WH KT20 238 F6
Banstead Clinic BNSTD SM7 239 K1
Banstead County Junior School BNSTD SM7 239 J1
Banstead County Primary School BNSTD SM7 239 J1
Banstead Downs Golf Club BELMT SM2 221 K7
Banstead Sports Centre KWD/TDW/WH KT20 238 F6
Banstead Village Clinic BNSTD SM7 239 L1
Barbara Castle Health Centre HLWW/ROY CM19 46 D5
Barber Surgeons' Hall BARB EC2Y 12 F4
Barbican Cinema BARB EC2Y 12 E3
The Barbican BARB EC2Y 12 E3
Barbican Theatre BARB EC2Y 12 F3
Barclay Junior & Infant School LEY E10 121 J4
Barham Primary School ALP/SUD HA0 135 H1
Baring Primary School LEE/GVPK SE12 183 M3
Baring Road Medical Centre LEE/GVPK SE12 183 M5
Barkantine Clinic POP/IOD E14 160 F1
Barking Abbey Comprehensive School
BARK IG11 122 G10
BARK IG11 143 J1
Barking Abbey Industrial Estate BARK IG11 142 E3
Barking College ROMW/RG RM7 124 E7
Barking FC BCTR RM8 123 L10
Barking Hospital BARK IG11 143 J2
Barking Industrial Park BARK IG11 143 J3
Barking RUFC DAGW RM9 143 N3
Barkingside Cemetery BARK/HLT IG6 122 E1
Barkingside FC BARK/HLT IG6 122 G2
Barlby Primary School NKENS W10 136 G6
Barley Lane Primary School GDMY/SEVK IG3 123 K5
Barnabas Medical Centre NTHLT UB5 134 B1
Barncroft JMI School HHNE HP2 35 N1
Barn Croft Primary School WALTH E17 120 D4
Barnehurst Primary School BXLYHN DA7 164 D7
Barnehurst Public Pay & Play Golf Club BXLYHN DA7 164 E9
Barn Elms Athletics Track BARN SW13 156 E8
Barn Elms Water Sports Centre BARN SW13 156 F8
Barnes Cray Primary School DART DA1 165 H10
Barnes Hospital MORT/ESHN SW14 156 B9
Barnes Sports Club BARN SW13 156 C7
Barnet College
BAR EN5 77 J8
NFNCH/WDSP N12 97 M6
Barnet Copthall Stadium HDN NW4 96 F9
Barnet County Court
BAR EN5 77 M8
FNCH N3 97 K9
Barnet FC (Underhill) BAR EN5 77 K9
Barnet General Hospital BAR EN5 76 G8
Barnet Health Centre BAR EN5 77 K9
Barnet Hill JMI School BAR EN5 77 J9
Barnet Hospital Chest Clinic BAR EN5 76 G8
Barnet Magistrates Court BAR EN5 77 J8
Barnet Museum BAR EN5 77 H8
Barnet Trading Estate BAR EN5 77 J7
Barnett Wood Infant School ASHTD KT21 237 J3
Barnfield Primary School EDGW HA8 95 P9
Barnhill Community High School YEAD UB4 133 J5
Barnsbury County School WOKS/MYFD GU22 232 A7
Barnsbury School for Girls IS N1 6 A3
Barn Theatre WGCW AL8 22 F5
Barnwood County First School GUW GU2 249 J9
Barons Court Theatre WKENS W14 14 B7
Barratt Industrial Park BOW E3 141 H6
Barrett Industrial Park STHL UB1 133 P10
Barrett Way Industrial Estate HRW HA1 114 C1
Barrington Primary School WELL DA16 163 N8
Barrow Hedges Primary School CAR SM5 221 P4
Barrow Hill Junior School STJWD NW8 3 N8
Barton House Health Centre STNW/STAM N16 119 L8
Barwell Business Park CHSGTN KT9 219 J4
Baston School HAYES BR2 205 N9
Bata Medical Centre TIL RM18 169 M3
Batchwood Golf Club STALW/RED AL3 38 A3
Batchwood School STALW/RED AL3 38 C3
Batchworth Park Golf Club RKW/CH/CXG WD3 92 A4
Bates Industrial Estate HARH RM3 105 P8
Bath Factory Estate HNHL SE24 181 K2
Battersea Business Centre BTSEA SW11 158 B9
Battersea Dogs' Home VX/NE SW8 158 C6
Battersea Power Station VX/NE SW8 16 F10
Battersea Sports Centre BTSEA SW11 157 N9
Battersea Technology College BTSEA SW11 158 A7
Battersea Tutorial College TOOT SW17 180 B5
Bayfordbury College of Hertfordshire HERT/BAY SG13 25 J10
Bayford Primary School HERT/BAY SG13 42 G4
Bayhurst Wood Country Park DEN/HRF UB9 112 A3
Baylis Business Centre SL SL1 129 J9
Baylis Court School SL SL1 129 J7
BBC Studios MV/WKIL W9 8 G1
BBC Television Centre SHB W12 136 F9
Beacon Hill Industrial Estate PUR RM19 166 A3
Beacon House School EA W5 135 L10
Beacon School BNSTD SM7 239 H3
The Beacon School AMS HP6 68 G1
Beaconsfield Cricket Club BEAC HP9 88 F10
Beaconsfield Golf Club BEAC HP9 89 H9
Beaconsfield High School BEAC HP9 88 C10
Beaconsfield RFC BEAC HP9 108 E1
Beaconsfield School BEAC HP9 88 D10
Beal High School REDBR IG4 122 B1
Beam Primary School DAGE RM10 144 D4
Bean Primary School RDART DA2 189 H6
Beatrix Potter Primary School WAND/EARL SW18 179 M4
Beauclerc Infant School SUN TW16 197 K3
Beaufort Primary School WOKN/KNAP GU21 231 L2
Beaumont Primary School
LEY E10 120 G5
PUR/KEN CR8 222 G10
Beaumont School STALE/WH AL4 39 J5
The Beavers Community Primary School HSLWW TW4 153 K9
Beaverwood School for Girls CHST BR7 185 H9
Beckenham Business Centre BECK BR3 182 D9
Beckenham Crematorium SNWD SE25 204 B3
Beckenham Cricket Club BECK BR3 182 G10
Beckenham Hospital BECK BR3 204 E2
Beckenham Leisure Centre BECK BR3 204 D1
Beckenham Place Park Golf Course BECK BR3 182 G9
Beckenham RFC BECK BR3 204 D4
Beckenham Town FC BECK BR3 204 F5
Becket Sports Centre DART DA1 187 K2
Beckford Primary School KIL/WHAMP NW6 117 J10
Beckmead School BECK BR3 204 F8
The Beck Theatre HYS/HAR UB3 132 G8
Beckton Ski Centre EHAM E6 142 D6
Beckton Special School CAN/RD E16 142 A7
Beckton Triangle Retail Park EHAM E6 142 E5
Beconscot Model Village BEAC HP9 88 C8
Becontree Day Hospital BCTR RM8 123 P7
Becontree Primary School BCTR RM8 123 L8
Bective House Clinic PUT/ROE SW15 157 J10
Beddington Infants School WLGTN SM6 202 D10
Beddington Medical Centre CROY/NA CR0 222 F1
Beddington Park Primary School WLGTN SM6 202 F10
Beddington Trading Estate CROY/NA CR0 202 F8
Bedelsford School KUT KT1 199 K3
Bedensfield Clinic SCUP DA14 185 P8
Bedfont Health Clinic EBED/NFELT TW14 174 F3
Bedfont Industrial Park ASHF TW15 174 E6
Bedfont Junior & Infant School EBED/NFELT TW14 174 F2
Bedfont Lakes Country Park EBED/NFELT TW14 174 D5
Bedington Infant School WLGTN SM6 222 D1
Bedmond JMI School ABLGY WD5 54 G4
Bedonwell Clinic ABYW SE2 163 P5
Bedonwell Medical Centre BELV DA17 164 A4
Bedonwell Primary School BELV DA17 163 P5
Beechcroft Farm Industrial Estate BGR/WK TN15 211 J10
Beechfield Junior Middle & Infant School WATN WD24 73 H3
Beech House School SAND/SEL CR2 223 N6
Beech Hyde Primary School STALE/WH AL4 21 J4
Beecholme First School MTCM CR4 202 C1
Beechwood School SLN SL2 128 G5
Beis Rochel D'satmar Girls School STNW/STAM N16 119 M5
Beis Yaakov Primary School CDALE/KGS NW9 116 A1
Belcon Industrial Estate HOD EN11 45 H3
Belfry Shopping Centre REDH RH1 258 A9
Belhus Golf Club & Leisure Centre SOCK/AV RM15 146 D8
Belhus Woods Country Park SOCK/AV RM15 146 C5
Bellamy's Wharf WAP E1W 140 C10
Bellenden Primary School PECK SE15 159 P9
Bellenden Road Business Centre PECK SE15 159 N8
Bellenden Road Retail Park PECK SE15 159 N7
Bellerbyth GU GU1 268 A1
Belleville Primary School BTSEA SW11 180 A1
Belle Vue Cinema
EDGW HA8 95 M7
WLSDN NW10 136 E2
Bell Farm Junior School WOT/HER KT12 217 K1
Bellgate JMI School HHNE HP2 35 P4

Bell Industrial Estate
CHSWK W4 155 P3
Bellingham Trading Estate
CAT SE6 182 G6
Bell Lane Combined School
AMS HP6 69 N4
Bell Lane JMI School
HDN NW4 116 C2
Belmont First & Middle School
KTN/HRWW/W HA3 94 E10
Belmont Junior & Infant School
WDGN N22 119 K1
Belmont Medical Centre
UX/CGN UB8 131 N2
Belmont (Mill Hill Junior School)
MLHL NW7 96 D4
Belmont Park School
LEY E10 121 H4
Belmont Primary School
BXLYHN DA7 164 B6
CHSWK W4 156 A3
Belmore Primary School
YEAD UB4 133 J5
Belswains Infant School
HHS/BOV HP3 36 A10
Belvedere Day Hospital
WLSDN NW10 136 D3
Belvedere Industrial Estate
BELV DA17 144 E10
Belvedere Link Business Park
BELV DA17 164 D2
Belvedere Primary School
BELV DA17 164 C3
Belvue Business Centre
NTHLT UB5 134 A2
Belvue School
NTHLT UB5 133 P3
Bengeo Junior & Infant School
HERT/WAS SG14 25 K2
Benhurst JMI School
HCH RM12 125 J8
Ben Jonson Primary School
WCHPL E1 140 D6
Bensham Manor School
THHTH CR7 203 K5
Benson Primary School
CROY/NA CR0 204 D10
Bentalls Shopping Centre
KUT KT1 199 J2
Benthal Primary School
STNW/STAM N16 119 P8
Bentley Golf Club
BRWN CM15 86 D5
Bentley Street Industrial Estate
GVE DA12 190 F2
Bentley Wood Girls School
STAN HA7 94 E6
Bentworth Primary School
SHB W12 136 E8
Benyon Primary School
SOCK/AV RM15 147 H4
Beormund School
STHWK SE1 18 G2
Berger Primary School
HOM E9 140 C1
Berkeley Clinic
RKW/CH/CXG WD3 91 M2
Berkeley Primary School
HEST TW5 153 L5
Berkhamstead Collegiate Preparatory School
BERK HP4 33 N5
Berkhamsted Castle (remains)
BERK HP4 34 A4
Berkhamsted Collegiate School
BERK HP4 33 N5
Berkhamsted FC
BERK HP4 33 N4
Berkhamsted Golf Club
BERK HP4 34 B2
Berkhamsted Health Centre
BERK HP4 33 M4
Berkhamsted School House
BERK HP4 33 P5
Berkhamsted Tennis Club
BERK HP4 33 P4
Berlitz Schools of Languages
LINN WC2A 11 P4
Bermondsey Town Hall
STHWK SE1 19 M4
Bermondsey Trading Estate
BERM/RHTH SE16 160 B3
Bernards Heath Infant School
STAL AL1 38 E4
Berrymede Junior School
ACT W3 155 N1
Bertram House School
TOOT SW17 180 B5
Bessemer Grange Junior & Infant School
CMBW SE5 159 M10
Bessemer Park Industrial Estate
HNHL SE24 159 J10
Beta Health Clinic
HHNE HP2 35 N6
Betchworth Park Golf Club
RDKG RH5 273 K1
Bethlem Royal Hospital
BECK BR3 204 F7
Bethnal Green Museum of Childhood
BETH E2 140 A5
Bethnal Green Technology College
BETH E2 7 M10
Beulah Junior & Infant School
THHTH CR7 203 K2
Bevendean Pre-Preparatory School
LHD/OX KT22 218 B9
Beverley School
NWMAL KT3 200 D5
Beverley Trading Estate
MRDN SM4 200 G7
Bevington Primary School
NKENS W10 8 B3
Bewbush Medical Centre
CRAWW RH11 283 H10
Bewbush Middle School
CRAWW RH11 283 H10
Bewhurst County First School
CRAWW RH11 283 J10
Bexley College
ABYW SE2 163 N5
ERITH DA8 164 D3
Bexley Cricket Club
BXLY DA5 186 B4
Bexley Erith Technical High School
BXLY DA5 186 B2
Bexley Grammar School
WELL DA16 163 L10
Bexleyheath Centre
BXLYHS DA6 163 P10
Bexleyheath Golf Club
BXLYHS DA6 185 P1
Bexleyheath School
BXLYHN DA7 164 B9
Bexley Hospital
BXLY DA5 186 F5
Bexley RFC
BXLY DA5 186 B3
BFI London IMAX Cinema
STHWK SE1 11 P10
The Bharani Medical Centre
SL SL1 128 C8
Bickley Park Cricket Club
BMLY BR1 206 B2
Bickley Park Prep School
BMLY BR1 206 A3
Bickley Park School
BMLY BR1 206 B3
Big Ben
WEST SW1P 17 M2
Biggin Hill Airport
BH/WHM TN16 226 A9
Biggin Hill Business Park
BH/WHM TN16 244 A1
Biggin Hill Primary School
BH/WHM TN16 244 B2
Bigham's Park Farm
HHW HP1 35 H1
Bigland Green Primary School
WCHPL E1 140 A8
Billingsgate Fish Market
POP/IOD E14 140 G10
Binscombe Medical Centre
RGODL GU7 267 J9
Birch Court Colindale Hospital
CDALE/KGS NW9 96 B10
Birchwood County Primary School
SWLY BR8 208 E1
Birchwood Leisure Centre
HAT AL10 40 E1
Birchwood Park Golf Club
RDART DA2 186 D10
Birchwood Primary School
HAT AL10 40 D2
Birkbeck College
STPAN WC1H 11 J1
Birkbeck Primary School
SCUP DA14 185 L6
Bishop Challoner Girls School
WCHPL E1 13 P7
Bishop Challoner RC Secondary School
WCHPL E1 140 B8
Bishop Challoner School
HAYES BR2 205 J2
Bishop David Brown School
WOKN/KNAP GU21 214 G9
Bishop Douglas RC School
EFNCH N2 97 M10
Bishop Gilpin Primary School
WIM/MER SW19 179 J8
Bishophalt School
UX/CGN UB8 132 A5
Bishop John Robinson CE Primary
THMD SE28 143 M9
Bishop Perrin CE Primary School
WHTN TW2 176 A3
Bishop Ramsey CE School
RSLP HA4 113 H5
RSLP HA4 112 G5
Bishop Reindorp CE School
GU GU1 249 P7
Bishopsgate Institute
WCHPL E1 13 K4
Bishopsgate School
EGH TW20 171 M6
Bishops Hatfield Girls School
HAT AL10 40 D4
Bishops Square Business Park
HAT AL10 40 B3
HAT AL10 40 D8
Bishop Stopford School
EN EN1 80 A6
Bishops Wood Hospital
RKW/CH/CXG WD3 92 B6
Bishop Thomas Grant School
STRHM/NOR SW16 180 G8
Bishop Wand CE Secondary School
SUN TW16 196 G2
Bishop Winnington-Ingram CE Primary School
RSLP HA4 112 E5
Bittacy Business Centre
MLHL NW7 97 H7
Blackburn Trading Estate
STWL/WRAY TW19 174 A2
Blackfen School for Girls
BFN/LL DA15 185 L2
Blackfriars Millennium Pier
EMB EC4Y 12 B7
Blackfriars Pier
BLKFR EC4V 12 D7
Blackfriars Station
BLKFR EC4V 12 C7
Blackheath Bluecoat CE School
BKHTH/KID SE3 161 N6
Blackheath Business Estate
GNWCH SE10 161 H7
The Blackheath Clinic
BKHTH/KID SE3 161 M10
Blackheath High School GDST
BKHTH/KID SE3 161 L8
Blackheath High Senior School
BKHTH/KID SE3 161 M6
Blackheath Hospital
BKHTH/KID SE3 161 L9
Black Park Country Park
DTCH/LGLY SL3 130 D4
Blackshots Leisure Centre
CDH/CHF RM16 168 A1
Blackthorn Junior School
WGCE AL7 23 K6
Blackwall Trading Estate
POP/IOD E14 141 J7
Blaire Peach School
STHL UB1 133 L10
Blake College
GTPST W1W 10 G3
Blanche Neville School
WDGN N22 99 H9
Blenheim Business Centre
MTCM CR4 202 A1
Blenheim High School
HOR/WEW KT19 220 A6
Blenheim Junior & Infant School
ORP BR6 207 M9
Blenheim Shopping Centre
PGE/AN SE20 182 B10
Blessed Dominic RC Primary School
CDALE/KGS NW9 96 B10
Blessed John Roche Catholic School
POP/IOD E14 140 F8
Blessed Sacrament RC Primary School
IS N1 5 M6
Bletchingley Golf Club
REDH RH1 259 L9
Blood Transfusion Centre
EDGW HA8 95 N8
Bloomfield Clinic (Guys Hospital)
STHWK SE1 19 H1
Bloomsbury College
FUL/PGN SW6 157 K6
Bloomsbury Theatre
STPAN WC1H 11 J1
Blossoms Inn Medical Centre
BLKFR EC4V 12 F7
Blue Gate Fields Primary School
WCHPL E1 140 B9
Bluewater Park
GRH DA9 188 E3
BMI Medical Centre
CAVSQ/HST W1G 10 D4
Bnois Jerusalem School
STNW/STAM N16 119 L5
The Bob Hope Theatre
ELTH/MOT SE9 184 C2
Bocketts Fm Park
LHD/OX KT22 254 E1
Bodywise Natural Health Centre
BETH E2 140 B5
Boleyn Cinema
EHAM E6 142 A4
Bolingbroke Hospital
BTSEA SW11 179 P1
Bolingbroke Primary School
BTSEA SW11 157 N7
Bond First School
MTCM CR4 202 A2
Bond Road School
MTCM CR4 202 A2
Bonner Primary School
BETH E2 140 C4
Bonneville Primary School
CLAP SW4 180 D2
Bonneygrove Junior & Infant School
CHESW EN7 61 P6
Bonnygate Primary School
SOCK/AV RM15 146 G7
Bon Secours Hospital
BEAC HP9 88 D9
Bonus Pastor School
BMLY BR1 183 K7
Bookham Industrial Estate
GT/LBKH KT23 235 N9
Boomes Industrial Estate
RAIN RM13 144 G6
Booster Cushion Theatre
WDGN N22 98 G10
Borehamwood FC
BORE WD6 75 N6
Borehamwood Industrial Park
BORE WD6 76 A6
Borers Business Park
CRAWE RH10 285 K2
Borough Market
STHWK SE1 12 G9
Boston Business Park
NWDGN UB2 154 D2
Botany Bay Cricket Club
ENC/FH EN2 78 E2
Botwell RC Primary School
HYS/HAR UB3 152 G1
Boulevard 25 Retail Park
BORE WD6 75 M7
Boundary Business Centre
WOKN/KNAP GU21 232 D1
Boundary Business Park
MTCM CR4 201 N2
Bounds Green Health Centre
FBAR/BDGN N11 98 E8
Bounds Green Industrial Estate
FBAR/BDGN N11 98 D7
Bounds Green Primary School
FBAR/BDGN N11 98 F8
Bourne Business Park
ADL/WDHM KT15 195 M9
Bourne CP School
RSLP HA4 113 K10
Bourne Hall Health Centre
EW KT17 220 C5
Bournehall Junior & Infant School
BUSH WD23 73 P9
Bourne Road Industrial Park
DART DA1 186 E1
Bourneside Sports Club
STHGT/OAK N14 98 F2
Bousfield Primary School
WBPTN SW10 15 J7
Boutcher CE Primary School
STHWK SE1 19 L4
Bovingdon Primary School
HHS/BOV HP3 52 E3
Bowater House
SKENS SW7 16 A2
Bow County Court
SRTFD E15 141 L1
Bow County Secondary School
BOW E3 140 F5
Bowden House Clinic
HRW HA1 114 D7
Bower Hill Industrial Estate
EPP CM16 65 K8
Bower Park School
ROM RM1 104 F7
Bowes Primary School
FBAR/BDGN N11 98 E6
Bowes Road Clinic
FBAR/BDGN N11 98 D6
Bow Industrial Park
SRTFD E15 140 F2
Bowman Trading Estate
CDALE/KGS NW9 115 M1
Bow Street Magistrates Court
HOL/ALD WC2B 11 M6
Bow Triangle Business Centre
BOW E3 140 F6
Boxgrove Primary School
ABYW SE2 163 M2
GU GU1 250 E9
Box Hill Country Park
KWD/TDW/WH KT20 255 K8
Box Hill School
RDKG RH5 254 G3
Boxmoor Golf Club
HHW HP1 35 H10
Boxmoor House Special School
HHS/BOV HP3 35 J9
Boxmoor Primary School
HHW HP1 35 K7
Boyd School
UPMR RM14 126 D7
Boys' Club
EDGW HA8 95 M8
Brackenbury Health Centre
HMSMTH W6 156 E2
Brackenbury Primary School
HMSMTH W6 156 E2
Bracken Industrial Estate
BARK/HLT IG6 103 J8
Bradbourne School
RSEV TN14 247 H7
Brady Primary School
RAIN RM13 145 K7
Brady Recreation Centre
WCHPL E1 13 N3
Braeside Junior School
BKHH IG9 101 P2
Braeside Senior School
BKHH IG9 101 N2
Braincroft Primary School
CRICK NW2 116 C8
Braintree Road Industrial Estate
RSLP HA4 113 J9
Bramah Tea & Coffee Museum
STHWK SE1 19 M1
Brambletye Junior School
REDH RH1 276 B2
The Bramley Business Centre
SHGR GU5 268 C10
Bramley Golf Club
SHGR GU5 268 B10
Bramley School
KWD/TDW/WH KT20 256 D1
Brampton Manor School
PLSTW E13 142 A6
Brampton Primary School
EHAM E6 142 B5
WELL DA16 163 N8
Brandlehow Primary School
PUT/ROE SW15 157 J10
Branfil Junior & Infant School
UPMR RM14 125 P9
Branollys Health Centre
PLSTW E13 141 M6
Brays Grove School
HLWS CM18 47 L3
Breakspear Crematorium
RSLP HA4 112 D3
Breakspeare School
ABLGY WD5 54 F7
Breakspear Primary School
HGDN/ICK UB10 112 B7
Breaside Pre Prep School
BMLY BR1 183 M10
Brecknock Primary School
HOLWY N7 5 K1
Bredinghurst School
PECK SE15 160 B10
Brent Adult College
WLSDN NW10 136 A3
Brent Arts Council
CRICK NW2 116 D8
Brent Child & Family Clinic
WLSDN NW10 116 C10
Brent Cross Shopping Centre
HDN NW4 116 F5
Brentfield Medical Centre
WLSDN NW10 136 A1
Brentfield Primary School
WLSDN NW10 136 A1
Brentford Business Centre
BTFD TW8 155 H6
The Brentford Clinic
BTFD TW8 155 K5
Brentford County Court
BTFD TW8 155 J6
Brentford FC (Griffin Park)
BTFD TW8 155 J5
Brentford Fountain Leisure Centre
CHSWK W4 155 M4
Brentford Health Centre
BTFD TW8 155 H5
Brentford Medical Centre
BTFD TW8 155 J6
Brentford School for Girls
BTFD TW8 155 J5
Brent Knoll School
SYD SE26 182 C6
Brent Magistrates Court House
WLSDN NW10 136 B1
Brent Park Industrial Estate
NWDGN UB2 153 J2
The Brent Primary School
RDART DA2 188 B3
Brentside First School
HNWL W7 134 D7
Brentside High School
HNWL W7 134 D6
Brentside Primary School
HNWL W7 134 D6
Brent Trading Estate
WLSDN NW10 116 B10
Brent Valley Golf Club
HNWL W7 134 D9
Brentwaters Business Park
BTFD TW8 155 H6
Brentwood Chiropody Surgery
BRW CM14 107 J3
The Brentwood Clinic
BRWN CM15 107 J2
Brentwood Community Hospital
BRWN CM15 107 K2
Brentwood County High School
BRW CM14 107 J4
Brentwood Preparatory School
BRWN CM15 107 K2
Brentwood RFC
BRW CM14 107 K5
Brentwood School
BRWN CM15 107 J3
Brentwood Sports Ground
BRWN CM15 107 J2
Brentwood Theatre
BRW CM14 107 J2
Brewers' Hall
CITYW EC2V 12 F4
Brewery Industrial Estate
IS N1 6 E8
Brewery Mews Business Centre
ISLW TW7 154 E9
Brickendon Grange Golf Club
HERT/BAY SG13 43 J5
Brickfields Industrial Estate
HHNE HP2 36 C2
Brick Lane Music Hall
SDTCH EC2A 7 K10
Brick Lane Music House
WCHPL E1 13 M2
Bricklayer Arms Industrial Estate
STHWK SE1 19 L6
The Bridewell Theatre
EMB EC4Y 12 C6
The Bridge Business Centre
NWDGN UB2 153 P1
Bridgegate Business Centre
WGCE AL7 23 J4
Bridge Industrial Estate
HORL RH6 280 C4
Bridge Lane Theatre
BTSEA SW11 157 P7
Bridge Medical Centre
CRAWE RH10 284 B6
Bridge View Industrial Estate
WTHK RM20 166 F5
Bridgewater School
BERK HP4 33 M3
Briggens House Hotel Golf Club
WARE SG12 27 P8
Bright Sparks Montessori School
WKENS W14 156 G1
Bright Sparks School
STRHM/NOR SW16 180 F7
The Brigidine School
WDSR SL4 149 J9
Brigstock Medical Centre
THHTH CR7 203 J5
Brimsdown Industrial Estate
PEND EN3 80 B6
Brimsdown Primary School
PEND EN3 80 C7
Brindishe Primary School
LEE/GVPK SE12 183 L1
Britannia Business Centre
CHES/WCR EN8 62 E10
CRICK NW2 116 G9
Britannia Industrial Estate
DTCH/LGLY SL3 151 H8
Britannia Sports Ground
WALTH E17 100 F8
Britannia Village Primary School
CAN/RD E16 141 N10
British Airways London Eye
WHALL SW1A 17 M1
British Dental Association
CAVSQ/HST W1G 10 E4
British Library
CAMTN NW1 5 K9
British Library Newspaper Library
CDALE/KGS NW9 116 B1
British Medical Association
STPAN WC1H 11 K1
British Museum
RSQ WC1B 11 L4
The British Museum Shop
HTHAIR TW6 174 C1
British Telecom Tower
GTPST W1W 10 G3
The Brit School
SNWD SE25 203 L6
Brittania Business Park
CHES/WCR EN8 62 E10
Brittons School
RAIN RM13 144 G2
Britwell Health Clinic
SLN SL2 128 F5
Brixton Academy BRXN/ST SW9 159 H9
Brixton College for Further Education
BRXS/STRHM SW2 180 G1
Brixton Recreation Centre
BRXN/ST SW9 159 H9
Broadfield Infant School
HHNE HP2 36 A6
Broadfield Junior School
HHNE HP2 35 P6
Broadfields Infant School
EDGW HA8 95 M3
Broadfields Junior School
EDGW HA8 95 N3
Broadfields Primary School
HLW CM20 29 H10
Broadford Park Business Centre
RGUE GU4 268 A7
Broadford Primary School
HARH RM3 105 L7
Broadgate
LVPST EC2M 13 H3
Broadgate Ice Arena
LVPST EC2M 13 J4
Broadhurst School
KIL/WHAMP NW6 3 J3
Broadmead Primary School
CROY/NA CR0 203 L6
The Broadmere Primary School
WOKN/KNAP GU21 214 G9
Broadwalk Shopping Centre
EDGW HA8 95 M7
Broadwater Farm Primary School
TOTM N17 99 L10
Broadwater Park Golf Club
RGODL GU7 267 M10
Broadwater Primary School
TOOT SW17 179 N7
Broadwater School
RGODL GU7 267 M9
Broadway Clinic
EDGW HA8 95 N9
Broadway Retail Park
CRICK NW2 116 G9
Broadway Shopping Centre
BXLYHS DA6 164 B10
HMSMTH W6 156 F4
Broadway Square Shopping Centre
BXLYHN DA7 164 B10
Brockham School
BRKHM/BTCW RH3 273 N2
Brocklebank Health Centre
WAND/EARL SW18 179 L3

Brocklebank Industrial Estate
GNWCH SE10 161 M3
Brockley Cross Business Centre
BROCKY SE4 160 D9
Brockley Primary School
BROCKY SE4 182 E1
Brockwell Lido
HNHL SE24 181 J2
Brockwell Primary School
BRXS/STRHM SW2 181 H2
Broke Hill Golf Club
RSEV TN14 228 A5
Bromet Primary School
OXHEY WD19 93 L1
Bromley Cemetery
BMLY BR1 183 L10
Bromley College of Further & Higher Education
BMLY BR1 205 M1
HAYES BR2 206 A6
Bromley County Court
BMLY BR1 205 M1
Bromley FC
HAYES BR2 205 N5
Bromley Golf Club
HAYES BR2 206 B7
Bromley High School
BMLY BR1 206 D4
Bromley Hospital
HAYES BR2 205 N4
Bromley Hospitals NHS Trust
ORP BR6 226 D1
ORP BR6 227 J1
Bromley Industrial Centre
BMLY BR1 206 A3
Bromley Mall Indoor Market
BMLY BR1 205 M2
Bromley Museum
ORP BR6 207 L7
Bromley Road Infant School
BECK BR3 204 G1
Bromley Road Retail Park
CAT SE6 182 G5
Brompton Cemetery
WBPTN SW10 15 H10
Brompton Medical Centre
WBPTN SW10 15 H7
Brompton Oratory
SKENS SW7 15 N4
Bromyard Leisure Centre
ACT W3 136 B10
Brondesbury College for Boys
KIL/WHAMP NW6 136 G2
Bronte School
GVW DA11 190 D3
Brook Business Centre
IVER SL0 131 K4
Brooke Trading Estate
ROM RM1 124 G5
Brook Farm Industrial Estate
ABR/ST RM4 104 E1
Brookfield Primary School
ARCH N19 118 C7
CHEAM SM3 201 H8
Brookfield Retail Park
CHES/WCR EN8 62 C3
Brook House FC
YEAD UB4 132 G5
Brook Industrial Estate
YEAD UB4 133 L10
Brookland Junior & Infant School
CHES/WCR EN8 62 D4
Brookland Primary School
GLDGN NW11 117 L2
Brooklands Business Park
WEY KT13 215 P6
Brooklands College
WEY KT13 216 A3
Brooklands Museum
WEY KT13 216 B5
Brooklands Primary School
BKHTH/KID SE3 161 M9
Brooklands School
REIG RH2 257 L8
Brook Lane Business Centre
BTFD TW8 155 J4
Brookmans Park Golf Club
BRKMPK AL9 59 K1
Brookmans Park Primary School
BRKMPK AL9 59 H2
Brookmarsh Trading Estate
DEPT SE8 160 G6
Brookmead Industrial Estate
MTCM CR4 202 D6
Brookside Junior & Infant School
YEAD UB4 133 K5
Brookside Primary School
HARH RM3 105 M6
Brookweald Cricket Club
BRW CM14 106 D2
Brookwood Cemetery
CHOB/PIR GU24 230 G8
Brookwood County Primary School
CHOB/PIR GU24 230 F6
Broomfield House School
RCH/KEW TW9 155 L7
Broomfield School
STHGT/OAK N14 98 E6
Broomsleigh Business Park
CAT SE6 182 E8
Broomwood Hall School
BAL SW12 180 B3
Brownlow Medical Centre
FBAR/BDGN N11 98 F6
Broxbourne Business Centre
CHES/WCR EN8 62 C2
Broxbourne Primary School
BROX EN10 44 F7
Broxbourne Sailing Club
HOD EN11 45 J6
The Broxbourne School
BROX EN10 44 D8
Broxbourne Sports Club
BROX EN10 44 E7
Bruce Castle Museum
TOTM N17 99 M9
Bruce Grove Primary School
TOTM N17 99 N10
Brunel Engine House
BERM/RHTH SE16 160 B1
Brunel University
ISLW TW7 154 D6
TWK TW1 154 G10
UX/CGN UB8 131 P5
Brunel University (Osterley Campus) Track
ISLW TW7 154 D6
Brunswick Health Centre
FBAR/BDGN N11 98 B3
Brunswick Housing & Shopping Centre
BMSBY WC1N 11 M2
Brunswick Industrial Park
FBAR/BDGN N11 98 C5
Brunswick Medical Centre
BMSBY WC1N 11 L1
Brunswick Park JMI School
FBAR/BDGN N11 98 B2
Brunswick Park Primary School
CMBW SE5 159 L6
Brushwood Junior School
CSHM HP5 51 K5
BT Centre
STBT EC1A 12 E5
Buckhurst Hill FC
BKHH IG9 102 B2
Buckhurst Hill Primary School
BKHH IG9 102 B3
Buckingham College School
HRW HA1 114 D3
Buckingham Palace
WHALL SW1A 16 F2
Buckingham Primary School
HPTN TW12 175 N8
Buckingham Road Cemetery
IL IG1 122 G7
Buckinghamshire Chilterns University College
CSTG HP8 90 D3
Buckinghamshire Golf Club
DEN/HRF UB9 111 M7
Buckland Infant School
CHSGTN KT9 219 L2
Buckland Primary School
STA TW18 173 M10
Building Centre
GWRST WC1E 11 J4
Bullers Wood School
CHST BR7 206 C1
Bullsbridge Industrial Estate
NWDGN UB2 153 J3
The Bull Theatre
BAR EN5 77 J8
Bupa Roding Hospital
REDBR IG4 122 A1
Burbage School
IS N1 7 J7
Burdett Coutts CE Primary School
WEST SW1P 17 J5
Burgess Industrial Park
CMBW SE5 159 L6
Burghwood Clinic
BNSTD SM7 239 J2
Burhill Golf Club
WOT/HER KT12 217 H5
Burhill Infant School
WOT/HER KT12 217 L3
Burleigh Primary School
CHES/WCR EN8 62 C6
Burlington Danes School
SHB W12 136 E8
Burlington Primary School
NWMAL KT3 200 C4
Burnham Abbey
MDHD SL6 128 B10
Burnham Beeches Golf Club
SL SL1 128 C3
Burnham Beeches (Nature Reserve)
SLN SL2 108 F10
Burnham FC
SL SL1 128 A5
Burnham Grammar School
SL SL1 128 C6
Burnham Health Centre
SL SL1 128 A5
Burnham Trading Estate
DART DA1 165 L10
Burnham Upper School
SL SL1 128 A6
Burnhill Business Centre
BECK BR3 204 F1
Burnley Road Clinic
WLSDN NW10 116 D10
Burnside Industrial Estate
BARK/HLT IG6 103 L6
Burnt Ash Infant School
BMLY BR1 183 M8
Burnt Ash School
BMLY BR1 183 L8
Burntmill Industrial Estate
HLW CM20 28 F8
Burnt Mill School
HLW CM20 29 H9
Burnt Oak Junior School
BFN/LL DA15 185 K4
Burntwood School
TOOT SW17 179 N5
Burpham Foundation Primary School
RGUE GU4 250 D6
Burrels Wharf
POP/IOD E14 160 G4
Bursted Woodprimary School
BXLYHN DA7 164 C8
Burstow Business Centre
HORL RH6 281 J2
Burstow Lodge Business Centre
HORL RH6 280 C6
Burstow Primary School
HORL RH6 281 H4
Burvale Cemetery
WOT/HER KT12 217 H3
Burwell Industrial Estate
LEY E10 120 D6
Burwood Park School & College
WOT/HER KT12 216 G3
Burwood School
ORP BR6 207 N9
Burys Court School
REIG RH2 274 G6
Bushey Golf & Country Club
BUSH WD23 73 P10
Bushey Hall Golf Club
BUSH WD23 73 N8
Bushey Hall School
BUSH WD23 73 N10
Bushey Hall Swimming Pool
BUSH WD23 73 N9
Bushey Health Centre
BUSH WD23 73 N10
Bushey Heath Primary School
BUSH WD23 94 C2
Bushey Manor Junior School
BUSH WD23 73 N9
Bushey Meads School
BUSH WD23 74 B9
Bushey Middle School
RYNPK SW20 200 E3
Bushey Museum & Art Gallery
BUSH WD23 73 P10
Bush Hill Park Golf Club
WCHMH N21 79 K9
Bush Hill Park Medical Centre
EN EN1 79 N10
Bush Hill Park Primary School
EN EN1 79 P9
Bush House (BBC)
HOL/ALD WC2B 11 N6
Bush Industrial Estate
ARCH N19 118 D8
WLSDN NW10 136 A5
Bushy Hill Junior School
GU GU1 250 G8
The Business Design Centre
IS N1 6 B6
Business Park 5
LHD/OX KT22 236 F6
The Business Village
SLN SL2 129 N10
Bute House Preparatory School for Girls
HMSMTH W6 156 F3
Butlers Court County First & Middle School
BEAC HP9 88 C10
Butlers Wharf
STHWK SE1 13 M10
Butler's Wharf Business Centre
STHWK SE1 19 M1
Butler's Wharf Pier
STHWK SE1 13 M10
Butterfly House
BTFD TW8 154 G7
Butterfly Sports Club
ELTH/MOT SE9 184 E2
Buxlow Preparatory School
WBLY HA9 115 K8
Buzzard Creek Industrial Estate
BARK IG11 143 J5
Byam Shaw School of Art
ARCH N19 118 D7
Byfleet Business Centre
BF/WBF KT14 215 N7
Byfleet CP School
BF/WBF KT14 215 N7
Byfleet Industrial Estate
BF/WBF KT14 215 N7
WATW WD18 92 D2
Bygrove JMI School
POP/IOD E14 140 G8
Byron Court Primary School
ALP/SUD HA0 115 H7
Byron Primary School
COUL/CHIP CR5 240 F3
Cabinet War Rooms
WHALL SW1A 17 K1
Cable House School
WOKN/KNAP GU21 232 B1
Cadogan Pier
CHEL SW3 15 P10
Calcot Medical Centre
CFSP/GDCR SL9 90 A9
Calder House School
BTSEA SW11 158 A7
Caldicott School
SLN SL2 128 G2
Caledonian Market
STHWK SE1 19 K3
Calverton Primary School
CAN/RD E16 142 A8
Cambell Primary School
DAGW RM9 143 N2
Camberwell Business Centre
CMBW SE5 159 L6
Camberwell College of Arts
CMBW SE5 159 M7
Camberwell New Cemetery
FSTH SE23 182 C2
Camberwell Trading Estate
CMBW SE5 159 J8
Cambridge Park Bowling & Sports Club
TWK TW1 177 H2
Cambridge School
HMSMTH W6 156 E3
Cambridge Theatre
LSQ/SEVD WC2H 11 L6
Camden House Clinic
BKHTH/KID SE3 161 K8
Camden Junior School
CAR SM5 222 A1
Camden Market
CAMTN NW1 4 D4
Camden Peoples Theatre
CAMTN NW1 4 G10
Camden School for Girls
CAMTN NW1 5 H2
Camden Theatre
CAMTN NW1 4 G7
Camden Town Hall & St Pancras Library
CAMTN NW1 5 L9
Camelot Primary School
PECK SE15 160 A6
Cameron House School
CHEL SW3 15 M9
Camperdown House
WCHPL E1 13 M6
Camphill Industrial Estate
ADL/WDHM KT15 215 L7
Camphill Road First School
BF/WBF KT14 215 L8
Campion House College
ISLW TW7 154 C6
The Campion School
EMPK RM11 125 N2
Camp Primary School
STAL AL1 38 G7
Campsbourne Infant School
CEND/HSY/T N8 118 F1
Campsbourne Junior School
CEND/HSY/T N8 118 F1
Campus West Cinema
WGCW AL8 22 G4
Campus West Leisure Centre
WGCW AL8 22 F4
Canada House
STJS SW1Y 11 K9
Canada House Business Centre
RSLP HA4 113 K6
Canada Square
POP/IOD E14 140 F10
Canada Water Retail Park
BERM/RHTH SE16 160 C2
Canada Wharf Museum
BERM/RHTH SE16 140 E10
Canal Cafe Theatre
BAY/PAD W2 9 H3
Canal Industrial Park
GVE DA12 190 G2
Canary Riverside
POP/IOD E14 140 E10
Canary Wharf Pier
POP/IOD E14 140 E10
Canary Wharf Tower
POP/IOD E14 140 G10
Canberra Primary School
SHB W12 136 E9
Canbury Business Centre
KUTN/CMB KT2 199 K1
Canbury 2000 Business Park
KUTN/CMB KT2 199 K1
Canbury Medical Centre
KUTN/CMB KT2 199 L1
Canbury School
RCHPK/HAM TW10 177 N9
Cann Hall Primary School
WAN E11 121 L8
The Canning School
KENS W8 14 E3
Cannock House School
ORP BR6 228 A2
Cannon Hill Clinic
STHGT/OAK N14 98 F4
Cannon Lane Primary School
PIN HA5 113 L4
Cannon Sports Club
CANST EC4R 12 F7
Cannon Street Station
CANST EC4R 12 G7
Cannon Trading Estate
WBLY HA9 115 N9
Cannon Wharf Business Centre
DEPT SE8 160 D3
Cannon Workshops
POP/IOD E14 140 F9
Canon Barnett Primary School
WCHPL E1 13 M5
Canonbury Business Centre
IS N1 6 F5
Canonbury JMI School
IS N1 6 C2
Canon Palmer RC High School
IL IG1 123 H6
Canons Brook Golf Club
HLW CM20 28 D10
Canons High School
EDGW HA8 95 L10
The Canons Leisure Centrel
MTCM CR4 202 A4
Canterbury Industrial Estate
PECK SE15 160 C5
Cantium Retail Park
STHWK SE1 19 N9
Capel Manor Primary School
EN EN1 79 P2
Capital Business Centre
ALP/SUD HA0 135 J4
MTCM CR4 202 A5
WATN WD24 73 L2
Capital Industrial Estate
BELV DA17 144 D10
BELV DA17 164 C3
Capital Radio
LSQ/SEVD WC2H 11 K8
Capital Wharf
WAP E1W 13 P10
Capitol Industrial Park
CDALE/KGS NW9 115 P1
Caplan Estate
MTCM CR4 202 D1
Capswood Business Centre
CFSP/GDCR SL9 110 F6
Cardiff Road Industrial Estate
WATW WD18 73 J10
Cardinal Hinsley High School
WLSDN NW10 136 D3
Cardinal Newman RC School
WOT/HER KT12 197 L10
Cardinal Pole RC School
HOM E9 140 D1
Cardinal Pole RC Secondary Lower School
HOM E9 140 C2
Cardinal Road Infant School
FELT TW13 175 J4
Cardinal Vaughan Memorial School
WKENS W14 14 A1
The Cardinal Wiseman ARC School Technology & Art College
GFD/PVL UB6 134 B7
Cardwell Primary School
WOOL/PLUM SE18 162 C3
Carew Manor School
WLGTN SM6 202 E10
Carlisle Infant School
HPTN TW12 176 A9
Carlton Gate Development
MV/WKIL W9 8 F3
Carlton House
STJS SW1Y 11 J10
Carlton Primary School
KTTN NW5 118 B10
Carlton Vale Infant School
MV/WKIL W9 2 D9
Carlyle Business Centre
CHERT KT16 195 K7
Carlyle's House
CHEL SW3 15 N10
Carnwath Road Industrial Estate
FUL/PGN SW6 157 L9
Carolyn School Shop
PIN HA5 113 M2
Carpenders Park Cemetery
OXHEY WD19 93 N5
Carpenters Business Park
HOM E9 140 F1
Carpenters' Hall
LVPST EC2M 13 H4
Carpenters Primary School
SRTFD E15 141 H3
Carrier Business Park
CRAWE RH10 284 C6
Carshalton AFC
SUT SM1 201 P10
Carshalton College of Further Education
CAR SM5 202 A10
Carshalton High School for Boys
CAR SM5 201 N9
Carshalton High School for Girls
CAR SM5 201 P10
Carshalton War Memorial Hospital
CAR SM5 222 A2
Carterhatch Primary School
EN EN1 80 A5
Caryl Thomas Clinic
HRW HA1 114 D2
Cascades Leisure Centre
GVE DA12 191 K7
The Cassel Hospital
RCHPK/HAM TW10 177 J7
Cassidy Medical Centre
FUL/PGN SW6 157 K6
Castilion Primary School
THMD SE28 143 M8
Castlebar Special School
WEA W13 134 F7
Castlecombe Primary School
ELTH/MOT SE9 184 B8
Castle Hall Theatre & Civic Centre
HERT/WAS SG14 25 K5
Castle Industrial Estate
WALW SE17 18 E5
Castle Montessore School
BERK HP4 34 A5
Castleview Combined School
DTCH/LGLY SL3 150 A3
The Caterham Dene Hospital
CTHM CR3 241 N9
Caterham High School
CLAY IG5 102 C10
Caterham Preparatory School
CTHM CR3 259 N2
Caterham School
CTHM CR3 259 N2
Catford Cricket & Sports Club
CAT SE6 182 G4
Catford Cyphers Cricket Club
CAT SE6 182 E5
Catford Girls School
CAT SE6 183 J6
Catford Trading Estate
CAT SE6 182 G5
Catford Wanderers Sports Club
CAT SE6 183 H7
Cathall Leisure Centre
WAN E11 121 J8
Cathedral
STALW/RED AL3 38 B6
Cathedral Hill Industrial Estate
GUW GU2 249 M9
Cathedral of St Mary & St Helen
BRWN CM15 107 J3
Cathedral School of St Saviour & St Mary Overie
STHWK SE1 18 F1
Catherington Special School
CRAWW RH11 283 N3
Cator Park School for Girls
BECK BR3 182 D10
Cavendish College
FITZ W1T 11 J4
Cavendish Primary School
CHSWK W4 156 B6
The Cavendish School
CAMTN NW1 4 E5
HHW HP1 35 L5
Cavendish Special School
HNWL W7 134 E8
Caxton Hall
STJSPK SW1H 17 J3
Caxton Trading Estate
HYS/HAR UB3 152 F1
Cayley Primary School
POP/IOD E14 140 D7
Cecil Park Clinic
PIN HA5 113 M2
Cecil Road Primary School
GVW DA11 190 C4
Cecil Sharpe House
CAMTN NW1 4 D5
The Cedar School
FSTGT E7 141 P1
Cedars First School
KTN/HRWW/W HA3 94 B9
Cedars Middle School
KTN/HRWW/W HA3 94 B9
The Cedars Primary School
HEST TW5 153 H6
Cedar Way Industrial Estate
CAMTN NW1 5 J4
Cenotaph
WHALL SW1A 17 L1
Centaurs Business Centre
BTFD TW8 154 F5
Centaurs RFC
ISLW TW7 154 E5
Central Business Centre
WLSDN NW10 116 B10
Central Criminal Court
STP EC4M 12 C5
Central Estate
E/WMO/HCT KT8 197 N5
Central Foundation Boys School
SDTCH EC2A 13 H1
Central Foundation Girls School
BOW E3 140 D5
Central Hall
STJSPK SW1H 17 K2
Central Hendon Clinic
HDN NW4 116 E2
Central London County Court
CAVSQ/HST W1G 10 E2
Central London Golf Club
TOOT SW17 179 N5
Central London Markets
FARR EC1M 12 C4
Central Medical Centre
MRDN SM4 201 M4
Central Middlesex Hospital
WLSDN NW10 135 P5
Central Park Arena
DART DA1 187 M4
Central Park Primary School
EHAM E6 142 A4
Central Park Swimming Pool
HARH RM3 105 M6
Central Primary School
WAT WD17 73 K8
Central St Martins College of Art & Design
RSQ WC1B 11 M4
Central School of Ballet
CLKNW EC1R 12 B2
Central School of Fashion
GTPST W1W 10 G4

Central School of Speech & Drama HAMP NW3 3 L3
Central School Speech & Drama CAMTN NW1 5 J6
Central Square Shopping Centre ALP/SUD HA0 135 K1
Centre Court Shopping Centre WIM/MER SW19 179 J9
Centre Point LSQ/SEVD WC2H 11 K5
Chace Community School EN EN1 79 M5
Chadwell Heath Hospital CHDH RM6 123 L3
Chadwell Heath Industrial Park BCTR RM8 123 P6
Chadwell Heath Luncheon & Leisure Centre CHDH RM6 123 N4
Chadwell Heath School CHDH RM6 123 L4
Chadwell St Mary Primary School CDH/CHF RM16 168 D3
Chadwell Springs Golf Club WARE SG12 26 B3
Chaffinch Business Park BECK BR3 204 C3
The Chafford Hundred Medical Centre CDH/CHF RM16 167 K2
Chaffords School RAIN RM13 145 K7
Chailey Industrial Estate HYS/HAR UB3 153 H1
Chalcot School CAMTN NW1 4 E3
Chalfont Leisure Centre CFSP/GDCR SL9 89 P9
Chalfont St Giles Infant School CSTG HP8 89 N3
Chalfont St Giles Junior School CSTG HP8 89 N4
Chalfont St Peter FC CFSP/GDCR SL9 90 A8
Chalfont St Peter Junior School CFSP/GDCR SL9 90 A8
Chalfont St Peters Infant School CSTG HP8 89 P8
The Chalfonts Community College CFSP/GDCR SL9 89 P8
Chalfonts & Gerrards Cross Health Clinic CFSP/GDCR SL9 90 A9
Chalgrove Primary School FNCH N3 117 H1
Chalkhill Primary School WBLY HA9 115 N8
Chambersbury JMI School HHS/BOV HP3 36 C9
Chambers Business Park WDR/YW UB7 152 B5
Chambers Wharf BERM/RHTH SE16 19 P1
Chancellors School BRKMPK AL9 59 L1
Chandlers Field Primary School E/WMO/HCT KT8 197 P5
Chandos Business Centre WLGTN SM6 222 D3
Channelsea Business Centre SRTFD E15 141 J4
Channing School HGT N6 118 C6
Chantry Primary School GVE DA12 190 F3
Chantry School WDR/YW UB7 131 P8
Chapel End Infant School WALTH E17 100 G10
Chapel End Junior School WALTH E17 100 G9
Chapel High Shopping Centre BRW CM14 107 H3
Chapman Park Industrial Estate WLSDN NW10 136 C1
Charing Cross Hospital HMSMTH W6 156 G5
Charing Cross & Westminster Medical School HMSMTH W6 156 G4
Charing Cross Station CHCR WC2N 11 M9
Charles Darwin School BH/WHM TN16 244 C1
Charles Dickens Primary School STHWK SE1 18 E2
Charles Edward Brook Lower School CMBW SE5 159 J7
Charles Edward Brook Upper School CMBW SE5 159 J7
Charles Lamb Primary School IS N1 6 E5
Charlotte Sharman Primary School LBTH SE11 18 C4
Charlton Athletic FC (The Valley) CHARL SE7 161 P4
Charlton House CHARL SE7 162 A5
Charlton RFC ELTH/MOT SE9 184 E3
Charlton School CHARL SE7 162 B5
Charlwood Place HORL RH6 279 H7
Charlwood Village Infant School HORL RH6 279 J8
Charrington Bowl SURB KT6 199 N9
Charrville Primary School YEAD UB4 132 F4
Charter Clinic CHEL SW3 16 A8
Charterhouse FARR EC1M 12 D3
Charterhouse School RGODL GU7 267 H10
Charterhouse School Students Residences RGODL GU7 266 G10
Charter Nightingale Hospital & Counselling Centre CAMTN NW1 9 P3
The Charter School HNHL SE24 181 L1
Charters School ASC SL5 192 C7
Chartfield School PUT/ROE SW15 178 E1
Chartridge Combined School CSHM HP5 50 B3
Chartridge Park Golf Club CSHM HP5 50 C4
Chartwell Business Centre BMLY BR1 206 A3
Chase Bridge Primary School WHTN TW2 176 D2
Chase Farm Hospital ENC/FH EN2 79 H4
Chase Lane Primary School CHING E4 100 E5
Chase Road Trading Estate WLSDN NW10 136 A6
Chase Side Junior & Infant School ENC/FH EN2 79 K6
Chaseville Clinic WCHMH N21 78 G10
Chater Infant School WATW WD18 73 H8
Chater Junior School WATW WD18 73 H8
Chatsworth Infant School BFN/LL DA15 185 K4
Chatsworth Junior & Infant School HSLW TW3 154 B10
Chaucer Clinic STHL UB1 154 C1
Chaulden Primary School HHW HP1 35 J7
The Chauncy School WARE SG12 26 A1
Cheam Common Infant School WPK KT4 200 E9
Cheam Common Junior School WPK KT4 200 E10
Cheam Fields Primary School CHEAM SM3 221 H2
Cheam High School CHEAM SM3 221 H1
Cheam Leisure Centre CHEAM SM3 220 G1
Cheam Park Farm Junior School CHEAM SM3 201 H10
Cheam Sports Club BELMT SM2 220 G4
Cheapside CE Primary School ASC SL5 192 D1
Chelsea Barracks BGVA SW1W 16 D8
Chelsea Bridge Business Centre VX/NE SW8 158 C6
Chelsea Centre & Theatre WBPTN SW10 157 N6
Chelsea Cinema CHEL SW3 15 P8
Chelsea College of Art & Design CHEL SW3 15 M8
Chelsea FC (Stamford Bridge) FUL/PGN SW6 157 L6
Chelsea Fields Industrial Estate WIM/MER SW19 201 N1
Chelsea Fire Station CHEL SW3 15 N8
Chelsea Old Town Hall CHEL SW3 15 P8
Chelsea Physic Garden CHEL SW3 16 A9
Chelsea Sports Centre CHEL SW3 15 P8
Chelsea & Westminster Hospital WBPTN SW10 15 K10
Chelsea Wharf WBPTN SW10 157 N6
Chelsfield Lakes Golf Centre ORP BR6 227 P4
Chelsfield Park Hospital ORP BR6 228 A2
Chelsfield Primary School ORP BR6 227 P2
Chenies Combined School RKW/CH/CXG WD3 70 D4
Chenies Cricket Club RKW/CH/CXG WD3 70 E5
Chennestone Community School SUN TW16 197 J2
Cherington House Health Centre HNWL W7 134 E10
Cherry Garden School BERM/RHTH SE16 19 P5
Cherry Lane Primary School WDR/YW UB7 152 A3
Cherry Lodge Golf Club BH/WHM TN16 244 D3
Cherry Orchard Primary School CHARL SE7 161 P6
Cherry Tree JMI School WATN WD24 73 H2
Chertsey Business Centre CHERT KT16 195 K7
Chertsey Cemetery ADL/WDHM KT15 195 K9
Chertsey Hall CHERT KT16 195 K7
Chertsey Museum CHERT KT16 195 K6
Chertsey Recreation Centre CHERT KT16 195 J8
Chertsey Town FC CHERT KT16 195 J6
Chesham Bois CE Combined School AMS HP6 69 K1
Chesham Community Hospital CSHM HP5 51 H8
Chesham Health Centre CSHM HP5 50 G8
Chesham High School CSHM HP5 51 J6
Chesham Leisure Centre CSHM HP5 51 J7
Chesham & Ley Hill Golf Club CSHM HP5 51 P7
Chesham Park Community College CSHM HP5 50 F6
Chesham Preparatory School CSHM HP5 51 M3
Chesham United FC CSHM HP5 50 G9
Cheshunt Community Hospital CHES/WCR EN8 62 D7
Cheshunt FC CHES/WCR EN8 62 B8
Cheshunt Golf Club CHESW EN7 62 A3
Cheshunt School CHES/WCR EN8 62 B6
Chessington Community College CHSGTN KT9 219 J4
Chessington Cricket Club CHSGTN KT9 219 H4
Chessington Golf Club CHSGTN KT9 219 J4
Chessington World of Adventures CHSGTN KT9 219 H6
Chesterfield Primary School PEND EN3 80 D3
Chesterton Primary School BTSEA SW11 158 B7
Chestnut Grove School BAL SW12 180 B4
Chestnut Lane First School AMS HP6 69 K2
Chevening Cross RSEV TN14 246 B6
Chevening Primary School RSEV TN14 246 C8
Cheyne Centre CHEL SW3 15 N10
Chigwell Golf Club CHIG IG7 102 D6
Chigwell Primary School CHIG IG7 102 F3
Chigwell Row Infants School CHIG IG7 103 L3
Chigwell School CHIG IG7 102 F3
Childerditch Industrial Park RBRW/HUT CM13 127 L1
Childeric Primary School NWCR SE14 160 D6
Childs Hill Clinic CRICK NW2 117 J7
Childs Hill Primary School CRICK NW2 117 H8
Childs Welfare Clinic DAGW RM9 123 M10
Chiltern Business Village IVER SL0 131 L4
Chiltern Open Air Museum CSTG HP8 90 C3
Chiltonian Industrial Estate LEE/GVPK SE12 183 L2
Chilworth CE Infant School RGUE GU4 268 G6
The Chimes Shopping Centre UX/CGN UB8 131 M2
Chimnocks Wharf POP/IOD E14 140 D9
Chingford CE Infant School CHING E4 101 J2
Chingford CE Junior School CHING E4 101 J2
Chingford Hall Primary School CHING E4 100 E7
Chingford Health Centre CHING E4 100 E5
Chingford Industrial Centre CHING E4 100 D6
Chingford RFC CHING E4 100 F2
Chingford School CHING E4 100 G2
Chinthurst School KWD/TDW/WH KT20 238 F9
Chipperfield Junior & Infant School KGLGY WD4 53 K7
Chipping Ongar Primary School CHONG CM5 67 N6
Chipstead Golf Club COUL/CHIP CR5 240 A4
Chipstead RFC COUL/CHIP CR5 240 A7
Chipstead Valley Primary School COUL/CHIP CR5 240 B2
Chisenhale Primary School BOW E3 140 D4
Chislehurst Caves CHST BR7 206 D1
Chislehurst Cemetery CHST BR7 185 H8
Chislehurst Golf Club CHST BR7 184 E10
Chislehurst Natural Health Centre CHST BR7 184 E9
Chislehurst & Sidcup Grammar School BFN/LL DA15 185 L5
Chiswick & Bedford Park Preparatory School CHSWK W4 156 B3
Chiswick Community School CHSWK W4 156 A6
Chiswick House CHSWK W4 156 A5
Chobham FC CHOB/PIR GU24 213 L8
Chobham Golf Club WOKN/KNAP GU21 231 J1
Chobham RFC CHOB/PIR GU24 213 K6
Chobham St Lawrence CE First & Middle School CHOB/PIR GU24 213 K7
Chorleywood Golf Club RKW/CH/CXG WD3 70 G8
Chorleywood Health Centre RKW/CH/CXG WD3 70 F8
Chorleywood Primary RKW/CH/CXG WD3 70 F10
Chrisp Street Health Centre POP/IOD E14 140 G8
Christ Church Bentinck CE Primary School CAMTN NW1 9 N3
Christ Church Brondesbury CE Primary School KIL/WHAMP NW6 2 C4
Christ Church CE Infant School NWMAL KT3 200 B3
Christchurch CE Infant School VW GU25 193 M3
Christ Church CE Junior School NWMAL KT3 200 A3
Christ Church Cemetery BRW CM14 107 H5
Christ Church CE Primary School BAR EN5 76 G6
BRXN/ST SW9 159 H7
BRXS/STRHM SW2 180 G4
BRYLDS KT5 199 M6
CHEL SW3 15 P9
FSTH SE23 182 C5
RKW/CH/CXG WD3 71 J8
WCHPL E1 13 M4
Christ Church CE Primary School WOOL/PLUM SE18 162 D7
Christchurch CE School NFNCH/WDSP N12 97 N6
Christ Church CE Middle School EA W5 135 J9
Christchurch Industrial Centre STHWK SE1 12 C9
Christchurch Junior School CHERT KT16 214 G3
Christ Church Primary School BTSEA SW11 157 P9
Christchurch Primary School IL IG1 122 F6
Christ Church Primary School PUR/KEN CR8 223 J6
WARE SG12 26 D2
Christ Church School CAMTN NW1 4 F8
Christian Meeting Hall BECK BR3 204 F1
Christopher Hutton Primary School FSBYW WC1X 12 A2
Christopher Place Shopping Centre STALW/RED AL3 38 C6
Christs College BKHTH/KID SE3 161 M7
EFNCH N2 117 L1
Christs College School EFNCH N2 117 L1
Christs School RCHPK/HAM TW10 177 L1
Christ the King RC First School STWL/WRAY TW19 173 N2
Christ the King RC Primary School FSBYPK N4 118 G7
Chrysalis Theatre BAL SW12 180 B4
Chrysanthemum Clinic CHSWK W4 155 P6
Church Down Adult School LEE/GVPK SE12 183 M5
Church End Medical Centre WLSDN NW10 136 B1
Church Farm House Museum HDN NW4 116 E1
Churchfield Primary School ED N9 99 N2
Churchfield School WOOL/PLUM SE18 163 J3
Churchfields Junior & Infant School SWFD E18 101 M9
Churchfields Primary School BECK BR3 204 C3
Churchgate CE Primary School HLWE CM17 30 A8
Church Hill Primary School EBAR EN4 98 A1
Churchill Business Park BH/WHM TN16 262 G2
Churchill CE Primary School BH/WHM TN16 262 F1
Churchill Clinic STHWK SE1 18 B3
Churchill College RYNPK SW20 200 F2
TOOT SW17 180 A5
Churchill Gardens Primary School PIM SW1V 16 G8
Churchill Theatre HAYES BR2 205 M2
Church Lane School UPMR RM14 126 G10
Church Langley Primary School HLWE CM17 47 M1
Church Mead Infant School LEY E10 120 F6
Church Mead Junior School LEY E10 120 F6
Churchmead School DTCH/LGLY SL3 149 N6
The Church School BTFD TW8 155 K5
Church Stairs WAP E1W 160 A1
Church Street Industrial Estate WARE SG12 26 C1
Church Trading Estate ERITH DA8 165 H6
Cineworld Cinema BXLYHS DA6 164 C10
FELT TW13 175 J5
WDGN N22 99 H10
Cippenham Infants School SL SL1 128 C9
Cippenham Junior School SL SL1 128 C9
Cippenham Medical Centre SL SL1 128 G10
Citizans Advice Bureau LHD/OX KT22 236 F7
City Banking College STHWK SE1 19 H1
City Business Centre BERM/RHTH SE16 160 B1
The City Business Centre CRAWE RH10 283 N3
City Business College FSBYE EC1V 6 D10
City Central Estate FSBYE EC1V 6 E10
City College of Higher Education IS N1 7 H9
City & Guilds of London Art School LBTH SE11 18 B8
City Health Centre FSBYE EC1V 12 G1
City & Islington College FSBYPK N4 119 J7
HOLWY N7 118 F9
IS N1 6 G5
STLK EC1Y 12 G2
City & Islington College Sixth Form Centre HOLWY N7 118 G9
City of London Cemetery MNPK E12 122 B7
City of London Crematorium MNPK E12 122 A8
City of London Club OBST EC2N 13 J5
City of London College WCHPL E1 13 N5
City of London Freemans School ASHTD KT21 237 N5
City of London Magistrates Court MANHO EC4N 12 G6
City of London Polytechnic Sports Ground ELTH/MOT SE9 183 P5
City of London School BLKFR EC4V 12 D7
City of London School for Girls BARB EC2Y 12 E3
City of Westminster Cemetery HNWL W7 134 E10
City of Westminster College BAY/PAD W2 9 L3
MV/WKIL W9 2 E10
City of Westminster Vehicle Pound BAY/PAD W2 9 K4
City Thameslink Station STP EC4M 12 C5
City University FSBYE EC1V 6 C9
FSBYE EC1V 6 C10
City University Business School BARB EC2Y 12 F3
Civic Centre & Bromley Palace BMLY BR1 205 N2
Civic Centre & Woodville Halls GVW DA11 190 E3
Civic Hall Cinema HOD EN11 44 E4
Civic Medical Centre HRW HA1 114 D3
Civil Service College ASC SL5 192 E5
Civil Service Recreation Centre WEST SW1P 17 K4
Civil Service Sports Ground ELTH/MOT SE9 183 P2
Clandon CE Infant School RGUE GU4 251 K7
Clandon Regis Golf Club RGUE GU4 251 L7
Clapham Common Clinic CLAP SW4 158 E10
Clapham Manor Primary School CLAP SW4 158 D9
Clapham Manor Street Public Baths CLAP SW4 158 E9
Clapham North Business Centre CLAP SW4 158 E9
Clapham Park School CLAP SW4 180 E1
Clapham Picture House CLAP SW4 158 D10
Clapton Girls' Technology College CLPT E5 120 B9
Clapton Jewish Boys School STNW/STAM N16 119 N5
Clara Grant Primary School BOW E3 140 F6
Clare House Primary School BECK BR3 205 H2
Claremont Clinic FSTGT E7 121 N10
Claremont Fan Court School ESH/CLAY KT10 218 A3
Claremont High School KTN/HRWW/W HA3 115 K3
Claremont Way Industrial Estate CRICK NW2 116 F6
Clarence House WHALL SW1A 17 H1
Clarendon Primary School ASHF TW15 174 A6
Clarendon Special School HPTN TW12 176 A9
Claridges Hotel MYFR/PKLN W1K 10 E7
Claverings Industrial Estate ED N9 100 B3
Claycots School SLN SL2 128 F6
Claygate Primary School ESH/CLAY KT10 218 D4
Clayhall Clinic CLAY IG5 122 B1
Clayponds Hospital BTFD TW8 155 K3
Cleeve Park School SCUP DA14 185 M6
Clementine Churchill Hospital HRW HA1 114 E8
Cleopatra's Needle CHCR WC2N 11 N9
Clerkenwell County Court IS N1 6 C7
Clerkenwell Heritage Centre FARR EC1M 12 C2
Clerkenwell Parochial CE Primary School CLKNW EC1R 6 A10
Cleveland Primary School IL IG1 122 E9
Cleves Junior School WEY KT13 216 G1
Cleves Primary School EHAM E6 142 A3
Clewer Green CE First School WDSR SL4 148 E9
C & L Golf & Country Club NTHLT UB5 133 K3
Clifton Hill School CTHM CR3 241 L10
Clifton Lodge School EA W5 135 J9
Clifton Primary School NWDGN UB2 153 M3
Clink Exhibition STHWK SE1 12 G9
Clissold Park Natural Health Centre STNW/STAM N16 119 M7

Clitterhouse Primary School
CRICK NW2 ... **116** G7
C & L Leisure Centre
NTHLT UB5 ... **133** J2
Clockhouse Industrial Estate
EBED/NFELT TW14 ... **174** C4
Clockhouse Primary School
CRW RM5 ... **104** C7
Clock Museum
CITYW EC2V ... **12** F5
Cloisters Business Centre
VX/NE SW8 ... **158** C6
Clore Gallery
WEST SW1P ... **17** L6
Clore Shalom School
RAD WD7 ... **57** K7
The Clore Tikva School
BARK/HLT IG6 ... **102** F10
Clothworkers' Hall
FENCHST EC3M ... **13** K7
Clouster's Green
WAP E1W ... **13** N9
Coach Museum
WDSR SL4 ... **149** K7
Coalhouse Fort
TIL RM18 ... **169** P7
Coates Way Primary School
GSTN WD25 ... **55** M9
Cobbold Estate
WLSDN NW10 ... **136** C1
Cobham Bus Museum
COB KT11 ... **216** D8
The Cobham Health Centre
COB KT11 ... **217** J9
Cobham RFC
COB KT11 ... **217** L8
Cobourg Primary School
CMBW SE5 ... **19** L8
Cochrane Theatre
GINN WC1R ... **11** N4
Cockfosters Sports Ground
EBAR EN4 ... **78** A7
The Cockpit Theatre
STJWD NW8 ... **9** N2
Coldharbour Industrial Estate
CMBW SE5 ... **159** K8
Coldharbour Sports Ground
ELTH/MOT SE9 ... **184** D5
Colebrooke Primary School
IS N1 ... **6** C7
Colegrave Primary School
SRTFD E15 ... **121** J10
Colehill Cricket Club
AMSS HP7 ... **68** G9
Coleraine Park Primary School
TOTM N17 ... **100** A9
Coleridge Primary School
HGT N6 ... **118** E5
Coleshill CE First School
AMSS HP7 ... **68** E10
Colfes Preparatory School
LEE/GVPK SE12 ... **183** N2
Colham Manor Junior & Infant School
UX/CGN UB8 ... **132** A8
Colindale Business Park
CDALE/KGS NW9 ... **115** P1
Colindale Hospital
CDALE/KGS NW9 ... **116** B1
Colindale Primary School
CDALE/KGS NW9 ... **116** C2
Coliseum Theatre
CHCR WC2N ... **11** L8
College Fields Business Centre
WIM/MER SW19 ... **201** P1
College Library & Civic Centre
SUT SM1 ... **221** L2
College of Arms
BLKFR EC4V ... **12** E6
College of Fuel Technology
HGT N6 ... **118** B4
College of Law
GWRST WC1E ... **11** J3
The College of Law
FLST/FETLN EC4A ... **12** A5
GWRST WC1E ... **11** J3
College of North East London
CEND/HSY/T N8 ... **119** H2
FBAR/BDGN N11 ... **98** D9
SEVS/STOTM N15 ... **119** N2
College of North West London
KIL/WHAMP NW6 ... **2** E5
WBLY HA9 ... **115** M8
WLSDN NW10 ... **116** C10
College of Organists
FLST/FETLN EC4A ... **12** B5
College of Teachers
EPP CM16 ... **82** G2
College Park School
BAY/PAD W2 ... **8** F6
Collett Special School
HHW HP1 ... **35** M5
Collier Row Clinic
ROMW/RG RM7 ... **104** C9
Collier Row FC
ROMW/RG RM7 ... **104** A9
Collingwood Business Centre
ARCH N19 ... **118** F8
Collingwood Preparatory School
WLGTN SM6 ... **222** C2
Collins Method School
CRICK NW2 ... **136** F1
Collis Primary School
TEDD TW11 ... **176** G9
Colnbrook CE Combined School
DTCH/LGLY SL3 ... **150** G6
Colnbrook School
OXHEY WD19 ... **93** K3
Colnbrook Sports Club
DTCH/LGLY SL3 ... **151** J7
Colne Bridge Retail Park
WAT WD17 ... **73** L9
Colne Valley Retail Park
WAT WD17 ... **73** L9
Colney Heath JMI School
STALE/WH AL4 ... **39** P8
Coln Industrial Estate
DTCH/LGLY SL3 ... **151** J6
Coloma Convent Girls School
CROY/NA CR0 ... **204** C10
Colonial Business Park
WATN WD24 ... **73** K5
The Colonnades Shopping Centre
BGVA SW1W ... **16** E5
Colours Sports Club
SUT SM1 ... **221** M2
Columbia Primary School
BETH E2 ... **7** M9
Colvestone Primary School
HACK E8 ... **119** N10
Colville Primary School
NTGHL W11 ... **8** C6
Colyers Lane Medical Centre
BXLYHN DA7 ... **164** E7
Colyers Primary School
BXLYHN DA7 ... **164** E7
Combe Bank School
RSEV TN14 ... **245** P9
Comber Grove Primary School
CMBW SE5 ... **159** K6
Combermere Barracks
WDSR SL4 ... **148** G9
Comedy Theatre
STJS SW1Y ... **11** J8
Comelle House Trading Estate
DEPT SE8 ... **160** D4
Commonside School
HLWS CM18 ... **47** H5
Commonswood JMI School
WGCE AL7 ... **23** L8
Commonwealth Institute
KENS W8 ... **14** D3
Community Arts Centre
GNWCH SE10 ... **160** G6
Community Care Centre
ENC/FH EN2 ... **79** L5
Community Centre (Island History Trust)
POP/IOD E14 ... **161** H3
Community College & School
GNWCH SE10 ... **161** H6
Community Mental Health Cen
BRXN/ST SW9 ... **159** H6
Community Mental Health Centre
GSTN WD25 ... **55** K10
HHNE HP2 ... **35** N5
Compass Theatre
HGDN/ICK UB10 ... **112** D8
Complementary Health Centre
LEW SE13 ... **183** K2
The Compton School
NFNCH/WDSP N12 ... **97** P7
Concord Business Centre
ACT W3 ... **135** N7
Concorde Business Park
BH/WHM TN16 ... **244** A1
Concord Shopping Centre
WKENS W14 ... **156** G1
Coney Hill School
HAYES BR2 ... **205** L9
Connaught Business Centre
CDALE/KGS NW9 ... **116** C3
CROY/NA CR0 ... **222** G3
MTCM CR4 ... **202** A5
Connaught Girls School
WAN E11 ... **121** K6
Connections Business Park
RSEV TN14 ... **247** J6
Consort Clinic
PECK SE15 ... **160** A9
Consulate General of Monaco
SKENS SW7 ... **15** L5
Consulate General of The Republic of Guinea Bissau
KENS W8 ... **15** J3
Consulate of Burkina Faso
BTSEA SW11 ... **157** M9
Consulate of Chile
CAVSQ/HST W1G ... **10** E2
Consulate of Colombia
GTPST W1W ... **10** G5
Consulate of Eritrea
IS N1 ... **6** B7
Consulate of Guinea
MYFR/PKLN W1K ... **10** C8
Consulate of Panama
MYFR/PICC W1J ... **10** E10
Convent of Jesus & Mary Infant School
CRICK NW2 ... **136** F1
Convent of Jesus & Mary Language College
WLSDN NW10 ... **136** C3
Convent of St John the Baptist
WDSR SL4 ... **148** F8
Convent Preparatory School
GVE DA12 ... **190** F5
Conway Hall
FSBYW WC1X ... **11** N3
Conway Medical Centre
WOOL/PLUM SE18 ... **162** G4
Conway Primary School
WOOL/PLUM SE18 ... **163** H3
Coombe Girls School
NWMAL KT3 ... **200** A2
Coombe Hill Golf Club
KUTN/CMB KT2 ... **178** A10
Coombe Hill Junior & Infant School
NWMAL KT3 ... **200** A1
Coombe Wood Golf Club
KUTN/CMB KT2 ... **177** N10
Coopersale Hall School
EPP CM16 ... **65** L10
Coopersale & Theydon Garnon CE Primary School
EPP CM16 ... **65** N5
Coopers Company & Coborn School
UPMR RM14 ... **126** C8
Coopers' Hall
LVPST EC2M ... **13** K4
Coopers Lane Primary School
LEE/GVPK SE12 ... **183** M5
Coopers School
CHST BR7 ... **206** F1
Copenhagen Primary School
IS N1 ... **5** M6
Copland Community School & Technology Centre
WBLY HA9 ... **115** L10
Coppermill Primary School
WALTH E17 ... **120** C3
Coppetts Wood Hospital
MUSWH N10 ... **98** A9
Coppetts Wood Primary School
MUSWH N10 ... **98** B9
Coppice Primary School
CHIG IG7 ... **103** K6
Copthall School
MLHL NW7 ... **96** E7
Copthorn CE Junior School
CRAWE RH10 ... **285** J2
The Copthorne Business Centre
CRAWE RH10 ... **285** J2
Copthorne Fairway Infant School
CRAWE RH10 ... **285** J2
Copthorne Golf Club
CRAWE RH10 ... **285** K2
Copthorne Junior School
CRAWE RH10 ... **285** J2
Copthorne Preparatoryschool
CRAWE RH10 ... **285** L2
Copthorne Squash Club
CRAWE RH10 ... **285** H3
Corbets Tey School
UPMR RM14 ... **126** A10
Cordwainers College
HOM E9 ... **140** B2
Corinium Industrial Estate
AMS HP6 ... **69** L4
Corinthian Casuals FC
CHSGTN KT9 ... **199** M10
Corinthian Sports Club
HART DA3 ... **211** J6
Corn Exchange
HERT/WAS SG14 ... **25** L5
Cornhill Sports Club
BECK BR3 ... **182** F8
Coronet Cinema
NTGHL W11 ... **8** E9
SEVS/STOTM N15 ... **119** J1
Corpus Christi RC Primary School
BRXS/STRHM SW2 ... **180** G1
Cosmopolitan College
IS N1 ... **5** N8
Coston Secondary Modern Girls School
GFD/PVL UB6 ... **134** B5
Coteford Infant School
RSLP HA4 ... **113** H4
Coulsdon CE Primary School
COUL/CHIP CR5 ... **240** G4
The Coulsdon Eye Clinic
COUL/CHIP CR5 ... **240** D1
Coulsdon High School
COUL/CHIP CR5 ... **241** J6
Coulsdon Manor Hotel Golf Club
COUL/CHIP CR5 ... **240** G2
Coulsdon 6th Form College
COUL/CHIP CR5 ... **241** H5
Counterpoint Theatre
STPAN WC1H ... **5** M9
Countess Anne Primary School
HAT AL10 ... **40** E3
Country Gardens Estate
BFOR GU20 ... **192** B9
County Mall
CRAWE RH10 ... **283** P7
County Oak Retail Park
CRAWE RH10 ... **283** N3
Courtauld Institute Galleries
HOL/ALD WC2B ... **11** N7
Court Farm Industrial Estate
STWL/WRAY TW19 ... **174** A2
Courtfield Medical Centre
ECT SW5 ... **15** H6
Courtland JMI School
MLHL NW7 ... **96** B3
Court Lodge County First School
HORL RH6 ... **280** A4
Courtwood Primary School
CROY/NA CR0 ... **224** E6
Covent Garden Flower Market
VX/NE SW8 ... **17** K10
Covent Garden Medical Centre
LSQ/SEVD WC2H ... **11** L6
Coward Industrial Estate
CDH/CHF RM16 ... **168** E4
Cowarth Park School
CHOB/PIR GU24 ... **212** G1
Cowley Business Park
UX/CGN UB8 ... **131** M5
UX/CGN UB8 ... **131** N9
Cowley Hill Primary School
BORE WD6 ... **75** N5
Cowley Mill Industrial Estate
IVER SL0 ... **131** K4
CPFC Soccer & Sports Centre
BRXN/ST SW9 ... **158** G9
Cp House Business Centre
GSTN WD25 ... **73** N5
Crabtree Infant School
HARP AL5 ... **20** B2
Crabtree Junior Mixed School
HARP AL5 ... **20** C2
Crampton Primary School
WALW SE17 ... **18** D6
Cranborne Industrial Estate
POTB/CUF EN6 ... **59** H6
Cranborne Primary School
POTB/CUF EN6 ... **59** H7
Cranbourne JMI School
HOD EN11 ... **26** G10
Cranbrook College
IL IG1 ... **122** D7
Crane Infant School
FELT TW13 ... **175** N5
Crane Junior School
FELT TW13 ... **175** M5
Cranford Community College
HEST TW5 ... **153** J5
Cranford Infant School
HSLWW TW4 ... **153** H8
Cranford Junior School
HSLWW TW4 ... **153** J8
Cranford Park Junior School
HYS/HAR UB3 ... **152** G3
Cranford Park Primary School
HYS/HAR UB3 ... **152** G1
Cranham Health Centre
UPMR RM14 ... **126** D5
Cranleigh Gardens Industrial Estate
STHL UB1 ... **133** N7
Cranmer School
MTCM CR4 ... **202** A5
Cranmore School
EHSLY KT24 ... **252** D5
The Craven Clinic
HMSMTH W6 ... **156** E3
Craven Park Health Centre
WLSDN NW10 ... **136** A3
Craven Park Medical Centre
WLSDN NW10 ... **136** A3
Craven Park Primary School
SEVS/STOTM N15 ... **119** P4
Crawford Primary School
CMBW SE5 ... **159** K7
Crawford Upper School
MBLAR W1H ... **10** A4
Crawley College
CRAWE RH10 ... **283** P7
Crawley College Annexe
CRAWW RH11 ... **283** M6
Crawley Down Health Centre
CRAWE RH10 ... **285** P5
Crawley Health Clinic
CRAWE RH10 ... **283** P7
Crawley Hospital
CRAWW RH11 ... **283** M7
The Crawley Lawn Tennis Club
CRAWE RH10 ... **284** C5
Crawley Leisure Centre Athletics Arena
CRAWE RH10 ... **284** A8
Crawley Museum (Goffs Park House)
CRAWW RH11 ... **283** L8
Crawley RFC
CRAWW RH11 ... **283** K3
Crayfield Industrial Park
STMC/STPC BR5 ... **207** M2
Crayfields Business Park
STMC/STPC BR5 ... **207** M1
STMC/STPC BR5 ... **207** M5
Crayford Commercial Centre
DART DA1 ... **186** F1
Crayford Industrial Estate
DART DA1 ... **186** G1
Crayford Leisure Centre & Greyhound Stadium
DART DA1 ... **186** F2
Crayford Medical Centre
DART DA1 ... **186** G1
Crayside Industrial Estate
DART DA1 ... **165** H9
Cray Valley Golf Club
STMC/STPC BR5 ... **207** P1
Creekmouth Industrial Estate
BARK IG11 ... **143** J6
Creek Road Health Centre
DEPT SE8 ... **160** F5
Creek Road Industrial Estate
DEPT SE8 ... **160** G5
Cremer Business Centre
BETH E2 ... **7** L8
Creswick Primary School
WGCE AL7 ... **22** G8
Crewe House
MYFR/PICC W1J ... **10** E9
Crews Hill Golf Club
ENC/FH EN2 ... **60** G10
The Cricket Club
SLN SL2 ... **129** H5
SLN SL2 ... **129** M6
Cricket Pavilion
WEST SW1P ... **17** J5
Cricklefield Stadium
IL IG1 ... **123** H7
Cricklewood Trading Estate
CRICK NW2 ... **117** H8
Crispin Industrial Centre
UED N18 ... **100** B6
Criterion Theatre
MYFR/PICC W1J ... **11** H8
Crockenhill Primary School
SWLY BR8 ... **208** D6
Crockham Hill County Primary School
EDEN TN8 ... **262** F9
Crofton Leisure Centre
BROCKY SE4 ... **182** F2
Crofton School
BROCKY SE4 ... **182** F2
Croham Hurst Golf Club
SAND/SEL CR2 ... **223** N3
Croham Hurst School
SAND/SEL CR2 ... **223** N2
Cromer Road JMI School
BAR EN5 ... **77** L7
Cromwell Business Centre
BARK IG11 ... **143** H5
Cromwell Hospital
KENS W8 ... **14** G5
Cromwell Industrial Estate
LEY E10 ... **120** D6
Crook Log Baths
BXLYHS DA6 ... **163** N10
Crook Log Primary School
BXLYHS DA6 ... **163** N10
Crook Log Sports Centre
WELL DA16 ... **163** N9
Crosby Hall
CHEL SW3 ... **15** M10
Crouch End Art School
CEND/HSY/T N8 ... **118** F3
Crouch End Health Centre
CEND/HSY/T N8 ... **118** F3
Crouch Hill Recreation Centre
ARCH N19 ... **118** F5
Crouch Industrial Estate
LHD/OX KT22 ... **236** F5
Crowland Primary School
SEVS/STOTM N15 ... **119** N3
Crowlands Primary School
ROMW/RG RM7 ... **124** D4
Crown Business Centre
WDR/YW UB7 ... **132** A10
Crown Business Estate
CSHM HP5 ... **51** H6
Crown Close Business Centre
BOW E3 ... **140** F3
Crown Court at the Borough
STHWK SE1 ... **18** D1
Crowndale Health Centre
CAMTN NW1 ... **5** H7
Crownfield Primary School
ROMW/RG RM7 ... **104** B10
Crown Lane Clinic
STHGT/OAK N14 ... **98** D2
Crown Lane Primary School
WNWD SE27 ... **181** J8
Crown Prosecution Service
STAL AL1 ... **38** C6
Crown Trading Centre
HYS/HAR UB3 ... **152** F1
Crown Woods School
ELTH/MOT SE9 ... **184** F1
Croydon Airport Industrial Estate
CROY/NA CR0 ... **223** H4
Croydon Cemetery
THHTH CR7 ... **202** G5
Croydon Clocktower Cinema
CROY/NA CR0 ... **203** K10
Croydon College
CROY/NA CR0 ... **203** L10
Croydon Fairfield Halls Cinema
CROY/NA CR0 ... **203** L10
Croydon FC
SNWD SE25 ... **204** B5
Croydon High School GDST
SAND/SEL CR2 ... **224** A7
Croydon Indoor Bowling Club
SAND/SEL CR2 ... **223** K2
Croydon Road Industrial Estate
SNWD SE25 ... **204** B4
Croydon Sports Arena
SNWD SE25 ... **204** B5
Crusader Industrial Estate
FSBYPK N4 ... **119** K4
Crusoe House School
IS N1 ... **6** G9
Crystal Palace
NRWD SE19 ... **181** P9
Crystal Palace Athletics Stadium
NRWD SE19 ... **181** P9
Crystal Palace FC (Selhurst Park)
SNWD SE25 ... **203** M4
Crystal Palace Museum
NRWD SE19 ... **181** N9
Cuaco Sports Ground
BECK BR3 ... **182** F9
Cubitt Town Primary School
POP/IOD E14 ... **161** H2
Cuddington Cemetery
WPK KT4 ... **200** E9
Cuddington CP School
HOR/WEW KT19 ... **200** C10
Cuddington Golf Club
BNSTD SM7 ... **221** H9
Cudham CE Primary School
BH/WHM TN16 ... **244** D2
Cuffley Primary School
POTB/CUF EN6 ... **60** G6
Culloden Primary School
POP/IOD E14 ... **141** J8
Culvers House Primary School
MTCM CR4 ... **202** B8
Cumberland Business Park
WLSDN NW10 ... **135** N5
Cumberland Comprehensive School
CAN/RD E16 ... **141** L7
Cumberland Park Industrial Estate
WLSDN NW10 ... **136** D5
The Cuming Museum
WALW SE17 ... **18** E6
Cumnor House School
SAND/SEL CR2 ... **223** J5
Cunningham Hill Junior Middle & Infant School
STAL AL1 ... **38** F8
Curwen Primary School
PLSTW E13 ... **141** M4
Curzon CE Primary School
AMSS HP7 ... **68** A8
Curzon Mayfair Cinema
MYFR/PICC W1J ... **10** E10
Curzon Soho Cinema
SOHO/SHAV W1D ... **11** K7
Cutlers' Hall
STP EC4M ... **12** D5
Cutty Sark
GNWCH SE10 ... **161** H5
Cygnet Clinic Beckton
EHAM E6 ... **142** E8
Cygnet Leisure Centre
GVW DA11 ... **190** B5
Cygnus Business Centre
WLSDN NW10 ... **116** C10
Cypress Infant School
SNWD SE25 ... **203** M2
Cypress Junior School
SNWD SE25 ... **203** M2
Cyprus College of Art
WNWD SE27 ... **181** J7
Cyril Jackson Primary School
POP/IOD E14 ... **140** E9
Dacorum Athletics Track
HHS/BOV HP3 ... **36** A8
Dacorum District Sports Centre
HHW HP1 ... **35** M8
Dacre Industrial Estate
CHES/WCR EN8 ... **62** E5
Dagenham Chest Clinic
BCTR RM8 ... **124** A8
Dagenham Priory Comprehensive School
DAGE RM10 ... **144** C2
Dagenham & Redbridge FC
DAGE RM10 ... **124** C10
Dagenham Superbowl
DAGE RM10 ... **144** C4
Dagenham Swimming Pool
BCTR RM8 ... **124** A7
Daiglen School
BKHH IG9 ... **101** P2
Daily Mirror Office
FLST/FETLN EC4A ... **12** B4
Daily Telegraph
POP/IOD E14 ... **160** F2
Dairy Meadow Primary School
NWDGN UB2 ... **153** N2
D'Albiac House
HTHAIR TW6 ... **152** B8
Dali Universal Exhibition
STHWK SE1 ... **17** M1
Dallington School
FSBYE EC1V ... **12** D1
Dalmain Primary School
FSTH SE23 ... **182** D4
Dame Alice Owens School
POTB/CUF EN6 ... **59** H9
Dame Tipping CE Primary School
ABR/ST RM4 ... **104** F4
Danegrove Primary School
EBAR EN4 ... **77** P10
Danesfield Manor School
WOT/HER KT12 ... **197** J9
Danes Hill School
LHD/OX KT22 ... **218** C10
Danetree School
HOR/WEW KT19 ... **219** P4
Danson Primary School
WELL DA16 ... **163** L10
Dapdune Wharf
GU GU1 ... **249** P10
Darell Primary School
RCH/KEW TW9 ... **155** M9
Darenth Primary School
RDART DA2 ... **188** E9
Darenth Valley Golf Club
RSEV TN14 ... **229** H8
Darenth Valley Hospital
RDART DA2 ... **188** C4
Darent Industrial Park
ERITH DA8 ... **165** L4

Darley Dene Infant School
ADL/WDHM KT15 .... 215 M1
Darrick Wood Primary School
ORP BR6 .... 226 E1
Darrick Wood Swimming Pool
ORP BR6 .... 206 E10
Dartford County Court
DART DA1 .... 187 M2
Dartford FC
EYN DA4 .... 209 P1
RDART DA2 .... 188 A4
Dartford Golf Club
DART DA1 .... 187 J5
Dartford Grammar School for Boys
DART DA1 .... 187 K2
Dartford Grammar School for Girls
DART DA1 .... 187 K3
Dartford Hospital School
HART DA3 .... 211 M3
Dartford Magistrates Court
DART DA1 .... 187 L2
Dartford Museum & Library
DART DA1 .... 187 M3
Dartford Natural Health Centre
DART DA1 .... 187 M3
Dartford West Health Centre
DART DA1 .... 187 K2
Dartford West Technology College
DART DA1 .... 187 K3
Datapoint Business Centre
CAN/RD E16 .... 141 J6
Datchet Golf Club
DTCH/LGLY SL3 .... 149 M6
Datchet St Marys Primary School
DTCH/LGLY SL3 .... 149 N6
Datchet Sports Club
DTCH/LGLY SL3 .... 149 N6
Daubeney Primary School
CLPT E5 .... 120 D9
Davenant Foundation School
LOU IG10 .... 82 F4
Davenies School
BEAC HP9 .... 88 D9
David Game College
KENS W8 .... 8 E9
David Game Tutorial College
SKENS SW7 .... 15 L6
David Livingstone Primary School
THHTH CR7 .... 203 K1
David Lloyd Leisure Centre
SKENS SW7 .... 15 H5
Davidson Junior & Infant School
CROY/NA CR0 .... 203 N7
Davies Lane Infant School
WAN E11 .... 121 L7
Davies's College
STHWK SE1 .... 18 F1
Dawlish Primary School
LEY E10 .... 121 H7
The Dawnay County Primary School
GT/LBKH KT23 .... 253 P2
Day Hospital
CAMTN NW1 .... 5 H3
PUR/KEN CR8 .... 223 H7
Days Lane Primary School
BFN/LL DA15 .... 185 J2
Deanesfield Primary School
RSLP HA4 .... 113 L9
Deansbrook Primary School
MLHL NW7 .... 95 P7
Deansfield Primary School
ELTH/MOT SE9 .... 162 D9
Deans Trading Estate
RAIN RM13 .... 145 L6
Debden House Residential Centre
LOU IG10 .... 82 E4
Debden Sports Club
LOU IG10 .... 82 F9
De Beauvoir Primary School
IS N1 .... 7 K2
De Bohun Primary School
STHGT/OAK N14 .... 78 B9
Debworth Green First School
WDSR SL4 .... 148 D8
Dedworth Clinic
WDSR SL4 .... 148 D7
Dedworth County Middle School
WDSR SL4 .... 148 D7
Deerswood School
CRAWW RH11 .... 283 K5
de Havilland Aircraft Heritage Centre
STAL AL1 .... 39 H7
Delrow School
GSTN WD25 .... 74 B5
Denbies Wine Estate
RDKG RH5 .... 254 G8
Deneholm Primary School
CDH/CHF RM16 .... 167 P1
Dene House Hospital
WDSR SL4 .... 149 H9
Denham Aerodrome
DEN/HRF UB9 .... 111 H3
Denham County Infant School
DEN/HRF UB9 .... 111 J7
Denham Golf Club
DEN/HRF UB9 .... 110 G4
Denmead School
HPTN TW12 .... 175 P10
Denver Industrial Estate
RAIN RM13 .... 144 G7
Department for Environment, Food & Rural Affairs
WHALL SW1A 11 L9
Department of Health
WHALL SW1A 17 L1
Department of Trade & Industry
STJSPK SW1H 17 K3
Deptford Business Centre
DEPT SE8 .... 160 C4
Deptford Green School
NWCR SE14 .... 160 E6
Deptford Park Business Centre
DEPT SE8 .... 160 D4
Deptford Park Primary School
DEPT SE8 .... 160 D4
Deptford Trading Estate
DEPT SE8 .... 160 D4
Dersingham Infant School
MNPK E12 .... 122 C10
Derwentwater Primary School
ACT W3 .... 135 P10
Design Museum
STHWK SE1 .... 13 M10
De Stafford College
CTHM CR3 .... 241 N7
Deutsche Schule
RCHPK/HAM TW10 .... 177 J4
Devonshire Hill Primary School
TOTM N17 .... 99 L7
Devonshire Hospital
MHST W1U 10 D3
Devonshire House Preparatory School
HAMP NW3 .... 117 M10
Devonshire House School
HAMP NW3 .... 117 M10
Devonshire Primary School
BELMT SM2 .... 221 M4
Dewhurst St Mary Junior Middle & Infant School
CHESW EN7 .... 62 A5
Diamond College
SOHO/SHAV W1D 11 K5
Diana Fountain
E/WMO/HCT KT8 .... 198 E2
Diane Matthews Clinic
ROMW/RG RM7 .... 124 E2
Diaspora Museum
KTTN NW5 .... 4 C2
The Dickens House Museum
BMSBY WC1N 11 N2
Dilkes Primary School
SOCK/AV RM15 .... 146 E8
Dilloway Industrial Estate
NWDGN UB2 .... 153 M1
Discover Bible School
GSTN WD25 .... 73 K1
Discovery Business Park
BERM/RHTH SE16 .... 19 P4
Divine Saviour RC Primary School
ABLGY WD5 .... 54 E8
Docklands Medical Centre
POP/IOD E14 .... 160 F3
Docklands Sailing Centre
POP/IOD E14 .... 160 F2
Docklands Sailing & Watersports Centre
POP/IOD E14 .... 160 E2
Dockley Road Industrial Estate
BERM/RHTH SE16 .... 19 N4
Dockmaster's House
POP/IOD E14 .... 140 F9
Dockwell's Industrial Estate
EBED/NFELT TW14 .... 175 J1
Dockyard Industrial Estate
WOOL/PLUM SE18 .... 162 B2
Doddinghurst Infant School
BRWN CM15 .... 86 G3
Doddinghurst Junior School
BRWN CM15 .... 86 G3
Dog Kennel Hill Primary School
CMBW SE5 .... 159 M9
Dokal Industrial Estate
NWDGN UB2 .... 153 M1
Dollis Infant School
MLHL NW7 .... 96 F8
Dollis Junior School
MLHL NW7 .... 96 F8
The Dolphin Leisure Centre
ROM RM1 .... 124 G2
Dolphin School
BTSEA SW11 .... 180 A1
Dome
GNWCH SE10 .... 141 K10
Dominion Business Park
ED N9 .... 100 C3
Dominion Theatre
NOXST/BSQ WC1A 11 K5
Dominoes Health Centre
GRAYS RM17 .... 167 M5
Donmar Warehouse Theatre
LSQ/SEVD WC2H 11 L6
Donnington Primary School
WLSDN NW10 .... 136 E2
Donyngs Recreation Centre
REDH RH1 .... 257 P9
Doods Brow School
REDH RH1 .... 258 G9
Dorchester Primary School
WPK KT4 .... 200 F8
The Dorking Business Park
DORK RH4 .... 272 F1
Dorking Cemetery
DORK RH4 .... 255 H10
Dorking FC
RDKG RH5 .... 255 H5
Dorking General Hospital
DORK RH4 .... 272 F3
Dorking Golf Club
RDKG RH5 .... 273 H3
Dorking Halls
DORK RH4 .... 273 H1
Dorking Lawn Tennis & Squash Club
DORK RH4 .... 272 F4
Dorking Museum
DORK RH4 .... 272 F1
Dorking RFC
BRKHM/BTCW RH3 .... 255 N10
Dorking Swimming & Sports Centre
DORK RH4 .... 273 H1
Dorma Trading Park
LEY E10 .... 120 C6
Dormers Wells Medical Centre
GFD/PVL UB6 .... 133 P8
Dormers Wells Primary School
STHL UB1 .... 134 A9
Dormers Wells School
GFD/PVL UB6 .... 133 P8
Dorney Court
WDSR SL4 .... 148 A2
Dorothy Barley Primary School
BCTR RM8 .... 123 L10
Dorset Road Infant School
ELTH/MOT SE9 .... 184 B5
Dorton College of Further Education
BGR/WK TN15 .... 247 M8
The Douay Martyrs RC School
HGDN/ICK UB10 .... 112 C9
Douglas Bader Foundation
PUT/ROE SW15 .... 178 D2
Dover Road Primary School
GVW DA11 .... 190 B4
Dovers Corner Industrial Estate
RAIN RM13 .... 144 G5
Dovers Green School
REIG RH2 .... 275 M4
Downderry Primary School
BMLY BR1 .... 183 K7
Downe Manor Primary School
NTHLT UB5 .... 133 J5
Downe Primary School
ORP BR6 .... 226 D7
Downfield Primary School
CHES/WCR EN8 .... 62 D7
Downham Health Centre
BMLY BR1 .... 183 K7
Downhills Primary School
TOTM N17 .... 119 L2
Down House - Home of Charles Darwin
ORP BR6 .... 226 C8
Down Lane Junior School
TOTM N17 .... 99 N10
Downsell Junior School
WAN E11 .... 121 J9
Downsend School
LHD/OX KT22 .... 237 J6
Downsend School - Ashtead Lodge
ASHTD KT21 .... 237 K4
Downside Primary School
CLPT E5 .... 119 P9
The Downs P & N School
HLW CM20 .... 46 G1
Downsview Infant School
SWLY BR8 .... 209 H3
Downsview Primary School
NRWD SE19 .... 181 K10
Downsview School
CLPT E5 .... 120 A9
Downs Way County Primary School
OXTED RH8 .... 261 K3
Drapers Hall
LOTH EC2R 13 H5
Drapers Sports Ground
SRTFD E15 .... 121 H9
Drayton Green Primary School
WEA W13 .... 134 F9
Drayton Manor High School
HNWL W7 .... 134 E9
Drayton Park Primary School
HBRY N5 .... 119 H10
DRCA Business Centre
BTSEA SW11 .... 158 B7
Dr Challoners Grammar School
AMS HP6 .... 69 H4
Dr Challoners High School
AMSS HP7 .... 69 N6
Drew Primary School
CAN/RD E16 .... 142 B10
Drift Golf Club
COB KT11 .... 234 G9
Driving School & Road Safety Centre
KTN/HRWW/W HA3 .... 114 F1
Dr Johnson's House
FLST/FETLN EC4A 12 B6
Dropmore Infant School
SL SL1 .... 108 B8
Dr Tripletts CE J & I School
HYS/HAR UB3 .... 132 G8
Drummond Shopping Centre
CROY/NA CR0 .... 203 K9
Drury Way Industrial Estate
WLSDN NW10 .... 116 A9
Dry Ski Slope
HGDN/ICK UB10 .... 112 A10
RBRW/HUT CM13 .... 107 H8
Duchess Theatre
COVGDN WC2E 11 N7
Duke of York Column
STJS SW1Y 11 J10
Duke of York's HQ
CHEL SW3 .... 16 B6
Duke of York Theatre
CHCR WC2N 11 L8
Duke's Dene Golf Club
WARL CR6 .... 242 C6
Dulverton Primary School
BFN/LL DA15 .... 184 G5
Dulwich College
DUL SE21 .... 181 M4
Dulwich College Preparatory School
DUL SE21 .... 181 M6
Dulwich College Track
DUL SE21 .... 181 M5
Dulwich Hamlet FC
CMBW SE5 .... 159 M10
Dulwich Hamlet Junior School
HNHL SE24 .... 181 L2
Dulwich Medical Centre
EDUL SE22 .... 181 P1
Dulwich Picture Gallery
DUL SE21 .... 181 L3
Dulwich & Sydenham Hill Golf Club
DUL SE21 .... 181 P5
Dulwich Village CE Infant School
DUL SE21 .... 181 M2
Dunbar Wharf
POP/IOD E14 .... 140 E9
Duncombe Primary School
ARCH N19 .... 118 F6
Duncombe School
HERT/WAS SG14 .... 25 K4
Dundee Wharf
POP/IOD E14 .... 140 E9
Dundonald First School
WIM/MER SW19 .... 179 J10
Dunningford Primary School
HCH RM12 .... 124 G10
Dunottar School
REIG RH2 .... 275 N1
Dunraven School (Lower School)
STRHM/NOR SW16 .... 180 G6
Dunraven School (Upper School)
STRHM/NOR SW16 .... 180 G6
Dunton Green Primary School
SEV TN13 .... 246 F6
Duppas Junior School
CROY/NA CR0 .... 223 J2
Durand Primary School
BRXN/ST SW9 .... 158 G7
Durants School
EN EN1 .... 80 B5
Durdans Park Primary School
STHL UB1 .... 133 N7
Durston House School
EA W5 .... 135 J8
Dycourts School
HARH RM3 .... 105 P5
Dyrham Park Country Club
BAR EN5 .... 76 D4
Dysart School
KUTN/CMB KT2 .... 177 J7
Dysart Special School
SURB KT6 .... 199 K7
Eaglesfield School
WOOL/PLUM SE18 .... 162 D7
Eagle Trading Estate
MTCM CR4 .... 202 A6
Ealdham Primary School
ELTH/MOT SE9 .... 161 P10
Ealing Abbey
EA W5 .... 135 H8
Ealing Abbey Scriptorium
WEA W13 .... 135 H8
The Ealing Broadway Centre
EA W5 .... 135 J9
Ealing Central Sports Ground
GFD/PVL UB6 .... 134 F4
Ealing College Upper School
WEA W13 .... 134 G8
Ealing Cricket Club
EA W5 .... 135 K8
Ealing Film Studios
EA W5 .... 135 H10
Ealing Golf Club
GFD/PVL UB6 .... 134 G5
Ealing Hospital
STHL UB1 .... 154 C1
Ealing Northern Sports Centre
NTHLT UB5 .... 114 C9
Ealing Park Health Centre
EA W5 .... 155 J3
Ealing Road Trading Estate
BTFD TW8 .... 155 J4
Ealing Sports Centre
EA W5 .... 135 K9
Ealing Tertiary College
EA W5 .... 135 H10
Ealing Tutorial College
EA W5 .... 135 H9
Eardley Primary School
STRHM/NOR SW16 .... 180 D9
Earlham Junior & Infant School
WDGN N22 .... 99 H8
Earlham Primary School
FSTGT E7 .... 121 L10
Earls Court Exhibition Centre
ECT SW5 .... 14 E8
Earlsfield Primary School
WAND/EARL SW18 .... 179 M5
Earlsmead First & Middle School
RYLN/HDSTN HA2 .... 113 N9
Earlsmead Primary School
SEVS/STOTM N15 .... 119 N2
Earlswood Infant School
REDH RH1 .... 276 B1
Earth Gallery (Geological Museum)
SKENS SW7 .... 15 L4
East Acton Primary School
ACT W3 .... 136 B9
East Barking Luncheon & Leisure Centre
BCTR RM8 .... 123 M10
East Barnet Health Centre
EBAR EN4 .... 77 N9
East Barnet School
EBAR EN4 .... 77 N7
EBAR EN4 .... 78 A10
East Beckton District Centre
EHAM E6 .... 142 C8
East Berkshire College
DTCH/LGLY SL3 .... 150 C1
WDSR SL4 .... 149 H8
Eastbrook Comprehensive School
DAGE RM10 .... 124 D9
Eastbrook End Cemetery
DAGE RM10 .... 124 F8
LOU IG10 .... 82 A8
Eastbrookend Country Park
DAGE RM10 .... 124 E9
Eastbrook Junior School
HHNE HP2 .... 36 A1
Eastbury Comprehensive
BARK IG11 .... 142 G2
Eastbury Comprehensive School
BARK IG11 .... 143 J3
Eastbury Farm JMI School
NTHWD HA6 .... 92 G5
Eastbury Infant School
BARK IG11 .... 143 J2
Eastcote Cricket Club
PIN HA5 .... 113 J3
Eastcote Health Centre
PIN HA5 .... 113 K5
Eastcote Industrial Estate
RSLP HA4 .... 113 K5
Eastcote Lane Cemetery
RYLN/HDSTN HA2 .... 114 A8
Eastcote Primary School
ELTH/MOT SE9 .... 162 G9
Eastcourt Independent School
GDMY/SEVK IG3 .... 123 K6
East Dulwich Baths
EDUL SE22 .... 159 N10
Eastern Business Park
HTHAIR TW6 .... 152 G8
Eastfield Primary School
PEND EN3 .... 80 C4
Eastfields High School
MTCM CR4 .... 202 C2
East Finchley Cemetery
EFNCH N2 .... 117 L1
East Finchley Medical Centre
EFNCH N2 .... 117 P2
East Finchley School of English
EFNCH N2 .... 117 P1
East Greenwich Christ Church CE Primary School
GNWCH SE10 .... 161 K3
East Ham Industrial Estate
CAN/RD E16 .... 142 A6
East Ham Jewish Cemetery
EHAM E6 .... 142 B5
East Ham Memorial Hospital
FSTGT E7 .... 142 A2
East Ham Nature Reserve
EHAM E6 .... 142 C6
East Lane Business Park
WBLY HA9 .... 115 J7
Eastlea Community School
CAN/RD E16 .... 141 K6
East London Business College
WAN E11 .... 121 K6
East London Cemetery
PLSTW E13 .... 141 L5
East London Crematorium
PLSTW E13 .... 141 L5
East London RFC
EHAM E6 .... 142 C7
East London RUFC
PLSTW E13 .... 141 L4
Eastman Dental Hospital
FSBYW WC1X 11 N1
East Molesey Cricket Club
E/WMO/HCT KT8 .... 198 B3
East Sheen Cemetery
RCHPK/HAM TW10 .... 177 M1
East Sheen Primary School
MORT/ESHN SW14 .... 156 B10
East Surrey College
REDH RH1 .... 258 B6
East Surrey Hospital
REDH RH1 .... 276 C4
East Surrey Museum
CTHM CR3 .... 241 N10
East Thamesmead Business Park
ERITHM DA18 .... 164 A1
East Wickham Primary School
WELL DA16 .... 163 J7
Eastwick Infant School
GT/LBKH KT23 .... 236 A10
Eastwick Junior School
GT/LBKH KT23 .... 236 A10
Eaton House School
KTBR SW1X 16 C5
Eaton Manor RFC
WAN E11 .... 121 P3
Eaton Square Preparatory School
BGVA SW1W 16 E5
Eaton Square School
PIM SW1V 16 G6
Ebbisham County Infants School
EPSOM KT18 .... 219 P10
Ebbisham Sports Club
HOR/WEW KT19 .... 219 P8
Ebbsfleet Industrial Estate
GVW DA11 .... 189 M1
Ecclesbourne Primary School
IS N1 .... 6 G3
THHTH CR7 .... 203 K5
Echelford Primary School
ASHF TW15 .... 174 C8
Eckerd College
GWRST WC1E 11 J3
Eclipse Estate
HOR/WEW KT19 .... 219 P9
Ecole De Mime Corporel Theatre De Lange Fou
ARCH N19 .... 118 F7
Eden College
STHWK SE1 .... 18 D3
Edenham High School
CROY/NA CR0 .... 204 E7
Eden Medical Centre
WKENS W14 .... 14 D6
Edenvale Child Health Clinic
TOOT SW17 .... 180 B10
Eden Walk Shopping Centre
KUT KT1 .... 199 K2
Edes Business Park
WLGTN SM6 .... 202 B9
Edgebury Primary School
CHST BR7 .... 184 F7
Edge Business Centre
CRICK NW2 .... 116 E7
Edge Grove School
GSTN WD25 .... 74 B3
Edgwarebury Cemetery
EDGW HA8 .... 95 M3
Edgware Clinic
EDGW HA8 .... 95 M7
Edgware College
HAMP NW3 .... 3 J2
Edgware Community Hospital
EDGW HA8 .... 95 N8
Edgware FC & Wealdstone FC
EDGW HA8 .... 95 M8
Edgware Infant School
EDGW HA8 .... 95 M7
Edgware Junior School
EDGW HA8 .... 95 M7
The Edgware School
EDGW HA8 .... 95 L5
Edinburgh Primary School
WALTH E17 .... 120 E3
Edith Neville Primary School
CAMTN NW1 .... 5 J8
Edmonton Cemetery
ED N9 .... 99 L3
Edmonton County Court
UED N18 .... 99 P6
Edmonton Green Shopping Centre
ED N9 .... 100 A3
Edmonton Leisure Centre
ED N9 .... 99 P4
Edmonton Upper School
EN EN1 .... 99 N1
Edmund Waller Primary School
NWCR SE14 .... 160 C8
Education Centre
UX/CGN UB8 .... 131 M1
WOOL/PLUM SE18 .... 162 E4
Edward Betham CE Primary School
GFD/PVL UB6 .... 134 C5
Edward Pauling School
FELT TW13 .... 174 F5
Edward Redhead Primary School
WALTH E17 .... 120 D1
Edward Wilson Primary School
BAY/PAD W2 .... 8 G3
Edwin Lambert School
EMPK RM11 .... 125 H4
Effingham Cricket Club
EHSLY KT24 .... 235 J10
Effingham Golf Club
EHSLY KT24 .... 253 L4
Effingham Park Golf Club
CRAWE RH10 .... 285 N1
Effra Primary School
BRXS/STRHM SW2 .... 181 H1
Effra Road Retail Park
BRXS/STRHM SW2 .... 181 H1
Egerton Rothesay School
BERK HP4 .... 33 L5
Egham Business Village
EGH TW20 .... 194 F2
Egham Cricket Club
EGH TW20 .... 172 E9
Egham Sports Centre
EGH TW20 .... 172 E9
Egham Town FC
EGH TW20 .... 172 F9

Eglinton Infant School WOOL/PLUM SE18 162 D6
Eglinton Junior School WOOL/PLUM SE18 162 D5
Elangeni Junior School AMS HP6 69 K2
Elbourne Trading Estate BELV DA17 164 C2
Eldenwall Industrial Estate BCTR RM8 123 P6
Eldon JMI School ED N9 100 B2
Eleanor Estate CHES/WCR EN8 62 E10
Eleanor Palmer Primary School KTTN NW5 118 D9
Eleanor Smith Special School & Primary Support Service PLSTW E13 141 M4
Electrical Trades Union College ESH/CLAY KT10 217 P1
Electric Cinema NTGHL W11 8 C6
The Electric Theatre GU GU1 267 P1
Elephant & Castle Shopping Centre STHWK SE1 18 D4
Elers Clinic HYS/HAR UB3 152 E3
Elfrida Primary School CAT SE6 182 G7
Eliot Bank Primary School FSTH SE23 182 A5
Elizabeth Garrett Anderson Hospital CAMTN NW1 5 K10
Elizabeth Garrett Anderson School IS N1 5 P7
Elizabeth Selby Infant School BETH E2 7 P9
Elizabeth Trading Estate NWCR SE14 160 C5
Ellen Wilkinson Primary School EHAM E6 142 A7
Ellen Wilkinson School for Girls ACT W3 135 L8
Ellerslie Square Industrial Estate CLAP SW4 158 F10
Ellingham Primary School CHSGTN KT9 219 J4
Elliott Foundation School PUT/ROE SW15 178 F2
Elliswick Lawn Tennis Club HARP AL5 20 A1
Elmbridge Leisure Centre WOT/HER KT12 197 J5
Elmbridge Museum WEY KT13 216 B1
Elm Court School WNWD SE27 181 J5
Elmgrove First & Middle School KTN/HRWW/W HA3 114 F2
Elmhurst Preparatory School BECK BR3 204 C4
Elmhurst Primary School FSTGT E7 141 N2
Elmhurst School CROY/NA CR0 223 L1
Elm Lea Trading Estate TOTM N17 99 P8
The Elms Health Centre POTB/CUF EN6 59 M7
Elms Industrial Estate HARH RM3 106 A8
The Elmsleigh Centre Shopping Precinct STA TW18 173 H7
Elmtree Infant School CSHM HP5 50 G6
Elmwood Primary School CROY/NA CR0 203 J7
Elm Wood Primary School WNWD SE27 181 L6
Elsdale Street Health Centre HOM E9 140 B2
Elsley Primary School WBLY HA9 135 L1
Elsley School BTSEA SW11 158 B9
Elstree Aerodrome BORE WD6 74 E7
Elstree Golf Club BORE WD6 75 J7
Elstree Studios BORE WD6 75 M7
Elstree Way Clinic BORE WD6 75 N6
Eltham Baths ELTH/MOT SE9 184 B1
Eltham Bus Station ELTH/MOT SE9 184 C1
Eltham Cemetery ELTH/MOT SE9 162 F10
Eltham CE Primary School ELTH/MOT SE9 184 C1
Eltham College ELTH/MOT SE9 184 A5
Eltham College Junior School ELTH/MOT SE9 184 A4
Eltham Crematorium ELTH/MOT SE9 162 G10
Eltham Green School ELTH/MOT SE9 184 A2
Eltham Health Clinic ELTH/MOT SE9 184 B1
Eltham Hill Technology College ELTH/MOT SE9 184 B2
Eltham Palace (remains) ELTH/MOT SE9 184 B3
Eltham Warren Golf Club ELTH/MOT SE9 184 E1
Elthorne Park High School HNWL W7 154 E2
Elystan Business Centre HYS/HAR UB3 133 K9
Emanuel School WAND/EARL SW18 179 N1
Embankment Pier CHCR WC2N 11 N9
Embass of Thailand SKENS SW7 15 K4
Embassy of Afghanistan SKENS SW7 15 L2
Embassy of Albania BGVA SW1W 16 F4
Embassy of Algeria NTGHL W11 8 B10
Embassy of Angola MYFR/PKLN W1K 10 C8
Embassy of Argentina MYFR/PKLN W1K 10 E7
Embassy of Armenia KENS W8 14 G3
Embassy of Austria KTBR SW1X 16 C3
Embassy of Bahrain SKENS SW7 15 J4
Embassy of Belarus KENS W8 15 H2
Embassy of Belgium KTBR SW1X 16 D4
Embassy of Bolivia KTBR SW1X 16 D4
Embassy of Bosnia-Herzegovina CAVSQ/HST W1G 10 F5
Embassy of Brazil MYFR/PKLN W1K 10 C7
Embassy of Bulgaria SKENS SW7 15 K3
Embassy of Cameroon WKENS W14 8 B10
Embassy of China CAVSQ/HST W1G 10 E3
Embassy of Costa Rica BAY/PAD W2 9 K7
Embassy of Cote d'ivoire KTBR SW1X 16 D3
Embassy of Croatia GTPST W1W 10 F2
Embassy of Cuba HHOL WC1V 11 L5
Embassy of The Democratic Republic of the Congo KTBR SW1X 16 B4
Embassy of Denmark KTBR SW1X 16 A3
Embassy of The Dominican Republic BAY/PAD W2 9 H6
Embassy of Ecuador KTBR SW1X 16 A3
Embassy of Egypt MYFR/PICC W1J 10 E9
Embassy of Estonia SKENS SW7 15 K2
Embassy of Ethiopia SKENS SW7 15 M2
Embassy of Finland KTBR SW1X 16 C3
Embassy of France KTBR SW1X 16 B1
Embassy of Gabon SKENS SW7 15 K4
Embassy of Georgia KENS W8 14 G2
Embassy of Germany KTBR SW1X 16 C3
Embassy of Ghana HGT N6 118 C6
Embassy of Greece KENS W8 8 C10
Embassy of Guatemala WBPTN SW10 15 J9
Embassy of Honduras MBLAR W1H 10 B3
Embassy of Hungary KTBR SW1X 16 D4
Embassy of Iceland KTBR SW1X 16 C5
Embassy of Indonesia MYFR/PKLN W1K 10 D8
Embassy of Iran SKENS SW7 15 M2
Embassy of Iraq SKENS SW7 15 K3
Embassy of Ireland KTBR SW1X 16 E2
Embassy of Israel KENS W8 15 H1
Embassy of Italy MYFR/PKLN W1K 10 D7
Embassy of Japan MYFR/PICC W1J 10 F10
Embassy of Jordan KENS W8 14 E2
Embassy of Korea WESTW SW1E 17 H3
Embassy of Krygyzstan MBLAR W1H 10 A4
Embassy of Kuwait KTBR SW1X 16 B1
Embassy of Latvia CAMTN NW1 10 C2
Embassy of Lebanon KENS W8 8 G9
Embassy of Liberia BAY/PAD W2 8 F7
Embassy of Lithuania MBLAR W1H 10 A4
Embassy of Luxembourg KTBR SW1X 16 C2
Embassy of Mexico MYFR/PICC W1J 10 E10
Embassy of Mongolia KENS W8 15 H2
Embassy of Morocco SKENS SW7 15 J5
Embassy of Mozambique FITZ W1T 10 G2
Embassy of Myanmar MYFR/PICC W1J 10 E9
Embassy of Nepal KENS W8 8 G9
Embassy of The Netherlands SKENS SW7 15 K2
Embassy of Norway KTBR SW1X 16 D3
Embassy of Paraguay SKENS SW7 15 H4
Embassy of Peru KTBR SW1X 16 B3
Embassy of Poland CAVSQ/HST W1G 10 E3
Embassy of Portugal KTBR SW1X 16 C2
Embassy of Qatar MYFR/PKLN W1K 10 D10
Embassy of Romania KENS W8 14 G1
Embassy of Russian Federation KENS W8 8 C10
Embassy of Saudi Arabia MYFR/PICC W1J 10 E9
Embassy of Slovak Republic KENS W8 8 C9
Embassy of Slovenia CAVSQ/HST W1G 10 E5
Embassy of South Vietnam KENS W8 15 H3
Embassy of Spain KTBR SW1X 16 D3
Embassy of Sudan WHALL SW1A 10 G10
Embassy of Sweden MBLAR W1H 10 A4
Embassy of Switzerland MBLAR W1H 10 A4
Embassy of Syria KTBR SW1X 16 C2
Embassy of The Philippines KENS W8 8 G10
Embassy of The Republic of Senegal CRICK NW2 136 F2
Embassy of Tunisia SKENS SW7 15 M2
Embassy of Turkey KTBR SW1X 16 D2
Embassy of Turkmenistan GTPST W1W 11 H4
Embassy of Ukraine NTGHL W11 8 B10
Embassy of The United Arab Emirates SKENS SW7 15 M1
Embassy of Uruguay SKENS SW7 15 P3
Embassy of USA MYFR/PKLN W1K 10 C7
Embassy of Uzbekistan NTGHL W11 8 C10
Embassy of Venezuela SKENS SW7 15 M4
Embassy of Yemen SKENS SW7 15 L5
Ember Sports Club ESH/CLAY KT10 198 B8
Embroidery World Business Centre WFD IG8 102 A10
EMD Walthamstow Cinema WALTH E17 120 F2
Emerson Park School EMPK RM11 126 A5
Emery Theatre POP/IOD E14 140 G8
Emmanuel CE Primary School KIL/WHAMP NW6 117 K10
Emmanuel CE School NTHWD HA6 92 G8
Empire Cinema LSQ/SEVD WC2H 11 K7
Endsleigh Industrial Estate NWDGN UB2 153 M3
Enfield Business Centre PEND EN3 80 B6
Enfield Chace Lower School ENC/FH EN2 79 M4
Enfield College PEND EN3 80 B7
Enfield County Upper School ENC/FH EN2 79 L7
Enfield Crematorium EN EN1 80 A3
Enfield Cricket Club EN EN1 79 M8
Enfield FC ED N9 100 B3
EN EN1 79 P7
Enfield Golf Club ENC/FH EN2 79 J8
Enfield Grammar School (Upper) ENC/FH EN2 79 L7
Enfield Lower Grammar School ENC/FH EN2 79 L6
Enfield School of Swimming FBAR/BDGN N11 98 E6
Engayne Junior School UPMR RM14 126 C4
Englefield Green County Infant School EGH TW20 171 P8
English Martyrs RC Primary School WALW SE17 18 G6
WCHPL E1 13 M6
Ennersdale Primary School LEW SE13 183 J1
Ensham Secondary School TOOT SW17 180 A8
Enterprise Business Park POP/IOD E14 160 G1
Enterprise Industrial Estate BERM/RHTH SE16 160 B4
Epping CE Primary School EPP CM16 64 E1
Epping County Infant School EPP CM16 65 H5
Epping Forest College Tertiary FE LOU IG10 82 E7
Epping Forest Conservation Centre LOU IG10 81 P4
Epping Forest District Museum WAB EN9 63 H9
Epping Forest Railway CHONG CM5 67 N3
EPP CM16 65 L6
The Epping Golf Club EPP CM16 65 L9
Epping House School HERT/BAY SG13 42 D7
Epping Junior School EPP CM16 65 J6
Epping Sports Centre EPP CM16 64 G10
EPP CM16 65 J7
Epsom Bowls EPSOM KT18 220 B10
Epsom Business Park EW KT17 220 B7
Epsom Cemetery EPSOM KT18 238 B2
Epsom College EW KT17 220 D10
Epsom County & Magistrates Court EPSOM KT18 220 A9
Epsom County Primary School HOR/WEW KT19 220 A7
Epsom Downs Racecourse EPSOM KT18 238 D4
Epsom & Ewell High School HOR/WEW KT19 219 P3
Epsom Ewell & St Hellier NHS Trust EPSOM KT18 237 P1
Epsom Golf Club EW KT17 238 D1
Epsom Health Clinic EPSOM KT18 220 B9
Epsom Sports Club EPSOM KT18 237 P1
Equestrian Centre NTHWD HA6 92 C8
Erith & Belvedere FC BELV DA17 164 C2
Erith Cemetery BELV DA17 164 C5
Erith & District Hospital ERITH DA8 164 E5
Erith Health Centre ERITH DA8 164 F5
Erith Library & Museum ERITH DA8 164 F4
Erith School ERITH DA8 164 D6
Erith Small Business Centre ERITH DA8 164 G5
Erith Sports Centre ERITH DA8 164 F5
Erith Stadium ERITH DA8 164 F5
Erith Theatre Guild ERITH DA8 164 G4
Ernest Bevin School TOOT SW17 179 P6
Eros MYFR/PICC W1J 11 J8
Esher Church School (Primary) ESH/CLAY KT10 218 B3
Esher College THDIT KT7 198 D7
Esher RFC WOT/HER KT12 197 M9
Essendine Primary School KIL/WHAMP NW6 2 F10
Essendon Primary School BRKMPK AL9 42 A3
The Essex Nuffield Hospital BRWN CM15 107 K2
Essex Primary School MNPK E12 142 B1
Ethelburga GM School BTSEA SW11 157 P7
Ethel Davis School CHDH RM6 123 L3
Eton College WDSR SL4 149 J4
Eton Wick CE First School WDSR SL4 148 F4
Eton Wick FC WDSR SL4 148 E4
Euro Business Centre SRTFD E15 141 L3
Eurolink Business Centre BRXS/STRHM SW2 159 H10
Europa Trading Estate ERITH DA8 164 E4
WTHK RM20 167 J4
European Business Centre CDALE/KGS NW9 116 A1
European School of Economics KTBR SW1X 16 D2
European Vocational College HDTCH EC3A 13 K6
Euro Way School CEND/HSY/T N8 119 H1
Euro Way School London FSBYPK N4 119 J5
Euston Centre CAMTN NW1 10 G1
Euston Station CAMTN NW1 5 J10
Euston Tower CAMTN NW1 10 G1
Eveline Lower Primary School STHWK SE1 19 N8
Evelyns School WDR/YW UB7 132 A8
Evendine College SOHO/SHAV W1D 11 J5
Everest Sports Club CHES/WCR EN8 62 A5
Eversley College SBW CM21 29 N1
Eversley Medical Centre THHTH CR7 203 H6
Eversley Primary School WCHMH N21 78 F9
Everyman Cinema HAMP NW3 117 M9
Evolution House RCH/KEW TW9 155 K8
Ewell Athletics Track HOR/WEW KT19 220 A3
Ewell Castle School EW KT17 220 D5
Ewell Grove Infant School EW KT17 220 C5
EW Fact/Emile Woolf Colleges HOLWY N7 5 M1
Excel Exhibition Centre CAN/RD E16 141 M9
Exchange Square SDTCH EC2A 13 J3
The Exchange IL IG1 122 E7
Executive Park Industrial Estate STAL AL1 38 G6
Exhibition Halls STLK EC1Y 12 F3
WBLY HA9 115 M9
Eye Clinic LSQ/SEVD WC2H 11 K5
Eye Hospital HHOL WC1V 11 L5
Eynsford Castle EYN DA4 209 M9
Eynsford Cricket Club EYN DA4 209 M9
Fairacres Industrial Estate WDSR SL4 148 B8
Fairbrook Medical Centre BORE WD6 75 N6
Faircharm Trading Estate DEPT SE8 160 G6
IS N1 6 E7
The Faircross Complementary Medical Centre BARK IG11 143 H1
Fairfield Clinic BKHH IG9 101 N2
Fairfield Industrial Estate KUT KT1 199 L3
Fair Field Junior School RAD WD7 74 D2
Fairfield Medical Centre GT/LBKH KT23 254 A2
Fairfield Pool & Leisure Centre DART DA1 187 M3
Fairfields Primary School CHESW EN7 61 P3
Fairholme Junior & Infant School EBED/NFELT TW14 174 E4
Fairlawn Primary School FSTH SE23 182 B3
Fairley House School WEST SW1P 17 J6
Fairlop Primary School BARK/HLT IG6 102 F9
Fairoaks Airport CHOB/PIR GU24 214 C7
Fairview Industrial Centre DAGW RM9 144 E8
Fairview Industrial Estate AMS HP6 69 L4
HYS/HAR UB3 152 G1
OXTED RH8 261 J6
OXTED RH8 261 M9
Fairview Medical Centre STRHM/NOR SW16 202 F1
Fairway JMI School MLHL NW7 96 A3
Fairway Primary School MLHL NW7 96 A3
Fairways Business Park LEY E10 120 D7
Falconbrook JMI School BTSEA SW11 157 N8
Falcon Business Centre BTSEA SW11 157 P10
Falconer School BUSH WD23 73 N9
Falcon Park Industrial Estate WLSDN NW10 116 B10
Falkner House School ECT SW5 15 K7
Fanmakers' Hall LVPST EC2M 13 J5
Fan Museum GNWCH SE10 161 H6
Faraday Building BLKFR EC4V 12 D6
Farleigh Court Golf Club WARL CR6 224 F8
Farleigh Rovers FC WARL CR6 242 E1
Farm Lane Trading Estate FUL/PGN SW6 14 E10
Farnborough Primary School ORP BR6 226 G2
Farncombe CE Infant School RGODL GU7 267 K10
Farncombe Cricket Club RGODL GU7 267 L10
Farnell House Medical Centre HSLW TW3 154 A7
Farnham Common Infant School SLN SL2 108 G9
Farnham Common Middle School SLN SL2 109 H9
Farnham Common Sports Club SLN SL2 109 H9
Farnham Green Primary School GDMY/SEVK IG3 123 K4
Farnham Park Golf Club SLN SL2 129 K3
Farnham Road Hospital GUW GU2 267 N2
Farnham Royal CE Combined School SLN SL2 129 H5
Farningham Woods (Nature Reserve) SWLY BR8 209 L4
Farringdon Station FARR EC1M 12 C3
Farrington & Stratford House School CHST BR7 184 G10
Fashion & Textile Design Museum STHWK SE1 19 K2
Fawbert & Barnards (Undl) Primary School HLWE CM17 29 M8
Fawkham CE Primary School HART DA3 210 F8
Fawkham Manor Hospital HART DA3 211 H8
Featherstone Industrial Estate NWDGN UB2 153 M1
Featherstone Primary School NWDGN UB2 153 M2
Featherstone Road Health Clinic NWDGN UB2 153 M2
Featherstone School NWDGN UB2 153 L3
Felnex Trading Estate WLGTN SM6 202 B9
Feltham Airparcs Leisure Centre FELT TW13 175 L5
Feltham Athletics Arena EBED/NFELT TW14 175 H3
Felthambrook Industrial Estate FELT TW13 175 J6
Feltham Community College FELT TW13 175 K5
Feltham Hill Infant School FELT TW13 174 F6
Feltham Hill Junior School FELT TW13 174 G6
Feltham & Hounslow Boro FC EBED/NFELT TW14 175 H3
Feltham Superbowl FELT TW13 175 J5
Feltonfleet School COB KT11 216 F9
Fenchurch Street Station MON EC3R 13 J6
Fenstanton Junior & Infant School BRXS/STRHM SW2 181 H4
Fenton House HAMP NW3 117 M8
Fern Hill Primary School KUTN/CMB KT2 177 K9
Ferrier Industrial Estate WAND/EARL SW18 157 L10
Ferry Island Retail Park TOTM N17 119 N1

Ferry Lane Industrial Estate
RAIN RM13 145 H7
WALTH E17 120 B1
Ferry Lane Primary School
WALTH E17 120 A2
Festival Pier
STHWK SE1 11 P9
Fetcham Social & Sports Club
LHD/OX KT22 236 C8
Fetcham Village Infant School
LHD/OX KT22 236 D7
Fiddlebridge Industrial Centre
HAT AL10 40 D3
Field End Primary School
RSLP HA4 113 L7
Fielding Primary School
WEA W13 154 G2
Field Junior School
WATW WD18 73 K9
Film House Cinema
RCH/KEW TW9 177 J1
Financial Times
POP/IOD E14 141 H8
STHWK SE1 12 F9
Finchley Catholic High School
NFNCH/WDSP N12 97 L4
Finchley Cricket Club
FNCH N3 97 L10
Finchley Golf Club
MLHL NW7 97 J7
The Finchley Industrial Centre
NFNCH/WDSP N12 97 M5
Finchley Memorial Hospital
FNCH N3 97 M8
Finchley Youth Theatre
EFNCH N2 117 P1
Fine Arts College
HAMP NW3 3 P2
Finsbury Circus Medical Centre
LVPST EC2M 13 H4
Finsbury Health Centre
CLKNW EC1R 12 A1
Finsbury Leisure Complex
FSBYE EC1V 12 E1
Finsbury Park Track
FSBYPK N4 119 J5
Finton House School
TOOT SW17 180 A5
Fircroft Primary School
TOOT SW17 180 A5
Fire Brigade Museum
STHWK SE1 18 E1
Firepower (Museum of Artillery)
WOOL/PLUM SE18 162 E2
Firs Farm Primary School
PLMGR N13 99 L4
First Quarter Business Park
HOR/WEW KT19 220 B7
Fisher Athletic FC
BERM/RHTH SE16 140 C10
Fisher Industrial Estate
WATW WD18 73 K9
Fishmonger's Hall
CANST EC4R 12 G8
Fitness Unlimited Leisure Centre
BOW E3 140 F4
Fitzjohns Primary School
HAMP NW3 117 N10
Fitzrovia Medical Centre
GTPST W1W 10 G2
Fitzroy Nuffield Hospital
MBLAR W1H 10 A5
Five Elms Primary School
DAGW RM9 124 A8
Five Oaks Primary School
HAT AL10 40 D6
Five Ways Business Centre
FELT TW13 175 J6
Flamstead End Infant School
CHESW EN7 61 P3
Flamstead End Junior School
CHESW EN7 61 P3
Flamsteed House Museum
GNWCH SE10 161 J6
Flaxman Sports Centre
CMBW SE5 159 K8
Fleecefield Primary School
ED N9 99 P5
Fleetdown Primary School
RDART DA2 188 B5
Fleet Primary School
HAMP NW3 118 A10
Fleetville Infant School
STAL AL1 38 F6
Fleetville Jm School
STAL AL1 38 F6
Fleetway Business Park
GFD/PVL UB6 134 G4
Fleetway Sports Club
GVE DA12 190 F4
Fleming Lab Museum
BAY/PAD W2 9 M5
Flexlands School
CHOB/PIR GU24 213 L7
Flora Gardens Primary School
HMSMTH W6 156 E3
Florance Nightingale
Health Centre
HLWE CM17 47 M1
Florence Nightingale Museum
STHWK SE1 17 N2
Florida State University
RSQ WC1B 11 K4
Flutters Leisure Centre
FUL/PGN SW6 157 K6
FOB School
CLPT E5 119 P5
Follys End Christian High School
SNWD SE25 203 M6
Fondu Sports Club
PUR RM19 166 B3
Fontigarry Farm Business Park
REIG RH2 275 M9
The Foot Clinic
WIM/MER SW19 179 H8
The Foot Health Centre
COUL/CHIP CR5 240 E1
Fordbridge Medical Centre
ASHF TW15 174 A7
The Ford College
CONDST W1S 10 F7
Ford Industrial Park
DAGW RM9 144 C5
Fordview Industrial Estate
RAIN RM13 144 E5
Fordwater Trading Estate
ADL/WDHM KT15 195 M8
Foreign & Commonwealth Office
WHALL SW1A 17 K1
Foreland Medical Centre
NTGHL W11 8 A7
Forest Business Park
WALTH E17 120 C5
Forestdale Primary School
CROY/NA CR0 224 D5
Foresters Primary School
WLGTN SM6 222 E3
Forest Gate Community School
FSTGT E7 121 M10
Forest Hill Business Centre
FSTH SE23 182 B5
Forest Hill Industrial Estate
FSTH SE23 182 B5
Forest Hill School
SYD SE26 182 C6
Forest House Business Centre
WAN E11 121 L5
Forest Industrial Park
BARK/HLT IG6 103 H8
Forest Medical Centre
LOU IG10 82 B9
Forest Road Medical Centre
WALTH E17 120 E1
Forest School
WALTH E17 121 K2
Forest Trading Estate
WALTH E17 120 C1
Forge Close Clinic
HAYES BR2 205 M8
Forge Lane Primary School
FELT TW13 175 M8
Forge Wood Industrial Estate
CRAWE RH10 284 C3
The Former Health Centre
CHARL SE7 162 A3
Forres CP School
HOD EN11 26 G10
Forster Park Primary School
CAT SE6 183 K6
Fortismere School
EFNCH N2 98 A10
Fortismere Secondary School
MUSWH N10 118 B1
Fortune Theatre
HOL/ALD WC2B 11 M6
Forty Hall Museum
ENC/FH EN2 79 N3
Forty Hill CE Primary School
EN EN1 79 P3
The Forum
EDGW HA8 95 M7
Forum Theatre
HAT AL10 40 C3
Fossdene Primary School
CHARL SE7 161 N4
Fosters Primary School
WELL DA16 163 M8
Foulds School
BAR EN5 76 G7
The Foundling Museum
BMSBY WC1N 11 M1
Fountayne Business Centre
SEVS/STOTM N15 119 P2
Fountayne Road Health Centre
CLPT E5 119 P7
Four Swannes Primary School
CHES/WCR EN8 62 D9
Foxborough Primary School
DTCH/LGLY SL3 150 D4
Foxhills Golf Club
CHERT KT16 214 C1
Fox Primary School
KENS W8 8 E10
Frances Bardsley School for Girls
ROM RM1 125 H3
Frances King School of English
SKENS SW7 15 J5
Francis Bacon School
STAL AL1 38 G9
Franciscan Primary School
TOOT SW17 180 B7
Francis Combe School
GSTN WD25 55 K8
Francis Holland School
BGVA SW1W 16 D6
CAMTN NW1 10 A2
Frank Barnes Primary School
HAMP NW3 3 M4
Franklin Industrial Estate
PGE/AN SE20 204 B1
Freehold Industrial Centre
HSLWW TW4 175 K1
Freemantles School
CHERT KT16 195 H7
Free Trade Wharf
WAP E1W 140 C9
Fresh Wharf Estate
BARK IG11 142 E3
Freuchen Medical Centre
WLSDN NW10 136 C4
Freud Museum
HAMP NW3 3 K1
Friars Primary
Foundation School
STHWK SE1 18 C1
The Friary Centre
GU GU1 267 P1
The Fridge
BRXS/STRHM SW2 158 G10
Friends House
CAMTN NW1 5 J10
Friends of Bar Ilan University
GLDGN NW11 117 K6
Friends of the
Hebrew University
CAMTN NW1 4 E6
Friern Barnet School
FBAR/BDGN N11 98 A6
Friern Bridge Retail Park
FBAR/BDGN N11 98 C7
Frithsden Vineyard
HHW HP1 34 E1
Frithwood Primary School
NTHWD HA6 92 G7
Frobisher Way Hatfield
Business Park
HAT AL10 40 C2
Froebel College
PUT/ROE SW15 178 D2
Frogmore House
WDSR SL4 149 L9
Frogmore Industrial Estate
HBRY N5 119 K9
HYS/HAR UB3 152 F1
WLSDN NW10 135 P5
Frogmore Road Industrial Estate
HHS/BOV HP3 35 N9
Fryent Country Park
WBLY HA9 115 M5
Fryent Medical Centre
CDALE/KGS NW9 115 P5
Fryent Primary School
CDALE/KGS NW9 115 P5
Fulham Clinic
WKENS W14 14 D9
Fulham Cross School
FUL/PGN SW6 156 G6
Fulham FC (Craven Cottage)
BARN SW13 156 F7
Fulham Medical Centre
FUL/PGN SW6 157 L6
Fulham Palace
FUL/PGN SW6 157 H8
Fulham Preparatory School
FUL/PGN SW6 157 H8
Fulham Primary School
FUL/PGN SW6 14 E10
Fulham Warner Village Cinema
FUL/PGN SW6 157 K6
Fullbrook School
ADL/WDHM KT15 215 K7
Fuller Smith & Turner
Sports Club
CHSWK W4 156 B7
Fullwell Cross Health Centre
BARK/HLT IG6 102 F10
Fullwood Primary School
BARK/HLT IG6 122 F2
Fulmer Infant School
DTCH/LGLY SL3 110 B9
Fulwell Golf Club
HPTN TW12 176 C7
Furness School
SWLY BR8 186 G9
Furness Swanley FC
SWLY BR8 208 E5
Furzedown Primary School
TOOT SW17 180 C9
Furze Field Leisure Centre
POTB/CUF EN6 59 H7
Furzefield Primary School
REDH RH1 258 E4
Furzehill School
BORE WD6 75 M8
Furze Infant School
CHDH RM6 123 P4
Future Business College
CONDST W1S 10 F6
Gade Valley JMI School
HHW HP1 35 L5
Gaflac Sports Ground Pavilion
SUN TW16 197 H1
Gainsborough Primary School
HOM E9 140 E1
SRTFD E15 141 K5
Gainsborouh Clinic
PLMGR N13 98 G5
Galleria Shopping Centre
HAT AL10 40 C4
The Gallery at Lakeside
WTHK RM20 166 G3
Galley Hill Industrial Estate
SWCM DA10 189 K1
Galleywall Primary School
BERM/RHTH SE16 160 A3
Galliard Primary School
ED N9 79 P10
Gallions Mount Primary School
WOOL/PLUM SE18 163 J4
Gants Hill Medical Centre
GNTH/NBYPK IG2 122 D4
The Garden City Practice
WGCW AL8 22 G4
Garden Court Business Centre
WGCE AL7 23 J5
Gardener Industrial Estate
BECK BR3 182 D8
Garden Fields Junior
Middle & Infant School
STALW/RED AL3 38 C3
Gardens of the Rose
(Royal National Rose)
LCOL/BKTW AL2 55 N2
Garden Suburb Primary School
GLDGN NW11 117 J3
Garfield Primary School
FBAR/BDGN N11 98 C6
WIM/MER SW19 179 M9
Garratt Park Secondary
Special School
WAND/EARL SW18 179 L6
Garrick Industrial Centre
CDALE/KGS NW9 116 C3
Garrick Theatre
LSQ/SEVD WC2H 11 L8
Garston Clinic
WATN WD24 73 J2
Garston JMI School
GSTN WD25 73 L1
Garston Manor Special School
GSTN WD25 55 K8
Garston Medical Centre
GSTN WD25 73 K2
Garth Primary School
MRDN SM4 201 N5
The Garth Road Industrial Centre
MRDN SM4 200 F7
Gascoigne Primary School
BARK IG11 142 F3
Gate Cinema
NTGHL W11 8 E9
Gatehouse School
BETH E2 140 C4
The Gatehouse Theatre
HGT N6 118 B5
The Gate Theatre
NTGHL W11 8 E9
Gateway
EHAM E6 142 E6
Gateway Industrial Estate
WLSDN NW10 136 C5
Gateway Primary School
STJWD NW8 9 M1
Gatton Park Business Centre
REDH RH1 258 C6
Gatwick Gate Industrial Estate
HORL RH6 279 P10
Gatwick Industrial Estate
HORL RH6 279 J9
Gatwick Medical Centre
HORL RH6 280 C8
Gatwick Park Hospital
HORL RH6 279 P5
Gatwick Zoo
HORL RH6 278 G9
Gayhurst Primary School
HACK E8 7 P3
Gayhurst School
CFSP/GDCR SL9 109 P2
Gaynes School
UPMR RM14 126 B10
Gazelda Industrial Estate
WAT WD17 73 K9
Gearies Infant School
GNTH/NBYPK IG2 122 D3
Gearies Junior School
GNTH/NBYPK IG2 122 E3
Geffrye Museum
BETH E2 7 K8
Gemini Business Estate
NWCR SE14 160 C4
General Medical Clinics
WCHPL E1 13 L3
Genesis Business Park
WOKS/MYFD GU22 232 F1
Genesis Cinema
WCHPL E1 140 B6
Geoffrey Chaucer School
STHWK SE1 18 G4
The Geoffrey Lloyd
Foulkes Clinic
IL IG1 122 D7
Geoffrey Whitworth Theatre
DART DA1 165 H10
George Abbot School
GU GU1 250 D8
George Elliot Primary School
STJWD NW8 3 K5
George Green Mixed School
POP/IOD E14 161 H4
George Lowe Court
BAY/PAD W2 8 G3
George Mitchell School
LEY E10 120 G6
George Mitchell School Annexe
LEY E10 120 G6
George Spicer Primary School
EN EN1 79 N7
George Tomlinson
Primary School
WAN E11 121 K6
The Gerrards Cross CE School
CFSP/GDCR SL9 110 B5
Gerrards Cross Golf Club
CFSP/GDCR SL9 110 C1
Gerrards Cross Sports Centre
CFSP/GDCR SL9 110 A5
Gibson Business Centre
TOTM N17 99 N7
The Gibson Business Centre
TOTM N17 99 N8
Gidea Park College
GPK RM2 125 H1
Gidea Park Primary School
GPK RM2 124 G2
Gidea Park Sports Ground
GPK RM2 105 K10
The Gielgud Theatre
SOHO/SHAV W1D 11 J7
Giffin Business Centre
DEPT SE8 160 F6
Gifford Primary School
NTHLT UB5 133 N4
Gilbert Collection
TPL/STR WC2R 11 N7
WAP E1W 140 A9
Gilbert Colvin Primary School
CLAY IG5 102 D9
Gilbert Scott Primary School
SAND/SEL CR2 224 D4
Gillespie Primary School
FSBYPK N4 119 J8
Girdlers' Hall
CITYW EC2V 12 F4
The Glade Business Centre
WTHK RM20 166 E4
Glade Primary School
CLAY IG5 102 C9
Gladesmore Community School
SEVS/STOTM N15 119 P3
The Glades Shopping Centre
BMLY BR1 205 M2
Gladstone Court
Business Centre
VX/NE SW8 158 D7
Gladstone Medical Centre
CRICK NW2 116 C9
Gladstone Park Primary School
WLSDN NW10 116 E10
Glaziers/Scientific
Instrument Makers Hall
STHWK SE1 12 G9
Glebe First & Middle School
KTN/HRWW/W HA3 115 J2
Glebe Primary School
HGDN/ICK UB10 112 E9
Glebe School
WWKM BR4 205 J8
Gleen Lecky Health Centre
PUT/ROE SW15 156 G10
Glenbrook Primary School
CLAP SW4 180 E2
Glencairn Sports Club
FBAR/BDGN N11 98 D8
Glendower Preparatory School
SKENS SW7 15 K5
Glenesk School
EHSLY KT24 252 E1
Glenham College
IL IG1 122 E7
Glenlyn Medical Centre
E/WMO/HCT KT8 198 B5
Glenthorne High School
CHEAM SM3 201 K8
Globe Industrial Estate
GRAYS RM17 167 P5
Globe Primary School
BETH E2 140 B5
Globe Theatre
STHWK SE1 12 D8
Globe Wharf
BERM/RHTH SE16 140 C9
Globe Works Industrial Estate
GRAYS RM17 167 P4
Gloucester Primary School
PECK SE15 19 L10
PECK SE15 159 M6
Glyn Technology School
EW KT17 220 C7
Goal Farm Golf Club
CHOB/PIR GU24 230 C7
Gobions JMI School
CRW RM5 104 E7
Godalming Leisure Centre
RGODL GU7 267 M10
Godolphin Infant School
SL SL1 129 J7
Godolphin & Latymer School
HMSMTH W6 156 E3
Godolphin Middle School
SL SL1 129 J8
Godwin Junior School
FSTGT E7 121 N9
Godwin Primary School
DAGW RM9 143 P2
Goffs Oak Primary School
CHESW EN7 61 J4
Goffs School
CHESW EN7 61 P5
Goldbeaters Primary School
EDGW HA8 96 A9
Golden Hinde
Educational Museum
STHWK SE1 12 G8
Golders Green Crematorium
GLDGN NW11 117 K5
Golders Green Health Centre
GLDGN NW11 117 L6
Golders Hill Health Centre
EFNCH N2 117 M4
Golders Hill School
GLDGN NW11 117 K5
Goldhawk Industrial Estate
SHB W12 156 E2
Goldings Hill Clinic
LOU IG10 82 D6
Goldsmiths College
BROCKY SE4 160 E9
DEPT SE8 160 F5
LEW SE13 161 K10
NWCR SE14 160 D7
Goldsmiths College
Sports Ground
SCUP DA14 186 A6
Goldsmiths Hall
STBT EC1A 12 E5
Goldsworth CP School
WOKN/KNAP GU21 231 P4
Goldsworth Park Health Centre
WOKN/KNAP GU21 231 M3
Goldsworth Park Trading Estate
WOKN/KNAP GU21 231 M2
Goldsworth Rd Industrial Estate
WOKN/KNAP GU21 232 A3
The Gomshall Gallery
SHGR GU5 270 E5
Gonville Primary School
THHTH CR7 202 G5
Goodinge Health Centre
HOLWY N7 5 L1
Goodmayes Retail Park
CHDH RM6 123 L5
Goodrich Junior & Infant School
EDUL SE22 181 P2
Good Shepherd RC
Primary School
BMLY BR1 183 L7
CROY/NA CR0 224 G4
The Good Shepherd RC
Primary School
SHB W12 156 C1
Goodwyn School
MLHL NW7 96 D6
Goose Green Trading Estate
EDUL SE22 159 P10
Gordonbrock Primary School
BROCKY SE4 182 F1
Gordon Hospital
WEST SW1P 17 J6
Gordon House Health Centre
WEA W13 135 H10
Gordon Infant School
IL IG1 122 G8
Gordon Primary School
ELTH/MOT SE9 162 C10
Gordons School
CHOB/PIR GU24 212 D8
Goresbrook Leisure Centre
DAGW RM9 143 N3
Gorhambury (Remains)
STALW/RED AL3 37 J5
Gorringe Park Middle School
MTCM CR4 202 B1
Gosai Cinema
WEA W13 134 G10
Gosbury Hill Health Centre
CHSGTN KT9 219 K1
Gosden House School
SHGR GU5 268 B9
Gosling Stadium
WGCW AL8 22 F7
Gospel Oak Primary School
HAMP NW3 118 B9
Gossops Green Clinic
CRAWW RH11 283 J9
Gossops Green First &
Middle School
CRAWW RH11 283 K8
Gower House School
CDALE/KGS NW9 115 P7
Grace Business Centre
MTCM CR4 202 A6
Grace Theatre at the Latchmere
BTSEA SW11 158 A8
Graduate School of Management
TOTM N17 99 N9
Grafton Primary School
BCTR RM8 123 P7
HOLWY N7 118 F8
Grahame Park Health Centre
CDALE/KGS NW9 96 B9
Grahame Park Junior &
Infant School
CDALE/KGS NW9 96 B9
Granard Business Centre
EDGW HA8 96 B7
Granard Primary School
PUT/ROE SW15 178 E2
Granby Sports Club
ELTH/MOT SE9 184 B8
Grand Avenue Primary School
BRYLDS KT5 199 P7
Grande Vitesse Industrial Centre
STHWK SE1 12 D10
Grand Union Industrial Estate
WLSDN NW10 135 N4
Grange CP School
ADL/WDHM KT15 215 K6
Grange First & Middle School
RYLN/HDSTN HA2 114 A6
Grange Infant School
CAN/RD E16 141 L5
The Grange Museum
CRICK NW2 116 C9
Grange Park Clinic
YEAD UB4 132 G6
Grange Park Preparatory School
WCHMH N21 79 J10

Grange Park Primary School *ENC/FH* EN2 79 H8
Grange Park Primary School *YEAD* UB4 132 G6
Grange Primary School *EA* W5 155 J1
STHWK SE1 19 J4
Grangewood Independent School *FSTGT* E7 142 A2
Grangewood School *RSLP* HA4 113 H3
Granton Primary School *STRHM/NOR* SW16 180 D10
Granville Road Industrial Estate *CRICK* NW2 117 J7
The Granville School *SEV* TN13 247 H9
Grasmere Primary School *STNW/STAM* N16 119 L9
Grasshoppers RFC *ISLW* TW7 154 E5
Grassroots School *HPTN* TW12 197 P1
Grasvenor Avenue Infant School *BAR* EN5 77 K10
Gravel Hill Primary School *BXLYHS* DA6 186 C1
Graveney School *TOOT* SW17 180 C9
Gravesend County Court *GVE* DA12 190 E2
Gravesend Cricket Club *GVW* DA11 190 D3
Gravesend Grammar School *GVE* DA12 190 G3
Gravesend Grammar School for Girls *GVW* DA11 190 D4
Gravesend Museum *GVW* DA11 190 E2
Gravesend & Northfleet FC *GVW* DA11 189 P2
Gravesend & North Kent Hospital *GVW* DA11 190 D2
Gravesend Rowing Club *GVE* DA12 190 F2
Gravesend Yacht Club *GVE* DA12 190 G2
Graves Yard Industrial Estate *WELL* DA16 163 K8
Grays Athletic FC *GRAYS* RM17 167 N5
Grays Business Centre *GRAYS* RM17 167 P2
Grays Convent School *GRAYS* RM17 167 N3
Grays County Court *GRAYS* RM17 167 M5
Grays Farm Primary School *STMC/STPC* BR5 207 L1
Grays Health Centre *GRAYS* RM17 167 M4
The Grays School *GRAYS* RM17 167 N2
Grazebrook Primary School *STNW/STAM* N16 119 M7
Great Bookham County Infant School *GT/LBKH* KT23 253 P2
Great Cambridge Industrial Estate *EN* EN1 80 A9
Great Chapel Street Medical Centre *SOHO/SHAV* W1D 11 J5
Greater London Authority Headquarters (City Hall) *STHWK* SE1 13 K10
Greatham Road Industrial Estate *BUSH* WD23 73 M8
Great Jubilee Wharf *WAP* E1W 140 B10
Greatness Park Cemetery *RSEV* TN14 247 L7
Great Stony School *CHONG* CM5 67 P3
Great Western Industrial Park *STHL* UB1 154 A1
Great West Trading Estate *BTFD* TW8 154 C5
Grebe House Wildlife Centre & Gardens *STALW/RED* AL3 38 A6
Greenacre School for Girls *BNSTD* SM7 221 M9
Greenacres Primary School *ELTH/MOT* SE9 184 D5
Green Business Centre *EGH* TW20 172 F7
The Green CE Primary School *TOTM* N17 119 N1
Green Dragon School *BTFD* TW8 155 K4
Green End Business Centre *RKW/CH/CXG* WD3 71 K3
Greenfield Medical Centre *CRICK* NW2 117 H8
Greenfield School *WOKS/MYFD* GU22 232 B5
Greenfields Junior School *SHB* W12 136 C9
Greenfields Primary School *OXHEY* WD19 93 K6
Greenfields Special School *MUSWH* N10 98 A9
Greenford Avenue Medical Centre *HNWL* W7 134 D7
Greenford Green Clinic *NTHLT* UB5 114 D10
Greenford High School *STHL* UB1 133 P5
Greenford Industrial Estate *GFD/PVL* UB6 134 A3
Greenford Park Cemetery *GFD/PVL* UB6 134 A7
Greenford Road Medical Centre *GFD/PVL* UB6 134 C4
Greengate Medical Centre *PLSTW* E13 141 N5
Greengrove College *STHGT/OAK* N14 98 F3
Greenheath Business Centre *BETH* E2 140 A5
Greenhill College *HRW* HA1 114 E3
Greenhill Park Medical Centre *WLSDN* NW10 136 B3
Greenhithe Health Clinic *GRH* DA9 188 G1
Greenland Pier *BERM/RHTH* SE16 160 E2
Green Lane Business Park *ELTH/MOT* SE9 184 D5
Green Lane Infant School *RGODL* GU7 267 K8
Green Lane Primary School *WPK* KT4 200 E7
Green Lanes Primary School *HAT* AL10 22 C10
Greenleaf Primary School *WALTH* E17 120 E1
Greenmead Primary School *PUT/ROE* SW15 178 E1
The Green School for Girls *ISLW* TW7 154 F6
Greenshaw High School *SUT* SM1 201 M9
Greenshields Industrial Estate *CAN/RD* E16 141 M10
CAN/RD E16 161 M1
Greenside Primary School *SHB* W12 156 D1
Greenslade Primary School *WOOL/PLUM* SE18 162 G5
Green Street Primary School *ORP* BR6 227 J3
Greenvale Primary School *SAND/SEL* CR2 224 C7
Greenway First School *BERK* HP4 33 M5
Greenway School *CSHM* HP5 50 G3
Greenwich Centre Business Park *DEPT* SE8 160 G6
Greenwich Cinema *GNWCH* SE10 161 H6
Greenwich College *GNWCH* SE10 161 H6
Greenwich Community College *WOOL/PLUM* SE18 162 E3
WOOL/PLUM SE18 162 G5
Greenwich Hospital *GNWCH* SE10 161 L4
Greenwich Industrial Estate *CHARL* SE7 161 N3
GNWCH SE10 160 G6
Greenwich Natural Health Centre *GNWCH* SE10 161 H6
Greenwich School of English *GNWCH* SE10 161 H5
Greenwich Theatre & Art Gallery *GNWCH* SE10 161 J6
Greenwich University Library *GNWCH* SE10 161 H5
Greenwood First School *MTCM* CR4 202 E3
Greenwood Park Leisure Centre *LCOL/BKTW* AL2 56 A1
Greenwood Primary School *NTHLT* UB5 114 B10
Greenwood School *WOOL/PLUM* SE18 163 H7
Greenwood Theatre *STHWK* SE1 19 H1
Green Wrythe Primary School *CAR* SM5 201 N6
Grenfell Primary School *WCHPL* E1 140 A8
Gresham College *FLST/FETLN* EC4A 12 A4
Gresham Primary School *SAND/SEL* CR2 223 N8
Gresham Way Industrial Estate *WIM/MER* SW19 179 L6
Greville Primary School *ASHTD* KT21 237 L3
The Greycoat Hospital *WEST* SW1P 17 J6
Grey Coat Hospital Upper School *WEST* SW1P 17 J4
Grey Court School *RCHPK/HAM* TW10 177 H6
Griffen Manor School *WOOL/PLUM* SE18 163 H7
Grimsdyke First & Middle School *PIN* HA5 93 N7
Grims Dyke Golf Club *PIN* HA5 93 P5
Grinling Gibbons Primary School *DEPT* SE8 160 E5
Grist Memorial Sports Club *E/WMO/HCT* KT8 198 D5
Grocers' Hall *CITYW* EC2V 12 G6
Grosvenor Hospitals *HDN* NW4 116 E3
Grove Health Centre *KENS* W8 8 F9
The Grove Health Centre *HMSMTH* W6 156 E1
Grovehill Medical Centre *HHNE* HP2 36 A2
Grove House School *WNWD* SE27 181 J5
The Grove Infant School *HARP* AL5 20 C3
The Grove Junior School *HARP* AL5 20 C3
Grovelands Business Centre *HHNE* HP2 36 D4
Grovelands Priory Hospital *STHGT/OAK* N14 98 F2
Grovelands School *WOT/HER* KT12 197 J6
Grove Medical Centre *DEPT* SE8 160 D3
The Grove Medical Centre *ARCH* N19 118 D7
Grove Park Industrial Estate *CDALE/KGS* NW9 116 A2
Grove Park Primary School *CHSWK* W4 155 P5
Grove Park School *CDALE/KGS* NW9 115 P2
Grove Primary School *CHDH* RM6 123 L3
Grove Road Primary School *HSLW* TW3 153 P10
The Groves Medical Centre *NWMAL* KT3 200 B3
Grove Vale Primary School *EDUL* SE22 159 N10
Grove Village Medical Centre *EBED/NFELT* TW14 174 F4
Grundy Park Leisure Centre *CHES/WCR* EN8 62 D6
The Gryphon Industrial Park *STALW/RED* AL3 38 E2
Guardian Angels RC Primary School *BOW* E3 140 D6
Guardian Business Centre *HARH* RM3 105 L8
Guardian Newspapers *POP/IOD* E14 160 G1
Guards' Chapel & Museum *WHALL* SW1A 17 J2
Guildford Castle *GU* GU1 268 A2
Guildford Cathedral *GUW* GU2 249 N10
Guildford College of Further & Higher Education *GU* GU1 250 A9
Guildford County School *GUW* GU2 267 N2
Guildford Crematorium *RGODL* GU7 267 N9
Guildford Golf Club *GU* GU1 250 F10
Guildford Grove Primary School *GUW* GU2 249 K10
Guildford High School *GU* GU1 250 B10
Guildford Hockey & Cricket Club *GU* GU1 249 P10
Guildford House Gallery *GU* GU1 268 A2
Guildford Industrial Estate *GUW* GU2 249 M9
Guildford Lido *GU* GU1 250 A9
Guildford Museum *GU* GU1 268 A2
The Guildford Nuffield Hospital *GUW* GU2 249 K10
Guildford Rowing Club *GU* GU1 268 A3
Guildford Spectrum *GU* GU1 250 B9
Guildford Spectrum Athletics Stadium *GU* GU1 250 B8
Guildhall School *BARB* EC2Y 12 F3
Guildhall School of Music & Drama *BARB* EC2Y 12 F4
STLK EC1Y 12 F2
Guildhall University *WCHPL* E1 13 P5
Gumley House Convent School *ISLW* TW7 154 F9
Gunnersbury Catholic School *BTFD* TW8 155 H4
Gunnersbury Park Museum *ACT* W3 155 M2
Gurnell Leisure Centre *WEA* W13 134 E5
Gurnell Middle School *WEA* W13 134 E7
Guru Gobind Singh Khalsa College *CHIG* IG7 102 C2
Guru Nanak Medical Centre *STHL* UB1 133 L10
Guru Nanak Sports Club *GVE* DA12 190 F3
Guys Hospital *STHWK* SE1 13 H10
Guys Kings & St Thomas School of Medicine *CMBW* SE5 159 K8
Gwyn Jones Primary School *WAN* E11 121 J5
GX Superbowl *EHAM* E6 142 D7
Gypsy Moth IV *GNWCH* SE10 161 H5
Haberdashers' Askes's Boys' School *BORE* WD6 74 G7
Haberdashers' Aske's Girls' School *BORE* WD6 74 G8
Haberdashers Askes Hatcham College *NWCR* SE14 160 D7
Haberdashers' Hall *CITYW* EC2V 12 F5
Haberdashers RUFC *BORE* WD6 75 L6
Hackbridge Primary School *WLGTN* SM6 202 B8
Hackney Business Centre *HACK* E8 140 A1
Hackney City Farm *BETH* E2 7 N8
Hackney Community College *CLPT* E5 120 A8
IS N1 7 J8
Hackney Empire Variety Theatre *HACK* E8 140 A1
Hackney Free & Parochial CE School *HOM* E9 140 B1
Hackney Hospital *HOM* E9 120 D10
The Hackney Museum *HOM* E9 140 B3
Hackney Sports Centre *HOM* E9 120 F9
Hacton JMI School *HCH* RM12 125 M9
Hadley Wood Golf Club *EBAR* EN4 77 P5
Hadley Wood Primary School *EBAR* EN4 77 M4
The Haelan Clinic *CEND/HSY/T* N8 118 E4
Haggerston School *BETH* E2 7 M7
Haggerston Swimming Pool *BETH* E2 7 M6
Hague Primary School *BETH* E2 140 A6
Haileybury College *HERT/BAY* SG13 26 C9
Haileybury College Track *HERT/BAY* SG13 26 C9
Hailey Hall Special School *HOD* EN11 26 E9
Hailey Road Business Park *ERITHM* DA18 164 B1
Haimo Primary School *ELTH/MOT* SE9 184 A1
Hainault Forest Country Park *CHIG* IG7 103 N4
Hainault Forest Golf Club *CHIG* IG7 103 N7
Hainault Forest High School *CHIG* IG7 103 K6
Hainault Industrial Estate *BARK/HLT* IG6 103 M6
Hakim Qureshi Clinic *NWDGN* UB2 153 M2
The Hale Clinic *REGST* W1B 10 F2
Half Moon Theatre *WCHPL* E1 140 C6
Haling Manor High School *CROY/NA* CR0 223 J4
Halley Primary School *POP/IOD* E14 140 D7
Hallfield Clinic *BAY/PAD* W2 9 J6
Hallfield Junior & Infant School *BAY/PAD* W2 9 H6
Halliford Health Clinic *SHPTN* TW17 196 F4
Halliford School *SHPTN* TW17 196 D7
The Hall Junior School *HAMP* NW3 3 M2
Hallmark Trading Estate *WBLY* HA9 115 P9
Hall Mead School *UPMR* RM14 126 C5
Hall Place *BXLY* DA5 186 D2
Halls Business Centre *HYS/HAR* UB3 153 H2
Hall School Wimbledon *PUT/ROE* SW15 178 D6
The Hall Senior School *HAMP* NW3 3 M2
Hallsville Primary School *CAN/RD* E16 141 M8
Halstead Place School *RSEV* TN14 227 P8
Halstead Preparatory School *WOKN/KNAP* GU21 232 C1
Halstead Primary School *RSEV* TN14 228 A8
Halstow Primary School *GNWCH* SE10 161 L4
Hambrough Primary School *STHL* UB1 133 M10
Hamer Indoor Market *BOW* E3 140 E4
Ham Health Clinic *RCHPK/HAM* TW10 177 H6
Ham House (NT) *RCHPK/HAM* TW10 177 H4
Hamilton Road Industrial Estate *WNWD* SE27 181 L7
Hamlet International Industrial Estate *ERITH* DA8 164 E4
Hamm Court *WEY* KT13 196 A10
Hammersmith Apollo *HMSMTH* W6 156 F4
Hammersmith Cemetery *HMSMTH* W6 14 A8
The Hammersmith Hospitals *SHB* W12 136 D8
Hammersmith Industrial Estate *HMSMTH* W6 156 F5
Hammersmith New Cemetery *RCH/KEW* TW9 155 N8
Hammersmith Palais *HMSMTH* W6 156 F3
Hammersmith Physio & Sports Injury Clinic *HMSMTH* W6 156 F3
Hammersmith & West London College *WKENS* W14 14 B5
WKENS W14 156 G3
The Hammond Junior Mixed Infant School *HHNE* HP2 36 A2
Hampden Gurney School *MBLAR* W1H 9 P5
Ham & Petersham Cricket Club *RCHPK/HAM* TW10 177 J7
The Hampshire School (Knightsbridge) *SKENS* SW7 15 N2
The Hampshire School *BAY/PAD* W2 9 H7
Hampstead Cricket Club *KIL/WHAMP* NW6 117 L10
Hampstead Golf Club *EFNCH* N2 117 M5
Hampstead Medical Centre *HAMP* NW3 117 M9
Hampstead Parochial CE School *HAMP* NW3 117 M9
Hampstead School *CRICK* NW2 117 H9
Hampstead School of English *KIL/WHAMP* NW6 117 K9
Hampton Cemetery *HPTN* TW12 175 P10
Hampton Community College *HPTN* TW12 175 P8
Hampton Court Palace *E/WMO/HCT* KT8 198 E3
Hampton Farm Industrial Estate *FELT* TW13 175 M6
Hampton FC *HPTN* TW12 198 A1
Hampton Hill Junior School *HPTN* TW12 176 B8
Hampton Infant School *HPTN* TW12 175 N10
Hampton Junior School *HPTN* TW12 197 P1
The Hampton Medical Centre *HPTN* TW12 175 P10
Hampton Road Industrial Park *CROY/NA* CR0 203 K6
Hampton School *HPTN* TW12 175 P8
Hampton Swimming Baths *HPTN* TW12 176 B10
Hampton Wick Infants School *KUT* KT1 177 H10
Hamsey Green County Junior School *WARL* CR6 242 A2
Hamsey Green Infant School *WARL* CR6 242 A2
Handsworth Health Clinic *CHING* E4 101 J7
Handsworth Primary School *CHING* E4 101 J7
Hanover Primary School *IS* N1 6 D7
Hanover Trading Estate *HOLWY* N7 118 F10
Hanover West Industrial Estate *WLSDN* NW10 135 P5
Hanworth Business Park *CHERT* KT16 195 J8
Hanworth Trading Estate *FELT* TW13 175 M6
Happy Valley Golf Club *CTHM* CR3 241 J9
Happy Valley Industrial Estate *KGLGY* WD4 54 C4
Harbinger Primary School *POP/IOD* E14 160 F3
Harborough School *ARCH* N19 118 E7
Harefield Cricket Club *DEN/HRF* UB9 91 N10
Harefield Health Centre *DEN/HRF* UB9 91 M9
Harefield Hospital *DEN/HRF* UB9 91 M9
Harefield Infant School *DEN/HRF* UB9 91 L9
Harefield Junior School *DEN/HRF* UB9 91 M9
Harefield Road Industrial Estate *RKW/CH/CXG* WD3 91 P5
Harenc School *SCUP* DA14 185 M8
Haresfoot School *BERK* HP4 33 N8
Haresfoot Senior School *BERK* HP4 34 D3
Hare Street Junior School *HLWW/ROY* CM19 46 F1
Harewood Down Golf Club *CSTG* HP8 69 N8
Hargrave Park Primary School *ARCH* N19 118 D7
Haringey Arts Council *ED* N9 99 P3
Haringey Community Health Clinic *SEVS/STOTM* N15 119 N2
Haringey Health Care *SEVS/STOTM* N15 119 N2
Haringey Magistrates Court *HGT* N6 118 B4
Harkness Industrial Estate *BORE* WD6 75 M8
Harland Primary School *WIM/MER* SW19 201 M2
Harlequin Shopping Centre *WAT* WD17 73 K8
Harlesden Primary School *WLSDN* NW10 136 B4
Harley Medical Centre *CAVSQ/HST* W1G 10 E5
The Harley Medical Centre *CANST* EC4R 12 F7
Harley Street Clinic *CAVSQ/HST* W1G 10 E4
The Harley Street Clinic *CAVSQ/HST* W1G 10 E3
Harlington Community School *HYS/HAR* UB3 152 E3
Harlowbury Primary School *HLWE* CM17 29 N7
Harlow Business Park *HLWW/ROY* CM19 46 B1
Harlow College *HLW* CM20 29 H10
HLW CM20 46 F1
Harlow Museum *HLWS* CM18 46 F2
Harlow RFC *HLW* CM20 28 E9
Harlow Sports Centre *HLW* CM20 28 F9
Harlyn Primary School *PIN* HA5 113 J1
Harold Court Primary School *HARH* RM3 105 P8
The Harold Macmillan Medical Centre *HRW* HA1 114 C5
Harold Wood Clinic *HARH* RM3 105 N10
Harold Wood JMI School *HARH* RM3 125 P1
Harp Business Centre *CRICK* NW2 116 D7
Harpenden Common Golf Club *HARP* AL5 20 A5
Harpenden Memorial Hospital *HARP* AL5 20 A1
Harperbury Hospital *RAD* WD7 57 H7
Harpley School *WCHPL* E1 140 B6
Harrington Hill Primary School *CLPT* E5 120 A6
Harris City Technology College *NRWD* SE19 203 N1
Harrodian School *BARN* SW13 156 C6
Harrods Store *CHEL* SW3 16 A3
Harrovian Business Village *HRW* HA1 114 C5
Harrow Arts Centre *PIN* HA5 94 A8
Harrow Borough FC *RYLN/HDSTN* HA2 113 P9
Harrow College *HRW* HA1 114 D5
Harrow Cricket Club *HRW* HA1 114 D9
Harrow Crown Courts *HRW* HA1 114 C1
Harrow Heritage Museum *RYLN/HDSTN* HA2 114 B1
Harrow High School *HRW* HA1 114 F4

Harrow Magistrates Court
HRW HA1 ... 114 E2
Harrow RFC
STAN HA7 ... 94 G4
Harrow Road Health Centre
BAY/PAD W2 ... 8 F3
Harrow School
HRW HA1 ... 114 D6
Harrow Superbowl
RYLN/HDSTN HA2 ... 114 A3
Harrow Town Cricket Club
RYLN/HDSTN HA2 ... 113 P6
Harrow Weald Cemetery
KTN/HRWW/W HA3 ... 94 D7
Harry Gosling Primary School
WCHPL E1 ... 13 P6
Hartley Primary School
EHAM E6 ... 142 B3
HART DA3 ... 211 K5
Hartsbourne Golf & Country Club
BUSH WD23 ... 94 B3
Hartsbourne JMI School
BUSH WD23 ... 94 C3
Hartspring Industrial Park
GSTN WD25 ... 73 P6
Hartspring Sports Centre
BUSH WD23 ... 73 P6
The Hartswood Clinic
RBRW/HUT CM13 ... 106 G7
Hartswood Golf Club
BRW CM14 ... 107 K5
Harvey Centre
HLW CM20 ... 46 G1
Harvey Road Primary School
RKW/CH/CXG WD3 ... 72 B10
Harvington School
EA W5 ... 135 H8
Haselrigge School
CLAP SW4 ... 158 E10
Haseltine Primary School
CAT SE6 ... 182 E7
Haslemere Business Centre
EN EN1 ... 80 A8
Haslemere Industrial Estate
EBED/NFELT TW14 ... 175 H1
HLWW/ROY CM19 ... 46 D2
WAND/EARL SW18 ... 179 L5
WGCE AL7 ... 23 J4
Haslemere Primary School
MTCM CR4 ... 201 N2
Haslewood Junior School
HOD EN11 ... 44 F2
Hasmonean High School
HDN NW4 ... 96 G10
MLHL NW7 ... 96 D9
Hasmonean Primary School
HDN NW4 ... 116 G3
Haste Hill Golf Club
NTHWD HA6 ... 92 F10
Hastings Clinic
BRXS/STRHM SW2 ... 180 G1
Hastingwood Business Centre
HLWE CM17 ... 47 M3
Hastingwood Trading Estate
UED N18 ... 100 D7
Hatcham Mews Business Centre
NWCR SE14 ... 160 C6
Hatch End High School
KTN/HRWW/W HA3 ... 94 A8
Hatfield Business Park
HAT AL10 ... 40 A1
HAT AL10 ... 40 B3
Hatfield House
BRKMPK AL9 ... 40 G4
Hatfield Leisure Centre
HAT AL10 ... 40 E6
Hatfield London Country Club
BRKMPK AL9 ... 42 A5
Hatfield Swim Centre
HAT AL10 ... 40 D3
Hatton School
REDBR IG4 ... 122 A1
Havering College
HARH RM3 ... 105 N5
Havelock Primary School
NWDGN UB2 ... 153 N2
Havenbury Industrial Estate
DORK RH4 ... 272 F1
Haven Green Clinic
EA W5 ... 135 J8
Havering College of Further & Higher Education
EMPK RM11 ... 125 J5
EMPK RM11 ... 125 M2
Havering Country Park
ABR/ST RM4 ... 104 E5
Havering Court Nursing Home
ROM RM1 ... 104 F6
Havering Cricket Club
ABR/ST RM4 ... 84 G7
Havering Hospitals
HARH RM3 ... 105 M9
Havering Magistrates Court
ROM RM1 ... 124 F2
Havering Sixth Form College
EMPK RM11 ... 125 N6
Haverstock School
CAMTN NW1 ... 4 C2
Hawes Down Clinic
WWKM BR4 ... 205 J9
Hawes Down primary School
WWKM BR4 ... 205 J8
Hawkedale GM School
SUN TW16 ... 196 G3
Hawkins Clinic
EW KT17 ... 238 F1
PUT/ROE SW15 ... 156 G10
RYNPK SW20 ... 200 C1
Hawksmoor Primary School
THMD SE28 ... 143 L9
Hawkswood School & Centre
CHING E4 ... 81 H9
Hawley Infant School
CAMTN NW1 ... 4 F4
Hawridge & Cholesbury CE Combined School
CSHM HP5 ... 32 D7
The Hawthorns Pre-Prep School
REDH RH1 ... 259 J7
The Hawth Theatre, Cinema & Conference Complex
CRAWE RH10 ... 284 A8
Haydon School
PIN HA5 ... 112 G1
Hayes Bridge Middle School
NWDGN UB2 ... 153 M1
Hayes Bridge Retail Park
HYS/HAR UB3 ... 133 K9
Hayes Cricket Club
HYS/HAR UB3 ... 132 G8
Hayes FC
HYS/HAR UB3 ... 132 G9
Hayes Grove Priory Hospital
HAYES BR2 ... 205 M9
The Hayes Manor School
HYS/HAR UB3 ... 132 E8
Hayes Park Junior & Infant School
YEAD UB4 ... 132 G6
Hayes Primary School
HAYES BR2 ... 205 N8
The Hayes Primary School
PUR/KEN CR8 ... 241 J2
Hayes School
HAYES BR2 ... 205 N9
Hayes Social & Sports Club
HYS/HAR UB3 ... 132 G9
Hayes Stadium
HYS/HAR UB3 ... 132 E8
Haymerle School
PECK SE15 ... 19 N10
Hays Galleria
STHWK SE1 ... 13 J9
Hayward Gallery
STHWK SE1 ... 11 P10
Hazelbury Primary School
ED N9 ... 99 M4
Hazeldene Medical Centre
WBLY HA9 ... 135 N1
Hazelgrove Primary School
HAT AL10 ... 40 C7
Hazelhurst School
RYNPK SW20 ... 200 G1
Hazelwick School
CRAWE RH10 ... 284 B5
Hazelwood Infant School
PLMGR N13 ... 99 J5
Hazelwood Junior School
PLMGR N13 ... 99 H5
Hazelwood School
OXTED RH8 ... 261 M7
Healy Medical Centre
CLPT E5 ... 120 A6
The Heart Hospital
CAVSQ/HST W1G ... 10 D4
Heathbrook Primary School
VX/NE SW8 ... 158 D8
Heath Business Centre
HSLW TW3 ... 154 B10
REDH RH1 ... 276 C10
Heathcote Medical Centre
KWD/TDW/WH KT20 ... 238 G8
Heathcote School
CHING E4 ... 101 K3
Heathermount School
ASC SL5 ... 192 C6
Heathfield College
HAYES BR2 ... 225 P3
Heathfield Primary School
WHTN TW2 ... 175 P4
Heathfield School (Senior)
PIN HA5 ... 113 L4
Heath House Preparatory School
BKHTH/KID SE3 ... 161 L8
Heathland School
HSLWW TW4 ... 175 N2
Heathlands Special School
STALW/RED AL3 ... 38 D3
Heathmere Primary School
PUT/ROE SW15 ... 178 D4
Heathpark Golf Club
WDR/YW UB7 ... 152 B2
Heathrow Airport
HTHAIR TW6 ... 152 A8
Heathrow Airport Central Bus & Coach Station
HTHAIR TW6 ... 152 B9
Heathrow International Trading Estate
HSLWW TW4 ... 153 J9
Heathrow Medical Centre
HYS/HAR UB3 ... 152 E4
Heathrow Primary School
WDR/YW UB7 ... 152 A5
Heathrow World Cargo Centre
HTHAIR TW6 ... 174 A1
Heathside Preparatory School
HAMP NW3 ... 117 M9
Heathside School
WEY KT13 ... 216 A2
Heathway Industrial Estate
DAGE RM10 ... 124 C9
Heathway Medical Centre
DAGW RM9 ... 124 A9
Heavers Farm Primary School
SNWD SE25 ... 203 N5
Heber Primary School
EDUL SE22 ... 181 N2
Heckford Street Business Centre
WAP E1W ... 140 C9
Hedges & Butler Estate
SRTFD E15 ... 141 H4
Hedgewood School
YEAD UB4 ... 132 F5
Hedley Walter High School
BRWN CM15 ... 107 H1
Helena Road Clinic
WLSDN NW10 ... 116 E9
Heliport Industrial Estate
BTSEA SW11 ... 157 N8
Hellenic College of London
KTBR SW1X ... 16 A4
Helston Court Business Centre
WIM/MER SW19 ... 178 E8
Hemel Hempstead (Camelot) RFC
HHW HP1 ... 35 J8
Hemel Hempstead General Hospital
HHNE HP2 ... 35 N7
Hemel Hempstead RLFC
HHNE HP2 ... 36 A3
Hemel Hempstead School
HHW HP1 ... 35 M7
Hemel Hempstead Town Cricket Club
HHS/BOV HP3 ... 35 M8
Hemel Hempstead United FC
HHNE HP2 ... 36 C6
Hemel Hempsted Silver Blades Ice Rink
HHS/BOV HP3 ... 36 A7
Henderson Hospital
BELMT SM2 ... 221 K5
Hendon Cemetery
HDN NW4 ... 96 G9
Hendon College
CDALE/KGS NW9 ... 96 C9
Hendon Crematorium
HDN NW4 ... 96 G8
Hendon FC
CRICK NW2 ... 116 G7
Hendon Golf Club
HDN NW4 ... 96 F8
Hendon Preparatory School
HDN NW4 ... 116 G1
Hendon School
HDN NW4 ... 116 G3
Hendon Secretarial College
HDN NW4 ... 116 E3
Hendon Youth Sports Centre
CRICK NW2 ... 116 G5
Henry Cavendish Primary School
BAL SW12 ... 180 D4
Henry Compton School
FUL/PGN SW6 ... 156 G7
Henry Fawcett Primary School
LBTH SE11 ... 18 A9
Henry Green Primary School
BCTR RM8 ... 123 N6
Henry Maynard Infant School
WALTH E17 ... 121 H3
Henry Maynard Junior School
WALTH E17 ... 121 H3
Henwick Primary School
ELTH/MOT SE9 ... 162 A9
Herbert Morrison Primary School
VX/NE SW8 ... 158 F6
The Hereward County School
LOU IG10 ... 82 F5
Hereward House School
HAMP NW3 ... 3 N2
Herington House School
RBRW/HUT CM13 ... 87 N10
Heritage Close Shopping Centre
STALW/RED AL3 ... 38 B6
Heritage House Special School
CSHM HP5 ... 51 J6
Her Majestys' Theatre
STJS SW1Y ... 11 K9
Hermitage County First School
WOKN/KNAP GU21 ... 231 K5
Hermitage Primary School
UX/CGN UB8 ... 131 N2
WAP E1W ... 13 N9
The Hermitage School
WOKN/KNAP GU21 ... 231 K5
Hermitage Stairs
WAP E1W ... 13 N10
Herne Hill School
HNHL SE24 ... 181 K1
Heron Industrial Estate
SRTFD E15 ... 140 G4
Heronsgate Primary School
THMD SE28 ... 162 G2
Heron Trading Estate
ACT W3 ... 135 N7
Herringham Primary School
CDH/CHF RM16 ... 168 E2
Herschel Grammar School
SL SL1 ... 129 H8
The Herschel Medical Centre
SL SL1 ... 149 L2
Hersham Trading Estate
WOT/HER KT12 ... 197 M9
Hertford County Hospital
HERT/WAS SG14 ... 25 J5
Hertford Museum
HERT/WAS SG14 ... 25 L5
Hertford Regional College
WARE SG12 ... 26 C3
Hertford St Andrew Primary School
HERT/WAS SG14 ... 24 G4
Hertfordshire Business Centre
LCOL/BKTW AL2 ... 57 J2
Hertfordshire Country Club
WGCE AL7 ... 22 G8
Hertfordshire County Constabulary
HHW HP1 ... 35 M6
Hertford Town FC
HERT/WAS SG14 ... 25 J6
Hertsmere Jewish Primary School
RAD WD7 ... 75 H4
Heston Community School
HEST TW5 ... 153 P6
Heston Industrial Mall
HEST TW5 ... 153 N6
Heston Infant School
HEST TW5 ... 153 P6
Heston Junior School
HEST TW5 ... 153 P5
Heston Park Cricket Club
HEST TW5 ... 153 N5
Heston Swimming Baths
HEST TW5 ... 153 N5
Hextable Comprehensive School
SWLY BR8 ... 208 G1
Hextable Primary School
SWLY BR8 ... 186 G9
HGS Institute Centre
GLDGN NW11 ... 117 L3
Higgs Industrial Estate
BRXN/ST SW9 ... 159 J9
Highams Lodge Business Centre
WALTH E17 ... 120 C1
Highams Park School
CHING E4 ... 101 J7
High Beech CE Primary School
LOU IG10 ... 81 M5
High Beeches Primary School
HARP AL5 ... 20 C3
High Beech Golf Club
LOU IG10 ... 81 N3
Highbridge Industrial Estate
DEN/HRF UB9 ... 131 M1
Highbridge Retail Park
WAB EN9 ... 62 G10
Highbury Corner Magistrates Court
HBRY N5 ... 6 B1
Highbury Fields School
HBRY N5 ... 119 J10
Highbury Grove School
HBRY N5 ... 119 K10
Highbury Park Clinic
HBRY N5 ... 119 J8
Highbury Quadrant Primary School
HBRY N5 ... 119 K9
Highclere Farm Country Touring Park
BEAC HP9 ... 89 K5
High Commission of Angola
MYFR/PKLN W1K ... 10 D7
High Commission of Antigua & Barbuda
MHST W1U ... 10 C5
High Commission of Bahamas
MYFR/PICC W1J ... 10 D9
High Commission of Bangladesh
SKENS SW7 ... 15 K3
High Commission of Barbados
FITZ W1T ... 11 J5
High Commission of Belize
CAVSQ/HST W1G ... 10 E5
High Commission of Botswana
OXSTW W1C ... 10 E6
High Commission of Brunei
BAY/PAD W2 ... 9 M5
KTBR SW1X ... 16 C3
High Commission of Cyprus
CONDST W1S ... 10 F6
MYFR/PKLN W1K ... 10 C7
High Commission of Dominica
ECT SW5 ... 15 H6
High Commission of Fiji
SKENS SW7 ... 15 J2
High Commission of Guyana
NTGHL W11 ... 8 G8
High Commission of Jamaica
SKENS SW7 ... 15 L2
High Commission of Kenya
CAVSQ/HST W1G ... 10 E3
High Commission of Lesotho
KTBR SW1X ... 16 C3
High Commission of Malawi
MYFR/PKLN W1K ... 10 E7
High Commission of Malaysia
KTBR SW1X ... 16 D2
MBLAR W1H ... 10 A5
High Commission of Malta
MYFR/PICC W1J ... 11 H8
High Commission of Mauritius
SKENS SW7 ... 15 K4
High Commission of Namibia
CAVSQ/HST W1G ... 10 F4
High Commission of New Zealand
STJS SW1Y ... 11 J9
High Commission of Nigeria
CHCR WC2N ... 11 L9
EMB EC4Y ... 12 B6
High Commission of Pakistan
KTBR SW1X ... 16 B3
High Commission of Papua New Guinea
STJS SW1Y ... 11 J9
High Commission of St Vincent & The Grenadines
KENS W8 ... 15 H2
High Commission of Seychelles
MBLAR W1H ... 10 B3
High Commission of Sierra Leone
OXSTW W1C ... 10 G5
High Commission of Singapore
KTBR SW1X ... 16 B2
KTBR SW1X ... 16 C4
STJS SW1Y ... 11 J9
WEST SW1P ... 17 H5
High Commission of South Africa
CHCR WC2N ... 11 K9
High Commission of Sri Lanka
BAY/PAD W2 ... 9 M7
High Commission of Swaziland
WESTW SW1E ... 16 G3
High Commission of the Gambia
KENS W8 ... 15 H2
High Commission of the Maldives
MHST W1U ... 10 C3
High Commission of Tonga
MBLAR W1H ... 9 P4
High Commission of Trinidad & Tobago
KTBR SW1X ... 16 C3
High Commission of Uganda
STJS SW1Y ... 11 K9
High Commission of Zambia
SKENS SW7 ... 15 J2
High Commission of Zimbabwe
CHCR WC2N ... 11 L8
High Cross Centre
SEVS/STOTM N15 ... 119 P2
High Elms Country Park
ORP BR6 ... 226 F4
High Elms Golf Club
ORP BR6 ... 226 F4
Highfield Infant School
HAYES BR2 ... 205 K4
Highfield Junior School
HAYES BR2 ... 205 K4
Highfield Primary School
WCHMH N21 ... 99 J2
Highfield School
HGDN/ICK UB10 ... 132 C5
WAND/EARL SW18 ... 179 P3
High Firs Primary School
SWLY BR8 ... 208 G4
Highgate Cemetery
HGT N6 ... 118 B6
Highgate Golf Club
HGT N6 ... 117 P4
Highgate Junior School
HGT N6 ... 118 A5
Highgate Pre-Preparatory School
HGT N6 ... 118 A5
Highgate Primary School
HGT N6 ... 118 A4
Highgate Private Hospital
HGT N6 ... 118 A4
Highgate School
HGT N6 ... 118 A5
Highgate Wood School
CEND/HSY/T N8 ... 118 D3
Highgrove Swimming Pool
RSLP HA4 ... 113 H5
Highlands Junior & Infant School
IL IG1 ... 122 C6
Highlands Primary School
IL IG1 ... 122 C6
High March School
BEAC HP9 ... 88 C7
High Road Swimming Baths
IL IG1 ... 122 G7
Highshore School
PECK SE15 ... 159 N7
High Street Business Park
CHES/WCR EN8 ... 62 D8
High View Primary School
BTSEA SW11 ... 157 N10
Highview Primary School
WLGTN SM6 ... 222 F2
The Highway Primary School
ORP BR6 ... 227 M2
The Highway Trading Centre
WAP E1W ... 140 C9
High Wood Hospital
BRWN CM15 ... 106 G2
Highwood Primary School
BUSH WD23 ... 73 M5
Hillbrook Primary School
TOOT SW17 ... 180 A7
Hillcroft College
SURB KT6 ... 199 K6
Hillcroft Primary School
CTHM CR3 ... 241 M9
Hilldene Primary School
HARH RM3 ... 105 K7
Hille Business Centre
WATN WD24 ... 73 J5
Hill Farm Industrial Estate
GSTN WD25 ... 54 G9
Hill Fort
STALE/WH AL4 ... 21 L4
Hillgrove Business Park
WAB EN9 ... 45 H8
Hill House International School
KTBR SW1X ... 16 A4
Hill House School
CHEL SW3 ... 15 P9
Hillingdon Borough FC
RSLP HA4 ... 112 C3
Hillingdon Golf Club
HGDN/ICK UB10 ... 132 A4
Hillingdon Hospital
UX/CGN UB8 ... 132 A6
Hillingdon Primary School
UX/CGN UB8 ... 132 B5
Hill Mead Infant School
HNHL SE24 ... 159 J10
Hillmead Primary School
BRXN/ST SW9 ... 159 J10
Hill School
BH/WHM TN16 ... 244 E9
Hills Grove Primary School
WELL DA16 ... 163 M6
Hillside Primary School
NTHWD HA6 ... 93 H8
Hillside School
BORE WD6 ... 75 P8
Hill Top First School
WDSR SL4 ... 148 D9
Hilly Fields Medical Centre
BROCKY SE4 ... 182 F1
The Hiltongrove Business Centre
WALTH E17 ... 120 F2
Hinchley Wood School
ESH/CLAY KT10 ... 198 F9
Hinley Clinic
LBTH SE11 ... 18 C6
Hispaniola
WHALL SW1A ... 11 M10
Hitherfield Primary School
STRHM/NOR SW16 ... 181 H5
Hither Green Cemetery
CAT SE6 ... 183 L5
Hither Green Primary School
LEW SE13 ... 183 J2
HM Prison
CLAP SW4 ... 180 F2
HOLWY N7 ... 5 N2
HOLWY N7 ... 118 F9
SHB W12 ... 136 D8
WAND/EARL SW18 ... 179 N2
HMS Belfast
STHWK SE1 ... 13 K9
HMS President
EMB EC4Y ... 12 B7
HM Young Offender Institution
FELT TW13 ... 174 E6
Hobbayne First & Middle School
HNWL W7 ... 134 E8
Hobbayne Primary School
HNWL W7 ... 134 D8
Hobbs Hill Wood Primary School
HHS/BOV HP3 ... 36 C8
Hobletts Manor Primary School
HHNE HP2 ... 36 A5
Hockley Industrial Centre
REDH RH1 ... 276 A1
Hoddesdon Health Centre
HOD EN11 ... 44 F4
Hoddesdon Industrial Estate
HOD EN11 ... 45 H2
Hoddesdon Lawn Tennis Club
HOD EN11 ... 44 E3
Hoddesdon St Pauls Infant School
HOD EN11 ... 44 G3
Hoebridge Golf Centre
WOKS/MYFD GU22 ... 232 F5
Hoe Bridge School
WOKS/MYFD GU22 ... 232 E5
Hogan Business Centre
WOKN/KNAP GU21 ... 232 B3
Hogarth Business Park
CHSWK W4 ... 156 B5
Hogarth Industrial Estate
WLSDN NW10 ... 136 D6
Hogarth Primary School
BRWN CM15 ... 107 L4
CHSWK W4 ... 156 B4
Hogarth's House
CHSWK W4 ... 156 A5
Holbeach Primary School
CAT SE6 ... 182 F3
Holborn College
WKENS W14 ... 14 B9
Holborn Medical Centre
BMSBY WC1N ... 11 N2
Holborn Town Hall
HHOL WC1V ... 11 M5
Holdbrook Primary School
CHES/WCR EN8 ... 62 E10
Holland & Holland Shooting School
DEN/HRF UB9 ... 92 B10
Holland House
KENS W8 ... 14 D2
Holland House School
EDGW HA8 ... 95 M5
Holland Park School
KENS W8 ... 8 D10
Holland Park Theatre
KENS W8 ... 14 D2
Holland Street Clinic
KENS W8 ... 14 F2
Hollickwood JMI School
MUSWH N10 ... 98 C8
Holloway School
HOLWY N7 ... 118 E10

Hollybush Business Centre *CRAWE* RH10 284 G1
Hollybush Primary School *HERT/WAS* SG14 25 H5
Hollydale Primary School *PECK* SE15 160 B8
The Hollyfield School *SURB* KT6 199 K5
Holly House Private Hospital *BKHH* IG9 101 N3
Holly Industrial Park *WATN* WD24 73 K5
Hollymount Primary School *RYNPK* SW20 200 F1
Holly Park JMI School *FBAR/BDGN* N11 98 B5
Hollytrees Junior School *BRW* CM14 106 G5
Holly Trees Primary School *BRW* CM14 107 H5
Hollywood Bowl *CRAWE* RH10 283 N6
Holmers First School *WDSR* SL4 148 C7
Holmesdale School *REIG* RH2 257 L8
The Holme *CAMTN* NW1 4 B10
Holmethorpe Industrial Estate *REDH* RH1 258 C7
Holmleigh Primary School *STNW/STAM* N16 119 N6
Holmshill School *BORE* WD6 75 P6
Holtsmere End Junior & Infant School *HHNE* HP2 36 C1
Holwell Junior & Infant School *WGCE* AL7 23 J6
Holy Cross Catholic Primary School *HLWS* CM18 47 K3
Holy Cross Convent School *CFSP/GDCR* SL9 90 A9
NWMAL KT3 200 A4
Holy Cross Preparatory School *KUTN/CMB* KT2 177 P10
Holy Cross RC Primary School *CAT* SE6 183 H4
SOCK/AV RM15 146 G9
Holy Family College *WALTH* E17 121 H1
Holy Family RC Primary School *ADL/WDHM* KT15 215 K2
ELTH/MOT SE9 161 N10
POP/IOD E14 140 F9
Holy Family RC School *DTCH/LGLY* SL3 150 C4
Holy Family Technology College *WALTH* E17 120 G2
Holy Ghost RC Primary School *BAL* SW12 180 A3
Holy Innocents Catholic Primary School *ORP* BR6 207 J10
Holy Rood Junior School *WAT* WD17 72 E2
Holy Rood RC Infant School *WAT* WD17 72 E2
Holy Trinity CE First School *WIM/MER* SW19 179 K9
Holy Trinity CE Junior School *GU* GU1 268 C2
WLGTN SM6 222 D1
Holy Trinity CE Primary School *ASC* SL5 192 F6
BGVA SW1W 16 C5
BRXS/STRHM SW2 180 G3
CHOB/PIR GU24 212 F8
DART DA1 187 K1
EFNCH N2 117 N1
FSTH SE23 182 B5
GVE DA12 190 F3
HAMP NW3 3 K2
NTHWD HA6 92 D7
RCHPK/HAM TW10 155 M10
The Holy Trinity CE School *CRAWW* RH11 283 K9
Holy Trinity College *BMLY* BR1 205 P1
Holy Trinity Haverstock Hill CE Primary School *CAMTN* NW1 4 E3
Holy Trinity Primary School *CHES/WCR* EN8 62 C8
HACK E8 7 L2
Holy Trinity School *CHEL* SW3 16 B5
Holywell School *WATW* WD18 72 G10
Home Farm Industrial Estate *WARE* SG12 27 L6
Home Park Golf Club *E/WMO/HCT* KT8 199 H5
Home Park Industrial Estate *KGLGY* WD4 54 C6
Homerswood Junior & Infant School *WGCW* AL8 22 G1
Homerton Hospital *CLPT* E5 120 C10
Homerton House School *HOM* E9 120 B10
Homewood Independent School *LCOL/BKTW* AL2 56 A4
Homoeopathic Health Centre *PLSTW* E13 141 M6
The Homoeopathic Health Centre *MLHL* NW7 96 C6
Honeypot Business Centre *STAN* HA7 95 K9
Honeypot Lane Centre *STAN* HA7 95 J9
Honeypot Medical Centre *STAN* HA7 95 K10
Honeywell Primary School *BTSEA* SW11 180 A2
Hong Kong & Shanghai Sports Club *BECK* BR3 182 D9
Honilands Primary School *EN* EN1 80 A2
Honor Oak Crematorium *FSTH* SE23 182 C1
Honor Oak Gallery *FSTH* SE23 182 C2
Honor Oak Health Centre *BROCKY* SE4 160 D10
Honourable Artillery Company HQ *STLK* EC1Y 12 G2
Hook Lane Primary School *WELL* DA16 163 K9
Hook Rise South Industrial Park *CHSGTN* KT9 199 M10
Horizon Business Centre *ED* N9 100 C3
Horizon Industrial Estate *PECK* SE15 19 N10
Horizon School *STNW/STAM* N16 119 M9
Horley Anderson Sports Centre *HORL* RH6 279 P4
Horley Health Centre *HORL* RH6 280 B4
Hornchurch Clinic *EMPK* RM11 125 M6
Hornchurch Country park *HCH* RM12 145 K1
Hornchurch Sports Centre *HCH* RM12 125 K7
Hornchurch Stadium *UPMR* RM14 125 P7
Horndon Industrial Park *RBRW/HUT* CM13 127 N4
The Horniman Museum & Gardens *FSTH* SE23 182 A4
Horniman Primary School *FSTH* SE23 182 A4
Horn Park Primary School *LEE/GVPK* SE12 183 N3
Hornsby House School *BAL* SW12 180 B4
Horns Cross *GRH* DA9 188 E2
Hornsey Central Hospital *CEND/HSY/T* N8 118 E3
Hornsey County School *FSBYPK* N4 119 J3
Hornsey Rise Health Centre *ARCH* N19 118 E5
Hornsey School for Girls *CEND/HSY/T* N8 118 G3
Horseferry Road Magistrates Court *WEST* SW1P 17 K4
Horse Guards Parade *WHALL* SW1A 11 K10
Horsell CE Junior School *WOKN/KNAP* GU21 231 P2
Horsenden Hill Golf Club *GFD/PVL* UB6 134 G1
Horsenden Primary School *GFD/PVL* UB6 134 D1
Horseshoe Business Park *LCOL/BKTW* AL2 56 A6
Horsley Sports Club *EHSLY* KT24 252 G3
Horton Country Park *HOR/WEW* KT19 219 M5
Horton Hospital *HOR/WEW* KT19 219 P7
Horton Industrial Park *WDR/YW* UB7 132 A10
Horton Kirby CE Primary School *EYN* DA4 210 B3
Horton Kirby Trading Estate *EYN* DA4 210 B2
Horton Park Golf & Country Club *HOR/WEW* KT19 219 P4
Horton Trading Estate *DTCH/LGLY* SL3 150 E9
Hortus Cemetery *NWDGN* UB2 153 N1
Hospital of St John & St Elizabeth *STJWD* NW8 3 L8
Hotham Primary School *PUT/ROE* SW15 156 G10
Hot Shots Ten Pin Bowling *HHS/BOV* HP3 36 A7
Hotspur Industrial Estate *TOTM* N17 100 A7
Houndsfield Primary School *ED* N9 99 P1
Hounslow Business Park *HSLW* TW3 153 P10
Hounslow Cemetery *HSLWW* TW4 175 N3
Hounslow College Independent School *FELT* TW13 175 L7
Hounslow Cricket Club *HSLW* TW3 153 N8
Hounslow Heath Golf Club *HSLWW* TW4 175 L1
Hounslow Heath Infant School *HSLWW* TW4 153 M9
Hounslow Heath Junior School *HSLWW* TW4 153 M9
Hounslow Manor School *HSLW* TW3 154 A9
Hounslow & Spelthorne Community & Mental Health NHS Trust *STA* TW18 173 K8
Hounslow Town Primary School *HSLW* TW3 154 B9
Household Cavalry Museum *WDSR* SL4 148 G9
House of Detention *CLKNW* EC1R 12 B1
House of St Barnabus *SOHO/SHAV* W1D 11 J6
Houses of Parliament *WEST* SW1P 17 M2
Houston Business Park *YEAD* UB4 133 K10
Howard Business Park *WAB* EN9 63 J10
The Howard Centre *WGCW* AL8 22 G5
Howard Industrial Estate *CSHM* HP5 51 H5
Howard of Effingham School *EHSLY* KT24 253 M3
Howard Primary School *CROY/NA* CR0 223 K1
Howe Dell Primary School *HAT* AL10 40 E4
Howland Quay *BERM/RHTH* SE16 160 C2
How Wood Primary School *LCOL/BKTW* AL2 56 B3
Hoxton Hall Community Theatre *IS* N1 7 J7
HQS Wellington (Master Mariners) *TPL/STR* WC2R 12 A8
HRH Princess Christians Hospital *WDSR* SL4 149 H7
Hubbinet Industrial Estate *ROMW/RG* RM7 124 D1
Hughesfields Primary School *DEPT* SE8 160 F5
Hugh Myddelton Primary School *CLKNW* EC1R 6 B10
The Humana Wellington Hospital *STJWD* NW8 3 M9
Humber Trading Estate *CRICK* NW2 116 E7
Hungerford Primary School *HOLWY* N7 5 K1
Huntercombe Manor Hospital *WDSR* SL4 128 B9
Hunters Hall Primary School *DAGE* RM10 124 C10
Hunter Street Health Centre *STPAN* WC1H 11 L1
Huntsman Sports Club *BKHTH/KID* SE3 161 M10
Hurlingham Business Park *FUL/PGN* SW6 157 K9
Hurlingham & Chelsea School *FUL/PGN* SW6 157 K9
Hurlingham House *FUL/PGN* SW6 157 J9
Huron College *SKENS* SW7 15 K5
Huron University *SKENS* SW7 15 M3
Hurricane Trading Centre *CDALE/KGS* NW9 96 C9
Hurst Drive Primary School *CHES/WCR* EN8 62 B10
Hurst Green School *OXTED* RH8 261 M8
Hurst Lodge School *ASC* SL5 192 A8
Hurstmere School *BFN/LL* DA15 185 L4
Hurst Park School *E/WMO/HCT* KT8 197 P3
Hurst Primary School *BXLY* DA5 185 N4
Hurtmore Golf Club *RGODL* GU7 266 E10
Hyde Heath Infant School *AMS* HP6 50 B10
The Hyde Industrial Estate *CDALE/KGS* NW9 116 C3
The Hyde School *CDALE/KGS* NW9 116 C3
Hyland Business Centre *REDH* RH1 258 A10
Hyland House School *WALTH* E17 101 J10
Hyleford Leavers Unit School *BARK/HLT* IG6 102 G10
Hyleford School *IL* IG1 123 H10
Hythe Road Industrial Estate *WLSDN* NW10 136 D6
The Hythe School *STA* TW18 172 G8
Ibstock Place School *PUT/ROE* SW15 178 B2
ICA Cinema *STJS* SW1Y 11 K10
Ichthus Primary School *CMBW* SE5 159 L6
Ickburgh School *CLPT* E5 120 A8
Ickenham Clinic *HGDN/ICK* UB10 112 D8
Ide Hill CE Aided Primary School *RSEV* TN14 263 P7
Ifield Community College *CRAWW* RH11 283 K6
Ifield First & Middle School *CRAWW* RH11 283 K7
Ifield Golf & Country Club *CRAWW* RH11 283 H7
Ifield School *GVE* DA12 190 F8
Ihlara Sport FC *HBRY* N5 119 K9
Ikra Primary School *STNW/STAM* N16 119 M9
Ilderton Primary School *BERM/RHTH* SE16 160 B5
Ilford County Court *IL* IG1 122 G7
Ilford County High School *BARK/HLT* IG6 102 F10
Ilford Golf Club *IL* IG1 122 C6
Ilford Jewish Primary School *BARK/HLT* IG6 122 G1
Ilford Medical Centre *IL* IG1 122 E8
Ilford Preparatory School *GDMY/SEVK* IG3 123 J6
Ilford Retail Park *IL* IG1 122 F7
Imber Court Trading Estate *E/WMO/HCT* KT8 198 C6
Immanuel CE Primary School *STRHM/NOR* SW16 180 F9
Immanuel College *BUSH* WD23 94 D1
Immanuel School *ROM* RM1 104 F7
Imperial Business Estate *GVW* DA11 190 C2
Imperial College *PUT/ROE* SW15 156 G8
SKENS SW7 15 L3
SKENS SW7 15 L8
Imperial College Athletic Ground *WDR/YW* UB7 152 D5
Imperial College of Science *FUL/PGN* SW6 14 E9
Imperial College of Science & Technology *SKENS* SW7 15 M2
Imperial College of Science Technology & Medicine *ASC* SL5 192 E3
SKENS SW7 15 K3
Imperial College School of Medicine *PIM* SW1V 17 J6
Imperial Retail Park *GVW* DA11 190 D2
Imperial Trading Estate *RAIN* RM13 145 K6
Imperial War Museum *STHWK* SE1 18 B4
Imperial War Museum Annexe *STHWK* SE1 18 B4
Independent Industrial Estate *WDR/YW* UB7 132 A10
India House *HOL/ALD* WC2B 11 N7
Indoor Sports Centre *STA* TW18 173 K7
Industrial Estate Annexe *RAIN* RM13 144 F8
Industrial Health Clinic *UX/CGN* UB8 131 L5
Industrial Park *TIL* RM18 169 L4
Infant College *IL* IG1 122 D7
Infant School *WOKN/KNAP* GU21 232 A2
The Infirmary Royal Hospital *CHEL* SW3 16 C8
Ingrave Johnstone CE Primary School *RBRW/HUT* CM13 107 P7
Ingrebourne Primary School *HARH* RM3 105 K5
Innellan House School *PIN* HA5 113 L1
Inner London Sessions House (Crown Court) *STHWK* SE1 18 E3
Innholders Hall *CANST* EC4R 12 F7
Innova Business Park *PEND* EN3 80 E2
Inns of Court & Chancery *TPL/STR* WC2R 12 A6
Inns of Court School of Law *GINN* WC1R 11 P3
Institut Francais *SKENS* SW7 15 L5
International Community School *CAMTN* NW1 10 C2
International Financial Centre *OBST* EC2N 13 J5
International Medical Centre *ECT* SW5 14 F6
International School of London *ACT* W3 155 M3
International Trading Estate *NWDGN* UB2 153 J2
International University *BUSH* WD23 73 N8
Invicta Industrial Estate *SRTFD* E15 141 H5
Invicta Primary School *BKHTH/KID* SE3 161 M5
Invicta Sports Club *DART* DA1 187 L1
Inwood Business Centre *HSLW* TW3 154 A10
Ironmongers Hall *STBT* EC1A 12 E4
Islamia Girls School *KIL/WHAMP* NW6 2 B5
Islamic College *WCHPL* E1 13 P5
Islamic College for Advanced Studies *WLSDN* NW10 136 E2
The Islamic Grammar School *WAND/EARL* SW18 179 J3
Island Clinic *POP/IOD* E14 161 H1
Isleworth Baths *ISLW* TW7 154 E10
Isleworth Blue CE Primary School *ISLW* TW7 154 F9
Isleworth Cemetery *ISLW* TW7 154 F8
Isleworth & Syon School for Boys *ISLW* TW7 154 D6
Isleworth Town Primary School *ISLW* TW7 154 E8
Islington Arts & Media School *FSBYPK* N4 118 G6
Islington Business Centre *IS* N1 6 E5
Islington Crematorium *EFNCH* N2 97 P9
Islington Green Medical Centre *IS* N1 6 C5
Islington Green School *IS* N1 6 D6
Islington Town Hall *IS* N1 6 C3
Ismaili Centre *SKENS* SW7 15 M5
Italia Conti Academy of Theatre Arts *BRXN/ST* SW9 158 F9
Italian Hospital *WEST* SW1P 16 G5
Iver Golf & Leisure Centre *IVER* SL0 130 E10
Iver Heath First School *IVER* SL0 130 G5
Iver Heath Health Centre *IVER* SL0 130 G4
Iver Heath Primary School *IVER* SL0 130 G4
Iver Village Infant School *IVER* SL0 131 J8
Iver Village Junior School *IVER* SL0 131 H8
Ivybridge Primary School *TWK* TW1 176 E2
Ivybridge Retail Park *ISLW* TW7 176 E1
Ivy Chimneys Primary School *EPP* CM16 65 J8
Ivydale Primary School *PECK* SE15 160 C10
Jack & Jill School *HPTN* TW12 175 P9
WHTN TW2 176 D5
Jack Lobley Primary School *TIL* RM18 168 C7
Jack Taylor School *STJWD* NW8 3 J5
Jack Tizzard School *FUL/PGN* SW6 156 G7
Jamahiriya School *CHEL* SW3 15 N9
James Allens Preparatory Girls School *HNHL* SE24 181 L1
James Dixon Primary School *PGE/AN* SE20 181 P10
James Elliman School *SL* SL1 129 K8
James Oglethorpe Primary School *UPMR* RM14 126 E7
Jamestown Mental Health Centre *HAMP* NW3 4 A3
James Wolfe Primary School *GNWCH* SE10 160 G6
Janet Adegoke Leisure Centre *SHB* W12 136 D9
The Japanese School *ACT* W3 135 M9
Japan Green Medical Centre *ACT* W3 135 N10
Jenner Health Centre *FSTH* SE23 182 D4
Jermyn Street Theatre *STJS* SW1Y 11 H8
Jerounds Junior & Infant School *HLWW/ROY* CM19 46 E4
Jessop Primary School *HNHL* SE24 159 J10
Jewel Tower *WEST* SW1P 17 L3
Jewish Community Theatre *CMBW* SE5 159 L9
The Jewish Museum *CAMTN* NW1 4 E6
FNCH N3 97 K10
Jews College London *HDN* NW4 116 G2
Johanna Primary School *STHWK* SE1 18 A2
John Ball Primary School *BKHTH/KID* SE3 161 K8
John Betts Primary School *HMSMTH* W6 156 D2
John Bramston Primary School *BARK/HLT* IG6 103 K7
John Burns Primary School *BTSEA* SW11 158 B8
John Chilton School *NTHLT* UB5 133 M2
John Dixon Clinic *BERM/RHTH* SE16 160 A2
John Donne Primary School *PECK* SE15 160 A7
John Fisher School *PUR/KEN* CR8 222 F6
John Fisher Sports Club *WARL* CR6 242 D4
John F Kennedy RC School *HHW* HP1 35 J5
John F Kennedy Special School *SRTFD* E15 141 J3
John Keble CE Primary School *WLSDN* NW10 136 C3
John Kelly Boys & Girls Technology College *CRICK* NW2 116 C8
The John Loughborough School *TOTM* N17 99 N10
John Lyon School *RYLN/HDSTN* HA2 114 C6
John Milton Primary School *VX/NE* SW8 158 D6
John Nightingale School *E/WMO/HCT* KT8 197 N3
John Paul II RC School *WIM/MER* SW19 178 G3
John Penrose School *DEN/HRF* UB9 91 N9
John Perryn Primary School *ACT* W3 136 B7
John Perry Primary School *DAGE* RM10 144 E1
John Roan Lower School *BKHTH/KID* SE3 161 L5
John Roan School *BKHTH/KID* SE3 161 K6
John Ruskin College *SAND/SEL* CR2 224 D4
John Ruskin Primary School *WALW* SE17 18 E9
John Scott Health Centre *FSBYPK* N4 119 K6
John Scurr JMI School *WCHPL* E1 140 B6
John Smith House *WALW* SE17 18 E6
Johnsons Industrial Estate *HYS/HAR* UB3 153 H2
John Stainer Primary School *BROCKY* SE4 160 D9
The John Warner School *HOD* EN11 26 G10
Jordans Quaker Meeting House *BEAC* HP9 89 K7
Jordans School *BEAC* HP9 89 L7
Joseph Clarke Special School *CHING* E4 101 J7
Joseph Hood Primary School *RYNPK* SW20 201 H2
Joseph Lancaster School *STHWK* SE1 18 F4
Joseph Tritton Primary School *BTSEA* SW11 157 M10
Joydens Wood Infant School *RDART* DA2 186 F7
Joydens Wood Junior School *BXLY* DA5 186 F7
Jubilee Centre *STALW/RED* AL3 38 C5
Jubilee Country Park *HAYES* BR2 206 E4
Jubilee Hall Clinic *CRAWE* RH10 284 B7
Jubilee JMI School *STNW/STAM* N16 119 P6
Jubilee Market *COVGDN* WC2E 11 M7
Jubilee Primary School *THMD* SE28 143 M9
Jubilee Sports Centre *NKENS* W10 2 B10
Jubilee Sports Ground *CHING* E4 101 J5
Julians Primary School *STRHM/NOR* SW16 181 H7
Junior & Youth Centre *POP/IOD* E14 140 E7
Juno Way Industrial Estate *NWCR* SE14 160 C5
Jupiter Drive JMI School *HHNE* HP2 36 A4
JVC Business Park *CRICK* NW2 116 D6

Kangley Business Centre SYD SE26 182 E8
Katella Trading Estate BARK IG11 143 H5
Katherine Road Medical Centre FSTGT E7 141 P1
Katherines Primary School HLWW/ROY CM19 46 C3
Keats House Museum HAMP NW3 117 N9
Keble Preparatory School WCHMH N21 99 H1
Keen Students Supplementary School WCHPL E1 13 N3
Keir Hardie Primary School CAN/RD E16 141 M7
Keith Davis Cue Sports Club DAGW RM9 143 N2
Kelmscott Leisure Centre WALTH E17 120 E4
Kelmscott School WALTH E17 120 E4
Kelrose Swimming Pool Centre RBRW/HUT CM13 127 K3
Kelsey Park School BECK BR3 204 F3
Kelvedon Hatch Primary School BRWN CM15 86 D2
Kelvin Business Centre CRAWE RH10 284 A4
Kelvin Grove Primary School SYD SE26 182 A6
Kelvin Industrial Estate GFD/PVL UB6 134 A3
GFD/PVL UB6 134 C5
Kemnal Technology College CHST BR7 184 G8
Kempton Park Racecourse SUN TW16 197 K1
Kemsing Primary School BGR/WK TN15 247 P3
Ken Barrington Centre LBTH SE11 17 P10
Kender Primary School NWCR SE14 160 B7
Kenilworth First School BORE WD6 76 A7
Kenley Primary School PUR/KEN CR8 241 M2
Kenley Sports Club PUR/KEN CR8 223 K10
Kenmont Primary School WLSDN NW10 136 D5
Kenmore Park Middle School KTN/HRWW/W HA3 115 J1
Kenneth More Theatre IL IG1 122 F8
Kenningtons Primary School SOCK/AV RM15 146 B8
Kensal Rise Primary School WLSDN NW10 136 G4
Kensington Ave Primary School THHTH CR7 203 H1
Kensington Business Centre SKENS SW7 15 P3
Kensington & Chelsea College NKENS W10 8 B3
WBPTN SW10 157 M6
Kensington & Chelsea Town Hall KENS W8 14 F2
The Kensington Clinic KENS W8 14 G4
Kensington Market KENS W8 14 G2
Kensington Palace State Apartments & Royal Ceremonial Dress Collection KENS W8 9 H10
Kensington Park School REGST W1B 10 F3
Kensington Preparatory School FUL/PGN SW6 157 J7
Kensington Primary School MNPK E12 142 C1
Kensington School of Business HCIRC EC1N 12 B3
Kensington Wharf WBPTN SW10 157 N6
Kensit Memorial College FNCH N3 97 H10
Kentish Town Church CE Primary School KTTN NW5 118 D10
Kentish Town Health Centre KTTN NW5 4 G2
Kentish Town Industrial Estate KTTN NW5 118 C10
Kent Kraft Industrial Estate GVW DA11 167 L10
Kenton Clinic KTN/HRWW/W HA3 115 K3
Kenton Cricket Club KTN/HRWW/W HA3 115 H2
Kent Park Industrial Estate PECK SE15 160 A5
Kenwood House HGT N6 117 P6
Kenyngton Manor Primary School SUN TW16 175 H9
Kerem House School EFNCH N2 117 M3
The Kerem School EFNCH N2 117 N3
Kestner Industrial Estate GRH DA9 188 F1
Keston CE Primary School HAYES BR2 226 A2
Keston Infant Schooll COUL/CHIP CR5 241 H5
Keston Junior School COUL/CHIP CR5 241 H5
Kew Bridge Steam Museum BTFD TW8 155 L4
Kew College RCH/KEW TW9 155 M6
Kew Gardens (Royal Botanic Gardens) RCH/KEW TW9 155 K7
Kew Palace RCH/KEW TW9 155 K6
Kew Retail Park RCH/KEW TW9 155 N7
Keyplan & Roxburghe College FITZ W1T 11 H2
Keyworth Primary School WALW SE17 18 C8
Khalsa College London HRW HA1 114 E4
Kidbrooke Park Primary School BKHTH/KID SE3 161 P8
Kidbrooke School BKHTH/KID SE3 162 A8
Kilburn Park Junior School KIL/WHAMP NW6 2 E8
Killick Street Medical Centre IS N1 5 N7
Killigrew Primary School LCOL/BKTW AL2 56 A1
Kilmorie Primary School FSTH SE23 182 D5
Kiln Park Business Centre EW KT17 220 B7
Kimberley Industrial Estate WALTH E17 100 E8
Kimpton Industrial Estate CHEAM SM3 201 J9
Kinetic Business Centre BORE WD6 75 L7
King Alfred School GLDGN NW11 117 L6
King Athelstan Primary School KUT KT1 199 L3
King Edward Court Shopping Centre WDSR SL4 149 H7
King Edwards Road Clinic RSLP HA4 112 E6
King Edward VII Hospital WDSR SL4 149 H9
King Edward VII Hospital for Officers MHST W1U 10 D3
Kingfield School WOKS/MYFD GU22 232 D6
The Kingfisher Medical Centre DEPT SE8 160 E5
Kingford Community School PLSTW E13 141 P6
King George Hospital GDMY/SEVK IG3 123 K3
Kingham Industrial Estate WLSDN NW10 136 A5
King Harold Gm School WAB EN9 63 K9
King Henry's Reach Dev BARN SW13 156 F5
King & Queen Wharf WAP E1W 140 C9
Kings Acre Primary School CLAP SW4 180 F1
Kings Avenue Medical Centre GFD/PVL UB6 134 B8
Kingsbury Green Primary School CDALE/KGS NW9 115 N3
Kingsbury High School CDALE/KGS NW9 115 N2
Kingsbury Hospital CDALE/KGS NW9 115 M2
Kingsbury Tamil School CDALE/KGS NW9 115 N1
Kingsbury Trading Estate CDALE/KGS NW9 115 P4
Kingsbury Watermill Museum & Waffle House STALW/RED AL3 38 A6
Kings College GUW GU2 249 K10
Kings College Hospital CMBW SE5 159 K9
Kings College Hospital EDUL SE22 159 M10
Kings College London CHEL SW3 15 N8
CMBW SE5 159 L8
HAMP NW3 117 K9
STHWK SE1 12 D9
STHWK SE1 12 F10
TPL/STR WC2R 11 P7
WBPTN SW10 157 M6
WEST SW1P 17 H5
King's College School WIM/MER SW19 178 F9
Kings College School of Medicine & Dentistry HNHL SE24 181 L2
Kings College Sports Ground RSLP HA4 112 F4
Kingscote School CFSP/GDCR SL9 110 B1
Kings Court First School WDSR SL4 171 M3
Kingscroft School STA TW18 173 K9
Kings Cross Station CAMTN NW1 5 L8
Kings Cross Thameslink Station FSBYW WCIX 5 N9
Kingsdale School DUL SE21 181 M6
Kings Estate HCH RM12 125 H9
Kings Farm Infant School GVE DA12 190 F8
Kings Farm Junior School GVE DA12 190 F7
Kingsfield Business Centre REDH RH1 276 B1
Kingsgate Business Centre KUTN/CMB KT2 199 K1
Kingsgate Infant School KIL/WHAMP NW6 2 E3
Kingsgate Junior School KIL/WHAMP NW6 2 E4
Kings Head Theatre IS N1 6 C5
Kings House School RCHPK/HAM TW10 177 L1
Kingsland Health Centre IS N1 7 K3
Kingsland School HACK E8 119 N10
Kingsland Shopping Centre HACK E8 7 L1
Kings Langley Primary School KGLGY WD4 54 A4
Kingsley Primary School CROY/NA CR0 202 G8
Kings Mall Shopping Centre HMSMTH W6 156 F3
Kingsmeadow Athletics Centre KUT KT1 199 M3
Kingsmead Primary School CLPT E5 120 D9
Kingsmead School EN EN1 79 P8
Kingsmoor Infant School HLWW/ROY CM19 46 F5
Kingsmoor Recreation Centre HLWW/ROY CM19 46 E5
The Kings Oak Private Hospital ENC/FH EN2 79 H4
King Solomon High School BARK/HLT IG6 102 G10
Kings Park Industrial Estate KGLGY WD4 54 C5
Kings Private Clinic GDMY/SEVK IG3 123 J6
MHST W1U 10 C3
Kings School of English BECK BR3 204 E2
Kings Stairs BERM/RHTH SE16 160 A1
Kingston Business Centre CHSGTN KT9 199 K10
Kingston College of Further Education KUT KT1 199 J3
Kingston Crematorium KUT KT1 199 M3
Kingston Crown Court KUT KT1 199 J3
Kingston Grammar School KUT KT1 199 L2
Kingston Hospital NHS Trust KUTN/CMB KT2 199 M1
Kingstonian FC NWMAL KT3 199 N3
Kingston Magistrates Court KUT KT1 199 J2
Kingston Museum & Art Gallery KUT KT1 199 K2
Kingston Sport & Recreation Centre NWMAL KT3 200 C4
Kingston University KUT KT1 199 K3
KUTN/CMB KT2 178 A10
KUTN/CMB KT2 178 A8
King Street College HMSMTH W6 156 F3
Kingsway Business Park HPTN TW12 197 N1
Kingsway College CLKNW EC1R 12 B1
KTTN NW5 4 E1
STPAN WC1H 5 N10
Kingsway Infant School GSTN WD25 55 H10
Kingswey Business Park WOKN/KNAP GU21 214 F10
Kingswood Golf Club KWD/TDW/WH KT20 239 K10
Kingswood House School HOR/WEW KT19 219 N9
Kingswood Primary School KWD/TDW/WH KT20 257 J4
WNWD SE27 181 L7
Kingswood School HARH RM3 105 P5
Kisharon School GLDGN NW11 117 J4
KLC School of Design WBPTN SW10 157 M7
Knaphill Junior School WOKN/KNAP GU21 231 H4
Knaphill Lower School WOKN/KNAP GU21 230 G4
Knightsbridge Barracks SKENS SW7 15 P2
Knightsbridge Medical Centre KTBR SW1X 16 B3
Knightsmead Special School SOCK/AV RM15 146 E9
Knockholt CE Primary School RSEV TN14 245 L3
Knole Park Golf Club BGR/WK TN15 247 K10
Knollmead Primary School WPK KT4 199 P9
Knowledge Point School HOLWY N7 5 N2
Knowle Park Infant School STA TW18 173 K8
Knowl Hill School CHOB/PIR GU24 230 D8
Knutsford Junior & Infant School WATN WD24 73 L4
Kobi Nazrul Primary School WCHPL E1 13 P5
KP Estate RAIN RM13 144 F9
KS Medical Centre STHL UB1 134 A9
Kubrick Business Estate FSTGT E7 121 N9
Laban Centre DEPT SE8 160 G6
Laburnum Health Centre DAGE RM10 124 B7
Laburnum Primary School HACK E8 7 L6
Ladbrooke JMI School POTB/CUF EN6 59 L8
Lady Bankes Primary School RSLP HA4 113 H7
Lady Boswells CE Primary School BGR/WK TN15 265 K1
Lady Edens School KENS W8 15 J3
The Lady Eleanor Holles School HPTN TW12 176 A8
Lady Margaret Primary School STHL UB1 133 N7
Lady Margaret School FUL/PGN SW6 157 K7
Ladywell Arena LEW SE13 182 G2
Ladywell Cemetery BROCKY SE4 182 E1
Ladywell Leisure Centre LEW SE13 183 H1
Laharna Trading Estate WATN WD24 73 K4
Laine Theatre Arts EW KT17 220 B9
Laings Sports Ground BAR EN5 76 B8
Lake Business Centre TOTM N17 99 P7
Laker Industrial Estate BECK BR3 182 D8
Lakeside Industrial Estate DTCH/LGLY SL3 151 H6
DTCH/LGLY SL3 151 K5
Lakeside Retail Park WTHK RM20 166 F3
Lakeside Shopping Centre WTHK RM20 166 G2
Lakeside Special School WGCW AL8 22 E7
Laleham CE Primary School STA TW18 195 M2
Laleham Golf Club CHERT KT16 195 L4
Lambeth Cemetery TOOT SW17 179 M8
Lambeth College CLAP SW4 180 D1
STHWK SE1 13 K10
Lambeth County Court LBTH SE11 18 B7
Lambeth Crematorium TOOT SW17 179 M7
Lambeth Palace STHWK SE1 17 N4
Lambourne Golf Club SL SL1 128 A1
Lambourne Primary School ABR/ST RM4 83 L8
Lambs Court POP/IOD E14 140 D9
Lamont Business Centre CROY/NA CR0 202 F7
Lamorbey Swimming Centre BFN/LL DA15 185 K5
Lampton School HEST TW5 153 P7
The Lanark Medical Centre MV/WKIL W9 3 H9
Lancaster House WHALL SW1A 16 G1
Lancasterian Primary School TOTM N17 99 M9
Lancaster Road Industrial Estate EBAR EN4 77 N9
Lancelot Medical Centre ALP/SUD HA0 115 J10
Lanford Obesity Clinic ED N9 100 A1
Langafel CE Primary School HART DA3 211 M3
Langbourne Primary School DUL SE21 181 M6
Langdon Park Secondary School POP/IOD E14 140 G8
Langdon School EHAM E6 142 E4
Langford Primary School FUL/PGN SW6 157 L8
The Langham School SEVS/STOTM N15 119 K2
Langhedge Lane Industrial Estate UED N18 99 N7
Langley Business Centre DTCH/LGLY SL3 150 D1
Langley Business Park DTCH/LGLY SL3 150 C1
Langley Grammar School DTCH/LGLY SL3 150 C3
Langley Green First School CRAWW RH11 283 N3
Langley Health Centre DTCH/LGLY SL3 150 D4
Langley Manor School DTCH/LGLY SL3 130 B10
Langley Park Country Park DTCH/LGLY SL3 130 D6
Langley Park Golf Club BECK BR3 205 J6
Langley Park School for Boys BECK BR3 204 G6
Langley Park School for Girls BECK BR3 204 G6
Langleywood School DTCH/LGLY SL3 150 B2
Langshott County Infant School HORL RH6 280 D4
Langthorne Health Centre WAN E11 121 J8
Langthorne Hospital WAN E11 121 J9
Langtons Junior & Infant School EMPK RM11 125 M6
The Lansbury Estate WOKN/KNAP GU21 231 J4
Lansbury Lawrence Primary School POP/IOD E14 140 G8
Lansdownecollege BAY/PAD W2 8 G8
Lansdowne Primary School TIL RM18 168 C8
Lansdowne School BRXN/ST SW9 158 G9
La Retraite RC Girls School BAL SW12 180 D3
Lark Hall Junior School CLAP SW4 158 E8
Lark Hall Primary School CLAP SW4 158 E8
Larkshall Business Centre CHING E4 101 J3
Larkswood Primary School CHING E4 100 G5
Larmenier Infant School HMSMTH W6 156 G3
La Sainte Union Convent School KTTN NW5 118 B8
La Salette RC Primary School RAIN RM13 145 H5
Laser Clinic CHESW EN7 62 A6
Latchmere Infant School KUTN/CMB KT2 177 L9
Latchmere Leisure Centre BTSEA SW11 158 A8
Lathom Junior School EHAM E6 142 B2
Latimer Industrial Estate SHB W12 136 F8
Latton Bush Business Centre HLWS CM18 47 J4
Latton Bush Recreation Centre HLWS CM18 47 H4
Latymer All Saints CE Primary School ED N9 99 N3
The Latymer School ED N9 99 M3
Latymer Upper School HMSMTH W6 156 D3
Launcelot Primary School BMLY BR1 183 M7
Laurel Clinic EA W5 155 H3
Laurence Haines School WATW WD18 73 H10
Lauriston Primary School HOM E9 140 C3
Lavender Primary School ENC/FH EN2 79 M4
Lawdale Junior School BETH E2 7 P9
Lawn Primary School GVW DA11 189 P2
Lawn Tennis Club HORL RH6 280 A4
REDH RH1 258 A8
Lawn Tennis School BEAC HP9 88 D8
Lawrence Trading Estate GNWCH SE10 161 K3
GRAYS RM17 167 P3
Lawrence University SKENS SW7 15 K6
Lawrence Wharf BERM/RHTH SE16 140 E10
Laycock Primary School IS N1 6 B2
Lazards Sports Club SUN TW16 197 J1
LBH Hayes Swimming Baths HYS/HAR UB3 132 G10
Lea Bridge Industrial Estate LEY E10 120 D6
Leadenhall Market BANK EC3V 13 J6
Lea Farm Junior School GSTN WD25 73 L2
Leah Manning Centre HLW CM20 28 G9
Lea Infant School SLN SL2 129 N9
Lea Junior School SLN SL2 129 M9
Lea Park Trading Estate LEY E10 120 E5
Lea Road Industrial Park CHES/WCR EN8 62 F10
Leaside Business Centre PEND EN3 80 E6
Leatherhead Business Park LHD/OX KT22 236 G5
Leatherhead Clinic LHD/OX KT22 237 H7
Leatherhead Cricket Club LHD/OX KT22 236 F8
Leatherhead FC LHD/OX KT22 236 F8
Leatherhead Golf Club LHD/OX KT22 236 F2
Leatherhead Hospital LHD/OX KT22 237 H8
Leatherhead Industrial Estate LHD/OX KT22 236 F7
Leatherhead Institute LHD/OX KT22 236 G7
Leatherhead Leisure Centre & Water Park LHD/OX KT22 236 F9
Leatherhead Museum LHD/OX KT22 236 G8
Leathermarket Gardens STHWK SE1 19 J2
Leathersellers Sports Ground ELTH/MOT SE9 183 P3
Leathers Hall HDTCH EC3A 13 J5
Lea Valley High School PEND EN3 80 B1
Lea Valley Primary School TOTM N17 99 P8
Lea Valley Trading Estate UED N18 100 B5
UED N18 100 C7
Leavesden Green Junior Middle & Infant School GSTN WD25 55 H10
Leavesden Hospital ABLGY WD5 55 H7
L'écoles Des Petits FUL/PGN SW6 157 L8
Lee Manor Primary School LEW SE13 183 K2
Leeside Court BERM/RHTH SE16 140 C10
Leeside Trading Estate TOTM N17 100 B8
Leesons Primary School STMC/STPC BR5 207 K3
Lee Valley Campsite CHING E4 80 G6
Lee Valley Caravan Park HOD EN11 45 H5
Lee Valley Leisure Centre Camping & Caravan ED N9 100 C2
Lee Valley Leisure Golf Club ED N9 100 D1
Lee Valley Park Farms WAB EN9 62 G3
Lee Valley Watersports Centre CHING E4 100 D7
Legoland Windsor WDSR SL4 170 C1
Leigh City Technology College DART DA1 187 P4
Leigh Close Industrial Estate NWMAL KT3 200 A4
Leigh Primary School REIG RH2 274 D6
Leighton House Museum & Art Gallery WKENS W14 14 D3
Lena Gardens Primary School HMSMTH W6 156 F2
Lent Rise Combined School SL SL1 128 A7
Leopold Primary School WLSDN NW10 136 C2
Leopold Street Clinic BOW E3 140 E7
Lesnes Abbey ABYW SE2 163 N3
Lesney Park Primary School ERITH DA8 164 E5
Lessness Heath Primary School BELV DA17 164 B4
Leverstock Green JMI School HHNE HP2 36 E7
Leverstock Green Lawn Tennis Club HHS/BOV HP3 36 C8

The Leverton Primary School *WAB* EN9 **63** L10
Lewin Mead Community Mental Health Centre *STRHM/NOR* SW16 **180** E9
Lewis Clinic *CAR* SM5 **222** B1
Lewisham Bridge Primary School *LEW* SE13 **160** C9
Lewisham Business Centre *NWCR* SE14 **160** C5
Lewisham Centre *LEW* SE13 **161** H9
Lewisham College *DEPT* SE8 **160** F7
Lewisham Crematorium *CAT* SE6 **183** L5
Ley Hill Cricket Club *CSHM* HP5 **51** P6
Ley Hill School *CSHM* HP5 **51** N6
Ley Park CP School *BROX* EN10 **44** E8
The Leys Primary School *DAGE* RM10 **144** D2
Leyton Business Centre *LEY* E10 **120** E7
Leyton Cross *DART* DA1 **187** H5
Leyton FC *LEY* E10 **120** E6
Leyton Industrial Village *LEY* E10 **120** C5
Leyton Orient FC (Matchroom Stadium) *LEY* E10 **120** C8
Leytonstone School *WAN* E11 **121** K4
Leyton VI Form College *LEY* E10 **121** J4
Leyton Youth Sports Ground *LEY* E10 **120** C6
The Liberty City Clinic *SDTCH* EC2A **13** J1
Liberty II Centre *ROM* RM1 **124** F2
Liberty Middle School *MTCM* CR4 **201** P2
Lifecare NHS Trust *CTHM* CR3 **241** M9
Light Industrial Estate *WDSR* SL4 **170** A5
Lilian Baylis School *LBTH* SE11 **17** P6
VX/NE SW8 **17** N10
Lillian Baylis Theatre *FSBYE* EC1V **6** C9
Lillian Bishop School of English *SKENS* SW7 **15** L5
Limehouse Town Hall *POP/IOD* E14 **140** E8
Limes Business Centre *HORL* RH6 **279** J9
Limes Farm Primary School *CHIG* IG7 **102** G7
The Limes Medical Centre *EPP* CM16 **65** L5
EPP CM16 **66** C2
Lime Trees Park Golf Club *NTHLT* UB5 **133** J2
Lime Walk JMI School *HHS/BOV* HP3 **36** A8
Limpsfield CE Infant School *OXTED* RH8 **261** N5
Limpsfield Chart Golf Club *OXTED* RH8 **261** P5
Limpsfield Grange School *OXTED* RH8 **261** M3
Limpsfield Lawn Tennis Club *OXTED* RH8 **261** M4
Lincoln Road Clinic *EN* EN1 **79** P9
Lincoln's Inn *LINN* WC2A **11** P5
Linden Bridge School *WPK* KT4 **200** B10
Linden Lodge School *WIM/MER* SW19 **179** H4
Lindon Bennett School *FELT* TW13 **175** L8
Linford Christie Stadium *SHB* W12 **136** D7
The Link Day Primary School *CROY/NA* CR0 **222** F1
The Link Secondary School *CROY/NA* CR0 **222** G1
Links Primary School *TOOT* SW17 **180** B9
Linley Sambourne House *KENS* W8 **14** E2
Linnet House Clinic *STJWD* NW8 **3** N8
Linton Mead Primary School *THMD* SE28 **143** L9
Lionel Road Primary School *BTFD* TW8 **155** K3
Lion House School *PUT/ROE* SW15 **156** G10
Lion Retail Park *WOKS/MYFD* GU22 **232** E2
Lismarrine Industrial Park *BORE* WD6 **74** G10
Lisson Grove Health Centre *STJWD* NW8 **9** N1
Lister Community School *PLSTW* E13 **141** N4
The Lister Hospital *BGVA* SW1W **16** E8
Lister House Clinic *CAVSQ/HST* W1G **10** E5
Lister Medical Centre *HLWS* CM18 **46** F4
Littlebrook Business Centre *DART* DA1 **166** B9
Little Chalfont CP School *AMS* HP6 **70** B5
Little Chalfont Golf Club *CSTG* HP8 **70** B6
Little Danson Welfare Clinic *WELL* DA16 **163** K10
Littledown Special School *SL* SL1 **129** L9
Little Furze School *OXHEY* WD19 **93** J4
Little Green Junior School *RKW/CH/CXG* WD3 **72** B7
Little Hands Theatre *HDN* NW4 **116** F2
Little Hay Golf Complex *HHW* HP1 **34** F10
Little Heath Primary School *POTB/CUF* EN6 **59** M6
Little Heath School *CHDH* RM6 **123** L2
Little Ilford School *MNPK* E12 **122** C10
Little Reddings Primary School *BUSH* WD23 **74** A9
Little St Helens School *NTHWD* HA6 **92** G7
Little Stanmore First & Middle School *EDGW* HA8 **95** K9
Little Thurrock Primary School *GRAYS* RM17 **168** A2
Littleton CE Infant School *SHPTN* TW17 **196** B3
Little Wandsworth School *TOOT* SW17 **180** B5
Liverpool Street Station *LVPST* EC2M **13** J4
Livesey Museum *PECK* SE15 **160** A5
Livingstone Hospital *DART* DA1 **187** N3
Livingstone Primary School *EBAR* EN4 **77** N7
Lloyd's *BANK* EC3V **13** J6
Lloyds Register Cricket Club *DUL* SE21 **181** L4
Lochinver House School *POTB/CUF* EN6 **59** L6
Lockers Park School *HHW* HP1 **35** L6
Locks View Court *POP/IOD* E14 **140** D9
Lockwood Industrial Park *TOTM* N17 **120** A1
Lodge School *PUR/KEN* CR8 **222** E8
Lodge Sun Sports Club *WAT* WD17 **72** F5
Log Church *CHONG* CM5 **67** L5
Lombard Business Centre *BTSEA* SW11 **157** N8
Lombard Business Park *CROY/NA* CR0 **202** G7
WAND/EARL SW18 **179** N2
WIM/MER SW19 **201** M2
Lombard Trading Estate *CHARL* SE7 **161** N3
Lombardy Retail Park *HYS/HAR* UB3 **133** J9
London Aquarium *STHWK* SE1 **17** N1
London Area Terminal Control Centre *WDR/YW* UB7 **152** A1
London Arena *POP/IOD* E14 **160** G2
London Ballet Theatre *HAMP* NW3 **3** M3
London Balloon *LBTH* SE11 **17** N8
London Bible College *NTHWD* HA6 **92** E7
London Bridge City Pier *STHWK* SE1 **13** J9
London Bridge Hospital *STHWK* SE1 **13** H9
London Bridge Sports Centre *CANST* EC4R **12** G8
London Bridge Station *STHWK* SE1 **13** J10
London Broncos RLFC *BTFD* TW8 **155** J5
London Bubble Theatre *BERM/RHTH* SE16 **160** A1
London Business School *CAMTN* NW1 **10** A1
The London Canal Museum *IS* N1 **5** M7
London Capital College *CAMTN* NW1 **4** F5
London City Airport *CAN/RD* E16 **142** C10
London City Mission *STHWK* SE1 **19** K1
The London Clinic *MHST* W1U **10** D2
London College of Business & Computing *BETH* E2 **140** A4
London College of Fashion *CAVSQ/HST* W1G **10** F5
MHST W1U **10** D6
SDTCH EC2A **13** K1
London College of Further Education *LBTH* SE11 **18** C6
London College of Higher Education *CLAP* SW4 **158** C9
London College of International Business Studies *HHOL* WC1V **11** M4
London College of Printing *LBTH* SE11 **18** D4
The London College *KENS* W8 **8** E9
London Colney JMI School *LCOL/BKTW* AL2 **57** J1
London Commodity Exchange *WAP* E1W **13** M8
London Dungeon *STHWK* SE1 **13** H9
London Electronics College *ECT* SW5 **14** G7
London Executive College *TOOT* SW17 **180** B6
London Eye Clinic *CAVSQ/HST* W1G **10** E4
London Fields Primary School *HACK* E8 **140** A3
London Foot Hospital *FITZ* W1T **10** G2
London Gatwick Airport *HORL* RH6 **280** A9
HORL RH6 **280** B8
HORL RH6 **280** D8
London Gender Clinic *HDN* NW4 **116** E4
London Group Business Park *CRICK* NW2 **116** C6
London Guildhall University *LVPST* EC2M **13** H4
TWRH EC3N **13** L6
London Guildhall University Sports Ground *LEE/GVPK* SE12 **183** P5
London Heart Clinic *CAVSQ/HST* W1G **10** E4
London Hospital Medical College *WCHPL* E1 **140** A7
The London Industrial Estate *EHAM* E6 **142** D7
London Industrial Park *EHAM* E6 **142** E7
London International Cruise Terminal *TIL* RM18 **168** D10
The London & International School of Acting *MV/WKIL* W9 **8** D2
London Irish RFC *SUN* TW16 **197** H1
The London Irish Youth Theatre *HGT* N6 **118** C6
London Ladies & Girls FC *CAT* SE6 **182** G8
London Lane Clinic *BMLY* BR1 **183** L10
London, Leyton - Lee Valley Ice Centre *LEY* E10 **120** C7
London Lighthouse *NTGHL* W11 **8** A6
London Living Theatre *SYD* SE26 **182** C7
London Nautical School *STHWK* SE1 **12** B9
London Open College *FSBYE* EC1V **6** D9
London Oratory School *FUL/PGN* SW6 **157** K6
London Pavilion *REGST* W1B **11** J8
London Road Medical Centre *THHTH* CR7 **203** H6
London School of Economics *HHOL* WC1V **11** L5
LINN WC2A **11** P6
STHWK SE1 **12** E9
London School of Hygiene & Tropical Medicine *GWRST* WC1E **11** K3
London Silver Vaults *LINN* WC2A **12** A4
The London Television Centre (LWT) *STHWK* SE1 **12** A9
London Tourist Board & Convention Centre *BGVA* SW1W **16** E3
London Toy & Model Museum *BAY/PAD* W2 **9** K7
SHB W12 **136** F8
London Transport Bus Depot *BXLYHN* DA7 **164** C9
London Transport Museum *COVGDN* WC2E **11** M7
London Underwriting Centre *MON* EC3R **13** K7
London Weather Centre *CLKNW* EC1R **12** A3
London Welsh FC *RCH/KEW* TW9 **155** K9
London Welsh School *CRICK* NW2 **136** F1
London Zoo *CAMTN* NW1 **4** C7
Lonesome First School *MTCM* CR4 **202** C2
Long Close School *DTCH/LGLY* SL3 **149** M3
The Longcroft Clinic *BNSTD* SM7 **221** M10
Longdean School *HHS/BOV* HP3 **36** C9
Long Ditton County Infant School *SURB* KT6 **199** H8
Longfield Primary School *RYLN/HDSTN* HA2 **113** P4
Longford Community School *EBED/NFELT* TW14 **174** C3
Longford Industrial Estate *HPTN* TW12 **176** A9
Longlands Primary School *BFN/LL* DA15 **185** H6
BROX EN10 **62** E1
Long Lane AFC *BKHTH/KID* SE3 **161** P8
Longley Trading Estate *CRAWE* RH10 **283** P8
Longmead Business Centre *HOR/WEW* KT19 **220** A7
Longmead Industrial Estate *HOR/WEW* KT19 **220** A7
Longmead Primary School *WDR/YW* UB7 **151** N2
Long Ridings Junior & Infant School *RBRW/HUT* CM13 **87** N9
Longshaw Primary School *CHING* E4 **101** J4
Longwood Business Park *SUN* TW16 **196** G5
Lord Lister Health Centre *FSTGT* E7 **121** M9
Lordship Lane Clinic *TOTM* N17 **99** M10
Lordship Lane Primary School *WDGN* N22 **99** K9
Lord's Tour & MCC Museum *STJWD* NW8 **3** L10
Loreto RC Girls College *STAL* AL1 **38** D6
Lorimar Business Centre *RAIN* RM13 **144** F8
Loseley House *RGUW* GU3 **267** L6
Loughborough Primary School *BRXN/ST* SW9 **159** J8
Loughton Cricket Club *LOU* IG10 **82** C7
Loughton Golf Club *LOU* IG10 **82** E5
Loughton Hall Clinic *LOU* IG10 **82** E8
Loughton Health Centre *LOU* IG10 **82** B7
Loughton Mental Health Centre *LOU* IG10 **82** B9
Lovelace Primary School *CHSGTN* KT9 **219** H2
Lower Clapton Health Centre *CLPT* E5 **120** B10
Lower Place Business Centre *WLSDN* NW10 **135** P4
Lower Sydenham Industrial Estate *CAT* SE6 **182** E8
Lowewood Museum *HOD* EN11 **44** F4
Lowfield Heath Industrial Estate *HORL* RH6 **279** P10
Lowfield Medical Centre *DART* DA1 **187** M3
Lowfield Sports Ground *HOD* EN11 **44** E3
Low Hall Sports Ground *WALTH* E17 **120** C4
Lowther Primary School *BARN* SW13 **156** D5
Loxford School of Science & Technology *IL* IG1 **122** G10
Loyola Preparatory School *BKHH* IG9 **101** P2
LPR Sports Club *BARK/HLT* IG6 **103** J9
LSE Sports Club *NWMAL* KT3 **200** A6
LT Lost Property Office *CAMTN* NW1 **10** B2
LTR Depot *SHB* W12 **136** G10
Lucas Vale Primary School *DEPT* SE8 **160** F7
Lucie Clayton Secretarial/Fashion Design College *SKENS* SW7 **15** J4
Lullingstone Castle *EYN* DA4 **229** K2
Lullingstone Park Golf Club *ORP* BR6 **228** E1
Lullingstone Roman Villa *EYN* DA4 **209** J10
Lutomer House Business Centre *POP/IOD* E14 **140** G10
Lux Cinema *IS* N1 **7** J10
Lycee Francais *SKENS* SW7 **15** L5
The Lyceum Theatre *TPL/STR* WC2R **11** N7
Lynch Hill School *SLN* SL2 **128** E5
Lyndean Industrial Estate *ABYW* SE2 **163** M2
Lyndhurst House Preparatory School *HAMP* NW3 **117** N10
Lyndhurst Middle School *BORE* WD6 **75** L5
Lyndhurst Primary School *CMBW* SE5 **159** L8
Lyne & Longcross CE Infant School *CHERT* KT16 **194** E9
Lynton Preparatory School *EW* KT17 **220** C7
Lyon Business Park *BARK* IG11 **143** H4
Lyon Park Junior & Infant School *ALP/SUD* HA0 **135** L2
Lyonsdown School *BAR* EN5 **77** M9
Lyons Industrial Estate *WDR/YW* UB7 **131** M8
Lyric Theatre *SOHO/SHAV* W1D **11** J7
Lyric Theatre Hammersmith *HMSMTH* W6 **156** F3
Mabwin Supplementary School *ED* N9 **100** A3
Macaulay CE Primary School *CLAP* SW4 **158** C10
Madame Tussaud's *CAMTN* NW1 **10** C2
Madeira Grove Clinic *WFD* IG8 **101** N6
Madison Bowl *NTHWD* HA6 **92** F8
Magna Carta School *EGH* TW20 **172** C9
Magnet Estate *WTHK* RM20 **167** H4
Mahatma Gandhi Industrial Estate *BRXN/ST* SW9 **159** J9
Maida Vale Hospital *MV/WKIL* W9 **9** K1
Maida Vale Medical Centre *MV/WKIL* W9 **2** G10
Maidenbower First & Middle School *CRAWE* RH10 **284** E9
Malcolm Primary School *PGE/AN* SE20 **182** B10
Malden Golf Club *NWMAL* KT3 **200** B2
Malden Manor Junior School *NWMAL* KT3 **200** B7
Malden Parochial Primary School *WPK* KT4 **200** B8
Malden Road Baths *CHEAM* SM3 **220** C1
Malham Road Industrial Estate *FSTH* SE23 **182** C4
Mall Galleries *STJS* SW1Y **11** K9
The Mall School *WHTN* TW2 **176** C6
Malmesbury Middle School *MRDN* SM4 **201** M6
Malmesbury Primary School *BOW* E3 **140** E5
MRDN SM4 **201** M7
Malorees Junior & Infant School *KIL/WHAMP* NW6 **136** G2
Malory School *BMLY* BR1 **183** M7
Maltings Arts Theatre *STAL* AL1 **38** C6
The Maltings Industrial Estate *SBW* CM21 **30** A1
WARE SG12 **27** J7
The Maltings Shopping Centre *STAL* AL1 **38** C6
Maltmans Green School *CFSP/GDCR* SL9 **109** P1
Malvern Way Infant School *RKW/CH/CXG* WD3 **72** D9
Manby Lodge Infant School *WEY* KT13 **216** C1
Mandeville Health Centre *STAL* AL1 **38** C9
Mandeville Primary School *CLPT* E5 **120** D8
STAL AL1 **38** C9
Mandeville Special School *NTHLT* UB5 **133** N1
Manford Industrial Estate *ERITH* DA8 **165** J5
Manford Way Health Centre *BARK/HLT* IG6 **103** J7
Manor Brook Medical Centre *BKHTH/KID* SE3 **161** N8
Manorcroft Primary School *EGH* TW20 **172** D9
Manor Drive Health Centre *WPK* KT4 **200** C8
Manorfield Primary School *POP/IOD* E14 **140** G7
Manor House Hospital *GLDGN* NW11 **117** L6
Manor House School *EHSLY* KT24 **253** M3
HNWL W7 **134** D9
Manor Lodge School *RAD* WD7 **57** P6
Manor Mead School *SHPTN* TW17 **196** C5
Manor Oak Primary School *STMC/STPC* BR5 **207** N5
The Manor of Groves *SBW* CM21 **29** J1
Manor Park Cemetery *FSTGT* E7 **122** A9
Manor Park Crematorium *FSTGT* E7 **121** P9
Manor Park Medical Centre *SL* SL1 **129** J7
Manor Park Methodist School *MNPK* E12 **122** B9
Manor Park Primary School *SUT* SM1 **221** M2
Manor Place Industrial Estate *BORE* WD6 **75** P7
Manor Primary School *SRTFD* E15 **141** K4
The Manor Primary School *ROM* RM1 **124** G3
The Manor School *BF/WBF* KT14 **215** P10
Manorside Primary School *FNCH* N3 **97** L9
Manor Special School *WLSDN* NW10 **136** C4
Manor Way Business Centre *DAGW* RM9 **144** E7
Manor Way Industrial Estate *GRAYS* RM17 **167** P6
Mansion House *MANHO* EC4N **12** G6
Manzoori Clinic *SWLY* BR8 **186** G10
Maple Cross Industrial Estate *RKW/CH/CXG* WD3 **91** H5
Maple Cross Junior Middle & Infant School *RKW/CH/CXG* WD3 **90** G6
Mapledown School *CRICK* NW2 **116** G5
Maple Grove Business Centre *HSLWW* TW4 **153** K10
Maple Industrial Estate *FELT* TW13 **175** H5
Maple Infant School *SURB* KT6 **199** J5
Maple Primary School *STAL* AL1 **38** D5
Maple River Industrial Estate *HLW* CM20 **29** L5
Maples Business Centre *IS* N1 **6** B5
Marble Arch *BAY/PAD* W2 **10** B7
Marble Hill House *TWK* TW1 **177** H3
Marden Lodge Primary School *CTHM* CR3 **242** A6
Margaret Roper RC Primary School *PUR/KEN* CR8 **222** G6
Margaret Wix JMI School *STALW/RED* AL3 **38** B2
Maria Fidelis Convent Lower School *CAMTN* NW1 **5** H10
Maria Fidelis Convent Upper School *CAMTN* NW1 **5** J9
Marillac Hospital *RBRW/HUT* CM13 **107** J7
Marion Richardson Primary School *WCHPL* E1 **140** C8
Marion Vian Primary School *BECK* BR3 **204** C5
Marish First School *DTCH/LGLY* SL3 **150** C2
Marist Convent Senior School *ASC* SL5 **192** C5
Marist Junior School *ASC* SL5 **192** C4
The Marist RC Primary School *BF/WBF* KT14 **215** J9
Maritime Industrial Estate *CHARL* SE7 **161** N3
Maritime Museum *GNWCH* SE10 **161** K3
The Marjory Kinnon School *EBED/NFELT* TW14 **174** F1
Market Trading Estate *NWDGN* UB2 **153** J3
Mark Hall Comprehensive School *HLWE* CM17 **29** M9
Mark Hall Cycle Museum *HLW* CM20 **29** L8
Marks Gate Junior School *CHDH* RM6 **123** P1
Marlborough Cricket Club *DUL* SE21 **181** P4
Marlborough Day Hospital *STJWD* NW8 **3** J7
Marlborough First & Middle School *HRW* HA1 **114** D2
Marlborough House *STJS* SW1Y **11** H10

Marlborough Park School
BFN/LL DA15 185 K4
Marlborough Primary School
CHEL SW3 15 P6
ISLW TW7 154 F7
Marlborough School
STAL AL1 38 B9
Marlborough Trading Estate
RCH/KEW TW9 155 N7
Marlin Montessori School
BERK HP4 33 N5
Marlowe Business Centre
NWCR SE14 160 D6
Marlowes Health Centre
HHW HP1 35 M6
Marlowes Shopping Centre
HHW HP1 35 M7
Marner Primary School
BOW E3 140 G6
Marshalls Park School
ROM RM1 104 F10
Marshall Street Leisure Centre
SOHO/CST W1F 10 G6
Marshfields CE School
ADL/WDHM KT15 215 H3
Marsh Gate Business Centre
SRTFD E15 141 H4
Marshgate Trading Estate
HERT/BAY SG13 25 M4
SRTFD E15 140 G2
Marsh Green School
DAGW RM9 144 B4
Marsh View Industrial Estate
RAIN RM13 145 N5
Martan College
HOL/ALD WC2B 11 M5
Martin Baker Sports Ground
DEN/HRF UB9 111 J5
Martinbridge Industrial Estate
EN EN1 79 P9
Martindale Industrial Estate
EN EN1 79 M9
Martindale JMI School
HHW HP1 35 J5
Martinfield Business Centre
WGCE AL7 23 J4
Martin Infant School
EFNCH N2 97 P10
Marvels Lane Primary School
LEE/GVPK SE12 183 P7
Maryland Industrial Estate
SRTFD E15 121 K10
Maryland Primary School
SRTFD E15 121 K10
Marylebone Health Centre
MHST W1U 10 D2
Marylebone Magistrates Court
CAMTN NW1 9 P3
Marylebone Station
CAMTN NW1 10 A2
Marymount International School
KUTN/CMB KT2 177 P10
Mary Wallace Theatre
TWK TW1 176 F4
Maswell Park Health Centre
HSLW TW3 176 B1
Matching Green CE Primary School
HLWE CM17 31 L9
Matilda Marks School
MLHL NW7 96 A6
Matrix Business Centre
DART DA1 187 M1
The Matthew Arnold School
STA TW18 173 M9
Maudlin's Green
WAP E1W 13 N9
The Maudsley Hospital
CMBW SE5 159 L8
Maunds Wood CP School
HLWS CM18 46 G5
Mawbrey Brough Health Centre
VX/NE SW8 158 F6
The Mawney School
ROMW/RG RM7 124 E3
May Avenue Industrial Estate
GVW DA11 190 C4
Maybury Business Centre
WOKS/MYFD GU22 232 D3
Maybury Infant School
WOKN/KNAP GU21 232 C2
Mayday University Hospital
THHTH CR7 203 J6
Mayesbrook Park Arena
BCTR RM8 123 K10
Mayespark Primary School
GDMY/SEVK IG3 123 K8
Mayfair Medical Centre
MYFR/PKLN W1K 10 D6
Mayfield Infant School
CHES/WCR EN8 62 D3
Mayfield Primary School
GFD/PVL UB6 134 C8
Mayfield School
PIN HA5 113 M1
Mayfield School & College
BCTR RM8 123 M6
Mayflower Primary School
POP/IOD E14 140 F8
Maylands Golf Club & Country Club
HARH RM3 106 A6
Mayplace Primary School
BXLYHN DA7 164 E10
Maypole Primary School
BXLY DA5 186 F5
Maytime School
IL IG1 122 D8
Mayville Infant School
WAN E11 121 K8
Mayville Junior School
WAN E11 121 K7
Maze Hill School
GNWCH SE10 161 K5
McEntee School
WALTH E17 100 E9
McKay Trading Estate
DTCH/LGLY SL3 151 H8
NKENS W10 8 A1
McMillan Clinic
HYS/HAR UB3 132 D9
The Mead Business Centre
HERT/BAY SG13 25 M4
Mead Industrial Park
HLW CM20 29 J7
The Mead Infant School
HOR/WEW KT19 200 C10
Mead JMI School
HARH RM3 105 N7
Meadlands Primary School
RCHPK/HAM TW10 177 H7
Meadowbrook Industrial Centre
CRAWE RH10 284 B4
Meadowcroft County Infant School
CHERT KT16 195 J10
Meadowgate School
PECK SE15 160 C9
Meadow School
UX/CGN UB8 131 P7
Meadow Wood School
BUSH WD23 74 B9
Mead Road Infant School
CHST BR7 184 F9
The Mead School
HLWS CM18 47 H3
Meath Green County Infant School
HORL RH6 280 A2
Meath Green Junior School
HORL RH6 280 A2
Meath School
CHERT KT16 214 G4
Medical Express Clinic
CAVSQ/HST W1G 10 E3
Mednurs Clinic
SEVS/STOTM N15 119 L4
Megabowl
BRXS/STRHM SW2 180 F5
Melcombe Primary School
HMSMTH W6 156 G5
Mellish Industrial Estate
WOOL/PLUM SE18 162 A2
Mellow Lane School
YEAD UB4 132 D6
Melrose Special School
MTCM CR4 201 P3
Memorial Hospital
WOOL/PLUM SE18 162 D8
The Menorah Foundation School
EDGW HA8 95 P8
Menorah Grammar School
GLDGN NW11 117 H5
Mercers College
WARE SG12 26 C1
Mercers' Hall
CITYW EC2V 12 F6
The Merchant Taylors Hall
BANK EC3V 13 H6
Merchant Taylors School
NTHWD HA6 92 F2
Mercury Theatre
LSQ/SEVD WC2H 11 L6
Meriden Primary School
GSTN WD25 73 L2
Meridian Clinic
BRXN/ST SW9 159 H9
Meridian Locality Mental Health Centre
CHARL SE7 161 P5
Meridian Primary School
GNWCH SE10 161 J4
Meridian Sports Club
CHARL SE7 162 B5
Meridian Trading Estate
CHARL SE7 161 N3
Merland Rise Primary School
KWD/TDW/WH KT20 238 F5
Merlin Primary School
BMLY BR1 183 M6
Merlin School
PUT/ROE SW15 178 G1
Mermaid Theatre
BLKFR EC4V 12 D7
Merrielands Retail Park
DAGW RM9 144 A3
Merrist Wood College
RGUW GU3 249 H4
Merrist Wood Golf Club
RGUW GU3 249 H5
Merrow Business Centre
RGUE GU4 250 G7
Merrow CE Infant School
RGUE GU4 250 G8
Merrow Clinic
GU GU1 250 E9
Merryfield Primary School
BORE WD6 75 L5
Merryhills Clinic
ENC/FH EN2 78 G7
Merryhills Primary School
ENC/FH EN2 78 G8
Merstham Primary School
REDH RH1 258 D4
Merton Abbey First School
WIM/MER SW19 201 L1
Merton Adult College
RYNPK SW20 201 H3
Merton College
MRDN SM4 201 J5
Merton Court Preparatory School
SCUP DA14 185 M7
Merton Industrial Park
WIM/MER SW19 201 M1
Merton Park Primary School
WIM/MER SW19 201 J2
Merton Road Industrial Estate
WAND/EARL SW18 179 K3
Metro Business Centre
SYD SE26 182 E9
The Metro Golf Centre
HDN NW4 96 F9
Metro Industrial Centre
ISLW TW7 154 D8
Metropolitan Business Centre
HACK E8 7 K4
Metropolitan Hospital
STHWK SE1 18 B3
Metropolitan Police
STJWD NW8 3 N8
Metropolitan Police FC
E/WMO/HCT KT8 198 C6
Metropolitan Police Hayes Sports Club
HAYES BR2 205 L9
Metropolitan Police (Hendon) Track
CDALE/KGS NW9 116 C1
Metropolitan Police Training School, Hendon
CDALE/KGS NW9 116 C1
Metropolitan Tabernacle
LBTH SE11 18 D5
Metro Trading Centre
WBLY HA9 115 N9
Michael Faraday Primary School
WALW SE17 19 H8
Michael Manley Industrial Estate
VX/NE SW8 158 D8
Michael Sobell Sinai School
KTN/HRWW/W HA3 115 M4
The Michael Tippett School
LBTH SE11 18 B6
Micheal Sobel Sports Centre
HOLWY N7 118 G8
Micklefield School
REIG RH2 257 K9
Micklem JMI School
HHW HP1 35 J5
Midas Business Centre
DAGE RM10 124 B9
Midas Industrial Estate
DAGE RM10 124 B9
UX/CGN UB8 131 L4
Middlegreen Trading Estate
DTCH/LGLY SL3 150 A1
Middle Park Primary School
ELTH/MOT SE9 184 A3
Middle Row Primary School
NKENS W10 8 A1
Middlesex Business Centre
NWDGN UB2 153 P1
Middlesex CCC (Lord's Cricket Ground)
STJWD NW8 3 M9
Middlesex Guildhall
WEST SW1P 17 K2
Middlesex Hospital
GTPST W1W 11 H4
Middlesex Hospital Medical School
FITZ W1T 11 H3
Middlesex Hospital Nurses Home
GTPST W1W 10 G3
Middlesex Hospital School of Physiotherapy
FITZ W1T 11 H3
Middlesex Hospital Sports Ground
CHST BR7 185 J8
Middlesex University
EBAR EN4 78 B10
GLDGN NW11 117 L6
TOTM N17 99 M7
WDGN N22 98 F10
Middlesex University Business School
HDN NW4 116 E2
Middle Temple Hall
TPL/STR WC2R 12 A7
Middleton Special School
WARE SG12 26 C4
Mid Essex Adult Community College
RBRW/HUT CM13 87 N10
Midfield Primary School
CHST BR7 185 K10
Mid Kent Golf Club
GVW DA11 190 E6
Midleton Industrial Estate
GU GU1 249 N9
Midway Mission Hospital
BETH E2 7 L10
Milbourne Lodge School
ESH/CLAY KT10 218 C3
Mile End & Bow Business Centre
WCHPL E1 140 A7
Mile End Hospital
WCHPL E1 140 C5
Mile End Stadium
BOW E3 140 E7
Milehams Industrial Estate
PUR RM19 165 P2
Miles Coverdale Primary School
SHB W12 156 F1
Milestone School
HART DA3 211 L8
Military Barracks
WOOL/PLUM SE18 162 D4
Military Cemetery
CHOB/PIR GU24 230 E7
Millbank Millennium Pier
WEST SW1P 17 L6
Millbank Primary School
WEST SW1P 17 K6
Millbank Tower
WEST SW1P 17 L6
Millbarn Medical Centre
BEAC HP9 88 E10
Millbourne Lodge Junior School
ESH/CLAY KT10 218 B2
Millbrook School
CHES/WCR EN8 62 D5
Millennium Arena
BTSEA SW11 158 B6
Millennium Balloon
STHWK SE1 13 K10
Millennium Harbour Development
POP/IOD E14 160 E1
Millennium Quay
DEPT SE8 160 G5
Millennium Wharf Development
POP/IOD E14 161 J2
Mill Farm Business Park
HSLWW TW4 175 M3
Millfields Junior & Infant School
CLPT E5 120 B9
Millfield Theatre
UED N18 99 L5
Mill Green Business Park
MTCM CR4 202 A7
Mill Green Golf Club
BRKMPK AL9 23 J10
Mill Hill Cemetery
MLHL NW7 96 F7
Mill Hill County High School
MLHL NW7 96 B3
The Mill Hill Cricket Club
MLHL NW7 96 F4
Mill Hill Golf Club
MLHL NW7 96 B3
Mill Hill Industrial Estate
MLHL NW7 96 C7
Mill Hill School
MLHL NW7 96 E5
Mill Lane Medical Centre
KIL/WHAMP NW6 117 K10
Mill Lane Trading Estate
CROY/NA CR0 202 G10
Mill Mead Junior & Infant School
HERT/WAS SG14 25 K5
Mill River Trading Estate
PEND EN3 80 D8
Millside Industrial Estate
DART DA1 165 L10
Mill Street Clinic
STHWK SE1 19 M1
Mill Studio Business Centre
WARE SG12 26 D2
Mill Trading Estate
WLSDN NW10 135 N4
Millwall FC (The New Den)
BERM/RHTH SE16 160 B4
Milmead Industrial Centre
TOTM N17 100 A10
Milton Mount School
CRAWE RH10 284 D5
Milton Natural Health Centre
HGT N6 118 D5
Milton Road Business Park
GVE DA12 190 F3
Milton's Cottage
CSTG HP8 89 N4
Milwards Primary School
HLWW/ROY CM19 46 E5
Minet Clinic
HYS/HAR UB3 133 H10
Minet Junior & Infant School
HYS/HAR UB3 133 J10
Ministry of Defence
WHALL SW1A 11 L10
Mini Town Hall
WOOL/PLUM SE18 163 J4
Mint Business Park
CAN/RD E16 141 M7
Mirravale Trading Estate
BCTR RM8 123 P5
Mission Grove Primary School
WALTH E17 120 E2
Mitcham Cricket Club
MTCM CR4 201 P4
Mitcham Golf Club
MTCM CR4 202 B5
Mitcham Industrial Estate
MTCM CR4 202 B1
Mitcham Road Crematorium
THHTH CR7 202 F5
Mitchell Brook Primary School
WLSDN NW10 136 A1
Mitre Bridge Industrial Park
WLSDN NW10 136 E6
Moatbridge School
ELTH/MOT SE9 184 A2
Mole Business Park
LHD/OX KT22 236 F7
Molesey Hospital
E/WMO/HCT KT8 197 P5
Molesey Lock
E/WMO/HCT KT8 198 D3
Mollison Drive Health Centre
WLGTN SM6 222 F4
Monega Primary School
MNPK E12 122 A10
Monken Hadley CE Primary School
EBAR EN4 77 K5
Monkfrith Primary School
EBAR EN4 98 B1
Monksmead School
BORE WD6 75 P7
Monks Orchard Primary School
CROY/NA CR0 204 C5
Monro Industrial Estate
CHES/WCR EN8 62 D10
Monson Primary School
NWCR SE14 160 C6
Montbelle Primary School
ELTH/MOT SE9 184 E6
Monteagle Primary School
DAGW RM9 143 L3
Montem Primary School
HOLWY N7 118 G8
SL SL1 148 G1
Montem Sports Centre
SL SL1 149 J1
The Montessori House School
MUSWH N10 118 C1
Montpelier Primary School
EA W5 135 J7
Monument Bridge East Industrial Estate
WOKN/KNAP GU21 232 E1
The Monument
MON EC3R 13 H8
Moorcroft School
UX/CGN UB8 132 C7
Moore Place Golf Club
ESH/CLAY KT10 217 P2
Moorfields Eye Hospital
FSBYE EC1V 6 C10
Moorfields Primary School
STLK EC1Y 12 G1
Moor House School
OXTED RH8 261 L8
Moor Lane Junior School
CHSGTN KT9 219 L2
Moor Park Golf Club
RKW/CH/CXG WD3 92 C4
Moor Park Industrial Estate
WATW WD18 92 D1
Mora Primary School
CRICK NW2 116 F9
Morden Cemetery
MRDN SM4 200 F6
Morden College Homes
BKHTH/KID SE3 161 M8
Morden First School
MRDN SM4 201 K5
Morden Hall Medical Centre
WIM/MER SW19 201 L3
Morden Mount Primary School
LEW SE13 160 G8
Morden Road Clinic
WIM/MER SW19 201 L3
More House School
ISLW TW7 154 D7
KTBR SW1X 16 B4
Moreland Primary School
FSBYE EC1V 6 D10
Moreton Bay Industrial Estate
GPK RM2 105 L10
Moreton CE Primary School
CHONG CM5 49 K6
Moreton Industrial Estate
SWLY BR8 209 J4
Morgans JMI School
HERT/BAY SG13 25 L7
Morgans Junior School
HERT/BAY SG13 25 L7
Morgans Walk Junior Mixed School
HERT/WAS SG14 25 H7
Moriah Jewish Day School
PIN HA5 113 M6
Morningside Primary School
HOM E9 140 B1
Mornington Leisure Centre
CAMTN NW1 4 F5
Morpeth School
BETH E2 140 B5
Mortimer Road Clinic
WLSDN NW10 136 F5
Mortimer School
STRHM/NOR SW16 180 E5
Mortlake Cemetery
MORT/ESHN SW14 156 B9
Mortlake Crematorium
RCH/KEW TW9 155 N8
Moselle School
TOTM N17 99 M10
Mosiah Foundation Supplementary School
STNW/STAM N16 119 M6
Mosquito Aircraft Museum
LCOL/BKTW AL2 57 N5
Mossford Green Primary School
BARK/HLT IG6 102 F10
Moss Hall Primary School
FNCH N3 97 L7
The Mother & Baby Clinic
HOM E9 140 B1
Mottingham Community Health Clinic
ELTH/MOT SE9 184 B7
Mottingham Primary School
ELTH/MOT SE9 184 C6
Mount Alvernia Hospital
GU GU1 268 B2
Mount Carmel RC Primary School
EA W5 155 H2
Mount Grace School
POTB/CUF EN6 59 L6
The Mount Infant School
NWMAL KT3 199 N3
Mount Medical Centre
FELT TW13 175 M5
Mount Pleasant J & I School
LCOL/BKTW AL2 55 M6
The Mount Primary School
NWMAL KT3 199 N3
Mount School
MLHL NW7 96 E6
Mount Stewart Primary School
KTN/HRWW/W HA3 115 J4
Mount Vernon Hospital
RKW/CH/CXG WD3 92 C6
Mowat Industrial Estate
WATN WD24 73 K4
Mowlem Primary School
BETH E2 140 B4
Mowlem Trading Estate
TOTM N17 100 B8
MS Business Centre
PIN HA5 113 L1
MSP Business Centre
WBLY HA9 115 N9
Mudchute City Farm
POP/IOD E14 161 H3
Mudlands Estate
RAIN RM13 144 F5
Mulberry Business Centre
BERM/RHTH SE16 160 C1
Mulberry House School
CRICK NW2 117 H10
Mulberry School for Girls
WCHPL E1 140 A8
Mulgrave Primary School
WOOL/PLUM SE18 162 E2
Murky Puddle Theatre
NWMAL KT3 200 C3
Murray Business Centre
STMC/STPC BR5 207 L3
Muschamp Primary School
CAR SM5 201 P9
Museum in Docklands
POP/IOD E14 140 F9
Museum of Artillery in the Rotunda
CHARL SE7 162 C4
Museum of Domestic Design & Architecture
EBAR EN4 78 A9
Museum of Fulham Palace
FUL/PGN SW6 156 G8
Museum of Garden History
STHWK SE1 17 M4
Museum of London
IS N1 6 F6
STBT EC1A 12 E4
Museum of Richmond
RCH/KEW TW9 177 J1
Museum of Rugby & Twickenham Stadium Tours
WHTN TW2 176 D2
Museum of the Order of St John
FARR EC1M 12 D2
Museums of the Royal College of Surgeons
LINN WC2A 11 P5
The Musical Museum
BTFD TW8 155 K5
Musley Infant School
WARE SG12 26 D1
Muswell Hill Bowling Club
MUSWH N10 118 B1
Muswell Hill Golf Club
FBAR/BDGN N11 98 C9
Myatt Garden Primary School
BROCKY SE4 160 E8
Myatts Field Clinic
BRXN/ST SW9 159 J7
Nagi Business Centre
ALP/SUD HA0 135 J4
Nags Head Shopping Centre
HOLWY N7 118 G9
Naima Jewish Preparatory School
KIL/WHAMP NW6 2 G7
Napsbury Hospital
LCOL/BKTW AL2 56 G3
Nascot Wood Junior School
WAT WD17 73 H4
Nash Mills Primary School
HHS/BOV HP3 54 A1
National Army Museum
CHEL SW3 16 B9
National Film Theatre
STHWK SE1 11 P9
National Film & TV School
BEAC HP9 88 D9
National Gallery
LSQ/SEVD WC2H 11 K8

National Hospital for Neurology & Neurosurgery
BMSBY WC1N 11 L2
National Hospital for Sick Children (Great Ormond St)
BMSBY WC1N 11 M2
National Maritime Museum
GNWCH SE10 161 J5
National Physical Laboratory
TEDD TW11 176 D9
National Portrait Gallery
LSQ/SEVD WC2H 11 K8
National Temperance Hospital
CAMTN NW1 5 H10
National Youth Theatre of GB
HOLWY N7 118 F8
Natural History Museum
SKENS SW7 15 L4
Natural Therapy Clinic
TOOT SW17 180 C8
Nature Reserve
CROY/NA CR0 224 D7
LCOL/BKTW AL2 57 K4
WALTH E17 120 B5
Natwest Sports Club
BECK BR3 182 E9
Navigation College
MANHO EC4N 12 F7
Nazeing CP School
WAB EN9 45 K9
Nazeing Golf Club
WAB EN9 45 P10
Nazeing Park (School)
WAB EN9 45 P8
NEC Harlequins RFC (The Stoop Memorial Ground)
WHTN TW2 176 D3
Nelmes Primary School
EMPK RM11 125 N2
Nelson Dock Museum
BERM/RHTH SE16 140 E10
Nelson Hospital
WIM/MER SW19 201 J2
Nelson Primary School
EHAM E6 142 D4
WHTN TW2 176 A2
Nelson's Column
CHCR WC2N 11 L9
Nelson Trading Estate
WIM/MER SW19 201 L1
Neo Clinic
PIM SW1V 16 G6
Netley Primary School
CAMTN NW1 4 G10
New Addington Swimming Pools
CROY/NA CR0 225 H6
The New Ambassadors Theatre
LSQ/SEVD WC2H 11 L6
New Ash Green Primary School
HART DA3 211 L9
New Atlas Wharf Development
POP/IOD E14 160 E2
The New Aylesbury Medical Centre
WALW SE17 19 H7
The New Beacon School
SEV TN13 264 G3
New Brentford Cemetery
HSLW TW3 153 N8
New Briars Primary School
HAT AL10 40 D4
Newbury Park Health Centre
GNTH/NBYPK IG2 122 G4
Newbury Park Primary School
GNTH/NBYPK IG2 122 G4
The New Business Centre
WLSDN NW10 136 C5
New Caledonian Wharf
BERM/RHTH SE16 160 E2
New Chiswick Swimming Pool
CHSWK W4 156 B6
New City Primary School
PLSTW E13 141 P5
The New College
WDSR SL4 149 J6
New Connaught Rooms
HOL/ALD WC2B 11 M5
New Covent Garden Market
VX/NE SW8 158 E6
New Crane Wharf
WAP E1W 140 B10
New Cross Sports Arena
NWCR SE14 160 D6
New Elgiva Theatre
CSHM HP5 50 G7
New End Primary School
HAMP NW3 117 M9
New End Theatre
HAMP NW3 117 M8
New England Industrial Estate
BARK IG11 142 F4
HOD EN11 45 H2
Newfield Primary School
WLSDN NW10 136 C2
The New Furness Primary School
WLSDN NW10 136 D4
Newham College of Further Education
EHAM E6 142 C4
SRTFD E15 141 K2
Newham Community College
CAN/RD E16 141 K6
Newham General Hospital
PLSTW E13 141 P6
Newham Leisure Centre
PLSTW E13 141 P7
Newham Medical Centre
PLSTW E13 141 P4
Newham Museum Service
SRTFD E15 141 J2
Newham Sixth Form College
PLSTW E13 141 N6
New Haw Therapy Clinic
ADL/WDHM KT15 215 L6
New Health Centre
TOTM N17 99 M9
Newington Court Business Centre
STHWK SE1 18 E4
Newington Green Primary School
STNW/STAM N16 119 M10
Newington Industrial Estate
WALW SE17 18 D6
New Kings Primary School
FUL/PGN SW6 157 J8
Newland House School
TWK TW1 176 E7
New London Theatre
LSQ/SEVD WC2H 11 M5
New Monument School
WOKS/MYFD GU22 232 F1
Newnham Junior & Infant School
RSLP HA4 113 K6
Newport Junior & Infant School
WAN E11 121 H7
New River Stadium
WDGN N22 99 J8
New River Trading Estate
CHES/WCR EN8 62 C2
New Rush Hall School
IL IG1 122 F7
New School
FUL/PGN SW6 157 J7
The New School at West Heath
SEV TN13 265 J5
New Scotland Yard
STJSPK SW1H 17 J3
News International
WAP E1W 13 P8
New Southgate Cemetery
FBAR/BDGN N11 98 C4
New Southgate Crematorium
FBAR/BDGN N11 98 C4
New Southgate Industrial Estate
FBAR/BDGN N11 98 D6
New Southgate Pain Clinic & Medical Centre
FBAR/BDGN N11 98 D6
Newstead Wood School for Girls
ORP BR6 206 G10
Newton Farm First & Middle School
RYLN/HDSTN HA2 113 N7
Newton Industrial Estate
CHDH RM6 123 N2
Newton Medical Centre
BAY/PAD W2 8 F5
Newton Preparatory School
VX/NE SW8 158 C6
Newtons Primary School
RAIN RM13 144 E4
New Victoria Hospital
KUTN/CMB KT2 178 B10
New Victoria Theatre
WOKN/KNAP GU21 232 B3
New Woodlands School
BMLY BR1 183 K7
New Zealand Golf Club
WOKN/KNAP GU21 215 H8
Nicholas Breakspear RC School
STALE/WH AL4 39 K7
Nicholas Hawksmoor School
BORE WD6 75 N5
Nightingale Clinic
PLSTW E13 141 P4
Nightingale Primary School
SWFD E18 121 P2
WDGN N22 98 F9
WOOL/PLUM SE18 162 E4
Nightingale School
STHWK SE1 17 N2
TOOT SW17 179 P5
Nineacres School
WOOL/PLUM SE18 162 G4
Nizels Hotel Golf & Leisure Club
RTON TN11 265 M10
Noel Park Primary School
WDGN N22 99 J10
Nomad Theatre
EHSLY KT24 252 G5
Nonsuch High School for Girls
EW KT17 220 G4
Nonsuch Industrial Estate
EW KT17 220 B7
Nonsuch Primary School
EW KT17 220 E2
Norbury Complementary Therapy Clinic
STRHM/NOR SW16 202 G1
Norbury First & Middle School
HRW HA1 114 D3
Norbury Health Centre
STRHM/NOR SW16 202 G2
Norbury Manor Primary School
STRHM/NOR SW16 202 F1
Norbury Manor Secondary Girls School
STRHM/NOR SW16 202 G1
Norbury Trading Estate
STRHM/NOR SW16 202 G2
Norfolk House School
MUSWH N10 98 C10
Norlington School
LEY E10 121 J6
Normand Park Primary School
FUL/PGN SW6 14 C9
Normandy Primary School
BXLYHN DA7 164 E7
Normanhurst School
CHING E4 101 J1
Norman Park Athletics Track
HAYES BR2 205 N6
Norman Shaw Building (MP's Offices)
WHALL SW1A 17 L1
North Acton Business Park
ACT W3 136 A8
Northaw Primary School
POTB/CUF EN6 60 B5
North Beckton Primary School
EHAM E6 142 C7
North Bridge House
HAMP NW3 3 K1
North Bridge House Senior School
CAMTN NW1 4 E6
Northbrook CE School
LEW SE13 183 K1
Northbury Primary School
BARK IG11 142 E1
Northchurch Cricket Club
BERK HP4 33 J2
North Clinic
BMLY BR1 205 M1
Northcote Lodge School
BTSEA SW11 179 P2
Northcourt Primary School
GVE DA12 191 H4
North Cray Primary School
SCUP DA14 185 P9
North Croydon Medical Centre
THHTH CR7 203 J6
North Downs Business Park
RSEV TN14 246 D2
North Downs Golf Club
GDST RH9 260 F1
North Ealing Primary School
WEA W13 134 G6
North East Surrey College of Technology
EW KT17 220 D7
North East Surrey Crematorium
NWMAL KT3 200 F6
Northend Primary School
ERITH DA8 164 G7
North End Trading Estate
ERITH DA8 164 F6
North Feltham Trading Estate
EBED/NFELT TW14 153 J10
Northfields Industrial Estate
ALP/SUD HA0 135 M3
Northfields Prospect Business Centre
WAND/EARL SW18 157 J10
Northfleet Cemetery
GVW DA11 189 P4
Northfleet Industrial Estate
GVW DA11 167 L10
Northfleet School for Boys
GVW DA11 190 A4
Northfleet School for Girls
GVW DA11 190 A5
Northgate Business Centre
EN EN1 80 A7
Northgate Clinic
CDALE/KGS NW9 116 B4
Northgate First & Middle School
CRAWE RH10 283 P5
Northgate Industrial Park
ROMW/RG RM7 104 A10
North Harringey Primary School
CEND/HSY/T N8 119 H2
North Havering College of Adult Education
ROM RM1 124 F2
North Holmwood Cricket Club
RDKG RH5 273 H7
North London Collegiate School
EDGW HA8 95 K7
North London School of Physiotherapy
ARCH N19 118 D6
North London Tutorial College
HDN NW4 116 F4
North Middlesex Golf Club
TRDG/WHET N20 97 N4
North Middlesex Hospital
UED N18 99 M6
North Mymms Cricket Club
BRKMPK AL9 58 D2
Northolt Aerodrome
RSLP HA4 133 H1
Northolt High School
NTHLT UB5 133 N1
Northolt Park Infant School
NTHLT UB5 114 A10
Northolt Primary School
NTHLT UB5 133 L2
Northolt Road Clinic
RYLN/HDSTN HA2 114 B8
North Orbital Trading Estate
STAL AL1 38 F10
North Peckham Civic Centre & Library
STHWK SE1 19 N9
North Primary School
STHL UB1 133 N9
Northside Primary
NFNCH/WDSP N12 97 L6
The North Street Health Centre
CLAP SW4 158 D9
Northumberland Heath Medical Centre
ERITH DA8 164 E6
Northumberland Heath Primary School
ERITH DA8 164 C6
Northumberland Park Industrial Estate
TOTM N17 100 A7
Northumberland Park School
TOTM N17 99 P8
Northview Primary School
WLSDN NW10 116 B9
North Watford Cemetery
GSTN WD25 73 H1
North Watford Health Clinic
GSTN WD25 55 K10
Northway School
MLHL NW7 95 P4
North Weald Golf Club
EPP CM16 48 B9
North & West Essex Adult Community College
HLW CM20 28 F9
North West Kent College of Technology
DART DA1 187 K3
GVE DA12 191 J4
North West London Jewish Primary School
CRICK NW2 2 A3
North West London Medical Centre
MV/WKIL W9 3 J8
North Westminster Community School
BAY/PAD W2 9 L4
STJWD NW8 9 N3
North Westminster Community Secondary School
MV/WKIL W9 8 F1
North Weylands Industrial Estate
WOT/HER KT12 197 M9
Northwick Park Hospital & Clinical Research Centre
HRW HA1 114 G5
Northwold Primary School
CLPT E5 119 P7
Northwood Cemetery
NTHWD HA6 92 G10
Northwood College
NTHWD HA6 92 E8
Northwood FC
NTHWD HA6 92 G10
Northwood Golf Club
NTHWD HA6 92 E8
Northwood & Pinner Community Hospital
NTHWD HA6 93 H9
Northwood Preparatory School
RKW/CH/CXG WD3 92 D3
Northwood School
NTHWD HA6 93 J9
Northwood Sports Centre
PIN HA5 93 J9
Norwegian/British Monument
BAY/PAD W2 9 P10
Norwood Green Infant School
NWDGN UB2 153 M4
Norwood Heights Shopping Centre
NRWD SE19 181 M9
Norwood Park Primary School
WNWD SE27 181 K7
Norwood School
WNWD SE27 181 K8
Notre Dame Preparatory School
WOT/HER KT12 216 G7
Notre Dame RC Girls School
STHWK SE1 18 C3
Notre Dame RC Primary School
WOOL/PLUM SE18 162 E5
Notting Hill & Ealing High School
WEA W13 134 G7
Novello Theatre
ASC SL5 192 C5
Nower Hill High School
PIN HA5 113 P2
Nower Lodge School
DORK RH4 272 F3
N1 Shopping Centre
IS N1 6 B7
NTGB Sports Ground
EHAM E6 142 D1
Nuffield Hospital
ENC/FH EN2 79 H6
Nugent Industrial Park
STMC/STPC BR5 207 M4
Nutfield Cemetery
REDH RH1 258 E9
Nutfield Church CE Primary School
REDH RH1 276 G1
Nutley Dean Business Park
HORL RH6 279 H1
Nutrition Clinic
MHST W1U 10 C3
NW5 Theatre School
KTTN NW5 118 D10
Oakdale Infant School
SWFD E18 101 N10
Oakdale Junior School
SWFD E18 101 P10
Oak Farm Clinic
HGDN/ICK UB10 132 C3
Oak Farm Junior & Infant School
HGDN/ICK UB10 132 C2
Oakfield First School
WDSR SL4 148 G8
Oakfield Junior School
LHD/OX KT22 236 B9
Oakfield Preparatory School
DUL SE21 181 L5
Oakfield Primary School
DART DA1 187 L5
Oakfield Road Industrial Estate
PGE/AN SE20 182 A10
Oakfield School
WOKS/MYFD GU22 233 J1
Oak Hill College
EBAR EN4 78 B10
Oak Hill Health Centre
SURB KT6 199 K6
Oakhill Primary School
WFD IG8 101 K7
Oakhyrst Grange School
CTHM CR3 259 L2
Oakington Manor School
WBLY HA9 115 N10
Oakland CP School
EBAR EN4 78 A10
Oakland Park Golf Club
CSTG HP8 89 L5
Oakland Primary School
BH/WHM TN16 243 P2
Oakland School
BNSTD SM7 221 K10
Oaklands College
BORE WD6 75 P6
HARP AL5 20 A2
HAT AL10 40 D4
STAL AL1 38 D6
STALE/WH AL4 39 K5
WGCW AL8 22 G4
Oaklands Primary School
HNWL W7 154 E1
Oaklands School
ISLW TW7 154 C9
LOU IG10 82 A9
Oak Lane Cemetery
TWK TW1 176 F3
Oak Lane Medical Centre
TWK TW1 176 G3
Oakleigh School
TRDG/WHET N20 97 P4
Oak Lodge JMI School
WWKM BR4 204 G7
Oak Lodge Medical Centre
EDGW HA8 95 N8
Oak Lodge School
BAL SW12 180 A3
EFNCH N2 117 M1
Oakmere Primary School
POTB/CUF EN6 59 N8
The Oaks First & Middle School
CRAWE RH10 284 A10
The Oaks Industrial Estate
HLW CM20 29 J8
Oaks Sports Centre
CAR SM5 222 A7
Oakthorpe Primary School
PLMGR N13 99 K6
Oak Tree Clinic
WOKN/KNAP GU21 231 J4
Oak Tree Medical Centre
GDMY/SEVK IG3 123 H7
Oakwood Business Park
WLSDN NW10 136 A5
Oakwood Estate
HLW CM20 29 K8
Oakwood Hill Industrial Estate
LOU IG10 82 E9
Oakwood Independent School
PUR/KEN CR8 223 J9
Oakwood Industrial Park
CRAWE RH10 284 B4
Oakwood JMI School
STALE/WH AL4 39 H5
Oakwood Medical Centre
STHGT/OAK N14 78 D9
Oakwood School
HORL RH6 280 C4
Oakwood Sports Centre
HORL RH6 280 D4
Oasis Sports Centre
LSQ/SEVD WC2H 11 L5
Oatlands School
WEY KT13 216 E1
The Observatory Shopping Centre
SL SL1 149 M1
Obstetrics Hospital
GWRST WC1E 11 H2
Occupational Health Centre
CROY/NA CR0 203 L10
Ockendon School
SOCK/AV RM15 146 F7
Odeon Cinema
BAR EN5 77 K9
BECK BR3 204 F2
CAMTN NW1 4 F5
CFSP/GDCR SL9 110 B3
ELTH/MOT SE9 162 B10
ESH/CLAY KT10 218 A1
EW KT17 220 B9
FITZ W1T 11 J4
GNTH/NBYPK IG2 122 D4
HAYES BR2 205 M2
HHS/BOV HP3 36 A7
HLW CM20 28 F10
HOLWY N7 118 F8
KENS W8 14 E3
KIL/WHAMP NW6 3 L4
MBLAR W1H 10 B6
MUSWH N10 118 B2
RCHPK/HAM TW10 177 J1
ROM RM1 124 G3
STJS SW1Y 11 J8
STRHM/NOR SW16 180 F6
SWFD E18 101 M10
UX/CGN UB8 131 M2
WIM/MER SW19 179 K10
Odeon Covent Gardens Cinema
LSQ/SEVD WC2H 11 K6
Odeon Multiplex Cinema
GU GU1 267 P1
Odeon Wardour Street Cinema
SOHO/SHAV W1D 11 J7
Odessa Infant School
FSTGT E7 121 M10
Odhams Industrial Estate
WATN WD24 73 K3
Odhams Trading Estate
WATN WD24 73 H2
WATN WD24 73 K2
Odyssey Business Park
RSLP HA4 113 J10
Old Actonians Sports Club
EA W5 155 L1
Old Admiralty
WHALL SW1A 11 K10
Old Bancroftians FC
BKHH IG9 102 A5
Old Barnes Cemetery
BARN SW13 156 E8
Old Barn Theatre
CRAWW RH11 283 J5
Old Beckenhamian RFC
WWKM BR4 205 J10
Old Bellgate Wharf Development
POP/IOD E14 160 E2
Old Bexley Business Park
BXLY DA5 186 C3
Old Bexley CE Primary School
BXLY DA5 186 A4
The Old Brickworks Business Centre
HARH RM3 105 P8
Old Brockleians Sports Ground
ELTH/MOT SE9 183 P2
Old Bromlians Cricket Club
HAYES BR2 205 N5
Old Cemetery
EDUL SE22 182 A2
Old Chigwellians Sports Club
CHIG IG7 102 E2
Oldchurch Hospital
ROMW/RG RM7 124 E4
Old Colfeian Sports Club
LEE/GVPK SE12 183 M1
The Old Cottage Hospital
EW KT17 220 C9
Old Curiosity Shop
LINN WC2A 11 N5
Old Elthamians Sports Club
CHST BR7 185 H9
Oldfield House Special School
HPTN TW12 197 N1
Oldfields Primary School
GFD/PVL UB6 134 C4
Oldfields Trading Estate
SUT SM1 201 K10
Old Fold Manor Golf Club
BAR EN5 77 H5
Old Ford Primary School
BOW E3 140 E4
Old Guildfordians RFC
GU GU1 250 C9
The Old Guild Theatre
GVW DA11 190 A4
Old Harlow Health Centre
HLWE CM17 29 M7
Oldhill Medical Centre
STNW/STAM N16 119 N6
Old Jamaica Business Estate
BERM/RHTH SE16 19 M3
Old Lyonian Sports Ground
RYLN/HDSTN HA2 114 B3
Old Merchant Taylors Sports Club
RKW/CH/CXG WD3 72 C8
Old Millhillians Sports Ground
PIN HA5 93 P9
Old Oak Primary School
SHB W12 136 C8
Old Operating Theatre Museum
STHWK SE1 12 G10
Old Owens Sports Ground
TRDG/WHET N20 97 N2
Old Palace Primary School
BOW E3 140 G5
Old Palace School
CROY/NA CR0 203 J10
Old Royal Naval College
GNWCH SE10 161 J5
Old Royal Observatory Greenwich
GNWCH SE10 161 J6
Old St Patricks School
WCHPL E1 13 N2

Old Station Museum
CAN/RD E16 162 D1
Old Sun Wharf
POP/IOD E14 140 D9
Old Tiffinians Sports Ground
E/WMO/HCT KT8 198 D5
Old Town Hall
CHERT KT16 195 K7
Old Treasury
WHALL SW1A 17 L1
Old Verulamians RFC
LCOL/BKTW AL2 57 H1
Old Vicarage School
RCHPK/HAM TW10 177 K2
Old Vic Theatre
STHWK SE1 18 B1
Old War Office
WHALL SW1A 11 L10
Old Wilsonians Sports Club
WWKM BR4 205 K8
Olga Primary School
BOW E3 140 D4
Oliver Business Park
WLSDN NW10 135 P4
Oliver Goldsmith Primary School
CDALE/KGS NW9 116 A3
CMBW SE5 159 M7
Olympia
WKENS W14 14 B4
Olympia Industrial Estate
WDGN N22 98 G10
Olympic Industrial Estate
WBLY HA9 115 N9
Olympic Retail Park
WBLY HA9 115 M9
Olympic Trading Estate
WBLY HA9 115 N9
The One Stanley Medical Centre
ALP/SUD HA0 135 K2
Ongar & District Sports Club
CHONG CM5 67 P4
Ongar Health Centre
CHONG CM5 67 P4
Ongar Leisure Centre
CHONG CM5 67 P2
Ongar Place Infant School
ADL/WDHM KT15 215 K3
Ongar War Memorial Hospital
CHONG CM5 67 P2
On Sai Clinic
ECT SW5 14 G6
Onslow County Infant School
GUW GU2 267 L2
Onslow St Audreys School
HAT AL10 40 E4
On the Road Tours CC
WAND/EARL SW18 179 M2
Open Air Theatre
CAMTN NW1 4 C10
The Open University
FSBYW WC1X 5 N9
KIL/WHAMP NW6 117 K9
Ophaboom Theatre
WLSDN NW10 136 E5
Optima Business Park
HOD EN11 45 H2
Optimax Laser Eye Clinic
HAMP NW3 3 K2
Orange Tree Theatre
RCH/KEW TW9 155 K10
Oratory RC Primary School
CHEL SW3 15 N7
Orchard Business Centre
REDH RH1 276 B9
SYD SE26 182 E8
The Orchard Health Centre
BARK IG11 142 F4
Orchard House Industrial Estate
CSHM HP5 51 H8
Orchard Infant School
REIG RH2 275 K3
The Orchard Junior School
HSLW TW3 153 P10
Orchard Primary School
HOM E9 140 B2
WATN WD24 72 G2
The Orchard School
E/WMO/HCT KT8 198 C5
Orchard Shopping Centre
DART DA1 187 M2
The Orchard Theatre
DART DA1 187 M2
Orchard Way Primary School
CROY/NA CR0 204 D7
Oriel Primary School
FELT TW13 175 M6
Orient Industrial Park
LEY E10 120 F7
Orion Business Centre
BERM/RHTH SE16 160 C4
Orleans House Gallery
TWK TW1 176 G4
Orleans Infant School
TWK TW1 176 G3
Orleans Park School
TWK TW1 176 G3
Orley Farm School
HRW HA1 114 C8
Orpington College of Further Education
ORP BR6 207 K8
The Orpington Halls
ORP BR6 207 K9
Orpington Mental Health Centre
ORP BR6 207 J10
Orpington Retail Park
STMC/STPC BR5 207 M4
Orpington Superbowl
ORP BR6 207 K8
Osidge JMI School
STHGT/OAK N14 98 D2
Osmani Primary School
WCHPL E1 13 P2
Osteopathic Clinic
HOR/WEW KT19 220 A2
Osterley RFC
NWDGN UB2 154 A2
Otford Primary School
RSEV TN14 247 H2
Our Lady Immaculate RC Primary School
BRYLDS KT5 199 N8
Our Lady of Dolours RC Primary School
BAY/PAD W2 8 G3
Our Lady of Grace RC Junior School
CRICK NW2 116 E8
Our Lady of Hartley RC Primary School
HART DA3 211 L5
Our Lady of Lourdes RC Primary School
FBAR/BDGN N11 98 D6
FNCH N3 97 M8
LEW SE13 161 J9
WAN E11 121 L4
WLSDN NW10 135 P3
Our Lady of Muswell RC Primary School
MUSWH N10 98 B10
Our Lady of St Johns
BTFD TW8 155 H4
Our Lady of the Rosary RC Primary School
BFN/LL DA15 185 H2
STA TW18 173 K9
Our Lady of the Sacred Heart School
HOLWY N7 5 P1
Our Lady of Victories RC Primary School
PUT/ROE SW15 156 G10
SKENS SW7 15 L6
Our Lady Queen of Heaven Catholic First School
CRAWW RH11 283 L5
Our Lady Queen of Heaven RC Primary School
WIM/MER SW19 178 G3
Our Lady RC Primary School
CAMTN NW1 5 H5
POP/IOD E14 140 E8
Our Lady & St Joseph Primary School
IS N1 7 J2
Our Lady & St Philip Neri RC Primary School
FSTH SE23 182 C6
Our Ladys Catholic Primary School
AMS HP6 68 G1
DART DA1 187 K2
Our Ladys Convent High School
STNW/STAM N16 119 M5
Our Ladys RC Primary School
WGCE AL7 23 H7
Outwood Windmill
REDH RH1 277 L9
Oval Business Centre
LBTH SE11 17 P8
Oval House Theatre
LBTH SE11 18 A10
Oval Primary School
CROY/NA CR0 203 M8
Overton Grange School
BELMT SM2 221 L4
Oxford Gardens Primary School
NKENS W10 136 G8
Oxford House College
SOHO/SHAV W1D 11 J5
Oxhey Infant School
BUSH WD23 73 M10
Oxhey Wood Primary School
OXHEY WD19 93 K5
Oxo Tower Wharf
STHWK SE1 12 B8
Oxted Health Centre
OXTED RH8 261 L5
Oxted & Limpsfield Hospital
OXTED RH8 261 J4
Oxted School
OXTED RH8 261 L4
Pachesham Park Golf Centre
LHD/OX KT22 236 D4
Paddington Bowling & Sports Club
MV/WKIL W9 8 G1
Paddington Community Hospital
MV/WKIL W9 8 E3
Paddington Green Primary School
BAY/PAD W2 9 L2
Paddington Recreation Ground Athletics Track
KIL/WHAMP NW6 2 F9
Paddington Station
BAY/PAD W2 9 L5
Paddock School
PUT/ROE SW15 156 C10
Pain Relief Clinic
HDN NW4 116 E4
Painshill Landscape Garden
COB KT11 216 G10
Painters Ash Primary School
GVW DA11 190 A6
Pakeman Primary School
HOLWY N7 118 G8
Palace Gardens Shopping Centre
ENC/FH EN2 79 L7
Palace Theatre
WAT WD17 73 J7
Palladium Theatre
REGST W1B 10 G6
Palmers College
GRAYS RM17 168 C3
Palmers Green High School
WCHMH N21 99 H3
Palmerston Business Centre
SUT SM1 221 M2
Palm House
RCH/KEW TW9 155 L7
Panorama Pier
STHWK SE1 12 D8
Panshanger Aerodrome
WGCE AL7 23 P5
Panshanger Golf & Squash Complex
WGCE AL7 23 M3
Panshanger JMI School
WGCE AL7 23 K4
Paradise Swimming Pools
MLHL NW7 96 B6
Paradise Wildlife Park
BROX EN10 43 N7
Paramount Industrial Estate
WATN WD24 73 K4
Parayhouse School
WBPTN SW10 157 M6
Parchmore Medical Centre
THHTH CR7 203 K3
Pardes House & Beis Yaakov Boys School
FNCH N3 97 J10
Parent Infant Clinic
HAMP NW3 117 M10
Paringdon Primary School
HLWS CM18 46 G5
Parish CE Primary School
BMLY BR1 183 M10
Parish Church CE Primary School
CROY/NA CR0 203 J10
Park Avenue Clinic
WAT WD17 73 H6
Park Business Centre
KIL/WHAMP NW6 2 E10
Parker Industrial Centre
RDART DA2 188 B3
Parkfield Industrial Estate
BTSEA SW11 158 B8
Parkfield JMI School
HDN NW4 116 E5
Parkfield Medical Centre
POTB/CUF EN6 59 L8
Parkgate House School
CLAP SW4 158 B10
Parkgate Infant School
WATN WD24 73 K3
Parkgate Junior School
WATN WD24 73 K3
Park Hall Trading Estate
WNWD SE27 181 K6
Park High School
STAN HA7 95 J10
Park Hill Junior School
CROY/NA CR0 203 L10
Parkhill Primary School
CLAY IG5 122 C1
Park House Medical Centre
KIL/WHAMP NW6 2 B7
Parkhouse Middle School
WIM/MER SW19 179 J7
Park House RFC
HAYES BR2 205 P9
Parkhurst Infant School
TOTM N17 99 N10
Park Industrial Estate
LCOL/BKTW AL2 56 D3
Parklands Primary School
ROM RM1 124 E1
Park Lane Primary School
WBLY HA9 115 K9
Park Medical Centre
BERM/RHTH SE16 160 C3
Park Mews Small Business Centre
HNHL SE24 181 K2
Park Primary School
SRTFD E15 141 L2
Park Road Clinic
CEND/HSY/T N8 118 E3
Park Road Industrial Estate
SWLY BR8 208 G3
Park Royal Business Centre
WLSDN NW10 135 P6
Park School
WOKS/MYFD GU22 232 D3
Park School for Girls
IL IG1 122 E6
Parks Golf Courses & Sports Grounds
STA TW18 173 L6
Parkside Business Estate
DEPT SE8 160 E5
Parkside Clinic
NTGHL W11 8 B5
Parkside Health
NTGHL W11 8 B6
Parkside Hospital
WIM/MER SW19 178 G6
Parkside Primary School
BORE WD6 75 L4
Parkside School
COB KT11 235 P4
Park Street CE Primary School
LCOL/BKTW AL2 56 C3
Park Walk Primary School
WBPTN SW10 15 L10
Parkway Primary School
ERITHM DA18 163 P2
Parkway Trading Estate
HEST TW5 153 K5
Park Wood Golf Club
BH/WHM TN16 244 B8
Parkwood Hall School
SWLY BR8 209 J3
Parkwood Primary School
FSBYPK N4 119 J7
Parlaunt Park Combined School
DTCH/LGLY SL3 150 E2
Parliament Hill Fields Athletics Track
KTTN NW5 118 A9
Parliament Hill School
KTTN NW5 118 B9
Parmiter Industrial Centre
BETH E2 140 A4
Parmiters School
GSTN WD25 55 K7
Parndon Wood
HLWS CM18 46 G7
Parndon Wood Cemetery
EPP CM16 46 F7
Parndon Wood Crematorium
HLWW/ROY CM19 46 F7
Parnells Sports Ground
KTN/HRWW/W HA3 115 L4
Parsloes Primary School
DAGW RM9 144 A1
Parsonage Farm Primary School
RAIN RM13 145 K5
Parsons Green Health Clinic
FUL/PGN SW6 157 K7
Parsons Mead School
ASHTD KT21 237 K5
Passmores School
HLWS CM18 46 G3
Passport Language Schools
BMLY BR1 205 N1
Patent Office
HHOL WC1V 12 A4
The Patrick Doody Clinic & Health Centre
WIM/MER SW19 179 K10
Pattinson Clinic
RCHPK/HAM TW10 177 J1
The Paul Robeson Theatre
HSLW TW3 154 A9
Pavilion Barclays Sports Ground
EA W5 135 K7
The Pavilion Leisure Centre
BMLY BR1 205 M2
Pavilion Restaurant
RCH/KEW TW9 155 K8
Paxton Primary School
NRWD SE19 181 N9
Payne Clinic
EW KT17 220 D9
PDSA Hospital
REDBR IG4 122 A1
Peace Pagoda
BTSEA SW11 158 A6
Peacock Cinema
WOKN/KNAP GU21 232 B3
Peacock Estate
TOTM N17 99 N7
Peacock Industrial Estate
TOTM N17 99 N8
The Peacocks Shopping Centre
WOKN/KNAP GU21 232 B3
The Peacock Theatre
HOL/ALD WC2B 11 N6
Peall Road Industrial Estate
CROY/NA CR0 202 G6
Peaslake School
SHGR GU5 270 F10
Peckham Park Primary School
PECK SE15 159 P6
The Peckham Pulse Health & Leisure Centre
PECK SE15 159 P7
Peckham Rye Primary School
PECK SE15 160 A9
Pedham Place Industrial Estate
SWLY BR8 209 H5
Peerglow Industrial Estate
WATW WD18 92 C1
Pelham Primary School
BXLYHN DA7 164 B9
WIM/MER SW19 179 K10
Pendragon Secondary School
BMLY BR1 183 M6
Pentavia Retail Park
MLHL NW7 96 C8
Penton Primary School
IS N1 6 B7
Penwortham Primary School
STRHM/NOR SW16 180 C9
Percival David Foundation of Chinese Art
STPAN WC1H 11 K1
Perivale Industrial Park
GFD/PVL UB6 134 F3
Perivale New Business Centre
GFD/PVL UB6 135 H4
Perivale Park Athletics Track
GFD/PVL UB6 134 D5
Perivale Park Golf Course
GFD/PVL UB6 134 D5
Perivale Primary School
GFD/PVL UB6 135 H4
Perrin Road Clinic
ALP/SUD HA0 114 G9
Perry Hall Primary School
ORP BR6 207 J6
Perrymount Primary School
FSTH SE23 182 C5
Perrywood Business Park
REDH RH1 276 C8
Perth Trading Estate
SL SL1 128 G7
Peterborough Primary School
FUL/PGN SW6 157 K8
Peterborough & St Margarets High School
STAN HA7 94 D4
Peter Hills School
BERM/RHTH SE16 140 C10
Peter James Business Centre
HYS/HAR UB3 153 H1
Peterley Business Centre
BETH E2 140 A4
Peter Pan Statue
BAY/PAD W2 9 L9
Pewley Down Infant School
GU GU1 268 B2
Pewterers' Hall
CITYW EC2V 12 F4
Phoenix Business Centre
CSHM HP5 50 G6
POP/IOD E14 140 F7
Phoenix Cinema
EFNCH N2 117 P2
Phoenix College
MRDN SM4 201 L5
TOOT SW17 179 P5
Phoenix Court
POP/IOD E14 160 F3
Phoenix High School
SHB W12 136 D9
Phoenix Industrial Estate
HRW HA1 114 E2
Phoenix Leisure Centre
CAT SE6 182 G3
Phoenix School
BOW E3 140 E5
HAMP NW3 3 L2
Phoenix Theatre
LSQ/SEVD WC2H 11 K6
Phoenix Trading Estate
GFD/PVL UB6 135 H3
Physical Energy Statue
BAY/PAD W2 9 L10
Piccadilly Theatre
SOHO/SHAV W1D 11 J7
Pickford Lane Medical Centre
BXLYHN DA7 163 P7
Pickhurst Infant School
HAYES BR2 205 K6
Pickhurst Junior School
HAYES BR2 205 L6
Picture House Cinema
SRTFD E15 141 J1
Pield Heath School
UX/CGN UB8 131 P6
Pilgrims Hatch County Primary School
BRWN CM15 86 F10
Pilgrims Way Junior & Infant School
PECK SE15 160 B5
Pilot Industrial Centre
WLSDN NW10 136 B6
Pilton Estate
CROY/NA CR0 203 J9
Pimlico School
PIM SW1V 17 H8
The Pines Primary School
HERT/BAY SG13 25 P4
The Pines Trading Estate
RGUW GU3 249 J8
Pine Trees Business Park
STA TW18 173 H8
Pinewood Film Studios
IVER SL0 130 E2
Pinewood Primary School
CRW RM5 104 C6
Pinewood Special School
WARE SG12 26 C4
Pinkwell Primary School
WDR/YW UB7 152 D3
Pinner Hill Golf Club
PIN HA5 93 J7
Pinner Park Primary School
RYLN/HDSTN HA2 114 A1
Pinner View Medical Centre
HRW HA1 114 B3
Pinner Wood Primary School
PIN HA5 93 K9
Pinn Medical Centre
PIN HA5 113 M2
Pioneers Industrial Park
CROY/NA CR0 202 F8
Pippins School
DTCH/LGLY SL3 151 J7
Pirbright Camp
CHOB/PIR GU24 230 A6
Pirbright Primary School
CHOB/PIR GU24 230 D8
Pitfarm Lawn Tennis Club
GU GU1 250 C10
Pitshanger Manor Museum
EA W5 135 H10
Pitwood Park Industrial Estate
KWD/TDW/WH KT20 238 G6
Pixham School
DORK RH4 255 H10
Pixies Hill JMI School
HHW HP1 35 J7
Plaisterers Hall
CITYW EC2V 12 E4
Plaistow Hospital
PLSTW E13 141 N4
Planetarium
CAMTN NW1 10 C2
Plantation House Medical Centre
LOTH EC2R 13 H5
Plashet Jewish Cemetery
MNPK E12 142 A1
Plashet Road Medical Centre
FSTGT E7 141 N2
Plashet School
EHAM E6 142 B2
Players Theatre
CHCR WC2N 11 L9
Playhouse
HLW CM20 46 F1
Playhouse Cinema
EPSOM KT18 220 A10
The Playhouse
CHCR WC2N 11 M9
Playhouse Theatre
EPSOM KT18 219 P9
Plaza Business Centre
PEND EN3 80 E6
Plaza Cinema
OXTED RH8 261 K5
Plough Industrial Estate
LHD/OX KT22 236 F6
Plumcroft Primary School
WOOL/PLUM SE18 162 F5
Plumstead Manor School
WOOL/PLUM SE18 162 G4
The Pointer School
BKHTH/KID SE3 161 M7
Police Cadet School
WAN E11 121 M6
The Polish Institute & Sikorski Museum
SKENS SW7 15 M2
Polka Theatre for Children
WIM/MER SW19 179 L9
Pollock's Toy Museum
FITZ W1T 11 H3
Polygon Business Centre
DTCH/LGLY SL3 151 J8
Ponders End Industrial Estate
PEND EN3 80 C6
PEND EN3 80 E8
Pond Meadow School
GUW GU2 249 K9
Ponsbourne St Marys JMI School
HERT/BAY SG13 42 F10
Ponsbourne Tunnel
HERT/BAY SG13 43 H8
Poole's Park Primary School
HOLWY N7 118 G7
Pope John Primary School
SHB W12 136 E9
Pope Paul RC Primary School
POTB/CUF EN6 59 J9
Pop In Business Centre
WBLY HA9 115 N10
Poplar Business Park
POP/IOD E14 141 H9
Poplar First School
WIM/MER SW19 201 K3
Pop Up Theatre
FSBYE EC1V 6 C8
Porchester Leisure Centre
BAY/PAD W2 8 G5
Porny CE First School
WDSR SL4 149 J5
Portcullis House
WHALL SW1A 17 M2
Porters Park Golf Club
RAD WD7 57 H10
Portland Business Centre
DTCH/LGLY SL3 149 N7
The Portland Hospital
REGST W1B 10 F2
Portland House Medical Centre
GFD/PVL UB6 134 A6
Portland Medical Centre
SNWD SE25 204 A5
Portland Place School
REGST W1B 10 F3
The Portman Clinic
HAMP NW3 3 L1
Portobello Medical Centre
NTGHL W11 8 B6
Portway Primary School
SRTFD E15 141 M3
Potten End First School
BERK HP4 34 E3
Potterells Medical Centre
BRKMPK AL9 58 G1
Potters Bar Cricket Club
POTB/CUF EN6 59 L8

Potters Bar Golf Club
POTB/CUF EN6 ... 59 K7
Potter Street Primary School
HLWE CM17 ... 47 L3
Pound Hill Middle School
CRAWE RH10 ... 284 D6
Pound Park Nursery School
CHARL SE7 ... 162 A4
The Pountney Clinic
HSLW TW3 ... 153 P9
Poverest Primary School
STMC/STPC BR5 ... 207 K5
Powell Corderoy CP School
DORK RH4 ... 272 E3
Powell Corderoy Primary School
DORK RH4 ... 272 E3
Powergate Business Park
WLSDN NW10 ... 136 A5
Power Industrial Estate
ERITH DA8 ... 164 G7
Prae Wood JMI School
STALW/RED AL3 ... 37 P7
Pratts Bottom Primary School
ORP BR6 ... 227 M7
Premier Cinema
DORK RH4 ... 273 H1
PECK SE15 ... 159 P8
Prendergast School
BROCKY SE4 ... 160 F10
Presdales School
WARE SG12 ... 26 C3
Preston Cross Hotel & Country Club
GT/LBKH KT23 ... 253 M2
Preston Manor School
WBLY HA9 ... 115 L7
Preston Medical Centre
WBLY HA9 ... 115 K8
Preston Park Primary School
WBLY HA9 ... 115 J6
PR for Schools
SYD SE26 ... 182 B6
Priestmead First & Middle Schools
KTN/HRWW/W HA3 ... 114 G1
Primrose Hill School
CAMTN NW1 ... 4 D5
Primrose Montessori School
HBRY N5 ... 119 K8
Prince Charles Cinema
SOHO/SHAV W1D ... 11 K7
Prince Edward Theatre
SOHO/SHAV W1D ... 11 J6
Prince of Wales Primary School
PEND EN3 ... 80 E3
Prince of Wales Theatre
STJS SW1Y ... 11 J8
Princes College
NOXST/BSQ WC1A ... 11 L5
Princes Court Business Centre
WAP E1W ... 140 A9
Princess Alexandra Hospital
HLW CM20 ... 28 E10
Princess Frederica CE J & I School
WLSDN NW10 ... 136 E4
Princess Grace Hospital
MHST W1U ... 10 C2
Princess Louise Hospital
NKENS W10 ... 136 F7
Princess Margaret Hospital
WDSR SL4 ... 149 J8
Princess Margaret Royal Free CE School
WDSR SL4 ... 149 H10
Princess of Wales Conservatory
RCH/KEW TW9 ... 155 L6
Prins Willem-Alexander School
WOKS/MYFD GU22 ... 232 F3
Priors Field School
RGODL GU7 ... 266 E8
Prior Western Primary School
STLK EC1Y ... 12 F2
Priory Boys & Infant School
ACT W3 ... 155 P1
Priory CE Middle School
WIM/MER SW19 ... 179 L8
Priory Hospital Group
KWD/TDW/WH KT20 ... 257 K4
Priory House School
CAT SE6 ... 182 G4
Priory Retail Park
WIM/MER SW19 ... 179 N10
Priory School
BNSTD SM7 ... 239 K1
SL SL1 ... 128 C7
STMC/STPC BR5 ... 207 M8
The Priory School
DORK RH4 ... 272 E3
Priory Shopping Centre
DART DA1 ... 187 L2
Priory Special School
SNWD SE25 ... 203 N4
The Priory
ORP BR6 ... 207 L7
Privy Council
STJS SW1Y ... 11 J10
Privy Council Office
WHALL SW1A ... 11 L10
Progress Business Centre
SL SL1 ... 128 C8
Progress Business Park
CROY/NA CR0 ... 202 G9
Pronto Trading Estate
HYS/HAR UB3 ... 132 F7
Prospect Business Park
LOU IG10 ... 82 G8
Prospect House School
PUT/ROE SW15 ... 178 C3
Prospect Industrial Estate
CSHM HP5 ... 51 H8
Prospect of Whitby
WAP E1W ... 140 B10
Proud Gallery
CHCR WC2N ... 11 L8
Providence Road School
WDR/YW UB7 ... 131 P10
Providence Square
STHWK SE1 ... 19 N1
Provident Industrial Estate
HYS/HAR UB3 ... 153 H1
Psychiatric Home
BRXN/ST SW9 ... 158 F9
Public Record Office
LINN WC2A ... 12 A5
Public Record Office Museum
RCH/KEW TW9 ... 155 N6
Pump House
BERM/RHTH SE16 ... 140 D10
Pump House Theatre
WAT WD17 ... 73 K9
Pump Lane Industrial Estate
HYS/HAR UB3 ... 153 J1
The Purcell School
BUSH WD23 ... 73 N6
HRW HA1 ... 114 C8
Purdy Hicks Gallery
STHWK SE1 ... 12 C9
Purfleet Industrial Park
PUR RM19 ... 145 N10
Purfleet Primary School
PUR RM19 ... 165 P3
Purford Green Primary School
HLWS CM18 ... 47 K3
Purley Community Health Clinic
PUR/KEN CR8 ... 223 H7
Purley & District War Memorial Hospital
PUR/KEN CR8 ... 223 H7
Purley Downs Golf Club
PUR/KEN CR8 ... 223 L7
Purley Gallery
PUR/KEN CR8 ... 223 H7
Purley John Fisher RFC
COUL/CHIP CR5 ... 241 H6
Purley Oaks Primary School
SAND/SEL CR2 ... 223 L4
Purley Secretarial & Language College
PUR/KEN CR8 ... 223 H7
Purley Sports Club
WLGTN SM6 ... 222 E6
Pursuit Centre
WAP E1W ... 140 B9
Putney Animal Hospital
PUT/ROE SW15 ... 156 G10
Putney Exchange Shopping Centre
PUT/ROE SW15 ... 156 G10
Putney High School
PUT/ROE SW15 ... 178 G1
Putney Hospital
PUT/ROE SW15 ... 156 F9
Putney Leisure Centre
PUT/ROE SW15 ... 156 F10
Putney Lower Common Cemetery
PUT/ROE SW15 ... 156 E8
Putneymead Medical Centre
PUT/ROE SW15 ... 156 F10
Putney Park School
PUT/ROE SW15 ... 156 E10
Putney School of Art
PUT/ROE SW15 ... 157 H10
Putney Vale Cemetery
PUT/ROE SW15 ... 178 D5
Putney Vale Crematorium
PUT/ROE SW15 ... 178 D5
Puttenham CE Infant School
RGUW GU3 ... 266 A5
Puttenham Golf Club
RGUW GU3 ... 266 C5
Pylon Trading Estate
CAN/RD E16 ... 141 J6
Pyrcroft Primary School
CHERT KT16 ... 195 H6
Pyrford County Middle School
WOKS/MYFD GU22 ... 233 J2
Pyrford Golf Club
RPLY/SEND GU23 ... 233 N3
Quadrant Business Park
KIL/WHAMP NW6 ... 2 B5
Quainton Hall School
HRW HA1 ... 114 C3
Quarry Hill Infant School
GRAYS RM17 ... 167 N4
Quarry Hill Junior School
GRAYS RM17 ... 167 N4
Quarryside Business Park
REDH RH1 ... 258 C6
Quebec House
BH/WHM TN16 ... 262 G2
Quebec Industrial Estate
BERM/RHTH SE16 ... 160 D1
The Queen Anne Royal Free CE First School
WDSR SL4 ... 149 J9
Queen Charlottes & Chelsea Hospital
HMSMTH W6 ... 156 D2
Queen Charlotte's Cottage
RCH/KEW TW9 ... 155 L6
Queen Eleanors CE Junior School
GUW GU2 ... 267 L1
Queen Elizabeth Centre
BAR EN5 ... 77 J8
Queen Elizabeth College
KENS W8 ... 14 E1
Queen Elizabeth Conference Centre
WEST SW1P ... 17 K2
Queen Elizabeth Foundation
BNSTD SM7 ... 239 M2
Queen Elizabeth Hall
STHWK SE1 ... 11 N9
Queen Elizabeth Hospital
BNSTD SM7 ... 239 M4
CHARL SE7 ... 162 C5
Queen Elizabeth II Hospital
BRKMPK AL9 ... 23 K9
Queen Elizabeth II School
MV/WKIL W9 ... 8 D2
Queen Elizabeth Museum
CHING E4 ... 101 L1
Queen Elizabeths Boys School
BAR EN5 ... 76 G7
Queen Elizabeths Girls School
BAR EN5 ... 77 J8
Queen Elizabeth Stadium
EN EN1 ... 79 N6
Queenhithe Stairs
BLKFR EC4V ... 12 E8
Queen Marys Hospital
SCUP DA14 ... 185 K8
Queen Marys Hospital for Children
CAR SM5 ... 222 A5
Queen Marys Hospital School
CAR SM5 ... 222 A6
Queen Mary's Hospital
HAMP NW3 ... 117 M8
Queen Mary's University Hospital
PUT/ROE SW15 ... 178 D2
Queen Mary & Westfield College
SWFD E18 ... 101 M9
WCHPL E1 ... 140 C6
Queen Mother Sports Centre
PIM SW1V ... 16 G5
Queensbridge Infant School
HACK E8 ... 7 M4
Queen's Building
HTHAIR TW6 ... 152 C9
Queens CE Primary School
RCH/KEW TW9 ... 155 L6
Queen's Club
HMSMTH W6 ... 14 A8
Queens College
CAVSQ/HST W1G ... 10 E4
Queen's Gallery
WHALL SW1A ... 16 F2
The Queens House
GNWCH SE10 ... 161 J5
Queens Ice Skating Club
BAY/PAD W2 ... 9 H8
Queens Manor Primary School
FUL/PGN SW6 ... 156 F6
Queensmead School
RSLP HA4 ... 113 L9
Queensmead Sports Centre
RSLP HA4 ... 113 H7
Queens Medical Centre
RCHPK/HAM TW10 ... 177 L1
Queensmere Shopping Centre
SL SL1 ... 149 L1
Queens Park Community School GM
WLSDN NW10 ... 136 F3
Queens Park Health Centre
NKENS W10 ... 2 B9
Queens Park Primary School
NKENS W10 ... 8 B1
Queens Park Rangers FC (Loftus Road Stadium)
SHB W12 ... 136 E9
Queen's Road Cemetery
CROY/NA CR0 ... 203 K6
Queens Road Practice
NWCR SE14 ... 160 C7
Queens School
BUSH WD23 ... 73 N7
Queens Schools
WDSR SL4 ... 149 H5
Queens Sports Centre
RGODL GU7 ... 266 G10
Queens Theatre
EMPK RM11 ... 125 L5
SOHO/SHAV W1D ... 11 J7
Queensway Business Centre
PEND EN3 ... 80 B8
Queensway Health Centre
HAT AL10 ... 40 E3
Queenswell Infant School
TRDG/WHET N20 ... 97 N3
Queenswood School
BRKMPK AL9 ... 59 N4
Queen Victoria Memorial
WHALL SW1A ... 16 G2
The Questors Theatre
EA W5 ... 135 H9
Quintin Kynaston School
STJWD NW8 ... 3 K6
Rabbsfarm Primary School
WDR/YW UB7 ... 131 N8
Racecourse Yacht Basin
WDSR SL4 ... 148 E6
Radcliffe College
SOHO/CST W1F ... 10 G6
Radlett Cricket Club
RAD WD7 ... 74 G3
Radlett Infant School
RAD WD7 ... 74 G2
Radlett Lodge School
RAD WD7 ... 56 G8
Radlett Preparatory School
RAD WD7 ... 75 H4
RAF Uxbridge
HGDN/ICK UB10 ... 131 P3
Ragged School Museum Trust
BOW E3 ... 140 D7
Raglan Infant School
EN EN1 ... 79 M10
Raglan Junior School
EN EN1 ... 99 M1
Raglan Primary School
HAYES BR2 ... 205 P4
Railton Road Clinic
HNHL SE24 ... 181 J1
Rainbow Industrial Estate
RYNPK SW20 ... 200 E2
WDR/YW UB7 ... 131 N9
Rainbow Leisure Centre
EW KT17 ... 220 B8
Rainbow Natural Health Centre
REDH RH1 ... 276 A1
Rainbow Quay
BERM/RHTH SE16 ... 160 D2
Raines Foundation School
BETH E2 ... 140 A5
Rainham Cemetery
RAIN RM13 ... 145 K5
Rainham Hall NT
RAIN RM13 ... 145 H6
Rainham Trading Estate
RAIN RM13 ... 144 F5
Rainham Village Primary School
RAIN RM13 ... 145 H6
The Raleigh School
EHSLY KT24 ... 252 D1
Ramac Industrial Estate
CHARL SE7 ... 161 M4
Ram Brewery & Visitor Centre
WAND/EARL SW18 ... 179 L1
Rams Episcopal Primary School
HACK E8 ... 120 B10
Randal Cremer Primary School
BETH E2 ... 7 L7
Randolph Medical Centre
DTCH/LGLY SL3 ... 149 N6
Ranelagh Gardens (site of Chelsea Flower Show)
CHEL SW3 ... 16 D8
Ranelagh Primary School
SRTFD E15 ... 141 K4
Rangefield Primary School
BMLY BR1 ... 183 K8
Rangers House
GNWCH SE10 ... 161 J7
Ransomes Dock Business Centre
BTSEA SW11 ... 157 P6
Raphael School
EMPK RM11 ... 125 H4
Rare Breeds Centre
FLKWH HP10 ... 108 A3
Rathfern Primary School
FSTH SE23 ... 182 E4
Ravenor Primary School
GFD/PVL UB6 ... 133 P5
Ravensbourne College of Design & Communication
CHST BR7 ... 184 C8
Ravensbourne School
HARH RM3 ... 105 L9
The Ravensbourne School
HAYES BR2 ... 205 N4
Ravensbourne Trust
COUL/CHIP CR5 ... 240 D3
Ravenscourt Park Preparatory School
HMSMTH W6 ... 156 D3
Ravenscroft Medical Centre
GLDGN NW11 ... 117 J5
Ravenscroft Primary School
PLSTW E13 ... 141 M6
Ravenscroft School
TRDG/WHET N20 ... 97 J1
Ravenside Retail Park
UED N18 ... 100 C6
Ravensquay Business Centre
STMC/STPC BR5 ... 207 L5
Ravenstone Primary School
BAL SW12 ... 180 B4
Ravenswood Industrial Estate
WALTH E17 ... 121 H2
Ravens Wood School
HAYES BR2 ... 206 A10
Ray Lodge Primary School
WFD IG8 ... 102 A7
Raynehurst Junior School
GVE DA12 ... 191 J6
Raynes Park High School
NWMAL KT3 ... 200 E3
Raynes Park Sports Ground
RYNPK SW20 ... 200 D2
Raynes Park Vale FC
RYNPK SW20 ... 200 G5
Raynham Primary School
UED N18 ... 99 P6
RCA
SKENS SW7 ... 15 K4
RCA Sculpture School
BTSEA SW11 ... 157 P6
Real Tennis Club
BRKMPK AL9 ... 40 G4
Reay Primary School
BRXN/ST SW9 ... 158 G6
Records Office
CLKNW EC1R ... 12 B1
Recreation Centre
LBTH SE11 ... 18 D5
Rectory Business Centre
SCUP DA14 ... 185 L7
Rectory Paddock School
STMC/STPC BR5 ... 207 M2
Redbridge College
CHDH RM6 ... 123 L3
Redbridge Museum Service
IL IG1 ... 122 F7
Redbridge Primary School
REDBR IG4 ... 122 B3
Redbridge Sports Centre Trust
BARK/HLT IG6 ... 102 G9
Redburn Industrial Estate
PEND EN3 ... 80 C10
Redcliffe School
WBPTN SW10 ... 15 H9
Redden Court School
HARH RM3 ... 125 N1
Reddiford School
PIN HA5 ... 113 M2
Reddings Primary School
HHS/BOV HP3 ... 36 B8
Redford Lodge Psychiatric Hospital
ED N9 ... 99 P3
Redhill Aerodrome
REDH RH1 ... 276 F5
Redhill Business Centre
REDH RH1 ... 258 A9
Redhill FC
REDH RH1 ... 276 A4
Redhill Junior School
CHST BR7 ... 184 E8
Redhill & Reigate Golf Club
REDH RH1 ... 275 N3
Redlands Primary School
WCHPL E1 ... 140 B7
The Redlands Primary School
RDKG RH5 ... 272 G5
Red Lion Business Park
SURB KT6 ... 199 L9
Redriff Community Primary School
BERM/RHTH SE16 ... 140 D10
Red Rose Trading Estate
EBAR EN4 ... 77 N9
Redstone Cemetery
REDH RH1 ... 276 C1
Reedham Park School
PUR/KEN CR8 ... 223 H10
Reed Place Business Park
SHPTN TW17 ... 196 A8
Reeds School
COB KT11 ... 217 P8
Regent Business Centre
HYS/HAR UB3 ... 153 J1
Regent Clinic
CAVSQ/HST W1G ... 10 E4
Regent's College
CAMTN NW1 ... 4 C9
Regent's Park Barracks
CAMTN NW1 ... 4 E7
Regents Park Clinic
CAMTN NW1 ... 10 A1
Regents Park Medical Centre
CAMTN NW1 ... 4 F9
Regina Coeli RC Primary School
CROY/NA CR0 ... 223 J4
Regional Sports Centre
TIL RM18 ... 168 E8
Reigate Cinema
REIG RH2 ... 257 K10
Reigate College
REIG RH2 ... 257 L9
Reigate Day Hospital
REIG RH2 ... 257 N10
Reigate Grammar School
REIG RH2 ... 257 M10
Reigate Heath Golf Club
REIG RH2 ... 256 F10
Reigate Hill Golf Club
REIG RH2 ... 258 B4
Reigate Parish Infant School
REIG RH2 ... 257 M10
Reigate Priory Junior School
REIG RH2 ... 257 K10
Reigate Priory & Museum
REIG RH2 ... 257 K10
Reigate St Marys Preparatory & Choir School
REIG RH2 ... 257 L10
Reigate School
REIG RH2 ... 275 M3
Renoir Cinema
BMSBY WC1N ... 11 M1
Renwick Industrial Estate
BARK IG11 ... 143 L4
The Retail Business Centre
EW KT17 ... 220 C6
Reynard Mills Trading Estate
BTFD TW8 ... 155 H4
RHM Medical Centre
WDSR SL4 ... 149 J7
Rhoda Mcgaw Theatre & Cinema
WOKN/KNAP GU21 ... 232 B3
Rhodes Avenue Primary School
FBAR/BDGN N11 ... 98 D9
Rhodes Farm Clinic
MLHL NW7 ... 96 F5
Rhs Gardens Wisley
RPLY/SEND GU23 ... 233 P4
Rhyl Primary School
KTTN NW5 ... 4 C1
Riba Drawings Collection & Heinz Gallery
MBLAR W1H ... 10 B5
Ricards Lodge High School
WIM/MER SW19 ... 179 J8
Richard Alibon Primary School
DAGE RM10 ... 124 B10
Richard Atkins Primary School
BRXS/STRHM SW2 ... 180 F3
Richard Cloudesley School
STLK EC1Y ... 12 E2
Richard Cobden Primary School
CAMTN NW1 ... 5 H6
Richard Hale School
HERT/BAY SG13 ... 25 L6
Rich Industrial Estate
PECK SE15 ... 160 A5
STHWK SE1 ... 19 K4
STHWK SE1 ... 19 M7
Richings Park Golf & Country Club
DTCH/LGLY SL3 ... 150 G3
Richings Park Sports Club
IVER SL0 ... 151 J2
Richmond Adult & Community College
RCH/KEW TW9 ... 155 J10
TWK TW1 ... 176 E4
The Richmond Clinic
RCHPK/HAM TW10 ... 155 L10
Richmond College
KENS W8 ... 14 G3
RCHPK/HAM TW10 ... 177 K3
Richmond FC
RCH/KEW TW9 ... 155 J10
The Richmond Golf Club
RCHPK/HAM TW10 ... 177 K5
The Richmond Green Medical Centre
RCH/KEW TW9 ... 177 J1
Richmond House School
HPTN TW12 ... 175 N8
Richmond Magistrates Court
RCH/KEW TW9 ... 155 J10
Richmond Park Golf Club
PUT/ROE SW15 ... 178 B3
Richmond Road Medical Centre
KUTN/CMB KT2 ... 177 K10
Richmond Theatre
RCH/KEW TW9 ... 155 J10
Richmond-upon-Thames College
WHTN TW2 ... 176 D3
Rickmansworth Public Golf Club
RKW/CH/CXG WD3 ... 92 A3
Rickmansworth School
RKW/CH/CXG WD3 ... 72 A10
Rickmansworth Sports Club
RKW/CH/CXG WD3 ... 71 P10
Riddlesdown High School
SAND/SEL CR2 ... 223 M10
Ridge House Clinic
WCHMH N21 ... 99 L1
Ridgeway Primary School
SAND/SEL CR2 ... 223 M5
Rio Cinema
HACK E8 ... 119 N10
Ripley CE School
RPLY/SEND GU23 ... 233 L7
Ripley Court School
RPLY/SEND GU23 ... 233 M7
Ripley Cricket Club
RPLY/SEND GU23 ... 233 M6
Ripple Junior & Infant School
BARK IG11 ... 142 G3
Risebridge Golf Club
ROM RM1 ... 104 G8
Rise Park Primary School
ROM RM1 ... 104 E9
Risley Avenue Primary School
TOTM N17 ... 99 M9
Ritzy Cinema
BRXN/ST SW9 ... 159 H10
River Brent Business Park
NWDGN UB2 ... 154 D2
Riverdene Industrial Estate
WOT/HER KT12 ... 217 L2
River Gardens Business Centre
EBED/NFELT TW14 ... 153 J10
Riverhead Infant School
SEV TN13 ... 246 G8
River Mole Business Park
ESH/CLAY KT10 ... 197 P8
River Park Industrial Estate
BERK HP4 ... 33 M4
River Place Health Centre
IS N1 ... 6 E4
River Road Business Park
BARK IG11 ... 143 H5
Riversdale Primary School
WAND/EARL SW18 ... 179 K4
Riverside Business Centre
WAND/EARL SW18 ... 179 L4
The Riverside Business Centre
GU GU1 ... 249 P10
Riverside Business Park
WIM/MER SW19 ... 201 M1
Riverside Community Health Care
NKENS W14 ... 156 G2
Riverside Golf Club
THMD SE28 ... 143 P8

Riverside Industrial Estate
BARK IG11 143 K5
DART DA1 187 M1
ED N9 80 D10
LCOL/BKTW AL2 57 K3
Riverside Primary School
BERM/RHTH SE16 19 P2
Riverside Retail Park
RSEV TN14 247 K5
Riverside Studios Cinema
BARN SW13 156 F4
Riverside Swimming Centre
ERITH DA8 164 F4
Riverside Wandle Trading Estate
MTCM CR4 202 A7
Riverston School
LEE/GVPK SE12 183 M1
Riverview CE Primary School
HOR/WEW KT19 219 P1
Riverview Clinic
GVE DA12 191 J8
Riverview Primary School
GVE DA12 191 H7
Riverway Industrial Estate
RGODL GU7 267 P9
R J Mitchell Primary School
HCH RM12 145 J1
Rnib Sunshine House School
NTHWD HA6 92 E7
Roan Industrial Estate
MTCM CR4 201 P1
Robert Blair Primary School
HOLWY N7 5 M2
Robert Browning Primary School
WALW SE17 18 F7
Robert Clack School
BCTR RM8 124 A6
Robertswood Combined School
CFSP/GDCR SL9 90 C8
Robin Hood Junior School
SUT SM1 221 L2
Robin Hood Lane Health Centre
SUT SM1 221 K2
Robin Hood Primary School
KUTN/CMB KT2 178 A8
Robinsfield Infant School
STJWD NW8 3 M7
The Roche School
WAND/EARL SW18 179 K1
Rockcliffe Manor Primary School
WOOL/PLUM SE18 163 H6
Rockmount School
NRWD SE19 181 K9
Rockware Business Centre
GFD/PVL UB6 134 C3
Rodd Estate
SHPTN TW17 196 D5
Roding Primary School
BCTR RM8 123 M9
WFD IG8 102 B8
Roding Valley High School
LOU IG10 82 B9
LOU IG10 82 E8
Roebuck Road Trading Estate
BARK/HLT IG6 103 L7
Roe Green Infant School
CDALE/KGS NW9 115 N2
Roehampton Church School
PUT/ROE SW15 178 E3
Roehampton Golf Club
PUT/ROE SW15 156 C10
Roehampton Institute
PUT/ROE SW15 178 C1
WAND/EARL SW18 179 H2
The Roehampton Priory Hospital
PUT/ROE SW15 156 C10
Roehampton Recreation Centre
PUT/ROE SW15 178 D3
Roger Ascham Primary School
WALTH E17 100 E9
Roger Bannister Sports Ground
KTN/HRWW/W HA3 94 B7
Rokeby School
KUTN/CMB KT2 177 P10
SRTFD E15 141 J2
Roke Primary School
PUR/KEN CR8 223 K10
Roker Park Golf Club
RGUW GU3 249 J5
Rokesly Primary School
CEND/HSY/T N8 118 F3
Roman Bath
TPL/STR WC2R 11 P7
Roman Industrial Estate
CROY/NA CR0 203 M7
Roman Road Primary School
EHAM E6 142 A6
Roman Theatre of Verlamivm
STALW/RED AL3 38 A6
Roman Wall Remains
BARB EC2Y 12 E4
Romford Cemetery
ROMW/RG RM7 124 D5
Romford Clinic
ROM RM1 124 G2
Romford County Court
ROM RM1 124 G2
Romford Golf Club
GPK RM2 125 H1
Romford Ice Rink
ROMW/RG RM7 124 F5
Ronald Rose Primary School
WIM/MER SW19 178 G3
Rood Lane Medical Centre
FENCHST EC3M 13 J7
Roosevelt Memorial
MYFR/PKLN W1K 10 D7
Ropery Business Park
CHARL SE7 161 P3
Rosary Priory High School
BUSH WD23 74 D10
Rosary RC Infant School
HEST TW5 153 N5
The Rosary RC Primary School
HAMP NW3 117 P10
Rosebery Industrial Park
TOTM N17 100 A10
Rosebery School
EPSOM KT18 219 P10
Rose Bruford College
DEPT SE8 160 F5
Rose Bruford College of Speech & Drama
BFN/LL DA15 185 L4
Rosedale Clinic
CHESW EN7 61 P3
Roseland Junior Middle & Infant School
HOD EN11 26 E10
Roselands Clinic
NWMAL KT3 199 P4
Rosemary Primary School
IS N1 6 E5
Rosemary Secondary School
CLKNW EC1R 12 C1
Rose McAndrew Clinic
BRXN/ST SW9 158 G8
Rosemead Preparatory School
DUL SE21 181 K5
Rosendale Primary School
DUL SE21 181 K3
Rose Theatre Exhibition
STHWK SE1 12 E9
Rosetta Primary School
CAN/RD E16 141 N7
Rosewood Medical Centre
HCH RM12 125 J10
Rosherville CE Primary School
GVW DA11 190 B2
Rosh Pinah Primary School
EDGW HA8 95 N3
Rossgate JMI School
HHW HP1 35 K4
Rosslyn Park RFC
PUT/ROE SW15 156 C10
Rotherhithe Primary School
BERM/RHTH SE16 160 B3
The Roundhouse Theatre
CAMTN NW1 4 C3
Roundwood Park Medical Centre
WLSDN NW10 136 D2
Rowan High School
CLAP SW4 180 E2
MTCM CR4 202 D2
Rowans Primary School
WGCE AL7 23 K2
Rowans School
RYNPK SW20 178 D10
Rowfant Business Centre
CRAWE RH10 285 M7
Rowhill School
RDART DA2 187 K7
Rowley Industrial Park
ACT W3 155 N2
Roxbourne Medical Centre
RYLN/HDSTN HA2 114 A7
Roxbourne Middle School
RSLP HA4 113 L7
Roxeth First & Middle School
RYLN/HDSTN HA2 114 C7
Roxeth Manor First School
RYLN/HDSTN HA2 113 P8
Roxeth Mead School
RYLN/HDSTN HA2 114 C7
Roxwell Trading Park
LEY E10 120 D5
Royal Academy of Arts
MYFR/PICC W1J 10 G8
Royal Academy of Dramatic Art
GWRST WC1E 11 K2
Royal Academy of Music
CAMTN NW1 10 D2
Royal Air Force Museum
CDALE/KGS NW9 96 D10
Royal Albert Hall
SKENS SW7 15 L2
The Royal Alexandra & Albert School
REIG RH2 257 P5
Royal Army Medical College
WEST SW1P 17 K7
Royal Arsenal
WOOL/PLUM SE18 162 E2
The Royal Ballet School
HMSMTH W6 156 G4
Royal Blackheath Golf Club
ELTH/MOT SE9 184 C3
Royal Brompton Hospital
CHEL SW3 15 N7
Royal College of Anaesthetists
RSQ WC1B 11 L3
Royal College of Art
SKENS SW7 15 K2
Royal College of Music
SHB W12 156 D2
SKENS SW7 15 L3
Royal College of Nursing
CAMTN NW1 11 H1
IS N1 6 C6
Royal College of Obstetricians & Gynaecologists
CAMTN NW1 10 A1
Royal College of Ophthalmologists
CAMTN NW1 10 C2
Royal College of Paediatrics & Child Health
GTPST W1W 10 F3
The Royal College of Pathology
STJS SW1Y 11 J10
Royal College of Physicians
CAMTN NW1 10 E1
Royal College of Surgeons
LINN WC2A 11 P5
Royal Courts of Justice
LINN WC2A 11 P6
Royal Court Theatre
BGVA SW1W 16 C6
Royal Court Young Peoples Theatre
NKENS W10 8 B4
The Royal Dock Community School
CAN/RD E16 141 P8
Royal Docks Medical Centre
EHAM E6 142 D8
Royal Epping Forest Golf Club
CHING E4 101 K1
Royal Exchange
LOTH EC2R 13 H6
Royal Festival Hall
STHWK SE1 11 N10
Royal Foundation of Grey Coat Hospital
WESTW SW1E 16 G3
Royal Free Hospital
HAMP NW3 117 P10
Royal Free Hospital School of Medicine
HAMP NW3 117 P10
Royal Geographical Soc
SKENS SW7 15 L2
Royal Grammar School
GU GU1 268 A1
Royal Holloway College
EGH TW20 172 A7
EGH TW20 194 A1
Royal Holloway University of London
EGH TW20 172 A9
Royal Horticultural Society New Hall
WEST SW1P 17 J4
Royal Horticultural Society Old Hall
WEST SW1P 17 J5
Royal Hospital
RCH/KEW TW9 155 K9
Royal Hospital Chelsea
CHEL SW3 16 C9
Royal Hospital for Neuro-Disability
PUT/ROE SW15 179 H2
Royal Hospital & Home
PUT/ROE SW15 178 E3
Royal Hospital Museum
CHEL SW3 16 C8
Royal Institute of British Architects
REGST W1B 10 F3
Royal Institution (Faraday Museum)
MYFR/PICC W1J 10 F8
The Royal Kent CE Primary School
LHD/OX KT22 218 B10
Royal Liberty School
GPK RM2 125 K1
The Royal London Estate
TOTM N17 100 A8
Royal London Homeopathic Hospital
BMSBY WC1N 11 M3
Royal London Hospital
BETH E2 140 B4
The Royal London Hospital
BOW E3 140 E5
The Royal London Hospital (Whitechapel) A & E
WCHPL E1 140 A7
Royal Marsden Hospital
BELMT SM2 221 M6
CHEL SW3 15 M7
The Royal Masonic School for Girls
RKW/CH/CXG WD3 71 N9
Royal Mews
WDSR SL4 149 K7
The Royal Mews
WHALL SW1A 16 F3
Royal Mid-Surrey Golf Club
RCH/KEW TW9 155 J9
Royal Mint Court
TWRH EC3N 13 M8
Royal National Orthopaedic Hospital
GTPST W1W 10 F2
STAN HA7 94 G2
Royal National Theatre
BRXN/ST SW9 159 H6
STHWK SE1 12 A9
Royal National Throat Nose & Ear Hospital
FSBYW WC1X 5 N9
Royal Observatory Greenwich
GNWCH SE10 161 J5
Royal Opera House
COVGDN WC2E 11 M6
Royal Park Primary School
SCUP DA14 185 P6
Royal Russell School
CROY/NA CR0 224 A3
The Royal School
HAMP NW3 117 N9
Royal Society of Arts
TPL/STR WC2R 11 M8
Royal Society of Medicine
CAVSQ/HST W1G 10 E5
Royal Surrey County Hospital
GUW GU2 249 K10
Royal Terrace Pier
GVE DA12 190 F1
Royal Veterinary College
BRKMPK AL9 58 G4
CAMTN NW1 5 H6
Royal Victoria Docks Watersports Centre
CAN/RD E16 141 M9
Royal Wimbledon Golf Club
WIM/MER SW19 178 E8
Roydonbury Industrial Estate
HLWW/ROY CM19 46 C1
Roydon CP School
HLWW/ROY CM19 45 N1
Roydon Leisure Park
HLWW/ROY CM19 27 M10
Roydon Mill Leisure Park
HLWW/ROY CM19 27 M10
Royston Primary School
BECK BR3 204 C1
RSPB Site
SLN SL2 109 J6
RSPCA Animal Hospital
HOLWY N7 118 G7
Rudolf Steiner School
KGLGY WD4 53 P5
Rudolph Steiner Hall
CAMTN NW1 10 A1
Rufus Business Centre
WAND/EARL SW18 179 L5
Ruislip Gardens Primary School
HGDN/ICK UB10 112 F9
Ruislip Golf Club
RSLP HA4 112 D7
Ruislip Manor FC
RSLP HA4 112 G7
Ruislip RFC
RSLP HA4 112 F7
Rumford Shopping Hall
ROM RM1 124 F2
Runnymede Hospital
CHERT KT16 194 G10
Rush Croft School
CHING E4 100 G8
Rushey Green Primary School
CAT SE6 182 G4
Rush Green Primary School
ROMW/RG RM7 124 E6
Rushmore Junior School
CLPT E5 120 B9
Ruskin House School
HNHL SE24 181 K1
Russell Clinic
STALW/RED AL3 38 C6
The Russell JMI School
RCHPK/HAM TW10 177 J5
The Russell School
RCHPK/HAM TW10 177 J4
RKW/CH/CXG WD3 70 E8
Russet House School
EN EN1 80 A5
Rutherford Way Industrial Estate
CRAWE RH10 284 B2
Rutlish School
RYNPK SW20 201 J2
Ruxley Corner Industrial Estate
SCUP DA14 185 N9
Ruxley Manor School
ELTH/MOT SE9 184 D7
Ruxley Park Golf Centre
STMC/STPC BR5 207 N1
Ryde College
WATW WD18 72 F10
Rydens School
WOT/HER KT12 197 K10
The Ryde Primary School
BRKMPK AL9 40 G1
Rydes Hill Preparatory School
GUW GU2 249 L8
Rydon Business Centre
LHD/OX KT22 236 F6
Ryebrook Business Park
LHD/OX KT22 236 F6
Ryefield Primary School
HGDN/ICK UB10 132 E3
Rye House Stadium
HOD EN11 45 J1
Ryelands JMI School
HOD EN11 44 G2
Ryelands Primary School
SNWD SE25 204 A5
Rye Park Industrial Estate
HOD EN11 45 H1
Ryvers Combined School
DTCH/LGLY SL3 150 A2
Saatchi Gallery
STJWD NW8 3 H6
Sacred Heart High School
HMSMTH W6 156 F3
Sacred Heart High School for Girls
KTN/HRWW/W HA3 94 D10
Sacred Heart Junior Middle & Infant School
OXHEY WD19 73 N10
Sacred Heart Junior School
HMSMTH W6 156 G3
The Sacred Heart of Mary RC School
UPMR RM14 126 A7
Sacred Heart RC Infant School
BTSEA SW11 157 P8
Sacred Heart RC Junior & Infant School
RSLP HA4 112 F7
Sacred Heart RC Junior & Middle School
BTSEA SW11 157 P9
Sacred Heart RC Primary School
NWMAL KT3 200 D4
TEDD TW11 176 G10
WARE SG12 26 B2
Sacred Heart RC School
CMBW SE5 159 K7
Sacred Heart School
HOLWY N7 118 G10
Saddlers Hall
CITYW EC2V 12 E6
Sadler's Wells Theatre
CLKNW EC1R 6 B9
SAE Technology College
HOLWY N7 118 F10
Safari Cinema
CROY/NA CR0 203 J7
Safari Cinema & Bingo
HRW HA1 114 E3
Saffron Green Primary School
BORE WD6 76 B8
Sai Medical Centre
POP/IOD E14 141 H10
St Adrians RC Primary School
STAL AL1 38 B9
St Agathas RC Primary School
KUTN/CMB KT2 177 L9
St Agnes RC Primary School
BOW E3 140 F5
CRICK NW2 117 H8
St Aidans Primary School
FSBYPK N4 119 H5
St Aidans RC Primary School
IL IG1 122 G6
St Albans CE Primary School
FSBYW WC1X 12 A3
St Albans City FC
STAL AL1 38 E6
St Albans City Hospital
STALW/RED AL3 38 B4
St Albans Girls School
STALW/RED AL3 38 D2
St Albans Health Clinic
KTTN NW5 118 B8
St Albans High School for Girls
STAL AL1 38 D5
St Albans Junior & Infant RC School
PECK SE15 159 N7
St Albans Lawn Tennis Club
STALE/WH AL4 39 H4
St Albans Museum
STAL AL1 38 D6
St Albans Musical Museum
LCOL/BKTW AL2 56 A4
St Albans Music School
STALW/RED AL3 38 C3
St Albans Organ Museum
STAL AL1 38 G7
St Albans Primary School
HLW CM20 29 J9
St Albans Principal Health Centre
STAL AL1 38 C6
St Albans RC Aided Primary School
E/WMO/HCT KT8 198 A5
St Albans RC Church & School Presbytery
HCH RM12 125 H10
St Albans RC JMI School
RAIN RM13 145 J2
St Albans Retail Park
STAL AL1 38 C8
St Albans Road Infant School
DART DA1 187 N2
St Albans & St Stephens RC Infant School
STAL AL1 38 F7
St Albans & St Stephens RC Junior & Middle School
STAL AL1 38 F6
St Albans School
STALW/RED AL3 38 B6
St Albert the Great RC Primary School
HHS/BOV HP3 36 B8
St Alfege with St Peter CE Primary School
GNWCH SE10 161 H5
St Aloysius College
ARCH N19 118 D6
St Aloysius RC Infant School
CAMTN NW1 5 J9
St Aloysius RC Junior School
CAMTN NW1 5 H8
St Andrew & St Francis CE JM & I School
CRICK NW2 136 D1
St Andrews CE Combined School
CRAWE RH10 284 B8
St Andrews CE JMI School
TRDG/WHET N20 97 J3
St Andrews CE Junior & Infant School
UX/CGN UB8 131 N3
St Andrews CE Primary School
EN EN1 79 L6
EPP CM16 66 D1
STHGT/OAK N14 98 E2
BRXN/ST SW9 159 H7
St Andrews Greek School
CAMTN NW1 4 F2
St Andrews Hospital
BOW E3 140 G6
St Andrews Primary School
BRXN/ST SW9 158 G8
COB KT11 217 K9
IS N1 5 P5
WARE SG12 27 J7
St Andrews RC School
LHD/OX KT22 237 H6
St Andrews School
RYLN/HDSTN HA2 114 A3
WLSDN NW10 136 E2
WOKN/KNAP GU21 232 A2
St Angelas RC School
FSTGT E7 141 N1
St Annes Catholic High School
PLMGR N13 99 H5
St Annes Catholic Primary School
BNSTD SM7 239 K2
CHERT KT16 195 K8
St Annes CE Primary School
WAND/EARL SW18 179 L1
St Annes Convent School
EN EN1 79 L8
St Annes Primary School
STWL/WRAY TW19 173 P3
St Annes RC Primary School
LBTH SE11 17 N9
WCHPL E1 13 N2
St Annes Special School
MRDN SM4 201 L5
St Anne's Trading Estate
POP/IOD E14 140 E8
St Anns CE Primary School
SEVS/STOTM N15 119 L3
St Ann's General Hospital
SEVS/STOTM N15 119 K3
St Anns Heath Junior School
VW GU25 194 C5
St Anns School
HNWL W7 134 D10
St Ann's Shopping Centre
HRW HA1 114 D4
St Anselms RC First & Middle School
HRW HA1 114 D5
St Anselms RC Primary School
DART DA1 187 P1
NWDGN UB2 153 N2
St Anslems RC Primary School
TOOT SW17 180 B6
St Anthonys Hospital
WPK KT4 200 G8
St Anthonys RC Junior School
WATW WD18 72 F9
St Anthonys RC Primary School
EDUL SE22 181 N2
FSTGT E7 141 M2
PGE/AN SE20 204 A1
SLN SL2 129 H5
St Antonys RC Primary School
WFD IG8 101 M5
St Aubyns School
WFD IG8 101 L8
St Augustines CE School
KIL/WHAMP NW6 2 F8
St Augustines Primary School
BELV DA17 164 A2
KIL/WHAMP NW6 2 F7
St Augustines RC Infant School
GNTH/NBYPK IG2 122 E3
St Augustines RC Primary School
CAT SE6 182 G8
FUL/PGN SW6 14 B10
GNTH/NBYPK IG2 122 E3
HOD EN11 44 G4
St Barnabas CE Primary School
BGVA SW1W 16 D7
St Barnabas & Philip CE Primary
KENS W8 14 E4
St Barnabas & St Philips CE Primary School
KENS W8 14 E4
St Bartholomews CE Primary School
SYD SE26 182 B7
St Bartholomews Hospital
STBT EC1A 12 D4
SWLY BR8 208 G3
St Bartholomews Medical School
FARR EC1M 12 D2
St Bartholomews RC Primary School
SWLY BR8 208 F3
St Bartholomews & Royal London School of Medicine
FARR EC1M 12 E3
St Bartholomew's the Great
STBT EC1A 12 D4
St Barts Hospital Sports Ground
CHST BR7 184 G9
St Bedes CE Junior School
RPLY/SEND GU23 232 G10

St Bedes RC Primary School
CHDH RM6 **123** M3
St Bede's School
REDH RH1 **257** P7
St Benedicts Junior School
EA W5 **135** H7
St Benedicts School
EA W5 **135** J7
St Bernadette RC Primary School
LCOL/BKTW AL2 **57** J3
St Bernadettes RC First & Middle School
KTN/HRWW/W HA3 **115** L2
St Bernadettes RC Primary School
HGDN/ICK UB10 **132** C3
St Bernards Convent School
DTCH/LGLY SL3 **149** N1
St Bonaventure's School
FSTGT E7 **141** M2
St Boniface RC Primary School
TOOT SW17 **180** A8
St Botolphs CE Primary School
GVW DA11 **190** A3
St Catherine of Sienna RC Primary School
GSTN WD25 **55** L8
St Catherine's Hospice
CRAWE RH10 **283** N9
St Catherines RC Girls School
BXLYHS DA6 **186** C1
St Catherines RC Middle School
NWMAL KT3 **200** F5
St Catherines RC Primary School
WDR/YW UB7 **151** N1
St Catherines School
SHGR GU5 **268** C10
TWK TW1 **176** E5
St Cecilias RC Primary School
WPK KT4 **200** G9
St Chads RC Primary School
SNWD SE25 **203** M5
St Chads School
TIL RM18 **168** D7
St Charles Hospital
NKENS W10 **136** G7
St Charles RC Primary School
WEY KT13 **196** B10
St Charles RC Sixth Form College
NKENS W10 **136** G7
St Christophers School
BECK BR3 **205** H2
EPSOM KT18 **220** B10
HAMP NW3 **117** N10
WBLY HA9 **115** L8
St Christopher House
STHWK SE1 **12** E9
St Clare Business Park
HPTN TW12 **176** B9
St Clement Danes CE Primary School
HOL/ALD WC2B **11** N6
St Clement Danes School
RKW/CH/CXG WD3 **70** G6
St Clement & James CE Primary School
NTGHL W11 **8** A9
St Clements Junior School
CHES/WCR EN8 **62** D3
St Clements RC Primary School
EW KT17 **220** C5
St Columbas College Preparatory School
STALW/RED AL3 **38** B8
St Columbas RC Boys School
BXLYHS DA6 **186** C1
St Cross RC Primary School
HOD EN11 **44** F5
St Cuthbert Mayne RC Primary School
HHW HP1 **35** L5
St Cuthberts CE Primary School
EGH TW20 **171** P10
St Cuthbert With St Matthias CE Primary School
ECT SW5 **14** F7
St Davids College
WWKM BR4 **204** G7
St Davids Health Centre
STWL/WRAY TW19 **173** N3
St Davids School
ASHF TW15 **174** A6
PUR/KEN CR8 **222** G7
St Dominic RC Primary School
HARP AL5 **20** A3
St Dominics RC Junior & Infant School
HOM E9 **140** C1
St Dominics RC Primary School
HAMP NW3 **118** A10
St Dominics 6th Form College
HRW HA1 **114** D7
St Dunstans CE Primary School
CHEAM SM3 **221** H4
St Dunstans College
CAT SE6 **182** E4
St Dunstans RC Primary School
WOKS/MYFD GU22 **232** D3
St Ebba's Hospital
HOR/WEW KT19 **219** P5
St Edmunds RC Primary School
ED N9 **100** A2
POP/IOD E14 **160** F3
WHTN TW2 **176** A3
St Edwards CE Comprehensive School
CHDH RM6 **124** B4
St Edwards CE Primary School
ROM RM1 **124** E2
St Edwards RC First School
WDSR SL4 **148** F7
St Edwards RC JMI School
STJWD NW8 **9** N2
St Edwards Royal Free Ecumenical Middle School
WDSR SL4 **148** F7
St Elizabeths RC Primary School
RCHPK/HAM TW10 **177** L2
St Elpheges RC Primary School
WLGTN SM6 **222** F3
St Ethelberts Catholic School
SLN SL2 **129** M8
St Eugene de Mazenod RC Primary School
KIL/WHAMP NW6 **2** F4
St Faiths CE School
WAND/EARL SW18 **179** L1
St Fidelis Catholic Primary School
ERITH DA8 **164** D5
St Francesca Cabrini Primary School
FSTH SE23 **182** B2
St Francis of Assisi Primary School
CRAWE RH10 **283** P8
NTGHL W11 **136** G9
St Francis RC Primary School
PECK SE15 **19** P10
SRTFD E15 **121** K10
St Francis RC School
CTHM CR3 **241** N7
St Francis Xavier College
BAL SW12 **180** C2
St Gabriels CE Primary School
PIM SW1V **16** G8
St Georges Business Park
WEY KT13 **216** B5
St George's Cathedral
STHWK SE1 **18** B3
St George's Cathedral RC Primary
STHWK SE1 **18** C3
St Georges CE Infant School
AMS HP6 **69** K4
St Georges Centre
GVW DA11 **190** E2
St Georges CE Primary School
BMLY BR1 **205** P2
PECK SE15 **19** J10
PECK SE15 **159** M6
VX/NE SW8 **158** D6
St Georges CE School
GVW DA11 **190** D5
St George's Chapel
WDSR SL4 **149** J6
St Georges College
ADL/WDHM KT15 **195** N10
HOLWY N7 **119** H8
St Georges College Junior School
WEY KT13 **196** C10
St George's College Track (under construction)
ADL/WDHM KT15 **195** N9
St Georges Elizabethan Theatre
HOLWY N7 **118** E9
St Georges Hanover Square CE Primary School
MYFR/PKLN W1K **10** D8
St George's Hill Golf Club
WEY KT13 **216** D7
St Georges Hospital
HCH RM12 **125** M9
TOOT SW17 **179** P8
St Georges Industrial Estate
AMSS HP7 **69** L5
KUTN/CMB KT2 **177** J8
WDGN N22 **99** J8
St Georges Medical Centre
HDN NW4 **116** E1
St Georges Preparatory School
WDSR SL4 **149** J6
St Georges RC First & Middle School
HRW HA1 **114** E8
St Georges RC Primary School
ENC/FH EN2 **79** L6
St Georges RC School
MV/WKIL W9 **3** H8
St Georges School
ASC SL5 **192** A4
HARP AL5 **20** A1
St Georges Shopping Centre & Cinema
HRW HA1 **114** C4
St George the Martyr CE Primary School
BMSBY WC1N **11** N2
St George Wharf
VX/NE SW8 **17** L8
St Gildas RC Junior School
CEND/HSY/T N8 **118** F5
St Giles CE (Aided) Infant School
ASHTD KT21 **237** L4
St Giles College London Central
RSQ WC1B **11** L3
St Giles Primary School
POTB/CUF EN6 **58** D8
St Giles School
CROY/NA CR0 **223** J3
St Gregorys High School
KTN/HRWW/W HA3 **115** J3
St Gregorys RC Primary School
EA W5 **135** H6
St Helens Catholic Infant School
WALTH E17 **121** H3
St Helens College
HGDN/ICK UB10 **132** B2
St Helens Primary School
STALE/WH AL4 **21** J3
St Helens RC Infant School
BRW CM14 **107** J3
St Helens RC Junior School
BRWN CM15 **107** J1
St Helens RC Primary School
BRXN/ST SW9 **159** H9
PLSTW E13 **141** L6
St Helens School for Girls
NTHWD HA6 **92** F7
St Helier Hospital
SUT SM1 **201** M8
St Hilarys School
SEV TN13 **247** J8
St Hildas School
BUSH WD23 **94** A1
St Hugh of Lincoln RCP School
WOKN/KNAP GU21 **231** J5
St Ignatius College
EN EN1 **79** P3
St Ignatius RC Primary School
SEVS/STOTM N15 **119** M4
SUN TW16 **197** H1
St James CE J & I School
BERM/RHTH SE16 **19** N3
St James CE Primary School
HLWS CM18 **46** G5
MUSWH N10 **118** B2
PEND EN3 **80** B6
WEY KT13 **196** D10
St James CE Junior School
FSTGT E7 **121** L10
St James Hatcham CE Primary School
NWCR SE14 **160** D7
St James Independent Boys Junior School
WKENS W14 **14** B5
St James Independent Girls School
WKENS W14 **14** B5
St James Independent School
TWK TW1 **176** F5
St James Medical Centre
CROY/NA CR0 **203** L7
St James RC Primary School
HAYES BR2 **206** E5
WHTN TW2 **176** D6
St James & St Michaels CE Primary School
BAY/PAD W2 **9** K7
St James's Health Centre
WALTH E17 **120** D3
St James's Palace
WHALL SW1A **11** H10
St James the Great RC Primary School
THHTH CR7 **203** J2
St Joan of Arc RC School
RKW/CH/CXG WD3 **91** P1
St John Fisher RC First & Middle School
RYLN/HDSTN HA2 **113** P2
St John Fisher RC JMI School
STALE/WH AL4 **39** H3
St John Fisher RC Primary School
ERITH DA18 **163** P2
GFD/PVL UB6 **135** H5
LOU IG10 **82** F6
NWMAL KT3 **200** F5
St John of Jerusalem CE Primary School
HOM E9 **140** B2
St John Rigby Catholic College
WWKM BR4 **225** J1
St Johns Ambulance Station
WEA W13 **134** G10
St Johns Angell Town CE Primary School
BRXN/ST SW9 **159** H8
St Johns Beaumont School
STWL/WRAY TW19 **171** P5
St Johns CE First School
STAN HA7 **94** F5
St Johns CE Infant School
CTHM CR3 **260** A1
St Johns CE Junior & Infant (Mixed) School
WGCW AL8 **22** C6
St Johns CE Middle School
STAN HA7 **94** F5
St Johns CE Primary School
BETH E2 **140** B4
BKHH IG9 **101** N2
ENC/FH EN2 **79** J2
FBAR/BDGN N11 **98** A5
KUT KT1 **199** K3
PGE/AN SE20 **182** B10
TRDG/WHET N20 **97** M3
WALW SE17 **18** F6
WLYN AL6 **23** J1
St Johns C E School
CDALE/KGS NW9 **116** B3
St John's CE Walham Green
FUL/PGN SW6 **157** H7
St Johns CE Infant School
HDN NW4 **116** E3
St John's Concert Hall
WEST SW1P **17** L4
St Johns CP School
WOKN/KNAP GU21 **231** K4
St Johns Highbury Vale CE Primary School
HBRY N5 **119** J8
St John's Hospital
SOHO/SHAV W1D **11** J7
St John's Hospital Day Centre
BTSEA SW11 **157** N10
St Johns Infant School
RAD WD7 **74** E1
St Johns Junior School
CTHM CR3 **260** A2
St Johns Primary School
REDH RH1 **275** P2
WEA W13 **134** F9
St Johns RC Comprehensive School
GVE DA12 **190** G4
St Johns RC Primary School
BERM/RHTH SE16 **160** D1
GVE DA12 **190** G4
RKW/CH/CXG WD3 **91** L2
St Johns RC Special School
WFD IG8 **102** D6
St Johns & St James CE School
UED N18 **99** N6
St Johns School
ENC/FH EN2 **79** H6
EPP CM16 **65** H6
LHD/OX KT22 **236** G7
NTHWD HA6 **93** J7
St Johns Upper Holloway CE Primary School
ARCH N19 **118** E8
St Johns Way Medical Centre
ARCH N19 **118** E6
St John the Baptist CE Junior School
KUT KT1 **177** J10
St John the Baptist CE Primary School
CAT SE6 **183** H7
IS N1 **7** J8
St John the Baptist Primary School
WARE SG12 **26** F6
St John the Baptist RC School
WOKS/MYFD GU22 **232** D5
St John the Divine CE Primary School
CMBW SE5 **159** J6
St John the Evangelist RC Primary School
IS N1 **6** C7
St John Vianney RC Primary School
SEVS/STOTM N15 **119** J2
St Joseph RC Primary School
DORK RH4 **272** F2
St Josephs Catholic High School
SLN SL2 **129** M8
St Josephs Catholic Infant School
LEY E10 **120** E6
St Josephs Catholic Primary Redhill
REDH RH1 **257** P9
St Josephs Catholic Primary School
BMLY BR1 **183** P10
EPSOM KT18 **219** P10
St Josephs CE Combined School
CFSP/GDCR SL9 **109** P1
St Josephs College
STRHM/NOR SW16 **181** J9
St Josephs Convent School
WAN E11 **121** M4
St Josephs Primary School
HDN NW4 **116** E2
PUT/ROE SW15 **179** K1
St Josephs RC First & Middle School
KTN/HRWW/W HA3 **94** F10
St Josephs RC Infant School
NRWD SE19 **181** K9
WBLY HA9 **135** L1
St Josephs RC JMI School
CHES/WCR EN8 **62** D9
St Josephs RC Junior School
CMBW SE5 **159** K6
LEY E10 **120** G6
NRWD SE19 **181** K9
WBLY HA9 **115** L10
St Josephs RC Primary School
ARCH N19 **118** C6
BARK IG11 **142** F3
BERM/RHTH SE16 **19** N2
BERM/RHTH SE16 **160** B2
CHEL SW3 **16** A6
DAGW RM9 **124** A9
DART DA1 **164** E10
DEPT SE8 **160** F6
GNWCH SE10 **161** K4
HNWL W7 **134** D10
HOL/ALD WC2B **11** M5
KUT KT1 **199** K2
MV/WKIL W9 **3** J10
STHWK SE1 **18** F1
WLSDN NW10 **136** B2
St Josephs RC School
GVW DA11 **190** A3
OXHEY WD19 **93** J4
St Josephs School
UPMR RM14 **126** A7
St Joseph the Worker RC Primary School
RBRW/HUT CM13 **87** P10
St Judes CE Junior School
EGH TW20 **171** P9
St Judes CE Primary School
STHWK SE1 **18** C4
St Judes & St Pauls CE Primary School
IS N1 **7** J1
St Katharine Pier
TWRH EC3N **13** M9
St Laurence CE Junior School
UX/CGN UB8 **131** M7
St Lawrence Business Centre
FELT TW13 **175** J5
St Lawrence Catholic School
FELT TW13 **175** J5
St Lawrence CE School
WAB EN9 **63** L9
St Lawrence Junior School
E/WMO/HCT KT8 **198** C3
St Lawrence Primary School
EHSLY KT24 **253** L3
St Lawrence University
FSBYW WC1X **11** P2
St Leonards CE Primary School
STRHM/NOR SW16 **180** E8
St Leonards Hospital
IS N1 **7** K7
St Lukes CE Primary School
CAN/RD E16 **141** L8
FSBYE EC1V **6** F10
KIL/WHAMP NW6 **2** D8
KUTN/CMB KT2 **199** L1
POP/IOD E14 **161** J3
WNWD SE27 **181** K8
St Luke's Health Centre
CAN/RD E16 **141** L8
St Lukes Hospital for the Clergy
FITZ W1T **10** G2
St Lukes RC Primary School
HLWW/ROY CM19 **46** F3
St Lukes School
THHTH CR7 **203** H4
St Lukes Special School
LOU IG10 **82** D8
St Lukes Woodside Hospital
MUSWH N10 **118** B2
St Margaret Clitherow RC Primary
THMD SE28 **143** L10
St Margaret Lee CE Primary School
LEW SE13 **161** K10
St Margarets Business Centre
TWK TW1 **176** F3
St Margarets CE First & Middle School
CRAWW RH11 **283** K6
St Margarets Clitherow RC Primary School
WLSDN NW10 **116** A8
St Margarets Hospital
EPP CM16 **65** L5
St Margarets Primary School
BARK IG11 **142** E3
St Margarets School
BUSH WD23 **93** P1
HAMP NW3 **117** L9
St Marks CE Primary School
ARCH N19 **118** F7
HAYES BR2 **205** M3
LBTH SE11 **17** P9
SNWD SE25 **203** P4
St Marks Industrial Estate
CAN/RD E16 **142** A10
St Marks Primary School
MTCM CR4 **202** A2
STHL UB1 **154** D1
St Marks RC Comprehensive School
HLWS CM18 **47** H2
St Marks RC School
HSLW TW3 **153** N9
St Marthas Convent Senior School
EBAR EN4 **77** K5
St Martin-in-the-Fields High School
BRXS/STRHM SW2 **181** J4
St Martin of Pores RC Primary School
FBAR/BDGN N11 **98** D7
St Martins CE Junior School
EPSOM KT18 **238** A1
St Martins CE Primary School
DORK RH4 **272** E1
St Martins Hospital
MYFR/PKLN W1K **10** C7
St Martins House Business Centre
EHSLY KT24 **252** F5
St Martins Medical Centre
RSLP HA4 **112** F5
St Martins School
MLHL NW7 **96** B6
NTHWD HA6 **92** E6
RBRW/HUT CM13 **107** P2
St Martins School of Art
SOHO/SHAV W1D **11** K6
St Martins Theatre
LSQ/SEVD WC2H **11** K7
St Martins Walk Shopping Centre
DORK RH4 **272** G1
St Mary Abbots CE Primary School
KENS W8 **14** G2
St Mary Abbots Church Hall
KENS W8 **14** G1
St Mary & All Saints CE Primary School
BEAC HP9 **88** D9
St Mary CE Primary School
PUT/ROE SW15 **156** G9
St Marylebone CE Secondary School
MHST W1U **10** D3
St Marylebone Crematorium
EFNCH N2 **117** L1
St Mary Magdalene CE Primary School
MV/WKIL W9 **8** G3
WOOL/PLUM SE18 **162** C3
PECK SE15 **160** A8
St Mary Magdalene Primary School
HOLWY N7 **6** A1
St Mary Magdalen RC Junior School
CRICK NW2 **136** E1
St Mary Magdalens RC Primary School
MORT/ESHN SW14 **156** A9
St Mary of the Angels RC Primary School
BAY/PAD W2 **8** E5
St Marys Abbey
MLHL NW7 **96** D4
St Mary & St Josephs GM School
SCUP DA14 **185** J8
St Mary & St Pancras CE Primary School
CAMTN NW1 **5** J8
St Marys Bryanston Square CE Primary School
MBLAR W1H **10** A4
St Marys Catholic Primary School
CHING E4 **101** J2
St Marys CE Combined School
AMSS HP7 **68** G5
St Marys CE High School
HDN NW4 **116** F1
St Marys CE Infant School
LHD/OX KT22 **237** H8
St Marys CE Junior School
CEND/HSY/T N8 **118** F2
OXTED RH8 **261** K4
STWL/WRAY TW19 **173** P2
THDIT KT7 **198** G8
St Mary's Cemetery
BTSEA SW11 **179** P1
St Marys CE Primary School
BF/WBF KT14 **215** P9
BRWN CM15 **87** L10
CHSGTN KT9 **219** K3
EBAR EN4 **77** P10
FNCH N3 **97** J9
IS N1 **6** D4
LEW SE13 **182** G1
St Mary's CE Primary School
SL SL1 **149** M2
St Marys CE Primary School
SWLY BR8 **208** F4
TWK TW1 **176** F3
WLSDN NW10 **136** B1
St Marys Church of England High School
HDN NW4 **116** F1
St Marys First School
BERK HP4 **33** K3
St Marys Greek Cathedral
WDGN N22 **98** G9
St Marys Hare Park School
GPK RM2 **125** K1
St Marys High School
CHESW EN7 **62** A6
CROY/NA CR0 **203** K8
St Marys Hospital
BAY/PAD W2 **9** M5
St Marys Hospital Medical School
BAY/PAD W2 **9** M5
St Marys Infant School
CAR SM5 **221** P1
St Mary's Kilburn Primary School
KIL/WHAMP NW6 **2** F5
St Marys Magdalens RC Primary School
BROCKY SE4 **160** D10
St Marys Primary School
BRKMPK AL9 **40** E9
St Mary's Primary School
WKENS W14 **156** G2
St Marys RC Infant School
CAR SM5 **222** A1
CROY/NA CR0 **203** L8
St Marys RC JMI School
HCH RM12 **125** H6
St Marys RC Junior School
CROY/NA CR0 **203** L8
WALTH E17 **121** H1
St Marys RC Primary School
BECK BR3 **183** H10
CHSWK W4 **156** A4

CLAP SW4 180 D1
ELTH/MOT SE9 184 D1
ISLW TW7 154 F9
KIL/WHAMP NW6 2 E7
NKENS W10 8 A2
PEND EN3 80 C8
SEVS/STOTM N15 119 L3
TIL RM18 168 C8
UX/CGN UB8 131 M3
VX/NE SW8 158 C7
WIM/MER SW19 179 K10
St Marys & St Peters CE Primary School
TEDD TW11 176 D8
St Marys School
CEND/HSY/T N8 118 G3
CFSP/GDCR SL9 110 B2
HAMP NW3 117 M10
St Marys School Ascot
ASC SL5 192 A7
St Marys Stoke Newington CE Primary School
STNW/STAM N16 119 M7
St Marys Tutorial College
GUW GU2 267 P3
St Marys University College
TWK TW1 176 E6
St Matthews CE (Aided) Infant School
COB KT11 235 J4
St Matthews CE Primary School
PEND EN3 80 B9
REDH RH1 258 A8
RYNPK SW20 200 D1
SURB KT6 199 K7
WDR/YW UB7 131 N10
WEST SW1P 17 K4
St Matthias CE Primary School
BETH E2 13 M1
STNW/STAM N16 119 M10
St Meryl Junior Middle & Infant School
OXHEY WD19 93 M4
St Michael At Bowes CE Junior School
PLMGR N13 99 H7
St Michaels Catholic Grammar School
NFNCH/WDSP N12 97 L6
St Michaels CE First School
RDKG RH5 255 H3
St Michaels CE JMI School
STALW/RED AL3 38 A6
St Michaels CE Primary School
ASC SL5 192 C5
CAMTN NW1 4 G5
ENC/FH EN2 79 K5
HGT N6 118 B5
WAND/EARL SW18 179 J3
WDGN N22 98 G9
St Michaels CE Aided Primary School Hall
WELL DA16 163 M7
St Michaels Primary School
STALW/RED AL3 38 A6
St Michaels RC Primary School
EHAM E6 142 C4
St Michaels RC School
ASHF TW15 174 B8
GSTN WD25 55 L8
St Michaels RC Secondary School
BERM/RHTH SE16 19 N2
St Michaels & St Martins RC Primary School
HSLWW TW4 153 N9
St Michaels Sydenham CE Primary
SYD SE26 182 D7
St Monicas RC Primary School
IS N1 7 J9
STHGT/OAK N14 98 F4
St Nicholas CE First & Middle School
SHPTN TW17 196 C6
St Nicholas Centre
SUT SM1 221 L2
St Nicholas House School
HHS/BOV HP3 54 C1
St Nicholas School
BORE WD6 75 K10
CHST BR7 184 F10
HLWE CM17 30 A8
PUR/KEN CR8 222 G9
REDH RH1 258 E5
St Nicolas CE Infant School
GUW GU2 267 P2
St Olaves Preparatory School
ELTH/MOT SE9 184 E5
St Olave's & St Saviour's Grammar School
ORP BR6 207 L10
St Osmunds RC Primary School
BARN SW13 156 C7
St Pancras Hospital
CAMTN NW1 5 J6
St Pancras & Islington Cemetery
EFNCH N2 97 P9
St Pancras Station
CAMTN NW1 5 L9
St Patricks Church School
STHWK SE1 12 A10
St Patricks Infants School
WAP E1W 140 A10
St Patricks International School
SOHO/CST W1F 11 H5
St Patricks RC JMI School
ROMW/RG RM7 104 C9
St Patricks RC Primary School
WALTH E17 120 D2
WAP E1W 140 A10
WOOL/PLUM SE18 162 G3
St Paulinus CE Primary School
DART DA1 164 F10
St Pauls & All Hallows CE Infant School
TOTM N17 99 P8
St Paul's Cathedral
STP EC4M 12 D6
St Paul's Cathedral School
STP EC4M 12 E6
St Pauls Catholic College
SUN TW16 197 H1
St Pauls CE Aided Primary School
DORK RH4 272 G2
St Pauls CE JMI School
MLHL NW7 96 E5
St Pauls CE Primary School
ADL/WDHM KT15 215 K1
BRWN CM15 86 C6
BTFD TW8 155 J5
CHSGTN KT9 219 K1
FBAR/BDGN N11 98 B6
HAMP NW3 3 P4
KGLGY WD4 54 C10
SWLY BR8 209 J1
WALW SE17 18 D8
WCHMH N21 99 J1
WCHPL E1 13 P7
St Pauls CE Junior School
KUTN/CMB KT2 177 M10
St Pauls Cray CE Primary School
STMC/STPC BR5 207 M3
St Pauls Cray Health Clinic
STMC/STPC BR5 207 K2
St Pauls Girls School
HMSMTH W6 156 G3
St Pauls Preparatory School
BARN SW13 156 D4
St Paul's Primary School
HMSMTH W6 156 F4
St Pauls RC Primary School
CHESW EN7 62 A3
THDIT KT7 198 D7
WDGN N22 98 G10
St Pauls RC School
WOOL/PLUM SE18 163 K5
St Pauls Road Medical Centre
IS N1 6 D1
St Pauls Way School
BOW E3 140 F6
St Pauls With St Lukes CE Primary School
BOW E3 140 E7
St Paul's with St Michael's CE Primary School
HACK E8 7 P5
St Paul with St Luke CE Primary School
POP/IOD E14 140 E7
St Peter Chanel RC Primary School
SCUP DA14 185 M8
St Peter & Pauls RC Primary School
IL IG1 122 G8
St Peter & St Paul CE Primary School
CTHM CR3 259 H1
St Peter & St Paul RC Primary School
MTCM CR4 202 A4
St Peter & St Pauls Primary School
FSBYE EC1V 12 D1
St Peters Catholic Primary School
ROM RM1 124 E1
St Peters Catholic School
GU GU1 250 F9
St Peters CE Combined School
SL SL1 128 A5
St Peters CE Middle School
WDSR SL4 171 L2
St Peters CE Primary School
BRW CM14 106 C3
GDST RH9 260 F9
HMSMTH W6 156 D4
MV/WKIL W9 8 E2
WALW SE17 18 G8
St Peters Eaton Square CE Primary School
BGVA SW1W 16 E4
St Peter's Hospital
COVGDN WC2E 11 M7
St Peters JMI School
STAL AL1 38 D7
St Peters Junior Middle & Infant School
RKW/CH/CXG WD3 91 L2
St Peters Primary School
SAND/SEL CR2 223 L3
WAP E1W 140 B10
St Peters RC Primary School
DAGW RM9 144 A3
LHD/OX KT22 237 H6
WOOL/PLUM SE18 162 E4
St Philip Howard Catholic Primary School
HAT AL10 40 E4
St Philips School
CHSGTN KT9 219 J3
SKENS SW7 15 K6
St Phillips Infant School
SYD SE26 182 A7
St Philomenas RC High School
CAR SM5 222 A2
St Philomenas RC Primary School
STMC/STPC BR5 207 M7
St Quintins Health Centre
NKENS W10 136 F7
St Raphaels Hospice
WPK KT4 200 G9
St Raphael's RC Primary School
NTHLT UB5 133 J4
St Raphaels Way Medical Centre
WBLY HA9 115 P10
St Richards with St Andrews CE Primary School
RCHPK/HAM TW10 176 G6
St Robert Southwell RC Primary School
CDALE/KGS NW9 115 P4
St Roses RC Infant School
HHW HP1 35 K8
St Saviour & St Olaves School
STHWK SE1 19 H4
St Saviours CE Infant School
EA W5 135 J10
St Saviours CE Primary School
HNHL SE24 159 K9
MV/WKIL W9 9 H2
POP/IOD E14 140 G7
St Saviours RC Primary School
LEW SE13 161 H10
St Scholastica's RC Primary School
STNW/STAM N16 119 P8
St Stephens CE Junior School
TWK TW1 176 F2
St Stephens CE Primary School
BAY/PAD W2 8 F4
DEPT SE8 160 F8
SHB W12 136 F10
St Stephens CE School
VX/NE SW8 158 F6
St Stephens Primary School
EHAM E6 141 P2
St Stephens RC Primary School
WELL DA16 163 K9
St Swithun Wells RC Primary School
RSLP HA4 113 L8
St Teresa RC Primary School
BCTR RM8 123 M9
St Teresas Preparatory School
EHSLY KT24 253 L4
St Teresa's RC Primary School
BORE WD6 75 N6
St Teresas RC School
KTN/HRWW/W HA3 94 B9
St Teresas School
RDKG RH5 253 L8
St Theresas RC Primary School
FNCH N3 117 K1
St Thomas CE Primary School
NKENS W10 8 A2
STNW/STAM N16 119 N6
St Thomas Childrens Day Hospital
LBTH SE11 17 P7
St Thomas' Hospital
STHWK SE1 17 N3
St Thomas' Hospital Operation Theatre
STHWK SE1 13 H10
St Thomas More RC Primary School
BERK HP4 33 M5
BXLYHN DA7 164 A8
ELTH/MOT SE9 162 B9
St Thomas More RC School
CHEL SW3 16 A6
ELTH/MOT SE9 184 D2
St Thomas More School
WDGN N22 98 G8
St Thomas of Canterbury J & I School
BRWN CM15 107 J1
St Thomas of Canterbury RC Middle School
MTCM CR4 202 B3
St Thomas of Canterbury RC Primary School
FUL/PGN SW6 157 J6
GRAYS RM17 167 N3
GU GU1 250 E10
St Thomas Primary School
SEV TN13 265 J1
St Thomas the Apostle College
PECK SE15 160 B7
St Ursulas Convent School
GNWCH SE10 161 J6
St Ursulas RC Infant School
HARH RM3 105 J7
St Ursulas RC Junior School
HARH RM3 105 J7
St Vincent de Paul RC Primary School
WEST SW1P 16 G4
St Vincents Catholic Primary School
ELTH/MOT SE9 184 B7
St Vincents Hospital
RSLP HA4 112 F1
St Vincents RC Primary School
ACT W3 135 N9
BCTR RM8 123 M7
MHST W1U 10 C4
MLHL NW7 96 F5
St Walter & St John Sports Ground
TOOT SW17 179 P4
St Wilfrids RC School
CRAWW RH11 283 L8
St William of York Primary School
FSTH SE23 182 D4
St Winefrides Catholic Primary School
MNPK E12 122 C10
St Winifreds Junior School
LEE/GVPK SE12 183 L2
St Winifreds RC Infant School
LEW SE13 183 K1
Salcombe School
STHGT/OAK N14 98 E1
Salesian College
BTSEA SW11 157 P7
CHERT KT16 195 K8
Salesian RC School
CHERT KT16 195 H9
Salford Primary School
REDH RH1 276 B6
Salfords Industrial Estate
REDH RH1 276 B8
Salisbury Hall
LCOL/BKTW AL2 57 N5
Salisbury Infant School
HAT AL10 40 E2
Salisbury Lawn Tennis Club
STAL AL1 38 G5
Salisbury Primary School
MNPK E12 122 A10
Salisbury School
ED N9 100 B2
Salisbury Upper School
ED N9 100 B1
Salters' Hall
BARB EC2Y 12 F4
Salusbury Primary School
KIL/WHAMP NW6 2 C6
Salvation Army Heritage Centre
BLKFR EC4V 12 E7
Salvatorian College
KTN/HRWW/W HA3 94 D10
Samaritan & Western Ophthalmic Hospital
MBLAR W1H 10 A3
Samuel Jones Industrial Estate
PECK SE15 159 M6
Samuel Rhodes School
IS N1 6 A5
Sandcross Junior School
REIG RH2 275 J3
Sanders Draper School
HCH RM12 125 L9
Sanderstead Junior School
SAND/SEL CR2 223 L5
Sandfield CP School
GU GU1 268 A1
Sandgate Trading Estate
BERM/RHTH SE16 160 A4
Sandhurst Primary School
CAT SE6 183 K3
Sandown Industrial Park
ESH/CLAY KT10 197 P9
Sandown Park Racecourse
ESH/CLAY KT10 198 B9
Sandown Road Industrial Estate
WATN WD24 73 K3
Sandridge Gate Business Centre
STALE/WH AL4 20 G10
STALW/RED AL3 38 E2
Sandridge School
STALE/WH AL4 21 J9
Sandridge Youth Club & Sports Centre
STALW/RED AL3 20 G10
Sandringham Primary School
FSTGT E7 141 P1
Sandringham School
STALE/WH AL4 38 G2
Sandy Lodge Golf Club
NTHWD HA6 92 E3
Sangers County Middle School
HORL RH6 280 A4
Sapcote Trading Centre
WLSDN NW10 116 C10
Saracen Industrial Area
HHNE HP2 36 C4
Sarah Bonnell School
SRTFD E15 141 K1
Sarbir Industrial Park
HLW CM20 29 M6
Sarrat School
RKW/CH/CXG WD3 71 K2
Sarum Hall School
HAMP NW3 3 P3
Satellite Business Village
CRAWE RH10 283 P3
Satmer Trust School
STNW/STAM N16 119 P7
Savill Garden (Windsor Great Park)
EGH TW20 171 K9
Savoy Pier
TPL/STR WC2R 11 N8
Savoy Theatre
TPL/STR WC2R 11 N8
Sawbridge Health Clinic
SBW CM21 29 P1
Saxeway Business Centre
CSHM HP5 50 D4
Saxon Business Centre
WIM/MER SW19 201 M2
Saxon CP School
SHPTN TW17 196 A5
Sayer Clinic
CROY/NA CR0 222 G1
Sayer Clinics
MBLAR W1H 10 B6
Sayes Court Junior School
ADL/WDHM KT15 215 L2
Scarsdale Place Medical Centre
KENS W8 14 G3
Schiller International School
STHWK SE1 12 A10
Schomberg House
STJS SW1Y 11 H10
School House Aveley School
SOCK/AV RM15 146 D10
Schooling Licensed Conveyancers
GRAYS RM17 167 N4
School of Art
RCH/KEW TW9 155 K10
School of Art & Design
HAT AL10 40 A1
REIG RH2 257 N10
School of English
GLDGN NW11 117 K6
School of Health
RDART DA2 188 A2
School of Oriental & African Studies
STPAN WC1H 11 K2
The School of Pharmacy
BMSBY WC1N 11 M1
The School of St David & St Katharine
CEND/HSY/T N8 118 F2
Science Museum Imax Cinema
SKENS SW7 15 L4
The Science Museum Library
SKENS SW7 15 L3
The Scott Gallery
HORL RH6 280 B5
Scott's Grotto
WARE SG12 26 C3
Scotts Park Primary School
BMLY BR1 205 P1
Scotts Primary School
HCH RM12 125 K10
Scott Wilkie Primary School
CAN/RD E16 141 P8
Screen Cinema
WOT/HER KT12 197 H8
Screen on Baker Street Cinema
MHST W1U 10 B3
Screen on the Green Cinema
IS N1 6 C6
Screen on the Hill Cinema
HAMP NW3 117 P10
Seaton House School
BELMT SM2 221 N6
Sebright Primary School
BETH E2 7 N7
Secombe Centre
SUT SM1 221 K2
Sedgehill School
CAT SE6 182 G8
Sedgewick Centre
WCHPL E1 13 M5
Sedleys CE Primary School
MEO DA13 189 M8
Seer Green CE Combined School
BEAC HP9 89 H7
Selborne Primary School
GFD/PVL UB6 134 E4
The Sele School
HERT/WAS SG14 24 G5
The Selhurst Medical Centre
SNWD SE25 203 L6
Sellincourt School
TOOT SW17 180 A9
Selsdon High School
SAND/SEL CR2 224 C4
Selsdon Park Hotel Golf Club
SAND/SEL CR2 224 B7
Selsdon Primary School
SAND/SEL CR2 224 B5
Selsdon Road Industrial Estate
SAND/SEL CR2 223 L4
Selwyn Primary School
CHING E4 101 H7
PLSTW E13 141 M3
Semaphore Tower
COB KT11 234 E3
Send CE Infant School
RPLY/SEND GU23 232 G10
Send Cricket Club
RPLY/SEND GU23 232 E10
Sergeant Industrial Estate
WAND/EARL SW18 179 L2
Serpentine Gallery
BAY/PAD W2 9 M10
Servite RC Primary School
WBPTN SW10 15 J9
Seven Islands Leisure Centre
BERM/RHTH SE16 160 B2
Seven Kings Health Centre
GDMY/SEVK IG3 123 H6
Seven Kings High School
GNTH/NBYPK IG2 122 G5
Seven Mills Primary School
POP/IOD E14 160 F1
Sevenoaks Business Centre
RSEV TN14 247 J6
Sevenoaks Hospital
SEV TN13 247 K7
Sevenoaks Museum & Library
BGR/WK TN15 265 K1
Sevenoaks Primary School
SEV TN13 247 J8
Sevenoaks RFC
BGR/WK TN15 265 K1
Sevenoaks School
BGR/WK TN15 265 K2
Sevenoaks School Track
BGR/WK TN15 265 K2
Sevenoaks Swimming Centre
BGR/WK TN15 265 K1
Sevenoaks Way Industrial Estate
STMC/STPC BR5 207 M3
Sevenoaks Weald Primary School
RSEV TN14 265 J8
Seven Sisters Primary School
SEVS/STOTM N15 119 M3
Seymour Gardens Medical Centre
IL IG1 122 C6
Seymour Leasure Centre
MBLAR W1H 10 A4
Shaare Zedek Medical Centre
GLDGN NW11 117 J4
Shacklewell Primary School
STNW/STAM N16 119 N9
Shaftesbury High School
KTN/HRWW/W HA3 94 A9
Shaftesbury Hospital
LSQ/SEVD WC2H 11 K6
Shaftesbury Medical Centre
RYLN/HDSTN HA2 114 B6
Shaftesbury Park Primary School
BTSEA SW11 158 B9
Shaftesbury Primary School
FSTGT E7 141 P2
Shaftesbury Theatre
LSQ/SEVD WC2H 11 L5
Shahjalal Medical Centre
WCHPL E1 13 P6
Shakespeare Business Centre
BRXN/ST SW9 159 J9
Shakespeare Globe Exhibition
STHWK SE1 12 E8
Shakespeare Industrial Estate
WATN WD24 73 H4
Shalford Infant School
RGUE GU4 268 B6
Shalford Mill (NT)
RGUE GU4 268 B5
The Shamrock Sports Club
ACT W3 135 P8
Shannon Corner Retail Park
NWMAL KT3 200 D4
Shapla Primary School
WCHPL E1 13 N7
Sharp Sports Centre
EDGW HA8 95 M7
Shawcroft School
STMC/STPC BR5 207 P5
Shawley Primary School
EPSOM KT18 238 F4
Shaw Primary School
SOCK/AV RM15 146 G8
Shears Green Primary School
GVW DA11 190 C6
Sheeji Medical Centre
SL SL1 129 J9
Sheen Lane Health Centre
MORT/ESHN SW14 155 P9
Sheen Mount Primary School
RCHPK/HAM TW10 177 N1
Sheen School
MORT/ESHN SW14 156 B10
Sheen Sports Centre
MORT/ESHN SW14 156 B10
Sheepcot Medical Centre
GSTN WD25 55 K10
Sheering CE Primary School
RBSF CM22 30 E2
Shell Centre
STHWK SE1 11 P10
Shelley Primary School
CHONG CM5 67 M2
Shelley School
CLAP SW4 158 D9
Shendish Manor Golf Club
HHS/BOV HP3 53 N2
Shenfield Cricket Club
BRWN CM15 87 L10
Shenfield High School
BRWN CM15 87 M9
Shenfield Sports Centre
BRWN CM15 87 M9
Shenley JMI School
RAD WD7 57 L10
Shenstone School
DART DA1 186 E1
Shenval Industrial Estate
HLW CM20 29 K7
Shepherd Primary School
RKW/CH/CXG WD3 91 K2
Shepherd's Bush Cricket Club
ACT W3 136 B9
Shepherd's Bush Empire
SHB W12 156 F1
Shepherds Community School YWAM
BROCKY SE4 160 F9
Shepperton Business Park
SHPTN TW17 196 D5
Shepperton Health Centre
SHPTN TW17 196 C5

Shepperton Studios SHPTN TW17 196 A3
Sheraton Business Centre GFD/PVL UB6 135 H4
Shere CE Infant School SHGR GU5 270 B5
Sheredes School HOD EN11 44 E4
Sheringdale Primary School WAND/EARL SW18 179 J4
Sheringham Junior School MNPK E12 122 C9
Sherington Primary School CHARL SE7 161 N5
Sherlock Holmes Museum CAMTN NW1 10 B2
Sherwood First School MTCM CR4 202 D4
Sherwood Park School WLGTN SM6 202 E10
Shire Horse Centre CFSP/GDCR SL9 90 D4
Shirley Clinic CROY/NA CR0 204 B8
Shirley High School CROY/NA CR0 204 C10
Shirley Medical Centre CROY/NA CR0 204 D9
Shirley Park Golf Club CROY/NA CR0 204 A9
Shirley Wanderers RFC WWKM BR4 225 H1
Shooters Hill Golf Club WOOL/PLUM SE18 162 F7
The Shopping Hall EHAM E6 142 B3
Shore Business Centre HOM E9 140 B2
Shoreditch Comprehensive School IS N1 7 K8
Shoreditch County Court STLK EC1Y 13 H1
Shoreham County Primary School RSEV TN14 228 G7
Shorne CE Primary School GVE DA12 191 P8
Shortlands Golf Club HAYES BR2 205 K1
Shortwood Infant School STA TW18 173 L6
Shotfield Health Clinic WLGTN SM6 222 C3
Showcase Bluewater Cinema GRH DA9 188 E4
Showcase Cinema WDGN N22 99 H10
Showcase Newham Cinema BARK IG11 142 F5
Show Jumping/Equestrian Circuit UPMR RM14 146 A1
Shrewsbury House School SURB KT6 199 J9
Shrewsbury Road Health Centre FSTGT E7 142 A2
Sidcup Cemetery BXLY DA5 185 N5
Sidcup Golf Club BFN/LL DA15 185 K5
Sidcup Health Centre SCUP DA14 185 K6
Sidcup Hill Primary School SCUP DA14 185 L8
Sidcup Sports Club SCUP DA14 185 J7
Sidney Russell School DAGW RM9 123 P9
Silicon Business Centre GFD/PVL UB6 135 H4
Silverdale Industrial Estate HYS/HAR UB3 133 H10
Silverglade Business Park CHSGTN KT9 219 H8
Silver Industrial Estate TOTM N17 99 N10
Silvermere Golf Club COB KT11 216 C9
Silver Street Medical Centre UED N18 99 M5
Silver Wing Industrial Estate CROY/NA CR0 222 G3
Simon Balle School HERT/BAY SG13 25 M6
Simon Marks Jewish Primary School STNW/STAM N16 119 N6
Simpson Health Centre BEAC HP9 88 B8
Singlegate First School WIM/MER SW19 179 N10
Singlewell Primary School GVE DA12 190 G9
Sion College EMB EC4Y 12 B7
Sion Manning RC Girls School NKENS W10 136 G7
Sir Francis Drake Primary School DEPT SE8 160 D4
Sir Frederic Osborn School WGCE AL7 23 L4
Sir George Monoux College WALTH E17 100 C10
Sir James Barrie School VX/NE SW8 158 D7
Sir John Cass College of Art WCHPL E1 13 N5
Sir John Cass Foundation/Redcoat School WCHPL E1 140 C7
Sir John Cass Foundation School TWRH EC3N 13 L6
Sir John Lillie Primary School FUL/PGN SW6 14 B10
Sir John Newsom School WGCE AL7 23 H8
Sir John Soane's Museum LINN WC2A 11 P5
Sir Thomas Abney Primary School STNW/STAM N16 119 L5
Sir Thomas Lipton Memorial Hospital STHGT/OAK N14 98 C1
Sir William Burrough Primary School POP/IOD E14 140 D8
Sir William Perkins School CHERT KT16 195 J8
Six Bridges Trading Estate STHWK SE1 19 P8
Sixth Form Centre FSTGT E7 141 N1
Ski Centre HHS/BOV HP3 35 P8
Skidmore Clinic RKW/CH/CXG WD3 91 P2
Skillion Business Park BARK IG11 143 J5
Skinners Company Lower Girls School CLPT E5 120 A6
Skinners Companys School For Girls STNW/STAM N16 119 M5
Ski Slope STMC/STPC BR5 207 N1
Sky Business Park EGH TW20 194 F2
Skyswood JMI School STALE/WH AL4 39 H3
Slade Green FC ERITH DA8 165 J7
Slade Green Primary School ERITH DA8 165 H6
Slade School of Fine Art STPAN WC1H 5 K10
Sleaford Industrial Estate VX/NE SW8 158 D6
Sloane Hospital BECK BR3 205 J1
Slough Cemetery SLN SL2 129 L8
Slough Community Mental Health Centre DTCH/LGLY SL3 150 D3
Slough Crematorium SLN SL2 129 L8
Slough & Eton CE School SL SL1 149 J2
Slough Grammar School DTCH/LGLY SL3 149 N2
Slough Ice Arena SL SL1 149 J1
Slough Museum SL SL1 129 J10
SL SL1 149 M1
Slough RFC DTCH/LGLY SL3 149 N4
Slough Sports Club SL SL1 149 K2
Slough Town FC SLN SL2 129 M7
Slough Trading Estate SL SL1 128 F7
SL SL1 128 G9
Slyfield Industrial Estate GU GU1 250 A5
Smallberry Green Primary School ISLW TW7 154 F8
Smallwood Primary School TOOT SW17 179 N7
SMA Medical Centre LEY E10 120 G5
Smitham Primary School COUL/CHIP CR5 240 D2
Smithy Street School WCHPL E1 140 B7
Smug Oak Green Business Centre LCOL/BKTW AL2 56 A5
Snaresbrook College SWFD E18 101 M10
Snaresbrook Crown Court WAN E11 121 L3
Snaresbrook Primary School SWFD E18 121 M2
Snowhill Business Centre CRAWE RH10 285 P1
Snowsfields Primary School STHWK SE1 19 J1
Sobel Medical Centre HOLWY N7 119 H9
Soho Parish CE Primary School SOHO/CST W1F 11 J7
Solefield School SEV TN13 265 K3
Solent Road Health Centre KIL/WHAMP NW6 2 E1
Somerset House COVGDN WC2E 11 N7
Somers Heath Primary School SOCK/AV RM15 146 F9
Somers Town Community Sports Centre CAMTN NW1 5 H8
Sopwell House Hotel & Country Club STAL AL1 38 E10
Sorsby Health Centre CLPT E5 120 C9
South Bank Business Centre BTSEA SW11 158 B7
Southbank Business Centre VX/NE SW8 17 K10
Southbank International School NTGHL W11 8 E8
Southbank University STHWK SE1 18 C2
STHWK SE1 18 E3
VX/NE SW8 158 E7
South Bookham School GT/LBKH KT23 254 B3
Southborough Primary School HAYES BR2 206 D5
Southborough School SURB KT6 199 K10
Southbury Primary School PEND EN3 80 A8
South Camden Community School CAMTN NW1 5 H7
South Chelsea College BRXN/ST SW9 158 G10
South Croydon Medical Centre SAND/SEL CR2 223 K4
South Croydon Sports Club SAND/SEL CR2 223 M2
Southdown Industrial Estate HARP AL5 20 B3
South Eastern University HOLWY N7 118 G8
Southern Clinic REIG RH2 275 M1
Southern Road Primary School PLSTW E13 141 N4
Southern Valley Golf Club GVE DA12 191 K7
South Essex Crematorium UPMR RM14 126 C10
Southfield First & Middle School CHSWK W4 156 B1
Southfield Medical Centre CHSWK W4 156 A1
The Southfields Clinic WAND/EARL SW18 179 K2
Southfields Community School WAND/EARL SW18 179 K4
Southfields School GVE DA12 190 F8
Southgate Cemetery STHGT/OAK N14 98 D3
Southgate College STHGT/OAK N14 98 D3
Southgate Compton Cricket Club EBAR EN4 78 A8
Southgate First & Middle School CRAWE RH10 283 N9
Southgate Leisure Centre STHGT/OAK N14 98 E1
Southgate Road Medical Centre IS N1 7 H3
Southgate School EBAR EN4 78 C9
Southgate West Middle School CRAWW RH11 283 M9
South Grove Primary School WALTH E17 120 D4
South Hampstead Cricket Club CRICK NW2 136 F2
South Hampstead High School (Senior) HAMP NW3 3 L2
South Harringay Junior School FSBYPK N4 119 H3
South Herts Golf Club TRDG/WHET N20 97 K2
South Hill JMI School HHW HP1 35 M7
Southlands College PUT/ROE SW15 156 C10
South Lewisham Health Centre CAT SE6 183 H7
South London Crematorium MTCM CR4 202 D2
South London Montessori School BTSEA SW11 157 P7
The South London Natural Health Centre CLAP SW4 158 D10
South London Tamil School CROY/NA CR0 203 K7
South London Theatre WNWD SE27 181 K6
Southmead Primary School WIM/MER SW19 179 H4
South Norwood Country Park SNWD SE25 204 B4
South Norwood Hill Medical Centre SNWD SE25 203 M2
South Norwood Medical Centre SNWD SE25 203 M4
South Norwood Primary School SNWD SE25 203 P4
South Nutfield Cricket Club REDH RH1 276 G2
South Park Business Centre IL IG1 123 H7
South Park Clinic IL IG1 123 H9
South Park Primary School GDMY/SEVK IG3 123 H8
South Quay Plaza POP/IOD E14 160 G1
South Rise Primary School WOOL/PLUM SE18 162 G4
Southside Industrial Estate VX/NE SW8 158 D6
South Terminal HORL RH6 280 B8
South Thames College PUT/ROE SW15 178 G1
South Thames College/Wandsworth Adult College PUT/ROE SW15 178 C2
Southville Junior School EBED/NFELT TW14 174 G4
Southwark Bridge Business Centre STHWK SE1 12 F10
Southwark Bridge Stairs BLKFR EC4V 12 E8
Southwark Cathedral STHWK SE1 12 G9
Southwark College BERM/RHTH SE16 160 A2
CMBW SE5 159 M6
STHWK SE1 18 C1
STHWK SE1 19 K3
Southwark Crown Court STHWK SE1 13 J9
Southwark Park Primary School BERM/RHTH SE16 160 A2
Southwark Park Running Track BERM/RHTH SE16 160 B3
Southwark Sports Ground DUL SE21 181 N4
South West Middlesex Crematorium FELT TW13 175 M4
Southwold Primary School CLPT E5 120 B7
South Woodford Health Centre SWFD E18 101 M9
Southwood Hospital HGT N6 118 B5
Southwood Primary School DAGW RM9 123 P9
Sovereign Business Centre PEND EN3 80 E7
The Space Arts Centre Cinema DEPT SE8 160 E3
Sparrow Farm County Junior School EW KT17 220 E2
Sparrow Farm Junior School EBED/NFELT TW14 175 K3
Sparrow Farm Nursery School EBED/NFELT TW14 175 K3
Spa School STHWK SE1 19 N6
Speakers Corner BAY/PAD W2 10 B7
Spectators Viewing Area HTHAIR TW6 152 C9
Speedway Industrial Estate HYS/HAR UB3 152 E1
Speke's Monument BAY/PAD W2 9 K9
Spelthorne Clinic ASHF TW15 174 E9
Spelthorne Leisure Centre STA TW18 173 K8
Spelthorne Museum STA TW18 173 H8
Spelthorne Primary School ASHF TW15 174 E9
Spelthorne Sixth Form College ASHF TW15 174 A7
Spelthorne Sports Club ASHF TW15 174 E10
Spencer House WHALL SW1A 10 G10
Spencer Junior School STALW/RED AL3 38 D3
Sphere Industrial Estate STAL AL1 38 F7
The Spinney Junior & Infant School HLW CM20 29 K10
The Spires Shopping Centre BAR EN5 77 H7
Spiritualist University WLSDN NW10 136 D2
Spitalfields Community Farm BETH E2 13 N1
Spitalfields Health Centre WCHPL E1 13 M4
Spitalfields Market LEY E10 120 F8
Spitalfields Market Hall WCHPL E1 13 L3
Sports & Conference Centre WGCW AL8 22 F7
Springfield Hospital TOOT SW17 179 P6
Springfield Primary School SUN TW16 196 F1
VX/NE SW8 158 E6
Spring Grove Primary School ISLW TW7 154 C8
Springhallow School HNWL W7 134 E8
Springmead JMI School WGCE AL7 23 M4
Spring Park Primary School CROY/NA CR0 204 F10
Springvale Retail Park STMC/STPC BR5 207 M3
STMC/STPC BR5 207 N5
Springwell Infant School HEST TW5 153 M6
Springwell Junior School HEST TW5 153 M6
Sprint Industrial Estate BF/WBF KT14 215 N7
Spurgeons College SNWD SE25 203 M2
Squerryes Court Manor House & Gardens BH/WHM TN16 262 F4
Squirrels Heath Junior School GPK RM2 125 J3
Squirrels Trading Estate HYS/HAR UB3 152 G2
The Stables Gallery & Art Centre CRICK NW2 116 D9
Stadium Business Centre WBLY HA9 115 N8
Stadium Industrial Estate WBLY HA9 115 N10
Stadium Retail Park WBLY HA9 115 M8
Stafford Cross Business Park CROY/NA CR0 222 G2
Stafford Industrial Estate EMPK RM11 125 L1
Stag Lane Medical Centre CDALE/KGS NW9 115 P1
Stag Lane Primary School EDGW HA8 95 M10
Stags School STALW/RED AL3 38 D2
Stag Theatre SEV TN13 265 J1
Staines County Court STA TW18 173 K8
Staines Preparatory School STA TW18 173 K8
Staines RFC FELT TW13 175 H8
Staines Town FC STA TW18 173 K10
Stamford Clinic HMSMTH W6 156 D3
Stamford Green County Primary School HOR/WEW KT19 219 N8
Stamford Hill Primary School SEVS/STOTM N15 119 L4
Stanborough School GSTN WD25 73 J1
WGCW AL8 22 E7
Stanburn Middle School STAN HA7 95 H8
Standard Industrial Estate CAN/RD E16 162 A1
CAN/RD E16 162 C1
Stanford Middle School STRHM/NOR SW16 202 E1
Stanhope Primary School GFD/PVL UB6 134 B6
Stanley Infant School TEDD TW11 176 D7
Stanley Junior School WHTN TW2 176 D7
Stanley Park High School CAR SM5 222 B3
Stanley Park Junior School CAR SM5 222 A4
Stanley Technical Boys High School SNWD SE25 203 N3
Stanmore College STAN HA7 94 G7
Stanmore Golf Club STAN HA7 94 G8
Stanton Square Industrial Estate CAT SE6 182 E7
Stanway School DORK RH4 254 G9
Stapleford Abbotts Golf Club ABR/ST RM4 105 H1
Stapleford Abbotts Primary School ABR/ST RM4 84 C9
Staple Inn Buildings HHOL WC1V 12 A4
Staples Corner Business Park CRICK NW2 116 D6
Staples Road Junior & Infant School LOU IG10 82 B7
Staple Tye Shopping Centre HLWS CM18 46 G4
Star Business Centre DAGW RM9 144 E7
Starhurst School RDKG RH5 273 H4
Star Primary School CAN/RD E16 141 K6
Stationers Hall STP EC4M 12 D6
Stationery Office GINN WC1R 11 P4
Station Yard KWD/TDW/WH KT20 239 J7
Stepgates Community School CHERT KT16 195 L7
Stephen Hawking Primary School POP/IOD E14 140 D8
Stepney Day Hospital WCHPL E1 140 B8
Stepney Greencoat CE Primary School POP/IOD E14 140 E8
Stepney Green School WCHPL E1 140 C7
Stepping Stone School HAMP NW3 3 K1
Ster Century Cinema ROM RM1 124 F3
Sterling Industrial Estate DAGE RM10 124 C9
Sterling Way Clinic UED N18 99 N6
Stewards School HLWS CM18 46 F5
Stewart Fleming Primary School PGE/AN SE20 204 B3
Stewart Headlam Primary School WCHPL E1 140 A6
Stifford Clays Health Centre CDH/CHF RM16 147 N10
Stifford Clays Primary School CDH/CHF RM16 147 N10
Stifford Primary School GRAYS RM17 167 K4
Stillness Primary School BROCKY SE4 182 D2
Stirling Industrial Centre BORE WD6 76 A9
Stirling Way Industrial Estates CROY/NA CR0 202 F7
Stock Exchange OBST EC2N 13 H5
Stockley Park Golf Club STKPK UB11 132 D9
Stockwell Lodge Medical Centre CHESW EN7 61 P4
Stockwell Park School BRXN/ST SW9 158 G7
Stockwell Primary School BRXN/ST SW9 158 G9
Stoke Hill CP School GU GU1 249 P7
Stoke Newington School STNW/STAM N16 119 L8
Stoke Park House SLN SL2 129 K5
Stoke Poges County Middle School SLN SL2 129 L2
Stoke Poges Golf Club SLN SL2 129 J5
Stoke Poges School SLN SL2 129 N2
Stompond Lane Track WOT/HER KT12 197 H9
The Stonebridge Primary School WLSDN NW10 135 P3
Stonebridge Shopping Centre WLSDN NW10 136 A3
Stonehill Business Centre UED N18 100 C7
Stonehill Business Park UED N18 100 C6
Stone House Hospital RDART DA2 188 B2
Stone Lake Retail Park CHARL SE7 161 P3
Stoneydown Park Primary School WALTH E17 120 D2
Stony Dean Special School AMSS HP7 69 L5
Storey Primary School CAN/RD E16 142 D10
Stormont House School CLPT E5 120 A9
Stormont School POTB/CUF EN6 59 M7
Stoughton County Junior School GUW GU2 249 N7
Stowford College BELMT SM2 221 M4
Strand on the Green Junior & Infant School CHSWK W4 155 M5
Strand Theatre HOL/ALD WC2B 11 N7
Stratford Magistrates Court SRTFD E15 141 J2
Stratford School FSTGT E7 141 M2
Stratford Shopping Centre SRTFD E15 141 J2
Strathmore School RCHPK/HAM TW10 177 J4
Strawberry Fields School BAY/PAD W2 8 F6
Strawberry Hill Golf Club WHTN TW2 176 D6
Stream Woods School HAT AL10 40 E5
Streatham Cemetery TOOT SW17 179 P6

Streatham & Clapham High School STRHM/NOR SW16 180 D6
Streatham & Clapham High School Preparatory Site BRXS/STRHM SW2 180 G4
Streatham & Croydon RFC THHTH CR7 203 H5
Streatham Ice Rink STRHM/NOR SW16 180 F8
Streatham Modern School STRHM/NOR SW16 180 F9
Streatham Park Cemetery MTCM CR4 202 D2
Streatham Swimming Pool STRHM/NOR SW16 180 F8
Streatham Vale Sports Club STRHM/NOR SW16 180 D10
Streatham Wells Primary School BRXS/STRHM SW2 180 G5
Streete Court School GDST RH9 260 D6
Strodes College EGH TW20 172 C8
Stroud Green Primary School FSBYPK N4 119 H6
Stroud Wood Business Centre LCOL/BKTW AL2 56 D3
Stubbers (Outdoor Pursuits Centre) UPMR RM14 146 E1
Studholme Medical Centre ASHF TW15 174 A7
The Study Preparatory School WIM/MER SW19 178 G8
The Study School NWMAL KT3 200 B5
Sturt Priory Hospital KWD/TDW/WH KT20 256 D2
Sudbourne Primary School BRXS/STRHM SW2 180 G1
Sudbury Court Sports Club ALP/SUD HA0 115 H8
Sudbury Golf Club GFD/PVL UB6 135 H1
Sudbury Primary School ALP/SUD HA0 114 G9
Suffolks Primary School EN EN1 80 A6
Sulivan Primary School FUL/PGN SW6 157 K8
Summerside JMI School NFNCH/WDSP N12 97 N7
Summerswood Primary School BORE WD6 75 N8
Summit Business Park SUN TW16 175 H10
Sumners Community Recreation Centre HLWW/ROY CM19 46 D5
Sunbury Business Centre SUN TW16 196 F1
Sunbury Court SUN TW16 197 L2
Sunbury Health Centre SUN TW16 197 H2
Sunbury Leisure Centre SUN TW16 196 G1
Sunbury Lock WOT/HER KT12 197 J3
Sunbury Manor School SUN TW16 196 G1
Sunderland Estate KGLGY WD4 54 C5
Sundridge & Brasted CE Primary School RSEV TN14 263 P1
Sundridge Park Golf Club BMLY BR1 183 P9
Sun Life Trading Estate EBED/NFELT TW14 153 H9
Sunningdale Golf Club ASC SL5 192 F8
Sunningdale Ladies Golf Club ASC SL5 192 E8
Sunningdale School ASC SL5 192 D6
Sunnydown School CTHM CR3 241 N7
Sunnyfields Primary School HDN NW4 116 E1
Sunnyhill Primary School STRHM/NOR SW16 180 G7
Super Bowl BXLYHS DA6 164 A10
Surbiton Business Centre SURB KT6 199 J6
Surbiton Cemetery BRYLDS KT5 199 M4
Surbiton Golf Club ESH/CLAY KT10 218 G1
Surbiton High School KUT KT1 199 K4
Surbiton Hospital SURB KT6 199 K6
Surbiton Natural Health Centre SURB KT6 199 K6
Surex Swimming Pools BH/WHM TN16 244 A1
Surrey Business Park EW KT17 220 B7
Surrey College GU GU1 268 B2
Surrey County Cricket Club (The Oval) LBTH SE11 17 P9
Surrey Docks Farm BERM/RHTH SE16 160 E1
Surrey Docks Health Centre BERM/RHTH SE16 160 D1
Surrey History Centre WOKN/KNAP GU21 232 A4
Surrey Institute of Art & Design EPSOM KT18 220 A10
HOR/WEW KT19 220 B8
Surrey Quays Leisure Park BERM/RHTH SE16 160 C2
Surrey Quays Shopping Centre BERM/RHTH SE16 160 C2
Surrey Square Primary School WALW SE17 19 J7
The Surrey & Sussex Crematorium CRAWE RH10 284 E2
Sussex House Preparatory School KTBR SW1X 16 A5
Sussex Manor Business Park CRAWE RH10 284 B3
Sutcliffe Park Athletics Track ELTH/MOT SE9 183 N1
Sutton Alternative Health Centre SUT SM1 221 L2
Sutton Arena CAR SM5 201 N7
Sutton at Hone CE Primary School EYN DA4 187 P10
Sutton Bowling Club BELMT SM2 221 K5
Sutton Cemetery CHEAM SM3 201 J9
Sutton General Hospital BELMT SM2 221 L6
Sutton Grammar School for Boys SUT SM1 221 M2
Sutton Green Golf Club WOKS/MYFD GU22 232 B9
Sutton High Junior School SUT SM1 221 L3
Sutton High School for Girls GDST SUT SM1 221 K3
Sutton House HOM E9 120 B10
Suttons Business Park RAIN RM13 144 E5
Suttons JMI School HCH RM12 125 L9
Suttons Manor Clinic ABR/ST RM4 84 F4
Sutton Superbowl SUT SM1 221 L2
Sutton United FC SUT SM1 221 K1
Sutton West Centre SUT SM1 221 K2
Swaffield Primary School WAND/EARL SW18 179 M2
Swakeleys School HGDN/ICK UB10 132 D4
Swaminarayan School WLSDN NW10 136 A1
Swan Business Centre CHSWK W4 156 A3
Swan Business Park DART DA1 165 L10
The Swan Centre LHD/OX KT22 236 G7
Swan Lane Pier CANST EC4R 12 G8
Swanlea School WCHPL E1 140 A6
Swanley School SWLY BR8 208 E3
Swanscombe Business Centre SWCM DA10 189 K1
Swansmere School WOT/HER KT12 197 K8
Swan Valley Community School SWCM DA10 189 L3
Swan Wharf Business Centre UX/CGN UB8 131 M4
Swedish School BARN SW13 156 D5
CRAWE RH10 284 A9
The Sweyne Junior School SWCM DA10 189 L3
Swing Gate First School BERK HP4 34 A6
Swiss Cottage School HAMP NW3 3 M4
Sybil Elgar School EA W5 135 K9
NWDGN UB2 153 N2
Sybourn Infant School LEY E10 120 D6
Sybourn Junior School WALTH E17 120 E5
Sydenham Girls School SYD SE26 182 A6
Sydenham High School SYD SE26 182 A8
Sydenham (Junior) High School SYD SE26 182 A7
Sydney Russell Comprehensive School DAGW RM9 123 N10
Syon House BTFD TW8 155 H7
Syon Park BTFD TW8 155 H8
Syon Park School ISLW TW7 154 G7
Syracuse University London Centre NTGHL W11 8 C8
Sythwood Primary School WOKN/KNAP GU21 231 N2
Tabard RFC RAD WD7 74 G3
Tabard Theatre CHSWK W4 156 B3
Taberner House CROY/NA CR0 203 K10
Tadworth Primary School KWD/TDW/WH KT20 238 G8
Tait Road Industrial Estate CROY/NA CR0 203 L7
Tamian Industrial Estate HSLWW TW4 153 K10
Tamworth Manor High School STRHM/NOR SW16 202 E3
Tandem Centre WIM/MER SW19 201 N1
Tandridge Golf Club OXTED RH8 261 H7
Tanners Wood Primary School ABLGY WD5 54 F8
Tanys Dell Primary School HLW CM20 29 K8
Tapling Trading Estate WDR/YW UB7 131 N9
Taplow Health Centre MDHD SL6 128 A8
Tate Britain WEST SW1P 17 L6
Tate Modern STHWK SE1 12 D9
Tatsfield Primary School BH/WHM TN16 244 A7
Tattenham Health Centre EPSOM KT18 238 E4
Tavistock Clinic HAMP NW3 3 L2
TAVR Centre KUT KT1 199 J4
Tavy Clinic ABYW SE2 163 M1
Taylor Trading Estate HERT/BAY SG13 26 A4
TCA Leisure Centre TIL RM18 168 D8
Teardrop Industrial Park SWLY BR8 209 K5
Teddington Business Park TEDD TW11 176 E8
Teddington Cemetery WHTN TW2 176 D7
Teddington Clinic TEDD TW11 176 D9
Teddington Lock TEDD TW11 176 G7
Teddington Memorial Hospital TEDD TW11 176 D9
Teddington School TEDD TW11 177 J9
Teddington Swimming Pool TEDD TW11 176 F8
The Teddington Theatre Club E/WMO/HCT KT8 198 C5
Teikyo School DTCH/LGLY SL3 130 A2
Telegraph Hill School BROCKY SE4 160 D8
Temperate House RCH/KEW TW9 155 L8
Temple Court Business Centre WOKN/KNAP GU21 232 C3
Temple Hill Primary School DART DA1 187 P1
Temple of Bacchus CMBW SE5 159 K8
Temple of Mithras MANHO EC4N 12 G6
Templewood Primary School WGCW AL8 22 F3
Tenby Road Clinic EDGW HA8 95 L10
Tenterden Sports Ground KTN/HRWW/W HA3 115 K5
Terence McMillan Stadium PLSTW E13 141 P6
Tewin Cowper Primary School WLYN AL6 23 P1
Tewin Road Business Centre WGCE AL7 23 H4
Tewin Water School WLYN AL6 23 K1
Thames Barrier CAN/RD E16 162 A1
Thames Barrier Visitor Centre WOOL/PLUM SE18 162 A2
Thames Ditton & Esher Golf Club ESH/CLAY KT10 198 A10
Thames Ditton Infant School THDIT KT7 198 E6
Thames Ditton Junior School THDIT KT7 198 E7
Thames House WEST SW1P 17 L5
Thameside Industrial Estate CAN/RD E16 142 A10
Thameside Primary School GRAYS RM17 167 P5
Thameside Theatre GRAYS RM17 167 M4
Thames Industrial Park TIL RM18 169 M3
Thames Magistrates Court BOW E3 140 F5
Thamesmead Community College ERITHM DA18 163 P1
Thamesmead School SHPTN TW17 196 E6
Thamesmead Shopping Centre THMD SE28 143 K9
Thames Valley Athletics Centre WDSR SL4 149 K4
Thames Valley Community Infant School SL SL1 149 H1
The Thames Valley Nuffield Hospital DTCH/LGLY SL3 129 P3
Thames Valley University EA W5 135 J10
SL SL1 129 K10
Thamesview Business Centre RAIN RM13 144 F7
Thames View Clinic BARK IG11 143 J4
Thames View Junior & Infant School BARK IG11 143 K4
Thamesview School GVE DA12 191 J6
Thames Water Tower NTGHL W11 156 G1
Theatre Centre BECK BR3 204 G2
Théâtre De Complicité HOLWY N7 118 G10
Theatre for Mankind FSBYPK N4 118 G6
Theatre Magenta LHD/OX KT22 236 F6
Theatre Museum Library & Archive COVGDN WC2E 11 M7
Theatre of the Dispossessed WIM/MER SW19 178 G4
The Theatre on the Hill CTHM CR3 241 M8
Theatre Royal SRTFD E15 141 J2
WDSR SL4 149 J6
Theatre Royal, Drury Lane HOL/ALD WC2B 11 M6
Theatre Royal Haymarket STJS SW1Y 11 K8
Therapia Trading Estate CROY/NA CR0 202 E7
Therfield School LHD/OX KT22 236 F5
Theydon Bois Primary School EPP CM16 83 H2
Thistlebrook Industrial Estate ABYW SE2 163 M2
Thomas Arnold Primary School DAGW RM9 144 A2
Thomas Becket RC Primary School SNWD SE25 203 P6
Thomas Bennett Community College CRAWW RH11 283 N10
Thomas Buxton Primary School WCHPL E1 13 N2
The Thomas Coram Middle School BERK HP4 34 A7
Thomas Fairchild Primary School IS N1 6 G7
Thomas Gamuel Primary School WALTH E17 120 F4
Thomas Harding Junior School CSHM HP5 50 G8
Thomas Rivers Medical Centre HLW CM20 29 M4
The Thomas Rivers Medical Centre SBW CM21 29 M2
Thomas Road Industrial Estate POP/IOD E14 140 F7
Thomas's Preparatory School BTSEA SW11 157 N7
Thomas Tallis School BKHTH/KID SE3 161 N9
WAB EN9 63 L9
Thomas Willingale Primary School LOU IG10 82 F7
Thorn Chase School GU GU1 250 F10
Thorncroft Manor LHD/OX KT22 236 F9
Thorndon Park RBRW/HUT CM13 107 M8
Thorndon Park Golf Club RBRW/HUT CM13 107 N7
Thorney Park Golf Club IVER SL0 151 L2
Thornhill Primary School IS N1 6 A4
Thornton Heath Baths THHTH CR7 203 L4
Thornton Heath Health Centre THHTH CR7 203 K4
Thornton Road Industrial Estate CROY/NA CR0 202 F6
Thorntree Primary School CHARL SE7 162 A4
Thorpe CE Infant School EGH TW20 194 F3
Thorpe Cricket Club EGH TW20 194 C4
Thorpe Hall Primary School WALTH E17 101 H9
Thorpe Industrial Park EGH TW20 194 G1
Thorpe Lea Primary School EGH TW20 172 G9
Thorpe Park EGH TW20 195 H4
Three Bridges Business Centre STHL UB1 154 B1
Three Bridges Cricket Club CRAWE RH10 284 B7
Three Bridges FC CRAWE RH10 284 B7
Three Bridges First School CRAWE RH10 284 B6
Three Bridges Middle School CRAWE RH10 284 A7
Three Bridges Primary School NWDGN UB2 153 K3
NWDGN UB2 154 A2
Three Mills Heritage Centre SRTFD E15 141 H5
Thumbswood Primary School WGCE AL7 23 K6
Thurlow Park School WNWD SE27 181 J5
Thurrock Athletics Stadium CDH/CHF RM16 168 A1
Thurrock Business Centre WTHK RM20 166 E5
Thurrock College CDH/CHF RM16 168 C3
Thurston Industrial Estate LEW SE13 160 G9
Tidemill Primary School DEPT SE8 160 F6
Tideway Industrial Estate VX/NE SW8 17 H10
Tiffin Girls School KUTN/CMB KT2 177 K9
Tiffin School KUTN/CMB KT2 199 L2
Tilbury Fort TIL RM18 168 F10
Tilbury/Gravesend Passenger Ferry TIL RM18 168 E10
Tilbury Manorjunior School TIL RM18 168 E6
Tilehouse Combined School DEN/HRF UB9 111 J4
Tiller Centre (Swimming Baths) POP/IOD E14 160 F2
Tiller Leisure Centre POP/IOD E14 160 F2
Tillingbourne Junior School RGUE GU4 268 E7
Timbercroft Primary School WOOL/PLUM SE18 163 H6
Timbers Clinic KTN/HRWW/W HA3 94 C7
Times Square Shopping Centre SUT SM1 221 L2
Titan Industrial Estate GRAYS RM17 167 M3
Tithe Barn Museum UPMR RM14 126 B5
Tiverton Primary School SEVS/STOTM N15 119 L4
Tobacco Dock WAP E1W 140 A9
Tokyngton Community Centre WBLY HA9 115 N10
Toldos School STNW/STAM N16 119 L6
Tollgate Primary School CROY/NA CR0 204 B6
PLSTW E13 141 P6
Tolworth CP School SURB KT6 199 L8
Tolworth Girls School & Centre for Continuing Education SURB KT6 199 L10
Tolworth Recreation Centre CHSGTN KT9 199 L10
Tolworth Tower SURB KT6 199 N9
Tom Hood School WAN E11 121 L8
Tomo Industrial Estate UX/CGN UB8 131 M8
Tonybee Hall & Curtain Theatre WCHPL E1 13 L5
Toot Hill Golf Club CHONG CM5 66 G7
Tooting Bec Athletics Track TOOT SW17 180 C7
Tooting & Mitcham United FC MTCM CR4 202 B1
Top Meadow Golf Club UPMR RM14 147 J1
Torells School CDH/CHF RM16 168 C1
Tormead School GU GU1 250 C10
Torriano Junior & Infant School KTTN NW5 118 D10
Torridon Primary School CAT SE6 183 J5
Torrington Clinic NFNCH/WDSP N12 97 M6
Torrington Park Health Centre NFNCH/WDSP N12 97 M5
Total Health Clinic SHB W12 156 E1
Tottenhall Infants School PLMGR N13 99 H6
Tottenham Hale Retail Park SEVS/STOTM N15 119 P2
Tottenham Hotspur FC (White Hart Lane) TOTM N17 99 N8
Tottenham Park Cemetery ED N9 100 A4
Totteridge Cricket Club TRDG/WHET N20 97 K3
The Tower Bridge Experience STHWK SE1 13 L10
Tower Bridge Museum STHWK SE1 13 L10
Tower Bridge Primary School STHWK SE1 19 L1
Tower Bridge Wharf WAP E1W 13 N10
Tower Hamlets College BETH E2 7 N10
POP/IOD E14 140 G9
WCHPL E1 140 B7
Tower House School MORT/ESHN SW14 155 P10
Tower Industrial Estate SNWD SE25 203 P4
Tower Millennium Pier MON EC3R 13 K9
Tower of London TWRH EC3N 13 L8
Tower Retail Park DART DA1 186 G1
Towers Business Park WBLY HA9 115 N9
Towers Infant School EMPK RM11 125 K5
Towers Junior School EMPK RM11 125 K5
Tower Stairs MON EC3R 13 J8
Town Farm Primary School STWL/WRAY TW19 173 N3
Townley Grammar School for Girls BXLYHS DA6 186 A2
Townmead Business Centre FUL/PGN SW6 157 M9
Town Medical Centre SEV TN13 265 J1
Townsend Industrial Estate WLSDN NW10 135 P3
Townsend Primary School STHWK SE1 19 J5
Townsend School STALW/RED AL3 38 B1
Trabzon Spor FC STNW/STAM N16 119 L9
Trade Union Congress NOXST/BSQ WC1A 11 K5
Traditions Golf Club WOKS/MYFD GU22 233 K1
Trafalgar Business Centre BARK IG11 143 J6
Trafalgar Primary School WHTN TW2 176 C5
Trafalgar Trading Estate PEND EN3 80 E8
Tramshed Theatre WOOL/PLUM SE18 162 E3
Trans Atlantic College BETH E2 7 L7
Transport House WEST SW1P 17 L4
Treasury WHALL SW1A 17 L2
The Treaty Centre HSLW TW3 154 A9
Tree Tops Special School GRAYS RM17 167 N3
Trent CE Primary School EBAR EN4 78 A8
Trent Country Park EBAR EN4 78 B6
Trent Park Cemetery EBAR EN4 78 B7
Trent Park Golf Club EBAR EN4 78 D8
Trevelyan Middle School WDSR SL4 148 F8
Trevor Roberts School HAMP NW3 3 M3
Tricor Business Park CHES/WCR EN8 62 D10
Tricor Trading Estate CHES/WCR EN8 62 D10
Tricycle Cinema KIL/WHAMP NW6 2 D4
Tricycle Theatre KIL/WHAMP NW6 2 D3
Trident Business Centre TOOT SW17 180 A8
Trident Industrial Estate DTCH/LGLY SL3 151 H9
HOD EN11 45 H2
Trinity Business Centre BERM/RHTH SE16 160 E1
Trinity Catholic Lower High School WFD IG8 101 M5
Trinity College Centre PECK SE15 19 J10
PECK SE15 159 M6
Trinity College of Music MHST W1U 10 D4

Trinity Hospital
GNWCH SE10 161 J4
Trinity House
TWRH EC3N 13 K7
Trinity RC High School (Upper)
WFD IG8 101 M5
Trinity St Marys Primary School
BAL SW12 180 B4
Trinity St Stephen CE First School
WDSR SL4 149 H7
Trinity School
CROY/NA CR0 204 B9
DAGE RM10 124 B8
Trinity School Belvedere
BELV DA17 164 D3
Trinity Trading Estate
HYS/HAR UB3 153 H2
Triumph Trading Estate
TOTM N17 99 P7
Trocadero Centre
MYFR/PICC W1J 11 J8
Trojan Business Centre
WLSDN NW10 136 C1
Troy Industrial Estate
HRW HA1 114 E3
True Buddha School
IS N1 5 N6
Trumps Green County Infant School
VW GU25 194 A6
Tudor Court Primary School
CDH/CHF RM16 167 L1
Tudor Lodge Health Centre
WIM/MER SW19 178 G3
Tudor Primary School
FNCH N3 97 M9
HHS/BOV HP3 35 P8
STHL UB1 133 M9
Tudors Business Centre
KWD/TDW/WH KT20 239 J8
Tufnell Park Primary School
HOLWY N7 118 E9
Tuke School
PECK SE15 160 A7
Tulloch Clinic
SHB W12 136 G10
Tunnel Avenue Trading Estate
GNWCH SE10 161 J1
Tunnel Industrial Estate
WTHK RM20 166 E3
WTHK RM20 166 E5
Turners Hill CE Primary School
CRAWE RH10 285 P10
Turney School
DUL SE21 181 K3
Turnford School
CHES/WCR EN8 62 D4
Turnham Primary School
BROCKY SE4 160 D10
Turtle Key Arts Centre
FUL/PGN SW6 14 F10
Tweeddale Infant School
CAR SM5 201 N7
Tweeddale Junior School
CAR SM5 201 N7
Twickenham Cemetery
WHTN TW2 176 A4
Twickenham Golf Club
FELT TW13 175 P6
Twickenham Park Health Centre
TWK TW1 177 H2
Twickenham Stadium
WHTN TW2 176 D2
Twickenham Trading Estate
TWK TW1 176 E2
Two Bridges Business Park
SAND/SEL CR2 223 L3
Two Rivers Retail Park
STA TW18 173 H7
Two Waters JMI School
HHS/BOV HP3 53 N1
Twyford CE High School
ACT W3 135 N10
Tyburn Infant School
STJWD NW8 9 M1
The Type Museum Operation Hannibal
BRXN/ST SW9 158 G7
Tyrrells Wood Golf Club
LHD/OX KT22 237 L10
UGC Cinema
CRAWE RH10 283 N6
CRICK NW2 116 E6
UCI Cinema
WTHK RM20 166 E3
BAY/PAD W2 9 H6
BERM/RHTH SE16 160 C2
ED N9 100 C1
HAT AL10 40 C3
SUT SM1 221 L2
UCI Empire Cinema
LSQ/SEVD WC2H 11 K8
UCI Filmworks Cinema
GNWCH SE10 161 L3
UCL Hospitals
FITZ W1T 11 H2
UGC Cinema
EA W5 135 J9
EN EN1 79 P8
HLW CM20 29 J7
HMSMTH W6 156 E3
SOHO/SHAV W1D 11 J7
WBPTN SW10 15 K8
CHEL SW3 15 M9
UGC Cinema Slough
SL SL1 149 L1
The Ullswater Business Park
COUL/CHIP CR5 240 F2
Ullswater Trading Estate
COUL/CHIP CR5 240 F2
Underhill Junior & Infant School
BAR EN5 77 H9
Unicorn School
RCH/KEW TW9 155 L7
Union Business Park
UX/CGN UB8 131 M2
United Medical & Dental Schools
STHWK SE1 17 N3
United Services Sports Ground
CHSWK W4 156 B7
Unity College
KTTN NW5 118 C9
Unity Trading Estate
WFD IG8 122 A1
University Church of Christ the King
STPAN WC1H 11 J2
University College Hospital
GWRST WC1E 11 H2
HAMP NW3 3 M2
University College Junior School
HAMP NW3 117 M9
University College London
GWRST WC1E 11 J2
STPAN WC1H 5 K10
University College London, Astor College
FITZ W1T 11 H3
University College London, Department of Clinical Haematology
GWRST WC1E 11 J2
University College London Medical School
FITZ W1T 10 G3
University College School
HAMP NW3 117 M10
University Hospital Lewisham
LEW SE13 182 G1
University of California
WHALL SW1A 10 G10
University of East London
BCTR RM8 123 K9
EHAM E6 142 D9
PLSTW E13 141 N5
University of Greenwich
DART DA1 187 K5
DART DA1 187 N5
GNWCH SE10 161 J4
WOOL/PLUM SE18 162 D2
University of Greenwich (Mansion Site)
ELTH/MOT SE9 184 F2
University of Greenwich (Southwood Site)
ELTH/MOT SE9 184 F2
University of Greenwich Sports Ground
ELTH/MOT SE9 162 B10
ELTH/MOT SE9 184 F3
University of Hertfordshire
GSTN WD25 74 A2
HAT AL10 40 C5
HAT AL10 40 D3
HERT/BAY SG13 25 N7
STAL AL1 38 E8
University of Herts Faculty of Law
STAL AL1 38 D5
University of London
BAY/PAD W2 9 L6
BMSBY WC1N 11 M2
ENC/FH EN2 79 P2
FITZ W1T 11 J5
GWRST WC1E 11 K3
NWCR SE14 160 D7
STPAN WC1H 5 L10
STPAN WC1H 11 K1
University of London Athletics Ground
NWMAL KT3 200 D5
University of Middlesex
EBAR EN4 78 D6
PEND EN3 80 A9
University of North London
HOLWY N7 118 G10
University of Notre Dame
LSQ/SEVD WC2H 11 K8
University of Surrey
GUW GU2 249 M10
University of Westminster
CAMTN NW1 10 G1
CHSWK W4 155 P7
GTPST W1W 10 F3
HGT N6 118 C6
MHST W1U 10 C3
University of Westminster (Harrow Campus)
HRW HA1 114 F5
University Vandals RFC
WOT/HER KT12 196 D7
Uphall Primary School
IL IG1 122 E10
Upland Primary School
BXLYHN DA7 164 A9
Uplands Business Park
WALTH E17 100 C10
Upminster Cemetery
UPMR RM14 126 C10
Upminster Golf Club
UPMR RM14 126 C5
Upminster Primary School
UPMR RM14 126 B8
Upminster Trading Park
UPMR RM14 127 J5
Upper Clapton RFC
EPP CM16 47 L10
Upper Montagu Street Clinic
MBLAR W1H 10 A3
Upper Tooting Independent High School
TOOT SW17 179 P5
Upshire Primary School
WAB EN9 63 N9
Upton Cross Primary School
PLSTW E13 141 N3
Upton Day Hospital
BXLYHS DA6 163 P10
Upton Hospital
SL SL1 149 L1
Upton House School
WDSR SL4 149 H8
Upton Lane Medical Centre
FSTGT E7 141 N1
Upton Primary School
BXLY DA5 185 P1
Upton Road School
BXLYHS DA6 185 P1
Ursuline Convent High School
BRW CM14 107 J4
Ursuline High School
IL IG1 122 E7
RYNPK SW20 178 G10
Uxbridge Cemetery
UX/CGN UB8 132 A5
Uxbridge College
HGDN/ICK UB10 131 P1
HYS/HAR UB3 133 H9
Uxbridge County Court
HYS/HAR UB3 132 F7
UX/CGN UB8 131 M1
Uxbridge Cricket Club
HGDN/ICK UB10 131 P1
Uxbridge FC
WDR/YW UB7 132 B9
Uxbridge Golf Club
HGDN/ICK UB10 111 P7
Uxbridge Health Centre
UX/CGN UB8 131 N2
Uxbridge High School
UX/CGN UB8 131 N4
Uxbridge Industrial Estate
UX/CGN UB8 131 L4
Uxbridge Swimming Pool
HGDN/ICK UB10 131 P1
Uxendon Manor JMI School
KTN/HRWW/W HA3 115 K3
Vale Farm Sports Centre
ALP/SUD HA0 114 G9
Vale Industrial Estate
WATW WD18 92 D2
The Vale Medical Centre
FSTH SE23 182 D5
Valence House Museum & Library
BCTR RM8 123 N7
Valence School
BH/WHM TN16 263 J2
Valentine High School
IL IG1 122 D4
Valentines High Lower School
GNTH/NBYPK IG2 122 E3
Vale Park Industrial
ACT W3 156 B1
Vale Primary School
EPSOM KT18 238 A5
The Vale School
SKENS SW7 15 J4
Vallance Road School
WCHPL E1 13 N3
Valley End CE Infant School
CHOB/PIR GU24 212 F3
Valley End Cricket Club
CHOB/PIR GU24 212 F4
The Valley Gardens
EGH TW20 193 L2
Valley Primary School
HAYES BR2 205 K2
Valmar Trading Estate
CMBW SE5 159 K7
Vanbrugh Theatre
GWRST WC1E 11 J2
Vanguard Trading Estate
SRTFD E15 141 H3
Vaudeville Theatre
COVGDN WC2E 11 M7
Vaughan First & Middle School
RYLN/HDSTN HA2 114 B4
Vauxhall Primary School
LBTH SE11 17 N7
Vernon House Special School
WLSDN NW10 115 P10
Verulam Golf Club
STAL AL1 38 E8
Verulam Industrial Estate
STAL AL1 38 E8
Verulam School
STAL AL1 38 F5
Verulamium Museum
STALW/RED AL3 38 A6
Verulamium Roman Town
STALW/RED AL3 37 P6
Vestry Hall
MTCM CR4 202 A3
Vestry House Museum
WALTH E17 120 G2
Vestry Industrial Estate
RSEV TN14 247 J5
Vicarage Fields Health Clinic
BARK IG11 142 F2
The Vicarage Field Shopping Centre
BARK IG11 142 F2
Vicarage Primary School
EHAM E6 142 C5
Vicarage Road Cemetery
WATW WD18 73 H8
Vicars Green Primary School
GFD/PVL UB6 135 H4
VI Components Industrial Park
ERITH DA8 164 F4
Victoria & Albert Museum
SKENS SW7 15 M4
Victoria Barracks
WDSR SL4 149 J7
Victoria Business Centre
WELL DA16 163 K8
Victoria Chiropractic Clinic
CHEL SW3 16 A2
Victoria Clinic
WOKN/KNAP GU21 232 C2
Victoria Coach Station
BGVA SW1W 16 E6
Victoria First School
BERK HP4 33 P5
Victoria Hall
FNCH N3 97 J9
Victoria Industrial Estate
ACT W3 136 A7
Victoria Industrial Park
DART DA1 187 L1
Victoria Junior School
FELT TW13 175 J4
Victoria Medical Centre
PIM SW1V 16 G6
Victoria Palace Theatre
WESTW SW1E 16 F4
Victoria Park Industrial Centre
HOM E9 140 E2
Victoria Place Shopping Centre
PIM SW1V 16 F5
Victoria Rail/Air Terminal
PIM SW1V 16 F5
Victoria Retail Park
RSLP HA4 113 L10
Victoria Square Business Area
STAL AL1 38 E7
Victoria Station
PIM SW1V 16 F5
Victoria Wharf
POP/IOD E14 140 D9
Victoria Wharf Industrial Estate
DEPT SE8 160 E4
Victor Seymour Infant School
CAR SM5 202 A10
Victory Business Centre
ISLW TW7 154 E10
Victory Primary School
WALW SE17 18 F5
Viking Business Centre
ROMW/RG RM7 124 D5
Viking Primary School
NTHLT UB5 133 L5
The Village Medical Centre
SL SL1 128 C10
The Village School
HAMP NW3 4 B1
Village Shopping Centre
SL SL1 149 L1
Villiers High School
STHL UB1 133 P10
The Vine Clinic
KUTN/CMB KT2 177 K9
Vine Medical Centre
E/WMO/HCT KT8 198 B3
The Vines School
BTSEA SW11 158 B10
The Vineyard Primary School
RCHPK/HAM TW10 177 K2
Vinopolis, City of Wine
STHWK SE1 12 F9
Vinters' Hall
BLKFR EC4V 12 F7
VIP Trading Estate
CHARL SE7 161 P3
Virginia Primary School
BETH E2 7 L10
Virgo Fidelis Convent Schools
NRWD SE19 181 K9
Viscount Industrial Estate
DTCH/LGLY SL3 151 H9
Voyager Business Estate
BERM/RHTH SE16 19 N3
Vulcan Business Centre
CROY/NA CR0 225 K5
Vyners School
HGDN/ICK UB10 112 A9
Waddon Clinic
CROY/NA CR0 223 H2
Waddon Infant School
CROY/NA CR0 223 H2
Wadham Lodge Sports Centre
WALTH E17 100 G9
Wadsworth Business Centre
GFD/PVL UB6 135 H4
The Waldegrave Clinic
TEDD TW11 176 E8
Waldegrave Girls School
WHTN TW2 176 C6
Waldo Industrial Estate
BMLY BR1 205 P3
Waldorf School of SW London
STRHM/NOR SW16 180 D5
Waldorf Steiner School of SW London
STRHM/NOR SW16 180 E7
Walford Secondary School
NTHLT UB5 133 M3
Walker Primary School
STHGT/OAK N14 98 E3
Wallace Collection
MHST W1U 10 C5
Wallace Fields County Infant School
EW KT17 220 D9
Wallace Fields Junior School
EW KT17 220 D8
Wallbrook Business Centre
HSLWW TW4 153 J9
Wallington County Grammar School
WLGTN SM6 202 C10
Wallington High School for Girls
WLGTN SM6 222 C5
Walmer Road Clinic
NTGHL W11 8 A7
Walm Lane Clinic
CRICK NW2 116 G10
Walnut Leisure Centre
ORP BR6 207 K8
Walnuts Shopping Centre
ORP BR6 207 K8
Walnut Tree Walk Primary School
LBTH SE11 18 A5
Waltham Abbey Gatehouse
WAB EN9 63 H9
Waltham Abbey Swimming Pool
WAB EN9 81 J1
Waltham Forest College
WALTH E17 100 C10
WALTH E17 120 G1
Waltham Forest Magistrates Court
WALTH E17 120 G1
Waltham Forest Theatre
WALTH E17 120 E1
Waltham Forest Track
WALTH E17 100 G10
Waltham Holy Cross Junior School
WAB EN9 63 J9
Walthamstow Business Centre
WALTH E17 101 H10
Walthamstow Greyhound Stadium
CHING E4 100 G8
Walthamstow School for Girls
WALTH E17 120 G2
Walton Business Centre
WOT/HER KT12 197 J7
Walton Casuals FC
WOT/HER KT12 197 J5
Walton Community Hospital
WOT/HER KT12 197 J9
Walton Heath Golf Club Shop
KWD/TDW/WH KT20 256 E1
Walton & Hersham FC
WOT/HER KT12 197 H9
Walton Leigh School
WEY KT13 216 F1
Walton-on-Thames Cricket Club
WOT/HER KT12 196 G8
Walton on the Hill CE Junior School
KWD/TDW/WH KT20 256 D1
Walton on the Hill Primary School
KWD/TDW/WH KT20 238 E10
Walton Swimming Pool
WOT/HER KT12 197 J8
Walworth Lower School
WALW SE17 19 H7
Walworth Town Hall
WALW SE17 18 E6
Walworth Upper School
WALW SE17 19 K8
Wandle Primary School
WAND/EARL SW18 179 L4
Wandle Recreation Centre
WAND/EARL SW18 179 L2
Wandle Trading Estate
MTCM CR4 202 A7
Wandsworth Adult College
TOOT SW17 179 P7
The Wandsworth Arndale Centre
WAND/EARL SW18 179 L2
Wandsworth Cemetery
WAND/EARL SW18 179 M4
Wandsworth Community Health Trust
TOOT SW17 180 B8
Wandsworth County Court
PUT/ROE SW15 179 H1
Wandsworth Public Baths
TOOT SW17 180 B5
Wandsworth Trading Estate
WAND/EARL SW18 179 L3
Wansfell College
EPP CM16 82 G1
Wanstead CE Primary School
WAN E11 121 M3
Wanstead Cricket Club
WAN E11 121 N5
Wanstead Golf Club
WAN E11 121 P5
Wanstead High School
WAN E11 121 P4
Wanstead Hospital
WAN E11 121 N2
Wapping
WAP E1W 140 B10
Wapping Pier Head
WAP E1W 13 P10
Wapping Sports Centre
WAP E1W 140 A10
Warehouse Theatre
CROY/NA CR0 203 L9
Warley Hill Business Park
RBRW/HUT CM13 107 H7
Warley Hospital
BRW CM14 106 G6
Warley Lodge Hospital
RBRW/HUT CM13 107 J9
Warley Park Golf Club
RBRW/HUT CM13 107 J10
Warley Primary School
BRW CM14 107 H6
Warlingham County Junior School
WARL CR6 242 C3
Warlingham Park Hospital
WARL CR6 242 F2
Warlingham Park School
WARL CR6 242 F2
Warlingham RFC
WARL CR6 242 E3
Warlingham School
WARL CR6 242 A2
Warlingham Sports Club
WARL CR6 242 C3
War Memorial Sports Ground
SUT SM1 221 P1
Warner Village Cinema
ACT W3 135 M6
CROY/NA CR0 202 G9
DAGW RM9 143 P3
GSTN WD25 55 K9
HRW HA1 114 D4
HAMP NW3 3 J1
NFNCH/WDSP N12 97 N9
SHB W12 156 G1
SOHO/SHAV W1D 11 K7
WTHK RM20 166 F2
Warnford Industrial Estate
HYS/HAR UB3 152 F1
Warren Comprehensive School
CHDH RM6 124 A3
Warren Dell Primary School
OXHEY WD19 93 K4
Warrender School
RSLP HA4 112 G5
Warren Junior School
CHDH RM6 124 A3
Warren Mead Infant School
BNSTD SM7 238 F1
Warren Mead Junior School
BNSTD SM7 238 F1
The Warren Medical Centre
YEAD UB4 133 J8
Warren Primary School
CDH/CHF RM16 167 H2
Warren Road Primary School
ORP BR6 227 J1
Warwick Estate
BAY/PAD W2 9 H4
Warwick Leadlay Gallery
GNWCH SE10 161 H5
Warwick Park School
PECK SE15 159 N7
Warwick Quadrant & Harlequin Theatre, Cinema & Library
REDH RH1 258 B9
Warwick School for Boys
WALTH E17 121 H2
The Warwick School
REDH RH1 258 C9
Watchlytes JMI School
WGCE AL7 23 L5
Waterden Road Private Medical Clinic
GU GU1 268 B1
Waterfield First School
CRAWW RH11 283 H9
Watergate School
LEW SE13 160 G10
Waterloo Health Centre
STHWK SE1 18 A2
Waterloo Station
STHWK SE1 18 A1
Watermans Arts, Cinema & Theatre Centre
BTFD TW8 155 K5
Watermans Business Park
STA TW18 173 H7
The Watermans Hall
MON EC3R 13 J8
Watermeads High School
MRDN SM4 201 N6
Watermill Business Centre
PEND EN3 80 E6
Water Rats Theatre
STPAN WC1H 5 M9
Waterside Business Centre
ISLW TW7 154 G10
Waterside Combined School
CSHM HP5 51 J9

Waterside Industrial Estate *HOD* EN11 45 J4
The Waterside Trading Centre *NWDGN* UB2 154 D2
Waterside Trading Estate *ADL/WDHM* KT15 215 P1
Watersmeet Centre *RKW/CH/CXG* WD3 91 P1
Water Sports Centre *BERM/RHTH* SE16 160 D2
Waterways Business Centre *PEND* EN3 80 E4
Waterways Heritage Museum *RKW/CH/CXG* WD3 91 P2
Watford Arches Retail Park *WATW* WD18 73 K9
Watford Business Centre *WATW* WD18 73 J7
Watford Central Swimming Bath *WAT* WD17 73 H7
Watford County Court *WAT* WD17 73 J6
Watford FC & Saracens RFC (Vicarage Road Stadium) *WATW* WD18 73 J9
Watford General Hospital *WATW* WD18 73 J9
Watford Grammar School for Boys *WATW* WD18 72 G8
Watford Grammar School for Girls *WATW* WD18 73 K9
Watford Museum *WAT* WD17 73 K9
Watford Sports & Leisure Centre *GSTN* WD25 55 K9
Watling Clinic *EDGW* HA8 96 A8
Watling Medical Centre *EDGW* HA8 95 P9
Watling View Special School *STAL* AL1 38 C10
Wattenden Primary School *PUR/KEN* CR8 241 H2
Waverley Industrial Estate *HRW* HA1 114 C1
Waverley Lower Secondary School *EDUL* SE22 182 A1
Waverley School *EDUL* SE22 182 B1
PEND EN3 80 B8
Waxchandlers' Hall *CITYW* EC2V 12 F5
Weald College *KTN/HRWW/W* HA3 94 D7
Weald First & Middle School *KTN/HRWW/W* HA3 94 E8
Weald Hall Lane *EPP* CM16 65 L1
Weald Park (Country Park) *BRW* CM14 106 D1
Weald Park Golf Club *BRW* CM14 85 P9
Weekend Arts College *KTTN* NW5 4 E1
Welbeck Clinic *CRICK* NW2 117 K8
Welbourne Primary School *SEVS/STOTM* N15 119 P2
Welfare Clinic *CMBW* SE5 159 L9
GNWCH SE10 161 H6
HGT N6 118 B4
Wellcome Institute *CAMTN* NW1 11 J1
Welldon Park Middle School *RYLN/HDSTN* HA2 114 B9
The Welling Clinic *WELL* DA16 163 K8
Welling Medical Centre *WELL* DA16 163 J10
Welling School *WELL* DA16 163 L7
Wellington Arch *MYFR/PICC* W1J 16 D1
Wellington Barracks *STJSPK* SW1H 17 H2
Wellington Primary School *BOW* E3 140 F5
HSLW TW3 153 N8
Welling United FC *WELL* DA16 163 M9
Wells Park School *CHIG* IG7 103 J5
Wells Primary School *WFD* IG8 101 N5
Welwyn Garden City Cricket Club *WGCW* AL8 22 F1
Welwyn Garden City Football & Social Club *WGCE* AL7 23 L3
Welwyn Garden City Golf Club *WGCW* AL8 22 E5
Welwyn RFC *WGCW* AL8 22 F6
Wembley Arena *WBLY* HA9 115 M9
Wembley Conference Centre *WBLY* HA9 115 L9
Wembley FC *ALP/SUD* HA0 114 G9
Wembley High School *ALP/SUD* HA0 115 H8
Wembley Hospital *ALP/SUD* HA0 135 J1
Wembley Manor Primary School *WBLY* HA9 115 K8
Wembley Park Business Centre *WBLY* HA9 115 N8
Wembley Stadium *WBLY* HA9 115 M10
Wembley Stadium Industrial Estate *WBLY* HA9 115 M9
WBLY HA9 115 P8
Wendell Park Primary School *SHB* W12 156 C1
Wennington Hall Farm Business Centre *RAIN* RM13 145 M8
The Wenta Business Centre *WATN* WD24 73 L3
Wentworth Club *VW* GU25 193 M5
Wentworth Primary School *DART* DA1 186 G3
Wentworth Tutorial College *GLDGN* NW11 116 G4
Wesley's Chapel, House & Museum *STLK* EC1Y 12 G1
Wessex Gardens Primary School *CRICK* NW2 117 H6
West Acton Primary School *ACT* W3 135 N8
West Ashtead Primary School *ASHTD* KT21 237 K6
West Becton Health Centre *CAN/RD* E16 142 A8
Westbourne Green Sports Complex *BAY/PAD* W2 8 F4
Westbourne Primary School *SUT* SM1 201 K10
Westbridge College *BTSEA* SW11 157 P7
Westbrooke School *WELL* DA16 163 N9
Westbrook Hay Preparatory School *HHW* HP1 34 G9
Westbury Medical Centre *WDGN* N22 99 K10
West Byfleet Golf Club *BF/WBF* KT14 215 J9
West Byfleet Health Centre *BF/WBF* KT14 215 K9
West Byfleet Physiotherapy Clinic *BF/WBF* KT14 215 K8
West Byfleet Primary School *BF/WBF* KT14 215 L8
Westcott CE First School *DORK* RH4 272 B3
Westcourt Primary School *GVE* DA12 191 H5
The Westcroft Leisure Centre *CAR* SM5 222 B1
West Dene School *PUR/KEN* CR8 222 G9
West Drayton Cricket Club *WDR/YW* UB7 151 M3
West Drayton Primary School *WDR/YW* UB7 151 P1
West Ealing Business Centre *WEA* W13 134 F9
Westerham Golf Club *BH/WHM* TN16 263 J2
Western Avenue Business Park *ACT* W3 135 N6
Western House First School *SL* SL1 128 E9
Western House Hospital *WARE* SG12 26 C1
Western Trading Estate *WLSDN* NW10 135 P6
West Essex Golf Club *LOU* IG10 81 K8
West Ewell County Infant School *HOR/WEW* KT19 220 A2
Westfield Community Primary School *HOD* EN11 44 E2
Westfield First School *BERK* HP4 33 L4
Westfield Primary School *WOKS/MYFD* GU22 232 B7
Westfield School *WATW* WD18 72 G10
Westfields Primary School *BARN* SW13 156 C8
Westgate Primary School *DART* DA1 187 L3
Westgate Retail Park *SL* SL1 128 F9
Westgate School *SL* SL1 128 F10
West Green First School *CRAWW* RH11 283 M7
West Grove Primary School *STHGT/OAK* N14 98 E1
West Ham Church Primary School *SRTFD* E15 141 L3
West Ham Lane Clinic *SRTFD* E15 141 K3
West Hampstead Clinic *KIL/WHAMP* NW6 2 F3
West Ham United FC (Upton Park) *EHAM* E6 142 A4
West Hatch High School *CHIG* IG7 102 C6
West Hendon Clinic *CDALE/KGS* NW9 116 C4
West Hertfordshire College *WAT* WD17 73 H4
West Hertfordshire Crematorium *GSTN* WD25 55 L7
West Herts Business Centre *BORE* WD6 75 N7
West Herts College *BUSH* WD23 73 L7
HHW HP1 35 M5
West Herts Golf Club *RKW/CH/CXG* WD3 72 E7
West Hill Golf Club *CHOB/PIR* GU24 230 G7
West Hill Primary School *DART* DA1 187 K2
WAND/EARL SW18 179 K1
West Hill School *LHD/OX* KT22 236 F4
West India Pier *POP/IOD* E14 160 E1
West India Shopping Centre *POP/IOD* E14 140 F10
West Kensington Sports Centre *NTGHL* W11 136 G9
West Kent Golf Club *ORP* BR6 226 B8
Westland Heliport *BTSEA* SW11 157 N9
West Lea School *ED* N9 99 M4
West Lodge Preparatory School *BFN/LL* DA15 185 J6
West Lodge Primary School *PIN* HA5 113 L2
West London County Court *WKENS* W14 14 B5
West London Magistrates Court *HMSMTH* W6 156 G4
West London Tamil School *WLSDN* NW10 136 C4
West Mead Clinic *RSLP* HA4 113 K8
West Middlesex Golf Club *STHL* UB1 134 B9
West Middlesex University Hospital *ISLW* TW7 154 F8
Westminster Abbey *WEST* SW1P 17 L3
Westminster Abbey Choir School *WEST* SW1P 17 K3
Westminster Business Square *LBTH* SE11 17 N8
Westminster Cathedral *WEST* SW1P 16 G4
Westminster Cathedral Choir School *WEST* SW1P 17 H5
Westminster Cathedral RC Primary School *PIM* SW1V 17 K7
Westminster City Hall *WESTW* SW1E 17 H3
Westminster City School *WESTW* SW1E 17 H3
Westminster College *BTSEA* SW11 158 B7
SOHO/SHAV W1D 11 H7
Westminster Gallery *STJSPK* SW1H 17 K2
Westminster Industrial Estate *WOOL/PLUM* SE18 162 A2
Westminster Lodge Sports Centre & Abbey View Golf Club *STALW/RED* AL3 38 A7
Westminster Natural Health Centre *PIM* SW1V 16 G6
Westminster Pier *WHALL* SW1A 17 M2
Westminster School *WEST* SW1P 17 L3
Westminster Technical College *WEST* SW1P 17 H5
Westminster Theatre *WESTW* SW1E 16 G3
Westminster Under School *WEST* SW1P 17 J6
Westmoor Community Clinic *PUT/ROE* SW15 178 D3
West Norwood Clinic *WNWD* SE27 181 K5
West Norwood Crematorium *WNWD* SE27 181 K6
West One Shopping Centre *MYFR/PKLN* W1K 10 D6
Weston Green School *THDIT* KT7 198 D8
Weston Park Clinic *CEND/HSY/T* N8 118 F3
Weston Park Primary School *CEND/HSY/T* N8 118 G3
West Park Hospital *HOR/WEW* KT19 219 K8
Westpoint Trading Estate *ACT* W3 135 N7
West Ramp Coach Park *WDR/YW* UB7 152 B7
West Ruislip Elementary School *HGDN/ICK* UB10 112 D8
West Thames College *ISLW* TW7 154 D7
West Thornton Primary School *CROY/NA* CR0 202 G7
West Thurrock Primary School *WTHK* RM20 166 F5
West Twyford Primary School *WLSDN* NW10 135 M4
Westway Business Centre *BAY/PAD* W2 8 G4
The Westway Clinic *REDH* RH1 257 P9
Westway Sports Centre *NKENS* W10 136 G8
West Wickham Swimming Baths *WWKM* BR4 205 H8
Westwood High School for Girls *NRWD* SE19 181 K10
Westwood Primary School *WELL* DA16 163 H10
Westwood School *BUSH* WD23 94 C3
Westwood Technology College *WELL* DA16 162 G10
The Wetlands Centre *BARN* SW13 156 E7
Wexham Court Primary School *SLN* SL2 129 P8
Wexham Park Golf Club *DTCH/LGLY* SL3 129 P4
Wexham School *SLN* SL2 129 N7
Weybridge Business Park *ADL/WDHM* KT15 215 P1
Weybridge Cricket Club *WEY* KT13 196 F9
Weybridge Hospital & Primary Care Centre *WEY* KT13 216 B1
Weyfield Primary School *GU* GU1 250 A7
Wey House School *SHGR* GU5 268 B9
Wey Retail Park *BF/WBF* KT14 215 P8
Whaddon House Clinic *CMBW* SE5 159 M9
Wheatcroft School *HERT/BAY* SG13 25 P4
Wheatfields Junior & Infant School *STALE/WH* AL4 38 G2
Whelpley Hill Park *CSHM* HP5 52 A2
Whipps Cross Hospital *WAN* E11 121 J4
White Bridge Primary School *LOU* IG10 102 B1
Whitechapel Art Gallery *WCHPL* E1 13 M5
Whitefield School *CRICK* NW2 116 G5
Whitefield School & Leisure Centre *WALTH* E17 101 J9
Whitefriars First & Middle School *KTN/HRWW/W* HA3 94 D10
Whitefriars Trading Estate *KTN/HRWW/W* HA3 94 C10
Whitehall Estate *HLWW/ROY* CM19 46 B2
Whitehall Primary School *CHING* E4 101 K3
UX/CGN UB8 131 M3
Whitehall Theatre *WHALL* SW1A 11 K9
White Hart Lane School *WDGN* N22 99 J8
Whiteheath Infant School *RSLP* HA4 112 C4
Whiteheath Junior School *RSLP* HA4 112 D4
Whitehill Junior School *GVE* DA12 190 F6
Whitehorse Manor Primary School *THHTH* CR7 203 L4
Whiteleys Shopping Centre *BAY/PAD* W2 8 C6
White Oak Primary School *SWLY* BR8 208 F2
Whiterose Trading Estate *EBAR* EN4 97 P1
The Whitewebbs Museum of Transport & Industry *ENC/FH* EN2 79 J1
Whitewebbs Park Golf Club *ENC/FH* EN2 79 L3
Whitgift School *SAND/SEL* CR2 223 K2
Whitgift Shopping Centre *CROY/NA* CR0 203 K9
Whitings Hill Primary School *BAR* EN5 76 F9
Whitmore High School *RYLN/HDSTN* HA2 114 B6
Whitmore Primary School *IS* N1 7 H6
Whittingham Community Primary School *WALTH* E17 100 D9
Whittington Hospital *ARCH* N19 118 C7
Whittle Business Centre *SL* SL1 128 C8
Whittlesea School *KTN/HRWW/W* HA3 94 B8
Whitton Health Centre *WHTN* TW2 176 B4
Whitton Health Clinic *WHTN* TW2 176 A4
Whitton School *WHTN* TW2 176 A5
Whybridge Infant School *RAIN* RM13 145 H3
Whybridge Junior School *RAIN* RM13 144 G3
Whyteleafe Business Village *CTHM* CR3 241 N3
Whyteleafe FC *CTHM* CR3 241 N5
Whyteleafe Primary School *CTHM* CR3 241 N4
Wickham Theatre *WWKM* BR4 205 J10
Widewater Business Centre *DEN/HRF* UB9 111 M3
Wide Way Health Clinic *MTCM* CR4 202 E3
Widmore Centre *BMLY* BR1 205 P2
Wigmore Hall *MHST* W1U 10 E5
Wilberforce Primary School *NKENS* W10 2 B9
Wilbury Primary School *UED* N18 99 L6
Wildernesse Golf Club *BGR/WK* TN15 247 P8
Wildernesse School *BGR/WK* TN15 247 M7
Wildernesse Sports Centre *BGR/WK* TN15 247 M7
Willesden Community Hospital *WLSDN* NW10 136 D2
Willesden County Court *WLSDN* NW10 136 B4
Willesden High School *WLSDN* NW10 136 E3
Willesden Medical Centre *CRICK* NW2 136 E1
Willesden Sports Stadium *WLSDN* NW10 136 E3
William Bellamy Junior & Infant School *DAGE* RM10 124 B7
William Byrd School *HYS/HAR* UB3 152 D5
William C Harvey Special School *TOTM* N17 99 L10
William Davies Primary School *FSTGT* E7 142 A1
The William Durrant Junior School *CSHM* HP5 50 G4
William Edwards School *CDH/CHF* RM16 147 P9
William Ellis School *KTTN* NW5 118 B8
William Ellis Sports Ground *EDGW* HA8 95 M9
William Ford CE Junior School *DAGE* RM10 144 B2
William Morris Gallery *WALTH* E17 120 F1
William Morris Middle School *MTCM* CR4 202 E3
William Morris School *WALTH* E17 100 D9
William Penn Leisure Centre *RKW/CH/CXG* WD3 91 J2
The William Penn School *SLN* SL2 129 J6
William Torbitt Junior & Infant School *GNTH/NBYPK* IG2 123 H3
William Tyndale Primary School *IS* N1 6 D3
Willington School *WIM/MER* SW19 179 J9
Willoughby Hall School *HAMP* NW3 117 N9
Willow Business Centre *MTCM* CR4 202 A5
Willow Business Park *SYD* SE26 182 B6
Willow Court Colindale Hospital *CDALE/KGS* NW9 96 A10
Willowfield Adult Education Centre *WALTH* E17 120 C1
Willowfield School *HNHL* SE24 159 K10
WALTH E17 120 D1
The Willows Clinic *CHST* BR7 184 D9
The Willows *YEAD* UB4 133 L6
Willow Tree Primary School *NTHLT* UB5 133 M1
Wilmington Boys Grammar School *RDART* DA2 187 J6
Wilmington Grammar School for Girls *RDART* DA2 187 J5
Wilmington Hall School *RDART* DA2 187 H6
Wilmington Primary School *RDART* DA2 187 J6
Wilsons School *WLGTN* SM6 222 F3
Wilton's Music Hall *WCHPL* E1 13 N7
Wimbledon Chase Middle School *RYNPK* SW20 201 H1
Wimbledon College High School *WIM/MER* SW19 178 G10
Wimbledon Common Golf Club *WIM/MER* SW19 178 D8
Wimbledon Common Pre-Preparatory School *WIM/MER* SW19 178 F9
Wimbledon FC (Selhurst Park) *SNWD* SE25 203 M4
Wimbledon (Gap Road) Cemetery *WIM/MER* SW19 179 L7
Wimbledon High School *WIM/MER* SW19 179 H9
Wimbledon House School *WIM/MER* SW19 201 K1
Wimbledon Magistrates Court *WIM/MER* SW19 179 K9
Wimbledon Park Athletics Track *WIM/MER* SW19 179 J5
Wimbledon Park Golf Club *WIM/MER* SW19 179 J6
Wimbledon Park Primary School *WIM/MER* SW19 179 K5
Wimbledon RFC *RYNPK* SW20 178 C10
Wimbledon School of Art *WIM/MER* SW19 179 K10
WIM/MER SW19 201 H1
Wimbledon School of English *WIM/MER* SW19 179 H9
Wimbledon Stadium *TOOT* SW17 179 L7
Wimbledon Stadium Business Centre *WIM/MER* SW19 179 L6
Wimbledon Theatre *WIM/MER* SW19 179 K10
Winchcombe Business Centre *PECK* SE15 19 K10
Winchmore Hill Clinic *WCHMH* N21 99 J2
Winchmore Hill Cricket Club *AMSS* HP7 68 A10
WCHMH N21 99 K2
Winchmore School *WCHMH* N21 99 K3
Windermere JMI Primary School *STAL* AL1 38 G8
Windlemere Golf Club *CHOB/PIR* GU24 212 D7
Windlesham Village Infant School *BFOR* GU20 212 A1
Windmill Business Centre *STHL* UB1 134 B10
Windmill School *BRXS/STRHM* SW2 180 F1
Windmill Trading Estate *MTCM* CR4 202 D5
SUN TW16 196 E1
Windrush Primary School *THMD* SE28 143 L10
Windsor Boys School *WDSR* SL4 148 G7
Windsor Business Centre *WDSR* SL4 148 E6
WDSR SL4 149 H6
Windsor Castle *WDSR* SL4 149 K6
Windsor Cemetery *WDSR* SL4 148 G9
Windsor & Eton FC *WDSR* SL4 148 G10
Windsor Girls School *WDSR* SL4 148 F9
Windsor Industrial Estate *HERT/BAY* SG13 26 A3
Windsor Leisure Centre *WDSR* SL4 148 G6
Windsor Racecourse *WDSR* SL4 148 F5
Winfield House *CAMTN* NW1 3 P9
Wingate & Finchley FC *NFNCH/WDSP* N12 97 N8
Wingate Trading Estate *TOTM* N17 99 N8
Wingfield Primary School *BKHTH/KID* SE3 161 M9
Winns Primary School *WALTH* E17 100 E10
Winsor Primary School *EHAM* E6 142 C8
Winston Churchill's Britain at War Experience *STHWK* SE1 13 H10
The Winston Churchill School *WOKN/KNAP* GU21 231 K4
Winterbourne Junior Girls School *THHTH* CR7 203 H4
Winton Primary School *IS* N1 5 N8
Wishmore Cross School *CHOB/PIR* GU24 213 K6
Witley Industrial Estate *NWDGN* UB2 153 N3
Witnitz School *STNW/STAM* N16 119 N6
Wix Primary School *BTSEA* SW11 158 C9

Woking Arts Council
WOKN/KNAP GU21 ... 232 B3
Woking Athletics Track
WOKN/KNAP GU21 ... 214 F9
Woking Business Park
WOKN/KNAP GU21 ... 232 E1
Woking College
WOKS/MYFD GU22 ... 232 D6
Woking Community Hospital
WOKS/MYFD GU22 ... 232 B4
Woking FC
WOKS/MYFD GU22 ... 232 C6
Woking Golf Club
WOKS/MYFD GU22 ... 231 M6
Woking High School
WOKN/KNAP GU21 ... 232 A1
Woking Hospice
WOKS/MYFD GU22 ... 232 B4
Woking Leisure Centre & Swimming Pool
WOKS/MYFD GU22 ... 232 C4
Woking Nuffield Hospital
WOKN/KNAP GU21 ... 214 B10
Woking St John's Crematorium
WOKN/KNAP GU21 ... 231 K5
Woldingham School
GDST RH9 ... 260 D1
Wolf Fields Primary School
NWDGN UB2 ... 153 N3
Wolfson-Hillel Primary School
STHGT/OAK N14 ... 78 E10
Wolfson Medical Centre
RYNPK SW20 ... 178 D10
Wolsey Business Park
WATW WD18 ... 92 E1
Wolsey Place Shopping Centre
WOKN/KNAP GU21 ... 232 B3
Women's Theatre Workshop
REGST W1B ... 11 H8
Woodacre Special School
SOCK/AV RM15 ... 146 E7
The Woodberry Clinic
MUSWH N10 ... 118 C1
Woodbridge Business Park
GU GU1 ... 249 P9
Woodbridge High School & Language College
WFD IG8 ... 101 N8
Woodbrook School
BECK BR3 ... 204 E1
Woodbury Down Primary School
FSBYPK N4 ... 119 K5
Woodcote High School
COUL/CHIP CR5 ... 222 E9
Woodcote House School
BFOR GU20 ... 212 A2
Woodcote Park Golf Club
COUL/CHIP CR5 ... 222 D10
Woodcotes Primary School
COUL/CHIP CR5 ... 222 E10
Woodcroft Primary School
EDGW HA8 ... 96 A8
Woodcroft School
LOU IG10 ... 82 C5
Wood End Junior School
NTHLT UB5 ... 114 C10
Wood End Park Junior School
UX/CGN UB8 ... 132 D9
Woodentops School
BAL SW12 ... 180 E4
Woodfield School
CDALE/KGS NW9 ... 116 B6
REDH RH1 ... 258 F5
Woodfield Special School
HHS/BOV HP3 ... 36 D8
Woodford County High School
WFD IG8 ... 101 L7
Woodford Golf Club
WFD IG8 ... 101 L6
Woodford Green Preparatory School
WFD IG8 ... 101 M7
Woodford Green Primary School
WFD IG8 ... 101 L6
Woodford Trading Estate
WFD IG8 ... 101 P10
Woodgrange Infant School
FSTGT E7 ... 121 N9
Woodgrange Park Cemetery
FSTGT E7 ... 122 A10
Wood Green Crown Court
WDGN N22 ... 99 H9
Wood Green Health Centre
WDGN N22 ... 98 G9
Wood Green Old Boys FC
WDGN N22 ... 99 H8
Woodhall School
OXHEY WD19 ... 93 M5
Woodhill Primary School
CHARL SE7 ... 162 B3
Woodhouse Sixth Form College
NFNCH/WDSP N12 ... 97 N6
Woodlands Infant & Junior School
IL IG1 ... 122 G10
Woodlands Park Primary School
SEVS/STOTM N15 ... 119 K3
Woodlands Preparatory School
RBRW/HUT CM13 ... 127 J2
Woodlands Primary School
BORE WD6 ... 75 M5
Woodlands School
LHD/OX KT22 ... 237 H8
Wood Lane Medical Centre
RSLP HA4 ... 112 F6
Wood Lane School
FUL/PGN SW6 ... 157 M7
Wood Lane Sports Centre
BCTR RM8 ... 124 C6
Woodlea Primary School
CTHM CR3 ... 242 E8
Woodman Road Cemetery
BRW CM14 ... 107 J6
Woodmansterne Primary School
BNSTD SM7 ... 222 A10
STRHM/NOR SW16 ... 202 E1
Woodmansterne Sports Club
BNSTD SM7 ... 239 P1
Woodridge Primary School
NFNCH/WDSP N12 ... 97 J4
Woodside Health Centre
SNWD SE25 ... 204 A5
Woodside Junior School
AMS HP6 ... 69 K4
CROY/NA CR0 ... 203 P7
Woodside Park Golf Club
NFNCH/WDSP N12 ... 97 K5
Woodside Park School
FBAR/BDGN N11 ... 98 A6
NFNCH/WDSP N12 ... 97 L5
Woodside Primary School
CDH/CHF RM16 ... 168 C2
CHESW EN7 ... 61 K5
Woodside School
BELV DA17 ... 164 C3
Woodside Stadium
GSTN WD25 ... 55 K9
Wood Street County Infant School
RGUW GU3 ... 249 H8
Wood Street Medical Centre
WALTH E17 ... 121 H1
Woodville Junior School
LHD/OX KT22 ... 236 G6
Wood Wharf
POP/IOD E14 ... 140 G10
Wood Wharf Business Park
POP/IOD E14 ... 161 H1
Woolmore Primary School
POP/IOD E14 ... 141 H9
Woolwich Cemetery
WOOL/PLUM SE18 ... 163 J6
Woolwich College
WOOL/PLUM SE18 ... 162 A3
WOOL/PLUM SE18 ... 162 F3
Woolwich County Court
WOOL/PLUM SE18 ... 162 D2
Woolwich Crown Court
THMD SE28 ... 163 H1
Woolwich Polytechnic School
THMD SE28 ... 143 K10
Worcesters Primary School
EN EN1 ... 79 N4
Working & Horsell Cricket Club
WOKN/KNAP GU21 ... 232 A3
Working Mens College
CAMTN NW1 ... 5 H7
World Business Centre Heathrow
HTHAIR TW6 ... 152 D7
World End
TIL RM18 ... 168 E10
World of Football Hall of Fame
STHWK SE1 ... 17 N2
Worlds End Place
WBPTN SW10 ... 157 M6
World Trade Centre
TWRH EC3N ... 13 M8
World University Service
STLK EC1Y ... 12 G2
Wormholt Park Primary School
SHB W12 ... 136 D9
Wormley Primary School
BROX EN10 ... 44 D9
Worple Primary School
ISLW TW7 ... 154 F10
Worplesdon CP School
RGUW GU3 ... 249 J6
Worplesdon Golf Club
WOKS/MYFD GU22 ... 231 K8
Worsley Bridge Junior School
BECK BR3 ... 182 F10
Worton Hall Industrial Estate
ISLW TW7 ... 154 D10
Wray Common County Middle School
REIG RH2 ... 257 N9
Wray Common Primary School
REDH RH1 ... 257 N9
Wraysbury Medical Centre
STWL/WRAY TW19 ... 172 C2
Wraysbury Primary School
STWL/WRAY TW19 ... 172 B2
Wrencote
CROY/NA CR0 ... 203 K10
Wrexham Park Hospital
SLN SL2 ... 129 P6
Wrotham Road Health Clinic
GVW DA11 ... 190 E4
Wrotham Road Primary School
GVW DA11 ... 190 E3
The Wroxham School
POTB/CUF EN6 ... 58 F7
Wyborne Primary School
ELTH/MOT SE9 ... 184 E4
Wyke Green Golf Club
ISLW TW7 ... 154 E5
Wykeham Primary School
HCH RM12 ... 125 H6
WLSDN NW10 ... 116 A8
The Wyllotts Centre Cinema
POTB/CUF EN6 ... 59 J8
Wyndhams Theatre
LSQ/SEVD WC2H ... 11 K7
Wyvil Primary School
VX/NE SW8 ... 17 M10
VX/NE SW8 ... 158 F6
Yale University Press
HAMP NW3 ... 117 P9
Yardley Primary School
CHING E4 ... 80 G9
Yattendon School
HORL RH6 ... 280 B3
Yeading FC
HYS/HAR UB3 ... 133 K10
Yeading Medical Centre
NTHLT UB5 ... 133 K5
Yeading Primary School
YEAD UB4 ... 133 K7
Yehudi Menuhin School
COB KT11 ... 235 P5

Notes

Notes

Notes

AA Street by Street QUESTIONNAIRE

Dear Atlas User
Your comments, opinions and recommendations are very important to us. So please help us to improve our street atlases by taking a few minutes to complete this simple questionnaire.

You do NOT need a stamp (unless posted outside the UK). If you do not want to remove this page from your street atlas, then photocopy it or write your answers on a plain sheet of paper.

Send to: The Editor, AA Street by Street, FREEPOST SCE 4598, Basingstoke RG21 4GY

ABOUT THE ATLAS...

Which city/town/county did you buy?

Are there any features of the atlas or mapping that you find particularly useful?

Is there anything we could have done better?

Why did you choose an AA Street by Street atlas?

Did it meet your expectations?

Exceeded ☐ **Met all** ☐ **Met most** ☐ **Fell below** ☐

Please give your reasons

continued overleaf

Where did you buy it?

For what purpose? (please tick all applicable)

To use in your own local area ☐ **To use on business or at work** ☐

Visiting a strange place ☐ **In the car** ☐ **On foot** ☐

Other (please state)

LOCAL KNOWLEDGE...

Local knowledge is invaluable. Whilst every attempt has been made to make the information contained in this atlas as accurate as possible, should you notice any inaccuracies, please detail them below (if necessary, use a blank piece of paper) or e-mail us at *streetbystreet@theAA.com*

ABOUT YOU...

Name (Mr/Mrs/Ms)

Address

Postcode

Daytime tel no

E-mail address

Which age group are you in?

Under 25 ☐ **25-34** ☐ **35-44** ☐ **45-54** ☐ **55-64** ☐ **65+** ☐

Are you an AA member? **YES** ☐ **NO** ☐

Do you have Internet access? **YES** ☐ **NO** ☐

Thank you for taking the time to complete this questionnaire. Please send it to us as soon as possible, and remember, you do not need a stamp (unless posted outside the UK).